July 7–11, 2012
Philadelphia, Pennsylvania, USA

Association for
Computing Machinery

Advancing Computing as a Science & Profession

GECCO

GECCO'12 Vol. 1 of 2

Proceedings of the Fourteenth International Conference on

Genetic and Evolutionary Computation

Sponsored by:

ACM SIGEVO

Association for
Computing Machinery

Advancing Computing as a Science & Profession

The Association for Computing Machinery
2 Penn Plaza, Suite 701
New York, New York 10121-0701

ISBN: 978-1-4503-1177-9 (Digital)

ISBN: 978-1-4503-1944-7 (Print Vol. 1)

Additional copies may be ordered prepaid from:

ACM Order Department
PO Box 30777
New York, NY 10087-0777, USA

Phone: 1-800-342-6626 (USA and Canada)
+1-212-626-0500 (Global)
Fax: +1-212-944-1318
E-mail: acmhelp@acm.org
Hours of Operation: 8:30 am – 4:30 pm ET

ACM Order Number: 910122

Printed in the USA

Welcome from General Chair

It is my pleasure to welcome you to Philadelphia for the 2012 Genetic and Evolutionary Computation Conference (GECCO-2012). This is the first time GECCO has been held in Philly. We very much you hope you enjoy this historic American city and all it has to offer.

This will be my 14th year attending GECCO. I have contributed a number of papers and have enjoyed many thought-provoking presentations over the years. GECCO has played a very important role in my research program and in the training of many of my students and postdocs. I agreed to serve as General Chair of GECCO-2012 because it was time to give back to the community I have enjoyed being a part of since 1999.

Terence Soule served as the editor-in-chief this year and did a very skillful job maintaining the high quality of the conference. GECCO-2012 accepted 172 full papers for oral presentation out of a total of 467 submitted. This is an acceptance rate of less than 37%. I am very thankful to Terry, Anne Auger, our Proceedings Chair, and all the track chairs for their hard work managing the review, selection and scheduling process for the scientific papers. Thanks to Mark Montague from Linklings and Lisa Tolles from Sheridan Printing Company for their assistance with the publication of the proceedings.

One of the highlights of every GECCO is the free tutorials and the free workshops held during the first two days of the conference. I found these to be incredibly helpful when I was still learning about the field. Thanks to Gabriela Ochoa for chairing the tutorials and Bill Rand for chairing the workshops.

In addition to the main program, there are many other parts that make GECCO a special and meaningful experience. Marylyn Ritchie served as Local Chair and was very helpful with planning our visit to Philly. Xavier Llorà did a superb job of publicity with the help of our webmaster and design consultant, Gerardo Valencia. Daniele Loiacono did a great job as Competitions Chair and, as Student Chair, Josh Bongard masterfully oversaw the process of awarding student travel grants. I would also like to thank Thomas Bartz-Beielstein, David Davis and Jörn Mehnen for their role as Evolutionary Computation in Practice Chairs.

I couldn't have planned GECCO-2012 without the generous time commitment of all the chairs mentioned above. I would also like to thank Wolfgang Banzhaf and Marc Schoenauer from the ACM SIGEVO Business Committee and Franz Rothlauf, the ACM SIGEVO Treasurer, for their encouragement and assistance navigating the enormous number of details from budgets to planning and execution. Additionally, I would like to thank Roxane Rose and Jill Skuba from Executive Events for their expert handling of the many logistical and registration-related details that are needed to make the conference a success.

Finally, I would like to thank you, the authors, presenters, reviewers, and all the other attendees. It is your participation that makes GECCO what it is, one of the premier conferences on evolutionary computation and a source of great discussions, ideas, and inspirations. Thank you all for your involvement.

Jason H. Moore, Ph.D.
Dartmouth College, USA

A Word from the Chair of SIGEVO

Welcome to the Proceedings of GECCO-2012, the fourteenth GECCO, and a "recombination" of the 21th International Conference on Genetic Algorithms (ICGA) and the 17th Genetic Programming Conference (GP). This year, Jason Moore has acted with great energy and diligence as General Chair of GECCO-2012. Terry Soule, the Editor-in-Chief of GECCO-2012 has done a terrific job at keeping the tracks on track and the reviewing process going and leading the effort to select papers for publication. Finally, as a first this year, we have created the position of a Proceedings Chair. Anne Auger did a great job tending to the details of this year's proceedings with results that you can inspect here.

GECCO is the premiere venue for presenting papers in the area of Genetic and Evolutionary Computation world-wide. The quality of the papers submitted to GECCO is very high, and GECCO has the most rigorous selection process in the field of Evolutionary Computation. The combined effect means that the best papers and most important work in the field of Evolutionary Computation is presented at the GECCO conference. If you were not able to attend GECCO-2012 in person, the Proceedings are in the ACM Digital Library; they are globally accessible and readily found, which benefits both readers and authors.

ACM SIGEVO

The members of ACM SIGEVO, sponsor of GECCO, continue to draw major benefits of becoming a part of ACM. In addition to being part of the ACM Digital Library, another key benefit is the outstanding newsletter, SIGEVOlutions, produced by editor Pier Luca Lanzi and an excellent editorial board. If you are accessing these proceedings and are not a member of SIGEVO, please consider joining (for the low price of $25/year for non-students, and $10/year for student members). This will help us a lot in promoting our community. In addition to SIGEVOlutions, members receive a substantial discount for GECCO registration.

Involvement in ACM SIGEVO

SIGEVO is now an established Special Interest Group (SIG) of the ACM. ACM considers its SIGs as the lifeblood of the organization. We are governed by bylaws available on the SIGEVO web pages. There, you also find a list of members of the 18-member Executive Committee. This past year, I was elected chair of SIGEVO, together with a new team of officers: Una-May O'Reilly (Vice-Chair), Marc Schoenauer (Secretary), and Franz Rothlauf (Treasurer). We have started our work and are dedicated to improve our organization. If you have any suggestions how to make GECCO or SIGEVO better, please let us know.

Wolfgang Banzhaf
SIGEVO Chair

Table of Contents

Bioinformatics, Computational, Systems and Synthetic Biology Track Papers

Digital Entertainment Technologies and Arts Track Papers

Estimation of Distribution Algorithms Track Papers

Evolution Strategies and Evolutionary Programming Track Papers

Evolutionary Combinatorial Optimization and Metaheuristics Track Papers

Evolutionary Multiobjective Optimization Track Papers

Generative and Developmental Systems Track Papers

Genetic Algorithms Track Papers

Genetics Based Machine Learning Track Papers

Integrative Genetic and Evolutionary Computation Track Papers

Parallel Evolutionary Systems Track Papers

Real World Applications Track Papers

Search-Based Software Engineering Track Papers

Self-* Search Track Papers

Theory Track Papers

GECCO 2012 Editors

Terence Soule *(University of Idaho, USA)*

Anne Auger *(INRIA Saclay - Île-de-France, France)*

Christian Blum *(Universitat Politècnica de Catalunya, Spain)*

Juergen Branke *(University of Warwick, UK)*

Nicolas Bredeche *(TAO / LRI, Univ. Paris-Sud, INRIA Saclay, CNRS, France)*

Will Neil Browne *(Victoria University of Wellington, New Zealand)*

John Andrew Clark *(University of York, UK)*

Kalyanmoy Deb *(Indian Institute of Technology Kanpur, India)*

Alan Dorin *(Monash University, Australia)*

Rene Doursat *(Institut des Systemes Complexes, CNRS)*

Aniko Ekart *(Aston University, UK)*

Tobias Friedrich *(Max-Planck-Institut Informatik, Germany)*

Steven Gustafson *(GE Global Research, USA)*

Gregory S. Hornby *(UC Santa Cruz, USA)*

Christian Igel *(University of Copenhagen, Denmark)*

Tim Kovacs *(University of Bristol, UK)*

Dario Landa-Silva *(University of Nottingham, UK)*

Fernando G. Lobo *(University of Algarve, Portugal)*

Gisele Lobo Pappa *(Federal University of Minas Gerais, Brazil)*

Jose A. Lozano *(University of the Basque Country, Spain)*

Silja Meyer-Nieberg *(Universitaet der Bundeswehr Muenchen, Germany)*

Alison Motsinger *(NC State University, USA)*

Frank Neumann *(University of Adelaide, Australia)*

Gabriela Ochoa *(University of Nottingham, UK)*

Gustavo Olague *(CICESE, USA)*

Yew-Soon Ong *(Nanyang Technological University, Singapore)*

Martin Pelikan *(University of Missouri in St. Louis, USA)*

David Pelta *(University of Granada, Spain)*

Clara Pizzuti *(Institute for High Performance Computing and Networking - ICAR National Research Council of Italy – CNR, Italy)*

Mike Preuss *(TU Dortmund, Germany)*

Jonathan Rowe *(University of Birmingham, UK)*

Stephen Leslie Smith *(University of York, UK)*

Christine Solnon *(LIRIS, University of Lyon 1, France)*

Giovanni Squillero *(Politecnico di Torino, Italy)*

Daniel Tauritz *(Missouri University of Science and Technology, USA)*

Man Leung Wong *(Lingnan University, Hong Kong)*

Shin Yoo *(University College London, UK)*

Tina Yu *(Memorial University, Canada)*

GECCO 2012 Conference Organizers

General Chair: Jason H. Moore *(Dartmouth College, USA)*

Editor-in-Chief: Terence Soule *(University of Idaho, USA)*

Business Committee: Wolfgang Banzhaf *(Memorial University of Newfoundland, Canada)*
Marc Schoenauer *(INRIA Saclay, France)*

Publicity Chair: Xavier Llorà *(Google Inc., USA)*

Proceedings Chair: Anne Auger *(INRIA, France)*

Local Chair: Marylyn Ritchie *(Vanderbilt University, USA)*

Tutorials Chair: Gabriela Ochoa *(University of Nottingham, UK)*

Workshops Chair: William Rand *(University of Maryland, USA)*

Students Chair: Josh Bongard *(University of Vermont, USA)*

Competitions Chair: Daniele Loiacono *(Politecnico di Milano, Italy)*

Late Breaking Papers Chairs: Katya Rodriguez-Vazquez *(IIMAS-UNAM, Mexico)*
Christian Blum *(Universitat Politècnica de Catalunya, Spain)*

Evolutionary Computation in Practice Chairs: Jörn Mehnen *(Cranfield University, UK)*
Thomas Bartz-beielstein *(Cologne University of Applied Sciences, Germany)*
David Davis *(VGO Associates, USA)*

GECCO 2012 Program Committee Members

Hussein Abbass, *UNSW@ADFA*
Ashraf Abdelbar, *American University in Cairo*
Ajith Abraham, *Machine Intelligence Research Labs*
Tarek Abudawood, *King Abdulaziz City for Science & Technology*
Berry Adam, *CSIRO*
Andrew Adamatzky
Chris Adami, *Keck Graduate Institute of Applied Life Sciences*
Michael Affenzeller, *Upper Austrian University of Applied Sciences*
Wasif Afzal, *Blekinge Institute of Technology*
Jesus S. Aguilar-Ruiz, *Pablo de Olavide University*
Hernan Aguirre, *Shinshu University*
Chang Wook Ahn, *Sungkyunkwan University*
Barry Ahrens, *Nova Southeastern University*
Juan-Manuel Ahuactzin, *PROBAYES*
Muhammad Ali Akbar, *nexGIN RC, FAST-NU, Islamabad, Pakistan*
Youhei Akimoto, *INRIA Saclay*
Enrique Alba, *University of Málaga*
Javier Alcaraz, *Universidad Miguel Hernández*
Ricardo Aler, *Universidad Carlos III de Madrid*
Eva Alfaro-Cid, *Instituto Tecnologico de Informatica*
Francisco Almeida
Lee Altenberg, *Associate Editor, BioSystems*
Ng Amos
Jason Ansel, *MIT*
Ricardo Araujo, *Informatics Center - Federal University of Pernambuco*
Alfredo Arias Montaño, *CINVESTAV-IPN*
Takaya Arita, *Nagoya University*
Dirk V. Arnold, *Dalhousie University*
Antonio D. Masegosa Arredondo
David Atienza, *Ecole Polytechnique Federale de Lausanne*
Anne AUGER, *INRIA*
Gideon Avigad, *Braude College of Engineering*
Nizamettin Aydin, *Yildiz Technical University*
Raja Muhammad Atif Azad, *University of Limerick*
Vladan Babovic, *National University Singapore*
B. V. Babu, *JK Lakshmipat University, Jaipur.*
Jaume Bacardit, *University of Nottingham*
Thomas Baeck, *Leiden University*
Rami Bahsoon, *The University of Birmingham*
Ruibin Bai, *University of Nottingham Ningbo*
Carsten Baldauf, *Fritz-Haber-Institut der MPG*
Pedro J. Ballester, *European Bioinformatics Institute*
Sunith Bandaru, *Indian Institute of Technology Kanpur*
Zorana Bankovic, *Technical University of Madrid*
Wolfgang Banzhaf, *Memorial University of Newfoundland*
Adam Banzi, *Federal University of Parana*
Ranieri Baraglia, *ISTI-CNR*
Helio J.C. Barbosa, *LNCC*
Gregory J. Barlow, *Carnegie Mellon University*
Marcio Barros, *UNIRIO*
Thomas Bartz-Beielstein, *Cologne University of Applied Sciences*
Jeffrey K. Bassett, *George Mason University*
Iain Bate, *University of York*
Benoit Baudry, *INRIA*
Jacob Beal, *BBN Technologies*
Mark A. Bedau, *Reed College; ProtoLife Inc.*
Randall Beer, *Case Western Reserve University*
Mohammad Behdad, *The University of Western Australia*
Theodore C. Belding, *Belding Consulting, Inc.*
Fevzi Belli, *Univ. Paderborn, EIM-ADT*
Gerardo Beni
Peter J. Bentley, *University College London*
Jean Berger, *Defence R&D Canada - Valcartier*
Matthias Bernt, *University Leipzig*
Rod Berry, *University of Technology Sydney*
Tom Bersano, *University of Michigan*
Hugurd Bersini, *IRIDIA-ULB*
Eva Besada-Portas, *Universidad Compluntense de Madrid*
Hans-Georg Beyer, *Vorarlberg Univ. of Applied Sciences*
Bir Bhanu, *University of California at Riverside, USA*
Marco Biazzini, *University of Nantes - France*
Concha Bielza, *Technical University of Madrid*
Mauro Birattari, *Université Libre de Bruxelles*
Bernd Bischl, *TU Dortmund*
Tim Blackwell, *Goldsmiths, University of London*
Jacek Blazewicz, *Poznan University of Technology*

Maria J. Blesa, *Universitat Politècnica de Catalunya*
Christian Blum, *Universitat Politècnica de Catalunya*
Danushka Bollegala, *The University of Tokyo*
Eric Bonabeau
Josh Bongard, *University of Vermont*
Lashon Booker, *The MITRE Corporation*
Jakramate Bootkrajang, *University of Birmingham*
Peter A.N. Bosman, *Centre for Mathematics and Computer Science*
Leonardo Bottaci, *University of Hull*
Lydia Boudjeloud, *LITA*
Amine Boumaza, *Univ. Littoral / LISIC*
Pascal Bouvry
Ollie Bown, *University of Sydney*
Juergen Branke, *University of Warwick*
Nicolas Bredeche, *TAO / LRI; Univ. Paris-Sud, INRIA Saclay, CNRS*
David E. Breen, *Drexel University*
Karl Bringmann, *Max Planck Institute for Informatics*
Dimo Brockhoff, *Ecole Polytechnique*
Gavin Brown, *University of Manchester*
Will Neil Browne, *Victoria University of Wellington*
Alexander Brownlee, *Loughborough University*
Arne Brutschy, *Universite Libre de Bruxelles*
Fernando Buarque, *University of Pernambuco*
Anthony Bucci, *Icosystem Corporation*
Lam Thu Bui, *Le Quy Don Technical University*
Thang Bui, *Penn State Harrisburg, USA*
Larry Bull, *University of the West of England*
John A. Bullinaria, *University of Birmingham, UK*
Seth Bullock, *University of Southampton*
Paolo Burelli, *IT-Universitet i København*
Will Bush, *Vanderbilt Medical Center*
Martin V. Butz, *University of Tübingen*
Leticia Cagnina, *Universidad Nacional de San Luis*
Stefano Cagnoni, *University of Parma, Italy*
Angelo Cangelosi, *University of Plymouth*
Bastos Filho Carmelo J A, *University of Pernambuco, Politechnic School of Pernambuco*
Andre Carvalho, *USP, Brazil*
Alberto Castellini, *Center for BioMedical Computing, University of Verona, Italy*
Mariano Ceccato, *Fondazione Bruno Kessler*
Uday Chakraborty, *University of Missouri*
Shamik Chaudhuri, *General Electric India Technology Center, Bangalore*
Ying-ping Chen, *National Chiao Tung University, Taiwan*
Marco Chiarandini, *University of Southern Denmark*
Francisco Chicano, *University of Malaga*
Raymond Chiong, *Swinburne University of Technology*
Darren Chitty, *QinetiQ*
Hwan-Gue Cho, *Pusan University*
Siang Yew Chong, *University of Nottingham*
Prabhas Chongstitvatana, *Chulalongkorn University*
David Johan Christensen, *Technical University of Denmark, Denmark*
Dominique Chu, *University of Kent, UK*
Chung-Yao Chuang, *Institute of Information Science, Academia Sinica, Taiwan*
Vic Ciesielski, *RMIT University*
Ozer Ciftcioglu
Christopher D. Clack, *University College London*
John Andrew Clark, *University of York*
Eddie Clemente, *CICESE*
Maurice Clerc, *Independent Consultant*
Jeff Clune, *Cornell University*
Leandro Coelho, *Pontifical Catholic University of Parana*
Carlos A. Coello Coello, *CINVESTAV-IPN*
Myra Cohen, *University of Nebraska-Lincoln*
Mitch K. Colby, *Oregon State University*
Pierre Collet, *LIL-ULCO*
J. Manuel Colmenar, *Complutense University of Madrid*
Simon Colton, *Imperial College London*
Clare Bates Congdon, *University of Southern Maine*
Philippa Conmy, *University of York*
Brian D. Connelly, *Michigan State University*
Ademir Constantino
Oscar Cordon, *European Centre for Soft Computing*
David Corne, *Heriot-Watt University*
Lino António Costa, *University of Minho*
Carlos Cotta, *University of Málaga*
Peter Cowling, *University of Bradford*
Bart G.W. Craenen, *University of Birmingham*
David Cuesta, *Complutense University*
Wei Cui, *University College Dublin*
Xiaohui Cui, *Oak Ridge National Laboratory*
Ronan Cummins, *National University of Ireland, Galway*

Dara Curran, *Cork Constraint Computation Centre*
Sylvain Cussat-Blanc, *University of Toulouse*
Keshav Dahal
Palle Dahlstedt, *University of Gothenburg & Chalmers University of Technology*
David B. D'Ambrosio, *University of Central Florida*
Angan Das, *Intel*
Swagatam Das, *Jadavpur University*
Rituparna Datta, *IIT Kanpur*
Cornforth David, *PC Member*
Jesica de Armas, *University of La Laguna*
Ivanoe De Falco, *ICAR - CNR*
Kenneth De Jong, *George Mason University*
Luis Gerardo de la Fraga, *CINVESTAV*
Luis de la Ossa
Anthony G. Deakin, *University of Liverpool*
Kalyanmoy Deb, *Indian Institute of Technology Kanpur*
Kusum Deep, *Indian Institute of Technology*
Gabriele D'Eleuterio, *University of Toronto*
Antonio Della Cioppa, *Natural Computation Lab - DIIIE, University of Salerno*
Ian Dempsey, *UCD/Virtu Financial Ireland*
Eelco den Heijer, *Vrije Universiteit*
Clarisse Dhaenens, *LIFL / CNRS / INRIA*
Saxena Dhish
Medha Dhurandhar, *Centre for Dev. of Advanced Computing*
Gianni Di Caro, *IDSIA*
Luca Di Gaspero, *University of Udine*
Giovanna Di Marzo Serugendo, *Birkbeck, University of London*
Ezequiel Di Paolo, *Ikerbasque - University of the Basque Country*
Massimiliano Di Penta, *RCOST - University of Sannio*
Ada Diaconescu, *Telecom ParisTech*
Peter Dittrich, *Friedrich-Schiller-Universität Jena*
Federico Divina, *Universidad Pablo de Olavide*
Karl F. Doerner, *University of Vienna*
Benjamin Doerr, *MPI Saarbruecken*
Stéphane Doncieux, *ISIR/UPMC*
Marco Dorigo, *IRIDIA, Université Libre de Bruxelles*
Alan Dorin, *Monash University*
Bernabe Dorronsoro, *University of Luxembourg*
Rene Doursat, *Institut des Systemes Complexes, CNRS*
León Dozal, *CICESE*
Scott Draves, *Electric Sheep*
Moshe Dror, *University of Arizona*
Jan Drugowitsch, *École normale supérieure*
Hai-Bin DUAN, *Beihang University*
Frederick Ducatelle, *IDSIA*
Peter Duerr, *EPFL*
Dan Dumitrescu
Yves Duthen, *Universite Toulouse 1 Capitole*
Marc Ebner, *Ernst-Moritz-Universitat Greifswald, Germany*
Narayanan Unny Edakunni, *University of Bristol*
Todd Edwards, *Vanderbilt Medical Center*
Peter Eggenberger Hotz
Jeroen Eggermont, *Leiden University Medical Center*
Aniko Ekart, *Aston University*
Neil Eklund, *GE Global Research*
Mohammed El-Abd, *American University of Kuwait*
Alice Eldridge, *University of the Arts London*
Mohammed El-Sharkawi
Michael T. M. Emmerich, *LIACS*
Andries P. Engelbrecht, *University of Pretoria*
Margaret J. Eppstein, *University of Vermont*
Anton V. Eremeev, *Omsk Branch of Sobolev Institute of Mathematics*
Daryl Essam, *UNSW@ADFA*
Lutton Evelyne, *INRIA Saclay*
Richard Everson, *University of Exeter*
Patrick Fan, *Virginia Tech*
Zhun Fan, *Tongji University, Shanghai, China*
Muddassar Farooq, *National University of Computer and Emerging Sciences*
Robert Feldt, *Chalmers University of Technology*
Thomas Fench, *University of Edinburgh*
Serge Fenet, *Université Lyon 1*
Carlos Fernandes, *Universidad de Granada*
Francisco Fernández de Vega, *Universidad de Extremadura*
Antonio J. Fernández Leiva, *University of Málaga*
Paola Festa, *Universitá degli Studi di Napoli*
Álvaro Fialho, *Nokia Institute of Technology*
Jonathan Edward Fieldsend, *University of Exeter*
Jose Figueira, *Instituto Superior Técnico*
Bogdan Filipic, *Jozef Stefan Institute*
Steffen Finck, *ESEP*
Ilias Flaounas, *University of Bristol*
Peter Fleming, *PCMEMBER*

James Foley, *Georgia Tech*
Gianluigi Folino, *ICAR-CNR*
James A. Foster, *University of Idaho*
Maria Auxiliadora Franco Gaviria, *University of Nottingham*
Gordon Fraser, *University of Saarland*
Regina Frei, *Cranfield University*
Bernd Freisleben, *Universität Marburg*
Alex A. Freitas, *University of Kent*
Tobias Friedrich, *Max-Planck-Institut Informatik*
Charlie Frowd, *University of Central Lancashire*
Alex Fukunaga, *University of Tokyo*
Matteo Gagliolo, *VUB*
Philip Galanter, *Texas A&M University*
Marcus R. Gallagher, *University of Queensland*
Edgar Galvan, *Trinity College Dublin*
Leo Galway, *University of Ulster*
Luca Maria Gambardella, *IDSIA*
José A. Gamez, *Universidad de Castilla-La Mancha*
Xavier Gandibleux, *Université de Nantes*
Yang Gao, *Nanjing University*
Maribel Garcia Arenas, *University of Granada*
Carlos García-Martínez, *University of Córdoba*
Vahid Garousi, *University of Calgary*
Josep Maria Garrell-Guiu, *La Salle - Ramon Llull University*
Deon Garrett, *Icelandic Institute for Intelligent Machines*
Antonio Gaspar-Cunha, *University of Minho*
Marco Gaudesi, *Politecnico di Torino*
Zong Woo Geem, *iGlobal University*
Michel Gendreau, *École Polytechnique de Montréal*
Monica Gentili, *University of Salerno*
Carlos Gershenson, *Universidad Nacional Autonoma de Mexico*
Osvaldo Gervasi, *University of Perugia*
Marian Gheorghe, *University of Sheffield, UK*
Mario Giacobini, *University of Torino*
Jean-Louis Giavitto, *CNRS - IRCAM, UPMC, Inria*
Acampora Giovanni, *University of Salerno*
Raul Giraldez Rojo, *Pablo de Olavide University of Seville*
Tobias Glasmachers, *IDSIA*
Chi Keong Goh, *National University of Singapore*
Marco César Goldbarg, *Universidade Federal do Rio Grande do Norte*
Brian W. Goldman, *Missouri University of Science and Technology*
Juan A. Gomez-Pulido, *University of Extremadura*
Juan Ramon Gonzalez Gonzalez, *University of Granada*
Erik Goodman, *Michigan State University*
Jose Luis Gordillo, *ITESM Monterrey*
Jens Gottlieb, *SAP AG*
Jörn Grahl, *University of Mainz*
Uli Grasemann, *UT Austin*
Marde Greeff, *Council for Scientific and Industrial Research, South Africa*
Casey Greene, *Princeton University*
Gary Greenfield, *University of Richmond*
David Greiner, *Universidad de Las Palmas de Gran Canaria*
Roderich Gross, *The University of Sheffield*
Paul Grouchy, *University of Toronto Institute for Aerospace Studies*
Yann-Gael Guéhéneuc, *École Polytechnique de Montréal*
Frederic Guinand
Michael Guntsch, *Eurobios*
Steven Gustafson, *GE Global Research*
Gregory Gutin, *Royal Holloway,University of London*
Walter J. Gutjahr, *University of Vienna*
Evert Haasdijk, *VU University Amsterdam*
Johan Hagelbäck, *Blekinge Tekniska Högskola*
Jennifer S. Hallinan, *Newcastle University*
Heiko Hamann, *University of Graz*
Lutz Hamel
Ali Hamzeh, *Shiraz University*
Hisashi Handa, *Okayama University*
Julia Handl, *University of Manchester*
Nikolaus Hansen, *INRIA Saclay*
Jin-Kao Hao, *University of Angers*
Simon Harding, *IDSIA*
Paul Harmer, *Air Force Institute of Technology*
Emma Hart, *Napier University*
William Hart, *Sandia National Laboratories*
Inman Harvey, *University of Sussex*
Geir Hasle, *SINTEF*
Erin Hastings, *University of Central Florida*
Sabine Hauert, *MIT*
Mark W. Hauschild, *University of Missouri-St. Louis*
Jun He, *University of Wales, Aberystwyth*

Robert B. Heckendorn, *University of Idaho*
Verena Heidrich-Meisner
Erik Hemberg, *UCD*
Hadi Hemmati, *Queen's University, Canada*
Tim Hendtlass, *Swinburne University of Technology*
Daniel Eduardo Hernandez, *CICESE*
Hugo Hernandez, *Technical University of Catalonia*
Benjamín Hernández, *Universidad Nacional Autónoma de México*
Arturo Hernández-Aguirre, *Centre for Research in Mathematics*
Alfredo G. Hernández-Díaz, *Pablo de Olavide University*
Francisco Herrera, *University of Granada*
Malcolm Heywood, *Dalhousie University*
J. Ignacio Hidalgo, *Complutense University of Madrid*
Ronald Hochreiter, *WU Vienna University of Economics and Business*
Tim Hohm, *University of Lausanne*
Ekaterina Holdener, *Exegy, Inc.*
Kenneth Holladay, *Southwest Research Institute*
John Holmes, *University of Pennsylvania*
Amy K. Hoover, *University of Central Florida*
Jeffrey Horn, *Northern Michigan University*
Gregory S. Hornby, *UC Santa Cruz*
Gerard Howard, *University of the West of England*
Bin Hu, *Technische Universität Wien*
Jianjun Hu, *University of South Carolina*
Ting Hu, *Dartmouth College*
Evan J. Hughes, *Cranfield University*
Phil Husbands, *Sussex University*
Frank Hutter, *UBC*
Matthew R. Hyde, *University of Nottingham*
Hitoshi Iba, *University of Tokyo*
Christian Igel, *University of Copenhagen*
Fumiya Iida, *ETH Zurich*
Takashi Ikegami, *University of Tokyo*
Iñaki Inza, *University of the Basque Country*
Pedro Isasi
Hisao Ishibuchi, *Osaka Prefecture University*
Juhos Istvan, *University of Szeged*
David Jackson, *University of Liverpool*
Cezary Z. Janikow, *UMSL*
Thomas Jansen, *University College Cork*
Mark Jelasity, *University of Szeged, Hungary*
Swan Jerry, *University of Nottingham, UK*
Yue Jia, *University College London*
Yaochu Jin, *University of Surrey*
Daniel Johannsen, *Tel Aviv University*
Stefan Johansson, *Blekinge Tekniska Högskola*
András Joó, *Sapientia University, Romania*
Laetitia Jourdan, *INRIA Lille Nord Europe*
Reyes Juarez, *UABC*
Bryant Arthur Julstrom, *St. Cloud State University*
Muhammad Bilal Junaid, *FAST National University of Computer & Emerging Sciences (NUCES)*
Andy Keane, *University of Southampton*
Maarten Keijzer, *Chordiant Software Inc.*
Markus Kemmerling, *TU Dortmund*
Graham Kendall, *University of Nottingham*
James Kennedy, *US Bureau of Labor Statistics*
Stefan Kern, *GE Global Research*
Didier Keymeulen, *NASA-Jet Propulsion Laboratory / CalTech*
Evan Kirshenbaum, *HP Labs*
Ronald Klazar, *University of Pretoria*
Joshua D. Knowles, *University of Manchester*
Gary Kochenberger, *University of Colorado*
Mario Koeppen, *Kyushu Institute of Technology*
Nate Kohl, *University of Texas at Austin*
Maciej Komosinski, *Poznan University of Technology*
Oliver Korb, *Cambridge Crystallographic Data Centre*
Bogdan Korel, *Illinois Institute of Technology*
Timo Kötzing, *MPI-INF*
Tim Kovacs, *University of Bristol*
Taras Kowaliw, *ISC-PIF, CNRS*
Oliver Kramer, *University of Dortmund*
Jozef Kratica, *Serbian Academy of Sciences and Arts*
Krzysztof Krawiec, *Poznan University of Technology*
Johannes Kruisselbrink, *LIACS Leiden University*
Jiri Kubalik, *CTU Prague*
Saku Kukkonen
Joerg Laessig
Gary Byron Lamont, *AF Institute of Technology*
Jouni Lampinen, *University of Vaasa*
Dario Landa-Silva, *University of Nottingham*
Leo H. Langenhoven, *University of Pretoria*
Pier Luca Lanzi, *Politecnico di Milano*
Adriana Lara, *CINVESTAV-IPN*
Pedro Larranaga, *Technical University of Madrid*
Antonio LaTorre, *Universidad Politécnica de Madrid*

Pierrick Legrand, *Université Bordeaux*
Guillermo Leguizamon, *Universidad Nacional de San Luis*
Per Kristian Lehre, *University of Nottingham*
Kenji Leibnitz, *Osaka University, Japan*
Coromoto Leon
Erwan Lepennec
Paul Anton Letnes, *Norwegian University of Science and Technology*
Kwong Sak Leung, *The Chinese University of Hong Kong*
Matthew Lewis, *Ohio State University*
Hui Li, *Xi'an Jiaotong University*
Jingpeng Li, *University of Nottingham*
Xiaodong Li, *RMIT University*
Claudio M. F. Lima, *University of Algarve*
Steffen Limmer, *University Erlangen*
Sean Lineaweaver, *Cochlear LTD.*
Alain Lioret, *Université Paris 8*
Piotr Lipinski, *University of Wroclaw*
Xavier Llorà, *Google Inc.*
Daniel Lobo, *Tufts University*
Fernando G. Lobo, *University of Algarve*
Gisele Lobo Pappa, *Federal University of Minas Gerais - UFMG*
Daniele Loiacono, *Politecnico di Milano*
Michael Lones, *University of York*
Moshe Looks, *Google*
Heitor S. Lopes, *UTFPR, Brazil*
Eunice Lopez-Camacho, *ITESM*
Manuel López-Ibáñez, *IRIDIA, Université Libre de Bruxelles*
Antonio López-Jaimes, *Centro de Investigación y de Estudios Avanzados (CINVESTAV)*
Jose A. Lozano, *University of the Basque Country*
Manuel Lozano, *University of Granada*
Simon Lucas, *University of Essex*
Martin Lukasiewycz, *TU Munich*
Sean Luke, *George Mason University*
Francisco Luna, *University of Málaga*
Rodica Ioana Lung, *Babes-Bolyai University*
Gabriel Luque, *University of Malaga*
Shingo Mabu, *Waseda University*
Penousal Machado, *University of Coimbra*
Nuria Macia, *ETSEEI La Salle, Universitat Ramon Llull*
Demetrio Macias, *Université de technologie de Troyes*
Ana Maria Madureira, *Institute of Engineering - Polytechnic Institute of Porto*
Domenico Maisto, *National Research Council of Italy (ICAR–CNR)*
Abhinav Malhotra, *NSIT*
Marco Mamei, *Universita degli Studi di Modena e Reggio Emilia*
Spiros Mancoridis, *Drexel University*
Bernard Kamiel Manderick, *Vrije Universiteit Brussel*
Gong Maoguo, *Xidian University*
Elena Marchiori
Yannis Marinakis
Dietmar Maringer, *University of Basel*
Robert E. Marmelstein, *East Stroudsburg University, USA*
Luis Martí, *Universidad Carlos III de Madrid*
Hector P. Martinez, *IT-Universitet i København*
Ivette C. Martinez, *Universidad Simon Bolivar*
Igor V. Maslov, *EvoCo Inc.*
Schillaci Massimiliano, *MGTech S.r.l.*
Shouichi Matsui, *SERL, CRIEPI*
Nicolini Matteo, *University of Udine*
Jorge Maturana, *Universidad Austral de Chile*
Helmut A. Mayer, *University of Salzburg*
John McCall, *IDEAS Research Institute*
James McDermott, *Massachusetts Institute of Technology*
Sean McGarraghy, *University College Dublin*
Bob McKay, *Seoul National University*
Brett McKinney, *University of Tulsa*
Bruce McLennan, *University of Tennessee*
Phil McMinn
Barry McMullin, *Dublin City University, Ireland*
Nicholas Freitag McPhee, *University of Minnesota, Morris*
Jorn Mehnen, *Cranfield University*
David Meignan, *University of Osnabrück*
Alexander Melkozerov, *Tomsk State University of Control Systems and Radioelectronics*
Drew Mellor
Rui Mendes, *CCTC/UM*
Eugenio Mendez, *CICESE*
Alexander Mendiburu, *The University of the Basque Country*
Juan-Julián Merelo-Guervós, *Dept. ATC-UGR*

Daniel Merkle, *University of Southern Denmark*
Ryan J. Meuth, *University of Advancing Technology*
Silja Meyer-Nieberg, *Universitaet der Bundeswehr Muenchen*
Efrén Mezura-Montes, *LANIA*
Zapf Michael
Olivier Michel, *LACL - U-PEC*
Martin Middendorf, *University of Leipzig*
Kaisa Miettinen, *University of Jyvaskyla*
Risto Miikkulainen, *The University of Texas at Austin*
Mitsunori Miki, *Doshisha University*
Ali Minai, *University of Cincinnati*
Luis Miramontes Hercog, *Self-Organizing Solutions*
Mustafa Misir, *KAHO Sint-Lieven - K.U. Leuven*
George Mitchell, *CCKF Ltd*
Kenji Mizuguchi, *National Institute of Biomedical Innovation*
Eric Mjolsness, *UC Irvine*
Hans Jonas Fossum Moen, *Norwegian Defence Research Establishment*
Chilukuri K. Mohan, *Syracuse University*
Julian Molina, *University of Malaga*
Nicolas Monmarche, *University of Tours*
David Montana, *BBN Technologies*
Jean-Marc Montanier, *Université Paris-Sud*
Marco A. Montes de Oca, *IRIDIA, Université Libre de Bruxelles*
Antonio Mora, *Dpto. Arquitectura y Tecnología de Computadores*
Pablo Moscato, *Hunter Medical Research Institute*
Sanaz Mostaghim, *Karlsruhe Institute of Technology*
Alison Motsinger, *North Carolina State University*
Jean-Baptiste Mouret, *ISIR - UPMC/CNRS*
Christian Lorenz Müller, *ETH Zurich*
Christine Lesley Mumford, *Cardiff University*
Masaharu Munetomo, *Hokkaido University*
Jorge Munoz, *Universidad Carlos III de Madrid*
Spencer Muse, *North Carolina State University*
Nysret Musliu, *Vienna University of Technology*
Yuichi Nagata, *Tokyo Institute of Technology*
Boris Naujoks, *Cologne University of Applied Sciences*
Antonio Nebro, *University of Málaga*
Chrystopher L. Nehaniv, *University of Hertfordshire*
Juan Neirotti, *Aston University, United Kingdom*
Ferrante Neri, *University of Jyväskylä*
Frank Neumann, *University of Adelaide*
Hoai Nguyen Xuan, *Hanoi University, Vietnam*
Giuseppe Nicosia, *University of Catania*
Julio Cesar Nievola, *PUCPR*
Yusuke Nojima, *Osaka Prefecture University*
Ann Nowe, *Vrije Universiteit Brussel*
Mel Ó Cinnéide, *National University of Ireland, Dublin*
Gabriela Ochoa, *University of Nottingham*
Charles Ofria, *Michigan State University*
Rehan O'Grady, *IRIDIA, Universite Libre de Bruxelles*
Choong Kun Oh, *U.S. Naval Research Laboratory*
Toby O'Hara, *University of the West of England*
Gustavo Olague, *CICESE*
Markus Olhofer, *Honda Research Institute Europe GmbH*
Pedro N. F. P. Oliveira, *University of Minho*
Pietro S. Oliveto, *University of Birmingham*
Tomasz Oliwa, *The University of Georgia*
Mohammed Omran, *Gulf University for Science & Technology*
Michael O'Neill, *University College Dublin*
Yew-Soon Ong, *Nanyang Technological University*
Colm O'Riordan, *NUI, Galway*
Michael Orlov, *Ben-Gurion University*
Albert Orriols-Puig
Julio Ortega, *PES PC Member*
Lisa Osadciw, *Syracuse University*
Conall O'Sullivan, *University College Dublin*
Ender Ozcan, *University of Nottingham*
Norman Packard
Nikhil Padhye, *IIT Kanpur*
Michael E. Palmer, *Stanford University*
Luis Paquete, *University of Coimbra*
Andrew J. Parkes, *University of Nottingham, UK*
Victor Parque, *Waseda University*
Konstantinos Parsopoulos, *University of Ioannina*
Chandana Paul, *Harvard University*
Castillo Pedro, *UGR*
Martin Pelikan, *University of Missouri in St. Louis*
Paola Pellegrini, *IRIDIA-CoDE ULB*
David Pelta, *University of Granada*
Jorge Peña, *University of Lausanne*
Jose-Maria Peña
Juan Peralta, *University Carlos III Madrid*

Francisco Baptista Pereira, *Instituto Superior de Engenharia de Coimbra*
Sanja Petrovic
Rolf Pfeifer, *University of Zurich*
Steve Phelps, *University of Essex, UK*
Andrew Philippides, *University of Sussex*
Clara Pizzuti, *ICAR National Research Council of Italy - CNR*
Daniel Polani, *University of Hertfordshire*
Silvia Poles, *EnginSoft*
Jordan Pollack, *Coevolution*
Carlo Poloni, *Esteco*
Petrica Pop, *North University of Baia Mare*
Elena Popovici, *Icosystem Corp.*
Petr Pošík, *Czech Technical University in Prague*
Walter Potter, *University of Georgia*
Simon Poulding, *University of York*
Richard J. Preen, *University of the West of England*
Steve Prestwich, *University College Cork*
Mike Preuss, *TU Dortmund*
Kenneth Price, *ESEP*
Christian Prins, *University of Technology of Troyes*
Adam Prugel-Bennett, *University of Southampton*
Przemyslaw Prusinkiewicz, *University of Calgary*
Jakob Puchinger, *AIT - Austrian Institute of Technology*
Cesar Puente, *Universidad Autónoma de San Luis Potosi*
Jose Miguel Puerta, *UCLM*
William F. Punch, *Michigan State University*
Rong Qu, *University of Nottingham*
Nguyen Quang Huy, *Singapore Institute of Manufacturing Technology*
M. Zubair Rafique, *King Saud University*
Günther R. Raidl, *Vienna University of Technology*
Helena Ramalhinho-Lourenço, *Universitat Pompeu Fabra*
Marcus Christian Randall, *Bond University*
Ranji S. Ranjithan, *North Carolina State Univ*
Steen Rasmussen
Tapabrata Ray, *School of Aerospace, Civil and Mechanical Engineering*
Tom Ray, *University of Oklahoma*
Patrick Michael Reed, *Pennsylvania State University*
David Reif, *U.S. Environmental Protection Agency*
Alan Reynolds
Craig Reynolds, *Sony Computer Entertainment*
Phill Kyu Rhee, *Inha University, Korea*
J. Neal Richter, *Rubicon Project*
John Rieffel, *Tufts University*
Marylyn Ritchie, *Penn State University*
Wille Robert, *University of Bremen*
Denis Robilliard, *Univ Lille-Nord de France*
Daniel Rodriguez, *The University of Alcala*
Daniel Roggen, *ETH Zurich*
Philipp Rohlfshagen, *University of Essex*
Andrea Roli, *Alma Mater Studiorum Universita di Bologna*
Marc Roper, *University of Strathclyde*
Brian J. Ross, *Brock University*
Peter M. Ross, *Napier University*
Franz Rothlauf, *University of Mainz*
Jonathan Rowe, *University of Birmingham*
Rajkumar Roy, *Cranfield University*
Guenter Rudolph, *TU Dortmund University*
Sarker Ruhul, *University of New South Wales*
Conor Ryan, *University of Limerick*
Ramon Sagarna, *University of the Basque Country*
Erol Sahin
Sancho Salcedo-Sanz, *Universidad de Alcala*
Michael Sampels, *Université Libre de Bruxelles*
Ernesto Sanchez, *Politecnico di Torino*
Luciano Sanchez, *Universidad de Oviedo*
Rian Sanderson, *Carnegie Mellon West*
Roberto Santana, *University of the Basque Country (UPV/EHU)*
Luis Vicente Santana-Quintero, *George Mason University*
Iván Santibáñez Koref, *Technical Univ. Berlin*
Hiroyuki Sato, *The University of Electro-Communications*
Yuji Sato, *Hosei University*
Fredéric Saubion, *University of Angers, France*
Hideyuki Sawada, *Kagawa University, Japan*
Daniel Sawitzki, *Nevigo GmbH, Bochum*
Hiroki Sayama, *SUNY Binghamton*
Andrea Schaerf, *University of Udine*
David Schaffer, *University of California, Berkeley*
Tom Schaul, *New York University*
Thomas Schmickl, *Karl-Franzens-Universitaet Graz*
Verena Schmid, *Universität Wien*
Marc Schoenauer, *INRIA Saclay*

Oliver Schuetze, *CINVESTAV-IPN*
Giovanni Sebastiani, *Sapienza University of Rome*
Carlos Segura, *Universidad de La Laguna*
Yann Semet, *yakaz.com*
Sandip Sen, *University of Tulsa*
Bernhard Sendhoff, *Honda Research Institute Europe*
Kevin Seppi, *Brigham Young University*
Martin Serpell, *University of the West of England*
Travis Service, *Vanderbilt University*
Marc Sevaux, *Université de Bretagne-Sud - Lab-STICC*
Kamran Shafi, *UNSW@ADFA*
Fatima Shaheen, *Loughborough University*
Siddhartha Shakya, *Business Modelling & Operational Transformation Practice, BT*
Jonathan Lee Shapiro, *University of Manchester*
Wei-Min Shen, *University of Southern California*
Yang Shengxiang, *Brunel University*
Yuhui Shi
Patrick Siarry, *University of Paris-Est Créteil*
Rodrigo Silva, *Universidade Federal de Minas Gerais*
Sara Silva, *INESC-ID Lisboa*
Anabela Simões, *DEIS/ISEC - Coimbra Polytechnic*
Harding Simon, *PES*
Martin Simonsen, *Aarhus University*
Moshe Sipper, *Ben-Gurion University*
Alexei N. Skurikhin, *Los Alamos National Laboratory*
Will Smart, *Victoria University of Wellington*
Alice Smith, *Auburn University*
Jim Smith, *University of the West of England*
Robert E. Smith, *UCL*
Stephen Leslie Smith, *University of York*
Christine Solnon, *LIRIS, University of Lyon 1*
Andy Song, *RMIT University*
Humberto Sossa, *Instituto Politécnico Nacional*
Jerffeson Souza, *State University of Ceara*
Lee Spector, *Hampshire College*
Giandomenico Spezzano, *ICAR-CNR*
Antoine Spicher, *Université Paris-Est Creteil*
Giovanni Squillero
Dipti Srinivasan, *National University of Singapore*
Patrick Oliver Stalph, *University of Tübingen*
Kenneth O. Stanley, *University of Central Florida*
Richard Stapenhurst, *University of Manchester*
Chris Stephens, *Instituto de Ciencias Nucleares, UNAM*
Susan Stepney, *University of York*
Adrian Stoica, *NASA-JPL*
Wolfgang Stolzmann, *Daimler AG*
Forrest Stonedahl, *Northwestern University*
Daniel W. Stouch, *Charles River Analytics*
Kasper Stoy, *University of Southern Denmark*
Umberto Straccia, *ISTI-CNR, Italy*
Juergen Stradner, *Univ. Graz, Austria*
Thomas Stützle, *Université Libre de Bruxelles*
Tatsuya Suda, *Consultant*
Dirk Sudholt, *University of Sheffield*
YI Sun, *IDSIA*
Reiji Suzuki
Gabriel Synnaeve, *INRIA LIG (Grenoble) and Collège de France LPPA (Paris)*
Keiki Takadama, *UEC*
El-Ghazali Talbi, *INRIA*
KC Tan, *NUS*
Ying Tan, *Peking University*
Kiyoshi Tanaka, *Shinshu University*
Ivan Tanev, *Doshisha University*
Ke Tang, *University of Science and Technology of China*
Ernesto Tarantino, *ICAR - CNR*
Daniel Tauritz, *Missouri University of Science and Technology*
Jorge Tavares, *University of Coimbra*
Tim Taylor, *Goldsmiths, University of London*
Jürgen Teich, *University of Erlangen-Nuremberg*
Hugo Terashima Marín, *ITESM - CSI*
German Terrazas Angulo, *University of Nottingham*
Andrea G. B. Tettamanzi, *Università degli Studi di Milano*
Christof Teuscher, *Portland State University*
Fabien Teytaud, *University of Paris-Dauphine / HEC Paris, CNRS*
Olivier Teytaud, *INRIA*
Lothar Thiele, *ETH Zurich*
Dirk Thierens, *Universiteit Utrecht*
Adrian Thompson, *University of Sussex*
Tricia Thornton-Wells, *Vanderbilt Medical Center*
Jonathan Timmis, *University of York*
Chuan-Kang Ting, *National Chung Cheng University*
Ashutosh Tiwari, *Cranfield University*
Santosh Tiwari, *Vanderplaats Research & Development Inc.*

Peter M. Todd, *Indiana University*
Julian Togelius, *IT University of Copenhagen*
Michael Tolley, *GDS*
Marco Tomassini, *University of Lausanne*
Alberto Paolo Tonda, *Politecnico di Torino*
Alexander Topchy, *Nielsen Media Research*
Jim Torresen, *University of Oslo*
Gregorio Toscano-Pulido, *Cinvestav-Tamaulipas*
Heike Trautmann, *TU Dortmund, Germany*
Martin Trefzer,
Vito Trianni, *ISTC-CNR*
Leonardo Trujillo, *Instituto Tecnológico de Tijuana*
Elio Tuci, *Aberystwyth University*
Gunnar Tufte, *NTNU*
Cem Celal Tutum, *Technical University of Denmark*
Jamie Twycross, *University of Nottingham*
Man Chon U, *The University of Georgia*
Shmuel Ur, *Ur Innovation*
Ryan Urbanowicz, *GBML-Track*
Neil Urquhart, *Edinburgh Napier University*
A. Sima Uyar, *Istanbul Technical University*
Frans van den Bergh, *Meraka, CSIR, South Africa*
H. Jaap Van den Herik, *Tilburg University*
Leonardo Vanneschi, *University of Milano-Bicocca*
Igor Vatolkin, *TU Dortmund*
Kalyan Veeramachaneni, *MIT*
Sebastian Ventura, *Universidad de Cordoba*
Sebastien Verel, *university of Nice Sophia Antipolis*
Alessandro Vespignani,
Francisco J. Vico, *Universidad de Malaga*
Paul Vogt, *Tilburg University*
Christoph von der Malsburg, *Goethe University Frankfurt am Main*
Tanja Vos, *Universidad Politecnica de Valencia*
Michael Vose, *University of Tennessee, Knoxville*
Michael N. Vrahatis, *University of Patras*
Markus Wagner, *The University of Adelaide*
Naoki Wakamiya, *Osaka University*
Antony Waldock, *BAE Systems*
James Alfred Walker, *University of York*
Paul Walsh, *Cork Institute of Technology*
Ray Walshe, *Dublin City University*
Jean-Paul Watson, *Sandia National Laboratories*
Richard A. Watson, *University of Southampton*
Karsten Weicker, *HTWK Leipzig*
Thomas Weise, *University of Science and Technology of China (USTC)*
Justin Werfel, *Harvard University*
Peter Alexander Whigham, *University of Otago*
Ronald Lyndon While, *The University of Western Australia*
David White, *University of Glasgow*
Tony White, *Carleton University*
Darrell Whitley, *Colorado State University*
R. Paul Wiegand, *Institute for Simulation and Training / UCF*
Janet Wiles, *The University of Queensland*
Josh Wilkerson, *Missouri University of Science and Technology*
Tiffani L. Williams, *Texas A&M University*
Garnett C. Wilson, *Memorial University of Newfoundland*
Stewart W. Wilson, *Prediction Dynamics*
Alan F. T. Winfield, *University of the West of England*
Stephan Winkler, *Upper Austrian University of Applied Sciences*
Carola Winzen, *Max-Planck-Institut fuer Informatik*
Carsten Witt, *Technical University of Denmark*
M. L. Dennis Wong, *Xi'an Jiaotong-Liverpool University*
Man Leung Wong, *Lingnan University, Hong Kong*
John Woodward, *Nottingham University*
Jonathan Wright, *Loughborough University*
Borys Wrobel, *Adam Mickiewicz University*
Annie S. Wu, *University of Central Florida*
Zheng Yi Wu, *Bentley Systems*
Rolf Wurtz, *Ruhr-Universitaet Bochum*
Huayang Xie, *Victoria University of Wellington*
Takeshi Yamada, *NTT Communication Science Labs.*
Lidia Yamamoto, *University of Strasbourg*
Masayuki Yamamura, *Tokyo Institute of Technology*
Weizhong Yan, *GE Global Research*
Georgios Yannakakis, *IT University of Copenhagen*
Zhang Yanqing, *Georgia State University*
Shin Yoo, *University College London*
Tian-Li Yu, *Taiwan Evolutionary Intelligence Lab*
Tina Yu, *Memorial University*
Daniela Zaharie, *West University of Timisoara*
Franco Zambonelli, *Universita degli Studi di Modena e Reggio Emilia*
Manuela Zanda, *Wellcome Trust Sanger Institute*

Saúl Zapotecas Martínez, *CINVESTAV-IPN*
Christine Zarges, *University of Warwick*
Andreas Zell
Zhu Zexuan
Byoung-Tak Zhang, *Seoul National University*
Mengjie Zhang, *Victoria University of Wellington*
Qingfu Zhang, *University of Essex*
Yi Zhang, *IESD, De Montfort University*
Yuanyuan Zhang, *University College London*
Ming-Jie Zhao, *University of Manchester*
Eckart Zitzler
Albert Zomaya

Is There a Computational Advantage to Representing Evaporation Rate in Ant Colony Optimization as a Gaussian Random Variable?

Ashraf M. Abdelbar
Dept. of Computer Science & Engineering
American University in Cairo
abdelbar@aucegypt.edu

ABSTRACT

We propose an ACO (Ant Colony Optimization) variation in which the evaporation rate, instead of being constant as is common in standard ACO algorithms, is a Gaussian random variable with non-negligible variance. In experimental results in the context of $\mathcal{MAX}$-$\mathcal{MIN}$ Ant System ($\mathcal{MM}$AS) and the Traveling Salesman Problem (TSP), we find that our variation performs considerably better than $\mathcal{MM}$AS when the number of iterations is small, and that its performance is slightly better than $\mathcal{MM}$AS when the number of iterations is large.

Categories and Subject Descriptors

I.2.8 [**Artificial Intelligence**]: Problem Solving, Control Methods, and Search—*Heuristic methods*

General Terms

Algorithms

Keywords

Ant Colony Optimization, Pheromone Decay

1. OVERVIEW

Ant Colony Optimization (ACO) algorithms [8, 9] are motivated by certain characteristics of the behavior of biological ants. The τ data structure, that is central to ACO algorithms, is a representation of the pheromone trails deposited by many species of ants. The evaporation step in the ACO paradigm is a representation of the physical evaporation process that occurs to biological pheromone trails. This evaporation step is typically implemented as a simple reduction by a fixed fraction ρ,

$$\tau_{ij} = \tau_{ij} \times (1 - \rho) , \quad (1)$$

where ρ is an external parameter called the *evaporation rate*.

Of course, in nature, the evaporation rate is not constant, but rather is dependent on myriad factors such as temperature, and humidity. A reasonable approximation, because of the Central Limit Theorem, might be to consider the evaporation rate to be a normal (Gaussian) random variable with mean ρ_m and variance ρ_s^2. Equation (1) can be considered a further approximation of this, where the variance is neglected, and the value of ρ_m is taken as the evaporation rate.

In this paper, we ask the question: might there be something to be gained performance-wise from treating the evaporation rate as a normal random variable with non-negligible variance instead of as a constant? In a set of experiments with $\mathcal{MAX}$-$\mathcal{MIN}$ Ant System applied to the traveling salesman problem (TSP), we find, perhaps surprisingly, that:

- Using a Gaussian evaporation rate with a fairly-high value of ρ_s, such as $\rho_s = 0.5$, can improve solution quality.
- This does not result in an increase in execution time, as the extra execution time spent generating Gaussian random numbers is offset by reductions in execution time in other parts of the algorithm.

2. BACKGROUND

Ant colony optimization (ACO) [8, 9] is a general-purpose biologically-motivated population-based discrete optimization paradigm.

In each iteration, each ant i generates a candidate solution x_i, and the set of solutions generated by all ants is used to update a central data structure, conventionally called τ, that can be thought of as representing the evolving collective wisdom of the group. The data structure τ is meant to model the pheromone trails deposited by biological ants. In generating its solution in a given iteration, each ant makes use of the τ data structure, and also makes use of a problem-dependent heuristic function η.

In the case of TSP, τ would be a two-dimensional $n \times n$ array, where n represents the number of cities; the entry τ_{ij} represents the extent to which the collective wisdom of the swarm is inclined towards edge e_{ij}. A common heuristic for TSP is for η_{ij} to simply represent the reciprocal of the distance d associated with the edge e_{ij}, i.e. $\eta_{ij} = 1/d(e_{ij})$.

A number of different algorithms [1, 3, 4, 6] have been introduced within the ACO paradigm. The following abstract skeleton describes most of these algorithms for a static combinatorial optimization problem such as the TSP:

Initialization
`while` (*termination criteria not reached*) do
SolutionConstruction
LocalSearch // optional
PheromoneUpdate

The different ACO algorithms that have been studied are generally similar in the **SolutionConstruction** step, and mostly differ in the **PheromoneUpdate** step. One of the earliest ACO algorithms was Ant System (AS) [7], and one of the currently best-performing ACO algorithms is $\mathcal{MAX}$-$\mathcal{MIN}$ Ant System ($\mathcal{MM}$AS) [14, 15]. Below, we expand some of the algorithmic skeleton given above for $\mathcal{MM}$AS in the context of TSP. For a fuller presentation of $\mathcal{MM}$AS, the reader is directed to [8].

SolutionConstruction: For each ant k, construct a tour $\mathcal{S}_k$ by adding one edge at a time until a full tour is constructed. We always maintain a current city i (starting off with a random choice of the first city), and, repeatedly, we choose the next edge e_{ij} to add to $\mathcal{S}_k$ from the feasible domain set $\mathcal{D}_i^{(k)}$, where $\mathcal{D}_i^{(k)}$ is the set of edges in which city i participates, excluding any edge connecting i to a city that has already been visited (because of the Hamiltonian cycle constraint). Once an edge e_{ij} is added to the solution, the city j then becomes the new current city and the process repeats. For the current city i:

$$\Pr\left[e_{ij} \in S_k^t\right] = \frac{[\tau_{ij}]^\alpha \cdot [\eta_{ij}]^\beta}{\sum_{h\in\mathcal{D}_i^{(k)}} [\tau_{ih}]^\alpha \cdot [\eta_{ih}]^\beta} \quad \text{for } j \in \mathcal{D}_i^{(k)} . \quad (2)$$

Thus, the probability that the edge e_{ij} is included in $\mathcal{S}_k$ is proportional to the product of the two terms of the numerator. As discussed earlier, the value τ_{ij} represents the extent to which the past experience of the colony indicates it is a good idea to include the edge e_{ij}, and η_{ij} represents a problem-dependent heuristic function that indicates the intrinsic "goodness" of the edge e_{ij}. The two parameters α and β are used to adjust the relative emphases of the two terms.

A commonly-used [8] implementation tradeoff is to precompute for each city, the set of its r nearest neighbors (where r is typically a value between 15 and 40), and then to restrict the feasible domain $\mathcal{D}_i^{(k)}$ in Equation (2) to city i's r nearest neighbors. If all r nearest neighbors have already been visited, the choice is made from the entire set of unvisited set. The reader is directed to [8] for more information.

LocalSearch. Once each ant has constructed a complete tour $\mathcal{S}_k$, it can optionally run a local-search procedure to improve the tour before proceeding to the next step. A common local search procedure for TSP is 2-opt, in which all tours that can be obtained from $\mathcal{S}_k$ by exchanging 2 edges are exhaustively considered.

PheromoneUpdate. The τ array is then updated to integrate the experience gained from the solutions constructed into the collective wisdom of the colony. First, every entry in the τ array is reduced by an evaporation parameter ρ, as described by Equation (1):

$$\tau_{ij} = \tau_{ij} \times (1 - \rho) .$$

The τ array is then updated by a solution $\mathcal{S}_{\hat{k}}$, where depending on the implementation, $\mathcal{S}_{\hat{k}}$ is either the best solution found so far in the history of the colony (called the "global-best" option) or the best solution found by an ant in the current iteration (called the "iteration-best" option).

Finally, in $\mathcal{MM}$AS, each τ_{ij} entry in the τ array is forced to be in the range $[\tau_{min}, \tau_{max}]$ by applying:

$$\tau_{ij} = \begin{cases} \tau_{max} & \text{if } \tau_{ij} > \tau_{max} \\ \tau_{ij} & \text{if } \tau_{min} \le \tau_{ij} \le \tau_{max} \\ \tau_{min} & \text{if } \tau_{ij} < \tau_{min} \end{cases} , \quad (3)$$

where τ_{min} and τ_{max} are two heuristically-set parameters. The purpose of these limits is to control the extent to which the collective wisdom of the colony is allowed to be biased towards or against a particular solution component.

3. GAUSSIAN RANDOM EVAPORATION

In this paper, we focus on the pheromone evaporation step described in the previous section. Equation (1) is used by most ACO algorithms, including Ant System, $\mathcal{MAX}$-$\mathcal{MIN}$ Ant System ($\mathcal{MM}$AS), and many others. As discussed in Section 1, this step is a representation of the physical reality that pheromone trails left by biological ants evaporate over time. In nature, the evaporation rate depends on many factors that are difficult to model precisely. A reasonable approximation, because of the Central Limit Theorem, might be to describe evaporation rate as a normal (Gaussian) random variable $\mathcal{N}(\rho_m, \rho_s)$, with mean ρ_m and variance ρ_s^2.

A rougher but computationally-faster approximation would be to neglect the variance (i.e. take ρ_s as zero) and simply treat evaporation rate as a constant. As mentioned above, this is the approach that is used in existing ACO methods.

In this paper, we ask the question: might there be a performance gain to be expected from representing evaporation rate as a Gaussian random variable? Further, will this result in an increase in run-time because of the computational cost of generating Gaussian random numbers? We will address these questions in Section 4.

In summary, what we are proposing is that Equation (1), repeated here for convenience,

$$\tau_{ij} = \tau_{ij} \cdot (1 - \rho) ,$$

be replaced by:

$$\tau_{ij} = \tau_{ij} \cdot [1 - \mathsf{gauss}(\rho_m, \rho_s)] , \quad (4)$$

where $\mathsf{gauss}(a, b)$ is a Gaussian random number generator function with mean a and standard deviation b that returns a different Gaussian random number *every* time it is called. In other words, each entry in the τ array will be reduced by an evaporation factor that, instead of being constant for all entries, will be a random number centered around ρ_m, with the degree of dispersion determined by ρ_s.

If a particular value of ρ has been experimentally found to produce good results for a particular problem (e.g. $\rho = 0.2$ has been found to be a good default value for $\mathcal{MM}$AS applied to TSP [8]), we would recommend this value be used as ρ_m. The parameter ρ_s determines the level of variation of $\mathsf{gauss}(\rho_m, \rho_s)$. In the extreme, if $\rho_s = 0$, then the random generator will always return ρ_m, and our variation will reduce to the standard model. In general, because of elementary properties of the Gaussian distribution, about 95.5% of the generated random numbers will be within the range $\rho_m \pm 2\rho_s$.

Because the function **gauss** must be called for every τ array entry, for every ant, for every iteration, its implementation must be very efficient. We use the polar-form of the Box-Muller transform [2], as implemented in *Numerical Recipes* [12].

Table 1: General parameters for all experiments

Parameter	Value
α	1
β	2
ρ	0.2
length of nearest-neighbor list	25
type of local search	2-opt
number of ants	50

4. EXPERIMENTAL RESULTS

4.1 Experimental Setup

We evaluate Gaussian evaporation in the context of the traveling salesman problem, using problem instances from TSPLIB. The TSPLIB naming convention is that the number of cities in a problem instance is included in the instance name. For example, `pcb1173` is an instance with 1,173 cities, and `rl5934` is an instance with 5,934 cities. The global optimal solutions are known for all problems in the TSPLIB library. Therefore, in presenting our results in this paper, we will express solution cost as the percentage by which the TSP tour exceeds the optimal. For example, the optimal solution cost for `rl5934` is known to be 556,045. If we wish to report a solution cost of 558,500, this will be reported as being 1.23% in excess of the optimal.

In all experiments, when we report execution time, we refer to CPU execution time as measured by the Linux `getrusage` function. All experimental results were obtained on a 2.83 GHz Intel processor.

Our implementation is based on Thomas Stützle's `acotsp` implementation [13], which is the companion open-source software to the Dorigo and Stützle book [8]. In order to implement Gaussian evaporation, we did not need to modify or add more than 30 lines of code to `acotsp`. Our modified code is available at `http://aucegypt.edu/faculty/abdelbar/acotspv1.02.tar.gz`.

In Experiment A, we use seven TSP instances of varying size from TSPLIB. In the two main experiments, Experiments B and C, we use all TSPLIB instances with number of cities between 300 and 6,000, excluding only three instances whose format is not supported by `acotsp`.

With `acotsp`, we use the default values (based on the recommendations in [8]) for most of the parameters, as shown in Table 1. We set the number of ants to 50, and use `2-opt` local search, as implemented in `acotsp`. Recent work [11, 16] has explored on-line parameter adaptation schemes for $\mathcal{MM}$AS. However, we use static parameter settings in this paper since our purpose is to isolate the effect of Gaussian evaporation.

4.2 Experiment A

Table 2: Experimental Setup for Experiment A

Parameter	Value
Problem instances	7 instances
Values of ρ_s	11 values
Number of iterations	200
Number of trials	30

The objective of Experiment A is to find a good working value of the parameter ρ_s for $\mathcal{MM}$AS. We use seven problem instances of gradually increasing size, as shown in Table 3. We ran each instance for 30 trials for each value of ρ_s in the set $\{0.0, 0.05, 0.1, 0.2, 0.3, 0.4, 0.5, 0.6, 0.7, 0.8, 0.9\}$, running each trial for 200 iterations. Of course, setting $\rho_s = 0$ reduces to the standard model, and we use this as the control setting.

Table 2 provides a summary of the experimental setup for this experiment, and Table 3 shows the results. For each instance, and each value of ρ_s, the table shows the mean and standard deviation of the solution cost (denoted in the table as μ_c and σ_c, respectively), and the mean and standard deviation of the execution time (denoted in the table as μ_t and σ_t, respectively). We can see from the table that $\rho_s = 0.5$ is a good working value, and we use this as the default value in Experiments B and C. We also observe that:

- For all instances, the worst mean solution cost is obtained without Gaussian evaporation (i.e. $\rho_s = 0$).
- For all instances, most values of $\rho_s > 0$ produce smaller run-times than $\rho_s = 0$.

4.3 Experiment B

Table 4: Experimental Setup for Experiment B

Parameter	Value
Problem instances	41 instances (as listed in Table 5)
Value of ρ_s	{ 0.0, 0.5 }
Number of iterations	200
Number of trials	100

The purpose of this experiment is to evaluate the performance of Gaussian evaporation, using the default value of $\rho_s = 0.5$ identified in Experiment A, against standard $\mathcal{MM}$AS, in the first 200 iterations of the computation. Table 4 provides a summary of the setup for this experiment, and the results are shown in Table 5. In this experiment, we use almost all instances at TSPLIB with number of cities between 300 and 6,000. Table 5 shows the mean and standard deviation of solution cost and of CPU execution time. The smallest solution cost and execution time for each instance are shown in bold. These results indicate the following:

- Gaussian evaporation reduces solution cost for 36 of the 41 instances. All 5 instances in which solution cost was not reduced are relatively small, with less than 500 cities.
- Gaussian evaporation has smaller run-time for all instances.

Table 5 also shows the results of applying a (one-tailed) non-parameteric Wilcoxon rank-sum test at the 95% confidence level to the solution cost with Gaussian evaporation versus without Gaussian evaporation, for each instance. The p-values resulting from these tests are shown in the last column of Table 5, and each p-value is shown in bold if it is statistically significant (i.e. less than 0.05). Note that p-values are shown to three decimal places, so p-values less

Table 3: Results of Experiment A

		0.0	0.05	0.1	0.2	0.3	0.4	0.5	0.6	0.7	0.8	0.9
rl5934	μ_c	5.15	5.07	4.98	4.66	4.59	4.59	4.46	4.54	4.52	4.35	4.58
	σ_c	0.20	0.22	0.27	0.34	0.28	0.26	0.29	0.37	0.30	0.40	0.37
	μ_t	92.5	91.3	90.1	89.0	86.9	86.3	85.4	84.6	84.2	83.1	85.5
	σ_t	0.29	0.45	0.34	0.49	0.48	0.63	0.78	0.70	0.74	1.28	1.05
fnl4461	μ_c	5.62	5.43	5.29	5.03	4.87	4.75	4.63	4.63	4.59	4.59	4.60
	σ_c	0.13	0.09	0.15	0.16	0.19	0.18	0.23	0.25	0.27	0.28	0.25
	μ_t	78.3	77.4	76.5	74.9	73.0	72.0	70.5	69.0	67.6	66.8	65.8
	σ_t	0.19	0.22	0.33	0.46	0.45	0.49	0.80	0.78	0.92	0.85	0.91
fl3795	μ_c	4.33	4.25	4.26	4.12	4.06	4.05	4.11	4.00	4.18	4.20	4.14
	σ_c	0.49	0.38	0.46	0.31	0.39	0.45	0.41	0.28	0.48	0.43	0.37
	μ_t	40.0	39.8	39.4	39.4	38.7	38.6	38.4	38.1	38.3	37.8	37.8
	σ_t	0.10	0.12	0.13	0.16	0.15	0.18	0.15	0.19	0.21	0.22	0.22
pcb3038	μ_c	5.84	5.64	5.42	5.10	4.81	4.54	4.49	4.14	4.11	3.82	4.09
	σ_c	0.12	0.22	0.25	0.29	0.31	0.38	0.41	0.47	0.48	0.47	0.55
	μ_t	31.0	30.7	29.4	28.3	27.6	27.0	26.4	25.6	24.8	24.6	24.5
	σ_t	0.26	0.38	0.64	0.17	0.29	0.37	0.47	0.54	0.48	0.59	0.63
pr2392	μ_c	5.45	5.15	5.03	4.67	4.47	4.11	3.66	3.41	3.23	3.04	3.25
	σ_c	0.21	0.25	0.25	0.30	0.43	0.54	0.63	0.62	0.80	0.64	0.63
	μ_t	19.4	19.7	18.7	18.3	18.0	17.6	17.2	16.8	16.7	16.3	16.2
	σ_t	0.30	0.18	0.18	0.25	0.36	0.27	0.46	0.47	0.55	0.50	0.33
pcb1173	μ_c	3.50	3.17	2.68	1.86	1.22	1.17	0.97	0.88	0.81	0.95	0.84
	σ_c	0.39	0.45	0.43	0.65	0.33	0.34	0.26	0.29	0.26	0.29	0.28
	μ_t	7.6	7.5	7.3	7.1	7.2	6.8	6.5	6.4	6.3	6.3	6.3
	σ_t	0.09	0.09	0.10	0.15	0.14	0.19	0.16	0.17	0.19	0.14	0.15
att532	μ_c	0.46	0.32	0.29	0.34	0.27	0.25	0.29	0.28	0.27	0.29	0.36
	σ_c	0.31	0.18	0.12	0.15	0.14	0.15	0.16	0.17	0.15	0.15	0.23
	μ_t	2.8	2.7	2.7	2.5	2.5	2.5	2.5	2.5	2.5	2.5	2.5
	σ_t	0.06	0.06	0.06	0.05	0.05	0.05	0.05	0.04	0.04	0.03	0.03

than 0.001 appear in the table as 0.000. As the table indicates, the difference in solution cost is significant for all instances with more than 500 cities.

Figure 1 shows the evolution of the difference in solution quality with and without Gaussian evaporation, for seven representative instances. In this figure, the x-axis represents the iteration number and the y-axis represents average solution cost without Gaussian evaporation minus average solution cost with Gaussian evaporation. For example, if at iteration 17, the average solution cost without Gaussian evaporation is 1.52% percent in excess of the optimal and the average solution cost with Gaussian evaporation is 1.21% percent, the average difference in performance at the 17th iteration would be 0.31%, and the point $(17, 0.31)$ would be a point on the plot. We see from the figure that the difference in performance is mostly positive, indicating that the performance gain produced by Gaussian evaporation is generally maintained throughout the first 200 iterations.

4.4 Discussion of Results of Experiment B

The results of Experiment B indicate that the use of Gaussian evaporation with a high setting of ρ_s results in a statistically-significant improvement in solution cost for all instances with more than 500 cities. Let us reflect briefly on what the setting $\rho_m = 0.2$ and $\rho_s = 0.5$ means. Based on well-known properties of the normal distribution, it means that:

1. The evaporation rate is within the range $[-0.3, 0.7]$ about 68.3% of the time, and within the range $[-0.8, 1.2]$ about 95.5% of the time.

2. The evaporation rate is negative about 34.5% of the time. A negative ρ means that instead of being reduced, the entry undergoing evaporation τ_{ij} would actually have its value increased—although of course it cannot become higher than τ_{max}.

3. The evaporation rate is greater than unity about 5.5% of the time. If $\rho > 1$, this means the relevant entry τ_{ij} would be made equal to a negative value. However, in practice, because τ_{min} is always positive, the actual effect of generating a value of ρ greater than unity is that the relevant entry τ_{ij} is driven to the value τ_{min}.

4.5 Run-Time Profiling

Table 5 indicates that using Gaussian evaporation reduces run-time for all instances. This is curious since one might expect the added burden of generating Gaussian random numbers in Equation (4) to increase run-time. To understand this phenomenon, we used the GNU profiler to examine the detailed run-time behavior of `acotsp`, with and without Gaussian evaporation, running on the instance `pcb1173` for 200 iterations, repeated for 100 trials. Note that because run-time profiling [10] relies on a sampling process, the execution time percentages are only an estimate.

We found that without our proposed variation, roughly 96% of the overall program's CPU execution time is accounted for by the following:

1. Roughly 43% is spent in the **SolutionConstruction** step. This 43% does not include the processing that is carried out when the nearest-neighbor list is exhausted (see Section 2).

2. In the profiled runs, the case that the nearest-neighbor list was exhausted occurred exactly 2.76% of the time, and the processing that was carried out in this case

Table 5: Results of Experiment B

	Standard $\mathcal{MMAS}$ ($\rho_s = 0.0$)				Modified $\mathcal{MMAS}$ ($\rho_s = 0.5$)				
	cost		time		cost		time		
	μ	σ	μ	σ	μ	σ	μ	σ	p-val
rl5934	5.24	0.24	113.0	1.45	**4.54**	0.38	**98.6**	7.74	**0.000**
rl5915	5.08	0.21	127.0	1.45	**4.51**	0.31	**115.0**	1.48	**0.000**
fnl4461	5.65	0.12	108.0	0.33	**4.70**	0.23	**91.4**	1.27	**0.000**
fl3795	4.26	0.38	53.5	0.14	**4.09**	0.43	**45.3**	0.32	**0.004**
pcb3038	5.79	0.20	37.4	0.60	**4.29**	0.43	**30.6**	0.71	**0.000**
pr2392	5.47	0.21	23.6	0.11	**3.71**	0.64	**19.5**	0.64	**0.000**
u2319	2.28	0.08	23.3	0.07	**1.62**	0.13	**18.1**	0.20	**0.000**
u2152	4.15	0.49	17.8	0.16	**1.20**	0.44	**13.2**	0.88	**0.000**
d2103	1.51	0.34	16.3	0.56	**0.82**	0.27	**14.0**	0.59	**0.000**
rl1889	3.91	0.41	26.2	0.19	**2.73**	0.58	**21.4**	0.31	**0.000**
u1817	3.31	0.45	14.6	0.15	**1.34**	0.51	**11.8**	0.36	**0.000**
vm1748	4.03	0.33	23.8	0.87	**2.23**	0.58	**19.7**	0.40	**0.000**
d1655	3.84	0.35	13.9	0.09	**2.55**	0.53	**11.3**	0.18	**0.000**
fl1577	2.44	0.27	11.3	0.07	**2.11**	0.32	**10.0**	0.08	**0.000**
u1432	4.06	0.27	10.7	0.05	**1.88**	0.49	**8.8**	0.16	**0.000**
fl1400	1.93	0.31	12.9	0.07	**1.62**	0.33	**11.4**	0.42	**0.000**
nrw1379	3.85	0.26	13.8	0.33	**1.77**	0.41	**11.1**	0.50	**0.000**
rl1323	1.88	0.44	12.6	0.23	**1.01**	0.35	**9.8**	0.24	**0.000**
rl1304	2.79	0.52	12.4	0.20	**1.12**	0.34	**9.0**	0.17	**0.000**
d1291	0.91	0.44	9.1	0.15	**0.53**	0.30	**7.3**	0.32	**0.000**
pcb1173	3.46	0.33	8.9	0.06	**0.98**	0.27	**7.1**	0.20	**0.000**
vm1084	2.33	0.45	9.1	0.12	**0.46**	0.19	**7.2**	0.14	**0.000**
u1060	4.65	0.32	7.9	0.03	**3.94**	0.39	**7.2**	0.06	**0.000**
pr1002	4.16	0.38	7.1	0.05	**1.88**	0.53	**6.1**	0.15	**0.000**
dsj1000	3.96	0.30	11.2	0.25	**2.78**	0.54	**9.4**	0.37	**0.000**
rat783	1.95	0.60	5.1	0.06	**0.60**	0.21	**4.2**	0.09	**0.000**
u724	0.92	0.39	4.4	0.07	**0.43**	0.14	**3.6**	0.04	**0.000**
gr666	1.75	0.40	4.0	0.03	**0.89**	0.32	**3.6**	0.09	**0.000**
d657	1.53	0.53	4.2	0.05	**0.54**	0.18	**3.6**	0.07	**0.000**
p654	0.89	0.18	4.2	0.02	**0.81**	0.19	**4.0**	0.03	**0.003**
rat575	1.29	0.54	3.4	0.05	**0.50**	0.21	**2.8**	0.04	**0.000**
u574	1.87	0.60	3.5	0.04	**0.71**	0.37	**3.0**	0.05	**0.000**
ali535	0.31	0.15	3.7	0.07	**0.20**	0.09	**3.4**	0.05	**0.000**
att532	0.56	0.31	3.2	0.07	**0.25**	0.12	**2.7**	0.05	**0.000**
d493	1.56	0.35	3.0	0.02	0.90	**0.27**	**2.8**	0.03	**0.000**
pcb442	**0.50**	0.19	2.3	0.04	0.50	0.17	**1.9**	0.02	0.474
pr439	0.16	0.09	2.3	0.03	**0.15**	0.08	**2.2**	0.02	0.066
gr431	**0.47**	0.22	2.5	0.04	0.50	0.39	**2.3**	0.06	0.088
fl417	**0.27**	0.10	2.2	0.02	0.30	0.10	**2.1**	0.02	**0.023**
rd400	**0.22**	0.19	2.3	0.04	0.26	0.21	**2.0**	0.02	0.090
lin318	**0.27**	0.18	1.5	0.02	0.28	0.18	**1.4**	0.02	0.320

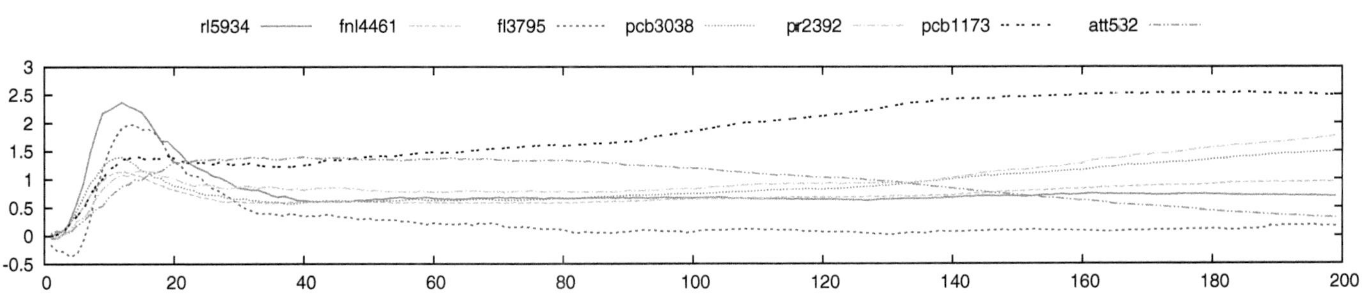

Figure 1: Experiment B: Plot of average difference in solution cost (y-axis) versus iteration number (x-axis), for seven representative problem instances.

accounted for roughly 13% of the overall program's execution time.

3. Roughly 38% of execution time was accounted for by the **LocalSearch** step.

4. The **Evaporation** step accounted for roughly 1.8% of the overall program's execution time.

In the profiled runs, the use of Gaussian evaporation (using $\rho_s = 0.5$) reduced the overall program's execution time by 13%. We found that the main causes of this reduction were the following:

1. The time spent in the **Solution Construction** step, excluding the case where the nearest-neighbor list is exhausted, remains roughly unchanged.

2. The frequency of nearest-neighbor list exhaustion is reduced by 36%, thus reducing overall program execution time by 5%.

3. The execution time consumed by **Local Search** is reduced by 17%, thus reducing overall program execution time by 7%. This is likely because the local search starts from a better solution and thus takes less time to find the nearest local optimum.

4. The execution time of the **Evaporation** step increases dramatically by 160%, but this results in an increase in the overall program execution time of only 3%.

In other words, the increase in execution time in the **Evaporation** step is more than offset by reductions in execution time elsewhere in the algorithm.

4.6 Experiment C

Table 6: Experimental Setup for Experiment C

Parameter	Value
Problem instances	41 instances (as listed in Table 7)
Value of ρ_s	{ 0.0, 0.5 }
Number of iterations	equal to number of cities
Number of trials	30

The purpose of Experiment C is to evaluate the performance of Gaussian evaporation against standard $\mathcal{MM}$AS beyond the first 200 iterations. In this experiment, we let the number of iterations be equal to the number of cities, as indicated in Table 6. The results are shown in Table 7. These tables follow a similar format to Table 5: each row corresponds to a problem instance and shows the mean and standard deviation of cost and of run-time, and also shows the result of applying a Wilcoxon rank-sum test at the 95% confidence level. For each row, the smallest solution cost and the smallest run-time are shown in bold. The last column shows the p-value resulting from applying the Wilcoxon rank-sum test; the p-value is shown in bold if it is statistically significant (i.e. less than 0.05).

Table 7 indicates that Gaussian evaporation improves solution cost for 19 of the 24 instances with more than a thousand cities. However, in nearly all cases, the difference in performance is not statistically significant. We can also see from the table that Gaussian evaporation has smaller runtime for the vast majority of instances.

We also observe from the table that the performance pattern is quite different when the number of cities is below a thousand: solution cost is better *without* Gaussian evaporation for 12 of the 17 instances with a thousand cities or less.

In addition to applying a Wilcoxon rank-sum test to the difference in solution cost for each problem instance individually, we also apply a Wilcoxon signed-rank test to determine if the overall difference in performance of the two methods is statistically significant over each collection of instances. We apply this test separately for instances with more than a thousand cities, and for instances with a thousand cities or less, because, as discussed above, the performance pattern appears to nearly reverse itself as the number of cities increases beyond a thousand.

The reason we apply the Wilcoxon signed-rank test at the level of the collection of instances, rather than just applying the rank-sum test for each individual instance, is based on the following argument by Demšar [5]:

> Some authors prefer to count only the significant wins and losses, where the significance is determined using a statistical test on each data set ... The reasoning behind this practice is that "some wins and losses are random and these should not count." This would be a valid argument if statistical tests could distinguish between the random and non-random differences. However, statistical tests only measure the improbability of the obtained experimental result if the null hypothesis was correct, which is not even the (im)probability of the null-hypothesis.
>
> For the sake of argument, suppose that we compared two algorithms on one thousand different data sets. In each and every case, algorithm A was better than algorithm B, but the difference was never significant. It is true that for each single case the difference between the two algorithms can be attributed to a random chance, but how likely is it that one algorithm was just lucky in all 1000 out of 1000 independent experiments?
>
> Contrary to the popular belief, counting only significant wins and losses therefore does not make the tests more but rather less reliable, since it draws an arbitrary threshold of $p < 0.05$ between what counts and what does not.

The results of the Wilcoxon signed-rank tests are shown in Table 8. The results indicate that, in terms of overall performance, solution cost is significantly better with Gaussian evaporation for instances where the number of cities, denoted n, is more than 1,000. On the other hand, the results indicate that, for instances with $n \leq 1{,}000$, solution cost is significantly worse with Gaussian evaporation.

Figure 2 shows the evolution of the difference in solution quality over the course of the algorithm, for seven representative instances. The format of this figure is similar to Figure 1, except that the iteration number is expressed as a percentage of the total number of iterations. We observe from the figure that the difference in solution cost is more pronounced in the first third of the computation, and we also

Table 7: Results of Experiment C

	Standard $\mathcal{MMAS}$ ($\rho_s = 0.0$)				Modified $\mathcal{MMAS}$ ($\rho_s = 0.5$)				
	cost		time		cost		time		
	μ	σ	μ	σ	μ	σ	μ	σ	p-val
rl5934	1.88	0.34	2,560.0	176.89	**1.83**	0.32	**1,930.0**	32.52	0.184
rl5915	1.50	0.26	2,350.0	276.47	**1.46**	0.40	**2,050.0**	101.26	0.263
fnl4461	0.80	0.10	1,340.0	44.49	**0.77**	0.09	**1,110.0**	110.44	0.199
fl3795	**2.26**	0.27	**609.0**	18.26	2.40	0.29	679.0	13.49	**0.041**
pcb3038	0.79	0.14	323.0	19.02	**0.77**	0.13	**282.0**	5.87	0.206
pr2392	0.75	0.18	177.0	4.66	**0.73**	0.18	163.0	3.37	0.282
u2319	0.41	0.04	167.0	5.38	**0.40**	0.05	147.0	6.21	0.440
u2152	0.45	0.16	127.0	5.05	**0.48**	0.14	**113.0**	3.90	0.168
d2103	0.32	0.15	**123.0**	4.66	**0.30**	0.11	124.0	3.58	0.421
rl1889	0.95	0.38	173.0	7.66	**0.84**	0.32	**141.0**	11.12	0.115
u1817	**0.48**	0.17	91.3	1.56	0.57	0.23	**86.0**	2.50	0.053
vm1748	0.57	0.17	139.0	18.44	**0.56**	0.20	**117.0**	10.22	0.450
d1655	0.77	0.27	**79.2**	1.52	**0.70**	0.18	79.7	2.70	0.215
fl1577	1.33	0.27	77.1	1.59	**1.30**	0.21	**64.0**	1.85	0.248
u1432	0.58	0.11	52.1	2.66	**0.58**	0.10	**46.1**	1.66	0.347
fl1400	1.20	0.20	74.7	1.90	**1.17**	0.20	**67.7**	0.81	0.282
nrw1379	0.57	0.12	78.8	1.38	**0.52**	0.14	**61.7**	1.31	0.062
rl1323	0.67	0.26	72.9	1.90	**0.57**	0.29	**64.1**	0.99	0.068
rl1304	0.56	0.28	**51.3**	2.80	**0.52**	0.23	56.4	0.52	0.272
d1291	**0.22**	0.13	49.4	0.40	0.34	0.25	**42.9**	1.26	**0.034**
pcb1173	0.45	0.21	39.3	1.35	**0.41**	0.23	**34.8**	0.38	0.177
vm1084	0.22	0.10	39.8	3.43	**0.21**	0.10	**37.8**	0.49	0.500
u1060	1.59	0.33	32.7	0.83	**1.47**	0.38	**32.2**	0.31	**0.041**
pr1002	**0.69**	0.22	27.3	0.20	0.72	0.25	**25.2**	0.22	0.358
dsj1000	**1.16**	0.37	42.2	0.50	1.26	0.37	**40.2**	0.49	0.097
rat783	**0.35**	0.14	16.5	0.44	0.38	0.20	**15.0**	0.25	0.410
u724	**0.28**	0.07	13.0	0.30	0.30	0.09	**12.3**	0.14	0.177
gr666	**0.41**	0.15	12.0	0.11	0.42	0.14	**10.7**	0.17	0.398
d657	0.39	0.10	11.7	0.13	**0.36**	0.12	**10.9**	0.09	0.174
p654	**0.47**	0.13	11.8	0.33	0.48	0.14	**11.3**	0.08	0.387
rat575	**0.28**	0.13	**7.8**	0.15	0.40	0.19	8.1	0.06	**0.007**
u574	**0.30**	0.19	8.4	0.09	0.38	0.28	**8.0**	0.10	0.156
ali535	0.10	0.07	8.9	0.09	**0.08**	0.05	**8.7**	0.10	0.119
att532	**0.18**	0.11	7.2	0.13	0.22	0.15	**6.7**	0.09	0.069
d493	0.53	0.15	6.9	0.04	**0.53**	0.16	**6.2**	0.08	0.485
pcb442	**0.40**	0.13	4.4	0.03	0.46	0.17	**4.2**	0.05	0.252
pr439	0.07	0.05	4.7	0.04	**0.07**	0.05	**4.7**	0.02	0.376
gr431	**0.17**	0.15	4.9	0.07	0.26	0.20	**4.7**	0.08	**0.024**
fl417	**0.16**	0.07	4.3	0.03	0.17	0.07	**4.1**	0.07	0.292
rd400	**0.11**	0.16	4.1	0.04	0.18	0.19	**3.6**	0.02	0.082
lin318	0.24	0.14	2.27	0.02	**0.15**	0.02	**1.33**	0.02	0.407

note that the y-axis value is generally positive throughout the computation for most instances.

5. DISCUSSION

In this paper, we have proposed an ACO variation in which the evaporation rate ρ is a Gaussian random variable. In the main experiments of this paper, Experiments B and C, we evaluated Gaussian evaporation in the context of $\mathcal{MMAS}$ with the mean ρ_m of the evaporation rate set to 0.2 and the standard deviation ρ_s set to 0.5. As discussed in Section 4.4, this setting means that ρ will be negative (which means that instead of reducing pheromone trails, the "evaporation" step will actually positively reinforce them) about a third of the time. This is certainly a radical proposal, and one would, at first examination, expect this to result in poor solution quality, as well as increased run-time because of the computational burden of generating a large number of Gaussian random numbers.

However, the results of this paper indicate that Gaussian evaporation improves solution cost significantly (and in some cases dramatically) in the early part of the computation. Even when the computation is allowed to run for a large number of iterations as in Experiment C, our proposal per-

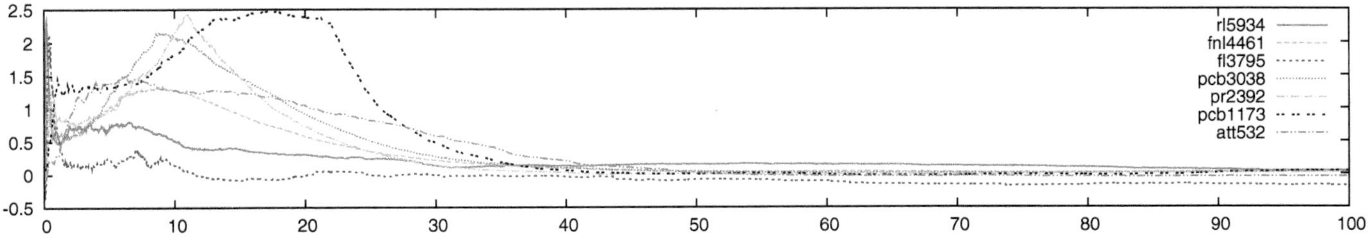

Figure 2: Experiment C: Plot of average difference in solution cost (y-axis) versus iteration number (x-axis), expressed as percentage of total number of iterations, for seven representative problem instances.

Table 8: Results of applying Wilcoxon signed-rank tests to the results of Experiment C

Hypothesis	p-value
Solution cost is *better* with Gaussian evaporation (for $n > 1{,}000$)	**0.032**
Solution cost is *worse* with Gaussian evaporation (for $n \leq 1{,}000$)	**0.020**

forms slightly better than standard $\mathcal{MM}$AS for larger problem instances. This is significant because it means that the extra search diversity that comes from such extreme values of ρ does not come at the expense of hindering exploitation of knowledge gained from past solutions. The results also indicate that Gaussian evaporation does not increase run-time.

6. CONCLUDING REMARKS

The results of this paper are curious. They indicate that, in at least one experimental context, there appears to be a computational advantage to using Gaussian evaporation, especially in the early part of an ACO computation. While we hypothesize that these performance gains are caused by the increased diversity arising from the Gaussian randomness, more research is needed to determine more conclusively the causes of these performance gains. Further investigation is also needed to determine whether the phenomenon observed in our experimental results carries over to other optimization problems.

7. ACKNOWLEDGEMENTS

We would like to thank Thomas Stützle for very valuable advice and guidance, and for useful discussions. We would also like to thank Fernando Otero for useful advice on statistical significance tests.

8. REFERENCES

[1] A.M. Abdelbar. Stubborn ants. *Proceedings IEEE Swarm Intelligence Symposium*, IEEE Press, Piscataway, NJ, pages 1-5, 2008.

[2] G.E.P. Box, and M.E. Muller. A note on the generation of random normal deviates. *Annals of Mathematical Statistics*, Vol. 29(2):610-611, 1958.

[3] B. Bullnheimer, R.F. Hartl, and C. Strauss. An improved ant system algorithm for the vehicle routing Problem. *Annals of Operations Research*, 89:319-328, 1999.

[4] O. Cordón, I.F. de Viana, and F. Herrera. Analysis of the best-worst ant system and its variants on the TSP. *Mathware and Soft Computing*, 9(2-3):177-192, 2002.

[5] J. Demšar. Statistical comparisons of classifiers over multiple data sets. *Machine Learning Research*, 7:1-30, 2006.

[6] M. Dorigo, and L.M. Gambardella. Ant colony system: a cooperative learning approach to the traveling salesman problem. *IEEE Transactions on Evolutionary Computation*, 1(1):35-66, 1997.

[7] M. Dorigo, V. Maniezzo, and A. Colorni. Ant system: optimization by a colony of cooperative agents. *IEEE Transactions on Systems, Man, and Cybernetics*, 26(1):29-41, 1996.

[8] M. Dorigo and T. Stützle. *Ant Colony Optimization.* MIT Press, Cambridge, MA, USA, 2004.

[9] M. Dorigo, and T. Stützle. Ant colony optimization: overview and recent advances. IRIDIA Technical Report 2009-013, Université Libre de Bruxelles, Brussels, Belgium, 2009.

[10] J. Fenlason, and R. Stallman. *GNU Gprof Manual.* Free Software Foundation, 2000.

[11] P. Pellegrini, T. Stützle, and M. Birattari. A critical analysis of parameter adaptation in ant colony optimization. *Swarm Intelligence* 6(1):23-48, 2012.

[12] W.H. Press, S.A. Teuskolsky, W.T. Vetterling, and B.P. Flannery. *Numerical Recipes: The Art of Scientific Computing.* Cambridge University Press, New York, 2007.

[13] T. Stützle. ACOTSP: a software package for various ant colony optimization algorithms applied to the symmetric traveling salesman problem. URL `http://aco-metaheuristic.org/aco-code`, 2002.

[14] T. Stützle, and H. Hoos. MAX-MIN Ant System and local search for the traveling salesman problem. *Proceedings IEEE 1997 International Conference on Evolutionary Computation*, pages 309-314, 1997.

[15] T. Stützle, and H.H. Hoos. MAX-MIN Ant System. *Future Generation Computer Systems*, 16(8):889-914, 2000.

[16] T. Stützle, M. López-Ibañez, P. Pellegrini, M. Maur, M. Montes de Oca, M. Birattari, and M. Dorigo. Parameter adaptation in ant colony optimization. In Y. Hamadi, E. Monfroy, and F. Saubion (Eds.): *Autonomous Search*, pages 191-215, Springer, Berlin, Germany, 2012.

Learning Fuzzy Cognitive Maps from Data by Ant Colony Optimization

Ye Chen
School of Electronic and Computing Systems
University of Cincinnati
2600 Clifton Ave., Cincinnati, OH 45221
chenye84@gmail.com

Lawrence J. Mazlack
Applied Computational Intelligence Laboratory
University of Cincinnati
2600 Clifton Ave., Cincinnati, OH 45221
mazlack@ucmail.uc.edu

Long J. Lu
Division of Biomedical Informatics
Cincinnati Children's Hospital Medical Center
3333 Burnet Ave., Cincinnati, OH 45229
Long.Lu@cchmc.org

ABSTRACT

Fuzzy Cognitive Maps (FCMs) are a flexible modeling technique with the goal of modeling causal relationships. Traditionally FCMs are developed by experts. We need to learn FCMs directly from data when expert knowledge is not available. The FCM learning problem can be described as the minimization of the difference between the desired response of the system and the estimated response of the learned FCM model. Learning FCMs from data can be a difficult task because of the large number of candidate FCMs. A FCM learning algorithm based on Ant Colony Optimization (ACO) is presented in order to learn FCM models from multiple observed response sequences. Experiments on simulated data suggest that the proposed ACO based FCM learning algorithm is capable of learning FCM with at least 40 nodes. The performance of the algorithm was tested on both single response sequence and multiple response sequences. The test results are compared to several algorithms, such as genetic algorithms and nonlinear Hebbian learning rule based algorithms. The performance of the ACO algorithm is better than these algorithms in several different experiment scenarios in terms of model errors, sensitivities and specificities. The effect of number of response sequences and number of nodes is discussed.

Categories and Subject Descriptors

I.2.8 [**Artificial Intelligence**]: Problem Solving, Control Methods, and Search – *heuristic methods.*

General Terms

Algorithms

Keywords

Fuzzy Cognitive Maps, Ant Colony Optimization, numerical optimization, data-driven learning algorithm

1. INTRODUCTION

Fuzzy Cognitive Maps (FCM) [1] are a modeling technique that is used in a variety of applications. A FCM is a graph consists of weighted edges and nodes. The nodes represent concepts. The edges are associated with weights to represent the strength of causal relations between two concepts. FCMs have several advantages, such as (a) the nodes in FCM represent real-world concepts and should be easier to be understood by human than other modeling techniques such as neural networks; (b) FCMs can represent cycles and recursive cycles. The traditional FCM learning approach is that experts build an initial network and then learning algorithms, such as Hebbian learning rule [2], can be used to improve the accuracy of the FCM. However, expert knowledge may not be available for all application areas for which FCMs might be desirable. For example, there is limited expert knowledge available if FCMs are used to describe the gene regulatory relation contains less studied genes. It follows that it may be difficult to build FCM models for gene regulatory networks as well as many other areas with only limited available expert knowledge. Consequently, it is useful to learn FCMs from data without prior knowledge.

Several computational intelligence algorithms have been proposed to learn FCMs directly from data. These computational intelligence algorithms include: genetic algorithm [3], particle swarm optimization [4], simulated annealing [5] as well as others. Stach [6] was able to solve problems with tens of nodes. The number of weights to be optimized increases quadratically as the number of nodes increases. The possible combination of different weights increases exponentially as the number of weights increases. Performance measured as out-of-sample data error [7] drops as the number of nodes increases. For practical problems, such as building gene regulatory network from gene expression data, the number of nodes ranges from several dozens to thousands; for these larger problems, previously used methods are computationally intractable. A more powerful learning algorithm is necessary to learn these networks.

Ant Colony Optimization (ACO) is a prominent algorithm for both combinatory and numerical optimization problems [8, 9]. It has been shown to outperform genetic algorithms, particle swarm optimizations and simulated annealing algorithms in many application areas [8, 10, 11]. It seems reasonable to consider applying ACO to the FCM learning problem.

An initial study has shown that ACO is capable of building an FCM model for a process control problem [12]. However, this prior research has several limitations:

(a) The learning algorithm was tested on a very small problem with only 5 nodes in the FCM model;

(b) The structure of the FCM model is pre-defined by domain experts and the number of un-determined weights is reduced;

(c) The ranges of several weights are pre-defined to reduce the size of solution space.

Because of the above three limitations, the dimension of the problem (i.e. the number of weights to be determined) is only 8. This is a relatively small dimension. Many recent optimization algorithms are able to solve problems with more than one hundred variables [10, 13].

In this paper, the ACO algorithm is used to build FCMs from data. The proposed algorithm is different from the previous ACO approach [12] in two aspects:

- First, the objective functions are different. The aim of Ding's approach is to maintain the values of the nodes in a reasonable interval and the objective function is to minimize the violation to the constraints on the range of several manually designated nodes [12]; while in our approach, the aim is to discover causal relations among the nodes from the observed data and the objective function is the difference between the observed value and estimated value of every node.
- Second, the scales of the problem are different. Ding's approach was applied to a problem with only 8 weights to be optimized; while in this paper, the proposed algorithm is applied to optimize 25 to 1600 weights.

The remainder of paper is organized as follows. Section 2 introduces FCMs and the problem of FCM learning. Section 3 introduces the proposed ACO based learning algorithm. Numerical experiments and results analysis are introduced in Section 4. Finally a conclusion is drawn in Section 5.

2. FUZZY COGNITIVE MAPS LEARNING

This section describes the basic concepts of FCM; briefly reviews FCM learning algorithms; and presents the mathematic formulation of the FCM learning problem used in this paper.

2.1 Fuzzy Cognitive Maps

Figure 1 shows an example of a FCM. A fuzzy cognitive map consists of N_n concept nodes C_i (i=1,2, ..., N_n) and the weighted edges between pairs of nodes $w_{ij} \in [-1,1]$. Every node represents a concept. The values of the concept nodes represent the activation degree of the concept. The activation degree is a fuzzy variable ranges from 0 to 1. The weighted edges represent the causal relations between pairs of nodes. The weight is a positive (negative) number if one concept has a positive (negative) causal effect on another concept. If two concepts have no causal relation, the corresponding weight should be 0.

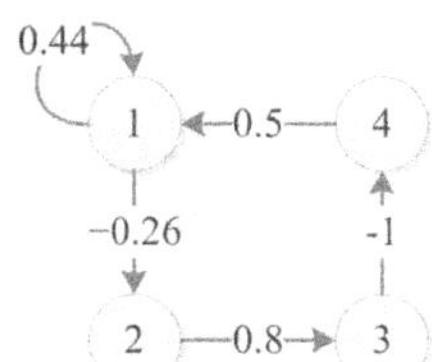

Figure 1. An example of a FCM

The dynamics of FCMs is determined by the following equation:

$$C_i^{(t+1)} = f\left(\sum_{i=1}^{N_n} w_{ij} C_i^{(t)}\right) \quad (1)$$

where $C_i^{(t)}$ is the activation degree of node i in iteration t, $f(\cdot)$ is a transfer function that is used to bound the activation degree in the range of [0,1]. There are many different transfer functions. Usually the transfer function should be chosen according to the nature of the problem. However comparison study carried out by Tsadiras [14] suggests that sigmoid transfer functions are better than the other transfer functions in general. In this paper, sigmoid transfer functions will be used and it is defined as follows:

$$f(x) = \frac{1}{1+e^{-\lambda x}} \quad (2)$$

where λ is a parameter used to characterize the steepness of the function around zero. λ should be chosen according to the nature of the problem. Usually it is chosen by performing experiments on different values for λ and the best value is chosen based on the performance of the overall model. In this paper, λ is set to 5 because this is a widely used value in many FCM learning research [7]. Another reason is that the value of this parameter does not change the nature of the FCM learning problem. The performance of the algorithms test on different λ value should be consistent. In practice, the value of λ should be determined according to the property of the system to be modeled. Usually a small λ is suitable for highly nonlinear system.

2.2 Data-driven Learning Algorithms

The learning of Fuzzy Cognitive Maps (FCM) from data is an important issue that has largely limited the application of FCM to many areas. For example, biologists need to study gene regulatory relations of genes related to diseases. In some cases, the mechanism of the diseases hasn't been well studied by biologists yet. They need to discover the gene regulatory relations from data. As there is only limited expert knowledge available, we need to learning regulatory networks from data.

Hebbian rule based learning algorithms [15] are designed to improve the accuracy of FCM generated by human experts. A good initial FCM model is required so that Hebbian rule based learning algorithms can be used to improve the initial FCM model. For some applications, domain knowledge is limited. It is hard to build a good initial FCM model by human experts for Hebbian rule based learning algorithms to improve.

Optimization algorithms based on computational intelligence were used to learn FCMs from data without domain knowledge.

Koulouriotis [16] proposed learning FCMs from data by using Evolution Strategy (ES). ES is similar to genetic algorithms except solutions in ES are represented by real numbers while solutions are represented in binary strings in genetic algorithms. ES algorithms are suitable for continuous domain optimization problems because the solutions are directly represented as real number. The problem of learning FCMs was stated as finding a suitable FCM so that for a given input the output should be the same as the observed data. Several input-output pairs are used. Evolution strategy algorithm is used to minimize the error between the output of the candidate FCM in the algorithm and the output that is observed from the to-be-modeled system.

Stach [17] proposed learning FCM from data by using the Real-Coded Genetic Algorithm (RCGA), an improved genetic algorithm for continuous domain problems. They assumed a sequence of values of every node (concept) has been observed from the to-be-modeled system. The sequence is broken down into several pairs. For example, assume the sequence is {V(1), V(2), V(3)}, where $V(t)$ is the values of all the nodes at time point t. This sequence implies that if the previous values of the nodes are V(1), the values should be V(2) in the next iteration. It is similar for the pair of V(2) and V(3). Therefore there will be two input-output pairs. The estimated values can be calculated with the following equation:

$$\hat{V}(n+1) = FCM\left(V(n)\right) \quad (3)$$

where $FCM(X)$ means the output of the FCM network given initial node value vector X. RCGA was used to minimize the errors between the estimated and the observed values. Stach [17] showed the advantage of RCGA over ES [16] through experiments.

A scalable divide and conquer based approach was proposed by Stach to learn large FCMs [6]. The division is performed on the response sequence that is being learnt from. It is divided into several small sequences. Each genetic algorithm focuses on minimizing the output error of one sequence. There will be several FCMs after all the genetic algorithms have finished their calculation. Every FCM is assigned a weight as 1−objective function value. Final result FCM is calculated as the weighted average of the individual FCMs.

Parsopoulos [18] introduced an approach of learning FCM by particle swarm optimization (PSO). PSO is an algorithm based on moving a set of solution in the solution space towards the presently found best solution. It has been shown by experiments that PSO can obtain an accurate FCM model.

Alizadeh [19] proposed learning FCM by Tabu search. Tabu search is a search algorithm that can remember some of the solutions that has been evaluated. This is proposed to avoid repeatedly evaluation of the same solution, which often happens in genetic algorithms and other computational intelligence algorithms. It is applied to the same optimization model as [17].

Alizadeh [20] proposed a Simulated Annealing (SA) based FCM learning algorithm. The problem formulation is the same as [19], except the optimization algorithm is changed to SA.

Although many computational intelligence algorithms have been applied to FCM learning problems, relatively few studies have been done on the application of ACO to FCM learning problems. Furthermore, many of the FCM learning algorithms are applied to learn small scale FCM learning problems with less than 100 weights to be determined. As discussed in Section 1, an initial study on the application of ACO to FCM learning problems shows the applicability of ACO based learning algorithm on small scale problems. This paper focuses on relatively large problems. A FCM learning algorithm based on ACO is proposed and it is used to learn FCMs with 40 nodes (i.e. 1600 weights to be determined).

2.3 Problem Formulation

FCMs can be used to model different problems. Different mathematical formulations of FCM learning are used in different modeling problems. For example, FCM models were used to design a proper fuzzy controller in some of the researches [4, 12, 18]. In these works, the concept nodes are divided into internal state nodes and output nodes. The FCM learning problem is formulated as minimizing the difference between the desired output values and the steady state values of the output nodes. Another example is that FCM models are used to study the causal relations among the concept nodes [6, 17, 19]. In these works, all the concept nodes are considered as output nodes, i.e. the objective of the optimization algorithm is to minimize the difference between the desired value of every concept node and the estimated activation degree based on the learnt FCM model. Ideally, the result FCM model should be able to generate the same sequence data as the system under study. The problem addressed in this paper is similar to the second example. It is more challenging than the first one because there are more weights to be optimized in the second example.

In this paper, a FCM is isomorphically represented by a weight matrix $W=[w_{ij}]$. The FCM itself is a graph. It is represented in an isomorphic matrix form for the convenience of writing equations. To learn a FCM, ACO algorithm is used to minimize the following error function:

$$Data\ Error = \frac{1}{(N_t-1)N_nN_s}\sum_{\substack{1\le t\le N_t-1\\ 1\le n\le N_n\\ 1\le s\le N_s}}\left(C_n^{(t)}(s)-\hat{C}_n^{(t)}(s)\right)^2 \quad (4)$$

where N_t is the length of the response sequence data, N_s is the number of response sequences, N_n is the number of nodes in the FCM network, $C_n^{(t)}(s)$ is the t-th value of node n in the s-th observed data series. $\hat{C}_n^{(t)}(s)$ is the t-th value of node n in the s-th data series generated by the FCM network.

3. LEARNING ALGORITHM

ACO is used to minimize the objective function, i.e. equation (4). ACO is first introduced to solve combinatory optimization problems [9, 21]. It is inspired from ants' behavior. Ants leave pheromone on their paths as they are moving between a food source and their nest. For the ants moving on short paths, they travel more times between the food source and the nest. Therefore more pheromone is left on the short paths. Ants tend to explore the space around the paths with high pheromone intensities. Over time, the ants will find a heuristically short path between the food source and the nest (the discovered path may or may not be optimal). In ACO algorithms, solutions to the problems are encoded as ant paths. Pheromone is used to guide the search process of the artificial ants. Because of the way the pheromone is stored, ACO algorithms are usually used in combinatory optimization problems.

Several extensions to ACO have been proposed to address continuous numerical optimization problems. One approach is to represent pheromone as Probability Density Functions (PDF) [10]. Another approach is to discretize the continuous space [11]. Both approaches have their advantages. The PDF approach represents pheromone intensities more accurate, while the discretization approach runs faster [11]. Discretization approach is used here.

3.1 Representation of the Candidate Solutions

The candidate solutions to the FCM learning problem are weight matrices. Since the problem is formulated as a numerical optimization problem, the candidate solutions are represented in vector form instead of the matrix form so that the notations can be fit into numerical optimization literature more easily. The vector form is

$$W_v = [w_{11}, w_{12}, \ldots, w_{1,N_n}, \ldots, w_{N_n,1}, w_{N_n,2}, \ldots w_{N_n,N_n}] \quad (5)$$

where w_{ij} is the weight on the edge from node i to j. The values in W_v are continuous values. They are represented as several decimal numbers according to the required precision:

$$w_{ij} = [d_{ij1}, d_{ij2}, \ldots, d_{ijk}, \ldots, d_{ijN_d}] \quad (6)$$

where d_{ijk} is the k-th digit for the weight w_{ij}, d_{ijk} ranges from 0 to 9, is the number of digits used to represent one weight. The digits for all the w_{ij}'s consist a candidate solution, i.e. a candidate FCM model. The digits are converted to the weights according to the following equation:

$$w_{ij} = g\left(\sum_{k=1}^{N_d} d_{ijk}\times 10^{-k}\right) \quad (7)$$

where function $g(x)$ is used to map the values in interval [0,1) to the interval of the weights [−1,1). It is defined as follows:

$$g(x) = 2\times(x-0.5) \quad (8)$$

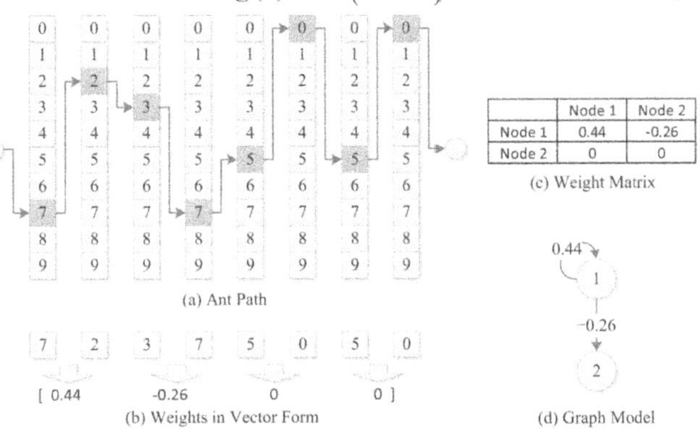

Figure 2. Different representations forms of FCMs

Examples of the different representation forms are shown in Figure 2. Ant paths are generated by ACO algorithm described in the following sub-sections. The ant paths are decoded according to equation (7) to obtain the vector form W_v. The weights in vector form can be rearranged according to the definition of W_v to obtain the weight matrix. The vector form of the weight matrix is used in the ACO algorithm. The weight matrix is the internal form used in the calculation of activation levels of the FCMs. Both vector form and matrix form are equivalent. We distinguish them because in the literature of optimization, variables to be optimized are usually represented in vector form, while the matrix form is usually used in the FCM simulations. The graph model is usually used as a user friendly representation form of FCMs.

3.2 Storage of Pheromone Intensities

As shown in Figure 2(a), the ants begin their search from a virtual starting node (the left-most circle). In every decision step, the ants will choose one node (the squares marked with numbers) from the next column of nodes. The pheromone intensities are stored on the edges between any two nodes in adjacent columns. The pheromone intensities are stored in a three-dimension matrix $\boldsymbol{\tau} = [\tau_{cn_1n_2}]$, where $\tau_{cn_1n_2}$ is the pheromone intensity stores on the edge from node n_1 in the c-th column to node n_2 in the (c+1)-th column. Both n_1 and n_2 range from 0 to 9. The initial values for $\boldsymbol{\tau}$ is set to the parameter τ_0. This parameter is usually chosen by experience. In this paper, experiments are performed on different values for τ_0 and then use the parameter that generates the minimum data error.

3.3 Ant Colony Optimization Algorithm

The ACO algorithm consists of several steps include (a) building ant tours; (b) decoding the ant tours to obtain candidate FCMs (in the form of weight matrices); (c) evaluate the candidate FCMs; and (d) update the pheromone intensities. These steps will be performed many times until either a satisfactory solution is found or the maximum number of iteration is reached.

3.3.1 Build ant tours

Usually there are several ants building individual tours simultaneously. Each ant starts from the virtual initial node and chooses one node from the first column of nodes. Then the ants start from their nodes in current column and choose their next nodes in the next column iteratively. The node in the next column is chosen according to the following equation:

$$T_{mc} = \begin{cases} argmax_{n_2}\left(\tau_{c-1,T_{m,c-1},n_2}\right) & ,q > p_0 \\ S_r & ,q \le p_0 \end{cases} \tag{9}$$

where T_{mc} is the node the m-th ant chose in the c-th column, $\tau_{c-1,T_{m,c-1},n_2}$ is the pheromone intensity from node $T_{m,c-1}$ (i.e. the node the m-th ant chose in the (c-1)-th column) to node n_2 in the c-th column. $argmax_{n_2}(\tau_{c-1,T_{m,c-1},n_2})$ is a function returns the value of n_2 which maximize the value of $\tau_{c-1,T_{m,c-1},n_2}$, $q\in[0,1]$ is a random number generated every time this equation is applied, p_0 is a pre-defined parameter, S_r is the node chosen by pseudo-random proportional rule. In this rule, a node is chosen randomly according to the probabilities defined as below:

$$P_{cn_2} = \frac{\tau_{c-1,T_{m,c-1},n_2}}{\sum_{n=0}^{9} \tau_{c-1,T_{m,c-1},n}} \tag{10}$$

where P_{cn_2} is the probability of node n_2 in column c being chosen. The probability is proportional to the corresponding pheromone intensity.

3.3.2 Local pheromone update

Local pheromone update performs as the ants move. In this step, the pheromone intensities on the ants' path will be decreased in order to encourage the ants exploring more paths. After the m-th ant chose a new node T_{mc}, the pheromone intensity on the edge from the ant's previous choice $T_{m,c-1}$ to its new choice T_{mc} will be updated according to the following equation:

$$\tau_{c-1,T_{m,c-1},T_{mc}} = (1-\rho)\times\tau_{c-1,T_{m,c-1},T_{mc}} + \rho\tau_0 \tag{11}$$

where $\rho\in[0,1]$ is a parameter represents the decay rate of pheromone.

3.3.3 Evaluate ant tours

After all the ants have chosen one node in every column, the choices of the ants are decoded to obtain FCM models as described in Section 3.1. The values of the objective function for the FCM models are calculated according to Section 2.3. The ant with minimum objective function value is called iteration-best ant. If the iteration-best ant in current iteration has a smaller objective function value than the iteration-best ant in any previous iteration, it is called global-best ant and its tour is denoted as

$$T^* = \left[T_1^*, T_2^*, \ldots, T_{N_c}^*\right] \tag{12}$$

where N_c is the number of columns.

3.3.4 Global pheromone update

Global pheromone update is performed after all the ants have been evaluated. The pheromone intensities on the best paths are rewarded. The update equation is shown as below:

$$\tau_{c,T_c^*,T_{c+1}^*} = (1-\alpha)\times\tau_{c,T_c^*,T_{c+1}^*} + \alpha/f_{fit}^* \tag{13}$$

where α is a parameter reflects the strength of the global update rule, f^*_{fit} is the fitness of the global-best ant. In this paper, objective function value is used as the fitness except when objective function equals zero. In order to avoid the error of being divided by 0, the objective function value is set to a very small number such as 10^{-6} when the objective function is zero.

3.3.5 Pseudo-code

The pseudo-code of the algorithm is listed as follows:

Algorithm 1: FCM learning algorithm based on ACO

```
Input: desired response sequence data C_n^(t)(s) .
Output: the best FCM model found.
   Initialize the parameters, pheromone intensities;
   while Maximum number of iteration is not reached do
      if this is the first iteration
         Assign random initial tours to the ants;
      else
         for m = 1 to N_a do
            Build tour for ant m according to Section 3.3.1;
            Update pheromone intensity of ant m's tour
               according to Section 3.3.2;
         end for
      end if
      Decode the ant tours into FCM models according to
         Section3.1;
      Calculate objective function values for the FCM models
         according to the problem formulation in Section 2.3;
      Update the pheromone intensity on the global best ant
         tour according to Section 3.3.4;
   end while
   Report the results.
```

In this pseudo-code, the ACO algorithm stops while the number of iterations reached a pre-defined maximum allowed number. This stop criterion is used because it is simply to compare algorithms if the number of objective function calculation (which equals number of iterations multiplied by number of ants) is the same. In practical problems, algorithm can be stopped if the solution did not improve over a number of iterations.

4. EXPERIMENTS AND RESULTS

4.1 Test Data Generation

Simulated data is used to test our algorithm. An FCM model is first generated randomly and then the data sequences are generated according to the FCM model.

The FCM model is generated by assigning random values to the weight matrix in the range of −1 to 1. In order to control the density of the random FCM model, a fraction of the edges are chosen according to the desired density. For example, if a density of 40% is expected for a 5-node FCM, 10 random edges (the total number of edges is 5×5=25, 40% of 25 edges is 10) will be selected and random values will be assigned to these edges. After the target edges are selected, random values are assigned to these edges. The value will be set to 0 if the absolute value of the generated random number is less than 0.05. This is because causal relation with strength less than 0.05 usually has no significance in practical problems [17].

The data sequences are generated by simulating the randomly generated FCM model with random initial concept activation degrees. The detail process is described in the following:

(a) Generate random initial values for all the nodes;

(b) Use equation (1) to calculate the values of the nodes in the next time points;

(c) Repeat step (b) until the length of the sequence reaches the desired value N_t;

(d) Repeat step (a) to (c) until the number of sequences reaches the desired value N_s.

4.2 Parameters

There are two categories of parameters: (a) problem related parameters, which are determined by the problem. For example, number of nodes N_n is determined by the number of concepts need to be modeled; number of digits N_d is determined according to the required precision of the weights; number of columns is determined by both N_n and N_d: $N_c=N_n^2 \times N_d$. (b) ACO algorithm related parameters. These parameters affect the performance of the algorithm and the relation between these parameters and the performance is complicated. In this paper, some of the parameters are chosen by grid search. As there are 6 parameters need to be determined, it is not time-efficient to search all the parameters. Even if only 10 different numbers are considered for every parameter, there would be 1,000,000 combinations. It will require too much computation. Some of the parameters are chosen based on experience and some of them by grid search. The initial pheromone intensity is chosen to be

$$\tau_0 = 1/f'_{fit} \tag{14}$$

where f'_{fit} is an estimated objective function value of a local best solution. In the ACO algorithm for Travelling Salesman Problem (TSP), f'_{fit} is calculated by nearest neighbor search. In the ACO algorithm for FCM learning, f'_{fit} is chosen by a random search. 100 random FCM models are generated and evaluated. Finally f'_{fit} is set to be a value slightly smaller than the local best objective function value.

As the parameters α, ρ and p_0 are related to the balance of exploration and exploitation, these three parameters are chosen by grid search. The other parameters are chosen based on experience. The other parameters are changed slightly around the chosen values to make sure it is at least a locally best parameter choice.

Number of iterations affects the number of objective function calculations. In order to compare with the other algorithms, the number of objective function calculations is kept the same. Stach compared several algorithms with 3,000,000 times of objective function calculations [7]. The maximum number of iterations is set to the number of objective function calculations divided by the number of ants.

The parameter settings are list in Table 1.

Table 1. Parameter settings

Parameter	Description	Value
N_d	Number of digits	2
N_n	Number of nodes	20*
N_c	Number of columns	800*
N_{iter}	Maximum number of iterations	60,000
N_a	Number of ants	50
α	Strength of global update	0.4
ρ	Pheromone decay rate	0.4
p_0	The probability of choosing the digit numbers deterministically	0.9
τ_0	Initial pheromone intensity	0.01

* These two parameter values are chosen for the problem of modeling the relation among 20 concepts. The values should be re-calculated if the number of concepts was changed.

4.3 Performance Measures

The performance is measured by model error, specificity, sensitivity, the mean value of specificity and sensitivity, and receiver operating characteristics.

4.3.1 Model error

Model error is used to measure the difference between the weight matrix of the learned FCM model and the weight matrix of the target FCM model. It is defined as follows.

$$Model\ Error = \frac{1}{N_n^2}\sum_{i=1}^{N_n}\sum_{j=1}^{N_n}\left|w_{ij} - \hat{w}_{ij}\right| \tag{15}$$

where $\hat{w}_{ij}$ is the estimated weight from node i to node j. Standard deviation of model error across different experiments is used to measure the stability of the proposed algorithm.

4.3.2 Specificity and sensitivity

For many application areas such as building gene regulatory networks, the goal of building network models is to identify plausible causal relation among genes. The learning algorithm is required to predict the existence of an edge between two nodes. In order to evaluate the performance of the proposed FCM learning algorithm for edge predicting problem, the FCM learning problem is extended and transformed to a binary classification problem. First, the target FCM model and the learned FCM model are transformed to binary networks (i.e. the weights are either zero or one). If the absolute weight between two nodes in the FCM model is larger than a pre-defined threshold ε_w, the weight between the corresponding nodes in the binary network will be set to one; otherwise the weight will be set to zero. In order to compare with the other algorithms, the same threshold value and the same definition of positive and negative results as defined by Stach [7] are used. The threshold is set to 0.05. The edges with absolute weights less than 0.05 are identified as positive edges; otherwise, they are identified as negative edges. These definitions are opposite to the definitions in bioinformatics literature. The sensitivity is defined as

$$Sensitivity = \frac{N_{TP}}{N_{TP} + N_{FN}} \quad (16)$$

where N_{TP} is the number of true positive edges (correctly identified positive edges), N_{FN} is the number of false negative edges (the positive edges that are incorrectly identified as negative edges).

The specificity is defined as

$$Specificity = \frac{N_{TN}}{N_{TN} + N_{FP}} \quad (17)$$

where N_{TN} is the number of true negative edges (correctly identified negative edges), N_{FP} is the number of false positive edges (the negative edges that are incorrectly identified as positive edges).

4.3.3 Mean value of specificity and sensitivity

SS mean is the mean value of specificity and sensitivity. It is defined as

$$SS\ mean = \frac{2 \times Specificity \times Sensitivity}{Specificity + Sensitivity} \quad (18)$$

4.3.4 Receiver operating characteristic

The specificity and sensitivity described above are determined under one threshold, i.e. an edge is classified as zero if the strength of the edge is larger than a predefined threshold; it is classified as one otherwise. They depend on the threshold. The Receiver Operating Characteristic (ROC) curve shows how the specificity and sensitivity changes as the threshold changes. It is a more accurate measure of how well the positive and negative edges can be identified. It is independent of the threshold.

4.4 Results

4.4.1 Comparison of different algorithms

For the purpose of comparison, the test data is generated in the same way as Stach used to compare 3 different algorithms [7]. Response sequences are generated randomly from FCM models with different number of nodes and different densities. For every given number of nodes and density, 10 random FCM models are generated as testing models. Several random response sequences are generated from the testing models with different random initial concept activation degrees. In order to compare the results with the other algorithms, appropriate number of sequences and length of the sequences is chosen so that the total volume of data is the same. Stach tested the algorithms on a sequence with 20 data points for each node in the FCM [7]. A sequence of the same size are used in the first set of experiments (denote as ACO-1,20 in Table 2) and 5 response sequences with 4 data points in each sequence are used to perform the second set of experiments (denote as ACO-5,4). We perform the third set of experiments with 40 sequences with 10 data points in each sequence (denote as ACO-40,10) in order to obtain results better than the first two set of experiments. The experiment results are compared with Real-Coded Genetic Algorithm (RCGA) [17], Data-Driven Nonlinear Hebbian Learning (DD-NHL) [2], and Nonlinear Hebbian Learning (NHL) [22]. The results are reported in Table 2.

It may be noticed that the SS mean of ACO-1,20 is better than the three non-ACO algorithms in the experiments with 5 nodes. However, it is worse than RCGA in the experiments with more

Table 2. Experiment results of different algorithms

Algorithm	Data Error	Model Error	Spec	Sens	SS mean	Data Error	Model Error	Spec	Sens	SS mean
	Number of Nodes = 5, Density = 20%					Number of Nodes = 5, Density = 40%				
ACO-1,20	0.000±0.000	0.362±0.132	0.92±0.16	0.17±0.11	0.27±0.17	0.000±0.000	0.324±0.108	0.93±0.08	0.11±0.10	0.19±0.15
ACO-5,4	0.000±0.000	0.064±0.058	0.95±0.09	0.68±0.24	0.76±0.21	0.000±0.000	0.075±0.066	0.97±0.06	0.58±0.32	0.67±0.30
ACO-40,10	0.000±0.000	**0.012**±0.014	**1.00**±0.00	**0.93**±0.07	**0.96**±0.04	0.000±0.000	**0.020**±0.012	**0.99**±0.03	**0.88**±0.09	**0.93**±0.05
RCGA		0.321	0.93	0.12	0.20		0.361	0.96	0.09	0.16
DD-NHL		0.317	0.96	0.06	0.11		0.381	0.96	0.07	0.12
NHL		0.345	0.94	0.07	0.13		0.346	0.93	0.05	0.10
	Number of Nodes = 10, Density = 20%					Number of Nodes = 10, Density = 40%				
ACO-1,20	0.001±0.001	0.449±0.041	0.92±0.08	0.09±0.03	0.16±0.05	0.001±0.000	0.485±0.034	0.93±0.04	0.09±0.04	0.17±0.06
ACO-5,4	0.004±0.001	0.319±0.057	0.93±0.08	0.13±0.06	0.23±0.09	0.002±0.001	0.302±0.040	0.92±0.05	0.13±0.05	0.22±0.08
ACO-40,10	0.003±0.001	**0.187**±0.040	0.93±0.04	**0.26**±0.06	**0.40**±0.07	0.002±0.001	**0.170**±0.049	0.93±0.05	**0.26**±0.07	**0.41**±0.08
RCGA		0.398	**0.96**	0.11	0.19		0.385	**0.94**	0.11	0.20
DD-NHL		0.412	**0.96**	0.07	0.13		0.423	0.93	0.05	0.10
NHL		0.420	0.93	0.07	0.12		0.435	0.93	0.06	0.11
	Number of Nodes = 20, Density = 20%					Number of Nodes = 20, Density = 40%				
ACO-1,20	0.002±0.001	0.513±0.026	0.93±0.04	0.07±0.01	0.13±0.02	0.001±0.001	0.517±0.022	**0.94**±0.02	0.07±0.02	0.14±0.03
ACO-5,4	0.011±0.005	0.461±0.019	0.93±0.03	0.09±0.02	0.16±0.03	0.006±0.002	0.473±0.020	0.92±0.02	0.08±0.02	0.14±0.03
ACO-40,10	0.009±0.002	**0.348**±0.017	0.92±0.03	**0.12**±0.02	**0.21**±0.04	0.006±0.002	**0.328**±0.031	0.92±0.02	**0.14**±0.03	**0.24**±0.04
RCGA		0.426	**0.94**	0.09	0.16		0.413	**0.94**	0.08	0.14
DD-NHL		0.464	0.93	0.08	0.14		0.436	**0.94**	0.07	0.13
NHL		0.461	0.93	0.07	0.13		0.468	0.93	0.05	0.10
	Number of Nodes = 40, Density = 20%					Number of Nodes = 40, Density = 40%				
ACO-1,20	0.006±0.006	0.525±0.011	0.94±0.01	0.07±0.01	0.13±0.01	0.004±0.002	0.562±0.010	0.94±0.01	0.06±0.01	0.12±0.01
ACO-5,4	0.020±0.005	0.508±0.010	0.94±0.01	0.07±0.00	0.12±0.01	0.014±0.005	0.538±0.007	0.94±0.01	0.07±0.01	0.13±0.01
ACO-40,10	0.019±0.006	**0.448**±0.021	0.94±0.02	**0.08**±0.01	**0.15**±0.01	0.019±0.004	0.437±0.012	0.93±0.01	**0.09**±0.01	**0.16**±0.01
RCGA		0.453	0.94	**0.08**	**0.15**		**0.436**	**0.96**	0.08	0.15
DD-NHL		0.468	**0.96**	0.07	0.12		0.465	0.93	0.06	0.12
NHL		0.489	0.95	**0.08**	**0.15**		0.498	0.94	0.06	0.12

Note: Spec means specificity. Sens means sensitivity. Data errors for RCGA, DD-NHL and NHL are not available.

than 5 nodes and it is worse than DD-NHL and NHL in the experiments with more than 10 nodes. Although the model errors and SS means are not satisfactory, the data error (i.e. the objective function value) is low (approximately 10^{-5}). It is possible that the low performance is because that only one response sequence does not provide enough information. So another two sets of experiments are performed (i.e. ACO-5,4, and ACO-40,10).

In ACO-5,4, the size of the input data sequence is the same as ACO-1,20, but the data contains more response sequences. Each of the response sequence provides an independent observation of the FCM model. The results suggest that ACO-5,4 is significantly improved over ACO-1,20 with the confidence level of 95%. ACO-5,4 is better than the three non-ACO algorithms in terms of both model error and SS mean for the problems with 5 nodes and 10 nodes. However ACO-5,4 is worse than RCGA for problems with 20 and 40 nodes.

The number of response sequences is further increased in order to obtain better results. The ACO-40,10 experiments use 40 response sequences with 10 data points in each sequence. The model errors, sensitivities and SS means are all better than the other three algorithms, except the case with 40 nodes and 40% of density (the model error is 0.001 higher than RCGA). Although specificity is slightly lower, SS mean should be considered as a more accurate measure of the performance because the balance between specificity and sensitivity can be adjusted as shown in Figure 3.

In many of the experiments, the sensitivity value is between 0.1 and 0.2. The low sensitivity value is partly due to the way of classifying the edges. ε_w=0.05 is used as the threshold for the weights to determine the class label of the edges. In practical problems, a larger threshold should be chosen. The ROC curve is usually used to show how the true positive rate (specificity) and false positive rate (1−sensitivity) changes as the threshold changes. The ROC curve for three randomly chosen experiments from Table 2 is shown in Figure 3. The curves are all above the reference line. The Area Under ROC Curve (AUC) is 0.98, 0.85, 0.72 and 0.65. These values are relatively high and it is possible to find a good balance between sensitivity and specificity.

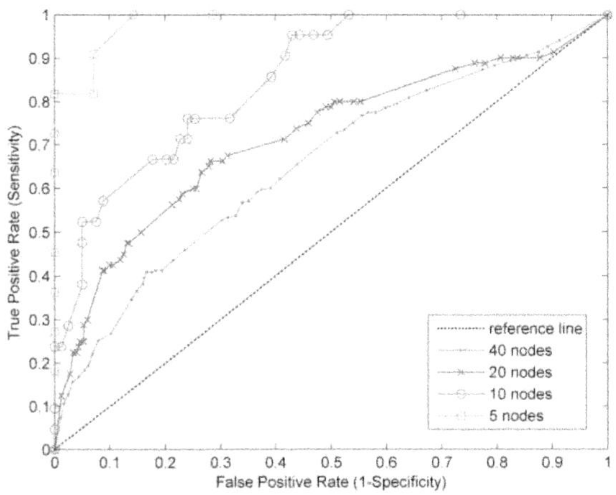

Figure 3. ROC curves of three randomly chosen experiments

From the experiment results we may conclude that ACO can learn FCM models more accurate than the other three non-ACO algorithms in some of the problems. However the ACO's performance drops as the number of nodes increases. The accuracy of the learned FCM models can be improved by providing more data to the ACO algorithm. As both the number of response sequences and the number of nodes affect the accuracy of the learned FCM models, more experiments are performed to show the effect of these two factors.

4.4.2 Effect of number of response sequences

In practical problems, multiple response sequences may be observed. The results in Table 2 suggest that the model error and SS mean improves as number of response sequences increases. More response sequences should be provided to the algorithm if they are available. Figure 4 and Figure 5 shows the box-plots of model errors and SS means for different number of response sequences respectively. The results are based on the experiments on FCMs with 20 nodes and a density of 40%. Every response sequence contains 10 data points. 10 experiments are performed for every number of response sequences. As shown in Figure 4, the maximum, minimum and average model errors decreases as the number of response sequences increases, with only three exceptions: the average model error for N_s=25 is slightly higher (than the average model error for N_s=20); the average model error for N_s=40 is slightly higher; and the minimum model error for N_s=40 is higher. These exceptions should be caused by random effect. The SS mean values shown in Figure 5 have a similar trend. The maximum SS mean increases as the number of response sequences increases, except for the case of N_s=40. However the trend for average values and minimum values of SS mean is not as clear as the trend for model errors. It should be clearer if more experiments are performed.

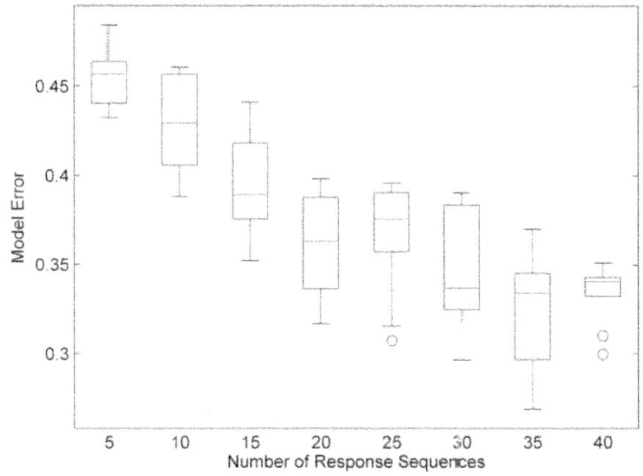

Figure 4. Effect of number of sequences on model errors

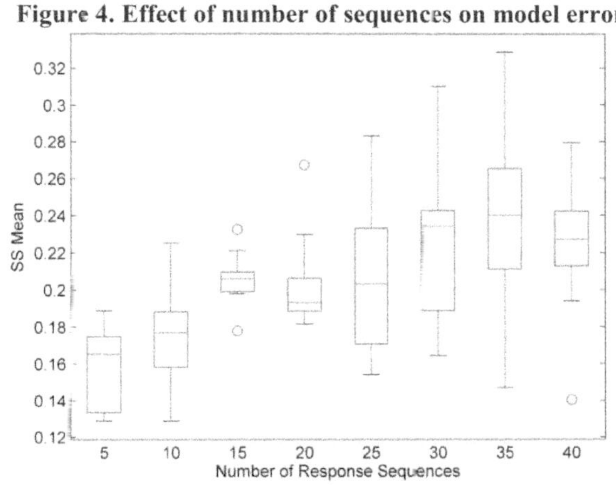

Figure 5. Effect of number of response sequences on SS means

4.4.3 Effect of number of FCM nodes

As the number of FCM nodes increases, the number of weights increases quadratically and the possible number of solutions increases exponentially. The performance of the algorithm drops because there are more solutions to be explored and the algorithm may be easier to be trapped in the increasing number of local optimums. Figure 6 shows how model error and

SS mean changes as the number of FCM nodes changes. The average, minimum and maximum values of both performance measures drops as the number of nodes increases.

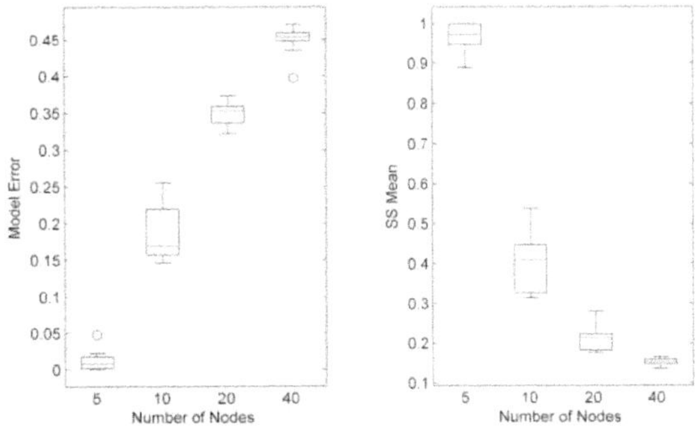

Figure 6. The effect of number of FCM nodes

5. CONCLUSION

Building causal models from data is an important problem with many applications. Fuzzy Cognitive Maps (FCMs) are a particular causal model. The aim of this paper is to present an Ant Colony Optimization (ACO) based algorithm to develop a FCM causal model from data.

A prior study proposed learning FCMs by an ACO. The algorithm was shown to be able to learn 8 weights of a FCM. A new ACO approach that is able to learn FCMs with at least 1600 weights (40 nodes) from several response sequences is proposed.

Several algorithms, such as Real-Coded Genetic Algorithm (RCGA), Nonlinear Hebbian Learning (NHL) and Data-Driven NHL (DD-NHL), were proposed to learn FCMs directly from data and applied to the same problem as this paper (i.e. recovering causal model from data). The ACO approach was compared to these algorithms through experiments. The proposed ACO algorithm outperforms RCGA, NHL and DD-NHL in terms of model error and SS mean measures when multiple response sequences are used in the learning process. However the ACO algorithm outperforms the three algorithms in only limited cases when only one response sequence is used in the learning process.

Because the basic ACO algorithm is used without any further improvements such as local search procedures, the performance of the ACO algorithm can be improved in the future studies.

6. REFERENCES

[1] Kosko, B. Fuzzy cognitive maps. *International Journal of Man-Machine Studies*, 24, 1 (1986), 65-75.

[2] Stach, W., Kurgan, L. and Pedrycz, W. Data-driven nonlinear Hebbian learning method for fuzzy cognitive maps. In *Proceedings of the 2008 IEEE International Conference on Fuzzy Systems, FUZZ 2008,* (Hong Kong, China, June 1 - June 6, 2008), 1975-1981.

[3] Stach, W., Kurgan, L., Pedrycz, W. and Reformat, M. Genetic learning of fuzzy cognitive maps. *Fuzzy Sets and Systems*, 153, 3 (2005), 371-401.

[4] Papageorgiou, E. I., Parsopoulos, K. E., Stylios, C. S., Groumpos, P. P. and Vrahatis, M. N. Fuzzy Cognitive Maps Learning Using Particle Swarm Optimization. *Journal of Intelligent Information Systems*, 25(2005), 95-121.

[5] Ghazanfari, M., Alizadeh, S., Fathian, M. and Koulouriotis, D. E. Comparing simulated annealing and genetic algorithm in learning FCM. *Applied Mathematics and Computation*, 192, 1 (2007), 56-68.

[6] Stach, W., Kurgan, L. and Pedrycz, W. A divide and conquer method for learning large fuzzy cognitive maps. *Fuzzy Sets and Systems*, 161, 19 (2010), 2515-2532.

[7] Stach, W. *Learning and Aggregation of Fuzzy Cognitive Maps - An Evolutionary Approach*. PhD Dissertation, University of Alberta, 2010.

[8] Chandra Mohan, B. and Baskaran, R. A survey: Ant Colony Optimization based recent research and implementation on several engineering domain. *Expert Systems with Applications*, 39, 4 (2012), 4618-4627.

[9] Dorigo, M., Maniezzo, V. and Colorni, A. Ant system: optimization by a colony of cooperating agents. *Systems, Man, and Cybernetics, Part B: Cybernetics, IEEE Transactions on*, 26, 1 (1996), 29-41.

[10] Liao, T., Oca, M. A. M. d., Aydin, D., Stützle, T. and Dorigo, M. An incremental ant colony algorithm with local search for continuous optimization. In *Proceedings of the 13th annual conference on Genetic and evolutionary computation* (Dublin, Ireland, 2011), 125-132.

[11] Xiao-Min, H., Jun, Z., Chung, H. S. H., Yun, L. and Ou, L. SamACO: Variable Sampling Ant Colony Optimization Algorithm for Continuous Optimization. *Systems, Man, and Cybernetics, Part B: Cybernetics, IEEE Transactions on*, 40, 6 (2010), 1555-1566.

[12] Ding, Z., Li, D. and Jia, J. First Study of Fuzzy Cognitive Map Learning Using Ants Colony Optimization. *Journal of Computational Information Systems*, 7, 13 (2011), 4756 - 4763.

[13] Chen, N. and Zhang, J. Index-based genetic algorithm for continuous optimization problems. In *Proceedings of the 13th annual conference on Genetic and evolutionary computation* (Dublin, Ireland, 2011), 1029-1036.

[14] Tsadiras, A. K. Comparing the inference capabilities of binary, trivalent and sigmoid fuzzy cognitive maps. *Information Sciences*, 178, 20 (2008), 3880-3894.

[15] Papageorgiou, E. I., Stylios, C. D. and Groumpos, P. P. Active Hebbian learning algorithm to train fuzzy cognitive maps. *International Journal of Approximate Reasoning*, 37, 3 (2004), 219-249.

[16] Koulouriotis, D. E., Diakoulakis, I. E. and Emiris, D. M. Learning fuzzy cognitive maps using evolution strategies: A novel schema for modeling and simulating high-level behavior. In *Proceedings of the Congress on Evolutionary Computation* (Soul, Korea, Republic of, 2001), 364-371.

[17] Stach, W., Kurgan, L., Pedrycz, W. and Reformat, M. Evolutionary development of fuzzy cognitive maps. In *Proceedings of the IEEE International Conference on Fuzzy Systems, FUZZ-IEEE 2005* (Reno, NV, United states, May 22 - May 25, 2005), 619-624.

[18] Parsopoulos, K. E., Papageorgiou, E. I., Groumpos, P. P. and Vrahatis, M. N. A first study of fuzzy cognitive maps learning using particle swarm optimization. In *Proceedings of the The 2003 Congress on Evolutionary Computation, 2003. CEC '03* (2003), 1440- 1447.

[19] Alizadeh, S., Ghazanfari, M., Jafari, M. and Hooshmand, S. Learning FCM by Tabu Search. *International Journal of Computer Science*, 2, 2 (2007), 142–149.

[20] Alizadeh, S. and Ghazanfari, M. Learning FCM by chaotic simulated annealing. *Chaos, Solitons & Fractals*, 41, 3 (2009), 1182-1190.

[21] Christian, B. Ant colony optimization: Introduction and recent trends. *Physics of Life Reviews*, 2, 4 (2005), 353-373.

[22] Papageorgiou, E. I., Stylios, C. D. and Groumpos, P. P. Fuzzy cognitive map learning based on nonlinear Hebbian rule. In *Proceedings of the Australian Conference on Artificial Intelligence* (2003), 256-268.

Ants Easily Solve Stochastic Shortest Path Problems

Benjamin Doerr
Max Planck Institute for Informatics
Saarbrücken, Germany
doerr@mpi-inf.mpg.de

Ashish Ranjan Hota
Indian Institute of Technology
Kharagpur, India
hota.ashish@acm.org

Timo Kötzing
Max Planck Institute for Informatics
Saarbrücken, Germany
koetzing@mpi-inf.mpg.de

ABSTRACT

The recent theoretical analysis (Horoba, Sudholt (GECCO 2010)) of an ant colony optimizer for the stochastic shortest path problem suggests that ant system experiences significant difficulties when the input data is prone to noise. In this work, we propose a slightly different ant optimizer to deal with noise.

We prove that, under mild conditions, it finds the paths with shortest expected length efficiently, despite the fact that we do not have convergence in the classic sense. To prove our results, we introduce a stronger drift theorem that can also deal with the situation that the progress is faster when one is closer to the goal.

Categories and Subject Descriptors

F.2 [**Theory of Computation**]: Analysis of Algorithms and Problem Complexity

General Terms

Theory, algorithms

Keywords

stochastic shortest path, running time analysis, theory

1. INTRODUCTION

Ant colony optimization (ACO) is a powerful bio-inspired optimization meta-heuristic. It has been applied successfully to a wide range of optimization problems, not restricted to the natural application area of graph algorithms. A key feature of these algorithms is that they do not stick to a fixed set (population) of solution candidates, but evolve a probability distribution whose mass ideally converges to favorable parts of the search space. For this reason, it seems likely that ACO approaches work robustly in computationally harder settings, for example, those involving uncertainty. Unfortunately, the seemingly first and still only rigorous run-time analysis of ACO on a problem with uncertainty [22] shows that a natural adaption of the Min-Max Ant System (MMAS) to the stochastic single-source shortest path problem experiences significant difficulties in finding (in expectation) optimal solutions.

In this work, we show how to overcome many of the difficulties demonstrated there. The key difference in this work is that we reevaluate the best-so-far solution whenever it is compared to a newly found one. This avoids being mislead by an exceptional, too optimistic evaluation. A consequence of the reevaluation is that we do not have convergence in the pheromone values anymore. From the view-point of application, this is not a problem, as taking a solution with close to maximum pheromone value safely identifies the optimum.

In the mathematical analysis performed in this paper, however, the absence of convergence poses some challenges. To overcome them, we use drift analysis [19, 20]. Since the drift we encounter is not monotone with the distance to the optimum, we prove the first drift theorem not needing this assumption. We are optimistic that this will find more applications in the near future.

1.1 Ant Colony Optimization

The ant colony optimization (ACO) method was suggested by Dorigo in his Ph.D. thesis [8] and has since found numerous applications, see, e.g., [9]. The basic idea is to mimic the foraging behavior of an ant colony, which builds on ant leaving pheromone traces on paths leading to food sources. Since paths to rich food sources are used more often, the pheromone trail becomes stronger here, attracting other ants to follow this route. While this paradigm naturally is suited for optimization problems involving shortest paths, routes, etc., it can also be applied to problems without a natural graph structure by adding a suitable *construction graph*. What is generally seen as a strength of ACO systems is that they do not keep a sample of the search space (population) as do many evolutionary algorithms, but rather evolve a probability space defined on the solution space.

The downside of this richer approach is that theoretical analyses of ACO systems are seemingly very difficult. While a well-developed theory of evolutionary algorithms exists for many years, it was not before the year 2000 that convergence results were proven [11, 12] and it took until 2007 for the first theoretical run-time analyses for ACO systems to appear [15, 16, 7, 17]. These results clearly show that analyzing even very simple ACO algorithms is much more difficult than analyzing simple evolutionary algorithms, and even more recent papers like [24] seemingly found no simple analysis method.

In this work, we consider ACO in the presence of noisy

GECCO'12, July 7–11, 2012, Philadelphia, Pennsylvania, USA.

data (optimization in the presence of stochastic uncertainties is sometimes called stochastic programming or stochastic combinatorial optimization). While there is good empirical evidence that using ACO in stochastic settings makes sense (for this we refer to the survey [3] and the references therein), a clear theoretical understanding of this aspect is still missing.

Indeed, Gutjahr in [13, 14] proposed the S-ACO algorithm for stochastic problems and proved convergence under moderate conditions. A main ingredient of this algorithm is that in the pheromone update, the observed quality of a new solution is not simply compared with the (at that time observed) quality of the best-so-far solution, but rather both solution candidates are re-sampled an increasing number of times to get more stable estimates.

On the other hand, the single rigorous run-time analysis for stochastic problems [22] does not suggest that ACO methods are particularly suitable in stochastic optimization. Let us describe their approach in more detail. The work [22] studies how shortest paths can be found using ACO when the edge lengths are stochastic, that is, there is random noise added to the evaluation of any edge length. Like previous works performing a run-time analysis on shortest path problems [1, 21], an ACO system was used where one ant starts in each node in parallel. Each of these ants only puts pheromone on the first edge of its walk (which is an outgoing edge from its starting node). Otherwise, the ACO system builds on the Max-Min Ant System [27], in which the current solution is compared to the best-so-far seen solution and the pheromone update is made with respect to the better of the two.

Also, to make ant walks and paths to be found lead into the same direction, not the classic single-source shortest path problem is regarded, but instead the single-destination version. This is no loss, since one variant can be turned into the other by reverting all directions. For this problem formulation, both [1] and [21] show good run-time results for the ACO system analyzed. Hence, the non-stochastic version seems to be well tractable with the ACO algorithm proposed.

For the stochastic setting, [22] basically uses the same ant system. Thus, when an ant produces a path, its stochastic length is evaluated and compared with the best-so-far seen length of a path from this starting point. The better of the two is reinforced by the pheromone system and stored as best-so-far solution and solution value. This system seems to have difficulties optimizing stochastic shortest paths. The authors present an example graph where, with high probability, the ants get stuck on an inferior solution (see Section 4 of this paper for a simple graph demonstrating the same effect). The authors also show that the ACO system suggested can compute approximate solutions. However, the approximation ratio, that is, the factor by which the solution computed is longer than the optimal one, is exponential in the length (number of edges) of the longest path. This makes no sense for most real-world graphs.

In this work, we overcome the difficulties seen in [22] via a simple modification. Analyzing the proofs there, we find the main difficulty is that an ant might be exceptionally lucky and evaluate a path to have a relatively small length. If this happens, the ant will prefer this path in the future, despite the actual quality of this solution not being so good. The simple way to overcome this is to reevaluate the best-so-far solution whenever it is compared to an actual solution. Clearly, this makes the comparison more fair, with both solutions "just having a single try" to evaluate shorter. This approach differs from the one of the S-ACO algorithm, where a relatively large number of reevaluations is done to not only get fairness, but also relatively stable evaluations. In a nutshell, the outcome of our work is that a single reevaluation often is enough.

The results we obtain justify this positive opinion. The ant system with reevaluation easily optimizes the example graph for which the previous approach failed. More generally, we show that for suitable choices of the system's parameters, the ACO system finds all shortest paths that, in direct comparison, have a chance of slightly more than $1/2$ of being evaluated shorter. For reasonable probability distributions for the noise, this implies that the ants find the paths with the shortest expected length.

While from the view-point of application the new system provides little difficulties, for the analysis this is different. Since the new system does not "lock in" the best-so-far solution (as often did the previous, whether actually better or not), we do not have such a strong convergence of the pheromone values. In fact, we do not have convergence at all, because it may always happen that the path which is better in expectation is evaluated to be longer than an alternative one. Of course, we do have the property that the aimed at solution often looks better than the alternatives, and this is enough to show that its pheromone values stay close to the maximum value. Hence, we may read off the optimal solution from those edges that carry close to maximum pheromone.

The true difficulty is in the mathematical analysis of the ACO process. Since we do not have convergence, we only observe a weaker drift behavior towards high pheromone values on preferred edges. *Drift analysis*, as introduced to our field by He and Yao [19, 20], is an advanced method to deal with such situations. Unfortunately, in our case the drift displays an uncommon behavior, being strongest for medium range pheromone values and weaker at the extremes. This makes all of the *additive drift* method of He and Yao, best for uniform drift, the *multiplicative drift* method by Doerr, Johannsen and Winzen [6], best for drift proportional to the distance from the optimum, and the *variable drift* method of Johannsen [23] (cited, e.g., in [5]), applicable whenever the drift is monotone with the distance from the optimum, give only bad run-time bounds. For this reason, we prove a generalization of the variable drift theorem (in a sense, of all drift theorems so far) that does not need the assumption that the drift is non-decreasing with the distance from the goal. This drift theorem might be useful for future research, in particular, in the ACO field.

Due to space constraints, some proofs are omitted.

2. PROBLEM DESCRIPTION AND ALGORITHM

In this section, we give a formal definition of the stochastic shortest path problem we regard and present the ACO algorithm we propose and analyze. We also describe how both relate to the well-known bandits learning problem.

2.1 Stochastic Shortest Path Problems

As most previous works, we regard a variant of the single-destination shortest path (SDSP) problem. Here, we are looking for shortest paths from any other vertex to a particular vertex called *sink*. Of course, by reverting the directions of all edges we can transform any problem instance (including the optimal solution) of the SDSP to the classic single-source shortest path problem and vice versa. So both problems are equivalent.

DEFINITION 1 (STOCHASTIC SDSP PROBLEM). *Let (V, E) be a directed acyclic graph (DAG). Assume that there is a unique sink (a vertex without edges going out), and that there is a path from every other vertex to the sink. For each edge $e \in E$, let X_e be a random variable describing the stochastic length of e. Denote by $X = (X_e)_{e \in E}$ the family of all these. Then the triple $G = (V, E, X)$ is called* graph with stochastic edge weights *or* stochastic-weight graph.

For any (directed) path p consisting of the edges $E_p \subseteq E$, we let $X_p = \sum_{e \in E_p} X_e$ be the (random) length of the path p.

The aim of this investigation is analyzing to what extent ACO systems are capable of finding a shortest path from any vertex in G to the sink. As pointed out in the introduction, in contrast with the deterministic setting, it is not so clear what "shortest path" means in the context of stochastic path lengths. One possible goal could be to find paths with minimal expected length. The performance measure could be the first hitting time. As we will see later, our ACO system only achieves the similar aim of finding paths with good probability of appearing shorter than other alternatives. While pathological examples show that there is little correlation between the two goals, for many natural distributions the difference is small.

We would like to stress that our focus is on understanding how natural ACO systems behave in situations of uncertainty. It is absolutely clear that custom-tailored methods are better suited to overcome the particular uncertainties in our setting. For example, by sufficiently often sampling the lengths of all edges separately, one can derive an arbitrarily close approximation of the underlying length distribution. This would allow, e.g., replacing the stochastic edge lengths with the approximate expected edge lengths and then running a classic shortest path algorithm to compute expected shortest paths.

2.2 Our ACO Algorithm

The common theme of all ACO algorithms is that artificial ants do a random walk over a given graph. The random decisions are heavily influenced by pheromone values attached to the edges. The outcome of each walk (in fact, it will be always a path) is interpreted as a solution of the underlying problem. Depending on the fitness of this solution, the pheromone values are updated in a way that (hopefully) makes this solution and similar ones more likely to be found in future ant walks.

In this subsection, we first make precise the construction of paths via ant walks, describe the way pheromones are updated, and finally give the ACO algorithm resulting from these and further design choices. The path construction and the pheromone update rule follow the usual standards. The ACO algorithm considered is the so-called Max-Min Ant System (MMAS) as first introduced in [27]. As in [22], we adopt it to the SDSP problem by having one ant start in each vertex in parallel. This is justified by the fact that we are looking for shortest paths from each vertex to the sink. What constitutes the crucial difference to [22] is that we reevaluate the best-so-far solution for each ant walk (see line 8 in Algorithm 2).

Path construction: As previously mentioned, we start (in parallel) one ant a_v from every non-sink vertex v and let it construct a path from v to the sink. When situated at a non-sink vertex, the ant randomly chooses one outgoing edge with a probability proportional to the pheromone on that edge, and then traverses this edge. The ants repeat this step until the sink is reached (since the graph is acyclic and has a unique sink, this always happens, without multiple visits to a vertex). This path construction procedure is made precise in Algorithm 1.

Algorithm 1: Path Construction from u to the sink

Input: DAG G, start vertex u, pheromones τ;
$i \leftarrow 0$, $p_0 \leftarrow u$;
$V_1 \leftarrow \{p \in V \mid (p_0, p) \in E\}$;
while $V_{i+1} \neq \emptyset$ **do**
  $i \leftarrow i + 1$;
  choose $p_i \in V_i$ with probability $\tau(p_{i-1}, p_i) / \sum_{p \in V_i} \tau(p_{i-1}, p_i)$;
  $V_{i+1} \leftarrow \{p \in V \mid (p_i, p) \in p\}$;
return $(p_0, \ldots, p_i)$;

Pheromone updates: Assume that the ant a_v has found a path p from v to the sink which we consider good. In this case, to increase the probability that this path is found again, we update the pheromone values on the edge outgoing from v, that lies on path p. We use the following rule for the pheromone update. Let $\tau : E \to [0, 1]$ describe our current pheromone values on the edges. Then the pheromone values $\tau' := \tau'(\tau, p)$ after this update satisfy

$$\tau'(e) = \begin{cases} \min((1-\rho)\tau(e) + \rho, \tau_{\max}), & \text{if } e \text{ is used in } p; \\ \max((1-\rho)\tau(e), \tau_{\min}), & \text{otherwise} \end{cases}$$

for all edges out-going from v. For all other edges e, we have $\tau'(e) = \tau(e)$. Note that $\tau_{\min}$ and $\tau_{\max}$ are parameters to the algorithm.

The MMAS ACO algorithm with reevaluation of stochastic lengths: The basic concept of the MMAS ACO algorithm is that after each run of an ant, a pheromone update is made. If the just-constructed path p is at least as good as the best-so-far seen path p^*, then the update is done with respect to p, otherwise with respect to p^*.

Since we have one ant a_v for each non-sink vertex v, we store a best-so-far solution p_v^* for each vertex and compare this with the solution constructed by a_v.

There is one difficulty to deal with for stochastic settings: there is no absolute quality of solutions. Due to the stochasticity, the same path may be evaluated with different lengths. Horoba and Sudholt [22] decided that they store the best-ever seen length with the best-so-far solution. However, as can be seen from analyzing their proofs, this leads to strange behavior. If a path was ever evaluated at an unexpectedly short length (as may rarely happen), then this path looks too good for the remainder of the ACO run.

To overcome this problem, we suggest to reevaluate the best-so-far solution whenever it is compared to another solution. By this we hope to better capture the typical quality of a solution.

Algorithm 2 gives the complete Max-Min Ant System with reevaluation of the best-so-far solution.

Algorithm 2: Max-Min Ant System

Parameter: ρ;
Input: DAG $G = (V, E)$;
initialize pheromones τ and best-so-far paths $p_1^*, \dots, p_n^*$;
while *termination criterion not met* **do**
  for $u = 1$ **to** n *in parallel* **do**
    construct a simple path p_u from u to the sink w.r.t. τ;
    $w \leftarrow$ evaluate(p_u);
    $w^* \leftarrow$ evaluate(p_u^*);
    if $w \leq w^*$ **then** $p_u^* \leftarrow p_u$;
    update pheromones τ on all edges outgoing from u w.r.t. p_u^*;
return $(p_0, \dots, p_i)$;

We will use the following lemma about pheromones in the MMAS taken from [21].

LEMMA 2 ([21, LEMMA 1]). *Let v be a vertex and τ be a the vector of pheromones in some iteration during some run of MMAS. Then the total pheromones τ_{total} on the edges going out from v is bounded from above by $1 + n\tau_{\min}$.*

In particular, any edge with pheromone τ is chosen with a probability at least $\tau/(1 + n\tau_{\min})$.

2.3 Bandit Setting

We consider the following definition for a stochastic online learning setting (see, for example, [4]). Given a finite set of possible *actions* and associated real-valued random variables $(X_a)_{a \in A}$ a *learner* is asked to repeatedly choose an action from A. With every choice $a \in A$, the learner incurs a *loss* drawn according to X_a (the draws of different iterations are assumed to be independent). The goal is to minimize the loss; the difference between the actual loss (after n iterations) and the loss of the optimal strategy of always choosing the action corresponding to the random variable with smallest expected value, is known as the *regret*.

Trivially, if the learner knows the distribution of the losses $(X_a)_{a \in A}$ at the start, then he can achieve an expected regret of 0. Instead, one looks at settings where only the set of possible actions and not the associated loss functions are given. There are several different settings for how a learner gathers information about the loss functions; the most interesting setting for our purposes is the *multi-armed bandit setting* [26], where, after each iteration, the learner gets to know the loss it incurred in the given iteration, but nothing about the alternatives. This poses a question regarding the exploration vs. exploitation trade off: should the learner choose an action known to have a small loss in order to keep the regret low, or try to find actions with even lower loss?

The case of finding the shortest link among m parallel links corresponds to choosing between one of m different actions. Since our ACO algorithm reevaluates its best-so-far solution, it requires choosing two actions for each iteration of the ACO.

The setting where several bandit problems are supposed to be solved in parallel, and feedback from one task might benefit the learner in other tasks (as in the stochastic single-destination shortest path problem), is called a *multitask bandit problem*.

For the multi-armed bandit setting, efficient algorithms are known which achieve a sublinear regret [25]. Furthermore, many variations of the settings of online learning have been studied, including with adversarial rather than stochastic loss [2], also in a setting of finding a shortest path [18]. One of the main interests of this work lies in finding efficient problem specific algorithms with low regret.

We consider MMAS optimizing m parallel links and compute the expected regret. Suppose one edge has deterministic weight 0 and all others deterministic weight 1. After an initial phase of finding the good edge and converging in pheromones to that edge, MMAS will sample a non-optimal edge with probability about $(1-n\tau_{\min})$ in every iteration. In each iteration where a non-optimal edge is chosen, MMAS incurs a regret of 1. Thus, the expected regret in t rounds is $\Theta(t(1 - \tau_{\max}))$, linear in the number of iterations. This shows that MMAS is inferior in the bandit setting to tailored algorithms.

Intuitively, MMAS focuses more strongly on exploration than problem specific algorithms. Note that MMAS will not converge to the right link at all if, for example, the link with highest expected value has a chance of less than 1/2 of coming out higher when compared with any other link (see the example given in Proposition 8).

For the remainder of this paper we will not consider the bandit setting, but focus on the questions of whether and how fast MMAS converges to paths that are good in expectation.

3. PARALLEL LINKS

In this section, we analyze the most simple case of two nodes connected by several parallel edges. This will be the cornerstone of the results in the following sections.

Roughly speaking, we will show that, if there is an edge that looks shorter than any other edge with probability strictly greater than 1/2, then this edge will attract the vast majority of the pheromone.

While seemingly a natural result, its proof is surprisingly hard. The main difference, e.g., compared to the previous work [22], is that now the preferred edge only gains pheromone at a higher rate than the other edges. In previous works, typically the MMAS once it found a good edge, it sticked to it and reinforced it until $\tau_{\max}$ was reached.

For this reason, we shall need arguments from drift analysis to bound the time needed until this process has brought the maximum pheromone to the preferred edge. Unfortunately, the progress of growth of pheromone on the preferred edge follows an uncommon pattern. It is strongest for mid-range pheromone values, but slow for both high and low pheromone values. To analyze such types of drift, we need to prove a variation of Johannsen's variable drift theorem that can deal with the situation that the drift is not monotonic with the distance to the optimum.

3.1 Result

In the remainder of this section, let $G = (V, E, X)$ be a stochastic-weight graph such that

- $V = \{v, s\}$,
- E consists of m parallel edges from v to the sink s,

- there is an $e \in E$ and a $\delta > 0$ such that for all $f \in E \setminus \{e\}$, $\Pr(X_e < X_f) \geq 0.5 + \delta$. We call e a *preferred* edge, since e looks shorter than each of the other edges with probability more than 0.5.

Note that the condition of being a preferred edge is more than just saying that X_e has the minimum expectation. Furthermore, it may also happen that none of the edges is preferred. Examples of this type can easily be constructed from the famous *non-transitive dice* example from elementary probability theory, see, e.g., Gardner [10].

Of course, we would hope that MMAS recognizes a preferred edge, if it exists, and ideally raises its pheromone value to the upper boundary $\tau_{\max}$. This is indeed true, though hard to prove.

THEOREM 3. *Suppose $\tau_{\max} + \tau_{\min} = 1$ and $2\rho \leq \tau_{\min}$. Then, after an expected number of $O(\frac{\log(1/\tau_{\min})}{\delta\rho})$ iterations, the pheromone value on the preferred edge e is $\tau_{\max}$.*

In Section 3.2 we give an important tool for our proof of Theorem 3, a new drift theorem allowing for drift which is not increasing with the distance to the optimum. Section 3.3 constitutes the proof of Theorem 3.

We will give a version of Theorem 3 applicable to arbitrary graphs in Section 5, namely Theorem 11; note, however, that Theorem 11 requires an additional restriction on δ which is not present in Theorem 3.

3.2 Proof via Improved Drift Analysis

The difficulty in proving Theorem 3 lies in the fact that, while e is preferred over other edges, this preference may be only slight. So, unlike with many proofs on the performance of MMAS, it does not happen that once e is found, MMAS does not reinforce the other alternatives anymore. Rather, with constant rate, it will happen that an alternative looks better, and that this is reinforced instead of e.

The current best method to deal with such situations is *drift analysis*, which was first introduced to the theory of evolutionary computation by He and Yao [19, 20]. In a nutshell, this method tries to suitably characterize the expected progress of a random process in one iteration. From this, via so-called drift theorems, one can deduce information about the expected time the process needs to reach a certain area in the state space.

While the (now so-called) *additive drift* of He and Yao is most suitable for situations in which the progress is uniform, the recently introduced multiplicative drift analysis [6] captures best the situation that the progress is proportional to the current distance from the goal. A generalization of this, applicable to the general situation that the progress is faster if the distance to the goal is larger, was proven in Johannsen's PhD thesis [23, Theorem 4.6] and is called *variable drift*.

Unfortunately, even this very general tool is not enough for our purposes. The problem is that the expected increase of the pheromone level of e is small both when e carries much pheromone (this stems from the pheromone update rule) and when e has little pheromone (because then the probability of sampling e is small). Hence, Johannsen's monotonicity assumption seems hard to fulfill.

We overcome this difficulty by proving a variable drift theorem that does not need the monotonicity assumption. We are optimistic that this new drift theorem will be useful both in other ACO problems and, more generally, for the analysis of other bio-inspired search heuristics.

THEOREM 4. *Let $(X_t)_{t\geq 0}$ be random variables describing a Markov process over a finite state space $0 \in S \subseteq \mathbb{R}_0^+$ and let $x_{\min} := \min\{x \in S \mid x > 0\}$. Furthermore, let T be the random variable that denotes the first point in time $t \in \mathbb{N}$ for which $X_t = 0$. Suppose that there exist $c \geq 1$, $d > 0$ and a continuous function $h : \mathbb{R}_0^+ \to \mathbb{R}^+$ such that*

- *for all $t < T$, $E(X_t - X_{t+1} \mid X_t) \geq h(X_t)$;*
- *for all $t < T$, $P(X_t - X_{t+1} \leq d) = 1$; and*
- *for all $x < y$ with $y - x \leq d$, we have $h(x) \leq c\,h(y)$.*

Then

$$E(T \mid X_0) \leq c \left(\frac{x_{\min}}{h(x_{\min})} + \int_{x_{\min}}^{X_0} \frac{1}{h(x)} dx \right).$$

Note that the case of $c = 1$ above just means that h is monotonic. For our purposes, we will need the statement for $c > 1$.

3.3 Analysis: Parallel Edges

Using the above new drift theorem, we can now analyze how the pheromone is accrued on the preferred edge e. As always in drift analysis, we have to define a suitable progress measure (potential function).

Recall that the state of the MMAS for our graph is fully described by the pheromone values of all edges and the best-so-far solution, which is one of the edges from E. For the purpose of our analysis, only the pheromone on e is important and whether e is the current best-so-far solution or not. We denote such a reduced state by a pair (τ, x), where τ is the present pheromone on e and x is set to 1 if e is the current best-so-far solution and 0 otherwise.

For such a state (τ, x), we define its *potential* by

$$g(\tau, x) = \tau + \rho x.$$

Hence, g basically measures the pheromone on e, giving a "bonus" of ρ when e is the current best-so-far solution. For this potential, we can show the following statement on its expected increase.

LEMMA 5. *Let $r = 1 + \varepsilon$ be an upper bound on the total pheromone on the edges of the graph. Let $\delta \geq \varepsilon$. Let MMAS be in a state with reduced state (τ, x). Let (τ', x') be (random variables denoting) the (reduced) state after one iteration, where the update of the pheromone values was made ignoring the pheromone boundaries $\tau_{\min}$ and $\tau_{\max}$. Then*

$$E[g(\tau', x') - g(\tau, x)] \geq \min(\tau, 1 - \tau)\rho\delta/2.$$

PROOF. To prove the lemma, we first make the underlying Markov chain precise, that is, given a state (τ, x), we find the transition probabilities of going to other states.

When $x = 1$, we sample e again with probability at least τ/r, which automatically implies $x = 1$ for the next state. If we sample some edge other than e (with probability at most $1 - \tau/r$), we can still have $x = 1$ in the next state with probability $p \geq 0.5 + \delta$, thanks to e having the better value in the direct comparison (see Definition 9). Thus, the probability of next going to a state with $x = 1$, given in the present state $x = 1$, is at least $\tau/r + (1 - \tau/r)p$. In this

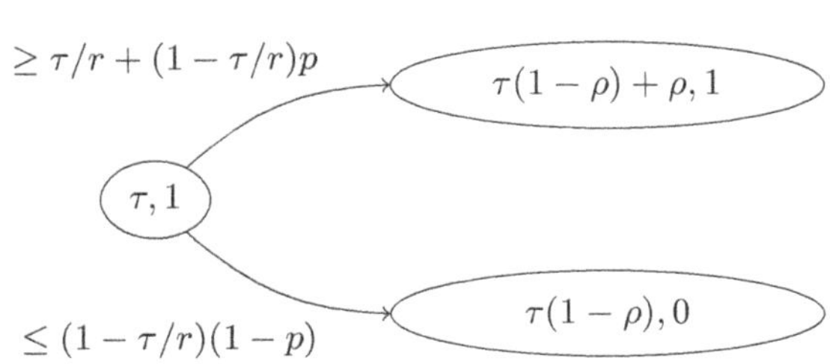

(a) Best-So-Far=1

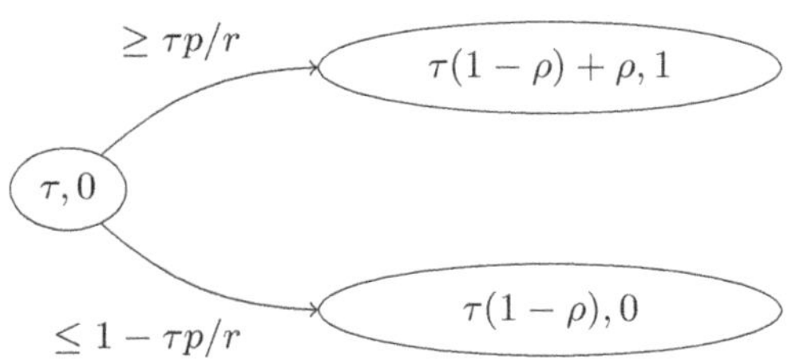

(b) Best-So-Far=0

Figure 1: Markov Chain

state, we have a positive reinforcement of the pheromone τ to $\tau(1-\rho)+\rho$.

With similar arguments, we find the probability of going to a state with $x=0$, given the present has $x=1$, is at most $(1-\tau/r)(1-p)$ and the pheromone value in that state is $\tau(1-\rho)$. In this case there is no positive reinforcement in the pheromone on e.

Similarly, if in the present state we have $x=0$, then the probability of going to a new state with $x=1$ is at least $\tau p/r$. With remaining probability of at most $1-\tau p/r$ we go to a state with $x=0$. The pheromone values of the next states are the same as in the cases of $x=1$. Fig. 1 depicts the different states and corresponding transitions of the Markov chain. The associated transition probabilities of going from one state to the other are also shown.

Given this chain, we can now prove the statement of the lemma. Assume first that $x=1$. Then

$$\begin{aligned}
&E[g(\tau',x')-g(\tau,x)]\\
&= P(x'=1)\,g(\tau(1-\rho)+\rho,1)+\\
&\quad P(x'=0)\,g(\tau(1-\rho),0)-\\
&\quad g(\tau,1)\\
&\geq (\tau/r+(1-\tau/r)p)(\tau(1-\rho)+2\rho)+\\
&\quad (1-\tau/r)(1-p)\tau(1-\rho)-(\tau+\rho)\\
&= \tau^2(1-\rho)/r+2\tau\rho/r+\tau(1-\tau/r)p(1-\rho)+\\
&\quad 2(1-\tau/r)p\rho+\tau(1-\tau/r)(1-p)(1-\rho)\\
&\quad -(\tau+\rho)\\
&= \tau^2(1-\rho)/r+2\tau\rho/r+\tau(1-\tau/r)(1-\rho)\\
&\quad +2(1-\tau/r)p\rho-(\tau+\rho)\\
&= 2\tau\rho/r+\tau(1-\rho)+2(1-\tau/r)p\rho-(\tau+\rho)\\
&= (2p-1+\tau(2/r-1-2p/r))\rho.
\end{aligned}$$

The last term is at least $(1-\tau)\rho\delta/2$ if the following two equations hold.

$$\begin{aligned}
2p-1 &\geq \delta/2;\\
2p/r+1-2/r &\geq \delta/2.
\end{aligned}$$

The first of these equations follows from $2p-1=\delta$; the second is implied by $\delta \geq \varepsilon$.

For $x=0$, we have

$$\begin{aligned}
&E[g(\tau',x')-g(\tau,x)]\\
&= P(x'=1)\,g(\tau(1-\rho)+\rho,1)+\\
&\quad P(x'=0)\,g(\tau(1-\rho),0)-\\
&\quad g(\tau,0)\\
&= (\tau p/r(\tau(1-\rho)+2\rho)+(1-\tau p/r)\tau(1-\rho)-\tau\\
&= \tau^2 p(1-\rho)/r+2\tau p\rho/r+\tau(1-\rho)-\tau^2 p(1-\rho)/r-\tau\\
&= 2\tau p\rho/r-\tau\rho\\
&= \tau\rho(2p/r-1).
\end{aligned}$$

The last term is at least $\tau\rho\delta/2$ if $2p/r-1 \geq \delta/2$, which is implied by $\delta \geq \varepsilon$.

Thus, the drift is lower bounded by $\min(\tau,1-\tau)\rho\delta/2$. □

For all t, let τ^t and x^t be the random variables denoting the pheromone in iteration t and the value of the best-so-far solution in iteration t, respectively. We define the random variables X^t by

$$X^t = \begin{cases} 1-g(\tau^t,x^t) & \text{if } \tau^t < \tau_{\max} \\ 0 & \text{else} \end{cases}$$

for all t.

We want to use Theorem 4 with the drift computed in Lemma 5. To that end we let h be such that, for all z,

$$h(z) = \min(z,1-z)\rho\delta/4.$$

Note that the drift computed in Lemma 5 does not directly apply to the Markov chain $(X^t)_t$, as the potential values of a state of the algorithm might be up to ρ different from its pheromone value τ. However, straightforward calculations with the result of Lemma 5 show that, for all z, $h(z)$ gives a lower bound for the drift of $(X^t)_t$.

The minimal x that we will use this on is $1-\tau_{\max}-\rho = \tau_{\min}-\rho$, since $\tau_{\max}+\rho$ is the largest potential value of g. Furthermore we have, for all t,

$$g(\tau^t,x^t)-2\rho \leq g(\tau^{t+1},x^{t+1}) \leq g(\tau^t,x^t)+2\rho.$$

This holds because, in one iteration, the pheromone value can change by at most ρ, and the value of x can change by at most 1, which changes the value of $g(\tau^{t+1},x^{t+1})$ by at most 2ρ from the value of $g(\tau^t,x^t)$. A special case occurs when $\tau^{t+1}=\tau_{\max}$, the boundary case of the Markov chain $(X^t)_t$; the additional distance is $1-\tau_{\max}-\rho=\rho$. However, it is easy to see that in this case we have $x^t=1$, which means that the potential cannot be decreased by changing x from 0 to 1, so the maximum change in potential is 2ρ also in this case.

Thus, for the preconditions of Theorem 4, we need to show that there is a c' such that, for all x,y with $0 \leq x < y \leq 1-\tau_{\min}=\tau_{\max}$ and $y-x \leq 2\rho$, $h(x) \leq c'h(y)$. We let $c'=2$. Let x,y with $1-\tau_{\max}-\rho \leq x < y \leq 1-\tau_{\min}$ be such that $y-x \leq 2\rho$. The claim is trivial if $y \leq 1/2$, so suppose $y > 1/2$. We have $2y - x \le y + 2\rho \le 1$; hence, $1 - x \le 2(1 - y)$. Therefore,

$$h(x) \le (1-x)\rho\delta/4 \le 2(1-y)\rho\delta/4 = 2h(y).$$

This fulfills the preconditions of Theorem 4 as desired.

By Theorem 4, the expected time until the pheromone value on the preferred edge e is at $\tau_{\max}$, is at most

$$2\left(\frac{1}{\rho\delta} + \int_{\tau_{\min}-\rho}^{\tau_{\max}} \frac{4}{\min(x,(1-x))\rho\delta}dx\right)$$
$$= \frac{2}{\rho\delta} + \frac{8}{\rho\delta}\left(\int_{\tau_{\min}-\rho}^{\frac{1}{2}} \frac{1}{x}dx + \int_{\frac{1}{2}}^{\tau_{\max}} \frac{1}{1-x}dx\right)$$
$$\le \frac{2}{\rho\delta} + \frac{16}{\rho\delta}\int_{\tau_{\min}-\rho}^{\frac{1}{2}} \frac{1}{x}dx$$
$$= O\left(\frac{\log(1/\tau_{\min})}{\rho\delta}\right).$$

4. EXAMPLES

Next we give some illustrative examples of stochastic-weight graphs, where MMAS converges as desired (using the result of the previous section). The first example concerns normally distributed random variables as edge lengths. Together with the previous section, Proposition 6 shows that, for parallel links with normally distributed lengths, MMAS will converge in pheromone to the edge with shortest expected value (given δ large enough).

PROPOSITION 6. *Consider two normal distributed random variables $X \sim N(\mu, \sigma_1^2)$ and $Y \sim N(\mu(1+\epsilon), \sigma_2^2)$, where μ, ϵ, σ_1 and $\sigma_2 \in \mathbb{R}^+$. Then, $P(X \le Y) = 0.5 + \delta$, where*

$$\delta = \Omega\left(\frac{\mu\epsilon}{\sqrt{\sigma_1^2 + \sigma_2^2}}\right).$$

We denote the gamma distribution with shape parameter $k > 0$ and scale parameter $\theta > 0$ as $\Gamma(k, \theta)$.

The paper [22] gives a family of instances for stochastic-weight graphs where MMAS *without* reevaluation of the best-so-far path requires a superpolynomial number of iterations for finding the paths that are shortest in expectation. The random weights in these instances are based on the gamma distribution. The core difficulty for these instances lies in differentiating correctly whether to use a single long edge to the goal, or many short edges, which are just a bit shorter than the long edge in total; see Figure 2 for an illustration of two cases with $n \in \{1, 4\}$ short edges. The edge weights w are subject to a gamma distributed noise, such that the stochastic length is $w(1 + \Gamma(k, \theta))$, where the parameters k and θ are the same over all edges of the graph.

In [22] it was shown that MMAS without reevaluation will be deceived by the variance of the single long edge, and converge to it in pheromone values. In Proposition 7 we show, for many relevant parameters, that the sum of the short edges (corresponding to the random variable X in the proposition) is likely to come out better than the long edge (corresponding to the random variable Y). Together with the result from Section 3, this implies that many of the instances given in [22] which MMAS cannot solve without reevaluation, *can* be solved using reevaluation. In particular, we have that MMAS with reevaluation on instances exemplified in Figure 2 will converge (as desired) to the lower edges (following the lower chain depicted in Figure 2).

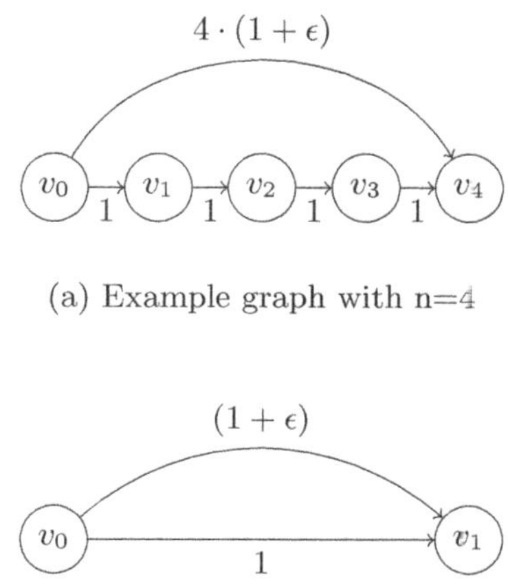

(a) Example graph with n=4

(b) Example graph with n=1

Figure 2: Example graphs

PROPOSITION 7. *Let m be a natural number and $k, \theta, \varepsilon > 0$. Suppose $k\varepsilon^2 \ge 16$. For $i \le m$, let $X_i \sim 1 + \Gamma(k, \theta)$ be i.i.d. and let $X \sim \sum_{i=1}^m X_i$. Furthermore, let $Y \sim m(1 + \varepsilon)(1 + \Gamma(k, \theta))$ be independent of all X_i. Then*

$$P(X \le Y) \ge 9/16.$$

In general, when comparing two random variables, a smaller expected value does not imply that it is more likely to come out smaller. Instead, there are two random variables where the first one has an expected value arbitrarily higher than the second, and still comes out better with an arbitrarily good probability. This is formalized in the following proposition.

PROPOSITION 8. *For all $c > 1$ and q with $0 < q < 1$, there are X, Y such that $E(X) = cE(Y)$ and $P(X < Y) = q$.*

5. GENERAL GRAPHS

In this section we formally analyze the behavior of MMAS on well-behaved stochastic-weight graphs.

DEFINITION 9. *Let $G = (V, E, X)$ be a stochastic-weight graph and let $\delta > 0$. For all $i \le n$, we inductively define sets of edges A_δ^i such that $A_\delta^0 = \emptyset$ and an edge e from v to w is an element of A_δ^{i+1} if and only if there is a path p from v to the sink using only edges from $A_\delta^i \cup \{e\}$ such that p contains e and, for any path p' from v to the sink where p' does not use e, $P(X_p < X_{p'}) \ge 0.5 + \delta$. We call edges from A_δ^n δ*-preferred edges.

In Theorem 11 below we will show that the name "preferred edge" has its justification in the fact that MMAS will prefer to take these edges (after an initial phase to find these edges). But first we will give an example of preferred edges in a stochastic-weight graph where all edge weights are normally distributed; Proposition 10 shows that, in this case, the set of preferred edges corresponds to the tree of paths of shortest expected length.

PROPOSITION 10. *Let $G = (V, E, X)$ be a stochastic-weight graph such that, for all edges $e \in E$, X_e is normally distributed. Furthermore, suppose that the graph derived from G by replacing all random weights by their expected value has a unique shortest path tree S. Then, for δ small enough, the set of δ-preferred edges A_δ^n is the tree S.*

We now get to the main theorem of the paper, concerning the behavior of MMAS on general graphs.

THEOREM 11. *Let $G = (V, E, X)$ be a stochastic-weight graph with n vertices and suppose $\tau_{\min} = O(1/n^3)$ and $\rho = \tau_{\min}/2$. Then there is a constant c such that, for δ such that the set of δ-preferred edges $A_\delta^n \subseteq E$ is a tree and $\delta \geq cn^2\tau_{\min}$, after*

$$O\left(\frac{n \log(1/\tau_{\min})}{\delta\rho}\right)$$

iterations, MMAS on G has a pheromone of $1 - O(n\tau_{\min})$ on all edges of A_δ^n and $O(n\tau_{\min})$ on all others.

Acknowledgement

We thank one anonymous reviewer for pointing us to Gutjahr's work [13, 14] on the S-ACO algorithm, which we (and the authors of [22]) unfortunately overlooked. Ashish Ranjan Hota was gratefully supported by the German Academic Exchange Services (DAAD) through a WISE stipend for undertaking an internship at the Max Planck Institute for Informatics, Saarbrücken, Germany.

6. REFERENCES

[1] N. Attiratanasunthron and J. Fakcharoenphol. A running time analysis of an ant colony optimization algorithm for shortest paths in directed acyclic graphs. *Information Processing Letters*, 105:88–92, 2008.

[2] P. Auer, N. Cesa-Bianchi, Y. Freund, and R. E. Schapire. The nonstochastic multiarmed bandit problem. *SIAM Journal of Computing*, 32:48–77, 2003.

[3] L. Bianchi, M. Dorigo, L. M. Gambardella, and W. J. Gutjahr. A survey on metaheuristics for stochastic combinatorial optimization. *Natural Computing*, 8:239–287, 2009.

[4] N. Cesa-Bianchi and G. Lugosi. *Prediction, Learning, and Games*. Cambridge University Press, 2006.

[5] B. Doerr, M. Fouz, and C. Witt. Sharp bounds by probability-generating functions and variable drift. In *Genetic and Evolutionary Computation Conference (GECCO'11)*, pages 2083–2090. ACM, 2011.

[6] B. Doerr, D. Johannsen, and C. Winzen. Multiplicative drift analysis. In *Genetic and Evolutionary Computation Conference (GECCO'10)*, pages 1449–1456. ACM, 2010.

[7] B. Doerr, F. Neumann, D. Sudholt, and C. Witt. On the runtime analysis of the 1-ANT ACO algorithm. In *Genetic and Evolutionary Computation Conference (GECCO'07)*, pages 33–40. ACM, 2007.

[8] M. Dorigo. *Optimization, Learning and Natural Algorithms (in Italian)*. PhD thesis, Dipartimento di Elettronica, Politecnico di Milano, Milan, Italy, 1992.

[9] M. Dorigo and T. Stützle. *Ant colony optimization*. MIT Press, 2004.

[10] M. Gardner. Nontransitive dice and other probability paradoxes. *Scientific American*, 223:110–114, 1970.

[11] W. J. Gutjahr. A graph-based ant system and its convergence. *Future Generation Comper Systems*, 16:873–888, 2000.

[12] W. J. Gutjahr. ACO algorithms with guaranteed convergence to the optimal solution. *Information Processessing Letters*, 82:145–153, 2002.

[13] W. J. Gutjahr. A converging ACO algorithm for stochastic combinatorial optimization. In *Symposium on Stochastic Algorithms: Foundations and Applications (SAGA'03)*, pages 10–25, 2003.

[14] W. J. Gutjahr. S-ACO: An ant-based approach to combinatorial optimization under uncertainty. In *ANTS*, pages 238–249. Springer, 2004.

[15] W. J. Gutjahr. Mathematical runtime analysis of aco algorithms: survey on an emerging issue. *Swarm Intelligence*, 1:59–79, 2007.

[16] W. J. Gutjahr. First steps to the runtime complexity analysis of ant colony optimization. *Computers and Operations Research*, 35:2711–2727, 2008.

[17] W. J. Gutjahr and G. Sebastiani. Runtime analysis of ant colony optimization with best-so-far reinforcement. *Methodology and Computing in Applied Probability*, 10:409–433, 2008.

[18] A. György, T. Linder, G. Lugosi, and G. Ottucsák. The on-line shortest path problem under partial monitoring. *Journal of Machine Learning Research*, 8:2369–2403, 2007.

[19] J. He and X. Yao. Drift analysis and average time complexity of evolutionary algorithms. *Artificial Intelligence*, 127:57–85, 2001.

[20] J. He and X. Yao. A study of drift analysis for estimating computation time of evolutionary algorithms. *Natural Computing*, 3:21–35, 2004.

[21] C. Horoba and D. Sudholt. Running time analysis of ACO systems for shortest path problems. In *Engineering Stochastic Local Search Algorithms (SLS'09)*, pages 76–91. Springer, 2009.

[22] C. Horoba and D. Sudholt. Ant colony optimization for stochastic shortest path problems. In *Genetic and Evolutionary Computation Conference (GECCO'10)*, pages 1465–1472. ACM, 2010.

[23] D. Johannsen. *Random Combinatorial Structures and Randomized Search Heuristics*. PhD thesis, Universität des Saarlandes, 2010. Available online at http://scidok.sulb.uni-saarland.de/volltexte/2011/3529/pdf/Dissertation_3166_Joha_Dani_2010.pdf.

[24] T. Kötzing, F. Neumann, D. Sudholt, and M. Wagner. Simple max-min ant systems and the optimization of linear pseudo-boolean functions. In *Foundations of Genetic Algorithms (FOGA'11)*, pages 209–218. ACM, 2011.

[25] T. Lai and H. Robbins. Asymptotically efficient adaptive allocation rules. *Advances in Applied Mathematics*, 6:4 – 22, 1985.

[26] H. Robbins. Some aspects of the sequential design of experiments. *Bulletin of the American Mathematical Society*, 58:527–535, 1952.

[27] T. Stützle and H. H. Hoos. MAX-MIN ant system. *Future Generation Computer Systems*, 16:889–914, 2000.

Why Six Informants Is Optimal in PSO

José García-Nieto
University of Malaga
Dept. Lenguajes y Ciencias de la Computación
Bulevar Louis Pasteur, 35
29071 Malaga- Spain
jnieto@lcc.uma.es

Enrique Alba
University of Malaga
Dept. Lenguajes y Ciencias de la Computación
Bulevar Louis Pasteur, 35
29071 Malaga- Spain
eat@lcc.uma.es

ABSTRACT

In a previous work, it was empirically shown that certain numbers of informants different from the standard "two" and the expensive "all" may provide the Particle Swarm Optimization (PSO) with new essential information about the search landscape, leading this algorithm to perform more accurately than other existing versions of it. Here, we extend this study by analyzing the internal behavior of PSO from the point of view of the evolvability. Our motivation is to find evidences of why such number of $6_{\pm 2}$ informant particles, perform better than other neighborhood formulations of PSO. For this task, we have evaluated different combinations of informants for an extensive set of problem functions. Using fitness-distance correlation and fitness-fitness cloud analyses we have tested the accuracy of the resulting landscape characterizations. The results suggest that, in spite of certain deviation to the global optimum, a number of 6 informants in PSO can generate new improved particles for a longer time, even in complex problems with multi-funnel landscapes.

Categories and Subject Descriptors

I.2.8 [**Problem Solving, Control Methods, and Search**]: Heuristic methods; G.1.6 [**Optimization**]: [Global Optimization]

General Terms

Algorithms

Keywords

Particle Swarm Optimization, Fully Informed PSO, fitness-distance correlation, fitness-fitness cloud

1. INTRODUCTION

Evolvability has first been introduced in theoretical Biology for the characterization of information landscapes [16], although it can be directly related to problem hardness for Evolutionary Algorithms (EAs), and metaheuristics in general [4]. Evolvability can be defined as the capacity of algorithms' operators to improve the fitness quality for a given problem [6]. From a complementary point of view, the outlined fitness traces (and distance to optimum) of different algorithms for a given problem can be also used to compute indicators in terms of their evolvability. In this way, it is possible to distinguish which algorithm has larger search capabilities for the tackled problem, and why.

In a previous work [3], an empirically study clearly shown that certain numbers of informant neighbors may provide Particle Swarm Optimization (PSO) with new essential information about the search landscape, leading this algorithm to perform more accurately than other existing versions of it (Standards [12] and FIPS [7] versions). Here, we contribute to this research line by analyzing the internal behavior of PSO from the point of view of the evolvability. Our main motivation is to find evidences of why certain unstructured neighborhoods, with $6_{\pm 2}$ informant particles, perform better than other neighborhood formulations.

With this aim, we have developed a new version of PSO called PSO-k (with k informant neighbors) that, ranging from the Standard PSO (2 informants) to the Fully Informed PSO (FIPS) allows to generalize the number of informant particles involved in the calculation of new particles. Then, the PSO-k with different combinations of informants has been evaluated over the CEC 2005 [13] Benchmark of functions, on which we have computed both, fitness and distance to optimum traces to calculate evolvability measures. We use this standard benchmark to avoid biasing the results and to have a high number of test problems with different complexities that endorse our claims. Since the CEC'05 Test Suite has been properly characterized in a recent work [11] by means of the Fitness Distance Correlation (fdc), we have decided to use this measure in this work together with the Fitness Cloud (fc) and Escape Probability (ep), to test the resulting landscape characterizations from all combinations of neighbors in PSO-k. With the outlined information, we expect to test the following hypothesis:

Work Hypothesis: a number of $6_{\pm 2}$ informants in the operation of PSO may compute new improved particles for longer than other PSO formulations in single and multi-funnel benchmarking problems.

In this article we will show that, on the one hand, few informants (one or two as in Standard PSO) could sometimes show high escaping probabilities and positive correlation, although evolving solutions with poor fitness values. On the

GECCO'12, July 7-11, 2012, Philadelphia, Pennsylvania, USA.

other hand, we will show that in PSO with more than 10 informants, solutions could concentrate on small regions whose sizes decrease as the neighborhood topology increases, thus confusing the search and again reducing the escape probability [9, 14].

The structure of this paper is as follows. In Section 2 we describe the PSO-k approach devoted to evaluate different combinations of number of informants. Section 3 presents the experimentation setup and the evolvability measures applied to PSO-k. In Section 4, resulted fitness-correlation and fitness-fitness indicators are analyzed. Concluding remarks are summarized in Section 5.

2. QUASY-OPTIMALLY INFORMED PSO

The canonical particle swarm optimization (PSO) [5], as well as recent standard versions of this algorithm (Standards 2006, 2007, and 2011) [12], work by iteratively generating new particles' positions located in a given problem search space. Each one of these new particles' positions are calculated using the particle's current position (solution), the particle's previous velocity, and two main informant terms: the particle's best previous location, and the best previous location of any of its neighbors.

Formally, in canonical PSO each particle's position vector $\mathbf{x}_i$ is updated each time step t by means of the Equation 1.

$$\mathbf{x}_i^{t+1} = \mathbf{x}_i^t + \mathbf{v}_i^{t+1} \tag{1}$$

where $\mathbf{v}_i^{t+1}$ is the velocity vector of the particle given by

$$\mathbf{v}_i^{t+1} = \omega\mathbf{v}_i^t + U^t[0,\varphi_1]\cdot(\mathbf{p}_i^t - \mathbf{x}_i^t) + U^t[0,\varphi_2]\cdot(\mathbf{b}_i^t - \mathbf{x}_i^t) \tag{2}$$

In this formula, $\mathbf{p}_i^t$ is the personal best position the particle i has ever stored, $\mathbf{b}_i^t$ is the position found by the member of its neighborhood that has had the best performance so far. Acceleration coefficients φ_1 and φ_2 control the relative effect of the personal and social best particles, and U^t is a diagonal matrix with elements distributed in the interval $[0, \varphi_i]$, uniformly at random. Finally, $\omega \in (0,1)$ is called the inertia weight and influences the tradeoff between exploitation and exploration.

An equivalent version of the velocity equation was reported in [2], where Clerc's constriction coefficient χ is used instead of inertia weight as shown in Equation 3.

$$\mathbf{v}_i^{t+1} = \chi\left(\mathbf{v}_i^t + U^t[0,\varphi_1]\cdot(\mathbf{p}_i^t - \mathbf{x}_i^t) + U^t[0,\varphi_2]\cdot(\mathbf{b}_i^t - \mathbf{x}_i^t)\right) \tag{3}$$

$$\chi = \frac{2}{|2-\varphi-\sqrt{\varphi^2-4\varphi}|},\ \textit{with}\ \varphi = \sum_i \varphi_i,\ \textit{and}\ \varphi > 4 \tag{4}$$

Constriction coefficient χ is calculated, by means of Equation 4, from the two acceleration coefficients φ_1 and φ_2, being the sum of these two coefficients what determines the χ to use. Usually, $\varphi_1 = \varphi_2 = 2.05$, giving as results $\varphi = 4.1$, and $\chi = 0.7298$. As stated by Mendes et al. [7], this fact implies that the particle's velocity can be adjusted by any number of informant terms, as long as acceleration coefficients sum to an appropriate value, since important information given by other neighbors about the search space may be neglected through overemphasis on the single best neighbor. With this assumption, Mendes et al. [7] proposed the Fully Informed Particle Swarm (FIPS), in which a particle uses information from all its topological neighbors. In FIPS, the value φ, that is, the sum of the acceleration coefficients, is equally distributed among all the neighbors of a particle. Therefore, for a given particle i with position $\mathbf{x}_i$, φ is broken up in several smaller coefficients $\varphi_j = \varphi/|\mathcal{N}_i|, \forall j \in \mathcal{N}_i$. Then, the velocity is updated as follows:

$$\mathbf{v}_i^{t+1} = \chi\left[\mathbf{v}_i^t + \sum_{j\in\mathcal{N}_i} U^t\left[0,\varphi_j\right]\cdot(\mathbf{p}_j^t - \mathbf{x}_i^t)\right], \tag{5}$$

where $\mathcal{N}_i$ is the set of neighbors of the particle i, and following the neighborhood a given structured topology (All or Fully-Connected, Ring, Square, Four-Clusters, and Pyramid). Their results show that the Square topology (with 4 informants) outperforms the other ones. Indeed, the fact of defining these neighborhoods in the swarm makes the particles to be influenced only by a certain number of neighbors and connected with static links in the graph. Once again, important information may be disregarded through overemphasis, in this case, of structured sets of neighbors. The number of informants seems to play also an important role, but with no clue on how many of them is the best choice or if even the influent issue is the neighborhood topology itself, forgetting the intermediate sources of information existing between Canonical/Standard PSO and FIPS versions.

As commented before, the possibility of adjusting the particle's velocity by an arbitrary number of terms enables us to generalize the number (k) of neighbors, from 1 to Ss (being Ss the swarm size). Therefore, a number Ss of different versions of PSO can be generated (selecting k particles of the swarm without replacement), each one of them with neighborhoods containing k particles. Obviously, if $k = Ss$ the resultant version is the FIPS algorithm with a fully connected neighborhood.

Nevertheless, since providing each k neighborhood with structured topologies is impractical due to the great number of graph combinations, we opted to simply selecting k random (uniform) informants of the swarm (S). In this way, for each particle i, and at each time step t, a different neighborhood ($\mathcal{N}_i^t$) with k elements is generated, and hence, the number of informants can be analyzed with independence of any structured topology. Formally, we can represent a given neighborhood as follows

$$\mathcal{N}_i^t = \{n_1,\ldots,n_k\} \mid \mathcal{N}_i^t \subset S^t,$$
$$\forall n_j, n_h \in \mathcal{N}_i^t, n_h \neq n_j \wedge n_h \neq i \wedge n_j \neq i \tag{6}$$

Following this scheme, our new PSO-k performs as formulated in Equation 5, and using sets of k random (uniform) informant particles as neighborhoods. Then, we can evaluate all the PSO-k versions (with $k: 1 \ldots Ss$) in order to discover whether an optimal value, or range of values, exists that allow to improve over the standard PSO and avoid the overhead of using topologies or computing contributions from all particles in the swarm which number of informant terms provides the new velocity vector with essential information, and discarding redundant one.

The pseudocode of PSO-k is introduced in Algorithm 1. After swarm initialization and φ_j value calculation (lines 1 to 3), the optimization process is repeated until reaching the stop condition. In this, at each iteration and for each particle, a new neighborhood is randomly (uniformly) generated by fulfilling conditions of Equation 6 (line 6). Then,

Table 1: **CEC'05 benchmark test suite with functions' properties: unimodal (U), basic multimodal (BM), Expanded (E), and Hybrid Composed (HC). Their fitness landscapes (FL) can be characterized as single-funnel (S) or multi-funnel (M) according to mean dispersion [10]**

f	Name	Kind	FL	Intervals	f^*
f1	Shifted Sphere	U	S	[-100, 100]	-450
f2	Shifted Schwefel 1.2	U	S	[-100, 100]	-450
f3	Shifted Rotated High Conditioned Elliptic	U	S	[-100, 100]	-450
f4	Shifted Schwefel's Problem 1.2 with Noise	U	S	[-100, 100]	-450
f5	Schwefel's Problem 2.6	U	S	[-100, 100]	-310
f6	Shifted Rosenbrock's	BM	S	[-100, 100]	390
f7	Shifted Rotated Griewank's. Global Optimum Outside of Bounds	BM	S	[0, 600]	-180
f8	Shifted Rotated Ackley's with Optimum on Bounds	BM	S	[-32, 32]	-140
f9	Shifted Rastrigin's	BM	S	[-5, 5]	-330
f10	Shifted Rotated Rastrigin's	BM	S	[-5, 5]	-330
f11	Shifted Rotated Weierstrass	BM	M	[-0.5, 0.5]	90
f12	Schwefel's Problem 2.13	BM	M	[$-\pi$, π]	-460
f13	Shifted Expanded Griewank's plus Rosenbrock's	E	M	[-3, 1]	-130
f14	Shifted Rotated Expanded Scaffer's F6	E	S	[-100, 100]	-300
f15	Hybrid Composition (f1-f2,f3-f4,f5-f6,f7-f8,f9-f10)	HC	M	[-5, 5]	120
f16	Rotated Version of Hybrid Composition f15	HC	M	[-5, 5]	120
f17	F16 with Noise in Fitness	HC	M	[-5, 5]	120
f18	Rot. Hybr. Comp. (f1-f2,f3-f4,f5-f6,f7-f8,f9-f10)	HC	M	[-5, 5]	10
f19	Rot. Hybr. Comp. Narrow Basin Global Optimum	HC	M	[-5, 5]	10
f20	Rot. Hybr. Comp. Global Optimum on Bounds	HC	M	[-5, 5]	10
f21	Rot. Hybr. Comp. (f1-f2,f3-f4,f5-f6,f7-f8,f9-f10)	HC	M	[-5, 5]	360
f22	Rot. Hybr. Comp. High Condition Number Matrix	HC	M	[-5, 5]	360
f23	Non-Continuous Rotated Hybrid Composition	HC	M	[-5, 5]	360
f24	Rot. Hybr. Comp. (f1,f2,f3,f4,f5,f6,f7,f8,f9,f10)	HC	M	[-5, 5]	260
f25	Rot. Hybr. Comp. Global Optimum Outside of Bounds	HC	M	[2, 5]	260

Algorithm 1 Pseudocode of PSO-k

```
1: t ← 0
2: φ_j = φ/k
3: initialize(S^t) /* Swarm S^0 with N particles */
4: while t < MAXIMUM_t) do
5:   for each particle i^t of the swarm S^t do
6:     N_i^t = generate_neighborhood(k, i, S^t) //Equation 6
7:     v_i^{t+1} = update_velocity(v_i^t, x_i^t, φ_j, N_i^t) //Equation 5
8:     x_i^{t+1} = update_possiton(x_i^t, v_i^{t+1}) //Equation 1
9:     p_i^{t+1} = update_local_best(p_i^t, x_i^{t+1})
10:  end for
11:  t ← t + 1
12: end while
13: Output: b /*The best solution found*/
```

particle's velocity, current position, and local best position are updated (lines 7 to 9). Finally, the best so far particle position is returned as output (line 13).

3. EXPERIMENTAL ANALYSIS

We have implemented our PSO-k using the MALLBA library [1] in C++, a framework of metaheuristics. Following the specifications proposed in CEC'05 [13] experimental procedure, we have performed 25 independent runs of PSO-k for each test function and for each $k \in \{1, \ldots, Ss\}$ neighborhood. For simplicity, our study is illustrated for dimension $D = 30$ (number of continuous variables) of all functions, although we have performed additional experiments showing that our claims hold for other dimensions ($D = 10$ and $D = 50$). In the results, we are reporting the Mean Error of the best solutions found in the 25 independent runs. For a solution $\mathbf{x}$, the error measure is defined as: $f(\mathbf{x}) - f^*$, where f^* is the optimum fitness of the function. The maximum number of fitness evaluations is $10,000 \times D$, which constitutes the stop condition.

The used test suite is composed by 25 functions (see Table 1) with different features [13]: unimodal, multimodal, separable, non-separable, shifted to biased optimum, rotated, single-funnel, multi-funnel, and hybrid composed. Functions f1 to f5 are unimodal, functions f6 to f12 are basic multimodal, functions f13 and f14 are expanded, and functions f15 to f25 are composed by several basic ones. Functions 11, 12, 13, and 15 to 25 are characterized to multi-funnel according to fdc and mean dispersion analyses in [10, 11].

The parameter setting applied to PSO-k follows the specification proposed in Clerc's approach [2]: the acceleration coefficient has been set to $\varphi = 4.1$, and constriction coefficient to $\chi = 0.7298$. The swarm size has been set to 30 particles in order to simplify the experimental procedure.

3.1 Evolvability on PSO

Before we start to discuss the results, we describe here the evolvability measures used in this work and their application to the particular case of PSO.

- *Fitness-distance* analysis quantifies the relation between the fitness of particles $f(\mathbf{x}_i)$ in the landscape and their distances to the nearest global optimum $\mathbf{x}_{min}$ [6]. Assuming that we are minimizing, correlation means that both, the fitness and the distance to the nearest optimum, decreases whereas anti-correlation is registered when the fitness decreases and the distance to the nearest optimum increases (or vice versa). Distance between points in continuous domains are measured using Euclidean distance d_E. Then, the *fitness-distance correlation* (fdc) can be quantified by the following coefficient (ratio of fdc):

$$r_{fdc} = \frac{c_{fd}}{s_f \cdot s_d}, being\ c_{fd} = \frac{1}{n}\sum_{i=1}^{n}(f_i - \overline{f}) \cdot (d_i - \overline{d}) \qquad (7)$$

where f_i is the fitness of solution $f(\mathbf{x}_i)$, d_i is the distance of the solution $\mathbf{x}_i$ to the optimum $d_i = d_e(\mathbf{x}_i, \mathbf{x}_{min})$, $\overline{f}$, $\overline{d}$, s_f, and s_d are the means and standard deviations of the fitness and distance samples, respectively.

In our experiments, for each function and for each PSO-k version, we have used all the samples of each one of the 25 independent runs to compose the r_{fdc}. The median value (25 runs) of this coefficient is then reported in the following section. In addition, a number of 10,000 uniform random samples have been also collected for each function with the aim of comparing the resulting r_{fdc} coefficients to those computed by PSO-k. In this way, as suggested in [4], it is possible to detect wrong correlation coefficients resulting from PSO samples trapped in large basins of attraction.

An interpretation of this coefficient can be as follows [11]: a positive r_{fdc} near to 1 means globally convex single-funnel topologies. A value around 0 of this coefficient may indicate plateau shape landscapes with tiny sharp basins and problems without any global structure. A negative value of r_{fdc} indicate the existence of "deceiving" landscapes, where an optimizer (PSO in our case) perceives poor objective function values closer to the minimum than farther away.

- *Fitness-fitness* or *Fitness Cloud* (fc) [15] analysis is basically a plot of fitness values of individuals against fitness values of their neighbors. By definition of fc, for each sampled individual $\mathbf{x}_i$ with fitness f_i, generate k neighbors by applying a genetic operator to $\mathbf{x}_i$, and let be $\overline{f_i}$ the mean fitness of all neighbors of $\mathbf{x}_i$. Then, the set of points $\{(f_1, \overline{f_1}), \ldots, (f_n, \overline{f_n})\}$ is taken as the fitness cloud. In our particular case, we are interested in computing the fitness cloud by plotting the fitness (f'_i) of a new particle ($\mathbf{x}'_i$) that is generated from their informants (using velocity rule in Equation 5), and the mean fitness $\overline{f_i}$ of all these particles of $\mathbf{x}_i$. Now, the set of points $\{(f'_1, \overline{f_1}), \ldots, (f'_n, \overline{f_n})\}$ can be analyzed as the fitness cloud of PSO-k for a problem.

- *Escape Probability* (*ep*) [8] analysis considers the number of steps required to escape from a local optimum. It is defined as $P(f_i) = \frac{1}{S_i}$, where S_i denotes the average number of steps required to find an improving move starting in an individual with fitness value f_i. In the context of our PSO, we will average the improving intervals (evaluation steps) computed by each particle of the swarm to calculate the escape probability through the iteration process. In next sections, several examples of *ep* are plotted for f24.

4. ANALYSIS AND DISCUSSION

Since in this study we have concentrated on a swarm size with 30 particles, the number of PSO-k's versions is 30, from PSO-1 to PSO-29, plus PSO-30 represented by the so called FIPS-All. Therefore, we have undergone the evaluation of each version of PSO-k with every function in the benchmark. Summing up, 25 independent runs for each algorithm version and for each function have been performed, resulting in a total number of $25 \times 25 \times 30 = 18,750$ experiments. The resulting r_{fdc} coefficients are summarized in Figure 1 as bar graphs. In this figure, the r_{fdc} coefficients computed from random samples are also plotted as dotted lines. Not surprisingly, these last r_{fdc} values agree with the ones computed in [11].

In the following, we make several observations about Figure 1. After this, we will focus on interesting observations concerning fc and *ep* indicators. Later, we will focus our analysis on different problem dimensions.

4.1 Fitness-Distance Analysis

In general, we can first observe from Figure 1 that PSO with k=6±2 informants shows $r_{fdc} > 0$ in single-funnel functions (f1-f10) and $r_{fdc} <= 0$ in multi-funnel ones (f11-f25). This means that using k=6±2 informants, our proposal is able to distinguish between globally convex and/or deceiving (multiple convexities) landscapes, and irrespectively of the problem modality. Nevertheless, three exceptions are registered: for f8, with plateau landscape and hence, highly dependent to the swarm initialization, and for f16 and f17, which were characterized as bi-funnel in [11]. For these two last functions, there is a certain probability of evolving samples (from initialization) on the funnel where the optimum is located [14], which contributes to compute a r_{fdc} higher than 0.

Second, when comparing PSO-6s' samples with random ones we can check in Figure 1 that there are few cases in which the resulting r_{fdc} coefficients (in these two cases) are closed to each other. Concretely for functions f7, f8, f11, f14, and f17, the median r_{fdc} of PSO-6 is practically similar to the dotted line of random samples. On the contrary, for the remaining twenty functions, the r_{fdc} coefficients of random samples show quite different values to those of PSO-k with 6 informants. For these last functions, PSO-6 seems to perform a guided search towards promising regions in the landscape, not visited by the random samples, and far from the reference global optimum in CEC'05 [13] source code. Probably, new particles in PSO-6 are guided towards other (different to the reference) global optima since the difference (in r_{fdc} coefficients) with random samples is particularly observed for multi-modal functions (with multiple global optima).

Third, for almost all the functions (excepting f8, f16, and f17) a number of informants close to 6 in PSO-k registered in general the lowest values of r_{fdc}. This suggests that using few (<4) or too much (>10) informants could create a tendency to move toward non interesting regions, leading the algorithm to show an early stagnation and obtaining fake correlated solutions with large fitness values and far from the optimum.

To see this last more in detail, Figure 2 shows the fitness-distance plots resulted from independent executions of PSO with 2, 6, 12, and 29 informants, for functions f5, f15, and f24. We can observe in this figure that using few informants (2 in this case), the algorithm shows correlation for the three functions, even though evolving solutions with poor fitness values since the low diversity of neighbors leads the early convergence of the algorithm. With more than 10 informants, solutions are again correlated, although concentrating on several small regions on multi-funnel landscapes (as plotted for f15 and f24) that may confuse the particles' decisions and may slow down their escape from these regions. Using 6 informants in PSO is the best trade-off between fitness-distance correlation and fitness quality. A special case can be observed for f24 (highly deceptive), where solutions are gradually improving although showing certain distance with regards to the global optimum provided by the CEC'05 test suite.

4.2 Fitness-Fitness Analysis

Figure 3 plots the Fitness Clouds of functions f5, f15, and f24, generated from independent executions of PSO with 2, 6, 12, and 29 informants. For the three functions, a number of 6 informants is able to keep for longer the generation of new better particles with improving fitness (f', see Section 3.1). In fact, regression lines calculated from dis-

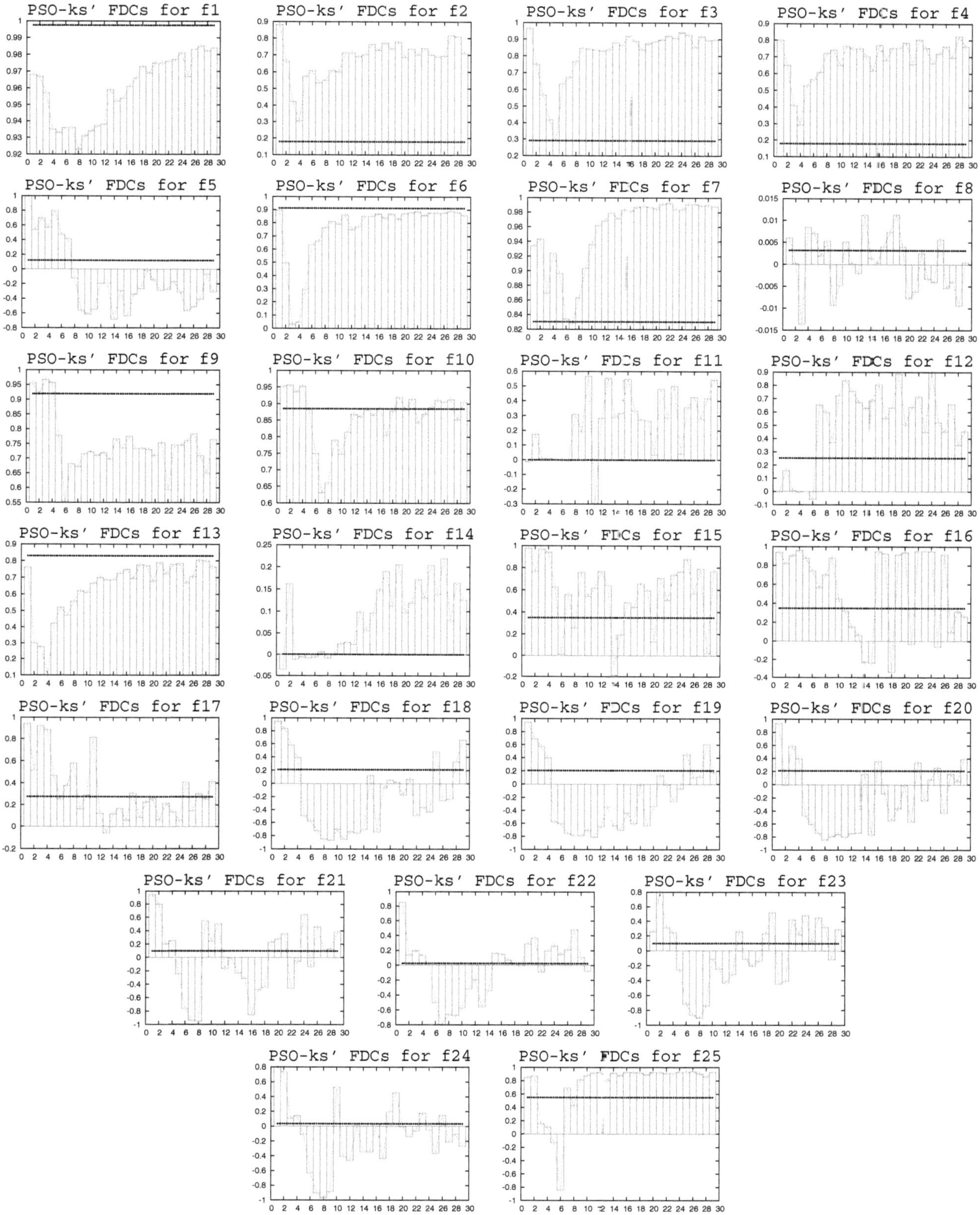

Figure 1: Each plot shows the median r_{fdc} coefficients in the Y-axis (out of 25 independent runs) of the different PSO-k versions (for the 30 possible values of k) in X-axis, for all benchmark functions with dimension $D = 30$. The dotted lines in these graphs represent the r_{fdc} coefficients computed from 10,000 uniform random samples for each function

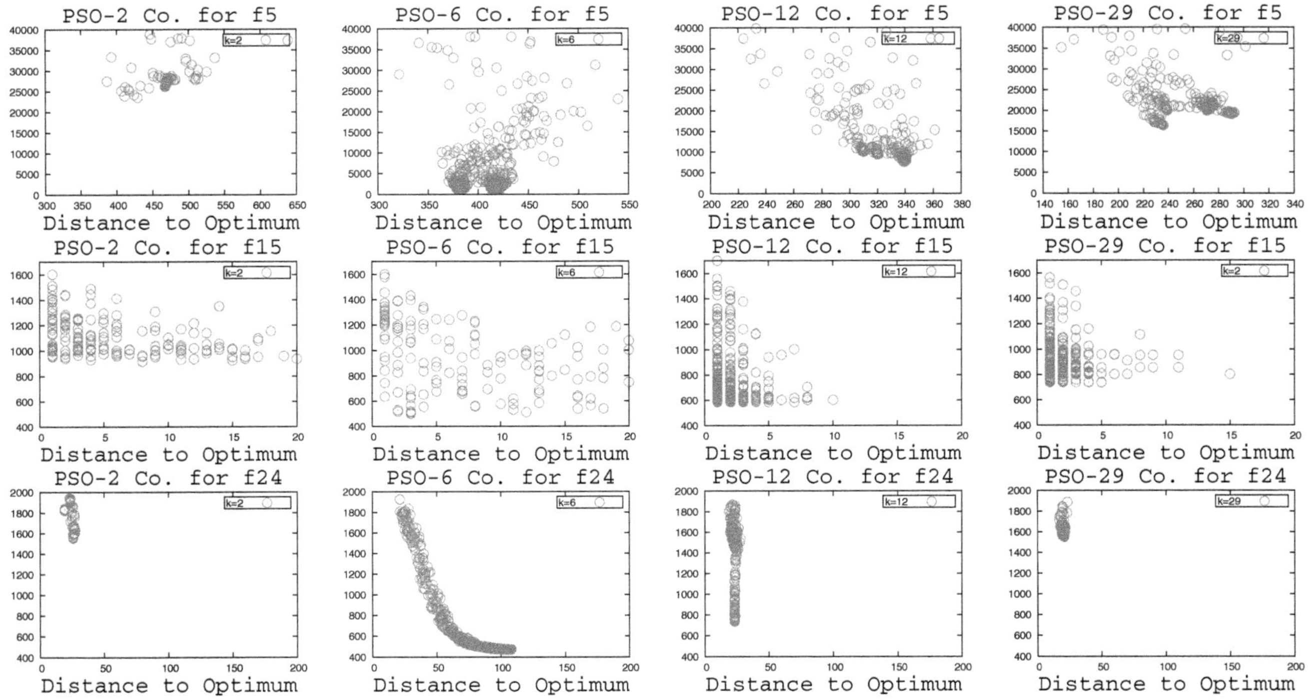

Figure 2: Fitness-distance plots of functions f5, f15, and f24, generated from independent executions of PSO with 2, 6, 12, and 29 informants (dimension D=30)

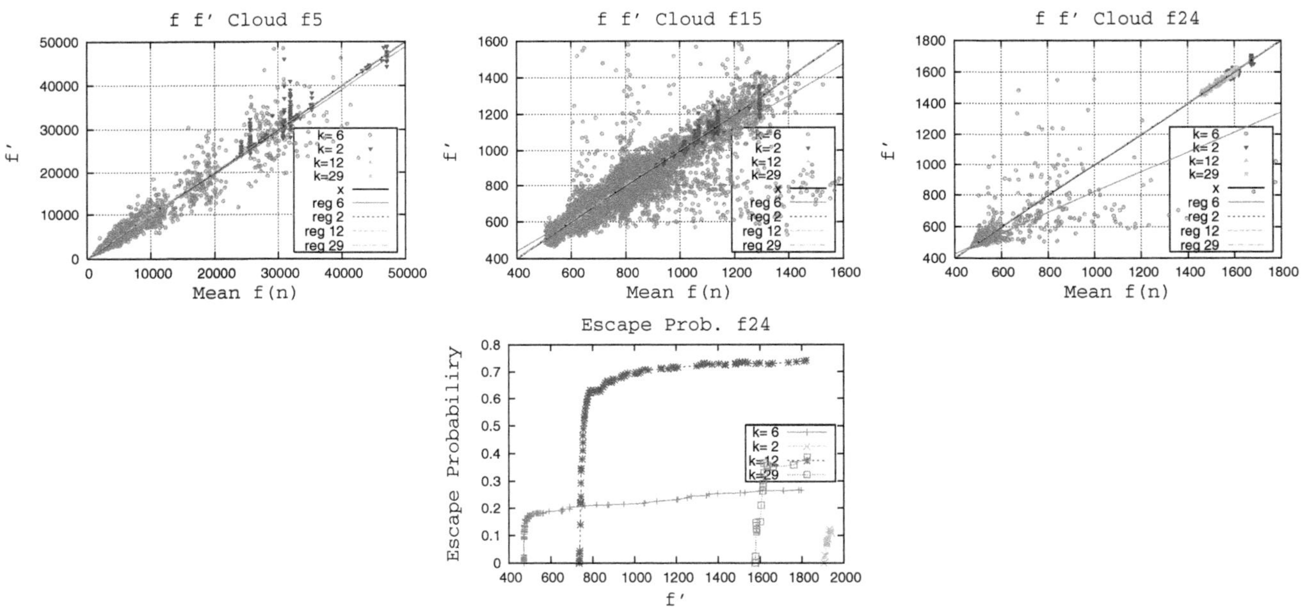

Figure 3: Illustrative fitness-fitness clouds $\{(f'_1, \overline{f_1}), \ldots, (f'_n, \overline{f_n})\}$ of functions f5, f15, and f24, generated from independent executions of PSO-k with 2, 6, 12, and 29 informants. Graph in bottom-right plots the Escape Probability with regards to the new fitness value f' concerning f24 (see this curve from right to left)

tribution clouds (of 2, 12, and 29 informants) generally fit the diagonal line of plots, whereas regression lines of 6 informants' clouds show positive slopes in final evolution steps, with regard to diagonal lines. This means that new fitness values f' calculated using 6 informants provokes a higher probability of mean fitness $\overline{f(n)}$ improvement of neighbors in the search landscape .

An illustrative example of this behavior can be explicitly observed in Figure 3 bottom-right, where the Escape Probability concerning f24 is progressively plotted. Solutions evolved by PSO-6 generally show a moderated *ep* progress, although reaching a deeper basin of local optimum, e.g., better fitness values. A different behavior is shown by PSO with 12 informants which initially shows high values of *ep*,

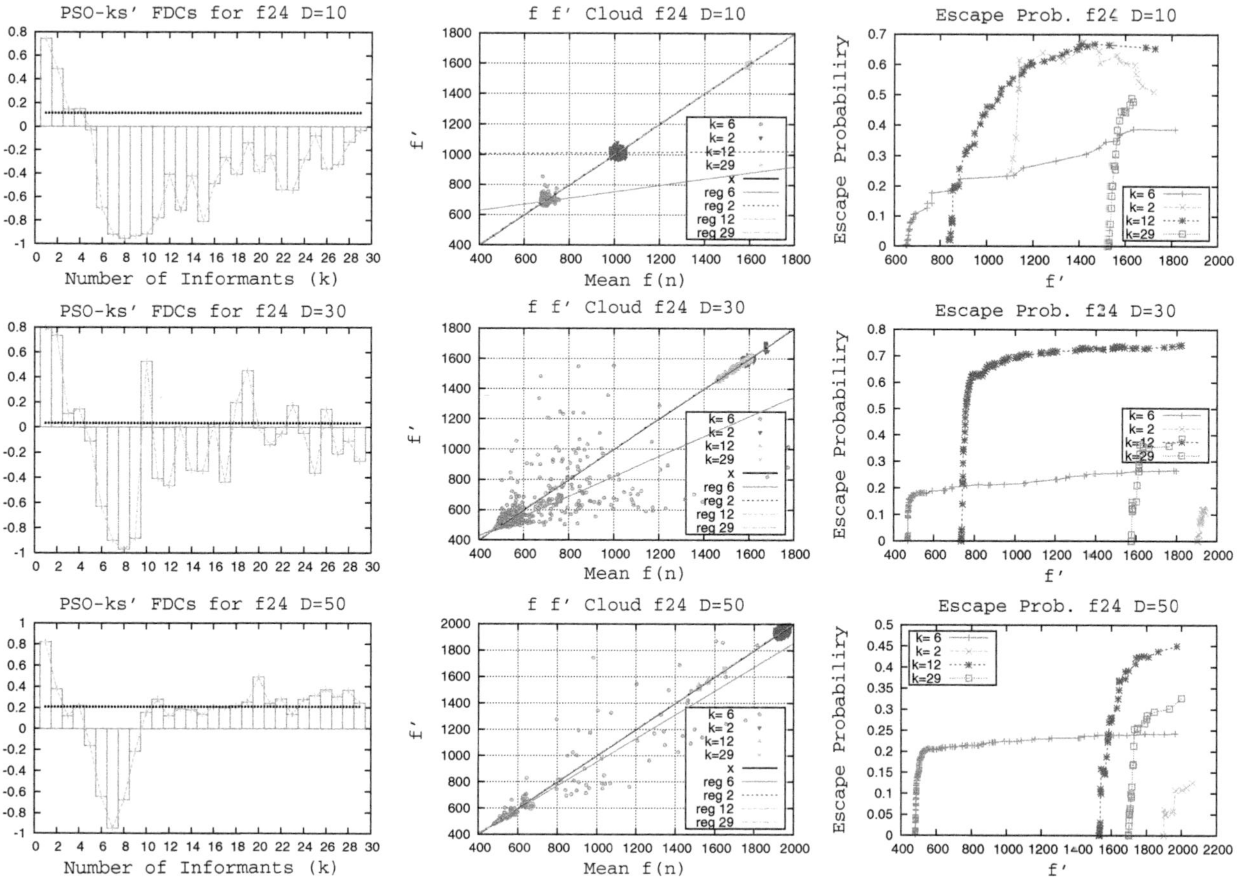

Figure 4: Plot graphs of the three studied evolvability measures: *fdc* (left), *fc* (center), and *ep* (right); and three different problem dimensions: 10 (top), 30 (center) and 50 (bottom) variables, for f24

although decreasing with fair fitness values. This means that 12 informants initially provides the PSO with high exploration ability, but tending to search in non interesting regions. PSO with 2 informants generally shows a low degree of *ep* with poor fitness quality, meaning that for f24, its particles are quickly trapped in local basins, and hence more informants are required for the movement (velocity calculation) of these particles.

4.3 Results Hold Over Different Dimensions

In this section, the influence that scaling to different problem dimensions may have on the selection of the number of informants (in PSO-k) is studied. In concrete, we illustrate with the interesting case of function 24 with dimensions $D =$ 10, 30, and 50 variables, although the same profiles can be got for the rest of functions. The swarm size was set to 30 particles as in initial experiments, and our goal is to see how sensible are all PSO-k versions to the problem size.

Figure 4 shows the graphs concerning the three studied evolvability measures: fdc (left), fc (center), and *ep* (right); and three different problem dimensions: 10 (top), 30 (center) and 50 (bottom) variables, for f24. From this figure, we can observe that in general the behavior of all PSO-k versions is kept constant along with the problem dimension. This means that our previous claims could be generalized for scaling problems. There are certain slight differences with regards to the fdc indicator in PSO-ks with more than 10 informants, which increases the r_{fdc} coefficient as the problem dimension is higher. Once again, more fitness-distance correlation (in $D = 50$) corresponds to solutions with poor fitness values and far from the global optimum, whereas a negative r_{fdc} represents solutions with better fitness values, although far from the reference global optimum. In this sense, the escape probability plots in Figure 4 illustrate this behavior since PSO-k with 12 informants reaches moderate fitness values in $D = 10$, and $D = 30$, but with poor fitness quality in $D = 50$. In the case of PSO-k with 6 informants, the *ep* indicator shows a similar curve for the three different problem dimensions (as well as similar r_{fdc}) with successful fitness values, which lead us to suggest 6 informants as the best option also when facing scaling problems.

4.4 Confirming the Initial Hypothesis

Once we have analyzed the evolvability of the different PSO-k versions performed here, and based on observations of the actual values of the algorithm, we make a summary of lessons learned and whether they confirm the initial hypothesis of this work:

Why a number of $6_{\pm 2}$ informants in the operation of PSO may compute new improved particles for longer than other PSO formulations in complex single and multi-funnel benchmarking problems?.

For this, we can argue the following:

1. Using few informants (<4) leads the PSO-k to show a positive fitness-distance correlation, although evolving solutions with poor fitness values and far from global optima. With more than 10 informants, solutions are again correlated, although concentrating on small non interesting regions of the landscape. Using 6 informants is the best trade-off between fitness-distance and fitness quality.

2. The regression lines calculated from 6 informants' clouds show positive slopes in final evolution steps, meaning that new fitness values f' calculated from 6 informant neighbors improve more frequently the mean fitness $\overline{f(n)}$ of these neighbors.

3. Solutions evolved by PSO-6 generally show a moderate but maintained *ep* progress, finally reaching a deeper basins, e.g., better fitness values than with other number of informants.

4. In general the behavior of all PSO-k versions is stable for different problem dimensions. In concrete, PSO-6 shows quite similar evolvability indicators for the three studied dimensions.

5. CONCLUSIONS

Based on the previous experience, in this work we have used different evolvability measures with the aim of shedding light on the question that a number of $6_{\pm 2}$ informants in the operation of PSO may compute new improved particles for longer, even in complex problems with single and multi-funnel landscapes. After the experimentation in the context of the CEC'05 benchmark suite and using different problem dimensions, we have tested our initial research question showing that 6 informants in PSO is the best trade-off between fitness-distance and fitness quality. This is noticeable since the algorithm is simple (Occam's razor), and these results together with the previous ones in [3] suggest that the benchmark should be updated with more varied functions.

We have shown why and who PSO works by using a new kind of probability of escape analysis that is useful for any PSO. We give a comprehensive analysis beyond a couple of functions or one dimension: we address classes of problems.

As future work, we are working on creating new evolvability measures well-adapted to the operation of PSO. We will also experiment with other standard benchmarks to test if $6_{\pm 2}$ informants in PSO is appropriated to be used on them.

Acknowledgments

Authors acknowledge funds from the CICE of the Junta de Andalucia, under contract P07-TIC-03044 (DIRICOM `http://diricom.lcc.uma.es`) and Spanish Ministry of Sciences and Innovation (MICINN) and FEDER under contracts TIN2011-28194 (RoadMe `http://roadme.lcc.uma.es`) and TIN2008-06491-C04-01 (M* `http://mstar.lcc.uma.es`). José García-Nieto is supported by grant BES-2009-018767 from the MICINN

6. REFERENCES

[1] E. Alba, G. Luque, J. García-Nieto, G. Ordonez, and G. Leguizamón. MALLBA: A software library to design efficient optimisation algorithms. *Int. Jour. of Innov. Comp. and Appl. (IJICA)*, 1(1):74–85, 2007.

[2] M. Clerc and J. Kennedy. The particle swarm - explosion, stability, and convergence in a multidimensional complex space. *IEEE Trans. Evol. Comp.*, 6(1):58 – 73, 2002.

[3] J. García-Nieto and E. Alba. Empirical computation of the quasi-optimal number of informants in particle swarm optimization. In *Proceedings of GECCO'11*, pages 147–154, New York, NY, USA, 2011. ACM.

[4] T. Jones and S. Forrest. Fitness distance correlation as a measure of problem difficulty for genetic algorithms. In *Proceedings of the 6th International Conference on Genetic Algorithms*, pages 184–192, San Francisco, CA, USA, 1995. Morgan Kaufmann Publishers Inc.

[5] J. Kennedy and R. C. Eberhart. *Swarm Intelligence*. Morgan Kaufmann, S. Fco., California, 2001.

[6] G. Lu, J. Li, and X. Yao. Fitness-probability cloud and a measure of problem hardness for evolutionary algorithms. In *EvoCOP'11*, volume 6622 of *LNCS*, pages 108–117. Springer, 2011.

[7] R. Mendes, J. Kennedy, and J. Neves. The Fully Informed Particle Swarm: Simpler, Maybe Better. *IEEE Tran. on Evol. Comp.*, 8(3):204 – 210, 2004.

[8] P. Merz. Advanced fitness landscape analysis and the performance of memetic algorithms. *Evol. Comput.*, 12:303–325, September 2004.

[9] M. A. Montes de Oca and T. Stützle. Convergence behavior of the fully informed particle swarm optimization algorithm. In *Proceedings of GECCO08*, pages 71–78, New York, NY, USA, 2008. ACM.

[10] C. L. Müller, B. Baumgartner, and I. Sbalzarini. Particle swarm cma evolution strategy for the optimization of multi-funnel landscapes. In *Evolutionary Computation, 2009. CEC '09. IEEE Congress on*, pages 2685 –2692, may 2009.

[11] C. L. Müller and I. F. Sbalzarini. Global characterization of the CEC 2005 fitness landscapes using fitness-distance analysis. In *Proceedings of EvoNUM*, EvoApplications'11, pages 294–303, Berlin, Heidelberg, 2011. Springer-Verlag.

[12] PSO-Central-Group. Standard PSO 2006, 2007, and 2011. Technical Report [online] http://www.particleswarm.info/, Particle Swarm Central, January 2011.

[13] P. N. Suganthan, N. Hansen, J. J. Liang, K. Deb, Y.-P. Chen, A. Auger, and S. Tiwari. Problem Definitions and Evaluation Criteria for the CEC'05 Special Session on Real-Parameter Optimization. Technical Report KanGAL Report 2005005, Nanyang Technological University, 2005.

[14] A. M. Sutton, D. Whitley, M. Lunacek, and A. Howe. PSO and multi-funnel landscapes: how cooperation might limit exploration. In *Proceedings of GECCO'06*, pages 75–82, New York, NY, USA, 2006. ACM.

[15] L. Vanneschi, M. Clergue, P. Collard, M. Tomassini, and S. Vérel. Fitness clouds and problem hardness in genetic programming. In *GECCO'04*, volume 3103 of *LCNS*, pages 690–701. Springer, 2004.

[16] A. Wagner. *Robustness and evolvability in living systems*. Princeton Studies in Complexity. Princeton University Press, 2005.

CGrAnt: A Swarm Intelligence-based Routing Protocol for Delay Tolerant Networks

Ana Cristina B. Kochem Vendramin, Anelise Munaretto, Myriam R. Delgado
DAINF, CPGEI. Federal Technological University of Parana (UTFPR). Curitiba, Brazil. +55 41 33104750
{criskochem, anelise, myriamdelg}@utfpr.edu.br

Aline Carneiro Viana
INRIA Saclay - Ile de France. Laboratoire d'Informatique de l'Ecole Polytechnique (LIX). Orsay, France. +33 1 69 33 41 01
aline.viana@inria.fr

ABSTRACT
This paper presents a new routing protocol for Delay Tolerant Networks (DTNs), based on a distributed swarm intelligence approach. The protocol is called Cultural Greedy Ant (CGrAnt), as it uses a Cultural Algorithm (CA) and a greedy version of the Ant Colony Optimization (ACO) metaheuristic. The term greedy implies the use of a deterministic transition rule to exploit previously found good paths or explore new paths by selecting, from among a set of candidates, the most promising message forwarders. CGrAnt chooses each next node toward the message destination based on pheromone concentration (i.e., global information) whenever it is available. However, as the pheromone is not always available due to connectivity partitions, local information (i.e., heuristic function) captured from DTN nodes also supports a routing decision. Specific metrics and information gathered from the evolution are stored in Situational, Domain, and Historical Knowledge. The knowledge composes the CA's belief space, which is used to guide and improve the search. CGrAnt is compared with two DTN routing protocols (Epidemic and PROPHET) in an activity-based scenario. The results show that CGrAnt achieves a higher delivery ratio and lower byte redundancy than Epidemic and PROPHET.

Categories and Subject Descriptors
I.2.11 [**Artificial Intelligence**]: Distributed Artificial Intelligence – *Intelligent agents.*
C.2.2 [**Computer-Communication networks**]: Network Protocols – *Routing protocols.*

Keywords
Ant colony optimization; cultural algorithms; social metrics, routing protocol; delay tolerant network.

1. INTRODUCTION
A Delay Tolerant Network (DTN) is a specific class of networks in which connectivity between neighboring nodes is intermittent due to either mobility or varying conditions of wireless communications. To achieve a minimum message delivery, intermediate DTN employ a store-carry-forward communication model [1, 2]. The nodes may need to store messages from other nodes in their buffers for long periods of time and carry these messages until a forwarding opportunity arises [3]. Additionally, message replications may be necessary to increase the probability of successfully delivered messages. However, some problems exist in a limited resource scenario: replications are undesirable, as they compete with valid data messages in the paths (set of nodes) toward destination, and due to limited buffer sizes, storing neighbors' data messages can be a problem.

Considering these challenges, maintaining an updated view of DTN dynamics is necessary and can be accomplished by periodically analyzing neighbors' information and selecting more than one path along which to forward each message while limiting message redundancy. Moreover, the network users' (nodes) behavior presents some similarities that can be explored by the belief space of a Cultural Algorithm (CA). Those premises characterize a DTN as an environment favorable for applying swarm intelligence-based paradigms, including Ant Colony Optimization (ACO) and CA [4-7]. The ACO is inspired by the collective behavior of real ants to find the shortest trail from their nests to food sources [4, 5]. The CA is derived from the cultural evolutionary process [6, 7]. The motivation for using ACO is to take advantage of its population-based search and adaptive learning framework. Conversely, CAs gather information during the evolutionary process and use it to guide the population and thus accelerate learning while providing more efficient solutions.

This paper proposes a Cultural Greedy Ant (CGrAnt) protocol that infers the most promising message forwarders in DTNs using opportunistic information about social connectivity between nodes and determines the best paths along which to forward each message while limiting message byte redundancy. To the best of our knowledge, this is the first routing protocol that employs ACO and CA to direct traffic in dynamic and complex networks.

2. THE ADDRESSED PROBLEM
DTNs suffer connectivity loss, long and variable delays, and large resource consumption when sending a message between the source and destination nodes. The problem of message forwarding in DTNs can thus be modeled like multimodal optimization problems, as we try to find not just one solution but a set of solutions (i.e., good paths between two nodes). The finite set of possible solutions (i.e., paths formed by a sequence of nodes, where each node permutation generates a new solution) features routing in DTNs as a combinatorial problem. The problem can also be modeled as dynamic, as the search space characteristics and the location and value of the solutions change over time.

The problem of routing in DTNs is then a complex challenge, with several aspects still unexplored by most approaches described in the literature. The most popular protocols for routing in DTNs are Epidemic [8] (a controlled flooding-based protocol, which sends messages to all or almost all encountered nodes without predicting the good message forwarders) and PROPHET [9] (a prediction-based protocol, which tries to predict which nodes are useful for delivering messages based on history of encounters). Though ACO has been extensively used in network environments, especially in MANETs [10, 11], routing in DTNs is challenging and few ACO protocols have been proposed: (i) DAR [11] does not consider local information from neighboring nodes and uses only the pheromone global information which is not always available in DTNs; (ii) ABMF [12] only aims to estimate the extra capacity of each node as a message forwarder depending on its buffer dynamics. Even if a node has a large storage capacity to maintain several messages from other nodes, in the case of a low connectivity range, it may not be able to continue forwarding those messages; (iii) ACRP [13] uses the Epidemic protocol to flood the network with control messages associated with Forward Ants (FAs) and Backward Ants (BAs). No approach considers important aspects of sparse and opportunistic networks: (i) analyzing node social metrics, including their degree and betweenness centralities to help select message forwarders; (ii) preventing the loss of previously found good paths caused by pheromone evaporation processes periodically performed (i.e., based on time, as in ABMF and ACRP) or the overuse of those paths due to the absence of an evaporation process (as in DAR); (iii) dynamically limiting the number of control and data messages forwarded in the network. Keeping these issues in mind, we proposed a first version of the swarm intelligence-based routing protocol for DTNs that uses only ACO [14]. Guided by pheromone concentration, heuristic function, and social metrics, the Greedy Ant protocol (GrAnt) performed better than the well-known DTN routing protocols [14].

In this paper, we propose a hybrid protocol called Cultural Greedy Ant (CGrAnt), which encompasses CA and ACO metaheuristics. It can be considered an extension of our previous method [14], as it improves the learning process gathering, during evolution, of high-level information to be stored in the CA belief space. To the best of our knowledge, there is no previous approach using both ACO and CA to route messages in mobile communication networks. Previous protocols [15, 16] use CA (the first protocol proposes a population space based on the simulated annealing algorithm, and the second uses ACO) for routing in a static topology with service quality constraints. The proposed protocols differ from CGrAnt in the following characteristics: (i) they operate in a static environment (i.e., the node topology is fixed) and do not analyze the dynamics on a social network of contacts to determine opportunities; (ii) they search for a single optimal path with a set of constraints; (iii) they use Situational and Normative knowledge only to increase the convergence speed; and (iv) they use a single and centralized belief space.

3. THE CGRANT PROTOCOL

This paper proposes the CGrAnt protocol as a solution to the problem of finding a set of nodes to route each message in DTNs. Using ACO and CA, CGrAnt provides a hybrid swarm intelligence system that can benefit from the specific advantages of each metaheuristic: the self-organizing nature and adaptation of the ACO learning structure and the CA ability to store and reuse experiences gathered during the search to guide new populations and thus accelerate the learning process. Moreover, the environment of opportunistic DTNs presents some similarities in the behavior patterns of nodes that compose each solution. These similarities can be well explored by joining CA and ACO, e.g., knowledge stored in the belief space can guide ants through new or already constructed paths, depending on nodes behavior, providing a good balance between search space *exploration* and *exploitation*.

To adapt to the large topology variations suffered by a DTN and reduce latency in message delivery, some modifications are incorporated into CGrAnt that differentiate it from traditional ACO and CA protocols: (i) FAs are encapsulated into data messages; (ii) the number of FAs created and forwarded is dynamically defined; (iii) CGrAnt adopts a greedy ACO transition rule that considers the heuristic function and/or pheromone concentration and either forwards messages to the most promising node(s) or exploits previously found good solutions. The search space exploration is still provided by the DTNs' dynamics; (iv) allowing redundant paths becomes more important than converging to the best path. Instead of using traditional time-based pheromone evaporation, CGrAnt performs an event-driven evaporation, which only occurs if a node detects that a new path toward a destination has just been found; (v) as there is no central element in DTNs, the knowledge components stored in the CA belief space are distributed among network nodes; and (vi) the information exchanged between the belief and population spaces always occurs in a distributed way, and this communication can be direct (through the influence function) or indirect (through acceptance and update functions). In the latter case, communication is mediated by specific metrics. The ACO and CA modifications seem more adapted to intermittently connected networks as DTNs, yet some may allow CGrAnt to operate in different dynamic scenarios.

3.1 Metrics and Components

The metrics incorporated into CGrAnt can be classified as *basic* (obtained directly from the population space or nodes) or *composite* (obtained from manipulating other metrics). The basic metrics can be classified into *local* (associated with each node and its neighborhood) and *global* (associated with complete paths constructed by ants). Part of the interaction between population and belief spaces is guided by the basic and composite metrics. Through these metrics, a more abstract model level (i.e., the belief space) can be updated according to the complexity and dynamic specifics of DTN environments to further influence the search process in a more appropriate way.

Figure 1 illustrates the basic metrics and their relationships with the composite metrics and other components used by CGrAnt.

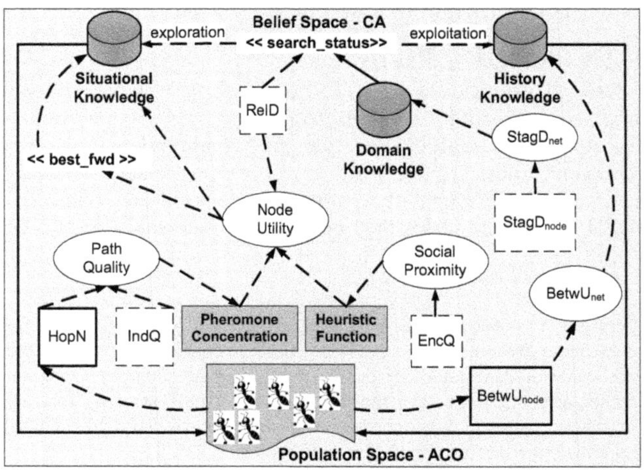

Figure 1. Components of Population and Belief Spaces.

The *Local Basic Metrics* used by the CGrAnt protocol include the following: (i) the Encounter Quality between a pair of nodes (*EncQ*); (ii) the Individual Quality of a node (*IndQ*), represented by its degree centrality [17]. To obtain its *IndQ*, each node stores the total number of contacts established per unit of time divided by (*N-1*), where *N* is the total number of nodes in the network; (iii) the Relationship Degree (*RelD*) of a node with respect to each of its buffered data messages (i.e., the node is the source (s_m) or an intermediate node (int_m) for each of its messages *m*); and (iv) the stagnation degree of a node ($StagD_{node}$), which considers its average movement speed ($\bar{v}$) and average pause time in each visited place ($\bar{\varrho}$) (i.e., $StagD_{node} = 1/ \bar{v} \times \bar{\varrho}$).

The *Global Basic Metrics* of CGrAnt include (i) the Number of Hops in a complete path (*HopN*) and (ii) the betweenness utility of a node ($BetwU_{node}$) in relation to each message destination *d*. The traditional betweenness centrality measures the frequency with which a node appears on the shortest paths linking any two other nodes [17]. As we are interested in different paths to each destination *d*, we compute the nodes' betweenness centrality in a slightly different way, referred to here as *betweenness utility*. To have a high betweenness utility in relation to *d*, a node must appear with a high frequency in paths between any source node and *d*. This requires no shortest-path verification, and, differing from related works [18], no list of all previously encountered contacts by a node is exchanged.

The *Composite Metrics* of CGrAnt include: (i) *Path Quality*, which measures the quality of each constructed path and encompasses *IndQ* and *HopN*; (ii) *Social Proximity*, represented by *EncQ* (*Social Proximity* = *EncQ* = *F*×*D*, i.e., it considers the frequency (*F*) and duration (*D*) of a contact between two nodes); (iii) *Node Utility*, which describes how well a node can perform as a message forwarder and encompasses *RelD*, *Path Quality*, and *Social Proximity*; (iv) the Stagnation Degree of the social network of a node ($StagD_{net}$); and (v) the Betweeness Utility of the social network of a node ($BetwU_{net}$).

The composite metric *Path Quality* measures the quality of a path between source(*s*)-destination(*d*) nodes ($Q(path_{s,d})$) and is directly associated with the ACO global operator *Pheromone Concentration*. The *Social Proximity* metric, which indicates the frequency and duration of a contact between node *x* and destination *d* ($SocialProx_{x,d}$), is directly associated with the ACO local operator *Heuristic Function* ($\eta_{x,d}$). The heuristic function and pheromone concentration, along with *RelD* (*x* is s_m or int_m), determine the utility of node *x* as a forwarder for data message *m* stored in node *i* according to the value resulting from:

$$U_x = \begin{cases} \eta_{x,d} & if\ i = s_m \\ \eta_{x,d} + \tau_{(i,y),d} & otherwise \end{cases} \quad (1)$$

The pheromone concentration ($\tau_{(i,y),d}$) is deposited on each link *(i,y)* belonging to a constructed path toward *d*, where *y* is the destination *d* of *m* (when calculating the utility of node *i*, which currently has custody of *m*) or *y* is node *j* (when calculating the utility of node *j*, which is a neighbor of *i* and a candidate to forward *m*). The utility of a node can then consider only local or both local and global information, depending on the relationship degree (*RelD*) of node *i* with message *m* to be forwarded.

The Betweenness Utility of node *x* in relation to message destination *d* ($BetwU_{x,d}$) initializes the betweenness utility of the social network of *i* in relation to *d* ($BetwU^i_{net,d}(t=0) = BetwU_{x,d}$). Node *x* can be either node *j* (*x*=*j*), through which *i* received the information that a complete path (global solution) toward *d* was constructed, or node *i* (*x*=*i*), if *i* received the information from *d*. $BetwU^i_{net,d}$ is always updated with $BetwU_{i,d}$, and, when node *j* is not destination *d*, $BetwU_{j,d}$ is also used to update $BetwU^i_{net,d}$:

$$\begin{cases} BetwU^i_{net,d}(t+1) = \frac{BetwU^i_{net,d}(t)+BetwU_{i,d}}{2} \\ BetwU^i_{net,d}(t+2) = \frac{BetwU^i_{net,d}(t+1)+BetwU_{j,d}}{2}, if j \neq d \end{cases} \quad (2)$$

In addition to the basic and composite metrics, CGrAnt uses two indicators: *best_fwd*, which stores the current best forwarder for a given message, and *search_status*, which decides if ants must explore or exploit the environment while seeking solutions for the DTN forwarding problem (Section 3.3.1).

3.2 Population and Belief Spaces

The population space is comprised of ants looking for sets of possible paths, one set for each pair (source-destination) associated with message *m*. We thus have a total of *M* messages to be forwarded and several sets $\{P_1, \ldots, P_m, \ldots, P_M\}$ being constructed simultaneously. Every set P_m represents a niche in the population space, which is generated when message *m*, originating in s_m, must be sent to destination d_m. Each complete path in P_m, represented by a sequence of nodes, is established when ant *k* reaches d_m and can be defined as $path^k_{s,d} = \{s_m, j1_m^k, \ldots, jc_m^k, \ldots, d_m\}$, $k = 1, \ldots, K_m$, where K_m defines the number of generated ants for *m*. In general, we have $|P_m| < K_m$ because some ants cannot find d_m. In CGrAnt, K_m is dynamically defined according to the belief space's knowledge and message delivery success. A new FA is created and sent only while the reception of its respective message remains unknown and when better forwarders appear. Due to CGrAnt's message custody copy, a new ant is generated to start a new path construction in each node encountered where the custody copy occurs (it has the same nodes from the source to the current custody copy point). From this point, however, the new ant is free to find the destination and can provide a different path to the population space. Dynamic ant generation is thus auto-adaptive, as is the number of constructed paths, and both depend on the network dynamics.

CGrAnt distributes information, as there is no element to centralize and share the best solution(s). The belief spaces are thus distributed over the network. Each belief space encompasses three types of knowledge: Situational, Domain, and History. Situational knowledge is introduced to provide a memory of the best solutions and, through these solutions, influence the search process. The Situational knowledge memory is partial instead of global, represented by the best forwarder of each message. Domain knowledge is introduced to support the analysis of local and specific DTN dynamics. In this paper, Domain knowledge keeps the CGrAnt protocol up-to-date about the local dynamics of the node's stagnation degree in relation to its social network. Based on this information and specific heuristics of the DTN forwarding problem, Domain knowledge can set the status of the path search (exploration or exploitation). History knowledge is introduced to adapt CGrAnt to changes in the environment, thus being able to reflect global network dynamics. This knowledge stores a history of important past events (in this case, the information that complete paths to the destination were found). As in the CGrAnt Situational knowledge, complete paths cannot be shared in the History knowledge. The betweenness utility metric (representing partial information of the global solution) is then used and may subsequently influence the search.

The Situational knowledge is distributed among network nodes ($Situat^i$, $i=1, ..., N$). In each node i, this knowledge is divided into M_i niches (i.e., $Situat^i_m$, $m = 1, ..., M_i$), with a niche for each message m stored in its buffer. The *Acceptance Function* in every Situational niche of node i considers that, if a new node j (partial solution) is found, it is accepted to update the belief space of i only if $U_j > U_{best\_fwd}$, where U_{best_fwd} is the current best forwarder utility for m stored in the niche $Situat^i_m$. After accepting a new solution, the *Update Function* is called. The new solution thus replaces the previous solution, and the new solution quality also updates the U_{best_fwd}. The *Influence Function* dictates the future of each path being built by each ant to a given pair (source-destination) of message m and thus constructs different sets in the population space (Section 3.3.1).

The Domain knowledge is also distributed among network nodes (Dom^i, $i=1, ..., N$). In each node i, there is only one niche associated with the local dynamics on the stagnation degree of node i ($StagD_i$) and its social network ($StagD^i_{net} = \Sigma_{j \in J} StagD_j$, where J is the set of nodes j encountered by node i). It thus assists CGrAnt in characterizing three types of nodes: (i) Dom^i = *high stagnation degree*, where node i is characterized as a high stagnation node when the following relation holds: $StagD_i > StagD^i_{net} + V_{sup}$ *if* $StagD^i_{net} \neq 0$, where V_{sup} is the value added to the social network's stagnation degree to allow detecting nodes with a stagnation degree higher than that of its social network; (ii) Dom^i = *low stagnation degree*, where node i has a low stagnation degree when the relation $StagD_i < StagD^i_{net} - V_{inf}$ *if* $StagD^i_{net} \neq 0$ holds, where V_{inf} is the value subtracted from the social network's stagnation degree to detect nodes with a stagnation degree lower than that of its social network; and (iii) Dom^i = *medium stagnation degree*, where node i is characterized as a medium stagnation node when the relations described above do not hold. The *Acceptance Function* of the Domain knowledge in each node i accepts information about the local dynamics of neighboring node j if the stagnation degree of j is greater than zero. After accepting a new solution, the *Update Function* is called to calculate $StagD^i_{net}$. Based on changes in node i's stagnation degree with respect to its social network, the *Influence Function* acts during the message forwarding phase by changing the value of the *search_status* indicator. The Domain knowledge can thus detect when an individual (ant) in node i should exploit or explore the search space while solving the DTN forwarding problem.

The History knowledge is distributed in each node i of the network ($Hist^i$, $i=1, ..., N$). The History knowledge of node i is represented by $Hist^i_d$, $d=1, ..., D_i$, where D_i ($D_i \leq N$) represents the number of destination nodes for which node i originated or intermediated a path. History knowledge helps each node i keep up-to-date on asynchronous events that characterize a change in the complete path construction dynamics. These events represent the global changes occurring in the network in relation to the best solutions for each message destination d. The *Acceptance Function* in each niche of node i ($Hist^i_d$) is called after receiving a Backward Ant (BA) from a node, indicating that a complete path to the destination d has just been found. After the node i receives a BA (from node j or d), its $BetwU_{i,d}$ is accepted to initialize or update its belief space. The BA reception initializes or updates the belief space of i with the betweenness utility of j ($BetwU_{j,d}$) if j is not the destination d. After accepting a new solution (j and/or i), the *Update Function* is called to calculate the average betweenness utility of node i's social network ($BetwU^i_{net,d}$, as in Eq. (2)). The *Influence Function* evaluates the movement directions ($dr=+1$, $dr=-1$ or $dr=0$) of each neighboring node j as a candidate forwarder for message m to d ($BetwU_{j,d}$) in relation to the $BetwU^i_{net,d}$ dynamics.

3.3 Forward and Backward Phases

The CGrAnt routing protocol contains two phases (Figure 2): *forward* or *path search* (provided by FAs) and *backward* (provided by BAs). The path search phase involves two functions to infer the best message forwarders: *path quality measuring* and *message forwarding*.

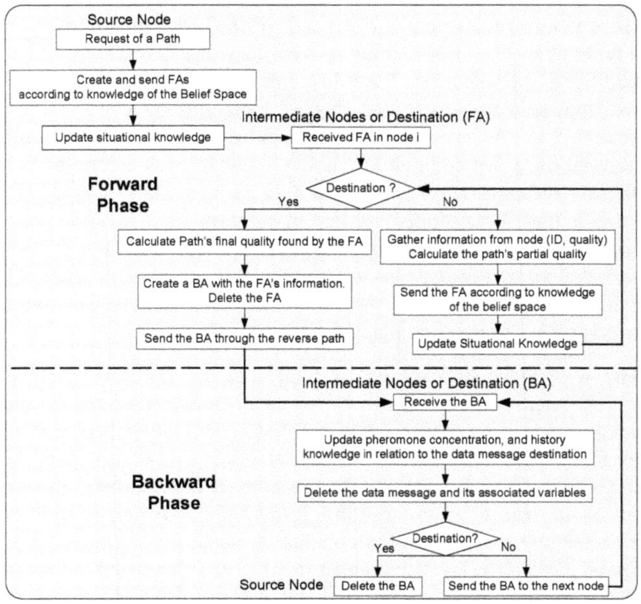

Figure 2. Forward and Backward Phases of CGrAnt.

The forward phase in CGrAnt is initialized on-demand, when a data message must be delivered to its destination d. FAs are then created, encapsulated into the data message, and sent toward the destination via one or more neighboring (intermediate) nodes. If more than one neighbor appears, the best one is accepted as the message forwarder according to the knowledge of the belief space. Control messages are periodically and locally exchanged between each node i and its neighboring nodes $j \in J$ to update node i's Domain knowledge. The search for new paths toward d continues until node i performs one of the following actions: (i) encountering the destination node, (ii) becoming aware of the successful delivery of the corresponding data message to its destination, or (iii) detecting that the Time to Live (TTL) field of the data message has expired.

Throughout its path search, an FA carries the following information: the ID of the node that originated the data message, the ID of the message destination, the nodes' ID through which it passes (between source and destination nodes), and the individual quality of each visited node j ($IndQ_j$). As j becomes more popular (high degree centrality), it has more opportunities to choose the best message forwarders ($IndQ_j$ = *degree centrality*). The individual quality updates the partial quality ($q(path^k_{s,d})$) of the path being constructed by the FA k ($path^k_{s,d}$) at time t:

$$q(path^k_{s,d}(t)) = \Sigma_j IndQ_j(t), \quad j \in path^k_{s,d} \tag{3}$$

When an FA (along with the data message) reaches the destination, the final quality of the constructed path ($Q(path^k_{s,d})$) is calculated, considering the average quality of its nodes and the reciprocal of the number of hops composing it:

$$Q(path^k_{s,d}(t)) = \frac{q(path^k_{s,d}(t))}{nHops} + \frac{1}{nHops} \quad (4)$$

When there are few hops in a path, fewer resources are consumed, and less interference is generated.

After calculating the quality of each new path, a new control message, the BA, is created from the information obtained by the FA, and the FA is deleted. During the backward phase, the BA returns to the node that originated the data message through the reverse path selected by the FA. The idea of using a reverse path even in DTN is motivated by wireless social networks in which (i) individuals are often linked by a short chain of acquaintances, (ii) some encounters have repetitive behavior, and (iii) nodes have routines that result in frequently visited locations and encounters.

In the reverse path, receiving a BA sent from node j to each neighboring node i produces three effects: (i) increasing by one the betweenness utility of node i to the message destination d (i.e., $BetwU_{i,d}$++); (ii) updating the betweenness utility of the social network of node i in relation to d ($BetwU^i_{net,d}$), as in Eq. (2); and (iii) updating the pheromone toward d according to:

$$\tau_{(i,j),d}(t) = (1 - \rho) \times \tau_{(i,j),d}(t - 1) + Q(path^k_{s,d}(t)), \quad (5)$$

where $\tau_{(i,j),d}(t - 1)$ is the pheromone on link (i, j) that was last updated at time (t - 1) and $Q(path^k_{s,d}(t))$, calculated as in Eq. (4), is the pheromone concentration deposited by the received BA k on link (i, j) (where $i, j \in path^k_{s,d}$). An evaporation process (1-ρ) is necessary for the ants "to forget" previous pheromone values deposited on a link to a specific destination d. This evaporation reduces the search history influence. When updating the pheromone, all concentrations that belong to the same destination d of the data message are evaporated in the considered node i.

Effects (i) and (ii) both represent the *Update Function* of the History Knowledge.

Even if the BA does not reach the node that originated the message (due to connection partitions), the message forwarding phase of the CGrAnt protocol is guided by a local search provided by the heuristic function information. Differing from other protocols that use only global (pheromone concentration) or local (heuristic function) information, CGrAnt has additional flexibility, as the decision is based on all available information (both ACO operators and knowledge stored in the CA belief space).

Additionally, the BA serves as an acknowledgment that the message achieved its destination node, allowing the nodes that maintain the message to delete it. A node that encounters another node that has already received a BA for a given data message deletes the corresponding message and its associated variables. When the source node receives it, the BA is deleted. Full paths are thus constructed for each destination using information gathered by ants during the search phase.

3.3.1 Message Forwarding Phase

CGrAnt message forwarding phase determines which route(s) a message must follow to eventually reach its destination. During message forwarding, an FA at a node i decides whether to forward data message m to a new neighboring node j according to the influence of the three types of knowledge stored in its belief space (Figure 3): Situational, History and Domain.

```
1 for each data message m in the buffer of node i
2   best_fwd_m = ∅;  {No forwarder is assigned to m}
3 endfor
4 {The History knowledge is updated during the backward phase}
5 for each data message m in the buffer of node i
6   U_i ← U_x;  {Node i utility, as in Eq. (1)}
7   if (best_fwd_m = ∅)
8      best_fwd_m ← i;  {Initializes the Situational Knowledge}
9      f(best_fwd_m) ← U_i; {Quality of the best forwarder for m}
10  endif
11  search_status exploration ← true;
12  search_status exploitation ← true;
13  {Domain Knowledge influence}
14  if (RelD^i_m = Int_m and Dom^i = medium stagnation degree)
15     search_status exploration ← false;
16  endif
17  if (RelD^i_m = Int_m and Dom^i = low stagnation degree)
18     search_status exploration ← false;
19     search_status exploitation ← false;
20  endif
21  for connections j do
22    U_j ← U_x; {Node j utility, as in Eq. (1)}
23    if (search_status exploration and best_fwd_m = i and U_i = U_j)
24       initial_exploration ← true;
25    else
26       initial_exploration ← false;
27    endif
28  if (search_status exploitation and Influence_Function( ))
29     Pair<Message, Forwarder> (m, j); {History Knowledge Influence}
30  else
31     if (initial_exploration or Accept_Function( ))
32        best_fwd_m ← j;         {Update Situational Knowledge}
33        f(best_fwd_m) ← U_j; {Update Situational Knowledge}
34     endif
35  endif
36  endfor
37  if (best_fwd_m ≠ ∅) {Situational Knowledge Influence}
38     Pair <Message, Forwarder> (m, best_fwd_m);
39  endif
40 endfor
41 Influence_Function( ) {History Influence Function}
42   if (BetwU_j,d > Hist^i_d)
43      return true;  {dr_j = +1}
44   else
45      return false;  {dr_j = −1 or dr_j = ∅}
46   endif
47 Accept_Function( ) {Situational Acceptance Function}
48   if (U_j > Situat^i_m)
49      return true; {Accept the solution j}
50   else
51      return false;
52   endif
```

Figure 3. Pseudo-code of CGrAnt Message Forwarding Phase.

As node i is the first candidate solution for forwarding message m, its identification and utility initialize the Situational knowledge (lines 8 and 9). The decision of forwarding m to j may be to explore (i.e., it is not required that node j has previously participated in a path to destination d of m) or exploit (i.e., node j has previously participated in a path toward d). The decision is guided by the following information about node i: its *RelD* with m (i.e., is it the source or an intermediate node of m?) and the *StagD* stored in the Domain knowledge (Dom^i). The status is initialized, enabling both exploitation and exploration of the search space (lines 11 and 12). These conditions can change in two situations: (i) node i is an intermediate node with a *medium* stagnation degree (in this case, the exploration stops (line 15)), or (ii) node i is an intermediate node with a *low* stagnation degree (in this case, both exploration and exploitation stop (lines 18 and 19)).

Aside from Domain knowledge, History and Situational knowledge also influence CGrAnt message forwarding. History knowledge influences it (line 29) when the decision is to exploit the solutions already found: node i forwards m to solution j if node j's betweenness utility ($BetwU_{j,d}$) is higher than the betweenness utility of node i's social network (the $BetwU^{i}_{net,d}$ stored in History Knowledge ($Hist^{i}_{d}$)), as observed in lines 42 and 43. Situational knowledge influences it (line 38) when the decision is to explore the environment or when better solutions appear. Node i only forwards m to a new solution j if one of the following two conditions is satisfied: (i) j's utility (U_j) is higher than the utility of the best forwarder previously found for m ($Ubest\_fwd_m$, which is stored in the Situational Knowledge ($Situat^{i}_{m}$)), as observed in lines 48 and 49. This condition tries to locate a new best forwarder for m among the current neighboring nodes of i; or (ii) at the beginning of the exploration (i.e., the data message was not forwarded to any other node, $best\_fwd_m = i$) and $U_j = U_i$ (lines 23-24, 31-33). Situational and History knowledge are important contributions of the CGrAnt protocol because, they dynamically control the number of created ants and data message redundancy by setting each new best message forwarder or forwarding m to already good known nodes, thus differing from pure ACO algorithms proposed for DTNs.

After analyzing the utility of every current contact j and inferring the best one, CGrAnt creates a new pair <*Message, forwarder*> (lines 29 and/or 38), which represents the corresponding data message and its designated forwarder.

4. SIMULATION SETUP AND RESULTS

The simulation scenario considers the Working Day movement model [19], which represents an activity-based environment that simulates the daily lives of people who go to work in the morning, spend the day working, may go to a public place for leisure activities with friends at the end of day, and return to their houses at night. The scenario is divided into meeting points, busses, houses, offices, and roads. Social relationships are formed when a group of people performs the same activity in the same location. Eight groups are created, denoted by the letters A to H. Groups A to D simulate only intra-group movements. Groups E, F, and G simulate movements between A and the other groups, and H simulates movements among all groups. The assignment of nodes per group is the following: A has 50 nodes, B has 15, C has 30, D has 30, E has 30 (i.e., nodes from A and B), F has 50 (i.e., nodes from A and C), G has 50 (i.e., nodes from A and D), and H has 70 (i.e., nodes from all groups). The traffic is generated every 100-150 s. The communication ranges are 10 and 100 m, and transmission speeds are 2 and 10 Mbps. The simulation lasts for 800,000 s. The nodes update their qualities after every 5,000 s of simulation. The node buffer size is 10 MB. Each message has a TTL of 1,800 minutes and size of 500 KB. In CGrAnt, each message encapsulates an FA with 8 bytes (i.e., a double number that represents its path quality). The BA size is 100 bytes (including the header, path quality, and path hops). The simulation experiments are conducted using the ONE Simulator [20].

To determine some CGrAnt parameters, experiments are conducted, and the performance is analyzed, focusing on the message delivery ratio. Due to space limitations, the detailed results are not presented here: (i) a pheromone evaporation rate of 0.1 provides the best results; (ii) to represent the individual quality ($IndQ$), the degree centrality of a node provides better results than a metric considering the percentage of a node's free buffer; and (iii) $V_{sup} = 8 \times \mathrm{StagD}^{i}_{net}$ and $V_{inf} = 0.9 \times \mathrm{StagD}^{i}_{net}$.

Initially, we evaluate the influence of CGrAnt's components in the message delivery and byte redundancy ratios. The latter performance metric represents the number of bytes transmitted to nodes (B_{transm}) with respect to the number of delivered message bytes ($B_{delivery}$). For this experiment, we adopt an additive methodology in which components are added one by one to previous configurations of the protocol until we reach its final version (configuration 6). Each configuration runs an entire simulation (800,000 s). Table 1 shows the mean results and confidence intervals (at a 95% confidence level) for 30 runs.

Table 1. Additive Analysis of CGrAnt's Components.

Configuration	Message Delivery	Byte Redundancy
1. Heuristic Function	53.38±0.60	85.87±0.94
2. Pheromone	54.97±0.61	68.62±0.96
3. Dom. Knowledge 1	64.26±0.63	43.18±0.41
4. Situational Knowledge	61.04±0.68	10.87±0.11
5. History Knowledge	63.70±0.69	19.04±0.23
6. Dom. Knowledge 2	63.19±0.72	12.43±0.12

The first two configurations in Table 1 represent the CGrAnt protocol when considering only the ACO metaheuristic. The pheromone slightly increases the delivery ratio and reduces the number of replicated bytes. In configurations 3 to 6, we can analyze the influence of the new component incorporated into CGrAnt (i.e., CA's belief space). Comparing the results obtained from the pure ACO metaheuristic (emphasized in Table 1) with the final performance of CGrAnt (configuration 6), we observe an increase of 14.95% in the delivery ratio with a reduction of 81.89% in the byte redundancy ratio. Situational knowledge (configuration 4) aims to dynamically restrict the number of FAs (and, consequently, the number of data messages) relayed only to the most promising forwarders. Its higher influence is thus in the number of bytes replicated. Historical knowledge (configuration 5) seeks to provide the exploitation of already known good solutions. Its higher influence is thus in the delivery ratio. Domain knowledge 1 (configuration 3) is responsible for determining when an individual (i.e., ant) must explore the search space and Domain knowledge 2 (configuration 6) determines when it must explore or exploit. According to the analysis of configurations 3 to 6, we conclude that, Domain knowledge thus aims to increase the message delivery and reduce byte redundancy ratio. Our previous ACO-based protocol, named GrAnt [14], performs better (i.e., it provides 60.25±0.75 of message delivery and 13.55±0.14 of byte redundancy) than configuration 2 (i.e., CGrAnt uses only the ACO metaheuristic). Additionally to ACO operators, GrAnt uses an external memory to store the best forwarder for each message. This, however, is modeled in CGrAnt as a situational knowledge of the CA's belief space.

After achieving its final configuration, CGrAnt is compared with two protocol categories for DTNs, which are usually considered in comparisons for DTN environments, as they are available in DTN simulators, such as ONE, and can operate in various environments with different node mobility models. Epidemic [8] and PROPHET [9] are used for performance gain comparisons with CGrAnt. Differing from Epidemic and PROPHET, CGrAnt conduct a global search and gather relevant information from DTN nodes.

CGrAnt can thus analyze the utilities of each node as a message forwarder and limit message byte replications.

Figures 4 and 5 show the performance gain of the three DTN routing protocols when varying buffer sizes and message TTLs, respectively. The dashed curves with empty points show the results when nodes operate at a communication range of 10 m and transmission speed of 2 Mbps; the solid curves with black points show results when nodes operate at a communication range of 100 m and transmission speed of 10 Mbps. We performed 30 runs, and the results represent the mean values.

Figures 4(a) and 4(b) show that as the buffer size and communication range increase, more messages are delivered and lower byte redundancy is generated by the three protocols. Nevertheless, for all buffer sizes and both communication ranges, CGrAnt provides a higher delivery ratio combined with a smaller redundancy ratio. For a buffer size of 8 MB, CGrAnt delivers 61.60±0.70% of the messages with a redundancy ratio of only 12.24±0.11 (using a 10 m range) and 98±0.09% with a 21.57±0.57 redundancy with a 100 m range. PROPHET delivers 28.25±0.32% (10 m) and 77.96±0.32% (100 m) of messages with a redundancy ratio of 116.33±1.10 (10 m) and 123.48±0.78 (100 m). Epidemic delivers 22.60±0.33% and 71.02±0.30% of messages with a redundancy ratio of 227.85±2.79 (10 m) and 278.88±1.73 (100 m). PROPHET and Epidemic performed poorly, as they do not have a dynamic mechanism for limiting the number of forwarded messages and choosing the best forwarding candidates, as CGrAnt does through its Situational knowledge. The results show that a node with an efficient routing protocol can abdicate only a small space of its buffer to message custodies. Figure 4(c) shows the message delivery delay for increasing buffer sizes. The PROPHET and Epidemic protocols provide lower delays for smaller buffer sizes. Instead, CGrAnt provides the lowest delay when using a higher buffer size (i.e., 10 MB to 16 MB). This is the only metric in which CGrAnt cannot provide the best results for all buffer sizes, which is justified by its ability to carefully analyze the node's utilities and forward a message to a new node only if it is more promising than the already established custodian node for that message.

Figure 5 shows the message delivery, byte redundancy, and delivery delay over different message TTLs. Figures 5(a) and 5(b) show that CGrAnt provides the best results for all message TTLs and communication ranges in message delivery and byte redundancy. Figure 5(c) shows that CGrAnt achieves shorter delays when using a 10 m range and similar delays, when compared to PROPHET and Epidemic, with a 100 m range.

Finally, we perform an experiment to evaluate the number of messages delivered by the three protocols over simulation time. The aim here is to demonstrate that a better delivery ratio can be achieved as time increases. Though the delivery ratio increases for the three protocols when increasing the simulation time from 400,000 s to 800,000 s (with a 10 m range), CGrAnt has higher performance gain (10.99±0.90%) than PROPHET (2.65±0.40%) and Epidemic (2.49±0.43%). This is justified by CGrAnt's ability to gather more updated information over time and make better choices concerning message forwarding candidates.

5. CONCLUSIONS

In this paper, we proposed a swarm intelligence-based routing protocol for DTNs, called CGrAnt. CGrAnt uses a greedy version of the ACO metaheuristic and CA to conduct local and global searches in a highly dynamic and complex environment by analyzing and gathering information on candidate nodes. Extracting information from the evolution and social behavior of nodes can improve searching and motivated the CA usage. Simulations show that for an activity-based scenario, CGrAnt achieved a higher message delivery ratio and generated lower byte redundancy when compared to the Epidemic and PROPHET protocols because CGrAnt can dynamically restrict the number of messages forwarded to the most promising nodes. Using the information stored in the CA belief space concerning the forwarding candidates, including their degree centrality, betweenness utility, and social proximity to other nodes, CGrAnt can save nodes' resources and provide better network utilization. In future work, we intend to compare CGrAnt with other ACO-based routing protocols. Additionally, we will test CGrAnt using other scenarios. We believe that its ability to extract information online from dynamic conditions can be explored in many different situations, from almost static to completely mobile and disconnected networking environments.

6. ACKNOWLEDGMENTS

This work is partially supported by the Brazilian National Research Council (CNPq), under research grants 301801/2008-8 to A. Munaretto and 307735/2008-7 to M.R. Delgado. Authors would like to thank INRIA-France and Fundação Araucária for their infrastructure and financial support.

7. REFERENCES

[1] Fall, K. 2003. A delay-tolerant network architecture for challenged internets. In *Proceedings of the 2003 conference on Applications, technologies, architectures, and protocols for computer communications*. ACM, New York, NY, USA, 27-34. DOI= http://doi.acm.org/10.1145/863955.863960.

[2] Fall, K. and Farrel, S. 2008. DTN: an architectural retrospective. *IEEE J. Sel. Areas in Commun.*, 26, 5 (June 2008), 828–836. DOI= http://dx.doi.org/10.1109/JSAC.2008.080609.

[3] Cerf, V. et al. 2007. *Delay-tolerant network architecture*, IETF RFC 4838, DTN Research Group. <http://www.ietf.org/rfc/rfc4838.txt>.

[4] Dorigo, M., Maniezzo, V., and Colorni, A. 1996. Ant system: optimization by a colony of cooperating agents. *IEEE Trans. Syst. Man Cybern. Part B Cybern.*, 26, 1 (Feb. 1996), 29-41. DOI= http://dx.doi.org/10.1109/3477.484436.

[5] Dorigo, M. and Caro, G. 1999. Ant colony optimization meta-heuristic. *New Ideas in Optimization*, McGraw-Hill, 11-32.

[6] Reynolds, R. 1994. An introduction to cultural algorithm. In *Proceedings of the 3rd Annual Conference on Evolutionary Programming*, World Scientific Publishing, River Edge, New Jersey, USA, 131-139.

[7] Saleem, S. M. 2001. *Knowledge-Based Solution to Dynamic Optimization Problems using Cultural Algorithms. PhD Thesis*, Wayne State University, Detroit, Michigan.

[8] Vadhat, A. and Becker, D. 2000. *Epidemic routing for partially connected ad hoc networks*. Technical Report CS-2000-06, Duke University.

[9] Lindgren, A., Doria, A, and Schelén, O. 2004. Probabilistic routing in intermittently connected networks. In *Lect. Notes*

Comput. Sci., 3126 (Jan. 2004), 239-254. DOI= http://dx.doi.org/10.1007/978-3-540-27767-5_24.

[10] Liu, L. and Feng, G. 2005. Swarm intelligence based node-disjoint multi-path routing protocol for mobile ad hoc networks. In *Proceedings of the 5th International Conference on Information, Communications and Signal Processing*, Bangkok, Thailand, 598-602. DOI= http://dx.doi.org/10.1109/ICICS.2005.1689117.

[11] Rosati L., Berioli, M., and Reali, G. 2008. On ant routing algorithms in ad hoc networks with critical connectivity. *Ad Hoc Networks*, 6, 6 (Aug. 2008), 827-859. DOI= http://dx.doi.org/10.1016/j.adhoc.2007.07.003.

[12] La, R. J., and Ranjan, P. 2009. Ant-based adaptive message forwarding scheme for challenged networks with sparse connectivity. In *Proceedings of the 28th IEEE Military Communications Conference*, Boston, MA, USA, 1-7. DOI= http://dx.doi.org/10.1109/MILCOM.2009.5379884.

[13] Zhang, P. et al. 2010. ACRP: Ant-colony-based routing protocol for DTMNs. In *Proceedings of the 2010 International Conference on Educational and Information Technology*, 2, Chongqing, China, 272-276. DOI= http://dx.doi.org/10.1109/ICEIT.2010.5607571.

[14] Vendramin, A. C. B. K., Munaretto, A., Delgado, M., and Viana, A. C. 2012. GrAnt: Inferring Best Forwarders from Complex Networks' Dynamics through a Greedy Ant Colony Optimization. *Computer Networks*, 56, 3 (Feb. 2012), 997-1015. DOI= http://dx.doi.org/10.1016/j.comnet.2011.10.028.

[15] Ma, J. et al. 2008. Research on cultural algorithm for solving routing problem of mobile agents. *The Journal of China Universities of Posts and Telecommunications*, 15, 4 (Dec. 2008), 121-125. DOI= http://dx.doi.org/10.1016/S1005-8885(08)60415-X.

[16] Zhang, M.-W., Sun, X.-M., and Lv, X.-Y. 2010. A QoS routing algorithm based on culture-ant colony algorithm. In *Proceedings of the International Conference on Computer Application and System Modeling*, Taiyuan, China, 198-201. DOI= http://dx.doi.org/10.1109/ICCASM.2010.5622234.

[17] Freeman, L. C. 1979. Centrality in social networks: conceptual clarification. *Social Networks*, 1, 3, 215-239. DOI= http://dx.doi.org/10.1016/0378-8733(78)90021-7.

[18] Daly, E. M. and Haahr, M. 2007. Social network analysis for routing in disconnected delay-tolerant MANETs. In *Proceedings of the 8th ACM International Symposium on Mobile Ad Hoc Networking and Computing*, ACM, New York, NY, USA, 32-40. DOI= http://doi.acm.org/10.1145/1288107.1288113.

[19] Ekman, F. et al. 2008. Working day movement model. In *Proceedings of 1st ACM SIGMOBILE Workshop on Mobility Models*, ACM, New York, NY, USA, 33–40. DOI= http://doi.acm.org/10.1145/1374688.1374695.

[20] Keränen, A., Kärkkäinen, T., and Ott, J. 2010. Simulating mobility and DTNs with the ONE. *Journal of Communications*, 5, 2, 92-105 (Feb. 2010). DOI= http://dx.doi.org/10.4304/jcm.5.2.92-105.

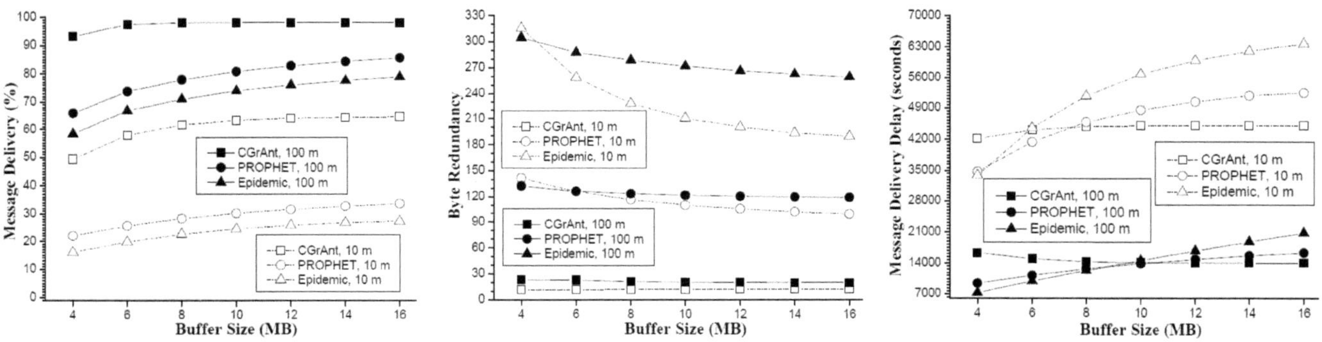

(a) **(b)** **(c)**

Figure 4. Protocols performance over different buffer sizes: (a) delivery ratio; (b) redundancy ratio; (c) delivery delay.

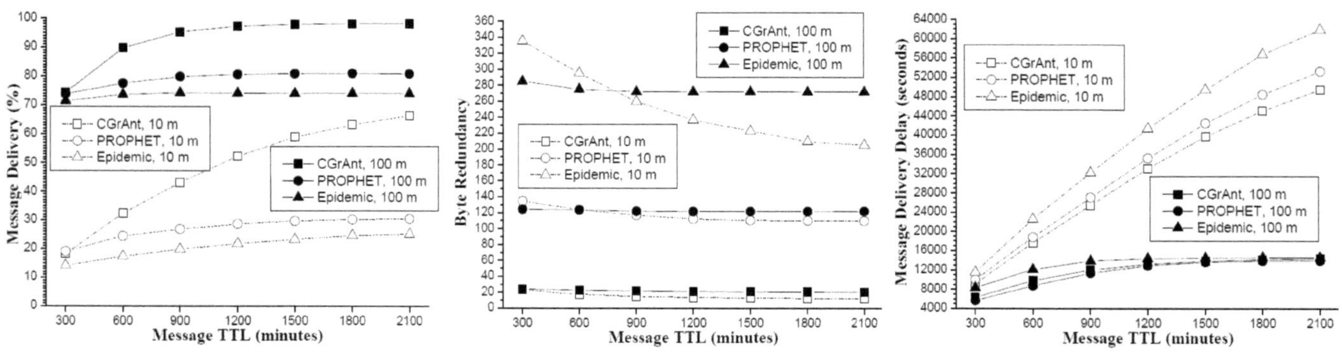

(a) **(b)** **(c)**

Figure 5. Protocols performance over different message TTL: (a) delivery ratio; (b) redundancy ratio; (c) delivery delay.

DACCO: A Discrete Ant Colony Algorithm to Cluster Geometry Optimization

Nuno Lourenço
CISUC, Department of Informatics Engineering
University of Coimbra, 3030 Coimbra, Portugal
naml@dei.uc.pt

Francisco B. Pereira
[1]CISUC, Department of Informatics Engineering
University of Coimbra, 3030 Coimbra, Portugal
[2]ISEC, Quinta da Nora, 3030 Coimbra, Portugal
xico@dei.uc.pt

ABSTRACT

We present a discrete ant colony algorithm to cluster geometry optimization. To deal with this continuous problem, the optimization framework includes functions to map solutions across the discrete and continuous spaces. Results obtained with short-ranged Morse clusters show that the proposed approach is effective, scalable and is competitive with state-of the-art optimization methods specifically designed to tackle continuous domains. A detailed analysis is presented to help to gain insight into the role played by several components of the ant colony algorithm.

Categories and Subject Descriptors

G.1.6 [**Numerical Analysis**]: Optimization—*Global Optimization*; I.2.8 [**Artificial Intelligence**]: Problem Solving, Control Methods, and Search—*Heuristic Methods*

General Terms

Algorithms

Keywords

Ant colony optimization, Cluster geometry optimization, Hybridization, Morse clusters

1. INTRODUCTION

Ant Colony Optimization (ACO) methods are population-based metaheuristics regularly applied in combinatorial and continuous optimization problems [7]. The original algorithm, Ant System (AS), was proposed by Dorigo in the early 1990's [5] and it is loosely inspired by the organization of natural ant societies. When foraging, ants deposit pheromone on the ground to guide co-workers towards promising areas. Then, individuals belonging to the colony communicate via stigmergy, an indirect way to exchange information mediated by modifications in the environment.

GECCO'12, July 7-11, 2012, Philadelphia, Pennsylvania, USA.

Following AS, many other ACO variants have been proposed in the literature. Relevant examples are the Ant Colony System (ACS) [6] and the Max-Min Ant System (MMAS) [19], two approaches that have been thoroughly tested on combinatorial optimization problems. Even though earlier ACO research focused on discrete problems, there are a number of variants for continuous optimization. Bilchev and Parmee pioneered the extension of an ant algorithm to explore real-valued search spaces [1] and, since then, several other approaches have been proposed [13, 18, 21].

In this paper we propose an ACO algorithm to solve the cluster geometry optimization problem. This is an important problem from the chemistry area, where the goal is to find the optimal structural organization for a set of particles in a 3D space [8, 23]. Estimating the most relevant properties of chemical clusters has immediate relevance in many areas, ranging from protein structure prediction to the study of the influence of stratospheric clouds in ozone destruction. Also, a proper understanding of cluster properties is crucial for the field of nanotechnology. In simple terms, a cluster is an aggregate of between a few and millions of atoms or molecules, which may present distinct physical properties from those of a single particle or bulk matter. The Potential Energy Function (PES) models the interactions between particles and it contains all the relevant information about the chemical system. PES are multidimensional functions generating highly roughed search landscapes, with a number of local minima increasing exponentially with the size of the cluster [22]. The goal of the optimization is to find the global minimum of the PES, i.e., to determine the relative position in the 3D space of all the atoms that correspond to the lowest potential energy. In our study we adopt the Morse function to describe interactions between atoms, a model potential that can accurately represent real materials [3, 9, 16]. Moreover, this is a difficult real-valued optimization function that has been regularly used as a benchmark to determine the performance of global search methods for cluster geometry optimization [4, 10, 11, 17].

We have developed DACCO (Discrete Ant Colony algorithm to Cluster geometry Optimization), a framework that follows an unusual approach to apply an ACO algorithm to seek for the optimal arrangement of atomic clusters. We discretize the problem and rely on the MMAS variant to find solutions on the discrete space. Then, a mapping function, consisting of a gradient-driven local optimization procedure, pushes the solutions obtained by the ants back to the original continuous space. The reasons for relying on this framework are twofold: first, there is a deeper insight into the main properties of existing discrete ACO algorithms, when compared to continuous variants; on the other hand, the problem consists in placing objects in a 3D space, subject to a minimal distance constraint. Then, discretizing the space is a straightforward strategy to ensure a valid arrangement of the cluster. A previous work from Korb et al. adopts a similar strategy to solve the protein-ligand docking problem [12].

We test the effectiveness of DACCO by seeking the global optima of short-ranged Morse clusters between 30 and 80 atoms. Results obtained show that the hybrid architecture composed by the discrete MMAS variant and the continuous local optimization procedure is competitive with current state-of-the-art metaheuristics for cluster geometry optimization. Additionally, we investigate how some specific components of DACCO help to enhance the likelihood of discovering good quality solutions.

The paper is structured as follows: in section 2 we provide a general description of ACO algorithms, including the main variants for continuous optimization. Section 3 comprises a presentation of DACCO and of the optimization problem to be addressed. Optimization results and the corresponding analysis are accomplished in section 4 and, finally, section 5 gathers the main conclusions and suggests directions for future work.

2. ANT COLONY OPTIMIZATION

The first ACO variants (e.g., AS or ACS) were proposed for combinatorial optimization, such as the traveling salesperson or the quadratic assignment problems [5, 6, 7]. The application of an ant algorithm to a specific problem requires the specification of a set of solution components. A graph is then created, where each vertex represents a component and edges link related vertices. The artificial ants construct solutions by traversing this graph. They start at a random vertex and iteratively collect new components. At each vertex of the path they build, ants stochastically select a new edge. The probability of choosing a specific edge (i.e., the desirability of adding a particular new component to the solution) depends on static heuristic information and on the pheromone level of that connection. Higher pheromone concentrations signal components that tend to appear in better solutions. When all artificial ants have completed their solutions, the pheromone levels are updated. To avoid stagnation, evaporation first decreases all pheromone values by a given factor. Then, a subset of ants deposits pheromone on the edges they crossed when building a solution. The amount placed by each ant is proportional to the quality of the solution found. ACO variants differ in the way ants build solutions and/or on the pheromone update step. For algorithmic details, consult the aforementioned references. By iterating these steps until a termination criterion is met, a solution to the problem will emerge from the cooperation made by the ants. In algorithm 1 we present the general structure of an ACO metaheuristic. The *Daemon actions* step identifies several optional actions, such as the application of local search or pheromone matrix restart.

Algorithm 1 General ACO Algorithm

```
Set parameters
Init pheromone trails
while termination condition not met do
    Construct solutions
    Update pheromones
    Daemon actions {optional}
end while
```

2.1 ACO for Continuous Optimization

There are several reports in the literature describing extensions of ACO architectures to continuous optimization. In 1995, Bilchev and Parmee [1] proposed an algorithm where the ants start from a given location in the search space (the nest) and explore the continuous neighborhood by selecting one from a set of vectors. These vectors depart from the nest and represent a set of possible search directions. The probability of selecting a vector reflects the likelihood that this direction leads to promising solutions. Tsutsui presented an approach based on the concept of aggregate pheromone density functions [21]. Each ant emits an aggregate pheromone amount, which is proportional to quality of the solution found. The total aggregate pheromone density is therefore biased towards promising areas of the search space and is used by a probability density function to generate new solutions. $ACO_{\mathbb{R}}$ is a recent approach from Socha and Dorigo to tackle continuous problems [18]. It relies on a set of solutions (the solution archive) to represents the pheromone model. The archive is used to bias the generation of new solutions. In this process, each variable is treated independently and its value is obtained by sampling a mixture of weighted Gaussian functions. Recently, this method was enhanced with the addition of a variable size solution archive and a local search procedure [13]. PLANTS is an ACO algorithm for protein-ligand docking proposed by Korb et al [12]. In this problem, the goal is to find the optimal settings for several real valued parameters defining the degrees of freedom and torsional degrees of freedom for the ligand and protein, respectively. The approach followed in PLANTS is similar to the one adopted in our research. The continuous variables are discretized and the MMAS variant is applied to solve the problem. PLANTS does not use heuristic information and relies on a local search algorithm to map solutions back to the continuous space.

3. DACCO

In this section we present DACCO, the Discrete Ant Colony algorithm that will be applied to Cluster geometry Optimization. First, we describe the problem to be addressed and then detail the main algorithmic components of the optimization framework.

3.1 Morse Clusters

A chemical cluster is an aggregate of between a few and millions of atoms or molecules. Understanding the properties of clusters is relevant for many areas, from protein structure prediction to the field of nanotechnology. The PES is a multidimensional function that contains all the relevant information about the chemical system [23]. The goal of cluster geometry optimization is to determine the optimal structural organization for the particles that compose a given aggregate, i.e., to discover the arrangement in the 3D space that corresponds to the global minimum of the PES. The Morse function [16] is a model potential regularly adopted in cluster geometry optimization, as it provides accurate approximations of real materials (e.g., alkalimetal clusters or C_{60} molecules) [3]. It is a pairwise additive

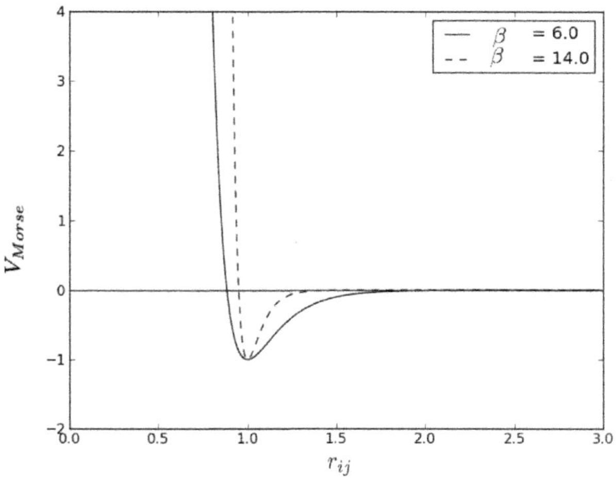

Figure 1: Morse Potential for different values of β

potential that considers the distance between every pair of particles to determine the energy of the cluster. In Morse clusters, all particles are identical. Then, the total potential energy of a N-cluster Morse aggregate is given by the following equation:

$$V_{Morse} = \epsilon \sum_{i=1}^{N-1} \sum_{j=i+1}^{N} \left(\exp^{-2\beta(r_{ij}-r_0)} - 2\exp^{-\beta(r_{ij}-r_0)} \right) \tag{1}$$

where r_{ij} is the Cartesian distance between atoms i and j, ϵ is the bond dissociation energy, r_0 is the equilibrium bond and β is the range exponent of the potential. Following [9], both ϵ and r_0 are set to 1.0, leading to a scaled version of the Morse function without specific atom interactions.

Hence, the potential has a single adjustable parameter β that determines the shape of the energy contribution of every pair of atoms [23]. The chart from figure 1 illustrates how this pairwise contribution is modeled as a function of the distance between atoms (displayed in the xx axis). Two different β values are exemplified: in both cases, the lowest potential energy is achieved when the two atoms are separated by a distance that is equal to the equilibrium bond. However,moving from a long ranged potential ($\beta = 6.0$) to a short ranged version ($\beta = 14.0$) leads to a narrower curvature, promoting the appearance of very roughed landscapes, with the number of local minima increasing exponentially as the number of atoms increases [8, 22]. In our study β is set to 14.0, as this creates optimization instances that are particularly challenging.

3.2 Optimization Framework

When solving a Morse cluster instance with N identical atoms, one must specify the location of each particle. The search space is defined as a cubic area in the first quadrant with side $N^{1/3}$, as this enables the cluster volume to scale correctly with N [11]. Additionally, small interatomic distances should not be allowed, because the potential tends to infinity when two atoms are too close (see figure 1). This minimum distance constraint creates a favorable environment for the application of discrete ACO variants. Ants build a solution by traversing the 3D space and placing atoms in selected locations. A careful definition of the discrete step length ensures that two atoms never stay too close to each other.

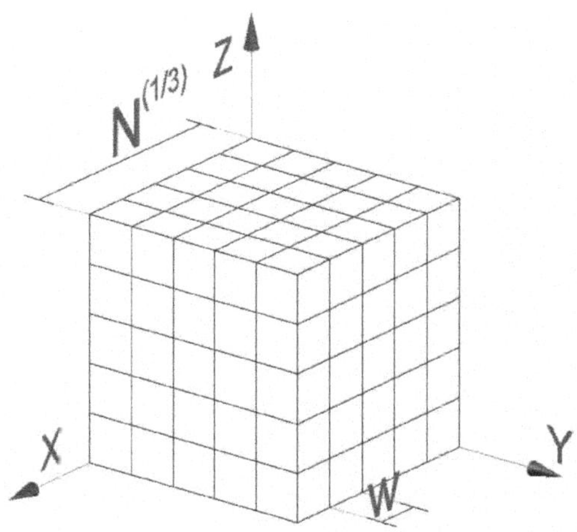

Figure 2: Discretized Cluster Geometry Optimization Space

In concrete, the problem of cluster geometry optimization is defined in a 3 dimensional space $(x, y, z) \in \mathbb{R}^3$, where $x, y, z \in [0, N^{1/3}]$. This cube is divided into cells of side w. The value selected for this parameter must ensure that it is possible to place atoms in neighbor locations, but it is not feasible to have two particles inside the same cell. Given the value of parameter r_0, for all experiments reported in this work, w is set to 0.6. We did some additional tests with different values and verified that this setting provides the best compromise. Figure 2 presents an overview of the discretized optimization space.

The well-known MMAS discrete variant [19] is adopted by DACCO to seek for the optimal configuration of different Morse cluster instances. The automatic rescaling approach proposed by the Hyper-Cube Framework (HCF) [2] is incorporated in the algorithm, in order to increase its robustness. Algorithm 2 presents a general overview of DACCO, with an identification of the steps required to move from the continuous space to the discrete one and vice-versa. In the next paragraphs we detail the operations involved in the application of this algorithm.

Algorithm 2 General Overview of DACCO

```
Construct Discrete Search Space
Initialize Pheromone Matrix
while termination condition not met do
    Construct Solutions in the Discrete Space
    Convert Solutions to the Continuous Space
    Evaluate Solutions in the Continuous Space
    Convert Solutions to the Discrete Space
    Apply Discrete Local Improvement
    Update Pheromone Values
end while
return best individual in the population
```

Initialize pheromones: In cluster geometry optimization, what is important is the relative position of the atoms in space, and not the order in which they are placed. Then, the structure of the pheromone matrix is identical to that of the discretized cube and it stores the desirability of placing an atom in a given cell. In the beginning of the optimization, all the cells from the pheromone matrix are initialized with the same value. Following the recommendations from [2], we set this value to 0.5.

Algorithm 3 Solution Construction

```
Given an ant do:
current_location = select_random_cell()
place_atom()
placed_atoms = 1
while placed_atoms < N do
  neighbors = find_feasible_neighborhood(ant)
  current_location = find_next_cell(neighbors, pher_matrix)
  place_atom()
  placed_atoms = placed_atoms + 1
end while
```

Construction of Solutions: Algorithm 3 details the actions performed by an ant to build a solution. When seeking for a good geometry of a Morse instance with N atoms, an ant starts in a randomly selected cell and must visit another N-1 locations to place one atom in each one of them. Ants consider both heuristic information and pheromone values to select the next cell to visit. The first component favors cells in the neighborhood of already occupied locations to place the next atom. Optimal configurations of clusters tend to correspond to compact structures, so heuristic information bias the formation of solutions where atoms are located in adjacent cells (the discretization of the space prevents atoms from being too close). We consider two alternatives for the definition of the heuristic neighborhood:

Current Moore Neighborhood It consists of all unoccupied cells that surround the current location of the ant. Different neighborhood ranges R can be considered, impacting the size of the cube around the current cell. In panel a) of figure 3 we illustrate a Current Moore Neighborhood with R=2. For simplicity, the example is presented in a 2D grid.

Full Moore Neighborhood It consists of all unoccupied cells surrounding atoms already placed in the grid. Just like in the previous alternative, different neighborhood ranges may be considered. Panel b) of figure 3 displays a Full Moore Neighborhood with R=1.

After determining the feasible neighborhood, an ant selects the next cell to place an atom by applying the MMAS selection rule. In this stage, only the pheromone values are considered (MMAS selection does not take into account any heuristic information). This process is repeated until all the atoms are placed in the grid.

Mapping Solutions to the Continuous Space and Evaluation: Mapping of a discrete solution into the continuous space consists in two steps: first, each atom is positioned in the geometric center of the cell in which it was placed during the construction of the solution. Afterwards, the positioning of atoms inside the cluster is refined by the application of a local optimization procedure. Most effective unbiased techniques for cluster geometry optimization are hybrid approaches combining a global optimization algorithm with a local search procedure [10, 11, 17]. In accordance, we

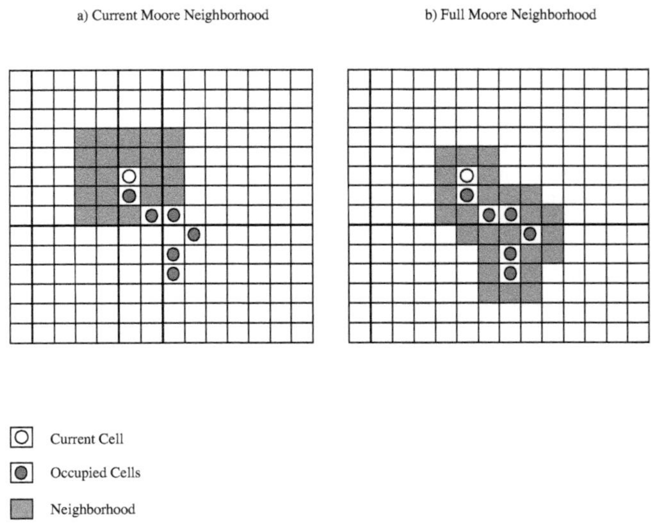

Figure 3: Examples of heuristic neighborhoods in a 2D grid: a) Current Moore neighborhood with R=2; b) Full Moore Neighborhood with R=1.

rely on the Broyden-Fletcher-Goldfarb-Shannon (L-BFGS) method [14], a conjugate gradient algorithm that efficiently guides the solution created by the ants into the nearest local minimum. Finally, the resulting solution is evaluated with equation 1.

Mapping Solutions to the Discrete Space After evaluation, clusters are mapped back to the discrete space. To accomplish this, atoms are simply moved to the geometric center of the cell where they were positioned by L-BFGS. Given the selected w value, it is highly unlikely that local optimization places two atoms in the same cell. Anyway, if this happens, then one of the particles is moved to the nearest unoccupied cell. There are two reasons to discretize the solutions after evaluation. The first is to apply a discrete local improvement method, that seeks for better configurations by iteratively perturbing existing solutions. The improvement strategy is straightforward: it seeks for the worst atom of the cluster (i.e., the one that has the highest contribution to the total potential energy) and moves it to an unoccupied cell randomly selected. The modified solution is locally optimized with L-BFGS and evaluated. If the resulting cluster has lower energy than the original one, then it is kept. The process is repeated for a predetermined number of iterations. The second reason to move the solutions back to the discrete space is to perform the update of the pheromone matrix. First, evaporation slightly decreases all values. Then, the rule described in [2] for MMAS is used to reinforce the pheromone of promising cells. Pheromone reinforcement adopts a diffusion model. If a cell is going to be reinforced with a given amount A, then it only receives $(A - p)$ and the quantity that is left over is distributed in equal parts among all adjacent cells. This procedure aims to smooth the transition between the discrete and continuous spaces and it was also adopted by [12].

4. EXPERIMENTS

In this section we present the results obtained by DACCO

in the optimization of short-ranged Morse clusters between 30 and 80 atoms. With these experiments we aim to determine the absolute optimization performance of the proposed approach and to gain insight into the role played by the different algorithmic components. The settings of the algorithm are the following: Number of runs: 30; Number of ants: equal to the number of atoms of the instance; Evaluations: 5,000,000; α: 4; Pheromone diffusion p: 0.5; Current Moore neighborhood with R=3; Discrete local improvement iterations: 10; L-BFGS accuracy: $1.0E-8$. Each iteration performed by the L-BFGS method counts as one evaluation.

Analysis of results focus on the ability of DACCO to find the putative global optimum (within a pre-specified computational effort), as this is the criterion regularly adopted in cluster geometry optimization studies. Therefore, for each instance we present the success rate (SR) of DACCO, i.e., the number of runs (out of 30) that discovered the best known solution. For completeness, we also provide the mean best fitness (MBF) of all reported experiments.

4.1 Optimization Results

Table 1 contains an overview of the optimization results. There is a line for each one of the instances selected. Column *Opt* displays the potential energy of the putative global optimum[1], whereas columns 3 and 4 present the SR and the MBF, respectively. The last column *Deviation* measures how the MBF deviates, in percentage, from the best-known solution. Results confirm that DACCO can effectively find good quality solutions. With just two exceptions, $N = \{47, 79\}$, it always discovers the putative global optima of short ranged Morse instances between 30 and 80 atoms. The effectiveness of DACCO is particularly relevant, since the global optima of different Morse instances correspond to distinct structural shapes (e.g. poly-tetrahedral, icosahedral or decahedral) [9]. The outcomes displayed in table 1 suggest that DACCO is not biased towards generating solutions with a particular geometry.

There is a trend for a decrease in the success rate achieved by DACCO as the clusters grow in size. This effect can be partially justified by the fixed number of evaluations granted to all experiments reported in this paper. Instances with more atoms define larger search spaces and, therefore, it is expected that the success rate of DACCO might be lower. Additionally, the optimal geometry for some specific Morse instances is particularly hard to discover, which helps to explain the variation in the success rate. Examples of magic numbers (*i.e.*, particularly hard Morse instances) are 38, 47, 61, 68 or 79 atoms [9, 10].

The MBF achieved by DACCO in all instances is always close to the value of the putative optima. The deviation rarely exceeeds 1% and, in most cases, is well below this threshold. This result shows that the proposed algorithm is robust, since, even when it does not discover the global optimum, it converges to good quality local optima.

4.2 Comparison with Other Approaches

It is essential to compare the results obtained by DACCO with those achieved by state-of-the-art methods for cluster geometry optimization. We selected two global optimization algorithms recently described in the literature: a hybrid

[1]Consult the Cambridge Cluster Database for an up to date list of Putative Optima: http://www-wales.ch.cam.ac.uk/CCD.html

N	Opt	SR	MBF	Deviation
30	-106.835790	28 / 30	-106.831095	0.004
31	-111.760670	30 / 30	-111.760670	0.000
32	-115.767561	30 / 30	-115.767561	0.000
33	-120.741345	30 / 30	-120.741345	0.000
34	-124.748271	30 / 30	-124.748271	0.000
35	-129.737360	30 / 30	-129.737360	0.000
36	-133.744666	30 / 30	-133.744666	0.000
37	-138.708582	28 / 30	-138.682731	0.019
38	-144.321054	25 / 30	-144.053535	0.185
39	-148.327400	26 / 30	-148.243303	0.057
40	-152.333745	25 / 30	-152.228797	0.069
41	-156.633479	11 / 30	-156.483040	0.096
42	-160.641020	5 / 30	-160.449243	0.119
43	-165.634973	6 / 30	-165.361457	0.165
44	-169.642441	3 / 30	-169.383463	0.153
45	-174.511632	3 / 30	-174.295931	0.124
46	-178.519320	2 / 30	-178.371855	0.083
47	-183.508227	0 / 30	-183.095976	0.225
48	-188.888965	19 / 30	-188.402414	0.258
49	-192.898412	15 / 30	-192.675230	0.116
50	-198.455632	12 / 30	-197.853115	0.304
51	-202.468274	13 / 30	-201.992636	0.235
52	-207.480764	18 / 30	-207.294088	0.090
53	-211.493405	14 / 30	-211.225485	0.127
54	-216.636864	5 / 30	-216.171684	0.215
55	-220.646208	10 / 30	-220.422433	0.101
56	-225.655136	11 / 30	-224.935830	0.319
57	-230.663986	15 / 30	-229.976103	0.298
58	-234.809078	9 / 30	-234.394252	0.177
59	-240.572493	6 / 30	-239.338941	0.513
60	-244.579066	5 / 30	-244.090244	0.200
61	-249.587740	3 / 30	-248.668557	0.368
62	-253.612942	11 / 30	-253.277141	0.132
63	-258.620607	7 / 30	-258.032594	0.227
64	-264.587042	6 / 30	-262.706618	0.711
65	-268.594702	11 / 30	-267.406606	0.442
66	-273.602343	6 / 30	-272.023822	0.577
67	-278.400953	2 / 30	-276.976700	0.512
68	-282.683003	2 / 30	-281.715729	0.342
69	-287.462110	8 / 30	-286.366826	0.381
70	-292.462856	10 / 30	-291.443945	0.348
71	-298.405353	3 / 30	-295.263173	1.053
72	-302.413229	5 / 30	-299.983942	0.803
73	-307.421094	5 / 30	-304.684859	0.890
74	-312.441302	4 / 30	-309.237024	1.026
75	-318.407330	6 / 30	-315.446093	0.930
76	-322.414257	4 / 30	-319.405598	0.933
77	-327.371999	4 / 30	-324.342238	0.925
78	-331.379143	2 / 30	-328.915871	0.743
79	-336.798725	0 / 30	-333.181307	1.074
80	-340.811371	2 / 30	-338.162647	0.777

Table 1: Results obtained by DACCO in the optimization of Morse clusters between 30 and 80 atoms.

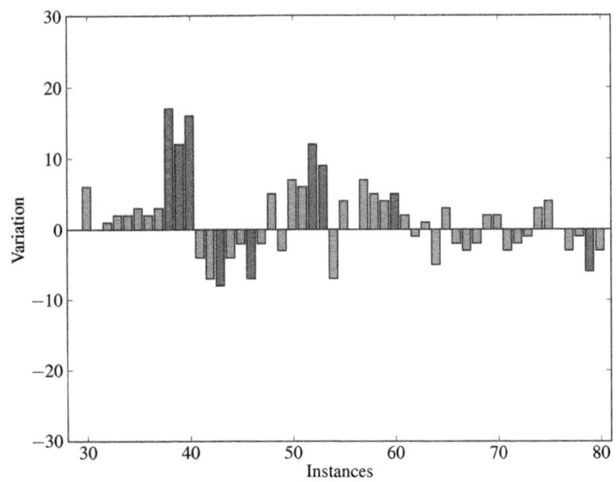

Figure 4: Comparison of the SR obtained by DACCO and the hybrid EA from [17] in the optimization of Morse clusters between 30 and 80 atoms. Darker columns highlight instances where significant differences were found.

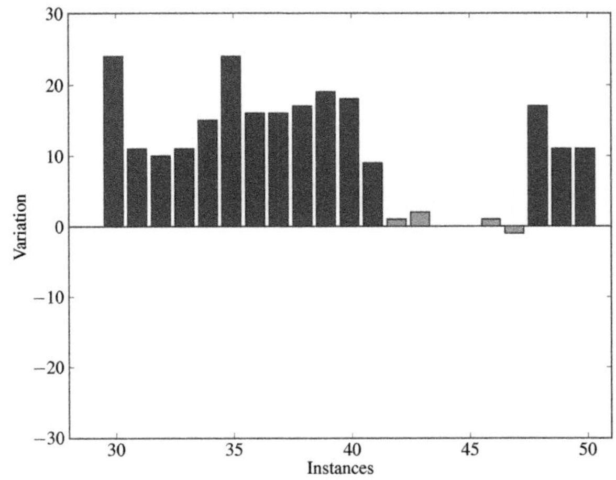

Figure 5: Comparison of the SR obtained by DACCO and the PSO from [15] in the optimization of Morse clusters between 30 and 50 atoms. Darker columns highlight instances where significant differences were found.

evolutionary algorithm (EA) [17] and a Particle Swarm Optimization (PSO) method [15]. The hybrid EA was the first completely unbiased algorithm to discover all putative global optima for short-ranged Morse clusters until 80 atoms. As for the PSO, it is the most effective swarm intelligence algorithm for this problem. Both algorithms incorporate a local procedure based on the L-BFGS method, similar to the one described for DACCO, and were granted the same number of evaluations to optimize the Morse instances selected for the comparison. For algorithmic details concerning both methods, consult the aforementioned references.

In figure 4 we display the SR difference between DACCO and the hybrid EA, across all instances. A positive (negative) variation corresponds to an instance where DACCO achieved a higher (lower) SR than the EA. In the same manner, figure 5 presents the comparison between DACCO and the PSO. Here, we only display results between 30 and 50 atoms, since the PSO was not applied to larger instances. A general overview of figure 4 reveals that the performance of DACCO and the EA is comparable. DACCO achieved a higher success rate on 27 instances, whereas EA was better on 21 instances (on the 3 remaining cases, both algorithms obtained the same SR). To strengthen the analysis, we applied a pairwise test to compare proportions, described in [20], to the results obtained by these two methods. Darker columns in the figure highlight instances where significant differences were found (significance level of 1%). The statistical analysis confirms the global equivalence of the two algorithms, as only in 9 instances a significant difference is identified (in 6 of them DACCO is better, whereas the EA achieves a higher SR in the remaining 3).

The chart from figure 5 clearly confirms that DACCO is more effective than the PSO when seeking for low energy Morse clusters. In 18 out of 21 instances the success rate achieved by DACCO is higher and, in most of them (15 instances), the difference if statistically significant. This is a relevant result, as it reveals that an adapted discrete ACO algorithm can outperform a PSO method in a hard continuous optimization problem.

As a final note, it is important to refer that both the EA and the PSO require the explicit application of a structural distance measure to help maintain the diversity in the population of solutions. Without this mechanism, both algorithms are likely to suffer from premature convergence. Results presented in this section show that DACCO is able to obtain results comparable to the hybrid EA without relying on an explicit and problem specific way to maintain diversity. Also, it does not require the computational overhead needed to calculate this measure.

4.3 DACCO Detailed Analysis

This last section aims to establish the impact of specific DACCO components on the performance of the algorithm. We focus our analysis on the definition of the heuristic neighborhood, on the pheromone diffusion model and on the application of the discrete local improvement method. Due to space constraints we present results obtained with a subset of instances $N = \{30, 50, 70, 79\}$, which help to gain insight into the relevance of specific design options. We did, however, additional tests with clusters with different sizes and verified that the results follow the same trend. Unless explicitly stated, experiments described in this section adopt the settings previously defined.

The heuristic is a greedy component that can play an important role in the behavior of an ACO algorithm. In what concerns DACCO, it bias the placement of atoms in the vicinity of already occupied positions. Recalling section 3, there are several options to define the neighbor cells that can be considered as viable options to place the next particle. Table 2 displays the optimization results obtained by several configurations in the selected instances. In concrete, we display the SR and the MBF of experiments done with the Current and Full Moore neighborhood and with $R = \{1, 2, 3, 4\}$. An overview of table 2 reveals that there

	Moore								Full Moore							
	1		2		3		4		1		2		3		4	
	SR	**MBF**	**SR**	**MBF**	**SR**	**MBF**	**SR**	**MBF**	**SR**	**MBF**	**SR**	**MBF**	**SR**	**MBF**	**SR**	**MBF**
30	25 / 30	-106.824	26 / 30	-106.826	28 / 30	-106.831	27 / 30	-106.828	25 / 30	-106.824	27 / 30	-106.828	27 / 30	-106.828	25 / 30	-106.824
50	0 / 30	-196.301	4 / 30	-196.958	12 / 30	-197.853	7 / 30	-197.898	2 / 30	-196.923	8 / 30	-197.620	7 / 30	-197.608	10 / 30	-197.819
70	0 / 30	-287.568	2 / 30	-289.673	10 / 30	-291.443	9 / 30	-291.483	0 / 30	-288.645	2 / 30	-290.621	8 / 30	-291.543	6 / 30	-291.487
79	0 / 30	-327.855	1 / 30	-332.482	0 / 30	-333.181	0 / 30	-333.618	0 / 30	-329.417	0 / 30	-332.539	1 / 30	-333.754	2 / 30	-334.085

Table 2: Optimization results obtained by different DACCO heuristic neighborhoods in selected Morse instances.

	No Pheromone Diffusion		With Pheromone Diffusion	
	SR	MBF	SR	MBF
30	26 / 30	-106.826	28 / 30	-106.831
50	7 / 30	-197.709	12 / 30	-197.853
70	10 / 30	-291.563	10 / 30	-291.443
79	0 / 30	-333.372	0 / 30	-333.181

Table 3: Impact of the pheromone diffusion model in the optimization results obtained by DACCO in selected Morse instances.

	No Local Improvement		With Local Improvement	
	SR	MBF	SR	MBF
30	2 / 30	-106.378	28 / 30	-106.831
50	0 / 30	-194.405	12 / 30	-197.853
70	0 / 30	-281.598	10 / 30	-291.443
79	0 / 30	-324.128	0 / 30	-333.181

Table 4: Impact of the discrete local improvement step in the optimization results obtained by DACCO in selected Morse instances.

are no noteworthy differences in the outcomes of the different heuristic neighborhoods (Current vs. Full). As for the range value, experiments done with $R = 3$ and $R = 4$ tend to obtain better results, suggesting that it is advantageous to define a neighborhood that is not too narrow. Overall, these tests show that DACCO is robust to small variations in the definition of the heuristic neighborhood.

Table 3 displays the optimization results obtained in the selected instances by two DACCO configurations: the standard algorithm with pheromone diffusion and a variant without this mechanism. An inspection immediately reveals that both variants obtained comparable results, suggesting that, with the framework proposed in this paper, it is not mandatory to adopt a diffusion model to smooth the transition between the discrete and continuous spaces. However, it is important to emphasize that this result was obtained with a specific experimental condition: Current Moore neighborhood with $R = 3$ and cell size $w = 0.6$. In future research we will verify if the similarity between results is maintained for other settings.

Table 4 shows the results obtained by DACCO with and without the discrete local improvement step. The number of evaluations is kept fixed in both configurations, so when DACCO is running alone it performs a higher number of iterations. A brief perusal of the table reveals the relevance of discrete local improvement. The version of DACCO that does not incorporate this component fails to discover the putative global optimum in nearly all runs of every selected instance. Also, the MBF values are clearly worse than those achieved by the full DACCO framework. These results show that DACCO clearly benefits from the addition of a discrete greedy perturbation of the solutions built by the ants. This performance improvement is in agreement with existing literature, as there are many reports describing the advantage of incorporating a local improvement step in the processing of an ACO algorithm [7].

5. CONCLUSIONS

We presented DACCO, a discrete ant colony algorithm for cluster geometry optimization. In this framework, the continuous 3D space where the cluster must be located is discretized and ants build a solution by iteratively traversing a 3D grid and placing atoms at selected cells. DACCO includes functions to map clusters between the discrete and continuous spaces and incorporates a discrete greedy local improvement step to further enhance solutions created by the ACO algorithm.

Results obtained with short-ranged Morse instances show that DACCO is competitive with state-of-the-art methods for cluster geometry optimization. It clearly outperforms a PSO approach recently proposed and its performance is comparable to the most effective hybrid EA for this problem. This outcome confirms that the application of discrete ACO variants to (discretized) hard continuous problems is a viable option and it allows the development of successful optimization methods.

There are several possible directions to follow in what concerns future work. On the one hand, our research efforts will be directed towards modifications that can further enhance the robustness and scalability of DACCO framework. This might allow its application to molecular aggregates (e.g, H_2O clusters), a particularly hard class of cluster geometry optimization problems. Also, we aim to investigate the generalization ability of DACCO, by applying it to other continuous optimization problems.

6. ACKNOWLEDGMENTS

This work was supported by Fundação para a Ciência e Tecnologia (FCT), Portugal, under project PTDC/QUI/69422/2006, which is financed by Programa Operacional Factores de Competitividade (COMPETE) of QREN and FEDER programs. The authors are grateful to the Laboratory for Advanced Computing of the University of Coimbra for the provision of supercomputer time on Milipeia (Project daion_10).

7. REFERENCES

[1] G. Bilchev and I. Parmee. The ant colony metaphor for searching continuous design spaces. In T. Fogarty, editor, *Evolutionary Computing*, Lecture Notes in Computer Science 993, pages 25–39. Springer, 1995.

[2] C. Blum and M. Dorigo. The hyper-cube framework for ant colony optimization. *IEEE Transactions on Systems, Man, and Cybernetics, Part B: Cybernetics*, 34(2):1161–1172, 2004.

[3] P. Braier, R. Berry, and W. D. How the range of pair interactions govern features of multidimensional potentials. *Journal of Chemical Physics*, 93:8745–8756, 1990.

[4] L. Cheng and J. Yang. Global minimum structures of morse clusters as a function of the range of the potential: $81 \leq n \leq 160$. *Journal of Physical Chemistry A*, 111:5287–5293, 2007.

[5] M. Dorigo. *Optimization, Learning and Natural Algorithms*. PhD thesis, Politecnico di Milano, Italy, 1992.

[6] M. Dorigo and L. Gambardella. Ant colony system: a cooperative learning approach to the traveling salesman problem. *IEEE Transactions on Evolutionary Computation*, 1(1):53–66, 1997.

[7] M. Dorigo and T. Stützle. *Ant Colony Optimization*. Bradford Company, 2004.

[8] J. P. K. Doye, R. H. Leary, M. Locatelli, and F. Schoen. Global optimization of morse clusters by potential energy transformations. *Informs Journal on Computing*, 16(4):371–379, 2004.

[9] J. P. K. Doye and D. J. Wales. Structural consequences of the range of the interatomic potential: a menagerie of clusters. *Journal of Chemical Society, Faraday Transactions*, 93:4233–4243, 1997.

[10] A. Grosso, M. Locatelli, and F. Schoen. A population-based approach for hard global optimization problems based on dissimilarity measures. *Mathematical Programming*, 110:373–404, 2007.

[11] R. L. Johnston. Evolving better nanoparticles: Genetic algorithms for optimising cluster geometries. *Dalton Transactions*, pages 4193–4207, 2003.

[12] O. Korb, T. Stützle, and T. Exner. An ant colony optimization approach to flexible protein-ligand docking. *Swarm Intelligence*, 1:115–134, 2007.

[13] T. Liao, M. Oca, D. Aydin, T. Stützle, and M. Dorigo. An incremental ant colony algorithm with local search for continuous optimization. In *Proceedings of the Genetic and Evolutionary Computation Conference (GECCO-2011)*, pages 125–132. ACM, 2011.

[14] C. D. Liu and J. Nocedal. On the limited memory bfgs method for large scale optimization. *Mathematical Programming*, 45:503–528, 1989.

[15] N. Lourenco and F. Pereira. PSO-CGO: A Particle Swarm Algorithm for Cluster Geometry Optimization. *International Journal of Natural Computing Research*, 2(1):1–20, 2011.

[16] P. M. Morse. Diatomic molecules according to the wave mechanics. ii. vibrational levels. *Physical Review*, 34(1):57–64, 1929.

[17] F. Pereira and J. Marques. A study on diversity for cluster geometry optimization. *Evolutionary Intelligence*, 2:121–140, 2009.

[18] K. Socha and M. Dorigo. Ant colony optimization for continuous domains. *European Journal of Operational Research*, 185(3):1155 – 1173, 2008.

[19] T. Stützle and H. H. Hoos. $\mathcal{MAX} - \mathcal{MIN}$ Ant system. *Future Generation Computer Systems*, 16(8):889 – 914, 2000.

[20] E. Taillard, P. Waelti, and J. Zuber. Few Statistical Tests for Proportions Comparison. *European Journal of Operational Research*, 185:1336–1350, 2008.

[21] S. Tsutsui. An enhanced aggregation pheromone system for real-parameter optimization in the aco metaphor. In *Ant Colony Optimization and Swarm Intelligence*, Lecture Notes in Computer Science 4150, pages 60–71. Springer, 2006.

[22] L. Wille and J. Vennik. Computational complexity of the ground-state determination of atomic clusters. *Journal of Physics A: Mathematical and General*, 18:419–422, 1985.

[23] A. Zaslavski and J. P. K. Doye. Physical perspectives on the global optimization of atomic clusters. In P. Pardalos and J. D. Pinter, editors, *Global Optimization*, volume 85 of *Nonconvex Optimization and Its Applications*, pages 103–139. Springer US, 2006.

A Study of Different Quality Evaluation Functions in the *c*Ant-Miner$_{\text{PB}}$ Classification Algorithm

Matthew Medland
School of Computing
University of Kent, Canterbury
Kent, CT2 7NF
mm443@kent.ac.uk

Fernando E. B. Otero
School of Computing
University of Kent, Canterbury
Kent, CT2 7NF
F.E.B.Otero@kent.ac.uk

ABSTRACT

Ant colony optimization (ACO) algorithms for classification in general employ a sequential covering strategy to create a list of classification rules. A key component in this strategy is the selection of the rule quality function, since the algorithm aims at creating one rule at a time using an ACO-based procedure to search the best rule. Recently, an improved strategy has been proposed in the *c*Ant-Miner$_{\text{PB}}$ algorithm, where an ACO-based procedure is used to create a complete list of rules instead of individual rules. In the *c*Ant-Miner$_{\text{PB}}$ algorithm, the rule quality function has a smaller role and the search is guided by the quality of a list of rules. This paper sets out to determine the effect of different rule and list quality functions in terms of both predictive accuracy and size of the discovered model in *c*Ant-Miner$_{\text{PB}}$. The comparative analysis is performed using 12 data sets from the UCI Machine Learning repository and shows that the effect of the rule quality functions in *c*Ant-Miner$_{\text{PB}}$ is different from the results previously presented in the literature.

Categories and Subject Descriptors

I.2.8 [**Artificial Intelligence**]: Problem Solving, Control Methods, and Search—*Heuristic methods*

General Terms

Algorithms

Keywords

ant colony optimization, classification, sequential covering, rule quality functions, list quality functions

1. INTRODUCTION

Data mining is, in essence, the automated search for useful and usable patterns in data. These patterns are used by scientists, marketing staff, CEOs, bankers and anyone with an interest in what their data holds. There are three main approaches to finding these patterns, and subsequently three separate data mining tasks. These are *classification*, *association rule learning* and *clustering* [13]. Of these tasks, classification is the most studied.

Classification aims to produce a model which can be used to group objects (physical or metaphorical) and assign a class value (group name). Therefore, classification problems can be viewed as optimisation problems, where the goal is to find the best model that represents the predictive relationships in the data. There are many different model representations, such as 'black-box' (not easily comprehensible) models produced by support vector machines (SVM) and artificial neural networks, and 'white-box' (comprehensible) decision tree and classification rule models.

The approach on which this paper focuses is stochastic based upon Ant Colony Optimization (ACO), a meta-heuristic inspired by the foraging behaviour of ants [2]. The first application of ACO for the classification task in data mining was reported by Parpinelli et al. [11], where an ACO algorithm—called Ant-Miner—is proposed for the discovery of classification rules. Ant-Miner aims at extracting a list of *IF-THEN* classification rules of the form *IF* antecedent *THEN* consequent from a data set—the antecedent is composed by predictor attribute-value conditions, while the consequent corresponds to the class value to be predicted.

Several extensions of Ant-Miner have been proposed in the literature, as reviewed in [8]. The majority of these extensions maintain the overall structure of the algorithm—i.e., the algorithm employs an ACO-based procedure to create individual rules in order to produce a complete classification model (list of rules). This strategy to obtain a list of classification rules is referred to as sequential covering (or separate-and-conquer), where each rule is discovered individually. Recently, an improved strategy has been proposed in the *c*Ant-Miner$_{\text{PB}}$ algorithm [10], where an ACO-based procedure is used to create a complete list of rules instead of individual rules, and it has been shown to outperform state-of-the-art rule induction algorithms. One of the main differences between the Ant-Miner and *c*Ant-Miner$_{\text{PB}}$ algorithms is that in Ant-Miner the search is performed (and optimised) to find the best individual rules at each step of the sequential covering, whereas in *c*Ant-Miner$_{\text{PB}}$ the search is performed (and optimised) to find the best list of rules. While in Ant-Miner the search is guided by the quality of an individual rule, in *c*Ant-Miner$_{\text{PB}}$ the search is guided by the quality of a candidate list of rules.

The importance of the rule quality function in sequential covering algorithms has been highlighted in [4, 6], and in the

GECCO'12, July 7–11, 2012, Philadelphia, Pennsylvania, USA.

context of ACO classification algorithm in [12]. In this paper we present a study of the effects of rule quality functions, as well as list quality functions, in the cAnt-Miner$_{PB}$ algorithm. Different than Ant-Miner and its extensions, cAnt-Miner$_{PB}$ employs two quality functions in its search procedure: a rule quality function, which is used to decide whether or not to prune an individual rule; and a list quality function, which guides the search (i.e., the pheromone update is based on the quality of a candidate list of rules). We evaluate different combinations of rule quality and list quality functions in terms of both predictive accuracy and size of the classification model, and compare the results against the default combination used in cAnt-Miner$_{PB}$.

The remainder of this paper is organised as follows. In Section 2 we discuss related works, focusing on the Ant-Miner family of algorithms and rule learning heuristics. In Section 3 we revisit the evaluation functions in greater depth, and define the functions used in our study. In Section 4 we describe both the steps for tuning our heuristics (Subsection 4.1) and our final results (Subsection 4.2). Section 5 then concludes this paper by assessing and aiming to explain our results.

2. BACKGROUND

Sequential covering, also called separate-and-conquer, is a classification rule learning approach with two main discrete steps [6]. In essence, the approach finds a rule with a high quality on the dataset (conquer), and then removes the examples which are covered by the rule (separate). This repeats until there are either no or few remaining training examples.

The effectiveness of a sequential covering algorithm stems from the quality of the rules that are produced [4, 6]. Some rules may only cover correctly classified examples (high consistency) but might only cover a small sample (low coverage). Conversely, a rule may cover a large portion of the dataset (high coverage) but mis-classify most of them (low consistency). Both of these results are undesirable, and rule quality functions tend to trade one off against the other. It is for this reason that the rule quality function needs to be carefully chosen to provide an optimal trade-off, and result in a list of rules with high predictive accuracy.

Ant-Miner [11] is a sequential covering rule learning metaheuristic based upon the foraging behaviour of a colony of ants. Ants, when searching for routes to food sources, drop pheromones. The ants tend to move towards areas with a higher concentration of pheromone, and as a result of the shortest route being travelled more often, it will have more pheromone and will therefore be reinforced. This behaviour has been observed, translated into optimisation algorithms and is referred to as Ant Colony Optimization (ACO) [2].

The Ant-Miner algorithm works as follows. First, a construction graph is created where each node is a value for a given variable, with every variable-value pair from the dataset represented. Each ant then moves from a start node (with an empty rule) and stochastically chooses a vertex with a probability based upon the pheromone value and a heuristic value. The visited vertex is a rule term as a variable-value pair. The ant will continue to add new terms until either all variables have been covered, or if by adding another term, it would decrease the number of covered examples bellow a predefined threshold. After a rule has been created, a pruning procedure removes irrelevant terms from the newly created rule. Once every ant in the colony (of predetermined size) has traversed the graph, the best rule (based on a rule quality function) is selected and the pheromone levels are adjusted. The pheromone on the terms included in the best rule increase and the pheromone on the others (unused terms) decrease. After a rule has been created, all of the examples covered by the rule are removed from the dataset and the next rule is created. The algorithm finishes once the training set has less than a predefined number of training examples remaining. Most of the proposed extensions of Ant-Miner follow this same strategy to create a list of rules [8].

Require: training examples
Ensure: best discovered list of rules

```
InitialisePheromones();
list_gb ← ∅;
m ← 0;
while m < maximum iterations and not stagnation do
   list_ib ← ∅;
   for n ← 1 to colony_size do
      examples ← all training examples;
      list_n ← ∅;
      while |examples| > maximum uncovered do
         ComputeHeuristicInformation(examples);
         rule ← CreateRule(examples);
         Prune(rule);
         examples ← examples − Covered(rule, examples);
         list_n ← list_n + rule;
      end while
      if Quality(list_n) > Quality(list_ib) then
         list_ib ← list_n;
      end if
   end for
   UpdatePheromones(list_ib);
   if Quality(list_ib) > Quality(list_gb) then
      list_gb ← list_ib;
   end if
   m ← m + 1;
end while
return list_gb;
```

Figure 1: High-level pseudocode of the cAnt-Miner$_{PB}$ algorithm [10].

cAnt-Miner$_{PB}$ [10] is an ACO classification algorithm that employs a different search strategy than Ant-Miner. The main difference in the search strategy of cAnt-Miner$_{PB}$ is that it aims to create the best list of rules rather than creating a list of best rules. This change is slight, but has a profound effect on the algorithm. The ants, rather than creating one rule each, create an entire model (list of rules) each. The best model (based on a list quality function) created in an iteration is used to update the pheromone values, and it is compared to the previous best model. If the new model is better, it survives and may end up being the final model.

The high-level pseudocode of the cAnt-Miner$_{PB}$ algorithm is presented in Figure 1 and works as follows. At each iteration, an ant in the colony starts with an empty list of rules and the full training set. The ant then creates a rule, prunes the rule, and removes all of the covered examples from the training set. It is important to note that the only stage at which the rule quality function is used is in the pruning step. The ant then repeats these steps until the number of examples remaining are below a given threshold. The list of rules created by the ant is then compared to the current iteration's best list of rules based on the list quality function, and if it is better than the current best, it replaces the previous best. Once the colony's best list of rules has been found, the pheromones of the construction graph are updated. This entire process repeats until either the maximum number of iterations have been reached or until the colony converges. The best list of rules found is returned at the end.

This highlights the main differences between Ant-Miner and cAnt-Miner$_{\text{PB}}$. The Ant-Miner algorithm is guided by the quality of the individual rule. The best rule found by the colony is always used, without regard for how this will affect the quality of the list of rules being created. The cAnt-Miner$_{\text{PB}}$, on the other hand, has the goal of producing the best list of rules, with less regard to how rules perform individually. The entire list of rules is created at once, and the best is chosen to guide the search.

In evaluating the rules in either algorithm, the quality of each individual rule is calculated, and in Ant-Miner the function which calculates this quality may have a large effect on the quality of the model as a whole. It has been suggested that traditional non-parametric rule quality functions, such as Sensitivity × Specificity, accuracy or precision, implement a fixed trade off [6]. That is, they either prefer consistency or coverage, with no means of modifying this bias. Parametric functions, such as the the m-estimate or Klösgen, allow the user to modify this trade off depending on their application.

Due to the importance of rule quality functions in sequential covering classification algorithms, there is significant interest in this field and a number of papers have been published. One is a mainly theoretical study [6], which looks at how rule quality functions affect a relatively simple sequential search algorithm. In this study, it was shown that the parametrized functions performed well. The m-estimate and Klösgen functions were amongst the best performing parametric functions. A further study [12] focuses on how the rule quality function can affect ACO-based classification algorithms, which follow the same strategy as Ant-Miner. The results presented in [12] show that sensitivity × specificity, used in Ant-Miner and also in cAnt-Miner$_{\text{PB}}$, is not amongst the best performing rule quality functions that have been evaluated. These studies, however, are focused on the effect of the rule quality function in traditional sequential covering algorithms. As cAnt-Miner$_{\text{PB}}$ employs a different strategy, where the rule quality function has a smaller role and the search is guided by the quality of a list of rules, it is interesting to evaluate the effects of different rule quality functions, as well as different list quality functions.

3. EVALUATION FUNCTIONS

The rule evaluation function is the keystone of sequential covering algorithms. In Ant-Miner (and its variations), every time an ant creates a rule, its quality is calculated and the rule is only considered if it has the best quality in that iteration. In cAnt-Miner$_{\text{PB}}$, however, the rule quality function has a less prominent role. It is only used during the pruning stage, as the search is guided by the quality of a list of rules. It is with these facts in mind that we are testing different rule quality functions to judge how much effect each has on cAnt-Miner$_{\text{PB}}$, and also testing different list quality functions.

3.1 Rule Quality Functions

This section presents the rule quality functions used in our study. A series of shorthands are being used in the equations below to condense the formulae and are defined as follows.

TP The number of examples covered by the rule that belong to the class predicted by the rule (true positives).

FP The number of examples covered by the rule that do not belong to the class predicted by the rule (false positives).

TN The number of examples not covered by the rule that do not belong to the class predicted by the rule (true negatives).

FN The number of examples not covered by the rule that belong to the class predicted by the rule (false negatives).

S The total number of examples (TP + FP + TN + FN).

Sensitivity × Specificity.

Sensitivity × Specificity is used in the original Ant-Miner and in the cAnt-Miner$_{\text{PB}}$. Sensitivity measures the fraction of true positives covered by the rule and the specificity measures the fraction of examples of different classes which were not covered [7]. The Sensitivity × Specificity is given by:

$$\underbrace{\frac{TP}{TP+FN}}_{\text{Sensitivity}} \cdot \underbrace{\frac{TN}{TN+FP}}_{\text{Specificity}} \quad (1)$$

Confidence + Coverage.

The Confidence + Coverage was used in AntMiner+ algorithm [9]. The confidence measures the fraction of examples covered by the rule correctly, and the coverage measures the importance of the rule by calculating the fraction of correctly covered examples against all remaining examples. The Confidence + Coverage is given by:

$$\underbrace{\frac{TP}{TP+FP}}_{\text{Confidence}} + \underbrace{\frac{TP}{S}}_{\text{Coverage}} \quad (2)$$

Jaccard Coefficient.

The Jaccard coefficient calculates the similarity between sample sets. In our case, the Jaccard coefficient is the fraction of correctly covered examples divided by the number of all but the examples not covered by the rule that do not belong to the class predicted by the rule. This rule quality function has been used in the study presented by Salama and Abdelbar [12], where it was one of the best performing functions. The Jaccard coefficient is given by:

$$\frac{TP}{TP+FP+FN} \quad (3)$$

Klösgen.

The Klösgen function, when $\omega = 0$, acts as the precision gain (the precision with respect to $\frac{(TP+FN)}{S}$). As ω increases the Klösgen acts in a manner similar to recall. The transition from one to the other is not linear, and as ω increases further it starts acting as coverage. An ω value of 0.4323 was found to be optimum by Janssen and Fürnkranz [6]. We have tested the neighbour values $\{0.3, 0.35, 0.4, 0.45, 0.5\}$ in a tuning step, as it will be discussed in Section 4. The Klösgen is given by:

$$\left(\frac{TP+FP}{S}\right)^{\omega} \cdot \left(\frac{TP}{TP+FP} - \frac{TP+FN}{S}\right) \quad (4)$$

m-estimate.

The m-estimate is a parametric function with the parameter m. The m value found to be the best by Janssen and Fürnkranz was 22.466, and this resulted in the best quality function overall in their study. We have tested the neighbour values $\{21, 22, 23, 24, 25\}$ in a tuning step, as it will be discussed in Section 4. The m-estimate is given by:

$$\frac{TP + m \cdot \frac{TP}{S}}{TP+FP+m} \quad (5)$$

3.2 List Quality Functions

This section presents the list quality functions used in our study. While we focus on lists of rules in this paper, the list quality functions presented in this section are in fact classification model evaluation functions.

Predictive Accuracy.

This is the standard list quality function used by cAnt-Miner$_{PB}$. It corresponds to the number of correct classification divided by the total number of examples. The accuracy is given by:

$$\frac{number\ of\ correct\ classification}{total\ number\ of\ examples} \quad (6)$$

Micro-Average F-Measure.

The micro-average F-Measure is a commonly used evaluation function in information retrieval and text classification systems. It involves the global precision (Pr_{mic}) and recall (Re_{mic}) values, given by:

$$Pr_{mic} = \frac{\sum_{i=0}^{|C|} TP_i}{\sum_{i=0}^{|C|} TP_i + \sum_{i=0}^{|C|} FP_i} \quad (7)$$

$$Re_{mic} = \frac{\sum_{i=0}^{|C|} TP_i}{\sum_{i=0}^{|C|} TP_i + \sum_{i=0}^{|C|} FN_i} \quad (8)$$

where $|C|$ corresponds to the total number of classes, TP_i, FP_i and FN_i correspond to the number of true positive (the number of examples of class i predicted as being in class i), false positive (the number of examples predicted as being in class i which are not of class i) and false negative (the number of examples of class i not predicted as being of class i) of the i-th class, respectively. Given the Pr_{mic} and Re_{mic}, the micro-average F-Measure is given by:

$$\frac{(1+\beta^2) \cdot Pr_{mic} \cdot Re_{mic}}{(\beta^2 \cdot Pr_{mic}) + Re_{mic}} \quad (9)$$

where β controls the importance of precision and recall: β values lower than 1 puts more emphasis on precision than recall; β values greater than 1 puts more emphasis on recall than precision; and a β equal to 1 puts the same emphasis on both precision and recall.

Macro-Average F-Measure.

The macro-average F-Measure is also a commonly used evaluation function in information retrieval and text classification systems. The main difference between the micro-average and macro-average is that in the former, global precision and recall values are used in the calculation of the F-Measure, while in the latter, individual precision and recall values for each class are used in the calculation. The precision (Pr_i) and recall (Re_i) values for the i-th class is given by:

$$Pr_i = \frac{TP_i}{TP_i + FP_i} \quad (10)$$

$$Re_i = \frac{TP_i}{TP_i + FN_i} \quad (11)$$

The macro-average F-Measure is given by:

$$\sum_{i=0}^{|C|} \left(\frac{1}{|C|} \cdot \frac{(1+\beta^2) \cdot Pr_i \cdot Re_i}{(\beta^2 \cdot Pr_i) + Re_i}\right) \quad (12)$$

Weighted Macro-Average F-Measure.

The macro-average F-Measure presented in Equation (12) gives an equal importance for every class. In order to take the number of examples of each class in the quality function, we have used a weighted macro-average F-Measure (where the weight corresponds to the fraction of examples belonging to the class) given by:

$$\sum_{i=0}^{|C|} \left(\frac{TP_i + FN_i}{|D|} \cdot \frac{(1+\beta^2) \cdot Pr_i \cdot Re_i}{(\beta^2 \cdot Pr_i) + Re_i}\right) \quad (13)$$

where $|D|$ corresponds to the total number of examples.

Inverse Weighted Macro-Average F-Measure.

Using the same idea of having different weights for classes, the inverse weighted macro-average puts more emphasis on classes with a smaller number of examples (the smaller the number of examples, the more important the class) and it is given by:

$$\sum_{i=0}^{|C|} \left(\left[1 - \frac{TP_i + FN_i}{|D|}\right] \cdot \frac{(1+\beta^2) \cdot Pr_i \cdot Re_i}{(\beta^2 \cdot Pr_i) + Re_i}\right) \quad (14)$$

4. COMPUTATIONAL RESULTS

In order to evaluate the different rule and list quality functions, we first determined optimal parameter values for the parametric functions in a tuning step, described in Subsection 4.1. These parameter values were then used in our final experiments, described in Subsection 4.2.

4.1 Experimental Setup

We split the process of finding the optimal combinations of rule and list quality functions into three distinct steps. Throughout these three experiments we used the automobile, blood transfusion, ecoli, heart-c, heart-h, hepatitis, horse-colic, voting records and zoo datasets from the UCI Machine Learning repository [3]. These data sets are only used for parameter tuning and comprise our training data sets.

1. **Rule Quality Functions:** With the aim of finding the optimal parameter values for the parametric rule quality functions—ω parameter for Klösgen (Equation 4) and m parameter for m-estimate (Equation 5), we ran the *c*Ant-Miner$_{PB}$ algorithm on our training data sets for each different rule evaluation function and parameter value (described in Section 3.1), repeating each experiment 10 times, each time using 10-fold cross validation. The list quality function was fixed to predictive accuracy, the default list quality function used in *c*Ant-Miner$_{PB}$.

2. **List Quality Functions:** Using a similar setup of the previous step, we have determined optimal values for the β parameter used in the list quality functions based on the F-Measure—micro-average F-Measure (Equation 9), macro-average F-Measure (Equation 12), weighted macro-average F-Measure (Equation 13) and inverse weighted macro-average F-Measure (Equation 14). In this step, the rule quality function was fixed to the Sensitivity × Specificity, the default rule quality function used in *c*Ant-Miner$_{PB}$.

3. **Determining the best combination of rule and list quality functions:** Finally, we then found the best combination of rule and list quality functions by testing each of the 5 different rule quality functions (using the optimised parameters found in the first step) with each of the 4 different list quality functions (using the optimised parameters found in the second step).

As a result of the experiments outlined above we have determined a group of optimal rule and list quality functions pairings, presented in Table 1. In that table, a row corresponds to a pair of rule and list quality functions. Pairing 1 is the default (baseline) used in *c*Ant-Miner$_{PB}$. Pairing 2 corresponds to the Klösgen function (with ω equal to 0.5) paired with the predictive accuracy list quality function. Pairing 3 corresponds to the m-estimate function (with m equal to 21) paired with the predictive accuracy list quality function. Pairings 3 and 4 are using the Jaccard and Confidence + Coverage functions, respectively, and are both paired with the weighted macro F-Measure list quality function (with β equal to 0.5).

4.2 Evaluating the Optimal Combinations

Once the optimal parameters and pairing (Table 1) had been determined, we aimed to find which combination is the most effective. To do this we used a separate set of data sets from the UCI Machine Learning repository [3]. The summary of the data sets used is presented in Table 2. During this experiment, we used 10-fold cross-validation (each fold having the same class distribution, i.e., stratified folds), and the default parameters of *c*Ant-Miner$_{PB}$ [10]: colony size of 5, 500 iterations and evaporation factor 0.90.[1] The only parameter that has been changed is the minimum number of examples, which was set to 2 (instead of 10) to test if any of the rule quality functions are prone to overfitting. Given the stochastic nature of *c*Ant-Miner$_{PB}$, we ran the algorithm 10 times for each fold of the cross-validation.

Table 1: Optimal combinations of rule and list quality functions.

Pair	Rule Function	List Function
1	Sensitivity × Specificity	Accuracy
2	Klösgen ($\omega = 0.5$)	Accuracy
3	m-estimate ($m = 21$)	Accuracy
4	Jaccard	Weighted Macro F-Measure ($\beta = 0.5$)
5	Confidence + Coverage	Weighted Macro F-Measure ($\beta = 0.5$)

Table 2: Summary of the data sets used in the experiments.

data set	attributes		classes	size
	nominal	continuous		
balance-scale	4	0	3	625
breast-l	9	0	2	286
breast-tissue	0	9	6	106
breast-w	0	30	2	569
credit-a	8	6	2	690
dermatology	33	1	6	366
glass	0	9	7	214
ionosphere	0	34	2	351
iris	0	4	3	150
liver-disorders	0	6	2	345
parkinsons	0	22	2	195
wine	0	13	3	178

Table 3 presents the results for each of the function pairings concerning the predictive accuracy and Table 4 presents the results concerning the size of the discovered list of rules (measured as the total number of rule conditions). Each value in those tables represents the average value calculated over the cross-validation procedure. Table 5 shows the results of the Friedman statistical test [1, 5] for predictive accuracy and size of the discovered list of rules. The information presented in Table 5 corresponds to the average rank (first column), where the lower the rank the better the pairing's performance, the p-value of the statistical test (second column), and Holm's post-hoc critical value (third column).

[1]The binaries and source-code of the *c*Ant-Miner$_{PB}$ algorithm implementation used in this paper can be found at http://sourceforge.net/projects/myra. The datasets partitions can be found at http://cs.kent.ac.uk/~febo.

Table 3: Average predictive accuracy (*average* [*standard error*]) in %, measured by 10-fold cross-validation. The value of the most accurate configuration for a given data set is shown in bold.

data set	Sen × Spe	Klösgen	m-estimate	Jaccard	Conf + Cov
balance-scale	76.99 [0.19]	78.54 [0.32]	**80.22 [0.37]**	77.05 [0.30]	73.96 [0.23]
breast-l	**69.77 [0.60]**	62.51 [0.66]	64.26 [0.62]	69.04 [0.57]	63.00 [0.86]
breast-tissue	**66.74 [0.91]**	62.76 [0.81]	64.30 [0.75]	63.65 [0.72]	62.97 [1.24]
breast-w	93.44 [0.28]	93.14 [0.28]	93.49 [0.25]	**93.72 [0.48]**	93.60 [0.32]
credit-a	84.49 [0.18]	83.10 [0.30]	82.97 [0.38]	**85.22 [0.23]**	79.16 [0.27]
dermatology	92.81 [0.44]	92.94 [0.19]	93.23 [0.35]	**93.38 [0.42]**	91.73 [0.48]
glass	**70.66 [0.70]**	69.16 [0.60]	68.78 [0.56]	69.74 [0.64]	67.11 [0.68]
ionosphere	**90.49 [0.21]**	88.45 [0.39]	89.04 [0.43]	90.09 [0.55]	88.70 [0.40]
iris	94.13 [0.29]	93.00 [0.40]	93.27 [0.48]	**94.33 [0.11]**	93.40 [0.32]
liver-disorders	**65.82 [0.38]**	64.91 [0.45]	63.57 [0.77]	63.25 [0.28]	64.50 [0.57]
parkinsons	**85.49 [0.64]**	83.51 [0.28]	83.07 [0.77]	84.43 [0.88]	84.53 [0.78]
wine	91.63 [0.52]	90.63 [0.79]	92.14 [0.56]	**92.59 [0.44]**	90.90 [0.56]

Table 4: Average number of terms (rule conditions) in the discovered list (*average* [*standard error*]) measured by 10-fold cross-validation. The value of the configuration with the lowest average for a given data set is shown in bold.

data set	Sen × Spe	Klösgen	m-estimate	Jaccard	Conf + Cov
balance-scale	**20.26 [0.30]**	105.21 [1.16]	77.42 [1.50]	20.56 [0.46]	332.07 [6.09]
breast-l	**62.96 [1.90]**	229.71 [2.51]	199.92 [2.53]	70.03 [1.55]	258.77 [1.52]
breast-tissue	**15.93 [0.31]**	26.88 [0.33]	21.21 [0.31]	17.72 [0.18]	32.80 [0.22]
breast-w	13.87 [0.20]	22.90 [0.46]	25.29 [0.42]	**12.11 [0.20]**	18.47 [0.33]
credit-a	**29.04 [0.51]**	111.82 [1.32]	104.19 [1.96]	29.14 [0.68]	228.96 [2.36]
dermatology	**52.13 [0.74]**	58.14 [0.98]	54.62 [0.99]	53.40 [0.92]	69.32 [1.70]
glass	**28.41 [0.23]**	58.86 [0.51]	48.03 [0.41]	29.70 [0.34]	75.68 [1.05]
ionosphere	20.06 [0.24]	30.09 [0.35]	29.15 [0.44]	**14.31 [0.18]**	24.30 [0.75]
iris	8.78 [0.20]	12.70 [0.22]	12.54 [0.31]	**7.32 [0.15]**	11.11 [0.26]
liver-disorders	24.31 [0.37]	93.12 [1.34]	79.13 [0.54]	**21.30 [0.26]**	152.21 [1.24]
parkinsons	12.05 [0.16]	22.29 [0.48]	21.25 [0.36]	**11.42 [0.28]**	18.50 [0.67]
wine	9.68 [0.31]	13.43 [0.37]	12.81 [0.42]	**9.25 [0.15]**	13.40 [0.43]

A row is shown in bold when there is a statistically significant difference between the average rank of a pairing and the control pairing (the pairing with the best average rank)—when the p-value is lower than the critical value—and shows that the control pairing is significantly better than the pairing in that row.

The Sensitivity × Specificity (Pair 1) and Jaccard (Pair 4) were the most successful, each achieving an average rank of 2.08 with regards to predictive accuracy. They were also the highest performing pairings with regards to the size of the list of rules, with Jaccard achieving an average rank of 1.49 and Sensitivity × Specificity achieving a rank of 1.5. Our results show that the parametric functions did not perform well in the cAnt-Miner$_{\text{PB}}$ algorithm. The m-estimate function (Pair 3) achieved the third ranking, while the Klösgen (Pair 2) achieved the lowest ranking and it was statistically significantly worse than Sensitivity × Specificity, in terms of both predictive accuracy and model size. This is different than the results presented by Janssen and Fürnkranz [6], where these parametric functions were amongst the best performing ones in a traditional sequential covering algorithm. Considering the results presented by Salama and Abdelbar [12], our results agree in respect to the use of Jaccard function, given that Jaccard is amongst the best performing ones. However, in Salama and Abdelbar study, Sensitivity × Specificity was amongst the worse performing ones, which is not the case in the cAnt-Miner$_{\text{PB}}$ algorithm.

While Klösgen (Pair 2) and Confidence + Coverage (Pair 5) were statistically significantly worse than Sensitivity × Specificity in terms of both predictive accuracy and model size, they achieved the highest predictive accuracy during training overall. Therefore, their poor performance in the test set is likely due to overfitting—the case where the list of rules created is too tailored to the training set and does not generalise well, i.e., it has a lower predictive accuracy in unseen test cases.

Table 5: Statistical test results according to the non-parametric Friedman test with the Holm's post-hoc test for $\alpha = 0.05$.

configuration	average rank	p	*Holm*
(i) Accuracy			
Sen × Spe (control)	2.08	–	–
Jaccard	2.08	0.999	0.0500
m-estimate	3.08	0.121	0.0250
Con + Cov	**3.83**	**0.007**	**0.0167**
Klösgen	**3.92**	**0.004**	**0.0125**
(ii) Model Size			
Jaccard (control)	1.49	–	–
Sen × Spe	1.50	0.999	0.0500
m-estimate	**3.42**	**0.003**	**0.0250**
Con + Cov	**4.25**	**2.04E-5**	**0.0167**
Klösgen	**4.33**	**1.14E-5**	**0.0125**

Although our results did not improve the predictive accuracy or the size of the discovered list of rules, they show that the rule quality functions which perform well in traditional sequential covering algorithms do not have the same performance in *c*Ant-Miner$_{PB}$. This suggests that other aspects of the algorithm (e.g., solution construction, pruning procedure, pheromone update) are more interesting to investigate in order to improve the overall performance of *c*Ant-Miner$_{PB}$.

5. CONCLUSION

Our findings show that, in contrast to the results found by Salama and Abdelbar [12], the Sensitivity × Specificity rule quality function is a good choice for *c*Ant-Miner$_{PB}$, and that it performs well alongside the accuracy list quality function. This is a useful discovery as it means that the current default selection for *c*Ant-Miner$_{PB}$ is adequate. In agreement with Salama and Abdelbar, we have also shown that the Jaccard coefficient performs well and is comparable to the rule quality function currently in use. The use of parametric rule quality functions, used in a similar study by Janssen and Fürnkranz [6], did not improve the predictive accuracy of the algorithm and in some cases were statistically significantly worse. The difference in results is likely to be an effect of the new strategy employed by *c*Ant-Miner$_{PB}$ to search for the best list of rules instead of the list of best rules.

In our study the optimal rule quality functions and their parameter values were optimised statically (prior to the run of the algorithm). It will be interesting to see if a dynamic selection technique will provide better results, and this is an interesting future research direction.

6. REFERENCES

[1] J. Demšar. Statistical Comparisons of Classifiers over Multiple Data Sets. *Machine Learning Research*, 7:1–30, 2006.

[2] M. Dorigo and T. Stützle. *Ant Colony Optimization.* The MIT Press, 2004.

[3] A. Frank and A. Asuncion. UCI machine learning repository, 2010.

[4] J. Fürnkranz and P. Flach. ROC 'n' Rule Learning—Towards a Better Understanding of Covering Algorithms. *Machine Learning*, 58:39–77, 2005.

[5] S. García and F. Herrera. An Extension on 'Statistical Comparisons of Classifiers over Multiple Data Sets' for all Pairwise Comparisons. *Machine Learning Research*, 9:2677–2694, 2008.

[6] F. Janssen and J. Fürnkranz. On the quest for optimal rule learning heuristics. *Machine Learning*, 78:343–379, 2010.

[7] H. S. Lopes, M. S. Coutinho, and W. C. Lima. An evolutionary approach to simulate cognitive feedback learning in medical domain. In E. Sanchez, T. Shibata, and L. A. Zadeh, editors, *Genetic Algorithms and Fuzzy Logic Systems*, volume 7, pages 193–207. 1997.

[8] D. Martens, B. Baesens, and T. Fawcett. Editorial survey: swarm intelligence for data mining. *Machine Learning*, 82:1–42, Jan 2011.

[9] D. Martens, M. De Backer, R. Haesen, J. Vanthienen, M. Snoeck, and B. Baesens. Classification with ant colony optimization. *Evolutionary Computation, IEEE Transactions on*, 11(5):651 –665, Oct 2007.

[10] F. Otero, A. Freitas, and C. Johnson. A new sequential covering strategy for inducing classification rules with ant colony algorithms. To appear in IEEE Transactions on Evolutionary Computation, 2012.

[11] R. Parpinelli, H. Lopes, and A. Freitas. Data mining with an ant colony optimization algorithm. *Evolutionary Computation, IEEE Transactions on*, 6(4):321 – 332, Aug 2002.

[12] K. Salama and A. Abdelbar. Exploring different rule quality evaluation functions in aco-based classification algorithms. In *Swarm Intelligence (SIS), 2011 IEEE Symposium on*, pages 1 –8, Apr 2011.

[13] I. H. Witten, E. Frank, and M. A. Hall. *Data Mining: Practical Machine Learning Tools and Techniques*. 3rd edition, 2011.

Optimal Cyclic Replacement Policy in MSS Maintenance via Binomial-PSO

Angel E. Muñoz-Zavala
Universidad Autónoma de Aguascalientes
Av. Universidad 940, Ciudad Universitaria, C.P. 20089
Aguascalientes, AGS, México
aemz@correo.uaa.mx

Evelyn J. Hernández-Ramos
Universidad Autónoma de Aguascalientes
Av. Universidad 940, Ciudad Universitaria, C.P. 20089
Aguascalientes, AGS, México
ejhernan@correo.uaa.mx

ABSTRACT

Several systems can perform their intended functions at more than two different levels, from perfectly working to completely failed. These kind of systems are known as multi-state systems. In many complex and sophisticated systems, reliability and maintainability theory plays a very important role in maintaining such systems. The purpose of MSS maintenance optimization is to extend system lifetime, or at least the mean time to the next failure whose repair may be costly. Furthermore, it is expected that effective maintenance policies can increase system availability and reduce the consequences of unavailability (unaccomplished demand). In this study, we consider cyclic replacement policy in a preventive maintenance planning for a component subject to failure. This paper introduces a new approach based on PSO with constraints handling for MSS maintenance optimization problems. The universal generating function is applied in this work to evaluate MSS reliability. Our approach is tested in a real MSS maintenance problem in full measure in the *state-of-the-art*. The main advantage of the suggested approach is that it can be easily implemented in practice for maintenance of real MSS.

Categories and Subject Descriptors

I.2.8 [**Artificial Intelligence**]: Problem Solving, Control Methods and Search—*Heuristic methods*; G.3 [**Probability and Statistics**]: [Reliability and life testing, Distribution functions]

General Terms

Algorithms, Reliability

Keywords

Combinatorial optimization, Replacement policy, Maintenance, MSS, PSO

1. INTRODUCTION

Real-world systems are becoming more and more complex and sophisticated. Several systems can perform their intended functions at more than two different levels, from perfectly working to completely failed. In such cases, the system failure can lead to decreased ability to perform the goal task, but not necessarily to a complete failure. These kind of systems are known as multi-state systems (MSS)[22].

Considering system attributes, quality has become a mandatory requirement for customer satisfaction and is playing an increasing role in determining the competitiveness of companies. The concept of reliability is relatively new in the engineering disciplines, but it is becoming increasingly important as part of the engineering design process, the establishment of preventive maintenance programs, and others. The common sense perception of reliability is the absence of failures. Therefore, reliability is sometimes referred as quality in the time dimension because is determined by the failures that may or may not occur during the life time of the product.

Reliability plays a very important role for manufacturers and users. A large reliability increases the production costs, affecting the final user. Thereby, the design reliability optimization problems seek to improve reliability at the minimum cost. The redundancy and reliability allocation problem is a classical optimization problem in the area of system reliability. In general, the objective of these problems is to optimize the system design in terms of the number of components and its reliabilities, subject to known constraints on resources as cost, weight, volume, availability, mean time to failure, etc.

An important subset of design optimization problems contains optimization tasks that are difficult to solve with traditional methods because objectives and constraints (in real world problems) may not be analytically treatable, great complexity, high dimensionality, multi-modal, without gradient information, etc. For these reasons, evolutionary algorithms may be an attractive alternative.

Evolutionary algorithms have been widely used to solve reliability optimization problems [18, 28, 29]. Nevertheless, no meta-heuristic is versatile, which could always outperform other meta-heuristics in solving all kinds of problems [33]. The problem becomes more complicated in the presence of a considerable number of linear and nonlinear inequality and equality constraints. The evolutionary algorithms are unconstrained search techniques which lack an explicit mechanism to deal with constrained search spaces. Therefore, introducing new good optimization approaches can be very helpful in some specific areas and benefit practitioners with more options.

The particle swarm optimization (PSO) algorithm, proposed for Kennedy and Eberhart in 1995 [12], has triggered a considerable amount of research regarding the development of mechanisms able to incorporate information about the constraints of a problem into the fitness function.

This paper introduces a new approach based on PSO with constraints handling for MSS maintenance optimization problems. The universal generating function (UGF)[30] is applied in this work to evaluate MSS reliability. The UGF technique allows one to find the entire MSS reliability based on the performance distributions of its components by using algebraic procedures. This technique is fast enough to be implemented in optimization procedures [17].

In the next section, we describe the basic concepts and techniques for MSS Reliability. In Section 3, we state the problem and review related literature. We then explain the Binomial PSO algorithm propoused in this paper to solve MSS maintenance in Section 4. Section 5 presents the experiment results. We conclude in Section 6, offering future research directions.

2. MSS RELIBILITY

In many complex and sophisticated systems, reliability and maintainability theory plays a very important role in maintaining such systems. The reliability of a entity (component, subsystem, system, production line, service, etc.) is the probability that it will perform its required function without failure under given conditions for an intended period of operation. The decision regarding the reliability characteristics of a system is taken during the drawing board stage of system development. The aim is to prevent the occurrence of failures and also to eliminate their effects on the operational capability of systems [14].

The maintainability of a entity can be defined as the probability that it will be restored to a specified condition within a given time period using specified resources. High maintainability performance is obtained when the system is easy to maintain and repair. In general, maintainability is measured by the mean repair time, often called the mean time to repair, which includes the total time for fault finding and the actual time spent carrying out the repair [4].Mathematical maintenance policies, centering preventive maintenance, have been developed mainly in the research area of operations management science, to generate an effective preventive maintenance schedule.

Statistically speaking, the uptimes and downtimes in a MSS are random variables and will have their distributions. Based on these distributions, one can compute mean uptime and mean downtime. Actually mean uptime reflects how good the inherent design or built-in reliability is, and mean downtime reflects how good the maintainability is. If the steady state availability is to be kept high, one should try to design for a high value of mean uptime (MUT) and mean down time (MDT) to be as low as possible, since availability is the ratio of mean uptime to mean cycle time which is the sum of mean uptime and mean downtime.

Availability is defined as the expected fraction of an interval of specified length that the equipment or system is in an up state. Thus availability is dependent on reliability and maintainability, and by clever manipulation one can get the desired value of availability. But the life cycle costs must not be lost sight of while designing a maintained equipment or system. There can be several combinations of MUT and MDT which can offer the same value of availability [4].

The purpose of MSS maintenance is to extend system lifetime, or at least the mean time to the next failure whose repair may be costly. Furthermore, it is expected that effective maintenance policies can increase system availability and reduce the consequences of unavailability (unaccomplished demand). Maintenance clearly impacts on component and system reliability: if too little is done, this may result in an excessive number of costly failures and poor system performance and, therefore, reliability is degraded; done often, reliability may improve but the cost of maintenance will sharply increase. In a cost-effective scheme, the two expenditures must be balanced [8].

Maintenance and repair problems have been widely investigated in the literature [9, 32]. Maintenance strategies addressed in most previous research works have been developed for improving reliability of binary-state systems. There is relatively limited number of research works focused on the maintenance strategies for MSS. The problem of perfect preventive maintenance optimization was considered for MSS by Levitin and Lisnianski [19].

Levitin and Lisnianski applied the UGF and genetic algorithm (GA) approach to the optimization of diverse MSS maintenance policies [22]. Lisnianski and Levitin systematically present the UGF approach for redundancy optimization for series-parallel multi-state systems, and describe in detail how GA can be used as the optimization engine. They deal with system optimization considering maintenance such as joint redundancy and maintenance optimization, imperfect preventive maintenance, and optimal replacement scheduling [22].

2.1 Universal Generating Function

The universal generating function (UGF) was introduced by Ushakov in 1986 [30]. In mathematics a *generating function* is a formal power series whose coefficients encode information about a sequence a_n that is indexed by the natural numbers. The ordinary generating function of a sequence a_n is

$$G(a_n; x) = \sum_{n=0}^{\infty} a_n x^n \quad (1)$$

If a_n is the probability mass function of a discrete random variable, then its ordinary generating function is called a *probability generating function*. Probability generating functions are often employed because they succinctly describe the sequence of probabilities $P(X = i)$. The UGF represents an extension of the widely known *moment generating function* [30].

In MSS reliability, the UGF $u_j(z)$ of the discrete random variable G_j, represents the probabilities $p_{j,i}$ and performances levels $g_{j,i}$ for every component j as follows:

$$u_j(z) = \sum_{i=0}^{n_j} p_{ji}(t) z^{g_{ji}} \quad (2)$$

where $g_{j,i}$ and $p_{j,i}$ represents the performance level and probability of the component j in state i, respectively. For modeling the entire performance of the MSS the u-function

$U(z)$ is used to represent the reliability and performance level of each system state

$$U(z) = \otimes_f(u_1(z), ..., u_N(z)) \quad (3)$$

where $\otimes_f$ represents the MSS structure function. The function f into the composition operator $\otimes_f$ expresses the entire performance of a subsystem in terms of the individual performance of their components. The definition of the function f strictly depends on the type of connection between the components in the reliability diagram sense (i.e. on the topology of the subsystem structure). Several composition operators $\otimes_f$ were determined for important types of MSS by Lisnianski and Levitin [22].

In his book chapter [17], Levitin describes the main advantages of the UGF method. Mainly, the UGF technique allows one to find the entire multi-state system reliability based on the performance distributions of its items by using algebraic procedures. It has been reported, that the UGF technique works fast in computational optimization procedures [17]. Besides, the UGF approach is universal. An analyst can use the same recursive procedures for systems with a different physical nature of performance and different types of element interaction. This approach enables one to obtain the performance distribution of complex MSS using a generalized reliability block diagram method (recursively aggregating multi-state elements and their replacement by single equivalent element).

The UGF method that allows for system performance distribution, and thereby its performance measures to be evaluated based on a fast procedure, opens new possibilities for solving MSS reliability optimization problems. Based on the UGF technique, the MSS reliability can be obtained as a function of the system structure and the performance distributions of its elements. Therefore, numerous optimization problems can be formulated in which the optimal composition of all or part of the factors influencing the entire MSS reliability has to be found subject to different constraints.

3. MSS MAINTENANCE OPTIMIZATION

Most technical systems are repairable. For many kinds of industrial systems, it is very important to avoid failures or reduce their occurrences and duration in order to improve system reliability and reduce the corresponding costs. With the increasing complexity of systems, only specially trained staff with specialized equipment can provide system service. In this case, maintenance service is provided by an external agent and the owner is considered a customer of the agent for maintenance service [21].

The main problem in mathematical maintenance policies is to design a maintenance plan with two maintenance options: preventive replacement and corrective replacement. In preventive replacement, the system or unit is replaced by a new one before it fails. On the other hand, with corrective replacement it is the failed unit that is replaced [5].

Preventative maintenance is a schedule of planned maintenance aimed to prevent future breakdowns and failures of a system that is functioning properly, namely, it is performed to prevent equipment failure before it actually occurs and to keep the system working. Usually, it is performed on system components on a regular basis based on the expected life of the components, and the frequency of the maintenance is generally constant.

The ideal preventive maintenance program would prevent all system failures before they occur [24]. Effective preventive maintenance planning is critical for cost-reduction in manufacturing environments. Besides the obvious aim of sustaining the production without interruptions, the planned preventive maintenance activities are also expected to bring reduced system failures and extended system lifetimes. It has been shown that a comprehensive preventive maintenance program can effectively improve system availability [23, 26]. In addition, the opportunity cost of production losses during the preventive maintenance times, and the direct costs and the overhead of the preventive maintenance activity should be considered when accounting for preventive maintenance costs.

All these cost components should be carefully included in the analysis when generating preventive maintenance plans. In literature, preventive maintenance planning or scheduling is usually studied as a stochastic decision problem. Very few papers handle the problem as a deterministic one, where the cyclic scheduling of maintenance activities is handled with a fixed cycle length and under a predetermined cost-structure [10].

In this paper, the aim is to find the optimal intervals between the maintenance activities of the component until replacement. We formulate the problem for a component with a known reliability function and compute the optimal solution when a reliability threshold is used for determining the schedules of the maintenance activities.

In general, preventive maintenance is carried out at discrete time instants. Many different types of preventive maintenance have been proposed to model the degradation and failure occurrence of systems, which involve optimal maintenance strategies subject to cost, availability and time repair constraints.

3.1 Cyclic Replacement Policy

Preventive maintenance planning for an unreliable component has received much attention in literature, since it has crucial practical importance. After the minimal repair model was presented by [1], a number of optimal strategies have been developed with the objective of improving reliability and preventing failures while reducing maintenance-related costs. In conventional preventive maintenance, the activities are scheduled periodically [25]. Under this policy, maintenance actions can be done at specified time instants.

This section describes a technique for optimal corrective maintenance planning during a life period T. The objective is to determine a series of component replacements for different operational periods that provides a minimal total expected cost accumulated during the system life cycle subject to cost, time repair and availability constraints. This approach assumes that the effect of preventive maintenance activities on the component is perfect, namely, they bring the component to an *as good as new* state every time they are performed. In other words, each time the component is perfectly maintained, it is as though we are starting over with a new piece of component. Then, if a perfect maintenance is performed at time τ, the reliability at any time $t \geq \tau$ depends only on the history of the system from τ up to t.

We define a system total cost TC as the cost incurred by the user in operations and maintenance of the system during its lifetime. In that case, TC will comprise operating costs, replacement costs, and penalty costs (unaccomplished demand), accumulated during the system life cycle.

We consider the determination of the optimal schedule of cyclic replacement for an MSS with a given series-parallel configuration and multi-state components. The times and costs of replacement are available for each system component. The objective is to provide the desired system availability by the minimal sum of maintenance cost and penalty costs caused by system performance deficiencies. The method presented presumes independence between replacement activities for different system components [16].

In his book [16], Levitin provides a complete problem formulation about cyclic replacement policy; in this section we describe the main elements of this problem. Assume a system consists of N components connected according to a structure function. Also, assume that for each component $j = 1, \cdots, N$, its nominal performance rate $g_{j,1}$, expected preventive time, corrective maintenance time and cost are given; as well as a renewal function $f_j(t)$ representing the expected number of components replacements in the time interval $(0, T)$.

Different components can have different possible numbers of preventive replacement actions during the system operation time T. The replacement interval can be estimated as $t_j = T/(x_j + 1)$, where x_j is the number of preventive replacement actions. Under the assumptions formulated, the expected time that the jth system element is unavailable can be estimated by the following expression:

$$\overline{A_j}(x_j) = (x_j + 1) f_j(t_j)\mu_j + x_j \lambda_j$$

where μ_j and λ_j are the minimal repair and preventive replacement times for component j, respectively. We can define the availability of each component as follows:

$$p_j(x_j) = \frac{T - \overline{A_j}(x_j)}{T}$$

The total expected maintenance time during the system operation time is:

$$\tau_m(x) = \sum_{i=1}^{N} \overline{A_j}(x_j)$$

The expected maintenance cost during the system operation can be calculated as:

$$C_m(x) = \sum_{i=1}^{N} (x_j + 1) f_j(t_j) cc_j + x_j cp_j$$

where cc_j and cp_j are the corrective and preventive maintenance costs, respectively. Applying the UGF and the reliability block diagram method to the system structure, we can obtain the entire system reliability.

For a given demand distribution w with associated probability q we can obtain the system availability $A(x, w, q)$ and the expected performance deficiency $D(x, w, q)$, where x is the system replacement policy vector. Thereby, we can estimated the total unsupplied demand cost during the system operation time T as:

$$C_d(x, w, q) = c_u D(x, w, q) T$$

where c_u is a cost of unsupplied demand per time unit. According to [16], in the general case, we can use the following formulation of the problem of system maintenance optimization:

$$min_x TC(x) = C_m(x) + C_d(x, w, q)$$

$$S.t. \quad A(x, w, q) \geq A^*, \quad \tau_m(x) \leq \tau^*$$

Namely, find the system replacement policy x that minimizes the total maintenance and unsupplied demand cost while provides the required MSS availability level A^* and the total maintenance time does not exceed preliminarily specified limitation τ^*.

The above formulation involves a combinatorial optimization process for finding the suitable tradeoff between reliability, cost and performance. In the next section, we explain the modified PSO algorithm applied in this paper to perform the required optimization.

4. PARTICLE SWARM OPTIMIZATION

The diversity of system structures, resource constraints, and options for reliability improvement has led to the construction and analysis of several optimization models. We are interested in the general *reliability allocation* problem. The objective for this combinatorial problem is to decide which replacement policy to use for each component. This problem has been shown to be NP-hard [2].

Many optimization approaches have previously been used to solve the reliability allocation problem [15]. Evolutio-nary algorithms, mainly, genetic algorithms (GAs) have been used in many works for solve reliability optimization pro-blems [20, 22, 29]. However, the tests performed in [7] showed that the particle swarm optimization algorithm (PSO) is able to get better results than those obtained by a GA for several reliability optimization problems.

Evolutionary algorithms are unconstrained search techniques which lack an explicit mechanism to deal with constrained search spaces. Therefore, introducing new good optimization approaches can be very helpful in some specific areas and can benefit practitioners by providing more choices [18]. This paper proposes to apply a modified version of the PSO algorithm to solve MSS maintenance optimization.

As it is reported in the PSO literature [11], this algorithm has several advantages compared to other meta-heuristics:

- It can be easily implemented and adapted to complex problems (for the continuous optimization problems, the encoding is straightforward and does not need extra conversion).
- It allows simple constraint handling.
- Its convergence properties are almost insensitive to the design of fitness functions.

The PSO algorithm is a population-based optimization technique inspired by the motion of a bird flock, or fish schooling [12]. In the PSO model, every particle flies over a real valued n-dimensional space of decision variables X. Each particle keeps track of its position X, velocity V, and remembers the best position ever visited, P_{Best}. The particle with the best P_{Best} value is called the leader, and its position is called global best, G_{Best}. The next particle's position is computed by adding a velocity term to its current position, as follows:

$$X_{t+1} = X_t + V_{t+1}$$

The velocity term combines the local information of the particle with global information of the flock, in the following way.

$$V_{t+1} = wV_t + U(0, c_1)(P_{Best} - X_t) + U(0, c_2)(G_{Best} - X_t)$$

The equation above reflects the socially exchanged information. It summarizes PSO three main features: distributed control, collective behavior, and local interaction with the environment [6, 13].The second term is called the cognitive component, while the last term is called the social component. w is the inertia weight, and c_1 and c_2 are called acceleration coefficients. The inertia weight regulates the mixture of the previous velocity with the current one.

When the flock is split into several neighborhoods the particle's velocity is computed with respect to its neighbors. The best P_{Best} value in the neighborhood is called the local best, L_{Best}.

$$V_{t+1} = wV_t + U(0, c_1)(P_{Best} - X_t) + U(0, c_2)(L_{Best} - X_t)$$

Originally developed for the optimization of continuous unconstrained functions, PSO did not attract much attention from the reliability community because most reliability optimization problems are of discrete nature and have constraints. As an emerging stochastic optimization method, PSO exhibits great potential in solving reliability engineering problems. [18].

In his work [18], Levitin, Hu and Dai talks about the possible directions of PSO performance improvement: *"...design of solution encoding schemes providing fitness function smoothness and combining the PSO with other heuristics and local search methods. The adaptation of PSO for solving sequencing, partition and scheduling problems that arise in reliability engineering is the main challenge for further research."*. In this paper we propose a novel PSO based on a simple modification applying a Binomial distribution in the velocity equation.

4.1 Binomial Particle Swarm Optimization

In probability theory and statistics, the binomial distribution $Bin(n, p)$ is the discrete probability distribution of the number of successes in a sequence of n independent Bernoulli experiments, each of which yields success with probability p. The parameter p controls the distribution behaviour and n defines the distribution domain.

Figure 1 shows the behaviour of the binomial distribution for diferent success probabilities and a sample size $n = 6$

The modification proposed is to use a Binomial distribution in the velocity equation to generate a discrete random number in the direction of the P_{Best} and L_{Best} particles.

$$\begin{aligned} V_{t+1} &= sign(V_t)Bin(|V_t|, w) \\ &+ sign([G_{Best} - X_t])Bin(|P_{Best} - X_t|, c_1) \\ &+ sign([L_{Best} - X_t])Bin(|L_{Best} - X_t|, c_2) \end{aligned}$$

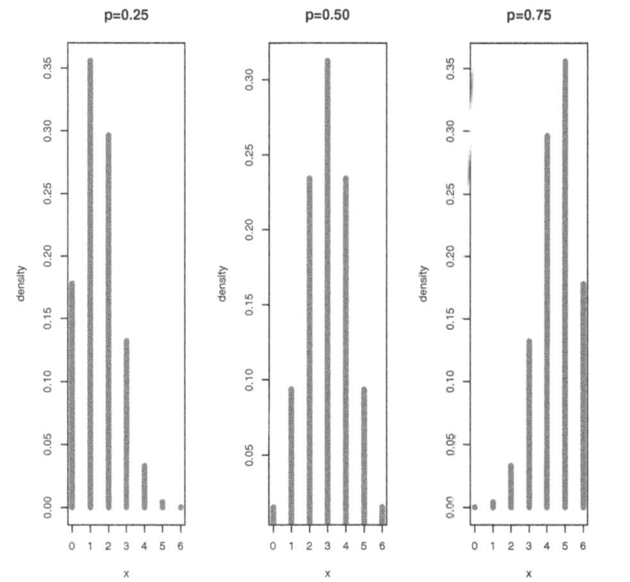

Figure 1: Density of a Binomial Distribution with sample size $n = 6$ and $p = \{0.25, 0.5, 0.75\}$

where $sign(a) = 1$ if $a \geq 0$ and $sign(a) = -1$ in other case. The Binomial PSO algorithm (BPSO) provides discrete values into the discrete domain $\{0, 1, \cdots, n\}$ where n represents the absolute value of the difference between P_{Best} and X_t or L_{Best} and X_t. The parameters $0 \leq w \leq 1$, $0 \leq c_1 \leq 1$ and $0 \leq c_2 \leq 1$ represents the success probablity of the binomial distribution for each term of the velocity equation.

A low value of w, c_1 or c_2 reduces the effect of the inertia, cognitive or social components, respectively. For instance, if we choose the next parameter values $w = 0.5$, $c_1 = 0.2$, and $c_2 = 0.7$ the particle velocity was influence, mainly, by its best neighbor. This help to the encoding schemes providing fitness function smoothness.

4.2 Constraint handling approach

Deb introduced the *superiority of feasible solutions* selection based on the idea that any individual in a constrained search space must first comply with the constraints and then with the function value [3]. BPSO adopted such popular tournament selection whose rules are the following:

1. Given two feasible particles, pick the one with better function value;
2. From a pair of feasible and infeasible particles, pick the feasible one;
3. If both particles are infeasible, pick the particle with the lowest sum of constraint violation.

The sum of constraint violations is, of course, the total value by which unsatisfied constraints are violated. The superiority of feasible solutions method does not require tuning parameters or applying special operators. Just a simple comparison is used to choose the best individual. Our approach applies this method, allowing feasible and infeasible solutions in the swarm. It enriches the information about the search space, especially at its boundaries.

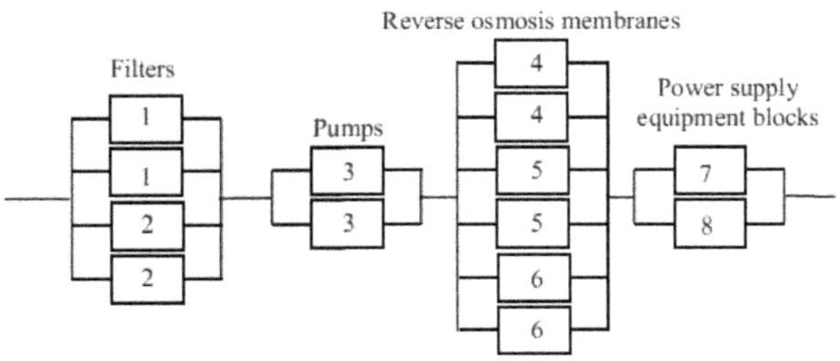

Figure 2: Series-parallel water desalination system

Table 2: Demand distribution

w	1.00	0.80	0.50	0.20
q	0.60	0.25	0.05	0.10

5. EXPERIMENTS AND RESULTS

The multi-state series-parallel system considered in [18], is a series-parallel water desalination system which consists of four subsystems containing 14 components. The structure of the system is presented in Figure 2.

Table 1 contains parameters of each component, including its renewal function $f_j(t)$ (replacement period t in months is given for each x), estimated using expert judgments. Times are measured in months. The component nominal performance is measured as a percentage of a maximal system demand.

All the replacement times in the system are equal to 0.5hrs (0.0007 month). The corrective maintenance includes a fault location search and tuning of the components, so it takes much more time than preventive replacement, but repairs are much cheaper than replacements. The demand distribution is presented in Table 2. The total operation time T is 120 months, and the cost of 1% of unsupplied demand during one month is $c_u = 10$.

For each experiment 100 runs were performed with the next parameters: $swarm = 50$, $c_1 = 0.5$, $c_2 = 0.5$ and $w = 0.5$. The experments were developed in a Laptop Alienware M17x Core i7 2830QM with 16GB Ram. The algorithm was implemented in the free software R [27] for Windows 7 (64 bits) in parallel (4 cores). The machine execution time for the 10,000 fitness evaluations perfomed in every run was 48 seconds.

5.1 Experiment I

In the first problem formulation, proposed by Levitin et al. [18], unsupplied demand cost was not considered $c_u = 0$ and the total maintenance time was not constrained $\tau^* = \infty$. The results for three different MSS availability levels A^* are presented in Table 3. The optimal values were provided in [18].

The replacement vector for the best result obtained in each experiment is shown in Table 4. According to the results reported in [18], we detect a mistake in the replacement vector when the $A^* = 0.97$, since the evaluation of the vector reported by Levitin et al. correspond to a higher cost $C_m = 314.4384$. The result obtained by BPSO in this experiment when the $A^* = 0.97$ is the optimal maintenance cost $C_m = 296.6412$ reported in [18]. The mistake is marked in the second line of Table 4.

5.2 Experiment II

In the second problem formulation, the unsupplied demand cost was introduced $c_u = 10$ per 1% of unaccomplished demand. The results for five different constraints are presented in Table 5. The optimal values were provided in [18].

The vector replacements for the best results obtained in these experiment are shown in Table 6.

The best results obtained by BPSO are the same that the results reported in [18]. The results obtained by BPSO reflect a robust performance of our proposal. A comparison between the GA applied in [18] and BPSO cannot be peformed due to there is not more information reported by the authors in [18]. In her thesis [31], Vargas-Serdio reported a poor performance of an ACO algorithm implemented in a computer cluster with 16 processors; she reports a machine execution time around 2 hours.

6. REMARKS AND FUTURE WORK

This work contributes to the fields of both evolutionary algorithm and MSS reliability. Succinctly, it can be described as a development of a discrete particle swarm optimization algorithm and its application to the MSS maintenance optimization.

In this study, we investigate the cyclic replacement policy for MSS. The applicability of the developed model in real life problems will be highly dependent on the estimation of problem parameters, such as replacement cost, unaccomplish demand cost, component reliabilities, and time of replacement of the components. With the correct estimation of such parameters, the model could be adapted to any environment.

In this paper we show that the BPSO algorithm can be an effective tool for solving some discrete constrained reliability optimization problems. The proposal was tested in a set of MSS maintenance problems under different availability and time repair constraints. BPSO shows a significant improvement in both performance and robustness.

The next step is to apply BPSO to other MSS maintenance problems (imperfect maintenance, corrective maintenence, etc.). Besides, BPSO could be tested in other fields to compare its performance against other PSO variants or other evolutionary algorithms.

7. ACKNOWLEDGMENTS

The first author acknowledges the support from National Council of Science and Technology (CONACYT) and from the Programa de Mejoramiento del Profesorado (PROMEP) to pursue this research at the Universidad Autónoma de Aguascalientes. The second author acknowledges the support from the Programa de Mejoramiento del Profesorado (PROMEP), to pursue graduate studies at the Universidad Autónoma de Aguascalientes.

8. REFERENCES

[1] R. Barlow and L. Hunter. Optimum preventive maintenance policies. *Operations Research*, 8(1):90–100, 1960.

[2] M. Chern. On the computational complexity of reliability redundancy allocation in a series system. *Operations Research Letters*, 11(5):309–315, 1992.

Table 1: Characteristics of the system components

Component	g_j	cp_j	cc_j	μ_j	Renewal function $f_j(t)$						
					t:	24	12	8	6	4.8	4
j					x:	5	10	15	20	25	30
1	0.40	3.01	0.019	0.002		25.00	10.00	5.00	2.0	1.00	0.50
2	0.30	2.21	0.049	0.004		26.00	9.00	2.00	0.6	0.20	0.05
3	0.60	2.85	0.023	0.008		20.00	4.00	1.00	0.3	0.08	0.01
4	0.15	2.08	0.017	0.005		36.00	14.00	9.00	6.0	4.00	3.00
5	0.15	1.91	0.029	0.003		55.00	15.00	7.00	4.0	0.32	0.30
6	0.25	0.95	0.031	0.009		31.00	9.50	5.60	4.0	2.70	2.00
7	1.00	5.27	0.050	0.002		13.00	3.20	1.40	0.8	0.50	0.10
8	0.70	4.41	0.072	0.005		5.00	2.00	1.00	0.4	0.10	0.01

Table 3: Minimal C_m obtained for experiment I

A^*	Optimal	Best	Mean	Median	Worst	Std. Dev.
0.96	263.1	263.061	263.061	263.061	263.061	0
0.97	296.6	296.6412	296.6412	296.6412	296.6412	0
0.98	384.4	384.4487	384.754	384.4487	388.0589	0.8053

Table 4: Replacement policies obtained for experiment I

A^*	Optimal	Best BPSO
0.96	5 5 5 5 5 5 5 5 10 10 10 10 5 5	5 5 5 5 5 5 5 5 10 10 10 10 5 5
0.97	5 5 5 5 10 10 5 5 10 10 25 25 5 5	5 5 5 5 10 10 5 5 10 10 15 15 5 5
0.98	5 5 5 5 15 15 10 10 25 10 25 25 5 5	5 5 5 5 15 15 10 10 25 10 25 25 5 5

Table 5: Minimal cost obtained for experiment II

Objective	A^*	τ^*	Optimal	Best	Mean	Median	Worst	Std. Dev.
min C_m	0	∞	249.1	249.084	249.084	249.084	249.084	0
min C_u	0	∞	156.4	156.3879	156.3879	156.3879	156.3879	0
min TC	0	∞	653.5	653.553	653.553	653.553	653.553	0
min TC	0	3	856.4	856.4096	856.4096	856.4096	856.4096	0
min TC	0.985	5.5	690.9	690.9552	692.4106	690.9552	695.567	2.0634

Table 6: Replacement policies obtained for experiment II

Objective	A^*	τ^*	Optimal	Best BPSO
min C_m	0	∞	5 5 5 5 5 5 5 5 5 5 5 5 5 5	5 5 5 5 5 5 5 5 5 5 5 5 5 5
min C_u	0	∞	30 30 30 30 30 30 30 30 25 25 30 30 30 30	30 30 30 30 30 30 30 30 25 25 30 30 30 30
min TC	0	∞	5 5 5 5 20 20 10 10 10 10 30 30 5 5	5 5 5 5 20 20 10 10 10 10 30 30 5 5
min TC	0	3	10 20 20 20 25 20 30 30 25 25 30 30 10 5	10 20 20 20 25 20 30 30 25 25 30 30 10 5
min TC	0.985	5.5	5 5 5 5 25 25 10 10 25 25 30 30 10 5	5 5 5 5 25 25 10 10 25 25 30 30 10 5

[3] K. Deb. An efficient constraint handling method for genetic algorithms. *Computer Methods in Appplied Mechanics and Engineering*, 186(2):311–338, 2000.

[4] B. Dhillon. *Engineering maintenance: a modern approach*. CRC Press LLC, Florida, U.S., 2002.

[5] T. Dohi, N. Kaio, and S. Osaki. *Preventive Maintenance Models: Replacement, Repair, Ordering, and Inspection*, pages 349–366. Engineering. Springer-Verlag, 2003.

[6] R. Eberhart, R. Dobbins, and P. Simpson. *Computational intelligence PC tools*. Academic Press Professional, San Diego, U.S., 1996.

[7] E. Elbeltagi, T. Hegazy, and D. Grierson. Comparison among five evolutionary-based optimization algorithms. *Operations Research Letters*, 19(1):43–53, 2005.

[8] J. Endrenyi. Impact of maintenance strategy on reliability. Final report, Reliability, Risk and Probability Applications Subcommittee.

[9] I. Gertsbakh. *Reliability Theory with Applications to Preventive Maintenance*. Springer-Verlag, Berlin, Germany, 2000.

[10] A. Grigoriev, J. van de Klundert, and F. Spieksma. Modeling and solving the periodic maintenance problem. *European Journal of Operational Research*, 172(3):783–797, 2006.

[11] X. Hu, Y. Shi, and R. Eberhart. Recent advances in particle swarm. In *Proceedings of IEEE Congress on Evolutionary Computation 2004*, pages 90–97. IEEE, June 2004.

[12] J. Kennedy and R. Eberhart. Particle swarm optimization. In *Proceedings of the IEEE International Conference On Neural Networks*, pages 1942–1948. IEEE, November 1995.

[13] J. Kennedy and R. Eberhart. *The particle swarm: social adaptation in information-processing systems*. McGraw-Hill, London, U.K., 1999.

[14] U. Kumar. *System Maintenance: Trends in Management and Technology*, pages 755–772. Engineering. Springer-Verlag, 2008.

[15] W. Kuo and R. Prasad. An annotated overview of system reliability optimization. *IEEE Transactions on Reliability*, 49(2):176–187, 2000.

[16] G. Levitin. *The Universal Generating Function in Reliability Analysis and Optimization*. Springer-Verlag, London, U.K., 2005.

[17] G. Levitin. *Universal generating function in analysis of multi-state systems*, pages 447–464. Engineering. Springer-Verlag, 2008.

[18] G. Levitin, X. Hu, and Y. Dai. *Particle swarm optimization in reliability engineering*, pages 83–112. Studies in Computational Intelligence. Springer-Verlag, 2006.

[19] G. Levitin and A. Lisnianski. Joint redundancy and maintenance optimization for multi-state series-parallel systems. *Reliability Engineering and System Safety*, 64(1):33–42, 1998.

[20] G. Levitin, A. Lisnianski, H. Ben-Haim, and D. Elmakis. Genetic algorithm and universal generating function technique for solving problems of power system reliability optimization. In *Proceedings of the International Conference on Electric Utility Deregulation and Restructuring and Power Technologies 2000*, pages 582–585. IEEE, April 2000.

[21] A. Lisnianski, I. Frenkel, L. Khvatskin, and Y. Ding. Maintenance contract assessment for aging systems. *Quality and Reliability Engineering International*, 24(5):519–531, 2008.

[22] A. Lisnianski and G. Levitin. *Multi-state system reliability: assessment, optimization and applications*. World Scientific, London, U.K., 2003.

[23] J. McCall. Maintenance policies for stochastically failing equipment: A survey. *Management Science*, 11(5):493–524, 1965.

[24] K. Misra. *Maintenance Engineering and Maintainability: An Introduction*, pages 755–772. Engineering. Springer-Verlag, 2008.

[25] T. Nakagawa. Optimal policy of continuous and discrete replacement with minimal repair at failure. *Naval Research Logistics*, 31(4):543–550, 1984.

[26] W. Pierskalla and J. Voelker. A survey of maintenance models: The control and surveillance of deteriorating systems. *Naval Research Logistics*, 23(3):353–388, 1976.

[27] R Development Core Team. *R: A Language and Environment for Statistical Computing*. R Foundation for Statistical Computing, Vienna, Austria, 2009. ISBN 3-900051-07-0.

[28] H. Taboada, J. Espiritu, and D. Coit. Design allocation of multi-state series-parallel systems for power systems planning: a multiple objective evolutionary approach. *Journal of Risk and Reliability*, 222(3):381–391, 2008.

[29] H. Taboada, J. Espiritu, and D. Coit. Moms-ga: a multi-objective multi-state genetic algorithm for system reliability optimization design problems. *IEEE Transactions on Reliability*, 57(1):182–191, 2008.

[30] I. Ushakov. A universal generating function. *Soviet Journal of Computer and Systems Sciences*, 24:37–49, 1986.

[31] L. Vargas-Serdio. Optimización de confiabilidad en sistemas multi-estado. Master's thesis, Centro de Investigación en Matemáticas, Guanajuato, Gto., México, 2010.

[32] H. Wang. A survey of maintenance policies of deteriorating systems. *European Journal of Operational Research*, 139(3):469–489, 2002.

[33] D. Wolpert and W. Macready. No free lunch theorems for optimization. *IEEE Transactions on Evolutionary Computation*, 1(1):67–82, 1997.

Integrating Particle Swarm Optimization with Reinforcement Learning in Noisy Problems

Grigoris S. Piperagkas
Department of Computer Science,
University of Ioannina,
GR–45110 Ioannina, Greece
gpiperag@cs.uoi.gr

George Georgoulas
Teorema Engineering Srl,
Area Science Park Basovizza,
Trieste, Italy
georgoul@gmail.com

Kostas E. Parsopoulos
Department of Computer Science,
University of Ioannina,
GR–45110 Ioannina, Greece
kostasp@cs.uoi.gr

Chrysostomos D. Stylios
Department of Informatics and Communications Technology,
Technological Educational Institute of Epirus,
GR–47100 Arta, Greece
stylios@teiep.gr

Aristidis C. Likas
Department of Computer Science,
University of Ioannina,
GR–45110 Ioannina, Greece
arly@cs.uoi.gr

ABSTRACT

Noisy optimization problems arise very often in real–life applications. A common practice to tackle problems characterized by uncertainties, is the re–evaluation of the objective function at every point of interest for a fixed number of replications. The obtained objective values are then averaged and their mean is considered as the approximation of the actual objective value. However, this approach can prove inefficient, allocating replications to unpromising candidate solutions. We propose a hybrid approach that integrates the established Particle Swarm Optimization algorithm with the Reinforcement Learning approach to efficiently tackle noisy problems by intelligently allocating the available computational budget. Two variants of the proposed approach, based on different selection schemes, are assessed and compared against the typical alternative of equal sampling. The results are reported and analyzed, offering significant evidence regarding the potential of the proposed approach.

Categories and Subject Descriptors

G.1.6 [**Optimization**]: Global optimization,Unconstrained optimization; G.3 [**Probability and Statistics**]: Probabilistic algorithms

General Terms

Algorithms, Performance, Experimentation

Keywords

Particle Swarm Optimization, Reinforcement Learning, Noisy Problems, Budget Allocation

1. INTRODUCTION

A plethora of algorithms for deterministic global optimization problems have been developed in the past years. However, sources of uncertainty may complicate the optimization process in real–life problems. Among the various types of uncertainty [9], the presence of noise in the evaluation of objective function is the most extensively investigated one due to its direct relation to the field of simulation optimization [8]. Such noisy objective functions may assign different values to the same input vector. These inconsistencies can be the outcome of possible errors in sensory measurements, games of chance or randomized simulations [9].

The uncertainty in objective values dictates the use of optimization heuristics. Evolutionary and swarm intelligence algorithms have been successfully applied to hard optimization tasks and appear as a powerful artillery for solving problems under uncertainty [9, 15, 16]. However, these algorithms have been primarily developed for deterministic problems and their operators are heavily based either on direct comparisons or rankings of the objective values of their population members. Thus, they can be easily misled by noisy environments that do not preserve the relative ordering between objective values. In such cases, proper modifications of the algorithms are needed.

A common practice in noisy objective functions is the multiple re–evaluation of each candidate solution. Then, the average of the obtained sample values is set as the objective value of the solution. The average constitutes a rough approximation of the actual objective value. Obviously, higher number of replications (larger sample) is expected to provide better approximations, although at higher computational cost. This trade–off gives raise to a crucial dilemma for the practitioner when a specific computational budget, in terms of the available function evaluations, has to be allocated during the optimization procedure. The dilemma subsumes to two crucial decisions. The first one is the homogeneous or inhomogeneous allocation of the budget to the candidate solutions, i.e., the allocation (or not) of the same number of replications to each candidate solution. The second question refers to the actual number of replications that will be allocated in the homogeneous case.

Various techniques have been proposed to tackle the aforementioned sampling problems. One of the first attempts to intelligently allocate replications among different solutions was proposed by Aizawa and Wah [1, 9], where higher sample size numbers are assigned to candidates with increased variance in their objective values. However, this approach neglects the mean of the candidate solution values. Chen [3] proposed the utilization of both the mean and the variance as a means to allocate replications originally for a restricted number of candidate solutions by optimizing the measure of *(Approximate–) Probability of Correct Selection* (A–PCS) [16]. This approach has proved to be asymptotically optimal and has been combined with different search procedures, such as the neighborhood random search, cross–entropy method, population–based incremental learning [4] and Particle Swarm Optimization (PSO) [21]. The identification of a superior solution can be performed either by quantifying its ranking among other solutions by using a measure such as the PCS or by taking into account differences in the fitness values using measures such as the *Expected Opportunity Cost* (EOC) [5]. Nevertheless, the homogeneous allocation of replications remains the most popular approach. This approach will be denoted as *equal sampling* (ES) throughout the rest of the present paper.

In the current work, we propose an alternative, hybrid approach for solving noisy problems. Our approach utilizes PSO and *Reinforcement Learning* (RL) for the efficient allocation of replications among candidate solutions. The corresponding reward for the learning procedure is based on the previously mentioned PCS concept [16]. The choice of RL was motivated by its significant contribution in the field of Machine Learning as well as on its smooth integration with metaheuristic algorithms [2, 13].

The rest of the paper is structured as follows: Section 2 constitutes a brief reference to the employed methodologies, i.e., PSO, PCS and the relative RL methodologies. The proposed approach is exposed in Section 3, while experimental results are reported in Section 4. Finally, the paper concludes in Section 5.

2. BACKGROUND INFORMATION

The main noisy optimization problem considered throughout the paper has the form:

$$\min_{x \in X \subset \mathbb{R}^n} f(x)(1+\eta), \tag{1}$$

where $f(x)$ is the actual (noiseless) objective function defined over the search space X, and η is a Gaussian random variable:

$$\eta \sim \mathcal{N}\left(0, \sigma^2\right),$$

with zero mean and standard deviation σ.

2.1 Particle Swarm Optimization

In recent years, *Particle Swarm Optimization* (PSO) has been placed in a salient position among the population–based algorithms [15]. The original PSO algorithm was introduced back in 1995 by Eberhart and Kennedy [7]. Its main concept includes a population, called a *swarm*, of potential solutions, called the *particles*, iteratively probing the search space. Each particle moves in the search space with an adaptable velocity, while retaining in a memory the *best position* it has ever visited, i.e., the position where its lowest function value was achieved (without loss of generality, only minimization problems are considered).

An additional feature of PSO is the *information exchange* that takes place among the particles. This aims at enhancing the search capability of a particle by exposing it to the experience of its mates in the swarm. Naturally, this may have tremendous impact on the overall *exploration* and *exploitation* capability of the swarm.

The information exchange is structured within the particles. For this purpose, communication schemes shall be defined among them. These schemes are called *neighborhood topologies* and they are usually represented as connected graphs where nodes represent the particles and edges represent the communication channels among them. We shall underline that the term "particle" is used here to express the general concept of a search unit rather than its actual position vector in the search space.

The neighborhood topologies determine a *neighborhood* for each particle, which is a set of other particles that will share their experience with it. If this set is strictly smaller than the whole swarm, then the local PSO model (also called *lbest*) is obtained. On the other hand, if the whole swarm is considered as the neighborhood of each particle, then the global PSO model (also called *gbest*) is obtained. Obviously, gbest can be considered as a special case of lbest. Various neighborhood topologies have been introduced in literature [10, 17]. A very popular one is the *ring*, where each particle is assigned a neighborhood consisting of the particles with indices adjacent to it.

Formalizing our description, consider the minimization problem of Eq. (1) and let:

$$S = \{x_1, x_2, \ldots, x_N\},$$

be a swarm of N particles with $x_i \in X \subset \mathbb{R}^n$, $i \in I = \{1, 2, \ldots, N\}$. Also, let v_i denote the velocity (position shift) of the i–th particle and $bp_i \in X$ denote the best position it has ever visited. A ring neighborhood of *radius* s for x_i, is defined as the set of indices:

$$B_i = \{i-s, i-s+1, \ldots, i, \ldots, i+s-1, i+s\}.$$

Assume that g_i is the index of the best position found in the neighborhood of x_i, and let t denote the iteration counter. Then, according to the popular *constriction coefficient* version of PSO [6], the swarm and velocities are updated as follows:

$$v_{ij}^{(t+1)} = \chi \left[v_{ij}^{(t)} + \varphi_1 \left(bp_{ij}^{(t)} - x_{ij}^{(t)} \right) + \varphi_2 \left(bp_{g_i j}^{(t)} - x_{ij}^{(t)} \right) \right], \tag{2}$$

$$x_{ij}^{(t+1)} = x_{ij}^{(t)} + v_{ij}^{(t+1)}, \tag{3}$$

where $i \in I$ and $j = 1, 2, \ldots, n$. The parameter χ is the constriction coefficient and offers a means of controlling the magnitude of the velocities. The other two parameters are defined as $\varphi_1 = c_1 \mathcal{R}_1$, $\varphi_2 = c_2 \mathcal{R}_2$, where c_1 and c_2 are positive constants, also called the *cognitive* and the *social* parameter, respectively, while $\mathcal{R}_1$, $\mathcal{R}_2$, are random variables uniformly distributed in the range $[0, 1]$, assuming different values for each i, j and t. Obviously, in the gbest model it holds that $g = g_1 = \cdots = g_N$.

The constriction coefficient is needed to restrict the magnitude of the velocities, promoting convergence and alleviating the *swarm explosion* effect that has been shown to be detrimental for the search procedure [6]. PSO's theoretical investigations due to Clerc and Kennedy [6] and Trelea [19] offered insight for its proper parameter setting. Based on these results, the values $\chi = 0.729$, $c_1 = c_2 = 2.05$, are commonly considered as an acceptable parameter set.

The iteration of PSO is completed with the best positions' update, as follows:

$$bp_i^{(t+1)} = \begin{cases} x_i^{(t+1)}, & \text{if } f\left(x_i^{(t+1)}\right) < f\left(bp_i^{(t)}\right), \\ bp_i^{(t)}, & \text{otherwise}, \end{cases} \tag{4}$$

followed by the corresponding update of the indices g_i, $i \in I$.

Although in deterministic environments the application of PSO is straightforward, several issues arise in the context of noisy optimization problems. Perhaps the most crucial question refers to the reliability of selecting best positions to drive the search towards the optimal solution(s) of the problem. Noisy objective values may promote inferior best positions, thereby misleading the algorithm.

In order to alleviate this problem, the typical procedure of re–evaluating each new particle position for a fixed number of replications has been used [14]. However, more sophisticated techniques can significantly improve the algorithm by allocating the computational budget more effectively. The proposed approach aims at introducing such a technique, utilizing the concept of PCS, which is sketched in the following section.

2.2 Probability of Correct Selection

In PSO there are two main procedures that need to be accomplished at each iteration. The one is the determination of the personal best position for each particle, and the other is the selection of the neighborhood's best particle. In noisy problems, the challenge lies at the main task of identifying the actual best particle among N candidates, with respect to the smallest mean objective function value, while minimizing the total number of replications needed for a precise and safe selection. To this end, the *Probability of Correct Selection* (PCS) can be very useful.

Let a set consist of N candidates (e.g, particles, best positions etc.), each one already assigned a number, M_l, of replications (not necessarily equal). Let f_{lm} be the output (objective value) of the m–th evaluation of candidate l, $l = 1, 2, \ldots, N$, $m = 1, 2, \ldots, M_l$. If μ_l and $\hat{\sigma}_l^2$ denote the sample mean and variance of the obtained objective values for candidate l, respectively, then:

$$\mu_l = \sum_{m=1}^{M_l} \frac{f_{lm}}{M_l}, \qquad \hat{\sigma}_l^2 = \sum_{m=1}^{M_l} \frac{(f_{lm} - \mu_l)^2}{(M_l - 1)}.$$

Apparently, the values of M_l, μ_l, $\hat{\sigma}_l^2$, change as long as additional replications are performed.

We assume that the means, μ_l, follow the Student's t–distribution:

$$St\left(\mu_l, M_l/\hat{\sigma}_l^2, M_l - 1\right).$$

Given the available replications data, Θ, the PCS_{Bayes} that the individual k with the best observed mean is the actual best, can be approximated with the Slepian inequality and Welch approximations, as follows [16]:

$$\begin{aligned} PCS_{\text{Bayes}} &= P\left(\mu_k \leqslant \min_{l \neq k} \mu_l \mid \Theta\right) \\ &\geqslant \prod_{l \neq k} P\left(\mu_k \leqslant \mu_l \mid \Theta\right) \\ &\approx \prod_{l \neq k} \Phi_{v_{kl}}\left(d_{lk}/s_{lk}\right), \end{aligned} \tag{5}$$

where Φ_v is the cumulative distribution function of Student's t–distribution; v_{lk} are the degrees of freedom; $d_{lk} = \mu_l - \mu_k$ are the observed differences; and $s_{lk} = \sqrt{\hat{\sigma}_l^2/M_l + \hat{\sigma}_k^2/M_k}$, is the variance of the difference of the estimated means. Further theoretical and practical details on the application of PCS can be found in [16].

2.3 Reinforcement Learning

Reinforcement Learning (RL) is a machine learning field that copes with decision–making, based on a reward maximization approach [18]. Among the numerous RL approaches, the *Parallel Recombinative Reinforcement Learning* (PRRL) technique [11, 12, 13] has been established as a population–based recombinative technique for the solution of binary optimization problems. It has also been extended to tackle discrete optimization problems through its Multivalued PRRL (MPRRL) variant, as well as to continuous problems by exploiting the concurrent operation of individual RL optimizers.

Based on the *Reinforce Theorem*, the *Multivalued Discrete Stochastic* (MDS) unit is defined, which is characterized by a set of adaptable parameters [11]. Using MDS or binary stochastic units in PRRL, results in efficient RL optimizers for discrete optimization tasks [11, 12, 13].

In binary problems, the scheme generates new candidate solutions, $y = (y_1, \ldots, y_n)$, using a group of n Bernoulli units, each one determining a component, y_j, of the binary output vector. The MDS unit generalizes the Bernoulli unit, providing discrete output values, $y \in \{a_1, \ldots, a_L\}$. Also, it is characterized by a parameter vector, $w = (w_1, \ldots, w_L)$, and a corresponding probability vector, $p = (p_1, \ldots, p_L)$, which is computed as follows:

$$p_i = \frac{\exp(w_i/T)}{\sum_{j=1}^{L} \exp(w_j/T)}, \tag{6}$$

where T is a positive control parameter. Obviously, it holds that $\sum_{i=1}^{L} p_i = 1$.

According to the *Reinforce Algorithm* [20], which possesses the stochastic hill–climbing property, the weights of an MDS unit are updated at each step according to the formula:

$$\Delta w_i = \alpha(r - \bar{r}) \frac{\partial \ln g}{\partial w_i}, \tag{7}$$

where α is the *learning rate factor*; r is the *reinforcement signal* delivered by the environment; $\bar{r}$ is the *reinforcement comparison*, defined as:

$$\bar{r}^{(t)} = \gamma \bar{r}^{(t-1)} + (1 - \gamma) r^{(t)}, \tag{8}$$

where γ is a decay rate in the range $[0, 1]$; and $g(a, w) = P\{y = a \mid w\}$ is the probability that the output y will be equal to a when the parameter vector is w

Algorithm 1 Pseudocode of PSO with RL and PCS.

```
INPUT: PSO, RL and PCS parameters; swarm size, N; objective
function, f; initial replications, M_0; maximum replications, M_p,
M_g; index of best particle, g.

/* INITIALIZATION */
for (i = 1,...,N) do
    initialize particle x_i within the search space X.
    evaluate x_i with M_0 initial replications.
    compute mean μ_{x_i} and standard deviation σ̂_{x_i}.
end for
duplicate all quantities to the best positions.

/* PSO ITERATIONS */
while (stopping criterion not met) do
    for (i = 1,...,N) do
        update x_i using Eqs. (2) and (3).
        evaluate x_i with M_0 replications.
        compute mean μ_{x_i} and standard deviation σ̂_{x_i}.

        /* Update Personal Best */
        call Algorithm 2 or 3 for C = {x_i, bp_i}, M ← M_p.
        if (μ_{x_i} < μ_{bp_i}) then
            bp_i ← x_i.
        end if
    end for

    /* Update Global Best */
    call Algorithm 2 or 3 for C = {bp_1,...,bp_N}, M ← M_g.
    g ← arg min_i {μ_{bp_i}}.
end while
return bp_g and f̂(bp_g).
```

Concerning the MDS unit, it holds that:

$$\frac{\partial \ln g}{\partial p_i} = \begin{cases} 1/p_i, & \text{if } y = a_i, \\ 0, & \text{otherwise.} \end{cases} \tag{9}$$

Moreover,

$$\frac{\partial \ln g}{\partial w_i} = \sum_{k=1}^{L} \frac{\partial \ln g}{\partial p_k} \frac{\partial p_k}{\partial w_i}, \tag{10}$$

and, from Eq. (6), it follows that:

$$\frac{\partial p_i}{\partial w_k} = \begin{cases} \frac{1}{T} p_i (1 - p_i), & \text{if } k = i, \\ -\frac{1}{T} p_i p_k, & \text{otherwise.} \end{cases} \tag{11}$$

Based on the above relations, it follows that:

$$\Delta w_i = \begin{cases} \alpha (r - \bar{r}) \frac{1}{T} p_i (1 - p_i) - \delta w_i, & \text{if } i = k, \\ -\alpha (r - \bar{r}) \frac{1}{T} p_i p_k - \delta w_i, & \text{otherwise,} \end{cases} \tag{12}$$

where $-\delta w_i$ is a decay term introduced to sustain search diversity, with $0 < \delta < 1$. Equation (12) is the main reinforcement update rule used in the MPRRL algorithm. This approach was also adopted in our algorithm. Further details on the MPRRL algorithm and the use of MDS units in discrete optimization environments can be found in [11].

3. THE PROPOSED APPROACH

As previously mentioned, the main issues of PSO in noisy problems are the correct update of the personal best of each particle with Eq. (4) as well as the correct determination of the globally best position. Both procedures require the best possible estimation of the objective values for both the particle's current and best position. In order to alleviate the computational burden that accompanies the equal sampling of each particle and best position, as described in the previous sections, we propose an approach that utilizes RL to intelligently allocate the available budget in terms of function evaluations.

Algorithm 2 Selection with Stochastic Independent Decisions (SID).

```
INPUT: Set of candidates, C = {z_1,...,z_K}; maximum replications, M.

set initial weights, w_{z_i} ← 1/K, i = 1,...,K.
compute selection probabilities p_{z_i}, i = 1,...,K, from Eq. (6).
i ← 0, l ← 0.
while (PCS < threshold) AND (l < M) do
    if (i = K) then
        i ← 1.
    else
        i ← i + 1.
    end if
    if (rand() < p_{z_i}) then
        evaluate candidate z_i and set l ← l + 1.
        update the corresponding mean and standard deviation of z_i.
        update PCS using Eq. (5).
    end if
    update weights w_{z_i}, i = 1,...,K, with Eq. (12).
    update selection probabilities p_{z_i}, i = 1,...,K, with Eq. (6).
end while
```

Algorithm 3 Selection with Roulette Wheel (RW).

```
INPUT: Set of candidates, C = {z_1,...,z_K}; maximum replications, M.

set initial weights, w_{z_i} ← 1/K, i = 1,...,K, and l ← 0.
compute selection probabilities p_{z_i}, i = 1,...,K, from Eq. (6).
while (PCS < threshold) AND (l < M) do
    R ← rand().
    find j ∈ {1,...K} such that R ⩽ p_{z_j} and R > p_{z_{j-1}}.
    evaluate candidate z_j and set l ← l + 1.
    update the corresponding mean and standard deviation of z_j.
    update PCS using Eq. (5).
    update weights w_{z_i}, i = 1,...,K, with Eq. (12).
    update selection probabilities p_{z_i}, i = 1,...,K, with Eq. (6).
end while
```

Specifically, let S be a swarm of N particles, M_0 be a fixed number of initial replications, M_p be the maximum number of replications to be allocated per particle for updating its personal best at each iteration, and M_g be the maximum number of available replications for the determination of the globally best position. Initially, each particle x_i, $i \in I = \{1, 2, \ldots, N\}$, is randomly positioned in the search space and it is evaluated M_0 times, deriving the corresponding mean and standard deviation, μ_{x_i} and $\hat{\sigma}_{x_i}$, of the obtained values. The same quantities are reproduced for the best positions since, initially, they coincide with the swarm.

Then, the iterative PSO scheme of Eqs. (2) and (3) is initiated and a new current position is produced for each particle. For each new position, M_0 replications are performed and the mean and standard deviation is derived. Now, the procedure of updating the personal best position of each particle is triggered. There are M_p replications (at maximum) available per particle that will be allocated using the RL scheme by maximizing the PCS.

Specifically, each particle, x_i, is isolated along with its best position, bp_i, and they are assigned equal weights, w_{x_i} and w_{bp_i}, respectively. These weights are used to produce the corresponding selection probabilities according to Eq. (6). Probabilistic selection is performed (we will refer to this procedure later) and either x_i or bp_i is selected to be assigned the next replication. After the new evaluation, the mean and standard deviation of the selected position (current or best) is updated. At this point, PCS is updated with Eq. (5), and the weights are updated through the learning rule of Eq. (12), assuming the obtained PCS values as reward. The

Table 1: Parameter values employed in the experiments.

Parameter	Value
Test problems	Sphere (TP1), Rosenbrock (TP2), Rastrigin (TP3), Griewank (TP4), Ackley (TP5)
Dimensions	5, 15, 40
Noise levels	0.01, 0.03, 0.05
Computational budget	2×10^5 function evaluations
PSO parameters	Swarm size $N = 25$, $\chi = 0.729$, $c_1 = c_2 = 2.05$ (gbest model)
RL parameters	$\alpha = 2.0$, $T = 0.02$, $\delta = 0.002$, $\gamma = 0.7$
PCS upper bound	0.9
Replications	$M_0 = 10$, $M_p = 25$, $M_g = 300$
Number of experiments	100 per algorithm, problem and noise instance

procedure is repeated by probabilistically selecting again between x_i and bp_i to allocate the next replication and so on. The procedure stops as soon as the PCS exceeds a maximum threshold or the maximum available replications, M_p, have been assigned. The same procedure is applied on all particles for the determination of their new best positions.

The next stage is the determination of the globally optimal solution. The same procedure as for the particles is used also in this stage. Specifically, the best positions of all particles are isolated and assigned, initially, equal weights. All best positions are assumed to be accompanied by the mean and standard deviations they have obtained in the previous steps of the algorithm. Then, probabilistic selection among them takes place, pointing the best position that will be assigned the next replication. After the replication, the corresponding mean and standard deviation are updated, along with the PCS, and new weights are computed according to the RL rule. The procedure is repeated until PCS reaches its maximum threshold or the maximum available replications, M_g, are exceeded. The pseudocode of the whole procedure is reported in Algorithm 1.

Regarding the probabilistic selection, two approaches were considered. The first one is called the *Stochastic Independent Decisions* (SID) and it individually examines each candidate, either selecting or neglecting it, based on its selection probability. The pseudocode of SID is provided in Algorithm 2. The second approach is the well–known *Roulette Wheel* (RW) selection. Its pseudocode is reported in Algorithm 3. The main difference between SID and RW, is that SID may not assign a replication before updating weights and selection probabilities, while RW will always assign a replication prior to the updates. Also, it shall be underlined that SID employs Bernoulli units, while RW employs the MDS units.

4. EXPERIMENTAL ANALYSIS

The proposed approach was tested on five widely used test problems, contaminated by multiplicative noise. The algorithm was compared with the typical equal sampling approach. The complete experimental setting is exposed in the following section, followed by the experimental results.

4.1 Experimental Setting

The test suite used in our experimental analysis consists of five test functions: Sphere (TP1), Rosenbrock (TP2), Rastrigin (TP3), Griewank (TP4) and Ackley (TP5). The problems are defined by Eqs. (13)–(17) in the Appendix at the end of the present paper. Each problem was considered in its 5–, 15– and 40–dimensional instance. The test functions were contaminated by multiplicative Gaussian noise with standard deviation (henceforth called *noise level*) equal to 0.01, 0.03 and 0.05, which correspond to distortions of 1%, 3% and 5%, respectively, of the actual objective functions.

The available computational budget was set to 2×10^5 function evaluations for each test problem. This value was proved to be satisfactory for all the considered approaches in preliminary experiments. Two variants of the proposed approach were considered, namely, PSO with RL using SID selection, henceforth denoted as RL, and its counterpart with RW selection, henceforth denoted as RLrw, both based on the gbest model of PSO. The two PSO–based approaches were compared to the typical equal sampling technique, henceforth denoted as ES.

The RL based approaches were based on the PCS maximization scheme, with upper PCS bound equal to 0.9. The swarm size was kept small, counting 25 particles in all cases. We avoided larger swarms due to our interest in observing the manipulation of the computational budget by the algorithm for lengthier runs. Also, the default PSO parameters' values, $\chi = 0.729$, $c_1 = c_2 = 2.05$, were used.

Regarding the RL parameters, α was initially considered in the set $\{2.0, 4.0, 6.0\}$. However, preliminary experiments revealed that $\alpha = 2.0$ was the most promising setting, hence, it was adopted in our study. Smaller values of α that are usually met in machine learning approaches, e.g., within the range $(0, 1)$, were proved to slow down the convergence speed of the algorithm to unacceptable levels. Thus, they were abandoned. The rest of RL parameters were set to the values:

$$T = 0.02, \qquad \delta = 0.002, \qquad \gamma = 0.7.$$

Regarding the replications, the initial number $M_0 = 10$ was used, while $M_p = 25$ and $M_g = 300$ were used for the determination of the personal and the global best, respectively. The same values were also used for the corresponding procedures of the ES approach, were all candidate solutions are assigned the same number of replications. Finally, 100 independent experiments were conducted per algorithm, problem and noise instance, recording the distance of the best detected solution from the actual solution of the corresponding problem. The results are reported and discussed in the next section. All parameter values are summarized in Table 1.

4.2 Experimental Results

A total number of 4500 independent experiments was performed per algorithm. At each experiment, the best solution detected by the algorithm was recorded, and its distance from the actual global minimizer of the corresponding (noiseless) objective function was computed. The obtained

Table 2: Results for all algorithm, problem and noise instances. The distance from the actual solution, averaged over 100 experiments, is reported. Best performance per case is boldfaced.

			RL		RLrw		ES	
Noise	Problem	Dim	Mean	StD	Mean	StD	Mean	StD
0.01	TP1	5	**6.2252e − 13**	**8.1178e − 13**	7.0565e − 13	1.9094e − 12	4.7264e − 09	9.6887e − 09
		15	**4.0689e − 06**	**4.2673e − 06**	7.0333e − 06	1.1233e − 05	3.4827e − 02	3.2550e − 02
		40	3.3334e + 02	1.7245e + 03	**2.2827e + 02**	**1.4078e + 03**	6.8298e + 02	1.0377e + 03
	TP2	5	1.0198e + 04	9.9501e + 04	**1.0046e + 04**	**9.9949e + 04**	1.0217e + 04	9.9647e + 04
		15	1.3018e + 05	3.3634e + 05	**1.0047e + 05**	**2.9989e + 05**	1.3118e + 05	3.3730e + 05
		40	1.3282e + 05	3.3945e + 05	**7.2018e + 04**	**2.5642e + 05**	1.3836e + 07	2.3744e + 07
	TP3	5	1.5188e + 00	1.2810e + 00	**1.4203e + 00**	**1.2250e + 00**	1.6418e + 00	1.2979e + 00
		15	2.5331e + 01	1.0185e + 01	**2.3429e + 01**	**1.0523e + 01**	2.7628e + 01	9.8925e + 00
		40	**1.5282e + 02**	**3.8680e + 01**	1.5611e + 02	3.5560e + 01	1.9527e + 02	3.3892e + 01
	TP4	5	6.3845e − 02	4.3811e − 02	**5.9517e − 02**	**3.5620e − 02**	8.9027e − 02	5.9574e − 02
		15	5.8112e − 02	5.5362e − 02	**5.3849e − 02**	**5.2725e − 02**	2.8362e − 01	2.1390e − 01
		40	3.1580e + 00	1.2744e + 01	**2.5672e + 00**	**9.6840e + 00**	6.6175e + 00	9.3756e + 00
	TP5	5	4.5802e − 09	5.4258e − 09	**3.8459e − 09**	**3.6731e − 09**	5.4689e − 09	5.5983e − 09
		15	**3.5321e − 10**	**3.0538e − 10**	3.9243e − 10	3.8634e − 10	3.6604e − 10	3.6604e − 10
		40	**2.2610e − 02**	**1.6037e − 01**	8.2413e − 02	3.4345e − 01	4.0950e − 02	2.4101e − 01
0.03	TP1	5	7.3003e − 13	1.2936e − 12	**6.2201e − 13**	**7.3231e − 13**	3.4001e − 09	6.0581e − 09
		15	**4.7440e − 06**	**8.0663e − 06**	6.1386e − 06	1.0164e − 05	3.3991e − 02	3.5064e − 02
		40	3.0869e + 02	1.5994e + 03	**2.3277e + 02**	**1.4267e + 03**	6.4756e + 02	1.0410e + 03
	TP2	5	**3.5473e + 02**	**1.6958e + 03**	2.9895e + 04	1.6998e + 05	1.0119e + 04	9.9430e + 04
		15	**1.0959e + 05**	**3.1031e + 05**	1.1879e + 05	3.2149e + 05	1.2071e + 05	3.2460e + 05
		40	1.2619e + 05	3.2951e + 05	**8.3097e + 04**	**2.7262e + 05**	1.0358e + 07	8.5382e + 06
	TP3	5	1.3932e + 00	1.3093e + 00	**1.2158e + 00**	**9.9188e − 01**	1.6210e + 00	1.1719e + 00
		15	**2.2651e + 01**	**1.1496e + 01**	2.8667e + 01	1.4427e + 01	2.7660e + 01	1.2799e + 01
		40	**1.4794e + 02**	**3.2793e + 01**	1.5511e + 02	3.8106e + 01	1.8990e + 02	3.8559e + 01
	TP4	5	5.7390e − 02	4.5452e − 02	**5.5932e − 02**	**4.0744e − 02**	8.6565e − 02	4.4118e − 02
		15	**4.4530e − 02**	**3.6157e − 02**	5.2763e − 02	4.4096e − 02	2.8537e − 01	1.9812e − 01
		40	**5.1072e + 00**	**1.8102e + 01**	5.9459e + 00	1.9931e + 01	7.8330e + 00	1.3196e + 01
	TP5	5	**5.6730e − 09**	**6.4548e − 09**	6.2441e − 09	6.7018e − 09	7.3606e − 09	1.0042e − 08
		15	**4.8670e − 09**	**5.1335e − 09**	6.0212e − 09	7.9248e − 09	4.8614e − 09	6.1410e − 09
		40	1.9340e + 00	5.1686e + 00	1.9927e + 00	4.9377e + 00	**1.5146e + 00**	**4.3447e + 00**
0.05	TP1	5	7.2314e − 13	1.2754e − 12	**7.0765e − 13**	**1.0996e − 12**	2.5668e − 09	3.5830e − 09
		15	**6.5432e − 06**	**9.6862e − 06**	1.4793e − 05	9.7763e − 05	3.9236e − 02	5.2710e − 02
		40	3.3011e + 02	1.7363e + 03	**2.3402e + 02**	**1.3896e + 03**	8.7819e + 02	1.7877e + 03
	TP2	5	**9.9304e + 03**	**9.7955e + 04**	1.9351e + 04	1.3586e + 05	9.9983e + 03	9.9507e + 04
		15	9.8164e + 04	2.9434e + 05	**8.9247e + 04**	**2.8166e + 05**	9.9632e + 04	2.9649e + 05
		40	**1.2437e + 05**	**3.2886e + 05**	2.0443e + 05	4.0698e + 05	1.1958e + 07	1.0061e + 07
	TP3	5	1.4061e + 00	1.2151e + 00	**1.3365e + 00**	**1.3578e + 00**	1.7680e + 00	1.4024e + 00
		15	**2.3576e + 01**	**1.1829e + 01**	2.3801e + 01	1.0679e + 01	2.9363e + 01	1.2676e + 01
		40	1.5642e + 02	3.5043e + 01	**1.5472e + 02**	**3.2447e + 01**	2.0052e + 02	4.1461e + 01
	TP4	5	5.6665e − 02	3.1438e − 02	**5.3956e − 02**	**3.3854e − 02**	8.6181e − 02	5.7802e − 02
		15	**5.5365e − 02**	**5.0899e − 02**	5.6809e − 02	4.9469e − 02	2.8920e − 01	1.9866e − 01
		40	7.2492e + 00	2.2179e + 01	**3.9561e + 00**	**1.3095e + 01**	1.2624e + 01	2.2924e + 01
	TP5	5	1.2196e − 08	1.5082e − 08	1.4285e − 08	1.9523e − 08	**1.0513e − 08**	**1.0318e − 08**
		15	2.6863e − 01	1.9230e + 00	2.4333e − 01	1.7848e + 00	**1.5637e − 01**	**1.5584e + 00**
		40	1.5814e + 01	1.1089e + 00	**1.5687e + 01**	**1.3739e + 00**	1.5713e + 01	1.2499e + 00

averaged results are reported in Table 2, where the best approach per case appears boldfaced.

A first inspection of the results offers a clear conclusion. The RL–based variants, outperformed the typical ES approach in almost all cases. Exceptions were observed in three instances of TP5 for higher noise levels, probably due to the structure of the specific problem. In all other cases, the best performance was observed with competitive frequencies either by RL or RLrw.

The statistical significance of performance differences between the algorithms was not very distinguishable in several instances, due to large standard deviations and marginal differences between the means. For this purpose, pairwise comparisons of the algorithms were conducted through Wilcoxon statistical tests for each one of the 45 different experimental configurations (5 problems $\times$ 3 dimensions $\times$ 3 noise levels), at a 95% level of significance. A pairwise comparison between two algorithms was considered as *positive* for the one that outperformed the other with statistical significance. Obviously, for the other algorithm the comparison was recorded as *negative*. If no statistical significance was observed in their differences, the comparison was characterized as *neutral* for both algorithms.

The percentages of positive, negative and neutral comparisons for the three algorithms are graphically illustrated in Fig. 1 for all test problems. In this figure, the superiority of RL and RLrw is apparent and statistically verified. As we can see, for almost 40% of the cases, RL and RLrw (individually) were statistically dominant. The majority of their neutral comparisons referred to comparisons between them, while the negative comparisons correspond to the exceptions of TP5 observed in Table 2, where ES achieved its best performance.

Further analysis to identify the cases where each algorithm was performing better, was based on the positive comparisons of the algorithms and their relative distributions with respect to the problems' dimensions and noise levels. Figure 2 depicts these distributions for the three algorithms. As we can see, RL outperforms (often marginally) the RLrw approach for all problems' dimensions. This holds also for the higher noise cases. However, lower noise levels provide an advantage to the RLrw approach.

A possible explanation for this may lie to the fact that RW selection assigns a replication whenever it is evoked, while SID may update several times the selection probabilities of the candidates before assigning a replication. Thus, in low noise levels where the expected noisy objective values lie

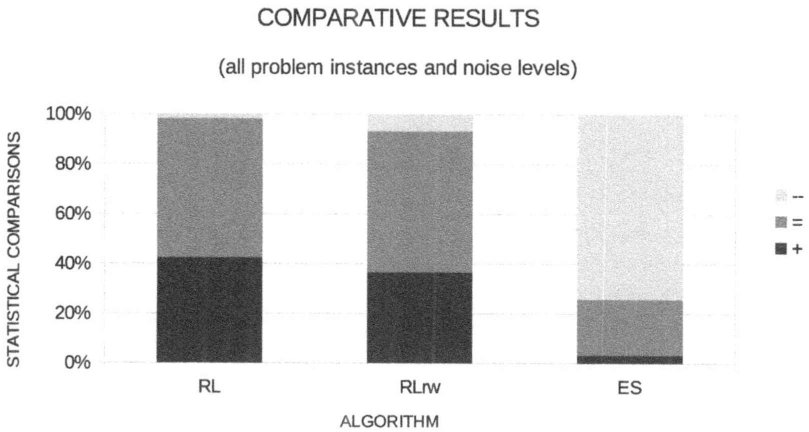

Figure 1: Percentage of positive (+), neutral (=) and negative (−) pairwise comparisons between the algorithms for all problem instances and noise levels.

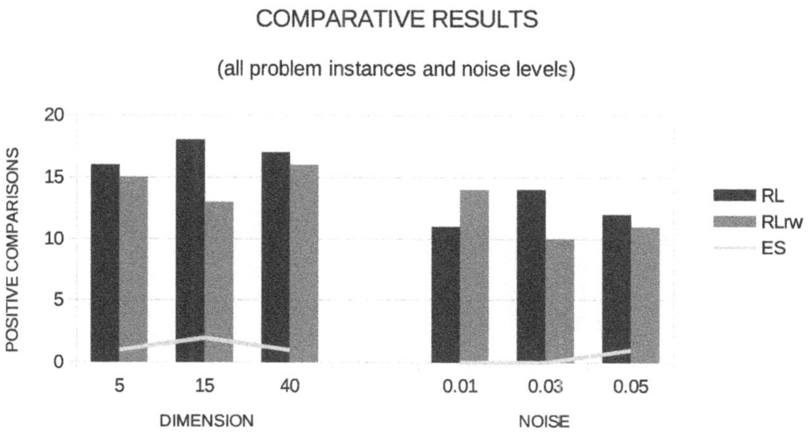

Figure 2: Number of positive pairwise comparisons per algorithm for the different dimensions and noise levels over all problems.

closer to the actual ones, RW may offer faster convergence towards candidate solutions that lie closer to the optimal one. On the other hand, higher noise levels can shadow this advantage, resulting in slower replications' allocation through the RL approach.

Finally, it is worth noting that ES performance, illustrated with a curve in Fig. 2, follows the trend of RL with respect to the problems' dimensions, i.e., it exhibits a noticeable increase for the 15–dimensional cases and decreases for the 40–dimensional ones. Contrary to this, when the analysis refers to the noise level, the performance of ES follows the trend of RLrw, i.e., it slightly declines for the case of 0.03 and then increases for 0.05.

5. CONCLUSIONS

We proposed a hybrid approach that integrates PSO with the RL methodology to efficiently allocate replications in noisy problems. The main algorithm was combined with two different selection schemes. Their performances were assessed on a set of widely used test functions and compared against the typical equal sampling approach.

The obtained results suggested that the proposed algorithms offer significant advantage against equal sampling. Both approaches were satisfactorily scaling with respect to the problems' dimension and noise level. Naturally, further work is required to fully reveal the potential of the proposed algorithms through extensive experimentation.

Acknowledgment

This work was partially supported by the E.U. FP7–PEOPLE–IAPP–2009, Grant Agreement No. 251589, Acronym: SAIL.

6. REFERENCES

[1] A. N. Aizawa and B. W. Wah. Dynamic control of genetic algorithms in a noisy environment. In *ICGA*, pages 48–55, 1993.

[2] R. Battiti and P. Campigotto. Reinforcement learning and reactive search: an adaptive max-sat solver. In

Proceedings of the 2008 conference on ECAI 2008: 18th European Conference on Artificial Intelligence, pages 909–910, Amsterdam, The Netherlands, The Netherlands, 2008. IOS Press.

[3] C.-H. Chen. An effective approach to smartly allocate computing budget for discrete event simulation. In *Proceedings of the 34th IEEE Conference on Decision and Control*, pages 2598–2605, 1995.

[4] C. H. Chen and L. H. Lee. *Stochastic Simulation Optimization: An Optimal Computing Budget Allocation.* World Scientific Publishing Co., 2010.

[5] S. Chick and K. Inoue. New two-stage and sequential procedures for selecting the best simulated system. *Operations Research*, 49:732–743, September 2001.

[6] M. Clerc and J. Kennedy. The particle swarm–explosion, stability, and convergence in a multidimensional complex space. *IEEE Trans. Evol. Comput.*, 6(1):58–73, 2002.

[7] R. C. Eberhart and J. Kennedy. A new optimizer using particle swarm theory. In *Proceedings Sixth Symposium on Micro Machine and Human Science*, pages 39–43, Piscataway, NJ, 1995. IEEE Service Center.

[8] M. Fu, C. Chen, and L. Shi. Some topics for simulation optimization. In *Winter Simulation Conference*, pages 27–38, 2008.

[9] Y. Jin and J. Branke. Evolutionary optimization in uncertain environments-a survey. *IEEE Trans. Evolutionary Computation*, 9(3):303–317, 2005.

[10] J. Kennedy. Small worlds and mega–minds: Effects of neighborhood topology on particle swarm performance. In *Proc. IEEE Congr. Evol. Comput.*, pages 1931–1938, Washington, D.C., USA, 1999. IEEE Press.

[11] A. Likas. Multivalued parallel recombinative reinforcement learning: A multivalued genetic algorithm. In *Proc. HERCMA'98 Conference, Athens, Greece*, 1998.

[12] A. Likas, K. Blekas, and A. Stafylopatis. Parallel recombinative reinforcement learning. In *Proc. 8th European Conference on Machine Learning (ECML-95), LNAI 912*, pages 311–314. Springer Verlag, 1995.

[13] A. Likas, K. Blekas, and A. Stafylopatis. Parallel recombinative reinforcement learning: A genetic algorithm. *Journal of Intellligent Systems*, 6:145–169, 1996.

[14] K. E. Parsopoulos and M. N. Vrahatis. Particle swarm optimizer in noisy and continuously changing environments. In M. Hamza, editor, *Artificial Intelligence and Soft Computing*, pages 289–294. IASTED/ACTA Press, 2001.

[15] K. E. Parsopoulos and M. N. Vrahatis. *Particle Swarm Optimization and Intelligence: Advances and Applications.* Information Science Publishing (IGI Global), 2010.

[16] C. Schmidt, J. Branke, and S. Chick. Integrating techniques from statistical ranking into evolutionary algorithms. *Lecture notes in computer science*, 3907/2006:752–763, 2006.

[17] P. N. Suganthan. Particle swarm optimizer with neighborhood operator. In *Proc. IEEE Congr. Evol. Comput.*, pages 1958–1961, Washington, D.C., USA, 1999.

[18] R. S. Sutton and A. G. Barto. *Reinforcement Learning: An Introduction.* MIT Press, 1998.

[19] I. C. Trelea. The particle swarm optimization algorithm: Convergence analysis and parameter selection. *Information Processing Letters*, 85:317–325, 2003.

[20] R. Williams. Simple statistical gradient-following algorithms for connectionist reinforcement learning. *Machine Learning*, 8:229–256, 1992.

[21] S. Zhang, P. Chen, L.-J. Lee, C.-E. Peng, and C.-H. Chen. Simulation optimization using the particle swarm optimization with optimal computing budget allocation. In *Winter Simulation Conference*, 2011.

APPENDIX

The employed test problems are defined as follows:

Test Problem 1 (TP1 – Sphere) [15]. This is a separable n–dimensional problem, defined as:

$$f(x) = \sum_{i=1}^{n} x_i^2. \tag{13}$$

It has a global minimizer, $x^* = (0, \dots, 0)^\top$, with $f(x^*) = 0$.

Test Problem 2 (TP2 - Generalized Rosenbrock) [15]. This is a non–separable n–dimensional problem, defined as:

$$f(x) = \sum_{i=1}^{n-1} \left(100 \left(x_{i+1} - x_i^2\right)^2 + (x_i - 1)^2\right). \tag{14}$$

It has a global minimizer, $x^* = (1, \dots, 1)^\top$, with $f(x^*) = 0$.

Test Problem 3 (TP3 - Rastrigin) [15]. This is a separable n–dimensional problem, defined as:

$$f(x) = 10n + \sum_{i=1}^{n} \left(x_i^2 - 10\cos(2\pi x_i)\right). \tag{15}$$

It has a global minimizer, $x^* = (0, \dots, 0)^\top$, with $f(x^*) = 0$.

Test Problem 4 (TP4 - Griewank) [15]. This is a non–separable n–dimensional problem, defined as:

$$f(x) = \sum_{i=1}^{n} \frac{x_i^2}{4000} - \prod_{i=1}^{n} \cos\left(\frac{x_i}{\sqrt{i}}\right) + 1. \tag{16}$$

It has a global minimizer, $x^* = (0, \dots, 0)^\top$, with $f(x^*) = 0$.

Test Problem 5 (TP5 - Ackley) [15]. This is a non–separable n–dimensional problem, defined as:

$$f(x) = 20 + \exp(1) - 20\exp\left(-0.2\sqrt{\frac{1}{n}\sum_{i=1}^{n} x_i^2}\right) - \exp\left(\frac{1}{n}\sum_{i=1}^{n}\cos(2\pi x_i)\right). \tag{17}$$

It has a global minimizer, $x^* = (0, \dots, 0)^\top$, with $f(x^*) = 0$.

Gaussian Mixture Modeling for Dynamic Particle Swarm Optimization of Recurrent Problems

Eduardo Vellasques
École de Technologie Supérieure
Université du Québec
1100 rue Notre-Dame Ouest
Montreal, Canada
evellasques@livia.etsmtl.ca

Robert Sabourin
École de Technologie Supérieure
Université du Québec
1100 rue Notre-Dame Ouest
Montreal, Canada
robert.sabourin@etsmtl.ca

Eric Granger
École de Technologie Supérieure
Université du Québec
1100 rue Notre-Dame Ouest
Montreal, Canada
eric.granger@etsmtl.ca

ABSTRACT

In dynamic optimization problems, the optima location and fitness value change over time. Techniques in literature for dynamic optimization involve tracking one or more peaks moving in a sequential manner through the parameter space. However, many practical applications in, e.g., video and image processing involve optimizing a stream of recurrent problems, subject to noise. In such cases, rather than tracking one or more moving peaks, the focus is on managing a memory of solutions along with information allowing to associate these solutions with their respective problem instances. In this paper, Gaussian Mixture Modeling (GMM) of Dynamic Particle Swarm Optimization (DPSO) solutions is proposed for fast optimization of streams of recurrent problems. In order to avoid costly re-optimizations over time, a compact density representation of previously-found DPSO solutions is created through mixture modeling in the optimization space, and stored in memory. For proof of concept simulation, the proposed hybrid GMM-DPSO technique is employed to optimize embedding parameters of a bi-tonal watermarking system on a heterogeneous database of document images. Results indicate that the computational burden of this watermarking problem is reduced by up to 90.4% with negligible impact on accuracy.

Categories and Subject Descriptors

I.2.8 [**Computing Methodologies**]: Artificial Intelligence—*Problem Solving, Control Methods, and Search*

General Terms

Experimentation

GECCO'12, July 7–11, 2012, Philadelphia, Pennsylvania, USA.

Keywords

Particle Swarm Optimization, Dynamic Optimization, Gaussian Mixture Models, Estimation of Distribution Algorithms

1. INTRODUCTION

In evolutionary computing (EC), populations of candidate solutions are evolved through a certain number of generations, driven by one or more fitness functions. Since EC allows the inherent optimization problem to be seen as a black box, it has led not only to an increased interest by researchers, but to a considerable increase in its practical applications. However, differently than the idealized static synthetic problems commonly seen in the literature, most practical applications have a dynamic nature.

In a dynamic optimization problem (DOP), the optimum (or optima) change with time. A change might be followed by a period of stasis [7]. As observed by Nickabadi et al [16], a change can be either of type I (optimum location changes with time), type II (optimum fitness changes with time but location remains fixed) or type III (both, the location and fitness change with time). A change in such context is subject to *temporal severity* and/or *spatial severity.* Some applications involve tracking one or more peaks moving in a sequential manner through the environment. In such scenario, changes can be of any of the three types above but the temporal severity is usually high (change occurs in short intervals of time) while spatial severity is usually low (peaks move in a smooth fashion, therefore stasis is small or inexistent).

Control applications usually involve such type of change. For example, moving a robot through a 3D space based on sensor data usually involves tracking small variations on the signals occurring in short intervals). In such cases, the most important issues to be addressed are diversity loss (in static optimization, the population tends to collapse towards a narrow region of the fitness landscape, making adaptation difficult) and outdated memory (past knowledge is very useful in EC, but it might be useless when a change occurs). Diversity loss can be mitigated by three different approaches – introducing diversity after a change occurs, maintaining diversity throughout the run or using multi-population – while outdated memory can be tackled by either erasing memory or re-evaluating memory and setting it to either previous or current value (which one is better) [4]. Another important issue for such type of DOP is detecting when a change occurs. The most common approach is to track the fitness value of one or more sentry particles [5, 10]. An alternative is to compute a running average of the fitness function for the best individuals over a certain number of iterations [23].

However, in some other applications (those that involve cyclic changes), the spatial severity is high (peaks "jump" from their previous locations) but the temporal severity is low. Moreover after a certain number of instances, a problem instance seen before can re-appear (in some cases with small distortions). This type of DOP is known as a recurrent (or cyclic) problem [1, 25, 13]. Such type of DOP is usually relied to applications involving optimizing system parameters for streams of data like machine learning [11] or digital watermarking [22].

In [22], it was observed that computational burden can be decreased for DOP involving recurrent problems with the use of a memory of selected solutions. Costly re-optimization operations can be avoided in some cases by properly matching new problems with their corresponding memory solutions and employing these solutions directly. The main reason is that a recurrent problem is a special case of a type III change where the spatial severity is minimal (or inexistent) in the parameter space and small in the fitness space. Moreover, time severity is small or inexistent – the exact moment a new problem instance arrives is known beforehand, e.g. the moment a new image is picked from a stream – that is, stasis can have an indefinite length. Such case of type III change can be considered as a pseudo-type II change. Therefore, even though an optimal solution obtained for a similar previous problem might not be exactly optimal for the new problem (they are near-optimal), there are several practical applications where the computational burden is an important constraint and an insignificant loss in precision is to be preferred as long as it results in a significant decrease in computational burden. Due to its fast convergence, Particle Swarm Optimization (PSO) is preferred in such time-constrained applications.

In this paper, a novel memory-based Dynamic PSO (DPSO) technique is proposed for fast optimization of recurrent dynamic problems. In this approach, a two-level memory of selected solutions and Gaussian Mixture Models (GMM) of their corresponding environments is incrementally built. For each new problem instance, solutions are sampled from this memory and re-evaluated. A statistical test compares the distribution of both fitness values and the best re-evaluated solutions is employed directly if both distributions are considered similar. Otherwise, DPSO [11] is employed in order to optimize parameters. The main research problem addressed in the given work is how to build a comprehensive model of the stream of optimization problems using representative instances of these problems. The research hypothesis is that density estimates of historical solutions found during the optimization phase provide a compact yet flexible representation of a given optimization problem and for this reason, are more suitable for high data rate applications where change in the streams of problems might require a fast adaptation of the given memory. Such flexibility is expected because a density estimate allows for more dynamic update operators than would be possible with a memory of static solutions. Moreover, sentry solutions sampled from this density estimate should provide a more general coverage of a given landscape than selected isolated solutions and are thus more appropriate for matching two problem instances.

A review of DPSO is provided in Section 2. The proposed hybrid GMM-DPSO technique for fast dynamic optimization of long streams of recurrent problems is proposed in Section 3. Section 4 provides proof of concept simulation results and discussions.

2. DYNAMIC PSO

PSO [12] is an optimization heuristics based on the concept of swarm intelligence. In its canonical form, a population (swarm) of candidate solutions (particles) is evolved through a certain number of generations. As its physics equivalent, each particle i in PSO has a position ($\mathbf{x}_i$) in a multidimensional search space and a velocity ($\mathbf{v}_i$). The velocity of the ith particle is adjusted at each generation according to the best location visited by that particle ($\mathbf{p}_i$) and the best location visited by all neighbors of particle i ($\mathbf{p}_g$):

$$\mathbf{v}_i = \chi \times (\mathbf{v}_i + c_1 \times r_1 \times (\mathbf{p}_i - \mathbf{x}_i) + c_2 \times r_2 \times (\mathbf{p}_g - \mathbf{x}_i)) \quad (1)$$

where χ is a constriction factor, chosen to ensure convergence [2], c_1 and c_2 are respectively the cognitive and social acceleration constants (they determine the magnitude of the random forces in the direction of $\mathbf{p}_i$ and $\mathbf{p}_g$ [19]), r_1 and r_2 are two different random numbers in the interval $[0, 1]$. PSO parameters c_1 and c_2 are set to 2.05 while χ is set to 0.7298 as it has been demonstrated theoretically that these values guarantee convergence [19]. The neighborhood of a particle can be restricted to a limited number of particles (L-Best topology) or the whole swarm (G-Best topology).

After that, the velocity is employed in order to update the position of that same particle:

$$\mathbf{x}_i = \mathbf{x}_i + \mathbf{v}_i \quad (2)$$

Issues like outdated memory, lack of change detection mechanism and diversity loss limit the use of the canonical PSO to static problems [3, 5]. It is important to mention that outdated memory can be easily tackled by re-evaluating the fitness function for the new problem instance [4, 10] while change detection can be tackled by the use fixed sentry particles, re-evaluated at each generation [5]. However, tackling diversity loss requires more elaborate techniques, which can be categorized as [24]: increasing diversity after a change, maintaining diversity throughout the run, memory-based schemes and multi-population approach.

The choice of diversity enhancement strategy is tied to properties of the dynamic optimization problem. Problems involving a single optimum drifting in the fitness landscape can be tackled by either increasing diversity after a change (e.g. re-initializing part of the swarm, a technique known as random immigrants [23]) or by maintaining diversity throughout the run. Problems involving multiple peaks drifting in the fitness landscape with the optimal position shifting between these peaks can be tackled with the use of multi-population and is for example, the assumption of the technique proposed by Parrot and Li [17].

Problems involving one or more states re-appearing over time are better tackled through the use of memory-based schemes [25]. The main reason is that in such type of DOP, the transition between one or more problem instances is not smooth as assumed in [17] and the three strategies described above are of no use when the optimum moves away from the area surveyed by the swarm. As observed by Yang and Yao [25], the main strategy to tackle such type of DOP is to preserve relevant solutions in a memory either by an implicit or an explicit memory mechanism and then, recall such solutions for similar future problems. In an implicit memory mechanism, redundant genotype representation (i.e. diploidy-based GA) is employed in order to preserve knowledge about the environment for future similar problems. In an explicit mechanism, precise representation of solutions is employed but an extra storage space is necessary to preserve these solutions for future similar problems. The three major concerns in memory-based optimization systems are: (1) what to store in the memory?; (2) how to organize and update the memory?; (3) how to retrieve solutions from the memory?

In this paper we propose a technique which is based on storing Gaussian Mixture Model of solutions in the optimization space along with their respective global best solutions. The use of probabilistic models in EC is not new. Such approach, known as Estimation of Distribution Algorithms (EDA) [18] is an active research topic. The main advantage of EDA is that such probabilistic models are more effective in preserving historical data than a few isolated high evaluating solutions.

3. FAST OPTIMIZATION OF RECURRENT PROBLEMS USING GAUSSIAN MODELING OF DPSO POPULATIONS

Figure 1 illustrates the proposed memory-based method. In the proposed approach, the basic memory unit is a **probe** and it contains a density estimate of solutions plus the global best solution, obtained after the optimization of a given problem instance. The first memory level is the Short Term Memory (STM) which contains a single probe, obtained during the optimization of a single problem instance and provides fast recall for situations where a block of similar problem instances appear sequentially (e.g. a sequence of practically identical frames in a video sequence, except for noise). The second memory level is the Long Term Memory (LTM) which contains multiple probes obtained in the optimization of different problem instances and allows recalling solutions for problems reappearing in an unpredictable manner.

Given a stream of optimization problems, an attempt to recall the STM is performed first. During a recall, solutions are re-sampled from the density estimate and re-evaluated (along with the global best solution) in the new problem instance. The Kolmogorov-Smirnov statistical test is employed in order to measure the difference between the sampled and re-evaluated sets of fitness values. If they are similar, this means that the given problem instance is a recurrent one and therefore, the best re-evaluated solution is employed right away, avoiding a costly re-optimization operation. If the distributions are not similar, the same process (sampling/re-evaluation/statistical test) is repeated for each probe in the LTM until either a similarity between both distributions of fitness values is found or all probes have been tested.

In such case, the solutions sampled from the STM probe are used as a starting point for a new round of optimization. The L-best DPSO algorithm described in [11] is used for this purpose. The change detection module was adapted to the memory recall mechanism employed in the proposed approach. Although each problem instance is static, this DPSO variant allows tackling multi-modal optimization problems and the motivation behind the proposed technique is tackling dynamic optimization of recurrent problems in practical applications (which might imply in multi-modal landscapes). After that, a mixture model of the fitness landscape is estimated using the GMM approach of Figueiredo and Jain [8]. The **position** and **fitness** data of all intermediary solutions, found in all generations are employed for this purpose. The reason for using all intermediary solutions and not selected solutions (e.g. best particle positions) is that these solutions allow a more general model of the fitness landscape. That is, local best data usually results in density estimates that are over-fit to a specific problem.

This mixture model along with the global best solution will form a probe, to be stored in the STM (replacing the previous probe) and updated into the LTM. The LTM update consists of either a merge between the new probe and a probe in the memory (if they are similar) or an insert (if either the LTM is empty or no similar probe has been found). In such case, if the memory limit has been reached, an older probe is deleted (we propose deleting the probe which resulted in the smallest number of successful recalls up to that instant).

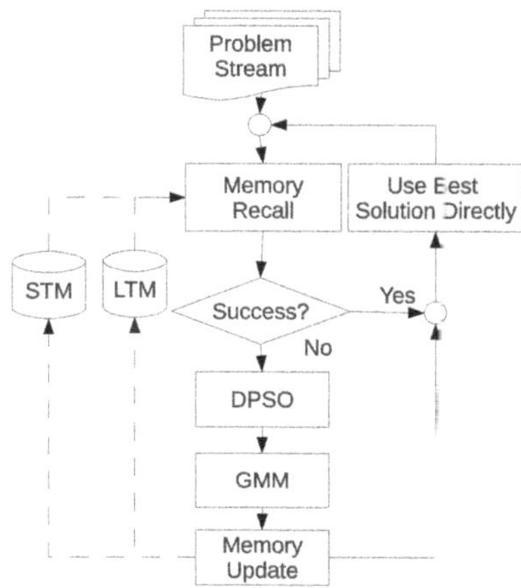

Figure 1: Diagram of the proposed method.

3.1 Gaussian mixture modeling of fitness landscapes

The main reason for building and storing a model of all solutions found during the optimization of a problem instance rather than storing selected solutions is that the former allows a more compact and precise representation of the fitness landscape than individual solutions. As explained before, GMM [8] is employed for this purpose since it is a powerful tool for modeling multi-modal data (which makes the proposed technique robust for multi-modal optimization as well). Different than other clustering techniques such as k-means, GMM allows to model overlap among data densities, and provides more accurate (complex) modeling of data distributions. A mixture model is a linear combination of a finite number of models

$$p(\boldsymbol{x}|\Theta) = \sum_{j=1}^{K} \alpha_j p(\boldsymbol{x}|\theta_j) \tag{3}$$

where $p(\boldsymbol{x}|\Theta)$ is the probability density function (pdf) of a continuous random vector $\boldsymbol{x}$ given a mixture model Θ,

K is the number of mixtures, α_j and θ_j are the mixing weights and parameters of the jth model (with $0 < \alpha_j \leq 1$ and $\sum_{j=1}^{K} \alpha_j = 1$). The mixture model parameters $\Theta = \{(\alpha_1, \theta_1), ..., (\alpha_K, \theta_K)\}$ are estimated using the particle position ($\boldsymbol{x}$) and fitness ($f(\boldsymbol{x})$) of all particles through all generations.

The use of density models in EC is not new. However, such strategy of using both phenotypic and genotypic data to estimate the models is novel. Another major difference between the proposed use of probabilistic models and those seen in the EDA literature is that in the proposed approach, all solutions found in the course of an optimization task are employed in order to estimate the model of the fitness landscape. In the EDA literature instead, selected (best fit) solutions at each generation are employed in model estimation, as a selection strategy. In the proposed approach, a density estimate is employed as a mean of matching new problems with previously seen problems.

3.2 Memory update

The memory is due to be updated after the mixture model has been created. As mentioned before, the basic memory element in the proposed approach is a probe. Updating the STM is trivial, it requires basically deleting the current probe and inserting the new probe since the STM should provide means of recalling the last case of optimization, for situations involving a block of similar optimization problems appearing in sequence.

The LTM instead, must provide a general model of the stream of optimization problems. Since all LTM probes must be recalled before optimization is triggered, the size of the LTM must be kept to a minimum in order to avoid a situation where the cost of an unsuccessful recall is greater than the cost of full optimization. For this reason, we propose an adaptive update mechanism. In the proposed mechanism, when the LTM is due to be updated, the $C2$ distance metric [21] (which provides a good balance between computational burden and precision) is employed in order to measure the similarity between the GMM of the new probe and that of each of the probes in the LTM. The new probe is merged with the most similar probe in LTM if this distance is smaller than a given threshold. Otherwise, the new probe is inserted (the probe with smallest number of successful recalls is deleted if the LTM size limit has been reached). The insert threshold is computed based on the mean minimum distance between new probes and probes on the LTM for the last T LTM updates (μ_δ^t). That is, an insert will only occur if $C2 - \mu_\delta^t$ is greater than the standard deviation for the same time-frame (σ_δ^t).

The Hennig [9] technique, which is based on the use of Bhattacharyya distance and does not require the use of historical data, is employed in order to merge two GMMs. The Bhattacharyya distance is defined as:

$$\bar{\boldsymbol{\Sigma}} = \frac{1}{2}(\boldsymbol{\Sigma}_1 + \boldsymbol{\Sigma}_2) \tag{4}$$

$$d_B(\Theta_1, \Theta_2) = (\boldsymbol{\mu}_1 - \boldsymbol{\mu}_2)^T \bar{\boldsymbol{\Sigma}}^{-1} (\boldsymbol{\mu}_1 - \boldsymbol{\mu}_2) + \frac{1}{2}\log\left(\frac{|\frac{1}{2}(\boldsymbol{\Sigma}_1 + \boldsymbol{\Sigma}_2)|}{\sqrt{|\boldsymbol{\Sigma}_1||\boldsymbol{\Sigma}_2|}}\right) \tag{5}$$

where μ_i is a mean vector and Σ_i is a covariance matrix.

In Hennig's approach, given a tuning constant $d^* < 1$, the two components with maximum Bhattacharyya distance are merged iteratively as long as $e^{-d_B} < d^*$ for at least one component. We propose a slight modification, which is to merge the two components with minimum distance instead, in order to get a more incremental variation in the mixture components.

If the number of mixture components after the merge operation is still greater than a limit, unmerged components from the older mixture are deleted (the old unmerged component with the highest Bhattacharyya distance from all other components is delete iteratively until the limit has been achieved).

Algorithm 1 summarizes the memory update mechanism. After the end of a round of re-optimization, a new mixture (Θ_N) is estimated based on position and fitness values of all particles from all generations during the optimization process (step 1). The estimated mixture plus the global best solution will form a probe to be added to the STM (any previous STM probe is deleted, step 2). Then, if the length of the vector containing the last n minimum $C2$ distances between new probes and probes in the LTM ($\boldsymbol{\delta}$) is smaller than T (step 3), its mean and standard deviation ($\mu_{\boldsymbol{\delta}}^t$ and $\sigma_{\boldsymbol{\delta}}^t$) are initialized based on pre-defined values ($\mu_{\boldsymbol{\delta}}^0$ and $\sigma_{\boldsymbol{\delta}}^0$, steps 4 and 5). Otherwise, $\mu_{\boldsymbol{\delta}}^t$ and $\sigma_{\boldsymbol{\delta}}^t$ are computed based on $\boldsymbol{\delta}$ (steps 7 and 8). After that, the minimum $C2$ distance between new probe and probes in the LTM is added to $\boldsymbol{\delta}$ (steps 10 and 11). The new probe is inserted into the memory if the difference between the minimum $C2$ distance and $\mu_{\boldsymbol{\delta}}^t$ is greater than the standard deviation ($\sigma_{\boldsymbol{\delta}}^t$, steps 12 to 16). It important to notice that before the insert, the LTM probe with smallest number of recalls is deleted if memory limit has been reached. Otherwise the new probe is merged with the most similar probe in the LTM (steps 18 and 19). If the limit of vector $\boldsymbol{\delta}$ has been reached, its first element is deleted (steps 21 to 23).

3.3 Memory recall

Basically, the recall mechanism is the same for both levels of memory. The only difference is that the LTM contains more probes than the STM and for this reason, this process might be repeated for many LTM probes until either all probes have been tested of a successful recall has occurred. For a given probe, N_s solutions are sampled from its mixture model:

$$\boldsymbol{X}_s = \boldsymbol{\mu}_j + \boldsymbol{\Lambda}_j^{\frac{1}{2}} \boldsymbol{U}_j \boldsymbol{R}_s \tag{6}$$

where $\boldsymbol{X}_s$ is a sampled solution, s is the index of a solution sampled for the component j in the mixture ($\lfloor (N_s \alpha_j) + 0.5 \rfloor$ solutions are sampled per component), $\boldsymbol{\Lambda}_j$ and $\boldsymbol{U}_j$ are the eigen-decomposition of $\boldsymbol{\Sigma}_j$ ($\boldsymbol{\Sigma}_j = \boldsymbol{U}_j \boldsymbol{\Lambda}_j \boldsymbol{U}_j^{-1}$) and $\boldsymbol{R}_s$ is a vector with the same length as $\boldsymbol{\mu}_j$ whose elements are sampled from a normal distribution $N(0, \mathbf{I})$, being $\mathbf{I}$ the identity matrix.

It is important to observe that both, position and fitness values are sampled simultaneously. Then, the sampled solutions (along with the corresponding global best) are reevaluated for the new problem instance. A Kolmogorov- Smirnov statistical test is employed in order to compare the sampled and re-evaluated fitness values. If they are below a critical value for a given confidence level, the recall is considered to be successful and the best recalled solution is employed right away, avoiding a costly re-optimization. If no probe (neither in the STM nor in the LTM) results in a successful recall, a

Algorithm 1 Memory update mechanism.

Inputs:

k_{max} – maximum number of components with $\alpha_j > 0$.

$\mathfrak{M}_S$ – Short Term Memory.

$\mathfrak{M} = \{\mathfrak{M}_1, ..., \mathfrak{M}_{|\mathfrak{M}|}\}$ – Long Term Memory.

$\mathfrak{D}$ – optimization history (set of all particle positions and fitness values for new problem instance).

$L_{\mathfrak{M}}$ – maximum number of probes in LTM.

$\boldsymbol{\delta}$ – last T minimum $C2$ distances between a new probe and probes in the LTM.

$|\boldsymbol{\delta}|$ – number of elements in $\boldsymbol{\delta}$.

T – maximum size of $\boldsymbol{\delta}$.

μ_{δ}^0, σ_{δ}^0 – initial mean and standard deviation of $\boldsymbol{\delta}$.

Output:

Updated memory.

```
Estimate Θ_N using 𝔇 [8].
Add Θ_N and p_g to 𝔐_S.
if |δ| < T then
    μ_δ^t ← μ_δ^0
    σ_δ^t ← σ_δ^0
else
    μ_δ^t ← (1/|δ|) Σ_{i=1}^{|δ|} δ_i
    σ_δ^t ← sqrt( Σ_{i=1}^{n} (δ_i − μ_δ^t)^2 / |δ| )
end if
i* ← argmin_i{C2(Θ_N, Θ_i)}, ∀Θ_i ∈ 𝔐
δ ← δ ∪ C2(Θ_N, Θ_i*)
if C2(Θ_N, Θ_i*) − μ_δ^t > σ_δ^t then
    if |𝔐| = L_𝔐 then
        Remove LTM probe with smallest number of successful recalls.
    end if
    Add Θ_N and p_g to 𝔐
else
    Merge(Θ_i*, Θ_N) (section 3.2)
    Purge merged mixture in case number of elements exceed k_max.
end if
if |δ| > T then
    Remove δ_1.
end if
```

part of STM re-sampled solutions is injected into the swarm and optimization is triggered for that problem instance.

4. EXPERIMENTAL RESULTS

4.1 Application

The proposed fast optimization technique will be validated in the optimization of embedding parameters for a bi-tonal watermarking system [22]. This is an interesting problem because a given watermark needs to be robust against attacks but at the same time result in minimum visual interference in the host image and this trade-off can be manipulated by carefully adjusting heuristic parameters in the watermark embedder. Generally speaking, in this watermarking system, a cover bi-tonal image is partitioned into several blocks, the flippability score of each pixel is computed using a moving window, the pixels are shuffled according to shuffling seed and each bit of the given bit stream is embedded into each block of the cover image through manipulation of the quantized number of black pixels. The quantization step size (Q) determines the robustness of the watermark and since this watermarking technique allows the embedding of multiple watermarks (with different levels of robustness), we will embed two watermarks a fragile one (which can be employed to enforce image integrity) with a fixed value for its quantization step size of ($Q_F = 2$) and robust one (which can be employed to enforce image authenticity) with an adjustable quantization step size $Q_R = Q_F + \Delta_Q$ where Δ_Q is a parameter to be optimized. More details can be found in [22]. Four parameters need to be optimized: the partition block size which is an integer between 1 and the maximum attainable size for the given image as seen in [15]; the size of the window used in the flippability analysis, which can be either 3×3, 5×5, 7×7 or 9×9; the difference between the quantization step size for the robust and fragile watermarks (Δ_Q), which is an even number between 2 and 150; and the index of the shuffling key (we proposed using a pool of 16 possible shuffling keys, thus this index is an integer between 1 and 16).

The fitness function is a combination of the Bit Correct Ratio (BCR) between the embedded and detected watermarks (both, robust and fragile), and Distance Reciprocal Distortion Measure (DRDM) [14], which measures the quality of the watermarked image (more details can be found in [22]). The three fitness values are aggregated using Chebyshev approach [6]:

$$F(\mathbf{x}) = max_{i=1,..,3}\{(1-\omega_1)(\alpha_s DRDM - r_1), \\ (1-\omega_2)(1 - BCR_R - r_2), \\ (1-\omega_3)(1 - BCR_F - r_3)\} \quad (7)$$

where α_s is the scaling factor of the quality measurement $DRDM$, BCR_R is the robustness measurement of the robust watermark, BCR_F is the robustness measurement of the fragile watermark, ω_i is the weight of the ith objective with $\omega_i = \frac{1}{3}, \forall_i$, r_i is the reference point of objective i.

4.2 Validation protocol

The BancTec logo (Figure 2a), which has 26×36 pixels will be employed as robust watermark and the Université du Québec logo (Figure 2b), which has 36×26 pixels will be employed as fragile watermark.

(a) (b)

Figure 2: Bi-tonal logos used as watermarks. (a) 26×36 BancTec logo. (b) 36×26 Université du Québec logo.

Oulu University's MediaTeam [20] (OULU-1999) database is employed as image stream. This database was scanned at 300 dpi with 24-bit color encoding. Since the baseline watermarking system is bi-tonal, the OULU-1999 database was binarized using the same protocol as in [22]. As some of its images lack the capacity necessary to embed the watermarks described above, a reject rule was applied: all images containing less than 1872 pixels with Structural Neighborhood

Distortion Metric (SNDM) [15] greater than zero were discarded. This rule resulted in the elimination of 15 of the original 512 images. The database was split in two subsets: a smaller one for development purposes, containing 100 images and a larger one, for validation purposes, containing 397 images. Images were assigned to these sets randomly. Table 1 shows the structure of both subsets.

Table 1: OULU-1999 database structure.

Category	Number of Images	
	TRAIN	TEST
Addresslist	0	6
Advertisement	5	19
Article	51	180
Businesscards	1	10
Check	0	3
Color Segmentation	1	7
Correspondence	6	18
Dictionary	1	9
Form	9	14
Line Drawing	0	10
Manual	6	29
Math	4	13
Music	0	4
Newsletter	4	37
Outline	4	13
Phonebook	4	3
Program Listing	2	10
Street Map	0	5
Terrainmap	2	7
Total:	**100**	**397**

As can be seen in Figure 3, the images in this database are considerably heterogeneous.

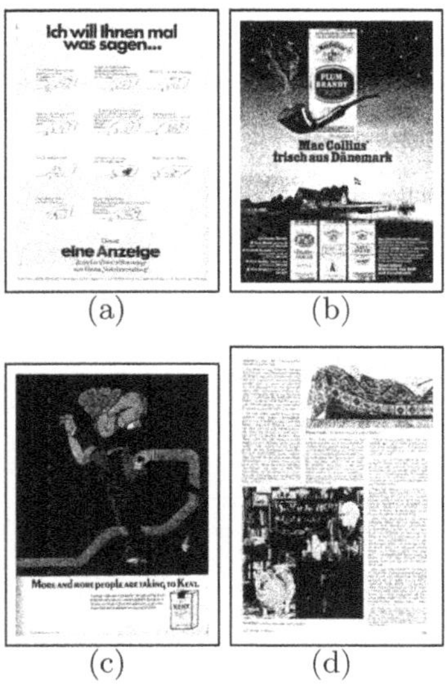

Figure 3: Images from OULU-1999-TRAIN. (a) Image 1. (b) Image 2. (c) Image 5. (d) Image 6.

The number of previous updates T employed to compute the adaptive threshold will be set to 10. The initial mean and standard deviation of the minimum distance were set to 361.7 and 172.3 respectively. These values were obtained by running the proposed technique in a "fill-up" mode (forcing re-optimization and LTM insert for every image in the OULU-1999-TRAIN subset). The resulting minimum $C2$ distances of these inserts were employed in order to compute these initial values.

The metrics employed in order to assess the computational performance are the average number of fitness evaluations per image ($AFPI$), the total number of fitness evaluations required to optimize the whole image stream (F_{Evals}) and the decrease in the number of fitness evaluations (DFE), computed as:

$$DFE = 1 - \frac{F_{Evals,M}}{F_{Evals,F}} \tag{8}$$

where $F_{Evals,M}$ is the cumulative number of fitness evaluations for the memory based approach and $F_{Evals,F}$ is the cumulative number of fitness evaluations for full optimization.

The reference points for the Chebyshev Weighted Aggregation were obtained through sensitivity analysis of the OULU-1999-TRAIN subset and were set to $r_1 = r_2 = r_3 = 0.01$. The scaling factor of the DRDM (α_r) was also obtained through sensitivity analysis using the training subset and was to 0.53.

During recall, 19 solutions are re-sampled from each probe, which are re-evaluated along with the global best solution, resulting in 20 sentry particles. The confidence level (α) of the KS statistic was set to the same value employed in [22], which is 0.95 and corresponds to a critical value (D_α) of 0.43. The LTM size is limited to 20 probes. The PSO parameters employed on full optimization are the same defined in [22] (20 particles, neighborhood size of 3, optimization stops if the global best has not improved for 20 generations). Cropping of 1% of the image surface was employed during the optimization since such attack can effectively remove a non-optimized watermark. The proposed approach is compared with a previous approach (case-based), which relies on a memory of selected solutions [22] to demonstrate the main advantages of employing a memory of mixture models.

4.3 Simulation results

The GMM-based approach resulted in a significant decrease in computational burden when compared to full optimization and even compared to the case-based approach (Table 2).

Despite the decrease in computational burden, the watermarking performance of the GMM-based approach is practically the same of the other two approaches (Table 3).

These results demonstrate that the memory of mixture models can cope better with the variations in the stream of optimization problems. Since the case-based probes are more tuned to the problems that generated them, they are more sensitive to small variations in a given recurrent landscape caused by noise. A clear sign of this is that the smaller number of fitness evaluations was obtained even though for two of the watermarking performance metrics there was even an improvement when compared to the case-based approach. Moreover, for both cases, the watermarking performance is similar to that of full optimization, which illustrates the applicability of the proposed technique. However it is important to notice that the basic assumption is that the application can be formulated as the problem of optimizing a stream of optimization problems with some of the problems re-appearing over time, subject to noise.

Table 2: Computational cost of the proposed technique compared to case-based approach and full optimization. $AFPI$ is the average number of fitness evaluations per image where the mean μ and standard deviation σ are presented as $\mu(\sigma)$. F_{Evals} is the cumulative number of fitness evaluations required to optimize the whole stream and DFE is the decrease in the number of fitness evaluations compared to full optimization.

Subset	Full PSO		Case-based			GMM-based		
	$AFPI$	F_{Evals}	$AFPI$	F_{Evals}	DFE	$AFPI$	F_{Evals}	DFE
TRAIN	887 (340)	88740	351 (455)	35100	60.5%	274 (447)	27420	69.1%
TEST	860 (310)	341520	177 (351)	70300	79.4%	83 (213)	32920	90.4%

Table 3: Watermarking performance of the proposed technique compared to case-based approach and full optimization. Here, † is the $DRDM$, ‡ is the BCR robust, § is the BCR fragile. For all values, the mean μ and standard deviation σ per image are presented in the following form: $\mu(\sigma)$. $DRDM$ is presented with two decimal points and BCR is presented in percentage (%) with one decimal point.

Subset	Full PSO			Case-based			GMM-based		
	†	‡	§	†	‡	§	†	‡	§
TRAIN	0.03 (0.03)	98.4 (2.1)	99.7 (0.6)	0.03 (0.03)	97.9 (2.6)	99.6 (1.0)	0.03 (0.03)	97.5 (2.8)	99.4 (1.0)
TEST	0.03 (0.04)	98.4 (2.2)	99.6 (0.6)	0.03 (0.03)	97.2 (3.6)	99 (1.6)	0.03 (0.03)	96.7 (4.0)	99.1 (1.5)

4.4 Discussion

The proposed technique was assessed in a proof of concept intelligent watermarking problem. These simulation results demonstrate that the proposed technique allows decreasing computational burden of dynamic optimization with little impact on precision for applications involving the optimization of a stream of recurrent problems. For example, in Figure 4, which shows the best fitness value for each generation for both, full optimization and the proposed approach, it is possible to observe that although the proposed technique resulted in less generations, the best recalled solutions (square and triangle marks) are very close to those obtained by full optimization.

The improvement compared with a previous (case-based) version of the proposed technique is also worth of notice and justifies the storage of GMM of solutions rather than selected solutions. Such improvement is mainly due to the fact that selected solutions tend to be over-fit to the optimization problems that generated them. For this reason, these sentries cover a limited region of the fitness landscape and tend to be more sensitive to small variations in the fitness values of the optimum caused by noise (as explained in our pseudo-type II formulation of such scenario).

Another advantage of the proposed approach is that it results in a more adaptive model than that created by the case-based approach and is thus more appropriate for applications where the stream of optimization problems to be optimized is heterogeneous (that is, the recurrent problems might be subject to noise). This is mainly due to the proposed adaptive memory management technique, which is novel and can be considered as one of the main contributions of this paper since it allows the memory to incrementally adapt to new trends on the stream of optimization problems.

5. CONCLUSION

A hybrid GMM/PSO dynamic optimization technique was proposed in this paper. The main objective of the proposed approach is to tackle optimization of streams of recurrent optimization problems. Such formulation of dynamic optimization is applicable to many practical applications, mainly those related to optimizing heuristic parameters of systems that process streamed data such as batch processing of images, video processing, incremental machine learning.

In the proposed technique, a two-level adaptive memory containing GMMs of solutions in the optimization space and global best solutions is incrementally built. For each new problem instance, solutions are re-sampled from this memory and employed as sentries in order to (1) measure the similarity between the new problem instance and previous instances that had already resulted in optimization; (2) provide ready-to-use solutions for recurrent problems, avoiding an unnecessary re-optimization.

It is worth noticing that the proposed technique resulted in a decrease of 90.4% in computational burden (compared to full optimization) with minimum impact on accuracy in an application involving a heterogeneous stream of document images. Although these results are still preliminary, they are comparable to results obtained in a previous version of the proposed approach already published, with the main difference that the experiments reported in this paper involved a much more challenging database which results in more varied (noisy) optimization problems.

As a future work we propose an evaluation in a larger stream of document images and also in synthetic benchmark functions which could allow a better understanding of the mechanisms behind the proposed approach.

6. ACKNOWLEDGMENTS

This work has been supported by National Sciences and Engineering Research Council of Canada and BancTec Canada Inc.

7. REFERENCES

[1] G. J. Barlow and S. F. Smith. Using memory models to improve adaptive efficiency in dynamic problems. In *IEEE Symposium on Computational Intelligence in Scheduling*, Nashville, March 2009.

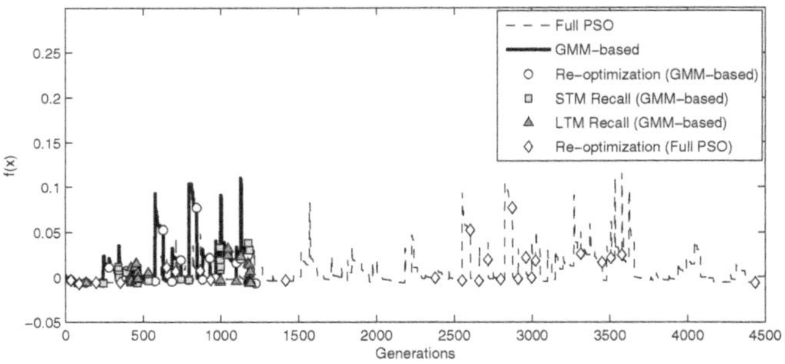

Figure 4: Tracking of best fitness for each generation using dataset OULU-1999-TRAIN.

[2] M. Blackwell. Particle swarms and population diversity. *Soft Comput.*, 9(11):793–802, 2005.

[3] T. Blackwell. *Evolutionary Computation in Dynamic Environments*, chapter Particle swarm optimization in dynamic environments. Springer, 2007.

[4] T. Blackwell and J. Branke. Multiswarms, exclusion, and anti-convergence in dynamic environments. *IEEE Trans. Evolutionary Computation*, 10(4):459–472, 2006.

[5] A. Carlisle and G. Dozier. Tracking changing extrema with adaptive particle swarm optimizer. *Proceedings of the 5th Biannual World Automation Congress, 2002.*, 13:265–270, 2002.

[6] Y. Collette and P. Siarry. On the sensitivity of aggregative multiobjective optimization methods. *CIT*, 16(1):1–13, 2008.

[7] M. Farina, K. Deb, and P. Amato. Dynamic multiobjective optimization problems: test cases, approximations, and applications. *IEEE Trans. Evolutionary Computation*, 8(5):425–442, 2004.

[8] M. A. T. Figueiredo and A. K. Jain. Unsupervised learning of finite mixture models. *IEEE Transactions on Pattern Analysis and Machine Intelligence*, 24:381–396, 2000.

[9] C. Hennig. Methods for merging gaussian mixture components. *Advanced Data Analysis and Classification*, 4:3–34, 2010.

[10] X. Hu and R. Eberhart. Adaptive particle swarm optimization: detection and response to dynamic systems. *Proceedings of the 2002 Congress on Evolutionary Computation. CEC '02.*, 2:1666–1670, 2002.

[11] M. N. Kapp, R. Sabourin, and P. Maupin. A dynamic model selection strategy for support vector machine classifiers. *Applied Soft Computing (accepted for publication)*, March 2011.

[12] J. Kennedy. Some issues and practices for particle swarm. In *Proc. IEEE Swarm Intelligence Symposium*, 2007.

[13] X. Li and K. H. Dam. Comparing particle swarms for tracking extrema in dynamic environments. In *Proceedings of the 2003 Congress on Evolutionary Computation. CEC '03.*, volume 3, pages 1772–1779, Dec. 2003.

[14] H. Lu, A. C. Kot, and Y. Q. Shi. Distance-reciprocal distortion measure for binary document images. *Signal Processing Letters, IEEE*, 11(2):228 – 231, February 2004.

[15] E. Muharemagic. *Adaptive Two-Level Watermarking for Binary Document Images.* PhD thesis, Florida Atlantic University, December 2004.

[16] A. Nickabadi, M. M. Ebadzadeh, and R. Safabakhsh. DNPSO: A dynamic niching particle swarm optimizer for multi-modal optimization. In *IEEE World Congress on Computational Intelligence*, pages 26–32, June 2008.

[17] D. Parrott and X. Li. A particle swarm model for tracking multiple peaks in a dynamic environment using speciation. In *Proceedings of the 2004 Congress on Evolutionary Computation. CEC '04.*, volume 1, pages 98–103, June 2004.

[18] M. Pelikan, D. E. Goldberg, and F. G. Lobo. A survey of optimization by building and using probabilistic models. *Comput. Optim. Appl.*, 21(1):5–20, 2002.

[19] R. Poli, J. Kennedy, and T. Blackwell. Particle swarm optimisation: an overview. *Swarm Intelligence Journal*, 1(1):33–57, June 2007.

[20] J. Sauvola and H. Kauniskangas. MediaTeam Document Database II, a CD-ROM collection of document images, University of Oulu, Finland, 1999.

[21] G. Sfikas, C. Constantinopoulos, A. Likas, and N. P. Galatsanos. An analytic distance metric for gaussian mixture models with application in image retrieval. In *Proceedings of the 15th international conference on Artificial neural networks: formal models and their applications - Volume Part II*, ICANN'05, pages 835–840, Berlin, Heidelberg, 2005. Springer-Verlag.

[22] E. Vellasques, R. Sabourin, and E. Granger. A high throughput system for intelligent watermarking of bi-tonal images. *Applied Soft Computing*, 11(8):5215–5229, December 2011.

[23] H. Wang, D. Wang, and S. Yang. Triggered memory-based swarm optimization in dynamic environments. In *EvoWorkshops*, pages 637–646, 2007.

[24] S. Yang. Population-based incremental learning with memory scheme for changing environments. In *GECCO '05: Proceedings of the 2005 conference on Genetic and evolutionary computation*, pages 711–718, New York, NY, USA, 2005. ACM.

[25] S. Yang and X. Yao. Population-based incremental learning with associative memory for dynamic environments. *IEEE Transactions on Evolutionary Computation*, 12(5):542–561, Oct. 2008.

Multi-Objective Particle Swarm Optimisation (PSO) for Feature Selection

Bing Xue Mengjie Zhang Will N. Browne

School of Engineering and Computer Science
Victoria University of Wellington
PO Box 600, Wellington 6140, New Zealand
{Bing.Xue, Mengjie.Zhang,Will.Browne}@ecs.vuw.ac.nz

ABSTRACT

Feature selection (FS) is an important data preprocessing technique, which has two goals of minimising the classification error and minimising the number of features selected. Based on particle swarm optimisation (PSO), this paper proposes two multi-objective algorithms for selecting the Pareto front of non-dominated solutions (feature subsets) for classification. The first algorithm introduces the idea of non-dominated sorting based multi-objective genetic algorithm II into PSO for FS. In the second algorithm, multi-objective PSO uses the ideas of crowding, mutation and dominance to search for the Pareto front solutions. The two algorithms are compared with two single objective FS methods and a conventional FS method on nine datasets. Experimental results show that both proposed algorithms can automatically evolve a smaller number of features and achieve better classification performance than using all features and feature subsets obtained from the two single objective methods and the conventional method. Both the continuous and the binary versions of PSO are investigated in the two proposed algorithms and the results show that continuous version generally achieves better performance than the binary version. The second new algorithm outperforms the first algorithm in both continuous and binary versions.

Categories and Subject Descriptors

I.2 [**Computing Methodologies**]: Artificial Intelligence

General Terms

Algorithm, Performance

Keywords

Feature selection, particle swarm optimisation, multi-objective optimisation

1. INTRODUCTION

In many problems such as classification, a large number of features are introduced to well describe the target concepts. However, the large number of features causes the problem of "the curse of dimensionality", which is a major obstacle in classification. Meanwhile, not all of the features are useful for classification. Irrelevant and redundant features may even increase the classification error rate. Feature selection (FS) could reduce the number of features by eliminating irrelevant and redundant features, and thus result in enhanced efficiency and/or increased classification performance [5].

Based on whether a learning algorithm is included in the training process or not, existing FS approaches can be broadly classified into two categories: filter and wrapper approaches. A filter FS approach is conducted as a preprocessing procedure and the search process is independent of a learning algorithm. In wrapper approaches, a learning algorithm is part of the evaluation function to determine the goodness of the selected feature subset. Wrappers can usually achieve better results than filters while filters are more general and computationally less expensive than wrappers [14].

A FS algorithm explores the search space of different feature combinations to reduce the number of features and simultaneously optimise the classification performance. In FS, the size of the search space for n features is 2^n. So in most situations, it is impractical to conduct an exhaustive search [14]. Therefore, the search strategy is the key part in FS. Different search techniques have been applied to FS such as greedy search, but most of them suffer from the problem of becoming stuck in local optima and/or high computational cost [25, 17]. Therefore, an efficient global search technique is needed to develop a good FS algorithm.

Evolutionary computation techniques are well-known for their global search ability, and have been applied to the FS problems. These include particle swarm optimisation (PSO) [23, 26], genetic algorithms (GAs) [27] and genetic programming (GP) [20]. Compared with GAs and GP, PSO is easier to implement, has fewer parameters, computationally less expensive, and can converge more quickly [12]. Due to these advantages, two versions of PSO, namely continuous PSO and binary PSO, have been used for FS problems [23, 26, 19]. However, no study has been conducted to investigate the difference of using continuous PSO and binary PSO for FS. FS problems have two goals, which are maximising the classification performance (minimising the classification error rate) and minimising the number of features. These two objectives are usually conflicting and there is a trade-off between them. However, most of the existing FS approaches, including PSO based approaches, aim to maximise the classification performance only. Therefore, it is sought to use

GECCO'12, July 7–11, 2012, Philadelphia, Pennsylvania, USA.

PSO to develop a multi-objective FS approach to simultaneously minimising the classification error rate and minimising the number of features selected.

1.1 Goals

The overall goal of this paper is to develop a PSO based multi-objective FS approach to classification problems with the expectation of obtaining a set of non-dominated solutions, which contain a small number of features and achieve better classification performance than using all features. To achieve this goal, we will firstly develop two single objective FS methods with a fitness function considering classification error rate and the number of features. We will then develop two new FS methods based on two multi-objective PSO algorithms, *non-dominated sorting PSO (NSPSO)* using the idea of non-dominated sorting based multi-objective genetic algorithm II (NSGAII) and *CMDPSO* using the ideas of crowding, mutation and dominance. These proposed FS algorithms will be examined on benchmark problems of varying difficulty. Specifically, we will investigate

- whether single objective PSO based FS algorithms can select a small number of features and improve classification performance over using all features,
- whether the NSPSO based multi-objective FS algorithm can evolve a Pareto front of non-dominated solutions with a smaller number of features and better classification performance than single objective FS algorithms,
- whether a CMDPSO based multi-objective FS algorithm can obtain a better set of non-dominated solutions than NSPSO and outperform the single objective FS algorithms, and
- which of the two versions of PSO, continuous PSO and binary PSO, can achieve better performance for FS.

2. BACKGROUND

2.1 Particle Swarm Optimisation (PSO)

PSO is an evolutionary computation technique proposed by Kennedy and Eberhart in 1995 [10, 21]. In PSO, a population, called a *swarm*, of candidate solutions are encoded as particles in the search space. PSO starts with the random initialisation of a population of particles. The whole swarm move in the search space to search for the best solution by updating the position of each particle based on the experience of its own and its neighbouring particles [10, 21]. During movement, the current position of particle i is represented by a vector $x_i = (x_{i1}, x_{i2}, ..., x_{iD})$, where D is the dimensionality of the search space. The velocity of particle i is represented as $v_i = (v_{i1}, v_{i2}, ..., v_{iD})$, which is limited by a predefined maximum velocity, v_{max} and $v_{id}^t \in [-v_{max}, v_{max}]$. The best previous position of a particle is recorded as the personal best *pbest* and the best position obtained by the population thus far is called *gbest*. Based on *pbest* and *gbest*, PSO searches for the optimal solution by updating the velocity and the position of each particle according to the following equations:

$$x_{id}^{t+1} = x_{id}^t + v_{id}^{t+1} \tag{1}$$

$$\begin{aligned} v_{id}^{t+1} &= w * v_{id}^t + c_1 * r_{1i} * (p_{id} - x_{id}^t) \\ &+ c_2 * r_{2i} * (p_{gd} - x_{id}^t) \end{aligned} \tag{2}$$

where t denotes the tth iteration. $d \in D$ denotes the dth dimension in the search space. w is inertia weight. c_1 and c_2 are acceleration constants. r_{1i} and r_{2i} are random values uniformly distributed in [0, 1]. p_{id} and p_{gd} represent the elements of *pbest* and *gbest* in the dth dimension.

PSO was originally proposed for solving continuous problems [10]. However, many problems, such as FS, occur in a discrete search space. Therefore, Kennedy and Eberhart [11] developed a binary PSO (BPSO) for discrete problems. In BPSO, x_{id}, p_{id} and p_{gd} are restricted to 1 or 0. The velocity in BPSO indicates the probability of the corresponding element in the position vector taking value 1. A sigmoid function $s(v_{id})$ is introduced to transform v_{id} to the range of (0, 1). BPSO updates the position of each particle according to the following formulae:

$$x_{id} = \begin{cases} 1, & \text{if } rand() < s(v_{id}) \\ 0, & otherwise \end{cases} \tag{3}$$

where

$$s(v_{id}) = \frac{1}{1 + e^{-v_{id}}} \tag{4}$$

where $rand()$ is a random number selected from a uniform distribution in [0,1].

BPSO preserves the fundamental concept of the PSO algorithm. However, not all important characteristics of the PSO algorithm are completely present in BPSO [11].

2.2 Multi-Objective Optimisation

Multi-objective optimisation involves simultaneously optimising two or more conflicting objective functions. In mathematical terms, the formulae for a minimisition problem with multiple objective functions can be written as:

$$minimise \quad F(x) = [f_1(x), f_2(x), \ ... \ , f_k(x)] \tag{5}$$

subject to

$$g_i(x) \leqslant 0, \ i = 1, 2, \ ... \ m \tag{6}$$

$$h_i(x) \leqslant 0, \ i = 1, 2, \ ... \ l \tag{7}$$

where x is the vector of decision variables, $f_i(x)$ is a function of x, k is the number of objective functions to be minimised, $g_i(x)$ and $h_i(x)$ are the constraint functions of the problem.

The quality of a solution in multi-objective problems is explained in terms of trade-offs between two or more conflicting objectives. Let y and z be two solutions of the above k-objective minimisation problem. If the following conditions are met, one can say y dominates z (or z is dominated by y, or y is better than z):

$$\forall i : f_i(y) \leqslant f_i(z) \quad and \quad \exists f_i(y) < f_i(z) \tag{8}$$

When y is not dominated by any other solutions, y is referred to as a Pareto-optimal solution. The set of all Pareto-optimal solutions forms the trade-off surface in the search space, the Pareto front. An multi-objective algorithm is designed to search for a set of non-dominated solutions.

FS can be expressed as a two-objective minimisation problems with the objectives of minimising the number of features and the classification error rate.

2.3 Recent Work Related to FS

2.3.1 Classical FS Approaches

Sequential forward selection (SFS) [25] and sequential backward selection (SBS) [17] are two popular wrapper FS approaches, but suffer from the so-called nesting effect and easily trapped into local optima.

The FOCUS algorithm [1], a classical filter algorithm, exhaustively examines all feature subsets, then selects the smallest feature subset. However, the FOCUS algorithm is computationally inefficient because of the exhaustive search. The Relief algorithm [13] assigns a relevance weight to each feature to denote the relevance of the feature to the target concept. However, Relief does not deal with redundant features, because it attempts to find all relevant features regardless of the redundancy between them.

2.3.2 Non-PSO Evolutionary computation Methods for FS

GP, GAs and ant colony optimisation (ACO) have been applied to FS. Based on GP and a variation of naïve Bayes, Neshatian and Zhang [20] propose a FS approach, where a bit-mask representation is used for feature subsets and a set of operators are used as primitive functions. GP is used to combine feature subsets and operators together to find the optimal subset of features. Experiments show that the dimensionality and processing time can be significantly reduced by the proposed algorithm.

Chakraborty [3] proposes a GA with fuzzy sets based fitness function to build a filter FS approach. This method have the same fitness function with BPSO based method in [4]. However, the performance of BPSO in [4] is better than that of this GA based algorithm.

Based on ACO and rough sets theory, He [18] proposes a filter based FS approach. The features included in the core of the rough sets is the starting point of the proposed method. Forward selection is adopted into the proposed method to search for the best feature subset. Experimental results show that the proposed approach achieves better classification performance with fewer features than a C4.5 based FS approach.

2.3.3 PSO based FS Approaches

PSO has recently gained more attention for solving FS problems. Based on continuous PSO and support vector machines (SVM), Azevedo et al. [2] propose a FS algorithm for keystroke dynamics systems. Experimental results show that the proposed algorithm produces better performance than a GA with SVM model regarding the classification error, processing time and feature reduction rate.

Mohemmed et al. [19] propose a hybrid method (PSOAdaBoost) which incorporated PSO with an AdaBoost framework for face detection. PSOAdaBoost aims to search for the best feature subset and determine the decision thresholds of AdaBoost simultaneously, which would also speed up the process of training and increase the accuracy of weak classifiers in AdaBoost.

Based on BPSO, Unler and Murat [23] propose a FS algorithm with an adaptive selection strategy, where a feature is chosen not only according to the likelihood calculated by BPSO, but also to its contribution to the features already selected. Experimental results suggest that the proposed BPSO method outperforms the tabu search and scatter search algorithms.

Based on PSO and SVM, Huang et al. [9] propose a FS method in which BPSO is used to search the optimal feature subset and continuous PSO is used to simultaneously optimise the parameters in the kernel function of SVM. Experiments show that the proposed algorithm could determine the parameters and search the optimal feature subset simultaneously, and also achieve good classification performance.

Liu et al. [16] introduce a multi-swarm BPSO (MSPSO) algorithm to search for the optimal feature subset and optimise the parameters of SVM simultaneously. Experiments show that the proposed FS method could achieve higher classification accuracy than grid search, standard BPSO and GA. However, the proposed algorithm is computationally more expensive than the other three methods because of the large population size and complicated communication rules between different subswarms.

Many studies have shown that PSO is an efficient search technique for FS. However, most of the existing work aims to minimise the classification error and not much work has been conducted for solving a FS task as a multi-objective problem. Therefore, development of a multi-objective FS algorithm using PSO to simultaneously minimise the classification error and minimise the number of features is still an open issue.

3. PROPOSED APPROACHES

3.1 Single Objective PSO for FS

FS can be performed by BPSO as a single objective problem to minimise the classification error rate. The goal is to see whether BPSO can select a subset of features to achieve a lower classification error rate than using all features, and the results will be used to as a baseline to compare the performance of newly developed algorithms. The fitness function (Equation 9) is to minimise the classification error rate obtained by the selected feature subset during evolution.

$$Fitness_1 = ErrorRate = \frac{FP + FN}{TP + TN + FP + FN} \tag{9}$$

where TP, TN, FP and FN stand for true positives, true negatives, false positives and false negatives, respectively.

The representation of a particle in BPSO is a n-bit binary string, where n is the number of available features in the dataset and also the dimensionality of the search space. In the binary string, "1" represents that the feature is selected and "0" otherwise.

3.2 Single Objective PSO for Weighting Two Objectives in FS

The feature subset selected by BPSO may still contain potential redundancy because the fitness function (Equation 9) does not intend to minimise the number of features. A new fitness function (Equation 10) is proposed with the goals of minimising both the classification error rate and the number of features selected.

$$Fitness_2 = \alpha * \frac{\#Features}{\#All\ Features} + (1 - \alpha) * \frac{ErrorRate}{Error_0} \tag{10}$$

where $\alpha \in [0, 1]$, α and $(1 - \alpha)$ show the relative importance of the number of features and the classification error rate. $(1 - \alpha)$ is set larger than α because the classification performance is assumed more important than the number of features. However, the number of selected features $\#Features$ is usually much larger than the classification error rate $ErrorRate$. In order to balance these two components, $\#Features$ is divided by the total number of features $\#All\ Features$, which transforms the value to the range of (0, 1]. Meanwhile, the classification error rate is normalised via dividing it by the error rate using all available features $Error_0$.

The representation of a particle in this algorithm is the same as the n-bit binary string described in Section 3.1.

Algorithm 1: NSBPSO for Feature Selection

```
begin
    divide Dataset into a training set and a test set; initialise each particle in the swarm (Swarm);
    while Maximum Iterations is not met do
        evaluate two objective values of each particle ;      /* number of features and the training error rate */
        identify the non-dominated particles (nonDomS) in Swarm;
        calculate crowding distance of each particle in nonDomS;
        Sort particles in nonDomS according to the crowding distance;
        copy all the particles in Swarm to a form temporary swarm (temSwarm);
        for i=1 to Population Size (P) do
            update the pbest of particle i;
            randomly selecting a gbest for particle i from the highest ranked (least crowded) solutions in nonDomS;
            update the velocity and the position of particle i;
            add the updated particle i to temSwarm;
        identify different levels of non-dominated fronts F = (F1, F2, F3, ...) in temSwarm;
        empty the current Swarm for the next iteration;
        i = 1;
        while |Swarm| < P do
            if (|Swarm| + |Fi| ⩽ P) then
                calculate crowding distance of each particle in Fi;
                add Fi to Swarm;
                i = i + 1;
            if (|Swarm| + |Fi| > P) then
                calculate crowding distance of each particle in Fi;
                sort particles in Fi;
                add the (P − |Swarm|) least crowded particles to Swarm;
    calculate the classification error rate of the solutions in the F1 on the test set ;    /* F1:achieved Pareto front */
    return the positions of particles in F1;
    return the training and test classification error rates of the solutions in F1;
```

3.3 NSPSO for FS

Equation 10 considers both the number of features and classification performance, but a proper value of α needs to be pre-determined. In most situations, users may want to make an informed decision from many available feature subsets. Therefore, it is needed to use multi-objective PSO to address FS problems with the objectives of minimising both the number of features and the classification error rate.

PSO was originally proposed as a single objective technique for continuous problems. In order to use PSO for multi-objective problems, we need to determine a good leader (*gbest*) for the swarm among a set of potential non-dominated solutions. Li [15] introduces the idea of non-dominated sorting in NSGAII [6] into PSO to develop a continuous multi-objective PSO algorithm and shows that the proposed algorithm can achieve promising results on the optimisation of several functions. However, this algorithm has never been applied to FS problems.

In this study we propose a multi-objective FS framework (NSPSO) and the continuous multi-objective PSO [15] is applied to search for the non-dominated solutions. Further, we propose a new binary multi-objective PSO using the idea of non-dominated sorting and applied in the proposed FS framework (NSPSO). Therefore, the FS framework, NSPSO, includes both the continuous and the binary versions of multi-objective PSO for FS. Algorithm 1 shows the pseudo-code of binary NSPSO for FS.

When using continuous NSPSO for FS, the representation of a particle is a vector of n real numbers and a threshold θ is needed to compare with the value x_i in the vector. Feature i is selected if $\theta > x_i$ and $\theta \leqslant x_i$ otherwise.

3.4 CMDPSO for FS

Although NSPSO has shown promising results on different problems [15], it has a potential limitation. By selecting particles from the combination of current swarm and the updated swarm, all non-dominated particles that share the same position will be added into the next iteration. Therefore, the diversity of the swarm might be lost during the evolutionary process. In order to better address FS problems, we develop another multi-objective FS framework, CMDPSO, based on multi-objective PSO using the ideas of crowding, mutation and dominance [22].

The ideas of crowding, mutation and dominance were used to in a continuous multi-objective PSO [22], but it has never been applied to FS and will employed in the proposed FS framework to develop a continuous versions of CMDPSO. Further, we develop a binary multi-objective PSO using the ideas of crowding, mutation and dominance to propose a binary CMDPSO FS algorithm. Except for the steps related to the selection of *gbest*, mutation and dominance, binay CMDPSO follows the basic steps of a PSO algorithm. In order to address the main issue of determining a good leader (*gbest*), a leader set is used to keep the non-dominated solutions as the potential leaders for each particle. The maximum size of the leader set is usually set as the number of individuals in the population. A crowding factor is employed to decide which non-dominated solutions should be added into the leader set and kept during the evolutionary process. Binary tournament selection based on the crowding factor is applied to choose a leader (*gbest*) for each particle from the leader set. A bit-flip mutation operator is adopted to keep the diversity of the swarm and improve the search ability of the algorithm. An archive is used to keep the non-dominated solutions and a dominance factor is adopt to determine the size of archive, which is also the number of non-dominated solutions that CMDBPSO reports.

In binary CMDPSO, the representation of each particle

Table 1: Datasets

Dataset	# features	# classes	# instances
Wine	13	3	178
Zoo	17	7	101
Vehicle	18	4	846
World Breast Cancer -Diagnostic (WBCD)	30	2	569
Sonar	60	2	208
Movementlibras	90	15	360
Hillvalley	100	2	606
Musk Version 1 (Musk1)	166	2	476
Isolet5	617	2	1559

is the same as the n-bit binary string described in Section 3.1. In continuous CMDPSO for FS, the representation of each particle is the same as the vector of n real numbers described in Section 3.3.

4. EXPERIMENTAL DESIGN

Table 1 shows the nine datasets used in the experiments, which are chosen from the UCI machine learning repository [7]. The nine datasets were selected to have different numbers of features (from 13 to 617), classes and instances as the representative samples of the problems that the proposed algorithms can address. In the experiments, the instances in each dataset are randomly divided into two sets: 70% as the training set and 30% as the test set.

All the algorithms are wrapper approaches, i.e. needing a learning algorithm in the evolutionary training process. Many learning algorithms can be used here and one of the simplest algorithms, K-nearest neighbour (KNN), was chosen in the experiments. We use K=5 in KNN (5NN) to simplify the evaluation process. The linear forward selection (LFS) [8] is used as a benchmark technique to examine the performance of the proposed approaches.

In both single objective and multi-objective algorithms, the parameters of PSO are set as follows: inertia weight $w = 0.7298$, acceleration constants $c_1 = c_2 = 1.49618$, maximum velocity $v_{max} = 6.0$, population size $P = 30$, maximum iteration $T = 100$. The fully connected topology is used in BPSO. These values are chosen based on the common settings in the literature [21, 24]. In the weighted single objective algorithm, $\alpha = 0.2$ is used in Equation 10 to give more weight to classification performance. The threshold used in the continuous version of PSO for FS is set to 0.6. For each dataset, each algorithm has been conducted for 40 independent runs.

In single objective algorithms, one single solution (feature subset) is obtained in each run while for multi-objective algorithms CMDPSO and NSPSO, a set of solutions (feature subsets) are obtained in each run. In order to compare these two kinds of algorithms, 40 results (from 40 runs) of each single objective algorithm are presented in the Section 5. 40 sets of feature subsets achieved by each multi-objective algorithm are firstly combined into one union set. In the union set, the classification error rate of feature subsets, which share the same number of features (e.g. m), are averaged. The average classification error rate is assigned as the classification performance of the subsets with m features. A set of average solutions is obtained by using the average classification error rates and the corresponding numbers. The set of average solutions is called the *average* Pareto front and presented in the Section 5. Besides the average Pareto front, the non-dominated solutions in the union set are also presented in the Section 5 to compare with the solutions achieved by single objective algorithms. Experiments have been conducted on nine datasets, but due to the page limit, results on six datasets are presented as other three datasets have similar results.

5. RESULTS AND DISCUSSIONS

Experimental results of the four algorithms on six of the nine datasets are shown in Figures 1 and 2 In each figure, the numbers in the brackets show the number of available features and the classification error rate using all features. In each chart, the horizontal axis shows the number of features selected for classification and the vertical axis shows the classification error rate.

In Figure 1, "NSB-Ave" ("NSC-Ave") stands for the average Pareto front resulted from binary (continuous) NSPSO for FS in the 40 independent runs. "NSB-Best" ("NSC-Best") represents the non-dominated solutions of all solutions resulted from binary (continuous) NSPSO for FS. "Stand" represents the solutions of BPSO with the overall classification performance as the fitness function. "Weights" shows the solutions of BPSO with the fitness function considering both the number of features and the classification performance. In Figure 2, "CMDB- " and "CMDC- " show the results of binary and continuous CMDPSO.

For "Stand" and "Weights", in some datasets, the algorithm may evolve the same feature subset in different runs and they are shown in the same point in the chart. Therefore, for "Stand" or "Weights", 40 results are presented, but there may be less than 40 points shown in each chart.

5.1 Results of Single Objective PSO for FS

According to Figures 1, in all datasets, both "Stand" and "Weights" can evolve many feature subsets, which selected around half of the available features and achieved a lower classification error rate than using all features.

Comparing "Stand" with "Weights", in all datasets, the number of features evolved by "Weights" is usually smaller than that of "Stand", which is caused by the weight factor in the fitness function (Equation 10). There is no significant difference between the classification error rates achieved by "Stand" and "Weights". This shows that feature subsets evolved by "Stand" still have redundancy because the number of features was not considered in the fitness function.

The results suggest that in all datasets, BPSO with the overall classification error rate as fitness function can effectively select a feature subset that contains around half of the available features and increases classification performance. By considering the number of features in the fitness function, "Weights" can further reduce the number of features while maintaining the classification performance.

5.2 Results of NSPSO for FS

5.2.1 Results of Binary NSPSO for FS

According to Figure 1, in almost all datasets, the average Pareto front of binary NSPSO ("NSB-Ave") contains two or more solutions, which selected a small number of features and achieved a lower classification error than using all features. For the same number of features, there are a variety of combinations of features with different classification error rates, the feature subsets obtained in different runs are usually different. Therefore, although the solutions obtained in

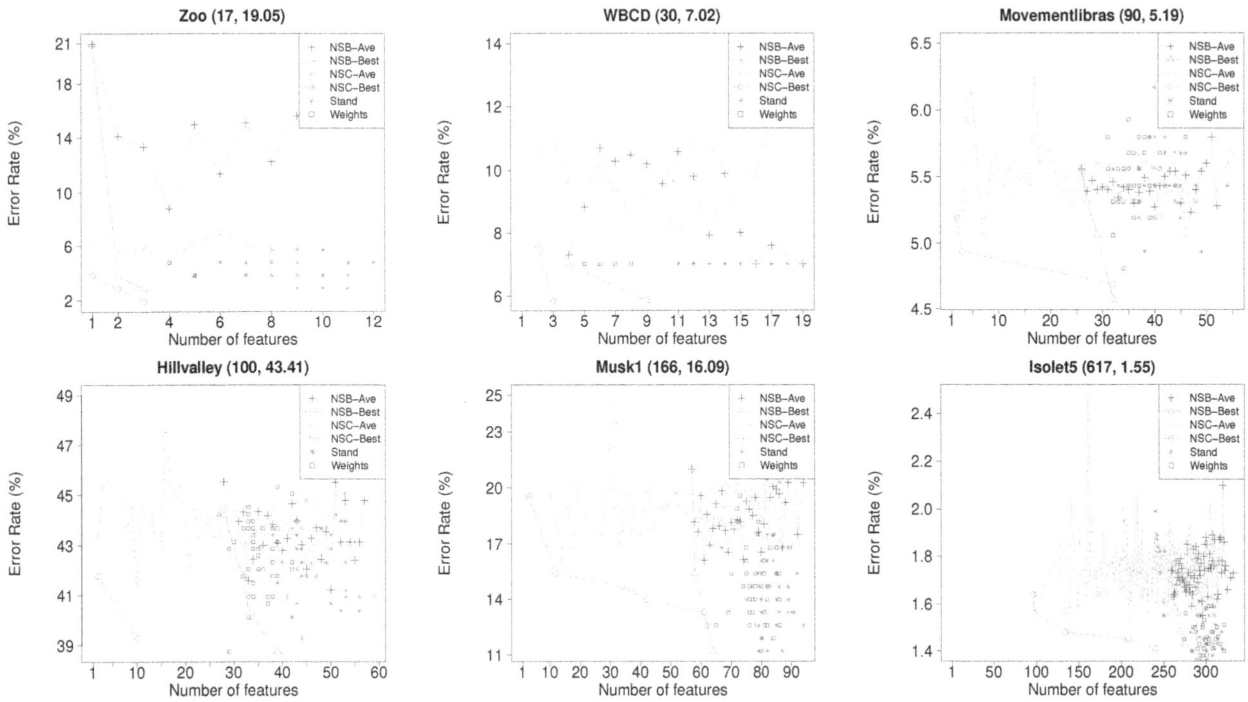

Figure 1: Results of continuous and binary NSPSO for FS and two single objective algorithms.

each run are non-dominated, some solutions in the average Pareto front may dominate others.

"NSB-Best" shows the non-dominated solutions of the binary NSPSO in the 40 independent runs. In almost all datasets, "NSB-Best" can evolve two or more feature subsets, which selected around only one third of the available features and achieved better classification performance than using all features (except for around 40% in the Isolet5 dataset).

Comparing binary NSPSO with "Stand" and "Weights", it can be seen that in some datasets, feature subsets obtained by "Stand" and "Weights" achieved a lower classification error rate than the average Pareto front ("NSB-Ave"). However, in almost all cases, the non-dominated solutions ("NSB-Best") of binary NSPSO are better than the feature subsets evolved by "Stand" and "Weights" in terms of both the number of features and the classification error rate.

5.2.2 *Results of Continuous NSPSO for FS*

According to Figure 1, in almost all cases, "NSC-Ave" contains two or more solutions, which selected a small number of features and achieved a lower classification error rate than using all features.

In all cases, "NSC-Best" evolved one or more feature subsets, which selected no more than 10% of the available features and achieved better classification performance than using all features (except for around 16% in the Isolet5 dataset). For example, in the Hillvalley dataset, by using the selected 1 or 10 features (from the available 100 features), 5NN can achieve a lower classification error rate than using all features.

Comparing continuous NSPSO with "Stand" and "Weights", it can be seen that in most cases, "NSC-Ave" successfully selected a smaller or much smaller number of features and achieved similar or better classification performance than "Stand" and "Weights". In all datasets, the solutions in "NSC-Best" are better than the feature subsets evolved by "Stand" and "Weights" in terms of both the number of features and classification performance.

The results suggest that in all datasets, both continuous and binary versions of NSPSO can evolve a set of feature subsets that selected only a small number of features but achieved better classification performance than using all features. The two versions of NSPSO as multi-objective techniques guided by two objectives can achieve better feature subsets than "Stand" and "Weights" in terms of the classification performance and the number of features.

5.3 Results of CMDPSO for FS

5.3.1 *Results of CMDPSO for FS*

According to Figure 2, in all datasets, "CMDB-Ave" contains two or more solutions, which successfully selected a small number of features and achieved better classification performance than using all features.

In most datasets, "CMDB-Best" contains one or more feature subsets, which selected around one third of the available features and achieved better classification performance than using all features.

Comparing the results of binary CMDPSO with that of "Stand" and "Weights", it can be seen that in almost all datasets, the classification error rate of "Stand" and "Weights" is similar with that of the solutions included in "CMDB-Ave". However, in all datasets, the non-dominated solutions ("CMDB-Best") of binary CMDPSO had a smaller number of features and achieved better classification performance than feature subsets evolved by "Stand" and "Weights".

5.3.2 *Results of Continuous CMDPSO for FS*

According to Figure 2, in all datasets, "CMDC-Ave" basically followed the same behaviours of "CMDB-Ave", but achieved better results than "CMDB-Ave" in most cases.

Comparing continuous CMDPSO with "Stand" and "Weights",

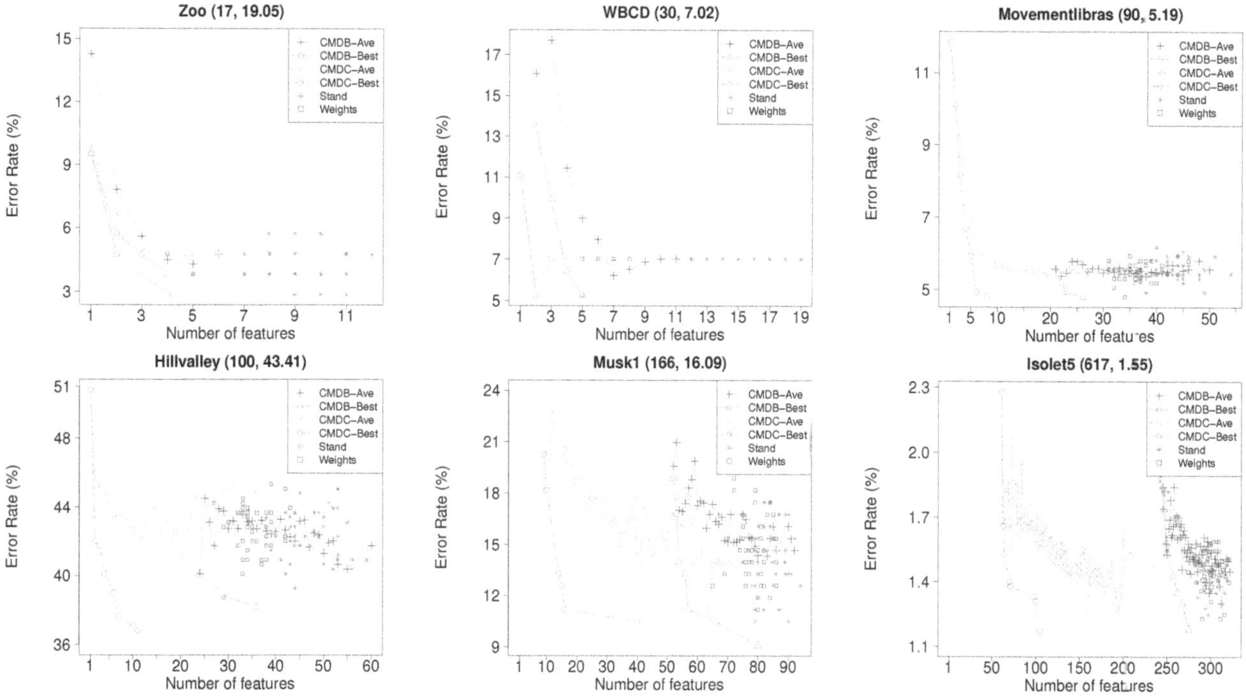

Figure 2: Results of continuous and binary CMDPSO for FS and two single objective algorithms

in almost all datasets, some of the feature subsets in "CMDC-Ave" selected a smaller number of features and achieved similar or even better classification performance than the feature subsets evolved by "Stand" and "Weights". In all datasets, the non-dominated solutions ("CMDC-Best") outperformed feature subsets evolved by "Stand" and "Weights".

The results suggest that in all datasets, both continuous and binary versions of CMDPSO can evolve a set of feature subsets with a small number of features and better classification performance than using all features. Although CMDPSO share the same parameter settings with "Stand" and "Weights", both versions of CMDPSO as multi-objective techniques can effectively explore the Pareto front and achieve better classification performance using fewer features than "Stand" and "Weights".

5.4 Comparisons Between Two Multi-objective Approaches

The results of "Stand" and "Weights" are shown in Figures 1 and 2. Therefore, "Stand" and "Weights" can be a baseline to compare the performance of the NSPSO with that of CMDPSO for FS.

Taking the WBCD dataset as an example, the average Pareto fronts of the two NSPSO algorithms could not achieve a lower classification error rate than "Stand" and "Weights". However, some solutions in the average Pareto fronts of the two CMDPSO algorithms have a smaller number of features and achieve better classification performance than "Stand" and "Weights". Comparing Figure 1 with Figure 2, in most cases, the performance of the average Pareto front of CMDPSO is better than that of NSPSO in both continuous and binary versions. In almost all cases, "CMDB-Best" and "CMDC-Best" outperformed "NSB-Best" and "NSC-Best", respectively, in terms of classification performance and the number of features.

Generally, CMDPSO can achieve better performance than NSPSO for FS. The reason may be that the way of setting the new positions for particles in NSPSO makes the swarm quickly loss diversity during the evolutionary training process and could not effectively search the solution space. We will investigate this in the future.

5.5 Comparisons Between Continuous and Binary PSO for FS

According to Figure 1, in almost all datasets, the average Pareto front, "NSC-Ave" outperformed "NSB-Ave". In the datasets with a relatively large number of features, continuous NSPSO can obtain a much smaller feature subset with similar or even better classification performance than binary NSPSO. The results of "NSC-Best" are also better than those of "NSB-Best" in most cases. According to Figure 2, continuous CMDPSO outperformed binary CMDPSO in almost all cases.

Generally, the two continuous versions of multi-objective PSO ("NSC","CMDC") achieved better performance than the two binary versions of multi-objective PSO ("NSB", "CMDB"). This might be because BPSO does not present all of the important characteristics of the PSO algorithm.

5.6 Comparisons with a Conventional FS Method

Taking the Zoo and WBCD datasets as examples, we check how well the four proposed algorithms perform compared with linear forward selection (LFS) [8]. LFS selected 6 features in Zoo with a classification error rate of 4.76% and 9 features in WBCD with a classification error rate of 11.70%. Comparing the results in Figures 1 and 2, "Stand", "Weights" can evolve two or more feature subsets that outperformed the subset selected by LFS. Results of NSPSO ("NSB-Ave", "NSB-Best", "NSC-Ave", and "NSC-Best") and CMDPSO ("CMDB-Ave", "CMDB-Best", "CMDC-Ave", and "CMDC-

Best") are much better than those of LFS. Other datasets have similar results, which show that PSO can effectively select a good feature subset with a small number of features and achieve high classification performance.

6. CONCLUSIONS

The goal of this paper was to develop a PSO based multi-objective FS approach to selecting a set of non-dominated feature subsets and achieving high classification performance. This goal was successfully achieved by developing two new multi-objective FS algorithms. The first algorithm employed multi-objective PSO using the idea of NSGAII to search for the Pareto front in FS problems. The second algorithm employed multi-objective PSO, which adopted the idea of crowding, mutation and dominance, as the seach technique for FS. The two proposed algorithms were examined and compared with two single objective FS algorithms and LFS on nine benchmark datasets of varying difficulty. The results suggest that two proposed algorithms can obtain a set of non-dominated solutions, which can successfully select a small number of features and achieve higher classification performance than using all features. In terms of both the number of features and classification performance, the two proposed algorithms outperformed the two single objective methods and LFS, and the second algorithm outperformed the first algorithm. In both two algorithms, using continuous PSO achieved better performance than using binary PSO, especially in the number of features selected.

The two propsed algorithms successfully reduced the number of features needed and achieved higher classification performance, but it is unknown whether the classification performance can be further increased without increasing the number of features, or whether the number of features can be further reduced with similar classification performance. In the future, we will further investigate the multi-objective PSO based FS approach to better exploring the Pareto front of non-dominated solutions in FS problems. We will intend to further investigate the why BPSO usually evolve a larger subset of features than continuous PSO, then develop a new BPSO algorithm to overcome the limitation of BPSO and address this problem.

7. REFERENCES

[1] H. Almuallim and T. G. Dietterich. Learning boolean concepts in the presence of many irrelevant features. *Artificial Intelligence*, 69:279–305, 1994.

[2] G. Azevedo, G. Cavalcanti, and E. Filho. An approach to feature selection for keystroke dynamics systems based on pso and feature weighting. In *IEEE Congress on Evolutionary Computation (CEC'07)*, pages 3577–3584, 2007.

[3] B. Chakraborty. Genetic algorithm with fuzzy fitness function for feature selection. In *IEEE International Symposium on Industrial Electronics (ISIE'02)*, volume 1, pages 315– 319, 2002.

[4] B. Chakraborty. Feature subset selection by particle swarm optimization with fuzzy fitness function. In *3rd International Conference on Intelligent System and Knowledge Engineering (ISKE'08)*, volume 1, pages 1038–1042, 2008.

[5] M. Dash and H. Liu. Feature selection for classification. *Intelligent Data Analysis*, 1(4):131–156, 1997.

[6] K. Deb, A. Pratap, S. Agarwal, and T. Meyarivan. A fast and elitist multiobjective genetic algorithm: Nsga-ii. *IEEE Transactions on Evolutionary Computation*, 6(2):182 –197, 2002.

[7] A. Frank and A. Asuncion. UCI machine learning repository, 2010.

[8] M. Gutlein, E. Frank, M. Hall, and A. Karwath. Large-scale attribute selection using wrappers. In *IEEE Symposium on Computational Intelligence and Data Mining (CIDM '09)*, pages 332–339, 2009.

[9] C. L. Huang and J. F. Dun. A distributed pso-svm hybrid system with feature selection and parameter optimization. *Application on Soft Computing*, 8:1381–1391, 2008.

[10] J. Kennedy and R. Eberhart. Particle swarm optimization. In *IEEE International Conference on Neural Networks*, volume 4, pages 1942–1948, 1995.

[11] J. Kennedy and R. Eberhart. A discrete binary version of the particle swarm algorithm. In *IEEE International Conference on Systems, Man, and Cybernetics, 1997. Computational Cybernetics and Simulation.*, volume 5, pages 4104–4108, 1997.

[12] J. Kennedy and W. Spears. Matching algorithms to problems: an experimental test of the particle swarm and some genetic algorithms on the multimodal problem generator. In *IEEE Congress on Evolutionary Computation (CEC'98)*, pages 78–83, 1998.

[13] K. Kira and L. A. Rendell. A practical approach to feature selection. *Assorted Conferences and Workshops*, pages 249–256, 1992.

[14] R. Kohavi and G. H. John. Wrappers for feature subset selection. *Artificial Intelligence*, 97:273–324, 1997.

[15] X. Li. A non-dominated sorting particle swarm optimizer for multiobjective optimization. In *GECCO*, pages 37–48, 2003.

[16] Y. Liu, G. Wang, H. Chen, and H. Dong. An improved particle swarm optimization for feature selection. *Journal of Bionic Engineering*, 8(2):191–200, 2011.

[17] T. Marill and D. Green. On the effectiveness of receptors in recognition systems. *IEEE Transactions on Information Theory*, 9(1):11–17, 1963.

[18] H. Ming. A rough set based hybrid method to feature selection. In *International Symposium on Knowledge Acquisition and Modeling (KAM '08)*, pages 585–588, 2008.

[19] A. Mohemmed, M. Zhang, and M. Johnston. Particle swarm optimization based adaboost for face detection. In *IEEE Congress on Evolutionary Computation (CEC'09)*, pages 2494–2501, 2009.

[20] K. Neshatian and M. Zhang. Dimensionality reduction in face detection: A genetic programming approach. In *24th International Conference Image and Vision Computing New Zealand (IVCNZ'09)*, pages 391–396, 2009.

[21] Y. Shi and R. Eberhart. A modified particle swarm optimizer. In *IEEE International Conference on Evolutionary Computation (CEC'98)*, pages 69–73, 1998.

[22] M. R. Sierra and C. A. C. Coello. Improving pso-based multi-objective optimization using crowding, mutation and epsilon-dominance. In *EMO*, pages 505–519, 2005.

[23] A. Unler and A. Murat. A discrete particle swarm optimization method for feature selection in binary classification problems. *European Journal of Operational Research*, 206(3):528–539, 2010.

[24] F. Van Den Bergh. *An analysis of particle swarm optimizers*. PhD thesis, Pretoria, South Africa, 2002.

[25] A. Whitney. A direct method of nonparametric measurement selection. *IEEE Transactions on Computers*, C-20(9):1100–1103, 1971.

[26] C. S. Yang, L. Y. Chuang, C. H. Ke, and C. H. Yang. Boolean binary particle swarm optimization for feature selection. In *IEEE Congress on Evolutionary Computation (CEC'08)*, pages 2093–2098, 2008.

[27] H. Yuan, S. S. Tseng, and W. Gangshan. A two-phase feature selection method using both filter and wrapper. In *IEEE International Conference on Systems, Man, and Cybernetics (SMC'99)*, volume 2, pages 132–136, 1999.

Impact of Neuron Models and Network Structure on Evolving Modular Robot Neural Network Controllers

Leo Cazenille
TAO/LRI
Univ. Paris-Sud, CNRS, INRIA
F-91405 Orsay, France
leo.cazenille@lri.fr

Nicolas Bredeche
TAO/LRI
Univ. Paris-Sud, CNRS, INRIA
F-91405 Orsay, France
nicolas.bredeche@lri.fr

Heiko Hamann
Art. Life Lab, Zoology,
Karl-Franzens University Graz
8010 Graz, Austria
heiko.hamann@uni-graz.at

Jürgen Stradner
Art. Life Lab, Zoology,
Karl-Franzens University Graz
8010 Graz, Austria
juergen.stradner@uni-graz.at

ABSTRACT

This paper investigates the properties required to evolve Artificial Neural Networks for distributed control in modular robotics, which typically involves non-linear dynamics and complex interactions in the sensori-motor space. We investigate the relation between macro-scale properties (such as modularity and regularity) and micro-scale properties in Neural Network controllers. We show how neurons capable of multiplicative-like arithmetic operations may increase the performance of controllers in several ways whenever challenging control problems with non-linear dynamics are involved. This paper provides evidence that performance and robustness of evolved controllers can be improved by a combination of carefully chosen micro- and macro-scale neural network properties.

Categories and Subject Descriptors

I.2.9 [**Computing Methodologies**]: Artificial Intelligence—*Robotics*

General Terms

Experimentations, Algorithms, Reliability

Keywords

Evolutionary Robotics, Artificial Neural Networks, Evolutionary Algorithms, Modular Robotics

1. INTRODUCTION

Evolving Artificial Neural Networks (ANN) for robotic control offers many interesting properties: ANN are easy to implement, easy to compute on-board, robust to noise, expressive and evolvable. In the recent years, several methods have been proposed to evolve ANN, through direct or indirect encodings, and with various macro-scale properties (e.g. regularity, modularity and hierarchy), either hand-crafted or obtained through spontaneous evolution (see next section for references).

However, properties at the level of a single neuron have been largely overlooked and most models proposed so far are based on variations of the seminal McCulloch and Pitts summing unit neuron (e.g. weighted sum of inputs, with a sigmoidal activation function). However, this original model is but a very basic interpretation of what can be observed in nature. Evidence from biology shows many cases of non-linear interactions between sensory inputs, which are addressed by unit (single neuron or population of neurons) performing multiplicative operations [12]. Multiplicative models have been introduced in Machine Learning [16, 4], and their benefits in term of expressivity have been thouroughly studied [17].

This is particularly relevant with modular robotics where non-linear interactions in the feature space are an important part of the problem of designing distributed controllers. This paper is related to our on-going research on this topic, where control is decentralized among autonomous robotic units assembled together into a larger robot, as illustrated in figure 1. In this setup, each robotic unit communicates with its direct neighbors and cooperation must be achieved so that the whole organism can address a given task [13].

This paper explores the benefits of macro-scale properties on network structure (regularity and modularity) and micro-scale properties at the level of a single neuron (summing vs. multiplicative operations) with respect to an evolutionary robotics problem involving non-linear dynamics and complex interactions between autonomous units. We consider an existing benchmark that is designed to match the properties of distributed control in modular robotics and we investigate the impact of several properties on control performance and robustness to generalization. We show that while modularity and regularity are important features for neural networks controllers, as advocated in other works, properties at the level of the neuron can also lead to an

GECCO'12, July 7-11, 2012, Philadelphia, Pennsylvania, USA.

Figure 1: Five modules connected together to form a larger organism in the Symbrion project. Each module embeds its own controller and communicates with its neighbors.

increase in performance, generalization and speed of convergence, under certain conditions.

The paper is organized as follows: the next Section provides some background regarding both micro-scale properties and macro-scale Neural Networks properties. Then Section 3 describes the task and the Neural Networks models under scrutiny. Results and Analysis are presented in Section 4. Then, the last Section concludes and sketches future directions.

2. BACKGROUND

This section provides background information on micro-scale (neuron models) and macro-scale properties (network structures).

2.1 Neuron Models

In this review, we exclusively consider discrete time neural networks, due to the ease of implementation within on-board micro-controller with limited computational power and memory (e.g. spiking neurons offer original computational properties but also require additional computational resource which can be a problem when low-cost hardware is considered).

In this context, the classic summing unit is the most commonly used neuron model in Artificial Neural Networks. It is expressed as:

$$a_i = f(\sum_{j=1}^{N} w_{ji} * x_j + w_0), \tag{1}$$

where a_i is the activation of a given neuron, which results from the application of an activation function f on the weighted sum of signals from incoming neurons x_j (with $w_{ji} \in \mathbb{R}$), plus bias. Depending on the nature of f, this may corresponds to the classic threshold, sigmoidal or Radial Basis Function neuron models.

Most published works in Neuro-Evolution rely on this summing unit model as being the standard for neuron computation. Some few exceptions exists, in particular with respect to periodic functions, such as Karl Sims complex function for locomotion [18] or Compositional Pattern Producing Networks [19] (CPPN), which is not restricted to any particular kind of function.

While the original motivation for the summing unit model is based on its relevance to early biological data, as the original McCulloch and Pitts model suggests, other models have been explored, both in Biology and Computer Science. Multiplicative operations have been observed in various animals and experimental evidence has been found both at the level of population of neurons and single neurons [12].

In Computer Science, various multiplicative unit models have been introduced: the Sigma-Pi model [16], the Pi-Sigma model and the more general Product-Unit model (PUNN). The PUNN model [4] can be described as follows:

$$a_i = f(\prod_{j=1}^{N} x_j^{w_{ji}}) \tag{2}$$

Notations are similar as before, including $w_{ji} \in \mathbb{R}$, which is of utmost importance as negative exponents enable division operations. The number of exponents to multiply gives the *order* of the unit, hence the general term Higher-Order Neural Networks (HONN). Figure 2 shows a classical HONN topology where the hidden layer uses HONN units while the read-outs are summing units.

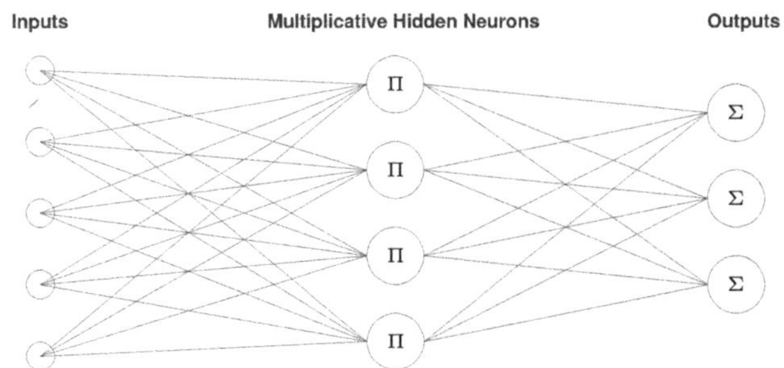

Figure 2: Example of Higher-Order Neural Network. The hidden layer embeds product units while the read-out neurons are summing units (possibly with sigmoid activation function).

Such models offer an increased computatioanal power as they can address non-linear interactions among sensory inputs. While multiplication and division can be accomplished using summing units, it would require much more neurons and layers just to match what a single multiplicative unit can do, in particular when real numbers and calculus precision are considered [17].

2.2 Network Structure

Several authors have highlighted the importance of topological structure for neuro-evolution [14, 9]. The main desired properties are modularity, regularity and hierarchy. These terms are defined as follow:

- Modularity: clearly identified localization of a specific element, either functional or structural;
- Regularity: repetitions of one or several patterns observed in the description;
- Hierarchy: recursive composition of a structure and/or function.

These properties have been studied both with respect to their functional relevance and possible spontaneous emergence during the evolutionary process. For example, early works with Cellular Encoding implemented regularity through recursive decomposition, and was successfully applied to a six-legged robot locomotion problem [5]. Recent works focused on how such properties emerge during evolution, either with direct encoding [11, 2] or indirect encoding approaches [22]. The trade-off between capturing regularity and irregularities with indirect encoding methods has also been studied [3].

Another important property is related to feature space design, that is how sensory inputs are processed within the neural network. On the one hand, independent features with few interactions may be processed through different pathways and recombined in the last step (e.g. weighted aggregation). On the other hand, features may be strongly interacting and higher-level feature construction may be required to capture the information needed for the decision process. In Machine Learning, this is sometimes addressed as feature extraction [6], through feature decomposition (non-correlated features are treated separately) or construction (new features are constructed as combination of previous features). The challenge is to come up with a well-balanced trade-off between expressiveness and complexity (size of the feature space). As with other properties, feature space decomposition may or may not be relevant depending on the problem at hand. In the following, modularity is defined to enforce feature space decomposition (i.e. each module gets only part of the feature space as input).

3. METHOD

This section introduces the robotic task and representation formalisms considered to model the control architecture, each with specific micro- and macro-scale properties. Evolutionary setups and parameters are also presented.

3.1 The Robotic Task

The Coupled Inverted Pendulums benchmark introduced in [7] (and termed "multipole benchmark" in the following) extends the standard inverted pendulum scenario with non-linear dynamics. The goal of the multipole benchmark is to provide a challenge that is close to what one would expect from modular robotics scenarios, with interactions between autonomous parts and non-linear dynamics.

In this benchmark, pendulums are started in lower positions, hence, the non-linear upswinging phase is included, and the cart track length is restricted. In combination with a limited acceleration of the cart motor the upswinging cannot be managed by just moving back and forth once. In addition sampling rates of all sensors are limited, which is documented by the relation between the pre-defined cycle length τ of the controller and the maximal angular velocity of $0.05\pi[1/\tau] = 9°[1/\tau]$ (pendulum motion of up to 9° between two calls of the controller). The sensors do not deliver actual angles and positions directly, but instead partition the original values onto several intervals and sensors (a total of 10 sensors). The controllers have two outputs, left actuator A_0 and right actuator A_1 and the acceleration control of the cart is determined by their difference. Therefore, there is a total of 10 sensory inputs and 2 motor outputs. For each ANN model, there are two additional inputs and outputs to enable communication between controllers of connected, neighboring carts. These communication channels corresponds to additional inputs/outputs in the controller

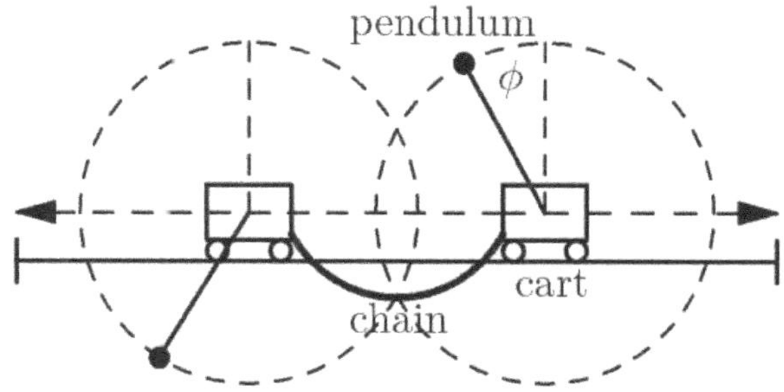

Figure 3: Coupled inverted pendulum benchmark with two carts, pendulums are free to move full 360° mounted on the carts that move in one dimension (left/right) bounded by walls (track ends) and other carts. Marked angle is pendulum angle ϕ.

for setups with more than one cart (the one-cart version has, of course, no communication).

In addition to the original definition of the benchmark, referred to as *multipole-velocity* from now, we consider an additional setup where the sensors for cart velocities and pendulum angular velocities are removed. This will be referred to as the *multipole-no-velocity* benchmark and it offers an increased challenge as velocities may be required, and thus reconstructed, to completely address the balancing problem. Due to the removal of velocity sensors, the multipole-no-velocity benchmark provides 6 (+2 for communication) sensory inputs instead of 10 (+2). An important fact is that when coupled carts are considered, it is theoretically possible to obtain memory-based behaviors even if the controllers are not capable of memorization as information can be transmitted back and forth between controllers of the carts.

The coupling of carts by chains is the most important difference to the standard inverted pendulum. Carts can move independently as long as they do not pull a chain or run into each other. Hence, each cart has to avoid other carts and walls (cart track ends) and has to balance its pendulum at the same time. In the following investigations, the cart number is increased without changing the track length so as to model problems of growing difficulty.

The fitness function is basically the percentage of time steps that all pendulums spent in the upper equilibrium position ($\phi = 0$) – the higher the fitness, the better the behavior. Deviations from $\phi = 0$ are linearly scaled, that is, $\phi = 0.5\pi$, for example, is evaluated as '50% in upper position'. If any constraint is violated (e.g., cart runs into other cart, cart runs into chain, cart runs into wall, pendulum velocity too high, etc.) an evaluation run is aborted and the fitness is reduced proportionally to the elapsed time. An extensive description can be found in [8].

3.2 The Controllers

Each pole is controlled by an Artificial Neural Networks, which can communicate with its direct neighbors. As with homogeneous distributed control in modular robotics, only one neural algorithm is evolved for control, which is considered as a template and duplicated within each cart. As a consequence, each cart will behave differently depending on its initial position, sensory inputs and past experience.

Controllers have been designed so that it can be possible

to evaluate the relevance of specific properties, both at the level of the network structure and neuron model. In particular, we aim to address the following questions: Is there a benefit in modularity in processing specific inputs through well identified group of neurons? Is there a benefit in regularity as evolving few patterns (i.e. groups of neurons with a given structure and weights), duplicated to form a final, larger, network? What is the benefit of using multiplicative neurons compared to summing units? The following models are devised to address these questions:

HONN and MLP: Higher-Order Neural Networks (HONN) and Multi-Layered Perceptron (MLP) are similarly defined as Multi-Layered Neural Networks: the input and output layers are fully connected to the hidden layer, and neurons for the output layer use a summing unit model with a sigmoidal activation function. They differ only in that MLP gets only one hidden layer of sigmoidal summing units while the HONN gets one hidden layer of multiplicative units.

C-MLP and C-HONN (i.e. with compartment): The notion of "compartment" (i.e. a structural module) refers to dedicated groups of neurons that are connected to only one input and one output. Figure 4 illustrates the structure of a Compartment Artificial Neural Networks. For C-MLP, a compartment is an MLP with one input, a hidden layer of sigmoid summing units, and one output with linear activation function. A C-HONN is similarly defined, except that there are two hidden layers, the first with multiplicative units, and the second with summing units, and a multiplicative unit as output (sigmoid activation functions are used for all neurons). In both cases, read-out neurons for the whole network are summing units with linear activation function. The number of compartments is fixed *a priori*, but the connection to one specific input and output is evolved, as well as the weights within each compartment. Weights connecting each compartment to its selected input and selected read-out neurons are also evolved. To some extent, this is an extreme case of feature space decomposition where the whole network may be considered as a mixture of experts, each expert specialized for processing a specific feature.

C-MLP-WP and C-HONN-WP (i.e. with pattern(s)): As previously, the neural network structure is organized into compartments with one input and one output. All compartments, however, may be identically defined as an instance of a reference evolved pattern. A pattern is defined as a compartment template, i.e. a neural network with one input, one output and one (MLP) or two (HONN) hidden layers. The motivation is to explore the impact of regularity in the network. In the extreme case, only one pattern may be evolved, and cloned during the actual construction of the neural network. As previously, weights connecting each compartment to its selected input and output are evolved.

In addition, we considered several well established neuro-evolution methods from the literature: Echo State Networks [10] (ESN), NEAT [21] and HyperNEAT [20] (used to generate an ANN which is then used for control). It should be noted that the original HyperNeat implementation used for this experiment has been shown to produce sub-optimal solutions whenever regularity is required [3]. Hence, different results may be obtained with further extensions of this algorithm that are able to deal with regularity [22]. However, we highlight that the goal here is to provide a baseline with well-known algorithms from the literature, so as to advocate for the relevance (or not) of micro- and macro-scale properties in various experimental setups.

We also considered the Artificial Homeostatic Hormone Systems (AHHS), initially used for the multipole-velocity version of the benchmark, and which provides the best solution so far (compared to NEAT) on performance and generalization. To some extent, AHHS also models several properties evoked earlier: feature space is decomposed as each feature is processed separately by specialized "rules" and multiplicative operations can be computed through virtual "hormones", that are used to transmit information in the system. An extensive description can be found in [8].

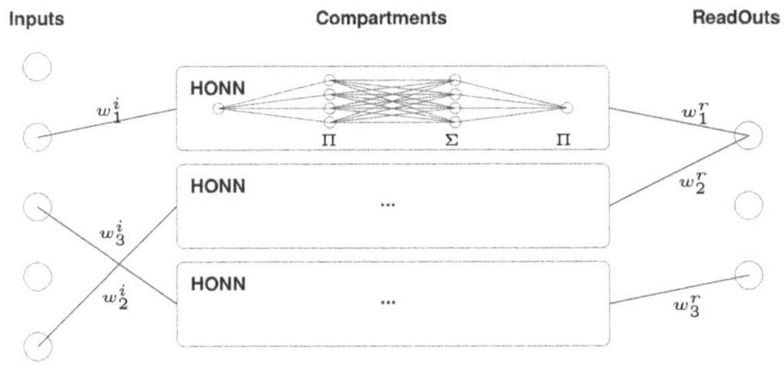

Figure 4: Structural description of a C-HONN. A C-MLP is described in a similar fashion by replacing the embedded HONN networks by MLP networks with one hidden layer. Similarly, C-HONN-WP, resp. C-MLP-WP, accept the same description, with embedded HONN, resp. MLP, as copies of a specific reference template (i.e. an evolved pattern).

3.3 Evolutionary Optimization

All models (except Neat, HyperNEAT and AHHS) are optimized using the state-of-the-art CMA-ES [1] algorithm. The official rtNeat and HyperNEAT-C++ implementations are used for the corresponding models. The original AHHS implementation is used [7].

A fixed budget of 20,000 (resp. 50,000) evaluations is set for the multipole-velocity (resp. multipole-no-velocity) benchmarks. 30 independent runs have been performed for each setup (NN model, cart number, with/without velocity information). In the next section, all claims consider statistically significant measure based on Wilcoxon tests (i.e. with p-value < 0.05).

A large number of preliminary experiments were performed to find operational experimental parameters for each approach. Table 5 summarizes parameters for each approach, as well as comments on robustness of parameters and genome size for each setup (except for Neat and HyperNEAT, which use variable-length genomes). Genome sizes vary to a large extent, depending on the structure of the controllers, but the evaluation budget remains the same to provide fair comparison. Note that the source code for running all the experiments is freely available[1].

4. RESULTS

Figure 7 show the results from experiments on the multipole-velocity and multipole-no-velocity benchmarks, using a sin-

[1]http://pages.isir.upmc.fr/evorob_db/

Method	Parameters	Comments	Genome sizes
MLP	20 hidden neurons (with bias)		262, 344, 182, 264
NEAT	Parameters as in [23]		n/a
HyperNEAT	HyperNEAT-C++ default parameters, recurrence and self-recurrence enabled		n/a
ESN	reservoir size=100, density=0.5, damping=0.88	robust to density (values of 0.1, 0.2, 1.0 provide similar results)	200, 400, 200, 400
AHHS	Parameters as in [7]. 2 compartments per controller, 30 rules, 1 (multipole-velocity) to 3 (multipole-no-velocity) hormones		363, 369, 363, 369
C-MLP	30 compartments, each compartment is an MLP(1:20:1) (i.e. 1 input, 20 hidden neurons, 1 output)	bias is not mandatory	1320,1320,1320,1320
C-MLP-WP	30 compartments, each compartment is an MLP(1:20:1) (same as previous), 1 pattern	increasing the number of patterns up to 60 does not make any difference, bias is not mandatory	190, 190, 190, 190
HONN	multipole-velocity: 1 layer of 20 hidden multiplicative neurons ; multipole-no-velocity: 1 layer of 100 hidden multiplicative neurons, no bias	multipole-no-velocity requires larger networks	160, 240, 800, 1200
C-HONN	30 Compartments of HONN(1:4:4:1) (i.e. 1 input, 4 multiplicative units, 4 summing units, 1 multiplicative unit as output)	two hidden layers is mandatory	840, 840, 840, 840
C-HONN-WP	30 Compartments of HONN(1:4:4:1) (same as previous), 5 patterns	requires 5 (or more) patterns	270, 270, 270, 270

Figure 5: Parameters for all the models. The third column gives genome size for (a) multipole-velocity with 1 cart; (b) multipole-velocity with >1 carts; (c) multipole-no-velocity with 1 cart; (d) multipole-no-velocity with >1 carts

gle cart, and then 3 and 5 coupled carts. Boxplots aggregate the best results from each run obtained from each models and setups (i.e. a total of 1800 runs - i.e. 30 runs, 10 models, 6 setups). The one-cart versions of the benchmark roughly corresponds to the traditional inverted pendulum benchmark while the 3- and 5-carts versions feature both non-linear dynamics and complex interactions between carts.

Figure 6: Snapshots of the best behaviors obtained for 5 carts in the (a) multipole-velocity and (b) multipole-no-velocity benchmarks.

Results on the multipole-velocity benchmark (see Figs. 7(a), 7(c), 7(e)) show that while well-established neuro-evolutionary algorithms (MLP, ESN, Neat, HyperNeat) perform extremely well on the simplest setup (1 cart), performance drops dramaticaly whenever more carts are considered. On the other hand, all other models (except for HONN) remain remarkably stable for any number of carts considered. For the more difficult multipole-velocity with 3 or 5 carts, models with compartments (incl. AHHS) dominate in term of average performance. It is even more true for pattern-enabled models (C-MLP-WP, C-HONN and C-HONN-WP) which provide the best results whenever more than one cart is involved.

Several observations can be drawn from these results: firstly, it appears that modularity (using compartments) and regularity (using duplicated patterns) are key features as difficulty grows. Secondly, multiplicative units (HONN) appears as a counter-productive property if used alone, while they yield to the best scores when combined with modularity (and regularity) on the more complex setups. Also, the good performance of decomposing the feature space, thanks to specialized compartments with one input each, may advocate that the multipole-velocity does not require complex interactions between inputs to be solved.

The fact that modularity and regularity are relevant properties is not a new idea and has been claimed elsewhere on many occasions (cf. section 2.2). However, it is interesting to note that both Neat and HyperNeat are unable to reach the best performance while they could theoretically evolve such properties in the controllers: this issue relates to the trade-off between expressivity and evolvability that have been addressed elsewhere (e.g. see [22] on enabling HyperNeat to generate regularity and modularity).

Let us now consider the multipole-no-velocity benchmark. Results with one cart are roughly the same as previously except for HONN controllers which go from the worst performing controllers (if velocity information is available) to the top performing controllers, implying that multiplicative units can be exploited in the current setup. Another surprising results is achieved with MLP, which successfully succeeds in balancing the pole. Looking carefully at the evolved strategies, we found that the one-cart multipole-no-velocity

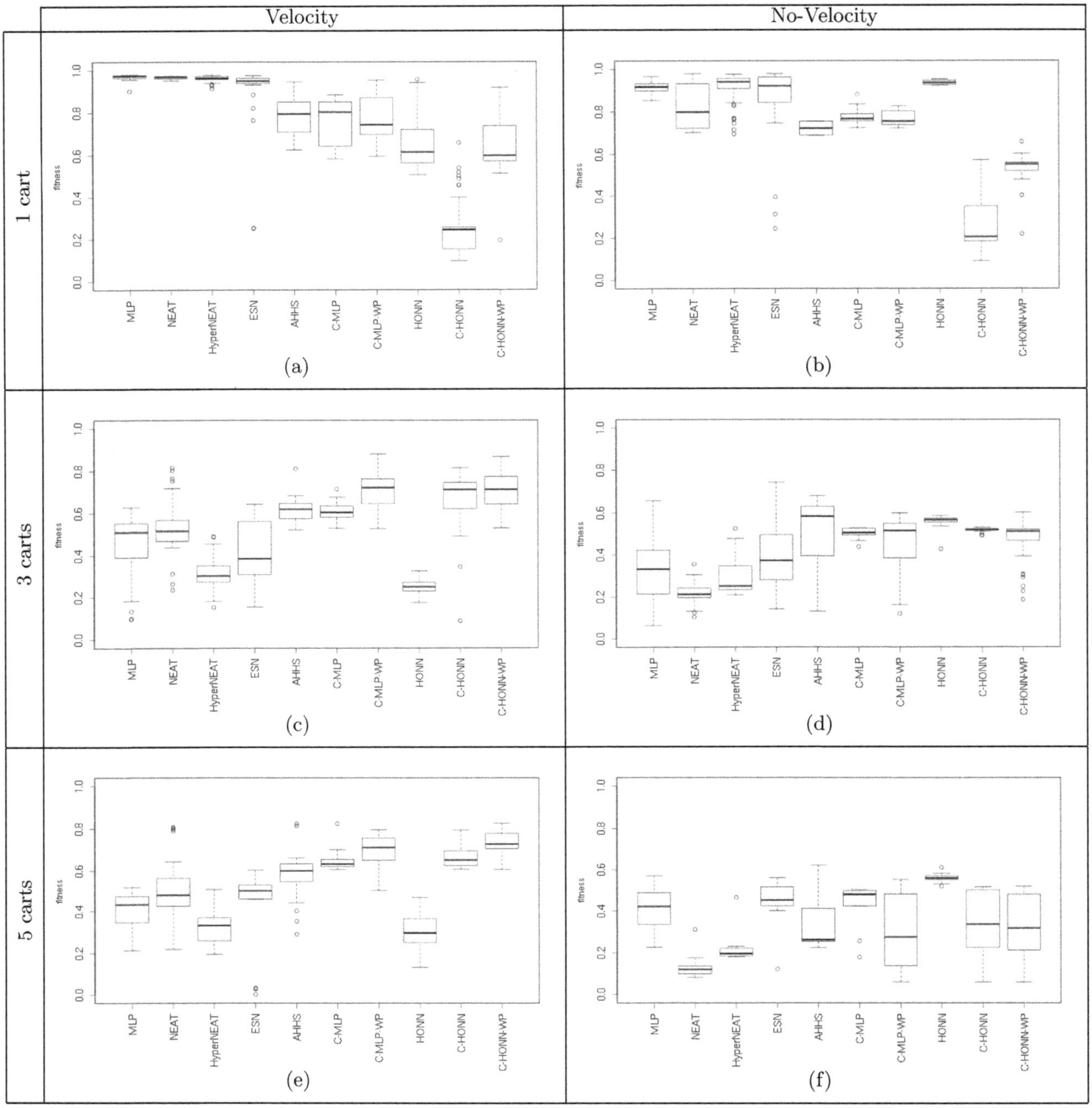

Figure 7: Performance of all controllers. For a given model and configuration, each boxplot aggregates the best individuals from 30 independant runs (i.e. 30 values).

can indeed be solved without memory capabilities: using the distance sensors to the wall, a simple MLP is able to learn a perfect trajectory from the cart initial position to the balanced position. While this trick is possible with one cart, the complex dynamics involved when several carts are considered did not permit to find such a solution in further experiments. At this point, an important fact to keep in mind is that a controller from a cart is able to communicate with its neighbors. As a consequence, memorizing information is possible even when the controller is a feed-forward neural network as information can be transmitted back and forth between carts.

Results are quite different when more than one cart is considered. HONN remains unchallenged, closely followed by AHHS, C-MLP, C-MLP-WP, C-HONN and C-HONN-WP when three carts are considered. On the 5-carts version, AHHS performance drops while C-MLP, ESN and MLP provide competitive results (still below those of HONN). The fact that MLP and C-MLP are still well ranked can be explained by looking at the resulting behaviors. Figure 6 illustrates the best behaviors for 5 carts obtained in both benchmarks. While the multipole-velocity benchmark is solved by most of the models with a median value > 0.6, no model achieves the optimal behavior whenever velocity information is removed. Instead, best behaviors correspond to swinging poles, accelerating or decelerating depending on the position

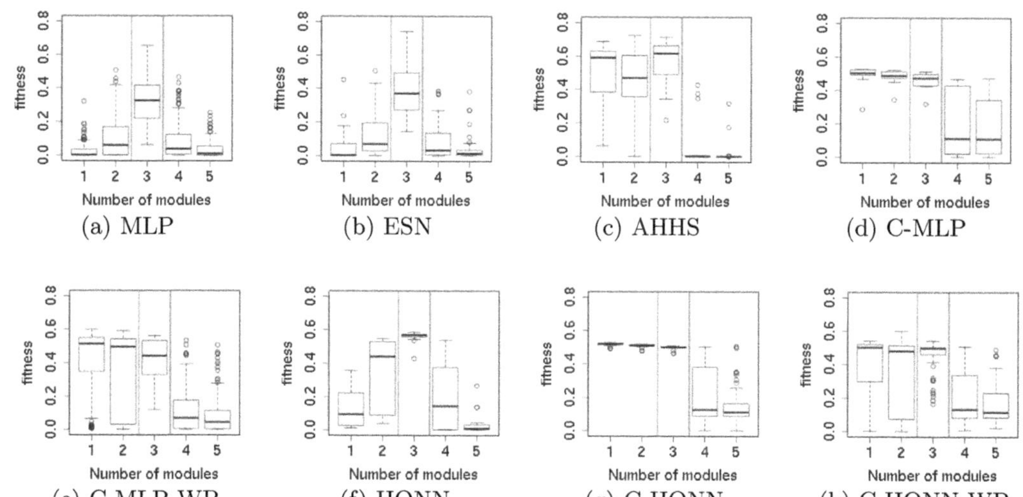

(a) MLP (b) ESN (c) AHHS (d) C-MLP (e) C-MLP-WP (f) HONN (g) C-HONN (h) C-HONN-WP

Figure 8: Generalization capability of the best controllers evolved for three carts, in the multipole-no-velocity benchmark. Each controller is re-evaluated with 1, 2, 4, and 5 carts to assert its transferability in a different setup. Neat and HyperNeat are omitted due to poor performance (similar to MLP and ESN).

of the pole with respect to the horizon so as to maximize the time spent near the equilibrium position while avoiding the other carts. In the 3-carts multipole-no-velocity, evolved behaviors are similar with some exceptions for some HONN and ESN controllers that achieve equilibrium for one cart, and adopt swinging behaviors for the two other carts.

What makes a significant difference between these approaches is to be found in their generalization capabilities. The goal is to evaluate how controllers for each model evolved for the 3-carts version of the multipole-no-velocity perform when tested with 1, 2, 4 or 5 carts. Firstly, in the multipole-velocity benchmark, 3-carts evolved controllers from all approaches yield similar good results with different number of carts, except for MLP, ESN, and Neat which completely fail the generalization test. Secondly, the multipole-no-velocity provides an increased challenge with respect to generalization, as shown in figure 8. The supposedly nearly best results in performance with HONN (and, to some extent, with MLP) are strongly counter-balanced by their very bad results in generalization. Then, only C-MLP and C-HONN controllers (and to less extent C-MLP-WP and C-HONN-WP controllers) produce similar perfomance with 1 or 2 carts while still performing quite well with 4 or 5 carts, at least for some individuals (cf. upper quartiles, maximum values and outliers).

From the results in performance and generalization, it appears that both macro-scale properties and micro-scale properties are relevant to achieve good performance and generalization. In the multipole-velocity benchmark, using modularity (i.e. with compartments) or, even better, modularity combined with regularity (i.e. with patterns) provide the best results, and using multiplicative unit neurons even increases performance as C-HONN and C-HONN-WP both improve over the performance of their MLP equivalents. In the multipole-no-velocity, generalization plays a key role for comparing the different models: this time, modularity alone provides the best controllers on performance *and* generalization, and using summing units leads to slightly better results than using multiplicative units. However, a closer look at the actual course of the evolutionary process advocates for the benefits of using multiplicative units: figure 9 shows progress throughout the evolutionary process for the various flavors of additive- and multiplicative-based models and establish that C-HONN and C-HONN-WP controllers improves *much* faster than any other methods on the most complex versions of the multipole-no-velocity benchmark, especially with respect to other models capable of generalization (results are similar for both the 3 and 5 carts configurations). As a matter of fact, C-HONN almost converged in less than 10,000 evaluations (followed by C-HONN-WP), while other methods require more than 40,000 evaluations to reach similar performance.

5. CONCLUSIONS

This work demonstrates the importance of micro-scale properties in Artificial Neural Networks, in particular with control problems that are characterized by non-linear dynamics and complex interactions between autonomous systems, as it is often the case in modular robotics. The benefits of neuron models that enable multiplicative operations have been demonstrated in combination with other macro-scales properties, in particular when modularity is involved. The take-home message advocates for the use of multiplicative units in neuro-evolutionary algorithms: multiplicative units used in conjunction with modularity, or modularity with regularity, always lead to at least similar or better results when complex dynamics are involved, in much less evaluations.

This work assumed a straight-forward approach to implementing modularity and regularity as explicit features of neural network controllers. This was justified as the goal was to evaluate the positive or negative impacts of such properties. However, and with respect to further use, relaxing this assumption may lead to more adaptive neuro-evolutionary algorithms that can exploit results obtained here. For example, recent works on spontaneous evolution of such network properties [2, 22] suggest that the decision to use summing and/or multiplicative units may be evolved as well, to match the requirements of the problem at hand.

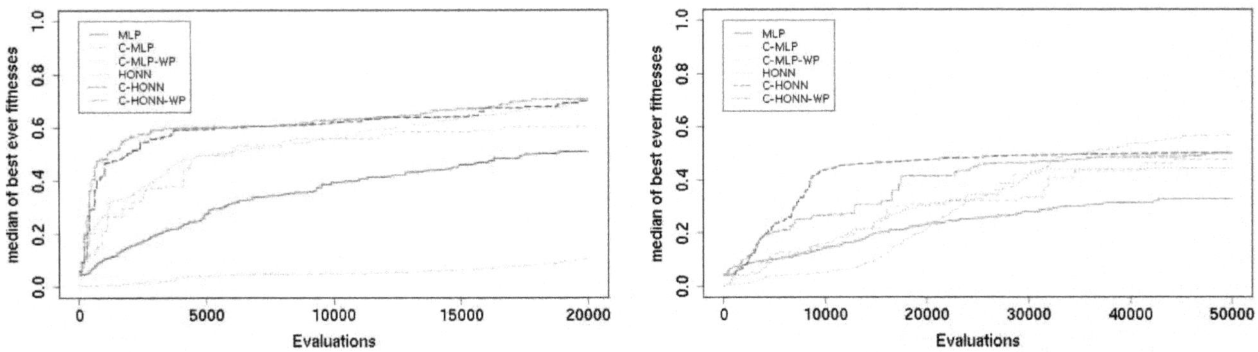

(a) multipole-velocity, 3 carts (b) multipole-no-velocity, 3 carts

Figure 9: Evolutionary runs: tracking improvements throughout evaluations using medians of the best-ever individuals from each runs. (a) multipole-velocity, 3 carts ; (b) multipole-no-velocity, 3 carts. Note that results with 5 carts are similar (not shown due to page limit restriction).

Hierarchy as a macro-scale property has not been discussed in this paper while it could be combined with the properties evoked earlier. Indeed, preliminary experiments yielded limited results, which are mostly due to the difficulty of defining an explicit encoding allowing for hierarchical organization of compartments. This also advocates for an indirect encoding representation, that is leaving the algorithm to decide on the structure of the controllers, rather than enforcing it. To this end, extensions of this work towards integration of evolving micro-scale properties in Cartesian GP [15] and/or HyperNeat-like methods are currently under investigation.

We conclude this paper with a last remark on the multipole benchmarks. The no-velocity version remains very challenging for all approaches as only sub-optimal solutions have been found whenever there is more than one cart. Moreover, it offers an interesting environment with regards to generalization because some methods appear to be much more efficient than others with respect to the transferability of the controllers. Also the memory issue is addressed because operations requiring memorization (such as reconstruction of velocity information) may be achieved through sharing information between several carts.

Acknowledgments

This work was made possible by the European Union FET Proactive Initiative: Pervasive Adaptation funding the Symbrion project under grant agreement 216342. Experiments presented in this paper were carried out using the Grid'5000 experimental testbed, being developed under the INRIA ALADDIN development action with support from CNRS, RENATER and several Universities as well as other funding bodies (see https://www.grid5000.fr). We also would like to thank Jean-Marc Montanier and Taras Kowaliw for many helpful scientific and technical discussions.

References

[1] A. Auger and N. Hansen. A restart cma evolution strategy with increasing population size. In *Proc. CEC 2005*, pages 1769–1776. IEEE Press, 2005.

[2] J. C. Bongard. Spontaneous evolution of structural modularity in robot neural network controllers hardware. In *GECCO*, pages 251–258, 2011.

[3] J. Clune, K. Stanley, R. Pennock, and C. Ofria. On the performance of indirect encoding across the continuum of regularity. *IEEE Transactions on Ev. Comp*, 2011.

[4] R. Durbin and D. Rumelhart. Product units: A computationally powerful and biologically plausible extension to backpropagation networks. *Neural Computation*, 1(1):133–142, 1989.

[5] F. Gruau. Modular genetic neural networks for six-legged locomotion. In *Artificial Evolution*, 1995.

[6] I. Guyon. *Feature extraction: foundations and applications*, volume 207. Springer Verlag, 2006.

[7] H. Hamann, T. Schmickl, and K. Crailsheim. Coupled inverted pendulums: a benchmark for evolving decentral controllers in modular robotics. In *GECCO*, pages 195–202, 2011.

[8] H. Hamann, T. Schmickl, and K. Crailsheim. A hormone-based controller for evaluation-minimal evolution in decentrally controlled systems. *Artificial Life*, 18(2), 2012.

[9] G. Hornby. Measuring, enabling and comparing modularity, regularity and hierarchy in evolutionary design. In *Proceedings of the 2005 conference on Genetic and evolutionary computation*, pages 1729–1736. AcM, 2005.

[10] H. Jaeger. Tutorial on training recurrent neural networks, covering bppt, rtrl, ekf and the echo state network approach. Technical report, Fraunhofer Institute AIS, 2002. GMD Report 159.

[11] N. Kashtan and U. Alon. Spontaneous evolution of modularity and network motifs. *Proceedings of the National Academy of Sciences of the United States of America*, 102(39):13773, 2005.

[12] C. Koch. *Biophysics of computation: information processing in single neurons*. Oxford University Press, USA, 2005.

[13] P. Levi and S. Kernbach, editors. *Symbiotic Multi-Robot Organisms*, volume 7 of *Cognitive Systems Monographs*. Springer Berlin Heidelberg, 2010.

[14] H. Lipson. Principles of modularity, regularity, and hierarchy for scalable systems. *Journal of Biological Physics and Chemistry*, 7(4):125, 2007.

[15] J. F. Miller and P. Thomson. Cartesian genetic programming. In *Proceedings of the European Conference on Genetic Programming*, pages 121–132, London, UK, 2000. Springer-Verlag.

[16] D. E. Rumelhart, G. E. Hinton, and J. L. McClelland. *A general framework for parallel distributed processing*, pages 45–76. MIT Press, Cambridge, MA, USA, 1986.

[17] M. Schmitt. On the complexity of computing and learning with multiplicative neural networks. *Neural Computation*, 14(2):241–301, 2002.

[18] K. Sims. Evolving virtual creatures. In *SIGGRAPH'94*, pages 15–22. ACM Press, July 1994.

[19] K. Stanley. Compositional pattern producing networks: A novel abstraction of development. *Genetic Programming and Evolvable Machines*, 8(2):131–162, 2007.

[20] K. Stanley, D. D'Ambrosio, and J. Gauci. A hypercube-based encoding for evolving large-scale neural networks. *Artificial Life*, 15(2):185–212, 2009.

[21] K. Stanley and R. Miikkulainen. Evolving neural networks through augmenting topologies. *Evolutionary Computation*, 10(2):99–127, 2002.

[22] P. Verbancsics and K. Stanley. Constraining connectivity to encourage modularity in hyperneat. In *GECCO*, pages 1483–1490, 2011.

[23] S. Whiteson and P. Stone. Evolutionary function approximation for reinforcement learning. *The Journal of Machine Learning Research*, 7:877–917, 2006.

Hierarchical Task Decomposition through Symbiosis in Reinforcement Learning

John A. Doucette
School of Computer Science,
University of Waterloo,
Waterloo, ON. Canada
j3doucet@cs.uwaterloo.ca

Peter Lichodzijewski
Faculty of Computer Science,
Dalhousie University,
Halifax, NS. Canada
piotr@cs.dal.ca

Malcolm I. Heywood
Faculty of Computer Science,
Dalhousie University,
Halifax, NS. Canada
mheywood@cs.dal.ca

ABSTRACT

Adopting a symbiotic model of evolution separates context for deploying an action from the action itself. Such a separation provides a mechanism for task decomposition in temporal sequence learning. Moreover, previously learnt policies are taken to be synonymous with meta actions (actions that are themselves policies). Should solutions to the task not be forthcoming in an initial round of evolution, then solutions from the earlier round represent the 'meta' actions for a new round of evolution. This provides the basis for evolving policy trees. A benchmarking study is performed using the Acrobot handstand task. Solutions to date from reinforcement learning have not been able to approach the performance of those established 14 years ago using an A* search and a priori knowledge regarding the Acrobot energy equations. The proposed symbiotic approach is able to match and, for the first time, better these results. Moreover, unlike previous work, solutions are tested under a broad range of Acrobot initial conditions, with hierarchical solutions providing significantly better generalization performance.

Categories and Subject Descriptors

I.2.6 [**Learning**]: Parameter Learning

General Terms

Algorithms, Experimentation, Performance

Keywords

Symbiosis, Reinforcement learning, Meta actions, Task decomposition, Genetic Programming

1. INTRODUCTION

Temporal sequence learning or reinforcement learning (RL) represents a generic class of decision making problems for which the state variables of the task domain change under the influence of actions suggested by the decision maker's policy. The states and actions are task specific. Naturally, the credit assignment process is subject to temporal discounting as it is not generally possible to provide definitive information regarding the impact of any one action on the eventual payoff of a policy [7], [21], [14]. Moreover, task domains of any practical interest generally encounter the 'curse of dimensionality' with regards to the enumeration of the state–action space. Various schemes have therefore been considered for addressing the 'scaling problem' of RL. That is, how to develop a decision maker that describes policies at a more abstract level.

One of the most frequently encountered metaphors is that of a hierarchical architecture for decision making in general. Such schemes have been recommended from many standpoints e.g., philosophy [18], cognition [16], [2] and complex systems [22]. Implicit in the assumption that such hierarchies are beneficial for building effective decision makers is that some form of abstraction takes place as the hierarchy is traversed. Thus, rather than always making decisions in terms of the task specific 'atomic' actions, meta actions are first developed that are appropriate for solving useful subtasks. We assume that such meta actions form the first level of the hierarchical policy learner. Decision making at the next level of the policy learner determines under what conditions to deploy the previously identified meta actions, thus potentially decoupling RL from the curse of dimensionality. Naturally, the above represents a motivation for the ensuing approach, developments in gradient based RL methods assume somewhat different solutions typically related to Markov Processes e.g., [5, 6].

In this work we present an entirely evolutionary framework for developing such a hierarchical policy learner without recourse to prior identification of appropriate subtasks and illustrate its application under the challenging domain of the Acrobot handstand task [1]. The resulting solution represents a *policy tree* in which each node represents a set of programs with decision making beginning at the root node. Leaf nodes deploy an atomic action whereas internal nodes correspond to meta actions. Programs establish whether child arcs are taken or not, with only a single arc being active at any layer of the decision tree i.e. winner takes all resolution across programs from the same node. The resulting policy tree is evolved 'bottom up' with no prior assumption regarding the number or type of meta actions necessary. The evolutionary basis for such a process is symbiotic bid-based genetic programming (SBB) [13]. This work emphasizes how SBB is extended to provide explicitly hierarchical solutions and applied to policy search. Task generalization is shown to

GECCO'12, July 7–11, 2012, Philadelphia, Pennsylvania, USA.

benefit significantly from the capacity to build hierarchical policies.

2. SYMBIOTIC BID-BASED GP

The generic architecture for SBB explicitly enforces symbiosis by separating host and symbiont into independent populations [13]. Each host represents a candidate solution in the form of a set of symbionts existing independently in the symbiont population. Performance is measured relative to the interaction between training scenarios (points) and host. A breeder model of evolution is assumed, thus a fixed number of hosts and points are deleted/ introduced at each generation. The respective properties of symbiont and host population are developed below. Note that space precludes a complete description of the algorithm [13]; instead we draw the reader's attention to the specific major differences introduced here for applying SBB to the temporal difference domain i.e., constructing policy trees. Interested readers are referred to online resources for further details [10, 11].

2.1 Representation and execution

2.1.1 Symbiont Population

Members of the symbiont population assume a Bid-Based GP representation [12]. As such, each symbiont, sym, is represented as a tuple $\langle a, p \rangle$; where a is an action as selected from the set of atomic actions associated with the task domain and p is the corresponding symbiont's program. Without loss of generality, a linear representation is assumed [3]. Execution of a symbiont's program results in a corresponding real-valued outcome in the output register, $R[0]$. In order to encourage a common bidding range from the outset, this is mapped to the unit interval through the sigmoid operator, or $sym(bid) = (1+\exp(-R[0]))^{-1}$. The linear representation leads to programs being defined by a simple register addressing language of the form: 1) Two argument instructions, or $R[x] := R[x] \langle op_2 \rangle R[y]; op_2 \in \{+, -, \div, \times\}$; 2) Single argument instructions, or $R[x] := \langle op_1 \rangle (R[y]); op_1 \in \{\cos, \ln, \exp\}$; 3) A conditional statement of the form "IF $(R[x] < R[y])$ THEN $(R[x] := -R[x])$. In addition, $R[y]$ can be either a register reference or index a state variable.

2.1.2 Host Population

Symbionts are explicitly limited to deploying a single action. Thus a host needs to identify relevant subsets of symbionts that are capable of collaborating or ***lateral task decomposition***. To do so, each host indexes a subset $[2, ..., \omega]$ of the symbionts currently existing in the symbiont population. Fitness evaluation is only performed for hosts, symbionts do not have a fitness. Thus, for each host, h_i, fitness is evaluated with respect to a set of initial configurations of the task domain, as defined by individuals from the point population, p_j. For each task initialization, p_j, a series of interactions – defining an episode – occur between task's state variables and action as suggested by the host presently under evaluation. Each training episode ends when a task specific end condition or a computational limit is encountered (see Section 3).

In the case of SBB, each interaction between task and host has the following form:

1. Present the state variables from the task domain at time step t_s, or $\vec{s}(t_s)$;
2. Execute all (symbiont) programs identified by host, h_i, resulting in a matching number of symbiont bids or $\forall sym \in h_i : sym(bid(t_s))$, where $sym(bid(t_s))$ is the bid value resulting from execution of a symbiont's program (Section 2.1.1);
3. Identify the 'winning' symbiont as that with the maximum bid from host h_i or, $sym^* = \arg_{sym \in h_i} \max(sym(bid(t_s)))$;
4. Present the action from the winning symbiont to the task domain and update the state variables accordingly or $\vec{s}(t_s + 1) \leftarrow task \leftarrow sym^*(a)$; where $sym^*(a)$ is the action of the winning symbiont identified at Step (3).

Symbionts therefore use bidding to establish the **context** for deploying their respective action. The number of symbionts per host and 'mix' of actions represented by a host are both an artifact of evolution. The relative uniqueness of the distribution of goal satisfaction across the host and point populations will be discounted under competitive fitness sharing [17], Section 2.2.2. Should a single dominant policy *not* emerge then fitness sharing represents the principal scheme for developing meta action diversity.

2.2 Selection and Replacement

2.2.1 Point Population

The role of the point population is to define a sample of initial task configurations with sufficient diversity to provide variation in the behaviours of hosts as measured through the fitness function. A tabula rasa approach is assumed in which a simple stochastic sampling heuristic is adopted. At each generation P_{gap} points are removed with uniform probability and a corresponding number of new points introduced. The process for initializing / generating points is naturally a function of the task domain itself and will be detailed within the context of the Acrobot handstand task (Section 3).

2.2.2 Host Population

As per the point population, a fixed number of hosts, H_{gap}, are removed at each generation. Host removal is applied deterministically with the worst H_{gap} hosts removed at each generation. However, assuming a competitive fitness sharing formulation [17] maintains diversity in the host population. Thus shared fitness, s_i, of host h_i takes the form:

$$s_i = \sum_k \left(\frac{G(h_i, p_k)}{\sum_j G(h_j, p_k)} \right)^3 \quad (1)$$

where $G(h_i, p_k)$ is the task dependent reward defining the quality of policy h_i on test point p_k (see Section 4).

Naturally, deleting the worst H_{gap} hosts may result in some symbionts no longer receiving (host) indexes. Given that such symbionts must have been associated with the worst performing hosts, these symbionts are also deleted. A secondary implication of this is that symbiont population size will vary whereas the host population size remains fixed.

2.3 Variation Operators

Symbiosis is an explicitly hierarchical coevolutionary process. From an exploration/ exploitation perspective it is important not to disrupt 'good' symbiont combinations while simultaneously continuing to search for better hosts. Moreover, variation needs to be maintained at the symbiont level without disrupting symbionts that are already effective. The process for maintaining exploration (diversity) without unduly disrupting the better host–symbiont relationships therefore follows an explicitly hierarchical formulation. Following the removal of H_{gap} hosts, the remaining $H_{size} - H_{gap}$ hosts are sampled for cloning with uniform probability. The resulting clones have both their host and symbiont content modified. As such, it is ensured that new symbionts are only associated with new hosts and therefore no disruption of previous host behaviour takes place. For a detailed presentation of this process see [10, 11, 13].

2.4 Evolving policy trees through SBB

The above description summarizes the process as applied to a single 'level' or round of evolution as conducted over a fixed number of generations t_{max}. However, the content of the host–symbiont population pair might not provide any outright solutions to the task domain. Rather than begin evolution afresh from a completely new host–symbiont parameterization/ initialization, the current host population is considered to represent a set of **meta actions** from which solutions can be more readily composed. That is to say, the hosts as previously evolved at level 'l' represent the set of new 'meta' actions for the symbiont population at level '$l + 1$'. Thus the only difference between evolution at each level is the declaration of the actions that symbionts may index. At level $l = 0$ symbiont actions are always defined by the task domain, or **atomic actions**. Thereafter, for symbionts at level $l > 0$ the action set is the set of all hosts from level $l - 1$ or $a \in \{H^l\}$. For simplicity we assume that evolution is only ever conducted at the highest 'level'; all earlier levels having their content 'frozen'. Moreover, there is no requirement for each host at level l to index all available actions from level $l - 1$. The subset of actions utilized by each host is a function of policy search.

Evaluating host i at level l (or h_i^l) now has the following hierarchical form:

1. Present the state variables describing the current state of the task domain, or $\vec{s}(t_s)$;
2. $\forall sym^l \in h_i^l$, identify the corresponding level set of l symbiont bids, or $sym^l(bid(t_s))$;
3. Identify the 'winning' symbiont for host h_i^l, or $sym^* = \arg_{sym^l \in h_i^l} \max(sym^l(bid(t_s)))$;
4. IF $l == 0$ THEN Step (5) ELSE
   (a) Update level: $l = l - 1$;
   (b) Let the action from the winning symbiont, $sym^*(a)$, in Step (3) identify the new host: $h_i^l \leftarrow sym^*(a)$;
   (c) RETURN to Step (2);
5. Present the atomic action from the winning symbiont to the task domain and update any state variables accordingly, or $\vec{s}(t_s + 1) \leftarrow task \leftarrow sym^*(a)$; where $sym^*(a)$ is the action of the winning symbiont as identified at Step (3).

Such a process represents a process for the bottom-up evolution of a **policy tree**. Conversely, evaluation of a policy tree is performed top-down relative to the host–symbiont population currently under evolution. Nodes in the tree are hosts, whereas symbionts define the branching factor of a node. The path from each branch is selected as per the action of a winning bid. Nodes at deeper levels represent hosts evolved at previous generations. Only the lowest level nodes (hosts) retain symbionts with actions specified in terms of the task domain's atomic actions.

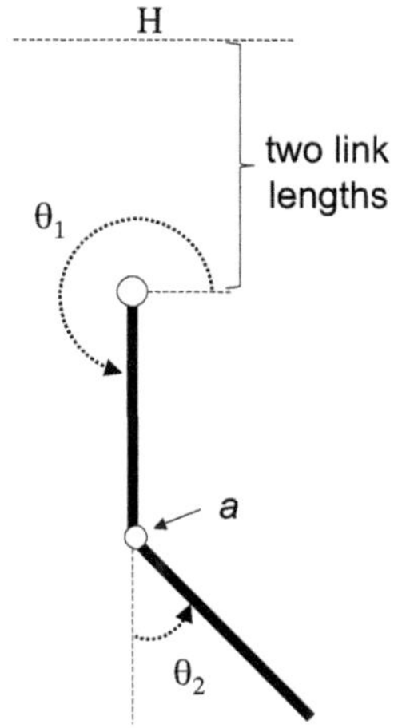

Figure 1: Acrobot 'handstand' domain. The controller is provided with state variable information in the form of the angular position θ_1, θ_2 and velocities $\dot{\theta}_1, \dot{\theta}_2$. The controller supplies the torque a to the acrobot 'waist,' the feet are at the free end of the second link whereas the 'hands' are connected to the rotating bar of the first link. Goal distance 'H' is set to two links above the axis of ϑ_1 in the handstand task. The force the control policy can apply is limited to one of three values: $a \in \{0, \pm 1\}$ N.

3. HANDSTAND ACROBOT

The Acrobot task domain represents a domain in which a two link 'body' has a control force applied to the 'waist' or middle link (Figure 1) [19], [21]; whereas the hands remain fixed at an axle and the feet are free to spin about the waist. The basic goal is to learn a policy that swings the feet to a goal height, H, above the hands. When this height is one link above the hands, this represents the easier *height* task [21]. An alternate definition for the goal state requires that the Acrobot perform a *handstand* [19]. Thus, a policy needs to be identified that is capable of balancing the 'feet' of the Acrobot such that the two links are aligned in the same vertical plane directly above the Acrobot's hands with a near-zero velocity. In this work we concentrate on the more difficult handstand task.

3.1 Previous Results under RL

Previous approaches to the handstand task using RL provided solutions that additionally made use of: simplifications to the goal condition (e.g., by not requiring any velocity reduction [15]); or increased the control force beyond the ±1 N permitted (e.g., real-valued forces over the interval ±30 N [23], [8] or ±2 N [4]). One recent development in which the Acrobot handstand task utilizes the original task constraints incorporates the concept of 'intrinsic util-

Table 1: Task Domain Parameterization. ***C. of M.*** **denotes Center of Mass;** ***M. of I.*** **denotes Moment of Inertia.**

Length of upper (lower) link	1.0m (1.0m)
Length to C. of M.: upper (lower) link	1.0m (1.0m)
M. of I.: upper (lower) link	1.0 (1.0)
Gravitational constant (g)	9.8
Control torque update freq.	5 Hz
Simulation step size	0.05 sec
Target capture region position	$\frac{\pi}{2} \pm 0.3$ rad
Target capture region velocity	± 0.3 rad/sec
Max simulation steps (D_{max})	200
Atomic actions (a)	$\{0, \pm 1N\}$

ity' [6]. Specifically, a Monti-Carlo approximation is used to provide a measure of intrinsic reward applicable to domains with continuous state spaces. The ensuing solution is able to provide solutions taking 17–18 seconds of simulated time (or 85 to 90 interactions).

3.2 Solution using exhaustive search

It is possible to utilize domain specific heuristics to simplify the problem to the extent that an A^* search represents a feasible approach for discovering solutions [1]. Specifically, information was utilized to establish constraints to the frequency of torque direction switches and speed–energy profiles, as well as emphasizing the use of 'singular arcs' during a trajectory. While this by no means detracted from the quality of solutions produced, it did leave several questions unanswered. First, it was still unclear whether general machine learning algorithms could discover solutions of equivalent quality. Boone's work included a comparison with the well known SARSA lambda RL algorithm (e.g., [21]), but found that it failed to converge to a solution after several days of training. Second, although Boone's work found a best case trajectory starting from the stable equilibrium position – or the **swing-up** task – the method produced no meaningful approximation of the state space. This solution is simply a sequence of torque values specific to the stable equilibrium starting point. As a consequence, varying the start position of the arm by even small amounts will require re-running the search algorithm to generate a new torque sequence. In this work we investigate the special case of the swing-up initial condition and generalizing to multiple Acrobot initializations.

3.3 Atomic action and state variables

The Acrobot parameterization explicitly follows that established in [1]. The goal of the handstand task is to identify control policies that successfully enter a ***target capture region*** while enforcing the 1 N magnitude limitation on the control force. The target capture region define specific conditions under which the goal state is satisfied i.e., a region in phase space corresponding to an (unstable) vertical equilibrium position (Table 1).[1] **State variables** take the form of angular position θ_1, θ_2 and velocities $\dot{\theta}_1, \dot{\theta}_2$ (Figure 1). Figure 1 and Table 1 also identify the available **atomic actions**.

[1]Established practice is to deploy a LQR controller once the target capture region is encountered [19].

3.4 Performance evaluation

The Acrobot handstand task will be considered from the perspective of two independent experiments: 1) rewarding solutions for the 'swing-up' formulation of the task i.e., the ultimate goal is to provide a controller capable of swinging the acrobot from the single at rest stable equilibrium position to the Acrobot entering the target capture region (defined in Section 3.3). Such an approach facilitates direct comparison with what still represents the best solution to the swing-up task (82 steps) [1]. 2) rewarding generalization properties; in which case the radii about the Acrobot 'hands' are set to twice the link length and initial Acrobot configurations sampled at 200 equally spaced intervals. Given the differing objectives of the two assessments, the process for initializing and replacing individuals from the point population assumes different biases (see Section 3.5).

3.5 Point population routines

Acrobot configurations defined by the point population always assume alignment of the two limbs ($\theta_2 = 0$, Figure 1) and zero initial velocity. Points differ with respect to their θ_1 values. Given the a priori knowledge regarding the significance of the $< \frac{\pi}{2}, 0 >$ configuration in the swing-up runs versus a requirement for generalization in the second Acrobot runs, we introduce a bias to ensure a greater frequency of encountering the swing-up configuration during this training. Thus, for the P_{gap} points replaced at each generation, the point replacement process has the following generic form. With frequency p_{pf} initialize points to the swing-up position. The remaining $1 - p_{pf}$ points are created by selecting a 'parent point' and adding an offset of 0.05 radians to θ_1 with sign selected stochastically.

At initialization, p_{pf} points are again set to the swing-up position, with the remainder initialized with θ_1 selected with uniform probability over the interval $[0, 2\pi)$. The only difference between point initialization processes as applied to the swing-up task versus that applied during the generalization test is the value used for p_{pf}. Thus, in the swing-up (generalization) runs the corresponding value for p_{pf} is 0.5 (0.0). Naturally, points corresponding to the swing-up position benefit from fitness caching.

3.6 Concluding comments

A complete description of the system dynamics may be found in several previous works (e.g., [19], [21]), but amount to a second order differential equation. However, the Acrobot is highly sensitive to the quality of the simulation used because small errors produce cascading effects. Commonly used techniques like the Euler-Cromer method are inappropriate for use in this task domain using conventional time step sizes. With this in mind, the 4th order Runge-Kutta method of integration was used to define the new position and velocity of the Acrobot at each time step.

4. EXPERIMENTAL METHODOLOGY

4.1 Lexicographic cost function

A hierarchy of properties within a single scalar fitness function is established. Thus, constraints on each of the measured properties are sequentially satisfied in order or 'incremental evolution'. Three properties are considered: position, velocity and time; with position and velocity enforcing constraints associated with the target capture region employed by Boone (Section 3) and provides a measure of solution quality; summarized as follows,

1. Position (F_p): expresses the need to first reach the target capture region and was motivated by the approach taken by Munos and Moore [15] or,

$$\begin{array}{ll} \frac{\sin(\theta_1)+\sin(\theta_1+\theta_2)+2}{4} & \leftarrow \text{IF } (\theta_1+\theta_2 \notin \{\pi/2 \pm 0.3\} \\ & \text{OR } \theta_1 \notin \{\pi/2 \pm 0.3\}) \\ 1 & \leftarrow \text{otherwise} \end{array} \tag{2}$$

2. Velocity (F_v): enforces the requirement to enter the target capture region at a sufficiently low velocity or,

$$\begin{array}{ll} 0 & \leftarrow \text{IF } (F_p < 1 \text{ OR } |\dot{\theta_1}| > 2 \text{ OR } |\dot{\theta_2}| > 2) \\ 1 & \leftarrow \text{IF } (|\dot{\theta_1}| < 0.3 \text{ OR } |\dot{\theta_2}| < 0.3) \\ \frac{4-|\dot{\theta_1}|-|\dot{\theta_2}|}{4} & \leftarrow \text{otherwise} \end{array} \tag{3}$$

3. Duration (F_d): distinguishes between the quality of solutions based on the number of steps, t_s, necessary to reach the target capture region, given a maximum duration to locate a solution, D_{max} (Table 1) or,

$$\begin{array}{ll} \frac{t_s}{D_{max}} & \leftarrow \text{IF } (F_v = 1) \\ 0 & \leftarrow \text{otherwise} \end{array} \tag{4}$$

The resulting reward function is merely the sum over contributions from each of the three properties (with the proviso that the properties are satisfied in order) or,

$$G(h_i, p_k) = \frac{1}{3} \max_{t_s}(F_p(t_s) + F_v(t_s) + F_d(t_s)) \tag{5}$$

where $0 \leq t_s \leq D_{max} - 1$ are the discrete time steps over which an interaction takes place. Thus, $G(\cdot)$ returns the best value encountered over the duration of a policy given a point–host pair (h_i, p_k). Naturally, if both position, F_p, and velocity, F_v, goals are satisfied, an interaction will terminate with the current value for the duration property, F_d. Such a reward function is of comparable complexity to functions designed by others for the swing-up task (e.g., [8], [4], [1]).

4.2 SBB Parameterization

Parameterization of SBB follows exactly the same form as used in the earlier supervised learning (classification task domain) benchmark study [13], and is summarized in Table 2. Needless to say, no claims are made regarding the optimality of these parameters.

4.3 NEAT Parameterization

The C++ distribution of NEAT [20] is employed to provide a baseline for the relative difficulty of the task domain; where NEAT represents one of the most widely utilized frameworks for policy search in RL. The original NEAT distribution is augmented with the point population to provide the same tabula rasa training dynamic as SBB receives. Thus, at each generation performance of NEAT individuals are evaluated over P_{size} points, with P_{gap} points replaced. The reward function – that is before application of NEAT specific speciation/ fitness sharing mechanisms – is the sum of rewards over all points, or Equation (5). Needless to say, both NEAT and SBB assume a common parameterization of the point population, with P_{size} and P_{gap} set to 120 and 20 respectively.

Table 2: Parameterization of Host and Symbiont populations. As per Linear GP, a fixed number of general purpose registers are assumed (*numRegisters*) and variable length programs subject to a max. instruction count (*maxProgSize*).

Host (solution) population			
Parameter	Value	Parameter	Value
t_{max}	1 000	ω	10
P_{size}, H_{size}	120	P_{gap}, H_{gap}	20, 60
p_{md}	0.7	p_{ma}	0.7
p_{mm}	0.2	p_{mn}	0.1
Symbiont (program) population			
numRegisters	8	*maxProgSize*	48
p_{delete}, p_{add}	0.5	p_{mutate}, p_{swap}	1.0

Table 3: Parameterization of NEAT.

Parameter	Value	Parameter	Value
Pop size	150	c_1	1.0
Survival thres.	0.2	c_2	1.0
weight mut. power	2.5	c_3	0.4
p(wt. link)	0.9	δ	3.0
p(toggle)	0.01	p(gene reint.)	0.001
p(add node)	0.03	p(add link)	0.05
p(recur. link)	0.1	p(mate only)	0.2
p(inter.spec.mate)	0.001	p(mutate only)	0.25
Dropoff age	15	New link tries	20

A base parameterization of NEAT was established from the original experiments with the inverted pendulum problem [20]. As per recommendations from the NEAT users page (http://www.cs.ucf.edu/~kstanley/neat.html), additional experimentation was then performed to tune the link weight mutation probabilities and assess the impact of permitting recurrent links. The resulting parameterization is summarized in Table 3. Naturally, no claims regarding the optimality of this selection is made.

Finally, the number of fitness evaluations between SBB and NEAT runs was designed to be as similar as possible, or 16,812,000 NEAT evaluations versus 16,800,000 SBB evaluations. This reflects the different population sizes for each algorithm and support for hierarchical SBB. Thus, hierarchical SBB assumes 8,400,000 evaluations per layer. In the case of each architecture 100 initializations are performed for each experiment.

5. RESULTS

Section 3 introduced a two part framework for evaluating solutions to the Acrobot handstand task: swing-up versus generalization. Results are first reported with respect to the Acrobot 'swing-up' task under the problem configuration established by Boone, Section 5.1. We then then go on to assess the "generalization properties" of the SBB approach by considering performance under an independent test set, as evolved under the second formulation of the point population, Section 5.2.

In all cases Shapiro-Wilk tests and visualization are used to verify the support for assuming a normal distribution in the data. Should normality be supported in all data involved in a hypothesis test, then 1-way ANOVA and stu-

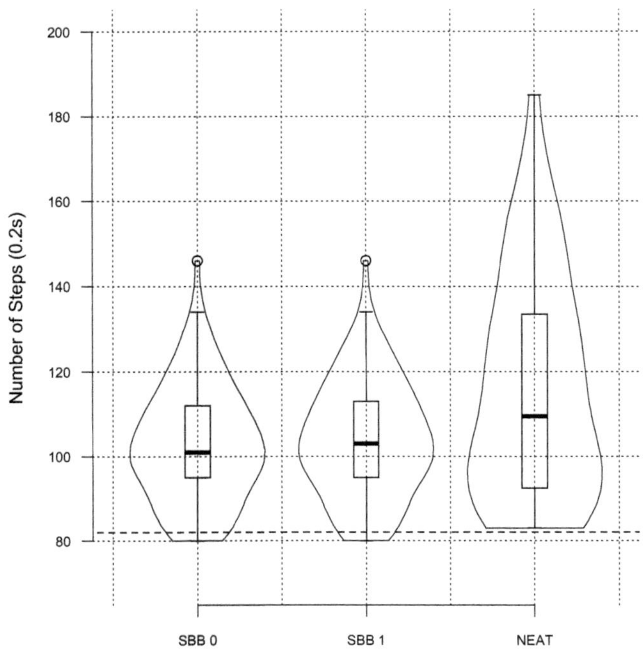

Figure 2: Number of steps necessary to solve the Acrobot swing-up task. The horizontal dashed line represents the case of the shortest previously known solution from Boone (82 steps) [1]. Box plot represents quartile statistic.

dent t-tests establish the corresponding statistical significance. Conversely, when data is not normally distributed then a Kruskal-Wallace test is employed. Bonferroni corrections were used to adjust p-values based on the number of hypothesis tested.

5.1 Experiment 1: Swing-up task

The basic objective is to evolve solutions to the swing-up initialization of the handstand task using the smallest number of steps as possible. NEAT found solutions on 70% of the runs, whereas SBB found solutions in 95% of runs. The following analysis is therefore performed relative to the runs that succeeded in solving the swing-up task. Figure 2 summarizes the time taken by a valid solution trajectories under the swing-up task. The distributions were not normal. No significant difference appeared between SBB levels 0 and 1, but both SBB results differed significantly from solutions identified by NEAT ($p < 0.05$ in both cases). Observed sample means were 102, 103 and 115 steps for SBB levels 0 and 1, and NEAT respectively.

In addition to constantly providing solutions to the swing-up task SBB was also able to match the previous best case 82 step trajectory on the swing-up task from Boone [1] in 3 cases and in 2 cases identified a faster solution utilizing 80 and 81 steps respectively for both non-hierarchical (SBB 0) and hierarchical policies (SBB 1) i.e., SBB 0 are reused as meta actions by SBB 1. Naturally, SBB 0 is already solving the swingup task, where this is achieved under half the evaluation count.

The principle reason for the existence of faster solutions under SBB than in the original work of Boone is that the policy is now non-greedy. Rather than always selecting actions to increase energy, actions are selected that initially result in less energy injected into the Acrobot. This actually results in more energy being pumped into the Acrobot at later time steps. In Section 5.2 we emphasize how hierarchical SBB is able to leverage this capability into better generalization performance.

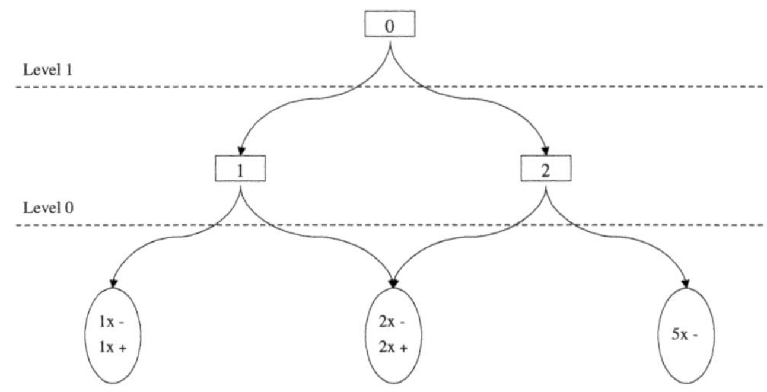

Figure 3: Breakdown of SBB architecture corresponding to the best Acrobot swing-up solution from level 1. A total of 169 instructions are distributed across 13 symbiont programs and 3 hosts.

The structure of the policy tree associated with the 80 step SSB 1 solution is summarized by Figure 3. Ellipses at the bottom of the figure represent sets of symbionts (and corresponding atomic action) *common* to a host. Thus, the left hand ellipse labeled '1x $-$, 1x $+$' denotes two symbionts, one with an atomic action of $-1N$ and the second with an atomic action of $+1N$. The arc connecting this pair of symbionts to the level 0 host with label '1' (left hand rectangle) implies that both symbionts are *unique* to this host. However, the two symbionts identified by the central ellipse are used by *both* hosts from level 0 (hosts carrying labels 1 and 2); as indicated by the two arcs pointing to the central set of symbionts. The last (right hand) set of symbionts consists of five symbionts all with a $-1N$ atomic action. Likewise, the single level 1 host (labeled 0) has two arcs, one to each level 0 host. Thus, there is a single level 1 symbiont associated with deploying the meta action associated with the behaviour of each level 0 host. Moreover, the solution policy is itself a combination of level 0 policies as opposed to merely the case of deploying one level 0 policy relative to a specific initial condition (Figure 4).

5.2 Experiment 2: Generalized Acrobot task

The focus of the Acrobot swing-up task of Section 5.1 was to evolve a solution with the smallest number of time steps relative to the single swing up test configuration. No advantage was demonstrated in the hierarchical formulation of SBB. In this section we are more interested in solutions that generalize, or provide solutions to as many test configurations as possible. From the perspective of the evolutionary framework, the only difference in the approach is with regard to the method for initializing/replacing members of the point population, everything else remains unchanged (Section 3.5). A total of 200 test cases are generated by sampled uniformly over the range of θ_1 or 2π. Each test case is therefore equivalent to rotating the feet to points on the circumference of a circle (radii equal to the two Acrobot links) and letting the Acrobat 'fall' under gravity. A point in the test set was deemed "solved" if the controller being tested

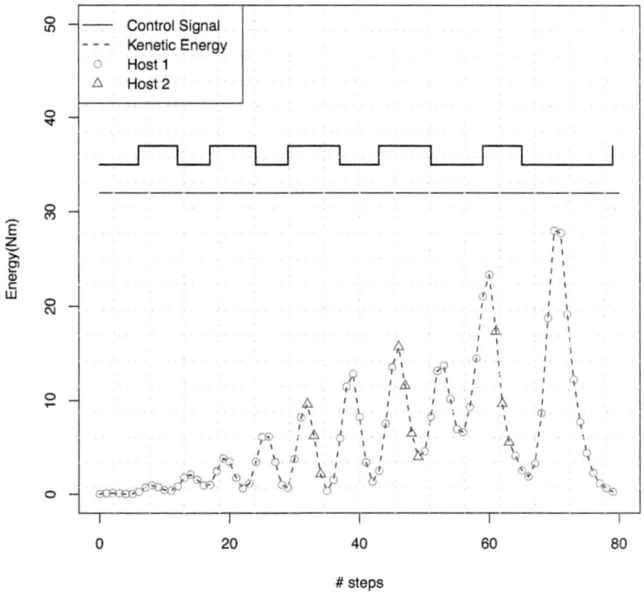

Figure 4: SBB 1 solution in 80 steps w.r.t. Acrobot swingup task . Different coloured icons differentiate between different level 0 host (meta action) deployed by level 1 symbionts.

successfully drove the Acrobot into the target capture region within 200 steps.

Naturally, test cases about the target capture region require a rather different behaviour than those elsewhere. Indeed, it transpired that such Acrobot configurations can be 'solved' through learning to do nothing. Figure 5 summarizes the frequency with which a test condition of a given initial θ_1 are solved. Given the offset in defining the 'origin' for θ_1 (Figure 1), then angles in the region of $\pi/2$ (≈ 1.571 radians) correspond to test cases in the target capture region.

In summary, NEAT solutions are dominated by those corresponding to test cases around the target capture region, in effect a mediocre stable state dominates the resulting solutions. Note also that there is no bias in the generation of training initializations in the point population to create initial Acrobot configurations in this region, all configurations are equally likely (Section 3.5). The addition of hierarchical SBB actually results in a redistribution of test cases solved away from those within the target capture region. Naturally, in the case of SBB, level 1 is limited to using behaviours previously learnt at level 0. Thus, in order for level 1 hosts to solve new test cases relative to those solved at level 0, as is the case here, then level 0 hosts must be redeployed to identify useful temporal abstractions at level 1.

The violin plot of Figure 6 summarizes the number of test cases solved when the 19 Acrobot configurations at or near the goal state are removed. The distributions are non-normal, and significant differences exist between samples ($p < 10^{-16}$). The observed average solution rates per point were 1.81%, 4.92% and 7.95% for NEAT and SBB levels 0 and 1 respectively. In short, for a given point, SBB level 1 is more than 4 times as likely as NEAT to have an individual capable of solving the test point or nearly twice as likely as a hosts at level 0.

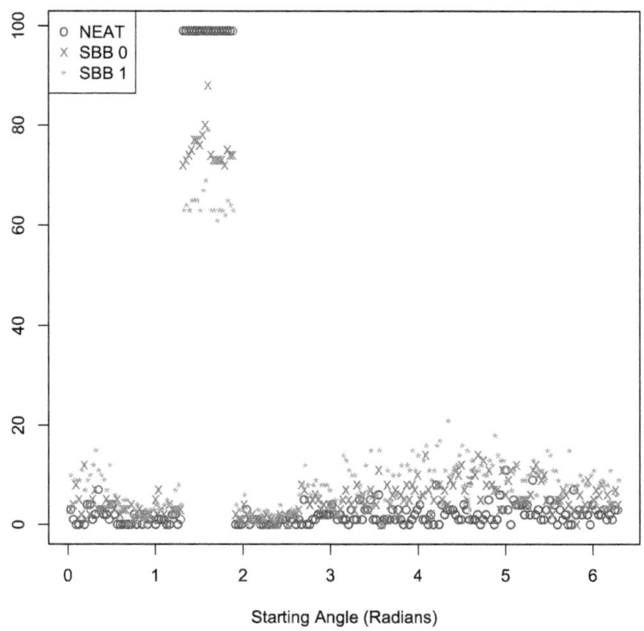

Figure 5: Scatter plot summarizes the percentage of runs for each method that solved an Acrobot initial state for a θ_1 initial condition. The plot requires viewing in colour. Test cases in the vicinity of 1.571 radians correspond to the target capture region and have a trivial solution. Cases in the vicinity of 4.712 radians correspond to the 'swing-up' task.

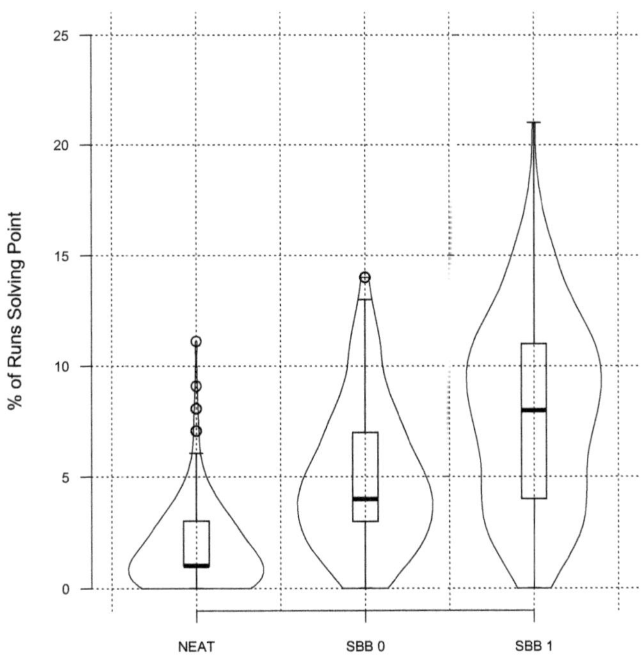

Figure 6: Percentage of individuals solving an Acrobot test configuration. The 19 test points within the vicinity of the target capture region leading to trivial policies are excluded. Box plot represents quartile statistic.

6. CONCLUSION

A symbiotic framework for evolving policy trees under RL is presented. Each round of evolution results in the construction of a new level to the policy tree. In the special case of the first round of SBB deployment actions take the form of the atomic actions of the task domain. Should solutions not be identified, then the content of the host population from the previous round of evolution are considered meta actions. The next round of evolution attempts to build hosts from symbionts that reference the meta actions as their actions; or policy construction at a more abstract level. A bottom up process for constructing policy trees is established where this has implications for addressing the scaling problem of RL. No a priori knowledge is necessary regarding what represent appropriate meta actions, the same generic cost function is employed throughout. Instead meta action discovery is a function of fitness sharing. The framework is demonstrated under the Acrobot handstand task. We establish for the first time solutions that match and better those identified under the A^* search heuristic and emphasize the contribution of hierarchical solutions to generalizing over multiple Acrobot configurations.

Future research will continue to benchmark the approach on additional task domains. Indeed, [10, 11] present results in a truck reversal domain[2] and [9] illustrates the approach using the 'Pinball' task. In all cases hierarchical SBB results in a significant improvement to the generalization performance. More generally a theme of particular interest is the interaction between ecology and the conditions under which new levels to the hierarchy are introduced.

Acknowledgements

The authors are grateful for support from MITACS, NSERC and CFI New Opportunities granting agencies and Killam Trust (Canada).

7. REFERENCES

[1] G. Boone. Minimum-time control of the acrobot. In *International Conference on Robotics and Automation*, pages 3281–3287, 1997.

[2] M. M. Botvinick, Y. Niv, and A. C. Barto. Hierarchically organized behavior and its neural foundations: A reinforcement learning perspective. *Cognition*, 113:262–280, 2009.

[3] M. Brameier and W. Banzhaf. A comparison of linear Genetic Programming and neural networks in medical data mining. *IEEE Transactions on Evolutionary Computation*, 5(1):17–26, 2001.

[4] R. Coulom. High-accuracy value-function approximation with neural networks applied to the Acrobot. In *European Symposium on Artificial Neural Networks*, pages 28–30, 2004.

[5] Y. Engel. *Gaussian process reinforcement learning*, pages 439–447. Springer, 2010.

[6] T. Jung, D. Polani, and P. Stone. Empowerment for continuous agent-environment systems. *Adaptive Behavior*, 19(1):16–39, 2011.

[2]A code distribution is available for this task at http://www.cs.dal.ca/~mheywood/Code/SBB/

[7] L. P. Kaelbling, M. L. Littman, and A. W. Moore. Reinforcement learning: A survey. *Journal of Machine Learning Research*, 4:237–285, 1996.

[8] K. Kawada, M. Obika, S. Fujisawa, and T. Yamamoto. Creating swing-up patterns of an Acrobot using Evolutionary Computation. In *IEEE International Symposium on Computational Intelligence in Robotics and Automation*, pages 261–266, 2005.

[9] S. Kelly, P. Lichodzijewski, and M. I. Heywood. On run time libraries and hierarchical symbiosis. In *IEEE Congress on Evolutionary Computation*, 2012.

[10] P. Lichodzijewski. *A symbiotic bid-based framework for problem decomposition using Genetic Programming*. PhD thesis, Faculty of Computer Science, Dalhousie University, 2011. http://www.cs.dal.ca/~mheywood/Thesis/PhD.html.

[11] P. Lichodzijewski, J. A. Doucette, and M. I. Heywood. A symbiotic framework for hierarchical policy search. Technical Report CS-2011-06, Dalhousie University, Faculty of Computer Science, 2011. http://www.cs.dal.ca/research/techreports/.

[12] P. Lichodzijewski and M. I. Heywood. Pareto-coevolutionary Genetic Programming for problem decomposition in multi-class classification. In *Proceedings of the ACM Genetic and Evolutionary Computation Conference*, pages 464–471, 2007.

[13] P. Lichodzijewski and M. I. Heywood. Symbiosis, complexification and simplicity under GP. In *Proceedings of the ACM Genetic and Evolutionary Computation Conference*, pages 853–860, 2010.

[14] D. Moriarty, A. C. Schultz, and J. J. Grefenstette. Evolutionary algorithms for reinforcement learning. *J. of Machine Learning Res.*, 11:241–276, 1999.

[15] R. Munos and A. Moore. Variable resolution discretization for high-accuracy solutions of optimal control problems. In *International Joint Conference on Artificial Intelligence*, pages 1348–1355, 1999.

[16] O. P. -Y, F. Kaplan, and V. V. Hafner. Intrinsic motivation systems for autonomous mental development. *IEEE Transactions on Evolutionary Computation*, 11(2):265–286, 2007.

[17] C. D. Rosin and R. K. Belew. New methods for competitive coevolution. *Evolutionary Computation*, 5:1–29, 1997.

[18] H. A. Simon. The architecture of complexity. In *The Sciences of the Artificial*, chapter 4. MIT Press, 1969.

[19] M. W. Spong. The swing up control problem for the Acrobot. In *IEEE Control Systems Magazine*, pages 49–55, 1995.

[20] K. O. Stanley and R. Miikkulainen. Evolving neural networks through augmenting topologies. *Evolutionary Computation*, 10(2):99–127, 2002.

[21] R. R. Sutton and A. G. Barto. *Reinforcement Learning: An introduction*. MIT Press, 1998.

[22] R. A. Watson and J. B. Pollack. Modular interdependency in complex dynamical systems. *Artificial Life*, 11(4):445–457, 2005.

[23] J. Yoshimoto, S. Ishii, and M. Sato. Application of reinforcement learning to balancing of acrobot. In *IEEE Int. Conf. Systems, Man and Cybernetics*, pages 516–521, 1999.

Exploring and Evolving Process-oriented Control for Real and Virtual Fire Fighting Robots

Kathryn Hardey
Centenary College
Shreveport, LA 71104
khardey@my.centenary.edu

Eren Corapcioglu
Centenary College
Shreveport, LA 71104
ecorapci@my.centenary.edu

Molly Mattis
Allegheny College
Meadville, PA 16335
mattism@allegheny.edu

Mark Goadrich
Centenary College
Shreveport, LA 71104
mgoadric@centenary.edu

Matthew Jadud
Allegheny College
Meadville, PA 16335
matthew.c@jadud.com

ABSTRACT

Current research in evolutionary robotics is largely focused on creating controllers by either evolving neural networks or refining genetic programs based on grammar trees. We propose the use of the dataflow languages for the construction of effective robotic controllers and the evolution of new controllers using genetic programming techniques. These languages have the advantages of being built on concurrent execution frameworks that lend themselves to formal verification along with being visualized as a dataflow graph. In this paper, we compare and contrast the development and subsequent evolution of one such process-oriented control algorithm. Our control software was built from composable, communicating processes executing in parallel, and we tested our solution in an annual fire-fighting robotics competition. Subsequently, we evolved new controllers in a virtual simulation of this parallel dataflow domain, and in doing so discovered and quantified more efficient solutions. This research demonstrates the effectiveness of using process networks as the basis for evolutionary robotics.

Categories and Subject Descriptors

I.2.9 [**Robotics**]: Autonomous vehicles; D.1.3 [**Concurrent Programming**]: Parallel Programming

General Terms

Experimentation, Algorithms

Keywords

Evolutionary Robotics, Concurreny, CSP, occam-pi

1. INTRODUCTION

Evolutionary robotics explores the use of genetic algorithms to learn controllers for autonomous robots. Recent surveys show that neural networks account for the basis of approximately 40% of such controllers, while genetic programming is used in another 30% [10]. Progress has been made in the learning of simple behaviors such as locomotion and obstacle avoidance [12], phototaxis [16], and searching and foraging [13]. As research has moved to attempting tasks involving multiple behaviors, tension has developed between learning controllers for these complex tasks and limiting the amount of *a priori* background knowledge used in the learning frameworks.

We show here how process networks written in dataflow languages can be used as a basis for evolutionary robotics, where the level of controller complexity can be tuned. Our work examines the creation of one such set of processes and their subsequent evolution to improve the performance of a robot within a task involving coordination of multiple simultaneous behaviors. We first describe process networks, and then contrast them with neural networks. We next demonstrate the use of process networks by detailing our creation of a real world controller for a robotic fire fighting competition. This task is then abstracted into a virtual simulation, where we employed an evolutionary algorithm using the basic control processes to improve our performance on the locomotion and object avoidance aspects of the fire fighting task. Finally, we discuss the results of this experiment, related work in evolutionary robotics, and directions for future work.

1.1 Dataflow Languages

A robot is continuously and simultaneously engaged in three activities: it reads inputs, computes over that data, and controls motors and other actuators. By using a parallel instead of a sequential language, these can be written as separate processes that execute concurrently and flow data from one process to the next. Recent research has explored the use of inherently parallel programming languages for writing robotic control systems [2, 7, 17].

Parallel, process-oriented dataflow languages such as occam-pi, Erlang, and Google's Go are based on the Communicating Sequential Processes (CSP) formalism described by Hoare [6]. Programs are written using two main structures, namely processes and channels. The processes involved are self-contained sequences of computation, typically looping forever. These processes only share data (or state) via communication over well-defined channels. This allows the compiler and/or runtime environment of the language to guarantee properties like freedom from deadlock or the absence of race hazards, thus greatly simplifying the process of writing concurrent programs. Another convenient aspect of these languages is that programs can be completely represented as a human-readable network that describes the flow of data from one independent process to another.

1.2 From Neurons to Brains

In comparison to evolutionary systems based on neural networks, dataflow networks can be composed of higher-order processes that have two distinct benefits. First, the complexity of individual nodes can be controlled and augmented beyond a simple activation threshold, and second, all stages of the evolution are understandable by humans for inspection and refinement.

For example, success in a complex locomotion domain could involve developing one set of behaviors to react in an XOR fashion to two input sensors. A neural network would need to refine the connections between individual activation nodes across multiple layers. In a process network, the connections in the neural network can be recreated as simple threshold processes connected with channels of communication, or (alternatively) the entire XOR function can be created as one process, to be connected as a building block in a larger process network of other programmed functions.

Because processes and channels are the primary abstraction mechanisms in dataflow languages, processes become the genetic material upon which evolution can act. In this manner, we can incorporate varying amounts of prior knowledge into the genome, from processes as simple as neurons, to more complicated circuit functions, and even complete programs for specific behaviors arranged in a complex process hierarchy.

2. THE PHYSICAL PROVING GROUND

Each year Trinity College hosts a fire fighting home robot contest (TCFFHRC) [1]. The purpose of this contest is to navigate an arena, locate a candle, and extinguish it. A sample arena is shown in Figure 1.

At the start of a trial, the robot is placed on the home circle. The robot then has a five minute time limit to extinguish the candle placed in one of the four rooms. A successful robot must be able to coordinate and execute the behaviors of locomotion, object avoidance, and phototaxis, along with some method of extinguishing the candle. Points are awarded based on the duration of the trial and whether the contestant chooses to participate in any optional point multiplier challenges. Our team participated in the Senior Division of the April 2011 contest using a system based on the Arduino (for hardware) and occam-pi (for software).

2.1 Hardware

Our hardware was a low-cost, differential-drive platform with a trailing caster. We used three infrared range sensors for obstacle sensing, three (tuned) infrared diodes for flame detection, a fan for extinguishing flame, and the commonly available Arduino platform to handle sensor processing and computation. Figure 2 shows our competition robot from the rear, and Figure 3 diagrams the placement of the sensors on the robot.

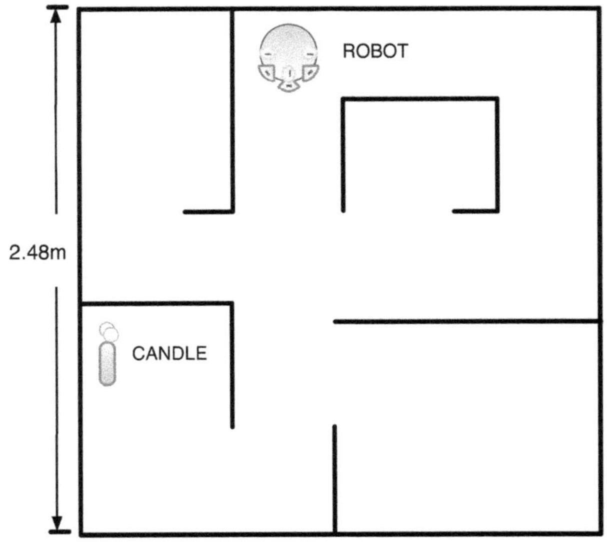

Figure 1: The TCFFHRC Competition Arena

Figure 2: The robot used in competition

The microcontroller board we used to control our robot was an Arduino Duemilanove[1] with an Adafruit Motor Shield[2] attached. The Arudino is open hardware, and uses a 16MHz processor with 32K of internal flash for program storage and 2K of RAM. The Arduino can read digital and analog inputs (via a built-in, 10-bit ADC) and produce output through these same pins.

2.2 Software

Our controller was hand-coded in occam-pi. Our process network is shown in Figure 4, and the full source to our controller is open and available for download[3]. We have

[1] http://www.arduino.cc/en/Main/ArduinoBoardDuemilanove
[2] http://www.ladyada.net/make/mshield/index.html
[3] http://code.google.com/p/occam-rescue/

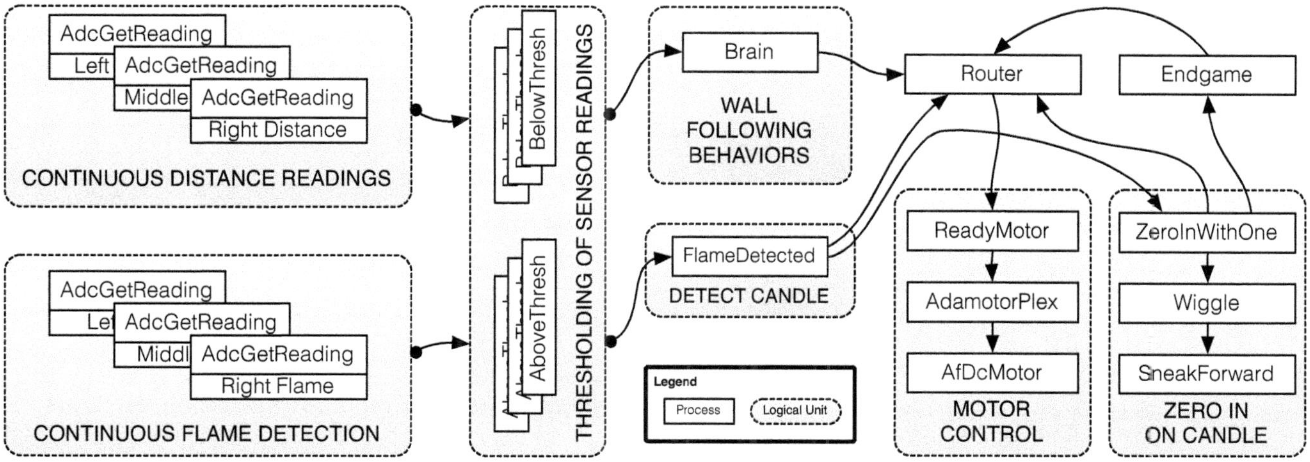

Figure 4: occam-pi process network for physical robot

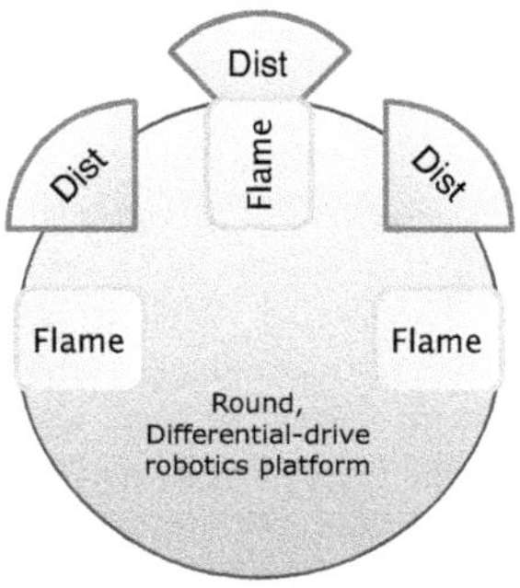

Figure 3: Placement of sensors on the robot

two main modes: a movement and wall-avoidance mode for wandering the arena, and a flame-detected mode for extinguishing the candle.

The Brain of the robot initializes the motor shield and begins giving the motors commands based on signals from multiple AboveThresh and BelowThresh processes. The threshold processes continuously take readings from the sensors using the AdcGetReading process and activate the correct motors such that the robot moves through the arena and avoids walls.

When one of the flame sensors detects a high reading, AboveThresh tells FlameDetected that it should send out signals, which lets other processes know the robot is switching into phototaxis mode. The Router manages this switch and begins listening to the ZeroInWithOne process, which closes in on the candle using the front flame sensor by moving toward the direction where the sensor detects the most light.

Once ZeroInWithOne gets a high enough reading, it signals the EndGame process which turns the robot 180 degrees and starts a fan on the top of the robot to hopefully extinguish the flame.

2.3 Evaluation

In the TCFFHRC, each contestant is given two chances to find and extinguish the candle. If the robot is able to accomplish this in at least one trial, a third trial is awarded. For our first two trials, our robot was able to find the candle. In the second trial, our robot extinguished the candle successfully, granting us a third trial.

Our robot visited most of the arena by following the right wall. However, by using this technique the upper right island room was inaccessible. Thus, if a candle was placed in that room, the robot could not locate and extinguish it. At the contest, the candle was placed in the island room for our third trial. Our flame sensors were unable to see the candle and our robot bypassed the room. Overall, our robot placed 15th out of 41 contestants in the Senior Division, a respectable showing for first-time contestants.

3. THE VIRTUAL PROVING GROUND

To demonstrate the utility of using process networks as a foundation for evolutionary robotics, we implemented each of the four possible TCFFHRC arenas in Simbad, an open-source and easily customizable Java 3D simulator [5]. Figure 5 is an example of an arena with one possible candle placement. Our simulations randomly chose one arena along with a random candle location for each run.

Our virtual robot in Simbad closely followed the specifications of our physical robot used in competition. The motors in Simbad simulated a two-wheeled robot, with the ability to control the speed of each motor independently, and the light and distance sensors in Simbad were altered to closely match the expected range of input from the physical sensors.

3.1 Communicating Processes in Java

As Simbad is written in Java, we chose to express our process network controller using Communicating Sequential Processes for Java (JCSP) [18]. Using this library, we created parallel processes for our virtual robots using message passing as opposed to the usual threads and shared memory. This enabled a near one-to-one mapping of our original control code into the simulator. Figure 6 shows the *wallbrain*

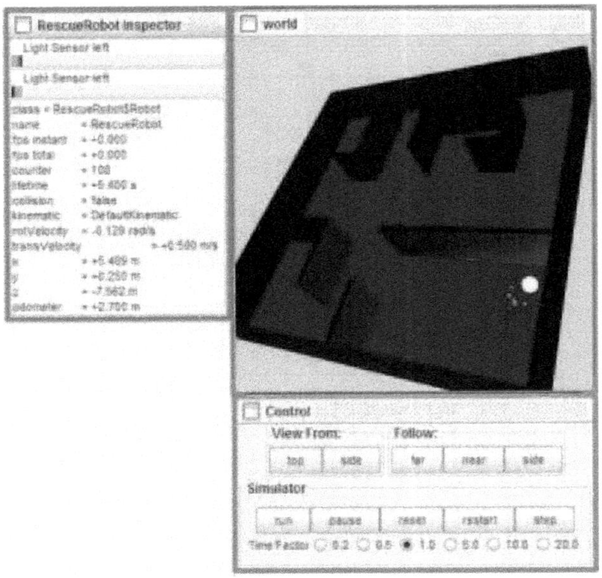

Figure 5: A sample arena in Simbad

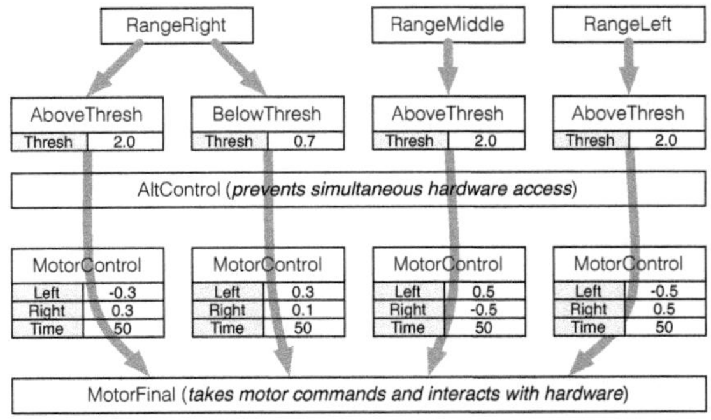

Figure 6: The wallbrain portion of our competition controller, reformulated for execution in Simbad

portion of our original occam-pi robot, now programmed using a JCSP process network to move and avoid the walls within the arena.

In JCSP, we recreated the AboveThresh and BelowThresh processes, which listened to a distance or light sensor and compared the sensor readings to a fixed threshold level. All processes send their signals to an AltControl process, which listens to and prioritizes the signals. This process takes the place of and abstracts our Brain and FlameDetected processes in the previous network so that our networks can be more flexible. Each AltControl listens for the threshold process signals and passes signals along to the next process stage.

In our setup, AltControl passes an incoming signal to the respective MotorControl process. The MotorControl process stores the direction and speed for the left and right motor along with the duration for the movement. All MotorControl processes feed into a MotorFinal process that guarantees motors are not controlled simultaneously from separate sources. If the MotorFinal has not received any signals, it will perform a default behavior of moving forward for a brief time interval.

4. EVOLVING PROCESS NETWORKS

To test the feasibility of evolving process networks, we focused on evolving networks capable of performing the locomotion and obstacle avoidance elements of the TCFFHRC task.

4.1 Initialization

Our population was initialized to twelve randomly generated robots. Each robot in the population was given one AltControl process. The AltControl is then augmented with a random number of *information pathways*. An information pathway can be seen as the flow of data starting from a sensor, and passing through a threshold process to a particular MotorControl (gray arrows, Figures 6, 7, and 8).

For each of these pathways, a threshold process was randomly chosen by creating an AboveThresh or BelowThresh process with a valid, random threshold level. Each threshold was then connected to a particular sensor from which to receive readings; in these experiments the possible sensors were the range sensors. In this way, sensors are allowed to send information to more than one threshold, which can allow for complex behaviors to emerge.

Next, MotorControl processes were created for each threshold. Random values are chosen for the left and right motors; negative values turn the wheels backwards, while positive values spin the wheels forward. The time interval for movement was selected from between ten and 99 milliseconds. This range was chosen based on our experience with the physical robot. Finally, a MotorFinal process is created and the MotorControl channels are connected to complete the flow of data.

4.2 Evaluation

The contest specifies that a robot has five minutes to complete the task of extinguishing the candle, with the score based on the time used in the arena. We found this to be an incomplete evaluation metric, where many robots would succeed in identification of the candle but fail to extinguish it properly, yet receive the same score as a robot that failed to move.

To increase the learnability of the task, we wanted to track the effectiveness of the robot scanning the whole arena. To calculate this, we overlaid a 20x20 grid on the arena, and recorded how many squares were left unseen at the end of the run as a percentage of the total number of squares. This forms the basis for our fitness function, and refer to it as the unseen grid.

Our uniform, unseen grid was improved by adding additional emphasis when the robot visited a room as opposed to a hallway, as candles will always be placed in rooms. The unconnected room in the upper-right corner of the arena is weighted even higher, since this room could not be easily found with our hand-crafted solution. Therefore, squares in a hallway are assigned one point, squares in the three wall-connected rooms earn two points, and squares in the unconnected room earn three points. Our weighted score is then the sum of the weights on unseen squares divided by the total of all the weighted squares, with the goal being to minimize this score.

4.3 Selection

We used tournament selection for all of our experiments. This incorporated the absolute ranking of the robots, as the *unseen* metrics of the robots were tightly clustered. We performed selection twelve times to keep our population size constant, discarding the original population completely.

4.4 Mutation

Our mutation methods were focused on altering individual processes or the flow of information between processes. For a given run of the evolutionary algorithm, we chose a mutation rate, and each mutation method in a process was performed with that probability. This mutation rate is applied to each individual in the selected population.

Above and Below Thresholds

- **Alter** the level for the threshold
- **Listen** to a different sensor
- **Toggle** between Above and Below threshold types

AltControl

- **Add information pathway** . Create a new Threshold, MotorControl, and necessary channels to connect to a sensor, the AltControl, and MotorFinal processes.
- **Delete information pathway** . If there is currently more than one pathway, delete a selected channel and pathway connected to it.
- **Switch pathways** . Select two Thresholds and switch which MotorControl process they activate by switching their channels.

MotorControl

- **Re-selected direction** values for left and/or right motor.
- **Reset time interval** for movement to another number between ten and 99.

Figure 7 provides an example of a brain being mutated using several of the above methods. In this example, each of the Threshold mutation methods were executed. The leftmost BelowThresh **altered** its value from 1.5 to 0.3. The rightmost threshold was mutated to **listen** to the RangeMiddle sensor rather than the original RangeLeft sensor. The leftmost threshold originally was a BelowThresh and was **toggled** to AboveThresh.

This mutation session did not **Add** nor **Delete** a pathway from the AltControl process. However, the middlemost and rightmost thresholds were **switched** to different MotorControl processes. The rightmost MotorControl's right **direction** was updated from -0.8 in the original brain to 0.7 in the mutated brain. The same MotorControl also mutated its **time interval** from 56 milliseconds to 23 milliseconds.

4.5 Crossover

To perform crossover, all individuals in our selected population were randomly paired, and then children were created by swapping all of the information pathways connected to one randomly chosen sensor. If one parent did not have a pathway attached to the chosen sensor, the sensor in the

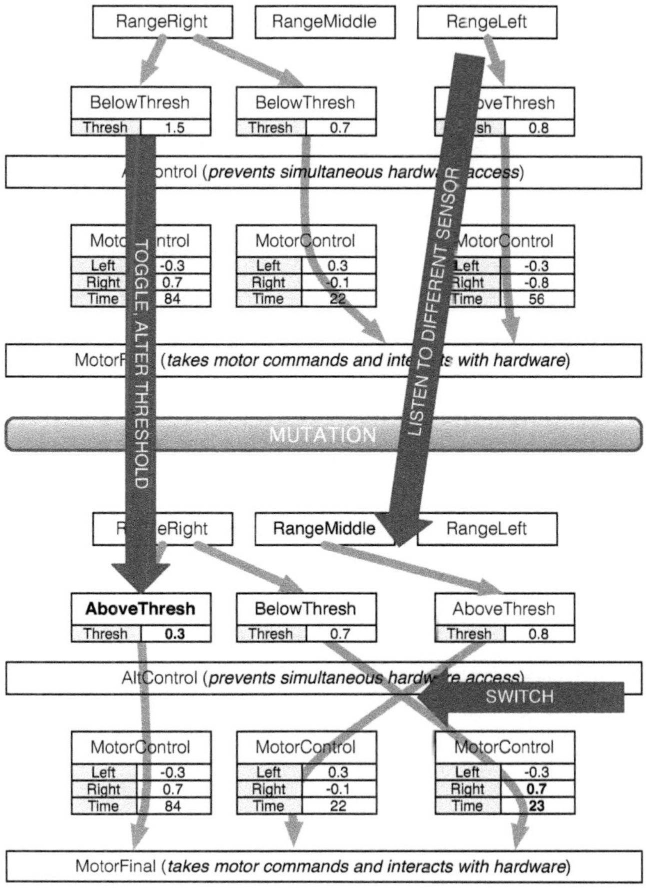

Figure 7: Example of mutation methods on sample brain

other parent now has no pathways. In cases when this leads to an empty robot, it was replaced with a new randomly generated robot.

Figure 8 demonstrates our crossover method applied to two sample parent brains. In this example, the RangeMiddle sensor has been selected for crossover. The first parent lacks a pathway attached to this sensor while the second parent has two pathways attached to RangeMiddle. This leads to two children, the child on the left having four pathways and the child on the right remaining with one.

5. EXPERIMENTS

Our experiments explored the effect of different mutation rates on our process networks, and compared the best results to our original process network written for the TCFFHRC. We investigated two different ways to specify the amount of mutation applied to each robot in the population:

1. We first set a mutation rate, and then applied the mutation methods with this probability for each process. We chose to vary the mutation rate from five to 45 percent, increasing in increments of five. A robot could potentially be mutated in multiple ways over one generation.

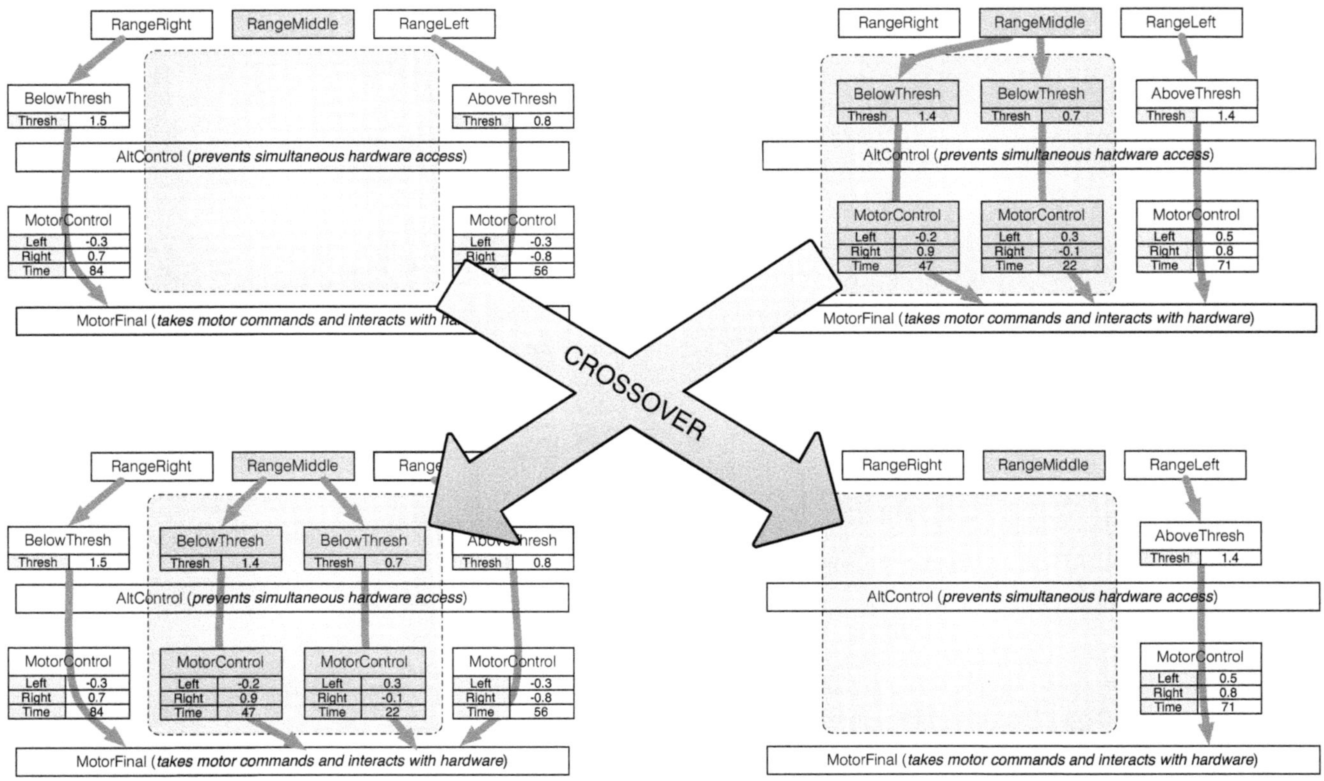

Figure 8: Example of crossover method on two brains, where the chosen swap involves the RangeMiddle sensor

2. To test the effects of this multiple mutation, we also ran experiments allowing only one randomly chosen mutation per robot.

Throughout all our experiments, we used a population of twelve robots and ran for twenty generations, repeated and averaged over five runs. The effectiveness of a given robot brain was evaluated using the the weighted *unseen* evaluation metric (described in Section 4.2). Due to limitations in Simbad, we were forced to run our experiments in real-time. Therefore, our experiment here used a time limit of 60 seconds, rather than the five minute limit for a trial at TCFFHRC. We also declared a trial complete when the robot collided with an arena wall, because our physical robot lacked bump sensors—a real-world crash would have resulted in failure in the contest.

6. RESULTS

Our experiments resulted in process networks that were more effective at covering more of the competition space than the original human-devised solution. The most effective solutions (covering the largest portion of the competition arena) evolved both obstacle avoidance (wall following) and locomotion (wiggling). Both behaviors are consistent with our original solution for the TCFFHRC task.

6.1 Locomotion and Obstacle Avoidance

We found that lower mutation rates produced robots that developed effective locomotion strategies faster. Figure 9 shows the average scores of all the mutation rates with tournament selection. By inspection, low mutation rates (< 15% mutation rate per generation) appear to be different from high mutation rates (> 15% mutation rate per generation). A one-way analysis of variance between results based on mutation rate per generation indicated a significant difference (p-value of 0.0000013), and pairwise t-tests between each experimental condition confirmed a significant difference between a robot evolved using 5% mutation rate per generation and all other mutation rates.

Notably, the *one mutation per brain* method was initially similar to the 5% mutation rate performance, but eventually degraded over time and did not produce statistically significant results: some mutation (but not too much) was good. With higher mutation, any progress toward finding a successful network is destroyed each generation.

6.2 Improved Arena Coverage

As part of this work, we translated our occam-pi contest solution into JCSP (Figure 6). Our contest solution achieved a score of 0.85 in Simbad using our weighted unseen evaluation metric. Guided by our previous results, we compared the best score (lowest weighted unseen metric) from each of the five runs of the brains evolved with five mutations/generation to our hand-crafted solution.

Figure 10 shows that, after twenty generations, the best (evolved) solutions do as much as 10% better than our hand-crafted solution. Controllers that achieve these scores either (1) moved at a faster pace (spending less time wiggling and

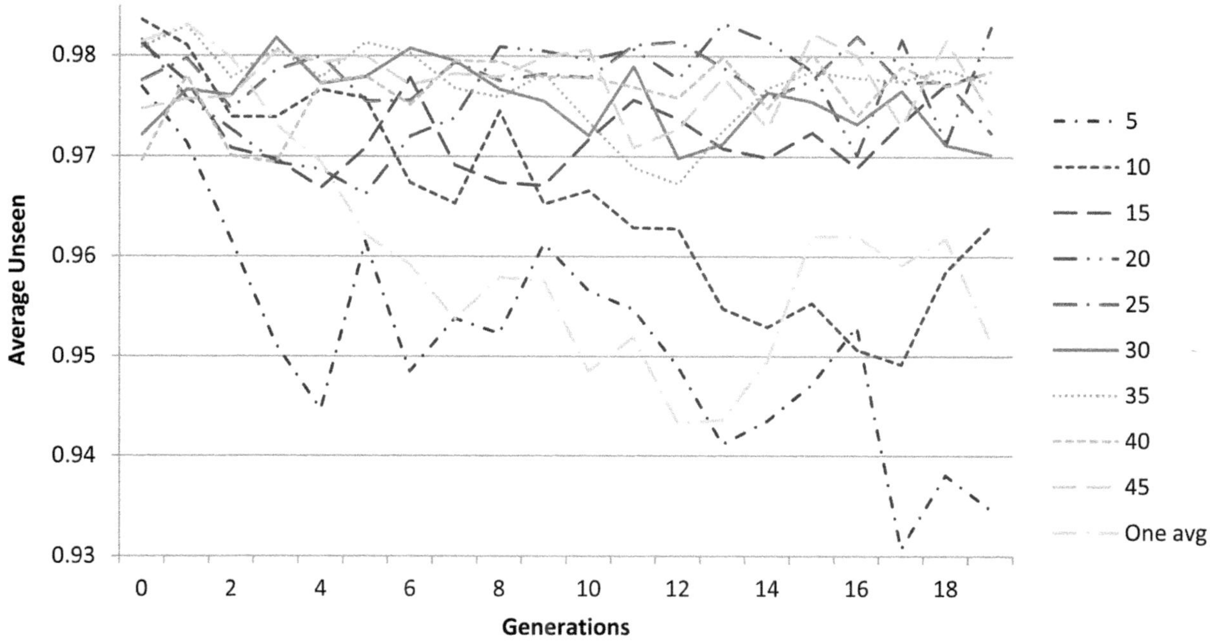

Figure 9: Average scores across five runs for various mutation rates

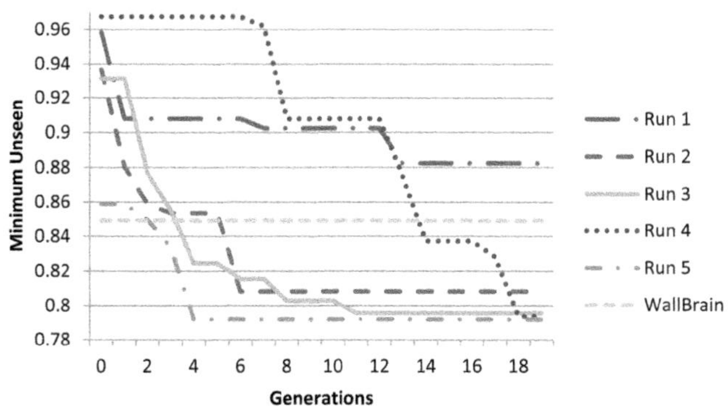

Figure 10: Minimum scores across five runs for 5% mutation rate

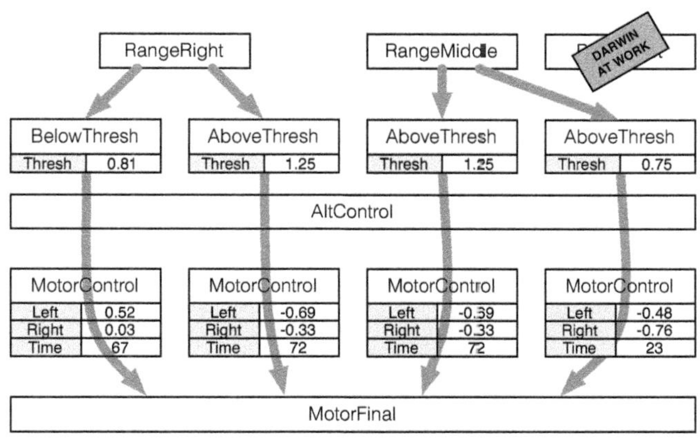

Figure 11: Successful evolved brain for wall navigation

more time moving forward), (2) followed paths that let them cover more ground in rooms (which are worth more in the weighted unseen metric), or (3) moved faster and covered ground in rooms.

6.3 A Successful Strategy: Wiggle and Avoid

We found there were two distinct movements among the best scoring evolved robots: obstacle avoidance was achieved through wall following and locomotion through wiggling. Figure 11 shows one such successful evolved network. The robots learned to use their distance sensors to follow either the right wall or the left wall. Also, for each robot there was some version of a wiggle motion (repeatedly moving slowly left then right while moving forward) with the use of the middle distance sensor. These behaviors align well with our successful implementation for the physical TCFFHRC task.

7. RELATED WORK

Research involving complex domains requiring multiple behaviors is currently on the rise in evolutionary robotics. Nelson and Grant [11] investigate a complex *Capture the Flag* game, and evolve feedforward and recurrent neural networks in a competitive environment for this task in both virtual and real robots. Capi [3] also uses recurrent neural networks to learn a parallel foraging and protection task, and find successful controllers through the use of a multi-objective function.

Ross [15, 14] used genetic programming to evolve concurrent programs capable of solving simple mathematical functions. Ross discusses the CCS algebra implementation, where the language primitives are much more suitable for mathematical functions than the complete programming languages discussed here.

Early work by Koza using a genetic algorithm to evolve a robotic controller [8] created virtual robots which followed the wall of an irregular shaped room. Liu and Iba [9] incorporated the subsumption architecture into evolutionary robotics. They divided a cooperative task into four levels, hand-coding some and allowing a genetic program to evolve the rest in a hierarchical procedure. Our approach differs from these by evolving the values of and connections between high-level parallel processes.

8. FUTURE WORK

Our current research has focused on learning process networks for locomotion and obstacle avoidance to successfully complete a complex fire-fighting task. The final portion of the task involves phototaxis (finding and extinguishing the candle), and we are currently investigating similar evolutionary methods for learning and refining networks for this behavior. We next plan to evolve the higher-level control structure, which will coordinate the actions of these separate behavior networks.

With our individual wall-following brain abstracted to read from sensors and control motors, we plan to port our learned JCSP process networks back to the occam-pi language for the physical Arduino framework. This will give us insight into the alignment between our Simbad simulator and the actual TCFFHRC arena.

We also plan to investigate the use of JCSP and our process network framework to learn in new and more realistic environments beyond the TCFFHRC. USARSim is a robotics simulation environment based on the Unreal game engine, and is currently used for the annual Robocup Rescue Virtual Simulation competition [4]. By developing an interface layer to make the information to and from the network sockets in USARSim look like our Arduino interface, our evolutionary framework should be easily transferred to this domain.

9. ACKNOWLEDGEMENTS

This research was supported through funding from the NSF CREU program. We would like to thank Centenary and Allegheny Colleges for the use of their facilities in preparation for the TCFFHRC.

10. REFERENCES

[1] D. J. Ahlgren and I. M. Verner. Fire-Fighting Robot International Competitions: Education Through Interdisciplinary Design. In *I*nternational Conference on Engineering Education, 2001.

[2] I. Armstrong, M. Pirrone-Brusse, A. Smith, and M. C. Jadud. The Flying Gator: Towards Aerial Robotics in occam-π. In P. H. Welch, A. T. Sampson, J. B. Pedersen, J. Kerridge, F. R. M. Barnes, and J. F. Broenink, editors, *C*ommunicating Process Architectures 2011, pages 329–340, jun 2011.

[3] G. Capi. Evolution of efficient neural controllers for robot multiple task performance - a multiobjective approach. In *I*CRA, pages 2195–2200, 2008.

[4] S. Carpin, M. Lewis, J. Wang, S. Balakirsky, and C. Scrapper. USARSIm: A Robot Simulator for Research and Education. In *I*EEE Internation Conference on Robotics and Automation, April 2007.

[5] C. Hartland and N. Bredeche. Evolutionary Robotics: From Simulation to the Real World using Anticipation. In *U*niversite de Paris-Sud, 2000.

[6] C. A. R. Hoare. Communicating sequential processes. *C*ommun. ACM, 21(8):666–677, Aug. 1978.

[7] M. Jadud, C. L. Jacobsen, J. Simpson, and C. G. Ritson. Safe parallelism for behavioral control. In *2008 IEEE Conference on Technologies for Practical Robot Applications*, pages 137–142. IEEE, November 2008.

[8] J. R. Koza. Evolution of subsumption using genetic programming. In F. Varela and P. Bourgine, editors, *Toward a Practice of Autonomous Systems: Proceedings of the First European Conference on Artificial Life*, pages 110–119. The MIT Press, 1993.

[9] H. Liu and H. Iba. Multi-agent learning of heterogeneous robots by evolutionary subsumption. In *P*roceedings of the 2003 international conference on Genetic and evolutionary computation: PartII, GECCO'03, pages 1715–1728, Berlin, Heidelberg, 2003. Springer-Verlag.

[10] A. L. Nelson, G. J. Barlow, and L. Doitsidis. Fitness functions in evolutionary robotics: A survey and analysis. *R*obotics and Autonomous Systems, 57(4):345–370, April 2009.

[11] A. L. Nelson and E. Grant. Using direct competition to select for competent controllers in evolutionary robotics. *R*obotics and Autonomous Systems, 54(10):840–857, 2006.

[12] A. L. Nelson, E. Grant, J. Galeotti, and S. Rhody. Maze exploration behaviors using an integrated evolutionary robotics environment. In *J*ournal of Robotics and Autonomous Systems, 2003, pages 159–173, 2004.

[13] S. Nolfi and D. Parisi. Evolving non-trivial behaviors on real robots: an autonomous robot that picks up objects. In *R*obotics and Autonomous Systems, pages 187–198. Springer Verlag, 1995.

[14] B. J. Ross. Pairwise Sequence Comparison and the Genetic Programming of Iterative Concurrent Programs. In *P*roc. Genetic Programming, pages 338–343. Morgan Kaufmann, 1998.

[15] B. J. Ross. The Evolution of Concurrent Programs. *A*pplied Intelligence, 8:21–32, 1998.

[16] H.-S. Seok, K.-J. Lee, and B.-T. Zhang. An on-line learning method for object-locating robots using genetic programming on evolvable hardware. In M. Sugisaka and H. Tanaka, editors, *P*roceedings of the Fifth International Symposium on Artificial Life and Robotics, volume 1, pages 321–324, Oita, Japan, 26-28 January 2000.

[17] J. Simpson, C. L. Jacobsen, and M. C. Jadud. Mobile Robot Control - The Subsumption Architecture and occam-pi. In P. Welch, J. Kerridge, and F. Barnes, editors, *Communicating Process Architectures 2006*, volume 64 of *C*oncurrent Systems Engineering, pages 225–236, Amsterdam, September 2006. IOS Press.

[18] P. Welch, N. Brown, J. Moores, K. Chalmers, and B. Sputh. Integrating and Extending JCSP. *C*ommunicating Process Architechtures, 2007.

Open-ended Coevolution and the Emergence of Complex Irreducible Functional Units in Iterated Number Sequence Games

Benjamin Inden
Artificial Intelligence Group, Bielefeld University
Universitätsstr. 25, 33615 Bielefeld, Germany
binden@techfak.uni-bielefeld.de

ABSTRACT

We present three related number sequence games as simple models of coevolution and demonstrate that they produce escalating arms races and irreducible functional units of unbounded size. We argue that our results imply that the models also show unbounded evolutionary activity according to a previous formal definition. Furthermore, we examine the robustness of the coevolutionary dynamics under different parameter regimes. We propose number sequence games as benchmarks for coevolutionary algorithms, and make some suggestions on adjusting task difficulty and choosing selection methods in coevolutionary algorithms.

Categories and Subject Descriptors

J.3 [**Computer Applications**]: Life and Medical Sciences—*Biology and genetics*

Keywords

coevolution, complexity, number sequence games

1. INTRODUCTION

Open-ended evolution is an interesting concept both from the perspective of theoretical biology and from the perspective of evolutionary robotics, which aims to automatically construct robot morphologies and controllers in an incremental way. A precise measure for evolutionary activity that was introduced several years ago has been used to demonstrate that many of the early artificial life systems do not have the potential for open-ended evolution [1]. Although it was later shown that a particular artificial life system called "Geb" does show unbounded evolutionary dynamics according to that measure [4], many questions remain about what exactly causes open-ended evolution to occur. One assumption that seems to be plausible is that coevolution can be open-ended provided the environment in which it occurs and the genetic system employed are sufficiently rich, whereas open-ended evolution seems to be hard to achieve using a static fitness function. However, a sufficiently simple model that can still produce open-ended evolution would certainly be helpful for more systematic investigations of the conditions necessary for open-ended evolution and sustained increases in complexity (complexification). The type of complexification that we are interested in is not just an increase in the number of components. We are interested in the number of components that, taken together, solve a particular problem arising as a consequence of the need to survive and reproduce, or in other words, that can be seen as performing a particular function.

Previous research on coevolutionary number games (starting with [16]) may provide some inspiration here. However, this research was targeted at other questions about coevolutionary dynamics, and the used encodings (single numbers or vectors of a few component numbers) do not provide the potential for complexification. Previous biological research on "Gene for Gene" coevolution models and various related extensions [14, 3] has focused on the dynamics of one gene or a fixed number of genes with several (typically 2) alleles each that can make a host resistant to infection, or a pathogen virulent. In these models, the more powerful alleles typically incur fitness costs, and the distributions of alleles over time in the two populations are studied. These models are not concerned with questions of complexification over time or the difficulties of finding powerful alleles in the first place, and "arms races" [6] arising in these models typically consist of cycles where the frequencies of a finite number of different strategies in the populations increase and decrease.

Another approach towards coevolution comes from the Webworld family of models [7]. In the basic Webworld model, a species is characterized by a fixed size list of features. It interacts with species that have other features as defined by a randomly initialized feature interaction matrix. The model consists of phases were species sizes are computed iteratively by means of differential equations until the food web becomes stable. In between these phases, new species are created by randomly changing the feature lists of existing species. This model has been extended such that the number of features of a species can vary within bounds, and a growth in complexity has been observed in the extended model, although the reasons for that growth were not entirely clear [11].

The Foodchain model [9] is perhaps closest to what we are going to present here. It models symmetric competitive coevolution between individuals that are strings of letters

GECCO'12 July 7-11, 2012, Philadelphia, Pennsylvania, USA.

with a fixed length. Some letters can be used for attack, others for defense, and the rest has no function. Matching is done between sequences of attack and defense letters present in the genome of two individuals to determine which one gains from the interaction. Point mutations and duplications are used in an evolutionary process that leads to complexification, i.e., a growth of functional subsequences in the genomes.

Paths of Darwinian evolution have previously been classified as serial direct evolution, parallel direct evolution, indirect evolution by redundancy removal, and indirect evolution by change of function (also known as *exaptation*) [15]. In response to claims by proponents of "Intelligent Design" that evolution cannot produce "irreducible complexity", i.e., functional units of many components with the property that removal of any one part destroys the function [2], the authors of the above classification have argued that the two indirect evolution paths can produce irreducible functional units. Exaptation, just like open-ended evolution, seems more likely to occur in a coevolutionary scenario than with a static fitness function. In an attempt to demonstrate the emergence of complex function by evolution with the artificial life system AVIDA [10], the authors have manually provided intermediate rewards for organisms performing a number of simple logical operations to finally arrive at an organisms that can perform the logical operation "EQU" (= "A equals B"). Of course, hand-designing intermediate rewards becomes very difficult once more complex domains are considered. Besides, it raises the question whether the most interesting issue is actually where these intermediate rewards come from. Here we intend to go beyond that approach and demonstrate that intermediate rewards can be provided by using coevolution.

Three related simple models of coevolution are presented in this article. The first is a model of competitive coevolution (parasitism), the second of cooperative coevolution (mutualism), and the third of commensal coevolution (where one species gains from the interaction whereas the other is indifferent to it). We demonstrate that the models can produce escalating arms races and irreducible functional units of unbounded size under certain conditions. (Here we use the term "arms races" in a loose sense such that everything used to gain from an interaction is considered part of the arms, regardless of the nature of the interaction, whereas originally the term was used for competitive interactions.) Although we do not directly measure evolutionary activity as defined previously [1], we argue that our results imply that the models also show unbounded evolutionary activity according to that definition. Furthermore, we examine the robustness of the coevolutionary dynamics under different parameter regimes. We discuss possible implications of our results for coevolutionary algorithms.

2. METHODS

2.1 Number sequence games

There are two populations in our number sequence games. In the parasitic and commensal model, individuals from the first population termed symbionts gain from the interaction, while those from the second, the hosts, are influenced in a negative way or not at all. In the mutualist model, individuals from both populations gain from the interactions provided they meet certain conditions.

The genotype — and the phenotype — of a member of either population is a sequence of numbers. What biological phenomena could be modeled by these number sequences? On a molecular level, the numbers could represent enzymes that need to be expressed in a particular temporal order to achieve a given function. On a behavioral level, they could represent behavioral primitives. Typical parasitic scenarios include host defense enzymes, and corresponding neutralizing parasite enzymes, or behavioral primitives in a pursuit and evasion scenario. Typical commensal scenarios include microbes that live on the waste products of other organisms, to the chemical composition of which they have to adapt. For typical mutualist scenarios, we may think of pollination, in which case individuals from the symbiont population correspond to pollinators, and those from the host population to plants.

In every generation, each organism in one population is tested against every organism in the other population. In the parasitic and commensal models, symbionts gain a fitness bonus for every host organism whose number sequence they completely match. This means that there must be pairwise matches between corresponding host and symbiont numbers. This pairwise matching is performed until either only the host sequence ends (the symbiont wins), only the symbiont sequence ends (the host wins), both sequences end (the symbiont wins), or a wrong number event occurs in the host sequence (the symbiont wins). A wrong number event means that the defense produced by the host is ineffective because it violates externally provided constraints. To use such constraints in the parasitic and commensal models has proved to be necessary because otherwise the search space of the symbionts (which have to exactly match the host numbers) is much more difficult than the search space of the hosts (which can choose any number), which lead to the hosts escaping from the symbionts early in evolution in preliminary experiments. We define a match between two numbers as equality here, but other relations (like complement) would be equivalent as long as they do not change the number of possible solutions. If the host wins, it gets the corresponding fitness bonus in the parasitic model. In the commensal model, the host always gets a fitness proportional to the length of the subsequence in its genome that fulfills the externally provided constraints, which effectively means that a simple fitness functions with intermediate rewards is provided to the hosts.

In the mutualist model, an organisms gains a fitness bonus if it matches the whole sequence of the organism from the other population. This means that if their sequences have equal length, both will obtain the fitness bonus, but if one has a longer sequence than the other, then only the one with the longer sequence will win (provided, of course, that it completely matches the shorter sequence). No external constraints are imposed in the mutualist model because it is by nature symmetric.

Each fitness bonus has a value of 1.0. To arrive at the final fitness of an organism, these bonuses are added, and then a fitness contribution due to genome length $f_l(o) = c_{lp} \exp(-0.1 \cdot [\textit{genome length}])$ is added, where c_{lp} is a constant that determines the costs of adding and maintaining further genes.

The nature of the constraint on the host number sequence in the parasitic and commensal model is as follows: The first number in the sequence must be 1, and a number at posi-

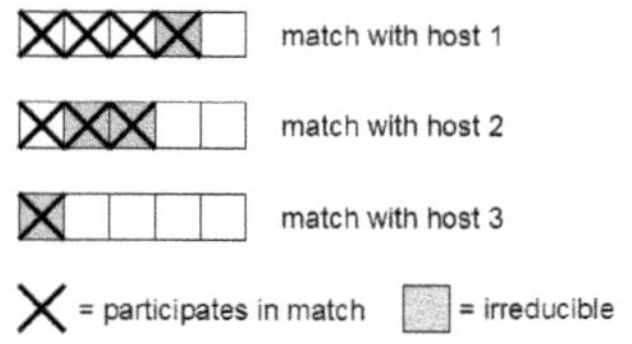

Figure 1: Measuring irreducible functional unit size (IFUS) in symbionts. In this example, the host population size is 3, and the symbiont sequence matches all host sequences. IFUS is defined as the maximum of the number of irreducible sites in a matching sequence, where irreducible means that there is no intermediate reward provided by other matches.

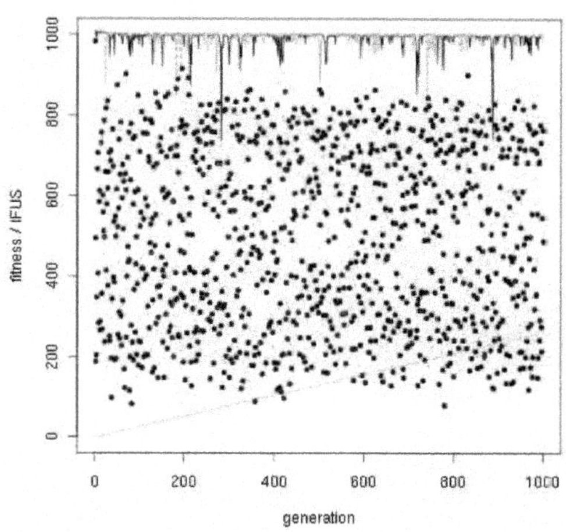

Figure 2: A typical run of the parasitic model. Maximal fitness of symbionts (solid black line) and hosts (dashed green line), mean fitness of symbionts (thick black dots) and hosts (thin green dots), maximal symbiont IFUS (red dotted line). IFUS increases linearly over time.

tion $n+1$ must have the value $v(n+1) = (v(n)+1)\%n_p$, where $0..n_p-1$ is the range of possible gene values and '%' denotes the modulo operation. This means that only a fraction $1/n_p$ of the newly added genes will be effective. So the space of host solutions is constrained exactly as much as the space of symbiont solutions (where also only one number will match at a given position), and the only effective gene sequence of length $n < n_p$ takes the form $[1,..,n]$. It should be noted that neither the genetic system nor the fitness function (apart from this constraint) use any notion of neighborhood of numbers, so we could equivalently use any other constraint as long as effective solutions have the same probability in the search space under that constraint. Another important point is that, while we do provide a gradual path towards more complex solutions here, we provide it only to the host population. Furthermore, the host population in the parasitic model can only exploit the fitness gradient if the parasite population is at the right place in the sequence space to provide this information (whereas the host population in the commensal model can exploit information about the gradient at any time because its fitness is directly dependent on matching the external constraints). In section 3.3, we will introduce a more sophisticated method of setting constraints.

Simple fitness proportional selection (without any elite mechanism) is used as a starting point. Unlike many other selection methods, this one is known to be well-behaved with regards to game theory in the sense that all Nash equilibria of a given game are fixed-points of systems using fitness proportional selection, and all point attractors of systems using it are Nash equilibria of the game [8]. All experiments use a well-mixed population without spatial structure.

2.2 Genetic representation and operators

As already mentioned, the genome is basically a sequence of numbers. (For administrative and statistical purposes, we also provide each gene with a unique identification number as introduced in [13], but this has no influence on the model behavior as presented here.) Three mutation operators are used on these sequences: add a number (with probability 0.2), delete a number (with probability 0.1), and change a number (with probability 0.2). Values are always randomly drawn with uniform probabilities over the whole range. By default, the operations are only applied at the end of the sequence. Of course, the order of numbers in the genome could also be arbitrary if each gene also contained some information about the time of its expression. These ways of encoding the phenotype are equivalent.

All populations are seeded with a common ancestor that has a random sequence of length 1. Recombination is not used in the experiments reported here.

2.3 Measuring outcomes of coevolution

We are most interested in calculating *irreducible functional unit size* (IFUS) for organisms in the first population. This is done by iterating over all cases where an organism from the symbiont population matches an organism from the host population in a given generation (see Fig. 1). The sites in the symbiont genome that participated in that match are marked. Next, all sites that also participated in shorter matches in the given generation are unmarked. IFUS is then defined as the maximum of the number of marked sites over all matches. The highest IFUS found in the population is recorded in every generation. This in turn leads to two measures related to coevolutionary complexification: the highest IFUS ever reached during a run, and the number of generations before the maximal IFUS in the population finally dropped to zero. The latter value is equal to the total number of generations if no such drop occurs, or the population can recover from a temporary drop. This measure indicates for how long the symbiont population can compete before the host population completely escapes from it. We call this *effective symbiont competition time*, or ESCT.

3. RESULTS

3.1 Evolutionary complexification

First we examine how the parasitic model behaves with different length punishment constants $c_{lp} = 0, 1, 10, 100, 1000$. As for all subsequent experiments, means of 20 runs with

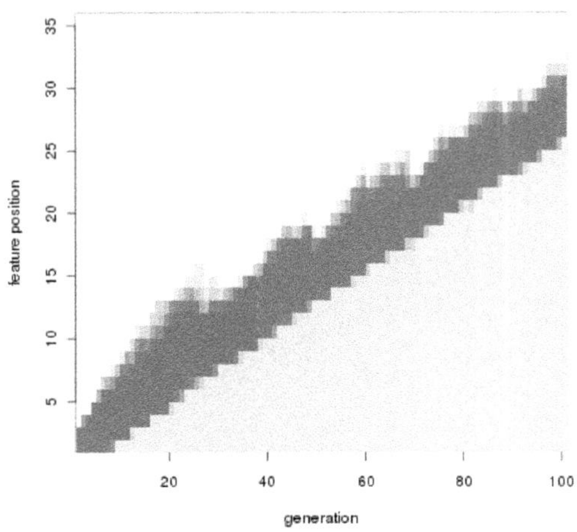

Figure 3: Sequence diversity in the host population for a typical run of the parasitic model. Diversity is color coded, with white corresponding to 0 and the most intense red corresponding to maximal diversity (in this case, 10) at a given position in the genome.

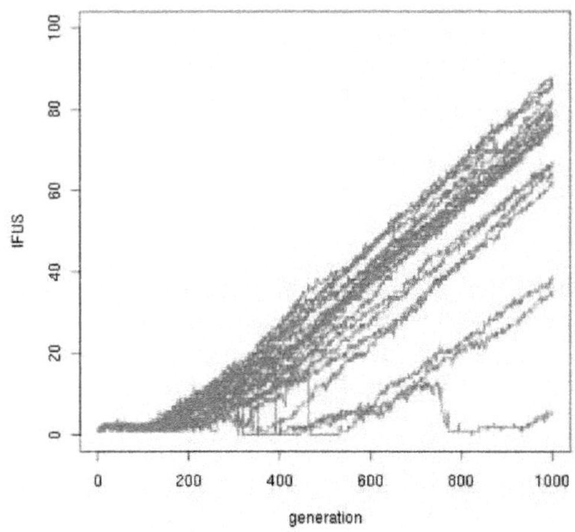

Figure 4: Complexification in 20 runs of the mutualist model. IFUS breaks down and builds up again in some runs. Otherwise, it grows linearly.

population sizes of 1000 and running for 1000 generations are reported. We set $n_p = 10$ for these experiments, so numbers can be in $\{0, 1, ..., 9\}$. The maximal IFUS reached during coevolution using the different length punishment constants is 261.4, 261.1, 260.9, 260.0, and 23.9, respectively. ESCT is 1000 generations in all cases. This means that the parasite population can catch up with the host population in all cases, and irreducible functional units of similar sizes are produced as long as the costs of genes are not too high. The growth of IFUS is linear and therefore unbounded in typical runs (see Fig. 2). The mean fitness of the two populations oscillates with high frequency, while the maximal fitness values only occasionally drop much below the maximally obtainable fitness. So this is a fast arms race where one population is never much behind the other. Experiments not reported in detail here indicate that moderate changes in mutation rate change the speed of the arms race and therefore the maximally obtainable IFUS, but do not change the dynamics qualitatively. By looking at the host diversity (see Fig. 3), it can be found that only the last few positions in the sequence are variable, while the initial positions converge rapidly. The reason for convergence is, of course, that only a single value at any given position satisfies the external constraints.

When the mutualist model is run with $c_{lp} = 10$, an IFUS of 69.8 is reached on average. ESCT is 1000 generations in all cases, but the dynamics of IFUS is different in different runs: some experience intermediate breakdowns in complexity before recovery and renewed complexification (see Fig. 4). When the commensal model is run with $c_{lp} = 1$, an IFUS of 40.2 is reached on average. The symbiont population often cannot keep pace with the hosts, so IFUS breaks down. Sometimes there is an immediate recovery, but if not, the IFUS stays at zero because the hosts have permanently escaped (Fig. 5), so ESCT is below 1000 in most cases, and IFUS does not grow unboundedly.

3.2 Robustness of complexification for different mutation and selection methods

Mutations have been implemented such that new numbers are always added at the end of a sequence. The justification for this is that the sequences represent not just the genotype, but features of the phenotype in this model, and it is certainly possible to conceive of genetic architectures where mutations are more or less strongly constrained to only add features without changing existing ones (on which they may depend), or situations where all other mutations are instantly removed by purifying selection. Nevertheless, one might wonder what happens in the more general case when numbers can be added anywhere in the sequence. In principle this should produce many individuals with a disrupted sequence and zero fitness, and make favorable mutations more rare. How does that affect coevolutionary dynamics?

In the parasitic model, complexification leads to average genome lengths of 97.8 in the final generation, and the symbionts remain competitive all the time. However, maximal IFUS remains close to zero. This can be explained by the effects of mutations: about 50% of the individuals are mutated, which means that about 500 mutations are introduced into the population in every generation. These are distributed randomly over the sequence length, so a host sequence in a given generation that satisfies the external constraints up to a position $p < length$ in the genome leads to many sequences in the next generation that satisfy the constraints up to positions $p_i \leq p$, thereby providing a path with many intermediate rewards towards the maximum for the symbiont population. This also results in a measurable increase in host diversity (see Fig. 6). Examination of the best individuals in the final generation reveals that evolution can maintain rather long correct initial sequences despite high mutation pressure. By contrast, the commensal model produces modest maximal IFUS (12.2), but permanent breakdowns occur in all runs, so complexification is bounded. The mutualist model reaches a maximal IFUS at

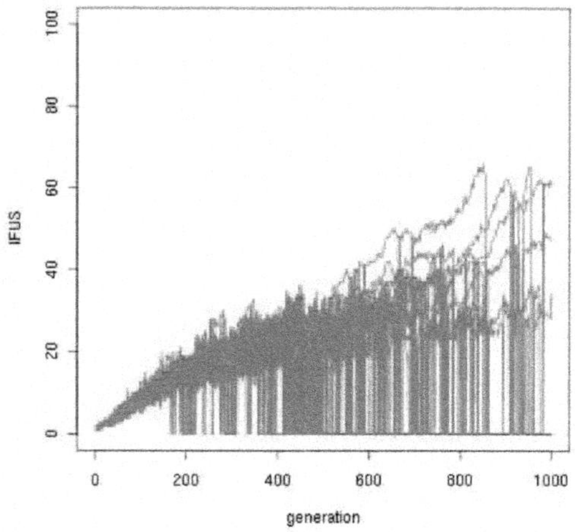

Figure 5: Complexification in 20 runs of the commensal model. IFUS frequently drops to zero, sometimes with immediate recovery, sometimes permanently.

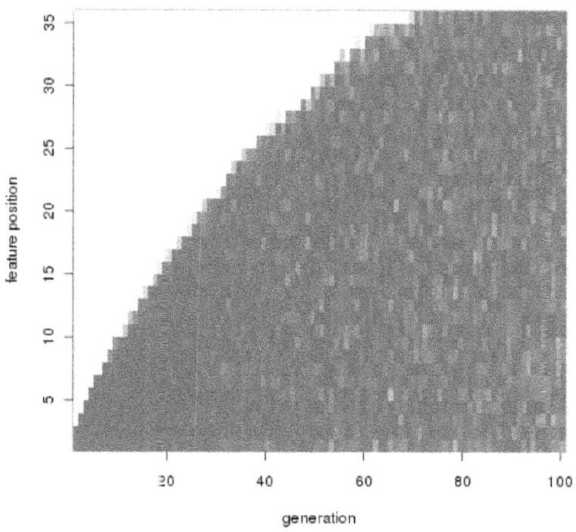

Figure 6: Host diversity for the parasitic model when mutations are allowed anywhere in the sequence. Compare with Fig. 3.

a chance level of 3.2 only, and ESCT is usually below 1000. Complexification does no longer occur in this model.

Because of the above considerations that mutations anywhere in the sequence would produce many dysfunctional individuals, one might wonder whether a stronger type of selection perhaps could filter out these individuals and make all of the three models return to a complexifying dynamics. We investigated the effect of truncation selection (selecting a fraction of the population with the best fitness values, and assigning an equal number of offspring to each of them) with a truncation threshold of 0.01, which corresponds to selecting just 10 individuals from a population of 1000. The dynamics in the parasitic model remains the same qualitatively.

However, compared with fitness proportional selection, truncation selection significantly ($p < 10^{-9}$, t-test) increases maximal IFUS to 45.6 on average in the commensal model, though complexification is still bounded (see Fig. 7). In the mutualist model, truncation selection leads to complexification with a maximal IFUS of 90.8 on average. Like before, complexification seems to be unbounded in principle, but there are occasional breakdowns of complexity (see Fig. 8).

3.3 Effects of different constraints on the coevolving populations

So far, both populations have had search spaces with the same difficulty, i.e., the ratio of viable choices to possible choices of numbers has been the same for both populations. Instead, we can also choose two different numbers n_{c1} and n_{c2} and set the range of possible numbers to $[1, n_{c1} \cdot n_{c2}]$. Previously, only a single number as specified by an external constraint was valid at each position in the host genome. For the experiments in this section, the host number $n \in [1, n_{c1} \cdot n_{c2}]$ is divided by n_{c2}, and the result must then be a single number. In other words, the host number must be in the correct bin out of n_{c1} bins. Similarly, the symbiont and host numbers are divided by n_{c1} each, and the results must be equal for a match. In other words, we require that host and symbiont number are in the same out of n_{c2}bins (see Fig. 9).

We examined complexification for several different constraint ratios using the parasitic model with $c_{lp} = 10$, truncation selection with a threshold of 0.01, and two populations of 1000 individuals each running for 1000 generations (see Table 1). It can be seen that as the task of the symbionts becomes easier relative to the task of the host, complexification speed increases. However, complexification is fastest when the constraint ratios are exactly equal. This is remarkable given that even constraint ratios very close to equality do not gain an advantage. Why this is so remains unclear. Nevertheless, there is considerable robustness with respect to the constraint ratio. However, breakdowns in complexity often occur (see Fig. 10). When using fitness proportional selection instead of truncation selection, a bin size ratio of 100:100 yields maximal IFUS of 140.1 and no complexification breakdowns in most of the runs, whereas only very modest amounts of IFUS are produced with bin size ratios of 100:101 and 101:100 (16.2 and 18.3, respectively) and complexification breaks down early in these configurations.

4. DISCUSSION

4.1 Irreducibility of functional units

These results demonstrate that irreducible functional units can in principle arise by coevolution — even if the individual elements have costs. The matching sequences are irreducible because deleting or changing a single number from one of these sequences in evolved individuals would make the whole sequence dysfunctional with regards to their environment. Furthermore, these functional units are often so complex that their emergence in direct evolutionary scenarios without intermediate rewards is practically impossible. For example, the probability of a sequence of numbers between 0 and 9 and of length 260 that evolves in a typical parasitic model to arise by pure chance is 10^{-260}. By contrast, a single run consists of only 10^6 evaluations here.

To make the competitive and mutualist task approximately

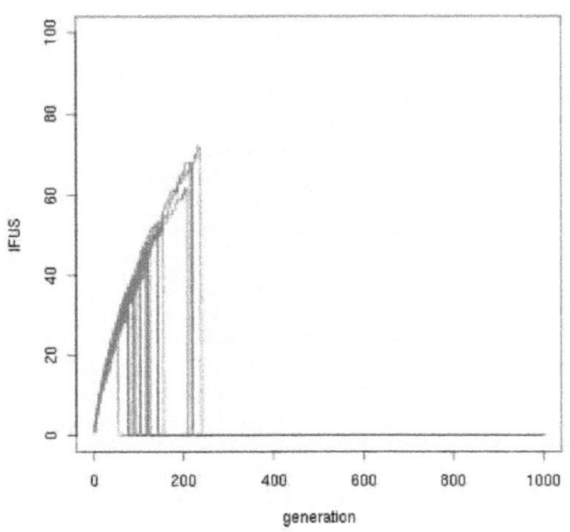

Figure 7: Complexification in 20 runs of the commensal model with mutations allowed anywhere in the sequence and truncation selection. IFUS eventually drops to zero in all runs because the symbionts cannot keep pace with the hosts.

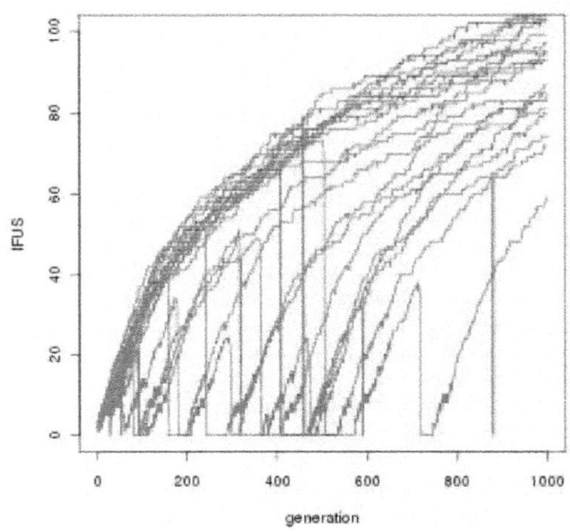

Figure 8: Complexification in 20 runs of the mutualist model with mutations allowed anywhere in the sequence and truncation selection. IFUS grows, although with occasional breakdowns.

bin size ratio	IFUS		bin size ratio
100:100	458.8		100:100
100:101	325.3	328.7	101:100
100:102	321.7	329.5	102:100
100:105	318.3	323.9	105:100
100:110	310.2	332.5	110:100
100:120	307.3	341.4	120:100
100:150	281.5	356.4	150:100
100:200	250.3	372.6	200:100

Table 1: Maximal IFUS reached for different constraint ratios in the parasitic model. Bin size ratios are given as (symbiont bin size ratio) : (host size ratio). A larger bin size means less bins and therefore makes the task easier for the respective population.

equally difficult for the host and symbiont populations, it has been necessary to constrain the solution space of the host population. One might think that makes the tasks equivalent to a simple evolutionary setup where a specified sequence has to be evolved and intermediate rewards are provided. But this is not the case for two reasons. Firstly, the information about the target sequence is provided only to the host population, but the sequence evolves in the parasite population as well. Secondly, the fitness function for the parasite population at any given time does not provide intermediate rewards for most of the sequence, but only for the latest additions to the sequence that have arisen in the host population. There are intermediate rewards only if all individuals that ever existed are taken into account (unless, of course, mutation provides intermediate rewards in every generations, as was the case in one of the models studied in section 3.2).

Furthermore, while we have implemented a simple identity function for matching between a host and a parasite, any different function would lead to the same results as long as the constraint ratio remains unchanged.

However, one limitation of the model is that complexification can only occur if the individual steps (in this case, adding a single valid number to the end of the sequence) are not too difficult. As the results in section 3.3 show, the parasitic model still produces large irreducible functional units if the range of possible numbers is extended to 100 or more, but complexification becomes less stable, and if the search space is further enlarged, at some point the probability of finding the next correct number by a mutation is too small given the total number of evaluations. Where this point is will certainly depend on the population size among other factors. The abstract models introduced in this article can of course not replace studies that examine whether basic assumptions of the models regarding the nature of the search space are met in particular biological systems. However, they extend previous theoretical models of coevolution such that studies on complexification and irreducible functional units become possible, and the time required for finding feasible genes can be taken into account.

4.2 Open-ended evolution

According to [1], evolutionary activity (EA) can be measured as follows: all components of the system (e.g., genes) have an activity counter that is increased every time the component is used. The diversity is then the number of components with non-zero activity. The total cumulative evolutionary activity (TCEA) is defined as the sum of all activity counts, and the mean cumulative evolutionary activity (MCEA) is defined as TCEA divided by diversity. In addition, two levels of activity are defined such that the first level is close to chance activity level and the second is slightly above it. All components with an activity in that range are new to the system and have adaptive value, so the sum of their activity divided by diversity is defined as new evolutionary activity (NEA). In order to determine chance levels for a given model, a *neutral shadow* model is created. It is like the original model with one exception: whenever

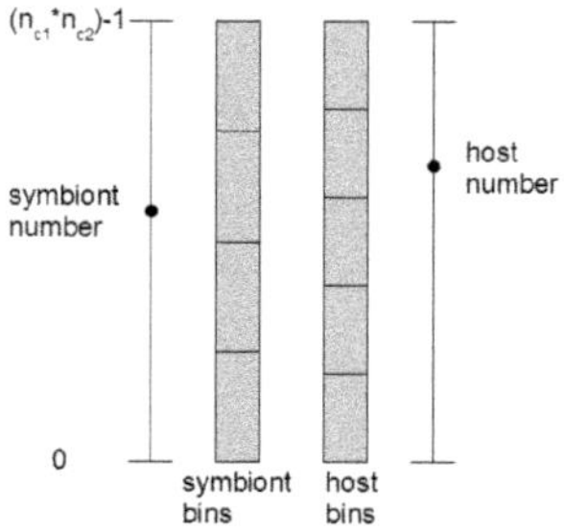

Figure 9: An example of how different constraint ratios can be achieved in number sequence tasks. A new number can have $n_{c1} \cdot n_{c2}$ different values. For the host population, it must be in the correct one out of $n_{c1} = 5$ bins. For the symbiont population, host and symbiont numbers must be in the same out of $n_{c2} = 4$ bins.

selection is applied in the original model, a random choice is made in the neutral shadow. Using theses statistics, a system can be classified as exhibiting unbounded evolutionary activity if its MCEA is unbounded and its NEA is positive (meaning that the limit of its integral over time, divided by time, is above zero). Modifications to these statistics proposed later [4] include resetting the neutral shadow periodically such that its population becomes identical to the population of the original model again, and using median cumulative evolutionary activity instead of the mean.

We have not measured evolutionary activity in our models, nor have we performed neutral shadow runs. Nevertheless, we argue that our models exhibit unbounded evolutionary activity if we define the components as genes and their usage as participation in a match. In the basic parasitic model (as in a number of other models and configurations), IFUS grows unboundedly. Because genes that participate in a match are considered active components with regards to EA statistics, that implies that the diversity of active components grows unboundedly. TCEA grows in an unbounded way, too (because old genes that participate in a match continue to be used), as does mean and median cumulative evolutionary activity (because most genes that participate in a match are old genes that continue to be used, so their activity counts keep increasing). Furthermore, NEA is positive because the chains are elongated all the time and the genes to be added at their ends will inevitably pass through the range of activity that has been determined for measuring NEA.

The neutral shadow run for our model can be performed as a thought experiment. In the neutral shadow, matches of longer sequences are extremely unlikely to occur because parasites with many matches have the same probability of survival as those with few matches. Therefore, component usage will be much lower. Furthermore, used components will be removed randomly over time due to deletions that destroy the match but have no effect in the neutral shadow. All in all, evolutionary activity in the neutral shadow will be much lower. The same applies even if the shadow is periodically reset — degeneration of matching sequences will inevitably occur, and elongation of sequences will drop to chance level.

From the arguments in this section it can be concluded that our coevolutionary models are simple (to our knowledge, the simplest described so far) examples of systems with unbounded evolutionary activity. On the other hand, if we had a direct evolutionary setup where a single population was evolved to match an infinite sequence and intermediate rewards were provided, perhaps the same argument for unbounded evolutionary activity could be made. So perhaps unbounded evolutionary activity, while providing a quantitative measure for evolutionary processes, is not the only desirable quality of artificial evolutionary systems. Emergence of structures that are not completely reducible to environmental conditions is another desirable feature in many cases. At least our mutualist model does have that feature, too, because here the sequence does not depend on external constraints (the others can be argued to have it to some degree if, as in section 3.3, constraints are relaxed).

Unlike the parasitic and mutual model, the commensal model does not show potentially unbounded complexification. A plausible explanation is that a fitness gradient is provided all the time to the host population in this model, so the host population can continue complexification very fast even if there is a temporary breakdown in symbiont complexity, which leads to the symbionts permanently falling behind the hosts. This problem could be ameliorated, but not completely eliminated, by slowing down evolutionary speed in the host population.

4.3 Implications for research on coevolutionary algorithms

Research on evolutionary algorithms has greatly benefited from the widespread use of benchmark functions. We propose number sequence games as benchmarks for coevolutionary algorithms here. They can be used to obtain an empirical understanding of how different coevolutionary algorithms work, and how well they work in different kinds of situations. Once the properties of standard coevolutionary algorithms are better understood they in turn can be used to better understand the properties of different coevolutionary problems, and in particular of coevolutionary robotics problems, which are often too complex for direct analysis.

The results reported here provide some support for two design heuristics for coevolutionary algorithms: First, asymmetric arms races in coevolution work best if the tasks difficulty for the symbionts is not much larger than for the hosts. Therefore, it could sometimes pay to make the task more difficult for the hosts artificially to obtain a more balanced coevolutionary dynamics and open-ended evolution. Second, while fitness proportional selection will make the system reach game theoretic equilibria, other selection methods seem to achieve more robust complexification. The particular method used here, truncation selection, can be said to take intraspecific competition into account to get from the separately calculated fitness potentials to the final fitness values of individuals in the context of their population [12]. Truncation selection is known to efficiently reduce mutation load [5]. Truncation selection can be approximated by other models of selection, but may perhaps often be a plausible model of natural selection in its own right. A more systematic investigation of the influence of different selection

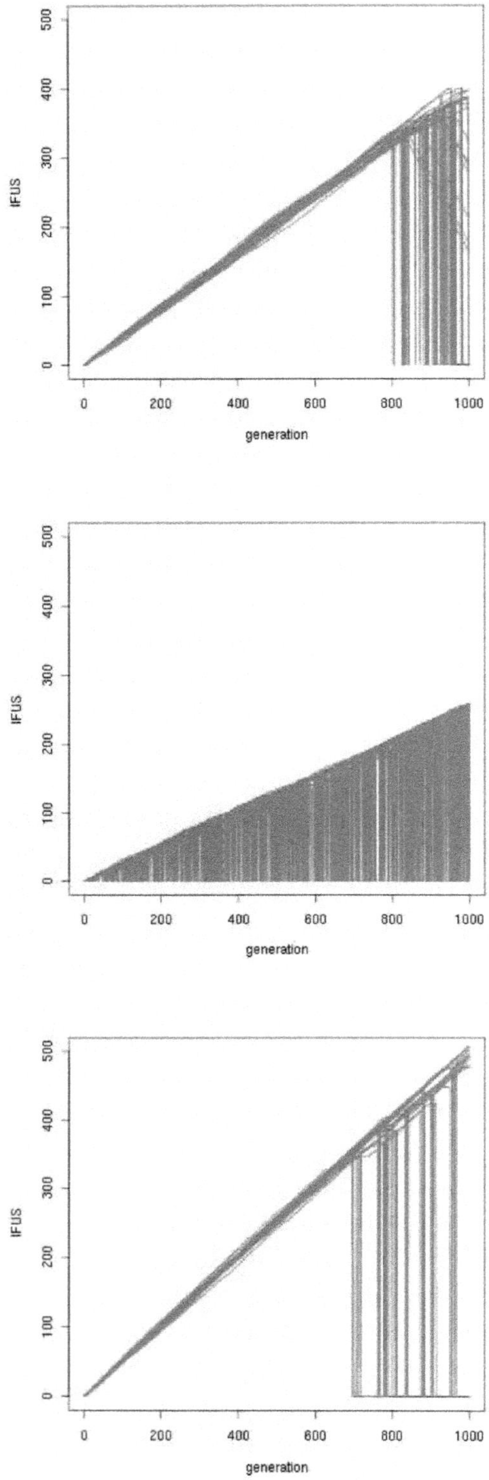

Figure 10: Complexification in 20 runs of the parasitic model with truncation selection and bin size ratios of (a) 200:100; (b) 100:200; (c) 100:100). Breakdowns of IFUS occur most often when bin size ratio makes the task more difficult for the symbionts as in (b).

methods and their parameters on coevolutionary complexification is one area of possible future studies.

Acknowledgments

The author would like to thank Ipke Wachsmuth and Helge Ritter for hosting him in their departments, and acknowledges present funding by the Deutsche Forschungsgemeinschaft (DFG) in the Collaborative Research Center 673.

5. REFERENCES

[1] M. A. Bedau, E. Snyder, and N. H. Packard. A classification of long-term evolutionary dynamics. In C. A. et al., editor, *Artificial Life VI*, 1998.

[2] M. Behe. *Darwin's Black Box: The Biochemical Challenge to Evolution*. Free Press, 1996.

[3] J. Bergelson, G. Dywer, and J. J. Emerson. Models and data on plant-enemy coevolution. *Annual Reviews of Genetics*, 35:469–499, 2001.

[4] A. Channon. Unbounded evolutionary dynamics in a system of agents that actively process and transform their environment. *Genetic Programming and Evolvable Machines*, 7:253–281, 2006.

[5] J. F. Crow and M. Kimura. Efficiency of truncation selection. *Proceedings of the National Academy of Sciences*, 76:396–399, 1979.

[6] R. Dawkins and J. R. Krebs. Arms races between and within species. *Proceedings of the Royal Society B*, 205:489–511, 1979.

[7] B. Drossel, P. G. Higgs, and A. J. McKane. The influence of predator-prey population dynamics on the long-term evolution of food web structure. *Journal of Theoretical Biology*, 208:91–107, 2001.

[8] S. G. Ficici, O. Melnik, and J. B. Pollack. A game-theoretic and dynamical-systems analysis of selection methods in coevolution. *IEEE Transactions on Evolutionary Computation*, 9:580–602, 2005.

[9] N. Guttenberg and N. Goldenfeld. Cascade of complexity in evolving predator-prey dynamics. *Physical Review Letters*, 100:058102, 2008.

[10] R. E. Lenski, C. Ofria, R. T. Pennock, and C. Adami. The evolutionary origin of complex features. *Nature*, 423:139–144, 2003.

[11] M. Maron and C. Fernando. Food webs and the evolution of organism complexity. In *Artificial Life X Workshop Proceedings*, 2006.

[12] R. Milkman. A competitive selection model. *Genetics*, 74:727–732, 1973.

[13] K. Stanley and R. Miikkulainen. Evolving neural networks through augmenting topologies. *Evolutionary Computation*, 10:99–127, 2002.

[14] J. N. Thompson and J. J. Burdon. Gene-for-gene coevolution between plants and parasites. *Nature*, 360:121–125, 1992.

[15] R. H. Thornhill and D. W. Ussery. A classification of possible routes of darwinian evolution. *Journal of Theoretical Biology*, 203:111–116, 2003.

[16] R. A. Watson and J. B. Pollack. Coevolutionary dynamics in a minimal substrate. In *Proceedings of the Genetic an Evolutionary Computation Conference*, 2005.

Evolving Axonal Delay Neural Networks for Robot Control

Francis Jeanson
Carleton University
1125 Colonel By Dr.
Ottawa, Ontario
fjeanson@connect.carleton.ca

Anthony White
Carleton University
1125 Colonel By Dr.
Ottawa, Ontario
arpwhite@scs.carleton.ca

ABSTRACT

This paper investigates the dynamical and control properties of a discrete spiking neural network model with axonal delays. After examining contemporary work on spike timing as a mechanism for neural coding, we introduce a simple axonal delay network model which, via coincidence detection, demonstrates the presence of biologically observed regimes such as sustained firing and the emergence of synchrony. We establish delay criteria allowing for the classification of three distinct regimes including global synchrony, complex firing, and dissipation. We then proceed to test this model in a robot light seeking task. Results show that evolving network delays is sufficient for solving the task. We conclude by hypothesizing that global synchronous firing is more suited to reactive behaviours while complex firing patterns may serve as an organizing mechanism for more indirect processing.

Categories and Subject Descriptors

I.2.6 [**ARTIFICIAL INTELLIGENCE**]: Learning—*Connectionism and neural nets*; I.2.10 [**ARTIFICIAL INTELLIGENCE**]: Vision and Scene Understanding—*Architecture and control structure, perceptual reasoning*

Keywords

Neural Coding, Spiking Neural Network, Axonal Delays, Coincidence Detection, Neural Adaptation, Embodied Cognition

1. INTRODUCTION

A growing consensus regarding the importance of spatiotemporal properties in neural processes suggests that firing rates are not the only form of neural coding in the brain. In the late 60's, Perkel & Bullock were amongst the first to demonstrate a variety of forms with which neural spikes can encode information [19]. Later, Abeles introduced the possibility of coincidence detection as a process by which neurones can exploit the precise millisecond timing of incoming spikes for coding [1]. Other temporal phenomena found both experimentally and developed theoretically, such as oscillations and synchrony, have also attracted much attention [27], [7], [28], [6]. More generally, it appears that a better understanding of neural coding mechanisms that take advantage of spatiotemporal effects may lead to important insights into the functional processes underlying intelligent adaptation in animals and humans.

Significant progress was recently made in interpreting the role of axonal and synaptic delays in the brain. Fujii et al. offered a comprehensive review of spatiotemporal characteristics of neural coding as it pertains to coincidence detection within their general *dynamic cell assembly* hypothesis [10]. Their work investigated the theoretical implications of coincidence detection to address long standing neural coding challenges such as the binding problem [27], [9]. Importantly, Fujii and colleagues noted that no strong evidence linking behavioural correlates of temporally linked neural assemblies with object or event representations have yet been demonstrated. Since the late 80's Thorpe and colleagues have also contributed to this area with a sparse temporal coding approach favouring rank order coding in visual recognition tasks [26], [25]. Recently, significant efforts in the investigation of neuronal properties of networks with axonal delays have led to the identification of 'neural groups' by Izhikevich and colleagues: subsets of neurones within a population which are not identified by their spatial location but by their transient participation in coordinated time-locked firing, which they call polychronization [13], [12]. These neural groups present the potential of performing collaborative encoding tasks offering a promising fit within Edelman's neural group selection theory [8]. The characteristics that polychronization provide for sensory classification when combined with synaptic plasticity has potentially important consequences for our understanding of neural coding. This, however, relies on spike time dependent plasticity (STDP) for the growth and maintenance of neural groups [13]. While this approach may be pertinent to our understanding of working memory and other long term cognitive processes, it does not seem adequate for rapid encoding in sensory memory. Fast encoding of novel stimuli, for instance, takes place within 50ms which is too short for metabolic processes such as STDP taking upwards of 500ms to settle [23], [24]. Furthermore, direct behavioural evidence for temporal coding in agent tasks and adequate formalisms is lacking. As suggested by Fujii et al. as well as Thorpe and others, the detection of spikes with millisecond precision may serve, in itself, as a bedrock for fundamental cognitive processes. We opt here to investigate the adaptability of spiking neural networks which exploit axonal delays alone in behavioural tasks.

At present, two important contributions can be made to adequately evaluate the potential that axonal delays represent. First, formal models of neural ensembles and mechanisms for information encoding must be developed; mechanisms that include the ability to support associative memory. Second, that investigating the coding features of axonal delays within spiking networks should greatly benefit from functional constraints that embodied tasks impose. This paper is motivated to investigate the latter problem. In particular, we show here that elementary neural controllers using axonal delays alone can efficiently solve the problem of light seeking in simple robots. By doing so we hope to contribute *direct evidence* that timing in neural ensembles may serve a functional purpose in cognition. Here, we begin by presenting the details of the neural and network model developed to investigate this and the dynamics that they offer under different parameter settings. We then present the experimental setting and results leading to light seeking behaviour in evolved simulated robots.

2. AXONAL DELAY NETWORK MODEL

A neurone typically fires a short lived spike when its soma reaches a particular voltage value. Although a large number of interesting activation dynamics have been observed in the sub-threshold and super-threshold conditions, such as resonation and bursting, this spiking behaviour is believed to be the primary method by which neurones communicate [11]. In the most common case, this threshold is reached when sufficient amounts of neurotransmitters activate a sufficiently large number of ion gates at the surface of dendritic trees or even the soma. If a sufficient number of afferent action potentials from a multitude of cells[1] reach the target within a small time interval, this threshold will be reached and the target cell will spike, transferring in turn an action potential to its own target cells. This coincidence of spikes on the target cell is at the crux of neural coding via axonal delays.

Although a number of interesting dynamical properties arise from differentially integrated spiking neurone models, we believe simple discrete state neurones will allow a clear isolation of the essential coding characteristics that axonal delay networks possess. For this reason, cells in our model have integer activation values with a negative or positive value. Axons have discretized lengths and either carry a value of 0 or 1 representing inactivity or a spike respectively. A single cell in the network behaves as an integer-valued coincidence detection and fire unit. When the activation of the node reaches its threshold value, a spike of value 1 is added to the beginning of the axonal paths leading to target nodes. If a node does not reach its threshold at given time step t then a 0 signal is set on the axonal spike train. Because nodes follow a basic coincidence detection scheme, we allow incoming signals to be either excitatory or inhibitory. Hence, an incoming spike can either cause the coincident activation to go up by 1 if the connection is excitatory or down by 1 if the connection is inhibitory. Excitation and inhibition are set to connections rather than cells; hence any given cell can have both excitatory or inhibitory effects on their targets depending on the connection type. While this violates Dale's principle[2], this fits with recently observed biological findings in cortical pyramidal cells [21] and has been found to significantly attenuate any global residual synchrony otherwise found in Dale-like networks [5] [15]. Importantly, a distinction is made between 'strict coincidence detection' where a target cell fires at time t if and only if the right number (the threshold) of incident spikes reach this cell at time t, and 'loose coincidence detection' where sub-threshold activation of the target cell may also contribute to total activation at time t. In the following description we restrict our model to the 'strict coincidence detection' scenario only. If a node's activation reaches a threshold T and spikes then the node's activation is reset to 0 for the duration of a refractory period R during which no change of activation can take place. Activation of cells thus obey the following equation:

$$A_i(t) = \sum_{j}^{N_{Ci}} s_{ji}(t), s \in \{-1, 0, 1\} \tag{1}$$

Where $A_i(t)$ is the activation value of cell i at time t, N_{Ci} the number of connections to cell i, and $s_{ji}(t)$ the spike value at the tail of the spike train (synapse) between source cell j and target cell i at time t. In the present models, the propagation of a spike through an axon with discrete delay D_{ij} from node i to node j advances by one location on the axon at every time step. In the following, we first introduce preliminary simulation results of our discrete axonal delay neural network (discrete ADNN) activity given a simple input, which we expect to elicit non-trivial sustained firing with the ability to support temporal coding. We then adapt this network model to work within the simulated context of a Khepera robot performing a light seeking task.

3. PRELIMINARY TEST MODEL

Spiking neural networks with axonal delays, like many other networks, will exhibit a wide number of spiking behaviours based on their parameter settings [11]. Although discretization of the network helps reduce the model's state space, a number of parameters will have a significant impact on the network's behaviour. By basing these settings as closely as possible on experimental knowledge of biological networks, we expected the appearance of sustained firing as well as predictable global spiking powers in the frequency domain. Our test model included the following parameters: number of neurones (N), connection probability (C), activation threshold (T), refractory period (R), minimum delay (D_{min}), and delay range (D_{range}). Connections could also be excitatory or inhibitory which we set to the cortically plausible ratio of 85% excitatory versus 15% inhibitory [20]. Keeping parsimony in mind, we decided to start with a very small number of $N = 25$ cells in the model. The connection probability was set high given the small number of cells to $C = 0.6$, resulting in an average of 375 total connections in the network. Each connection had a connection weight of one, meaning that unlike other neural network models, connection weighting had no variable influence on network behaviour. Activation threshold was in contrast set to the minimally interesting condition where at least two spikes

[1]An average of 5000 afferent connections exist per neurone [1].

[2]A cell's target connections are either all excitatory or all inhibitory.

($T = 2$) had to coincide on a target at a point in time to trigger a spike on a target; this also promoted a greater chance of observing coincidence detection events given the small number of neurones. Simulation time was discretized where we interpreted 10 time steps to correspond to 1ms; hence temporal resolution was one order of magnitude below the biological time scale of neuronal spiking events (1ms)[3]. Discretization has the advantage of significantly reducing computation. However, the lack of noise produces artificially many spikes with identical spike times. In fact, from the sample run in Figure 1 we found that with short delays a majority of cells spiked simultaneously until delay ranges reach about 6 time steps above the minimum 15 time steps. Using this, the period during which cells could not be excited or depressed, including the absolute refractory period, was set to reflect a biologically realistic duration of 1ms, i.e., $R = 10$. Axonal delays were also scaled within this time scale in order to reflect realistic delay ranges above 1.5ms ($D_{min} = 15$) but never over 10ms ($D_{max} = 100$). A minimum delay above the refractory period R was chosen because the presence of delays below R reduces the probability of coincidence which is already relatively limited in such small networks. Given that axonal delays were of central interest in our investigation, we varied the delay range (D_{range}) that axons were uniformly randomly assigned from 0 to 30 time steps. Thus, a network with $D_{range} = 9$, for example, had a random distribution of connection delays between D_{min} to $D_{min} + 9$ time steps (i.e., 1.5ms to 2.4ms in our model). Overall connections and their delays were assigned with uniform random probability.

3.1 Simulation Results

As input to the network, 30% of the 25 cells were randomly selected at the start of every run and set to fire upon network initialization. No further input was provided during a run. Simulation runs lasted 10,000 time steps. By varying the delay ranges in the network from 0 to 30 by increments of 3 we obtained three noticeably distinct spiking regimes in the network. Spike count plots and spike rasters show that with little or no variation in the delays, networks exhibited strong synchronous and sustained spiking during the entire simulation run. This took place with a D_{range} of 0, 3 and 6 as seen in a single sample run in Figure 1. We observed that synchronous firing of all cells took place after 100 time steps of 'start-up time' when all delays were equal at $D_{range} = 0$. With $D_{range} = 3$, 14 to 16 cells consistently fired at very regular intervals. When $D_{range} = 6$, strong synchrony was still present but spike count peaks varied more widely between 6 and 10 spikes after an initial 100 time step start-up period. These spike count ranges varied within narrow ranges on every run. When averaged over 30 trials with randomly re-initialized input and network connections, the average number of spikes in each condition was: 15,487.5 spikes (std dev. 233.2) at $D_{range} = 0$, 15,500.4 spikes (std dev. 182.5) at $D_{range} = 3$, and 14,874 spikes (std dev. 285.4) at $D_{range} = 6$. Average power spectral plots computed over 30 trials for each condition are shown as inlays in Figure 1. From the averaged power spectra we found that the firing frequency was nearly identical between $D_{range} = 0$ and $D_{range} = 3$ with a large 620Hz component and 750Hz secondary component, reaching nearly 79dB and 22dB respectively for $D_{range} = 0$ and 78dB and 17dB respectively for $D_{range} = 3$. This rate reduced to about 600Hz at about 36dB for $D_{range} = 6$ with a small secondary component of about 6dB at 800Hz.

[3]No significant differences in dynamics was found in simulations with 100 time steps per millisecond.

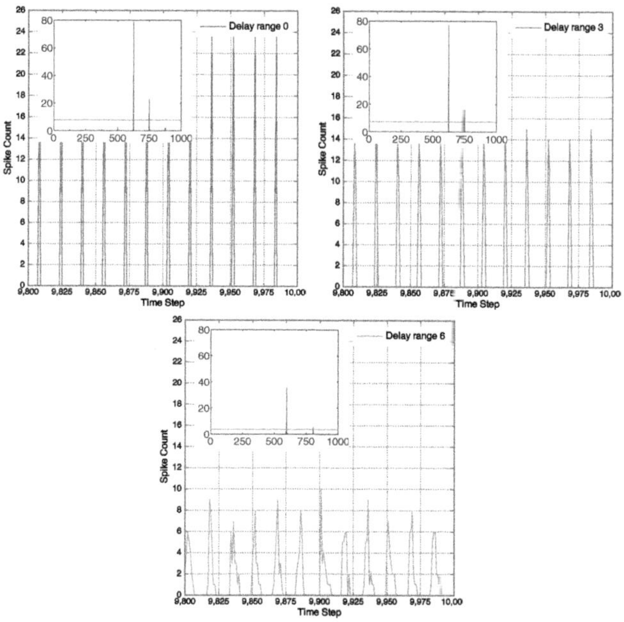

Figure 1: Sample spike counts in a population of 25 neurones over 200 time steps for small delay ranges. Top left: $D_{range} = 0$. Top right: $D_{range} = 3$. Bottom $D_{range} = 6$. Inlay: Respective average power-spectra over 30 trials.

By further increasing the variability of delays in the network three effects were observed: spiking became less synchronous, not every simulation run led to sustained firing, and overall spike counts increased. The predictability of spikes was reduced (increased spike timing complexity) and rapid dissipation to an inactive state was more likely. Figure 2 illustrates the spiking activity for $D_{range} = 9$, $D_{range} = 12$, and $D_{range} = 15$. Although spike count plots revealed no distinctive differences between these 3 scenarios, the probability of obtaining sustained activity reduced as the delay range increased. Out of 60 runs $D_{range} = 9$ achieved sustained activity on 82% of the runs, $D_{range} = 12$ reached sustained firing 66% of the time, and $D_{range} = 15$ fired sustainably 36% percent of the time. A broader comparison of the average dissipation times between networks with delay ranges is shown in Figure 3. From this dissipation analysis, we found that networks were much less likely to fire sustainably beyond a D_{range} of 15. Figure 2 shows only cases where firing was sustained throughout the simulation. Compared to smaller delay ranges seen above, spike counts were noticeably higher in all three scenarios. The average number of spikes in sustained firing runs was: 19,966.6 spikes (std dev. 1875.6) at $D_{range} = 9$, 19,784.5 spikes (std dev. 955.9) at $D_{range} = 12$, and 19,557.5 spikes (std dev. 1030.9) at $D_{range} = 15$. Hence both spike counts and variation in the number of spikes increased in these broader delay conditions in comparison to the shorter delay ranges seen above. The complex nature of the spike count patterns at these delay ranges made it difficult to estimate if any frequency compo-

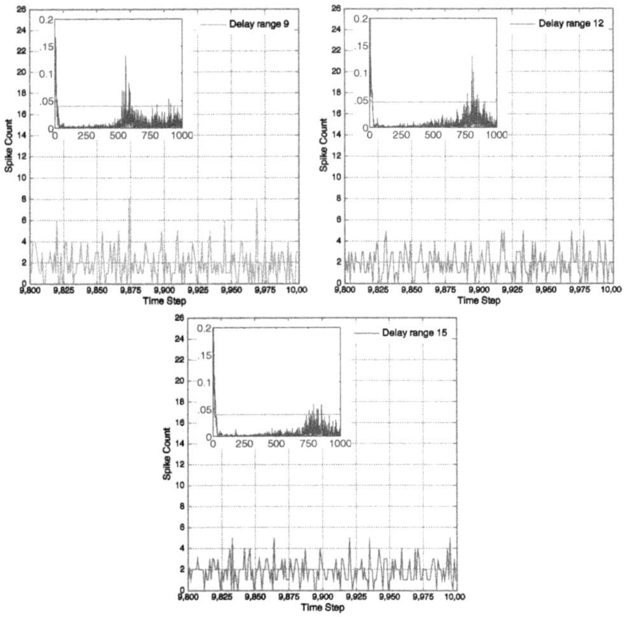

Figure 2: Spike counts in a population of 25 neurones over 200 time steps for medium delay ranges. Top left: $D_{range} = 9$. Top right: $D_{range} = 12$. Bottom $D_{range} = 15$. Inlay: Respective average power-spectra over 30 trials.

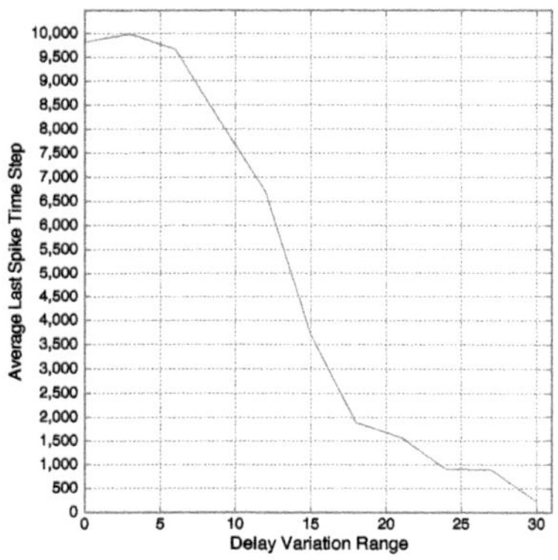

Figure 3: Comparison of the averaged dissipation times (last spike time step) between networks with delay ranges from 0 to 30 in increments of 3. Averages were computed over 60 runs in each case.

nent was present via visual inspection alone. However, as revealed by the average power spectra over 30 sustained firing trials, as seen in the inlays of Figure 2, significant frequency components in comparison to the standard deviation of the signal (horizontal line at $3 * stddev.$) were found, despite reaching powers below 0.2dB and being more widely spread over the frequency ranges. At $D_{range} = 9$, a broad, yet significant, component was present in the 530Hz to 600Hz range of up to 0.13dB. For $D_{range} = 12$, a significant component centred at 820Hz took place also around 0.13dB. At $D_{range} = 15$, a significant yet more modest, component centred at 800Hz with approximately 0.06dB was obtained on average.

When simulations led to dissipating activity, this occurred very rapidly within the first few dozen time steps. Overall these results suggest that neural networks with axonal delays possess three distinct regimes: sustained strong synchrony when assigned a small range distribution of delays, sustained complex activity with considerable asynchronous firing when the delay distribution is medium, and rapid dissipation when the variation in delays is large. Interestingly, the distinction between strong synchrony and the onset of complex firing seems to lie between the delay ranges $6 < D_{range} < 9$.

3.2 Model Discussion

Despite the sustained synchronous entrainment of most neurones in the short delay scenarios ($D_{range} \leq 6$) at high frequencies ($> 600Hz$), the complex firing with partial synchrony in the broader delay ranges ($D_{range} \geq 9$) demonstrated larger spike counts with a near 30% increase, suggesting that more neurones can participate in the neural dynamics in this regime. Furthermore, the higher standard deviation of these averaged spike counts indicates the presence of greater variation in these broader delay conditions, making it more difficult to predict the firing pattern. Connectivity with a sufficiently broad range of delays thus appears to have a greater coding potential than do networks with more homogeneous delay ranges. This potentially greater coding capacity fits well with the existing hypothesis that neural coding via coincidence detection can lead to complex processing [14]. Due to small network modelling constraint, the frequencies obtained were much higher than that typically observed in biological networks (usually in the range of 10hz to 100Hz). However, by demonstrating that delay dynamics will give rise to detectable frequency components in narrow *but also* broad delay conditions lends support to the hypothesis that spatio-temporal dynamics may, in part, address existing neurophysiological data on cortical cell activity in cognitive tasks such as attention [2], perception [7], and sensorimotor control [17]. While we did not, for this first stage, investigate the variable dynamics of the network under various input conditions, results support the potential applicability of coincidence detection networks under specific axonal delay conditions to more complex tasks.

Quantifying the three obtained regimes can be achieved for the present model by taking into account the standard deviation of delays as a means to indicate which category a network belongs to (see Table 1). Delay distribution ranges are selected from the firing dynamics and dissipation results discussed above (see Figure 3). These values, however, are only known to work given the simple initial 30% input to the neural network and the other fixed network parameters. The application of this kind of network to continuous stimulation may achieve greater functionality by taking advantage of complex firing states via adjustments of firing threshold and connectivity. However, the results on the preliminary discrete axonal delay neural network model encourage the exploration of its use in a simple robot light seeking task.

4. EMBODIED NEURAL MODEL

To test whether the axonal delays of a network can alone account for behaviour based information coding, we adapted the previous network model to control a simulated Khepera robot [16] in a simple sensorimotor task: light seeking. Although no known complexity measure has been formally established to determine the difficulty for embodied tasks

Delay Distribution	Delay Std. Dev.	Behaviour
$D_{range} < 7$	$0 \leq D_{SD} < 2$	Synchrony
$7 \leq D_{range} < 15$	$2 \leq D_{SD} < 5$	Complexity
$15 \leq D_{range}$	$5 \leq D_{SD}$	Dissipation

Table 1: Network behavioural categories based on standard deviation of delays

given sensory, motor, body and environmental conditions the evolutionary robotics approach has provided a number of insights since the mid 1980's. One precursor to this approach is Braitenberg's 'vehicles' experiments which introduced simple agents capable of solving a number of tasks with varying complexity [3].

Developments in the evolutionary robotics field have demonstrated that classical connectionist network controllers can take advantage of environmental, bodily, and multi-sensory regularities to perform tasks of higher orders, such as resolving perceptual aliasing and object categorization [22] [18]. As we see it, these results have begun to pave a pragmatic scientific approach to the isolation of the fundamental principles underlying basic cognitive capacities found in animals and humans. In a similar spirit we aim to explore the capability of axonal delay spiking networks at solving these fundamental sensorimotor problems. Here we demonstrate the ability of delay networks to solve a simple light seeking behaviour by adjusting axonal delays alone.

4.1 Evolving Axonal Delay Neural Networks for Light Seeking

A population of 25 neural controllers were initialized with random axonal delays. Two of the robot's 8 light sensors were used as sensory input, one placed at the front left (-45 degs from median) and front right (+45 degs from median). Sensory input and motor output had 5% added noise. Robot neural networks had 25 discrete spiking cells, with similar properties to the model presented above, except for the following variations. Connections were excitatory only, so as to test for the simplest condition. Connection probability was set to 30% upon initialization of a robot; these connections remained fixed throughout an agent's lifetime. All neurone thresholds were set to 3. Sensory neurones had no refractory period which was found necessary[4] to provide sufficient stimulation for mobility - all other cells had a refractory period of 10 time steps. This suggests that up to 10 spikes could be lost between a continuously firing sensory source and a non-sensory target due to that target's refractory period. A total of 4 sensory neurones per light sensor were used, and 4 neurones per wheeled motor effector were used. Light sensing was transduced using an inverse stimulation function which excited target sensory neurones more given less light input in order to promote explorative behaviour. When no light was presented to a sensor a noisy input of 1 was multiplied by the firing threshold (in this case 3) to the sensory cell thereby enabling it to send a spike downstream. The maximum presence of light reduced stimulation to a noisy input of 0 also multiplied by the firing threshold. Hence sensory neurones could only send spikes under the condition of nearly complete darkness if no coinciding afferent inputs from other cells in the network were providing supplementary excitation. Each motor effector received positive input from three dedicated neurones and negative input from one dedicated neurone. Hence motor speeds could vary between -10 to 30 by increments of 10 depending on the number and type of motor neurones firing at any given time step.

Each Khepera robot was tested over three random initial positions per life cycle. A life cycle lasted 4000 time steps. The world had dimensions of 90cm * 90cm with wrap around borders. A light source was placed in the centre of the arena. Robot fitness was evaluated based on the average distance to the centre of the light source over its lifetime. A floating point valued genotype with 625 loci encoded delay values between 0 and 1, which were later scaled to the delay ranges explored in the three conditions described below. As noted above, only 30% of these connections were used per individual. This connectivity mapping was preserved over generations and unaffected by mutation. Amongst the most successful individuals per generation, 20% were selected (the elite) from which two were randomly chosen for 50% crossover and 50% mutation to form a single new individual which replaced one non-elite population member for the subsequent generation. Mutation was applied by adding or subtracting (with 50% chance) a gaussian distributed value with mean 0 and standard deviation 0.03.

We tested a number of network configurations, with either full (4 neurones per sensor) positive excitation of sensory cells in the presence of light, partial excitation with light and inverse excitation in the absence of light (3-1 and 1-3 neurones per sensor), and full (4 neurones per sensor) inverse excitation in the absence of light. Highest fitness was obtained in the last scenario where sensors were only excited in the absence of light, which we believe promoted a greater degree of exploration and faster movement. In this 'explorative' sensory scenario, three delay ranges were tested: 0 to 3 time steps ($D_{range} = 3$, with no minimum delay), 60 to 63 time steps ($D_{range} = 3$, with a minimum delay of 60), and 15 to 23 time steps ($D_{range} = 8$, with a minimum delay of 15).

4.2 Simulation Results

Overall, the fitness achieved by each type of robot population improved rapidly within the first 300 generations as shown in Figure 4. The first population with delays in the range 0-3 time steps (population A) reached on average an inverse fitness of about 219 (219mm from the light; based on the last 100 generations). For the population with delay ranges 15-23 (population B), which was just above the refractory period, individuals did not perform as well illustrating a greater variance in fitness over time and a final average inverse fitness of about 244. In the final population (population C), delays in the range 60-63 implied very similar low variation in delay as in the first condition (0-3) but with much greater delay. This resulted in the highest fitness of all three conditions with an average inverse-fitness of about 196 by the last generations. A one-way ANOVA between population fitnesses revealed that the evolved performance between these three types of delay scenarios was significant with $F(2, 2997) = 735.2$, $p < 0.001$. Before exploring the reasons behind these inter-population differences, we first explored the details of individual population network characteristics and robot behaviours.

A typical network in population A possessed an overall

[4]Subsequent experiments showed that sensory refractoriness ≤ 5 time steps was sufficient for adequate network activity.

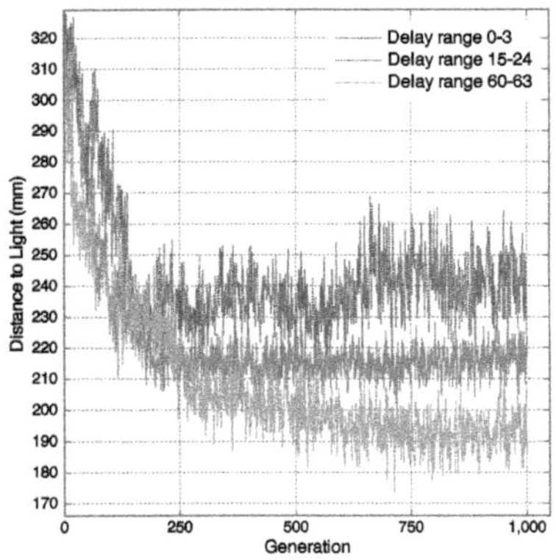

Figure 4: Inverse fitness results for three delays distribution cases: A (0-3), B (15-23) , and C (60-63).

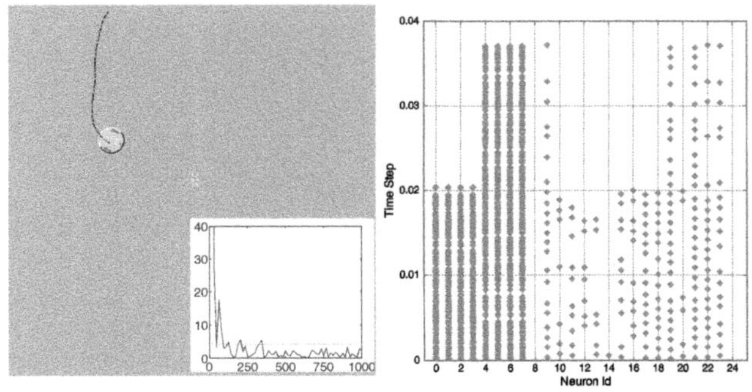

Figure 5: Left: typical behaviour of a last generation robot with axonal delays between 0 and 3 times steps (population A). Inlay is the power spectrum during the activity. Right: corresponding spike raster.

network delay mean of 1.39ts with standard deviation 0.97ts by the final generation. With respect to behaviour, robots wandered at moderate to swift speeds in straight lines with some random shift right or left and very little jitter. When the light source was sensed the robot aligned itself with the light and often stopped quickly. This typically resulted in an end position relatively far from the light on the edge of perceptible input. This is explained by the inhibitory effect light had on the sensory neurones. Occasionally, a robot passed over the light if it got close enough thereby situating the light within its frontal 'blind-spot'. Figure 5 illustrates the typical behaviour of a last generation robot along with the corresponding network's spike count. From the raster plot one can note how the 'inverse' input on neurones 0 to 7 led to high activity when the robot was far from the light, causing it to move forward which correlated with the activity of the last 8 neurones (16 to 24). Since the robot approached the light from its left the firing of the four left sensor neurones (0 to 3) stopped as soon as the light was in range while the right sensory neurones continued to fire. This had the effect of reducing left motor neurone activation (neurones 16 to 20) causing the robot to veer to the left while maintaining activation of the right motor neurones (21 to 24). By the 370'th time step the robot faced the light causing both left and right sensory neurones to stop firing, which induced a cessation of activity within motor cells resulting in the stopping of the robot relatively close to the light source. Analysis of the frequency components for this robot did not reveal any significant power despite the expected synchrony in networks with narrow axonal delay ranges found in the pure network analysis above. This could be due to the small number of collected samples during the robot's recorded behaviour, but also due to the sensory input causing an important amount of fluctuation in network firing.

The higher fitness variation found in the 15-23 delay range population can be explained by the higher degree of variation in delays and the contingent effect it had on the global firing activity in each robot. In particular, as seen in the previous section, networks of this type with greater delay ranges tend to exhibit complex spiking activity. As predicted by our network analysis, broad delay ranges resulted in a wider range of behaviours during evolution. However, by the final generation, most individuals exhibited similar light seeking behaviour suggesting that a sufficiently optimal strategy was found for genotypic convergence within 1000 generations. Typical networks for population B robots had mean delay of approximately 19.3ts with standard deviation 2.3ts. As seen in Figure 6, final generation individuals wandered swiftly with slight jiggle and a bias towards left turns. When the light source was sensed the robot aligned itself with the light and moved forward towards it. Similar to population A, these robots often stopped far from the light source at the limit of perceptual input. This is primarily due to the inhibitory input that the light exercised on sensory cells. Here, the agent passed the light on its right without turning towards it and stopped when in sensory range. From the spike raster plot we notice that the lack of firing for right sensor neurones (4 to 7) at the 1230'th time step caused some targets as well as right motor neurones (20 to 24) to reduce their firing, thereby allowing the left motor neurones to slightly take over which caused the robot to move in a relatively straight line with slight veering to the right. However, as the robot passed the light, sensory inhibition no longer took place causing the robot to resume its left turn behaviour by time step 1850. This allowed the robot to reposition itself and face the light by causing the left sensory neurones to stop firing at time step 2300, inducing a sharp extinction of left motor neurone firing (16 to 20) while maintaining firing of the right motor neurone 21. This caused the robot to turn left more sharply and face the light source completely by time step 3010, at which point right sensory cells were completely inhibited thereby preventing any further movement. Interestingly, as the agent got closer to the light from its right, left sensory cells began firing once no more light impinged on the left sensory cells. This, however, did not have a sufficient spiking effect to alter behaviour. This suggests that right sensory firing along with a history of left sensory and internal network firing was necessary for this agent to move but not vice-versa. Spectral analysis in this particular behavioural sample did not reveal any significant frequency component despite the greater number of recorded samples than from our population A sample. This network, however, possessed greater axonal variation (std dev. 2.3ts) which we believe led to fewer oscillations and less synchrony within the network.

Given the higher fitness found within the small delay variability of population A we were interested in exploring the effect of small delay variability at a much greater mean delay. Population C consisted of robots controlled by net-

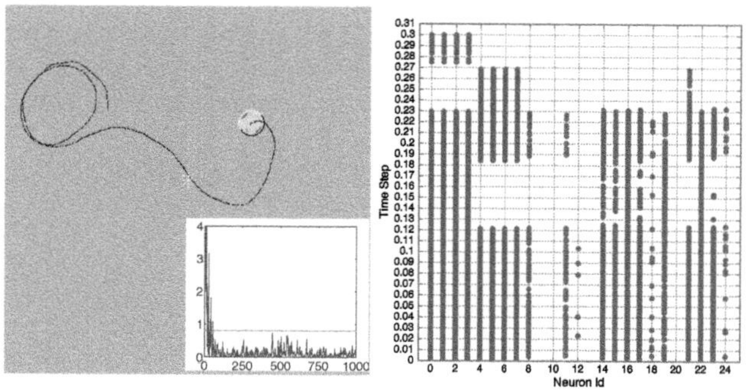

Figure 6: Left: typical behaviour of a last generation robot with axonal delays between 15 and 23 times steps (population B). Inlay is the power spectrum during the activity. Right: corresponding spike raster.

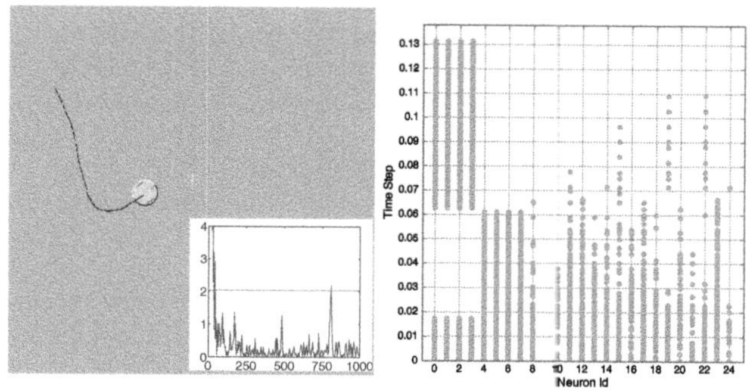

Figure 7: Left: typical behaviour of a last generation robot with axonal delays between 60 and 63 times steps (population C). Inlay is the power spectrum during the activity. Right: corresponding spike raster.

works with axonal delays with mean 61.5ts and standard deviation of 0.97ts. In contrast to agents from population A, networks from population C had axonal delays above the refractory period of non-sensory cells (recall, $R = 10$). As noted above, overall fitness of population C did improve substantially compared to both populations A and B despite the very similar rectilinear behavioural motion of robots to those of population A. Generally, the advantage that these robots possessed in accomplishing the task was a delayed stop when moving towards the light source, which enabled them to get closer on average to the target than did final generation robots from other populations. From Figure 7 we notice that when left sensory cells stopped firing at time step 180, the continued firing of the right sensory cells caused the agent to make a sharp left turn especially driven by right motor neurone 23. At time step 620, right sensory cells ceased to receive input while left sensory cells resumed firing as the light became imperceptible by left sensory neurones. At this point, however, continued firing took place within the network enabling the robot to move slightly closer to the light until about time step 1130. Similar to agents in population B, the sole firing of left sensory neurones was not enough to trigger substantial firing within the network. Instead, right sensory cells along with a history of sensory and network cell firing seemed necessary to enable motion. The delayed firing attenuation in agents of population C appeared to be the direct cause of the improved fitness by enabling agents to get closer to the light source despite the inhibitory effect the light source exercised on sensory cells. Interestingly, in this particular run, a significant 800Hz power component was found from spectral analysis. In addition to the larger number of samples when compared to the sample from population A, this is likely explained by the small axonal delay variation between 60ts and 63ts, causing increased synchrony in the network.

4.3 Discussion

The present results support the view that small delay ranges are best suited in a reactive task such as light seeking. Given the relatively little amount of time to find the light source, this scenario enabled a more direct response to sensory input. Agents could move in an overall linear fashion but also perform sharp turns and stops as soon as the light source was sensed. In contrast, the complexity of broader axonal delay ranges led to greater behavioural diversity across the population and increased complexity within an agent's control network by the final generation. As seen with population B, the most suited agents spun in a circular motion with slight drift over time, enabling them to accomplish the task, but not always in a timely fashion. We hypothesize, however, that the complexity that such networks possess may prove to be essential for more sophisticated behaviours. In particular, a network's ability to exploit subtle time-based variations from sensory stimuli could vary greatly depending on connectivity and delay characteristics. This remains to be explored in more complex tasks. A good candidate for this, could be solving the perceptual aliasing problem via sensorimotor coordination [22], [18].

With respect to evolutionary influence, although delays were selected for, the genotype consisted of real values between 0 and 1. Transcription to axonal delays was done by multiplying a gene by the delay range and adding a minimum delay, if any. This had the effect of preventing evolution from having to explore a very broad range of delays; however, this also precluded the possibility for the network to find potential useful delay configurations constituted by a mix of small delay range sub-populations and broader delay range sub-populations. This could be an important feature to explore in future experiments. In the broad delay case (population B), however, nothing prevented a network from converging towards narrow delay variation, although visibly, some performance improvement was found when smaller variation was set manually as in population A and population C. This may be due to rapid fitness convergence in the genetic landscape and lack of genotypic specialization in population B. Further examination of this would require alternate evolutionary approaches.

The investigation presented here is supportive of the hypothesis that distinct functional categories of axonal delay neural networks using coincidence detection exist. While strong synchronous activity may suit an automatic or reactive response, complex spike timing may serve both cooperation via partial synchrony, but also the formation of active memories or other processing functions. The coordination of these elementary mechanisms may thus organize into larger units serving global functions. In contrast to a pure network dynamics analysis, this hypothesis is supported by a simple, yet pertinent, embodied task. While the level of representation achieved by the robot is simply instantiated in the ability to distinguish inputs and achieve a reactive response, these results contribute a preliminary answer to providing direct evidence for the functional role of spike timing in cognition. Furthermore, this approach is not remote to the principal ideas behind the subsumption theory, whereby the aggregation of distinct functional units self-organize into general behaviours, which in turn subsume these units [4]. In contrast, however, we aim to minimize our assumptions regarding the individual role of specific network structures and focus instead on defining their uniqueness in terms of their dynamics and participation in solving adaptive tasks. By identifying classes of time coding networks and improving our understanding of how these are formed we hope to develop a greater understanding of neural organization and function for cognition as an adaptive phenomenon.

5. REFERENCES

[1] M. Abeles. *Corticonics: Neural circuits of the cerebral cortex.* Cambridge University Press, 1991.

[2] J. Bouyer, M. Montaron, and A. Rougeul. Fast fronto-parietal rhythms during combined focused attentive behaviour and immobility in cat: cortical and thalamic localozations. *Electroencephalography and Clinical Neurophsysiology*, 51:244–252, 1981.

[3] V. Braitenberg. *Vehicles: Experiments in synthetic psychology.* Cambridge, MA: MIT Press, 1984.

[4] R. Brooks. Intelligence without representation. *Artificial Intelligence*, 47:139–159, 1991.

[5] N. Brunel. Dynamics of sparsely connected networks of excitatory and inhibitory spiking neurons. *Computational Neuroscience*, 8(3):183–208, 2000.

[6] G. Buszaki. *Rhythms of the Brain.* Oxford University Press, 2006.

[7] R. Eckhorn, R. Bauer, W. Jordan, M. Brosch, W. Kruse, M. Munk, and H. Reiboek. Coherent oscillations: A mechanism for feature linking in the visual cortex? *Biological Cybernetics*, 60:121–130, 1988.

[8] G. M. Edelman. *Neural Darwinism: The theory of neuronal group selection.* New York: Basic Books, 1987.

[9] K. Engel and W. Singer. Temporal binding and the neural correlates of sensory awareness. *Trends in Cognitive Sciences*, 5(1):16–25, 2001.

[10] H. Fujii, H. Ito, K. Aihara, N. Ichinose, and M. Tsukada. Dynamical cell assembly hypothesis - theoretical possibility of spatio-temporal coding in the cortex. *Neural Networks*, 9(8):1303–1350, 1996.

[11] E. Izhikevich. Simple model of spiking neurons. *IEEE Transactions on Neural Networks*, 14(6):1569–1572, 2003.

[12] E. M. Izhikevich. Polychronization: Computation with spikes. *Neural Computation*, 18:245–282, 2006.

[13] E. M. Izhikevich, J. A. Gally, and G. M. Edelman. Spike-timing dynamics of neuronal groups. *Cerebral Cortex*, 14(8):933–944, 2004.

[14] P. König, A. Engel, and W. Singer. Integrator or coincidence detector? the role of the cortical neuron revisited. *Trends in Neurosciences*, 19(4):130–137, 1996.

[15] B. Kriener, T. Tetzlaff, A. Aertsen, M. Diesmann, and S. Rotter. Correlations and population dynamics in cortical networks. *Neural Computation*, 20:2185–2226, 2008.

[16] O. Michel. Khepera simulator package version 2.0. freeware mobile robot simulator, 1995.

[17] N. Murthy and E. Fetz. Coherent 25- to 35-hz oscillations in the sensorimotor cortex of awake behaving monkeys. *Proceedings of the National Acedemy of Sciences*, 89:5670–5674, 1992.

[18] S. Nolfi. Adaptation as a more powerful tool than decomposition and integration. In T. Fogarty and G. Venturini, editors, *Proceedings of the Workshop on Evolutionary Computing and Machine Learning, 13th International Conference on Machine Learning.* University of Bari, 1996.

[19] D. Perkel and T. Bullock. Neural coding. *Neurosciences Research Program Bulletin*, 6:221–348, 1968.

[20] A. Peters and E. Yilmaz. Neuronal organization in area 17 of cat visual cortex. *Cerebral Cortex*, 3:49–68, 1993.

[21] M. Ren, Y. Yoshimura, N. Takada, S. Horibe, and Y. Komatsu. Specialized inhibitory synaptic actions between nearby neocortical pyramidal neurons. *Science*, 316:758–761, 2007.

[22] C. Scheier and R. Pfeifer. Classification as sensory-motor coordination: A case study on autonomous agents. In F. Moran, A. Moreno, J. Merelo, and P. Chacon, editors, *Advances in Artificial Life: Proceedings of the Third European Conference on Artificial Life*, pages 862–875. Springer Verlag, 1995.

[23] G. Sperling. The information available in brief visual presentations. *Psychological Monographs*, 74:1–29, 1960.

[24] F. Stevens and F. Wesseling. Augmentation is a potentiation of the exocytotic process. *Neuron*, 22:139–146, 1999.

[25] S. Thorpe, A. Delorme, and R. V. Rullen. Spike-based strategies for rapid processing. *Neural Networks*, 14:715–725, 2001.

[26] S. Thorpe and M. Imbert. *Connectionism in Perspective*, chapter Biological constraints on connectionist models, pages 63–92. Elsevier Science Publishers, 1989.

[27] C. von der Marlsburg. The correlation theory of brain function. *(Internal Report): Goettingen: Max-Planck Institute for Biophysical Chemistry*, 2, 1981.

[28] L. M. Ward. Synchronous neural oscillations and cognitive processes. *Trends in Cognitive Sciences*, 7(12):553–559, 2003.

How to be a Successful App Developer: Lessons from the Simulation of an App Ecosystem

Soo Ling Lim
Department of Statistical Science
University College London
United Kingdom
s.lim@cs.ucl.ac.uk

Peter J. Bentley
Department of Computer Science
University College London
United Kingdom
p.bentley@cs.ucl.ac.uk

ABSTRACT

App developers are constantly competing against each other to win more downloads for their apps. With hundreds of thousands of apps in these online stores, what strategy should a developer use to be successful? Should they innovate, make many similar apps, optimise their own apps or just copy the apps of others? Looking more deeply, how does a complex app ecosystem perform when developers choose to use different strategies? This paper investigates these questions using AppEco, the first Artificial Life model of mobile application ecosystems. In AppEco, developer agents build and upload apps to the app store; user agents browse the store and download the apps. A distinguishing feature of AppEco is the explicit modelling of apps as artefacts. In this work we use AppEco to simulate Apple's iOS app ecosystem and investigate common developer strategies, evaluating them in terms of downloads received, app diversity, and adoption rate.

Categories and Subject Descriptors

I.6.3 [**Simulation and Modelling**]: Applications
I.6.5 [**Simulation and Modelling**]: Model Development

General Terms

Algorithms, Experimentation, Human Factors.

Keywords

App developers, strategies, app ecosystems, Artificial Life, mobile apps, agent-based simulation, app store, software ecosystems.

1. INTRODUCTION

It pays to be an app developer. Some of the world's most recent millionaires made their money from mobile apps. For example, Ethan Nicholas made his million from his iShoot app in less than a year [1]. Rovio, the developer of Angry Birds, made a revenue of $100 million in 2011 [2]. The revenue generated from app sales is estimated to surpass $15 billion in 2011 and reach $58 billion by 2014 [3]. However, not all app developers are so lucky. In fact, the majority of developers make little or no profit from their apps. Reports suggested that 80% of paid apps in the Android Market have been downloaded less than 100 times [4].

While such problems may be familiar to those in the music or publishing industries, app ecosystems (comprising developers, users, and apps) face challenges that are brand new to the software industry. App store owners face the challenges of presenting the rapidly increasing app store content to the users and encouraging users to download apps. App users have difficulty in finding good apps amongst the vast number of alternatives. App developers find it increasingly difficult to make their apps stand out among hundreds of thousands of other apps in the app store, achieve downloads, and make profit.

Competition is so fierce and advertising space so congested that the question of how to be a successful app developer is now on the lips of thousands of programmers around the world. But which strategy is best? One approach to answering this question might be to experiment with a real app store: flood the store with thousands of new apps developed using specific strategies and measure their success. However, some strategies, such as copying the apps of others, are difficult to try in the real world. One developer faced a $12.5 million lawsuit for allegedly copying a $3 beer-drinking novelty app that allows users to virtually drink a pint by tilting their iPhone[1]. Consequently for this work we present an Artificial Life (Alife) agent-based model as an experimental tool to address such questions. Alife methods have proven their worth with many previous simulations of ecosystems.

In this paper, we present AppEco, a model of app ecosystems. AppEco models developers (agents that build apps) and users (agents that download apps). It simulates the app store environment, which hosts and organises content created by the developers, and enables users to browse and download apps. Significantly, AppEco also models apps – artefacts produced by the developers and downloaded by users – and their features. AppEco allows us to conduct experiments, test hypothesis about various processes in the ecosystem, and ask "what if" questions, all of which are difficult if not impossible to conduct in a real-world setting. Here, we use AppEco to simulate Apple's iOS app ecosystem and investigate common strategies adopted by developers.

The rest of the paper is organised as follows. Section 2 describes existing work. Section 3 describes AppEco. Section 4 describes the application of AppEco to simulate the iOS app ecosystem, the experiments and results. Section 5 provides our conclusions based on the results.

[1] http://www.wired.com/gadgetlab/2008/10/indie-iphone-de/

2. BACKGROUND

While the study of mobile app ecosystems is a current and significant topic for researchers, to date there has been little work focussing on the topic [5, 6]. However there is much related work that contextualises and informs our study.

One area related to app ecosystems is the study and prediction of app sales and usage. For example, Garg and Telang developed strategies to infer the current sales of an app based on its ranking on Apple's iOS App Store Top Apps Chart [7]. Such work may enable investors to estimate likely profits should an app reach a specific rank, however there is no certainty that a new app will appear on the chart. Bohmer et al. developed a mobile app to collect mobile app usage information from over 4,100 users of Android devices [8]. Their research revealed interesting app usage behaviours among the users. For example, although users spend almost an hour a day using their phones, an average session with an app lasts less than a minute. They also found that news apps are most popular in the morning and games are at night, but communication apps dominate through most of the day [8]. These studies are informative, but they are limited to studying what is already out there, and "what-if" questions cannot be answered.

In the fields of Alife, Evolutionary Computing and Agent-Based Simulation, researchers have modelled various aspects of ecosystems such as evolutionary dynamics within interacting populations. Classic works in this area include studies by Axelrod and Hamilton on the evolution of cooperation [9] and Maynard Smith and Price on conflicts between animals of the same species [10]. More recently, Holland created Echo, a generic ecosystem model in which evolving agents are situated in a resource-limited environment [11]. Pachepsky et al. investigated the effect of ecological interactions between organisms on the evolutionary dynamics of a community [12]. There are also a growing number of studies on the emergent effects of human interaction at the population level. For example, Kohler et al. used models to understand the environmental and social factors that led to the disappearance of the Puebloan peoples of the North American Southwest [13]. Lux and Marchesi showed that the scaling of financial prices arises from interactions between a large number of market participants [14]. App stores have large populations of apps, developers, and users, and can benefit from similar studies.

Indirect interaction through mechanisms such as stigmergy is commonly studied by Alife researchers. In human society different kinds of objects and tools are often built, adopted, shared and used to support people in their work [15]. It is common for such artefacts to become media for communication (e.g., books, music, and software). One study relating to this topic is the use of robots to create music. In this work, Miranda developed a group of interactive autonomous singing robots that imitate each other to create music [16]. Despite such studies, which often focus on the evolution of human culture with reference to artefacts [17], there is a lack of models that study the development and consumption of artefacts by agents, and how the success of the artefact depends on the preferences of the agents.

3. APPECO

In an app ecosystem, coevolving systems of apps, developers, and users form complex relationships, filling niches, competing and cooperating, similar to species in a biological ecosystem [6]. The health of the app ecosystem is largely determined by the communities of developers that create innovative solutions that users want to buy [5, 18]. In an app ecosystem, application software (such as games, medical applications, and productivity tools) that is built for a mobile platform is sold via an app store running on the platform. The app store concept has democratised the software industry – almost anyone can build and sell apps. Once built, an app quickly becomes available to a worldwide market. Mobile device users can download the apps, use them immediately and provide feedback to the developers.

AppEco is an Artificial Life simulation of mobile app ecosystems. The model consists of agents that are abstractions of app users and developers, as well as artefacts that are abstractions of apps. Developer agents build and upload apps to the app store; user agents browse the store and download the apps, see Figure 1. Each download corresponds to a new sale. A distinguishing feature of the AppEco model compared to more traditional agent-based models is the explicit modelling of artefacts as well as the agents that produce and use the artefacts. Different from agents, artefacts are not autonomous, they represent passive entities of the system that are intentionally created and used by agents [15]. App artefacts are important in a model of an app ecosystem because the agents interact with one another via the apps.

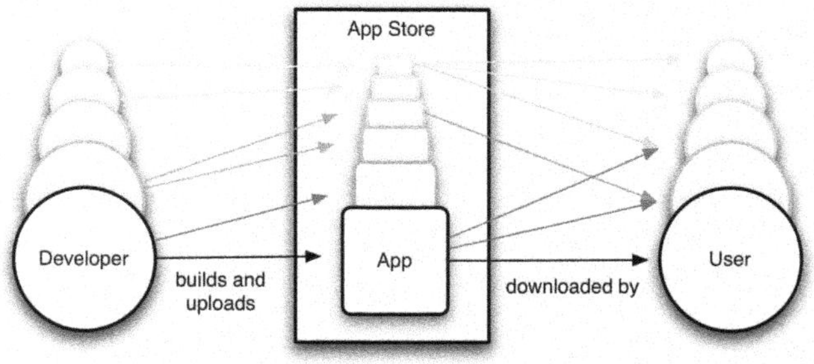

Figure 1. The interaction between developers, apps, and users in AppEco.

3.1 AppEco Components

AppEco consists of app developers, apps, users, and the app store. Each component is described as follows.

3.1.1 Developers

In AppEco, a developer agent represents a solo developer or a team of developers working together to produce an app. Each developer agent has a development duration (*devDuration*, a random value between [dev_{min}, dev_{max}]), which specifies the number of days it needs to build an app. Each developer also records the number of days it has already spent building the app (*daysTaken*). Each developer is initially active (it continuously builds and upload apps to the app store) but may become inactive (it stops building apps) with probability $P_{Inactive}$. This enables the modelling of part-time developers, hobbyists, and the tendency of developers to stop building apps[2]. Every developer records the number of apps it has already developed and the number of downloads it has received. Each developer uses one of the following strategies to build apps:

- **S0 Innovator**: Builds an app with random features each time. This strategy models innovative developers. For example, iOS developer Shape Services produces different apps in a variety of categories such as social networking, business, utilities, and productivity[3].

---

[2] http://t-machine.org/index.php/2009/06/11/may-2009-survey-of-iphone-developers/

[3] http://www.shapeservices.com/

- **S1 Milker**: Makes a variation of own most recent app each time. This strategy models developers who "milk" a single app idea repeatedly. An extreme example is Brighthouse Labs which produced thousands of similar apps[4], such as an app to provide news for each region in each country, and an app about each sports team for each sport.
- **S2 Optimiser**: Makes a variation of own best app each time. This strategy models developers who learn from downloads and improve on their best app. For example, Rovio developed many game apps before hitting the jackpot with Angry Birds. They then built on their success, releasing new apps such as Angry Birds Seasons, and Angry Birds Rio[5].
- **S3 Copycat**: Copies an app in the Top Apps Chart. This strategy models developers who are less creative but want to achieve many downloads quickly. Angry Chickens and Angry Dogs are two example copycats of Angry Birds[6].
- **S* Flexible**: Developers begin with one of the strategies S0-S3. Each developer then has a 0.99 probability to randomly select an app from the Top Apps Chart and change strategy to be the same as the developer of the selected app. There is a 0.01 probability that a strategy is randomly selected.

These strategies are abstracted after consultation with app literature and developers. Few app developers perform market research before developing.

3.1.2 Apps

Each app artefact is built and uploaded by a developer agent. The features of the app are abstracted as a 10x10 feature grid (**F**) for each app. If a cell in **F** is filled, then the app offers that particular feature. A grid is used so that feature similarity can be represented in the future, e.g., features that are similar can be represented as cells that are near to one another on the grid. For ranking purposes, each app keeps a record of the total number of downloads it has received to date and the number of downloads it has received on each of the previous seven days. For simplicity, the model currently assumes that all apps are sold at the same price; the model of variations in app pricing and categories of apps is left for future work. Each app also records the time when it is being uploaded.

The app feature grid **F** is filled depending on the strategy used by the app's developer:

- **S0**: The cells in **F** are filled probabilistically, such that each cell in the grid has a probability P_{Feat} of being filled.
- **S1**: The cells in **F** are filled probabilistically as in S0 if this is the developer's first app. Otherwise, the developer copies the features of his own latest app with random mutation.
- **S2**: The cells in **F** are filled probabilistically as in S0 if this is the developer's first app. Otherwise, the developer copies the features in his own best app (as determined by the highest daily average downloads) with random mutation. The choice of which app to copy occurs when the developer is starting to build the app. If no apps by this developer have downloads, the developer just copies his most recent app.
- **S3**: An app is randomly selected from the Top Apps Chart and its features are copied with random mutation. The choice of app to copy occurs when the developer is starting to build the app.

There is a 0.5 probability that mutation occurs during a copy. Mutation is implemented by randomly selecting a filled cell in **F** and randomly "moving" it to an empty cell in **F**.

3.1.3 Users

Inspired by the recommender systems literature [19], each user agent has preferences (or taste information) that determine the app features that it prefers. The preferences of a user agent are abstracted as a 10x10 preference grid (**P**). The cells in **P** are filled probabilistically, such that each cell in the grid has a probability P_{Pref} of being filled. If a cell in **P** is filled, then the user agent desires the feature represented by that cell. If the feature grid **F** of an app has a cell in the same location filled, then it means the app offers a feature desired by the user agent. For example, in Figure 2, all four of the features offered by App 1 match the user agent's preferences, but only two of the features offered by App 2 match the user agent's preferences. For simplicity, preference matching is binary: filled cells either match or do not match. The top right quadrant in **P** is always empty in order to model some features that are undesirable to all users, see Figure 2. For example, no users want an app to have the features of a difficult-to-use or malicious program. Using the AppEco model, a popular app such as Angry Birds can be abstracted as an app with **F** that matches **P** of many users, while a less popular app has **F** that matches few or no users' **P**. The developers are unaware of the users' preferences.

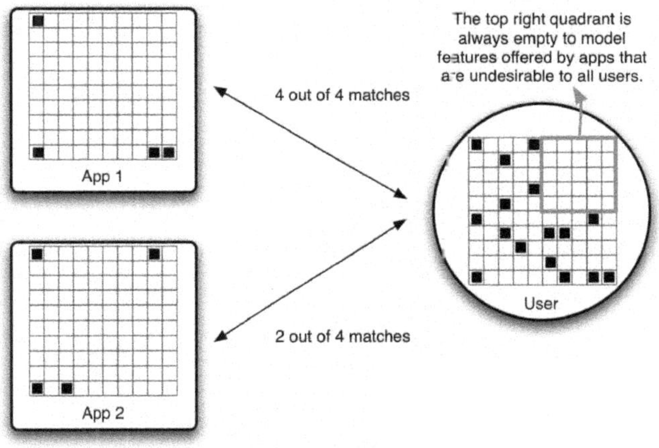

Figure 2. Matching app features with user preferences.

Finally, a user agent keeps a record of the apps it has downloaded, the number of days between each browse of the app store (*daysBtwBrowse*, a random value between $[bro_{min}, bro_{max}]$), and the number of days that have elapsed since it last browsed the app store (*daysElapsed*). *daysElapsed* is recorded so that the user agent knows when to browse the app store next. When users are initialised, *daysElapsed* is set to be a random number between [0, *daysBtwBrowse*] so that users don't all browse at the same time when they start.

3.1.4 App Store

The app store is the environment used by the agents to store and access apps. Its primary function is to provide a shop front for users and enable them to locate and download apps that match their preferences. To achieve this, it provides three browsing methods: the Top Apps Chart, the New Apps Chart, and Keyword Search. These three methods are modelled because they are

[4] http://isource.com/2009/05/27/app-store-hall-of-shame-brighthouse-labs/

[5] http://www.wired.co.uk/magazine/archive/2011/04/features/how-rovio-made-angry-birds-a-winner

[6] http://techcrunch.com/2011/12/06/can-we-stop-the-copycat-apps/

common to many app stores, such as iOS, Android, and BlackBerry. The Top Apps Chart ranks apps based on the number of downloads the apps have received. The New Apps Chart displays new apps that have recently been uploaded by developer agents; only a small subset of new apps is chosen for this chart. Keyword Search returns a list of apps that match the keyword entered by the user agent. In AppEco, Keyword Search is abstracted as a random search for a random number of apps. It is implemented in this way because keywords may not correspond to features, so a matching keyword does not mean the app has desirable features for the user.

3.2 AppEco Algorithm

The AppEco algorithm models the daily interactions between the AppEco components described in the previous section. Each timestep in the algorithm represents a day in the real ecosystem.

Inspired by the ecology literature [20, 21], the population growth of user and developer agents is modelled using a sigmoid growth function commonly used to model the population growth in natural systems. The equation models the growth rate of user and developer agents in an app ecosystem declining as their population density increases, with the size of the ecosystem limited by the market share of the mobile platform. The population size at timestep t, pop_t, is defined by Eq. 1.

$$pop_t = \text{MinPop} + \frac{(\text{MaxPop-MinPop})}{1+e^{S*t-D}} \qquad \text{(Eq. 1)}$$

where MinPop is the minimum population, MaxPop is the maximum population, S determines the slope of the growth curve (S is negative for a growth curve), and D shifts the curve from left to right. Different growth formulas can be used to model different ecosystems [20, 21].

The AppEco algorithm, see Figure 3, is detailed as follows.

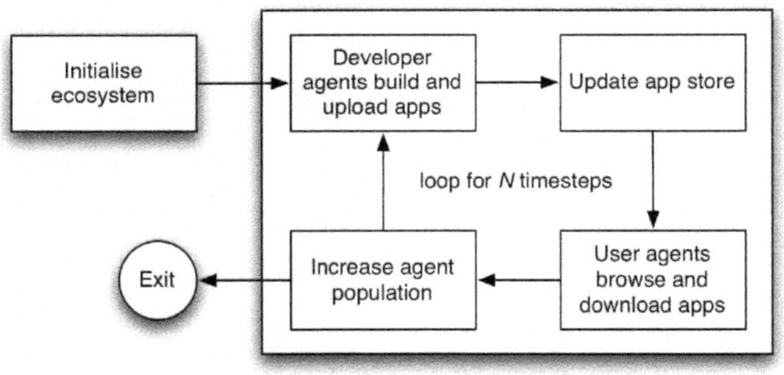

Figure 3. The AppEco algorithm.

Initialise ecosystem. This step launches AppEco with the population of developer and user agents as defined in Eq. 1, with timestep $t = 0$. It is common for app stores to have apps before it is opened. For example, the iOS App Store had 500 apps the day it was launched[7]. As such, this step also creates an initial number of app artefacts ($N_{InitApp}$). The developers of these initial apps are randomly selected from the pool of initial developers of strategy S0, S1 or S2 (S3 waits for apps to be on Top Apps Chart before it builds apps). The attributes of initial developers, apps, and users are set as described in the previous section.

Developer agents build and upload apps. For each active developer, *daysTaken* is incremented by 1. If *daysTaken* exceeds this developer's *devDuration*, the app is completed. The developer then uploads the app to the store, resets *daysTaken* to 0, and decides on the next app to build. The feature grid **F** of the app is set depending on the developer's strategy.

Update app store. The New Apps Chart is updated. When timestep $t = 0$, the New Apps Chart consists of a random selection of initial apps. In each following timestep, each new app has a probability $P_{OnNewChart}$ of appearing on the New Apps Chart. Apps are randomly selected here because the selection criteria are not the focus of this work and real app stores do not reveal how they select apps for the New Apps Chart. The maximum number of apps in the chart is defined by $N_{MaxNewChart}$. As newly selected apps are added to the chart, older apps appear lower in the chart and are no longer listed when their position exceeds the chart size. The Top Apps Chart is also updated. When timestep $t = 0$, the Top Apps Chart is empty because no apps have been downloaded yet. In each following timestep, apps are ranked in the order of decreasing score, calculated as $8*D_1+5*D_2+5*D_3+3*D_4$ where D_n is the number of downloads received by the app on the nth day before the current day [22]. The maximum number of apps in the Top Apps Chart is defined by $N_{MaxTopChart}$.

User agents browse and download apps. For each user, *daysElapsed* is incremented by 1. If *daysElapsed* exceeds *daysBtwBrowse*, then the user browses the app store, and resets *daysElapsed* to 0. The user browses the New Apps Chart and the Top Apps Chart, and conducts Keyword Search (which returns a random number of apps between [key_{min}, key_{max}]). The user browses each app that it has not previously downloaded: the feature grid of the app is compared with the preference grid of the user. If all the features offered by the app match the user's preferences, then the user downloads the app. For example, in Figure 2, the user downloads App 1 but not App 2.

Increase agent population. This step increases the number of user and developer agents in the ecosystem for the next timestep, using Eq. 1.

AppEco is implemented in C++ and the code can be requested from the authors via email. It is developed to be highly configurable so that it can simulate various app ecosystems, such as iOS, Android, and BlackBerry.

4. EXPERIMENTS

In order to investigate the effects of developer strategies in AppEco, we must first calibrate the simulation to match, as much as is feasible, the behaviour of a real app store. We select Apple's iOS App Store for our experiments, as it is one of the oldest and most established app stores. The calibration of AppEco to the iOS App Store is described in Section 4.1. We then investigate how different developer strategies affect individual and collective success in AppEco. Two experiments are conducted. Experiment 1 (E1) in Section 4.2 investigates the success of each individual strategy S0, S1, S2, and S3. Experiment 2 (E2) in Section 4.3 investigates the more realistic scenario of competing strategies by having developers select their own strategies over time. Thus in E2, developers have strategy S*, and the overall success of the App Store is compared against E1.

4.1 Calibrating AppEco for iOS

We collected the following iOS data over a period of three years, from the start of the iOS ecosystem in July 2008 (Q4 2008) until the end of June 2011 (Q3 2011):

[7] http://www.apple.com/pr/library/2008/07/10iPhone-3G-on-Sale-Tomorrow.html

- **Number of iOS developers**. The number of iOS developers is based on the number of worldwide iOS developers month over month compiled by Gigaom[8].
- **Number of iOS apps and downloads**. The number of apps and downloads is based on statistics provided in Apple press releases and Apple Events[9]. For example, in the Apple Special Event on 9th September 2009, Apple CEO Steve Jobs announced the App Store to reach 75,000 apps and 1.8 billion downloads, and Apple's press release on 28th September 2009 announced that the App Store has achieved more than 85,000 apps and 2 billion downloads[10].
- **Number of iOS users**. The number of iOS users is based on the number of iOS devices (iPod Touch, iPhone, and iPad) sold by Apple over time. The sales figures are available from Apple's quarterly financial data[10], and for simplicity the calculation assumes that each user has one iOS device.

We calibrated AppEco to simulate the iOS app ecosystem. Table 1 summarises the calibrated values for the system constants. Most constants were set from publicly available data. For example, the total number of people in the world who use mobile devices is approximately 4 billion [23]. According to the International Data Corporation (IDC), Apple had 2.8% of the mobile device market share in Q1 2010 and 5% in Q1 2011[11]. By assuming a maximum increase of market share to be 10%, our calculation gives us a $MaxIncrease_{User}$ of 400 million users. In order to match (curve-fit) the iOS user and developer growth rates, values such as D and S for users and developers were determined through tuning experiments. To ensure that the system is computationally feasible, one app represents one real app, and one developer agent represents one real developer, but one user agent represents 10,000 real users. This is because it is computationally infeasible in terms of memory to simulate hundreds of millions of users.

Table 1. Constant Values Resulting from iOS Calibration

$[Pop_{minUser}, Pop_{maxUser}]$	[1500, 40000]	$[dev_{min}, dev_{max}]$	[1, 180]
D_{User}	-4.0	P_{Pref}	0.45
S_{User}	-0.0038	P_{Feat}	0.04
$[Pop_{minDev}, Pop_{maxDev}]$	[1000, 120000]	$P_{OnNewChart}$	0.001
D_{Dev}	-4.0	$N_{MaxNewChart}$	40
S_{Dev}	-0.005	$N_{MaxTopChart}$	50
$N_{InitApp}$	500	$P_{Inactive}$	0.0027
$[bro_{min}, bro_{max}]$	[1, 360]	$[key_{min}, key_{max}]$	[0, 50]

Figure 4 illustrates the actual and simulated number of users, developers, apps, and downloads. As can be seen, the behaviour of AppEco closely resembles the behaviour of the iOS ecosystem, including emergent rates such as the number of apps and downloads. A run of the simulation takes approximately 16 seconds CPU time on a MacBook Air with a 1.8GHz Intel Core i7 Processor and 4GB of 1333 MHz DDR3 memory. After three years (1080 timesteps assuming 30 days a month), the model typically contains more than 100,000 developer agents, 500,000 apps, 20,000 user agents (corresponding to 200m real users), and 1.5 million downloads (corresponding to 15bn real downloads).

[8] http://gigaom.com/apple/infographic-apple-app-stores-march-to-500000-apps/

[9] http://www.apple.com/apple-events/

[10] http://www.apple.com/pr/library/

[11] http://www.idc.com/getdoc.jsp?containerId=prUS22808211

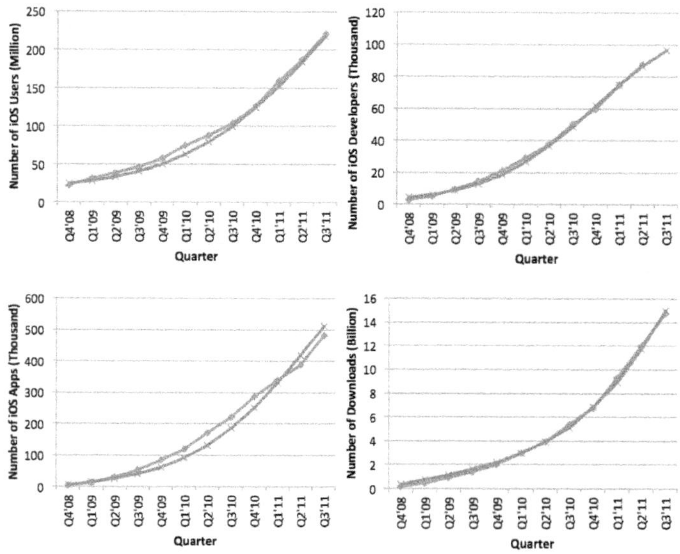

Figure 4. Actual vs. simulated number of iOS users, developers, apps, and downloads (blue is actual, red is simulated).

4.2 E1: Comparing Strategies

4.2.1 Objective and Setup

In a mobile app ecosystem, developers compete with each other to earn more downloads. Some developers try many different ideas, some produce many similar apps, some gain experience from their previous successful apps, and some copy successful apps created by other developers. To learn how each strategy performs relative to one another, we ask the following research questions:

RQ1: Which developer strategy enables individual developers to be most successful?

RQ2: What is the diversity of apps produced by each strategy?

RQ3: Which developer strategy enables the developer to become more successful as they develop more apps?

To answer **RQ1**, the following measurements are used: (1) ***Average Downloads per App (AvgDl)***: For each strategy S0 to S3, *AvgDl* is the total number of downloads received by the developers of the strategy, divided by total number of apps built by the developers of the same strategy. (2) ***Top 20 Total Downloads (Top20TotDl)***: The developers of all strategies are ranked based on the total number of downloads they received. For each strategy S0 to S3, *Top20TotDl* is the proportion of developers in the top 20 of this list that belong to the current strategy. (3) ***Top 20 Average Downloads (Top20AvgDl)***: The developers are ranked based on the average number of downloads they received per app. For each strategy S0 to S3, *Top20AvgDl* is the proportion of developers in the top 20 of this list that belong to the current strategy. Developers can receive more total downloads by building more apps – this measure identifies efficient developers who have many downloads with few apps. (4) ***Zero Downloads (ZeroDl)***: For each strategy S0 to S3, *ZeroDl* is the proportion of developers that belong to the current strategy who have received no downloads for any of their apps so far.

To answer **RQ2**, the ***Feature Coefficient of Variation (FeatCV)*** is used to measure the app coverage of features that are desired by users. For each cell in the desired region of feature grid **F**, we calculate the number of apps that offer that feature, forming a combined feature grid $\mathbf{F}^C$. *FeatCV* is the coefficient of variation of grid $\mathbf{F}^C$. *FeatCV* is defined in Eq. 2 and expressed as a percentage.

$$FeatCV = \sigma / \mu \qquad \text{(Eq. 2)}$$

where σ is the standard deviation and μ is the mean of values in grid $\mathbf{F}^C$. In this simulation, the user preference coefficient of variation in the desired region of **F** is 0.68%, indicating that the mean preferences for the user population are evenly distributed over the mean **F** feature grid. As such, a good strategy should have a low *FeatCV*, which means that all the apps have features that cover the desired region in **F** evenly (in combination they better meet all the users' needs).

To answer **RQ3**, we measure the ***Fitness*** of each strategy as its developers gain more experience in app development. For each strategy, we categorised the apps into classes corresponding to their developers' first apps, second apps, third apps, and so on. These correspond to the apps created by the developers at experience level 1, 2, 3, and so on. For each app, we "survey" the users and ask if they would download the app: if all the features in the app match the user's preferences then they would download the app. For each strategy, the *Fitness* of the strategy at experience level *L* is defined in Eq. 3.

$$Fitness_L = \frac{AvgDl_L}{NumUsers} \qquad \text{(Eq. 3)}$$

where $AvgDl_L$ is the number of potential downloads as reported by users in the survey for all the apps in experience level *L* divided by the number of apps in *L*, and *NumUsers* is the number of users who participated in the survey. $Fitness_L$ ranges from 0 to 1. The higher the value, the fitter the strategy.

AppEco was run with the settings described in Section 4.1. Throughout each run, developers in the ecosystem were randomly assigned strategies S0, S1, S2 or S3 in equal proportions to enable direct comparison of relative performance. AppEco was run for 1080 timesteps (corresponding to three years in the real world, assuming 30 days a month). The experiment was repeated 100 times. The results were averaged over the 100 runs.

4.2.2 Results and Analysis

RQ1: Which developer strategy enables individual developers to be most successful? As can be seen in Table 2, the Copycat strategy S3 is the most successful, receiving the highest *AvgDl*, *Top20TotDl* and *Top20AvgDl*, and the lowest *ZeroDl*. (The success of Copycats is well known in the real world – several Copycats who have parasitised Angry Birds have risen high in the Top Apps Chart[6].) Although the Innovator strategy S0 performed the worst with the lowest *AvgDl* and *Top20TotDl*, it has a lower number of developers with zero downloads (*ZeroDl*) compared to strategies S1 and S2. This is because by randomly trying different ideas for apps, creative S0 avoids dwelling on ideas that do not work, unlike S1 Milker and S2 Optimiser that keep working on similar apps. S1 Milker has the lowest *Top20AvgDl*, illustrating that a strategy that produces many similar apps results in poor performance. (In the real App Store this strategy is also heavily criticised by other developers and users for its exploitative approach[4].)

Studies of individual runs show that although S3 Copycat dominates the top developers lists, individual developers from other strategies can become the most successful developer in the ecosystem, achieving either the highest number of downloads or the highest average downloads per app. However, the occurrence is by chance: the developer has to build the right app at the right time (e.g., the app has features preferred by many users, appears on the New Apps Chart, is downloaded by many users, appears on the Top Apps Chart, and continues to attract downloads). Developers with high *Top20AvgDl* tend to develop one app in the entire three years. This shows that it is difficult to repeat success (a fact well-known to app developers in the real world[12]). The more apps a developer builds, the lower the average downloads tends to be. As such, the same developers rarely appear on both average and top downloads lists. In many runs, we observe that developers who built many apps can have the highest total number of downloads, but often have a low average.

Table 2. Results for RQ1 and RQ2 (Std. Dev. in Brackets)

	AvgDl	*Top20TotDl*	*Top20AvgDl*	*ZeroDl*	*FeatCV*
S0 Innovator	1.18	3.85%	9.10%	26.51%	**1.40%**
	(0.14)	(4.20%)	(5.52%)	(0.23%)	(0.13%)
S1 Milker	1.19	5.95%	8.80%	32.85%	4.27%
	(0.14)	(5.16%)	(6.52%)	(0.26%)	(0.35%)
S2 Optimiser	1.41	7.40%	9.25%	32.90%	6.50%
	(0.15)	(6.05%)	(7.30%)	(0.27%)	(0.62%)
S3 Copycat	**8.22**	**82.80%**	**72.85%**	**7.74%**	54.36%
	(0.41)	(8.30%)	(10.03%)	(0.23%)	(6.78%)

RQ2: What is the diversity of apps produced by each strategy? Developers who use the S0 Innovator strategy offer the most even coverage of features. Despite being the most successful strategy in terms of downloads, S3 Copycat has the highest *FeatCV*, which suggests that it only partially covers the preference space of users. Analysis shows that S3 produces an average of about 1 feature per app, while the other strategies have an average of 4 features per app. This is because users only download an app when all the features of the app matches their preference, and as a result apps with fewer features will have a higher chance to be downloaded by many users and appear on the Top Apps Chart. Since S3 Copycat copies from Top Apps Chart, the Copycat developers are likely to copy apps with very few features. (This is consistent with the advice from successful app developers – apps with fewer features have a higher chance of being downloaded[13].)

To investigate further, we group the apps by the experience level of their developers when the apps are built. We aggregate the features of the apps with the same strategy and experience level. We find that the coverage of features using S3 Copycat is worse than other strategies indicating that developers following this strategy are not satisfying as many users' needs (Figure 5). In contrast, the developers using S2 Optimiser correctly avoid the top right corner as they become more experienced, while also consistently covering the features desired by the users.

RQ3: Which developer strategy enables the developer to become more successful as they develop more apps? The only strategy that shows clear improvement as the developers become more experienced is S2 Optimiser. While S3 Copycat is the clear winner in terms of downloads, developers using the strategy are plagiarising the work of other developers rather than improving their own work. In S2 developers release new apps based on mutated copies of their most successful apps. As such this is similar to a (1 + λ) Evolutionary Strategy. Figure 6 illustrates that among the four strategies, S2 shows a classic evolutionary curve. This demonstrates that developers who improve their own apps

[12] http://www.fastcompany.com/1792313/striking-it-rich-in-the-app-store-for-developers-its-more-casino-than-gold-mine

[13] http://www.zdnet.com/blog/mobile-news/the-common-error-of-overloading-mobile-apps-with-features/5686

based on download feedback should increasingly meet the needs of the users. In addition, among all four strategies, S2 also offers the highest number of features desired by the users.

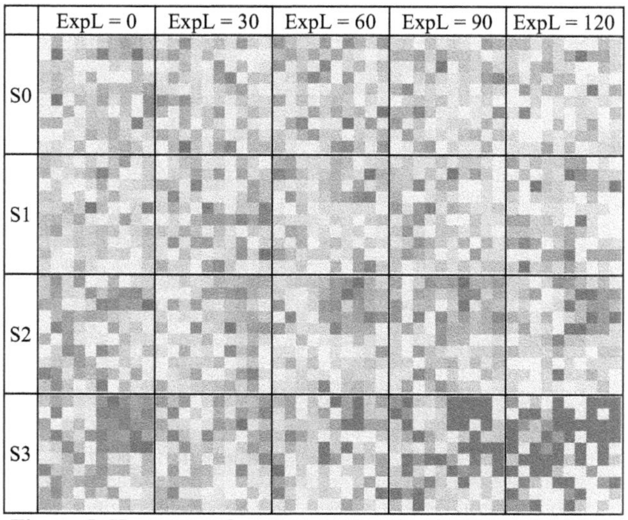

Figure 5. Heat maps for one run showing total app features over experience level.

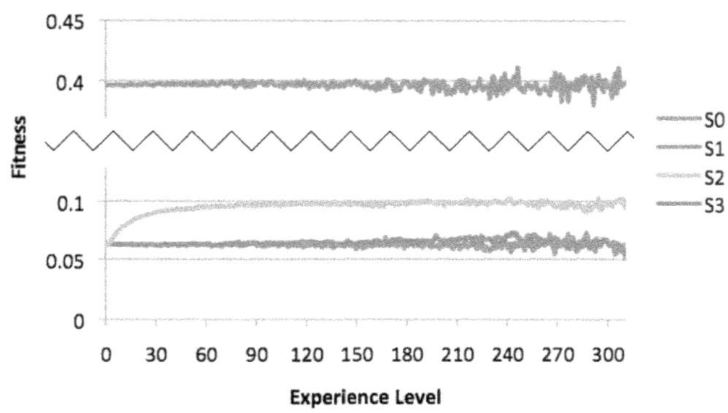

Figure 6. Fitness of a strategy as its developers become more experienced. Later data is more sparse as fewer developers create large number of apps, resulting in more noise.

4.3 E2: Ecosystem Health

4.3.1 Objective and Setup

In real life, there are no fixed strategies. Developers can choose the strategy they want to use. With all developers free to choose, the strategies directly compete with each other in the ecosystem. If a strategy were more effective then it might quickly dominate all others; less effective strategies might become a tiny minority. However, in many ecosystems, individual success is not always reproducible for many [9]. It is therefore of great interest to study how the number of developers using each strategy varies over time. Our research questions are thus:

RQ4: When strategies compete, how often is each strategy chosen by developers?

RQ5: What is the diversity of apps produced?

RQ6: Is an app ecosystem that comprises competing strategies able to improve its performance in the long term?

To answer **RQ4**, we measure the proportion of developers using each strategy over time. To answer **RQ5**, we use *FeatCV* (Eq. 2) on the aggregated app features in E2 and compare the results with the aggregated app features in E1. To answer **RQ6**, we use the *Fitness* measure (Eq. 3) on E2 and compare the outcome with E1. AppEco was run with the settings described in Section 4.1, with all developers initialised with Flexible strategy S*. E2 was also run for 1080 timesteps and repeated 100 times. The results were averaged over the 100 runs.

4.3.2 Results and Analysis

RQ4: When strategies compete, how often is each strategy chosen by developers? The choice of strategy depends on the proportion of other strategies in the population, but S3 Copycat is the least frequently chosen strategy (Table 3), despite appearing to be the best strategy from E1. When developers have a choice, very quickly the Copycat strategy is dropped in favour of the other strategies. As is evident from Table 3, strategy S0 Innovator is the most popular choice, followed by S2 Optimiser and then S1 Milker. However, the standard deviations for S0, S1 and S2 are very high, indicating that the percentage of developers from those strategies differs greatly in different runs (Table 3).

Table 3. Proportion of Developers at timestep $t = 1080$ (RQ4)

	Proportion of Developers	Standard Deviation
S0 Innovator	**33.51%**	19.74%
S1 Milker	26.57%	17.17%
S2 Optimiser	29.26%	18.94%
S3 Copycat	10.67%	7.65%

Indeed, studies from individual runs reveal that while S3 Copycat consistently falls quickly to 10% of the developer population, the winning strategies fluctuate unpredictably, at times with S0 Innovator, S1 Milker or S2 Optimiser each dominating the population, see Figure 7. It is interesting to note that the two most widely hated strategies in real life: S1 Milker and S3 Copycat, appear to be used the least in the ecosystem, with S3 Copycat clearly in the minority. To assess whether S3 could ever become widely adopted, we repeated E2 by only allowing developers to change strategies after 2 months in order to give S3 more opportunity to work. There was no change to the result: S3 again becomes unpopular. Even when E2 is repeated with 50% developers using S3 Copycat, most developers subsequently avoid choosing S3. In fact, in E2, the only way to guarantee that S3 will dominate the ecosystem is to force developers not to change strategies until after 1 year, by which time there are plenty of good apps to copy. This demonstrates that S3 is only viable as a minority strategy in a healthy ecosystem. Copycats rely on good apps created by other strategies; it is extremely difficult for an ecosystem to support a large proportion of Copycats. The result mirrors the app stores in the real world – Copycat developers regularly appear and take advantage of the success of others, but nevertheless their strategy remains in the minority.

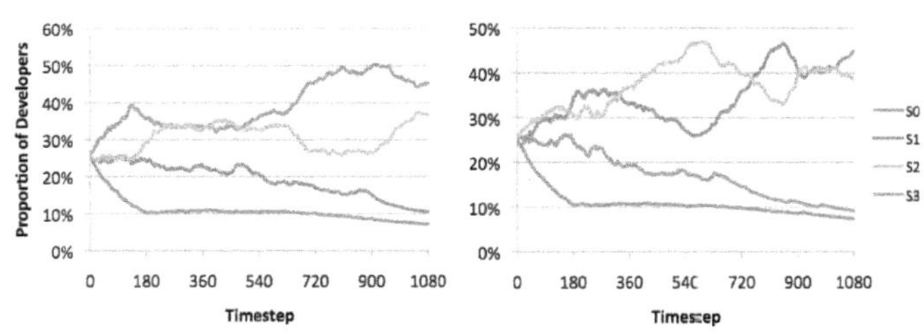

Figure 7. Proportion of developers in two example runs.

RQ5: What is the diversity of apps produced? When developers can choose their strategy, the app ecosystem has a higher diversity of apps. E1 resulted in a *FeatCV* of 6.28% with a standard deviation of 0.72%; E2 resulted in *FeatCV* of 2.87% with a standard deviation of 2.33%. This shows that in E2, the apps evenly cover the users' preference space. Analysis of all features for E1 and E2 shows that E2 has a more evenly distributed feature set. This means that in E1, users may find that the app store does not have any apps that meet some of their preferences.

RQ6: Is an app ecosystem that comprises competing strategies able to improve its performance in the long term? When we plot total fitness against developer experience level, there is a clear improvement evident for the more realistic ecosystem where developers are free to choose their strategies. Figure 8 illustrates that the developers in E2 improve more as they become more experienced, indicating that flexible developers who are not all locked into one development strategy will collectively perform better as they develop more apps.

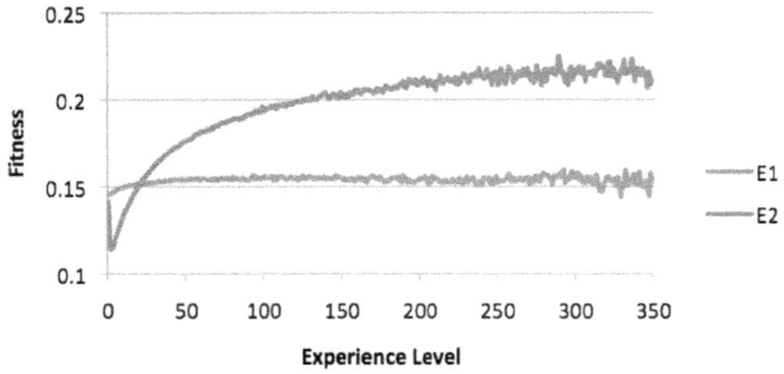

Figure 8. Fitness as developers become more experienced.

5. CONCLUSIONS

It is the dream of many developers to make their fortune with a clever app. But when the chances of success are now similar to the chances of winning the lottery – and falling daily as new apps are released – how can anyone be a successful app developer?

In this work, we presented AppEco, an Artificial Life agent-based model that simulates app ecosystems, and investigated these issues. AppEco models developers (agents that build apps) and users (agents that download apps). It simulates the app store environment and the population growth of the agents and apps. Significantly, AppEco also models apps (artefacts produced by the developers and downloaded by users) and their features. AppEco is a complex ecosystem where developers, users and apps increase continuously, and interaction strategies may continuously change. Our experiments investigated different developer strategies: Innovators, Milkers, Optimisers, and Copycats.

In a complex ecosystem no strategy can be a guaranteed winner, but our results indicate that some strategies should be chosen more frequently than others. Innovators produce diverse apps, but they are hit or miss – some apps will be popular, some will not. Milkers may dwell on average or bad apps as they churn out new variations of the same idea. Optimisers produce diverse apps and tailor their development towards users' needs. Finally, Copycats may seem like the best strategy to guarantee downloads in an app ecosystem, but the strategy can only work when there are enough other strategies to copy from. In addition, this strategy can only exist in a minority, otherwise app diversity will decrease (many duplicated apps result in a scarcity of some features desired by users) and the fitness of the ecosystem will suffer.

This study is one of many we will be undertaking with AppEco. We plan to study the effect of publicity on app downloads, and understand how a user might best locate desirable apps and communicate their requirements and feedback about the apps to developers, and how these feedback can influence app development. AppEco can also be calibrated to study other app ecosystems, such as Android and Blackberry, and extended to model web-based platforms such as Facebook and Chrome.

6. REFERENCES

[1] Chen, B. X. 2009. Coder's Half-Million-Dollar Baby Proves iPhone Gold Rush Is Still On. *Wired.* (12 Feb).

[2] Dredge, S. 2012. Angry Birds bags 6.5m Christmas Day downloads. *The Guardian.* (4 Jan).

[3] Baghdassarian, S., and Milanesi, C. 2010. *Forecast: Mobile Application Stores, Worldwide, 2008-2014.* Gartner.

[4] Distimo. 2011. *In-depth view on download volumes in the Google Android Market.* Utrecht, Netherlands.

[5] Jansen, S., Finkelstein, A., and Brinkkemper, S. 2009. A sense of community: a research agenda for software ecosystems. In *Proc. of 31st Int. Conf. on Software Engineering (ICSE) - Companion Volume*, p. 187-190.

[6] Lin, F., and Ye, W. 2009. Operating System Battle in the Ecosystem of Smartphone Industry. In *Int. Symp. on Information Engineering and E-Commerce*, p. 617-621.

[7] Garg, R., and Telang, R. 2011. *Estimating App Demand from Publicly Available Data.* School of Information Systems and Management, Heinz College, Carnegie Mellon University.

[8] Bohmer, M., Hecht, B., Schoning, J., Kruger, A., and Bauer, G. 2011. Falling asleep with Angry Birds, Facebook and Kindle: a large scale study on mobile application usage. In *MobileHCI 2011*, p. 47-56.

[9] Axelrod, R., and Hamilton, W. D. 1981. The evolution of cooperation. *Science.* 211(4489): p. 1390.

[10] Smith, J. M., and Price, G. 1973. The Logic of Animal Conflict. *Nature.* 24615.

[11] Holland, J. H. 1992. *Adaptation in natural and artificial systems.* MIT Press, Cambridge, MA.

[12] Pachepsky, E., Taylor, T., and Jones, S. 2002. Mutualism promotes diversity and stability in a simple artificial ecosystem. *Artificial Life.* 8(1): p. 5-24.

[13] Kohler, T. A., Gumerman, G. J., and Reynolds, R. G. 2005. Simulating ancient societies. *Scientific American.* 293(1): p. 76-84.

[14] Lux, T., and Marchesi, M. 1999. Scaling and criticality in a stochastic multi-agent model of a financial market. *Nature.* 397(6719): p. 498-500.

[15] Omicini, A., Ricci, A., and Viroli, M. 2008. Artifacts in the A&A meta-model for multi-agent systems. *Autonomous Agents and Multi-Agent Systems.* 17(3): p. 432-456.

[16] Miranda, E. R. 2008. Emergent songs by social robots. *Journal of Experimental & Theoretical Artificial Intelligence.* 20(4): p. 319-334.

[17] Wheeler, M., Ziman, J., and Boden, M. A. 2002. *The Evolution of Cultural Entities.* OUP/British Academy.

[18] Cusumano, M. A. 2010. Platforms and services: Understanding the resurgence of Apple. *Communications of the ACM.* 53(10): p. 22-24.

[19] Adomavicius, G., and Tuzhilin, A. 2005. Toward the next generation of recommender systems: A survey of the state-of-the-art and possible extensions. *IEEE Trans. on Knowledge and Data Engineering.* 17(6): p. 734-749.

[20] Kingsland, S. E. 1995. *Modeling nature: episodes in the history of population ecology.* University of Chicago Press.

[21] Gershenfeld, N. A. 1999. *The nature of mathematical modeling.* Cambridge University Press.

[22] Lanfranchi, M.-C., Benezet, B., and Perrier, R. 2010. *How to Successfully Market your iPhone Application.* faberNovel.

[23] International Telecommunication Union. 2009. *Yearbook of Statistics - Chronological Time Series 2000-2009.* p. 302.

Evolving Network Motifs based Morphogenetic Approach to Self-Organizing Robotic Swarms

Yan Meng
Stevens Institute of Technology
Hoboken, NJ 07670, USA
yan.meng@stevens.edu

Hongliang Guo
Almende Organizing Networks
Westerstraat 50, 3016 DJ Rotterdam, Netherlands
scott@almende.org

ABSTRACT
In order to traverse through a complex environment, swarm robotic systems need to self-organize themselves to form different yet suitable shapes dynamically to adapt to unknown environments. Biological morphogenetic networks, such as gene regulatory networks (GRNs), are modular with independent units and often show the reuse of recurring patterns termed network motifs. Inspired by biological morphogenesis and evolution and structure of network motifs in biology, in this paper, we propose an evolving GRN-based approach for self-organizing robotic swarms to autonomously generate dynamic patterns in unknown environments. The basic idea of this GRN-based model is: first, several network motifs are predefined as the basic building blocks for GRNs, then an evolutionary algorithm is applied to evolve parameters and the structures of the GRNs model. Then a previously proposed bio-inspired pattern formation algorithm is applied to move robots to generated patterns automatically in a distributed manner. Simulation and experimental results demonstrate that the proposed bio-inspired model is effective for complex shape generation and formation and robust to environmental changes in complex unknown environments.

Categories and Subject Descriptors
I.2.9 [**Computing Methodologies**]: Artificial Intelligence – *Robotics, Autonomous vehicles*

General Terms
Algorithms, Experimentation, Reliability.

Keywords
Evolutionary Robotics, Swarm Robots, Biological Morphogenesis, Gene Regulatory Networks.

1. INTRODUCTION
Distributed swarm robotic systems have some obvious advantages over traditional monolithic robot systems, such as robustness, flexibility, and adaptability for tasks that are inherently distributed in space and/or time. Examples of real-world applications of swarm robotic systems include collaborative search and rescue, aggregation and segregation, pattern formation, collective construction, target tracking and observation, etc.

In this paper, we will mainly focus on the self-organization and distributed control of swarm robots for complex shape generation and formation. Multi-robot pattern formation has been studied extensively, such as heuristic rule-based methods[1, 3], geometrical methods, potential field-based methods, or leader-following based methods [4, 8, 12, 13, 15], and biological inspired methods [18, 19, 20]. For example, Shen [20] proposed a digital hormone model (DHM) as a decentralized control method for robot swarms, which is inspired from biological hormone diffusion systems. They applied Turing's reaction-diffusion model [21] to describe the interactions between the hormones.

Recently, inspired by biological morphogenesis, some distributed gene regulatory network based approaches have been proposed in our previous work [9, 10] for swarm robots in pattern formation and boundary coverage. However, the major limitations of our previous work [9, 10] and other above mentioned alternative methods include: (1) the target shapes have to be predefined, which cannot be applied to dynamic unknown environments; and (2) the rule-based or dynamic equation based methods have been applied to describe the motion dynamics of each robot, which is only efficient for specific tasks. If the environment and tasks change, new differential equations have to be developed from scratch, which is not robust enough for dynamic environments.

To address these issues, in this paper, we aim to develop a bio-inspired distributed self-organization algorithm for swarm robots, which is able to automatically generate adaptive patterns to respond to environmental changes. As we know, biological morphogenesis is biological process guided by complex gene regulatory networks (GRN) that causes an organism to develop its shapes showing amazing self-organizing and robustness capability[5]. Although various mathematical models of GRNs have been proposed by biological researchers [2, 7] to describe the relationship between GRNs and the organism's developmental process, these models always have some specific assumptions or only focus on some specific aspects of the GRNs. More universal or generic model development for GRNs remains to be solved. Recently, Milo et al. [14, 16] found out that network motifs are simple universal building blocks for most complex networks.

Inspired by these biological studies, a generic development method for GRNs is proposed in this paper. This GRN-based controller is applied to pattern generation for robotic swarms by evolving some predefined network motifs as basic building blocks using an evolutionary algorithm. Compared to other state-of-the-art algorithms in swarm robot pattern formation, major advantage of this proposed framework is that robotic swarms can automatically generate suitable patterns to adapt to dynamic unknown environments (with various physical constraints, such as obstacles) only based on their on-board sensing systems.

The rest of the paper is organized as follows. Section 2 describes the proposed GRN-based pattern generation model. The algorithm for pattern formation proposed in our previous work [9, 10] is introduced in Section 3. Simulation results are provided in Section 4. Conclusions and future works are discussed in Section 5.

2. THE PATTERN GENERATION MODEL

2.1 Assumptions

The objective of this study is to develop a decentralized controller for swarm robots so that they can automatically generate suitable patterns to traverse dynamic unknown environments with various physical constraints (e.g. obstacles). To this end, we need to make some assumptions on the system. First, the environment is partitioned into discrete grids. It is assumed that each robot only occupies one grid at a time within the environment, and the distance between the robots is one grid away from each other. Since the number of robots does not change during the traversing process (assuming no robots fail), the overall size of the area covered by robots should keep the same even though different shapes may be generated. In addition, the generated shapes should not be too close to the obstacles, in which case robots may easily collide with obstacles, or too far away from the obstacles, in which case a thin line may be generated all the time to traverse all the paths.

It is assumed the robots know the traversing direction (i.e., which direction to go) but don't know physical constraints of the environment along the traversing path. The traversing path is a curve which is defined as $path = p(u)$, where u is the path parameter within the range (0, 1). $p(0)$ denotes the starting point of the path and $p(1)$ denotes the destination. In this paper, we mainly focus on how to generate the suitable shapes for robots. In other words, the robots can occupy all grids within the generated shape automatically using our previous work in [9, 10]. It is also assumed that robots have a limited sensing and communication range; they can only detect their local environment and communicate with their local neighbors within their communication range.

We assume that there is one organizing robot in the swarm which will initiate the pattern generation process. For example, in a 2D environment, the robot's current position is $pos = (x, y)$, since we know the path representation $p(u)$, the path parameter for the robot can be calculated as $u = \underset{\min}{\arg}(\| p(u) - pos \|)$. Where $\| . \|$ is the norm of a vector. Only the robot with the largest path parameter will be selected as the organizing robot. Once the organizing robot is selected, it will generate a local coordinate system, where the organizing robot is located at the origin of this local coordinate system and the orientation of the local coordinate system is decided by the heading direction of the organizing robot. Then, the organizing robot will develop/grow the target shape from a single robot to an appropriate shape (with predefined number of robots) to adapt to the current environment.

2.2 The Generic GRN Framework

In biological systems, when the DNA is expressed, information stored in the genome is transcribed into mRNAs and then translated into proteins. Some of these proteins are transcription factors (TFs) that can regulate the expression of their own or other genes, thus resulting in a complex network of interacting genes termed as a gene regulatory network (GRN). In this sense, TFs can be used to denote the inputs of the GRN framework, which are responsible to collect the environmental information and/or represent the internal states of the robots. Genes can be used as the processors of the GRN framework, which are responsible to process the inputs of the GRN framework and send signals to trigger the outputs of the GRN framework. Proteins can be adopted as the outputs of the GRN framework, which represent the robot behaviors. Fig. 1 shows the general regulations among TFs, genes and proteins.

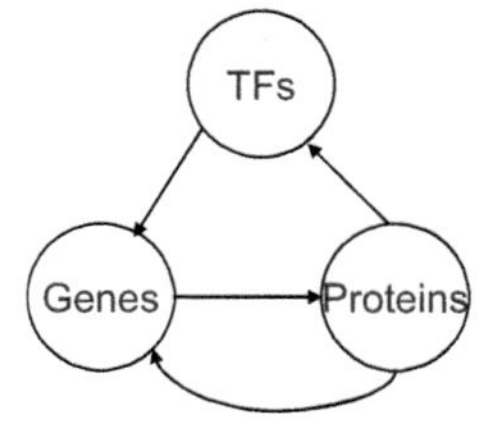

Figure 1. General regulations among TFs, genes and proteins.

To develop the GRN-based controller for each robot in a robotic swarm, more specific definitions for genes, TFs, and proteins are needed for robotic systems. TF1 is used to collect environmental information, which will gauge the minimal distance from the current robot to the nearest obstacle. TF1 can be defined as

$$TF1 = e^{-\min(d)} \tag{1}$$

Where d is the collection of the minimal distances to all the detected obstacles in the environment by the robot.

As we mentioned before, once robots start the traversing process, the total number of the robots in the swarm is predefined and will keep the same during traversing. When the organizing robot initiates the shape generation process, the number of robots will be increased from 1 till the predefined number of robots. TF2 is used to represent this internal state (i.e., the number of robots within the shape at the current moment) during the shape growing phase. To reduce the system complexity and computational cost while improve the system robustness, only two genes are applied as the processors of the GRN framework, called G1 and G2, respectively. A robot may have three different actions: growing into an area (denoted by P1), skipping an area and try to grow into another area (denoted by P2), or stopping growing (denoted by P3).

Since a robot can only perform one action at a time, regulations among P1, P2 and P3 must be negative. It is assumed that the environment does not change while the robot is performing any action, and can be changed after the action is conducted. TF2 (the number of robots) only changes when the robot performs action P1 (grow into this area). With these assumptions, the general GRN framework can be depicted in Fig. 2. This general GRN framework is embedded into each robot in a distributed manner in the system. However, *only the organizing robots will activate the framework and generate the suitable shapes virtually in its own mind.* Then, this generated shape will be sent to all the other robots through local communication so that they can merge to this shape automatically using the controller we proposed in our previous work [9, 10].

In summary, the organizing robot will first evaluate the neighboring grids in the local environment in an anticlockwise order. If the neighboring grids are open, it will grow into that area. If there are some obstacles in the neighboring grids, it will skip those grids and try to grow toward other open grids. Once the stop-growing condition is reached (i.e., reaching the predefined number of robots), the growing process is stopped and the current shape is the target shape for the robotic swarm.

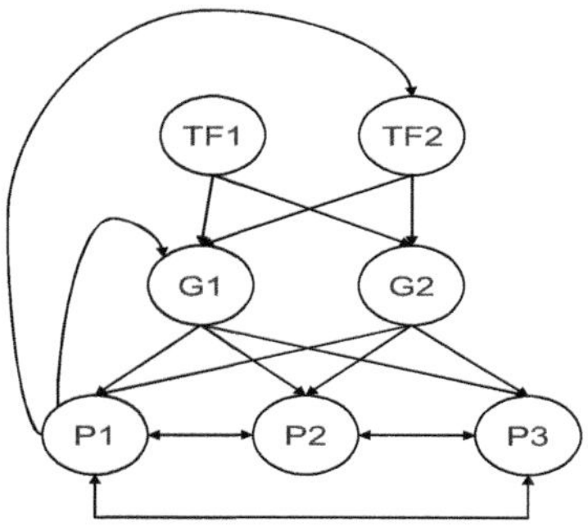

Figure 2. The General Gene Regulatory Network Framework.

2.3 Basic Building Blocks

Recent biological studies suggest that some "network motifs" occur significantly more frequently than other structures in the GRNs in a multi-cellular organism [14], and in most cases GRNs are largely composed of these network motifs. Inspired by these studies, we propose six basic regulations, namely, positive, negative, band, OR, AND, and XOR regulations, shown in Fig. 3, as the basic network motifs to construct the generic GRN framework. Note that these regulations can be applied to any regulation among genes, proteins, and TFs, for example, gene-gene, gene-protein, gene-TFs, protein-protein, TFs-TFs, protein-TFs, etc. In the following description, to make it simple, we use gene-gene regulations as examples.

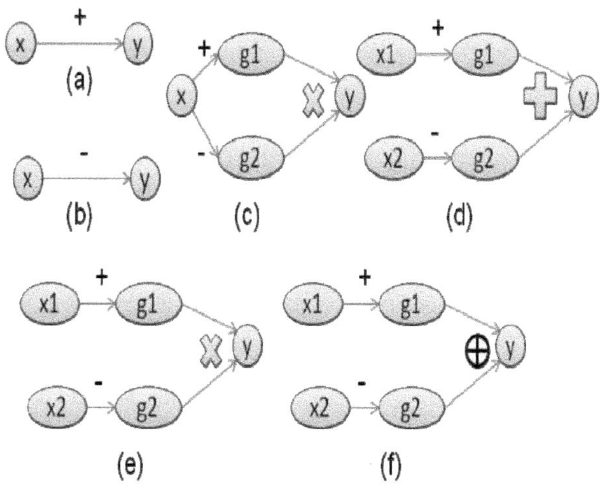

Figure 3. Basic regulations: (a) positive regulation; (b) negative regulation; (c) OR regulation; (d) AND regulation; (e) XOR regulation.

2.3.1 Positive Regulation

When gene X activates gene Y or gene X poses a positive feedback to gene Y, this is defined as a positive regulation relationship from X to Y, which is depicted in Fig. 3(a). The mathematical description of positive regulation from X to Y is defined as follows:

$$\frac{dy}{dt} = -y + sig(x,\theta) \quad (2)$$

$$sig(x,\theta) = \frac{1}{1+e^{-k(x-\theta)}} \quad (3)$$

Where y is the expression level of gene Y; x is the expression level of gene X. θ is a regulatory parameter which will be optimized later by an evolutionary algorithm in our model.

2.3.2 Negative Regulation

When gene X inhibits gene Y or gene X poses a negative feedback to gene Y, this is defined as negative regulation from X to Y, which is depicted in Fig. 3(b). The mathematical description of the negative regulation from X to Y is defined as follows:

$$\frac{dy}{dt} = -y + (1 - sig(x,\theta)) \quad (4)$$

Where the definitions of x, y and θ are the same as we described in the positive regulation.

2.3.3 Band Regulation

When gene X is within a range (e.g., $a \le x \le b$) that causes gene Y to be expressed, we call this "band" regulation between gene X and gene Y, as shown in Fig. 3(c). The corresponding mathematical model is:

$$\frac{dg_1}{dt} = -g_1 + sig(x_1,\theta_1) \quad (5)$$

$$\frac{dg_2}{dt} = -g_2 + sig(x_2,\theta_2) \quad (6)$$

$$\frac{dy}{dt} = -y + sig(g_1,\theta)\cdot sig(g_2,\theta) \quad (7)$$

Where g_1 and g_2 are expression levels of gene X1 and X2, respectively. x_1 and x_2 are the inputs to g_1 and g_2, respectively. y is the expression level of gene Y. θ_1 and θ_2 are the lower and upper threshold factors, respectively.

2.3.4 OR-Regulation

Gene Y expresses only if either gene X1 or gene X2 expresses, this is called OR-regulation from X1 and X2 to Y, which is depicted in Fig. 3(d). The mathematical description of the OR-regulation is defined as follows:

$$\frac{dg_1}{dt} = -g_1 + sig(x_1,\theta_1) \quad (8)$$

$$\frac{dg_2}{dt} = -g_2 + (1 - sig(x_2,\theta_2)) \quad (9)$$

$$\frac{dy}{dt} = -y + (sig(g_1,\theta) + sig(g_2,\theta)) \quad (10)$$

Where g_1 and g_2 are expression levels of gene X1 and X2, respectively. x_1 and x_2 are the inputs to g_1 and g_2, respectively. y is the expression level of gene Y. θ_1, θ_2, and θ are regulatory parameters.

2.3.5 AND-Regulation

Gene Y will express only if both genes X1 and X2 express, this is defined as the AND-regulation from X1 and X2 to Y, which is depicted in Fig. 3(e). The mathematical description of the AND-regulation relationship is as follows:

$$\frac{dg_1}{dt} = -g_1 + sig(x_1, \theta_1) \quad (11)$$

$$\frac{dg_2}{dt} = -g_2 + (1 - sig(x_2, \theta_2)) \quad (12)$$

$$\frac{dy}{dt} = -y + (sig(g_1, \theta) \otimes sig(g_2, \theta)) \quad (13)$$

Where the definitions of all the variables are the same with the ones described in the OR-regulation.

2.3.6 XOR-Regulation

Gene Y will express only if gene X1 and X2 have disparate expression levels. For example, if gene X1 expresses and gene X2 does not express or the other way around, gene Y expresses. The XOR-regulation is depicted in Fig. 3(f), and defined as follows:

$$\frac{dg_1}{dt} = -g_1 + sig(x_1, \theta_1) \quad (14)$$

$$\frac{dg_2}{dt} = -g_2 + (1 - sig(x_2, \theta_2)) \quad (15)$$

$$\frac{dy}{dt} = -y + (sig(x_1, \theta_3) \cdot (1 - sig(x_2, \theta_4))) + ((1 - sig(x_1, \theta_3) \cdot sig(x_2, \theta_4)) \quad (16)$$

Where the definitions of all the variables are the same with the ones described in the OR-regulation.

2.4 Evolutionary Optimization of the GRN Model

2.4.1 Simplifications and Parameterization of the Generic GRN Framework

Now we need to construct a generic GRN framework using these predefined network motifs as building blocks. To this end, an evolutionary algorithm is applied to tune the regulation structure of GRN framework. In this manner, each connection in the GRN framework can be mathematically modeled by one of basic network motifs, however, this would make fitness landscapes of the evolutionary algorithm very large. As a result, it may affect the searching efficiency for the optimal parameter combination for the GRN structure. Therefore, the following realistic simplifications have been made. Since there are three types of robot actions (P1, P2, and P3), a robot must respond to any output sent from the combinations of G1 and G2 processors (as shown in Fig. 2). There are four possible combinatory regulations of G1 and G2, i.e., positive-positive, positive-negative, negative-positive, and negative-negative regulations. For example, positive-positive regulation means that both G1 and G2 have a positive regulation on the target protein. Meanwhile, the combinatory regulation is an AND-regulation. Other types of regulations can be deducted accordingly.

For each robot, actions P1 (grow into the evaluation area) and P2 (skip the evaluation area and grow into another area) must respond to one of four combinatory regulations. Action P3 (stop growing) must respond to other two unselected combinatory regulations. The regulatory parameters θ_1 and θ_2 introduced in the basic network motifs are the same for P1, P2, and P3.

Before applying the evolutionary algorithm to the optimization of the structure of GRN framework, we need to parameterize the proposed GRN framework. With the above simplifications, we have 17 parameters need to be optimized, i.e., $\theta_{11}, \theta_{12}, \theta_{21}, \theta_{22}, t_{11}, t_{12}, t_{21}, t_{22}, c_1, c_2, \theta_1, \theta_2, t_1, t_2, p_{12}$, p_{13}, and p_{23}.

θ_{ij} and t_{ij} refer to regulation parameters and regulation types from TF_i to G_j (i, j = 1, 2). t_{ij} can be 1 (positive regulation) or 2 (negative regulation). For example, if $\theta_{11} = 2.5$ and $t_{11} = 1$, which means that it is a positive regulation (the meaning of t_{ij} will be specified in next subsection). The partial dynamics (not considering the effect of TF2) of G1 can be described as:

$$\frac{dg_1}{dt} = -g_1 + sig(TF1, \theta_{11}) \quad (17)$$

Where c_i (i = 1, 2) denotes the combinatory regulation type from TF1 and TF2 to G_i. c_i can be 1 (AND-regulation) or 2 (OR-regulation).

θ_1 and θ_2 are shared common regulatory parameters for the regulations between genes and proteins. t_i denotes the responding combinatory regulation of P_i, where t_i can be 1 (positive-positive), 2 (negative-positive), 3 (negative-negative), or 4 (positive-negative). p_{ij} denotes the regulatory parameter for the negative regulation between proteins P_i and P_j.

2.4.2 Evolving the Structure of GRN Framework

To meet two system requirements, i.e., keep the shape size the same during traversing and keep certain distance from the obstacles), we need to apply an evolutionary algorithm to optimize the structure of generic GRN framework. To this end, first, we need to setup an appropriate fitness function for the evolutionary algorithm. Suppose the expected size of the generated shape covered by swarm robots is denoted by s_0. The shortest distance from the generated shape to the nearest obstacle should be as close as possible to a predefined distance d_0 but not smaller than d_0. To this end, the fitness function can be set up as:

$$f = (TF2 - s_0)^2 + (\max(TF1) - e^{-d_0})^2 \quad (18)$$

Where f is the fitness value, and max(*TF1*) represents the maximum distance from the generated shape to all obstacles. TF2 denotes the number of robots within the shape (where one robot occupies on grid) during the shape growing phase.

In our simulation, we adopt the Covariance Matrix Adaptation Evolution Strategy (CMA-ES)[11] to optimize these 17 parameters so that the fitness value in Eqn. (18) can be minimized. Evolution strategies are stochastic, derivative-free methods for numerical optimization of nonlinear or non-convex continuous optimization problems. In an evolution strategy, new candidates solutions are sampled according to a multivariate normal distribution in the $\mathbf{R}^n$. Pairwise dependencies between the variables in this distribution are represented by a covariance matrix. The covariance matrix adaptation (CMA) is a method to update the covariance matrix of this distribution (from Wikipedia). Since CMA-ES needs to perform parameter optimization in a continuous domain, we need to transform the discrete numbers (such as t_{ij}) into continuous values. For example, t_{ij} can be assigned as real values from 0 to 1. If t_{ij} <0.5, it can be treated as 1. If t_{ij} >0.5, it can be treated as 2. Similar procedure will be applied for c_i and t_i. t_i can be assigned to be real values from 0 to 1. If t_i <0.25, we treat it as 1; if $0.25 < t_i < 0.5$, we treat it as 2, if $0.5 < t_i < 0.75$, we treat it as 3, if $0.75 < t_i < 1$, we treat it as 4.

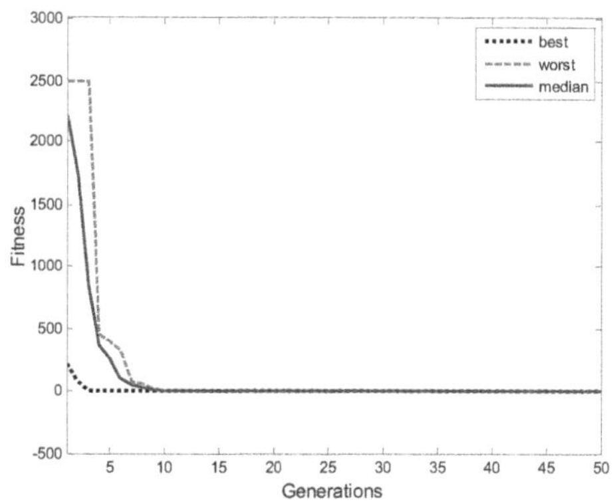

Figure 4. The evolutionary fitness value versus generations.

The parameters are setup as follows: θ_{21} and θ_{22} were assigned to be real numbers from 0 to 400. All other parameters were assigned to real numbers from 0 to 1. Due to the large parameter space, the population size was set to 400. The evolutionary algorithm runs for 50 generations. During the evolutionary process, the expected size of the generate shape is set as 200, and the shortest distance from the shape to the obstacles is set as 1. Fig. 4 shows that the fitness value will eventually converge to a stable value (close to zero) over generations. Since the objective is to minimize the fitness value defined in Eqn. (18), we can conclude that the behaviors of robots are getting better over time.

After the evolutionary process, we select the best individuals in the last generation as the optimal parameter combination for the generic GRN framework. The optimized parameter combination is listed as follows: $\theta_{11} = 0.3668$, $\theta_{12} = 0.0032$, $\theta_{21} = 0.0891$, $\theta_{22} = 199.8601$, $t_{11} = 1$ (positive regulation between TF1 and G1), $t_{12} = 2$ (negative regulation between TF1 and G2), $t_{21} = 2$ (negative regulation between TF2 and G1), $t_{22} = 1$ (positive regulation between TF2 and G2), $c_1 = 1$, $c_2 = 1$, $\theta_1 = 0.2786$, $\theta_2 = 0.0021$, $t_1 = 3$, $t_2 = 4$, $p_{12} = 0.3755$, $p_{13} = 0.4025$, and $p_{23} = 0.2486$. These parameters are applied to the GRN framework that is used in the following simulations and experiments.

From the above evolved parameters, the final GRN framework can be constructed as follow. $c_1 = 1$ and $c_2 = 1$ suggest that the combinatory regulation from TF1 and TF2 to G1 and G2 are both OR-regulations. $t_1 = 3$ suggests a negative-negative combinatory regulation from G1 and G2 to P1; $t_2 = 4$ suggests a positive-negative combinatory regulation from G1 and G2 to P2. Based on the aforementioned deduction, the final GRN framework is depicted in Fig 9. Since P1 and P2 will respond to the negative-negative regulation and positive-negative regulation from G1 and G2, P3 will respond to the remaining regulation relationships (positive-positive and negative-positive), we can deduct that G1 will not have any effect on P3, so only G2 will have a positive regulation on P3.

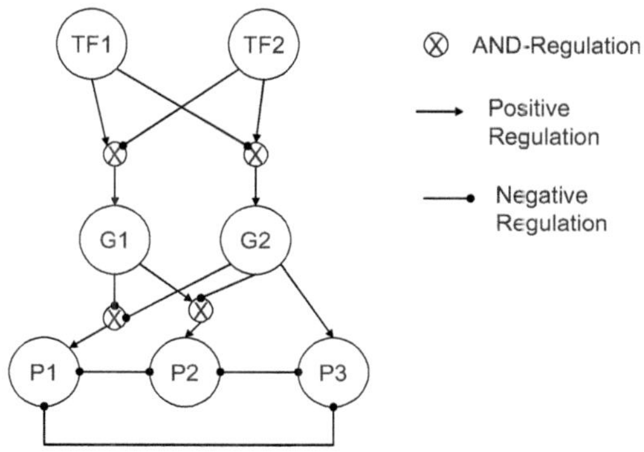

Figure 5. The evolved generic GRN framework.

The evolved generic GRN framework is to generate the target patterns for robot swarms. To efficiently represent the generated target pattern, we employed the Non-Uniform Rational B-Spline (NURBS)[17] model, which is used to represent the generated pattern as well as the environment, as shown in Fig. 6. NURBS is a mathematical model commonly used in computer graphics and structural design for generating and representing curves and surfaces. NURBS can offer one common mathematical form for both analytic and freeform shapes. A NURBS curve is defined by its order, a set of weighted control points, and a knot vector. The control points define the shape of the curve, and the knot vector is a set of parameters that determines where and how the control points affect the NURBS curve. A NURBS model can represent both curve and surface in a two- or three-dimensional Cartesian space. Please refer to [17] for the more detailed description of NURBS.

3. PATTERN FORMATION MODEL

With the generated pattern represented in NURBS, our next step is to move the robots to the target pattern automatically. To this end, we applied a distributed bio-inspired approached we proposed in our previous work [9,10]. We outlined the approach here to make it easier for the readers to understand the whole self-organization process. The movement dynamics of each robot can be described by the following model:

$$dg_{i,x}/dt = -a \cdot z_{i,x} + m \cdot p_{i,x}$$
$$dg_{i,y}/dt = -a \cdot z_{i,y} + m \cdot p_{i,y} \quad (19)$$

$$dp_{i,x}/dt = -c \cdot p_{i,x} + k \cdot f(z_{i,x}) + b \cdot D_{i,x}$$
$$dp_{i,y}/dt = -c \cdot p_{i,y} + k \cdot f(z_{i,y}) + b \cdot D_{i,y} \quad (20)$$

where i = 1,2,…,n, and n is the total number of robots in the system. $g_{i,x}$ and $g_{i,y}$ are x and y positions of robot i respectively. $p_{i,x}$ and $p_{i,y}$ are the internal states of robot i along x and y coordinates, respectively. $D_{i,x}$ and $D_{i,y}$ are sum of distances between i-th robot and its neighbors, which are defined as

$$D_{i,x} = \sum_{j=1}^{N_i} D_{i,x}^j, \quad D_{i,y} = \sum_{j=1}^{N_i} D_{i,y}^j \quad (21)$$

where Ni denotes the number of neighbors of robot i, and $D_{i,x}^j$ and $D_{i,y}^j$ are the protein concentrations diffused from neighboring robot j received by robot i, which is defined as:

$$D_{i,x}^j = \frac{(g_{i,x} - g_{j,x})}{\sqrt{(g_{i,x} - g_{j,x})^2 + (g_{i,y} - g_{j,y})^2}}, \quad (22)$$

$$D_{i,y}^j = \frac{(g_{i,y} - g_{j,y})}{\sqrt{(g_{i,x} - g_{j,x})^2 + (g_{i,y} - g_{j,y})^2}}. \quad (23)$$

In order to embed the target shape represented by NURBS method into this robot motion model, we define $f(z_i)$ as the following sigmoid functions:

$$f(z_{i,x}) = \frac{1 - e^{-z_{i,x}}}{1 + e^{-z_{i,x}}}, \quad f(z_{i,y}) = \frac{1 - e^{-z_{i,y}}}{1 + e^{-z_{i,y}}} \quad (24)$$

where $z_{i,x}$ and $z_{i,y}$ can be defined as

$$z_{i,x} = -(g_{i,x} - g_{i,x}(u)), \quad z_{i,y} = -(g_{i,y} - g_{i,y}(u)) \quad (25)$$

where $g_{i,x}(u)$ and $g_{i,y}(u)$ are x and y coordinates of a point on the NURBS curve depending on the parameter u, respectively Note that robot i may need to change its goal point on the target shape dynamically depending on its current local environment.

In Eqn. (25), u is the parameter in the NUBRS model, which ranges from 0 to 1. Driven by the regulatory dynamics defined in Eqns. (19) and (20) and a fixed $u \in (0, 1)$, robots will converge to the target shape. To enhance the efficiency of the system, it is desired that each robot moves to the closest point on the target shape. Specifically, for robot i, we can find the optimal u_i if the following objective is minimized:

$$u_i = \arg \min_{0 \le u \le 1} \left(z_{i,x}^2 + z_{i,y}^2 \right) \quad (26)$$

Since we do not have an analytic function to calculate $g_{i,x}(u)$ or $g_{i,y}(u)$, we can discretize u in the range of (0,1) according to the number of robots in the environment. For example, if we have n robots, u can be discretized as u = (0, 1/(n-1), 2/(n-1), …, 1). A $u_i \in u$ that minimizes Eqn. (26) will be chosen for robot i, where i = 1, 2…, n. As mentioned above, it may happen that more than one robot choose the same value for u and tends to converge to the same point on the target shape. However, the diffusion dynamics will push robots away from one another and in the end only one of the robots will converge to a certain point on the target shape.

Five parameters a, m, c, k, and b in Eqns. (19) and (20) have been optimized using NSGA-II [6]. The goal of the optimization is to minimize the robots' travel distance and the convergence time, while ensuring that the system's convergence property is not violated. From the Pareto-optimal solutions achieved by NSGA-II, we pick out one solution that has a balanced performance with respect to travel distance and convergence time for the following case studies: a=62.6459, m=63.9489, c=70.2715, k=45.5208, and b=380.4215. Please refer [9, 10] for more details on the pattern formation model and the parameter adjustments.

4. SIMULATION RESULTS

To evaluate the automatic pattern generation capability of the proposed GRN framework, we will let swarm robots to traverse through a complex unknown environment. More specifically, we want to verify whether the proposed GRN framework is able to automatically generate the desired shape for swarm robots to adapt to the environment during the traversing process. The parameters of the proposed GRN framework for pattern generation in Section 2.4 and the pattern formation model with parameters in Section 3 have been applied for the following simulations.

4.1 The Developmental Process of Shape Generation

To simulate the shape developmental (growing) process, the organizing robot needs to grow to final target shape from a single robot based on the current environmental constrains. Please note that this shape growth process is actually executed virtually in the organizing robot's mind (instead of physically implemented by real robots). Once the target shape is generated, the robots need to self-organize into the target shape using the pattern formation method introduced in Section 3.

Fig. 6 shows this developmental (growing) process of shape generation executed by an organizing robot from a single robot till the final circular shape with and without nearby obstacles. From Fig. 6, we can see that our proposed GRN framework is able to generate and grow into different yet suitable shapes given different environmental conditions. When the environment is wide enough, the algorithm will perform a 'normal' growth, and develop into a circular shape; while if the environment is 'narrow', the algorithm can adapt to the environment, and grow into a suitable shape that fits into the environment. The reason why a circular shape is desired in an open space is because it can cover the largest area.

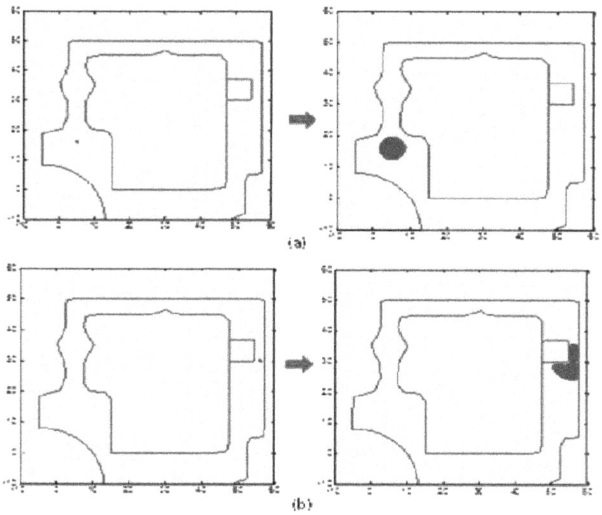

Figure 6. The developmental (growing) process of shape generation.

4.2 Adaptive Shape Generation in a Dynamic Environment

Now we need to evaluate whether the proposed GRN framework can generate different suitable shapes (with the same size of the initial shape) for robots so that robots can traverse through a complex dynamic environment. To this end, a case study of swarm robots to traverse a complex environment is conducted, where there are different environmental constraints along the traversing path of the robots. With the generated shapes, the GRN-based controller developed in our previous work [7, 8] and discussed in Section 3 is applied to move the robots to the target shapes automatically. A set of snapshots of this simulation is shown in Fig. 7.

We conducted the simulation with 40 robots, and each robot will occupy one grid. Since it is very congested to show individual robot, we only show the constructed shape in Fig. 7. From Fig. 7, we can see that the robots can automatically generate various suitable shapes to adapt to different environmental constraints using the proposed GRN framework.

5. CONCLUSION AND FUTURE WORK

Inspired by the biological morphogenesis and the evolution and structure of network motifs in biological networks, in this paper, we propose a new distributed GRN-based control model for swarm robot pattern generation in complex unknown environments based on biological network motifs. More specifically, several network motifs are predefined as the basic building blocks for the GRN based framework, then an evolutionary algorithm is applied to evolve parameters and the structures of the GRN-based model. Experimental results demonstrate that the proposed model can automatically generate suitable patterns for swarm robots to adapt to complex unknown environments. In the current model, we assume that the size of the target shape is always the same during traversing, which means there is no robot failure. However, this is a strong assumption in robotic systems, where robot failure may happen at any time. We plan to investigate this issue in our future work. Another future study we would like to investigate is how to automatically generate more combined network motifs from basic network motifs and use them for the GRN framework construction.

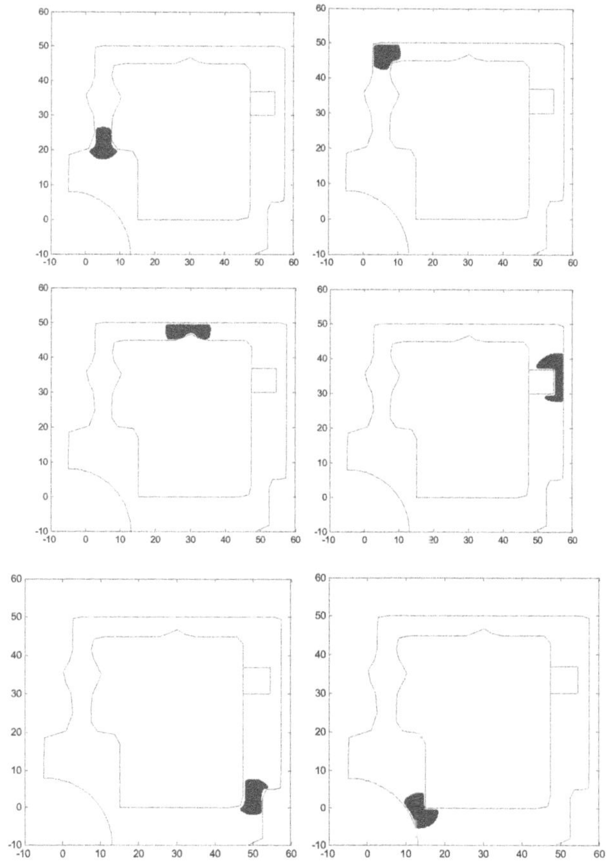

Figure 7. Dynamically generated shapes in an unknown environment.

6. REFERENCES

[1] Albayrak, O., *Line and circle formation of distributed autonomous mobile robots with limited sensor range.* Master Thesis of Naval Postgraduate School, Naval Postgraduate School, 1996.

[2] Alon, U., *An introduction to systems biology: design principles of biological circuits.* Chapman and Hall/CRC, 2006.

[3] Balch, T. and Arkin, R.C., Behavior-based formation control for multirobot teams, *IEEE Transactions on Robotics and Automation*, vol. 14, 926-939, 1998.

[4] Choi, J. and Kim, Y., Fuel efficient three dimensional controller for leader-follower UAV formation flight, 2007 International Conference on Control, Automation and Systems (ICCAS), 2007.

[5] S. Ciliberti, O. C. Martin, and A. Wagner, "Innovation and robustness in complex regulatory gene networks," Proceedings of the National Academy of Sciences, vol. 104, 13591-13596, 2007.

[6] Deb, K., Pratap, A., Agarwal, S., and Meyarivan, T., A Fast and Elitist Multiobjective Genetic Algorithm: NSGA-II. IEEE Transactions on Evolutionary Computation, vol. 6, no. 2,182-197, 2002.

[7] de Jong, H., Modeling and simulation of genetic regulatory systems: a literature review, *Journal of Cmputational Biology*, vol. 9, 67-103, 2002.

[8] Ekanayake, S. W., and Pathirana, P. N., Geometric formations in swarm aggregation: An artificial formation force based approach, *3rd International Conference on Information and Automation for Sustainability*, 2007, 82-87.

[9] Guo, H., Meng, Y., and Jin, Y., A cellular mechanism for multi-robot construction via evolutionary multi-objective optimization of a gene regulatory network, *Biosystems*, vol. 98, 193-203, 2009.

[10] Guo, H., Meng, Y., and Jin, Y., Swarm robot pattern formation using a morphogenetic multi-cellular based self-organization algorithm, *2011 IEEE International Conference on Robotics and Automation (ICRA)*, Shanghai, China, May 9-13, 2011.

[11] Hansen, H. and Ostermeier, A., Completely derandomized self-adaptation in evolution strategies, *Evolutionary Computation*, vol. 9, 159-195, 2001.

[12] Hsieh, M., Kumar, V., and Chaimowicz, L., Decentralized controllers for shape generation with robotic swarms, *Robotica*, vol. 26, 691-701, 2008.

[13] Jadbabaie, A., Jie, L., and Morse, A. S., Coordination of groups of mobile autonomous agents using nearest neighbor rules, *IEEE Transactions on Automatic Control*, vol. 48, 988-1001, 2003.

[14] Kashtan, N. and Alon, A., Spontaneous evolution of modularity and network motifs, P*roceedings of the National Academy of Sciences*, vol. 102, 13773-13778, 2005.

[15] Masoud, A., Decentralized self-organizing potential field-based control for individually motivated mobile agents in a cluttered environment: a vector-harmonic potential field approach, *IEEE Trans. on Systems, Man, and Cybernetics – Part A: Systems and Humans,* vol. 37, 372-390, 2007.

[16] Milo, R., Shen-Orr, S., Itzkovitz, S., Kashtan, N., Chklovskii, D., and Alon, U., Network Motifs: Simple Building Blocks of Complex Networks, *Science*, vol. 298, 824-827, 2002.

[17] Piegl L. and Tiller, W., *The NURBS Book,* 2nd ed.: Springer, 1997.

[18] Pugh, J. and Martinoli, A., Distributed Adaptation in Multi-robot Search Using Particle Swarm Optimization, *From Animals to Animats 10.* vol. 5040, M. Asada, et al., Eds., ed: Springer Berlin / Heidelberg, 2008, pp. 393-402.

[19] Schmickel, R. D., Gonzalez, I. L., and Erickson, J. M., Nucleolus Organizing Genes on Chromosome 21: Recombination and Nondisjunction, *Annals of the New York Academy of Sciences*, vol. 450, 121-131, 1985.

[20] Shen, W., Will, P., Galstyan, A., and Chuong, C., Hormone-Inspired Self-Organization and Distributed Control of Robotic Swarms, *Autonomous Robots*, vol. 17, 93-105, 2004.

[21] Turing, A., The chemical basis of morphogenesis, *Bulletin of Mathematical Biology*, vol. 52, 153-197, 1990.

Evolving Flexible Joint Morphologies

Jared M. Moore and Philip K. McKinley
Department of Computer Science and Engineering
Michigan State University
East Lansing, Michigan, USA
moore112@msu.edu

ABSTRACT

Transferring virtual robotic designs into physical robots has become possible with the development of 3D printers. Accurately simulating the performance of real robots in a virtual environment requires modeling a variety of conditions, including the physical composition of the robots themselves. In this paper, we investigate how modeling material flexibility through the use of a passive joint affects the resulting arm morphology and gait of a crawling virtual robot. Results indicate that flexibility can be a beneficial characteristic of robotic morphology design while also providing insight into the benefits of modeling material properties in a simulation environment.

Categories and Subject Descriptors

I.2.9 [**Computing Methodologies**]: Artificial Intelligence—*Robotics*

General Terms

Experimentation

Keywords

Evolutionary Robotics, Morphology, Morphological Evolution, Simulation

1. INTRODUCTION

The field of evolutionary robotics has produced many effective robotic designs that address a variety of tasks. Previous works have focused on controller evolution [1, 3, 5, 6, 7, 15, 23, 32], morphological evolution [11, 16, 29], and the co-evolution of morphology and control [7, 31] in virtual simulated environments. In some cases, these designs have been transferred into real robots for validation [14, 18, 24]. Designing robots with morphologies capable of accomplishing different tasks has presented both technical design and fabrication challenges. Recent developments in 3D printer technology now enable the rapid fabrication of robotic designs at finer levels of detail. It is possible to evolve a design in simulation and validate the results in a real robot in a short period of time.

Despite their potential to advance the field, 3D printers bring their own set of issues, including how to model the properties of physical materials and their interactions with each other and the external environment. Early studies addressing this "reality-gap" [10, 22] found that evolving controllers only in simulation can lead to solutions that are not transferable due to exploitation of the simulation environment [24]. When considering the morphology of a robot, accurately modeling the material properties is a vital component for simulations. High fidelity simulations will allow for better representations of physical properties that can reduce the differences between simulation and reality.

As a first step in addressing the reality gap with respect to physical materials, we need to demonstrate that the relevant characteristics can be modeled and subjected to selective pressures. Using these physical properties, we may be able to simplify robotic designs in the future by exploiting the material properties themselves. Robots often contain motorized joints, powered by actuators, to move various parts in order to accomplish tasks. However, material flexibility makes *passive* joints possible, which can increase performance and simplify controller complexity, since they do not require a dedicated motor. Harnessing the inherent properties of passive joints such as flexibility and the restorative properties of a material may allow for unique characteristics to evolve that improve the efficiency of a robot.

In this paper, we investigate the property of material flexibility in a morphological evolution experiment by implementing a passive joint and evaluating its movement characteristics. Results indicate that passive flexibility is a potentially useful characteristic in morphological evolution. Solutions exhibiting both semi-flexible and flexible joints exhibit increased performance when compared to more rigid morphologies. The flexibility demonstrated in the evolved solutions appears to be realistic and can be transferred into physical robots. This work helps to address the reality gap and the use of 3D printers in fabricating evolved robotic designs. The background and related work are presented in Section 2. Section 3 provides an overview of the virtual robot used in this experiment, a discussion of the simulation environment, as well as a description of the evolutionary process used. Results from the experiment are presented in Section 4 with a discussion following in Section 5. Conclusions and future directions are discussed in Section 6.

2. BACKGROUND

Evolutionary computation borrows concepts from biology to address complex computational tasks. By employing a process of development similar to natural evolution, novel solutions to problems can be found through optimization directed by fitness functions. Although these fitness functions are normally provided by a researcher, the actual process of evolution is left to a combination of mutation, crossover, and selection operations in order to minimize human bias. Solutions discovered through evolutionary computation often yield results that would not have been considered using traditional engineering methods. In the field of evolutionary robotics [5, 10, 17, 28], evolutionary computation is used to develop the aspects of control of a robot, both at the individual and group level, as well to optimize physical structures comprising the morphology of the robot. Employing these evolutionary concepts has yielded robots capable of bipedal walking [4, 29] as well as other types of robots used in the study of biological organisms [18, 19, 20, 21].

Many evolutionary approaches to robotics address the development of controllers for fixed morphology robots. Utilizing concepts and control patterns found in biology, controllers often emulate the neural architecture of natural creatures [9, 12, 18, 19, 20, 21]. Such works have laid the foundation for many of the concepts currently in use and provided insight into how natural organisms' neural controllers function. Research on morphology has been conducted mostly by applying co-evolution, in which controllers and morphology have been evolved concurrently [8]. This model closely resembles natural evolution, as organisms do not evolve new structures or locomotion strategies independently. This approach typically starts from a very primitive template which evolves into a complex final form capable of locomotion and other behaviors [27, 30]. Studies using co-evolution have investigated movement patterns using a predesigned initial robot, which was then subjected to evolution and resulted in solutions capable of effective locomotion with unique body structures and controllers [2, 7]. These co-evolution experiments have shown promise in producing robots capable of executing both simple and complex tasks [11, 16].

The ultimate goal of evolutionary robotics is synthesis [25, 26], in which a machine is capable of creating other machines in a process that mimics natural evolution. Realizing this goal depends in part on being able to model physical material properties in a realistic manner in simulation. New issues related to bridging simulation and reality have emerged with the introduction of 3D printing technologies. The reality gap appeared when controllers were evolved in simulation and transferred to real systems [10, 22]. Koos et al. [24] recently introduced a simulation-reality disparity measure to account for the differences in performance between the virtual and physical worlds. Moving from simulation to reality can further be refined by developing accurate models for physical conditions such as friction, gravity and material properties. 3D printing technologies increase the need for accurate material modeling, as new types of morphologies are possible that exploit properties of the constituent materials. In this paper, one of the properties, material flexibility, is explored in a simulated robot morphology.

3. METHODS

This section describes the various components of the study. An overview of the virtual robot is presented followed by a discussion of the simulation environment. Finally, a description of the evolutionary process is presented along with a discussion of the experimental procedures.

Virtual Robot.

A depiction of the virtual robot used in this study is presented in Figure 1. *Oxudercinae*, an amphibious fish commonly referred to as the mudskipper, was the inspiration for this two-armed model. Crawling locomotion is achieved by movement of the arms in a circular pattern. Each arm is connected to the main body by a joint with two degrees of freedom, allowing for a circular path of motion while preventing rotation of the arm in the third dimension. The angle between the arm and body is fixed at 23 degrees throughout the range of motion. In this study, movement of the arms is synchronous with a constant rate of oscillation.

Figure 1: Initial morphology of the virtual robot. Body is fixed to accommodate motor and batteries in a real robot. The flexible joint is located between the arm and cylindrical foot. Different flexibilities allow for a variable contact area of the foot and ground.

Initial morphological design of the virtual robot was completed by hand allowing the body cavity to accommodate two motors and a battery required for realizing the robot in a real environment. Figure 2 depicts a prototype of the initial design that was printed using an Objet Connex 350 multi-material 3D printer. The prototype was printed to assess robot operation and properties of the constituent materials. Physical realization of the movement pattern required the use of two single-axle DC motors with a custom ball-and-socket joint interface with the arm. This design allowed for translating the rotational movement of the motor's drive shaft into an offset rotational motion. The initial prototype, upon which the virtual robot was based, was 14.8 centimeters long and 7.6 centimeters wide.

In the study described here, various aspects of the arm morphology are subjected to selective pressures to determine the most effective configuration for basic locomotion. The dimensional characteristics, arm length and foot radius are evolvable. Arm length is measured as the distance from

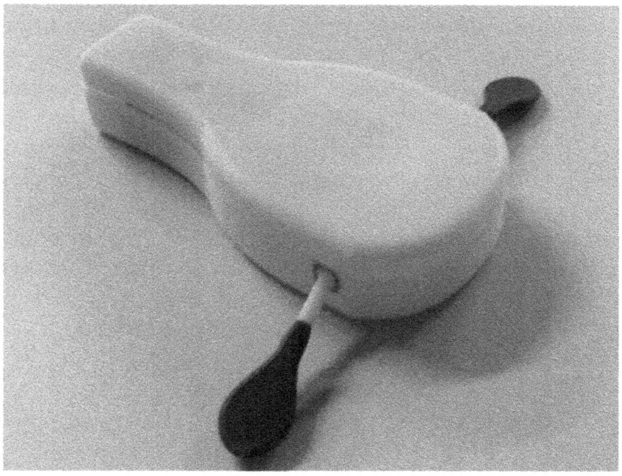

Figure 2: A hand-designed prototype of the robot produced with multiple materials. The feet are composed of both soft and rigid materials. This initial prototype had a completely rigid arm which resulted in a small contact area between the foot and surface during movement producing slippage of the feet on the surface.

the main body to the end of the foot. In the initial hand-designed robot, the joint between the arm and foot was not included and led to a rigid connection with a very small contact area between the arm and ground. This property created a higher chance of slippage when compared to a foot with an increased contact area. Flexibility is an important evolvable characteristic in this study and is modeled as a joint between the arm and foot. Two dimensions of flexibility are considered for this joint, enabling an ankle-like behavior. The flexibility of this joint determines what portion of the foot can come into contact with the ground potentially changing the amount of forward locomotion possible by the robot. In a flexible joint, the foot can come into full contact with the ground, maximizing the surface area, whereas, a rigid joint allows only for a very small part of the foot to contact the ground. Differing contact areas affect the traction that a robot is able to achieve, which can result in performance variation.

Simulation Environment.

A simulation using the Open Dynamics Engine (ODE) [13], was used to evaluate the performance of the various morphologies. The simulation parameters are presented in Table 1. Two separate environments were modeled using the simulator. In the primary environment, a flat plane was used with friction values set to approximate a slick surface, allowing for slippage of the feet during locomotion. The gravity and scale used in the simulation were set to model real world conditions. A secondary environment was introduced halfway through the evolutionary run that was also a flat plane. However, in this environment, friction values were set to be more like those found in a normal surface such as a countertop or floor, with a reduced chance of slippage due to the higher friction. Preliminary testing found that these two environments produced conflicting selective pressure upon the morphologies. Each individual was given 10 seconds of simulation time to travel as far as possible.

Table 1: The simulation parameters used in the experiment.

Parameter	Value
Timestep	.005 sec.
Evaluation Time	10 sec.
Primary Friction	0.6
Secondary Friction	1.0

Flexibility is modeled using two parameters, error reduction parameter (ERP) and constraint force mixing (CFM). Although these are simulation specific parameters, together they correlate to spring and damper constraints found in a mechanical model. ERP indicates the restorative force produced by a flexible joint that has moved away from its neutral position. This parameter ranges from 0 to 1, with values under 0.25 indicating that a minimal restorative force is applied to a deflected joint. In morphologies with these low values, the joint is returned to its neutral state only after the force that caused it to deform in the first place is removed. For example, in the simulation described here, the opposing force would be introduced when the foot comes into contact with the surface. A deflected foot would return to its neutral state only after the foot was no longer in contact with the surface. When ERP values exceed 0.25, a noticeable restorative force is present that returns a joint to its neutral position even as an opposing force is still acting upon the body.

The second component of flexibility is the CFM parameter, which determines how likely a joint is to move away from its neutral position. The value of CFM is strictly greater than 0. Generally, the larger the CFM value, the greater the joint will deflect under load. For purposes of this study, combinations of ERP less than 0.25 and CFM values greater than 0.8 resulted in flexible morphologies, while ERP values greater than 0.25 and CFM values greater than 0.8 resulted in morphologies that would be considered semi-flexible. In this paper, we consider flexible joints to be those that deformed upon contact with the ground and returned to a neutral state once the arm no longer was in contact with the surface. Semi-flexible joints were considered to be those that would deform upon contact with the surface but would return to neutral as the joint was still in contact with the ground. These semi-flexible joints can be thought of as a spring-like system in which the joint not only flexes to increase contact area, but also demonstrates a new component of the gait that is not present in fully rigid or flexible morphologies.

Evolutionary Setup.

Table 2 summarizes the parameters used for the evolutionary trials conducted in this study. Four separate treatments were conducted with 30 replicate runs each. With the exception of Treatment 1, a control with no evolution, each replicate run contained a population of 250 randomly generated individuals that were allowed to evolve for 100 generations. A simple genome was used in this study which contained the six parameters: arm length, foot radius, and ERP and CFM values for each of the two dimensions of the passive joint. A binary encoded genome was used for this study. Mutation and crossover operations were therefore subject to differing levels of impact depending on the location of the operation.

Crossover could occur at any point in the binary encoded genome. A representation of the genome can be seen in Figure 3. Selection was performed using a combination of elitism and tournament selection with a tournament size of 5. Specifically, the best performing individual per generation was carried over to the next generation with the remaining slots filled by tournament selection using parent individuals from the previous generation. Single-point crossover was used with a crossover probability of 20% and randomly selected crossover point using two parent solutions selected from the previous generation. Mutation was performed at the bit level with a probability of 2.3%, which equated to one mutation per genome.

Table 2: The evolutionary parameters used in the experiment.

Parameter	Value
Population Size	250
Generations	100
Replicate Runs	30
Tournament Size	5
Crossover Probability	20%
Mutation Rate	2.3%

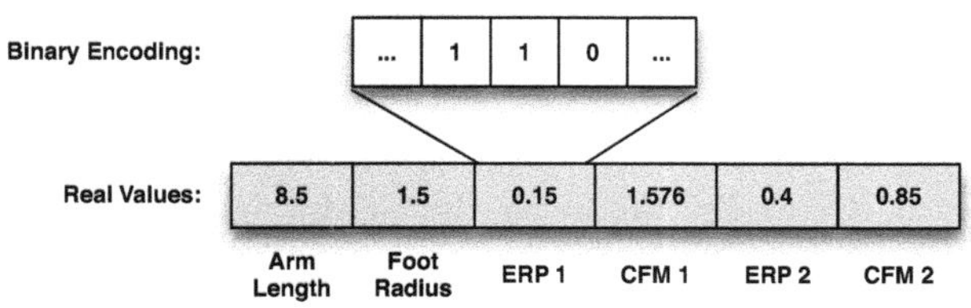

Figure 3: An example of the genome used in this study with sample values. Genome is encoded in binary values for purposes of mutation and crossover. As such, different mutation sites can result in higher or lower impact to the phenotype based on the position of the mutated bit.

Individual morphologies were evaluated by measuring the forward progress of the robot through the difference in the location of the main body segment at the start and finish of each individual replicate run. Equations (a) and (b) give the two fitness functions used in this experiment. For the first fifty generations, fitness was based only on performance in the primary environment as shown in Equation (a). Equation (b) was used for the simulations conducted after generation 50. Performance in these simulations was based on the forward progress from both environments which were added together and averaged to give a combined fitness value representing the two environments.

$$\text{fitness} = \text{prim\_fitness} \quad \text{(a)}$$
$$\text{fitness} = (\text{prim\_fitness} + \text{sec\_fitness}) \;/\; 2 \quad \text{(b)}$$

Experimental Setup.

Flexibility was evaluated through a set of four unique treatments that provide insight into its effect on a virtual robot's morphology and gait. The primary environment was a flat plane with low friction values. A secondary environment, introduced after 50 generations, was a similar flat plane with friction values more closely resembling that found on a normal surface. The two-environment approach is used to introduce competing pressures on the morphology. Introducing the secondary environment after 50 generations allows for a morphology to become near-optimal in one environment before being introduced to a different selective pressure from the second environment. This approach was based on the assumption that the robot is designed to perform tasks in a specific environment for the majority of its effective lifespan, occasionally interacting in a second type of environment. Once the second environment is introduced, fitness is treated as the average performance across both environments.

The evolvable parameters for each treatment are presented in Table 3. Treatment 1 is a control run that uses the initial hand-designed morphology prototyped prior to this study. The morphology of this creature is given an arm length of 8.5 centimeters and a foot radius of 1.0 centimeter with a rigid joint connecting the two parts of the arm. Flexibility of the passive joint is allowed to evolve in Treatment 2, while the dimensional characteristics of the arm morphology remain fixed at the values from Treatment 1. In Treatment 3, the dimensional characteristics of the arm morphology, arm length and foot radius, are placed under selective pressure while keeping the joint fixed. This run provides insight as to how morphologies evolve and perform without the influence of passive flexibility. Treatment 4 allows all aspects of the morphology to evolve under selective pressures providing feedback into how a complete morphology behaves in the two environments.

Table 3: Parameters subject to evolutionary pressure per treatment. X indicates a parameter subjected to selective pressures.

Parameters:	Arm Length	Foot Radius	Flexibility
Treatment 1			
Treatment 2			X
Treatment 3	X	X	
Treatment 4	X	X	X

4. RESULTS

Forward progress was the primary fitness measure used to assess the performance of the passive joint. Table 4 summarizes the fitnesses of the four treatments conducted in the study, providing the average forward progress achieved by each treatment in both environments along with the standard deviation, minimum, and maximum fitnesses found for the replicate runs. Treatments 2 and 3 have standard deviations of 0.0, as the replicate runs converged on similar performing solutions with small variations between the fitnesses of the replicate runs. Given the nature of these treatments, where at most one condition is subject to selective pressures, this is expected as there exists a small set of possible morphologies that optimize the fitness of the virtual robot. When more parameters were subjected to evolutionary pressures in Treatment 4, variation in the morphologies was seen with different competing morphologies gaining prevalence.

Table 4: Fitness summary for all treatments after the evolutionary runs.

Treatment:	1	2	3	4
Primary	26.8	28.3	32.0	44.6
Std. Dev.	0.0	0.0	0.0	0.1
Min.	26.8	28.3	32.0	42.9
Max.	26.8	28.3	32.0	46.5
Secondary	59.1	59.2	71.8	73.2
Std. Dev.	0.0	0.0	0.0	0.2
Min.	59.1	59.2	71.6	68.6
Max.	59.1	59.2	71.9	77.5
Distance traveled in cm.				

The average fitness for each treatment is presented visually in Figure 4. Error bars displayed in the graph are not visible for Treatments 1-3 as the variation in the replicate runs was minimal, however, Treatment 4 exhibits variation in performance in both environments. Performance in the secondary environment is significantly better than that of the primary environment, as the higher friction values found in the second environment allow the robot to move forward with less slippage. Evaluating the effect of flexibility on the performance of the various treatments is best seen by comparing Treatment 1 to Treatment 2 and Treatment 3 to Treatment 4. These comparisons demonstrate how a flexible joint performs against a rigid joint as well as how flexibility complements other aspects of morphology to improve performance.

When considering the effect of flexibility alone in Treatments 1 and 2, passive joints offer only a minimal improvement over a completely fixed arm morphology. In the primary environment, all trials in Treatment 2 performed better than Treatment 1, with an average improvement of 1.5 centimeters. Performance in the second environment was similar between the treatments. Greater friction rewards longer arms as opposed to a flexible joint in the secondary environment, explaining the lack of performance improvement for flexible joints. As the joint flexes, the effective arm length of the robot is reduced, resulting in a shorter distance of travel per arm stroke. Reviewing the resulting morphology of Treatment 2 showed a solution that uses a large restorative force to aid locomotion by giving the arm stroke an extra kick of the foot as the arm moved away from the ground. In this instance, the passive flexibility was directly responsible for an increase in the forward progress of the arm by exerting a force propelling the virtual robot forward.

Effect of flexibility on a fully evolvable morphology can be seen in the performance differences between Treatments 3 and 4. In the primary environment, an increased performance of at least 34% is achieved between the worst performing solution in Treatment 4 and the best performing solution in Treatment 3. Interestingly, the performance in the secondary environment is mixed, with some solutions performing worse than those with inflexible joints found in Treatment 3. These performance differences relate to the two different morphologies that became prevalent in the solutions for Treatment 4. Generally speaking, when friction is high, there is less pressure to increase contact area with the surface. Consequently, morphologies that are highly flexible tend to perform worse in the secondary environment due to the reduced effective arm length.

The evolved morphologies of the individual treatments exhibited similar dimensional morphology characteristics between replicate runs. Table 5 displays the morphological characteristic values found in this study. Treatments 2 and 3 generally resulted in replicate runs that evolved the same morphologies per treatment. The single evolvable traits in both treatments led to a single morphology giving optimal fitness. In Treatment 2, only flexibility is evolvable and Treatment 3 allows for evolving the dimensional morphological traits. Given these reduced parameters, evolution arrives at an optimal morphology relatively quickly. Treatment 4 yielded the most variable morphology likely due to the increased numbers of parameters that were subject to the evolutionary process.

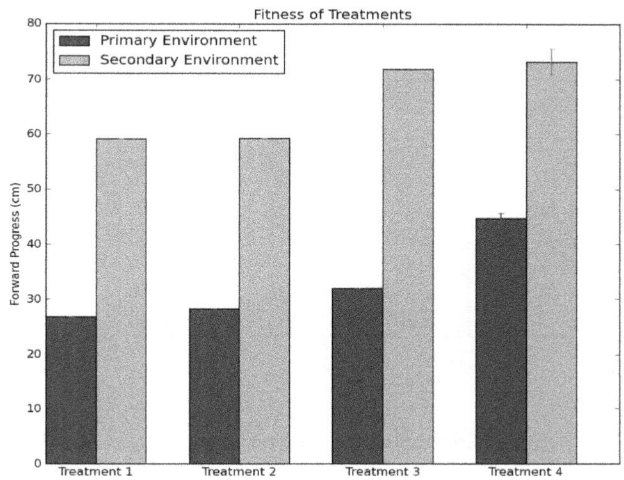

Figure 4: Forward progress of the various treatments in both environments. The primary environment fitness is generally lower due to the reduced friction environment resulting in increased slippage during locomotion.

When considering the morphologies that evolved in Treatment 4, two general patterns emerged. Figure 5 shows one of the solutions from Treatment 4, a morphology with high flexibility of the passive joint. This morphology tended to do well in the primary environment as it had a large contact area with the ground due to its high flexibility. However, the performance in the primary environment came at a cost, as the flexibility hindered performance in the secondary environment. A second morphology that came from Treatment 4 excelled in the secondary environment by having a semi-flexible morphology with a greater foot radius. These solutions utilized a small kicking motion of the foot during the period in which the foot contacted the ground to aid in propelling the robot forward. The joint did not deflect as far from the neutral position in these morphologies, which provided for a larger effective arm length than the highly flexible morphologies. This lower joint deflection resulted in the better performance observed in the secondary environment. Such behaviors illustrate the need for high fidelity simulations that account for the nuances of the constituent materials to better simulate material behaviors that can aid the performance of robots. In this case, the gaits of the dif-

Table 5: Evolved Morphology Characteristics

Treatment 1				
Attribute	Average	Std. Dev.	Min.	Max.
Arm Length	8.5	0.0	8.5	8.5
Foot Radius	1.0	0.0	1.0	1.0
No flexibility in this treatment.				
Treatment 2				
Attribute	Average	Std. Dev.	Min.	Max.
Arm Length	8.5	0.0	8.5	8.5
Foot Radius	1.0	0.0	1.0	1.0
ERP 1	0.767	0.000	0.767	0.767
CFM 1	1.968	0.000	1.938	1.984
ERP 2	0.100	0.000	0.100	0.100
CFM 2	2.307	0.136	2.16	2.6
Treatment 3				
Attribute	Average	Std. Dev.	Min.	Max.
Arm Length	10.275	0.000	10.275	10.275
Foot Radius	5.000	0.008	4.932	5.086
No flexibility in this treatment.				
Treatment 4				
Attribute	Average	Std. Dev.	Min.	Max.
Arm Length	10.275	0.000	10.275	10.275
Foot Radius	4.413	0.080	2.261	5.086
ERP 1	0.691	0.163	0.191	0.767
CFM 1	1.372	0.485	0.620	1.984
ERP 2	0.557	0.179	0.140	0.735
CFM 2	0.297	0.439	0.040	1.440

ferent morphologies benefitted from the small but important characteristics relating to flexibility. Increased simulation capabilities modeling these inherent material properties may result in further increases in robotic performance. Moreover, exploiting the properties of the constituent materials in this manner is complementary to other facets of robot design.

Figure 5: Evolved morphology demonstrating flexibility of the passive joint as it makes contact with the surface. In this morphology, the foot comes into full contact with the ground with the aid of a flexible joint at the arm-foot junction. The foot size also increased giving the morphology a greater contact area with the surface.

Further insight into the evolutionary process of Treatment 4 can be gained through Figure 6. The performance over evolutionary time is indicated for each environment by highlighting the best performing individual in a single environment and the best individual with respect to performance in both environments. Variation among the replicate runs is indicated by the error bars. The variation is due to the two different resultant morphologies that emerged over the course of this evolutionary run. In this case, the error bars also illustrate how the two separate general morphologies performed. When considering the secondary environment, the high error bar indicates solutions that utilized the semi-flexible morphology, as these excelled in the higher friction environment. The lower error bars indicate the solutions that harnessed more flexible morphologies to excel in the primary environment. For the primary environment lines, the inverse is true, with the high error bars indicating more flexible morphologies and the lower error bars indicating semi-flexible morphologies. This graph also demonstrates clearly the compromise made by the final solutions, in that the best performing individuals in one environment were not necessarily the solutions selected for their performance across both environments. The evolutionary path taken by the two morphologies is illustrated and provides insight as to how different morphologies can result from the same set of initial conditions to meet a fitness goal.

5. DISCUSSION

Visual observations of the behavior of the individual evolved solutions indicate that a variety of different flexibility characteristics arose in the final evolved morphologies for Treatment 4. The best performers in the primary environment had a combination of smaller foot radii and more flexible joints, enabling the feet to lie flat against the ground, increasing the contact area in the low friction environment. The majority of the solutions in Treatment 4 tended to evolve semi-flexible joints and larger foot radii to gain an advantage in the secondary environment, where performance gains were greater than those of the primary environment. Given the contribution of both environments to the fitness function, greater performance differences in the secondary environment results led to the semi-flexible morphologies being selected, as they performed better in a full friction environment. Regardless of the degree of flexibility evolved, all best performers selected in Treatment 4 exhibited at least a moderate amount of flexibility, with none of the trials resulting in an inflexible joint as the best performing individual.

Not only was flexibility beneficial to the virtual robots in this experiment, but the evolved solutions exhibited characteristics that is transferable to physical robots. Specifically, visual observation of the resulting evolved morphologies indicated that the solutions did not exploit flexibility in the simulation environment to develop unrealistic movement patterns, as has been noted in other research pertaining to the reality gap [10, 22, 24]. Transferring these designs into physical materials will require further analysis of material properties, but the initial findings of this study demonstrate that flexibility can be modeled adequately in a simulation environment. Of course, further verification will be necessary for new materials as the physical characteristics vary.

Modeling physical material properties in simulation can produce morphologies that make use of these characteristics to increase a robot's performance. Implementation of pas-

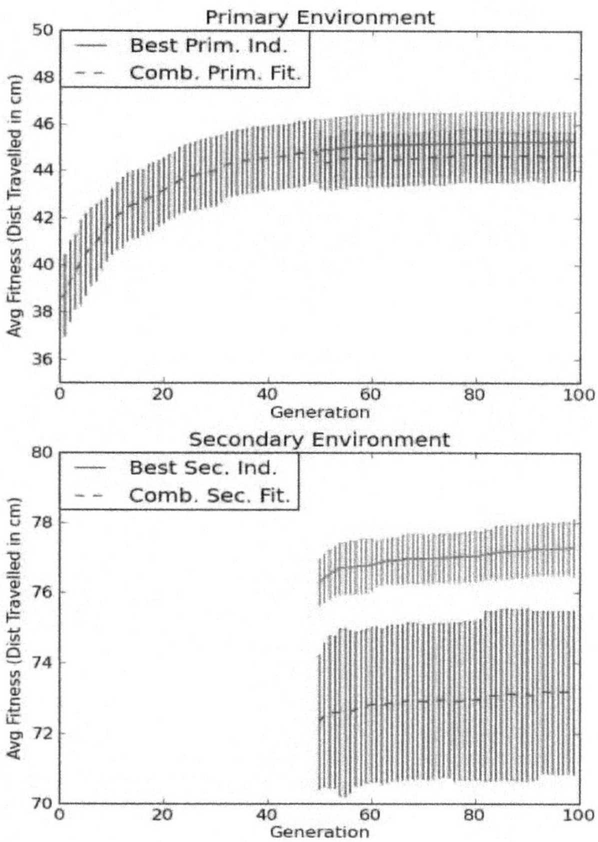

Figure 6: Treatment 4: Forward progress in both environments with all parameters subject to selective pressures. Compromise between the best individual in an environment and the individual morphology that is selected for its performance in both environments can be seen in the disparity between the two lines for each respective environment.

sive joints in physical robots could have positive effects such as increasing battery life and reducing weight due to the need for fewer motors. In the study described here, material flexibility aided the forward progress of the two resultant morphologies by either allowing the foot to increase its contact area with the ground, or by adding in a small kicking motion to aid in forward locomotion. These characteristics evolved through the use of evolutionary computation without the need for direct intervention during the testing phase. Providing a method for evolution to exploit these material properties may result in new characteristics emerging that increase performance in ways not considered *a priori*. It is therefore important to provide a simulation environment with the capabilities to make full use of these material properties when conducting evolutionary experiments concerned with morphology.

6. CONCLUSION

In this study, material flexibility was investigated through modeling the property in a virtual robot and evaluation in two separate simulated environments. The four treatments used in this experiment addressed passive joint flexibility both alone and coupled with dimensional characteristics of the arm morphology. Flexibility was found to be a beneficial characteristic, with evolved solutions exhibiting both semi-flexible joints that emphasized a forceful restorative force, and more pliable joints that increased the contact area with the ground. In the case of this study, evolved morphologies exhibited realistic characteristics that demonstrated the feasibility of modeling flexibility in a simulation environment. High quality simulations are necessary to model the material properties and allow evolution to incorporate these benefits into the morphological design of a robot.

Future experiments will refine the modeling of flexibility in passive joints. Additional work will focus on addressing material properties that help to close the reality gap. Further modeling of flexibility is planned in order to develop a more in-depth method of evaluating flexibility, such as devising a measure of flexibility based on deformation between parts. Using the capabilities of the 3D printer described earlier, fabricating evolved virtual robotic designs using the results of this study will help reduce the need for modification between simulated designs and physical realizations. Accurate simulation models will also allow for reduced transfer time between virtual and real robots.

7. ACKNOWLEDGMENTS

The authors gratefully acknowledge the contributions to this work of Anthony Clark, Jianxun Wang and Professor Xiaobo Tan. This research has been supported in part by National Science Foundation grants CNS-1059373, CNS-0915855, CNS-0751155, CCF-0820220, and DBI-0939454, and by U.S. Army Grant W911NF-08-1-0495. Any opinions, findings, and conclusions or recommendations expressed in this material are those of the author(s) and do not necessarily reflect the views of the National Science Foundation or other research sponsors.

8. REFERENCES

[1] J. Auerbach and J. C. Bongard. How robot morphology and training order affect the learning of multiple behaviors. In *Proceedings of the 2009 IEEE Congress on Evolutionary Computation* pages 39–46, Trondheim, Norway, May 2009. IEEE.

[2] J. Auerbach and J. C. Bongard. Dynamic resolution in the co-evolution of morphology and control. In *Proceedings of the Twelfth International Conference on Artificial Life (ALIFE XII)*, pages 451–458, Odense, Denmark, 2010.

[3] J. Auerbach and J. C. Bongard. Evolving monolithic robot controllers through incremental shaping. In S. Doncieux, N. Bredeche, and J.-B. Mouret, editors, *New Horizons in Evolutionary Robotics*, volume 341 of *Studies in Computational Intelligence*, pages 55–65. Springer Berlin / Heidelberg, 2011.

[4] A. G. Baydin. Evolution of central pattern generators for the control of a five-link planar bipedal walking mechanism. *PALADYN Journal of Behavioral Robotics*, 2008.

[5] R. D. Beer and J. C. Gallagher. Evolving dynamical neural networks for adaptive behavior. *Adaptive Behavior*, 1(1):91–122, 1992.

[6] J. C. Bongard. Behavior chaining: Incremental behavioral integration for evolutionary robotics. In S. Bullock, J. Noble, R. Watson, and M. A. Bedau, editors, *Artificial Life XI: Proceedings of the Eleventh International Conference on the Simulation and Synthesis of Living Systems*, pages 64–71, Winchester, UK, 2008.

[7] J. C. Bongard. The utility of evolving simulated robot morphology increases with task complexity for object manipulation. *Artificial Life*, 16(3):201–223, 2010.

[8] J. C. Bongard and H. Lipson. Once more unto the breach: Co-evolving a robot and its simulator. In *Proceedings of the Ninth International Conference on the Simulation and Synthesis of Living Systems*, pages 57–62, Boston, MA, USA, 2004.

[9] V. Braitenberg. *Vehicles: Experiments in Synthetic Psychology.* The MIT Press, February 1986.

[10] R. A. Brooks. Artificial life and real robots. In F. J. Varela and P. Bourgine, editors, *Proceedings of the First European Conference on Artificial Life*, pages 3–10. MIT Press, Cambridge, MA, 1992.

[11] N. Chaumont, R. Egli, and C. Adami. Evolving virtual creatures and catapults. *Artificial Life*, 13(2):139–157, 2007.

[12] D. Cliff, P. Husbands, and I. Harvey. Explorations in Evolutionary Robotics. *Adaptive Behavior*, 2(1):73–110, June 1993.

[13] R. S. et al. Open Dynamics Engine, http://www.ode.org/, 2012.

[14] H. Feng and R. Wang. Construction of central pattern generator for quadruped locomotion control. In *Proceedings of the IEEE/ASME International Conference on Advanced Intelligent Mechatronics*, pages 979–984, Xi'an, China, July 2008. IEEE.

[15] D. Floreano, P. Husbands, and S. Nolfi. Evolutionary Robotics. In *Handbook of Robotics.* Springer Verlag, Berlin, 2008.

[16] P. Funes and J. Pollack. Evolutionary body building: Adaptive physical designs for robots. *Artificial Life*, 4(4):337–357, 1998.

[17] I. Harvey, E. D. Paolo, R. Wood, M. Quinn, and E. Tuci. Evolutionary robotics: A new scientific tool for studying cognition. *Artificial Life*, 11(1-2):79–98, 2005.

[18] A. Ijspeert, A. Crespi, and J. Cabelguen. Simulation and robotics studies of salamander locomotion. *Neuroinformatics*, 3(3):171–195, 2005.

[19] A. J. Ijspeert. A connectionist central pattern generator for the aquatic and terrestrial gaits of a simulated salamander. *Biological Cybernetics*, 84(5):331–48, May 2001.

[20] A. J. Ijspeert. Central pattern generators for locomotion control in animals and robots: A review. *Neural networks : The Official Journal of the International Neural Network Society*, 21(4):642–53, May 2008.

[21] K. Inoue, T. Sumi, and S. Ma. CPG-based control of a simulated snake-like robot adaptable to changing ground friction. In *Proceedings of the IEEE/RSJ International Conference on Intelligent Robots and Systems*, pages 1957 –1962, 2007.

[22] N. Jakobi. Running across the reality gap: Octopod locomotion evolved in a minimal simulation. In *Proceedings of the First European Workshop on Evolutionary Robotics: EvoRobot'98*, pages 39–58, Paris, France, 1998. Springer-Verlag.

[23] L. Konig and H. Schmeck. A completely evolvable genotype-phenotype mapping for evolutionary robotics. In *Proceedings of the Third IEEE International Conference on Self-Adaptive and Self-Organizing Systems*, San Francisco, California, 2009.

[24] S. Koos, J. B. Mouret, and S. Doncieux. Crossing the reality gap in evolutionary robotics by promoting transferable controllers. In *Proceedings of the 12th Annual Conference on Genetic and Evolutionary Computation*, GECCO '10, pages 119–126, New York, NY, USA, 2010. ACM.

[25] H. Lipson. Evolutionary robotics and open-ended design automation. In B. Cohen, editor, *Biomimetics*, pages 129–155. CRC Press, 2005.

[26] H. Lipson and J. B. Pollack. Automatic design and manufacture of robotic lifeforms. *Nature*, 406(6799):974–978, August 2000.

[27] M. Mazzapioda, A. Cangelosi, and S. Nolfi. Evolving morphology and control: A distributed approach. In *Proceedings of the 2009 IEEE Congress on Evolutionary Computation*, pages 2217–2224, Trondheim, Norway, May 2009. IEEE.

[28] S. Nolfi and D. Floreano. *Evolutionary Robotics: The Biology, Intelligence and Technology of Self-Organizing Machines.* The MIT Press, 2000.

[29] C. Paul and J. C. Bongard. The road less travelled: Morphology in the optimization of biped robot locomotion. In *Proceedings of the 2001 IEEE/RSJ International Conference on Intelligent Robots and Systems*, volume 1, pages 226 – 232, Maui, Hawaii, USA, 2001.

[30] L. Schramm, Y. Jin, and B. Sendhoff. Emerged coupling of motor control and morphological development in evolution of multi-cellular animats. In *Proceedings of the 10th European conference on Advances in artificial life: Darwin meets von Neumann - Volume Part I*, ECAL'09, pages 27–34, Berlin, Heidelberg, 2011. Springer-Verlag.

[31] K. Sims. Evolving 3d morphology and behavior by competition. *Artificial Life*, 1(4):353–372, 1994.

[32] T. Ziemke, N. Bergfeldt, G. Buason, T. Susi, and H. Svensson. Evolving cognitive scaffolding and environment adaptation: A new research direction for evolutionary robotics. *Connection Science*, 16(4):339–350, 2004.

A Comparison of a Communication Strategies in Cooperative Learning

Michael Solomon
Department of Computer Science
University of Idaho
83844-1010
solo4857@vandals.uidaho.edu

Robert B. Heckendorn
Department of Computer Science
University of Idaho
83844-1010
heckendo@cs.uidaho.edu

Terence Soule
Department of Computer Science
University of Idaho
83844-1010
tsoule@cs.uidaho.edu

ABSTRACT

In the wild, groups of hyenas are often observed to cooperate in driving lions away from a kill in order to claim it for themselves. Because lions are much larger and can easily injure or kill a single hyena, this is a difficult, high risk/high reward behavior requiring complex cooperation by the hyenas. The hyenas depend on communication to coordinate their attack. In this paper, we attempt to evolve hyena behaviors that successfully drive-off simulated lions. We are particularly interested in how the type of communication influences the evolution of successful strategies. Several forms of communication are tested including two inspired by hyena behavior. The first is a generalized vocalization or "call" that can be either local or global and used by any hyena. The second mimics the recognition of a special hyena, which we refer to as the "flag-bearer". Our results show that the presence of a flag-bearer leads to the evolution of significantly more effective coordination than either purely local or name based communication. These results suggest that there may be a "sweet spot" between too little information, which makes coordination difficult, and too much information which makes both evolutionary learning and coordination difficult.

Categories and Subject Descriptors

I.2.9 [**Robotics**]: Autonomous vehicles

Keywords

Cooperation, communication, multi-agent

1. INTRODUCTION

To successfully solve difficult problems requiring cooperation between multiple agents, agents must be able to effectively coordinate their actions. Communication is a critical component of successful coordination. Fundamentally, communication is the exchange of information. An effective method of communication must make sure that the right information is exchanged between the right individuals at the right time. This introduces a problem of information filtering, either the sender or the receiver must decide which information is most useful to send and when to send it. Too little information impedes cooperation and, especially in the context of evolutionary learning, too much information might make learning more difficult by introducing a signal-to-noise problem.

Evolutionary methods have proven effective at evolving behaviors exhibiting coordination and cooperation. However, research on comparative communication strategies among agents has been surprisingly limited, focusing on only a few, standard communication forms. To date, most research has focused on either fully distributed swarms in which members can communicate locally, or fully centralized systems in which a central controller coercively directs all of the agents (see [4, 13, 12] for summaries of recent results with multi-agent swarms). In both models, communication plays a critical role and the range and density of the communication network has a significant effect on the success of the evolutionary process. In contrast, many different types of communication are observed in nature, where evolution has evolved specific types of communication to meet specific problem requirements.

In this paper, we examine how the amount of information and range of communication effects the evolution of cooperation. We focus on two very different forms of communication inspired by African spotted hyenas (*Crocuta crocuta*). The first is a generalized vocalization or "call" which can be either local or global and can be used by any hyena. The second mimics the recognition of a special hyena, which we refer to as the "flag-bearer". The flag-bearer is heard by the entire group, but cannot coerce agent actions. Our results show that the presence of a flag-bearer leads to the evolution of significantly more effective cooperation and coordination than either the local or global call based communication. These results suggest that there may be a "sweet spot" between too little information, which makes coordination difficult, and too much information which makes both evolutionary learning and coordination difficult thereby causing the evolution of successful solutions to take significantly longer or to get stuck in local optima. Interestingly, a similar relationship has been suggested between the amount and quality of information available early in the learning process and the effectiveness of the learning process [6].

GECCO'12, July 7-11, 2012, Philadelphia, Pennsylvania, USA.

2. BACKGROUND

Often communication is interpreted as implying *intent* by the sender. For example, if agent A learns the location of agent B because agent B intentionally broadcast its location, that is typically considered communication. In contrast if agent A learns the location of agent B through a passive medium, e.g. agent A sees agent B, that is often considered *sensing* as distinct from communication. However, this distinction is often unclear. If every agent has an RFID chip or a transponder that continually broadcasts its location is it communicating its location, are other agents sensing its location, or both? Further, from an information flow perspective this distinction may be irrelevant, one agent is learning information about another agent regardless of whether the exchange was intentional or not.

We explore how the type and quantity of *information* that one agent receives regarding another agent affects the evolution of successful cooperation. Because we are primarily interested in information exchange, we choose not to distinguish between sensing and communication and we will refer to both as communication.

2.1 Background: Multi-Agent Communication

Early research suggests that for evolved cooperation name based approaches to communication are more successful than deictic approaches, particularly for teams of heterogeneous agents [10]. In name based communication agents receive information from (or about) other agents by name: "Joe is at location x,y", "Agent 7 is attacking", etc. In contrast, in deictic communication agents receive information based on relative roles or positions that can change of overtime: "the closest agent is at location x,y", "the highest agent is attacking", etc.

Despite the early promise of name based communication, more recent research has primarily focused on local communication or centralized communication. In systems using local communication, such as fully distributed systems, agents only exchange information with their nearest neighbors. This is a form of deictic communication, as the communication links change with location. These systems have produced a number of impressive results (see, for example [7, 9, 12, 13]). However, there also is growing empirical and theoretical evidence that for many problems centralized communication and control can significantly improve performance (see for example [11, 8, 2]). Unfortunately, in most centralized communication systems the central agent forms both a bottleneck and weak point largely nullifying the advantages in robustness and scalability of fully distributed systems.

The shift away from name based communication towards either local and distributed communication or centralized communication is largely due to the increasing size of the teams being studied. In a named based system any agent has the potential to communicate with any other agent, thus the number of possible interactions grows exponentially with the number of participating agents. Learning which interactions are beneficial appears to become increasingly infeasible as team size increases, although this has not been rigorously tested.

Here we compare local communication, name based communication, and two novel communication strategies based on the behavior of spotted hyenas. The first novel strategy allows one agent to learn how many other agents are in a particular state, in this case the number of "calling" or "vocalizing" agents. The second strategy denotes one agent as a "flag-bearer", all of the other agents can immediately hear when the flag-bearer calls and then become aware of its location. However, the flag-bearer does not have any coercive capabilities typical associated with a centralized control and communication strategy. Further, because the flag-bearer can only broadcast its own location, it does not create a communication bottleneck.

2.2 Background: Hyena-Lion Interactions

Hyenas and lions exhibit a number of complex interactions involving multiple members of both species [15, 3, 14]. We are modeling hyenas cooperative attempts to drive-off one or more lions from a kill. In the wild, a single lion can easily defeat several hyenas and often several lions will defend a kill. So, safely taking a kill requires a coordinated effort by a large number of hyenas.

In the process of taking a kill the hyenas exhibit considerable vocalization, which is assumed to aid the cooperation and coordination required to drive off the lions. Our "number calling" strategy (described below) reflects the hyenas ability to estimate the number of participating hyenas based on the overall volume of vocalization. Rank is also known to play an important role in the cooperative process for the hyenas, with lower rank members often being more active participants and taking higher risks in approaching the lions [15]. Our flag-bearer is a simplified approach that can be interpreted as assigning a rank to one of the hyenas, although given the more aggressive behavior of lower ranked hyenas in the wild it is unclear whether our flag-bearer more accurately represents a high or low ranked individual.

Overall the process of hyenas stealing a lion kill is interesting because it represents a difficult, high risk/high reward, cooperative behavior. Individual lions can easily injure or kill individual hyenas and are fairly aggressive in defending their kills. Thus, the hyenas must be very careful and well coordinated in attempting to drive the lions away.

3. MODEL

Our model is designed to reflect the basic hyena-lion interaction. In a 2 dimensional world with real valued coordinates, lions are guarding a kill (e.g. a zebra) and hyenas are attempting to drive the lions away without undue risk to themselves. The lions' behavior is fixed, whereas the hyenas' behaviors evolve. Each hyena evolves its own, potentially unique, behavior, so the hyena clan is heterogeneous.

3.1 Lion Behavior

The lions' behaviors are fixed. Initially the lions are placed randomly within 1 unit of the kill, which we'll refer to as a zebra. Lions do not move unless forced out of position by being outnumbered by more than 3 to 1, a ratio suggested by field studies. Specifically, if the hyenas within 5 units of a lion outnumber the lions within that range by more than 3 to 1 then the lion moves directly away from the nearest hyena. E.g., for a given lion L if there is one other lion (for a total of 2 lions) and at least 7 hyenas within 5 units of lion L then lion L will move directly away from the nearest hyena which typically will force it away from the zebra. If a hyena ends its move within 3 units of a lion then that hyena risks injury by the lion and is penalized (see Section 4 below).

This represents the potential of being injured by getting too close to a lion.

3.2 Hyena Behavior

Hyenas begin at random locations. All but one hyena start at least 8 units from the zebra, i.e. outside of the range in which they can sense the zebra (see Figure 1). One hyena, but not the flag-bearer if one is used, starts within sensing range, 8 units, of the zebra. Each hyena's behavior is determined by that hyena's evolved control structure. Each control structure is a vector expression tree representing a vector function. Inputs to the function (e.g. leaves of the vector expression tree) represent environmental factors the hyena can "sense" (see Table 1). For example, hyenas can "sense" the distance and direction to the nearest other hyena and to the nearest other hyena that is "calling". The output of the vector function (also a vector) is the hyena's move for that timestep.

Note that the hyenas can only move at most 1.0 units in a single timestep. If the returned movement vector is longer than 1.0, the hyena moves a distance of 1.0 in the given direction. Each hyena's vector function is re-evaluated every timestep to determine the hyena's movement in that timestep. The functions used in the hyenas' control structure are given in Table 2. Each function takes 2 to 4 vector inputs and returns a vector. Hyenas within 8 units of the zebra are within the "calling area" and call automatically.

As noted in Table 1 some of the input vectors have a maximum range. For example, hyenas can only sense the zebra if they are within 8 units of it and lions if they are within 5. If objects are out of range (e.g. a hyena is more than 8 units from the zebra or more than 10 units from the next nearest hyena) then that input vector is set to the zero vector: zero angle and zero magnitude.

Two features of our model make this problem particular difficult. First, because the hyenas start each trial at random locations and distances from the lions they cannot simply charge the lions. If they did then they would arrive at different times and the early arriving hyenas would suffer large penalties from being near the lions, at least until enough hyenas converged to drive the lions away. Second, if the hyenas surround the lions the lions will simply "bounce" back and forth between the hyenas inflicting considerable damage. Thus, to be maximally successful the hyenas must coordinate both the timing of their rush, to make sure sufficient numbers of hyenas rush at the same time, and the direction of the rush, to make sure they are not simply pushing the lions into other hyenas.

3.2.1 Hyena Communication - Calling Behavior

Hyenas can "hear" calling hyenas at unlimited distance, i.e. we assume that all hyenas begin and remain within hearing range of each other. A hyena can sense the zebra when it is within 8 units of the zebra (see Table 1). If a hyena is within sensing range of the zebra then that hyena automatically begins "calling". This is a fixed behavior. How the other hyenas can interpret the calling hyena is varied across the trials and represents the major communication variable being tested. Several possible inputs based on calling are tested, each allowing a different form of communication:

- Nearest hyena - hyenas can "hear" the nearest calling hyena. This is represented as an available input vector that points from the active hyena to the nearest calling hyena. This is local, deictic communication.

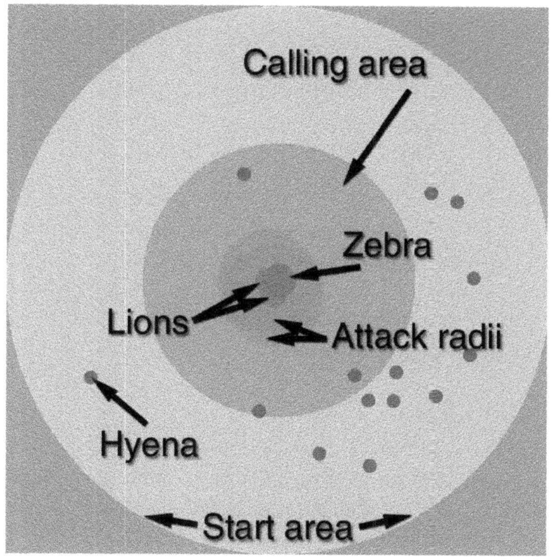

Figure 1: Example layout, with hyenas, lions, and key areas labeled. There are 14 hyenas (smallest circles), two lions, and one zebra kill. Hyenas can only "see" the zebra from within the 8 unit calling area. Hyenas within this area call automatically. In each simulation one hyena (randomly selected, but not the flag-bearer) starts within the calling circle, all other hyenas start outside of the calling circle and within the starting area, i.e. close enough to hear a calling hyena, but too far away to see the zebra. The circles around the lions in the figure are the area in which they attack hyenas.

- All hyenas - hyenas can "hear" any calling hyena. Effectively, each hyena's call is a broadcast signal that can be received by any interested hyena. This is represented as 14 available input vectors, one for each hyena (e.g. $calling_1$, $calling_2$, etc.), the input vector points towards the numbered hyena if it is calling and is zero otherwise. This is high density, name based communication.

- Flag-bearer - there is one unique hyena, the flag-bearer, that all other hyenas can hear as soon as it starts calling. This is represented by an available input vector ($calling_{f}lag$) that points towards the flag-bearer if it is calling and is zero otherwise. This is somewhat similar to a centralized system, but the flag-bearer has no coercive ability and because it does not transmit messages between other hyenas it does not create a communication bottleneck. Arbitrarily the first hyena in the clan is the flag-bearer.

- Number calling - hyenas know how many other hyenas are calling. This is represented by an available input vector whose magnitude is the number of calling hyenas and whose direction is fixed.

- Landmark - all hyenas know the location of (have a vector to) a fixed landmark (e.g. a stump) located somewhere within the calling radius - it is placed randomly in each trial. This is used, as discussed below, as a comparison to the flag-bearer to determine whether the advantage of the flag-bearer is simply that it represents a piece of shared information.

It is important to note that while the act of calling is fixed (hyenas always call if within 8 units of the zebra) the hyenas' response to hearing another hyena calling is purely evolved: hyenas may evolve to ignore all calling, approach callers, avoid callers, etc. depending on how they evolve to use, or not use, the available inputs.

4. FITNESS

For the evolutionary step each hyena and each clan of hyenas is assigned a fitness. At each timestep a hyena is given a fitness based on its distance (d) to the zebra:

$$f_{zebra}(d) = \frac{1}{1+d} \quad (1)$$

and its distance d to *each* lion:

$$f_{lion}(d) = \sum_{for\ each\ lion} \begin{cases} 3(d-3) & \text{if } d < 3, \\ 0 & \text{otherwise} \end{cases} \quad (2)$$

I.e. if the hyena is within 3 units of a lion it **loses** fitness proportional to how close it is to the lion. The total fitness of a hyena is the sum of its fitness at each timestep. So, the best fitness is achieved by quickly getting close to the zebra without getting too close to the lion. The fitness of a hyena clan is simply the sum of the fitnesses of all members of the clan.

5. EXPERIMENTAL PARAMETERS

As noted previously, each hyena has its own evolved control structure represented by a vector expression tree. These trees evolve following a generational, island model algorithm [5] with a population size of 100. In the island model there is a single population of individuals, each of the individuals actually represents a clan of 14 hyenas.

During the selection step, tournament selection is applied to each hyena role. I.e. a tournament is carried out between the hyenas in the role defined by position number 1, then a tournament is carried out between the hyenas in the number 2 position, etc. until a new "parent" clan is created of the winning hyenas. The process is repeated to create a second parent clan. These two clans then undergo crossover to create two offspring clans. Crossover uses the 90/10 rule [1] and is applied between hyenas in the same position: the two number 1 hyenas cross, the two number 2 hyenas cross, etc.

After crossover each of the hyenas in the two new offspring clans undergoes mutation. Each node in the expression tree has a 1% chance of being mutated. Internal nodes are mutated into other nodes with the same arity. If a leaf node representing a constant is selected for mutation the constant value is mutated by a random real value selected uniformly in the range -2 to 2.

Each hyena clan is evaluated by testing it 5 times. In each test the hyenas start in random positions with one hyena (not the flag-bearer) within sensing range of the zebra (see Figure 1). Each evaluation lasts for 100 timesteps. At the end of each trial the best clan is retested 2000 times and the final fitness is based on the average performance over those 2000 tests. All results are the average of 40 independent trials. The GP parameters are summarized in Table 3.

Table 3: Summary of the GP parameters.

Population Size	100
Clan/Team Size	14
Crossover Rate	100%
Mutation Rate	1%
Selection	Tournament (Size 3)
Trials	40

6. RESULTS

Table 4 shows the average fitness of the best clans across all 40 trials. The true or false values in columns 2 through 5 represent whether a particular communication type is available to the hyenas. E.g. in the experiment represented in row 2 hyenas know the number of calling hyenas, but there is no flag-bearer, no landmark, and they can only hear the nearest calling hyena, not all calling hyenas. Column 6 gives the average fitness (and standard deviation) of the best hyena clans from each of the forty trials. The last nine columns show the results of a two-tailed Student's t-test between each pairs of conditions, *'s represent significant differences at the $P = 0.01$ level, -'s are non-significant. E.g. The difference in average fitness between rows 3 and 1 is significant, but not the difference between rows 2 and 1. $P = 0.01$ is chosen to be conservative because of the multiple tests.

Perhaps most surprisingly, the data in Table 4 suggests that just knowing the number of calling hyenas is not beneficial (e.g. row 1 versus row 2). As noted previously to effectively drive off the lions without injury the hyenas must coordinate their charge so that enough hyenas are present to drive off the lions without injury. This is a numbers game. We had hypothesized that knowing the number of calling hyenas, i.e. the number of hyenas within the calling range of the zebra (Figure 1) would be useful, but the results do not support this conclusion.

In contrast, having a flag-bearer is highly beneficial (rows 5 to 8), unless hear-all is enabled (rows 9 to 10). Observation of the hyenas' behavior suggests that with a flag-bearer the hyenas usually evolve the same general behavior, which consists of four rules:

1. all hyenas except the flag-bearer remain stationary until the flag-bearer begins calling
2. the flag bearer begins by moving towards the nearest calling hyena and then stops (as noted previously at least one hyena always begins within sensing range of the zebra)
3. once the flag-bearer begins calling all other hyenas converge on it
4. once a *sufficient* number of hyenas have converged on the flag-bearer, all of the hyenas move to drive away the lions

This pattern of behavior meets the timing and positioning requirements described previously for a successful attack.

Table 1: List of allowed inputs to the hyenas' control structures. Each of these can be a leaf node in the evolved vector expression trees that are used to control the hyenas' movements. These nodes represent what the hyenas can "sense".

Name	Description	Maximum Range
Nearest Hyena	Vector to the nearest hyena	10
Nearest Calling	Vector to the nearest calling hyena	No maximum
All Calling	Separate vector for each calling hyena	No maximum
Flag-bearer	Vector to the flag-bear, if its calling	No maximum
Nearest Lion	Vector to the nearest lion	5
Zebra	Vector to the zebra	8
North	North, magnitude 1	No maximum
Num. Calling	Vector whose magnitude is the number of currently calling hyenas and whose direction is always north	No maximum
Random	Vector randomized every time step	No maximum
Last Move	Vector used last time step	No maximum
Constant	Vector randomized exactly once	No maximum
Mirror Nearest	Vector used last time step by the nearest hyena	10

Table 2: List of functions used in the hyenas' control structure.

Function	Description	Number of Inputs
Sum	Sums 2 input vectors	2
Invert	Inverts a vector	1
LessThanMagnitude	Compares the *magnitude* of the first 2 input vectors. Returns the 3rd vector if the 1st vector is smaller else returns the 4th vector	4
LessThanClockwise	Compares the *direction* of the first 2 input vectors. Returns the 3rd vector if the 1st vector is smaller, otherwise returns the 4th vector	4
VectorZero	If the first input has 0 for direction and magnitude, return the 2nd vector, otherwise return the 3rd.	3

The hyenas don't attack until sufficient numbers have converged and they usually all attack from the same direction. In one instance, we observed hyenas attacking in two groups from roughly opposing sides of the lions, which still successfully forced the lions away from the zebra without inflicting additional damage.

Although this pattern of behavior appears frequently when a flag-bearer is used, there are still several features of the evolved strategy that are unclear. It is unclear exactly how the hyenas determine that a sufficient number have converged to drive away the lions as the data shows that number calling is not contributing. Our current hypothesis is that the hyenas use the lions themselves as the determinant. That is they 'push' up against the lions and only advance as when the lions begin to move away - an indication that sufficient hyenas are present. It is also unclear how the hyenas guide their approach to drive off the lions. In some cases it appears that they approach the zebra and drive off the lions as a side-effect, but in other cases they appear to focus on the lions, briefly moving past the zebra to push the lions away before returning to the zebra.

The data also shows that having a common landmark as a reference point is beneficial (rows 1 and 2 versus rows 3 and 4). However, this benefit is not as great as having a flag-bearer and is not additive with having a flag-bearer. This implies that while there is some benefit to having a static reference (the landmark) this benefit is superseded by having an "intelligent" reference, i.e. the flag-bearer.

We also observed an interesting intermediate behavior in the earlier generations of many of the runs. In this intermediate behavior the hyenas would approach the zebra, apparently drawn by a calling hyena, but would stop as soon as they were inside the calling radius. This allowed the hyenas to get closer to the zebra, but also kept them a safe distance away from the lions. It was only much later in the evolutionary process that they began to learn to coordinate their attack on the lions and move further toward the zebra. This intermediate behavior emphasizes the importance of the available information about the environment in determining agent behaviors. The calling radius is an identifiable landmark, which is both closer to the zebra than most of the hyenas' starting points (only one hyena begins within the calling radius), but is also far enough away from the lions to be safe.

To further understand the role of the different inputs we performed "knock-out" experiments on the best clans from each of the 40 trials with the flag-bearer, landmark, and number calling (row 8 in Table 4. In these experiments one or more of the inputs were disabled in the most fit clan from each of the 40 trials and the clans were then retested. Disabled inputs consistently returned a zero vector instead of the correct input. (This is analogous to taking an animal,

Table 4: Results, averaged over 40 trials, with different forms of communication. The true or false values in columns 2 through 5 represent whether a particular communication type is available to the hyenas. E.g. in the experiment represented in row 2 hyenas know the number of calling hyenas, but there is no flag-bearer, no landmark, and they can only hear the nearest calling hyena not all calling hyenas. The best results are observed with a flag-bearer (rows 5 to 8), but not hear-all (rows 9 and 10). The last nine rows show the results of a Student's two-tailed t-test, * denotes significance at the $P = 0.01$ level, - represents non-significance. For example, rows 5 to 8 are significantly better than rows 1 to 4.

	Flag Bearer	Land-mark	Number Calling	Hear All	Avg. Fit (std. dev.)	1	2	3	4	5	6	7	8	9
1	False	False	False	False	860.4 (326.9)	-								
2	False	False	True	False	836.1 (318.5)	-	-							
3	False	True	False	False	991.9 (123.6)	*	*	-						
4	False	True	True	False	992.0 (119.4)	*	*	-	-					
5	True	False	False	False	1056.9 (149.0)	*	*	*	*	-				
6	True	False	True	False	1066.6 (97.9)	*	*	*	*	-	-			
7	True	True	False	False	1066.1 (101.5)	*	*	*	*	-	-	-		
8	True	True	True	False	1055.3 (95.5)	*	*	*	*	-	-	-	-	
9	False	True	False	True	939.7 (151.4)	-	-	-	-	*	*	*	*	-
10	True	True	False	True	954.7 (155.4)	-	*	-	-	*	*	*	*	-

knocking-out a specific gene, e.g. to degrade its hearing, and re-examining its fitness or behavior.) Table 5 shows the results of this experiment.

The knock-out data in Table 5 confirms that the flag-bearer input is the most important input for the evolved clans. When it is disabled, average fitness becomes negative (negative fitness occurs when the lion attacks out-weight the fitness obtained by being close to the zebra). However, decreases in fitness are also observed when either number calling or landmark are disabled. This suggests that at least in some trials the clans are evolving to use those inputs. Interestingly, Table 4 show that the clans can evolve equally successful strategies even when the landmark and number calling inputs are not available during evolution (row 5 versus rows 6, 7 ,and 8). So, they are often used when available, but are not essential to maximizing fitness.

Overall these results suggest that in different trials the hyenas evolve different strategies for attacking the lions and that these strategies depend on different inputs. When it is available, the flag-bear based communication always plays a critical role. Without a flag-bearer evolution cannot find as successful solutions (in the given number of generations) and knocking it out has a significant negative effect in teams that evolved with it. In contrast, the landmark and number calling inputs are somewhat useful on their own, but can be superseded by the having a flag-bearer. Finally, when a flag-bearer is used it appears to sometimes take advantage of either the landmark, the number calling, or both - hence the decrease in fitness in Table 5 from row 8 to rows 5, 6, and 7 when landmark or number calling is knocked-out.

Interestingly, Table 4 shows that hear-all (the name based case) is generally detrimental (row 3 versus row 9 and row 7 versus row 10). Further, hear-all negates the benefits of having a flag-bearer (rows 3 and 7 versus row 10). It is important to note that with hear-all the hyenas could evolve to only "listen" to hyena 1, thereby perfectly replicating the flag-bearer case. However, we hypothesize that with 14 hyenas, it takes considerable evolutionary time for the clans to "agree" on which hyena to listen to. Figure 2 shows the evolutionary curves (averaged across all 40 trials) with a flag-bearer and with and without hear-all. The improvement in fitness is much slower with hear-all than without. This supports the hypothesis that learning with name based communication is difficult when there are many named individuals to consider.

7. CONCLUSIONS

In this paper we used a model of hyena-lion interactions to explore several different and nontraditional communication strategies for a cooperative, multi-agent teams. Our results show that having a single, global identifiable individual - a flag-bearer - significantly improves the evolution of cooperative, coordinated behavior. This benefit arises even though the flag-bearer has none of the coercive ability typically associated with a centralized control structure. Importantly the flag-bearer also does not form a communication bottleneck by acting as a central communication node for the other agents. Thus, a limited number of flag-bearers holds promise as an effective coordination method even for very large swarms where a more typical centralized communication structure would be infeasible.

We studied two other sources of shared information: number calling, which gives general information about the state of the swarm; and landmark, which represents a shared reference similar to the flag-bearer, but static. Number calling generally did not improve fitness while the inclusion of a landmark improved fitness, but not as much as flag-bearer. This suggests that while a shared reference point, the landmark, can be useful, if that reference point is also an evolving agent the potential benefits are much greater.

We also studied traditional name based communication, in which each agent could listen *by name* to the calls of any other agent (referred to in the paper as "hear-all"). This increased performance slightly, but not by a statistically significant amount. It also significantly hindered the performance with a flag-bearer. In our model there are 14 agents, we hypothesize that the difficulty with name based calling arises because each agent most learn which of the other agents it is beneficial to listen while the other agents' behaviors are themselves evolving.

Overall the results support the idea that there is a "sweet spot" in communication bandwidth. Small, tailored increases

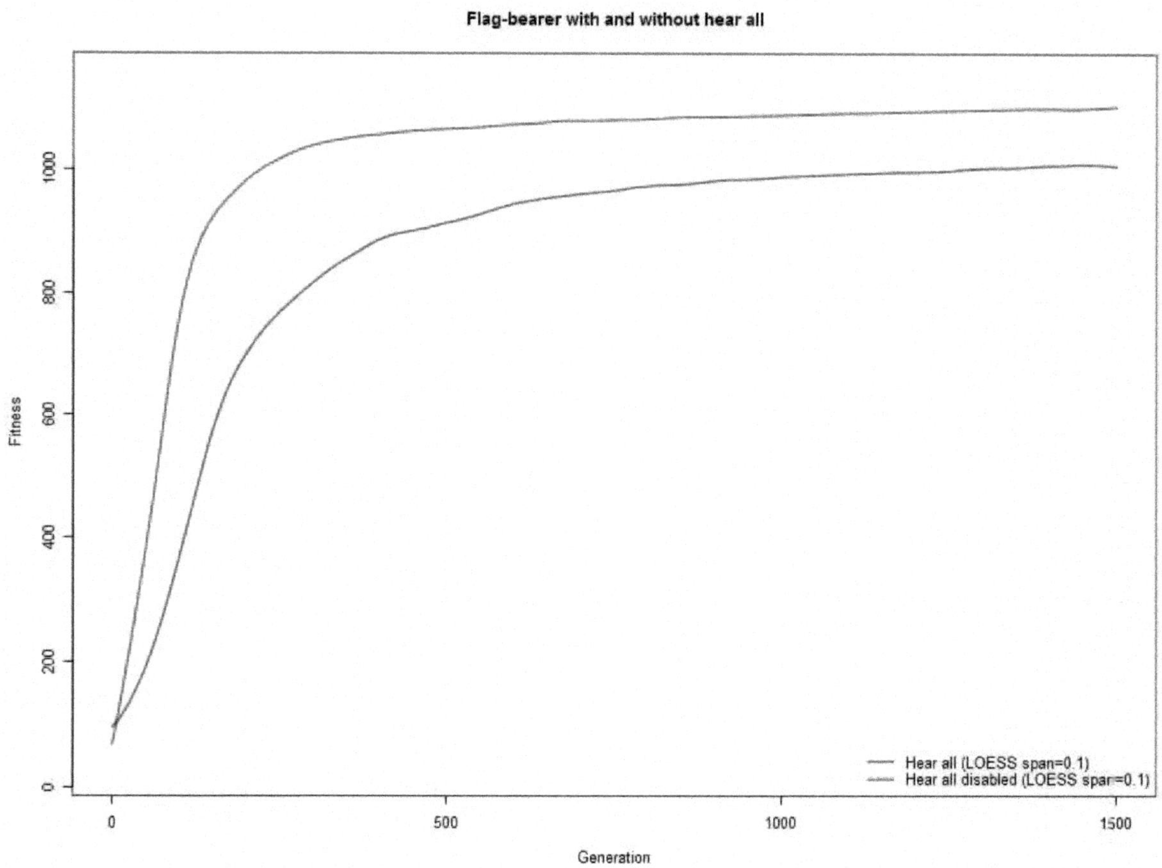

Figure 2: Average best teams over 40 trials with a flag-bearer and with and without hear-all. Under the hear-all condition the hyenas can evolve to listen to only one hyena, thereby replicating the flag-bearer cases. However, the data shows that evolution is faster and achieves better results with the more limited communication case

Table 5: Knockout results, averaged over 40 trials. False means that input was "knocked-out" of the best evolved clan and the clan was retested with that input returning a zero vector. Negative fitness is possible with repeated lion attacks. (The results in row 8 are for the same case as in Figure 4 row 8, differences are due to retesting the clans.) The last eight columns show the results of a Student's 2-tailed t-test between the respective rows, * denotes significance at the conservative 0.01 level, - represents non-significance. For example, the average fitness given in row 8 is significantly better than any of the other rows, but the fitness in row 7 is not significantly better than row 5 or 6. Knocking out the landmark, number calling, or both inputs have a small, but significant affect on fitness. Knocking out the flag-bearer input has a very large affect on fitness (rows 1-4), confirming that it is the most significant form of communication when we tested. Knocking out the other inputs has a smaller, but significant effect when the flag-bearer is available (row 8 versus 5, 6, or 7), but without the flag-bearer changing the other inputs does not significantly influence fitness.

	Flag Bearer	Land-mark	Number Calling	Avg. Fit (std. dev.)	1	2	3	4	5	6	7
1	False	False	False	-162.5 (658.2)	-						
2	False	False	True	-157.4 (816.2)	-	-					
3	False	True	False	-128.6 (788.8)	-	-	-				
4	False	True	True	-123.7 (664.4)	-	-	-	-			
5	True	False	False	668.3 (510.5)	*	*	*	*	-		
6	True	False	True	888.9 (382.8)	*	*	*	*	*	-	
7	True	True	False	842.4 (387.5)	*	*	*	*	-	-	-
8	True	True	True	1064 (95.12)	*	*	*	*	*	*	*

in communication, e.g. the flag-bear, can improve the rapid evolution of cooperation and coordination. In contrast, allowing unlimited communication, e.g. hear-all, has much smaller benefits, if any, and can interfere with the evolution of more limited and successful communication methods by overwhelming the useful signal with noise from other agents and thereby impeding the evolution of successful solutions.

8. REFERENCES

[1] W. Banzhaf, P. Nordin, R. E. Keller, and F. D. Francone. *Genetic Programming: An Introduction.* 1998.

[2] D. Braess, A. Nagurney, and T. Wakolbinger. On a paradox of traffic planning. *Transportation Science*, 39(4):446–450, 2005.

[3] S. Cooper. Optimal hunting group size: the need for lions to defend their kills against loss to spotted hyaenas. *African Journal of Ecology*, 29(2):130–136, 1991.

[4] G. Dudek, M. Jenkin, E. Milios, and D. Wilkes. A taxonomy for multi-agent robotics. *Autonomous Robots*, 3(4):375–397, 1996.

[5] A. E. Eiben and J. E. Smith. *Introduction to Evolutionary Computing.* Springer, 2003.

[6] J. Elman. Learning and development in neural networks: The importance of starting small. *Cognition*, 48(1):71–99, 1993.

[7] M. Ghavamzadeh, S. Mahadevan, and R. Makar. Hierarchical multi-agent reinforcement learning. *Autonomous Agents and Multi-Agent Systems*, 13(2):197–229, 2006.

[8] M. Land and R. Belew. No perfect two-state cellular automata for density classification exists. *Physical Review Letters*, 74(25):5148–5150, 1995.

[9] V. Lesser. Reflections on the Nature of Multi-Agent Coordination and Its Implications for an Agent Architecture. *Autonomous Agents and Multi-Agent Systems*, 1(1):89–111, 1998.

[10] S. Luke and L. Spector. Evolving teamwork and coordination with genetic programming. In *Proceedings of the first annual conference on genetic programming*, pages 150–156. MIT Press, 1996.

[11] M. Mitchell, J. Crutchfield, and R. Das. Evolving cellular automata with genetic algorithms: A review of recent work. In *Proceedings of the First International Conference on Evolutionary Computation and Its Applications (EvCAŠ96).* Citeseer, 1996.

[12] L. Panait and S. Luke. Cooperative Multi-Agent Learning: The State of the Art. *Autonomous Agents and Multi-Agent Systems*, 11(3):387–434, 2005.

[13] L. E. Parker. Current state of the art in distributed autonomous mobile robotics. In *Distributed Autonomous Robotic Systems*, pages 3–12. Springer, 2000.

[14] J. E. Smith, R. C. Van Horn, K. S. Powning, A. R. Cole, K. E. Graham, S. K. Memenis, and K. E. Holekamp. Evolutionary forces favoring intragroup coalitions among spotted hyenas and other animals. *Behavioral Ecology*, 21(2):284–303, 2010.

[15] H. Watts, L. Blankenship, S. Dawes, and K. Holekamp. Responses of spotted hyenas to lions reflect individual differences in behavior. *Ethology*, 2010.

On the Cumulative Effect of Bloat and Genetic Transposition on the Efficiency of Incremental Evolution of Snake-like Robot

Ivan Tanev, Tüze Kuyucu, Katsunori Shimohara
Department of Information Systems Design
Doshisha University, Kyotanabe, Japan
{itanev, tkuyucu, kshimoha}@mail.doshisha.ac.jp

ABSTRACT

We present a study on the cumulative effect of the bloat and the seeding of the initial population, inspired by genetic transposition (GT), on the efficiency of incremental evolution of simulated snake-like robot (Snakebot). In the proposed incremental genetic programming (IGP), the task of coevolving the locomotion gaits and sensing of the bot in a challenging environment is decomposed into two subtasks, implemented as two consecutive evolutionary stages. First, we use genetic programming (GP) with two ways of bloat management, (i) parsimony pressure which penalizes the bloat and (ii) no bloat control, to evolve two pools of sensor-less Snakebots. During the second stage of IGP, we use these pools to seed the initial population of Snakebots applying two methods of seeding: canonical seeding and GT-inspired seeding. The empirical results indicate that the efficiency of the first stage of IGP for both bloat control techniques is similar. However, the bloated bots contribute to a much more efficient second stage of evolution. Compared to the canonical seeding with parsimony bots, the GT-inspired seeding with bloated Snakebots yields about five times higher probability of success and similar decrease of computational effort of the second stage of IGP.

Categories and Subject Descriptors

I.2 [**Computing Methodologies**]: Artificial Intelligence

General Terms

Algorithms, Design, Experimentation

Keywords

Snakebot, genetic programming, bloat, genetic transposition, incremental GP

GECCO'12, July 7–11, 2012, Philadelphia, Pennsylvania, USA.

1. INTRODUCTION

The insufficient efficiency of the genetic programming (GP), together with its non-determinism are among the most important drawbacks that still hinder the wide adoption of the evolutionary paradigm for solving challenging real-world problems. The overall efficiency of GP depends on the cumulative effect of two major, relatively independent factors: (i) the computational effort, i.e., the number of genetic programs that should be evaluated in order to achieve a given probability of success, and (ii) the computational performance, i.e., the average run-time, required to evaluate a single genetic program. Therefore, most of the efforts of researchers and practitioners in evolutionary computation (EC) community are aligned along the two orthogonal directions–improving the computational effort and computational performance of GP.

The computational effort of GP could be improved in several ways, such as, incorporating a domain-specific knowledge into the key attributes of GP (e.g., genetic representation, genetic operations, etc.), imposing problem-specific syntax constrains (i.e., grammar) on the evolved genetic programs, employing probability-distribution models, etc. These approaches are usually intended to steer the simulated evolution towards the most promising areas in the explored (presumably rugged) fitness landscapes.

Another approach of improving computational effort of GP stems from the assumption that the main genetic operations (crossover and mutation), due to their randomness, are often damaging the partially constructed building blocks of the solution. Thus, the destructive effects of these operations could be limited if they are occasionally allowed to operate on the neutral genetic code, i.e., the code, that is irrelevant to the quality (fitness) of the corresponding genetic program. Moreover, such a neutral code might provide the simulated evolution with a "playground" where the latter can experiment with developing either novel-, or better-than-existing genotypic traits without the risk of damaging the already evolved ones.

In biology, the constructive role of neutrality has been well recognized, and noted to be a conducive mechanism in the evolution of many successful traits in biological organisms [8, 22]. The presence of neutral genes in Nature is often associated with smoother fitness landscapes, more robust genotypes and a support mechanism for discovering new phenotypes [8, 21, 22]. Similarly, the neutrality has also been a topic of interest and discussion in EC. In a recent article, Galvan-lopez et al. [6], provide a good overview of the role of neutrality in EC. The authors conclude their work with the open issues in this area and with their opinion on the studies that would be beneficial to a better understanding of the role of neutrality in EC. Due to the complex and, to some extent, unpredictable nature of the latter, it is often difficult to achieve an in-depth theoretical analysis of the effects of mechanisms and parameters on the performance of these algorithms.

The work of Ebner [5] suggests that the neutrality induced by the "junk code" provides better performance for the evolution of genetic programs. It was also reported that the neutrality contributes to a better efficiency of evolution in Cartesian Genetic Programming (CGP) [20, 23]. This conclusion remains to be a controversial one, however, as in a follow-up study Collins reported that the latter work is being flawed and that the effects of neutrality could in fact be degrading the overall performance of evolution [3]. This ongoing discussion on the possible beneficial effect of neutrality on the overall efficiency of GP is also stated by Galvan-lopez et al. [6], who note that "one needs to find ways of predicting when the addition of neutrality can be beneficial in practical situations." Although neutrality has been shown to be beneficial in complex, rugged landscapes with multiple optima [1, 4, 12], it also has adverse effects on the evolution of simple problems with a small number of optima and a smooth landscape.

Despite the beneficial effects of neutrality on the computational effort of GP, its implications on the overall performance of GP are highly controversial. One of the most important drawbacks of neutral code is that it often causes a degradation of computational performance of GP. Indeed, the neutral code in GP is often associated with the resulting bloat [2], or, with a sharp increase of the size (and complexity) of genetic programs in due course of the simulated evolution. Usually, the increased size of the evolved genetic programs does not correlate well with the convergence of the respective fitness values. Moreover, due to the cache memory effects, the runtime overhead of interpreting the genetic programs (represented in the computer memory as highly fragmented parse trees) grows faster than linear with the increase of their size. Therefore, applying parsimony pressure in order to limit the growth of the size of genetic programs is often seen as a natural way to alleviate bloat-induced degradation of computational performance of GP [7, 14].

In our previous work we developed an incremental approach in order to improve the efficiency of evolution of complex robotic artifacts in challenging environment. In the proposed incremental genetic programming (IGP), the task of coevolving the locomotion gaits and sensing of a simulated Snake-like robot (Snakebot) in a challenging environment is decomposed into two subtasks, implemented as two consecutive evolutionary stages. First, we use genetic programming to evolve a pool of sensorless Snakebots that move fast in a smooth, open terrain. Then, during the second stage, we use these pools to seed the initial population of Snakebots that are further subjected to coevolution of their locomotion control and sensing morphology in a challenging environment. Moreover, we also demonstrated a mechanism, inspired by the genetic transposition (GT) seen in nature, to create redundant, neutral genetic spaces by artificially bloating the bots at the stage of seeding the second stage of IGP. This mechanism was shown to provide better performance in terms of the computational effort required to evolve high quality Snakebots [11]. The resulting approach provided a valuable gain in the overall performance due to the negligible decrease in the computational performance–since the main contributor to the computational overhead is the simulation of the Snakebots during the evaluation phase. However, the effect of neutral code in the bots, evolved during the first stage of IGP, on the efficiency of the second stage was considered beyond the scope of the considered work.

The objective of this work is to investigate the cumulative effects of both the bloat and GT on the efficiency of IGP used for incremental evolution of locomotion of sensing Snakebot in a challenging environment with obstacles. The successful bots should feature the evolved (emergent) know-how about how to clear a narrow corridor by (i) moving fast, (ii) following the walls of the corridor, (iii) overcoming a number of randomly scattered small boxes, and (iv) circumnavigating large obstacles. In the proposed incremental GP (IGP), the task of coevolving the locomotion and the sensing of Snakebot in a challenging environment is decomposed into two sub-tasks, implemented as two consecutive evolutionary stages. First we employ GP to evolve a pool of simple, sensor-less bots that are able to move fast in a smooth, open terrain. Then, during the second stage, we use this pool to seed the initial population of the bots that are further subjected to coevolution of their locomotion control and sensing in the challenging environment. We are especially interested on how the degree of bloat (and, consequently, the associated neutrality), introduced during the fist stage of the incremental evolution, effects the overall performance of IGP.

Our choice of the application of GP is motivated by two arguments that, as we believe, are in favour of the neutrality. First, the considered problem is rather challenging, as it features a large and highly rugged fitness landscape [11]. Shipman demonstrated that neutrality helps the discovery of multiple phenotypes, but reduces the evolutionary performance for achieving faster solutions in simpler problems [15]. Within this context, we would like to investigate if, during the second stage of IGP, the neutrality would decrease the computational effort of evolving novel traits (e.g., the sensory abilities of the bot) in addition to the already evolved locomotion of the bots. And second, as in the most of the tasks in evolutionary robotics, it is the realistic simulation of the physics of moving complex robotic artefact, rather than the parsing of the genetic programs that consumes the most of the run-time of GP. Therefore, we anticipate no major bloat-induced degradation of the computational performance of GP, as experienced with GT.

The remaining of this document is organized as follows. Section 2 introduces the morphology and the moving abilities of the Snakebot. In Section 3 we discuss the key attributes of the proposed evolutionary framework. Section 4 presents the empirical result on the effect of bloat on the efficiency of incremental evolution of the bot in a challenging environment. Section 5 draws a conclusion.

2. SIDEWINDING AND SENSING SNAKE-LIKE MODULAR ROBOT

Snake-like robots feature potential robustness characteristics beyond the capabilities of most wheeled and legged vehicles, such as: the ability to traverse challenging terrain and insignificant performance degradation when partial damage is inflicted. Some useful features of snake-like robots include smaller size of the cross-sectional areas, stability, ability to operate in difficult terrain, good traction, and complete sealing of the internal mechanisms. Moreover, due to the modularity of their design, the snake-like robots feature high redundancy and fault tolerance [17]. Robots with such properties can be valuable for applications that involve exploration, reconnaissance, medicine and inspection. Designing a controller that can achieve optimal locomotion of a modular Snakebot is a challenging task due to the large number of degrees of freedom in the movement of segments of a Snakebot. The locomotion gait of such bots is often seen as an emergent property; observed at a higher level of consideration of complex, nonlinear, hierarchically organized systems, comprising many relatively simply-defined entities (morphological segments). In such complex systems the higher-level properties of the system and the lower-level properties of comprising entities cannot be directly induced from each other [13]. Therefore even if an effective incorporation of sensing information in fast and robust locomotion gaits might emerge from intuitively defined sensing morphology and simple motion patterns of morphological segments, neither the degree of optimality of the developed code nor the way of how to incrementally improve this code is evident to the human designer [10].

The previous research demonstrates that the control for a fast moving modular robotic organism could be automatically developed through various nature-inspired paradigms, based on models of learning and evolution. The work, presented in [17] demonstrates the use of GP for evolution of sensor-less sidewinding Snakebots in various environmental conditions. Furthermore, the coevolution of active sensing and the control of the locomotion gaits was demonstrated to be achievable, albeit difficult [11]. The control of a modular Snakebot with sensors for locomotion through a maze with obstacles was shown to be a challenging task to achieve via canonical GP even when ADFs were used. The use of incremental GP was shown to be a better approach, where initially the locomotion of the Snakebot in an obstacle free environment was achieved before evolving these Snakebots for a second time to utilize sensors. Furthermore, the use of a GT inspired incremental GP, which utilizes the addition of neutral code into the genotype of the seeding individuals for the second stage of the incremental GP runs had higher success rates as well as more robust solutions [11].

The morphology of the sensors, attached to each of the segments of the bot, coevolves with the way to incorporate the sensory readings into the control of locomotion of the bot. The genetically optimized morphological traits of the bot include the initial orientation, the timing of switching on, and the range of the simulated proximity sensors (e.g., laser range finders, LRF) attached to each of the segments of the bot. The emergent features of the evolved gaits include both the contact and contact-less wall-following navigation accomplished via adaptive, sensory-controlled differential steering of the fast moving sidewinding bot.

In this paper we investigate the coevolution of the active sensing and locomotion control of sidewinding Snakebot in the same environment presented in [11], which features a narrow corridor with several large obstacles and many randomly placed small obstacles constituting a rugged terrain. The sensors on the Snakebot used in this paper follow the same model as proposed in [18]: each segment of the Snakebot is provided with a fixed, immobile LRF with evolvable initial orientation, range and timing of firing. The most efficient locomotion gaits of Snakebot are not necessarily associated with the forward, rectilinear motions (and sidewinding might emerge as a fast and robust locomotion). Therefore, the eventual fusion of the readings of many sensors mounted in all the segments of the bot would provide Snakebot with the capability to perceive the features of surrounding environment along its whole body. In addition to the widening of the area of the perceived surroundings, multiple sensors offer the potential advantages of robustness to damage of some of them, dependability of the sensory information, and an ability to perceive the spatial features of the surrounding environment due to the motion parallax.

Scalable approaches that can handle multiple tasks are important in the evolution of Snakebot, as the complexity of evolving a controller for the described set up can become an issue. The size of evolutionary search space can be seen as a multiplication of the sizes of the search spaces of the following interdependent evolutionary sub-tasks:

- Evolution of the *control of locomotion*: the time patterns of turning angles of actuators that result in a fast locomotion of the bot.
- Evolution of the *morphology of the active sensing*: initial orientation of the sensors, their range, and timing of their activation.
- Evolution of the *incorporation of the sensor signals* into the control of locomotion of the bot.

The evolution of both the morphology and the incorporation of the signals from many sensors face the challenge of dealing with the uncertain sensor readings as they move synchronously with the coupled segments of the snake. Figure 1 illustrates how the initial orientation of the axes of the internal coordination systems of the segments of a bot dramatically differs from a sample instant orientation of these axes in a moving bot. A sensor fixed to the segment of a moving Snakebot would constantly change its spatial orientation, and consequently it might alternatively perceive no signal, a signal from the ground surface or from another segment of the snake (in both cases the sensory reading should be ignored), or eventually from an obstacle. Moreover, in the targeted environment the obstacle could be either a wall (to be followed), a large box (to be circumnavigated), or a small box (to be overcome).

The large search space of the evolution of the considered Snakebot results in an intractable computational effort, and as it was demonstrated in [11], canonical GP with Automat-

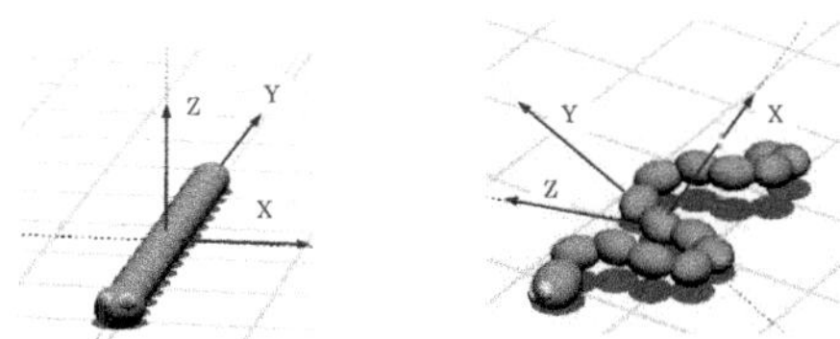

(a) Initial Orientation. (b) Intermediate Orientation.

Figure 1: Orientation of the axes of the internal coordination systems of the central segment at two different Snakebot positions.

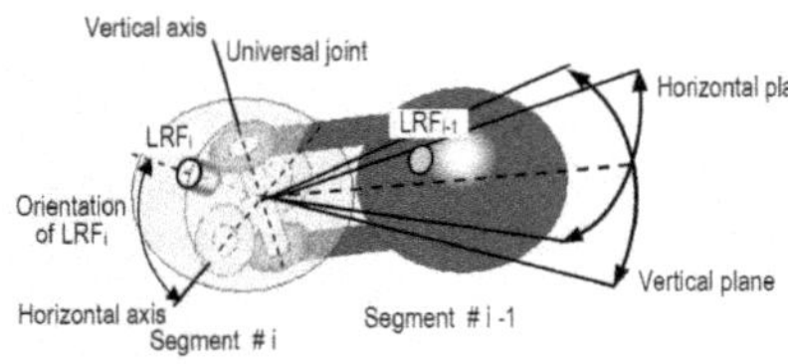

Figure 2: Morphological segments of Snakebot are linked via universal joint. Horizontal and vertical actuators attached to the joint perform rotation of the segment #i-1 in vertical and horizontal planes respectively. A single LRF is attached to each of the segments in the plane of the axes of the universal joint.

ically Defined Functions (ADF) is unable to effectively explore the emerging search space in a reasonable time frame.

3. EVOLUTIONARY FRAMEWORK AND THE SIMULATION ENVIRONMENT

For the experiments presented in this work we employ open dynamics engine (ODE) as a simulation platform for the Snakebot. ODE is a free, industrial quality software library for simulating articulated rigid body dynamics [16]. It is fast, flexible and robust, and it has built-in collision detection. Therefore, ODE is suitable for a realistic simulation of the physics of an entire Snakebot when applying actuating forces to its segments. The main ODE related parameters of the simulated Snakebot are same as elaborated in [17].

Snakebot is simulated in ODE as a set of 15 identical spherical morphological segments ("vertebrae"), linked together via universal (Cardan) joints (Figure 2). All joints feature identical angle limits and each joint has two attached actuators ("muscles"). A single LRF sensor, with a limited range is rigidly attached to each of the segments.

The functionality of the LRF can be defined by the values of the following set of parameters: (i) orientation, measured as an angle between the longitudinal axis of the sensor and the horizontal axis of the joint, (ii) range of the sensor (in cm), and (iii) the timing of activation, expressed as a threshold value of the turning angle of the horizontal actuator. The reading of LRF is a scalar value which corresponds inversely to the distance between the sensor and an object (if any within the sensor's range), measured along the longitudinal axis of the LRF. In the initial standstill position of Snakebot (as depicted in Figure 1(a)) the rotation axes of the actuators are oriented vertically (vertical actuator) and horizontally (horizontal actuator) and perform rotation of the joint in the horizontal and vertical planes respectively.

Considering the representation of Snakebot, the task of designing the fastest locomotion can be rephrased as developing temporal patterns of desired turning angles of horizontal and vertical actuators of each segment that result in fastest overall locomotion of Snakebot. The proposed representation of Snakebot as a homogeneous system comprising identical morphological segments is intended to significantly reduce the size of the search space of the GP.

For the evolution of the Snakebot, the genotype is represented as a triple consisting of a linear chromosome containing the encoded values of the three relevant parameters of LRF, and two parse trees corresponding to the algebraic expressions of the temporal patterns of the desired turning angles of both the horizontal and vertical actuators, respectively (Figure 3).

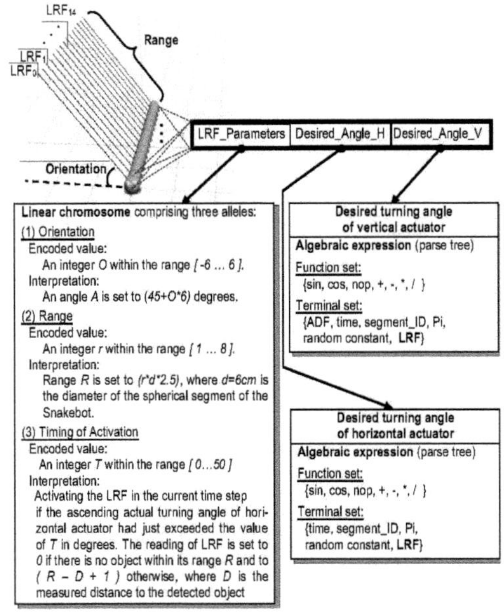

Figure 3: Genotype of the Snakebot consist of a triple containing the values of the parameters of LRF and two algebraic expressions of the temporal patterns of the desired turning angles of horizontal and vertical actuators, respectively. The genotype of Snakebot is homogeneous: therefore all segments feature the same triple.

The Snakebot is genotypically homogeneous in that the same triple is applied for the setup of the LRF and for the control of actuators of all morphological segments. The encoding of the parameters of LRF is as elaborated in Figure 3. The same figure also illustrates the function set and the terminal set of the GP, employed to evolve the control sequences of both actuators. Since the locomotion gaits by definition are periodical, the periodic functions sine and cosine are included in the function set of GP in addition to the basic algebraic functions. Terminal symbols include the variables time, segment_ID, an ADF, the reading of the sensor (LRF), and two constants: pi, and a random constant within the range [0, 2]. The incorporation of the terminal symbol segment_ID (a unique index of morphological segments of Snakebot) provides GP with an effective way to specialize (by phase, amplitude, frequency etc.) the genetically identical motion patterns of actuators of each of the morphological segments of the Snakebot.

The rationale of employing ADFs is based on the observation that the evolvability of straightforward, independent encoding of desired turning angles of both horizontal and vertical actuators is rather poor. Even without ADFs, GP is able to adequately explore the potentially large search space and ultimately discover the areas that correspond to fast locomotion gaits in the solution space. However, it was observed in the previous work of Tanev et al. [17] that not only the motion patterns of adjacent segments are correlated, but the motion patterns of horizontal and vertical actuators of each segment in fast locomotion gaits are highly correlated too. Moreover, discovering and preserving such correlation by GP is associated with enormous computational effort. ADFs, which provide a way of introducing modularity and reuse of code in GP [9], are employed in our approach to allow GP to explicitly evolve the correlation between motion patterns of horizontal and vertical actuators as shared fragments in algebraic expressions of desired turning angles of both actuators. Furthermore, we observed that the best results are obtained by; (i) allowing the use of ADF as a terminal symbol in algebraic expression of desired turning angle of vertical actuator only, and (ii) evaluating the value of ADF by equalizing it to the value of currently evaluated desired turning angle of horizontal actuator.

Table 1: Main parameters of GP.

Category	Value
Genotype	LRF parameters (linear chromosome) Horizontal actuator control (parse tree) Vertical actuator control(parse tree)
Population Size	200 individuals
Selection	Binary Selection ratio: 0.1 Reproduction ratio: 0.9
Elitism	4 individuals
Mutation Rate	0.01
Trial Interval	16s (400 time steps of 40ms per step)
Termination Criteria	(Fitness=120) or (Tot. No. of generations=80)

The main GP (hence the EA) parameters are summarized in Table 1. We use a DOM/XML-based implementation of GP [19], with binary tournament selection and a single point crossover. The crossover point is randomly selected between the three components of the genotype (as shown in Figure 3), unless stated otherwise. The mutation randomly alters either a value of an allele in the linear chromosome representing the parameters of LRF, or a sub-tree in one of the two parse tress that correspond to the temporal patterns of the control sequences of actuators.

4. EXPERIMENTAL SETUP

The experimental setup of employing IGP for evolution of Snakebot is illustrated in Figure 4. During the first stage of IGP, the locomotion of sensor-less bot is evolved in a smooth terrain with two cases of bloat control: parsimony pressure penalizing bloat (case 1a, pBC) and no bloat control (case 1b, noBC), respectively. In the former case, the fitness value is penalized by $\frac{1}{10}$ times the number of tree nodes in the genotype of the bot. In the case of no bloat control, the fitness value is not altered with respect to the complexity of the genotype of the bot. Each of these two cases are executed for 40 independent evolutionary runs. The target fitness value is 100, which corresponds to the velocity of locomotion that displace the Snakebot during the simulated trial of 16s a distance equal to twice its length.

The best six bots from each of these two cases are then used as seeding bots for the stage 2 of IGP, initialized by the following two seeding mechanisms: canonical seeding (stage 2a) and seeding via GT (stage 2b) respectively. In canonical seeding, 6 individuals from stage 1 are used "as is", while the remaining 194 individuals in the population are created randomly. In the seeding via GT all 200 individuals in population are created by incorporating the entire genomes of the 6 best bots from stage 1: 6 individuals being used "as is", and the remaining 194 individuals created using the GT inspired method described in Figure 4.

For the second stage of IGP, there are two experimental cases as well (shown in Figure 4 as stage 2a and 2b, respectively). These two stages differ in the mechanism of seen only, and feature identical evolutionary conditions. The experimental cases of both stages 2a and 2b feature the same parsimony pressure conditions - a penalty to the fitness of by $\frac{1}{10}$ times the number of tree nodes in the genotype. By applying bloat control in the second stage of IGP we could obtain good, yet genetically simple bots (i.e., Occam razor). These simple genotypes could be better comprehended and modified (if needed) by human, and efficiently implemented in the controller of the bot.

The difference in stages 2a and 2b is in the used two mechanisms of seeding: canonical seeding (stage 2a) and seeding via GT (stage 2b), respectively (Figure 4). In canonical seeding, 6 individuals from stage 1 are used "as is", while the remaining 194 individuals in the population are created randomly. In the seeding via GT all 200 individuals in population are created by incorporating the entire genomes of the 6 best bots from stage 1 (shown as Transposon A) in the randomly initialized genotype (Transposons B and C).

The fitness function is based on distance the Snakebot travels during the trial. The normalized fitness of 120 corresponds to the distance required to be traveled during the trial in order to clear a narrow corridor covered with obstacles of various sizes. The evolution is terminated if the bot clears the corridor (fitness is 120) or if the maximum number of generations is reached.

4.1 Stage 1: Evolution of Locomotion of Sensorless Snakebot

We executed 40 independent runs for both the Stage 1a (pBC) and 1b (noBC) of IGP, respectively. The aggregated fitness convergence characteristics are shown in Figure 5. As the figure illustrates, the use of a simple parsimony pressure, as described earlier, has no implications significant on the fitness convergence characteristics, and therefore, on the overall computational effort of the first stage of IGP. We also visually inspected the locomotion gaits of the successful Snakebots from each of these two cases and confirmed that

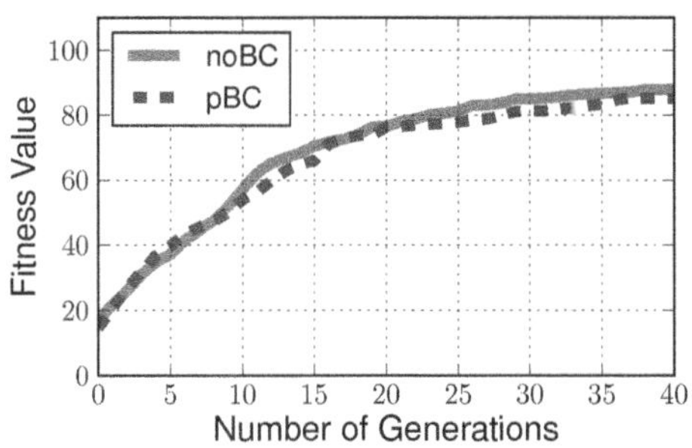

Figure 5: The convergence of average fitness during the first stage of IGP with two cases of bloat control - parsimony pressure (pBC) and no bloat control (noBC), respectively. The results are aggregated over 40 independent runs.

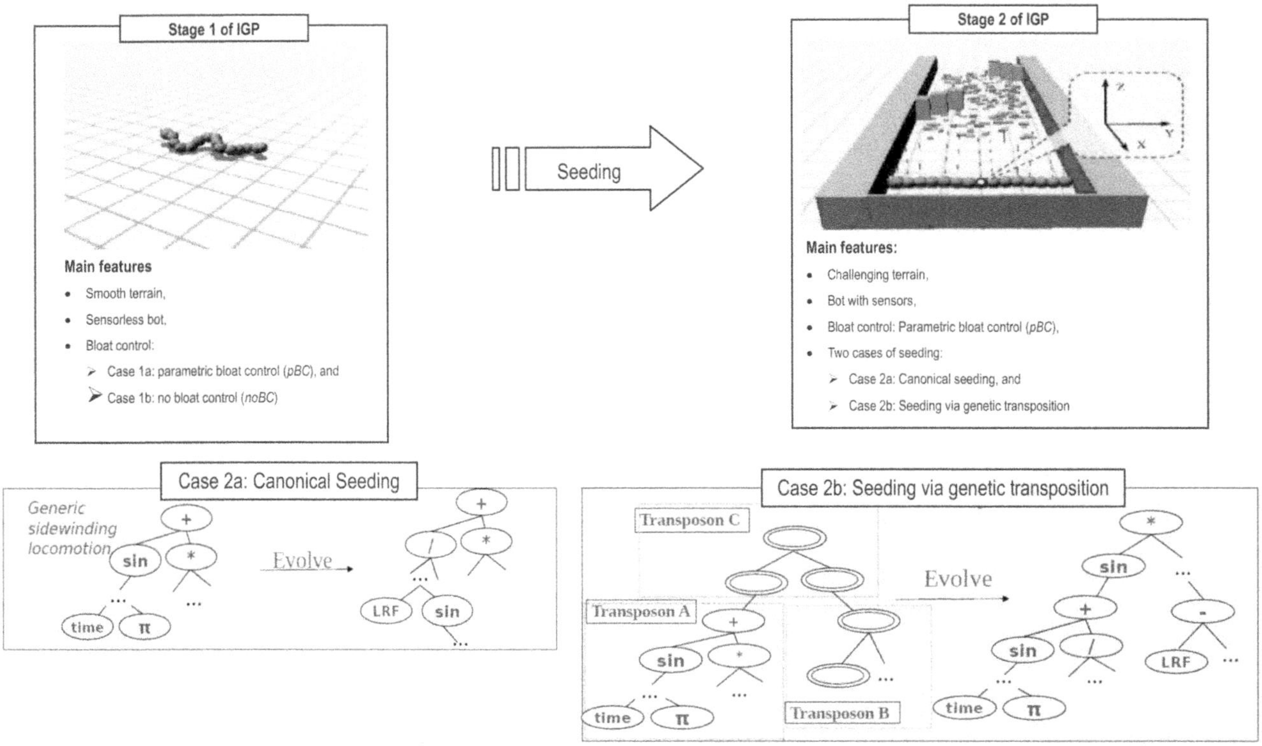

Figure 4: The two stages of IGP. In stage 1, the locomotion of senssorless bot is evolved in a smooth terrain with two cases of bloat control: parsimony pressure penalizing bloat (case 1a, pBC) and no bloat control (case 1b, noBC), respectively. The best six bots from each of these two cases are then used as seeding bots for the stage 2 of IGP, initialized by the following two seeding mechanisms: canonical seeding (stage 2a) and seeding via GT (stage 2b) respectively. In canonical seeding, 6 individuals from stage 1 are used "as is", while the remaining 194 individuals in the population are created randomly. In the seeding via GT all 200 individuals in population are created by incorporating the entire genomes of the 6 best bots from stage 1 (shown as Transposon A) in the randomly initialized genotype (Transposons B and C).

they are similar. The use of parsimony pressure did exactly what it is supposed to: the only significant difference between the two experimental cases was in the average tree sizes, and the use of parsimony pressure provided solutions with smallest tree sizes. The statistical results are shown in Table 2.

4.2 Stage 2a: Coevolution of Sensing and Locomotion via Canonical Seeding

We executed 40 independent evolutionary runs using canonical seeding with two different pools (of six best Snakebots each) of seeding bots, obtained from stages 1a (pBC) and 1b (noBC), respectively (Figure 4). The six bots from these pools are used as elite individuals and the remaining 194 individuals of the initial population are generated randomly. The average fitness convergence characteristics are shown in Figure 6(a). Unlike the runs from the first stage, there is a significant difference in the performance of the evolutionary runs using different seeds. The best evolutionary performance is obtained when seeds that were previously evolved with no bloat control are used, and the worst performance is observed when seeds with parsimony pressure are used. In average, the seeds with no bloat control reaches the best fitness values of the parsimony seeds about five times faster.

Table 2: Results of evaluation of IGP. Stages 2a and 2b are initialized via canonical and GT-inspired seeding, respectively. F_{avr} is the average fitness of population in the final generation, R_{succ} is the number of successful runs of the second stage (of 40), S_{avr} is the average size of genetic programs (number of tree nodes) in the final generation, and $SSeed_{avr}$ is the average size of genetic programs in the pool of the six seeding bots, respectively.

Stage of IGP		F_{avr}	R_{succ}	S_{avr}	$SSeed_{avr}$
Stage 1	noBC	101	NA	105.3	NA
	pBC	100.5	NA	82.4	NA
Stage 2a	noBC	87.3	8	197	131
	pBC	68	3	122	85
Stage 2b	noBC	95	16	220	131
	pBC	89.5	6	135	85

The probability of successful runs (i.e., the bot clears the narrow corridor) is shown in Figure 6(b) for the two cases of IGP runs. As the figure illustrates, a clearer distinction between the runs using no bloat control (noBC) and the parsimony pressure (pBC) can be seen; the former case feature both a better convergence of the fitness and higher probability of success. Moreover, because the realistic simulation of the physics of the bot (rather than the parsing of the genotype) consumes most of the run-time of GP, no major bloat-induced degradation of the computational performance of IGP is observed.

The statistical information from these experiments is summarized in Table 2.

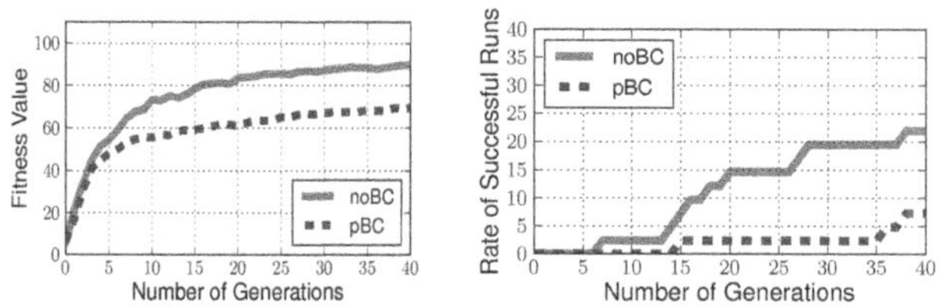

(a) (b)

Figure 6: The convergence of average fitness (a), and the probability of successful runs (b) of stage 2a (with canonical seeding) of IGP. pBC and noBC denote the results, obtained from the pool of seeding bots evolved during stages 1a and 1b, respectively. The results are aggregated over 40 independent runs.

4.3 Stage 2b: Sensing and locomotion via IGP with GT

We conducted 40 independent evolutionary runs using GT-inspired seeding from two different pools of bots (of six best Snakebots each), obtained from stages 1a (pBC) and 1b (noBC) of IGP, respectively (Figure 4). Analogically to the experimental setup of stage 2a, six bots from the two pools are used as elite individuals. However, the remaining 194 individuals of the population are created via the GT-inspired seeding mechanism as detailed in [11] and illustrated in Figure 4. The genome of the seeding bot is used to form only a part of the new individual, where the rest of the genetic structure is generated randomly. As shown in Figure 7(a), the average fitness convergence of the seeds, evolved without bloat control (noBC) during stage 1b of IGP, is much faster than the seed with parsimony pressure (pBC). The runs with seeds evolved with no bloat control reach the best fitness values of the parsimony seeds almost three times faster (fitness of 90 is achieved in 15 vs 40 generations).

As Figure 7(b) illustrates, the probability of success of the runs using seeds evolved under parsimony pressure have success chances of 20% after 40 generations. The same probability of success is reached in 13 generations (i.e., three times faster) by runs using seeds evolved with no bloat control. The best probability of success of 40% after 40 generations is achieved by seeds evolved with no parsimony pressure.

5. CONCLUSIONS

In this work we studied the cumulative effect of bloat and seeding inspired by genetic transposition (GT) on the efficiency of incremental evolution of simulated sensing snake-like robot in a challenging environment. As the experimental results suggest, the use of a simple parsimony pressure has

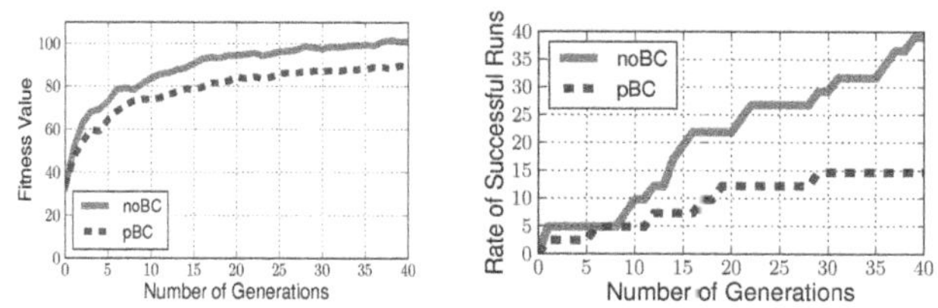

(a) (b)

Figure 7: The convergence of average fitness (a), and the probability of successful runs (b) of stage 2b (with GT-inspired seeding) of IGP. pBC and noBC denote the results, obtained from the pool of seeding bots evolved during stages 1a and 1b, respectively. The results are aggregated over 40 independent runs.

no immediate effect on the efficiency of evolution of the first stage of incremental genetic programming (IGP) - evolution of fast moving sensor-less bots in a smooth terrain. However, when, during the second stage of IGP, evolved genetic programs are reused for further development under different conditions than the first stage, the neutrality caused by the bloated genetic programs are beneficial for the more efficient evolution of the sensing abilities of the bot. We assume that this is due to the presence of a neutral code (i.e., a code which has no immediate effect on the fitness), that could be utilized by IGP as an evolutionary playground to develop the needed sensory abilities without the risk of damaging the already evolved, fast locomotion.

Furthermore, we demonstrate that the best performance is achieved when bloated seeds are used with GT-inspired seeding. In average, the GT-inspired seed with bloated bots features about five times higher probability of success and similar decrease of computational effort of the second stage of IGP than canonical seed with parsimony bots. GT aims to introduce additional neutrality to the seeding genome in order to provide a safe playground for the genetic operators. The success of GT was demonstrated to significantly surpass the performance shown by canonical seeding in an earlier work [11]. In the experiments presented here, the neutrality introduced by GT is shown to complement the neutrality from bloated seeds, providing the best evolutionary performance as a result. The experimental results suggest that evolution benefits from the presence of different forms of neutrality introduced by both GT and bloated seeds when a two-stage IGP is used. Conversely, the explicit parsimony pressure negatively affects the computational effort of evolution.

The presented findings could be applied for the domains where the implementation of the side effects, rather than the parsing of genetic representation, is by far the most computationally expensive aspect of fitness evaluation. However, the overall effect of the interplay between (i) the bloat-induced degradation of the computational performance, and (ii) the possible improvement of the computational effort should be carefully considered before applying the proposed approach in domains where the parsing and evaluating the very genetic programs dominate the run-time overhead of the evolutionary system.

6. ACKNOWLEDGMENTS

The presented work is part of a project funded by Japan Society for the Promotion of Science (JSPS).

7. REFERENCES

[1] W. Beaudoin, S. Verel, P. Collard, and C. Escazu. Deceptiveness and neutrality: The nd family of fitness landscapes. In *GECCO 2006: Proceedings of the 2006 conference on genetic and evolutionary computation*, pages 507–514, 2006.

[2] M. Brameier and W. Banzhaf. Neutral variations cause bloat in linear gp. In *Proceedings of the 6th European conference on Genetic programming*, EuroGP'03, pages 286–296. Springer-Verlag, 2003.

[3] M. Collins. Finding needles in haystacks is harder with neutrality. In *GECCO 2005: Proceedings of the 2005 conference on Genetic and evolutionary computation*, volume 2, pages 1613–1618, 2005.

[4] B. Doerr, M. Gnewuch, N. Hebbinghaus, and F. Neumann. A rigorous view on neutrality. In *Evolutionary Computation, 2007. CEC 2007. IEEE Congress on*, pages 2591 –2597, sept. 2007.

[5] M. Ebner. On the search space of genetic programming and its relation to nature's search space. In *Proceedings of the 1999 Congress on Evolutionary Computation. CEC 99*, pages 1357–1361, 1999.

[6] E. GalvÃąn-LÃşpez, R. Poli, A. Kattan, M. OâĂŹNeill, and A. Brabazon. Neutrality in evolutionary algorithmsâĂę what do we know? *Evolving Systems*, 2:145–163, 2011.

[7] S. Gelly, O. Teytaud, N. Bredeche, and M. Schoenauer. Universal Consistency and Bloat in GP. *Revue d'Intelligence Artificielle*, 20:805–827, 2006.

[8] M.A. Huynen, P.F. Stadler, and W. Fontana. Smoothness within ruggedness: the role of neutrality in adaptation. In *Proceedings of the National Academy of Sciences of the United States of America*, volume 93, pages 397–401, 1996.

[9] J.R. Koza. *Genetic programming II: automatic discovery of reusable programs.* MIT Press, Cambridge, MA, USA, 1994.

[10] J.R. Koza, M.A. Keane, J. Yu, F.H. Bennett, and W. Mydlowec. Automatic creation of human-competitive programs and controllers by means of genetic programming. *Genetic Programming and Evolvable Machines*, 1:121–164, 2000.

[11] T. Kuyucu, I.T. Tanev, and K. Shimohara. Incremental genetic programming via genetic transpositions for efficient coevolution of locomotion and sensing of simulated snake-like robot. In *European Conference on Artificial Life*, pages 439–446, 2011.

[12] J. Lobo, J. H. Miller, and W. Fontana. Neutrality in technological landscapes. *Santa Fe Working Paper*, 2004.

[13] H.J. Morowitz. *The Emergence of Everything: How the World Became Complex.* Oxford Uni. Press, 2002.

[14] R. Poli and N.F. McPhee. Covariant parsimony pressure for genetic programming. Technical Report CES-480, Department of Computing and Electronic Systems, University of Essex, UK, 2008.

[15] R. Shipman. Genetic redundancy: Desirable or problematic for evolutionary adaptation. In *4th International Conf. on Artificial Neural Networks and Genetic Algorithms (ICANNGA'99)*, pages 1–11, 1999.

[16] R. Smith. *Open Dynamics Engine*, 2004.

[17] I. Tanev, T. Ray, and A. Buller. Automated evolutionary design, robustness and adaptation of sidewinding locomotion of simulated snake-like robot. *IEEE Transactions on Robotics*, 21:632–645, 2005.

[18] I. Tanev and K. Shimohara. Co-evolution of active sensing and locomotion gaits of simulated snake-like robot. In *Proceedings of the 10th annual conference on Genetic and evolutionary computation*, GECCO '08, pages 257–264, New York, NY, USA, 2008. ACM.

[19] I.T. Tanev. Dom/xml-based portable genetic representation of the morphology, behavior and communication abilities of evolvable agents. *Artificial Life and Robotics*, 8:52–56, 2004.

[20] V.K. Vassilev and J.F. Miller. The advantages of landscape neutrality in digital circuit evolution. In *Proceedings of the 3rd International Conference on Evolvable Systems: From Biology to Hardware*, pages 252–26. Springer, 2000.

[21] A. Wagner. Robustness, evolvability, and neutrality. *FEBS Letters*, 579(8):1772–1778, 2005.

[22] C.O. Wilke, J.L. Wang, C. Ofria, R.E. Lenski, and C. Adami. Evolution of digital organisms at high mutation rates leads to survival of the flattest. *Nature*, 412:331–333, 2001.

[23] T. Yu and J.F. Miller. The role of neutral and adaptive mutation in an evolutionary search on the onemax problem. In *GECCO Late Breaking Papers'02*, pages 512–519, 2002.

Efficient Algorithms for Extracting Biological Key Pathways with Global Constraints

Jan Baumbach
Max Planck Institute for Informatics
Saarbrücken, Germany

Tobias Friedrich
Max Planck Institute for Informatics
Saarbrücken, Germany

Timo Kötzing
Max Planck Institute for Informatics
Saarbrücken, Germany

Anton Krohmer
Saarland University
Saarbrücken, Germany

Joachim Müller
Max Planck Institute for Informatics
Saarbrücken, Germany

Josch Pauling
Max Planck Institute for Informatics
Saarbrücken, Germany

ABSTRACT

The integrated analysis of data of different types and with various interdependencies is one of the major challenges in computational biology. Recently, we developed KeyPathwayMiner, a method that combines biological networks modeled as graphs with disease-specific genetic expression data gained from a set of cases (patients, cell lines, tissues, etc.). We aimed for finding all maximal connected sub-graphs where all nodes but K are expressed in all cases but at most L, i.e. key pathways. Thereby, we combined biological networks with OMICS data, instead of analyzing these data sets in isolation. Here we present an alternative approach that avoids a certain bias towards hub nodes: We now aim for extracting all maximal connected sub-networks where all but at most K nodes are expressed in all cases but in total (!) at most L, i.e. accumulated over all cases and all nodes in a solution. We call this strategy GLONE (global node exceptions); the previous problem we call INES (individual node exceptions). Since finding GLONE-components is computationally hard, we developed an Ant Colony Optimization algorithm and implemented it with the KeyPathwayMiner Cytoscape framework as an alternative to the INES algorithms. KeyPathwayMiner 3.0 now offers both the INES and the GLONE algorithms. It is available as plugin from Cytoscape and online at `http://keypathwayminer.mpi-inf.mpg.de`.

Categories and Subject Descriptors

J.3 [**Life and Medical Sciences**]: Biology and genetics

General Terms

Algorithms, Experimentation

Keywords

Ant Colony Optimization, Systems Biology, Gene Expression, Epigenetics

1. INTRODUCTION

Since the introduction of the so-called next generation sequencing technology it appears that we have finally arrived in the post-genome era. At the web site of the National Center for Biotechnology Information we find registered sequencing projects for 1520 eukaryotes, 8604 prokaryotes and 2987 viruses [21]. However, we still lack fundamental knowledge about crucial genetic programs, the interplay of genes and their products (the proteins) and their biochemical regulations and fine-tuning. We know very little about how cells, organs and tissues regulate survival, reproduction, movement, etc. in response to changing environmental conditions [20, 7]. The most important control mechanisms are transcriptional gene regulations and protein-protein interactions [8, 17]. They are typically modeled as graphs, where nodes correspond to genes/proteins and edges to biological interactions between them [9, 10]. In this regard, we may study statistical network properties [13], discuss node degree distributions [5], investigate network centrality node lists [4], or identify protein complexes [26], to name a few possibilities. On the other hand, we use so-called OMICS technologies for measuring the activity of biological entities within living cells under different conditions (stimuli, diseases, infections, etc.). The most prominent examples for such technologies are microarrays or RNA-seq (transcriptomics), genome-wide promoter/gene methylation assays (epigenetics), mass spectrometry (proteomics), and ion mobility spectrometry (metabolomics). A typical example for high-throughput OMICS data analysis (with relation to this paper) is cancer sub-typing based on the identification of genome-wide gene expression similarities [24, 25], to give only one of many possible examples. Recent advances in large-scale systems biology wet lab machinery provided us with huge amounts of both network data and OMICS data. In the Gene Expression Omnibus (GEO), the standard repository for microarray, RNA-seq and methylation profiling data, we have 630,000 samples measured at almost 10,000 platforms available for public download [12]. The most impressive number on the network side comes from the PSICQUIC platform, a SOAP-based online querying interface and meta-database that covers 16 interactome databases and provides access to 16 million protein-protein interactions of various evidence levels and for several species [3].

Although the integrated analysis of data from different types and with various interdependencies is one of the major challenges in computational biology, both kinds of data types, the rather static network data as well as the quite dynamic, case-specific OMICS data are usually studied in isolation. Therefore, we recently developed KeyPathwayMiner [2, 1], a method that combines biological networks modeled as graphs with disease-specific genetic expression data gained from a set of cases (patients, cell lines, tissues, etc.). Our approach aims to find all maximal connected subgraphs, w.r.t. the number of nodes, where all nodes but K are expressed in all cases but at most L. We refer to these maximal connected components as key pathways. First, we checked, for each node individually, whether the L-condition was fulfilled (expressed in all cases but L). If not, we marked the corresponding nodes as exception nodes, of which we allow at most K in a valid solution. We call this strategy INES (individual node exceptions). Using INES means, however, that we tend to prefer nodes with high degrees (hub nodes) as exception nodes, since they are more likely to maximize the sub-graph by connecting it with others. Depending on the underlying real world question, this bias may or may not be desired. Here we present an alternative approach that tackles this problem by slightly varying the optimization problem: Now we aim to extract all maximal connected sub-networks where all but at most K nodes are expressed in all cases but in total (!) at most L, i.e. accumulated over all cases and all nodes in a solution. In other words, a solution is valid when it is maximal w.r.t. the number of nodes and for all nodes but K we have at most L nonexpressed cases. We call this strategy GLONE (global node exceptions). Since finding such GLONE-components is NP-hard, we developed an Ant Colony Optimization algorithm and implemented it with the KeyPathwayMiner Cytoscape framework as an alternative to the INES algorithms. We demonstrate the power of GLONE by utilizing the same data sets that were used for evaluating the INES algorithms of the previous KeyPathwayMiner release [1] as well as related computational tools [23, 14, 2, 11]: the human protein-protein interaction network together with gene expression data of Huntington's disease patients.

2. DESCRIPTION OF ALGORITHMS

The formal model for the problem is as follows. Given an undirected graph $G = (V, E)$ and a node labeling function $f\colon V \to \mathbb{N}$, as well as parameters L and K, find a set of nodes $S \subseteq V$ *of maximal cardinality* such that

- S in G is connected;
- the sum over $f(v)$ for all $v \in S$, except the K nodes with highest $f(v)$, is at most L.

We call such a set S a *GLONE-component*. This problem is NP-hard (see [23] for a discussion). Intuitively, the nodes of the graph correspond to genes/proteins and the edges to biological interactions between them. For each node v, $f(v)$ corresponds, for example, to the number of *not* differentially expressed cases.

Algorithm 1: Max-Min Ant System

Input: $G = (V, E)$; f; L; K;
initialize all pheromones to 1/2 ;
foreach *v in the start node list* **do**
  let $S^* = \{V\}$;
  while *some improvement recently* **do**
    construct a solution S according to Algorithm 2;
    apply local search to S;
    if $|S^*| < |S|$ **then** $S^* = S$
return *best solution found*;

In [16] an ACO algorithm framework for finding solutions to subset problems was given. To find GLONE-components, we follow the general ideas inherent in this framework (as we are looking for a subset of nodes), but in pheromone update rules, follow an approach according to a Max-Min Ant System [22]. In what follows, we give a detailed description of our algorithm; an overview is given in Algorithm 1.

A list of all parameters to the algorithm, as well as the default values used for testing, can be found in Table 1. Experimentation showed that the default parameter values result in good solutions; careful adjustments of the values can lead to much faster termination, but possibly at the cost of a somewhat lower quality of the solutions (see also Figure 1).

Parameter	Value
ALPHA (Pheromone intensity)	2.0
BETA (Edge desirability importance)	5.0
RHO (Pheromone decay rate)	0.1
MAX_RUNS_WITHOUT_CHANGE (Max. iterations without change)	100
NUM_STARTNODES (Number of starting nodes)	100
TAU_MIN (Minimum node pheromone value)	0.1

Table 1: Parameter specification (default values).

The algorithm maintains a single best-so-far solution, which is the only solution used to update the pheromones. Pheromones are deposited on the nodes of the input graph. The algorithm makes a number of independent runs with different start nodes (the number is specified by a parameter of the algorithm). In each iteration, each ant grows a connected subgraph of the input graph beginning at the current start node until no node can be added without exceeding the limit in cumulative L-value (ignoring the K most costly nodes). After this, a local search is applied: We try all nodes u from the subgraph of the ant such that removing this node will not make the subgraph disconnected; we now remove u and add neighboring nodes in a greedy fashion until no nodes can be added without violating the constraint imposed by the K and L values. The number of ants per iteration is a parameter of the algorithm.

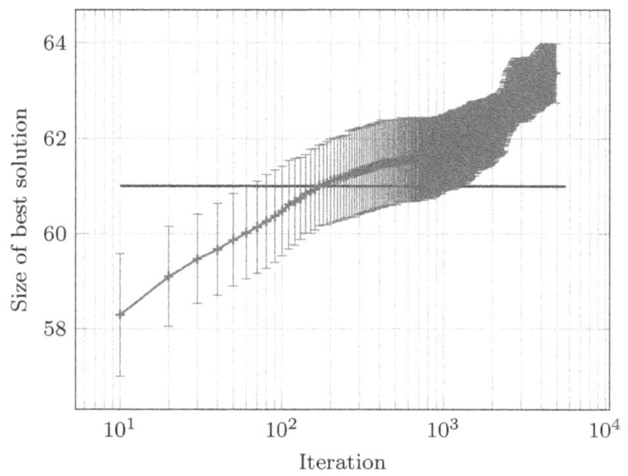

Figure 1: Comparison of the greedy algorithm (blue line) and our ACO algorithm (red chart with standard deviations).

Let a node v be given. The amount of pheromone on v is denoted by $\tau(v)$; we also associate a *heuristic value* with v, denoted by $\eta(v)$, equal to $1/f(v)$. This heuristic value is fixed during a run of the algorithm and is aimed at directing the algorithm to promising areas (low f-value). We make a multiplicative trade-off between pheromone value and heuristic value and choose node v proportional to

$$\tau(v)^{\alpha} \cdot \eta(v)^{\beta}.$$

Both α and β are parameters of the algorithm. Note that only nodes connected to the component constructed so far are considered.

All pheromones values are kept between the *pheromone borders* $\tau_{\min}$ and $\tau_{\max} = 1 - \tau_{\min}$ and initialized to 0.5, following the scheme of a Max-Min Ant System. When updating with the best-so-far solution S, the pheromone τ is updated according to the following rule. For all nodes v,

$$\tau_{\text{new}}(v) = \begin{cases} \min((1-\rho)\tau(v) + \rho, \tau_{\max}), & \text{if } v \in S; \\ \max((1-\rho)\tau(v), \tau_{\min}), & \text{otherwise.} \end{cases}$$

The algorithm stops the run for the current start node when there were no improvements in a fixed number of iterations (a parameter to the algorithm). The list of start nodes is deterministically created by choosing the nodes with the smallest average f-value of their neighborhood. Other heuristics are possible here, this one has shown a good performance in experiments.

Algorithm 2: Component Construction from v

Input: start vertex v;
$S = \{v\}$;
while $FN(S) \neq \emptyset$ **do**
  let $R = \sum_{u \in FN(S)} \tau(u)^{\alpha} \cdot \eta(u)^{\beta}$;
  choose $u \in FN(S)$ with probability $\tau(u)^{\alpha} \cdot \eta(u)^{\beta} / R$;
  $S = S \cup \{u\}$;
return S;

The construction of a solution is an iterative procedure detailed in Algorithm 2. For any set S of nodes of the input graph, we let $N(S) = \{u \mid u \notin S \wedge \exists v \in S \text{ s.t. } \{u, v\} \in E\}$ be the set of all nodes in the graph which have a neighbor in S. For a connected set S, a node $u \in N(S)$ can be added to S, if $S \cup \{u\}$ is a feasible solution. We call such nodes *feasible neighbors*, and denote the set of all feasible neighbors by $FN(S)$.

We observed that after a few hundred iterations our ACO algorithm always outperforms the greedy solution. Figure 1 shows an experimental comparison for $L = 400$ and $K = 2$ on the Ulitskty *et al.* data set [23]. The size of the solution of the greedy algorithm is the blue line. The quality of the best-so-far solution after each iteration and the respective standard deviations for 100 runs is shown in red. Note that the horizontal axis is scaled logarithmically. For this parameter setting, the best-so-far solution of our ACO algorithm is better than the solution of the greedy algorithm after 160 iterations on average. The behavior is similar for other parameter combinations. However, the greedy approach is significantly faster than the ACO.

3. EXPERIMENTS

In this chapter we elucidate the GLONE algorithm's characteristics and performance. We first compare the results to our previous algorithm INES (KPM 2.0 ACO) [1]. Subsequently, we present a comparison regarding identified known relevant genes to other software approaches. In the closing section we provide an analysis showing the running times and behavior of the GLONE algorithm in relation to varying parameter specifications.

3.1 Data

For evaluation purposes we use a human PPI network containing 7.384 nodes and 23,462 interactions extracted and compiled from several interaction databases. For the extraction of disorder-specific key pathways, we used gene expression data taken from the Gene Expression Omnibus (GEO) which was obtained using oligonucleotide arrays [6]. This data set consists of 38 affected samples taken from the caudate nucleus region of the brain. Since there is no commonly accepted gold standard data, we used the same data that was used by Ulitsky *et al.* [23]. To ensure comparability, we also used the same thresholds and p-values to determine differential gene expressions in our pre-processing. Note that generating an artificial gold standard is not feasible. We would be able to see that our algorithms solve the combinatorial optimization problem but not if the optimization model itself is appropriate. Hence, we work with real world data instead.

3.2 Evaluation

We tested the applicability of GLONE by comparing the found relevant genes to the following sources of already known and published HD-relevant genes:

- KEGG HD Pathway: The KEGG HD Pathway is part of the KEGG Pathway database [18] which consists of most of the known metabolic pathways and some of the known regulatory pathways.
- Calcium Signaling Pathway: This pathway is related to the KEGG HD Pathway and is also available at the KEGG Pathway database. It plays an important role in the development of HD.

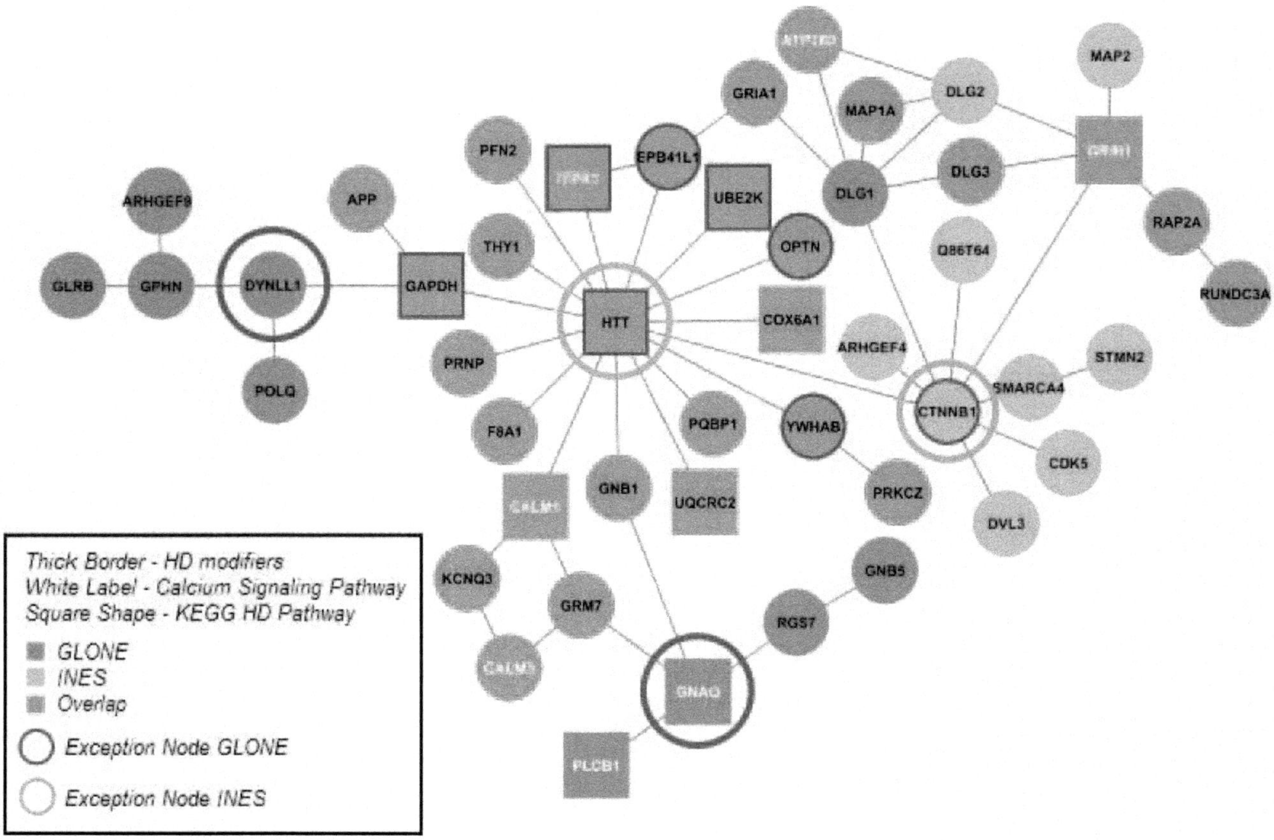

Figure 2: Merged networks from both GLONE and INES.

- HD Modifiers: These genes have been reported in the work of Kaltenbach and Romero [15] as important modifier genes playing key roles in the development of HD.

Since the GLONE approach requires a slight reformulation of the optimization problem, the L parameter now shows significantly higher values when compared to previous INES parameterization. We determined the overall network cost induced by our former INES approach (KPM 2.0 ACO) by accumulating all case exceptions over all nodes contained in the INES solution to determine new values for L. However, exception nodes were excluded. This strategy assures that both algorithms' computations are based on the same preconditioning, resulting in very similar and comparable solution networks that differ from each other only due to corresponding algorithmic characteristics.

Therefore, we set L=164 with K=2 which resembles the (now deprecated) INES parameter specification of L=8 and K=2 for the previously described HD gene expression data. We left the remaining parameters at their default values (Table 1). Since ant colony optimization is non-deterministic (random seeding), we report the worst as well as the best solution found. However, when comparing GLONE to INES we show the best solutions for both. Please note that all test runs resulted in finding key pathways of very similar sizes, varying by one node. This is an indicator for the algorithm's robustness and reliability.

3.2.1 GLONE versus INES

While INES could only use nodes that did not exceed the L parameter, GLONE is able to include more expensive nodes to maximize the sub-graph as long as the overall cost threshold (the new L) for the network is not exceeded. We evaluated the results of the GLONE algorithm and compared them to our previous approach INES implemented by the KPM 2.0 ACO algorithm and published under [1]. We visualized both the GLONE and the INES solution networks in Figure 2. The figure depicts the GLONE network (blue nodes), the INES network (green nodes) and their overlap (red nodes). The GLONE network consists of 38 nodes, compared to 37 nodes in the INES network, although the construction of both networks involved the same overall costs. It is noteworthy that GLONE selects fairly distributed nodes with lesser degrees as exception nodes, while the INES algorithm tends to have a bias towards picking hub-nodes in order to maximize the sub-graph. Depending on the data and local characteristics within the human PPI network this bias may or may not be desired.

By comparing the genes contained in the reported pathway solution to all combined known relevant genes (KEGG HD Pathway, Calcium Signaling Pathway, HD Modifiers), GLONE outperforms INES by two genes in the KEGG HD Pathway and in the Calcium Signaling Pathway (Gene Symbols: GNAQ, PLCB1), please refer also to Table 2. However, with INES we found one gene in the HD modifiers that was not identified using GLONE (Gene Symbol: CTNNB1).

	INES	GLONE (worst)	GLONE (best)	CUSP	GiGA	jActive-Modules	t-test top
Number of genes	37	37	38	34	34	282	34
Contains *HTT* ?	Yes	Yes	Yes	Yes	No	No	No
HD modifiers	8	6	7	7	3	12	2
KEGG HD pathway	8	8	10	4	0	4	0
Calcium pathway	5	5	7	6	5	10	3

Table 2: Table comparing the largest affected pathways found for $K = 2$ and $L = 8$ by the ACO 2.0, the worst and best results from the ACO 3.0 and other pathway extraction methods such as CUSP [23], GiGA [11], jActiveModules [14] and the top 34 active genes with the most significant t-scores.

Furthermore, even though INES included the Huntingtin gene (Gene Symbol: HTT) in the network, it was an exception node. Using GLONE the Huntingtin gene is added to the pathway as a regular node in the process.

3.2.2 *Comparing GLONE with other approaches*

We also evaluated the GLONE algorithm by comparing its performance to four additional software approaches respectively: CUSP, GiGA, jActiveModules, and t-test top. Table 2 shows the evaluation results. We used equal parameterization for each evaluation step regarding the allowed number of case exceptions K and the cost threshold for gene exceptions L. The GLONE algorithm found the highest overall amount of known HD-relevant genes, except for the jActiveModules, which finds a very large pathway. Apparently, the larger the pathway the higher the probability that it also contains one or many of the known relevant genes. However, large networks contain a lot of noise and thus are far from representing a key pathway. To address this, we use a metric (overlap) that accounts for the number of genes in relation to the network size. This is important since it is a measure for the key pathway's significance. Figure 3 showcases this

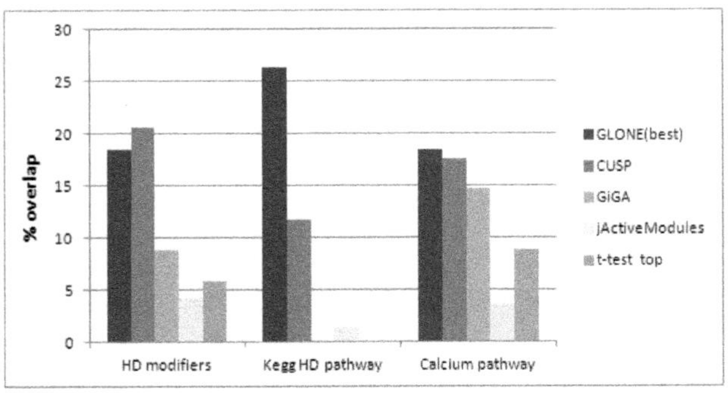

Figure 3: Bar diagram showing the % overlap of the reported found key pathway of each approach with each of the three control sets of known HD-relevant genes

relationship. We illustrate the overlap of each key pathway with the three control data sets of known relevant genes. Compared to the HD modifiers and the Calcium Signaling Pathway, the GLONE pathway reaches an 18% overlap and a 27% overlap with the KEGG HD Pathway. With CUSP having a slightly larger overlap with the HD modifiers control dataset, the GLONE algorithm outperforms any other approach having the greatest differences with respect to the KEGG HD Pathway.

To summarize the comparisons' results, GLONE is able to find the most significant key pathway regarding the number of identified known relevant genes from the three control datasets with respect to the size of the key pathway.

3.2.3 *GLONE Running Times*

All running time analyses were executed on an ordinary personal computer. Table 3 shows detailed hardware specifications. We varied the parameters K and L in a common value spectrum. Note that these values are always data specific and it could in some cases be desirable to use significantly smaller or higher values. Figure 4 shows these results.

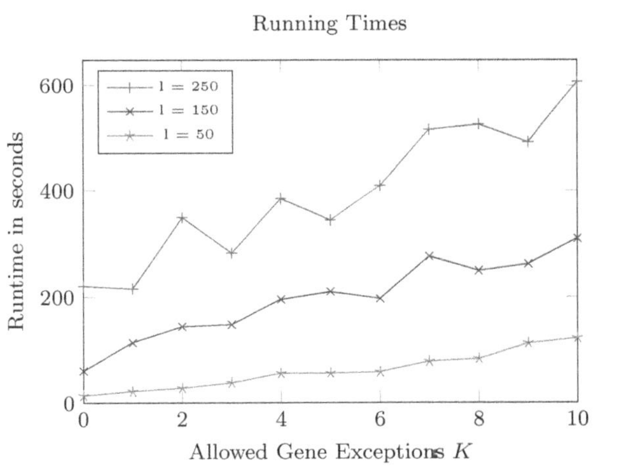

Figure 4: GLONE running time behavior for varying K and L using the HD data sets

When the solution space is extended by increasing both K and L, each iteration is more complex, as more nodes become available. However, while this increases the computation time to find the best solution it is noticeable that the margin of deviation is also increased. For a fixed L value, the amount of iterations and the computational cost per iteration can vary between different values of K in such a way that, to a limited extend, the algorithm may converge faster towards the best solution even for higher values of K or more slowly for lower values, thus, increasing the margin of deviation. This is due to both changing random seeds determining different starting conditions for the ACO and corresponding local characteristics of the PPI network.

Model:	Dell Latitude E6510
CPU:	Intel Core i5 CPU M540 @2.53GHz
RAM:	3.24GB
Operating System:	Windows XP Prof. 2002 SP 3

Table 3: System specifications

4. CONCLUSIONS

In this paper we presented KeyPathwayMiner 3.0, a set of algorithms tackling the computational problem of finding maximal sub-networks where all nodes but K are active in all studied cases but L.

Here, we complement the INES (individual node exceptions) approach from the previous KeyPathwayMiner release by addressing a potential bias regarding hub nodes with our GLONE (global node exceptions) approach. Now we aim to extract all maximal connected sub-networks where all but at most K nodes are active in all cases but in total (!) at most L, i.e., accumulated over all cases and all nodes in a solution. Since finding such solutions is computationally intensive we implemented and described a sophisticated ACO algorithm, which we compared to the KeyPathwayMiner release 2.0 as well as to similar software solutions. For our comparison, we used data sets previously utilized for the CUSP algorithm where our method performs as well as or better than the other methods.

In summary, our main contribution in comparison to release 2.0 is an alternative method for avoiding a potential bias towards hub/exception nodes. Regarding other methods, our main contribution is a method that requires minimal user input of two intuitive parameters that control the noise that we wish to allow in the network data (K) as well as the expression data (L). No prior knowledge regarding these two parameters is necessary. Besides methodological considerations, our implementation has some benefits over other approaches: KeyPathwayMiner 3.0 comes as an easy-to-use, easy-to-install Cytoscape plug-in, and its parallel implementation allows for speedups on multi-core computers.

In the future we plan to extend our approach to directed networks, such as metabolic networks and gene regulatory networks. Furthermore, we aim to integrate the method into CoryneRegNet [19, 9]. We are also working on a dedicated web server for online-only computations as well as a SOAP-based web service provider. Algorithmically, we will evaluate if a hybrid approach of using the results of our greedy strategy as seeding for the ACO algorithm will improve convergence (lower compute time) without running into local optima (similar accuracy).

5. ACKNOWLEDGMENT

JB, TF, TK, JM, and JP are grateful for financial support from the Cluster of Excellence for Multimodal Computing and Interaction (MMCI), Germany. TF and TK received support from the German Research Foundation (DFG, grant NE 1182/5-1).

6. REFERENCES

[1] N. Alcaraz, T. Friedrich, T. Kötzing, A. Krohmer, J. Mueller, J. Pauling, and J. Baumbach. Efficient key pathway mining - Combining networks and OMICS data. *Integr Biol*, in press, 2012.

[2] N. Alcaraz, H. Kucuk, J. Weile, A. Wipat, and J. Baumbach. KeyPathwayMiner - Detecting case-specific biological pathways by using expression data. *Internet Mathematics*, 7(4):299–313, 2011.

[3] B. Aranda, H. Blankenburg, S. Kerrien, F. S. L. Brinkman, A. Ceol, E. Chautard, J. M. Dana, J. De Las Rivas, M. Dumousseau, E. Galeota, A. Gaulton, J. Goll, R. E. W. Hancock, R. Isserlin, R. C. Jimenez, J. Kerssemakers, J. Khadake, D. J. Lynn, M. Michaut, G. O'Kelly, K. Ono, S. Orchard, C. Prieto, S. Razick, O. Rigina, L. Salwinski, M. Simonovic, S. Velankar, A. Winter, G. Wu, G. D. Bader, G. Cesareni, I. M. Donaldson, D. Eisenberg, G. J. Kleywegt, J. Overington, S. Ricard-Blum, M. Tyers, M. Albrecht, and H. Hermjakob. PSICQUIC and PSISCORE: accessing and scoring molecular interactions. *Nat Methods*, 8(7):528–9, Jul 2011.

[4] Y. Assenov, F. Ramírez, S.-E. Schelhorn, T. Lengauer, and M. Albrecht. Computing topological parameters of biological networks. *Bioinformatics*, 24(2):282–4, Jan 2008.

[5] S. Balaji, L. M. Iyer, L. Aravind, and M. M. Babu. Uncovering a hidden distributed architecture behind scale-free transcriptional regulatory networks. *J Mol Biol*, 360(1):204–12, Jun 2006.

[6] T. Barrett, D. B. Troup, S. E. Wilhite, P. Ledoux, C. Evangelista, I. F. Kim, M. Tomashevsky, K. A. Marshall, K. H. Phillippy, P. M. Sherman, R. N. Muertter, M. Holko, O. Ayanbule, A. Yefanov, and A. Soboleva. NCBI GEO: archive for functional genomics data sets–10 years on. *Nucleic Acids Res*, 39(Database issue):D1005–D1010, Jan 2011.

[7] J. Baumbach. On the power and limits of evolutionary conservation–unraveling bacterial gene regulatory networks. *Nucleic Acids Res*, Aug 2010.

[8] J. Baumbach, K. Brinkrolf, T. Wittkop, A. Tauch, and S. Rahmann. CoryneRegNet 2: an integrative bioinformatics approach for reconstruction and comparison of transcriptional regulatory networks in prokaryotes. *Journal of Integrative Bioinformatics*, 3(2):24, 2006.

[9] J. Baumbach, A. Tauch, and S. Rahmann. Towards the integrated analysis, visualization and reconstruction of microbial gene regulatory networks. *Briefing in Bioinformatics*, 10(1):75–83, Jan 2009.

[10] J. Baumbach, T. Wittkop, C. K. Kleindt, and A. Tauch. Integrated analysis and reconstruction of microbial transcriptional gene regulatory networks using CoryneRegNet. *Nat Protoc*, 4(6):992–1005, 2009.

[11] R. Breitling, A. Amtmann, and P. Herzyk. Graph-based iterative group analysis enhances microarray interpretation. *BMC Bioinformatics*, 5(1):100+, jul 2004.

[12] R. Edgar, M. Domrachev, and A. E. Lash. Gene expression omnibus: NCBI gene expression and hybridization array data repository. *Nucleic Acids Res*, 30(1):207–10, Jan 2002.

[13] M. L. Hartsperger, R. Strache, and V. Stümpflen. HiNO: an approach for inferring hierarchical organization from regulatory networks. *PLoS One*, 5(11):e13698, 2010.

[14] T. Ideker, O. Ozier, B. Schwikowski, and A. F. Siegel. Discovering regulatory and signalling circuits in molecular interaction networks. *Bioinformatics*, 18 Suppl 1:S233–40, 2002.

[15] L. Kaltenbach and E. Romero. Huntingtin interacting proteins are genetic modifiers of neurodegeneration. *PLoS Genet*, 2007.

[16] G. Leguizamon, Z. Michalewicz, and M. Schutz. An ant system for the maximum independent set problem. In *Proceedings of the 2001 Argentinian Congress on Computer Science*, pages 1027–1040, 2001.

[17] H. Neuweger, J. Baumbach, S. Albaum, T. Bekel, M. Dondrup, A. T. Hüser, J. Kalinowski, S. Oehm, A. Pühler, S. Rahmann, J. Weile, and A. Goesmann. CoryneCenter - an online resource for the integrated analysis of corynebacterial genome and transcriptome data. *BMC Syst Biol*, 1:55, 2007.

[18] H. Ogata, S. Goto, K. Sato, W. Fujibuchi, H. Bono, and M. Kanehisa. KEGG: Kyoto encyclopedia of genes and genomes. *Nucleic Acids Res*, 27(1):29–34, Jan 1999.

[19] J. Pauling, R. Röttger, A. Tauch, V. Azevedo, and J. Baumbach. Coryneregnet 6.0–updated database content, new analysis methods and novel features focusing on community demands. *Nucleic Acids Res*, 40(1):D610–4, Jan 2012.

[20] R. Röttger, U. Rückert, J. Taubert, and J. Baumbach. Towards the size of gene regulatory networks – how little do we actually know? *IEEE/ACM Transactions on Computational Biology and Bioinformatics*, in press, 2012.

[21] E. W. Sayers, T. Barrett, D. A. Benson, E. Bolton, S. H. Bryant, K. Canese, V. Chetvernin, D. M. Church, M. DiCuccio, S. Federhen, M. Feolo, I. M. Fingerman, L. Y. Geer, W. Helmberg, Y. Kapustin, D. Landsman, D. J. Lipman, Z. Lu, T. L. Madden, T. Madej, D. R. Maglott, A. Marchler-Bauer, V. Miller, I. Mizrachi, J. Ostell, A. Panchenko, L. Phan, K. D. Pruitt, G. D. Schuler, E. Sequeira, S. T. Sherry, M. Shumway, K. Sirotkin, D. Slotta, A. Souvorov, G. Starchenko, T. A. Tatusova, L. Wagner, Y. Wang, W. J. Wilbur, E. Yaschenko, and J. Ye. Database resources of the National Center for Biotechnology Information. *Nucleic Acids Res*, 39(Database issue):D38–51, Jan 2011.

[22] T. Stützle and H. H. Hoos. Max-min ant system. *Future Generation Comp. Syst.*, 16(8):889–914, 2000.

[23] I. Ulitsky, R. Karp, and R. Shamir. Detecting disease-specific disregulated pathways via analysis of clinical expression profiles. *Proceedings of RECOMB, Research in Computational Molecular Biology*, 4955:347–359, 2008.

[24] T. Wittkop, D. Emig, S. Lange, S. Rahmann, M. Albrecht, J. H. Morris, S. Böcker, J. Stoye, and J. Baumbach. Partitioning biological data with transitivity clustering. *Nat Methods*, 7(6):419–20, Jun 2010.

[25] T. Wittkop, D. Emig, A. Truss, M. Albrecht, S. Böcker, and J. Baumbach. Comprehensive cluster analysis with transitivity clustering. *Nat Protoc*, 6(3):285–95, Mar 2011.

[26] T. Wittkop, S. Rahmann, R. Röttger, S. Böcker, and J. Baumbach. Extension and robustness of transitivity clustering for protein-protein interaction network analysis. *Internet Mathematics*, 7(4):255–273, 2011.

Evolving Bio-PEPA Process Algebra Models Using Genetic Programming

David Marco
Carron Shankland
David Cairns
Computing Science & Mathematics
School of Natural Sciences
University of Stirling, UK
{dem,ces,dec}@cs.stir.ac.uk

ABSTRACT

This paper presents initial results of applying a Genetic Programming (GP) approach to the evolution of process algebra models defined in Bio-PEPA. An incomplete model of a system is provided together with target behaviour. GP is then used to evolve new definitions that complete the model while ensuring a good fit to target data. Our results show that a set of effective models can be developed with this approach that can either be used directly or further refined using a modeller's domain knowledge. Such an approach can greatly reduce the time taken to develop new models, enabling a modeller to focus on the subtler modelling aspects of the problem domain. Although the work presented here concerns the modelling of biological systems, the approach is generally applicable to systems for which appropriate target behaviour can be captured and that can be formalised as a set of communicating processes.

Categories and Subject Descriptors

I.2.2 [**Artificial Intelligence**]: Automatic Programming; I.6.5 [**Simulation and Modeling**]: Modelling Methodologies

General Terms

Experimentation, Reliability

Keywords

Process Algebra, Genetic Programming, Time-series

1. INTRODUCTION

In the last decade there has been an increase in the use of computational modelling techniques in biology [7, 17]. This approach formalises a biological system, allowing a range of analyses to be performed and different hypotheses about the biological system to be explored *in silico*. A significant bottleneck in this process is the construction of an appropriate model. Most formal modelling techniques require significant training and it can take some time to gain relevant expertise.

The viability of applying evolutionary techniques to optimising process algebra models has been pioneered by Ross and Imada [18]. They apply a grammar-based Genetic Programming (GP) technique to a subset of stochastic π-calculus to evolve the models. The focus of their early work concerned the most appropriate way to measure the fitness of candidate solutions via a suite of statistical tests. Their approach has been applied to a genetic circuit and chemical reaction model, evolving both the parameters and the model itself. This interdisciplinary field of research is in its infancy. Work to this point is far from exhaustive and still holds potential.

Our previous work [14] focused on the application of GAs to parameter matching problems for models defined in *Performance Evaluation Process Algebra* (PEPA) [11]. The work presented here tackles the more complex challenge of using GP to evolve the structure of process algebra models themselves. We assume the reader will be familiar with GP techniques but related reading can be found in Bäck *et al* [1, 2], De Jong [8] and Koza [12].

The paper is organised as follows: Section 2 contains an introduction to Bio-PEPA [6], the process algebra used in this study, and justification for that choice. The experimental framework developed for this work is presented in Section 3. The systems used to test the method are introduced in Section 3.2, and the results of evolving models are presented in Section 4. Finally, we conclude in Section 5 with some observations concerning the current results and thoughts about the potential for this approach.

2. BACKGROUND

2.1 Process Algebra

Process algebra was developed to model distributed computation systems in the early 1970s. For a historical overview, see Baeten [3]. Process algebras describe complex systems by the composition of multiple parallel agents, called processes. This feature makes them highly suitable for modelling of biological systems [5, 7, 15, 16]. Each process carries out modeller-defined actions, which may require communication with other processes to complete. Choices between actions can be made in a variety of ways: deterministically, probabilistically or non-deterministically.

Process algebras are usually very compact languages with a small number of operators to combine actions with pro-

GECCO'12, July 7-11, 2012, Philadelphia, Pennsylvania, USA.

cesses, and processes with other processes. The constrained nature of their syntax makes them a suitable candidate for use with GP techniques. They are mathematically based and allow rigorous analysis, meaning it is possible to effectively evaluate the fitness of candidate solutions during the selection process.

2.2 Bio-PEPA

Earlier work [14] successfully evolved numeric rate parameters for PEPA models. PEPA is a concise language with a small grammar. Significant advantages of PEPA are that it is well established and that models are built from the perspective of agents and their activities. Furthermore, it is capable of expressing complex systems with a small number of semantic building blocks.

For this work, the Bio-PEPA [6] variant of PEPA is more suitable. Bio-PEPA is aimed specifically at biological models, but this is not its main advantage in this context. Bio-PEPA models are based on a different view of a system than PEPA: instead of considering agents, the activities in which they may participate, and the paths they may follow as they execute, the focus is of the changing *concentrations* of those agents.

For example, consider the model in Figure 1 which represents the biochemical reaction $2X + Y \rightarrow 3Z$ [6]. A standard PEPA view of the system would require that molecule Y can change state to behave like molecule Z. Similarly, molecule X can also change state to behave like molecule Z. This interpretation doesn't really make sense in the context of biochemistry, therefore the Bio-PEPA view of the system is that concentration of species Y and X decrease as concentration of species Z increases. Concentrations are represented in terms of *levels* of concentration; in the limit case these can be thought of as numbers of molecules (or other individuals), depending upon what is being modelled.

$$\begin{array}{rcl} r & = & 0.001; \\ \mathit{kineticLawOf\ alpha} & : & \mathit{fMA}\ (r); \\ \\ X & = & (\mathit{alpha}, 2) \ll X; \\ Y & = & \mathit{alpha} \ll Y; \\ Z & = & (\mathit{alpha}, 3) \gg Z; \end{array}$$

$$X[200] < \mathit{alpha} > Y[100] < * > Z[0]$$

Figure 1: Reactant-Product Bio-PEPA Model

The simple model of Figure 1 demonstrates the core components of a Bio-PEPA model. A system modelled in Bio-PEPA will have numeric rates (r) and species definitions (X, Y and Z). There are inbuilt kinetic laws which define rates of activity for a given action (e.g. *alpha*) based on numeric rates, stoichiometry coefficient, and potentially also species concentration.

This last point is a key abstraction tool in Bio-PEPA, allowing rates to depend functionally on the species concentration (and thereby eliminating the need to code counting mechanisms in the species definition). This example uses the kinetic law of mass action and the information that two units of X are needed for every unit of Y to create three units of Z. There are additional inbuilt laws for other standard biochemical rates, including Hill kinetics and Michaelis-Menten kinetics. Further, the modeller may define kinetic rates by a mathematical expression which can involve arithmetic and trigonometric functions.

The operators $\gg$ and $\ll$ indicate that the species concentration either increases in the interaction (a product), or decreases in the interaction (a reactant). Additional operators shown in the other examples of this paper are $(+)$ and $(-)$ to indicate an activator or an inhibitor. For example, in the above, if the definition for Y were replaced by $\mathit{alpha}(+)Y$ then this indicates that Y is an enzyme in the reaction, required for the reaction to proceed, but not depleted by the reaction. In addition there is a generic modifier (.) which is neither an activator nor an inhibitor. If a species uses one of these operators in a reaction then its quantity remains unchanged: these operators only modify the behaviour of other species involved in the reaction via the kinetic law.

The last line of the model is the model component, defining communication paths and initial population sizes. In this example, X and Y can communicate only over action *alpha* while Z can communicate over any action (a moot point in this example, since *alpha* is the only action). The populations start at size 200, 100 and 0 respectively. In this paper, the ASCII notation for Bio-PEPA used by the Bio-PEPA plug-in is adopted to facilitate easier reproduction of our experiments.

Bio-PEPA syntax supports further complexity which is not shown in this example. Each species definition can contain multiple statements separated by the choice operator (a plus: '+'). For example, in the above, if the definition for the species Y were replaced by $\mathit{alpha} \ll Y + \mathit{beta} \ll Y$ this indicates a choice between actions *alpha* and *beta*. Which path is chosen is dictated by the rates of each action involved: actions with faster rates are more likely to occur, assuming the activities in which they take part are both enabled. That is, if the action requires a partner then there is a partner available to participate in the action. Bio-PEPA also supports compartments: these allow a notion of separate (physical) spaces where species can exist.

Bio-PEPA has a more expressive grammar than PEPA, giving it a larger number of semantic building blocks. Consequently, models described in Bio-PEPA tend to be more compact than those described in PEPA, although the components themselves are more complex. This makes Bio-PEPA a suitable language for defining process algebra models with GP as it saves time by not having to evolve complicated models from scratch. Bio-PEPA is also less susceptible to bloat because a well-formed Bio-PEPA process cannot have choices between repeated actions, thereby limiting the already compact notation further.

Here we present the EPA framework evolving the species in a Bio-PEPA model without compartments. We aim to investigate the addition of these elements in further work.

3. EXPERIMENTAL METHOD

3.1 The EPA Framework

We envisage the EPA framework as an experimental system in which process algebras can be combined with a range of evolutionary techniques. The first step combined PEPA with a GA for parameter fitting for the numeric activity rate values (e.g. the simple r in the above model). This second stage work applies GP to systems defined as Bio-PEPA models. For our implementation, we have combined the

ECJ evolutionary computing framework [13] and the Bio-PEPA Plug-in developed at the University of Edinburgh [9]. ECJ is designed for large and complex experimental systems and supports many different evolutionary computing approaches. The Bio-PEPA Plug-in allows direct access to, and control of, Bio-PEPA models and their evaluation.

Only species definitions are being evolved in this initial stage of the work. The species grammar S for Bio-PEPA (taken from Ciocchetta and Hillston [6]) is

$$S ::= (\alpha,\kappa) \text{ op } S \mid S + S \mid C$$

where op $= \ll \mid \gg \mid (+) \mid (-) \mid (.)$ and C is a constant (i.e. the name of a species). Figure 2 shows the slightly restricted version of Bio-PEPA species definition used here as a tree. Each potential GP solution contains multiple instances of these trees; one for each species definition flagged for optimisation. The GP solution tree is specific to the Bio-PEPA grammar and does not change. It is the values inside this tree which change. For example, a tree with only one Definition terminal represents $(alpha, 2) \ll X$ (from Figure 1). The parts of the tree may be manipulated to give other, one Definition, species, e.g. varying just one part of the tree: $(beta, 2) \ll X$, $(alpha, 42) \ll X$, $(alpha, 2)(.)X$, or $(alpha, 2) \ll Y$. Similarly, solutions may be manipulated by adding more choices. For example, $alpha \ll X + beta \gg X$.

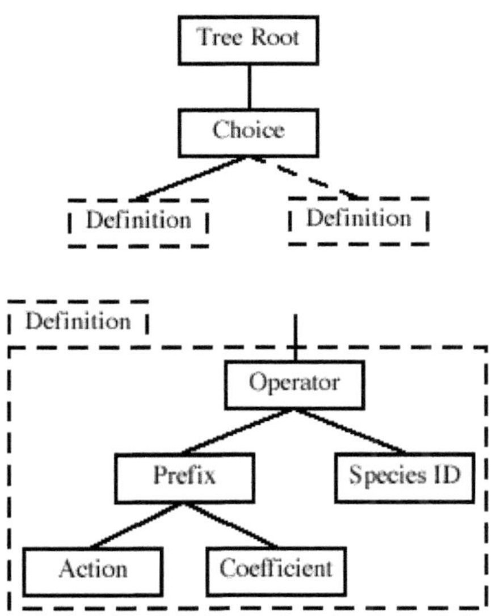

Figure 2: Bio-PEPA Species Definition Tree: A solid line indicates a single required element and a dashed line indicates 0 or more optional elements.

Numeric rates, kinetic laws and the model component of the Bio-PEPA models are fixed during this stage of work. This assures the findings are based solely on the evolution of the species definition.

Using the experimental set-up presented in Table 1 the main execution loop for the EPA system consists of the following steps:

1. *Model.* The input to the system is a pre-defined Bio-PEPA model developed in the Bio-PEPA Plug-in. One or more of the species definitions within the model are flagged to be evolved. Generated candidate solutions contain a definition for each flagged species as a tree.

Genetic Programming Variables	
Populations Size	100
Generations	100
Tournament Pool	10%
Elitism	1%
Bloat penalty	5%
Crossover rate	100%
Mutation rate	5%
Bio-PEPA Variables	
Simulation algorithm	Gibson-Bruck [10]
Internal replications	10
Failure timeout	10s
EPA System Variables	
Independent runs	50

Table 1: Experimental Values

2. *Simulate.* Each candidate solution is simulated via the Bio-PEPA Plug-in for a user-specified duration and granularity. Each simulation produces a stochastic time-series trace of results; these are averaged over multiple internal replications to reduce stochastic noise and produce a mean behaviour for each species.

3. *Score.* A fitness score is assigned to each individual according to a given desired behaviour. For the three models presented here, fitness is measured as the Euclidean distance from the simulated time-series trace and a target trace. An optimal score is zero, or no difference; indicating the behaviour of the solution's species definition tree provided an exact match to the model's desired behaviour. An evolutionary pressure is applied to individuals to lower bloat by having more concise definitions; each fitness score is penalised proportionately to its size based on the number of terms used in the species definition.

4. *Select.* Individuals from the current population are chosen for breeding the next generation using tournament selection. A single high scoring solution has the opportunity to be a parent more than once; however, the members of a tournament pool are selected randomly, therefore the highest scoring individuals may never be chosen to breed. Elitism is used to ensure the best candidate solutions have the opportunity to pass on their attributes to the generated offspring.

5. *Breed.* A new generation is bred using the parents selected in the previous step. Each offspring has variation added through crossover and a chance of mutation; this increases diversity and reduces the chance of premature convergence. The breeding process can produce poorly-formed Bio-PEPA models which could be removed at this stage and new individual generated. Rather than spend time analysing the model, we allow this to happen and rely on selection to remove these individuals. Once breeding is complete, the offspring generation replaces the parent generation.

6. *Termination.* Steps 2 to 5 are repeated until a specified number of generations have been completed.

3.2 Examples

Three Bio-PEPA models are used to demonstrate the ability of the EPA framework to evolve parts of model definitions. The models and experiments are described here, and results can be found in Section 4. The models are presented in order of increasing complexity or perceived difficulty for the EPA framework. Each model is known and in the public domain; we selectively remove parts of the model (species definitions) and challenge the EPA framework to discover a species description that produces the target behaviour. The target behaviour is obtained by simulating the known and complete model in the Bio-PEPA plug-in to obtain a time-series trace for some or all of the species of the model. We use the Gibson-Bruck simulation, and average the result of 1000 simulations to obtain a reliable target time-series.

3.2.1 Biochemical Reaction

To demonstrate the general method, a simple model is first chosen: the $2X + Y \rightarrow 3Z$ model discussed earlier. The complete, original model can be seen in Figure 1. The simple structure contains only one rate (r), one action ($alpha$), three species to define (X, Y and Z) and zero choices. The target solution only uses two Bio-PEPA operators; reactant ($\ll$) and product ($\gg$).

Two experiments are carried out. Initially, only the Y species is flagged to be defined by the EPA system. The second experiment increases difficulty by flagging all species X, Y and Z to determine if the EPA system can evolve three interlinked species simultaneously.

3.2.2 G-Protein

The G-Protein model describes the activation cycle of G-proteins that regulate cellular signalling events downstream of G-protein-coupled receptors. This activation cycle and accompanying computational models are presented by Bao *et al* [4]. For convenience, the Bio-PEPA model is shown in Figure 3.

This example demonstrates increased complexity over the previous model: there are seven species definitions comprising up to four choices. There are eight possible actions to choose from to build these definitions. Also, the target solution utilises another available Bio-PEPA operator: the activator or enzyme (+).

As described in the source literature [4], there are two linked cyclic processes inside the G-protein activation system. One involves R, L and RL; the other involves G, Ga, Gd and Gbg; these two loops are linked over a connection between RL and G. A single experiment is proposed to evolve the definition of RL.

3.2.3 Generic SEIR

Bio-PEPA is suitable for examples outside biochemistry. An example is the *Susceptible Exposed Infected Recovered* (SEIR) model, a generic model that describes disease communication through an epidemiological system. This is a system which could apply to many infectious behaviours, given appropriate numeric rate parameters. Figure 4 shows the Bio-PEPA syntax for this model. This was developed based on our group's extensive experience in modelling epidemiology using process algebra [15].

$$
\begin{aligned}
rl &= 3.32E-6;\\
rlm &= 0.01;\\
ga &= 1.0E-5;\\
gd1 &= 0.11;\\
g1 &= 1.0;\\
rd1 &= 4.0E-3;\\
rs &= 4.0;\\
rd0 &= 4.0E-4;
\end{aligned}
$$

$$
\begin{aligned}
kineticLawOf\ bindRL &: fMA\ (rl);\\
kineticLawOf\ bindAB &: fMA\ (g1);\\
kineticLawOf\ disRL &: fMA\ (rlm);\\
kineticLawOf\ activ &: fMA\ (ga);\\
kineticLawOf\ hydro &: fMA\ (gd1);\\
kineticLawOf\ degRL &: fMA\ (rd1);\\
kineticLawOf\ degR &: fMA\ (rd0);\\
kineticLawOf\ proR &: rs;
\end{aligned}
$$

$$
\begin{aligned}
L &= disRL \gg L + bindRL \ll L;\\
R &= disRL \gg R + bindRL \ll R + degR \ll R\\
&\quad + proR \gg R;\\
RL &= bindRL \gg RL + activ(+)RL\\
&\quad + disRL \ll RL + degRL \ll RL;\\
G &= bindAB \gg G + activ \ll G;\\
Ga &= activ \gg Ga + hydro \ll Ga;\\
Gd &= bindAB \ll Gd + hydro \gg Gd;\\
Gbg &= bindAB \ll Gbg + activ \gg Gbg;
\end{aligned}
$$

$$
\begin{aligned}
&L[603300] <*> R[10000] <*> RL[0] <*> G[7000]\\
&<*> Gd[3000] <*> Gbg[3000] <*> Ga[0]
\end{aligned}
$$

Figure 3: G-Protein Bio-PEPA Model

The SEIR model contains four species definitions, each of which comprises up to three choices. There are four actions available to build these species definitions. Furthermore, the target solution utilises another Bio-PEPA operator: the generic modifier (.).

Two experiments are carried out for this example. The first is to flag the most complex definition I for evolution. The second is to flag both species E and I for evolution. These two species control the majority of the complex behaviour in the system. Conversely, S is only responsible for contact actions and R can only be recovered.

4. RESULTS

We present the results of evolving the above three models using GP where the populations are seeded with partial models with the relevant species definitions left undefined. Performance is measured both quantitatively by comparing the time-series of the target and the proposed solution (fitness score), and qualitatively by manually comparing the original model and the evolved definitions. Only those solutions with a fitness deviation of less than 0.5% are considered since a modeller would only be interested in definitions that accurately reproduced the observed behaviour.

4.1 Biochemical Reaction

Correct definitions were found when only Y was flagged for optimisation. Results remained encouraging with species

$$
\begin{aligned}
crw &= 6.015;\\
ir &= 0.133;\\
rr &= 0.154;
\end{aligned}
$$

$$
\begin{aligned}
kineticLawOf\ contact &: (crw * S * I)\\
&\quad /(S + E + I + R);\\
kineticLawOf\ incubation &: (ir * E);\\
kineticLawOf\ recover &: (rr * I);
\end{aligned}
$$

$$
\begin{aligned}
S &= contact \ll S;\\
E &= contact \gg E + incubation \ll E;\\
I &= contact(.)I + incubation \gg I + recover \ll I;\\
R &= recover \gg R;
\end{aligned}
$$

$$
I[5] <*> S[508000] <*> E[0] <*> R[0]
$$

Figure 4: Generic SEIR Bio-PEPA Model

X, *Y* and *Z* being flagged together. These are a strong initial proof of concept.

The top 50% of EPA system runs return with exact matches to the $2X + Y \rightarrow 3Z$ structure. Their fitness scores are <0.005%, where 0% indicates no deviation from the target time-series trace. This demonstrates that obtaining a perfect 0% fitness is infeasible; the slight deviations can be attributed to the stochastic noise of Bio-PEPA simulations.

The lower 50% of solutions contain example solutions of the right format, but with different stoichiometry. For instance, $4X + 2Y \rightarrow 6Z$ is a sensible solution which scored a good fitness value, but which a human modeller would refine because the more elegant version is obvious. Given more time for evolution, a larger population size, or higher evolutionary stress on low stoichiometric coefficients the system could be made to push solutions towards a simpler definition.

4.2 G-Protein

In this example, a single experiment was carried out, flagging species *RL* for evolution. The target behaviour is shown in Figure 5 and includes data for just four of the species (*Ga* follows *Gbg* exactly). The remaining three species are not shown as two remain at 0 and the third is fixed at ≈ 600,000 and only varies slightly. Note that even though the system is trying to evolve a definition that reproduces the decreasing behaviour of *RL*, the levels of the other species will be affected by this definition and their traces would be subsequently distorted by a poor definition for *RL*. Figure 6 shows the trace produced by the best evolved model from this series and indicates a very a good match to the target time-series (less than 0.37% deviation from the limit). This is despite producing a different Bio-PEPA definition to the original model. The associated target and evolved Bio-PEPA definitions are shown below.

$$
\begin{aligned}
RL_{target} &= bindRL \gg RL + activ(+)RL\\
&\quad + disRL \ll RL + degRL \ll RL
\end{aligned}
$$

$$
\begin{aligned}
RL_{evolved} &= bindRL \gg RL + activ(.)RL\\
&\quad + degRL \ll RL
\end{aligned}
$$

The best solution omitted one action altogether (*disRL*) and has the wrong modifier for *activ* (a (.) instead of (+)). At first glance these results are surprising: surely all components would be required?

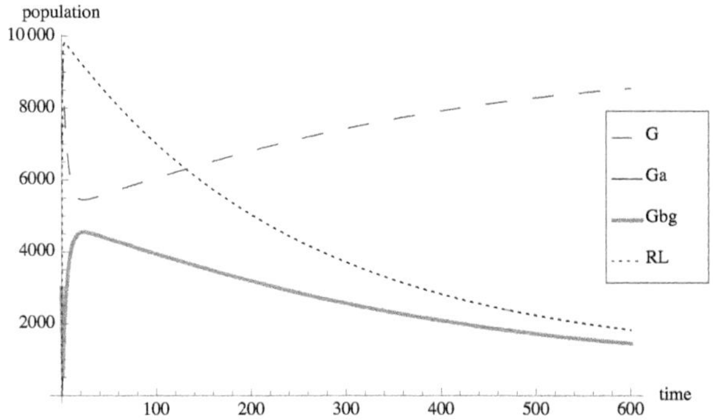

Figure 5: Target trace for the G-protein model showing species levels over time

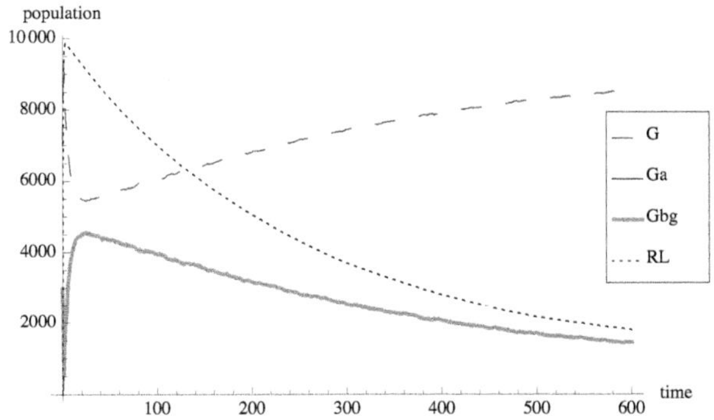

Figure 6: Best solution trace for the G-protein model showing species levels over time

An explanation may be found by examining the Bio-PEPA model more closely, and considering the semantics of the generic operator: (.). Behaviour in the model is driven both by the species definition and the kinetic rate definition. Here, the kinetic rate is a mass action rate. Since the quantity of *RL* does not change in the *activ* action, strictly this action need not appear in its definition. From a modelling perspective, the inclusion of *activ* in *RL* simply serves to remind the modeller that this species is involved in the kinetic rate.

The omission of $disRL \ll RL$ is more surprising since from Figure 5 it can be seen that the main behaviour of RL is to steadily deplete, and this is the function of *disRL*. This is also the function of *degRL* so it may be that in the short run, this action dominates the behaviour.

4.3 Generic SEIR

In this final example, two experiments were carried out. In the first case, only species *I* was flagged for evolution with the target levels of the four species involved shown in Figure 7. The correct definition was rediscovered with an excellent fitness of 0.03% deviation. An alternative, and equally fit, definition was also evolved. In this, the generic modifier

(.) is replaced by the activator (+). Other fit solutions omit the *contact* action from the species altogether.

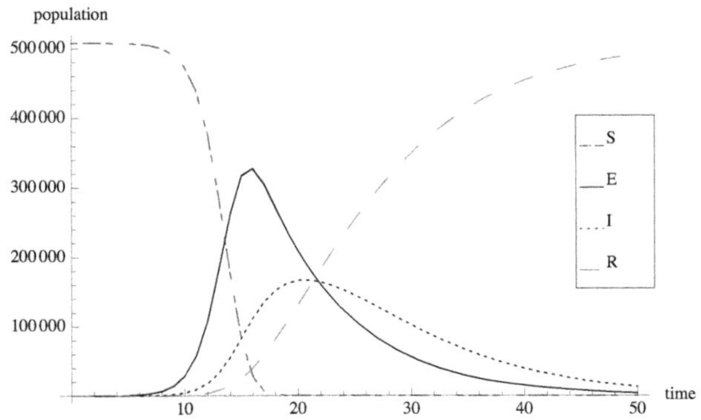

Figure 7: Target trace for the SEIR model showing species levels over time

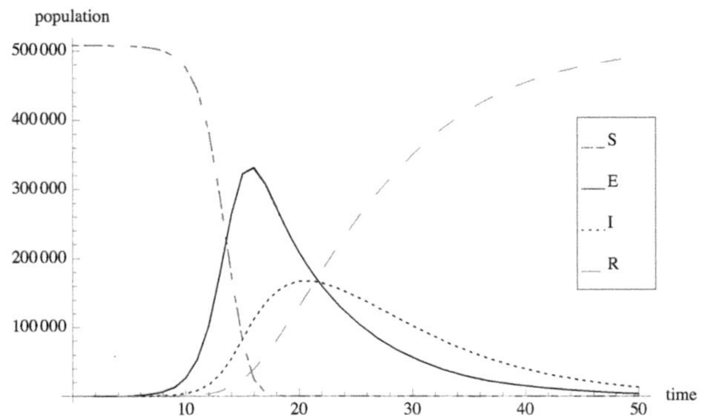

Figure 8: Best solution trace for the SEIR model showing species levels over time

As above, these alternative solutions (with excellent fitness) may be explained by the semantics of the (.) and (+) operators, and the reliance on the model of both kinetic laws and species definitions.

Given the promising results obtained for evolving I alone, a second experiment was then run that challenged the system by flagging both E and I for development. A definition that was very similar to the original unseen specification was evolved with a fitness of less than 0.31% deviation. The species level traces over time for this model can be seen in Figure 8 and show that the evolved *Exposed* and *Infected* curves closely match the original model. As above, the levels of all four traces for each species are interrelated and would be affected by poor definitions for E and I.

The associated target and evolved Bio-PEPA definitions are shown below.

$$\begin{aligned} E_{target} &= contact \gg E + incubation \ll E \\ I_{target} &= contact(.)I + incubation \gg I + recover \ll I \end{aligned}$$

$$\begin{aligned} E_{evolved} &= contact \gg E + incubation \ll E \\ &\quad + recover(.)E \\ I_{evolved} &= contact(.)I + incubation \gg I + recover \ll I \end{aligned}$$

In this case, the best solution has an additional choice term in the solution for E of '*+ recover (.) E*'. The correct definition for I was discovered. As described above, these modifiers do not alter the quantity of the species, and therefore this does not affect the overall time-series output of the model. This action implies a relation between E and recovery which does not exist, and which is not represented in the kinetic rate and therefore does not affect the outcome.

5. CONCLUSIONS AND FUTURE WORK

In this paper we have presented promising results indicating the potential of using a GP approach to evolving models specified in a process algebra suited to the modelling of biological systems. The approach has produced viable species definitions and in two examples, co-evolved species definitions that interact with each other. The results of such exercises can provide useful insights to a modeller. Future work will include more comprehensive testing, repeating the experiment with a higher population, and with more runs.

There is great scope to extend this work further, initially by increasing the number of species definitions that are evolved simultaneously, then expanding to kinetic laws and rate parameters. The approach is probably of most benefit where a modeller can provide the values or definitions of the system they are reasonably sure of and then letting the GP approach evolve the remaining components. If all elements are left unconstrained then the degrees of freedom will rise rapidly and an overly diverse set of models could be produced.

There is also further scope to limit the type of models produced as a result of the breeding process. At present, little effort is made to constrain this process since selection removes inappropriate choices eventually. This is not efficient and knowledge of syntax and structures could be incorporated to reduce this effect. A trade-off would need to be made between the computational effort required to analyse models versus the overhead of running weak models.

It is worth noting that some of the best solutions evolved using this approach were somewhat different from the published versions of the model, even though they had very similar outward behaviour. In some cases this is due to inappropriate actions being included in species definitions. For example, the modeller may know that *degR* is not a suitable action for *RL*, but this information has not been given to the EPA framework. Knowledge of these constraints could be added in a similar manner to the above to prevent the production of inefficient definitions.

Rather than eliminating the modeller from model construction altogether, the goal of this work is to maximise synergy between the automated and manual sides of this activity. The EPA framework provides a range of definitions with a good fit to data. The modeller can then use their experience to select the most appropriate of these definitions for the application domain. These definitions can act as the basis for a new round of modelling or even further refinement via evolution of the model using the described GP approach.

Acknowledgments

David Marco is grateful to the Scottish Informatics and Computer Science Alliance (SICSA), a research initiative of the Scottish Funding Council, for their financial support of his PhD studies. The authors thank the Bio-PEPA Plug-in development team at the University of Edinburgh. Erin Scott, PhD student at the University of Stirling, provided the SEIR Bio-PEPA model. We are grateful to the anonymous reviewers for their comments.

6. REFERENCES

[1] T. Bäck, D. B. Fogel, and Z. S. Michalewicz. *Evolutionary Computation 1: Basic Algorithms and Operators.* Taylor & Francis, 2000.

[2] T. Bäck, D. B. Fogel, and Z. S. Michalewicz. *Evolutionary Computation 2: Advanced Algorithms and Operators.* Taylor & Francis, 2000.

[3] J. Baeten. A brief history of process algebra. *Theoretical Computer Science*, 335(2/3):131–146, 2005.

[4] Y. Bao, A. Compagnoni, J. Glavy, and T. White. Computational Modeling for the Activation Cycle of G-proteins by G-protein-coupled Receptors. *Electronic Proceedings in Theoretical Computer Science*, 40:39–53, 2010.

[5] M. Bernardo, P. Degano, and G. Zavattaro, editors. *Formal Methods for Computational Systems Biology*, volume 5016 of *Lecture Notes in Computer Science*. Springer-Verlag, 2008.

[6] F. Ciocchetta and J. Hillston. Bio-PEPA: a framework for the modelling and analysis of biological systems. *Theoretical Computer Science*, 410:3065–3084, 2009.

[7] J. Cohen. The crucial role of CS in systems and synthetic biology. *Communications of the Association for Computing Machinery*, 51:15–18, 2008.

[8] K. A. De Jong. *Evolutionary Computation: A Unified Approach.* MIT Press, 2006.

[9] A. Duguid, S. Gilmore, M. Guerriero, J. Hillston, and L. Loewe. Design and development of software tools for Bio-PEPA. In *Proc. of Winter Simulation Conference 2009*, pages 956–967, 2009.

[10] M. A. Gibson and J. Bruck. Efficient exact stochastic simulation of chemical systems with many species and many channels. *J. Phys. Chem. A*, 104:1876–1889, 2000.

[11] J. Hillston. *A Compositional Approach to Performance Modelling.* Cambridge University Press, 1996.

[12] J. R. Koza. *Genetic Programming: On the Programming of Computers by Means of Natural Selection.* MIT Press, 1993.

[13] S. Luke. Essentials of Metaheuristics. http://cs.gmu.edu/~sean/book/, 2009.

[14] D. Marco, D. Cairns, and C. Shankland. Optimisation of Process Algebra Using Evolutionary Computation. In *IEEE Congress on Evolutionary Computation*, pages 1296–1301. IEEE, 2011.

[15] C. McCaig, M. Begon, R. Norman, and C. Shankland. A rigorous approach to investigating common assumptions about disease transmission: Process algebra as an emerging modelling methodology for epidemiology. *Theory in Biosciences*, 130:19–29, 2011. Special issue on emerging modelling methodologies.

[16] C. Priami. Process Calculi and Life Science. *Electronic Notes in Theoretical Computer Science*, 162:301–304, 2006.

[17] C. Priami. Algorithmic Systems Biology. *Communications of the ACM*, 52(5):80–88, 2009.

[18] B. Ross and J. Imada. Evolving stochastic processes using feature tests and genetic programming. In *11th Annual Conference on Genetic and Evolutionary Computation*, pages 1059–1066. ACM, 2009.

Reverse Engineering of GRNs: An Evolutionary Approach based on the Tsallis Entropy

Mariana R. Mendoza
Institute of Informatics
Federal University of Rio Grande do Sul
Porto Alegre, RS, Brazil
mrmendoza@inf.ufrgs.br

Fabrício M. Lopes
Federal University of Technology - Paraná
Cornélio Procópio, PR, Brazil
fabricio@utfpr.edu.br

Ana L. C. Bazzan
Institute of Informatics
Federal University of Rio Grande do Sul
Porto Alegre, RS, Brazil
bazzan@inf.ufrgs.br

ABSTRACT

The discovery of gene regulatory networks is a major goal in the field of bioinformatics due to their relevance, for instance, in the development of new drugs and medical treatments. The idea underneath this task is to recover gene interactions in a global and simple way, identifying the most significant connections and thereby generating a model to depict the mechanisms and dynamics of gene expression and regulation. In the present paper we tackle this challenge by applying a genetic algorithm to Boolean-based networks whose structures are inferred through the optimization of a Tsallis entropy function, which has been already successfully used in the inference of gene networks with other search schemes. Additionally, wisdom of crowds is applied to create a consensus network from the information contained within the last generation of the genetic algorithm. Results show that the proposed method is a promising approach and that the combination of a criterion function based on Tsallis entropy with an heuristic search such as genetic algorithms yields networks up to 50% more accurate when compared to other Boolean-based approaches.

Categories and Subject Descriptors

J.3 [**Computer Applications**]: Life and Medical Sciences – Biology and genetics

General Terms

Algorithms

Keywords

Gene Regulatory Networks, Inference, Mutual Information, Tsallis Entropy, Boolean Networks, Genetic Algorithms

1. INTRODUCTION

A recent and challenging goal in bioinformatics research is to understand the nature and control of cellular function and the reasons why cellular systems fail in disease. This can be accomplished (at least partially) by revealing the structure of the organisms' underlying gene regulatory networks. Nowadays scientists are attempting to perform this task by investigating the behavior of genes in a holistic way, based on large-scale gene expression profiles. A major motivation is the believe that genes' activity is not isolated or independent of each other [25]. Indeed, genes compose intricated networks through which they work in concert to promote life sustainability. Therefore, the discovery of gene regulatory networks' structure through reverse engineering is at the same time an appealing and complex approach.

Gene regulatory networks (GRNs) are graph models that reflect the mechanisms and dynamics of gene expression and regulation by mapping the physical or influence interactions between genes of a particular organism. The nodes of this graph represent genes or genes' products, while the wiring describe the regulatory interactions between these elements. Once modeled, gene networks explain how genes are over- or under-expressed in response to perturbation signals and environmental changes. This is particularly interesting, for instance, for new drugs and treatments development. Additionally, this model represents an important tool for in silico experiments. Thus, there is a strong motivation for improving and developing new reverse engineering algorithms.

Several approaches have been already explored for modeling and inference of GRNs. On the graph-based course, one may consider, for instance, Bayesian networks [9, 11], Boolean networks [2, 14, 15], weight matrices [4, 20], among others. Regardless the model applied, in general, reverse engineering algorithms try to reveal the regulatory interactions that compose the networks' topology from experimental data. The main goal is to recover gene interactions in a global and simple way, by identifying the most significant connections [18]. However, there is an important challenge involved in this context: as experiments usually produce sparse data sets, the interactions between hundreds of genes must be learned from a few available samples [11], which not only raises the complexity of the inference problem, but also impairs its accuracy. For this reason, the use of heuristic procedures has been recently explored.

Previous works [4, 7, 20, 23] have implemented a reverse engineering method based on genetic algorithms (GA) to reconstruct GRNs. In [4] and [20], authors represented the GRNs as weight matrices and aimed at minimizing the divergence between the expression patterns of the inferred network and the target network. Although the algorithms have

GECCO'12, July 7–11, 2012, Philadelphia, Pennsylvania, USA.

helped in the identification of networks with several dozen genes to significant accuracy, the large set of parameters to be inferred limits their application to realistic problems. In [7], the networks were modeled as Bayesian networks and evaluated based on metric scoring functions implemented by Weka[1], namely the Akaike Information Criterion (AIC) score and the Minimum Description Length (MDL) score. In this work, the correct topological ordering of nodes was predicted by the algorithm but the set of relationships between nodes could not be completely reconstructed. GAs were also explored in [23], in which a Boolean modeling framework was applied and the GAs' fitness function was implemented following the concepts of the *consistency problem*[2]. Authors have found the accuracy of the inferred networks to be satisfactory, but the generated models had the disadvantage of containing many false positives interactions. Furthermore, the fitness function applied in this work was not able to cope with self-loops, which are known to be prominent in real GRNs.

In the present paper we address some open questions raised by [23] and improve the previous approach in several different directions. First, a distinct encoding scheme is applied, based on integer representation, in order to reduce the length of GAs' individuals and therefore memory requirements. Second, a new, but still random initialization method is introduced, which aims at preventing the introduction of a high rate of false positives within the first generations of the algorithm. Third, GA operators of crossover and mutation are performed considering the network syntax. Finally, we evaluate candidate solutions by means of Tsallis entropy [26], which generalizes the Boltzmann entropy and has be shown to be a promising approach for inferring GRNs [18]. In contrast to the fitness function proposed by [23], the Tsallis entropy is able to cope with self-loops.

This paper is organized as follows. In the next section we will briefly describe the Boolean-based modeling framework and dynamics, the principles of Tsallis entropy, as well as the data set used in experiments. In the sequence, the proposed model is described. Finally, in Sections 5 and 6 we present and discuss the results of our work and point out future research directions.

2. METHODS

2.1 Random Boolean Networks

Random Boolean networks (RBNs) are one of the most well-known discrete modeling frameworks for GRNs. Albeit extremely simple, they are efficient in extracting meaningful biological information when the interest lies in a qualitative investigation of the regulatory interactions within a gene network [14]. A RBN is a directed graph $G(V, F)$ defined by a set of nodes $V = \{v_1, v_2, \dots, v_N\}$ and a set of Boolean transitional functions $F = \{f_1, f_2, \dots, f_N\}$. Each node v_i, $i = 1, \dots, N$, is a Boolean device that stands for the state of variable (gene) i: in GRNs context, $v_i = 1$ denotes that gene i is expressed, while $v_i = 0$ means that it is not expressed The network state at time t is thus given by a N-dimensional

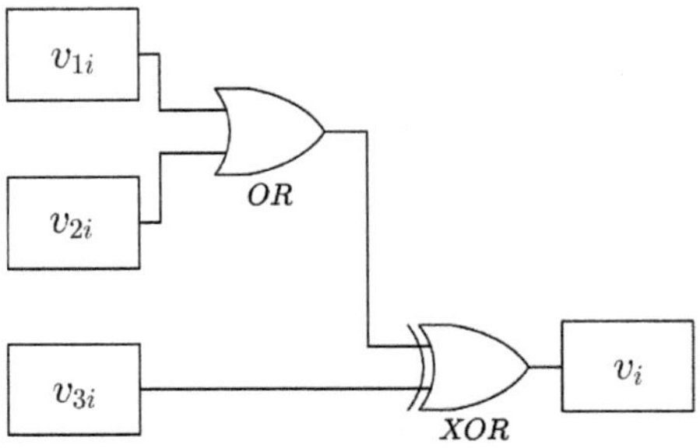

(a)

(t)			(t+1)
v_{1i}	v_{2i}	v_{3i}	v_i
0	0	0	0
0	0	1	1
0	1	0	1
0	1	1	0
1	0	0	1
1	0	1	0
1	1	0	1
1	1	1	0

(b)

Figure 1: An example of a Boolean function for node v_i, with predictors v_{1i}, v_{2i} and v_{3i} ($K_i = 3$), represented as a (a) logical circuit and (b) a state transition table. The state of v_i at time step $t + 1$ is obtained by applying the Boolean function to its predictors' state at the previous step, i.e., $v_i(t+1) = f_i(v_{ki}(t))$. For instance, this example indicates that when the predictors v_{1i}, v_{2i} and v_{3i} equal {0, 1, 1}, v_i will assume value 0. Adapted from [17].

vector $s(t) = [v_1(t), \dots, v_N(t)]$. Since each node is a Boolean device, the system has a finite state space of size 2^N.

Each node v_i has its value determined by a Boolean function $f_i \in F$, which represents the rules of regulatory interactions between nodes, and K_i specific inputs, denoting its regulatory factors or predictors. The function f_i is a logical circuit that, given the state of gene v_i's predictors, $v_{ki}(t)$ with $k = 1, \dots, K_i$, at time t, generates the network states $s(t + 1)$ by mapping $v_i(t + 1) = f_i(v_{ki}(t))$. An example is given in Figure 1. Thus, being K_i the number of predictors of a given node, which can be either at state 1 or 0, the number of possible states for the set of K_i predictors is 2^{K_i}. Furthermore, for each of these combinations, the output of gene v_i defined by its Boolean function f_i must be either 1 or 0. Therefore, the total number of Boolean functions over K_i predictors is $2^{2^{K_i}}$. When $K_i = 2$, some of these functions are well-known (AND, OR, XOR, NAND, etc.), but in the general case functions have no obvious semantics.

The groundbreaker suggestion of studying the behavior of gene regulatory systems by means of networks of Boolean functions was introduced by Kauffman in [13]. Kauffman's experiments suggested that large randomly connected feedback networks of binary nodes behave with stability comparable to that in living organisms. The author asserts that "*It seems unlikely that Nature has made no use of such probable and reliable systems, both to initiate evolution and protect its progeny*". Since Kauffman's seminal work, most of research on Boolean networks has focused on unraveling the structure of GRNs from gene expression data.

[1]http://www.cs.waikato.ac.nz/ml/weka/

[2]Identify a network consistent with the observations in the given gene expression profile or determine if this network exists at all.

2.2 Inference by Tsallis entropy

In the context of information theory, Shannon's entropy [24] was considered a suitable measure for GRNs inference from expression data [15]. In general, when the entropy is adopted in the inference process, the conditional dependence of a target gene given its potential predictors and their expression profiles is performed and as a result, the mean conditional entropy is applied as a criterion function [19], i.e., to evaluate the subset of predictors and their suitability to predict a target gene. This process has been recognized as an appropriated statistical tool to infer direct interactions between genes [6]. However, the inference depends on the accuracy of the information available and the appropriateness of its use.

Moreover, the conditional entropy is commonly used to estimate the relationships among a group of multivariate predictors genes and a given target gene, i.e., N-to-1. The criterion functions based on information theory (entropy and mutual information) are also frequently applied in GRNs inference methods. However, these criterion functions are used to detect relationships of both 1-to-1, replacing the Pearson correlation, and N-to-1 relationships [15, 19, 22], in which the uniformity of the conditional probability distributions of a target gene, given its predictors, is considered as a whole.

On the other hand, C. Tsallis proposed a new entropy form in 1988, which became known as generalized Tsallis entropy or just Tsallis entropy, which is defined as follows:

$$H_q(X) = k\frac{(1-\sum_{x\in X} P(x)^q)}{q-1}, \quad (1)$$

in which k is a positive constant (which defines the size and scale), x is a possible configuration of the random variable X, $P(x)$ is the probability of x and $q \in \mathbb{R}$ is the entropic parameter.

The entropic parameter q characterizes the degree of nonextensivity of the system, which in the limit $q \to 1$ recovers the Shannon entropy. Therefore, the entropic form of H_q is not additive for any $q \neq 1$, and the connection between the entropic parameter q and the nonextensivity of the entropy is given by the rule [26]:

$$H_q(A+B) = H_q(A)+H_q(B)+(1-q)\times H_q(A)\times H_q(B), \quad (2)$$

in which A e B are two independent systems, i.e., $P(A,B) = P(A) \times P(B)$. From Equation 2 it was generated the expression "nonextensive entropy". Some properties can be observed in this equation such as nonnegativity for $H_q \geq 0$, superextensivity (superadditivity) for $q < 1$, extensivity (additivity) for $q = 1$ and subextensivity (subadditivity) for $q > 1$.

This new functional form of entropy allows the generalization of Boltzmann's statistical mechanics, which has been successful in presenting the properties of the statistical physics theory [27]. Besides that, the Tsallis entropy has emerged in recent years as a generalization of the Shannon entropy, because of their applications [12] and its theoretical foundation [1]. Its use becomes important in systems with long-range interactions, which cause long-range correlations, a particular feature of the nonextensive systems. In order to investigate the possibility of non-extensiveness of GRNs, and hence its interpretation in this context, it was proposed a new criterion function for the inference of GRNs based on the generalized Tsallis entropy [18], which produced better results compared to the Shannon entropy. Therefore, in order to infer the relationships among genes from its temporal expression profiles we adopt the criterion function proposed in [18], which is defined as follows:

$$\begin{aligned} S_q(v_i \mid g) &= \frac{\alpha(m-n)}{\alpha m + d} S_q(v_i) + \\ & \sum_{g=1}^{n} \frac{r_g+\alpha}{\alpha m + d}\frac{1-\sum_{v_i} P(v_i|g)^q}{q-1}, \end{aligned} \quad (3)$$

where $\alpha \geqslant 0$ is the penalty weight, m is the number of possible instances of the gene group g (predictors), n is the number of observed instances, d is the total number of samples, r_g is the number of each observed instance of g and $q \in \mathbb{R}$ is the entropic parameter of the Tsallis entropy.

2.3 Artificial gene networks

Despite the increasing availability of large-scale gene expression patterns, the reverse engineering of GRNs still suffers from an important limitation: the difficulty to evaluate results due to the restricted knowledge about the biological systems that generated these data sets. Therefore, the use of artificial networks and simulated expression signals is a common practice to assess algorithms performance. In the present paper, we resort to an Artificial Gene Network (AGN) validation and simulation model[3] [16, 17] to compose an artificial set of 100-node networks adopting the Boolean network approach. In order to verify the sensibility of the method on the topology class, we generate AGNs with the uniformly-random Erdös-Rényi (ER, [8]) and the Barabási-Albert (BA,[5]) models. The latter is currently known to be one of the most similar models to real gene networks [3].

Following the upper limit of stability for Boolean networks discussed in [13], we set the upper bound of nodes' average connectivity to $\langle k \rangle = 3$. Also, we consider two distinct approaches for the Boolean modeling: a deterministic (RBN) and a probabilistic (PBN) one. While the first approach considers a single Boolean function per gene to generate network dynamics, the former relax the deterministic rigidity by allowing each gene to have more than one Boolean function, each of which have a particular usage probability [25]. This probabilistic class of Boolean model offers a more flexible and powerful modeling framework at the cost of a greater difficulty of inference.

For each possible configuration of network topology, i.e., ER or BA, and network class, i.e., deterministic or probabilistic, we generated a random 100-node network and simulated 10 temporal expression signals of length 30, each one starting from a randomly chosen initial state [18]. The dynamics of the AGN is obtained by applying the Boolean transition functions to the network's initial state. Furthermore, we concatenated these signals generating a single time series of size 300, which is used for network inference.

3. PROPOSED MODEL

3.1 Representation

Following the approach described in [23], we model the GRNs as RBNs: genes are Boolean devices whose expression is regulated by a Boolean function and a set of predictors. However, we are not interested in recovering the whole set of transitional functions, but solely the network topology.

[3]http://code.google.com/p/jagn/

Thus, each individual of the GA codifies the network wiring of a candidate solution. An example is given in Figure 2. Figure 2(a) depicts a 5-node network, in which each node is regulated by two predictors at most. Node 1's predictor is node 5, node 2's predictor are node 4 and 5, and so on. The corresponding representation of this network as a GA individual is given in Figure 2(b).

A GA individual is codified as an integer string containing the full network wiring specification. The string length is given by $N \times K_{max}$ digits, in which N is the number of nodes in the network and K_{max} is an user-configurable upper bound limit for the cardinality of the nodes' predictor set. It is important to stress that the K_{max} parameter is independent of the average connectivity ($\langle k \rangle$) used for AGNs generation (see Section 2.3): it is applied during network inference to standardize individuals' size and restrict the search space, and may assume a value either equal, lower or higher than the latter. Each digit of the integer string contains either a zero or a non-zero value: while a non-zero value refers to the unique ID of a node's predictor, a zero value is used to allow a cardinality lower than K_{max}, i.e., $K_i < K_{max}$. Note that as node 5 has an empty predictor set (Figure 2(a)), both digits corresponding to its predictors assume a zero value (N5 in Figure 2(b)).

3.2 Initialization

Each individual from the GA population is randomly initialized in such a way that every single node of the encoded network has one parent at most. This allows the heuristic search to start from a low-complex solution and gradually increase its complexity through GA operators, e.g., crossover and mutation, whenever this change results in a higher fitness value. Also, this strategy aims to reduce the frequency of false positive connections in the initial population.

3.3 Selection

The fittest individuals of a generation were selected based on the roulette wheel selection operator. The function to be optimized is implemented in terms of the Tsallis entropy, as defined in Equation 3, and aims to minimize the entropy of a single node regarding its predictors set. Elitism is applied in order to preserve the best found individuals in subsequent generations and maintain the monotonic convergence of the algorithm.

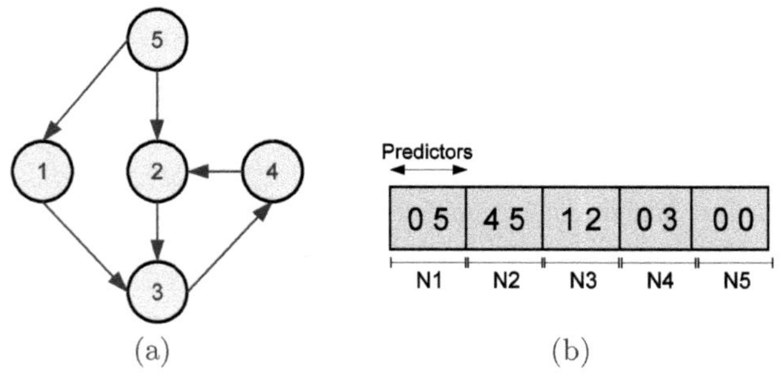

Figure 2: **A 5-node network (a) topology and its corresponding (b) representation as a GA individual. In this example, nodes have a maximum in-degree of 2 ($K_{max} = 2$) and predictors are denoted by non-zero node IDs. Since we are interested in reconstructing the GRNs' topology, we do not encode the nodes' Boolean functions in candidate solutions.**

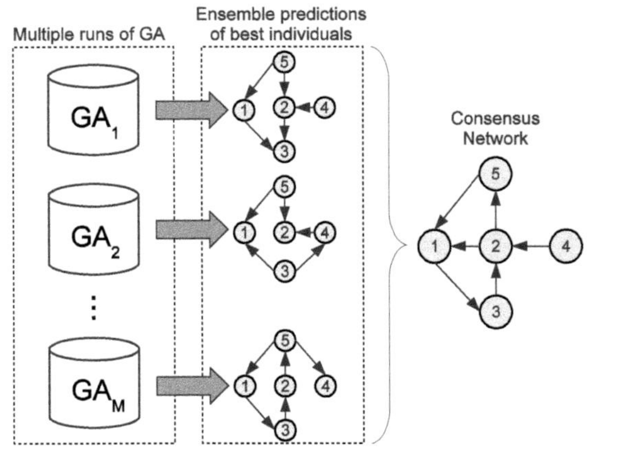

Figure 3: As multiple runs of GA may yield different results, wisdom of crowds is applied to construct a consensus network. The best individuals of the final generation perform a majority voting, generating an ensemble prediction for each simulation run. In the sequence, ensemble predictions are combined into a single consensus network.

3.4 Crossover and Mutation

In the context of exploring the solution space of RBNs with GAs, the operations of crossover and mutation are performed over the network wiring. As the number of nodes in the network is known and constant (it corresponds to the number of genes covered by the expression profile), the heuristic search must find the optimal connections between these nodes. This is achieved by varying the connections between the network's nodes and looking for the combination that maximizes the fitness function.

Therefore, in crossover operator, a pair of GA individuals exchange between themselves a set of connections placed between a randomly chosen point and the rightmost digit of the string (one-point crossover). Suppose we have two individuals of length 10 comprising a network of $N = 5$ nodes and $K_{max} = 2$, similar to the representation shown in Figure 2(b): `0545120300` and `2534102340`. If the random choice of the operator is to start the crossover on point 3, all connections regarding nodes 3 to N will be exchanged between the pair of mates to generate the offspring, which in this example will be `0545122340` and `2534100300`.

With respect to the mutation operator, which aims to promote diversity, the offspring may suffer eventual changes in their genetic material. In short, the network topology is varied by changing each digit of the integer string to a new random value with a small probability (P_{mut}). This operator may either remove (replace a non-zero digit by a zero digit) a node's connection, decreasing network complexity, or simply change (make a random swap between digits) a node's predictor. In order to allow some GA individuals to have its network complexity decreased and hence to explore in a controlled fashion sparse topologies within the search space, which are known to be GRNs' representative [11], the mutation operator performs a removal change in 10% of the mutations.

3.5 Wisdom of crowds

As genetic algorithms are a stochastic optimization approach [10], multiple runs of the algorithm may yield distinct results, such that an important question arises: how to compose the algorithm's final answer? One possible approach, applied in the present paper, is to combine the information carried by the best individuals in the last generation of each run [21]. Thus, we let the best individuals of the final generation to perform a majority voting on the network structure, generating an ensemble prediction. In the sequence, all ensembles are combined into a final consensus network, as depicted in Figure 3. This strategy has the benefit of improving results accuracy in the final network structure when compared to individual predictions [21].

4. EXPERIMENTS

In order to test the algorithm's sensibility to different network topologies, we run our method with networks based on the uniformly-random Erdös-Rényi (ER) and the Barabási-Albert (BA) models and on both deterministic (RBN) and probabilistic (PBN) classes. The simulations were set up by varying K_{max} between 2 and 3. These values were chosen based on the knowledge that biological gene networks are sparsely connected [11]. We performed 30 simulations for each network in our test set and combine their results in ensemble solutions, which in turn are used to build a final consensus network, as explained in Section 3.5. Also, we apply a reinforcement step to strengthen those interactions in the final consensus network whose inverse relationships are also present in the model with a lower confidence level (the ratio used is 0.5). We justify this operation with the fact that sometimes the reverse engineering algorithm is able to detect a significant correlation between two genes but the data or the score function are not fine enough to specify the sense of this influence.

The GA parameters were configured according to Table 1. We evolved a population of 30 individuals over 800 generations, applying one-point crossover and an elitist selection with elite size of four individuals. Mutation operator was applied with probability $P_{mut} = 0.001$ and edge removal operations were performed in 10% of cases. In what concerns the parameters from Tsallis entropy, defined in Equation 3, we used $\alpha = 1$ and $q = 2.5$. The choice of the q value is due to the good reconstruction accuracy attached to this configuration in [18].

5. RESULTS

The main results in terms of the ROC curve and the area under the curve (AUC score) are summarized in Table 2 and Figure 4. Table 2 shows the mean and standard deviation over 30 runs for the AUC score of ensemble predictions drawn from the final generation of each single simulation. Complementarily, the ROC curves for the final consensus network, i.e., the one assembled from the set of ensemble predictions, are plotted by varying the threshold used to create the consensus (Figure 4). Figures 4(a) to 4(d) refer to simulations for the ER model, while Figures 4(e) to 4(h) depict the results for simulations for the BA model. Furthermore, graphs on the right half concern the probabilistic Boolean model (PBN), while graphs on the left half are related to the deterministic one (RBN).

Observing the ROC curves in Figure 4, one can conclude that the proposed method has performed well relative to a random classifier. These graphs also bare the benefits of combining ensemble predictions into a single consensus network by means of wisdom of crowds: the AUC scores of the final consensus matrices are higher than the average AUC score for ensemble predictions in every case tested. Regarding the topology class, a comparison of results through 95% confidence intervals suggest there is no significant difference in the method performance in terms of the AUC score when comparing the ER and BA models. On average, the proposed method has achieved very similar scores for both topologies, 0.649 for ER against 0.647 for BA simulations, which let us conclude that the method's success does not depend on the network topology. Moreover, in general, simulations run with the probabilistic model (PBN, right half of Figure 4) have performed slightly poorer than those involving the deterministic ones (RBN, left half of Figure 4), but the difference is also not significantly different at the 0.05 significance level. This corroborates the idea that the reverse engineering of probabilistic models is harder due to the larger set of parameters to be inferred.

In what concerns the effects of the K_{max} parameter, except for simulations with the probabilistic ER model (Figures 4(c) and 4(d)), the use of $K_{max} = 2$ has yield better AUC scores. The improvement in performance was statistically significant ($p < 0.05$) and greater for networks based on the BA model, especially for the one with probabilistic nature. Table 3 shows a distinct results analysis, comparing the AGNs and the inferred consensus networks in terms of a similarity measure. This measure is obtained by combining both true positive rate (TPR, sensitivity) and true negative rate (TNR, specificity), as detailed in the following equations:

$$TPR = \frac{TP}{TP + FN} \qquad TNR = \frac{TN}{TN + FP} \tag{4}$$

$$similarity(N_1, N_2) = \sqrt{TPR \times TNR} \tag{5}$$

The analysis of results by the similarity measure confirms the better performance of $K_{max} = 2$ over $K_{max} = 3$. This indicates that high K_{max} values may degrade the method's performance, which is probably due to the inclusion of more

Table 1: Parameters used in simulations run.

Parameter	Description	Value
G_{max}	Number of generations	800
P_{size}	Population size	30
E	Elite size	4
P_{mut}	Mutation probability	0.001
P_{cross}	Crossover probability	1
K_{max}	Maximum predictors for node	{2, 3}

Table 2: Means and deviations of ensemble predictions' AUC scores over 30 runs of the GA.

Model	RBN				PBN			
	$K_{max} = 2$		$K_{max} = 3$		$K_{max} = 2$		$K_{max} = 3$	
	avg	std	avg	std	avg	std	avg	std
ER	520	.0097	.524	.0080	.513	.0087	.524	.0114
BA	.519	.0085	.525	.0082	.515	.0078	.518	.0106

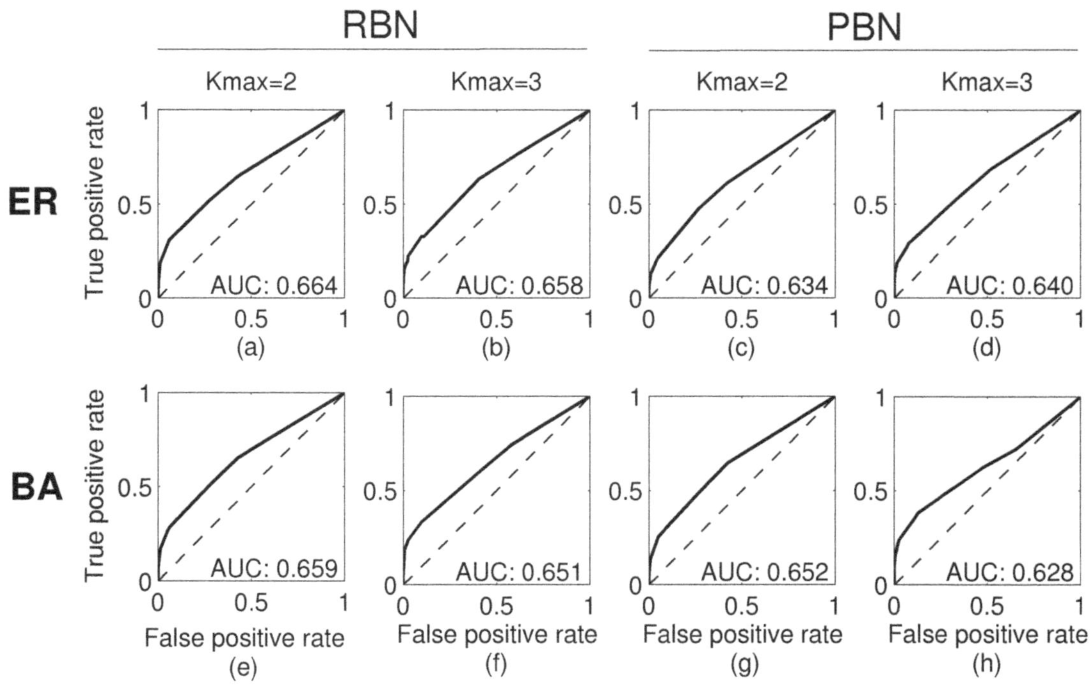

Figure 4: Results in terms of ROC curves and AUC scores for the different combinations of network topology, class and K_{max} value. Graphs on the top line (a to d) show the results for simulations with the ER model, while the graphs on the bottom line (e to h) depict the results for simulations with the BA model. Results suggest that the proposed method is not sensitive to network topology and that a more accurate inference is achieved with $K_{max} = 2$. Furthermore, the average AUC score for the probabilistic models is smaller than the average value found for the deterministic ones, which agrees with the common sense that probabilistic networks are of harder inference due to their more complex nature.

Table 3: Similarity between AGNs and inferred consensus networks for $q = 2.5$.

Model	RBN		PBN	
	$K_{max} = 2$	$K_{max} = 3$	$K_{max} = 2$	$K_{max} = 3$
ER	.6107	.5639	.5977	.5755
BA	.6123	.5609	.6098	.5005

false positive connections. Once again, the improvement was specially notable for the probabilistic BA model. In contrast, the impact over performance was modest for the probabilistic ER model. This finding agrees with the analysis by AUC score in the sense that the effect of K_{max} value is not very significant for the case of the probabilistic ER model. Moreover, the similarity values on Table 3 are close to results reported in [18] for ER and BA network models with average connectivity $\langle k \rangle = 3$.

In order to compare the reverse engineering method proposed in the current work with the solution discussed in [23], we followed the procedure described in Section 2.3 to generate an artificial 50-node probabilistic network and simulate its expression signal. Since previous results have shown that our method's performance is not dependent on the network topology, we compare solely the BA model, as this is currently known to be the closest topology to real gene regulatory networks [3]. At this point, we stress the main changes of the present work when compared to the approach in [23], namely the initialization procedure and the fitness function. These changes have the goal of smoothing false positive rates. For the opposite method, the fitness function was defined according to the Equation 4 in [23]. Regarding the GA parameters, simulations were set up following values on Table 1.

Table 4 shows the analysis of results by means of the similarity measure between inferred consensus networks and target GRNs, as defined in Equation 5. We identify our method by *Tsallis entropy*, while the approach suggested in [23] is referred to as *Inconsistency Ratio* (IR). The superior performance of the proposed method is clear: for a maximum connectivity of two ($K_{max} = 2$), the similarity measure is up to 50% higher than the results obtained with the IR fitness function – 0.5451, against 0.3512 for the latter. This is explained by the good balance between false positive and true positive connections recovered by our method when a maximum set of two predictors per gene is allowed. An improvement was also perceived for $K_{max} = 3$, although not in such a large scale: the similarity measure for networks obtained with the Tsallis entropy is equal to 0.5962, while the use of the IR fitness function has yield a consensus network with similarity rate equal to 0.5178.

An analysis by AUC scores confirms the higher robustness of the proposed method based on Tsallis entropy in relation to the minimization of an inconsistency ratio. For both $K_{max} = 2$ and $K_{max} = 3$, our method outperforms the approach introduced by [23], as shown in Figure 5. Ad-

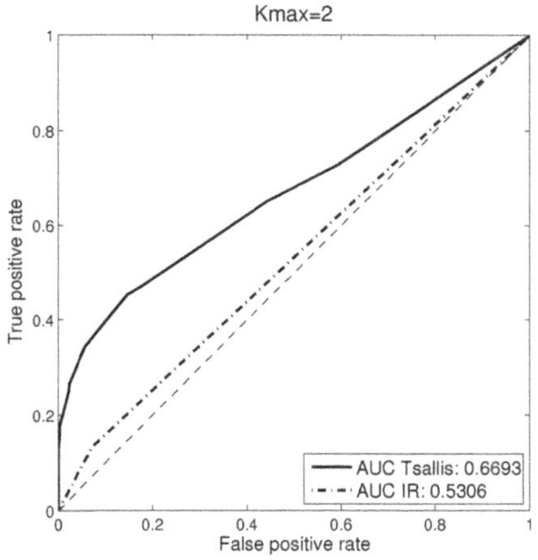

(a)

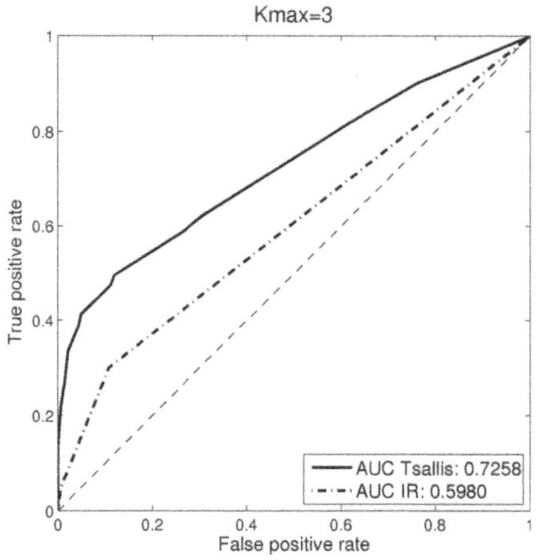

(b)

Figure 5: Network inference accuracy in terms of ROC curve and AUC scores for the two approaches compared: Tsallis entropy (Tsallis) and Inconsistency Ratio (IR). The left graph refers to the results obtained with $K_{max} = 2$, while the right graph reports the results for $K_{max} = 3$. The improvement achieved with the Tsallis criterion function is clear: for both values of K_{max} it has outperformed the inference by the minimization of an Inconsistency Ratio.

Table 4: Comparison between network inference by means of Tsallis entropy and through an inconsistency ratio fitness function for a 50-node AGN.

Fitness Function	Similarity $K_{max} = 2$	Similarity $K_{max} = 3$
Tsallis entropy	.5451	.5962
Inconsistency Ratio	.3512	.5178

ditionally, both methods have achieved a better score for networks inferred with $K_{max} = 3$ in contrast to simulations with $K_{max} = 2$. This is explained by the fact that a higher maximum connectivity increases the chance of recovering the whole set of true positive connections. However, this also makes the algorithm more vulnerable to false positive interactions, which in turn increases the need for more powerful criterion functions and GA operators. This balance between power and robustness has been better achieved by the proposed method: the evaluation of candidate solutions by Tsallis entropy not only recovers more interactions from the target network, but also causes a significant reduction of false positive rates.

6. CONCLUSION

In the present paper we introduced the application of the Tsallis entropy as a fitness function to reverse engineering gene networks by means of genetic algorithms. Although the idea of using entropy or mutual information to infer gene networks is not new, the inference of gene networks by means of Tsallis entropy was recently proposed in [18]. Authors have defined a new criterion function, which aimed at extending the Boltzmann entropy and allowing the recovery of networks whose genes do not follow linear relationships and short-range interactions. Moreover, while recent papers have covered the topic of applying genetic algorithms to uncover gene networks [4, 7, 20, 23], they all have issues that limit their application: bad scalability, need for many parameters tuning, high vulnerability to false positive connections and not so accurate results. Thus, improvements in the area are still necessary.

The proposed solution combines the robustness of Tsallis entropy, which is known for reducing false positive rates [18], with the benefits of ensemble predictions provided by the wisdom of crowds, which have been previously shown to yield more accurate results in the context of gene network inference [21]. Furthermore, as gene networks are known to have a sparse topology [11], GA operators are implemented in order to prioritize the exploration of sparser networks within the search space. For results assessment, we have generated deterministic and probabilistic artificial Boolean networks following two distinct models: uniformly-random Erdös-Rényi (ER) and the Barabási-Albert (BA). Simulations were run by varying the number of maximum allowed predictors per node, given by parameter K_{max}, for each network within the test set.

Results have shown that the performance of the proposed method does not hold any dependence on network topology. No significant difference in terms of the AUC score was noticed for simulations with the ER model in contrast to the BA model, as shown in Figure 4. Furthermore, simulations with $K_{max} = 2$, which allow a set of two predictors per gene at most, have yield more accurate results. This is due by the fact that when $K_{max} = 3$, as the set of predictors is larger, more false positives may be contained within the inferred networks, which in turn degrades reconstruction accuracy. In what concerns network classes, deterministic networks were more accurately inferred than probabilistic ones, due to the nonlinearity and higher complexity attached to the latter. When compared to similar approaches, such as the inference by minimization of an inconsistency ratio as described in [23], the proposed method has been shown to be more robust and have a better balance between true positive and false positive rates, as depicted in Figure 5.

Despite the satisfactory performance, there is still space and need for improvements. For future works, we believe that a promising direction for enhancement is to review and improve implementation details of genetic algorithm, specially regarding crossover and mutation operators. The goal is to bring them even closer to network syntax and thus promote better convergence. Additionally, there are still some parameters to be tested and optimized, such as the percentage of removal operations in mutations. As this has a direct influence over the rate of false positive connections, it may improve results when tuned. Moreover, we would like to investigate how the introduction of partial consensus networks within the generations would help to improve convergence to accurate networks. We are confident that these refinements would make the proposed solution even more robust and useful for knowledge discovery from gene expression patterns.

7. ACKNOWLEDGMENTS

We thank the reviewers for their comments and suggestions and the CNPq for its support to the authors.

8. REFERENCES

[1] S. Abe. Tsallis entropy: how unique? *Continuum Mechanics and Thermodynamics*, 16(3):237–244, 2004.

[2] T. Akutsu, S. Miyano, and S. Kuhura. Identification of genetic networks from a small number of gene expression patterns under the boolean network model. In *Proceedings of the Pacific Symposium on Biocomputing*, pages 17–28, 1999.

[3] R. Albert. Scale-free networks in cell biology. *J Cell Sci*, 118(21):4947–4957, 2005.

[4] S. Ando and H. Iba. Inference of gene regulatory model by genetic algorithms. In *Proceedings of the 2001 IEEE Congress on Evolutionary Computation*, pages 712–719. IEEE CS, 2001.

[5] A. L. Barabasi and R. Albert. Emergence of scaling in random networks. *Science*, 286(5439):509–512, 1999.

[6] C. Charbonnier, J. Chiquet, and C. Ambroise. Weighted-LASSO for Structured Network Inference from Time Course Data. *Statistical Applications in Genetics and Molecular Biology*, 9(1):15, 2010.

[7] C. Davidson. Identifying gene regulatory networks using evolutionary algorithms. *J. Comput. Small Coll.*, 25:231–237, May 2010.

[8] P. Erdös and A. Rényi. On random graphs, I. *Publicationes Mathematicae*, 6:290–297, 1959.

[9] N. Friedman, M. Liniar, I. Nachman, and D. Peer. Using Bayesian networks to analyse expression data. In *Journal of Computational Biology*, volume 7, pages 601–620. Mary Ann Liebert, Inc., 2000.

[10] D. E. Goldberg. *Genetic Algorithms in Search, Optimization and Machine Learning*. Addison-Wesley Longman Publishing Co., Inc., 1989.

[11] D. Husmeier. Sensitivity and specificity of inferring genetic regulatory interactions from microarray experiments with dynamic Bayesian networks. *Bioinformatics*, 19:2271–2282, 2003.

[12] S. Issue. Nonextensive statistical mechanics: new trends, new perspectives. *Europhysics News*, 36(6):185–231, 2005.

[13] S. A. Kauffman. Metabolic stability and epigenesis in randomly constructed genetic nets. *J Theor Biol*, 22(3):437–467, March 1969.

[14] H. Lähdesmäki, I. Shmulevich, and O. Yli-Harja. On learning gene regulatory networks under the Boolean network model. In *Machine Learning*, volume 52, pages 147–167. Kluwer Academic Publishers, 2003.

[15] S. Liang, S. Fuhrman, and R. Somogyi. REVEAL, A Generak Reverse Engineering Algorithm for Inference of Genetic Network Architectures. In *Proceedings of the Pacific Symposium on Biocomputing*, volume 3, pages 18–29, 1998.

[16] F. M. Lopes, R. M. Cesar-Jr, and L. da F. Costa. AGN Simulation and Validation model. In *Proceedings of Advances in Bioinformatics and Computational Biology*, volume 5167 of Lecture Notes in Bioinformatics, pages 169–173. Springer-Verlag Berlin, 2008.

[17] F. M. Lopes, R. M. Cesar-Jr, and L. da F. Costa. Gene Expression Complex Networks: Synthesis, Identification, and Analysis. *Journal of Computational Biology*, 18(10):1535–1367, 2011.

[18] F. M. Lopes, E. de Oliveira, and R. Cesar. Inference of gene regulatory networks from time series by Tsallis entropy. *BMC Systems Biology*, 5(1):61, 2011.

[19] F. M. Lopes, D. C. Martins-Jr, and R. M. Cesar-Jr. Feature selection environment for genomic applications. *BMC Bioinformatics*, 9(1):451, October 2008.

[20] M. Mamakou, C. Sirakoulis, I. Andreadis, and I. Karafyllidis. Adaptive reverse engineering of gene regulatory networks using genetic algorithms. In *Computer as a Tool, 2005. EUROCON 2005.The International Conference on*, volume 1, pages 401–404, nov. 2005.

[21] D. Marbach, C. Mattiussi, and D. Floreano. Combining Multiple Results of a Reverse Engineering Algorithm: Application to the DREAM Five Gene Network Challenge. *Ann N Y Acad Sci*, 1158:102–113, 2009.

[22] A. Margolin, K. N. Basso, C. Wiggins, G. Stolovitzky, R. Favera, and A. Califano. ARACNE: An algorithm for the reconstruction of gene regulatory networks in a mammalian cellular context. *BMC Bioinformatics*, 7(Suppl 1):S7, 2006.

[23] M. R. Mendoza and A. L. C. Bazzan. Evolving Random Boolean Networks with Genetic Algorithms for Regulatory Networks Reconstruction. In *Proceedings of the 13th annual Conference on Genetic and Evolutionary Computation*, GECCO '11, pages 291–298, New York, NY, USA, July 2011. ACM.

[24] C. E. Shannon. A mathematical theory of communication. *Bell System Technical Journal*, 27:379–423, 623–656, July, October 1948.

[25] I. Shmulevich, E. R. Dougherty, S. Kim, and W. Zhang. Probabilistic Boolean networks: a rule-based uncertainty model for gene regulatory networks. *Bioinformatics*, 18(2):261–274, 2002.

[26] C. Tsallis. I. Nonextensive Statistical Mechanics and Thermodynamics: Historical Background and Present Status. *Lecture Notes in Physics*, 560(3):3–98, 2001.

[27] C. Tsallis. What should a statistical mechanics satisfy to reflect nature? *Physica D: Nonlinear Phenomena*, 193(1-4):3–34, 2004.

Experimental Evaluation of Topological-based Fitness Functions to Detect Complexes in PPI Networks

Clara Pizzuti
National Research Council of Italy, CNR
ICAR
Via P. Bucci 41C, 87036 Rende(CS), Italy
pizzuti@icar.cnr.it

Simona Rombo
National Research Council of Italy, CNR
ICAR and DEIS, Univ. della Calabria
Via P. Bucci 41C, 87036 Rende(CS), Italy
simona.rombo@deis.unical.it

ABSTRACT

The detection of groups of proteins sharing common biological features is an important research issue, intensively investigated in the last few years, because of the insights it can give in understanding cell behavior. In this paper we present an extensive experimental evaluation campaign aiming at exploring the capability of Genetic Algorithms (GAs) to find clusters in protein-protein interaction networks, when different topological-based fitness functions are employed. A complete experimentation on the yeast network, along with a comparative evaluation of the effectiveness in detecting true complexes on the yeast and human networks, reveals GAs as a feasible and competitive computational technique to cope with this problem.

Categories and Subject Descriptors

H.2.8 [**Database Managment**]: Database Applications —*Data Mining*; J.3 [**Computer Applications**]: Life and Medical Science—*Biology and Genetics*; I.5.3 [**Computing Methodologies**]: Pattern Recognition—*Clustering*

General Terms

Algorithms

Keywords

Protein-Protein Interaction Networks, Complex Detection, Genetic Algorithms

1. INTRODUCTION

The molecular characterization of cellular activity is a challenging issue, thus, in the last few years, an increasing number of scientists, such as biologists, computer scientists and mathematicians, have been working to model and analyze biological processes. The most common assumption in this context is understanding the cell as a complex and dynamic system of interacting components, that cannot be analyzed independently [32]. In particular, the discovery and study of interactions between proteins is receiving great attention, also due to both high-throughput (e.g., yeast two-hybrid and coimmunoprecipitation) and computational techniques [14, 15] exploited to obtain a large amount of available interactions.

A powerful way of modeling the whole set of protein-protein interactions of a given organism is the protein-protein interaction (PPI) network. A PPI network is an undirect graph where nodes represent proteins and each edge is associated with a physical interaction (actual or predicted) between two proteins.

PPI networks can also be viewed as sets of interacting complexes, i.e. groups of physically or functionally related proteins joining together to accomplish distinct functions [6]. Thus, proteins can be grouped in clusters such that the proteins in the same cluster share common biological features, such as participating in the same processes, having similar functions, belonging to the same cellular compart. The detection of such clusters provides important knowledge about biological processes, giving a valuable help in understanding the behavior of the cell. This pushed for the proposal of several clustering techniques applied to PPI networks, most of which can be broadly categorized as distance-based and graph-based ones [19]. Distance-based clustering approaches apply traditional clustering techniques, such as hierarchical clustering, by employing the concept of distance between two proteins (e.g., [7, 4, 25]). Graph-based clustering techniques consider instead the topology of the PPI network under analysis (e.g., [31, 23, 2, 9, 27, 12]).

The clustering techniques proposed in the literature are based on various strategies, for example searching for subgraphs having maximum density [23, 2, 12], partitioning the graph by optimizing a cost function [31], exploiting the concept of flow simulation [9] or co-clustering approaches [27]. However, at the best of our knowledge, very few evolutionary techniques have been applied to cluster PPI networks. In particular, in [20] the authors proposed an algorithm based on evolutionary computation for enumerating maximal cliques and apply it to the yeast genomic data. This approach uses chaotic variables to initialize the population of individuals and adds chaotic disturbance in the fitness computation. The method needs to set some threshold values that bias it in the search for an optimal solution, but how to set these thresholds is neither discussed nor investigated. More recently, an immune genetic algorithm to find dense subgraphs based on efficient vaccination method, variable-

GECCO'12, July 7-11, 2012, Philadelphia, Pennsylvania, USA.

length antibody schema definition and new local and global mutations has been proposed in [28] and applied to clustering protein-protein interaction networks.

In this paper, we present an extensive experimental evaluation campaign aiming at exploring the capability of Genetic Algorithms (GAs) to find clusters in PPI networks, when different topological-based fitness functions are employed. The representation of individuals we adopted is the graph-based adjacency representation, originally proposed in [24], and particularly apt for the detection of dense groups of nodes in networks [26]. A complete experimentation on the *Saccaromycaes Cerevisiae* (yeast) PPI network has been performed, and a comparative evaluation of their effectiveness in detecting complexes is reported by using various evaluation metrics, currently adopted to assess computational methods for complex detection. In particular, the clusters predicted by the genetic algorithm using each fitness function are compared with the true known complexes stored in the MIPS databases [21], according to some validation measures widely exploited in the literature [3, 5, 17]. Furthermore, a comparison with the well known $MCODE$ method [5] to detect protein complexes has been performed. The analysis shows that evolutionary computational methods can constitute a valid alternative to state of the art approaches.

The paper is organized as follows. The next section formalizes the problem of complex detection, introduces the fitness functions that will be used, and briefly describes the adopted genetic operators. Section 3 describes the evaluation measures used for comparison. In Section 4 the results of the experiments are reported. Finally, Section 5 concludes the paper and suggests future developments.

2. METHODS

A PPI network N can be modeled as an undirected graph $G = (V, E)$ where V is a set of $n =\mid V \mid$ nodes, each corresponding to a specific protein, and E is a set of $m =\mid E \mid$ undirected edges corresponding to the pairwise interactions. The problem of clustering PPI networks may be interpreted as that of finding dense regions, that is, finding sub-graphs of the graph G associated with N having high density of edges within them, and lower density of edges between groups. This definition of clustering is rather intuitive and vague, thus several criteria have been introduced in order to understand at the best its intrinsic meaning, and heuristics to optimize them have been proposed. However, different criteria can generate different groupings of nodes, thus it is difficult to choose what is deemed the best.

Recently, Leskovec et al. [16] observed that the concept of *good cluster* relies on two criteria. The first is the number of edges between the members of the cluster, the second is the number of edges between the members of the cluster and the rest of the network. Thus they group quality indices in two categories: multi-criterion scores, that combine both criteria, and single criterion scores, that are based on only one criterion. The authors used these criteria to compare a range of community detection methods. In the following we propose to use these quality indices as fitness functions with the aim of detecting complexes in PPI networks, and to perform an experimental evaluation of the obtained results by comparing the complex predicted by using these measures with respect to the true complexes. In the following the definition of these measures is first reported, then the adopted genetic representation and variation operators are described.

2.1 Fitness Functions

Let $G = (V, E)$ be the graph modeling a PPI network, S be a cluster of nodes having n_s nodes and m_s edges, and $c_s = \{(u, v) \mid u \in S, v \notin S\}$ be the number of edges on the boundary of S. Let $\{S_1, \ldots, S_k\}$ be a partition of G in k clusters. The following metrics, reported from [16], that catch the concept of quality of a clustering, are defined.

Conductance: $Co = \sum_{s=1}^{k} \frac{c_s}{2m_s+c_s}$ measures the fraction of edges pointing outside the clustering.

Expansion: $Ex = \sum_{s=1}^{k} \frac{c_s}{n_s}$ measures the number of edges per nodes that point outside the clustering.

Cut Ratio: $CR = \sum_{s=1}^{k} \frac{c_s}{n_s(n-n_s)}$ measures the fraction of all possible edges leaving the clustering.

Normalized Cut: $NC = \sum_{s=1}^{k} \frac{c_s}{2m_s+c_s} + \frac{c_s}{2(m-m_s)+c_s}$ measures the fraction of total edge connections to all the nodes in the graph.

The lower the values of these scores, the better the quality of the clustering obtained. All the above measures are considered multi-criterion scores since they take into account both the edges inside a cluster and those crossing between groups. A single criterion score is the well known concept of *modularity* introduced by Girvan and Newman [22].

Modularity: $Q = \sum_{s=1}^{k} [\frac{2m_s}{m} - (\frac{d_s}{2m})^2]$ measures the expected number of edges between the nodes of a cluster S in a random graph with the same degree sequence, where d_s is the sum of degrees of the nodes of s.

Thus the first term of each summand is the fraction of edges inside a cluster, and the second one is the expected value of the fraction of edges that would be in the network if edges fall at random without regard to the cluster structure. Values approaching 1 indicate high quality clustering. However, it has been proved [11] that the optimization of modularity has a topological resolution limit that depends on both the total size of the network and the interconnections of groups. This implies that small, tightly connected clusters could not be found. This limit implies the drawback that, searching for partitioning of maximum modularity, may lead to solutions in which important structures at small scales are not discovered. To overcome this problem, Granell et al. [13] introduced a resolution control parameter γ in the modularity formulation, $Q_R = \sum_{s=1}^{k} [\frac{2m_s}{m} - \gamma(\frac{d_s}{2m})^2]$. When $\gamma = 1$ the original formulation is obtained and, for increasing values of γ, smaller groups of nodes can be found.

2.2 Genetic representation and operators

The genetic algorithm uses locus-based adjacency representation proposed in [24]. In this graph-based representation an individual of the population consists of n genes $g_1, \ldots, g_n$ and each gene can assume allele values j in the range $\{1, \ldots, n\}$. Genes and alleles represent nodes of the graph $G = (V, E)$ modelling a PPI network, and a value j assigned to the ith gene is interpreted as a link between the proteins i and j. This means that in the clustering solution found i and j will be in the same cluster. The initialization process assigns to each node i one of its neighbors j. This guarantees a division of the network in connected groups of nodes. The kind of adopted crossover operator is uniform crossover. Given two parents, a random binary vector is created. Uniform crossover then selects those genes where the vector is a 0 from the first parent, and those genes where the vector is a 1 from the second parent, and combines genes to generate the child. The mutation operator, analogously to the initialization process, randomly assigns to each node i one of its neighbors.

3. EVALUATION MEASURES

Available interaction data stored in public databases are not always reliable, since they are often obtained by prediction and computational techniques. MIPS databases [21] provide a collection of manually curated high-quality PPI data, collected from the scientific literature by expert curators. Only data from individually performed experiments are included, since they usually provide the most reliable evidence for physical interactions. By considering curated protein complexes stored in MIPS databases [21], the effectiveness of a method in detecting such known complexes can be evaluated by comparing the predicted clusters with the true known complexes.

In the following we describe some validation measures widely exploited in the literature [3, 5, 17] that will be used for the comparative analysis presented in this work. For the generic predicted cluster P_i and the generic known complex K_j, let $\mid P_i \mid$ and $\mid K_j \mid$ be their sizes, respectively. Furthermore, let $\mid P_i \cap K_j \mid$ be the size of the intersection set of the predicted cluster and the known complex. To evaluate how a predicted cluster P_i matches a known complex K_j, the *overlapping score* between P_i and K_j is defined as $OS(P_i, K_j) = \frac{|P_i \cap K_j|^2}{|P_i| \cdot |K_j|}$.

A known complex and a predicted cluster are considered a *match* [17] if $OS(P_i, K_j) \geq \sigma_{OS}$, i.e. their overlapping score is equal to or larger than a specific threshold σ_{OS}. To estimate the performance of algorithms for detecting protein complexes w.r.t. the overlapping score, the notions of *sensitivity* and *specificity*, commonly used in information retrieval and machine learning (also known as *recall* and *precision*), as well as a cumulative measure called *f-measure* are introduced.

Sensitivity: $S_n = \frac{TP}{TP+FN}$ is the fraction of the true-positive predictions out of all the true predictions, where TP (true positive) is the number of the predicted clusters matched by the known complexes with $OS(P_i, K_j) \geq \sigma_{OS}$, and FN (false negative) is the number of the known complexes that are not matched by the predicted clusters.

Specificity: $S_p = \frac{TP}{TP+FP}$ is the fraction of the true-positive predictions out of all the positive predictions, where FP (false positive) equals the total number of the predicted clusters minus TP.

F-measure: $F_m = \frac{2 \cdot S_n \cdot S_p}{S_n + S_p}$ is a measure that summarizes sensitivity and specificity. High values of f-measure means that both sensitivity and specificity are sufficiently high.

4. EXPERIMENTAL RESULTS

In this section we present the results of an extensive experimentation of the genetic algorithm to evaluate prediction capability when different topological measures, described above, are used as fitness functions. It is known that setting parameter values is a challenging research problem in evolutionary algorithms [10]. Though recently Smith and Eiben [30] found that good parameter values can be obtained for a set of problems, general tuning allowing for good performance on a wide range of problems raises specific difficulties. In particular, there are no studies regarding the application domain of PPI networks. Thus a complete experimental campaign has been performed by running the genetic algorithm for all combinations of values of crossover fraction and mutation rate, ranging from 0.2 to 1, with an increment step of 0.2. Furthermore we set elite reproduction 10% of the population size, roulette selection function, population size 50, and number of generations 50. For all the experiments, the statistical significance of the obtained results has been checked by performing a t-test at the 5% significance level. The p-values returned are very small, thus the significance level is very high since the probability that a complex could be obtained by chance is very low. The implementation has been written in MATLAB 4.3 R2010a, using Genetic Algorithms and Direct Search Toolbox 2. We run the GA method on a publicly available benchmark, namely the Database of Interacting Proteins, DIP, consisting of 17,203 interactions among 4,930 proteins. In order to evaluate the predicted complexes, a benchmark set of 428 gold standard complexes coming from different sources, such as MIPS and SGD database based on Gene Ontology annotations, have been used. Both the network and the true complexes have been provided by Li et al. [18].

Figure 1, Figure 2, and Figure 3 show the sensitivity, specificity, and f-measure values obtained for all the fitness functions, when crossover fraction and mutation rate vary in the range of values [0.2, 0.4, 0.6, 0.8, 1]. The first observation that can be done is that the values computed by using the evaluation measures do not show a high variation at the varying of crossover and mutation values, the differences being of the order of at most one decimal digit. For example, in Figure 1(a) the highest value of sensitivity is 0.393, obtained with mutation rate and crossover fraction both equal to 0.4, while the lowest value is 0.35 when mutation rate is 1 and crossover fraction is 0.6, differing only of 0.04 with respect to the second decimal digit. Thus the genetic approach seems to be rather stable as regards the choice of the parameter values that could give improved performance on the yeast network. The best value of sensitivity is obtained when the fitness function is modularity with resolution parameter $\gamma = 3$, mutation rate 0.2, and crossover fraction 0.8 (see Figure 1(b)). Actually, the differences with modularity are not very high, but the resolution parameter allows to partition the network in a larger number of smaller clusters. This can be seen in Table 1, where the number of complexes predicted by using each fitness function is shown, together with the number of predicted complexes that match at least a true complex. From the table it can be observed that, when the fitness function is Q_R, the number of both predicted clusters and matched complexes are the highest with respect to the other measures. However, looking at Figure 2, modularity is not the best performing measure. In fact, in such a case, all the other fitness functions obtain higher values of specificity. This means that modularity partitions the network such that the fraction of proteins correctly predicted is higher than the other scores. On the other hand, higher values of specificity, means lower number of false positive, that is in the same cluster the fraction of proteins effectively belonging to that cluster is higher However, since maximizing both scores is often difficult, a tradeoff between the two, i.e. the f-measure, allows to choose a model with good values of both sensitivity and specificity. To this end, Figure 3 shows that modularity obtains the best values of f-measure.

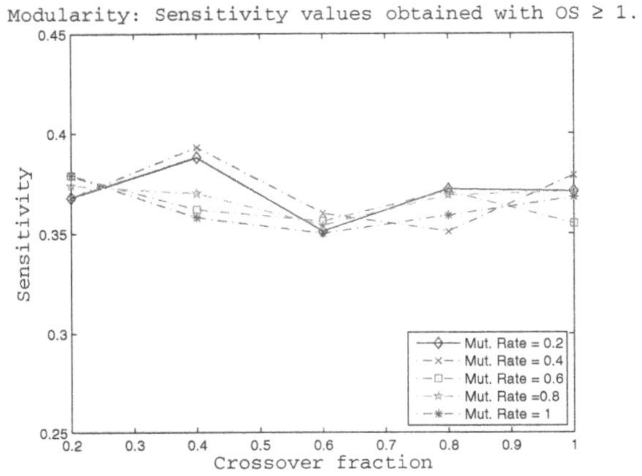

(a)

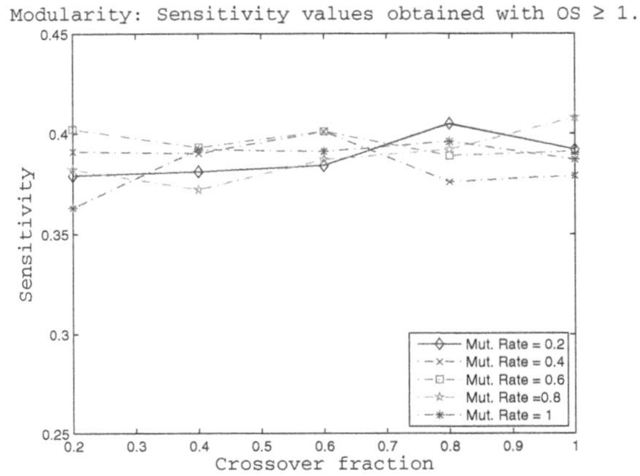

(b)

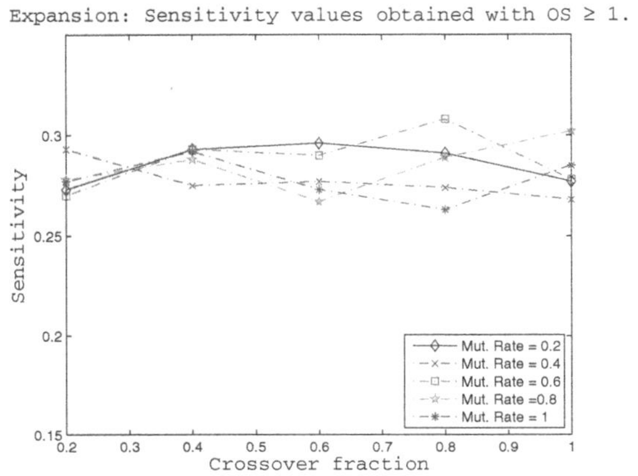

(c)

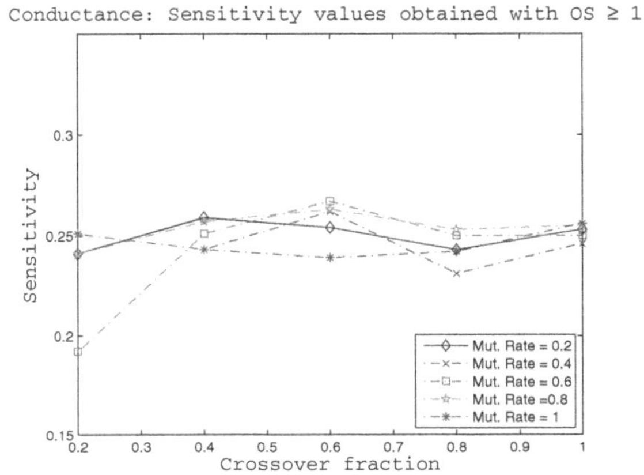

(d)

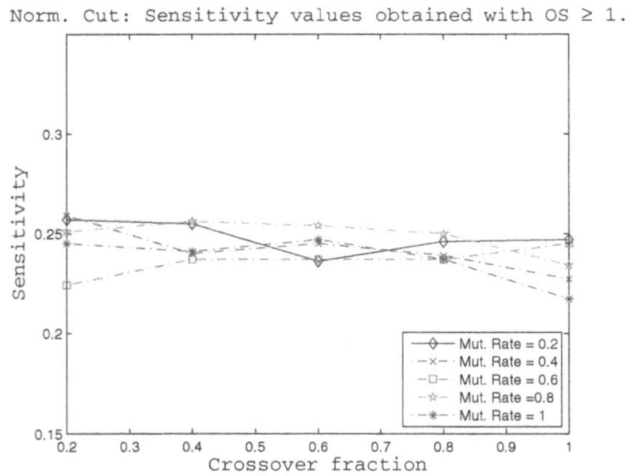

(e)

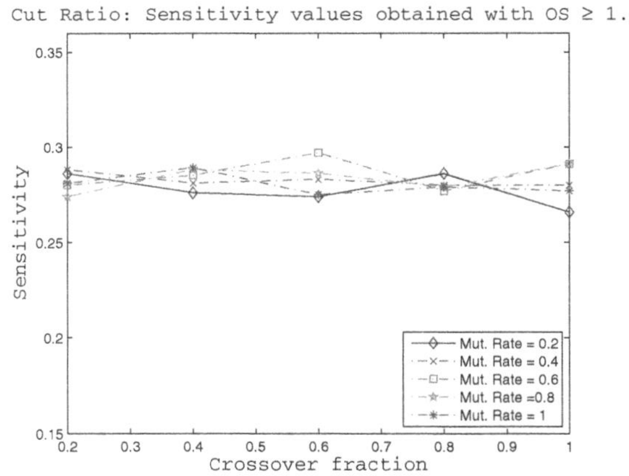

(f)

Figure 1: Sensitivity values for different values of crossover and mutation rate, with $\sigma_{OS} \geq 1$, for: (a) modularity (b) modularity with γ=3, (c) expansion, (d) conductance, (e) Normalized Cut, (f) CutRatio.

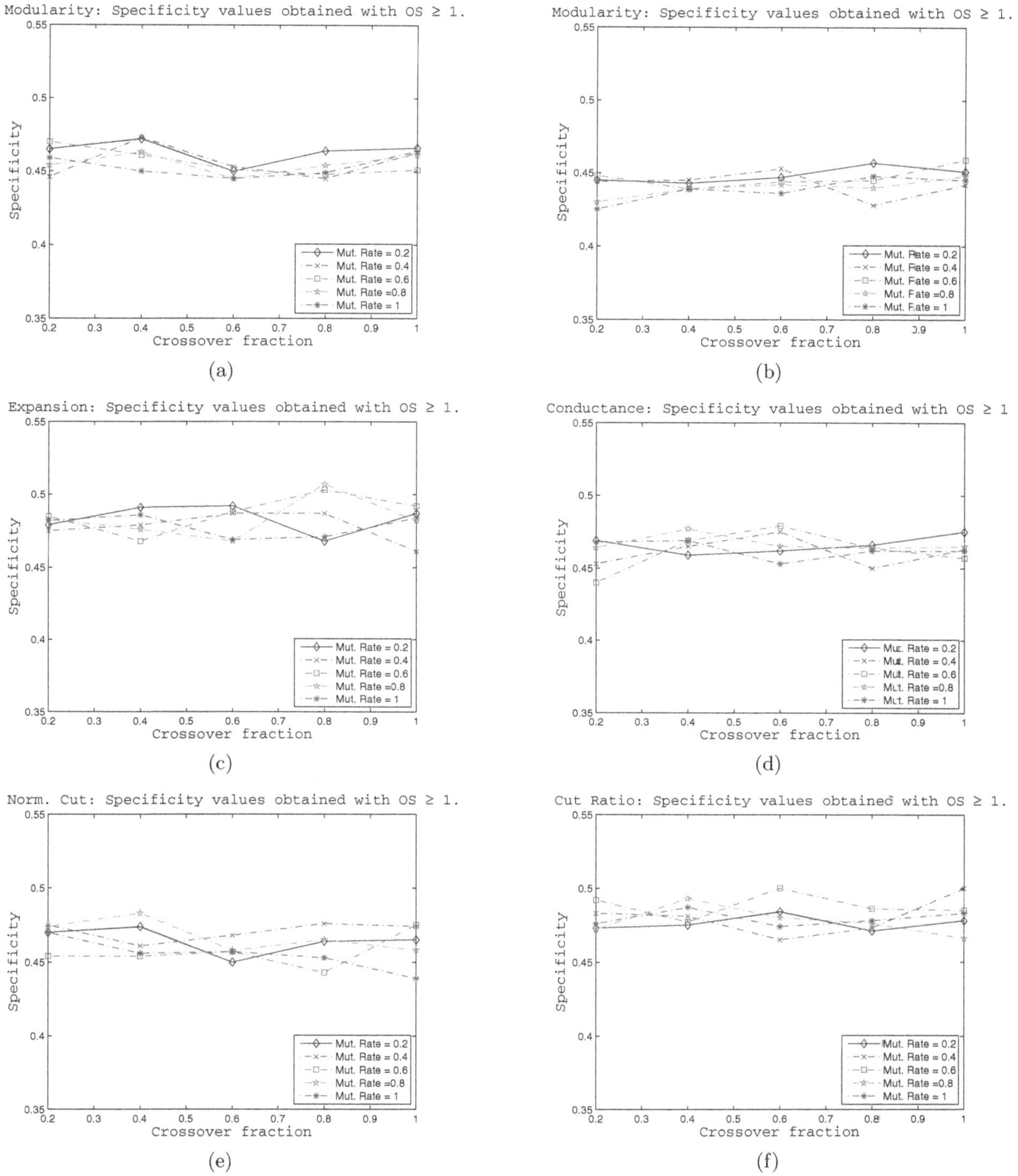

Figure 2: Specificity values for different values of crossover and mutation rate, with $\sigma_{OS} \geq 1$, for: (a) modularity (b) modularity with γ=3, (c) expansion, (d) conductance, (e) Normalized Cut, (f) CutRatio.

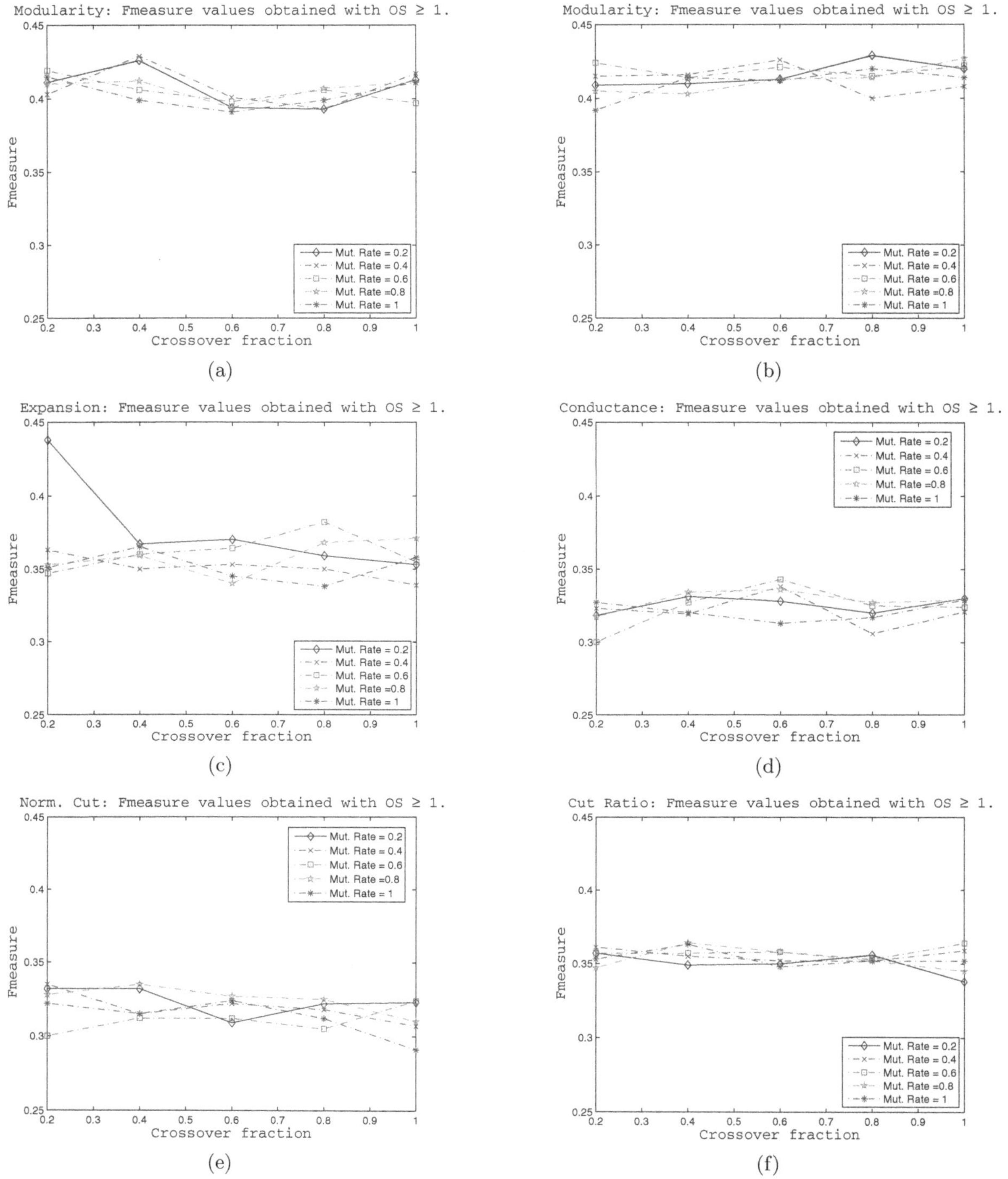

Figure 3: Fmeasure values for different values of crossover and mutation rate, with $\sigma_{OS} \geq 1$, for: (a) modularity (b) modularity with γ=3, (c) expansion, (d) conductance, (e) Normalized Cut, (f) CutRatio.

Table 1: Results with the various fitness functions on the DIP network.

Fitness	Co	Ex	CR	NC	Q	Q_R
# predicted complexes	221.8 (15.2)	242.2 (13.4)	242.4 (11.9)	215.6 (15.7)	329.8(11.8)	360.4 (13.6)
# matched complexes	116.9 (6.5)	112.6 (9.1)	130.7 (3.4)	114.3 (4.9)	167.7 (5.5)	177.6 (5.03)

Table 2: Comparative performance between the GA approach with modularity as fitness function, and *MCODE*, both non overlapping and overlapping (MCODE-OV) on the Human network.

Algorithms	MCODE	MCODE-OV	GA
Specificity	0.252	**0.306**	0.153
Sensitivity	0.141	0.176	**0.461**
F-measure	0.181	0.224	**0.23**

Another important consideration about the results we obtained is that the number of predicted clusters is lower than the number of true complexes. This means that the genetic approach, endowed with the topological measures previously described, finds clusters of larger size that could include some true complex. Considering that the benchmark set of 428 gold standard complexes do not cover all the proteins of the DIP network, thus many proteins are not assigned to any group, the detection of clusters of larger size, including a true complex, could be exploited for functional annotation of proteins. In fact, as pointed out by Sharan et al. [29], an approach to functional annotation of proteins is based on assigning the function that is prevalent in a group of proteins, obtained by dividing the PPI network in dense clusters. Figure 4 shows an example of a cluster predicted constituted by 7 proteins, namely YAL003W, YBR118W, YKL081W, YPL048W, YCR042C, YHL034C, YPL226W, that contains true MIPS complex composed by the first four proteins. It is interesting to note that the protein YPL226W is not assigned in the benchmark set of true complexes, though it is connected with the proteins YKL081W and YDR142C. Because of the above observations, YPL226W could be annotated with the same function of the 4-proteins MIPS complex.

Finally, we compare the GA approach, when modularity is used as fitness function, with one of the most known clustering technique proposed in the literature for PPI networks, i.e. the algorithm *MCODE* [5]. This method allows to detect also overlapping clusters, i.e. a protein can belong to more than one cluster, thus we report the results for both the versions of *MCODE*. For such a comparison, we used a different PPI network that is, the *Homo Sapiens* (human) network by setting mutation rate to 0.2, crossover fraction to 0.4, and by choosing the modularity as fitness function. The choice of another network has been done to test the performance of the better parameter values obtained by the previous experimentation on the yeast network. The human network, consisting of 6,716 nodes and 16,322 interactions, has been downloaded from the MINT database [8], while the benchmark set of 1,083 known and curated complexes for human has been taken from [1]. Table 2 points out that the genetic approach is comparable with *MCODE*. In fact, it obtains higher values of sensitivity and f-measure, while specificity is lower than both non-overlapping *MCODE* and overlapping *MCODE* (denoted as *MCODE-OV*).

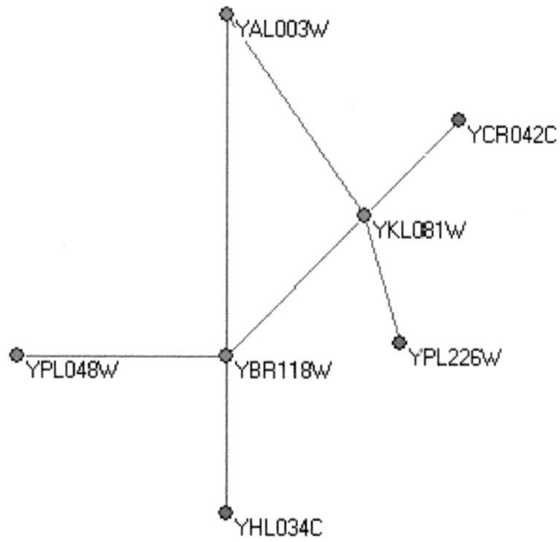

Figure 4: An example of predicted cluster containing the true MIPS complex YAL003W, YBR118W, YKL081W, YPL048W (red nodes).

5. CONCLUSIONS

This paper presented an extensive experimentation by using Genetic Algorithms endowed with six topological-based fitness functions, for the detection of dense groups of proteins in PPI networks. The results showed that this computational method is a viable choice to obtain significative solutions. It is worth to point out that a main drawback of the proposed approach is that a protein can be assigned to only one cluster. However, many proteins present the characteristic of being connected to a high number of other proteins, thus often participating in multiple biological processes and performing different functions. The incapability of detecting overlapping clusters is due to the genetic representation, that does not allow a node to be connected to more than one other node. Future work aims at extending the graph-based representation to allow for the detection of overlapping clusters, such that a protein can belong to several clusters, and to compare the approach with other state of the art clustering methods.

6. ACKNOWLEDGMENTS

This work has been partially supported by the project *MERIT : MEdical Research in Italy*, funded by MIUR.

7. REFERENCES

[1] Website title: http://mips.helmholtz-muenchen.de/genre/proj/corum.

[2] B. Adamcsek, G. Palla, I. J. Farkas, I. Dernyi, and T. Vicsek. Cfinder: locating cliques and overlapping modules in biological networks. *Bioinformatics*, 22(8):1021–1023, 2006.

[3] M. Altaf-Ul-Amin, Y. Shinbo, K. Mihara, K. Kurokawa, and S. Kanaya. Development and implementation of an algorithm for detection of protein complexes in large interaction networks. *BMC Bioinformatics*, 7(207), 2006.

[4] V. Arnau, S. Mars, and I. Marìn. Iterative cluster analysis of protein interaction data. *Bioinformatics*, 21(3):364–378, 2005.

[5] G. Bader and H. Hogue. An automated method for finding molecular complexes in large protein-protein interaction networks. *BMC Bioinformatics*, 4(2), 2003.

[6] A. Barabási and Z. N. Oltvai. Network biology: Understanding the cell's functional organization. *Nature Review Genetics*, 5:101–113, 2004.

[7] M. Blatt, S. Wiseman, and E. Domany. Superparamagnetic clustering of data. *Phisical Review Letters*, 76(18):3251–3254, 1996.

[8] A. Ceol et al. Mint, the molecular interaction database: 2009 update. *Nucleic Acids Research*, 38(Database issue):D532–D539, 2010.

[9] Y.-R. Cho, W. Hwang, M. Ramanathan, and A. Zhang. Semantic integration to identify overlapping functional modules in protein interaction networks. *BMC Bioinformatics*, 8(265), 2007.

[10] A. E. Eiben, R. Hinterding, and Z. Michalewicz. Parameter control in evolutionary algorithms. *IEEE Transactions on Evolutionary Computation*, 3(2):124–141, 1999.

[11] S. Fortunato and M. Barthélemy. Resolution limit in community detection. *Proc. National Academy of Science, USA*, 104(1):36–41, 2007.

[12] E. Georgii, S. Dietmann, T. Uno, P. Pagel, and K. Tsuda. Enumeration of condition-dependent dense modules in protein interaction networks. *Bioinformatics*, 25(7):933–940, 2009.

[13] C. Granell, S. Gómez, and A. Arenas. Unsupervised clustering analisys: A multiscale complex network approach. *Journal of Bifurcation and Chaos, in press*, 2012.

[14] T. Ito, T. Chiba, R. Ozawa, M. Yoshida, M. Hattori, and Y. Sakaki. A comprehensive two-hybrid analysis to explore the yeast protein interactome. *Proceedings of the National Academy of Science of the United States of America*, 98(8):4569–4574, 2001.

[15] N. J. Krogan et al. Global landscape of protein complexes in the yeast Saccharomyces cerevisiae. *Nature*, 440(7084):637–643, 2006.

[16] J. Leskovec, K. Lang, and M. Mahoney. Empirical comparison of algorithms for network community detection. In *Proc. Int. World Wide Web Conference (WWW 2010)*, pages 631–640, 2010.

[17] M. Li, J. Chen, J. Wang, B. Hu, and G. Chen. Modifying the DPClus algorithm for identifying protein complexes based on new topological structures. *BMC Bioinformatics*, 9(398), 2008.

[18] X. Li, M. Wu, C. Kwoh, and S. Ng. Computational approaches for detecting protein complexes from protein interaction network: a survey. *BMC Genomics*, 11(Suppl 1): S3, 2010.

[19] C. Lin, Y. Cho, W. Hwang, P. Pei, and A. Zhang. Clustering methods in protein-protein interaction network. *in Knowledge Discovery in Bioinformatics: Techniques, Methods and Application, John Wiley & Sons,Inc*, pages 319–355, 2006.

[20] H. Liu and J. Liu. Clustering protein interaction data through chaotic genetic algorithm. In *Simulated Evolution and Learning*, volume 4247 of *Lecture Notes in Computer Science*, pages 858–864. Springer Berlin / Heidelberg, 2006.

[21] H. W. Mewes and al. MIPS: a database for genomes and protein sequences. *Nucleic Acids Res.*, 30(1):31–34, 2002.

[22] M. E. J. Newman and M. Girvan. Finding and evaluating community structure in networks. *Physical Review*, E69:026113, 2004.

[23] G. Palla, I. Derenyi, I. Farkas, and T. Vicsek. Uncovering the overlapping community structure of complex networks in nature and society. *Nature*, 435:814–818, 2005.

[24] Y. Park and M. Song. A genetic algorithm for clustering problems. In *Proc. of 3rd Annual Conference on Genetic Algorithms*, pages 2–9, 1989.

[25] P. Pei and A. Zhang. A two-step approach for clustering proteins based on protein interaction profiles. In *IEEE Int. Symposium on Bioinformatics and Bioengeneering (BIBE'2005)*, pages 201–209, 2005.

[26] C. Pizzuti. GA-Net: a genetic algorithm for community detection in social networks. In *Proc. of the 10th International Conference on Parallel Problem Solving from Nature (PPSN 2008)*, pages 1081–1090. LNCS 5189, Springer, 2008.

[27] C. Pizzuti and S. E. Rombo. A Coclustering Approach for Mining Large Protein-Protein Interaction Networks. *IEEE/ACM Transactions on Compututational Biology and Bioinformatics*, 9(3): 717–730, 2012.

[28] H. Ravaee, A. Masoudi-Nejad, S. Omidi, and A. Moeini. Improved immune genetic algorithm for clustering protein-protein interaction network. In *Proceedings of the 2010 IEEE International Conference on Bioinformatics and Bioengineering*, BIBE '10, pages 174–179. IEEE Computer Society, 2010.

[29] R. Sharan, I. Ulitsky, and R. Shamir. Network-based prediction of protein function. *Molecular Systems Biology*, 3(88), 2007.

[30] S. K. Smit and A. E. Eiben. Parameter tuning of evolutionary algorithms: Generalist vs. specialist. In *Applications of Evolutionary Computation, Springer*, pages 542–551, 2010.

[31] V. Spirin and L. A. Mirny. Protein complexes and functional modules in molecular networks. *PNAS*, 100:12123–12128, 2003.

[32] D. von Mering, C. Krause, and *et al.* Comparative assessment of a large-scale data sets of protein-protein interactions. *Nature*, 31:399–403, 2002.

Bee Algorithms for Solving DNA Fragment Assembly Problem with Noisy and Noiseless data

Jesun Sahariar Firoz *
AℓEDA group
Department of CSE, BUET
Dhaka, Bangladesh
jesunsahariar@gmail.com

M. Sohel Rahman
AℓEDA group
Department of CSE, BUET
Dhaka, Bangladesh
msrahman@cse.buet.ac.bd

Tanay Kumar Saha
AℓEDA group
Department of CSE, BUET
Dhaka, Bangladesh
tanay@cse.jnu.ac.bd

ABSTRACT

DNA fragment assembly problem is one of the crucial challenges faced by computational biologists where, given a set of DNA fragments, we have to construct a complete DNA sequence from them. As it is an NP-hard problem, accurate DNA sequence is hard to find. Moreover, due to experimental limitations, the fragments considered for assembly are exposed to additional errors while reading the fragments. In such scenarios, meta-heuristic based algorithms can come in handy. We analyze the performance of two swarm intelligence based algorithms namely Artificial Bee Colony (ABC) algorithm and Queen Bee Evolution Based on Genetic Algorithm (QEGA) to solve the fragment assembly problem and report quite promising results. Our main focus is to design meta-heuristic based techniques to efficiently handle DNA fragment assembly problem for noisy and noiseless data.

Categories and Subject Descriptors

F.2.2 [**Analysis of Algorithms and Problem Complexity**]: Nonnumerical Algorithms and Problems—*Sequencing*

General Terms

Algorithm

Keywords

Bioinformatics, Genetic algorithms, DNA computing, Metaheuristics, Combinatorial optimization

1. INTRODUCTION

In DNA (Deoxyribonucleic Acid) fragment assembly problem (FAP), we are given a set of large number of DNA fragments with errors and are asked to find the correct sequence of the DNA by finding the permutation of fragments that best represents the DNA sequence. This problem finds its motivation from the limitation of current technology, which enables us to read only several hundreds of base pairs (bps) of a single DNA at a time. Consequently, we need to read fragments of the DNA but not the whole sequence at a time. During this process base pairs may be removed, misread or inserted.

To read the DNA fragments, a process named shotgun sequencing [31] is used. In this method, multiple copies of the DNA sequence are first generated through a process called amplification. Then we cut these sequences at random points keeping in mind that we can only directly read a sequence of several hundreds bps long. With these fragments, we try to reconstruct the overlapping DNA sequence as accurately as possible. This is called shotgun sequencing. A lot of tools have been invented to automate DNA sequencing. Among these tools, PHRAP [12], TIGR assembler [32], STROLL [7], CAP3 [13], Celera assembler [24] and EULER [26] may be cited. All of these tools focus on coping with different problems faced during fragment assembly.

To the best of our knowledge, the first work on solving the fragment assembly problem with meta-heuristics can be found in [20]. In this paper, approaches based on Ant Colony System (ACS) are proposed to solve FAP. Later, in [18], the authors presented several methods - a canonical genetic algorithm, a CHC (Cross generational elitist selection, Heterogeneous recombination and Cataclysmic mutation) method, a scatter search algorithm and a simulated annealing method - to solve accurately some problem instances that are 77K base pairs long. Since the work of [18], the problem of DNA fragment assembly has been tackled with different other heuristics and meta-heuristics in the literature [6, 8, 23]. However, the quest for new more accurate and faster techniques still continues.

Classical assemblers use fitness functions favoring solutions with strong overlaps between adjacent fragments in the layouts. But we also need to obtain an order of the fragments that minimizes the number of contigs, with the goal of reaching one single contig, i.e., a complete DNA sequence composed of all the overlapping fragments. PALS [6] (Problem Aware Local Search) is a simple, fast and accurate heuristic solution that is recently proposed with the objective of achieving this criteria. In PALS, the number of contigs is used as a high-level criterion to judge the whole quality of the results since it is difficult to capture the dy-

*This work is part of the M.Sc. Engg. thesis work of Firoz under the supervision of Rahman at the Department of CSE, BUET.

GECCO'12, July 7-11, 2012, Philadelphia, Pennsylvania, USA.

namics of the problem into other mathematical functions. However, the calculation of the number of contigs is quite time-consuming, and this fact definitely precludes any algorithm to use such calculation. A solution to this problem was introduced in [6] as the utilization of a method which should not need to know the exact number of contigs and thus be computationally light. The key contribution of PALS [6] is to indirectly estimate the number of contigs by measuring the actual number of contigs that are created or destroyed when tentative solutions are manipulated. The authors in [6] used a variation of a heuristic algorithm for TSP for the DNA field, which does not only use the overlaps among the fragments, but also takes into account (in an intelligent manner) the number of contigs that has been created or destroyed.

In [8], the authors proposed a new method combining a general purpose meta-heuristic with a local search method specifically designed for this problem, namely, PALS of [6]. They presented a new approach of cellular genetic algorithms (cGA) that regulates the intensity on the search while solving a problem, outperforming the compared cGAs with static populations. Another paper [17] proposed evolutionary-based iterative optimization method called Prototype Optimization with Evolved Improvement Steps (POEMS) to solve the DNA fragment assembly problem. POEMS is an iterative algorithm that seeks for the best modification of the current solution in each iteration. The modifications are evolved by means of an evolutionary algorithm.

All of the above mentioned previous works consider operations on noiseless data. Recently, in [23], performance of various meta-heuristic based algorithms were discussed where a uniform random error model was introduced in the fitness score matrix.Very recently in [11] several hybrid meta-heuristics were proposed to tackle the fragment assembly problem with noisy data taking into consideration different error models (e.g. Sanger,454 etc).

1.1 Our Contribution

In this paper, we focus on solving FAP for noisy and noiseless instances of DNA sequences. We have used fragments generated by GenFrag [9] to simulate noiseless instances. For noisy case, we first observe an important drawback of the recent work of [23]. The drawback of this technique is that no particular sequencing model was taken into consideration to incorporate the corresponding error model. To overcome this drawback and for the construction of a realistic read data set, here we use a sequencing simulator MetaSim [29]. In this simulator, the user is able to choose from different (adaptable) error models of current sequencing technologies (e.g. Sanger [21, 22], Rochei's 454 [19] and Illumina (former Solexa) [28]). In Sanger sequencing, the error model is based on the following two assumptions:

1. the probability of an error occurring at position i of a read increases linearly with i, and
2. if an error occurs at position i, then with some fixed probabilities, it is either a substitution, a deletion or an insertion.

In 454 sequencing, the intensity of emitted light is used to estimate the length of homopolymers, i.e. , runs of identical nucleotides in a sequence. During sequencing, the four DNA composing nucleotides are periodically flowed over the inserts to be sequenced. Within each flow, the intensity of the signal emitted reflects the number of nucleotides incorporated and thus the length of the homopolymer under consideration. For chemical and technical reasons, this signal is subject to fluctuations that lead to sequencing errors.

After generating realistic dataset with errors, we have implemented Artificial Bee Colony (ABC) algorithm and Queen Bee Evolution Based on Genetic Algorithm (QEGA) to solve the DNA fragment assembly problem as accurately as possible and compared the relative fitness achieved in each case.

As has been mentioned before, in most of the related works it was assumed that, the fragments being read are correct. We have eliminated this assumption by incorporating error models in generating artificial fragments to be sequenced and exploit the probabilistic behavior of ABC or QEGA so that worse individuals in the population are taken into consideration. In this way, the chance of completely eliminating a probably misread fragment is minimized and we are bound to find more realistic solutions. Simultaneously, we also analyze the behavior of these two algorithms for noiseless cases. Also, using forward and backward read technique of MetaSim [29], we have been able to emulate a more realistic input sequence mimicking experimental output. These facts give us a promising insight about the feasibility of using meta-heuristics to solve DNA fragment assembly problem.

The rest of the paper is organized as follows: In Section 2, we give an overview of DNA fragment assembly problem and error models used in fragment generation. In Section 3, we present the details of Artificial Bee Colony (ABC) algorithm and Queen Bee Evaluation based on genetic algorithm (QEGA) and the adaptation of these two algorithms to solve DNA FAP. Section 4 presents the experimental results achieved by executing our algorithms on several standard instances of DNA that are widely used in the literature. We briefly conclude in Section 5.

2. BACKGROUND

In this section, we present some background and preliminaries. Most of the definitions and procedures presented in this section follow from [18].

The input of the DNA fragment assembly problem is a set of fragments that are randomly cut from a DNA sequence. The DNA is a double helix of two anti-parallel and complementary nucleotide sequences. One strand is read from $5'$ to $3'$ and the other from $3'$ to $5'$. There are four kinds of nucleotides in any DNA sequence, namely, Adenine (A), Thymine (T), Guanine (G), and Cytosine (C).

To further understand the problem, we need to know the following basic terminology:

- *Fragment:* A short sequence of DNA with length up to 1000 bps.
- *Shotgun data:* A set of fragments.

- *Prefix:* A substring comprising the first n characters of a fragment f.
- *Suffix:* A substring comprising the last n characters of a fragment f.
- *Overlap:* Common sequence between the suffix of one fragment and the prefix of another fragment.
- *Layout:* An alignment of a collection of fragments based on the overlap order, i.e., the fragment order in which the fragments must be joined.
- *Contig:* A layout consisting of contiguous overlapping fragments, i.e., a sequence in which the overlap between adjacent fragments is greater than a predefined threshold.
- *Consensus:* A sequence or string derived from the layout by taking the majority vote for each column of the layout.

To measure the quality of a consensus, we can look at the distribution of the coverage. Coverage at a base position is defined as the number of fragments at that position. It is a measure of the redundancy of the fragment data. It denotes the number of fragments, on average, in which a given nucleotide in the target DNA is expected to appear and is computed as follows [30]:

$$Coverage = \frac{\sum_{i=1}^{g} \text{length of the fragment } i}{\text{target sequence length}}, \quad (1)$$

where g denotes the no. of fragments.

2.1 DNA Sequencing Process

To determine the function of specific genes, scientists read the sequence of nucleotides comprising a DNA sequence in a process called DNA sequencing. The fragment assembly starts with breaking the given DNA sequence into small fragments. To do that, multiple exact copies of the original DNA sequence are made. Each copy is then cut into short fragments at random positions (*duplicate and sonicate phases*). Then this biological material is "converted" to computer data (*sequence and call bases phases*). These steps take place in the laboratory. After the fragment set is obtained, traditional assembly approach is followed in the following phases in the given order: overlap, layout, and then consensus. In overlap phase, the best or longest match between the suffix of one sequence and the prefix of another are found. Layout phase consists of finding the order of fragments based on the computed similarity score. Consensus phase consists of deriving the DNA sequence from the layout. The most common technique used in this phase is to apply the majority rule in building the consensus.

2.2 Sanger Sequencing Error Model

In Sanger Sequencing [1] the following parameters concerning different probability values, P must be set because of the two assumptions mentioned earlier:

1. P (error at i) for positions $i = 1$ and $i = 1000$
2. P (deletion | error)
3. P (insertion | error)
4. P (subtitution | error) = 1 - P (deletion | error) - P (insertion | error)

2.3 454 Sequencing Error Model

For 454 sequencing [1] error model, let r denote the length of a given homopolymer. The emitted light intensity can be modeled by a normal distribution $N(\mu, \sigma)$, with mean $\mu = \sigma$ and standard deviation $\sigma = k * \sqrt{r}$, where k is a fixed proportionality factor ($k \approx 0.15$). Although basic statistics imply that the standard deviation should grow with the square root of r, for the light intensity emitted during 454-sequencing, it is reported to be $\sigma = k * r$. In 454 model, a *negative flow* is a flow of nucleotides in which the sequence to synthesize is not elongated. Light intensities of negative flows follow a lognormal distribution, with mean $\mu = 0.23$, and standard deviation $\sigma = 0.15$. A random variable X is said to be lognormally distributed, if the random variable $\ln X$ is normally distributed. Let μ and σ be the mean and standard deviation of X and let m and s be the mean and standard deviation of $\ln(X)$. Then,

$$m = \ln(\frac{\mu^2}{\sqrt{\sigma^2 + \mu^2}}),\ s = \sqrt{\ln((\frac{\sigma}{\mu})^2 + 1)} \quad (2)$$

The base-calling intensities of negative flows can be based on this and the misinterpretation of a base can be modeled as homopolymers of length = 1. A simulator take the order of the sequencing flows into account. The nucleotides are cyclicly flowed in the order T, A, C, G and thus only two specific negative flows in a specific order are allowed after any given base. Now comes the base-calling process. As the details of the base-calling algorithm are not known in detail, and are presumably subject to constant improvements, there may occur a loss of accuracy here. First, the intersections of the density functions of the normal distributions for different homopolymer lengths r_1 and r_2 are calculated and stored in an intersection matrix M. Then, these values are used to decide which homopolymer length is called.

2.4 Exact Error Model

The Exact Error Model is suitable for sampling reads without modifying any bases, i.e. in contrast to the other provided error models, no substitution, insertion or deletion is applied to the read sequences. But orientations may be changed during reading.

3. BEE ALGORITHMS

The Bee Colony meta-heuristic algorithms are nature-inspired algorithms based on various biological and natural processes observed in honeybee. Some of these algorithms are inspired by the foraging behavior of honeybee. One of them, Artificial Bee Colony (ABC) Algorithm, is a meta-heuristic designed upon the concept of the intelligent behavior of honey bee swarm. Honey bees use techniques like waggle dance that can be used to develop new intelligent search algorithms. Another class of Bee Colony algorithms is inspired by the queen bee evolution process and has used it to enhance the optimization capability of genetic algorithms. The queen-bee evolution makes it possible for genetic algorithms to quickly reach the global optimum as well as decreasing the probability of premature convergence.

3.1 Artificial Bee Colony (ABC) Algorithm

In the ABC algorithm [16], the colony of artificial bees contains three groups of bees: employed bees, onlookers and scouts. A bee which waits at the dance area for making decision to choose a food source depending on waggle dance of employed bee, is called an onlooker and a bee going to the food source visited by itself previously is named an employed bee. A bee which performs random search for food is called a scout. In the ABC algorithm (Algorithm 1), first half of the colony consists of employed artificial bees and the second half constitutes the onlookers. For every food source around the hive, there is only one employed bee. The employed bee whose food source is exhausted by the employed and onlooker bees becomes a scout.

For our DNA FAP, given a set of fragments, our target is to generate a permutation of fragments that minimizes the number of contigs and maximizes the fitness. The solution achieving these two objectives best represents the DNA sequence instance.

In our ABC algorithm, each of the food sources represents a permutation of fragments of a DNA sequence. The position of a food source represents a possible solution and the nectar amount of a food source corresponds to the quality (fitness) of the associated solution. Initially we generate the food source positions (i.e. permutations) randomly. We do not assume that the initial seeds are taken from the best of previous execution of any other algorithm. This is a more realistic assumption compared to [23] where the authors use seeding strategies to find good solution beforehand to exploit promising regions, for both noisy and noiseless data. Our algorithm is robust in the sense that, although we do not make any such preprocessing, our algorithm converges to almost same fitness compared to them in reasonable time.

After the initialization, the food sources are repeatedly searched by employed bees, onlooker bees and scout bees. A employed or onlooker bee produces a modification of the solution for finding a new food source and tests the nectar amount (fitness value) of the new solution. For the modification, we have used problem aware local search (PALS) [6] on the permutation μ under consideration. We have done so because, besides considering fitness value, we also take no. of contigs of a solution into consideration. In all cases, we have used a fitness function (calculation of the amount of nectar) that sums the overlap score for adjacent fragments ($f[i]$ and $f[i+1]$) in a given solution. Let us denote the overlap score by $w(f[i], f[i+1])$ and fitness function by F_μ. Then,

$$F_\mu = \sum_{i=0}^{g-2} w(f[i], f[i+1]), \tag{3}$$

where g is the no. of fragments in the solution.

If the nectar amount of the new modified source is higher than that of the previous one, the bee memorizes the new solution and forgets the old one. Otherwise it keeps the position of the previous one. Onlooker bees choose the food source for modification probabilistically, depending on the nectar amount of the food source. The probability, p_μ is calculated as follows:

$$p_\mu = \frac{F_\mu}{global_{max}}, \tag{4}$$

where $global_{max}$ denotes the maximum fitness value among all food sources. If the nectar amount of a food source increases, the probability with which that food source is chosen by an onlooker increases, too. The dance of employed bees carrying higher nectar has higher probability of being selected by onlookers for exploitation.

Algorithm 1 ABC Algorithm

1: Initialize potential food sources for employed bees.
2: **while** Requirements are not met **do**
3: Each employed bee goes to a food source in her memory and determines a neighbour source, then evaluates its nectar amount and dances in the hive
4: Each onlooker watches the dance of employed bees and chooses one of their sources depending on the dances, and then goes to that source. After choosing a neighbour around that, she evaluates its nectar amount.
5: Abandoned food sources are determined and are replaced with the new food sources discovered by scouts.
6: The best food source found so far is registered
7: **end while**

3.2 Queen-bee Evaluation Based On Genetic Algorithm (QEGA)

Conventional genetic algorithm sometimes become unsuccessful to find a globally optimal solution within a limited no. of evolutions. To overcome this disadvantage, a queen-bee evolution based on genetic algorithm (QEGA) ([15], [27]) is employed for solving the DNA FAP.

Algorithm 2 QEGA Algorithm

Input: time t, population size k, populations P, normal mutation rate σ, normal mutation probability p_m, strong mutation probability p'_m, a queen-bee I_q, selected bees I_m
Output: best fitness solution
1: Initialize $P(t)$
2: Evaluate $P(t)$
3: **while** Condition not met **do**
4: $t \leftarrow t + 1$
5: Select $P(t)$ from $P(t-1)$. So, $P(t) = \{I_q(t-1), I_m(t-1)$.
6: Recombine $P(t)$
7: Crossover
8: **for** $i = 0$ to k **do**
9: **if** $i \leq (\sigma * k)$ **then**
10: Mutate with p_m
11: **else**
12: Mutate with p'_m
13: **end if**
14: **end for**
15: Evaluate $P(t)$
16: **end while**

The population of QEGA consists of several permutations of fragments of a DNA sequence. To determine the fitness value of each individual in the population, we have used Equation 3 as the fitness calculating function in Steps 2 and 15 of QEGA (Algorithm 2).

There are two major differences between conventional genetic algorithm (CGA) and QEGA. Firstly, the parents $P(t)$ in CGA are composed of the k individuals selected by a selection algorithm such as tournament selection. On the other hand, parents $P(t)$ in QEGA consist of the $\frac{k}{2}$ copies of a queen-bee $I_q(t-1)$, where $q = arg\ max\ \{F_\mu, 1 \leq \mu \leq k\}$ and $\frac{k}{2}$ copies of bees $I_m(t-1)$ selected by a selection algorithm, where $1 \leq m \leq \frac{k}{2}$. Secondly, all individuals in conventional genetic algorithm are mutated with small mutation probability p_m, while in QEGA only a part of the individuals are mutated with normal mutation probability p_m and the others are mutated with strong mutation probability p'_m. The ratio between p_m and p'_m is denoted by σ in QEGA. Generally, p_m is less than 0.1 and p'_m is greater than p_m.

So, In QEGA, the fittest individual in a generation, cross-breeds with the bees selected as parents by means of a selection algorithm. This feature of queen-bee evolution reinforces the exploitation of genetic algorithms. That is, fitness of the offsprings mainly rely on the crossover operation and the fittest individual. Consequently, it also increases the probability of premature convergence. Nonetheless, the second feature of QEGA helps genetic algorithms search new space, i.e., it increases the exploration of genetic algorithms through strong mutation. These two features enable genetic algorithms to evolve quickly and simultaneously maintain good solutions. In other words, the queen-bee evolution makes it possible for genetic algorithms to quickly approach the global optimum as well as decreasing the probability of premature convergence.

Ordered two-point crossover has been used as crossover operator in Step 7 of Algorithm 2. In this scheme, given two parents, two random crossover points are selected partitioning them into a left, middle and right portion. Then ordered crossover is carried out in the following way: Child 1 inherits its left and right sections from Parent 1, and its middle section is determined by the fragments in the middle section of Parent 1 in the order these appear in Parent 2. A similar process is applied to determine Child 2. Notably, the Ordered crossover operator is a pure recombination operator [33]. For strong mutation, we have used problem aware local search (PALS) [6]. For normal mutation, we have done random mutation on the offsprings.

4. EXPERIMENTS

In this section, we present our experimental setup and the results obtained by our algorithms. The experiments were conducted in Ubuntu 11.04 running on an Intel core i3 Processor with 2GB RAM.

We have used GenFrag and MetaSim for generating noiseless and noisy artificial fragments respectively. For this, we collected the DNA sequences from NCBI [2, 3, 4, 5]. We give a summary on the different features of the datasets in Table 1.

Table 1: Information of datasets. Accession numbers are used as the name of the instances

Instances (abbreviated form)	Coverage	Mean fragment length	Number of fragments	Original sequence length (in bps)
acin1 (a_1)	26	182	307	2170
acin2 (a_2)	3	1002	451	147200
acin3 (a_3)	3	1001	601	200741
acin5 (a_5)	2	1003	751	329958
acin7 (a_7)	2	1003	901	426840
acin9 (a_9)	7	1003	1049	156305
x60189_4 (x_1)	4	395	39	3835
x60189_5 (x_2)	5	386	48	
x60189_6 (x_3)	6	343	66	
x60189_7 (x_4)	6	387	68	
m15421_5 (m_1)	5	398	127	10089
m15421_6 (m_2)	6	350	173	
m15421_7 (m_3)	7	383	177	
j02459_7 (j_1)	7	700	352	48502
BX842596_4 (b_1)	4	708	442	77292
BX842596_7 (b_2)	5	703	773	

4.1 Noisy Input Data Generation

We have used MetaSim [29] for noisy input data generation. The motivation behind using Metasim is briefly discussed as follows:

We have consulted different DNA sequence simulators like FASIM [14], GenFrag [9] and Celsim [25]. In [14], the authors have showed various problems associated with Celsim and GenFrag version 1.0 and 2.1. Mainly, these programs are designed on the assumption that fragments are equally distributed on genome. That is, clone sampling is uniformly carried out during fragment generation. Thus, these programs do not sufficiently reflect actual conditions of WGSS (Whole Genome Shotgun Sequencing). For FASIM, current release of the software is only available upon request. On the other hand, MetaSim is a freely available sequencing simulator for genomic and metagenomics. It can be utilized to simulate fragments of real read experiments by incorporating errors which occur at the Layout phase, i.e., unknown orientation, base call errors, incomplete coverage, repeated regions, chimeras and contamination. Here we have used three error models, namely, 454, Sanger and exact error models considering configuration of all parameters. These configurations are presented in Table 2.

4.2 Score Matrix Calculation

As the exact orientation of the generated fragments are not predictable, to tackle the problem of unknown orientation, we have checked fragment overlapping in both forward and backward orientation during calculation of the score matrix. For example, let us assume that we want to calculate overlap between Fragment 1 and Fragment 2. We first calculate normal overlap between these two segments (suffix-prefix) and then compare the obtained value with the overlap value calculated from the reverse direction of Fragment 2 (suffix-suffix). We take the best value from the above two options.

4.3 ABC Control Parameters

ABC algorithm has a few control parameters. We set

Table 2: Configuration of MetaSim for different error models and no. of generations used by the algorithms

Parameter Considered	Error Model	Instances								
		acin1	acin2	acin3	acin5	acin7	acin9	x60189_6	m15421_7	j02459_7
Number of reads or Mate pair	454, Sanger, Exact	307	451	601	751	901	1049	68	177	352
DNA clone size distribution type [a]	-do-	Normal								
Mean	-do-	190	1020	1001	1003	1003	1003	387	387	700
Second Parameter	-do-	10	30	100						
Mate pair Probability	-do-	0								
Expected read length	454	190	1020	1007	1007	1005	1005	388	388	700
Mate pair read length	-do-	20								
Number of flow cycles	-do-	75	400	395	395	394	394	152	152	275
Mean negative flow cycles[b]	-do-	0.23								
Std. deviation for negative flow cycle[c]	-do-	0.15								
Signal std. deviation multiplier	-do-	0.15								
Read length distribution type	Sanger	Normal								
Error rate at read start	-do-	0.01								
Error rate at end of read	-do-	0.02								
Insertion error rate	-do-	0.2								
Deletion error rate	-do-	0.2								
Insertion	454	1330	10460	13651	17146	20882	23872	604	1571	5694
	Sanger	146	1433	1643	2147	2480	2860	71	157	666
Deletion	454	369	2758	3687	4438	5396	6373	125	388	1469
	Sanger	162	1370	1679	2131	2467	2965	70	165	621
Substitutions	Sanger	532	4095	5094	6409	7642	8969	216	537	1988
No. of base pair processed	454	57857	458964	594676	738514	889923	1034189	23719	63688	233127
	Sanger	56414	452401	567768	710617	852423	997708	23145	61276	223168
	Exact	55915	461288	596036	755338	903193	1050247	23719	69562	243163
No. of base pair generated	454	58818	466666	604640	751222	905409	1051688	24198	64871	237352
	Sanger	56398	452464	567732	710633	852436	997603	23146	61268	223213
	Exact	55915	461288	596036	755338	903193	1050247	24198	69562	243163

[a] A Clone in MetaSim is a DNA fragment that is randomly extracted from the source genome sequence for read/mate-pair sampling.

[b] A negative flow is a flow of nucleotides in which the sequence to synthesize is not elongated. Light intensities of negative flows follow a lognormal distribution. The default value ($\mu = 0.23$) is taken from [10].

[c] The default value (0.15) is taken from [10].

Maximum number of cycles (MCN), i.e., maximum number of generation to 4000 and the colony size, i.e., population size to 256. The percentage of onlooker bees was set to 50% of the colony, the employed bees were 50% of the colony and the number of scout bees was selected as one. Notably, an increase in the number of scouts encourages the exploration whereas that in onlookers of a food source increases the exploitation.

4.4 Results

Now, we present the results obtained by our ABC algorithm and QEGA for solving different DNA instances. We measure the quality of the solution by considering the fitness value achieved as well as the number of contigs. The significance of contig calculation is to ensure that the solution best represents a continuous assembled sequence. We have tested our algorithms for both noisy and noiseless fragments.

For noiseless instances, we set a cutoff value, i.e., required overlap between two adjacent fragments, to thirty. Table 3 shows the results obtained for noiseless instances by our algorithms as well as by simulated annealing (SA), Problem aware local search (PALS) and Genetic algorithm (GA). In Table 3, A, Q, S, P and G denotes ABC, QEGA, SA, PALS and GA respectively. In this case we have found that our implementation of ABC and QEGA perform very competitively with the best algorithm in the literature which is based on simulated annealing (SA) for noiseless instances [23]. Similar behavior is observed in comparison to PALS [6], a defacto standard to compare genome assemblers, in all cases. These experiments validate our algorithms' good performance. Moreover, QEGA algorithm performs better than ABC algorithm for most of the instances. Notably, QEGA produces better results for longer instances. In terms of no. of contigs, QEGA does a better job at contig reduction than the ABC algorithm.

Table 3: Best final contig number and fitness for noiseless data

Ins.	Best Fitness					Best Contig				
	ABC	QEGA	SA	PALS	GA	A	Q	S	P	G
x_1	11478	11476	11478	11204	11478	1	1	1	1	1
x_2	14016	14027	14027	12898	13502	1	1	1	1	1
x_3	18339	18266	18301	16992	17688	1	1	1	1	1
x_4	21184	21208	21271	20424	20884	1	1	1	1	1
m_1	38423	38578	38583	36540	37714	3	1	1	1	1
m_2	47515	47882	48048	45773	46949	2	1	1	1	2
m_3	54607	55020	55048	51454	52695	2	1	1	1	2
j_1	114774	116222	116257	108744	111103	3	1	1	1	1
b_1	225431	227252	226538	211792	220558	13	8	1	1	6
b_2	440187	443600	436739	412374	416414	12	3	1	1	3
a_1	45403	47115	46955	44656	45565	8	4	1	1	5
a_2	142539	144133	144705	138423	143444	237	233	1	1	236
a_3	155413	156138	156630	151928	154947	362	358	1	1	358
a_5	144339	144541	146607	143835	145332	556	552	1	1	552
a_7	155182	155322	157984	155089	155873	726	722	1	1	722
a_9	321397	322768	324559	310235	313203	552	552	1	1	552

Next, We execute ABC and QEGA for noisy instances. It is to be noted that, in noisy instances, a lot of insertions, deletions or substitutions can occur. For instance, if we refer to Table 2, there are 5694 insertions, 1469 deletions and 1988 substitutions on *j02459_7* instance in 454 error model. So, empirically we set the cutoff value for noisy instances to lower values but ensure overlapping adjacent fragments. The results obtained by our algorithms (ABC and QEGA) are presented in Table 4 along with three other algorithms from [11] namely Genetic Algorithms (GA), Genetic Algorithm with Simulated Annealing (GA+SA)and Genetic Algorithm with Hill Climbing(GA+HC). We have given the comparison of our result with [11] because the authors of [11] have used the same error models and parameters as ours to present results. More importantly, there is no way to compare our results with [23] because the authors of [23] have only told that they have introduced random error but there was no indication of how much error was being introduced. As opposed to them, we have clearly mentioned the parameters of our noisy dataset generation in Table 2. Instead of introducing random error in score matrix [23], we generated fragments with three error models (454, Sanger and Exact). We execute our algorithms on these instances. We also take into consideration that DNA FAP is an off-line problem. So, instead of emphasizing on execution time of the algorithms, we concern ourself with assessment of the solution quality, based on number of contigs and fitness value.

As can be seen from Table 4, for most of the instances, QEGA outperforms all previously proposed algorithms as well as the ABC algorithm because of the elitist selection method imposed by QEGA. Our implementation of QEGA breeds fittest parent (i.e. queen bee) with other parents. The strong mutation in Step 12 of Algorithm 2 employs PALS to get the fittest mutants from the offspring. So we perform exploitation in the vicinity of the best solution of the current cycle. On the other hand, although ABC algorithm performs analogous action of mutation, but it does not do so with the fittest ones. Exploitation can sometime leads to local minima and QEGA countermeasures this by random mutation. All the fitness values for QEGA and ABC algorithm shown in Table 4 are obtained for a single contig i.e. one continuous sequence with some exceptions. These exceptions can not reach single contig value and the final contig value for each of these instances are shown in brackets just beside their fitness in Table 4. For GA, GA+HC and GA+SA, the authors in [11] did not mention the final contigs obtained by these algorithms. So we are unable to comment about these three algorithms in terms of contig value.

Figure 1 and 2 show the progressive improvement of fitness values for the instance j02459_7 for noiseless and noisy data by applying QEGA. As can be seen from the figures, final fitness values for the noisy cases is significantly smaller than that of noiseless cases. Figure 1 also shows that QEGA is able to overcome any local minima as is evident from the transition of lower fitness value at almost 1100-th iteration to higher fitness value at almost 1200-th iteration.

5. CONCLUSION

In this paper, we have used Artificial Bee Colony (ABC) algorithm and Queen-bee Evaluation based on Genetic Algorithm (QEGA) to tackle the DNA fragment assembly problem for noisy and noiseless instances. In particular, we have recorded the results obtained by our algorithm, taking into consideration various standard error models normally used by DNA sequencing experiments. Previous works on DNA FAP report their results for noiseless cases mostly. We have observed that, although our algorithms perform very well for noiseless data just like others, for noisy instances their obtained fitness value decrease significantly for different error models. We have pointed out the fact that errors in DNA fragments significantly impact the performance of standard algorithms. Future works should take this into account.
In future, we intend to design algorithms to achieve near-optimal fitness for noisy instances. We also wish to implement the parallel versions of our algorithms.

Table 4: Best fitness obtained by the algorithms for noisy data

Instances	Error Model	Best Fitness				
		ABC	QEGA	GA	GA+SA	GA+HC
acin1	454	4323	4631	162	3738	4611
	Sanger	7758	8512	178	6744	8394
	Exact	17354	160007(4)	214	14157	17914
acin2	454	2271	2418	260	1778	2208
	Sanger	2981	3142	264	2413	2924
	Exact	20570	20884	267	19140	20677
acin3	454	2960	3170	326	1972	2657
	Sanger	3281	3661	344	2199	3095
	Exact	26611	10605(237)	374	12865	13694
acin5	454	3759	3994	405	2220	3113
	Sanger	4223	4533	430	2384	3540
	Exact	14694	16182	431	7069	15001
acin7	454	3759(2)	4792	490	2528	3487
	Sanger	3964	5177	516	2651	3817
	Exact	15052(4)	18864	522	8212	16029
acin9	454	4671	6315	608	2838	3828
	Sanger	5204	7881	623	2982	4735
	Exact	31914(2)	48154(107)	625	11816	38262
x60189_6	454	353	363	41	358	362
	Sanger	609	623	36	622	624
	Exact	2292	2303	36	2289	2302
m15421_7	454	978	1029	88	939	1026
	Sanger	1429	1467	97	1380	1455
	Exact	7028	7181	93	6840	7170
j02459_7	454	1670	1776	183	1429	1673
	Sanger	2466	2563	188	2095	2443
	Exact	13353	13607	179	12659	13526

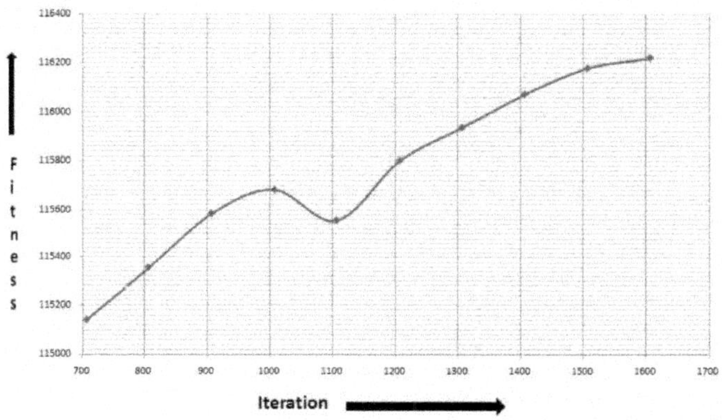

Figure 1: Iteration vs Fitness graph for j02459_7 noiseless data using QEGA

6. REFERENCES

[1] http://ab.inf.uni-tuebingen.de/teaching/ss07/albi2/script/readsim_2July2007.pdf. [Online; accessed 16-November-2011].

[2] http://www.ncbi.nlm.nih.gov/nuccore/178817?report=fasta(M15421.1). [Online; accessed 20-November-2011].

[3] http://www.ncbi.nlm.nih.gov/nuccore/34645?report=fasta(X60189.1. [Online; accessed 20-November-2011].

[4] http://www.ncbi.nlm.nih.gov/nuccore/215104?report=fasta(J02459.1. [Online; accessed 20-November-2011].

[5] http://0-www.ncbi.nlm.nih.gov.ilsprod.lib.neu.edu/Traces/wgs/?hide_master*=\&val=ACIN02000001\#9(ACIN_ALL). [Online; accessed 20-November-2011].

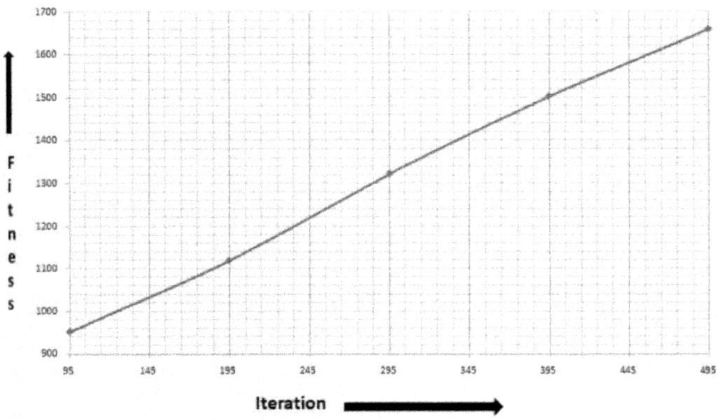

Figure 2: Iteration vs Fitness graph for j02459_7 noisy data(454 error model) using QEGA

[6] E. Alba and G. Luque. A new local search algorithm for the DNA fragment assembly problem. In *Evolutionary Computation in Combinatorial Optimization, EvoCOP'07*, Lecture Notes in Computer Science 4446, pages 1–12, Valencia, Spain, April 2007. Springer.

[7] T. Chen and S. S. Skiena. Trie-based data structures for sequence assembly. In *The Eighth Symposium on Combinatorial Pattern Matching*, pages 206–223. Springer-Verlag, 1997.

[8] B. Dorronsoro, E. Alba, G. Luque, and P. Bouvry. A self-adaptive cellular memetic algorithm for the DNA fragment assembly problem. In *IEEE Congress on Evolutionary Computation*, pages 2651–2658, 2008.

[9] M. L. Engle and C. Burks. Artificially generated data sets for testing DNA sequence assembly algorithms. *Genomics*, 16(1):286–8, 1993.

[10] M. M. et al. Genome sequencing in microfabricated high-density picolitre reactors. *Nature*, 437(7057):376–80, 2005.

[11] J. S. Firoz, M. S. Rahman, and T. k. Saha. Analyzing memetic algorithm behavior in DNA fragment assembly problem for noisy data. In *4th International Conference on Bioinformatics and Computational Biology (BICoB),Las Vegas, Nevada, USA*, 2012.

[12] P. Green. Phrap. `http://www.phrap.org/`. [Online; accessed 20-November-2011].

[13] X. Huang and A. Madan. Cap3: A DNA sequence assembly program. *Genome Research*, 9:868–877, 1999.

[14] C. G. Hur. Fasim: Fragments assembly simulation using biased-sampling model and assembly simulation for microbial genome shotgun sequencing.

[15] S. H. Jung. Queen-bee evolution for genetic algorithms. *Electronics Letters*, 39:575–576, March 2003.

[16] D. Karaboga and B. Basturk. A powerful and efficient algorithm for numerical function optimization: artificial bee colony (abc) algorithm. *J. of Global Optimization*, 39:459–471, November 2007.

[17] J. Kubalik, P. Buryan, and L. Wagner. Solving the dna fragment assembly problem efficiently using iterative optimization with evolved hypermutations. In *Proceedings of the 12th annual conference on Genetic and evolutionary computation*, GECCO '10, pages 213–214, New York, NY, USA, 2010. ACM.

[18] G. Luque and E. Alba. Metaheuristics for the DNA Fragment Assembly Problem. *International Journal of Computational Intelligence Research*, 1(1-2):98–108, 2005.

[19] M. Margulies, M. Egholm, W. E. Altman, S. Attiya, J. S. Bader, L. A. Bemben, J. Berka, M. S. Braverman, Y.-J. Chen, Z. Chen, and et al. Genome sequencing in microfabricated high-density picolitre reactors. *Nature*, 437(7057):376–380, 2005.

[20] P. Meksangsouy and N. Chaiyaratana. DNA fragment assembly using an ant colony system algorithm. In *Proceedings of Congress on Evolutionary Computation*, volume 3, pages 1756–1763, 2003.

[21] D. Meldrum. Automation for genomics, part one: Preparation for sequencing. *Genome Research*, 10(8):1081–1092, 2000.

[22] D. Meldrum. Automation for genomics, part two: Sequencers, microarrays, and future trends. *Genome Research*, 10(9):1288–1303, 2000.

[23] G. Minetti and E. Alba. Metaheuristic assemblers of DNA strands: Noiseless and noisy cases. In *IEEE Congress on Evolutionary Computation'10*, pages 1–8, 2010.

[24] E. W. Myers. Toward simplifying and accurately formulating fragment assembly. *Journal of Computational Biology*, 2:275–290, 1995.

[25] G. Myers. A dataset generator for whole genome shotgun sequencing. In *Proceedings of the Seventh International Conference on Intelligent Systems for Molecular Biology*, pages 202–210. AAAI Press, 1999.

[26] P. Pevzner. *Computational molecular biology: An algorithmic approach.* MIT Press, 2000.

[27] L. Qin, Q. Jiang, Z. Zou, and Y. Cao. A queen-bee evolution based on genetic algorithm for economic power dispatch. In *39th International Universities Power Engineering Conference*, volume 1, pages 453–456, September 2004.

[28] D. R and Bentley. Whole-genome re-sequencing. *Current Opinion in Genetics and Development*, 16(6):545 – 552, 2006.

[29] D. C. Richter, F. Ott, A. F. Auch, R. Schmid, and D. H. Huson. Metasim:a sequencing simulator for genomics and metagenomics. *PLoS ONE*, 3(10):e3373+, 2008.

[30] J. Setubal and J. Meidanis. Fragment assembly of DNA. *Introduction to Computational Molecular Biology*, pages 105–139, 1997.

[31] J. C. Setubal and J. Meidanis. *Introduction to Computational Molecular Biology.* PWS Publishing Company, 1997.

[32] G. Sutton, W. O., A. M.D., and K. A.R. Tigr assembler: A new tool for assembling large shotgun sequencing projects. *Genome Science and Tech*, pages 9–19, 1995.

[33] E. G. Talbi. *Metaheuristics from design to implementation.* WILEY, 2009.

ProRank: A Method for Detecting Protein Complexes

[ProRank]

Nazar Zaki*
Intelligent Systems
Faculty of Info. Technology
UAEU, Al Ain 17551, UAE
nzaki@uaeu.ac.ae

Jose Berengueres†
Intelligent Systems
Faculty of Info Technology
UAEU, Al Ain 17551, UAE
jose@uaeu.ac.ae

Dmitry Efimov‡
Department of Mathematics
Moscow State University,
Moscow
diefimov@gmail.com

ABSTRACT

Detecting protein complexes from protein-protein interaction (PPI) network is becoming a difficult challenge in computational biology. Observations show that genes causing the same or similar diseases tend to lie close to one another in a network of protein-protein or functional interactions. This paper introduces a novel method for detecting protein-complexes from PPI by using a protein ranking algorithm (ProRank) and incorporating an evolutionary relationships between proteins in the network. The method successfully predicted 57 out of 81 benchmarked protein complexes created from the Munich Information Center for Protein Sequence (MIPS). The level of the accuracy achieved using ProRank in comparison to other recent methods for detecting protein complexes is a strong argument in favor of our proposed method. Datasets, programs and results are available at http://faculty.uaeu.ac.ae/nzaki/ProRank.htm

Categories and Subject Descriptors

J. [**Computer Applications**]: LIFE AND MEDICAL SCIENCES—*Biology and genetics, Bioinformatics*

General Terms

Algorithms.

*Dr. Nazar Zaki is a Director of the Bioinformatics Laboratory and a Coordinator of Intelligent Systems Program with the Faculty of Information Technology, United Arab Emirates University, Al Ain, P. O. Box 17551, UAE, Email: nzaki@uaeu.ac.ae

†Dr. Jose Berengueres directs the Media Lab, Faculty of Information Technology, United Arab Emirates University, Al Ain, P. O. Box 17551, UAE, Email: jose@uaeu.ac.ae

‡Dr. Dmitry Efimov is an Assistant Professor at the Department of Applied Mathematics, Moscow State University, Moscow, Russia, Email: diefimov@gmail.com

GECCO'12, July 7–11, 2012, Philadelphia, Pennsylvania, USA.

Keywords

protein-protein interaction, protein complex detection, pairwise similarity, PageRank algorithm.

1. INTRODUCTION

A fundamental challenge in human health is the identification of disease-causing genes. One way to overcome this challenge is to study the network of protein-protein or functional interactions. Most of the biological processes are mediated via protein complexes. A protein complex is a group of two or more associated polypeptide chains which play a central role in disease development. In cancer for instance, the molecular analysis of events underlying tumor genesis could lead to the development of novel methods in cancer diagnosis and treatment, therefore, the identification and characterization of protein complexes involved is crucial to understanding the molecular events under normal and abnormal physiological conditions.

Several methods have recently been developed to predict protein complexes from a protein-protein interaction network (PPI). PPI networks possess valuable information and special structures regarding intra-cellular processes. Protein complexes are one example of these structures. They are assemblies of proteins that have various functions inside the cell, such as cellular machines, rigid structures, dynamic signaling or metabolic networks and post-translational modification systems.

Protein complexes are commonly modeled as dense protein subnetworks. One of the most commonly used algorithms for predicting protein complexes via the dense protein subnetworks model is the Molecular Complex Detection (MCode) algorithm [1]. Other clustering methods for inferring protein complexes include: Markov clustering (MCL) [2], restricted neighboringhood search clustering (RNSC) [3, 4], super paramagnetic clustering (SPC) and CFinder [5]. A comparative assessment made by Sylvain et al. [6] to evaluate the robustness of the above mentioned algorithms revealed that MCL is remarkably robust for graphing alterations. Guimei et al. [7] recently developed an algorithm called Clustering-based on Maximal Cliques (CMC) to discover complexes from weighted PPI networks. They used an iterative scoring method to assign weight to protein pairs, which indicates the reliability of the interaction between proteins. CMC showed that the iterative scoring method can considerably improve the performance of CMC and other well known protein complex prediction methods. Leung et al. [8] utilized the core-attachment concept to develop an algorithm called "Core" to identify complexes from PPI network. The evaluation of the effectiveness of their proposed algorithm showed that Core can predict many more complexes and with higher accuracy than other cluster based methods. However, all of the above mentioned methods for predicting protein complexes suffers from the following common limitations:

1. They are based on the idea of finding dense subgraphs, however, they differ in the definition of a dense subgraph and the procedure to cluster the nodes into dense subgraphs. In order to achieve a breakthrough, we need a deeper understanding of the proteins within these complexes.
2. They are unable to detect complexes which contain few proteins or few interactions.
3. They have not incorporated biological knowledge such as structural or evolutionarily relationships between proteins.

This paper introduces a novel method to detect protein-complexes from PPI by using protein ranking algorithm (ProRank), employing a novel PPI network filtering process and incorporating the evolutionary relationships between proteins in the network.

ProRank quantifies the importance of each protein based on the interaction structure of the protein network. The method identifies "central proteins" which we believe they are crucial in the structure of the complexes. This is somewhat analogous to PageRank algorithm [9, 10, 11, Ishii *et al.*, 2008] at Google which is one of the most successful algorithms used to quantify and rank the importance of web pages. The ProRank algorithm is based solely on the interaction structure inherent in the PPI network. More concretely, each protein is considered to be voting for the proteins with which it interacts. Next, in the ranking of a protein, the total number of votes as well as the importance of the voters are reflected. This problem is mathematically formulated as finding the eigenvector corresponding to the eigenvalue of a certain stochastic matrix associated with the PPI structure.

Unlike the PageRank algorithm, ProRank, uses the evolutionarily relationships (in terms of homology and structural similarity) to indicate the importance of the protein in the network. The fundamental idea is that the interesting characteristics of each protein sequence in the network are effectively captured by measuring similarities of this protein to those of a large collection of other proteins. Therefore, a given protein is compared to every protein in the network in terms of similarity. Sequence similarity often suggests evolutionary relationships between protein sequences that can be important for inferring similarity of structure or function [12].

2. METHOD

The ProRank method consists of five major steps:

- Assigning weights to protein pairs and determine the reliable interactions.
- Analyzing the PPI network to identify "bridge", "shore" and "fjord" proteins. All the three types of proteins add noise to the PPI dataset when detecting complexes.
- Calculating the similarity between proteins in the network.
- Ranking proteins and eliminating the noise in the PPI network (by removing bridge, shore and fjord proteins).
- Detecting protein complexes.

In the subsequent sections, we describe the above mentioned steps.

2.1 Assigning weights to protein pairs

To remove unreliable protein interaction pairs the AdjustCD iterative algorithm [13, 14, 15] is employed which is mainly based on the number of common neighbors for protein pairs in the network. If two neighbor proteins are denoted as u and v then the CD-distance [14] between these proteins is defined as:

$$CD(u,v) = 1 - \frac{2|N_u \cap N_v|}{|N_u| + |N_v|}, \quad (1)$$

where N_u and N_v are the numbers of neighbors of proteins u and v, respectively. Equation 1 was further modified by [15] to decrease the CD-distance for proteins with few number of interactions:

$$AdjustCD(u,v) = \frac{2|N_u \cap N_v|}{max(|N_u|, n_{avg}) + max(|N_v|, n_{avg})}, \quad (2)$$

where $n_{avg} = \frac{\sum_{x \in V} |N_x|}{n}$ is the average number of neighbors in the network, n is the total number of nodes in the network.

Equations 1 and 2, clearly show how many 3-cliques are based on edges between proteins u and v, but do not take into account the 3-cliques based on other edges going from nodes u and v. To solve this problem, Chua et al. [15] have suggested the iterative method which considers all 3-cliques based on edges from all neighbor nodes of u and v:

$$w^k(u,v) = \frac{\sum_{x \in N_u \cap N_v} (w^{k-1}(x,u) + w^{k-1}(x,v))}{max(\sum_{x \in N_u} w^{k-1}(x,u), w_{avg}^{k-1}) + max(\sum_{x \in N_v} w^{k-1}(x,v), w_{avg}^{k-1})} \quad (3)$$

where $w^0(x,u) = 1$, if x and u interact, $w^0(x,u) = 0$, otherwise; $w_{avg}^{k-1} = \frac{\sum_{x \in V} \sum_{y \in N_x} w^{k-1}(x,y)}{n}$ is the average number of weights on $(k-1)^{th}$ step; $w^1(x,u) = AdjustCD(x,u)$ and eventually $w^k(u,v)$ will show reliability of interaction between proteins u and v.

2.2 Analyzing the PPI

In this step bridge, shore and fjord proteins are identified. Bridge protein is a protein in the PPI network, which has disconnected subgraph of neighbors as shown in Figure 1 (a). Fjords protein is a protein with neighbors which have a small number of connections between each other as shown in Figure 1 (b). Shore protein is a protein with at least one special neighbor, which has significantly less connections with others as shown in Figure 1 (c).

The identification and removal of these types of proteins will assist us in cleaning the PPI network.

2.3 Calculating the similarity between proteins

In this step, the similarity score between all proteins in the network is calculated. It's assumed that interacting protein

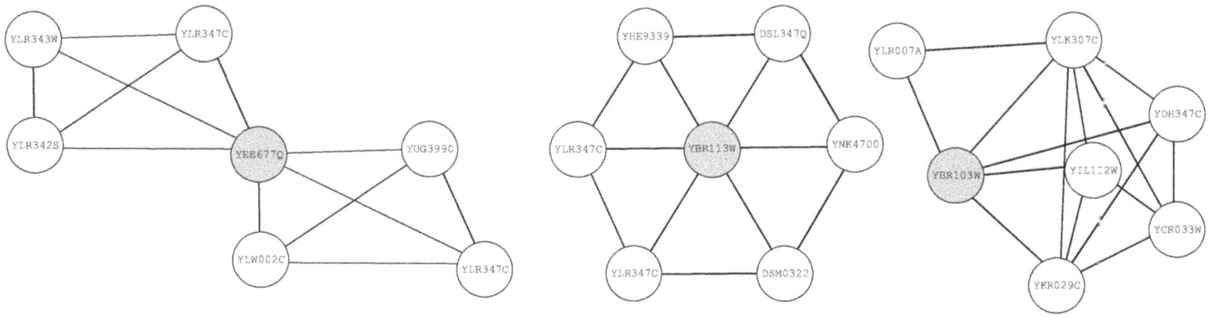

(a) Bridge protein (b) Fjiord protein (c) Shore protein

Figure 1: Types of proteins to be removed from the PPI network.

pairs within the same complex may have a high similarity score [16]. A motivating observation is that the pairwise alignment score provides a relevant measure of similarity between protein sequences [17]. This similarity may incorporate biological information about the proteins' evolutionarily structural relationships [18]. The expectation is that proteins within the same complex may share evolutionarily structural relationships which could be reflected by the similarity scores calculated using Smith-Waterman algorithm as implemented in Fasta [19]. Smith-Waterman [20] has undergone two decades of empirical optimization in the field of bioinformatics and thus, considerable prior knowledge is implicitly incorporated into the pairwise sequence similarity scores and hence into the PPI network. The Smith-Waterman score $SW(v_0, v_1)$ between protein sequences v_0 and v_1 is the score of the best local alignment with gaps between the two protein sequences, computed by the SW dynamic programming algorithm [20].

All protein sequences in the PPI network are scored against each other. For instance, if we have a protein sequence v then the corresponding score will be $F_v = f_{v_0}, ..., f_{v_n}$ where n is the total number of the proteins in the network and f_{v_i} is the $s_{v,i}$ score (E-value) between protein v and the ith protein sequence. In this case, the default parameters are used; gap opening penalty and extension penalties of 11 and 1, respectively, and the BLOSUM62 matrix. We suppose $s_{v,i} = 0$ if there is no interaction exists between proteins v and i. This process will result in generating the similarity matrix S between proteins in the PPI network:

$$S = \begin{bmatrix} s_{1,1} & s_{1,2} & \dots & s_{1,n} \\ s_{2,1} & s_{2,2} & \dots & s_{2,n} \\ \vdots & \vdots & \vdots & \vdots \\ s_{n,1} & s_{n,2} & \dots & s_{n,n} \end{bmatrix} \tag{4}$$

Furthermore, we create a new matrix S^* which is basically the normalized matrix S (by columns) such that $\sum_{i=1}^{n} s_{i,j} = 1$ for every $j = 1..n$.

2.4 Ranking the proteins

Consider a network of n proteins indexed by integers from 1 to n. This network is represented by the directed graph $G = (V, E)$. Here, $V := 1, 2, ..., n$ is the set of nodes (proteins) and E is a set of edges (interactions) among the proteins.

The protein i is connected to the protein j by an edge, i.e., $(i, j) \in E$, if protein i interacts with j.

The objective of the ProRank algorithm is to provide some measure of importance to each protein in the network. The ProRank value of protein $i \in V$ is a a real number in $[0, 1]$; we denote this by x_i.

The values are ordered such that $x_i > x_j$ implies that protein i is more important than protein j. The basic idea in ranking the proteins in terms of biological values is that a protein having interactions from important proteins is also important. This is realized by determining the value of one protein as a sum of the contributions from all proteins that have interactions to it. In particular, the value x_i of protein i is defined as:

$$x_i = \sum_{j \in \tau_i} s^*_{i,j} \cdot x_j \tag{5}$$

where $\tau_i := \{j : (j, i) \in E\}$, i.e., this is the index set of proteins interacting to protein i, and n_j is the number of outgoing links of protein j. It is customary to normalize the total of all values so that $\sum_{i=1}^{n} x_i = 1$

Let the values be in the vector form as $x \in [1, 0]^n$. Then, from what we described so far, the PageRank problem can be restated as:

$$x = S^* x, x \in [1, 0]^n, \sum_{i=1}^{n} x_i = 1 \tag{6}$$

where S^* is the normalized similarity matrix calculated in section 2.3.

Note that the vector x is a nonnegative eigenvector corresponding to the eigenvalue 1 of the nonnegative matrix S^*. In general, for this eigenvector to exist and to be unique, it is critical that the PPI network is strongly connected.

To find the eigenvector corresponding to the eigenvalue 1 a modified version of the values has been introduced in [9] as follows:

Let m be a parameter such that $m \in (0, 1)$, and let the modified interaction matrix $M \in \Re^{n \times n}$ be defined by:

$$M := (1 - m)S^* + \frac{m}{n}\mathbf{1} \tag{7}$$

where $\mathbf{1}$ is a $n \times n$ matrix with all elements equal to 1.

In the original algorithm in [9], a typical value for m is reported to be $m = 0.15$; The value of m is too small and it does not really influence the results. It is rather important in avoiding convergence problems. Notice that M is a positive stochastic matrix. Thus, according to Perron theorem [21], this matrix is primitive; in particular, $|\lambda| = 1$ is the unique maximum eigenvalue. To find corresponding eigenvector x we apply the following formula:

$$x(k+1) = Mx(k) = (1-m)S^{*}x(k) + \frac{m}{n}\mathbf{1}, \qquad (8)$$

where $x(k) \in \Re^{n\times 1}$ and the initial vector $x(0) \in \Re^{n\times 1}$ is a probability vector.

Now expand on the convergence rate of this scheme. Denote by $\lambda_1(M)$ and $\lambda_2(M)$ the largest and the second largest eigenvalues of M in magnitude. Then, for the power method applied to M, the asymptotic rate of convergence is exponential and depends on the ratio $|\lambda_2(M)/\lambda_1(M)|$. Since M is a positive stochastic matrix, we have $\lambda_1(M) = 1$ and $|\lambda_2(M)| < 1$. Furthermore, it is shown in [11] that the structure of the link matrix M leads us to the bound

$$|\lambda_2(M)| \leq 1 - m. \qquad (9)$$

We next provide a simple example for illustration.

Consider the PPI with four proteins shown in Figure 2.

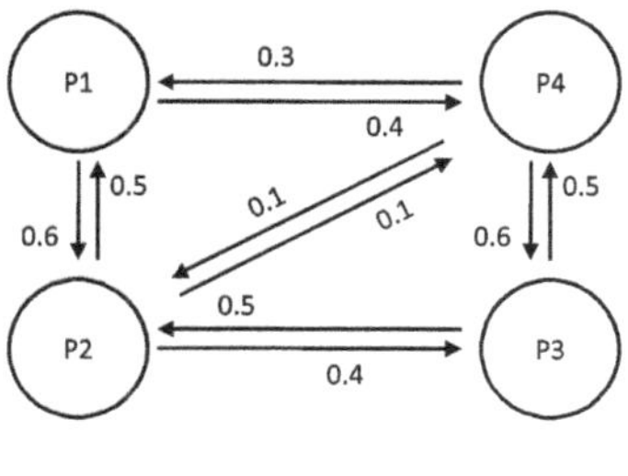

Figure 2: A hypothetical PPI network with four proteins.

The link matrix S^{*} and the modified link matrix M can easily be constructed by (2) and (3), respectively, as:

$$S^{*} = \begin{bmatrix} 0 & 0.5 & 0 & 0.3 \\ 0.6 & 0 & 0.5 & 0.1 \\ 0 & 0.4 & 0 & 0.6 \\ 0.4 & 0.1 & 0.5 & 0 \end{bmatrix}, M = \begin{bmatrix} 0.038 & 0.463 & 0.038 & 0.293 \\ 0.548 & 0.038 & 0.463 & 0.123 \\ 0.038 & 0.378 & 0.038 & 0.548 \\ 0.378 & 0.123 & 0.463 & 0.038 \end{bmatrix} \qquad (10)$$

Using power method, the eigenvector x can be computed as $x = [0.214, 0.283, 0.259, 0.244]^T$ with $m = 0.15$. Notice that the protein (P2) has the largest value since it interacts with three other proteins. On the other hand, protein (P2) and (P4) appear to have a similar number of interactions however P2 yielded a larger value since the similarities to other proteins (P1 and P3) are higher. This indicates that similarity evidence has a major effect in ranking proteins in the PPI network.

Following the ranking step, the bridge, shore and fjords proteins are excluded from the PPI network.

2.5 Detect protein complexes

Once all proteins in the network are ranked we used the spoke clustering model to identify the protein complexes. All of the previous methods have used matrix clustering model to identify protein complexes. The difference between the two models is shown in Figure 3.

In this case, once the highly ranked protein is identified, we can simply detect all neighbors connected to it. Following the complexes identification we check all predicted

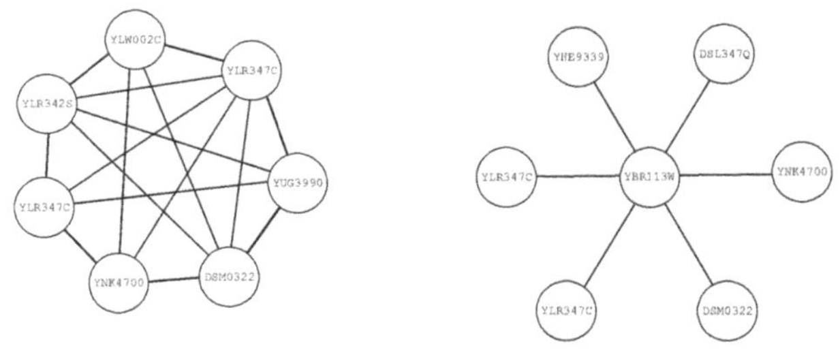

((a) Matrix model (b) Spoke model

Figure 3: Types of clustering models.

complexes. If more than 50% of the neighbors of each proteins from complex 1 are in complex 2 we merge the two complexes.

2.6 Evaluation measures

To evaluate the accuracy of the ProRank the Jaccard index measure is introduced and it is defined as follows:

$$Acc(K,P) = \frac{|K \cap P|}{|K \cup P|}, \qquad (11)$$

where K and P are the known and predicted complexes respectively, and $|.|$ is the number of proteins. The complex P is defined to match K if $Acc(K,P) \geq 0.5$.

To estimate the cumulative quality of the prediction, we compare the number of matching complexes with the number of known complexes using recall ($Rec_c = \frac{N_{MK}}{N_K}$) and precision ($Prec_c = \frac{N_{MP}}{N_P}$), where N_{MK} is a number of matching known complexes, N_{MP} is a number of predicted known complexes, N_K is a number of known complexes and N_P is the number of predicted complexes.

In some cases (for example, at a wide scatter of the sizes of predicted complexes) it is necessary to consider the quantity of proteins in the known and predicted complexes for prediction accuracy estimation. As before two characteristics are used:

$$Rec_N = \frac{\sum_{i=1}^{N_{MK}}|C_i|}{\sum_{i=1}^{N_K}|K_i|}, where|C_i| = max_{P_j:Acc(K_i,P_j)\geq 0.5}|K_i \cap P_j| \qquad (12)$$

and

$$Prec_N = \frac{\sum_{i=1}^{N_{MP}}|C_i|}{\sum_{i=1}^{N_P}|P_i|}, where|C_i| = max_{K_j:Acc(P_i,K_j)\geq 0.5}|P_i \cap K_j| \qquad (13)$$

Calculations were made of the precision and recall at complex and complex-protein levels.

3. EXPERIMENTAL WORK AND RESULTS

We evaluated the effectiveness of ProRank using two different yeast PPI datasets. The first dataset (PPI-D1) is prepared by Gavin et al. [22] and the second dataset (PPI-D2) is a combined PPI dataset containing yeast protein interactions generated by six individual experiments, including interactions characterized by mass spectrometry technique by [23], [24, 22] and [25], and interactions produced using two-hybrid techniques by Uetz et al. [26] and Ito et al. [27].

Two reference sets of protein complexes are used in these experiments. The first set (Cmplx-D1) comprises of 162 hand-curated complexes (size no less than 4 proteins) from MIPS [28]. This dataset was used by [7] to evaluate the CMC method. The second set of complexes (Cmplx-D2) is created from MIPS [29]. In this case only complexes that were manually annotated independently from DIP interaction data are considered. Furthermore, all complexes predicted based on high-throughput experiments are excluded. We considered complexes of sizes at least 5 [8] and there are 81 such complexes.

Employed first was the AdjustCD method [13, 14, 15] to assign weights to the PPI protein pairs in PPI-D1 and PPI-D2 to determine reliable interactions. The influence of using only reliable PPI interaction pairs is shown in Tables 1 and 2.

Table 1: Influence of using reliable PPI interaction pairs based on Cmplx-D1.

Threshold	Matched Cmplx	Rec_c	Prec_c
0	48	0.296	0.195
0.05	49	0.302	0.219
0.1	54	0.333	0.280
0.125	53	0.327	0.294
0.15	**59***	0.364	0.364
0.2	55	0.34	0.404
0.25	51	0.315	0.415
0.3	49	0.302	0.402

Table 2: Influence of using reliable PPI interaction pairs based on Cmplx-D2.

Threshold	Matched Cmplx	Rec_c	Prec_c
0	56	0.691	0.421
0.05	54	0.667	0.429
0.1	56	0.691	0.452
0.125	**57***	0.704	0.514
0.15	54	0.667	0.514
0.2	55	0.679	0.557
0.25	52	0.642	0.584
0.3	50	0.617	0.595

The tables clearly shows that better results are achieved by using threshold values of 0.15 and 0.125 for PPI-D1 and PPI-D2, respectively. Pairs with weight below the above mentioned threshold values are eliminated from the two PPI networks. Table 3, shows details of the two different PPI datasets and the number of proteins and interactions before and after the filtering process.

Table 3: Details of the number of interactions (Int.) and number of proteins (Prot.) in the two PPI datasets before and after the weighting process.

	Before weighting		After weighting	
Datasets	Int.	Prot.	Int.	Prot.
PPI-D1	6,531	1,430	4,687	990
PPI-D2	23,399	3,869	6,993	1,443

Following the filtering step, we calculate the similarity matrix S. In this case, the default parameters are used; gap opening penalty and extension penalties of 11 and 1, respectively, and the scoring matrix BLOSUM62. Table 4 and Table 5 show detailed results based on Cmplx-D1 and Cmplx-D2. Table 4 shows the performance based on different overlapping threshold values t. If the number of overlapping proteins found in known and predicted complexes is greater or equal to $t = \{0.6, 0.7, 0.8, 0.9\}$, we assume that the complex has been found. Table 5 records the complex detection accuracy in terms of Rec_c, $Prec_c$, Rec_N and $Prec_N$.

Table 4: Matched complexes detected for $t \geq (0.5, 0.6, 0.7, 0.8, 0.9)$.

Dataset	0.5	0.6	0.7	0.8	0.9	Matched Cmplx
Cmplx-D1	59	47	33	18	9	167
Cmplx-D2	57	50	41	29	20	115

Table 5: Complex detection accuracy in terms of Rec_c, $Prec_c$, Rec_N and $Prec_N$ ($t = 0.5$).

Dataset	Rec_c	$Prec_c$	Rec_N	$Prec_N$
Cmplx-D1	0.364	0.353	0.238	0.279
Cmplx-D2	0.716	0.504	0.647	0.563

3.1 Comparison to the existing methods

This section compares the performance of ProRank to other recent methods for detecting protein complexes. The comparison was conducted based on Cmplx-D1 and Cmplx-D2. In Figure 4 ProRank is compared to CMC [7], CFinder [5], MCL [2] and MCode [1] based on Cmplx-D1. It is clear that ProRank is able to detect more matched complexes (59 complexes) than any of the other state-of-the-art methods with higher Rec_c and $Prec_c$ accuracies.

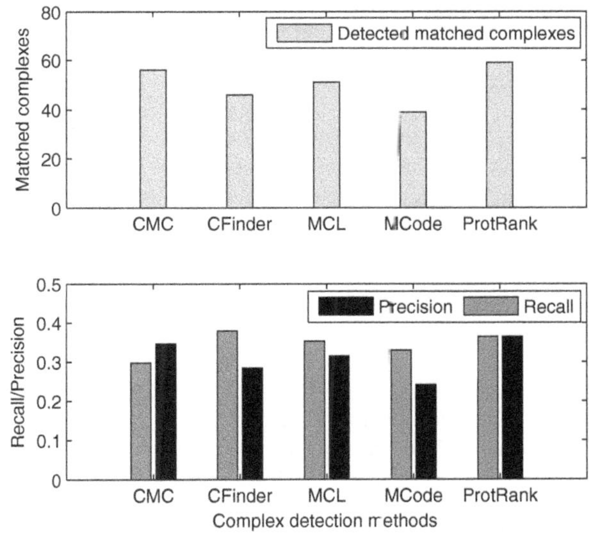

Figure 4: Compare ProRank to CMC [7], CFinder [5], MCL [2] and MCode [1].

For general purposes ProRank is compared to MCL [2]

and Core [8] based on Cmplx-D2. Figure 5 shows the ability of ProRank to detect more complexes than the other two methods.

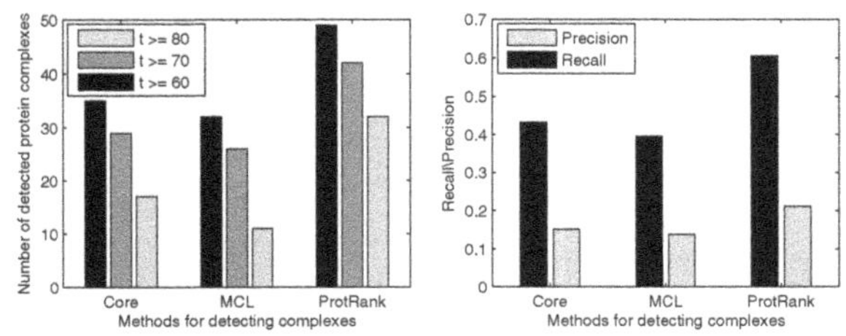

Figure 5: Comparison of ProRank to MCL [2] and Core [8].

4. CONCLUSION AND DISCUSSION

In this paper we introduce a novel method called ProRank used for detecting protein complexes from a PPI network of yeast. The level of accuracy achieved using ProRank for detecting protein complexes is a strong argument in favor of this proposed method. The improvement exhibited by ProRank in detecting protein complexes is due to three main reasons. Firstly, the utilization of a powerful method which is based on a PageRank algorithm. Secondly, the incorporation of the evolutionary relationships between proteins in the PPI network. Thirdly, utilizing a solid methods to analyze the topology of the network which assists in the removal of noise and unreliable interacting protein pairs from the network. Therefore, ProRank has a great potential to identify novel complexes.

The experimental comparisons have shown that ProRank is better than or competitive to other existing methods in many aspects. Unlike the existing methods ProRank focuses on identifying important proteins with great influence in the PPI network. As shown in Figure 6, ProRank is able to identify the protein YPR029C as a central protein with a high ranking score. Based on this information other proteins in the complex (highlighted in Grey) can easily be identified such as YLR170C, YPL259C, YKL135C and YHL019C. However, its worth mentioning that two more proteins in this case will be wrongly predicted to be members of the complex namely YBR196C and YFR043C. To solve this problem we propose to analyze the second rank neighbor. The two proteins in this case do not have more interactions with other members of the complex and should be ignored.

One weakness in ProRank is that some proteins may have a high ranking score but are not, in fact, central (hub) proteins in the complex. They could be attachment proteins which interact with many other proteins in the other complexes. Figure 7 shows such a case. Proteins YBR079C, YNL244C, YMR146C, YDR429C, YOR361C, YMR309C, YLR192C, YPR086W and YPR041W (all in Grey) should be members of one complex. This is a kind of a complex which is difficult to be detected by almost all the existing methods. In this case all members in the complex have less interactions among themselves than what they have with proteins out of the complex. One way to address this problem is to incorporate additional biological information of protein complexes, e.g., gene ontology (GO) annotation.

A probabilistic calculation of the affinity score between two proteins [30] and incorporating co-immunoprecipitation data to identify sets of preys that significantly co-associate with the same set of baits [31] could further improve the performance of ProRank.

Acknowledgment

The authors would like to acknowledge the assistance provided by the Research Support and Sponsored Projects Office and the Faculty of Information Technology at the United Arab Emirates University (UAEU). Special thanks to Piers Campbell and Maighdlin McKean for their valuable comments. Wu Min and Liu Guimei for providing the datasets.

5. REFERENCES

[1] G.D. Bader and W.H. Christopher. An automated method for finding molecular complexes in large protein interaction networks. *BMC Bioinformatics*, 4:2, 2003.

[2] S. Dongen. *Graph clustering by flow simulation.* University of Utrecht, 2000.

[3] D.K. Andrew, N. Przulj, and I. Jurisica. Protein complex prediction via cost-based clustering. *Bioinformatics*, 20(17):3013–3020, 2004.

[4] N. Przulj, D.A. Wigle, and I. Jurisica. Functional topology in a network of protein interactions. *Bioinformatics*, 20(3):340–348, 2004.

[5] B. Adamcsek, G. Palla, I.J. Farkas, I. Derenyi, and T. Vicsek. CFinder: locating cliques and overlapping modules in biological networks. *J. Bioinformatics*, 22(8):1021–1023, 2006.

[6] B. Sylvain and H. Jacques. Evaluation of clustering algorithms for protein-protein interaction networks. *BMC Bioinformatics*, 7(7):488, 2006.

[7] L. Guimei, L. Wong, and H.N. Chua. Complex discovery from weighted PPI networks. *Bioinformatics*, 25(15):1891–1897, 2009.

[8] H. Leung, Q. XIANG, S.M. Yiu, and F. Chin. Predicting protein complexes from ppi data: A core-attachment approach. *Journal of Computational Biology*, 16(2):133–139, 2009.

[Ishii *et al.*, 2008] H. Ishii and R. Tempo A distributed randomized approach for the PageRank computation: Part 1. *47th IEEE Conference on Decision and Control*, 3523-3528, 2008.

[9] S. Brin and L. Page. The anatomy of a large-scale hypertextual web search engine. *Computer Networks Systems*, 30:107–117, 1998.

[10] K. Bryan and T. Leise. The $25,000,000,000 eigenvector: the linear algebra behind Google. *SIAM Review*, 48(3):569–581, 2006.

[11] A.N. Langville, C.D. Meyer, and C. Meyer. *Matrix Analysis.* Princeton University Press, 2006.

[12] R. Kuang, J. Weston, W.S. Noble, and C.S. Leslie. Motif-based protein ranking by network propagation. *Bioinformatics*, 21(19):3711–3718, 2005.

[13] C. Brun Functional classification of proteins for the prediction of cellular function from a protein-protein interaction network. *Genome Biol.*, 5:R6, 2003.

[14] N.C. Hon, W.K. Sung, and L. Wong. Exploiting indirect neighbours and topological weight to predict

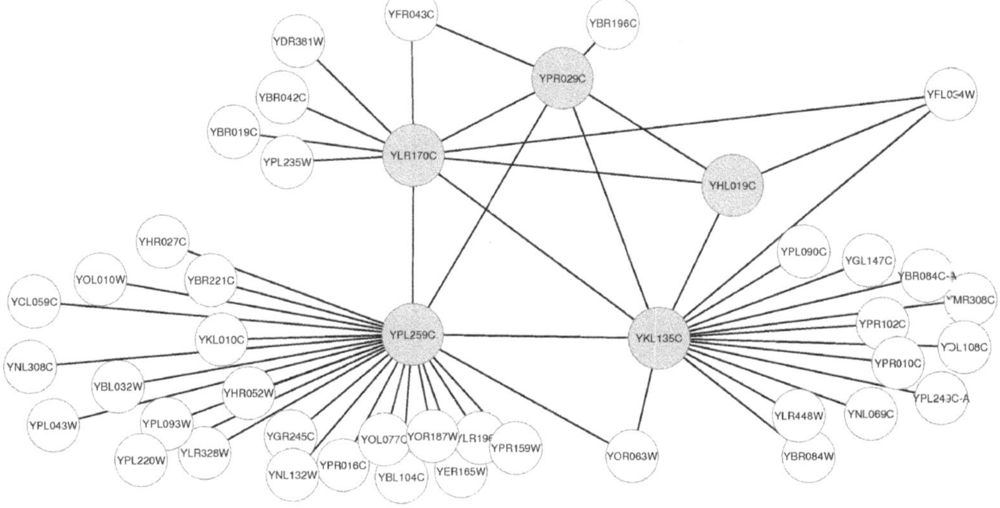

Figure 6: A complex which could easily be detected using ProRank.

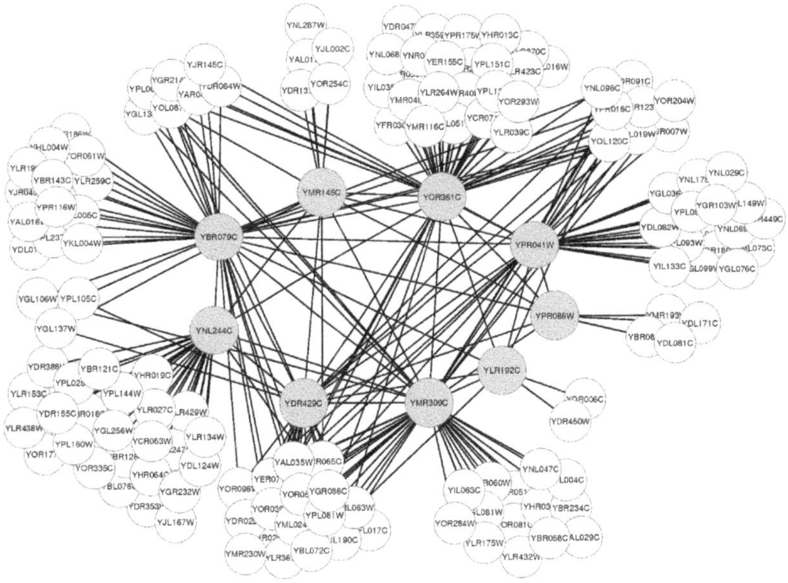

Figure 7: A complex which could not be detected using ProRank.

protein function from protein-protein interactions. *Bioinformatics*, 22(13):1623–1630, 2006.

[15] H.N. Chua, K. Ning, W.K. Sung, H.W. Leong, and L. Wong. Using indirect protein-protein interactions for protein complex prediction. *J. Bioinformatics and Computational Biology*, 6(3):435–466, 2008.

[16] N.M. Zaki, S. Lazarova-Molnar, W. El-Hajj, and P. Campbell. Protein-protein interaction based on pairwise similarity. *BMC Bioinformatics*, 10:150, 2009.

[17] N.M. Zaki, S. Wolfsheimer, G. Nuel, and S. Khuri. Conotoxin protein classification using free scores of words and support vector machines. *BMC Bioinformatics*, 12:217, 2011.

[18] H. Saigo, J. Vert, N. Ueda, and T. Akutsu. Protein homology detection using string alignment kernels. *Bioinformatics*, 20(11):1682–1689, 2004.

[19] W.R. Pearson and D,L. Lipman. Improved tools for biological sequence comparison. In *Proc. Natl. Acad. Sci.*, volume 85, pages 24444–24448, 1988.

[20] T.F. Smith and M.S. Waterman. Identification of common molecular subsequences. *Journal of Molecular Biology*, Vol. 147:195–197, 1981.

[21] R.A. Horn and C.R. Johnson. *Matrix Analysis.* Cambridge Univ. Press, 1985.

[22] A.C. Gavin et al. Proteome survey reveals modularity of the yeast cell machinery. *Nature*, 440:631–636, 2006.

[23] Y. Ho. Systematic identification of protein complexes

in saccharomyces cerevisiae by mass spectrometry. *Nature*, 415:180–183, 2002.

[24] A.C. Gavin et al. Functional organization of the yeast proteome by systematic analysis of protein complexes. *Nature*, 415:141–147, 2002.

[25] N.J. Krogan. Global landscape of protein complexes in the yeast saccharomyces cerevisiae. *Nature*, 440:637–643, 2006.

[26] P. Uetz et al. A comprehensive analysis of protein-protein interactions in saccharomyces cerevisiae. *Nature*, 403:623–627, 1999.

[27] T. Ito et al. A comprehensive two-hybrid analysis to explore the yeast protein interactome. *Proc. of The National Academy of Sciences*, 98:4569–4574, 2001.

[28] H.W. Mewes et al. MIPS: analysis and annotation of proteins from whole genomes in 2005. *Nucleic Acids Research*, 34(Database-Issue):169–172, 2006.

[29] H.W. Mewes et al. Mips: a database for genomes and protein sequences. *Nucleic Acids Res.*, 28:37–40, 2000.

[30] Z. Xie, C.K. Kwoh, X.L. Li, and M. Wu. Construction of co-complex score matrix for protein complex prediction from ap-ms data. *Bioinformatics*, 27:i159–i166, 2011.

[31] G. Geva and R. Sharan. Identification of protein complexes from co-immunoprecipitation data. *Bioinformatics*, 27:111–117, 2011.

HyperNEAT-GGP: A HyperNEAT-based Atari General Game Player

Matthew Hausknecht, Piyush Khandelwal, Risto Miikkulainen, Peter Stone
Department of Computer Science
University of Texas at Austin
{mhauskn,piyushk,risto,pstone}@cs.utexas.edu

ABSTRACT

This paper considers the challenge of enabling agents to learn with as little domain-specific knowledge as possible. The main contribution is HyperNEAT-GGP, a HyperNEAT-based General Game Playing approach to Atari games. By leveraging the geometric regularities present in the Atari game screen, HyperNEAT effectively evolves policies for playing two different Atari games, Asterix and Freeway. Results show that HyperNEAT-GGP outperforms existing benchmarks on these games. HyperNEAT-GGP represents a step towards the ambitious goal of creating an agent capable of learning and seamlessly transitioning between many different tasks.

Categories and Subject Descriptors

I.2.6 [**Artificial Intelligence**]: Learning, Intelligent Agents

General Terms

Algorithms, Experimentation, Performance

Keywords

HyperNEAT, General Game Playing, Atari, Learning Agents, Neuroevolution

1. INTRODUCTION

A major challenge for AI is to develop agents that can learn and perform many different tasks. To this end, this paper aims at developing a learning agent capable of playing a large number of games with as little domain specific knowledge as possible. Famous game playing AI systems such as Deep Blue for chess [1], Watson for Jeopardy [6], and TD-Gammon for backgammon [17] all demonstrate that with enough manpower and ingenuity it is possible to tackle AI challenges that may have previously seemed insurmountable. Unlike these game intelligences which were created and tuned specifically for a single task, the game playing agent described herein must be general enough to tackle many different Atari 2600 games. This requires general intelligence to be built into the agent itself rather than just imparted by the programmer of the agent in the form of clever single-purpose algorithms.

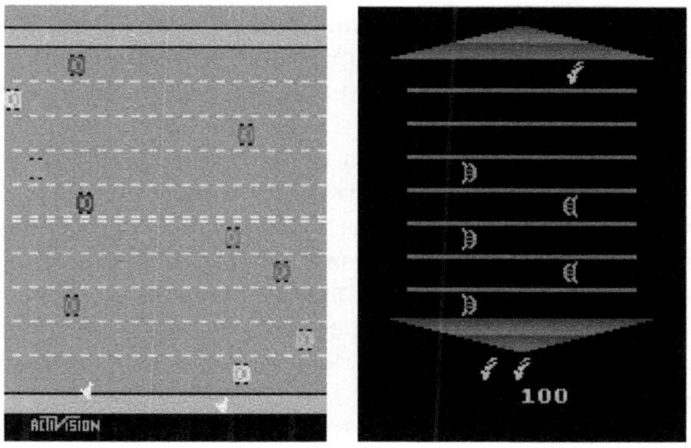

Figure 1: Freeway and Asterix, two of the many games available for the Atari 2600.

This work focuses on learning to play Atari 2600 games, a middle ground between classic board games and newer, graphically intensive video games. The Atari 2600 includes many different games, including complex ones such as chess and checkers, yet lacks the complex 3-D graphics of newer video games. Like traditional board games, the Atari provides opportunities for agents to benefit from a solid understanding of the game's dynamics and allows for careful planning while at the same time incorporating simple visual representations that can be processed and interpreted. Dynamics of Atari games vary wildly from Checkers to Space Invaders, necessitating the use of general learning algorithms.

Despite the variability of game dynamics, all Atari games share a standard interface designed for humans to interact with and enjoy. Game state is conveyed to the player through a 2D game screen, and in response, the player controls game elements by manipulating a joystick and pressing a single button. This standard interface, combined with the large number of available games, makes Atari a convenient platform for AI researchers.

This paper presents HyperNEAT-GGP, an agent which uses an evolutionary algorithm called Hypercube-based NeuroEvolution of Augmenting Topologies (HyperNEAT) [7]. Unlike most other approaches, HyperNEAT is capable of exploiting geometric regularities present in the 2D game screen in order to evolve highly effective game playing poli-

GECCO'12, July 7–11, 2012, Philadelphia, Pennsylvania, USA.

cies. This paper applies HyperNEAT-GGP to the two Atari games shown in Figure 1, Freeway and Asterix.

The next section contains related work. Section 3 discusses the merits of the Atari 2600 console as a research platform and describes the two games used in this paper. Section 4 covers the basics of HyperNEAT and how it is able to take advantage of game geometry. Next, Section 5 presents our visual processing architecture and parallel computing framework. Experiments are presented in Section 6, followed by future work and conclusions.

2. RELATED WORK

The study of general intelligence through the development of general game playing agents is not unique to this paper. Organizers in the field of General Game Playing (GGP) hold annual competitions for general game playing agents [8]. These agents are typically given a declarative description of an arbitrary game including a complete description of the game dynamics. They have no prior knowledge of this description and must formulate strategies to play this game on the fly. Unlike specialized game players, general game playing agents cannot rely on algorithms designed in advance for specific games. Successful agents typically incorporate artificial intelligence technologies such as knowledge representation, reasoning, learning, rational decision making and automatic theorem proving.

While motivations are similar, the work reported in this paper differs from GGP in that Atari games are not formalized in such an abstract representation. Atari games convey state through a visual representation, and the dynamics of the game must first be learned before strategies can be formulated. Additionally, HyperNEAT-GGP currently only considers single player games as opposed to GGP players who compete against each other.

Another class of game playing agents is found at the annual Ms. Pac-Man competition. Like HyperNEAT-GGP, Ms. Pac-Man agents utilize actual screen representations [9] and must deal with non-determinism introduced by delays in processing the game screen. Successful entries in this competition have now far exceeded novice human players [10]. HyperNEAT-GGP uses an approach similar to the Ms. Pac-Man agents in that both agents extract objects from the game screen. However, the object detection and game playing machinery used by HyperNEAT-GGP must be generally applicable enough to handle multiple games rather than specialized toward a single game such as Ms. Pac-Man.

In 3D environments, backpropagation and Lamarckian neuroevolution were used to train a neural network visual controller for agents in the Quake II environment [12]. In order to process the 3D game screen, the agents used an artificial retina consisting of 28 grayscale blocks arranged into a grid spanning the width of the game screen. Like the human retina, more blocks were clustered near the center of the visual field to allow the agent to better recognize if the target was directly ahead. The resulting agent was able to navigate a room with a large central pillar, seek out an enemy, and shoot it. However, how these techniques could be used to implement general game playing was not addressed.

To the best of the authors' knowledge, the first work on Atari game playing was an R-Max learning agent which employed an Object-oriented MDP representation [4]. Objects were detected in the game screen of the popular Atari game, *Pitfall*. The agent was able to make it past the first screen. Subsequent work on learning in Atari games includes that of Naddaf [11]. Naddaf modified the popular Atari 2600 emulator, Stella, in order to allow it to be easily controlled by computer programs such as learning agents. Naddaf quantified the performance of several reinforcement learning and search agents over 50 different Atari games. Reinforcement learning agents included a gradient descent Sarsa(λ) agent with linear function approximation, capable of learning from feature vectors generated from either the game screen or the console RAM. Search tree agents include full tree search and UCT-based agents. Also motivated by the desire to create general game playing agents, Naddaf compiled experimental results of RL and search tree agents in over 50 Atari games. More than just a experimental benchmark, this work served as the inspiration for much of the visual processing described in Section 5.

Learning to play games based on overhead representations has been previously attempted by Verbancsics and Stanley [18] who focused on the RoboCup Keepaway Soccer domain [14]. In this domain a number of *keeper* agents must maneuver and pass a soccer ball so that it is not captured by one of the *taker* agents. Verbancsics and Stanley encode the state of the game using an overhead representation of the objects on the playing field – namely the keepers, takers, and the ball. HyperNEAT is used to exploit the geometric regularities present in this overhead representation of the field. The learned policy is competitive with top learning algorithms for this task [15]. Additionally, the learned policy can be effectively transferred with no further learning to the same task at a higher resolution or a different number of players on the field. This successful transfer is a result of the indirect encoding of HyperNEAT. HyperNEAT has also been successfully applied to other domains such as checkers [7], multi-agent predator prey [3], and quadruped locomotion [2].

While HyperNEAT-GGP is quite similar to Verbancsics and Stanley's approach, in many ways Atari games represent a more challenging learning target than RoboCup Keepaway. In Keepaway there are a fixed number of object classes such as takers, keepers, and the ball. On the other hand, Atari games may contain an arbitrary number of object classes that interact with each other in unexpected ways, requiring HyperNEAT-GGP to be more general. Additionally, the dynamics in any given Atari game are highly variable, ranging from simple games in which the agent must reach the goal while avoiding cars to highly complex games in which the agent must shoot fish while attempting to rescue five swimmers, all before the oxygen in the player's submarine is depleted. Though this paper only demonstrates results on two of the many Atari games, the successful results represent an important step towards the long-term goal of testing the approach on, and refining it to generalize to, the full range of Atari games.

3. ATARI FOR RESEARCH

The Atari 2600 video game console was released in October 1977. It was the first console to create game cartridges that decoupled game code from console hardware (previous devices all contained dedicated hardware with games already built in). Selling over 30 million consoles [5], Atari was considered wildly successful as an entertainment device. Today, while Atari is no longer at the forefront of entertainment, the console has good research potential for three reasons:

First, the Atari console has a large collection of games. These games vary greatly from board games such as chess to action-exploration games like Pitfall to shooting games such as Asteroids and Space Invaders. Many games have support for a second player, opening the possibility of multi-agent learning. Having such a large number of games allows AI researchers to develop a single learning agent and then quickly and easily apply it to a large set of domains, facilitating the development of general game playing agents.

Second, a number of open-source Atari emulators exist, including projects such as Atari Learning Environment (ALE)[1] that are designed specifically to accommodate learning agents. Furthermore, since the Atari 2600 CPU ran at 1.19 megahertz, modern emulators can run at high speeds of up to 2000 frames per second, expediting the evaluation of agents and algorithms.

Third, the Atari state and action interface is simple enough for learning agents, but complex enough to control many different games. The state of an Atari game can be described relatively simply by its 2D graphics (containing between 8 and 256 colors depending on the color mode and a native resolution of 160×210), elementary sound effects, and 128 bytes of console RAM. The discrete action space for Atari consists of eight directions of movement for the joystick (up, down, left, right, up&left, up&right, etc) as well as a single button. This button can be pressed alone or simultaneously with any of the joystick movements. Including *NO-OP* (no action), this yields a total of 18 possible actions.

This work evaluates two Atari 2600 games – Freeway and Asterix. The objectives and controls of these games are as follows: In Freeway the player controls a chicken as it crosses a ten lane highway filled with traffic in an effort to "get to the other side." The chicken is allowed to move only up, down, or remain in place. Colliding with a car results in the chicken being thrown a distance towards the bottom of the screen. Each time a chicken reaches the top of the screen, the player is rewarded a point and the chicken respawns at the bottom of the screen. Gameplay continues for two minutes and sixteen seconds.

In Asterix the player controls a unit called Asterix in his quest to collect as many objects as possible while avoiding deadly lyres. Asterix can move in any of the four cardinal directions and receives 50 score whenever he collects a magic potion. Asterix loses a life when he touches a lyre and when Asterix has exhausted his supply of lives the game ends. Lyres and collectible objects spawn along the edges of the screen and move horizontally. Objects gain speed as the game progresses, necessitating quick reflexes and decisions.

Freeway and Asterix were selected as representative Atari 2600 games because their game dynamics were sufficiently different from each other, and both have been studied in the past [11].

Having motivated the Atari as a suitable research platform for the development of general game playing agents, the next challenge is developing a capable HyperNEAT-based learning agent.

4. HYPERNEAT

This section reviews the fundamentals of the HyperNEAT learning algorithm. HyperNEAT is an extension of the Neuro Evolution of Augmenting Topologies (NEAT) algorithm [13]. NEAT evolves the topology and weights of an Artificial Neural Network (ANN) that is applied directly to the problem of interest. In contrast, HyperNEAT, introduced by Gauci and Stanley [7], evolves an *indirect encoding* called a Compositional Pattern Producing Network (CPPN). The CPPN is then used to define the weights of an ANN that produces a solution for the problem. Furthermore, because the CPPN is aware of domain geometry, the ANN it encodes implicitly contains knowledge about geometric relationships present in a given domain. In comparison to standard NEAT, HyperNEAT's encoding allows it to take advantage of geometric regularities present in many board and 2D games, such as those in Atari 2600.

[1] http://yavar.naddaf.name/ale/

Specifically, HyperNEAT works in four stages:

1. The weights and topology of the CPPN are evolved. Internally a CPPN consists of functions such as Gaussians and sinusoids connected in a weighted topology (see Figure 2).
2. The CPPN is used to determine the weights for every pair of *(input,output)* nodes in a fully connected ANN.
3. With fully specified weights, the ANN is applied to the problem of interest. The performance of the ANN determines the fitness of the CPPN that generates it.
4. Based on fitness scores, the population of CPPNs is maintained, evaluated, and evolved via NEAT.

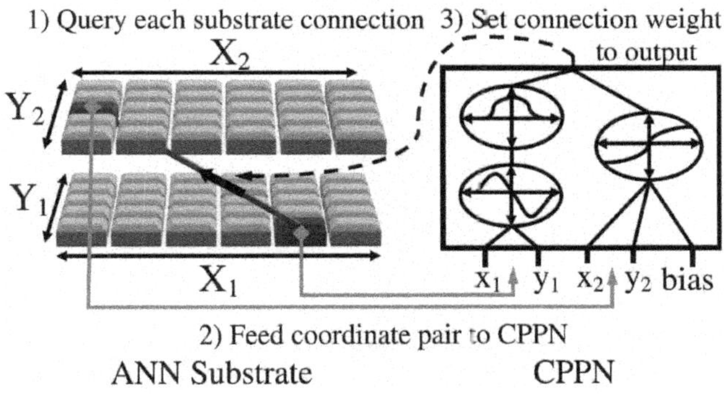

Figure 2: HyperNEAT evolves the weights and topology of a CPPN (right). This CPPN is subsequently used to determine all of the weights between substrate nodes in the ANN (left). Finally, the ANN is used to compute the solution to the desired problem. CPPNs are said to be geometrically aware because when they compute the weights of the associated ANN, they are given as input the x,y location of both the input and output node in the ANN. Figure duplicated from [18].

The ANN's input representation will be discussed further in Section 5.3. For more information on HyperNEAT, refer to [7].

5. APPROACH

This section describes the components of HyperNEAT-GGP. The main points are the manner in which the raw Atari game screen is processed, the self-agent is identified, and HyperNEAT is interfaced with the detected objects.

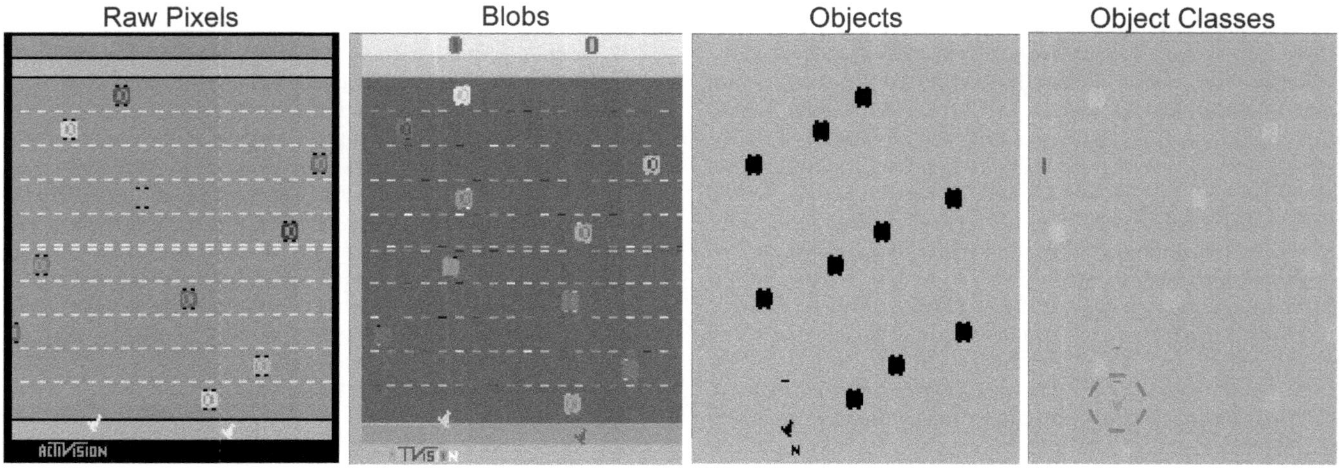

Figure 3: Visual Processing Architecture applied to the game Freeway. Raw pixels from the game screen are displayed on the left. Next, contiguous pixels of the same color are merged into blobs. Objects are then extracted by merging adjacent blobs which exhibit constant velocity over the last two frames. Next, objects are clustered into object classes based on a pixel similarity score. Three main object classes are found – cars facing left, cars facing right, and the chicken. This approach is similar to that of Naddaf [11]. Finally, self detection successfully identifies the chicken blob as the agent and colors it gray (circled in a red dashed line in rightmost screen).

5.1 Visual Processing

For nearly any machine learning problem, the question of how to encode the state space is of great importance. Similar to Verbancsics and Stanley's example, HyperNEAT-GGP uses an overhead object representation of the current game screen. Since the Atari provides only the raw pixels of the screen as input, a visual processing stack identifies objects and game entities without a priori knowledge of a specific game [11]. A graphical depiction of this stack is shown in Figure 3. While it is likely possible to learn from the raw screen's pixels, object detection requires little work and reduces the complexity of the learning task by eliminating pixels not directly relevant to playing the game.

Visual processing begins at the raw pixels of the game screen. Image segmentation groups adjacent raw pixels with similar colors into blobs. Next, blob merging occurs, outputting a set of current objects on screen. This process examines all of the recently discovered blobs and compares them with equivalent blobs in the last frame in order to compute a velocity for each blob. Blobs are matched between screens using pixel similarity. Velocity is computed by measuring the displacement of blob centroids. Once each blob is assigned a velocity, adjacent blobs with the same non-zero velocity are merged into objects. Objects that are too small or become stationary are thrown out. This check helps reduce the number of false positives in the object-detection process.

Finally, objects are clustered into object classes or prototypes. Specifically, the shape of each pair of objects is compared and if found to exceed a similarity threshold (97% pixel match in these experiments), the objects are grouped into the same class. Pixel similarity between two objects is computed by comparing the presence of pixels relative to each object's bounding box. As Figure 3 indicates, different object classes are discovered for the cars at the bottom half of the screen, cars at the top half of the screen, and the chicken.

To reduce the number of spurious prototypes, prototypes are passed to the next stage of the approach only when a number of instances of that prototype are seen within successive frames. In the example in Figure 3, this check helps remove prototypes for objects created when the cars are at the edges of the screen. Prototypes failing this check are removed while those which pass are assigned a unique real number (see Section 5.3 for more details).

Objects are assigned to the same class if their shape is relatively similar without taking color into consideration. This assumption has a potential drawback in certain games if different objects have similar shapes but different colors.

5.2 Self-Identification

The self identification step is meant to identify the location of an on-screen entity that is being controlled by the agent. In the vast majority of Atari games, the player's actions affect the movement of some on-screen entity, here termed the *self*. Knowledge of the location of the *self* is crucial to selecting an action, as described below. HyperNEAT-GGP uses an approach based on information gain to identify a blob most likely to correspond to the *self*. Pseudocode is given in Algorithm 1.

At the high level, this approach makes certain assumptions about the self entity. First, it is assumed that the self blob will move similarly whenever the same action is performed. That is, whenever an action, say Joystick Up, is taken, the resulting velocity of the self blob should have a similar value (e.g. blob.y_velocity = -1).

As input, in lines 1-3, the algorithm has access to the set of possible joystick and button actions applicable to the current game (this is typically a subset of the 18 possible actions present on the Atari console), a list of blobs detected in the current frame, and a history of the actions taken by the agent. Additionally, line 5 assumes access to the (x, y) velocity history $vHist$ of every blob. Next, Algorithm 1 computes the entropy of blob b's velocity his-

Algorithm 1 Identify Self

```
1: actions ← set of actions applicable to this game
2: current_blobs ← set of blobs in the current game frame
3: ActionHist ← Set of actions at time 0...n
4: for blob b ∈ current_blobs do
5:     vHist_b ← Set of velocities of blob b at time 0...n
6:     H_b ← H(vHist_b)
7:     for action a ∈ actions do
8:         vHist_(b|a) ← [vHist_b[t] ∀_t : ActionHist[t−1] == a]
9:         H_(b|a) ← H(vHist_(b|a))
10:    end for
11:    InfoGain_b ← H_b − sum_(a∈actions)(p_a * H_(b|a))
12: end for
13: return arg_max_(b∈current_blobs)(InfoGain_b)
```

tory. Entropy is calculated using the standard formulation: $H(X) = -\sum_{i=1}^{n} p(x_i) * ln(p(x_i))$. Taking entropy over a velocity history involves computing the distribution over blob b's velocity values. This computation is done using the empirically observed frequencies of each observed (x, y) velocity value in b's velocity history. A blob with highly random movement will exhibit a high information entropy over its full velocity history while a blob with highly regular movement will yield low entropy.

Having computed the information entropy over b's full velocity history, Algorithm 1 next examines each action individually and, in line 8, create b's selective velocity history $vHist_{(b|a)}$. The selective velocity history simply filters the full velocity history by including only velocities that were observed in frames after which action a was taken. For example, if $a =$ joystick left, then $vHist_{(b|a)}$ would only contain resultant velocities for frames in which a was the action selected. In line 9, entropy is computed over b's selective velocity history. This selective entropy $H_{(b|a)}$ should be low if a given action reliably causes the blob to move in a certain direction.

Finally, information gain is computed in line 11 by subtracting a frequency weighted sum of a blob's selective velocity entropies from the blob's full velocity entropy. If each of the selective entropies is low, as should be the case for the self blob, a high information gain results. In line 13, the algorithm concludes by returning the blob with maximum information gain.

While Algorithm 1 is generally successful in identifying the self blob, sometimes game dynamics break the assumption that actions result in similar velocities. For example, in the Freeway game, after colliding with a car, control is taken from the player and the chicken inadvertently is moved down for several frames regardless of which actions the agent is executing. This temporary lack of control results in irregular selective velocity histories and temporarily poorer identification of the self. However, in some sense the algorithm is correct in losing confidence in an object over which it no longer has control. In practice, since the chicken is still the most controlled blob, it remains the self.

5.3 Atari-HyperNEAT Interface

After extracting object classes as well as the location of the self from the raw game screen, this information needs to be sent to HyperNEAT. As discussed in Section 4, HyperNEAT evolves a CPPN that encodes an ANN. This section assumes access to a fully connected 2-layer ANN whose weights have been specified by the CPPN. At a high level, information from the game screen needs to be translated to activations of nodes in the input layer of the ANN. Then, after the network has been run in the standard feed-forward fashion, the activation of nodes on the output layer must be interpreted in order to select an action.

Figure 4 shows an example of how object classes are given as input to the substrate layer of the ANN. Since the ANN input nodes can only take real-valued activations, each class of objects must be mapped to a real number. Thus a mapping from object classes to real values is maintained. Upon discovery of new object classes, real values are incrementally added to the map in a non-decreasing fashion. The raw game screen of the Atari console displays a native resolution of 160×210, which is discretized by a factor of 10 in each dimension to produce a 16×21 grid of ANN input nodes. Figure 4b shows an example discretization. Following this step, each cell that contains an object is fed as input to the ANN with a real valued activation corresponding to the mapping of that object class. Cells devoid of objects are given input activations of zero. The ANN is run in a standard feed-forward manner, producing activations of the nodes in the 16×21 output layer (Figure 4d). Action selection involves locating the cell corresponding to the detected self object (colored blue in Figure 4d). The activation of this cell as well as the activations of the four adjacent cells (shown with red arrows) are compared and the action corresponding to the arrow in the highest of these five cells is returned (or no-op if the self square has the highest value). This method of action selection supports up to five possible actions. Future work involves extending this framework to support more complex actions such a button presses and combinations of joystick and button-press actions.

6. EXPERIMENTAL SETUP

The experimental setup was the same for both Freeway and Asterix: HyperNEAT-GGP was run for 250 generations, with 100 individuals in each generation and a substrate resolution of 16×21. All individuals learn from scratch and were evaluated on the Atari simulator using the same random seed. Evaluations of the 100 individuals in each generation were performed in parallel on a Condor cluster, resulting in each generation taking several minutes of wall-clock time to evaluate. Results are averaged across five runs of HyperNEAT-GGP evolution and compared with previous results obtained using gradient descent Sarsa(λ) with linear function approximation[11].

Sarsa(λ) was implemented as follows. Due to the large size of the state space, the Sarsa(λ) agent uses linear function approximation in which each state is represented by a vector of n values, $\Phi(s)$, known as the feature vector, where $n \ll |S|$. An additional vector of parameters θ is used to estimate the value of a state as follows: $V_t(s) = \sum_{i=1}^{n} \theta_t(i)\Phi(s)(i)$. Thus the objective is to find values for θ such that, when combined with the feature vector for any state, the estimated state value is close to the actual state value. This is accomplished by updating θ at each timestep as follows: $\theta_{t+1} = \theta_t + \alpha\delta e_t$ where α is the learning rate, δ is the temporal difference error, and e_t is the eligibility trace. More information about Sarsa(λ) can be found in Sutton and Barto [16].

Three different variations of the Sarsa(λ) agent were included, each using different feature vectors to represent the state of the Atari game. First, Sarsa(λ)-BASS (Basic Ab-

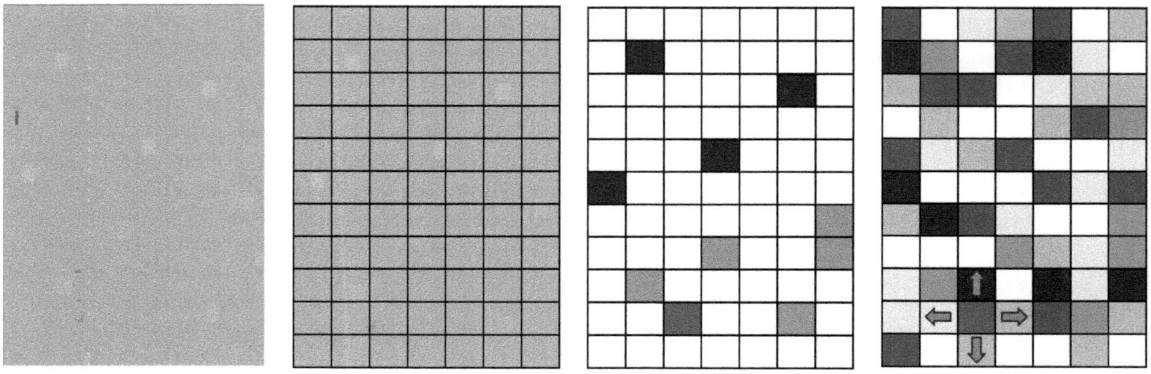

(a) Object Classes (b) Grid Overlay (c) ANN Input (d) ANN Output

Figure 4: The interface between visual processing framework and the HyperNEAT ANN. Classes of objects are discretized into a grid whose cells are fed to the input nodes of the ANN via a map from object classes to real numbers. After running the ANN, activations of the output layer in cells adjacent to the detected self are used to select which action the agent should take. In this case, the agent would move up since that adjacent cell has the highest activation.

straction of Screen Shots) discretizes the screen into a binary vector v_l of length 14x18x8 where 14 and 18 are the width and height of the discretized screen and 8 is the number of possible colors in SECAM mode. Next it creates another binary vector v_q which contains the pairwise ANDs of all items in v_l. Thus the full feature vector Φ_a is a $(|v_l|+|v_q|) \times |A|$ bit binary vector representing an abstraction of the raw game screen.

Second, Sarsa(λ)-DISCO (Detecting Instances of Class Objects) uses an object detection framework similar to the one outlined in Section 5 to detect classes of objects present in the current screen. To generate Φ it encodes the absolute location of each object class on the screen as well as the tile-coded relative position and velocity for each pair of object classes. Since there may be multiple instances of each object class present on a given screen and Φ is required to have a fixed length, tile-coded positions and velocities are found for each instance and summed.

Third, Sarsa(λ)-RAM uses a state representation based on the 1024 bits of random access memory (RAM) available to the Atari console. A binary vector v_l is created which contains each of the 1024 bits of memory. Next another binary vector v_q encodes the ANDs of all bits in v_l. Φ is a direct concatenation of v_l and v_q. For detailed descriptions of these learning agents, see Chapter 2 of [11].

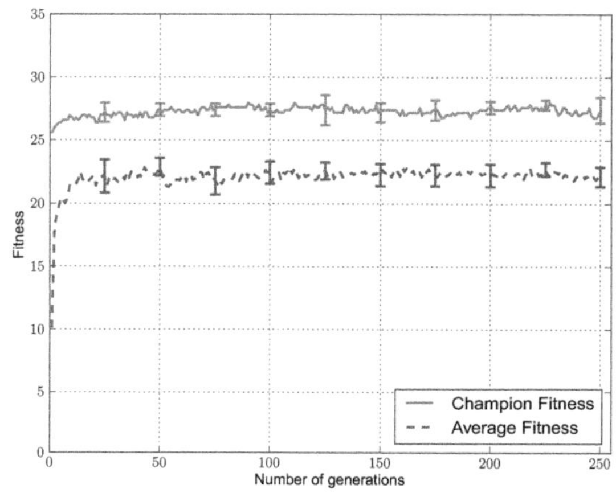

Figure 5: HyperNEAT-GGP learning performance on the Freeway game. Average fitness of the population along with the champion fitness for each generation are displayed. Error bars represent standard deviation. The fitness of an individual corresponds exactly to its game score. As the figure shows, effective Freeway policies are found in early generations.

7. RESULTS

This section provides experimental results obtained from applying HyperNEAT-GGP on two Atari games, *Freeway* and *Asterix*. Table 1 presents the fitness values of the best individual averaged across all the runs, as well as the overall best individual found. Previously published performances of BASS, DISCO, and RAM gradient descent Sarsa(λ) agents are also presented as well as an agent taking random actions each step [11].

7.1 Freeway

In Freeway the player controls a chicken as it attempts to cross the road. Average fitness of the population and the champion fitness throughout the learning process can be seen in Fig. 5. The most striking observation from these results is that the Sarsa(λ) agents are unable to find a solution to the problem (evident in the zero scores in Table 1), whereas even the first generation in HyperNEAT-GGP produces a champion with a very high fitness (starting average champion fitness = 26.4). Sarsa(λ) agents exhibit zero score due to the sparse reward on this domain. An agent would have had to perform a large number of exploratory actions before stumbling on the goal state at the top of the screen and receiving a reward. On the other hand, all individuals in HyperNEAT are produced by randomly initialized CPPNs. Due to the nature of CPPNs, at least a few individuals have the propensity to always take the *Up* action and obtain a large fitness at the outset. Evolution helps individuals to learn quickly to avoid cars over the next 50 generations, which can be seen by the slight increase in champion and average fitness.

7.2 Asterix

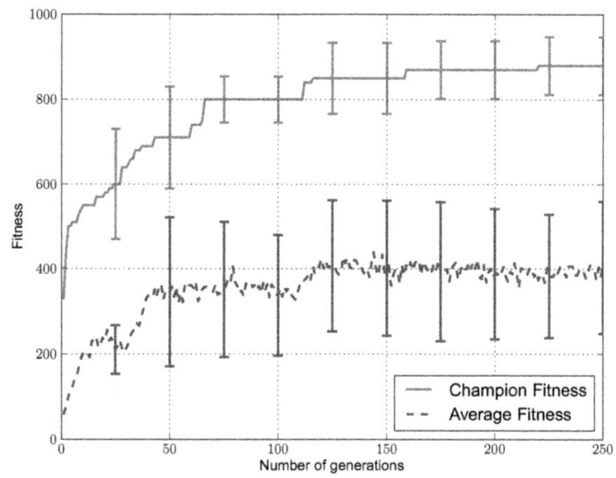

Figure 6: HyperNEAT-GGP learning performance on the Asterix game. The average fitness of the population along with the champion at each generation in the Asterix game. Error bars represent standard deviation. Fitness of an individual corresponds exactly to their game score. As the figure shows, policies are continually improved throughout the course of the 250 generations.

In Asterix, the player controls a unit called Asterix with the objective of collecting magic potions and avoiding *lyres*. Average fitness of the population and the champion fitness throughout the learning process can be seen in Fig. 6. Results for Asterix were averaged across five runs of HyperNEAT-GGP evolution. Table 1 contrasts our approach with previous results. The results for Asterix are qualitatively different from Freeway in a number of ways: First, random exploration obtains non-zero reward in Asterix as Asterix inadvertently collects magic potions. The Sarsa(λ) agents can bootstrap from this information and learn to become statistically better than random. Additionally, champions from HyperNEAT evolution start at close to random performance (starting average champion fitness = 80) and improve their performance to the same level as Sarsa(λ) within 50 generations. Finally, the learning process steadily improves the fitness through the entirety of 250 generations. This steady improvement demonstrates the power of using CPPNs at representing good policies for this game.

Results show excellent performance by HyperNEAT-GGP on the Asterix and Freeway games. Informal comparisons with agents controlled by the authors of this paper indicate that HyperNEAT-GGP achieves scores on par with human play. However, to extend HyperNEAT-GGP to play arbitrary games in the Atari simulator, some future work is required.

8. FUTURE WORK

The most pressing direction for future work is to extend HyperNEAT-GGP to a larger set of games. There are three

	Freeway	Asterix
Sarsa(λ)-BASS	0	402
Sarsa(λ)-DISCO	0	301
Sarsa(λ)-RAM	0	545
Random	0	156
HyperNEAT-GGP (Average)	27.4	870
HyperNEAT-GGP (Best)	29	1000

Table 1: Game scores obtained in the Freeway and Asterix games. HyperNEAT-GGP substantially outperforms Sarsa(λ) on both Freeway and Asterix. The last two lines report the average and best champion's score at generation 250.

main challenges: large numbers of possible actions, many different object classes, and robust visual processing.

In Freeway and Asterix, like in Robocup Keepaway, there are relatively few classes of objects that matter: cars and the chicken for Freeway, potions and lyres for Asterix, and takers and keepers for Keepaway. With a limited number of object classes it is easy to map from objects to substrate activations. For example, in Keepaway, keepers can be assigned values of 1 and takers values of -1. Having such few values allows HyperNEAT to easily differentiate between classes of objects and exhibit appropriate behaviors for each, such as avoiding lyres and collecting potions.

It is more difficult to differentiate between object classes as the number of classes increases and crowds the map of object class to substrate values. Accordingly, HyperNEAT becomes increasingly unable to distinguish between and formulate appropriate strategies for dealing with each class.

The second area of future work involves developing a better way to handle a large number of actions. In games like Freeway in which there are only a few actions (up, down, no-op), it is possible to choose which action to take by examining values of the output nodes adjacent to the self node (as described in Section 5.3). This issue becomes more complicated when other actions such as button presses are involved. For example, which node's value should be examined to decide if the button press action should be taken?

Finally, the visual processing stack could be made more robust. Specifically, objects are sometimes lost when they change shape or rotate. Additionally unmoving objects such as walls are not detected. This introduces difficulties in games such as Pac-man where static objects are essential to the game dynamics. Finally self-identification could also be improved by incorporating additional information about how long each object has been on-screen, with the assumption that the self object remains on screen while other objects are transitory. Further changes are encountered with self objects which retain velocity – such as the spaceship in Asteroids.

Addressing these areas of future work will go a long way towards making HyperNEAT-GGP more generally applicable to Atari games.

9. CONCLUSION

This paper introduces HyperNEAT-GGP, a HyperNEAT-based general Atari game playing agent. Many Atari games contain geometric regularities in the two-dimensional space of the game screen. This structure allows HyperNEAT to quickly learn effective policies. To reduce the complexity of learning from the raw game screen, HyperNEAT-GGP employs a game-independent visual processing hierarchy designed to identify classes of objects as well as the entity that the player controls on the game screen. Identified objects are provided as input to HyperNEAT. Due to the computational overhead of visual processing applied to each game screen, a parallel architecture is used to evaluate multiple individuals simultaneously. Results were presented for two Atari games, *Freeway* and *Asterix*. In both cases, HyperNEAT-GGP was shown to outperform previous reinforcement learning benchmarks [11]. While no single Atari game, if studied in isolation and given extensive feature engineering, likely poses too great a challenge for modern AI techniques, the full collection of over 900 Atari games presents a daunting task for a single learning agent. HyperNEAT-GGP represents a first step towards the ambitious goal of creating an agent capable of learning and seamlessly transitioning between many different tasks.

10. ACKNOWLEDGMENTS

This research is supported in part by NSF (IIS-0917122,DBI-0939454,IIS-0915038), ONR (N00014-09-1-0658), and FHWA (DTFH61-07-H-00030).

11. REFERENCES

[1] M. Campbell, A. J. H. Jr., and F. hsiung Hsu. Deep blue. *Artif. Intell.*, 134(1-2):57–83, 2002.

[2] J. Clune, B. E. Beckmann, C. Ofria, and R. T. Pennock. Evolving coordinated quadruped gaits with the hyperneat generative encoding. In *Proceedings of the Eleventh conference on Congress on Evolutionary Computation*, CEC'09, pages 2764–2771, Piscataway, NJ, USA, 2009. IEEE Press.

[3] D. B. D'Ambrosio and K. O. Stanley. Generative encoding for multiagent learning. In *GECCO '08: Proceedings of the 10th annual conference on Genetic and evolutionary computation*, pages 819–826, New York, NY, USA, 2008. ACM.

[4] C. Diuk, A. Cohen, and M. L. Littman. An object-oriented representation for efficient reinforcement learning. In *Proceedings of 25th International Conference on Machine Learning (ICML)*, pages 240–247, 2008.

[5] G. Edgers. Atari and the deep history of video games. `http://www.boston.com/bostonglobe/ideas/articles/2009/03/08/a_talk_with_nick_montfort/`.

[6] D. Ferrucci, E. Brown, J. Chu-Carroll, J. Fan, D. Gondek, A. A. Kalyanpur, A. Lally, J. W. Murdock, E. Nyberg, J. Prager, N. Schlaefer, and C. Welty. Building Watson: An Overview of the DeepQA Project. *AI Magazine*, 31(3), 2010.

[7] J. Gauci and K. O. Stanley. A case study on the critical role of geometric regularity in machine learning. In *Proceedings of the 23rd National Conference on Artificial Intelligence (AAAI)*, 2008.

[8] M. Genesereth and N. Love. General game playing: Overview of the aaai competition. *AI Magazine*, 26:62–72, 2005.

[9] S. M. Lucas. Ms pac-man competition (screen capture mode). `http://dces.essex.ac.uk/staff/sml/pacman/CIG2011Results.html`.

[10] S. M. Lucas. Ms pac-man competition. *SIGEVOlution*, 2(4):37–38, 2007.

[11] Y. Naddaf. Game-independent AI agents for playing atari 2600 console games. Master's thesis, University of Alberta, 2010.

[12] M. Parker and B. Bryant. Backpropagation without human supervision for visual control in quake II. *Proceedings of the 2009 IEEE Symposium on Computational Intelligence and Games (CIG'09)*, pages 287–293, 2009.

[13] K. O. Stanley and R. Miikkulainen. Evolving neural networks through augmenting topologies. *Evolutionary Computation*, 10(2):99–127, 2002.

[14] P. Stone and R. S. Sutton. Scaling reinforcement learning toward RoboCup soccer. In *Proceedings of the Eighteenth International Conference on Machine Learning*, pages 537–544. Morgan Kaufmann, San Francisco, CA, 2001.

[15] P. Stone, R. S. Sutton, and G. Kuhlmann. Reinforcement learning for RoboCup-soccer keepaway. *Adaptive Behavior*, 13(3):165–188, 2005.

[16] R. S. Sutton and A. G. Barto. Reinforcement learning: An introduction. *IEEE Transactions on Neural Networks*, 9(5):1054–1054, 1998.

[17] G. Tesauro. Td-gammon, a self-teaching backgammon program, achieves master-level play. *Neural Comput.*, 6:215–219, March 1994.

[18] P. Verbancsics and K. O. Stanley. Evolving static representations for task transfer. *J. Mach. Learn. Res.*, 11:1737–1769, August 2010.

Accelerating Human-Computer Collaborative Search through Learning Comparative and Predictive User Models

Gregory S. Hornby
University of California Santa Cruz
NASA Ames Research Center, MS 269-3
Moffett Field, CA USA
gregory.s.hornby@nasa.gov

Josh C. Bongard
Department of Computer Science
University of Vermont
Burlington, VT USA
josh.bongard@uvm.edu

ABSTRACT

Interactive Evolutionary Algorithms (IEAs) have much potential for allowing a human user to guide a search algorithm, but have struggled to overcome the limitations of slow, easily-fatigued human users. Here we describe The Approximate User (TAU) system in which these limitations are overcome by using a model of the user's preferences – which are continuously built and refined during the search process – to drive the search algorithm. Two variations of a user-modeling approach are compared to determine if this approach can accelerate IEA search. The two user-modeling approaches compared are: 1. learning a classifier which correctly determines which of two designs is better; and 2. learning a model which predicts a fitness score. Rather than having people do the user-testing, we propose the use of a simulated user as an easier means to test IEAs. Both variants of the TAU IEA are compared against a basic IEA and it is shown that TAU is up to 2.7 times faster and 15 times more reliable at producing near optimal results. In addition, we see TAU as a step toward building a more general Human-Computer Collaborative system.

Categories and Subject Descriptors

I.2.6 [**Artificial Intelligence**]: Learning

General Terms

Algorithms, Design

Keywords

Evolutionary Design, Interactive Evolutionary Algorithm, Preference Learning, User Fatigue, User Modeling

1. INTRODUCTION

An IEA is an interactive search algorithm that utilizes human input to make subjective decisions on potential problem solutions [5, 9, 13, 14]. In traditional interactive evolution, a human user is presented with one or more candidate individuals being evolved for selection. The human user directly performs selection and then the favored individuals are selected for propagation of offspring into the next generation. Current examples of this work on the Web are Picbreeder [12] and EndlessForms [7], both of which are based on using neural networks to encode 2D images (Picbreeder) or 3D shapes (EndlessForms).

Reliance on human input, however, induces a couple of major challenges. First, users suffer *user fatigue*: the quality and accuracy of human input greatly degrades with repeated prompts for input [14]. In addition, for typical non-interactive EAs, tens of thousands of evaluations are necessary to achieve interesting results, which is orders of magnitude more evaluations then can be expected from a single user. Finally, humans are generally far slower at evaluating designs than computer software is. To make IEAs viable, some method must be developed for overcoming these limitations of human users.

Given the limited number of human interactions possible with an IEA, it must strive to make the most of what little data the user has provided. The approach we are analyzing is that of learning a model of the human user and using this model as the fitness function rather than having the human user directly select parents. This idea came from the Estimation-Exploration Algorithm [2, 3], and was first applied to IEAs by Schmidt and Lipson [11].

The system we have developed is called **TAU**, for *The Approximate User*. Two different methods of user-modeling are described and compared: 1. learning a classifier which correctly determines which of two designs is better; and 2. learning a model which predicts a fitness score. Since the implementation used in this work is still in its preliminary stages, we hope that demonstrating a speedup on one domain is sufficient to show that it has potential.

In addition, TAU a step toward turning an IEA into a more general Human-Computer Collaborative Search system where the strengths of each system are better utilized. Traditionally, either a person does all the work or a computer search or optimization algorithm does all the work. With IEAs, a human is doing all the evaluations and the software is deciding what to be evaluated. We are working toward a system in which a human user is using their intelligence and experience to guide a search algorithm, taking advantage of the computer's speed to perform most of the evaluations.

The rest of this paper is organized as follows. In Section 2 we review related work in IEAs and user-modeling, followed by a description of the TAU algorithm in Section 3. To demonstrate that TAU algorithm can accelerate IEA search we use a simulated human user, which is described in Section 4. The setup for the experiments is described in Section 5. Then in Section 6 we present experimental results which show that fitness-predictive user modeling accelerates IEAs over that of a basic IEA, although are not as fast as an IEA accelerated with comparative user modeling. Finally, we present our conclusions in Section 7.

2. BACKGROUND

Quite recently there has been promising initial work toward addressing the user fatigue problem. One approach that has been used is to hardcode mathematical heuristics of aesthetics, and this has found some success for the interactive evolution of jewelry [15]. This system has several heuristics of beauty built in and reduces the amount of feedback needed from the user by two orders of magnitude. It can be thought of as a hybrid approach in which evaluations are partially done by an encoded fitness function – the heuristics of aesthetics – and partially done by the human user. Limitations of this approach are that it still requires a hard-coded fitness function and that results are somewhat dependent on it. Of interest are approaches in which there is no such dependence on a hard-coded fitness function.

An alternative to hard-coding heuristics is to build a model of the user's preferences with ideas from statistical Machine Learning. One system is to treat user feedback as inputs to a traditional parameter estimation system [1]. This leverages the speed of existing statistical machine learning systems but is limited to parameterized design spaces. To move beyond parameterized encodings, another approach is to learn weights on grammatical rules for constructing a design [6]. While allowing for search through a topological space of designs, this does not scale to systems with large sets of rules, or which require large derivation trees to produce a design, or in which multiple sets of rules can produce acceptable solutions.

Our approach is to build a model of what the user wants to drive search, and to continuously learn and refine this model of the user's preferences concurrent with the design process. The idea behind our approach comes from prior work with the Estimation-Exploration Algorithm [2, 3], in which a coevolutionary system is used to evolve an *estimation* population, which evolves improvements to models of the hidden system, given pairs of input/output data obtained from the physical model(s) being approximated; and an *exploration* population, which evolves intelligent tests to perform on the hidden target system using the best models so far. In this case, the "hidden system" is the human user, of whom the computer is trying to build a model.

By having a computer model of the human's desires, this model can be used tirelessly to perform thousands or millions of evaluations and thereby circumvent the limitations of having human users act as the fitness function. Already a version of this approach has been tried on IEAs and it seemed to work well [11]. We have implemented our own variant, which we have called The Approximate User (TAU), with two ways of modeling the user and here we are performing a more rigorous comparison of this approach against a basic IEA.

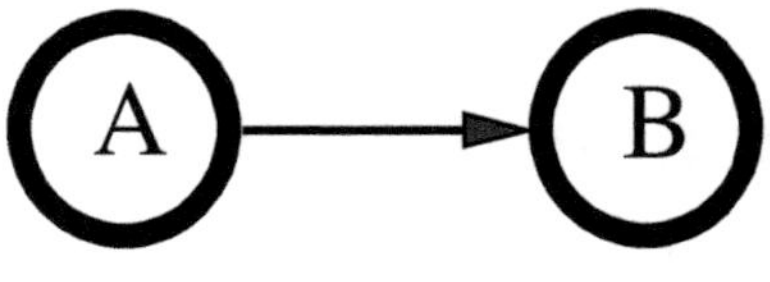

Figure 1: A simple relations graph showing that design `A` is preferred over design `B`.

3. OVERVIEW OF TAU

The TAU algorithm differs from a Basic IEA in that it uses a model of the user to perform its fitness evaluations rather than having the user manually evaluate each candidate solution. A user-model is built from a relations graph, which is a directed graph which stores every preference provided as input by the user. From this relations graph, modern machine learning techniques are used to train a model which can accurately match the user's preferences stored in this graph. This model of the user is then used as the evaluation function for a traditional optimizer to create a new set of solutions. Once a new set has been produced, a subset of them are presented to the user and the process repeats until a satisfactory result is produced.

An initial version of The Approximate User (TAU) algorithm for user-modeling has been implemented and an IEA augmented with TAU operates as follows:

1. Use the existing User Model to generate a set of candidate designs to present to the user. If the User Model is empty, generate random designs. This set of designs should be both good and diverse.

2. After the user has indicated their preference, update the relations graph by inserting the designs which were presented along with the user's preferences.

3. Do one of 3a (Comparator) or 3b (Fitness-Predictor):

   3a. Create a newer User Model by training a classifier to correctly predict each relation in the relations graph.

   3b. Sort the designs into layers of preferences, assign a fitness to each layer and then create a newer User Model by training a function approximator to match this.

4. Quit if a satisfactory solution has been produced.

For Step 1, we have implemented an Evolutionary Algorithm (EA) to create a set of designs using the User Model from Step 3 to either rank (3a) or score (3b) individuals. The EA used is configured to have a population size of 5 times the size of the grid shown to the user and a generational EA is run for 25 generations. Individuals are selected using tournament selection, with a tournament size of 2. New individuals are created using either mutation (65% of the time) or recombination (35% of the time) and are inserted into the population using Deterministic Crowding [10] to maintain genotypic diversity.

The data structure from which user models are built is the *relations graph*. The relations graph (Step 2) is a directed graph in which each node represents a design which has been shown to the user and each edge represents a user preference. For example, if a user is shown designs `A` and `B` and indicates that s/he prefers design `A`, then the relations

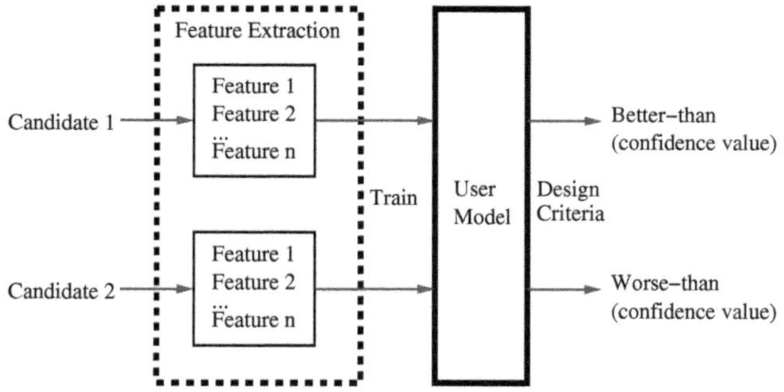

Figure 2: The basic structure of a Comparator user model. Features are extracted from two candidate designs and are fed into the Comparator, which then uses these features to predict which one is better.

graph will have two nodes, `A` and `B`, and a directed edge from `A` to `B` (Figure 1). The difference between the two variants of TAU is in how this relations graph is used to model a user.

The first variant of TAU models a user with a *Comparator* (Step 3a.), which takes the features of two designs as inputs and as an output it indicates which design is preferred (Figure 2). This user model is trained on the relations in the relations graph to predict, for any pair of designs, which one is better. In determining dominance from the relations graph, it is assumed that the dominance relation is transitive. Consider a population of candidate solutions (called *individuals* by those in the field of Evolutionary Computation) ind_A, ind_B and ind_C. If ind_A is better than ind_B, and ind_B is better than ind_C, it is assumed that ind_A is also better than ind_C.

Thus two key advantages of the Comparator approach are that more relations can be derived from the graph than there are elements in the graph, and the number of relations grows faster than the size of the graph. For example, the relations graph in Figure 3(a) contains six individuals (`A` through `F`) and represents a subset of the entire relations graph that might exist after a couple of prompts to the user. There are nine relations that can be derived from this graph – indicating the user's preference from past queries – with the first five relations being the arrows that are shown. The rest are: `A` is better than `E`; `A` is better than `F`; `C` is better than `E`; and `C` is better than `F`. If, after being presented with new designs `G` and `H` and previously seen designs `B` and `C`, the user indicates that s/he prefers `B` and `G` (Figure 3(b)), then two new nodes and four edges are added to the relations graph (Figure 3(c)). In addition to this, four additional relations can be derived: `G` is preferred over `D`, `E` and `F`, and `A` is preferred over `H`. It is this set of relations which can be derived from the relations graph which the Comparator user-model is trained to match.

The comparator user-model used here is quite similar to that of Schmidt and Lipson [11] with a few key differences. In Schmidt and Lipson's implementation, a population of ANNs was evolved using EAs, and the Estimation-Exploration Algorithm was used to determine a pair of designs to present to the user to evaluate and indicate their preference. Here, an ensemble of ANNs is trained using backpropagation and several designs are presented to the user with designs selected by using the ensemble to identify the better candidates in the population.

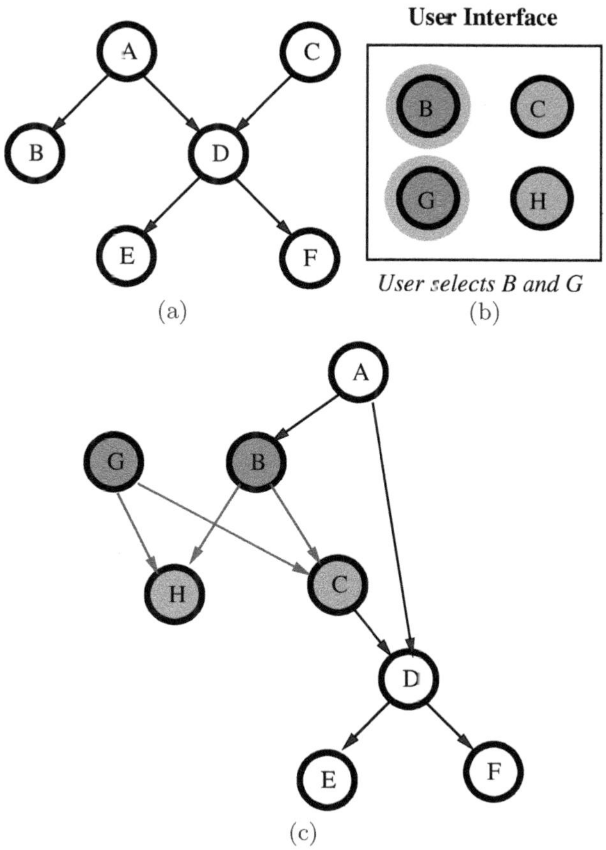

Figure 3: An example of how an update of the relations graph works: (a) shows the current relations graph consists of candidate solutions A through F; (b) two of these "old" candidates are shown to the user as well as two new ones, G and H, of which the user selects B and G; (c) based on the user's selection, the relations graph is now updated.

The other approach to user modeling is that of fitness prediction (Step 3b.). With this approach, the nodes in the relations graph are organized into layers of dominance, a fitness value is assigned to the nodes in each layer, and function approximator is trained to match the features of the designs to the appropriate fitness value. To put nodes into layers, all nodes which are not dominated by any other nodes are put into a layer and removed from the graph. This step of removing all non-dominated nodes to create a layer is repeated until all the nodes are removed from the relations graph. Applying this method to the relations graph in Figure 3(c) produces the layers in Figure 4.

To implement both user models the Fast Artificial Neural Network (FANN) library is used. ANNs are used because they have robust regression power with excellent interpolation and extrapolation characteristics [8]. Their classification output also corresponds to their statistical confidence in their prediction. In other words, noisy samples or conflicting samples reduce prediction confidence but in general maintain prediction accuracy [4]. The basic structure of a comparator neural net is shown in Figure 2. To improve performance, we are using an ensemble of three ANNs to

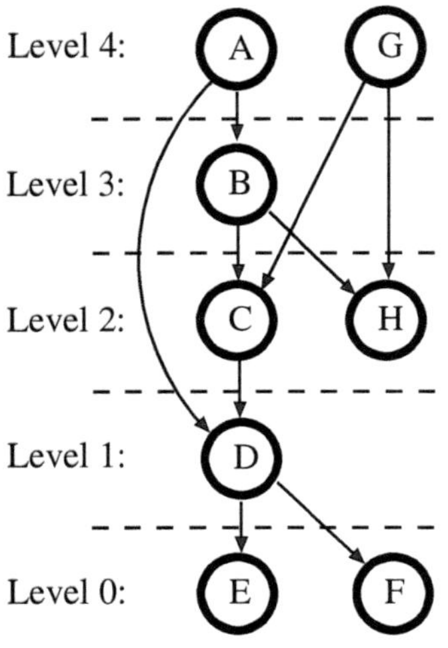

Figure 4: The result after taking the relations graph in Figure 3(c) and assigning levels to each node.

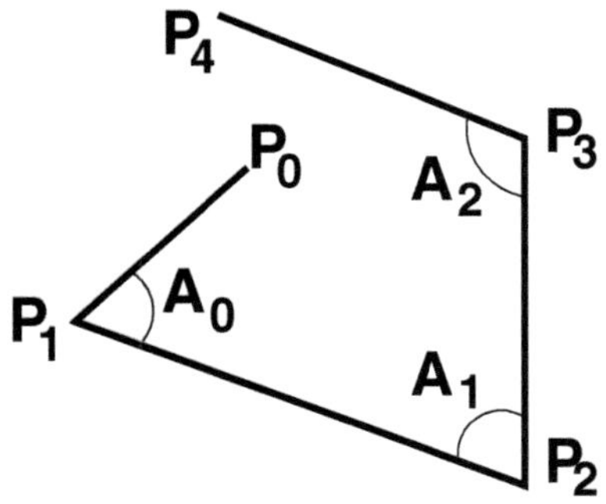

Figure 5: An example drawing that is scored for its closeness to a square.

create a User Model. Each ANN in the ensemble has a single hidden layer of 7 hidden units, a 40% connection density of the available, with weights randomly selected in the range of -0.1 to 0.1. Each ANN is trained using backpropagation for at most 50 iterations through the training data or until the training error is less than 0.001.

4. SIMULATING A HUMAN USER

Instead of performing comparison studies with real people, in this work a simulated person is used to drive the IEAs. The advantage of a simulated person is that comparisons between different versions of the TAU IEA and the Basic IEA can be done as often as desired. The simulated person is implemented as a combination of a scoring function for how well candidate designs match a target shape and a method for using this to drive the IEA. This scoring function could be used as a fitness function in a regular EA but in this case it is used as the target function which the TAU algorithm is trying to learn. Since it is not directly used to drive the EA we choose not to call it a fitness function to avoid confusion.

Here, designs are constructed from a contiguous sequence of connected line segments. The design-scoring function used by the simulated human user takes as input the endpoints of these line-segments – P_0, P_1, P_2, ... – and computes how close these line segments are to the target shape.

For these experiments, the test problem used is that of creating a square out of a sequence of four connected line segments. The four line segments are contiguous and are encoded as a real-valued vector with five x and y coordinates for the 5 end points, P_0, P_1, ... P_4, Figure 5. This scoring function has three distinct components: a score on the gap between P_0 and P_4; a score on how similar in length each line segment is to each other; and a score on how similar each of the three angles, A_0, A_1 and A_2 is to a right angle. Each of these three scoring-components has a range of 0 to 1 and the overall score is a product of these three sub-functions.

When creating a square from the five points which specify four contiguous line segments the first and last points, P_0 and P_4, must be the same. To score for this result the gap score function, S_{gap}, divides the distance between points P_0 and P_4 by the sum of the lengths for each of the four line segments:

$$S_{gap} = 1 - \frac{\text{distance from } P_0 P_4}{\text{sum of the length of all line segments}} \tag{1}$$

Another characteristic of a square is that all four sides have the same length. The score for this, the sub-function $S_{lengths}$ takes the length of each line segment and divides this by the average length of the four line segments. The ratio of the length of each side to the average length, L_i, is compared against the desired ratio, $L_{desired}$. For a square $L_{desired}$ is 1 for all line segments. To create a value between 0 and 1, the smaller of these two values is divided by the larger. This is done for each line segment and all four of these values are multiplied together:

$$S_{lengths}(L_{desired}) = \prod_{i=0}^{4} \begin{cases} \frac{|L_{desired}|}{|L_i|} & \text{if } L_i > L_{desired} \\ \frac{|L_i|}{|L_{desired}|} & \text{otherwise} \end{cases} \tag{2}$$

The third characteristic that is scored for is to score for the angles being right angles using the sub-function S_{angles}. Here, each angle A_i is compared against the desired angle, $A_{desired}$ and a value between 0 and 1 is computed similar to with $S_{lengths}$. For a square $A_{desired}$ is either $-\pi/2$ for all three angles or $+\pi/2$ for all three angles. The result for all three angles is multiplied together and returned:

$$S_{angles}(A_{desired}) = \prod_{i=0}^{2} \frac{|A_{desired}|}{|A_i - A_{desired}| + |A_{desired}|} \tag{3}$$

The overall score for how well a given shape matches the target shape is a product of the previous three sub-functions. For a square, the two options are for all line segments to have the same length and all three angles must be positive 90° turns ($\pi/2$) or they must all be negative 90° turns ($-\pi/2$):

$$S = S_{gap} S_{lengths}(1) max(S_{angles}(-\pi/2), S_{angles}(\pi/2)) \tag{4}$$

This approach to scoring how well a given shape matches a target shape is generic and can be used for scoring for different shapes by supplying the desired line-segment ratios and angles for the target shape. Because of symmetries, there are often multiple ways of producing a given shape from a sequence of line segments so the function returns the maximum of the different options.

In addition to the scoring function, the simulated user has a simple algorithm for driving the IEA to try and produce a desired drawing. The user interface for the IEA allows the user to: select and de-select designs; create a new set of candidate designs based on the current selections; discard all of the existing designs and create a new set of candidate designs based on the previous selections; and back-track to the previous set of designs. Roughly, the algorithm for the simulated human user requests a set of randomly generated designs until it finds one that scores higher than 0.25. It then iterates over selecting the top design, along with up to 2 other drawings which have a score within 10% of the top drawing. If the top drawing is not as good as the best drawing from the previous iteration, the algorithm requests an alternative set of candidates. If after three tries a new best drawing is not found, it backs up a level and tries again.

More precisely, the algorithm for the simulated user is as follows:

```
 1: Level = 0
 2: Set existing best to 0.
 3: repeat      ▷ Starting with randomly generated designs.
 4:     Request new random designs.
 5:     Score each design.
 6: until Best score is > 0.25
 7: repeat
 8:     if New best > previous best. then
 9:         Level = Level + 1
10:         Tries[Level] = 0
11:         Select the best design.
12:         Select next 2 best with score within 10% of best.
13:         Submit selections and request new designs.
14:         Score each design.
15:         continue.
16:     else
17:         Tries[Level] = Tries[Level] + 1.
18:         if Tries[Level] > 3 then
19:             Go back to previous generation.
20:             Level = Level - 1
21:             if Level = 0 then
22:                 Goto line 1.          ▷ Move to initial state.
23:             end if
24:         end if
25:         Request an alternative set of design.
26:         Score each design.
27:     end if
28: until Best score is 1.
```

5. EXPERIMENTAL SETUP

To demonstrate that concurrent construction of a user-model can accelerate search we compare the TAU algorithm – using both the Comparator (TAU-C) and Fitness Predictive (TAU-FP) approaches to user modeling – against a Basic IEA. The Basic IEA has the designs selected by the user being the parent designs for creating the next set of designs to present to the user. The configuration of TAU was described in Section 3, and both types of user modeling were tested. All of these IEAs are driven by the simulated human user described in Section 4.

An example of the application with a 3x5 grid of designs is shown in Figure 6. This has a sequence of pages shown to the user in interactively designing a square. The top page (Figure 6(a)) shows an initial set of randomly generated line drawings along with the simulated user's selections (in green). The next three images (Figures 6(b) to 6(d)) show the subsequent iterations of presenting the [simulated] user with new designs and their selections. In this exam-

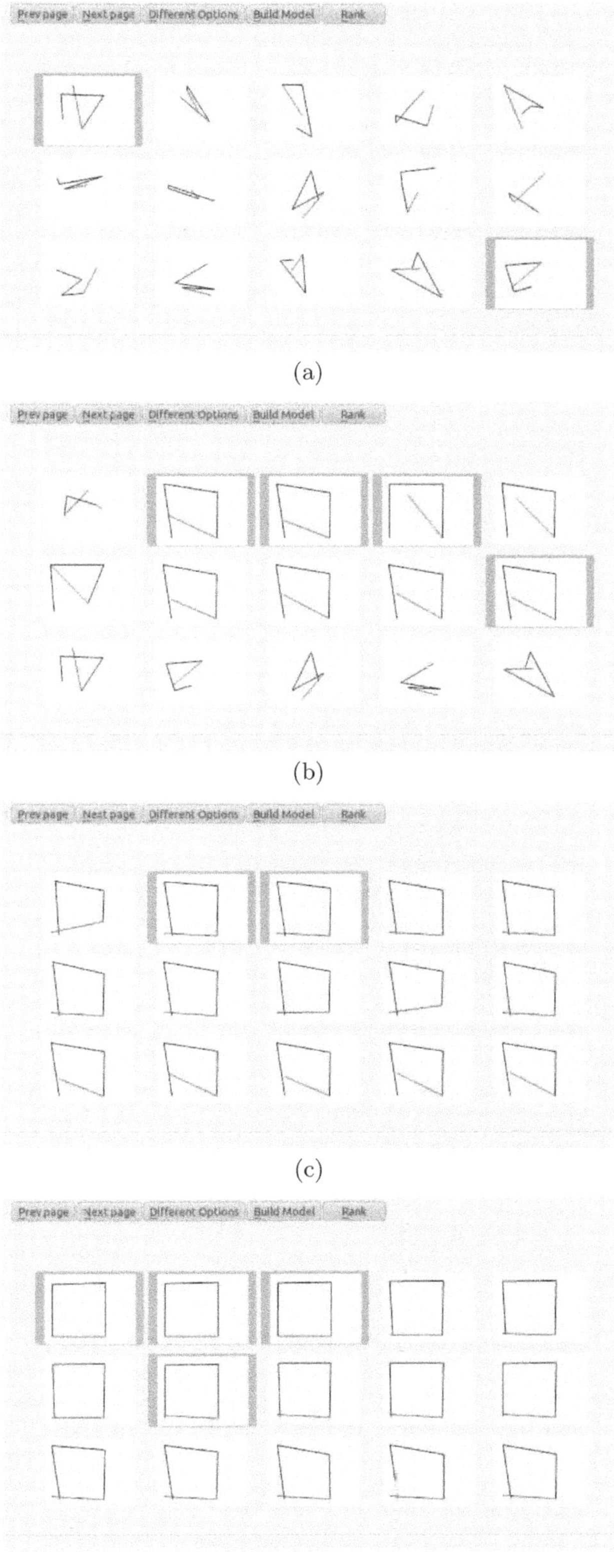

(a) (b) (c) (d)

Figure 6: A sequence of pages in interactively designing a square using the TAU Fitness Predictive user-modeling system.

ple the TAU algorithm is used with the fitness predictive user-modeling system.

An important point to note is that with TAO, the features being used to build and utilize user-models are different from the features used by the simulated human user to score designs. For the TAO IEAs, the features for a given design have the ratio of the length of each line segment to the average length of line segments in that design and the angle between each line segment. Also, the angle of the first line segment to the horizon is included to indicate the overall orientation of the design and the size of the average line segment is included to provide an indicator for the overall size of the drawing.

6. EXPERIMENTAL RESULTS

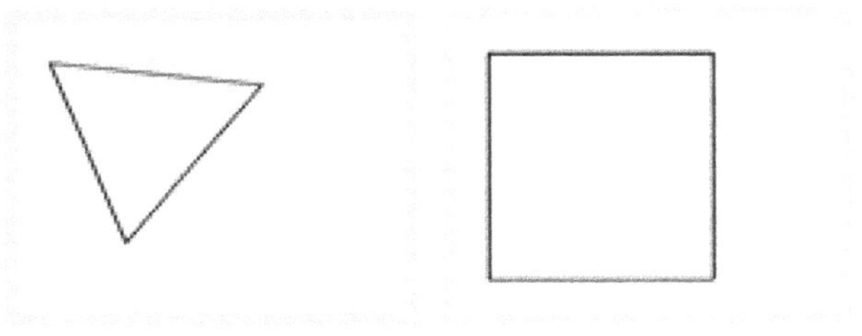

(a) (b)

Figure 7: The two test problems tried are to interactively evolve an equilateral triangle (a) and a square (b).

For these experiments 250 trials were run with each of the Basic IEA, and TAU with both the Comparator (TAO-C) and the Fitness Predictive (TAU-FP) user models on grid sizes of 3x3, 3x4 and 3x5. These were tried on two test problems: 1. producing an equilateral triangle; and 2. producing a square (Figure 7). Results of our experiments for the 3x3 and 3x5 grid sizes are shown graphically in Figure 8 and also in tabular form for the 3x5 grid in Table 1. Results for the 3x4 grid are not shown, but for all three systems these fall roughly in between results for the 3x3 and for the 3x5.

The graphs in Figure 8 show that all variants of IEAs perform better with a larger grid size and do better on the easier problem (creating a triangle out of three lines) than on the harder problem (creating a square out of four lines). The left set of graphs shows the frequency (out of the 250 trials) in which a given IEA reached a given degree of optimality in the design problem. In all cases TAO-C had the greatest likelihood of success, and only had a steep dropoff after the 95% range. The TAU-FP approach was not as reliable and tended to have a moderate dropoff in likelihood to succeed starting at around the 35% range, with a steep dropoff happening around 90% to 95%. Both variants of TAU were able to achieve 100% designs (75% of the time with TAU-C and 33% of the time with TAU-FP). The least reliable is the Basic IEA which, while more reliable than TAU-FP up to around 85%, then had a large drop in reliability and struggled to make even 98% of optimal with any regularity.

The set of graphs on the right side of Figure 8 show another important difference between TAU and the Basic IEA. With the Basic IEA, the number of selection iterations needed to achieve a given level of optimality seems to be growing at a polynomial rate. Combine this with the Basic IEA's rapidly decreasing success rate and it suggests that the Basic IEA will not be able to scale to achieving good results on more challenging problems. In contrast, with the TAU IEA it seems that a few selection rounds are needed for the algorithm to learn a reasonable model of what the user wants and, after this, it has a fairly flat, linear growth in the number of selection rounds needed to achieve a given level of design optimality. Here, TAU-C is about twice as fast as TAU-FP, and both have a slight upward inflection in the number of search iterations to get the last few percent of optimality. Overall, both variants of TAU show accelerated search over the basic IEA.

7. CONCLUSION

In this paper the method of accelerating IEAs through user-modeling was analyzed with The Approximate User (TAU) algorithm. With TAU, a relations graph of the user's preferences is updated after each interaction and this relations graph is used to build either a Comparative or Fitness Predictive model of the user. It is these user models which are used to drive an EA, thereby accelerating search by allowing many search evaluations to take place much more rapidly than by a human user.

To validate the effectiveness of TAU, we developed an artificial human user to drive search using a basic IEA and with the TAU IEA. Experiments were run comparing a Basic IEA against both variants of TAU. Overall, TAU was up to 15 times more reliable at achieving near optimal results and and more than 75 times more reliable at achieving optimal results. In addition to being more reliable, TAU achieved near-optimal results up to 2.7 times faster. In the best case, some trials with the TAU IEA achieved an optimal designs in 4-8 selection iterations. With a much a higher success rate at finding good solutions and the ability to find these solutions faster, the TAU algorithm has considerable promise in overcoming user fatigue.

We expect that by developing better approaches to modeling a human user's preferences that the TAU IEA can be made faster and able to scale to more difficult problems. In addition, this work is a step toward turning an IEA into a truly Human-Computer Collaborative Search system where the strengths of both the human and the computer are better utilized.

Acknowledgments.

This research was supported in part by the NSF Creative-IT grant 0757532 and DARPA M3 grant W911NF-1-11-0076. In addition, thanks to Grace Lin for her work on an early prototype.

8. REFERENCES

[1] G. J. Barnum and C. A. Mattson. A computationally assisted methodology for preference-guided conceptual design. *Journal of Mechanical Design*, 132, 2010.

[2] J. Bongard and H. Lipson. Nonlinear system identification using coevolution of models and tests. *IEEE Transactions on Evolutionary Computation*, 9:361–384, 2005.

[3] J. Bongard and H. Lipson. Automated reverse engineering of nonlinear dynamical systems. *Proceedings of the National Academy of Sciences*, 104:9943–9948, 2007.

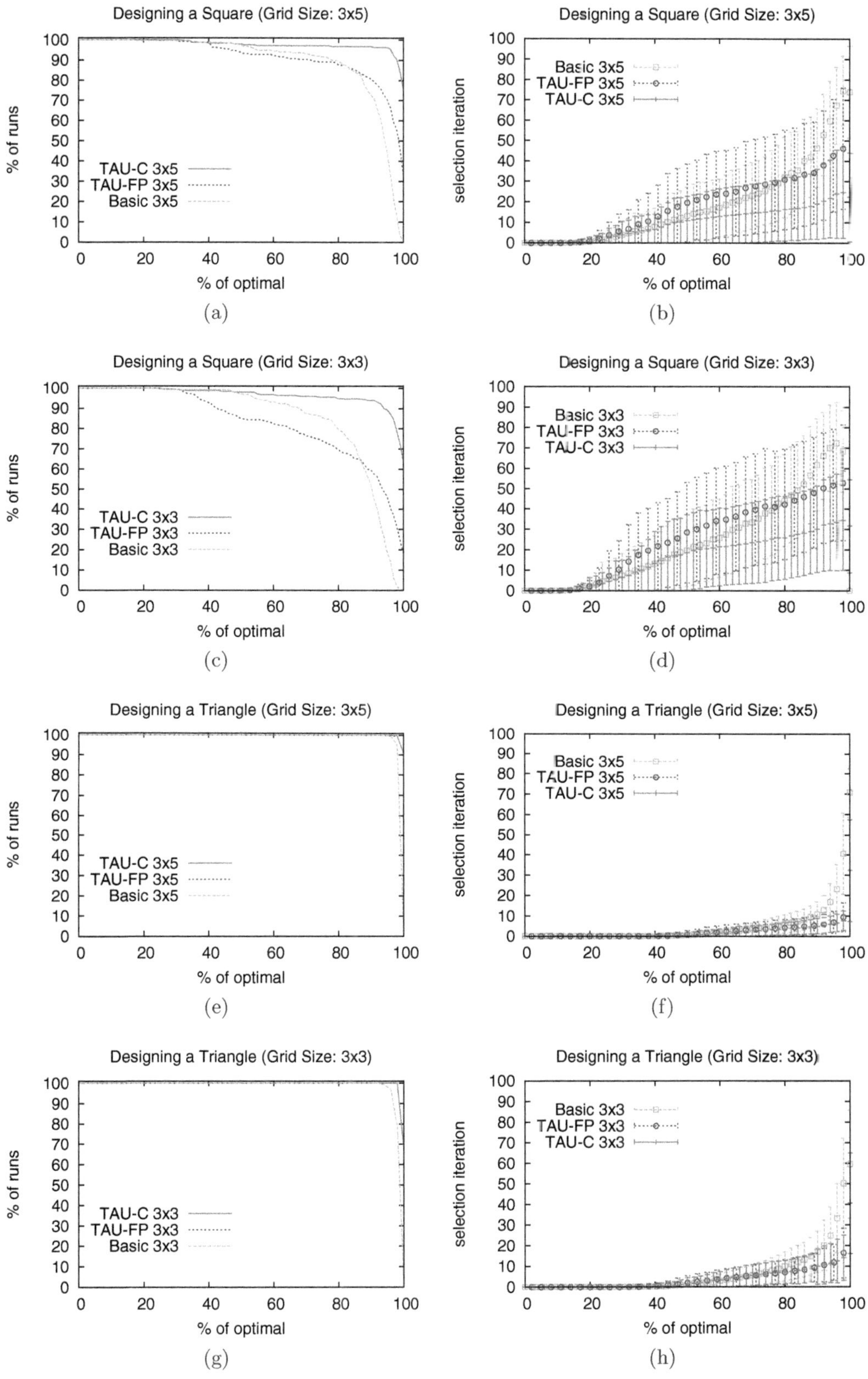

Figure 8: This figure shows graph which have plots of the performance of the Basic IEA and TAU using both a Comparator user-model (TAU-C) and a Fitness-Predictive user-model (TAU-FP). The graphs on the left show the probability of reaching a given percentage of optimal and the graphs on the right are the expected number of iterations to reach a given degree of optimality. This shows that the Comparator user models are better than the Fitness-Predictive ones, and both are better than the Basic IEA.

	Square					
	Basic IEA		TAU Fitness-Predictive		TAU Comparator	
% of Optimal	Prob Success	Avg Iterations	Prob Success	Avg Iterations	Prob Success	Avg Iterations
80	0.896	32.317 ± 19.8847	0.876	30.9726 ± 24.3431	0.968	16.4339 ± 15.2793
90	0.728	46.544 ± 19.4014	0.808	35.604 ± 25.29	0.968	19.2727 ± 17.2324
95	0.44	62.7455 ± 20.1492	0.704	42.8182 ± 27.6687	0.964	22.971 ± 19.9527
98	0.112	73.5357 ± 16.8907	0.54	45.7111 ± 29.7705	0.904	24.7522 ± 22.3901
99	0.028	68.5714 ± 12.6867	0.456	46.2632 ± 30.6672	0.836	24.8612 ± 23.7368
100	0.008	74 ± 22.6274	0.328	41.5732 ± 30.1236	0.756	22.3704 ± 21.6112

	Triangle					
	Basic IEA		TAU Fitness-Predictive		TAU Comparator	
% of Optimal	Prob Success	Avg Iterations	Prob Success	Avg Iterations	Prob Success	Avg Iterations
80	1	6.084 ± 4.54042	1	4.2 ± 4.04294	1	3.672 ± 3.07151
90	1	10.836 ± 6.15864	1	5.46 ± 4.76352	1	5.084 ± 3.74554
95	1	19.452 ± 10.1443	1	6.896 ± 5.3283	1	6.168 ± 4.0105
98	0.952	41.0252 ± 20.315	0.996	9.42972 ± 7.0628	1	7.828 ± 4.81531
99	0.696	57.431 ± 22.2958	0.996	13.2008 ± 9.83287	1	9.4 ± 5.88579
100	0.012	70.6667 ± 11.9304	0.732	43.8525 ± 25.7719	0.908	32.37 ± 25.087

Table 1: Summary of results for evolving a square on the 3x5 grid using the Basic IEA and the TAU algorithm with both Fitness-Predictive user-modeling and Comparative user-modeling. The top shows the results on interactively evolving a square, and the bottom are results on evolving a triangle. Both variants of TAU are more than 15 times more likely to reach 99% of optimal than the Basic IEA and up to 2.7 times faster.

[4] J. Bridle. Probabilistic interpretation of feedforward classification network outputs, with relationships to statistical pattern recognition. In Fogelman-Soulie and Herault, editors, *Neurocomputing: Algorithms, Architectures and Applications*, NATA ASI Series. Springer, 1990.

[5] C. Caldwell and V. S. Johnston. Tracking a criminal suspect through 'face-space' with a genetic algorithm. In R. K. B. L. B. Booker, editor, *Proc. of the Fourth Intl. Conf. on Genetic Algorithms*, pages 416–421, San Mateo, CA, 1991. Morgan Kaufmann.

[6] M. I. Campbell, R. Rai, and T. Kurtoglu. A stochastic graph grammar algorithm for interactive search. In *14th Design for Manufacturing and the Life Cycle Conference*, pages 829–840. ASME, 2009.

[7] J. Clune and H. Lipson. Evolving three-dimensional objects with a generative encoding inspired by developmental biology. *Lecture Notes in Computer Science*, 2011.

[8] G. Cybenko. Approximations by superpositions of a sigmoidal function. *Math. Contrl., Signals, Syst.*, 2:303–314, 1989.

[9] R. Dawkins. *The Blind Watchmaker*. Harlow Longman, 1986.

[10] S. W. Mahfoud. Crowding and preselection revisited. In R. Männer and B. Manderick, editors, *Parallel Problem Solving from Nature, 2*, pages 27–36. North-Holland, 1992.

[11] M. Schmidt and H. Lipson. Actively probing and modeling users in interactive co-evolution. In M. K. et al., editor, *Proc. of the Genetic and Evolutionary Computation Conference, GECCO-2006*, pages 385–386, Seattle, WA, 2006. ACM Press.

[12] J. Secretan, N. Beato, D. B. D. Ambrosio, A. Rodriguez, A. Campbell, J. T. Folsom-Kovarik, and K. O. Stanley. Picbreeder: A case study in collaborative evolutionary exploration of design space. *Evolutionary Computation*, 2011.

[13] K. Sims. Artificial Evolution for Computer Graphics. In *SIGGRAPH 91 Conference Proceedings*, Annual Conference Series, pages 319–328, 1991.

[14] H. Takagi. Interactive evolutionary computation: fusion of the capabilities of EC optimization and human evaluation. In *Proceedings of the IEEE*, pages 1275–1296, 2001.

[15] S. Wannarumon, E. L. J. Bohez, and K. Annanon. Aesthetic evolutionary algorithm for fractal-based user-centered jewelry design. *Artificial Intelligence for Engineering Design, Analysis and Manufacturing*, 22:19–39, 2008.

Photogrowth: Non-Photorealistic Renderings Through Ant Paintings

Penousal Machado
machado@dei.uc.pt

Luís Pereira
lcper@student.dei.uc.pt

CISUC, Department of Informatics Engineering
Polo II of the University of Coimbra
3030 Coimbra, Portugal

ABSTRACT

We introduce photogrowth, an evolutionary approach to the production of non-photorealistic renderings of images. The painting algorithm – inspired by ant colony approaches – is described and explained, giving emphasis to its novel aspects: the evolution of the sensory parameters of the ants; the production of resolution independent images; the rendering lines of variable width. The experimental results highlight the range of imagery that can be evolved by the system and show the potential of the approach for the production of large-format artworks.

Categories and Subject Descriptors

I.2.2 [**Artificial Intelligence**]: Automatic Programming; I.3.3 [**Computer Graphics**]: Picture/Image Generation—*Non-Photorealistic Rendering*

General Terms

Algorithms

Keywords

Evolutionary Art, Non-Photorealistic Rendering, Ant Colony

1. INTRODUCTION

The main goal of the research presented in this paper is the creation of large-scale non-photorealistic renderings (NPRs) of input images. The predominant artistic sources of inspiration for this work are ornamentation techniques. From a scientific point of view, areas such as evolutionary NPR and artistic filter evolution are of particular relevance.

Our approach can be seen as the evolution of a filter that transforms an input source image. The approach is inspired on ant colony approaches: the trails of artificial ants are used to produce an artistic rendering of the original. A interactive Genetic Algorithm (GA) is used to evolve the parameters that govern the behavior of ants' species, allowing the user to guide the algorithm to areas of the search space that she/he finds promising.

The novel characteristics of our approach derive, directly and indirectly, from the adoption of a scalable vector graphics, which contrasts with the pixel based approaches used in most ant colony painting algorithms. This enables the creation of resolution independent images and, as such, large-format artworks. The rendering algorithm represents the trail of each ant through a continuous line of varying width, which contributes to the expressiveness of the artworks.

We begin with a short survey of related work. Next, in the third section, we make a description of the photogrowth system, focusing on the behavior of the ants, on the evolutionary algorithm, and on the previewing and rendering modes. In the fourth section we present experimental results, making a brief analysis. Finally, we draw some conclusions and discuss aspects to be addressed in future work.

2. STATE OF THE ART

In this section we make a survey of related works, focusing on systems that use artificial ants for image generation purposes and on systems where evolutionary computation is employed for NPR purposes.

Tzafestas [20] presents a system where artificial ants pick-up and deposit food, which is represented by paint, and studies the self-regulation properties and complexity of the system and resulting images. Ramos and Almeida [18] explore the use of ant systems for pattern recognition purposes. The artificial ants successfully detect the edges of the images producing stylized renderings of the originals and smooth transitions between different images. The artistic potential of these approaches is explored in later works (e.g. [17]) and thorough his collaboration with the portuguese artist Leonel Moura, which resulted in several robotic swarm drawings (see e.g. [14]). Urbano [21, 22, 23, 24] presented several multi-agent systems based on artificial ants.

Aupetit et al. [1] present an interactive evolutionary computation system for the creation of ant paintings. They employ a GA to evolve parameters of the rules that govern the behavior of the ants. The artificial ants deposit paint on the canvas as they move thus producing a painting. In a later study, Monmarché [13] refines this approach exploring different rendering modes. Greenfield [5] presents an evolutionary approach to the production of ant paintings and explores the use of behavioral statistics of the artificial ants to automatically assign fitness. In [6] Greenfield adopted a multiple pheromone model where ants movements and behaviors are influenced (attracted or repelled) by both an en-

GECCO'12, July 7-11, 2012, Philadelphia, Pennsylvania, USA.
Copyright 2012 ACM 978-1-4503-1177-9/12/07 ...$10.00.

vironmentally generated pheromone and an ant generated pheromone.

The use of evolutionary algorithms to create image filters and NPRs of source images has been explored by several researchers. Focusing on the works where there was an artistic goal, we can mention the research of: Neufeld and Ross ([19, 15]), where Genetic Programming (GP, [8]), multi-objective optimization techniques, and an empirical model of aesthetics are used to automatically evolve image filters; [9], which evolved live-video processing filters through interactive evolution; [10], where GP is used to evolve image coloring filters from a set of examples; [25], which employs Genetic Algorithms (GAs) to evolve filters that produce images that match certain features of a target image; Collomosse ([4, 3, 2]), which uses image salience metrics to determine the level of detail for portions of the image, and GAs to search for painterly renderings that match the desired salience maps; [7] uses GP to evolve procedural textures for 3D objects; [11] employ GP to evolve assemblages of 3D objects that are an artistic representation of an input image.

3. PHOTOGROWTH

Photogrowth is composed of three main modules:

1. Evolutionary engine;
2. Previewing engine;
3. Rendering engine;

The evolutionary module is an interactive GA that allows the evolution of a series of parameters that govern the behavior of the ants. The previewing module is responsible for the production of the ant paintings during the evolutionary runs. The rendering engine is typically used offline to produce high quality renderings of specific ant paintings.

A graphic user interface gives access to these modules. It is composed of two windows (see Fig. 1: one depicts the paintings produced by the ants of the current population and allows the user to assign fitness to them, indicating a value between 0 and 10); the other, allows the user to navigate through populations, change the input image, inspect and edit the genotype of a given individual, save and load experiments and individuals, invoke the rendering engine, etc.

The following sections present the photogrowth system. We begin by describing the behavior of our painting ants. Next we present the evolutionary algorithm, focusing on the representation and genetic operators. Finally we highlight the differences between the previewing and rendering modes.

3.1 Painting Ants

Our painting ants live on the 2D world provided by the input image and they paint on a painting canvas that is initially empty (i.e., black in the experiments reported in this paper). Both living and painting canvas have the same dimensions and the ants move simultaneously on both canvas. The painting canvas is used exclusively for depositing ink. It has no interference with the behavior of the ants. They share these worlds with other artificial ants of the same species. Each ant has a position, color, deposit transparency and energy, all the remaining parameters are shared by the entire species. If the energy of an ant is bellow a given energy threshold it dies, if is is above a given threshold it generates offspring.

Figure 2: An ant with five sensory vectors.

The luminance of an area of the living canvas represents the available energy at that point. Therefore, ants may gain energy by traveling through light areas. The energy of an ant is updated as follows:

$$energy = (energy + b(x, y) * gain) * decay \quad (1)$$

where $b(x, y)$ is a function that returns the luminance (in the [0,1] interval) of the area where the ant is placed, *gain* is a scalar that represents the energy gain rate, and *decay* is a scalar in the $[0, 1[$ interval that represents the energy decay rate. The energy consumed by the ant is removed from the environment, as will be explained later in detail.

The ants' movement are determined by how they react to light. Each ant senses the environment by "looking" in several directions (see Fig. 2). In the experiments described in this paper we use 10 sensory vectors, each vector has a given direction relative to the current direction of the ant and a length. The sensory organs return the luminance value of the area where each vector ends. To update the position of an ant one calculates: the sum of the sensory vectors divided by their norms, multiplied by the luminance of their end point and by the weight the ant gives to each sensor, the result is multiplied by a scaling scalar that represents the ant's base speed:

$$\Delta\vec{p} = vel * \sum_{i=1}^{10} \frac{\vec{v}_i}{|\vec{v}_i|} * b((x, y), \vec{v}_i) * w_i \quad (2)$$

where, $\Delta\vec{p}$ is the displacement vector, (x, y) is the current position of the ant, *vel* is the ant's base velocity; $\vec{v}_i$ is the sensory vector i; $b((x, y), \vec{v}_i)$ a function that returns the luminance of the area at coordinates $(x, y) + \vec{v}_i$; w_i is the weight associated with $\vec{v}_i$.

Subsequently, to represent inaccuracy of movement and sensory organs, the direction $\Delta\vec{p}$ is perturbed by the addition Perlin noise [16] to its angle. Therefore, the position of the ant at instant $t + 1$ is given by the following formula:

$$(x, y)_{t+1} = (x, y)_t + perlin_{noise}(t, \Delta\vec{p}) \quad (3)$$

The ant simulation algorithm follows the following steps:

1. Initialization: n ants are placed on the canvas on pre-established positions; Each ants assumes the color of the area where it was placed; Their energy and deposit transparencies are initialized using the species parameters;

Figure 1: Screenshot of the graphic user interface. Control panel on the left and current population of ant paintings on the right.

2. For each ant:
   (a) Update the ant's energy following formula 1;
   (b) Update the energy of the environment;
   (c) Place ink on the painting canvas;
   (d) If the ant's energy is bellow the death threshold remove the ant from the colony;
   (e) If the ant's energy is above the reproduction threshold generate an offspring; The offspring assumes the color of the position where it was created and a percentage of the energy of the progenitor (which loses this energy); The offspring inherits the velocity of the parent, but a perturbation is added to the angular velocity by randomly choosing an angle between $descvel_{min}$ and $descvel_{max}$ (both values are species' parameters); Likewise, the deposit transparency is inherited from the progenitor but a perturbation is included by adding a randomly choosen a value between $dtransp_{min}$ and $dtransp_{max}$;
   (f) Update ant's position following formulas 2 and 3;
3. Repeat since 2 until no living ants exist;

Steps (b) and (c) require further explanation. The consumption of energy of the environment is attained by drawing on the living canvas a black circle of size equal to $energy * cons_{rate}$ of given transparency. $cons_{rate}$ and $cons_{trans}$ are parameters of the species. In previewing mode ink is deposited on the paining canvas by drawing a circle of the color of the ant – which is attributed when the ant is born – with a size given by $energy * deposit_{rate}$ and of given transparency. $deposit_{rate}$ is a species parameters, the deposit transparency is a parameter of the ant.

3.2 Evolutionary Engine

An interactive GA is used to evolve the ant species' parameters. The genotypes are tuples of floating point numbers which encode the parameters of the ant species. The size of the genotype depends on the experimental settings. Table 1 presents an overview of the encoded parameters. We use a two point crossover operator for recombination purposes and a Gaussian mutation operator. We employ tournament selection and an elitist strategy, the highest ranked individuals proceed, unchanged, to the next population.

3.3 Preview and Rendering Modes

We use scalable vector graphics in both preview and rendering modes. This allows the generation of resolution independent ant paintings, which, to the best of our knowledge, is a novel feature of our approach. As previously stated, in preview mode, the ants draw circles while they move. In rendering mode the ants behave similarly in every way. However, when the painting is finished, the trail of each ant is converted into a single line of variable width. This is attained by calculating external tangents to each pair of consecutive circles drawn by the ant, drawing polygons among these points and performing a shape union between all circles and polygons belonging to the same trail. In Fig. 3 we present a graphical portrayal of this process.

The differences between preview and rendering modes are usually not visible on screen, however, they have a significant impact when the artworks are printed or at high zoom rates. Fig. 4 highlights the differences.

It is also important to notice that the color of an ant is determined at birth, thus the ants may carry this color to areas of the screen that possess different colors in the original image, making the ant paintings further deviate from the original image (see Fig. 7). As a consequence of this

Table 1: Parameters encoded by the genotype

Name	#	Comments
gain	1	scaling for energy gains
decay	1	scaling for energy decay
$cons_{rate}$	1	scaling for size of circles drawn on the living canvas
$cons_{trans}$	1	transparency of circles drawn on the living canvas
$deposit_{rate}$	1	scaling for size of circles drawn on the painting canvas
$deposit_{transp}$	1	base transparency of circles drawn on the painting canvas
$dtransp_{min}$	1	limits for perturbation of deposit transparency when offsprings are generated
$dtransp_{max}$	1	
$initial_{energy}$	1	initial energy of the starting ants
$death_{threshold}$	1	death energy treshold
$birth_{threshold}$	1	generate offspring energy threshold
$descvel_{min}$	1	limits for perturbation of angular velocity when offsprings are generated
$descvel_{max}$	1	
vel	1	base speed of the ants
$noise_{min}$	1	limits for the perlin noise generator function
$noise_{max}$	1	
$initial_{positions}$	$2*n$	initial coordinates of the n ants placed on the canvas
$sensory_{vectors}$	$2*m$	direction and length of the m sensory vectors
$sensory_{weights}$	$2*m$	direction and length of the m sensory vectors

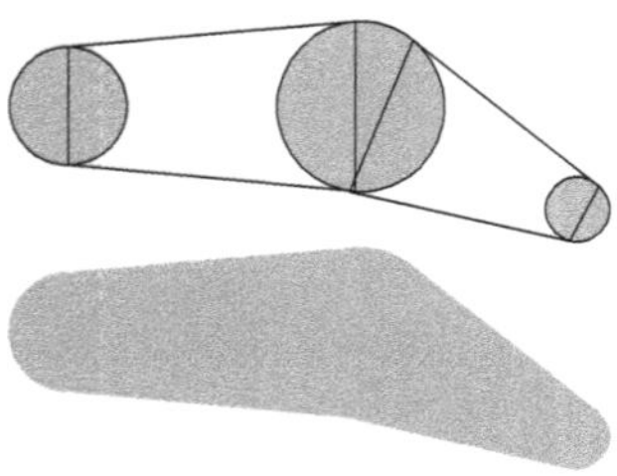

Figure 3: On the top, three circles belonging to the same trail and the polygons produced by tracing lines between the points of the external tangents to each consecutive pair. On the bottom, the shape resulting from the union of the three circles and two polygons

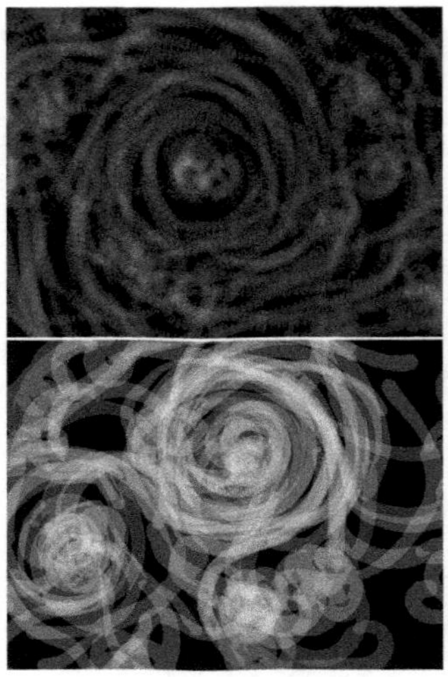

Figure 4: Details of images produced in preview(top) and rendering (bottom) modes depicting the differences in the rendering of the ants' trails.

coloring method, trails of progenitor ants become interlaced with those of descendants.

4. EXPERIMENTAL RESULTS

The results presented in this section were obtained by conducting a series of informal experiments with the following experimental setup: Population Size = 15; Tournament size = 3; Crossover probability = 0.9; Mutation Probability = 0.1 (per gene); Initial Position of the ants = center of the canvas; Initial number of ants = 1. Thus, when the drawing stage starts each ant specie is represented by a single ant. However, due to the abundance of energy this ant tends to generate offspring quickly. The length of each evolutionary run varied, typical runs had 30 to 40 generations.

The analysis of the experimental results of evolutionary art systems, specially user driven ones, is subjective by nature. As such, more than presenting measures of performance that would be meaningless when considering the goals of our system, we aim to:

1. Convey the overall feeling of the user experience when working with photogrowth through the presentation of different steps of the evolutionary process;
2. Highlight the different types of imagery that can be evolved with the system;
3. Show that the application of the same individual (ant colony) to different input images produces stylistically similar renderings;

In Fig 5 we present snapshots of the 1st, 2nd, 20th and 40th population of a typical evolutionary run. As it can be observed, most of the individuals of the initial population fail to portray the input image. In the second population, the percentage of images that depict the input image significantly increases. Nevertheless, the overall quality of the images is relatively low, in the sense that they do not convey the aesthetic preferences of the user. In the 20th population we observe the emergence of elliptical and organic ant trails

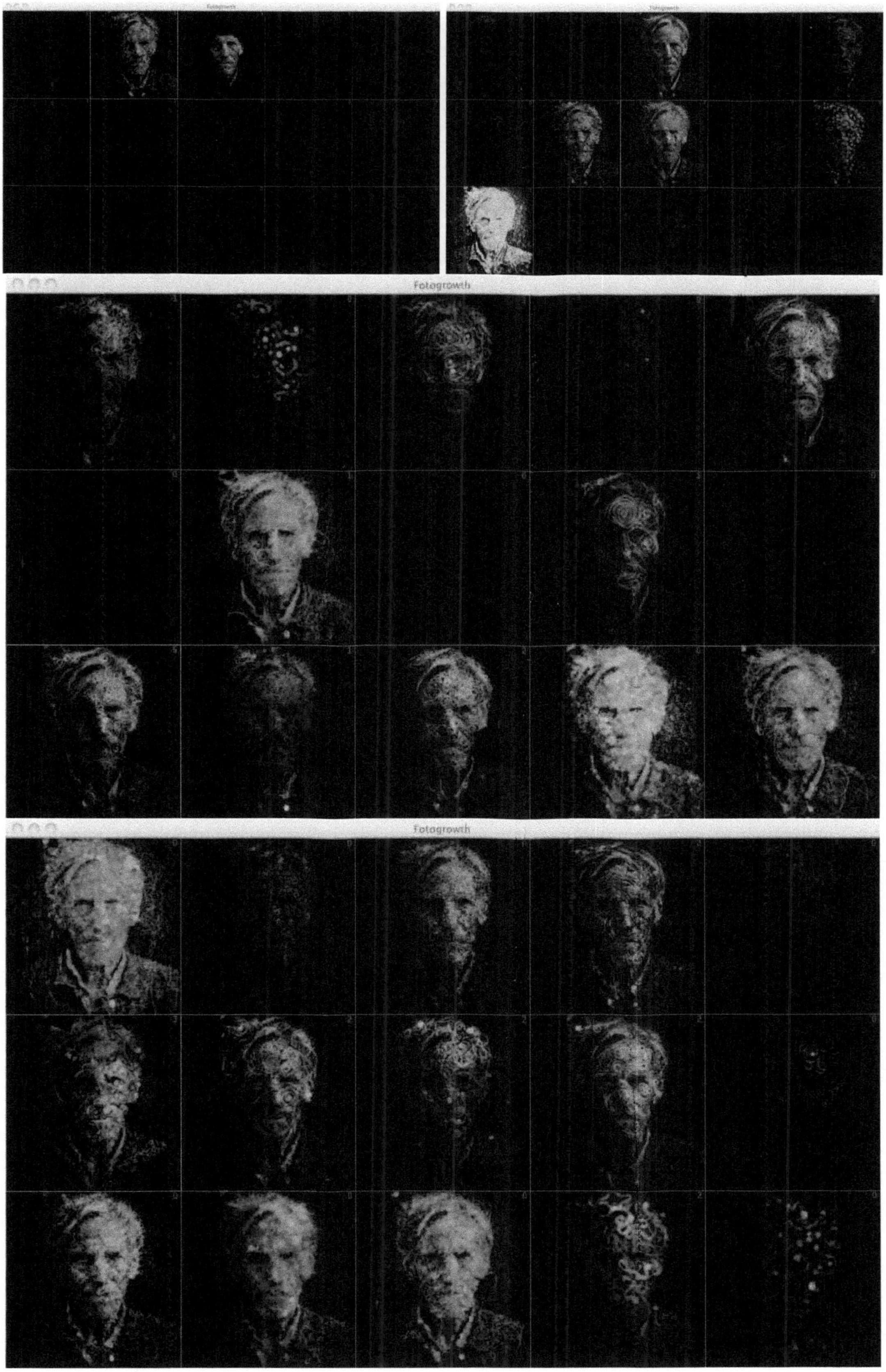

Figure 5: On the top row, snapshots of the 1st and 2nd populations of an evolutionary run. On the middle row, the 20th population. On the bottom row, snapshot of the 40th population.

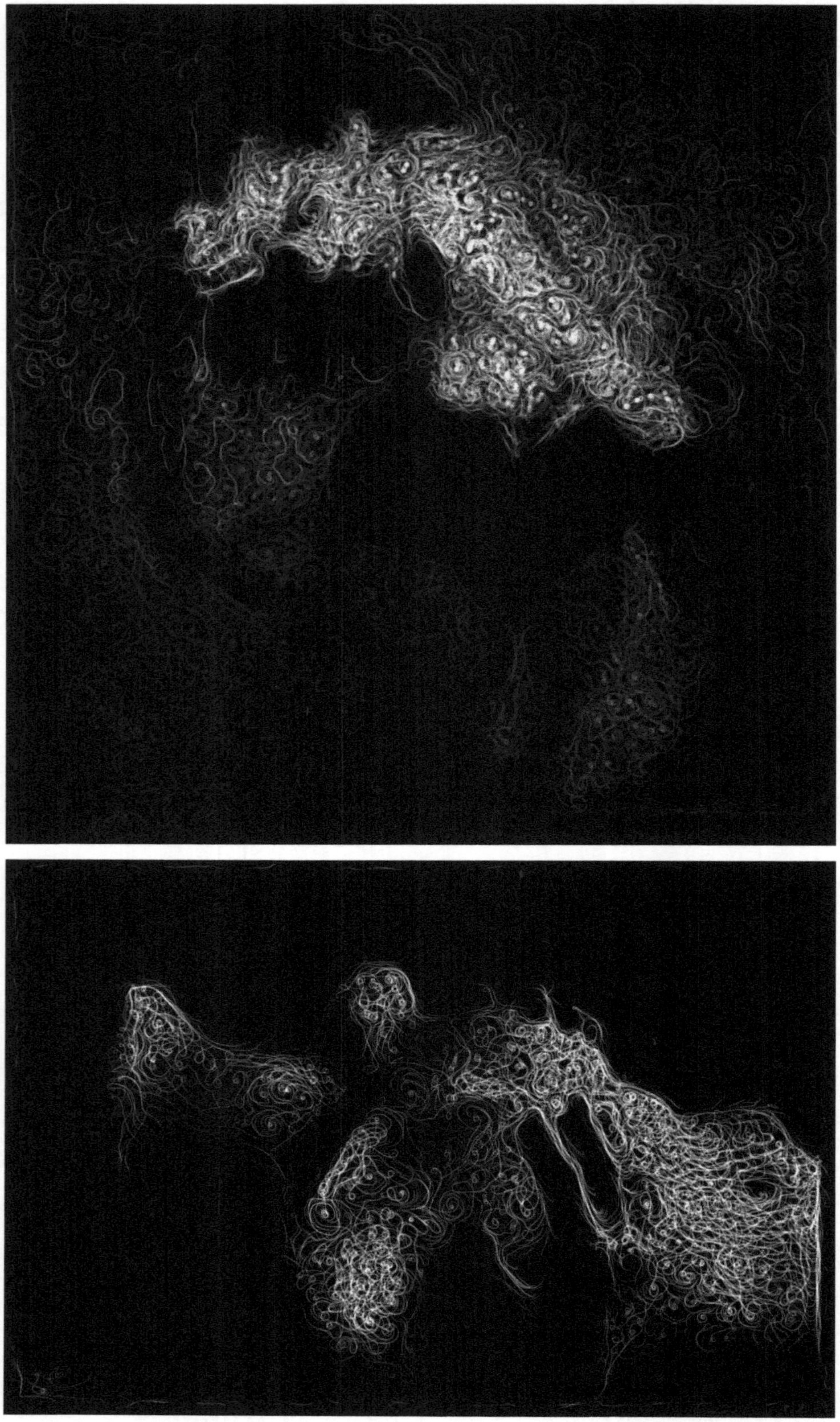

Figure 6: NPRs of two different images using the same evolved ant species.

(e.g., 3rd and 9th images of this population), a trait that will be favored by the user in subsequent runs. The 40th population presents an wide variety of images of contrasting line widths and trail curvature scales. The organic ant trails that emerged on the 20th population are still present on most of these images (although in some cases this is only observable at higher resolutions). At this generation we also observe the emergence of "abstract" portrayals of the original image (see figure 14th of this population). Progress from this point onwards tends to be slow and unsteady since, like in other interactive evolutionary art approaches, the user tends to often rewards novelty, resulting in frequent changes of selection criteria.

Fig. 6 presents the results of applying the same evolved ant species to two different images. As it can be observed the distinguishing traits of the ant colony are preserved, resulting in renderings that share stylistic characteristics.

In Fig. 7 we present two color images produced by different ant species to highlight the range of imagery that can be produced by photogrowth. The top image explores the use of thick organic lines of varying width to produce an abstract rendering of the original image. The bottom image is composed of thiner lines which become more intertwined. Both images take advantage of the coloring approach – the color of the ants is determined at birth – to transport the color of a region of the image to surrounding areas. This effect is particularly noticeable in the bottom image.

5. CONCLUSIONS

We presented photogrowth, a novel evolutionary approach to the production of NPRs of input images. The distinguishing characteristics of the system rest on the evolution of the sensorial organs of the ants, on the production of a scalable vector graphics output and on the rendering engine which represents the ant trails through continuous lines of variable width. The experimental results illustrate the range of imagery that can be produced by the system and demonstrate its adequacy for the production of large-format artworks.

Future research will focus on: (i) the improvement of the efficiency of the rendering engine – the production of an artwork in rendering mode can take from hours to days – which can be easily attained through parallelization since each ant trail can be independently processed; (ii) the development of automatic fitness assignment schemes. For this purpose, and considering the nature of our painting algorithm, we are particularly interested in the use of statistics of the behavior of the ants to assign fitness [5] and in the combination of this approach with ones that take into account the complexity and fractal dimension of the produced artwork (see e.g. [12]).

6. ACKNOWLEDGMENTS

This research is partially funded by the Portuguese Foundation for Science and Technology. Project PTDC/EIA-EIA/115667/2009.

7. REFERENCES

[1] S. Aupetit, V. Bordeau, N. Monmarché, C. Slimane, and G. Venturini. Interactive Evolution of Ant Paintings. In *IEEE Congress on Evolutionary Computation*, volume 2, pages 1376–1383, Canberra, 8-12 december 2003.

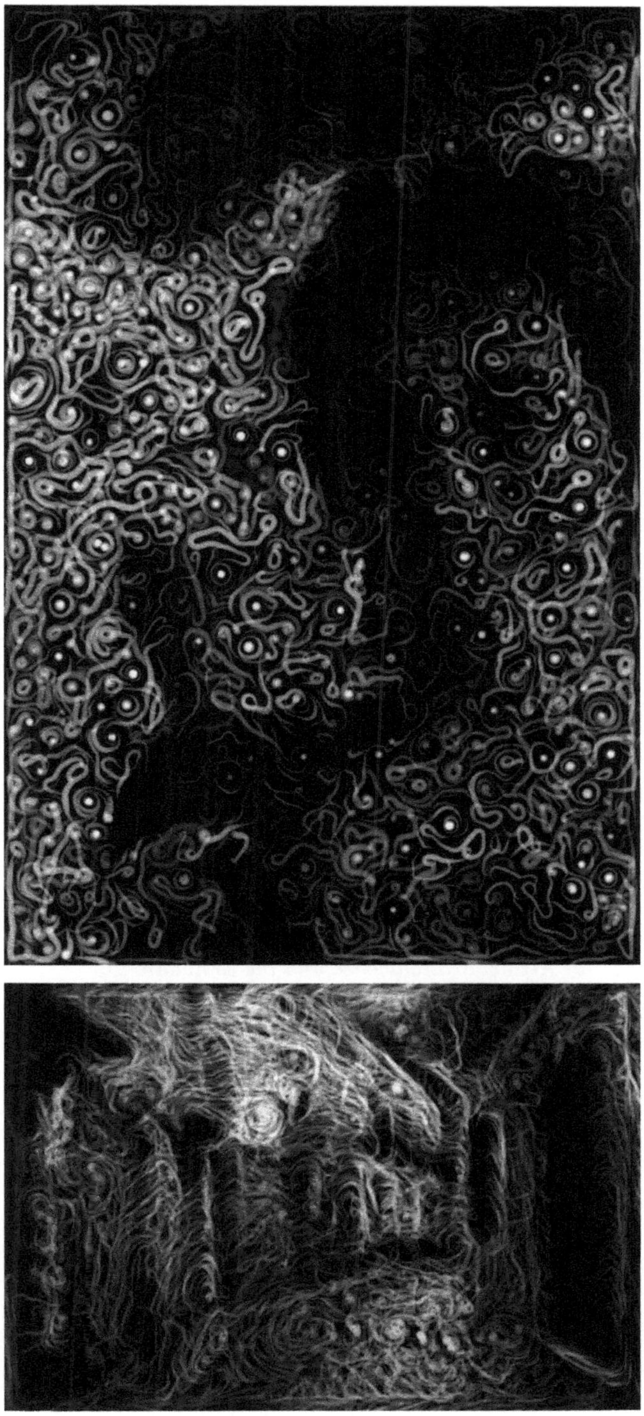

Figure 7: Examples of evolved color images.

[2] J. Collomosse. Evolutionary search for the artistic rendering of photographs. In J. Romero and P. Machado, editors, *The Art of Artificial Evolution: A Handbook on Evolutionary Art and Music*, pages 39–62. Springer Berlin Heidelberg, 2007.

[3] J. P. Collomosse. Supervised genetic search for parameter selection in painterly rendering. In *Applications of Evolutionary Computing,*

EvoWorkshops 2006, pages 599–610, Budapest, Hungary, 2006.

[4] J. P. Collomosse and P. M. Hall. Genetic paint: A search for salient paintings. In *Applications of Evolutionary Computing, EvoWorkshops 2005*, pages 437–447, Lausanne, Switzerland, 2005.

[5] G. Greenfield. Evolutionary methods for ant colony paintings. In F. Rothlauf, J. Branke, S. Cagnoni, D. W. Corne, R. Drechsler, Y. Jin, P. Machado, E. Marchiori, J. Romero, G. D. Smith, and G. Squillero, editors, *Applications of Evolutionary Computing, EvoWorkshops2005: EvoBIO, EvoCOMNET, EvoHOT, EvoIASP, EvoMUSART, EvoSTOC*, volume 3449 of *LNCS*, pages 478–487, Lausanne, Switzerland, 30 Mar.-1 Apr. 2005. Springer Verlag.

[6] G. Greenfield. Ant Paintings using a Multiple Pheromone Model. In *Bridges*, London, England, 2006.

[7] A. Hewgill and B. J. Ross. Procedural 3d texture synthesis using genetic programming. *COMPUTERS AND GRAPHICS*, 28:569–584, 2003.

[8] J. R. Koza. *Genetic Programming: On the Programming of Computers by Natural Selection.* MIT Press, Cambridge, MA, 1992.

[9] M. Lewis. Aesthetic video filter evolution in an interactive real-time framework. In *Applications of Evolutionary Computing, EvoWorkshops2004: EvoBIO, EvoCOMNET, EvoHOT, EvoIASP, EvoMUSART, EvoSTOC*, volume 3005 of *LNCS*, pages 409–418, Coimbra, Portugal, 5-7 Apr. 2004. Springer Verlag.

[10] P. Machado, A. Dias, and A. Cardoso. Learning to colour greyscale images. *The Interdisciplinary Journal of Artificial Intelligence and the Simulation of Behaviour – AISB Journal*, 1(2):209–219, 2002.

[11] P. Machado and F. Graça. Evolutionary pointillist modules: Evolving assemblages of 3d objects. In M. Giacobini, A. Brabazon, S. Cagnoni, G. D. Caro, R. Drechsler, A. Ekárt, A. Esparcia-Alcázar, M. Farooq, A. Fink, J. McCormack, M. O'Neill, J. Romero, F. Rothlauf, G. Squillero, S. Uyar, and S. Yang, editors, *Applications of Evolutionary Computing, EvoWorkshops 2008: EvoCOMNET, EvoFIN, EvoHOT, EvoIASP, EvoMUSART, EvoNUM, EvoSTOC, and EvoTransLog, Naples, Italy, March 26-28, 2008. Proceedings*, volume 4974 of *Lecture Notes in Computer Science*, pages 453–462. Springer, 2008.

[12] P. Machado, J. Romero, and B. Manaris. Experiments in computational aesthetics: An iterative approach to stylistic change in evolutionary art. In J. Romero and P. Machado, editors, *The Art of Artificial Evolution: A Handbook on Evolutionary Art and Music*, pages 381–415. Springer Berlin Heidelberg, 2007.

[13] N. Monmarché, I. Mahnich, and M. Slimane. Artificial art made by artificial ants. In J. Romero and P. Machado, editors, *The Art of Artificial Evolution: A Handbook on Evolutionary Art and Music*, pages 227–247. Springer Berlin Heidelberg, 2007.

[14] L. Moura. Swarm paintings – non-human. In *ARCHITOPIA Book, Art, Architecture and Science*, pages 1–24. 2002.

[15] C. Neufeld, B. Ross, and W. Ralph. The evolution of artistic filters. In J. Romero and P. Machado, editors, *The Art of Artificial Evolution: A Handbook on Evolutionary Art and Music*, pages 335–356. Springer Berlin Heidelberg, 2007.

[16] K. Perlin. An image synthesizer. In P. Cole, R. Heilman, and B. A. Barsky, editors, *Proceedings of the 12st Annual Conference on Computer Graphics and Interactive Techniques, SIGGRAPH 1985*, pages 287–296. ACM, 1985.

[17] V. Ramos. On the implicit and on the artificial - morphogenesis and emergent aesthetics in autonomous collective systems. In *ARCHITOPIA Book, Art, Architecture and Science*, pages 25–57. 2002.

[18] V. Ramos and F. Almeida. Artificial ant colonies in digital image habitats - a mass behaviour effect study on pattern recognition. In *In Dorigo, M., Middendorf, M., Stuzle, T. (Eds.): From Ant Colonies to Artificial Ants - 2 nd Int. Wkshp on Ant Algorithms*, pages 113–116, 2000.

[19] B. J. Ross, W. Ralph, and Z. Hai. Evolutionary image synthesis using a model of aesthetics. In G. G. Yen, S. M. Lucas, G. Fogel, G. Kendall, R. Salomon, B.-T. Zhang, C. A. C. Coello, and T. P. Runarsson, editors, *Proceedings of the 2006 IEEE Congress on Evolutionary Computation*, pages 1087–1094, Vancouver, BC, Canada, 16–21 July 2006. IEEE Press.

[20] E. Tzafestas. Integrating drawing tools with behavioral modeling in digital painting. In S. Ghandeharizadeh, S.-F. Chang, S. Fischer, J. A. Konstan, and K. Nahrstedt, editors, *ACM Multimedia Workshops*, pages 39–42. ACM Press, 2000.

[21] P. Urbano. Playing in the pheromone playground: Experiences in swarm painting. In F. Rothlauf, J. Branke, S. Cagnoni, D. W. Corne, R. Drechsler, Y. Jin, P. Machado, E. Marchiori, J. Romero, G. D. Smith, and G. Squillero, editors, *EvoWorkshops*, volume 3449 of *Lecture Notes in Computer Science*, pages 527–532. Springer, 2005.

[22] P. Urbano. Consensual paintings. In F. Rothlauf, J. Branke, S. Cagnoni, E. Costa, C. Cotta, R. Drechsler, E. Lutton, P. Machado, J. H. Moore, J. Romero, G. D. Smith, G. Squillero, and H. Takagi, editors, *EvoWorkshops*, volume 3907 of *Lecture Notes in Computer Science*, pages 622–632. Springer, 2006.

[23] P. Urbano. Mimetic variations on stigmergic swarm paintings. In N. Monmarché, E.-G. Talbi, P. Collet, M. Schoenauer, and E. Lutton, editors, *Artificial Evolution*, volume 4926 of *Lecture Notes in Computer Science*, pages 62–72. Springer, 2007.

[24] P. Urbano. The *t. albipennis* sand painting artists. In C. D. Chio, A. Brabazon, G. A. D. Caro, R. Drechsler, M. Farooq, J. Grahl, G. Greenfield, C. Prins, J. Romero, G. Squillero, E. Tarantino, A. Tettamanzi, N. Urquhart, and A. S. Etaner-Uyar, editors, *EvoApplications (2)*, volume 6625 of *Lecture Notes in Computer Science*, pages 414–423. Springer, 2011.

[25] C. Yip. Evolving Image Filters. Master's thesis, Imperial College of Science, Technology, and Medicine, September 2004.

Incremental Gaussian Model-Building in Multi-Objective EDAs with an Application to Deformable Image Registration

Peter A.N. Bosman
Centrum Wiskunde & Informatica (CWI)
P.O. Box 94079
1090 GB Amsterdam
The Netherlands
Peter.Bosman@cwi.nl

Tanja Alderliesten
The Netherlands Cancer Institute - Antoni van Leeuwenhoek Hospital (NKI-AVL)
P.O. Box 90203
1006 BE Amsterdam
The Netherlands
T.Alderliesten@nki.nl

ABSTRACT

Estimation-of-Distribution Algorithms (EDAs) build and use probabilistic models during optimization in order to automatically discover and use an optimization problems' structure. This is especially useful for black-box optimization where no assumptions are made on the problem being solved, which is characteristic of many cases in solving complex real-world problems. In this paper we consider multi-objective optimization problems with real-valued variables. Although the vast majority of advances in EDA literature concern single-objective optimization, advances have also been made in multi-objective optimization. In this paper we bring together two recent advances, namely incremental Gaussian model building to reduce the required population size and a mixture-based multi-objective framework that has specific methods to better facilitate model-building techniques that span multiple generations. Significantly faster convergence to the optimal Pareto front is achieved on 6 out of 7 artificial benchmark problems from literature. Although results on two of these problems show that building models with higher-order interactions between variables is required, these problems are still artificial. We therefore also consider a more realistic optimization problem in image processing, namely deformable image registration. For this problem too, our results show the need for processing interactions between problem variables, stressing the importance of studying the use of such models. Furthermore, the number of problem variables in the deformable image registration problem can be very large. The building of models with higher-order interactions, especially mixture-based models, then requires very large population sizes. The use of incremental model building is therefore of high importance. This claim is supported by our results that show a huge reduction in the number of required evaluations on this problem.

Categories and Subject Descriptors

G.1 [**Numerical Analysis**]: Optimization; I.2 [**Artificial Intelligence**]: Problem Solving, Control Methods, and Search

General Terms

Algorithms, Performance, Experimentation

Keywords

Evolutionary Algorithms, Estimation-of-Distribution Algorithms, Multi-Objective Optimization, Incremental Model Building, Deformable Image Registration

1. INTRODUCTION

Many optimization problems in practice are actually multi-objective optimization (MO) problems [6]. In such problems more than one objective functions must be optimized simultaneously without an expression of weights or other means of scalarizing these objectives. A typical example is the design of a product where one objective is the quality of the design and another objective is the associated cost. Minimizing the cost will in general lead to products of inferior quality, while maximizing the quality will give rise to an increasing cost. As a consequence, there are many optimal solutions to a MO problem, all of which represent a trade-off between the two objectives. The notion of searching a search space through maintaining a set of solutions is a key characteristic of evolutionary algorithms (EAs). EAs are commonly accepted to be well-suited for solving MO problems [6]. Because a set of solutions is used, EAs can spread their search bias along the Pareto front and thereby prevent many re-computations that are involved if a single point on the Pareto front is repeatedly targeted using a single-solution based approach.

The efficiency of variation operators when used in a multi-objective EA (MOEA) can often be improved by employing restricted mating such that solutions that are closer to each other in objective space have a higher probability of being combined. In EDAs a natural way to achieve this is by building mixture distributions that spread the mixture components throughout objective space [4, 8, 11]. Such an approach allows EDAs to spread the search intensity along the Pareto front, allowing more focused exploitation of problem structure in different regions of the objective space.

Recently, a specific way of building and using mixture models in EDAs was introduced that can be used to extend single-objective EDAs to MO [4]. Particular to this work is that it explicitly allows mixture components to overlap in the objective space in order to cover the entire Pareto front and prevent convergence of mixture components to singular points on the front. Furthermore, the progression of mixture components in objective space is explicitly tracked so as to increase the efficiency of adaptive distribution enhancement techniques that span over multiple generations such as adaptive variance scaling techniques [4] to prevent premature convergence. The downside to this approach to using mixture distributions is that for a mixture distribution with k mixture components, a population size is required that is $\mathcal{O}(k)$ times larger. Especially when building higher-order probabilistic models, as is common in EDA literature, the required population size tends to be quite large. The additional requirement imposed by the aforementioned approach to using mixture distributions for MO then can become problematic. However, some studies have shown that probabilistic models can be learned effectively in EDAs over multiple generations [3, 9]. This can greatly reduce the required population size. Such an approach therefore is a good candidate to reduce the number of required evaluations in mixture-based EDAs for MO. Moreover, the recent work on tracking mixture components across generations fits perfectly with the idea of building models incrementally over multiple generations. Therefore, in this paper we combine incremental model building with this approach, and experimentally validate the performance resulting from the reduction in required population size. Specifically, we consider the use of a recent Gaussian EDA named AMaLGaM [3] and its incremental model-building counterpart, iAMaLGaM.

In addition to experimentally validating the merits of EDAs on well-understood and well-known artificial benchmark problems, it is important to also consider non-artificial benchmark problems. Besides obtaining realistic insights about the potential real-world performance of EDAs, it is important to validate issues such as whether key research efforts in EDA literature, such as the building of probabilistic models that cover interactions between problem variables, is really needed and leads to better performance in practice as well. In addition to well-known artificial benchmark problems, in this paper we therefore also consider a non-artificial problem, namely deformable image registration.

The remainder of this paper is organized as follows. In Section 2 we provide an overview of the most important concepts and definitions in multi-objective optimization. Then, in Section 3 we outline the single-objective AMaLGaM and the multi-objective mixture-based EDA framework. In Section 4 we discuss the iAMaLGaM approach to incremental Gaussian model building and its use in the multi-objective mixture-based EDA framework. We perform an experimental analysis on 7 well-known benchmark problems from the literature and a deformable image registration problem in Section 5 and draw our final conclusions in Section 6.

2. MULTI-OBJECTIVE OPTIMIZATION

We assume to have m objective functions $f_i(\boldsymbol{x})$, $i \in \{0, 1, \dots, m-1\}$ and, without loss of generality, we assume that the goal is to *minimize* all objectives.

A solution $\boldsymbol{x}^0$ is said to (Pareto) *dominate* a solution $\boldsymbol{x}^1$ (denoted $\boldsymbol{x}^0 \succ \boldsymbol{x}^1$) if and only if $f_i(\boldsymbol{x}^0) \leq f_i(\boldsymbol{x}^1)$ holds for all $i \in \{0, 1, \dots, m-1\}$ and $f_i(\boldsymbol{x}^0) < f_i(\boldsymbol{x}^1)$ holds for at least one $i \in \{0, 1, \dots, m-1\}$. A *Pareto set* of size n then is a set of solutions $\boldsymbol{x}^j$, $j \in \{0, 1, \dots, n-1\}$ for which no solution dominates any other solution, i.e. there are no $j, k \in \{0, 1, \dots, n-1\}$ such that $\boldsymbol{x}^j \succ \boldsymbol{x}^k$ holds. A *Pareto front* corresponding to a Pareto set is the set of all m-dimensional objective function values corresponding to the solutions, i.e. the set of all $\boldsymbol{f}(\boldsymbol{x}^j)$, $j \in \{0, 1, \dots, n-1\}$.

A solution $\boldsymbol{x}^0$ is said to be *Pareto optimal* if and only if there is no other $\boldsymbol{x}^1$ such that $\boldsymbol{x}^1 \succ \boldsymbol{x}^0$ holds. Further, the *optimal Pareto set* is the set of all Pareto-optimal solutions and the *optimal Pareto front* is the Pareto front that corresponds to the optimal Pareto set. We denote the optimal Pareto set by $\boldsymbol{\mathcal{P}_S}$ and the optimal Pareto front by $\boldsymbol{\mathcal{P}_F}$.

3. GENERATIONAL MODEL-BUILDING

In this section we briefly describe the single-objective EDA that we consider as well as the extension thereof to MO via a specific use of mixture distributions.

3.1 AMaLGaM

The Adapted Maximum-Likelihood Gaussian Model (AMaLGaM) is a Gaussian EDA that estimates a Gaussian distribution from the selected solutions with maximum likelihood (ML) and subsequently adaptively changes this estimate on the basis of observations regarding improvements that were found after sampling the Gaussian. For details about these adaptive techniques, we refer the interested reader to the literature [3]. Here we only point out that the main parameters to be estimated in a Gaussian EDA are the mean vector $\boldsymbol{\mu}$ and the covariance matrix $\boldsymbol{\Sigma}$, or, if the distribution is factorized so that the variables are all considered to be independent, the variance vector. Moreover, ML parameter estimates for the Gaussian distribution are well-known. Let $\boldsymbol{\mathcal{S}}$ denote a vector of data. A ML estimation for parameters of the Gaussian probability distribution is obtained from $\boldsymbol{\mathcal{S}}$ if $\boldsymbol{\mu}$ and $\boldsymbol{\Sigma}$ are estimated by the sample average and sample covariance matrix respectively [1]:

$$\hat{\boldsymbol{\mu}} = \frac{1}{|\boldsymbol{\mathcal{S}}|} \sum_{j=0}^{|\boldsymbol{\mathcal{S}}|-1} (\boldsymbol{\mathcal{S}}_j), \quad \hat{\boldsymbol{\Sigma}} = \frac{1}{|\boldsymbol{\mathcal{S}}|} \sum_{j=0}^{|\boldsymbol{\mathcal{S}}|-1} ((\boldsymbol{\mathcal{S}}_j) - \hat{\boldsymbol{\mu}})((\boldsymbol{\mathcal{S}}_j) - \hat{\boldsymbol{\mu}})^T.$$

Although the variance is adaptively scaled up in AMaLGaM to prevent premature convergence, the use of ML estimates aligns the principle axis of variance with the density contours of the search space because of selection. It is however in the perpendicular direction that the most improvement can be obtained in the local fitness landscape. To overcome this misalignment problem, the Anticipated Mean Shift is used in AMaLGaM [3]. The AMS is computed as the difference between the means of subsequent generations, i.e. $\hat{\boldsymbol{\mu}}^{\text{Shift}}(t) = \hat{\boldsymbol{\mu}}(t) - \hat{\boldsymbol{\mu}}(t-1)$. A part of the newly sampled solutions is then moved in the direction of the AMS: $\boldsymbol{x} \leftarrow \boldsymbol{x} + 2\hat{\boldsymbol{\mu}}^{\text{Shift}}(t)$.

3.2 MAMaLGaM-X

A specific extension of single-objective EDAs to MO on the basis of mixture distributions was recently studied and applied to AMaLGaM, resulting in the Multi-objective AMaLGaM-miXture (MAMaLGaM-X) [4]. Using a clustering technique, the selected solutions are clustered into k overlapping clusters of identical size. Specifically, for an overall population size n and selection size τn where $\tau \in [\frac{1}{n}; 1]$, each cluster will have $(2\tau n)/k$ solutions. Subsequently, distribution estimation and sampling proceeds as normally done in the EDA, but independently per cluster.

The problem with solutions aligning with contours of the fitness landscape also exists in MO [4]. For this reason, techniques such as AMS are important in MO as well. However, to ensure that AMS works well, there needs to be a meaningful progression in the Gaussian distribution in subsequent generations. In the mixture distribution this means that individual clusters need to be associated with each other in a sensible manner across subsequent generations. This is however not automatically the case by clustering the selected solutions anew in each generation. Therefore, in MAMaLGaM-X an explicit cluster registration step is performed that computes the overall most likely association between clusters of subsequent generations by minimizing the sum of all distances between associated clusters [4].

An elitist archive is maintained, storing all currently non-dominated solutions. Because the objectives are real-valued, there are typically infinitely many non-dominated solutions possible. To prevent the archive from growing to an extreme size, the objective space is discretized into hypercubes by discretizing each objective separately. Only one solution per hypercube is allowed in the archive. Newly generated solutions are compared to the solutions in the archive. If a new solution is dominated by any archive solution, it is not entered. If a new solution is not dominated, it is added to the archive if the hypercube that it resides in does not already contain a solution or if it dominates that particular solution. When a new solution is entered, all archive solutions that are dominated by it, are removed.

3.3 MAMaLGaM-X$^+$

An extension of MAMaLGaM-X called MAMaLGaM-X$^+$ was shown to exhibit the most robust performance on a set of well-known benchmark problems. The difference between MAMaLGaM-X$^+$ and MAMaLGaM-X is that m additional clusters are maintained, one for each objective. Selection in these clusters is done completely independently on the basis of each respective individual objective, thereby specifically targeting convergence at the extreme regions of the Pareto front. Solutions from these specific clusters are furthermore also integrated into the selection procedure on the basis of which the k clusters are computed for the mixture distribution in MAMaLGaM-X. For details, see [4].

4. INCREMENTAL MODEL-BUILDING

Estimating the probability distribution in AMaLGaM and in MAMaLGaM-X is done anew from scratch each generation. However, subsequent generations have much in common, which allows the required population size to be reduced using incremental learning, i.e. combining the probability distribution that is estimated from the selected solutions in this generation with the distribution that was used in the previous generation. A specific approach to doing this is provided in the incremental AMaLGaM (iAMaLGaM).

4.1 iAMaLGaM

In iAMaLGaM a memory-decay approach is taken for the covariance matrix and the AMS. The equations for incrementally estimating the covariance matrix and the AMS in generation t are:

$$\begin{aligned}\hat{\mathbf{\Sigma}}(t) &= (1-\eta^{\mathbf{\Sigma}})\hat{\mathbf{\Sigma}}(t-1)+ \\ &\quad \eta^{\mathbf{\Sigma}}\tfrac{1}{|\mathcal{S}|}\textstyle\sum_{i=0}^{|\mathcal{S}|-1}(\mathcal{S}_i-\hat{\boldsymbol{\mu}}(t))(\mathcal{S}_i-\hat{\boldsymbol{\mu}}(t))^T\end{aligned}$$

$$\begin{aligned}\hat{\boldsymbol{\mu}}^{\text{Shift}}(t) &= (1-\eta^{\text{Shift}})\hat{\boldsymbol{\mu}}^{\text{Shift}}(t-1)+ \\ &\quad \eta^{\text{Shift}}(\hat{\boldsymbol{\mu}}(t)-\hat{\boldsymbol{\mu}}(t-1)).\end{aligned}$$

Values for the learning-rate parameters $\eta^{\mathbf{\Sigma}}$ and η^{Shift} were determined empirically [3].

4.2 iMAMaLGaM-X$^{(+)}$

We combine the use of incremental model learning with the specific mixture-based EDA extension as outlined above. This means that for every cluster, including the ones in which selection is done separately on the basis of individual objectives (e.g. as in MAMaLGaM-X$^+$), we have a separate incremental Gaussian model that is updated using the incremental updates provided above. The explicit cluster registration in MAMaLGaM-X was shown to work well in combination with the AMS technique. It is therefore expected that the so-established relation between clusters in subsequent generations is sufficiently meaningful for incremental model building to work as well. We will identify the resulting multi-objective EDAs as incremental MAMaLGaM-X (iMAMaLGaM-X) and incremental MAMaLGaM-X$^+$ (iMAMaLGaM-X$^+$).

5. EXPERIMENTS

In this section we present our experimental analysis of iMAMaLGaM-X and iMAMaLGaM-X$^+$. First, we describe the optimization problems that we consider, both the common benchmark problems and the deformable image registration problem. Next, we describe how we evaluate performance and then we present our results.

5.1 Common Benchmark Problems

The definitions of the problems in our multi-objective optimization problem test suite are presented in Table 1.

We used the well-known problems[1] EC_i, $i \in \{1,2,3,4,6\}$. The initialization ranges (IRs) of the EC_i problems are also hard constraints. The reason for this is that otherwise some objectives can not always be evaluated. Such rigid constraints can be hard for a numerical optimizer. EC_1 and EC_2 are continuous and do not have any local fronts. EC_1 has a convex Pareto front whereas EC_2 has a concave Pareto front. These problems differ from the GM problems in that the objectives are not similarly defined and not similarly scaled. EC_3 is similar to EC_1 but has a discontinuous Pareto front. EC_4 has many locally optimal Pareto fronts. Finally, the Pareto front of EC_6 is non-uniformly distributed. For more details about these functions, see [12].

Two additional problems come from more recent literature on real-valued MO optimization [5] and are labeled BD_i, $i \in \{1,2\}$. Both problems make use of Rosenbrock's function. Premature convergence on this function is likely without proper induction of the structure of the search space. Function BD_2 is harder than BD_1 in that the objective functions overlap in all variables instead of only in x_0. Further, the IR of x_0 in function BD_1 is also a constraint. Finally, we

[1]These problems are also known as ZDT_i.

have scaled the objectives of BD_2 to ensure that the optimum of all problems is in approximately the same range. By doing so, using the same value-to-reach for the $\boldsymbol{D_{\mathcal{P}_F \to S}}$ indicator (which is explained in the next Section) on all problems corresponds to a similar front quality on all problems.

Name	Objectives	IR
EC_1	$f_0 = x_0, \quad f_1 = \gamma\left(1 - \sqrt{f_0/\gamma}\right)$ $\gamma = 1 + 9\left(\sum_{i=1}^{l-1} x_i/(l-1)\right)$	$[0;1]^{30}$ $(l = 30)$
EC_2	$f_0 = x_0, \quad f_1 = \gamma\left(1 - (f_0/\gamma)^2\right)$ $\gamma = 1 + 9\left(\sum_{i=1}^{l-1} x_i/(l-1)\right)$	$[0;1]^{30}$ $(l = 30)$
EC_3	$f_0 = x_0, \quad f_1 = \gamma\left(1 - \sqrt{f_0/\gamma} - (f_0/\gamma)\sin(10\pi f_0)\right)$ $\gamma = 1 + 9\left(\sum_{i=1}^{l-1} x_i/(l-1)\right)$	$[0;1]^{30}$ $(l = 30)$
EC_4	$f_0 = x_0, \quad f_1 = \gamma\left(1 - \sqrt{f_0/\gamma}\right)$ $\gamma = 1 + 10(l-1) + \sum_{i=1}^{l-1}\left(x_i^2 - 10\cos(4\pi x_i)\right)$	$[-1;1]\times$ $[-5;5]^9$ $(l = 10)$
EC_6	$f_0 = 1 - e^{-4x_0}\sin^6(6\pi x_0), \quad f_1 = \gamma\left(1 - (f_0/\gamma)^2\right)$ $\gamma = 1 + 9\left(\sum_{i=1}^{l-1} x_i/(l-1)\right)^{0.25}$	$[0;1]^{10}$ $(l = 10)$
BD_1	$f_0 = x_0, \quad f_1 = 1 - x_0 + \gamma$ $\gamma = \sum_{i=1}^{l-2}\left(100(x_{i+1} - x_i^2)^2 + (1 - x_i)^2\right)$	$[0;1]\times$ $[-5.12;5.12]^9$ $(l = 10)$
BD_2^s	$f_0 = \frac{1}{l}\sum_{i=0}^{l-1} x_i^2$ $f_1 = \frac{1}{l-1}\sum_{i=0}^{l-2}\left(100(x_{i+1} - x_i^2)^2 + (1 - x_i)^2\right)$	$[-5.12;5.12]^{10}$ $(l = 10)$

Table 1: The MO problem test suite.

It is important to note that for the EC_i problems and for x_0 in function BD_1, this IR is a constraint. If these variables move outside of their IR, some objective values can become non-existent. It is therefore important to keep these variables within their IRs. However, a simple repair mechanism that changes a variable to its boundary value if it has exceeded this boundary value gives artifacts. If for instance the search on problem EC_6 probes a solution that has a negative value for each of the variables x_i with $i \geq 1$, then the repair mechanism sets all these variables to 0. The solution that results after boundary repair lies on the Pareto front. To avoid artifacts resulting from boundary-repair methods, the sampling procedure in all MOEDAs is constructed such that solutions that are out of bounds are rejected.

5.2 Deformable Image Registration

Medical imaging is of great value in healthcare. There are a variety of imaging modalities available nowadays (e.g. CT, MRI, PET, etc.), all with different purposes and characteristics. When multiple images are available, either acquired with different imaging techniques or using the same technique but acquired at different points in time, for example for follow-up purposes, important information about the state of a patient lies in comparing and relating these images to one another in order to obtain a more complete picture or see how things changed over time.

The general idea of image registration is to find a transformation that transforms a source image to a target image. By means of rigid registration, only rigid transformations such as rotations and translations are considered. However, for medical applications, *deformable* image registration is of far greater value. This is because in many cases the anatomy that is imaged has changed for various reasons, including changes as a result of treatment, disease progression or simply a difference in patient orientation during image acquisition, resulting in anatomical changes due to different effects of gravity. Although deformable image registration is of great value, it is also generally a hard problem.

For the task of deformable image registration two issues are of prime interest: 1) intensity similarity, i.e. the degree of similarity between intensity patterns in the target image and the transformed source image, and 2) transformation effort, i.e. the amount of energy required to accomplish the transformation. Even within specific real-world problems such as this, competent BBO optimizers such as (most) EDAs can play an important role. Not only is the problem multi-objective, which already makes a set-based approach such as EDAs of interest, also there are many different ways possible to compute similarities and there are many transformation models possible. For more advanced transformation models, as typically required for deformable image registration, optimization already becomes harder to do problem-specifically, but moreover, it is undesirable to have to laboriously design specific optimization algorithms for each different combination of transformation model and similarity model. It is however not the main purpose of this paper to provide a rigorous study into different models for image registration. Therefore, in the following we provide rudimentary, but computationally useful models.

5.2.1 Representation

The transformation model, i.e. the representation of possible transformations, is a square grid of size $n_g \times n_g$. The grid overlays the source image in a regular manner, meaning that it corresponds to a subdivision of the source image into $(n_g - 1)(n_g - 1)$ equally-sized axes-parallel rectangles (see Figure 1). The actual transformation then is given by the association of coordinates with each point in the grid. A means of interpolation is required to extend the so-established correspondence between grids to create the transformed source image. We use bi-linear interpolation in each rectangle.

5.2.2 Similarity measure

We model similarity in intensity with a measure (to be maximized) that is commonly adopted in registration literature, namely normalized mutual information:

$$\frac{(H(T[s]) + H(t))}{H(T[s], t)} - 1,$$

where $H(T[s])$, $H(t)$ and $H(T[s], t)$ denote the entropy of the probability distribution of the grey values in the transformed source image, the entropy of the probability distribution of the grey values in the target image and the entropy of the joint probability distribution of the grey values (i.e. for the registered pairs of pixels) in the transformed source image and the target image, respectively [10]. Because we will consider minimization of all objectives, we will consequently minimize the negative normalized mutual information.

5.2.3 Deformation energy

To associate physical characteristics with transformations, Hooke's law is used [2]. Because we are interested in non-rigid transformations, transformations such as rotations and translations of the entire grid should not correspond to an increase in energy. The required energy is therefore computed on the basis of changes in the lengths of edges in the grid. To ensure that the physical changes we are interested in, i.e. non-rigid deformations of subrectangles, are always

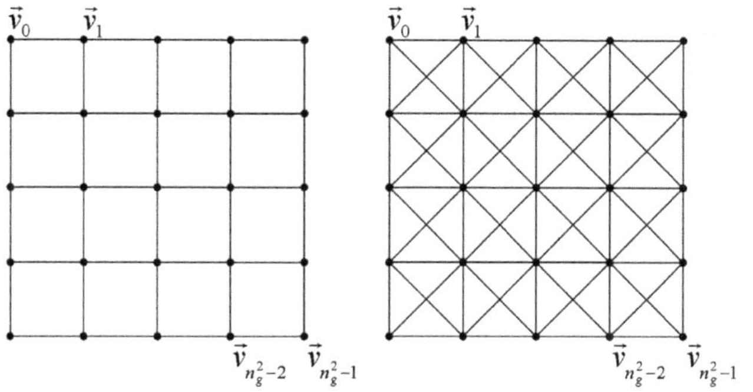

Figure 1: Left: grid of points used as a basis for the transformation model. Right: grid of points with all connections taken into account in the calculation of the required energy to accomplish a transformation.

associated with an increase in required energy, we also include the diagonal edges in each subrectangle (see Figure 1). Now, if we denote the grid coordinates in the source and target images by vectors $\boldsymbol{v}_i^{before}, \boldsymbol{v}_i^{after}, i \in \{0, 1, \ldots, n_g^2 - 1\}$ and the set of considered edges by E, we can define the total energy $U_{total\text{-}deform}$ to be minimized as follows:

$$U_{total\text{-}deform} = \sum_{(i,j) \in E} U_{deform}(i,j)$$

where

$$U_{deform}(i,j) =$$

$$\frac{1}{2} l_{ij} \left(\| \boldsymbol{v}_i^{before} - \boldsymbol{v}_j^{before} \| - \| \boldsymbol{v}_i^{after} - \boldsymbol{v}_j^{after} \| \right)^2$$

where l_{ij} is an elasticity constant associated with the tissue that edge (i, j) crosses.

5.2.4 *Optimization*

In theory, the goal now becomes to find the transformation that corresponds to minimal energy while obtaining perfect similarity between the images, i.e. a constrained single-objective optimization problem. However, in practice, due to issues such as noise in image acquisition, inaccuracy in the determination of the parameters of the physical model (i.e. segmentation and values for material properties) and the inability to mathematically compactly represent all possible transformations, a transformation that results in perfect similarity may not exist. Moreover, transformations that result in a larger similarity are not necessarily preferable. Therefore, the underlying problem in practice is actually multi-objective, i.e. find transformations that on the one hand maximize the similarity between source and target image (objective 1) and on the other hand minimize the amount of required energy (objective 2). In addition to these objectives, constraints are required that are well-known to be important in deformable image registration such as prohibiting transformations that fold the grid. We incorporated these constraints into the multi-objective optimization approach using constraint domination by means of which a solution is always preferred in selection if it doesn't violate any constraints [7]. Finally, we used a single problem instance in

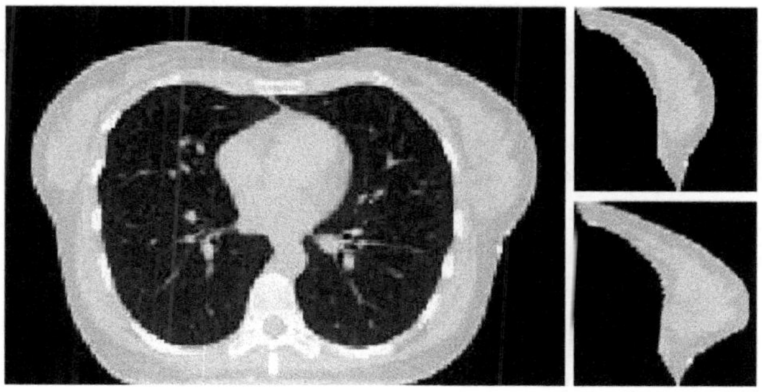

Figure 2: Left: axial slice of a CT scan. Right top: segmented left breast (source image). Right bottom: artificially deformed left breast (target image).

terms of pairs of images to perform deformable image registration on with $n_g = 5$, giving a 50-dimensional real-valued constrained multi-objective optimization problem. The pair of images to be registered is shown in Figure 2. Both images have a dimensionality of 125×125 pixels.

5.3 Measuring performance

We consider the Pareto set that can be computed from the elitist archive combined with the population upon termination to be the outcome of running an EDA and refer to it as an approximation set, denoted $\mathcal{S}$. To measure performance the $\boldsymbol{D}_{\mathcal{P}_F \to \mathcal{S}}$ performance indicator is computed. This performance indicator computes the average distance over all points in the optimal Pareto front $\boldsymbol{\mathcal{P}_F}$ to the nearest point in $\mathcal{S}$:

$$\boldsymbol{D}_{\mathcal{P}_F \to \mathcal{S}}(\mathcal{S}) = \frac{1}{|\mathcal{P}_F|} \sum_{\boldsymbol{f}^1 \in \mathcal{P}_F} \min_{\boldsymbol{f}^0 \in \mathcal{S}} \{d(\boldsymbol{f}^0, \boldsymbol{f}^1)\}$$

where $\boldsymbol{f}$ is a point in objective space and $d(\cdot, \cdot)$ computes Euclidean distance. A smaller $\boldsymbol{D}_{\mathcal{P}_F \to \mathcal{S}}$ value is preferable and a value of 0 is obtained if and only if the approximation set and the optimal Pareto front are identical. This indicator is useful for evaluating performance if the optimum is known because it describes how well the optimal Pareto front is covered and thereby represents an intuitive trade-off between the diversity of $\mathcal{S}$ and its proximity (i.e. closeness to the optimal Pareto front). Even if all points in $\mathcal{S}$ are on the optimal Pareto front the indicator is not minimized unless the solutions in the approximation set are spread out perfectly. Because the optimal Pareto front may be continuous, there are infinitely many solutions possible on the optimal Pareto front. Therefore, we computed 5000 uniformly sampled solutions along the optimal Pareto front to use as a discretized version of $\boldsymbol{\mathcal{P}_F}$ for a high-quality approximation.

For the problems in our test-suite, given the ranges of the objectives for the optimal Pareto front configurations, a value of 0.01 for the $\boldsymbol{D}_{\mathcal{P}_F \to \mathcal{S}}$ indicator corresponds to fronts that are quite close to the optimal Pareto front. Fronts that have a $\boldsymbol{D}_{\mathcal{P}_F \to \mathcal{S}}$ value of 0.01 can be seen in Figure 3.

5.4 Results

MAMaLGaM-X, MAMaLGaM-X$^+$, iMAMaLGaM-X and iMAMaLGaM-X$^+$ were run using an unfactorized Gaussian, i.e. with a full covariance matrix, and a univariately factorized Gaussian, i.e. with all variables modeled as independent. All presented results are averaged over 10 independent runs. The subpopulation or cluster sizes were set according to guidelines from recent literature on SO [3]:

- Full covariance matrix
  generational: $n^{sub} = 17 + 3l^{1.5}$
  incremental: $n^{sub} = 10l^{0.5}$
- Univariate factorization
  generational: $n^{sub} = 10l^{0.5}$
  incremental: $n^{sub} = 4l^{0.5}$

The overall population size is $\frac{1}{2}k$ times the cluster size. Furthermore, we used $k = 20$ clusters as this number was previously found to provide excellent results [4]. The discretization of the objectives into hypercubes for the elitist archive is set to 10^{-2}.

We observe the average convergence of the $\boldsymbol{D}_{\mathcal{P}_F \rightarrow \mathcal{S}}$ metric to study the impact of incremental model building in combination with estimating Gaussian distributions. The average convergence results are shown in Figure 4. It is clear from the results that overall, iMAMaLGaM-X$^+$ performs the best as it converges to the lowest $\boldsymbol{D}_{\mathcal{P}_F \rightarrow \mathcal{S}}$ score on all problems except EC_4 and does so with the least number of function evaluations, with the exception of problem BD_2^s. Moreover, the higher the dimensionality of the problem, the bigger the difference. This is the clearest on the deformable registration (DR) problem, which has the largest dimensionality of all problems in our test suite, when the full covariance matrix is used. The difference in required number of function evaluations before convergence is huge. In the case of a problem like DR this is of prime importance because function evaluations take much more time than is the case for the artificial benchmark problems. Consequently, using MAMaLGaM-X$^{(+)}$ on DR with the full covariance matrix takes hours to run whereas with the incremental variants useful answers are already found within 30 minutes.

The results also show that the use of incremental model building narrows the gap between use of the full covariance matrix and the univariate factorization in the mixture-based MO setting. However, on problems where modelling dependencies between problem variables is not required (i.e. on EC_1, EC_2, EC_3 and EC_6, use of the univariately factorized Gaussian distribution is still far more efficient. This indicates that there is still a performance gain to be achieved by online deciding whether to process dependencies.

Finally, the results show that modeling dependencies can be of importance to reliably converge to the optimal Pareto front. On both problem BD_1 and BD_2^s the use of a univariately factorized Gaussian distribution leads to convergence to worse $\boldsymbol{D}_{\mathcal{P}_F \rightarrow \mathcal{S}}$ values, although this convergence does proceed much faster for incremental model building on the BD_2^s problem. A similar observation can be made for the DR problem. Although it is not easy to see in the logarithmic convergence graphs in Figure 4, the univariate models all converge to worse $\boldsymbol{D}_{\mathcal{P}_F \rightarrow \mathcal{S}}$ values than do their unfactorized counterparts. This can be better observed in Figure 5 where the Pareto front is shown computed for each algorithm over all runs. The difference between the unfactorized Gaussian models and the factorized Gaussian models is clear as there is a part of the Pareto front, corresponding to larger deformations of the grid and better similarity values, that cannot be reached (efficiently) by the univariate models. This stresses the need for considering dependencies also in real-world problems.

For completeness, in Figure 6 we show the transformation that was found with the best similarity value. Given the degrees of freedom in the transformation model, a perfect match cannot be obtained, but the match is already close enough to be of real-world clinical relevance. Considering that a black-box approach to solving this problem was taken, this further illustrates how EDAs can find high-quality solutions and make a solid contribution to real-world problem solving. Also, in image registration literature, a linear combination is always made of the two objectives. Not only is there no theoretical underpinning available for selecting a weight for such as a linear combination, it is known from multi-objective optimization theory that if part of the Pareto front is concave, no solutions on this part of the Pareto front can be found using a weighted linear combination [6], which speaks in favor of using a multi-objective approach instead, like the one studied in this paper.

6. CONCLUSIONS

In this paper, we have combined the use of Gaussian mixture distributions in an EDA for multi-objective optimization with an approach to incremental model building spanning multiple generations. The use of mixture distributions is very useful in multi-objective optimization as it allows spreading the search bias of the optimization algorithm across the Pareto front in a natural manner. We found that using mixture-component registration that associates the nearest mixture components in subsequent generations with each other, incremental model-building techniques that span multiple generations can successfully be applied. The reduction in required population size is k-fold larger compared to the single-objective case if k mixture components are used. As a result, we observed a substantial reduction in the required number of function evaluations on a set of common multi-objective benchmark problems as well as on a higher-dimensional multi-objective application problem: deformable image registration. Taken over all results, the multi-objective EDA that was introduced as iMAMaLGaM-X$^+$ (incremental Multi-objective AMaLGaM-miXture with parallel single-objective optimization clusters) was found to be the most promising variant to consider in future research.

7. REFERENCES

[1] T. W. Anderson. *An Introduction to Multivariate Statistical Analysis.* John Wiley & Sons Inc., New York, 1958.

[2] G. Arfken. *Mathematical methods for physicists.* Academic Press, Inc., San Diego, 1985.

[3] P. A. N. Bosman. On empirical memory design, faster selection of Bayesian factorizations and parameter-free Gaussian EDAs. In G. Raidl et al., editors, *Proc. of the Genetic and Evolutionary Comp. Conf. — GECCO–2009,* pages 389–396, New York, 2009. ACM Press.

[4] P. A. N. Bosman. The anticipated mean shift and cluster registration in mixture-based EDAs for multi-objective optimization. In J. Branke et al., editors, *Proc. of the Genetic and Evolutionary Comp. Conf. — GECCO–2010,* pages 351–358, New York, 2010. ACM Press.

[5] P. A. N. Bosman and D. Thierens. Adaptive variance scaling in continuous multi–objective estimation–of–distribution algorithms. In D. Thierens et al., editors, *Proceedings of the Genetic and Evolutionary Computation Conference — GECCO–2007,* pages 500–507, New York, 2007. ACM Press.

[6] K. Deb. *Multi-Objective Optimization Using Evolutionary Algorithms.* John Wiley & Sons Inc., New York, 2001.

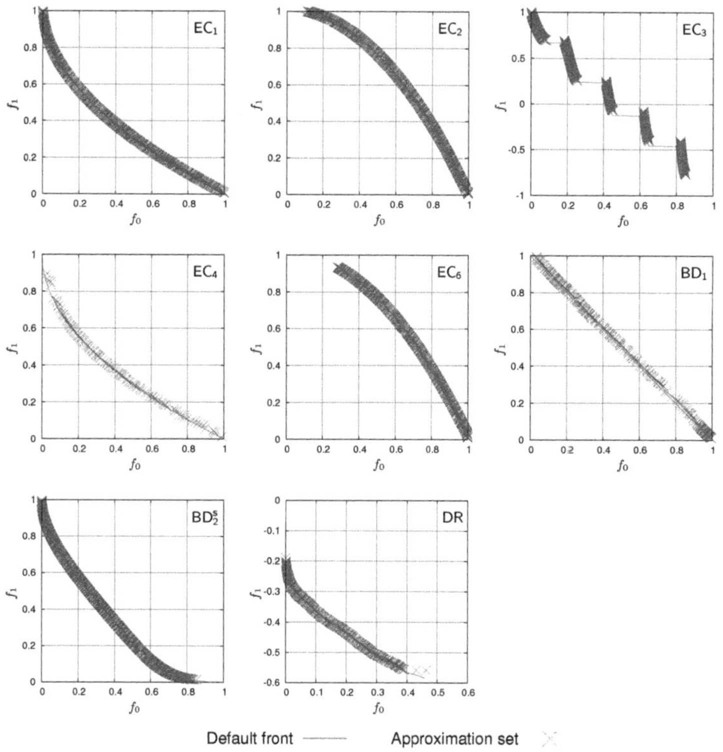

Figure 3: Default fronts and approximation sets obtained with iMAMaLGaM-X$^+$ ($D_{\mathcal{P}_F \rightarrow \mathcal{S}} = 0.01, k = 20$).

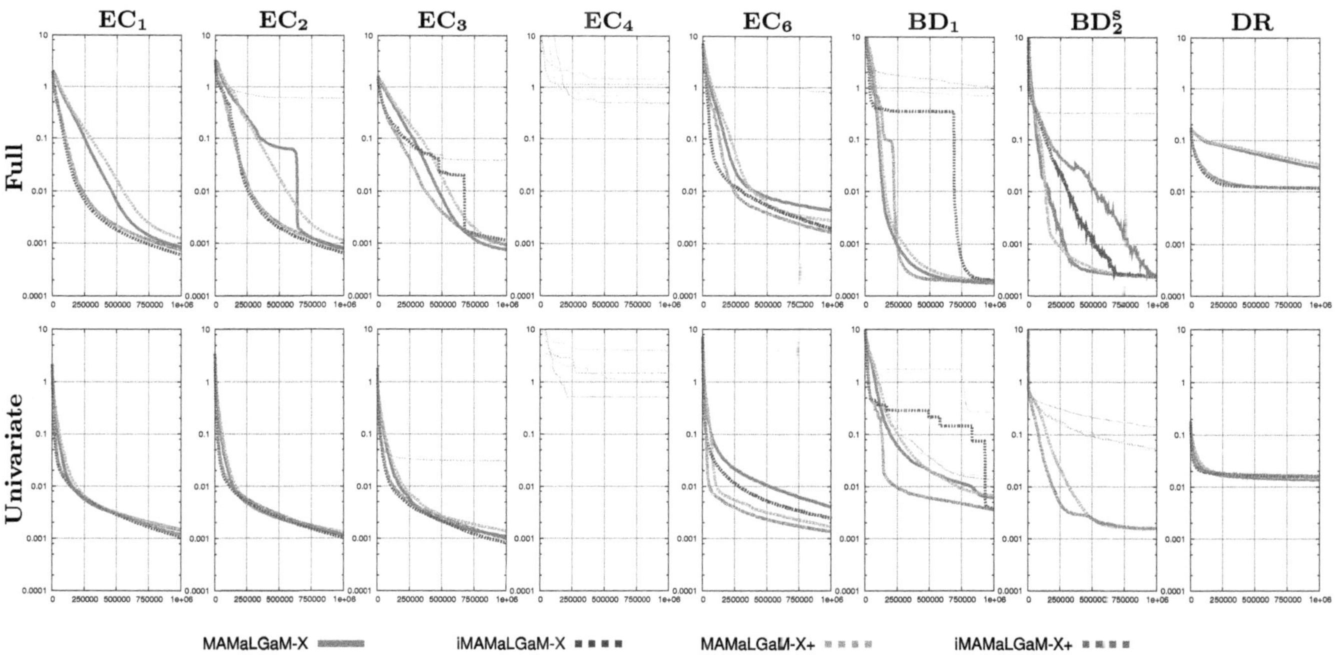

Figure 4: Average performance of various MOEDAs on all problems, estimating full covariance matrices in each cluster. Horizontal axis: number of evaluations (both objectives per evaluation). Vertical axis: $D_{\mathcal{P}_F \rightarrow \mathcal{S}}$. For each algorithm averages are shown both for successful runs (bold) and unsuccessful runs, giving double occurrences of lines if some runs were unsuccessful.

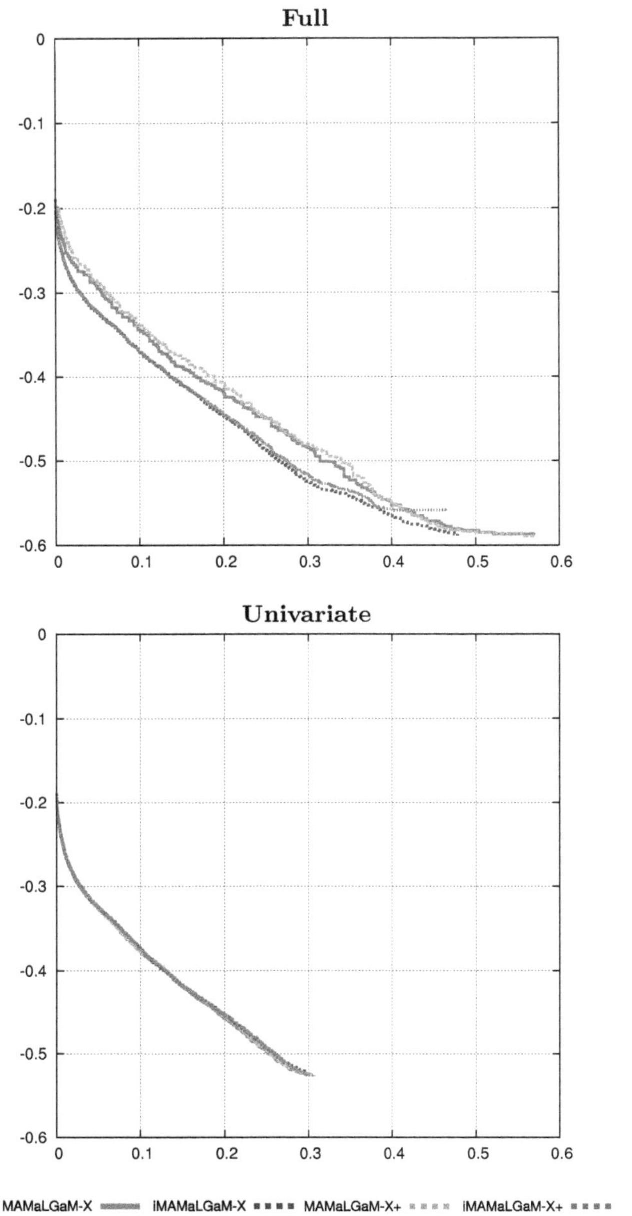

Figure 5: Pareto fronts computed over all runs on the deformable image registration problem instance. Horizontal axis: energy objective. Vertical axis: similarity objective.

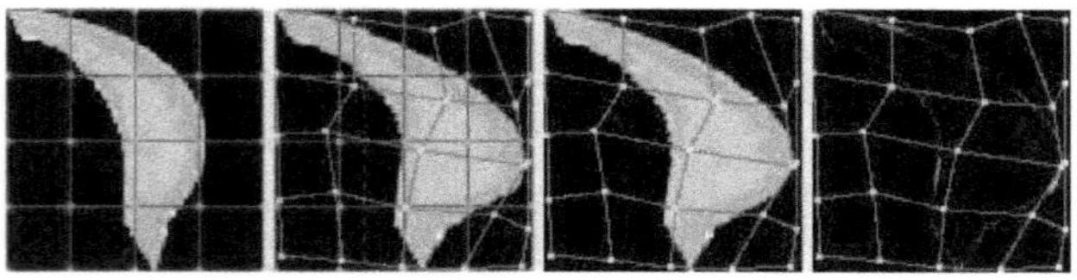

Figure 6: Best similarity result for the deformable image registration problem instance. From left to right: source image, target image, transformed source image, absolute difference of target and transformed source image. Green: initial regular grid. Yellow: transformed grid.

[7] K. Deb, A. Pratap, and T. Meyarivan. Constrained test problems for multi–objective evolutionary optimization. In E. Zitzler et al., editors, *Evolutionary Multi–Criterion Optimization — EMO–2001*, pages 284–298, Berlin, 2001. Springer–Verlag.

[8] M. Pelikan, K. Sastry, and D. E. Goldberg. Multiobjective hBOA, clustering, and scalability. In H.-G. Beyer et al., editors, *Proceedings of the Genetic and Evolutionary Computation Conference — GECCO–2005*, pages 663–670, New York, 2005. ACM Press.

[9] M. Pelikan, K. Sastry, and D. E. Goldberg. iBOA: the incremental bayesian optimization algorithm. In *Proceedings of the Genetic and Evolutionary Computation Conference — GECCO–2008*, pages 455–462, New York, 2008. ACM Press.

[10] J. P. W. Pluim, J. B. A. Maintz, and M. A. Viergever. Mutual-information-based registration of medical images: a survey. *IEEE Trans Med Imag*, 22:986–1004, 2004.

[11] D. Thierens and P. A. N. Bosman. Multi–objective mixture–based iterated density estimation evolutionary algorithms. In L. Spector et al., editors, *Proceedings of the Genetic and Evolutionary Computation Conference — GECCO–2001*, pages 663–670, San Francisco, California, 2001. Morgan Kaufmann.

[12] E. Zitzler, K. Deb, and L. Thiele. Comparison of multiobjective evolutionary algorithms: Empirical results. *Evolutionary Computation*, 8(2):173–195, 2000.

Influence of Selection on Structure Learning in Markov Network EDAs: An Empirical Study

Alexander E.I. Brownlee
School of Civil and Building Engineering
Loughborough University
Leicestershire, UK
a.e.i.brownlee@lboro.ac.uk

John A. W. McCall
IDEAS Research Institute
Robert Gordon University
Aberdeen, UK
j.mccall@rgu.ac.uk

Martin Pelikan
Missouri Estimation of Distribution Algorithms Laboratory (MEDAL)
Dept. of Mathematics and Computer Science
Univ. of Missouri in St. Louis
St. Louis, MO, USA
martin@martinpelikan.net

ABSTRACT

Learning a good model structure is important to the efficient solving of problems by estimation of distribution algorithms. In this paper we present the results of a series of experiments, applying a structure learning algorithm for undirected probabilistic graphical models based on statistical dependency tests to three fitness functions with different selection operators, proportions and pressures. The number of spurious interactions found by the algorithm are measured and reported. Truncation selection, and its complement (selecting only low fitness solutions) prove quite robust, resulting in a similar number of spurious dependencies regardless of selection pressure. In contrast, tournament and fitness proportionate selection are strongly affected by the selection proportion and pressure.

Categories and Subject Descriptors

I.2.8 [**Artificial Intelligence**]: Problem Solving, Control Methods, and Search—*Heuristic methods*

General Terms

Algorithms, Experimentation, Performance

Keywords

Selection, structure learning, spurious dependencies, Markov network, EDA

1. INTRODUCTION AND CONTEXT

Estimation of Distribution Algorithms (EDA) [9, 13, 16] construct and sample a probability distribution to generate new solutions and move towards an optimum for a problem. A major issue in this field of research is the exploration of factors which influence the quality of the model [30, 31]. This includes the interactions between variables in the model (structure) [8, 10, 12, 19, 28, 29, 31]. Many EDAs are able to learn the structure of the probabilistic model, and in the discrete domain there are two potential sources of error in the structures learned: missing important dependencies and including erroneous (spurious) dependencies [19]. In [37] it was shown that spurious dependencies can negatively impact on performance; recent works including [15, 25] have explored the impact of such errors on the scalability and efficiency of EDAs and the latter of these showed that spurious dependencies can hamper performance, particularly when niching is added to the algorithm.

EDAs effectively use observed likelihoods of variable value combinations in a selected sample of relatively high fitness as an estimate of a distribution that generates high fitness solutions with high probability. Dependencies generated by selection may genuinely reflect such a distribution or may simply be due to a sampling bias imposed by the selection (in [24] this was demonstrated for tournament selection). We term the latter "spurious" dependencies. As well as introducing a potential source of error into the probabilistic model, these are a problem because more complex models require more effort to estimate parameter values – both in population size and estimating the parameters from the data in the population.

There has been some interest over the past few years in EDAs using undirected probabilistic graphical models, or Markov networks [3, 27, 32, 33, 35]. This paper investigates the impact of selection on the discovery of spurious dependencies in this context. Specifically, we apply a simple dependency test structure learning algorithm from [5, 26, 34] to three well-known fitness functions (onemax, checkerboard and trap-5) and measure the number of spurious dependencies found when using one of nine selection operators including truncation, tournament and fitness proportionate selection. Similar to ref. [24], in this study we focus on the first generation, allowing us to gain better understanding of the operators in the easily comprehended conditions of a uniformly distributed population. The focus of this work on undirected networks contrasts with much of the previous work on selection and structure learning, which has focused on directed (Bayesian) networks. The requirements for the structure types are quite different: an undirected

```
Initialise dependency graph (fully connected)
Generate a random population P of size N
Select proportion p of P to form σ, where σ ⊆ P
for all possible pairs (X_i, X_j) of variables in the problem do
  Compute the Chi-square value χ for (X_i, X_j) over σ
  if χ^2 < T then
    Remove edge connecting (X_i, X_j) from the dependency graph
  end if
end for
```

Figure 1: Structure learning algorithm

network simply needs to coincide with the additively decomposable function structure of the problem (for example, Ising-DEUM [35]), whereas a directed model structure may need interactions covering distances of 2 nodes or more [10]. Further, in contrast to ref. [6], in this study we focus on the effect of selection on structure learning rather than model parameters, and cover a wider range of commonly-used selection operators.

Related work on selection in EDAs includes a number of methods for selecting low-fitness solutions alongside high-fitness ones or the whole population [6,11,14,18,21,36]. In this study we also include two variants of truncation selection (taken from ref. [6]) designed to explicitly include low-fitness solutions in structure learning.

The rest of the paper is structured as follows. Section 2 introduces the structure learning algorithm at the centre of our experiments. Section 3 summarises the selection operators studied, and Section 4 outlines the experimental procedure. Sections 5 to 7 present the results. Finally, in Section 8 we draw our conclusions.

2. STRUCTURE LEARNING

The structure learning algorithm is given in Figure 1. Selection is performed to obtain a subset of the population; using the selected solutions as a dataset, pairs of variables are subjected to a statistical independence test to determine whether they are independent of each other. There are many methods which may be used to determine such independence; examples of this are the joint entropy of the pair as used in MIMIC [7] and the Chi-square independence test [17], as used in BMDA [23] and MN-FDA [26]. Each starts with a fully connected graphical model and removes edges where the independence score is below some threshold.

The Chi-square (χ^2) test is a comparison between the joint distribution of a pair of variables and the product of their marginal distributions. If these are equal then the χ^2 value is zero and the variables are said to be independent. Normally, rather than comparison to zero, a threshold T is used to reduce false dependencies caused by noise in the sample data. The threshold we use is 3.84, where the variables may be said to be independent with 95% confidence [2]. For each possible interaction, the test between a pair of variables X_i and X_j is calculated over all values x_i and x_j in a population of N points as in (1).

$$\chi^2_{i,j} = \sum_{x_i,x_j} \frac{(Np(x_i,x_j) - Np(x_i)p(x_j))^2}{Np(x_i)p(x_j)} \qquad (1)$$

Chi-square may also be extended to test higher order interactions by testing for conditional probabilities, but that is not covered further here.

Once completed, the dependency graph will include a set of bivariate dependencies which can be used as the structure for the undirected probabilistic model. In [27], the graph is refined (some dependencies removed) and a search for higher-order cliques is run prior to fitting model parameters. In our experiments we omit these stages as we are only interested in the effect of selection on introducing spurious dependencies to the graph.

3. SELECTION OPERATORS

Several variants of well-known selection operators were implemented in this study.

3.1 Truncation selection

Truncation selection is often used in EDAs, and we implemented the three variants of it described in [6]. In the unaltered form of truncation selection [20], the population is sorted in descending order of fitness, and the top $p*N$ solutions are selected, where $0 < p \leq 1$ and N is the population size. Truncation selection selects a solution only once (unless it is duplicated in the population), and poor fitness individuals are never selected. In this unaltered form, truncation selection is referred to here as *top selection*, as it selects the top part of the population.

As a number of studies [6,11,14,18,21,36] have shown that including low-fitness solutions can be beneficial to model building, we have included two variants of truncation selection which explicitly include such solutions. These are *bottom* selection and *top+bottom selection*. Bottom selection is a duplicate of top selection, but the population is sorted in ascending order of fitness, so it selects the least fit members of the population. Top+bottom selection selects the fittest $(p/2)*N$ and least fit $(p/2)*N$. In [6], it was found that in some situations, top+bottom selection helped to sharpen the information held within a population, resulting in a better model.

3.2 Tournament selection

Several variants of tournament selection (with replacement) are implemented, with tournament sizes of 2, 3, 5 and 10. These are referred to as TS_2, TS_3, TS_5 and TS_{10}. The tournament size provides direct control on selection pressure. The tournament was repeated N times to fill the pool of solutions, with the possibility that solutions could be selected more than once.

3.3 Fitness proportionate selection

Two variants of fitness proportionate (or roulette wheel) selection were implemented for the study. For both, the draw was repeated N times to fill the pool of solutions. Straight fitness proportionate selection has the probability p_i of a solution being directly proportional to its fitness f_i, relative to the fitnesses f_1 to f_N of all other solutions in the population. The probability of selection is explicitly defined in (2).

$$p_i = \frac{f_i}{\sum_{j=1}^{N} f_i} \qquad (2)$$

```
for each selection operator S do
    for each selection proportion p do
        Run the structure learning algorithm, using S with
        proportion p
        Compare learned structure with known true structure – how many false interactions were found?
    end for
end for
```

Figure 2: Experimental procedure

Rank selection is the same as fitness proportionate selection, but with the raw fitness values replaced by the fitness ranks for all solutions. Selection pressure for fitness proportionate selection is controlled by how the raw fitness values are treated; in this case, whether raw fitnesses or ranks are used.

3.4 No selection

When the number of selected solutions equals the population size, with the truncation selection variants we effectively have no selection. This does not apply for the other selection operators: there will be some duplication or bias among the selected population in this case as they do not guarantee against selecting the same solution more than once.

4. EXPERIMENTS

In order to explore the issue of spurious dependencies introduced by selection, we apply the structure learning algorithm using different selection operators to three well-known fitness functions which have known variable (in)dependencies. We compare the learned structure with the "true" structure; variables known to interact from the definition of the problem. The true structures are described with each problem. The experiments are designed to simultaneously measure the effect of selection operator, selection proportion, and selection pressure on the number of spurious dependencies found.

All three benchmark problems have a bit string representation. These are onemax, checkerboard and trap-5, and they are briefly summarised with the results for each. These problems are selected for their simplicity: they are well understood and have clearly defined variable interactions. The experiments covered a range of problem sizes from 10 bits to 1000 bits for onemax and trap-5, and 16 bits to 400 bits for checkerboard. The results here are for 100 bit versions of both problems – reflecting the broader trend seen across the wider range of sizes covered by the experiments. A technical report [4] features the full set of results.

The experiments followed the steps given in Figure 2, and were repeated over 30 runs. We report mean numbers of spurious interactions detected over all these runs. In the figures, error bars showing one standard deviation have been omitted for clarity, because these were small enough in most cases to be obscured by the data points.

In all experiments, the proportions p of the population selected were 0.01, 0.02, 0.05, 0.1, 0.2, 0.28, 0.5, 0.67, 0.83 and 1 (that is, no selection). The starting population size N was always 10000, allowing us to maintain some diversity in the selected set even when selection pressure is high. Results show the different selection operators, for increasing selection proportion (that is, selecting progressively more of the starting population).

Figure 3: "True" structure for a 5-bit instance of onemax; no dependencies between variables

5. RESULTS - ONEMAX

This is one of the simplest and most commonly used benchmarks. In this problem the fitness is simply the number of bits with the value 1, expressed formally in (3).

$$f(x) = \sum_{i=1}^{n} x_i \tag{3}$$

The onemax problem has no interactions between variables (Figure 3), which makes it an excellent candidate for measuring an algorithm's tendency to learn false dependencies. Any dependencies found by the structure learning algorithm for this problem are counted as false dependencies. The raw number of false interactions found for 100 bit onemax for the different selection operators and selection proportions is illustrated in Figure 4.

Several trends can be observed. With a small selection proportion, all the operators produce a similar number of false positives; 200-300 spurious dependencies, and is in line with the demonstration of tournament selection resulting in discovery of dependencies in [24]. Truncation selections seems to perform best; top selection and bottom selection has around the same number of false positives for any selection proportion. This reinforces the findings of works including [6,11,14,18,21,36] that low fitness solutions can be useful in constructing the model.

T+B selection appears to be worst among all the operators with a small selection proportion (high pressure). As selection pressure decreases more spurious dependencies are found, peaking around selection of 0.1 of the population before improving as selection pressure drops further. This is in contrast to the results seen in [6], where T+B selection was found to help produce a good model when estimating model parameters. The poorer performance of T+B selection can be explained – in that work, the model incorporated fitness during the parameter estimation phase, so the low and high fitness solutions were still distinguishable. In contrast, here once the selection is performed the difference between high and low fitness solutions is lost – this would imply that the structure learning algorithm would need modified to make proper use of top+bottom selection.

The other operators result in increasing numbers of false interactions as selection proportion increases. This will be for two reasons. When applying these operators with a selection proportion of 1.0 (selecting the whole population) there will be more duplicated individuals in the selected set (the population size being the same as the number to be selected). For TS_2, selecting a set equal to the population size results in 70% of the selected set being solutions with at least one duplicate. For TS_{10} (higher selection pressure than TS_2), this figure is 92%. This creates higher frequencies of specific value pairs which skew the Chi-square values. In contrast, truncation selection of the whole population has no duplication.

More crucially, as the selection proportion increases with

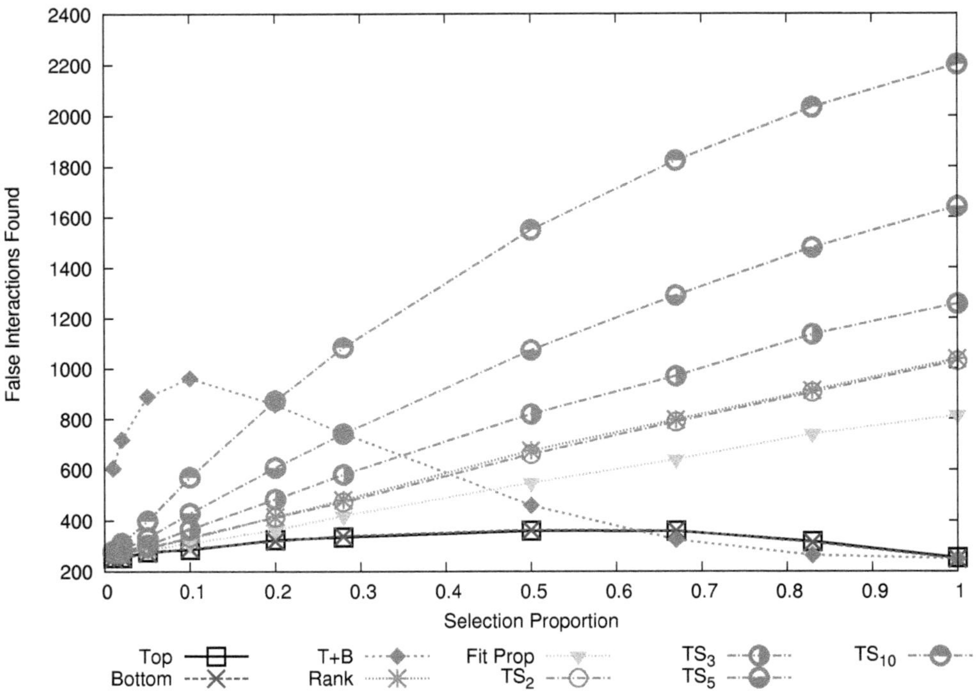

Figure 4: False interactions found for 100 bit onemax with different selection operators and proportions. For clarity, from top to bottom the plots are for TS_{10}, TS_5, TS_3, TS_2 and rank (near identical), fit prop, and finally top selection and bottom selection (near identical). The plot for T+B selection starts high, increases, then falls after a selection proportion of 0.1.

tournament selection, the sample size increases but the selection pressure remains the same. As the statistical test is dependent on the sample size, increasing sample size increases the chance of spurious dependencies. When changing the selection proportion with the truncation selection variants, the selection pressure is also changed, which appears to have a cancelling effect.

6. RESULTS - CHECKERBOARD

The checkerboard problem [1, 13] introduces bivariate interactions. Chromosomes are a square number of bits in length; they represent the rows of a s x s grid concatenated into one string. The objective is to realise a grid with a checkerboard pattern with alternating 1s and 0s; thus each 1 should be surrounded by 0s and vice versa, not including corners. Formally this is written as in (4).

$$f(x) = 4(s-2)^2 - \sum_{i=2}^{s-1}\sum_{j=2}^{s-1} \left\{ \begin{array}{c} \delta\left(x_{ij}, x_{i-1j}\right) \\ +\ \delta\left(x_{ij}, x_{i+1j}\right) \\ +\ \delta\left(x_{ij}, x_{ij-1}\right) \\ +\ \delta\left(x_{ij}, x_{ij+1}\right) \end{array} \right\}, \quad (4)$$

where:

$$\delta_{ij} = \left\{ \begin{array}{lll} 1 & if & i = j \\ 0 & if & i \neq j \end{array} \right. \quad (5)$$

This problem is useful as it has a simple underlying 2D lattice structure which is easily understood and visualised. The true structure is perfectly aligned with fitness independence, and for 100 bit checkerboard has 144 interactions:

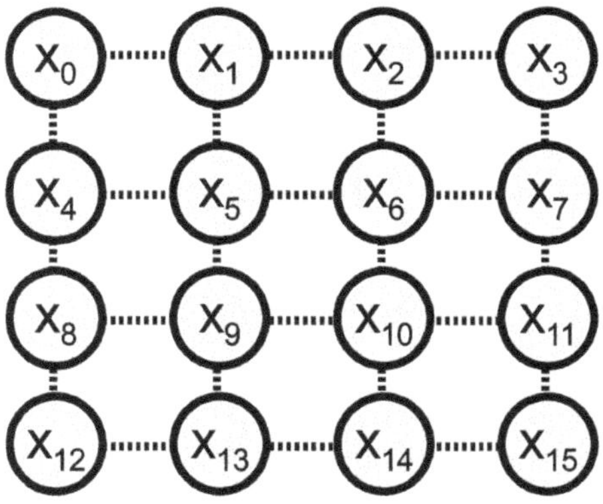

Figure 5: "True" structure for a 16-bit instance of checkerboard; dependencies (dotted lines) between variables form a lattice

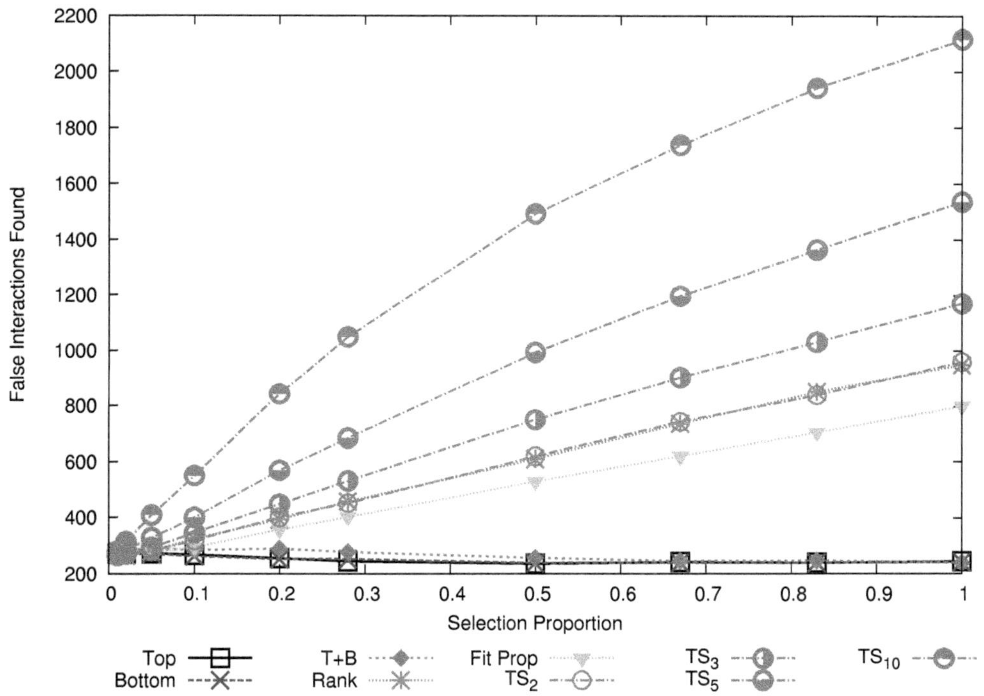

Figure 6: False interactions found for 100 bit checkerboard with different selection operators and proportions. For clarity, from top to bottom the plots are for TS_{10}, TS_5, TS_3, TS_2 and rank (near identical), fit prop, T+B selection, and finally top selection and bottom selection (near identical).

a 2D lattice, with no wrapping around the edges (Figure 5). Any interactions found by the structure learner which were not connecting neighbouring nodes in the lattice were counted as spurious. We can do this for undirected graphical models because such a model simply needs to coincide with the additively decomposable function structure of the problem to be able to generate high fitness solutions with high probability. In contrast, a directed model structure may need interactions covering distances of 2 nodes or more (this at least being the case for Ising spin glasses, which have a similar lattice structure [10]).

The results are illustrated in Figure 6. As with onemax, top selection and bottom selection perform very similarly, resulting in around 200-300 spurious interactions being found regardless of selection proportion.

The other selection operators decrease in performance (more spurious interactions) as the chance of duplicates in the selected set increases – both as the selected proportion increases to select the same number of solutions as the population size, and for tournament selection as the tournament size (selection pressure) increases.

One difference to the trends seen for onemax, is that top+bottom selection does not show the same poor performance when selecting a small proportion of the population – instead resulting in a similar number of spurious dependencies as top selection and bottom selection. A possible explanation for this is that the two optima for checkerboard contain alternating patterns of 0 and 1. Thus, in the selected set there will be lots of alternating patterns at the top (but in different positions), and lots of patterns with adjacent pairs the same at the bottom. This will mean Chi-square often sees little difference from the product of the marginals and thus detects few spurious dependencies.

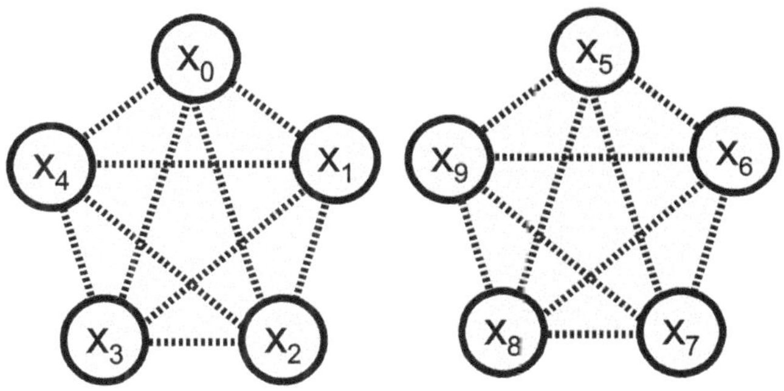

Figure 7: "True" structure for a 10-bit instance of trap-5; dependencies (dotted lines) between variables in each group of five form a fully connected graph, with no dependencies between groups

7. RESULTS - TRAP-5

The trap functions [22] are designed to deceive evolutionary algorithms into converging on a local optimum. This is particularly a problem for algorithms which do not consider interactions between variables. The trap function of order k is defined in (6). It computes fitness by dividing the bit string into blocks.

$$f(x) = \sum_{i=1}^{n/k} trap_k(x_{b_i,1} + ... + x_{b_i,k}) \qquad (6)$$

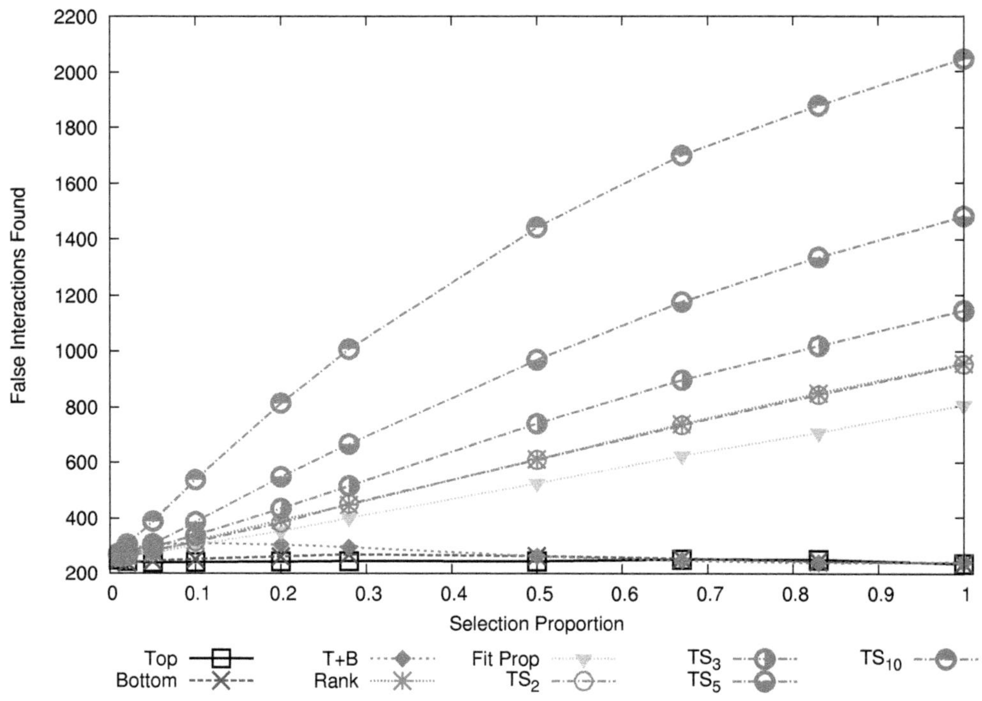

Figure 8: False interactions found for 100 bit trap-5 with different selection operators and proportions. For clarity, from top to bottom the plots are for TS_{10}, TS_5, TS_3, TS_2 and rank (near identical), fit prop, T+B selection, top selection and finally bottom selection.

Each block ($x_{b_i,1}, +... + x_{b_i,k}$) gives a fitness, calculated as in (7), where u is the number of 1s in the block of k bits. Trap-5, which is the specific instance used in this paper, has $k = 5$, $f_{high} = 5$ and $f_{low} = 4$.

$$trap_k(u) = \begin{cases} f_{high} & \text{if } u = k \\ f_{low} - u\frac{f_{low}}{k-1} & otherwise \end{cases} \quad (7)$$

The functions are designed to mislead or *trap* algorithms which do not account for interactions between variables, so is also useful for testing a structure learning algorithm. As u increases, fitness decreases, which leads the algorithm away from the global optimum. Algorithms which do find interactions should be able to determine that groups of k variables being switched to all 0 improves fitness.

For trap-5, we considered the true interactions to be a fully connected graph within each groups of five bits (Figure 7). This means that for each group there are 10 interactions, and 1000 interactions for a 100 bit instance of the problem. We count as spurious interactions falling outside these groups.

The results are similar to those for onemax and checkerboard, and are illustrated in Figure 8. Top selection and bottom selection perform similarly, with 200-300 spurious interactions being found regardless of selection proportion.

As before, the other selection operators result in more spurious interactions being found as the sample size and along with it the chance of duplicates in the selected set increase – as the proportion of the population selected increases. Further, as the tournament size (selection pressure) increases, so does the number of spurious dependencies.

Similar to checkerboard but not onemax, top+bottom selection shows a similar number of spurious dependencies as top selection and bottom selection. Here this is possibly caused by the deceptiveness of the problem – solutions quite close to the optimum (at least within the groups) will have a low fitness, so will appear in the bottom part of the population. This will mean that top+bottom selection effectively becomes top selection for this problem.

8. CONCLUSIONS

We have presented an empirical study of the effect of different selection operators, proportions and pressures on an algorithm for learning the structure of an undirected probabilistic model. Several conclusions can be drawn from these results.

Truncation selection for structure learning return similar number of false interactions for wide range of selection proportions. In addition, the number found is similar for each of the problems. This may seem curious given that all the problems examined have different numbers of true interactions. However, the true interactions make up a small fraction of the total number of possible variable pairs and assuming an even distribution of false interactions among the set of those possible, it is reasonable that there would be a similar number found for each problem. This consistency allows fine tuning of the operator to find as high a number of true interactions as possible, without the issue of introducing more false ones into the model structure. We conclude that truncation selection is quite a robust operator (at least in the context of these problems), further justifying its common use among EDAs. This is a similar conclusion to that in ref. [15], where Lima et al found that truncation selection performs well because the distribution of solutions it selects is uniform, which is more suitable for metrics like K2.

Top selection and bottom selection perform similarly for all the test problems, reinforcing similar results [6,11,14,18, 21,36] that show the usefulness of including low fitness solutions in model construction. Fitness proportionate and rank selection are quite poor for structure learning, particularly as selection proportion is increased. Tournament selection shows a similar pattern: increasing the tournament size (a higher selection pressure) leads to the number of spurious interactions found increasing. This is undesirable as having a small selection proportion necessitates a large population, which will require many fitness evaluations. A likely explanation for this is given in [24], that most selection methods introduce nonlinearities between bits regardless of whether or not these bits are correlated in the fitness function (an exception being Boltzmann selection, which preserves independence between the bits that are not related in the fitness). This problem grows as selection pressure increases. It may also be due to a combination of the increased sample size and a large number of duplicates in the selected set.

Although in this study we used a large population size to allow us to keep some diversity in the selected set with high selection pressures, producing more consistent results, we believe that the insights carry over to smaller population sizes. If the sample size is reduced, the Chi-square values also reduce and so the threshold for the structure learning algorithm must be lowered in order to find the true interactions. In [29], Santana used a population size of 1000 and threshold of 0.75. A repeat of our trap-5 experiment with this population size and threshold showed similar results. Further exploration of this and the wider issues of the interplay between the population size, selection operator or the selection pressure and minimum population size for finding an accurate enough model present an interesting direction for further work. This relates to other similar lines of current research in EDAs such as [25,38].

In this paper, we have focused on the first generation only (similar to ref. [24]). There are many other considerations when choosing a selection operator in an EDA beyond the quality of the model in the first generation. The initial study here does provide some insight into the selection operators studied, and in the easily understood conditions of a uniformly distributed starting population. With these foundations, the logical next step is to study selection in the same way over the course of an evolutionary run, and in parallel explore how selection affects the overall algorithm performance in terms of function evaluations required to find an optimum.

We intend to explore these issues on a much wider range of fitness functions with different characteristics, with the goal of determining approaches to choosing the appropriate selection for a given problem. The series of experiments in this paper provides the basis for a more extensive study which will help to inform the current research on improving model quality and efficiency in EDAs.

9. ACKNOWLEDGEMENT

Martin Pelikan was supported by the National Science Foundation under grants ECS-0547013 and IIS-1115352. Any opinions, findings, and conclusions or recommendations expressed in this material are those of the authors and do not necessarily reflect the views of NSF.

10. REFERENCES

[1] S. Baluja and S. Davies. Using optimal dependency-trees for combinational optimization. In *ICML '97: Proceedings of the Fourteenth International Conference on Machine Learning*, pages 30–38. Morgan Kaufmann Publishers Inc, 1997.

[2] S. Boslaugh and P. A. Watters. *Statistics: A Desktop Quick Reference.* O'Reilly, 2008.

[3] A. E. I. Brownlee. *Multivariate Markov Networks for Fitness Modelling in an Estimation of Distribution Algorithm.* PhD thesis, Robert Gordon University, Aberdeen, May 2009.

[4] A. E. I. Brownlee, J. A. W. McCall, and M. Pelikan. Influence of selection on structure learning in Markov network EDAs: An empirical study. Technical Report MEDAL Report No. 2012006, Missouri Estimation of Distribution Algorithms Laboratory, Univ. of Missouri in St. Louis, 2012. Online: http://medal-lab.org/files/2012006.pdf.

[5] A. E. I. Brownlee, J. A. W. McCall, S. K. Shakya, and Q. Zhang. Structure Learning and Optimisation in a Markov-network based Estimation of Distribution Algorithm. In *Proceedings of the IEEE Congress on Evolutionary Computation (CEC 2009)*, pages 447–454, Trondheim, Norway, 2009. IEEE Press.

[6] A. E. I. Brownlee, J. A. W. McCall, Q. Zhang, and D. Brown. Approaches to Selection and their effect on Fitness Modeling in an Estimation of Distribution Algorithm. In *Proc. of the IEEE World Congress on Computational Intelligence (CEC 2008)*, pages 2621 –2628, Hong Kong, China, 2008. IEEE Press.

[7] J. S. de Bonet, C. L. Isbell Jr., and P. Viola. MIMIC: Finding optima by estimating probability densities. In M. C. Mozer, M. I. Jordan, and T. Petsche, editors, *Advances in Neural Information Processing Systems*, 1997.

[8] C. Echegoyen, J. Lozano, R. Santana, and P. Larranaga. Exact Bayesian network learning in estimation of distribution algorithms. In *Proceedings of the IEEE Congress on Evolutionary Computation (CEC 2007)*, pages 1051–1058, sept. 2007.

[9] M. Hauschild and M. Pelikan. An introduction and survey of estimation of distribution algorithms. *Swarm and Evolutionary Computation*, 1(3):111 – 128, 2011.

[10] M. Hauschild, M. Pelikan, K. Sastry, and C. Lima. Analyzing probabilistic models in hierarchical BOA. *IEEE Transactions on Evolutionary Computation*, 13:1199–1217, December 2009.

[11] Y. Hong, G. Zhu, S. Kwong, and Q. Ren. Estimation of distribution algorithms making use of both high quality and low quality individuals. In *IEEE International Conference on Fuzzy Systems (FUZZ-IEEE 2009)*, pages 1806–1813, August 2009.

[12] L. Kallel, B. Naudts, and R. Reeves. Properties of fitness functions and search landscapes. In L. Kallel, B. Naudts, and A. Rogers, editors, *Theoretical Aspects of Evolutionary Computing*, pages 177–208. Springer Verlag, 2000.

[13] P. Larrañaga and J. A. Lozano. *Estimation of Distribution Algorithms: A New Tool for Evolutionary Computation.* Kluwer Academic Publishers, Boston, 2002.

[14] X. Li, S. Mabu, and K. Hirasawa. Use of infeasible individuals in probabilistic model building genetic network programming. In *Proc. of the 13th Genetic and Evolutionary Computation COnference (GECCO 2011)*, pages 601–608, New York, NY, USA, 2011. ACM.

[15] C. F. Lima, F. G. Lobo, M. Pelikan, and D. E. Goldberg. Model accuracy in the Bayesian optimization algorithm. *Soft Computing*, 15(7):1351–1371, 2010.

[16] J. A. Lozano, P. Larrañaga, I. Inza, and E. Bengoetxea. *Towards a New Evolutionary Computation: Advances on Estimation of Distribution Algorithms (Studies in Fuzziness and Soft Computing)*. Springer-Verlag, 2006.

[17] L. A. Marascuilo and M. McSweeney. *Nonparametric and Distribution-Free Methods for Social Sciences.* Brooks / Cole Publishing Company, California, 1977.

[18] T. Miquélez, E. Bengoetxea, and P. Larrañaga. Evolutionary computation based on Bayesian classifiers. *Int'l Jnl. of Applied Mathematics and Computer Science*, 14(3):101–115, 2004.

[19] H. Mühlenbein and T. Mahnig. Evolutionary optimization using graphical models. *New Gen. Comput.*, 18(2):157–166, 2000.

[20] H. Mühlenbein and D. Schlierkamp-Voosen. Predictive models for the breeder genetic algorithm I. continuous parameter optimization. *Evolutionary Computuation*, 1(1):25–49, 1993.

[21] M. Munetomo, N. Murao, and K. Akama. Introducing assignment functions to Bayesian optimization algorithms. *Info. Sciences*, 178(1):152 – 163, 2008.

[22] M. Pelikan. *Bayesian optimization algorithm: from single level to hierarchy.* PhD thesis, University of Illinois at Urbana-Champaign, Urbana, IL, 2002.

[23] M. Pelikan and H. Mühlenbein. The bivariate marginal distribution algorithm. In R. Roy, T. Furuhashi, and P. K. Chawdhry, editors, *Advances in Soft Computing - Engineering Design and Manufacturing*, pages 521–535, 1999.

[24] M. Pelikan, K. Sastry, and D. E. Goldberg. Scalability of the Bayesian optimization algorithm. *Int'l. Jnl. of Approximate Reasoning*, 31(3):221 – 258, 2002.

[25] E. Radetic and M. Pelikan. Spurious dependencies and EDA scalability. In *Genetic and Evolutionary Computation Conference*, pages 303–310, 2010.

[26] R. Santana. A Markov network based factorized distribution algorithm for optimization. In *Proceedings of the 14th European Conference on Machine Learning; Lecture Notes in Artificial Intelligence*, volume 2837, pages 337–348, Berlin, 2003. Springer-Verlag.

[27] R. Santana. Estimation of distribution algorithms with Kikuchi approximations. *Evolutionary Computation*, 13(1):67–97, 2005.

[28] R. Santana, C. Bielza, J. A. Lozano, and P. Larrañaga. Mining probabilistic models learned by EDAs in the optimization of multi-objective problems. In *Proceedings of the 11th Annual conference on Genetic and evolutionary computation (GECCO 2009)*, pages 445–452, New York, NY, USA, 2009. ACM.

[29] R. Santana, P. Larrañaga, and J. A. Lozano. Interactions and dependencies in estimation of distribution algorithms. In *Proc. of the IEEE Congress on Evolutionary Computation (CEC 2005)*, volume 1, pages 1418–1425. IEEE Press, 2-4 Sept. 2005.

[30] R. Santana, P. Larrañaga, and J. A. Lozano. Challenges and open problems in discrete EDAs. Technical Report EHU-KZAA-IK-1/07, Department of Computer Science and Artificial Intelligence, University of the Basque Country, October 2007.

[31] R. Santana, P. Larrañaga, and J. A. Lozano. Research topics on discrete estimation of distribution algorithms. *Memetic Computing*, 1(1):35–54, 2009.

[32] S. Shakya and R. Santana. An EDA based on local Markov property and Gibbs sampling. In *Proceedings of the Genetic and Evolutionary Computation COnference (GECCO 2008)*, pages 475–476. ACM Press, 2008.

[33] S. Shakya and R. Santana, editors. *Markov Networks in Evolutionary Computation.* Springer, 2012.

[34] S. K. Shakya, A. E. I. Brownlee, J. A. W. McCall, F. Fournier, and G. Owusu. A fully multivariate DEUM algorithm. In *Proceedings of the IEEE Congress on Evolutionary Computation (CEC 2009)*, pages 479–486. IEEE Press, 2009.

[35] S. K. Shakya and J. A. W. McCall. Optimization by estimation of distribution with DEUM framework based on Markov random fields. *International Journal of Automation and Computing*, 4(3):262–272, 2007.

[36] D. Wallin and C. Ryan. Using over-sampling in a Bayesian classifier EDA to solve deceptive and hierarchical problems. In *Proc. of the IEEE Congress on Evolutionary Computation*, pages 1660 –1667, 2009.

[37] T.-L. Yu, K. Sastry, and D. E. Goldberg. Linkage learning, overlapping building blocks, and systematic strategy for scalable recombination. In *Proceedings of the 2005 conference on Genetic and evolutionary computation*, GECCO '05, pages 1217–1224, New York, NY, USA, 2005. ACM.

[38] T.-L. Yu, K. Sastry, D. E. Goldberg, and M. Pelikan. Population sizing for entropy-based model building in discrete estimation of distribution algorithms. In *Proceedings of the 9th annual conference on Genetic and evolutionary computation*, GECCO '07, pages 601–608, New York, NY, USA, 2007. ACM.

A Test Problem with Adjustable Degrees of Overlap and Conflict among Subproblems

Wei-Ming Chen
Department of Electrical Engineering
National Taiwan University
r00921044@ntu.edu.tw

Chung-Yu Shao
Department of Electrical Engineering
National Taiwan University
r00921046@ntu.edu.tw

Po-Chun Hsu
Department of Electrical Engineering
National Taiwan University
r00921034@ntu.edu.tw

Tian-Li Yu
Department of Electrical Engineering
National Taiwan University
tianliyu@cc.ee.ntu.edu.tw

ABSTRACT

In the field of genetic algorithms (GAs), some researches on overlapping building blocks (BBs) have been proposed. To further study on overlapping BBs, we need to measure the performance of an algorithm to solve problems with overlap among subproblems. Several test problems have been proposed, but the controllability over the degree of overlapping is not yet fully satisfactory. Our new test problem is designed with full controllability of overlapping as well as conflict, a specific type of overlap, among BBs. We present a framework for building the structure of this problem in this paper. Some model-building GAs are tested by the proposed problem. This test problem can be applied to further researches on overlapping and conflicting BBs.

Categories and Subject Descriptors

F.2.m [**Analysis of Algorithms and Problem Complexity**]: Miscellaneous; I.2.8 [**Artificial Intelligence**]: [Problem Solving, Control Methods, and Search]

Keywords

Genetic Algorithms, Building Blocks, Non-separable Problems, Performance Measures

1. INTRODUCTION

The building block (BB) hypothesis states that the complexity of a problem could be reduced by identifying and recombining BBs in the problem [9, 5]. Goldberg [5] described BBs as low order, low defining-length schemata with above average fitness. Recent researches have also shown that a genetic algorithm (GA) works well with efficient BB mixing [16]. One approach to identifying BBs is decomposing a problem into subproblems [7]. That is, a GA could find the global optimum by combining solutions to these subproblems. Different approaches to find linkages of highly correlated variables in a problem have been proposed in competent GA designs. Some of those competent GAs are known to be capable of identifying overlapping BBs [6, 20].

The concept of overlap among BBs is essential because it is not practical to assume real-world problems consist of only separable BBs. Moreover, a specific type of overlap exists. If two overlapping BBs cannot both reach their own optimal solution at the same time, this type of overlap is called *conflict* by Chang *et al.* [3] Overlapping BBs are common in a real-world problem. Among these overlapping BBs, conflict is also common. Hence, we believe that an investigation on overlapping and conflicting BBs is important to studies on GAs. For a GA researcher to measure the ability of a GA to solve such problems, a test problem with controllable degrees of overlap and conflict among BBs is needed.

In this paper, we propose a new test problem and present the building step of the structure. A researcher can implement this problem and freely set the degree of overlap and conflict among BBs. Some model-building GAs are tested by this test problem. The experimental results show that this test problem can practically measure the performances of the GAs.

This paper continues as follows. In Section 2, we describe some relevant researches on overlapping BBs and some shortcomings of the former test problems. In Section 3, we propose our test problem with controllable degrees of overlap and conflict to overcome these shortcomings. In Section 4, we apply this problem to test three model-building GAs and present the experimental results. Finally, we conclude this paper with discussions and possible future work.

2. RELATED WORK

Considering a test problem for researches on overlapping BBs, some properties are required. First, the degree of overlap among BBs should be adjustable. Second, we need to observe whether a GA finds a optimal solution, so a known global optimum, or a global optimum can be calculated in polynomial time, is required. Moreover, we do not want that

GECCO'12, July 7–11, 2012, Philadelphia, Pennsylvania, USA.

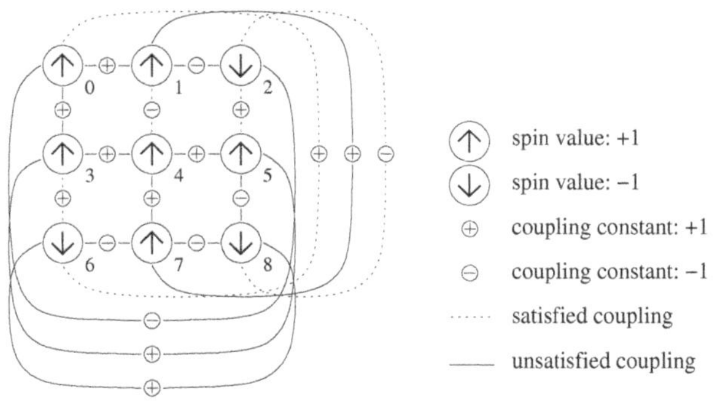

Figure 1: The 3×3 Ising spin-glass system.

some part of the problem is especially hard for a GA to solve than other parts are. Unexpected difficulties in the problem may add noise to the experiments. In the other words, we require that the difficulties of all the parts of the problem are the same, or approximately the same. Hence, Chang *et al.* [4] proposed three criteria: A practical test problem should have (1) controllability of the degree of overlap, (2) a known global optimum and (3) an uniform overlap structure. The following are some test problems which have been published, but all of them have shortcomings with regard to these criteria.

The Ising spin-glass problem [15] has been applied to test the performance of GAs [12, 18]. The simplest spin-glass system can be described by an energy function, H, defined over a set of spin variables $\sigma = \{\sigma_0, \sigma_1, \ldots, \sigma_{\ell-1}\}$ and a set of coupling constants J as

$$H(\sigma) = -\sum_{i=0}^{\ell-1}\sum_{j=0}^{\ell-1} J_{ij}\sigma_i\sigma_j.$$

Each spin variable σ_i can be either -1 or $+1$. Each coupling constant, $J_{ij} \in \{-1, +1\}$, relates a pair of spins σ_i and σ_j. If $J_{ij}\sigma_i\sigma_j = 1$, the coupling of σ_i and σ_j is satisfied. Given a set of coupling constants J, the objective is to find a set of spin values σ that minimizes the energy function H, or maximizes the number of satisfied couplings. Researchers have worked on a two-dimensional special case, where each spin variable interacts only with its neighbouring variables on a toroidal lattice, as in Figure 1. Each pair of interactive spin variables is regarded as a BB. As Figure 1 shows, the BB structure is always highly overlapping and is not adjustable. This is a shortcoming for further researches on the effect of varying overlap. Besides the two-dimensional special case, Pelikan *et al.* [13] used the Sherrington-Kirkpatrick (SK) spin-glass model with Gaussian couplings to show the performance of hBOA. However, finding ground states of the SK spin-glass model is an NP-complete problem. If we want to test how an arbitrary algorithm performs, using the SK spin-glass model is not convenient.

Yu *et al.* [20] proposed a test problem with circularly overlapping BBs only for theoretical developments. Based on this problem, Tsuji *et al.* [17] proposed a practical test problem with a known optimum and adjustable degrees of overlap. However, the overlap structure of this problem is based on samples from normal distributions and is non-uniform, so unexpected difficulties could be induced.

Pelikan *et al.* [14] used NK landscapes with nearest neighbor interactions and tunable overlap for performance testing. The problem formula is

$$f_{nk}(X_0, X_1, , X_{n-1}) = \sum_{i=0}^{\lfloor \frac{n-1}{step} \rfloor} f_i(X_{i \times step}, \Pi(X_i)).$$

This problem applies three parameters, n, k and $step$, which respectively represent the number of bits, the number of neighbors per bit and the step with which the basis bits are selected. X_i is the i-th bit, and $\Pi(X_i)$ is a set of k neighbors for X_i. The subfunction f_i defines a real value for each combination of values of X_i and $\Pi(X_i)$ as a lookup table with 2^{k+1} values. The parameter $step$ is used to tune the extend of overlap. By restricting neighborhoods to nearest neighbors, the problem can be solved in polynomial time using a dynamic programming algorithm. However, Lee and Yu [10] proposed a method to detecting the existence of building blocks. In their experiments, the probability that a random generated NK landscape problem forms a BB is about 50%.

Chang *et al.* designed a test problem [4] with a known global optimum, a uniform overlap structure and controllability of the degree of overlap. They claimed that it helps in further researches on overlapping BBs. Here is their approach. They reduce the procedure of building the overlap structure into a well-known problem, bipartite matching, which can be solved easily by the maximum flow algorithm [1]. To clearly define the concept of overlap, they define a variable, ω, as the number of subproblems to which a bit belongs. We can specify the size of a subproblem (k), the problem length (ℓ) and the desired ω ($\omega_{Desired}$). The problem consists of ℓ bits. If there are k different bits in each subproblem, with ℓ and $\omega_{Desired}$ given, the number of subproblems should be $m = \lfloor \ell \cdot \omega_{Desired}/k \rfloor$. In the bipartite matching problem, there are m nodes representing subproblems and ℓ nodes representing bits. An edge between the source and any node representing a subproblem has capacity of k. Because a bit could belong to any subproblem, every node representing a subproblem has ℓ edges, with capacity of 1, linked to all the nodes representing bits. In addition, every node representing a bit has an edge linked to the sink. By constricting the difference between any two flows on these edges to be 1 at most, we can find a solution of the maximal flow, as in Figure 2. Therefore, the uniformity is achieved and the average of ω among bits is always closed to $\omega_{Desired}$. The fitness function of the subproblems are specially designed so that if a GA cannot identify these subproblems, it requires an exponentially large population size for solving the problem. Thus, we can regard the subproblems as BBs of the test problem.

Chang *et al.* also mentioned that with overlapping BBs, local optima might not compose the global optimum [3]. They called this phenomenon conflict. Although their test problem has great features on investigating overlap among BBs, the experimental results show that the effects of conflict become minor as the degree of overlap increases. To illustrate the concept of conflict, take the two-dimensional Ising spin-glass system shown in Figure 1 as an example. In this example, spin variables 2 and 8 form an unsatified coupling. If we try to change the two values such that the coupling is satisfied, some satisfied coupling must become unsatisfied. That is, if the BB consisting of these two variables achieves its optimum, some other BBs must give up the optima. The BB has conflict with other BBs.

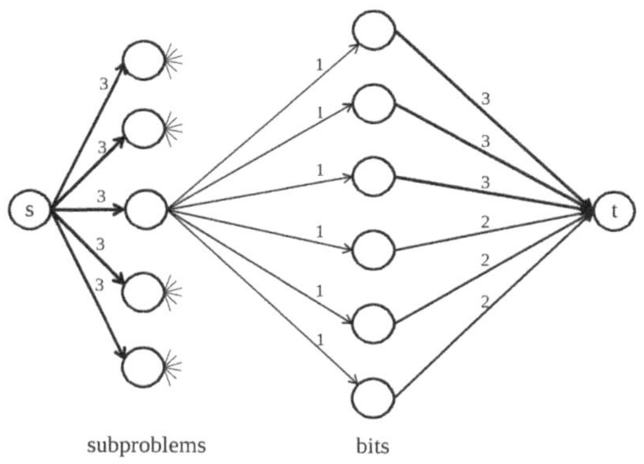

Figure 2: The flow graph of $\ell = 6$, $k = 3$, $\omega_{Desired} = 2.5$ proposed by Chang *et al.*

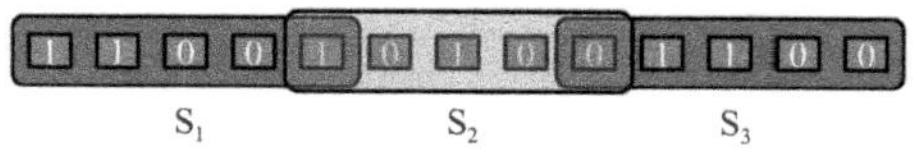

Figure 3: An example of fitness evaluation. This problem consists of three subproblems S_1, S_2 and S_3. Either S_1 or S_3 has fitness function V_1, and S_2 has fitness function V_0. The fitness value of the solution shown in this figure is $V_1(3) + V_0(2) + V_1(2)$.

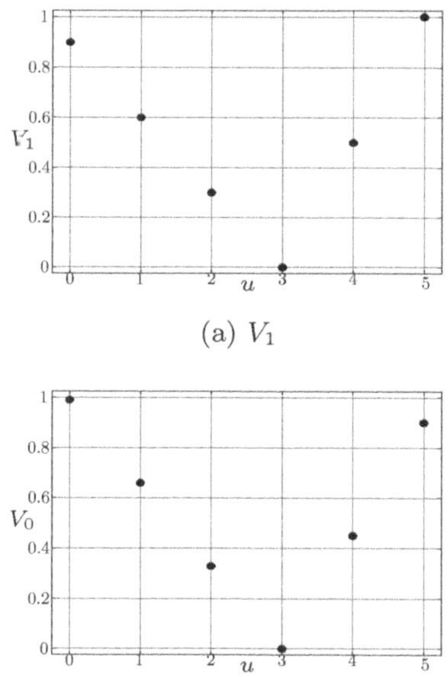

(a) V_1

(b) V_0

Figure 4: Functions V_1 and V_0 with $k = 5$, $t = 3$, $q = 0.9$ and $\epsilon = 0.01$.

Intuitively, a real-world problem with higher degree of either overlap or conflict is more difficult to solve. Hence, we design a new test problem with a different structure, which is described in the next section.

3. PROPOSED TEST PROBLEM

In this section, we first introduce our definitions of overlap and conflict among subproblems. After that, a new test problem with controllable degrees of overlap and conflict is proposed. This test problem still keeps the merits of a known global optimum and the uniformity.

3.1 Subproblems in the Test Problem

Our test problem consists of ℓ bits. Any bit in the problem belongs to at least one subproblem. Let u be the number of bits with a value of 1 in a solution to a subproblem. Here we define two functions V_1 and V_0 with respect to u as

$$V_1(u) = \begin{cases} \frac{t-u}{t} \cdot q & \text{if } u \le t \\ \frac{u-t}{k-t} & \text{if } u > t \end{cases}$$

and

$$V_0(u) = \begin{cases} \frac{t-u}{t} \cdot (1-\epsilon) & \text{if } u \le t \\ \frac{u-t}{k-t} \cdot q & \text{if } u > t \end{cases},$$

where k is the number of bits in each subproblem, t is an integer satisfying $0 < t < k$, q and ϵ are two real numbers satisfying $0 < q < 1$ and $0 < \epsilon < (1-q)$.

The fitness function of each subproblem is either V_1 or V_0. Given a set of bits, as a solution to a subproblem, we can compute u and find the fitness value of this set of bits. The fitness value of a solution to the test problem is the sum of the fitness values of all the solutions to subproblems, as in Figure 3.

When $t > k/2$, V_1 is a trap function which can mislead a GA. The power of misleading is controlled by the values of t and q. If a GA cannot identify trap functions in the problem, the GA theoretically needs an exponentially large population size. Subproblems with fitness function V_0 are used for confusing the GA. The optimal solution to V_0 is that all the bits are 0. Note that V_0 is not a trap function. If V_0 is also a trap function, it leads a GA to its local optimum, where all the bits are 1, and helps a GA search for the global optimum of the test problem instead. That is, the effects of confusion decrease if V_0 is a trap function. In addition, we also want that the global optimum of the problem is achieved when values of all the bits are 1 for convenience of analysis. The constant ϵ is defined for this purpose.

In our works, we set $k = 5$. This setting of the size of a subproblem has been practically applied to some former test problems mentioned above [20, 17, 4]. With $k = 5$, we find that $t = 3$, $q = 0.9$ and $\epsilon = 0.01$ bring out reasonably high difficulties. If the test problem is way too difficult for any GA to solve in polynomial time, we cannot observe the effects of overlap or conflict among BBs.

To sum up, in this paper, we have $k = 5$, $t = 3$, $q = 0.9$ and $\epsilon = 0.01$ in all the experiments. Functions V_1 and V_0 in this setting are shown in Figure 4. Researchers can use other values for further investigation.

3.2 Overlap and Conflict among Subproblems

Our definition of the degree of overlap, ω, is the average number of subproblems to which a bit belongs minus 1. This definition is similar to that of Chang *et al.* mentioned above, but we normalize the minimum value of ω to 0. Moreover, we need to define the degree of conflict, c, appropriately so that the difficulty of test function increases when c increases.

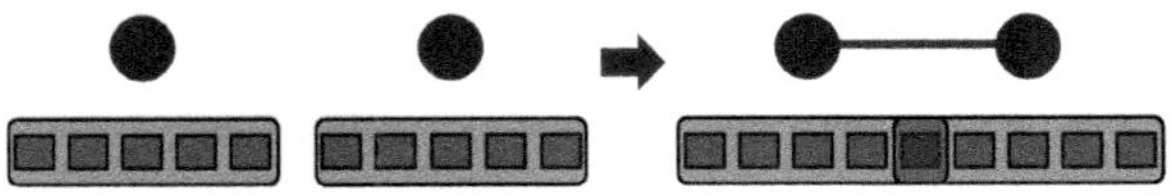

Figure 5: Representation of overlap relations. A node represents a subproblem, which consists five bits. An edge between two nodes indicates that the two corresponding subproblems share a bit.

Hence, we make subproblems with fitness function V_1 and subproblems with fitness function V_0 overlap. We let the degree of conflict, c, be the percentage of subproblems with fitness function V_0.

With l, the length of the problem, ω and c given, we can start to build the test problem. The structure of our test problem is transferred to a graph for convenience of understanding. In the graph, each subproblems is represented by a node. If two subproblems overlap each other, we use an edge to link the two corresponding nodes as in Figure 5. Moreover, a subproblem with fitness function V_1 is represented by a black node and a subproblem with fitness function V_0 is represented by a white node.

The following are some important equations we need to build the structure of the desired problem. According to the definition of ω, the number of subproblems each bit expectedly belongs to, we have

$$\omega = \frac{mk}{\ell} - 1, \tag{1}$$

where m is the number of subproblems and k is the number of bits in each subproblem.

Next, if we add an edge between two nodes, that is, to make two subproblems overlap on a bit, the number of bits decreases by 1. Initially, the number of bits is mk when the subproblems do not overlap. The value should be decreased to ℓ, the given problem size. Let the number of edges that we need on the graph be e, and we thus have

$$e = m \cdot k - \ell. \tag{2}$$

Now we consider conflict among subproblems. Let m_1 be the number of subproblems with fitness function V_1 and m_0 be the number of problems with fitness function V_0. We know

$$m_1 + m_0 = m \tag{3}$$

and

$$c = \frac{m_0}{m}, \tag{4}$$

according the definition of the degree of conflict c.

With $k = 5$ fixed, given ℓ and ω, we can compute m, rounded to the nearest integer, in Equation 1. We can also compute e in Equation 2. Given c, Equations 3 and 4 can help us find m_1 and m_0.

3.3 Building the Problem

After the values of m, m_0 and e are computed, we can build the main structure of the problem. We should add e edges among the m nodes and make the edges uniformly distributed on the graph. We also need to assign m_0 nodes to be white and the others are assigned to be black. Moreover, every white node must share an edge with a different black node in order that this problem has a known global optimum, which is described later. The steps of building the structure are listed in Algorithm 1 and are illustrated in Figures 6 and 7. With this algorithm, if we have $m_0 \leq m_1$, or $2m_0 \leq m$, we can make sure that the first m_0 edges connect $2m_0$ different nodes. Thus, each of the m_0 chosen white nodes shares an edge with a different black node.

Algorithm 1 Steps of building the test problem

Require: k, the size of a subproblem; m, the number of nodes; m_0, the number of white nodes; e, the required number of edges.

Ensure: A test problem with the required structure.

1: Create a graph G with m nodes representing subproblems. (See Figure 6(a).)
2: Create mk disjoint sets, each of which contains one bit. Let each of the mk bits belong to only one subproblem.
3: **while** (the number of edges on G) $< e$ **do**
4: Among all the pairs of two nodes which do not share an edge, choose a pair of nodes with the lowest number of edges linked to other nodes. Ties in the numbers are broken at random. (We assume $e \leq m(m-1)/2$.)
5: Choose one bit in each corresponding subproblem of the two nodes determined in the previous step such that the set to which the bit belongs has the lowest number of elements. Ties in the numbers are broken at random.
6: Add an edge between the two chosen nodes and union the two sets to which the two chosen bits belong. (See Figure 6(b).)
7: **end while**
8: For each of the first m_0 added edges, assign one of its two ends to be white. Assign the other nodes to be black. (We assume $e \leq m(m-1)/2$. See Figure 6(c).)
9: Now the number of disjoint sets is ℓ. Index all the sets in an arbitrary order. The index of each disjoint set represents a position on the test problem.
10: As in Figure 7, if two or more bits belong to one disjoint set, they actually represent only one bit which is shared by two or more subproblems. We have the required problem structure.

Here are some constraints on the values of ℓ, ω and c, which should be satisfied due to the assumptions in Algorithm 1.

1. Practically, the value of ℓ should not be less than 20 since the problem could be easily solved by an exhaustive search method.

2. We assume $e \leq m(m-1)/2$ so that any pair of subproblems could overlap on at most one bit. If we have $k = 5$ and $l \geq 20$, we can show that the assumption always holds, by solving the quadratic inequality

$$mk - \ell \leq \frac{m(m-1)}{2}$$

with respect to m.

3. If the inequality above holds, the value of ω only has to satisfy $\omega \geq 0$. However, if the degree of overlap is unrealistically large, the problem might lose the meaning of BBs to some extent.

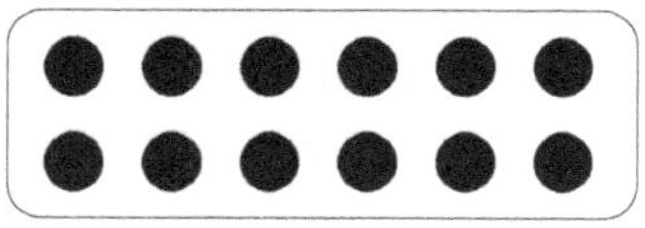

(a) We have $k = 5$, $\ell = 50$, $\omega = 0.2$ and $c = 0.25$ for example. First, we create $m = \ell(\omega + 1)/k = 12$ nodes on G.

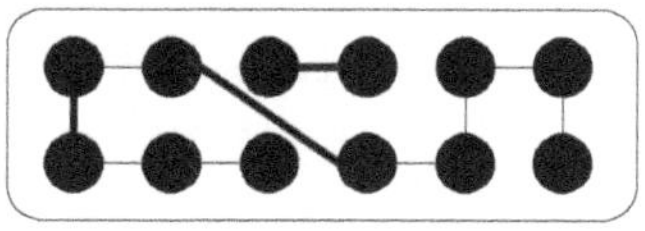

(b) Second, we make $e = mk - \ell = 10$ edges uniformly distributed among the nodes. The thicker lines represent the first m_0 added edges, where $m_0 = cm = 3$.

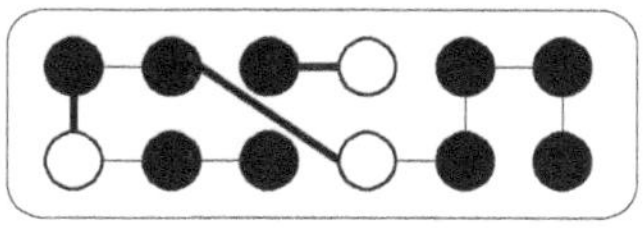

(c) Finally, we choose one end for each of the first m_0 added edges and assign these m_0 nodes to be white.

Figure 6: An example graph building process.

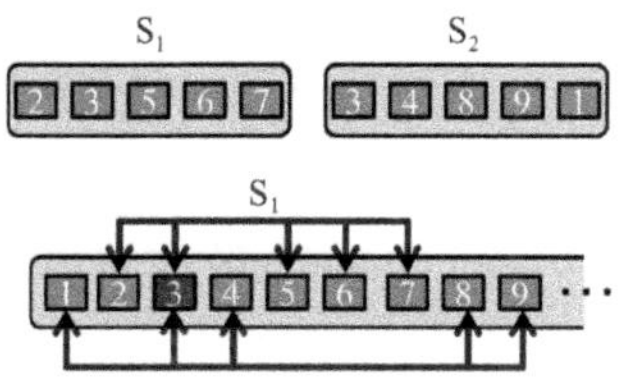

Figure 7: An example of the indices of sets. S_1 and S_2 are two subproblems. Either S_1 or S_2 has a bit which belongs to disjoint set 3. That is, the two subproblems share the third bit in the test problem.

4. We assume $0 \leq m_0 \leq m_1$. Since $m_0 = cm$ and $m_1 = (1 - c)m$ the value of c have to satisfy

$$0 \leq c \leq 0.5.$$

5. Assuming $e \geq m_0$, we have $mk - \ell \geq cm$. Substituting $m = \ell(\omega + 1)/k$ in it, we get a constraint

$$c \leq k(1 - \frac{1}{\omega + 1}).$$

For example, if we set ω to be 0, the value of c can only be 0. It is reasonable because we cannot induce conflict when no overlap exists.

3.4 The Computation of the Global Optimum

Whenever we use this test problem to test the ability of a GA, we need to know the global optimum of this problem. Given the setting of constants k, t, q and ϵ above, we can easily find the global optimum. If a different setting is applied, this test problem may have a different optimum.

In the structure mentioned above, there are black nodes $p_1, p_2, \ldots, p_{m_1}$ and white nodes $q_1, q_2, \ldots, q_{m_0}$ on the graph, where $m_1 \geq m_0$. We know that every white node is linked to one different black node at least. Without loss of generality, let q_i be linked to p_i for $1 \leq i \leq m_0$. Here we prove that the global optimum of this test function is $m_1 + 0.9 \cdot m_0$. Recall that p_i has fitness function V_1 and q_i has fitness function V_0, and the two functions are shown in Figure 4. The upper bound of the fitness value of a pair (p_i, q_i) is $1+0.9 = 1.9$, which can be verified by enumerating the possibilities. Hence, the global optimum of the whole graph is not greater than $1.9 \cdot m_0 + 1 \cdot (m_1 - m_0) = m_1 + 0.9 \cdot m_0$. Moreover, when we set all the values of the bits to 1, the overall fitness is $m_1 + 0.9 \cdot m_0$. Thus, if all the bits in the problem have the values of 1, the GA achieves the global optimum.

4. EXPERIMENTS

In this section, we briefly describe the mechanism for three model building GAs and the experiments we have done. hBOA [11] and DSMGA [19] are known to be able to cope with overlapping BBs, with the reasons described below. We also introduce a crossover method, SBS proposed by Yu *et al.* [18]. We use DSMGA with SBS and hBOA to solve our test problem to see the relation between their performance and the degrees of overlap and conflict among BBs. In addition, ECGA [8], which has no ability to store information about overlapping BBs in its model, is tested as comparison.

In our experiment, we set the upper bound for ω to be 1. We find that the problem is hard for the three GAs to solve when ω is larger than 1. Therefore, we examine previous works to find the reasonable range.

For the circular overlapping test function with 5-bit trap subfunction proposed by Yu *et al.* [20], ω would be $(\frac{5\ell-2}{3\ell} - 1)$, which is less than 1. The overlapping test function proposed by Tsuji *et al.* [17] has the same ω value as the circular overlapping test function above. The degree of overlap defined by us is different from that defined by Tsuji *et al.* The higher σ value in their test problem makes the positions of overlapped bits more scattered throughout the whole problem. However, σ does not affect how many subproblem a bit belongs averagely.

For a instance of NK landscape problems with nearest neighbor interactions [14], there exists $\frac{n-k}{step}$ subproblems with a length of $(k+1)$, and k subproblems with lengths which range from k to 1. Therefore, we can calculate the degree of overlap, ω, of this problem as

$$\frac{1}{n}\left(\frac{(k+1)(n-k)}{step}+\frac{(k+1)k}{2}\right)-1.$$

This NK landscape problem have the highest degree of overlap when the parameter $step$ is set to be 1. However, we consider the reasonable overlap degree to be at most 2 bits for subproblems with a length of 5 bits. With this assumption, we set k to be 4 and $step$ to be 3 in an NK landscape problem. Therefore, we can get ω of this problem to be $(\frac{5}{3}+\frac{10}{3n}-1)$, which is less than 1 even if n is set to be 20, let alone larger problem sizes. Consequently, we think that setting the upper bound for ω to be 1 is sufficient.

4.1 Extended Compact Genetic Algorithm (ECGA)

ECGA is proposed by Harik. To learn the BB model, Shannon's entropy is utilized to indicate the interactions among genes. To prevent from overfitting, the minimum description length (MDL) principle [2] is taken as the criterion. We want to minimize the length, in bits, to describe the model and the data. Shannon's entropy is taken as length in the sense that if there are fewer interactions among variables, we become more uncertain for their relationship, and the entropy among them is higher, which means that the length of an effective description of one variable is longer. The reason for minimizing the description length is from the philosophy of Occam's razor. If there are two models describing the data with the same accuracy, we choose the simpler one. To sum up, the model building process in ECGA is just like simple hill climbing. Initially each variable forms a separate group. Then two groups are merged for the best reduction of the description length, iteratively.

Since the model building process of ECGA does not have the mechanism that makes one variable belong to two or more building blocks, it might be difficult for ECGA to solve the problem with overlapping and conflicting BBs.

4.2 Hierarchical Bayesian Optimization Algorithm (hBOA)

hBOA, a modified version of the Bayesian optimization algorithm (BOA), is proposed by Pelikan and Goldberg. hBOA has shown its ability to solve the Ising spin-glass problem, a problem which has highly overlapping BBs [12]. The essential part of the ability lies in the Bayesian network (BN) structure. It is widely used to represent the dependencies among variables. In hBOA, the BN is learned from the selected candidate populations and is applied to describe the dependencies among genes. Every generation is sampled by the forward algorithm from the BN.

4.3 Dependency Structure Matrix Genetic Algorithm (DSMGA) and Strength-Based Sampling (SBS)

DSMGA is proposed by Yu *et al.* The concept of a dependency structure matrix (DSM) is borrowed from organization theories. DSMGA represents dependencies among variables by mutual information, and each entry in the DSM describes whether or not dependencies between two variables exceed some threshold. By the technique of DSM clustering, we can rearrange the order so that genes corresponding to dependent variables become closer on a chromosome. The DSM clustering method also utilizes the concept of MDL. Given a DSM, this method finds a model that minimizes the sum of the model description length and the mismatched data description length. The DSM structure can contain the information of overlap between two BBs. DSMGA is thus capable of dealing with problems that have overlapping BBs.

In our experiments, we select the strength-based sampling (SBS) as the crossover operator in DSMGA. SBS is proposed by Yu *et al.* They define the strength of a BB as the degree of disruption when the BB is crossed in the middle. With the definition of the strength, SBS works as follows to decide the alleles of genes. A BB is defined to be decided if it contains at least one decided gene. If no undecided BB is overlapped with a decided BB, we select the strongest BB. Otherwise, we choose the strongest undecided BB which is overlapped by some decided BB. After deciding a BB, an undecided gene, g_x, in the BB is randomly select. If any gene related to g_x has not been decided, the allele of g_x is sampled by the marginal probability, which is generated from the mating pool. Otherwise, the allele is sampled by conditional probability given the alleles of decided neighbors of g_x. As a result, genes in a stronger BB are decided earlier, whereas genes in a weaker BB are decided according the conditional probability distribution given the decided alleles. Therefore, SBS can achieve higher information exchange rate and reduce the disruption of overlap.

4.4 The Experimental Results

The purpose of our test problem is to find the relationships between the performance of GAs and the degrees of overlap and conflict among BBs. Thus, we conduct some experiments to find the number of function evaluations (NFE) required for each of the three GAs to solve the test problem. For each of the GAs, the following experiments are done.

We fix ℓ at 100. Given different settings of ω and c, we can build several different graphs, which represent problems with different degrees of overlap and conflict among BBs. We first use bisections with 10 successive runs to ensure the required population size for each problem. The convergent criterion is that the GA finds out the global optimum. With the required population size, we have the average NFE required for 10 successive runs. For each setting of ω and c, we generate 10 different problems since there is randomness in the graph building process, and repeat the above procedures for each of these problems. Finally, we compute the average NFE, with the maximum and the minimum eliminated, as the results of this experiment. The maximum NFE in our experiments is set to 10^7.

The experimental results are shown in Tables 1, 2 and 3 and Figures 8 and 9. The minus symbols in these tables represent that we cannot create such problems with the desired values of ω and c due to the constraints which are mentioned in Section 3.3. The abbreviation CNS in Tables 1 and 3 means that the GA cannot solve the problem under the constraint on the NFE.

The results show that ECGA, which lacks the ability to deal with an overlapping sturcture, cannot solve problems with ω more than 0.1 or c more than 0.05. For the other two GAs with ability to cope with overlapping and conflicting

Table 1: NFE required by ECGA.

ω	c = 0.0	0.05	0.1
0.0	286,395	–	–
0.05	586,434	752,295	CNS
0.1	CNS	CNS	CNS

Table 2: NFE required by hBOA.

ω	c = 0.0	0.1	0.2	0.3	0.4	0.5
0.0	37,046	–	–	–	–	–
0.1	34,232	36,056	41,559	49,264	56,946	–
0.2	30,607	40,929	42,391	46,635	55,845	58,894
0.3	34,607	42,198	51,593	53,676	52,254	67,478
0.4	42,235	49,853	51,667	57,711	65,915	79,650
0.5	46,554	54,138	63,205	76,150	80,235	90,954
0.6	56,705	61,586	77,255	86,044	101,476	126,051
0.7	65,495	77,713	93,363	103,109	137,605	171,947
0.8	73,842	90,798	104,938	145,536	181,004	234,095
0.9	94,034	110,372	148,089	174,829	231,098	318,008
1.0	107,882	140,830	177,426	224,878	314,090	374,988

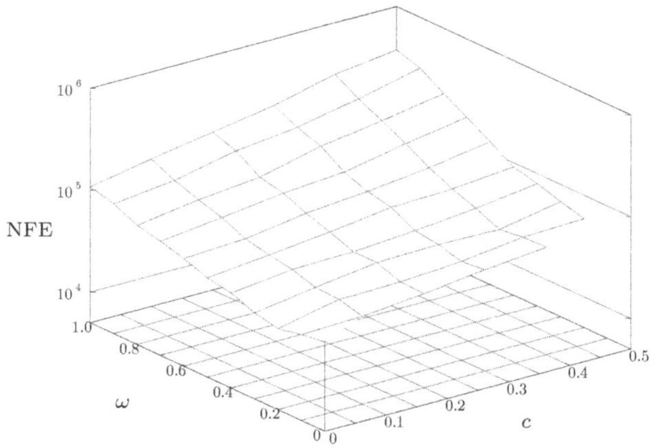

Figure 8: NFE required by hBOA.

BBs, the results show that the difficulty increases as the degree of overlap or conflict increases.

5. CONCLUSION

The main purpose for this paper is to design a test problem as a robust and flexible benchmark to evaluate GAs. We first take a second thought on the definition of the degrees of overlap and conflict among subproblems. Then we design a new test problem structure in order to overcome shortcomings of previous works. We define the degree of overlap, which is the average subproblems to which a gene belongs minus 1, and the degree of conflict, which is the percentage of subproblems with fitness function V_0. Experiments on any desired degree of overlap and conflict can be easily implemented, under clean constraints on the input parameters ℓ, ω and c. With this new test problem, three GAs are tested. The experimental results indicate that our test problem becomes more difficult when the degree of overlap or conflict becomes higher. With those attributes, the proposed test problem is more scalable for further researches on overlapping and conflicting BBs than previous works are.

One of the key topics for future work is to discover how overlapping and conflicting subproblems affect problem difficulties for different GAs. Second, although the parameter ω is a possible definition for the concept of overlap, it is an approximation in terms of using average number of

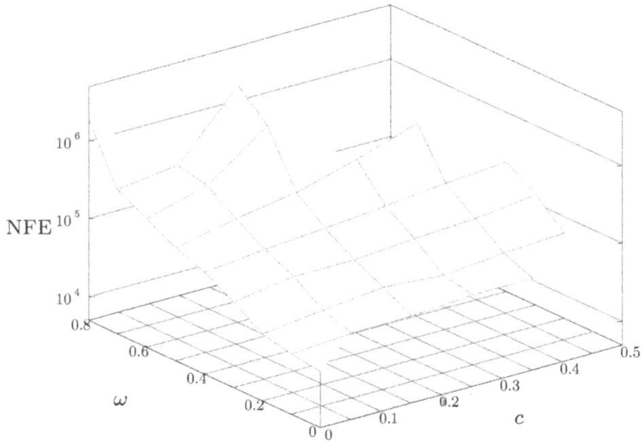

Figure 9: NFE required by DSMGA with SBS.

Table 3: NFE required by DSMGA with SBS.

ω	c = 0.0	0.1	0.2	0.3	0.4	0.5
0.0	26,028	–	–	–	–	–
0.1	29,522	33,427	33,879	39,200	39,572	–
0.2	35,466	44,170	53,939	47,475	55,522	61,444
0.3	61,522	80,612	82,076	92,664	102,607	129,107
0.4	100,762	121,310	137,454	165,044	197,575	231,017
0.5	138,493	200,774	265,900	441,474	778,403	CNS
0.6	217,776	359,813	1,304,350	CNS	CNS	CNS
0.7	350,595	444,066	2,860,840	CNS	CNS	CNS
0.8	1,830,910	CNS	CNS	CNS	CNS	CNS

subproblems to which a variable belongs. Tsuji *et al.* [17] proposed another view to describe overlap, which indicates how complex the overlapping structure is rather than how many subproblems a variable belongs to. We could find a more proper description to define this phenomenon because different factors that affect problem difficulties might exist. Finally, another possible direction for extending our proposed model is to consider non-binary functions. Many discrete real-world problems are non-binary and difficult to model.

6. REFERENCES

[1] R. K. Ahuja, T. L. Magnanti, and J. B. Orlin. *Network Flows: Theory, Algorithms, and Applications.* Prentice Hall, Englewood Cliffs, NJ, 1993.

[2] A. Barron, J. Rissenen, and B. Yu. The MDL principle in coding and modeling. *IEEE Transactions on Information Theory*, 44(6):2743–2760, 1998.

[3] J.-H. Chang, C.-H. Hsueh, H. Lee, T.-L. Yu, and T.-Y. Ho. A test function with full controllability over overlapping and confliction between sub-problems. TEIL Report No. 2011003, National Taiwan University, Taipei, Taiwan, July 2011.

[4] J.-H. Chang, C.-H. Hsueh, H. Lee, T.-L. Yu, and T.-Y. Ho. A test function with full controllability over overlapping: estimation of distribution algorithms. In *GECCO (Companion)*, pages 61–62. ACM, 2011.

[5] D. E. Goldberg. *Genetic Algorithms in Search, Optimization, and Machine Learning.* Addison-Wesley, Reading, MA, 1989.

[6] D. E. Goldberg. *The design of innovation: Lessons from and for competent genetic algorithms.* Kluwer Academic Publishers, Boston, MA, 2002.

[7] D. E. Goldberg, K. Deb, and J. H. Clark. Genetic algorithms, noise, and the sizing of populations. *Complex Systems*, 6:333–362, 1992.

[8] G. Harik. Linkage learning via probabilistic modeling in the ECGA. IlliGAL Report No. 99010, University of Illinois at Urbana-Champaign, Urbana, IL, February 1999.

[9] J. H. Holland. *Adaptation in natural and artificial systems.* University of Michigan Press, Ann Arbor, MI, 1975.

[10] H. Lee and T.-L. Yu. Off-line building block identification: Detecting building blocks directly from fitness without genetic algorithms. *Proceedings of the Genetic and Evolutionary Computation Conference (GECCO-2012)*, 2012.

[11] M. Pelikan and D. E. Goldberg. Escaping hierarchical traps with competent genetic algorithms. *Proceedings of the Genetic and Evolutionary Computation Conference (GECCO-2001)*, pages 511–518, 2001.

[12] M. Pelikan and D. E. Goldberg. Hierarchical BOA solves Ising spin glasses and MAXSAT. *Proceedings of the Genetic and Evolutionary Computation Conference (GECCO-2003)*, pages 1271–1282, 2003.

[13] M. Pelikan, K. G. Helmut, and S. Kobe. Finding ground states of sherrington-kirkpatrick spin glasses with hierarchical boa and genetic algorithms. *Proceedings of the Genetic and Evolutionary Computation Conference (GECCO-2008)*, pages 447–454, 2008.

[14] M. Pelikan, K. Sastry, D. E. Goldberg, M. V. Butz, and M. Hauschild. Performance of evolutionary algorithms on nk landscapes with nearest neighbor interactions and tunable overlap. *Proceedings of the Genetic and Evolutionary Computation Conference (GECCO-2009)*, pages 851–858, 2009.

[15] D. Sherrington and S. Kirkpatrick. Solvable model of a spin-glass. *Phys. Rev. Lett.*, 35:1792–1796, 1975.

[16] D. Thierens and D. E. Goldberg. Mixing in genetic algorithms. *Proceedings of the Fifth International Conference on Genetic Algorithms*, pages 38–45, 1993.

[17] M. Tsuji, M. Munetomo, and K. Akama. A crossover for complex building blocks overlapping. *Proceedings of the Genetic and Evolutionary Computation Conference (GECCO-2006)*, pages 1337–1344, 2006.

[18] T.-L. Yu, D. E. Goldberg, K. Sastry, C. F. Lima, and M. Pelikan. Dependency structure matrix, genetic algorithms ,and effective recombination. *Evolutionary Computation*, vol. 17, no. 4, pp. 595–626, 2009.

[19] T.-L. Yu, D. E. Goldberg, A. Yassine, and Y.-p. Chen. Genetic algorithm design inspired by organizational theory: Pilot study of a dependency structure matrix driven genetic algorithm. *Proceedings of Artificial Neural Networks in Engineering (ANNIE 2003)*, pages 327–332, 2003.

[20] T.-L. Yu, K. Sastry, and D. E. Goldberg. Linkage learning, overlapping building blocks, and systematic strategy for scalable recombination. *Proceedings of the Genetic and Evolutionary Computation Conference (GECCO-2005)*, pages 1217–1224, 2005.

Higher-Order Linkage Learning in the ECGA

David Iclănzan
Babes-Bolyai University, Department of Computer Science
Str. Mihail Kogalniceanu no. 1, Cluj-Napoca, Romania
david.iclanzan@gmail.com

ABSTRACT

In this paper, we present a higher-order dependency identification algorithm for binary variables that employs a novel metric to detect linkages. The proposed method applies an entropy distillation operation over bounded groups of variables. Lack of increase in randomness signals an underlaying statistical dependence between the inputs.

We incorporate the higher order linkage learning in the Extended Compact Genetic Algorithm (ECGA). Experiments show that the extended linkage learning enables the ECGA to correctly model and solve problems with bounded-order building-blocks that do not contain pairwise dependencies.

Categories and Subject Descriptors

I.2.8 [**Artificial Intelligence**]: Problem Solving, Control Methods and Search

General Terms

Algorithms, Design, Theory

Keywords

linkage learning, higher order statistics, entropy distillation

1. INTRODUCTION

Successful solving of nearly-decomposable problems by competent selecto-recombinative algorithms depends on the proper processing of the partial sub-solutions, also referred as building-blocks [5]. Estimation of Distribution Algorithms (EDAs) [14, 17, 16] or probabilistic model-building genetic algorithms (PMBGAs) [20] use interaction detection techniques designed to decompose the boundedly difficult problems on the fly by adapting the linkage model.

Always finding an accurate model is not a trivial endeavor as exploration of higher order dependencies is a computationally expensive task being exponential in the size of interactions covered. A common approach and efficient computational shortcut employed by linkage learning methods is to begin the construction of higher order models by exploiting pairwise dependencies. Therefore, decomposable problems lacking or exhibiting only a low degree of pairwise dependencies are hard for current linkage learning mechanisms and consequently can be very hard to optimize [10, 1, 2].

The "innovation time" (linkage learning) of recombinative algorithms must be less than the "takeover or convergence time" (mixing and decision making between competing building-blocks) [6]. Thus, the precision of the linkage model in early iterations is highly critical for problems where the repeated mixing of sub-solutions is required [10]. Without a proper linkage model, the takeover and convergence mechanism will operate on an incomplete set of building-blocks, leading to allelic premature convergence.

In this paper we introduce a novel higher order interaction detection technique for binary variables and incorporate it in the Extended Compact Genetic Algorithm (ECGA) [8, 7]. Our method exploits the property of the exclusive or (XOR) operator to produce randomness from a non-deterministic source. The method searches for groups of variables where entropy distillation does not occur, signaling a non-determinism in the source - statistical dependence between the variables.

The ECGA with higher-order linkage learning is used to solve instances of problems containing bounded-order building-blocks exhibiting pairwise allelic independence.

Albeit a costly search for the groups of variables must be performed, this approach can solve problems that are intractable by pairwise linkage exploitation. For other cases it can facilitate a fast convergence, requiring an order of magnitudes less objective function evaluations, than approaches that do not correctly model the higher-order dependencies.

The rest of the paper is organized as follows: in section 2 we discuss the issue of detecting higher-order linkages for functions that do not contain pairwise low-order dependencies. Section 3 introduces a novel multivariate linkage detection method, where a bounded order search is performed for variables where the XOR operation does not lead to entropy distillation. Section 4 presents the ECGA and the incorporation of the new linkage detection mechanism. The test functions are described in section 5, while section 6 presents the experimental results. Conclusions and further work is outlined in section 7.

2. DETECTING GROUPS OF DEPENDENT VARIABLES

Binary problems of real interest may have many variables with complicated multivariate interactions among them. For these problem pairwise dependencies might be very small or lacking altogether. Finding the adequate linkage model for problems containing such dependencies is a hard task. Prospective methods must combine an extensive higher order model search guided by a criteria that evaluates the quality of the model in rapport with the evidence, like the Minimum Description Length (MDL) principle [21] or Bayesian-Dirichlet metric [18].

2.1 Complexity of multivariate linkage detection

The complexity of the model determination is a product of the complexity of the search and candidate model evaluation.

For problems where statistical dependence can only be detected by considering at least k variables, the search must enumerate at least all combinations of variables taken k at the time. Thus the run-time cost of the model determination will be:

$$T(M_{(n,k)}) = O(n^k)T_E(m_k) \tag{1}$$

where n is the number of variables and $T_E(m_k)$ is the run-time cost of the model quality discriminant function.

2.2 Model discriminant function

An ordered tuple of binary random variables $X = (X_1, X_2, \ldots, X_n)$ is independent iff the joint distribution $Pr(X_1 = x_1, X_2 = x_2, \ldots, X_n = x_n)$ and the product of the independent ones $\prod_{k=1}^{n} Pr(X_k = x_k)$ is equal for all $x = (x_1, x_2, \ldots, x_n) \in \{0,1\}^n$.

Relative entropy or *Kullback-Leibler divergence* [3] can be used to measure the "distance" between these two distributions:

$$D_{KL}(p||q) = \sum_{x \in X} p(x) \log_2 \left(\frac{p(x)}{q(x)} \right) \tag{2}$$

Measuring the D_{KL} between the observed joint distribution of some variables and the product of independent joint distribution one can measure the information gain by considering a group of variables linked.

The complexity of calculating D_{KL} is exponential in k with a base equal to the cardinality of the random variables. Thus, for the binary case $T_E(m_k) = O(2^k)$.

In the following we consider ways in which the complexity of the model discriminatory function can be heavily reduced for the binary case.

3. XOR BASED MULTIVARIATE LINKAGE DETECTION

Most practical sources of randomness, be it hardware or pseudo-random number generators, exhibit a certain level of imperfection or bias. A perfectly random bit has an entropy of one bit and bias of 0. To obtain a highly random bit, there are algorithms that combine multiple, streams of imperfect random bits, each with entropy less than one, to create a single bit with entropy one and bias 0. This process is called entropy distillation or entropy extraction.

3.1 Exclusive OR and entropy distillation

Exclusive OR (XOR, also denoted by $\otimes$) is commonly used to reduce the bias from imperfectly random bits, provided that the random bits are statistically independent.

The reduction in bias by repeatedly applying the XOR on non-deterministic inputs can be computed using the Piling-Up Lemma [15].

LEMMA 3.1. *Let X_i for $i \in \overline{1,n}$ be statistically independent random binary variables, where p_i is the probability that $X_i = 0$ and $\epsilon_i = p_i - 1/2$ are the biases. Then the probability that $X_1 \otimes X_2 \otimes \ldots \otimes X_n = 0$ is*

$$\frac{1}{2} + 2^{n-1} \prod_{i=1}^{n} \epsilon_i \tag{3}$$

Note that as biases $\epsilon_i \in [0,1]$ their product is a monotonically decreasing function. If any of the ϵ's is zero, that is, one of the binary variables is unbiased, the resulting probability function will be unbiased. Also, performing an XOR with a constant variable having $p_i = 0$ or $p_i = 1$ i.e a maximum bias of $\epsilon_i = \pm 1/2$ will not reduce the bias.

In our algorithm we will apply the XOR operation in a sequential manner, performing in each step the operation between a variable X_i and the result $Y = X_1 \otimes X_2 \otimes \ldots \otimes X_{i-1}$ of the repeated XOR up to that variable i. Therefore, we take a closer look on the expected result of XOR for two variables.

LEMMA 3.2. *If X and Y are independent random binary variables with expectations $E(X) = \mu$ and $E(Y) = \nu$ then*

$$E(X \otimes Y) = \mu + \nu - 2\mu\nu \tag{4}$$

$$= \frac{1}{2} - 2(\mu - \frac{1}{2})(\nu - \frac{1}{2}) \tag{5}$$

PROOF. Following from the logical table of the XOR, for two bits a and b, $a \otimes b$ equals 1 if $a = 0$ and $b = 1$ or if $a = 1$ and $b = 0$.

Thus, $E(X \otimes Y)$ can be written as

$$\begin{aligned} E(X \otimes Y) &= (1-\mu)\nu + \mu(1-\nu) \\ &= \mu + \nu - 2\mu\nu\nu \\ &= \mu + \nu - 2\mu\nu + \frac{1}{2} - \frac{1}{2} \\ &= \frac{1}{2} - 2\left[\mu\nu - \frac{\mu}{2} - \frac{\nu}{2} + \frac{1}{4}\right] \\ &= \frac{1}{2} - 2(\mu - \frac{1}{2})(\nu - \frac{1}{2}) \end{aligned}$$

□

3.2 XOR based dependency detection

The Piling-Up Lemma is successfully used in linear cryptanalysis to construct linear approximation to the action of non-linear block ciphers. In this application, the X_i-s are approximations to the substitution-boxes of block ciphers for which the biases are trivial to measure. The attack relies on performing a costly search for finding combinations of input and output values that have very high biases i.e probabilities very close of zero or one.

In our vision a similar approach can also be used for linkage detection: a search is performed to find groups of variables for which the actual probability mass of the result obtained by performing the XOR greatly differs from the value predicted by the Piling-Up Lemma. For these cases the high bias must come from the fact that the assumption of non-determinism is not satisfied. Thus, there is an underlaying statistical dependence between the inputs. If the absolute

```
function
FindLinkages(st,idx,k,n,xr,xi,
            f,X,pX,thr,LinkageModel)
{
  /*compute start index, and
    initialize XOR results on the 1'st level*/
  if (idx == 0)
  {
    si = 0;  xr(:,0) = X(:,0); xi(0) = pX(0);
  }
  else
    si = st(idx-1) + 1;

  for (i = si; i < n; i++)
  {
    st(idx) = i;
    if (idx > 0)
    {
      //compute XOR result
      xr(:,idx) = xr(:,idx-1) ⊗  X(:,i);

      /*if variables are independent
        this should be the expected
        nr. of 0's as of Eq.  ?? */
      xi(idx) = xi(idx-1) + pX(i)
            - 2*xi(idx-1)*pX(i);

      //compute the actual nr. of 0's
      f(idx) = nrZerosIn(xr(:,idx));
      f(idx) /= nrRowsIn(X);

      //compute the difference
      diff = xi(idx) - f(idx);

      /*if it is significant, retain
        the interdependent variables*/
      if (|diff| > thr)
        LinkageModel.Add(st,idx);
    }
    if (idx < k)
      //recursive call
      FindLinkages(st,idx+1,k,n,xr,xi
                  f,X,pX,thr,LinkageModel);
  }
}
```

Figure 1: The proposed search implemented as a recursive backtracking algorithm.

value of the resulting bias is greater than a threshold, then we will consider the variables as linked in our linkage model.

The proposed metric has a great complexity advantage, as performing k consecutive XOR operations in linear.

While the approach is efficient in detecting multivariate dependences, we still have to perform an ample search to find the groups of variables that are linked.

3.3 Searching for the linkage structure

In order to enable the solving of boundedly difficult problems, we must be able detect multivariate dependencies from n variables up to order k ($k << n$). For this we perform a search over all combinations up to order k and we use the measure in the previous subsection to detect dependencies.

The proposed search algorithm is presented in Fig. 1.

The notations, parameters and variables used in the search algorithms are detailed in the following:

- the ":" denotes the colon operator as used in Matlab or Octave colon notation for selecting ranges of a dimension. Thus, $X(:,i)$ denotes the ith column of X.
- n, k - n is the number of variables while k is the size limit on the order of dependencies explored.
- st, idx - represent the stack and the actual level in the stack, variables needed for the recursive backtracking.
- X - is a binary matrix of size $m \times n$, where m is the number of observations. Thus each column of X corresponds to one of the n variables.
- pX - is a vector containing the approximated probability mass functions of the n variables. $pX(i)$ is just the number of ones in the ith column of X, divided by the number of observations m.
- thr - is a predefined threshold used to decide if the detected amount of dependency should be deemed relevant or not.
- $LinkageModel$ - is a list that collects the detected building-blocks.
- xr - is a binary matrix of m rows and idx columns. Each column i contains the result of applying repeatedly XOR to the variables contained in st up to the level i. For example, if $idx = 4$, thus the stack contains for values $st = 2, 6, 7, 9$, then the first column of xr just equals $X_{st(0)} = X_2$ as there are no lower levels to XOR with. The second column will be $X_2 \otimes X_6$, the third $X_2 \otimes X_6 \otimes X_7$ and finally, the last column will be the result of $X_2 \otimes X_6 \otimes X_7 \otimes 9$. There is no need to recompute the entire series of XOR-s at each level, as for columns greater than one the $xr(:,i) = xr(:,i-1) \otimes X(:,st(i))$ recursive relation holds.
- xi - is a vector of length idx, containing for each level i the *expected* probability mass function of the result of applying repeatedly XOR to the variables contained in st up to the level i *under the assumption of statistical independence.*
- f - is a vector of length idx, containing for each level i the *actual* probability mass function of the result of applying repeatedly XOR to the variables contained in st up to the level i.
- $diff$ - is the difference between the expected and actual probability mass functions of the result.

The algorithm explores all combination of variables up to level k. As the XOR operation is associative, each combination is generated and analyzed only once. This is achieved by enforcing an increasing order of the elements in the stack. Hereby, each dependent group of variables is detected and added to the linkage model only once.

The presented backtracking algorithm often recomputes large subtrees. However, trying to cache partial results in order to avoid recomputation would quickly hit the available memory barrier for large problems.

In a post processing step, in order to minimize disruption, we process the resulting building-block list $LinkageModel$ and remove the nodes containing building-blocks that are subsets of any other building-block. Also in this step, if an allele is not contained in any linkage group, it is added to the list as an elementary building-block. Thus, for 10 variables and the linkage model { (1,3,5), (0,4,6,8), (5,7,9), (1,3,5,7),

(3,5,7,9) } the post processing eliminates $(1,3,5)$ and $(5,7,9)$ as they are subsets of $(1,3,5,7)$ respectively $(3,5,7,9)$. Also we add (2) as an elementary building-block, as it is not contained in any linkage-group of the model. The resulting linkage model is $\{(0,4,6,8),(1,3,5,7),(3,5,7,9),(2)\}$.

In the following section we detail how the proposed higher order linkage detection can be incorporated in the ECGA.

4. THE EXTENDED COMPACT GENETIC ALGORITHM

The ECGA [7] is a multivariate extension of the Compact Genetic Algorithm [8] based on the key principle that learning a good probability distribution of the population is equivalent to the linkage learning process. The measure of a good distribution is quantified based on minimum description length (MDL) models. MDL is pillared on the concept that any regularity in a given set of data can be used to compress the data. The best hypothesis for a given set of data is the one that leads to the largest compression. Consequently, a tradeoff between model accuracy and complexity must be found.

MDL restriction reformulates the problem of finding a good distribution as minimizing both population representation (population complexity – C_p) and the cost of representing the model itself (model complexity – C_m). Hence the combined complexity criterion C_c to be minimized is given by:

$$C_c = C_p + C_m \tag{6}$$

The probability distribution used by the ECGA belongs to the Marginal Product Model (MPM), a class of probability model. Subsets of variables can be modeled jointly as partitions, providing a direct linkage map. Partitions together with the products of marginal distributions over them they form the MPMs.

The MPM concept is illustrated in Table 1 over a 3 bit problem with $[1,3],[2]$ as partitions. The first and third bit are jointly distributed while variable [2] is independent. The compound partition [1,3] can have four settings: {00, 01, 10, 11}. The probability distribution for the partitions is given by the frequency of the individuals in the population with those bit values.

Starting from a random population, the ECGA applies the process of evaluation, selection, MPMs based model-building and sampling until a halting criterion is met.

In its model-building phase, the ECGA greedily searches the space of possible partitions guided by the C_c, evaluating all pairwise partition merges and always retaining the best one until no more improvements can be made. Given

$[X_1, X_3]$	$[X_2]$
$P(X_1 = 0 \text{ and } X_3 = 0) = 0.0$	$P(X_2 = 0) = 0.25$
$P(X_1 = 0 \text{ and } X_3 = 1) = 0.5$	$P(X_2 = 1) = 0.75$
$P(X_1 = 1 \text{ and } X_3 = 0) = 0.5$	
$P(X_1 = 1 \text{ and } X_3 = 1) = 0.0$	

Table 1: MPM over 3 variables. X_1 and X_3 are linked together defining a joint distribution where X_1 having the same values as X_3 has probability 0.0. This, together with the information that X_2 is three times more likely to be 1 than 0 helps focusing the search.

Algorithm 1: Model-building in the ECGA

1 Build initial model m where each variable is an independent partition;
2 **repeat**
3 $\quad m_{best} \leftarrow m$;
4 $\quad$ **foreach** $[p,q]$ *from the* $\binom{|m|}{2}$ *set of possible pair partitions of* m **do**
5 $\quad\quad$ Form new model m' based on m but with p and q merged into a joint partition;
6 $\quad\quad$ Evaluate combined complexity criterion $C_c(m')$;
7 $\quad\quad$ **if** m' *improves over* m_{best} **then**
8 $\quad\quad\quad m_{best} \leftarrow m'$;
9 $\quad m \leftarrow m_{best}$;
10 **until** *No improvement was found*;

a partition configuration, their probability distribution are estimated by counting the frequencies of each different partition setting in the population.

The model building process is outlined in Algorithm 1. The method has $O(n^3)$ complexity over the combined complexity criterion evaluations as line 5 iterates over pairs of variables. This can be intuitively seen as $\binom{n}{2}$ has complexity $O(n^2)$. Implementing a cache to avoid recomputation of MPMs, can decrease the model by one factor.

Enabling the higher order dependency search in the ECGA is simple: we only need to replace the initial model m formed by all variables as independent partitions, with the building-block list *LinkageModel* obtained by running the function **FindLinkages** described in Fig. 1 and performing the post processing step. This adds an $O(n^k)$ overhead to the algorithm.

Another effect of the higher order dependency search is that the initial model will no longer be restricted to partitions, allowing an initial building-block setup containing overlaps. Therefore, when sampling overlapping building-blocks, in order to make the effect of the potential disruption non-deterministic, the sampling mechanism enumerates the building-blocks in a random order.

5. TEST FUNCTIONS

5.1 Pairwise independent test functions

One of the simplest ways to design an allelic-pairwise independent function for the binary case is to assign the same fitness to the individuals with the same parity of unitation. The parity function is the generalization of the exclusive or operator and the Walsh transform, being:

$$parity(X) = \begin{cases} C_{even} & \text{if } u(X) \text{ is even} \\ C_{odd} & \text{otherwise} \end{cases} \tag{7}$$

where $u(X)$ is the unitation or bit count of string X, and C_{even} and C_{odd} are constants.

Coffin and Smith [2] defined the *concatenated parity function (CPF)* and the *concatenated parity/trap function (CP/TF)* in their work.

CPF is defined as a concatenation of parity functions:

$$CPF(X) = \sum_{i=0}^{m-1} parity(X_{ik}, X_{ik+1} \dots X_{ik+(k-1)}) \tag{8}$$

where m is the number of concatenated parity functions.

A more difficult problem can be derived from the parity function by concatenating deceptive traps with the CPF, resulting in the CP/TF:

$$CP/TF(X) = \sum_{i=0}^{m-1} \begin{cases} parity(x_{ik} \dots x_{ik+(k-1)}) & \text{if } i \text{ is even} \\ trap(x_{ik} \dots x_{ik+(k-1)}) & \text{otherwise} \end{cases} \tag{9}$$

In concatenated trap functions [4], the fitness gradient leads search away from the solution to each block. Each block of length k is maximally rewarded if it is contains all but ones; for the other cases, the fitness of the block is directly proportional with the number of zeros, the string of all zeros being a strong local optima:

$$trap(X) = \begin{cases} k & \text{if } u(X) = k \\ k - 1 - u(X) & \text{otherwise} \end{cases} \tag{10}$$

Certain EDAs can solve these problems in polynomial time, without a correct linkage model by randomly stumbling upon one of the global optima [1, 2]. However, the search is inefficient, requesting many objective function evaluations as the problem structure is not exploited. Competent optimization algorithms must solve boundedly difficult problems with modularity, hierarchy, and overlap quickly, reliably, and accurately [6]. Here, we focus on achieving these goals, therefore the correct modelling and sampling of the building-blocks is critical.

5.2 Pairwise weakly dependent test functions

Relying the model building just on pairwise dependency exploitation is not problematic only for the cases when these dependencies are lacking. A higher-order dependency might be present at pairwise level but the signal it provides might be weak and be suppressed by the exogenous noise coming from other building-blocks.

To study this phenomena we introduce a test function called $halfones$, which rewards a building-block if it has half of it genes set to one. For odd length building-block sizes, we overcome the fact that the half is not an integer by taking the ceiling, rounded-up value of the length divided by 2; thus for these cases, the building-block must have exactly one more gene set to one than there are genes set to zero.

The function is formalized as:

$$halfones(X) = \begin{cases} 1 & \text{if } u(X) = \lceil \frac{length(X)}{2} \rceil \\ 0 & \text{otherwise} \end{cases} \tag{11}$$

where $u(X)$ is the unitation or bit count of the string X.

While pairwise dependencies are present between the variables of $halfones$, their strength is inversely proportional with the length of the building-block and the number of other building-blocks.

6. RESULTS

6.1 Linkage detection performance

In a first step, we tested how the higher-order linkage measurement can be used to detect and quantify multivariate dependencies. We were interested in seeing if it can (1) reliably detect higher-order linkage groups that do not contain pairwise dependencies and (2) aid performance for cases where pairwise dependencies are present but weak.

For the first scenario we relied on the CPF as the parity function is allelic pairwise independent. For the second test objective we used a concatenated $halfones$ function.

To account for the effect of both building-block length and building-block numbers, we varied the parameters in the following ranges: k from 5 to 20 by increments of 1, m from 10 to 200 by increments of 10.

For each pair of k and m we randomly generated a population of $n = 10000$ individuals with uniform distribution and selected the top 2500. Next we measured the average pairwise dependence $pw(bb)$ between genes belonging to the same building-block and the average pairwise dependence $pw(non-bb)$ between genes belonging to different building-blocks. We also measured the average bias $bXOR(bb)$ obtained by performing XOR based entropy distillation on the genes belonging to the same building-blocks. Similarly, $bXOR(non-bb)$ averages the bias obtained by performing XOR based entropy distillation on genes belonging to different building-blocks. When calculating the statistics for non related genes, to be able to trace the results, we averaged the results obtained from 10000 randomly generated blocks containing genes from different linkage groups.

For the CPF, as expected, there was no significant difference between $pw(bb)$ and $pw(non-bb)$ since the parity function is pairwise allelic independent. However, the XOR based entropy distillation signaled a high bias for the building-blocks, while for the non-linked groups of variables the bias was less than 0.009. The biases on CPF for all k-s and m-s are presented in Fig. 2. For the building-blocks, the bias is almost as high as 0.2 on the easiest case. When the problem size is increased, this value decreases to about 0.04.

In the case of concatenated $halfones$ there are pairwise dependencies, thus the values for $pw(bb)$ and $pw(non-bb)$ differ. Their value for the different pairs of k and m is presented in Fig. 3. As seen in the figure, the pairwise dependency measure might be useful only for limited problems sizes, where both k and m are small. Once these values increases the pairwise dependency measure quickly looses its ability to discriminate the real underlaying linkages. Again, as depicted in Fig. 4, the XOR based entropy distillation bias measure can discriminate between linked and non-linked groups of variables. Albeit now the bias for the hardest instance is about 0.02, this approach is much more robust to the exogenous noise coming from the other building-blocks in the problem. Increasing the selection pressure can reduce the inter building-block noise. For example by selecting only the top 500 out of 10000 individuals, the bias for the hardest problem increases from 0.02 to 0.0425.

From Fig. 2 and 4 results that the XOR based entropy distillation bias measure is mostly insensitive to the building-block size, as for the same m values the bias is almost constant for all k-s.

We conclude that the proposed linkage detection mechanism can detect allelic pairwise independent building-blocks and it also useful in amplifying and aggregating low pairwise dependency signals.

6.2 ECGA scalability

We conducted scalability experiments on the shuffled CPF and CP/TF for the ECGA with higher order linkage learning, where the minimal population sizes were determined with the bisection method [19], requiring 50 out of 50 successful runs. As already discussed, we put emphasis on the correct linkage learning, thus we counted as successful run those instances where the global optima is found and the correct building-block structure is detected. A model is considered correct if the dependent alleles are modelled in same linkage groups.

The bias threshold used in the higher order linkage learning was set to 0.04;

Similarly to previous works [1, 2] we set the block size $k = 5$, $C_{odd} = 5$ and $C_{even} = 0$ for the parity function. In the ECGA we used truncation selection, where the top quarter of the population was selected for learning.

The ECGA with higher-order linkage detection easily solved all instances of the test suite detecting also the correct building-blocks. The minimal population sizes for the two test functions are presented in Fig. 5 while the scaling of objective function evaluations is presented in Fig. 6.

The inclusions of the trap function makes the task of linkage learning harder, making more difficult the separation of different building-blocks. Therefore, the minimal population sizes and number of objective function evaluations are significantly larger in the case of the CP/TF.

As it exploited the problem structure, the minimal population sizes and number of objective function evaluations are a magnitude of order smaller than those reported for EDAs that solve these problems without correct linkage structures. On the CP/TP with $m = 100$ building-blocks, the ECGA without higher-order linkage learning, requires more than double in population size and several hundred-thousand objective function evaluations to find the global optima [1].

For these problems, the computational investment for a higher-order linkage model yields a high return by requiring a much smaller number of objective function evaluations. This gain is especially important for complex problems where the objective functions can be very slow to evaluate, restricting the optimization process to only a few hundred or thousand objective calculations [11, 12]. Besides the increased speed in convergence, another important advantage is that the correct linkage structure is identified and explicitly modeled. This description of higher-order dynamics exhibited by the problem can help advancing knowledge by providing valuable insights about the problems and their structure.

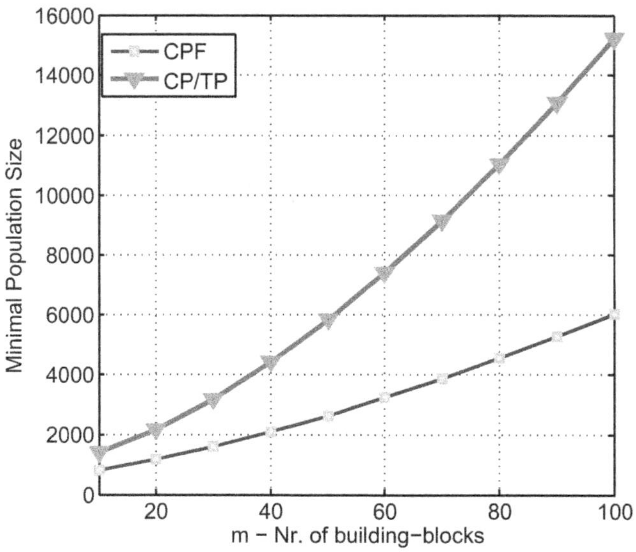

Figure 5: Minimal population sizes found by bisection method for ECGA with higher order linkage learning on the CPF and CP/TP.

The explicit linkage models derived not only helps in speeding up the convergence, but it also describes the higher-order dynamics exhibited by the problem and can help researchers gain important insights and better understanding of the studied processes and systems.

Searching for k-bounded interactions has a complexity of $O(n^k)$, which limits the applicability of the method on a single central processing unit for larger k-s. Fortunately, backtracking algorithms are very ease to parallelize as processing different paths in the search tree is an embarrassingly parallel task, with no communication overhead [13, 9, 22]. Thus, parallel backtracking scales very well with the number of available processors. In a future effort, we will focus on parallelizing the higher-order linkage learning procedure.

The classical ECGA is limited to the identification of non-overlapping building-blocks only. As the higher order dependency search allows the identification of overlapping building-blocks, we will also investigate if the transition of the model from partitions to clusters of variables has a beneficial effect in the case of problems containing overlapping dependencies.

7. CONCLUSIONS AND FUTURE WORK

Current multivariate EDAs rely on computationally efficient pairwise linkage detection mechanisms to identify higher order linkage blocks. This may lead to poor performance for problems where such pairwise dependencies are not available for exploitation.

In this paper we introduced a higher-order linkage detection mechanism, where we search for groups of variables from which randomness can not be extracted, signaling an underlaying dependency. Albeit we must perform the highly combinatorial search, the complexity of measuring the entropy distillation is just linear.

Experiments performed on various allelic-pairwise independent of bounded order confirms that the method is able to learn the correct linkage groups for these hard functions and optimize them efficiently. To best of our knowledge, so far no other EDA applies higher order model search, thus no method is known to infer the correct linkage model for these types of problems.

Acknowledgments

This research is supported by Grant PN II TE 320, Emergence, auto-organization and evolution: New computational models in the study of complex systems, funded by CNCSIS, Romania. We also acknowledge the financial support of the Sectoral Operational Program for Human Resources Development 2007-2013, co-financed by the European Social Fund, within the project POSDRU 89/1.5/S/60189 with the title "Postdoctoral Programs for Sustainable Development in a Knowledge Based Society".

8. REFERENCES

[1] S.-C. Chen and T.-L. Yu. Difficulty of linkage learning in estimation of distribution algorithms. In *Proceedings of the 11th Annual conference on Genetic*

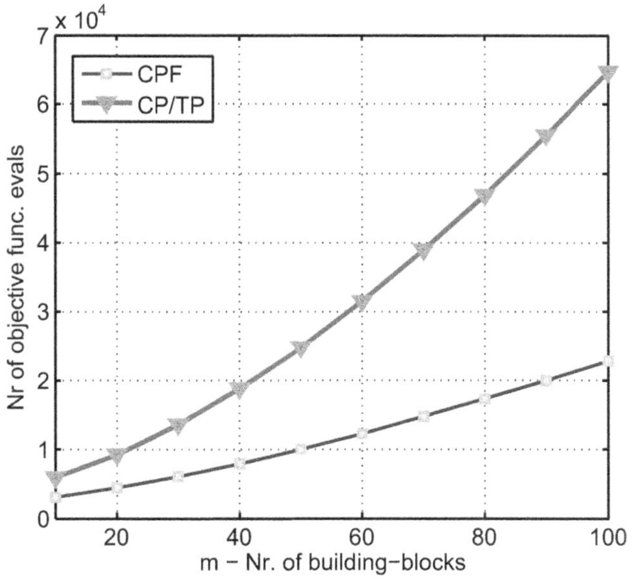

Figure 6: Objective function evaluation scalability of the ECGA with higher order linkage learning on the CPF and CP/TP.

and evolutionary computation, GECCO '09, pages 397–404, New York, NY, USA, 2009. ACM.

[2] D. J. Coffin and R. E. Smith. Why is parity hard for estimation of distribution algorithms? In *GECCO '07: Proceedings of the 9th annual conference on Genetic and evolutionary computation*, pages 624–624, New York, NY, USA, 2007. ACM.

[3] T. M. Cover and J. A. Thomas. *Elements of information theory.* Wiley-Interscience, New York, NY, USA, 1991.

[4] K. Deb and D. E. Goldberg. Analyzing deception in trap functions. In L. D. Whitley, editor, *Foundations of Genetic Algorithms 2*, pages 93–108, San Mateo, 1993. Morgan Kaufmann.

[5] D. E. Goldberg. *Genetic Algorithms in Search, Optimization and Machine Learning.* Addison Wesley, 1989.

[6] D. E. Goldberg. *The Design of Innovation: Lessons from and for Competent Genetic Algorithms.* Kluwer Academic Publishers, Norwell, MA, USA, 2002.

[7] G. Harik. Linkage learning via probabilistic modeling in the ECGA. Technical Report IlliGAL Report no. 99010, Illinois Genetic Algorithms Laboratory, University of Illinois at Urbana-Champaign, Feb. 04 1999.

[8] G. R. Harik, F. G. Lobo, and D. E. Goldberg. The compact genetic algorithm. *IEEE-EC*, 3(4):287, Nov. 1999.

[9] K. T. Herley, A. Pietracaprina, and G. Pucci. Deterministic parallel backtrack search. *Theor. Comput. Sci.*, 270:309–324, January 2002.

[10] D. Iclanzan. Hierarchical allelic pairwise independent functions. In *GECCO '11: Proceedings of the 13th Annual conference on Genetic and evolutionary computation*, page (accepted), New York, NY, USA, 12-16 July 2011. ACM.

[11] Y. Jin. A comprehensive survey of fitness approximation in evolutionary computation. *Soft Computing*, 9(1):3–12, 2005.

[12] Y. Jin, M. Olhofer, and B. Sendhoff. A framework for evolutionary optimization with approximate fitness functions. *IEEE Trans. Evolutionary Computation*, 6(5):481–494, 2002.

[13] M. Kouril and J. L. Paul. A parallel backtracking framework (bkfr) for single and multiple clusters. In *Proceedings of the 1st conference on Computing frontiers*, CF '04, pages 302–312, New York, NY, USA, 2004. ACM.

[14] P. Larranaga and J. A. Lozano. *Estimation of Distribution Algorithms: A New Tool for Evolutionary Computation.* Kluwer, Norwell, MA, USA, 2001.

[15] M. Matsui. Linear cryptanalysis method for DES cipher. In T. Helleseth, editor, *Advances in Cryptology—EUROCRYPT 93*, volume 765 of *Lecture Notes in Computer Science*, pages 386–397. Springer-Verlag, 1994, 23–27 May 1993.

[16] H. Mühlenbein and R. Höns. The estimation of distributions and the minimum relative entropy principle. *Evol. Comput.*, 13(1):1–27, 2005.

[17] H. Muhlenbein and G. PaaB. From recombination of genes to the estimation of distributions: I. binary parameters. In H.-M. Voigt, W. Ebeling I. Rechenberg, and H.-P. Schwefel, editors, *Parallel Problem Solving From Nature-PPSN IV (4th PPSN'96)*, volume 1141 of *Lecture Notes in Computer Science (LNCS) September 1996*, pages 178–187. Springer-Verlag, Berlin, 96.

[18] M. Pelikan. *Hierarchical Bayesian optimization algorithm: Toward a new generation of evolutionary algorithms.* Springer Verlag, 2005.

[19] M. Pelikan, D. E. Goldberg, and E. Cantú-Paz. Bayesian optimization algorithm, population sizing, and time to convergence. In L. D. Whitley, D. E. Goldberg, E. Cantú-Paz, L. Spector, I. C. Parmee, and H.-G. Beyer, editors, *GECCO*, pages 275–282. Morgan Kaufmann, 2000.

[20] M. Pelikan, D. E. Goldberg, and F. G. Lobo. A survey of optimization by building and using probabilistic models. *Comput. Optim. Appl.*, 21:5–20, January 2002.

[21] J. Rissanen. Modelling by the shortest data description. *Automatica*, 14:465–471, 1978.

[22] P. Sanders. Better algorithms for parallel backtracking. In *Proceedings of the Second International Workshop on Parallel Algorithms for Irregularly Structured Problems*, IRREGULAR '95, pages 333–347, London, UK, 1995. Springer-Verlag.

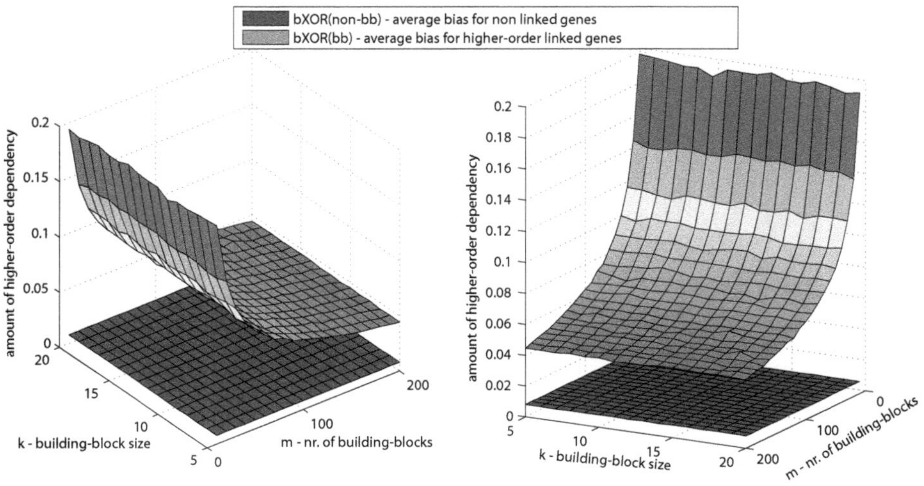

Figure 2: Average bias of the XOR based distillation for groups of dependent and independent variables on the CPF.

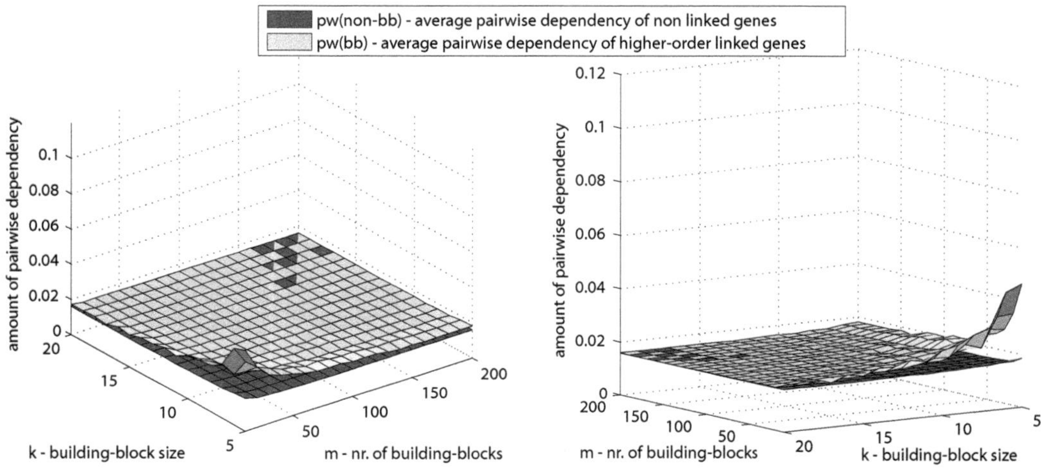

Figure 3: Average pairwise correlation coefficient for variables belonging to groups of dependent and independent variables on the concatenated *halfones*.

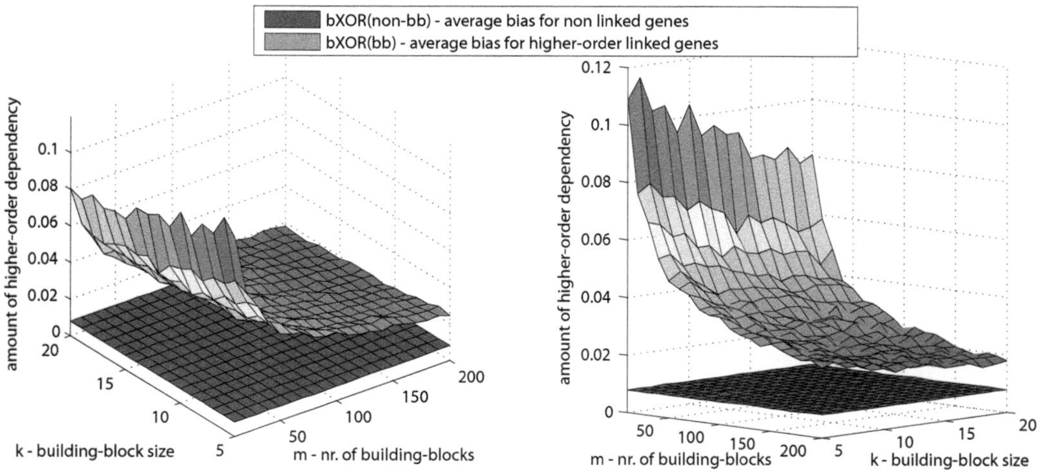

Figure 4: Average bias of the XOR based distillation for groups of dependent and independent variables on the concatenated *halfones*.

Distance-Based Bias in Model-Directed Optimization of Additively Decomposable Problems

Martin Pelikan
Missouri Estimation of Distribution Algorithms Laboratory (MEDAL)
University of Missouri, St. Louis, MO
martin@martinpelikan.net

Mark W. Hauschild
Missouri Estimation of Distribution Algorithms Laboratory (MEDAL)
University of Missouri, St. Louis, MO
mwh308@umsl.edu

ABSTRACT

For many optimization problems it is possible to define a distance metric between problem variables that correlates with the likelihood and strength of interactions between the variables. For example, one may define a metric so that the dependencies between variables that are closer to each other with respect to the metric are expected to be stronger than the dependencies between variables that are further apart. The purpose of this paper is to describe a method that combines such a problem-specific distance metric with information mined from probabilistic models obtained in previous runs of estimation of distribution algorithms with the goal of solving future problem instances of similar type with increased speed, accuracy and reliability. While the focus of the paper is on additively decomposable problems and the hierarchical Bayesian optimization algorithm, it should be straightforward to generalize the approach to other model-directed optimization techniques and other problem classes. Compared to other techniques for learning from experience put forward in the past, the proposed technique is both more practical and more broadly applicable.

Categories and Subject Descriptors

I.2.6 [**Artificial Intelligence**]: Learning; I.2.8 [**Artificial Intelligence**]: Problem Solving, Control Methods, and Search; G.1.6 [**Numerical Analysis**]: Optimization

General Terms

Algorithms, Performance

Keywords

Estimation of distribution algorithms, hierarchical Bayesian optimization algorithm, decomposable problems, inductive transfer, learning from experience, efficiency enhancement

1. INTRODUCTION

Even for optimization problems that are extremely difficult to solve, it may be straightforward to extract information about important dependencies between variables and other problem regularities directly from the problem definition [2, 6, 12, 32, 34]. Furthermore, when solving many problem instances of similar type, it may be possible to gather information about variable interactions and other problem features by examining previous runs of the optimization algorithm, and to use this information to bias optimization of future problem instances to increase its speed, accuracy and reliability [10, 14]. The use of information from previous runs to introduce bias into future runs of an evolutionary algorithm is often referred to as *learning from experience* [10, 14, 21]. The use of bias based on the results of other learning tasks in the same problem domain is also commonplace in machine learning where it is referred to as *inductive transfer* or *transfer learning* [3, 29]. Numerous studies have shown that using prior knowledge and learning from experience promise improved efficiency and problem solving capabilities [2, 6, 12, 14, 30, 32, 34]. However, most prior work in this area was based on hand-crafted search operators, model restrictions, or representations.

This paper describes an approach that combines prior problem-specific knowledge with learning from experience. The basic idea of the proposed approach comprises of (1) defining a problem-specific distance metric, (2) analyzing previous EDA models to quantify the likelihood and nature of dependencies at various distances, and (3) introducing bias into EDA model building based on the results of the analysis using Bayesian statistics. One of the key goals of this paper is to develop an automated procedure capable of introducing bias based on a distance metric and prior EDA runs, without requiring much expert knowledge or hand-crafted model restrictions from the practitioner. Furthermore, the proposed approach is intended to be applicable in a more practical manner than other approaches to learning from experience. For example, the proposed approach makes it feasible to use prior runs on problems of a smaller size to introduce bias when solving problem instances of a larger size, and the bias can be introduced even when the importance of dependencies between specific pairs of variables varies significantly across the problem domain. Although this paper focuses on the hierarchical Bayesian optimization algorithm (hBOA) and additively decomposable functions (ADFs), the proposed approach can also be applied to other model-directed optimization techniques and other problem types. The paper outlines a framework that can be used to adapt the proposed approach to a different context.

The paper is organized as follows. Section 2 describes hBOA. Section 3 outlines the framework for introducing bias

GECCO'12, July 7–11, 2012, Philadelphia, Pennsylvania, USA.

based on prior runs on similar problems in model-directed optimization. Section 4 presents the proposed approach to introducing bias into hBOA model building for additively decomposable problems. Section 5 presents experimental results. Section 6 summarizes and concludes the paper.

2. HIERARCHICAL BOA

The hierarchical Bayesian optimization algorithm (hBOA) [22, 24, 25] is an estimation of distribution algorithm (EDA) [1, 13, 18, 19, 26, 28]. hBOA works with a population of candidate solutions represented by fixed-length strings over a finite alphabet. In this paper, candidate solutions are represented by n-bit binary strings. The initial population of binary strings is generated at random according to the uniform distribution over candidate solutions. Each iteration starts by selecting promising solutions from the current population; here binary tournament selection without replacement is used. Next, hBOA (1) learns a Bayesian network with local structures for the selected solutions and (2) generates new candidate solutions by sampling the distribution encoded by the built network [4, 7]. To maintain useful diversity in the population, the new candidate solutions are incorporated into the original population using restricted tournament selection (RTS) [9]. The run is terminated when termination criteria are met. In this paper, each run is terminated either when the global optimum is found or when a maximum number of iterations is reached. Since the basic understanding of probabilistic models used in hBOA is necessary for the remainder of the paper, the rest of this section discusses the class of probabilistic models used in hBOA.

hBOA represents probabilistic models of candidate solutions by Bayesian networks with local structures [4, 7]. A Bayesian network is defined by two components: (1) an acyclic directed graph over problem variables specifying direct dependencies between variables and (2) conditional probabilities specifying the probability distribution of each variable given the values of the variable's parents. A Bayesian network encodes a joint probability distribution as $p(X_1, \ldots, X_n) = \prod_{i=1}^{n} p(X_i|\Pi_i)$ where X_i is the ith variable and Π_i are the parents of X_i in the underlying graph.

To represent conditional probabilities of each variable given the variable's parents, hBOA uses decision trees. Each internal node of a decision tree specifies a variable, and the subtrees of the node correspond to the different values of the variable. Each leaf of the decision tree for a particular variable defines the probability distribution of the variable given a condition specified by the constraints given by the path from the root of the tree to this leaf (constraints are given by the assignments of the variables along this path).

To build probabilistic models, hBOA typically uses a greedy algorithm that initializes the decision tree for each problem variable X_i to a single-node tree that encodes the unconditional probability distribution of X_i. In each iteration, the model building algorithm tests how much a model would improve after splitting each leaf of each decision tree on each variable that is not already located on the path to the leaf. The algorithm executes the split that provides the most improvement, and the process is repeated until no more improvement is possible.

Improvement of the model after a split is often evaluated using the Bayesian-Dirichlet (BDe) metric with penalty for model complexity. Bayesian measures evaluate the goodness of a Bayesian network structure given data D and background knowledge ξ as [5, 16]

$$p(B|D,\xi) = cp(B|\xi)p(D|B,\xi), \tag{1}$$

where c is a normalization constant. For the Bayesian-Dirichlet metric, the term $p(D|B,\xi)$ is estimated as [4]

$$p(D|B,\xi) = \prod_{i=1}^{n} \prod_{l \in L_i} \frac{\Gamma(m'_i(l))}{\Gamma(m_i(l) + m'_i(l))} \prod_{x_i} \frac{\Gamma(m_i(x_i,l) + m'_i(x_i,l))}{\Gamma(m'_i(x_i,l))}, \tag{2}$$

where L_i is the set of leaves in the decision tree T_i for X_i; $m_i(l)$ is the number of instances in the selected population which end up the traversal through the tree T_i in the leaf l; $m_i(x_i,l)$ is the number of instances that have $X_i = x_i$ and end up the traversal of the tree T_i in the leaf l; $m'_i(l)$ represents the prior knowledge about the value of $m_i(i,l)$; and $m'_i(x_i,l)$ represents the prior knowledge about the value of $m_i(x_i,l)$. Without any prior knowledge, an uninformative prior $m'_i(x_i,l) = 1$ is typically used. To favor simpler networks to the more complex ones, the prior probability of each network decreases exponentially fast with respect to the description length of this network's parameters [7, 22]:

$$p(B) = c2^{-0.5(\sum_i |L_i|) \log_2 N}, \tag{3}$$

where c is a normalization constant required for the prior probabilities of all network structures to sum to one.

3. BIAS BASED ON PREVIOUS EDA RUNS

Building an accurate probabilistic model in hBOA and other EDAs based on complex probabilistic models can be time consuming and it may require rather large populations of solutions. That is why much effort has been put into enhancing efficiency of model building in EDAs and improving quality of EDA models even with smaller populations of candidate solutions [2, 10, 11, 14, 20]. Learning from experience [10, 11, 14, 22] represents one approach to dealing with this issue. In learning from experience, models discovered by EDAs in previous runs are mined to identify regularities and the discovered regularities are used to bias model building in future runs on problems of similar type. Since learning model structure is often the most challenging task in model building, learning from experience often focuses on identifying regularities in model structure and using these regularities to bias structural learning in future runs.

It is straightforward to collect statistics on the most frequent dependencies in EDA models. Nonetheless, for the collected statistics to be useful, it is important to ensure that the statistics are meaningful with respect to the problem being solved. For example, consider optimization of NK landscapes [17], in which the fitness function is defined as the sum of n subfunctions $\{f_i\}_{i=1}^{n}$, and the subfunction f_i is applied to the ith bit and its k neighbors. The neighbors of each bit are typically chosen at random for each problem instance. Therefore, if we consider 1,000 problem instances of NK landscapes, looking at the percentage of models that included a dependency between the first two bits for the first 999 instances will not say much about the likelihood of the same dependency for the last instance. A similar observation can be made for many other important problem classes, such as MAXSAT or the quadratic assignment problem. That is why it is important to develop a more general framework that allows one to learn and use statistics on dependencies in EDA models across a range of problem domains of different structure and properties. In the remainder of this section we describe one such framework.

To formalize the proposed framework to identifying structural regularities in EDA models, let us define a set of m dependency categories $D = \{D_1, \ldots, D_m\}$ and denote the background knowledge about the problem by ξ. Then, we can define a function $\gamma(i, j, \xi)$ that, given ξ, maps any dependency (i, j) covered by the probabilistic model into one of the m categories so that $\gamma(i, j, \xi) = k$ if and only if $(i, j) \in D_k$. Two straightforward possibilities for defining γ function were proposed in refs. [10, 11]: (1) Each pair of problem variables X_i and X_j defines a special category, and (2) categories are defined using a discretization of a problem-specific distance metric between variables. The first approach is useful especially when solving a number of instances of a problem where each variable has a fixed meaning across the entire set of instances; this is the case for example in spin glasses defined on a regular lattice, where every pair of variables in the lattice can be assigned a special category because the structure of the problem does not change from one instance to another [15]. The latter approach is useful especially when one can define a distance metric on variables so that the distance between two variables correlates strongly with the likelihood or strength of their interaction; for example, one may define a distance metric such that variables that interact more strongly are closer to each other according to the metric. Such a distance metric can be defined for example in the quadratic assignment problem, traveling salesman problem or, more generally, classes of additively decomposable functions. While these two approaches are applicable to many important classes of problems, one may envision many other approaches based on this framework. The key issue in defining γ is that the categories should be related to the problem, so that each category contains pairs of variables that have a lot in common and that can be expected to be either correlated or independent most of the time.

The statistics obtained from previous EDA models can be used to bias the search operators of model-directed optimization methods using either a soft bias or a hard bias. A soft bias allows one to define preference to some models using a prior distribution over network structures or partial variable assignments [11, 32]. A hard bias encodes hard restrictions on model structure or variable assignments, restricting the class of allowable models [2, 10, 20]. While in most prior work on bias in EDAs the bias was based on expert knowledge, in learning from experience the focus is on *automated learning* of a bias from past EDA runs.

In this paper we describe one way of using the above framework to facilitate learning from experience in hBOA for additively decomposable problems based on a problem-specific distance metric. However, note that the framework can be applied to other EDAs based on graphical models.

4. DISTANCE-BASED BIAS

4.1 Additively Decomposable Functions

For many optimization problems, the objective function (fitness function) can be expressed in the form of an additively decomposable function (ADF) of m subproblems:

$$f(X_1, \ldots, X_n) = \sum_{i=1}^{m} f_i(S_i), \tag{4}$$

where $(X_1, \ldots, X_n)$ are problem's decision variables, f_i is the ith subfunction, and $S_i \subset \{X_1, X_2, \ldots, X_n\}$ is the subset of variables contributing to f_i. While there may often exist multiple ways of decomposing the problem using additive decomposition, one would typically prefer decompositions that minimize the sizes of subsets $\{S_i\}$. It is of note that the difficulty of ADFs is not fully determined by the order of subproblems, but also by the definition of the subproblems and their interaction. In fact, there exist a number of NP-complete problems that can be formulated as ADFs with subproblems of order 2 or 3, such as MAXSAT for 3CNF formulas. On the other hand, one may easily define ADFs with subproblems of order n that can be solved by a simple bit-flip hill climbing in low-order polynomial time.

4.2 Measuring Variable Distances for ADFs

The definition of a distance between two variables of an ADF used in this paper follows the refs. [10, 14]. Given an additively decomposable problem, we define the distance between two variables using a graph G of n nodes, one node per variable. For any two variables X_i and X_j in the same subset S_k, that is, $X_i, X_j \in S_k$, we create an edge in G between the nodes X_i and X_j. Denoting by $l_{i,j}$ the number of edges along the shortest path between X_i and X_j in G (in terms of the number of edges), we define the distance between two variables as

$$D(X_i, X_j) = \begin{cases} l_{i,j} & \text{if a path between } X_i \text{ and } X_j \text{ exists} \\ n & \text{otherwise} \end{cases}$$

The above distance measure makes variables in the same subproblem close to each other, whereas for the remaining variables, the distances correspond to the length of the chain of subproblems that relate the two variables. The distance is maximal for variables that are completely independent (the value of a variable does not influence the contribution of the other variable in any way).

Since interactions between problem variables are encoded mainly in the subproblems of the additive problem decomposition, the above distance metric should typically correspond closely to the likelihood of dependencies between problem variables in probabilistic models discovered by EDAs. Specifically, the variables located closer with respect to the metric should more likely interact with each other. Figure 1 illustrates this on two ADFs discussed later in this paper— the NK landscape with nearest neighbor interactions and the two-dimensional Ising spin glass (for a description of these problems, see section 5.1). The figure analyzes probabilistic models discovered by hBOA in 10 independent runs on each of the 1,000 random instances for each problem and problem size. For a range of distances d between problem variables, the figure shows the proportion of splits on a variable located at distance d. The results clearly support the fact that hBOA models indicate strongest dependencies between variables located close to each other according to the aforementioned metric and that there is a clear correlation between the distance metric and the likelihood of dependencies. Furthermore, the figure indicates that the likelihood of dependencies at a specific distance does not change much from one problem size to another, indicating that the bias based on these statistics should be applicable across a range of problem sizes.

It is important to note that other approaches may be envisioned to defining a distance metric for ADFs. For example, a weight may be added on each edge that would de-

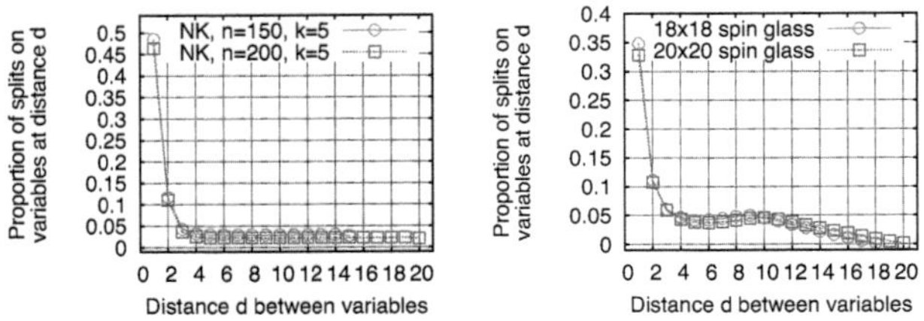

(a) Nearest-neighbor NK. (b) 2D spin glass.

Figure 1: Dependencies between variables that are closer to each other are stronger than the dependencies between other variables. Furthermore, the proportion of splits capturing dependencies between variables at a given distance changes only little between instances of various sizes. This indicates that the statistics acquired from models of one size should be useful for biasing hBOA runs on problems of another size. The results are based on 979,020 models obtained from hBOA on 1,000 unique problem instances of each problem, 10 runs per instance.

crease with the number of subsets that contain the two connected variables. Another interesting possibility would be to consider the subfunctions themselves in measuring the distances, so that only correlations that lead to nonlinearities are considered or that some correlations are given a priority over others. Finally, the distance of variables may depend on the problem definition itself, not on the decomposition only. For example, in the quadratic assignment problem, a distance between two facility locations is specified directly by the problem instance. The key is to use problem-specific information to specify a distance metric so that the distance between a pair of variables correlates with the likelihood or strength of their interaction.

4.3 Using Distance-Based Bias in hBOA

The basic idea of incorporating the distance-based bias based on prior runs into hBOA is inspired mainly by the work of Hauschild et al. [11]. Hauschild et al. proposed to incorporate learning from experience into hBOA by modifying prior probabilities of network structures using the statistics that capture the number of splits on each variable in the decision tree for each other variable in past hBOA runs on similar problems. Nonetheless, the approach of Hauschild et al. [11] is only applicable to problems where the strength of interactions between any two variables is not expected to change much from instance to instance. That is why this approach can only be applied in a limited set of problem domains and it is difficult to use this approach when problem size is not fixed in all runs. In this paper, we propose to capture the *nature of dependencies between variables with respect to their distance* using the distance metric defined for ADFs or another distance metric. This allows one to apply the technique in more problem domains and also allows models from problem instances of one size to be useful in solving problem instances of different sizes (see figure 1).

Recall that the BDe metric used to evaluate probabilistic models in hBOA contains two parts: (1) prior probability $p(B|\xi)$ of the network structure B, and (2) posterior probability $p(D|B,\xi)$ of the data (population of selected solutions) given B. Prior probabilities of network structures are typically set to represent the uniform distribution over admissible network structures or to provide a bias toward simple models regardless of the problem. However, the prior probability distribution of network structures can also be used to specify preferable structures. In this paper, we will use the prior probability distribution of network structures to introduce bias toward models that resemble models obtained in previous runs on problems of similar type with the focus on distance-based statistics. An analogous approach can be used to incorporate bias into hBOA for a different mapping γ of pairs of variables into dependency categories $\{D_i\}$.

Let us assume a set M of hBOA models from prior hBOA runs on similar ADFs. Before applying the bias by modifying the prior probability distribution of models in hBOA, the models in M are first processed to generate data that will serve as the basis for introducing the bias. The processing starts by analyzing the models in M to determine the number $s(m,d,j)$ of splits on any variable X_i such that $D(X_i,X_j)=d$ in a decision tree T_j for variable X_j for a model $m\in M$. Then, the values $s(m,d,j)$ are used to compute the probability $P_k(d,j)$ of a kth split on a variable at distance d from X_j in a dependency tree T_j given that $k-1$ such splits were already performed in T_j:

$$P_k(d,j)=\frac{|\{m\in M : s(m,d,j)\geq k\}|}{|\{m\in M : s(m,d,j)\geq k-1\}|}. \quad (5)$$

Given the terms $P_k(d,j)$, we can now define the prior probability of a network B as

$$p(B,\xi)=c\prod_{d=1}^{n}\prod_{j=1}^{n}\prod_{k=1}^{n_s(d,j)}P_k^{\kappa}(d,j), \quad (6)$$

where $n_s(d,j)$ denotes the number of splits on any variable X_i such that $D(X_i,X_j)=d$ in T_j, $\kappa>0$ is used to tune the strength of bias (the strength of bias increases with κ), and c is a normalization constant. Since log-likelihood is typically used to evaluate model quality, to evaluate the contribution of any particular split, the main difference from the standard version of the BDe metric with the complexity penalty is that instead of reducing the metric according to the additional complexity of $\log_2(N)/2$ for each new split, we reduce the metric by the corresponding $\kappa\log_2 P_k(d,j)$. Therefore, the computation of the change of the prior probability of the network structure can still be done in constant time. Of course, the change in $p(D|B,\xi)$ requires computation of marginal frequencies, so it cannot be done in constant time.

It is important to note that the prior probability of hBOA models defined in eq. (6) is certainly not the only possible approach to incorporating learning from experience using distance-based statistics into hBOA. The main source of inspiration for the proposed approach is the work on incorporating bias in learning Bayesian networks using Bayesian metrics [16] and the prior work on learning from experience in hBOA by Hauschild et al. [11]. The experimental results presented in the next section confirm that this approach leads to substantial speedups in both problem classes considered in this paper and preliminary experiments in other problem domains including MAXSAT and minimum vertex cover indicate that substantial speedups can be obtained also in other problem classes defined as ADFs.

5. EXPERIMENTS

5.1 Test Problems

To test the proposed approach to biasing hBOA model building, we consider two problem classes: shuffled nearest-neighbor NK landscapes and two-dimensional spin glasses.

Both these problem classes were shown to be challenging for conventional genetic algorithms and many other optimization techniques due to the rugged landscape, strong epistasis, and complex structure of interactions between problem variables [17, 23, 27, 35]. However, for both problem classes, it is straightforward to generate a large number of problem instances with known optima. For each problem class and problem size, we use 1,000 unique problem instances; the reason for using such a large number of instances is that for these problem classes, algorithm performance often varies substantially from one instance to another and the results would thus be unreliable if only a few instances were used.

An NK fitness landscape [17] is fully defined by the following components: (1) The number of bits, n, (2) the number of neighbors per bit, k, (3) a set of k neighbors $\Pi(X_i)$ of the ith bit for every $i \in \{1, \ldots, n\}$, and (4) a subfunction f_i defining a real value for each combination of values of X_i and $\Pi(X_i)$ for every $i \in \{1, \ldots, n\}$. Typically, each subfunction is defined as a lookup table. The objective function f_{nk} to maximize is defined as $f_{nk}(X_1, X_2, \ldots, X_n) = \sum_{i=1}^{n} f_i(X_i, \Pi(X_i))$. The difficulty of optimizing NK landscapes depends on all components defining an NK problem instance. In this paper, we consider nearest-neighbor NK landscapes, in which neighbors of each bit are restricted to the k bits that immediately follow this bit. The neighborhoods wrap around; thus, for bits which do not have k bits to the right, the neighborhood is completed with the first few bits of solution strings. The reason for restricting neighborhoods to nearest neighbors was to ensure that the problem instances can be solved in polynomial time even for $k > 1$ using dynamic programming [23]. The subfunctions are represented by look-up tables (a unique value is used for each instance of a bit and its neighbors), and each entry in the look-up table is generated with the uniform distribution from $[0, 1)$. The used class of NK landscapes with nearest neighbors is thus the same as that in ref. [23]. In all experiments, we use $k = 5$ and $n \in \{100, 150, 200\}$. For each n, we use 1,000 unique, independently generated instances; overall, 3,000 unique instances of NK landscapes were tested.

Ising spin glasses are prototypical models for disordered systems [35]. A simple model to describe a finite-dimensional Ising spin glass is typically arranged on a regular 2D or 3D grid where each node i corresponds to a spin s_i and each edge $\langle i, j \rangle$ corresponds to a coupling between two spins s_i and s_j. Each edge has a real value $J_{i,j}$ associated with it that defines the relationship between the two connected spins. To approximate the behavior of the large-scale system, periodic boundary conditions are often used that introduce a coupling between the first and the last elements in each dimension. For the classical Ising model, each spin s_i can be in one of two states: $s_i = +1$ or $s_i = -1$. Given a set of coupling constants $J_{i,j}$, and a configuration of spins C, the energy can be computed as $E(C) = -\sum_{\langle i,j \rangle} s_i J_{i,j} s_j$, where the sum runs over all couplings $\langle i, j \rangle$. Here the task is to find a spin configuration for a given set of coupling constants that minimizes the energy of the spin glass. The states with minimum energy are called *ground states*. The spin configurations are encoded with binary strings where each bit specifies the value of one spin (0 for a spin +1, 1 for a spin -1). One generally analyzes a large set of random spin glass instances for a given distribution of the spin-spin couplings. In this paper we consider the $\pm J$ spin glass, where each spin-spin coupling is set randomly to either $+1$ or -1 with equal probability. We use instances arranged on square grids of sizes 10×10, 12×12, 14×14, 16×16, 18×18 and 20×20 spins; that is, the problem sizes range from 100 to 400 spins. We consider periodic boundary conditions. For each problem size, we use 1,000 unique, independently generated problem instances; overall, 6,000 unique instances of the 2D spin glass were tested. All instances were obtained from the Spin Glass Ground State Server [33].

5.2 10-Fold Crossvalidation

To ensure that the same problem instances were not used for defining the bias as well as for testing it, 10-fold crossvalidation was used. For each problem size and each problem, 1,000 random problem instances were used in the experiments. The 1,000 instances in each set were randomly split into 10 equally sized subsets of 100 instances each. In each round of crossvalidation, 1 subset of 100 instances was left out and hBOA was run on the remaining 9 subsets of 900 instances total. The runs on the 9 subsets produced a number of models that were analyzed in order to obtain the probabilities $P_k(d, j)$ for all d, j, and k. The bias based on the obtained values of $P_k(d, j)$ was then used in hBOA runs on the remaining subset that was left out. The same procedure was repeated for each subset; overall, 10 rounds of crossvalidation were performed for each set of 1,000 instances. Each problem instance was used exactly once in the test of the proposed approach to biasing hBOA models and in every test, models used to generate statistics for hBOA bias were obtained from hBOA runs on different problem instances.

While the experiments were performed across a variety of computer architectures and configurations, it was always ensured that the base case with no bias and the case with bias were both run on the same computational node and the results of the two runs can therefore be compared against each other with respect to the actual CPU time.

5.3 Experimental Setup

The maximum number of iterations for each problem instance was set to the overall number of bits in the problem; according to preliminary experiments, this upper bound substantially exceeded the actual number of iterations required to solve each problem. Each run was terminated either when the global optimum was found, when the population consisted of copies of a single candidate solution, or when the maximum number of iterations was reached. For each problem instance, we used bisection [22, 31] to ensure that the population size was within 5% of the minimum population size to find the optimum in 10 out of 10 independent runs.

Bit-flip hill climbing (HC) is incorporated into hBOA to improve its performance. HC takes a candidate solution represented by an n-bit binary string on input. Then, it performs one-bit changes on the solution that lead to the maximum improvement of solution quality. HC is terminated when no single-bit flip improves solution quality and the solution is thus locally optimal. Here, HC is used to improve every solution in the population before the evaluation is performed. Without HC, the number and size of problem instances would have to substantially reduce due to the increased computational requirements. However, preliminary results indicate that even without HC the benefits of the proposed approach would be substantial.

The proposed approach to distance-based bias in hBOA is tested for $\kappa = \{1, 2, 3, 4, 5, 6, 7\}$ to assess how the strength of the bias represented by κ affects hBOA performance.

To evaluate hBOA performance, we focus on (1) the execution time per run, (2) the number of steps of HC, (3) the number of evaluations, and (4) the required population size. The steps of HC are not counted as evaluations in order to distinguish between evaluations and HC steps, because for many additively decomposable problems, performing a HC step is much less computationally expensive than evaluating a solution. To evaluate the benefits of distance-based bias, the paper uses *multiplicative speedups*, where the speedup is defined as a multiplicative factor by which a particular complexity measure improves by using the distance-based bias compared to the base case with no distance-based bias. For example, an execution-time speedup of 2 indicates that the bias allowed hBOA to find the optimum twice as fast as without the bias. Although the code could be further optimized for efficiency, the primary focus of our experiments concerning the execution times was on the *speedups* of the CPU times rather than their absolute values. We have used the most efficient implementation of hBOA available for the base case with no bias and we only modified it for the remaining cases to incorporate the bias.

5.4 Results

Fig. 2(a) shows the effects of κ on the multiplicative speedups with respect to the execution time, the number of evaluations, the number of HC steps, and the population size. The results confirm that, for adequate values of κ, the speedups in terms of execution time are substantial for both NK landscapes as well as 2D spin glasses; the maximum speedup for NK landscapes was over 2.26 whereas for spin glasses it was over 1.66. For NK landscapes, the speedups in terms of execution time grow both with problem size n and with κ, and they can be expected to increase further for even larger values of n or κ. For spin glasses, the speedups seem nearly independent of problem size and best speedups are obtained for $\kappa = 3$. The multiplicative speedups in terms of the number of evaluations, the number of HC steps and the population size indicate that the reduction in the population sizes appears to be one of the most important factors reducing the overall computational cost, although improvements can be observed also in most other statistics.

Fig. 2(b) shows the speedups obtained with respect to the problem size for a range of values of κ; these results are useful for visualizing the relationship between the problem size and the speedups obtained with the distance-based bias. The results confirm that for NK landscapes, the speedups appear to grow at least linearly with the problem size, regardless of the value of κ. However, for the 2D spin glass, the speedups fluctuate around the same value for all problem sizes. The speedups obtained on NK landscapes are thus not only better, but they further improve with problem size, unlike for the 2D spin glass. On one hand, one may argue that this is due to the fact that NK landscapes with nearest neighbor interactions have a simpler structure than the 2D spin glass due to the short-range interactions. On the other hand, the interactions in 2D spin glasses are of much smaller order (subproblems in problem decomposition have 2 bits each instead of 6). We are currently evaluating the distance-based bias on other classes of nearly decomposable problems such as MAXSAT and the minimum vertex cover in order to provide more empirical evidence that would help explain when the distance-based bias works better and when it has limitations.

In summary, fig. 2 provides solid empirical evidence that the speedups obtained are substantial and that the proposed approach to learning from experience is useful in practice.

6. SUMMARY AND CONCLUSIONS

This paper introduced a practical approach to incorporating bias in estimation of distribution algorithms (EDAs) based on models built in previous EDA runs on problems of similar type. The approach was demonstrated on the hierarchical Bayesian optimization algorithm (hBOA) and additively decomposable functions, although the framework can be applied also to other EDAs based on graphical models and other problem types. For example, it should be straightforward to adapt this framework to the extended compact genetic algorithm [8] or classes of facility location problems. The key idea of the proposed approach was to define a distance metric that corresponds to the likelihood of dependencies between variables, and to use the statistics on dependencies at various distances in previous hBOA runs as the basis for introducing bias in future hBOA runs. The bias was introduced using prior probabilities of Bayesian network structures. The models were thus learned using a combination of the selected population of candidate solutions and the prior knowledge extracted from previous hBOA models. The strength of the bias can be tuned with a user-defined parameter $\kappa > 0$. The proposed approach was tested on two challenging additively decomposable functions, the NK landscapes with nearest-neighbor interactions and the two-dimensional Ising spin glass. The results on 9,000 unique problem instances from the two problem classes provided empirical evidence that the proposed approach provides substantial speedups across a variety of settings. Specifically, speedups of over 2.26 were achieved for NK landscapes, and speedups of over 1.66 were achieved for spin glasses. Furthermore, the speedups for NK landscapes grew with problem size and the parameter κ, and it can thus be expected that higher speedups can be achieved in practice. Preliminary experiments on other problem classes, including MAXSAT and minimum vertex cover, indicate that the approach provides substantial benefits also in other important classes of additively decomposable functions.

The results thus reaffirm that one of the key advantages of EDAs is that EDAs provide practitioners with a rigorous framework for incorporating prior knowledge and for automated learning from solving instances of similar type so that future problem instances can be solved with increased speed, accuracy, and reliability. EDAs thus not only allow practitioners to scalably solve problems with high levels of epistasis (variable interactions), but they also allow effective inductive transfer (transfer learning) in optimization.

In future work, the approach should be tested on other additively decomposable problems. Experiments should also be done to confirm the hypothesis that models obtained on problems of one size can be used to bias model building on problems of another size. Furthermore, the approach should be adapted to other model-directed optimization techniques, including other EDAs and genetic algorithms with linkage learning. The approach should also be modified to introduce bias on problems that cannot be formulated using an additive decomposition in a straightforward manner. Finally, it is important to study the limitations of the proposed approach, and create theoretical models to automatically tune the strength of the bias and predict expected speedups.

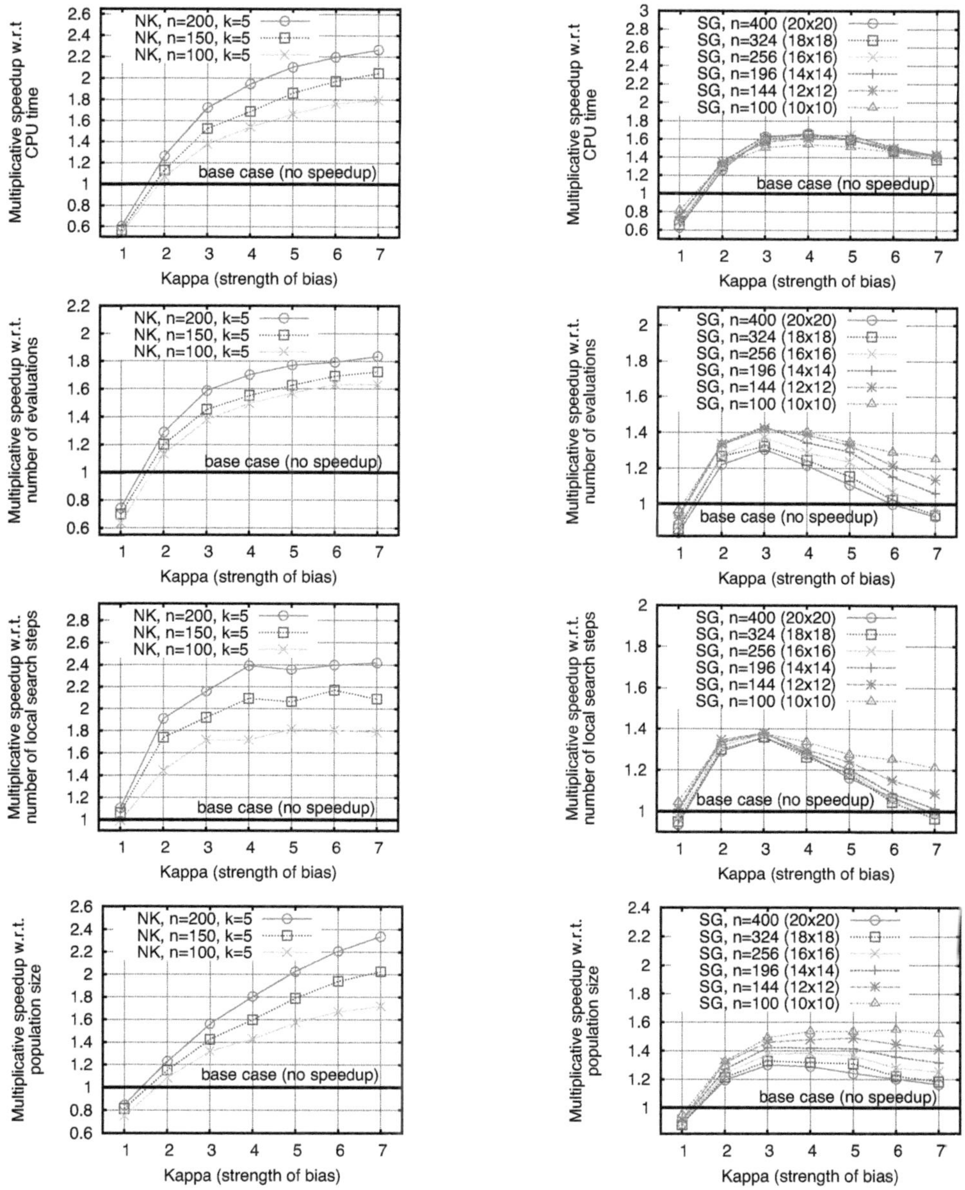

(a) Effects of κ on the reduction of the execution (CPU) time, the number of evaluations, the number of steps of local search, and the population size.

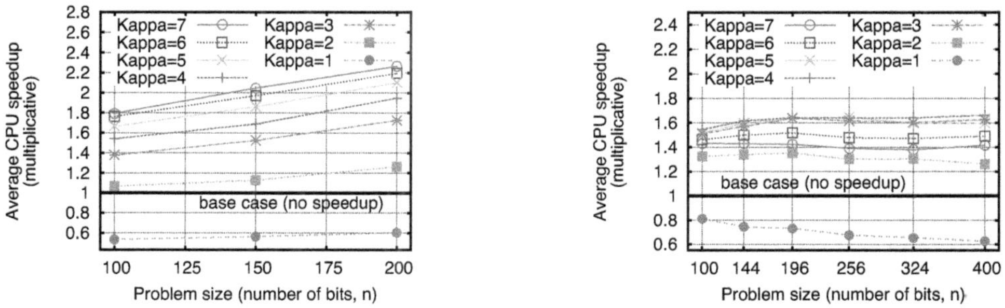

(b) Effects of problem size on execution-time speedups.

Figure 2: Effects of the distance-based bias based on models from hBOA runs on other problem instances measured by multiplicative speedups. The speedup for a particular statistic is the ratio of the value of the statistic without the bias and its value with the bias. Thus, the greater the speedup, the better the effects of the bias. For example, if CPU speedup is 2, hBOA with the distance-based bias is twice as fast as hBOA without it in terms of the total execution time. The results for NK landscapes are shown on the left, the results for 2D spin glasses are shown on the right.

Acknowledgments

This project was sponsored by the National Science Foundation under grants ECS-0547013 and IIS-1115352, and by the Univ. of Missouri in St. Louis through the High Performance Computing Collaboratory sponsored by Information Technology Services. Most experiments were performed on the Beowulf cluster maintained by ITS at the Univ. of Missouri in St. Louis and the HPC resources at the Univ. of Missouri Bioinformatics Consortium. Any opinions, findings, and conclusions or recommendations expressed in this material are those of the authors and do not necessarily reflect the views of the National Science Foundation.

7. REFERENCES

[1] S. Baluja. Population-based incremental learning: A method for integrating genetic search based function optimization and competitive learning. Tech. Rep. No. CMU-CS-94-163, Carnegie Mellon University, Pittsburgh, PA, 1994.

[2] S. Baluja. Incorporating a priori knowledge in probabilistic-model based optimization. In E. Cantú-Paz, M. Pelikan, and K. Sastry, editors, *Scalable optimization via probabilistic modeling: From algorithms to applications*, pages 205–219. Springer, 2006.

[3] R. Caruana. Multitask learning. *Machine Learning*, 28:41–75, 1997.

[4] D. M. Chickering, D. Heckerman, and C. Meek. A Bayesian approach to learning Bayesian networks with local structure. *The 13th Conference on Uncertainty in Artificial Intelligence (UAI'97)*, pages 80–89, 1997.

[5] G. F. Cooper and E. H. Herskovits. A Bayesian method for the induction of probabilistic networks from data. *Machine Learning*, 9:309–347, 1992.

[6] Z. Drezner and S. Salhi. Using hybrid metaheuristics for the one-way and two-way network design problem. *Naval Research Logistics*, 49(5):449–463, 2002.

[7] N. Friedman and M. Goldszmidt. Learning Bayesian networks with local structure. In M. I. Jordan, editor, *Graphical models*, pages 421–459. MIT Press, 1999.

[8] G. Harik. Linkage learning via probabilistic modeling in the ECGA. IlliGAL Report No. 99010, University of Illinois at Urbana-Champaign, Illinois Genetic Algorithms Laboratory, Urbana, IL, 1999.

[9] G. R. Harik. Finding multimodal solutions using restricted tournament selection. *Proc. of the Int. Conf. on Genetic Algorithms (ICGA-95)*, pages 24–31, 1995.

[10] M. W. Hauschild and M. Pelikan. Enhancing efficiency of hierarchical BOA via distance-based model restrictions. *Parallel Problem Solving from Nature*, pages 417–427, 2008.

[11] M. W. Hauschild and M. Pelikan. Intelligent bias of network structures in the hierarchical BOA. *Genetic and Evol. Comp. Conf. (GECCO-2009)*, pages 413–420, 2009.

[12] M. W. Hauschild and M. Pelikan. Network crossover performance on NK landscapes and deceptive problems. *Genetic and Evol. Comp. Conf. (GECCO-2010)*, pages 713–720, 2010.

[13] M. W. Hauschild and M. Pelikan. An introduction and survey of estimation of distribution algorithms. *Swarm and Evolutionary Computation*, 1(3):111–128, 2011.

[14] M. W. Hauschild, M. Pelikan, K. Sastry, and D. E. Goldberg. Using previous models to bias structural learning in the hierarchical BOA. *Evolutionary Computation*, 2011. In Press.

[15] M. W. Hauschild, M. Pelikan, K. Sastry, and C. F. Lima. Analyzing probabilistic models in hierarchical BOA. *IEEE Transactions on Evolutionary Computation*, 13(6):1199–1217, 2009.

[16] D. Heckerman, D. Geiger, and D. M. Chickering. Learning Bayesian networks: The combination of knowledge and statistical data. Technical Report MSR-TR-94-09, Microsoft Research, Redmond, WA, 1994.

[17] S. Kauffman. Adaptation on rugged fitness landscapes. In D. L. Stein, editor, *Lecture Notes in the Sciences of Complexity*, pages 527–618. Addison Wesley, 1989.

[18] P. Larrañaga and J. A. Lozano, editors. *Estimation of Distribution Algorithms: A New Tool for Evolutionary Computation*. Kluwer, Boston, MA, 2002.

[19] J. A. Lozano, P. Larrañaga, I. Inza, and E. Bengoetxea, editors. *Towards a New Evolutionary Computation: Advances on Estimation of Distribution Algorithms*. Springer, 2006.

[20] H. Mühlenbein and T. Mahnig. Evolutionary optimization and the estimation of search distributions with applications to graph bipartitioning. *International Journal of Approximate Reasoning*, 31(3):157–192, 2002.

[21] M. Pelikan. *Bayesian optimization algorithm: From single level to hierarchy*. PhD thesis, University of Illinois at Urbana-Champaign, Urbana, IL, 2002.

[22] M. Pelikan. *Hierarchical Bayesian optimization algorithm: Toward a new generation of evolutionary algorithms*. Springer, 2005.

[23] M. Pelikan. NK landscapes, problem difficulty, and hybrid evolutionary algorithms. *Genetic and Evol. Comp. Conf. (GECCO-2010)*, pages 665–672, 2010.

[24] M. Pelikan and D. E. Goldberg. Escaping hierarchical traps with competent genetic algorithms. *Genetic and Evol. Comp. Conf. (GECCO-2001)*, pages 511–518, 2001.

[25] M. Pelikan and D. E. Goldberg. A hierarchy machine: Learning to optimize from nature and humans. *Complexity*, 8(5):36–45, 2003.

[26] M. Pelikan, D. E. Goldberg, and F. Lobo. A survey of optimization by building and using probabilistic models. *Computational Optimization and Applications*, 21(1):5–20, 2002.

[27] M. Pelikan and A. K. Hartmann. Searching for ground states of Ising spin glasses with hierarchical BOA and cluster exact approximation. In E. Cantú-Paz, M. Pelikan, and K. Sastry, editors, *Scalable optimization via probabilistic modeling: From algorithms to applications*. Springer, 2006.

[28] M. Pelikan, K. Sastry, and E. Cantú-Paz, editors. *Scalable optimization via probabilistic modeling: From algorithms to applications*. Springer-Verlag, 2006.

[29] L. Y. Pratt, J. Mostow, C. A. Kamm, and A. A. Kamm. Direct transfer of learned information among neural networks. In *Proceedings of the Ninth National Conference on Artificial Intelligence*, pages 584–589, 1991.

[30] F. Rothlauf. *Representations for Genetic and Evolutionary Algorithms*. Springer, 2006.

[31] K. Sastry. Evaluation-relaxation schemes for genetic and evolutionary algorithms. Master's thesis, University of Illinois at Urbana-Champaign, Department of General Engineering, Urbana, IL, 2001.

[32] J. Schwarz and J. Ocenasek. A problem-knowledge based evolutionary algorithm KBOA for hypergraph partitioning. In *Proc. of the Fourth Joint Conf. on Knowledge-Based Software Engineering*, pages 51–58, Brno, Czech Republic, 2000. IO Press.

[33] Spin Glass Ground State Server. `http://www.informatik.uni-koeln.de/ls_juenger/research/sgs/sgs.html`, 2004. University of Köln, Germany.

[34] F. Stonedahl, W. Rand, and U. Wilensky. Crossnet: a framework for crossover with network-based chromosomal representations. *Genetic and Evol. Comp. Conf. (GECCO-2008)*, pages 1057–1064, 2008.

[35] A. Young, editor. *Spin glasses and random fields*. World Scientific, Singapore, 1998.

A Memory Efficient and Continuous-valued Compact EDA for Large Scale Problems

Sergio Rojas-Galeano
Engineering School
District University of Bogota
Bogota, Colombia
srojas@udistrital.edu.co

Nestor Rodriguez
Engineering School
District University of Bogota
Bogota, Colombia
nearodriguezg@correo.udistrital.edu.co

ABSTRACT

This paper considers large-scale `OneMax` and `RoyalRoad` optimization problems with up to 10^7 binary variables within a *compact* Estimation of Distribution Algorithms (`EDA`) framework. Building upon the compact Genetic Algorithm (`cGA`), the continuous domain Population-Based Incremental Learning algorithm ($\texttt{PBIL}_c$) and the arithmetic-coding `EDA`, we define a novel method that is able to compactly solve regular and noisy versions of these problems with minimal memory requirements, regardless of problem or population size. This feature allows the algorithm to be run in a conventional desktop machine. Issues regarding probability model sampling, arbitrary precision of the arithmetic-coding decompressing scheme, incremental fitness function evaluation and updating rules for compact learning, are presented and discussed.

Categories and Subject Descriptors

I.2.8 [**Computing Methodologies**]: Artificial Intelligence—*Problem Solving, Control Methods and Search*

General Terms

Algorithms

Keywords

EDA, compact GA, large scale optimization, arithmetic coding

1. INTRODUCTION

Estimation of Distribution Algorithms (`EDA`) [11, 16] approximately optimizes a cost function by building a probabilistic model of a pool of promising sub-optimal solutions over a given search space. For very-high dimensional search spaces, storing and updating a large population of candidates may imply a computational burden in both time and memory. The *compact* approach circumvents storage limitations by incrementally updating the probability model using just two candidates at any step of the algorithm, instead of the entire population. This feature makes the compact `EDA` framework practical for large-scale optimization, a soon-to-be commonplace setting in scientific domains such as bioinformatics, particle physics, chemical crystallography, or social network analysis, to name a few.

This study reports on a new efficient, continuous-valued, compact `EDA` aimed at optimization of large-scale problems of up to 10^7 binary decision variables, nevertheless requiring low-cost computational resources. The method is tailored to optimization of decomposable cost functions in terms of the contribution of individual variables, that is, to problems where incremental fitness evaluation is feasible. Although at present no second- or higher-order dependencies within the variables are considered in our method, its value as an early-stage data analysis tool in high dimensional spaces might be relevant, for example to carry out feature selection for subsequent dependencies estimation on smaller variable subsets, as other models with independence assumptions have shown [17]. Even so, we anticipate modeling multivariate dependencies will widen the applicability of our method. In this respect, incorporating memory and time efficiencies such as fitness evaluation relaxation [19] would be an interesting avenue of future work.

Our findings are organized as follows: a short review of methods related to our research is presented in section 2; a description of the techniques involved in the design of the algorithm is given in section 3; the algorithm itself is discussed in section 4; empirical arguments are provided in section 5 and closing remarks are highlighted in section 6.

Notation. Lower-case boldface is used to denote vector arrays (e.g. $\boldsymbol{\mu} \in \mathbb{R}^2, \mathbf{s} \in \mathbb{R}^\ell$) whereas plain font denotes scalar values (e.g. $\gamma, p, q \in \mathbb{R}$). Capital letters refer to sets of elements. We use n to denote the size of a given population, and ℓ represents the size of the search problem, that is, its dimensionality.

2. LITERATURE REVIEW

The compact Genetic Algorithm (`cGA`) [8] was proposed as a memory-efficient variant of the canonical genetic algorithm [5]. The idea behind the `cGA` is to consider the population of candidates as a sample from which a probability model of Bernoulli trials can be estimated. The algorithm performs successive binary tournaments of two sampled candidates from the current distribution and also updates the model parameters with a frequentist rule based on only those two candidates; thus it avoids the need to keep the entire population in memory. As a result, the `cGA` reduces the storing capacity needed to evolve the population from $O(n\ell)$ to $O(\ell(\log_2 n + 2))$. This property enabled the algorithm to solve problems with dimensionality up to one billion binary variables, as subsequently reported in [20]. In such problems ($\ell = 10^9, \log_2 \ell \approx 30$), the memory size required for running the algorithm would roughly reach $(10^9 \times 32)$bits $\approx 3,72$Gb, yet a stringent amount for a conventional machine; in fact, some efficacies including distributed computing, vectorized and integer operations, and tailored random number generation were necessary to solve large scale problems with a `cGA` running in a 256-processor cluster machine [20].

`cGA` works in discrete domains where variables take binary values. Other non-compact `EDA`s have been proposed to address optimization in both discrete [2,14] and continuous domains [6,21]. Particularly, continuous-domain Population-Based Incremental Learning ($\texttt{PBIL}_c$) [21] is an algorithm that assumes variables are independently normally distributed. The mean and variance parameters are updated using the maximum likelihood marginal estimates from a sample population. Since the population is used at every iteration of the algorithm, $\texttt{PBIL}_c$ is more demanding in terms of memory when compared to `cGA`, and would be difficult to apply to large scale problems in conventional machines.

It is also worth mentioning a recent study [22] where an encoding technique known as arithmetic-coding [18], was used within a continuous domain population-based `EDA` to solve large scale problems of up to one billion variables. The encoding technique allows compressing a binary string of arbitrary length using a couple of double precision numbers. Although the fitness evaluation still requires $\ell/8$ bytes of memory per active candidate, the compression scheme enabled the algorithm to solve the problem with a population size of 3200 candidates in a regular PC-computer in about 36 hours. Regrettably, the study did not provide details on the mechanics of the algorithm, motivation of the updating rules of the distribution parameters, or issues related to the precision of arithmetic-coding.

In this paper we build upon the above algorithms and propose a novel method to solve canonical and noisy versions of large-scale `OneMax` and `RoyalRoad` problems by using a compact and continuously-valued representation, which is further enhanced with an arithmetic-coding scheme. For this kind of additively-separated tasks and with the assumption of independently-distributed binary variables, the new method demands minimal memory consumption ($O(1)$), regardless of the problem dimension or population size. The insights are reported in the following sections.

3. TOOLS

3.1 TILDA

The basis of this study is an algorithm we devised as a mix of `cGA` and $\texttt{PBIL}_c$. The underlying idea is to model the pool of solution candidates with a multivariate marginal joint Gaussian distribution whose parameters are estimated within a compact framework. The estimates of marginal parameters $(\mu_i, \sigma_i)_{i=1}^{\ell}$ for both the mean and standard deviation of each input variable, are periodically updated with information from the fittest candidates selected by means of 2-way tournaments, as explained next[1]. Let us assume we have a population P of $2n$ candidates were n simple 2-way tournaments are performed (two candidates from P are randomly chosen without replacement, and the the winner substitutes the loser). Let W and L be the sets of tournament's winners and losers, respectively. The new population is then $\widetilde{P} = (P \setminus L) \cup W$. Then, the maximum likelihood mean estimate of the new population, that is $\boldsymbol{\mu} = (\mu_1, \ldots, \mu_\ell)$, can be computed in vectorized form as:

$$\begin{aligned} \boldsymbol{\mu} &= \frac{1}{2n} \sum_{\mathbf{x}_k \in \widetilde{P}} \mathbf{x}_k = \frac{1}{2n} \left(\sum_{\mathbf{x}_k \in P} \mathbf{x}_k - \sum_{\mathbf{x}_k \in L} \mathbf{x}_k + \sum_{\mathbf{x}_k \in W} \mathbf{x}_k \right) \\ &= \frac{1}{n} \sum_{\mathbf{x}_k \in W} \mathbf{x}_k, \end{aligned}$$

since $P = W \cup L$. Now, assuming that variables are mutually independent, and defining the unordered set of winner indexes as $\mathcal{W} = \{k_t : t = 1, \ldots, n;\ \mathbf{x}_{k_t} \in W\}$, the estimate can be re-casted in terms of its components as:

$$\mu_i = \frac{1}{n} \sum_{t=1}^{n} x_i^{k_t},$$

where $x_i^{k_t}$ is the i-th component of the candidate $\mathbf{x}_{k_t}$. We observe that if we initialise $\mu_i = 0$, then the estimate can be updated incrementally with a fraction of each tournament's winner, as the formula in Equation (1) indicates.

$$\mu_i := \mu_i + \tfrac{1}{n} x_i^{k_t}; \quad t = 1, \ldots, n. \tag{1}$$

Now, the same rationale can be applied to the variance estimate $\boldsymbol{\Sigma} = (\sigma_1^2, \ldots, \sigma_\ell^2)$:

$$\begin{aligned} \sigma_i^2 &= \frac{1}{n} \sum_{t=1}^{n} (x_i^{k_t} - \mu_i)^2 = \frac{1}{n} \left(\sum_{t=1}^{n} (x_i^{k_t})^2 - 2\mu_i \sum_{t=1}^{n} x_i^{k_t} + n\mu_i^2 \right) \\ &= \frac{1}{n} \sum_{t=1}^{n} (x_i^{k_t})^2 - \mu_i^2. \end{aligned}$$

Then again, an incremental update can be obtained by first setting a temporal variable $\tilde{\sigma}_i^2 = 0$, then accumulating deviations of each tournament's winner in this variable using Equation (2), and finally subtracting the square of the previously computed mean estimate to obtain the variance estimate, as in Equation (3).

$$\tilde{\sigma}_i^2 := \tilde{\sigma}_i^2 + \tfrac{1}{n} (x_i^{k_t})^2; \quad t = 1, \ldots, n. \tag{2}$$

$$\sigma_i^2 = \tilde{\sigma}_i^2 - \mu_i^2 \tag{3}$$

Equations (1-3) outline the compact updating rules of the new method, named the Tiny Incremental Learning Density Estimation Algorithm (`TILDA`) – see Algorithm 1.

The aim of the algorithm is to approximately find a solution to the unconstrained optimisation problem:

$$\boldsymbol{\beta}^\star = \underset{\mathbf{x} \in \mathbb{R}^\ell}{\mathsf{argmax}}\, f(\mathbf{x}),$$

where $f(\cdot)$ is the fitness or cost function to be optimised. The algorithm models a population of promising solutions using a multivariate marginal joint Gaussian distribution with parameters $\boldsymbol{\mu}$ and $\boldsymbol{\Sigma}$. The main loop (line 2) runs for a number of generations or until the parameters converge. The inner loop (line 4) simulates the breeding of one population by sampling two candidates at a time (line 5), carrying out 2-way tournaments to determine the winner $\hat{\mathbf{x}}$ (line 6), and also keeping temporary parameter estimates for the current

[1] A similar reasoning was followed in [12, Appendix A].

Algorithm 1 TILDA

Requires: $\ell > 0$, fitness function $f(\cdot)$
Outputs: best candidate $\boldsymbol{\beta}$
1: $\boldsymbol{\mu} = \mathbf{0}, \boldsymbol{\Sigma} = \mathbf{1}, \boldsymbol{\beta} = \mathbf{0}, \gamma = 0.5, \epsilon = 0.01$
2: **repeat until ending citeria not met**
3: $\quad \tilde{\boldsymbol{\mu}} = \tilde{\boldsymbol{\Sigma}} = \mathbf{0}$
4: $\quad$ **repeat** n **times**
5: $\quad\quad \{\mathbf{x}', \mathbf{x}''\} \sim \mathcal{N}(\boldsymbol{\mu}, \boldsymbol{\Sigma})$
6: $\quad\quad \hat{\mathbf{x}} = \mathsf{argmax}(f(\mathbf{x}'), f(\mathbf{x}''))$
7: $\quad\quad \boldsymbol{\beta} = \mathsf{argmax}(f(\boldsymbol{\beta}), f(\hat{\mathbf{x}}))$
8: $\quad\quad \tilde{\boldsymbol{\mu}} = \tilde{\boldsymbol{\mu}} + \frac{1}{n}(\hat{x}_1, \hat{x}_2, \ldots, \hat{x}_\ell)$
9: $\quad\quad \tilde{\boldsymbol{\Sigma}} = \tilde{\boldsymbol{\Sigma}} + \frac{1}{n}(\hat{x}_1^2, \hat{x}_2^2, \ldots, \hat{x}_\ell^2)$
10: $\quad \boldsymbol{\mu} = \boldsymbol{\mu} - \gamma(\boldsymbol{\mu} - \frac{1}{2}(\boldsymbol{\beta} + \tilde{\boldsymbol{\mu}}))$
11: $\quad \boldsymbol{\Sigma} = \boldsymbol{\Sigma} - \gamma(\boldsymbol{\Sigma} - (\tilde{\boldsymbol{\Sigma}} - (\tilde{\mu}_0^2, \tilde{\mu}_1^2, \ldots, \tilde{\mu}_\ell^2))) + \epsilon$

population (lines 8-9) using Equations (1-2). Notice that the algorithm stores the best solution found up to a certain generation in the variable $\boldsymbol{\beta}$ (line 7). The actual updates of the overall estimates are performed at the end of the main loop (lines 10-11). The overall mean estimate is computed with a memory-preserving rule with decay factor γ, incorporating an elitist mechanism that shifts the estimate towards the average of the population mean and the best candidate. Similarly, the overall variance estimate uses the population mean, as stated in Equation (3), plus a small constant intended to prevent premature convergence[2]. When the ending criteria is met, the approximate optimal solution found by the algorithm can be retrieved from $\boldsymbol{\beta}$.

3.2 Arithmetic coding of binary strings

Given the alphabet $S = \{0, 1\}$ and a probability distribution $\Phi = \{P(0)=p, P(1)=1-p\}$, the idea of arithmetic coding is to represent an arbitrary binary string of length ℓ using distribution Φ and a single real number $q \in [0, 1]$ known as a *code value* (see details in [18]). Decoding is achieved by performing a Bernoulli trial for each bit in the sequence, that is, flipping an unfair coin with bias p, where q represents the chance of a face-up outcome. For this purpose, the decoder builds nested intervals and biases $\{[a_i, b_i], p_i\}_{i=1}^{\ell}$ that re-define the support and probability distributions throughout consecutive bits along the sequence. Thus, a decoded string $\mathbf{s}_p^q$ corresponds to $\mathbf{s}_p^q = (s_i^q)_{i=1}^{\ell} = (s_1^q, \ldots, s_\ell^q)$, where the outcome for each bit i is determined by the indicator function:

$$s_i^q = \begin{cases} 0 & q \le p_i \\ 1 & q > p_i \end{cases}, \; i \ge 1, \tag{4}$$

and the bias p_i is updated iteratively according to the outcome of the preceding bit and the bounds a_i, b_i of the nested support intervals, following the recursions:

$$\begin{aligned} [a_1, b_1] &= [0, 1]\,, \\ [a_i, b_i] &= \begin{cases} [a_{i-1}, p_{i-1}] & q \le p_{i-1} \\ [p_{i-1}, b_{i-1}] & q > p_{i-1} \end{cases}, \; i > 1, \\ p_i &= a_i + (b_i - a_i)p\,, \; i \ge 1. \end{aligned} \tag{5}$$

Equation (5) implies that the support interval for a subsequent trial is replaced by the subinterval chosen from the comparison of the code value and the bias of the current trial. As a result, the length of nested intervals shrinks away as the decoding progresses, with the values of these variables growing in precision digits. In theory, one may obtain an arbitrary number of bits with this decoding scheme. In practice, however, the number of bits is limited by machine-dependent floating point arithmetic, in other words, due to round-off errors the supporting interval (and the bias p_i too) eventually collapses and yields the code value q, resulting in a constant zero-output from that trial onwards.

In an attempt to circumvent this shrinking-interval limitation, we contemplated an alternative decoding scheme, as explained next. Firstly, observe that during the shrinking procedure the nested probability distributions obtained with the successive updates of $[a_i, b_i]$ and p_i, preserve the proportions of the original distribution defined by p in Φ. In fact, these are just shrunk replica distributions repeatedly shifted to different locations along the unit interval. Within these distributions, the *global* (fixed) code value q defines a *local* chance of outcome that is relative to the location of the supporting interval and bias of the respective trial. Bearing in mind this observation, we sought to switch roles and keep distribution Φ *global*, that is, fixed to the unit interval, whereas the otherwise constant code value is repeatedly shifted to mirror the *local* chance of outcome at each trial of the shrinking procedure. In this way, for all i we fixed $[a_i = 0, b_i = 1]$ and $p_i = p$ and rescaled the value of the now variable q_i using the following recursive rules:

$$\begin{aligned} q_1 &= q\,, \\ q_i &= \begin{cases} \dfrac{q_{i-1}}{p} & q_{i-1} \le p \\ \dfrac{(q_{i-1} - p)}{(1 - p)} & q_{i-1} > p \end{cases}, \; i > 1 \end{aligned} \tag{6}$$

In this new scheme, the values of q_i shift around the unit interval resembling the cursor of an old-fashion sliding rule, thus the name *sliding-pin* arithmetic decoding. Since the length and bias of the supporting interval are in a normal scale, the relocated values of q_i are not machine-precision dependent. Additionally, it is worth noting that the sliding-pin procedure only maintains one parameter (q_i) as opposed to three parameters (a_i, b_i, p_i) for the shrinking decoding. The decoded string $\mathbf{s}_p^q$ would be now obtained as:

$$\mathbf{s}_p^q = (s_i^p)_{i=1}^{\ell} = (s_1^p, \ldots, s_\ell^p), \tag{7}$$

where the indicator function becomes:

$$s_i^p = \begin{cases} 0 & q_i \le p \\ 1 & q_i > p \end{cases}, \; i \ge 1. \tag{8}$$

The two decompression schemes are illustrated in Figure 1.

[2]It is interesting to remark that more sophisticated mechanisms to prevent premature convergence such as adaptive variance scaling from EDA and Evolutionary Strategies literature (e.g. [1, 3, 10]), are worthy of further study in future extensions.

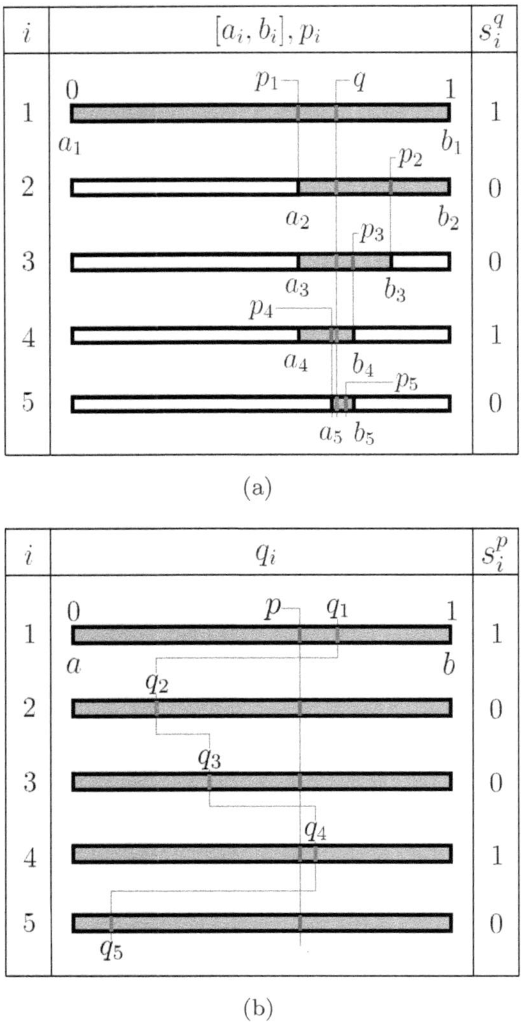

Figure 1: Illustration of the operation of two arithmetic-decoding techniques for a string of length $\ell = 5$. The leftmost column i of each illustration indicates the decoding step. The corresponding output bit for each step is depicted in the rightmost column. (a) *Shrinking-interval* decoding [18]: The values of $\{[a_i, b_i], p_i\}_{i=1}^{5}$ are updated recursively using Equations (5) for a given fixed q whilst the output bit s_i^q is obtained with Equation (4); the shaded area within the nested subintervals shrinks away as the decoding progresses. (b) *Sliding-pin* decoding: The support interval and p are now fixed, while $\{q_i\}_{i=1}^{5}$ is subsequently shifted throughout the unit interval using Equation (6), thus resembling the strip of a sliding-rule; the output bit s_i^p in this case is given by Equation (8).

3.3 Truncated-normal random numbers

Algorithm 1 is designed to work in continuous domains where variables are assumed to be Gaussian-distributed over the real line. In an arithmetic coding scheme, however, the search of a feasible set of values for a pair (p, q) requires the evolutionary algorithm to generate random numbers bounded within the $[0, 1]$ interval[3]. For this reason we adapted the algorithm to a *truncated* Gaussian model with support on the unit interval only, following [4, page 39]: given a random variable X with cumulative probability distribution Φ, the truncated random variable X^T with distribution Φ^T and support $[a, b]$ is defined as

$$\Phi^\mathsf{T}(x) = \begin{cases} 0 & x < a \\ \frac{\Phi(x)-\Phi(a)}{\Phi(b)-\Phi(a)} & a \leq x \leq b \\ 1 & x > b \end{cases}. \qquad (9)$$

We define $\Phi \equiv \mathcal{N}(\mu, \sigma), a = 0, b = 1$ and normalise $x' = \frac{x-\mu}{\sigma}$, $a' = \frac{a-\mu}{\sigma} = \frac{-\mu}{\sigma}$ and $b' = \frac{b-\mu}{\sigma} = \frac{1-\mu}{\sigma}$. Let $u \sim [0, 1]$ be a uniformly distributed random number; hence we use the inversion method for random number generation (see e.g. [4]), that is, assume $u = \Phi^\mathsf{T}(x')$ and work out the resulting x bounded to [0,1]. Since $0 \leq x' \leq 1$ from Equation (9) we get:

$$\Phi(x') = u(\Phi(b') - \Phi(a')) + \Phi(a'),$$

which in turn implies that,

$$x = \sigma(\Phi^{-1}(u(\Phi(b') - \Phi(a')) + \Phi(a')) + \mu. \qquad (10)$$

Since $\Phi(a')$ and $\Phi(b')$ are constant terms, Equation (10) can be used to generate a truncated random number by computing a uniform random number and one evaluation of the inverse normal distribution with given parameters (μ, σ).

4. ALGORITHM

To begin with, let us recall the arithmetic-coded EDA proposed in [22]. It is a continuous domain population-based EDA that takes advantage of the shrinking-interval arithmetic decoding, defined in Equations (4-5), in order to search for a solution string $\mathbf{s}_p^q$ in a high dimensional space of size ℓ. The compression scheme reduces the memory requirements needed to store and maintain the population of candidates, enabling the algorithm to solve large-scale problems in a standard desktop machine. Here we present an algorithm that further improves memory usage by means of a compact representation.

The new algorithm is an adaptation of TILDA (as described in Section 3.1). The idea is to search for the best $(p, q) \in \mathbb{R}^2$ that determines the string $\mathbf{s}_p^q$ whose fitness function is evaluated in $\{0, 1\}^\ell$. For this purpose, we let $\boldsymbol{\mu}, \tilde{\boldsymbol{\mu}}, \boldsymbol{\Sigma}, \tilde{\boldsymbol{\Sigma}}, \boldsymbol{\beta} \in \mathbb{R}^2$ in Algorithm 1 and we chose the sliding-pin scheme of Equations (6-8) to decompress $\mathbf{s}_p^q$. Likewise, we decided on using the truncated Gaussian random generator of Equation (10) for sampling. The resulting method (@TILDA: *arithmetic-coding* TILDA) is shown in Algorithm 2.

The time complexity of the algorithm is dependent on the convergence speed, the population size n, and the cost needed to decompress and evaluate the candidate (usually linear in ℓ). More specifically, neglecting the cost of random number generation, each inner loop iteration incurs $O(\ell)$ for the two fitness evaluations in line 6 (the fitness evaluations in line 7 can be spared by caching previous calls). So, assuming t_c iterations are needed to converge, the running time is in $O(n\ell t_c)$.

[3]Let us mention that mechanisms for truncated pseudorandom number generation in other support intervals has been also highlighted in previous EDA studies (e.g. [7, 12])

Algorithm 2 @TILDA

Requires: $\ell > 0$, fitness function $f(\cdot)$
Outputs: best candidate $\boldsymbol{\beta}$
$\boldsymbol{\beta} = \boldsymbol{\mu} = (0.5, 0.5), \boldsymbol{\Sigma} = (10, 10), \gamma = 0.9, \epsilon = \ell^{-1}$
repeat until convergence
  $\tilde{\boldsymbol{\mu}} = \tilde{\boldsymbol{\Sigma}} = (0, 0)$
  repeat n **times**
    $\{(p', q'), (p'', q'')\} \sim \mathcal{N}^{\mathsf{T}}(\boldsymbol{\mu}, \boldsymbol{\Sigma})$ //sampling (Eq.(10))
    $(\hat{p}, \hat{q}) = \mathsf{argmax}(f(\mathbf{s}^{p'}_{q'}), f(\mathbf{s}^{p''}_{q''}))$ //decoding (Eq.(6-8))
    $\boldsymbol{\beta} = \mathsf{argmax}(f(\mathbf{s}^{\hat{p}}_{\hat{q}}), f(\mathbf{s}^{\beta_1}_{\beta_2}))$ // update best
    $\tilde{\boldsymbol{\mu}} = \tilde{\boldsymbol{\mu}} + \frac{1}{n}(\hat{p}, \hat{q})$
    $\tilde{\boldsymbol{\Sigma}} = \tilde{\boldsymbol{\Sigma}} + \frac{1}{n}(\hat{p}^2, \hat{q}^2)$
  $\boldsymbol{\mu} = \boldsymbol{\mu} - \gamma(\boldsymbol{\mu} - \frac{1}{2}(\boldsymbol{\beta} + \tilde{\boldsymbol{\mu}}))$
  $\boldsymbol{\Sigma} = \boldsymbol{\Sigma} - \gamma(\boldsymbol{\Sigma} - (\tilde{\boldsymbol{\Sigma}} - (\tilde{\mu}_0^2, \tilde{\mu}_1^2)) + \epsilon$

Now we discuss an interesting memory saving mechanism obtainable with this new algorithm. Observe that its memory cost is dominated by the size of the problem ℓ. This is because the working memory consists of nine bi-dimensional variables in $O(1)$ plus the temporal buffer needed to decompress $\mathbf{s}^q_p$, which is in $O(\ell)$. However, if we constrain the application domain to additively-separable problems exhibiting modularity of fitness evaluation to the level of single variables, that is, problems where the fitness function aggregates independent contributions in each dimension of the solution, then the memory cost can be $O(1)$. The latter is possible by incrementally evaluating and disposing bits obtained during the stream decompression of $\mathbf{s}^q_p$. And given that the best solution can be retrieved at any point of the evolutionary loop from the arithmetic code $\boldsymbol{\beta} = (\beta_1, \beta_2)$, corresponding to $\mathbf{s}^{\beta_2}_{\beta_1}$, no string buffering is actually needed. As mentioned earlier, even if bits are not discarded (i.e. buffering them into a string) the fitness evaluation requires $O(\ell)$ time to scan the string, so the memory savings using streaming implies no additional time overload. It is in this sense that the algorithm is well suited for large scale problems, ensuring minimal memory consumption, regardless of the problem and population size. The memory efficiency of @TILDA compares favorably with arithmetic-coded EDA [22], which requires $O(\ell + n)$ for the evolutionary loop (although it could be lowered to $O(n)$ by using the same streaming technique), and also with cGA [8], which requires $O(\ell(\log_2 n + 2))$.

It may be noted in passing that, by using the sliding-pin arithmetic-coding technique and the truncated random number generator, @TILDA is able to always decompress feasible solutions notwithstanding the problem size ℓ. The latter contrasts with the difficulties found for the arithmetic-coded EDA, where some (p, q) codes where unable to produce the desired string length due to precision issues [22].

5. EMPIRICAL STUDY

We conducted an empirical study of @TILDA applied to the OneMax [15] and RoyalRoad [13] problems (including noisy variations). Fitness functions for a candidate solution ($\mathbf{s} \in [0, 1]^\ell$) to these problems are defined in Table 1. For the case of RoyalRoad functions, the parameter c represents a score added to a candidate for each succeeding schema of order c that can be found within its bit string, starting at bit 1 (in contrast to the original definition given in [13], here only a single block scan of ℓ/c schemas is carried out to compute

Problem	Fitness function
OneMax	$f(\mathbf{s}) = \sum_{i=1}^{\ell} s_i$
Noisy OneMax	$\hat{f}(\mathbf{s}) = f(\mathbf{s}) + \mathcal{N}(0, \sigma_N^2)$
RoyalRoad	$f_c(\mathbf{s}) = \sum_{i=0}^{(\ell/c)-1} c \left(\prod_{k=ic+1}^{(i+1)c} s_k\right)$
Noisy RoyalRoad	$\hat{f}_c(\mathbf{s}) = f_c(\mathbf{s}) + \mathcal{N}(0, \sigma_N^2)$

Table 1: Fitness functions used in the empirical study for a candidate $\mathbf{s} = \{s_1, \ldots, s_\ell\}$, $s_i \in \{0, 1\}$. $\mathcal{N}(0, \sigma_N^2)$ denotes a normally distributed random variable of variance σ_N^2.

Requires: $(p, q), \ell, noise$
Outputs: f
  $f = 0$
  repeat ℓ **times**
    $bit = q > p$
    if bit **then**
      $q = (q - p)/(1 - p)$
      $f = f + 1$
    else $q = q/p$
  end-repeat
  if $noise$ **then** $f = f + \mathcal{N}(0, \sigma_N^2)$

(a) OneMax

Requires: $(p, q), \ell, c, noise$
Outputs: f
  $f = 0; k = 1; block =$ **true**
  repeat ℓ **times**
    $bit = q > p;\ block = block \wedge bit$
    if bit **then** $q = (q - p)/(1 - p)$
    else $q = q/p$
    if $k = c$ **then**
      $k = 0$
      if $block$ **then** $f = f + c$
      else $block =$ **true**
    end-if
    $k = k + 1$
  end-repeat
  if $noise$ **then** $f = f + \mathcal{N}(0, \sigma_N^2)$

(b) RoyalRoad

Table 2: Stream algorithms for string decompression and fitness evaluation. (a) OneMax: this algorithm is a variation of the sliding-pin arithmetic decoder of Equations (6-8), where the fitness f is increased every time the current *bit* is set to true; inputs are: arithmetic code (p, q), problem size ℓ, and a *noise* flag to activate the noisy version. (b) RoyalRoad: based on the OneMax code above, and using c as an additional input defining the order of the schema, this algorithm keeps a *block* flag that is successively updated with the conjunction of the decoded *bit* variable; for every succeeding schema, whose extent is controlled with counter k, score c is added to f if the schema *block* flag is set, otherwise this flag is readjusted.

fitness; no additional hierarchical scans of higher -doubled-order schemas follow up).

Let us observe that the evaluation of these fitness functions allows additively-separable computations. Hence we implemented stream decompression/fitness-evaluation algorithms (see Table 2) in order to take advantage of the memory savings of @TILDA[4]. Instead of **s**, these stream algorithms take an arithmetic code (p, q) as their input, which implicitly defines the bit string $\mathbf{s}_p^q$ of Equation (7), and simultaneously decompress the candidate and compute its fitness value f. In this way we were able to run the experiments in a conventional laptop Intel® Core™ i7 machine with 6GB memory. Algorithm 2 and test-bed scripts were implemented in both Octave version 3.2.4 with QtOctave version 0.9.1 and Matlab R2011. Fitness routines in Table 2 were implemented in C with the MEX interface for faster evaluation.

5.1 Results on noiseless problems

The first set of experiments were aimed at testing the behaviour of the algorithm on noise-free (regular) problems. We set the number of maximum generations to 1000 for all experiments, with an early-stopping condition whenever a candidate decoding a number of bits equals to the problem size ℓ was found. In order to set the appropriate population size needed to find a solution with respect to ℓ, we carried out a grid-search [9] over $n \in \{2^3, 2^4, \ldots, 2^{12}\}$; the search was stopped when, for a given n, at least 90% of 100 runs were successful. For the RoyalRoad case, the schema order c was set to 100 for all experiments. The values of learning rate and premature convergence parameters ($\gamma = 0.9$ and $\epsilon = \ell^{-1}$) were chosen from empirical evidence of preliminary experiments. Results of the final experiments are listed in Table 3.

In summary, these results show that the algorithm succeeded in solving both problems from medium- to large-scale lengths (10^3 to 10^7 variables). Interestingly enough, it can be seen that a small population size $n \leq 32$ was needed to solve the problems, even for the large dimensionalities. The average generation of solution emergence was much smaller than the maximum setting of 1000. On the other hand, a comparable trend of performance is visible in the OneMax and RoyalRoad instances, except that a bigger population size was needed in the smaller problems for the latter. This finding may drop a hint on the potential effectiveness of the algorithm to tackle basic levels of structure in the problem (recall that RoyalRoadfitness function assigns score only to entire schemas of length c, that is, contiguous chunks of variables).

5.2 Results on noisy problems

The second set of experiments focused on testing the robustness of the algorithm when exogenous noise was added to the original fitness function. We followed the same settings as before but with 30 runs. Again the population size was obtained by a grid-search. The level of noise was controlled with a exogenous-noise-variance to deterministic-fitness-variance ($\frac{\sigma_N^2}{\sigma_f^2}$) parameter as defined in [20]. We tested the algorithm using a corruption $\frac{\sigma_N^2}{\sigma_f^2}$ ratio of 10^{-2}. Results of this set of experiments are listed in Table 4.

[4]We remark that the algorithm is suitable as well for non-decomposable fitness functions, or problems where no stream decompressing algorithm is available. In the worst of these cases its memory complexity, as mentioned earlier, would be in $O(\ell)$, still a favourable scenario for large-scale applications.

Problem size	Solution	OneMax	RoyalRoad
$\ell = 10^3$	n	8	16
	Success rate	100/100	96/100
	Age (avg.)	29.62	58.22
$\ell = 10^4$	n	8	16
	Success rate	99/100	92/100
	Age (avg.)	77.21	42.33
$\ell = 10^5$	n	8	16
	Success rate	98/100	99/100
	Age (avg.)	146.58	93.24
$\ell = 10^6$	n	16	16
	Success rate	94/100	94/100
	Age (avg.)	229.95	207.27
$\ell = 10^7$	n	32	32
	Success rate	95/100	91/100
	Age (avg.)	214.88	235.59

Table 3: Noise-free experiments. For each problem (OneMax, RoyalRoad) and dimension ℓ, results are reported on n (population size required to solve it), success rate (successful runs over 100 repetitions) and average age of the solution (generation where optimal candidate emerged).

In these experiments, the results on both problems are dissimilar. For the Noisy OneMax problem the incidence of noise in medium-size instances causes no difficulty to the algorithm in solving it. In larger instances, however, ($\ell = \{10^5, 10^6\}$) the algorithm struggles and demands higher population sizes of up to $n = 2048$ but still obtains success rates inferior to 50%. In contrast, a small population size $n = 32$ seems appropriate to solve all instances of Noisy RoyalRoad problems. We reason that in this case, the block-structure of the fitness score diminishes the effect external noise may have in misguiding the algorithm during its search.

6. CONCLUSIONS

We introduced a new compact EDA algorithm that is able to solve to optimality additively-separable bit-string problems of up to 10^7 dimensions with minimum memory requirements, both at individual or block contribution of variables to the fitness score. In the presence of noise, the algorithm is suitable to solve medium to large-size instances of Noisy RoyalRoad problems but struggles with large scale Noisy OneMax problems. On this topic we are considering exploring different ideas for noise tolerance such as the effect of using a combination of best candidates obtained from independent shorter, quicker runs, and also analysing in depth the role of elitism in such scenario.

In addition we are planning to study the role of the learning rate and premature convergence parameters within more elaborated mechanisms as those proposed in existing EDA literature. Moreover, it would be interesting to study the behaviour of the algorithm in different kinds of fitness landscapes, for example, uneven (not all-ones) optimal solutions and also, deceptive functions. Yet another exciting avenue of

Problem size	Solution	OneMax	RoyalRoad
$\ell = 10^3$	n	8	32
	Success rate	28/30	30/30
	Age (avg.)	59.93	32.20
$\ell = 10^4$	n	64	32
	Success rate	30/30	30/30
	Age (avg.)	48.17	48.47
$\ell = 10^5$	n	2048	32
	Success rate	19/30	27/30
	Age (avg.)	134.37	133.90
$\ell = 10^6$	n	2048	32
	Success rate	12/30	28/30
	Age (avg.)	168.87	153.80

Table 4: Noisy experiments. An exogenous noise rate of $\frac{\sigma_N^2}{\sigma_f^2} = 0.01$ was used in both test problems. For each each problem (OneMax, RoyalRoad) and dimension ℓ, results are reported on n (population size required to solve it), success rate (successful runs over 30 repetitions) and average age of the solution (generation where optimal candidate emerged).

future research is extending the memory and time efficiency ideas here presented to models of higher-order variable interaction.

As a concluding remark we anticipate that a parallel implementation of the algorithm would improve running times, although at present, an average run to solve a one-million bit problem in a regular laptop with a population size of 2048 is 1 hour. Our current work aims to validate and extend these findings to very-high dimensional problems of up to one-billion variables.

7. ACKNOWLEDGMENTS

We would like to thank the anonymous reviewers for their insightful comments and suggestions.

8. REFERENCES

[1] T. Bäck and H.-P. Schwefel. An overview of evolutionary algorithms for parameter optimization. *Evolutionary Computation*, 1(1):1–23, 1993.

[2] S. Baluja and R. Caruana. Removing the genetics from the standard genetic algorithm. Technical Report CMU-CS-95-141, Carnegie-Mellon University, 1995.

[3] Y. Cai, X. Sun, H. Xu, and P. Jia. Cross entropy and adaptive variance scaling in continuous EDA. In *Proceedings of the 9th annual conference on Genetic and evolutionary computation*, GECCO '07, pages 609–616, New York, NY, USA, 2007.

[4] L. Devroye. *Non-Uniform Random Variate Generation.* Springer-Verlag, 1986.

[5] D. E. Goldberg. *Genetic Algorithms in Search, Optimization, and Machine Learning.* Addison-Wesley Professional, 1 edition, 1989.

[6] C. Gonzáles, J. A. Lozano, and P. Larrañaga. Mathematical modelling of $UMDA_c$ algorithm with tournament selection. *International Journal of Approximate Reasoning*, 31(3):313–340, 2002.

[7] J. Grahl and F. Rothlauf. Polyeda: Combining estimation of distribution algorithms and linear inequality constraints. In *Proceedings of the 6th Annual Conference on Genetic and Evolutionary Computation*, GECCO '04, pages 1174–1185, 2004.

[8] G. R. Harik and F. G. Lobo. The compact genetic algorithm. *IEEE Transactions on Evolutionary Computation*, 3:523–528, 1999.

[9] C. W. Hsu, C. C. Chang, and C. J. Lin. *A practical guide to support vector classification.* Department of Computer Science, National Taiwan University, 2003.

[10] O. Kramer and F. Gieseke. Variance scaling for EDAs revisited. In *KI 2011: Advances in Artificial Intelligence*, volume 7006 of *Lecture Notes in Computer Science*, pages 169–178. Springer, 2011.

[11] P. Larrañaga and J. A. Lozano, editors *Estimation of Distribution Algorithms: A New Tool for Evolutionary Computation.* Springer, 2001.

[12] E. Mininno, F. Cupertino, and D. Naso. Real-valued compact genetic algorithms for embedded microcontroller optimization. *IEEE Transactions on Evolutionary Computation*, 12(3):203–219, 2008.

[13] M. Mitchell, S. Forrest, and J. H. Holland. The royal road for genetic algorithms: Fitness landscapes and GA performance. In *Proceedings of the First European Conference on Artificial Life*, pages 245–254, 1991.

[14] H. Mühlenbein. The equation for response to selection and its use for prediction. *Evolutionary Computation*, 5(3):303–346, 1997.

[15] M. Pelikan and K. Sastry. Initial-population bias in the univariate estimation of distribution algorithm. In *Proceedings of the 11th Annual Conference on Genetic and Evolutionary Computation*, GECCO '09, pages 429–436, New York, NY, USA, 2009. ACM.

[16] M. Pelikan, K. Sastry, and E. Cantú-Paz, editors. *Scalable Optimization via Probabilistic Modeling: From Algorithms to Applications.* Springer-Verlag New York, Inc., Secaucus, NJ, USA, 2006.

[17] S. Rojas-Galeano, E. Hsieh, D. Agranoff, S. Krishna, and D. Fernandez-Reyes. Estimation of relevant variables on high-dimensional biological patterns using iterated weighted kernel functions. *PLoS ONE*, 3(3), 2008.

[18] A. Said. Introduction to arithmetic coding - theory and practice. Technical Report HPL-2004-76, Imaging Systems Laboratory, HP Laboratories Palo Alto, 2004.

[19] K. Sastry. Evaluation-relaxation schemes for genetic and evolutionary algorithms. Technical report, 2002.

[20] K. Sastry, D. E. Goldberg, and X. Llora. Towards billion-bit optimization via a parallel estimation of distribution algorithm. In *Proceedings of the 9th Annual Conference on Genetic and Evolutionary Computation*, GECCO '07, pages 577–584, 2007.

[21] M. Sebag and A. Ducoulombier. Extending Population-Based incremental learning to continuous search spaces. *Lecture Notes in Computer Science*, 1498, 1998.

[22] W. Suwannik and P. Chongstitvatana. Solving one-billion-bit noisy onemax problem using estimation distribution algorithm with arithmetic coding. In *IEEE Congress on Evolutionary Computation*, pages 1203–1206, 2008.

Predetermined versus Learned Linkage Models

Dirk Thierens
Institute of Information and Computing Sciences
Utrecht University, The Netherlands
D.Thierens@uu.nl

Peter A. N. Bosman
Centre for Mathematics and Computer Science
Amsterdam, The Netherlands
Peter.Bosman@cwi.nl

ABSTRACT

The *linkage tree genetic algorithm* (LTGA) learns, each generation, a linkage model by building a hierarchical cluster tree. The LTGA is an instance of the more general *gene-pool optimal mixing evolutionary algorithm* (GOMEA) that uses a family of subsets (FOS) linkage model. We compare the performance of the linkage model learning LTGA with several predetermined FOS linkage models applied by GOMEA. The predetermined models are matched to the underlying problem structure of four benchmark functions: onemax, deceptive trap functions, maximal overlapping nearest-neighbor NK-landscapes, and weighted MAXCUT problems. Although the a priori fixed models are specifically designed to capture the interactions between the problem variables, experimental results show that - for problems with intricate interaction structure - they are actually less efficient than LTGA that dynamically learns a hierarchical tree model. Some of these observations were unexpected and raise the question of what exactly is the optimal linkage structure for a given problem as used by GOMEA. In the case of the NK-problem a linkage model that is an accurate description of the underlying additively decomposable fitness structure is clearly not an optimal linkage model. Being able to rebuild the linkage model each generation has clear benefits above using fixed, predetermined linkage models.

Categories and Subject Descriptors

I.2 [**Artificial Intelligence**]: Problem Solving, Control Methods, and Search

General Terms

Algorithms, Performance, Experimentation

Keywords

Evolutionary Computation, Genetic Algorithms, Estimation-of-Distribution Algorithms, Linkage Learning, Optimal Mixing Algorithm.

1. INTRODUCTION

Linkage learning evolutionary algorithms aim to identify interacting or dependent problem variables that contribute to highly fit solutions [1]. The goal hereby is to build a linkage model of these interactions and use this model to generate, with high probability, new, highly fit solutions. In previous work we have classified a large group of linkage models as family of subsets (FOS) [11]. Depending on the specific family of subsets used, we obtain linkage learning algorithms with different modeling capability and thus a different search bias. In this paper we reflect on what would be a proper - let alone, optimal - structure that a linkage learning algorithm should learn in order to efficiently solve a given problem. In other words, what would be a good or even optimal predetermined linkage model ?

The FOS linkage models specify interactions between problem variables, they do not specify how these interactions are used to explore the search space. Therefore, in previous work we have introduced an evolutionary algorithm that uses a FOS model to define its search bias [11]. Here, we apply this algorithm - called, *Gene-pool Optimal Mixing Evolutionary Algorithm* (GOMEA) - on four benchmark problems with different predetermined FOS linkage models. We are also interested in investigating how well GOMEA with predetermined FOS linkage models performs compared to a linkage learning GOMEA algorithm, namely the *Linkage Tree Genetic Algorithm* (LTGA) [10, 11] ? The LTGA is a GOMEA algorithm that learns a hierarchical cluster tree as FOS model. It would seem that when the predetermined linkage model is an accurate description of the underlying structure of the fitness function then the GOMEA algorithm should perform better than the LTGA that has to learn the structural information. It turns out that this is not the case when the structure is non-trivial, like for instance for the nearest-neighbor NK-landscape with maximal overlap (NK-S1).

The paper is organized as follows. In Section 2 we discuss the family of subsets concept and describe the predetermined models that we will use in the rest of the paper. We also explain the GOMEA and the LTGA algorithms. Section 3 first specifies the four benchmark functions used, and then describes the experimental observations made. In Section 4 we discuss our findings, while Section 5 concludes the paper.

2. LINKAGE MODELS AND GOMEA

Linkage learning evolutionary algorithms aim to identify groups of problem variables that together make an important contribution to highly fit solutions. We consider a general class of linkage models, called the *Family Of Subsets* (FOS) model. Thereafter, we specify the *Gene-pool Optimal Mixing Evolutionary Algorithm* (GOMEA) that uses a FOS model to explore the search space.

2.1 The Family Of Subsets (FOS) model

2.1.1 Definition

The model we use for representing linkage between groups of problem variables is the *family of subsets*, denoted $\mathcal{F}$. A FOS contains subsets of a certain set S. Moreover, subsets may appear more than once, making a FOS a multiset that consists of elements of the powerset $\mathcal{P}(S)$ of the set S. Here, the main set S is the set of all problem variable indices, i.e. $\{0, 1, \ldots, l-1\}$. A FOS $\mathcal{F}$ can be written as $\mathcal{F} = \{\boldsymbol{F}^0, \boldsymbol{F}^1, \ldots, \boldsymbol{F}^{|\mathcal{F}|-1}\}$ where $\boldsymbol{F}^i \subseteq \{0, 1, \ldots, l-1\}$, $i \in \{0, 1, \ldots, |\mathcal{F}|-1\}$. To represent variable linkage to be applied in a mixing process, we use families that are complete in the sense that every problem variable index is contained in *at least* one subset in $\mathcal{F}$, i.e. $\forall i \in \{0, 1, \ldots, l-1\} : (\exists j \in \{0, 1, \ldots, |\mathcal{F}|-1\} : i \in \boldsymbol{F}^j)$. This way, when performing variation using the subsets in the FOS $\mathcal{F}$, no problem variable is left out of the process.

2.2 Predetermined Family of Subsets

Before we discuss how the linkage tree genetic algorithm learns a hierarchical tree as its FOS model, we first specify four predetermined models that we will test with four benchmark functions. The benchmark functions - onemax, deceptive trap function, nearest neighbor NK-landscape problem with maximal overlap (NK-S1), and weighted MAXCUT problem - will be detailed in Section 3.

1. **Marginal Product Model (MPM).** The MPM linkage model is a family of subsets where all subsets are mutually exclusive and matched to the structure of the subfunctions that defined the problem. It was first used in the Extended Compact Genetic Algorithm [4]. For the onemax problem the MPM model is simply the set of all singletons $[0][1]\ldots[95][99]$ (when $\ell = 100$), while for the deceptive trap function the model becomes: $[0\ldots4][5\ldots9]\ldots[90\ldots94][95\ldots99]$.

   For the NK-landscape problem (NK-S1) the MPM linkage model cannot represent the overlapping variables, and the best approximation of the underlying additively decomposable structure is to match as many mutually exclusive subfunctions as possible. We will use the same MPM model as for the deceptive trap function shown above.

2. **Additively Decomposable Model (ADM).** When the family of subsets is an exact mirror of the additively decomposable structure of the problem definition, we call the model an ADM model. For the onemax problem and the deceptive trap function the ADM is equal to the MPM. For the nearest neighbor NK-S1 problem however the model becomes ($\ell = 100$):

   $$[0\ldots4][1\ldots5]\ldots[94\ldots98][95\ldots99].$$

3. **Linkage Neighbors Model (LN).** In the LN model we group each variable together with all the variables it shares a subfunction with. Again this makes no difference with the MPM and ADM models for the onemax problem and the deceptive trap function. For the NK-S1 problem the subsets are now larger than the defining subfunctions because all variables that are k positions away from the start and end position of the problem string are a member of $2k-1$ subfunctions:

   $$[0\ldots4][0\ldots5][0\ldots6][0\ldots7][0\ldots8]$$
   $$[1\ldots9][2\ldots10]\ldots[90\ldots98][91\ldots99]$$
   $$[92\ldots99][93\ldots99][94\ldots99][95\ldots99].$$

4. **Linkage Tree Model (LT).** The predetermined linkage tree model is a balanced tree obtained by recursively splitting the subsets in two equal length subsets starting from the full string length. Whenever the length of a subset is odd, the split is made by giving the left half one variable less than the right half. For the trap function we do this splitting on problems with length equal to $k.2^j$ with $j \in \{0, 1, \ldots, \log_2(\ell/k)\}$ in order to ensure that the subsets of length k that match the problem structure are part of the hierarchical tree. For instance for $k = 5$ and $\ell = 80$:

   $$[0\ldots79][0\ldots39][40\ldots79]$$
   $$[0\ldots19][20\ldots39][40\ldots59][60\ldots79]$$
   $$[0\ldots9][10\ldots19]\ldots[60\ldots69][70\ldots79]$$
   $$[0\ldots4][5\ldots9]\ldots[70\ldots74][75\ldots79]$$
   $$[0,1][2\ldots4][5,6][7\ldots9]\ldots[75,76][77\ldots79]$$
   $$[0][1][2][3,4]\ldots[75][76][77][78,79][3][4]\ldots[78][79]$$

In the experiments described below, these four predetermined FOS linkage models are used by GOMEA to optimize four benchmark functions. To exclude any bias in the order we defined the FOS set, the order in which GOMEA goes through the set of predetermined structures is randomized.

2.3 Learned Linkage Tree

The linkage tree (LT) is a specific type of FOS. The LT is a hierarchical model that represents the outcome of a hierarchical clustering procedure started from all l singleton sets, with the exception that the top level, i.e. all variables in a single cluster, is excluded [2, 10]. For any subset $\boldsymbol{F}^i$ with more than one variable, there are subsets $\boldsymbol{F}^j$ and $\boldsymbol{F}^k$ such that $\boldsymbol{F}^j \cap \boldsymbol{F}^k = \emptyset$, $|\boldsymbol{F}^j| < |\boldsymbol{F}^i|$, $|\boldsymbol{F}^k| < |\boldsymbol{F}^i|$ and $\boldsymbol{F}^j \cup \boldsymbol{F}^k = \boldsymbol{F}^i$. Different from most linkage models in the literature, variables can thus both be independent and dependent in the same model. A LT somewhat represents a path through dependency space, from the univariate, all-independent state to the full, all-jointly-dependent state.

To learn a LT from data, we use a bottom-up or hierarchical agglomerative clustering procedure that iteratively merges the two sets that are the most similar. Both the combined subset as well as its constituent subsets are then in the LT FOS. As measure of similarity of subsets we typically apply measures from information theory such as Variation of Information (VI) or Mutual Information (MI). It should be noted that VI is actually a distance and should therefore be minimized, whereas MI is a similarity and should therefore be maximized. In this paper we will use MI to build the LT. The MI similarity between two sets of random variables $X_{\boldsymbol{F}^i}$ and $X_{\boldsymbol{F}^j}$ is defined as $I(X_{\boldsymbol{F}^i}, X_{\boldsymbol{F}^j}) = H(X_{\boldsymbol{F}^i}) + H(X_{\boldsymbol{F}^j}) - H(X_{\boldsymbol{F}^i \cup \boldsymbol{F}^j})$, where $H(X_{\boldsymbol{F}^i})$ denotes the well-known definition of entropy, i.e. $H(X_{\boldsymbol{F}^i}) = -\sum_{\boldsymbol{x} \in \Omega(X_{\boldsymbol{F}^i})} P(X_{\boldsymbol{F}^i} = \boldsymbol{x}) \log_2 P(X_{\boldsymbol{F}^i} = \boldsymbol{x})$ where $\Omega(X_{\boldsymbol{F}^i})$ is the sample space for random variables $X_{\boldsymbol{F}^i}$, i.e. all $2^{|\boldsymbol{F}^i|}$ binary strings of length

$|\boldsymbol{F}^i|$. For large subsets of variables, i.e. high up in the LT, this however requires counting the frequencies of instances for many variables, which is computationally costly. Moreover, instead of computing measures such as VI or MI for the purpose of building a LT an alternative approach can be used to computing similarities that is well-known in clustering literature, namely average linkage clustering or unweighted pair group method with arithmetic mean (UPGMA) [11, 8]. UPGMA involves only looking at similarities between pairs of variables. In the case of the LT, the use of MI, and the similarity of two subsets of variables this comes down to

$$I(X_{\boldsymbol{F}^i}, X_{\boldsymbol{F}^j}) = \frac{1}{|X_{\boldsymbol{F}^i}||X_{\boldsymbol{F}^j}|} \sum_{X \in X_{\boldsymbol{F}^i}} \sum_{Y \in X_{\boldsymbol{F}^j}} I(X, Y).$$

Given a data set of size n, a straightforward implementation of the above described clustering procedure requires $\mathcal{O}(nl^3)$ time, which is asymptotically similar to to the model complexity of most well-known EDAs that are capable of effectively processing higher-order linkage information. However, using the reciprocal nearest-neighbor chain algorithm the LT can also be built in $\mathcal{O}(nl^2)$ time with a provable equivalent result [3, 6, 7].

2.4 Optimal Mixing

In general, learning can be defined as finding the best possible instance of a certain class. This is often synonymously called building a model. Such model building is characteristic of the specific type of EA known as the Estimation-of-Distribution Algorithm (EDA). In an EDA a probability distribution is estimated and resampled to generate new solutions. Equivalently, the model being built is a probabilistic one. For efficient representation, probability distributions are often factorized in some way. A factorization can be seen as a linkage model. In some cases, this correspondence is very clear, as is the case in the Extended Compact Genetic Algorithm (ECGA) that uses mutually exclusive subsets of variables as a basis for factorization the probability distribution. Such subsets are clearly an instance of the FOS model described in Section 2.

The LT however does not correspond to a probability distribution that can be sampled in an equally trivial manner. In general, this is the case if any two subsets in the FOS overlap. A traditional crossover operator that respects the linkage information in the FOS is then arguably impossible to design. A straightforward crossover operator that exchanges all subsets in the FOS between two parent solutions for instance potentially involves many meaningless operations as for every problem variable the last subset in the FOS that contains this problem variable overwrites the action of any earlier subsets that contain this problem variable. In the case of the LT, moving from root to leaves this means that essentially uniform crossover is always performed. Therefore, a procedure called Optimal Mixing (OM) [11] is used to construct new solutions instead.

The idea of OM can be applied to any variation operator. Instead of fully creating new solutions first and only then evaluating fitness, in OM an existing parent solution is chosen and cloned first. Then, during variation, each time a partial solution is generated, such as is the result of crossing over a part from another parent as reminiscent of GAs or sampling values for a subset of variables as reminiscent of EDAs, this part is used in the full solution that was cloned. If this leads to the solution being improved, the improved solution is kept, otherwise the solution is left unchanged. Variation continues, each time testing whether newly generated partial solutions lead to improvements. Thus, during variation the quality of a solution monotonically improves. The reason for calling this operation optimal mixing is due to its inception in the original LTGA [10] where a two-parent crossover operator was used following the LT with intermediate evaluations to check for improvements. Given only two parents, traversing a FOS while performing crossover then ensures that all building blocks as described in the FOS wind up in one of the two parents and mixing therefore can be said to be optimal. However, it was recently shown that considering a randomly selected new donor parent for each element in the FOS while performing crossover, which was called Gene-pool Optimal Mixing (GOM) is overall a more efficient manner of mixing because this removes the covariance in mixing that is inherent in using the same two parents for the entire crossover operation [11].

The use of OM allows making use of the linkage information as provided by all subsets in the FOS. OM further strongly increases the selection pressure in a building-block-wise manner instead of on an entire solution basis, the latter of which is a source of noise in deciding well between building blocks that increases the population size. It is through OM that the LTGA is capable of working with very small population sizes compared to most linkage learning EAs of the EDA type.

2.5 Forced Improvements

Using the ingredients of the above subsections, a canonical EA can be constructed. Recently, such a canonical EA was formulated and coined Optimal Mixing Evolutionary Algorithm (OMEA). However, the canonical setup that was used included a selection step on top of the selection inherent in OM. At the end of each generation, a tournament selection operation with tournament size 2 was performed on the offspring. This was done in order to ensure convergence by logistic growth of the optimal solutions over multiple generations and in order to be able to ensure similar convergence properties as a GA approach without OM and an EDA approach that was used to compare the results with. However, the additional selection step continuously reduces the diversity in the population faster than needed. We therefore propose to not use this additional selection step after optimal mixing. However, we do continue to perform selection to select the solutions on the basis of which we will perform learning. Optimal mixing then proceeds to work on the original population, not on the selection. The reason for having an additional tournament selection phase for learning is to increase the frequencies of the best solutions further. Although existing results on common linkage benchmark problems inspire confidence, it is important to realize that (real-world) problems may contain (many) local optima and/or symmetries. Solutions in the population may then become divided over multiple basins of attraction and progress may be slow to none in each of these basins because variation is attempted between solutions located in different basins. Overall, convergence can become very slow and it is hard to detect when the algorithm should halt. One approach to deal with this is to introduce niching. Although potentially effective, it is however nontrivial to select the right number of niches or, alternatively, the niche radius. We therefore consider an alternative, which is a means of breaking symme-

```
GOMEA //population size n, problem size l
for i ∈ {0,1,...,n−1} do
  P_i ← CreateRandomSolution()
  EvaluateFitness(P_i)
while ¬TerminationCriterionSatisfied do
  x^best ← arg max_{x∈P}{fit[x]}
  S ← TournamentSelection(P, n, 2)
  LearnModel(S)
  for i ∈ {0,1,...,n−1} do
    O_i ← FI-GOM(P_i)
  P ← O
```

```
FI-GOM(x)
b ← o ← x; fit[b] ← fit[o] ← fit[x]; improved ← false
for i ∈ {0,1,...,|F|−1} do
  p ← Random({P_0, P_1, ..., P_{n−1}})
  o_{F^i} ← p_{F^i}
  if o_{F^i} ≠ b_{F^i} then
    EvaluateFitness(o)
    if fit[o] > fit[b] then
      b_{F^i} ← o_{F^i}; fit[b] ← fit[o]; improved ← true
    else
      o_{F^i} ← b_{F^i}; fit[o] ← fit[b]
if ¬improved then
  for i ∈ {0,1,...,|F|−1} do
    o_{F^i} ← x^best_{F^i}
    if o_{F^i} ≠ b_{F^i} then
      EvaluateFitness(o)
      if fit[o] > fit[b] then
        b_{F^i} ← o_{F^i}; fit[b] ← fit[o]; improved ← true
      else
        o_{F^i} ← b_{F^i}; fit[o] ← fit[b]
    if improved then breakfor
if ¬improved then
  o ← x^best; fit[o] ← fit[x^best]
```

Figure 1: Pseudo-code for GOMEA where FI-GOM is the gene-pool optimal mixing operator with forced improvement for a single solution.

tries and focusing selection on a single optimum to pursue. To do so, whenever a solution could not be improved by optimal mixing, an additional optimal mixing operation is performed on that solution but now with the currently known best solution as the donor. However, as soon as an improvement is detected, this forced-improvement optimal mixing operation is stopped. One advantage of this approach is that it doesn't continuously increase the selection pressure and reduce population diversity further. This only happens if a solution couldn't be improved anymore anyway. Also, it puts a very specific additional pressure on the convergence phase, namely a directed convergence, through dependency space following the linkage tree, toward the best solution found so far.

3. EXPERIMENTAL ANALYSIS

3.1 Benchmark Functions

We consider three additively decomposable benchmark problems and one $\mathcal{NP}$-hard combinatorial optimization problem.

3.1.1 Onemax Problem

The first is the well known onemax or bit counting where fitness is simply the number of ones:

$$f_{\text{Onemax}}(\boldsymbol{x}) = \sum_{i=0}^{l-1} x_i, \qquad x_i \in \{0,1\}.$$

Of course there is no interacting structure to detect in this problem, but we have still included it here to see what the computational cost is of the overhead of learning a linkage model when none is actually needed.

3.1.2 Deceptive Trap functions

The second function is the non-overlapping, additively decomposable composition of the order-k deceptive trap functions. We consider subfunctions with $k = 5$:

$$f_{\text{Trap5}}(\boldsymbol{x}) = \sum_{i=0}^{(l/k)-1} f^{\text{sub}}_{\text{Trap-k}}\left(\sum_{j=ki}^{ki+k-1} x_j\right)$$

where

$$f^{\text{sub}}_{\text{Trap-k}}(u) = \begin{cases} 1 & \text{if } u = k \\ \frac{k-1-u}{k} & \textit{otherwise} \end{cases}$$

It has been shown that an EA needs to detect and process the linkage groups pertaining to the deceptive subfunctions in order for optimization to proceed efficiently. Specifically, using univariate structures, the minimally required population size and number of function evaluations scale up exponentially [12]. It is clear that for this problem the MPM structure is a perfect fit.

3.1.3 Nearest-Neighbor NK landscape

The third function is the nearest-neighbor overlapping, additively decomposable composition of predetermined, but completely random subfunctions of length k, which is essentially a NK-landscape [9]. This type of NK-landscape problem where the overlap between subfunctions is exactly defined rather than randomly defined as in traditional NK-landscapes has the advantage that the optimum can be computed using dynamic programming [9]. This is important as we want to use this type of function to determine the minimally required resources for an EA to find the optimum. We consider subfunctions of length 5 and the maximum overlap of 4 (corresponding to a shift of 1 where the next subfunction starts). No wraparound is used:

$$f_{\text{NK-S1}}(\boldsymbol{x}) = \sum_{i=0}^{l-k} f^{\text{sub}}_{\text{NK}}\left(\boldsymbol{x}_{(i,i+1,\ldots,i+k-1)}\right)$$

where $f^{\text{sub}}_{\text{NK}}\left(\boldsymbol{x}_{(i,i+1,\ldots,i+k-1)}\right)$ is a randomly chosen constant value in $[0;1]$.

3.1.4 MAXCUT problem

The combinatorial optimization problem we consider is weighted MAXCUT that is defined given an weighted undirected graph with a set of l vertices $V = \{v_0, v_1, \ldots, v_{l-1}\}$, a set of edges E between the vertices, and a weight w_{ij} for each edge $(v_i, v_j) \in E$. The goal in weighted MAXCUT is to split V into two sets such that the combined weight of all edges that are thereby cut, i.e. running between vertices in different sets, is maximized. By introducing a single binary variable x_i for every vertex that indicates if vertex v_i is either in set 0 or set 1, the function to be optimized can be written as follows:

$$f_{\text{weighted MAXCUT}}(\boldsymbol{x}) = \sum_{(v_i,v_j)\in E} \begin{cases} w_{ij} & \text{if } x_i \neq x_j \\ 0 & \textit{otherwise} \end{cases}$$

We encode this problem in a straightforward manner, i.e. using the binary problem variables x_i directly in the representation that the EA optimizes over.

Benchmark sets of various types and sizes of problem instances exist in literature, but because we want to be able to perform a controlled scalability analysis, we have generated our own instances. For problem sizes $l \in \{6, 12, 25, 50, 100\}$ we have generated fully connected graphs, i.e. graphs having precisely $\frac{1}{2}l(l-1)$ edges. The weights set randomly chosen following a β distribution with parameters $\alpha = 100$, $\beta = 1$ and scaled to the range of $[1; 5]$. For each problem size, we generate 10 instances. The maximum problem size was chosen such that a freely available highly performant exact optimization algorithm (BIQMAC) was still able to find the optimal solutions to these problems within a reasonable time. Knowing the optimum is convenient to test the performance of our EAs.

3.2 Experimental setup

For every problem and every population size we consider, we always perform 100 independent runs of an EA. We say that an algorithm solved the problem if at least 99 of these runs converged to either the global optimum or a predefined sufficiently close approximation of the global optimum. Moreover, instead of halting an EA when the optimum is reached, we let it run until convergence (all solutions are the same) because we feel this is more realistic in practice where the optimum is usually not known beforehand either and one typically collects the answer of a run once it has terminated.

For the NK-S1 problem, we have generated 100 instances per problem size randomly beforehand. This means that on NK-S1 the 100 independent runs are performed on 100 different, but always the same, 100 instances per problem dimensionality. For the weighted MAXCUT problem however, we followed an approach that is more typical of combinatorial optimization literature, namely every problem instance is considered separately because the properties of a specific instance may be interesting to study separately due to the fact that some instances can be very hard and some relatively simple to solve. In effect therefore, for weighted MAXCUT 100 independent runs are performed per problem instance per problem dimensionality. It should be noted that this does alter the interpretation of the min-max error bars that we will show in the graphs where we aggregate over all experiments per problem size. Specifically, for weighted MAXCUT these min-max error bars will be much larger.

A key performance indicator for the performance of EAs on a certain type of problem is scalability, i.e. how do the required resources (population size and number of required evaluations) increase as the problem gets bigger. In this paper we therefore mostly study performance using this performance indicator. We determine, for various problem sizes, the minimally required population size for the EA to solve the problem at that problem size. To do so, we perform a bisection search in which, starting from population size 1, the population size is doubled until the problem is solved and subsequently a binary search is performed in the range between the last two tested population sizes. Because this process is still subject to noise rooted in the stochastic nature of EAs, we perform 10 independent bisection searches for every problem size (and in case of weighted MAXCUT, for every problem instance).

3.3 Experimental observations

3.3.1 Onemax problem.

Figures 2 and 3 show that when no dependencies exist between the problem variables the MPM model is the most efficient. The MPM model has in this case exactly ℓ subsets in the linkage model - each a singleton of the variables - while the predetermined and learned tree structure both have $2\ell-2$ subsets. For the onemax problem the higher order subsets are not only not necessary but they are also inefficient in terms of additional function evaluations. The learned tree model also requires a slightly larger population size than the predetermined tree which results in a slightly larger number of function evaluations.

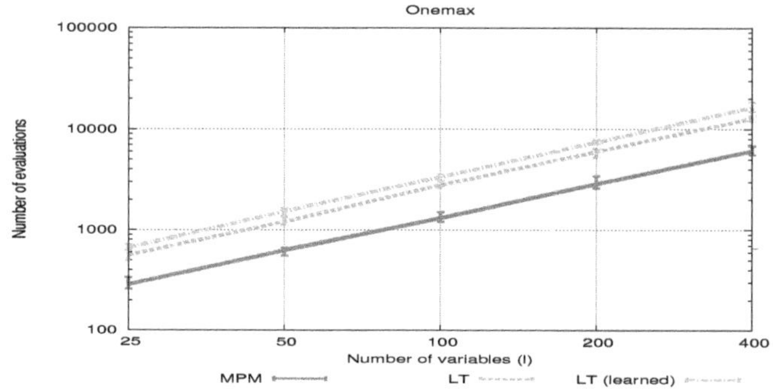

Figure 2: Onemax: number of function evaluations for the predetermined models MPM and LT versus the learned LT model.

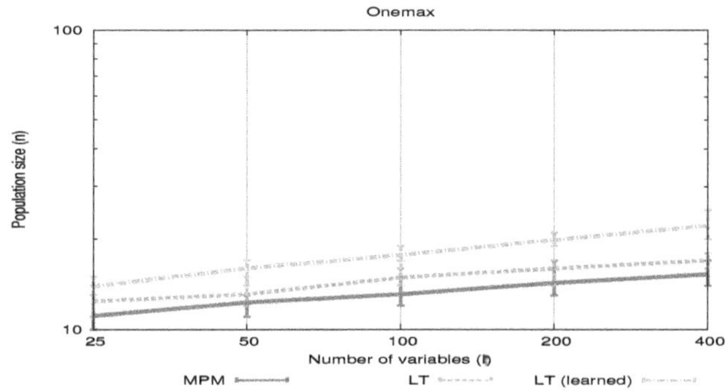

Figure 3: Onemax: minimal population size for the predetermined models MPM and LT versus the learned LT model.

3.3.2 Deceptive trap problem.

Figure 4 shows that for the trap function the MPM model is again the most efficient in terms of function evaluations. This is as expected since here too the MPM model has a very limited number of subsets - namely, the number of subfunctions $\frac{\ell}{k}$ - while both tree models have much more: $2\ell - 2$. For the trap function it is sufficient to be able to exchange the building blocks of the problem since there is no further interaction between them. It is interesting to see however that the learned tree model is now more efficient than the predetermined model. Looking at figure 5 we see that this is caused by the fact that the learned tree requires a much smaller population size than the predetermined tree model, actually even smaller than for the MPM model. This observation is a first indication that the learned model is capable to adapt its linkage model in such a way that it makes better use of the current state of the population than an a priori fixed tree model can, even though the predetermined model has been given the structural information of the problem.

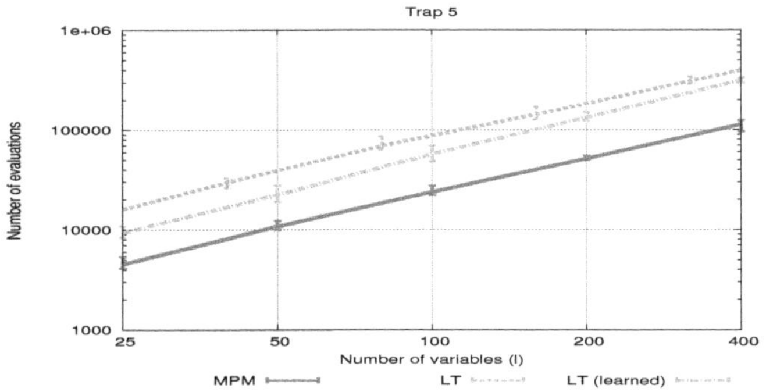

Figure 4: Trap: number of function evaluations for the predetermined models MPM and LT versus the learned LT model.

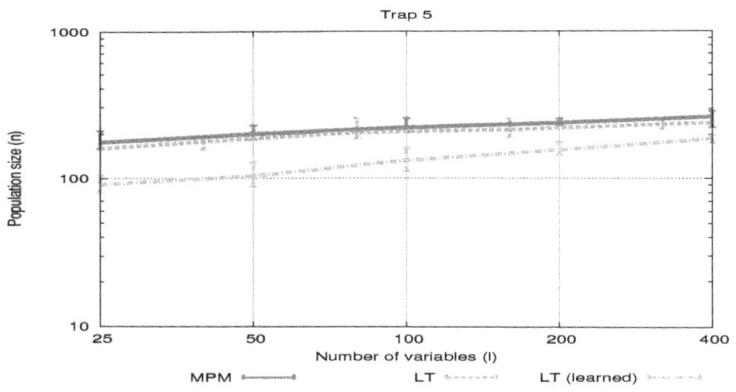

Figure 5: Trap: minimal population size for the predetermined models MPM and LT versus the learned LT model.

3.3.3 *Nearest-neighbor NK-landscape problem.*

The onemax and the deceptive trap functions are both functions with a very simple dependency structure. Therefore simple predetermined linkage models that capture this structure - especially, the MPM model - are very efficient. The nearest-neighbor NK-landscape however has a more intricate dependency structure. The maximal overlap between the subfunctions make it much harder for the linkage models to represent the required non-linear interactions between the problem variables. In figures 6 and 7 we can see that the predetermined MPM linkage model requires a very large number of function evaluations and a very large population size to solve even the small NK-S1 problems ($\ell = 25$ and 50). Of course the MPM model cannot represent any overlap information. On the contrary the predetermined ADM model that mirrors the actual structure of the subfunctions of the NK-S1 problem is perfectly capable of representing interactions as defined by the problem definition. Surprisingly however, figures 6 and 7 show that it too is not very effective at solving the problem. Again, only the small problems can be solved and this with a rapidly increasing computational effort - both in the number of function evaluations as in the required population size. It seems that being able to represent the overlapping subfunctions accurately is not enough for efficiently solving the problem. Both figures also show that the predetermined tree model performs a lot better than the accurate ADM model. It is not clear why this is actually the case, since the tree model is not capable of perfectly representing overlapping linkage groups. It can however represent certain combinations of linkage groups that include more variables than the number of variables k used in the definition of the subfunctions of the NK-S1 problem. The predetermined linkage neighbors model (LN) does represent both the overlapping linkage groups and the higher order interactions between the variables. Figures 6 and 7 show that this model performs best of all the predetermined linkage models tested here.

Finally, the figures show that the learned linkage tree model is capable of solving the NK-S1 problem very efficiently. For problem lengths up to $\ell = 100$ its performance is a little below the predetermined LN linkage model, but for larger problems - especially from $\ell = 400$ - the required number of function evaluations and the minimal population size is significantly less than any of the predetermined linkage models. These results show that it is definitely an advantage to be able to adapt the linkage model to the current state of the population. This conclusion is also supported by the fact that the learned MPM linkage model is also capable of solving the NK-S1 landscape problem with much greater efficiency than the predetermined MPM model, although less efficient than the learned linkage tree model [11].

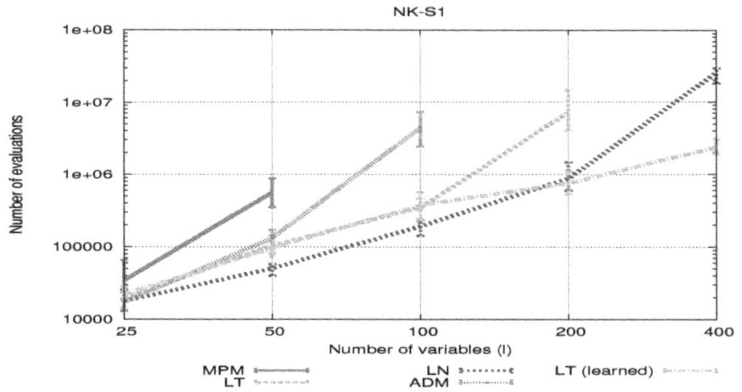

Figure 6: NK-S1: number of function evaluations for the predetermined models MPM, LT, LN, and ADM versus the learned LT model.

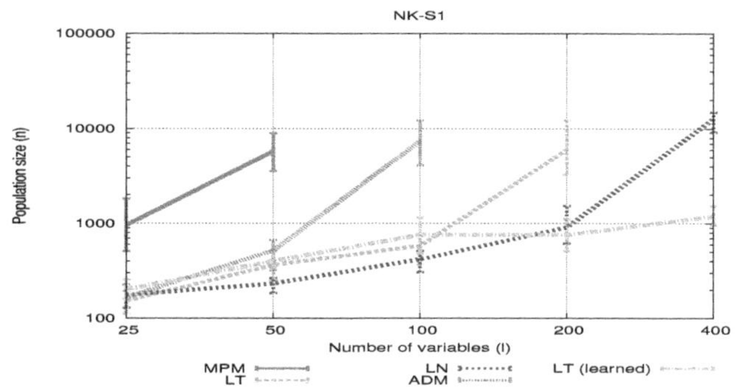

Figure 7: NK-S1: minimal population size for the predetermined models MPM, LT,LN, and ADM versus the learned LT model.

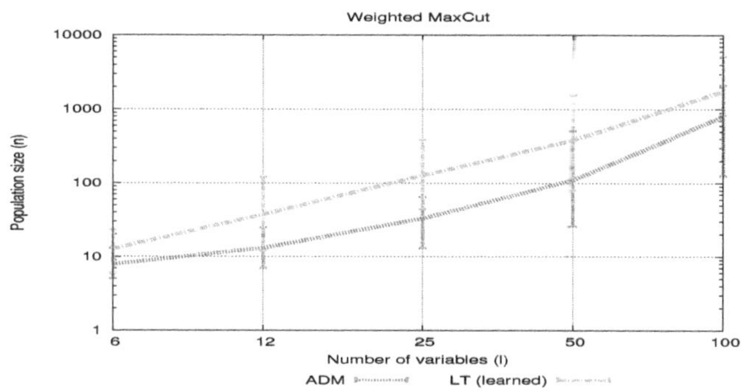

Figure 9: MAXCUT: minimal population size for the predetermined model ADM versus the learned LT model.

3.3.4 MAXCUT problem.

The onemax, deceptive trap function, and nearest-neighbor NK-landscape problem are all additively decomposable functions and thus have a well-defined structure that can be matched by a predetermined linkage model. This is not the case for our weighted MAXCUT problem where a fully connected, weighted graph has to be partitioned in two parts. Because the graph is fully connected, we take as predetermined model the family of subsets consisting of all pairs of variables - this is, all edges. The learned model is again the linkage tree model. Figures 8 and 9 show the results for reaching the global optimal solution computed with the BIQMAC algorithm. We see that the learned LT model requires a larger population size but needs less function evaluations when the graph becomes larger. Once again we observe that learning a linkage tree model is more efficient than a predetermined linkage model, even when the learned model is limited to a hierarchical tree of the problem variables.

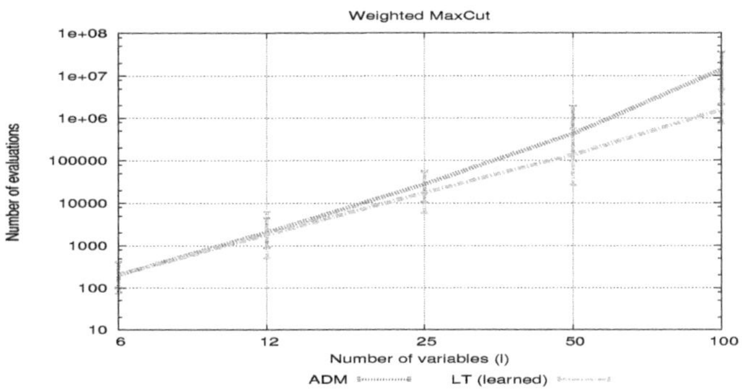

Figure 8: MAXCUT: number of function evaluations for the predetermined model ADM versus the learned LT model.

4. DISCUSSION

The results on the nearest-neighbor problem with maximal overlap (NK-S1) are the most intriguing and unexpected. Figures 6 and 7 show that all predetermined linkage models perform worse than the LTGA that learns a new linkage tree each generation. The predetermined MPM and ADM model perform even much worse and need a rapidly increasing population size to solve the NK-S1 problem. The MPM model cannot represent the structure of the NK-S1 problem so its poor performance is not a surprise. The ADM model however is an exact copy of the underlying structure of the additively decomposable fitness function. From a static point of view it has been given all the structural information of the problem but it nevertheless scales very badly with increasing problem length. Apparently, exploring new solutions by exchanging building blocks defined by the static structure of the problem definition is not enough to ensure good performance. The LN model represents linkage groups that go beyond the individual subfunctions. It takes into account that variables not only interact when they belong to the same subfunction but that they also interact because they have a common third variable with which they share a subfunction. Capturing this higher order interaction in the linkage model does indeed lead to better performance. Both the required number of function evaluations and the minimal population size are much lower than with the ADM model. The predetermined linkage tree (LT) seems to behave in a similar way as the LN model, indicating that it is indeed necessary to be able to exchange groups of variables of larger size than the size of the subfunctions that define the problem. An important observation to be made is that the a priori fixed linkage tree model (LT) performs much worse for large problems than the dynamically learned linkage tree model. This again is an unexpected result as one would assume that the fixed tree structure has the best possible matching of a hierarchical tree to the problem structure and therefore should have an advantage above the learned linkage tree model. Clearly this is not the case at all. Being able to learn a different linkage tree each generation and thus being able to represent different interacting groups of variables at different stages of the search process is a vital ingredient for the GOMEA algorithm.

5. CONCLUSIONS

We have discussed the notion of the optimal linkage model used by GOMEA for a given problem. Predetermined linkage models were designed to capture the underlying structure of four benchmark functions: onemax problem, deceptive trap functions, maximal overlapping nearest-neighbor NK-landscapes, and weighted MAXCUT problems. Experimental results showed that for problems with a non-trivial interaction structure - such as the NK-S1 problem - the use of a priori fixed linkage models was nevertheless less efficient than the use of a dynamically learned hierarchical cluster tree model. These results were unexpected and raise the question of what exactly is an optimal linkage model, and does there even exist a predetermined model that outperforms an online learned linkage model ? Answering these questions will be the topic of future research.

6. REFERENCES

[1] Y.-P. Chen and M.-H. Lim, editors. *Linkage in Evolutionary Computation*, volume 157 of *Studies in Computational Intelligence*. Springer, 2008.

[2] T. S. Duque and D. E. Goldberg. A new method for linkage learning in the ECGA. In *GECCO '09: Proceedings of the 11th Annual conference on Genetic and evolutionary computation*, pages 1819–1820, New York, NY, USA, 2009. ACM.

[3] I. Gronau and S. Moran. Optimal implementations of UPGMA and other common clustering algorithms. *Inf. Process. Lett.*, 104(6):205–210, 2007.

[4] G. R. Harik, F. G. Lobo, and K. Sastry. Linkage learning via probabilistic modeling in the extended compact genetic algorithm. In M. Pelikan, K. Sastry, and E. Cantú-Paz, editors, *Scalable Optimization via Probabilistic Modeling*, volume 33 of *Studies in Computational Intelligence*, pages 39–61. Springer, 2006.

[5] N. Krasnogor and P. L. Lanzi, editors. *13th Annual Genetic and Evolutionary Computation Conference, GECCO 2011, Proceedings, Dublin, Ireland, July 12-16, 2011*. ACM, 2011.

[6] F. Murtagh. Complexities of hierarchic clustering algorithms: state of the art. *Computational Statistics Quarterly*, 1(2):101–113, 1984.

[7] F. Murtagh and P. Contreras. Algorithms for hierarchical clustering: an overview. *WIREs Data Mining and Knowledge Discovery*, (1):86–97, 2012.

[8] M. Pelikan, M. Hauschild, and D. Thierens. Pairwise and problem-specific distance metrics in the linkage tree genetic algorithm. In Krasnogor and Lanzi [5], pages 1005–1012.

[9] M. Pelikan, K. Sastry, D. E. Goldberg, M. V. Butz, and M. Hauschild. Performance of evolutionary algorithms on NK landscapes with nearest neighbor interactions and tunable overlap. In G. Raidl et al., editors, *Proceedings of the Genetic and Evolutionary Computation Conference — GECCO-2009*, pages 851–858, New York, New York, 2009. ACM Press.

[10] D. Thierens. The linkage tree genetic algorithm. In R. Schaefer et al., editors, *Parallel Problem Solving from Nature — PPSN XI*, pages 264–273, Berlin, 2010. Springer–Verlag.

[11] D. Thierens and P. A. N. Bosman. Optimal mixing evolutionary algorithms. In Krasnogor and Lanzi [5], pages 617–624.

[12] D. Thierens and D. E. Goldberg. Mixing in genetic algorithms. In *International Conference on Genetic Algorithms (ICGA)*, pages 38–47, 1993.

A (1+1)-CMA-ES for Constrained Optimisation

Dirk V. Arnold
Faculty of Computer Science
Dalhousie University
Halifax, Nova Scotia
Canada B3H 1W5
dirk@cs.dal.ca

Nikolaus Hansen
INRIA Saclay – Île-de-France
Machine Learning and Optimization Group (TAO)
Université Paris-Sud, LRI, Bât. 490
91405 Orsay Cedex, France
Nikolaus.Hansen@lri.fr

ABSTRACT

This paper introduces a novel constraint handling approach for covariance matrix adaptation evolution strategies (CMA-ES). The key idea is to approximate the directions of the local normal vectors of the constraint boundaries by accumulating steps that violate the respective constraints, and to then reduce variances of the mutation distribution in those directions. The resulting strategy is able to approach the boundary of the feasible region without being impeded in its ability to search in directions tangential to the boundaries. The approach is implemented in the $(1+1)$-CMA-ES and evaluated numerically on several test problems. The results compare very favourably with data for other constraint handling approaches applied to unimodal test problems that can be found in the literature.

Categories and Subject Descriptors

I.2.8 [**Problem Solving, Control Methods, and Search**]; I.2.6 [**Learning**]: Parameter Learning; G.1.6 [**Optimization**]: Constrained Optimization

General Terms

Algorithms

Keywords

Stochastic optimisation, constraint handling, variable metric algorithm, evolution strategy

1. INTRODUCTION

Numerous constraint handling approaches have been proposed for use in evolutionary algorithms (EAs). A list of references[1] to constraint handling techniques used with EAs compiled by Coello Coello at the time of this writing contains more than one thousand entries. Among the most commonly employed approaches are algorithms that rely on immediate resampling of infeasible candidate solutions, penalty functions, or multiobjective techniques. A recent survey [15] provides a comprehensive overview.

Despite their strong performance in black box optimisation benchmarking exercises focusing on unconstrained real-valued problems [6], little research has been done on constraint handling techniques for covariance matrix adaptation evolution strategies (CMA-ES). The objective of this paper is to develop a simple and robust constraint handling approach for use in CMA-ES, and to incorporate it in the $(1+1)$-CMA-ES. We consider the problem of minimising $f(\mathbf{x})$ subject to inequality constraints $g_j(\mathbf{x}) \leq 0$ for $j = 1, \ldots, m$. Function $f : \mathbb{R}^n \rightarrow \mathbb{R}$ is referred to as the objective function; functions $g_j : \mathbb{R}^n \rightarrow \mathbb{R}$ are the constraint functions. In contrast to many existing constraint handling approaches, we do not make the assumption that it is possible to obtain meaningful objective function values for infeasible candidate solutions. Moreover, our strategy does not make use of constraint function values other than for the purpose of determining feasibility of a candidate solution. That is, even though the constraint functions yield real values, our algorithm only makes use of the binary information whether a constraint is violated or not. As a result, our approach enjoys invariance properties that algorithms that rely on quantifying the degree of constraint violation do not. See Hansen et al. [7] for a discussion of the importance of invariance properties in black box optimisation.

The key idea underlying our algorithm is to approximate the directions of the normal vectors of the constraint boundaries in the vicinity of the current candidate solution by accumulating steps that violate the respective constraints. Subsequently reducing variances of the distribution of offspring candidate solutions in those directions enables the strategy to closely approach the boundary of the feasible region without inhibiting its ability to search in orthogonal directions.

The remainder of this paper is organised as follows. Section 2 discusses constraint handling techniques used in connection with evolution strategies and then summarises the main ideas underlying the $(1+1)$-CMA-ES for unconstrained optimisation. Section 3 introduces the novel constraint handling approach that is the subject of this paper and describes its incorporation in the $(1+1)$-CMA-ES. Section 4 experimentally evaluates the algorithm on several test functions and compares its performance with that of other EAs for constrained optimisation. Section 5 concludes with a discussion of the results and directions for future research.

[1] http://www.cs.cinvestav.mx/~constraint/

GECCO'12, July 7–11, 2012, Philadelphia, Pennsylvania, USA.

2. BACKGROUND

This section first reviews constraint handling techniques proposed in connection with evolution strategies. It then provides a brief review of the $(1+1)$-CMA-ES, which forms the basis of the approach introduced in Section 3.

2.1 Related Work

Two of the simplest constraint handling techniques used in connection with evolution strategies are discussed by Oyman et al. [17]. One approach resamples infeasible candidate solutions until a feasible one has been generated. The other approach prefers feasible candidate solutions over infeasible ones, and it prefers those candidate solutions with smaller overall degrees of constraint violation in comparisons among infeasible candidate solutions. Neither approach requires computing objective function values for infeasible candidate solutions. In the case of the $(1+1)$-ES, which adapts its step size based on observed success probabilities, the difference between the two approaches is highly significant. Fig. 1(a) illustrates a linear problem with a linear constraint. We refer to the angle between the normal vector of the constraint boundary and the gradient vector of the objective function as the constraint angle. If the parental candidate solution is in close proximity to the constraint plane, then small constraint angles result in a small probability of generating successful offspring. The approach that resamples infeasible candidate solutions does not consider those in the calculation of the success probability and thus does not reduce the step size in response to infeasible candidate solutions. In situations where there are multiple constraints active at the same time, this may result in generating very large numbers of infeasible candidate solutions before a feasible one is found. The approach that ranks feasible candidate solutions higher than infeasible ones does consider infeasible candidate solutions in its calculation of the success probability and systematically reduces the step size, resulting in convergence to a non-stationary point of the objective. This issue was first pointed out by Schwefel [19] and has since been studied analytically by Arnold and Brauer [1]. Fig. 1(b) illustrates that small constraint angles may arise in connection with nonlinear constrained optimisation problems.

Runarsson and Yao [18] propose stochastic ranking as an approach for weighting differences in objective function values and constraint violations against each other. The approach requires the ability to obtain objective function values for infeasible candidate solutions.

Kramer et al. [14] propose the use of biased mutations for solving constrained optimisation problems. They do not evaluate their approach in an evolution strategy that is invariant with regard to rotations of the coordinate system.

Kramer and Schwefel [13] propose and experimentally evaluate several constraint handling techniques for evolution strategies, ranging from adaptively lowering a lower bound on the global step size of the strategy to an algorithm evolving populations of feasible and infeasible candidate solutions in tandem and one that involves a nested strategy that adapts rotation angles of the mutation ellipsoid. All of those have in common that no objective function values are computed for infeasible candidate solutions.

Kramer et al. [12] are the first to propose a constraint handling approach specifically for CMA-ES. Similar to our approach, they learn a model of the constraint function and use that model to adapt the covariance matrix that governs

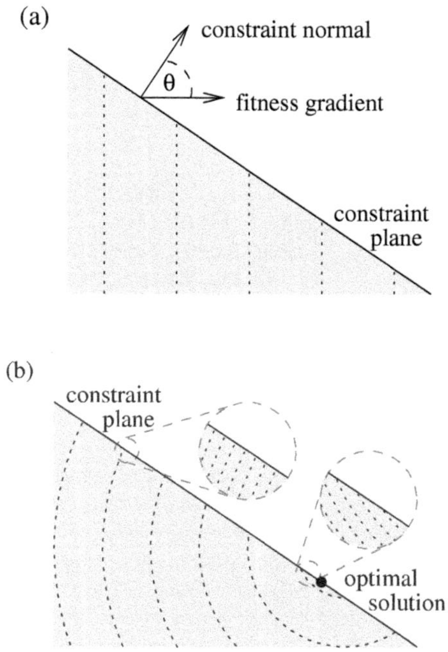

Figure 1: (a) Linear problem with a single linear constraint. The two-dimensional subspace spanned by the normal vector of the constraint plane and the gradient vector of the objective function is shown. The feasible region is shaded. (b) Two-dimensional quadratic problem with a linear constraint where the optimal solution lies on the boundary of the feasible region. Constraint angles decrease as the optimal solution is approached.

the distribution of offspring candidate solutions. However, both the nature of the model for the constraint functions and the covariance matrix update differ. Our model is simpler and obtained on the fly, without the need for additional constraint function evaluations. The covariance matrix update in [12] aims to rotate the covariance matrix, whereas ours acts to reduce variances in directions where constraint violations have been observed.

Collange et al. [3] introduce a constraint handling approach for CMA-ES that strives to ensure that within some given number of iterations the population contains at least one feasible candidate solution. Their approach relies on constraint function values and a user defined constraint value threshold. No results from an evaluation of the approach on test functions are provided.

2.2 (1+1)-CMA-ES

The $(1+1)$-CMA-ES introduced by Igel et al. [10] is a variant of the $(1+1)$-ES that adapts the entire covariance matrix of its offspring distribution in addition to its global step size. As the covariance matrix $\mathbf{C}$ is positive definite, Cholesky decomposition yields $n \times n$ matrix $\mathbf{A}$ such that $\mathbf{C} = \mathbf{A}\mathbf{A}^{\mathrm{T}}$, and offspring candidate solutions $\mathbf{y}$ are generated as

$$\mathbf{y} = \mathbf{x} + \sigma \mathbf{A}\mathbf{z} \tag{1}$$

where $\mathbf{x}$ is the parental candidate solution, $\mathbf{z} \in \mathbb{R}^n$ has standard normally distributed components, and σ is the global step size of the strategy. The strategy maintains an exponentially fading record $\mathbf{s} \in \mathbb{R}^n$ of successful steps that is referred to as the search path. Upon generating a successful offspring candidate solution it performs covariance matrix update

$$\mathbf{C} \leftarrow (1 - c_{\text{cov}}^{+})\mathbf{C} + c_{\text{cov}}^{+}\mathbf{s}\mathbf{s}^{\mathrm{T}} \tag{2}$$

where $c_{\text{cov}}^{+} \in (0, 1)$ is a constant. Rather than working with the covariance matrix and performing a Cholesky decomposition in every iteration of the algorithm, Igel et al. [10] show that equivalently, matrix $\mathbf{A}$ can be updated according to

$$\mathbf{A} \leftarrow \sqrt{1 - c_{\text{cov}}^{+}}\mathbf{A} + \frac{\sqrt{1 - c_{\text{cov}}^{+}}}{\|\mathbf{w}\|^2}\left(\sqrt{1 + \frac{c_{\text{cov}}^{+}\|\mathbf{w}\|^2}{1 - c_{\text{cov}}^{+}}} - 1\right)\mathbf{s}\mathbf{w}^{\mathrm{T}} \tag{3}$$

where $\mathbf{w} = \mathbf{A}^{-1}\mathbf{s}$. Suttorp et al. [20] provide an analogous update of the inverse of $\mathbf{A}$ that removes the need for matrix inversion and makes it possible to implement the update with $\Theta(n^2)$ cost per iteration.

A variant of the (1 + 1)-CMA-ES proposed by Arnold and Hansen [2] incorporates the active covariance matrix update due to Jastrebski and Arnold [11] into the strategy. The key observation is that in situations where there are isolated large eigenvalues of the Hessian matrix of the objective function, many iterations are required before the update in Eq. (2) yields appropriate step sizes in the directions of the corresponding eigenvectors. Rather than letting variances in those directions decay through repeated multiplication with $(1 - c_{\text{cov}}^{+}) < 1$, in situations where the offspring candidate solution is especially unsuccessful (in the sense that it is inferior to its kth order ancestor for some $k > 1$), the strategy performs covariance matrix update

$$\mathbf{C} \leftarrow (1 + c_{\text{cov}}^{-})\mathbf{C} - c_{\text{cov}}^{-}(\mathbf{A}\mathbf{z})(\mathbf{A}\mathbf{z})^{\mathrm{T}} \tag{4}$$

where $c_{\text{cov}}^{-} \in (0, 1)$ is a constant. Arnold and Hansen [2] show that the update can equivalently be accomplished by updating matrix $\mathbf{A}$ according to

$$\mathbf{A} \leftarrow \sqrt{1 + c_{\text{cov}}^{-}}\mathbf{A} + \frac{\sqrt{1 + c_{\text{cov}}^{-}}}{\|\mathbf{z}\|^2}\left(\sqrt{1 - \frac{c_{\text{cov}}^{-}\|\mathbf{z}\|^2}{1 + c_{\text{cov}}^{-}}} - 1\right)\mathbf{A}\mathbf{z}\mathbf{z}^{\mathrm{T}} \tag{5}$$

and they also provide an update of the inverse of $\mathbf{A}$ that allows performing updates with $\Theta(n^2)$ cost per iteration.

3. ALGORITHM

The key idea underlying our constraint handling approach is to reduce variances of the distribution of offspring candidate solutions in the directions of the normal vectors of constraint boundaries in the vicinity of the current parental candidate solution. For that purpose, for each of the m constraints we maintain an exponentially fading record $\mathbf{v}_j$, $j = 1, \ldots, m$, of steps that have violated the constraint. Those vectors are initialised to be zero and, in those iterations where the jth constraint is violated, updated according to

$$\mathbf{v}_j \leftarrow (1 - c_c)\mathbf{v}_j + c_c\mathbf{A}\mathbf{z} \ . \tag{6}$$

We refer to the $\mathbf{v}_j$ as constraint vectors. Accumulation acts as a low-pass filter and ensures that components of $\mathbf{A}\mathbf{z}$ that are tangential to the local constraint boundary average out in the mean. Parameter $c_c \in (0, 1)$ determines how quickly the information present in the constraint vectors fades.

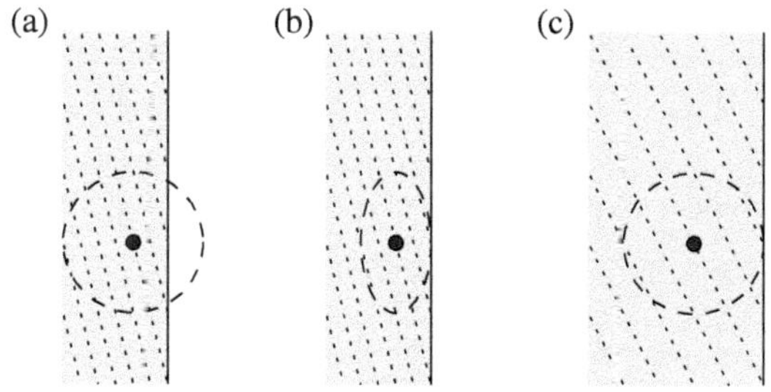

Figure 2: Effect of reducing the variance of the offspring distribution in the direction of the normal vector of the constraint boundary. The parental candidate solution is marked by a dot. (a) The original distribution is indicated by the dashed circle. Dotted lines are contour lines of the objective function. (b) The variance of the distribution in the horizontal direction is reduced. (c) Situation from (b) shown with the variables transformed by $\mathbf{A}^{-1}$.

In those iterations where the offspring candidate solution is infeasible, the Cholesky factor of the covariance matrix is updated according to

$$\mathbf{A} \leftarrow \mathbf{A} - \frac{\beta}{\sum_{j=1}^{m} \mathbb{1}_{g_j(\mathbf{y})>0}} \sum_{j=1}^{m} \mathbb{1}_{g_j(\mathbf{y})>0} \frac{\mathbf{v}_j\mathbf{w}_j^{\mathrm{T}}}{\mathbf{w}_j^{\mathrm{T}}\mathbf{w}_j} \tag{7}$$

where $\mathbf{w}_j = \mathbf{A}^{-1}\mathbf{v}_j$ and $\mathbb{1}_{g_j(\mathbf{y})>0}$ equals one if $g_j(\mathbf{y}) > 0$ and zero otherwise. The update is akin to that in Eq. (5) with the constraint vectors $\mathbf{v}_j$ replacing $\mathbf{A}\mathbf{z}$. Parameter β in Eq. (7) controls the size of the updates similar to the way that c_{cov}^{-} does in Eq. (5). However, while the update in Eq. (5) is of rank one, that in Eq. (7) is a multiple-rank update if multiple constraints are violated. In contrast to the update in Eq. (5), there is no multiplication of matrix $\mathbf{A}$ with a scalar greater than one in order to increase variances in directions other than those implicit in the constraint vectors. Also in contrast to the active covariance matrix update described in Section 2.2, we do not have an update of the inverse of matrix $\mathbf{A}$ that would allow performing a step with cost quadratic in n. Instead, the computational cost of the update is in $\mathcal{O}(n^3 + mn^2)$.

Fig. 2 illustrates the effect of reducing the variance of the distribution of offspring candidate solutions in the direction of the normal vector of the constraint plane for a linear problem. Fig. 2(a) shows a parental candidate solution in the vicinity of the constraint boundary. The dashed circle indicates a contour line of the offspring density. Fig. 2(b) depicts the same situation with the variance of the offspring distribution reduced in the direction of the normal vector of the constraint plane as a result of the transformation implicit in matrix $\mathbf{A}$. Fig. 2(c) considers the same situation as in (b), but uses a coordinate system transformed by $\mathbf{A}^{-1}$. See Hansen [5] for a discussion of coordinate transformations and adaptive encodings. Notice that the change in offspring distribution results in an increase in the constraint angle in the transformed space in Fig. 2(c) compared to Fig. 2(a). If capable of learning an appropriate coordinate transformation, the algorithm will be able to avoid the pitfalls associated with small constraint angles discussed in Section 2.1.

1. Generate offspring candidate solution $\mathbf{y}$ according to Eq. (1).

2. For $j = 1, \ldots, m$, determine whether $g_j(\mathbf{y}) > 0$ and update $\mathbf{v}_j$ according to Eq. (6) if it is.

3. If $\mathbf{y}$ is infeasible, then compute $\mathbf{w}_j = \mathbf{A}^{-1}\mathbf{v}_j$ for all $j = 1, \ldots, m$ and update the transformation matrix $\mathbf{A}$ according to Eq. (7). The iteration is complete.

4. Otherwise, evaluate $f(\mathbf{y})$, update the success probability estimate according to

$$P_{\text{succ}} \leftarrow (1 - c_P)P_{\text{succ}} + c_P \mathbb{1}_{f(\mathbf{y}) \leq f(\mathbf{x})}$$

and update the global step size according to

$$\sigma \leftarrow \sigma \exp\left(\frac{1}{d}\frac{P_{\text{succ}} - P_{\text{target}}}{1 - P_{\text{target}}}\right).$$

5. If $f(\mathbf{y}) \leq f(\mathbf{x})$, then replace $\mathbf{x}$ with $\mathbf{y}$, update the search path according to

$$\mathbf{s} \leftarrow (1 - c)\mathbf{s} + \sqrt{c(2 - c)}\mathbf{A}\mathbf{z}$$

and update matrix $\mathbf{A}$ according to Eq. (3). The iteration is complete.

6. Otherwise, if $f(\mathbf{y})$ is inferior to its fifth order ancestor, update matrix $\mathbf{A}$ according to Eq. (5).

Figure 3: Single iteration of the $(1 + 1)$-CMA-ES with constraint handling through active covariance matrix adaptation.

Incorporating the idea of constraint handling through active covariance matrix adaptation in the $(1 + 1)$-CMA-ES yields an algorithm the state of which is described by parental candidate solution $\mathbf{x}$ along with its objective function value $f(\mathbf{x})$ and those of its five most recent ancestors, global step size σ, success probability estimate P_{succ}, transformation matrix $\mathbf{A}$, search path $\mathbf{s}$, and constraint vectors $\mathbf{v}_j$ for $j = 1, \ldots, m$. Each iteration of the algorithm updates those quantities as described in Fig. 3. For $\beta = 0$, the algorithm is identical to the $(1+1)$-CMA-ES as described in [2], with constraints handled using the simple resampling scheme described by Oyman et al. [17]. All parameter settings are summarised in Table 1. Values for parameters c_c and β have been obtained by optimising the performance of the strategy applied to linearly constrained sphere functions and then reducing β by a factor of about six in order to achieve robust performance on other test problems. All other parameter settings are identical to those given in [2].

4. EXPERIMENTAL EVALUATION

This section experimentally evaluates the performance of the algorithm proposed in Section 3 using several constrained test problems. Section 4.1 considers constrained sphere functions that serve to examine basic scaling properties. Section 4.2 considers several test problems frequently used to evaluate the performance of algorithms for constrained optimisation, and it compares results observed for the $(1+1)$-CMA-ES with constraint handling through active covariance matrix adaptation with published work.

Table 1: Parameter settings.

$$d = 1 + \frac{n}{2} \qquad c = \frac{2}{n+2} \qquad c_P = \frac{1}{12} \qquad P_{\text{target}} = \frac{2}{11}$$

$$c_{\text{cov}}^{+} = \frac{2}{n^2 + 6} \qquad c_{\text{cov}}^{-} = \min\left(\frac{0.4}{n^{1.6} + 1}, \frac{1}{2\|\mathbf{z}\|^2 - 1}\right)$$

$$c_c = \frac{1}{n+2} \qquad \beta = \frac{0.1}{n+2}$$

4.1 Constrained Sphere Functions

Consider the problem of minimising function

$$f(\mathbf{x}) = \sum_{i=1}^{n} x_i^2$$

subject to constraints $x_i \geq 1$ for $i = 1, \ldots, m \leq n$. The optimal solution has components $x_i = \mathbb{1}_{i \leq m}$ and objective function value m. Fig. 4 shows the number of objective and constraint function evaluations required to locate a solution with an objective function value that differs from the optimal one by no more than 10^{-8} plotted against the dimension of the search space. In the counting of constraint function evaluations it is assumed that one function call yields information for all constraints. The upper graph shows results for $m = 1$, the lower one for $m = n/2$.

Two variants of the $(1 + 1)$-CMA-ES are considered: one that employs constraint handling through active covariance matrix adaptation as described in Section 3, and one that relies on the simple resampling approach described by Oyman et al. [17] (which is recovered from the former for $\beta = 0$). In every run the initial candidate solution is sampled uniformly from the feasible subregion of $[-100, 100]^n$. The global step size σ and Cholesky factor $\mathbf{A}$ are initialised to 0.1 and the $n \times n$ identity matrix, respectively. Runs are terminated when either the optimal solution has been found to within the desired accuracy, or when 10^6 iterations have failed to locate it. We have conducted 99 runs of either strategy in each case and ordered the runs by the number of objective function evaluations and constraint function calls. The bars in the figure indicate the 10th, 50th, and 90th smallest values observed. The thin dotted lines have slopes corresponding to linear and quadratic growth, respectively.

In the case of a single constraint, the strategy variant that employs active covariance matrix adaptation for constraint handling locates the optimal solution to within the desired accuracy in every run and for every value of n considered. Both the number of objective function evaluations and the number of of constraint function calls appear to grow linearly with the dimension n. The number of objective function evaluations is less than twice that required on unconstrained sphere functions of the same dimension. The strategy variant that simply resamples infeasible candidate solutions locates the optimal solution to within the desired accuracy in every run up to $n = 40$. However, it requires more function evaluations, with the gap between the two variants widening as n increases. For $n = 100$, the resampling approach regularly fails to reach the termination condition within 10^6 iterations.

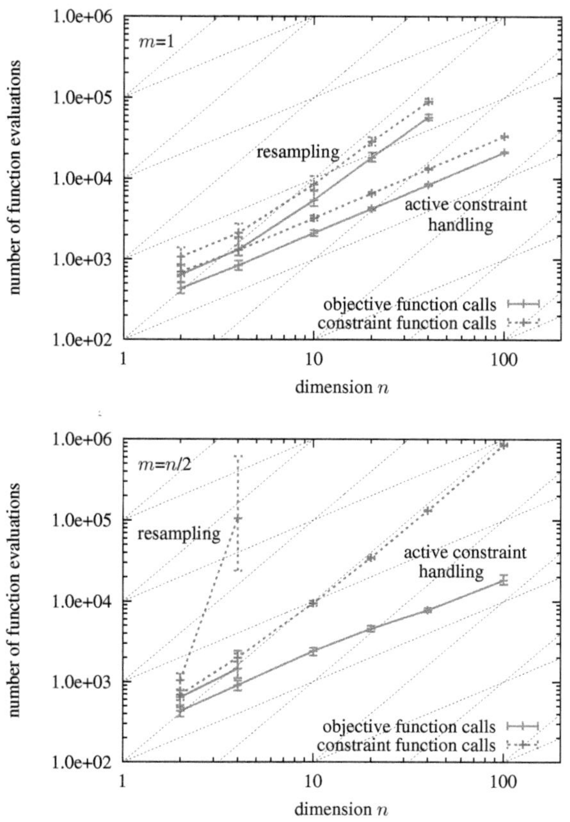

Figure 4: Comparison of the number of objective and constraint function evaluations required to optimise constrained sphere functions with $m = 1$ (top) and $m = n/2$ (bottom). The curves show results for the (1+1)-CMA-ES with and without constraint handling through active covariance matrix adaptation.

In the case of $m = n/2$ constraints, the strategy variant that employs active covariance matrix adaptation for constraint handling again locates the optimal solution to within the desired accuracy in every run and for every value of n considered. The growth of the number of objective function evaluations again appears linear in n, with overall numbers very similar to those observed for $m = 1$. The growth of the number of constraint function calls appears to be quadratic in the dimension of the problem. Results for the strategy variant that resamples infeasible candidate solutions are incomplete as for $n \geq 10$ the strategy regularly fails to locate the optimal solution to within the desired accuracy.

4.2 Other Test Functions

In order to perform a comparison of our algorithm with published results, we have evaluated its performance on several test functions that are commonly used to evaluate EAs for constrained optimisation. Specifically, we have considered the test functions collected by Michalewicz and Schoenauer [16] as well as those employed by Kramer and Schwefel [13]. However, a comparison is difficult for several reasons:

- Many test problems have multiple local minima. The (1 + 1)-ES is a poor global optimiser and not usefully applied to multimodal problems. We have restricted ourselves to test functions g06, g07, g09, and g10 from the test suite in [16] as all others are multimodal. When comparing our results with those found in the literature, it is important to keep in mind that other EAs may sacrifice speed of convergence for improved global search performance, and that our choice of test functions is biased in favour of fast local optimisers. We expect that this caveat will be addressed as we incorporate the approach of handling constraints through active covariance matrix adaptation in the $(\mu/\mu, \lambda)$-CMA-ES.

- Many algorithms for which results are reported in the literature compute objective function values for infeasible candidate solutions. While this is possible for commonly used artificial test problems relying on the ability to obtain meaningful objective function values for infeasible candidate solutions limits the applicability of the algorithms for some practical problems. Presumably, being able to compute objective function values for infeasible candidate solutions can simplify the task of locating near optimal solutions. At the same time, those algorithms that evaluate infeasible candidate solutions incur computational costs that those that evaluate only feasible candidate solutions do not.

- Our algorithm requires a feasible candidate solution as starting point. Some test problems include recommended starting points, and we have used those. For those test problems where no starting point is given, we uniformly sample candidate solutions from the volume defined by the bound constraints until the first feasible candidate solution is encountered. Notice that no objective function evaluations are required for this process. The number of constraint function calls required to generate starting points is highly dependent on the choice of bound constraints and is not included in the figures given below. Algorithms that evaluate infeasible candidate solutions may have a bias in the first feasible candidate solutions that they encounter as the objective function landscape in the infeasible region may act as a funnel.

- Performance measures employed in different papers vary. Many authors only report objective function values after a number of objective function evaluations that far exceeds the computational budget required by our algorithm to locate near optimal solutions.

We have performed 99 runs of the (1 + 1)-CMA-ES with constraint handling through active covariance matrix adaptation on each of the eight test problems described in Appendix A. For test problems g06, g07, g09, g10, and HB, runs were terminated when a solution was obtained that, when rounded to the accuracy with which the optimal values are given in Appendix A, was identical to the optimal value. For the remaining problems, runs were terminated when optimal objective function values were attained to within a factor of 10^{-8}. Table 2 lists the problems' dimensions n, the number m_{act} of constraints active at the location of the optimal solution, and the 10th, 50th, and 90th smallest numbers of objective and constraint function evaluations in each case. All runs have located the respective optimal solutions

Table 2: Function evaluations required to solve test problems.

problem	n	m_{act}	objective function			constraint function		
			10th	50th	90th	10th	50th	90th
g06	2	2	272	308	364	827	1060	1223
g07	10	6	1939	2211	2703	10435	11283	12704
g09	7	2	1430	1674	2074	3626	4106	5075
g10	8	6	2794	3976	5369	15621	18781	23088
TR2	2	1	376	443	510	616	708	839
2.40	5	5	1326	1990	3326	4551	6994	11114
2.41	5	5	1483	2271	3581	5235	8108	12056
HB	5	4	623	768	1150	2338	2912	3970

to within the desired accuracy. We have conducted analogous experiments with the strategy that employs the simple resampling scheme and observed failure to converge to the optimal solutions in many cases for all test problems but g06 and TR2. In those cases where optimal solutions were attained, the number of constraint function calls was very significantly higher than for the strategy that employs active covariance matrix adaptation for constraint handling.

While a comparison with published work is difficult for the reasons outlined above and the figures need to be interpreted with care, some results from the literature are as follows:

- Runarsson and Yao [18] use stochastic ranking in a relatively basic evolution strategy that evaluates infeasible candidate solutions. They report the median number of function evaluations required to attain the best values encountered in each run. Those values are in some cases less accurate than those used as termination conditions here. For test problems g06, g07, g09, and g10 they report figures of 108,000, 143,000, 124,000, and 128,000 objective and as many constraint function calls, respectively. These values exceed the median values reported in Table 2 by factors of 350.6, 64.7, 74.1, and 32.2 for objective function calls and by factors of 101.9, 12.7, 30.2, and 6.8 for constraint function calls.

- In a paper that was ranked first in the 2006 IEEE Congress on Evolutionary Computation Special Session on Constrained Real-Parameter Optimization, Takahama and Sakai [21] report the number of function calls required by ϵ constrained differential evolution with gradient-based mutation and feasible elites to obtain solutions within 10^{-4} of optimal solutions for g06, g07, g09, and g10 to be 7,381, 74,303, 23,121, and 105,234 in the mean, respectively. These values exceed the median values reported in Table 2 by factors of 24.0, 33.6, 13.8, and 26.5 for objective function calls and by factors of 7.0, 6.6, 5.6, and 5.6 for constraint function calls.

- Takahama and Sakai [22] report to have reached optimal solutions for problems g06, g07, g09, and g10 using ϵ constrained adaptive differential evolution after 15,846, 38,402, 25,400, and 24,815 objective function calls on average, respectively. These values exceed the median values reported in Table 2 by factors of 51.4, 17.4, 15.2, and 6.2. The corresponding numbers of constraint function calls are 36,112, 99,896, 50,766, and 99,866 and exceed the median values reported in Table 2 by factors of 34.1, 8.9, 12.4, and 5.3.

- Kramer and Schwefel [13] apply evolution strategies with several constraint handling mechanisms to problems TR2, 2.40, 2.41, and HB. The best figures they report for any of the evolution strategies are 796,201, 79,566, 51,660, and 54,344 objective function calls and 1,100,872, 770,334, 379,268, and 211,499 constraint function calls, respectively. These values exceed the median values reported in Table 2 by factors of 1,797.3, 40.0, 22.7, and 70.8 for objective function calls and by factors of 1,554.9, 110.1, 46.8, and 72.6 for constraint function calls.

- Kramer et al. [12] employ a CMA-ES that learns constraint function models and rotates mutation distributions accordingly. They report figures of 3,249 and 11,216 objective function calls and 3,650 and 30,068 constraint function calls for problems TR2 and 2.40, respectively. These figures exceed the median numbers of objective function calls reported in Table 2 by factors of 7.3 and 5.6. The corresponding numbers of constraint function calls differ by factors of 5.2 and 4.3.

Keeping the caveats mentioned above in mind, these results suggest the (1 + 1)-CMA-ES with constraint handling through active covariance matrix adaptation as a relatively capable EA for solving unimodal constrained optimisation problems.

5. DISCUSSION AND FUTURE WORK

We have proposed a novel approach for handling constraints in covariance matrix adaptation evolution strategies. Our algorithm does not assume that meaningful objective function values can be obtained for infeasible candidate solutions. It does not make use of constraint function values other than for determining feasibility of candidate solutions and thus has desirable invariance properties. The key idea of the approach is to obtain approximations to the directions of normal vectors of constraint boundaries in the vicinity of the location of current candidate solutions by low-pass filtering steps that violate the respective constraints, and to then reduce variances of the offspring distribution in those directions. The scaling implicit in the transformation that is learned in the process has the effect of increasing local constraint angles. We have presented experimental evidence that if incorporated in the (1 + 1)-CMA-ES, the proposed constraint handling approach outperforms a simple resampling scheme. Further experiments on several unimodal test problems suggest that the approach may be significantly more efficient than other approaches for constrained evolutionary optimisation.

In future work we will conduct comparisons of the performance of the evolution strategy introduced here with further algorithms for constrained optimisation, such as mesh adaptive direct search algorithms and generating set search methods. Furthermore, we will incorporate the idea of constraint handling through active covariance matrix adaptation in the $(\mu/\mu, \lambda)$-CMA-ES and evaluate its potential for solving constrained multimodal optimisation problems.

ACKNOWLEDGEMENTS

This research was supported by the Natural Sciences and Engineering Research Council of Canada (NSERC) and the Canada Foundation for Innovation (CFI).

6. REFERENCES

[1] D. V. Arnold and D. Brauer. On the behaviour of the $(1+1)$-ES for a simple constrained problem. In G. Rudolph et al., editors, *Parallel Problem Solving from Nature — PPSN X*, pages 1–10. Springer Verlag, 2008.

[2] D. V. Arnold and N. Hansen. Active covariance matrix adaptation for the $(1+1)$-CMA-ES. In *Genetic and Evolutionary Computation Conference — GECCO 2010*, pages 385–392. ACM Press, 2010.

[3] G. Collange, N. Delattre, N. Hansen, I. Quinquis, and M. Schoenauer. Multidisciplinary optimisation in the design of future space launchers. In P. Breitkopf and R. F. Coelho, editors, *Multidisciplinary Design Optimization in Computational Mechanics*, pages 487–496. Wiley, 2010.

[4] C. Floudas and P. Pardalos. *A Collection of Test Problems for Constrained Global Optimization Algorithms*. Springer Verlag, 1987.

[5] N. Hansen. Adaptive encoding: How to render search coordinate system invariant. In G. Rudolph et al., editors, *Parallel Problem Solving from Nature — PPSN X*, pages 205–214. Springer Verlag, 2008.

[6] N. Hansen, A. Auger, R. Ros, S. Finck, and P. Pošík. Comparing results of 31 algorithms from the black-box optimization benchmarking BBOB-2009. In *Genetic and Evolutionary Computation Conference Companion — GECCO 2010*, pages 1689–1696. ACM Press, 2010.

[7] N. Hansen, R. Ros, N. Mauny, M. Schoenauer, and A. Auger. Impacts of invariance in search: When CMA-ES and PSO face ill-conditioned and non-separable problems. *Applied Soft Computing*, 11(8):5755–5769, 2011.

[8] D. M. Himmelblau. *Applied Nonlinear Programming*. McGraw-Hill, 1972.

[9] W. Hock and K. Schittkowski. *Test Examples for Nonlinear Programming Codes*. Springer Verlag, 1981.

[10] C. Igel, T. Suttorp, and N. Hansen. A computational efficient covariance matrix update and a (1+1)-CMA for evolution strategies. In *Genetic and Evolutionary Computation Conference — GECCO 2006*, pages 453–460. ACM Press, 2006.

[11] G. A. Jastrebski and D. V. Arnold. Improving evolution strategies through active covariance matrix adaptation. In *IEEE World Congress on Computational Intelligence — WCCI 2006*, pages 9719–9726. IEEE Press, 2006.

[12] O. Kramer, A. Barthelmes, and G. Rudolph. Surrogate constraint functions for CMA evolution strategies. In B. Mertsching et al., editors, *KI 2009: Advances in Artificial Intelligence*, pages 169–176. Springer Verlag, 2009.

[13] O. Kramer and H.-P. Schwefel. On three new approaches to handle constraints within evolution strategies. *Natural Computing*, 5(4):363–385, 2006.

[14] O. Kramer, C.-K. Ting, and H. Kleine Büning. A new mutation operator for evolution strategies for constrained problems. In *IEEE Congress on Evolutionary Computation — CEC 2005*, pages 2600–2606. IEEE Press, 2005.

[15] E. Mezura-Montes and C. A. Coello Coello. Constraint-handling in nature-inspired numerical optimization: Past, present, and future. *Swarm and Evolutionary Computation*, 1(4):173–194, 2011.

[16] Z. Michalewicz and M. Schoenauer. Evolutionary algorithms for constrained parameter optimization problems. *Evolutionary Computation*, 4(1):1–32, 1996.

[17] A. I. Oyman, K. Deb, and H.-G. Beyer. An alternative constraint handling method for evolution strategies. In *Proceedings of the 1999 IEEE Congress on Evolutionary Computation*, pages 612–619. IEEE Press, 1999.

[18] T. P. Runarsson and X. Yao. Stochastic ranking for constrained evolutionary optimization. *IEEE Transactions on Evolutionary Computation*, 4(3):274–283, 2000.

[19] H.-P. Schwefel. *Evolution and Optimum Seeking*. Wiley, 1995.

[20] T. Suttorp, N. Hansen, and C. Igel. Efficient covariance matrix update for variable metric evolution strategies. *Machine Learning*, 75(2):167–197, 2009.

[21] T. Takahama and S. Sakai. Constrained optimization by the ϵ constrained differential evolution with gradient-based mutation and feasible elites. In *IEEE World Congress on Computational Intelligence — WCCI 2006*, pages 308–315. IEEE Press, 2006.

[22] T. Takahama and S. Sakai. Efficient constrained optimization by the ϵ constrained adaptive differential evolution. In *IEEE World Congress on Computational Intelligence — WCCI 2010*, pages 2052–2059. IEEE Press, 2010.

APPENDIX

A. TEST PROBLEMS

Problem g06: (Floudas and Pardalos [4]) Minimise

$$f(\mathbf{x}) = (x_1 - 10)^3 + (x_2 - 20)^3$$

subject to

$$g_1(\mathbf{x}) = -(x_1 - 5)^2 - (x_2 - 5)^2 + 100 \leq 0$$
$$g_2(\mathbf{x}) = (x_1 - 6)^2 + (x_2 - 5)^2 - 82.81 \leq 0$$

and bound constraints $13 \leq x_1 \leq 100$ and $0 \leq x_2 \leq 100$. Both constraints other than the bound constraints are active at the optimum, which has an objective function value of -6961.81381.

Problem g07: (Hock and Schittkowski [9]) Minimise

$$\begin{aligned}f(\mathbf{x}) &= x_1^2 + x_2^2 + x_1x_2 - 14x_1 - 16x_2 + (x_3 - 10)^2 \\ &+ 4(x_4 - 5)^2 + (x_5 - 3)^2 + 2(x_6 - 1)^2 + 5x_7^2 \\ &+ 7(x_8 - 11)^2 + 2(x_9 - 10)^2 + (x_{10} - 7)^2 + 45\end{aligned}$$

subject to

$$\begin{aligned}g_1(\mathbf{x}) &= 4x_1 + 5x_2 - 3x_7 + 9x_8 - 105 \le 0 \\ g_2(\mathbf{x}) &= 10x_1 - 8x_2 - 17x_7 + 2x_8 \le 0 \\ g_3(\mathbf{x}) &= -8x_1 + 2x_2 + 5x_9 - 2x_{10} - 12 \le 0 \\ g_4(\mathbf{x}) &= -3x_1 + 6x_2 + 12(x_9 - 8)^2 - 7x_{10} \le 0 \\ g_5(\mathbf{x}) &= 3(x_1 - 2)^2 + 4(x_2 - 3)^2 + 2x_3^2 - 7x_4 - 120 \le 0 \\ g_6(\mathbf{x}) &= x_1^2 + 2(x_2 - 2)^2 - 2x_1x_2 + 14x_5 - 6x_6 \le 0 \\ g_7(\mathbf{x}) &= 5x_1^2 + 8x_2 + (x_3 - 6)^2 - 2x_4 - 40 \le 0 \\ g_8(\mathbf{x}) &= (x_1 - 8)^2 + 4(x_2 - 4)^2 + 6x_5^2 - 2x_6 - 60 \le 0\end{aligned}$$

and bound constraints $-10 \le x_i \le 10$ for $i = 1, \ldots, 10$. Six of the eight constraints other than the bound constraints are active at the optimum, which has an objective function value of 24.3062091.

Problem g09: (Hock and Schittkowski [9]) Minimise

$$\begin{aligned}f(\mathbf{x}) &= (x_1 - 10)^2 + 5(x_2 - 12)^2 + x_3^4 + 3(x_4 - 11)^2 \\ &+ 10x_5^6 + 7x_6^2 + x_7^4 - 4x_6x_7 - 10x_6 - 8x_7\end{aligned}$$

subject to

$$\begin{aligned}g_1(\mathbf{x}) &= -127 + 2x_1^2 + 3x_2^4 + x_3 + 4x_4^2 + 5x_5 \le 0 \\ g_2(\mathbf{x}) &= -196 + 23x_1 + x_2^2 + 6x_6^2 - 8x_7 \le 0 \\ g_3(\mathbf{x}) &= -282 + 7x_1 + 3x_2 + 10x_3^2 + x_4 - x_5 \le 0 \\ g_4(\mathbf{x}) &= 4x_1^2 + x_2^2 - 3x_1x_2 + 2x_3^2 + 5x_6 - 11x_7 \le 0\end{aligned}$$

and bound constraints $-10 \le x_i \le 10$ for $i = 1, \ldots, 7$. Two of the constraints other than the bound constraints are active at the optimum, which has an objective function value of 680.630057.

Problem g10: (Hock and Schittkowski [9]) Minimise

$$f(\mathbf{x}) = x_1 + x_2 + x_3$$

subject to

$$\begin{aligned}g_1(\mathbf{x}) &= 0.0025(x_4 + x_6) - 1 \le 0 \\ g_2(\mathbf{x}) &= 0.0025(x_5 + x_7 - x_4) - 1 \le 0 \\ g_3(\mathbf{x}) &= 0.01(x_8 - x_5) - 1 \le 0 \\ g_4(\mathbf{x}) &= -x_1x_6 + 833.33252x_4 + 100x_1 - 83333.333 \le 0 \\ g_5(\mathbf{x}) &= -x_2x_7 + 1250x_5 + x_2x_4 - 1250x_4 \le 0 \\ g_6(\mathbf{x}) &= -x_3x_8 + 1250000 + x_3x_5 - 2500x_5 \le 0\end{aligned}$$

and bound constraints $100 \le x_1 \le 10000$, $1000 \le x_i \le 10000$ for $i = 2.3$, and $10 \le x_i \le 1000$ for $i = 4, \ldots, 8$. All six constraints other than the bound constraints are active at the optimum, which has an objective function value of 7049.2480.

Problem TR2: (Kramer and Schwefel [13]) Minimise

$$f(\mathbf{x}) = x_1^2 + x_2^2$$

subject to

$$g_1(\mathbf{x}) = 2 - x_1 - x_2 \le 0.$$

The constraint is active at the optimum, which has an objective function value of 2. Point $(50, 50)^{\mathrm{T}}$ serves as the starting point.

Problem 2.40: (Schwefel [19]) Minimise

$$f(\mathbf{x}) = -\sum_{i=1}^{5} x_i$$

subject to

$$g_1(\mathbf{x}) = \sum_{i=1}^{5} (9 + i)x_i - 50000 \le 0$$

and bound constraints $0 \le x_i$ for $i = 1, \ldots, 5$. Constraint g_1 as well as four of the bound constraints are active at the optimum, which has an objective function value of -5000. Point $\mathbf{x} = (250, 250, 250, 250, 250)^{\mathrm{T}}$ serves as the starting point.

Problem 2.41: (Schwefel [19]) Minimise

$$f(\mathbf{x}) = -\sum_{i=1}^{5} ix_i$$

subject to

$$g_1(\mathbf{x}) = \sum_{i=1}^{5} (9 + i)x_i - 50000 \le 0$$

and bound constraints $0 \le x_i$ for $i = 1, \ldots, 5$. Constraint g_1 as well as four of the bound constraints are active at the optimum, which has an objective function value of $-125000/7$. Point $\mathbf{x} = (250, 250, 250, 250, 250)^{\mathrm{T}}$ serves as the starting point.

Problem HB: (Himmelblau [8]) Minimise

$$\begin{aligned}f(\mathbf{x}) &= 5.3578547x_3^2 + 0.8356891x_1x_5 \\ &+ 37.293239x_1 - 40792.141\end{aligned}$$

subject to

$$\begin{aligned}g_1(\mathbf{x}) &= -h_1(\mathbf{x}) \le 0 \\ g_2(\mathbf{x}) &= h_1(\mathbf{x}) - 92 \le 0 \\ g_3(\mathbf{x}) &= 90 - h_2(\mathbf{x}) \le 0 \\ g_4(\mathbf{x}) &= h_2(\mathbf{x}) - 110 \le 0 \\ g_5(\mathbf{x}) &= 20 - h_3(\mathbf{x}) \le 0 \\ g_6(\mathbf{x}) &= h_3(\mathbf{x}) - 25 \le 0\end{aligned}$$

where

$$\begin{aligned}h_1(\mathbf{x}) &= 85.334407 + 0.0056858x_2x_5 \\ &+ 0.00026x_1x_4 - 0.0022053x_3x_5 \\ h_2(\mathbf{x}) &= 80.51249 + 0.0071317x_2x_5 \\ &+ 0.0029955x_1x_2 + 0.0021813x_3^2 \\ h_3(\mathbf{x}) &= 9.300961 + 0.0047026x_3x_5 \\ &+ 0.0012547x_1x_3 + 0.0019085x_3x_4\end{aligned}$$

and bound constraints $78 \le x_1 \le 102$, $33 \le x_2 \le 45$, and $27 \le x_i \le 45$ for $i = 3, 4, 5$. One of the constraints other than the bound constraints as well as three of the bound constraints are active at the optimum, which has an objective function value of -30665.539.

Mutation Strength Control by Meta-ES on the Sharp Ridge

Hans-Georg Beyer
Research Center PPE
Vorarlberg University of Applied Sciences
Dornbirn, Austria
Hans-Georg.Beyer@fhv.at

Michael Hellwig
Research Center PPE
Vorarlberg University of Applied Sciences
Dornbirn, Austria
Michael.Hellwig@fhv.at

ABSTRACT

This paper investigates mutation strength control using Meta-ES on the sharp ridge. The asymptotical analysis presented allows for the prediction of the dynamics in ridge as well as in radial direction. Being based on this analysis the problem of the choice of population size λ and isolation parameter γ will be tackled. Remarkably, the qualitative convergence behavior is not determined by γ alone, but rather by the number of function evaluations $\lambda\gamma$ devoted to the inner ES.

Categories and Subject Descriptors

I.2.8 [**Problem Solving, Control Methods, and Search**]: Control theory

General Terms

Algorithms

Keywords

Adaption, Evolution Strategies, Meta-ES, Mutation Strength, Sharp Ridge Function

1. INTRODUCTION

Controlling the strategy parameters of an Evolutionary Strategy (ES) by hierarchically organized ESs, also referred to as Meta-ESs, is a common practice in the field of ESs. Formally Meta-ESs are described by the generalized ES bracket notation according to Rechenberg [8]

$$[\mu'/\rho', \lambda'(\mu/\rho, \lambda)^{\gamma}]. \tag{1}$$

The Meta-ES (1) runs λ' parallel inner $(\mu/\rho, \lambda)$-ESs over γ generations. Each of these ESs are equipped with different initial strategy parameters such as different initial mutation strengths or population sizes. Selection on the higher level then chooses the μ' best for recombination with respect to a previously defined fitness criterion. While there is experimented evidence that Meta-ES can tune the inner ES to optimal performance [5], the control investigations are still scarce. There are basically two papers on that topic: In [4] the performance of the $[1, 2(\mu/\mu_I, \lambda)^{\gamma}]$-Meta-ES on the sphere model has been analyzed. In [1] Arnold presented an analysis of the mutation strength adaption by $[1, 2(\mu, \mu_I, \lambda)^{\gamma}]$-Meta-ES on the family of ridge functions

$$F(\mathbf{x}) = -x_1 + d\left(\sum_{i=2}^{N} x_i^2\right)^{\frac{1}{2}\beta}, \quad \beta \geq 2. \tag{2}$$

His analysis did not include the sharp ridge. However, the sharp ridge is especially interesting since this fitness landscape poses a challenge on any mutation adaption mechanism including cumulative step-size adaption and self-adaption, see also [6]. Furthermore the sharp ridge can be regarded as a model for linear constraint optimization where standard methods are known to show a premature convergence behavior. Therefore, this paper will particularly investigate Meta-ES in the fitness environment defined by the sharp ridge function which is defined as

$$F(\mathbf{x}) = -x_1 + d\left(\sum_{i=2}^{N} x_i^2\right)^{\frac{1}{2}} = -x_1 + dR \tag{3}$$

for $\mathbf{x} = (x_1, \ldots, x_N) \in \mathbb{R}^N$. The parameter d is called the nonlinearity strength parameter of the ridge function.

The x_1-axis also referred to as the ridge axis is in this definition identified with an axis of the coordinate system. While this is a special choice, an arbitrary coordinate transformation would not have any effect to the strategy's performance. This is so because the inner ES uses isotropically distributed mutations.

The term $R := \sqrt{\sum_{i=2}^{N} x_i^2}$ describes the distance of the argument $\mathbf{x} \in \mathbb{R}^N$ to the ridge axis.

Without loss of generality we assume a minimization problem. The sharp ridge function has no finite optimum, thus minimization steadily decreases the F-value. Fitness improvement can be achieved in two

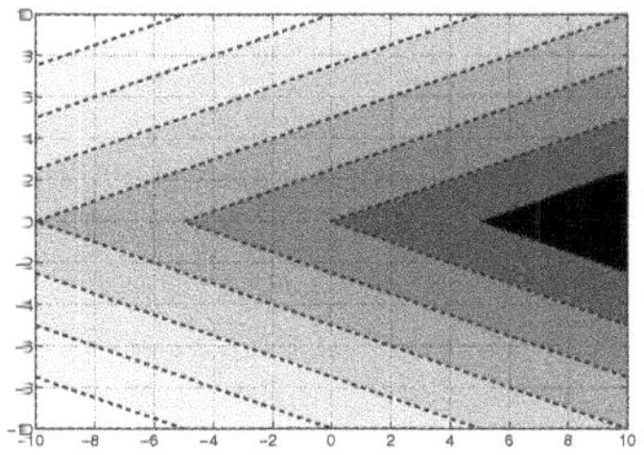

Figure 1: The contour plot of the 2-dimensional Sharp Ridge function with $d = 2$. Notice that darker regions correspond to lower function values.

GECCO'12, July 7-11, 2012, Philadelphia, Pennsylvania, USA.

ways: either by reducing the distance R to the ridge axis or by increasing the x_1-value, i.e. making progress in direction of the ridge axis. In the short run this is realized fastest by reducing the distance to the ridge axis. However, the convergence to the ridge axis also results in a stagnation of the progress in direction of the ridge axis. Thus a long term improvement is achieved better by enlarging the x_1 value and accepting an increasing radius R, see [1].

This paper is organized as follows: Section 2 contains a description of the investigated $[1, 2(\mu/\mu_I, \lambda)^\gamma]$-Meta-ES algorithm. In Section 3 we work on the theoretical analysis of the inner ES for three cases depending on the initial distance to the ridge axis R. Resulting in a rule for the choice of the isolation length parameter γ which allows for the control of the mutation strength σ. The analysis of the Meta-ES behavior over multiple isolation periods is presented in Section 4. For sufficiently long isolation length γ we provide an asymptotic solution for the expected results. Section 5 investigates the impact of small dimensionalities N on the Meta-ES dynamics. Finally, Section 6 sums up our results and offers an outlook on future research.

2. CONTROLLING THE MUTATION STRENGTH BY [1, 2]-META-ES

This section recaps the simple $[1, 2(\mu/\mu_I, \lambda)^\gamma]$-Meta-ES which is used to control the mutation strength σ. The outer ES, see Fig. 2, generates two $(\mu/\mu_I, \lambda)$ populations. The inner ESs start from the same initial $\mathbf{y_p}$ but with different mutation strengths $\tilde{\sigma}$ which are kept constant during the isolation period of γ generations. As one

```
[1, 2(μ/μ_I, λ)^γ]-ES                     line
Initialize(y_p, σ_p, α, μ, λ, γ, N);      1
t = 0;                                    2
Repeat                                    3
  σ̃_1 := σ_p α;                           4
  σ̃_2 := σ_p α^{-1};                      5
  [ỹ_1, f̃_1] := ES(μ, λ, γ, σ̃_1, y_p);    6
  [ỹ_2, f̃_2] := ES(μ, λ, γ, σ̃_2, y_p);    7
  σ_p := σ̃_{1;2};                         8
  y_p := ỹ_{1;2};                         9
  t := t + 1;                             10
Until(termination condition)              11
```

Figure 2: Pseudo code of the [1, 2]-Meta-ES. The Code of the inner ES is displayed in Fig. 3.

can see in Line 4 and 5 the two different $\tilde{\sigma}$ values are computed by increasing respectively decreasing the parental mutation strength by the factor $\alpha > 1$. As a result there is always one $(\mu/\mu_I, \lambda)^\gamma$-ES running with mutation strength $\tilde{\sigma}_1 = \alpha\sigma_p$ and one with $\tilde{\sigma}_2 = \sigma_p/\alpha$. Selection is explained in lines 8 and 9 using the standard notation "$m; \lambda'$" indicating the m-th best population out of all λ' populations. The populations are ordered by the function value returned by the respective inner standard ES, displayed in Fig. 3, after having evolved independently over γ generations. The inner ES generates a population of λ offspring by adding the product of the mutation strength σ and a vector of independent, standard normally distributed components to the centroid $\mathbf{y}$ of the parental generation. The μ best candidates (in terms of their function values $\tilde{F}_l$) out of these λ offsprings are used to build the new parental centroid $\mathbf{y}$. Proceeding this way over γ generations the inner ES returns the tuple $[\mathbf{y}, F(\mathbf{y})]$.

As a termination criterion for the outer ES one can for example choose an upper bound for the number of function evaluations or specify a fixed number of isolation periods.

```
Function: ES(μ, λ, γ, σ, y)
g=1;
While g ≤ γ
  For l = 1 To λ
    ỹ_l := y + σN_l(0, I);
    F̃_l := F(ỹ_l);
  End For
  y := (1/μ) Σ_{m=1}^{μ} ỹ_{m;λ};
  g := g + 1;
End While
Return [y, F(y)];
```

Figure 3: The inner $(\mu/\mu_I, \lambda)^\gamma$-ES

3. THEORETICAL ANALYSIS

In what follows, we examine the dynamics of the inner $(\mu/\mu_I, \lambda)$-ES over a period of γ generations. The theoretical analysis is based on mean value dynamics which is a common practice in the field of ES. Taking into account the selection mechanism of the Meta-ES we can derive directives for the mutation strength control depending on the population size and the fitness environment in terms of the dimensionality N and the nonlinearity strength d. The theoretical results are finally compared with the empirical analysis of the algorithm.

The analysis is based on the deterministic mutation rule that produces exactly two inner $(\mu/\mu_I, \lambda)$-ES, i.e. one with $\sigma_+ = \alpha\sigma^{(g)}$ and one with $\sigma_- = \sigma^{(g)}/\alpha$. Note that $\sigma_\pm$ corresponds to $\tilde{\sigma}_1$ and $\tilde{\sigma}_2$ mentioned in Section 2. We take a look at the expected value $F^{(g)}$ of the sharp ridge function at generation $g+1$ which is already constituted in [1] by the recurrence equation

$$F^{(g+1)} = -x^{(g+1)} + dR^{(g+1)}, \tag{4}$$

where the distance in direction of the ridge axis is given by

$$x^{(g+1)} = x^{(g)} + \frac{\sigma c_{\mu/\mu,\lambda}}{\sqrt{1+d^2}} \tag{5}$$

and the distance to the ridge axis is constituted by

$$R^{(g+1)} = R^{(g)} + \frac{\sigma^2 N}{2\mu R^{(g)}} - \frac{d\sigma c_{\mu/\mu,\lambda}}{\sqrt{1+d^2}}. \tag{6}$$

For the definition of the so called progress coefficient $c_{\mu/\mu,\lambda}$ we refer the reader to [3]. We can see that $x^{(g+1)}$ scales up linearly with the number of generations, thus we can transform it to

$$x^{(g+1)} = x^{(0)} + \frac{\sigma c_{\mu/\mu,\lambda}}{\sqrt{1+d^2}}(g+1). \tag{7}$$

In order to investigate the behavior of the $[1, 2(\mu/\mu, \lambda)^\gamma]$-Meta-ES we need a similar expression for $R^{(g+1)}$. Because of the nonlinearity of the recurrence equation (6) we are not able to find a closed analytical solution for $R^{(g+1)}$. Hence we switch to the continuous time limit to approximate the difference equation (6) by a differential equation which is formally obtained by expanding $R(g+1)$ into a Taylor series at g and breaking off after the linear part

$$R(g+1) = R(g) + \frac{\mathrm{d}R}{\mathrm{d}g}1 + \dots. \tag{8}$$

Identifying $R(g+1)$ with $R^{(g+1)}$ and $R(g)$ with $R^{(g)}$ in (6) we get the nonlinear differential equation

$$\frac{\mathrm{d}R}{\mathrm{d}g} = \frac{\sigma^2 N}{2\mu R} - \frac{d\sigma c_{\mu/\mu,\lambda}}{\sqrt{1+d^2}}. \tag{9}$$

Equation (9) describes the basis of the further theoretical analysis. If the isolation period γ is sufficiently large, $\gamma \to \infty$, the expected distance reaches a steady state R denoted by R_∞. This is equivalent to $\frac{dR}{dg} \to 0$, i.e. $R^{(g)} = R^{(g-1)} = R_\infty$ for $g \to \infty$. That is, the inner ES with constant mutation strength σ approaches the expected residual steady state distance R_∞ to the sharp ridge axis which is obtained by resolving (9) for $\frac{dR}{dg} = 0$

$$R_\infty(\sigma) := \frac{N\sigma}{2\mu c_{\mu/\mu,\lambda}} \frac{\sqrt{1+d^2}}{d}. \tag{10}$$

Due to mathematical difficulties solving (9) for R we have to consider three special cases depending on the choice of the initial distance R of the starting point from the ridge axis:

$$\text{a) } R \approx R_\infty, \quad \text{b) } R \ll R_\infty, \quad \text{and c) } R \gg R_\infty.$$

3.1 Analysis of the $R \approx R_\infty$ Case

First we explore the situation in which the initial distance to the ridge axis lies in the vicinity of the residual distance R_∞. In this case we are able to replace the rhs of the differential equation (9) with its Taylor series around R_∞. With the derivation of (9) with respect to R

$$\frac{d}{dR}\Big(\frac{dR}{dg}\Big) = \frac{-\sigma^2 N}{2\mu R^2} \tag{11}$$

and by considering again only the linear terms we get

$$\frac{dR}{dg} \approx \frac{dR}{dg}\Big|_{R=R_\infty} + \frac{d}{dR}\Big(\frac{dR}{dg}\Big)\Big|_{R=R_\infty}(R - R_\infty) \tag{12}$$

$$= \frac{-2c^2_{\mu/\mu,\lambda} d^2 \mu}{(1+d^2)N}(R - R_\infty) \tag{13}$$

This differential equation can be solved for g by separating the variables, in the first step yielding

$$\int_{R^{(0)}}^{R^{(g)}} \frac{1}{R' - R_\infty} dR' = \int_0^g \frac{-2c^2_{\mu/\mu,\lambda} d^2\mu}{(1+d^2)N} dg'. \tag{14}$$

The integration leads to the equation

$$\ln\Big(\frac{R^{(g)} - R_\infty}{R^{(0)} - R_\infty}\Big) = \frac{-2c^2_{\mu/\mu,\lambda} d^2\mu}{(1+d^2)N} g. \tag{15}$$

This can be solved for $R^{(g)}$

$$R^{(g)} = R_\infty + (R^{(0)} - R_\infty) e^{\frac{-2c^2_{\mu/\mu,\lambda} d^2\mu}{(1+d^2)N} g} \tag{16}$$

$$= R^{(0)} e^{-g/\tau} + R_\infty\left(1 - e^{-g/\tau}\right), \tag{17}$$

where τ is defined as

$$\tau := \frac{(1+d^2)N}{2c^2_{\mu/\mu,\lambda} d^2\mu}. \tag{18}$$

Taking into account Eq. (4), (7), and (17) we obtain an expression for the expected value of the sharp ridge function at generation g

$$\boxed{F^{(g)} = F^{(0)} - \frac{\sigma c_{\mu/\mu,\lambda}}{\sqrt{1+d^2}} g - d\left(R^{(0)} - R_\infty\right)(1 - e^{-g/\tau}).} \tag{19}$$

The $F^{(g)}$-dynamics of the inner ES is governed by a linearly decreasing term and a term proportional to the initial $\left(R^{(0)} - R_\infty\right)$ difference which reaches a saturation value $d\left(R^{(0)} - R_\infty\right)$ exponentially fast. The latter is approached with the time constant τ, see Eq. (18). The approach is slower for decreasing d and increasing dimensionality N. The parental population size μ decreases the time constant (provided that $c_{\mu/\mu,\lambda} \approx const$).

Now we are able to investigate the γ-dependency of the Meta-ES. Starting with a random point at generation G with initial values $F^{(G)}$, $x^{(G)}$, $R^{(G)}$, and $\sigma^{(G)}$ the inner ES generates two σ-values from the parental $\sigma^{(G)}$

$$\sigma_+ = \alpha\sigma^{(G)} \quad \text{and} \quad \sigma_- = \sigma^{(G)}/\alpha. \tag{20}$$

Thus there are two expected function values $F^{(G+\gamma)}$ after γ generations of the inner $[(\mu/\mu_I, \lambda)^\gamma]$-ES

$$F_+^{(G+\gamma)} := F^{(G+\gamma)}(\alpha\sigma^{(G)}) \quad \text{and} \quad F_-^{(G+\gamma)} := F^{(G+\gamma)}(\sigma^{(G)}/\alpha). \tag{21}$$

Using (19) we obtain

$$F_+^{(G+\gamma)} = F^{(G)} - \frac{\alpha\sigma^{(G)} c_{\mu/\mu,\lambda}}{\sqrt{1+d^2}}\gamma - d\left(R^{(G)} - R_\infty(\alpha\sigma^{(G)})\right)(1 - e^{-\gamma/\tau}) \tag{22}$$

$$F_-^{(G+\gamma)} = F^{(G)} - \frac{\sigma^{(G)} c_{\mu/\mu,\lambda}}{\alpha\sqrt{1+d^2}}\gamma - d\left(R^{(G)} - R_\infty(\sigma^{(G)}/\alpha)\right)(1 - e^{-\gamma/\tau}) \tag{23}$$

The sign of the function $\delta(\gamma)$ defined as the difference of the above constructed function values

$$\delta(\gamma) := F_+^{(G+\gamma)} - F_-^{(G+\gamma)} \tag{24}$$

determines whether to increase or to decrease the mutation strength in the outer [1, 2]-ES. Since we are aiming at fast F-decrease we get the conditions

$$\begin{aligned} \delta(\gamma) < 0 \quad &\Rightarrow \quad \sigma^{(G+\gamma)} = \alpha\sigma^{(G)} \\ \delta(\gamma) > 0 \quad &\Rightarrow \quad \sigma^{(G+\gamma)} = \sigma^{(G)}/\alpha. \end{aligned} \tag{25}$$

Combining (22) and (23) one gets

$$\delta(\gamma) = \Delta(\gamma)\sigma^{(G)}\left(\alpha - \frac{1}{\alpha}\right) \tag{26}$$

with

$$\Delta(\gamma) := \frac{N\sqrt{1+d^2}}{2\mu c_{\mu/\mu,\lambda}}(1 - e^{-\gamma/\tau}) - \frac{c_{\mu/\mu,\lambda}}{\sqrt{1+d^2}}\gamma. \tag{27}$$

Since $\alpha - \frac{1}{\alpha} > 0$ the condition (25) becomes

$$\begin{aligned} \Delta(\gamma) < 0 \quad &\Rightarrow \quad \sigma^{(G+\gamma)} = \alpha\sigma^{(G)} \\ \Delta(\gamma) > 0 \quad &\Rightarrow \quad \sigma^{(G+\gamma)} = \sigma^{(G)}/\alpha. \end{aligned} \tag{28}$$

Considering the long-term behavior of the F-evolution in (19) one sees that this behavior is mainly governed by the linear g term. Aiming at fast F-decrease, i.e. minimization, the mutation strength σ should be increased by the outer ES implying $\Delta(\gamma) < 0$ in (28). Thus, using (27) we obtain a rule for the choice of the γ-value

$$\frac{c_{\mu/\mu,\lambda}}{\sqrt{1+d^2}}\gamma > \frac{N\sqrt{1+d^2}}{2\mu c_{\mu/\mu,\lambda}}(1 - e^{-\gamma/\tau}) \tag{29}$$

$$\Leftrightarrow \quad \gamma > \frac{N(1+d^2)}{2\mu c^2_{\mu/\mu,\lambda}}\left(1 - e^{-\gamma/\tau}\right). \tag{30}$$

This causes the Meta-ES to steadily increase the mutation strength σ. Since $(1 - e^{-k\gamma}) < 1$ the inequality (30) is surely fulfilled for an isolation period $\gamma = \hat{\gamma}$

$$\hat{\gamma} = \left\lceil \frac{N(1+d^2)}{2\mu c^2_{\mu/\mu,\lambda}} \right\rceil. \tag{31}$$

If we consider (31) as well as the truncation ratio $\nu = \frac{\mu}{\lambda}$ and assuming $c_{\mu/\mu,\lambda} \approx 1$, Eq. (30) can be transformed to

$$\boxed{\gamma\lambda > \frac{N(1+d^2)}{2\nu}.} \tag{32}$$

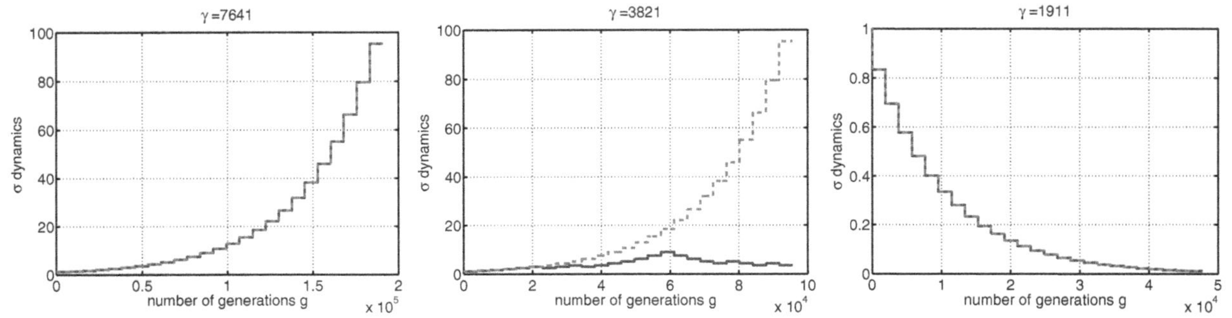

Figure 4: Illustration of the mutation strength behavior for three different choices of the isolation length. The σ-dynamics of a $[1, 2(3/3, 10)^\gamma]$-Meta-ES with $\gamma \approx 2\hat{\gamma}$, $\gamma = \hat{\gamma}$ and $\gamma \approx \hat{\gamma}/2$ are shown for $N = 1000$, $\sigma^{(0)} = 1$, $\alpha = 1.2$ on the sharp ridge with $d = 5$ over 25 isolation periods ($\hat{\gamma} = 3821$).

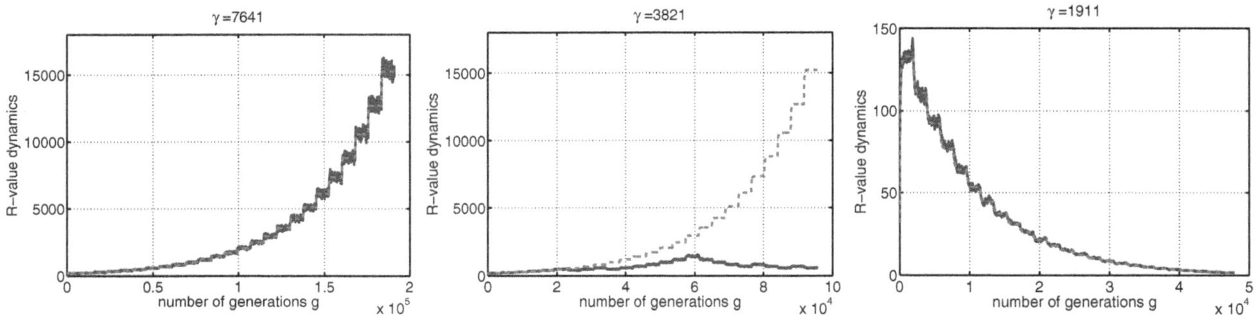

Figure 5: On the R-value dynamics of a $[1, 2(3/3, 10)^\gamma]$-Meta-ES with $\gamma \approx 2\hat{\gamma}$, $\gamma = \hat{\gamma}$ and $\gamma \approx \hat{\gamma}/2$ for $N = 1000$, $\sigma^{(0)} = 1$, $\alpha = 1.2$ on the sharp ridge with $d = 5$ over 25 isolation periods ($\hat{\gamma} = 3821$). The distance R to the ridge axis is displayed according to the σ dynamics presented in Fig. 4.

Note, $\gamma\lambda$ is the number of function evaluations during the inner ES. Equation (32) suggests that the divergence behavior of the Meta-ES can be controlled either by choosing a sufficiently large isolation length γ or by increasing the size of the population parameter λ (and μ proportionally).

Now we focus on the precision of our theoretical predictions from Eq. (6) and (7) compared to the results of a experimental run of the Meta-ES algorithm described in Section 2. For that reason the theoretical equations are iterated over γ generations in two runs with different constant mutation strengths $\alpha\sigma$ and σ/α. Then the resulting σ, R, and x values which lead to the best fitness function value $F = -x + dR$ are selected and used as starting points for the next iteration over γ generations. The σ dynamics and the R-value dynamics of the Meta-ES are illustrated for different choices of the isolation length parameter γ in Fig. 4, and Fig. 5 respectively. In each plot the experimental results of a run over 25 isolation periods, or 25γ generations, of the Meta-ES are represented by the solid blue lines whereas the iteratively computed analytical results are depicted as dashed red lines.

There is a good agreement between theoretical predictions and experiments. For long choices of the isolation length γ relative to $\hat{\gamma}$ in (31) we observe overlapping graphs of theoretical and experimental results for the σ dynamics in Fig. 4. That is, the Meta-ES steadily increases the mutation strength after each isolation period. According to the σ-dynamics the strategy increases the distance to the ridge axis with every isolation period, see Fig. 5 for the R dynamics, which leads the Meta-ES to gain constantly better fitness. Even for very short isolation periods $\gamma \ll \hat{\gamma}$ the experimental results suit our predictions. Thus we observe a permanent decrease of the mutation strength in Fig. 4 which is linked to the behavior of the R dynamics to get reduced to zero. This leads the Meta-ES to converge to the ridge axis. That is, choosing γ too small, the ES exhibits premature convergence behavior.

Only the vicinity of the critical γ-value we can observe distinct deviations between theory and experimental results. While the isolation length $\gamma = \hat{\gamma}$ is theoretically sufficient to cause a steady increase of the σ and R dynamics, the experimental run departs from the theoretical results. This does not come as surprise, since we replaced the stochastic dynamics by mean value dynamics.

3.2 Analysis of the $R \ll R_\infty$ Case

If the initial point of the Meta-ES lies near the ridge axis we again start the analysis with Eq. (9) and by using (10) one obtains

$$\frac{\mathrm{d}R}{\mathrm{d}g} = \frac{\sigma^2 N}{2\mu}\left(\frac{1}{R} - \frac{1}{R_\infty}\right) = \frac{-\sigma d c_{\mu/\mu,\lambda}}{\sqrt{1+d^2}}\left(\frac{R - R_\infty}{R}\right). \tag{33}$$

By separating the variables this leads to the integral equation

$$\int_{R^{(0)}}^{R^{(g)}} \frac{R'}{R' - R_\infty}\mathrm{d}R' = \frac{-\sigma d c_{\mu/\mu,\lambda}}{\sqrt{1+d^2}} \int_0^g \mathrm{d}g'. \tag{34}$$

While (34) can be integrated in closed form, it is not possible to solve the resulting equation for $R^{(g)}$. Thus we consider the limit cases of small $R^{(0)}$ and large $R^{(0)}$ states separately. The former case allows for a neglection of R in the denominator of the lhs in (34)

$$\int_{R^{(0)}}^{R^{(g)}} \frac{R'}{R_\infty}\mathrm{d}R' = \frac{\sigma d c_{\mu/\mu,\lambda}}{\sqrt{1+d^2}} \int_0^g \mathrm{d}g'. \tag{35}$$

by the use of the condition $R' \ll R_\infty$. Taking into account (10) and solving both integrals yields

$$\frac{1}{2R_\infty}\left(R^{(g)2} - R^{(0)2}\right) = \frac{2\sigma d c_{\mu/\mu,\lambda}}{\sqrt{1+d^2}} g \tag{36}$$

$$\left(R^{(g)2} - R^{(0)2}\right) = \frac{\sigma^2 N}{\mu} g \tag{37}$$

$$R^{(g)} = \sqrt{R^{(0)2} + \frac{\sigma^2 N}{\mu} g}. \tag{38}$$

Considering the case that the ES is initialized at the ridge axis, $R^{(0)} = 0$, one obtains

$$R^{(g)} = \sigma \sqrt{Ng/\mu} \propto \sqrt{g}. \tag{39}$$

That is, the ES departs with a random walk $\sqrt{g}$-law from the ridge axis. Using (4), (7), and (39) the fitness at generation g becomes

$$\boxed{F^{(g)} = -x^{(0)} - \frac{\sigma c_{\mu/\mu,\lambda}}{\sqrt{1+d^2}} g + \frac{d\sigma\sqrt{N}}{\sqrt{\mu}}\sqrt{g}.} \tag{40}$$

For sufficiently large g (keeping $\sigma = const.$) $F^{(g)}$ decreases linearly. This is similar to (19), however, due to the $\sqrt{g}$ term it happens slower.

Considering the difference between $F_+^{(G+\gamma)}$ and $F_-^{(G+\gamma)}$, (21), the σ-learning behavior of the Meta-ES can be analyzed. Using (24) and (40) one gets

$$\delta(\gamma) = \left(\frac{d\sqrt{N}}{\sqrt{\mu}}\sqrt{\gamma} - \frac{c_{\mu/\mu,\lambda}}{\sqrt{1+d^2}}\gamma\right)\sigma^{(G)}\left(\alpha - \frac{1}{\alpha}\right). \tag{41}$$

Now we can define

$$\tilde{\Delta}(\gamma) := \left(\frac{d\sqrt{N}}{\sqrt{\mu}}\sqrt{\gamma} - \frac{c_{\mu/\mu,\lambda}}{\sqrt{1+d^2}}\gamma\right). \tag{42}$$

Similar to (28) we conclude that the Meta-ES increases the mutation strength σ if $\tilde{\Delta}(\gamma) < 0$

$$\tilde{\Delta}(\gamma) < 0 \quad \Leftrightarrow \quad \frac{c_{\mu/\mu,\lambda}}{\sqrt{1+d^2}}\gamma > \frac{d\sqrt{N}}{\sqrt{\mu}}\sqrt{\gamma}. \tag{43}$$

Resolving for the isolation period duration parameter γ, we obtain

$$\gamma \geq \left\lceil \frac{d^2(1+d^2)N}{\mu c^2_{\mu/\mu,\lambda}} \right\rceil \tag{44}$$

$$\Rightarrow \quad \sigma^{(G+\gamma)} = \alpha\sigma^{(G)}. \tag{45}$$

Compared to $\hat{\gamma}$ from Eq. (31) one sees that the isolation period has to be chosen by a factor $2d^2$ larger in order to lead the strategy to diverge from the ridge axis in the case that the Meta-ES starts very close to the ridge axis. However, this result must be taken *cum grano salis*. The bound derived in (44) is based on the R-dynamics (39) that assumed $0 = R^{(0)} \ll R_\infty$. That is, $\sigma\sqrt{Ng/\mu} \ll R_\infty$ must hold. This puts a constraint on the number of generations g the approximation can be used. Taking (10) into account, we see

$$g \ll \frac{N}{4\mu c^2_{\mu/\mu,\lambda}}\left(1 + \frac{1}{d^2}\right) \tag{46}$$

If this condition is violated, the ES already enters the $R \approx R_\infty$ region. Comparing the rhs of (46) with the rhs of (44) we get $d \ll \frac{1}{\sqrt{2}}$. In other words the $R \ll R_\infty$ is left rather fast for sufficient large d and the bound (44) is rather pessimistic. Similar to Section 3.1 we are able to compute the R dynamics iteratively by the use of Eq. (39) and we compare them to the results of an experimental run of the Meta-ES algorithm, see Fig. 6. Again the iterative result is depicted as dashed red line whereas the experiment is represented by the solid blue line and we observe a very good correspondence between the theory and experiments. Even for choices of small d and σ values the strategy is leaving the initial state on the ridge axis relatively fast. That is, after a few generations the special state of $R \ll R_\infty$ is left and the further dynamics can be described by the theory presented in Section 3.1.

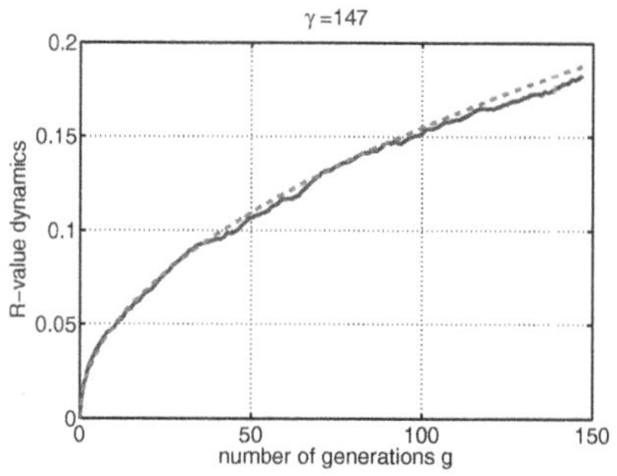

Figure 6: On the R dynamics of the inner strategy of the $[1, 2(3/3, 10)^\gamma]$-Meta-ES initialized on the ridge axis, $R^{(0)} = 0$, with $N = 500$, $d = \frac{1}{100}$, $\sigma^{(0)} = 0.001$ and $\alpha = 1.2$. The distance to the ridge axis is illustrated over the first isolation period of $\gamma = 147$ generations.

3.3 Analysis of the $R \gg R_\infty$ Case

In the case that the radius R of the initial point is considerably larger than R_∞ we start just like in the previous section. But Eq. (34) now can be simplified to

$$\int_{R^{(0)}}^{R^{(g)}} 1 \mathrm{d}R' = \frac{-\sigma dc}{\sqrt{1+d^2}} \int_0^g \mathrm{d}g' \tag{47}$$

which leads directly to

$$R^{(g)} = R^{(0)} - \frac{d\sigma c_{\mu/\mu,\lambda}}{\sqrt{1+d^2}} g. \tag{48}$$

Using (4), (7), and (48) the fitness dynamics of the inner ES become

$$\boxed{F^{(g)} = F^{(0)} - \sigma c_{\mu/\mu,\lambda}\sqrt{1+d^2} g.} \tag{49}$$

Considering the fitness difference in the Meta-ES (24), we immediately obtain

$$F_+^{(G+\gamma)} - F_-^{(G+\gamma)} = -\gamma c_{\mu/\mu,\lambda}\sqrt{1+d^2}\left(\alpha - \frac{1}{\alpha}\right)\sigma \tag{50}$$

which is equivalent to

$$\delta(\gamma) < 0 \quad \forall \gamma \in \mathbb{N}. \tag{51}$$

That is, each choice of γ is leading the Meta-ES to a steady increase of the mutation strength σ until the strategy reaches the steady state distance R_∞ and the dynamics described in Section 3.1 hold again.

Fig. 7 compares the R-value dynamics of two runs of the Meta-ES algorithm with the iteratively computed predictions of Eq. (9). In both cases we observe a good agreement of analytical and experimental results. The lhs of the illustration shows the strategy with a rather short isolation length γ, i.e. $\gamma \approx \hat{\gamma}/2$ whereas on the rhs of Fig. 7 a long isolation time of $\gamma \approx 2\hat{\gamma}$ generations has been chosen.

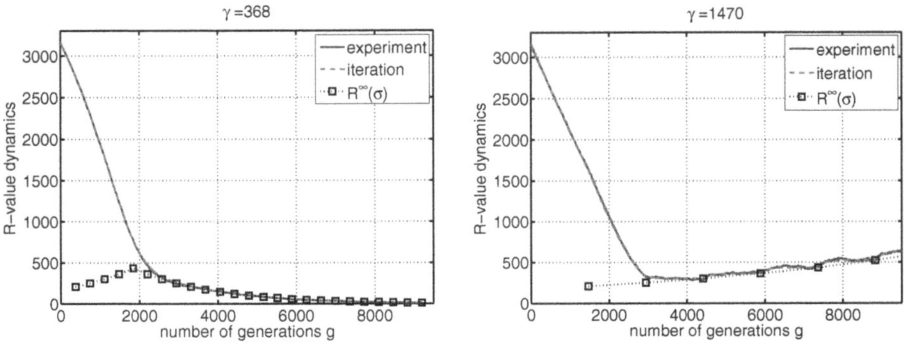

Figure 7: On the R dynamics of the $[1, 2(3/3, 10)^{\gamma}]$-Meta-ES initialized for $R^{(0)} \gg R_{\infty}$, with $N = 1000$, $d = 2$, $\sigma^{(0)} = 1$ and $\alpha = 1.2$. The distance to the ridge axis is displayed over 9500 generations with an isolation length of $368 = \gamma < \hat{\gamma}$ generations on the lhs and of $1470 = \gamma > \hat{\gamma}$ on the rhs of the figure. The black squares symbolize the location of the steady state distance R_{∞} of the respective isolation period which depends on the previously selected mutation strength σ, see also Fig. 8 for the respective σ dynamics.

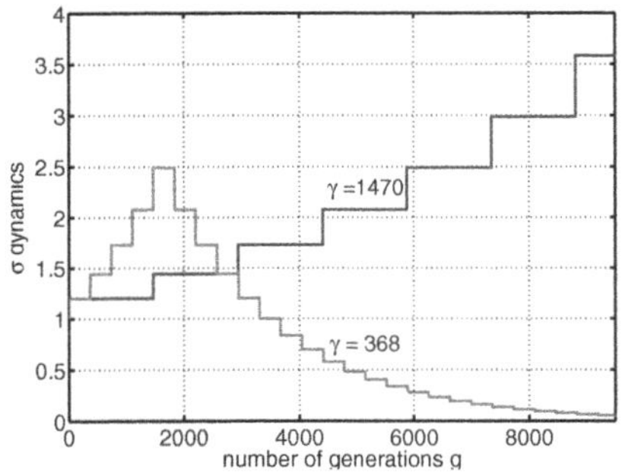

Figure 8: On the σ dynamics of the $[1, 2(3/3, 10)^{\gamma}]$-Meta-ES initialized with $R^{(0)} \gg R_{\infty}$, with $N = 1000$, $d = 2$, $\sigma^{(0)} = 1$ and $\alpha = 1.2$. For the respective R dynamics see Fig. 7. The blue line represents iteratively generated results of the σ-dynamics for long isolation time $\gamma = 1470$ whereas the red line depicts these results for the choice of a short isolation length parameter ($\gamma = 368$). Because the experimental results correspond to the iterative ones for both choices of γ, in this figure we disregard them for reasons of clarity.

As we can see in the respective σ dynamics, Fig. 8, the strategy increases the mutation strength until a sufficient vicinity to the steady state distance is reached in a certain isolation period. That is, we observe a great compliance with the theoretical results, see Eq. (51). Afterwards the Meta-ESs behaviors continue as described in Section 3.1, i.e., for short isolation time the strategy converges to the ridge axis and decreases the mutation strength. Conversely it diverges and steadily increases the mutation strength for long isolation periods.

4. BEHAVIOR OVER MULTIPLE ISOLATION PERIODS

Since in Section 3 the dynamics of the inner ES were already illustrated over several isolation periods and compared to the experimental results of the algorithm we are now going to theoretically investigate the behavior of the Meta-ES over multiple isolation periods. Taking $G + \gamma$ instead of g, defining

$$b := \frac{N\sqrt{1+d^2}}{2\mu c_{\mu/\mu,\lambda} d} \tag{52}$$

and remembering (18), Eq. (17) becomes

$$R^{(G+\gamma)} = R^{(G)} e^{-\gamma/\tau} + b\sigma^{(G)}\left(1 - e^{-\gamma/\tau}\right). \tag{53}$$

Our analysis is based on the results derived for the $R \approx R_{\infty}$ case in Section 3.1. That is sufficient because in both other cases, i.e. $R \ll R_{\infty}$ or $R \gg R_{\infty}$, the initial state is left rather fast with the strategy making progress towards the steady state distance R_{∞}. Assuming the choice of γ big enough, i.e. $\gamma > \hat{\gamma}$ in (31), the Meta-ES is supposed to increase the mutation strength after each isolation period. Thus, after the first isolation over γ generations the algorithm picks the parental $\mathbf{y}_p$ out of the inner ES with the distance to the ridge axis given by

$$R^{(G+\gamma)} = R^{(G)} e^{-\gamma/\tau} + b\alpha\sigma^{(G)}\left(1 - e^{-\gamma/\tau}\right). \tag{54}$$

After the second isolation period with

$$\sigma_p := \sigma^{(G+\gamma)} = \alpha\sigma^{(G)} \tag{55}$$

again the inner ES with increased mutation strength is chosen

$$\begin{aligned} R^{(G+2\gamma)} &= R^{(G+\gamma)} e^{-\gamma/\tau} + b\alpha\sigma^{(G+\gamma)}\left(1 - e^{-\gamma/\tau}\right) && (56)\\ &= R^{(G)} e^{-2\gamma/\tau} + b\alpha\sigma^{(G)}\left(1 - e^{-\gamma/\tau}\right)\left(e^{-\gamma/\tau} + \alpha\right). && (57)\end{aligned}$$

Continuing this way we are able to predict the expected distance to the ridge axis $R^{(G+t\gamma)}$ after t isolation periods

$$R^{(G+t\gamma)} = R^{(G)} e^{-t\gamma/\tau} + b\alpha\sigma^{(G)}\left(1 - e^{-\gamma/\tau}\right) e^{-(t-1)\gamma/\tau} \sum_{i=0}^{t-1} \alpha^i e^{i\gamma/\tau}. \tag{58}$$

Applying the geometric series formula this equation becomes

$$R^{(G+t\gamma)} = R^{(G)} e^{-t\gamma/\tau} + b\alpha\sigma^{(G)}\left(1 - e^{-\gamma/\tau}\right) e^{-(t-1)\gamma/\tau} \frac{\alpha^t e^{t\gamma/\tau} - 1}{\alpha e^{\gamma/\tau} - 1}. \tag{59}$$

Rewriting the second term,

$$\begin{aligned} & b\alpha\sigma^{(G)}\left(1 - e^{-\gamma/\tau}\right) e^{-(t-1)\gamma/\tau} \frac{\alpha^t e^{t\gamma/\tau} - 1}{\alpha e^{\gamma/\tau} - 1} && (60)\\ =\; & b\sigma^{(G)}\left(1 - e^{-\gamma/\tau}\right) \alpha^t \frac{1 - \alpha^{-t} e^{-t\gamma/\tau}}{1 - \alpha^{-1} e^{-\gamma/\tau}} && (61)\end{aligned}$$

and using (10), the R-dynamics becomes

$$R^{(G+t\gamma)} = R^{(G)} e^{-t\gamma/\tau} + R_{\infty}^{(G)} \alpha^t \left(1 - e^{-\gamma/\tau}\right) \frac{1 - \alpha^{-t} e^{-t\gamma/\tau}}{1 - \alpha^{-1} e^{-\gamma/\tau}}, \tag{62}$$

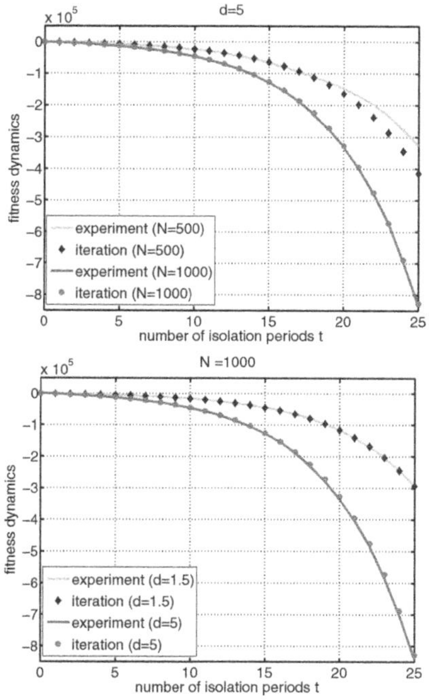

Figure 9: The upper graphs show the fitness dynamics of an $[1, 2(3/3, 10)^{2\hat{\gamma}}]$-Meta-ES with $\sigma^{(0)} = 1$, $\alpha = 1.2$ and two different choices of the dimension N and the nonlinearity strength d each. The dynamics are illustrated over 25 isolation periods of $2\hat{\gamma}$ generations with $\hat{\gamma}$ from (31) depending on N and d.

with $R_\infty^{(G)} = \frac{N\sqrt{1+d^2}}{2\mu c_{\mu/\mu,\lambda} d}\sigma^{(G)}$.

Equation (62) simplifies when taking into account $e^{-\gamma/\tau} \ll 1$

$$R^{(G+t\gamma)} \simeq R_\infty^{(G)}\alpha^t. \tag{63}$$

In order to have this dynamics, we have to demand $e^{-\gamma/\tau} \ll 1$, i.e. $\gamma/\tau \gg 1$. Using an isolation period (31) and τ given by (18), this transfers to the condition

$$\gamma/\tau = d^2 \gg 1 \tag{64}$$

which is approximately fulfilled for sufficiently large nonlinearity parameter d in (4). In the same manner we can derive a formula for the progress of the Meta-ES in direction of the ridge axis. Using (7) and (55) one gets

$$x^{(G+\gamma)} = x^{(G)} + \frac{c_{\mu/\mu,\lambda}}{\sqrt{1+d^2}}\alpha\sigma^{(G)}\gamma \tag{65}$$

$$x^{(G+2\gamma)} = x^{(G+\gamma)} + \frac{c_{\mu/\mu,\lambda}}{\sqrt{1+d^2}}\gamma\alpha\sigma^{(G+\gamma)} \tag{66}$$

$$= x^{(G)} + \frac{c_{\mu/\mu,\lambda}}{\sqrt{1+d^2}}\gamma\sigma^{(G)}\alpha(1+\alpha). \tag{67}$$

After t isolation periods we have

$$x^{(G+t\gamma)} = x^{(G)} + \frac{c_{\mu/\mu,\lambda}}{\sqrt{1+d^2}}\gamma\sigma^{(G)}\alpha\sum_{i=0}^{t-1}\alpha^i. \tag{68}$$

By use of the geometric series formula this can be simplified to

$$x^{(G+t\gamma)} = x^{(G)} + \frac{c_{\mu/\mu,\lambda}}{\sqrt{1+d^2}}\gamma\sigma^{(G)}\alpha\frac{\alpha^t - 1}{\alpha - 1}. \tag{69}$$

Using (63), (68), and (4) the approximate F-dynamics of the Meta-ES reads ($x^{(G)} = 0$)

$$F^{(G+t\gamma)} \simeq -\frac{c_{\mu/\mu,\lambda}}{\sqrt{1+d^2}}\gamma\sigma^{(G)}\alpha\frac{\alpha^t - 1}{\alpha - 1} + dR_\infty^{(G)}\alpha^t. \tag{70}$$

This leads to an asymptotic dynamics

$$F^{(G+t\gamma)} \sim -\alpha^t\sigma^{(G)}\frac{N\sqrt{1+d^2}}{2\mu c_{\mu/\mu,\lambda}}\left(\frac{2\mu c_{\mu/\mu,\lambda}^2}{N(1+d^2)}\frac{\gamma\alpha}{\alpha - 1} - 1\right). \tag{71}$$

That is, the Meta-ES diverges exponentially fast at a rate of $\ln\alpha$.

The fitness value dynamics predicted in Eq. (70) compared to three different Meta-ES runs are displayed in Fig. 9 for $N = 500$ and $N = 1000$. We observe an increasing compliance of iteratively computed and experimental results by increasing the dimensionality N. On the lower depiction of Fig. 9 the influence of the nonlinearity strength parameter d is shown, i.e. the fitness dynamics of two Meta-ESs on different fitness landscapes are illustrated. The use of a bigger nonlinearity strength d causes longer isolation periods, see (31), letting the Meta-ES reach better fitness. For long isolation periods and high dimensionalities the predictions agree with the experiments.

5. FINITE SEARCH SPACE DIMENSIONALITY EFFECTS

The inequality (32) offers an astonishing interpretation: The progress on the ridge function only depends on the number of function evaluations being larger than the constant term on the rhs of (32). That is, in the asymptotic limit case ($N \to \infty$) isolation periods > 1 are unnecessary. This conclusion calls for an examination of the Meta-ES dynamics in low-dimensional spaces. From the progress rate analysis of the sphere model and also the ridge function we know that the progress rate does not linearly scale with the population size. That is, the increase of μ does only make sense if $\mu \ll N$. If this condition is violated, $\gamma > 1$ might be of use.

Therefore, we investigate the Meta-ES behaviors for a constant number of function evaluations but with different choices of population size parameters (μ, λ) and isolation length parameter γ under the condition of small N. Using (32) with $\nu = 0.25$ we consider

$$\frac{N(1+d^2)}{2} < \mu\gamma = 2^\beta = 2^{\beta_1}2^{\beta_2} = const. \tag{72}$$

with $\mu := 2^{\beta_1}$, $\gamma := 2^{\beta_2}$ and $\beta = \beta_1 + \beta_2 \in \mathbb{N}$. As we can see in the illustrations for small dimensional spaces, see Fig. 10 ($\beta = 8$, $N = 30$, $d = 0.9$) and Fig. 11 ($\beta = 8$, $N = 30$, $d = 3$), the use of isolation within the Meta-ES leads to a great improvement in the case of small search space dimensions. In Fig. 10 the inequality in (32) is relatively high because of the small choice of d which results in similar mutation strength dynamics and therefore overlapping graphs of the illustrated five Meta-ES settings with ($\mu = 1, \gamma = 256$), ($\mu = 4, \gamma = 64$), ($\mu = 16, \gamma = 16$), ($\mu = 64, \gamma = 4$) and ($\mu = 256, \gamma = 1$). While the σ dynamics are equal we can observe that the Meta-ESs with longer isolation periods and smaller populations outperform the conversely constructed ones with respect to their R-value and fitness dynamics compared against the same number of function evaluations (or isolation periods respectively). The situation illustrated in Fig. 11 describes a low inequality in Eq. (32). In contrast to Fig. 10 the R-value dynamics of the Meta-ES settings with short isolation periods and larger population sizes tend to converge to the ridge axis. This leads to premature convergence behavior while longer isolation periods still lead to increase the distance to the ridge axis and gain greater progress of the fitness values. Regarding the σ dynamics in Fig. 11, we see that no Meta-ES setting steadily increases the mutation strength under the

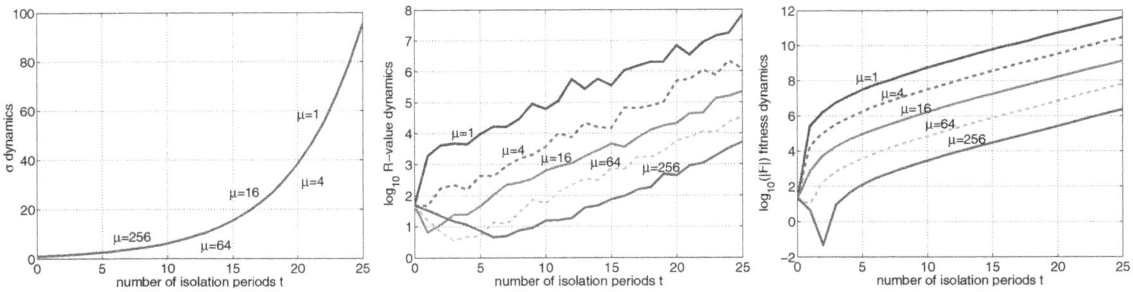

Figure 10: Illustration of the $[1, 2(\mu/\mu, \lambda)^\gamma]$-Meta-ES dynamics for dimension $N = 30$, nonlinearity strength parameter $d = 0.9$ and truncation ratio $\nu = 0.25$. The mutation strength σ, the distance to the ridge axis R and the fitness function value F are compared for five different combinations of $\gamma\mu = 2^8 = 256$ over a time of 25 isolation periods.

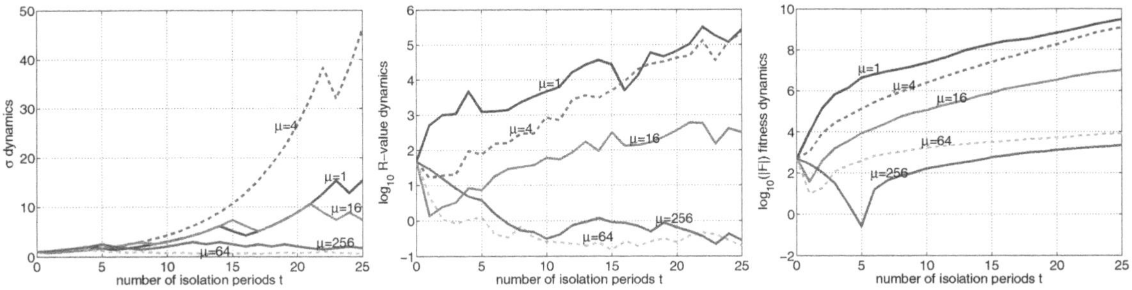

Figure 11: Depiction of the $[1, 2(\mu/\mu, \lambda)^\gamma]$-Meta-ES dynamics for dimension $N = 30$, $d = 3$ and $\nu = 0.25$. Again the dynamics of the five Meta-ES runs with $\gamma\mu = 2^8 = 256$ are compared over 25 isolation periods. Note that Fig. 10 only differs from Fig. 11 by the choice of the nonlinearity strength parameter d.

condition that the inequality (32) is not sufficiently satisfied. But again rather the settings with longer isolation periods and smaller population sizes tend to increase the mutation strength. That is, leaving the asymptotic limit case we can infer advantages from the use of a sufficiently long isolation period.

6. CONCLUSIONS AND OUTLOOK

In this paper we examined the σ-control of the $[1, 2(\mu/\mu, \lambda)^\gamma]$-Meta-ES on the sharp ridge. Our theoretical analysis allows for a deeper understanding of the influence of the isolation length γ on the performance of the Meta-ES. We derived an estimate for the choice of γ which depends on the population sizes λ and μ and the dimensionality N as well as d being the nonlinearity strength parameter determining the "hardness" of the sharp ridge. From earlier empirical investigations [5] it was conjectured that the isolation parameter γ has considerable influence on the performance of the Meta-ES. The asymptotical analysis done here, however, revealed that it is not γ alone that determines the qualitative behavior (whether there is premature convergence or not), but the number of function evaluations $\gamma\lambda$ devoted to the inner ES. That is, similar convergence effects can be obtained by either increasing the population size or the isolation period. This is a very remarkable results, since it predicts Meta-ES functioning even for $\gamma = 1$ provided that the population size has been chosen sufficiently large, see Inequality (32). The result has been obtained for $N \to \infty$ assuming that the population size is much smaller than the search space dimensionality N. This still leaves room for $\gamma > 1$ advantages. Considering small dimensionalities, we have found indeed experimental evidence for advantages of longer isolation periods.

The investigations should be extended to other test problems where the choice of the populations size versus the isolation time might have a much greater impact on the ES performance, as perhaps for noisy problems. The theoretical analysis performed will be also the basis for the design of theoretically motivated population size control rules.

7. ACKNOWLEDGMENTS

This work was supported by the Austrian Science Fund (FWF) under grant P22649-N23.

8. REFERENCES

[1] D. V. Arnold and A. MacLeod. Step length adaption on ridge functions. *Evolutionary Computation*, 16:151–184, 2008.

[2] H.-G. Beyer. On the Performance on $(1, \lambda)$-Evolution Strategies for the Ridge Function Class. *IEEE Transactions on Evolutionary Computation*, 5(3), June 2001.

[3] H.-G. Beyer. *The Theory of Evolution Strategies*. Natural Computing Series, Springer, Heidelberg, 2001.

[4] H.-G. Beyer, M. Dobler, C. Hämmerle, and P. Masser. On Strategy Parameter Control by Meta-ES. GECCO'09, 2009.

[5] M. Herdy. Reproductive Isolation as Strategy parameter in Hierarchically Organized Evolution Strategies. In *R. Männer and B. Manderick, editors, Parallel Problem Solving from Nature*, volume 2, pages 207–217. Elsevier, 1992.

[6] M. Lunacek and D. Whitley. Searching for Balance: Understanding Self-Adaption on Ridge Functions. PPSN, 2006.

[7] S. Meyer-Nieberg. *Self-Adaptation in Evolution Strategies*. PhD thesis, Dortmund, 2007.

[8] I. Rechenberg. *Evolutionsstrategie '94*. Frommann-Holzboog Verlag, Stuttgart, 1994.

Algorithm Selection Based on Exploratory Landscape Analysis and Cost-Sensitive Learning

Bernd Bischl*
TU Dortmund, Germany
bischl@statistik.tu-dortmund.de

Olaf Mersmann
TU Dortmund, Germany
olafm@statistik.tu-dortmund.de

Heike Trautmann
TU Dortmund, Germany
trautmann@statistik.tu-dortmund.de

Mike Preuss
TU Dortmund, Germany
mike.preuss@tu-dortmund.de

ABSTRACT

The steady supply of new optimization methods makes the algorithm selection problem (ASP) an increasingly pressing and challenging task, especially for real-world black-box optimization problems. The introduced approach considers the ASP as a cost-sensitive classification task which is based on Exploratory Landscape Analysis. Low-level features gathered by systematic sampling of the function on the feasible set are used to predict a well-performing algorithm out of a given portfolio. Example-specific label costs are defined by the expected runtime of each candidate algorithm. We use one-sided support vector regression to solve this learning problem. The approach is illustrated by means of the optimization problems and algorithms of the BBOB'09/10 workshop.

Categories and Subject Descriptors

G.1.6 [**Optimization**]: Global Optimization, Unconstrained Optimization; G.3 [**Probability and Statistics**]: Statistical Computing; I.2.6 [**Learning**]: Knowledge Acquisition

General Terms

Experimentation, Algorithms, Performance

Keywords

algorithm selection, evolutionary optimization, fitness landscape, exploratory landscape analysis, BBOB test set, benchmarking, machine learning

*Corresponding author

GECCO'12, July 7–11, 2012, Philadelphia, Pennsylvania, USA.

1. INTRODUCTION

The *algorithm selection problem* (ASP) (Rice, 1976) resembles the old desire to choose the right optimization algorithm for a not well-known optimization task without enumerating all available techniques. Although there are algorithms coping well with many problems, a cleverly constructed portfolio provides better efficiency than any single algorithm even on a small set of problems as, e.g., the BBOB test set, see the results of the related 2009 and 2010 competitions in Hansen et al. (2010) and Auger et al. (2010). Thus, the ASP can be regarded as still important and largely unsolved.

We suggest to employ *Exploratory Landscape Analysis* (ELA) techniques to approach this problem. The low-level features presented in Mersmann et al. (2011) are a first step to automatically and numerically characterize the landscape of a given fitness function. Section 2 gives an introduction into the ELA background and describes the employed features. The long term goal is to provide a method that is able to select a good algorithm for an arbitrary problem. As a first approach we use the 24 BBOB functions as a representative benchmark set.

Taking into account that some of the tested algorithms are not really competitive on any of the BBOB functions and that a practical portfolio should be as small as possible, we select 4 diverse optimizers from the ones that have been run in 2009 and 2010. Assuming we had an oracle, which would always select the correct algorithm for us given a test function, the chosen subset is optimal among all subsets of the same size. Furthermore, its performance is not far off from the one we would obtain by considering a selection oracle for all available algorithms.

Now a machine learning model has to be constructed that selects a well-performing algorithm from the portfolio based on the extracted ELA features. Usually this problem is tackled either by standard classification (given the features, predict the best algorithm) or regression (given the features, predict the performance measure for each algorithm, then select the algorithm with the best predicted value). But in our opinion both approaches fail to optimally solve the problem at hand: How do we score suboptimal selections and how can this information best be incorporated into the model fitting process? It is neither satisfying to minimize the classification error (because the penalty we incur for a wrong selection should depend on the gap in performance to the optimal choice), nor do we have to accurately predict performance values given a feature vector (this will in general be impossible and we only care about the order of the predicted performances). For practical applications, we need to minimize the loss in runtime for the predicted algorithm when compared with the optimal available candidate. This implies some form of cost-sensitive learning. As the costs in the discussed scenario are different for each single data point, not many machine learning models are currently available that can solve such tasks with example-specific costs. We propose to use the recently published method of one-sided support vector regression (Tu and Lin (2010)), which is discussed in more detail in Section 3.

We are currently unaware of other work that combines automatically computed, numerical features with a selection strategy that incorporates the relevant costs of wrong selections for optimization.

Some interesting questions can be asked concerning the performance of our approach, and they are answered in the experimental study presented in Section 4:

- Can we generalize over instances? Meaning, can we train our model on only some of the BBOB function instances and predict well-performing algorithms for the remaining ones that we have never seen?
- Can we even generalize over functions? Not only generalizing over instances but transferring knowledge to completely unseen function types would be a much stronger result than generalizing only over instances. If the former can be done successfully but not the latter, this might indicate that the BBOB set is too small and its test functions are too different for effective usage in such learning problems as considered in this study.
- Do we also need the expensive ELA features, e.g., local searches, or can satisfying results also be achieved with only "cheap" features?

We feel that we probably have reached the limit of what can be achieved with the BBOB data alone with respect to algorithm selection and that more extensive experimental data is needed to move beyond the results presented here. This and related aspects are discussed in Section 5. Further discussion and an outlook on future research are given in 6.

2. EXPLORATORY LANDSCAPE ANALYSIS: USED FEATURES

Exploratory Landscape Analysis (ELA) aims at extracting characteristics for a given optimization problem prior to optimization which, in this work, form the basis for an algorithm recommendation. Preliminary approaches date back to measures related to fitness distance correlation (Jones and Forrest (1995)) but did not lead to satisfying results. The reason was mainly that only a single feature was used, which is by far not enough to capture and explain all possible differences in optimization problems. Consequently, the ELA approach is set-based and much more pragmatic: We define many features and then experimentally determine the ones that are actually useful for a given classification problem.

In Mersmann et al. (2010a) and Bartz-Beielstein and Preuss (2012) high-level features specified by human experts such as the level of modality or separability are introduced to reflect the problem characteristics. As these features depend on subjective assessment, experimental low-level features which are presented in Mersmann et al. (2011) can be automatically extracted by using systematic sampling of the decision space using a suitable space filling design. It was shown that these features not only match the expert designed high-level features but that they can be used to successfully predict the predefined function groups of the BBOB'09/10 function set with negligible errors.

The starting point for computing our low-level features is a data set of s different decision variable settings X^s with respective objective values Y^s generated by a random Latin hypercube (LH) design covering the decision space. We will denote the combination of search points and corresponding function values by $D^s = [X^s, Y^s]$. The size of the LH design increases linearly with the dimension d of the problem which is one suitable heuristic possibility to account for the increasing problem complexity, i.e., the number of initial points is chosen as $s = c \cdot d$, where c is a predefined constant.

The features can be grouped into five classes related to characteristics of the distribution of the objective function values (y - Distribution), the relative position of each objective value compared to the median of all values (Levelset), meta-modeling of the initial data set (Meta-Model), the estimated degree of convexity of the function (Convexity) as well as the assessment of multimodality by local searches starting from the initial design points (Local Search). Details are given in Mersmann et al. (2011). Each class contains several lower level sub-features which, in each case, can be generated using the same experimental data pool. All of these sub-features are listed in Table 1. The first three feature classes can be computed directly on the sample without additional evaluations and are denoted as "cheap" features in the following. The last two feature classes require additional function evaluations. In order to limit the required computational effort we strive to restrict the analysis to a low-level feature set which can be computed solely based on the initial design. However, it is currently not clear if using only "cheap" features is feasible when tackling the algorithm selection.

3. COST-SENSITIVE LEARNING AND ONE-SIDED REGRESSION

In this section we briefly introduce a general definition of cost-sensitive learning and present a solution based on one-sided support vector regression proposed by Tu and Lin (2010). The following section will show how to facilitate this modeling technique in order to select an efficient algorithm for continuous black-box optimization.

Supervised classification is concerned with creating predictors mapping from a feature space $\mathcal{X}$ (here $\mathbb{R}^p$) to a set of classes $\mathcal{Y} = \{1, \ldots, k\}$, also called labels. We usually assume a stochastic data-generating process, a distribution $\mathcal{P}$ on $\mathcal{X} \times \mathcal{Y}$, and a data set $\{(\mathbf{x}^i, y^i)\}_{i=1}^n$, whose observations have been independently drawn from $\mathcal{P}$. This data shall be used to learn the predictor.

Given a parametrized classification model $f(\mathbf{x}, \boldsymbol{\theta})$, where the vector $\boldsymbol{\theta}$ denotes the parameters to be determined, our task can be described as the minimization of the expected number of misclassifications

$$\min_{\boldsymbol{\theta}} \int_{\mathcal{X} \times \mathcal{Y}} [y \neq f(\mathbf{x}, \boldsymbol{\theta})] \, d\mathcal{P}(\mathbf{x}, y) \, . \tag{1}$$

A multitude of different machine learning algorithms exists for multiclass-classification (see Hastie et al. (2001)), and of

Feature group and name	Description
y distribution features:	
4 distr.skewness_y	skewness of the distribution of the function values
4 distr.kurtosis_y	kurtosis of the distribution of the function values
4 distr.n_peaks	estimation of the number of peaks in the distribution of the function values
Levelset features:	
5 levelset.lda_mmce_{10,25,50}	mean LDA misclassification error for function values split by 0.1, 0.25, 0.5 quantile (estimated by CV)
5 levelset.lda_vs_qda_{10,25,50}	levelset.lda_mmce_{10,25,50} divided by levelset.qda_mmce_{10,25,50}
6 levelset.qda_mmce_{10,25,50}	mean QDA misclassification error for function values split by 0.1, 0.25, 0.5 quantile (estimated by CV)
7 levelset.mda_mmce_{10,25,50}	mean MDA misclassification error for function values split by 0.1, 0.25, 0.5 quantile (estimated by CV)
Meta-model features:	
1 approx.{linear,lineari}_ar2	adjusted R^2 of the estimated linear regression model without and with interaction
1 approx.linear_{min,max}_coef	minimum and maximum value of the absolute values of the linear model coefficients
2 approx.{quadratic,quadratici}_ar2	adjusted R^2 of the estimated quadratic regression model without or with interaction
2 approx.quadratic_cond	maximum absolute over minimum absolute value of the quadratic term coefficients in the quadratic model
Convexity features:	
3 convex.{linear,convex}_p	estimated probability of linearity and convexity
3 convex.linear_dev	mean deviation from linearity
Local search features:	
8 ls.n_local_optima	number of local optima estimated by the number of identified clusters
8 ls.best_to_mean_contrast	minimum value of cluster centers divided by the mean value of cluster centers
8 ls.{best}_basin_size	proportion of points in the best cluster
8 ls.mean_other_basin_size	mean proportion of points in all clusters but the cluster with the best cluster center
8 ls.{min,lq,med,uq,max}_feval	0, 0.25, 0.5, 0.75 and 1 quantile of the distribution of #function evaluations performed during a single local search

Table 1: Low-level features; summary of sub-features within the feature classes. Leading numbers refer to the feature group the low-level feature belongs to. LDA, QDA and MDA denote linear, quadratic resp. mixture discriminant analysis. The two groups below the double line require additional evaluations.

course it is usually impossible to tackle (1) directly. As we do not know $\mathcal{P}$, we have to fit w.r.t. the training data; minimizing the number of misclassified examples is computationally intractable, so we have to approximate the idea expressed in (1) with something more efficient; and we often combine it with regularization to restrict the complexity of the model.

A more realistic scenario – especially if we associate specific actions with our predictions – might be to assume individual costs for a predicted class depending on the true label. The standard examples, where this is obviously reasonable and necessary, are labeling patients as "sick" or "healthy" and granting / rejecting credit applications. In such a case we assume a cost matrix G, where $G(i, j)$ expresses the cost of classifying an object of class i as class j. Now we naturally try to minimize

$$\min_{\boldsymbol{\theta}} \int_{\mathcal{X}\times\mathcal{Y}} G(y, f(\mathbf{x}, \boldsymbol{\theta}))\, d\mathcal{P}(\mathbf{x}, y) \tag{2}$$

instead of (1). Optimally solving this cost-sensitive problem for the multiclass case $k > 2$ is quite hard, and although a lot of proposed approaches exist, no consensus seems to have been reached what works best in the general case.

A further generalization allows the costs to depend on the example $\mathbf{x}$ and its features which is the scenario we are interested in. This is sometimes referred to as cost-sensitive learning with example-specific costs, see Turney (2000) for a very extensive taxonomy of cost-sensitive problems. Here, each observed $\mathbf{x}$ has an associated cost vector $\mathbf{c}$, so the available data set has the form $\{(\mathbf{x}^i, \mathbf{c}^i)\}_{i=1}^n$, where c_j^i specifies the cost of labeling example i as class j. Therefore, our distribution $\mathcal{P}$ is now defined on $\mathcal{X} \times \mathbb{R}^k$ and, as our goal still is to obtain a cost-optimal predictor, (2) changes to

$$\min_{\boldsymbol{\theta}} \int_{\mathcal{X}\times\mathbb{R}^k} c(f(\mathbf{x}, \boldsymbol{\theta}))\, d\mathcal{P}(\mathbf{x}, \mathbf{c})\,. \tag{3}$$

Tu and Lin (2010) have proposed to solve the problem (3) via one-sided support vector regression. They compare their method to the most common alternatives (not that many exist) and present convincing empirical results in addition to some theoretical guarantees. For these reasons we select it as our method of choice in this paper. We report the main ideas and formulas of their approach in the following paragraphs.

Construct k regression problem sets $S_j = \{(\mathbf{x}^i, c_j^i)\}_{i=1}^n$ from the observed data where $j \in \{1, \ldots, k\}$. Define $z_j^i = 1$, if c_j^i is the minimal entry in the vector $\mathbf{c}^i$, and therefore labeling $\mathbf{x}^i$ as class j is the best possible action, otherwise set $z_j^i = -1$. Our goal is to construct k regression models f_j, one for each S_j. Then we can estimate the cost vector $\hat{\mathbf{c}} = (f_1(\mathbf{x}), \ldots, f_k(\mathbf{x}))^T$, given a feature vector $\mathbf{x}$, and select $\operatorname{argmin}_j \hat{c}_j$ as our predicted, hopefully not too pricey, label.

The important observation now is that we do not necessarily have to minimize the difference between $\hat{\mathbf{c}}$ and $\mathbf{c}$, e.g., by minimizing the squared loss $||\mathbf{c} - \hat{\mathbf{c}}||_2^2$ or absolute loss $||\mathbf{c} - \hat{\mathbf{c}}||_1$ in the regression. We only have to be concerned with the property that the true cost of the minimal entry of $\hat{\mathbf{c}}$ is as close as possible to the minimal entry of $\mathbf{c}$, because their difference expresses how much we score worse if we use our predictors f_j instead of directly accessing the unknown true cost vector $\mathbf{c}$ to build our decision. Therefore we choose $L(c_j^i, z_j^i, \hat{c}_j^i) = \max(0, z_j^i(\hat{c}_j^i - c_j^i))$ as our loss function. Meaning, we do not penalize underestimating the true cost of the optimal decision, which can never have a negative effect on selection, and we penalize overestimation linearly. For non-optimal labels we proceed vice versa for a similar reason. Tu and Lin (2010) prove that the true cost of the predicted label for an example $\mathbf{x}^i$ is always bounded from above by $\sum_{j=1}^k L(c_j^i, z_j^i, \hat{c}_j^i) + \min(\mathbf{c})$, further motivating this choice of L. As L is either 0 to the left or right of the origin of the real line, we call a regression based on such L "one-sided". Note, that L is not very different from the hinge loss used in binary support vector classification.

Let us now fix j and construct a regression model for S_j based on the above motivated loss L. Assuming (for now) a linear model $f(\mathbf{x}, \mathbf{w}) = \mathbf{w}^T\mathbf{x}+b$ and that L_2-regularization of $\mathbf{w}$ makes sense, we define the following primal optimization problem:

$$\min_{\mathbf{w},b} \sum_{i=1}^{n} L(c_j^i, z_j^i, \mathbf{w}^T\mathbf{x}^i + b) + \frac{\lambda}{2}||\mathbf{w}||_2^2 \qquad (4)$$

Encoding the non-differentiability of L in constraints results in:

$$\begin{cases} \min_{\mathbf{w},b} & \frac{\lambda}{2}||\mathbf{w}||_2^2 + \sum_{i=1}^{n} \xi_i \\ \text{s.t.} & \xi_i \geq z_j^i(\mathbf{w}^T\mathbf{x}^i + b - c_j^i) \\ & \boldsymbol{\xi} \geq 0 \,. \end{cases} \qquad (5)$$

Note that both (4) and (5) are equal to respective formulations in binary support vector classification, if we use $z_j^i \in \{+1, -1\}$ for positive / negative labels and set all $c_j^i = 1$. Converting (5) into its dual version and employing the kernel trick by substituting all scalar products with a kernel function $k(\cdot, \cdot)$, we finally arrive at

$$\begin{cases} \min_{\mathbf{w},b} & \frac{1}{2}\boldsymbol{\alpha}^T \text{diag}(\mathbf{z}) K \text{diag}(\mathbf{z}) \boldsymbol{\alpha} + \mathbf{z}^T\boldsymbol{\alpha} \\ \text{s.t.} & \mathbf{z}^T\boldsymbol{\alpha} = 0 \\ & 0 \leq \boldsymbol{\alpha} \leq \frac{1}{\lambda} \,. \end{cases} \qquad (6)$$

Here, K is the kernel matrix with $K(i, j) = k(\mathbf{x}^i, \mathbf{x}^j)$, $\boldsymbol{\alpha}$ is the vector of Lagrange multipliers and $\text{diag}(\mathbf{z})$ is a diagonal matrix with entries $\mathbf{z} = (z_j^1, \dots, z_j^n)$. Again, this is very similar to the dual problem of the standard support vector machine. It is a quadratic program that we can solve with the same techniques as the "classic" Support Vector Machine (SVM) problem. And as usual we obtain a formula for the intercept b from the Karush-Kuhn-Tucker conditions. Finally, a prediction for a new point $\mathbf{x}$ can be obtained by

$$f(\mathbf{x}, \boldsymbol{\alpha}, b) = \sum_{i \in \text{SV}} -\alpha_i z_j^i k(\mathbf{x}, \mathbf{x}^j) + b \,, \qquad (7)$$

where the set SV indexes the support vectors, i.e., $\text{SV} = \{i : \alpha_i > 0\}$. As always, the kernel trick allowed us to transform an essentially linear model into a powerful non-linear one. We use an interior point solver provided by the R package kernlab (Karatzoglou et al. (2004)) to optimize (6).

4. ALGORITHM SELECTION FOR BBOB FUNCTIONS

A detailed description of the BBOB setup can be found in Hansen et al. (2009). It uses a balanced and unbiased sample of the published set of test functions from the field of black-box optimization. To assess the performance of an algorithm, the BBOB team proposes the use of the so called *expected running time* (ERT). This measure estimates the expected number of function evaluations required to achieve an accuracy of $\epsilon > 0$. For a given ϵ the ERT is defined as

$$\mathbf{E}\{RT(\epsilon)\} := \mathbf{E}\{N_{\text{eval}}^{\text{succ}}(\epsilon)\} + \frac{1 - \pi^{\text{succ}}(\epsilon)}{\pi^{\text{succ}}(\epsilon)} \mathbf{E}\left\{N_{\text{eval}}^{\text{fail}}(\epsilon)\right\},$$

where $N_{\text{eval}}^{\text{succ}}(\epsilon)$ denotes the number of function evaluations until the algorithm reaches the desired accuracy of ϵ, $N_{\text{eval}}^{\text{fail}}(\epsilon)$ denotes the number of function evaluations until the algorithm terminates without reaching the desired accuracy level (unsuccessful run) and $\pi^{\text{succ}}(\epsilon)$ is the probability of a successful run. Note that the maximum number of function evaluations for each algorithm is set by the resp. BBOB contestant and thus varies within the algorithm set. We will estimate the ERT from the r runs performed by every algorithm on each test function by plugging in the empirical equivalents of the unknown parameters. For a thorough motivation of the ERT see Hansen and Auger (2005).

In order to estimate the ERT, each contestant is required to submit 15 runs of his or her algorithm for each of the 24 test functions. It was required to submit results for 2, 3, 5, 10, 20 and optionally 40 dimensional parameter spaces. The results of each run are automatically stored in a file by the BBOB framework. From this file it is possible to infer the number of function evaluations used for almost any accuracy level ϵ. There is one small difference in the way the 15 runs are composed between the 2009 and 2010 competition. In the 2009 competition the 15 runs were divided among 5 different test function instances[1] for each of which 3 runs had to be performed. In 2010, instead of 5 instances, 15 instances with just one run per instance were required.

4.1 Experimental Setup

The 24 BBOB test functions (Hansen et al. (2009)) are subdivided into four classes, basically with respect to modality, separability and global structure. As already shown in Mersmann et al. (2010a) and Mersmann et al. (2011a) the algorithm performance is not consistent enough within the specified function groups to justify the selection of a reduced set of representative test problems. Therefore, we concentrate on the individual functions rather than selecting a representative function of each algorithm group.

In order to ensure distinguishable performance results of the algorithms the analysis focuses on a precision level of 10^{-3} to be reached. This coincides with the requirements of many practical applications in which a sufficient decrease of the fitness function is acceptable and it is not necessary to discover the global optimum. Furthermore, problem dimensionality is exemplary set to ten dimensions as a representative of the practically relevant dimensions 5-20.

The outline of the analysis is as follows: Based on the raw data, graciously provided by BBOB team on their website[2], and the benchmarking concepts of Mersmann et al. (2010) and Mersmann et al. (2011a), we determine the best algorithm for each BBOB function w.r.t. ERT which is presented in Table 2.

As can be seen in Table 2, there is no global "best" algorithm. In fact, no algorithm is best on more than three functions. In addition, the relative ERT (rel. ERT) values, i.e., the ERT of the specific algorithm divided by the ERT of the optimal algorithm for the respective function, are computed. Table 2 lists the respective median and maximum statistics, computed across all functions. However, the computation of the individual rel. ERT values faces some problems as almost none of the competing BBOB algorithms succeeded in solving all functions for the chosen (minimal) precision level. In many cases even half of the ERT data was missing. The number of solved functions of the considered algorithms together with the unsolved functions are presented in Table 3. The ERT values for a specific unsolved function are imputed by assigning ten times the maximal ERT value of all 14 algo-

[1]Slight reparameterizations of the test function obtained by rescaling, rotating or otherwise transforming the parameter vector before applying the function.

[2]`http://coco.gforge.inria.fr/doku.php`

Algorithm	Best on Function	med (rel. ERT)	max (rel. ERT)
AVGNEWUOA	8	29.67	58731.09
BFGS	1, 10	31.55	58731.09
BIPOP-CMA-ES	17	3.83	5873.11
DE-F-AUC	18	41.13	11867.07
FULLNEWUOA	6	39.36	58731.09
GLOBAL	12, 21, 22	22.60	58731.09
iAMALGAM	23	10.02	2287.43
IPOP-ACTCMA-ES	7, 11, 13	3.72	2655.55
IPOP-CMA-ES	15, 16, 19	3.40	5743.86
Line Search-fminbnd	2	172.23	58731.09
Line Search - STEP	3, 4	417.47	13494.28
MCS	5, 9	39.55	58731.09
MOS	20, 24	4.27	1186.71
NEWUOA	14	28.01	58731.09

Table 2: All BBOB algorithms which performed best on at least one of the 24 functions w.r.t. ERT. The functions are listed in the 2nd column. In addition, median and maximum rel. ERT values over all functions are given.

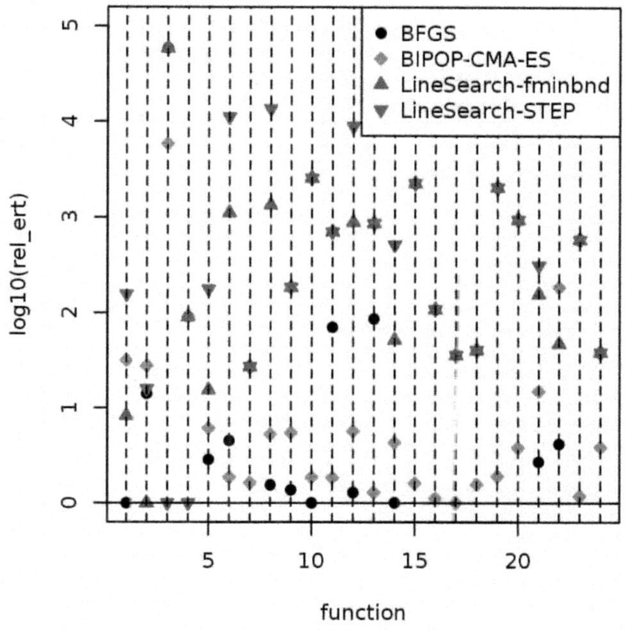

Figure 1: Rel. ERT value (logscale) of the algorithms in the portfolio for the 24 BBOB functions

rithms listed in Table 3 on this function. The worst imputed value equals 58731.09 for the third function.

We can observe that each algorithm performs very badly on at least one function or is not able to solve specific functions at all. This observation underscores the importance of the ASP. However, it turns out that a smaller subset of the 14 algorithms is sufficient to ensure a very good performance of the resulting algorithm portfolio.

We select a representative algorithm pool as follows. We consider an oracle that always selects the optimal algorithm out of the portfolio given a test function. This results in 24 rel. ERT values when the portfolio is applied to all BBOB functions and we use the maximum of these values to describe the worst-case behavior of the portfolio combined with the oracle. We then minimize this value over all possible portfolios. For a portfolio of size four this "oracle performance" drops down to a maximal rel. ERT of 4.169, and further increasing the algorithm set only lowers it insubstantially.

Hence, we select four algorithms for our portfolio: BFGS, BIPOP-CMA-ES, LineSearch-fminbnd and LineSearch-STEP, which also ensure a sufficiently high variety of algorithm concepts. The median rel. ERT value of the portfolio (combined with an oracle) is 1.454, meaning that our portfolio is in principle constructed well enough to allow for an excellent selection strategy: If we would reach the performance of the oracle, we would on average score only 1.5 times worse than the best available algorithm for each function. This value serves as a lower bound and comparison value for our learned selection strategies.

Figure 1 visualizes the rel. ERT values of the selected algorithms for each function. It becomes obvious that in most cases at least one of the algorithms is either optimal or almost optimal within the BBOB algorithm set. On the other hand considerable variance of the algorithms' performance becomes visible.

Two different values of baseline performance of the individual algorithms are given in Table 3 relating to the median rel. ERT value of an individual algorithm applied to all 24 functions. The first column only includes the rel. ERT values of the solved functions while the second one accounts for the whole data with imputed values. Both values are biased but the best option is to refer to the imputed data as the bad performance of an algorithm on an unsolved function has to be taken into account as well. Therefore, the BIPOP-CMA-ES shows the best baseline performance in the portfolio which however is roughly twice as bad as the optimal value which can be reached based on the whole portfolio.

In the present situation an adequate measure of classification performance is required. Instead of the misclassification rate often used in machine learning, a specific indicator related to the performance loss incurred by suboptimal predictions should be used. In case the best performing algorithm is not correctly identified the classifier is supposed to predict the algorithm with minimal possible loss w.r.t. the optimal ERT. With regard to the cost-sensitive learning approach explained in Section 3 we use the above mentioned four algorithms, therefore $k = 4$. As each x^i relates to a specific test function, we simply define the example-specific cost value c_j^i as the rel. ERT value of algorithm j on this test function. On this learning data we apply one-sided support vector regression with a radial basis function (RBF) kernel. For internal modeling, the rel. ERT values are transformed to logarithmic scale. As the support vector machine is sensitive w.r.t. its hyperparameter settings, both λ and σ (the latter belonging to the RBF kernel) are optimized by grid search on a logarithmic scale by using the values $\{2^{-16}, 2^{-15}, \ldots, 2^{16}\}$.

The low-level features listed in Table 1 are repeatedly computed in five runs for each of the five instances of the 24 functions using an initial budget of 5000 points for the LH design. This results in 600 observations in the data set used for learning the predictor. Note that the feature levels vary for each run and instance whereas the relative ERT value is constant over all runs and instances per function. Only one

Algorithm	# solved	Unsolved Functions	Baseline # solved	Performance Imputed
BFGS	13	3, 4, 7, 15-20, 23, 24	2.70	31.55
BIPOP-CMA-ES	23	4	3.81	3.83
LineSearch-fminbnd	9	3, 7, 9-11, 11, 13, 15-20, 23	51.8	172.23
LineSearch-STEP	6	6-20, 22-24	86.4	417.47

Table 3: Summary of the algorithm portfolio. The number of solved functions, the unsolved functions as well as the baseline performance for the solved functions and included imputed unsolved functions performance are given.

(BBOB 2010) or three (BBOB 2009) repeated algorithm runs on each function are available so that the estimation of the probability of a successful run is only possible in case the individual runs are aggregated for each function. In addition to the whole feature set a subset of the features which do not require additional function evaluations compared to the LH design is considered, and it will be investigated if similar classification accuracy can be achieved.

4.2 Results

Summarizing, the task is to predict a well-performing algorithm within the portfolio for each function based on the extracted low-level features of a specific function instance.

A crucial aspect of classification tasks is the necessity to (cross-) validate the trained model on unseen data. In the considered setting two different options are possible. Ideally, in each sequence of the cross-validation one function is completely discarded for training, and the remaining 25 observations are only used for testing. However, as the BBOB set is rather diverse in feature space (Mersmann et al. (2011)) the characteristics of the discarded functions might be not sufficiently covered by the feature space of the training set. The second option is to cross-validate on function instances, i.e., a five-fold cross-validation is carried out where in each sequence one of the five instances of each function is used for model validation, i.e., in total 120 observations. In both approaches the median of the rel. ERT values of the total 600 observations is used as the overall performance measure. In addition, the maximum rel. ERT value is presented.

Cross-Validation Omitting Instances.

In case of an instance-based cross-validation strategy the cost-sensitive classification approach succeeds in reaching a very high prediction accuracy. Many combinations of λ and σ lead to a median rel. ERT smaller than 1.6. The best classification result is generated based on the settings listed in Table 4. Here, the median of the rel. ERT values is very close to the optimal reference value of 1.454, even if the subset of "cheap" features is used. In case the whole feature set is considered even the worst prediction only takes a rel. ERT value of 86 whereas in the latter situation at least one function, in this case the third, is assigned the worst performing algorithm.

	med(rel. ERT)	max(rel. ERT)
optimum	1.454	4.169
all features	1.540835	86.76449
cheap features	1.606443	58731.08

Table 4: Classification results of cross-validation strategy based on omitting instances depending on the support vector regression parameters in case all features or only the "cheap" features are used.

	med(rel. ERT)	max(rel. ERT)
optimum	1.454	4.169
all features	1.901808	58731.08
cheap features	2.700301	58731.085

Table 5: Classification results of cross-validation strategy based on omitting functions depending on the support vector regression parameters in case all features or only the "cheap" features are used.

Cross-Validation Omitting Functions.

As already discussed before, it is of high interest if the highly qualitative results reported in the previous subsection can also be achieved in case whole functions, not only function instances, are omitted in the training set.

A high number of combinations of λ and σ resulted in a better performance than the best baseline algorithm BIPOP-CMA-ES. The best result out of the tested svm parameterizations for all features as well as the subset of "cheap" features are listed in Table 5.

However, in spite of the different characteristics of all BBOB functions related to the structure of the BBOB test set, the result is quite satisfying. In case all features are used, even 34 different parameterizations generate the same best result reported which is quite close to the optimum achievable value and only 1.9 times worse than the optimum ERT when all 60 BBOB algorithms are considered. The result gets worse in case the prediction is only based on the "cheap" features which, however, is still considerably better than the best baseline algorithm, i.e., the BIPOP-CMA-ES with a median rel. ERT of 3.83.

Figure 2 shows the euclidean distances between the functions in feature space based on all respectively on only the "cheap" features while the median of the scaled feature values over all runs and instances per function form the basis for the computation. Both the median rel. ERT of the predicted as well as the best algorithm of the portfolio for each BBOB function are related to the distance in feature space.

It becomes obvious that the degree of classification performance tends to correlate with the proximity in feature space if it is based on all features which is not that straightforward for the "cheap" features. However, this analysis might be improved by performing feature selection and changing the distance function with regard to the influence that the features have on the classification boundary.

Summarizing, the presented cost-sensitive classification approach proves to be highly successful for the addressed algorithm selection task despite of some limitations due to the structure of the BBOB test set and the results data set. These issues will be discussed in detail in the next section.

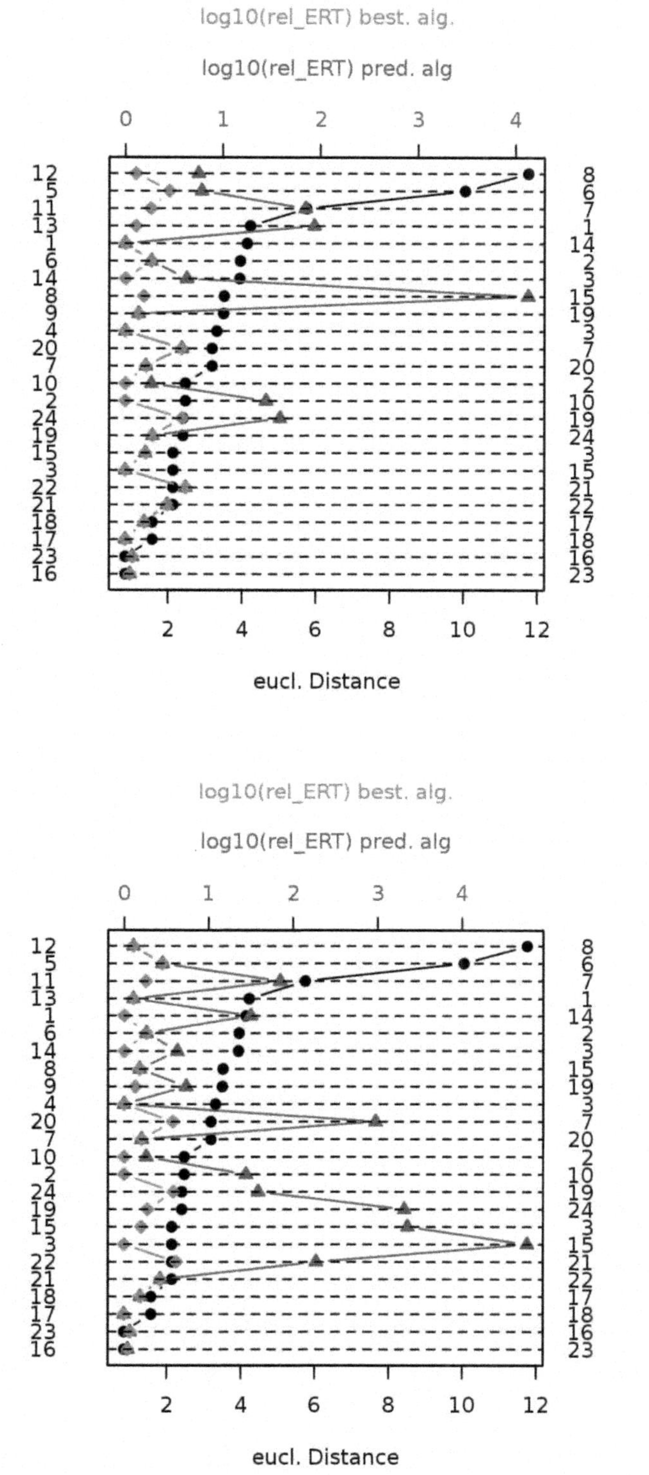

Figure 2: Per function in leave-one-out cross-validation: Median rel. ERT of predicted (blue) and best algorithm (red) of the portfolio and euclidean distance to nearest neighbor in feature space (black). Function removed in leave-one-out is given on the left, its nearest neighbor on the right side. Top: all features, bottom: "cheap features".

5. COMMENTS REGARDING BBOB DATA

One of the achievements of the two BBOB workshops that have been held so far is a wealth of data on a slew of different optimization algorithms and their relative performance. This data is the basis of our ERT calculations and without it, this study would not have been possible. The experimental setup of BBOB has been designed to be as lean as possible to reduce the burden on individual teams. This has lead to a function set that is very heterogeneous, i.e., each function is "very different" from every other function. While good in the context of the BBOB workshop, in the scenario under consideration it makes the machine learning task much more difficult. On the one hand, we have a very limited number of functions to cross-validate over, thus requiring the machine learning algorithm to extrapolate to vastly different functions. While we do want to see that the learning algorithm can generalize, this may in fact be too hard a task for it, given that some functions lie rather isolated in feature space. One way out would be to cross-validate over different instances of the same function instead. The difficulty here is that for each instance we only have three (2009) or one (2010) algorithm results and thus no chance to calculate a decent per-instance ERT estimate.

Another aspect which could be improved is the data storage format. While the BBOB workshop publishes all submitted results, these are stored in either cryptic text files or Python specific binary files. Neither solution is ideal. While both contain all the relevant data, what is missing or hidden in both cases is the relevant metadata. This also includes such simple things as a consistent naming scheme and directory structure for the result files, unique and meaningful algorithm names and a safe way to identify different runs of the same algorithm on the same function instance. Improving this would serve the whole community since the BBOB datasets are also a record of the evolution of the state of the art in our field.

Lastly, the number of algorithms will continue to grow, and this will make it increasingly more difficult to set up the algorithm portfolio. Which CMA-ES variant do I want? Do we want to use FULL_NEWUOA or AVG_NEWUOA? Is there a state of the art Nelder-Mead type algorithm in the dataset? What would help here are two things. First, a taxonomy of the different algorithms as well as a machine-readable classification for each and second, a repository of, again machine-readable, comparison results. The taxonomy would make it much easier for a non-expert to group the different algorithms and to pick a candidate from each group. Furthermore, it would allow us to easily examine hypotheses such as: "Similar algorithms perform similar". The long term goal here would be to arrive at a benchmarking framework in the spirit of the PISA (Bleuler et al., 2003) setup for multi-objective optimization which allows researchers to compare combinations of building blocks of algorithms instead of monolithic algorithm designs. This would greatly aid the understanding of why some algorithms perform well on some functions and others do not. Regarding the suggestion concerning a repository of machine-readable results, this could foster further collaboration between different groups and reduce redundant efforts of duplicated results.

6. DISCUSSION AND OUTLOOK

Notwithstanding the above remarks, we have introduced a novel solution to the ASP and shown that it works in different scenarios. In the first scenario, we showed that we can generalize to new instances of the same function for all functions in the BBOB test set. Depending on which ELA features are used, we can predict the optimal or close to optimal portfolio candidate (w.r.t. the median rel. ERT). It is noteworthy that such a portfolio would be a valid entry to the BBOB workshop and might outperform single algorithms (but see the remark about feature costs below). It could even trump a perfect oracle for the two algorithms recommended in Hansen and Ros (2010) (NEWUOA and BIPOP-CMA-ES).

On the other hand, we showed that the approach works remarkably well if we wish to generalize to new functions. This is astonishing given that the BBOB functions were designed to be quite different and unique. The poor worst case performance (max(rel. ERT)) of our approach does mean that the BBOB function set is, for our purposes, too small and would benefit from more functions. Given such a larger set our approach will likely generalize even better and provide further insights into how "landscape" features can be mapped to efficient algorithms.

Of course, for a proper evaluation when comparing such a selection procedure against single algorithms the costs for calculating the features must now be added to the function evaluations of the selected algorithm. For the "cheap" feature set in 10 dimensions this would result in 5000 evaluations. Note that here the median ERT of all the algorithms in the BBOB data is about 10^5, so the additional costs for the feature computation might be amortized in most cases.

However, both the selection of algorithms for the portfolio as well as the selection of the features used could be improved. Ideally, we would like to perform both selections at the same time. This could be done using a binary coded GA that selects both features and algorithms while minimizing the rel. ERT of the selection strategy. If one also considers the additional feature costs, this feature and portfolio optimization might be approached in a multi-criteria fashion similar to what we have already presented in Mersmann et al. (2011). But for all such endeavors a larger benchmark data set is required as well.

In the future we would like to explore ways to generate more test functions in a systematic fashion. This would allow us to apply experimental design methodologies to the problem to generate "unbiased" sets of test functions. For such an analysis it would be beneficial to have a learner that allows some more insight into the selection strategy.

Acknowledgements.
This work was partly supported by the Collaborative Research Center SFB 823 (B4), the Graduate School of Energy Efficient Production and Logistics and the Research Training Group "Statistical Modelling" of the German Research Foundation.

References

AUGER, A., FINCK, S., HANSEN, N., AND ROS, R. 2010. BBOB 2010: Comparison Tables of All Algorithms on All Noiseless Functions. Technical Report RT-388, INRIA. 09.

BARTZ-BEIELSTEIN, T. AND PREUSS, M. 2012. Experimental analysis of optimization algorithms: Tuning and beyond. In *Theory and Principled Methods for Designing Metaheuristics*, Y. Borenstein and A. Moraglio, Eds. Springer, New York.

BLEULER, S., LAUMANNS, M., THIELE, L., AND ZITZLER, E. 2003. PISA — a platform and programming language independent interface for search algorithms. In *Evolutionary Multi-Criterion Optimization (EMO 2003)*, C. M. Fonseca, P. J. Fleming, E. Zitzler, K. Deb, and L. Thiele, Eds. Lecture Notes in Computer Science. Springer, Berlin, 494 – 508.

HANSEN, N. AND AUGER, A. 2005. Performance evaluation of an advanced local search evolutionary algorithm. In *In Proceedings of the IEEE Congress on Evolutionary Computation*. IEEE Press, 1777–1784.

HANSEN, N., AUGER, A., FINCK, S., AND ROS, R. 2009. Real-parameter black-box optimization benchmarking 2009: Experimental setup. Tech. Rep. RR-6828, INRIA.

HANSEN, N., AUGER, A., ROS, R., FINCK, S., AND POŠÍK, P. 2010. Comparing results of 31 algorithms from the black-box optimization benchmarking bbob-2009. In *GECCO '10: Proceedings of the 12th annual conference comp on Genetic and evolutionary computation*. ACM, New York, NY, USA, 1689–1696.

HANSEN, N., FINCK, S., ROS, R., AND AUGER, A. 2009. Real-parameter black-box optimization benchmarking 2009: Noiseless functions definitions. Tech. Rep. RR-6829, INRIA.

HANSEN, N. AND ROS, R. 2010. Black-box optimization benchmarking of NEWUOA compared to BIPOP-CMA-ES: on the bbob noiseless testbed. In *Proceedings of the 12th annual conference on Genetic and evolutionary computation*. GECCO '10. ACM, New York, NY, USA, 1519–1526.

HASTIE, T., TIBSHIRANI, R., AND FRIEDMAN, J. 2001. *The Elements of Statistical Learning*. Springer, New York.

JONES, T. AND FORREST, S. 1995. Fitness distance correlation as a measure of problem difficulty for genetic algorithms. In *Proceedings of the Sixth International Conference on Genetic Algorithms*. Morgan Kaufmann, 184–192.

KARATZOGLOU, A., SMOLA, A., HORNIK, K., AND ZEILEIS, A. 2004. kernlab – an S4 package for kernel methods in R. *Journal of Statistical Software 11*, 9, 1–20.

MERSMANN, O., BISCHL, B., TRAUTMANN, H., PREUSS, M., WEIHS, C., AND RUDOLPH, G. 2011. Exploratory landscape analysis. In *Proceedings of the 13th annual conference on Genetic and evolutionary computation*. GECCO '11. ACM, New York, NY, USA, 829–836.

MERSMANN, O., PREUSS, M., AND TRAUTMANN, H. 2010a. Benchmarking evolutionary algorithms: Towards exploratory landscape analysis. In *PPSN XI: Proceedings of the 11th International Conference on Parallel Problem Solving from Nature*, R. Schaefer et al., Eds. Lecture Notes in Computer Science 6238. Springer, 71–80.

MERSMANN, O., PREUSS, M., TRAUTMANN, H., BISCHL, B., AND WEIHS, C. 2011a. Analyzing the BBOB Results by Means of Benchmarking Concepts. *Evolutionary Computation Journal, accepted*.

MERSMANN, O., TRAUTMANN, H., NAUJOKS, B., AND WEIHS, C. 2010. Benchmarking evolutionary multiobjective optimization algorithms. In *Congress on Evolutionary Computation (CEC)*, H. Ishibuchi et al., Eds. IEEE Press, Piscataway NJ.

RICE, J. R. 1976. The algorithm selection problem. *Advances in Computers 15*, 65–118.

TU, H.-H. AND LIN, H.-T. 2010. One-sided support vector regression for multiclass cost-sensitive classification. In *ICML*, J. Fürnkranz and T. Joachims, Eds. Omnipress, 1095–1102.

TURNEY, P. 2000. Types of cost in inductive concept learning. In *Workshop on Cost-Sensitive Learning at the Seventeenth International Conference on Machine Learning*. 15–21.

Self-Adaptive Surrogate-Assisted Covariance Matrix Adaptation Evolution Strategy

Ilya Loshchilov
TAO, INRIA Saclay

Marc Schoenauer
TAO, INRIA Saclay

Michèle Sebag
CNRS, LRI UMR 8623

LRI, Univ. Paris-Sud, Orsay, France
firstname.lastname@inria.fr

ABSTRACT

This paper presents a novel mechanism to adapt surrogate-assisted population-based algorithms. This mechanism is applied to ACM-ES, a recently proposed surrogate-assisted variant of CMA-ES. The resulting algorithm, ^{s*}ACM-ES, adjusts online the lifelength of the current surrogate model (the number of CMA-ES generations before learning a new surrogate) and the surrogate hyper-parameters.

Both heuristics significantly improve the quality of the surrogate model, yielding a significant speed-up of ^{s*}ACM-ES compared to the ACM-ES and CMA-ES baselines. The empirical validation of ^{s*}ACM-ES on the BBOB-2012 noiseless testbed demonstrates the efficiency and the scalability w.r.t the problem dimension and the population size of the proposed approach, that reaches new best results on some of the benchmark problems.

Categories and Subject Descriptors

I.2.8 [**Computing Methodologies**]: Artificial Intelligence Problem Solving, Control Methods, and Search

General Terms

Algorithms

Keywords

Evolution Strategies, CMA-ES, self-adaptation, surrogate-assisted optimization, surrogate models, ranking support vector machine, black-box optimization

1. INTRODUCTION

Evolutionary Algorithms (EAs) have become popular tools for optimization mostly thanks to their population-based properties and the ability to progress towards an optimum using problem-specific variation operators. A search directed by a population of candidate solutions is quite robust with respect to a moderate noise and multi-modality of the optimized function, in contrast to some classical optimization methods such as quasi-Newton methods (e.g. BFGS method [25]). Furthermore, many bio-inspired algorithms such as EAs, Differential Evolution (DE) and Particle Swarm Optimization (PSO) with rank-based selection are comparison-based algorithms, which makes their behavior invariant and robust under any monotonous transformation of the objective function. Another source of robustness is the invariance under orthogonal transformations of the search space, first introduced into the realm of continuous evolutionary optimization by Covariance Matrix Adaptation Evolution Strategy (CMA-ES) [9]. CMA-ES, winner of the Congress on Evolutionary Computation (CEC) 2005 [5] and the Black-Box Optimization Benchmarking (BBOB) 2009 [8] competitions of continuous optimizers, has also demonstrated its robustness on real-world problems through more than one hundred applications [7].

When dealing with expensive optimization objectives, the well-known surrogate-assisted approaches proceed by learning a surrogate model of the objective, and using this surrogate to reduce the number of computations of the objective function in various ways. The best studied approach relies on the use of computationally cheap polynomial regression for the line search in gradient-based search methods, such as in the BFGS method [25]. More recent approaches rely on Machine Learning algorithms, modelling the objective function through e.g. Radial Basis Functions (RBF), Polynomial Regression, Support Vector Regression (SVR), Artificial Neural Network (ANN) and Gaussian Process (GP) a.k.a. Kriging. As could have been expected, there is no such thing as a best surrogate learning approach [14, 20]. Experimental comparisons also suffer from the fact that the results depend on the tuning of the surrogate hyper-parameters. Several approaches aimed at the adaptive selection of surrogate models during the search have been proposed [27, 28, 1]; these approaches focus on measuring the quality of the surrogate models and using the best one for the next evolutionary generation.

This paper, aimed at robust surrogate-assisted optimization, presents a surrogate-adaptation mechanism (^{s*}) which can be used on top of any surrogate optimization approach. ^{s*} adapts online the number of generations after which the surrogate is re-trained, referred to as the surrogate lifelength; further, it adaptively optimizes the surrogate hyper-parameters using an embedded CMA-ES module. A proof of principle of the approach is given by implementing ^{s*} on top of ACM-ES, a surrogate-assisted variant of CMA-ES, yielding the ^{s*}ACM-ES algorithm. To our best knowledge, the self-adaptation of the surrogate model within CMA-ES and by

CMA-ES is a new contribution. The merits of the approach are shown as ^{s*}ACM-ES show significant improvements compared to CMA-ES and ACM-ES on the BBOB-2012 noiseless testbed.

The paper is organized as follows. Section 2 reviews some surrogate-assisted variants of Evolution Strategies (ESs) and CMA-ES. For the sake of self-containedness, the ACM-ES combining CMA-ES with the use of a Rank-based Support Vector Machine is briefly described. Section 3 discusses the merits and weaknesses of ACM-ES and suggests that the online adjustment of the surrogate hyper-parameters is required to reach some robustness with respect to the optimization objective. The ^{s*}ACM-ES algorithm, including the online adjustment of the surrogate lifelength and hyper-parameters on top of ACM-ES, is described in section 4. The experimental validation of ^{s*}ACM-ES is reported and discussed in section 5. Section 6 concludes the paper.

2. SURROGATE MODELS

This section discusses the various techniques used to learn surrogate models, their use within EAs and specifically CMA-ES, and the properties of surrogate models in terms of invariance w.r.t. monotonous transformations of the objective function [24], and orthogonal transformations of the instance space [21].

2.1 Surrogate-assisted Evolution Strategies

As already mentioned, many surrogate modelling approaches have been used within ESs and CMA-ES: RBF network [11], GP [29, 4], ANN [6], SVR [30, 19], Local-Weighted Regression (LWR) [18, 3], Ranking SVM [24, 21, 12]. In most cases, the surrogate model is used as a filter (to select λ_{Pre} promising pre-children) and/or to estimate the objective function of some individuals in the current population. The impact of the surrogate, controlled by λ_{Pre}, should clearly depend on the surrogate accuracy; how to measure it ? As shown by [15], the standard Mean Square Error (MSE) used to measure a model accuracy in a regression context is ill-suited to surrogate-assisted optimization, as it is poorly correlated with the ability to select correct individuals. Another accuracy indicator, based on the (weighted) sum of ranks of the selected individuals, was proposed by [15], and used by [30, 11].

2.2 Comparison-based Surrogate Models

Taking advantage of the fact that some EAs, and particularly CMA-ES, are comparison-based algorithms, which only require the offspring to be correctly ranked, it thus comes naturally to learn a comparison-based surrogate. Comparison-based surrogate models, first introduced by Runarsson [24], rely on learning-to-rank algorithms, such as Ranking SVM [17]. Let us recall Ranking SVM, assuming the reader's familiarity with Support Vector Machines [26].

Let $(x_1, \ldots, x_N)$ denote an N-sample in instance space X, assuming with no loss of generality that point x_i has rank i. Rank-based SVM learning [17] aims at a real-valued function $\widehat{f}$ on X such that $\widehat{f}(x_i) < \widehat{f}(x_j)$ iff $i < j$. In the SVM framework, this goal is formalized through minimizing the norm of $\widehat{f}$ (regularization term) subject to the $N(N-1)/2$ ordering constraints. A more tractable formulation, also used in [24, 21], only involves the $N-1$ constraints related to consecutive points, $\widehat{f}(x_i) < \widehat{f}(x_{i+1})$ for $i = 1 \ldots N-1$.

Using the kernel trick[1], ranking function $\widehat{f}$ is defined as a linear function w w.r.t. some feature space $\Phi(X)$, i.e. $\widehat{f}(x) = \langle w, \Phi(x) \rangle$. With same notations as in [26], the primal minimization problem is defined as follows:

$$\text{Minimize}_{\{w,\,\xi\}} \tfrac{1}{2}||w||^2 + \textstyle\sum_{i=1}^{N} C_i \xi_i$$
$$\text{subj. to} \begin{cases} \langle w, \Phi(x_i) - \Phi(x_{i+1}) \rangle \geq 1 - \xi_i \;\; (i = 1, \ldots N-1) \\ \xi_i \geq 0 \;\; (i = 1 \ldots N-1) \end{cases} \tag{1}$$

where slack variable ξ_i (respectively constant C_i) accounts for the violation of the i-th constraint (resp. the violation cost). The corresponding dual problem, quadratic in the Lagrangian multipliers α, can be solved easily by any quadratic programming solver. The rank-based surrogate $\widehat{f}$ is given as

$$\widehat{f}(x) = \textstyle\sum_{i=1}^{N-1} \alpha_i (K(x_i, x) - K(x_{i+1}, x))$$

By construction, $\widehat{f}(x)$ is invariant to monotonous transformations of the objective function, which preserve the ranking of the training points.

2.3 Invariance w.r.t. Orthogonal Transformations

As already mentioned, CMA-ES is invariant w.r.t. orthogonal transformations of the search space, through adapting a covariance matrix during the search. This invariance property was borrowed by ACM-ES [21], using the covariance matrix C learned by CMA-ES within a Radial Basis Function (RBF) kernel K_C, where C^{-1} is used to compute Mahalanobis distance:

$$K_C(x_i, x_j) = e^{-\frac{(x_i - x_j)^t C^{-1} (x_i - x_j)}{2\sigma^2}} \tag{2}$$

For the sake of numerical stability, every training point x is mapped onto x' such as

$$x' = C^{-1/2}(x - m), \tag{3}$$

where m is the mean of the current CMA-ES distribution. The standard RBF kernel with Euclidean distance is used on top of this mapping. By construction, ACM-ES inherits from CMA-ES the property of invariance under orthogonal transformations of the search space; the use of the covariance matrix C brings significant improvements compared to standard Gaussian kernels after [21].

3. DISCUSSION

This section analyzes the weaknesses of ACM-ES. Following the characterization proposed in [16], ACM-ES is a surrogate-assisted optimizer with an individual-based evolution control. As in other pre-selection methods, at each generation ACM-ES generates λ_{Pre} individuals, where λ_{Pre} is much larger than population size λ. Then λ_{Pre} pre-children are evaluated and ranked using surrogate model $\widehat{f}$. The most promising λ' pre-children are selected and evaluated using the true expensive function, yielding new points $(x, f(x))$. When the objective function of λ' individuals is known, the ranking of other $\lambda - \lambda'$ points can be approximated.

[1]The so-called kernel trick supports the extension of the SVM approach from linear to non-linear model spaces, by mapping instance space X onto some *feature space* $\Phi(X)$. The actual mapping cost is avoided as the scalar product in feature space $\Phi(X)$ is computed on instance space X through a *kernel* function K: $\langle \Phi(x), \Phi(x') \rangle =_{def} K(x, x')$.

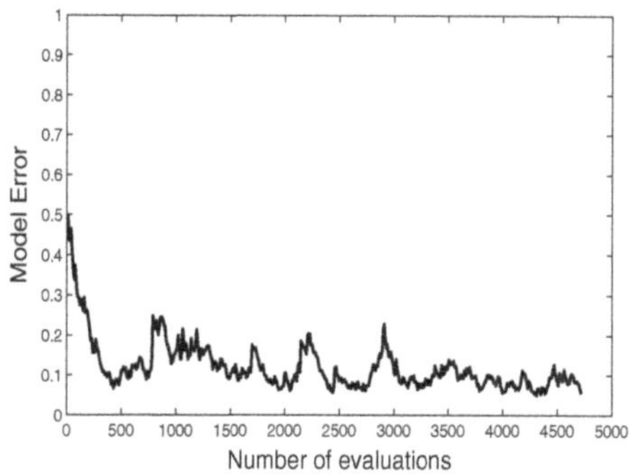

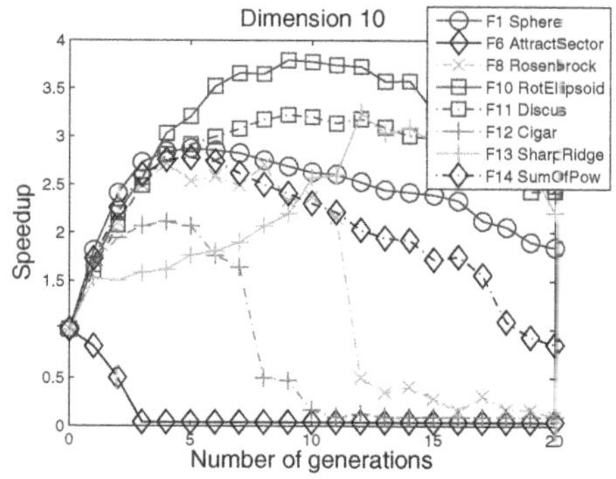

Figure 1: Left: Rank-based surrogate error vs number of evaluations, during a representative run of active CMA-ES on 10-D Rotated Ellipsoid. Right: The speedup of IPOP-aACM-ES over IPOP-aCMA-ES, where speedup = 2.0 means that IPOP-aACM-ES with a given lifelength $\widehat{n}$ of the surrogate model requires 2.0 times less computational effort SP1 (i.e. average number of function evaluations of successful runs divided by proportion of successful runs) than IPOP-aCMA-ES to reach the target objective value of $f_t = f_{\text{opt}} + 10^{-8}$.

While our experimental results confirm the improvements brought by ACM-ES on some functions (about 2-4 times faster than CMA-ES on Rosenbrock, Ellipsoid, Schwefel, Noisy Sphere and Ackley functions up to dimension 20 [21]), they also show a loss of performance on the multi-modal Rastrigin function. Complementary experiments suggest that:

1. on highly multi-modal functions the surrogate model happens to suffer from a loss of accuracy; in such cases some control is required to prevent the surrogate model from misleading the search;
2. surrogate-assisted algorithms may require a larger population size for multi-modal problems.

The lack of surrogate control appears to be an important drawback in ACM-ES. This control should naturally reflect the current surrogate accuracy. A standard measure of the rank-based surrogate error is given as the fraction of violated ranking constraints on the test set [17]. Accuracy 0 (respectively .5) corresponds to a perfect surrogate (resp. random guessing).

However, before optimization one should be sure that the model gives a reasonable prediction of the optimized function. Fig. 1 (Left) illustrates the surrogate model error during a representative run of active CMA-ES (with re-training at each iteration, but without any exploitation of the model) on 10 dimensional Rotated Ellipsoid function. After the first generations, the surrogate error decreases to approximately 10%. This better than random prediction can be viewed as a source of information about the function which can be used to improve the search.

Let $\widehat{n}$ denote the number of generations a surrogate model is used, referred to as surrogate lifelength. In so-called generation-based evolution control methods [16], the surrogate $\widehat{f}$ is directly optimized for $\widehat{n}$ generations, without requiring any expensive objective computations. The following generation considers the objective function f, and yields instances to enrich the training set, relearn or refresh the surrogate and adjust some parameters of the algorithm. The surrogate lifelength $\widehat{n}$ is fixed or adapted.

The impact of $\widehat{n}$ is displayed on Fig. 1 (Right), showing the speedup reached by direct surrogate optimization on several 10 dimensional benchmark problems *vs* the number of generations $\widehat{n}$ the surrogate is used. A factor of speedup 1.7 is obtained for $\widehat{n}= 1$ on the Rotated Ellipsoid function, close to the optimal speedup 2.0. A speedup ranging from 2 to 4 is obtained for IPOP-aCMA-ES with surrogates for $\widehat{n}$ *in* $[5, 15]$. As could have been expected again, the optimal value of $\widehat{n}$ is problem-dependent and widely varies. In the case of the Attractive Sector problem for instance, the surrogate model is not useful and $\widehat{n} = 0$ should be used (thus falling back to the original aCMA-ES with no surrogate) to prevent the surrogate from misleading the search.

4. SELF-ADAPTIVE SURROGATE-BASED CMA-ES

In this section we propose a novel surrogate adaptation mechanism which can be used in principle on top of any iterative population-based optimizer without requiring any significant modifications thereof. The approach is illustrated on top of CMA-ES and ACM-ES. The resulting algorithm, ^{s*}ACM-ES, maintains a global hyper-parameter vector $\theta = (\theta_{opt}, \theta_{sur}, \widehat{n}, \mathcal{A}, \alpha)$, where:
• θ_{opt} stands for the optimization parameters of the CMA-ES used for expensive function optimization;
• θ_{sur} stands for the optimization parameters of the CMA-ES used for surrogate model hyper-parameters optimization;
• $\widehat{n}$ is the number of optimization generations during which the current surrogate model is used;
• $\mathcal{A}$ is the archive of all points $(x_i, f(x_i))$ for which the true objective function has been computed, exploited to train the surrogate function;
• α stands for the surrogate hyper-parameters.
All hyper-parameters are indexed by the current generation g; by abuse of notations, the subscript g is omitted when clear from the context.

The main two contributions of the paper regard the adjustment of the surrogate hyper-parameters (section 4.2) and of the surrogate lifelength $\widehat{n}$ (section 4.3).

4.1 Overview of ^{s*}ACM-ES

Let *GenCMA*$(h,\theta_h,\mathcal{A})$ denote the elementary optimization module (here one generation of CMA-ES), where h is the function to be optimized (the true objective f or the surrogate $\widehat{f}$), θ_h denotes the current optimization parameters

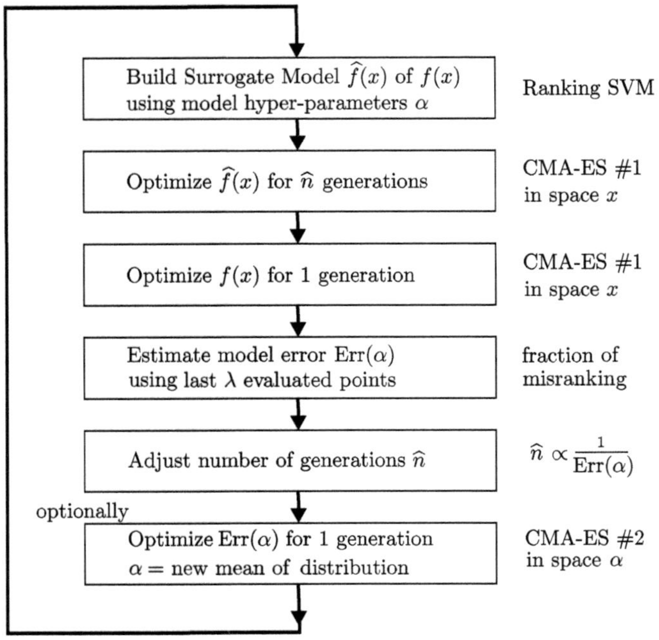

Figure 2: Optimization loop of the ^{s*}ACM-ES.

Algorithm 1 ^{s*}ACM-ES

1: $g \leftarrow 0$; Err $\leftarrow 0.5$; $\mathcal{A}_g \leftarrow \emptyset$;
2: $\theta_{opt} \leftarrow$ InitializationCMA(); { to optimize $f(x)$ }
3: $\theta_{sur} \leftarrow$ InitializationCMA(); { to optimize $h(\alpha)$ }
4: **repeat**
5: $\quad \{\theta_{opt}, \mathcal{A}_{g+1}\} \leftarrow$ GenCMA(f,θ_{opt}, $\mathcal{A}_g$);
6: $\quad g \leftarrow g+1$;
7: **until** $g = g_{start}$;
8: **repeat**
9: $\quad \widehat{f}(x) \leftarrow$ BuildSurrogateModel(α, $\mathcal{A}_g$, θ_{opt});
10: $\quad g_{prev} \leftarrow g$;
11: $\quad$ **for** $i = 1, \ldots, \widehat{n}$ **do**
12: $\quad\quad \{\theta_{opt}, \mathcal{A}_{g+1} = \mathcal{A}_g\} \leftarrow$ GenCMA($\widehat{f}$,θ_{opt}, $\mathcal{A}_g$);
13: $\quad\quad g \leftarrow g+1$;
14: $\quad \{\theta_{opt}, \mathcal{A}_{g+1}\} \leftarrow$ GenCMA(f,θ_{opt}, $\mathcal{A}_g$);
15: $\quad g \leftarrow g+1$;
16: $\quad$ Err(α) $\leftarrow$ MeasureSurrogateError($\widehat{f}$,θ_{opt});
17: $\quad$ Err $\leftarrow (1-\beta_{\text{Err}})$Err $+ \beta_{\text{Err}}$Err(α);
18: $\quad \widehat{n} \leftarrow \left\lfloor \frac{\tau_{err} - \text{Err}}{\tau_{err}} \widehat{n_{max}} \right\rfloor$;
19: $\quad$ // adjust surrogate hyperparameters
20: $\quad \theta_{sur} \leftarrow$ GenCMA(Err,θ_{sur});
21: $\quad \alpha \leftarrow \theta_{sur}.m$;
22: **until** stopping criterion is met ;

Algorithm 2 Objective function Err(α) of surrogate model

1: Input: α
2: $\widehat{f}(x) \leftarrow$ BuildSurrogateModel(α, $\mathcal{A}_{g_{prev}}$, $\theta_{sur,g_{prev}}$);
3: Err(α) $\leftarrow$ MeasureSurrogateError($\widehat{f}$, $\theta_{opt,g_{prev}}$);
4: Output: Err(α);

(e.g. CMA-ES step-size and covariance matrix) associated to h, and $\mathcal{A}$ is the archive of f. After each call of *GenCMA*, optimization parameters θ_h are updated; and if *GenCMA* was called with the true objective function f, archive $\mathcal{A}$ is updated and augmented with the new points $(x, f(x))$. Note that *GenCMA* can be replaced by any black-box optimization procedure, able to update its own optimization parameters and the archive.

^{s*}ACM-ES starts by calling *GenCMA* for g_{start} number of generations with the true objective f, where θ_{opt} and $\mathcal{A}$ are respectively initialized to the default parameter of CMA-ES and the empty set (lines 4-7). In this starting phase, optimization parameter θ_{opt} and archive $\mathcal{A}$ are updated in each generation.

Then ^{s*}ACM-ES iterates a three-step process (Algorithm 1, illustrated on Fig. 2):

1 learning surrogate $\widehat{f}$ (procedure BuildSurrogateModel, line 9; section 4.2);

2 Optimizing surrogate $\widehat{f}$ during $\widehat{n}$ generations (lines 11-13). This step classically calls *GenCMA*($\widehat{f}$,θ_{opt},$\mathcal{A}$) for $\widehat{n}$ consecutive generations; θ_{opt} is updated accordingly while $\mathcal{A}$ is unchanged since this step does not involve any computation of the expensive f.

3 Adjusting the surrogate lifelength $\widehat{n}$ (section 4.3).

4.2 Learning a Surrogate and Adjusting its Hyper-parameters

The surrogate model learning phase proceeds as in ACM-ES (section 2.3). *GenCMA*(f,θ_{opt},$\mathcal{A}$) is launched for one generation with the true objective f, updating and augmenting archive $\mathcal{A}$ with new $(x, f(x))$ points.

$\widehat{f}$ is built using Ranking SVM [17] with archive $\mathcal{A}$ as training set, where the SVM kernel is tailored using the current optimization parameters θ_{opt} such as covariance matrix C.

The contribution regards the adjustment of the surrogate hyper-parameters α (e.g. the number and selection of the training points in $\mathcal{A}$; the weights of the constraint violations in Ranking SVM, section 2.3), which are adjusted to optimize the quality of the surrogate Err (Eq. 4). Formally, to each surrogate hyper-parameter vector α is associated a surrogate error Err(α) defined as follows: hyper-parameter α is used to learn surrogate $\widehat{f}_\alpha$ using $\mathcal{A}_{g-1}$ as training set, and Err(α) is set to the ranking error of $\widehat{f}_\alpha$, using the most recent points ($\mathcal{A}_g - \mathcal{A}_{g-1}$) as test set.

Letting Λ denote the test set and assuming with no loss of generality that the points in Λ are ordered after f, Err($\widehat{f}_\alpha$) is measured as follows (procedure MeasureSurrogateError, line 16):

$$\text{Err}(\alpha) = \frac{2}{|\Lambda|(|\Lambda|-1)} \sum_{i=1}^{|\Lambda|} \sum_{j=i+1}^{|\Lambda|} w_{ij}.1_{\widehat{f}_\alpha,i,j} \tag{4}$$

where $1_{\widehat{f}_\alpha,i,j}$ holds true iff $\widehat{f}_\alpha$ violates the ordering constraint on pair (i,j). In all generality, the surrogate error can be tuned using weight coefficients w_{ij} to reflect the relative importance of ordering constraints. Only $w_{ij} = 1$ will be used in the remainder of the paper. For a better numerical stability, the surrogate error is updated using additive relaxation, with relaxation constant β_{Err} (lines 16-17).

Finally, the elementary optimization module *GenCMA*(Err,θ_{sur}) (in this study we do not use archive parameter here) is launched for one generation (line 20), and

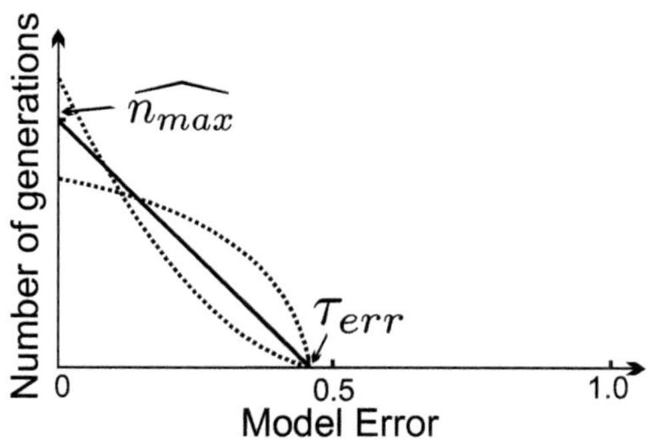

Figure 3: Number of generations $\widehat{n}$ versus surrogate error Err. Linear interpolation (bold curve) has been used in the experimental validation.

the mean of the CMA-ES mutation distribution is used (line 21) as surrogate hyper-parameter vector in the next surrogate building phase (line 9).

4.3 Adjusting Surrogate Lifelength

Lifelength $\widehat{n}_g$ is likewise adjusted depending on the error made by the previous surrogate $\widehat{f}_{g-1}$ on the new archive points ($\mathcal{A}_g - \mathcal{A}_{g-1}$). If this error is 0, then $\widehat{f}_{g-1}$ is perfectly accurate and could have been used for some more generations before learning $\widehat{f}_g$. In this case lifelength $\widehat{n}_g$ is set to the maximum value $\widehat{n_{max}}$, which corresponds to the maximum theoretical speedup of the ^{s*}ACM-ES.
If the error is circa .5, surrogate $\widehat{f}_{g-1}$ provides no better indications than random guessing and thus misleads the optimization; $\widehat{n}_g$ is set to 0. More generally, considering an error threshold τ_{err}, $\widehat{n}$ is adjusted between $\widehat{n_{max}}$ and 0, proportionally[2] to the ratio between the actual error and the error threshold τ_{err} (line 18, bold curve on Fig. 3).

5. EXPERIMENTAL VALIDATION

The experimental validation of the approach proceeds by comparing the performance of ^{s*}ACM-ES to the original [9] and active [13] CMA-ES versions, considering the restart scenario with increasing population size (IPOP [2, 10]).

The active IPOP-aCMA-ES [10] with weighted negative covariance matrix update is found to perform equally well or better than IPOP-CMA-ES, which is explained as it more efficiently exploits the information of the worst $\lambda/2$ points. We use IPOP-aCMA-ES as challenging baseline, more difficult to speed up than the original IPOP-CMA-ES.

Specifically, ^{s*}ACM-ES is validated on the noiseless BBOB testbed by comparing IPOP-aACM-ES with fixed hyper-parameters, and IPOP-^{s*}aACM-ES with online adaptation of hyperparameters of the surrogate model[3].

After detailing the experimental setting, this section reports on the offline tuning of the number $N_{training}$ of points used to learn the surrogate model, and the online tuning of the surrogate hyper-parameters.

[2]Complementary experiments omitted for brevity, show that the best adjustment of $\widehat{n}$ depending on the surrogate error is again problem-dependent.
[3]For the sake of reproducibility we used the Octave/MatLab source code of IPOP-CMA-ES with default parameters, available from its author's page, with the active flag set to 1. The ^{s*}ACM-ES source code is available at
`https://sites.google.com/site/acmesgecco/`.

Parameter	Range for online tuning	Offline tuned value
$N_{training}$	$[4d, 2(40+\lfloor 4d^{1.7}\rfloor)]$	$40+\lfloor 4d^{1.7}\rfloor$
C_{base}	$[0, 10]$	6
C_{pow}	$[0, 6]$	3
c_{sigma}	$[0.5, 2]$	1

Table 1: Surrogate hyper-parameters, default value and range of variation

5.1 Experimental Setting

The default BBOB stopping criterion is reaching target function value $f_t = f_{opt} + 10^{-8}$. Ranking SVM is trained using the most recent $N_{training}$ points (subsection 5.2); its stopping criterion is arbitrarily set to a maximum number of $1000N_{training}$ iterations of the quadratic programming solver.

After a few preliminary experiments, the Ranking SVM constraint violation weights (Eq. 1) are set to

$$C_i = 10^{C_{base}}(N_{training} - i)^{C_{pow}}$$

with $C_{base} = 6$ and $C_{pow} = 3$ by default: the cost of constraint violation is thus cubically higher for top-ranked samples. The σ parameter of the RBF kernel is set to $\sigma = c_{sigma}\sigma_x$, where σ_x is the dispersion of the training points (their average distance after translation, Eq. 3) and c_{sigma} is set to 1 by default. The number g_{start} of CMA-ES calls in the initial phase is set to 10, the maximum lifelength $\widehat{n_{max}}$ of a surrogate model is set to 20. The error threshold τ_{err} is set to .45 and the error relaxation factor is set to .2.

The surrogate hyper-parameters θ_{sur} are summarized in Table 1, with offline tuned value (default for IPOP-aACM-ES) and their range of variation for online tuning, (where d stands for the problem dimension). Surrogate hyper-parameters are optimized with a population size 20 (20 surrogate models), where the Err function associated to a hyper-parameter vector is measured on the most recent λ points in archive $\mathcal{A}$, with λ the current optimization population size.

5.2 Offline Tuning: Number of Training Points

It is widely acknowledged that the selection of the training set is an essential ingredient of surrogate learning [16]. After some alternative experiments omitted for brevity, the training set includes simply the most recent $N_{training}$ points in the archive. The study thus focuses on the tuning of $N_{training}$. Its optimal tuning is of course problem- and surrogate learning algorithm-dependent. Several tunings have been considered in the literature, for instance for 10-dimensional problems: 3λ for SVR [30]; 30 for RBF [29]; 50 for ANN [6]; $\lambda, 2\lambda$ for Ranking SVM[24, 12]; $\frac{d(d+1)}{2} + 1 = 66$ for LWR in the lmm-CMA-ES [3]; $70\sqrt{d} = 221$ for Ranking SVM in the ACM-ES [21].

In all above cases but ACM-ES, the surrogate models aim at local approximation. These approaches might thus be biased toward small $N_{training}$ values, as a small number of training points are required to yield good local models (e.g. in the case of the Sphere function), and small $N_{training}$ values positively contribute to the speed-up. It is suggested

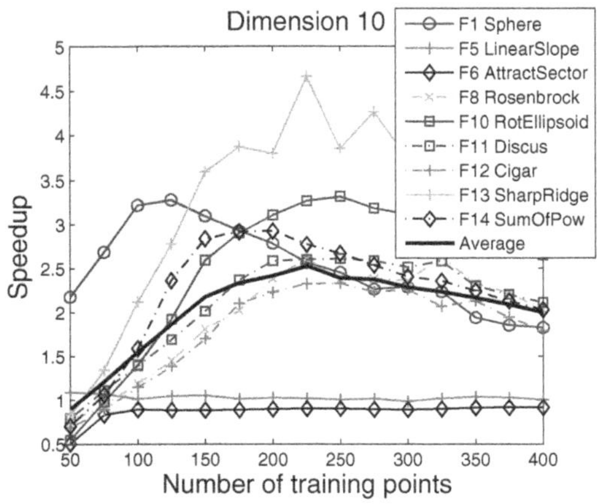

Figure 4: The speedup of IPOP-aACM-ES over IPOP-aCMA-ES w.r.t. (fixed) number of training points.

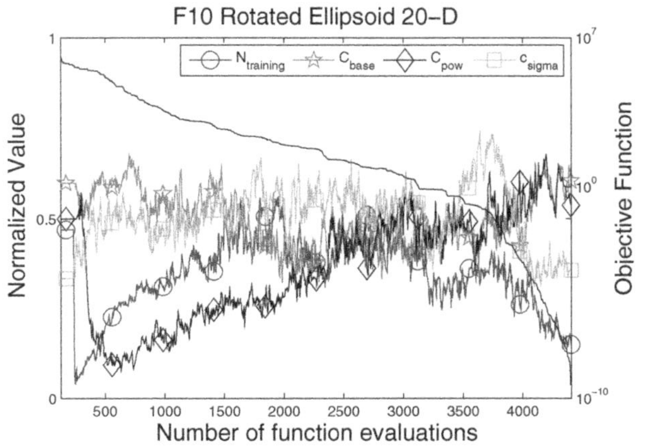

Figure 5: The median trajectories of normalized surrogate hyper-parameters estimated on 15 runs of the IPOP-^{s*}aACM-ES on Rotated Ellipsoid 20-D.

however that the Sphere function might be misleading, regarding the optimal adjustment of $N_{training}$.

Let us consider the surrogate speed-up of IPOP-aACM-ES w.r.t. IPOP-CMA-ES depending on (fixed) $N_{training}$, on uni-modal benchmark problems from the BBOB noiseless testbed (Fig. 4 for $d = 10$). While the optimal speed-up varies from 2 to 4, the actual speed-up strongly depends on the number $N_{training}$ of training points.

Complementary experiments on d-dimensional problems with $d = 2, 5, 10, 20, 40$ (Fig. 4) yield to propose an average best tuning of $N_{training}$ depending on dimension d:

$$N_{training} = \lfloor 40 + 4d^{1.7} \rfloor \tag{5}$$

Eq. (5) is found to empirically outperform the one proposed in [21] ($N_{training} = \lfloor 70\sqrt{d} \rfloor$), which appears to be biased to 10-dimensional problems, and underestimates the number of training points required in higher dimensions. Experimentally however, $N_{training}$ must super-linearly increase with d; eq. (5) states that for large d the number of training points should triple when d doubles.

Further, Fig. 4 shows that the optimal $N_{training}$ value is significantly smaller for the Sphere function than for other functions, which experimentally supports our conjecture that the Sphere function might be misleading with regard to the tuning of surrogate hyper-parameters.

5.3 Online Tuning: Surrogate Hyper-parameters

The IPOP-^{s*}ACM-ES achieves the online adaptation of the surrogate hyper-parameters within a specified range (Table 1), yielding the surrogate hyper-parameter values to be used in the next surrogate learning step.

Note that a surrogate hyper-parameter individual might be non-viable, i.e. if it does not enable to learn a surrogate model (Ranking SVM fails due to an ill-conditioned kernel). Such non-viable individual is heavily penalized ($\text{Err}(\alpha) >> 1$). In case no usable hyper-parameter individual is found (which might happen in the very early generations as it is shown on Fig. 5), θ_{sur} is set to its default value.

The online adaptation of surrogate hyper-parameters however soon reaches usable hyper-parameter values. The trajectory of the surrogate hyper-parameter values vs the number of generations is depicted in Fig. 5, normalized in $[0, 1]$ and considering the median out of 15 runs optimizing 20 dimensional Rotated Ellipsoid function.

The trajectory of $N_{training}$ displays three stages. In a first stage, $N_{training}$ increases as the overall number of evaluated points (all points are required to build a good surrogate). In a second stage, $N_{training}$ reaches a plateau; its value is close to the one found by offline tuning (section 5.2). In a third stage, $N_{training}$ steadily decreases. This last stage is explained as CMA-ES approaches the optimum of f and gets a good estimate of the covariance matrix of the Ellipsoid function. At this point the optimization problem is close to the Sphere function, and a good surrogate can be learned from comparatively few training points.

The trajectories of other surrogate hyper-parameters are more difficult to interpret, although they clearly show non-random patterns (e.g. C_{pow}).

5.4 Comparative Performances

The comparative performance of ^{s*}ACM-ES combined with the original and the active variants of IPOP-CMA-ES is depicted on Fig. 6, on the 10-d Rotated Ellipsoid (Left) and Rosenbrock (Right) functions. In both cases, the online adaptation of the surrogate hyper-parameters yields a quasi constant speed-up, witnessing the robustness of ^{s*}ACM-ES. On the Ellipsoid function, the adaptation of the covariance matrix is much faster than for the baseline, yielding same convergence speed as for the Sphere function. On the Rosenbrock function the adaptation is also much faster, although there is clearly room for improvements.

The performance gain of ^{s*}ACM-ES, explained from the online adjustment of the surrogate hyper-parameters, in particular $N_{training}$, confirms the fact that the appropriate surrogate hyper-parameters vary along search, and can be adjusted based on the accuracy of the current surrogate model. Notably, IPOP-^{s*}ACM-ES almost always outperforms IPOP-ACM-ES, especially for $d > 10$.

5.5 Scalability w.r.t Population Size

The default population size $\lambda_{default}$ is suggested to be the only CMA-ES parameter to possibly require manual tuning. Actually, $\lambda_{default}$ is well tuned for uni-modal problems and only depends on the problem dimension. Increasing the pop-

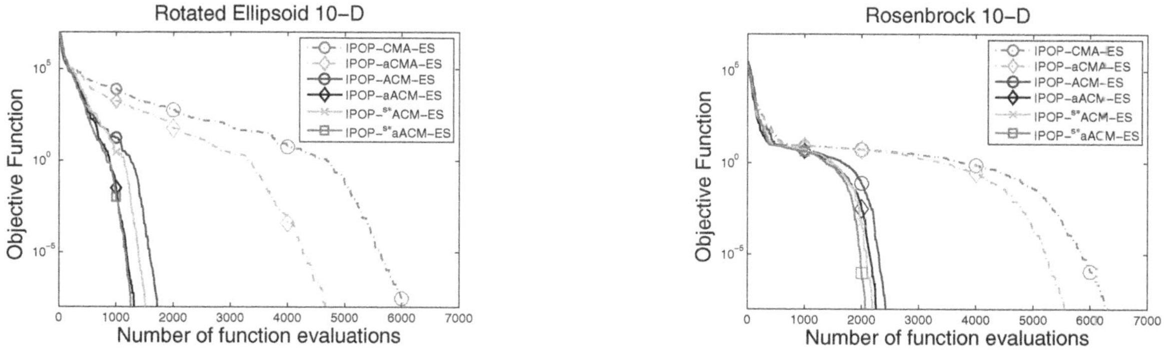

Figure 6: Comparison of the proposed surrogate-assisted versions of the original and active IPOP-CMA-ES algorithms on 10 dimensional Rotated Ellipsoid (Left) and Rosenbrock (Right) functions. The trajectories show the median of 15 runs.

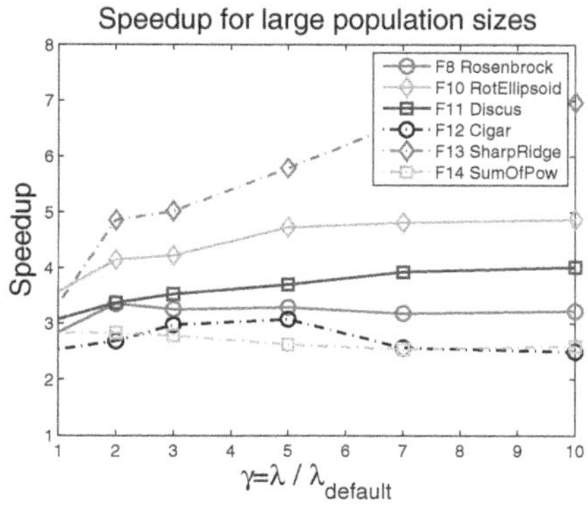

Figure 7: Speedup of the IPOP-^{s*}aACM-ES over IPOP-aCMA-ES for large population sizes $\lambda = \gamma\lambda_{default}$ on 10-D problems.

ulation size does not decrease the overall number of function evaluations needed to reach an optimum in general. Still, it allows one to reach the optimum after fewer generations. Increasing the population size and running the objective function computations in parallel is a source of speed-up, which raises the question of ^{s*}ACM-ES scalability w.r.t. the population size.

Fig. 7 shows the speedup of the IPOP-^{s*}aACM-ES compared to IPOP-aCMA-ES for unimodal 10 dimensional problems, when the population size λ is set to γ times the default population size $\lambda_{default}$. For F8 Rosenbrock, F12 Cigar and F14 Sum of Different Powers the speedup remains almost constant and independent of γ, while for F10 Rotated Ellipsoid, F11 Discus and F13 Sharp Ridge, it even increases with γ. We believe that with a larger population size, "younger" points are used to build the surrogate model, that is hence more accurate.

The experimental evidence suggests that ^{s*}ACM-ES can be applied on top of parallelized versions of IPOP-^{s*}aACM-ES, while preserving or even improving its speed-up. Note that the same does not hold true for all surrogate-assisted methods; for instance in trust region methods, one needs to sequentially evaluate the points.

It is thus conjectured that further improvements of CMA-ES (e.g. refined parameter tuning, noise handling) will translate to ^{s*}ACM-ES, without degrading its speed-up.

6. CONCLUSION AND PERSPECTIVES

This paper presents a generic framework for adaptive surrogate-assisted optimization, which can in principle be combined with any iterative population-based optimization, and surrogate learning, algorithms. This framework has been instantiated on top of surrogate-assisted ACM-ES, using CMA-ES as optimization algorithm and Ranking SVM as surrogate learning algorithm. The resulting algorithm, ^{s*}ACM-ES, inherits from CMA-ES and ACM-ES the property of invariance w.r.t. monotonous transformations of the objective function and orthogonal transformations of the search space.

The main contribution of the paper regards the online adjustment of i) the number $\widehat{n}$ of generations a surrogate model is used, called surrogate lifelength; ii) the surrogate hyper-parameters controlling the surrogate learning phase. The surrogate lifelength is adapted depending on the quality of the current surrogate model; the higher the quality, the longer the next surrogate model will be used. The adjustment of the surrogate hyper-parameters is likewise handled by optimizing them w.r.t. the quality of the surrogate model, without requiring any prior knowledge on the optimization problem at hand.

IPOP-^{s*}aACM-ES was found to improve on IPOP-aCMA-ES with a speed-up ranging from 2 to 3 on uni-modal d-dimensional functions from the BBOB-2012 noiseless testbed, with dimension d ranging from 2 to 40. On multi-modal functions, IPOP-^{s*}aACM-ES is equally good or sometimes better than IPOP-aCMA-ES, although the speed-up is less significant than for uni-modal problems. Further, IPOP-^{s*} aACM-ES also improves on IPOP-aCMA-ES on problems with moderate noise from BBOB-2012 noisy testbed. All these results as well as the computational complexity of the algorithm are discussed in details in BBOB-2012 workshop papers [22] and [23].

A long term perspective for further research is to better handle multi-modal and noisy functions. A shorter-term perspective is to consider a more comprehensive surrogate learning phase, involving a portfolio of learning algorithms and using the surrogate hyper-parameter optimization phase to achieve portfolio selection. Another perspective is to design a tighter coupling of the surrogate learning phase, and the CMA-ES optimization, e.g. using the surrogate model $\widehat{f}$ to adapt the CMA-ES hyper-parameters during the optimization of the expensive objective f.

7. ACKNOWLEDGMENTS

The authors would like to acknowledge Anne Auger, Zyed Bouzarkouna, Nikolaus Hansen and Thomas P. Runarsson for their valuable discussions. This work was partially funded by FUI of System@tic Paris-Region ICT cluster through contract DGT 117 407 *Complex Systems Design Lab* (CSDL).

8. REFERENCES

[1] G. T.-P. Alan Diaz-Manriquez and W. Gomez-Flores. On the selection of surrogate models in evolutionary optimization algorithms. In *Proc. CEC'2011*, pages 2143–2150. IEEE Press, 2011.

[2] A. Auger and N. Hansen. A restart CMA evolution strategy with increasing population size. In *Proc. CEC'2005*, pages 1769–1776. IEEE Press, 2005.

[3] Z. Bouzarkouna, A. Auger, and D. Ding. Investigating the local-meta-model CMA-ES for large population sizes. In C. Di Chio et al., editor, *Proc. EvoNUM'10*, pages 402–411. LNCS 6024, Springer, 2010.

[4] M. T. Emmerich, K. C. Giannakoglou, and B. Naujoks. Single- and Multiobjective Evolutionary Optimization Assisted by Gaussian Random Field Metamodels. *IEEE TEC*, 10(4):421–439, 2006.

[5] S. García, D. Molina, M. Lozano, and F. Herrera. A study on the use of non-parametric tests for analyzing the evolutionary algorithms' behaviour: a case study on the CEC'2005 special session on real parameter optimization. *Journal of Heuristics*, 15:617–644, 2009.

[6] L. Graning, Y. Jin, and B. Sendhoff. Efficient evolutionary optimization using individual-based evolution control and neural networks: A comparative study. In *Proc. ESANN'2005*, pages 27–29, 2005.

[7] N. Hansen. References to CMA-ES applications. http://www.lri.fr/ hansen/cmaapplications.pdf, 2009.

[8] N. Hansen, A. Auger, R. Ros, S. Finck, and P. Pošík. Comparing results of 31 algorithms from the BBOB-2009. In *GECCO Workshop Proc.* ACM, 2010.

[9] N. Hansen and A. Ostermeier. Completely derandomized self-adaptation in evolution strategies. *Evolutionary Computation*, 9(2):159–195, 2001.

[10] N. Hansen and R. Ros. Benchmarking a weighted negative covariance matrix update on the bbob-2010 noiseless testbed. In *In GECCO Workshop Proc.*, pages 1673–1680. ACM, 2010.

[11] F. Hoffmann and S. Holemann. Controlled model assisted evolution strategy with adaptive preselection. In *International Symposium on Evolving Fuzzy Systems*, pages 182–187. IEEE, 2006.

[12] H. Ingimundardottir and T. Runarsson. Sampling strategies in ordinal regression for surrogate assisted evolutionary optimization. In *Proc. ISDA'2011*, page To appear, 2011.

[13] G. A. Jastrebski and D. V. Arnold. Improving evolution strategies through active covariance matrix adaptation. In *Proc. CEC'2006*, pages 2814–2821, 2006.

[14] R. Jin, W. Chen, and T. W. Simpson. Comparative studies of metamodeling techniques under multiple modeling criteria. *Structural and Multidisciplinary Optimization*, 23:1–13, 2000.

[15] Y. Jin. Quality measures for approximate models in evolutionary computation. In *GECCO Workshop Proc.*, pages 170–173. AAAI, 2003.

[16] Y. Jin. A Comprehensive Survey of Fitness Approximation in Evolutionary Computation. *Soft Computing*, 9(1):3–12, 2005.

[17] T. Joachims. A support vector method for multivariate performance measures. In L. D. Raedt and S. Wrobel, editors, *Proc. ICML'05*, volume 119 of *ACM ICPS*, pages 377–384. ACM, 2005.

[18] S. Kern, N. Hansen, and P. Koumoutsakos. Local meta-models for optimization using evolution strategies. In Th. Runarsson et al., editor, *PPSN IX*, pages 939–948. LNCS 4193, Springer, 2006.

[19] O. Kramer. Covariance matrix self-adaptation and kernel regression - perspectives of evolutionary optimization in kernel machines. *Fundam. Inf.*, 98:87–106, 2010.

[20] D. Lim, Y.-S. Ong, Y. Jin, and B. Sendhoff. A study on metamodeling techniques, ensembles, and multi-surrogates in evolutionary computation. In *Proc. GECCO'2007*, pages 1288–1295. ACM, 2007.

[21] I. Loshchilov, M. Schoenauer, and M. Sebag. Comparison-Based Optimizers Need Comparison-Based Surrogates. In J. K. R. Schaefer, C. Cotta and G. Rudolph, editors, *Proc. PPSN XI*, pages 364–373. LNCS 6238, Springer, 2010.

[22] I. Loshchilov, M. Schoenauer, and M. Sebag. Black-box optimization benchmarking of IPOP-saACM-ES and BIPOP-saACM-ES on the BBOB-2012 noiseless testbed. In *In GECCO Companion*, page To appear. ACM, 2012.

[23] I. Loshchilov, M. Schoenauer, and M. Sebag. Black-box optimization benchmarking of IPOP-saACM-ES on the BBOB-2012 noisy testbed. In *In GECCO Companion*, page To appear. ACM, 2012.

[24] T. P. Runarsson. Ordinal regression in evolutionary computation. In Th. Runarsson et al., editor, *PPSN IX*, pages 1048–1057. LNCS 4193, Springer, 2006.

[25] D. F. Shanno. Conditioning of Quasi-Newton methods for function minimization. *Mathematics of Computation*, 24(111):647–656, 1970.

[26] J. Shawe-Taylor and N. Cristianini. *Kernel Methods for Pattern Analysis.* Cambridge Univ. Press, 2004.

[27] L. Shi and K. Rasheed. Asaga: an adaptive surrogate-assisted genetic algorithm. In *Proc. GECCO'2008*, pages 1049–1056, 2008.

[28] Y. Tenne and S. W. Armfield. A versatile surrogate-assisted memetic algorithm for optimization of computationally expensive functions and its engineering applications. In *Success in Evolutionary Computation*, pages 43–72. Springer, 2008.

[29] H. Ulmer, F. Streichert, and A. Zell. Evolution strategies assisted by gaussian processes with improved pre-selection criterion. In *Proc. CEC'2003*, pages 692–699, 2003.

[30] H. Ulmer, F. Streichert, and A. Zell. Evolution strategies with controlled model assistance. In *Proc. CEC'2004*, pages 1569 – 1576, 2004.

Natural Evolution Strategies Converge on Sphere Functions

Tom Schaul
Courant Institute of Mathematical Sciences
New York University
715, Broadway, New York, NY 10003
schaul@cims.nyu.edu

ABSTRACT

This theoretical investigation gives the first proof of convergence for (radial) natural evolution strategies, on d-dimensional sphere functions, and establishes the conditions on hyper-parameters, as a function of d. For the limit case of large population sizes we show asymptotic linear convergence, and in the limit of small learning rates we give a full analytic characterization of the algorithm dynamics, decomposed into transient and asymptotic phases. Finally, we show why omitting the natural gradient is catastrophic.

Categories and Subject Descriptors

F.1.2 [**Analysis of Algorithms and Problem Complexity**]: Numerical Algorithms and Problems

General Terms

Algorithms, Theory

Keywords

black-box optimization, evolution strategies, stability theory, sphere function, convergence proof, natural gradient

1. INTRODUCTION

One of the most widely used algorithm classes for continuous black-box optimization are evolution strategies (ES). Their modern variants adapt multi-variate search distributions and include covariance matrix adaptation (CMA-ES [9]) and natural evolution strategies (NES [16]). While these methods were widely adopted for practical applications, and successfully so, theoretical work has lagged behind their developments, because it remained mostly focused on (1+1) ES (and its self-adaptive variant). For a recent review of the state of the field, see [4], and references therein. A noteworthy (negative) result for the broader category of purely comparison-based algorithms is that convergence can at best be linear [15].

The present paper aims to establish first positive convergence results for a popular class of evolutionary optimization algorithms, by studying the convergence properties of a canonical version of NES on d-dimensional sphere functions, a problem class which serves as a minimal condition for convergence to arbitrary precision.

Our approach consists in studying the dynamics of the algorithm as a stochastic process using tools from stability theory (resembling the dynamic systems approach taken in [6], and to a lesser degree related to the phi-irreducible Markov chains used in [3]). We make use of a novel type of utility function (section 2.2) that delivers manageable analytic expressions. Beyond establishing convergence itself, we obtain an explicit characterization of the dynamics, and exact convergence rates, in the limit cases of large populations sizes or small learning rates. Apart from the numerous technical results, in section 3.3 we also provide the (more casual) reader with visualizations of the dynamics, and intuitions for why the algorithm dynamics are composed of three distinct regimes.

Our investigation also includes a number of practical ramifications, giving new guidelines for hyper-parameter settings (and validating existing heuristics) in section 6.

It is a notable strength of the NES framework that the user may choose among many types of search distributions, and weighting functions for the samples, properties that were prerequisites for our explicit analysis. Nevertheless, we expect the techniques from this paper to be applicable to studying other, related algorithms.

2. NATURAL EVOLUTION STRATEGIES

In real-valued optimization, we call $f : \mathcal{S} \subset \mathbb{R}^d \mapsto \mathbb{R}$ the *fitness* function on some search space $\mathcal{S}$, which admits an optimum $f^* = f(\mathbf{z}^*)$.

Natural evolution strategies (NES) [16] are a class of evolutionary algorithms for this type of problems, which maintain a search distribution π and adapt the distribution parameters θ towards higher expected fitness J, that is, maximizing

$$J(\theta) = \mathbb{E}_\theta[f(\mathbf{z})] = \int f(\mathbf{z})\ \pi(\mathbf{z}\,|\,\theta)\ d\mathbf{z} \tag{1}$$

Each iteration the algorithm produces n samples $\mathbf{z}_i \sim \pi(\mathbf{z}|\theta)$, $i \in \{1, \dots, n\}$, i.i.d. from its search distribution, which is parameterized by θ. The gradient w.r.t. the parameters θ can be rewritten (see [16]) as

$$\nabla_\theta J(\theta) \;= \nabla_\theta \int f(\mathbf{z})\ \pi(\mathbf{z}\,|\,\theta)\ d\mathbf{z} \;= \mathbb{E}_\theta\left[f(\mathbf{z})\ \nabla_\theta \log \pi(\mathbf{z}\,|\,\theta)\right]$$

from which we obtain a Monte Carlo estimate

$$\nabla_\theta J(\theta) \approx \frac{1}{n}\sum_{i=1}^{n} f(\mathbf{z}_i)\, \nabla_\theta \log \pi(\mathbf{z}_i \mid \theta)$$

of the search gradient. The key step then consists in replacing this gradient by the *natural gradient* [1], defined as $\mathbf{F}^{-1}\nabla_\theta J(\theta)$ where $\mathbf{F} = \mathbb{E}\left[\nabla_\theta \log \pi\left(\mathbf{z}|\theta\right) \nabla_\theta \log \pi\left(\mathbf{z}|\theta\right)^\top\right]$ is the Fisher information matrix. The search distribution is iteratively updated using natural gradient ascent

$$\theta \leftarrow \theta + \eta \mathbf{F}^{-1}\nabla_\theta J(\theta) \tag{2}$$

with learning rate parameter η.

This general formulation is applicable to arbitrary parameterizable search distributions [16, 12], including multivariate Gaussians [8] and Cauchy distributions [13].

2.1 Radial NES

To facilitate our study, we consider the simple but useful case of NES with radial Gaussian distributions (as in [5]), with search distribution $\pi_t = \mathcal{N}(\boldsymbol{\mu}_t, \sigma_t^2\mathbb{I})$, where $\mathbb{I}$ is the d-dimensional identity matrix. The distribution parameters are a mean vector $\boldsymbol{\mu}_t \in \mathbb{R}^d$ and a scale coefficient $\sigma_t \in \mathbb{R}^+$. The update equations at time-step t follow from equation 2 and read:

$$\begin{aligned} \boldsymbol{\mu}_{t+1} &= \boldsymbol{\mu}_t + \eta_\mu \sigma_t \sum_{i=1}^{n} u_i \mathbf{s}_i \\ \sigma_{t+1} &= \sigma_t \cdot \exp\left(\frac{\eta_\sigma}{2}\sum_{i=1}^{n} u_i(\|\mathbf{s}_i\|^2 - d)\right) \end{aligned} \tag{3}$$

where a utility weight u_i has substituted the fitness $f(\mathbf{z}_i)$, and where the $\mathbf{s}_i$ are standard multi-normal sample points in the *natural coordinate system*, that is $\mathbf{z}_i = \boldsymbol{\mu}_t + \sigma_t \mathbf{s}_i$. Operating on natural coordinates is the reason for the multiplicative update on σ_t (see also [8] for a more extensive discussion of natural coordinate systems). Besides the initial distribution $\langle \boldsymbol{\mu}_0, \sigma_0\rangle$, the algorithm has three effective parameters:

- the population size n,
- the two learning rates $\eta_\mu > 0$ and $\eta_\sigma > 0$, and
- the function u_i, which assigns 'utility' weights to each sample $\mathbf{z}_i$, based exclusively on the rank of its fitness. It satisfies $\sum^n |u_i| = 1$, which helps disentangle the effects of the learning rate from those of redistributing sample utility. It is also rank-preserving: $f(\mathbf{z}_i) > f(\mathbf{z}_j) \Rightarrow u_i > u_j$.

Using a rank-based utility function, instead of the raw fitness values f, increases robustness [16, 12] and makes the algorithm invariant under monotone transformations of the fitness function.

2.2 Gaussian utility functions

One way to simplify the subsequent analysis, is to choose a utility function that has the property of becoming a Gaussian density in the limit of infinitely many samples.

Under the search distribution π_t, the values of the sphere function $f_i = f(\mathbf{z}_i) \propto \|\mathbf{z}_i/\sigma_t\|^2$ follow a noncentral χ^2-distribution with d degrees of freedom and noncentrality parameter $\lambda = \Delta_t^2/\sigma_t^2$, where $\Delta_t = \|\boldsymbol{\mu}_t\|$. Thus, the (normalized) rank function $\text{rank}(f_i)$ coincides with the corresponding cumulative distribution function (CDF; with value 0 for the best point, 1 for the worst):

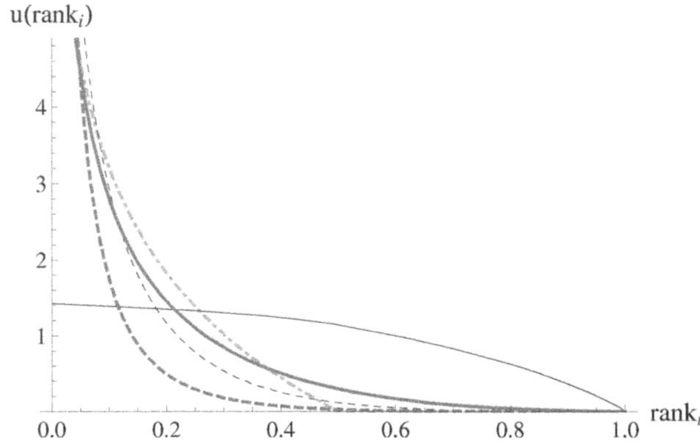

Figure 1: Different utility functions. With $\Delta_t^2/\sigma_t^2 = r_t \gg 1$, the utilities resemble the classical exponential decay from best to worst (dashed lines; thin black is for $d = 1$, thick red is for $d = 10$). At the other extreme, with $r_t \ll 1$, the utilities decay exponentially for large dimensions (solid thick red, $d = 10$), but are very flat for $d = 1$ (solid thin black). For comparison, we also show the most common utility function used in previous work, which is proportional to $\log(\text{rank}_i)$, but uses a cutoff (dashed-dotted, green): the approximation by the Gaussian utilities is close if r_t is not too small, which is the case as $r_t \to r_* \approx d$. Also note that in all cases the plots are normalized to an area under the curve of 1; in practice this normalization constant depends on the number of samples n.

$$\text{rank}(f_i) = \text{CDF}\left[\chi^2_{\nu=d,\lambda=\Delta_t^2/\sigma_t^2}\right](f_i)$$

In order to numerically[1] compute $\text{rank}^{-1}(x)$, we need to estimate Δ_t somehow. One option is to take the distance to the currently best sample as a reasonable (but underestimating) proxy: $\Delta_t \approx \|\boldsymbol{\mu}_t - \mathbf{z}_b\|$, where $\mathbf{z}_b$ is the best sample of the iteration: $b = \arg\max_{1\leq i\leq n}(f_i)$. This requires using a utility function that changes in time, and is similar to an existing (successful) speedup technique, called 'distance-weighted' NES (DX-NES [7]), which adapts learning rates online (which has a similar effect to adjusting the utility function), to one of three discrete settings, based on an estimated value of Δ_t^2/σ_t^2.

In section 3.3, we will see that the quantity Δ_t^2/σ_t^2 reaches an equilibrium point near d, and we thus take that point as default value, if a static utility function is desired.

Using this inverse rank function, we constrain $u_i(\text{rank}(f_i))$ to be approximately Half-Gaussian:

$$\begin{aligned} u_i(\text{rank}(f_i)) &= 2\phi_{\langle 0,1\rangle}\left(\sqrt{f_i}/\sigma_t\right) \\ \Leftrightarrow u_i(x) &= 2\phi_{\langle 0,1\rangle}\left(\sqrt{\text{rank}^{-1}(x)}/\sigma_t\right) \end{aligned}$$

where $\phi_{\langle\mu,\sigma^2\rangle}$ denotes the Gaussian density function. Now, in the limit of many samples, $u_i(\text{rank}(f_i)) \cdot \pi_t(\mathbf{z}_i)$ is again

[1]There is no closed form for the inverse, but numerical approximations can be based on [11], for example.

normally distributed. In the natural coordinates we obtain

$$u(\mathbf{z}) \cdot \pi_t(\mathbf{s}) \approx \phi_{\left\langle \frac{-\boldsymbol{\mu}_t}{\sigma_t}, \mathbb{I} \right\rangle}(\mathbf{s}) \cdot \phi_{\langle \mathbf{0}, \mathbb{I} \rangle}(\mathbf{s}) = \phi_{\langle \boldsymbol{\mu}', \sigma'^2 \mathbb{I} \rangle}(\mathbf{s})$$

where the resulting distribution has parameters

$$\boldsymbol{\mu}'_t = \frac{1 \cdot \frac{-\boldsymbol{\mu}_t}{\sigma_t} + \mathbf{0}}{1+1} = \frac{-\boldsymbol{\mu}_t}{2\sigma_t}, \quad \sigma'^2 = \frac{1}{2} \tag{4}$$

Figure 1 shows how the function u_i varies with rank, for different values of the ratio $r_t = \Delta_t^2/\sigma_t^2$ and different problem dimensions d. Note that this new utility function closely resembles the most popularly used (and heuristically chosen) utility function [8] (shown as dashed-dotted green line on Figure 1); we expect this approximation to be sufficient because empirical results indicate that the precise utility function does not affect performance substantially [12].

3. CONVERGENCE ON SPHERE

The goal of any stochastic search algorithm is to find a solution that is arbitrarily close in value to the optimum $f(\mathbf{z}^*)$. Given the stochastic nature of algorithms with search distributions, an appropriate success criterion can be formulated as follows: For any given $\epsilon > 0$, at least half of the samples $\mathbf{z} \sim \pi_t$, drawn from the search distribution (at iteration $t = T$) have a fitness value not worse than ϵ from the optimal one. Or more concisely:

Criterion 1 (Stochastic convergence).

$$\exists T \in \mathbb{N}, \forall t > T, \mathbf{z} \sim \pi_T \Rightarrow P(|f(\mathbf{z}^*) - f(\mathbf{z})| < \epsilon) > \frac{1}{2}$$

If we further assume that the fitness function has bounded curvature around the optimum:

$$|f(\mathbf{z}^*) - f(\mathbf{z})| < \epsilon \Rightarrow \frac{|f(\mathbf{z}^*) - f(\mathbf{z})|}{\|\mathbf{z}^* - \mathbf{z}\|} < K$$

for some constant $K < \infty$, then criterion 1 is also implied by convergence based on distance:

$$\forall \mathbf{z} \in \mathcal{S}, \|\mathbf{z}^* - \mathbf{z}\| < \epsilon' \Rightarrow |f(\mathbf{z}^*) - f(\mathbf{z})| < \epsilon \tag{5}$$

for any $\epsilon' < \frac{\epsilon}{K}$. That is, if the distribution is close enough to the optimum, then the fitness will also be good enough.

3.1 Sphere functions

Let f be the simple but common *sphere function*, in d dimensions:

$$\forall \mathbf{z} \in \mathbb{R}^d, f(\mathbf{z}) = \mathbf{z}^\top \mathbf{z},$$

where the objective is to minimize it. The sphere function is commonly used as a test function for optimization algorithms, because any smooth function is locally quadratic near its optimum, and thus convergence on the sphere function is a necessary condition for convergence on any smooth function.

Translation invariance: For convenience of notation, we use the sphere function centered at zero, but all our results can trivially be generalized to the translated variant $f(\mathbf{z}) = (\mathbf{z} - \mathbf{z}^*)^\top (\mathbf{z} - \mathbf{z}^*)$.

Intrinsic one-dimensionality: The sphere function is rotation-symmetric (around $\mathbf{z}^* = \mathbf{0}$), and the search distribution is also rotation symmetric (around $\boldsymbol{\mu}_t$). Without loss of generality, we can therefore rotate the coordinate system at each iteration, such that $\boldsymbol{\mu}_t = (\Delta_t, 0, \cdots, 0)$, where $\Delta_t = \|\boldsymbol{\mu}_t - \mathbf{0}\|$, the distance of the current distribution's center to the optimum.

We can now reformulate criterion 1 for the case of the sphere function:

$$\begin{aligned}
\frac{1}{2} &< \int_{\|\mathbf{z}\| < \epsilon'} \frac{1}{(2\pi\sigma_t^2)^{d/2}} \exp\left(-\frac{1}{2\sigma_t^2}\|\mathbf{z} - \boldsymbol{\mu}_t\|^2\right) d\mathbf{z} \\
&= \int_{\|\mathbf{z}\|^2 < \epsilon'^2} \frac{1}{(2\pi\sigma_t^2)^{d/2}} \exp\left(-\frac{1}{2\sigma_t^2}\|\mathbf{z} - \boldsymbol{\mu}_t\|^2\right) d\mathbf{z} \\
&= \int_{\|\mathbf{z}'\|^2 < \epsilon'^2/\sigma_t^2} \frac{1}{(2\pi)^{d/2}} \exp\left(-\frac{1}{2}\|\mathbf{z}' - \boldsymbol{\mu}_t/\sigma_t\|^2\right) d\mathbf{z}' \\
&= \int_0^{\frac{\epsilon'^2}{\sigma_t^2}} \chi^2_{\nu=d, \lambda=\Delta_t^2/\sigma_t^2}(x)\, dx
\end{aligned} \tag{6}$$

where $\chi^2_{\nu,\lambda}$ is the density of the noncentral χ^2-distribution, with $\nu = d$ degrees of freedom and noncentrality parameter $\lambda = \Delta_t^2/\sigma_t^2$. In other words, the inequality holds if and only if ϵ'^2/σ_t^2 is larger than the distribution's median $m_{\nu,\lambda}$. From [14] we know that

$$\nu - 2 + \lambda < m_{\nu,\lambda} \leq \nu + \lambda,$$

therefore the inequality 6 is verified if

$$d + \frac{\Delta_t^2}{\sigma_t^2} < \frac{\epsilon'^2}{\sigma_t^2} \Leftrightarrow \Delta_t^2 + \sigma_t^2 d < \epsilon'^2 \tag{7}$$

Thus, we find that criterion 1 together with equations 5 and 7 lead to a simple new success criterion for the sphere function:

Criterion 2 (Convergence on sphere).

$$\exists T \in \mathbb{N}, \forall t > T, \Delta_T^2 + \sigma_T^2 d < \epsilon'^2$$

In other words, both Δ_t and σ_t must converge to zero.

3.2 Update dynamics

This section contains a number of auxiliary derivations of the expectations of parameter updates, required for the analysis in the subsequent sections.

Using the Gaussian utilities from section 2.2, we can rewrite the update equations 3 as

$$\boldsymbol{\mu}_{t+1} = \boldsymbol{\mu}_t + \eta_\mu \sigma_t \sum_{i=1}^n u_i \mathbf{s}_i = \boldsymbol{\mu}_t + \eta_\mu \sigma_t \frac{1}{n} \sum_{i=1}^n \mathbf{s}'_i$$

where the samples $\mathbf{s}'_i$ are now drawn from $\mathcal{N}(\boldsymbol{\mu}', \sigma'^2 \mathbb{I})$, with parameters from equation 4. We can decompose the sample vectors $\mathbf{s}_i$ into their components $\mathbf{s}_{i,j}$ with $j \in \{1, \ldots, d\}$:

$$\begin{aligned}
\Delta_{t+1}^2 &= \|\boldsymbol{\mu}_{t+1}\|^2 = \left\| \boldsymbol{\mu}_t + \eta_\mu \sigma_t \frac{1}{n} \sum_{i=1}^n \mathbf{s}'_i \right\|^2 \\
&= \left(\Delta_t + \eta_\mu \sigma_t \frac{1}{n} \sum_{i=1}^n \mathbf{s}'_{i,1}\right)^2 + \eta_\mu^2 \sigma_t^2 \sum_{j=2}^d \left(\frac{1}{n} \sum_{i=1}^n \mathbf{s}'_{i,j}\right)^2
\end{aligned}$$

So, denoting by ξ_k independent standard normal (1-dimensional) samples we can explicitly separate the stochastic parts from the deterministic ones: The intrinsic one-dimensionality gives us $\mathbf{s}_{i,1} = \frac{-\Delta_t}{2\sigma_t} + \frac{1}{\sqrt{2}}\xi_1$ and $\mathbf{s}_{i,j} = \frac{1}{\sqrt{2}}\xi_j$ for $j > 1$; therefore

$$\begin{aligned}\Delta_{t+1}^2 = & \left(\eta_\mu \sigma_t \tfrac{1}{n} \sum_{i=1}^n \left(\tfrac{\Delta_t}{\eta_\mu \sigma_t} + \tfrac{-\Delta_t}{2\sigma_t} + \tfrac{1}{\sqrt{2}}\xi_i\right)\right)^2 \\ & + \eta_\mu^2 \sigma_t^2 \sum_{j=2}^d \left(\tfrac{1}{n\sqrt{2}} \sum_{i=1}^n \xi_{jd+i}\right)^2 \\ = & \tfrac{(2-\eta_\mu)^2}{4}\Delta_t^2 + \tfrac{\eta_\mu(2-\eta_\mu)\sigma_t \Delta_t}{n\sqrt{2}} \sum_{i=1}^n \xi_i + \tfrac{\eta_\mu^2 \sigma_t^2}{2n^2} \sum_{j=1}^{nd} \xi_j^2\end{aligned}$$

giving, in expectation

$$\mathbb{E}[\Delta_{t+1}^2] = \frac{(2-\eta_\mu)^2}{4}\Delta_t^2 + \frac{\eta_\mu^2 d}{2n}\sigma_t^2 \quad (8)$$

$$\mathbb{V}\mathrm{ar}[\Delta_{t+1}^2] = \frac{\eta_\mu^2(2-\eta_\mu)^2}{2n}\sigma_t^2\Delta_t^2 + \frac{\eta_\mu^4 d}{2n^2}\sigma_t^4 \quad (9)$$

Similarly, we rewrite the update of σ_t (from equation 3):

$$\begin{aligned}\sigma_{t+1}^2 &= \sigma_t^2 \exp\left(\eta_\sigma \sum_{i=1}^n u_i(\|\mathbf{s}_i\|^2 - d)\right) \\ &= \sigma_t^2 \exp\left(-\eta_\sigma d + \frac{\eta_\sigma}{n}\sum_{i=1}^n \|\mathbf{s}'_i\|^2\right) \\ &= \sigma_t^2 \exp\left(-\eta_\sigma d + \frac{\eta_\sigma}{2n}\sum_{i=1}^n \left[\left(-\frac{\Delta_t}{\sigma_t} + \xi_i\right)^2 + \sum_{j=2}^d \xi_j^2\right]\right) \\ &= \sigma_t^2 \exp\left(-\eta_\sigma d + \frac{\eta_\sigma \Delta_t^2}{2\sigma_t^2} - \frac{\eta_\sigma \Delta_t}{n\sigma_t}\sum_{i=1}^n \xi_i + \frac{\eta_\sigma}{2n}\sum_{j=1}^{nd}\xi_j^2\right)\end{aligned}$$

To compute the expectation, we can decompose this into a product, because all the ξ_i are independent of each other. Using the auxiliary results

$$\mathbb{E}\left[\exp\left(\tfrac{\eta_\sigma}{2n}\xi^2\right)\right] = \left(1 - \tfrac{\eta_\sigma}{n}\right)^{-1/2}$$

$$\mathbb{E}\left[\exp\left(-\tfrac{\eta_\sigma \Delta_t}{n\sigma_t}\xi + \tfrac{\eta_\sigma}{2n}\xi^2\right)\right] = \left(1 - \tfrac{\eta_\sigma}{n}\right)^{-1/2} \exp\left(\tfrac{\eta_\sigma^2 \Delta_t^2}{2n\sigma_t^2(n-\eta_\sigma)}\right)$$

we obtain

$$\begin{aligned}\mathbb{E}[\sigma_{t+1}^2] = & \sigma_t^2 \exp\left(-\eta_\sigma d + \tfrac{\eta_\sigma \Delta_t^2}{2\sigma_t^2}\right) \\ & \cdot \mathbb{E}\left(\exp\left[-\tfrac{\eta_\sigma \Delta_t}{n\sigma_t}\xi_i + \tfrac{\eta_\sigma}{2n}\xi_i^2\right]\right)^n \mathbb{E}\left(\exp\left[\tfrac{\eta_\sigma}{2n}\xi_j^2\right]\right)^{n(d-1)} \\ = & \sigma_t^2\left(1 - \tfrac{\eta_\sigma}{n}\right)^{-nd/2} \exp\left(-\eta_\sigma d + \tfrac{\eta_\sigma \Delta_t^2}{2\sigma_t^2} + \tfrac{\eta_\sigma^2 \Delta_t^2}{2\sigma_t^2(n-\eta_\sigma)}\right) \\ \approx & \sigma_t^2 \exp\left(-\tfrac{\eta_\sigma}{2}d + \tfrac{n\eta_\sigma}{2(n-\eta_\sigma)}\tfrac{\Delta_t^2}{\sigma_t^2}\right) \quad (10)\end{aligned}$$

where we used $\log(1 - \frac{\eta_\sigma}{n}) \approx -\frac{\eta_\sigma}{n}$, with the assumption $\eta_\sigma \ll n$. Similarly, the variance of the update becomes:

$$\begin{aligned}\mathbb{V}\mathrm{ar}[\sigma_{t+1}^2] = & -\mathbb{E}[\sigma_{t+1}^2]^2 + \sigma_t^4 \exp\left(-2\eta_\sigma d + \tfrac{\eta_\sigma \Delta_t^2}{\sigma_t^2}\right) \\ & \cdot \mathbb{E}\left(\exp\left[-\tfrac{2\eta_\sigma \Delta_t}{n\sigma_t}\xi_i + \tfrac{\eta_\sigma}{n}\xi_i^2\right]\right)^n \mathbb{E}\left(\exp\left[\tfrac{\eta_\sigma}{n}\xi_j^2\right]\right)^{n(d-1)} \\ = & \sigma_t^4 \exp\left(-2\eta_\sigma d + \tfrac{n\eta_\sigma}{n-\eta_\sigma}\tfrac{\Delta_t^2}{\sigma_t^2}\right) \\ & \cdot \left[\left(1 - \tfrac{2\eta_\sigma}{n}\right)^{-nd/2} - \left(1 - \tfrac{\eta_\sigma}{n}\right)^{-nd}\right] \\ \approx & \sigma_t^4 \exp\left(-\eta_\sigma d + \tfrac{n\eta_\sigma}{n-\eta_\sigma}\tfrac{\Delta_t^2}{\sigma_t^2}\right)\left[\exp\left(\tfrac{\eta_\sigma^2 d}{2n-4\eta_\sigma}\right) - 1\right] \quad (11)\end{aligned}$$

3.3 Phase plane analysis

The fixed points of the dynamics are those values for which the expected update is the identity function. As a prerequisite for our stability analysis, we thus determine the fixed point for each variable. We have a fixed point for Δ_t^2 if the equality holds in

$$\begin{aligned}\mathbb{E}[\Delta_{t+1}^2] &\leq \Delta_t^2 \\ \Leftrightarrow \frac{\eta_\mu^2 d}{2n}\sigma_t^2 + \frac{\eta_\mu^2 - 4\eta_\mu}{4}\Delta_t^2 &\leq 0 \\ \Leftrightarrow \frac{\Delta_t^2}{\sigma_t^2} &\geq \frac{2\eta_\mu}{n(4-\eta_\mu)}d \quad (12)\end{aligned}$$

Note that we only have a fixed point only if $\eta_\mu < 4$, so for larger values, we have divergence. Similarly, we have a fixed point of σ_t^2 if the equality holds in

$$\begin{aligned}\mathbb{E}[\sigma_{t+1}^2] &\leq \sigma_t^2 \\ \Leftrightarrow \exp\left(-\frac{\eta_\sigma}{2}d + \frac{n\eta_\sigma}{2(n-\eta_\sigma)}\frac{\Delta_t^2}{\sigma_t^2}\right) &\leq 1 \\ \Leftrightarrow \frac{\Delta_t^2}{\sigma_t^2} &\leq \frac{n-\eta_\sigma}{n}d \quad (13)\end{aligned}$$

Given that the left term is positive, we only have a fixed point for σ_t if $\eta_\sigma < n$.

Thus, it is clear that under these conditions, the *single* fixed point for the joint updates is where these two lines intersect, namely at $\langle \Delta_t^2 = 0, \sigma_t^2 = 0 \rangle$.

Based on the inequalities 12 and 13, we find that the dynamics can be divided into three distinct regimes:

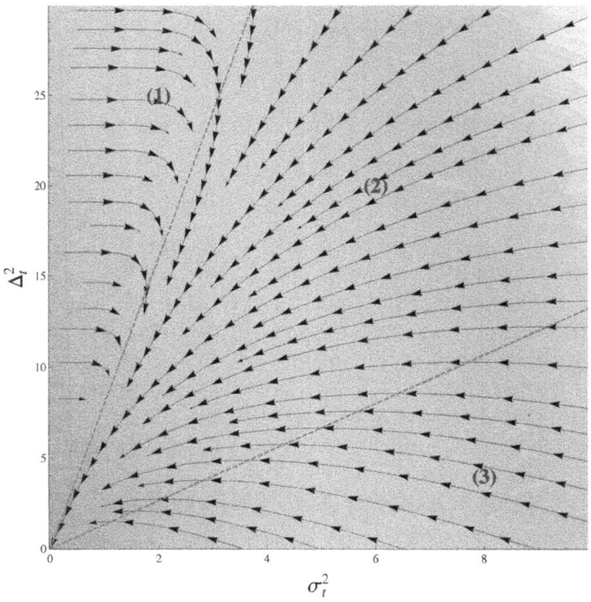

Figure 2: NES phase plane. Black arrows give the directions of the expected combined update of Δ_t^2 and σ_t^2 (magnitudes are not to scale). The settings used are $d = 10$, $n = 5$, $\eta_\mu = 1$ and $\eta_\sigma = 1$. The dashed red lines indicate the null clines (fixed points) for the two variables, and at the same time delimit the three dynamic regimes. The underlaid color gradient is corresponds to the objective from criterion 2. Visibly, regimes (1) and (3) are transient, and all updates in (2) lead toward the optimum (at the origin). Note also the very drastic increase of σ_t^2 whenever it is much smaller than Δ_t^2/d, in regime (1).

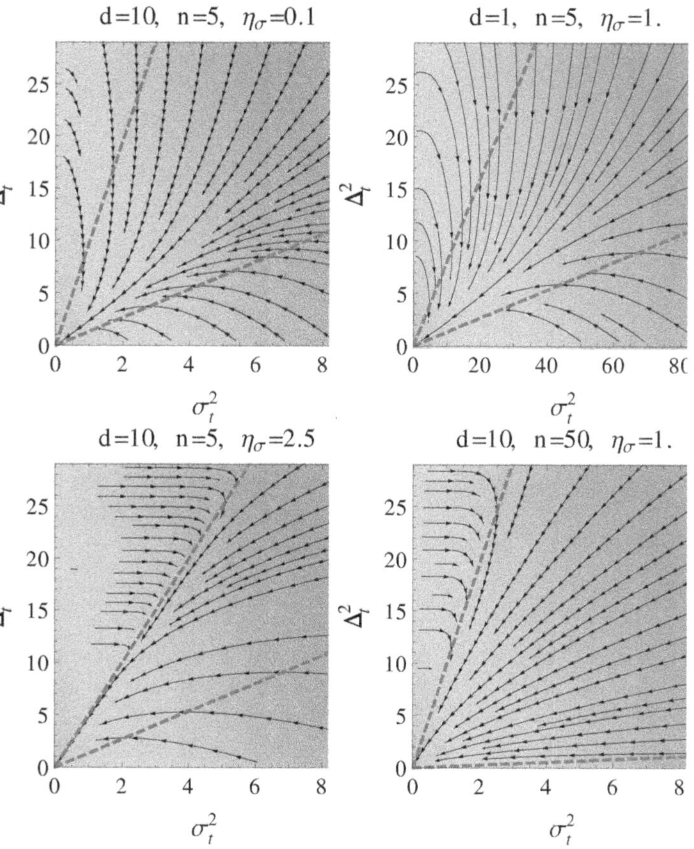

Figure 3: Additional NES phase planes. Compared to figure 2, we varied d, n and η_σ. In the top left, we see that reducing η_σ by a factor 10 smoothens the transition between regimes (1) and (2). On the top right, we illustrate how similar the dynamics remain (as compared to the corresponding settings top left), even when reducing the dimension by a factor 10. The bottom left plot shows how increasing η_σ substantially changes both the borders of the regimes, narrowing regime (2), and the dynamics within. Finally, the bottom right plot reduces the noise by increasing n by a factor 10; as expected, regime (3) almost vanishes.

(1) If $\frac{\Delta_t^2}{\sigma_t^2} \geq \frac{n-\eta_\sigma}{n} d$, then σ_t^2 increases, Δ_t^2 decreases, so $\frac{\Delta_t^2}{\sigma_t^2}$ decreases and we approach regime (2).

(2) If $\frac{n-\eta_\sigma}{n} d > \frac{\Delta_t^2}{\sigma_t^2} \geq \frac{2\eta_\mu}{n(4-\eta_\mu)} d$, then σ_t^2 decreases, Δ_t^2 decreases, and we approach the goal of $\Delta_t^2 + \sigma_t^2 d < \epsilon'$, and thus converge according to criterion 2.

(3) If $\frac{2\eta_\mu}{n(4-\eta_\mu)} d > \frac{\Delta_t^2}{\sigma_t^2} > 0$, then σ_t^2 decreases, Δ_t^2 increases so $\frac{\Delta_t^2}{\sigma_t^2}$ increases and we approach regime (2).

From this, we can deduce that regimes (1) and (3) are transient[2], and that the asymptotic regime is (2). Therefore, the algorithm will always converge according to criterion 2 in expectation.

The intuitive interpretations of these are that when Δ_t is much larger than σ_t (regime 1), the algorithm is far from the solution, and consequently increases the scale of the search distribution; which then allows it to reduce Δ_t with increasingly larger steps. On the other hand, if Δ_t is much smaller than σ_t (regime 3), it is so close to the optimum that the noise effects tend to temporarily lead it further away. Otherwise (regime 2), both Δ_t and σ_t decrease to obtain convergence.

The phase planes in figures 2 and 3 visualize the update directions in the different regimes, for a number of different dimensions and parameter settings.

3.4 Noise-free discrete dynamics

In our first limit case we study the dynamics in the absence of noise, which we can obtain by taking $n \to \infty$. We start by looking at the ratio $r_t = \frac{\Delta_t^2}{\sigma_t^2}$, which is omnipresent because it corresponds to the scale-invariant part of the state variables. We have:

$$\begin{aligned}\mathbb{E}\left[\frac{\Delta_{t+1}^2}{\sigma_{t+1}^2}\right] &= \mathbb{E}\left[\exp\left(\eta_\sigma d - \frac{\eta_\sigma \Delta_t^2}{2\sigma_t^2}\right)\left[\frac{(2-\eta_\mu)^2}{4}\Delta_t^2\right.\right.\\ &\quad \left. + \frac{\eta_\mu(2-\eta_\mu)\sigma_t\Delta_t}{n\sqrt{2}}\sum_{i=1}^n \xi_i + \frac{\eta_\mu^2\sigma_t^2}{2n^2}\sum_{j=1}^{nd}\xi_j^2\right]\\ &\quad \left. \cdot\, \sigma_t^{-2}\exp\left(\frac{\eta_\sigma\Delta_t}{n\sigma_t}\sum_{i=1}^n \xi_i - \frac{\eta_\sigma}{2n}\sum_{j=1}^{nd}\xi_j^2\right)\right]\end{aligned}$$

which, following a derivation analogous to the one for 10, and using $n \to \infty$ gives

$$\mathbb{E}[r_{t+1}] = \mathbb{E}\left[\frac{\Delta_{t+1}^2}{\sigma_{t+1}^2}\right] = \frac{(2-\eta_\mu)^2}{4}\exp\left(\frac{1}{2}\eta_\sigma(d-r_t)\right) r_t$$

and thus the following expression for the fixed point r_*:

$$\begin{aligned}\mathbb{E}[r_{t+1}] &= r_t\\ \Leftrightarrow r_* &= d - \frac{4\log(2) - 4\log(2-\eta_\mu)}{\eta_\sigma} \qquad (14)\end{aligned}$$

under the constraint that

$$\begin{aligned} r_* &\geq 0\\ \Leftrightarrow \eta_\sigma d &\geq 4\log(2) - 4\log(2-\eta_\mu)\\ \Leftrightarrow (2-\eta_\mu)^2 &\geq 4\exp(-1/2\eta_\sigma d) \qquad (15)\\ \Leftarrow \eta_\mu &\leq 2(1-\exp(-1/4\eta_\sigma d))\end{aligned}$$

Replacing in 10, this gives the asymptotic expected update

$$\begin{aligned}\mathbb{E}[\sigma_{t+1}^2] &= \sigma_t^2 \exp\left(\frac{\eta_\sigma^2 d}{2(n-\eta_\sigma)} - \frac{2n\log(2) - 2n\log(2-\eta_\mu)}{n-\eta_\sigma}\right)\\ &\approx \frac{(2-\eta_\mu)^2}{4}\sigma_t^2\end{aligned}$$

Thus there exists a time τ, for which

$$\sigma_{\tau+t}^2 = \left(\frac{(2-\eta_\mu)^2}{4}\right)^t \sigma_\tau^2 \;\geq\; \exp\left(-\frac{\eta_\sigma d}{2}t\right)\sigma_\tau^2$$

(from condition in equation 15), decay is analogously for $\Delta_{\tau+t}^2$. In other words, in the absence of noise, we have asymptotic linear convergence with a convergence rate $\exp\left(-\frac{\eta_\sigma d}{4}\right)$, which could in principle be boosted to arbitrary values by increasing η_σ. However, we will see below that for finite n the quantity $\eta_\sigma d$ should be bounded.

[2] A technical condition is that the updates are small enough to avoid oscillation between regimes (1) to (3), while regime (2) is 'over-jumped'. It can be shown that $\eta_\sigma < \frac{2}{d}\log\frac{4n}{\eta_\mu^2(n+2)}$ is a sufficient condition to avoid such oscillations (assuming $\eta_\mu \leq 1$).

4. CONTINUOUS-TIME DYNAMICS

Taking the learning rates to smaller values $\eta_\mu \to dt \cdot k_\mu$ and $\eta_\sigma \to dt \cdot k_\sigma$ while doing more iterations smoothens the updates of the algorithm. In the limit of infinitesimal steps, we obtain a stochastic continuous-time flow in $\mathbb{R}^2$ (as in [2]). Using our calculations in section 3.2, we can express it as a system of stochastic differential equations:

$$d\Delta_t^2 = -k_\mu \Delta_t^2 dt + k_\mu \sqrt{\frac{2}{n}}\, \sigma_t \Delta_t \, dW \quad (16)$$

$$d\sigma_t^2 = k_\sigma \left(\frac{1}{2}\Delta_t^2 - \frac{d}{2}\sigma_t^2\right) dt + k_\sigma \sqrt{\frac{d}{2n}} \sigma_t^2 dW \quad (17)$$

where dW denotes standard Brownian motion. Unlike in the discrete-time case, we can now explicitly compute the stability matrix from the Itō drift terms:

$$\begin{pmatrix} -k_\mu & 0 \\ \frac{k_\sigma}{2} & -\frac{k_\sigma d}{2} \end{pmatrix}$$

which has two negative eigenvalues[3], which implies that the dynamics correspond to an asymptotically stable (i.e., absorbing) node at the origin.

The joint density $p(x, y, t)$ at time t of the coupled stochastic process (where $x = \Delta_t^2$ and $y = \sigma_t^2$) is described by the Fokker-Planck equation [10]:

$$\begin{aligned} \frac{\partial p}{\partial t} &= k_\mu \frac{\partial}{\partial x}[xp] + \frac{k_\sigma}{2}\frac{\partial}{\partial y}[(yd - x)p] \\ &\quad + \frac{1}{n}\frac{\partial^2}{\partial x^2}[xyp] + \frac{k_\sigma^2 d}{2n}\frac{\partial^2}{\partial y^2}[y^2 p] \\ &= \left[k_\mu + \frac{n + 2k_\sigma}{2n} k_\sigma d\right] f + \left[k_\mu x + \frac{2}{n}\right]\frac{\partial f}{\partial x} + \frac{1}{n} xy \frac{\partial^2 f}{\partial x^2} \\ &\quad + \frac{k_\sigma}{2}\left[-x + d\frac{n + 4k_\sigma}{n} y\right]\frac{\partial f}{\partial y} + \frac{k_\sigma^2 d}{2n} y^2 \frac{\partial^2 f}{\partial y^2} \end{aligned} \quad (18)$$

These full dynamics appear to not be analytically tractable[4], but the differential equation can be numerically simulated, which shows qualitatively that there is a transient phase where x may grow, and after the ratio $r_t = x/y$ stabilizes the densities converge exponentially to a δ-function above the origin.

In the next subsections, we attempt to formally characterize these dynamical properties. First, we study the exponential convergence after the transient adaptation of r_t has taken place (section 4.1). Second, we look at infinite population sizes (i.e., noise-free dynamics as in section 3.4, but now for the continuous case), which is a proxy for characterizing the dynamics of the mean of the distribution, in section 4.2.

4.1 Geometric Brownian motion

In the discrete (noisy) case, there is no analytical solution for r_* (the fixed point of r_t)[5], but here, with continuous dynamics, we can identify it:

$$\begin{aligned} \frac{\Delta^2}{\sigma_t^2} &= \frac{\Delta^2 + d\Delta^2}{\sigma_t^2 + d\sigma_t^2} \\ \Leftrightarrow \frac{\Delta^2}{\sigma_t^2} &= \frac{\Delta^2 - k_\mu \Delta^2 dt}{\sigma_t^2 + \frac{k_\sigma}{2}(-\sigma_t^2 d + \Delta^2)\, dt} \\ \Leftrightarrow \frac{k_\sigma}{2}(-\sigma_t^2 d + \Delta^2)\, dt &= -k_\mu \sigma_t^2 dt \\ \Leftrightarrow \frac{\Delta^2}{\sigma_t^2} &= d - \frac{2k_\mu}{k_\sigma} \equiv r_* \end{aligned} \quad (19)$$

which is stable, but exists only if $k_\sigma > \frac{2}{d}k_\mu$. Under this condition, we call the *transient* phase the early part of the run until r_t has (approximately) converged to this fixed point[6].

If the adaptation of r_t is transient, then there is a time τ such that $\forall t \geq \tau$, $r_t \approx r_*$. We can study the asymptotic dynamics by just considering the updates of σ_t^2, because $\Delta_t^2 \approx r_* \sigma_t^2$, simply. The system of stochastic differential equations 17 becomes a single equation

$$d\sigma_t^2 \approx -k_\sigma \frac{d - r_*}{2}\sigma_t^2 dt + k_\sigma \sqrt{\frac{d}{2n}}\sigma_t^2 dW \quad (20)$$

This has the well-known form of a *geometric Brownian motion*, which is known to converge linearly to zero in expectation, if the drift term is negative (which is always true, because $r_* < d$ is guaranteed by equation 19). Thus, following [10] and replacing the value of r_*, we have

$$\sigma_{\tau+t}^2 = \sigma_\tau^2 \exp\left[-\left(k_\mu + \frac{k_\sigma^2 d}{4n}\right)t + k_\sigma \sqrt{\frac{d}{2n}} dW\right]$$

and

$$\begin{aligned} \mathbb{E}(\sigma_{t+\tau}^2) &= \sigma_\tau^2 \exp(-k_\mu t) \\ \mathbb{V}\text{ar}(\sigma_{t+\tau}^2) &= \sigma_\tau^4 \exp(-k_\mu t)\left[\exp\left(\frac{k_\sigma^2 d}{2n}t\right) - 1\right] \\ &< \sigma_\tau^4 \exp\left[\left(-k_\mu + \frac{k_\sigma^2 d}{2n}\right)t\right] \end{aligned}$$

Thus, we also have an exponential decrease in variance if

$$\begin{aligned} -k_\mu + \frac{k_\sigma^2 d}{2n} &< 0 \\ \Leftrightarrow k_\sigma &< \sqrt{\frac{2nk_\mu}{d}} \end{aligned} \quad (21)$$

which is in turn a guarantee that the density $p(x, y, t)$ will converge to a δ-peak above the origin.

4.2 Noise-free continuous dynamics

An alternative avenue to characterize convergence explicitly is taking $n \to \infty$, then the noise effects vanish, and from equation 16 we immediately obtain the expression of the exponential decay for Δ_t^2

$$\Delta_t^2 = \Delta_0^2 \exp(-k_\mu \cdot t) \quad (22)$$

which, when replacing in 17, gives the following inhomogeneous differential equation for σ_t^2:

$$\frac{d\sigma_t^2}{dt} = \frac{-k_\sigma d}{2}\sigma_t^2 + \frac{k_\sigma \Delta_0^2}{2}\exp(-k_\mu \cdot t)$$

[3]The eigenvalues can be identical, but the node remains asymptotically stable.

[4]A good candidate guess for p would be the two-dimensional Wishart distribution where the three scale parameters and the degrees-of-freedom parameter are a function of time. But our attempts at identifying the explicit form failed due to the last (y^2) term in equation 18.

[5]It always exists, because for $r_t \ll 1$, we have $\mathbb{E}[r_{t+1}] \gg 0$ while for $r_t \gg 1$, we have $\mathbb{E}[r_{t+1}] \ll 1$, so they must intersect.

[6]A possible heuristic for bypassing this transient phase, is to initialize the algorithm with $\sigma_0^2 \approx \hat{\Delta}_0^2/d$, if the user can provide a guess $\hat{\Delta}_0$ of the initial distance to the optimum.

Using the method of underdetermined coefficients, and assuming $\frac{k_\sigma d}{2} \neq k_\mu$, we guess at the form

$$\sigma_t^2 = C_1 \exp(-\frac{k_\sigma d}{2} t) + C_2 \exp(-k_\mu t)$$

Differentiating and identifying the coefficients, we find:

$$C_1 = \sigma_0^2 - C_2 \quad , \quad C_2 = \frac{k_\sigma \Delta_0^2}{k_\sigma d - 2k_\mu}$$

Otherwise, if $\frac{k_\sigma d}{2} = k_\mu$, we guess at the form

$$\sigma_t^2 = (C_3 + C_4 t) \exp(-k_\mu t)$$

and identify

$$C_3 = \sigma_0^2 \quad , \quad C_4 = \frac{k_\sigma \Delta_0^2}{2}$$

Clearly, Δ_t^2 converges to zero in $\mathcal{O}(e^{-k_\mu t})$. For the convergence of σ_t^2 we distinguish three cases: if $\frac{k_\sigma d}{2} > k_\mu$ then the convergence is in $\mathcal{O}(e^{-k_\mu t})$, if we have equality it is in $\mathcal{O}(t \cdot e^{-k_\mu t})$, otherwise it is in $\mathcal{O}(e^{-\frac{k_\sigma d}{2} t})$. The asymptotically best of these cases is when $\frac{k_\sigma d}{2} > k_\mu$, and for which we obtain the total convergence rate on the relevant quantity $\sigma_t^2 d + \Delta_t^2$ of $\mathcal{O}(e^{-k_\mu t})$. Explicitly:

$$\begin{aligned} \sigma_t^2 &= \sigma_0^2 \exp\left(-\frac{k_\sigma d}{2} t\right) \\ &\quad - \frac{k_\sigma \Delta_0^2}{k_\sigma d - 2k_\mu} \left(\exp\left(-\frac{k_\sigma d}{2} t\right) - \exp\left(-k_\mu t\right) \right) \quad (23) \end{aligned}$$

Note that this holds for all $t > 0$, unlike the strictly asymptotic characterization in section 3.4. We may see transient growth in σ_t^2, depending on the initial ratio $r_0 = \frac{\Delta_0^2}{\sigma_0^2}$, before the dominant term takes over, and the algorithm converges exponentially.

5. OMITTING THE NATURAL GRADIENT

It is not obvious at first sight that NES would perform qualitatively differently, were one to remove the natural gradient, as that would still optimize the right objective (equation 1). It is known [12] that this 'vanilla' version is not scale-invariant. With the tools introduced here, we can now characterize its contrasting convergence properties. The vanilla update equations are

$$\begin{aligned} \boldsymbol{\mu}_{t+1} &= \boldsymbol{\mu}_t + \frac{\eta_\mu}{\sigma_t} \sum_{i=1}^n u_i \mathbf{s}_i = \boldsymbol{\mu}_t + \frac{\eta_\mu}{n\sigma_t} \sum_{i=1}^n \mathbf{s}_i' \\ \sigma_{t+1} &= \sigma_t + \frac{\eta_\sigma}{2\sigma_t} \sum_{i=1}^n u_i (\|\mathbf{s}_i\|^2 - d) \\ &= \sigma_t - \frac{\eta_\sigma d}{2\sigma_t} + \frac{\eta_\sigma}{2n\sigma_t} \sum_{i=1}^n \|\mathbf{s}_i'\|^2 \end{aligned}$$

leading to the expectations

$$\begin{aligned} \mathbb{E}[\Delta_{t+1}^2] &= \frac{(2\sigma_t^2 - \eta_\mu)^2}{4\sigma_t^4} \Delta_t^2 + \frac{\eta_\mu^2 d}{2n\sigma_t^2} \quad (24) \\ \mathbb{E}[\sigma_{t+1}] &= \sigma_t - \frac{\eta_\sigma d}{4\sigma_t} + \frac{\eta_\sigma \Delta_t^2}{4\sigma_t^3} \end{aligned}$$

The fixed points are

$$\Delta_t^2 = \frac{2\eta_\mu d}{n(\eta_\mu + 4\sigma_t^2)} \sigma_t^2 \quad , \quad \sigma_t = \frac{\Delta_t}{\sqrt{d}}$$

which hold simultaneously if

$$\Delta_t^2 = \sigma_t^2 d \quad = \quad \frac{\eta_\mu d(n-2)}{4n}$$

As this equilibrium is not at the origin (as it is for NES), this implies that we need to choose

$$\eta_\mu < \frac{2n}{d\,(n-2)} \epsilon'^2$$

in order for the convergence condition from criterion 2 to hold eventually (at the equilibrium). This η_μ is an infinitesimal quantity for any ambitious ϵ', so equation 24 becomes

$$\mathbb{E}[\Delta_{t+1}^2] \quad \approx \quad \left(1 - \frac{\eta_\mu}{\sigma_t^2}\right) \Delta_t^2$$

which clearly shows that even if the algorithm converges (i.e., when noise effects are sufficiently attenuated with a large value of n), convergence must be very slow.

6. PARAMETER GUIDELINES

From the above results we can deduce guidelines for hyperparameter choices. Note that all of these, while useful, are to be taken with a grain of salt, because they result from the analysis of idealized scenarios, and not the exact algorithm.

- Section 5 justifies always using the natural gradient.
- Section 4.1 recommends the initialization $\sigma_0^2 \approx \frac{\hat{\Delta}_0^2}{d}$.
- Section 3.3 recommends setting $n > \frac{2d+6}{3d}$, where the larger n is, the closer the dynamics will be to those describes in section 3.4.
- Sections 4.1 and 4.2 recommend choosing $\frac{2}{d} < \eta_\sigma < \sqrt{\frac{2n}{d}}$, and section 3.4 showed that (at least if n is large) η_σ should be as large as possible[7].
- Section 3.4 recommends η_μ to be as large as possible with $\eta_\mu \leq 2 - 2\exp(-\frac{1}{4}\eta_\sigma d)$.

For example, given the often desirable choice of a minimal n, easy to remember learning rates (that satisfy the above) are $\eta_\sigma = \frac{2}{\sqrt{d}}$ and $\eta_\mu = 1$.

A common choice in previous work on NES [12] has been $n = 4 + \lfloor 3\log(d) \rfloor$, $\eta_\mu = 1$ and $\eta_\sigma = \frac{3+\log(d)}{5\sqrt{d}}$. These settings satisfy the constraint in equation 21 only for $d < 10^{63}$, but it is safe to say that includes all realistic cases.

7. DISCUSSION AND CONCLUSIONS

This paper has established a number of novel convergence results for natural evolution strategies. Using stability theory, we determined the parameter settings for which radial NES is guaranteed to converge on the sphere function.

For the most general case (section 3.3), we established a qualitative decomposition into three distinct regimes. For the limit case of large population sizes (section 3.4), we proved asymptotic linear convergence; for the orthogonal

[7]Note that in practice, choices of $\eta_\sigma < \frac{2}{d}$ often give robust empirical performance (especially on problems more difficult than sphere functions, see [8]), despite the absence of a distinct transient phase.

limit case of small learning rates (section 4.1), we determined the conditions for which both the mean and the variance of the diffusion converge linearly. Finally, combining both limit cases (section 4.2), we gave a full characterization of the dynamics, for both the transient and the asymptotic phases.

7.1 Generalizations

The performance on the sphere function generalizes to any function that is *strictly* monotonous in the distance to the optimum $f(\mathbf{z}) = g(\|\mathbf{z} - \mathbf{z}^*\|)$ (i.e., that has circular contour lines). The next milestone will be to determine whether convergence can be proven for general quadratic functions, or possibly even for all smooth convex functions.

All our results for the convergence or radial NES on sphere functions also carry over to *separable* multivariate Gaussian search distributions (SNES, [13]). This is because SNES can be seen as a collection of d independent radial NES algorithms that optimize parameters in each dimension separately; for each dimension, our convergence results hold separately, so they must hold for the composite case.

7.2 Future work

The presented may lend themselves to an extension for NES variants that adapt the full covariance matrix (e.g., xNES [8]), which must converge if none of the eigenvalues of the normalized covariance matrix vanish, (which holds trivially if $\eta_{\mathbf{B}} = 0$). Other interesting cases are non-Gaussian search distributions; here the full analysis will probably be limited to members of the exponential family (which admit conjugate priors).

A different direction is to develop improved algorithms using well-founded schemes for adapting the learning rates η_σ depending on the current regime (as in [7]), or time-dependent the population sizes n_t, based on the presented analysis.

Acknowledgments

I would like to thank Tobias Glasmachers for providing the motivation for this work, and Claudia Clopath for many helpful comments. I am also grateful to the anonymous reviewers for the careful proofreading.

This work was funded in part through AFR postdoc grant number 2915104, of the National Research Fund Luxembourg.

References

[1] S. I. Amari. Natural Gradient Works Efficiently in Learning. *Neural Computation*, 10:251–276, 1998.

[2] L. Arnold, A. Auger, N. Hansen, and Y. Ollivier. Information-Geometric Optimization Algorithms: A Unifying Picture via Invariance Principles. Technical report, June 2011.

[3] A. Auger. Convergence results for the (1,λ)-SA-ES using the theory of phi-irreducible Markov chains. *Theoretical Computer Science*, 334(1-3):35–69, 2005.

[4] A. Auger and N. Hansen. Theory of Evolution Strategies: a New Perspective. In A. Auger and B. Doerr, editors, *Theory of Randomized Search Heuristics: Foundations and Recent Developments*, chapter 10, pages 289–325. World Scientific Publishing, 2011.

[5] G. Cuccu, F. Gomez, and T. Glasmachers. Novelty-based restarts for evolution strategies. In *Evolutionary Computation (CEC), 2011 IEEE Congress on*, pages 158–163, 2011.

[6] S. Finck and H.-G. Beyer. Performance analysis of the simultaneous perturbation stochastic approximation algorithm on the noisy sphere model. *Theoretical computer science*, 419(C):50–72, Feb. 2012.

[7] N. Fukushima, Y. Nagata, S. Kobayashi, and I. Ono. Proposal of distance-weighted exponential natural evolution strategies. In *2011 IEEE Congress of Evolutionary Computation*, pages 164–171. IEEE, 2011.

[8] T. Glasmachers, T. Schaul, Y. Sun, D. Wierstra, and J. Schmidhuber. Exponential Natural Evolution Strategies. In *Genetic and Evolutionary Computation Conference (GECCO)*, Portland, OR, 2010.

[9] N. Hansen and A. Ostermeier. Completely derandomized self-adaptation in evolution strategies. *IEEE Transactions on Evolutionary Computation*, 9:159–195, 2001.

[10] N. Ikeda and S. Watanabe. Stochastic differential equations and diffusion processes. 1989.

[11] M. Sankaran. Approximations to the non-central chi-square distribution. *Biometrika*, 1963.

[12] T. Schaul. *Studies in Continuous Black-box Optimization*. Ph.D. thesis, Technische Universität München, 2011.

[13] T. Schaul, T. Glasmachers, and J. Schmidhuber. High Dimensions and Heavy Tails for Natural Evolution Strategies. In *Genetic and Evolutionary Computation Conference (GECCO)*, Dublin, Ireland, 2011.

[14] P. K. Sen. The Mean-Median-Mode Inequality and Noncentral Chi Square Distributions. *Sankhya: The Indian Journal of Statistics, Series A (1961-2002)*, 51 (1):pp. 106–114, 1989.

[15] O. Teytaud and S. Gelly. General lower bounds for evolutionary algorithms. *Parallel Problem Solving from Nature-PPSN IX*, 2006.

[16] D. Wierstra, T. Schaul, J. Peters, and J. Schmidhuber. Natural Evolution Strategies. In *Proceedings of the IEEE Congress on Evolutionary Computation (CEC)*, Hong Kong, China, 2008.

Towards a Population-Based Framework for Improving Stochastic Local Search Algorithms*

Ignacio Araya
Universidad Técnica Federico Santa María (UTFSM)
Av. España 1680, Valparaíso, Chile
iaraya@inf.utfsm.cl

Leslie Pérez
Université Libre de Bruxelles & UTFSM
50, Av. F. Roosevelt, CP 194/6
B-1050 Brussels, Belgium
leslie.perez.caceres@ulb.ac.be

María-Cristina Riff
Universidad Técnica Federico Santa María (UTFSM)
Av. España 1680, Valparaíso, Chile
mcriff@inf.utfsm.cl

ABSTRACT

Stochastic Local Search algorithms have already shown a good performance for solving large scale combinatorial optimization problems. In this paper, we introduce a method which goal is to help the search done by a Stochastic Local Search algorithm. Given a set of initial configurations, our algorithm dynamically discriminates the ones that seems to give more promising solutions, discarding at the same time those which did not help. The concept of diversity is managed in our framework in order to both avoid stagnation and to explore the search space. To evaluate our method, we use a well-known local search algorithm. This algorithm has been specially designed for solving instances of the challenging Traveling Tournament Problem. We compare the performance obtained running different configurations of the local search algorithm to the ones using our framework. Our results are very encouraging in terms of both the quality of the solutions and the execution time required.

Categories and Subject Descriptors

I.2.8 [**Problem Solving, Control Methods, and Search**]: Heuristic methods

General Terms

Algorithms

Keywords

Stochastic Local Search, Dynamic Search, Parameter Control, Traveling Tournament Problem

1. INTRODUCTION

Stochastic Local Search algorithms (SLS) can solve large scale combinatorial optimisation problems in an efficient way, [14]. However, as it is mentioned in [8] "Effective techniques for overcoming search stagnation are crucial components of high-performance SLS". In the same article the authors suggest that a way to prevent stagnation is to use multiple independent runs parallelisation. It allows the algorithm to explore different parts of the search space. SLS performance strongly depends on the initial executions conditions, as the initial candidate solution or the parameter values that control its components. Moreover, different random seeds will usually produce different searching path for the algorithm. Interesting works already exist for improving SLS. In [16] a hybrid randomised neighborhoods strategy has been proposed for DNA code design. This strategy enables the algorithm to explore regions of the search space that could not be reached by the underlying SLS algorithm. It includes three types of neighborhoods which are randomly used to avoid search stagnation. Their algorithm found word sets that are better than the best known constructions. Belov et al. [3] proposed a method for improving a SLS that solves SAT problems. Their method is based on the search history in order to dynamically modify the selection of the candidate variables, as well as to produce various modifications at one step of the search. Inc^* is an incremental approach proposed in [2]. It was evaluated for solving SAT instances. The algorithm constructs a chain of instances to be solved. In this framework the SLS begins by solving simplest instances, the solver continues solving instances without stopping it.

In this work we propose P-LS, a population-based approach for Stochastic Local Search algorithms. The key idea of our work is to generate a competition among different initial configurations of the local search algorithm. In our population-based approach, the members of the population are the same local search algorithm, but each of them uses different configurations. The main hypothesis of our work is that our approach will be able to find solutions with a better or the same quality in less time than the underlying local search method. Moreover, it is more efficient than to use multiple independent runs parallelisation in both quality of the solutions and CPU time. We compare P-LS to a set of quasi-parallel runs of the underlying local search method. The strategies are compared using instances of the Traveling Tournament Problem (TTP). To perform the local search, our approach uses a simple method proposed in [10] that obtains good solutions in a small amount of time. This paper is structured as follows: In section 2 we introduce our framework. A brief description of the TTP is presented in section 3. The local search method that solves instances of the TTP and its integration into the framework are de-

*Partially supported by Fondecyt Project 1120781

GECCO'12, July 7-11, 2012, Philadelphia, Pennsylvania, USA.

scribed in Section 4. Experimental results are shown and discussed in Section 5. Remarks about the related work are done in section 6. Finally, conclusions and future work are given in the last section.

2. POPULATION-BASED FRAMEWORK

In this section we describe P-LS (Population-based framework for Stochastic Local Search methods). The idea is mainly inspired by the PBSA algorithm proposed in [17]. Our approach uses an underlying local search method as a black-box. Individuals of the population represent runs of the local search method with different initial configurations. At each generation, a single individual is selected and executed by the local search during a very small amount of time. At the end of the execution, the final state of the run updates the individual state. This state will allow to continue the run at the same point where it was stopped. Copies with the states of the best runs (those runs that found the best solution) are stored into a memory structure (*retrieval* mechanism). Worst runs are removed from the population and replaced by ones from the memory (*injection* mechanism). The main objective of the retrieval and injection mechanisms are:

- to force the local search to compete according to the quality of the runs.
- to give more chances to promising to obtain better solutions.

To avoid that the runs converge to the same solution, special care is taken to maintain a diversity among the states in the memory.

Roughly speaking, the framework consists in a population of individuals that represent runs of the stochastic local search algorithm (SLS) with different initial configurations. Each individual is evaluated according to the quality of the candidate solution found. The framework also uses a memory where the best individuals (runs) from the population are saved, including both their current configuration and evaluation. This memory is used to filter the population in order to discard the runs that have shown a poor performance compared to the ones in memory. The poor performance runs are replaced by individuals from memory, given thus a new chance for searching to these members.

In the following subsections we explain the components of our framework.

2.1 Structures

2.1.1 Representation

An *individual* is a structure containing a valid state for a local search method, i.e., it contains all the required data to begin or resume a paused execution of the method. For instance, if the local search is performed by a simulated annealing, then the individual will contain at least the current solution and the current temperature value. An individual represents a *run* of the local search method. To continue a run, the local search takes the corresponding individual state and resume the search. When an execution is paused, the local search method updates the individual using its last reached state. Three methods must be implemented for the individual structure:

- The `fitness`(I) function indicates the quality of an individual. It can be computed, for example, by evaluating the quality of the best solution found by I.
- The `distance`(I_1, I_2) function quantitatively indicates, how much different is the individual I_1 from the individual I_2. It can be computed, for example, by using the Hamming distance between the corresponding current solutions.
- The `generate_new_individual` method that is used to generate new individuals, e.g., for the simulated annealing this method should create an individual including an initial solution for the specific problem and the initial temperature.

2.1.2 Population and Memory

The population (**P**) corresponds to a set of individuals that are constantly modified by the local search method in order to improve them. The memory (**M**) corresponds to a set of high quality individuals that are used replace worst ones in **P**. The population, as well as the memory, has a fixed size. Thus, each time that a new individual is added into the population (or into the memory), another one must be removed from it. Algorithm 1 shows the basic structure of the framework. In this case the individuals of the population are copied from **P** using the round-robin selection method. Best individuals are copied first.

Algorithm 1 P-LS(**in:** τ, n, m; **in-out:** **P**, **M**)

```
P ← generate_population(n)
M ← generate_memory(P,m)
repeat
  I ← select_individual(P)
  local_search_method(I, max_iter|max_time)
  retrieval(copy(I), M, τ)
  injection(M, P)
until termination_criterion
```

Until the termination criterion is reached, the following process is repeated. An individual I is selected from **P** (randomly). Then, the local search method uses I to continue the search. After *max_iter* iterations the search is *paused* and the current configuration of the individual I is saved. Then the `retrieval` and `injection` methods are called. Retrieval procedure selects individuals from the population to be included into memory. The individual is added only if it is good enough. The `injection` operation consists in replacing all the individuals from the population that are worse than the worst one from the memory. In the following section we give the details about the retrieval and injection methods.

2.2 Population and Memory Management

2.2.1 Retrieval

The `retrieval` method (algorithm 2) selects individuals from the population and puts them into the memory. The procedure is focused on:

- Identifying the best candidates, according to the quality of the solution found, to be included into memory.
- Selecting the candidates that are quite different of those currently in memory

The method attempts to retrieve good individuals such that they keep enough memory diversity. The notion of memory diversity is inspired from the work presented in [13] for immune algorithms. The symbol $\rhd$ indicates a *better than* comparison. The method first verifies if the individual I is better than the worst one in the memory (otherwise no retrieval is done: I is not good enough). Then, the method finds the individual I_c closest to I in the memory. When the distance between I_c and I is greater than τ (a user-defined threshold), we consider that I is far from I_c, then I is far from any individual in the memory. In this case, I replaces I_w, the worst individual in the memory. Otherwise, I_c is replaced by I if and only if I is better than I_c.

Algorithm 2 `retrieval`(**in:** I, τ; **in-out:** $\mathbf{M}$)

```
I_w ← worst_individual(M)
if fitness(I) ▷ fitness(I_w) then
  /* gets the memory individual closest to I */
  I_c ← arg min_{I_m ∈ M} distance(I, I_m)
  if distance(I, I_c) ≥ τ then
    /* all the memory individuals are far from I */
    replace(I → I_w, M)
  else
    /* I and I_c are close to each other */
    if fitness(I) ▷ fitness(I_c) then
      replace(I → I_c, M)
    end if
  end if
end if
```

Each individual I in memory has also associated a parameter called *age*. It is set to 0 the first time that the individual I is inserted into the memory. The age value is modified by the injection procedure.

2.2.2 Injection

The injection procedure modifies the members of the population. The idea is to have at each iteration a population with individuals with a fitness better or equal than the worst individuals in memory. It is a procedure that eliminates individuals from the population and replaces them by some members from the memory. Algorithm 3 details the `injection` procedure. The symbol $\rhd$ indicates *better than*. The age indicates the number of times that the individual has been injected from the memory into the propulation. The key idea of this parameter is to prevent too much copies of the same individual into the population. When two individuals from the memory have the same evaluation, the method will prefer to inject the youngest one into the population. The age of an individual is incremented each time it is injected into the population. The procedure replaces worst individuals in the population by the youngest ones currently in memory. Worst individuals are those which have a worse fitness than the worst individual from the memory (I_w). When there are two individual in the memory with the same age, the youngest method returns the one with the best fitness. The individuals are alternately injected from the memory (similar as a round-robin selection).

Consider, for example, a maximization problem and a population of size 5 ($I_1, ..., I_5$) and fitness 10, 6, 6, 5 and 2 respectively. Also consider a memory of the same size ($Im_1, ..., Im_5$), fitness 12, 11, 9, 7, 6 and ages 2, 1, 0, 2 and 1 respectively. The injection procedure will eliminate the individuals with a fitness lower than 6 (the worst in the memory). First, I_4 is eliminated ($\texttt{fitness}(I_4) = 5$) and replaced by the youngest memory individual, i.e., Im_3. The age of Im_3 is increased to 1. Then, I_5 is eliminated ($\texttt{fitness}(I_5) = 2$) and replaced by the current youngest memory individual. There are 3 candidates now: Im_2, Im_3 and Im_5. The algorithm selects the best, i.e., Im_2, which increases its age to 2.

Algorithm 3 `injection`(**in:** $\mathbf{M}$; **in-out:** $\mathbf{P}$)

```
I_w ← worst(M)
for all I ∈ P do
  if Fitness(I) ▷ Fitness(I_w) then
    I_m ← youngest(M)
    replace(P, s → copy(I_m))
    SetAge(I_m, Age(I_m) + 1)
  end if
end for
```

3. TRAVELING TOURNAMENT PROBLEMS

The Traveling Tournament Problem (TTP) was introduced by Easton et al. [7]. It has been treated by numerous heuristics-based approaches, such as simulated annealing [9], hybrid algorithms [18], genetic algorithms [5], population-based simulated annealing [17], hyperheuristics [10], ant colony-based approaches [4] and artificial immune algorithms [11] among others. An input for the TTP consists in t teams (t even) and a $t \times t$ symmetric matrix d, such that d_{ij} represents the distance between the homes of teams T_i and T_j. A solution is a schedule in which each team plays with each other twice, once in each team's home. It is trivial that such tournament has $2t-2$ rounds. For a given solution S, the cost of a team is the total distance that it has to travel starting from home, playing the scheduled games, and returning back home. The objective is to find a solution with a minimum cost satisfying two different constraints: (c_1) a team cannot play more than three consecutive games at home (or away) and (c_2) a game of T_i at T_j's home cannot be followed by a game of T_j at T_i's home.

3.1 Relaxed Travel Tournament Problems

The Relaxed TTP (RTTP) is a variant of the Traveling Tournament Problem and it was proposed by Renjun Bao and Michael Trick [15]. In this variant, the schedule is not compact: teams have byes in their schedule. A parameter K indicates the number of byes per team. $K = 0$ corresponds to the classical TTP.

4. THE LOCAL SEARCH METHOD

`ILTA` (Iteration Limited Threshold Accepting-based local search) was proposed by Misir et al. [10]. We selected this method because of its simplicity. It has just two parameters (k and R) and it is able to obtain high-quality solutions for the TTP.

4.1 ILTA for solving TTP

A solution is represented by a matrix indicating the opponents of the teams. Each line corresponds to a team and each column corresponds to a round. The opponent of team T_i at round r is given by the absolute value of element (T_i,r).

If (T_i, r) is positive, the game takes place at T_i's home, otherwise at its opponent home. Consider for instance the solution S_1 for 4 teams (and thus 6 rounds):

T/R	1	2	3	4	5	6
T_1	2	3	4	-2	-3	-4
T_2	-1	-4	-3	1	4	3
T_3	-4	-1	2	4	1	-2
T_4	3	2	-1	-3	-2	1

S_1 specifies, for instance, that T_4 successively plays against team T_3 at home, T_2 at home, T_1 away, etc. The traveling cost of team T_4 is thus $d_{41} + d_{13} + d_{32} + d_{24}$.

Neighbourhood

The neighbourhood of a solution is defined as the set of solutions which can be obtained by applying one of five types of moves. These moves are well-known and has been extensively applied to the TTPs (specific details about the moves may be found in [1]):

- SwapHomes: Swap home/away games between teams T_i and T_j.
- SwapTeams: Swap the schedule of teams T_i and T_j.
- SwapRounds: Swap two rounds by exchanging the assigned matches to the round $r1$ with round $r2$.
- PartialSwapTeams: Swap matches of T_i and T_j for a given round r.
- PartialSwapRounds: Swap matches of a team t in rounds $r1$ and $r2$.

The moves may create infeasible solutions. To lead with them, the constraint violations are managed using penalties in the cost function.

The cost function

The cost of a solution is the sum of the traveling costs for all the teams, plus a penalty multiplied by $\texttt{vc}(S)$, the number of violated constraints :

$$\texttt{cost}(S) = \sum_{i=1}^{t} \texttt{traveling\_cost}(T_i) + M.\texttt{vc}(S)$$

where M is a big number. Using this function the algorithm is able to discriminate between feasible and unfeasible solutions.

Algorithm 4 shows the basic structure of the method. It attempts to improve a current solution S by applying few changes using the **random_neighbor** method. In our case, this method selects, at random, one of the five moves defining the neighborhood of S. When a new solution S_{new} improves or maintains the quality of the solution S then S_{new} replaces S. Otherwise, a counter of unsuccessful attempts is increased by 1 (*w_iterations*). When the number of unsuccessful attempts is greater than a user-defined parameter k, a new acceptance criterion is considered: changes that decrease the quality of S are accepted if they are good enough, i.e., if $\texttt{cost}(S_{new}) < R.\texttt{cost}(S_{best})$. $R \geq 1$ is a user-defined parameter and S_{best} is the best solution already found by the local search.

Algorithm 4 $\texttt{ILTA}_{k,R}$**(in:** I, *max_iter*)

```
S ← current_solution(I)
S_best ← best_solution(I)
for all i = 1..max_iter do
  S_new ← random_neighbor(S)
  if cost(S_new) < cost(S) then
    S ← S_new
    w_iterations ← 0
    if cost(S_new) < cost(S_best) then
      S_best ← S_new
      break /*premature termination*/
    end if
  else if cost(S_new) = cost(S) then
    S ← S_new
  else if w_iterations ≥ k and cost(S_new) <
  R.cost(S_best) then
    S ← S_new
    w_iterations ← 0
  else
    w_iterations ← w_iterations + 1
  end if
end for
set_current_solution(I, S)
set_best_solution(I, S_best)
```

4.2 ILTA for solving RTTP

The representation of a RTTP solution is almost the same as for a TTP solution. We use the same matrix indicating the opponents of the teams, however in this case the number of rounds is $2t - 2 + K$. In our representation, byes are denoted by a 0 in the corresponding element of the matrix. For instance, if the team T_i has a bye at round r, then the element (T_i, r) is equal to 0. The *neighborhood* is defined by 6 moves. The same 5 moves used in the TTP and one move involving the byes (SwapByes). The new move, proposed in [11], searches two teams having byes in the same round, then, one of the two matches in the schedule, that involves these two teams, is moved to this round. The *cost function* is the same. Byes are not considered in this computation.

4.3 Integrating the local search into P-LS

To integrate **ILTA** into the **P-LS** framework, we need to define the individual structure and its associated methods: the fitness function, the distance measure and the procedure to generate a new individual. An individual for the **ILTA** is composed of two elements: the current solution and the best solution. Note that at the beginning of Algorithm 4 both elements of the individual I are equally setted. At the end, these elements are modified and the individual I is updated.

fitness

The **fitness** method returns the fitness of an individual. In the case of the **ILTA**, the fitness is the cost function of the best solution already found by the individual. Thus,

$$\texttt{fitness}(I) = -\texttt{cost}(\texttt{best\_solution}(I))$$

Note that the same function can be used if other local search techniques, such as simulated annealing or tabu search, are considered. More sophisticated fitness functions can be defined. For instance, we could include a penalty related to the time spent by an individual without improving its best solution found or the distance between the current and best solutions.

The following `distance` and `generate_new_individual` methods depend on the specific problem (the TTP in our case).

distance(I_1, I_2)

To compute the distance between two individuals we compute a Hamming distance-based function between the best solutions related to each of them. The *Hamming distance* between two solutions computes the number of positions at which their corresponding matrix are different. Consider for instance the solutions S_1 (up) and S_2 (down):

T/R	1	2	3	4	5	6
T_1	2	3	4	-2	-3	-4
T_2	-1	-4	-3	1	4	3
T_3	-4	-1	2	4	1	-2
T_4	3	2	-1	-3	-2	1

T/R	1	2	3	4	5	6
T_1	2	-4	3	-1	-3	4
T_2	-1	3	-4	2	4	-3
T_3	-4	-2	-1	4	1	2
T_4	3	1	2	-3	-2	-1

The Hamming distance between S_1 and S_2 is 14 . If we divide the distance by the size of the matrix $t.(2\,t-2) = 24$, then we obtain a normalized Hamming distance belonging to the interval $[0, 1]$: `norm_hamming`(S_1, S_2)$=\frac{14}{24} = 0.583$. We use this function to compute the distance of two individuals in the `P-LS` framework, i.e.,
`distance`(I_1, I_2) =
`norm_hamming`(`best_solution`(I_1), `best_solution`(I_2))

generate_new_individual()

The well-known *polygon method* [6] is used to build initial solutions for the TTP. This method generates a simple round robin schedule, that is, a tournament in which the teams play with each other once (for details see [12]). The second half of the tournament is generated replicating the first half of it. Finally, home and away matches are randomly assigned, taking into account that for all matches one team is at home and the other is away and a team plays once at home and once away with each other team. To generate initial solutions for solving RTTP, a solution for the TTP is generated first. Then, K columns (rounds) of 0s (byes) are added at the end of the TTP solution matrix. The `generate_new_individual` method, used by the `P-LS` framework, generates an individual with two elements: the *current solution*, initialized using the polygon-based method; and the *best solution*, which is a copy of the current solution.

5. EXPERIMENTS

This section describes the experimental results to evaluate our approach. All experiments were carried out on Pentium Quad 2.66 GHz with 4 GB memory. The codes were implemented in the C++ library. The TTP benchmarks that we used were derived from the US National League Baseball (NL instances) and the Super 14 Rugby League (Super instances). They can be found at the website `http://mat.gsia.cmu.edu/TOURN/`. We only used instances involving 10 teams or more. For the *ILTA* algorithm we used the same parameter values proposed by Misir et al. [10], i.e., $k = 100$ for all the instances and the value of R was set to 1.04, 1.02, 1.02, 1.01, 1.02, 1.015 and 1.01 for the instances NL10, NL12, NL14, NL16, Super10, Super12 and Super14 respectively. The stop criteria for the `P-LS` is a maximum number of iterations performed inside the `ILTA` procedure. For the TTP instances this limit is fixed to $5*10^8$ iterations. We used an iteration limit criteria because of allows us to always obtain, for a given strategy and random seed, the same results. Finally, we set the parameter *max_iter* to 10000. This parameter indicates the number of iterations performed by each run of the `ILTA` procedure. Using this value the algorithm controls the number of times that the injection and retrieval procedures are called. *max_iter* = 10000 is a good value because it does not imply overheads and it corresponds to a small fraction of the total number of iterations performed by the framework.
In this case P-LS requires less than 0.05% of the time used by ILTA. In all the experiments, the following three strategies were used:

- `ILTA x n`: An implementation of the framework without the retrieval and injection procedures. This variant can be seen as n *quasi-parallel* runs of the underlying local search method (`ILTA` in our case) returning the best found solution among all the runs.
- `P-LS`: The basic implementation of the framework.
- `P-LS+`: In this version, each time an individual improves its fitness, P-LS+ stops the local search procedure, updates both the memory and the population. In the next iteration, it restarts SLS using the same individual.

REMARK 5.1. *The idea of P-LS+ is to test if the algorithm convergence can be improved when the search is strongly focused on quickly obtaining better solutions.*

5.1 Solving the TTP

Plots of Figures 1 show the boxplots of the results obtained in each NL instance by ILTA and PL-S using different values for τ. Each strategy was run 10 times. Each run was restricted to $5*10^8$ iterations of the `ILTA` method.

The average performance of `P-LS+` outperforms the other two strategies when it works with $\tau = 0.5$. Thus, we note that the diversity plays an important rôle for improving the search of the algorithm. Figure 2 shows that the two strategies, using the injection and retrieval procedures, improve the results obtained by `ILTA x n`. Moreover, in some cases, the quality of the solution found by `P-LS+` is not reached by `ILTA x n` before several times the number of iterations (up tp 10 in some cases). In the first iterations ($< 5*10^6$), `P-LS+` shows to be much better than the other strategies. For larger number of iterations however, its performance is similar to `P-LS`. It is because of `P-LS+` exploits *promising* individuals (those improving their fitness). Fitness improvements are produced the most in the first iterations of the search. Thus, in further iterations, when fitness improvements does not occur frequently, `P-LS+` behaves similar to `P-LS`. The plots in figure 2 show the evolution over the iterations of the average of the relative costs. The relative cost corresponds to the cost of the best solution found by the strategy, in the given number of iterations, divided by

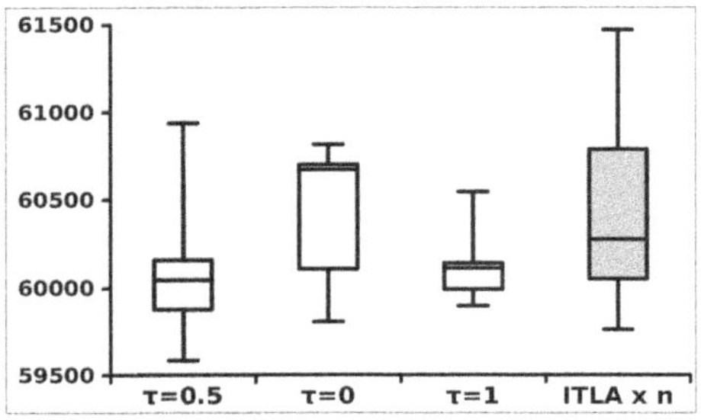

(a) $NL10$

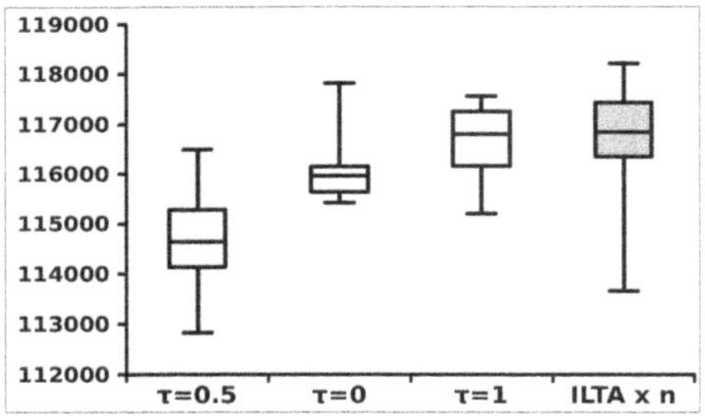

(b) $NL12$

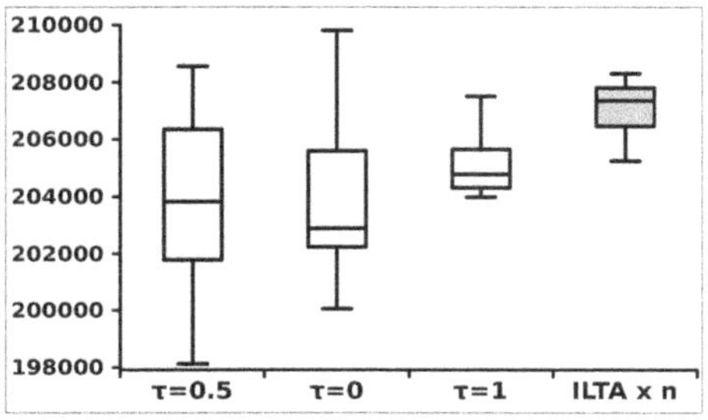

(c) $NL14$

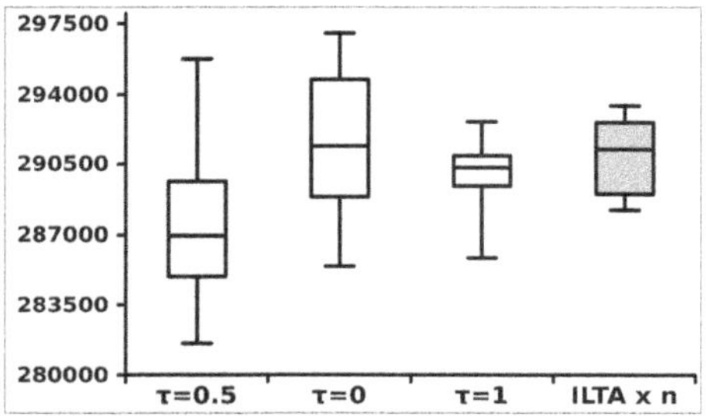

(d) $NL16$

Figure 1: Boxplots costs for NL instances with PL-S using different τ values and ILTA

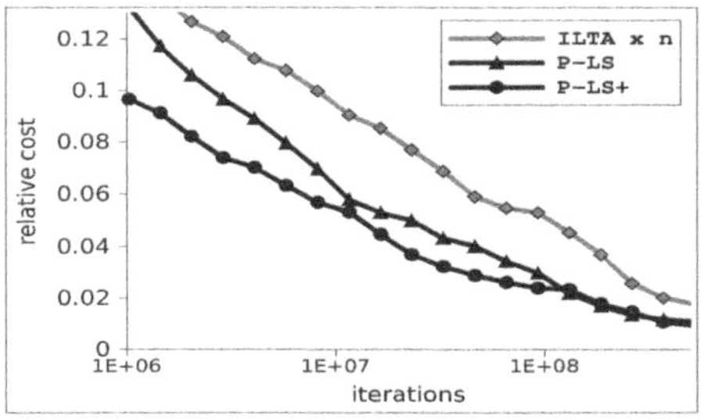

(a) $NL10$

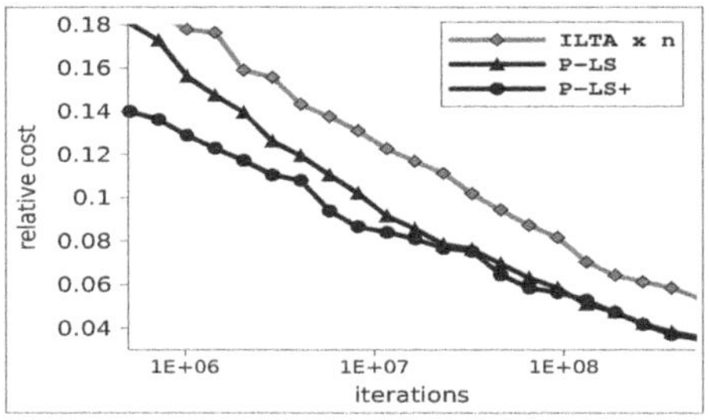

(b) $NL12$

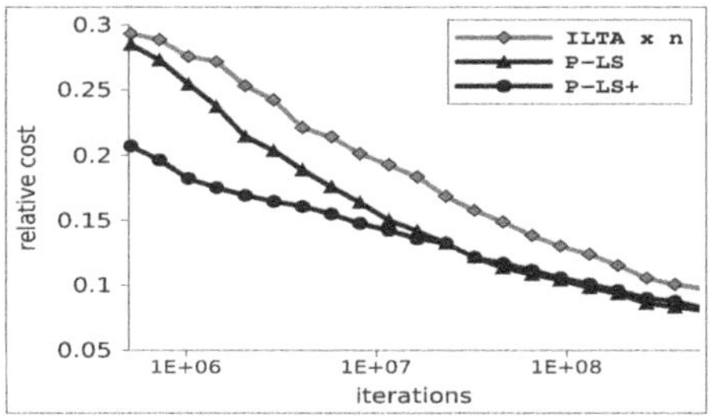

(c) $NL14$

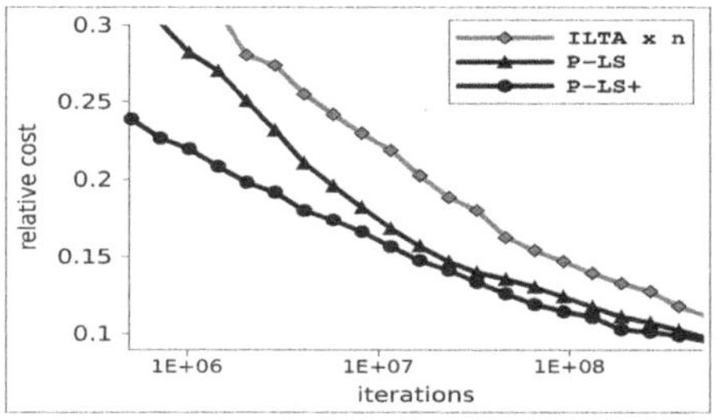

(d) $NL16$

Figure 2: Convergence of the relative cost for NL instances ($n = m = 50$).

the best already known solution. Note that the relative cost axis follows a logarithmic scale.

Finally, note that the performance of `ILTA x n` is comparable to the other strategies' performance only for a large number of iterations. We conclude that `P-LS` and `P-LS+` improve the convergence velocity of `ILTA x n`.

Comparison with the best known solutions

Compared to other approaches, the results provided in this paper were produced using small execution times. Table 1 shows a comparison of the best solution found by our algorithm strategies with respect to the best known solution for each instance of the benchmarks. The best known results for the NL instances were obtained by PBSA [17] (briefly described in the introduction section). The comparison is not fair enough, mainly because `P-LS` uses a much more simpler underlying method than PBSA. The best known solution for the Super instances were found by Langford [9]. He uses a variant of the TTSA algorithm and a sophisticated variant of the PartialSwapTeams move.

Table 2 reports the results obtained by the analysis-of-variances (ANOVA) in order to compare the results obtained by the three strategies.Only the case $K = 0$ was considered. The iteration limit was set to 10^8 iterations. Each strategy was run 30 times on each instance.Results show that there

Instance	ILTA x n	P-LS	P-LS+	Best known
NL10	59762	**59583**	**59583**	59436
NL12	113663	**112827**	113514	110729
NL14	205237	198115	**195256**	188728
NL16	287879	**281904**	283701	261687
Super10	319642	318595	**318258**	316329
Super12	468259	469205	**464640**	463876
Super14	603006	595864	**591649**	571632

Table 1: Comparison between the best solutions obtained by our population-based approaches and the best known solutions

Instance	NL10	NL12	NL14	NL16	Super10	Super12	Super14
F(2,87)	108.28	77.45	51.28	108.46	4.62	17.29	14.89
p	0.000	0.000	0.000	0.000	0.012	0.000	0.000

Table 2: Results provided by ANOVA. The difference between the algorithms is significant at the $p < .05$ level.

exist significant differences between the mean fitness reached by the strategies at the $p < .05$ level.

5.2 Solving the RTTP

Table 3 summarizes the results obtained by the studied strategies using $n = m = 10$. All the other values for the parameters were set equal to the TTP. The stop criteria is given by a limit in the total number of iterations inside the ILTA procedure and it is equal to 10^8.

Each cell in the table shows two values. The median of the costs for the best found solutions (above) and the *interquartile range* of these costs (below) for the given strategy and instance. The interquartile range is a well-known measure of statistical dispersion. It is equal to the difference between the upper and lower quartiles. Also the best known solution is indicated for each instance and K value. When it is the case, we include in parentheses a new best solution found by our indicated strategy. For example in the instance NL10 with $K = 1$ we found a new best solution ($cost = 58505$) by using the P-LS approach. The results are similar to those in the TTP. The median costs obtained by P-LS+ are almost always less than the median costs obtained by P-LS. Furthermore, in all the cases, the median costs obtained by P-LS+ and P-LS are less than the median costs obtained by ILTA x n. We also report in table 4 the average CPU time, in seconds, spent by the strategies for each instance size. The times are quite similar among the strategies, thus the use of our rejection/injection methods does not imply a high overhead. An iteration to solve relaxed instances uses more CPU time than a normal instance, because of the number of columns in the representation matrix is increased in K.

6. COMPARISON WITH EXISTING WORK

Population Based Simulated Annealing (PBSA), [17] has been proposed to solve instances of the TTP. It uses an underlying simulated annealing method (TTSA [1]) as a blackbox. The approach consists in a population-based simulated annealing which performs series of waves, each consisting in N parallel executions of the TTSA during a time t. The first series of executions simply executes TTSA(S,T), N times, where S is an initial solution and T the initial temperature. At the end of a wave, the runs producing the k best solutions so far continue their executions. The $N - k$ remaining runs are restarted from the best solution found at temperature T. All this process is into a loop that progressively decreases the initial temperature T. Compared to PBSA, several differences should be noted: to deal with diversity, P-LS maintains a diversified memory structure, while PBSA maintains a subset of k elite individuals continuously running. The worst individuals in PBSA are those that do not belong to the elite. They are only removed between two waves (N executions of the local search during a time t). In P-LS the individual quality is dynamically evaluated and depends on the memory quality: worse individuals are those having worse quality than the worst individual in the memory. Moreover, the memory is updated after each execution of the local search. Finally, all the worse individuals in PBSA are replaced by the best one. In our approach, worse individuals are replaced by individuals in memory respecting diversity.

strategy, inst.	$5 * 10^8$ it.	10^8 it. ($K = 1$)	10^8 it. ($K = 2$)	10^8 it. ($K = 3$)
P-LS, NL10	3340	705	721	730
P-LS+, NL10	3345	699	717	734
ILTA, NL10	3337	697	717	730
P-LS, NL12	4990	1020	1041	1070
P-LS+, NL12	4999	1021	1040	1067
ILTA, NL12	5001	1022	1037	1071
P-LS, NL14	6817	1351	1418	1460
P-LS+, NL14	6805	1350	1412	1465
ILTA, NL14	6812	1349	1406	1461
P-LS, NL16	8904	1808	1905	1995
P-LS+, NL16	8900	1805	1907	2001
ILTA, NL16	8901	1799	1906	2000
P-LS, Super10	3342	698	721	730
P-LS+, Super10	3345	700	715	740
ILTA, Super10	3340	700	712	738
P-LS, Super12	4992	1027	1041	1067
P-LS+, Super12	4999	1025	1031	1061
ILTA, Super12	5001	1022	1044	1060
P-LS, Super14	6817	1342	1419	1465
P-LS+, Super14	6805	1350	1421	1460
ILTA, Super14	6812	1355	1418	1455

Table 4: CPU time spent by the strategies for the different sizes of the instance problems.

7. CONCLUSIONS

In this paper we introduced a population-based framework to control the execution of a set of runs of an underlying local search method. It gives more chances to initial configurations that obtain promising solutions. It also dynamically discards configurations that show a poor performance. Memory diversity is a key concept of our framework. P-LS outperforms the convergence velocity of the underlying method when it is applied to the TTP and RTTP instances. This observation is clearly shown by most of the performed experiments. Applied to the RTTP problem, the approach also improves ILTA. Furthermore, we found new upper bounds in 5 instances for this problem: NL10 with $K = 1, 2, 3$ and NL12 with $K = 2, 3$.

Our approach can be applied to any local search method

	K=1			K=2			K=3		
Inst.	ILTAn	P-LS	P-LS+	ILTAn	P-LS	P-LS+	ILTAn	P-LS	P-LS+
NL10	60909 587	59168 602	59059 342	59806 611	59416 1030	58708 670	59840 450	59668 386	59321 307
Best known	59425 (**58505**, P-LS)			59373 (**58505**, P-LS)			59373 (**58505**, P-LS)		
NL12	116702 1119	114837 678	114782 773	115015 1255	112805 793	113016 1723	114024 399	112971 760	112476 971
Best known	110729			110729 (**110338**, P-LS+)			110729(**110338**, P-LS+)		
NL14	205681 2021	204180 4479	203431 3572	202972 1026	201289 1125	199088 2301	200801 1111	199915 469	198183 1353
Best known	188728			188728			188728		
NL16	288039 1951	285402 4070	284273 2779	281654 1333	278390 2012	277861 1251	277437 2027	274610 4574	271317 2504
Best known	261687			261687			261687		

Table 3: Results of the strategies for the NL instances with 3 different values for K.

with a small amount of additional work. For a future work, we intend to add a control mechanism to change the underlying method's parameter values as the search goes on. The basic idea consists in generating a performance predictor function $f(p)$ for any given parametrization p of the underlying method, that could be updated by using information of the current runs.

8. REFERENCES

[1] A. Anagnostopoulos, L. Michel, P. Van Hentenryck, and Y. Vergados. A simulated annealing approach to the traveling tournament problem. *Journal of Scheduling*, 9(2):177–193, 2006.

[2] M. Bader-El-Den and R. Poli. Inc*: an incremental approach for improving local search heuristics. In *Proceedings of the 8th European conference on Evolutionary computation in combinatorial optimization*, pages 194–205. Springer-Verlag, 2008.

[3] A. Belov and Z. Stachniak. Improving variable selection process in stochastic local search for propositional satisfiability. In *Proceedings of the 12th International Conference on Theory and Applications of Satisfiability Testing*, pages 258–264. Springer-Verlag, 2009.

[4] P. Chen, G. Kendall, and G. Berghe. An ant based hyper-heuristic for the travelling tournament problem. In *Computational Intelligence in Scheduling SCIS'07. IEEE Symposium on*, pages 19–26. IEEE, 2007.

[5] N. Choubey. A Novel Encoding Scheme for Traveling Tournament Problem using Genetic Algorithm. *International Journal of Computer Applications IJCA*, (2):1–7, 2010.

[6] J. Dinitz, E. Lamken, and W. Wallis. Scheduling a tournament. In *C.J. Colbourn, J. Dinitz (Eds.), Handbook of Combinatorial Designs, CRC Press*, pages 578–584, 1995.

[7] K. Easton, G. Nemhauser, and M. Trick. The traveling tournament problem description and benchmarks. In *CPâĂŹ99*, pages 580–589, Paphos, Cyprus, 2001. Springer-Verlag, LNCS 2239.

[8] H. H. Hoos and T. Stützle. *Stochastic Local Search : Foundations & Applications (The Morgan Kaufmann Series in Artificial Intelligence)*. Morgan Kaufmann, 2004.

[9] G. Langford. An Improved Neighbourhood for the Traveling Tournament Problem. *arXiv:1007.0501v1*, 2010.

[10] M. Misir, T. Wauters, K. Verbeeck, and G. Berghe. A new learning hyper-heuristic for the traveling tournament problem. In *Proceedings Of The VIII Metaheuristics International Conference*, 2009.

[11] L. Pérez and M. Riff. New bounds for the Relaxed Traveling Tournament Problems using an artificial immune algorithm. In *Evolutionary Computation (CEC), 2011 IEEE Congress on*, pages 873–879. IEEE, 2011.

[12] C. Ribeiro and S. Urrutia. Heuristics for the mirrored traveling tournament problem. *European Journal of Operational Research*, 179(3):775–787, 2007.

[13] M.-C. Riff and E. Montero. Managing diversity on an ais that solves 3-colouring problems. In *ICARIS, Lecture Notes in Computer Sciences*, pages 248–259. Springer-Verlag, 2009.

[14] T. Stützle, M. Birattari, and H. H. Hoos, editors. *Engineering Stochastic Local Search Algorithms. Designing, Implementing and Analyzing Effective Heuristics, 2nd. International Workshop, Belgium*, volume 5752 of *Lecture Notes in Computer Science*. Springer, 2009.

[15] M. Trick and R. Bao. Challenge Traveling Tournament Instances (Relaxed). `http://mat.gsia.cmu.edu/TOURN/relaxed/`.

[16] D. C. Tulpan and H. H. Hoos. Hybrid randomised neighbourhoods improve stochastic local search for dna code design. In *Proceedings of the 16th Canadian society for computational studies of intelligence conference on Advances in artificial intelligence*, AI'03, pages 418–433, Berlin, Heidelberg, 2003. Springer-Verlag.

[17] P. Van Hentenryck and Y. Vergados. Population-based simulated annealing for traveling tournaments. In *AAAI 2007*, pages 269–283, 2007.

[18] W. Wei, S. Fujimura, X. Wei, and C. Ding. A hybrid local search approach in solving the Mirrored Traveling Tournament Problem. In *Industrial Engineering and Engineering Management (IE&EM), IEEE 17Th International Conference on*, pages 620–624. IEEE, 2010.

From Neighbors to Global Neighbors in Collaborative Filtering: an Evolutionary Optimization Approach

Amine Boumaza
Univ. Lille Nord de France, F-59000 Lille, France,
ULCO, LISIC, F-62100 Calais, France
boumaza@lisic.univ-littoral.fr

Armelle Brun
LORIA - Université de Lorraine
Campus Scientifique
54506 Vandœuvre les Nancy, France
brun@loria.fr

ABSTRACT

The accuracy of recommendations of collaborative filtering based recommender systems mainly depends on which users (the neighbors) are exploited to estimate a user's ratings. We propose a new approach of neighbor selection, which adopts a global point of view. This approach defines a unique set of possible neighbors, shared by all users, referred to as Global Neighbors (GN). We view the problem of defining GN as a combinatorial optimization problem and propose to use an evolutionary algorithm to tackle this search. Our aim is to find a relatively small GN as the size of the resulting model, as well as the complexity of the computation of recommendations highly depend on the size of GN. We present experiments and results on a standard benchmark data-set from the recommender system community that support our choice of the evolutionary approach and show that it leads to a high accuracy of recommendations and a high coverage, while dramatically reducing the size of the model (by 84%). We also show that the evolutionary approach produces results able to generate accurate recommendations to unseen users, while easily allowing the insertion of new users in the system with little overhead.

Categories and Subject Descriptors

I.2.8 [**Artificial Intelligence**]: Problem Solving, Control Methods, and Search—*Heuristic methods*

General Terms

Algorithms

Keywords

Iterated Local Search, Recommender Systems

1. INTRODUCTION

With the emergence of the Web 2.0, finding the right piece of information is becoming challenging for users, due to the huge amount of information they can access. Personalization, which is the "ability to provide content and services tailored to individuals" [1], is one answer to this problem and one way to achieve personalization is through Recommender Systems (RS) [9]. RS aim at increasing users' satisfaction by recommending them items that fit their needs and preferences. RS are used in many domains such as e-commerce, tourism, e-learning, etc. Collaborative Filtering (CF) is a recommendation approach which relies on users' preferences (the ratings they assigned to items). To compute the recommendations to be suggested to a given user, called the active user (denoted a), CF exploits the ratings (preferences) of other users. The neighborhood approach, which is the one of interest in this paper, exploits the ratings of users similar to a: his/her neighbors.

Many works have focused on the adequate way to identify the active user's neighborhood. Neighbor selection is usually performed locally [20]: each active user a has his/her own neighborhood and the traditional criterion for selecting these neighbors is their similarity with a. Most of the neighborhood based approaches are labeled as memory-based as they use the entire set of ratings to define at the same time the neighborhood and to compute recommendations. This approach is accurate, intuitive, simple to implement and able to immediately integrate new user ratings in the recommendation process, which are the reasons why it is still of high interest for researchers [14]. However, this approach suffers from scalability issues.

In this paper, we propose a new CF approach, which alleviates scalability issues, while maintaining high quality recommendations. This approach leads to a small size recommendation model, and requires a small time to generate recommendations. Unlike classical approaches which select neighborhoods locally and independently for each active user, we propose to identify a global and unique set of neighbors, shared by all users. This set is referred to as the set of Global Neighbors ($GN = \{gn_1, \cdots, gn_g\}$), which is a subset of the entire set of users. Once the set GN is identified offline, the recommender system can estimate the preferences of each active user on each item, by managing only the ratings of users in GN, which depends neither on the active user nor on the item. The resulting recommendation process is based on the same principle as classical neighborhood approaches. As only the preferences of the set GN are used to compute recommendations, only these preferences need to be stored, which results in a decrease of the size of the model. In addition, the computational complexity of recommendations is also decreased as the neighbors of an active user a are selected within the small subset of users GN.

GECCO'12, July 7–11, 2012, Philadelphia, Pennsylvania, USA.

The question we face is: how to identify the set GN, which is at the same time small (to decrease the space and time complexities of the model), leads to accurate recommendations and to a high coverage. As GN is unique and its size has to be minimized, each $gn_i \in GN$ can not be selected independently of the others, nor locally. GN has to be selected as a whole. To ensure accurate recommendations, we propose to select GN based on its associated accuracy of recommendations, at the opposite of classical approaches that select each neighbor independently, based only on its similarity with the active user. We formulate the problem of selecting GN as a combinatorial optimization problem. This optimization problem has the characteristics to be a large scale problem in which optimal solutions are hard to find. Since it is impossible to exhaustively explore the space (exponential with the number of users) of all possible GN, we propose to use an evolutionary algorithm, more precisely an iterated local search method (ILS), to construct a set GN that is a good estimation of the optimal solution. Here the search algorithm optimizes a global objective function, which takes into account the following three elements: the recommendation error (MAE) which has to be minimized, the coverage which has to be maximized and the size of the set GN which has to be minimized also.

This paper is organized as follows. Section 2 presents related work on collaborative filtering. Section 3 introduces the global neighbors based collaborative filtering we propose and the evolutionary approach we use to construct the set of global neighbors. In Section 4, the experiments we have conducted and the corresponding results are presented and discussed. Finally, section 5 concludes this paper and presents perspectives.

2. RELATED WORK ON CF

2.1 Description

A collaborative filtering (CF) based recommender system, also called social recommender system [9], produces recommendations of items to users, based on the intuition that people who share common likes and dislikes with the active user, are likely to be a good source for recommendations. The set of items is denoted $I = \{i_1, \dots, i_m\}$, the set of users $U = \{u_1, \dots, u_n\}$, and the active user a. The input data is the set of ratings $r(u,i)$ that users $u \in U$ have assigned to some items $i \in I$, stored in a rating matrix $R = U \times I$. Let us notice that the number of users and items may be large and that a large portion of the rating matrix may be unknown.

To make recommendations to a, CF first estimates, for each item i that a has not rated, the rating $r^*(a,i)$ that he/she would assign to i if he/she rated it. Second, given this set of estimated ratings, the system recommends the items with the highest rating values. Several approaches are used to compute these ratings: neighborhood approaches, matrix factorization models, Bayesian networks, latent factor models [1].

Most of the neighborhood approaches, which are the focus of this paper, estimate $r^*(a,i)$ as presented in equation (1).

$$r^*(a,i) = \overline{r(a)} + \frac{\sum_{u \in U_{ai}} sim(a,u) * (r(u,i) - \overline{r(u)})}{\sum_{u \in U_{ai}} sim(a,u)}, \quad (1)$$

where U_{ai} are a's neighbors who rated item i. A neighbor of a is a like-minded user. $\overline{r(u)}$ (resp. $\overline{r(a)}$) is the average rating of user u (resp. a). $sim(a,u)$ is an interpolation weight and is usually instantiated by the similarity of ratings between users a and u. The more a neighbor is similar to a, the higher his/her weight in the estimation of $r^*(a,i)$ is. A common choice for computing this similarity is the Pearson Correlation Coefficient [6], presented in Equation (2).

$$corr(a,u) = \frac{\sum_{j \in I_{a \cap u}} (r(a,j) - \overline{r(a)}) * (r(u,j) - \overline{r(u)})}{\sqrt{\sum_{j \in I_{a \cap u}} (r(a,j) - \overline{r(a)})^2} * \sqrt{\sum_{j \in I_{a \cap u}} (r(u,j) - \overline{r(u)})^2}} \quad (2)$$

This correlation is computed on $I_{a \cap u}$, the set of items commonly rated by users a and u.

2.2 Neighbor Selection

In CF, there are two main approaches for neighbor selection. Both rely on the similarity between users, defined previously. Memory based approaches exploit the entire set of ratings to select neighbors and compute rating estimates. Model based approaches use the set of ratings to learn a model and then apply this model to select neighbors and estimate ratings.

The memory based approach, such as the K-nearest neighbor algorithm (K-NN) [2], defines a's neighborhood as the set of the K most similar users to a, within the set of those who have rated item i. This approach has the advantage to generate accurate recommendations, mainly due to the fact that a's neighborhood is centered around a. In addition, it requires no training stage as a's neighborhood is defined on-line. It however has one main drawback, is scalability: not only the whole set of ratings has to be kept in memory (space complexity), but also one neighborhood for each pair $(user, item)$ has to be built (time complexity). Notice that a's neighbors are selected by exploiting only the similarity between a and each user: this selection is performed locally. As a consequence, two neighbors may be highly similar, thus redundant and one of them is useless. This local point of view may limit the accuracy and diversity of recommendations. Nevertheless, memory based algorithms remain a popular baseline algorithm today.

The model based approach [17] learns off-line a model of the data, and uses this model to predict ratings. In neighborhood approaches, the most commonly used is clustering [22]. It computes clusters of similar users offline, by exploiting the predefined similarity between users (equation 2). The well-known K-means [16] computes K clusters so that the average similarity within clusters is maximized. The neighborhood of the active user a is made up of the set of users who belong to the same cluster than a. Clustering models have better scalability than memory based approaches as they make predictions from much smaller sets of users (a cluster), rather than the entire user set. The complex and expensive clustering computation is run off-line. However, its recommendation quality is generally lower than that of memory based approaches [19].

Notice that the issue of the choice of the value of K in the K-NN algorithm or the number of clusters in the K-means algorithm is usually handcrafted and often optimized on the testing set [11].

3. THE GLOBAL NEIGHBORS BASED CF

3.1 Description

In this paper, we aim at defining a scalable neighborhood based CF: small size model and recommendations generated within a small time, which leads to a high accuracy of recommendations. This issue of reducing the size of neighborhood based models has been rarely studied in the literature. To reach these objectives, we propose to reduce the set of possible neighbors of active users. We define a set of neighbors shared by all active users, called the set of Global Neighbors GN. Whichever the active user, his/her neighborhood is included in the set GN. This set is computed off-line and is unique.

The resulting recommender estimates ratings as a classical neighborhood based approach (equation 1), with the difference that the neighbors are chosen only in GN. This reduces the complexity of the recommendation process as neighbors are chosen in this reduced set. The smaller GN, the larger the reduction. In terms of space complexity, the model exploits and needs to store only the ratings of the users in GN and the similarity between each user $u \in GN$ and each active user a. The smaller GN, the smaller the model.

This new approach can seem to be similar to the approaches that perform instance selection [23]. However, in these approaches, as in classical ones, the neighbors of an active user are selected independently of the others. As a consequence, two neighbors may be highly similar with an active user but the second may not provide any additional information to the first one, thus may be useless for the recommendation, while being stored by the model. We want to minimize the size of GN, thus each $gn_i \in GN$ has to be useful. We propose to consider this set as a whole, so that the $GN - CF$ selects the optimal set of neighbors GN. Each $gn_i \in GN$ is not independent of others, and only neighbors gn_i that provide added value are retained in GN. As GN is defined as a whole, we propose to not evaluate the quality of each $gn_i \in GN$, but to evaluate the quality of the entire set. This quality is defined as its ability to provide high quality recommendations and a high coverage. Notice that evaluating the quality of a neighborhood on its predicted performance has already been proposed in [4], but it was computed on each neighbor independently.

In the following, we propose to formulate the search for the set of global neighbors among all possible users in the system as a combinatorial optimization problem and which we propose to solve using an evolutionary approach.

3.2 Evolutionary Search for GN

Evolutionary algorithms are usually applicable in many domains where the search problem can be expressed as an optimization problem. They only require an evaluation function that measures the value of a potential solution, or its fitness, a mean to represent solutions *i.e* the search space, and search operators to explore the space. Evolutionary algorithms are good candidates to tackle problems in high dimensions when exact methods fail and good approximate solutions are acceptable.

The use of evolutionary computation has already been proposed in CF, but with different purposes. For example, it has been used to compute the similarity between two users, in this case the weight of each feature in the similarity measure is user-dependent [21], or to define clusters of users [8], etc. However, none of these works has used evolutionary computation to select the adequate set of neighbors.

The identification of the best set GN can be formulated as an optimization problem where we aim to minimize the size of the set GN while maximizing the accuracy and coverage. More precisely this problem is a combinatorial optimization problem where we search among all possible subsets of a larger set for good subsets. The following section presents how to employ an evolutionary computation method namely stochastic local search (SLS) to construct this set GN. The details of the objective function used can be found in section 4.4. There are several advantages as to use an evolutionary computation method to tackle this problem, most of which is the prohibitive size of the search space, since the search space consists of all possible subsets (sets GN) of the entire set of users U. The number of possible solutions can be easily computed as 2^n, n being the number of users in total. Another advantage is the choice of the size of GN, one does not need to fix this size a priori but leaves it to the search algorithm.

In this study, we choose an Iterated Local Search algorithm or ILS [15] to search for the set GN. ILS is an evolutionary computation method that explores the space of local optima, by applying iteratively a naive local search algorithm. It can be thought of as a randomized walk in the space of local optima. This approach has proved very effective in many combinatorial optimization problems, like the traveling salesman problem [13], quadratic assignment problems [18], and scheduling problems [3], which motivates our choice.

3.3 The Search Algorithm

A detailed description of the search algorithm can be found in algorithm 1. At each iteration, a local search procedure (algorithm 2) is applied to the current search point after a perturbation to generate a new candidate solution. Based on the objective function value, this new solution is either accepted in which case it replaces the current solution or is discarded.

Algorithm 1 Procedure IteratedLocalSearch

```
Input (f, N, max_iter)
x := GenIntialSol()
x := LocalSearch(x, f, N)
x̂ := x, stuck := 0
while stuck ≤ max_iter do
    x' := Perturb(x, ⌊ps⌋)
    x' := LocalSearch(x', f, N)
    if f(x') < f(x) and not InHist(x') then
        AddToHist(x') /* better and unseen solution */
        x := x'
        ps := max (2.0, (1/β) × ps)
        if f(x') < f(x̂) then
            x̂ := x' /* better than the current best */
            stuck := 0
        end if
    else
        with probability p_worse
            x := x' /* keep worse solution */
        stuck := stuck + 1
        ps := max (β × ps, ps_max)
    end if
end while
return x̂
```

In order to select a subset of users (the set GN), a natural representation of the search space is to use a bit string of a size equal to the total number of users (n). The value of each bit determines if the user belongs (1) or not (0) to the set GN. The initial search point is fixed to a solution with some selected users whose proportion is fixed by the parameter P_{active}. This helps to boot-strap the search.

The local search procedure (algorithm 2) we use is an iterated descent algorithm, it is chosen to be very simple. At each iteration the algorithm samples N_s random solutions by flipping N_r (the neighborhood radius in the solution space) bits from the current solution thus adding and removing users from the current solution. This one is replaced by the best neighbor in the sample if the neighbor improves the current solution. This is repeated until no better neighbors are found, in which case we may consider that we have reached a local minimum.

Algorithm 2 Procedure LocalSearch

```
Input (x, f, N)
found_better := true
while found_better do
    found_better := false
    t := arg max_{x' ∈ N(x)}(f(x')) /* sample neighbors of x */
    if f(t) < f(x) then
        found_better := true
        x := t
    end if
end while
return x
```

We chose the above neighborhood operator experimentally making a compromise between the number of evaluations required at each sampling and the exactitude of the neighborhood. In experiments not reported here, a choice of a full size neighborhood where $N_s = n$ and $N_r = 1$ implementing thus a hill-climbing local search algorithm, produced very small improvements in the overall response of the algorithm, but at a prohibitive cost.

After each application of the local search procedure, the algorithm performs a jump in the search space. The produced solution is perturbed by flipping ps (perturbation strength) of its bits. As in variable neighborhood search [10], the strength of the perturbation ps is adapted according to the progress of the algorithm (lines 11 and 20) within the range of $[2, ps_{max}]$ using the adaptation rate $\beta > 1$. If consecutive applications of the local search procedure do not improve the current best solution, ps is increased. Otherwise, it is decreased. This helps the algorithm to escape "wide valleys" in the search space.

The algorithm accepts a new solution depending on its objective value and on the history of the search. If the solution produced by the local search procedure is better than the current solution then it is selected, otherwise it is disregarded. However, to increase exploration, the algorithm accepts with probability p_{worse} worsening solutions, giving thus a simulated annealing behavior. Furthermore, the algorithm uses a history archive (the procedure `InHist` in line 8) to memorize the improving solutions it encounters avoiding thus circling between previously visited local minima. This archive is implemented as a FIFO of a fixed length and when full, the older solutions are forgotten.

The overall search stops if no improvements are made *i.e.* when the best solution is not improved for a given number of consecutive iterations. Section 4.4 gives the values used in the experiments of all the above parameters.

4. EXPERIMENTS

This section is dedicated to the presentation of the experiments we conducted to evaluate the accuracy of the GN based collaborative filtering.

4.1 Metrics and Dataset

The approaches and experiments we conduct here will be evaluated with three classical metrics. The first one is the **Mean Absolute Error** (MAE) [12], which estimates the accuracy of the estimated ratings. The MAE represents the average error between the estimated ratings $r^*(a, i)$ and the actual ratings $r(a, i)$. The lower the MAE, the better the model. The second metric is the **coverage**, which represents the capacity of the system to be able to estimate ratings, whichever are the user and the item. The coverage is computed as the ratio between the number of ratings the system can estimate and the number of ratings he is asked to estimate. The higher the ratio, the better the model. The third metric is the **size of the resulting model**, which, in the GN based approach, is the size of the set GN. The smaller GN the smaller the size of the model.

We choose to conduct our experiments on the MovieLens dataset[1], a common benchmark dataset in the CF community. This dataset contains $100,000$ explicit ratings, on $1,682$ movies (items) from 943 anonymous users. The ratings take values in the range from 1 (dislike) to 5 (like). Each user has rated at least 20 movies. The data sparsity (missing ratings) on this dataset is 96%. Following the commonly used test procedures, we divide this dataset into 3 non-intersecting subsets: training (80%), optimization (15%) and testing (5%), and perform a 20-fold cross-validation. The **training set** used to compute the similarities between the users (equation 2). The **optimization set** is used in the fitness function of the ILS algorithm. Finally the **testing set** is used to compute the performance of the model in terms of MAE and coverage. The results reported below are computed on this set.

4.2 State of the Art Approaches

To assess the accuracy of the evolutionary GN based collaborative filtering, we compare it to the neighborhood based state of the art approaches discussed above: the **memory based K-NN** and the **model based K-means** clustering. Notice that, to improve the accuracy (here the MAE) of the approaches presented, a rating $(r^*(a, i))$ is estimated only if the number of neighbors who have actually rated i is greater than a predefined number. This number has been experimentally set to 4.

For the K-NN approach, a value of $K = 30$ has produced the lowest MAE value, 0.6809. The associated coverage is 85.22%. The union of these sets of neighbors reaches more than 98% of entire set of users U. Thus this approach requires the storage of almost the entire set of ratings .

With the K-means clustering approach, we have clustered users, and we found the optimal (with respect to the MAE and coverage) number of clusters to be 4. As expected, the accuracy of this model is lower than that of the K-NN approach, the MAE is 0.6934. The coverage is also slightly lower than that of K-NN: 82.1%. As each user is in the neighborhood of at least one user, this approach requires, as for the K-NN approach, the storage of almost the entire set of ratings. The MAE of both approaches are presented in Figure 1 and are used as baseline values.

4.3 Heuristic Based GN Selection

To evaluate the relevance of our stochastic search approach, we first conduct two experiments with two heuristics for selecting the set GN. Both of these algorithms build the set GN incrementally by incorporating users that maximize a certain heuristic. Initially the users are sorted from best to worst with

[1]http://movielens.org

respect to the value of the heuristic. At each iteration we evaluate the MAE and the coverage of the set GN constructed in increments of 10 from the sorted set, starting with the first 10 users. The algorithm stops when no more improvements are made. The idea behind this is to find the smallest set GN that minimizes the MAE.

The first heuristic is the **centrality** of distance, which assumes that the more a user is similar to the entire set of users U, the better a global neighbor he/she is. This heuristic aims at minimizing the MAE value. The second heuristic is the **connectivity**, it assumes that users who have the greater number of non-null similarity values with other users are good choices of global neighbors. This heuristic aims at maximizing the coverage. These two heuristics are inspired from measures used in the frame of social networks [7] and that have been already used in collaborative filtering to alleviate the cold-start (how to recommend unrated items) problem [5].

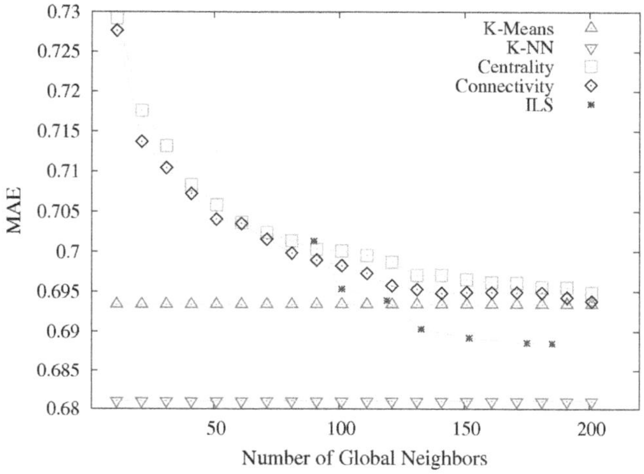

Figure 1: MAE with respect to the size of GN

Figure 1 presents the MAE value as a function of the size of GN for both of these heuristics. We can see that neither one of both heuristics give better results than the K-NN or the clustering approaches. Surprisingly, the connectivity heuristic, which has been chosen for its ability to increase the coverage, performs slightly better than the average similarity heuristic in terms of MAE. This conclusion makes us believe that highly connected users are also highly similar to those they are connected to. With this heuristic, starting at 140 global neighbors, the MAE reached is similar to that of the clustering based approach. The associated coverage value is 84.24, which is greater than that of the clustering based approach. The associated size of the model is smaller than that of the state of the art approaches, as it is of the order of the size of GN, here 140.

4.4 Stochastic Based GN Selection

The stochastic search aims at discovering the set GN which maximizes a predefined fitness function. We aim to find a relatively small set GN that gives a low value in MAE and a high coverage. The fitness function we use minimizes the size of the set GN (the number of bits at one in the bit-string), minimizes the MAE measured on the optimization dataset and maximizes the coverage measured on the optimization dataset too. Notice that, in all the above approaches the optimization set was not used, the set of neighbors or the set GN were determined on the training set. Similarly to the previous experiments, the performance presented below is evaluated on the testing set.

For the sake of simplicity, we decide to mix both MAE and coverage into one single value. We consider that, for each rating that the system cannot estimate, an error equivalent to a predefined value has been made. On the MovieLens dataset, the maximal error the system can make is 4 (the difference between the maximum rating value and the minimum rating value), and the state of the art average error is below 1. We fix this error experimentally to 2.5. Thus, the more a given GN has a low coverage, the more the average error is increased. The resulting estimated error is referred to as e. Therefore, only two parameters are incorporated in the fitness function: $e(s)$ which combines the MAE and the coverage of the potential solution s and $|s|$ the number of global neighbors in s. Each of these have to be minimized:

$$f(s) = \alpha \cdot e(s) + (1 - \alpha) \cdot |s| \tag{3}$$

In the experiments presented below, we fix the size of the sample $N_s = 10$ and the radius $N_r = 1$. The admissible values for the perturbation strength belong to the interval $[2, P_{active} \times n]$ and the adaptation rate $\beta = 1.01$. The size of the history archive was set experimentally to 50.

The proportion of users selected in the initial solution (initial size of GN) was set to $P_{active} = 15\%$ of the $n = 943$ total number of users. This choice ensures to start the search at a relatively small number of users. Furthermore we select these initial users from the ones that have a large connectivity (which corresponds to the heuristic that conducted to the lowest MAE). By this we hypothesize that such users are good representatives and thus will help to bootstrap the search. Experimental results support this hypothesis.

We tested different values of the weight α in the fitness function: $\alpha \in \{0.3, 0.4, 0.5, 0.6, 0.65, 0.7, 0.8\}$. For each of these values we conducted 30 independent runs, in each one of them ILS is run until it stops (when no improvement is made for 50 consecutive steps).

Figure 1 presents the performance of ILS for the different values of α. Each point represents the average MAE value (computed on the testing set) of the 30 independent runs and the number of users selected in the GN. For example, when $\alpha = 0.3$, the resulting number of global neighbors is 90 and the associated MAE is 0.702. When $\alpha = 0.65$, the number of global neighbors is 152 and the MAE is 0.6893.

We can see that starting at 100 global neighbors, the MAE is better than that of both heuristic based GN. Moreover, the larger the number of global neighbors, the more it tends to improve the heuristic based GN. As expected, ILS does not improve the K-NN approach that forms neighborhoods centered around each active user a. Nevertheless, it slightly improves the MAE of the clustering based approach when the number of GN exceeds 120 ($\alpha > 0.5$). Starting at 152 global neighbors ($\alpha >= 0.65$), the MAE of ILS stabilizes at around 0.6893, maintaining the slight improvement over the clustering based approach. In addition, it improves both heuristic based approaches by more than 1%. The coverage associated with the ILS approach and a value $\alpha = 0.65$ is slightly higher than 84%, which is also higher than that of the clustering based approach.

Focusing on the number of evaluations required to reach the convergence, we can see that it increases with the value of α

(thus the size of GN), by 15% between $\alpha = 0.3$ and $\alpha = 0.8$. Notice also that when the initial solution is initialized with randomly chosen users, the algorithm takes about 20% longer to converge.

In the GN based approach (whether heuristic or stochastic), the total set of neighbors involved in the recommendation process (all active users) is drastically reduced compared to the state of the art approaches. In our experiments, the lowest MAE is reached by ILS with only 16% of global neighbors (152 users), associated with an accuracy slightly better than that of the clustering based approach and a higher coverage. Recall that a reduction of the number of neighbors corresponds to a decrease, of the same rate, in the size of the model. Thus, the stochastic based approach decreases the complexity of the model by 84%. In comparison, the best possible model reduction with a K-NN approach is only 47% (with $K = 1$). In this case the value of MAE is 0.7634 (increase of 10% of the error). Table 1 presents an overview of MAE, coverage and complexity of the different approaches.

Table 1: The model size, MAE and coverage of different neighbor selection approaches

Approach	Model size	MAE	Cov. (%)
K-NN (reference)	923	0.6809	85.22
Clustering	943	0.6934	82.10
Avg Similarity	150	0.6965	84.52
# Connections	150	0.6949	84.85
Stochastic search	152	0.6893	84.12

If we look at the users in the set GN provided by ILS, when $|GN| = 90$ ($\alpha = 0.3$), we notice that they are almost identical to those of the heuristic based approaches for the same size. Which suggest that for small sets GN, the most highly connected users are the best candidates to be global neighbors. Beyond 90, the sets tend to be different and ILS identifies global neighbors that improve the MAE more than the highly connected ones. When comparing the initial set GN (the most connected ones) with $\alpha = 0.65$, and those in the set after convergence, only 27% remain in the final GN set while decreasing MAE, the rest are discarded to the benefit of new ones.

4.5 Recommending to New Users

In the previous experiments, the set GN has been identified on the entire set of users and evaluated with respect to its ability to generate accurate recommendations for these users. We conducted additional experiments with the aim to study if GN can be used to generate accurate recommendations for unseen users *i.e.* which are not in the optimization set.

To conduct these experiments, we randomly select a set of users, which represents the *New Users*. GN is optimized on the remaining users (referred to as *Users*) and we measure its ability to generalize to unseen users from the set *New Users*.

To implement this experiment, we removed 20% of the users from the entire set of users, these 20% constitute the set *New Users*. GN is constructed using the ILS algorithm as presented previously using only the ratings of the remaining 80% of users (the set *Users*). This was done 5 times to test with different combinations of sets *New Users* and *Users*.

As in the previous experiments, the set *Users* is split into 3 non-intersecting sets: the training set (80% of the ratings) which is used to compute similarities between users, the optimization set (15% of the ratings), on which GN is optimized and finally the testing set (5% of the ratings). Note that this last set will not be considered to evaluate the accuracy of the approach as accuracy will actually be evaluated on unseen users from the *New Users* set.

To perform rating estimation on the *New Users* set, the system has to compute the similarity of the corresponding users with each $gn_i \in GN$. Thus, the *New Users* set is split, in a similar fashion as the *Users* set: 80% of the ratings to compute these similarities, 15% for the optimization set and 5% for the testing set. Finally, the accuracy of GN on the *New Users* set is evaluated on the testing set. Notice that, in this experiment, the optimization set from *New Users* is not used as the evolutionary search is not performed on *New Users*.

Figure 2 presents the resulting MAE (average of 30 runs), with respect to the size GN. To make the MAE values comparable to those of the previous experiment, the same values of α have been used $\alpha = \{0.3, 0.4, 0.5, 0.6, 0.65, 0.7, 0.8\}$. The ILS line is the reference MAE, that corresponds to the previous experiment.

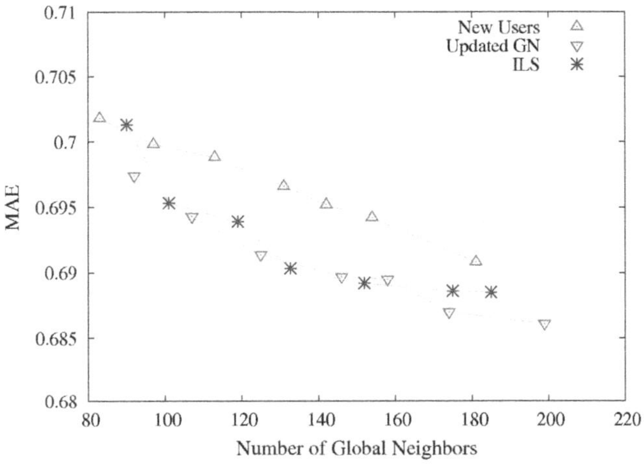

Figure 2: MAE with respect to the size of GN

First, we can see that the sizes of GN are decreased on average by 5% in this new experiment, compared to those of the previous experiment, probably due to the number of users on which GN is optimized, which is 20% smaller. Second, and as expected, the MAE is slightly higher than in the previous experiment as GN has been optimized on a set of users not intersecting with the set on which the MAE is evaluated. This increase is about 1%, except for extreme values of α, where it is smaller than 1%. The MAE obtained here is roughly equal to that one of the connectivity heuristic-based approach. Thus, for high values of α, it is lower than that of the clustering based approach. In addition to the increase in MAE, the average coverage is decreased by almost 2%. For high values of α, this coverage is similar to that of the clustering based approach.

As in the previous experiment, the number of total evaluations until convergence varies with the value of α, by 15% between $\alpha = 0.3$ and $\alpha = 0.8$.

In conclusion, we can say that the set GN resulting from the stochastic approach is quite generic as the MAE on new users is equivalent to that of heuristic based approaches and lower than that of the clustering based approach.

4.6 Updating GN

We have shown that building the set GN with the ILS algorithm provides high quality recommendations to new users, not involved in the optimization step. We are now interested in the way to update this set GN, so as to take into account these new users and provide them with higher quality recommendations. We aim at not recomputing GN from scratch, but taking advantage of the previously computed GN, so as to speed up the update. The advantage of this update is the possibility to include new data in the recommendation process as this new data arrives, thus reducing data latency.

Let us recall that the ILS algorithm is initialized with a set GN (in the previous experiments it has been chosen as the set of most connected users), which is iteratively improved. Thus, when additional ratings or users are known, ILS can be rerun while being initialized with the GN set resulting from a previous run.

We conduct here an additional experiment to study the way this update behaves on our dataset. In this experiment, the similarities between users are computed on a training set resulting from the union of the training sets of both the *Users* set and the *New Users* set. The optimization set is the union of the optimization sets of both the *Users* set and the *New Users* set. To make the MAE values comparable to the previous experiment, the testing set remains the same. Notice that in this experiment, both training and optimization sets are the same than those in the first experiment.

Figure 2 presents the evolution of the resulting MAE according to the size of GN (deduced from the value of α). As expected, the MAE is decreased, as the optimization process is run on additional data, from the *New Users* set. We can see that the resulting MAE is similar to that obtained in the first experiment (from section 4.4, and represented with the blue line), as well as the coverage. In addition, we can notice that the average size of GN according to α is slightly increased compared to the previous experiment (section 4.5), but is similar to that of the first experiment. As a consequence, we can say that the sets GN are quite equivalent when trained from scratch or incrementally when additional users or ratings are integrated in the system.

In terms of computation time of this update process, the number of evaluations used to update GN (till convergence) is lower than that required in the first experiment. This decrease varies according to the value of α. For example, it is decreased by 35% when $\alpha = 0.3$ while being similar when $\alpha = 0.8$. Thus, in the worst case, updating GN takes as much time as recomputing it from scratch.

We now focus on the members of the set GN resulting from this update. The question we ask is: to what extend the new users are included in the new GN sets after the update? When comparing the sets GN before and after the update process, we observe that on average 20% of its members have changed. This rate, which includes the 5% increase in size of GN, is stable and does not depend on α. When focusing on which users are in the final set GN, we can see that between 5% and 7% of the users from *New Users* are actually included in the final GN sets, which corresponds to the average increase in size of GN. As a result, in the 20% of changes in the members of GN, 15% represent users from the initial set *Users* that are no more present in GN.

We can conclude that, as new users are integrated in the system, recomputing GN improves the accuracy of the recommendations. As ILS starts with an initial state, we proposed to fix this initial state as the state resulting from a preceding execution (the one executed before the new users are integrated in the system). This allows to update GN instead of recomputing it from scratch. The size of the resulting GN is increased, while reaching a MAE and coverage, similar to the ones resulting from an optimization from scratch. In addition, the computation time required to form this new set is greatly reduced.

5. DISCUSSION AND CONCLUSION

We have proposed a new approach of neighbor selection which selects a unique set of neighbors, the global neighbors GN, shared by all active users. We view the problem of finding the set GN as a combinatorial optimization problem in which solutions must be small while leading to accurate recommendations and a high coverage. We propose to solve this optimization problem using an evolutionary approach, namely ILS.

The experiments have shown that this evolutionary approach produces small sets GN, with high accuracy of recommendations and high coverage. The associated performance is even higher than that of the state of the art clustering approach and that of heuristic based approaches. The resulting model size is decreased by 84%, compared to that of state of the art approaches. When considering the computation time of recommendations, a decrease is also reached. Indeed, to compute recommendations, the choice of neighbors of a given active user for a given item is conducted on the reduced set GN. Thus, compared to a classical K-NN approach, the time required to compute recommendations is decreased by the same rate as the decrease in size of the model.

Recall that the GN based collaborative filtering exploits both a set GN and the similarities between each user in GN and the active user. When new items/ratings are integrated in the system, these similarities should be updated, even though GN is not recomputed. As only the users in GN are used to compute recommendations, the similarities to be updated are only those related to GN. Thus, the time required to update the matrix is also reduced. When we aim at updating the set GN, the evolutionary approach can also be used The resulting recommendations are as accurate as if the set GN were built from scratch and the updating process is faster than a rerun from scratch.

In addition to the decrease in the model size, in the computation time and in the time required for updates, this new model has the advantage to be privacy compliant. Let us recall that the data required by classical approaches is the set of preferences/ratings of all users. The more information a recommender knows about users, the lower the users' privacy is. In the GN based collaborative filtering, only the preferences of the small set of users GN need to be stored (supposing an active user's profile is stored on the client side). In addition, these users can remain anonymous. Thus, privacy is increased as the risk to reveal sensitive data is decreased.

Finally, the set GN can be viewed as a set of delegates of the whole set of users. Their preferences can be considered as a summary of the preferences of all users. Managing the set GN can facilitate the estimation of information about the whole set of users, such as the average preference on a given item. Furthermore, GN can also be used to monitor the preferences of a population on new items, or as the "target" users to whom a new item should be proposed so as to get a quick overview of the global opinion of the population. In addition,

GN can also be used as a way to alleviate the new user cold start problem: they can be used as stereotype users to estimate the preferences of a new user.

In the future, we plan to study the stability of GN when users' preferences evolve through time. We also plan to design a new way to define and use GN: a user in GN may not be a neighbor of all users with who he/she has a non-null similarity. Thus the question is: how to define the set of users he/she will be a neighbor of? In parallel, we aim to tackle the optimization of the objectives independently with more suited multi-objective evolutionary algorithms (MOEA) techniques. Indeed the three objectives we combine in our fitness function are conflicting objectives and we believe that MOEA should provide better solutions, or at least sample enough pareto optimal solutions for an expert user to chose from.

6. REFERENCES

[1] G. Adomavicius and A. Tuzhilin. Toward the next generation of recommender systems: A survey of the state-of-the-art. *IEEE transactions on knowledge and data engineering*, 17(6):734–749, 2005.

[2] G. Amati, C. Carpineto, and G. Romano. An effective threshold-based neighbor selection in collaborative filtering. In *European Conference on Information Retrieval (ECIR 2007)*, pages 712–715, 2007.

[3] E. Balas and A. Vazacopoulos. Guided local search with shifting bottleneck for job shop scheduling. *Management Science*, 44(2):262–275, 1998.

[4] A. Bellogín and P. Castells. A performance prediction approach to enhance collaborative filtering performance. In *ECIR*, pages 382–393, 2010.

[5] A. Brun, S. Castagnos, and A. Boyer. Social recommendations: mentor and leader detection to alleviate the cold-start problem in collaborative filtering. In I. Ting *et al*, editor, *Social Network Mining, Analysis and Research Trends: Techniques and Applications*, pages 270–290. IGI Global, 2011.

[6] L. Candillier, F. Meyer, and M. Boullé. Comparing state-of-the-art collaborative filtering systems. In *Proc. of 5th Int. Conf. on Machine Learning and Data Mining in Pattern Recognition, MLMD'07*, pages 548–562, 2007.

[7] L. Freeman. A set of measures of centrality based on betweenness. *Sociometry*, 40:35–41, 1977.

[8] O. Georgiou and N. Tsapatsoulis. Improving the scalability of recommender systems by clustering using genetic algorithms. In *Proc. 20th Int. Conf. on Artificial Neural Networks (ICANN)*, pages 442–449, 2010.

[9] D. Goldberg, D. Nichols, B. Oki, and D. Terry. Using collaborative filtering to weave an information tapestry. *Communications of the ACM*, 35(12):61–70, 1992.

[10] P. Hansen and N. Mladenović. An introduction to variable neighborhood search. In S. Voss, S. Martello, I. H. Osman, and C. Roucairol, editors, *Meta-heuristics, Advances and trends in local search paradigms for optimization*, pages 433–458. 1998.

[11] J. Herlocker, J. Konstan, and J. Riedl. An empirical analysis of design choices in neighborhood-based collaborative filtering algorithms. *Journal of Information Retrieval*, 5(4):287–310, 2002.

[12] J. L. Herlocker, J. A. Konstan, L. G. Terveen, and J. T. Riedl. Evaluating collaborative filtering recommender systems. *ACM Transactions on Information Systems*, 22(1):5–53, 2004.

[13] D. Johnson and L. McGeoch. Experimental analysis of heuristics for the STSP. In A. P. G. Gutin, editor, *The Traveling Salesman Problem and Its Variations*, pages 369–443. Kluwer Academic Publishers, 2002.

[14] Y. Koren. Factor in the neighbors: Scalable and accurate collaborative filtering. *Transactions on Knowledge Discovery from Data*, 4(1):1–24, 2010.

[15] H. Lourenço, O. Martin, and T. Stützle. Iterated local search. In F. G. et. al., editor, *Handbook of Metaheuristics*, volume 57 of *International Series in Operations Research & Management Science*, pages 320–353. Springer New York, 2003.

[16] B. Mobasher, R. Burke, and J. Sandvig. Model-based collaborative filtering as a defense against profile injection attacks. In *Conference of the American Association for Artificial Intelligence (AAAI2006)*, pages 1388–1393, 2006.

[17] B. M. Sarwar, G. Karypis, J. Konstan, and J. Reidl. Item-based collaborative filtering recommendation algorithms. In *World Wide Web*, pages 285–295, 2001.

[18] T. Stützle. Iterated local search for the quadratic assignment problem. *European Journal of Operational Research*, 174(3):1519–1539, 2006.

[19] X. Su and T. Khoshgoftaar. A survey of collaborative filtering techniques. *Adv. in Artif. Intell.*, 2009:4:2, Jan. 2009.

[20] G. Takács, I. Pilászy, B. Németh, and D. Tikk. Scalable collaborative filtering approaches for large recommender systems. *JMLR*, 10:623–656, 2009.

[21] S. Ujjin and P. J. Bentley. Learning user preferences using evolution. In *Proc. of the 4th Asia-Pacific Conf. on Simulated Evolution And Learning (SEAL'02)*, 2002.

[22] L. Ungar and D. Foster. Clustering methods for collaborative filtering. In *AAAI Workshop on Recommendation Systems*, 1998.

[23] K. Yu, X. Xu, J. Tao, M. Ester, and H. Kriegel. Instance selection techniques for memory-based collaborative filtering. In *Proc. of the 2nd SIAM International Conference on Data Mining*, 2002.

On the Efficiency of an Order-based Representation in the Clique Covering Problem

David Chalupa
Institute of Applied Informatics
Faculty of Informatics and Information Technologies
Slovak University of Technology
Ilkovičova 3
84216 Bratislava, Slovakia
chalupa@fiit.stuba.sk

ABSTRACT

Although the (vertex) clique covering problem (CCP) is a classical NP-hard problem, it is still overlooked in the fields of heuristics and evolutionary algorithms. We present two main results concerning this problem. First, we propose a genotype-phenotype mapping algorithm for an order-based representation of the CCP, called greedy clique covering (GCC), and prove that for an arbitrary graph, there is a permutation, for which GCC constructs the optimal solution. Although the greedy graph coloring can also be used as genotype-phenotype mapping, we show that GCC is much more efficient for sparse graphs. Secondly, we adapt a mutation-based metaheuristic algorithm using the order-based representation - iterated greedy (IG), to solve the CCP. On sparse graphs with planted cliques, we provide empirical evidence that IG outperforms an exact algorithm. This result is supported by a runtime analysis of IG on several subclasses of graphs with planted cliques. We include experimental results of IG on random graphs, several DIMACS instances and social graphs. Its comparison to the related existing approaches shows that our IG algorithm outperforms the standard approaches in almost all instances.

Categories and Subject Descriptors

I.2.8 [**Problem Solving, Control Methods, and Search**]: Heuristic methods; G.2.3 [**Discrete Mathematics**]: Applications

General Terms

Algorithms, Experimentation

Keywords

Clique Covering, Order-based Representation, Permutation Mutations, Iterated Greedy, Graph Coloring

1. INTRODUCTION

Let $G = [V, E]$ be an undirected graph and let $d = \frac{|E|}{\binom{|V|}{2}}$ be its density, i.e. the number of edges, divided by the number of all possible connections. We will refer to $V_i \subset V$ as a *class* in V. Then, an *induced subgraph* $G(V_i) = [V_i, E_i]$ is a graph that contains only the edges between vertices in class V_i, i.e. $E_i = \{[v, w] \in E \mid v, w \in V_i\}$. The aim of the *(vertex) clique covering problem* (abbr. CCP, also known as the *clique cover* or the *clique decomposition* problem) is to find a partitioning of V into k classes, formally $S = \{V_1, V_2, ..., V_k\}$, such that each class V_i induces a clique, i.e. $\forall\ i = 1..k\ d(G(V_i)) = 1$. We will refer to the minimal k, for which CCP can be solved, as the *clique covering number* of G and denote it as $\vartheta(G)$.

It can be easily proved that the clique covering problem in G is equivalent to the graph coloring in the complementary graph $\overline{G}$. The clique covering number is equal to the chromatic number of the complement, i.e. $\vartheta(G) = \chi(\overline{G})$. Although the decision problem for the CCP is one of the classical Karp's 21 NP-complete problems [9], CCP is still overlooked in the heuristic and evolutionary algorithm fields.

Despite this fact, the applications of the CCP can be found in important fields such as data mining, network analysis, community detection [15] and especially in large sparse graphs, such as social networks, research citation networks or gene regulatory networks [16].

In this work, we propose a *genotype-phenotype mapping algorithm - greedy clique covering* (GCC), designed specifically for the CCP. The reason is that, when G is a very sparse graph, it might be desirable to perform the optimization over G, instead of coloring the dense graph $\overline{G}$. In addition, we study a *mutation-based metaheuristic algorithm* using the *order-based representation* - the iterated greedy (IG), on the CCP. On sparse graphs with planted cliques, we provide empirical evidence that it outperforms an exact algorithm. Using a combination of fitness-based partitions method of nature inspired algorithm analysis [13] and graph theory, we prove that under certain circumstances, IG solves the problem optimally in $\mathcal{O}(|V|^4)$ time.

2. RELATED WORK

Most of the current heuristics that are usable for the CCP, are the graph coloring heuristics over the complementary graph. In the greedy coloring, vertices are taken in a certain order and the *First Fit* method for color choice is generally used, when the first available color is assigned [17]. In

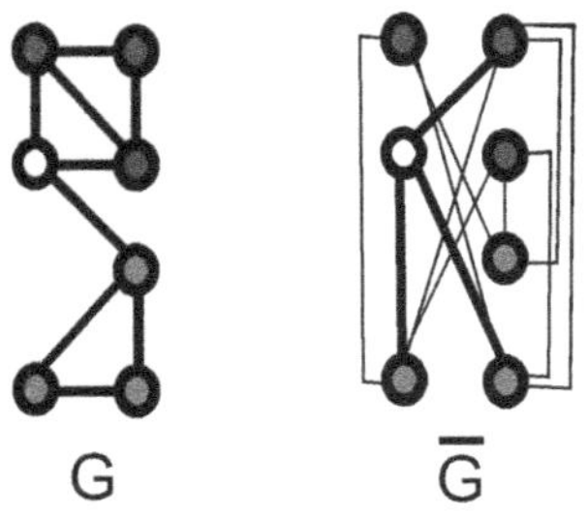

Figure 1: Illustration of the CCP in G and graph coloring in $\overline{G}$.

the terms of metaheuristics and evolutionary computation, using permutations of vertices is often referred to as the order-based representation of the problem.

An upper bound for the chromatic number $\chi(\overline{G})$ can be found using several variants of the greedy coloring. A typical method for vertex ordering is the *largest degree first* (LDF), when the vertices with more neighbors are colored first [17]. Brélaz extended this concept in an algorithm, often called *DSatur* or simply the Brélaz's heuristic, in which at each iteration, a vertex with highest *saturation* - the number of colors already used in the neighbors of a vertex, is colored next. If there are more vertices with highest saturation, LDF is used to break the tie [1]. Another interesting heuristic - RLF was proposed by Leighton, where the problem was tackled by iterative removal of large independent sets from the graph [11].

A problem is that a vast majority of modern graph coloring heuristics tackles the k-colorability decision problem, i.e. the number of colors is fixed to a constant k in the problem instance [7]. For benchmarking graphs, we know, what the k should be and this fixation significantly reduces the search space. However, for unknown instances, this would hardly be an appropriate way, how to estimate. Indeed, the problem can be solved by tackling the graph coloring for k, $k-1$, $k-2$, etc. However, when the estimate for the initial value k is very far away from the optimum, this strategy might be too exhaustive. Furthermore, when G is a sparse graph, the estimation of $\vartheta(G)$ through $\chi(\overline{G})$ might be computationally inefficient, since the computational complexity of greedy coloring for the complement with a predefined permutation of vertices is $\mathcal{O}(|E(\overline{G})|)$, where $|E(\overline{G})|$ will be very close to $\binom{|V|}{2} = \Theta(|V|^2)$ for the much denser graph $\overline{G}$. This complexity is impractical for large graphs.

Heuristics that allow a non-fixed number of colors represent a minority in the literature. Culberson and Luo have extensively studied the IG heuristic on the classical graph coloring problem [3, 4]. The IG heuristic evolves a greedy component using a neighborhood search procedure. The IG heuristic for the graph coloring relies on the fact that for every graph, there is a permutation, for which the greedy coloring produces the optimal solution with $\chi(G)$ colors. This permutation can be constructed from the optimal coloring in the way that the vertices with the same colors that form the independent sets, are adjacent in the permutation. However, when performing this transformation for a suboptimal coloring, if the independent sets are placed in a favorable order, the permutation may lead to a reduced coloring. Therefore, when beginning with a random permutation, with a sequence of permutation changes, Culberson's and Luo's method can evolve gradually better solutions. They obtained remarkable results especially for k-colorable graphs with embedded independent sets [4].

In another work, an evolutionary algorithm with non-fixed number of colors was presented, where the authors applied several types of problem-specific mutations [5], working with the order-based representation of the problem. A large spectrum of memetic algorithms for the graph coloring is also available. However, the k-fixed strategy is strongly preferred in these approaches [6, 12, 14]. In this paper, we pay special attention to sparse graphs. Previous work using heuristics designed specifically for sparse graphs can be found in [10].

3. THE ORDER-BASED REPRESENTATION OF THE CCP AND ITS EFFICIENCY

In this section, we propose our genotype-phenotype mapping algorithm and prove that for an arbitrary graph, there is a genotype, which leads to an optimal phenotype. In addition, we compare the algorithm to the existing approach to the genotype-phenotype mapping - the greedy coloring and show that our approach is much more efficient for sparse graphs, regarding both time and space complexity.

3.1 The Genotype-Phenotype Mapping Using Greedy Clique Covering (GCC)

We have already indicated that there are two different approaches available to tackle the estimation of $\vartheta(G)$. The first one is to use a graph coloring heuristic on $\overline{G}$. When using this approach, it is more efficient to store only the original graph G and handle the coloring of $\overline{G}$ by first sorting the adjacency lists (technically, when loading the graph) and then skipping the edges in G during the greedy coloring. Since G is much sparser than $\overline{G}$, this minor technical detail allows one to handle much larger graphs, due to the memory limitations. However, when using this approach, we have to take into account that for a dense graph like $\overline{G}$, complexity of $\mathcal{O}(|V|^2)$ should be accepted even for the greedy coloring.

The second way is to use a greedy algorithm that operates only on the edges of G. When looking at the graph G itself, e.g. a large social network, we can assume that it is much sparser than $\overline{G}$. The drawback, however, is that the edges in G have different interpretation than the edges in $\overline{G}$, since they do not technically represent the constraints of the problem. This is a big difference between the classical graph coloring and clique covering. However, an efficient heuristic can still be obtained to estimate the clique covering using just the original graph G.

In Figure 1, we show a simple example of the graph for the CCP (G) and the graph coloring ($\overline{G}$). In both graphs, there is a single uncolored vertex. In $\overline{G}$, we can see that it is enough to scan its neighbors to be sure that a new color will be needed, since the vertex has both a blue and a red neighbor. In G, the situation is different. The vertices that define the constraints are not adjacent to the uncolored vertex. However, suppose that we want to assign a color to the vertex in Figure 1. When we have only the graph G, it is enough to know that there are actually 3 blue and 3 red vertices. Then, if the vertex is not adjacent to all vertices of a particular color, it cannot be assigned this color. Therefore, with this additional information, a greedy heuristic would know that it needs a new color. This is the basic idea of the

Algorithm 1: Greedy Clique Covering

```
Greedy Clique Covering
Input: graph G = [V, E]
permutation P = [P_1, P_2, ..., P_|V|] of vertices in V
Output: clique covering S of G
1 for c = 1..|V|
2     sizes(c) = 0
3 for i = 1..|V|
4     j = P_i
5     c = find_equal(Γ(v_j, c), sizes(c))
6     V_c = V_c ∪ {v_j}
7 return S = {V_1, V_2, ..., V_k}
```

greedy clique covering (GCC), specified in the pseudocode of Algorithm 1.

The greedy clique covering is very similar to the greedy coloring. GCC processes the vertices iteratively, taking i-th component of permutation P as the current vertex in the step 4. In contrast to greedy coloring, we explicitly store an array $sizes$, in which $sizes(c)$ contains, how many vertices are already labeled with c. In this context, we will refer to colors as labels, since CCP is not a traditional perspective on the coloring problem.

Let $v_j \in V$ be a vertex to be labeled, $c \in C$ be a label and let $S = \{V_1, V_2, ..., V_k\}$ be a partial clique covering induced by the current labeling of G. Then, we define a function $\Gamma : V \times C \rightarrow N_0$ as a function, which returns the number of neighbors of v_j, which are colored with c, i.e.: $\Gamma(v_j, c) = |\{v_l \in V \mid [v_j, v_l] \in E \wedge v_l \in V_c\}|$.

When choosing a color for vertex v_j in the step 5, we verify, whether it is adjacent to all vertices that already have label c. Thus, by assigning label c to v_j, subgraph $G(V_c)$ induced by label c will still remain a clique. Practically, this means that value $\Gamma(v_j, c)$ must be equal to $sizes(c)$. If there is no such value, a new label must be chosen. The key issue in greedy clique covering is that, while scanning only the edges in G, the labeling can be constructed very quickly, even in very large graphs.

The only problem is the Γ function, used in the step 5 to determine the label to be assigned. This operation should be implemented by scanning the neighbors of the currently labeled vertex. Memorizing values of Γ is inefficient, we use it only as a formal concept.

Suppose that we implement the $find\_equal$ operator in the step 5 in the following way. We scan the neighbors of v_j. If the neighbor is already labeled, we decrement the corresponding value in $sizes()$. If the first decrementation is performed, we store the original value to be able to restore the initial values in $sizes()$. Then, if, during this process, some value $sizes(c)$ reaches 0, then c is a candidate for the label for v_j. From these candidates, we choose the lowest c, to ensure the conformity with the First Fit strategy. After this, we repeatedly scan the neighbors of v_j and restore the values in $sizes()$ that were present there before the decrementation process.

This strategy leads to an interesting complexity, since the operation in the step 4 costs $\mathcal{O}(1)$ time per iteration and the choice of label costs only $\mathcal{O}(\deg(v_j))$ time per iteration, since we iterate only over the neighbors. By using the well-known formula that $\sum_{v \in V} \deg(v) = 2|E|$, we obtain that the complexity of greedy clique covering is only $\mathcal{O}(|E|)$, which is highly favorable for sparse graphs.

Another issue is the genotype-phenotype mapping. The main question is, whether there is a permutation (genotype), for which Algorithm 1 will construct the optimal covering (phenotype). The idea here is similar to the theorem and proof of the same property for the greedy coloring [4].

Theorem 1.

For an arbitrary graph $G = [V, E]$, there is a permutation, for which the greedy clique covering will produce the optimal solution with $\vartheta(G)$ cliques.

Proof.

Let $S = \{V_1, V_2, ..., V_{\vartheta(G)}\}$ be the optimal solution to the CCP. Then, the optimal permutation P can be constructed in the way that the vertices from the same classes are next to each other in P, i.e. $P = [V_{s_1}, V_{s_2}, ..., V_{s_{\vartheta(G)}}]$, where $s_1, s_2, ..., s_{\vartheta(G)}$ is an arbitrary permutation of integers from 1 to $\vartheta(G)$. Since vertices of each of the subpermutations form the correct cliques, this permutation will surely lead to the optimal clique covering. □

3.2 A Comparison to Greedy Graph Coloring

We have shown that GCC and greedy graph coloring are equivalent in the suitability as genotype-phenotype mapping algorithms. At this point, we wonder, which of the two approaches is more suitable for which type of graphs. We briefly compare the time and space complexities of these approaches.

When we look on the number of operations needed by the algorithms in more detail, we obtain the following. In the greedy graph coloring, when performed over $\overline{G}$, both the color choice and updates in an auxiliary matrix, which is needed, require an amount of operations proportional to $|V| - \delta(G) - 1$, where $\delta(G)$ is the average degree of a vertex in G. The exact number of operations depends on a particular implementation. However, for our implementation we obtained $|V|[4|V| - 4\delta(G)]$ operations, when omitting the constant factor. In addition, greedy coloring needs $|V|[|V| - \delta(G)]$ additional storage space, to store the auxiliary matrix. For more details on this approach, the reader may refer to [1, 17].

In GCC, the amount of operations depends on the implementation details, too. Our currently best implementation performs $|V|[17\delta(G)]$ operations, where $17\delta(G)$ is the average number of operations, which are done during the neighbor scans. Again, we omitted the constant factor. In addition, instead of an auxiliary matrix, GCC uses the $sizes()$ array, which needs additional storage space only of size $|V|$.

Therefore, GCC always uses less space than the greedy graph coloring and performs faster, when $\delta(G) < \frac{4|V|}{21}$. This occurs, when the graph has a density lower than approximately $\frac{4}{21}$. However, better implementation strategies might be able to improve this factor.

4. A MUTATION-BASED APPROACH: THE IG ALGORITHM

At this point, we present an adaptation of a mutation-based stochastic search algorithm in the order-based representation - the iterated greedy (IG). In addition, a brief empirical study of the performance of IG is presented on

Algorithm 2: The IG Algorithm for the CCP

The IG heuristic for the CCP

Input: graph $G = [V, E]$
Output: clique covering S of G

1 $P = random\_permutation(1, 2, ..., |V|)$
2 for $i = 1..I_{max}$
3     $\{V_1, V_2, ..., V_k\} = greedy\_clique\_covering(G, P)$
4   if $\vartheta^*(G)$ is known and $k = \vartheta^*(G)$
5   return $S = \{V_1, V_2, ..., V_k\}$
6   with p_{rev} probability
7         $P = [V_k, V_{k-1}, ..., V_1]$
8   else
9         $P = random\_permutation(V_1, V_2, ..., V_k)$
10 return $S = \{V_1, V_2, ..., V_k\}$

graphs with planted cliques, which represent a simple model of clustered graphs.

4.1 The IG Algorithm

In the IG for the graph coloring, Culberson and Luo used three different mutations - moves of the independent sets - *random*, *reverse* and *largest first* [4]. The random move reordered the independent sets entirely randomly. The reverse move reordered them from the last to the first in the previous coloring. And the largest first move reordered them according to their size, from the largest to the smallest. They used a probabilistic choice of the move to be performed, generally a ratio of *50:50:30* (*largest first:reverse:random*) was shown to be efficient [3].

These moves can be easily reused to solve the CCP, by simply using the reorderings on cliques, instead of independent sets. For the clique covering, reverse and random moves require only $\mathcal{O}(|V|)$ time. The largest first would require sorting of the cliques to a non-increasing sequence according to their size, which can be done in $\mathcal{O}(|V| \log |V|)$ time using Merge sort or Heap sort or, with some additional space, $\mathcal{O}(|V|)$ time can be also achieved with Counting sort [2]. However, for simplicity, we have decided to use only the reverse and random moves. These were verified in our preliminary experiments to provide enough dynamics to use the IG as a neighborhood search algorithm.

In Algorithm 2, our IG for the CCP is specified. First, a random permutation P of vertices is generated. Then, at each iteration, P is used in greedy clique covering to generate a solution. Building blocks V_1, V_2, ..., V_k, representing the clique-inducing classes, are identified in the constructed solution (the index of the class represents the label of the clique). If we know the optimal number of cliques - $\vartheta^*(G)$, we verify the current k in the step 4. With probability p_{rev}, the reverse move is performed on the classes in the step 7, where the new permutation is generated in the way that the vertices of the clique labeled with the highest index come first and the vertices of the clique labeled with the lowest index come last. Otherwise, the cliques in the permutation are reordered randomly in the step 9, in the way that the equally labeled vertices should be still adjacent in P. We note that I_{max} is used in Algorithm 2 only as a formal concept. In the following, we use a similar symbol I to refer to the number of iterations, which are in fact performed by IG to obtain the optimal solution.

At this point, let us move on to the amount of operations, needed by IG. A random permutation of vertices can be generated in $\mathcal{O}(|V|)$ time. In the iterative procedure, the greedy clique covering takes $\mathcal{O}(|E|)$ time and the moves require no more than $\mathcal{O}(|V|)$ time per iteration. Therefore, if the IG for the CCP converges to the optimal solution, it will do so in $\mathcal{O}(I(|E| + |V|))$ time, which can be further reduced to $\mathcal{O}(I|E|)$ if $|E| \geq |V|$.

4.2 IG on the Graphs with Planted Cliques

The previous analysis implies an interesting question. If we fix the instance type to a topology, for which the IG will converge to the optimal clique covering, then we wonder, how does the computational complexity of IG behave.

For this purpose, we consider the *graphs with planted r-cliques*. Suppose that the graph contains cliques of size r and each vertex is in exactly one clique. Then, r must be a divisor of $|V|$ and the number of cliques is $\vartheta = \frac{|V|}{r}$. The edges between vertices in different cliques are generated with some relatively small probability p_{out}, to be able to practically guarantee that no pair of cliques will be merged during the edge generation process. This occurs when $p_{out}^{r^2}|V|(|V|-r)/2 << 1$, where $<<$ means "much smaller".

For simplicity, suppose that no pairs of cliques were merged and suppose that we know r. Under these circumstances, a simple exact algorithm can be found to solve the CCP. It just scans each r-tuple of vertices in the graph and verifies, whether they form a clique. It can be easily seen that this approach needs $\binom{|V|}{r} = \Theta(|V|^r)$ time and is polynomial, when r is a known constant.

Now, let us move on to the behavior of IG on the graphs with planted r-cliques. Generally, when r is small enough, IG has no problems converging to the global optimum within a small number of iterations. An interesting property is that if p_{out} is small, i.e. the graph is sparse, then the larger the cliques are, the stronger are also the attractors in the search space of IG. Therefore, for sparse graphs, smaller cliques require more "sorting", until the optimal permutation is found. However, when p_{out} is larger, the region of hard instances of the problem, which was a called a ridge by Culberson and Luo [4], moves to higher values of r.

Since for the graphs with planted r-cliques, we can generally say that $|E| \geq |V|$ and $|E| = \Theta(|V|^2)$, the complexity of IG on this type of graphs can be expressed as $\mathcal{O}(I|V|^2)$. The only question here is, how does the number of iterations I grow with $|V|$, under the consideration that p_{out} is small enough. Figures 2 and 3 shed a bit more light on the I function. It displays the growth of I as $|V|$ grows from 3×10^3 to 30×10^3 (with 3×10^3 intervals). We used the IG on graphs with planted r-cliques. These graphs were generated for $r = 3, 4, 5, 6$ and 8 with inter-clique edge generation probability $p_{out} = 10^{-3}$. The ratio for the reverse and random moves was 50 : 30 and the values displayed are the average values over 20 runs.

Figures 2 and 3 show that the growth of I is apparently very slow, enough to consider IG to be a promising tool for locating high local density anomalies in graphs with low global density (this is a very important property, especially for applications in data mining). For $r > 4$, IG required only tens of iterations to find the optimal covering. With growing r, the number of iterations decreases, which can be explained by the fact that larger cliques in a sparse graph tend to be more "visible" and therefore, are easier to be located. This also corresponds to the results presented by

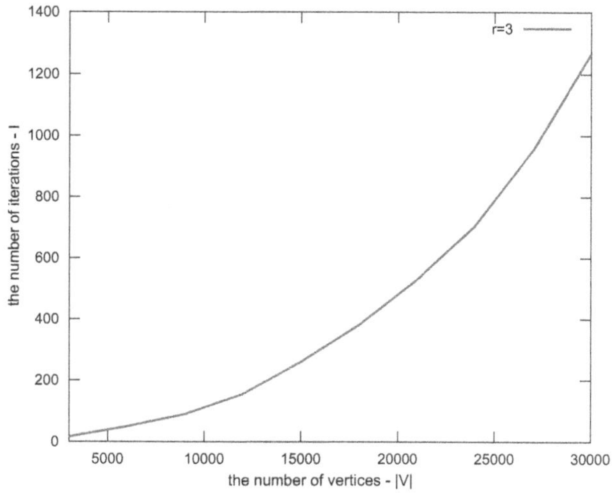

Figure 2: The number of iterations required by IG to solve the CCP over graphs with planted 3-cliques, as a function of $|V|$.

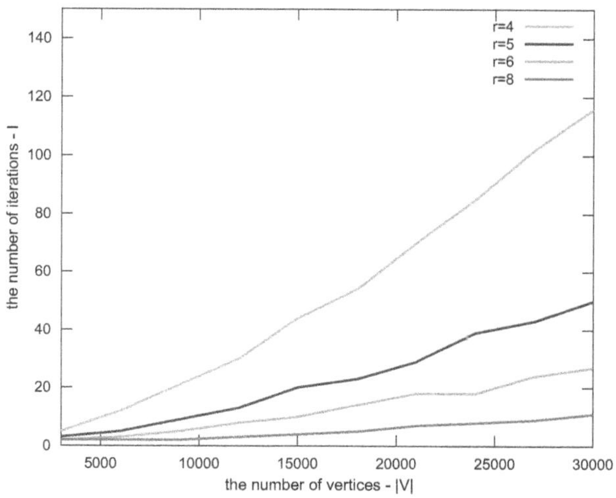

Figure 3: The number of iterations required by IG to solve the CCP over graphs with planted r-cliques ($r \geq 4$), as a function of $|V|$.

Culberson and Luo [4]. However, on the contrary, it is a reverse result to the complexity of the exact algorithm we were discussing before, where the degree of the polynomial grows with r. Perhaps an interesting observation is that the differences in $I(|V|)$ indicate mild convex behavior but with occasional local non-convex intervals, which may be caused by randomness. Maybe a more interesting information is that the quotients of the sequence, we measured for $I(|V|)$, tend to decrease with growing $|V|$. Thus, they do not indicate an exponential outbreak. A special case is $r = 3$, which seems to be on a boundary of a region of harder instances (that, in the case of small p_{out} seems to be very small). However, although this function grows fastest, the quotients here still do not indicate any exponential outbreak.

5. ANALYSIS OF IG ON GRAPHS WITH PLANTED CLIQUES

At this point, we wonder, whether it is possible to find an upper bound for the number of iterations analytically. In fact, IG is a variant of a stochastic neighborhood search algorithm. Therefore, it might be possible to analyze its behavior using the methods of evolutionary computation theory.

5.1 The Fitness-based Partitions of Planted Clique Landscapes

The appropriate method for analysis of this algorithm is the method of fitness-based partitions. In this method, the search space is divided into several partitions, according to the fitness function [13]. There are two key aspects that are important to be established for this method:

- *proper fitness-based partitions* - levels in the optimization, where the last level contains only optimal solutions
- *probability of augmentation to a new level* - the smallest probability that a mutation will lead the algorithm to augment the current solution to a higher fitness-based partition

IG is a typical algorithm for this method of analysis, since it uses only one individual and the objective function is monotonous in the search process - the algorithm never causes a degradation of fitness (in this sense, it is very similar to hill climbing). We will need the following lemma from [13]:

Lemma 1 [13].

The expected optimization time of a stochastic search algorithm that works at each time step with a population of size 1 and produces at each time step a new solution from the current solution is upper bounded by:

$$I \leq \sum_{i=1}^{m-1} \frac{1}{p_i}.$$

In this lemma, m is the number of fitness-based partitions and p_i is the smallest probability that in time step i, the mutation will cause an augmentation.

5.2 Analysis of IG on Sparse Biclique Graphs

Graphs with planted cliques can be formalized as a triple $[r, \vartheta, p_{out}]$, where r is the size of the clique, ϑ is the number of cliques and p_{out} is a probability that an inter-clique edge is generated. Indeed, for these graphs $|V| = r\vartheta$, so the number and size of cliques are divisors of the number of vertices. The expected number of inter-clique edges will be denoted as $|E|_{out}$.

In this section, we begin with the most basic case - complements of bipartite graphs, i.e. $\vartheta = \frac{|V|}{r} = 2$. For this type of graphs, the expected value of $|E|_{out} \approx p_{out}r^2$. An important assumption is that $|E|_{out} < r$. We will explain this later in more detail. For simplicity, we will refer to these graphs as sparse biclique graphs.

For practical purposes, we suppose that $r > 2$, so we consider the cliques to be at least triangles.

For the most simple situation, where $r = 3$ and $|E|_{out} = 0$, any permutation of vertices would generate the optimum. There is only one way, how to add an inter-clique edge (the other ways would always lead to isomorphic graphs). Figure

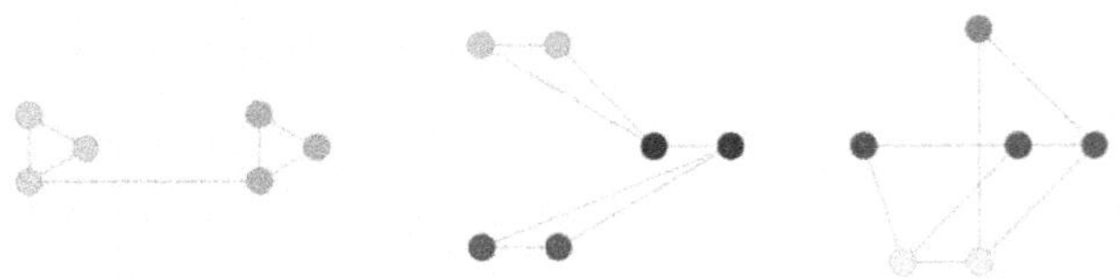

Figure 4: Two triangles with 1 inter-clique edge and their coverings with 2 and 3 cliques (on the left and in the middle) and two triangles with 2 inter-clique edges and their covering with 4 cliques (on the right).

4 shows this bridged graph with its covering with two cliques (on the left) and three cliques (in the middle).

We note that the suboptimal clique covering can be generated, when a couple of vertices, connected by the bridge (the dark green vertices in the middle of Figure 4), precedes all intra-clique couples of vertices. Therefore, it makes sense to re-represent a vertex ordering $[v_1, v_2, v_3, ..., v_{|V|}]$ as an ordering $[[v_1, v_2], [v_2, v_3], ..., [v_{|V|-1}, v_{|V|}]]$, where, instead of the vertices themselves, we have their couples. Then, a couple $[v_i, v_{i+1}]$ can fall exactly into one of the three following cases:

- (v_i, v_{i+1}) is an intra-clique edge; there are $|V|(r-1)/2$ such cases
- (v_i, v_{i+1}) is an inter-clique edge; there are $p_{out}|V|(|V|-r)/2$ such cases on average
- (v_i, v_{i+1}) is an inter-clique couple, without an edge between them; there are $(1-p_{out})|V|(|V|-r)/2$ such cases on average

When we aim our attention specifically at sparse graphs, there are two possibilities, how GCC can overestimate:

- When, in the ordering, an inter-clique edge between two cliques precedes all intra-clique edges from the cliques it connects.
- When an inter-clique couple $[v_i, v_{i+1}]$ without an edge precedes a vertex adjacent to both v_i and v_{i+1}, which is in the same clique as v_{i+1}, but the First Fit strategy will falsely put in the same clique as v_i.

Both of the cases are illustrated in Figure 4. A typical example of the first case was depicted on the left and in the middle. The second case can be illustrated by a two inter-clique edge scenario on the right.

These are the most basic worst-case scenarios for the GCC over two triangles. Now, let us move on to a formalization of these concepts.

Lemma 2.
Let $G = [V, E]$ be a graph with planted cliques for $\vartheta = \frac{|V|}{r} = 2$ and $|E|_{out} < r$. Then, GCC will be off by at most $r-1$ cliques.

Proof.
Suppose that $r = 3$. Then, there are $r^2 = 9$ inter-clique vertex couples. With the restriction that $|E|_{out} < r$, there are only 46 possible graphs and for each graph, there are $6! = 720$ permutations of vertices. This amount can be verified using an exhaustive evaluation. A typical example of the worst case is the two inter-clique edge scenario we discussed above. For this case, we have already shown that GCC uses at most $|V|/r + r - 1 = 4$ cliques.

We proceed by induction. By adding a new vertex into each of the cliques, one will obtain an analogous graph, for which, without adding a new inter-clique edge, GCC will be off by $r-2$ cliques. Similarly, the worst case here can be constructed by introducing a new inter-clique edge between the new vertices. This would cause GCC to be off by $r-1$ cliques. The non-existence of worse cases can be similarly verified using exhaustive evaluation of the possible positions of the new inter-clique edge. □

Lemma 3.
Let $G = [V, E]$ be a graph with planted cliques for $\vartheta = \frac{|V|}{r} = 2$ and $|E|_{out} < r$. Then, for each clique covering generated by GCC, a random reordering of its cliques will lead to the optimum with probability at least $\frac{1}{|V|/r+r-1}$.

Proof.
As we have shown, for this type of graphs, GCC cannot use more than $|V|/r + r - 1$ cliques. Therefore, there are $(|V|/r + r - 1)!$ possible reorderings. The property that $|E|_{out} < r$ is important, since it implies that, in the current solution, there must be at least one clique that is inside one of the expected cliques.

An important property of the reordering operators is that, when the reordering starts with a clique, that is a subclique of any optimal one (i.e. does not contain any inter-clique edge and it does not contain all vertices of the expected clique), then the reordering will surely lead to a correct labeling of the two cliques being involved.

Since there surely is such a clique, we put it first and reorder the rest in any way. There are $\frac{(|V|/r+r-2)!}{(|V|/r+r-1)!}$ such permutations. Therefore, the probability of a direct jump to the optimum is at least $\frac{1}{|V|/r+r-1}$. □

Theorem 2.
Let $G = [V, E]$ be a graph with planted cliques for $\vartheta = \frac{|V|}{r} = 2$ and $|E|_{out} < r$. Then, IG with GCC and random reorderings will converge to the optimal solution in $\mathcal{O}(|V|^3)$ time.

Proof.
The expected running time of IG on graphs with planted cliques is $\mathcal{O}(I|V|^2)$. By using Lemma 1, the number of iterations is upper bounded by $I(|V|) = |V|/r + r - 1 = |V|/2 + 1$. Therefore, the running time of IG is $\mathcal{O}(|V|^3)$. □

5.3 Analysis of IG on Other Cases of Graphs with Planted Cliques

The properties that $\vartheta = 2$ and $|E|_{out} < r$ lead us always to graphs, for which GCC will leave some clique to be a subclique of an expected one. This is an important property, which we can use in the running time analysis of IG.

Suppose that we have two triangles bridged by 3 inter-clique edges (each connecting a different couple). It can be easily seen that if GCC constructs a covering consisting of the three inter-clique edges, then any reordering of the initial cliques would always result in a suboptimal solution. This graph is an example of instance, for which $I = \infty$ in the worst case and the generic IG would not converge to the optimum. However, such problems can be easily overcome, e.g. by extending the clique-based reordering with a random swap of vertices in the resulting permutation. On the other hand, such extensions would make the analysis of IG even more complicated. Therefore, since these situations do not practically occur very often, we aim our attention at the more favorable scenario, when IG can improve the covering.

There are other subclasses of graphs with planted cliques, for which polynomial time upper bounds for the IG seem to be obtainable. For example, for graphs, that consist of several disjunct sparse biclique graphs, there clearly are $\vartheta/2 = |V|/2r$ fitness-based partitions. When we fix r to a constant, then we obtain an $\mathcal{O}(|V|^4)$ upper bound of the complexity.

The conditions, under which we are able to obtain an upper bound for IG analytically, can be summarized in the following theorem.

Theorem 3.

Let $G = [V, E]$ be a graph with planted cliques $K_{r,1}, K_{r,2}, ..., K_{r,|V|/r}$. Suppose that $S_i = \{V_{1,i}, V_{2,i}, ..., V_{k_i,i}\}$ is the current clique covering at the i-th iteration of IG. Furthermore, suppose that at each iteration i, there are j and m, such that there is a clique $G(V_{k_i,j}) \in S_i$, which is a subgraph of some expected clique $K_{r,m}$ ($G(V_{k_i,j}) \neq K_{r,m}$). Then, IG with GCC and random reorderings will converge to the optimal solution in $\mathcal{O}(|V|^4)$ time.

Proof.

At each iteration, there is a clique $G(V_{k_i,j})$ that is a subgraph of some of the expected cliques. Therefore, at each iteration, by putting the vertices of $V_{k_i,j}$ first in the permutation, GCC will be able to generate the whole expected clique $K_{r,m}$, because its intra-clique edges will precede the inter-clique edges being involved. This implies that each of the expected cliques is constructed in one step of IG. Thus, there are at most $|V|/r + 1$ fitness-based partitions of such landscape.

To keep the proof simple, we upper bound the current number of cliques in i-th iteration by $k_i \leq |V|$. Thus, there are at most $(|V|)!$ permutations and the probability of fitness augmentation is at least $\frac{(|V|-1)!}{(|V|)!} = \frac{1}{|V|}$. By using Lemma 1, we obtain that the number of iterations is upper bounded by $|V|^2/r$ and therefore, IG converges to the optimal solution in $\mathcal{O}(|V|^4)$ time. □

It is interesting to see that these analytical results tend to correlate well with the empirical evidence. The number of iterations really shows signs of being upper bounded by a polynomial, most probably of a second degree. Secondly, a factor of $|V|/r$ really seems to play a role in the number of fitness-based partitions of the landscape. The trend displayed in Figure 3 corresponds to this result, the number of iterations increases with $|V|$ and decreases with r.

Finally, we emphasize the fact that the complexities of IG we obtained, were never exponentially dependent on r for these sparse graphs. To obtain a polynomial-time complexity with an exact algorithm, we would have to fix r to a constant. With IG, this does not seem to be necessary. In addition, we have empirically demonstrated that the time needed by IG decreases with r, while in the exact algorithm, it is reversed. We also emphasize the fact that whenever, for a subclass of graphs with planted cliques, we can prove the $\mathcal{O}(|V|^4)$ upper bound analytically, it implies that IG outperforms the exact approach for $r > 4$.

6. EXPERIMENTAL EVALUATION

In this section, we briefly present experimental results of IG on several synthetic and real-world graphs[1]. Table 1 shows the experimental results of IG with GCC and 2 other approaches on several graphs we have chosen for the experimental evaluation. The Erdős-Rényi uniform random graphs are the most typical random graphs, generated by iterating through all couples of vertices and assigning an edge with some probability. The Leighton graphs from DIMACS instances [8] are instances, consisting of embedded cliques of different sizes[2]. These graphs are abstractions of large scheduling problems [11]. Last but not least, we have also used a sample of data from a local social network, to evaluate the performance of IG on some real-world data in the complex network domain.

The first column of the table contains the name of the graph, the other columns contain the minimal numbers of cliques obtained by the methods over 30 independent runs. BRE denotes the Brélaz's graph coloring heuristic we discussed in Section 2. This method was in fact applied to the complementary graph (using implicit mechanisms). The SAT-GCCH is a saturation-based version of GCC, in which, after assignment of a vertex into a clique, for each of its neighbors, which are adjacent to all of the vertices of the current clique, its saturation is incremented. Finally, the IG-GCC method is the IG using GCC with 50 : 30 ratio of reverse and random mutations of the clique orderings. This method was limited to 10^4 iterations.

These results demonstrate, how strongly IG outperforms the related approaches. On the random and Leighton graphs, IG shows major improvements, without fixing the number of cliques to a constant. The results on the social network data are also encouraging. Despite the fact that the difference is relatively small, IG still is able to achieve an improvement in the estimate of ϑ. These results emphasize the practical impact of this work.

7. CONCLUSION AND DISCUSSION

In this paper, we presented two contributions to the fields of heuristics and evolutionary algorithms for a classical, but still overlooked NP-hard problem [9] - the (vertex) clique covering problem (CCP).

We proposed a genotype-phenotype mapping algorithm for an order-based representation of the clique covering problem (CCP). For this algorithm - the greedy clique covering (GCC), we proved that for an arbitrary graph, there is a permutation, for which GCC constructs the optimal solution. We also showed that GCC is faster than the existing approach - greedy graph coloring, for sparse graphs. In our cur-

[1]All instances are publicly available at: `http://www.fiit.stuba.sk/~chalupa/benchmarks/ccp`.

[2]In Table 1, we present the approximations of $\vartheta(G) = \chi(\overline{G})$ for all graphs, including Leighton graphs. These numbers are different from the approximations of $\chi(G)$, which can be found in the graph coloring literature.

rently best implementation, this occurs for graphs with density less than approximately $\frac{4}{21}$. In addition, GCC always uses $\mathcal{O}(|V|)$ additional space, instead of $\mathcal{O}(|V|^2)$ needed by the greedy graph coloring. Therefore, it is highly suitable for large sparse graphs, which are typical for many real-world applications, i.e. in data mining [16], web engineering and analysis of clustered graphs [15].

In addition, we adapted a mutation-based stochastic metaheuristic approach to the CCP - iterated greedy (IG). Following-up the work by Culberson and Luo [3], we investigated the convergence ability of IG on graphs with planted cliques. We obtained interesting empirical evidence, showing that if the graph is sparse enough, IG practically guarantees the convergence to the optimum on a large spectrum of these graphs, without an evidence of an exponential outbreak in the complexity. We investigated this complexity analytically and, using the methods of evolutionary algorithm analysis, we found upper bounds for several specific types of graphs with planted cliques, mostly of $\mathcal{O}(|V|^4)$. With these results, we supported the empirical evidence that IG outperforms the exact algorithm, described in Section 4.2, on this type of graphs.

We also presented experimental evaluation of IG and its comparison to related existing approaches on random graphs, Leighton graphs and social graphs. The results show that IG in combination with GCC is a very promising method in handling large sparse graphs, regarding both the quality of results and the time needed to obtain them.

Acknowledgement

The author would like to thank prof. Jiří Pospíchal for his very helpful comments and the anonymous referees, whose remarks helped to improve this work. This contribution was supported by Grant Agency VEGA SR under the grant 1/0553/12.

Table 1: The comparison of the approximations of $\vartheta(G) = \chi(\overline{G})$ for each graph obtained by the Brélaz's heuristic (BRE), saturation-based GCC (SAT-GCC) and the IG heuristic with GCC (IG-GCC).

G	BRE	SAT-GCC	IG-GCC
Erdős-Rényi uniform random graphs			
*unif*1000_0.1	299	310	**243**
*unif*5000_0.1	1241	1288	**1066**
*unif*10000_0.1	2326	2389	**2025**
*unif*20000_0.01	7640	7817	**6387**
Leighton graphs from DIMACS instances.			
*le*450_15*a*	85	89	**80**
*le*450_15*b*	92	90	**82**
*le*450_15*c*	68	74	**57**
*le*450_15*d*	73	73	**57**
*le*450_25*a*	**91**	92	**91**
*le*450_25*b*	81	82	**80**
*le*450_25*c*	61	59	**54**
*le*450_25*d*	60	59	**51**
Social graphs			
*soc*2000	**1471**	1473	**1471**
*soc*10000	6619	6633	**6618**
*soc*20000	12770	12804	**12764**

8. REFERENCES

[1] D. Brélaz. New methods to color vertices of a graph. *Communications of the ACM*, 22(4):251–256, 1979.

[2] T. H. Cormen, C. E. Leiserson, R. L. Rivest, and C. Stein. *Introduction to Algorithms (3rd ed.)*. MIT Press, 2009.

[3] J. C. Culberson. Iterated greedy graph coloring and the difficulty landscape. Technical report, University of Alberta, 1992.

[4] J. C. Culberson and F. Luo. Exploring the k-colorable landscape with iterated greedy. In *Cliques, Coloring, and Satisfiability: Second DIMACS Implementation Challenge*, pages 245–284. American Mathematical Society, 1996.

[5] N. Drechsler, W. Günther, and R. Drechsler. Efficient graph coloring by evolutionary algorithms. In *Proceedings of the 6th International Conference on Computational Intelligence, Theory and Applications: Fuzzy Days*, pages 30–39. Springer, 1999.

[6] P. Galinier and J. K. Hao. Hybrid Evolutionary Algorithms for Graph Coloring. *Journal of Combinatorial Optimization*, 3(4):379–397, 1999.

[7] P. Galinier and A. Hertz. A survey of local search methods for graph coloring. *Computers & Operations Research*, 33(9):2547–2562, 2006.

[8] D. S. Johnson and M. Trick. *Cliques, Coloring, and Satisfiability: Second DIMACS Implementation Challenge*. American Mathematical Society, 1996.

[9] R. M. Karp. Reducibility among combinatorial problems. In *Complexity of Computer Computations*, pages 85–103. Plenum Press, 1972.

[10] M. Laguna and R. Martí. A grasp for coloring sparse graphs. *Computational Optimization and Applications*, 19(2):165–178, 2001.

[11] F. T. Leighton. A graph coloring algorithm for large scheduling problems. *Journal of Research of the National Bureau of Standards*, 84(6):489–503, 1979.

[12] Z. Lü and J. K. Hao. A Memetic Algorithm for Graph Coloring. *European Journal of Operational Research*, 203(1):241–250, 2010.

[13] F. Neumann and C. Witt. *Bioinspired Computation in Combinatorial Optimization - Algorithms and Their Computational Complexity*. Springer, 2010.

[14] D. C. Porumbel, J. K. Hao, and P. Kuntz. An evolutionary approach with diversity guarantee and well-informed grouping recombination for graph coloring. *Computers & Operations Research*, 37(10):1822–1832, 2010.

[15] S. E. Schaeffer. Graph clustering. *Computer Science Review*, 1(1):27–64, 2007.

[16] J. Sun, Y. Xie, H. Zhang, and C. Faloutsos. Less is more: Sparse graph mining with compact matrix decomposition. *Statistical Analysis and Data Mining*, 1(1):6–22, February 2008.

[17] D. J. A. Welsh and M. B. Powell. An upper bound for the chromatic number of a graph and its application to timetabling problems. *The Computer Journal*, 10(1):85–86, 1967.

An Efficient Genetic Algorithm for Subgraph Isomorphism

Jaeun Choi
School of Computer Science & Engineering
Seoul National University
1 Gwanak-ro, Gwanak-gu
Seoul, 151-744 Korea
eunue@soar.snu.ac.kr

Yourim Yoon
Future IT R&D Lab.
LG Electronics
19 Yangjae-daero 11gil
Seocho-gu
Seoul, 137-130 Korea
yryoon@soar.snu.ac.kr

Byung-Ro Moon
School of Computer Science & Engineering
Seoul National University
1 Gwanak-ro, Gwanak-gu
Seoul, 151-744 Korea
moon@snu.ac.kr

ABSTRACT

In this paper we propose a multi-objective genetic algorithm for the subgraph isomorphism problem. Usually, the number of different edges between two graphs has been used as a fitness function. This approach has limitations in that it only considers directly-visible characteristics of current solutions, not considering the potential for being an optimal solution. We designed a fitness function in which solutions with higher potential can be rated high. This new fitness function has good properties such as transforming the solution space globally convex and improving the performance of local heuristics and genetic algorithms. Experimental results show that the suggested approach brings a considerable improvement in performance and efficiency.

Categories and Subject Descriptors

G.1.6 [**Numerical Analysis**]: Optimization—*Global optimization*; G.2.2 [**Discrete Mathematics**]: Graph Theory—*Graph algorithms*

General Terms

Algorithms

Keywords

Genetic algorithm, subgraph isomorphism, fitness function, multi-objective genetic algorithm

1. INTRODUCTION

Graphs are a powerful data representation model in various fields. Computer networks, digital circuits, and chemical structures can be modeled into graphs. Finding a common structure in two graphs arises in many applications such as social network analysis, chemical structure matching, and digital circuit analysis. The *subgraph isomorphism* problem is a decision problem that is known to be NP-complete [5]. The input to the decision problem is a pair of graphs G_1 and G_2. The answer to the problem is positive if G_1 is *isomorphic* to a subgraph of G_2, and negative otherwise. Two graphs G and H are isomorphic if there is a bijection between the vertex sets of G and H such that any two vertices u and v of G are adjacent in G if and only if the corresponding vertices of u and v are adjacent in H. Since the subgraph isomorphism problem is a special case of the *maximum common subgraph* (MCS) problem, the methodologies to solve the two problems are closely related. The MCS problem is an optimization problem which aims to find the largest subgraph of two given graphs that are isomorphic to each other. The MCS problem is known to be NP-hard [10]. A typical object function is the ratio of the number of edges in the common subgraph against the number of edges in the smaller graph. If the size of the MCS equals the size of the smaller graph, it means that the pair of graphs satisfies subgraph isomorphism.

There are many algorithms for the two problems, but none of them runs on large size problems within reasonable time complexity. Ullmann [16] described a recursive backtracking procedure for the subgraph isomorphism problem, which has exponential time complexity in general. The running time can be reduced to linear time only under limited conditions [8]. The McGregor algorithm [12] and the Durand-Pasari algorithm [7] are two representative algorithms for the MCS problem [3] [4] [14], but they spend hours to find the MCS for graphs with fewer than 100 vertices. Rutgers et al. [14] proposed an approximate algorithm for graphs of up to 200,000 vertices, but it only works when graphs have specific properties of digital circuits.

Genetic algorithm (GA) has also been used for these problems, although not abundant like in other combinatorial optimization problems such as traveling salesman problem and graph partitioning problem. Brown et al. [2] and Wagener et al. [17] applied GA to chemical structure matching. They implemented pure GAs without local optimization algorithm. Fröhlich et al. [9] used GA to approximate the MCS, but it took more than 9 hours to match graphs of 200 vertices.

Kim and Moon [11] proposed a hybrid GA for the subgraph isomorphism problem as a part of malware detection process, where graphs of under 70 vertices were tested. They used directed graphs because a malware's structure is expressed in a dependency graph with directed edges. Based on the GA structure presented in [11], we propose a multi-objective GA for the subgraph isomorphism problem by introducing a new fitness function. The new fitness function compares the degree of each vertex of two graphs and ex-

GECCO'12, July 7-11, 2012, Philadelphia, Pennsylvania, USA.

ploit the information. Experimental results show that this approach improves the performance of GA to a significant extent.

The remainder of this paper is organized as follows. We explain the fitness function of previous work and it's limitation in Section 2. In Section 3, a new fitness function is described with examples and multi-objective GA is explained. Genetic framework is given in Section 4. Section 5 provides experimental results and discussion, and the conclusion is given in Section 6.

2. PREVIOUS WORK

2.1 Two-Vertex Exchange Heuristic

Kim and Moon [11] used a two-vertex exchange heuristic for the subgraph isomorphism problem. The two-vertex exchange heuristic is similar to 2-OPT in the traveling salesman problem.

Algorithm 1 Two-vertex exchange heuristic

```
Input: a permutation P of vertices in G(V,E)
for v1 ∈ V do
  for v2 ∈ V and v2 ≠ v1 do
    Copy and make P' from P
    Exchange the location of v1 and v2 on P'
    if P' is more attractive than P then
      Copy P' into P
    end if
  end for
end for
```

This heuristic works differently depending on the fitness function, which determines the direction of the search path of the heuristic. If the fitness function can reflect more characteristics of excellent solutions in relation to the current solution, the heuristic may take a more efficient path to find the optimal solution. Since local search algorithms have to terminate in a reasonable number of steps, they usually make a sequence of greedy choices based on the state of a solution. They move from one solution to another according to certain criteria. In Algorithm 1, the sixth line provides a criterion and it is up to the fitness function. The heuristic compares the fitness value of the current solution with the fitness value of an adjacent solution. It does not take a path which makes the fitness function value lower, even though taking that path eventually leads to an optimal solution. So if we can design a fitness function such that a solution with the potential is rated high, it will help in taking a better search path.

2.2 Fitness Function

In previous work [11], the number of different edges between two graphs over the mapping was used as a fitness function. Counting the number of common edges is an alternative [2] [17]. The former aims to minimize the value while the latter aims to maximize the value. We give the formal representation of the former case. Let $G_1 = (V_1, E_1)$, $G_2 = (V_2, E_2)$, where $|V_1| \leq |V_2|$, and $G_s = (V_s, E_s)$ be a subgraph of G_2 mapped to G_1. Then

$$f_1 = \sum_{e \in E_1} I(e, E_s) + \sum_{e \in E_s} I(e, E_1) \quad (1)$$

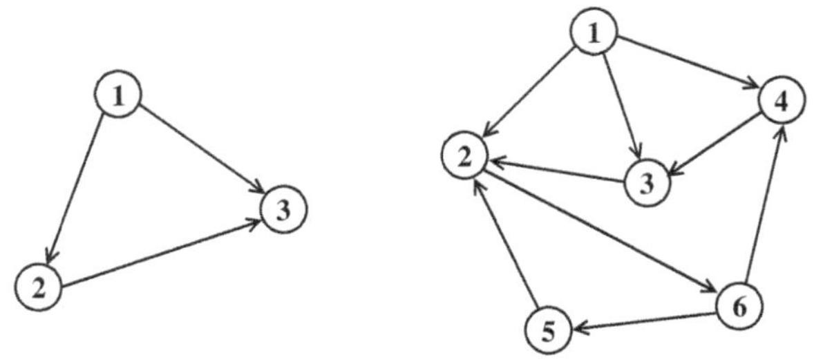

Figure 1: G_1 and G_2

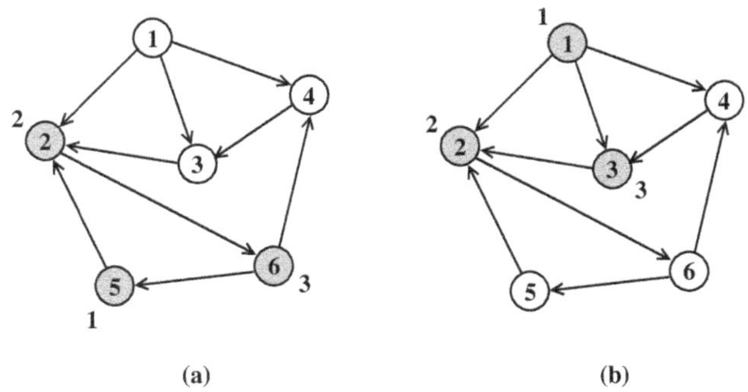

Figure 2: Two possible mappings between G_1 and G_2. (b) is a better solution than (a).

where

$$I(e, E) = \begin{cases} 0 & \text{if } e \in E \\ 1 & \text{otherwise} \end{cases}$$

If the value of f_1 is 0, it means that G_1 is a complete subgraph of G_2 and the attractiveness is the highest possible.

This function has limitations in that it only computes the number of different edges as a whole and does not consider the degree of each vertex. One can screen out unattractive candidate permutations in a heuristic by exploiting the degrees of vertices [6]. For example, in the problem of graph isomorphism, a vertex of one graph cannot be mapped onto a vertex of the other graph if the degrees of the two vertices are not equal. We extend this property; a pair of vertices, each from one of the two graphs, are not probable to match if the vertex from the smaller graph has a higher degree than the one from the larger graph. We devise another function to reflect this idea in the next section.

3. NEW FITNESS FUNCTION

3.1 Main Idea

In designing heuristics or evolutionary algorithms for an optimization problem, we have to choose an appropriate fitness function which leads to an effective search path. In that respect, f_1 is not an eventual fitness function. The fitness of a solution can be measured differently by comparing the degrees of any two vertices that are mapped to each other. Figure 1 shows two graphs, a 3-vertex graph G_1 and a 6-vertex graph G_2. Figure 2 shows two different mappings between G_1 and G_2. The number of different edges between G_1 and G_2 is two in both cases. However, Figure 2b is a better solution. In Figure 2a, two vertices out of three are mapped to unsuitable vertices. Vertex 5 of G_2 has only one

	d_{out}	d_{in}
1	2	0
2	1	1
3	0	2

	d_{out}	d_{in}
1	3	0
2	1	3
3	1	2
4	1	2
5	1	1
6	2	1

	1	2	3
1	0	1	1
2	1	0	0
3	1	0	0
4	1	0	0
5	1	0	1
6	0	0	1

Figure 3: First two tables show the degree of each vertex in G_1 and G_2. d_{out} denotes out-degree and d_{in} denotes in-degree.

outgoing edge, while vertex 1 of G_1 has two outgoing edges. Vertex 6 of G_2 has one incoming edge, while vertex 3 of G_1 has two incoming edges. As we discussed above, a vertex of the smaller graph with more outgoing (incoming) edges cannot be mapped to a vertex of the larger graph with fewer outgoing (incoming) edges. So vertex 1 of G_1 and vertex 5 of G_2 are better not to be a match. Vertex 3 of G_1 and vertex 6 of G_2 are better not to be a match either. On the other hand, no such case exists in Figure 2b. Vertices 1, 2, and 3 of G_2 have more or equal outgoing and incoming edges than vertices 1, 2, and 3 of G_1. It can become an optimal solution by mapping vertex 2 of G_1 to vertex 4 of G_2 and keeping the rest of vertices as they are. In the following section, we describe how to calculate the new fitness value based on this simple idea.

3.2 Formal Representation

We present the formal definition of the new fitness function in this section, and give an example with detailed explanation in the next section. When G_1 is mapped to a subgraph of G_2 by a function

$$g : V(G_1) \rightarrow V(G_2)$$

we calculate the new fitness function value as follows

$$f_2 = \sum_{v \in V(G_1)} J(v) \tag{2}$$

where

$$J(v) = \begin{cases} 0 & \text{if } d_{out}(g(v)) \geq d_{out}(v) \text{ and } d_{in}(g(v)) \geq d_{in}(v) \\ 1 & \text{otherwise} \end{cases}$$

We will call this function f_2 the 2nd fitness function through this paper. The fitness function f_1 presented in Section 2.2 will be called the 1st fitness function.

3.3 Example

We present how to calculate the new fitness function value associated with Figure 2. Figure 3 shows three tables. The first table has the degree of each vertex in G_1, and the second one has the degree of each vertex in G_2. Then we make the third table using the first two. Let a_{ij} denote the value of i_{th} row and j_{th} column of the table. a_{ij} equals 0 if vertex i of G_2 has more or equal outgoing and incoming edges than vertex j of G_1. It means that vertex i of G_2 can be mapped to vertex j of G_1. a_{ij} equals 1 otherwise. We calculate the new fitness value by adding the value of table entries corresponding to each vertex mapping. The 2nd fitness value of Figure 2a is

$$a_{22} + a_{51} + a_{63} = 2$$

The value of Figure 2b is

$$a_{11} + a_{22} + a_{33} = 0$$

A smaller value of f_2 indicates a better solution. So we can say that Figure 2b shows a better solution than Figure 2a according to the 2nd fitness function.

3.4 Multi-objective GA

The 2nd fitness function has no meaning by itself and needs to be combined with the 1st fitness function. It is clear that both of the f_1 value and the f_2 value equal zero when the smaller graph is a subgraph of the larger graph. If the f_1 value equals zero, then it indicates an optimal solution. It is a sufficient condition for an optimal solution. But the f_2 value being zero is a necessary condition.

In order to use the two fitness functions together, a multi-objective GA is needed. Multi objective GA is used when more than one object function need to be optimized [15]. A basic method for multi-objective GA is applying weighted sum method. Let w_1 be the relative weight of the 1st fitness function and w_2 be the relative weight of the 2nd fitness function. The united fitness function is

$$f(w_1, w_2) = w_1 f_1 + w_2 f_2$$

Still, the goal is to minimize the f_1 value. Since $f(w_1, w_2) = 0$ means $f_1 = 0$, optimizing $f(w_1, w_2)$ results in optimizing f_1. When $w_1 = 0.5$ and $w_2 = 0.5$, the fitness values of Figure 2a and 2b are

$$f(0.5, 0.5) = 0.5 \cdot 2 + 0.5 \cdot 2 = 2$$

$$f(0.5, 0.5) = 0.5 \cdot 2 + 0.5 \cdot 0 = 1$$

respectively.

4. GENETIC FRAMEWORK

A hybrid GA we used for the subgraph isomorphism problem is described below. It generates a set of initial solutions, evolves over generations, and terminates when meeting the stopping condition. The best solution is returned as a consequence. We used the same parameter values as in [11] and compared the consequences in order to focus on the effect of the 2nd fitness function.

Algorithm 2 Genetic algorithm

```
create initial population of fixed size
repeat
  for i = 0 to n do
    choose parent_1 and parent_2 from population;
    offspring_i ← crossover( parent_1, parent_2 );
    mutation( offspring_i );
    local-optimization( offspring_i );
  end for
  replace n chromosomes with n offspring;
until stopping condition
return the best chromosome;
```

- Representation
  The vertices of the two graphs are numbered. A chromosome is a permutation of the vertices of the larger graph. When the smaller graph has n vertices, n vertices of a chromosome are matched to the vertices of the smaller graph in order.

Table 1: The result of local optimization

M	η	Before	f_1	$f(0.5, 0.5)$
10	0.01	3.95	0.87	**0.45**
	0.05	6.41	0.01	0.01
	0.1	18.69	2.44	2.44
	0.2	27.57	4.91	4.91
30	0.01	17.46	2.89	**1.95**
	0.05	79.50	**23.65**	23.87
	0.1	163.96	72.99	**72.64**
	0.2	270.15	140.12	140.12
50	0.01	48.52	12.84	**10.78**
	0.05	222.66	**98.56**	100.32
	0.1	451.08	261.53	**261.20**
	0.2	759.21	486.85	**483.87**
70	0.01	88.87	28.24	**23.73**
	0.05	453.83	263.01	**262.44**
	0.1	862.62	573.93	**573.17**
	0.2	1461.46	**1032.58**	1036.10
90	0.01	154.34	70.68	**62.89**
	0.05	760.57	520.01	**503.87**
	0.1	1397.63	1038.23	**1005.13**
	0.2	2392.51	1841.27	**1831.05**

- Fitness Function
  We use $f(w_1, w_2)$ with different values of w_1, w_2 and compare the consequences.
- Initialization
  When GA starts, a hundred chromosomes are created at random.
- Selection
  The roulette-wheel-based proportional selection is used. The probability that the best chromosome is chosen was set to four times higher than the probability that the worst chromosome is chosen.
- Crossover and Mutation
  We used cycle crossover [13] which is applicable to permutational representation. We produce two offspring and choose the better one as the final offspring. After crossover, chromosomes are mutated with 20 percents chance. We select two genes at random and exchange them.
- Replacement
  We generate 20 offspring per generation and replace the worst members of the population with them.
- Local Optimization
  Algorithm 1 is used, changing the fitness function into $f(w_1, w_2)$.
- Stopping Criterion
  The GA stops when it finds a solution with $f_1 = 0$.

5. EXPERIMENTAL RESULTS

In this section, we provide our experimental results. We generated 200 pairs of graphs at random. Larger graphs have 100 vertices, and smaller graphs have 10, 30, 50, 70, or 90 vertices. The edge density of a larger graph is 0.01, 0.05, 0.1, or 0.2. The density of a larger graph is denoted by η,

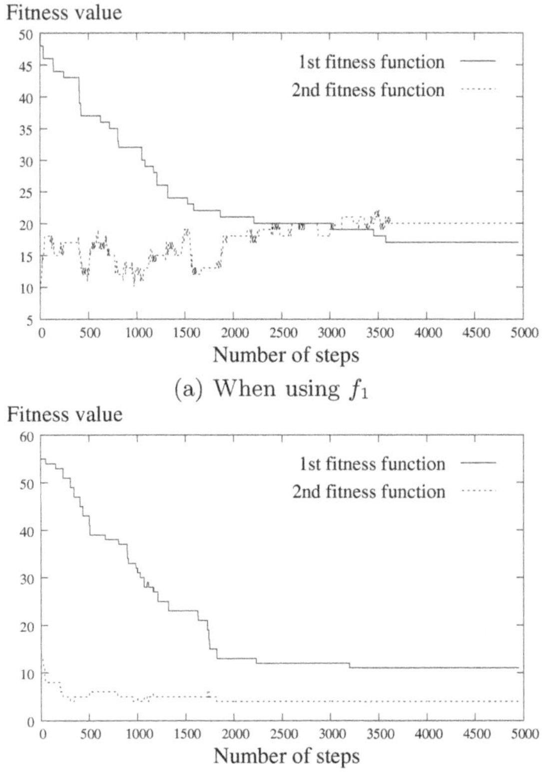

(a) When using f_1

(b) When using $f(0.5, 0.5)$

Figure 4: Local optimization path plotting

and the size of a smaller graph is denoted by M. The pairs of graphs are divided into 20 classes according to η and M, so each class contains 10 pairs of graphs. A smaller graph is a complete subgraph of the corresponding larger graph in each case, which means the optimal value of f_1 equals zero.

The code was programmed in C++ language and compiled using GNU's g++ compiler. The program was executed on a Xeon CPU 2.4GHz computer.

5.1 Local Optimization

We firstly used $f(1, 0) = f_1$ as the fitness function in Algorithm 1, and then used $f(0.5, 0.5)$ as the fitness function, and compared the consequences. Table 1 shows the average value of f_1 before and after optimization. We generated 100 chromosomes for each pair of graphs and applied local optimization once. Using $f(0.5, 0.5)$ gave better solutions in 13 cases out of 20. The results of using f_1 and $f(0.5, 0.5)$ were the same mostly when M was small. In most part of the other cases, the results of using $f(0.5, 0.5)$ were better.

Figure 4a and 4b plot the two fitness function values changing over local optimization process. Comparing the final value of the 1st fitness function in the two cases, the latter gives a better solution. In Figure 4a, the value of f_1 declines over time, but the value of f_2 roughly increases. It means that the output is far from satisfying the necessary condition to be an optimal solution. On the other hand, both of the f_1 value and the f_2 value decline in Figure 4b. This shows the synergetic power of the two fitness functions. Introducing and exploiting the 2nd fitness function helps optimize the value of the 1st fitness function.

Table 2: Test Instances

M	η	f_1	$f(0.5, 0.5)$
10	0.01	**0.2192**	0.1282
	0.05	**0.1061**	0.0919
	0.1	**0.4857**	0.4646
	0.2	**0.2384**	0.1871
30	0.01	0.2554	**0.3798**
	0.05	0.0593	**0.1532**
	0.1	0.1208	**0.1393**
	0.2	0.1491	**0.1535**
50	0.01	0.2282	**0.4033**
	0.05	0.0451	**0.1510**
	0.1	0.0713	**0.2078**
	0.2	0.1154	**0.1437**
70	0.01	0.2213	**0.5545**
	0.05	0.0604	**0.2989**
	0.1	0.1916	**0.4743**
	0.2	0.2940	**0.3247**
90	0.01	0.2625	**0.6018**
	0.05	0.3307	**0.6365**
	0.1	0.4005	**0.7366**
	0.2	0.4365	**0.5807**

5.2 Global Convexity of the New Fitness Landscape

Given a set of local optima, Boese et al. plotted, for each local optimum, the relationship between the cost and the average distance from all the other local optima [1]. They conducted experiments for the graph bisection and the traveling salesman problem, and showed strong positive correlations in both problems. This fact hints that the best local optimum is highly probably located near the center of the local-optimum space and, roughly speaking, the local-optimum space is globally convex.

We conducted their experiments for the subgraph isomorphism problem with different fitness functions and the corresponding local optimization methods. The solution space for the experiment is selected as follows. For both of $f(1,0) = f_1$ and $f(0.5, 0.5)$, we obtained the corresponding sets of local optima by choosing five-hundred random solutions and applying the corresponding local optimization methods. Then for each local optimum, we plotted the relationship between cost on each fitness function and the average distance from all the other local optima. Here, we used Hamming distance as the distance measure between two solutions. Table 2 shows the results. Each value means cost-distance correlation for each fitness function and each instance. Figure 5 shows a sample plotting of an instance with $\eta = 0.05$ and $M = 90$. For all instances except instances with $M = 10$, the results of $f(0.5, 0.5)$ showed stronger positive cost-distance correlation than those of f_1. Instances with $M = 10$ are too small for fitness functions to affect the structure of solution space.

From this experiment, we can infer that the fitness landscape with $f(0.5, 0.5)$ is more globally convex than that with f_1 for sufficiently large subgraph isomorphism instances.

5.3 GA Performance

In our experiments, the number of generations is limited to 100. If GAs find an optimal solution, they terminate instantly. For investigating the appropriate values of w_1 and w_2, we tested over six different pairs of (w_1, w_2), (1, 0), (0.9, 0.1), (0.7, 0.3), (0.5, 0.5), (0.3, 0.7), and (0.1, 0.9).

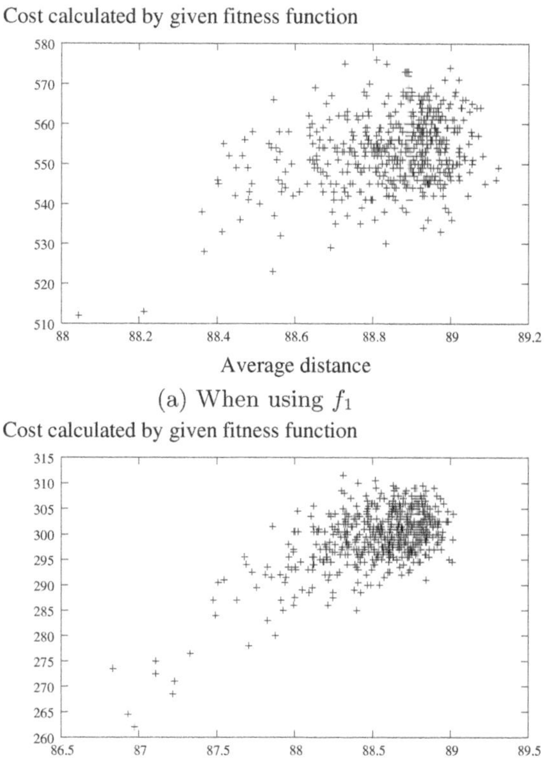

(a) When using f_1

(b) When using $f(0.5, 0.5)$

Figure 5: The relationship between cost and distance

From the experimental results, we observed that the solution qualities were not so different. However, the results showed clear differences in running time. The average running time tended to decrease as w_2 increased. Also, the difference between the average running times increased as M increased, i.e., as the size of instances increased. Figure 6a shows the average running time of GAs tested on 200 pairs of graphs. The running time decreased as w_2 increased except for the range [0, 0.1]. Figure 6b for the largest instance ($M = 90$) shows the tendency better. This tendency seems to be due to the difference of the two fitness values' ranges. Generally, the value of f_2 was much smaller than the value of f_1, especially when the value of f_1 was large. So f_1 exerts stronger influence even when $w_1 = w_2$. Further analysis of the normalization between the two fitness functions is needed.

Table 3 shows the total results of GAs using $f(1,0) = f_1$ and $f(0.1, 0.9)$. The table contains the average f_1 value, the CPU time, and the ratio of finding an optimal solution for each class. The ratio values are in percentage and the CPU time is in seconds. GA with $f(0.1, 0.9)$ gave much better solutions than that with f_1. GA with $f(0.1, 0.9)$ found optimal solutions without exception in 12 cases out of 20. For small graphs ($M = 10$), both GAs showed similar results. For medium size graphs ($M = 30$ and 50), the performance of both GAs were relatively unsatisfactory compared to other cases; however, GA with $f(0.1, 0.9)$ showed surely better re-

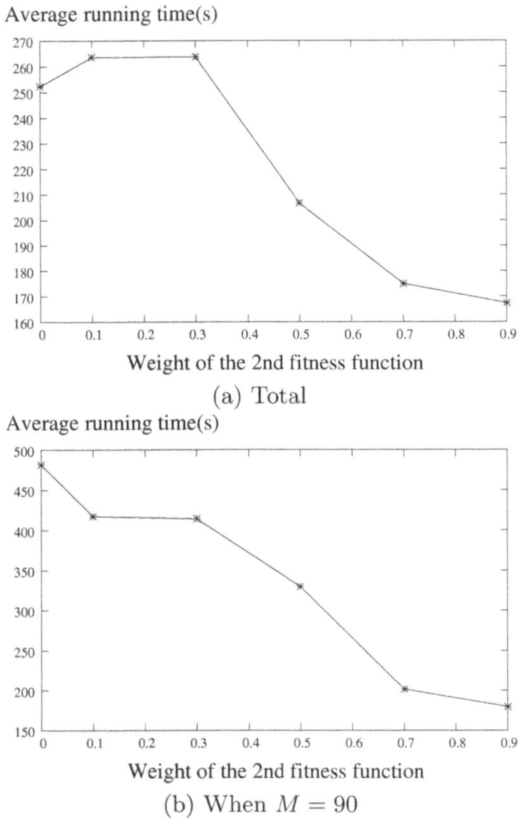

(a) Total

(b) When $M = 90$

Figure 6: The average running time of GA

sults. It found optimal solutions in more cases than GA with f_1. For large graphs ($M = 70$ and 90), GA with $f(0.1, 0.9)$ showed superior performance in the average value of f_1 and the ratio of hitting optimal solutions.

Moreover, the running time was reduced significantly when using $f(0.1, 0.9)$. This means that the new fitness function made the genetic search more efficient. The GA with the new fitness function found the optimal solution more quickly.

6. CONCLUSIONS

In this paper, we proposed a multi-objective GA for the subgraph isomorphism problem. We introduced an additional fitness function which reflects the potential of a solution. The new fitness function considers whether a solution satisfies the necessary condition to be an optimal solution, and put a high valuation on such solutions. By computing cost-distance correlation, we verified that the new fitness function makes the solution space more globally convex than the previous one. This property is good for local heuristics and GAs to find the optimal solution efficiently. We also observed that the running time of GAs decreased as the relative weight of the new fitness function increased. Based on these observations we designed an efficient GA with the best suitable fitness function and local optimization algorithm. Experimental results showed that the proposed GA improves the performance and efficiency.

Even though we only dealt with directed graphs in this paper, the idea can be applied to undirected graphs. The effect of this approach on undirected graphs will be worth examining. As another issue for future study, the normalization between the weight of each fitness function is required. We did not analyze the relation between the relative weight of the two fitness functions, but experimental results show that the distribution of weights affects the consequences.

7. ACKNOWLEDGEMENTS

This work was supported by the National Research Foundation of Korea (NRF) grant funded by the Korea government (MEST) (No. 2011-0018006), Brain Korea 21 Project in 2012, and Engineering Research Center of Excellence Program of Korea Ministry of Education, Science and Technology (MEST) / National Research Foundation of Korea (NRF) (Grant 2012-0000463). The ICT at Seoul National University provided research facilities for this study.

8. REFERENCES

[1] K. D. Boese, A. B. Kahng, and S. Muddu. A new adaptive multi-start technique for combinatorial global optimizations. *Operations Research Letters*, 15:101–113, 1994.

[2] R. Brown, G. Jones, P. Willett, and R. Glen. Matching two-dimensional chemical graphs using genetic algorithms. *Journal of Chemical Information and Computer Sciences*, 34(1):63–70, 1994.

[3] H. Bunke, P. Foggia, C. Guidobaldi, C. Sansone, and M. Vento. A comparison of algorithms for maximum common subgraph on randomly connected graphs. *Structural, Syntactic, and Statistical Pattern Recognition*, pages 85–106, 2002.

[4] D. Conte, P. Foggia, and M. Vento. Challenging complexity of maximum common subgraph detection algorithms: A performance analysis of three algorithms on a wide database of graphs. *Journal of Graph Algorithms and Applications*, 11(1):99–143, 2007.

[5] S. Cook. The complexity of theorem-proving procedures. In *Proceedings of the Third Annual ACM Symposium on Theory of Computing*, pages 151–158. ACM, 1971.

[6] D. Corneil and C. Gotlieb. An efficient algorithm for graph isomorphism. *Journal of the ACM (JACM)*, 17(1):51–64, 1970.

[7] P. Durand, R. Pasari, J. Baker, and C. Tsai. An efficient algorithm for similarity analysis of molecules. *Internet Journal of Chemistry*, 2(17):1–16, 1999.

[8] D. Eppstein. Subgraph isomorphism in planar graphs and related problems. In *Proceedings of the Sixth Annual ACM-SIAM Symposium on Discrete Algorithms*, pages 632–640. Society for Industrial and Applied Mathematics, 1995.

[9] H. Fröhlich, A. Košir, and B. Zajc. Optimization of FPGA configurations using parallel genetic algorithm. *Information Sciences*, 133(3):195–219, 2001.

[10] M. Garey and D. Johnson. *Computers and Intractability*, volume 174. Freeman San Francisco, CA, 1979.

[11] K. Kim and B. Moon. Malware detection based on dependency graph using hybrid genetic algorithm. In *Proceedings of the 12th Annual Conference on Genetic and Evolutionary Computation*, pages 1211–1218. ACM, 2010.

Table 3: The result of optimization by GA

M	η	f_1			$f(0.1, 0.9)$		
		f_1	CPU(s)	Ratio(%)	f_1	CPU(s)	Ratio(%)
10	0.01	0.00	0.32	**100**	0.00	0.28	**100**
	0.05	0.00	0.25	**100**	0.00	0.24	**100**
	0.1	0.00	1.26	**100**	0.00	3.45	**100**
	0.2	1.33	19.58	47	1.23	30.31	47
30	0.01	0.00	18.05	**100**	0.00	8.54	**100**
	0.05	12.57	194.38	7	12.00	359.96	10
	0.1	28.37	133.18	43	21.77	235.84	57
	0.2	43.73	92.08	60	25.70	153.58	77
50	0.01	2.97	469.52	10	0.30	493.49	70
	0.05	56.70	412.92	23	7.45	228.06	90
	0.1	21.80	129.80	90	9.70	167.71	95
	0.2	27.70	94.95	93	41.40	167.59	90
70	0.01	11.00	936.93	0	0.00	464.26	**100**
	0.05	43.27	388.58	80	0.00	126.65	**100**
	0.1	16.17	132.15	97	0.00	79.29	**100**
	0.2	0.00	95.25	**100**	0.00	110.03	**100**
90	0.01	8.37	1379.68	43	0.00	485.13	**100**
	0.05	14.93	240.13	97	0.00	81.96	**100**
	0.1	0.00	134.92	**100**	0.00	61.00	**100**
	0.2	0.00	170.88	**100**	0.00	90.31	**100**

[12] J. McGregor. Backtrack search algorithms and the maximal common subgraph problem. *Software: Practice and Experience*, 12(1):23–34, 1982.

[13] I. Oliver, D. Smith, and J. Holland. A study of permutation crossover operators on the traveling salesman problem. In *Proceedings of the Second International Conference on Genetic Algorithms and Their Application*, pages 224–230. L. Erlbaum Associates Inc., 1987.

[14] J. Rutgers, P. Wolkotte, P. Holzenspies, J. Kuper, and G. Smit. An approximate maximum common subgraph algorithm for large digital circuits. In *2010 13th Euromicro Conference on Digital System Design: Architectures, Methods and Tools (DSD)*, pages 699–705. IEEE, 2010.

[15] J. Schaffer and J. Grefenstette. Multi-objective learning via genetic algorithms. In *Proceedings of the Ninth International Joint Conference on Artificial Intelligence*, pages 593–595. Citeseer, 1985.

[16] J. Ullmann. An algorithm for subgraph isomorphism. *Journal of the ACM (JACM)*, 23(1):31–42, 1976.

[17] M. Wagener and J. Gasteiger. The determination of maximum common substructures by a genetic algorithm: Application in synthesis design and for the structural analysis of biological activity. *Angewandte Chemie International Edition in English*, 33(11):1189–1192, 1994.

Local Optima Networks and the Performance of Iterated Local Search

Fabio Daolio
Faculty of Business and Economics, DESI
University of Lausanne
fabio.daolio@unil.ch

Sébastien Verel
Université Nice-Sophia Antipolis
INRIA Lille Nord Europe
verel@i3s.unice.fr

Gabriela Ochoa
School of Computer Science, A.S.A.P. Group
University of Nottingham
gxo@cs.nott.ac.uk

Marco Tomassini
Faculty of Business and Economics, DESI
University of Lausanne
marco.tomassini@unil.ch

ABSTRACT

Local Optima Networks (LONs) have been recently proposed as an alternative model of combinatorial fitness landscapes. The model compresses the information given by the whole search space into a smaller mathematical object that is the graph having as vertices the local optima and as edges the possible weighted transitions between them. A new set of metrics can be derived from this model that capture the distribution and connectivity of the local optima in the underlying configuration space.This paper departs from the descriptive analysis of local optima networks, and actively studies the correlation between network features and the performance of a local search heuristic. The NK family of landscapes and the Iterated Local Search metaheuristic are considered. With a statistically-sound approach based on multiple linear regression, it is shown that some LONs' features strongly influence and can even partly predict the performance of a heuristic search algorithm. This study validates the expressive power of LONs as a model of combinatorial fitness landscapes.

Categories and Subject Descriptors

F.2.m [**Analysis of Algorithms and Problem Complexity**]: Miscellaneous; G.2.2 [**Discrete Mathematics**]: Graph Theory—*Network problems*; I.2.8 [**Artificial Intelligence**]: Problem Solving, Control Methods, and Search—*Heuristic methods*

General Terms

Algorithms, Measurement, Performance

Keywords

Combinatorial Fitness Landscape, Local Optima Network, Local Search Heuristics

1. INTRODUCTION

One of the most conspicuous limitations of heuristic search methods in combinatorial optimization, is the ability to become trapped at a local optimum [9]. The number and distribution of local optima in a search space have, therefore, an important impact on the performance of heuristic search algorithms. A recently proposed model: Local Optima Networks [22, 25], provides an intermediate level of description for combinatorial fitness landscapes. The model has a higher descriptive power than a single statistical metric or set of metrics; but it also compresses the search space into a more manageable mathematical object. Specifically, a graph having as vertices the optima configurations of the problem and as edges the possible weighted transitions between these optima. This network representation allows the application of new analytical tools and metrics to study combinatorial landscapes, namely, those of complex networks analysis (e.g. degree distribution, clustering coefficient, assortativity, and community structure, to name a few). In previous work, alternative definitions of edges have been studied, and some of these metrics have been computed on the network extracted for two combinatorial problems: the NK family of landscapes [22, 16, 17, 25, 24], and the Quadratic Assignment problem [7, 6]. Those studies have been mainly descriptive, although distinctive correlations between some network features and previous knowledge about search difficulty in these landscapes had been found. A previous related work [18], explored the relationships between NK landscape features and the performance of a hybrid EA. The authors use standard landscape metrics, and conduct a study based mainly on scatter plots. They suggest that: "further work is necessary to gain better understanding of the escape rate on the actual problem difficulty". The present study, addresses exactly this point. The goal is to systematically explore correlations between local optima network features and the performance of a stochastic local search algorithm (Iterated Local Search) running on the underlying combinatorial optimization problem (in this study the NK family of landscapes). The 'escape rate' is a property related to the local optimum, and the LON could be considered as a new tool to better understand problem difficulty. The ultimate goal is to have predictive models of the performance of specific local search heuristics when solving a given combinatorial optimization problem. This paper proposes an initial predictive model of performance based on the most influential LON features.

2. METHODS

The local optima network model of combinatorial landscapes, and the iterated local search metaheuristic are considered in this study. The relevant definitions and experimental setup are given below.

2.1 Local Optima Network

A *fitness landscape* [20] is a triplet (S, V, f) where S is a set of potential solutions i.e. the *search space*, $V : S \longrightarrow 2^S$ is a function that assigns to every $s \in S$ a set of neighbors $V(s)$ i.e the *neighborhood structure*, and $f : S \longrightarrow \mathbb{R}$ is the evaluation of the corresponding solutions i.e. the *fitness function*.

The present study uses the well-known NK-landscapes [12] as a benchmark set. It is a problem-independent model for constructing combinatorial landscapes that are tunably rugged. In the model, N refers to the number of (binary) genes in the genotype, i.e. the string length, and K to their epistatic interaction, i.e. the number of other loci (chosen at random here) that influence the fitness contribution of a particular gene. Starting from this N-loci 2-allele additive model, by increasing the non-linearity K from 0 to $N-1$, the landscapes can be tuned from smooth to rugged. Hence, S is the search space of all N-bit binary strings, and its size is $\sharp S = 2^N$. The neighborhood is defined by the minimum possible move on it, which is the single bit-flip operation, and the neighborhood size is $\sharp V(s) = N$. The fitness function evaluates each genotype s as $f(s) = \frac{1}{N}\sum_{i=1}^{N} f_i(s_i, s_{i1}, \ldots, s_{iK})$, where the values of loci contributions $f_i : \{0,1\}^{K+1} \rightarrow [0,1]$ are drawn uniformly at random in $[0,1]$.

A *local optimum* (*LO*), which is taken to be a maximum here, is a solution s^* such that $\forall s \in V(s)$, $f(s) \leq f(s^*)$. All optima are determined through exhaustive search by recursively running the 1-bit-flip best-improvement hill-climber, as in Algorithm 1. Let us denote by $h(s)$ the operator that associates to each solution $s \in S$, the solution obtained after applying that algorithm until convergence to a LO. Since S is of finite size and there is no neutrality in $f(s)$ values, this produces a partition of the landscape in a finite number of basins of attraction, which we can denote by $LO_1, LO_2, LO_3 \ldots, LO_{nv}$, the local optima.

Algorithm 1: Best-Improvement Hill-Climber

```
Choose initial solution s ∈ S ;
repeat
    choose s' ∈ V(s), such that f(s') = max_{x∈V(s)} f(x);
    if f(s) < f(s') then
        s ← s';
until s is a Local Optimum;
```

The connections among them account for the chances of escaping from a LO and jumping into another one with a controlled move [24]. There exists a directed transition e_{ij} from LO_i to LO_j if it exists a solution s such that $d(s, LO_i) \leq D$ and $h(s) = LO_j$, where the distance $d(s_i, s_j)$ can be measured in "number of moves" (i.e Hamming distance in the bit-flip operator case). The distance-threshold $D \in \mathbb{N}$ can be chosen accordingly to the applied perturbation; in this work, it is set to $D = 2$. The weight w_{ij} of such a transition is then: $w_{ij} = \sharp\{s \in S \mid d(s, LO_i) \leq D$ and $h(s) = LO_j\}$, i.e. the number of paths at distance D starting at LO_i and reaching the basin of LO_j. This can be normalized by the number of solutions within reach w.r.t. the given distance threshold, i.e. $\sharp\{s \in S \mid d(s, LO_i) \leq D\}$.

The weighted and directed graph $G = (V, E)$ having the set of vertices $V = \{LO_1, \ldots, LO_{nv}\}$ and the set of edges $E = \{e_{ij} | w_{ij} > 0\}$, is the *Local Optima Network* (LON) [24].

2.2 Iterated Local Search

Iterated local search is a relatively simple but successful algorithm. It operates by iteratively alternating between applying a move operator to the incumbent solution and restarting local search from the perturbed solution. This search principle has been rediscovered multiple times, within different research communities and with different names [3, 14]. The term *iterated local search* (ILS) was proposed in [13]. Algorithm 2 outlines the procedure.

Algorithm 2: Iterated Local Search

```
s0 ← GenerateInitialSolution;
s* ← LocalSearch(s0);
repeat
    s' ← Perturbation(s*);
    s'* ← LocalSearch(s');
    s* ← AcceptanceCriterion(s*, s'*);
until termination condition met;
```

In the present study, the base LocalSearch heuristic is the same best-improvement hill-climber of Algorithm 1, which stops on a LO. This heuristic uses the single bit-flip move operator. Therefore, a 2-bit-flip mutation is chosen as a Perturbation operator. When a different LO is found after that, the search process accepts the move if its fitness is higher (we are assuming maximization). With these settings, ILS is performing a first-improvement hill-climbing in the configuration space of the LON with the escape-edges at distance $D = 2$, as defined in section 2.1.

The search terminates at the global optimum, which for benchmark problems is known *a priori*, or when reaching a pre-set limit of fitness evaluations FE_{max}.

2.3 Performance Evaluation

As the performance criterion, we selected the expected number of function evaluations to reach the global optimum (*success*) after independent restarts of the ILS algorithm (Algorithm 2) [1]. This measure accounts for both the success rate ($p_s \in (0,1]$) and the convergence speed. In theory, after $(N-1)$ unsuccessful runs stopped at T_{us}-steps and the final successful one running for T_s-steps, the total running time would be $T = \sum_{k=1}^{N-1} (T_{us})_k + T_s$. Taking the expectation and considering that N follows a geometric distribution[1] with parameter p_s, it gives:

$$\mathbb{E}(T) = \left(\frac{1-p_s}{p_s}\right)\mathbb{E}(T_{us}) + \mathbb{E}(T_s)$$

where in the present case $\mathbb{E}(T_{us}) = FE_{max}$, the ratio of successful to total runs is an estimator for p_s, and $\mathbb{E}(T_s)$ can be estimated by the average running time of those successful runs.

The ILS variant detailed in Sec. 2.2 is *essentially incomplete*, i.e. there are soluble problem instances for which the success probability is < 1 even in the limit of an infinite running time [11]. Given the chosen acceptance criterion, the search will eventually get stuck. Indeed, out of the test runs, 1 instance with $K = 16$ and 3 instances with $K = 17$ were not solved. This theoretical limitation could be overcome by performing as many random restart as to cover the whole search space, but such a solution is of limited

[1] probability distribution of the number $N-1$ of failures before the first success (*Bernoulli trials*)

Table 1: Group averages of all the observed variables, aggregated by the epistasis K of the corresponding NK-landscape. Standard deviations are given in subscripts. nv = number of vertices (Local Optima), lo = average shortest path to reach the global optimum, lv = average path length ($d_{ij} = 1/w_{ij}$), fnn = Spearman coefficient for the nearest-neighbors fitness-fitness correlation, wii = average non-normalized weight of self-loops, cc global clustering coefficient, $zout$ = average out-going degree, $y2$ = average weight disparity for out-going edges, knn = degree assortativity, ets = estimated time to succeed.

aggregate	nv	lo	lv	fnn	wii	cc	zout	y2	knn	ets ($\times 10^4$)
$K = 2$	43_{28}	33.5_{14}	187_{51}	$0.703_{0.19}$	105_{11}	$0.425_{0.086}$	$6.9_{1.8}$	$0.392_{0.075}$	$0.155_{0.4}$	$2.16_{3.3}$
$K = 4$	221_{39}	53.7_{12}	214_{15}	$0.587_{0.07}$	83.9_{3}	$0.263_{0.013}$	14.3_{1}	$0.219_{0.016}$	$-0.536_{0.13}$	$8.39_{7.74}$
$K = 6$	748_{70}	66.7_{13}	$188_{4.8}$	$0.535_{0.041}$	$67.5_{1.9}$	$0.19_{0.005}$	$24.8_{0.86}$	$0.124_{0.0059}$	$-0.778_{0.035}$	$32.6_{36.1}$
$K = 8$	1669_{73}	$76.6_{9.1}$	$171_{1.9}$	$0.431_{0.025}$	$53.3_{0.88}$	$0.159_{0.0012}$	$35.7_{0.57}$	$0.0769_{0.002}$	$-0.856_{0.022}$	$51.8_{61.1}$
$K = 10$	3148_{110}	$90.7_{8.4}$	$166_{1.2}$	$0.342_{0.016}$	$40.7_{0.78}$	$0.143_{0.00085}$	$47.2_{0.57}$	$0.0491_{0.0011}$	$-0.904_{0.011}$	$81.5_{70.6}$
$K = 12$	5270_{104}	108_{12}	$170_{0.64}$	$0.255_{0.015}$	$30.8_{0.35}$	$0.133_{0.00054}$	$57.8_{0.39}$	$0.0334_{0.00046}$	$-0.928_{0.0093}$	276_{544}
$K = 14$	8100_{121}	$125_{8.6}$	$181_{0.6}$	$0.19_{0.011}$	$23.5_{0.25}$	$0.128_{0.00032}$	$66.9_{0.33}$	$0.0245_{0.00022}$	$-0.944_{0.0063}$	300_{288}
$K = 16$	11688_{101}	146_{11}	$197_{0.42}$	$0.143_{0.0073}$	$18.2_{0.11}$	$0.125_{0.00023}$	$74.6_{0.17}$	$0.0196_{7.8e-05}$	$-0.948_{0.0055}$	414_{632}
$K = 17$	13801_{74}	156_{12}	$205_{0.42}$	$0.133_{0.01}$	$16.1_{0.06}$	$0.125_{0.00021}$	$78.2_{0.13}$	$0.0179_{6.5e-05}$	$-0.944_{0.0063}$	793_{844}

practical interest for large problems. In the present study, the success performance has been estimated on all the instances that had been solved at least once.

The benchmark set consists of NK-landscapes with $N = 18$ and $K \in \{2, 4, 6, 8, 10, 12, 14, 16, 17\}$. Those are the largest possible parameter combinations for which we could afford the exhaustive extraction of the local optima networks. In order to minimize the influence of the random generation of landscapes, 30 independent problem instances are considered for each combination of N and K, which accounts for a total of 270 instances in the problem set. The function-evaluations limit is set to $1/5$ of $\sharp S$, i.e. $FE_{max} \simeq 5.2 \cdot 10^4$, success rate p_s and running time of successful runs T_s are estimated on 500 random restarts per instance.

3. RESULTS

3.1 Descriptive Statistics

Table 1 summarises the LON metrics. Results are grouped according to the K value of the corresponding NK-landscapes, and present averages and standard deviations over 30 independent realizations per group. The number of local optima nv, is a metric familiar to any description of a rugged landscape. The other metrics are particular to the complex-network perspective provided by the LON model [15].

From left to right in the table, lo represents the average length of the shortest paths that reach the global optimum starting from any other local optimum. The cost associated to an edge $\vec{ij}$ of the LON graph, is $d_{ij} = 1/w_{ij}$. This measure can be interpreted as the expected number of random perturbations for escaping LO_i and entering exactly the basin of LO_j. lv gives the average path length for the whole graph, which accounts for the weighted network *characteristic length*. lo is intuitively more directly related to the search difficulty. Indeed, lo increases steadily with the landscape ruggedness K, whilst the trend with lv is less clear. As a possible explanation, the network growth in terms of nodes might be counteracted by a growth in nodes connectivity: the number of weighted outgoing transitions from a given LO, i.e. its out-degree in the LON, increases with K (cf. column $zout$ in Tab. 1).

Column fnn measures the correlation between the fitness of a node and the weighted average of the fitness of its nearest neighbors [2]. This is relevant as the ILS acceptance criterion takes the fitness values of LO into account. With respect to this metric, NK-landscapes behave at the LO level as they do at the solution level: they become the more and more uncorrelated with K approaching $N - 1$ (see column fnn). In general, it is expected that a high and positive fnn correlation would help the search process.

Column wii reports the average number of perturbations that remain in the same basin of attraction, which is a proxy for the basin size. The larger the basins, the more difficult it is to escape them. Table 1 shows that average wii value decreases with the landscape ruggedness.

Column cc, reports the *clustering coefficient* [15], which measures the ratio of connected triples in the LON graph. In a social network, this coefficient measures the probability for one's friends to be friends among each other. In the LO networks, it provides an index of topological locality for the transitions between local optima. Table 1 suggest that cc values decrease steadily with increasing K, but so does the LON density [24] and that might be the reason.

Column $zout$ counts the number of transitions departing from a given LO. It is relevant to know whether all the transitions have the same rate, or if there is a preferred direction. To this aim, the *disparity* score $y2$ gauges the weight heterogeneity of out-going edges [2]. When all connections e_{ij} leaving a given LO_i have the same probability w_{ij}, the disparity will be close to the inverse of the out-degree $1/zout_i$ otherwise it will be higher than this value. Column $y2$ shows that the disparity monotonically decreases with increasing K. From the point of view of a metaheuristic dynamic, a low disparity means that transitions are almost equiprobable. The LON topology does not preferentially guide the search trajectory, which makes the search process harder.

Column knn, reports the nearest-neighbors degree correlation or *assortativity*, a classical description of the mixing pattern of nodes in a network. The assortativity measures the affinity to connect with high or low-degree neighbors. The LONs of NK-landscapes are strongly disassortative, i.e. LO with few connections tend to link to others with many, and conversely. The implications of this observation on the search difficulty are worth further investigation.

The last column in Table 1 gives the values of the success performance indicator $\mathbb{E}(T)$ detailed in Sec 2.3, which we abbreviate to ets in the following. Clearly, the expected running time increases with the landscape ruggedness (problem non-linearity) K. In order to analyze the inter-correlations between all the studied metrics, Figure 1 displays a *correlogram* of the whole data set. The figure depicts any possible pairing among the observed variables with a scatter plot in the panel below the diagonal, and the corresponding

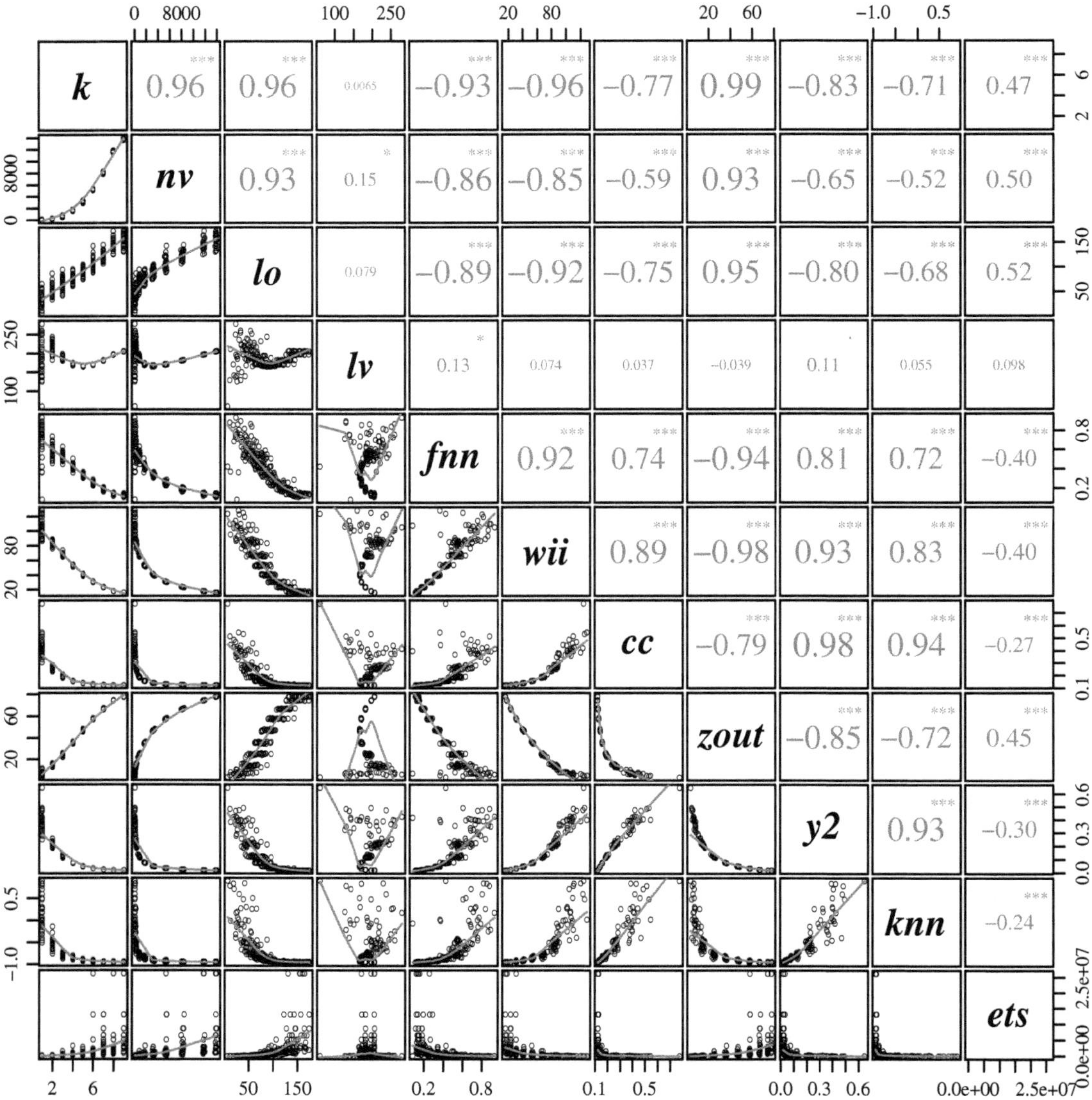

Figure 1: Correlation matrix for all pairs of the observed variables, to be read from the diagonal. The lower panel displays scatter plots and smoothing splines for every possible pairing; the upper panel gives the corresponding Pearson correlation coefficient, with text size proportional to its absolute value. In the lower panel, the smoothing is done through locally-weighted polynomial regressions [5]. In the upper panel, the correlation coefficient is tested against the null hypothesis and the resulting p-value is symbolically encoded at the levels of 0.1 **(')**, 0.05 **(*)**, 0.01 **(**)**, **and** 0.001 **(***).**

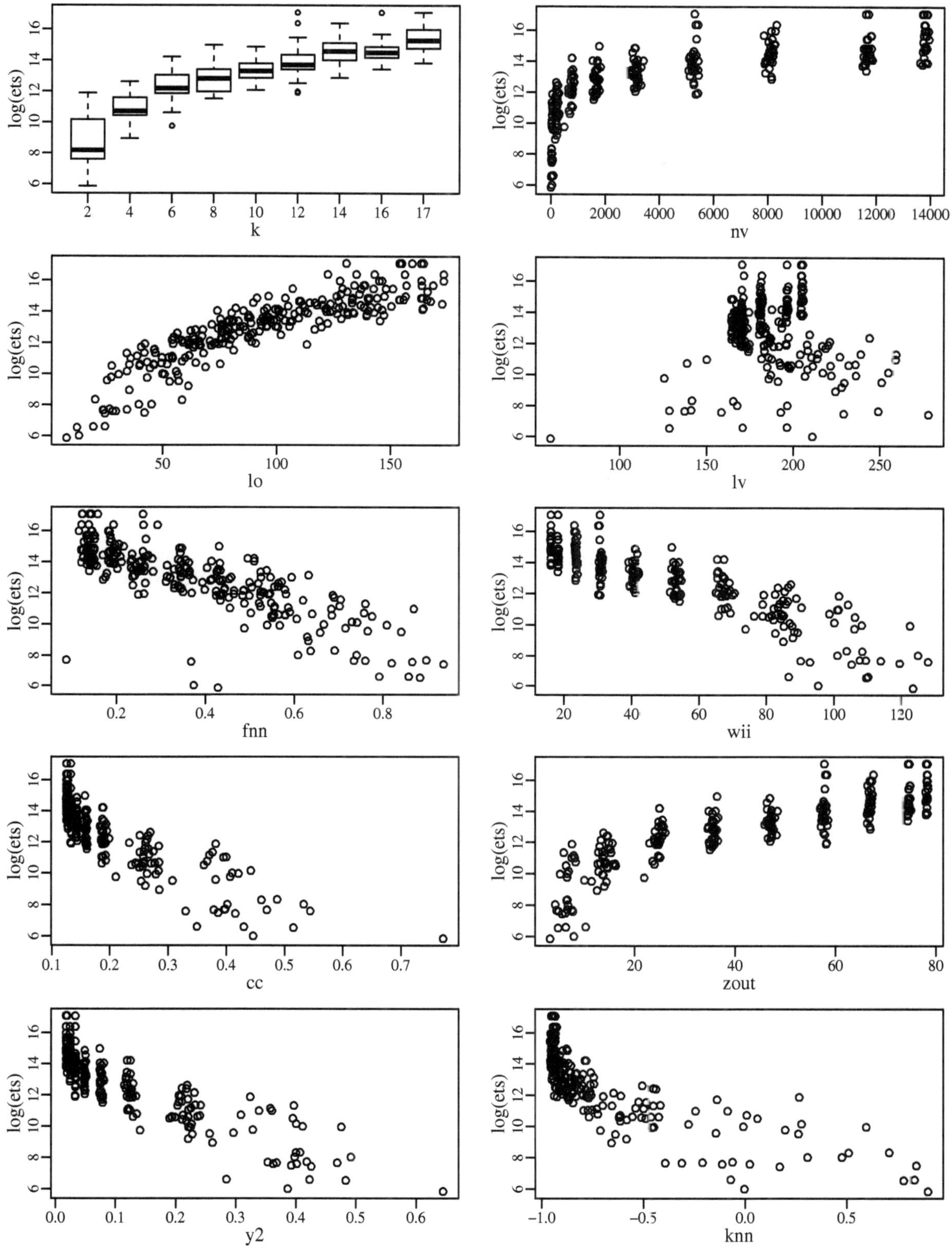

Figure 2: Scatter plots of the logarithm of the estimated time to succeed against all measured variables (see labels on x-axis). The epistasis value K is treated as a category, thus results are in a box-and-whisker diagram per group (fist plot on the top-left corner).

correlation coefficient in the upper panel. Table 1 corresponds to the first column of the correlation matrix, i.e. the one showing how the different network metrics shape against the epistasis K.

We are mostly interested in the correlations with the performance metric ets. Thus, the most relevant scatter plots are those in the last row of Figure 1 together with the respective Pearson coefficients in the last column. By inspecting these values, the highest positive correlation is with the average length of the shortest path climbing to the global optimum ($r(ets, lo) \simeq 0.52$). and with the total number of LO ($r(ets, nv) \simeq 0.50$). This observation seems reasonable: the more rugged the landscape (i.e. the larger its LON), the higher the number of hops through the LON to reach the global optimum, and thus the longer the expected running time of a restarting local search. Conversely, the larger the LO basins, and the higher the nearest-neighbors fitness-fitness correlation, the shorter the running time (($r(ets, wii) \simeq r(ets, fnn) \simeq -0.40$)). The catch here, is that those metrics are in turn correlated among themselves (e.g. $r(fnn, wii) \simeq 0.92$), which prevents one from drawing relationships of causality from simple pair-wise correlations.

The last column plots also suggest a strong non-linearity of the performance estimator w.r.t. the LON metrics. In order to further analyze these relationships, Figure 2 zooms on the relevant scatter plots, and displays the logarithm of ets as a function of the considered landscape measures. The log-transformation allows to approach linearity, highlighting and confirming the results in the last column of Figure 1. Namely, the relationships between ets and all the metrics but lv appear clearly. The picture suggests a positive exponential trend with lo and $zout$, and a negative exponential trend with fnn, wii, cc, and $y2$. In the case of nv, the relation could also be close to power-law.

Since data are far from being normal bivariate, a more robust measure of association would be the rank-based Spearman's ρ statistic, reported in Table 2. These results complement the visual inspection of scatter plots and confirm the previous observations.

Table 2: Spearman's ρ statistic for the correlation between ets and the LON metrics (p-value $< 2.2e-16$ for all pairings).

nv	lo	lv	fnn	wii	cc	zout	y2	knn
0.885	0.915	0.006	−0.830	−0.883	−0.875	0.885	−0.883	−0.850

3.2 Statistical Modeling

Figures 1 and 2, along with Table 2, address already some of the research questions asked in Section 1, but do not provide an explanatory model for the algorithm performance as a function of the landscape features. To this end, we perform a multiple linear regression on the data, which has the general form:

$$y_i = \beta_0 + \beta_1 x_{i,1} + \beta_2 x_{i,2} + \cdots + \beta_p x_{i,p} + \epsilon_i \quad (1)$$

where the response variable y in our case would be ets and p different predictors x_j are to be chosen among the LON metrics; ϵ is the usual random noise term.

The least square regression produces estimates $\hat{\beta}_j$ for the β_j model coefficients; the difference between the predicted values and the actual, observed values, are the regression residuals: $e_i = y_i - \hat{y}_i = y_i - \hat{\beta}_1 x_{i1} - \hat{\beta}_2 x_{i2} - \cdots - \hat{\beta}_p x_{ip}$.

The difficulty of this analysis is that there are several possible explanatory variables, which are in turn intercorrelated. In consequence, some of them could have a confounding effect on the regression. In general, when confounders are known, measurable, and measured, it is a good practice to include them in the model. We, therefore, start by fitting the following formula:

$$\log(ets) = \beta_0 + \beta_1 k + \beta_2 \log(nv) + \beta_2 lo + \cdots + \beta_{10} knn + \epsilon \quad (2)$$

where, w.r.t the general expression 1, the response and one of the predictors have been log-transformed in order to better approach linearity, as seen in Figure 2. Moreover, the variable k is qualitative and enters the model as a fixed effect, which translates in one appropriate dummy variable for each class $K = 2, K = 4, \ldots, K = 17$.

The summary statistics for this model are reported in Table 3. In the table caption, the multiple R^2 represents the proportion of variance explained by the linear regression. R^2 would be equal to 1 if all observed data points were lying on the regression plane. When comparing models with a different number of predictors, the adjusted R^2 should be used instead. The F statistic is the ratio of the variance explained by the parameters in the model, to the residual or unexplained variance. The p-value is the probability of achieving an F that large under the null hypothesis of no effect [4].

The estimated coefficient $\hat{\beta}_j$ and their estimated standard error $\hat{\sigma}_j$ are given in the 2nd and 3rd columns, respectively. Their ratio is the t-statistic (4th column) that is used to calculate a p-value for the significance of the estimation (last column).

Table 3: Summary statistics of the linear regression model on all variables. Residual standard error: 0.8702 on 248 degrees of freedom (4 observations deleted due to missingness). Multiple R-squared: 0.8585, Adjusted R-squared: 0.8488. F-statistic: 88.52 on 17 and 248 DF, p-value: $< 2.2e-16$.

summary	Estimate	Std. Error	t value	Pr(>|t|)
(Intercept)	16.06966	7.39640	2.1726	$3.08e-02$
k4	0.01542	0.63987	0.0241	$9.81e-01$
k6	−1.08926	1.39976	−0.7782	$4.37e-01$
k8	−3.14529	2.46616	−1.2754	$2.03e-01$
k10	−5.67316	3.76828	−1.5055	$1.33e-01$
k12	−8.19327	5.04638	−1.6236	$1.06e-01$
k14	−10.34765	6.17715	−1.6751	$9.52e-02$
k16	−12.85523	7.14074	−1.8003	$7.30e-02$
k17	−13.40456	7.59325	−1.7653	$7.87e-02$
log(nv)	−1.91370	1.12656	−1.6987	$9.06e-02$
lo	0.04882	0.00499	9.7919	$2.37e-19$
lv	0.00198	0.00376	0.5265	$5.99e-01$
fnn	0.54148	0.89574	0.6045	$5.46e-01$
wii	−0.00302	0.02739	−0.1104	$9.12e-01$
cc	−7.22853	5.00042	−1.4456	$1.50e-01$
zout	0.29514	0.15838	1.8636	$6.36e-02$
y2	−3.46837	5.00914	−0.6924	$4.89e-01$
knn	−0.88961	0.49062	−1.8132	$7.10e-02$

In this initial model, the average length of paths to the global optimum lo is the only predictor with a regression coefficient that is statistically-significant at the 0.05 threshold ($\beta_{lo} = 0.04882$, p-value = $2.37e-19$).

Therefore, we proceed to perform a step-wise model selection by *backward elimination* [23]. From the initial formula, at each step we compute what change in the fit could be produced by dropping each predictor in turn, and then we eliminate the one that minimizes the AIC score of the resulting model [21]. By iterating until all predictors become significant, we obtain the final model:

$$\log(ets) = \beta_0 + \beta_{lo} lo + \beta_{zout} zout + \beta_{y2} y2 + \beta_{knn} knn + \epsilon \quad (3)$$

which is detailed in Table 4.

Table 4: Summary statistics of the final linear regression model. Residual standard error: 0.8751 **on** 261 **degrees of freedom** (4 **observations deleted due to missingness). Multiple R-squared:** 0.8494**, Adjusted R-squared:** 0.8471**. F-statistic:** 368.1 **on** 4 **and** 261 **DF,** p**-value:** $< 2.2e-16$**.**

summary	Estimate	Std. Error	t value	Pr(>|t|)
(Intercept)	10.3838	0.58512	17.75	$9.24e-47$
lo	0.0439	0.00434	10.11	$1.67e-20$
zout	-0.0306	0.00831	-3.68	$2.81e-04$
y2	-7.2831	1.63038	-4.47	$1.18e-05$
knn	-0.7457	0.40501	-1.84	$6.67e-02$

This final model is able to explain 84.94% of the variance observed in $\log(ets)$ with a linear regression on four variables that are all LON network metrics. Among these metrics, the length of the paths to the global optimum, and the weight disparity have the highest relative importance [10].

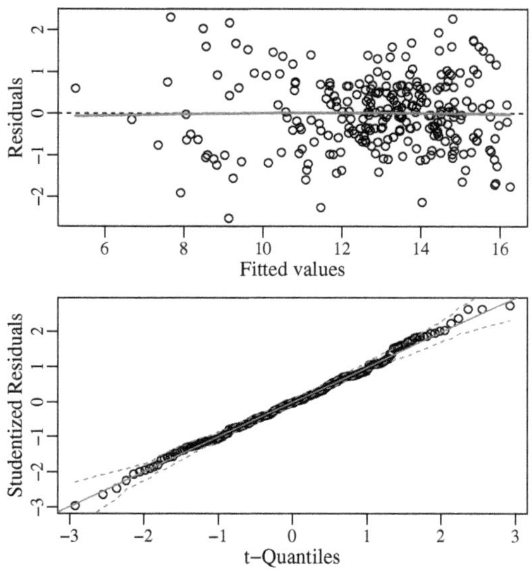

Figure 3: Top: residual plot, to asses the hypothesis of zero-mean and constant-variance of the regression residuals (circle dots) around the fitted values (dotted line); no visually-significant deviation appears (red smooth line). Bottom: quantile-quantile comparison of the studentized regression residuals (circle dots) against the theoretical quantiles (red thick line), to inspect the distribution of residuals; no significant deviation from normality appears (confidence intervals as dotted red lines).

Without a check on the model assumptions, this would remain an observational study and could not be used to make predictions. To this end, a combination of parametric tests (not reported for space reasons) provided a positive confirmation [19]. However, a visual diagnostics is more informative. In particular, Figure 3 helps to assess if the regression residuals follow a normal distribution with zero mean and homogeneous variance, whereas Figure 4 displays the contributions to the model of each predictor in turn, highlighting possible violations of the linearity hypothesis [8]. All assumptions seem acceptable. Therefore, formula 3 could be used to make inferences. In other words, formula 3 coefficients can be interpreted as conditional expectations for the average change in the response when one predictor undergoes a unitary change, and all the others remain fix. Since the dependent variable is log-transformed, this effect would be multiplicative.

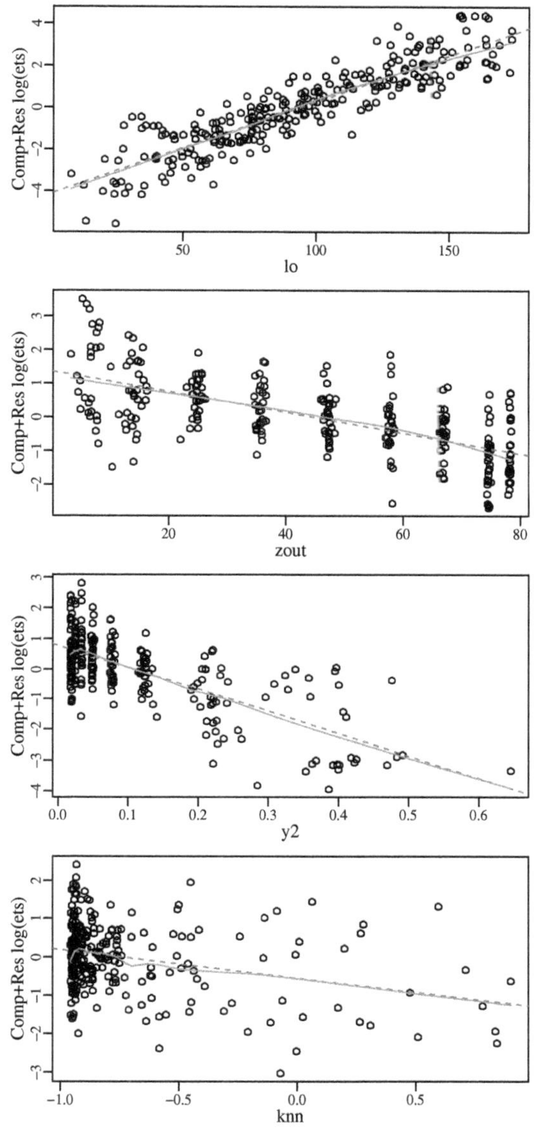

Figure 4: Component+residual plots for the linear regression model. Circle dots are, for each observation, the corresponding residual error from the regression plus the value fitted by one explanatory variable alone, plotted against that variable (see labels on x-axis). No significant deviation from linearity appears (smooth green line against the red dotted line of the partial regression).

The only important limitation of the proposed model is *multicollinearity*: due to the complex intercorrelations among LON metrics (cf. Figure 1), predictors are not really independent. This does not invalidate the multiple linear regression analysis, but it inflates the variance of its coefficients and makes it harder to disentangle their respective contributions [8].

4. CONCLUSIONS

This article explored correlations between local optima network features and the performance of a stochastic local search algorithm running on the underlying combinatorial optimization problem. The NK family of landscapes and the iterated local search meta-heuristic were considered. It has been shown in previous work e.g. [22, 25] that some features of the LON networks are related to the NK-landscapes ruggedness, and thus to problem difficulty. However, no statistically testable model was presented. The contribution of this study was to investigate, with a statistically-sound approach, which features of the LONs have a strong influence on the search performance, expressed as expected running times to success. The results obtained through the use of a multiple linear regression model show that some LON metrics are more important than others. These are: the average length of the shortest paths to the optimum, the average out-degree, the average disparity, and the degree assortativity. This study confirms and provides significant evidence that LON modeling is a compressed-but-relevant view of the fitness landscape, and can be used to understand and predict search difficulty.

It is worth noticing that some network metrics can be estimated without knowing the global optimum beforehand, such as the average out-degree, the fitness-fitness correlation, the average disparity and assortativity. Using these metrics and an adequate statistical model, as we have done in this work, opens up exciting possibilities. With standard sampling methods, larger search spaces could be studied. Thereafter, using the performance model based on the estimated LON metrics, the search heuristic parameters or its operators can be off-line tuned, or even on-line controlled. We plan to continue working in this direction and to extend this analysis to other combinatorial problems such as QAP.

5. ACKNOWLEDGMENTS

Fabio Daolio and Marco Tomassini gratefully acknowledge the Swiss National Science Foundation for financial support under grant number 200021-124578.

6. REFERENCES

[1] A. Auger and N. Hansen. Performance evaluation of an advanced local search evolutionary algorithm. In *Evolutionary Computation, 2005. The 2005 IEEE Congress on*, volume 2, pages 1777–1784. IEEE, 2005.

[2] M. Barthélemy, A. Barrat, R. Pastor-Satorras, and A. Vespignani. Characterization and modeling of weighted networks. *Physica A: Statistical Mechanics and its Applications*, 346(1):34–43, 2005.

[3] J. Baxter. Local optima avoidance in depot location. *Journal of the Operational Research Society*, 32:815–819, 1981.

[4] J. Chambers, T. Hastie, et al. Linear models. In *Statistical models in S*, chapter 4. Chapman & Hall London, 1992.

[5] W. Cleveland. Lowess: A program for smoothing scatterplots by robust locally weighted regression. *The American Statistician*, 35(1):54–54, 1981.

[6] F. Daolio, M. Tomassini, S. Vérel, and G. Ochoa. Communities of minima in local optima networks of combinatorial spaces. *Physica A Statistical Mechanics and its Applications*, 390:1684–1694, 2011.

[7] F. Daolio, S. Verel, G. Ochoa, and M. Tomassini. Local Optima Networks of the Quadratic Assignment Problem. In *Evolutionary Computation (CEC), 2010 IEEE Congress on*, pages 1–8. IEEE, 2010.

[8] J. Fox and S. Weisberg. *An R Companion to Applied Regression*. Sage, Thousand Oaks CA, second edition, 2011.

[9] F. Glover. Future paths for integer programming and links to artificial intelligence. *Computers & Operations Research*, 13(5):533–549, 1986.

[10] U. Groemping. Relative importance for linear regression in R: The package relaimpo. *Journal of Statistical Software*, 17(1):1–27, 2006.

[11] H. Hoos and T. Stützle. *Stochastic local search: Foundations and applications*. Morgan Kaufmann, 2005.

[12] S. A. Kauffman. *The Origins of Order*. Oxford University Press, New York, 1993.

[13] H. R. Lourenço, O. Martin, and T. Stützle. Iterated local search. In *Handbook of Metaheuristics*, volume 57 of *International Series in Operations Research & Management Science*, pages 321–353. Kluwer Academic Publishers, 2002.

[14] O. Martin, S. W. Otto, and E. W. Felten. Large-step Markov chains for the TSP incorporating local search heuristics. *Operations Research Letters*, 11(4):219–224, 1992.

[15] M. Newman. The structure and function of complex networks. *SIAM review*, pages 167–256, 2003.

[16] G. Ochoa, M. Tomassini, S. Verel, and C. Darabos. A study of NK landscapes' basins and local optima networks. In *Genetic and Evolutionary Computation Conference, GECCO 2008*, pages 555–562. ACM, 2008.

[17] G. Ochoa, S. Verel, and M. Tomassini. First-improvement vs. best-improvement local optima networks of nk landscapes. In *Parallel Problem Solving from Nature - PPSN XI*, volume 6238 of *Lecture Notes in Computer Science*, pages 104–113. Springer, 2010.

[18] M. Pelikan. Nk landscapes, problem difficulty, and hybrid evolutionary algorithms. In *Proceedings of the 12th annual conference on Genetic and evolutionary computation*, GECCO '10, pages 665–672, New York, NY, USA, 2010. ACM.

[19] E. A. Pena and E. H. Slate. *gvlma: Global Validation of Linear Models Assumptions*, 2010. R package version 1.0.0.1.

[20] C. Reidys and P. Stadler. Combinatorial landscapes. *SIAM review*, 44(1):3–54, 2002.

[21] Y. Sakamoto and G. Kitagawa. *Akaike information criterion statistics*. Kluwer Academic Publishers, 1987.

[22] M. Tomassini, S. Verel, and G. Ochoa. Complex-network analysis of combinatorial spaces: The NK landscape case. *Phys. Rev. E*, 78(6):066114, 2008.

[23] W. N. Venables and B. D. Ripley. *Modern Applied Statistics with S*. Springer, New York, fourth edition, 2002. ISBN 0-387-95457-0.

[24] S. Verel, F. Daolio, G. Ochoa, and M. Tomassini. Local Optima Networks with Escape Edges. In *Procedings of International Conference on Artificial Evolution (EA-2011)*, pages 10 – 23, Angers, France, Oct 2011.

[25] S. Verel, G. Ochoa, and M. Tomassini. Local optima networks of NK landscapes with neutrality. *Evolutionary Computation, IEEE Transactions on*, 6(15):783 – 797, 2011.

An Evolutionary Approach for the Dubins' Traveling Salesman Problem with Neighborhoods

Douglas G. Macharet
Armando Alves Neto
Vilar F. da Camara Neto*
Mario F. M. Campos
Computer Vision and Robotics Laboratory (VeRLab)
Department of Computer Science
Universidade Federal de Minas Gerais
Belo Horizonte - MG - Brazil
{doug,aaneto,neto,mario}@dcc.ufmg.br

ABSTRACT

In this work we propose an efficient and simple three-stage evolutionary algorithm to tackle the difficult problem of planning shorter paths through regions of an environment which are feasible for a nonholonomic vehicle with curvature constraints (*e.g.* Dubins' vehicle). Our method is able to efficiently solve both the combinatorial and the continuous steps of the problem in a combined manner. In the first phase, the method varies the position of the waypoints within the boundaries of each region, it then optimizes the path orientation at each waypoint, and finally it chooses the best actual sequence of visit. Numerous trials, under different scenarios in a simulated environment, were executed providing a thorough evaluation and validation of the methodology. The results show that a substantial improvement was obtained on the search for optimal paths in the Dubins' Traveling Salesman Problem with Neighborhoods (DTSPN) over current works in the literature. Numerical simulations also exhibit a significant performance improvement when compared with classical solutions that use the Alternating Algorithm, and they also show that our method outperforms a random sampling based technique. Our results present a reduction on the final path length of about 25% on average when compared to paths generated by the aforementioned methods.

Categories and Subject Descriptors

I.2.9 [**Artificial Intelligence**]: Robotics—*autonomous vehicles*; I.2.9 [**Artificial Intelligence**]: Robotics—*kinematics and dynamics*

*Vilar F. da Camara Neto is also with the Fundação Centro de Análise, Pesquisa e Inovação Tecnológica (FUCAPI), Manaus, AM, Brazil. E-mail: vilar.neto@fucapi.br.

GECCO'12, July 7-11, 2012, Philadelphia, Pennsylvania, USA.

General Terms

Algorithms, Performance, Experimentation

Keywords

TSP, Dubins' path, Nonholonomic vehicles

1. INTRODUCTION

Finding paths that are either length or time optimized has been the goal of several research fields, and throughout the years, several important results have been published. More than ever, parsimonious use of energy is paramount, and the search for energy efficient motion planning approaches are fundamental. Broadly speaking, the well known Traveling Salesman Problem (TSP) has been much investigated, and several important results have been made available.

As it happens with several hard problems, the first solutions were concerned with finding the best possible route, without taking into account the characteristics of the vehicle that would eventually perform it. In other words, several such approaches were designed for holonomic vehicles, for which mobility restrictions are imaterial. However, when motion constraints are present, due to the kinematic characteristic of the vehicle, the motion optimization tasks may turn out to be very difficult or even impossible to solve. It happens to be that the large majority of real world vehicles are non-holonomic, and are based on platforms with several motion constraints, in which case the classical TSP becomes more than just a combinatorial problem.

Car-like vehicles, for example, are unable to instantaneously move orthogonally to the rolling plane of their wheels due to kinematic constraints. Fixed-wing airplanes have limitations in their admissible curvature, climb angle and speed, which may even prevent them from following straight line paths produced by classical Euclidean TSP planners.

As far as the environment model is concerned, it is usually assumed that the vehicle is required to reach an exact position (*e.g.* cities in the TSP formulation, or a given waypoint for a robot). However, this is hardly the case in real world applications, where such precision may be unattainable or may not be even necessary. Therefore, when a vehicle does not have to reach a pre-defined set of points, but a group of regions instead, the difficulty of the problem becomes even greater. This is the type of problem we deal with in this paper.

This work describes our approach to tackle the problem of planning shorter paths through regions of an environment which are feasible for a non-holonomic vehicle with curvature constraints, based on an efficient and simple three-stage evolutionary algorithm.

Our robot is modeled as Dubins' vehicle, that is, a vehicle whose constraints are satisfied by paths modeled as Dubins' curves [6]. In that work, Dubins proved that optimal paths for vehicles with limited curvature radius in $\mathbb{R}^2$ are composed by three subcurves, tangent to the initial and final points with orientation angles previously specified.

Even though there exists a closed form solution to compute the length of a Dubins' curve, the problem of calculating a circuit through a set of points turns out to be quite difficult, since the orientation at each visited "city" must be taken into account. Actually, this is the description of the Dubins' TSP (DTSP), a variant of the TSP in a manifold space $SE(2)$, which is one order greater than the conventional two-dimensional space.

Further extending the idea, we may also consider the use of Dubins' vehicles in even more complex scenarios, such as the Traveling Salesman Problem with Neighborhoods (TSPN). In the Dubins' Traveling Salesman Problem with Neighborhoods (DTSPN) problem, there exist regions surrounding the waypoints that the Dubins' robots have to reached with any orientation, and finding an optimal solution for this case is quite expensive. Furthermore, the final path must be as short as possible in order to increase the vehicle's autonomy.

In this paper we present a solution to the problem of generating efficient (by efficient we mean *short*) paths for visiting regions in a known environment using a Dubins' vehicle. Combinatorial (referring to the sequence of visitation) and continuous (as far as the values of position and orientation at the waypoints is concerned) steps are treated in a combined manner using an Evolutionary Algorithm, in order to minimize the overall length of the complete tour, thereby reducing power consumption of the vehicle.

Our approach, which will be described later in the paper, produces tour lengths that are statistically ($\approx$ 25%, with confidence interval of 95%) shorter than those provided by state of the art algorithms in the literature.

The remainder of this paper is organized as follows: Section 2 discusses the works previously reported in the literature that have dealt with the related problems. Our methodology is detailed in Section 3 and validated by several experiments whose results are shown in Section 4. Finally, Section 5 discusses the results and indicate future directions for this investigation.

2. RELATED WORK

The generation of paths for nonholonomic vehicles is a topic of great relevance, especially in robotics. Numerous techniques that address this problem have been proposed in the literature.

Several shortest path algorithms for vehicles with no constraints have been reported. As an example, the Traveling Salesman Problem (TSP) is a fundamental optimization problem and has been widely studied [3]. The fundamental objective of the TSP is to determine the shortest path that passes through a set of points ("cities"), starting from and returning to any given point after having visited all other points exactly once. Formally, the problem can be posed as how to determine the shortest Hamiltonian cycle, which is known to be NP-hard.

Several papers dealing with this problem, but considering the constraints of the vehicle, are based of probabilistic algorithms. In [2] the authors propose a trajectory planning technique for fixed-wing UAVs in environments with obstacles based on Rapidly-Exploring Random Tree (RRT). In [12], path generation is obtained using Genetic Algorithms and Bézier curves.

However, most of the above methods have as their main focus the paths' feasibility (*e.g.* which satisfies the kinematic constraints of the vehicle), and usually neglect the length of the generated path.

In its seminal work, Dubins showed a way to calculate the shortest path between two points with assigned orientations in the two-dimensional space, considering a vehicle with a curvature constraint [6]. The resulting path is composed of line segments (S) and arcs (C) that respect the curvature radius of the vehicle. Figure 1 shows examples of Dubins' curves connecting different configurations. There are basically two types of paths: the short case (CCC) and the long case (CSC), or a subpath of a path of either of these two types. The first one is a composition of three arcs with the minimum curvature radius, while the other includes a straight line between arcs.

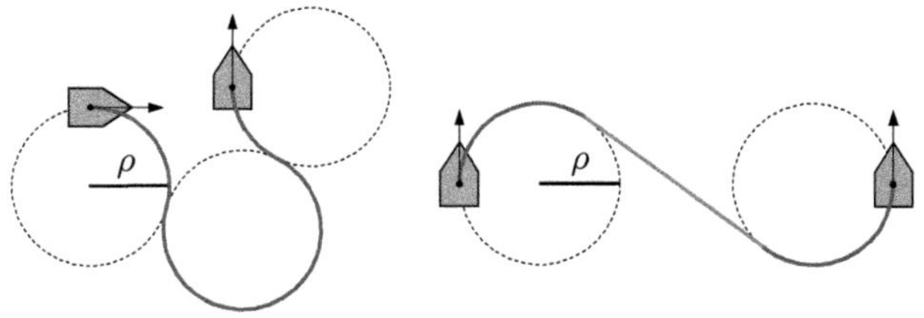

(a) (b)

Figure 1: Examples of Dubins' curves connecting configurations in two different cases: (a) the short case and (b) the long case.

The problem of generating the minimum length circuit visiting a set of points and considering the curvature constraint of the vehicle and making use of Dubins' curves, was initially introduced in [15]. This problem was named DTSP. Figure 2 shows the difference between the results given by the classical TSP and the DTSP. As it can be observed in the figure, curvature restriction and distribution of points in the environment may severely impact the length of the generated path.

Another generalization of the TSP is known as TSPN, and was presented in [4]. In this problem the salesman continues to possess a circuit of visits to be made. However, it is assumed that each point has a given associated neighborhood. So both the salesman and the buyer may meet in any place within this neighborhood. The problem can then be defined as how to generate the shortest path that intersects every neighborhood at least once.

In [7], an algorithm is proposed for the TSPN with non-overlapping regions. In [8] this restriction is lifted, and neighborhoods are allowed to have intersecting regions. The TSPN is often used to model problems related to the generation of tours to collect data from a wireless sensors network [18, 5].

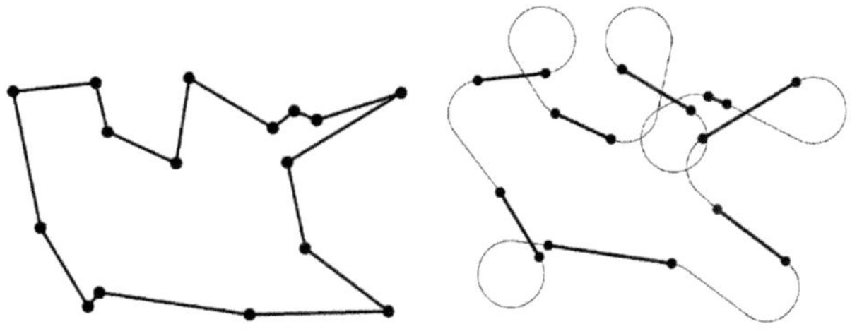

Figure 2: Comparison between the circuits obtained by the (a) TSP and the (b) DTSP with orientations given by the Alternating Algorithm [15].

A similar problem related to the TSPN is called Euclidean Group Traveling Salesman Problem (EGTSP) [9]. In this problem, the points of interest are grouped into clusters, and the shortest path generated passing through *at least one* of the points in each cluster must be calculated. This is an important difference from the TSPN, in which *any* part of the cluster can be visited (and not the exact position of a point). Figure 3 shows this difference between EGTSP and TSPN.

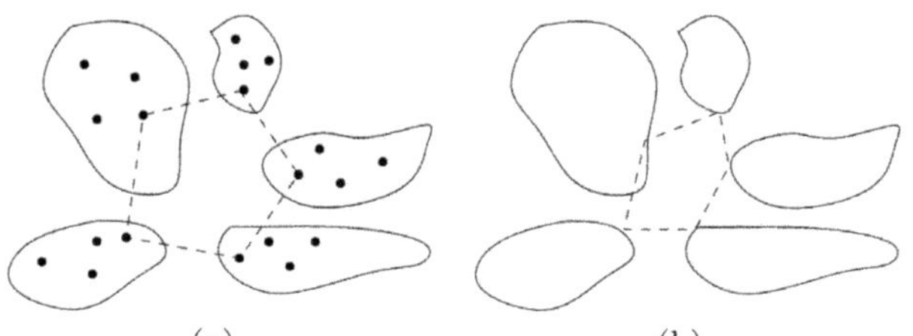

Figure 3: Comparison between the circuits obtained by the (a) EGTSP and the (b) TSPN [9].

Only recently, the union of the restrictions imposed by the DTSP and TSPN problems began to be considered as part of the same problem, which will be referred here as DTSPN. In [13] a Genetic Algorithm is proposed, while in [14, 11] a sampling based approach is used.

For both DTSP and TSPN, most of the techniques solve the combinatorial step (visiting sequence) first, and uses the sequence in subsequent calculations. It has been shown that although this approach produces good results, the sequence has great impact on the final result. Hence, we propose here to jointly consider both steps. We show that the use of a simple evolutionary algorithm to solve both combinatorial and continuous steps of the problem in a combined manner statistically produces better results.

3. METHODOLOGY

3.1 Theoretical formalization

As we stated before, we are dealing with the path planning problem for Dubins' vehicles in the context of the TSPN. Then, we first define the vehicle's nonholonomic constraint before formally presenting our problem. In this paper, we model the robot as a classical Dubins' vehicle [6], which has a maximum curvature ($\kappa_{\max}$) as well as a velocity constraint. This representation encompasses a large class of nonholonomic vehicles that range from Ackerman steering cars to fixed-wing airplanes.

As far as the underlying physics of the system is concerned, the curvature may be defined as a quantity that is directly proportional to the lateral acceleration of the robot in the plane. The value of $\kappa_{\max}$ is inversely proportional to the minimum curvature radius (ρ) of the curve that the vehicle is capable to execute. This is also related to the maximum lateral acceleration of the vehicle.

The DTSP is a TSP problem for which the path is composed by a Dubins' curves. This implies two requirements: (i) between any two points, the path is a Dubins' curve and (ii) orientations of two Dubins' curves that meet at the same point are equal.

Taking into account the formalization of the DTSPN problem, let $\mathcal{H} = \{\mathcal{H}_1, \mathcal{H}_2, \dots, \mathcal{H}_n\} \subset \mathbb{R}^2$ be a set of n closed regions representing waypoint areas to be reached by the vehicle. These regions are centered at coordinates $\mathbf{n}_i = (x_i, y_i)$, which forms a set of n nodes. For simplicity, in this paper we define the i-th neighborhood as a circular region centered on the i-th node, or:

$$\mathcal{H}_i = \{\mathbf{p} \in \mathbb{R}^2 : \|\mathbf{p} - \mathbf{n}_i\| \leq r_i\}, \quad (1)$$

where $\mathbf{p}$ are positions in the two-dimensional space and r_i is the radius of each circular region.

In the kinematic of the Dubins' vehicle, not only position $\mathbf{p}$, but also the orientation ψ of the robot is important to the problem. We use a configuration vector $\mathbf{q}_i = \langle \mathbf{p}_i, \psi_i \rangle$ to represent the complete state of the vehicle in the $SE(2)$ domain. Then, the goal of the DTSPN is to find a configuration $\mathbf{q}_i$ inside each $\mathcal{H}_i$ of the n regions and also a sequence Σ of visiting configurations that minimize the total circuit length $\mathcal{L}_\rho$ composed of Dubins' curves among those configurations. In other words, we may find a configuration set $\mathcal{Q}_\Sigma$ composed of $\mathcal{P}_\Sigma = \langle \mathbf{p}_1, \dots, \mathbf{p}_n \rangle$ (a set of positions) and $\Psi_\Sigma = \langle \psi_1, \dots, \psi_n \rangle$ (a set of corresponding orientations) in a sequence $\Sigma = \langle 1, \dots, n \rangle$ that generates the shortest Hamiltonian tour.

In this case, the following constraints hold:

1. each neighborhood $\mathcal{H}_i$ contains at least one of the waypoints; and

2. a predefined cost function (*e.g.*, the total traveled distance) is minimized.

With this approach, we can define the problem at hand as finding the shortest Hamiltonian path through a set of waypoint regions for robots with Dubins' kinematic constraints. Formally:

PROBLEM 3.1. *Dubins' Traveling Salesman Problem with Neighborhoods: Let $\mathcal{Q}_\Sigma = \langle \mathcal{P}_\Sigma, \Psi_\Sigma \rangle$ be some permutation Σ of configurations $\mathbf{q}$ that reach n regions $\mathcal{H}$. And let $\mathcal{P}_\Sigma$ be the position vector and Ψ_Σ the orientation vector of this permutation. Let also $P : SE(2) \to \mathbb{R}^2$ be the projection function that transforms the robot's configuration into the workspace. Then, we must optimize the Dubins' circuit length accordingly to*

$$\underset{\mathcal{P},\, \Psi,\, \Sigma}{\arg\min}\, \mathcal{L}_\rho(\mathcal{Q}_\Sigma) \quad (2)$$

$$\textit{subject to } P(\mathbf{q}_i) \in \mathcal{H}_i, i = 1, \dots, n,$$

with

$$\mathcal{L}_\rho(\mathcal{Q}_\Sigma) = \mathcal{D}_\rho(\mathbf{q}_n, \mathbf{q}_1) + \sum_{i=1}^{n-1} \mathcal{D}_\rho(\mathbf{q}_i, \mathbf{q}_{i+1}) \qquad (3)$$

where $\mathcal{D}_\rho : SE(2) \times SE(2) \to \mathbb{R}^+$ *represents the length of the shortest path feasible by a Dubins' vehicle with minimum curvature radius* ρ.

3.2 Evolutionary algorithm

Even though several methods to approach each individual subproblem of the larger problem posed here have been reported in the literature, we have not identified a suitable methodology that combines both the generation of the visiting sequence and the subsequent optimization steps. Clearly the problem is quite untractable, and finding good methodologies is a quite challenging task. Among the solutions for similar problems, evolutionary based ones have shown to be a very good choice.

The field of evolutionary computing encompasses a large literature describing techniques for solving problems in complex search spaces, based on simulation of processes ascribed to the evolutionary theory. The fundamental goal of these techniques is not simply an attempt to reproduce phenomena that occur in nature, but to use them as a model for the development of algorithms which *evolve* in pursuit of better solutions.

The methodology we propose in this paper consists of three basic optimization steps that aims to solve both combinatorial and continuous phases of Problem 3.1 in a combined manner. These steps will be further discussed in the next sections, but an overview of each step is presented here:

1. Position update: Moves the waypoint $\mathbf{q}_i$ inside the boundaries of a neighborhood $\mathcal{H}_i$ searching for the placement that best helps minimize the cost function of Equation 3;
2. Orientation update: Varies the orientation ψ_i assigned to each waypoint $\mathbf{q}_i$ in order to find a shorter Dubins' curve connecting them;
3. Visiting sequence update: Checks if there is a better visiting sequence Σ that produces a shorter Dubins' circuit.

Our technique uses, as optimization process, one of the simplest evolutionary algorithms found in the literature, the (1+1)-Evolution Strategy [17]. The main characteristics of this method are: (i) it mantains a population of size one through generations, and (ii) a new candidate is generated accordingly to a mutation process based on a Gaussian distribution. The optimization steps previously mentioned are then grouped to form Algorithm 1.

Let $\mathcal{P}$ be a set of position waypoints, with each $\mathbf{p}_i$ initially corresponding to the center $\mathbf{n}_i$ of a region $\mathcal{H}_i$, and $i = 1, \ldots, n$. With this as input, the algorithm starts by determining a initial sequence of visit Σ and orientation angles Ψ at each waypoint to compute the corresponding Dubins' circuit.

The sequence and the orientation are initially estimated by using a classical technique called Alternating Algorithm (AA) [15] (Algorithm 2), which is actually a straightforward heuristic. In short, it builds the circuit in such a way that consecutive pairs of waypoints are linked together with

Algorithm 1 Evolutionary-DTSPN($\mathcal{P}$)

$\Sigma, \Psi \leftarrow$ AA ($\mathcal{P}$)
$\mathcal{L}_\rho^* \leftarrow \mathcal{L}_\rho(\mathcal{P}_\Sigma, \Psi_\Sigma)$
while stopping criteria not met **do**
  $\hat{\mathcal{P}} \leftarrow$ positionUpdate($\mathcal{P}$)
  if $\mathcal{L}_\rho(\hat{\mathcal{P}}_\Sigma, \Psi_\Sigma) < \mathcal{L}_\rho^*$ **then**
    $\mathcal{P} \leftarrow \hat{\mathcal{P}}$
    $\mathcal{L}_\rho^* \leftarrow \mathcal{L}_\rho(\hat{\mathcal{P}}_\Sigma, \Psi_\Sigma)$
  end if
  $\hat{\Psi} \leftarrow$ orientationUpdate(Ψ)
  if $\mathcal{L}_\rho(\mathcal{P}_\Sigma, \hat{\Psi}_\Sigma) < \mathcal{L}_\rho^*$ **then**
    $\Psi \leftarrow \hat{\Psi}$
    $\mathcal{L}_\rho^* \leftarrow \mathcal{L}_\rho(\mathcal{P}_\Sigma, \hat{\Psi}_\Sigma)$
  end if
  $\hat{\Sigma} \leftarrow$ ATSP($\mathcal{M}$)
  if $\mathcal{L}_\rho(\mathcal{P}_{\hat{\Sigma}}, \Psi_{\hat{\Sigma}}) < \mathcal{L}_\rho^*$ **then**
    $\Sigma \leftarrow \hat{\Sigma}$
    $\mathcal{L}_\rho^* \leftarrow \mathcal{L}_\rho(\mathcal{P}_{\hat{\Sigma}}, \Psi_{\hat{\Sigma}})$
  end if
end while
return $\mathcal{P}, \Psi, \Sigma$

straight line segments. The remaining (non-straight line) links are completed with Dubins' curves based on the orientations previously assigned to the respective waypoints.

Algorithm 2 Alternating Algorithm($\mathcal{P}$) [15]

$\Sigma \leftarrow$ ETSP($\mathcal{P}$)
$\psi_1 \leftarrow \text{atan2}(\mathbf{p}_1, \mathbf{p}_2)$
for $i = 2$ to $n - 1$ **do**
  if i is even **then**
    $\psi_i \leftarrow \psi_{i-1}$
  else
    $\psi_i \leftarrow \text{atan2}(\mathbf{p}_i, \mathbf{p}_{i+1})$
  end if
end for
if n is even **then**
  $\psi_n \leftarrow \psi_{n-1}$
else
  $\psi_n \leftarrow \text{atan2}(\mathbf{p}_n, \mathbf{p}_i)$
end if
return Σ, Ψ

The objective function being optimized here corresponds to the length of the circuit $\mathcal{L}_\rho$ composed by Dubins' curves and computed according to Equation 3.

While a stop criteria is not met, Algorithm 1 iterates executing the three steps previously described, optimizing the sets containing the values of the position of the waypoints ($\mathcal{P}$), the values of orientation (Ψ) and the permutation of the visit sequence (Σ). The variable $\mathcal{L}_\rho^*$ represents the best (shortest) path found so far.

It is important to note that our approach is different from those in the literature, where a new candidate solution is evaluated only at the end of a generation. In our case, we evaluate each each new candidate after the execution of each optimization step. Therefore, if the overall path length obtained by a candidate solution is shorter than the current best solution, the modification made would be already assigned to the best solution. The reasoning behind this decision is to avoid *wasting* an entire iteration when a candidate solution is affected by a single step. This simple modification is very important since small modifications in each step can severely impact the final outcome.

3.2.1 Position Update

The main objective of this optimization step is to vary the position of previously estimated waypoints that lie within their corresponding regions, thus reducing the overall length of the generated path.

As it can be observed in Figure 3(b), a good solution for the TSPN has a great possibility of having points to be visited on the border of a region and also nigh to its central point (centroid).

Considering the above assumption, we propose a heuristic to improve the initial solution which allocates the waypoint in the center of the region. On every iteration of the algorithm, each waypoint $\mathbf{p}_i$ moves toward the centroid of the region set $\mathcal{H}$, providing a new position $\hat{\mathbf{p}}_i$ according to the equation:

$$\begin{aligned} \hat{\mathbf{p}}_i^x &= \mathbf{p}_i^x + |r|\cos(\alpha_i) \\ \hat{\mathbf{p}}_i^y &= \mathbf{p}_i^y + |r|\sin(\alpha_i) \end{aligned} \tag{4}$$

where r is a random variable normally distributed with mean μ and variance σ^2, and α_i defines the direction of motion, computed as

$$\alpha_i = \text{atan2}(\mathbf{n}_i, \mathbf{p}_m) \; + \; \nu, \tag{5}$$

with $\nu \in [-\pi/2, \pi/2]$ being a uniform random variable. The point $\mathbf{n}_i$ represents the center of $\mathcal{H}_i$, and $\mathbf{p}_m$ is the centroid position of all regions.

Figure 4 exemplifies this step with a sample instance. The dashed circles are the regions and the black dot in the center represents the centroid considering the position of the central point of all regions. The arrow indicates the initial direction of motion. In order to find a shorter path, the point being visited can be freely moved in the search space, represented by the gray area.

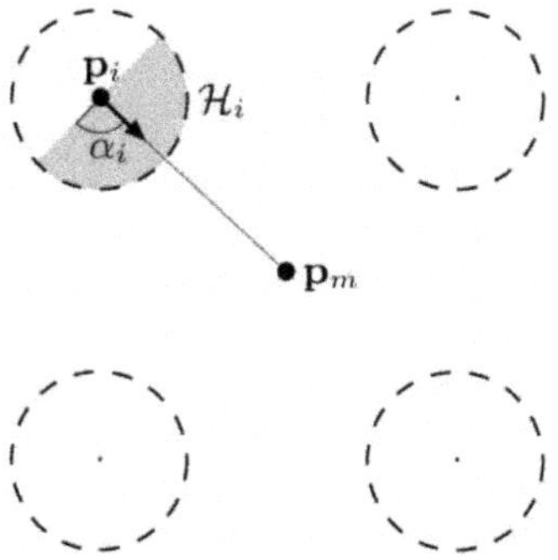

Figure 4: Position update step: the position $\mathbf{p}_i$ of a waypoint inside region $\mathcal{H}_i$ moves towards the centroid of $\mathcal{H}$. The gray semi-circle area represents the searching space.

3.2.2 Orientation Update

As presented in the previous sections, the Alternating Algorithm is used to assign the initial orientation at each point. However, the assigned orientations are usually very different from the value that would make it possible to find the shortest path.

Small variations in the orientation of the waypoint greatly impact the path's length, as depicted in Figure 5.

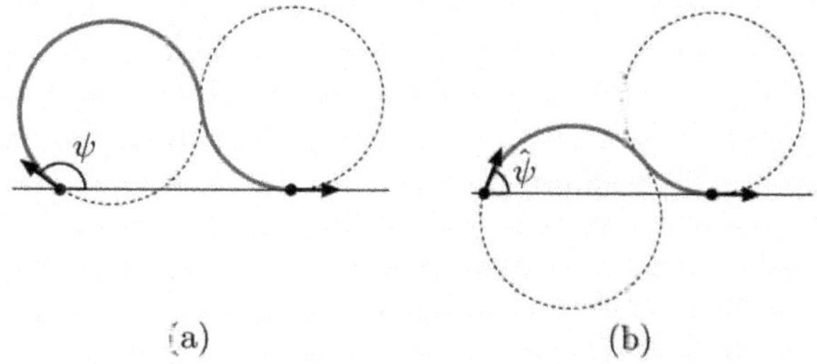

Figure 5: Orientation update step: impact of the orientation angle in the length of the Dubins' path.

Consequently, the main objective of this step is to optimize the orientation angles produced by the AA, having as consequence the overall shortening of the already found path's length. Each angle is modified according to:

$$\hat{\psi}_i = \psi_i + r \tag{6}$$

where r is a random variable normally distributed with mean μ and variance σ^2.

3.2.3 Visiting Sequence Update

Although the sequence based on the Euclidean distance obtained from the execution of the AA is a good initial estimation, it does not mean that the corresponding sequence will produce the shortest path based on a metric that uses Dubins' curves to connect the points. Therefore, the main objective of this step is to find the actual best visiting sequence based on the positions ($\mathcal{P}$) and the orientations (Ψ) calculated in the previous steps.

The visiting sequence also plays an important role, since two different Dubins' curves will be generated for the paths $\mathbf{p}_i \rightarrow \mathbf{p}_j$ and $\mathbf{p}_j \rightarrow \mathbf{p}_i$ (Figure 6).

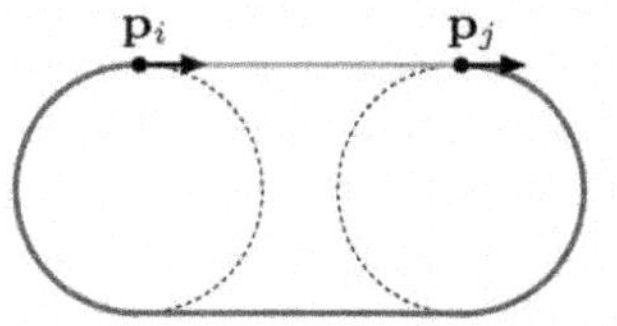

Figure 6: Visiting sequence update step: a different visiting sequence generates different Dubins' curves.

Therefore, we will use the Asymmetric TSP (ATSP), a technique capable of handling this asymmetry between the costs. There are reports in the literature of ATSP considering the cost of Dubins' curves has already been used, but we have not found it being used in an optimization context like the one proposed in this paper.

Hence, we create a cost matrix $\mathcal{M}$ by computing all the $n(n-1)$ Dubins' curves between all pairs of configurations, which produces a matrix that is used as input to an ATSP solver.

3.3 Complexity analysis

In this section, we bring a brief analysis of the computational complexity of the proposed technique, and we also present relevant bounds regarding both the execution time and the path's length.

The first two steps of the methodology (position and orientation update) run in linear time $O(n)$, where n is the number of waypoints. The third step is the most costly one, since it takes $O(n^2)$ to compute the cost matrix and $O(n^3)$ is the worst case time complexity for solving the ATSP [10]. Since the stop criterion of the algorithm is the number β of generations (iterations), algorithm has a final time complexity of $O(\beta n^3)$, or simply $O(n^3)$.

The length of the path generated by our methodology has the same upper bound as the Alternating Algorithm, since we use it in the initialization step, and the final result is updated only if a better solution is found.

Theorem 3.4 from [16] demonstrates that the Dubins' distance between two configurations is bounded by

$$\mathcal{D}_\rho(\mathbf{q}_i, \mathbf{q}_j) \leq \|\mathbf{p}_i - \mathbf{p}_j\| + \tau\rho\pi, \tag{7}$$

where $\tau \in [2.657, 2.658]$. Then, one may directly observe that a not tight upper bound for the length of the path is

$$\mathcal{L}_\rho(\mathcal{P}, \Psi) \leq \text{ETSP}(\mathcal{P}) + \left\lceil \frac{n}{2} \right\rceil \tau\rho\pi, \tag{8}$$

with $n > 2$ and $\rho > 0$, since we can consider that half of the connecting links are lines and the other half are Dubins' curves.

4. EXPERIMENTS

In this section, we describe our experiments and the corresponding statistical analysis, showing the improvement (path reduction) obtained with the proposed methodology when compared with other techniques in the literature. All ETSP and ATSP problems instances were solved to optimality using the well-known TSP solver **Concorde** [1].

Initially, as depicted in Figure 7, we show an example of possible results given by the techniques that will be used in our comparison. In this first example we have an environment with dimensions 500 m × 500 m and 10 regions uniformly randomly distributed, and a vehicle with minimum curvature radius of $\rho = 50$ m. The radius (area) of a region was chosen randomly from the interval [25 m, 75 m]. Figure 7(a) presents a path obtained by the classical DTSP solution (AA), which uses the Alternating Algorithm considering the exact center of each region (dashed blue line) and Figure 7(b) shows the path computed by a random sampling technique presented in [11] (Random), both techniques will be used for comparison. Finally, Figure 7(c) is the result produced by our methodology (Evolutionary).

One may clearly observe in Figure 7(c), the effect of each step of our methodology on the final outcome. The visiting positions have moved towards the center of the regions (red triangle), while the orientation and visiting sequence have also changed. The stop criterion used here was defined as 100 iterations, and we set $\sigma = 1$ (position update step) and $\sigma = 0.5$ (orientation update step), with $\mu = 0$ for both steps. For this initial example, it was possible to obtain a path reduction of $\approx 27\%$ and $\approx 40\%$ when compared to the results of AA and Random, respectively.

As the proposed technique is a probabilistic method, in order to perform a thorough statistical analysis, we present, next, an overall analysis with a significant number of experiments. We run 200 experiments in an environment with dimensions 500 m × 500 m containing a total of 25 regions whose positions were uniformly randomly distributed. Each region had a fixed radius chosen randomly from the inter-

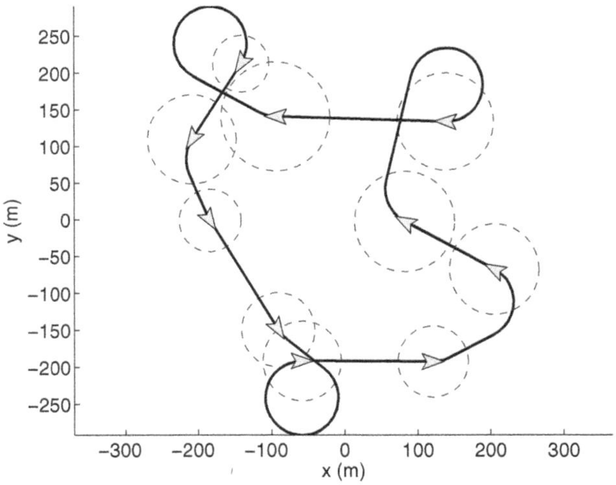

(a) AA (2 335.2 m)

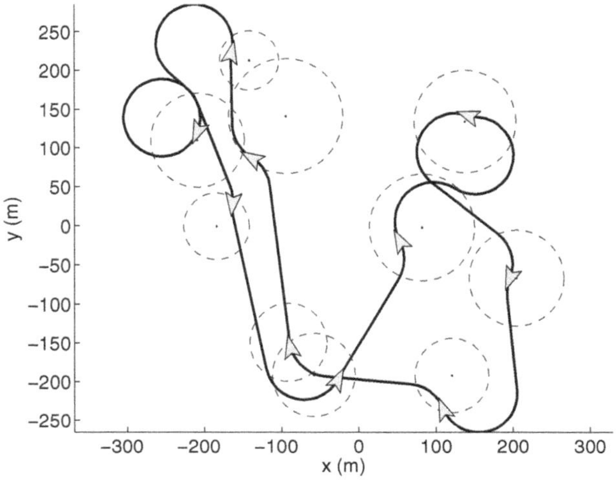

(b) Random (2 813 m)

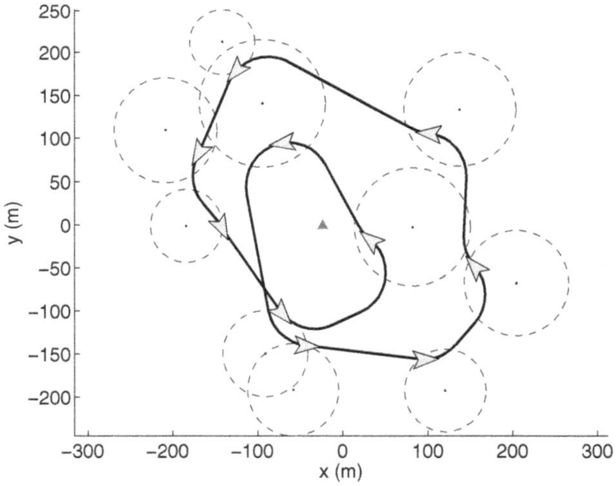

(c) Evolutionary (1 694.1 m)

Figure 7: Example solutions obtained by the compared techniques.

val [30 m, 60 m]. We also defined a simulated vehicle with a minimum curvature radius of $\rho = 50\,\text{m}$, which is adequate when compared to the dimensions of the environment. For each instance, all techniques (AA, Random and Evolutionary) were executed 15 times (the average path length is used for comparison). The parameters of the proposed methodology were the same as described earlier.

Figure 8 presents a histogram of the path reduction obtained by the proposed methodology compared to the results given by the AA. We can see that the mean percentage of length reduction is approximately 25%, with a standard deviation of about 4.9%. The mean path reduction is significantly larger than zero, $t(199) = 59.15$, two-tail $p = 0$. The average path lengths obtained for each technique were 5 078.05 m (AA) and 3 798.63 m (Evolutionary), a 95% C.I. about path reduction is (1236.76, 1322.07).

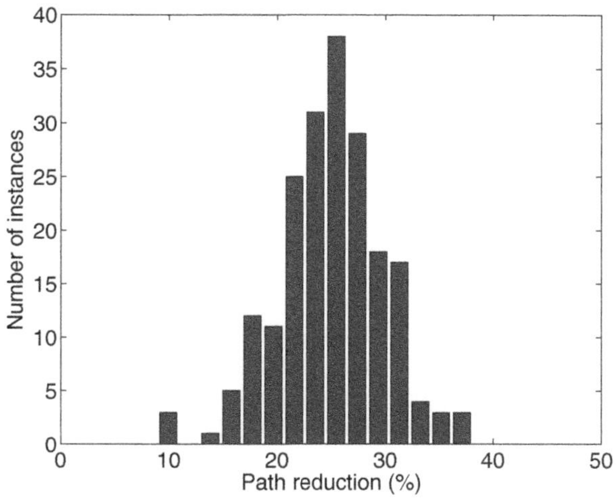

Figure 8: Path reduction histogram between AA versus Evolutionary.

Figure 9 presents a histogram of the path reduction obtained with our methodology compared to the results produced by the Random algorithm. The reduction reaches a mean value of 28.3% and a standard deviation of 4.4%. The mean path reduction is significantly greater than zero, $t(199) = 86.22$, two-tail $p = 0$. The average path length obtained by the Random algorithm was 5 302.40 m, a 95% C.I. about path reduction is (1469.38, 1538.17).

We also deseigned an experiment with a varying number of targets in the environment in order to analyze the impact of this variable in the performance of the algorithm. The number of targets varied in the interval [5, 10, 15, ..., 100], and for each specified value, 10 random instances were generated (all techniques were executed 15 times for each instance). The parameters of the algorithms were the same as those used in the previous experiment.

Figure 10 presents the results comparing the actual performance of the three different algorithms. The DTSP asymptotic lower bound shown was taken from [16] and is given by $Cn^{2/3}$ for any $\rho > 0$, with

$$C = \left(\frac{3}{4}\right) \sqrt[3]{3\rho WH}, \tag{9}$$

where W and H represent the width and height of the environment, respectively. Considering the parameters used in our experiment, we have $C \approx 251$.

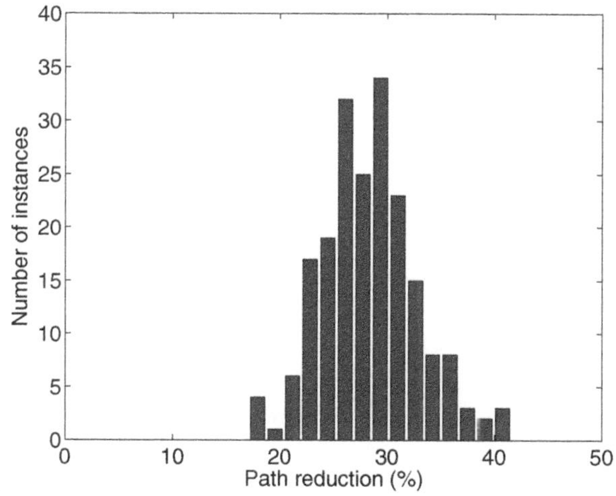

Figure 9: Path reduction histogram between Random versus Evolutionary.

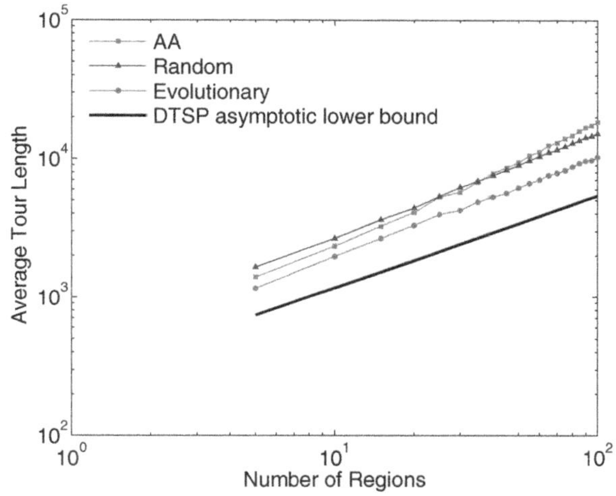

Figure 10: Average tour length behavior accordingly to the number of regions, plot on a log-log scale.

As it can be readily noted, the Evolutionary technique produced better results than the others two algorithms for all different number of regions used in the experiment. A noteworthy result is that the AA method had better performance than the Random for low region densities, but as the number of regions increase (≈ 40), the latter starts to show a better performance.

Table 1 presents the empirical growth rates for the different algorithms obtained by a linear regression based on the simulation results presented in Figure 10. The proposed methodology presented a good asymptotic performance, significantly lower than the trivial solution (AA), and slightly above the lower bound curve.

We also executed some experiments in order to verify the gain obtained by increasing the number of iterations. Although it is evident that running for more iterations will produce better results, we concluded that the improvement wasn't significant. However, it is up to the user to decide on the trade off between computation time and solution quality by adjusting the number of iterations.

Table 1: **Experimental growth rate of the average tour length, with uniform randomly distributed regions in a 500x500 environment.**

Algorithm	Average Tour Length
AA	$5.7 \times n^{0.88}$
Random	$6.2 \times n^{0.75}$
Evolutionary	$5.9 \times n^{0.71}$
Lower bound	$5.5 \times n^{0.67}$

5. CONCLUSION AND FUTURE WORK

In this work we described a three-stage optmization process based on an evolutionary algorithm to solve the Dubins' Traveling Salesman Problem with Neighborhoods (DTSPN). The results were satisfactory and show a significant improvement when compared to the general solution using the classical DTSP approach (AA) and a technique based on a random sampling method.

Several issues will be addressed in the future to improve the proposed methodology. As observed during the experiments, there are several overlapping areas among regions. We intend to take advantage of this fact, by choosing waypoints that belong to several regions at the same time (intersection among areas).

Future directions also include the extension of the proposed methodology to multi-robot ensambles and to environments containing obstacles, which is a better representation of real world scenarios.

One of the main problems concerning the use of Dubins' curves is the discontinuity on the curvature profile, which leads to abrupt lateral accelerations resulting in paths that are not feasible by a real robots. Therefore, we intend to study possible techniques for generating smoother variations of acceleration, for example, the use of other types of curves such as clothoids.

6. REFERENCES

[1] Concorde TSP Solver. Available at: `http://www.tsp.gatech.edu/concorde/index.html`.

[2] A. Alves Neto, D. G. Macharet, and M. F. M. Campos. Feasible RRT-based path planning using seventh order Bézier curves. In *Proceedings of the IEEE/RSJ International Conference on Intelligent Robots and Systems (IROS'2010)*, pages 1445–1450, oct. 2010.

[3] D. L. Applegate, R. E. Bixby, V. Chvatal, and W. J. Cook. *The Traveling Salesman Problem: A Computational Study (Princeton Series in Applied Mathematics)*. Princeton University Press, Princeton, NJ, USA, 2007.

[4] E. M. Arkin and R. Hassin. Approximation algorithms for the geometric covering salesman problem. *Discrete Applied Mathematics*, 55:197–218, dec 1994.

[5] G. Comarela, K. Gonçalves, G. L. Pappa, J. Almeida, and V. Almeida. Robot routing in sparse wireless sensor networks with continuous ant colony optimization. In *Proceedings of the 13th Annual Conference Companion on Genetic and Evolutionary Computation (GECCO'2011)*, pages 599–606, New York, NY, USA, 2011. ACM.

[6] L. E. Dubins. On Curves of Minimal Length with a Constraint on Average Curvature, and with Prescribed Initial and Terminal Positions and Tangents. *American Journal of Mathematics*, 79(3):497–516, 1957.

[7] A. Dumitrescu and J. S. Mitchell. Approximation algorithms for TSP with neighborhoods in the plane. *Journal of Algorithms*, 48(1):135–159, 2003. Twelfth Annual ACM-SIAM Symposium on Discrete Algorithms.

[8] K. Elbassioni, A. Fishkin, and R. Sitters. On Approximating the TSP with Intersecting Neighborhoods. In T. Asano, editor, *Algorithms and Computation*, volume 4288 of *Lecture Notes in Computer Science*, pages 213–222. Springer Berlin / Heidelberg, 2006.

[9] K. M. Elbassioni, A. V. Fishkin, N. H. Mustafa, and R. Sitters. Approximation Algorithms for Euclidean Group TSP. In L. Caires, G. Italiano, L. Monteiro, C. Palamidessi, and M. Yung, editors, *Automata, Languages and Programming*, volume 3580 of *Lecture Notes in Computer Science*, pages 1115–1126. Springer Berlin / Heidelberg, 2005.

[10] A. M. Frieze, G. Galbiati, and F. Maffioli. On the worst-case performance of some algorithms for the asymmetric traveling salesman problem. *Networks*, 12(1):23–39, 1982.

[11] J. T. Isaacs, D. J. Klein, and J. P. Hespanha. Algorithms for the traveling salesman problem with neighborhoods involving a dubins vehicle. In *Proceedings of the IEE American Control Conference (ACC'2011)*, pages 1704–1709, 2011.

[12] D. G. Macharet, A. Alves Neto, and M. F. M. Campos. Feasible UAV path planning using genetic algorithms and Bézier curves. In *Proceedings of the 20th Brazilian Conference on Advances in Artificial Intelligence (SBIA'2010)*, pages 223–232, Berlin, Heidelberg, 2010. Springer-Verlag.

[13] K. J. Obermeyer. Path planning for a UAV performing reconnaissance of static ground targets in terrain. In *Proceedings of the AIAA Conference on Guidance, Navigation and Control*, Chicago, IL, USA, Aug. 2009.

[14] K. J. Obermeyer, P. Oberlin, and S. Darbha. Sampling-based roadmap methods for a visual reconnaissance UAV. In *Proceedings of the AIAA Conference on Guidance, Navigation and Control*, Toronto, ON, Canada, Aug. 2010.

[15] K. Savla, E. Frazzoli, and F. Bullo. On the point-to-point and traveling salesperson problems for dubins' vehicle. In *Proceedings of the IEE American Control Conference (ACC'2005)*, volume 2, pages 786–791, june 2005.

[16] K. Savla, E. Frazzoli, and F. Bullo. Traveling salesperson problems for the dubins vehicle. *IEEE Transactions on Automatic Control*, 53(6):1378–1391, july 2008.

[17] H.-P. Schwefel. *Evolution and Optimum Seeking*. Sixth-generation computer technology series. Wiley, 1995.

[18] B. Yuan, M. Orlowska, and S. Sadiq. On the optimal robot routing problem in wireless sensor networks. *IEEE Transactions on Knowledge and Data Engineering*, 19(9):1252–1261, sept. 2007.

A Genetic and Insertion Heuristic Algorithm for Solving the Dynamic Ridematching Problem with Time Windows

Wesam Herbawi and Michael Weber
Institute of Media Informatics
University of Ulm
Ulm, Germany
firstname.lastname@uni-ulm.de

ABSTRACT

In this paper, we address the dynamic ridematching problem with time windows in dynamic ridesharing. The dynamic ridesharing is a special type of ridesharing where the participants form ridesharing on short notice. The ridematching problem is to assign riders to drivers and to define the ordering and timing of the riders' pickup and delivery. Because not all information is known in advance, the problem is dynamic. This is an optimization problem where we optimize a multicriteria objective function. We consider minimizing the total travel distance and time of the drivers and the total travel time of the riders and maximizing the number of the transported riders.

We propose a genetic and insertion heuristic algorithm for solving the addressed problem. In the first stage, the algorithm works as a genetic algorithm while in the second stage it works as an insertion heuristic that modifies the solution of the genetic algorithm to do ridematching in real-time. In addition, we provide datasets for the ridematching problem, derived from realistic data, to test the algorithm. Experimentation results indicate that the algorithm can successfully solve the problem by providing answers in real-time and it can be easily tuned between response time and solution quality.

Categories and Subject Descriptors

I.2.8 [**Problem Solving, Control Methods, and Search**]: Scheduling, Heuristic methods; G 1.6 [**optimization**]: Combinatorial optimization

General Terms

Algorithms

Keywords

Ridesharing, ridematching, genetic algorithms, heuristics

1. INTRODUCTION

The shared use of vehicle by its driver and one or more passengers (riders) is called ridesharing. Recently, there is an increasing interest in ridesharing as response to the environmental pollution and climate change, traffic congestion and oil cost [4]. The increasing ubiquity of mobile handheld devices also made the idea of ridesharing to be more appealing. It takes the idea of ridesharing from static to dynamic ridesharing where a rideshare can be formulated on very short notice [1].

In this study, we are interested in the ridematching problem with time windows (RMPTW) in dynamic ridesharing. The problem consists of a set of drivers' offers (representing a set of vehicles) and riders' requests. Each participant (driver or rider) specifies a source and a destination location for her/his trip. In addition, each participant specifies an earliest departure time and a latest arrival time which we use to define a time window at each location as we show later. Drivers define maximum travel time and distance for their trips and they are willing to detour to serve some riders. Riders define maximum travel time for their trips. The RMPTW is to assign riders to drivers and determine the timing and order of the pickup and delivery of riders in real-time. Because information about the drivers' offers and riders' requests is available only after their arrival to the system, the problem is dynamic.

The RMPTW is an optimization problem and it is subject to multicriteria optimization. In this study we consider the following criteria to optimize (We use the word vehicle instead of driver):

c_1. The total distance of vehicles' trips (to be minimized)

c_2. The total time of vehicles' trips (to be minimized)

c_3. The total time of the trips of the matched riders' requests (to be minimized)

c_4. The number of matched (served) riders' requests (to be maximized)

Note that the trip's time might include some waiting time (A vehicle with possibly some riders is waiting to pick up a rider when time allows). Criterion c_4 is conflicting with the other three criteria. Also criteria c_1 and c_2 could be conflicting with criterion c_3 as vehicles might tend to take riders for longer time to reduce their own time and distance.

The RMPTW could be seen as a pickup and delivery problem with time windows (PDPTW) which is a hard optimization problem. In this study we propose an algorithm alternating between a genetic algorithm and an insertion heuristic to solve static snapshots of the problem. In addition we provide real world datasets for the dynamic RMPTW extracted from a travel and activity survey for northeastern Illinois conducted by Chicago Metropolitan Agency for Planning. The datasets are used to test the proposed algorithm and could be used as benchmarks.

To the best of our knowledge, the only work that considers a similar ridematching problem is the one by Agatz et al. [2]. However, in their problem definition, a driver can make only one pickup and one delivery. While this assumption makes the problem easier to solve, it prevents the driver from serving some riders even if they are on his exact way. The problem is represented using a maximum-weight bipartite matching model and the optimization software CPLEX is used to solve it. In this work, we consider the possibility of making more than one pickup and delivery where we could simply put a constraint on the number of such operations.

The rest of the paper is organized as follows. In Section 2, we formally describe the problem and provide the mathematical model. The proposed algorithm is explained in Section 3 followed by the experimentation and results in Section 4. Finally we outline the conclusions of the paper.

2. FORMAL PROBLEM DEFINITION AND THE MATHEMATICAL MODEL

The ride matching problem with time windows is similar to the PDPTW especially the dial-a-ride problem (DAR). Therefore the formulated mathematical model is very similar to the DAR problem model in [6] which in turn is an extension to the pickup and delivery problem model in [9] and [3]. The main difference between the RMPTW problem and the DAR problem is that, in RMPTW the vehicles are not free to move everywhere\when and limited by the vehicles' sources and destinations (with possible detour flexibility) and time windows. We adapt the model of DAR problem for the RMPTW and modify the definition of the objective function and add additional constraints on it (Constraints 12, 13 and 14 in the model).

The problem consists of a set $R = \{1, 2, ..., n\}$ of n riders' requests and a set $V = \{2n+1, 2n+2, ..., 2n+v\}$ of v vehicles representing drivers' offers, $R \cap V = \varnothing$. For each rider's request $i \in R$, we have a pickup point i, a delivery point $i+n$, demand dm_i defining the numbers of persons to be delivered from point i to point $i+n$, earliest departure time ED_i from point i, latest arrival time LA_i to point $i+n$ and constants AT_i and BT_i to define the rider's maximum travel time MTT_i. Let $t_{i,j}$ be the direct travel time between points i and j. We compute MTT_i as done in [5]: $MTT_i = AT_i + BT_i \cdot t_{i,i+n}$. For each pickup point i and delivery point $i+n$, we compute a time window as follows: $[a_i, b_i] = [ED_i, LA_i - t_{i,i+n}]$ denoting the earliest and latest pickup time and $[a_{i+n}, b_{i+n}] = [ED_i + t_{i,i+n}, LA_i]$ denoting the earliest and latest delivery time. Figure 1 shows the calculation of the time windows.

For each vehicle $k \in V$ we have a source point k, destination point $k+v$, a maximum capacity C^k, earliest departure time ED_k from point k, latest arrival time LA_k to point $k+v$, and constants AT_k, BT_k, AD_k and BD_k to define the vehicle's maximum travel time MTT_k and distance MTD_k. The calculation of the time windows for the points k and $k+v$ ($[a_k, b_k]$ and $[a_{k+v}, b_{k+v}]$) that denote the earliest and

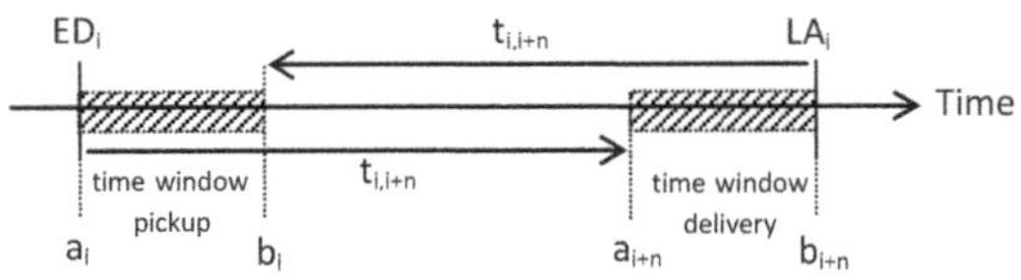

Figure 1: Time window calculation at pickup point i and delivery point $i+n$ for request i

latest departure time and the earliest and latest arrival time of vehicle k respectively is the same as for riders' points. The calculation of the maximum vehicle's travel time MTT_k is the same as for riders. Let $d_{i,j}$ denote the direct travel distance between points i and j, then the maximum vehicle's travel distance is $MTD_k = AD_k + BD_k \cdot d_{k,k+v}$.

Let $P = \{1, ..., n\}$ denote the set of pickup points and $D = \{n+1, ...2n\}$ denote the set of delivery points. The set of all pickup and delivery points is $N = P \cup D$ and the set of all points including the vehicles' sources and destinations is $A = N \cup \{k, k+v\}\ \forall k \in V$. Let $l_i = dm_i$ and $l_{i+n} = -dm_i$ represent the load change at points i and $i+n$ respectively. The load after servicing point i is L_i^k. Let T_i^k denote the service starting time at point i by vehicle k. It denotes the pickup and delivery times for riders and the departure and arrival times for vehicles (drivers). The service time at point $i \in N$ (time for pickup or delivery) is s_i and $\forall i \in A \setminus N$, $s_i = 0$. A binary decision variable $x_{i,j}^k$ is set to 1 if vehicle k services point i and travels directly to point j to service it. it is set to 0 otherwise. The multicriteria objective function that minimizes the total distance and time of the vehicles' trips and the total time of the trips of the matched riders' requests and maximizes the number of matched riders' requests r is provided in Equation 1. The weights α, β, γ and δ define the relative importance of the different components.

$$min\ \alpha \sum_{k \in V} \sum_{i,j \in A} x_{i,j}^k d_{i,j} + \beta \sum_{k \in V} (T_{k+v}^k - T_k^k) + \gamma \sum_{k \in V} \sum_{i \in P} (T_{i+n}^k - s_i - T_i^k) + \delta(n-r) \quad (1)$$

subject to:

$$\sum_{k \in V} \sum_{j \in P \cup \{k+v\}} x_{k,j}^k = v \quad (2)$$

$$\sum_{k \in V} \sum_{i \in D \cup \{k\}} x_{i,k+v}^k = v \quad (3)$$

$$\sum_{k \in V} \sum_{j \in A} x_{i,j}^k \leq 1, \forall i \in N \quad (4)$$

$$\sum_{j \in N} x_{i,j}^k - \sum_{j \in N} x_{j,i+n}^k = 0, \forall k \in V, i \in P \quad (5)$$

$$x_{i,j}^k (T_i^k + s_i + t_{i,j} - T_j^k) \leq 0, \forall k \in V, i,j \in A \quad (6)$$

$$a_i \leq T_i^k \leq b_i, \forall k \in V, i \in A \quad (7)$$

$$T_i^k + s_i + t_{i,i+n} \leq T_{i+n}^k, \forall k \in V, i \in P \quad (8)$$

$$x_{i,j}^k(L_i^k + l_j - L_j^k) = 0, \forall k \in V, i,j \in A \tag{9}$$

$$l_i \leq L_i^k \leq C^k, \forall k \in V, i \in P \tag{10}$$

$$L_k^k = L_{k+v}^k = 0, \forall k \in V \tag{11}$$

$$\sum_{i,j \in A} x_{i,j}^k d_{i,j} \leq MTD_k, \forall k \in V \tag{12}$$

$$(T_{k+v}^k - T_k^k) \leq MTT_k, \forall k \in V \tag{13}$$

$$(T_{i+n}^k - s_i - T_i^k) \leq MTT_i, \forall i \in P \tag{14}$$

$$x_{i,j}^k \in \{0,1\}, \forall i,j \in A \tag{15}$$

Constraints (2) and (3) ensure that the number of vehicles leaving their sources is equal to the number of vehicles arriving to their destinations. Constraint (4) ensures that a rider's request is matched at most once and constraint (5) ensures that both the pickup and delivery of the rider are performed by the same vehicle. Constraint (6) ensures that the minimal travel time between two consecutive points is not violated and constraint (7) ensures that the time windows are not violated. Constraint (8) is a precedence constraint where a pickup point has to be visited before its corresponding delivery point. Constraint (9) ensures that if vehicle k has a load L_i^k after servicing point i, it must have a load of $l_j + L_i^k$ after servicing point j and therefore it ensures that the number of loaded riders at a pickup point should be equal to the number of unloaded riders at its corresponding delivery point.

Constraint (10) ensures that the vehicles' capacities are not exceeded and the load of the vehicle is at least l_i after servicing a pickup point i. Constraint (11) ensures that vehicles depart without having riders onboard and arrive to their destinations without having riders onboard (Note that riders and vehicles might share the same geographic sources and destinations, however we consider them to be distinct points). Constraints (12) and (13) ensure that the maximum distance and time, respectively, for each vehicle's trip is within a defined value. Constraint (14) ensures that the time of the trip of each rider is within his defined value.

3. THE PROPOSED ALGORITHM

To solve the dynamic RMPTW, we divide the day into a set of time periods. Each period starts with executing a genetic algorithm to solve a static version of the problem given all known requests and offers. After the execution of the genetic algorithm we utilize an insertion heuristic very similar to the one proposed by Jaw et al. [5] to give an online answer, by updating the solution produced by the genetic algorithm, in real-time for each newly received request/offer until the end of the period. All non-matched requests by the genetic algorithm and the insertion heuristic are stored for future matching and to be as an input for the genetic algorithm in the next time period if not already matched. The

A^+	5^+	5^-	4^+	7^+	4^-	7^-	A^-		
B^+	1^+	3^+	3^-	1^-	B^-				
C^+	8^+	2^+	8^-	2^-	C^-				
D^+	6^+	6^-	D^-						
E^+	10^+	10^-	9^+	11^+	9^-	11^-	12^+	12^-	E^-

Figure 2: Solution representation. Five Vehicles (A-E) and twelve matched riders' requests (1-12). + - denote the pickup and delivery points of riders' requests and the vehicles' sources and destinations

genetic algorithm as a metaheuristic is supposed to produce better quality matches and to better optimize the objective function as compared to the insertion heuristic that is subject to local optima. However, the insertion heuristic is more suitable for the dynamic RMPTW as it can give answers in real-time.

The shorter the time period, the more often the genetic algorithm is executed resulting in better results on the cost of longer execution time. On the other hand, if the time period is long, then we put more pressure on the insertion heuristic resulting in a more responsive algorithm with probably lower quality solutions.

3.1 The Genetic Algorithm

In this section, we describe the different components of the proposed genetic algorithm. The proposed algorithm is a generational genetic algorithm gGA that follows the general skeleton of gGAs (with binary tournament selection).

3.1.1 Solution Representation

A solution is represented as a schedule of v routes, one route for each vehicle. Each route starts with the source point of the vehicle followed by a list of pickup and delivery points and ends with the destination point of the vehicle. The pickup and delivery points are inserted satisfying the constraints defined in the model. A solution may not match all riders' requests and therefore we keep a list of all non-matched requests. Figure 2 shows an example solution representation matching 5 vehicles (A - E) and 12 riders' requests (1 - 12). To speed up the genetic algorithm, we keep for each vehicle a list of matchable rider's requests taking time and distance feasibility into consideration.

3.1.2 Solution Initialization

An initial solution is created as follows. We randomly select a route to initialize among the v routes. The first two points to be inserted in the route are the source and destination points of the vehicle. Initially the two points are scheduled at their earliest time a_i (to take advantage of the maximum possible push forward as below). Then we continuously select a random pair of pickup and delivery points from the list of matchable rider's requests of the vehicle of the selected route and try to insert them in the route. The process repeats for all routes.

During the initialization process, we adopt the Solomon's insertion method [8]. Let $p = (p_1, p_2, ..., p_u)$ be a partially created route for vehicle k. The service time at p_i is $T_{p_i}^k = max\{a_{p_i}, T_{p_{i-1}}^k + s_{p_{i-1}} + t_{p_{i-1},p_i}\}$. If the vehicle arrives too early at point p_i, then it should wait before servicing p_i and the waiting time at p_i is $w_{p_i} = max\{0, a_{p_i} - T_{p_{i-1}}^k - s_{p_{i-1}} - t_{p_{i-1},p_i}\}$.

Now we discuss the necessary conditions for time feasibility when inserting a new point between the points p_{i-1} and p_i, $1 < i \leq u$. Let $newT^k_{p_i}$ denote the new service time by vehicle k for point p_i after inserting the new point before p_i. Assuming that the triangular inequality holds both on time and distance between the points, then the insertion of the new point will result in a time push forward (PF) in the route at p_i such that $PF_{p_i} = newT^k_{p_i} - T^k_{p_i} \geq 0$. It will also result in a time push forward at the points after p_i such that $PF_{p_{j+1}} = max\{0, PF_{p_j} - w_{p_{j+1}}\}$, $i \leq j < u$. After the time push forward, the time window and/or the maximum travel time constraints of some point p_j, $i \leq j \leq u$, might be violated. We sequentially check these two time feasibility constraints until we reach a point p_j with $PF_j = 0$ or its time window or maximum travel time constraint is violated or in the worst case until $j = u$.

In addition to time feasibility, we check the driver's maximum distance constraint after inserting the new point p. The distance should be less than MTD_k. For the precedence constraint, we always insert the pickup point before it corresponding delivery point and we search for a feasible insertion position for the delivery point in the route to the right of its pickup point.

3.1.3 Crossover Operator

We have defined a single point crossover operator. Given two parent solutions, we randomly select a crossover position (route index) and we make crossover by exchanging the routes among the parents starting from the crossover position upwards as in Figure 3. Note that the resulting children do not violate any of the defined constraints except constraints (4) and (5) (a riders' request could be matched twice with different vehicles). Example violation points are shaded in the child solutions. In addition to the constraints violation, some pairs of pickup and delivery points that exist in the parents might disappear in the children because of the crossover (e.g. points 10^+ and 10^- in child 1).

After the crossover operation, we apply a repair operation for the children. The repair operation removes all the pickup and delivery points in the routes after the crossover position whenever they exist in any route before the crossover position. Besides the repair operation, we also try to insert the pickup and delivery points of the riders' requests that are not matched in the resulting children after each crossover in a process similar to the one during solutions initialization.

3.1.4 Mutation Operators

We have defined five different mutation operators. All of them are on the route level (gene level). A mutation operation that violates any of the constraints is rejected.

The first mutation operator is the push backward. In this operator, we randomly select a point p_i from the route and define the push backward (PB_i) value as a random percentage of the time difference between the service time of the selected point and its earliest service time: $PB_i = random(T^k_{p_i} - a_{p_i})$. We also push backward all the points after p_i in the route: $PB_{p_{j+1}} = min\{PB_j, T^k_{p_{j+1}} - a_{p_{j+1}}\}$, $i \leq j < u$. We stop the push backward operation when we reach a point j with $PB_j = 0$ or when $j = u - 1$

The second mutation operator is the push forward (very similar to initialization push forward). In this operator, we randomly select a point p_i from the route and define the push forward (PF_i) value as a random percentage of the time difference between the latest service time of the selected point and its service time: $PB_i = random(b_{p_i} - T^k_{p_i})$. We also push forward all the points after p_i in the route: $PF_{p_{j+1}} = max\{0, PF_{p_j} - w_{p_{j+1}}\}$, $i \leq j < u$. We stop the push forward operation when we reach a point j with $PF_j = 0$ or when $j = u - 1$.

The third mutation operator is the remove-insert operator. We randomly select a pair of pickup and delivery points to delete from the route (and mark their request as non-matched). After the delete operation, we perform a push backward operation in the positions of the deleted points. By the end of the delete operations, we try to insert as much pairs of pickup and delivery points as possible from the points of the non-matched requests.

The fourth mutation operator is the transfer mutation. In this operator, we randomly select a pair of pickup and delivery points from the route and try to insert them in another route. The last mutation operator is the swap mutation operator. In this operator, we swap a randomly selected point p_i in the route and its neighbor point p_{i+1}.

We noticed that the push forward and push backward mutation operators are the most important among the mutation operators. However, still the other three mutation operators participate in the quality of the solution.

3.2 The Insertion Heuristic

Given a solution from the genetic algorithm, the insertion heuristic answers each newly received offer or request by modifying the solution when possible. If a driver offer is received, then a route is added to the solution and the heuristic tries to match as much as possible from the non-matched riders' requests. If a rider's request is received, then the heuristic tries to insert it in one of the routes. Finding a match for a given request involves finding all possible insertions for the pickup and delivery points of the request in all routes and selecting the best insertion. The best insertion is defined as the one that adds the minimum value to the heuristic objective function. The heuristic objective function is the weighted sum of the total distance and time of vehicles' trips and the total time of the trips of the matched riders' requests. We do not consider the number of matched riders in the heuristic's objective function because each insertion possibility adds one rider.

To find a feasible insertion, the same insertion method that is used in solution initialization is used here. By the time of receiving a new request x, parts of the solution might have been executed (points already visited). Therefore we apply an additional constraint when finding an insertion position for the pickup point of the new request. The constraint states that the scheduled time of the point just before the candidate insertion position i of the new pickup in the route p of vehicle k should be greater than the arrival time inT_x of the new request x, $T^k_{p_{i-1}} > inT_x$.

4. EXPERIMENTATION AND RESULTS

In this section, we describe the proposed real world datasets for ridematching and the experimentation methodology and discuss the experimentation results.

4.1 Experimentation data

To test the behavior of the proposed algorithm for solving the dynamic RMPTW, we have utilized a travel and activity survey for northeastern Illinois conducted by Chicago

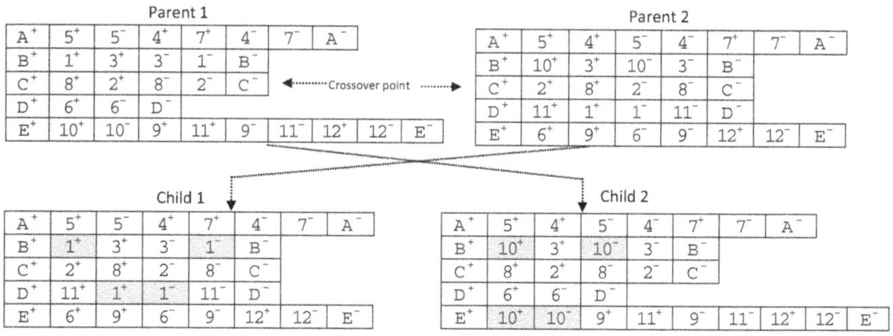

Figure 3: Single point crossover operator. Shaded points violate constraints (4) and (5)

Table 1: Problem instances. DMD = divers with maximum distance, TW= time window, DTD and DTT are the total direct travel distance and time respectively of the vehicles (drivers) without ridesharing.

Instance	No. drivers	No. riders	DMD	Earliest departure	Latest departure	TW ± min	DTD (km)	DTT (min)
RM744_R15	268	476	no	10:00	16:40	15	2621.8	2737
RM744_L15	268	476	yes	10:00	16:40	15	4468.2	4582
RM744_R60	268	476	No	10:00	16:40	60	2621.8	2737
RM744_L60	268	476	yes	10:00	16:40	60	4468.2	4582
RM698_R15	250	448	No	00:30	23:30	15	2451.9	2565
RM698_L15	250	448	yes	00:30	23:30	15	4602.6	4717
RM698_R60	250	448	No	00:30	23:30	60	2451.9	2565
RM698_L60	250	448	yes	00:30	23:30	60	4602.6	4717

Metropolitan Agency for Planning CMAP [1]. Data collection took place between January 2007 and February 2008 and covered a total of 10,552 households participant. A trip in the study is defined as a pair of source and destination positions (using latitude and longitude) with departure and arrival timestamps.

Our datasets are mainly based on two travel patterns. The first consists of a total of 698 trips (RM698) among them 469 trips with participants travel with their own vehicles and the rest rely on other forms of transportation. The second consists of a total of 744 trips (RM744) among them 533 trips with participants travel with their own vehicles and the rest rely on other forms of transportation. We select from the trips with participants traveling with their own vehicles what constitutes 36% of the total trips in each pattern to be as drivers and the rest as riders. The drivers are either selected randomly or those with the maximum travel distance. A time window is engineered for each trip. We consider a vehicle speed of 60km/h.

The distance between two points is measured using the Haversin formula [7] and the travel time between them is the ceil of the computed travel time (always integer). Table 1 shows the eight problem instances used in this study. For each one of the eight instances, we study the behavior of the algorithm in case of the percent of known riders' requests (KRR) by the time of executing the genetic algorithm is 20%,60% and 100% . We consider that all drivers' offers are known in advance by the time of executing the genetic algorithm.

4.2 Experiment settings

The parameters' settings (defined in Sec. 2) of the problem instances are $AT_i = 0$ and $BT_i = 1.3$ for all riders' requests and vehicles (drivers' offers), $C^k = 5$, $AD_i = 0$ and $BD_i = 1.3$ for all vehicles and $s_i = 0$ and $dm_i = 1$ for all riders' requests. The criteria weights are: $\alpha = 0.7$ and $\beta = \gamma = \delta = 0.1$.

[1]http://www.cmap.illinois.gov/travel-tracker-survey.

Table 2: Wilcoxon rank-sum test comparing different configurations G_i with 30 independent runs for each configuration. ▲ = row element is better than column element regarding the value of the objective function and the opposite for ▽.

crossover	mutation		G_1	G_2	G_3	G_4	G_5	G_6	G_7	G_8	G_9	G_{10}	G_{11}
1.0	1.0	G_0	–	–	▲	▲	▲	▲	–	▲	▲	▲	▲
1.0	0.7	G_1		–	▲	▲	▲	▲	▲	▲	▲	▲	▲
1.0	0.4	G_2			▲	▲	▲	▲	▲	▲	▲	▲	▲
1.0	0.1	G_3				▽	▽	–	▽	▽	▲	▽	–
0.7	1.0	G_4					▲	▲	–	–	▲	–	▲
0.4	1.0	G_5						▲	▽	▽	▲	▽	▲
0.1	1.0	G_6							▽	▽	▲	▽	–
0.7	0.7	G_7								–	▲	–	▲
0.7	0.3	G_8									▲	–	▲
0.7	0.1	G_9										▽	▽
0.4	0.7	G_{10}											▲
0.1	0.7	G_{11}											

The parameters' settings of the genetic algorithm are: population size = 100, number of generations = 100, crossover probability = 1.0 and mutation probability =0.4. The selection of the probabilities of the crossover and mutation is based on a study result summarized in Table 2. The algorithm is executed 30 independent times for each problem instance and percentage of KRR.

Experiments are performed on a computer with 4G RAM and 2.4GHz AMD 64bit dual core processor running Windows XP x64. JRE 1.6.0_22 is the runtime environment

4.3 Results discussion

Table 3 shows the results of the 30 independent runs of the algorithm for each instance and percentage of KRR (mean and standard deviation). The results include the value of the objective function and each of its components, the runtime of the genetic algorithm and the runtime per request of the insertion heuristic. To avoid scaling problems, the values of the different criteria are normalized before computing the

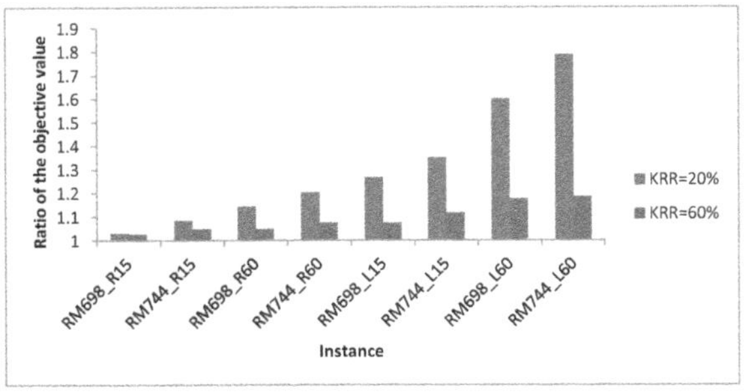

Figure 4: The ratio of the value of the objective function (OF) under the percentages 20% and 60% of the KRR to its value under percentage 100%.

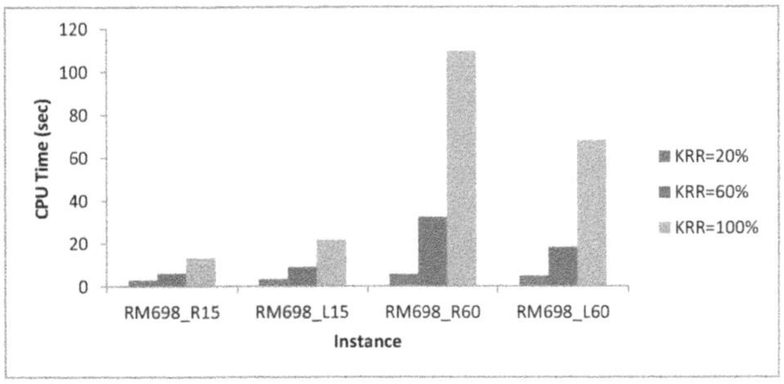

Figure 5: The average execution time of the genetic algorithm for instances RM698 under different percentages of KRR

value of the objective function. Note that the direct travel time and distance and the maximum allowed travel time and distance can provide us with upper and lower bounds for the total travel time and distance. The number of the riders' requests gives us an upper bound for the number of matched riders' requests.

We make use of figures to further discuss our findings. Figure 4 shows for each instance the ratio of the value of the objective function under percentages 20% and 60% of the KRR to its value under percentage 100%. In other words, it shows how worse the value of the objective function if we rely on the insertion heuristic than if we totally rely on the genetic algorithm.

We see that by decreasing the percentage of the known riders' requests at the time of executing the genetic algorithm we get wore final values of the objective function (larger ratio). Also we notice that the ratio is larger for instances with $DMD = yes$. This is because for instances with $DMD = yes$, the vehicles travel for longer distances and are supposed to serve larger number of riders requests. Therefore, there is larger room for optimization considering the ordering and timing of the riders' points where the insertion heuristic gets stuck in local optima and the genetic algorithm performs better. Within each group with $DMD = yes$ or $DMD = no$, instances with time windows of $\pm$ 60 minutes showed larger ratio than instances with time windows of $\pm$ 15 minutes. Increasing the time windows increases the search space by increasing the matchable riders' requests list of each vehicle. Also we notice that for each two instances with the same DMR and the same time window, we notice that the ratio is larger for the instances $RM744$.

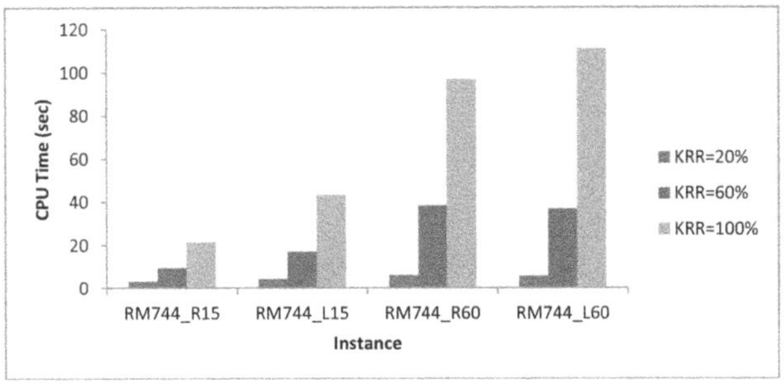

Figure 6: The average execution time of the genetic algorithm for instances RM744 under different percentages of KRR

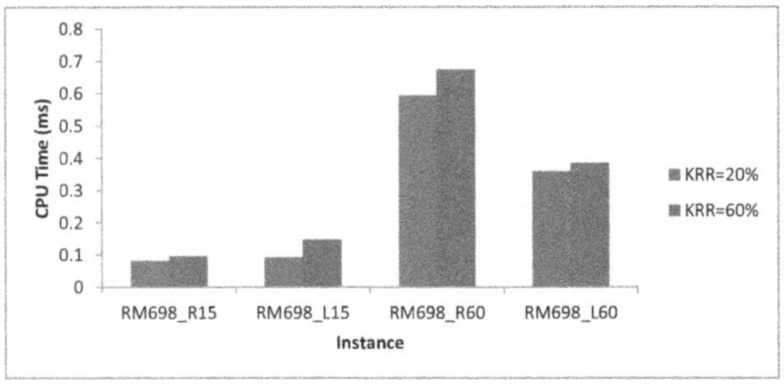

Figure 7: The average execution time of the insertion heuristic per request for instances RM698 under different percentages of KRR

This is because for instances $RM744$ we have more trips and the trips' departures are closer to each other as compared to instances $RM698$. This means that there is larger search space and riders' requests can be served with larger number of vehicles.

Figure 5 shows the runtime of the genetic algorithm for the instances RM698 under different percentages of the KRR. Obviously the runtime of the genetic algorithm increases with the increase of the percentage of the KRR at the time of its execution. Also we notice that the length of the time window plays a major rule in the runtime of the genetic algorithm. Longer time windows increase the size of the list of the matchable riders' requests of each vehicle which is used often after each crossover and remove-insert mutation to try to match additional non-matched requests. This leads

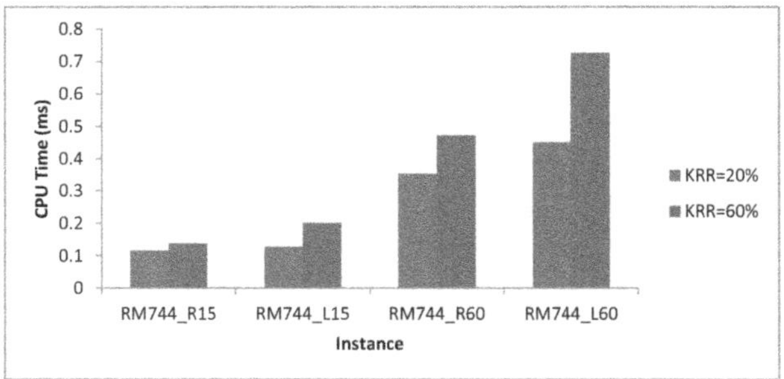

Figure 8: The average execution time of the insertion heuristic per request for instances RM744 under different percentages of KRR

Table 3: Results summary. %KRR= percentage of the known riders' requests, OF= objective function, No. MRR= No. of matched riders' requests, GRT= genetic alg. run time, HRT = heuristic run time per request.

Instance	%KRR	OF	No. MRR	vehicles' distance	vehicles' time	riders' time	GRT (sec)	HRT (ms)
RM744_R15	20	$0.605_{\sigma=0.0050}$	$105.333_{\sigma=4.671}$	$2786.127_{\sigma=8.524}$	$2932.833_{\sigma=10.453}$	$834.233_{\sigma=38.518}$	$3.15_{\sigma=0.17}$	$0.116_{\sigma=0.024}$
	60	$0.585_{\sigma=0.0030}$	$119.367_{\sigma=2.168}$	$2786.254_{\sigma=4.507}$	$2947.667_{\sigma=4.643}$	$901.267_{\sigma=9.889}$	$9.443_{\sigma=0.251}$	$0.137_{\sigma=0.039}$
	100	$0.558_{\sigma=0.0010}$	$138.7_{\sigma=0.69}$	$2784.907_{\sigma=2.259}$	$2953.8_{\sigma=2.701}$	$952.967_{\sigma=6.374}$	$21.509_{\sigma=0.431}$	$0.0_{\sigma=0.0}$
RM744_L15	20	$0.585_{\sigma=0.0020}$	$115.8_{\sigma=2.072}$	$4736.434_{\sigma=6.795}$	$4902.6_{\sigma=8.048}$	$1026.8_{\sigma=6.6}$	$4.188_{\sigma=0.073}$	$0.127_{\sigma=0.012}$
	60	$0.483_{\sigma=0.0050}$	$199.2_{\sigma=4.261}$	$4849.71_{\sigma=15.703}$	$5072.8_{\sigma=15.01}$	$1194.167_{\sigma=12.662}$	$17.004_{\sigma=0.705}$	$0.201_{\sigma=0.041}$
	100	$0.433_{\sigma=0.0030}$	$234.9_{\sigma=2.856}$	$4872.177_{\sigma=15.818}$	$5104.2_{\sigma=16.138}$	$1298.133_{\sigma=17.043}$	$43.301_{\sigma=1.628}$	$0.0_{\sigma=0.0}$
RM744_R60	20	$0.576_{\sigma=0.0050}$	$134.567_{\sigma=4.295}$	$2820.904_{\sigma=9.317}$	$2985.433_{\sigma=11.635}$	$1019.567_{\sigma=24.415}$	$5.892_{\sigma=0.472}$	$0.352_{\sigma=0.023}$
	60	$0.515_{\sigma=0.0040}$	$182.667_{\sigma=2.675}$	$2861.524_{\sigma=8.328}$	$3050.867_{\sigma=8.755}$	$1203.467_{\sigma=23.581}$	$38.229_{\sigma=1.82}$	$0.472_{\sigma=0.048}$
	100	$0.479_{\sigma=0.0040}$	$207.933_{\sigma=2.502}$	$2863.787_{\sigma=11.109}$	$3062.367_{\sigma=10.88}$	$1270.1_{\sigma=24.701}$	$96.662_{\sigma=4.273}$	$0.0_{\sigma=0.0}$
RM744_L60	20	$0.484_{\sigma=0.0070}$	$197.2_{\sigma=6.172}$	$4794.537_{\sigma=19.037}$	$4997.067_{\sigma=21.695}$	$1384.2_{\sigma=27.165}$	$5.641_{\sigma=0.321}$	$0.45_{\sigma=0.029}$
	60	$0.321_{\sigma=0.0060}$	$326.5_{\sigma=4.395}$	$4990.478_{\sigma=13.664}$	$5278.2_{\sigma=13.531}$	$1660.9_{\sigma=27.795}$	$36.614_{\sigma=2.223}$	$0.726_{\sigma=0.043}$
	100	$0.271_{\sigma=0.0050}$	$363.933_{\sigma=3.316}$	$5010.591_{\sigma=13.59}$	$5316.367_{\sigma=14.538}$	$1802.667_{\sigma=33.336}$	$110.767_{\sigma=8.226}$	$0.0_{\sigma=0.0}$
RM698_R15	20	$0.575_{\sigma=0.0030}$	$96.8_{\sigma=2.821}$	$2543.046_{\sigma=7.241}$	$2670.867_{\sigma=8.838}$	$557.8_{\sigma=10.028}$	$2.84_{\sigma=0.023}$	$0.081_{\sigma=0.01}$
	60	$0.573_{\sigma=0.0030}$	$110.533_{\sigma=3.096}$	$2593.739_{\sigma=8.929}$	$2730.133_{\sigma=9.976}$	$671.8_{\sigma=13.088}$	$6.072_{\sigma=0.156}$	$0.095_{\sigma=0.034}$
	100	$0.558_{\sigma=0.0010}$	$124.4_{\sigma=1.083}$	$2605.949_{\sigma=5.883}$	$2750.433_{\sigma=7.149}$	$685.467_{\sigma=8.913}$	$13.079_{\sigma=0.943}$	$0.0_{\sigma=0.0}$
RM698_L15	20	$0.584_{\sigma=0.0080}$	$106.6_{\sigma=6.859}$	$4796.58_{\sigma=21.38}$	$4947.433_{\sigma=26.087}$	$1050.233_{\sigma=17.701}$	$3.323_{\sigma=0.057}$	$0.092_{\sigma=0.018}$
	60	$0.495_{\sigma=0.0030}$	$174.3_{\sigma=1.754}$	$4973.511_{\sigma=12.49}$	$5170.5_{\sigma=13.455}$	$1198.4_{\sigma=13.827}$	$8.795_{\sigma=0.361}$	$0.147_{\sigma=0.018}$
	100	$0.461_{\sigma=0.0030}$	$198.267_{\sigma=1.459}$	$4983.294_{\sigma=11.52}$	$5195.0_{\sigma=12.565}$	$1264.9_{\sigma=10.888}$	$21.718_{\sigma=1.657}$	$0.0_{\sigma=0.0}$
RM698_R60	20	$0.551_{\sigma=0.0060}$	$135.633_{\sigma=4.963}$	$2651.593_{\sigma=14.225}$	$2799.333_{\sigma=17.034}$	$786.4_{\sigma=46.253}$	$5.657_{\sigma=0.23}$	$0.593_{\sigma=0.021}$
	60	$0.505_{\sigma=0.0030}$	$170.6_{\sigma=2.715}$	$2677.996_{\sigma=8.112}$	$2841.667_{\sigma=8.42}$	$1054.267_{\sigma=37.865}$	$32.277_{\sigma=2.622}$	$0.673_{\sigma=0.048}$
	100	$0.482_{\sigma=0.0030}$	$187.867_{\sigma=2.68}$	$2679.89_{\sigma=13.82}$	$2853.967_{\sigma=15.096}$	$1014.733_{\sigma=41.151}$	$109.378_{\sigma=10.636}$	$0.0_{\sigma=0.0}$
RM698_L60	20	$0.472_{\sigma=0.0090}$	$194.067_{\sigma=6.011}$	$4937.461_{\sigma=15.07}$	$5130.933_{\sigma=17.16}$	$1448.0_{\sigma=36.303}$	$4.824_{\sigma=0.13}$	$0.358_{\sigma=0.017}$
	60	$0.347_{\sigma=0.0060}$	$291.667_{\sigma=3.037}$	$5140.778_{\sigma=14.842}$	$5398.133_{\sigma=17.627}$	$1681.267_{\sigma=27.566}$	$18.235_{\sigma=0.983}$	$0.385_{\sigma=0.04}$
	100	$0.295_{\sigma=0.0070}$	$326.067_{\sigma=3.855}$	$5158.488_{\sigma=21.662}$	$5438.733_{\sigma=22.044}$	$1798.033_{\sigma=38.815}$	$68.063_{\sigma=3.992}$	$0.0_{\sigma=0.0}$

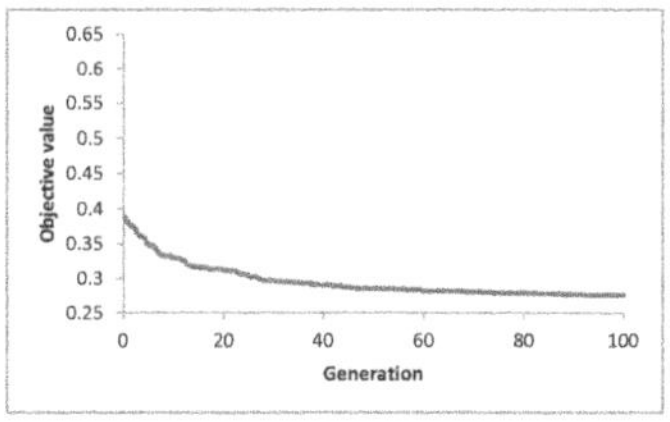

(a) RM744_L60

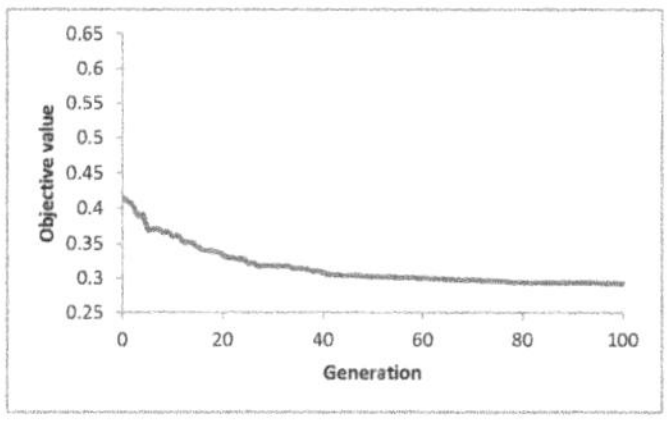

(b) RM698_L60

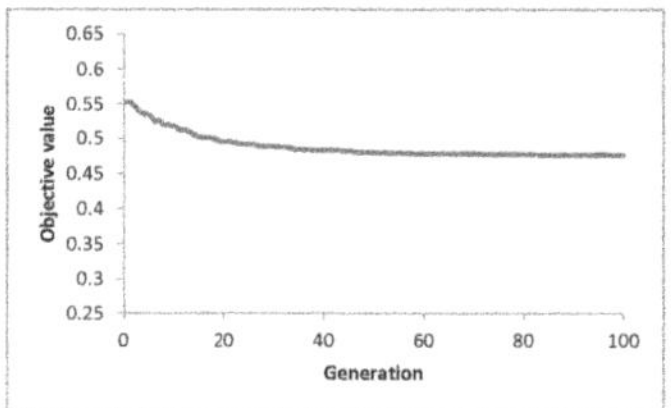

(c) RM744_R60

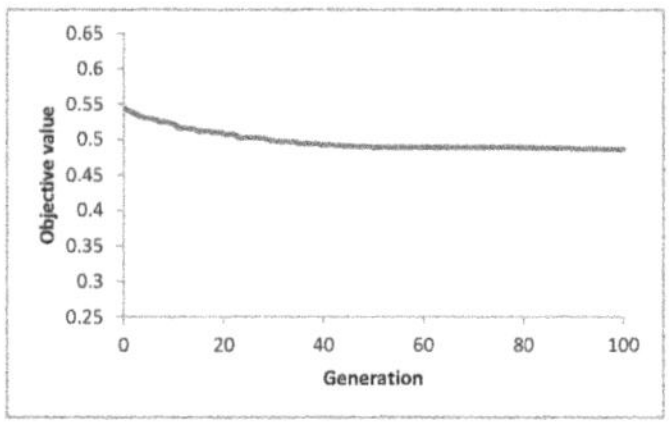

(d) RM698_R60

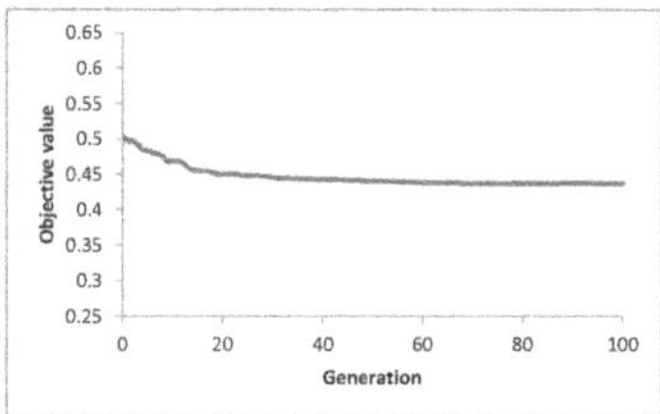

(e) RM744_L15

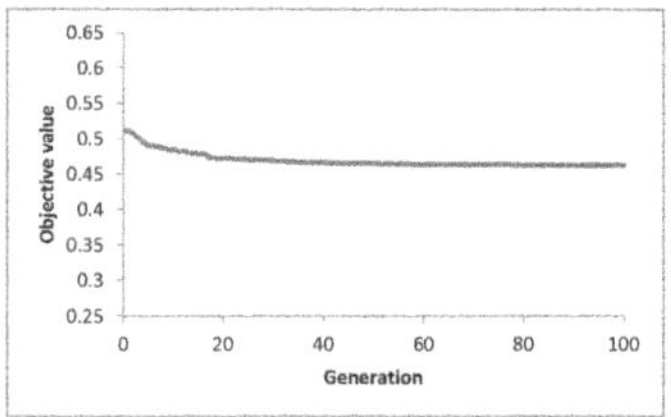

(f) RM698_L15

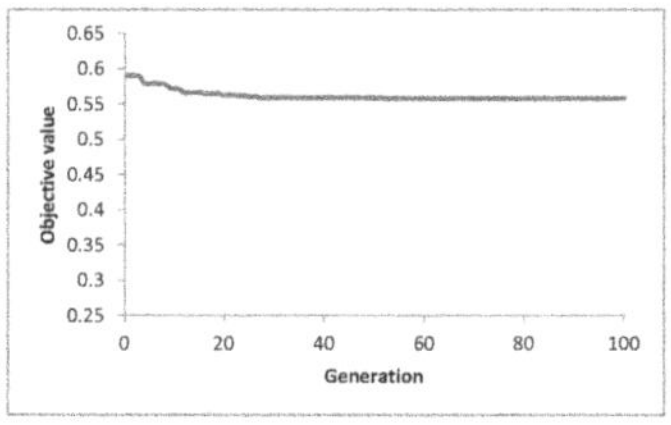

(g) RM744_R15

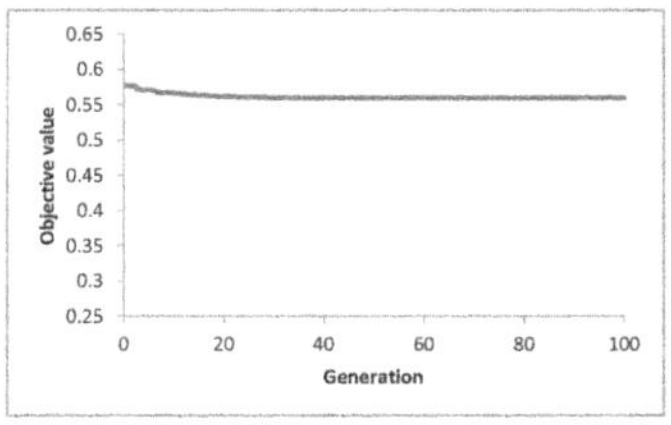

(h) RM698_R15

Figure 9: The best fitness at different generations of the genetic algorithm for the instances with KRR=100%

to increase the runtime of the genetic algorithm. Figure 6 shows a similar runtime pattern of the genetic algorithm on the instances RM744.

Figures 7 and 8 show the run time of the insertion heuristic per rider's request on the instances RM698 and RM744 under different percentages of KRR respectively. The runtime increases for instances with higher percentages of KRR as the solution of the genetic algorithm contains routes with more served requests. This results in larger number of possible insertions which needs to be considered by the heuristic.

It takes the insertion heuristic fractions of millisecond to answer a request on all datasets and percentages of KRR which is a real-time answer and in the worst case it takes the genetic algorithm 110.767 seconds. The runtime of the genetic algorithm is justifiable as we run it only once per time period and we rely on the insertion heuristic for the rest of the period. The results in Table 3 and Figure 4 indicate that the genetic algorithm helps to better optimize the objective function.

Figure 9 shows the optimization of the objective function by the genetic algorithm under different generations for each instance with all riders' requests being known (KRR = 100%). The most optimization is for instances with $DMD = yes$ and for time windows ±60 as in Figures 9(a) and 9(b). Figure 9(h) shows the least optimization for the instance RM698_R15 with time window ±15 and $DMD = no$ where the algorithm converges after near about 20 generations.

By dividing the entry of the vehicles' distance in table 3 on the DTD entry of the corresponding instance in table 1 we get the percentage of the travel distance (with serving riders) relative to the distance that would have been traveled without serving riders. The same applies for the travel time. For example, the DTD = 2451.9km for the instance RM698_R15 and the vehicles' distance = 2543.046km at KRR =20% for the same instance, so the total vehicle's travel distance that includes serving in average 96.8 riders is 1.037% of the DTD.

To see how the trips of the vehicles look like, we have created a GPX file for some of the vehicles' trips and used a GPX visualizer to visualize it on Google maps. The visualization result is provided in Figure 10.

5. CONCLUSIONS AND OUTLOOK

In this work, we have proposed a genetic and insertion heuristic algorithm for solving the dynamic ridematching problem with time windows. In addition, we have introduced eight datasets extracted from real world data for testing the behavior of the proposed algorithm. We conclude that the proposed algorithm can successfully solve the dynamic ridematching problem by providing answers to ridesharing requests in real-time. The algorithm is flexible and can be easily tuned to balance between the solution's quality and the responsiveness of the algorithm.

There are many interesting ideas to extend this work. First, we might move to a more realistic scenario. This implies adding more constraints such as limiting the number of pickup and delivery operations for each driver, putting a maximum detour distance per rider's request and considering realistic travel times and routes using Google APIs. An interesting direction is to extend the problem definition to solve the ridematching problem with time windows in dynamic multihop ridesharing where riders can share rides with multiple drivers.

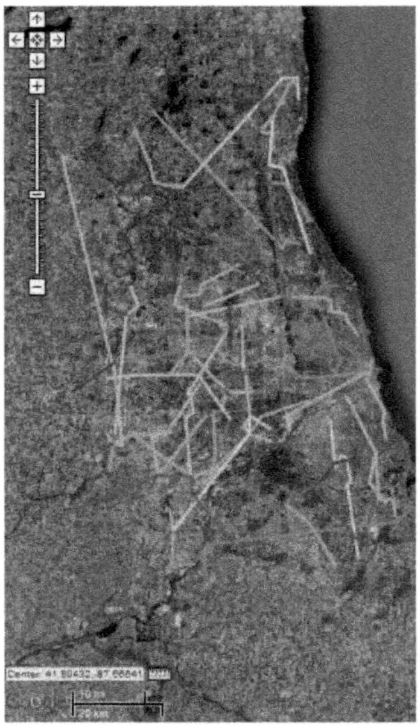

Figure 10: A color coded visualization of some vehicles' trips for instance RM744_L60 with KRR = 100%. The used GPX visualization service is: http://www.gpsvisualizer.com.

For the reproducibility of the results, the instances and the source code will be available on the authors' website.

6. REFERENCES

[1] Agatz, N., Erera, A., Savelsbergh, M., and Wang, X. Sustainable passenger transportation: Dynamic ride-sharing. Tech. rep., Erasmus Research Inst. of Management (ERIM), Erasmus Uni., Rotterdam, 2010.

[2] Agatz, N. A., Erera, A. L., Savelsbergh, M. W., and Wang, X. Dynamic ride-sharing: A simulation study in metro atlanta. *Transportation Research Part B: Methodological 45*, 9 (2011), 1450 – 1464.

[3] Baugh, J., Kakivaya, G., and Stone, J. Intractability of the dial-a-ride problem and a multiobjective solution using simulated annealing. *Engineering Optimization 30*, 2 (1998), 91–123.

[4] Chan, N., and Shaheen, S. Ridesharing in north america: Past, present, and future. *Transportation Research Board Annual Meeting* (2011).

[5] Jaw, J., Odoni, A., Psaraftis, H., and Wilson, N. A heuristic algorithm for the multi-vehicle advance request dial-a-ride problem with time windows. *Transportation Research Part B: Methodological 20*, 3 (1986), 243 – 257.

[6] Jorgensen, R. *Dial-a-Ride.* PhD thesis, Technical University of Denmark, 2002.

[7] Sinnott, R. W. Virtues of the haversine. *Sky and Telescope, Vol.68:2, P.158, 1984 62*, 2 (1984), 158.

[8] Solomon, M. Algorithms for the vehicle routing and scheduling problems with time window constraints. *Operations Research 35* (1987), 254–265.

[9] Toth, P., and Vigo, D., Eds. *The vehicle routing problem.* Siam, 2002.

An Evolutionary Algorithm with Solution Archives and Bounding Extension for the Generalized Minimum Spanning Tree Problem

Bin Hu and Günther R. Raidl

Institute of Computer Graphics and Algorithms
Vienna University of Technology
Favoritenstrasse 9-11
1040 Vienna, Austria
{hu|raidl}@ads.tuwien.ac.at

ABSTRACT

We consider the recently proposed concept of enhancing an evolutionary algorithm (EA) with a complete solution archive. It stores evaluated solutions during the optimization in order to detect duplicates and to efficiently transform them into yet unconsidered solutions. For this approach we introduce the so-called bounding extension in order to identify and prune branches in the trie-based archive which only contain inferior solutions. This extension enables the EA to concentrate the search on promising areas of the solution space. Similarly to the classical branch-and-bound technique, bounds are obtained via primal and dual heuristics. As an application we consider the generalized minimum spanning tree problem where we are given a graph with nodes partitioned into clusters and exactly one node from each cluster must be connected in the cheapest way. As the EA uses operators based on two dual representations, we exploit two corresponding tries that complement each other. Test results on TSPlib instances document the strength of this concept and that it can compete with the leading metaheuristics for this problem in the literature.

Categories and Subject Descriptors

I.2.8 [**Artificial Intelligence**]: Problem Solving, Control Methods, and Search—*Heuristic methods*; G.1.6 [**Numerical Analysis**]: Optimization

General Terms

Algorithms

Keywords

evolutionary algorithm, solution archive, network design, branch-and-bound

1. INTRODUCTION

Lots of complex combinatorial optimization problems (COPs) are nowadays approached by (hybrid) evolutionary algorithms (EA), which belong to the family of population based metaheuristics. In contrast to exact algorithms, they frequently scale better with increasing problem size and are able to find good approximate solutions in relatively short computation times. However, a common drawback is that they usually do not keep track of the search history, and already evaluated solutions are often revisited. When the selection pressure is rather high, the population size only moderate, or the genetic operators do not introduce much innovation, the population's diversity drops strongly and in the extreme case the EA gets stuck by creating almost only duplicates of a small set of leading candidate solutions, called "super-individuals". In such a situation of premature convergence, the heuristic obviously does not perform well anymore. There are several established approaches for handling this problem, such as duplicate elimination or population management. These are well-known techniques for maintaining a necessary degree of diversity in the current population.

We go one step further and investigate the recently introduced *complete solution archive* as a more powerful extension for EAs that not only considers the current population, but also detects already evaluated candidate solutions over the whole search history and efficiently transforms them into similar but yet unvisited solutions by means of an "intelligent mutation". Figure 1 illustrates the cooperation between the EA and the archive.

This concept has been successfully applied to some benchmark problems where solutions are encoded as binary strings [18, 14]. In our preliminary work [9], it was applied to a complex network design problem for the first time. Now we further extend the functionality of the solution archive by introducing the so-called *bounding extension* for detecting branches in the archive which only contain inferior solutions. These branches can be pruned similarly to classical branch-and-bound (B&B) algorithms in order to focus the search on more promising regions and to limit the memory overhead. For storing already considered solutions we use the *trie* data structure [4] that allows a fast duplicate-detection and an efficient transformation into unvisited solutions. Tries are typically used for effectively storing and searching large amounts of strings, e.g., in language dic-

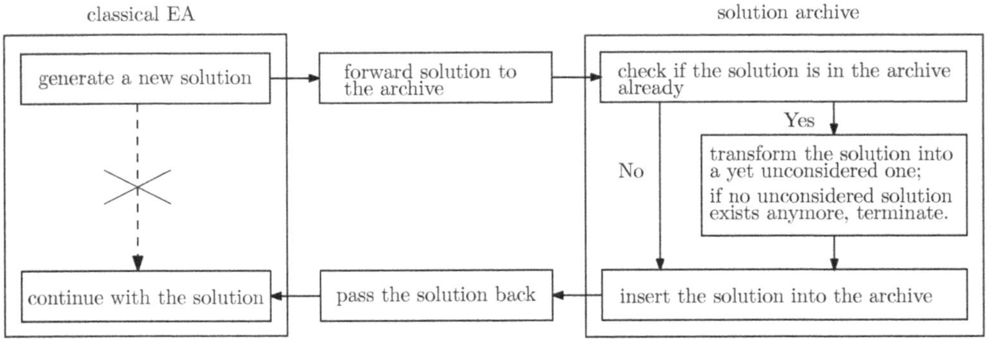

Figure 1: Cooperation between EA and trie.

tionary applications. Main advantages are that the memory effort is relatively low and that the costs for insertion and search operators essentially only depend on the word lengths, but not on the number of strings stored in the trie.

1.1 The Generalized Minimum Spanning Tree Problem

We apply our archive-enhanced EA to the generalized minimum spanning tree problem (GMSTP) which is defined as follows: Given an undirected weighted complete graph $G = \langle V, E, c\rangle$ with node set V partitioned into r pairwise disjoint clusters $V_1, \ldots, V_r$, edge set E and edge cost function $c : E \rightarrow \mathbb{R}^+$, a solution $S = \langle P, T\rangle$ is defined as $P = \{p_1, \ldots, p_r\} \subseteq V$ containing exactly one node from each cluster, i.e., $p_i \in V_i$, $i = 1, \ldots, r$, and $T \subseteq E$ being a spanning tree on the nodes in P, see Figure 2. The costs of S are the total edge costs, i.e., $C(T) = \sum_{(u,v)\in T} c(u, v)$ and the objective is to identify a solution with minimum costs.

The GMSTP was introduced in [11] and has been proven to be NP-hard. Beside our previous work [9], many successful exact methods [2, 13, 3] and metaheuristic approaches [5, 6, 8, 10, 12] were developed for this problem in the recent years. There are several real world applications of the GMSTP, e.g., in the design of backbones in large communication networks. Devices belonging to the same existing local area network correspond to nodes within the same cluster, and the backbone is required to connect one device per local network.

From the point of view of the EA, P is encoded as a vector. Therefore we use the notation $P = \langle p_1, \ldots, p_r\rangle$ in the remaining sections.

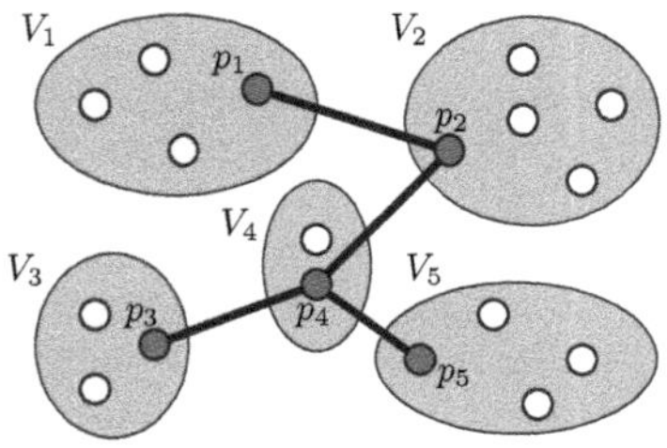

Figure 2: Example for a solution to the GMSTP.

2. EVOLUTIONARY ALGORITHM FOR THE GMSTP

We use a classic steady-state EA where the archive is consulted each time after a new solution is generated by crossover and mutation. In the following we describe the EA components.

2.1 Solution Encodings

Following [9], we utilize a dual-representation, i.e., two incomplete solution representations which complement each other are used together. On the one hand, the *Spanned Nodes Representation* (SNR) characterizes a solution by its spanned nodes P. Decoding such a genotype means to find a classical minimum spanning tree (MST) on P which can be done in polynomial time. On the other hand, the *Global Structure Representation* (GSR) characterizes solutions by the so-called global tree structure T^g where $T^g \subseteq V^g \times V^g$ and $V^g = \langle V_1, \ldots, V_r\rangle$. It defines which clusters are adjacent in the solution without specifying the actually spanned nodes. A decoding procedure calculates the optimal spanned node for each cluster via dynamic programming in $O(|V|^2)$ time [13]. Since T^g always describes a tree structure between the clusters, we store for each cluster its predecessor in the vector $\Pi = \langle \pi_2, \ldots, \pi_r\rangle$ when rooting the tree at V_1.

2.2 Genetic Operators

As selection we use tournament selection of size 2. Crossover is implemented for both representations separately. For SNR we apply uniform crossover on P and edge recombination [15] on the global tree structure is used for GSR. Each time a new offspring is created, we decide randomly which representation to use. Mutation is based on the same considerations, i.e., depending on the representation, we either exchange the spanned node in a randomly chosen cluster in SNR or a global connection in GSR. In fact, mutation is not absolutely necessary since duplicate solutions are transformed in the solution archive anyway. However, during our tests it turned out to be beneficial to include a fast and simple mutation with some low probability so that less duplicates arise and we do not need to transform so often.

3. SOLUTION ARCHIVES FOR THE GMSTP

The solution archive is implemented by two indexed tries [4], storing solutions for each representation, respectively.

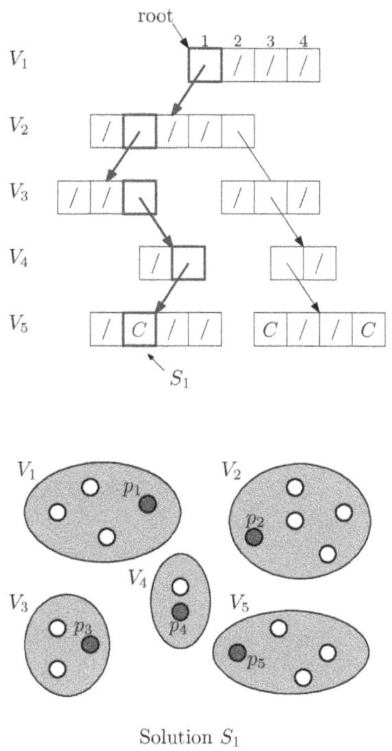

Figure 3: Example of how solution S_1 is stored in trie T_{SNR} already containing two solutions. The bold path marks the way of inserting or searching S_1.

Each trie is able to identify duplicate solutions and transforms them into new solutions in its associated solution encoding. We have to be aware though that it is possible that a new solution created by one trie becomes a duplicate in the other trie. Therefore the transformation procedures must be carried out in turn by the two tries so that a newly derived solution is re-checked in the opposite trie until it is new w.r.t. both tries. The specific implementations for the tries have been described in the previous work [9], but we summarize the essential parts in order to better understand the additional features in this work, namely the bounding extensions.

3.1 Trie Based on SNR

The trie T_{SNR} is based on the vector of spanned nodes $P = \langle p_1, \ldots, p_r \rangle$ and has maximal height r. Each trie-node at level $i = 1, \ldots, r$ corresponds to cluster V_i and contains entries $next[j]$, $j = 1, \ldots, |V_i|$, each being either a reference to a trie-node on the next level, a *complete*-flag, or an *empty*-flag. The empty-flag '/' means that none of the solutions in the subtree that would start at this point has been considered yet, while the complete-flag 'C' indicates that all solutions in the subtree have already been visited by the EA. When inserting a solution, we follow in each level i the entry that corresponds to the value of p_i. In the trie-node of the last level, $next[p_r]$ is set to 'C', indicating the presence of the solution at this point. Figure 3 shows an example of how a solution S_1 is stored in T_{SNR}. Since we want to keep the trie as compact as possible, subtries where all solutions have been visited are pruned. This is done by removing trie-nodes that only contain C-flags and changing the entry in the previous level that pointed towards it into a C-flag.

One essential feature of the solution archive is to transform duplicates upon detection. When the solution $P = \langle p_1, \ldots, p_r \rangle$ would be revisited, it is efficiently transformed into a yet unconsidered candidate solution P'. The basic idea of transformation is to backtrack to a previous trie-node on the path to the root that contains at least one yet unconsidered solution. In that trie-node on level i, $i = 1, \ldots, r$ we randomly choose an alternative entry not marked as complete and go down this subtrie following the remaining data $\langle p_{i+1}, \ldots, p_r \rangle$ whenever possible, i.e., unless we encounter a C-flag in which case we choose an alternative branch again that must contain at least one unconsidered solution. We follow a randomized transformation strategy [9] in order to avoid a strong biasing, i.e., that some positions are subject to changes more frequently than others.

We now add the new bounding extension as an additional feature based on the following idea: Since the solution archive covers the entire solution space, choosing a branch at a particular trie-node corresponds to choosing a subspace. If reasonable bounds can be computed in these nodes for the corresponding solutions' objective values, we are able to prune whole subtries that only contain inferior solutions without explicitly considering each of them. Note that this corresponds to the underlying idea of classical B&B where primal and dual heuristics are used to compute lower and upper bounds in each B&B node, aiming at pruning subtrees that exclusively consist of invalid and/or suboptimal solutions.

For calculating a lower bound at a particular entry in a trie-node corresponding to cluster V_x, we consider the graph $G^{\text{SNR}} = \langle V^{\text{SNR}}, E^{\text{SNR}} \rangle$ which is defined as follows. V^{SNR} is composed of two sets of clusters V^{f} and V^{o}. The fixed set V^{f} consists of clusters from the trie-root to cluster V_x where the spanned nodes are fixed. We denote by $p(V_i)$, $V_i \in V^{\text{f}}$, the spanned node of cluster V_i. The open set V^{o} consists of the remaining clusters that have no fixed nodes yet. For these clusters the condition to connect exactly one node will be relaxed by allowing arbitrary edges to any, even multiple, of its nodes. E^{SNR} is composed of three sets of connections E^{ff}, E^{fo}, and E^{oo}. Set E^{ff} contains connections between clusters of set V^{f}, i.e., $E^{\text{ff}} = \{(V_i, V_j) \mid V_i, V_j \in V^{\text{f}}\}$. The costs of such a connection corresponds to the actual edge cost $c(p(V_i), p(V_j))$. Set E^{fo} contains connections between a cluster of set V^{f} and a cluster of set V^{o}, i.e., $E^{\text{fo}} = \{(V_i, V_j) \mid V_i \in V^{\text{f}}, V_j \in V^{\text{o}}\}$. The costs of such a connection is defined as $\min\{c(p(V_i), v) \mid v \in V_j\}$. Finally, E^{oo} contains connections between clusters of set V^{o}, i.e., $E^{\text{oo}} = \{(V_i, V_j) \mid V_i, V_j \in V^{\text{o}}\}$. The costs of such a connection is defined as $\min\{c(u, v) \mid u \in V_i, v \in V_j\}$. Now the lower bound is obtained by applying a greedy MST algorithm on G^{SNR}.

Figure 4 shows an example for this procedure. Assume that a previously obtained solution $S_1 = \langle 1, 2, 3, 2, 2 \rangle$ has objective value $C(S_1) = 12$. A lower bound for all solutions starting with $\langle 1, 5, 2, \ldots \rangle$ is calculated on the graph G^{SNR}. The dashed lines represent the whole set of considered connections in E^{SNR} and the bold lines are the actually selected ones by the MST algorithm. Note that neither does only one node has to be connected per cluster, nor does the structure has to be connected. Assume the heuristic obtains a lower bound of 13, then there is no need to consider any further solutions in the corresponding subtrie and it is pruned.

Building up E^{SNR} can be computationally expensive if it is done every time from scratch when calculating a lower

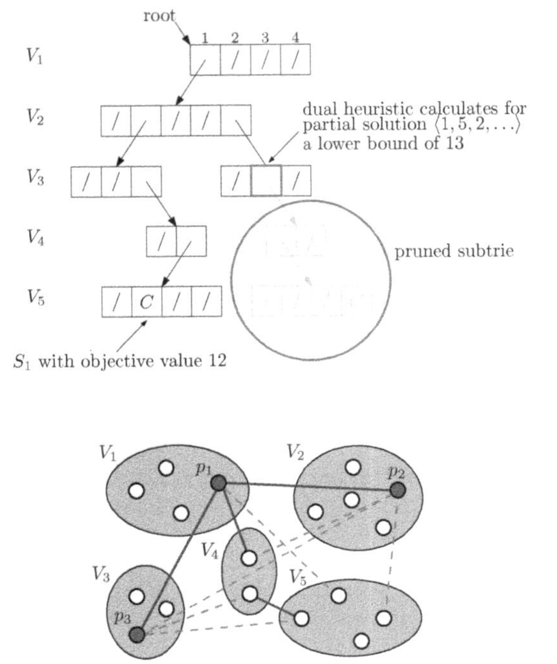

Graph G^{SNR} for determining a lower bound for partial solution $\langle 1, 5, 2, \ldots \rangle$

Figure 4: Example of how a lower bound is obtained for a partial solution in SNR and the corresponding subtrie is pruned due to the bound being larger than the objective value of a known solution (S_1).

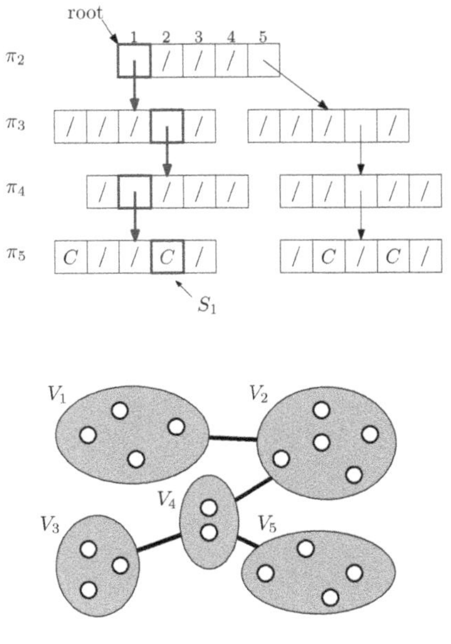

Solution S_1

Figure 5: Example of how solution S_1 is stored in trie T_{GSR} containing four solutions. The bold path marks the way of inserting or searching S_1.

bound. Fortunately, the sets E^{fo} and E^{oo} for all possible solutions can be computed once in advance in $O(|V|^2)$ time during preprocessing. Therefore the time-complexity of the bound calculation for a partial solution is dominated by applying the MST algorithm on E^{SNR} which requires $O(r^2 \log r)$ time. Nonetheless it is not convenient to do it at each level when inserting a new solution or transforming a duplicate. On the one hand, being able to prune a subtrie at high levels means that more inferior solutions are excluded at once, thus more space and time may be saved. On the other hand, the lower bounds in these situations with relatively few fixed clusters usually are not tight enough to let this happen. In our experiments there was not a single case where such a pruning could be performed in the upper half of the trie. Therefore during insertion and transformation, the bounding procedure is only applied in the lower half of the trie. Still it is too expensive to do it too often, so we apply the procedure only with a certain probability whenever the insertion or transformation operator accesses a trie node.

3.2 Trie Based on GSR

The trie T_{GSR} is based on the predecessors vector $\Pi = \langle \pi_2, \ldots, \pi_r \rangle$ and has maximal height $r-1$. Each trie-node at level $i = 1, \ldots, r-1$ corresponds to the predecessor π_{i+1} and contains entries $next[j]$, $j = 1, \ldots, r$. Figure 5 shows an example of how the solution S_1 is stored in T_{GSR}.

Inserting, searching and transforming a solution in this trie follows the same scheme as for T_{SNR}. While the first two operators require $O(r)$ time, the complexity of transformation is $O(r^3)$. This is due to the difficulties when modifying the predecessor vector. Changing one value of Π may result in an invalid tree structure. Therefore an additional repair-mechanism based on depth-first-search is required to ensure validity. Due to the larger trie-nodes, T_{GSR} is in general substantially larger than T_{SNR}.

The bound calculation for T_{GSR} works as follows. Without fixing the full predecessor vector $\Pi = \langle \pi_2, \ldots, \pi_r \rangle$, the global structure in general represents a forest $F^{\text{g}} = \bigcup_{i=1,\ldots,l} K_i^{\text{g}}$ where $K_i^{\text{g}} = \langle V_i^{\text{g}}, T_i^{\text{g}} \rangle$, $i = 1, \ldots, l$, are the l global tree components in F^{g} and V_i^{g} denotes the set of clusters that are contained in component K_i^{g}. For every K_i^{g}, $i = 1, \ldots, l$, that is not a single cluster we apply the dynamic programming procedure that is also used for decoding genotypes in GSR. As a result we obtain for each K_i^{g} the actual nodes to be spanned for the clusters in V_i^{g} that minimize the connection costs. After all global tree components are decoded, they are connected by using the same MST heuristic as in case of SNR. For this purpose the cheapest connections between all components are considered and the condition to connect exactly one node in each cluster is relaxed again. Since each component K_i^{g} is connected in the cheapest way, we obtain a lower bound.

Figure 6 shows an example for this procedure. Assume we want to compute the lower bound for all solutions starting with $\langle 5, 1, 5, \ldots \rangle$. Forest F^{g} contains two global tree components: K_1^{g} with clusters V_1 and V_3 as well as K_2^{g} with clusters V_2, V_4, and V_5. In the next step they are decoded via dynamic programming and connected using the cheapest connections. Assuming we obtain a lower bound of 14 and a previously known solution (S_1) with objective value of 12 exists, the subtrie starting at this point is pruned.

The complexity of calculating lower bounds in GSR is higher than for doing so in SNR. The cheapest connections

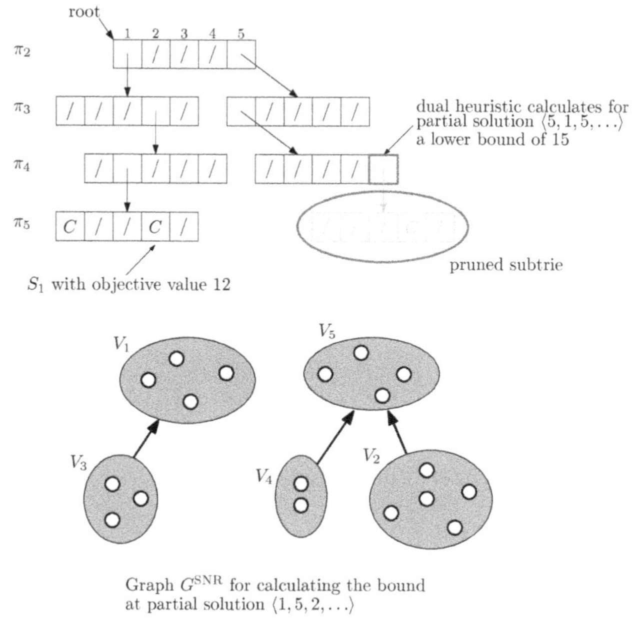

Figure 6: Example of how a lower bound is obtained for a partial solution in GSR and how the corresponding subtrie is pruned.

between clusters and/or nodes are the same which are precomputed for SNR. However, additional effort is necessary for decoding the l global tree components. In overall this requires at most $O(|V|^2)$ time since it will not take longer than decoding a complete genotype in GSR. In preliminary experiments we tried not to decode the components exactly but to use the estimated cheapest connections between clusters instead. Although this was much faster, the obtained bounds were too inaccurate and pruning happened only rarely.

Aside from the higher computational complexity, GSR's lower bounds are typically tighter than those from SNR. On the one hand this is due to the more sophisticated bounding calculation where runtime is not spent in vain. On the other hand decisions in GSR are more powerful per se, since fixing a connection between two widely separated clusters has a larger impact on solution quality than fixing a bad spanned node in a cluster in SNR. While pruning in SNR is typically only possible in the lower half of trie, this does not hold for the lower bounds calculated in GSR. Here we observe that pruning happens on nearly any arbitrary level in the trie, so all levels are considered. However, as in SNR, the bounding calculation is only performed with a certain probability.

4. COMPUTATIONAL RESULTS

We tested our approach on TSPlib[1] instances using geographical center clustering [1]. For each instance we performed 30 independent runs with each considered algorithm variant in order to derive average objective values and standard deviations. When generating new solutions, recombination was always performed and the mutation rate was set to 10%. The population contained 100 solutions. These parameters are relatively standard for an EA. We tested different settings, but the impact on the solution qualities were insignificant. This indicates that the solution archive is able to compensate changes in the primary parameters of the EA and makes it more robust. Archive specific parameters such as the probability for bounding calculations have larger effects. The time and memory overhead can become very large when they are set too high. The appropriate values are derived from extensive testings in [7].

First we show in Table 1 the impact on time and memory consumption with respect to the bounding extension. For this purpose we terminated the EA after a fixed number of 10000 iterations, and we either only used the SNR archive or the GSR archive. This way we are able to see the differences more clearly. The first column lists the instance names with the last three digits indicating $|V|$. For each variant we show average CPU-times required on a single core of an Intel Core 2 quad PC with 2.4GHz and 4GB memory and the average sizes of the archives at the end. Solution qualities are not listed here since they are not the focus of this table. The probability of the bound calculation at a trie node when it is accessed was set to 0.05. Even with this low probability, the time overhead is substantial and in many cases the runtime was doubled. We also observe an increased memory consumption when applying bounding. This might be counterintuitive at first glance since one goal of this technique is to save memory by pruning subtries with inferior solutions. However, a new solution must be generated each time when this happens. So we essentially perform a transformation after pruning which in general introduces new branches in the trie. As pointed out in Section 3.2, the GSR trie is substantially larger than the SNR trie.

Next we extend the results previously published in [9] in order to show the impact of the bounding extension on the solution quality. In Table 2 the EA was tested in the following variants: EA without archive, EA with SNR archive based on trie T_{SNR}, EA with GSR archive based on trie T_{GSR}, EA with full archive, i.e., using both tries, and EA with full archive and bounding. As termination criterion we now used a fixed CPU-time since the overhead caused by the archive and/or the bounding extension must be considered. The first two columns list the instance names and the time limit. For each EA variant we show the average final solution values $\overline{C(T)}$ and corresponding standard deviations (sd). Best results are marked bold. We observe that the EA variant without archive performs worst in general. Among the two variants where the archive only uses one representation, GSR is more often the better choice. By combining both tries in the archive we are able to get even better results, but including bounding further increases the solution qualities on all except one instance. This indicates that the solution archive and the bounding have a positive impact on the EA, and the time overhead is compensated. Since the differences on $\overline{C(T)}$ for the last two EA variants are relatively small, we performed one-sided Wilcoxon rank sum tests for the assumption that the variant with bounding performs better than the variant without bounding. On the five instances where the results differ, the error probabilities are between 0.07 and 0.50, so we conclude that the differences are not significant.

In order to obtain a more meaningful picture, we compare in Table 3 the last two EA variants on an extended TSPlib instance set[2] introduced in [12]. These instances

[1] elib.zib.de/pub/Packages/mp-testdata/tsp/tsplib/tsplib.html

[2] neumann.hec.ca/chairedistributique/data/gmstp

Table 1: Time and memory consumption by the archive.

	SNR archive				GSR archive			
	no bounding		with bounding		no bounding		with bounding	
Instance	$\overline{\text{time}}$	$\overline{\text{mem}}$	$\overline{\text{time}}$	$\overline{\text{mem}}$	$\overline{\text{time}}$	$\overline{\text{mem}}$	$\overline{\text{time}}$	$\overline{\text{mem}}$
kroa150	23s	6.7 MB	36s	8.0 MB	24s	28.9 MB	37s	32.8 MB
d198	39s	10.7 MB	75s	12.5 MB	41s	55.4 MB	58s	59.5 MB
krob200	49s	8.2 MB	82s	9.7 MB	49s	49.0 MB	99s	54.1 MB
gr202	42s	10.0 MB	68s	11.6 MB	44s	58.3 MB	55s	61.2 MB
ts225	49s	17.3 MB	73s	19.0 MB	53s	84.7 MB	61s	85.3 MB
pr226	64s	6.8 MB	126s	7.7 MB	61s	76.1 MB	100s	89.3 MB
gil262	74s	17.9 MB	123s	21.3 MB	78s	111.4 MB	93s	115.8 MB
pr264	80s	15.1 MB	139s	17.8 MB	83s	108.5 MB	106s	115.9 MB
pr299	101s	18.8 MB	174s	22.1 MB	105s	133.6 MB	129s	137.4 MB
lin318	113s	17.8 MB	217s	22.1 MB	116s	163.5 MB	152s	174.2 MB
rd400	168s	25.8 MB	318s	31.9 MB	178s	264.7 MB	212s	276.9 MB
fl417	204s	18.1 MB	499s	20.5 MB	196s	265.0 MB	326s	302.5 MB
gr431	243s	28.9 MB	466s	34.3 MB	248s	309.3 MB	267s	315.3 MB
pcb442	217s	34.4 MB	406s	41.1 MB	229s	360.0 MB	244s	367.4 MB

Table 2: Results of different EA variants.

		no archive		SNR archive		GSR archive		full archive		with bounding	
Instance	time	$\overline{C(T)}$	sd	$\overline{C(T)}$	sd	$\overline{C(T)}$	sd	$\overline{C(T)}$	sd	$\overline{C(T)}$	sd
kroa150	150s	9830.6	31.4	9831.3	30.1	**9815.0**	0.0	**9815.0**	0.0	**9815.0**	0.0
d198	300s	7055.1	8.7	7059.6	9.0	7044.6	2.3	**7044.0**	0.0	**7044.0**	0.0
krob200	300s	11275.0	45.6	11248.9	7.5	**11244.0**	0.0	**11244.0**	0.0	**11244.0**	0.0
gr202	300s	242.1	0.3	242.2	0.4	**242.0**	0.2	**242.0**	0.0	**242.0**	0.0
ts225	300s	62290.8	40.4	62299.1	50.9	62268.6	0.5	62268.4	0.5	**62268.3**	0.5
pr226	300s	**55515.0**	0.0	**55515.0**	0.0	**55515.0**	0.0	**55515.0**	0.0	**55515.0**	0.0
gil262	450s	945.5	4.0	945.0	3.7	942.4	2.0	**942.0**	0.0	**942.0**	0.0
pr264	450s	21893.2	7.7	21898.4	20.9	**21886.0**	0.0	**21886.0**	0.0	**21886.0**	0.0
pr299	450s	20352.1	37.4	20349.7	24.9	20318.5	11.3	20318.1	11.3	**20316.0**	0.0
lin318	600s	18545.9	29.2	18547.3	25.6	18525.8	12.4	**18511.0**	10.8	18513.8	9.9
rd400	600s	5953.0	15.4	5959.4	20.2	5946.4	10.8	5940.2	6.5	**5939.7**	6.7
fl417	600s	**7982.0**	0.0	**7982.0**	0.0	**7982.0**	0.0	**7982.0**	0.0	**7982.0**	0.0
gr431	600s	1034.1	1.4	1033.4	0.9	1033.3	0.7	**1033.0**	0.0	**1033.0**	0.0
pr439	600s	51921.4	60.7	51888.5	56.3	51810.5	26.5	**51791.0**	0.0	**51791.0**	0.0
pcb442	600s	19717.0	59.5	19708.1	70.2	19632.6	21.1	19623.7	15.9	**19617.0**	12.4

Table 4: Comparison with other state-of-the-art approaches on the standard TSPlib instances.

	TS		VNS			DCS			EA + archive		
Instance	C(T)	time	$\overline{C(T)}$	sd	time	$\overline{C(T)}$	sd	time	$\overline{C(T)}$	sd	time
kroa150	**9815.0**	150s	**9815.0**	0.0	150s	**9815.0**	0.0	133s	**9815.0**	0.0	39s
d198	7062.0	300s	**7044.0**	0.0	300s	**7044.0**	0.0	265s	**7044.0**	0.0	78s
krob200	11245.0	300s	**11244.0**	0.0	300s	**11244.0**	0.0	265s	**11244.0**	0.0	78s
gr202	**242.0**	300s	**242.0**	0.0	300s	**242.0**	0.0	265s	**242.0**	0.0	78s
ts225	62366.0	300s	62268.5	0.5	300s	**62268.3**	0.5	265s	62268.5	0.5	78s
pr226	**55515.0**	300s	**55515.0**	0.0	300s	**55515.0**	0.0	265s	**55515.0**	0.0	78s
gil262	**942.0**	450s	942.3	1.0	450s	**942.0**	0.0	398s	**942.0**	0.0	118s
pr264	**21886.0**	450s	21886.5	1.8	450s	**21886.0**	0.0	398s	**21886.0**	0.0	118s
pr299	20339.0	450s	20322.6	14.7	450s	20317.4	1.5	398s	**20316.0**	0.0	118s
lin318	18521.0	600s	**18506.8**	11.6	600s	18513.6	7.8	531s	18519.3	8.4	157s
rd400	5943.0	600s	5943.6	9.7	600s	5941.5	9.9	531s	**5939.5**	5.2	157s
fl417	7990.0	600s	**7982.0**	0.0	600s	7982.7	0.5	531s	**7982.0**	0.0	157s
gr431	1034.0	600s	**1033.0**	0.2	600s	**1033.0**	0.0	531s	**1033.0**	0.0	157s
pr439	51852.0	600s	51847.9	40.9	600s	51833.8	36.1	531s	**51791.0**	0.0	157s
pcb442	19621.0	600s	19702.8	52.1	600s	19662.5	39.8	531s	**19626.0**	17.0	157s

Table 5: Comparison with other state-of-the-art approaches on the extended TSPlib instances.

	GA		TS2		EA + archive			
Instance	$C^*(T)$	time	$C^*(T)$	time	$C^*(T)$	$\overline{C(T)}$	sd	time
ali535	114379	492s	**114303**	683s	**114303**	114419.1	96.6	243s
att532	12007	500s	**12001**	597s	**12001**	12007.8	6.3	115s
d493	16526	388s	**16493**	587s	**16493**	16501.0	18.3	154s
d657	19465	969s	**19427**	1056s	**19427**	19456.6	32.5	335s
fl417	7936	218s	**7935**	233s	**7935**	7935.0	0.0	2570s
gil262	**887**	73s	**887**	74s	**887**	887.0	0.0	13s
gr431	86899	266s	**86885**	233s	**86885**	86903.4	42.3	80s
gr666	144918	2866s	144756	1365s	**144737**	144747.7	40.8	237s
lin318	18476	105s	**18471**	130s	**18471**	18486.3	4.3	46s
p654	22214	881s	22208	1045s	**22207**	22207.0	0.0	1634s
pa561	868	559s	**864**	702s	865	870.7	2.7	107s
pcb442	19670	284s	**19571**	266s	**19571**	19593.9	22.1	66s
pr264	21886	57s	**21872**	72s	**21872**	21872.0	0.0	20s
pr299	20307	86s	**20290**	94s	**20290**	20290.0	0.0	21s
pr439	51808	981s	51760	574s	**51749**	51749.9	3.6	84s
rat575	2189	627s	**2170**	762s	**2170**	2180.0	6.3	125s
rat783	3044	1653s	3017	1916s	**3015**	3027.4	7.4	292s
rd400	5880	205s	**5868**	208s	**5868**	5875.9	8.9	56s
si535	**12791**	458s	**12791**	573s	**12791**	12791.0	0.0	123s
u574	15069	620s	15037	517s	**15034**	15058.1	14.3	155s
u724	16015	1281s	15905	1290s	**15904**	15947.4	26.6	324s

Table 3: Results of different EA variants on the extended TSPlib instances.

		no bounding		with bounding		sign.diff.
Instance	time	$\overline{C(T)}$	sd	$\overline{C(T)}$	sd	error
ali535	600s	114581.1	95.8	**114404.9**	90.7	<0.001
att532	600s	12008.1	7.4	**12004.9**	4.5	0.051
d493	600s	16516,8	14,5	**16494.9**	3.1	<0.001
d657	600s	19504.0	42.2	**19451.7**	31.3	<0.001
fl417	600s	**7935.0**	0.0	**7935.0**	0.0	N.A.
gil262	450s	**887.0**	0.0	**887.0**	0.0	N.A.
gr431	600s	86889.2	18.0	**86888.2**	17.3	0.500
gr666	600s	144837.3	109.1	**144790.6**	77.1	0.037
lin318	600s	18485.9	13.9	**18485.1**	8.6	0.468
p654	600s	**22207.0**	0.0	**22207.0**	0.0	N.A.
pa561	600s	870.6	2.9	**866.7**	2.4	<0.001
pcb442	600s	19589.0	21.5	**19584.1**	15.0	0.109
pr264	450s	**21872.0**	0.0	**21872.0**	0.0	N.A.
pr299	450s	20301.2	16.3	**20290.0**	0.0	<0.001
pr439	600s	51754.3	15.1	**51749.0**	0.0	0.050
rat575	600s	2184.0	6.3	**2178.5**	4.8	<0.001
rat783	600s	3033.6	13.2	**3028.5**	8.3	0.076
rd400	600s	**5874.9**	11.2	5875.0	5.4	0.670
si535	600s	**12791.0**	0.0	**12791.0**	0.0	N.A.
u574	600s	15063.0	15.1	**15051.4**	8.9	<0.001
u724	600s	15965.1	35.4	**15949.2**	29.4	0.046

are larger and have also been derived by geographical center clustering. Note that some of these instances have the same names as those in the first set, but the clustering data and/or the distance data are different. Beside the average final solution values and corresponding standard deviations, we also list for each instance the error probability (error) of the one-sided Wilcoxon rank sum test for the assumption that the variant with bounding performs better than the variant without bounding. Besides five instances where both variants perform equally well and one instance where the EA variant without bounding performs slightly better, we observe that the bounding extension now consistently increases the solution quality. On nine instances these improvements are statistically significant with error probabilities less than 5%.

In Table 4 we compare our EA using the full archive and bounding with several leading state-of-the-art approaches from literature consisting of a tabu search approach (TS1) by Ghosh [5], a hybrid variable neighborhood search approach (VNS) by Hu et al. [8], and an algorithm based on dynamic candidates sets (DCS) by Jiang and Chen [10]. Using a fixed CPU-time as termination criterion, TS1 and VNS ran on a Pentium 4 PC with 2.8GHz, DCS ran on a Pentium D PC with 2.66GHz and the EA ran on an Intel Core i7 PC with 3.4GHz (in contrast to the preliminary tests where an Intel Core 2 quad PC was used). Since the different approaches used different hardware, we scaled the time limits according to the the well-known Standard Performance Evaluation Corporation (SPEC) benchmark[3]. It indicates that Core i7 (score 47.1) is around 332% faster than Pentium D (score 14.2) which is then again around 15% faster than Pentium 4 (score 12.3). After compensating the heterogeneous testing environments by using the appropriate time limits, we observe that our EA can compete well with the other approaches, especially on larger instances.

In Table 5 we compare our approach with a genetic algorithm (GA) by Golden et al. [6] and a tabu search approach (TS2) by Oencan et al. [12] on the extended TSPlib instances. GA ran on a Xeon workstation with 2.66GHz and TS2 ran on a Pentium 4 PC with 3GHz. Since these authors did not use a fixed CPU-time as termination criterion, we terminated our EA after 2000 iterations without improvement. Because only best solutions are listed for GA and

[3]www.spec.org/cpu2006

TS2 in [12], we also focused on the best solutions obtained by 30 runs of our EA (but we nevertheless added the average values and the standard deviations). We observe that our approach competes well with TS2 and outperforms the GA. By means of the SPEC benchmarks for the different hardwares on which TS2 and our EA were tested, we can see that the required CPU-times are comparable for most of the instances. On the instance fl417 our EA consumes an exceptionally large amount of runtime. The reason is that the final best solution can be found extremely easily, therefore the solution archive spends much time on converting all the duplicates which arise.

5. CONCLUSIONS AND FUTURE WORK

In this paper we proposed a novel bounding extension for a solution archive enhanced EA for the GMSTP. Since the EA uses operators based on two dual representations, we introduced two different bounding heuristics, respectively. Tests on TSPlib instances show that the extension, particularly when combining both representations, is able to improve the search behavior significantly. Compared with several leading state-of-the-art approaches from literature, the archive-enhanced EA is able to keep up with the very top candidates.

For future work, we want to investigate another extension for solution archives where the transformation of duplicate solutions is guided by estimation heuristics. This approach complements the bounding extensions so that the solution archive not only cuts off inferior solutions, but puts more focus on promising ones. We also believe that the concept of solution archives is a powerful addition to EAs in a more general sense, when it is implemented adequately for appropriate combinatorial optimization problems. Hence we want to further pursue this concept also for other problems.

Acknowledgements

We thank Markus Wolf, Mika Sonnleitner, and Christian Gruber, who helped in the implementation of the described concepts and did the testing as part of their master theses [17, 16, 7].

6. REFERENCES

[1] C. Feremans. *Generalized Spanning Trees and Extensions.* PhD thesis, Universite Libre de Bruxelles, Belgium, 2001.

[2] C. Feremans, M. Labbe, and G. Laporte. A comparative analysis of several formulations for the generalized minimum spanning tree problem. *Networks*, 39(1):29–34, 2002.

[3] C. Feremans, M. Labbe, and G. Laporte. The generalized minimum spanning tree problem: Polyhedral analysis and branch-and-cut algorithm. *Networks*, 43(2):71–86, 2004.

[4] E. Fredkin. Trie memory. *Communications of the ACM*, 3:490–499, 1960.

[5] D. Ghosh. Solving medium to large sized Euclidean generalized minimum spanning tree problems. Technical Report NEP-CMP-2003-09-28, Indian Institute of Management, Research and Publication Department, Ahmedabad, India, 2003.

[6] B. Golden, S. Raghavan, and D. Stanojevic. Heuristic search for the generalized minimum spanning tree problem. *INFORMS Journal on Computing*, 17(3):290–304, 2005.

[7] C. Gruber. Ein Lösungsarchiv mit Branch-and-Bound-Erweiterung für das Generalized Minimum Spanning Tree Problem. Master's thesis, Vienna University of Technology, 2011.

[8] B. Hu, M. Leitner, and G. R. Raidl. Combining variable neighborhood search with integer linear programming for the generalized minimum spanning tree problem. *Journal of Heuristics*, 14(5):473–499, 2008.

[9] B. Hu and G. R. Raidl. An evolutionary algorithm with solution archive for the generalized minimum spanning tree problem. In R. Moreno-Díaz, F. Pichler, and A. Quesada-Arencibia, editors, *Proceedings of the 13th International Conference on Computer Aided Systems Theory: Part I*, volume 6927 of *LNCS*, pages 287–294. Springer, 2012.

[10] H. Jiang and Y. Chen. An efficient algorithm for generalized minimum spanning tree problem. In *GECCO '10: Proceedings of the 12th annual conference on Genetic and evolutionary computation*, pages 217–224, New York, NY, USA, 2010. ACM.

[11] Y. S. Myung, C. H. Lee, and D. W. Tcha. On the generalized minimum spanning tree problem. *Networks*, 26:231–241, 1995.

[12] T. Öncan, J.-F. Cordeau, and G. Laporte. A tabu search heuristic for the generalized minimum spanning tree problem. *European Journal of Operational Research*, 191(2):306–319, 2008.

[13] P. C. Pop. *The Generalized Minimum Spanning Tree Problem.* PhD thesis, University of Twente, The Netherlands, 2002.

[14] G. R. Raidl and B. Hu. Enhancing genetic algorithms by a trie-based complete solution archive. In *Evolutionary Computation in Combinatorial Optimisation – EvoCOP 2010*, volume 6022 of *LNCS*, pages 239–251. Springer, 2010.

[15] G. R. Raidl and B. A. Julstrom. Edge-sets: An effective evolutionary coding of spanning trees. *IEEE Transactions on Evolutionary Computation*, 7(3), 2003.

[16] M. Sonnleitner. Ein neues Lösungsarchiv für das Generalized Minimum Spanning Tree-Problem. Master's thesis, Vienna University of Technology, 2010.

[17] M. Wolf. Ein Lösungsarchiv-unterstützter evolutionärer Algorithmus für das Generalized Minimum Spanning Tree-Problem. Master's thesis, Vienna University of Technology, 2009.

[18] S. Y. Yuen and C. K. Chow. A non-revisiting genetic algorithm. In *IEEE Congress on Evolutionary Computation (CEC 2007)*, pages 4583–4590. IEEE Press, 2007.

PSO Based on Surrogate Modelling as Meta-Search to Optimise Evolutionary Algorithms Parameters

Ahmed Kattan
Um Al Qura University
AI Real-World Applications Lab
Department of Computer Science
Kingdom of Saudi Arabia
ajkattan@uqu.edu.sa

Muhammad Arif
Um Al Qura University
AI Real-World Applications Lab
Department of Computer Science
Kingdom of Saudi Arabia
mahamid@uqu.edu.sa

ABSTRACT

The problem of setting suitable parameters for population-based Evolutionary Algorithms (EA) is not new. However, the process of tuning the EA parameters is still challenging, since their sensitivity to the given problem is highly non-linear. This paper proposes a framework that uses Particle Swarm Optimisation (PSO) based on Surrogate Modelling (SM) to optimise population-based EA parameters before they can be applied to solve problems. The proposed framework is comprised of two components; PSO that searches the parameters space and a Radial Basis Function Networks (RBFN) surrogate model to guide it. The main advantage of our model is that it optimises the EA parameters in a way that ensures that EA searches the problem within a limited number of evaluations. Experiments with three different benchmark problems demonstrate that our proposed framework managed to assist a Genetic Algorithm (GA) in order to optimise its parameters and achieves better solutions than the use of Standard PSO without surrogate assistance to optimise the GA parameters, Standard GA that is applied directly to the problem with fixed parameters settings, Standard 1+1 Evolutionary Strategy (ES) applied directly to the problem and simple Random Search.

Categories and Subject Descriptors

I.2 [**Artificial Intelligence**]; I.2.8 [**Heuristic Methods**]

General Terms

Algorithms

Keywords

Parameters Tuning,Particle Swarm Optimisation, Evolutionary Algorithms, Surrogate, Radial Basis Function Networks.

1. INTRODUCTION

The problem of setting suitable parameters for population-based EAs has been the focus of an active research area in the past few decades [1]. However, tuning the EA parameters is still a challenging task since their sensitivity to the given problem is highly non-linear. A common parameter setting strategy involves running the algorithm multiple times with different settings, using a human-in-the-loop approach, in an attempt to fine-tune the EA approach to the given problem [1]. This can be a wearisome process; therefore, oftentimes, one is tempted to use default settings or settings in the literature that address similar problems.

The problem of parameter tuning can be seen as a classical optimisation problem. However, it requires a considerable amount of computational resources especially when the fitness function is computationally expensive (which is the case with most real-world problems). In such a circumstance, the process of tuning the parameters can become infeasible. Furthermore, in order to validate the goodness of a parameters set one may need to run the EA several times due to their stochastic nature. Thus, it is attractive to automate this process. One solution is to use "parameters sweep" strategy [2]. However, a proper parameters sweep can easily grow exponentially due to its combinatorial search space size. Another existing solution in the literature is to use an optimisation method as a top-level (or meta-search) [3]. This scenario raises an interesting question of how to tune the parameters of the top-level optimiser? This question does not seem to have any obvious answer [1]. Back to the computational intensity problem, one possible solution to reduce the computational cost of the top-level EA when optimising the low-level EA's parameters is to use approximation models, which are known as surrogate models, that can predict the fitness or objective function evaluation [4]. This can expedite the search by generating many candidate solutions in the search space at a smaller evaluation cost. The selection of these models is based on two main assumptions: *(a)* that their evaluation cost of the fitness function is much cheaper in comparison to the original evaluation (i.e., running the EA to validate the goodness of a parameters set), and *(b)* that they can successfully approximate the search space of the problem.

In this paper, we propose a framework that is based on PSO and RBFN surrogate to automatically optimise the EA parameters. The contributions of this paper are twofold:

1. We propose the use of PSO as a meta-search for other EA techniques. To the best of our knowledge, PSO-based on SM has never been used to search population-based EA's parameters space.

2. Unlike other parameters optimisation methods, the proposed framework ensures that EA searches the problem within a limited number of evaluations. Thus, our framework suggests the best settings under a pre-defined maximum number of evaluations.

GECCO'12, July 7–11, 2012, Philadelphia, Pennsylvania, USA.

Experiments with three different benchmark problems demonstrate that our proposed framework managed to assist GA to optimise its parameters and achieves better solutions than other standard systems (details in Section 5).

The remaining of this paper is organised as follows: Section 2 briefly presents some of the previous work that is related to EA parameters optimisation via surrogate and PSO based surrogate systems. Section 3 details our proposed framework. Experiments' settings and results are presented Sections 4 and 5, respectively. Section 6 present some discussion on the results. Finally, Section 7 presents some conclusive remarks and future work.

2. RELATED WORK

2.1 Parameter Optimisation Techniques

In terms of performance or the convergence of the EA, the parameter tuning of the evolutionary algorithms showed promising results. Eiben et al. [5] described two kinds of strategies for parameter setting in the evolutionary algorithms. In parameter control, the parameters of an algorithm are constantly updated during a single run according to a certain control strategy. Conversely, in the parameter tuning approach, for a particular run of an algorithm, a single set of parameters is used and its performance is assessed according to some performance measure. A comparison of parameter tuning methods can be found in [6, 1]. Preuss et al [7] demonstrated the efficacy of surrogate models in tuning the parameters of the optimisation algorithm. Rudolph et al. [8] proposed a two-layered optimisation mechanism to optimise the meta models at two different levels; at level-1, surrogate model is used based on true objective function calculations and at level-2 another surrogate model is used as meta-model. In [1], the author reviewed parameters tuning mechanisms at different stages of EA and pointed out that there is no universal strategy with which to tune the internal parameters of an evolutionary algorithm for all types of applications.

None of the above work defines a limit of evaluations before optimising the EA parameters. The proposed framework suggests the best settings under a pre-defined maximum number of evaluations.

2.2 PSO-Based Surrogate

For computationally expensive optimisation, various meta-models for fitness approximation are proposed to accelerate the convergence of PSO. Bird et al [9] used least square regression to estimate the local fitness function and location of peak is predicted which is later used in PSO. They claimed that, which such an approach, the convergence speed is greatly improved. Gorshy et al [10] applied the quadratic surface method to approximate the fitness function and applied it in the ship design. Seirra and Coello [11] used various types of fitness approximation techniques in multi-objective particle swarm optimisation. Further, Robert et al. [12] used inexpensive surrogate models in multi-objective particle swarm optimisation to reduce the computational cost. He used kriging method for fitness approximation in engineering design problems. Parno et al. [13] has proposed a framework to incorporate the surrogate models into particle swarm optimisation. They showed that surrogate model can be built by using the objective function values that are already available during optimisation process and this model can guide the optimisation algorithm in the search space.

To the best of our knowledge, PSO based on SM has never been used before as meta-models to optimise the parameters for the EA. In this paper, we explore the potentials of PSO-Surrogate as meta search for population-based EAs' parameters.

3. PROPOSED META SEARCH

As mentioned previously, PSO has been used as a top-level search to explore the parameters space for population-based EA, and RBFN surrogate is used to guide the search. Note that the landscape that is defined by the EA's parameters have the same unknown properties as the problem given to the EA itself. An interesting future study is to investigate the relationship between the problem's difficulty that suggested the use of an EA and the sensitivity of the parameters settings.

Here, PSO automatically adjusts the size of population and number of generations in the EA system as well as the search operators' rates in such a way as to keep the whole process under control and facilitate the best possible results. For this task, the EA is associated with a numerical set of weights $W = \{u_0, u_1\}$, which is used to identify its settings. Hence, u_0 is used to set the size of population and number of generations, while u_1 is used to set the search operators' rates. During the optimisation process of the particles, the system applies a constraint to ensure the validity of all settings. Thus, to prevent the PSO from setting a large number for the population size and the number of generations (that potentially may be computationally infeasible), the total number of evaluations should not be allowed to exceed a predefined maximum number of evaluations. Hence,

$$\text{Population\_Size} \times Number\_of\_Generations \leq max\_explorations$$

The "max _explorations" is the upper limit of evaluations for the EA system. The reason why this upper limit of evaluations is set is to allow the user to define an upper boundary of the computational costs before using this framework to tune the parameters. Here, the framework will search for the optimal settings under this boundary.

Each $u_i \in W$ is a real number from the interval $(0, 1)$. EA parameters are calculated as follows:

- $Population_= max\_explorations \times u_0$
- $Number\_of\_Generations = \frac{max\_explorations}{Population}$
- $Crossover\_rate = u_1$
- $Mutation\_rate = 1 - u_1$

The weights of the EA parameters form a two-dimensional vector $V = \{u_0, u_1\}$, which in turn corresponds to an individual/particle in a swarm population $P_{pso} = \{V_0, V_1, ..., V_n\}$, where n is the size of the swarm. Hence, swarm population (i.e., collection of weights) is used to optimise the parameters of the EA systems in such a way as to find the optimal solution under a limited number of evaluations.

3.1 PSO Parameters Optimisation

The proposed framework works as follows. First, the system randomly initialises a swarm population of size n, according to the constraint mentioned in the previous section. For each particle $V_i \in P_{pso}$ the system runs the EA by using the settings from the V_i. This raises the question of how to evaluate a set of EA's settings? In other words, what it the fitness measure of the PSO. In this work, we run the EA several times and report the best evolved solution across all of runs. The formal notation of the PSO fitness measure is defined as follows:

$$Fitness = \arg\max_{P_{pso}[V_i]} EA(P_{pso}[V_i]), V_i \in P_{pso} \quad (1)$$

Here, $EA(P_{pos}[V_i])$ refers to the function that runs the EA using the parameters set V_i in the P_{pso} population and returns the fitness of the best solution.

Once the system evaluates all V_i particles in P_{pso}, it allocates the best particle (i.e., the one which provided the best adjustment to the EA in such a way as to return the best solution) as a centre and all other particles in the P_{pso} move toward the centre by using a velocity value $V_i[u_i]$. Velocities were adjusted according to their difference from the best known location, as in [14], for each u_i in V_i particle as follows:

$if(centre_{u_i} < V_i[u_i])$

$$V_i[u_i] = V_i[u_i] - vFactor \times rand_1 \times [|centre_{u_i} - V_i[u_i]|]$$

else if($centre_{u_i} > V_i[u_i]$)

$$V_i[u_i] = V_i[u_i] + vFactor \times rand_1 \times [|centre_{u_i} - V_i[u_i]|] \quad (2)$$

Thus, each particle in P_{pso} remembers the globally best position (which is found by a member in the flock). Each particle moves into the two-dimensional weights space (or parameters space). The *"vFactor"* is a predefined constant and used to set the max step of any V_i particle in the P_{pso}. Preliminary experiments show that the best value for vFactor is 0.1. The particles optimisation process can be envisaged as birds flock flying in a 2D grid: as each particle moves into the 2D weights space, its weights u_0 and u_1 are adjusted in a simple manner: u_0 moves right or left by adding or subtracting a random amount weighted by the parameter *vFactor* and, similarly, u_1 moves up or down. At each move, the system checks whether the particles' values satisfy the constraint mentioned in Section 3. If the particles do not satisfy these constraints, then a new $rand_1$ value is placed in Equation 2 until the constraint is satisfied. The process of velocity adjustment iterates until the maximum number of moves.

Algorithm 1 broadly outlines the whole process. In **line 1**, the system generates P_{pso}, of size n particles, according to the constraint defined in Section 3. In **line 2**, the system defines the $max\_explore$ limit of evaluations. In **lines 3 - 14**, the system iterates over P_{pso}. For each V_i, it calculates the parameters set, namely, population size, number of generations, and search operators' rates (**lines 6 - 9**). Thereafter, the system runs the EA based on its new settings and stores fitness of the best solution found by the EA into $Best\_Sol\_Fitness$ (**line 11**). In **line 12**, the best V_i treated as a centre and all other individuals in P_{pso} update their velocity values (as explained in Equation 2) in order to move toward the centre (**line 13**). As previously stated, running the EA multiple times can be computationally expensive, therefore we replace (**line 11**) with RBFN surrogate to speed up the PSO search.

The size of the swarm population and number of moves is related to the problem difficulty (more details on the parameters' setting are provided in Section 4).

3.2 Radial Basis Function Networks Surrogate

There are a number of known approaches to learn a function that belongs to a certain class of functions from existing data-points [1] (i.e., finding a function in that class that interpolates and best fits the data-points according to some criteria). Some of these include Genetic Programming (GP), RBFN Interpolation, Artificial Neural Networks and Gaussian Process Regression (also known as Kriging) [4].

GP is a powerful method for approximating unknown functions. However, one major drawback of GP is its well-known expensive learning process. Gaussian Process Regression is a very powerful method with a solid theoretical foundation, which not only can make a rational extrapolation about the location of the global optimum, but also gives an interval of confidence about the prediction

[1] Data-point is the pair of solution and its real fitness value.

Algorithm 1: PSO tuning EA settings

1 Random-Generate-Swarm(V[u_0, u_1], n)
2 Integer $max\_explore$;
3 **repeat**
4   **foreach** V_i **do**
5   *Parameters_Set:*
6   *{ Pop_Size* = $u_0 \times max\_explore$;
7   *Number_of_Gen* = $max\_explore/Pop\_Size$;
8   *Crossover* = u_1;
9   *Mutation* = $1 - u_1$;
10   *}*
    `// Here we replace the real evaluation with a cheap RBFN surrogate`
11   *Best_Sol_Fitness = Run_EA(Parameters_Set);*
12   $centre_{best}[u_0, u_1] = Best\_Sol\_Fitness$
13   *Update-All*($V_0, \ldots, V_n$)
14 **until** *max-moves* ;

made. RBFN Interpolation is conceptually simpler than Gaussian Process Regression and can extrapolate the global optimum from the known data-points. In this paper, we focus on RBFNs as surrogate models.

RBFNs can be seen as variants of an artificial neural network that uses radial basis functions (RBF) as activation functions [15]. Typically, RBFN consists of three layers: input, hidden, and output layer. The relationship between the input and the hidden layer is determined by the RBF activation function. The nodes in the output layer usually perform a simple summation for the linear weights of these activations. RBFNs have successfully been used in function approximation, time series prediction, and control [15].

A RBF is a real-valued function $\phi : \mathbf{R}^n \rightarrow \mathbf{R}$; its value depends only on the distance from a known point in the search space c, called *centre*, so that $\phi(V_q) = \phi(\|V_q - c\|)$. The point c is a parameter of the function and the point V_q is the query point in the PSO to be estimated. The norm is usually Euclidean, so $\|V_q - c\|$ is the Euclidean distance between c and V_q.

There are several types of RBF functions, including: Gaussian, Multiquadric, Inverse Quadratic and Inverse Multiquadric. In this paper we use the Gaussian function of the form:

$$\phi(V_q) = \exp(-\beta\|V_q - c\|^2)$$

where $\beta > 0$ is the width parameter. Radial basis functions are typically used to build function approximations of the form:

$$y(V_q) = w_0 + \sum_{i=1}^{N} w_i\, \phi(\|V_q - c_i\|) \quad (3)$$

Thus, $y(V_q)$ is used to approximate the real-objective function, (i.e., running the EA multiple times with particular parameters set in our case), when evaluating a PSO particle. The approximating function $y(V_q)$ is represented as a sum of N radial basis functions, each associated with a different centre c_i, a different width β_i, and weighted by an appropriate coefficient w_i, plus a bias term w_0. In principle, any continuous function can be approximated with arbitrary accuracy by a sum of this form, if a sufficiently large number N of radial basis functions is used [15]. The bias w_0 can be set to the mean of the values of the training set fitnesses that are used to train the surrogate model, or set to 0.

Training the RBFNs requires three parameters to be found: *(a)* the centres c_i, *(b)* the values of w_i in such a way that the predictions on the training set minimises the errors and, finally, *(c)* the RBF width parameter β.

The centres can be chosen to coincide with the training set and evaluate them with the real fitness evaluation. The β value can be either fixed for all N linear RBFs (global) or it can be customised for each RBF (local). In this work, we set the β value as $1/D^2$ where D is the maximum pairwise distance between the query point and all of the points in the training set. The value of β controls the radius of each RBF (spreading on the search space to cover all the other centres), so that each known function value at a centre can potentially contribute significantly to the prediction of the function value of any point in space.

Finally, the weights vector can be calculated by solving the system of N simultaneous linear equations in w_i by requiring that the unknown function exactly predicts the training. Formally, we have:

$$y(V_i) = b_i,\ i = 1 \ldots N.$$

Setting $g_{ij} = \phi(||\mathbf{V}_j - \mathbf{V}_i||)$, the system can be written in a matrix form as $\mathbf{Gw} = \mathbf{b}$ where $\mathbf{b}$ is a vector of the true fitness values of the data-points that have been used to train the surrogate. The matrix $\mathbf{G}$ is non-singular, because we guarantee that the points V_i are distinct, so the weights w can be solved by simple linear algebra:

$$\mathbf{w} = \mathbf{G}^{-1}\mathbf{b}$$

The value of the bias term w_0 in Equation 3 is set to the mean value of the training set real fitnesses, i.e., the mean of vector $\mathbf{b}$. In this way, the predicted function value of a point which is out of reach of the influence of all centres is by default set to the average of their function values.

Once the RBF parameters are determined, the model is ready to estimate the fitness of any unseen point. Thus, the fitness $EA(P_{pos}[V_q])$ (defined in Equation 1) of a query point V_q in the search space is predicted by weighted linear combination of:

$$EA(P_{pos}[V_q]) \approx w_0 + \textstyle\sum_{i=1}^{N}[w_i * \phi(d(V_q, c_i))]$$

where, w_i is a vector of weights that has been calculated during the training phase and ϕ is the kernel function which is defined in Equation 3. Finally, $d(V_q, c_i)$ is the distance between the new point V_q and the training set points c_i.

3.3 Surrogate Implementation

Similar to traditional procedure of surrogate model based optimisation (SMBO) [4], the framework constructs an initial surrogate model by using the real fitness measure (defined in Equation 1) on a small set of solutions and replaces the real fitness measure in Algorithm 1 - **line 11**. The remaining expensive objective function evaluations out of a limited budget are applied to candidate solutions in which the surrogate model predicts to have promising performance. The process interleaves search of the surrogate model to obtain its optimum, evaluation of the optimum solution of the model by using the expensive objective function, and update of the surrogate model with the new point.

Here, we used PSO to optimise the surrogate model. We refer to this version of the PSO as *cheap PSO*, because it uses a computationally inexpensive surrogate model. The best solution that the cheap PSO has found is then compared with the best point of the training set (that are used to train the surrogate). If the newly suggested point is better than than the best existing point in the training set, then the system successfully managed to extrapolate from the training set. It updates the training set with the new point and re-trains the surrogate. Otherwise, the system adds a new random point to the training set, in a step to collect more information about the under-sampled search space. This procedure coincides with our main hypothesis that RBFN surrogate can successfully approximate the parameters search space.

Note that the role of surrogate is to infer the location of a promising solution, and it is not directly applied to the original problem with the expensive objective function. This is feasible because the computational cost of a complete run of the EA on the surrogate model is negligible (i.e., in the order of few seconds) with regard to the cost of evaluating a solution using the expensive objective function of the problem (in the order of minutes, hours, or even days, depending on the problem).

4. EXPERIMENT SETUP

Experiments have been conducted in order to validate our framework. The main aim of the experiments is to evaluate the performance of the framework and to assess its behaviour under a variety of circumstances. In principle, the proposed framework can optimise the parameters of any population-based EA. In this paper, we felt that GA is a good example with which to demonstrate the capabilities of our framework. The experiments included testing the framework on three different problems, namely, NK-Landscape [16] (unimodal problem), Hamming Centres [17], (multimodal problem), and three different continuous optimisation problems. For each problem we tested all systems under different chromosomes size m.

We compared the framework in terms of the best evolved solution with *(a)* Standard PSO without surrogate assistance to optimise the GA parameters, in order to verify whether surrogate can acutely find the best setting within a limited number of explorations in the parameters space, *(b)* Standard GA applied directly to the problem with fixed parameters settings to check whether parameters tuning has added any extra advantages to the search, *(c)* Standard 1+1 Evolutionary Strategy (ES) applied directly to the problem, to compare our framework performance against a standard search algorithm, and, finally, *(d)* simple Random parameters generator, to prove that surrogate sampling is better than random search in suggesting data-points in the search space.

Since the problem complexity is related to the the size of the GA chromosome (i.e., m value), here, we relate the value of $max\_explorations$ (the upper limit of evaluations as explained in Section 3) to problem complexity. Thus, $max\_explorations = m^2$. So, essentially our aim is to find the best solution to the problem the algorithm can produce in linear time out of an exponential number of candidate solutions in the problem space. Table 1 illustrates the settings used in our experiments for standard GA with fixed parameters and 1+1 ES.

Table 1: Settings used in the experiments

Operator	*Standard GA with fixed settings*	1+1 ES
Mutation	30%	100%
Crossover	70%	0%
Tournament size	2	N/A
Population Size	m	1
Generations	m	m^2

As for the PSO without surrogate assistance, the size of P_{pso} is equal to $\frac{m \times 2}{10}$ and the number of moves for each particle in the swarm is 5. Thus, each particle in the P_{pso} effectively evaluates 5 different parameters sets in a process of tuning the GA parameters. Note that the total number of evaluations performed by the GA in any settings of $V_i \in P_{pso}$ will not exceed the $max\_explorations$ value. Each particle runs the GA 10 times to validate the goodness of the V_i parameters set. Thus, each particle will effectively run the GA 10×5 times. Hence, to allow a fair comparison, when each individual in the P_{pso} runs the GA systems, we run both standard GA with fixed settings and 1+1 ES exactly 10×5. Obviously, this approach is not completely fair because the PSO, here, has the advantage of exploring different parameters sets while both standard GA and 1+1 ES searches the problem using a fixed parameters. However, it is also unfair to give them fewer number of problem evaluations than PSO. There is no clear method of comparing these algorithms.

Our proposed framework, PSO that uses a RBFN surrogate, received exactly the same number of parameters explorations $\frac{m \times 2}{10} \times 5$, and the same PSO fitness function to measure the parameters sets (i.e., running the GA 10 times and report the best fitness). The difference here is that PSO particles are evaluated using cheap RBFN surrogate rather than a complete real fitness measure (i.e., running the GA 10 times with each parameters set). Therefore, we were generous with the the cheap PSO settings. The number of particles in the cheap PSO is $10m$ and number of moves was set also to $10m$. Once the surrogate suggests a new promising point in the parameters space, it evaluates it using the real fitness measure and updates the surrogate model. Our aim is to utilise the RBFN surrogate to optimise the GA parameters using very small number of explorations in the parameters space (i.e., $5\frac{2m}{10} = m$)

5. RESULTS

5.1 Continuous Optimisation

In our experiments, we evaluated the framework using three different well-known benchmark problems. Namely, Rastrigin function, Dixson & Price function and, finally, Michalewics function [18]. The reason for choosing these three functions in particular is because they represent different landscapes with different levels of difficulty. The Rastrigin function has the overall structure of a hyper-parabola with many bumps, whereas the other two functions have a smoother, albeit deceptive, landscape (i.e., the best optima are on different sides of the search space). For each function, we investigate the performance of the system under $m = 20, 30, 40$, and 50. Each system was tested using 20 independent runs. Table 2 summarises the results of 1200 runs (20 independent runs for each system for each m value). It is clear that our framework comes in the first place in almost all cases with significant performance margins. The model failed to outperform the standard PSO only in two cases (when $m = 20$ and 30 in the Michalewics function). Note the the Std of our framework shows different levels of stability. This outcome is expected because PSO particles are searching for the best settings for the GA in the parameters space. Thus, depending on the PSO's initial population, each V_i particle explores different area in the search space, and thus, each V_i tries different settings which is not necessary to the best in a process of optimising the solution. However, in standard GA and 1+1 ES we used the same settings in all runs and thus, they tend to have more stability as shown by their Std.

5.2 NK-Landscape

NK-Landscape was established by Stuart Kauffman in [19]. The fitness of a gene could depend solely on its own state. At its most complex, the fitness of a gene could depend on the state of all others. Thus, there are N genes in which each gene's fitness depends of the state of K others.

We investigated the performance of our framework under different values of N. Namely, we used $N = 20$, 30, and 40. For each N value we tested three different K values $K = \frac{N}{5}$ *(easy problem)*, $\frac{N}{2}$ *(hard problem)*, and $\frac{N}{2} + 5$ *(very hard problem)*. [2] For each N, K combination we tested the system using 20 independent runs using the settings mentioned in Section 4.

Table 3 summarises the results of 900 independent runs (20 independent runs for each system for each N,K combination). As can be seen in the table, PSO-Surrogate managed to adjust the GA parameters in a way that makes the search achieves better results. It is clear that PSO-Surrogate is ranked first place both in terms of average (i.e., average of best solutions in the 20 runs) and best (i.e., best achieved solution across the entire 20 runs) in almost all test cases. The only time PSO-Surrogate did not manage to outperform PSO (that tunes the parameters directly without surrogate assistance) and Standard GA was when the problem was too easy ($N = 20$ and $K = 4$) so all algorithms can perform equally well.

5.3 Hamming Centres

Hamming centres is an NP-hard problem defined in [17] as follows. Lets a set S of k_i binary strings, where $i \in \{1, 2...I\}$, each of length m, and r is a positive integer. The objective is to find $m-$bits string y such that for every string k_i in S, the Hamming distance, $H(k_i, y) \leq r$.

We investigated the performance of our proposed framework under different values of $m-$bits ($m = 50$, 75, 100, and 125). For each m value we performed 20 independent runs for each system. The size of the set S was 20 in all experiments. The fitness value was measured as the number of cases that string y satisfied the condition of $H(k_i, y) \leq r$. Thus, the optimal solution is equal to the size of S (which is 20 in our case). The r value was set to $\sqrt{m}$. Table 4 illustrates the results of 400 runs (20 independent runs for each system for each m value). Clearly, PSO-Surrogate comes in first in all test cases in both average fitness (in 20 runs) and best fitness across all runs. Surprisingly, standard GA with fixed parameters settings outperformed PSO (applied directly to tune the GA parameters) in two test cases, namely, when $m = 100, 125$. This suggests that the allowed explorations in the parameters space is very low (i.e., m trials only where m is the GA chromosomes size) and it is not enough to allow PSO to converge to an optimum solution in this particular problem. This is also an indication that the use of SM has assisted the PSO in exploring potential areas in the parameters space.

6. DISCUSSION

It is a well-known fact in the field of optimisation that it is very difficult to determine an efficient optimisation algorithm for all types of functions of optimisation problems. The same is true for our proposed PSO-surrogate method. We have reported optimisation results for three different types of functions,including three continuous functions, Hamming centre and NK landscape. We have used RBFN as surrogate model which is well suited for approximation of continuous functions. Hence as expected our proposed algorithm has shown better results for all three continuous functions. In Table 5, improvement percentage is reported

[2] In [20] the authors provided an indication of NK-landscape hardness under different settings.

Table 2: Summary of 1200 **runs of Continuous Optimisation (20 independent runs for each system for each** m **size)**

	Mean	*Best*	*Std*	*Mean*	*Best*	*Std*	*Mean*	*Best*	*Std*	*Mean*	*Best*	*Std*
Dixon&Price Function												
	m=20			*m=30*			*m=40*			*m=50*		
PSO-Surrogate	**14063.7**	**15481.6**	795.8	**33328.1**	**35830.8**	2462.3	**63745.9**	**66033.8**	1709.9	**100863.8**	**105515.0**	3858.6
PSO	13428.1	14239.8	542.4	32487.1	35176.9	1999.5	60723.8	64666.9	2187.2	93936.8	103205.0	4462.5
Standard GA (Fixed settings)	12039.4	12919.7	579.1	27963.9	29972.9	1231.5	51728.3	55155.3	1232.8	82155.0	86391.2	1812.6
1+1 ES (Fixed settings)	10484.8	12215.1	775.0	22915.5	25598.9	903.3	39411.4	41936.5	1444.7	59656.4	64101.2	2416.6
Random Parameter search	9891.2	10851.6	496.8	21815.4	23319.3	886.7	38174.9	46156.5	2346.8	57476.1	60739.9	1596.5
Michalewics Function												
	m=20			*m=30*			*m=40*			*m=50*		
PSO-Surrogate	**8.7**	**10.5**	*0.9*	**13.8**	16.4	1.8	**22.3**	**25.2**	2.4	**29.2**	**33.7**	4.3
PSO	8.5	**10.5**	0.9	13.0	**17.0**	1.7	17.8	23.2	2.8	22.9	31.9	4.5
Standard GA (Fixed settings)	6.0	7.1	0.7	10.1	12.3	1.1	14.1	15.7	0.9	18.3	20.0	0.9
1+1 ES (Fixed settings)	4.4	5.1	0.4	6.2	7.3	0.6	7.1	9.0	0.7	8.6	11.0	0.9
Random Parameter search	4.1	5.5	0.6	5.4	7.3	0.7	6.5	7.3	0.5	7.9	9.9	0.9
Rastrigin Function												
	m=20			*m=30*			*m=40*			*m=50*		
PSO-Surrogate	**518.0**	**598.1**	*52.6*	**838.6**	**920.4**	60.9	**1142.9**	**1260.0**	114.1	**1466.8**	**1576.8**	139.3
PSO	478.0	552.3	36.0	748.5	875.4	92.5	931.3	1156.4	144.8	1247.7	1532.5	197.7
Standard GA (Fixed settings)	374.7	490.1	69.3	547.7	639.5	64.4	789.9	854.4	40.4	998.1	1142.0	71.2
1+1 ES (Fixed settings)	248.4	313.2	36.5	286.2	403.8	51.5	269.7	441.0	73.2	287.1	398.5	62.8
Random Parameter search	221.0	317.1	42.3	215.5	329.1	48.3	217.5	329.8	57.7	181.8	305.3	53.9

**Bold* numbers are the highest.

Table 3: Summary of 900 runs of NK-Landscape (20 independent runs)

Algorithm	*Mean*	*Best*	*Std*	*Mean*	*Best*	*Std*	*Mean*	*Best*	*Std*
	N20 K4			*N20 K10*			*N20 K15*		
PSO-Surrogate	**0.757**	0.775	0.017	**0.739**	**0.778**	0.017	**0.737**	**0.771**	0.013
PSO	0.743	0.775	0.020	0.737	0.770	0.015	0.729	0.756	0.019
Standard GA (Fixed settings)	0.725	0.775	0.025	0.714	0.755	0.023	0.687	0.750	0.018
1+1 ES (Fixed settings)	0.709	0.752	0.017	0.726	0.745	0.014	0.719	0.737	0.012
Random Parameters search	0.679	0.732	0.025	0.681	0.711	0.017	0.689	0.748	0.027
	N30 K6			*N30 K15*			*N30 K20*		
PSO-Surrogate	**0.766**	**0.798**	*0.019*	**0.724**	**0.760**	0.016	**0.710**	**0.757**	0.018
PSO	0.762	0.782	0.012	0.719	0.743	0.016	0.708	0.734	0.015
Standard GA (Fixed settings)	0.733	0.772	0.018	0.693	0.724	0.017	0.687	0.727	0.019
1+1 ES (Fixed settings)	0.697	0.721	0.011	0.701	0.728	0.014	0.698	0.731	0.011
Random Parameters search	0.670	0.700	0.014	0.673	0.708	0.017	0.663	0.697	0.015
	N40 K8			*K40 K20*			*N40 K25*		
PSO-Surrogate	**0.769**	**0.791**	*0.009*	**0.717**	**0.746**	0.014	**0.706**	**0.734**	0.013
PSO	0.767	0.782	0.008	0.716	0.731	0.010	0.702	0.724	0.012
Standard GA (Fixed settings)	0.721	0.757	0.014	0.689	0.713	0.016	0.683	0.714	0.015
1+1 ES (Fixed settings)	0.685	0.703	0.010	0.684	0.736	0.016	0.686	0.704	0.007
Random Parameters search	0.653	0.720	0.023	0.652	0.674	0.011	0.648	0.678	0.015

*__Bold__ numbers are the highest.

for all functions. Improvement in percentage is calculated between PSO-surrogate and second best result. For Michalewics and Rastrigin functions, optimisation results are improved by more than 20%. In Table 5, an increasing trend of improvement in the case of continuous functions is evident as the complexity of functions increase. This observation is very encouraging and makes our proposed algorithm a good candidate for very complex optimisation problems. Dixon & Price function is a unimodal function. Hence, all the algorithms have performed well and we have seen a maximum of 7% improvement by using PSO-surrogate method. But Michalewics and Rastrigin functions are multimodal functions and hence optimising these function is difficult. In these functions, our PSO-surrogate method outperformed all other algorithms by a wide margin.

In case of Hamming centre problem, our proposed algorithm has shown good improvement of about 7% for cases of $m = 75$ to $m = 125$. Hamming centre problem is a binary problem. Although the improvement is considerable but it is less than the continuous functions.

Hence, in order to get the best out of our proposed method, we have to select the type of surrogate model which is well suited for function approximation in a particular type of optimisation problem.

7. CONCLUSION

This paper proposes a framework for automatically tuning population-based EA. The proposed framework is comprised of two components; PSO that searches the parameters space and a RBFN surrogate model to guide it. The main advantage of our model is that it optimises the EA parameters in a way to ensure that EA searches the problem within a limited number of evaluations. We use PSO as a top-level search to explore the parameters space for population-based EA, and RBFN surrogate is used to guide the search. The framework tune the population size, number of generation and search operators rates.

In our experiments we have used GA as an example of population-based EA to demonstrate our framework capabilities. Experiments with three different benchmark problems, namely, NK-landscape, Hamming Centres and three different continuous optimisation problems demonstrate that our proposed framework managed to assist the GA to optimise its parameters and achieves better solutions than, using Standard PSO without surrogate assistance to optimise the GA parameters, Standard GA applied directly to the problem with fixed parameters settings, Standard 1+1 Evolutionary Strategy (ES) applied directly to the problem and simple Random Search. The results confirms that parameter tuning is useful and a key factor of the success of the search. In addition, our experiments confirm that the use of SM has assisted the PSO because it makes sense of the available information and point out promising areas in the parameters space. Thus, our framework was able to successfully optimise the parameters using a very small number of exploration in the parameters space.

There are many directions where we can extend this research. As mentioned previously, an interesting future study is to investigate the relationship between the problem's difficulty (that suggested the use of an EA) and the sensitivity of the parameters settings. We would also like to explore the model behaviour with different EA representations (e.g., optimising the parameters of GP) as each EA has different level of parameters sensitivity to its performance. Another direction of this research is to allow the model to tune the parameters of the EA during the run as to maintain its diversity and prevent the premature convergence problem.

8. REFERENCES

[1] K. DeJong, "Parameter setting in eas: a 30 year perspective." in *Parameter Setting in Evolutionary Algorithms*, ser. Studies in Computational Intelligence, F. G. Lobo, C F. Lima, and Z. Michalewicz, Eds. Springer, 2007, vol. 54, pp. 1–18.

[2] M. E. Samples, J. M. Daida, M. Byom, and M. Pizzimenti, "Parameter sweeps for exploring GP parameters," in *GECCO 2005: Proceedings of the 2005 conference on Genetic and evolutionary computation*, vol. 2. Washington DC, USA: ACM Press, 2005, pp. 1791–1792.

[3] T. Bäck and H. Schwefel, "An overview of evolutionary algorithms for parameter optimization," *Evolutionary computation*, vol. 1, no. 1, pp. 1–23, 1993.

Table 4: Summary of 400 runs of Hamming Centres (20 independent runs)

Algorithm	*Mean*	*Best*	*Std*
m = 50			
PSO-Surrogate	**8.600**	**10.000**	0.883
PSO	8.350	9.000	0.587
Standard GA (Fixed settings)	6.500	8.000	0.827
1+1 ES (Fixed settings)	4.500	6.000	0.607
Random Parameter search	3.400	4.000	0.503
m = 75			
PSO-Surrogate	**10.950**	**12.000**	*0.759*
PSO	10.100	11.000	0.718
Standard GA (Fixed settings)	9.450	11.000	0.759
1+1 ES (Fixed settings)	5.250	6.000	0.444
Random Parameter search	4.150	5.000	0.366
m = 100			
PSO-Surrogate	**14.000**	**12.905**	*0.700*
PSO	13.000	11.286	0.956
Standard GA (Fixed settings)	13.000	11.857	0.793
1+1 ES (Fixed settings)	7.000	6.000	0.447
Random Parameter search	6.000	5.095	0.625
m = 125			
PSO-Surrogate	**15.000**	**13.048**	*1.244*
PSO	13.000	11.238	1.221
Standard GA (Fixed settings)	14.000	11.619	1.322
1+1 ES (Fixed settings)	6.000	5.238	0.436
Random Parameter search	5.000	4.333	0.577

*__Bold__ numbers are the highest.

Table 5: Improvement in percentage

Chromosome Size	*Problem*			
	Continuous Optimisation			
	Discon&Price	*Michalewics*	*Rastrigin*	
m=20	4.7%	2.4%	8.4%	
m=30	2.6%	6.2%	12%	
m=40	5.0%	25.3%	22.8%	
m=50	7.4%	27.5%	17.6%	
	Hamming Centres			
m=50	3%			
m=75	8.4%			
m=100	7.7%			
m=125	7.1%			
	NK-Landscape			
NK(20,4)	1.9%	NK(30,15)	0.7%	
NK(20,10)	0.3%	NK(30,20)	0.3%	
NK(20,15)	1.1%	NK(40,8)	0.3%	
NK(30,6)	0.5%	NK(40,20)	0.14%	
NK(40,25)	0.6%			

[4] A. Forrester, A. Sóbester, and A. Keane, *Engineering design via surrogate modelling: a practical guide*. Wiley, 2008, vol. 226.

[5] A. Eiben, R. Hinterding, and Z. Michalewicz, "Parameter control in evolutionary algorithms," *Evolutionary Computation, IEEE Transactions on*, vol. 3, no. 2, pp. 124–141, 1999.

[6] S. Smit and A. Eiben, "Comparing parameter tuning methods for evolutionary algorithms," in *Evolutionary Computation, 2009. CEC'09. IEEE Congress on*. IEEE, 2009, pp. 399–406.

[7] M. Preuss, G. Rudolph, and S. Wessing, "Tuning optimization algorithms for real-world problems by means of surrogate modeling," in *Proceedings of the 12th annual conference on Genetic and evolutionary computation*, ser. GECCO '10. New York, NY, USA: ACM, 2010, pp. 401–408.

[8] G. Rudolph, M. Preuss, and J. Quadflieg, "Two-layered Surrogate Modeling for Tuning Optimization Metaheuristics," Faculty of Computer Science, Algorithm Engineering (Ls11), Technische Universität Dortmund, Germany, Algorithm Engineering Report TR09-2-005, Sep. 2009.

[9] S. Bird and X. Li, *Improving local convergence in particle swarm by fitness approximation using regression*. Springer Berlin Heidelberg, 2010.

[10] H. Gorshy, X. Chu, L. Gao, and P. Li, "An approach combined response surface method and particle swarm optimization to ship multidisciplinary design and optimization," in *Industrial Engineering and Engineering Management, 2009. IEEM 2009. IEEE International Conference on*. IEEE, 2009, pp. 1810–1814.

[11] M. Reyes-Sierra and C. Coello, "A study of fitness inheritance and approximation techniques for multi-objective particle swarm optimization," in *Evolutionary Computation, 2005. The 2005 IEEE Congress on*, vol. 1, 2005, pp. 65–72.

[12] R. Carrese, A. Sóbester, H. Winarto, and X. Li, "Swarm heuristic for identifying preferred solutions in surrogate-based multi-objective engineering design," *AIAA journal*, vol. 49, no. 7, 2011.

[13] M. Parno, K. Fowler, and T. Hemker, "Framework for particle swarm optimization with surrogate functions," Technical Report TUD-CS-2009-0139, Department of Computer Science, Technische Universität Darmstadt, Tech. Rep., 2009.

[14] J. Kennedy and R. Eberhart, "Particle swarm optimization," in *Neural Networks, 1995. Proceedings., IEEE International Conference on*, vol. 4. IEEE, 1995, pp. 1942–1948.

[15] A. G. Bors, "Introduction of the radial basis function (rbf) networks," Department of Computer Science, University of York, UK, Tech. Rep., 2001.

[16] S. A. Kauffman, *The Origins of Order – Organization and Selection in Evolution*. New York: Oxford University Press, 1993.

[17] M. Frances and A. Litman, "On covering problems of codes," *Theory of Computing Systems*, vol. 30, pp. 113–119, 1997, 10.1007/BF02679443.

[18] M. Molga and C. Smutnick, "Test functions for optimization needs," *Test functions for optimization needs*, 2005.

[19] S. Kauffman, *The origins of order*. Oxford University Press New York, 1993, vol. 209.

[20] T. Jones and S. Forrest, "Fitness distance correlation as a measure of problem difficulty for genetic algorithms." in *ICGA*, L. J. Eshelman, Ed. Morgan Kaufmann, 1995, pp. 184–192.

Challenging Heuristics: Evolving Binary Constraint Satisfaction Problems

Jorge H. Moreno-Scott
Tecnológico de Monterrey
Monterrey, Mexico
jorge.moreno@motorola.com

José Carlos Ortiz-Bayliss
Tecnológico de Monterrey
Monterrey, Mexico
jcobayliss@gmail.com

Hugo Terashima-Marín
Tecnológico de Monterrey
Monterrey, Mexico
terashima@itesm.mx

Santiago Enrique Conant-Pablos
Tecnológico de Monterrey
Monterrey, Mexico
sconant@itesm.mx

ABSTRACT

In computer science it is a common practice to evaluate the performance of algorithms using a set of benchmark or randomly generated instances. However, following that approach, the weaknesses of the algorithms may not be exposed. This work is the first phase of research project on coevolution of solutions methods versus problem instances. The goal of study is to generate a method to find difficult to solve problem instances capable of challenging the solution methods or algorithms under analysis, helping to discover opportunities for improvement. An evolutionary model is proposed to find hard binary constraint satisfaction problem instances for different variable ordering heuristics. We characterize the search space by generating random instances with different values for the constraint density and tightness. For all the heuristics, the most difficult problems are located in the same region of the space near to the phase transition. However, there are certain regions of the search space where a heuristic dominates the others, especially where the problems are solvable. Finally, we compare the hardest instances found during the search space exploration with the outcome instances of the evolutionary model. The results show that evolved instances are harder to solve than the ones randomly generated.

Categories and Subject Descriptors

I.2.8 [**Artificial Intelligence**]: Problem Solving, Control Methods, and Search—*Heuristic methods, Graph and tree search strategies*

General Terms

Algorithms

Keywords

Constraint Satisfaction, Heuristics, Evolutionary Computation

1. INTRODUCTION

A Constraint Satisfaction Problem (CSP) is defined as follows: given a set V which contains the variables in the problem, where each variable $v_i \in V$ has its respective domain of possible values D_i, and a set of constraints C that restricts the values a subset of variables can take simultaneously, find an instantiation of the $|V|$ variables satisfying all the constraints. For this research we have only considered CSP in which the domains are discrete, finite sets and the constraints involve only one or two variables (binary constraints).

Recent years have witnessed the rapid development of new search methods for constraint satisfaction. An important factor in the success of these algorithms is the availability of good sets of benchmark problems to evaluate and fine-tune them [2]. There are two main sources of benchmark problems. One class is based on real-world applications and the other is from random instance generators. Real-world instances are arguably the best source, but unfortunately are often short in supply. Then, random problem generators therefore provide a good additional source of problem instances. These generators also have the advantage of a more direct control over the problem characteristics, such as size and expected hardness [1, 5]. Random CSP are useful for systematic analysis of algorithms [14]. Also, random CSP have become a standard for testing constraint satisfaction solving and heuristic algorithms because of its randomness [17]. Many strategies and models for random CSP generation have been developed and they have been used in various investigations [16, 12, 3, 23, 22].

In most of the generation models presented in the literature, the generation process and the solving process were independent from each other. For each generation model, there are certain control parameters that, when provided the right values, produce instances which are hard to solve. A generation model that incorporates the solving process during the generation process is the approach described by van Hemert, who showed that an evolutionary algorithm can be used to detect problem instances that are hard to solve [20,

21]. The approach used by van Hemert searches the space of binary CSP looking for hard to solve instances and the fitness of each problem is defined as the number of consistency checks required by a solution technique to solve the problem or prove the problem unsolvable. The evolutionary algorithm maintains a population of binary CSP of which it changes the structure over time. Basically, its genetic operators alter the individual conflict pairs between two values of a pair of variables. The set of variables and their domains are kept unchanged during the process. Only the ratio of forbidden pairs of values can vary.

Nevertheless the approach presented by van Hemert produces hard to solve instances [20], it omits one important aspect when solving constraint satisfaction: the role of variable ordering heuristics during the search. Variable ordering heuristics have the task to dynamically order the variables during the search, according to some criteria, with the goal of reducing the search cost (usually measured in consistency checks). Because each heuristic uses a different criterion to decide the next variable to instantiate, their results vary from instance to instance because they tend to be very specialized. In this investigation, we want to exploit this specialization to generate instances which are harder for specific heuristics (and not necessarily for others). The idea is that a genetic algorithm is capable of generating instances with the properties that would make such instances difficult to solve under the guidance of one specific set of heuristics. With this, we want to identify instances which would be useful to specifically test some kinds of heuristics which we think would be helpful for the better understanding of the heuristics and how they make their decisions.

In this investigation, we propose to extend the use of evolutionary computation to create difficult to solve binary CSP instances for specific variable ordering heuristics. In our approach, the chromosomes represent instances and the evolutionary algorithm maintains a population of these instances and, as the evolutionary process takes place, it changes the structure of the instances over time. The goal of the evolutionary algorithm becomes to maximally aggravate the algorithm by trying to increase the search effort that it requires to solve the instances within the population, by using an specific set of variable ordering heuristics.

The paper is organized as follows. Section 2 presents the background about CSPs. Section 3 describes binary CSP instances representation suggested and the genetic algorithm employed to evolve the problem instances. Experiments, results and discussion are outlined in section 4. Finally, in section 5 are included the conclusions and some ideas for future work.

2. BACKGROUND

In this section we present a brief survey of the most common generation models that have been applied in previous CSP investigations. Also, a description of the variable ordering heuristics used in this research is presented.

2.1 Random CSP Generation

The generation of a random instance of CSP was originally divided into two stages: first, the generation of the constraint graph, governed by the parameter p_1, and secondly, the generation of the relation matrix for each pair of variables linked by a constraint, using p_2 [18]. This two-step approach gives place to four models of random problems (models A to D), where model B has been extensively used in most experimental and theoretical studies about random CSP. Model B, we generates a constraint graph G, and then for each edge in this graph, choose pairs of incompatible values. We can describe problems generated with model B by the tuple $\langle n, m, p_1, p_2 \rangle$, where n is the number of variables, d is he uniform domain size, p_1 is a measure of the density of the constraint graph (the proportion of constraints within the instance), and p_2 is a measure of the tightness of the constraints (the proportion of conflicts among the constraints). The original four models A to D are not the only way to generate random instances of CSP, and now the state of the art includes more elaborated models like: E [3], F [9] RB [23], RD [24] and the evolutionary model based on a genetic algorithm described by van Hemert [20], to cite the most relevant.

2.2 Variable Ordering Heuristics

In this section we will describe the variable ordering heuristics used in this investigation.

- **Rho**. This heuristic was used for the first time by Ian P. Gent [7]. It is based on the approximated calculation of the solution density ρ. The basic idea is to select a variable that enters in the subproblem which contains the largest fraction of solution states. This is, the subproblem with the largest solution density. If the constraints in which the variable v_i is involved are C_{v_i}, then to maximize ρ we have to select the variable that minimizes:

$$\rho(v_i) = \prod_{c_j \in C_{v_i}} (1 - p_{c_j}) \quad (1)$$

  where C_{v_i} represents the subset of constraints where the variable v_i is involved.

- **Expected Number of Solutions (E[N])**. The E[N] heuristic selects the variable in such a way that the subproblem maximizes the expected number of solutions. To maximize the expected number of solutions of the remaining instance, we branch on the variable that reduces $E[N]$ the least:

$$E[N](v_i) = d_{v_i} \times \prod_{c_j \in C_{v_i}} (1 - p_{c_j}) = d_{v_i} \times \rho(v_i) \quad (2)$$

  where d_{v_i} represents the domain size of variable v_i.

- **Kappa** (K). This heuristic selects the variable in such a way that the resulting subproblem minimizes the kappa factor, κ [8]. The constrainedness parameter κ represents a notion of how restricted a problem is. κ is defined as follows:

$$\kappa = \frac{-\sum_{c_i \in C} \log_2(1 - p_{c_i})}{\sum_{v_i \in V} \log_2(d_{v_i})} \quad (3)$$

  where p_{c_i} is the constraint tightness of constraint c_i (the proportion of forbidden pairs among the constraint). It is known that problems with $\kappa \ll 1$ are less restricted and may have many solutions, while the problems with $\kappa \gg 1$ are likely to be highly restricted and may not be solved [7]. With this heuristic, we branch on a variable that is estimated to be the most constrained, giving the least constrained subproblem.

3. EVOLVING BINARY CSP INSTANCES

A genetic algorithm was implemented to evolve the binary CSP instances. The chromosomes represent the problem instances. A population of problem instances is evolved by the algorithm over the time. The fitness of the chromosomes is directly related to difficulty of the problems and it is measured when solving the problems with a particular heuristic. Hence, the most difficult instances are the ones that remain until the end of the evolutionary process.

3.1 Binary CSP Instances Representation

We know that all non-binary CSP can be converted into a binary CSP [15]. For this reason we focused our investigation only on binary CSP. In this investigation, we introduce the array CSP representation. To use the evolutionary algorithm to evolve CSP instances, we propose to represent any binary CSP as an array of three dimensions. The first dimension in the array represents the pair of variables that may hold a constraint between them. The second and third dimensions are used to represent the tuples that restrict the variables indicated by the first dimension in the array. The size of the array depends on the number of variables and the uniform domain size. The length of the first dimension is $|V|^2-1$, where $|V|$ is the number of variables in the instance. Then, any CSP instance is represented as an array of matrices, in other words, an array of constraints. In Figure 1, a constraint is illustrated, represented as a two-dimensional matrix. As we mentioned before, the pair of variables that hold such constraint are encoded in the index of the first dimension of the array. For example, the index 0 in the first dimension corresponds to the pair of variables $\{v_0, v_0\}$, the index 1 corresponds to $\{v_0, v_1\}$ and so on. Hence, under this scheme there are indexes that are not used because of the pairs they correspond to. For example, the constraint between the pair $\{v_3, v_2\}$ can be represented also as $\{v_2, v_3\}$, but following the rule that the index of the first variable must always be smaller than the index of the second one, the first constraint will be ignored (and the corresponding index in the array will never be used).

The constraint tuples are represented by the second and third dimension, which can be seen as a square matrix of size $|D| \times |D|$, where $|D|$ is the uniform domain size of the instance. In that matrix, forbidden and valid tuples are represented with 1's or 0's, respectively. For example, a problem with three variables and domain size of four for all the variables, the constraint with the tuples $\{0, 1\}\{1, 3\}\{2, 3\}$ is represented as shown in Figure 1. Notice that domain values are indicated by the indexes of the constraint matrix.

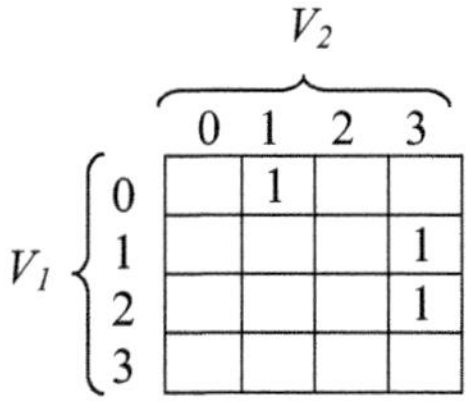

Figure 1: Constraint representation as a square matrix. The cells with 1's represent forbidden tuples (0's that represent supported tuples are omitted to make the image clearer).

For example, a tuple $\{1, 3\}$ contained in a constraint for variables v_0 and v_1 will be represented as $CSP(1, 1, 3)$, in the array CSP representation. This representation utilizes more memory space than required, which is not a limitation in this case and it keeps the implementation cleaner and easier to maintain. In future developments we plan to improve the representation to minimize the use of the memory.

3.2 Genetic Algorithm Implementation

The genetic algorithm evolves a population of binary problem instances, represented as a boolean array. The chromosome is a boolean array of three dimensions as explained earlier. The genetic operators are implemented in such way that number of variables and domain size are never changed, from the first generation to the last, these properties remain constant. Two properties of the problem instances can be changed: the number of constraints in the problem, and the number of forbidden tuples per constraint. These properties are also known as constraint density (p_1) and constraint tightness (p_2), respectively.

The genetic algorithm process is structured as follows.

1. Generate the initial population.
2. Calculate the initial fitness of the whole population using a particular solution method or heuristic.
3. Apply selection, crossover and mutation to produce the offspring. If the new individuals are identical to an individual in the population then are deleted and new random individuals are created.
4. Calculate the fitness of the new individuals.
5. Replace the two worst individuals of the population with the new offspring.
6. Repeat from step 3 until the termination criterion is reached.

The initial population is created using model B [12] to generate random CSP instances. This algorithm generates the CSP based in four variables $\langle n, m, p_1, p_2 \rangle$, where n is the number of variables, m is the uniform domain size, p_1 is the estimated constraint density of the instance, and p_2 is the estimated constraint tightness of the instance generated. The initial population is created with a specific number of variables and uniform domain size, however the density and tightness are randomly determined with a uniform distribution. The tightness at each instance generated is uniform across all the constraints within the same instance.

The type of selection used is tournament. First, three individuals are randomly picked and the one with largest fitness is selected, which becomes the first parent. For the second parent the same procedure is followed.

The genetic operators were designed to operate over the problem instances represented as an array CSP. We use simple one-point crossover (which is equivalent to a swap operation between the constraints of two instances). In more detail, the crossover point cx is one random index of the first dimension in the array representation and interchanges the arrays of both parents to produce two offspring. If $|C_A|$ constraints exist in parent A and $|C_B|$ constraints exist in parent B, the first offspring will contain constraints $C_A[0]$ to $C_A[cx-1]$ from the first parent and constraints $C_B[cx]$

Table 1: Genetic Algorithm Settings

Feature	*Setting*
Chromosome	Boolean Array
Population Initialization	Model B
Population Size	50
Crossover Type	One Cross-Point
Crossover Probability	1.0
Mutation Probability	0.2
Selection	2-Tournament
Generations	3000
Model	Steady State
Goal	Maximization

to $C_B[|C_B|]$ from the second parent. The second offspring will contain the constraints that were not selected to be part of the first offspring. This crossover implementation deals perfectly with problems of different density and tightness. However, it cannot work over problems with different number of variables and domain sizes, which is beyond the scope of this investigation. The mutation operator adds or deletes a random number of constraints, or modifies an existing constraint. When an individual is selected for mutation, the probability of adding or deleting a constraint is 25% for each operation, and the modification of a constraint has 50% of probability. The modification of constraint is divided into two operations, which are addition or removal of random number of tuples, each with equal probabilities of been performed. Deleting a constraint, means that all the tuples in the constraint are to be removed, replacing all the 0's with 1's for the corresponding matrix. Adding a constraint is done by adding tuples, this means adding 0's into the matrix that codes the constraint. The modification of a constraint is fairly similar: first, an existing constraint is selected and then, we randomly decide the number of tuples that will be added or removed from that particular constraint. The mutation probability remains constant during the whole process.

The fitness of the individuals is calculated solving them with one of the heuristics described in Section 2.2. The fitness of an individual is the number of consistency checks required to find the first solution or to determine that the instance is not solvable. The goal of the genetic algorithm is to maximise the fitness, in order to focus the search over the most difficult to solve instances.

We used a steady state genetic algorithm with only two individuals replaced in case the offspring are better than the worst two individuals of the population. Table 3.2 shows a summary of the components and settings of the genetic algorithm used to evolve the binary CSP.

4. EXPERIMENTS AND RESULTS

The experiments were divided into two stages. The first stage is related to the characterization of the search space where the genetic algorithm will work. The second part is the test of the performance of the genetic algorithm evolving CSP instances. Finally a comparison is performed between problem instances generated during the search space characterization and the instances generated by the genetic algorithm.

4.1 Search Space Characterization

In order to have an idea of the search space that the genetic algorithm will explore, a landscape characterization of the search space was made. The search space considered has two dimensions: constraint density (p_1) and constraint tightness (p_2). The number of variables and domain sizes are kept constant. The search space mapping was obtained generating random problems, with model B, varying the tightness and density in steps of 0.02, from 0.02 to 1.0. The result is a grid of 50×50 points. For each point in the grid 50 problems were randomly generated. All the problems were solved with three variable ordering heuristics: E[N], K and Rho. The average, maximum and minimum number of consistency checks required per heuristic at each point of the grid were recorded. The characterization was performed with problems instances of 10, 20 and 25 variables with a uniform domain size of 10 values. The results are similar with the three types of problems, but due space limitations we only show results of problem instances with 20 variables.

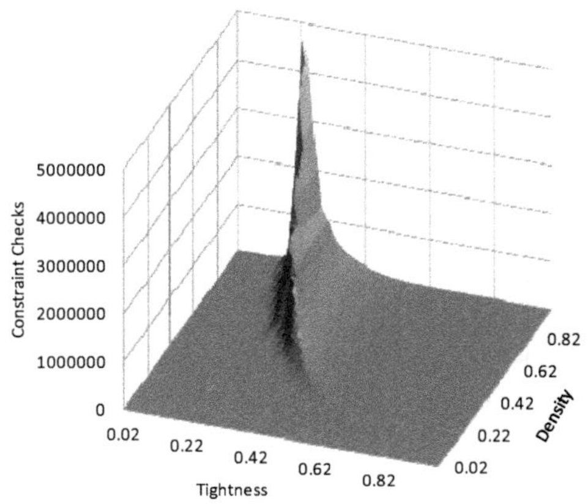

Figure 2: Search space landscape: average consistency checks vs. density and tightness for problems with 20 variables and domain size = 10, solved with the Rho heuristic.

Figure 2 shows the shape of the search space according to the average consistency checks required to solve the 50 problem instances per point in the grid, with heuristic Rho. A similar surface with same hill shape is obtained for the E[N] and K heuristics, the difference lays in the magnitude of consistency checks required to solve the instances. Table 2 shows the 30 hardest problem instances found during the search space mapping for the three heuristics. It can be observed the location of the most difficult problems is around the same area, independently of the heuristic, with values of density and tightness in average of 0.91 and 0.24, respectively. However, the effort required to solve the instances (in number of consistency checks) is considerably different between heuristics, where the best heuristic in that case was the E[N] and the worst was K. Figure 3 is a sectional view of Figure 2 from the perspective of tightness of the maximum of consistency checks required. This figure shows that most difficult problems are located at a tightness of 0.22, independently of the heuristic employed to solve the instances. Again, it can be noticed that best heuristic is, in average, E[N] and the worst is K, in that region. Similarly, Figure 4

Table 2: **Average of consistency checks required by the 30 hardest instances found during the search space mapping versus each heuristic. Density and tightness are the average over the cluster of instances.**

Heuristic	Density (Avg.)	Tightness (Avg.)	Consistency Checks (Avg.)
Rho	0.91	0.24	5024806
$E[N]$	0.91	0.24	4043282
K	0.91	0.24	9846912

shows a sectional view of the Figure 2 from the perspective of the axis density, where the hardest problems are located at density close to 1.0.

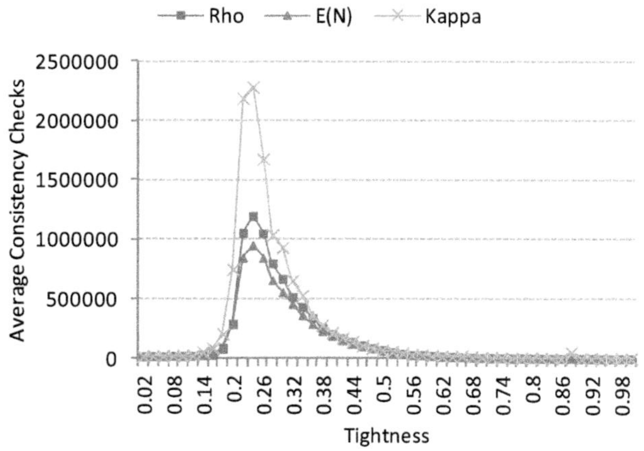

Figure 3: Maximum consistency checks required for three heuristics vs Tightness of instances with 20 variables and 10 values in their domains, generated during the search space exploration.

The region where the hardest problems are located is also the edge that divides the solvable and non-solvable instances. This region is known as the phase transition, studied by Cheeseman [4] and exhibited in NP complete problems when an order parameter varies certain features of the problem. The phase transition was also detected in binary CSP and reported by Prosser [11, 13, 19, 6]. Looking at Figure 2, the edge at the top of the hill is where the transition phase is located and divides the search space in two regions: the solvable and unsolvable problems. Figure 5, a top view of the search space, clearly illustrates the phase transition for the problems when solved with heuristic Rho. The curve that divides the region coincide with the shape of the upper level edge of the hill in the search space showed in Figure 2.

The heuristic with best performance (minimum average of consistency checks) at each point of the search space visited is shown in Figure 6. For this purpose, the average consistency checks required by each of the three heuristics for the 50 problem instances at each point of the search space was calculated. Notice that are certain regions in the space where some heuristics behave better than the others, especially in the left side of the graph, where the problems are solvable. It can be observed that heuristics behaviour somehow follows the phase transition curve. According to the results of the K heuristic, it showed a good performance

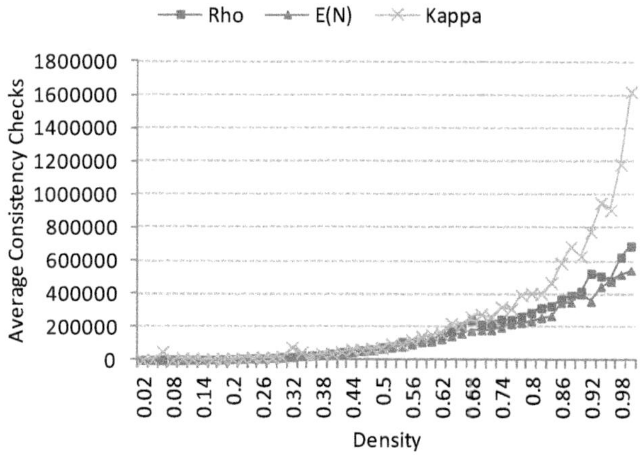

Figure 4: Maximum consistency checks required for three heuristics vs Density of instances with 20 variables and 10 values in their domains, generated during the search space exploration

in the solvable region where the tightness and density are low. This region is shared with Rho, which works better than K in the region with a bit higher tightness. The $E[N]$ heuristic behaves better in phase transition, as was previously observed in Figures 3 and 4. In the region where the problems become unsolvable, there is no pattern that indicates the one heuristic outperforms the others. Is important to notice there are instances in the regions dominated in average by a certain heuristic that can be solved with fewer consistency checks by other 'weaker' heuristic for the same region region. This indicates that are other parameters, apart from the tightness and the density, which can be also utilized to get additional information about the problem structure, and useful to distinguish more clearly for which problem instances the heuristics would behave better.

4.2 Hardness of Evolved Instances

The problem instances were evolved against the three heuristics: Rho, E[N] and K. We ran the genetic algorithm five times for each heuristic during 3000 generations, replacing two individuals at each generation. Figure 8 shows an example of the performance of the genetic algorithm over the generations, evolving problem instances against the heuristic E[N]. The average performance of distinct runs was not presented due the time required to produce enough runs to present a meaningful picture. The other two heuristics, E[N] and K, presented a similar performance, however are less efficient to solve problems when population is reaching the phase transition, specially heuristic K, hence the time required by those runs was greater.

The instances evolved by the genetic algorithm are located in the area where the most difficult instances are located, with a value close to 0.9 in density and around 0.2 in tightness, the same area as the hardest random generated instances found during the search space characterization. Figure 7 shows the 30 hardest instances found by the genetic algorithm, against each heuristic, as well as the 30 hardest instances generated during the search space characterization. The 30 hardest evolved instances are the best six individuals of the five runs, then we have 30 evolved instances per heuristic. The round markers in the figure are

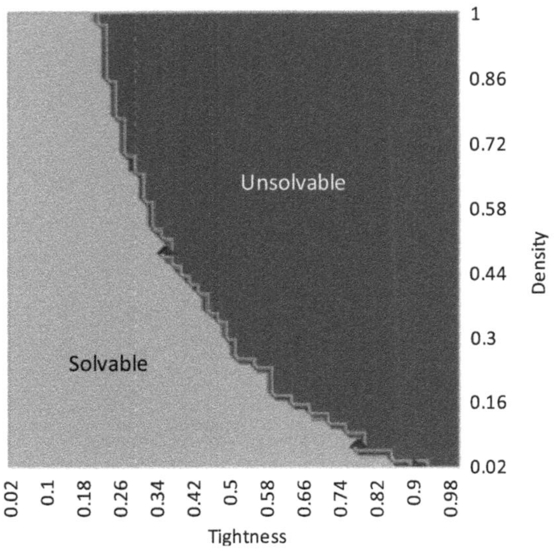

Figure 5: Phase transition for instances solved with heuristic Rho. The phase transition is similar when solved with heuristics E[N] and K

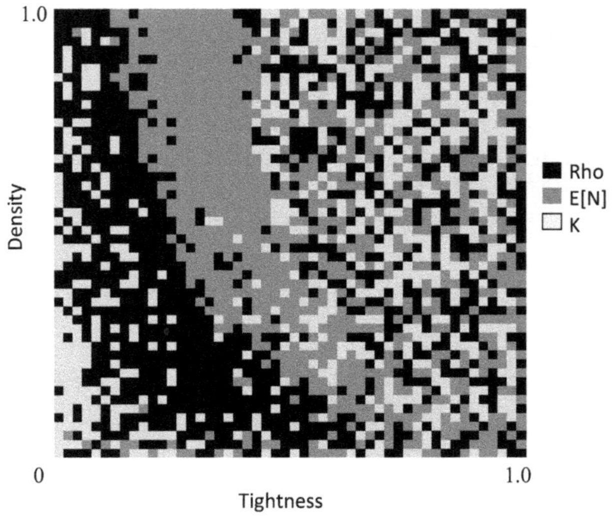

Figure 6: Best heuristic found for each point of the search space explored, using the average consistency checks required for instances with 20 variables and 10 values in their domains

Table 3: Average consistency checks required by the 30 hardest evolved instances for each heuristic. Density and tightness are the average over the cluster of instances.

Heuristic	Density (Avg.)	Tightness (Avg.)	Consistency Checks (Avg.)
Rho	0.89	0.24	6873922
E[N]	0.92	0.23	6080808
K	0.84	0.24	59395792

the random instances generated during search space characterization. Notice that they are aligned due the steps resolution used of 0.02 for tightness and density. The evolved instances are shown with square markers; they are located close to the hardest random generated instances. The genetic algorithm produces instances which are hard to solve for specific heuristics, however the most difficult evolved instances are located in the same area independently of the heuristic against they were evolved. It is important to notice that individuals at the end of the each run are very similar, in some cases with equal values of tightness and density, but they are never identical. Identical individuals are the ones with exactly the same boolean array representation. In order to avoid redundant individuals in the population, when the crossover operator produces an individual that is identical to an existing one in the population, the new individual is deleted and replaced with a randomly generated individual.

In Table 3 we present a summary of the average consistency checks required for the evolved instances for the three heuristics. In all the cases, the evolved instances outperformed the average difficulty of the random instances generated during the search characterization. The evolved instances have slightly different values in average for tightness and density; however we can see they are located in the same region where the hardest randomly generated instances were found.

We can argue against evolutionary algorithms to find hard instances: why all the extra effort? Why not to simply map the search spaces to find where are located the most difficult instances and then produce instances around that area? Of course that may be possible for small instances, however as soon as we increment size of the instances the time to explore the search space increases exponentially. Not to mention that the search space grows exponentially as the problem size increases and the points visited during mapping are quite less than total of possible problems in the search space, so it would be very likely that we miss areas of interest regarding hard instances. Considering those circumstances, the evolutionary model is a more efficient tool to find difficult instances, since it can save time just visiting the points of the space where the hard problems are located, independently of the size of the problems under analysis. In this study, we have demonstrated that a considerable less effort in terms of consistency checks is required by the genetic algorithm compared against the evaluations done during the characterization of the search space. The search space characterization required 50^3 evaluations, this is 50 steps for density, 50 steps for tightness and 50 random instances per point, which gives a total of 125000 evaluations, a really huge effort. However, the genetic algorithm required only 6000 evaluations (2 evaluations per generation in 3000 generations) to find harder problem instances than the instances randomly generated.

5. CONCLUSIONS

We have proposed an evolutionary approach as a tool to find difficult to solve problem instances to challenge the solutions methods, when the last are under analysis or development. The study was focused on evolving binary constraint satisfaction problems against three variable ordering heuristics: Rho, E[N] and K. The experiments were divided into two parts: search space characterization and the application of the evolutionary model to problem instances. During the search space mapping it was found that hardest instances,

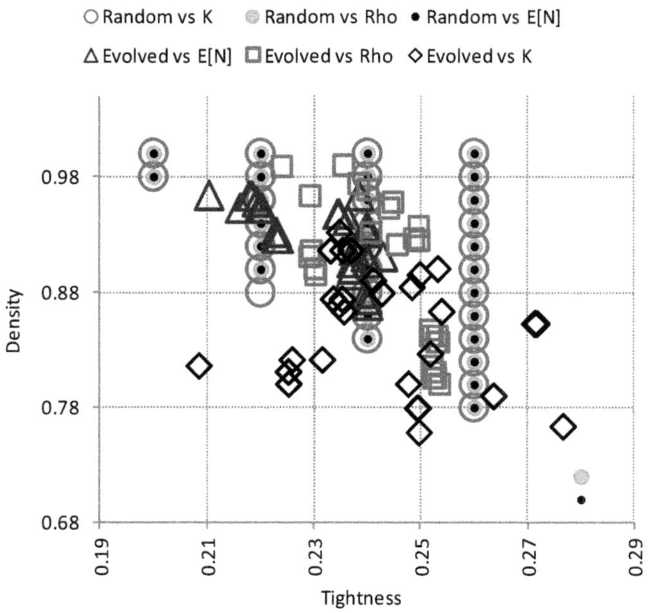

Figure 7: The 30 hardest instances found during the search space mapping and the 30 hardest evolved instances for each heuristic

for the three heuristics, are located on the same region of the search space. However, it was found that efficiency of the heuristics varies along the search space. A very interesting finding is that, in the region where the instances are solvable and around the phase transition, areas dominated by one heuristic were observed. On the other hand, in the area of the search space where the problems are unsolvable, there is no dominance of one heuristic over the others. This information can be used to create more complex solving strategies, such heuristics to choose heuristics, known as hyperheuristics, capable of decide when it is more efficient to use a particular heuristic depending of the features of the problem instances to be solved. Finally, the evolved problem instances were located in the same area where the difficult random instances were found during the search space exploration. The evolved instances outperformed the difficulty of the randomly generated instances, independently of the heuristic against they were evolved to be difficult for, but with a lot less effort. This indicates that the evolutionary model is a powerful tool to find hard to problem instances. The next step of this research is to implement a coevolutionary model, where solution strategies and problem instances will evolve against each other, expecting to find more efficient and robust solution methods. Additionally, we plan to extend the application of the evolutionary model to other combinatorial problems; the requisite is to find a representation that allows the genetic operator to work on them. Also, another topic for research is the usage of simulated annealing as an alternative tool to find hard to solve problem instances, considering that the nature of the bi-dimensional search space (density-tightness), at least on binary CSP, could be tackled by simulated annealing.

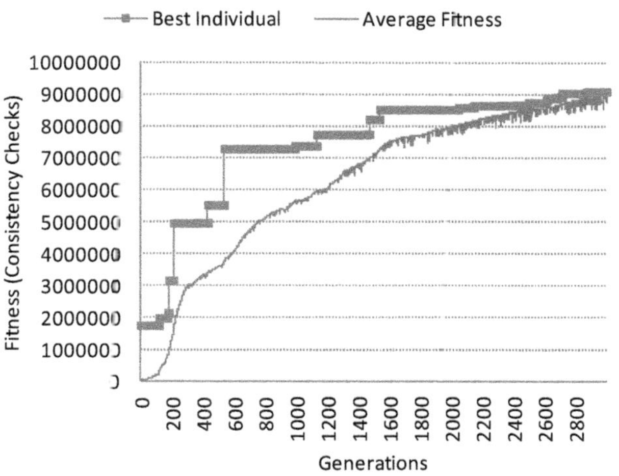

Figure 8: Genetic algorithm progress performance example of one run, evolving instances of 10 variables to be hard for heuristic $E[N]$

6. ACKNOWLEDGMENTS

This research was supported in part by ITESM under the Research Chair CAT-144 and the CONACYT Project under grant 99695.

7. REFERENCES

[1] D. Achlioptas, C. Gomes, H. Kautz, and B. Selman. Generating satisfiable problem instances. In *Proceedings of AAAI'00*, pages 256–301, 2000.

[2] D. Achlioptas, H. Jia, and C. Moore. Hiding satisfying assignments: Two are better than one. In *Proceedings of AAAI'ï£¡04*, pages 131–136, 2004.

[3] D. Achlioptas, M. S. O. Molloy, L. M. Kirousis, Y. C. Stamatiou, E. Kranakis, and D. Krizanc. Random constraint satisfaction: A more accurate picture. *Constraints*, 6(4):329–344, 2001.

[4] P. Cheeseman, B. Kanefsky, and W. M. Taylor. Where the really hard problems are. In *Proceedings of International Joint Conferences on Artificial Intelligence (IJCAI'91)*, pages 331–337, 1991.

[5] J. Culberson. Hidden solutions, tell-tales, heuristics and anti-heuristics. In *Workshop on Empirical Methods in Artificial Intelligence (IJCAI'01)*, 2001.

[6] Y. Fan and J. Shen. On the phase transitions of random k-constraint satisfaction problems. *Artif. Intell.*, 175(3-4):914–927, mar 2011.

[7] I. Gent, E. MacIntyre, P. Prosser, B. Smith, and T.Walsh. An empirical study of dynamic variable ordering heuristics for the constraint satisfaction problem. In *Proceedings of the International Conference on Principles and Practice of Constraint Programming (CP'96)*, pages 179–193, 1996.

[8] I. P. Gent, P. Prosser, and T. Walsh. The constrainedness of search. In *Proceedings of AAAI'96*, pages 246–252, 1999.

[9] E. MacIntyre, P. Prosser, B. M. Smith, and T. Walsh. Random constraint satisfaction: Theory meets practice. In *Proceedings of the 4th International Conference on Principles and Practice of Constraint Programming (CP 98)*, pages 325–339. Springer, 1998.

[10] M. Mouhoub and B. Jafari. Heuristic techniques for variable and value ordering in csps. In *Proceedings of the 13th annual conference on Genetic and evolutionary computation*, GECCO '11, pages 457–464, New York, NY, USA, 2011. ACM.

[11] P. Prosser. Hybrid algorithms for the constraint satisfaction problem. *Computational Intelligence*, 9:268–299, 1993.

[12] P. Prosser. Binary constraint satisfaction problems: Some are harder than others. In *Proceedings of the European Conference in Artificial Intelligence*, pages 95–99, 1994.

[13] P. Prosser. An empirical study of phase transitions in binary constraint satisfaction problems. *Artificial Intelligence*, 81(1-2):81 – 109, 1996. Frontiers in Problem Solving: Phase Transitions and Complexity.

[14] I. Rish and D. Frost. Statistical analysis of backtracking on inconsistent CSPs. In G. Smolka, editor, *Principles and Practice of Constraint Programming (CP'97)*, volume 1330 of *Lecture Notes in Computer Science*, pages 150–162. Springer, 1997.

[15] F. Rossi, C. Petrie, and V. Dhar. On the equivalence of constraint satisfaction problems. In *Proceedings of the 9th European Conference on Artificial Intelligence*, pages 550–556, 1990.

[16] B. Selman, D. Mitchell, and H. J. Levesque. Generating hard satisfiability problems. *Artificial Intelligence*, 81:17–29, 1996.

[17] Z. shan Li, H. ying Du, S. mei Xing, and F. wei Meng. Value ordering heuristic for solving algorithm based on the AC-4 algorithm. In *2nd International Workshop on Intelligent Systems and Applications (ISA'10)*, pages 1–4, 2010.

[18] B. M. Smith. Locating the phase transition in binary constraint satisfaction problems. *Artificial Intelligence*, 81:155–181, 1996.

[19] B. M. Smith. Constructing an asymptotic phase transition in random binary constraint satisfaction problems. *Theoretical Computer Science*, 265:265–283, 2001.

[20] J. I. van Hemert. Evolving binary constraint satisfaction problem instances that are difficult to solve. In *Proceedings of the 2003 IEEE Congress on Evolutionary Computation (CEC'03)*, pages 1267–1273. IEEE Press, 2003.

[21] J. I. van Hemert. Evolving combinatorial problem instances that are difficult to solve. *Evolutionary Computation*, 14(4):433–462, 2006.

[22] K. Xu, F. Boussemart, F. Hemery, and C. Lecoutre. Random constraint satisfaction: Easy generation of hard (satisfiable) instances. *Artificial Intelligence*, 171(8-9):514–534, 2007.

[23] K. Xu and W. Li. Exact phase transitions in random constraint satisfaction problems. *Journal of Artificial Intelligence Research*, 12:93–103, 2000.

[24] K. Xu and W. Li. Many hard examples in exact phase transitions. *Theorical Computer Science*, 355(3):291–302, 2006.

A Hybrid Heuristic for the k-medoids Clustering Problem

Mariá C. V. Nascimento*
Instituto de Ciência e Tecnologia - UNIFESP
Rua Talim, 330, CEP: 12230-280, São José dos Campos - SP
mcv.nascimento@unifesp.br

Franklina M. B. Toledo
Instituto de Ciências Matemáticas e de Computação, Universidade de São Paulo,
Caixa Postal 668, São Carlos-SP, CEP 13560-970, Brazil
fran@icmc.usp.br

André C. P. L. F. de Carvalho
Instituto de Ciências Matemáticas e de Computação, Universidade de São Paulo,
Caixa Postal 668, São Carlos-SP, CEP 13560-970, Brazil
andre@icmc.usp.br

ABSTRACT

Clustering is an important tool for data analysis, since it allows the exploration of datasets with no or very little prior information. Its main goal is to group a set of data based on their similarity (dissimilarity). A well known mathematical formulation for clustering is the k-medoids problem. Current versions of k-medoids rely on heuristics, with good results reported in the literature. However, few methods that analyze the quality of the partitions found by the heuristics have been proposed. In this paper, we propose a hybrid Lagrangian heuristic for the k-medoids. We compare the performance of the proposed Lagrangian heuristic with other heuristics for the k-medoids problem found in literature. Experimental results presented that the proposed Lagrangian heuristic outperformed the other algorithms.

Categories and Subject Descriptors

I.2.8 [**Problem Solving, Control Methods, and Search**]: Heuristic methods; I.5.3 [**Clustering**]: Metrics—*Algorithms*

Keywords

clustering, bioinformatics, heuristic, PAM, integer programming

1 Introduction

Clustering deals with the unsupervised classification of patterns (observations, data items or feature vectors) into groups (clusters) (14). Clustering algorithms can be roughly divided into two main approaches: partitioning clustering algorithms and hierarchical clustering algorithms. Partitioning clustering algorithms look for a partition that optimizes a given clustering criterion (14). Hierarchical clustering algorithms produce a nested series of partitions based on a criterion that either combines (agglomerative algorithms) or divides clusters (divisive algorithms) based on a similarity measure. There are many areas where clustering algorithms have been successfully used, such as pattern recognition, grouping, decision making, data mining and pattern classification (1; 4; 27).

Several clustering algorithms have been proposed in the last decades (19; 9; 21). Good surveys on clustering algorithms can be found, e.g., in (14; 28). Most of these algorithms are either deterministic or based on hill-climbing and can get trapped into local optimal solutions. Some heuristics may reduce the occurrence of this problem, by searching for multiple possible solutions.

Mathematical programming can be also employed in cluster analysis. Earlier studies have explored a mathematical formulation for the clustering problem, like, for example, (23; 19; 10; 24). One advantage of using mathematical programming is its easier validation, since it enables the generation of good bounds for a optimization problem by methods like Lagrangian relaxation. The Lagrangian relaxation is able to find lower (upper) bounds for a minimization (maximization) mathematical model by relaxing some of its constraints. The process works by multiplying relaxed constraints by a constant penalty and adding the result to the objective function. Lagrangian relaxation has been adopted by many researchers with interesting results for different kinds of optimization problems (19; 26).

This paper proposes a hybrid heuristic based on a Lagrangian heuristic (19) and a local search method (Partition Around Medoids, PAM) (15). PAM is a widely used heuristic for solving for the k-medoids problem for data clustering. To evaluate the solutions achieved by the proposed heuristic, called LPAM, we compare it with the Lagrangian heuristic proposed by Mulvey and Crowder (19) and with the original PAM. As a result, the gap relaxation of the proposed heuristic is very low for all partitions, outperforming the other Lagrangian heuristic. The comparison of LPAM with PAM showed that, particularly in datasets with the largest number of objects, LPAM presented much better results. The results from this experiment show a very good efficiency of the heuristic considering the objective function as the parameter of comparison.

This paper is structured as follows. Section 2 presents a

*Corresponding author.

GECCO'12, July 7-11, 2012, Philadelphia, Pennsylvania, USA.

mathematical model for the k-medoids clustering problem. In Section 3, the algorithms and strategies proposed in the literature to solve the studied problem are investigated. Section 4 presents the proposed heuristic to solve the k-medoids problem, LPAM. Section 5 reports the experimental results obtained in the computational tests and Section 6 concludes the paper presenting the final remarks.

2 k medoids problem

This section presents a mathematical model for the k-medoids clustering problem. This formulation is a p-median problem (which consists in locating p facilities in order to minimize the customer demands regarding these facilities) (17; 8) and it can be formulated as:

$$min \sum_{i=1}^{N} \sum_{j=1}^{N} d_{ij} x_{ij}$$

subject to:

$$\sum_{j=1}^{N} x_{ij} = 1 \qquad i = 1, \ldots, N \tag{1}$$

$$x_{ij} \leq x_{jj} \qquad i, j = 1, \ldots, N \tag{2}$$

$$\sum_{j=1}^{N} x_{jj} = M \tag{3}$$

$$x_{ij} \in \{0, 1\} \qquad i, j = 1, \ldots, N \tag{4}$$

where N is the number of objects; M is the number of clusters; d_{ij} is the distance between objects i and j; x_{ij} is a binary variable which assumes value 1, if the object i belongs to the cluster whose medoid is the object j and 0, otherwise. The objective function of this formulation aims to minimize the dissimilarity of the objects regarding their medoid. Constraints (1) assure that a object i is associated with one medoid, i.e., it belongs to one cluster. Constraints (2) force the object i to be associated with the medoid j only if j is really a medoid, i.e., if $x_{jj} = 1$. Constraints (3) assure that the number of medoids of the partition is M and Constraints (4) obligate all the variables to be binaries.

According to Cornuejols et al. (3), the problem of finding the optimal solution for this problem is NP-hard. In the next section we present some algorithms to solve heuristically the k-medoids formulation.

3 Related work

One of the most popular heuristics for the investigated problem is the Partition Around Medoids, PAM (15). PAM is a deterministic algorithm composed of two stages. While the first stage (known as BUILD) defines a set of initial medoids, the second stage (known as SWAP) fine tunes the medoids by swapping objects between the clusters. Kaufman and Rousseeuw (15) also proposed a variation of PAM, Clustering large Applications named CLARA, to make the algorithm manageable for large datasets. Large datasets mean datasets of order of thousands of objects. In this strategy, subsamples of the original dataset are clustered by PAM, instead of the whole original data. The best solution found through these subsample strategy is kept, producing the final partition.

A modified version of CLARA was proposed by Ng and Han (22), named CLARANS. This strategy uses a graph to represent the sets of medoids, indicated in its nodes. A local search with restricted neighbors is performed to find the nodes with the best medoids. The main difference between CLARA and CLARANS is that, the former limits the search for the medoids to the objects from the sorted subsample, whereas the latter, restricts the neighborhood of the local search for the medoids, which can be any object of the dataset.

Another method to solve the k-medoids formulation for large datasets was presented in (25). It consists in a hybrid genetic algorithm (GA) that does not require the definition of the number of clusters a priori.

A solution method to solve the k-medoids formulation, strongly related to the proposed methodology, is the Lagrangian relaxation presented in (19). This methodology is detailed in Section 4, together with the proposed hybrid heuristic.

4 Lagrangian Relaxation

The Lagrangian relaxation is a technique of relaxing some constraints of hard optimization problems. This relaxation enables the study of an easier (relaxed) problem, for which it is possible to propose exact solution methods. Moreover, it is a powerful technique to provide bounds for the original problem.

A Lagrangian relaxation of a minimization problem yields lower bounds for the original problem. The lower bound enables the assessment of the quality of the feasible solution found by some strategy. The quality of these lower bounds depends on the trait of the relaxation. The Lagrangian relaxation employed in this paper aims to dualize Constraints (1) of the previous model, resulting in a trivial problem, as proposed in (19). This relaxation is carried out in the following way:

Let μ be a N-vector of real numbers of Lagrangian multipliers and let $L(\mu)$ be the Lagrangian function defined as:

$$L(\mu) = \{\min \sum_{i=1}^{N} \sum_{j=1}^{N} d_{ij} x_{ij} + \sum_{i=1}^{N} \mu_i (1 - \sum_{j=1}^{N} x_{ij}) : s.t. (2-4)\}. \tag{5}$$

For our purpose, it is necessary to get the best lower bound, which is obtained by maximizing the $L(\mu)$ function. Therefore, consider the following problem:

$$\max_{\mu} \{\min \sum_{i=1}^{N} \sum_{j=1}^{N} (d_{ij} - \mu_i) x_{ij} + \sum_{i=1}^{N} \mu_i : s.t. \ (2-4)\}. \tag{6}$$

Notice that the function (5) was rearranged in order to make its solution simpler. The solution of the maximization problem (6) provides the best lower bound for the proposed mathematical model. In order to get the best μ that maximizes $L(\mu)$, we use the subgradient algorithm. This algorithm is an iterative method that produces a μ for each iteration k, μ^k, guided by the subgradient of the relaxed constraints, with $k = 1, \ldots, Max\_iterations$, where $Max\_iterations$ is a fixed number of iterations. Therefore, for each Lagrangian iteration k, a vector μ^k is supplied for the calculation of a new lower bound. Generally, the initial value μ^0 is a null vector. When $k > 0$, μ^k is calculated by the following equation:

$$\mu^k = \mu_{k-1} + \alpha_k * g^k, \tag{7}$$

where α_k indicates the step size in the subgradient direction in the iteration k and the N-dimensional vector g^k is the subgradient of the model, being given by: $g_i^k = 1 - \sum_{j=1}^{N} x_{ij} + \theta g_i^{k-1}$, for $i = 1, \ldots, N$.

Initially, g^0 is a null vector, g_i^k is the i-th component of g^k, and $\theta \in [0, 1]$. The α_k parameter can assume many distinct values and be updated by different rules. In this paper, we adopted the step rule from (11). We also tested two other rules for updating α_k: keeping it constant or randomly changing it at each iteration using a value in the range $[0, 1]$. Its formulation is given by: $\alpha_k = \alpha_0 \rho^k$, where α_0 is the initial value of α and $\rho < 1$. Different parameter values were tested with this formulation, but their results were not as good and stable as those obtained using the step rule proposed in (11). In (11), the step size rule, α_k, is updated at each Lagrangian iteration as follows.

$$\alpha_k = \lambda_k \frac{(best_{upper} - best_{lower})}{\sum_{i=1}^{N} g_i^k g_i^k}, \quad (8)$$

where $best_{lower}$ and $best_{upper}$ are, respectively, the best lower bound and the best upper bound found until iteration k. The λ_k parameter is generated by a decreasing sequence that depends on other parameters: n_{it}, r and MAX. The calculation of λ_k is given by the following steps:

***Calculating* $\lambda_k(k)$**

Step 1: Define $(\lambda_0, r, n_{it}, MAX)$.

Step 2: For each n_{it} iterations do:

- If $k < MAX$, then $n_{it} = \frac{n_{it}}{r}$ and $\lambda_k = \frac{\lambda_k}{r}$.
- If $k \geq MAX$, then the parameters n_{it} and λ_k will be equal to n_{it} in its previous iteration and λ_{MAX-1}, respectively.

Therefore, the solution of maximizing $L(\mu^k)$ is determined by the following steps.

***Maximization of* $L(\mu^k)$**

Step 1: (Definition of the medoids) Make $x_{jj} = 1$ for every $j \in S$, where S is the set of the M indexes $1 \leq j \leq N$ that provides the smallest values among $\sum_{i=1}^{N} \min(d_{ij} - \mu_i^k, 0)$.

Step 2: (Assignment of the objects) For every $i \in \{1, \ldots, N\}$, such that $d_{ij} - \mu_i^k < 0$ for $j \in S$, make $x_{ij} = 1$; otherwise, $x_{ij} = 0$.

As can be observed, the relaxation of some model constraints turns the model easy to solve. Nevertheless, this solution is just a lower bound for the original problem and its feasibility is not guaranteed.

Meanwhile, the knowledge of an effective lower bound has the advantage of estimating how acceptable is the upper bound that is a feasible solution for the original model. To find upper bounds, this paper proposes a novel Lagrangian heuristic (LPAM) based on the Lagrangian relaxation found in (19). In this heuristic, the medoids provided by each step of the Lagrangian relaxation are used as initial medoids for PAM. Giving the initial medoids for PAM, one of its two phases, the BUILD, is not used. Each step of the proposed Lagrangian heuristic is detailed as follows.

Procedure LPAM(x,d,μ)

Step 1: $k \leftarrow 0$, $\mu_0 \leftarrow 0$.

Step 2: (Lagrangian Evaluation) Find the solution of $L(\mu^k)$, the k-th lower bound, according to the routine *Maximization of* $L(\mu^k)$. Replace the best lower bound by the k-th lower bound if $k = 0$ or the best lower bound is lower than this found in iteration k.

Step 3: (Find the upper bound by LPAM) Perform PAM, defining its initial medoids those found in the Lagrangian step to produce lower bound of the current iteration.

Step 4: (Solution Update) Replace the best solution by the solution found in iteration k if it is lower than the current best solution or if $k = 0$.

Step 5: (Lagrangian Parameters Update) Update the Lagrangian parameters according to the routine *Calculating* $\lambda_k(k)$. Calculate α_k and μ_k using, respectively, Equations 8 and 7.

Step 6: $k \leftarrow k + 1$. If $k > Max\_iterations$ or $gap = 0$, where gap is calculated according to Equation 10, then return the best solution and lower bound. Else, go to *Step 2*.

In the Lagrangian heuristic proposed by (19), named LH, the *Step 2* is replaced by:

Step 2: (Find the upper bound by LH) Define as medoids of the upper bound those from the relaxed solution of the actual iteration. To produce the upper bound, assign each object from the dataset to its nearest medoid.

Next section reports the computational experiments performed using some biological datasets.

5 Computational Experiments

The first experiment compares the proposed LPAM with the other k-medoids algorithms, LH and PAM. In this experiment, all parameters of the Lagrangian heuristics, LPAM and LH, are set according to their performance in the tests. In another experiment, we evaluate the clustering partitions found by LPAM according to the real classification of the data sets using an external validation index. In this experiment, we compare LPAM with three other clustering algorithms: k-means (15), k-medians (15) and PAM.

5.1 Data sets

Progresses in biology research have lead to the production of a large amount of data, which needs to be analyzed. Clustering algorithms have become an important tool in the analysis of biological data, because they can discover useful patterns to support the understanding of biological processes. One of these processes is observed in gene expression data, where tumor tissues can be grouped by the identification of their underline patterns.

To evaluate the use of LPAM for clustering, we carried out experiments using: six cancer tissues data sets, another biological data set and one artificial data set. The real classification of these data sets is known. In some cases, there is more than one classification structure for the data set. Each classification is defined as a structure. Moreover, each one of these structures may have a different number of groups or classes. The main characteristics of these eight data sets can be seen in Table 1, which illustrates, for each data set, the number of objects (♯Obj.), the number of different structures (♯Str.) and the number of groups for each different structure between parenthesis (♯Groups), the number of attributes (♯Attrib.) and the main paper reference (Reference).

The objective function of the k-medoids problem requires a dissimilarity measure between pairs of objects from the data sets. To supply this dissimilarity matrix, $D = [d_{ij}]_{N \times N}$, this paper evaluates the Manhattan and Euclidean distances.

Table 1: **Data sets main characteristics. This table shows the main characteristics of each data set used in the experiments.**

Data set	Main characteristics			
	♯Obj.	♯Str. (♯groups)	♯Attrib.	Reference
Golub	72	4 (2,3,4)	3571	(7)
Leukemia	327	2 (3,7)	271	(29)
Novartis	103	1 (4)	1000	(12)
MultiA	103	1 (4)	5565	(12)
MiRNA	218	6 (2,3,4,9, 20)	217	(16)
Breast	699	1 (8)	9	(2)
Simulated6	60	1 (6)	600	(18)
Ecoli	336	1 (8)	7	(20)

Both are special cases of the *p-distance* metric and can be represented by equation (9):

$$d_{ij} = (\sum_{k=1}^{N_a} |a_{ik} - a_{jk}|^p)^{\frac{1}{p}}, \qquad (9)$$

where a_{ik} and N_a represent, respectively, the k-th attribute of the object i and the number of attributes of the objects, and p is an integer number that depends on the studied metric. If $p = 1$, the distance is known as the Manhattan distance; if $p = 2$, the distance is defined as the Euclidean distance, which is the most frequently used dissimilarity metric.

5.2 Experiment I

We implemented LH and LPAM using the R language from the R-project v.2.8.1. The implementation of PAM used in the LPAM was obtained from the R-project package *cluster*. This implementation enables the user to define the initial medoids for the PAM algorithm.

To check and compare the performance of the Lagrangian heuristics, a quantitative measure is adopted: the gap between the lower bound and upper bound. This gap indicates how far is the feasible solution obtained by LPAM and by LH from the best lower bound found by the relaxation of the mathematical model. It is calculated in the following way:

$$gap = \frac{(z_{upper} - z_{lower})}{z_{lower}} * 100 \qquad (10)$$

where
z_{upper} is the upper bound, i.e., the feasible solution;
z_{lower} is the Lagrangian lower bound.

Given that the subgradient method has a profound impact on the performance of the Lagrangian heuristics, we investigated the effect of different parameter values in them. For such, we considered the following range values for the parameters: $MAX \in \{5, 10, 15\}$; $n_{it} \in \{20, 25, 30\}$; $r \in \{1, 2, 3\}$; and $\lambda_0 \in [0.70, 2.0]$. The step size used for the interval of the last parameter, λ_0, was 0.05. For the data sets used in this paper, we found the best values adopting the following parameter values: $MAX = 15$, $n_{it} = 25$, $r = 2$ and $\lambda_0 = 1.75$. Other values were tested, but the gaps outside the previous parameter ranges achieved very high values. We also adopted $\alpha_0 = 0$ and a null value for the vector μ_0. The number of maximum Lagrangian iterations, *Max_iterations* parameter, was set to 100 for LPAM and 500 for LH. The number of maximum iterations fixed to LH was set according to the elapsed time that LPAM took to perform its 100 iterations. The number of iterations for LPAM was set after

Table 2: Mean and standard deviation of the gaps in percentage of LPAM considering the Euclidean distance metric.

Data set	LPAM		LH	
	Mean	SD	Mean	SD
Simulated6	0.046	0.102	0.149	0.232
Golub	0.039	0.045	0.335	0.288
MultiA	0.057	0.080	0.445	0.567
Novartis	0.059	0.104	0.411	0.518
MiRNA	0.126	0.064	1.591	1.819
Leukemia	0.040	0.028	0.314	0.412
Ecoli	0.281	0.146	4.966	4.141
Breast	2.869	1.585	25.387	13.278

Table 3: Mean and standard deviation of the gaps in percentage of LPAM considering the Manhattan distance metric.

Data set	LPAM		LH	
	Mean	SD	Mean	SD
Simulated6	0.034	0.120	0.160	0.295
Golub	0.150	0.269	0.608	0.562
MultiA	0.104	0.122	0.501	0.521
Novartis	0.153	0.276	0.679	0.766
MiRNA	0.089	0.074	1.304	2.182
Leukemia	0.150	0.085	0.905	0.641
Ecoli	0.448	0.167	5.405	4.213
Breast	4.435	2.203	30.860	17.570

tests that showed that the gap reduction is not so significant after 100 iterations for most of the data sets. The value for the parameter θ was defined 0.0 after preliminary tests. In these tests, we took into account the performance of both Lagrangian heuristics, LPAM and LH.

Initially, we present, in Tables 2 and 3 the mean gap values of the proposed Lagrangian heuristic, LPAM, and the Lagrangian heuristic found in the literature, LH. These values are the average gap results for LPAM and LH considering the Euclidean and Manhattan distances. This table also presents the standard deviation of the gaps. For each data set, we consider $M \in \{2, \ldots, 30\}$. We display these results in Figures 1 and 2 for every data set. These results refer to $M = 15$, considering the Euclidean distance as the dissimilarity between the pairs of objects. We used $M = 15$ because we wanted the heuristics found partitions with a reasonable number of medoids. The adopted time interval refers to 0 and the least elapsed time between LPAM and LH to achieve the last best gap, in the considered number of iterations.

Figure 1 presents the behavior of the data sets with the lowest number of objects. It can be noticed that, except for the MultiA, Figure1(d), LPAM achieved much better results than LH in the considered time interval. The inset subplots present the behavior of the gaps in the last period, discriminating their differences in such period.

Figure 2 clearly shows the superior performance of LPAM over LH. Although for MiRNA, Leukemia and Breast there were some intervals that LH was superior to LPAM, LPAM was more robust than LH, always achieving better final gaps for all data sets. It can also be observed that the differences between the final gaps of LPAM and LH were very significant in the last two data sets.

It can be observed from Tables 2 and 3 that, in all data sets, the mean gaps of LPAM outperformed the mean gaps of LH. Moreover, the standard deviations of the gaps of LPAM

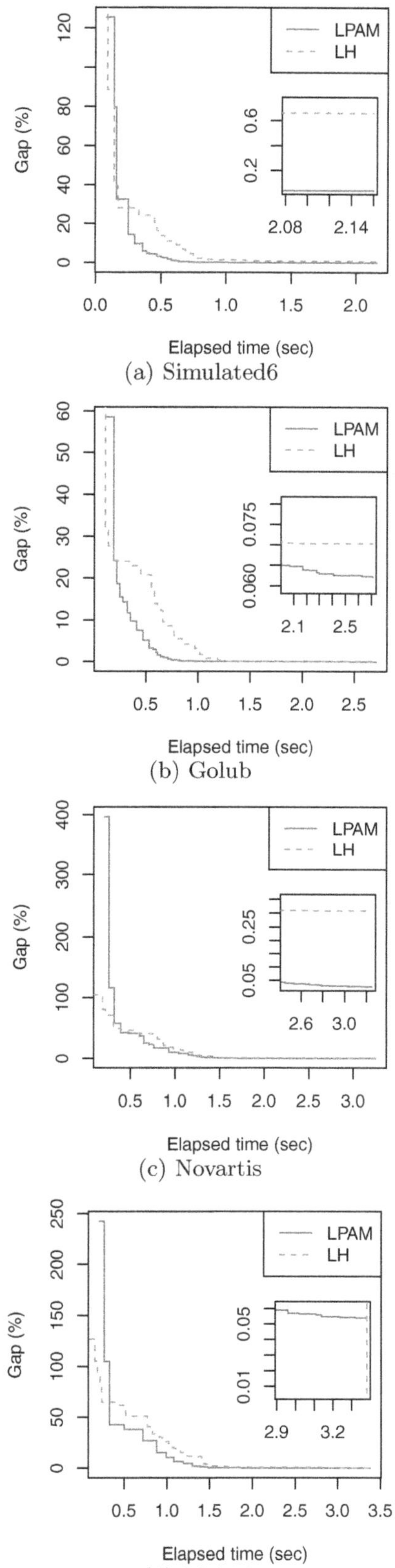

(a) Simulated6

(b) Golub

(c) Novartis

(d) MultiA

Figure 1: Relation gap versus elapsed time of LPAM and LH for, respectively, Simulated6, Golub, Novartis and MultiA data sets.

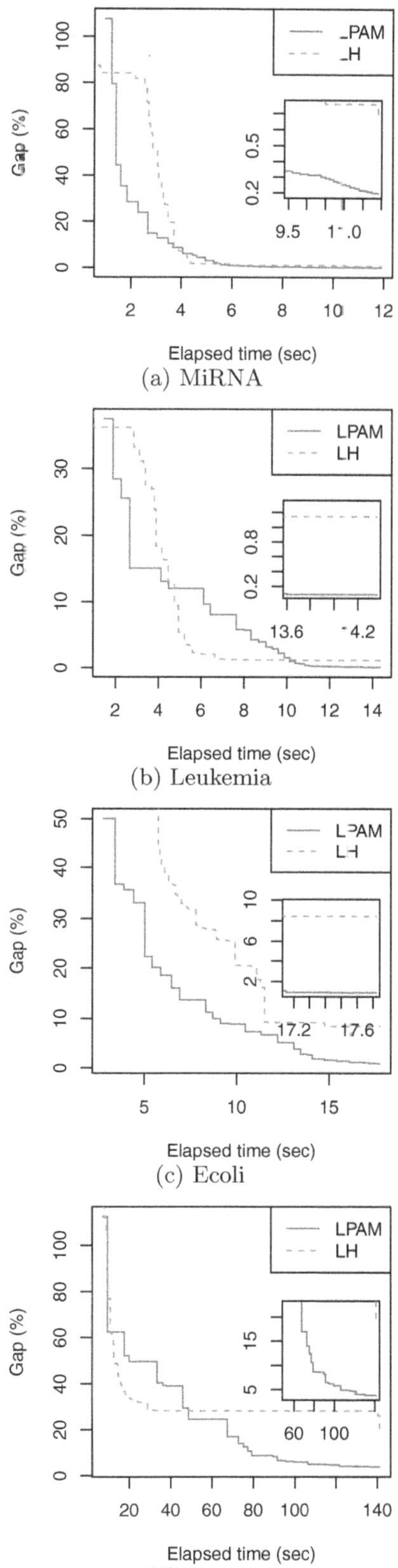

(a) MiRNA

(b) Leukemia

(c) Ecoli

(d) Breast

Figure 2: Relation gap versus elapsed time of LPAM and LH for, respectively, MiRNA, Leukemia, Ecoli and Breast data sets.

were much lower than those from LH. These results evidence the best performance of LPAM over LH. It is worth mentioning that, although the number of data sets is 8, 29 runs corresponding to different numbers of clusters were carried out. Moreover, two different dissimilarity metrics were used. Therefore, the total number of test cases was 464.

In order to compare the results from the original PAM with LPAM, we confronted their objective function solutions. For such, we calculated how far are the solutions found by PAM and LPAM using the following equation.

$$gap = \frac{z_{PAM} - z_{LPAM}}{z_{LPAM}} \tag{11}$$

In this equation, z_{PAM} and z_{LPAM} correspond to, respectively, the PAM solution and the LPAM solution. This gap is presented in percentage in the experiments. It is worth mentioning that the LPAM solutions were always better than or equal to the PAM solutions. Figure 3 presents the results of this comparison. Table 4 present the results of these comparisons.

Table 4: Mean and standard deviation of the gaps in percentage for LPAM.

Dataset	Euclidean		Manhattan	
	Mean	SD	Mean	SD
Simulated6	0.029	0.027	0.006	0.014
Golub	0.038	0.039	0.075	0.080
MultiA	0.002	0.005	0.002	0.011
Novartis	0.041	0.049	0.048	0.107
MiRNA	0.106	0.192	0.242	0.212
Leukemia	0.022	0.030	0.028	0.057
Ecoli	0.251	0.229	0.282	0.228
Breast	0.287	0.476	0.283	0.310

Note that, in Table 4, the higher the number of objects, the better the solutions found by LPAM over PAM. This is an indicative of a good performance of the proposed heuristic, since the higher the dimension of the matrices, the more difficult is to find good quality solutions for them.

In Figure 3, the data sets were divided into two sets. The set 1 refers to the data sets with the lowest number of objects, whereas the set 2 has the 4 data sets with the highest number of objects. Figures 3(a) and 3(c) show the results for the set 1, when the Euclidean and Manhattan distances between objects were used, respectively. It can be noticed that both Golub and MultiA presented the highest gaps. Moreover, the gaps were more significant when the Manhattan distance was used.

For the set 2, Figure 3(b) and 3(d) indicates that Breast, the data set with the highest number of objects, achieved the highest gaps. Moreover, considering the Figure 3(d), it can be observed that all data sets presented gaps higher than the previous analyzed data. Therefore, all these results demonstrate the superiority of LPAM over LH and PAM for the k-medoids problem.

5.3 Experiment II

In this experiment, we compare LPAM with three well known clustering algorithms from literature: k-means (15), k-medians (15) and PAM. The software implementation of the two first algorithms was obtained from (5). The use of the k-means and the k-medians for comparison is due to, as well as the k-medoids problem, they produce cluster with spherical shape.

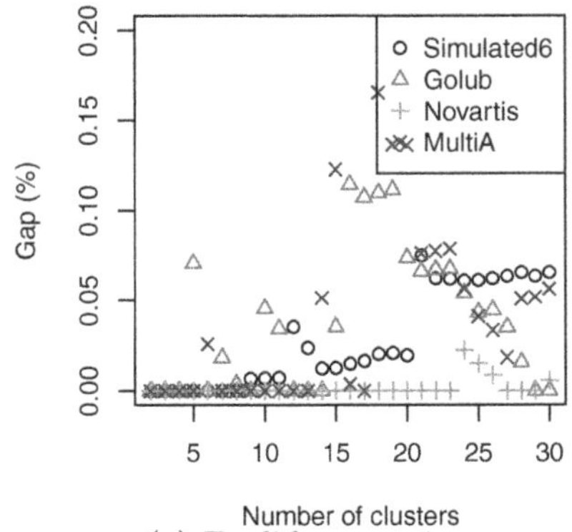

(a) Euclidean-set 1

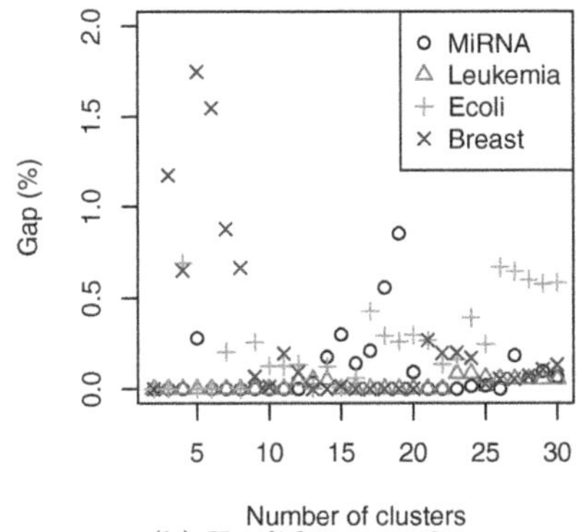

(b) Euclidean-set 2

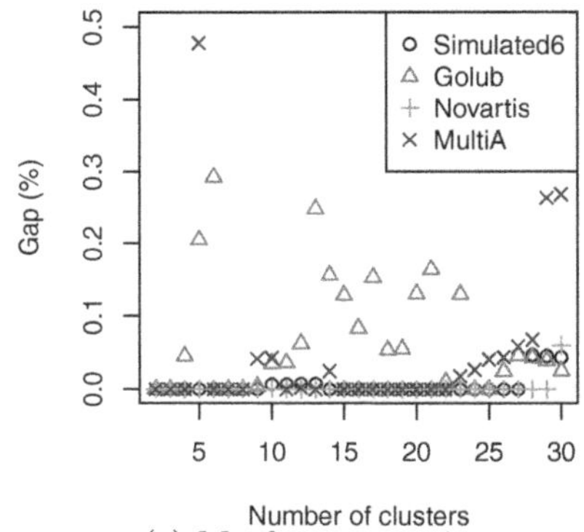

(c) Manhattan-set 1

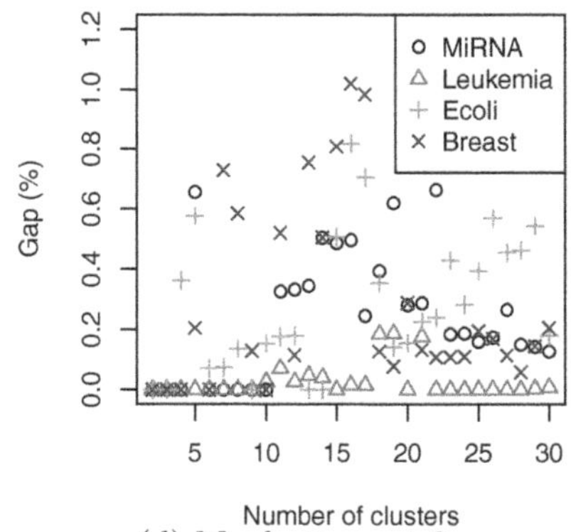

(d) Manhattan-set 2

Figure 3: These graphs present the gaps between LPAM and PAM regarding their number of clusters.

We evaluated the partitions produced by the four algorithms using the CRand measure (13), which is based on the real data classification. Thus, CRand provides an external evaluation criterion that estimates how much the partitions determined match the real classification. The CRand varies from -1 to 1, and the larger the CRand, the more accurate is the partition regarding the true classification. It is worth to remind that this is a classification index and it is just a validation measure for evaluating partitions found by a clustering algorithm. It indicates the agreement between a partition found and the real classification.

The experimental results present the CRand values with respect to the Euclidean and the Manhattan distances. Alike (9), we performed tests by firstly generating partitions with cluster numbers in the set $\{2, \ldots, 30\}$ for each data set. The partitions with the highest CRand are reported. This procedure was followed for every clustering algorithm used in this experiment.

A performance profile analysis proposed by Dolan and Moré (6) was employed to compare the CRand values of the four different algorithms. Let S and P be, respectively, the set of n_s algorithms to be analyzed and the set of n_p problems (data sets) into consideration. A factor, known as *performance ratio*, evaluates the performance of the algorithm s with regard to the problem (or instance) p. It is given by the following equation:

$$r_{ps} = \frac{t_{ps}}{min\{t_{ps} | s \in S\}} \tag{12}$$

The value of t_{ps}, used in the comparison of the algorithms, gives the performance of the algorithm s in the problem p. According to Dolan and Moré (6), the lower this value, the better. Regarding Equation 12, it must be observed that the best r_{ps} is 1, which occurs when t_{ps} has the minimum value among all algorithms.

Another factor considered in (6) is the ratio: the number of problems that an algorithm s presented a *performance ratio* equal to or better than an coefficient τ divided by the total number of problems ($\rho_s(\tau) = \frac{1}{n_p} size\{p \in P | r_{ps} \leq \tau\}$).

This ratio $\rho_s(\tau)$ represents the probability that an algorithm s has a *performance ratio* within a factor τ. In this performance analysis graph, the curves of the graph are plotted according to the values of τ and $\rho_s(\tau)$.

In this paper, S is composed by the four algorithms analyzed according to the CRand value: LPAM, k-means, k-medians and PAM. The distance matrix associated with each data set was considered an instance. Every CRand was taken into account for analysis, which means that a total of 34 instances composes the set P.

Figure 4 displays the results from this analysis. $\tau = 1$ shows the percentage that an algorithm s achieved results better than the other algorithms. Both LPAM and PAM achieved the best results in more than 60% of the problems. However, LPAM presented a slightly higher percentage than PAM, as can be observed in the subplot of Figure 4. Each one of the other algorithms achieved the best results in a little more than 20% of the instances. The robustness of the algorithms in the instances analysed can be observed when $\tau > 1$. For example, for $\tau = 1.2$, y-axis indicates the percentage of instances that an algorithm s achieved results at most 20% worse than the best results. It can be noticed that LPAM achieved the best results for almost every value of τ.

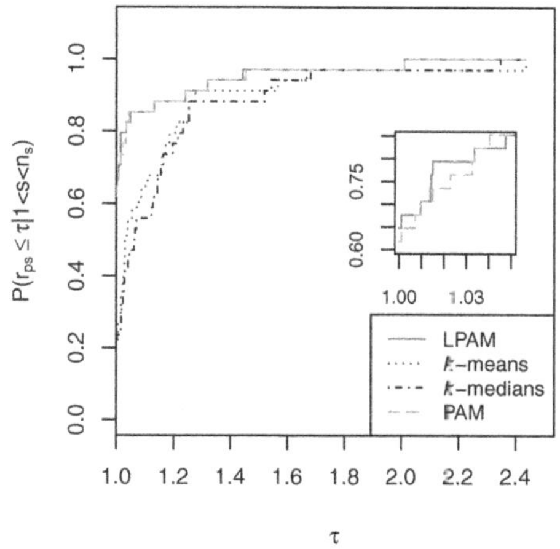

Figure 4: This graph shows the performance profile of all distance metrics, algorithms and data sets relating to the CRand index.

The subplot in Figure 4 highlights the superior performance of LPAM over PAM for small values of τ.

6 Final Remarks

This paper investigated a hybridization of a Lagrangian based heuristic with a known local search clustering method, PAM for the k-medoids problem. The first experiment investigated the efficiency of LPAM, comparing it with another k-medoids heuristics found in literature for the same problem. According to the experimental results, LPAM outperformed the other heuristics, mainly in the data sets with high number of objects. In the second experiment, the proposed heuristic was compared with the real partitions using the CRand index. In this experiment, LPAM was compared with the k-means, k-medians and PAM algorithms. The proposed algorithm performed better in most of the partitions, considering the Euclidean and Manhattan distances. Furthermore, LPAM is deterministic, in contrast to k-means and k-medians methods, known for the variation of the partitions obtained in different runs. PAM achieved, for some cases, the same clustering partitions as LPAM, however, the medoids were different, presenting worse solutions than LPAM. Regarding the computational time, LPAM took just some few seconds to find its solutions, even for medium sized data sets.

Acknowledgments

The authors would like to thank FAPESP and CNPq for the research funding.

References

[1] U. Alon, N. Barkai, D. A. Notterman, K. Gish, S. Ybarra, D. Mack, and A. J. Levine. Broad patterns of gene expression revealed by clustering analysis of tumor and normal colon tissues probed by oligonucleotide arrays. *Proc. Natl. Acad. Sci. USA*, 96(12):6745–6750, 1999.

[2] K. P. Bennett and O. L. Mangasarian. Robust linear programming discrimination of two linearly inseparable sets. *Optimization Methods and Software*, 1:23–34, 1992.

[3] G. Cornuejols, M. L. Fisher, and G. L. Nemhauser. Location of bank accounts to optmize float: an analytic study of exact and approximate algorithms. *Management Science*, 23:789–810, 1977.

[4] F. Corpet. Multiple sequence alignment with hierarchical clustering. *Nucleic Acids Research*, 22:10881–10890, 1988.

[5] M. J. L. de Hoon, S. Imoto, J. Nolan, and S. Miyano. Open source clustering software. *Bioinformatics*, 20(9):1453–1454, 2004.

[6] E. D. Dolan and J. J. Moré. Benchmarking optimization software with performance profiles. *Math. Program., Ser. A*, 91:201–213, 2002.

[7] T. R. Golub, D. K. Slonim, P. Tamayo, C. Huard, M. Gaasenbeek, J. P. Mesirov, H. Coller, M. L. Loh, J. R. Downing, M. A. Caligiuri, C. D. Bloomfield, and E. S. Lander. Molecular classification of cancer: class discovery and class prediction by gene expression monitoring. *Science*, 286(5439):531–537, 1999.

[8] S. L. Hakimi. Optimum distributions of switching centers in a communication network and some related graph theoretic problems. *Operations Research*, 13:462–475, 1965.

[9] J. Handl and J. Knowles. An evolutionary approach to multiobjective clustering. *IEEE Transactions On Evolutionary Computation*, 11:56–76, 2007.

[10] P. Hansen and B. Jaumard. Cluster analysis and mathematical programming. *Mathematical Programming*, 79:191–215, 1997.

[11] M. Held, P. Wolfe, and P. Crowder. Validation of subgradient optimization. *Mathematical Programming*, 6:62–88, 1974.

[12] Y. Hoshida, J.-P. Brunet, P. Tamayo, T. R. Golub, and J. P. Mesiro. Subclass mapping: Identifying common subtypes in independent disease data sets. *PLOS one*, 2(11):e1195, 2007.

[13] L. Hubert and P. Arabie. Comparing partitions. *Journal of Classification*, 2:193–218, 1985.

[14] A. K. Jain, M. N. Murty, and P. J. Flynn. Data clustering: a review. *ACM Comput. Surv.*, 31:264–323, 1999.

[15] L. Kaufman and P. J. Rousseeuw. *Finding groups in data: an introduction to cluster analysis.* New York: Wiley, 1990.

[16] J. Lu, G. Getz, E. A. Miska, E. Alvarez-Saavedra, J. Lamb, D. Peck, A. Sweet-Cordero, B. L. Ebert, R. H. Mak, A. A. Ferrando, J. R. Downing, T. Jacks, R. R. Horvitz, and T. R. Golub. Microrna expression profiles classify human cancers. *Nature*, 435(7043):834–838, 2005.

[17] F. Maranzana. On the location of supply points to minimize transport costs. *Operational Research Quarterly*, 15:261–270, 1964.

[18] S. Monti, P. Tamayo, J. Mesirov, and T. Golub. Consensus clustering: A resampling-based method for class discovery and visualization of gene expression microarray data. Technical report, Broad Institute/MIT - Kluwer Academic Publishers, 2003.

[19] J. M. Mulvey and H. P. Crowder. Cluster analysis: an application of lagrangian relaxation. *Management Science*, 25:329–340, 1979.

[20] K. Nakai and M. Kanehisa. Expert system for predicting protein localization sites in gram-negative bacteria. *PROTEINS: Structure, Function, and Genetics*, 11:95–110, 1991.

[21] M. C. V. Nascimento, F. M. B. Toledo, and A. C. P. L. F. Carvalho. Investigation of a new GRASP-based clustering algorithm applied to biological data. *Computers & Operations Research*, 37:1381–1388, 2010.

[22] R. Ng and J. Han. CLARANS: A method for clustering objects for spatial data mining. *IEEE Transactions Knowledge of Data Engineering*, 14:1003–1016, 2002.

[23] M. R. Rao. Cluster analysis and mathematical programming. *Journal of the American Statistical Association*, 66(335):622–626, 1971.

[24] B. Sağlam, F. S. Salman, S.l Sayin, and M. Türkay. A mixed-integer programming approach to the clustering problem with an application in customer segmentation. *European Journal of Operational Research*, 173:866–879, 2006.

[25] W. Sheng and X. Liu. A genetic k-medoids clustering algorithm. *J Heuristics*, 12:447–466, 2006.

[26] W. W. Trigeiro, L. J. Thomas, and J. O. McClain. Capacitated lot sizing with setup times. *Management Science*, 35:353–366, 1989.

[27] A. Ushioda and J. Kawasaki. Hierarchical clustering of words and application to nlp tasks. In E. Ejerhed and I. Dagan, editors, *Fourth Workshop on Very Large Corpora*, pages 28–41, Somerset, New Jersey, 1996. Association for Computational Linguistics.

[28] R. Xu and D. Wunsch. Survey of clustering algorithms. *IEEE Transactions on neural networks*, 16:645–678, 2005.

[29] E.-J. Yeoh, M. E. Ross, S. A. Shurtleff, W. K. Williams, D.Patel, R. Mahfouz, F.G. Behm, S. C. Raimondi, M. V. Relling, A. Patel, C. Cheng, D. Campana, D. Wilkins, X. Zhou, J. Li, H. Liu, C.-H. Pui, W. E. Evans, C. Naeve, L. Wong, and J.R. Downing. Classification, subtype discovery, and prediction of outcome in pediatric acute lymphoblastic leukemia by gene expression profiling. *Cancer cell*, 1:133–143, 2002.

A Hybridization between Memetic Algorithm and Semidefinite Relaxation for the Max-Cut Problem

Bo Song
Dept. of Electrical and Electronic Engineering
The University of Hong Kong, Hong Kong
bsong@hku.hk

Victor O. K. Li
Dept. of Electrical and Electronic Engineering
The University of Hong Kong, Hong Kong
vli@eee.hku.hk

ABSTRACT

The Max-Cut problem is a classical NP-hard combinatorial optimization problem. It consists of dividing the vertices of a weighted graph into two subsets, such that the sum of the weights of the edges connecting the two subsets is maximized. Although semidefinite relaxation algorithms for Max-Cut have been proved to be of high quality and offer performance guarantees, in practice, metaheuristic algorithms are still the first option to solve large Max-Cut instances. In this paper, we present the first effort at combining semidefinite programming (SDP) with metaheuristic algorithm (Memetic Algorithm) to solve the Max-Cut problem. Based on the solution of semidefinite relaxation, we use Goemans-Williamson Algorithm to seed high quality solutions to the initial population for the memetic algorithm. Experimental results on well-known benchmark problems show that our new hybrid algorithm is capable of obtaining better solutions in the initial population generation stage than previous algorithms, and the overall performance of our algorithm is better than one of the best existing algorithms. Besides, new best solutions for 14 benchmark problems were found by our algorithm.

Categories and Subject Descriptors

I.2.8 [**ARTIFICIAL INTELLIGENCE**]: Problem Solving, Control Methods, and Search—*heuristic methods*

General Terms

Algorithms

Keywords

Max-Cut, Hybrid Algorithms, Memetic Algorithm, Semidefinite Programming

1. INTRODUCTION

Given an undirected graph $G(V, E)$ with the vertex set $V = \{1, 2, \ldots n\}$ and the edge set E. Let w_{ij} be the weight of edge (i, j). The Max-Cut problem is to partition the vertex set V into two sets $S \subset V$ and $S' = V - S$, such that the sum of the weight of the edges connecting S and S' is maximized. Formally, it can be formulated as

$$max \sum_{i \in S, j \in S'} w_{ij} \tag{1}$$

Max-Cut is an important combinatorial optimization problem. It has applications in many areas, including VLSI design and statistical physics. Despite its simple description, Max-Cut is difficult to solve in practice and has been proved to be NP-hard [9]. To meet the computational challenge, a lot of research has been dedicated to design approximation algorithms for Max-Cut. The outcome can be classified in two categories: approximation algorithms with a proven performance guarantee and those without. In the first category, the real breakthrough came when Goemans and Williamson [11] devised a randomized approximation algorithm based on semidefinite relaxation and proved that their algorithm has a .878 approximation ratio for the Max-Cut problem. Their work led to important theoretical research [6, 15, 21] in recent years which eventually proved that if the Unique Games Conjecture [14] holds the Goemans-Williamson algorithm is optimal. Although of much theoretical importance, in practice Goemans-Williamson algorithm was found less efficient compared to other heuristic methods when solving Max-Cut. However, the idea of utilizing semidefinite relaxation for Max-Cut was proved quite valuable and it has been adopted in designing several other kinds of algorithms, such as a recent exact algorithm [23].

Different from Goemans-Williamson algorithm and its descendants, another category of approximation algorithms to solve Max-Cut is metaheuristic algorithms. Though without a proven approximation ratio, metaheuristic algorithms are generally efficient in obtaining high quality solutions in practice within a reasonable amount of time. There have been many studies on applying metaheuristic algorithms to solve Max-Cut [5, 8, 16, 17, 19]. Experimental results showed that these metaheuristics have similar or slightly better performance in terms of solution quality compared to the state-of-the-art specifically designed heuristics [4].

Given previous work, it is natural to ask whether semidefinite relaxation can be utilized by metaheuristic algorithms to get better overall performance. In fact, the idea of hybridizing metaheuristics with other optimization techniques to exploit problem knowledge is not new. As an example, local improvement as a problem domain heuristic has long been incorporated into metaheuristic algorithm design such

GECCO'12, July 7–11, 2012, Philadelphia, Pennsylvania, USA.

as in Scatter Search [24]. In this regard, Memetic Algorithm (MA) [20], as a denomination of a broad class of metaheuristics incorporating other techniques (e.g. heuristics, approximation algorithms, etc.), has attracted many research efforts and became a significant field. MA distinguishes itself by intrinsically seeking to exploit all available knowledge the target problem entails. Besides MA, there is also research on hybrid approaches conducted in the recent growing area of Hybrid Metaheuristics (see [2] for a recent survey). However, to the best of our knowledge, there is no study on combining semidefinite relaxation with metaheuristic algorithm to solve Max-Cut or any other combinatorial optimization problems. Therefore, our goal is to provide a first study on how to utilize semidefinite relaxation to enhance metaheuristics and also to develop a competing hybrid memetic algorithm capable of providing high-quality solutions for Max-Cut within reasonable computation time.

In this paper, we propose a new memetic algorithm exploiting semidefinite relaxation to solve Max-Cut. This hybrid algorithm uses Goemans-Williamson algorithm as a sub procedure to seed the initial population with high quality solutions. Care has been given in algorithm design to strike a balance between exploration and exploitation. More specifically, we designed a restart mechanism to overcome premature convergence and escape from local optima. We also intentionally use large parent and offspring population sizes to balance the intensification effect from the semidefinite programming (SDP) seeds in initial population and local search. We compare our algorithms with another state-of-the-art algorithm on the common benchmark problems. Experimental results show that

1. The initial population generation procedure in our algorithm can produce better solutions (in terms of average fitness value) than previous procedures, while at the same time maintaining a moderate diversity (in terms of average distance between candidate solutions) to cover the solution space.
2. The overall performance of our algorithm is better than another state-of-the-art algorithm in terms of solution quality and runtime.
3. In our experiment new best solutions for 14 benchmark problems were found.

The rest of this paper is structured as follows. In Section 2 we give a more detailed review on hybrid approaches in metaheuristic algorithm design, existing state-of-the-art algorithms for Max-Cut and initial population generation procedures. In reviewing initial population generation procedures, we have discovered two problems of an existing procedure. In Section 3 we present our proposed initial population generation algorithm. A detailed description of our overall hybrid memetic algorithm is given in Section 4. In Section 5 we report computational results. Finally, in Section 6 we conclude the paper and suggest possible future work.

2. RELATED WORK

2.1 Hybridizing Metaheuristics with Problem Relaxation

In recent years, the approach of combining mathematical programming with metaheuristic algorithm has become a research field in its own right under the name "Matheuristic Algorithm" [18]. In this field, utilizing problem relaxation to enhance metaheuristic algorithms is a popular hybridization approach. A relaxation of an optimization problem is obtained by modifying or removing some of the constraints (e.g. dropping the integer constraint) of the original problem. In this process, the feasible set of the original problem becomes a subset of the feasible set of the relaxed problem. Therefore, by solving the relaxed problem one is able to obtain a bound and/or approximate solution(s) to the original problem. As most relaxed problems can be solved efficiently, it is reasonable to take advantage of the bound/approximate solutions in the hope that they may facilitate solving the original problem.

In the literature, there exist hybrid metaheuristic algorithms on various combinatorial optimization problems using a similar methodology to that of this paper, i.e., using problem relaxation to generate feasible solutions in the algorithm. In [7] for the Generalized Assignment Problem (GAP), the authors designed a hybrid genetic algorithm integrating a "Linear Programming Initialization" procedure to generate initial population for the genetic algorithm. First, the procedure solves the linear programming (LP) relaxation to the GAP, then it adopts a rounding heuristic and repair and improvement operator to make the usually fractional LP solution integral and feasible. In [22], the authors also adopted a similar approach combining memetic algorithm with LP relaxation to solve the Multidimensional Knapsack Problem (MKP). Though dealing with different optimization problems, both of these studies showed that problem relaxation is helpful in producing high quality candidate solutions. However, it is proved that for Max-Cut SDP relaxation can provide better performance guarantee than LP relaxation.

2.2 Algorithms for Max-Cut

Practical algorithms for Max-Cut can be roughly categorized into three classes: exact algorithms, specifically designed heuristics, and metaheuristics. Exact algorithms are guaranteed to solve the problem to optimality (see [23] for a recent study). The runtime of exact algorithms are usually hours or days even on small Max-Cut instances with no more than a few hundred nodes.

Specifically designed heuristics are approximation algorithms that are specifically designed to solve Max-Cut. In this category, the approach proposed by Burer et al. [4] is the cutting edge one. Their algorithm CirCut restricted the semidefinite relaxation to a rank-two relaxation, and transformed the relaxed problem into a non-convex optimization problem with n (number of vertices in the graph) variables. By establishing the connection between discrete solutions to the original problem and stationary points to the relaxed problem, the authors developed a specialized heuristic to solve Max-Cut. Computation results showed that CirCut is efficient in producing high quality solutions. However, as shown in [19], when the runtime is long enough, the performance of CirCut in terms of solution quality is no better than that of metaheuristic methods.

The third category is metaheuristics. A brief summary of previous research is given in Table 1. Due to their reported superiority in performance, we give more detailed review on the two recent studies [16, 19].

In [19], the authors proposed several new heuristics to

Table 1: Summary of Metaheuristics for Max-Cut

Reference	Brief Description
Festa(2002) [8]	Various algorithms based on VNS, GRASP and path relinking
Durate(2005) [5]	A hybrid algorithm between VNS and memetic algorithm
Laguna(2009) [17]	A hybrid cross-entropy method combined with local search
Martí(2009) [19]	A scatter search algorithm enhanced by several advanced techniques
Kochenberger(2011) [16]	Tabu search algorithm effective for large Max-Cut instances

enhance the Scatter Search (SS) algorithm. The improvements include new diversification generation method, new local search method and new combination method. On the strategy level, several adaptive features were introduced and the authors proposed a method using GRASP to solve the Maximum Diversity Problem (MDP) to insert the reference set with most diverse candidate solutions. Besides, they also inserted learning mechanisms to local search and combination procedures. Experimental results showed that their advanced SS algorithm can produce slightly better solutions than CirCut with similar computation time. Compared to a previously developed metaheuristic algorithm (VNSPR) [8] however, the SS algorithm converges at a much faster speed and produces better solutions. In [16], the authors took a different approach. They proposed to solve Max-Cut by solving an equivalent Unconstrained Binary Quadratic Problem (UBQP). UBQP can be solved efficiently by Diversification Driven Tabu Search (DDTS) [10] which was designed by the same authors. Experimental results showed that the tabu search algorithm is capable of finding new best solutions for most of the test problems, and solving problem instances with up to 10000 nodes which were not dealt with before by previous algorithms.

2.3 Initial Population Generation Procedure

In metaheuristic algorithm design, successful initial population generation procedures usually maintain a balance between solution quality and diversity. For the Max-Cut problem, previous studies mainly used heuristic methods to construct high-quality solutions and used randomization or memory structures to maintain diversity. In this section, we review the deterministic method C_3 proposed in [19]. As indicated in the paper, C_3 produces initial population of reasonable diversity and best solution quality compared to other methods. It is adopted in the leading algorithm SS for Max-Cut. However, as will be shown in the following paragraphs, we discovered two problems with this method.

The C_3 procedure works as follows. To generate a solution, first all vertices are put in the set S'. Then at each step, the procedure selects the vertex with the largest $\Delta cut_f(v)$ value and moves it from S' to S, where

$$\Delta cut_f(v) = \Delta cut(v) - \beta \frac{freq(v)}{MaxFreq} \Delta cut(v),$$

and $\Delta cut(v)$ is the increase in fitness value when moving vertex v from S' to S; $freq(v)$ counts the number of times that vertex v has been moved to S in previous constructions; $MaxFreq$ is the maximum $freq(v)$ among all vertices; $beta$ is an input parameter in the range $[0, 1]$. Conceptually this deterministic algorithm incorporates a greedy heuristic to select the vertex which is likely to bring the maximum increase in fitness value; at the same time it also introduces a discount in preference if one vertex is selected many times. In this way a balance between solution quality and diversity is obtained. However, this approach has two problems:

1. For graphs consisting of homogeneous vertices, such as complete graph or toroidal grid with identical edge weights, C_3 is likely to loop among a few candidate solutions, thereby failing to generate a population of a predefined size. For example, consider a 4-vertex complete graph $K4$ with all edge weights equal to 1. The initial $freq(v)$ are all 0 and $MaxFreq = 1$. It is obvious that C_3 loops between two solutions, 1100 and 0011 (1 for vertex in S, 0 in S') for $K4$. This failure is also observed when using the SS algorithm to solve benchmark problems $g48$ to $g50$ (see Section 5).

2. The second problem of C_3 associates with the value $MaxFreq$. After many constructions, $MaxFreq$ becomes large, which makes it possible that changes in $freq$ may have little effect in reordering the preference of vertices. In other words, it is likely that C_3 generates many same solutions before changes in $freq$ can lead to a different solution. This problem may incur a failure if the number of iterations to generate a new solution is limited (which is usually the case). We observed early termination of SS algorithm on some benchmark problems due to this failure (see Section 5 for details).

3. INITIAL POPULATION GENERATION ALGORITHM

In this section we propose our new initial population generation algorithm. It utilizes semidefinite relaxation for Max-Cut. First, the semidefinite relaxation for Max-Cut and the Goemans-Williamson Algorithm, which serves as the basis of our algorithm, are introduced. Then the outline of our algorithm is presented.

3.1 Semidefinite Relaxation for Max-Cut

It is well known that the original Max-Cut problem (1) can be formulated into an equivalent Quadratic Integer Programming (QIP) problem

$$\begin{aligned} max\ \frac{1}{4} \sum_{1 \le i,j \le n} w_{ij}(1 - x_i x_j) \\ s.t.\ |x_i| = 1,\ i = 1, 2, \ldots, n \end{aligned} \qquad (2)$$

In (2) n is the number of nodes, w_{ij} is the weight of edge (i, j) with $w_{ij} = 0$ if $(i, j) \notin E$. As only undirected graph is of interest, $w_{ij} = w_{ji}$.

The semidefinite relaxation of (2) relaxes the scalar x_i to an n-dimensional vector $v_i \in R^n$ such that the Euclidean norm $\|v_i\| = 1$. By transforming to an equivalent matrix form, the Semidefinite Programming (SDP) relaxation for

Max-Cut is shown in (3).

$$\begin{aligned} & min\ W \bullet X \\ & s.t.\ diag(X) = e \\ & X \succeq 0 \\ & X \in R^{n \times n} \end{aligned} \tag{3}$$

In (3), $W = [w_{ij}] \in R^{n\times n}$, $W \bullet X = \sum_{1\leq i,j\leq n} w_{ij}x_{ij}$, i.e. the trace of WX. $diag(X)$ is the n-dimensional vector consisting of the diagonal elements of X. e is an all-one n-dimensional vector. $X \succeq 0$ is the constraint that X should be a symmetric positive semidefinite matrix. This SDP problem is a convex optimization problem and can be solved numerically by the interior point algorithm (see [25] for example).

3.2 The Goemans-Williamson Algorithm

The Goemans-Williamson (GW) algorithm is designed to round the solution of SDP relaxation back to cuts, i.e. to solution to the QIP formulation (2). GW-algorithm is presented in Algorithm 1. In the algorithm sgn(x) is a function whose value equals 1 if $x \geq 0$ and -1 if $x < 0$.

Algorithm 1: The Goemans-Williamson Algorithm

Input: Optimal solution $X = V^TV$ to the relaxation of the Max-Cut problem, the number of vertices n
Output: approximate cut vector x

begin
  Randomly generate a vector r uniformly from the unit sphere $S_n = \{y \in R^n \mid \|y\| = 1\}$;
  Compute $z = V^Tr$;
  Set x_i =sgn(z_i), $i = 1, 2, \ldots, n$;
end

The GW algorithm works as follows. Before being invoked, the SDP relaxation (3) should be solved and the optimal solution X to the SDP relaxation is obtained. Notice that as X is a positive semidefinite matrix, X can be decomposed to $X = V^TV$, $V = [v_1, v_2, \ldots, v_n]$. To generate valid cuts, GW randomly produces a hyperplane with norm vector r to separate the points v_i into two subsets, and assigns the corresponding discrete vector x according to the separation.

3.3 The New Initial Population Generation Algorithm

Our new initial population generation algorithm is illustrated in Algorithm 2. We call it GW+Random since it uses GW to generate high quality solutions and uses random generation method to maintain diversity. In this algorithm the function GWALG is the GW algorithm shown in Algorithm 1; Fitness is a function which evaluates fitness value to the solution. GW+Random works as follows. It repeatedly invokes GW to generate candidate solutions until P solutions are generated and these P solutions have been stable (i.e. no better solutions generated) for at least K_{SDP} iterations. Then to maintain diversity, Q additional candidate solutions are randomly generated and inserted into the initial population.

Since GW is a randomized algorithm, a least number of stable iterations K_{SDP} is necessary to overcome the variability of the algorithm in order to consistently generate high quality solutions. Also the values of P and Q can be adjusted to strike a balance between diversity and solution quality in the population, so as to accommodate different stages of the algorithm. Finally, it is worth noting that our algorithm uses a sampling *with replacement* strategy. This is because GW is a randomized algorithm for which is unlikely to generate duplicate solutions. Besides, as we intend to use large parent/offspring population sizes to increase the parallel search in the overall hybrid algorithm, using this strategy saves the computation time of comparing newly generated solutions to previously generated ones in the population.

Algorithm 2: GW+Random

Input: Num. of SDP generated solutions P, Num. of randomly generated solutions Q, least num. of stable iterations K_{SDP}, optimal solution $X = V^TV$ to the SDP relaxation, the number of vertices n
Output: a population POP of size $P + Q$

begin
  Set POP={};
  for $k \leftarrow 1$ **to** P **do**
    POP[k] $\leftarrow$ GWALG(V, n);
  end
  Set $j \leftarrow 0$;
  while $j \leq K_{SDP}$ **do**
    $j \leftarrow j + 1$;
    $x \leftarrow$GWALG(V, n);
    $y \leftarrow \text{argmin}_{i=1,2,\ldots,P}$Fitness($POP[i]$);
    if Fitness(x) > Fitness($POP[y]$) **then**
      POP[y]$\leftarrow x$;
      $j \leftarrow 0$;
    end
  end
  Randomly generate Q solutions and insert them to POP;
end

4. HYBRID MEMETIC ALGORITHM

In this section we describe our new hybrid memetic algorithm. The flow of the algorithm follows the standard MA framework, as shown in Algorithm 3. We use a binary encoding scheme to represent an individual solution. In such encoding $b_i = 1$ indicates that the vertex i is in subset S while $b_i = 0$ indicates it is in S'. To fully specify our algorithm, we describe it in three parts: operators, selection mechanism, and restart procedure.

4.1 Operators

4.1.1 Local Search

Our hybrid MA uses a simple local search heuristic to improve candidate solutions. It is shown in Algorithm 4. In this algorithm the function value of $\Delta(v)$ is the increase in fitness value when moving vertex v to the opposite set. This value is negative if such a move leads to a decrease in fitness value. Basically the local search operator looks through all vertices according to a predefined order and moves vertices to the opposite set if it brings an increase in fitness value. It only stops when such improvement movements do not exist for the current solution. Notice that though we use a first pivoting rule to move vertices, at the start of this procedure we generate a random permutation of vertex order for the procedure to look through, thereby eliminating potential bias on vertex position.

Algorithm 3: Hybrid Memetic Algorithm

```
begin
    Solve the SDP relaxation;
    Initialize parentPOP using GW+Random();
    parentPOP ← LocalSearch(parentPOP);
    while TerminationCondition() = false do
        if RestartCondition() = true then
            Preserve %preserve best solutions in parentPOP;
            Regenerate the remaining part of parentPOP
            using GW+Random();
            parentPOP ← LocalSearch(parentPOP);
        end
        candidateParents ←
        LinearRankingSelect(parentPOP);
        offspringPOP ← CrossOver(candidateParents);
        offspringPOP ← Mutation(offspringPOP);
        offspringPOP ← LocalSearch(offspringPOP);
        parentPOP ← LinearRankingSelect(parentPOP ∪
        offspringPOP)
    end
end
```

Algorithm 4: LocalSearch

```
begin
    Generate a random permutation P of {1, 2, ..., n};
    improved ← true;
    while improved do
        improved ← false;
        for i ← 1 to n do
            if Δ(P[i]) > 0 then
                x_P[i] ← 1 − x_P[i];
            end
        end
    end
end
```

4.1.2 Crossover and Mutation

We use the standard Uniform Crossover (UX) to generate two offsprings from two parents. The crossover operator looks through each gene in the pair of parents and exchange it with probability $p_{crossover}$. The mutation operator is a unary operator. It looks through all genes and flips each gene with a small probability $p_{mutation}$.

We implemented the crossover operator and the mutation operator by first using a binomial distribution to select the number of genes to exchange/mutate (say m), and then using a random permutation P of $\{1, 2, \ldots, n\}$ to choose the location of these genes (which are $P[1], P[2], \ldots, P[m]$).

4.2 Selection Mechanism

In the hybrid MA we use Linear Ranking Selection (LRS) for both parent selection and survival selection (see [13] for details). In parent selection, to generate an offspring population of size n, n parents are selected by LRS from parent population (duplicates allowed). For survival selection, from a parent population of size m and an offspring population of size n, m individuals are selected without duplicate to form a new parent population. In this process an elitism policy is adopted, always keeping the best solution among all candidate $(m+n)$ solutions in the next parent population. The remaining $m-1$ individuals of the next parent population are chosen by LRS from the remaining $n+m-1$ candidate solutions without duplicate. The hybrid MA uses two parameters ϕ_{parent} and $\phi_{survival}$ to control the selection pressure of parent selection and survival selection. The selection pressure is the ratio between the probability that the best solution is selected and the probability the median solution is selected by LRS. It is in the range of $(1, 2)$. A larger value indicates a larger selection pressure.

4.3 Restart Procedure

When the fitness value of the best solution in the current parent population has not changed for $K_{restart}$ iterations, the parent population is considered converged, and a restart procedure is invoked. The aim of the restart procedure is to escape from premature convergence and to perform further search on the solution space. The restart procedure works as follows. First a fraction ($\%preserve$) of the best solutions in the current population is retained, then SDP+Random is invoked to generate the remaining part of the population (with $\%SDP_{restart}$ generated by SDP and $\%Random_{restart}$ generated randomly). The newly generated population becomes the initial population and the hybrid algorithm restarts. Notice that the fraction parameters need not be the same as that of the first run. In fact in the first run we generate all initial population by SDP to speed up convergence, and when restart is needed we use small values of $\%preserve$ and $\%SDP_{restart}$ to include more randomly generated candidate solutions to the population.

5. COMPUTATIONAL RESULTS

5.1 Benchmark Problems

We use two well-known benchmark problem sets to evaluate the performance of our algorithm. The first set, G-set, is generated by Helmberg and Rendl [12]. It consists of 54 Max-Cut instances with density varying from 0.2% to 6% and graph size (number of vertices) varying from 800 to 3000. G-set includes various types of graphs such as random graphs, modified planar graphs and toroidal grids. The edge weights are chosen from $\{1, 0, -1\}$. The two leading algorithms SS [19] and DDTS [16] use this set to test their algorithms. The second set (DIMACS-set) comes from the 7th DIMACS Implementation Challenge (available at http://dimacs.rutgers.edu/Challenges/Seventh/Instances/). It consists of 2 instances of 512 nodes and 2 instances of 3375 nodes. SS and CirCut [4] used DIMACS-set in their experiments. In this paper, the best known objective function values for G-set are obtained from the more recent DDTS research. For DIMACS instances, the best known objective function values are extracted from the research of SS and CirCut.

5.2 Experimental Setup

The hybrid MA has been implemented in C++. In our algorithm, the SDP relaxation is solved by a parallel version of CSDP [3] version 6.1.1, which is one of the state-of-the-art SDP solvers. In the implementation of our GW+Random algorithm, we used a parallel version of LAPACK [1] to perform matrix calculations.

For comparison between our GW+Random and C_3, we implemented C_3 in C++ according to the description in the authors' original paper and their implementation code. This is for conformity with the underlining data structure and it also facilitates automatic comparison. For comparison between hybrid MA and SS, we use the SS code directly obtained from the authors and compiled it using the same compiler option as for our algorithm. The parameters of SS are set to the recommendation configuration in their paper.

All experiments are conducted on a PC with an Intel Core i5 750 2.67GHz CPU and 4GB memory.

5.3 Comparing GW+Random with C3

In the first experiment we compare our population generation procedure GW+Random with C_3 of SS. Our algorithm depends on three parameters, P, Q and K_{SDP}. As we are more interested in studying the SDP generated population, we experiment on 7 configurations of GW+Random with P set to the population size and Q set to 0 (therefore all solutions are generated by SDP), and K_{SDP} are chosen from 0, 10, 25, 50, 75, 90, 100 for the 7 configurations respectively. We denote these configurations as $GW(K_{SDP})$. For C_3 we study three configurations with parameter $\beta = 0.25, 0.5, 0.75$ denoted as $C_3(0.25)$, $C_3(0.5)$ and $C_3(0.75)$. The G-set is used as the benchmark set.

To evaluate an algorithm configuration, we are interested in four characteristics of the generated population: the fitness value of the best and worst solution f_{best} and f_{worst}; the average fitness value of the population f_{avg}; and the average distance among pairs of solutions d_{avg}, where the distance between two solutions is defined as the Hamming distance. As these four values can be treated as random variables (although C_3 is deterministic, the outcome is unpredictable beyond a few steps, exhibiting randomness to an observer), we compare them by conducting statistical tests. In our experiment, the population size is 100. For each problem, each algorithm configuration generates 50 populations, and the above four values associated with the generated populations are recorded. Under each measure (say f_{best}) for each pair of algorithm configurations (say A and B), we use one-sided Welch's t-test with 95% confidence level to compare them on each problem. Then we count the number of problems $\#_{A>B}$ on which t-test accepted $E(f^A_{best}) > E(f^B_{best})$ and the number of problems $\#_{A<B}$ on which t-test accepted $E(f^A_{best}) < E(f^B_{best})$. Conceptually, these two numbers count for the number of test problems in which A outperforms B and vice versa.

Due to space limitations and as indicated in [19], $C_3(0.75)$ attains best solution quality and best diversity compared to the other two configurations, we only report the comparison between GW+Random and $C_3(0.75)$. For $C_3(0.5)$ and $C_3(0.25)$ the trend is similar. Since $C_3(0.75)$ failed 10 test problems, the comparison is made only on the remaining 44 problems. The result is summarized in Figure 1. The four sub figures summarize the comparison results under the four measures respectively. In each sub figure the x-axis is the K_{SDP} value for GW+Random; the y-axis is the number of problems on which one algorithm outperforms another. Each dot (a, b) on the solid line represents that the algorithm configuration $GW(a)$ outperforms $C_3(0.75)$ by b problems. Similarly, each star (a, b) on the dashed line represents $C_3(0.75)$ outperforms $GW(a)$ by b problems.

First it can be seen that in each sub figure the solid line is always above the dashed line, indicating that for every measure GW+Random always outperforms $C_3(0.75)$. Secondly as $k = K_{SDP}$ increases, $\#_{GW(k)>C_3(0.75)}$ also increases for f_{best}, f_{worst} and f_{avg} while $\#_{GW(k)<C_3(0.75)}$ decreases for the above 3 measures, indicating that the increase in K_{SDP} consistently improves the population in terms of solution

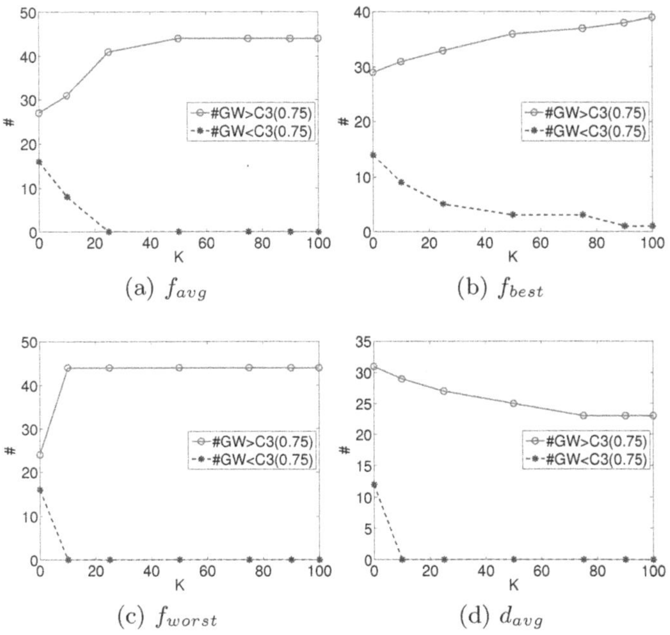

Figure 1: Comparing GW+Random with $C_3(0.75)$

quality. Finally, as $k = K_{SDP}$ increases, $\#_{GW(k)>C_3(0.75)}$ decreases for d_{avg}, indicating that the increase in K_{SDP} decreases the diversity of the population. However, as k increases, $\#_{GW(k)<C_3(0.75)}$ also decreases for d_{avg}. This may be caused by a reduction of variability of $GW(k)$. In other words, as k increases, the number of instances on which $GW(k)$ performs extremely poorly is reduced.

We also measured the average time to generate a population for each algorithm configuration. $K_{SDP} = 25$ is a good choice as it produces more diverse solutions with higher quality, and the computation time is similar to that of $C_3(0.75)$.

5.4 Comparing Hybrid MA with SS

We compare our algorithm with SS on G-set and DIMACS-set. Before making the comparison we use 12 representative problems of G-set to manually tune our algorithm. The resulting configuration is shown in Table 2, in which L is the number of vertices in the graph. Note that the parent and the offspring population sizes are set large to maintain diversity and fully exploit the parent population. We also set the mutation probability to $2/L$ to reduce the chance that the outcome of mutation is reverted by local search. We fix this configuration and use our algorithm and SS to solve all instances of G-set and DIMACS-set. For G-set, each algorithm solves each problem 10 times, each time running for 30 minutes. For each problem in DIMACS-set, each algorithm performs a single 3-hour run to solve it. Table 3 and 4 summarize the results.

In Tables 3 and 4 the column n stands for problem size; OBJ are the best known objective function values for each problem; HMA is our proposed hybrid memetic algorithm; f_{best} is the best solution returned by the corresponding algorithm (for G-set, it is the best solution returned over the 10 runs); f_{avg} (only in Table 3) is the average objective value of solutions returned over the 10 runs. We mark the corresponding f_{best}/f_{avg} in boldface if it is larger than the

Table 2: Parameters of Hybrid MA

Parameter	Value	Description
m	2000	Parent population size
n	4000	Offspring population size
$\%SDP_{init}$	1	Fraction of SDP generated solutions in initial population
$\%SDP_{restart}$	0.005	Fraction of SDP generated solutions in restart
$\%preserve$	0.005	Fraction of best solutions to retain in restart
ϕ_{parent}	1.1	Parent selection pressure
$\phi_{survival}$	1.8	Survival selection pressure
$p_{crossover}$	0.2	Crossover probability
$p_{mutation}$	2/L	Mutation probability
K_{SDP}	25	Least number of stable iterations for GW+Random
$K_{restart}$	60	Number of no improve iterations to invoke restart

f_{best}/f_{avg} of another algorithm. If an algorithm comes with better solution than the best known solution, its f_{best} is in square bracket.

For G-set, comparing f_{best}, our HMA outperforms SS on 36 instances while SS outperforms HMA on 5 instances; HMA attains 22 best known solutions while SS attains 13; HMA comes up with 12 new best solutions while SS comes up with 3. If comparing f_{avg}, HMA outperforms SS on 45 instances while SS outperforms HMA on 5 instances. It is also observed that for both HMA and SS, the standard deviation of objective function value of solutions found over the 10 runs for each problem is very small, thus f_{avg} is suitable for comparing the performance of HMA and SS. For DIMACS-set, apart from pm3-15-50, for the remaining 3 instances HMA found new best solutions for 2 instances and attains best known solution for the remaining one. Like HMA, SS also found the new best solution for pm-8-50. However, for the other 3 problems, the results of SS are worse than HMA. To summarize, HMA outperforms SS on both benchmark problem sets.

Finally, as already discussed in Section 2.3, C_3 may cause failure or early termination in SS. This is also observed in our experiment on G-set. For g48, g49, g50, which are all toroidal 2D grid with highly homogeneous vertices, C_3 failed to generate an initial population with predefined size. We also observed early termination of SS on several other problems. The f_{best} and f_{avg} values of these problems are underlined.

6. CONCLUSION

In this paper we demonstrated a hybrid memetic algorithm incorporating semidefinite relaxation to solve Max-Cut. Our work is the first study on integrating semidefinite relaxation into metaheuristic algorithms. The hybrid MA algorithm is simple in the sense that it does not adopt any advanced adaptive features or specially designed heuristics. It only uses the GW algorithm to seed the initial population and follows the common memetic algorithm framework. Computational results showed that the seeding procedure in our algorithm can produce better solutions than existing methods, and our hybrid MA is competitive with cutting edge metaheuristic algorithm SS. Besides, 14 new best solutions for the well-known benchmark problems are found.

As shown in the computational results, we only used manual tuning to set the parameters of our algorithm, and our algorithm got 14 new best known solutions to the benchmark problems. In the future, we intend to incorporate adaptive features to our algorithm and use automatic tuning to set the parameters, in the hope of getting better results. The recent algorithm DDTS [16] will also be included in our empirical study. Besides, though modern SDP solvers are very efficient, the computational cost is still high when dealing with large problems. On the other hand, to seed the initial population the SDP relaxation may not need to be solved to optimality. Therefore, it is possible to investigate the trade-off between solution quality of SDP relaxation and the seeded initial population.

7. REFERENCES

[1] E. Anderson, Z. Bai, C. Bischof, L. S. Blackford, J. Demmel, J. J. Dongarra, J. Du Croz, S. Hammarling, A. Greenbaum, A. McKenney, and D. Sorensen. *LAPACK Users' guide (third ed.).* Society for Industrial and Applied Mathematics, Philadelphia, PA, USA, 1999.

[2] C. Blum, J. Puchinger, G. R. Raidl, and A. Roli. Hybrid metaheuristics in combinatorial optimization: A survey. *Appl. Soft Comput.*, 11:4135–4151, September 2011.

[3] B. Borchers. CSDP, a C library for semidefinite programming. *Optimization Methods & Software*, 11-2(1-4):613–623, 1999.

[4] S. Burer, R. D. C. Monteiro, and Y. Zhang. Rank-Two relaxation heuristics for MAX-CUT and other binary quadratic programs. *SIAM J. on Optimization*, 12(2):503–521, 2002.

[5] A. Duarte, A. Sánchez, F. Fernández, and R. Cabido. A low-level hybridization between memetic algorithm and VNS for the max-cut problem. In *Proceedings of the 2005 conference on Genetic and evolutionary computation*, GECCO '05, pages 999–1006, New York, NY, USA, 2005.

[6] U. Feige and G. Schechtman. On the optimality of the random hyperplane rounding technique for MAX CUT. *Random Structures & Algorithms*, 20(3):403–440, 2002.

[7] H. Feltl and G. R. Raidl. An improved hybrid genetic algorithm for the generalized assignment problem. In *Proceedings of the 2004 ACM symposium on Applied computing*, SAC '04, pages 990–995, New York, NY, USA, 2004.

[8] P. Festa, P. M. Pardalos, M. G. C. Resende, and C. C. Ribeiro. Randomized heuristics for the MAX-CUT problem. *Optimization Methods & Software*, 17(6):1033–1058, 2002.

[9] M. R. Garey and D. S. Johnson. *Computers and intractability : A guide to the theory of NP-completeness.* W.H. Freeman, San Francisco, 1979.

[10] F. Glover, L. Zhipeng, and J.-K. Hao. Diversification-driven tabu search for unconstrained binary quadratic problems. *4OR: A Quarterly Journal of Operations Research*, 8:239–253, 2010.

[11] M. X. Goemans and D. P. Williamson. Improved approximation algorithms for maximum cut and satisfiability problems using semidefinite

programming. *Journal of the ACM*, 42(6):1115–1145, 1995.

[12] C. Helmberg and F. Rendl. A spectral bundle method for semidefinite programming. *SIAM Journal on Optimization*, 10(3):673–696, 2000.

[13] K. Jong. *Evolutionary computation: A unified approach.* Bradford Books. MIT Press, 2006.

[14] S. Khot. On the power of unique 2-prover 1-round games. In *Proceedings of the thiry-fourth annual ACM symposium on Theory of computing*, STOC '02, pages 767–775, New York, NY, USA, 2002.

[15] S. Khot, G. Kindler, E. Mossel, and R. O'Donnell. Optimal inapproximability results for MAX-CUT and other 2-variable CSPs? *SIAM Journal on Computing*, 37(1):319–357, 2007.

[16] G. Kochenberger, J.-K. Hao, Z. Lü, H. Wang, and F. Glover. Solving large scale Max Cut problems via tabu search. *Journal of Heuristics*, to appear in 2012.

[17] M. Laguna, A. Duarte, and R. Marti. Hybridizing the cross-entropy method: An application to the Max-Cut problem. *Computers & Operations Research*, 36(2):487–498, 2009.

[18] V. Maniezzo, T. Stützle, and S. Voss. *Matheuristics : hybridizing metaheuristics and mathematical programming.* Annals of information systems,. Springer, New York, 2009.

[19] R. Martí, A. Duarte, and M. Laguna. Advanced scatter search for the Max-Cut problem. *INFORMS J. on Computing*, 21(1):26–38, 2009.

[20] P. Moscato and C. Cotta. A modern introduction to memetic algorithms. In M. Gendreau and J.-Y. Potvin, editors, *Handbook of Metaheuristics*, volume 146 of *International Series in Operations Research & Management Science*, pages 141–183. Springer US, 2010.

[21] R. O'Donnell and Y. Wu. An optimal SDP algorithm for Max-Cut, and equally optimal long code tests. In *Proceedings of the 2008 ACM International Symposium on Theory of Computing*, Stoc'08, pages 335–344, 2008.

[22] J. Puchinger, G. R. Raidl, and U. Pferschy. The core concept for the multidimensional knapsack problem. *Evolutionary Computation in Combinatorial Optimization*, 3906:195–208, 2006.

[23] F. Rendl, G. Rinaldi, and A. Wiegele. Solving Max-Cut to optimality by intersecting semidefinite and polyhedral relaxations. *Mathematical Programming*, 121(2):307–335, 2010.

[24] M. G. C. Resende, C. C. Ribeiro, F. Glover, and R. Martí. Scatter search and path-relinking: Fundamentals, advances, and applications. In M. Gendreau and J.-Y. Potvin, editors, *Handbook of Metaheuristics*, volume 146 of *International Series in Operations Research & Management Science*, pages 87–107. Springer US, 2010.

[25] H. Wolkowicz, R. Saigal, and L. Vandenberghe. *Handbook of semidefinite programming: theory, algorithms, and applications.* International series in operations research & management science. Kluwer Academic Publishers, 2000.

Table 3: Computational Results for G-set

Prob	n	OBJ	HMA		SS	
			f_{best}	f_{avg}	f_{best}	f_{avg}
g1	800	11624	11624	11624	11624	11624
g2	800	11620	11620	11620	11620	11620
g3	800	11622	11622	**11622**	11622	11619.5
g4	800	11646	11646	**11646**	11646	11638.5
g5	800	11631	11631	**11631**	11631	11630.4
g6	800	2178	2178	**2178**	2178	2174.1
g7	800	2006	**2006**	**2006**	1996	1988.9
g8	800	2005	**2005**	**2005**	1996	1994.7
g9	800	2054	2054	**2053**	2054	2051.2
g10	800	2000	2000	1999.1	2000	1999.1
g11	800	564	558	558	**564**	**563.8**
g12	800	556	**556**	**552**	554	550.6
g13	800	580	578	**578**	578	575.8
g14	800	3061	3060	3058.1	[**3063**]	**3060.8**
g15	800	3050	**3049**	**3048.8**	3040	3036.8
g16	800	3052	**3050**	**3048.8**	3044	3043.7
g17	800	3046	**3045**	**3043.6**	3040	3038.4
g18	800	991	989	**986.9**	**991**	985.8
g19	800	904	[**906**]	**904.1**	[905]	898.9
g20	800	941	941	941	941	941
g21	800	931	931	930.9	931	**931**
g22	2000	13359	**13358**	**13349.8**	13349	13314.8
g23	2000	13342	**13337**	**13329.3**	13323	13312.6
g24	2000	13337	**13330**	**13321.8**	13318	13307.8
g25	2000	13332	**13330**	**13322**	13320	13313.8
g26	2000	13328	**13323**	**13310**	13308	13299.7
g27	2000	3336	**3334**	**3325.8**	3332	3312
g28	2000	3295	**3294**	**3286.9**	3275	3264.9
g29	2000	3391	[**3404**]	**3386.5**	3385	3376
g30	2000	3403	[**3407**]	**3402.8**	3395	3384.5
g31	2000	3288	[**3305**]	**3296.3**	3275	3265.8
g32	2000	1406	1396	1392.2	**1400**	**1393.2**
g33	2000	1378	**1372**	**1368.4**	1364	1359.4
g34	2000	1378	**1378**	**1375**	1368	1361.6
g35	2000	7678	[**7680**]	**7673**	7654	7648.5
g36	2000	7670	**7670**	**7665.7**	7667	7654.5
g37	2000	7682	**7682**	**7674.6**	7667	7660.3
g38	2000	7683	**7678**	**7669.9**	7668	7659.8
g39	2000	2397	[**2406**]	**2396.9**	2395	2388
g40	2000	2390	[**2393**]	**2389.2**	2380	2375.9
g41	2000	2400	[**2405**]	**2401.7**	2391	2385.7
g42	2000	2469	[**2478**]	**2469.1**	2462	2458.1
g43	1000	6660	6660	**6658.7**	6660	6656.2
g44	1000	6648	[6650]	**6649.7**	[6650]	6648.8
g45	1000	6652	[**6654**]	**6650.1**	6646	6643
g46	1000	6649	**6649**	**6645.8**	6647	6640.4
g47	1000	6665	**6656**	**6655.2**	6655	6652.9
g48	3000	6000	**6000**	**6000**	-	-
g49	3000	6000	**6000**	**6000**	-	-
g50	3000	5880	**5880**	**5880**	-	-
g51	1000	3847	**3847**	**3843.9**	3843	3839.4
g52	1000	3849	**3848**	**3844.8**	3841	3836.1
g53	1000	3848	[**3849**]	**3844.9**	3845	3844.3
g54	1000	3851	3845	3842.5	**3849**	**3846.4**

Table 4: Computational Results for DIMACS-set

Prob	n	OBJ	HMA	SS
pm-8-50	512	454	[458]	[458]
pm3-15-50	3375	2964	**919**	914
g3-8	512	41,684,814	**41,684,814**	41,634,364
g3-15	3375	281,029,888	[**284,527,624**]	282,692,960

A Parameterized Runtime Analysis of Evolutionary Algorithms for MAX-2-SAT

Andrew M. Sutton Jareth Day Frank Neumann

School of Computer Science
University of Adelaide
Adelaide, SA 5005, Australia
{andrew.sutton, jareth.day, frank.neumann}@adelaide.edu.au

ABSTRACT

We investigate the MAX-2-SAT problem and study evolutionary algorithms by parameterized runtime analysis. The parameterized runtime analysis of evolutionary algorithms has been initiated recently and reveals new insights into which type of instances of NP-hard combinatorial optimization problems are hard to solve by evolutionary computing methods. We show that a variant of the (1+1) EA is a fixed-parameter evolutionary algorithm with respect to the standard parameterization for MAX-2-SAT. Furthermore, we study how the dependencies between the variables affect problem difficulty and present fixed-parameter evolutionary algorithms for the MAX-(2,3)-SAT problem where the studied parameter is the diameter of the variable graph.

Categories and Subject Descriptors

F.2 [**Theory of Computation**]: Analysis of Algorithms and Problem Complexity

General Terms

Theory, Algorithms, Performance

Keywords

Combinatorial Optimization, MAXSAT, Theory, Runtime Analysis

1. INTRODUCTION

Bio-inspired computing methods such as evolutionary algorithms [5] and ant colony optimization [3] have been widely used for problems from combinatorial optimization. The mentioned algorithms iteratively try to improve currently best solutions during the optimization process and heavily rely on the use of randomness for creating new solutions and/or selecting solutions for the next iteration. Treating evolutionary algorithms as a special type of randomized algorithms allows them to be analyzed in a rigorous way. We contribute to this line of research which has been very successful during the last 15 years. This includes results on artificial functions that rigorously point out the working principles of bio-inspired algorithms as well as results for a wide range of classical combinatorial optimization problems. A comprehensive presentation of such results can be found in [1, 11].

Recently, evolutionary algorithms have been analyzed in the framework of fixed-parameter tractability [4]. Here an additional parameter to measure the hardness of an instance is taken into account. Initial results in the field of evolutionary algorithms have been obtained for two NP-hard combinatorial optimization problems, namely the vertex cover problem [10] and the problem of computing a spanning tree with a maximal number of leaves [9]. We want to push forward this relatively young line of research as it allows one to figure out which type of instances of a given (NP-hard) combinatorial optimization problem is provably easy to solve by evolutionary algorithms. Consequently, our runtime analysis will take into account the size of the given problem denoted by n (as usual for the analysis of algorithms) and an additional parameter k which measures the difficulty of an instance.

We study the well-known MAX-SAT problem. MAX-SAT is already NP-hard if the clauses have two variables as this corresponds to the optimization of quadratic pseudo-Boolean functions. We consider MAX-2-SAT and analyze the runtime behavior of evolutionary algorithms for this problem with respect to the standard parameterization, i.e. the value of an optimal solution. Our analysis takes into account results on the fitness landscape of such instances [13] by introducing a mutation operator that obeys Grover's wave equation [8] for MAX-2-SAT which has the interesting side-effect of an existence proof of an *elementary landscape* for the MAX-2-SAT problem. To our knowledge, this result is novel. We employ this difference equation to show that the (1+1) EA is a fixed-parameter algorithm for the standard parameterization of MAX-2-SAT. This bridges for the first time the field of runtime analysis and the study of landscapes in the field of theory of evolutionary computation.

Afterwards, we turn our attention the MAX-(2,3)-SAT problem which is an NP-hard subclass of MAX-2-SAT. We consider a parameterization which takes into account the degree of dependencies between the different variables. In the variable graph of a given MAX-(2,3)-SAT problem, the nodes are given by the Boolean variables of the problem and there is an edge between any pair of variables if they are present in the same clause. The parameter that we analyze is the diameter of the variable graph. We show that the (1+1) EA is a randomized XP-algorithm for this problem and show how a more global search behavior taking into account the variable graph can lead to fixed-parameter randomized algorithms. Furthermore, we explore different more local evolutionary algorithms working on the variable graph and show that these are fixed-parameter evolutionary algorithms for MAX-(2,3)-SAT.

The content of the paper is as follows. In Section 2, we introduce the MAX-2-SAT problem and the concept of parameterized analysis. In Section 3, we show that the classical (1+1) EA is a fixed-parameter evolutionary algorithm with respect to the standard parameterization. Section 4 analyzes the MAX-(2,3)-SAT problem parameterized by the diameter of the variable graph and shows that evolutionary algorithms are fixed-parameter algorithms for this problem. Furthermore, we present additional fixed-parameter evolutionary algorithms acting more locally for the MAX-(2,3)-SAT in Section 5. We summarize our findings with some concluding remarks.

2. PRELIMINARIES

The maximum 2-satisfiability problem (MAX-2-SAT) is a classic optimization problem in which, given a Boolean formula in conjunctive normal form where each clause is of cardinality exactly two,[1] one must find an assignment to its variables that satisfies the maximum number of clauses. Despite its apparent simplicity, the MAX-2-SAT problem belongs to the class of NP-hard problems [7].

An instance of a MAX-2-SAT problem is represented as a collection of m unique clauses

$$\mathscr{C} = \{(\ell_{1,1} \vee \ell_{1,2}), (\ell_{2,1} \vee \ell_{2,2}), \ldots, (\ell_{m,1} \vee \ell_{m,2})\}$$

where each $\ell_{i,j}$ is a Boolean variable or its negation. The set of all assignments to a set of n Boolean variables is isomorphic to $\{0,1\}^n$ by interpreting each position of the string as the state of exactly one Boolean variable v_i (i.e., a 1 corresponds to $v_i = \mathit{true}$; a 0 corresponds to $v_i = \mathit{false}$). Thus, given a MAX-2-SAT instance with n variables and m clauses, we represent candidate solutions to the instance as length-n bitstrings and define the function[2] $f : \{0,1\}^n \to \{0\} \cup [m]$ where $f(x)$ counts the elements in $\mathscr{C}$ that are satisfied under the assignment corresponding to $x \in \{0,1\}^n$. The task is then reduced to the optimization of a pseudo-Boolean function f.

In this paper we rigorously analyze the runtime character of the (1+1) EA maximizing the pseudo-Boolean function f. The (1+1) EA is defined as follows.

Algorithm 1: The (1+1) EA.

```
Choose x uniformly at random from {0,1}^n;
repeat forever
    x' ← mutate(x);
    if f(x') ≥ f(x) then x ← x'
```

[1]Some authors refer to this as MAX-E2-SAT.

[2]For a natural number n, throughout the paper we denote the set $\{1, \ldots, n\}$ as $[n]$.

The `mutate()` procedure is a randomized operator that negates some elements of the current string to produce a new string. Since the (1+1) EA relies on random decisions, we consider it as a special case of a *randomized algorithm*. We view the (1+1) EA as an infinite stochastic process $(x^{(1)}, x^{(2)}, \ldots)$ where $x^{(t)}$ denotes the string that the (1+1) EA produces in iteration t. For a given instance of MAX-2-SAT, let $f^{\max} = \max_{x \in \{0,1\}^n} f(x)$. We denote as T the lowest value of t such that $f(x^{(t)}) = f^{\max}$. T is a discrete random variable over $\mathbb{N}$, and we can measure the expected *optimization time* of the (1+1) EA as $E(T)$, the expectation of T.

Recently, the concept of *parameterized analysis* has been introduced into the theoretical analysis of evolutionary algorithms [10, 9]. Parameterized analysis allows for a more detailed understanding of the source of runtime complexity for NP-hard combinatorial optimization problems. A parameterized analysis expresses the runtime of an algorithm not only in terms of the size of the problem, but also as a function of a parameter that somehow measures the difficulty of the problem.

A *parameterized problem* (L, κ) consists of a language L over a finite alphabet Σ and a *parameterization* $\kappa : \Sigma^* \to \mathbb{N}$. (L, κ) is *fixed-parameter tractable* if there is an algorithm that decides $x \in L$ in time bounded by $g(\kappa(x)) \cdot |x|^{O(1)}$ where $g : \mathbb{N} \to \mathbb{N}$ is an arbitrary recursive function. Such an algorithm is called an *fpt-algorithm* and the problem class FPT consists of all decision problems that can be decided by an fpt-algorithm. A problem L is in the class XP if there is an algorithm that decides $x \in L$ in time bounded by $|x|^{g(\kappa(x))}$ for some computable function g.

A *Monte Carlo fpt-algorithm* for (L, κ) is a randomized fpt-algorithm such that for all $x \in \Sigma^*$ that in time bounded by $g(\kappa(x)) \cdot |x|^{O(1)}$ will accept x with probability at least $1/2$ if $x \in L$ and with probability 0 if $x \notin L$. Similarly, a *Monte Carlo* XP-*algorithm* for (L, κ) is a randomized algorithm that, for all $x \in \Sigma^*$, if $x \in L$ accepts x with probability at least $1/2$ in time $|x|^{g(\kappa(x))}$, otherwise it accepts with probability 0.

An evolutionary algorithm is a *fixed-parameter evolutionary algorithm* for a parameterized problem (L, κ) if its expected optimization time $E(T)$ is bounded above by $g(\kappa(x)) \cdot |x|^{O(1)}$. Similarly, an evolutionary algorithm is an XP *evolutionary algorithm* if its runtime is bounded above by $|x|^{g(\kappa(x))}$. We will later see that when the parameterization is related to the optimal solution of a combinatorial optimization problem, then a fixed-parameter evolutionary algorithm can be transformed into a Monte Carlo fpt-algorithm.

3. MAX-2-SAT

We now introduce a simple parameterized result for the (1+1) EA that connects the field of runtime analysis to the study of fitness landscapes. We devise a particular mutation operator that allows the (1+1) EA to at least make local improvements in such a way that it is guaranteed to reach a solution of a specific fitness in expected polynomial time.

3.1 Uniform-complement mutation

The standard (uniform) mutation operator in the traditional implementation of the (1+1) EA generates an offspring of $x \in \{0,1\}^n$ by flipping each bit of x with probability $1/n$. In *uniform-complement* mutation, we proceed similarly, except we also include with constant probability the *complement* of x, that is, the string obtained by flipping all bits of x.

Function `uniform-complement-mutate(x)`

```
y ← x;
choose r ∈ [0,1] uniformly at random;
if r < 1/2 then
    flip each bit of y with probability 1/n;
else
    flip each bit of y with probability 1;
return y;
```

We point out that uniform mutation can also generate the complement of x with finite probability. The distinction is that the probability of obtaining the complement of x under uniform-complement mutation is a constant, whereas it is $O(n^{-n})$ under uniform mutation. This constant probability to generate the complement is vital to our analysis.

The uniform-complement operator induces a connectivity on $\{0,1\}^n$ which obeys a strict difference equation from the theory of landscapes usually attributed to Grover [8] on MAX-2-SAT. This property will allow us to prove that the (1+1) EA discovers solutions of a certain quality in polynomial time.

Consider a MAX-2-SAT problem with n variables and m clauses. Given an element $x \in \{0,1\}^n$, we denote $N(x)$ as the set constructed from taking the union of immediate Hamming neighbors of x and the complement of x. We have the following result

Lemma 1. *For all $x \in \{0,1\}^n$,*

$$\sum_{y \in N(x)} f(y) = 3m + (n-3)f(x).$$

PROOF. Denote as $c_i : \{0,1\}^n \to \{0,1\}$ the indicator function that evaluates to 1 if and only if clause i is satisfied by the assignment corresponding to x.

If the i-th clause is not satisfied by x, then there are exactly three elements $y \in N(x)$ under which it is satisfied: the two distinct Hamming neighbors that negate each variable appearing in the clause, and the element corresponding to the complement of x, which negates both variables in the clause.

If the i-th clause is satisfied by x then at least one of its literals evaluates to true under x. In the case that exactly one of its literals evaluates to true, then there is exactly one element $y \in N(x)$ in which the clause is not satisfied (corresponding to the negation of the variable involved in the true literal). If both its literals evaluate to true under x, then there is exactly one element in $N(x)$ such that the clause is not satisfied (corresponding to the complement of x). Hence we can write c_i as

$$\sum_{y \in N(x)} c_i(y) = 3(1-c_i(x)) + (|N(x)|-1)c_i(x) = 3 + (n-3)c_i(x).$$

Since $f(x) = \sum_{i=1}^m c_i(x)$, we have

$$\sum_{y \in N(x)} f(y) = \sum_{i=1}^{m} (3 + (n-3)c_i(x)) = 3m + (n-3)f(x).$$

This completes the proof. □

Lemma 1 states that Grover's equation holds for MAX-2-SAT under uniform-complement mutation. Equivalently, this means that the fitness landscape induced by the uniform-complement operator and that MAX-2-SAT fitness function corresponds to an *elementary landscape* [14]. The existence of a move operator that induces an elementary landscape for the MAX-2-SAT problem was, to our knowledge, previously unknown. One immediate result we can obtain from this condition is that solutions of certain quality can be generated in polynomial time by making local improvements. This is due to the fact that, on such a landscape, local optima (with respect to N) cannot have arbitrarily poor fitness.

Lemma 2. *The (1+1) EA using uniform-complement mutation finds a solution x' where $f(x') \geq \frac{3}{4}m$ after an expected $O(mn)$ iterations.*

PROOF. We first prove that after a polynomial number of mutation steps, the (1+1) EA has reached a solution x' such that for all $y \in N(x')$, $f(y) \leq f(x')$. Let x be the current state generated by the (1+1) EA . If there are no states $y \in N(x)$ with strictly improving fitness, then clearly $x' = x$.

On the other hand, suppose there exists at least one state $y \in N(x)$ with $f(y) > f(x)$. We show that in this case, the probability that mutation generates the specific improving state in $N(x)$ is $\Omega(1/n)$. We make the following case distinction.

Case 1. The complement of x is an improving state. In this case, uniform-complement mutation generates an improving state with probability at least 1/2.

Case 2. A Hamming neighbor of x is an improving state. The mutation operator generates a specific Hamming neighbor with probability

$$\frac{1}{2}\left[\frac{1}{n}\left(1-\frac{1}{n}\right)^{n-1}\right] \geq \frac{1}{2en} = \Omega(1/n).$$

It follows that the waiting time to make an improvement from such a state is at most $O(n)$. The number of improvements made by the (1+1) EA is bounded by the cardinality of the codomain. Hence the (1+1) EA can reach a state x' such that no improving moves exist in $N(x')$ in expected time bounded by $O(mn)$.

It is now straightforward to show that Lemma 1 entails a bound on the fitness of x'. In particular, consider

$$\frac{1}{|N(x')|} \sum_{y \in N(x)} f(y) \leq f(x'),$$

since otherwise the assumption that no improving states exist in $N(x')$ would be contradicted. By Lemma 1,

$$\frac{1}{|N(x')|}(3m + (n-3)f(x')) \leq f(x'),$$

and since $|N(x')| = n+1$,

$$\frac{3m}{(n+1)} + \frac{(n-3)}{(n+1)} f(x') \leq f(x').$$

It follows from simple algebraic manipulation of the above inequality that $f(x') \geq \frac{3}{4}m$ which completes the proof. □

The above result depends on the fact that, on MAX-2-SAT, the complement operation can escape certain lower-quality states that the Hamming neighborhood cannot. It is possible to have a state with no improving Hamming neighbors that *does not* satisfy the quality bound of $\frac{3}{4}m$. As an example, consider a Boolean formula constructed as follows. Let $A_{i,j}$ be the 3-set of clauses defined on two variables v_i and v_j

$$A_{i,j} = \{(\neg v_i \vee \neg v_j), (\neg v_i \vee v_j), (v_i \vee \neg v_j)\}.$$

We construct a MAX-2-SAT instance on $2q$ variables by taking the union of q 3-sets of clauses

$$A_{1,2} \cup A_{3,4} \cup \cdots \cup A_{2q-1,2q}.$$

Thus for this instance, $m = 3q$. Let $\hat{x} = (111 \cdots 1)$ be the length-$2q$ bitstring of all ones. The assignment corresponding to $\hat{x}$ satisfies the two clauses in each set $A_{i,j}$ that contain non-negated variables.

Consider a Hamming neighbor of $\hat{x}$ that is generated by flipping some bit i that, without loss of generality, corresponds to variable v_i of the instance. Since v_i only appears in clauses that are in $A_{i,j}$, it suffices to inspect the effect on $A_{i,j}$. In this case, the clause $(\neg v_i \vee \neg v_j)$ becomes satisfied, while the clause $(v_i \vee \neg v_j)$ becomes unsatisfied. The clause $(\neg v_i \vee v_j)$ remains satisfied and so the number of satisfied clauses of the instance remains the same under the Hamming neighbor. Hence no Hamming neighbor of $\hat{x}$ can be an improving state. Since $\hat{x}$ satisfies 2 clauses in each set $A_{i,j}$, we have

$$f(\hat{x}) = 2q = \frac{2}{3}m < \frac{3}{4}m.$$

In this example, however, the state generated by taking the complement of $\hat{x}$ satisfies all m clauses.

3.2 Standard parameterization

Assuming maximization, given a combinatorial optimization problem Q with maximum evaluation OPT_Q, the *standard parameterization* of Q is the parameterized problem where, given an instance of Q of size n and a parameter k, the task is to decide whether $OPT_Q \geq k$ [6]. Using the previous results, we now show that the (1+1) EA, under uniform-complement mutation, is a fixed-parameter evolutionary algorithm with respect to the standard parameterization of MAX-2-SAT.

Theorem 1. *The (1+1) EA using uniform-complement mutation solves the standard parameterization of MAX-2-SAT with n variables and m clauses in $O\left(\max\{mn, k^{2.67 \cdot k}\}\right)$ expected time.*

Furthermore, after $O(\max\{mn^2, nk^{2.67 \cdot k}\})$ iterations, the (1+1) EA using uniform-complement mutation has solved the standard parameterization of MAX-2-SAT almost surely.

Proof. Let T denote the random variable that corresponds to the first time that the (1+1) EA using uniform-complement mutation has solved the standard parameterization of MAX-2-SAT.

We make the following case distinction. First, suppose that $m \geq \frac{4}{3}k$. In this case, by Lemma 2, (1+1) EA has found a solution $f(x) \geq \frac{3}{4}m \geq k$ after an expected $O(mn)$ steps and hence $E(T) = O(mn)$. Now suppose that $m < \frac{4}{3}k$. Since there are at most $2m$ variables, the number of variables n is bounded by $\frac{8}{3}k$. The probability that the (1+1) EA transforms an arbitrary assignment into an optimal assignment is at least $(1/n)^n \geq ((8/3)k)^{-(8/3)k}$. In this case $E(T) = O(k^{2.67 \cdot k})$ which is a function that depends only on k.

For the tail bound, we need only to appeal to the Markov inequality (see, e.g., [2]) which states that, for a non-negative random variable T, $\Pr(T \geq \lambda E(T)) \leq \lambda^{-1}$ for all $\lambda \geq 1$. Suppose $m \geq \frac{4}{3}k$. Letting $c \geq 1$ be an arbitrary constant, by the Markov inequality we have

$$\Pr(T \geq cmn^2) \leq 1/cn.$$

In the case that $m < \frac{4}{3}k$,

$$\Pr(T \geq cnk^{2.67 \cdot k}) \leq 1/cn.$$

Hence the probability that the (1+1) EA has solved the standard parameterization in $O(\max\{mn^2, nk^{2.67 \cdot k}\})$ steps is $1 - o(1)$. □

Note that in the case of the standard parameterization, a fixed-parameter evolutionary algorithm can be transformed into a Monte Carlo fpt-algorithm as follows. If $OPT_Q \leq k$, then the probability that the fixed-parameter evolutionary algorithm finds the optimal solution in $2E(T)$ is at least 1/2 by the Markov inequality. On the other hand, if $OPT_Q > k$, no solution of fitness at most k exists. Therefore running the evolutionary algorithm for twice the expected runtime yields a Monte Carlo fpt-algorithm for the decision problem.

4. MAX-(2,3)-SAT

We now turn our attention to more interesting parameterizations. In particular, we introduce a variant of MAX-2-SAT that we can analyze with respect to a parameter that somehow measures the source of complexity inherent in the structure of the problem itself.

The MAX-(2,3)-SAT problem is a restricted class of MAX-2-SAT in which each variable appears in at most 3 clauses of the formula. Though slightly more restrictive, the MAX-(2,3)-SAT problem is still NP-hard [12]. Thus, assuming P ≠ NP, the expected runtime of an evolutionary algorithm must be superpolynomial. We now perform a parameterized analysis of the (1+1) EA on the MAX-(2,3)-SAT problem in order to express the runtime as a function that isolates the source of the exponential complexity in a parameter.

Denote as $G(V, E)$ the *variable graph* of an instance where V corresponds to the set of variables and

$$E = \{\{u, v\} \subset V : u \text{ and } v \text{ appear together in a clause}\}.$$

We define the *diameter* of a (possibly disconnected) graph $G(V, E)$ as the maximum shortest-path distance in any of its connected components.

Lemma 3. *Consider a MAX-(2,3)-SAT formula in which the diameter of the variable graph is bounded by k. Then for any variable $v \in V$, the size of the connected component in $G(V, E)$ which contains v is bounded by $3 \cdot 2^k - 2$.*

Proof. Let v be an arbitrary variable. Denote as $C(v) \subseteq V$ the set of all nodes reachable on a path from v in G. Consider the breadth-first tree in G rooted at v. Since the degree of each vertex is bounded by 3 and the depth of the tree is bounded by k, there can be at most 3 children of the root, and each internal node can have at most 2 children. The number of nodes in this tree is hence bounded by

$$1 + 3 + 3 \cdot 2 + \cdots + 3 \cdot 2^{k-1} = 3 \cdot 2^k - 2 \geq |C(v)|.$$

Since the subgraph of $G(V,E)$ induced by $C(v)$ corresponds to the connected component containing v, the proof is complete. □

4.1 An XP evolutionary algorithm

Using Lemma 3, we can prove that as long as the diameter k of the variable graph is not too large, improving mutations are somehow close by in terms of Hamming distance. This results in an XP evolutionary algorithm in the parameter k, meaning that the expected runtime is bounded by a function of the form $n^{g(k)}$ where g depends only on k. We point out that the following theorem also follows from a result due to Wegener and Witt [15, Theorem 5.2] on separable quadratic functions with the slight modification that the size of the codomain of the fitness function can be restricted to $O(m)$.

Theorem 2. *Let F be a MAX-(2,3)-SAT formula where the diameter of the variable graph is bounded by k. Then the expected runtime of the (1+1) EA on F is bounded by $O(mn^{3\cdot 2^k-2})$. In other words, the (1+1) EA is an* XP *evolutionary algorithm for MAX-(2,3)-SAT.*

PROOF. The set of variables can be partitioned into sets $\mathcal{C} = \{C_1, C_2, \ldots, C_q\}$ representing the connected components in G. Consider the i-th component C_i. Denote as $f_i(x)$ the number of clauses containing a variable from C_i satisfied by the assignment corresponding to x and let

$$a_i = \max_{z\in\{0,1\}^n} f_i(z).$$

Since $\mathcal{C}$ partitions the clause set, optimal value of f is $a_1 + a_2 + \cdots + a_q$.

As long as $f(x)$ is suboptimal, there exists a component C_i such that $f_i(x) < a_i$. We show that in this case there always exists an improving move within a bounded Hamming distance. Let $z \in \{0,1\}^n$ be a string such that $f_i(z) = a_i$. Denoting as $x[j]$ the j-th component of the bitstring x and v_j the corresponding Boolean variable in V, we define the bitstring x' as follows.

$$x'[j] = \begin{cases} z[j] & \text{if } v_j \in C_i; \\ x[j] & \text{otherwise.} \end{cases}$$

It follows that $f_i(x') = f_i(z) = a_i$. Moreover, $\mathcal{C}$ partitions V, so $f_j(x) = f_j(x')$ for all $j \in [q] \setminus \{i\}$. Thus we have $f(x') = f(x) - f_i(x) + a_i$ and therefore $f(x') > f(x)$.

Let d denote the number of bits that differ between x and x'. The probability that the (1+1) EA transforms x into x' under uniform mutation is $(1/n)^d(1-1/n)^{n-d}$. Invoking Lemma 3, $d \le |C_i| \le 3 \cdot 2^k - 2$. Hence, as long as x is suboptimal, the probability of making an improving move is bounded below by $e^{-1}n^{-(3\cdot 2^k-2)}$. The number of steps until an improving move is found is thus distributed geometrically with expectation bounded by $O(n^{3\cdot 2^k-2})$. Finally, there are at most m suboptimal values of f, providing the claimed bound. □

4.2 A fixed-parameter evolutionary algorithm

In this section, we investigate a method to produce a fixed-parameter tractable algorithm for the MAX-(2,3)-SAT problem, yielding a runtime exponential in k but polynomial in n.

Following the format of the previous section, we consider the sets $\mathcal{C} = \{C_1, C_2, \ldots, C_q\}$ representing the connected

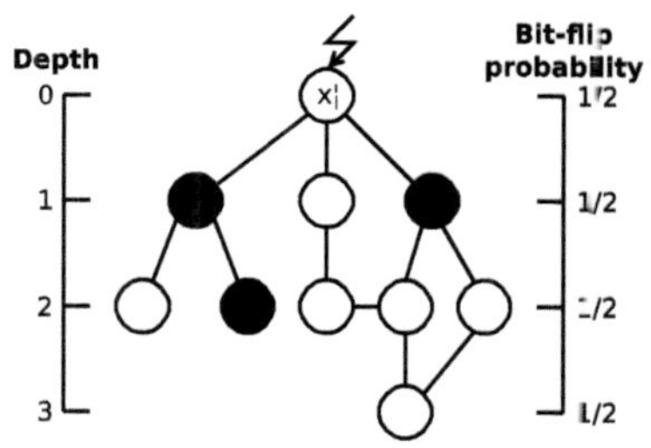

Figure 1: Probability characteristics of the Simple FPT (1+1) EA . Variable x'_i at depth 0 is the selected variable. White variables are flipped, black variables are unflipped.

components in $G(V,E)$. We use $f_i(x)$ to represent the number of clauses in component C_i satisfied by x, and a_i to represent the optimum value of f_i. We define the component which contains the Boolean variable v_j to be $C(v_j)$.

Algorithm 3: The FPT (1+1) EA.

1 Choose x uniformly at random from $\{0,1\}^n$;
2 **repeat** *forever*
3 $x' \leftarrow x$;
4 Select $i \in [n]$ uniformly at random;
5 Let v_i be the Boolean variable corresponding to element i of x;
6 Flip all bits of x' corresponding to $v_j \in C(v_i)$ with probability $\frac{1}{2}$;
7 **if** $f(x') \ge f(x)$ **then** $x \leftarrow x'$

Algorithm 3 uses the (1+1) EA structure as defined in Section 2. The mutation used in this FPT algorithm selects a bit of the solution uniformly at random and flips all bits within the selected variable's set with probability 1/2, as demonstrated by Figure 1. If the resultant solution is at least as fit as the original solution, the new solution replaces the original solution.

Theorem 3. *Let F be a MAX-(2,3)-SAT formula in which the diameter of the variable graph is bounded by k. Then the expected runtime of the FPT (1+1) EA on F is bounded by $O(n \log n \cdot 2^{(3\cdot 2^k-2)})$.*

PROOF. We analyze the waiting time to generate a solution that satisfies all the clauses in each connected component. Given a state x, a component C_i is *solved* by x if $f_i(x) = a_i$. Otherwise, it is *unsolved* by x. A solution is optimal if and only if it solves all the connected components of $G(V,E)$. From line 5 of Algorithm 3, if a variable is selected for flipping, each variable in its connected component in $G(V,E)$ will also be flipped with probability 1/2. If the mutation process selects a variable in an unsolved component C_i, the probability of generating a state that also solves C_i (and thus increases the overall fitness) is at least

$$(1/2)^{|C_i|} \ge (1/2)^{3\cdot 2^k-2}$$

since Lemma 3 appropriately bounds $|C_i|$.

Suppose that $j > 0$ connected components are unsolved by x. The probability that mutation selects a variable that belongs to an unsolved component is j/n. Hence the probability of producing a state that also solves at least one unsolved component is

$$\frac{j}{n} \cdot 2^{-(3 \cdot 2^k - 2)}.$$

Since only monotonically improving moves are accepted and $G(V, E)$ has at most n connected components, the total waiting time until all components are solved is bounded above by the series

$$\sum_{j=1}^{n} \frac{n}{j} \cdot 2^{3 \cdot 2^k - 2} = O(n \log n \cdot 2^{3 \cdot 2^k - 2}),$$

yielding the claimed result. □

5. ALTERNATIVE FPT ALGORITHMS

When the connected components of the variable graph are large, flipping all the variables within a component with constant probability is somewhat disruptive and thus contradicts the philosophy of a localized mutation operator since many variables are likely to be changed at once. Indeed, when there is a single connected component, Algorithm 3 essentially resorts to a uniform random search in $\{0, 1\}^n$. To address this, we introduce in this section three alternative fixed-parameter evolutionary algorithms which make less disruptive changes by attenuating the probability of changing variables that are further away in $G(V, E)$ from the variable selected for mutation.

5.1 Modified FPT (1+1) EA

The Modified FPT (1+1) EA utilizes probability attenuation in order to achieve a more natural solution that flips nodes with a lesser probability the further they are from the selected variable. This creates a more practical approach, albeit one with a greater upper bounds on the expected time to completion.

Algorithm 4: The Modified FPT (1+1) EA.

```
Choose x uniformly at random from {0,1}^n;
repeat forever
    x' ← x;
    Select i ∈ [n] uniformly at random;
    Let v_i be the Boolean variable corresponding to
    element i of x';
    S_u ← {v_i};
    S_v ← ∅;
    c ← 1;
    while S_u ≠ ∅ do
        Flip all bits of x' with corresponding variables in
        S_u with probability (1/2)^c;
        S_v ← S_v ∪ S_u;
        c ← c + 1;
        S_u ← {v ∈ V \ S_v : ∃({v, v'} ∈ E ∧ v' ∈ S_v)};
    if f(x') ≥ f(x) then x ← x'
```

The Modified FPT (1+1) EA detailed in Algorithm 4 has a decreasing probability of flipping bits the further they are from the selected bit. The mutation maintains a set of visited nodes S_v, and determines the set of unvisited adjacent nodes S_u. The bits in x' corresponding to Boolean variables in S_u are flipped with probability $1/2$ raised to the power of the distance from the originally selected variable v_i, as demonstrated by Figure 2. If the modified solution is at least as fit as the original solution, the new solution replaces the original solution.

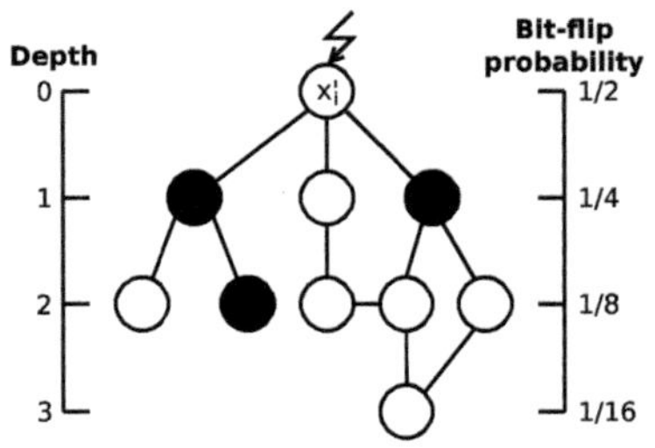

Figure 2: Probability characteristics of the Modified FPT (1+1) EA . Variable x_i' at depth 0 is the selected variable. White variables are flipped, black variables are unflipped.

Theorem 4. *Let F be a MAX-(2,3)-SAT formula in which the diameter of the variable graph is bounded by k. Then the expected runtime of the modified FPT (1+1) EA on F is bounded by $O(n \log n \cdot 2^{(3k \cdot 2^k - 2k)})$.*

Proof. As the diameter of the variable graph is bounded by k, the maximum graph distance from any selected variable to any other variable within the component is k. Thus, the probability to flip each bit is bounded below by $(1/2)^k$. With this, we may determine the runtime in the same manner as in Theorem 3.

Again, we say a connected component C_i is solved by a state x if $f_i(x) = a_i$. Suppose a variable in an unsolved component C_i is selected during mutation. The probability in this case of generating a state which solves C_i is at least

$$((1/2)^k)^{|C_i|} \geq (1/2)^{(3 \cdot 2^k - 2)k}$$

where the bound on $|C_i|$ comes from Lemma 3.

If $j > 0$ components are unsolved by x, the probability of producing a state that solves at least one of the components is

$$\frac{j}{n} \cdot 2^{(-(3 \cdot 2^k - 2)k)}.$$

Since there are at most n connected components in $G(V, E)$, the waiting time until all components are solved is bounded by the series

$$\sum_{j=1}^{n} \frac{n}{j} \cdot 2^{(3 \cdot 2^k - 2)k} = O(n \log n \cdot 2^{3k \cdot 2^k - 2k}),$$

thus providing the claimed runtime bound. □

5.2 Propagation FPT (1+1) EA

In this section, we propose two final FPT (1+1) EAs for the MAX-(2,3)-SAT problem. The algorithms presented by Algorithm 5 and 6 utilize probability propagation. Rather than flipping arbitrary nodes based on their distance from the selected variable, these algorithms flip only variables adjacent to previously flipped variables. This results in an algorithm with an easier implementation.

Algorithm 5, the Propagation FPT (1+1) EA, uses a local probability for each variable of $1/2$ rather than the global

Algorithm 5: The Propagation FPT (1+1) EA.

Choose x uniformly at random from $\{0,1\}^n$;
repeat *forever*
  $x' \leftarrow x$;
  Select $i \in [n]$ uniformly at random;
  Let v_i be the Boolean variable corresponding to element i of x';
  $S_u \leftarrow \{v_i\}$;
  $S_v \leftarrow \emptyset$;
  while $S_u \neq \emptyset$ **do**
    $S_f \leftarrow \emptyset$;
    foreach $v \in S_u$ **do**
      Choose $r \in [0,1]$ uniformly at random;
      if $r < \frac{1}{2}$ **then**
        Flip the bit of x' corresponding to v;
        $S_f \leftarrow S_f \cup \{v\}$;
    $S_v \leftarrow S_v \cup S_u$;
    $S_u \leftarrow \{v \in V \setminus S_v : \exists(\{v,v'\} \in E \wedge v' \in S_f)\}$;
  if $f(x') \geq f(x)$ **then** $x \leftarrow x'$

calculation from Algorithm 4. As before, the mutation maintains a set of visited nodes S_v, and determines the set of unvisited adjacent nodes S_u. In Algorithm 5, however, bits are flipped with probability 1/2, with flipped bits stored in a third set S_f. Propagation to the adjacent unvisited nodes only occurs if the current bit flips. The bits in x' corresponding to Boolean variables in S_u are thus flipped with probability 1/2 raised to the power of the distance from the originally selected variable v_i only if the previous bit was flipped. An example of this behaviour can be seen in Figure 3. If the modified solution is as least as fit as the original solution, the new solution replaces the original solution.

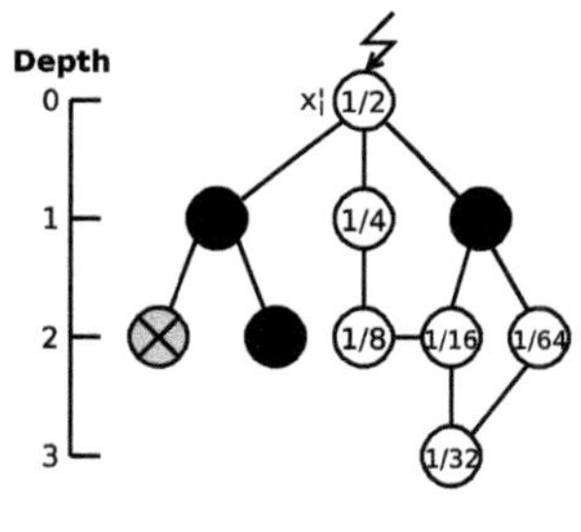

Figure 3: Probability characteristics of the Propagation FPT (1+1) EA . Variable x_i' at depth 0 is the selected variable. White variables are flipped, black variables are unflipped. The gray variable at depth 2 is unreachable and hence can not be flipped.

Theorem 5. *Let F be a MAX-(2,3)-SAT formula in which the diameter of the variable graph is bounded by k. Then the expected runtime of the propagation FPT (1+1) EA on F is bounded by $O(n \log n \cdot 2^{(3 \cdot 2^k - 2)^2})$.*

Proof. Suppose a variable v is selected for mutation. The variable negation process propagates out from v such that each subsequently flipped variable lies on a simple path of already-flipped variables of length d to v in $G(V,E)$. During this process, the variable is flipped only if its neighbor on the path to v was flipped, and in that case with probability 1/2. Therefore, the probability that the variable is flipped is $(1/2)^{d+1}$ for some $d > 0$. Since the length of a simple path in $G(V,E)$ is bounded above by the cardinality of its largest connected component, Lemma 3 applies and the probability the process flips a variable in the same connected component as v is at least $(1/2)^{3 \cdot 2^k - 2}$.

Let x be a suboptimal solution. If a variable in an unsolved component C_i is selected during mutation, the probability of generating a state which also solves C_i is at least

$$((1/2)^{3 \cdot 2^k - 2})^{|C_i|} \geq (1/2)^{(3 \cdot 2^k - 2)^2}.$$

The remainder of the proof follows the proof of Theorem 4 by imposing a bound on the probability of generating a new state x' in which at least one more component is solved than x. Again, if there are j unsolved components, the waiting time until such an improving move is generated is at most $(n/j) \cdot 2^{(3 \cdot 2^k - 2)^2}$. Since the number of connected components in $G(V,E)$ is at most n, summing over the waiting times yields the bound $O(n \log n \cdot 2^{(3 \cdot 2^k - 2)^2})$. □

This result is undesirable since it is somewhat larger than the runtime bound on Algorithm 4 given by Theorem 4. This can be solved by imposing a limit on the length of the path to the initial variable. Algorithm 6 performs this function by continuing to visit but not flipping variables along the path after an unflipped variable.

Algorithm 6: The Modified Propagation FPT (1+1) EA.

Choose x uniformly at random from $\{0,1\}^n$;
repeat *forever*
  $x' \leftarrow x$;
  Select $i \in [n]$ uniformly at random;
  Let v_i be the Boolean variable corresponding to element i of x';
  $S_u \leftarrow \{v_i\}$;
  $S_v \leftarrow \emptyset$;
  $S_d \leftarrow \emptyset$;
  while $S_u \neq \emptyset$ *and* $S_u \not\subset S_d$ **do**
    $S_f \leftarrow \emptyset$;
    foreach $v \in S_u \setminus S_d$ **do**
      Choose $r \in [0,1]$ uniformly at random;
      if $r < \frac{1}{2}$ **then**
        Flip the bit of x' corresponding to v;
        $S_f \leftarrow S_f \cup \{v\}$;
    $S_v \leftarrow S_v \cup S_u$;
    $S_u \leftarrow \{v \in V \setminus S_v : \exists(\{v,v'\} \in E \wedge v' \in S_v)\}$;
    $S_d \leftarrow S_d \cup (S_u \setminus S_f)$;
  if $f(x') \geq f(x)$ **then** $x \leftarrow x'$

This modification is implemented simply by marking the children of unflipped nodes as disallowed, unable to flip. By maintaining another set of disallowed variables S_d, the propagation algorithm investigates the variables in a tree-like search, maintaining the k bounds for the distance from the selected variable to any other. This modification creates a much stricter behaviour as demonstrated in Figure 4. Note that the probability propagation follows a directed acyclic path from the root to strictly deeper nodes. The probability of any node being flipped is dependent on at least one of its parents being flipped. The joint distribution of any component (or indeed any set of components) C can thus be written as

$$p(C) = \prod_{v \in C} p(v|\text{pa}(v)),$$

where $\text{pa}(v)$ is the set of parents of v, demonstrating that the graph is a Bayesian network.

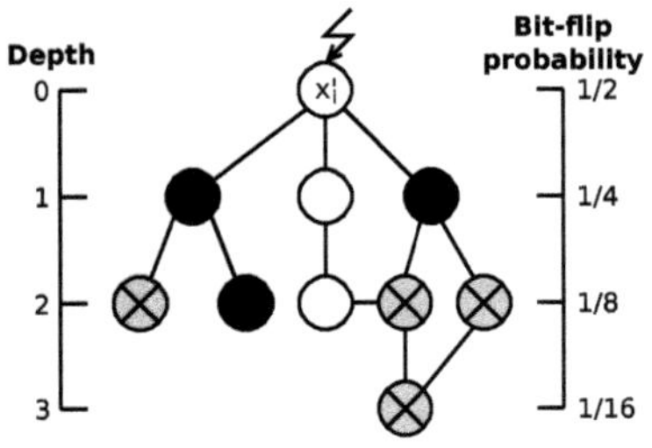

Figure 4: Probability characteristics of the Modified Propagation FPT (1+1) EA . Variable x'_i at depth 0 is the selected variable. White variables are flipped, black variables are unflipped. The gray elements at depth 2 and 3 are located after an unflipped variable and hence will also not be flipped. Note that one of the gray variables has an adjacent flipped node; to be viable for flipping, a variable must have a flipped parent at one depth shallower.

Theorem 6. *Let F be a MAX-(2,3)-SAT formula in which the diameter of the variable graph is bounded by k. Then the expected runtime of the modified propagation FPT (1+1) EA on F is bounded by $O(n \log n \cdot 2^{(3k \cdot 2^k - 2k)})$.*

PROOF. Each variable within a component is flipped with probability 1/2 if and only if its parent was also flipped. As the maximum path length of the propagation is bounded by k, this provides a lower bound on the probability for each bit flip of $(1/2)^k$. Using this probability, the rest of this proof proceeds exactly as in Theorem 4. □

6. CONCLUSION

The MAX-SAT problem is one of the most famous NP-hard optimization problems. The parameterized runtime analysis of evolutionary algorithms provides new insights into the behavior of evolutionary algorithms because it allows one to measure the difficulty of instances of an NP-hard combinatorial optimization problem by taking an additional parameter into account. In this paper, we have carried out a parameterized analysis of evolutionary algorithms for the MAX-2-SAT problem. Using results from the field of elementary landscapes, we have shown that the well-known (1+1) EA is a fixed-parameter algorithm with respect to the standard parameterization. Furthermore, we have analyzed the class of MAX-(2,3)-SAT problems with respect to the diameter of the variable graph. Our results show that the classical (1+1) EA is an XP-algorithm for this problem. Furthermore, we have shown that a mutation operator based on the structure of the variable graph leads to fixed-parameter evolutionary algorithms for this problem.

7. REFERENCES

[1] A. Auger and B. Doerr, editors. *Theory of Randomized Search Heuristics: Foundations and Recent Developments.* World Scientific, 2011.

[2] B. Doerr. Analyzing randomized search heuristics: Tools from probability theory. In Auger and Doerr [1].

[3] M. Dorigo and T. Stützle. *Ant Colony Optimization.* MIT Press, 2004.

[4] R. G. Downey and M. R. Fellows. *Parameterized Complexity.* Springer, 1999.

[5] A. Eiben and J. Smith. *Introduction to Evolutionary Computing.* Springer, 2nd edition, 2007.

[6] J. Flum and M. Grohe. *Parameterized complexity theory.* Springer-Verlag, 2006.

[7] M. R. Garey, D. S. Johnson, and L. J. Stockmeyer. Some simplified NP-complete graph problems. *Theoretical Computer Science,* 1(3):237–267, 1976.

[8] L. K. Grover. Local search and the local structure of NP-complete problems. *Operations Research Letters,* 12:235–243, 1992.

[9] S. Kratsch, P. K. Lehre, F. Neumann, and P. S. Oliveto. Fixed parameter evolutionary algorithms and maximum leaf spanning trees: A matter of mutation. In R. Schaefer, C. Cotta, J. Kolodziej, and G. Rudolph, editors, *Eleventh International Conference on Parallel Problem Solving from Nature (PPSN XI),* volume 6238 of *Lecture Notes in Computer Science,* pages 204–213. Springer, 2010.

[10] S. Kratsch and F. Neumann. Fixed-parameter evolutionary algorithms and the vertex cover problem. In *Proceedings of the Eleventh Annual Conference on Genetic and Evolutionary Computation,* GECCO '09, pages 293–300, New York, NY, USA, 2009. ACM.

[11] F. Neumann and C. Witt. *Bioinspired Computation in Combinatorial Optimization – Algorithms and Their Computational Complexity.* Springer, 2010.

[12] V. Raman, B. Ravikumar, and S. S. Rao. A simplified NP-complete MAXSAT problem. *Information Processing Letters,* 65(1):1–6, 1998.

[13] C. M. Reidys and P. F. Stadler. Combinatorial landscapes. *SIAM Review,* 44:3–54, 2002.

[14] P. F. Stadler. Toward a theory of landscapes. In R. Lopéz-Peña, R. Capovilla, R. García-Pelayo, H. Waelbroeck, and F. Zertruche, editors, *Complex Systems and Binary Networks,* pages 77–163. Springer Verlag, 1995.

[15] I. Wegener and C. Witt. On the analysis of a simple evolutionary algorithm on quadratic pseudo-Boolean functions. *Journal of Discrete Algorithms,* 3(1):61–78, 2005.

A Hybrid Metaheuristic Algorithm for Flexible Job-Shop Scheduling Problems with Transportation Constraints

Qiao Zhang
University of Technology of Belfort-Montbéliard
90000 Belfort, France
qiao.zhang@utbm.fr

Hervé Manier
University of Technology of Belfort-Montbéliard
90000 Belfort, France
herve.manier@utbm.fr

Marie-Ange Manier
University of Technology of Belfort-Montbéliard
90000 Belfort, France
marie-ange.manier@utbm.fr

ABSTRACT

In this paper, we aim at solving flexible job shop scheduling problems with transportation constraints and bounded processing times. We propose a hybrid method of genetic algorithm, tabu local search and a modified shifting bottleneck procedure. The genetic algorithm is used to generate and evolve assignment for each task (processing tasks and transportation tasks). The modified shifting bottleneck procedure is used to generate initial solutions and regenerate solutions when no improvement occurs during some generations. The tabu local search is then used to improve initial solutions during a limited number of iterations. To evaluate solutions, we elaborate a modified disjunctive graph which contains not only processing nodes, but also transportation and storage nodes. There are positive and negative arcs for bounded processing times, transportation times and minimum and maximum allowed storage time before and after each processing task. Our objective is to minimize makespan. Various types of instances with fixed or bounded processing times are tested. Computational results show that this hybrid method is able to solve efficiently these kinds of problems.

Categories and Subject Descriptors

I.2.8 [**Problem Solving, Control Methods, and Search**]: Scheduling

Keywords

Job shop scheduling problem, bounded processing times, transportation constraint, genetic algorithm, tabu search, shifting bottleneck procedure

GECCO'12, July 7-11, 2012, Philadelphia, Pennsylvania, USA.

1. INTRODUCTION

During the last decades, more and more complex production systems have been used for various types of productions. These automatized systems can be mainly classified as Flexible Manufacturing Systems (FMSs), Robotic Cells (RCs) and Surface Treatment Facilities (STF). The scheduling problems in these systems may have different characteristics: fixed or bounded processing times, transportation constraints, existence of buffers among machines or not, and so on. Most previous researches were dedicated to solve one associated type of problems. [3] considered a job shop problem in FMS with two available transport resources. A time window approach is proposed to schedule machines and material handling system. [10] studied the same problem by using a simple metaheuristic approach. [11] extended this problem with flexible machines which means that each processing task can be assigned to one among two machines. A dynamic heuristic is proposed to solve this flexible job shop problem (FJSP) with transportation. [8] and [7] analyzed the complexity of finding cyclic schedules in robotic flowshop cells. [14] proposed a two-stage local search for solving a job shop problem with a single robot in a robotic cell. In surface treatment facilities, Hoist Scheduling Problems (HSPs) are considered. [18] were the first ones to study 1-degree cyclic HSP (CHSP) with a single hoist. A branch and bound based mixed integer linear programming was applied to solve it. [20] considered the same problem but with dissociated loading and unloading stations. [6] applied a branch and bound method to find multi-degree cyclic schedules for CHSP with one hoist. [16] considered one part-type CHSP with two hoists. A multi part-type CHSP problem was treated by [17]. [13] extended this problem for more complex lines and also to find n-degree cycles ([12]). [5] studied the predictive HSP by using a disjunctive graph representation and a modified shifting bottleneck procedure. But the number of hoists was unlimited. We previously applied this shifting bottleneck for multi-hoists HSP ([21]). A modified disjunctive graph was proposed. It contains transportation nodes for taking into account schedules of hoists.

In recent literature, few researches consider a general model which can incorporate various kinds of problems encountered in those different systems. We have already used a hybrid method of genetic algorithm and tabu search for several kinds of problems ([22]). But it is less efficient for hoist scheduling problem which requires zero storage strictly. In this paper, we improve our initial disjunctive graph representation so as to model and solve not only the problems in

FMS, but also in RC and STF. This graph will be described in section 2. A hybrid metaheuristic method is proposed to solve these problems (section 3). Various types of instances are tested and results are shown and analyzed in section 4. The conclusion and perspective are given in section 5.

2. PROBLEM REPRESENTATION

In this section, we first describe the considered general model and then a proposed disjunctive graph representation is presented.

2.1 Description of a general model

The considered problem consists in a set of n jobs ($J = J_1, J_2, ..., J_n$), a set of m machines ($M = M_1, M_2, ..., M_m$), a set of h transport resources ($R = R_1, R_2, ..., R_h$) and a set of buffers allowing storage before and after each processing task ($S = S^-_{ij} \cup S^+_{ij}, i \in [1, n], j \in [1, n_i]$). Each job J_i follows a set of successive operations ($O_{i1}, O_{i2}, ..., O_{i,n_i}$). Each operation O_{ij} can be performed on one machine chosen from a set $MR_{ij} \subset M$ without preemption and its processing times is bounded $[p^-_{ij}, p^+_{ij}]$. The lower bounds may equal the upper bounds or not. The upper bounds may take infinite or finite values. The loaded transportation task after O_{ij} is labeled T_{ij}, and its duration is v_{ij}. It can be performed by any transport resource. Loaded travel time t^+_{ij} and empty travel time t^-_{ij} from M_i to M_j are given. A transportation resource must have enough time to travel empty between two loaded moves. Capacities of machines and transport resources are unitary and each job can only be treated on one resource for each task.

The objective is to solve both assignment and scheduling problems for the various considered systems, while respecting processing time constraints, travel time constraints, and/or storage requirement, and/or no wait constraint. The main objective to minimize is the makespan. The whole notation and mathematical model can be found in [22]. Considering the complexity of such a model, we chose to adopt a metaheuristic solving algorithm. This one is coupled with other technics to address the various kinds of considered scheduling problems.

2.2 Disjunctive graph representation

There exist already researches using disjunctive graphs for dedicated problems. Most applications of disjunctive graphs are for scheduling problems with fixed processing times. [4] used a classical disjunctive graph machine representation for the job shop scheduling problem. [14] proposed a graph containing nodes of processing and transport tasks for the job-shop problem in a robotic cell with a single transport resource. [15] extended it for problems with several robots. Other researches considered bounded processing times. [19] proposed a modified disjunctive graph containing processing nodes and adding negative arcs for representing maximum processing times. It can represent HSPs encountered in surface treatment facilities (STF). However the number of hoists is unlimited and empty travel times are not taken into account in a realistic way. In [21] and [23], we modified this graph by adding transportation nodes. This representation can easily model HSP solutions both for machines and transport resources. However, it is not adapted for solutions with storage, which are feasible for other production systems (FMS and RC). Until now, no graph representation exists to model various kinds of scheduling problems encountered in various systems, like flexible manufacturing systems (FMS), robotic cells (RC) and STF. For this purpose, we propose a new modified disjunctive graph. It contains three types of nodes: processing nodes, transportation tasks nodes and storage nodes.

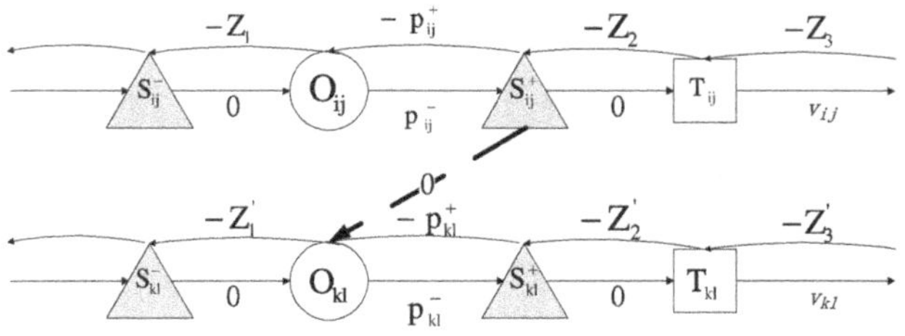

Figure 1: Arbitration of the disjunction between two processing tasks

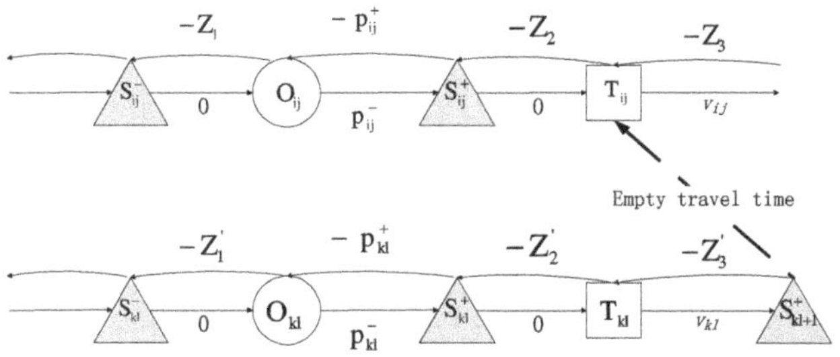

Figure 2: Arbitration of the disjunction between two transportation tasks

Figures 1 and 2 show the way to arbitrate a disjunction in our proposed graph. In this graph, round, squared and triangular nodes represent processing tasks, transportation tasks and storage respectively. Right forward arcs with zero or positive values on them represent constraints on job processing sequences. Values on inverse arcs represent maximum time limit constraints for processing times, transportation times, and storage times. Table 1 shows various possibilities for those values according to the systems and associated constraints. This flexibility allows the graph to represent various types of problems.

Table 1: Various values according to constraints

Constraints	associated systems	Z_1	p^+_{ij}	Z_2	Z_3
bounded processing times	some RCs STF		$> p^-_{ij}$		
fixed processing times	FMS some RCs		$= p^+_{ij}$		
unbounded processing times	FMS,STF some RCs		$\infty[$		
no wait	some RC,STF	$= 0$		$= 0$	$= v_{ij}$
no storage	some RC,STF	$= 0$		$= 0$	
transport ress. with storage	FMS				$\infty[$
transport ress. without storage	FMS				$= v_{ij}$

3. HYBRID METHOD

3.1 Hybrid global algorithm

Our objective is to propose a method which enables us to handle various types of problems while minimizing makespan. In searching space, solutions can be mainly classified into two types: solutions with storage and solutions without storage. Most of existing algorithms are dedicated to specific cases. [14],[10] applied local search techniques which are efficient for solutions with storage, but not for solutions without storage. We proposed a hybrid method to find solutions with storage configuration ([22]). However it is not so efficient to find solutions strictly without storage, especially for big size problems. In another way, methods which are efficient for finding solutions without storage may not generate very interesting makespan while storage is unlimited. In this paper, we combine the hybrid genetic and tabu search with the shifting bottleneck procedure with repair (initially more dedicated to HSPs).

In order to keep both types of solutions (with or without storage) in a same population during evolution, we use makespan and storage as two objectives. A Pareto ranking is applied so that any solution with optimal values for either criteria will survive. At the beginning, the modified shifting bottleneck procedure with repair is applied to generate feasible initial solutions. A tabu search algorithm is used at each generation to improve solutions. In order to keep the diversity of population, we regenerate initial solutions for individuals which have not been improved during a given number of generations. Fig. 3 shows the whole proposed procedure that we detail in the following.

3.2 Genetic algorithm with Tabu search

Most of previous researches were dedicated to solve sched uling problems with totally or partially fixed assignment of resources. Few of them consider both assignment and scheduling for processing and transport resources. Our hybrid me thod is designed to solve such problems which can be found in various systems. The tabu search heuristic is inspired by [10] and has been proved to be efficient in this field.

The chromosome is encoded in two parts: processing tasks and transportation tasks. Values of each bit represent assignment of operations to processing and transport resources. During the initialization stage, a population of individuals is generated randomly. A solution without deadlock is generated using the modified shifting bottleneck procedure. This one may modify the initial assignment.

Starting from the resulting assignment and sequence, the tabu search heuristic is then used to improve the schedule during a limited number of iterations. The genetic algorithm works as a superior level method to handle the assignment problem and make the whole population evolve, based on the fitness. The tabu search approach solves sequencing problems based on given assignments.

Furthermore, three moves are defined in tabu search to explore the neighbourhood:

- internal exchange move: for the same resource, exchange one task with another one whose processing time window increases the most waiting time. This reducing criterion is inspired by [10]. It is useful to reduce the makespan with unnecessary waiting time.

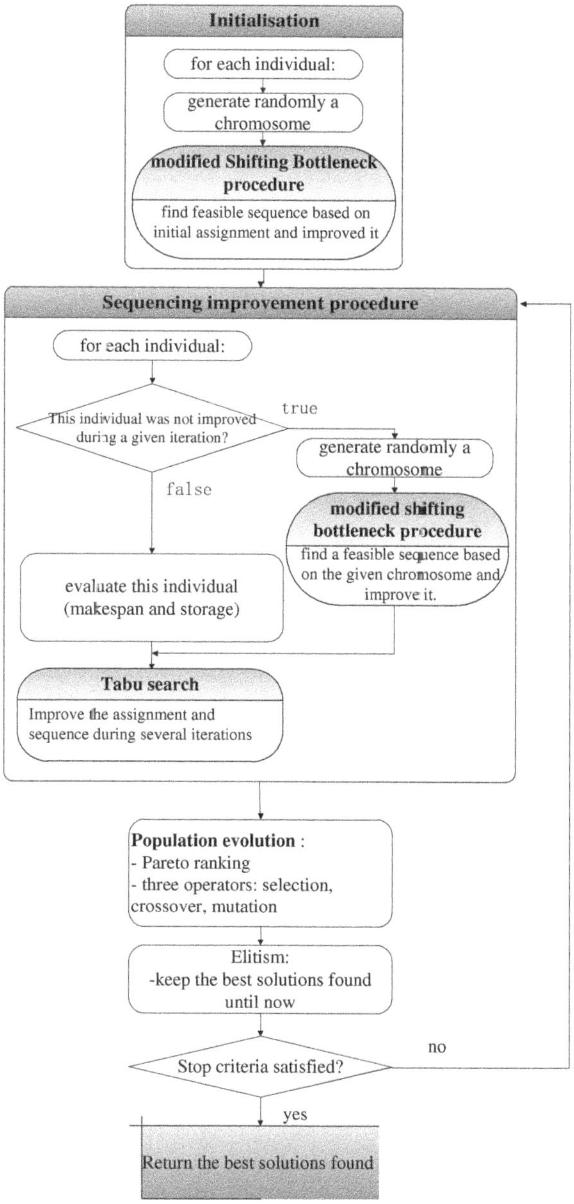

Figure 3: The global procedure of the proposed hybrid algorithm

But this is not very efficient when the solution contains no/less storage;

- external exchange move: exchange two tasks whose time intervals have non empty intersection. This criterion reduces the chance to get infeasible sequences;

- insert move: assign one task to another resource which is available during the time interval associated with this task. This re-assignment aims at processing this task as soon as possible. This will repair the original unbalanced assignment: for example, one resource is overloaded compared with other ones.

These moves may also be considered as an additional operator of the genetic algorithm which can change not only the sequence but also the original assignment. The principle of Tabu search heuristic is detailed in algorithm 1.

Algorithm 1 Tabu Local Search

Initial solution s0
$s^* \leftarrow s_0$
while stopping criteria is not met **do**
  LocaSearch (s_0), find all the neighbours based on the defined neighbour system
  evaluate neighbours
  choose the best s' among all the neighbours that are not in the tabu list
  $s_0 \leftarrow s'$
  if s_0 is better than s^* **then**
    $s^* \leftarrow s_0$
    if length of the tabu list = l **then**
      delete the head of tabu list.
    end if
    put s^* in tail of tabu list.
  end if
end while
return s^*

In order to apply this method for various problems, two objectives are considered: makespan (C_{max}) and storage ($Stor$). Makespan is defined as the time needed to complete a set of jobs. The storage is the total waiting time for each processing task before and after its treatment. It is interesting for some systems, where storage is not allowed. It enables to find the feasible solutions (with zero storage) among the possible ones. In the Tabu procedure, one solution is said to be better than another one if it is not dominated. During each iteration, the best solution is chosen randomly among all non dominated solutions which are not in the tabu list.

Instead of evaluating makespan and minimum storage of an individual, we develop an evaluation based on a disjunctive graph. The makespan corresponds to the longest path in a graph without positive cycle. As there are storage nodes (before and after each processing node) in the graph, we can calculate the waiting time of each task based on the earliest starting dates of storage nodes and processing nodes. Algorithm 2 shows the calculation procedure. L_{ij} / L'_{ij} represent longest paths from the starting node to the processing/transport node of O_{ij}/T_{ij}. S^-_{ij}, S^+_{ij} represent the longest path from the starting node to the storage node before and after O_{ij} respectively.

The crossover operator is a single point crossover. Mutation operator is to change one or several bit(s) in the chromosome which corresponds to the assignment of tasks. It is useful to keep the diversity of population. All these genetic operators perform on chromosome, which means they modify the assignment of processing and transport tasks. Tabu search procedure not only improves the sequence for a given assignment but also may impact the initial assignment. At each generation, a Pareto ranking is applied to the population, then crossover and mutation operations give birth to offspring which will compose the new population for the next generation. In order to keep the convergence, the best individual (for makespan criteria) found during the past generation is always kept in the population to replace the worst one in the new population. For the systems where no storage is allowed, only those solutions with zero storage are

---

Algorithm 2 Evaluation of an individual based on disjunctive graph representation

---

Apply Dantzig's algorithm to evaluate the longest path from the starting node to each task node in graph
C_{max} = the longest path from the starting node to the finishing node.
$Stor_{input} = Stor_{output} = 0$;
for each processing node O_{ij} in the graph **do**
  if $L_{ij} > S^-_{ij}$ **then**
    $Stor_{input} = Stor_{input} + L_{ij} - S^-_{ij}$
  end if
  if O_{ij} is not the last processing task of a job **then**
    if $L'_{ij+1} > S^+_{ij}$ **then**
      $Stor_{output} = Stor_{output} + L'_{ij} - S^+_{ij}$
    end if
  end if
end for
$Stor = Stor_{input} + Stor_{output}$

---

feasible. So the best and and the worst solutions are chosen among those ones with zero storage. The evolution improves both assignments and sequences. This hybrid method can solve several types of job shop problems with transportation: with fixed or minimum or bounded processing times, with or without storage allowed, with or without assignment problems.

3.3 Shifting Bottleneck heuristic

The shifting bottleneck heuristic (SBH) has been first proposed by [2] for job shop problems. It finds iteratively the bottleneck machine and then solves each single machine subproblem until all machines are scheduled. The bottleneck resource is the resource which impacts the most on the performance (makespan). The determination of the bottleneck resource among all resources which are not scheduled yet, is based on release dates and due dates of tasks. These ones are calculated by the associated disjunctive graph during each iteration.

The procedure starts with a set of machines whose sequences are fixed. A task's release date corresponds to the longest path from the starting node to its associate node in the graph. The longest path is calculated by Dantzig's algorithm ([9]), which can also to detect positive cycles. A task's due date equals to its release date plus its maximum processing time. If the schedule proposed by this procedure is not valid, then a repair is applied. It consists in searching feasible solutions by swapping any pair of tasks in the current sequence. This repair is not efficient enough when there is a big amount of tasks on a resource, especially in STF for the hoists which have many transportation tasks to perform. However, it is mainly effective for small cases, especially for transport resources.

In order to improve the solving of bigger instances, another heuristic is used to assign and schedule transportation tasks one by one while taking into account current release dates. At each step, it chooses the task with the smallest release date and assigns it to the hoist with the latest available date. Once a new task is assigned, new disjunctions may be arbitrated. The arbitrated disjunction will be the one corresponding to the latest release date. Then the associated arc in the graph is oriented. The new graph obtained is then verified and evaluated by Dantzig's algorithm. The procedure continues to assign a next task proposed by new calculated graph and then arbitrate a new disjunction. It continues until all tasks are assigned and no disjunction remains. The proposed heuristic is integrated with the modified shifting bottleneck procedure with repair when unfeasible schedules on transport resources are generated. The whole modified shifting bottleneck procedure is shown in algorithm 3. The procedure of the heuristic is shown in algorithm 4.

Algorithm 3 The whole procedure of modified SBN

```
{initial condition}
M0 contains already sequenced processing resources.
Construct a graph G which contains conjunctive arcs and
arbitrated arcs corresponding to sequences in M0
repeat
  for each machine Mi ∈ (M − M0) do
    minimize Lmax by using EDD rules for each instance
    1/rj/Lmax. Lmax(i) is the minimal Lmax found for
    the sub-problem associated Mi
  end for
  {find bottleneck resource}
  Lmax(k) ← max_{i∈[1,m]} Lmax(i)
  add arcs corresponding to the sequence of Mk in graph
  G.
  if Danzig(G) = −1 then
    delete the added arcs
    repair the sequence of Mk by testing all possible per-
    mutations
    if do not successful to repair then
      return −1
    else
      add arcs associated to the first feasible sequence
      found
    end if
  end if
  M0 ← M0 ⋃ Mk
until M0 ≠ M
using the heuristic (algorithm 4) for scheduling transport
resources)
if feasible solution found then
  return the solution
else
  return −1
end if
```

Algorithm 4 Assign and schedule transportation tasks

```
apply Dantzig's algorithm to evaluate the longest path
from the starting node to each task node in graph G
calculate the latest ending time for each hoist
increasing order of all transportation tasks according to
their release date (longest path)
repeat
  for each task in the increasing order do
    if current task is not assigned yet then
      assign current task to the most available hoist
      based on hoists' ending time and empty travel time
      update the ending time of the chosen hoist
      break;
    end if
  end for
  find increasing order of tasks which are already assigned
  for each hoist
  for each hoist do
    in its tasks order, find the pair of tasks with smallest
    release date and their disjunction is not fixed
  end for
  if all tasks are assigned and no new disjunction needs
  to be fixed then
    return G
  else
    among all pairs of tasks chosen for each hoist, choose
    the one with latest release date
    if the arc associated with the chosen pair can update
    release date then
      add this arc
      if Dantizig (G) = −1 then
        delete this arc
        add inverse arc
        if Dantizig (G) = −1 then
          return −1
        end if
      end if
      update ending times of hoists
    end if
  end if
until true
```

4. COMPUTATIONAL RESULTS

4.1 Instances

Four kinds of instances are tested. They could be seen as special cases of our considered general problem.

- First kind contains instances in [14] for robotic cells. These instances are characterized by : a single available machine for each processing task, a single transport resource and fixed processing times. No assignment problem needs to be considered.
- Second kind contains instances of Bilge and Ulusoy for FMS in [3]. They are characterized by only one available machine for each processing task, fixed processing times and two transport resources. So the assignment of transport tasks needs to be considered.
- Third kind is an extension of FJSP (flexible job shop scheduling problem) with transportation. It was proposed by Deroussi et al. in [11]. These instances include two available machines for each processing task, fixed processing times and two transport resources. There are assignment problems for both processing and transport tasks.
- Fourth kind is a set of HSP instances proposed by Mateo and Companys ([17]). Instances are characterized by: a single available machine for each processing task, bounded processing times, no storage allowed between two operations or during transportation task, and one or several transport resource(s). No wait and no storage are allowed. These instances consider various transportation times (hoist speeds) and contain two types of jobs which alternatively enter the line. Those jobs follow the same processing sequence but

Table 2: Cmax for RC instances ([14])

Instance	TS	GTS	Gap%	standard deviation
P01D1d1	87	98	12.64	4.22
P01D1t1	81	89	9.88	1.7
P01T2t1	74	81	9.46	1.2
P01T3t0	92	94	2.17	0.71
P01D3d1	216	220	1.85	1.03
P01D2d1	148	158	6.76	0.52

with different processing time windows. [17] use these instances to solve a 2-degree cyclic HSP. They search the optimal cycle time T of a repetitive hoist moving sequence for two kinds of jobs and one hoist. Because there are few benchmarks adapted to our considered predictive problem, we extend these instances to predictive problems with 5 jobs (3 jobs of type one and 2 jobs of type two) and 1 or 2 robots. Then we leave the cyclic environment to solve job shop one. But a cycle time T is not comparable directly with the makespan we obtain. Moreover the time between two successive inputs at the loading station and the real processing times for obtained solutions are not provided in [17]. For the 5 jobs case, the fifth job J_5 (type 1) enters the system last. The total processing time of J_5 is noted as $tt1$. So the total makespan for 5 jobs is $2 \times T + tt1$. But $tt1$ is no less than total minimum processing time plus associated loaded transportation times. Also it is no bigger than total maximum processing time plus associated loaded transportation times. So we compare our results with a lower bound (LB) and an upper bound (UB) for makespan which we have calculated as $LB = 2 \times T + \sum_{j \in [1,n_1]} p^-_{1j} + \sum_{j \in [1,n_1-1]} v_{1j}$, $UB = 2 \times T + \sum_{j \in [1,n_1]} p^+_{1j} + \sum_{j \in [1,n_1-1]} v_{1j}$. The makespan we consider as the reference and which corresponds to results of [17], will be between the lower bound and upper bound.

4.2 Results

Results are obtained by running ten times our algorithm and the best results are shown in the following tables. The size of population is 50, the maximum generation time is 1000. Programs are written in language C++, and are tested on a 2.8GHz CPU (AMD Phenom X2). CPU times vary according to various kinds of instances: from several minutes for small instances, to one hour for bigger instances (HSP instances).

Tables 2 to 6 compare the performance our method in terms of makesp an (Cmax) of and those methods found in literature which provide the best results. In those tables, our algorithm is labeled GTS (Genetic algorithm with Tabu search and Shifting bottleneck). The gap between GTS and any reference method (Ref) is calculated as: $G_{Ref} = (GTS - Ref)/Ref(\%)$. The reference methods vary according to the four classes of instances, and are respectively:

- TS: Tabu Search developped by [14], for RC in table 2;
- for FMS, in table 3: GAA (genetic algorithm in [1]) and SALS (simulated annealing local search in [10]);

Table 3: Cmax for FMS instances ([3])

Inst.	SALS	GAA	GTS	Gap %		std.
				G_{SALS}	G_{GAA}	dev
Ex11	96	96	96	0.00	0.00	0
Ex12	82	82	82	0.00	0.00	0
Ex13	84	84	84	0.00	0.00	0
Ex14	103	103	103	0.00	0.00	0
Ex21	100	102	103	3.00	0.98	0.71
Ex22	76	76	76	0.00	0.00	0
Ex23	86	86	86	0.00	0.00	0
Ex24	108	108	108	0.00	0.00	2.67
Ex31	99	99	99	0.00	0.00	2.8
Ex32	85	85	85	0.00	0.00	0
Ex33	86	86	86	0.00	0.00	0
Ex34	111	111	115	3.60	3.60	1.05
Ex41	112	112	114	1.79	1.79	2.08
Ex42	87	88	90	3.45	2.27	1.15
Ex43	89	89	89	0.00	0.00	1.78
Ex44	121	126	129	6.61	2.38	1.66
Ex51	87	87	87	0.00	0.00	0.48
Ex52	69	69	69	0.00	0.00	0
Ex53	74	74	74	0.00	0.00	0
Ex54	96	96	96	0.00	0.00	0
Ex61	118	118	122	3.39	3.39	0
Ex62	98	98	98	0.00	0.00	0.63
Ex63	103	104	103	0.00	-0.96	0
Ex64	120	120	126	5.00	5.00	1.58
Ex71	111	115	114	2.70	-0.87	2.12
Ex72	79	79	79	0.00	0.00	1.69
Ex73	83	86	85	2.41	-1.16	1.52
Ex74	126	127	130	3.17	2.36	2.83
Ex81	161	161	161	0.00	0.00	0
Ex82	151	151	151	0.00	0.00	0
Ex83	153	153	153	0.00	0.00	0
Ex84	163	163	163	0.00	0.00	0
Ex91	116	118	116	0.00	-1.69	0.97
Ex92	102	104	102	0.00	-1.92	0.84
Ex93	105	106	105	0.00	-0.94	0.48
Ex94	120	122	122	1.67	0.00	0.32
Ex101	147	147	148	0.68	0.68	1.29
Ex102	135	136	135	0.00	-0.74	1.51
Ex103	138	141	139	0.72	-1.42	2
Ex104	159	159	162	1.89	1.89	2.15

- for FJSP, ILS (Iterated Local Search in [11]) in table 4; and GATS (a more simple genetic algorithm and tabu search procedure we developped in [22]) in table 5. Table 4 provides results in terms of exit time of the last job of the system, instead of in terms of makespan.
- BB: Branch and Bound in [17] dedicated to cyclic HSP in STF;

For RC instances, GTS is not more efficient than the reference method (gap between 1.85% and 12.64%, mean gap equals 7.13%) (table 2). This can be explained as we use a method which is not dedicated to this kind of problems, and one only part of the algorithm is used (as no assignment problem and fixed processing times).

For FMS instances, SALS and GAA remain better than GTS in respectively 14 and 10 cases out of 40 (table 3). But we obtain the same best results as SALS and GAA in

Table 4: Exit time criterion for FJSP instances ([11])

Instance	ILS	GTS	Gap%	standard deviation
fjsp1	160	170	6.25	2.31
fjsp2	138	138	0.00	1.58
fjsp3	142	148	4.23	1.65
fjsp4	138	146	5.80	1.65
fjsp5	112	106	-5.36	2.35
fjsp6	158	164	1.27	1.7
fjsp7	150	160	6.67	1.89
fjsp8	197	197	0.00	2.06
fjsp9	166	170	2.41	1.35
fjsp10	188	202	7.45	1.89

Table 5: Cmax for FJSP instances ([11])

Instance	GATS	GTS	Gap%	standard deviation
fjsp1	144	146	1.39	1.07
fjsp2	118	118	0.00	1.14
fjsp3	124	124	0.00	2.5
fjsp4	124	124	0.00	1.75
fjsp5	94	94	0.00	0.97
fjsp6	144	144	0.00	1.7
fjsp7	124	122	-1.61	1.35
fjsp8	180	181	0.56	1.83
fjsp9	150	146	-2.67	1.58
fjsp10	178	178	0.00	2.49

respectively 65% and 75% of cases. Compared with GAA, we even improve Cmax for 8 instances (gain from 0.74% to 1.92%). The mean gaps are respectively 1% and 0.37%. This is rather satisfying considering that those reference methods are dedicated to a single class of instances.

In the same way for FJSP instances, we obtain rather good results. The mean gap for exit time criterion is weak (2.87%) (table 4). And GTS improves ILS results for one instance (gap equals 5.36%). For the makespan criterion, GTS provides a mean gain of 0.23%, and obtains at least the same results for 80% of cases (table 5).

For STF, table 6 shows our results for instances with one and two hoists. For a single hoist problem, our Cmax is less than the lower bound LB in 83% of instances. This means that GTS provides better results than those ones obtained with a 2-degree cycle time. Among the five remaining cases, if GTS is nearer LB than UB, then it involves that we have good chance to be better too. It is the case for three instances. For the two remaining ones, it is difficult to be sure as Cmax is between LB and UB.

The gain when adding one hoist, is calculated as $(GTS2hoists - GTS1hoist)/GTS1hoist$. GTS gives better results for 2 hoists (mean improvement about 35%). It is not surprising that adding one hoist can improve greatly the productivity, whatever the method is. However those results may be used as reference ones in further researches.

Let us note that, except for robotic cell instances, our algorithm GTS generally has better performance than our previous method GATS (see [22]).

5. CONCLUSION

In this paper, different kinds of job shop scheduling problems with transportation are considered For this purpose, we defined a generic problem which gathers all characteristics identified in each system (bounded processing times, transportation constraints, ...), knowing that each individual problem is known as NP-hard one. In order to represent these ones, we use a new disjunctive graph. In particular, this one contains nodes for processing tasks, transportation tasks and storage. To solve efficiently those problems, we propose a hybrid algorithm coupling genetic algorithm, tabu local search and a modified shifting bottleneck procedure. The idea was to take advantage of several methods which were proved to be individually efficient for dedicated cases. Various tests on benchmarks of the literature were performed. Our method gives results which are not so far from the best ones. We can conclude that our hybrid metaheuristic algorithm provides a good compromise between best results and flexibility (capacity to address several kinds of complex job shop scheduling problems).

Table 6: Results for instances of [17] with 5 jobs, 1 and 2 hoist(s)

Inst.	LB	UB	GTS 1hoist	Gap% G_L	Gap% G_U	GTS 2hoist	gain%	std. dev
501	1106	1509	1115	0.81	-26.11	735	-34.08	0
502	982	1357	906	-7.74	-33.24	639	-29.47	0
503	1294	1605	1207	-6.72	-24.80	670	-44.49	0
504	989	1309	937	-5.26	-28.42	586	-37.45	0
505	1144	1483	1105	-3.41	-25.49	690	-37.55	0
506	1085	1468	1059	-2.40	-27.86	653	-38.33	0
507	1248	1559	1240	-0.64	-20.46	692	-44.19	0
508	961	1281	910	-5.31	-28.96	663	-27.14	0
509	971	1291	960	-1.13	-25.64	660	-31.25	0
510	1029	1299	949	-7.77	-26.94	588	-38.04	0
511	1246	1632	1107	-11.16	-32.17	765	-30.89	0
512	862	1227	837	-2.90	-31.78	686	-18.04	0
513	1096	1447	1022	-6.75	-29.37	716	-29.94	0
514	1110	1497	1046	-5.77	-30.13	705	-32.60	0
515	903	1154	943	4.43	-18.28	587	-37.75	0
516	1274	1501	1314	3.14	-12.46	755	-42.54	0
517	1110	1436	1098	-1.08	-23.54	678	-38.25	0
518	1092	1479	1007	-7.78	-31.91	722	-28.30	0
519	1224	1610	1107	-9.56	-31.24	727	-34.32	0
520	903	1154	895	-0.89	-22.44	530	-40.78	0
521	1135	1469	1078	-5.02	-26.62	728	-32.46	0
522	1710	2226	1516	-11.35	-31.90	974	-35.75	0
523	1559	1892	1551	-0.51	-18.02	904	-41.71	0
524	992	1339	972	-2.02	-27.41	697	-28.29	0
525	1554	1995	1387	-10.75	-30.48	814	-41.31	0
526	1486	1927	1339	-9.89	-30.51	794	-40.70	0
527	1127	1461	1259	11.71	-13.83	739	-41.30	0
528	1008	1355	977	-3.08	-27.90	687	-29.68	0
529	1156	1546	1322	14.36	-14.49	776	-41.30	0
530	1523	1856	1495	-1.84	-19.45	1005	-32.77	0

6. REFERENCES

[1] T. Abdelmaguid, A. Nassef, B. Kamal, and M. Hassan. A hybrid ga/heuristic approach to the simultaneous scheduling of machines and automated guided vehicles. *International journal of production research*, 42(2):267–281, 2004.

[2] J. Adams, E. Balas, and D. Zawack. The shifting

bottleneck procedure for job shop scheduling. *Management science*, 34(3):391–401, Mar. 1988.

[3] Ü. Bilge and G. Ulusoy. A time window approach to simultaneous scheduling of machines and material handling system in an FMS. *Operations Research*, 43(6):1058–1070, 1995.

[4] J. Blazewicz, E. Pesch, and M. Sterna. The disjunctive graph machine representation of the job shop scheduling problem. *European Journal of Operational Research*, 127(2):317–331, 2000.

[5] C. Bloch, C. Varnier, and P. Baptiste. Stochastic methods combined with a modified shifting bottleneck heuristic for solving a blocking scheduling problem with bounded processing times. In *Proceedings of the 15th Triennal Conference of the International Federation of Operational Research Societies IFORS'99*, pages 125–126, Beijing (China), 1999.

[6] A. Che, C. Chu, and F. Chu. Multicyclic hoist scheduling with constant processing times. *IEEE Transactions on Robotics and Automation*, 18(1):69–80, 2002.

[7] Y. Crama, V. Kats, J. V. de Klundert, and E. Levner. Cyclic scheduling in robotic flowshops. *Annals of Operations Research*, 96(1):97–124, 2000.

[8] Y. Crama and J. Van de Klundert. Robotic flowshop scheduling is strongly np-complete. Technical Report 010, Maastricht : METEOR, Maastricht Research School of Economics of Technology and Organization, 1997.

[9] G. Dantzig and M. Thapa. *Linear programming: theory and extensions*, volume 2. Springer Verlag, 2003.

[10] L. Deroussi, M. Gourgand, and N. Tchernev. A simple metaheuristic approach to the simultaneous scheduling of machines and automated guided vehicles. *International Journal of Production Research*, 46(8):2143–2164, 2008.

[11] L. Deroussi and S. Norre. Simultaneous scheduling of machines and vehicles for the flexible job shop problem. In *International Conference on Metaheuristics and Nature Inspired Computing*, 2010.

[12] A. El Amraoui, M.-A. Manier, A. El Moudni, and M. Benrejeb. Heuristic for the resolution of the cyclic hoist scheduling problem with multi-items. In *The 18th World Congress of the International Federation of Automatic Control (IFAC)*, volume 18, pages 8195–8200, 2011.

[13] A. El Amraoui, M.-A. Manier, A. El Moudni, and M. Benrejeb. Hoist scheduling for multi-part chsp in complex lines' configuration. In *2011 IEEE International Conference on Industrial Technology (ICIT)*, pages 270–275. IEEE, 2011.

[14] J. Hurink and S. Knust. Tabu search algorithms for job-shop problems with a single transport robot. *European journal of operational research*, 162(1):99–111, 2005.

[15] P. Lacomme, M. Larabi, and N. Tchernev. A disjunctive graph for the job-shop with several robots. In *MISTA Conference*, pages 285–292, 2007.

[16] J. Liu and Y. Jiang. An efficient optimal solution to the two-hoist no-wait cyclic scheduling problem. *Operations Research*, pages 313–327, 2005.

[17] M. Mateo and R. Companys. New computational experiences on the hoist scheduling problem for cyclic manufacturing of different products. Technical report, Universitat Politècnica de Catalunya. Departament d'Organització d'Empreses Sense grup de recerca, 2007.

[18] L. Phillips and P. Unger. Mathematical programming solution of a hoist scheduling program. *AIIE Transactions*, 8(2):219–225, 1976.

[19] C. Rosse Bloch and P. Baptiste. *Contribution à l'ordonnancement dynamique de lignes de traitement de surface*. PhD thesis, Franche-Comté university, 1999.

[20] G. Shapiro and H. Nuttle. Hoist scheduling for a pcb electroplating facility. *IIE transactions*, 20(2):157–167, 1988.

[21] Q. Zhang, H. Manier, and M.-A. Manier. A disjunctive graph and shifting bottleneck heuristics for multi hoists scheduling problem. In *18th World Congress of the International Federation of Automatic Control (IFAC)*, volume 18, pages 6963–6968, 2011.

[22] Q. Zhang, H. Manier, and M.-A. Manier. A genetic algorithm with tabu search procedure for flexible job shop scheduling with transportation constraints and bounded processing times. *Computers & Operations Research*, 39:1713–1723, 2012.

[23] Q. Zhang, H. Manier, M.-A. Manier, and C. Bloch. Procédure de shifting bottleneck avec graphe disjonctif pour le hoist scheduling problem. In *12e congrès annuel de la société française de recherche opérationnelle et d'aide à la décision, ROADEF*, Mar. 2011.

Adaptive Multi-objective Genetic Algorithm using Multi-Pareto-Ranking

Wahabou Abdou
Christelle Bloch
Damien Charlet
François Spies

FEMTO-ST Institute
University of Franche-Comté
1 Cours Leprince-Ringuet, 25200 Montbéliard, France
{firstname.lastname}@univ-fcomte.fr

ABSTRACT

This paper extends an elitist multi-objective evolutionary algorithm, named GAME, based on several Pareto fronts corresponding to various fitness definitions. An additional operator is defined to create an adaptive version of this algorithm, called aGAME. This new operator alternates different modes of exploration of the search place all through aGAME execution. Mode switching is controlled according to the values of two performance indicators, in order to maintain a good compromise between the quality and diversity of the returned solutions. aGAME is compared with the previous version (GAME) and with the three best-ranking algorithms of the CEC 2009 competition, using five bi-objective benchmarks and the rules of this competition. This experimental comparison shows that aGAME outperforms these four algorithms, which validates both the efficiency of the proposed dynamic adaptive operator and the algorithm performance.

Categories and Subject Descriptors

I.2.8 [**Problem Solving, Control Methods, and Search**]: Heuristic methods

General Terms

Algorithms, Experimentation

Keywords

Adaptive multi-objective evolutionary algorithm, Quality and diversity indicators, Pareto ranking

1. INTRODUCTION

Over the last decade, many research works dealing with evolutionary algorithms (EA) have focused on multi-objective algorithms. They are often based on very famous algorithms using Pareto ranking and non-dominated archives. Besides, designing adaptive algorithms is one of the most-studied topics in this area. Section 2 gives a brief survey of these subjects. In the same way, this paper proposes a new adaptive multi-objective algorithm, called aGAME. It extends the previous version of an archive-based multi-objective algorithm called Genetic Algorithm with Multiple parEto fronts (GAME) [1]. The main parts of GAME are succinctly described in Section 3. GAME relies on a ranking process in which population is separated into several Pareto fronts. Associated selection strategies and several fitness definitions are also used. A parametric study based on the design of experiments allowed GAME to outperform three algorithms in an experimental comparison based on the procedure of CEC 2009 competition. In aGAME, an adaptive mechanism is added in order to improve both performance and robustness. This new contribution is presented in section 4. Both the selection probabilities of non-dominated individuals and mutation rate vary during the evolutionary process. This makes aGAME regularly switch between four behavior modes: initialization, normal search, exploration and exploitation. These changes are activated according to the values of two metrics measuring both the quality and the diversity of individuals. Finally, in section 5, the resulting algorithm behavior is analyzed and compared to the behavior of the previous static version GAME. This shows the impact of the proposed dynamic adaptation operator (DAO). Besides, all the constrained bi-objective benchmarks of the CEC 2009 competition are used to measure the provided benefits and to validate aGAME performance. Section 6 ends the paper by giving the main conclusions of this work and developing several promising prospects.

2. RELATED WORK

2.1 Elitist Pareto-based MOEAs

Many multi-objective evolutionary algorithms (MOEAs) use the concept of Pareto dominance to rank solutions and to apply selection strategies based on non-domination ranks. Generally, such algorithms are elitist: the best solutions (i.e.

non-dominated solutions) are kept either in the population itself or in a separate archive. In the first case, they participate in the reproduction process which guides the exploration of the search space towards interesting areas. But the number of non-dominated solutions might greatly increase with the number of objectives, which limits the number of places reserved for new individuals. Therefore, such algorithms generally use a specific operator to preserve diversity. **Elitist Non-dominated Sorting Genetic Algorithm (NSGA-II)** [2], is certainly one of the most famous algorithms belonging to this first category. The second class of MOEAs uses an archive of non-dominated solutions, which does not necessary takes part in reproduction. Besides, even if they use dominance to define the fitness of individuals, they usually use indicators rather than ranking in the strict sense of Pareto fronts. **Strength Pareto Evolutionary Algorithm 2 (SPEA2)** [3], as famous as NSGA-II, is certainly the reference algorithm in this class of MOEAs, known in literature as Indicator-based evolutionary algorithms [4]. Therefore, several recent MOEAs were inspired either by NSGA-II or by SPEA2. This subsection cannot give an exhaustive survey of such approaches. It briefly describes some of them, in order to give the main elements required to position GAME, the algorithm on which this contribution is based, in section 3. **NSGA-II** uses an elitist selection strategy for replacement (with respect to fitness and spread). For each generation, parents and offsprings are gathered in a mating pool. A fast non-dominated sorting approach is used to rank these individuals in subsequent Pareto fronts. Then the next generation is built by prefering the individuals with the lower non-domination ranks. In case of rank equality, the selection depends on a diversity preservation mechanism. A density measure, called crowding distance, is computed in the objective space. For each point, it represents the largest cuboid enclosing it without including any other point in the population. Thus, when two individuals have the same rank, the selection process favors the individual with the largest cuboid. The tournament used to select parents for reproduction is also based on this density measure. **SPEA2** preserves elitism by using an archive of non-dominated solutions. This set stores the best individuals found by the algorithm. But it also participates in genetic operations in order to guide the exploration of the search space. For each generation, the non-dominated solutions of the population are copied in this archive. This may eliminate some other solutions in the archive (if they are dominated by the entering ones). The fitness used in SPEA2 is based both on dominance and neighborhood density. The algorithm assigns a weight to each $\overrightarrow{x}$ solution, based on the number of non-dominated individuals (in the archive and in the current population) which dominate $\overrightarrow{x}$. A density estimation is computed using the k-th nearest neighbor method [12]. Finally, the fitness of $\overrightarrow{x}$ sums this distance and the weight of the solutions which dominate $\overrightarrow{x}$. Only the solutions of the archive participate in the reproduction selection. More recently, **FastPGA (Fast Pareto Genetic Algorithm)** [9] combined the ideas introduced in NSGA-II and SPEA2. FastPGA ranks parents and offsprings into two sets: non-dominated solutions and dominated ones. For non-dominated solutions, fitness is computed by using the crowding distance defined in NSGA-II. For dominated solutions, the calculation of fitness looks like the one used in SPEA2. FastPGA generalizes the weight computation: the fitness of any dominated solution $\overrightarrow{x}$ is the sum of the weight of individuals dominating $\overrightarrow{x}$ minus the sum of the weight of individuals dominated by $\overrightarrow{x}$. This allows to limit the number of solutions which have the same fitness value. Both non-domination rank and fitness are used in the selection for reproduction. Besides, an additional mechanism dyamically controls the population size. This allows FastPGA to keep good performance in optimization problems with complex objective functions (particularly those the evaluation of which requires a long computation time or simulation). **Indicator-based Evolutionary Algorithm (IBEA)** [4] was proposed in 2004. Its selection process explicitely relies on the computation of performance indicators. The optimization goal is defined as one or several metrics used to measure both the quality and diversity of solutions (such as those presented in section 4). Initially, such metrics were defined to assess the performance of MOEAs at the end of their execution. In IBEA, two metrics are used to define individual fitness, but the authors indicate that any other indicator may be used. Given that these metrics assess both the quality and diversity of solutions, no additional diversity preservation mechanism is needed. In keeping with IBEA, many EAs [5] and local search approaches [6] were developed, principally using hypervolume indicator to define their selection process. Indeed, this indicator allows both the estimates of the quality and diversity of individuals. Besides, it has the advantage that it is the only quality indicator known to be fully sensitive to Pareto dominance: if a set of solutions entirely dominates another set of solutions, then the dominating set will have the best value of hypervolume indicator [7].

2.2 Adaptive MOEAs

Another way is explored in literature to increase both the quality and diversity of the solutions returned by EAs. Indeed, such algorithms are often criticized because they involve several parameters, the values of which are difficult to choose. Inadequate values might significantly decrease the algorithm performance. Therefore, a lot of recent research work focuses either on statistical tuning approaches [8, 9] or on adaptive algorithms. Such algorithms dynamically adapt their parameter values. They can be classified according to the type of adaptation they perform - i.e. how are the parameters modified ? - or to the adaptation level - i.e. where are the modifications performed (on each individual or on the whole population)? These two classes may be combined into a hierarchical classification. Eiben et al. [10] first distinguish approaches which use parameter tuning from those which focus on parameter monitoring. Then, they separate this last category into three sub-classes: deterministic, adaptive and self-adaptive approaches. Deterministic monitoring modifies parameters independently from the intermediate results provided by the algorithm. Typically, some indicators, such as the generation number, are used to make the values of parameters vary according to a given range of values or to a deterministic function. For instance, the population size periodically varies in Saw-Tooth GA, the algorithm proposed by Koumousis and Katsaras [11]. Tan et al. [12] also presented such a method for binary genetic algorithms. It associates a crossover rate and a mutation rate with each bit. The variations of the most significant bits are favored at the beginning of execution to allow a large exploration of the search space. This probability then decreases in the course of the execution. But according to De Jong [13], deterministic methods can hardly be applied, because predicting the behavior an algorithm will have at a given generation is a difficult task. Adaptive methods explore another way. They modify the evolution process of the optimization algorithm by monitoring some of its characteristics. Deb et al. [14] proposed a crossover operator which adapts the algorithm evolution according to both the fitness of parents and the fitness of the resulting offsprings. It is an adaptive version of SBX (Simulated Binary Crossover) [15]. Zeng et al. [16] extended this contribution in such a way that the probability distribution used by SBX is dynamically adjusted according to diversity measures. Hippolyte et al. propose a multi-agent-based EA in which the population size results from interactions between the solutions (each of them being represented as an agent) [17]. Finally, self-adaptive algorithms insert the information which defines the adaptation strategy, the parameters to be controlled for instance, in the chromosomes themselves. These additional genes participate in the reproduction operations (in particular crossover). Solutions with efficient adaptation strategies are more likely to survive and to transmit this information to offsprings. Hinterding et al. [18] introduced the gaussian mutation, which is based on this principle: the parameter which permits to control the gaussian function is added to the chromosome.

The new MOEA proposed in this paper, aGAME, belongs to the second category: some of its parameters, such as mutation rate, vary in the course of its execution. These variations depend on performance indicators, which are periodically computed to assess the quality and the diversity of solutions. This is an adaptive version of GAME [1], an MOEA which includes several pareto fronts to rank individuals, a fitness function depending on the pareto set and a specific selection mechanism. The following section gives a rundown on the main GAME's principles required to describe the improvements brought in the adaptive version clearly.

3. GAME: STATIC MOEA WITH MULTIPLE PARETO FRONTS

GAME is an elitist MOEA which includes several pareto fronts to rank individuals, like NSGA-II. But it defines several fitness functions, like FastPGA. Indeed the fitness of individuals depends on the pareto set they belong to. Besides, a specific 2-step selection mechanism is also proposed. All these particularities of GAME are detailed in this section.

3.1 Ranking and fitness assignment

GAME (Genetic Algorithm with Multiple parEto sets) splits the population into several Pareto fronts. This permits to progressively rank individuals from non-dominated ones (first Pareto front PF_1) to dominated ones (last Pareto front). An PF_0 archive is also used to store non-dominated solutions found since the beginning of the execution in order to preserve elitism. When the optimization problem to be solved includes constraints, this is taken into account while building the successive Pareto fronts, using a penalty strategy. Solutions which do not satisfy constraints (i.e. unfeasible solutions) are not allowed to enter PF_1. Nevertheless, when this set is empty, such solutions may be accepted by default. Such a case may occur during the first generations of the algorithm. But this is fastly corrected, as soon as feasible solutions are found. They are more likely to survive, they transmit their characteristics to their descendants, and then unfeasible solutions naturally leave PF_1.

Individual fitness depends on the Pareto front the evaluated solution belongs to. GAME distinguishes three fitness definitions. Given that the algorithm must return solutions as close as possible to the PF^* optimal front while preserving their diversity, the fitness of the solutions contained in PF_0 and PF_1 is a diversity indicator: the crowding distance [2]. This indicator gives information about the distribution of solutions within the front. GAME uses a normalized *crowding distance* in order to avoid bias which might be involved by the sizes of the different objective ranges. In the second PF_2 front, GAME favours the solutions which are closest to PF_1. The used indicator is *generational distance*. It measures the proximity between the solutions belonging to the two fronts. Using fitness based on this indicator increases the selection probability of the solutions near PF_1, for reproduction and survival. Finally, for solutions in all the remaining fronts, the fitness is defined as an indicator called **gain**. The gain of solution $\overrightarrow{x_i}$ in relation to $\overrightarrow{x_j}$ for objective function f_k is called $gain(\overrightarrow{x_i}, \overrightarrow{x_j}, k)$. It represents the improvement brought by $\overrightarrow{x_i}$ in comparison to $\overrightarrow{x_j}$ for the considered function. This gain, defined by equation 1, reaches value of between -1 and 1. Negative value indicates that the second solution is better than the first one for this objective. The gain equals zero when the two solutions are equivalent.

$$gain(\overrightarrow{x_i}, \overrightarrow{x_j}, k) = \frac{\lambda(f_k(\overrightarrow{x_i}) - f_k(\overrightarrow{x_j}))}{Max(f_k(\overrightarrow{x_i}), f_k(\overrightarrow{x_j}))} \tag{1}$$

where λ is a coefficient equal to 1 for maximization problems and -1 for minimization. The fitness of each individual is the sum of its gains (for all the objective functions) in relation to the other solutions belonging to the same front (see equation 2).

$$fitness(\overrightarrow{x_i}) = \sum_{j=1}^{|PF|} \sum_{k=1}^{m} gain(\overrightarrow{x_i}, \overrightarrow{x_j}, k) \tag{2}$$

where

- $|PF|$ is the size of the front to which $\overrightarrow{x_i}$ belongs;
- m is the number of objective functions of the tackled problem;

Each of these fitness definitions only makes sense within the same front. Selection works in two steps. The first one selects a front, while adapting to the number of fronts and to their sizes. Indeed, a great selection probability assigned to a front the size of which is low should give too much strength to the individuals it contains. This would reduce diversity rate in the next generation. The selection probability $Proba(PF_i)$ GAME assigns to each front PF_i takes into account both its rank i and its size, in order to overcome this problem. Finally, in the second selection step, a fitness-based tournament is used to select an individual among those belonging to the selected front.

An experimental study was conducted to show the usefulness and the efficiency of the proposed ranking and selection process. GAME compared favorably against the three best-ranking algorithms of the CEC 2009 competition [19]. Nevertheless, for this static version, the tuning of parameters was performed in a preliminary parametric study based on statistical tools. Although the tuned value provided promising results, it is certainly not adequate in all kinds of problems. Constant parameter value hardly allows algorithms to adapt to search spaces which might have very different characteristics. This motivated the design of an adaptive version of GAME, called aGAME, in which a new dynamic adaptation operator (DAO) is added to increase robustness. The following section describes this contribution.

4. DYNAMIC ADAPTATION OPERATOR

Dynamic adaptation must allow MOEAs to adapt to various search spaces, particularly to detect local optima and to climb out of them. It must also increase the algorithm performance by making it find final solutions that are both very various and as close as possible to global optima.

According to [20], an efficient MOEA must satisfy two conflicting goals: ensuring a wide exploration of the search space while guiding the algorithm towards one (or several) global optimum(a). In literature, many works [12, 21, 22, 23] show that a wide exploration should be favored at the beginning of the algorithm execution. This strategy is known as ***explore first, exploit later***. Exploration permits to identify good solutions. Then, in the second phase, exploitation, the neighborhood of these solutions is more intensively examined. The performance of the various proposed approaches is generally compared using some indicators which measure both the quality and diversity of solutions. This work proposes a new way to maintain the equilibrium between exploration and exploitation phases. The proposed dynamic adaptation operator periodically alternates various modes of exploration all through aGAME execution. Mode switching occurs according to the values of quality and diversity indicators. The following subsection presents the chosen metrics and motivates this choice.

4.1 Quality indicators

In literature, many indicators were proposed to assess the quality of the solutions returned by MOEAs. As in some previous adaptive approaches, aGAME uses such measures to control the algorithm behavior. But the proposed dynamic adaptation operator uses two separate indicators, rather than a single metric to measure both the diversity and quality of solutions, like hypervolume indicator. First, this choice was made to ensure the scalability of aGAME. Indeed, since the computation of hypervolume indicator is NP-hard, using it would complicate the extension of aGAME to solve optimization problems involving more than four objective functions. Besides, Deb and Jain [24] explain that it is best to use an indicator to measure the diversity of solutions and another one to assess the convergence of solutions to the Pareto-optimal front. Therefore, the proposed operator, DAO, uses the **Inverted generational distance** (IGD) to measure the proximity between solutions and the optimal Pareto front, when the latter is known. Otherwise, the non-dominated archive, which constitutes the best estimation of this reference front, is used instead. IGD relies on the computation of a euclidean distance to assess the mean of the minimal distance between all the points of PF^* and those of PF (see equation 3).

$$IGD = \frac{\left(\sum_{i=1}^{|PF^*|} d_m^*(\overrightarrow{x_i^*})\right)^{1/m}}{|PF^*|} \tag{3}$$

where

$$d_m^*(\overrightarrow{x_i^*}) = \min_{j=1}^{|PF|} \sqrt{\sum_{k=1}^{m}(f_k(\overrightarrow{x_i^*}) - f_k(\overrightarrow{x_j}))^2} \tag{4}$$

$\overrightarrow{x_i^*}$ is a solution belonging to PF^* and $\overrightarrow{x_j}$ is a PF solution.

DAO also uses a diversity indicator proposed by Deb and Jain, and named ***diversity running performance metric*** (DM) [24]. It evaluates the distribution of solutions in a given front, in relation to one objective function. DM is computed, for each generation, by projecting the non-dominated solutions (belonging to the first PF_1 Pareto front) onto a hyperplane. The latter is then divided into n hypercubes [1]. The diversity measure depends on the presence, or the absence, of solutions in each hypercube. The DM value is maximal when each hypercube contains at least one solution.

Zeng et al. [25, 26] propose to define n (the total number of hypercubes) as the ratio between the size of the population and the number of objective functions.

DAO periodically calculates the values of IGD and DM. IGD is used to detect if aGAME does not manage to reduce the proximity between the population and the reference front. DM is used to check if this is due to a lack of diversity, which could indicate that aGAME is trapped in a local optimum. According to these elements, aGAME chooses the best mode of exploration to be used during the next period. This is detailed in the following subsection.

4.2 Adaptation mechanism

Sticking with in the *explore first, exploit later* strategy, DAO first uses an **initial exploration** phase, widely exploring the search space, at the beginning of aGAME execution. This phase duration is t_{init}, expressed in number of generations. During this phase, the mutation rate (p_m) depends on the diversity level within the population (see equation 5).

$$p_m = 1 - DM(population) \tag{5}$$

$DM(population)$ reaches a value of between 0 and 1. The closer to 1 it is, the better the diversity level of the population. When $DM(population)$ is near 0, representing a low diversity within the population, p_m increases in order to favor mutations.

Beyond t_{init}, exploitation must be strengthened while keeping aGAME from being trapped in possible local optima. DAO regularly supervises the algorithm behavior (with a $t_{monitoring}$ period). It guides its evolution, when necessary. Figure 1 illustrates the general working of DAO.

When the IGD of the archive does not vary between two successive monitorings, this indicates that a stagnation phase of IGD has begun [2]. The correction to be applied depends on the diversity level within the best solutions evaluated at

[1]Hypercubes whose dimension is $m-1$, m being the number of objective functions of the tackled problem.

[2]Computing the IGD of the archive is only possible when the

t: generation number
t_{init}: duration of the initialization phase
$t_{monitoring}$: monitoring period of the algorithm
t_d: number of the generation during which the latest monitoring occurred
$P(t)$: population at t generation
$PF_1(t)$: first Pareto front of the population at t generation
$A(t)$: non-dominated archive built until generation t
mode: behavior the algorithm must choose (*normal*, *exploration*, *initial exploration*, or *exploitation*)
if $t < t_{init}$ **then**
    mode ← *initial exploration*
else
    if $t \% t_{monitoring} = 0$ **then**
        if $IGD(A(t)) = IGD(A(t_d))$ **then**
            if $DM(PF_1(t)) > DM(PF_1(t-1))$ **then**
                mode ← *exploitation*
            else
                mode ← *exploration*
            end if
        else
            mode ← *normal*
        end if
    end if
    $t_d \leftarrow t$
end if
return *mode*

Figure 1: Dynamic adaptation algorithm

time t. If these solutions are more various than those belonging to the previous generation, there is certainly no diversity loss in the current population. The behavior to adopt, **exploitation mode**, consists in intensifying the search for new solutions in the neighborhood of the best-known solutions. The archive of non-dominated solutions then participates in reproduction operations. During the selection of parents, it has a greater selection probability than any other set of solutions. Consequently the solutions it contains have priority when aGAME selects some parents.

If IGD stagnates and the diversity of the best-found solutions do not change or decrease, the algorithm might be trapped in an optimum, which may be either local or global. In case of a global optimum, finding no more improvement in the quality of the solutions is normal. All the behavior corrections brought by DAO will be unsuccessful, but this will not damage the archive quality. Otherwise, if the algorithm is in a local optimum, increasing its mutation rate could allow it to escape from this trap. The strategy to be used is then the **exploration mode**. Equation 6 specifies the formula used to control the mutation rate variation.

$$p_m = DM(PF_1) \tag{6}$$

If DAO does not detect any IGD stagnation at the time of monitoring, it selects the **normal mode** which works as GAME. In this case, the mutation rate equals the value usually used in literature (equation 7).

$$p_m = \frac{1}{number\ of\ variables} \tag{7}$$

Thus, periodical monitorings based on the proposed DAO permit to guide aGAME throughout its execution.

5. VALIDATION AND PERFORMANCE ASSESSMENT

The specific characteristics of aGAME are validated in this section. The impact of multiple Pareto fronts was illustrated in previous work [1]. This paper focuses on the influence of the dynamic adaptation operator and the comparison of aGAME with other algorithms in literature.

5.1 Experimental procedure

The experimentations carried out in this paper are based on all constrained bi-objective problems proposed for the CEC 2009 competition [19]. It consists in seven minimization problems with 10 real-valued decision variables.

In accordance with the experimental procedure indicated for the CEC 2009 competition, each evolutionary algorithm executes thirty independent runs for each addressed problem. The maximum number of evaluations is 30,000. In order to meet this requirement, GAME and aGAME use a population size equal to 100 and a number of generations equal to 300. Moreover, they use a 2-point crossover and bitflip mutation operators. The crossover rate is 0.8 and the mutation rate is $\frac{1}{number\ of\ variables}$ (it may vary during aGAME execution, due to DAO).

The parameters of each algorithm should be the same in all the problems with the same number of objective functions.

The performance indicator to be used as a comparison criterion is the IGD (see Equation 3). The IGD is to be minimized.

5.2 Influence of the dynamic adaptation operator

Since evolutionary algorithms are stochastic processes, they are usually carried out several times before one draws conclusions based on statistically reliable results. The first constrained problem of the CEC 2009 competition has been solved in thirty independent runs by GAME (non-adaptive algorithm) and aGAME, in order to assess the impact of the proposed dynamic adaptation operator. The evolution of the IGD over generations for the two algorithms is shown in Figure 2. In this figure, each point represents the average of thirty IGDs (30 runs) for the corresponding generation number.

At the end of 300 generations, aGAME provides lower value of IGD than GAME. The curve of the IGD by aGAME decreases slower than the one by GAME This is due to the initial phase of exploration which favors a quick scan of the search space. The two curves in Figure 2 are obtained by computing the average of the IGD (of each generation) for thirty executions. A detailed examination of the progress of GAME for a randomly selected execution shows that the curve of the IGD is a staircase curve, with relatively long periods of stagnation. This is illustrated in Figures 3 (a) to (f), which are representative of the evolution of the IGD over

optimal solutions are known. Otherwise, the archive is used as a reference front, because it represents the best known assessment of the optimal Pareto front. Therefore, the instruction **If** $IGD(A(t)) = IGD(A(t_d))$ must be replaced by **If** $IGD(PF_1(t)) \leq IGD(PF_1(t_d))$ in the algorithm given in figure 1.

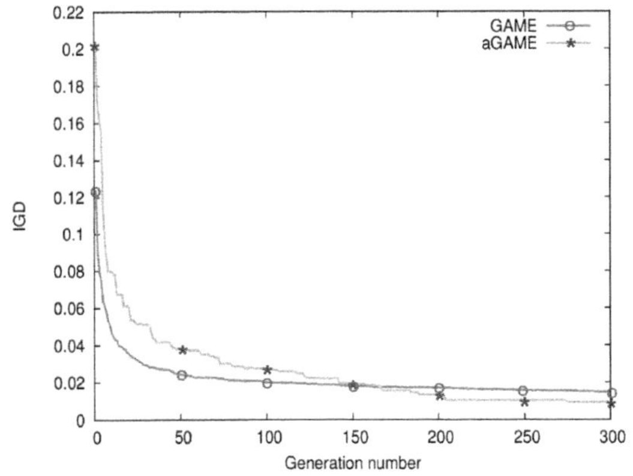

Figure 2: Average IGD for 30 independent runs of GAME and aGAME on the CEC 2009 first constrained problem

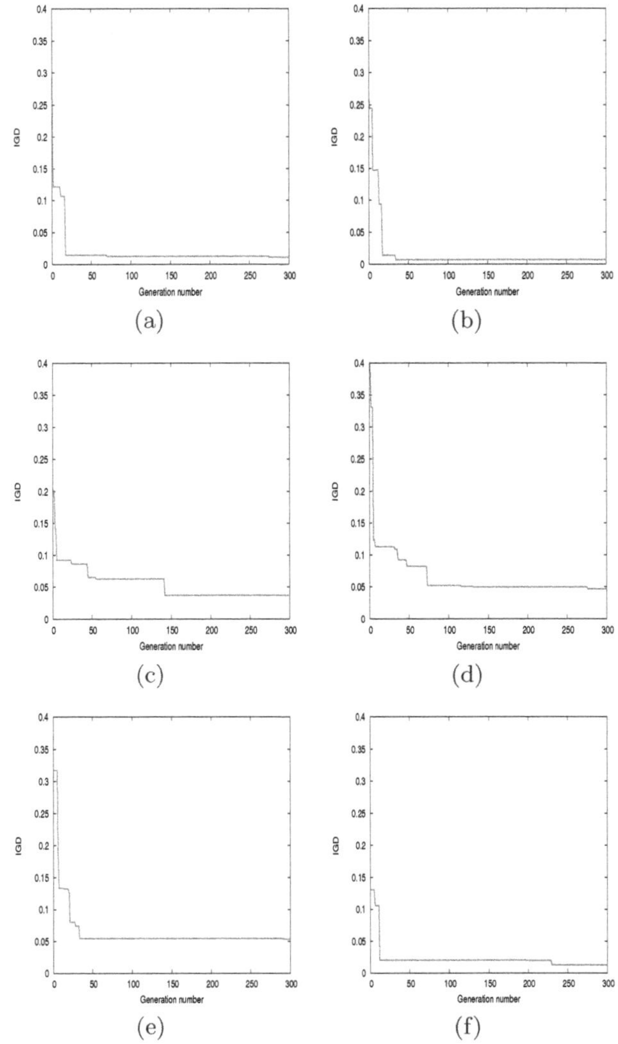

Figure 3: IGD value for six independent runs of GAME on the first constrained problem of the CEC 2009 competition

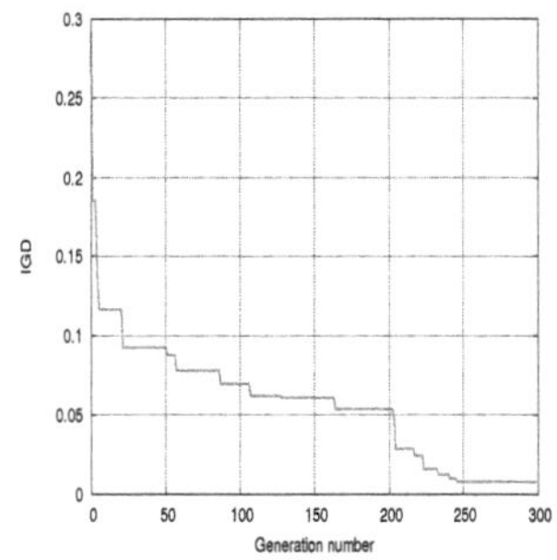

Figure 4: Improvement of the results of Fig. 3(a) with the DAO

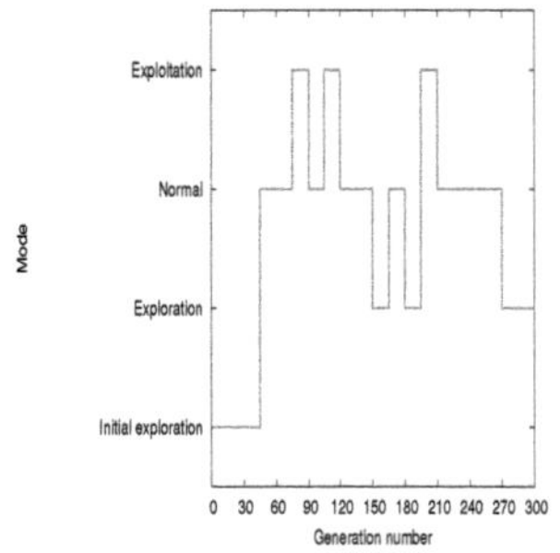

Figure 5: Dynamic mode switching associated to the results of Fig. 4

300 generations during 6 independent trials (with 5 Pareto fronts).

The experience that allowed to plot Figure 3 (a) was taken with aGAME (using the same algorithmic parameters and the same set of random numbers) in order to illustrate the influence of DAO on the progress of aGAME. The following values were arbitrarily set to the parameters required by DAO:

- t_{init} = 15% of the total number of generations
- $t_{monitoring}$ = 5% of the total number of generations

The IGD of the archive of the non-dominated solutions of aGAME (Figure 4) does not decline as rapidly as in the case of GAME (Figure 3 (a)). Indeed, aGAME begins with an initial exploration phase during which the probability of mutations is generally higher than in the GAME version. The goal is to enable a broad scan of the search space during the early generations and gather as much information as possible. The best solutions are added to the archive and their characteristics can be used during the exploitation phase.

In this example, the initial exploration phase is 45 generations long. After the expiration of t_{init}, aGAME alternates between three modes: normal, exploitation and exploration (see Figure 5). This dynamic change strategy allows aGAME to steadily improve its convergence indicator. This enables aGAME to reach lower IGD value at the end of the optimization process.

5.3 Comparison with other MOEAs

aGAME is compared to some algorithms of the literature. This comparative study is based on constrained bi-objective problems proposed for the CEC 2009 competition. Thus, it is compared to the three best-ranking algorithms in this category (*Constrained problems*)during the CEC 2009 competition: DMOEA-DD [27], LiuLi [28] and MTS [29].

DMOEAD-DD (Dynamical Multiobjective Evolutionary Algorithm - Domain Decomposition) improves DMOEA [30] that uses an aggregated *fitness* function including the notion of Pareto dominance, entropy and density (based on *crowding distance*). In the improved variant, the authors split the search space into several subsets. DMOEA computes Pareto fronts for each of them. Genetic operators permit information exchange between these subsets.

LiuLi (concatenation of the authors'name: Hai-Lin Liu and Xueqiang Li) splits the search space into sub-areas in order to reduce algorithm complexity. Genetic operations, particularly reproduction, are performed in a single subarea. Information exchange between areas is based on children, because they may be assigned to other areas.

MTS (Multiple Trajectory Search) is an algorithm based on three local search methods. For each solution, MTS determines the method which corresponds to its neighborhood. This algorithm begins with a large search. The size of neighborhood is progressively reduced until it reaches a given minimal size. Then its size is set to its initial value and the regression re-starts.

To illustrate the gain brought by the dynamic adaptation operator (DAO), aGAME performance is also compared to that of its non-adaptive version (GAME). The comparison is made in accordance with the experimental conditions defined in the competition. For each algorithm, Table 1 presents the average of the IGD value computed in the sets of final solutions, in 30 independent executions.

This study shows that, globally, GAME reaches solutions which are quite close to the reference front. This results in low IGD value in table 1. Moreover the adaptive version, aGAME, performs better than GAME.

6. CONCLUSION

To sum up, GAME is an elitist multi-objective genetic algorithm, based on the building of multiple Pareto fronts. This ranking strategy and the associated 2-step selection provided gains both in terms of proximity with optimal solutions and in terms of diversity in the set of final solutions returned by GAME.

Moreover, aGAME improves the results of GAME adding an adaptive strategy (DAO). Each loop is more efficient by selecting the right mode (exploration or exploitation) at the right time.

Finally, using the experimental conditions of the CEC 2009 competition showed that aGAME would have been quite well ranked in this competition, which constitutes a promising result. In addition, aGAME uses a parallel evaluation procedure based on a master-slave model. This model allowed to reduce the experimentation duration in previous work in the field of mobile networks [31]. In this context, a previous version of the algorithm allowed to solve constrained problems with four objectives, the evaluation of which was done using a network simulator. Nevertheless, designing an asynchronous version of aGAME would be very interesting. Such a version would no longer rely on architecture where the master must wait until all the slaves have finished their task before building the next generation.

7. REFERENCES

[1] Wahabou Abdou, Christelle Bloch, Damien Charlet, and François Spies. Multi-pareto-ranking evolutionary algorithm. In *12th European Conference on Evolutionary Computation in Combinatorial Optimisation (EvoCOP 2012)*, volume 7245 of *LNCS*, pages 194–205, Malaga, Spain, 2012. Springer.

[2] Kalyanmoy Deb, Amrit Pratap, Sameer Agarwal, and T. Meyarivan. A Fast Elitist Multi-Objective Genetic Algorithm: NSGA-II. *IEEE Transactions on Evolutionary Computation*, 6:182–197, 2000.

[3] E. Zitzler, M. Laumanns, and L. Thiele. SPEA2: Improving the strength pareto evolutionary algorithm. Technical Report 103, Computer Engineering and Networks Laboratory (TIK), Swiss Federal Institute of Technology (ETH), Zurich, Switzerland, 2001.

[4] E. Zitzler and S. Künzli. Indicator-Based Selection in Multiobjective Search. In *Conference on Parallel Problem Solving from Nature (PPSN VIII)*, pages 832–842. Springer, 2004.

[5] Aimin Zhou, Bo-Yang Qu, Hui Li, Shi-Zheng Zhao, Ponnuthurai Nagaratnam Suganthan, and Qingfu Zhang. Multiobjective evolutionary algorithms: A survey of the state of the art. *Swarm and Evolutionary Computation*, 1(1):32 – 49, 2011.

[6] Matthieu Basseur, Rong-Qiang Zeng, and Jin-Kao Hao. Hypervolume-based multi-objective local search. *Neural Computing & Applications*, pages 1–13, 2011. 10.1007/s00521-011-0588-4.

[7] Johannes Bader and Eckart Zitzler. Hype: an algorithm for fast hypervolume-based many-objective optimization. *Evolutionary Computation*, 19(1):45–76, 2011.

[8] Thomas Bartz-Beielstein, Marco Chiarandini, Luís Paquete, and Mike Preuss, editors. *Experimental Methods for the Analysis of Optimization Algorithms*. Springer, Germany, November 2010.

[9] Jean-Laurent Hippolyte, Christelle Bloch, Pascal Chatonnay, Christophe Espanet, Didier Chamagne, and Geneviève Wimmer. Tuning an evolutionary algorithm with taguchi methods. In Richard Chbeir, Youakim Badr, Ajith Abraham, Dominique Laurent, and Fernando Ferri, editors, *CSTST'08, 5th Int. Conf. on Soft Computing as Transdisciplinary Science and Technology*, pages 265–272. ACM Press, 2008.

[10] Agoston Endre Eiben, Robert Hinterding, and Zbigniew Michalewicz. Parameter control in evolutionary algorithms. *IEEE Transations on Evolutionary Computation*, 3(2):124–141, July 1999.

[11] V. K. Koumousis and C. P. Katsaras. A saw-tooth genetic algorithm combining the effects of variable population size and reinitialization to enhance performance. *IEEE Trans. Evolutionary Computation*, 10(1):19–28, 2006.

[12] Kay Chen Tan, Swee Chiang Chiam, Abdullah Al Mamun, and Chi Keong Goh. Balancing exploration and exploitation with adaptive variation for evolutionary multi-objective optimization. *European Journal of Operational Research*, 197(2):701–713, 2009.

[13] Kenneth De Jong. Parameter Setting in EAs: a 30 Year Perspective. pages 1–18. 2007.

[14] Kalyanmoy Deb, Karthik Sindhya, and Tatsuya Okabe. Self-adaptive simulated binary crossover for real-parameter optimization. In *Proceedings of the 9th annual conference on Genetic and evolutionary computation*, GECCO '07, pages 1187–1194, New York, NY, USA, 2007. ACM.

[15] Kalyanmoy Deb and Ram B. Agrawal. Simulated Binary Crossover for Continuous Search Space. *Complex Systems*, 9(2):115–148, 1995.

[16] Fanchao Zeng, Malcolm Yoke Hean Low, James Decraene, Suiping Zhou, and Wentong Cai. Self-Adptive Mechanism for Multi-objective Evolutionary Algorithms. In *Proceedings of the*

Problem	DMOEADD	LiuLi	MTS	GAME	aGAME
Constrained Problem 1	0.01131	0.00085	0.01918	0.01489	0.00828
Constrained Problem 2	0.0021	0.004203	0.02677	0.00042	0.00039
Constrained Problem 3	0.056305	0.182905	0.10446	0.03462	0.03385
Constrained Problem 4	0.00699	0.014232	0.01109	0.00742	0.00700
Constrained Problem 5	0.01577	0.10973	0.02077	0.01227	0.01129
Constrained Problem 6	0.01502	0.013948	0.01616	0.00181	0.00138
Constrained Problem 7	0.01905	0.10446	0.02469	0.00545	0.00373
Average Ranking	3rd	4th	5th	2nd	1st

Table 1: Mean value of IGD returned by aGAME, GAME and the 3 best-ranking algorithms in CEC 2009 competition

InternationalMultiConforence of Engineers and Computer Scientists 2010, IMECS 2010.

[17] Jean-Laurent Hippolyte, Christelle Bloch, Pascal Chatonnay, Christophe Espanet, and Didier Chamagne. A self-adaptive multiagent evolutionary algorithm for electrical machine design. In Dirk Thierens et al., editors, *GECCO'07, 9th annual conference on Genetic and evolutionary computation*, volume 2, pages 1250–1255, New York, United States, 2007. ACM Press.

[18] Robert Hinterding, Zbigniew Michalewicz, and Thomas C. Peachey. Self-adaptive genetic algorithm for numeric functions. In *Proceedings of the 4th International Conference on Parallel Problem Solving from Nature*, PPSN IV, pages 420–429, London, UK, 1996. Springer-Verlag.

[19] Qingfu Zhang, Aimin Zhou, Shizheng Zhao, Ponnuthurai Nagaratnam Suganthan, Wudong Liu, and Santosh Tiwari. Multiobjective optimization test instances for the cec 2009 special session and competition. Technical report, The School of Computer Science and Electronic Engineering, 2009.

[20] K. Deb. *Multi-Objective Optimization using Evolutionary Algorithms.* Wiley-Interscience Series in Systems and Optimization. John Wiley & Sons, Chichester, 2001.

[21] Kay Chen Tan, Chi Keong Goh, Y. J. Yang, and Tong Heng Lee. Evolving better population distribution and exploration in evolutionary multi-objective optimization. *European Journal of Operational Research*, 171(2):463–495, 2006.

[22] Kay Chen Tan, Tong Heng Lee, and Eik Fun Khor. Evolutionary algorithms with dynamic population size and local exploration for multiobjective optimization. *IEEE Trans. Evolutionary Computation*, 5(6):565–588, 2001.

[23] Neal K. Bambha, Shuvra S. Bhattacharyya, Jürgen Teich, and Eckart Zitzler. Systematic integration of parameterized local search into evolutionary algorithms. *IEEE Trans. Evolutionary Computation*, 8(2):137–155, 2004.

[24] Kalyanmoy Deb and Sachin Jain. Running Performance Metrics for Evolutionary Multi-Objective Optimization. In Lipo Wang, Kay Chen Tan, Takeshi Furuhashi, Jong-Hwan Kim, and Xin Yao, editors, *Proceedings of the 4th Asia-Pacific Conference on Simulated Evolution and Learning (SEAL'02)*, volume 1, pages 13–20, Orchid Country Club, Singapore, November 2002. Nanyang Technical University.

[25] Fanchao Zeng, James Decraene, Malcolm Yoke Hean Low, Suiping Zhou, and Wentong Cai. Diversity-driven self-adaptation inăevolutionary algorithms. 70:95–106, 2011.

[26] Fanchao Zeng, Malcolm Yoke Hean Low, James Decraene, Suiping Zhou, and Wentong Cai. Self-adaptive mechanism for multi-objective evolutionary algorithms. In S. I. Ao, Oscar Castillo, Craig Douglas, David Dagan Feng, and Jeong-A Lee, editors, *Proceedings of the International MultiConference of Engineers and Computer Scientists (IMECS 2010)*, pages 7–12. Newswood Limited, March 2010.

[27] Minzhong Liu, Xiufen Zou, Yu Chen, and Zhijian Wu. Performance assessment of dmoea-dd with cec 2009 moea competition test instances. In *IEEE Congress on Evolutionary Computation*, pages 2913–2918, 2009.

[28] Hai-Lin Liu and Xueqiang Li. The multiobjective evolutionary algorithm based on determined weight and sub-regional search. In *Proceedings of the Eleventh conference on Congress on Evolutionary Computation*, CEC'09, pages 1928–1934, Piscataway, NJ, USA, 2009. IEEE Press.

[29] Lin-Yu Tseng and Chun Chen. Multiple trajectory search for unconstrained/constrained multi-objective optimization. In *Proceedings of the Eleventh conference on Congress on Evolutionary Computation*, CEC'09, pages 1951–1958, Piscataway, NJ, USA, 2009. IEEE Press.

[30] Xiufen Zou, Yu Chen, Minzhong Liu, and Lishan Kang. A new evolutionary algorithm for solving many-objective optimization problems. *IEEE transactions on systems, man, and cybernetics. Part B, Cybernetics : a publication of the IEEE Systems, Man, and Cybernetics Society*, 38(5):1402–1412, October 2008.

[31] Wahabou Abdou, Adrien Henriet, Christelle Bloch, Dominique Dhoutaut, Damien Charlet, and François Spies. Using an evolutionary algorithm to optimize the broadcasting methods in mobile ad hoc networks. *Journal of Network and Computer Applications*, 34(6):1794 – 1804, 2011.

Convergence of Hypervolume-Based Archiving Algorithms II: Competitiveness

Karl Bringmann
Max-Planck-Institut für Informatik
Saarbrücken, Germany

Tobias Friedrich
Max-Planck-Institut für Informatik
Saarbrücken, Germany

ABSTRACT

We study the convergence behavior of $(\mu + \lambda)$-archiving algorithms. A $(\mu + \lambda)$-archiving algorithm defines how to choose in each generation μ children from μ parents and λ offspring together. Archiving algorithms have to choose individuals online without knowing future offspring. Previous studies assumed the offspring generation to be best-case. We assume the initial population and the offspring generation to be worst-case and use the competitive ratio to measure how much smaller hypervolumes an archiving algorithm finds due to not knowing the future in advance. We prove that all archiving algorithms which increase the hypervolume in each step (if they can) are only μ-competitive. We also present a new archiving algorithm which is $(4 + 2/\mu)$-competitive. This algorithm not only achieves a constant competitive ratio, but is also efficiently computable. Both properties provably do not hold for the commonly used greedy archiving algorithms, for example those used in SIBEA, SMS-EMOA, or the generational MO-CMA-ES.

Categories and Subject Descriptors

F.2 [**Theory of Computation**]:
Analysis of Algorithms and Problem Complexity

Keywords

Multiobjective Optimization, Theory,
Performance Measures, Selection

1. INTRODUCTION

As many real-world optimization problems have multiple objectives (like time vs. cost), they have in general no unique optimum, but an often very large (or even infinite) set of incomparable solutions which form the Pareto front. Multi-objective optimizers deal with this by trying to find a small set of trade-off solutions which approximate the Pareto front. They typically keep a bounded archive of μ points (population) in order to capture the output of the search process. In each round they generate λ new points (offspring) by mutation and crossover. The key question is then how to select μ individuals from a larger population. We consider the so-called plus selection strategy, where the next population is chosen out of the λ offspring and μ parents together. We call a specific replacement strategy a $(\mu + \lambda)$-*archiving algorithm* which defines how to choose a new population of μ children from the union of μ parents and λ offspring.

The goal for hypervolume-based multi-objective evolutionary algorithms (MOEAs) is to maximize the hypervolume indicator of the output population, which is the volume of the dominated portion of the objective space (see Section 2 for a formal definition). For this type of MOEA, two archiving algorithms are known in the literature:

- A *locally optimal* archiving algorithm returns a subset of μ points from the given $\mu + \lambda$ points such that the hypervolume indicator is maximized.
- A *greedy* archiving algorithm deletes a point such that the hypervolume of the remaining points is maximal. This is repeated until only μ points are left.

We prove in this paper that all locally optimal and all greedy archiving algorithms are NP-hard (cf. Theorem 3.1 and Observation 2.8) and therefore not efficiently computable unless P=NP. Many hypervolume based algorithms like SIBEA [12], SMS-EMOA [1], or the generational MO-CMA-ES [8] use greedy archiving algorithms. As locally optimal algorithms have to choose the best out of a large number, $\binom{\mu+\lambda}{\mu}$, of subsets of the given points, they are generally considered to be computationally infeasible. Note that a locally optimal archiving algorithm in general does not maximize the hypervolume over multiple generations. However, it still seems to have superior theoretical properties: It has long been known that the resulting point sets of both algorithms differ [3], and that the deleted hypervolume (the contribution of the deleted points) can even be arbitrarily larger for greedy archiving algorithms compared to locally optimal algorithms [5].

We want to study the intrinsic limitations of and the potential provided by hypervolume-based archiving algorithms. Beyond the smaller classes of locally optimal and greedy archiving algorithms we thus also consider the following two natural classes of archiving algorithms:

- A *non-decreasing* archiving algorithm chooses the population of children such that the dominated hypervolume does not decrease compared to the parent generation.
- An *increasing* archiving algorithm chooses the population of children such that the dominated hypervolume increases compared to the parent generation, unless there is no subset of population and offspring with larger dominated hypervolume.

GECCO'12, July 7–11, 2012, Philadelphia, Pennsylvania, USA.

Both are intuitively desirable properties for hypervolume-based archiving algorithms. We will see that there are algorithms which are non-decreasing, but not increasing (cf. Algorithms 3 and 4). Moreover, we prove that both classes significantly differ. There are non-decreasing archiving algorithms which are better and faster than all increasing archiving algorithms (see Sections 1.2 and 1.3 for more detailed statements).

To rigorously study the impact of archiving algorithms on convergence, we cannot concentrate only on single iterations, but have to consider multiple generations of populations. We model this long run behavior with the initial population being worst-case input to the archiving algorithm, followed by some kind of offspring generation, and we then ask whether we arrive at a population with large hypervolume. There are two natural assumptions on the offspring generation: best-case and worst-case. Each assumption corresponds to one of the following result sections.

1.1 Known results on effectiveness

All previous work in this setting [7, 10, 13] assumes a best-case perspective on the offspring generation. This means that we ask whether, for each population, there exists a sequence of offspring sets such that the archiving algorithm ends up in a population maximizing the hypervolume. This was formalized by Bringmann and Friedrich [7] with the notion of effectiveness: An archiving algorithm is *effective* if there is a sequence of offspring such that the algorithm reaches an optimum. Zitzler et al. [13] proved that all non-decreasing $(\mu + 1)$-archiving strategies are ineffective and all locally optimal $(\mu + \mu)$-archiving strategies are effective. Bringmann and Friedrich [7] proved that all non-decreasing $(\mu + \lambda)$-archiving strategies are ineffective for $\lambda < \mu$.

In order to measure how close to an optimal set the best reachable sets for $\lambda < \mu$ are, we call an archiving algorithm *α-approximate* if it can always reach a set with a hypervolume at least $1/\alpha$ times the largest possible hypervolume. Bringmann and Friedrich [7] proved that no non-decreasing $(\mu + \lambda)$-archiving algorithm can be better than $\left(1 + 0.1338\left(\frac{1}{\lambda} - \frac{1}{\mu}\right)\right)$-approximate. This bound can be tightened if the hypervolume is defined relative to a reference set instead of a single reference point. For this more general definition of the hypervolume indicator, Ulrich and Thiele [10] showed a lower bound of $1 + \frac{1}{2\lambda}$ for $\lambda < \mu$.

On the other hand, Bringmann and Friedrich [7] showed that every increasing $(\mu + \lambda)$-archiving algorithm reaches a 2-approximation. Ulrich and Thiele [10] showed that every increasing $(\mu + 1)$-archiving algorithm reaches a $\left(2 - \frac{1}{\mu}\right)$-approximation. More precisely, they showed that every non-decreasing $(\mu + \lambda)$-archiving algorithm reaches a $\left(2 - \frac{\lambda - p}{\mu}\right)$-approximation, where $\mu = q\lambda - p$ with $p < \lambda$ and $p, q \in \mathbb{N}_{\geqslant 0}$. Note that in these results we omitted all summands and factors of arbitrarily small $\varepsilon > 0$.

1.2 New results on competitiveness

In this paper we assume a worst-case perspective on the offspring generation. This corresponds to the well-known concept of *competitive analysis*. It has already been observed that archiving algorithms fit nicely in this classical theory developed for online algorithms [2]. López-Ibáñez, Knowles, and Laumanns [9, p. 59] suggested it as an open problem "to use competitive analysis techniques from the field of online algorithms to obtain worst-case bounds, in terms of a measure of 'regret' for archivers."

We consider the initial population and offspring as worst-case input and ask again how large a hypervolume we can get. In this case, however, the adversary, who selects the offspring, can limit the search to a very small part of the search space, and it is therefore impossible in general to reach the optimum hypervolume. This motivates the following definition. We say an archiving algorithm is *α-competitive* if for all initial populations and offspring it reaches a hypervolume which is only a factor $1/\alpha$ smaller than the hypervolume of the *best μ points seen* (cf. Definition 2.9).

On the negative side, we prove that all increasing archiving algorithms are exactly μ-competitive (see Theorem 3.2 for the upper bound and Theorem 3.3 for the lower bound). This means that there is a sequence of offspring such that the hypervolume of the μ individuals chosen iteratively by an algorithm which maximizes the hypervolume in each step is μ times larger than the maximum hypervolume achievable by another choice of μ individuals. This result seems to suggest that the notion of competitiveness does not help in comparing archiving algorithms, as all reasonable archiving algorithms meet exactly the same bound.

However, on the positive side, we are able to design an archiving algorithm that is $4 + 2/\mu$-competitive (cf. Theorem 4.1), which implies a constant competitive ratio compared to the unbounded ratio of μ. It is a non-decreasing archiving algorithm which is not increasing, i.e., there are populations and offspring where we stay with the current population, although the offspring allows an increase in hypervolume. This proves that significantly better competitive ratios can be achieved for archiving algorithms which are not increasing compared to the typically used increasing archiving algorithms. The algorithm works as follows (for details see Algorithm 3): It adds offspring one by one to the current population. Considering the population and an offspring, we compute the hypervolume for exchanging the offspring with any other point in the population. We take the best exchange only if it increases the population's hypervolume by at least a certain minimal factor.

1.3 New results on computational efficiency

We prove that all increasing archiving algorithms are NP-hard to compute (cf. Theorem 3.1). This also implies that all common greedy archiving algorithms are not efficiently computable unless P=NP (cf. Observation 2.8). This still allows archiving algorithms which are not increasing to be efficiently computable. Indeed, we also prove that a randomized variant of our aforementioned archiving algorithm can be made to run efficiently (cf. Theorem 4.3). Note that this is in sharp contrast to the large set of increasing archiving algorithms, which all have a worse competitive ratio (cf. Theorem 3.3) and a worse computational complexity (cf. Theorem 3.1) compared to the proposed new archiving algorithm. The underlying reason why the new algorithm can beat all increasing archiving algorithms is that approximating the hypervolume is tractable [4] and for the new algorithm it is sufficient only to approximate the hypervolume, as it checks only for constant factor increases. Although the new archiving algorithm might not be used as-is in any practical MOEAs, it is a proof of concept that there are efficiently computable archiving algorithms which can beat the competitive ratio of the thus far typically used locally optimal and greedy archiving algorithms.

The outline is as follows. In Section 2 we introduce the basic concepts and notation. Section 3 presents the tight bound on the competitiveness of increasing archiving algorithms and proves that all of them are NP-hard. We propose a non-decreasing algorithm with constant competitiveness in Section 4, and show that it can even be computed efficiently.

2. PRELIMINARIES

This section formally introduces all necessary notation. The two most fundamental concepts are the hypervolume indicator (Section 2.1) and archiving algorithms (Section 2.2). The combination of both, i.e. hypervolume-based archiving algorithms, are introduced in Section 2.3. These first three parts of this section closely follow [7]. Our new quality measure of competitiveness is then defined in Section 2.4.

We consider maximization problems with vector-valued objective functions $f\colon \mathcal{X} \to \mathbb{R}^d$, where $\mathcal{X}$ denotes an arbitrary search space. The feasible points $\mathcal{Y} := f(\mathcal{X})$ are called the objective space. Consider the following abstract framework of a MOEA:

Algorithm 1: General $(\mu + \lambda)$-MOEA

```
1  P^0 ← initialize with μ individuals
2  for i ← 1 to N do
3      Q^i ← generate λ offspring
4      P^i ← select μ individuals from P^{i-1} ∪ Q^i
```

We make no assumptions about the specific search space $\mathcal{X}$. We assume that both the initialization (cf. line 1 of Algorithm 1) and the offspring generation (cf. line 3 of Algorithm 1) are worst-case. Our main concern is how the population of children is chosen (cf. line 4 of Algorithm 1). We will formally define and discuss different *archiving algorithms* in Sections 2.2 and 2.3.

We use the terms archive and population synonymously for the set of current solutions P^i of Algorithm 1. In concrete MOEAs, populations are subsets of the search space. As we do not want to assume any structural properties of the search space, we abstract from the search space and will *only work on the objective space* $\mathcal{Y} \subseteq \mathbb{R}^d$ in the remainder. We therefore also identify individuals with points in the d-dimensional Euclidean space.

DEFINITION 2.1. *A population P is a finite multiset and a subset of $\mathbb{R}^d$. If an objective space $\mathcal{Y} \subseteq \mathbb{R}^d$ is fixed, we require $P \subseteq \mathcal{Y}$. We call P a μ-population if $|P| \leqslant \mu$.*

2.1 Hypervolume indicator

The hypervolume indicator HYP(P) [11] of a population P is the volume of the union of regions of the objective space which are dominated by P and bounded by a reference point R. Here domination refers to the following dominance relation for points in the objective space $\mathcal{Y} \subseteq \mathbb{R}^d$:

$$(x_1, x_2, \ldots, x_d) \preceq (y_1, y_2, \ldots, y_d)$$
$$\text{iff } x_1 \leqslant y_1, x_2 \leqslant y_2, \ldots, \text{and } x_d \leqslant y_d.$$

Formally, the hypervolume HYP(P) of a population P is defined as

$$\mathrm{HYP}(P) := \int_{\mathbb{R}^d} A_P(x)\,dx$$

where the attainment function $A_P\colon \mathbb{R}^d \to \{0,1\}$ is an indicator function on the objective space that describes the space above the reference point R which is dominated by P, that is, $A_P(x) = 1$ if $R \preceq x$ and there is a $p \in P$ such that $x \preceq p$, and $A_P(x) = 0$ otherwise.

We fix the reference point w.l.o.g. to $R = 0^d$, since translations do not change any of our results. This means that the reference point is globally fixed and known to the archiving algorithm.

The aim of a hypervolume-based MOEA is finding a set P^* of size μ which maximizes the hypervolume, that is,

$$\mathrm{HYP}(P^*) = \mathrm{maxHYP}_\mu(\mathcal{Y})$$

where we define for all $Y \subset \mathbb{R}^d$,

$$\mathrm{maxHYP}_\mu(Y) := \sup_{\substack{P \subseteq Y \\ |P| \leqslant \mu}} \mathrm{HYP}(P).$$

In the remainder of the paper, the set Y will often be finite. In these cases, the supremum in the definition of maxHYP$_\mu(Y)$ becomes a maximum. However, for infinite sets the supremum is necessary in general.

The *contribution* of a point p to a population P is

$$\mathrm{CON}_P(p) := \mathrm{HYP}(P) - \mathrm{HYP}(P - p),$$

where we use the notation $P - p$ for $P \setminus \{p\}$. We also use $P + p$ to shortcut $P \cup \{p\}$ throughout the paper.

Note that according to the definition of CON$_P(p)$, the contributing hypervolume of a dominated individual is zero.

2.2 Archiving algorithms

We now specify more formally how to choose the μ offsprings in line 4 of Algorithm 1. For this, we consider the following general framework of an archiving algorithm.

Algorithm 2: General $(\mu + \lambda)$-archiving algorithm

input : μ-population P, λ-population Q
output: μ-population P' with $P' \subseteq P \cup Q$

Note that any $(\mu + \lambda)$-archiving algorithm is also a $(\mu + \lambda')$-archiving algorithm for any $\lambda' < \lambda$, as we then allow only a subset of the inputs, namely with smaller offspring population Q. We do not make any assumptions on the runtime of an archiving algorithm. In fact, as hypervolume computation is #P-hard [4], most hypervolume-based archiving algorithms are not computable in polynomial time in the number of objectives d. We will use the following notation to describe an archiving algorithm.

DEFINITION 2.2. *A $(\mu+\lambda)$-archiving algorithm $\mathcal{A}$ is a partial mapping $\mathcal{A}\colon 2^{\mathbb{R}^d} \times 2^{\mathbb{R}^d} \mapsto 2^{\mathbb{R}^d}$ such that for a μ-population P and a λ-population Q, $\mathcal{A}(P,Q)$ is a μ-population and $\mathcal{A}(P,Q) \subseteq P \cup Q$.*

For convenience, we sometimes drop the prefix $(\mu + \lambda)$ and just refer to an archiving algorithm (or even shorter: *algorithm*) without specifying μ and λ. With this notation, we can now formally describe the generation process of Algorithm 1 as follows.

DEFINITION 2.3. *Let P^0 be a μ-population and $Q^1, \ldots, Q^N$ a sequence of λ-populations. Then*

$$P^i := \mathcal{A}(P^{i-1}, Q^i) \qquad \text{for all } i = 1, \ldots, N.$$

With slight abuse of notation we also set

$$\mathcal{A}(P^0, Q^1, \ldots, Q^i) := P^i \qquad \text{for all } i = 1, \ldots, N.$$

2.3 Hypervolume-based archiving algorithms

We now specify three classes of hypervolume-based archiving algorithms. The first one only requires the archiving algorithms to never return a solution with a smaller hypervolume:

DEFINITION 2.4. *A $(\mu + \lambda)$-archiving algorithm $\mathcal{A}$ is* non-decreasing, *if for all inputs P and Q we have*

$$\mathrm{HYP}(\mathcal{A}(P,Q)) \geqslant \mathrm{HYP}(P).$$

All reasonable hypervolume-based archiving algorithms are non-decreasing. However, the class also contains ineffective algorithms like the algorithm which always returns P.

The second, slightly smaller class of hypervolume-based archiving algorithms is defined as follows.

DEFINITION 2.5. *A $(\mu + \lambda)$-archiving algorithm $\mathcal{A}$ is* increasing, *if it is non-decreasing and for all inputs P and Q with*

$$\text{maxHYP}_\mu(P \cup Q) > \text{HYP}(P)$$

we have

$$\text{HYP}(\mathcal{A}(P, Q)) > \text{HYP}(P).$$

Moreover, we define locally optimal and greedy archiving algorithms. Note that for both classes there are more than one archiving algorithm fulfilling the respective definition, as ties may be broken arbitrarily.

DEFINITION 2.6. *A $(\mu + \lambda)$-archiving algorithm $\mathcal{A}$ is* locally optimal, *if for all inputs P and Q we have*

$$\text{HYP}(\mathcal{A}(P, Q)) = \text{maxHYP}_\mu(P \cup Q).$$

DEFINITION 2.7. *A $(\mu + \lambda)$-archiving algorithm $\mathcal{A}$ is* greedy, *if there are functions $\mathcal{A}'(P) = P \setminus \{\text{argmin}_{p \in P} \text{CON}_P(p)\}$ such that for all inputs P and Q we have*

$$\mathcal{A}(P, Q) = \underbrace{\mathcal{A}' \circ \ldots \circ \mathcal{A}'}_{\lambda \text{ times}}(P \cup Q).$$

The rest of the paper focuses on increasing and non-decreasing archiving algorithms. Their relation to locally optimal and greedy archiving algorithms is as follows.

OBSERVATION 2.8. *Greedy $(\mu + 1)$-archiving algorithms and locally-optimal $(\mu+\lambda)$-archiving algorithms are increasing archiving algorithms. Greedy $(\mu + \lambda)$-archiving algorithms are not necessarily non-decreasing archiving algorithms for $\lambda > 1$.*

This observation allows us to translate all forthcoming bounds for increasing archiving algorithms to locally-optimal archiving algorithms. Observation 2.8 also implies that all our negative results hold for greedy algorithms, since the computational hardness (cf. Theorem 3.1) and the lower bound for the competitive ratio (cf. Theorem 3.2) apply to the restriction of a greedy algorithm to $\lambda = 1$ and, thus, also to greedy algorithms in general. There is only one result for increasing algorithms which does not directly apply to greedy algorithms, which is the upper bound for the competitive ratio (cf. Theorem 3.3). As we are more interested in the lower bound for the competitive ratio of greedy algorithms, we do not prove an additional upper bound, but conjecture that the bound is still tight for greedy archiving algorithms for arbitrary λ.

2.4 Competitiveness

We take a worst-case view on the initial population as well as offspring generation, so we want to bound $\mathcal{A}(P^0, Q^1, \ldots, Q^N)$ for any initial population P^0 and any offspring generations $Q^1, \ldots, Q^N$. Observe that in this setting all results have to be independent of the specific objective space $\mathcal{Y}$ and we cannot hope to reach $\text{maxHYP}_\mu(\mathcal{Y})$ in general. The only aim can be achieving a hypervolume as good as the maximum hypervolume among all μ-populations which are subsets of the points we have seen so far, that is,

$$\text{maxHYP}_\mu\left(P^0 \cup \bigcup_{i=1}^{N} Q^i\right),$$

which can be arbitrarily smaller than $\text{maxHYP}_\mu(\mathcal{Y})$.

This allows us to view archiving algorithms as an online problem where the algorithm is fed with new offspring in a serial fashion and has to decide which individual it should keep in the population without knowing the entire input. To measure the 'regret' of an archiving algorithm we define its competitive ratio α as follows.

DEFINITION 2.9. *Let P^0 be a μ-population and Q^i be λ-populations for $1 \leqslant i \leqslant N$. Then $I := (P^0, Q^1, \ldots, Q^N)$ is an* instance. *We also set*

$$\text{Obs}(I) := P^0 \cup \bigcup_{i=1}^{N} Q^i.$$

An archiving algorithm $\mathcal{A}$ is α-competitive (for some $\alpha \geqslant 1$) if for all instances $I = (P^0, Q^1, \ldots, Q^N)$ we have

$$\mathcal{A}(P^0, Q^1, \ldots, Q^N) \geqslant \frac{1}{\alpha} \text{maxHYP}_\mu(\text{Obs}(I)).$$

3. INCREASING ALGORITHMS

We first study the large class of increasing archiving algorithms, which also includes locally optimal and greedy archiving algorithms (cf. Observation 2.8). We prove that all increasing archiving algorithms are NP-hard to compute (Section 3.1) and only achieve a competitive ratio of μ (Section 3.2).

3.1 Increasing algorithms are inefficient

By reduction from the known hardness of computing a least contributor of a set of points, we show the following theorem.

THEOREM 3.1. *All increasing archiving algorithm are NP-hard to compute (in $\mu + d$).*

Proof. We reduce from the problem of computing a least contributor of a set of points: Given $P \subseteq \mathbb{R}^d$ of size n, compute a point $p \in P$ with $\text{CON}_P(p)$ minimal (see Section 2.1 for the definition). This problem is NP-hard according to [6].

Let P be an instance to the least contributor problem, and let $\mathcal{A}$ be an efficiently computable increasing archiving algorithm. We compute $A(p) := P \setminus \mathcal{A}(P - p, \{p\})$ for each $p \in P$. This is the point with which the archiving algorithm $\mathcal{A}$ exchanges p given population $P - p$ and offspring $\{p\}$.

Consider the graph with vertex set P and directed edges $(p, A(p))$ for each $p \in P$. This graph may have self-loops. It includes a directed cycle as a subgraph: Starting at any point and always following the unique out-edge we will at some point see an already visited point again; this means we traversed a cycle (after some initial path).

Let $(p_0, \ldots, p_{k-1})$ be such a cycle. It can have length $k = 1$, if the cycle is a self-loop. Since $A(p_i) = p_{i+1}$ (with indices modulo k) and the archiving algorithm is increasing — thus also non-decreasing — we have $\text{HYP}(P - p_{i+1}) \geqslant \text{HYP}(P - p_i)$ for all $i \in \{0, \ldots, k - 1\}$. Hence, all $\text{HYP}(P - p_i)$ are equal; in particular $\text{HYP}(P - p_0) = \text{HYP}(P - A(p_0))$. Since the archiving algorithm is increasing, this means that no increase was possible given population $P - p_0$ and offspring $\{p_0\}$, and, hence, that $\text{HYP}(P - p_0) = \text{HYP}(P) - \text{CON}_P(p_0)$ is maximal among all $\text{HYP}(P - p)$. In other words, $\text{CON}_P(p_0)$ is minimal and p_0 is a least contributor. The same holds for all other points $p \in P$ that lie on a directed cycle in the constructed graph. Thus, we can compute a least contributor efficiently. □

3.2 Increasing algorithms are not competitive

It is easy to show an upper bound on the competitive ratio of μ for a very large class of archiving algorithms. It applies to all non-decreasing archiving algorithms with the following property: If a single offspring point $q \in Q$ alone dominates a larger hypervolume than all points in the current population together, then the algorithm should take this point q (or do something even better). Note that all increasing — and thus also all locally optimal — archiving algorithms satisfy this condition.

THEOREM 3.2. *Let $\mathcal{A}$ be a non-decreasing archiving algorithm such that for all inputs P and Q and points $q \in Q$ we have*

$$\mathrm{HYP}(\mathcal{A}(P,Q)) \geqslant \mathrm{HYP}(\{q\}).$$

Then $\mathcal{A}$ is μ-competitive.

In particular: All increasing $(\mu + \lambda)$-archiving algorithms are μ-competitive.

Proof. Let $I := (P^0, Q^1, \ldots, Q^N)$ be an instance and $P^* \subseteq \mathrm{Obs}(I)$ be a μ-population with $\mathrm{HYP}(P^*) = \mathrm{maxHYP}_\mu(\mathrm{Obs}(I))$. We have

$$\mathrm{HYP}(P^*) \leqslant \sum_{p \in P^*} \mathrm{HYP}(\{p\}),$$

so there is a point $p^* \in P^*$ with

$$\mathrm{HYP}(\{p^*\}) \geqslant \frac{1}{|P|}\mathrm{HYP}(P^*) \geqslant \frac{1}{\mu}\mathrm{HYP}(P^*).$$

Either $p^* \in P^0$ (in which case we set $r := 0$) or $p^* \in Q^r$ for some r. Consider $P^i = \mathcal{A}(P^0, Q^1, \ldots, Q^i)$. We have $\mathrm{HYP}(P^r) \geqslant \mathrm{HYP}(\{p^*\})$ by the extra assumption and $\mathrm{HYP}(P^r) \leqslant \mathrm{HYP}(P^{r+1}) \leqslant \ldots \leqslant \mathrm{HYP}(P^N)$ by $\mathcal{A}$ being non-decreasing. Taken together these prove the claim. □

Observe that even a very simple algorithm fulfills the premises of the above theorem: It considers the offspring one-by-one and replaces its current population P^i with $\{q\}$, if the offspring point q has greater hypervolume than P^i. This requires only one costly computation of $\mathrm{HYP}(P^0)$; all other populations consist of only a single point in the objective space.

Perhaps surprisingly, no increasing archiving algorithm is better than this simple algorithm in the worst case: For them, the bound of Theorem 3.2 is tight.

THEOREM 3.3. *No increasing $(\mu + \lambda)$-archiving algorithm is $(\mu - \varepsilon)$-competitive for any $\varepsilon > 0$.*

Proof. We construct an instance $I = (P^0, Q^1, \ldots, Q^N)$ as follows. For reals $a, A > 0$ to be chosen later and $j \in \{1, \ldots, \mu-1\}$, we set

$$p_j = (A + j\,a, (\mu - j)a),$$

and $B := (\mu - 1)a$. Moreover, for $\delta, \rho > 0$, $\rho < 1$ to be chosen later and $i \in \{0, \ldots, N\}$, we set $q_i = (x_i, y_i)$ with

$$x_i := A\rho^i,$$
$$y_i := B + \frac{1 + \delta\, i}{x_i}.$$

These points are depicted in figure Figure 1. Setting $P^0 := \{q_0, p_1, \ldots, p_{\mu-1}\}$ and $Q^i := \{q_i\}$ (or λ copies of q_i), we get an instance I.

We show that $\mathcal{A}(P^{i-1}, Q^i) = P^i$ with $P^i = \{q_i, p_1, \ldots, p_{\mu-1}\}$ for $\mathcal{A}$ being an increasing archiving algorithm. To do this, we have to show that the exchange of q_{i-1}

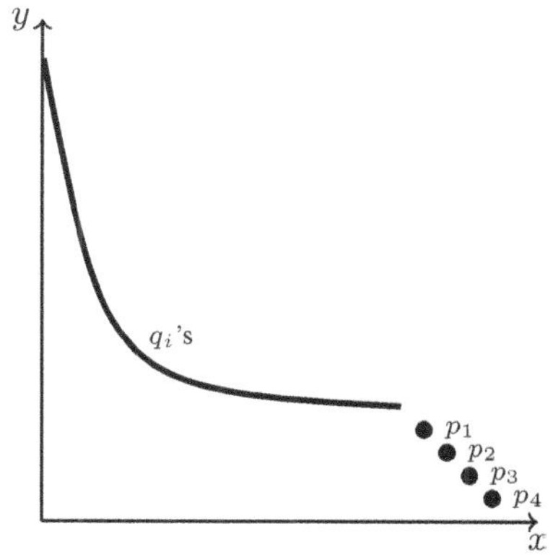

Figure 1: Illustration of the example used in the proof of Theorem 3.3.

with q_i is increases the hypervolume and is the only increasing exchange. This means we have to show $\mathrm{HYP}(P^i) > \mathrm{HYP}(P^{i-1})$ and $\mathrm{HYP}(P^{i-1}) \geqslant \mathrm{HYP}(P^{i-1} + q_i - p_j)$ for any $1 \leqslant j \leqslant \mu - 1$, as those are the only possible exchanges. We have

$$\mathrm{HYP}(P^i) = \mathrm{HYP}(\{p_1, \ldots, p_{\mu-1}\}) + \mathrm{CON}_{P^i}(q_i),$$

where $\mathrm{CON}_{P^i}(q_i) = x_i(y_i - B) = 1 + \delta i$, and $p_1, \ldots, p_{\mu-1}$ are collinear points, so that their hypervolume can be easily calculated, yielding

$$\mathrm{HYP}(P^i) = A\,B + \tbinom{\mu}{2}a^2 + 1 + \delta\, i. \tag{1}$$

This gives $\mathrm{HYP}(P^i) > \mathrm{HYP}(P^{i-1})$ right away. Moreover, we have

$$\begin{aligned}&\mathrm{HYP}(P^{i-1} + q_i - p_j)\\ &= \mathrm{HYP}(P^{i-1}) - \mathrm{CON}_{P^{i-1}}(p_j) + \mathrm{CON}_{P^{i-1}+q_i}(q_i),\end{aligned}$$

with $\mathrm{CON}_{P^{i-1}}(p_j) \geqslant a^2$ and

$$\begin{aligned}\mathrm{CON}_{P^{i-1}+q_i}(q_i) &= x_i(y_i - y_{i-1})\\ &= 1 + \delta\, i - \rho(1 + \delta(i-1))\\ &= (1-\rho)(1 + \delta(i-1)) + \delta.\end{aligned}$$

Hence, for

$$a^2 \geqslant (1-\rho)(1 + \delta\, N) + \delta, \tag{2}$$

we have $\mathrm{HYP}(P^{i-1}) \geqslant \mathrm{HYP}(P^{i-1} + q_i - p_j)$ for any $1 \leqslant j \leqslant \mu - 1$, and $P^i = \mathcal{A}(P^{i-1}, Q^i)$ indeed holds.

Lastly, we need a lower bound on $\mathrm{maxHYP}_\mu(\mathrm{Obs}(I))$. For this we require that μ divides N and consider $P = \{q_{iN/\mu} \mid 0 \leqslant i \leqslant \mu - 1\}$. If we consider instead $P' = \{q'_{iN/\mu} \mid 0 \leqslant i \leqslant \mu - 1\}$, with $q'_i = (x_i, y'_i)$, $y'_i = B + 1/x_i$, the hypervolume decreases only, as we decrease the y-coordinates. Hence, we have $\mathrm{maxHYP}_\mu(\mathrm{Obs}(I)) \geqslant \mathrm{HYP}(P) \geqslant \mathrm{HYP}(P')$. All that is left to show is

$$\mathrm{HYP}(P') > (\mu - \varepsilon)\mathrm{HYP}(P^N). \tag{3}$$

We compute $\mathrm{HYP}(P')$ to be

$$\begin{aligned}\mathrm{HYP}(P') &= \mathrm{HYP}(\{q_0'\}) + \sum_{i=1}^{\mu-1} x_{iN/\mu}(y'_{iN/\mu} - y'_{(i-1)N/\mu}) \\ &= A(B + 1/A) + \sum_{i=1}^{\mu-1} (1 - \rho^{N/\mu}) \\ &= A\,B + \mu - (\mu - 1)\rho^{N/\mu}. \end{aligned} \quad (4)$$

Then equation (3) is fulfilled (using equations (1) and (4)) if

$$\begin{aligned} &A\,B + \mu - (\mu-1)\rho^{N/\mu} > \\ &(\mu - \varepsilon)\left(A\,B + \tbinom{\mu}{2}a^2 + 1 + \delta\,N\right). \end{aligned}$$

Rearranging this, we get

$$\begin{aligned} \varepsilon >& (\mu - 1 - \varepsilon)A\,B + (\mu - \varepsilon)\tbinom{\mu}{2}a^2 + \\ & (\mu - 1)\rho^{N/\mu} + (\mu - \varepsilon)\delta\,N. \end{aligned}$$

This inequality is fulfilled by setting $A := \varepsilon/(4\mu B)$, $a^2 := \varepsilon/(4\mu^3)$, $\delta := \min\{\varepsilon/(4\mu N), a^2/2\}$, and $N := \mu\lceil\log_\rho(\varepsilon/(4\mu))\rceil$. As we can assume $\varepsilon \leqslant 1$, we have $\delta \leqslant \min\{1/N, a^2/2\}$, so that requirement (2) can be simplified to $a^2 \geqslant 2(1-\rho) + a^2/2$. We set $\rho := 1 - a^2/4$ to satisfy it. Noting that there is no cyclic dependence in these definitions, we conclude the proof. □

In the proof of Theorem 3.3, we explicitly construct a bad 2-dimensional instance; see Figure 1 for an example with $\mu = 5$. The initial population consists of the points $p_1, \dots, p_4$ and the rightmost point of the q_i's. Then every offspring consists of (λ copies of) a q_i slightly to the left and above the old one, so that any increasing algorithm has to exchange the two points. This way, the population will always consist of the points $p_1, \dots, p_4$ and one of the q_i's, with the latter point being dragged to the left. The optimal population, however, consists of 5 nicely spaced q_i's, which has (by choosing the free parameters correctly) a hypervolume that is nearly a factor μ larger than the hypervolume of the population of the increasing algorithm.

4. NON-DECREASING ALGORITHMS

Section 3 showed that increasing archiving algorithms are NP-hard to compute and only achieve an unbounded competitive ratio of μ. We now present a non-decreasing (and not increasing) archiving algorithm which achieves constant competitiveness (cf. Section 4.1). Afterwards, we present a randomized variant of the algorithm which is also efficiently computable (cf. Section 4.2).

4.1 A competitive non-decreasing algorithm

The results of Section 3.2 show that all increasing archiving algorithms have a very bad competitive ratio, and, even worse, that the notion of competitiveness is not suited for comparing different increasing archiving algorithms: All of them have the same competitiveness. This leaves open whether there are non-decreasing, but not increasing archiving algorithms with, say, a constant competitive ratio. This would imply that some archiving algorithm, that is not locally optimal, achieves a better competitive ratio than all locally optimal archiving algorithms. We show that this is indeed the case.

THEOREM 4.1. *There is a $(4 + 2/\mu)$-competitive non-decreasing $(\mu + 1)$-archiving algorithm.*

Note that we can easily build a $(\mu + \lambda)$-archiving algorithm with the same competitiveness from the $(\mu + 1)$-archiving algorithm guaranteed by Theorem 4.1 by feeding the λ offspring one by one to the $(\mu + 1)$-archiving algorithm.

We do not prove Theorem 4.1 directly, as it follows from the proof of Theorem 4.3 below. However, one such archiving algorithm $\mathcal{A}_{\text{comp}}$ is given in Algorithm 3. This non-locally-optimal algorithm improves on the locally optimal algorithms with respect to the competitive ratio and hence is is better suited for hypervolume-based selection in the worst case. Note that this does not imply that this algorithm should be used in practice, as worst-case optimality is usually not needed.

Algorithm 3: Competitive $(\mu + 1)$-archiving algorithm $\mathcal{A}_{\text{comp}}$

input : μ-population P, offspring $\{q\}$
output: μ-population P'

1 **foreach** $p \in P + q$ **do**
2 $\quad H_p \leftarrow \mathrm{HYP}(P + q - p)$
3 $p' \leftarrow \operatorname{argmax}\{H_p \mid p \in P\}$
4 **if** $H_{p'} > (1 + 1/\mu)\,H_q$ **then**
5 $\quad$ **return** $P + q - p'$
6 **else**
7 $\quad$ **return** P

Unfortunately, the runtime of $\mathcal{A}_{\text{comp}}$ cannot be polynomial in $\mu + d$ (unless P = NP) as the exact hypervolume calculation in line 2 of Algorithm 3 is #P-hard [4]. However, this also holds for all increasing archiving algorithms as shown in Theorem 3.1.

4.2 An efficient randomized competitive non-decreasing archiving algorithm

We now propose a randomized variant of $\mathcal{A}_{\text{comp}}$ which improves on all increasing algorithms not only with respect to the competitive ratio, but also the runtime. It is a randomized algorithm which meets the competitive ratio bound only with a certain high probability. Hence, we need to redefine competitiveness to include randomized algorithms.

DEFINITION 4.2. *Let $\alpha \geqslant 1$ and $p\colon \mathbb{N} \to [0,1]$. A randomized archiving algorithm $\mathcal{A}$ is α-competitive with probability p if for all instances $I = (P^0, Q^1, \dots, Q^N)$ we have*

$$\mathcal{A}(P^0, Q^1, \dots, Q^N) \geqslant \frac{1}{\alpha}\,\mathrm{maxHYP}_\mu(\mathrm{Obs}(I))$$

with probability $\geqslant p(N)$.

Our proposed algorithm $\mathcal{A}_{\text{eff}}$ is given in Algorithm 4. It takes additional parameters $\varepsilon, \delta > 0$ and is $(4 + 2/\mu + \varepsilon)$-competitive with probability $p(N) = 1 - N\delta$.

The critical feature of $\mathcal{A}_{\text{eff}}$ is line 4. It makes use of the hypervolume approximation scheme of Bringmann and Friedrich [4] which computes with probability at least $1 - \delta$ a $(1 + \varepsilon)$-approximation of the hypervolume of a given set of μ points in $\mathbb{R}^d$ in time $\mathcal{O}(\log(1/\delta)\mu d/\varepsilon^2)$. It is clear from the hypervolume approximation algorithm used here that $\mathcal{A}_{\text{eff}}$ is efficiently computable, namely with a run-time of at most $\mathcal{O}(\log(\mu/\delta)\mu^4 d/\varepsilon^2)$. Note that we aimed only for a polynomial runtime and did not try to optimize the algorithm for a better runtime bound.

We can prove that $\mathcal{A}_{\text{eff}}$ is competitive. The following theorem states our result.

Algorithm 4: Randomized Efficient Competitive $(\mu + 1)$-archiving algorithm $\mathcal{A}_{\text{eff}}$

input : μ-population P, offspring $\{q\}$, error bound ε, error probability δ
output: μ-population P'

$\varepsilon' \leftarrow \varepsilon/104$
$c \leftarrow 1 + 2\varepsilon'$
foreach $p \in P + q$ **do**
    $H_p \leftarrow$ compute $(1 + \varepsilon'/\mu)$-approximation of $\text{HYP}(P + q - p)$ with error probability $\delta/(\mu + 1)$
$p' \leftarrow \text{argmax}\{H_p \mid p \in P\}$
if $H_{p'} > (1 + \frac{c}{\mu})\, H_q$ **then**
    return $P + q - p'$
else
    return P

THEOREM 4.3. *Let* $0 < \varepsilon \leqslant 1$. *Algorithm* $\mathcal{A}_{\text{eff}}$ *is a randomized* $(\mu+1)$*-archiving algorithm which is non-decreasing and* $(4 + 2/\mu + \varepsilon)$*-competitive with probability* $p(N) = 1 - N\delta$ *and has a deterministic runtime polynomial in* μ, λ, d, $\log(1/\delta)$, *and* $1/\varepsilon$.

Proof. Let $I = (P^0, Q^1, \ldots, Q^N)$ be an instance. Consider the probability that every hypervolume approximation of $\mathcal{A}_{\text{comp}}$ on I indeed lies in the specified bounds, i.e., we have

$$(1-\varepsilon'/\mu)\text{HYP}(P+q-p) \leqslant H_p \leqslant (1+\varepsilon'/\mu)\text{HYP}(P+q-p)$$

for every computation of a H_p in $\mathcal{A}_{\text{comp}}$. For a single call, this happens with probability at least $1-\delta/(\mu+1)$. Furthermore, we have at most $N(\mu+1)$ hypervolume approximations running $\mathcal{A}_{\text{comp}}$ on I, as in every invocation of $\mathcal{A}_{\text{comp}}$, at most $\mu+1$ hypervolume approximations are computed. With the union bound, we arrive at a probability of at least $1 - N\delta$ that all the hypervolume approximations lie within the specified bounds.

Either we stay with the current population or the hypervolume increases by a constant factor, in which case

$$\begin{aligned}\left(1+\frac{\varepsilon'}{\mu}\right)\text{HYP}(P^i) &\geqslant H_{p'} \\ &\geqslant \left(1+\frac{c}{\mu}\right)H_q \geqslant \left(1-\frac{\varepsilon'}{\mu}\right)\left(1+\frac{c}{\mu}\right)\text{HYP}(P^{i-1}).\end{aligned}$$

For $c = 1 + 2\varepsilon' \geqslant 1$, $\mu \geqslant 1$ and $\varepsilon' \leqslant 1/3$, which is true by assumption, we have $\left(1-\frac{\varepsilon'}{\mu}\right)\left(1+\frac{c}{\mu}\right) \geqslant \left(1+\frac{\varepsilon'}{\mu}\right)$, implying that the algorithm is non-decreasing.

We prove that $\mathcal{A}_{\text{comp}}$ is $(4 + 2/\mu + \varepsilon)$-competitive if all the hypervolume approximations lie in the specified bounds. To do this, let $P^i = \mathcal{A}_{\text{comp}}(P^{i-1}, Q^i)$ for $i = 1, \ldots, N$. Consider $\hat{P} := \bigcup_{i=0}^{N} P^i$, the set of all points in $\text{Obs}(I)$ that were taken by $\mathcal{A}_{\text{comp}}$ at some point. Let $P^* \subseteq \text{Obs}(I)$ be a μ-population with $\text{HYP}(P^*) = \max\text{HYP}_\mu(\text{Obs}(I))$. We have

$$\begin{aligned}\max\text{HYP}_\mu(\text{Obs}(I)) &= \text{HYP}(P^*) \leqslant \text{HYP}(\hat{P} \cup P^*) \\ &\leqslant \text{HYP}(\hat{P}) + \sum_{q \in P^* \setminus \hat{P}} \text{CON}_{\hat{P}+q}(q) \qquad (5)\end{aligned}$$

To continue, we bound $\text{HYP}(\hat{P})$ as well as the contribution of any point $q \in P^* \setminus \hat{P}$ to $\hat{P}$ in terms of $\text{HYP}(P^N)$. This will yield the desired bound for $\text{HYP}(P^N)$. We start with the latter.

Consider a point not chosen by the algorithm, $q \in \text{Obs}(I) \setminus \hat{P}$. We have $Q^i = \{q\}$ for some $1 \leqslant i \leqslant N$. Let $\tilde{p} \in P^{i-1} + q$ with $\text{CON}_{P^{i-1}+q}(\tilde{p})$ minimal among all $p \in P^{i-1} + q$. Then we have

$$\begin{aligned}\text{CON}_{P^{i-1}+q}(\tilde{p}) &\leqslant \frac{1}{\mu+1}\sum_{p \in P^{i-1}+q}\text{CON}_{P^{i-1}+q}(p) \\ &\leqslant \frac{1}{\mu+1}\text{HYP}(P^{i-1}+q) \\ &= \frac{1}{\mu+1}\left(\text{HYP}(P^{i-1}) + \text{CON}_{P^{i-1}+q}(q)\right). \qquad (6)\end{aligned}$$

Let $p' = \text{argmax}\{H_p \mid p \in P^{i-1}\}$, see Algorthm 4. The point q was not taken by the algorithm, so we have

$$\begin{aligned}&(1-\frac{\varepsilon'}{\mu})\text{HYP}(P^{i-1}+q-\tilde{p}) \\ &\leqslant H_{\tilde{p}} \leqslant H_{p'} \leqslant (1+\frac{c}{\mu})H_q \\ &\leqslant (1+\frac{c}{\mu})(1+\frac{\varepsilon'}{\mu})\text{HYP}(P^{i-1}),\end{aligned}$$

where the factors $(1 \pm \varepsilon'/\mu)$ stem from the H_p being approximations. Using $\text{HYP}(P^{i-1} + q - \tilde{p}) = \text{HYP}(P^{i-1}) + \text{CON}_{P^{i-1}+q}(q) - \text{CON}_{P^{i-1}+q}(\tilde{p})$, equation (6) and $\frac{1}{1-\varepsilon'/\mu} \leqslant 1 + \frac{2\varepsilon'}{\mu}$ for $\varepsilon' \leqslant 1/2$, this can be simplified to

$$\text{CON}_{P^{i-1}+q}(q) \leqslant \beta\text{HYP}(P^{i-1}),$$

where

$$\beta = \frac{\mu+1}{\mu}\left(\left(1+\frac{c}{\mu}\right)\left(1+\frac{\varepsilon'}{\mu}\right)\left(1+\frac{2\varepsilon'}{\mu}\right)-1\right)+\frac{1}{\mu}.$$

As $\text{HYP}(P^N) \geqslant \text{HYP}(P^{i-1})$ and $\hat{P} \supseteq P^{i-1}$, this implies

$$\text{CON}_{\hat{P}+q}(q) \leqslant \beta\text{HYP}(P^N). \qquad (7)$$

Plugging in the definition of $c = 1 + 2\varepsilon'$, simplifying and roughly bounding the number of terms involving ε'/μ together with their coefficients, and using $\mu \geqslant 1$, we get

$$\beta \leqslant \frac{2}{\mu} + \frac{1}{\mu^2} + 64\frac{\varepsilon'}{\mu}. \qquad (8)$$

Now we bound $\text{HYP}(\hat{P})$. Consider $I = \{i \mid P^i \neq P^{i-1}, 1 \leqslant i \leqslant N\}$, the indices where P^i changed, and let p^i be the unique point in $P^{i-1} \setminus P^i$, i.e., the point we deleted in round $i \in I$. Then we have for $i \in I$ and every $p \in P^i + p^i$

$$\begin{aligned}\left(1+\frac{\varepsilon'}{\mu}\right)\text{HYP}(P^i) &\geqslant H_{p_i} \geqslant H_p \\ &\geqslant \left(1-\frac{\varepsilon'}{\mu}\right)\text{HYP}(P^i+p^i-p).\end{aligned}$$

Since $\text{HYP}(P^i + p^i - p) = \text{HYP}(P^i) + \text{CON}_{P^i+p^i}(p^i) - \text{CON}_{P^i+p^i}(p)$, this is equivalent to

$$\frac{2\varepsilon'}{\mu}\left(1-\frac{\varepsilon'}{\mu}\right)^{-1}\text{HYP}(P^i) + \text{CON}_{P^i+p^i}(p) \geqslant \text{CON}_{P^i+p^i}(p^i).$$

Summing over all $p \in P^i + p^i$ and using $\text{HYP}(P) \geqslant \sum_{p \in P}\text{CON}_P(p)$ we get

$$\begin{aligned}&2\varepsilon'\left(1+\frac{1}{\mu}\right)\left(1-\frac{\varepsilon'}{\mu}\right)^{-1}\text{HYP}(P^i) + \text{HYP}(P^i+p^i) \\ &\geqslant (\mu+1)\text{CON}_{P^i+p^i}(p^i),\end{aligned}$$

which yields, after substituting $\text{HYP}(P^i + p^i) = \text{HYP}(P^i) + \text{CON}_{P^i+p^i}(p^i)$ again,

$$\text{CON}_{P^i+p^i}(p^i) \leqslant \gamma \text{HYP}(P^i),$$

with $\gamma = \frac{1}{\mu}\left(1 + 2\varepsilon'\left(1+\frac{1}{\mu}\right)\left(1-\frac{\varepsilon'}{\mu}\right)^{-1}\right)$. Now,

$$\begin{aligned} \text{HYP}(\hat{P}) &= \text{HYP}(P^N) + \sum_{i\in I} \text{CON}_{P^N\cup\ldots\cup P^i+p^i}(p^i) \\ &\leqslant \text{HYP}(P^N) + \sum_{i\in I} \text{CON}_{P^i+p^i}(p^i) \\ &\leqslant \text{HYP}(P^N) + \gamma \sum_{i\in I} \text{HYP}(P^i). \end{aligned}$$

As we go to a new population only if we have an improvement of a factor $(1 + c/\mu)$, but we have approximations, we get $\delta \cdot \text{HYP}(P^i) \geqslant \text{HYP}(P^{i-1})$ for $i \in I$ and $\delta := (1+c/\mu)^{-1}(1-\varepsilon'/\mu)^{-1}(1+\varepsilon'/\mu)$, yielding

$$\begin{aligned} \text{HYP}(\hat{P}) &\leqslant \text{HYP}(P^N)\left(1+\gamma\sum_{i=0}^{N-1}\delta^i\right) \\ &\leqslant \text{HYP}(P^N)\left(1+\frac{\gamma}{1-\delta}\right). \end{aligned} \quad (9)$$

Plugging in the definition of $c = 1 + 2\varepsilon'$, δ and γ, simple calculations and rough estimations using $\mu \geqslant 1$ and $\varepsilon' \leqslant 1/6$ show that

$$\frac{\gamma}{1-\delta} \leqslant 1 + \frac{1}{\mu} + 40\varepsilon'. \quad (10)$$

Now we can take equation (5), plug in equations (7) and (9), and simplify using equations (8) and (10) to get

$$\begin{aligned} \text{HYP}(P^*) &\leqslant \text{HYP}(\hat{P}) + \sum_{q\in P^*\setminus\hat{P}} \text{CON}_{\hat{P}+q}(q) \\ &\leqslant \left(1+\frac{\gamma}{1-\delta}+\mu\beta\right)\text{HYP}(P^N) \\ &\leqslant \left(4+\frac{2}{\mu}+104\varepsilon'\right)\text{HYP}(P^N) \\ &= \left(4+\frac{2}{\mu}+\varepsilon\right)\text{HYP}(P^N). \end{aligned}$$

□

Observe that by setting $\varepsilon = 0$, so that all hypervolume approximations are in fact exact computations, Algorithm 4 becomes the same as Algorithm 3. This implies that the proof of Theorem 4.3 is a proof of Theorem 4.1, too.

The perhaps surprising probability bound is caused by the (necessary) assumption that every call to the hypervolume approximation algorithm indeed returns a $(1+\varepsilon'/\mu)$-approximation. The factor N in the probability can be easily canceled out by a sufficiently small δ, as the runtime depends only logarithmically on $1/\delta$.

5. CONCLUSION

Hypervolume based MOEAs like SIBEA [12], SMS-EMOA [1], and the generational MO-CMA-ES [8] use greedy archiving algorithms. We have proven that such increasing archiving algorithms are computationally inefficient, and achieve only an unbounded competitive ratio of μ. In sharp contrast to this, we presented a non-decreasing archiving algorithm which not only achieves a constant competitive ratio of $4 + 2/\mu$, but is also efficiently computable.

References

[1] N. Beume, B. Naujoks, and M. T. M. Emmerich. SMS-EMOA: Multiobjective selection based on dominated hypervolume. *European Journal of Operational Research*, 181:1653–1669, 2007.

[2] A. Borodin and R. El-Yaniv. *Online computation and competitive analysis*, Vol. 2. Cambridge University Press Cambridge, 1998.

[3] L. Bradstreet, L. Barone, and L. While. Maximising hypervolume for selection in multi-objective evolutionary algorithms. In *Proc. IEEE Congress on Evolutionary Computation (CEC '06)*, pp. 6208–6215, 2006.

[4] K. Bringmann and T. Friedrich. Approximating the volume of unions and intersections of high-dimensional geometric objects. *Computational Geometry: Theory and Applications*, 43:601–610, 2010.

[5] K. Bringmann and T. Friedrich. An efficient algorithm for computing hypervolume contributions. *Evolutionary Computation*, 18:383–402, 2010.

[6] K. Bringmann and T. Friedrich. Approximating the least hypervolume contributor: NP-hard in general, but fast in practice. *Theoretical Computer Science*, 425:104–116, 2012.

[7] K. Bringmann and T. Friedrich. Convergence of hypervolume-based archiving algorithms I: Effectiveness. In *Proc. 13th Annual Conference on Genetic and Evolutionary Computation Conference (GECCO '11)*, pp. 745–752. ACM Press, 2011.

[8] C. Igel, N. Hansen, and S. Roth. Covariance matrix adaptation for multi-objective optimization. *Evolutionary Computation*, 15:1–28, 2007.

[9] M. López-Ibáñez, J. D. Knowles, and M. Laumanns. On sequential online archiving of objective vectors. In *Proc. 6th International Conference on Evolutionary Multi-Criterion Optimization (EMO '11)*, Vol. 6576 of *LNCS*, pp. 46–60. Springer, 2011.

[10] T. Ulrich and L. Thiele. Bounding the effectiveness of hypervolume-based $(\mu + \lambda)$-archiving algorithms. In *Proc. 6th International Conference on Learning and Intelligent Optimization (LION '12)*, 2012. To appear.

[11] E. Zitzler and L. Thiele. Multiobjective evolutionary algorithms: A comparative case study and the strength Pareto approach. *IEEE Trans. Evolutionary Computation*, 3: 257–271, 1999.

[12] E. Zitzler, D. Brockhoff, and L. Thiele. The hypervolume indicator revisited: On the design of Pareto-compliant indicators via weighted integration. In *Proc. Fourth International Conference on Evolutionary Multi-Criterion Optimization (EMO '07)*, Vol. 4403 of *LNCS*, pp. 862–876. Springer, 2007.

[13] E. Zitzler, L. Thiele, and J. Bader. On set-based multiobjective optimization. *IEEE Trans. Evolutionary Computation*, 14:58–79, 2010.

On the Properties of the $R2$ Indicator

Dimo Brockhoff
INRIA Lille Nord-Europe
Dolphin Team
Villeneuve d'Ascq, France
dimo.brockhoff@inria.fr

Tobias Wagner
Institute of Machining Technology
TU Dortmund
Dortmund, Germany
wagner@isf.de

Heike Trautmann
Statistics Department
TU Dortmund, Germany
trautmann@statistik.uni-dortmund.de

ABSTRACT

In multiobjective optimization, set-based performance indicators are commonly used to assess the quality of a Pareto front approximation. Based on the scalarization obtained by these indicators, a performance comparison of multiobjective optimization algorithms becomes possible. The $R2$ and the Hypervolume (HV) indicator represent two recommended approaches which have shown a correlated behavior in recent empirical studies. Whereas the HV indicator has been comprehensively analyzed in the last years, almost no studies on the $R2$ indicator exist. In this paper, we thus perform a comprehensive investigation of the properties of the $R2$ indicator in a theoretical and empirical way. The influence of the number and distribution of the weight vectors on the optimal distribution of μ solutions is analyzed. Based on a comparative analysis, specific characteristics and differences of the $R2$ and HV indicator are presented.

Categories and Subject Descriptors

G.1.6 [**Mathematics of Computing**]: Numerical Analysis—*Optimization*

General Terms

Algorithms

Keywords

Performance assessment, Hypervolume indicator, $R2$ indicator, Multiobjective optimization

1. INTRODUCTION

Multiobjective optimization comprises the optimization of a vector of m objective functions $\vec{f} = (f_1(\vec{x}), \ldots, f_m(\vec{x}))$. We assume minimization tasks in the following, as maximization problems can easily be transferred to those by negation. A solution $\vec{x}$ in the decision space $\mathbb{S}$ is said to dominate a solution $\vec{y} \in \mathbb{S}$ ($\vec{x} \prec \vec{y}$), iff $\vec{f}(\vec{x})$ is better than or equal to $\vec{f}(\vec{y})$ in all objectives ($\forall i \in \{1, \ldots, m\} : f_i(\vec{x}) \leq f_i(\vec{y})$) and better than $\vec{f}(\vec{y})$ in at least one ($\exists j \in \{1, \ldots, m\} : f_j(\vec{x}) < f_j(\vec{y})$). Only the first condition is necessary for $\vec{x}$ to weakly dominate $\vec{y}$ ($\vec{x} \preceq \vec{y}$). The aim of multiobjective optimization is to detect the Pareto optimal set $P = \{\vec{x} \in \mathbb{S} \mid \nexists \vec{x}' \in \mathbb{S} : \vec{x}' \prec \vec{x}\}$. The Pareto front is the corresponding mapping $\vec{f}(P)$ to the objective space $\mathbb{R}^m$.

Evolutionary multiobjective algorithms are a specific class of solvers for multiobjective problems. They basically aim at approximating the true Pareto front of the problem at hand by minimizing the distance to the true Pareto front (convergence) and simultaneously covering all its parts (spread) in a well-defined way (distribution) [12]. Several performance indicators were introduced [14, 16] to assess one or all of these quality aspects of Pareto front approximations.

The Hypervolume (HV) [15] and the $R2$ indicator [7] are two recommended approaches which simultaneously evaluate all desired aspects of a Pareto front approximation. The HV is so far the only known indicator which fulfills the property of strict monotonicity, i.e., the indicator value $I(A)$ of a set A that dominates the set B has to be higher than the indicator value $I(B)$ for the set B, assuming that the indicator is to be maximized. In contrast, the $R2$ indicator is only weakly monotonic, i.e., $I(A) \geq I(B)$ in case A weakly dominates B. Nevertheless, the $R2$ indicator is often preferred over the HV for two reasons. On the one hand, the runtime of the HV is exponential with respect to the number of objectives m [4]. On the other hand, the distributions obtained using the HV are biased towards the knee regions of the Pareto front [1]. The $R2$ indicator is assumed to result in a more uniform distribution.

As monotonicity of both, the HV and the $R2$ indicator, is guaranteed [16], a similar behavior of the indicators can be expected. However, as the preferred distributions seem to be different, the degree of similarity might vary in different settings. In [10, 11], optimal parameterizations of the multiobjective optimizer SMS-EMOA [5] were investigated. Correlation structures between the evaluations of Pareto fronts based on different quality indicators were analyzed in order to select the most suitable indicator for the used Sequential Parameter Optimization (SPO) approach. It was shown that the HV and $R2$ indicator are highly correlated on a huge number of randomly generated populations in different dimensions. Pearson's correlation coefficient [9] takes a statistically significant value of 0.76. However, the indicators are different enough that they led to statistically distinguishable results when used individually in the SPO framework.

In this paper, we aim at a more detailed understanding of the properties of the $R2$ indicator. We perform an analysis about *how* it differs from the HV indicator for which several theoretical properties are already known [1, 2]. Furthermore, the finite sets of μ solutions maximizing the $R2$ indicator among all feasible sets of μ solutions—the so-called *optimal μ-distributions of the R2 indicator*—are generated for standard test functions with different Pareto front shapes. The effect of the distribution of the weight vectors is analyzed by alternatively investigating a uniform coverage of the angle space in addition to the standard uniform coverage of the weight space.

The paper is organized as follows. Details of the indicators are given in Sec. 2. Properties of the $R2$ indicator are discussed in Sec. 3, followed by an analysis and comparison of the optimal μ-distributions for both, the $R2$ and the HV indicator, in Sec. 4. Finally, conclusions are drawn and an outlook is given in Sec. 5.

2. $R2$ AND HV INDICATORS

The R indicator family [7] is based on utility functions which map a vector $\vec{y} \in \mathbb{R}^m$ to a scalar utility value $u \in \mathbb{R}$ for assessing the relative quality of two Pareto front approximation sets.

Definition 1. *For a set U of general utility functions, a probability distribution p on U, and a reference set R, the $R2$ indicator of a solution set A is defined as the expected utility [7]*

$$\begin{aligned} R2(R, A, U, p) &= \int_{u \in U} \max_{r \in R}\{u(r)\}p(u)du \\ &\quad - \int_{u \in U} \max_{a \in A}\{u(a)\}p(u)du \ . \end{aligned}$$

Definition 2. *For a discrete and finite set U and a uniform distribution p over U, the original $R2$ indicator can be written as [14]*

$$R2(R, A, U) = \frac{1}{|U|}\sum_{u \in U}\left(\max_{r \in R}\{u(r)\} - \max_{a \in A}\{u(a)\}\right).$$

Since the first summand is a constant if we assume R to be constant, we delete the first summand and call the resulting unary indicator also $R2$ for simplicity.

Definition 3. *For a constant reference set, the $R2$ indicator can be defined as a unary indicator*

$$R2(A, U) = -\frac{1}{|U|}\sum_{u \in U}\max_{a \in A}\{u(a)\} \ .$$

Note that we assume R to be constant throughout the paper and will only refer to Definition 3 when we use the term $R2$ indicator.

Different choices of the required utility function exist, e.g., based on weighted sum and weighted Tchebycheff functions or a combination of both. As suggested in [7], we use the standard weighted Tchebycheff function $u(z) = u_\lambda(\vec{z}) = -\max_{j \in \{1 \ldots m\}} \lambda_j |z_j^* - z_j|$ within the $R2$ indicator in the following where $\lambda = (\lambda_1, \ldots, \lambda_m) \in \Lambda$ is a given weight vector and z^* is a utopian point[1].

[1]An objective vector that is not dominated by any feasible search point.

Definition 4. *The $R2$ indicator of a solution set A for a given set of weights Λ and a utopian point z^* is defined as*

$$\begin{aligned} R2(A, \Lambda, z^*) &= \frac{1}{|\Lambda|} - \sum_{\lambda \in \Lambda} \max_{a \in A}\{- \max_{j \in \{1,\ldots,m\}}\{\lambda_j |z_j^* - a_j|\}\} \\ &= \frac{1}{|\Lambda|}\sum_{\lambda \in \Lambda} \min_{a \in A}\{\max_{j \in \{1,\ldots,m\}}\{\lambda_j |z_j^* - a_j|\}\} \ . \end{aligned}$$

Usually, the weight vectors are chosen uniformly distributed over the weight space [14], for example for $m = 2$ objectives,

$$\Lambda_{w,k} = \left(0, 1; \frac{1}{k-1}, 1 - \frac{1}{k-1}; \frac{2}{k-1}, 1 - \frac{2}{k-1}; \ldots; 1, 0\right).$$

denotes k uniformly distributed weights in the space $[0, 1]^2$. Alternatively, a uniform distribution over the angle space

$$\Phi_k = \left(0; \frac{\pi}{(2(k-1)}; \frac{2\pi}{2(k-1)}; \ldots; \frac{\pi}{2}\right)$$

can be considered for $m = 2$ objectives. In this case, rays from the utopian point with different slopes $\tan(\varphi)$ for $\varphi \in \Phi_k$ are constructed and then mapped to weight vectors

$$\Lambda_{\varphi,k} = \left\{ \left(\frac{1}{\tan(\varphi) + 1}, \frac{\tan(\varphi)}{\tan(\varphi) + 1}\right) \middle| \ \varphi \in \Phi_k \right\}$$

by normalization.[2] A weight vector corresponding to a ray which directly crosses a point $a \in A$ is defined as λ^a.

In addition to an overall quality assessment of an approximation set A, the contribution of an individual solution to the $R2$ value can be of interest.

Definition 5. *The contribution of a solution $a \in A$ to the $R2$ indicator is defined as*

$$C_{R2}(a, A, \Lambda, z^*) = R2(A, \Lambda, z^*) - R2(A \setminus \{a\}, \Lambda, z^*)$$

which can be written as

$$\begin{aligned} C_{R2}(a, A, \Lambda, z^*) &= \frac{1}{|\Lambda|}\sum_{\lambda \in \Lambda}\left(\min_{b \in A}\left\{\max_{j \in \{1 \ldots m\}}\{\lambda_j |z_j^* - b_j|\}\right\}\right. \\ &\quad \left. - \min_{b \in A \setminus \{a\}}\left\{\max_{j \in \{1 \ldots m\}}\{\lambda_j |z_j^* - b_j|\}\right\}\right). \end{aligned}$$

In the remainder, we only consider the bi-objective case, i.e., $m = 2$. We furthermore assume that the Pareto front is given by a continuous function $f : \mathbb{R} \rightarrow \mathbb{R}$ such that every point $(x, y = f(x))$ on the front can be uniquely described by a real value $x \in \mathbb{R}$. Finding the optimal μ-distribution then reduces to a μ-dimensional optimization problem

$$(x_1^\mu, \ldots, x_\mu^\mu) = \underset{(x_1, \ldots, x_\mu) \in \mathbb{R}^\mu}{\operatorname{argmin}} \ R2(\{(x_i, f(x_i)) \,|\, 1 \leq i \leq \mu\}, \Lambda, z^*)$$

where we refer to the resulting set of x-values $(x_1^\mu, \ldots, x_\mu^\mu)$ as optimal μ-distribution [1].

The HV indicator [15, 14] describes the hypervolume of a bounded space dominated by an approximation set.

Definition 6. *Based on an anti-optimal reference point r, the HV indicator of an approximation set A is defined as*

$$HV(A, r) = \mathcal{L}\Big(\bigcup_{a \in A}\{a' | a \prec a' \prec r\}\Big)$$

with $\mathcal{L}(.)$ denoting the Lebesgue measure of a set.

[2]The normalized weight vector to the slope (x, y) is given by $(\frac{1/y}{1/x+1/y}, \frac{1/x}{1/x+1/y})$ as long as $x, y \neq 0$, and by $(0, 1)$ if $x = 0$ or $(1, 0)$ if $y = 0$. In our case, $x = 1$ and $y = \tan(\varphi)$.

Analogously to Definition 5, the HV-contribution of an individual solution reflects the influence of a single point on the quality of the approximation set.

DEFINITION 7. *The HV contribution of a solution $a \in A$ is defined as*

$$C_{HV}(a, A, r) = HV(A, r) - HV(A \setminus \{a\}, r).$$

As mentioned in Sec. 1, the HV indicator is the only known performance indicator which is strictly compliant with the dominance relation. Implementations and a comprehensive overview of the state-of-the art research w.r.t. the HV indicator are provided on [3].

3. PROPERTIES OF THE $R2$ INDICATOR

In order to interpret the values of a quality indicator during the performance assessment of multiobjective optimizers, it is crucial to understand the inherent preferences expressed by the choice of this indicator. To be more precise, it is a fundamental information to know which solution sets of size μ achieve the maximum indicator values among all possible sets of a given size μ [1]. Only with this knowledge, it is then possible to interpret the resulting indicator values of different multiobjective optimizer outcomes also absolutely instead of only relatively as the *achieved* indicator values can be compared with the *maximum achievable* values. For the optimum sets of size μ, the term *optimal μ-distribution* was introduced and such sets have already been characterized theoretically for the standard, as well as for the weighted, HV indicator [1, 2]. Before we investigate the concrete optimal μ-distributions on specific test functions also for the $R2$ indicator in Sec. 4, we first prove some general theoretical statements about the $R2$ indicator.

3.1 Locality of the $R2$ Indicator Contribution

At first, we prove that for bi-objective problems the optimal placement of a point according to the $R2$ indicator only depends on its two neighbors and only on a subset of the weight vectors. Note that also for the HV indicator such a locality property has been proven [1]. Before formalizing the general locality property of the $R2$ indicator, let us prove two preliminary statements.

LEMMA 1. *Given a specific weight vector $\lambda \in \Lambda$ and a specific solution $a \in A$ where A only contains nondominated solutions. Then all points $b \in A$ to the left of a (to the right of a) are resulting in a worse Tchebycheff utility than a if $D_1 = \lambda_1|z_1^* - a_1| < D_2 = \lambda_2|z_2^* - a_2|$ (if $D_1 > D_2$).*

PROOF. All nondominated points b that are to the left of a have an f_1 value that is smaller than a ($b_1 < a_1$) and their f_2 value is larger than the one of a ($b_2 > a_2$). These points lie in the filled box in the left plot of Fig. 1—otherwise, b would not be nondominated with respect to a and lie to the left. In case that $D_1 = \lambda_1|z_1^* - a_1| < D_2 = \lambda_2|z_2^* - a_2|$, this means that for all other points b

$$\lambda_1|z_1^* - b_1| < \lambda_1|z_1^* - a_1| < \lambda_2|z_2^* - a_2| < \lambda_2|z_2^* - b_2|$$

and thus for the Tchebycheff utility function, it holds that $\max\{\lambda_1|z_1^* - b_1|, \lambda_2|z_2^* - b_2|\} = \lambda_2|z_2^* - b_2| > \lambda_2|z_2^* - a_2| = \max\{\lambda_1|z_1^* - a_1|, \lambda_2|z_2^* - a_2|\}$, i.e., a is better since we minimize the maximum weighted component. The proof of the other case $D_1 > D_2$ follows a symmetric argumentation and is visualized in the right plot of Fig. 1. □

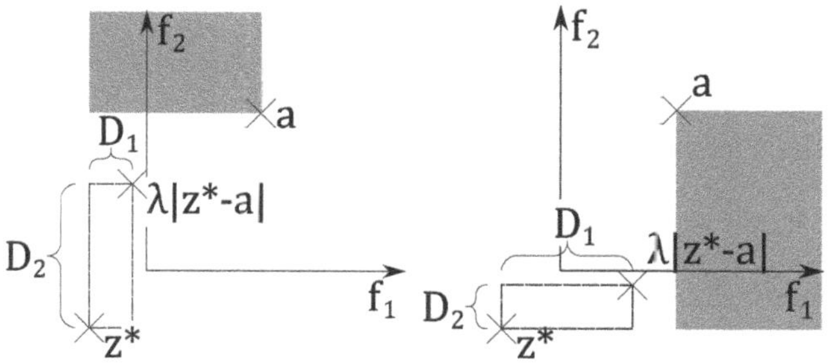

Figure 1: Sketch of idea for the proof of Lemma 1.

As a special case, we can investigate the specific weight vector λ^a that corresponds to a ray starting in the utopian point z^* and going through a (cf. Sec. 2).

LEMMA 2. *For each solution $a \in A$, there exists a specific weight $\lambda^a = (\lambda_1^a, \lambda_2^a)$ with $\lambda_1^a = \frac{|a_2 - z_2^*|}{|a_1 - z_1^*| + |a_2 - z_2^*|}$ and $\lambda_2^a = 1 - \lambda_1^a$ such that all other solutions $b \in A$ which do not dominate the point a have a worse weighted Tchebycheff value $\max\{\lambda_1^a|b_1 - z_1^*|, \lambda_2^a|b_2 - z_2^*|\}$ compared to a.*

PROOF. The proof follows the same ideas than the previous one. For $\lambda_1^a = \frac{|a_2 - z_2^*|}{|a_1 - z_1^*| + |a_2 - z_2^*|}$ and $\lambda_2^a = 1 - \lambda_1^a = \frac{|a_1 - z_1^*|}{|a_1 - z_1^*| + |a_2 - z_2^*|}$, it follows that $D_1 = \lambda_1^a|a_1 - z_1^*| = \lambda_2^a|a_2 - z_2^*| = D_2$. But then, for all solutions a' that do not dominate a and are left of a, $a'_1 < a_1$ and $a'_2 > a_2$ holds, such that $\lambda_1^a|a'_1 - z_1^*| < \lambda_1^a|a_1 - z_1^*| = \lambda_2^a|a_2 - z_2^*| < \lambda_2^a|a'_2 - z_1^*|$ which is equivalent to the fact that also the max in the weighted Tchebycheff for a' is larger and thus worse than the weighted Tchebycheff function for a. With a symmetric argument, we can prove that also all solutions a' that do not dominate a and are to the right of it are worse. □

As a result of the above lemmas, it follows that the optimal placement of a point according to the $R2$ indicator, given that all other points are already placed optimally, only depends on its neighbor(s) as well as on a subset of weight vectors.

COROLLARY 1. *The optimal placement of a point x_i with $x_{i-1}^\mu \le x_i \le x_{i+1}^\mu$ that maximizes the $R2$ indicator, given that all other points $x_1^\mu, \ldots, x_{i-1}^\mu, x_{i+1}^\mu, \ldots, x_\mu^\mu$ are already known, only depends on x_{i-1}^μ and x_{x+1}^μ and the weight vectors between these two points. Likewise, the optimal placements of x_1 and x_μ only depend on their single neighbor.*

PROOF. According to the above lemmas, for all weight vectors to the left of x_{i-1}^μ, x_{i-1}^μ is better than x_i and, analogously, for all weight vectors to the right of x_{i+1}^μ, x_{i+1}^μ is better than x_i. Consequently, the optimal placement of x_i only depends on these vectors. □

3.2 Optimal μ-Distributions for the $R2$ Indicator

With the above lemmas, we can now prove a few general statements about the optimal distribution of μ points with respect to the $R2$ indicator. In particular for the special case of more points than weight vectors ($\mu \ge |\Lambda|$), the optimal μ-distributions turn out to contain the intersection points of the rays corresponding to the weight vectors with the Pareto front.

THEOREM 1. *In the case that $\mu \geq |\Lambda|$, optimal μ-distributions for the R2 indicator with given weight vectors Λ contain all intersection points $\{a \in A | \lambda^a \in \Lambda\}$ between the rays defined by the weights and the actual Pareto front.*

PROOF. As we have seen in Lemma 2, no nondominated solution is better with respect to a given weight vector than the solution actually lying on the corresponding ray. Together with the weak monotonicity of the $R2$ indicator, this means that for a given weight vector, no other (feasible) solution can have a better $R2$ indicator contribution for this weight than the intersection between the corresponding ray and the Pareto front. Assuming $\mu \geq |\Lambda|$, the optimal μ-distribution consequently will include all those intersection points. □

Note here that the optimal μ-distribution is unique in the case $\mu = |\Lambda|$ and that all rays have to intersect with the Pareto front. In the case where μ is larger than the number N of intersection points between the rays and the Pareto front, the $R2$ indicator has no influence on $\mu - N$ points. On the opposite, we can show that the optimal μ-distributions in the case $\mu < |\Lambda|$ are also not always unique.

THEOREM 2. *In case $\mu < |\Lambda|$, there are examples where the optimal μ-distributions are not unique.*

PROOF. Let us investigate an example with $\mu = 3$ points and $N = 4$ weights. The problem is DTLZ1 [6], i.e., the front is described by $f(x) = 0.5 - x$. Let the four weights be $\lambda_1 = (\frac{1}{7}, \frac{6}{7})$, $\lambda_2 = (\frac{3}{7}, \frac{4}{7})$, $\lambda_3 = (\frac{4}{7}, \frac{3}{7})$, and $\lambda_4 = (\frac{6}{7}, \frac{1}{7})$. With the utopian point in $(-0.1, -0.1)$, this gives the scenario depicted in Fig. 2.

Let us assume for the moment that the two extreme points are used and that we have to place the third point in between them. We can then compute the $R2$ indicator value with respect to the weight vectors λ_2 and λ_3 dependent on the x-value of the third point while the $R2$ indicator contributions with respect to λ_1 and λ_4 are fixed to their optimal value by the other two points lying on the extremes. With simple calculus, we obtain

$$\begin{aligned} R2(x) &= \min\left\{\max\left\{\frac{3}{7}|-0.1-x|, \frac{4}{7}|-0.6+x|\right\}, \frac{18}{70}\right\} \\ &\quad + \min\left\{\max\left\{\frac{4}{7}|-0.1-x|, \frac{3}{7}|-0.6+x|\right\}, \frac{18}{70}\right\} \\ &= \min\left\{\max\left\{\frac{3}{70}+\frac{3}{7}x, \frac{12}{35}-\frac{4}{7}x\right\}, \frac{9}{35}\right\} \\ &\quad + \min\left\{\max\left\{\frac{2}{35}+\frac{4}{7}x, \frac{9}{35}-\frac{3}{7}x\right\}, \frac{9}{35}\right\} \end{aligned}$$

for the $R2$ indicator value depending on the x-value of the third point with $0 \leq x \leq 0.5$. The previous equation can be rewritten as

$$R2(x) = \begin{cases} \frac{36}{70} - \frac{3}{7}x & \text{for } 0 \leq x < 0.15 \\ 0.6 - x & \text{for } 0.15 \leq x < 0.2 \\ 0.4 & \text{for } 0.2 \leq x \leq 0.3 \\ 0.1 + x & \text{for } 0.3 < x \leq 0.35 \\ 0.3 + \frac{3}{7}x & \text{for } 0.35 < x \leq 0.5 \end{cases}$$

with the minimum value of 0.4 reached for $x \in [0.2, 0.3]$, see also the righthand plot of Fig. 2. Hence, the optimal 3-distribution is not unique in this case and not even a finite number of distinct optimal 3-distributions exist, but infinitely many solution sets are optimal.

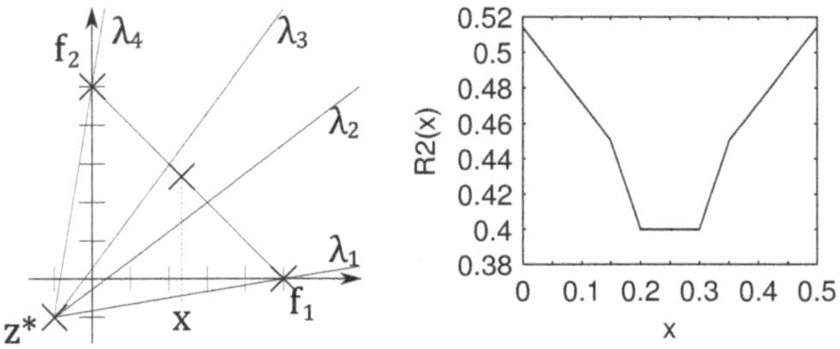

Figure 2: An example where the optimal μ-distribution for the $R2$ indicator is not unique: scenario (left) and corresponding $R2$ indicator (w.r.t. λ_2 and λ_3) when the third point moves from $x = 0$ on the left of the front to $x = 0.5$ on the right of the front (right).

Let us briefly comment on the leftmost and rightmost solutions and the above assumption to place them on the boundaries of the Pareto front. Due to symmetry reasons, we only consider the placement of the leftmost point. With x_2^μ in the optimal interval $[0.2, 0.3]$, we know that the placement of the leftmost point x_1^μ is only influenced by λ_3 and λ_4. Hence, we can compute the contribution of x_1^μ which results, again with simple calculus, in $\frac{6}{7}x_1^\mu + \frac{18}{70}$ and which is minimized for $x_1^\mu = 0$. □

4. APPROXIMATIONS OF OPTIMAL μ-DISTRIBUTIONS FOR THE $R2$ INDICATOR

The above theoretical results already gave some insights into the optimal distribution of μ points regarding the $R2$ indicator. In this section, these insights are enhanced with empirical observations with respect to the optimal μ-distributions of this indicator and an analysis of the difference to the optimal μ-distributions of the HV indicator. To accomplish this, we chose the three established test problems ZDT1 [13], DTLZ1, and DTLZ2 [6] with different Pareto front shapes—convex, linear (as a special case of convexity), and concave. Their exact Pareto front definitions are $f(x) = 1 - \sqrt{x}$ (ZDT1), $f(x) = 0.5 - x$ (DTLZ1), and $f(x) = \sqrt{1 - x^2}$ (DTLZ2). On each of these test problems, we approximated the optimal μ-distributions for $\mu = 10$ and the ideal point $(0, 0)$ as utopian using CMA-ES [8] on the ten respective x values. To also analyze the effect of the number of weight vectors N and to approximate the integral in Definition 1 which resembles an infinite number of weight vectors, the different multiples $N = \{\mu, 2\mu, 3\mu, 4\mu, 5\mu, 10\mu, 20\mu, 50\mu, 100\mu\}$ were considered. The same holds for different weight distributions by using uniform distributions in weight and angle space. On each combination of test problem, number of weight vectors, and weight distribution, 10 restarts of the CMA-ES are performed in order to have a more accurate estimate of the optimum distribution and to also analyze the variability in the results.

For a smart initialization, we used the theoretical result of Theorem 1. Based on the given distribution, μ weight vectors were generated and the corresponding intersections between the rays and the Pareto front were computed using standard calculus. The intersections' x-coordinates were then used as initial mean vector for the CMA-ES runs.

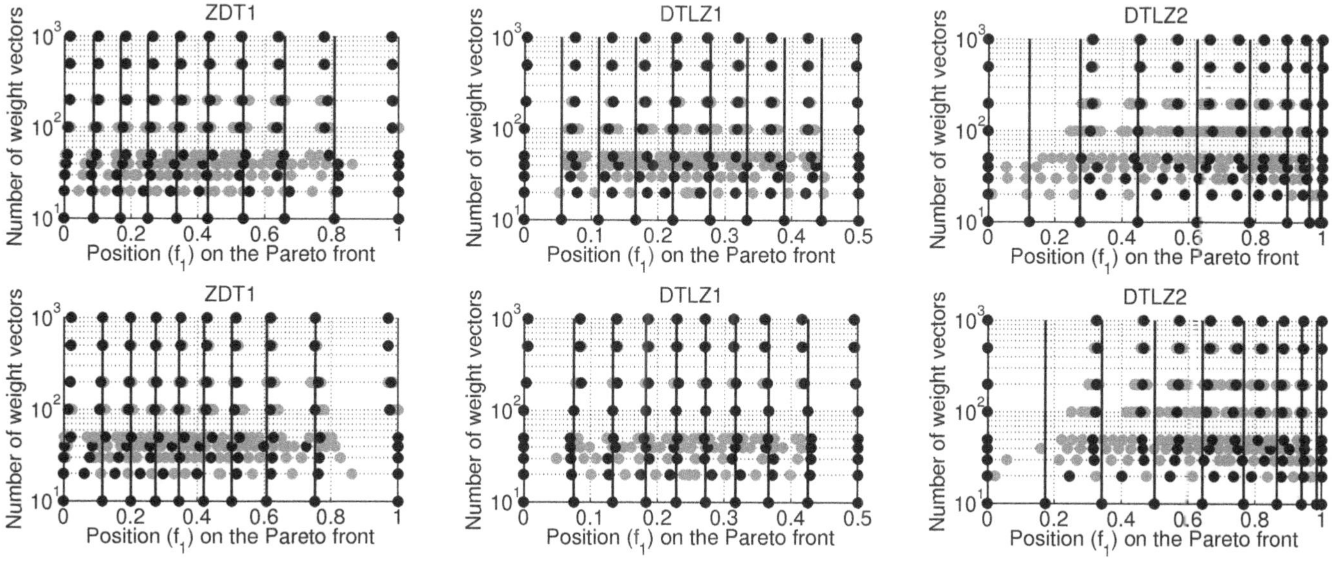

Figure 3: Positions (f_1-values) of the approximated optimal 10-distributions of the $R2$ indicator with increasing number of weight vectors uniformly distributed in weight space (top) and in angle space (bottom). Three different front shapes are considered: convex (ZDT1, $f_2 = 1 - \sqrt{f_1}$), linear (DTLZ1, $f_2 = 0.5 - f_1$), and concave (DTLZ2, $f_2 = \sqrt{1 - f_1^2}$). The final results of each CMA-ES run are depicted by gray dots. The run obtaining the best R2 value is highlighted in black. The positions of the initial points are indicated by the black lines. The utopian point was chosen as $(0, 0)$.

4.1 Effect of the Number of Weight Vectors

The results of the different runs of the CMA-ES are shown in Fig. 3. The positions of the initial solutions, i.e., the optimum distribution for $N = \mu$, is highlighted using black vertical lines. The final positions after each restart of the CMA-ES are depicted using gray dots. The best result for each setting is printed in black.

As a general observation, it can be stated that the variance of the results is higher for a lower number of weight vectors. In particular for $N < 10\mu$, it can hardly be distinguished between the result distributions of the different positions. For $N \geq 50\mu$, in contrast, the results of the CMA-ES hardly show any variance. It seems like each intersection point being a local optimum position, making the optimization hard for fewer weight vectors and higher distances between these local optima. With an increasing number of weights, the local basins become so small that the CMA-ES can easily jump from one to another.

With respect to the approximated optimal positions, the increase of N shows no significant effect for the convex Pareto front of ZDT1 and—given a uniform distribution in angle space—for the linear front of DTLZ1. The final points lie all close to the black lines indicating the optimal position for $N = \mu$. For uniform weights on DTLZ1, the points tend to become denser in the center of the Pareto front, as they all move towards the center from their initial position. Interestingly, for DTLZ2 it is shown that the optimal positions of the points extremely change with increasing N, i.e., for more than 100 weight vectors the distribution of the points is highly biased towards the right part of the front. No points but the extreme point at $f_1 = 0$ are placed within the interval $[0, 0.3]$. This may be caused by the possibility to strongly improve f_2 without deteriorating f_1 too much (cf. Fig. 5).

Even for the scenarios, in which the optimum distribution changes with increasing N, this distribution stabilizes after a specific number $N_{\text{threshold}}$ of weight vectors is exceeded. In our bi-objective experiments, this threshold lies at about $N_{\text{threshold}} = 10\mu = 100$. For higher N, the actual integral seems to be well approximated by the discretization by means of the sum over a finite set of N weight vectors.

4.2 Comparing the Hypervolume and the $R2$ Indicators

Despite of the empirically shown correlated behavior [10, 11], the indicators show specific preferences regarding the optimal distribution of the solutions on the Pareto front. For this purpose, it is analyzed how the R2 indicator would rearrange the points of the optimal μ-distribution w.r.t. the HV indicator and vice versa. In Fig. 4, the results for $\mu = 10$ on the considered test problems are shown. Starting from the optimal points on the x-axis (black dots), the contributions to the other indicator in case the least-contributing point (see Definitions 5 and Definition 7) is shifted to the respective x are shown on the y-axis.

For the optimal μ-distributions of the HV indicator, it becomes obvious that the R2 contributions tend to shift the points to the center of the front in order to reach a denser distribution in this region. The opposite tendency can be seen for the contributions to the HV indicator starting from the optimal μ-distribution of the R2 indicator. For the linear front of DTLZ1, for which the contributions are symmetric, the size of this shift decreases towards the center. This result is consistent for both kinds of weight distributions in the R2 indicator.

We now analyze the differences between the optimal distributions based on Fig. 5, in which we plot the 10-optimal distributions in objective space. For illustrating these dif-

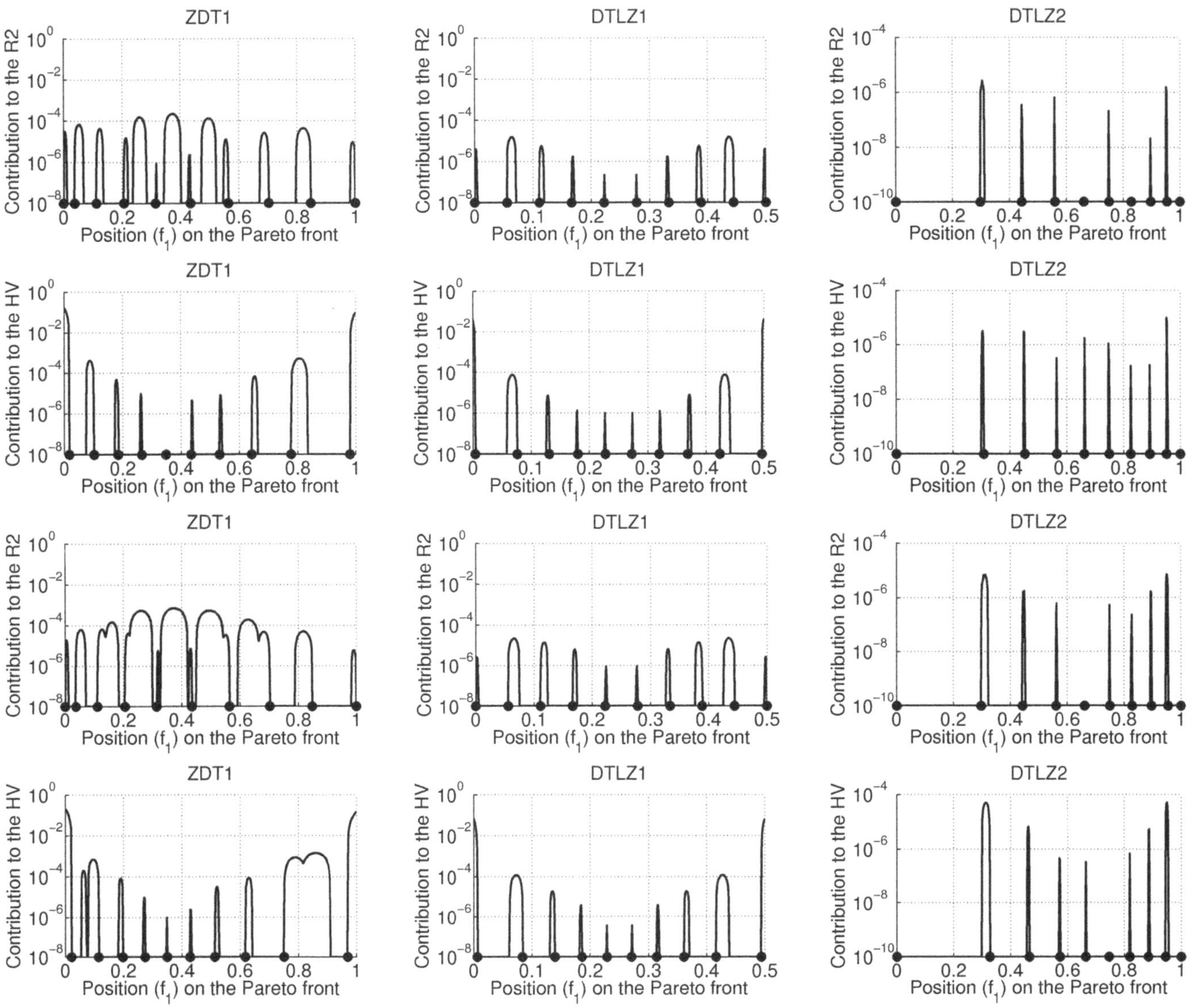

Figure 4: Contributions to either the R2 or the hypervolume (log-scale) when shifting the f_1 values of the optimal 10-distribution of the respective other indicator. The indicator to which the contributions are computed is indicated on the y-axis. The R2 indicator is calculated using 500 weights uniformly distributed in weight space (two lines on the top) or in angle space (two lines on the bottom) and the utopian point (0,0). The hypervolume is bounded using the reference point (11,11). Three different front shapes are considered: convex (ZDT1, $f_2 = 1 - \sqrt{f_1}$), linear (DTLZ1, $f_2 = 0.5 - f_1$), and concave (DTLZ2, $f_2 = \sqrt{1 - f_1^2}$).

ferences between the approximations of the optimal μ-distributions for the $R2$ indicator and the theoretically proven optimal ones for the HV indicator, we plot the individual differences between the x-values of corresponding points, i.e., $x^{\mu}_{1,R2} - x^{\mu}_{1,HV}, x^{\mu}_{2,R2} - x^{\mu}_{2,HV}, \ldots$, from left to right (on the bottom of Fig. 5). What can be seen is that in all cases, the optimal μ-distributions of the $R2$ indicators have a tendency towards the middle of the front, i.e., the distances between neighboring points compared to the HV indicator are larger at the extremes and smaller in the middle of the front. These distances turn out to be higher in angle space than in weight space. Sine-shaped curves of difference values result in the bottom of Fig. 5. It is caused by the higher influence of balanced weight vectors, i.e., vectors having almost similar weight components for each objective.

To understand the increase of influence for these weight vectors, consider the linear front of DTLZ1, $N = 101$ weight vectors, and a significantly lower number of points. For a uniform distribution in weight space, we know (cf. initial distributions of Fig. 3) that the intersection points of the vectors with the linear front are also uniformly distributed. Due to the selection of the best solution for each weight vector of the R2 indicator, each point covers a subset of weight vectors in its direct neighborhood. Thereby, the optimum point $(0.5, 0)$ for the extreme weight vector $(0, 1)$ has a value of $\max(0 \cdot 0.5, 1 \cdot 0.0) = 0$. Even for the

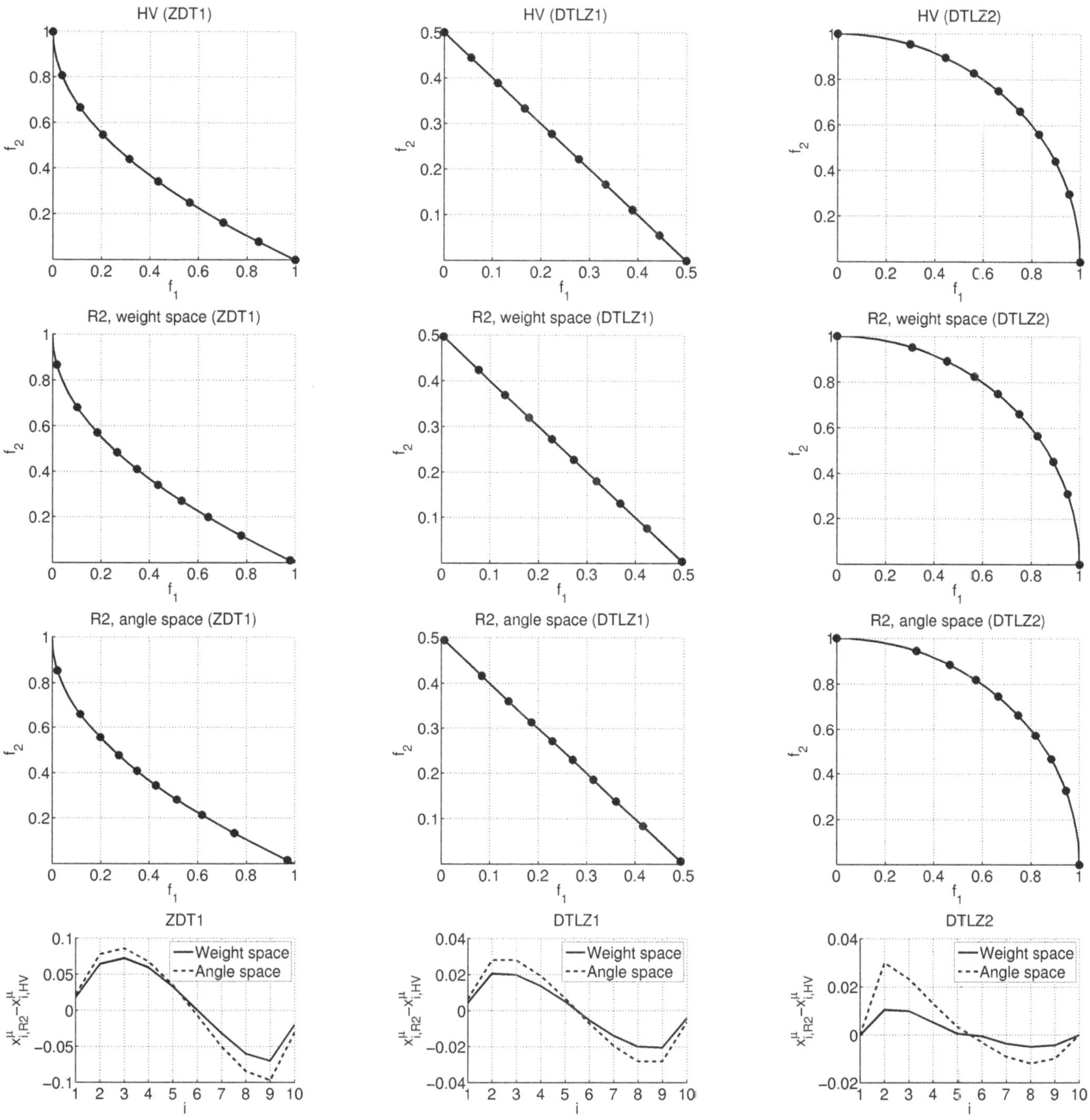

Figure 5: Comparison between approximations of the optimal 10-distributions for both $R2$ indicators and the theoretically known optimal 10-distributions for the hypervolume indicator on the ZDT1 (convex), DTLZ1 (linear) and DTLZ2 (concave) Pareto fronts. In the R2 indicator, 500 weight vectors and the utopian point $(0,0)$ are used. On the top, the distributions are plotted in objective space, whereas the distances between the f_1-values of corresponding points in each distribution are plotted in the second row.

next weight vector $(0.01, 0.99)$, this point obtains a value of $\max(0.01 \cdot 0.5, 0.99 \cdot 0.0) = 0.005$ compared to the optimum value of $\max(0.01 \cdot 0.495, 0.99 \cdot 0.005) = 0.00495$. In contrast, the optimum point $(0.25, 0.25)$ for the balanced weight vector $(0.5, 0.5)$ has a value of $\max(0.5 \cdot 0.25, 0.5 \cdot 0.25) = 0.125$. For the next weight vector $(0.49, 0.51)$, the corresponding value of this point is $\max(0.49 \cdot 0.25, 0.51 \cdot 0.25) = 0.1275$ compared to the optimum value of $\max(0.49 \cdot 0.255, 0.51 \cdot 0.245) = 0.12495$. Whereas we loose 0.0005 at the extremes, we loose 0.00255 in the center—the loss is more than five times greater in this region. As a consequence, the density of points becomes higher to compensate for this effect.

5. CONCLUSIONS

As addition to the hypervolume (HV) indicator, the $R2$ indicator has been recommended as an indicator for performance assessment of multiobjective optimizers [16, 14]. Although the $R2$ indicator is only weakly monotonic with respect to the dominance relation, while the HV indicator is strictly monotonic, it has been reported that both indicators show a correlated behavior in practice [11].

In this paper, we introduced a unary, completely equivalent, version of the $R2$ indicator and investigated its properties and its differences to the HV indicator. Such kind of study was performed for the first time in this detail. It assisted in obtaining a deeper understanding of those popular indicators. In particular, it was shown that in the bi-objective case the $R2$ indicator has a bias towards the center of the Pareto front when compared to the HV indicator, which we demonstrated to be caused by the maximum operation of the Tchebycheff function. This finding is in contrast to the common assumption of a more uniform coverage obtained by the $R2$ indicator. We proved that the optimal placement of a point according to the $R2$ indicator only depends on its two neighbors and a subset of the weight vectors. Furthermore, approximations of the optimal μ-distributions for the $R2$ indicator based on uniform weight distributions in weight as well as in angle space were generated for standard test functions with different Pareto front shapes. They showed different characteristics compared to the optimal μ-distributions of the HV indicator [1], whereby the bias towards the center is even more pronounced for the uniform distribution in angle space.

Although the comparisons between the two indicators obtained important insights into their specific characteristics, several open questions need to be addressed in future studies. Besides investigating other problems with different, in particular discontinuous front shapes, one important aspect is the scaling of the indicators with the number of objectives. It is expected that the differences between the indicators become larger with three and more objectives, as it is known that the HV indicator tends towards the extremes of the Pareto front if the reference point is far enough away. In contrast, a uniform distribution of the $R2$ indicator's weight vectors should still have the effect of focusing on the center of the front, as observed in the bi-objective case. Also additional theoretical results on the optimal μ-distributions for the $R2$ indicator would be valuable, e.g., characterizing the exact optimal placements of μ solutions depending on the number and distribution of the weight vectors in terms of a density as in [1, 2]. These results may improve the design of multi-objective optimization algorithms, as well as their performance assessment.

6. ACKNOWLEDGMENTS

This paper is based on investigations of the project D5 "Synthesis and multi-objective model-based optimization of process chains for manufacturing parts with functionally graded properties" as part of the collaborative research center SFB/TR TRR 30, which is kindly supported by the Deutsche Forschungsgemeinschaft (DFG).

7. REFERENCES

[1] A. Auger, J. Bader, D. Brockhoff, and E. Zitzler. Theory of the Hypervolume Indicator: Optimal μ-Distributions and the Choice of the Reference Point. In *Foundations of Genetic Algorithms (FOGA 2009)*, pages 87–102, New York, NY, USA, 2009. ACM.

[2] A. Auger, J. Bader, D. Brockhoff, and E. Zitzler. Hypervolume-based Multiobjective Optimization: Theoretical Foundations and Practical Implications. *Theoretical Computer Science*, 425:75–103, 2012.

[3] N. Beume et al. Hypervolume, 2 2012. `http://www.hypervolume.org`.

[4] N. Beume, C. M. Fonseca, M. Lopez-Ibanez, L. Paquete, and J. Vahrenhold. On the Complexity of Computing the Hypervolume Indicator. *IEEE Transactions on Evolutionary Computation*, 13(5):1075–1082, 2009.

[5] N. Beume, B. Naujoks, and M. Emmerich. SMS-EMOA: Multiobjective selection based on dominated hypervolume. *European Journal of Operational Research*, 181(3):1653–1669, 2007.

[6] K. Deb, L. Thiele, M. Laumanns, and E. Zitzler. Scalable Multi-Objective Optimization Test Problems. In *Congress on Evolutionary Computation (CEC 2002)*, pages 825–830. IEEE Press, 2002.

[7] M. P. Hansen and A. Jaszkiewicz. Evaluating The Quality of Approximations of the Non-Dominated Set. Technical report, Institute of Mathematical Modeling, Technical University of Denmark, 1998. IMM Technical Report IMM-REP-1998-7.

[8] N. Hansen and A. Ostermeier. Completely Derandomized Self-Adaptation in Evolution Strategies. *Evolutionary Computation*, 9(2):159–195, 2001.

[9] G. W. Snedecor and W. G. Cochran. *Statistical Methods.* Iowa State University Press, Iowa, 1989.

[10] S. Wessing. Towards Optimal Parameterizations of the S-Metric Selection Evolutionary Multi-Objective Algorithm. Diploma Thesis, Technical Report TR 09-06, TU Dortmund, 2009.

[11] S. Wessing and B. Naujoks. Sequential parameter optimization for multi-objective problems. In *IEEE Congress on Evolutionary Computation*, pages 1–8. IEEE, 2010.

[12] E. Zitzler. *Evolutionary Algorithms for Multiobjective Optimization: Methods and Applications.* PhD thesis, ETH Zurich, Switzerland, 1999.

[13] E. Zitzler, K. Deb, and L. Thiele. Comparison of Multiobjective Evolutionary Algorithms: Empirical Results. *Evolutionary Computation*, 8(2):173–195, 2000.

[14] E. Zitzler, J. Knowles, and L. Thiele. Quality Assessment of Pareto Set Approximations. In *Multiobjective Optimization: Interactive and Evolutionary Approaches*, pages 373–404. Springer, 2008.

[15] E. Zitzler and L. Thiele. Multiobjective Optimization Using Evolutionary Algorithms - A Comparative Case Study. In *Conference on Parallel Problem Solving from Nature (PPSN V)*, pages 292–301, 1998.

[16] E. Zitzler, L. Thiele, M. Laumanns, C. M. Fonseca, and V. Grunert da Fonseca. Performance Assessment of Multiobjective Optimizers: An Analysis and Review. *IEEE Transactions on Evolutionary Computation*, 7(2):117–132, 2003.

Locality-based Multiobjectivization for the HP Model of Protein Structure Prediction

Mario Garza-Fabre Gregorio Toscano-Pulido Eduardo Rodriguez-Tello

Information Technology Laboratory, CINVESTAV-Tamaulipas. Parque Científico y Tecnológico TECNOTAM
Km. 5.5 carretera Cd. Victoria-Soto La Marina, Cd. Victoria, Tamaulipas 87130, MÉXICO
{mgarza, gtoscano, ertello}@tamps.cinvestav.mx

ABSTRACT

Even under the rather simplified HP lattice model, protein structure prediction remains a challenging problem in combinatorial optimization. Recently, the multiobjectivization of this problem was proposed. By decomposing the original objective function, a two-objective formulation for the HP model was defined. Such an alternative formulation showed very promising results, leading to an increased search performance in most of the conducted experiments. This paper introduces a novel multiobjectivization for the HP model which is based on the locality notion of amino acid interactions. Using different evolutionary algorithms, this proposal was compared with respect to both the conventional single-objective formulation and the previously reported multiobjectivization. The new proposed formulation scored the best results in most of the cases. Statistical significance testing and a large set of test cases support the findings of this study. Results are provided for both the two-dimensional square lattice and the three-dimensional cubic lattice.

Categories and Subject Descriptors

I.2.8 [**ARTIFICIAL INTELLIGENCE**]: Problem Solving, Control Methods, and Search—*Heuristic methods*

Keywords

Multiobjectivization, protein structure prediction, HP model

1. INTRODUCTION

Proteins are fundamental elements of living organisms. These chain-like molecules are composed from a set of 20 different building blocks called amino acids. The specific sequence of amino acids determines how proteins fold into unique three-dimensional structures defining their biological functions [1]. The *protein structure prediction* problem, PSP, is the problem of finding the native (energy-minimizing) conformation for a protein given only its amino acid sequence.

The *hydrophobic-polar* (HP) *model* [12] is an abstraction of the PSP. This model captures the fact that the hydrophobicity of amino acids is one of the main driving forces determining the functional conformation of proteins. The prediction of protein structures using the HP model is a hard combinatorial optimization problem [3, 7]. Such a complexity has motivated the use of evolutionary algorithms and a variety of other metaheuristics to address this problem [25, 35].

Multiobjectivization refers to the process of reformulating a single-objective optimization problem as a multiobjective one [23]. This transformation has been successfully used to deal with difficult problems, such as the PSP [2, 8, 10, 16, 32]. However, it was not until recently that this concept was applied to the particular HP model of this problem for the first time [14]. In [14], the conventional energy (objective) function of the HP model was decomposed into two separate objectives based on the parity of amino acid positions in the protein sequence. This approach was named the *parity decomposition* (PD). Experimental results reported in [14] indicate that an important improvement in the search performance can be obtained by using such an alternative formulation, motivating further research in this direction.

In this paper, an improved multiobjectivization strategy for the HP model is proposed: the *locality decomposition* (LD). In LD, the decomposition of the HP model's energy function is carried out by segregating local from nonlocal amino acid interactions. This locality notion is based on the sequence distance between the interacting amino acids. The suitability of the proposed LD is investigated by comparing it with respect to both the conventional single-objective formulation and the preceding PD multiobjectivization [14].

The remainder of this document is organized as follows. Background concepts and notation are covered in Section 2. Section 3 summarizes related work. In Section 4, the new proposed formulation is described. Section 5 details the implemented algorithms, test cases and the performance assessment methodology. The results are presented in Section 6. Finally, Section 7 provides the conclusions of this study.

2. BACKGROUND AND NOTATION

2.1 The Hydrophobic-Polar (HP) Model

Amino acids can be classified either as *hydrophobic* (H) or *polar* (P) on the basis of their affinity for water. While the H amino acids tend to clump together on the inside of proteins, the P ones are usually found at the outer surface interacting with the aqueous environment. Hydrophobicity is, therefore, a dominant force in the protein folding process.

In the HP model [12], proteins are abstracted as chains of H- and P-type beads. Protein sequences, which are originally defined over a 20-letters alphabet, are thus of the form $S \in \{H, P\}^L$, where L is the number of amino acids. Valid protein conformations are modeled as *Self-Avoiding Walks* of the HP chain on a lattice. That is, each lattice node can be assigned to at most one amino acid and consecutive amino acids in S are to be also adjacent in the lattice.

By emulating the hydrophobic effect, the HP model aims to maximize the interaction among H amino acids in the lattice. Formally, protein structure prediction under the HP model is defined as the problem of finding $c^* \in C$ such that $E(c^*) = \min\{E(c) \mid c \in C\}$, being C the set of all valid conformations. $E(c)$ denotes the energy of conformation c:

$$E(c) = \sum_{s_i, s_j \in S} e(s_i, s_j) \quad (1)$$

where $e(s_i, s_j) = -1$ if s_i and s_j form a *hydrophobic topological contact*, denoted by $htc(s_i, s_j)$. Otherwise, $e(s_i, s_j) = 0$. A hydrophobic topological contact occurs when two H amino acids $s_i, s_j \in S$ are nonconsecutive in S but adjacent in the lattice. An example conformation for an HP chain of length $L = 20$ on the square lattice is shown in Figure 1.

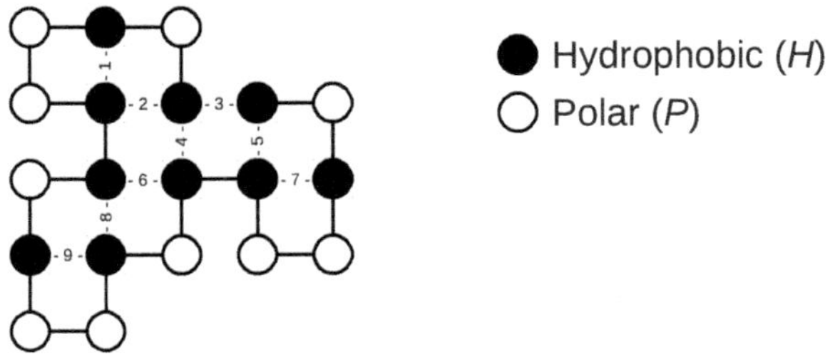

Figure 1: Hydrophobic topological contacts are numbered. The energy of this structure is $E(c) = -9$.

2.2 Single- and Multiobjective Optimization

A *single-objective optimization problem* can be stated as the problem of minimizing an *objective function* $f : \mathcal{F} \rightarrow \mathbb{R}$, where $\mathcal{F}$ is the set of all feasible solutions. The aim is to find the solution(s) $x^* \in \mathcal{F}$ such that $f(x^*) = \min\{f(x) \mid x \in \mathcal{F}\}$.

Similarly, a *multiobjective optimization problem* can be defined as the problem of minimizing an *objective vector* $\mathbf{f}(x) = [f_1(x), f_2(x), \ldots, f_k(x)]^T$, where $f_i : \mathcal{F} \rightarrow \mathbb{R}$ is the i-th objective function, $i \in \{1, 2, \ldots, k\}$. The goal is to find a set of *Pareto-optimal solutions* $\mathcal{P}^* \subset \mathcal{F}$, such that $\mathcal{P}^* = \{x^* \in \mathcal{F} \mid \nexists x \in \mathcal{F} : x \prec x^*\}$. The symbol "$\prec$" denotes the *Pareto-dominance* relation, which is given by:

$$\begin{aligned} x \prec y \quad \Leftrightarrow \quad & \forall i \in \{1, 2, \ldots, k\} : f_i(x) \leq f_i(y) \ \wedge \\ & \exists j \in \{1, 2, \ldots, k\} : f_j(x) < f_j(y) \end{aligned} \quad (2)$$

If $x \prec y$, then x is said to *dominate* y. Otherwise ($x \nprec y$), y is said to be *nondominated* with respect to x. The image of $\mathcal{P}^*$ in the objective space is called the *Pareto-optimal front*.

2.3 Multiobjectivization

Multiobjectivization concerns the reformulation of single-objective optimization problems in terms of two or more objective functions [23]. This can be done either by adding *supplementary* (also called artificial or helper) objectives [4, 21], or through the *decomposition* of the original objective function [17, 23]. In either case, multiobjectivization introduces fundamental changes in the search landscape, usually leading algorithms to perform a more efficient exploration. However, the goal remains to solve the original problem, so that the original optima are to be also Pareto-optimal with regard to the multiobjectivized version of the problem.

This work is based on the decomposition approach. A single-objective problem, with a given objective function $f : \mathcal{F} \rightarrow \mathbb{R}$, is restated in terms of $k \geq 2$ objectives $f_i : \mathcal{F} \rightarrow \mathbb{R}, i \in \{1, 2, \ldots, k\}$ such that $f(x) = \sum_{i=1}^{k} f_i(x)$, for all $x \in \mathcal{F}$. As the only possible effect [17], plateaus may be defined in the search landscape. That is, originally comparable solutions may become incomparable (mutually nondominated) with regard to the decomposed formulation. Multiobjectivization by decomposition has been proven to be effective as a means of escaping from local optima [17, 23].

3. RELATED WORK

There has been a great deal of research on the use of metaheuristics to solve the HP model of the PSP. This includes genetic algorithms [18, 33], memetic and hybrid algorithms [6, 19], immune-based algorithms [9], ant colony optimization [31], particle swarm optimization [5], differential evolution [28] and estimation of distribution algorithms [27]. Some of the literature in this regard is reviewed in [25, 35].

Multiobjectivization has been successfully applied in order to solve difficult optimization problems. Among them, there can be mentioned well-known combinatorial problems such as the traveling salesman problem [20, 21, 23], job-shop scheduling [21, 24] and bin packing problems [30], as well as important problems in the fields of mobile communications [29], computational mechanics [15] and computer vision [34]. Multiobjectivization has also been proposed for the PSP [2, 8, 10, 16, 32]. However, it was not until recently that the first multiobjectivized formulation for the particular HP model of this problem was reported [14]. Such an HP model's formulation is briefly described in Section 3.1.

3.1 The Parity Decomposition

In the two-dimensional square and the three-dimensional cubic lattices, topological contacts are only possible between amino acids whose sequence positions are of opposite parity. Based on this fact and following the multiobjectivization by decomposition approach, Garza-Fabre *et al.* [14] proposed a two-objective formulation, $\mathbf{f}(c) = [f_1(c), f_2(c)]^T$, for $c \in C$:

$$f_1(c) = \sum_{s_i, s_j \in S} e(s_i, s_j) \qquad \text{for } \boldsymbol{i \equiv 0 \pmod 2}, i < j \quad (3)$$

$$f_2(c) = \sum_{s_i, s_j \in S} e(s_i, s_j) \qquad \text{for } \boldsymbol{i \equiv 1 \pmod 2}, i < j \quad (4)$$

where both $f_1(c)$ and $f_2(c)$ are to be minimized and $e(s_i, s_j)$ was defined in Section 2.1. Function f_1 accounts only for hydrophobic topological contacts $htc(s_i, s_j)$ where i, the sequence position of amino acid s_i, is even. On the contrary, f_2 is defined for those cases where such the i-th sequence position is odd. Notice that $E(c) = f_1(c) + f_2(c)$ for all $c \in C$.

4. THE LOCALITY DECOMPOSITION

In this section, a novel multiobjectivization strategy for the HP model is proposed. The conventional energy (objective) function of the HP model is decomposed based on the locality notion of amino acid interactions. A hydrophobic topological contact $htc(s_i, s_j)$ can be considered to represent either a *local* or a *nonlocal* interaction. It depends on whether or not the sequence distance between the amino acids s_i and s_j (*i.e.*, $|j-i|$) is within a given maximum δ. From this, a two-objective formulation, $\mathbf{f}(c) = [f_1(c), f_2(c)]^T$, is defined over the set of valid protein conformations $c \in C$:

$$f_1(c) = \sum_{s_i, s_j \in S} e(s_i, s_j) \qquad \text{for } j - i \leq \delta, i < j \tag{5}$$

$$f_2(c) = \sum_{s_i, s_j \in S} e(s_i, s_j) \qquad \text{for } j - i > \delta, i < j \tag{6}$$

where $f_1(c)$ and $f_2(c)$ are both to be minimized and $e(s_i, s_j)$ has been previously defined in Section 2.1.

That is, f_1 is defined for local interactions, whereas f_2 accounts for the nonlocal ones. Note that the sum of the two proposed objectives equals the conventional energy function defined in Section 2.1 ($E(c) = f_1(c) + f_2(c)$, $\forall c \in C$). This is in accordance with the decomposition approach for multiobjectivization. It should also be noted that δ plays a decisive role for the behavior of this proposal. Thus, the impact of varying this parameter needs to be investigated.

5. EXPERIMENTAL SETUP

5.1 Test Cases

A total of 30 HP instances were considered. Out of them, 15 are for the two-dimensional square lattice and the other 15 are for three-dimensional cubic one. Tables 1 and 2 present the full sequences, their length (L) and the optimal or best known energy value (E^*), to the authors' knowledge.

Table 1: HP instances for the 2D square lattice.

	Sequence	L	E^*
2d1	$H_2P_5H_2P_3HP_3HP$	18	-4
2d2	$HPHPH_3P_3H_4P_2H_2$	18	-8
2d3	$PHP_2HPH_3PH_2PH_5$	18	-9
2d4	$HPHP_2H_2PHP_2HPH_2P_2HPH$	20	-9
2d5	$H_3P_2HPHPHP_2HPHPHP_2H$	20	-10
2d6	$H_2P_2HP_2HP_2HP_2HP_2HP_2HP_2H_2$	24	-9
2d7	$P_2HP_2H_2P_4H_2P_4H_2P_4H_2$	25	-8
2d8	$P_3H_2P_2H_2P_5H_7P_2H_2P_4H_2P_2HP_2$	36	-14
2d9	$P_2HP_2H_2P_2H_2P_5H_{10}P_6H_2P_2H_2P_2HP_2H_5$	48	-23
2d10	$H_2(PH)_4H_3P(HP_3)_3(P_3H)_3PH_4(PH)_4H$	50	-21
2d11	$P_2H_3PH_8P_3H_{10}PHP_3H_{12}P_4H_6PH_2PHP$	60	-36
2d12	$H_{12}PHPH(P_2H_2P_2H_2P_2H)_3PHPH_{12}$	64	-42
2d13	$H_4P_4H_{12}P_6(H_{12}P_3)_3HP_2H_2P_2H_2P_2HPH$	85	-53
2d14	$P_6HPH_2P_5H_3PH_5PH_2P_4H_2P_2H_2PH_5PH_{10}$ $PH_2PH_7P_{11}H_7P_2HPH_3P_6HPH_2$	100	-48
2d15	$P_3H_2P_2H_4P_2H_3PH_2PH_2PH_4P_8H_6P_2H_6P_9$ $HPH_2PH_{11}P_2H_3PH_2PHP_2HPH_3P_6H_3$	100	-50

Table 2: HP instances for the 3D cubic lattice.

	Sequence	L	E^*
3d1	$HPHP_2H_2PHP_2HPH_2P_2HPH$	20	-11
3d2	$H_2P_2HP_2HP_2HP_2HP_2HP_2HP_2H_2$	24	-13
3d3	$P_2HP_2H_2P_4H_2P_4H_2P_4H_2$	25	-9
3d4	$P_3H_2P_2H_2P_5H_7P_2H_2P_4H_2P_2HP_2$	36	-18
3d5	$P_2H_3PH_3P_3HPH_2PH_2P_2HPH_4PHP_2H_5PHPH_2P_2H_2P$	46	-32
3d6	$P_2HP_2H_2P_2H_2P_5H_{10}P_6H_2P_2H_2P_2HP_2H_5$	48	-31
3d7	$H_2(PH)_4H_3P(HP_3)_3(P_3H)_3PH_4(PH)_4H$	50	-32
3d8	$PH(PH_3)_2P(PH_2PH)_2H(HP)_3(H_2P_2H)_2PHP_4(H(P_2H)_2)_2$	58	-44
3d9	$P_2H_3PH_8P_3H_{10}PHP_3H_{12}P_4H_6PH_2PHP$	60	-52
3d10	$H_{12}PHPH(P_2H_2P_2H_2P_2H)_3PHPH_{12}$	64	-55
3d11	$P(HPH_2PH_2PHP_2H_3P_3)_3(HPH)_3P_2H_3P$	67	-56
3d12	$P(HPH)_3P_2H_2(P_2H)_6H(P_2H_3)_4P_2(HPH)_3$ $P_2HP(PHP_2H_2P_2HP)_2$	88	-72
3d13	$P_2H_2P_5H_2P_2H_2PHP_2HP_7HP_3H_2PH_2P_6HP_2HP$ $HP_2HP_5H_3P_4H_2PH_2P_5H_2P_4H_4PHP_8H_5P_2HP_2$	103	-56
3d14	$P_3H_3PHP_4HP_5H_2P_4H_2P_2H_2(P_4H)_2P_2HP_2H_2P_3H_2PHPH_3$ $P_4H_3P_6H_2P_2HP_2HPHP_2HP_7HP_2H_3P_4HP_3H_5P_4H_2(PH)_4$	124	-71
3d15	$HP_5HP_4HPH_2PH_2P_4HPH_3P_4HPHPH_4P_{11}HP_2HP_3HPH_2P_3$ $H_2P_2HP_2HPHPHP_8HP_3H_6P_3H_2P_2H_3P_3H_2PH_5P_9HP_4HPHP_4$	136	-80

5.2 Algorithms

The simplest version of an EA, the so-called (1+1) EA, is described in Algorithm 1. First, an initial individual c is generated at random. At each generation, a new individual c' is created by means of mutation. If c' is at least as good as c, then c' is accepted as the starting point for the next generation. Depending on the problem formulation, this acceptance criterion is to be based either on the conventional energy evaluation or on the Pareto-dominance relation.

Algorithm 1 Basic (1+1) Evolutionary Algorithm.

choose $c \in C$ *uniformly at random*
repeat
  $c' \leftarrow mutate(c)$
  if c' *not worse than* c **then**
    $c \leftarrow c'$
  end if
until < *stop condition* >

A variant of the above described (1+1) EA is presented in Algorithm 2. An external archive stores the nondominated solutions found along the evolutionary process. The archiving strategy influences the search behavior of the algorithm in such a way that the mutant c' is only accepted if it is not dominated by any individual in the archive. If accepted, c' is included in the archive and all individuals dominated by c', and those mapping to the same objective vector $\mathbf{f}(c')$, are removed. Note that this archiving strategy makes only sense for the multiobjectivized problem formulations.

Algorithm 2 Archiving (1+1) Evolutionary Algorithm.

choose $c \in C$ *uniformly at random*
$A \leftarrow \{c\}$
repeat
  $c' \leftarrow mutate(c)$
  if $\nexists \hat{c} \in A : \hat{c} \prec c'$ **then**
    $A \leftarrow \{\hat{c} \in A : c' \not\prec \hat{c} \wedge \mathbf{f}(\hat{c}) \neq \mathbf{f}(c')\} \cup \{c'\}$
    $c \leftarrow c'$
  end if
until < *stop condition* >

It was also considered a genetic algorithm (GA), whose general structure is given in Algorithm 3. First, an initial parent population P of size N is randomly generated. At each generation, the fittest individuals in P are selected for mating (*selection-for-variation*). Then, a children population P' is created by applying the variation operators. Finally, parents and children compete for a place in the new population (*selection-for-survival*). When applied to the single-objective problem formulation, selection is driven by the conventional energy value of the candidate conformations. Regarding the multiobjective formulation, the discrimination among individuals is to be based on *nondominated sorting* and *crowding distance*, as in the NSGA-II [11].

Algorithm 3 Genetic Algorithm.

choose $P \subset C : |P| = N$ *uniformly at random*
while < *stop condition* > **do**
  $\hat{P} \leftarrow$ *selection-for-variation*(P)
  $P' \leftarrow$ *variation*$(\hat{P})$
  $P \leftarrow$ *selection-for-survival*$(P \cup P')$
end while

A representation of absolute moves was adopted. Conformations are encoded as sequences in $\{U, D, L, R, F, B\}^{L-1}$, denoting the up, down, left, right, forward and backward lattice positions for an amino acid with regard to the preceding one. Only directions $\{U, D, L, R\}$ are used in the two-dimensional case. The implemented genetic operators are as follows. One-point crossover (only for the GA) is applied with a given probability p_c. In mutation, each encoding position is randomly perturbed with probability p_m. In all cases, only valid solutions are accepted during the search.

5.3 Performance Assessment

For all the experiments, 100 independent executions were performed. The results are evaluated in terms of the best obtained energy value (β), the number of times that this solution was found (f) and the arithmetic mean (μ). Additionally, the *overall average performance* (OAP) measure [13] was adopted in order to assess the overall behavior of the studied approaches. OAP is defined as the average ratio of the obtained mean values to the optimum (E^*). Formally:

$$\text{OAP} = \frac{100\%}{|T|}\left(\sum_{t \in T} \frac{\mu(t)}{E^*(t)}\right) \quad (7)$$

where T is the set of all test cases. Thus, OAP = 100% suggests the ideal situation where the optimum solution for each instance was reached during all the performed executions.

Statistical significance analysis was conducted as follows. First, *D'Agostino-Pearson's omnibus* K^2 test was used to evaluate the normality of data distributions. For normally distributed data, either *ANOVA* or the *Welch's t* parametric tests were used depending on whether the variances across the samples were homogeneous (*homoskedasticity*) or not. This was investigated using the *Bartlett's* test. For non-normal data, the nonparametric *Kruskal-Wallis* test was adopted. A significance level of $\alpha = 0.05$ was considered.

6. RESULTS

6.1 Results for the (1+1) EA

In this section, the (1+1) EA is used for comparing among the three studied HP model's formulations: the conventional single-objective formulation (SO), the parity decomposition (PD) [14], and the locality decomposition (LD) being proposed. Results are also presented for the archiving version of the (1+1) EA, which applies only for PD and LD. A fixed mutation probability of $p_m = \frac{1}{L-1}$ and a stopping condition of 100,000 evaluations were considered in all cases.

Given the importance that parameter δ has on the behavior of the LD approach (see Section 4), the best adjustment for this parameter is first investigated. A total of 10 odd values for δ have been evaluated, starting from 3.[1] Figure 2 presents the overall average performance (OAP) obtained using LD for the different values of δ. Results are provided for both the basic and the archiving (1+1) EA. Also, the performance of the SO formulation is shown as a baseline.

It is evident from this figure that an important increase in performance has been obtained by using the new proposed multiobjectivization. For the different values of δ, LD reached the best results when using the basic, non-archiving variant of the algorithm. However, even using the archiving

[1]In the 2D square and the 3D cubic lattices, a topological contact can only occur if the sequence distance between the amino acids is odd and at least equal to 3.

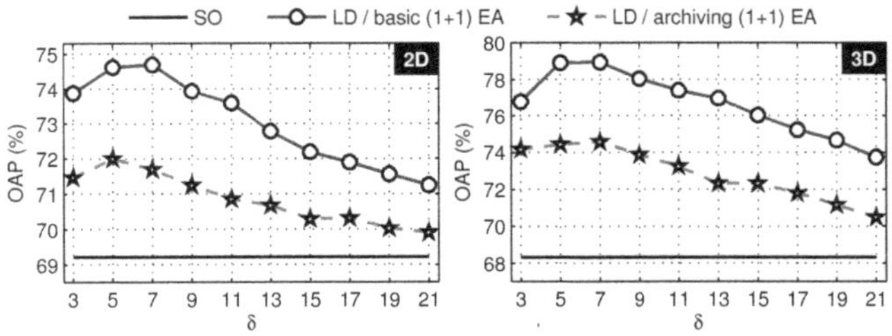

Figure 2: Varying the distance parameter δ.

(1+1) EA, LD performed better in all cases compared to the conventional SO formulation. It can be seen that the highest OAP values were obtained at $\delta = 7$, in most of the cases. In addition, notice that the performance of the algorithms gradually declined with the increasing value for δ.

The distance parameter δ was set to 7 for further analysis. Tables 3 and 4 detail the obtained results for all the two-dimensional and three-dimensional test cases, respectively. For each instance, these tables show the best energy (β), the frequency (f) and the mean (μ) achieved using the different formulations. The lowest μ obtained for each instance has been **shaded**. Finally, the OAP measure evaluates the overall performance of the formulations, see Section 5.3.

From these tables, it is possible to note that the proposed LD outperformed both the conventional SO formulation and the previously reported PD multiobjectivization in most of the cases. By using LD, the basic (1+1) EA reached the lowest average energy for 12 out of the 15 two-dimensional instances, leading to an OAP increase of (74.70 − 69.22) = 5.48% with regard to the SO formulation (see Table 3). As previously stated, the use of the archiving strategy within the (1+1) EA seemed not to be favorable for the proposed LD multiobjectivization. Nevertheless, even using this algorithm it was possible for LD to obtain better results than the SO and PD formulations for most of the instances.

As shown in Table 4, the proposed LD scored the best average performance for all the three-dimensional instances when using the basic (1+1) EA. This was also reflected as an OAP increase of 10.65% with respect to the conventional SO formulation. Just as it happened for the two-dimensional instances, the advantages of LD were not as remarkable when using the archiving (1+1) EA. However, the results of LD for this algorithm were still competitive; the OAP measure was improved by 6.28% over the SO, being this the second best performance achieved for the three-dimensional test cases.

Finally, Tables 5 and 6 outline how the SO, PD and LD formulations compare statistically with respect to each other in all the test cases. Each row in these tables compares two formulations, say A and B, which is denoted as "A/B". If a significant performance difference exists between A and B, the corresponding cells are marked either as + or − depending on whether such a difference was in favor of or against A. Empty cells indicate that there was not a statistically important difference between the approaches. The rightmost column shows the overall results of this analysis.

As can be seen from Table 5, both PD and LD significantly outperformed the conventional SO formulation in most of the cases when using the basic (1+1) EA. The proposed LD achieved statistically better results than SO in 28 out of the 30 adopted test cases. PD performed significantly better than SO for 20 of the instances. By comparing the multiobjectivized formulations, there was a significant performance difference in favor of LD for 23 of the test cases.

Table 3: Results for the basic and the archiving (1+1) EA on the two-dimensional benchmarks.

	Basic (1+1) EA						Archiving (1+1) EA			
	SO		PD		LD		PD		LD	
Seq.	β (f)	μ	β (f)	μ	β (f)	μ	β (f)	μ	β (f)	μ
2d1	-4 (4)	-2.70	-4 (6)	**-2.71**	-4 (3)	-2.69	-4 (5)	-2.69	-4 (2)	-2.67
2d2	-8 (18)	-6.81	-8 (24)	-7.04	-8 (31)	**-7.16**	-8 (21)	-7.00	-8 (21)	-6.99
2d3	-8 (11)	-7.00	-8 (48)	**-7.45**	-9 (2)	-7.39	-8 (24)	-7.12	-8 (22)	-7.05
2d4	-9 (8)	-6.84	-9 (4)	-6.95	-9 (11)	**-7.23**	-9 (6)	-6.88	-9 (14)	-7.13
2d5	-9 (3)	-6.92	-10 (2)	**-7.08**	-9 (1)	-7.06	-9 (1)	-6.99	-8 (14)	-6.89
2d6	-8 (14)	-6.81	-9 (1)	-6.87	-9 (2)	**-7.30**	-9 (1)	-6.89	-9 (1)	-6.95
2d7	-7 (26)	-5.79	-8 (6)	-5.90	-8 (7)	**-6.17**	-8 (5)	-5.80	-8 (10)	-6.08
2d8	-13 (1)	-9.97	-13 (1)	-10.23	-13 (4)	**-10.61**	-13 (1)	-10.12	-13 (1)	-10.13
2d9	-18 (5)	-14.23	-19 (2)	-15.20	-20 (2)	**-16.29**	-18 (5)	-15.02	-21 (1)	-15.64
2d10	-18 (2)	-13.79	-18 (1)	-14.06	-19 (1)	**-15.07**	-17 (4)	-13.76	-18 (1)	-14.40
2d11	-30 (2)	-24.39	-30 (7)	-25.43	-32 (1)	**-27.80**	-31 (1)	-25.32	-32 (1)	-25.80
2d12	-29 (1)	-23.82	-30 (1)	-25.12	-30 (4)	**-26.61**	-30 (1)	-24.63	-29 (2)	-24.91
2d13	-41 (1)	-33.81	-41 (1)	-34.54	-44 (1)	**-38.09**	-42 (1)	-34.18	-41 (1)	-35.34
2d14	-41 (1)	-30.80	-39 (3)	-32.18	-39 (2)	**-34.41**	-41 (1)	-31.72	-39 (1)	-32.58
2d15	-40 (1)	-31.71	-40 (3)	-32.70	-39 (7)	**-34.97**	-40 (1)	-32.57	-41 (1)	-33.60
OAP	69.22%		71.39%		**-74.70%**		70.47%		71.70%	

Table 4: Results for the basic and the archiving (1+1) EA on the three-dimensional benchmarks.

	Basic (1+1) EA						Archiving (1+1) EA			
	SO		PD		LD		PD		LD	
Seq.	β (f)	μ	β (f)	μ	β (f)	μ	β (f)	μ	β (f)	μ
3d1	-11 (57)	-10.48	-11 (69)	-10.64	-11 (94)	**-10.94**	-11 (64)	-10.51	-11 (60)	-10.52
3d2	-13 (23)	-11.30	-13 (34)	-11.70	-13 (66)	**-12.53**	-13 (27)	-11.59	-13 (42)	-11.87
3d3	-9 (57)	-8.48	-9 (70)	-8.65	-9 (95)	**-8.95**	-9 (62)	-8.51	-9 (73)	-8.66
3d4	-18 (10)	-15.19	-18 (13)	-15.74	-18 (46)	**-16.97**	-18 (8)	-15.30	-18 (15)	-15.96
3d5	-30 (2)	-23.87	-30 (1)	-25.38	-31 (1)	**-27.53**	-30 (1)	-24.56	-32 (1)	-25.68
3d6	-29 (1)	-22.79	-29 (2)	-24.42	-31 (1)	**-26.66**	-28 (3)	-23.64	-31 (1)	-24.64
3d7	-25 (6)	-20.64	-27 (1)	-22.07	-28 (1)	**-24.31**	-27 (1)	-21.22	-27 (4)	-22.77
3d8	-35 (1)	-27.34	-36 (1)	-29.02	-36 (2)	**-31.98**	-35 (1)	-27.96	-35 (5)	-29.98
3d9	-46 (1)	-37.20	-47 (1)	-40.03	-47 (3)	**-42.88**	-47 (1)	-38.81	-49 (1)	-41.59
3d10	-45 (1)	-35.59	-46 (1)	-37.69	-50 (1)	**-43.29**	-43 (2)	-36.51	-49 (1)	-40.28
3d11	-38 (2)	-30.17	-39 (2)	-32.65	-41 (1)	**-36.10**	-38 (2)	-31.17	-40 (3)	-34.82
3d12	-47 (1)	-36.22	-49 (1)	-39.85	-53 (1)	**-46.13**	-48 (1)	-38.09	-50 (1)	-42.55
3d13	-40 (1)	-29.97	-41 (1)	-31.31	-40 (1)	**-35.42**	-38 (1)	-29.94	-45 (1)	-33.52
3d14	-43 (4)	-34.51	-48 (1)	-36.97	-50 (2)	**-43.98**	-47 (1)	-35.04	-49 (2)	-40.83
3d15	-51 (1)	-37.26	-52 (1)	-42.11	-57 (1)	**-47.42**	-50 (1)	-40.43	-54 (1)	-44.90
OAP	68.31%		72.20%		**-78.96%**		70.00%		74.59%	

Table 5: Statistical analysis for comparing the three HP model's formulations. Basic (1+1) EA.

	2D benchmarks															3D benchmarks															
	2d1	2d2	2d3	2d4	2d5	2d6	2d7	2d8	2d9	2d10	2d11	2d12	2d13	2d14	2d15	3d1	3d2	3d3	3d4	3d5	3d6	3d7	3d8	3d9	3d10	3d11	3d12	3d13	3d14	3d15	Overall
PD/SO			+						+		+	+		+	+		+	+	+	+	+	+	+	+	+	+	+	+	+	+	20+ 0−
LD/SO		+	+	+		+	+	+	+	+	+	+	+	+	+	+	+	+	+	+	+	+	+	+	+	+	+	+	+	+	28+ 0−
LD/PD						+			+	+	+	+	+	+	+	+	+	+	+	+	+	+	+	+	+	+	+	+	+	+	23+ 0−

Regarding the archiving (1+1) EA, Table 6 shows that the proposed LD significantly improved the search performance in 22 and 15 of the instances when compared to SO and PD, respectively. PD's results for 8 of the test cases were statistically superior to those obtained by the SO formulation.

6.2 Results for the Genetic Algorithm

In this section, the results for the implemented genetic algorithm (GA) are analyzed. Three different problem formulations are compared: the conventional single-objective (SO), the recently proposed parity decomposition (PD) [14], and the locality decomposition (LD) proposed in this paper.

LD is sensitive to the distance parameter δ (see Section 4). Preliminary testing was conducted in order to investigate the value of δ providing the best performance for the GA. Due to space limitations, details of such an analysis were not included in this document, but the obtained results suggest that $\delta = 7$ is a convenient adjustment for this parameter.

Table 6: Statistical analysis for comparing the three HP model's formulations. Archiving (1+1) EA.

	2D benchmarks															3D benchmarks															
	2d1	2d2	2d3	2d4	2d5	2d6	2d7	2d8	2d9	2d10	2d11	2d12	2d13	2d14	2d15	3d1	3d2	3d3	3d4	3d5	3d6	3d7	3d8	3d9	3d10	3d11	3d12	3d13	3d14	3d15	Overall
PD/SO									+		+	+		+							+			+			+			+	8+ 0−
LD/SO							+		+	+	+	+	+	+	+		+	+	+	+	+	+	+	+	+	+	+	+	+	+	22+ 0−
LD/PD									+	+			+						+	+	+	+	+	+	+	+	+	+	+	+	15+ 0−

Furthermore, different settings for the GA are evaluated in order to identify the most appropriate conditions for the compared approaches. Three different recombination and mutation probabilities were considered: $p_c = \{0.8, 0.9, 1.0\}$ and $p_m = \{\frac{1}{L-1}, 0.01, 0.05\}$. Also, the effects of preventing duplicate individuals (clones) from the population are analyzed. Thus, 18 parameter configurations for the GA are investigated. The population size was fixed to $N = 100$ in all cases, and the algorithm was allowed to run until a maximum number of 100,000 evaluations was reached. Figures 3 and 4 present (2D and 3D, respectively) the overall average performance (OAP) measure obtained by the studied formulations when varying the different parameters of the GA.

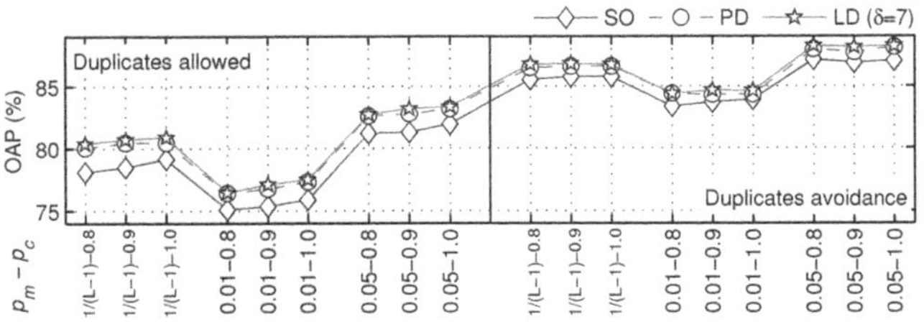

Figure 3: Settings for the GA, 2D benchmarks.

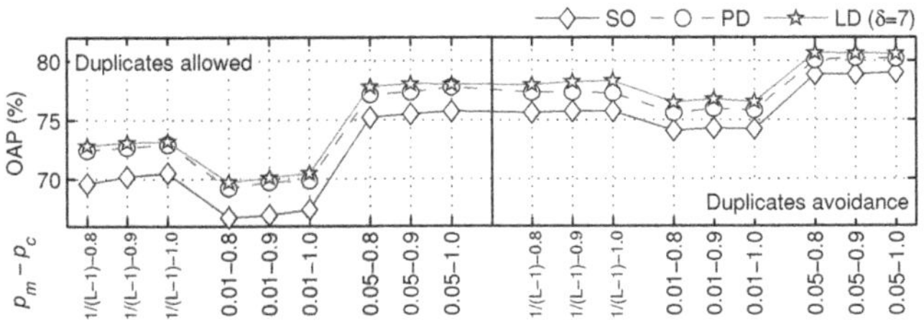

Figure 4: Settings for the GA, 3D benchmarks.

From these figures, both LD and PD performed better than the conventional SO formulation for all the different parameter configurations of the GA. By comparing between LD and PD, it can be noted that there was a performance difference in favor of the proposed LD, in all the cases. Some general observations can be made concerning the behavior of the GA. On the one hand, the algorithm seemed not to be seriously affected when varying the recombination probability. On the other hand, it responded positively to the increased mutation rate, being $p_m = 0.05$ the fixed value which provided the best performance in all the cases. Finally, the results were significantly improved in all the cases when duplicate individuals were removed from the population.

For a more detailed analysis, the parameters adjustment which allowed each of the formulations to reach the highest OAP value was selected. The obtained results are presented in Tables 7 and 8. These tables show the best energy (β), the frequency (f) and the mean (μ) obtained for each instance when using the different formulations. The lowest average energy achieved for each test case has been **shaded**. Also, the OAP measure is given at the bottom of the tables.

As shown in Table 7, the previously reported PD achieved the lowest average energy for 8 out of the 15 two-dimensional instances. The proposed LD presented the best performance for only 7 of the test cases. However, LD allowed the GA to reach the highest OAP value, which represents an increase of $(88.25 - 87.13) = 1.12\%$ over the SO formulation.

Regarding the three-dimensional instances, it can be seen from Table 8 that the best average performance of the algorithm was scored in most cases when using the proposed LD multiobjectivization. An OAP increase of 1.67% was obtained with regard to the conventional SO formulation.

Table 9 points out how the SO, PD and LD formulations are statistically compared to each other in all the instances. Each row in these tables compares two formulations, say A and B, which is denoted as "A/B". If a statistically significant difference exists between A and B, the corresponding cells are marked either as + or − depending on whether such a difference favors A or not. Empty cells indicate that there was not a significant difference between the approaches. The rightmost column presents the overall results of this analysis.

Table 7: Results for the GA, 2D benchmarks.

	SO		PD		LD	
Seq.	β (f)	μ	β (f)	μ	β (f)	μ
2d1	-4 (69)	-3.69	-4 (78)	**-3.78**	-4 (77)	-3.77
2d2	-8 (92)	**-7.92**	-8 (91)	-7.91	-8 (90)	-7.90
2d3	-9 (68)	-8.68	-9 (73)	-8.73	-9 (75)	**-8.75**
2d4	-9 (99)	-8.99	-9 (93)	-8.93	-9 (100)	**-9.00**
2d5	-10 (87)	-9.75	-10 (94)	**-9.89**	-10 (93)	-9.87
2d6	-9 (62)	-8.60	-9 (69)	-8.69	-9 (75)	**-8.75**
2d7	-8 (47)	-7.40	-8 (49)	**-7.47**	-8 (51)	**-7.47**
2d8	-13 (12)	-11.45	-14 (2)	-11.49	-13 (16)	**-11.62**
2d9	-21 (2)	-17.85	-23 (1)	-18.30	-22 (2)	**-18.45**
2d10	-21 (4)	-18.27	-21 (1)	**-18.54**	-21 (3)	-18.50
2d11	-34 (1)	-30.27	-34 (1)	**-30.54**	-34 (1)	-30.41
2d12	-36 (2)	-30.94	-35 (3)	-30.75	-36 (5)	**-31.56**
2d13	-49 (1)	-41.75	-48 (1)	**-42.57**	-47 (3)	-42.05
2d14	-44 (1)	-36.74	-43 (1)	**-37.74**	-41 (2)	-37.31
2d15	-43 (2)	-37.14	-43 (1)	**-38.28**	-43 (1)	-38.12
OAP	87.13%		88.13%		**88.25%**	

Table 8: Results for the GA, 3D benchmarks.

	SO		PD		LD	
Seq.	β (f)	μ	β (f)	μ	β (f)	μ
3d1	-11 (100)	**-11.00**	-11 (100)	**-11.00**	-11 (100)	**-11.00**
3d2	-13 (95)	**-12.94**	-13 (97)	**-12.94**	-13 (95)	-12.91
3d3	-9 (72)	-8.71	-9 (87)	-8.87	-9 (92)	**-8.92**
3d4	-18 (12)	-15.91	-18 (31)	**-16.54**	-18 (22)	-16.37
3d5	-32 (1)	-27.72	-32 (1)	-28.12	-31 (8)	**-28.37**
3d6	-31 (1)	-26.59	-30 (3)	-26.89	-31 (3)	**-27.24**
3d7	-30 (1)	-26.43	-29 (12)	-26.70	-31 (1)	**-26.85**
3d8	-37 (1)	-32.39	-37 (3)	-33.03	-40 (1)	**-33.53**
3d9	-50 (1)	-43.46	-50 (1)	**-44.56**	-49 (2)	-44.43
3d10	-52 (1)	-46.12	-53 (1)	-46.15	-52 (2)	**-46.95**
3d11	-41 (1)	-36.39	-43 (1)	-37.36	-43 (1)	**-37.62**
3d12	-50 (5)	-44.02	-54 (1)	-44.85	-52 (1)	**-45.26**
3d13	-41 (1)	-34.99	-43 (1)	**-35.78**	-42 (1)	-35.69
3d14	-51 (1)	-41.83	-50 (1)	-42.80	-49 (2)	**-43.09**
3d15	-52 (2)	-45.51	-56 (2)	-46.43	-54 (1)	**-47.17**
OAP	79.01%		80.26%		**80.68%**	

Table 9: Statistical analysis for comparing the three HP model's formulations. Genetic Algorithm.

	2D benchmarks															3D benchmarks															
	2d1	2d2	2d3	2d4	2d5	2d6	2d7	2d8	2d9	2d10	2d11	2d12	2d13	2d14	2d15	3d1	3d2	3d3	3d4	3d5	3d6	3d7	3d8	3d9	3d10	3d11	3d12	3d13	3d14	3d15	Overall
PD/SO				−					+				+	+	+			+	+				+	+		+	+	+	+		12+ 1−
LD/SO						+			+			+			+			+	+	+	+		+	+	+	+	+	+	+	+	16+ 0−
LD/PD				+								+													+						3+ 0−

Table 9 shows that PD obtained significantly better results than the SO problem formulation for 12 of the instances. Note, however, that PD was statistically inferior to SO in solving the 2d4 instance. For 16 out of the 30 adopted test cases, the proposed LD significantly increased the performance of the GA with respect to SO. Finally, the statistical analysis indicates that for only 3 of the adopted test cases there was a significant performance difference between PD and LD, all cases in favor of the proposed LD.

7. CONCLUSIONS AND FUTURE WORK

A novel multiobjectivization proposal for the HP model of protein structure prediction (PSP) was presented. In the proposed approach, called the locality decomposition, topological interactions on the lattice are classified either as local or nonlocal depending on the distance (in the sequence) between the amino acids involved. By grouping and isolating local interactions from the nonlocal ones, an alternative two-objective formulation of the problem was defined.

Different evolutionary algorithms (EAs) were implemented in order to investigate the suitability of the proposed locality decomposition. This approach was evaluated and compared with respect to both the conventional single-objective problem formulation and the recently proposed parity decomposition [14]. Experiments were conducted on both the two-dimensional square and the three-dimensional cubic lattices, and a large set of 30 HP model's instances was considered.

The proposed locality decomposition provided the best average performance of the implemented algorithms in most of the cases. Thus, the suitability of this approach was demonstrated. This supports previous evidence on the effectiveness of multiobjectivization to overcome search difficulties such as that of becoming trapped in local optima [17, 23].

Although competitive, both the parity and the locality decompositions were negatively affected by the use of the archiving strategy within the (1+1) EA. This is contrary to what is expected in multiobjective optimization, where archiving is essential for converging towards a set of trade-offs among the conflicting problem objectives [22, 26]. Nevertheless, in spite of being alternatively modeled and treated as a multiobjective problem, the HP model is actually a single-objective problem. Therefore, maintaining an approximation set of nondominated solutions becomes not as important. In addition, the archiving strategy influences the acceptance criterion of the algorithm in such a way that the introduction of plateaus, the only achievable effect of decomposition, may be partially reversed [17]. That is, some of the mutually incomparable solutions can be comparable to those in the archive. This could lead some parts of the plateaus to become inaccessible, thus restricting the exploration.

Even when the best results for the genetic algorithm were reached in most of the cases by using the proposed locality decomposition, the performance differences among the three compared formulations were not as impressive as those observed for the (1+1) EA. This can be explained by the fact that population-based approaches are inherently less susceptible to get stuck in local optima. On the other hand, the use of a multiobjective problem formulation enabled diversity promotion in the objective space (through the *crowding distance* operator [11]). This enhanced exploration and, to some extent, gives an explanation to the improvements that the parity and the locality decompositions achieved with respect to the conventional single-objective formulation.

To the best of authors' knowledge, the parity and the locality decompositions represent the first attempts on the use of multiobjective optimization techniques to solve PSP under the HP model. It is important to remark that the aim of this study was not to improve the state-of-the-art results, but rather to investigate the impact of using the proposed multiobjectivization on the resolution of this problem. From the obtained results, it is expected that the locality decomposition can be successfully incorporated in order to improve the performance of established state-of-the-art algorithms (such as those mentioned in Section 3). This issue needs to be investigated in order to derive more general conclusions. Also, the conflicting relationship between the objectives of the proposed formulation has to be analyzed. Finally, the multiobjectivization of the HP model by means of the addition of supplementary objectives remains unexplored. This can be seen as an interesting issue for future research.

8. ACKNOWLEDGMENTS

We would like to acknowledge support from CONACyT projects 105060 and 99276. Also, this research was partially funded by project 51623 from "Fondo Mixto Conacyt-Gobierno del Estado de Tamaulipas". Finally, we would like to thank to "Fondo Mixto de Fomento a la Investigación científica y Tecnológica CONACyT - Gobierno del Estado de Tamaulipas" for their support to publish this paper.

9. REFERENCES

[1] C. Anfinsen. Principles that Govern the Folding of Protein Chains. *Science*, 181(4096):223–230, 1973.

[2] D. Becerra, A. Sandoval, D. Restrepo-Montoya, and L. Nino. A Parallel Multi-Objective Ab Initio Approach for Protein Structure Prediction. In *IEEE International Conference on Bioinformatics and Biomedicine*, pages 137–141, 2010.

[3] B. Berger and T. Leighton. Protein Folding in the Hydrophobic-Hydrophilic (HP) Model is NP-complete. In *International Conference on Research in Computational Molecular Biology*, pages 30–39, New York, NY, USA, 1998. ACM.

[4] D. Brockhoff, T. Friedrich, N. Hebbinghaus, C. Klein, F. Neumann, and E. Zitzler. Do Additional Objectives Make a Problem Harder? In *Genetic and Evolutionary Computation Conference*, pages 765–772, London, England, 2007. ACM.

[5] A. Băutu and H. Luchian. Protein Structure Prediction in Lattice Models with Particle Swarm Optimization. In *Swarm Intelligence*, volume 6234 of *Lecture Notes in Computer Science*, pages 512–519. Springer Berlin / Heidelberg, 2010.

[6] C. Chira. A Hybrid Evolutionary Approach to Protein Structure Prediction with Lattice Models. In *IEEE Congress on Evolutionary Computation*, pages 2300–2306, New Orleans, LA, USA, 2011.

[7] P. Crescenzi, D. Goldman, C. Papadimitriou, A. Piccolboni, and M. Yannakakis. On the Complexity of Protein Folding. In *ACM Symposium on Theory of Computing*, pages 597–603, Dallas, TX, USA, 1998. ACM.

[8] V. Cutello, G. Narzisi, and G. Nicosia. A Multi-Objective Evolutionary Approach to the Protein Structure Prediction Problem. *Journal of The Royal Society Interface*, 3(6):139–151, 2006.

[9] V. Cutello, G. Nicosia, M. Pavone, and J. Timmis. An Immune Algorithm for Protein Structure Prediction on Lattice Models. *IEEE Transactions on Evolutionary Computation*, 11(1):101–117, 2007.

[10] R. Day, J. Zydallis, and G. Lamont. Solving the Protein Structure Prediction Problem Through a Multi-Objective Genetic Algorithm. In *IEEE/DARPA International Conference on Computational Nanoscience*, pages 32–35, 2002.

[11] K. Deb, S. Agrawal, A. Pratab, and T. Meyarivan. A Fast Elitist Non-Dominated Sorting Genetic Algorithm for Multi-Objective Optimization:

NSGA-II. In *Parallel Problem Solving from Nature*, pages 849–858, Paris, France, 2000. Springer. Lecture Notes in Computer Science No. 1917.

[12] K. Dill. Theory for the Folding and Stability of Globular Proteins. *Biochemistry*, 24(6):1501–9, 1985.

[13] M. Garza-Fabre, E. Rodriguez-Tello, and G. Toscano-Pulido. Comparing Alternative Energy Functions for the HP Model of Protein Structure Prediction. In *IEEE Congress on Evolutionary Computation*, pages 2307–2314, New Orleans, LA, USA, 2011.

[14] M. Garza-Fabre, E. Rodriguez-Tello, and G. Toscano-Pulido. Multiobjectivizing the HP Model for Protein Structure Prediction. In *European Conference on Evolutionary Computation in Combinatorial Optimisation*, volume 7245 of *Lecture Notes in Computer Science*, pages 182–193. Springer Berlin / Heidelberg, Málaga, Spain, 2012.

[15] D. Greiner, J. Emperador, G. Winter, and B. Galván. Improving Computational Mechanics Optimum Design Using Helper Objectives: An Application in Frame Bar Structures. In *Evolutionary Multi-Criterion Optimization*, volume 4403 of *Lecture Notes in Computer Science*, pages 575–589. Springer Berlin / Heidelberg, Matshushima, Japan, 2007.

[16] J. Handl, S. Lovell, and J. Knowles. Investigations into the Effect of Multiobjectivization in Protein Structure Prediction. In *Parallel Problem Solving from Nature*, volume 5199 of *Lecture Notes in Computer Science*, pages 702–711. Springer Berlin / Heidelberg, Dortmund, Germany, 2008.

[17] J. Handl, S. Lovell, and J. Knowles. Multiobjectivization by Decomposition of Scalar Cost Functions. In *Parallel Problem Solving from Nature*, volume 5199 of *Lecture Notes in Computer Science*, pages 31–40. Springer Berlin / Heidelberg, Dortmund, Germany, 2008.

[18] M. Hoque, M. Chetty, A. Lewis, and A. Sattar. Twin Removal in Genetic Algorithms for Protein Structure Prediction Using Low-Resolution Model. *IEEE/ACM Transactions on Computational Biology and Bioinformatics,*, 8(1):234–245, 2011.

[19] M. Islam, M. Chetty, and M. Murshed. Novel Local Improvement Techniques in Clustered Memetic Algorithm for Protein Structure Prediction. In *IEEE Congress on Evolutionary Computation*, pages 1003–1011, New Orleans, LA, USA, 2011.

[20] M. Jähne, X. Li, and J. Branke. Evolutionary Algorithms and Multi-Objectivization for the Travelling Salesman Problem. In *Genetic and Evolutionary Computation Conference*, pages 595–602, Montreal, Canada, 2009. ACM.

[21] M. Jensen. Helper-Objectives: Using Multi-Objective Evolutionary Algorithms for Single-Objective Optimisation. *Journal of Mathematical Modelling and Algorithms*, 3:323–347, 2004.

[22] J. Knowles and D. Corne. Properties of an Adaptive Archiving Algorithm for Storing Nondominated Vectors. *IEEE Transactions on Evolutionary Computation*, 7(2):100–116, 2003.

[23] J. Knowles, R. Watson, and D. Corne. Reducing Local Optima in Single-Objective Problems by Multi-objectivization. In *Evolutionary Multi-Criterion Optimization*, pages 269–283, London, UK, 2001. Springer-Verlag.

[24] D. Lochtefeld and F. Ciarallo. Helper-Objective Optimization Strategies for the Job-Shop Scheduling Problem. *Applied Soft Computing*, 11(6):4161–4174, 2011.

[25] H. Lopes. Evolutionary Algorithms for the Protein Folding Problem: A Review and Current Trends. In *Computational Intelligence in Biomedicine and Bioinformatics*, volume 151 of *Studies in Computational Intelligence*, pages 297–315. Springer Berlin / Heidelberg, 2008.

[26] M. López-Ibáñez, J. Knowles, and M. Laumanns. On Sequential Online Archiving of Objective Vectors. In *Evolutionary Multi-Criterion Optimization*, volume 6576 of *Lecture Notes in Computer Science*, pages 46–60. Springer Berlin / Heidelberg, 2011.

[27] R. Santana, P. Larranaga, and J. Lozano. Protein Folding in Simplified Models With Estimation of Distribution Algorithms. *IEEE Transactions on Evolutionary Computation*, 12(4):418–438, 2008.

[28] J. Santos and M. Diéguez. Differential Evolution for Protein Structure Prediction Using the HP Model. In *Foundations on Natural and Artificial Computation*, volume 6686 of *Lecture Notes in Computer Science*, pages 323–333. Springer Berlin / Heidelberg, 2011.

[29] E. Segredo, C. Segura, and C. Leon. A Multiobjectivised Memetic Algorithm for the Frequency Assignment Problem. In *IEEE Congress on Evolutionary Computation*, pages 1132–1139, New Orleans, LA, USA, 2011.

[30] C. Segura, E. Segredo, and C. León. Parallel Island-Based Multiobjectivised Memetic Algorithms for a 2D Packing Problem. In *Genetic and Evolutionary Computation Conference*, pages 1611–1618, Dublin, Ireland, 2011. ACM.

[31] A. Shmygelska and H. Hoos. An Ant Colony Optimisation Algorithm for the 2D and 3D Hydrophobic Polar Protein Folding Problem. *BMC Bioinformatics*, 6(1):30, 2005.

[32] C. Soares Brasil, A. Botazzo Delbem, and D. Ferraz Bonetti. Investigating Relevant Aspects of MOEAs for Protein Structures Prediction. In *Genetic and Evolutionary Computation Conference*, pages 705–712, Dublin, Ireland, 2011. ACM.

[33] R. Unger. The Genetic Algorithm Approach to Protein Structure Prediction. In *Applications of Evolutionary Computation in Chemistry*, volume 110 of *Structure & Bonding*, pages 2697–2699. Springer Berlin / Heidelberg, 2004.

[34] I. Vite-Silva, N. Cruz-Cortés, G. Toscano-Pulido, and L. de la Fraga. Optimal Triangulation in 3D Computer Vision Using a Multi-objective Evolutionary Algorithm. In *Applications of Evolutionary Computing*, volume 4448 of *Lecture Notes in Computer Science*, pages 330–339. Springer Berlin / Heidelberg, Valencia, Spain, 2007.

[35] X. Zhao. Advances on Protein Folding Simulations Based on the Lattice HP models with Natural Computing. *Applied Soft Computing*, 8(2):1029–1040, 2008.

Effects of Discrete Objective Functions with Different Granularities on the Search Behavior of EMO Algorithms

Hisao Ishibuchi, Masakazu Yamane and Yusuke Nojima
Graduate School of Engineering, Osaka Prefecture University
1-1 Gakuen-cho, Naka-ku, Sakai, Osaka 599-8531, Japan
Phone: +81-72-254-9350

{hisaoi@, masakazu.yamane@ci., nojima@}cs.osakafu-u.ac.jp

ABSTRACT

Objective functions in combinatorial optimization are discrete. The number of possible values of each discrete objective function is totally different from problem to problem. Optimization of a discrete objective function is often very difficult. In the case of multiobjective optimization, a different objective function has a different number of possible values. This means that each axis of the objective space has a different granularity. Some axes may have fine granularities while others are coarse. In this paper, we examine the effect of discrete objective functions with different granularities on the search behavior of EMO (evolutionary multiobjective optimization) algorithms through computational experiments. Experimental results show that a discrete objective function with a coarse granularity slows down the search of EMO algorithms along that objective. An interesting observation is that such a slow-down along one objective often leads to the speed-up of the search along other objectives. We also show that the search of some EMO algorithms on test problems is often improved by adding a small random noise to each discrete objective.

Categories and Subject Descriptors

I.2.8 [**Artificial Intelligence**]: Problem Solving, Control Methods, and Search – *Heuristic Methods.*

General Terms

Algorithms.

Keywords

Evolutionary multiobjective optimization (EMO), combinatorial optimization, discrete objective functions, genetic algorithms.

1. INTRODUCTION

In the implementation of evolutionary multiobjective optimization (EMO) algorithms [4]-[6], objective values are often normalized so that each objective function has the same range of objective values. The normalization is important in many EMO algorithms when the ranges of objective functions are totally different from each other. This is because fitness evaluation in EMO algorithms often includes distance calculations in the objective space. For example, Pareto dominance-based EMO algorithms such as NSGA-II [7] and SPEA2 [21] have a distance-based secondary criterion in addition to a Pareto dominance-based main criterion. Scalarizing function-based EMO algorithms such as MOEA/D [18] more directly depends on distance calculations. Whereas the necessity of the normalization seems to have been well-known in the EMO community (e.g., NSGA-II [7] has a normalization mechanism, and the normalization was mentioned in [18]), much attention has not been given to the handling of the difference in granularities of discrete objective functions. The goal of this paper is to clearly demonstrate how the difference in the granularities affects the search behavior of EMO algorithms.

Objective functions in combinatorial optimization are discrete (see [1], [3], [16] for various combinatorial optimization problems, their difficulties, and their optimization algorithms). The number of possible values is totally different from problem to problem. Some objectives such as the tour length in travelling salesman problems and the profit in knapsack problems have a large number of possible values. However, other objectives have only a small number of possible values. For example, the number of selected features in feature selection with 30 features has only 31 possible values including 0 to 30 whereas there exist more than one billion (i.e., 2^{30}) combinations of feature selection.

Optimization of a discrete objective function with a small number of possible values is often very difficult for search algorithms. This is because many different solutions have the same objective value (i.e., because the landscape of the objective function is like a stairway with a small number of large flat stairs). For example, local search will not work well when all neighbors of the current solution have the same objective value. When all solutions in the current population have the same fitness, it is difficult for genetic algorithms to efficiently generate promising solutions from the current population. Thus the ability of search algorithms is likely to be deteriorated when they are applied to a discrete objective function with a small number of possible values.

When combinatorial optimization involves multiple objectives, each discrete objective function has a different number of possible values. Let us assume that the above-mentioned feature selection problem with 30 features has the following two objectives: to minimize the error rate and the number of selected features. We also assume that 10,000 training patterns are given to calculate the error rate. In this case, the error rate has 10,001 possible values (from 0% to 100%) whereas the number of selected features has only 31 possible values (from 0 to 30). This means that each axis

GECCO'12, July 7-11, 2012, Philadelphia, Pennsylvania, USA.

of the objective space has a totally different granularity: One axis has a fine granularity with 10,001 possible values while the other has a coarse granularity with only 31 possible values.

The existence of an axis with a coarse granularity (i.e., a discrete objective function with a small number of possible values) will deteriorate the search ability of EMO algorithms along that axis for the above-mentioned reason (i.e., because many different solutions have the same objective value). Such an axis with a coarse granularity may also have a negative effect on the overall search ability of EMO algorithms since it decreases the number of different non-dominated objective vectors in the objective space. In this paper, we examine these effects of discrete objective functions with different granularities on the search behavior of EMO algorithms. Computational experiments are performed using discrete objective functions with a wide range of granularities.

This paper is organized as follows. In Section 2, we explain our test problems with a wide range of granularities. In Section 3, we report experimental results on each test problem. We use the following four EMO algorithms in computational experiments: NSGA-II [7], SPEA2 [21], MOEA/D [18] and SMS-EMOA [2]. NSGA-II and SPEA2 are well-known frequently-used Pareto dominance-based EMO algorithms. MOEA/D can be viewed as a representative of scalarizing function-based EMO algorithms. SMS-EMOA can be a representative of indicator-based EMO algorithms [19], [20]. Its high search ability was demonstrated in [17]. Finally, this paper is concluded in Section 4.

2. TEST PROBLEMS

We generate six test problems with different granularities from a two-objective 500-item 0/1 knapsack problem in Zitzler and Thiele [22]. Multi-objective 0/1 knapsack problems in [22] have been frequently used in the literature to evaluate the search ability of EMO algorithms for combinatorial multiobjective optimization (e.g., Jaszkiewicz [12], [13]). In Fig. 1, we show the Pareto front of the two-objective 500-item 0/1 knapsack problem together with an initial population of randomly generated 200 solutions. Since the initial population is not close to the Pareto front, a high convergence ability is needed to efficiently search for Pareto optimal solutions. At the same time, a diversity improvement ability is also needed since the width of the initial solution is smaller than that of the Pareto front. That is, both the convergence and the diversity are important for EMO algorithms to efficiently search for a good solution set that well approximates the entire Pareto front of the two-objective 500-item 0/1 knapsack problem.

As shown in Fig. 1, let $f_1(\mathbf{x})$ and $f_2(\mathbf{x})$ be the objective functions of the two-objective 500-item 0/1 knapsack problem. In [22], $f_1(\mathbf{x})$ and $f_2(\mathbf{x})$ were explained as being the total profit for each of the two knapsacks. The minimum possible difference in objective values of each objective function is 1 because the profit of each item is given as an integer in [22]. Thus each objective function can be viewed as having the discretization interval of size 1 (i.e., width 1). We use the size of the discretization interval as an index of the granularity of each objective function. Using this index, we refer to the two-objective 500-item 0/1 knapsack problem in [22] as the G1-G1 2-500 knapsack problem where G1 means the granularity with the discretization interval of size 1.

We generate six test problems by rounding up the first or second digit of objective values of $f_1(\mathbf{x})$ and/or $f_2(\mathbf{x})$. For example, let us assume that the first digit of objective values of $f_1(\mathbf{x})$ is rounded up (e.g., all objective values in the interval [19321, 19330] are changed to 19330). In this case, the minimum possible difference in objective values of $f_1(\mathbf{x})$ is 10 while that of $f_2(\mathbf{x})$ is 1 (because we do not round up objective values of $f_2(\mathbf{x})$). We refer to the generated test problem as the G10-G1 knapsack problem using the granularity G10 of $f_1(\mathbf{x})$ and G1 of $f_2(\mathbf{x})$. In another test problem, the first and second digits of objective values of $f_1(\mathbf{x})$ are rounded up (e.g., all objective values in the interval [19301, 19400] are changed to 19400). Since the minimum possible difference in objective values of $f_1(\mathbf{x})$ is 100, the generated test problem is referred to as the G100-G1 knapsack problem. In this manner, we generate the following six test problems from the original G1-G1 knapsack problem: the G10-G1, G100-G1, G1-G10, G1-G100, G10-G10 and G100-G100 knapsack problems.

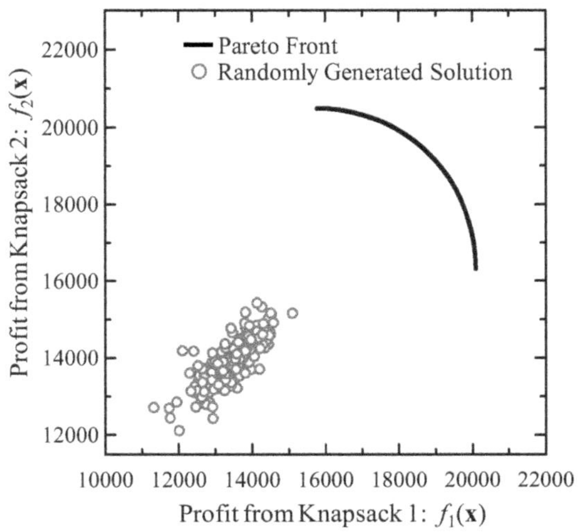

Figure 1. Pareto front and randomly generated 200 solutions.

For visually illustrating the difference between the original G1-G1 problem and the generated ones, we show the Pareto optimal solutions of the G100-G1 and G1-G100 problems together with those of the G1-G1 problem in Fig. 2 and Fig. 3, respectively. From these figures, we can see that the number of different Pareto optimal solutions in the objective space (i.e., different Pareto optimal objective vectors) is decreased by the use of a coarse granularity for one objective. In Fig. 2, our G100-G1 problem has no Pareto optimal solutions around the bottom-right edge of the Pareto front of the original G1-G1 problem. The distribution of different Pareto optimal objective vectors of the G100-G1 problem is sparse in the bottom-right area of Fig. 2 (i.e., this problem does not have many different Pareto optimal objective vectors around the best solution of $f_1(\mathbf{x})$ with the very coarse granularity). From this observation, one may expect difficulties in searching for good solutions in the bottom-right area of the objective space (i.e., good solutions with large values of $f_1(\mathbf{x})$).

On the other hand, in Fig. 3, the distribution of different Pareto optimal objective vectors of our G1-G100 test problem is sparse around the top-left edge of the Pareto front of the original G1-G1 problem. From this observation, one may expect difficulties in searching for good solutions in the top-left area of the objective space (i.e., good solutions with large values of $f_2(\mathbf{x})$).

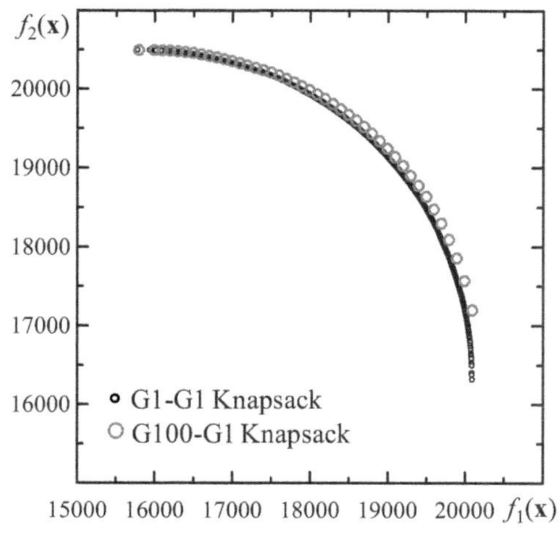

Figure 2. Pareto optimal solutions of the G1-G1 and G100-G1.

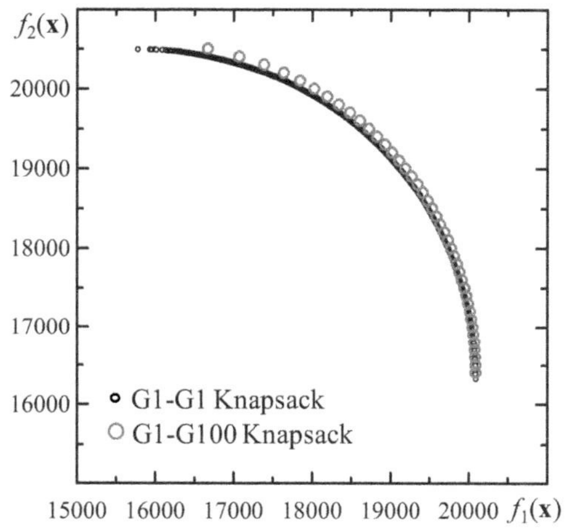

Figure 3. Pareto optimal solutions of the G1-G1 and G1-G100.

The biased distribution of the Pareto optimal objective vectors of each test problem in Fig. 2 and Fig. 3 is due to the convex shape of the Pareto front of the original G1-G1 knapsack problem. For examining test problems with a different shape of the Pareto front, we use a 500-bit one-max zero-max problem. This problem has two objectives to be maximized: the number of "1" and the number of "0" in a binary string of length 500. That is, $f_1(\mathbf{x})$ is the number of "1" while $f_2(\mathbf{x})$ is the number of "0". All binary strings of length 500 are Pareto optimal. In the objective space, this problem has 501 different Pareto optimal objective vectors uniformly distributed on the line between (0, 500) and (500, 0). The shape of the Pareto front of the one-max zero-max problem is a straight line. We refer to this problem as the linear G1-G1 one-max zero-max problem where "linear" means the linear Pareto front. In the same manner as our six knapsack problems (i.e., by rounding up the first or second digit of objective values), we generate the following six problems from the linear G1-G1 one-max zero-max problem: the linear G10-G1, G100-G1, G1-G10, G1-G100, G10-G10 and G100-G100 one-max zero-max problems.

For examining convex and concave Pareto fronts, we generate the following two test problems from the original 500-bit one-max zero-max problem with $f_1(\mathbf{x})$ and $f_2(\mathbf{x})$:

Convex Problem: $g_i(\mathbf{x}) = 500\sqrt{f_i(\mathbf{x})/500},\ i = 1,2$. (1)

Concave Problem: $h_i(\mathbf{x}) = 500(f_i(\mathbf{x})/500)^2,\ i = 1,2$. (2)

We refer to the generated two test problems as the convex and concave G1-G1 one-max zero-max problems, respectively. From each test problem, we generate six problems in the same manner as our six knapsack problems and six linear one-max zero-max problems (e.g., the convex G10-G1, G100-G1, G1-G10, G1-G100, G10-G10 and G100-G100 one-max zero-max problems are generated by rounding up $g_1(\mathbf{x})$ and/or $g_2(\mathbf{x})$ of the convex G1-G1 one-max zero-max problem in (1)).

In Fig. 4, we show the Pareto optimal objective vectors of the convex G1-G1 and G10-G1 one-max zero-max problems. We can observe similar distributions of the Pareto optimal objective vectors in Fig. 2 and Fig. 4. For comparison, we show the Pareto optimal objective vectors of the concave G1-G1 and G10-G1 one-max zero-max problems in Fig. 5. Since the shape of the Pareto front is different between Fig. 4 and Fig. 5, the distribution of their Pareto optimal objective vectors is different.

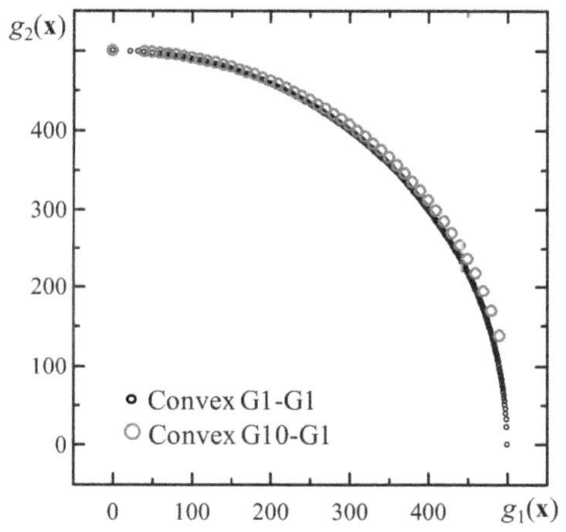

Figure 4. Pareto optimal solutions of the convex G1-G1 and G10-G1 one-max zero-max problems.

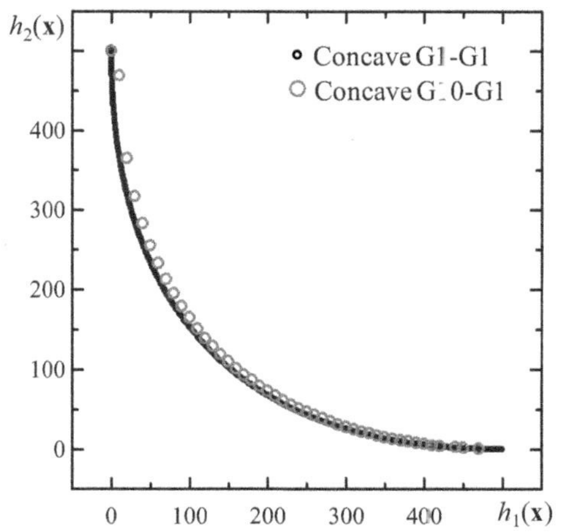

Figure 5. Pareto optimal solutions of the concave G1-G1 and G10-G1 one-max zero-max problems.

3. EXPERIMENTAL RESULTS

3.1 Setting of Computational Experiments

We apply NSGA-II, SPEA2, MOEA/D and SMS-EMOA to our test problems using the following parameter specifications:

Coding: Binary string of length 500 (i.e., 500-bit string),
Population size: 200,
Termination condition: 2000 generations,
Parent selection: Binary tournament selection with replacement,
Crossover: Uniform crossover (Probability: 0.8),
Mutation: Bit-flip mutation (Probability: 1/500),
Number of runs for each test problem: 100 runs.

The 50% attainment surface is calculated over 100 runs of each algorithm for each test problem. In SMS-EMOA, (0, 0) is used as a reference point for hypervolume calculation. In MOEA/D, the weighted Tchebycheff function with the following reference point $\mathbf{z}^*$ is used as a scalarizing function:

$$\text{Knapsack: } z_i^* = 1.1 \cdot \max\{f_i(\mathbf{x}) \mid \mathbf{x} \in \Omega(t)\},\ i = 1, 2, \quad (3)$$

$$\text{One-Max Zero-Max: } z_i^* = \max\{f_i(\mathbf{x}) \mid \mathbf{x} \in \Omega(t)\},\ i = 1, 2, \quad (4)$$

where $\Omega(t)$ shows the population at the t-th generation. The same scalarizing function was used in Zhang and Li [18].

3.2 Results on Knapsack Problems

In Fig. 6, we show experimental results of a single run of NSGA-II on the G1-G1 and G100-G1 knapsack problems. All solutions at the 20th, 50th and 2000th generations are shown in Fig. 6. We can see from Fig. 6 that the use of the very coarse granularity G100 for $f_1(\mathbf{x})$ in the G100-G1 problem biases the search towards the top-left area of the objective space as expected from Fig. 2.

In Fig. 7, we show the 50% attainment surface over 100 runs of each EMO algorithm for the G1-G1, G10-G1 and G100-G1 problems using the "rounded-up" objective functions of each test problem. The effect of the coarse granularity G10 (i.e., the G10-G1 problem) on each EMO algorithm is very small. However, the use of the much coarser granularity G100 (i.e., the G100-G1 problem) clearly biases the search by all the four EMO algorithms towards the top-left area of the objective space in Fig. 7.

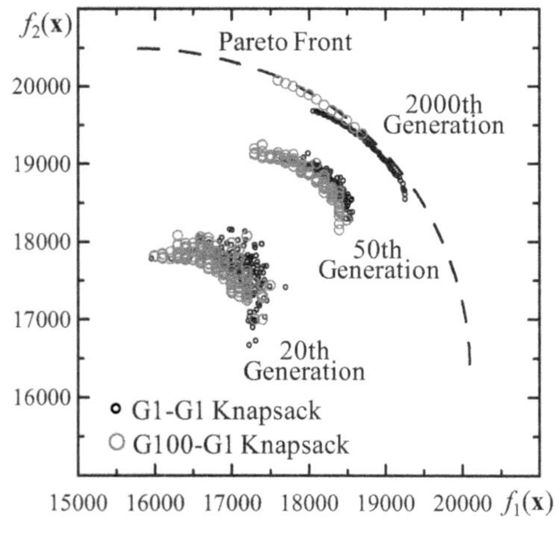

Figure 6. Experimental results of a single run of NSGA-II on the G1-G1 and G100-G1 knapsack problems.

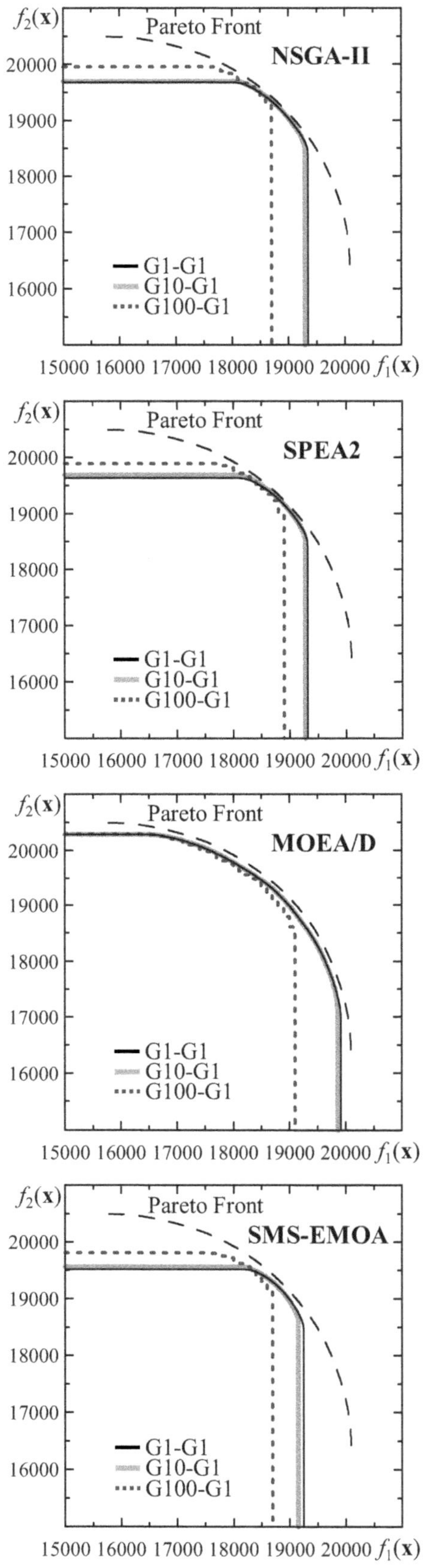

Figure 7. 50% attainment surface of each algorithm for the G1-G1, G10-G1 and G100-G1 knapsack problems.

For comparison, we show experimental results of a single run of NSGA-II on the G1-G100 knapsack problem with the very coarse granularity G100 for the second objective $f_2(\mathbf{x})$ in Fig. 8. We can see from Fig. 8 that the use of the very coarse granularity G100 in $f_2(\mathbf{x})$ biases the search by NSGA-II towards the bottom-right area of the objective space as expected from Fig. 3.

In Fig. 9, we show experimental results of NSGA-II on the G100-G100 problem with the very coarse granularity G100 for both $f_1(\mathbf{x})$ and $f_2(\mathbf{x})$. As shown in Fig. 9, the use of the very coarse granularity G100 in both of the two objectives clearly degrades the performance of NSGA-II. This is because many different solutions have the same objective value, which makes it very difficult to efficiently search for good solutions (as we have already mentioned in this paper). Another possible reason is the decrease in the number of different Pareto optimal objective vectors. To examine this issue, we perform computational experiments on the G100-G100 problem and its noisy version where a small noise (a real random number in the interval [0, 1]) is added to each of the calculated values of $f_1(\mathbf{x})$ and $f_2(\mathbf{x})$. Experimental results are summarized in Fig. 10 where the 50% attainment surface over 100 runs of each algorithm is shown.

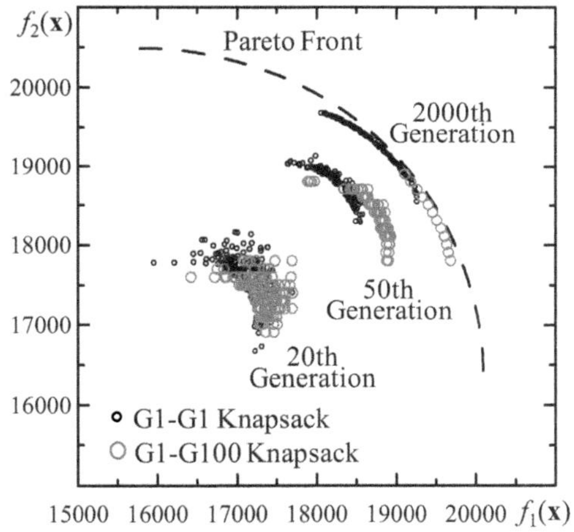

Figure 8. Experimental results of a single run of NSGA-II on the G1-G1 and G1-G100 knapsack problems.

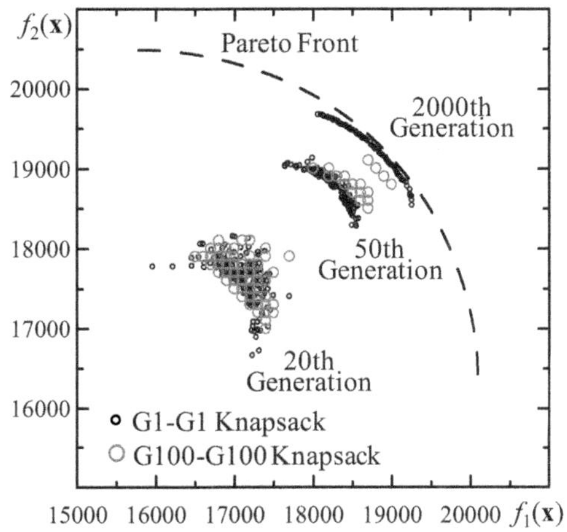

Figure 9. Experimental results of a single run of NSGA-II on the G1-G1 and G100-G100 knapsack problems.

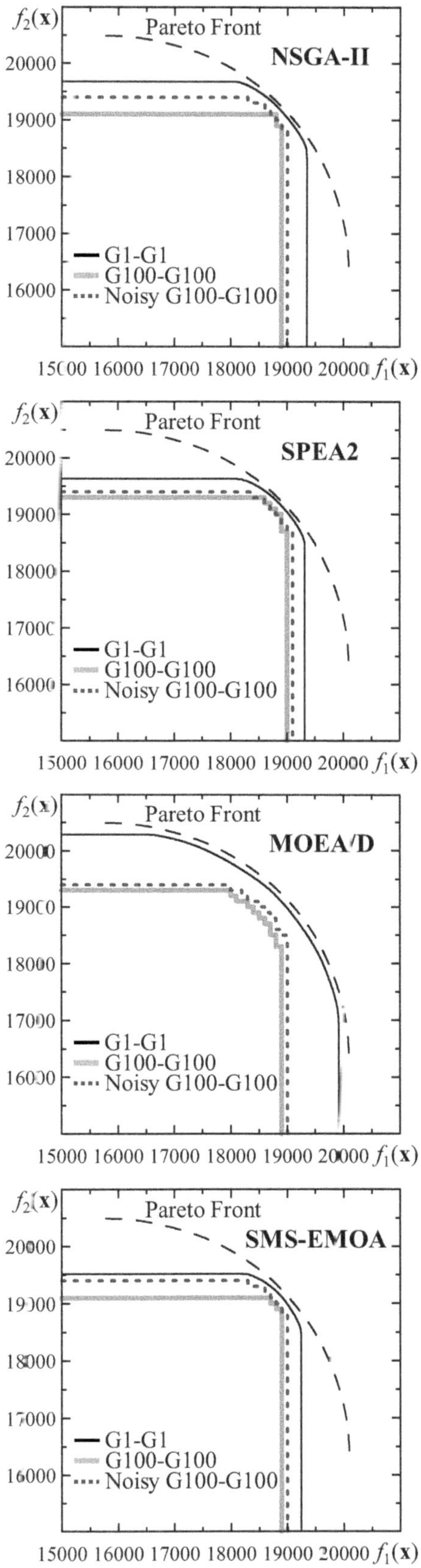

Figure 10. 50% attainment surface of each algorithm for the G1-G1, G100-G100 and noisy G100-G100 knapsack problems.

In Fig. 9 and Fig. 10, the use of the very coarse granularity G100 in $f_1(\mathbf{x})$ and $f_2(\mathbf{x})$ deteriorates the performance of all the four EMO algorithms (i.e., from results on G1-G1 to those on G100-G100).

In Fig. 10, the addition of a small random noise to $f_1(\mathbf{x})$ and $f_2(\mathbf{x})$ improves the performance of all the four EMO algorithms. A small random noise is not likely to make the search easier because it includes no information on the search direction. However, it actually improves the performance of the EMO algorithms in Fig. 10. This improvement may be due to the increase in the number of different non-dominated objective vectors.

3.3 Results on One-Max Zero-Max Problems

First, we show all solutions at the 2000th generation of a single run of NSGA-II on the linear G1-G1 and G10-G1 one-max zero-max problems in Fig. 11. The search by NSGA-II on the linear G10-G1 problem with the coarse granularity G10 in $f_1(\mathbf{x})$ is biased towards the top-left area in Fig. 11. For comparison, we show all solutions at the 2000th generation of a single run of NSGA-II on the concave G1-G1 and G10-G1 one-max zero-max problems in Fig. 12. This figure shows that the use of the coarse granularity G10 for the first objective of the concave G10-G1 problem biases the search of NSGA-II towards the top-left area (whereas the distribution of the different Pareto optimal objective vectors is sparse around the top-left area as shown in Fig. 5).

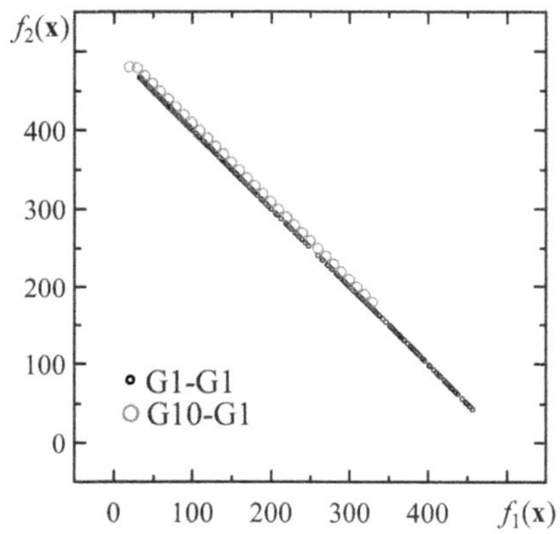

Figure 11. Solutions at the 2000th generation of NSGA-II on the linear G1-G1 and G10-G1 one-max zero-max problems.

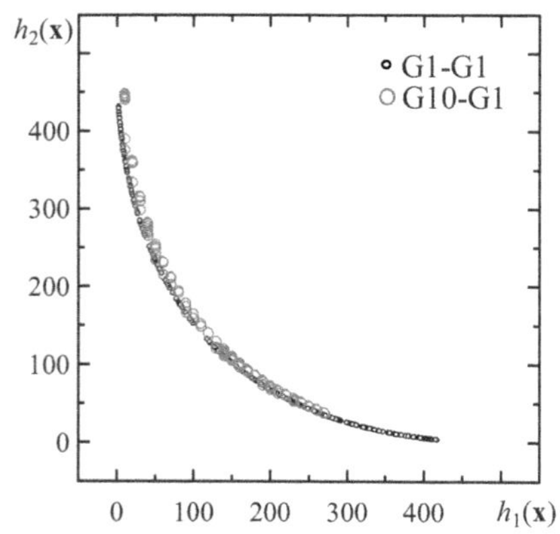

Figure 12. Solutions at the 2000th generation of NSGA-II on the concave G1-G1 and G10-G1 one-max zero-max problems.

In Figs. 13-15 in the next page, the 50% attainment surface over 100 runs of each EMO algorithm is shown for each test problem. As in Fig. 11, the search by each EMO algorithm in Fig. 13 is biased towards the top-left area by the use of the coarse granularity G10 in the first objective of the G10-G1 problem. In this case, we observe a clear improvement of the search towards the best solution of the second objective in the experimental results by SPEA2 and MOEA/D in Fig. 13. When we use the coarse granularity G10 in both objectives, the performance of all the four EMO algorithms is degraded in Figs. 13-15 (i.e., from results on G1-G1 to those on G10-G10).

In all experimental results in Figs. 13-15, we have the following two observations in common:

(i) The coarse granularity G10 in the first objective of the G10-G1 problem biases the search towards the top-left area.
(ii) The coarse granularity G10 in both objectives of the G10-G10 problem degrades the performance of the EMO algorithms.

That is, we have these two observations by all the four EMO algorithms for the three types of the one-max zero-max problems independently of the shape of their Pareto fronts (i.e., linear, convex and concave). This is interesting because the distribution of the Pareto optimal objective vectors is totally different between the convex and concave G10-G1 problems (see Fig. 4 and Fig. 5).

We also examine the performance of each EMO algorithm on the noisy versions of the three types of the G10-G10 problems. The addition of a small noise to each of the two objective functions improves the performances on the following cases:

NSGA-II on the concave G10-G10 problems,
SPEA2 on the convex and concave G10-G10 problems,
SMS-EMOA on all the three G10-G10 problems.

In the other cases (e.g., NSGA-II on the linear and convex G10-G10 problems), the addition of a small noise shows almost no effects on the performance of each EMO algorithm.

In Fig. 16, we show the experimental results of SMS-EMOA on the concave G1-G1, G10-G10 and noisy G10-G10 problems. This figure clearly shows that the addition of a small noise to each of the two objective functions improves the performance of SMS-EMOA on the concave G10-G10 one-max zero-max problem.

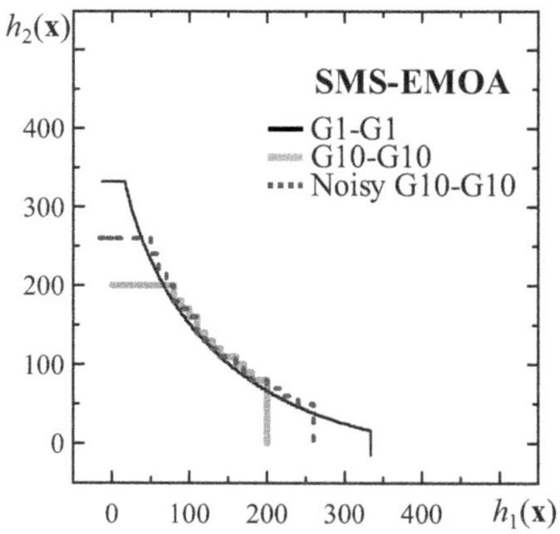

Figure 16. 50% attainment surface of SMS-EMOA for the concave G1-G1, G10-G10 and noisy G10-G10 one-max zero max problems.

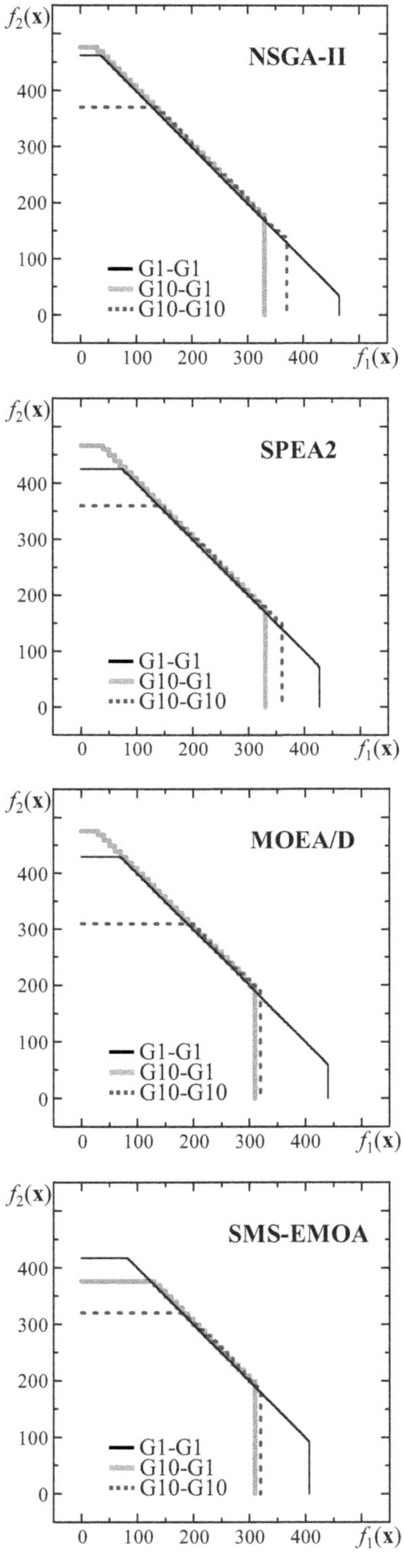

Figure 13. 50% attainment surface for the linear G1-G1, G10-G1, G10-G10.

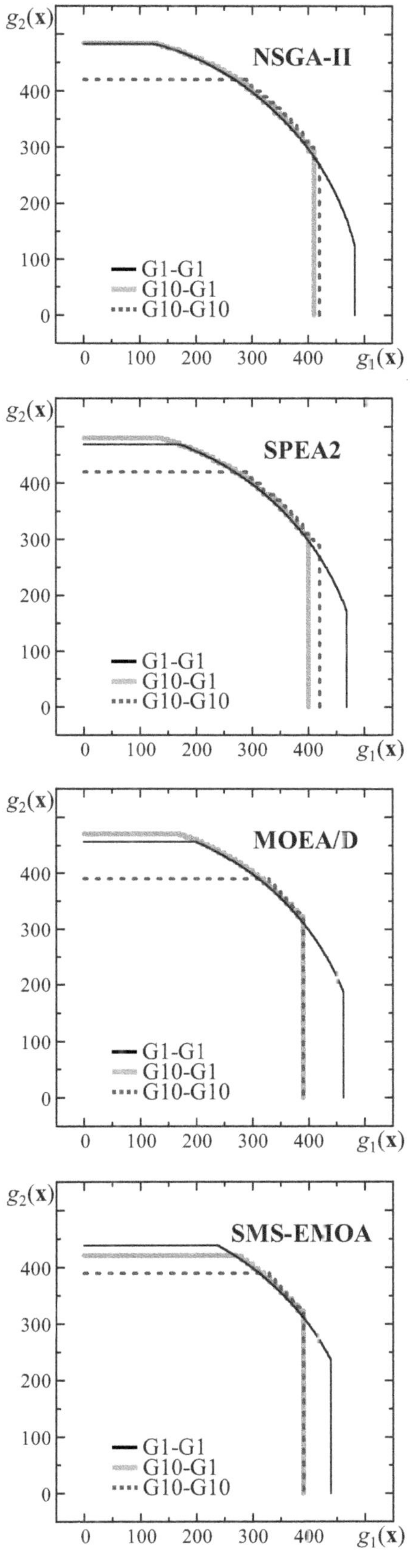

Figure 14. 50% attainment surface for the convex G1-G1, G10-G1, G10-G10.

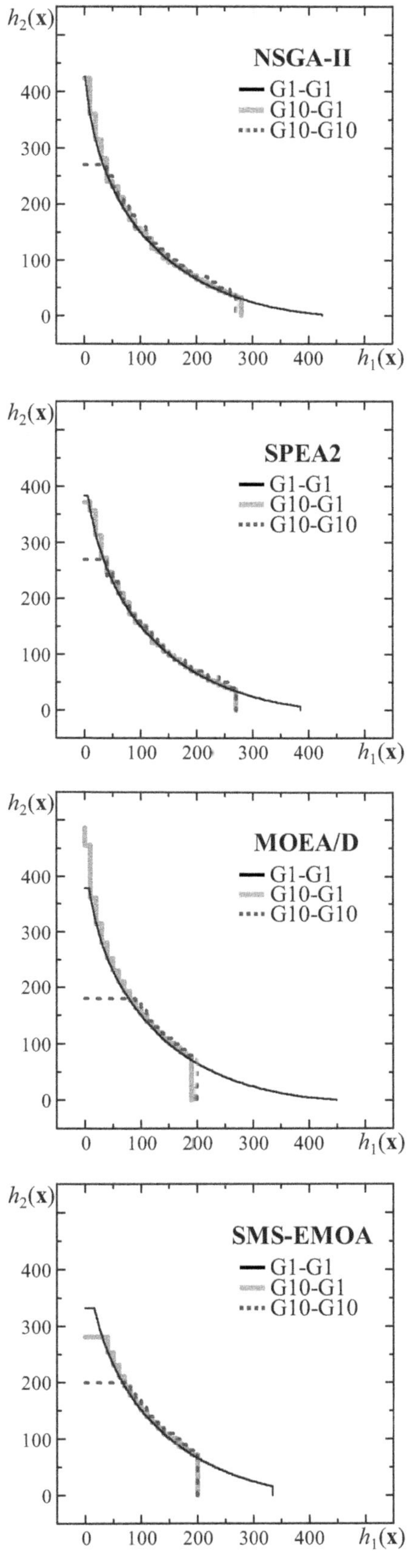

Figure 15. 50% attainment surface for the concave G1-G1, G10-G1, G10-G10.

4. CONCLUSIONS

In this paper, we examined the search behavior of the four well-known and frequently-used EMO algorithms (NSGA-II, SPEA2, MOEA/D and SMS-EMOA) on the two-objective combinatorial optimization problems with different granularities in their discrete objective functions. Through computational experiments, we clearly demonstrated that the difference in the granularities of discrete objective functions biased the search by those EMO algorithms towards a certain area of the objective space. To the best of our knowledge, the effect of the difference in the granularities of discrete objective functions has not been clearly demonstrated in the literature in the EMO community. We also demonstrated that the addition of a small noise to each discrete objective function with a coarse granularity (e.g., a random number in the interval [0, 1] to an objective function with the discretization interval of the width 100) improved the search ability of some EMO algorithms.

While these interesting observations were clearly demonstrated through computational experiments in this paper, the reason for such an interesting behavior of EMO algorithms was not clearly explained. A lot of empirical and theoretical studies may be needed to analyze and explain the behavior of EMO algorithms on multiobjective combinatorial optimization problems with different granularities in their discrete objective functions. While the effect of granularity difference in discrete objective functions on the behavior of EMO algorithms had not been discussed in the literature, a number of studies seem to be potentially related to our work in this paper. Among them are studies on the use of epsilon dominance [8], [10], the handling of overlapping solutions in the objective space [15], the evolutionary search with plateaus of constant fitness [11] and the landscape analysis based on neutral networks [9], [14].

5. REFERENCES

[1] Korte, B., and Vygen, J. *Combinatorial Optimization: Theory and Algorithms* (Fourth Edition). Springer, Berlin (2010).

[2] Beume, N., Naujoks, B., and Emmerich, M. SMS-EMOA: multiobjective selection based on dominated hypervolume. *European Journal of Operational Research* 181, 3 (2007) 1653-1669.

[3] Blum, C., and Roli, A. Metaheuristics in combinatorial optimization: Overview and conceptual comparison. *ACM Computing Surveys* 35, 3 (2003) 268-308.

[4] Coello, C. A. C., and Lamont, G. B. *Applications of Multi-Objective Evolutionary Algorithms*. World Scientific, Singapore (2004).

[5] Coello, C. A. C., Van Veldhuizen, D. A., and Lamont, G. B. *Evolutionary Algorithms for Solving Multi-Objective Problems*. Kluwer, Boston (2002).

[6] Deb, K. *Multi-Objective Optimization Using Evolutionary Algorithms*. John Wiley & Sons, Chichester (2001).

[7] Deb, K., Pratap, A., Agarwal, S., and Meyarivan, T. A fast and elitist multiobjective genetic algorithm: NSGA-II. *IEEE Trans. on Evolutionary Computation* 6, 2 (2002) 182-197.

[8] Giel, O., and Lehre, P. K. On the effect of populations in evolutionary multi-objective optimisation. *Evolutionary Computation* 18, 3(2010) 335-356.

[9] Harvey, I., and Thompson, A. Through the labyrinth evolution finds a way: A silicon ridge. *Lecture Notes in Computer Science 1259: ICES 1996*, 406-422.

[10] Horoba, C., and Neumann, F. Benefits and drawbacks for the use of epsilon-dominance in evolutionary multi-objective optimization. *Proc. of 2008 Genetic and Evolutionary Computation Conference* (2008) 641-648.

[11] Jansen, T., and Wegener, I. Evolutionary algorithms - How to cope with plateaus of constant fitness and when to reject strings of the same fitness. *IEEE Trans. on Evolutionary Computation* 5, 6 (2001) 589-599.

[12] Jaszkiewicz, A. On the performance of multiple-objective genetic local search on the 0/1 knapsack problem - A comparative experiment. *IEEE Trans. on Evolutionary Computation* 6, 4 (2002) 402-412.

[13] Jaszkiewicz, A. On the computational efficiency of multiple objective metaheuristics. The knapsack problem case study. *European Journal of Operational Research* 158, 2 (2004) 418-433.

[14] Katada, Y., and Ohkura, K. Analysis on topologies of fitness landscapes with both neutrality and ruggedness based on neutral networks. *Proc. of 2009 Genetic and Evolutionary Computation Conference* (2009) 1855-1856.

[15] Nojima, Y., Narukawa, K., Kaige, S., and Ishibuchi, H. Effects of removing overlapping solutions on the performance of the NSGA-II Algorithm. *Lecture Notes in Computer Science 3410: EMO 2005*, 341-354.

[16] Papadimitriou, C. H., and Steiglitz, K. *Combinatorial Optimization: Algorithms and Complexity*. Dover, Mineola (1998).

[17] Wagner, T., Beume, N., and Naujoks, B. Pareto-, aggregation-, and indicator-based methods in many-objective optimization. *Lecture Notes in Computer Science 4403: EMO 2007*, 742-756.

[18] Zhang, Q., and Li, H. MOEA/D: A multiobjective evolutionary algorithm based on decomposition. *IEEE Trans. on Evolutionary Computation* 11, 6 (2007) 712-731.

[19] Zitzler, E., Brockhoff, D., and Thiele, L. The hypervolume indicator revisited: On the design of Pareto-compliant indicators via weighted integration. *Lecture Notes in Computer Science 4403: EMO 2007*, 862-876.

[20] Zitzler, E., and Künzli, S. Indicator-based selection in multiobjective search. *Lecture Notes in Computer Science 3242: PPSN VIII* (2004) 832-842.

[21] Zitzler, E., Laumanns, M., and Thiele, L. SPEA2: Improving the strength Pareto evolutionary algorithm, *TIK-Report 103*, Computer Engineering and Networks Laboratory (TIK), ETH, Zurich (2001).

[22] Zitzler, E., and Thiele, L. Multiobjective evolutionary algorithms: A comparative case study and the strength Pareto approach. *IEEE Trans. on Evolutionary Computation* 3, 4 (1999) 257-271.

Lorenz Equilibrium: Equitability in non-Cooperative Games

Réka Nagy
Babes Bolyai University,
Cluj Napoca
reka@cs.ubbcluj.ro

Mihai Suciu
Babes Bolyai University,
Cluj Napoca
mihai.suciu@ubbcluj.ro

D. Dumitrescu
Babes Bolyai University,
Cluj Napoca
ddumitr@cs.ubbcluj.ro

ABSTRACT

The most popular solution concept in game theory, Nash equilibrium, has some limitations when applied to real life problems. Nash equilibrium rarely assures maximal payoff. A possibility is to consider Pareto equilibrium, inspired from the standard solution concept in multi-criteria optimization, but the obtained equilibria often consists of a large set of solutions that is too hard to process. Our aim is to find an equilibrium concept that provides a small set of efficient solutions, equitable for all players. The Lorenz dominance relation is investigated in this respect. A crowding based differential evolution method is proposed for detecting the Lorenz-optimal solutions. Based on the Lorenz dominance relation, the Lorenz equilibrium for non-cooperative games is proposed. The Lorenz equilibrium consists of those Pareto-optimal solutions that are the most balanced and equitable solutions for all players. We propose to use Lorenz equilibrium for selecting one Nash equilibrium for games having several Nash equilibria.

Categories and Subject Descriptors

I.2.8 [**Artificial Intelligence**]: Problem Solving, Control Methods, and Search - Heuristic Methods

General Terms

Algorithms, Experimentation

Keywords

Games, Equilibrium, Lorenz dominance, Multiple Nash Equilibrium

1. INTRODUCTION

A problem often encountered in classical multi-criteria optimization is the existence of a large (often infinite) set of optimal solutions. The decision making based on selecting a unique preferred solution becomes difficult.

GECCO'12, July 7–11, 2012, Philadelphia, Pennsylvania, USA.

The Lorenz dominance, also called equitable dominance relation, has been introduced by Kostreva and Ogryczak in [6, 7]. Lorenz domination, a refinement of the Pareto domination, is used in decision theory and fair optimization problems. Considering models with equitable efficiency relieves some of the burden from the decision maker by shrinking the solution set. It turns out that the set of equitably efficient solutions is contained within the set of efficient solutions for the same problem.

Having noticed the favourable properties of the Lorenz dominance, we consider that the Lorenz dominance relation could be successfully applied to address some limitations of the classical game theory.

The most commonly used solution concepts in game theory are Nash and Pareto equilibria. Nash equilibrium presumes that all the players in the game are completely rational agents, that have common knowledge of the structure of the game and they choose their strategies as best responses to the strategies of the adversary players. The outcome assured by Nash equilibrium is not always Pareto optimal. In many cases a more favorable outcome could be reached if all the players changed their strategies. On the other hand, Pareto equilibrium assures the greatest possible payoffs for the players, but the distribution of the payoffs is uneven and rarely equitable.

To overcome the above mentioned inefficiencies we propose a solution concept called Lorenz equilibrium, that assures the maximal possible payoffs and is equitable for all players.

Classical game theory has another major drawback, namely the multiplicity of Nash equilibria. The goal of game theory is to predict the outcome of games but when it comes to games with multiple equilibria it is impossible to give such a prediction. We propose Lorenz equilibrium for selecting the most favorable Nash equilibrium in case of multiple Nash equilibria.

The article is structured as follows. The Lorenz dominance relation is presented in Section 2. An evolutionary method for detecting the Lorenz-optimal solutions is proposed and we illustrate the Lorenz efficient solutions on some classical multiobjective problems. In Section 3 some basic notions of game theory is presented, and in Section 4 an evolutionary method for detecting the Lorenz equilibrium is proposed. We introduce the concept of Lorenz equilibrium for games in Section 5. In Section 6 the equilibrium selection problem in case of multiple Nash equilibria is addressed.

2. LORENZ DOMINANCE RELATION

The Lorenz dominance, also called equitable dominance relation, has been defined in [6] and extended in [7]. In this section we reuse the definitions to construct the Lorenz dominance relation.

Let us consider a multicriteria maximization problem with m objectives and n decision parameters. The problem can be formulated as follows:

$$\begin{array}{ll} \text{Maximize} & y = f(x) = (f_1(x), ..., f_m(x)) \\ \text{where} & x = (x_1, ..., x_n) \in X, \\ & y = (y_1, ..., y_m) \in Y, \end{array}$$

where x is the decision vector, X is the parameter space, y is the objective vector and Y the objective space.

Multicriteria optimization solution concepts may be defined by properties of the corresponding preference model. Let the relation of weak preference be denoted by $\succeq$. The corresponding relations of strict preference $\succ$ and indifference $\cong$ are defined as follows:

$$y' \succ y'' \Leftrightarrow (y' \succeq y'' \text{ and not } y'' \succeq y').$$

$$y' \cong y'' \Leftrightarrow (y' \succeq y'' \text{ and } y'' \succeq y').$$

The most common multicriteria optimization solution concept is Pareto-optimality. Let x' and x'' be two solutions.

Definition 1. x' is weakly preffered over x'' if $f(x')$ weakly Pareto dominates $f(x'')$:

$$f(x') \succeq_P f(x'') \Leftrightarrow f_i(x') \geq f_i(x''), \forall i \in \{1, ..., m\}.$$

Definition 2. x' is preffered over x'' if $f(x')$ Pareto dominates $f(x'')$:

$$f(x') \succ_P f(x'') \Leftrightarrow$$
$$\Leftrightarrow f(x') \succeq_P f(x'') \text{ and } \exists j : f_j(x') > f_j(x'').$$

Lorenz dominance is a refinement of Pareto dominance used in fair optimization problems. In addition to the initial objective aiming at maximizing individual utilities, fairness refers to the idea of favoring well-balanced solutions [7]. Hence, in fair optimization problems, we are interested in working with a preference relation $\succeq$ satisfying the following axioms:

(1) P-Monotonicity: For all $x', x'' \in X$:

$$f(x') \succeq_P f(x'') \Rightarrow f(x') \succeq f(x'')$$

and

$$f(x') \succ_P f(x'') \Rightarrow f(x') \succ f(x'').$$

(2) Impartiality: While dealing with uniform criteria, we want to focus on the distribution of outcome values while ignoring their ordering. In other words, a solution generating individual outcomes: 4, 2, 0 for criteria f_1, f_2 and f_3 respectively, should be considered equally good as a solution generating outcomes 0, 2 and 4. Hence we assume that the preference model is impartial (anonymous, symmetric). More formally:

$$(f_{\tau(1)}(x), f_{\tau(2)}(x), ..., f_{\tau(m)}(x)) \cong$$
$$(f_1(x), f_2(x), ..., f_m(x))$$

for any permutation τ of $\{1, 2, ...m\}$, $x \in X$.

(3) Principle of transfers: The (Pigou-Dalton) principle of transfers [13] states that a transfer of any small amount from an outcome to any other relatively worse-off outcome results in a more preferred outcome vector. More formally:

$$f_i(x) > f_j(x) \Rightarrow$$
$$((f_1(x), ..., f_i(x) - \epsilon, ..., f_j(x) + \epsilon, ..., f_m(x)) \succ$$
$$(f_1(x), ..., f_m(x))$$

for $0 < \epsilon < f_{i'}(x) - f_{i''}(x)$.

Thus a solution generating all three outcomes equal to 2 is better than any solution generating individual outcomes 4, 2 and 0.

The preference relation satisfying axioms (1)-(3) are called equitable (Lorenz) preference relations [6, 7].

Let us consider $f_{(1)}(x) \leq f_{(2)}(x) \leq ... \leq f_{(m)}(x)$ as the components of $f = (f_1(x), f_2(x), ..., f_m(x))$ sorted by increasing order.

Definition 3. Let $x \in X$ be a solution vector.
The generalized Lorenz vector associated to x is

$$L(x) = (l_1, ..., l_m),$$

where

$$l_1 = f_{(1)}(x),$$

$$l_2 = f_{(1)}(x) + f_{(2)}(x),$$

$$...$$

$$l_m = \textstyle\sum_{i=1}^{m} f_{(i)}(x).$$

Definition 4. For $x', x'' \in X$ weakly Lorenz dominates if:

$$x' \succeq_L x'' \Leftrightarrow L(x') \succeq_P L(x'').$$

Definition 5. For $x', x'' \in X$ Lorenz dominates if:

$$x' \succ_L x'' \Leftrightarrow L(x') \succ_P L(x'').$$

If a solution $x \in X$ is a Lorenz-optimal solution (or simply Lorenz solution) of a multiple criteria problem, it is also a Pareto-optimal solution [7].

2.1 Evolutionary Detection of Lorenz Solutions

We consider that multiobjective evolutionary algorithms are suitable tools for detecting the set of Lorenz-optimal solutions. In [2] an evolutionary algorithm for this purpose, L-NSGA, is proposed. We considered a different approach based on a differential evolution technique [14].

Differential evolution (DE) has been proposed in [14] to solve real-parameter optimization problems. DE is a simple evolutionary algorithm that creates new candidate solutions by combining the parent individual and several other individuals of the same population $\mathcal{P}$. A candidate replaces the parent only if it has better fitness. This is a rather greedy selection scheme that often outperforms standard evolutionary algorithms.

There are different schemes available for constructing a candidate $v = (v_1, ..., v_n)$ from the parent x_i. The most frequently used method can be summarized as follows:

For $j \in \{1, ..., n\}$,, the component v_j is defined as:

$$v_j = \begin{cases} x_{r_{3_j}} + F(x_{r_{1_j}} - x_{r_{2_j}}), & \text{with probability } CR, \\ x_{i_j}, & \text{with probability } 1 - CR \end{cases}$$

where r_1, r_2, r_3 are distinct indices randomly selected from $1, ..., pop\_size$, parameter $F \in (0, 2)$ is the differential weight and parameter $CR \in [0, 1]$ is the crossover probability.

Several multiobjective DE algorithms have been proposed [11, 15, 16]. The multiobjective method considered for our numerical experiments is based on the Crowding Differential Evolution algorithm [15]. In order to detect the Lorenz solution, the Lorenz dominance relation is used for the comparison of two solutions. The L-crowding DE is summarized in Algorithm 1.

Algorithm 1 L-Crowding DE

```
initialize population P
repeat
  for all i ∈ {1, 2, ..., pop_size} do
    create candidate v
    find the element w most similar to v in the design
    space
    if w ≻_L v then
      replace v with w
    end if
  end for
until a stopping condition is met
```

2.2 Lorenz Solutions in Multiobjective Optimization Problems

In order to illustrate the detection of Lorenz solution set we consider two of the classic multiobjective optimization test functions introduced in [17] and [5]. Both test functions have two objectives and are structured as follows:

$$\text{Maximize } T(x) = (-f_1(x_1), -f_2(x)),$$

$$\text{subject to } f_2(x) = g(x_2, ..., x_n)h(f_1(x_1), g(x_2, ..., x_n))$$

$$\text{where } x = (x_1, ..., x_n).$$

The function f_1 is a function of the first decision variable only, g is a function of the remaining $n-1$ variables, and the parameters of h are the function values of f_1 and g.

The first test function considered, T_1, is defined as:

$$f_1(x_1, ..., x_n) = x_1,$$

$$f_2(x_1, ..., x_n) = 1 - \sqrt{\frac{x_1}{g}},$$

$$g(x_2, ..., x_n) = 1 + 9 \sum_{i=2}^{n} \frac{x_i}{n-1}$$

where $n = 30$ and $x_i \in [0, 1]$. The function T_1 has a convex Pareto front, formed with $g(x) = 1$ [17].

In our numerical experiments we have considered the above described method with the following parameter settings: $CR = 0.3$, $F = 0.5$, $pop\_size = 100$.

The detected Pareto front and the detected Lorenz-optimal front are represented in Figure 1. We can observe, that the Lorenz front is exactly in the middle of the Pareto front, and contains the most balanced elements of the Pareto front.

The second test function considered, T_2, is defined as:

$$f_1(x_1, ..., x_n) = 1 - e^{s_1(x_1, ..., x_n)},$$

$$f_2(x_1, ..., x_n) = 1 - e^{s_2(x_1, ..., x_n)},$$

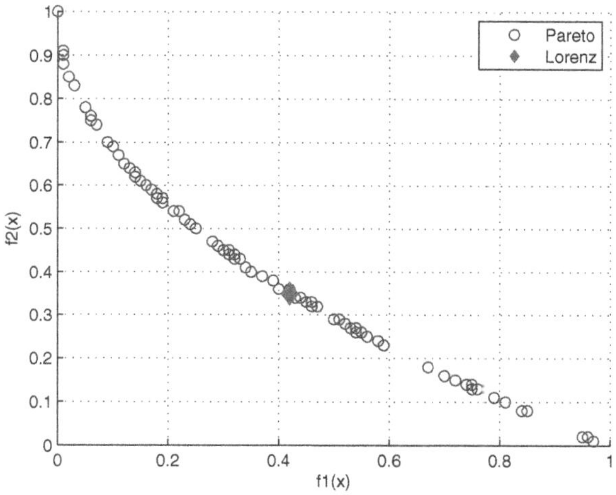

Figure 1: Objective space - The detected Pareto- and Lorenz-optimal solutions for test function T_1. The Lorenz front lies on the middle of the Pareto fornt.

where

$$s_1(x_1, ..., x_n) = \sum_{i=1}^{n} (a_i - \tfrac{1}{\sqrt{n}})^2 \text{ and}$$

$$s_2(x_1, ..., x_n) = \sum_{i=1}^{n} (a_i + \tfrac{1}{\sqrt{n}})^2.$$

where $n = 5$ and $x_i \in [-4, 4]$. The function T_2 has a concave Pareto front [5].

The detected Pareto front and the detected Lorenz-optimal set of solutions are represented in Figure 2.

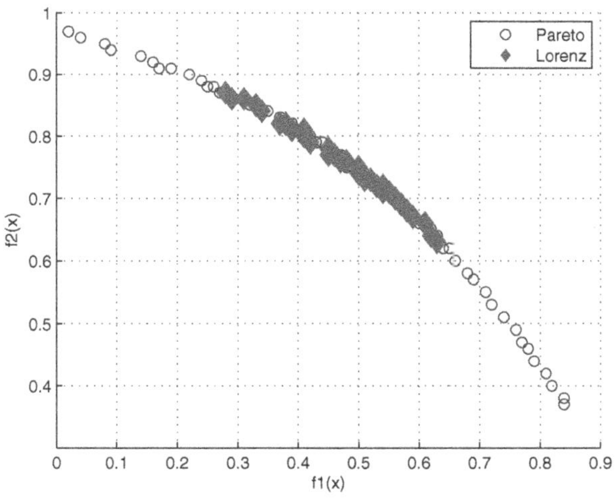

Figure 2: The detected Pareto- and Lorenz-optimal solutions for test function T_2

As expected, in both cases the set of Lorenz-optimal solutions is a subset of the Pareto-optimal solutions. The Lorenz dominance provides a stronger selection of the non-dominated solutions, the set of Lorenz optimal is less numerous and this provides intensification. Due to the fact that it explores only the equitable solutions one drawback of Lorenz dominance in multi-objective optimization is that it does not explore all the Pareto front, all solutions concentrate in the equitable area of the front.

3. GAME THEORY PREREQUISITES

For the seek of completeness, some basic notions related to game theory are presented.

A finite strategic game is defined as a system

$$\Gamma = ((N, S_i, u_i), i = 1, n),$$

where:

- N represents a set of n players, $N = \{1, ..., n\}$;
- for each player $i \in N$, S_i represents the set of actions available to her, $S_i = \{s_{i_1}, s_{i_2}, ..., s_{i_m}\}$;

  $$S = S_1 \times S_2 \times ... \times S_n$$

  is the set of all possible strategies (situations of the game);
- for each player $i \in N$, $u_i : S \to R$ represents the payoff function.

Denote by (s_{i_j}, s^*_{-i}) the strategy profile obtained from s^* by replacing the strategy of player i with s_{i_j} i.e.

$$(s_{i_j}, s^*_{-i}) = (s^*_1, s^*_2, ..., s^*_{i-1}, s_{i_j}, s^*_{i+1}, ..., s^*_n).$$

A strategy is a *Nash equilibrium* [1, 8, 10] if each player has no incentive to unilaterally deviate i.e. it can not improve the payoff by modifying its strategy while the others do not modify theirs.

More formally, the strategy s^* is a Nash equilibrium if and only if the inequality

$$u_i(s_i, s^*_{-i}) - u_i(s^*) \leq 0, \ \forall s_i \in S_i, \forall i \in N$$

holds.

A strategy s' Pareto-dominates the strategy s'' if and only if each player has a better payoff for s' than for s'' (and we write $s' \leq_P s''$ or $(s', s'') \in P_d$).

Formally: $(s', s'') \in P_d$ if and only if

$$u_i(s') \geq u_i(s''), \forall i \in \{1, ..., n\}, and$$
$$\exists j \in \{1, ..., n\} : u_j(s') > u_j(s'').$$

A strategy s'' is Pareto-non dominated, or Pareto-efficient, if does not exist $s' \in S$ such that $(s', s'') \in P_d$. The *Pareto equilibrium* of the game is represented by the set of Pareto-efficient strategies.

4. EVOLUTIONARY EQUILIBRIA DETECTION

Games can be viewed as multiobjective optimization problem, where the payoffs of the participating players are to be maximized. All of the objectives to be optimized are uniform and equally important. A solution of the game is called an equilibrium. At equilibrium all players are happy with their outcome, and they are not willing to switch their strategies. So, we can say, that the ideal equilibrium of a game is an outcome, where the total payoff for the players is maximal and is distributed fairly among the players.

An appealing technique is the use of generative relations and evolutionary algorithms for detecting equilibrium strategies. The payoff of each player is treated as an objective and the generative relation induces an appropriate dominance concept, which is used for fitness assignment purpose. Evolutionary multiobjective algorithms are thus suitable tools in searching for game equilibria.

A population of strategies is evolved. A chromosome is an n-dimensional vector representing a strategy profile $s \in S$. The initial population is randomly generated. Population model is generational. The non-dominated individuals from the population of strategy profiles at iteration t may be regarded as the current equilibrium approximation. Subsequent application of the search operators is guided by a specific selection operator induced by the generative relation. Successive populations produce new approximations of the equilibrium front, which hopefully are better than the previous ones.

The multiobjective method considered for our numerical experiments is based on the Crowding Differential Evolution algorithm described in section 2.1.

5. LORENZ EQUILIBRIUM

Lorenz equilibrium is defined in the framework of non-cooperative game theory using Lorenz dominance as its generative relation.

5.1 Generative Relation of Lorenz Equilibrium

Game equilibria may be characterized by generative relations on the set of game strategies [4]. The idea is that the non-dominated strategies with respect to the generative relation equals (or approximate) the equilibrium set.

Let us consider a relation $\mathcal{R}$ over $S \times S$.

A strategy s' is non dominated with respect to relation $\mathcal{R}$ if

$$\nexists s'' \in S : (s', s'') \in \mathcal{R}.$$

Let us denote by NDR the set of non-dominated strategies with respect to relation $\mathcal{R}$. A subset $S' \subset S$ is non-dominated with respect to $\mathcal{R}$ if and only if $\forall s \in S'$, $s \in NDR$.

Relation $\mathcal{R}$ is said to be a *generative relation* for the equilibrium E if and only if the set of non-dominated strategies with respect to $\mathcal{R}$ equals the set E of strategies i.e. $NDR = E$.

Definition 6. The *Lorenz equilibrium* of a game is the the set of non-dominated strategies with respect to the $\succ_L$ relation.

Therefore we may consider $\succ_L$ as a *generative relation for Lorenz equilibrium.*

For the generative relations for Nash and Pareto equilibria see [4].

5.2 Properties of Lorenz Equilibrium

The most studied equilibrium concepts in game theory are the Nash and Pareto equilibria. However, when applied in real-world situations these theoretical concepts have some limitations. Nash equilibrium presumes that players are rational agents choosing their strategies as best response to strategies chosen by other players. This equilibrium rarely assures maximal payoffs for all players. In contrary, Pareto equilibrium assures the optimal payoffs for the players but the set of Pareto-optimal solutions is often too large, while in game theory it is useful to find a unique preferred solution of the game. Moreover, payoffs of Pareto solutions may be highly unequal.

The advantage of the Lorenz equilibrium is that it preserves the qualities of Pareto equilibrium and the set of solutions is considerably smaller. Moreover the resulting solutions assure the maximal payoffs that are equitable for all players.

6. GAMES WITH MULTIPLE NASH EQUILIBRIA

An interesting question arises when there are multiple Nash equilibria in a game [1, 12]. In this case, classical game theory can say nothing about the outcome of the game and in case of multiple equilibria there is no particular reason to eliminate one out of these equilibria. We propose the use of Lorenz equilibrium for the selection of one Nash equilibrium.

Our assumption is, that because of its favorable properties, Lorenz equilibrium can be applied in the process of selecting the most equitable Nash equilibrium. Lorenz equilibrium is Pareto-optimal (it assures maximal payoffs) and provides the most fair payoff distribution to the players. Our assumption is, that in case of multiple equilibria, selecting the Nash equilibrium that is the closest to the Lorenz equilibrium is a natural choice. The distance is considered int the payoff space.

In the case when the Lorenz equilibrium is a subset of the Nash solutions, the selection is trivial. Since this is not always the case, the closest distance in the payoff space is considered.

Below we present several games with multiple equilibria that will be considered in our numerical experiments.

6.1 Bargaining Game

The bargaining game [9], or Nash demand game, is a simple two player game, where each player demands a portion of some good. If the total amount demanded by the players is less or equal than the available good, each player get their request, otherwise neither players get anything.

The function to be maximized is the following:

$$u_i(x_1, x_2, ..., x_n) = \begin{cases} x_i, & \text{if } \sum_{i=1}^{n} x_i < 1, \\ 0, & \text{otherwise} \end{cases}$$

6.2 X game

The X game is a theoretical game with infinite Nash equilibria that was introduced in [3].

The payoff function for this game is the following:

$$u_i(x_1, ..., x_n) = x_i[10 - sin(\sum_{i=1}^{n} x_i^2)],$$

where $x_i \in [0, 10]$.

6.3 Cournot oligopoly

A single good is produced by n firms. The cost to firm i of producing q_i units of the good is $C_i(q_i)$, where C_i is an increasing function (more output is more costly to produce). All the output is sold at a single price, determined by the demand for the good and the firms total output. If the firms total output is Q, than the market price is $P(Q)$. Market price can be expressed as

$$P(Q) = \begin{cases} a - Q, & \text{if } Q \leq a, \\ 0, & \text{otherwise} \end{cases}$$

If the output of each firm is q_i, then the price is $P(q_1 + q_2 + ... + q_n)$ and the firm i' revenue is $q_i P(q_1 + q_2 + ... + q_n)$.

The payoff function for the player i is:

$$u_i(q_1, ..., q_n) = q_i P(q_1 + ... + q_n) - C_i(q_i)$$

Suppose each firm's cost function is $C_i(q_i) = cq_i$ for all q_i. The profit of the ith firm is:

$$u_i(q_1, ..., q_n) = q_i[a - (q_1 + ... + q_n) - c].$$

It is known, that this linear version of the Cournot game has one single symmetric Nash equilibrium, $(\frac{1}{n+1}(a-c), \frac{1}{n+1}(a-c))$, however this equilibrium point is not Pareto-optimal. On the other hand in a non-linear version of the oligopoly model there might be multiple equilibria.

6.4 Non-linear Cournot Oligopoly

In this section, we consider a version of the Cournot game with the following payoff functions:

$$u_i(q_1, ..., q_n) = q_i P(q_1 + ... + q_n) - C_i(q_i)$$

, where

$$P(q_1 + ... + q_n) = a + b - \sum_{i=1}^{n} qi,$$

$$C(q_i) = \frac{1}{4}(q_i - a)^4 - q_i^2 + bq_i - d,$$

where $a, b, d > 0$.

This non-linear version of the Cournot game has exactly three Nash equlibria, the points: (a, a), $(a - 1, a + 1)$, $(a + 1, a - 1)$, so it is difficult to predict the market price.

7. NUMERICAL EXPERIMENTS

In our numerical experiments, in order to detect the Lorenz equilibrium, we used the evolutionary method described in Section 4. The multiobjective algorithm used is the differential evolution algorithm (Section 2.1) with the following parameter settings: $CR = 0.3$, $F = 0.5$, $pop\_size = 100$.

7.1 Experiment 1: Cournot game

In order to illustrate the Lorenz equilibrium, we consider the Cournot game described in Section 6.3, with the following parameter settings: $a = 24$, $c = 9$. The Nash, Pareto and Lorenz equilibria are illustrated in Figure 3. We can observe that the set of Pareto-optimal solutions is too large, while the Lorenz equilibrium consists of a single solution - the one that provides the maximum possible payoff for all players. Similar to the Lorenz equilibrium, the Nash equilibrium also consists of a single solution that is also a fair one, but compared to the Lorenz solution, it provides a lower payoff for both players. So we can conclude that the Lorenz equilibrium is the most equitable and most profiting choice for both players.

7.2 Experiment 2: Bargaining game

In case of the bargaining game (Section 6.1 the payoff values for the players are the same as chosen strategies. As illustrated on Figure 4, the game has an infinity of Nash and Pareto solutions.

The Nash and Pareto fronts are identical, they consist of all the solutions $(x, 1 - x), x \in [0, 1]$.

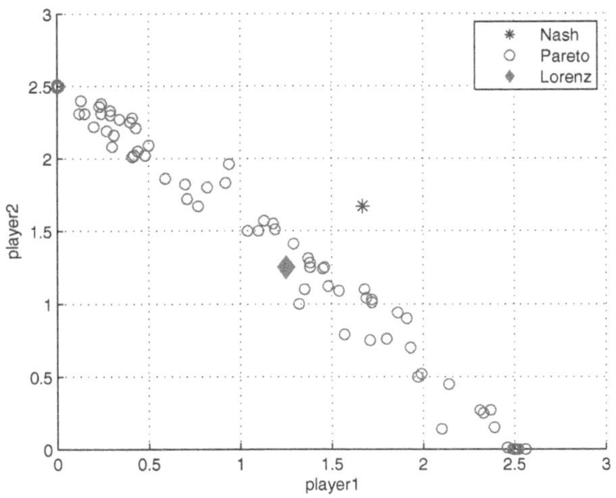

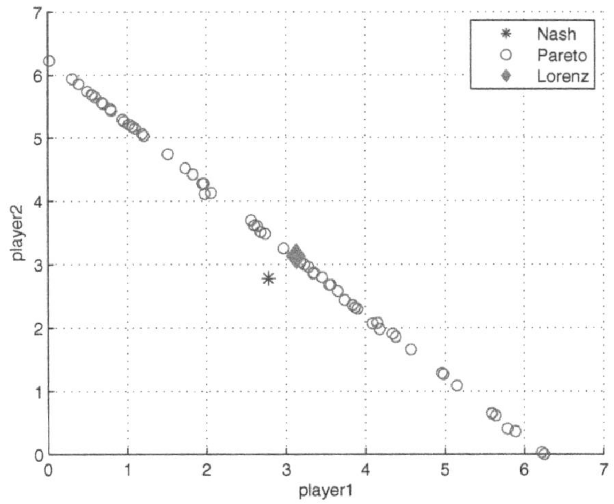

Figure 3: Experiment 1: The strategies (left) and payoffs (right) for the evolutionary detected Nash, Pareto and Lorenz equilibria for the two player Cournot game. The Lorenz equilibrium is in the middle of the Pareto-front, and assures higher payoffs than the Nash equilibrium.

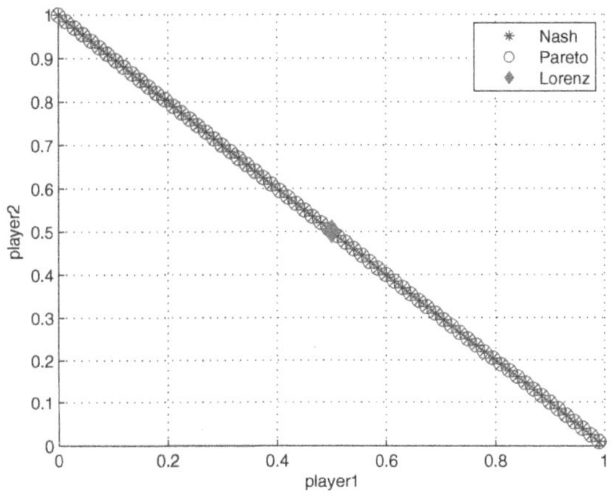

Figure 4: Experiment 2: The strategies for the evolutionary detected Nash, Pareto and Lorenz equilibria for the two player Bargaining game. The game has two identical Nash and Pareto fronts. The Lorenz fornt lies exactly in the middel of the Nash and Pareto front, and assures the most fair solution for both palyers. Since the Lorenz equilibrium is also a Nash equilibrium, the selection of a single Nash solution is trivial.

Because of the infinity of the equilibruim points, based on the Nash or Pareto equilibrium, no prediction can be made about the outcome of the game. The Lorenz equilibrium solves the problem, consisting of a unique symmetric and Pareto-optimal equilibrium point, it is clearly the most profitable outcome of the game for all players.

7.3 Experiment 3: X game

In cases when some of the Nash equilibrium points are Pareto-optimal, and the Lorenz equilibrium is a subset of the Nash equilibrium, the selection of equilibria is trivial. As Figure 5 shows, the X game has a more complex equilibria structure.

There are two Nash fronts, and one Pareto front. The Pareto front is identical with one of the Nash fronts. The Lorenz equilibrium is exactly on the middle of this front, and as in the previous experiments it provides the most equilibrated and fair solution for both players.

7.4 Experiment 4: Non-linear Cournot game

As Figure 6 shows, the non-linear version of the Cournot game has exactly three Nash equlibria, but none of these equilibrium points are Pareto-optimal. The Pareto front, similarly to the simplified version, has infinite solutions. So, based on the Nash and Pareto equilibria it is difficult to predict the market price. The Lorenz equilibrium, similarly as in case of the linear Cournot game, is the unique symmetric and optimal solution.

Since the Lorenz equilibrium is not a subset of Nash equilibria, the selection process is not that trivial. The equilibrium point that is closest to the Lorenz solution is the point $(1, 1)$. This outcome corresponds to the strategy (3, 3), which is clearly the most profitable solution if we consider both player's interest.

8. CONCLUSIONS

The Lorenz dominance relation is considered. The set of Lorenz solutions is a subset of the Pareto set. The Lorenz optimal set consists of the most equitable and balanced solutions. An evolutionary detection of the Lorenz-optimal solution is proposed. The Lorenz dominance solution is successfully tested on some classical multiobjective problems. The Lorenz dominance provides a stronger selection of the non-dominated solutions.

We propose a new game theoretical solution concept based on the Lorenz dominance relation: Lorenz equilibrium. This equilibrium overcomes some limitations of the Nash and Pareto equilibria. The Lorenz equilibrium solutions are optimal and fair for all players. In our numerical experiments we illustrate the Lorenz equilibrium on different types of

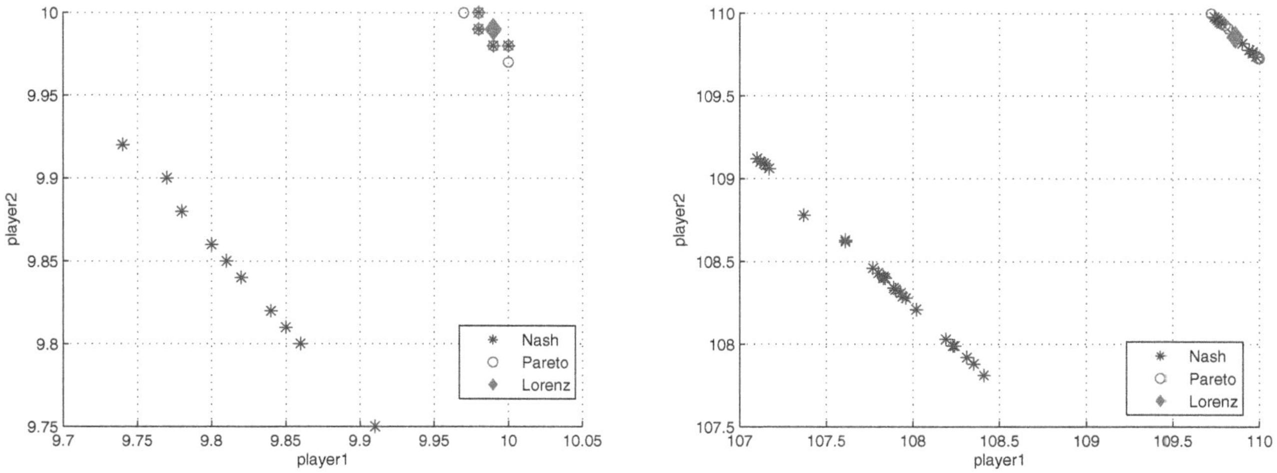

Figure 5: Experiment 3: The strategies (left) and payoffs (right) for the evolutionary detected Nash, Pareto and Lorenz equilibria for the two player X game. The game has two Nash front and one Pareto front, that is identical with one of the Nash fronts. The lorenz equilibrium lies in the middle of the Pareto front. Since the Lorenz equilibrium is also a Nash equilibrium, the selection of a single Nash solution is trivial.

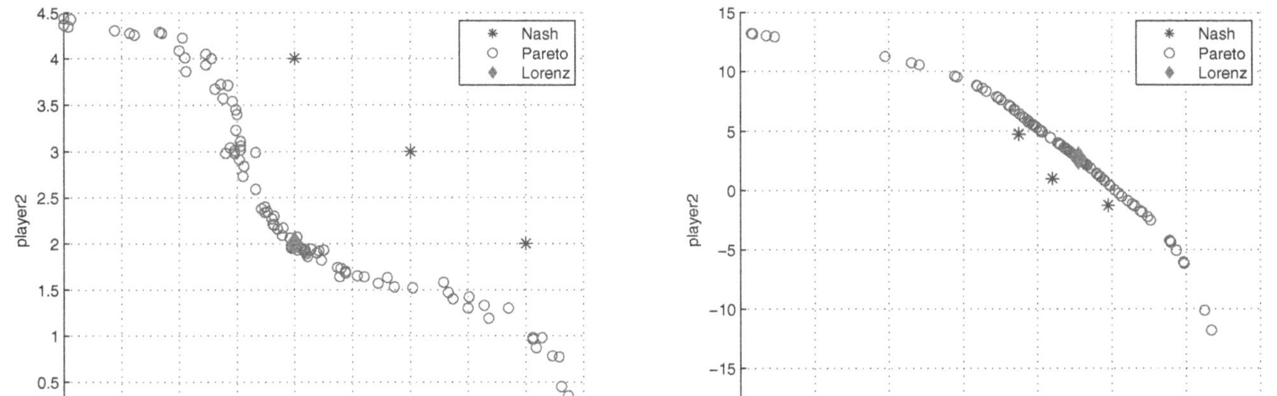

Figure 6: Experiment 4: The strategies (left) and payoffs (right) for the evolutionary detected Nash, Pareto and Lorenz equilibria for the two player, non-linear Cournot game. The game has three Nash equilibria. The Lorenz equilibrium lies on the middle of the Pareto front, assuring an optimal and equitable solution. The Nash equilibrium closest to the Lorenz equilibrium is the symmetric Nash solution.

games. The results show, that Lorenz equilibrium is a powerful and natural solution concept: it is both Pareto-optimal and assures a fair payoff distribution for all players. Lorenz equilibrium can also be applied in the process of selecting a single Nash equilibrium when multiple Nash equilibria are present in the game. This possibility is illustrated for several games having multiple Nash equilibria.

9. ACKNOWLEDGEMENTS

Authors have equal contributions.

This publication was made possible through the support of a grant from the John Templeton Foundation. The opinions expressed in this publication are those of the authors and do not necessarily reflect the views of the John Templeton Foundation.

This research was partially supported by the Romanian national program PN II TE, code TE 252, financed by CNCS-UEFISCDI.

The first and second authors wish to thank for the financial support provided from programs co-financed by the Sectoral Operational Programme Human Resources Development, Contract POSDRU/88/1.5/S/60185 - Innovative Doctoral Studies in a Knowledge Based Society, and POSDRU/107/1.5/S/76841 with the title Modern Doctoral Studies: Internationalization and Interdisciplinarity.

10. REFERENCES

[1] S. Bade, G. Haeringer, and L. Renou. More strategies, more nash equilibria. *Journal of Economic Theory*, 135(1):551–557, 2009.

[2] F. Dugardin, F. Yalaoui, and L. Amodeo. New multi-objective method to solve reentrant hybrid flow shop scheduling problem. *European Journal of Operational Research*, 203(1):22–31, May 2010.

[3] D. Dumitrescu, R. I. Lung, N. Gaskó, and D. T. Mihoc. Evolutionary detection of aumann equilibrium. In *Proceedings of the 12th annual conference on Genetic and evolutionary computation*, GECCO '10,827–828. ACM, 2010.

[4] D. Dumitrescu, R. I. Lung, and T. D. Mihoc. Generative relations for evolutionary equilibria detection. In *GECCO '09: Proceedings of the 11th Annual conference on Genetic and evolutionary computation*,1507–1512. ACM, 2009.

[5] C. M. Fonseca and P. J. Fleming. Multiobjective optimization and multiple constraint handling with evolutionary algorithms. ii. application example. *IEEE Transactions on Systems Man and Cybernetics Part A Systems and Humans*, 28:38–47, 1998.

[6] M. M. Kostreva and W. Ogryczak. Linear optimization with multiple equitable criteria. *RAIRO - Operations Research*, 33(03):275–297, 1999.

[7] M. M. Kostreva, W. Ogryczak, and A. Wierzbicki. Equitable aggregations and multiple criteria analysis. *European Journal of Operational Research*, 158(2):362 – 377, 2004.

[8] R. D. McKelvey and A. McLennan. Computation of equilibria in finite games. In *Handbook of Computational Economics*, volume 1, chapter 2, 87–142. Elsevier, December 1996.

[9] J. Nash. The bargaining problem. *Econometrica*, 18(2):155–162, April 1950.

[10] J. Nash. Non-cooperative games. *The Annals of Mathematics*, 54(2):286–295, September 1951.

[11] T. Robiè and B. Filipiè. Demo: Differential evolution for multiobjective optimization. In *In Proceedings of the 3rd International Conference on Evolutionary MultiCriterion Optimization (EMO 2005)*, 520–533. Springer. LNCS, 2005.

[12] Y. Sekiguchi, K. Sakahara, and T. Sato. Uniqueness of nash equilibria in quantum cournot duopoly game. *Journal of Physics A: Mathematical and Theoretical*, 43:7, 2009.

[13] T. Stephen, L. Tuncel, and H. Luss. On equitable resource allocation problems: a lexicographic minimax approach. *Operational Research*, 47:361–376, 1999.

[14] R. Storn and K. Price. Differential evolution - a simple and efficient heuristic for global optimization over continuous spaces. *Journal of Global Optimization*, 11:341–359, 1997.

[15] R. Thomsen. Multimodal optimization using crowding-based differential evolution. In *IEEE Proceedings of the Congress on Evolutionary Computation (CEC 2004)*, 1382–1389, 2004.

[16] D. Zaharie and D. Petcu. Adaptive pareto differential evolution and its parallelization. In *Parallel Processing and Applied Mathematics*, volume 3019 of *Lecture Notes in Computer Science*, 261–268. 2004.

[17] E. Zitzler, K. Deb, and L. Thiele. Comparison of Multiobjective Evolutionary Algorithms on Test Functions of Different Difficulty. In *Genetic and Evolutionary Computation Conference (GECCO 1999)*, July 1999.

Leveraging Indicator-based Ensemble Selection in Evolutionary Multiobjective Optimization Algorithms

Dung H. Phan
Dept. of Computer Science
University of Massachusetts, Boston
Boston, MA, USA 02125-3393
phdung@cs.umb.edu

Junichi Suzuki
Dept. of Computer Science
University of Massachusetts, Boston
Boston, MA, USA 02125-3393
jxs@cs.umb.edu

Isao Hayashi
Faculty of Informatics
Kansai University
Osaka, Japan 569-1095
ihaya@res.kutc.kansai-u.ac.jp

ABSTRACT

Various evolutionary multiobjective optimization algorithms (EMOAs) have replaced or augmented the notion of dominance with quality indicators and leveraged them in selection operators. Recent studies show that indicator-based EMOAs outperform traditional dominance-based EMOAs. This paper proposes and evaluates an ensemble learning method that constructs an ensemble of existing indicators with a novel boosting algorithm called Pdi-Boosting. The proposed method is carried out with a training problem in which Pareto-optimal solutions are known. It can work with a simple training problem, and an ensemble of indicators can effectively aid parent selection and environmental selection in order to solve harder problems. Experimental results show that the proposed method is efficient thanks to its dynamic adjustment of training data. An ensemble of indicators outperforms existing individual indicators in optimality, diversity and robustness. The proposed ensemble-based evolutionary algorithm outperforms a well-known dominance-based EMOA and existing indicator-based EMOAs.

Categories and Subject Descriptors

I.2.8 [**Artificial Intelligence**]: Problem Solving, Control Methods, and Search—*Heuristic methods*

General Terms

Algorithms

Keywords

Evolutionary multiobjective optimization algorithms, Quality indicators, Indicator-based ensemble selection, Boosting

1. INTRODUCTION

A recent research trend in the design space of evolutionary multiobjective optimization algorithms (EMOAs) is to adopt *indicator-based selection* operators that augment or replace traditional dominance ranking with *quality indicators* [4]. A quality indicator measures the goodness of each individual. Recent research findings (e.g., [2, 18, 21]) show that indicator-based EMOAs outperform traditional EMOAs that use dominance ranking in selection.

Many quality indicators have been proposed with the intention to capture different preferences in optimization [1,3, 19,21]. Therefore, indicator-based selection operators tend to have biased selection pressures that evolve individuals toward particular regions in the objective space. For example, the hypervolume indicator favors *balanced* individuals that equally balance the trade-offs among all objectives, while the weighted hypervolume indicator favors *extreme* individuals that yield superior performance only in a limited number of objectives [19]. A research question in this context is whether a set of existing indicators can create a single indicator that outperforms those existing ones.

The authors of the paper have addressed this question with the notion of *indicator-based ensemble selection*, which means selection with an ensemble of indicators, and verified that an ensemble of indicators outperforms each of those indicators [15,16]. In [15,16], a traditional boosting algorithm called AdaBoost [9] was used to construct ensembles.

This paper enhances the prior work by replacing AdaBoost with a novel boosting algorithm called Pdi-Boosting (Probabilistic data interpolation-Boosting). Pdi-Boosting interpolates data around misclassified data using a given probability density function, while AdaBoost labels misclassified data with associated weights.

Designed with Pdi-Boosting, the proposed boosting method constructs an ensemble of indicators for two types of selection operators in EMOAs: (1) *parent selection*, which chooses parent individuals from the population to reproduce offspring and (2) *environmental selection*, which chooses a set of individuals used in the next generation from the union of the current population and its offspring. The proposed boosting method is carried out with a training problem in which Pareto-optimal solutions are known. It can work with a simple training problem, and an ensemble of indicators can effectively aid to solve harder problems.

This paper also proposes a new EMOA, called BIBEA-P, which uses an ensemble selection operator constructed with the proposed boosting method. It is designed as a variant of an existing indicator-based EMOA: IBEA [21].

Experimental results show that the proposed boosting method outperforms its previous AdaBoost-based method in optimality, diversity and convergence metrics. It is 44% faster than the AdaBoost-based method thanks to its dynamic adjustment of training data. Experimental results also demonstrate that an ensemble of indicators outperforms existing individual indicators in optimality and diversity. The ensemble exhibits higher robustness than existing indicators against different characteristics in different problems and yields more stable performance to solve a wider range of problems. Moreover, BIBEA-P outperforms a well-known traditional EMOA (NSGA-II [5]) and existing indicator-based EMOAs (IBEA [21] and SMS-EMOA [2]).

2. RELATED WORK

This paper extends the authors' prior work [15,16], which investigated indicator-based ensemble selection with AdaBoost. As discussed in the previous section, this paper leverages a new boosting algorithm, Pdi-Boosting, in order to construct more efficient and effective ensembles of indicators.

Several existing work have integrated ensemble methods, including boosting algorithms, with evolutionary algorithms (EAs) although they have never used ensemble methods for selection operators in EAs. For example, boosting algorithms have been integrated with genetic algorithms (GAs) to solve classification problems [12,13]. The Boosting Genetic Algorithm integrates boosting with a GA to discover classification rules [12]. The GA is used as a base classifier in which each individual represents a classification rule. A boosting algorithm aggregates multiple base classifiers (i.e., GAs) to build a more accurate classifier than them.

Liu et al. integrate boosting with a GA for feature selection [13]. (Feature selection aims to identify the features that strongly contribute to classification accuracy.) The GA evolves a set of individuals, each of which encodes a feature selection candidate, and seeks the optimal feature selection that minimizes classification error. A feature selection candidate represents a set of boosted classifiers, each of which considers a single feature to perform classification. Boosted classifiers are constructed on a feature by feature basis.

Naujoks et al. propose an online statistical technique to determine the termination condition (i.e., the maximum number of objective function evaluations) for an indicator-based EMOA: SMS-EMOA [14]. This paper does not focus on dynamic adjustment of the termination condition, but uses statically-fixed termination conditions.

3. QUALITY INDICATORS

This section describes 19 representative quality indicators that the proposed boosting method uses.

3.1 Hypervolume Indicator

I_H measures the volume of a hypercube that an individual dominates in the objective space [22]. The hypercube is formed with the individual and the reference point representing the highest (or worst) possible objective values $\vec{r} = (r_1, r_2, .., r_n)$ where n denotes the number of objectives. I_H of an individual $\vec{x}$ is calculated as follows where $f_i(\vec{x})$ denotes the i-th objective function value of $\vec{x}$.

$$I_H(\vec{x}) = \prod_{i=1}^{n} |r_i - f_i(\vec{x})| \quad (1)$$

I_H is intended to favor balanced individuals in the objective space rather than extreme ones [22].

3.2 Weighted Hypervolume Indicators

I_W is an extension to I_H in that I_W places different weights on different regions in the objective space while I_H places the uniform weight on all regions [19]. I_W of an individual $\vec{x} = (x_1, x_2, ..., x_n)$ is computed as follows.

$$I_W(\vec{x}) = \int_{(x_1,x_2,\ldots,x_n)}^{(r_1,r_2,\ldots,r_n)} w(\vec{a})dz \quad (2)$$
$$where\ w(\vec{a}) = \frac{\sum_{i=1}^{n} e^{k_i(r_i - a_i)}}{\sum_{i=1}^{n} e^{k_i}}$$

$w(\vec{a})$ denotes the weight of a point $\vec{a} = (a_1, a_2, ..., a_n)$ in the objective space. It is calculated by applying a weight distribution $\vec{k} = (k_1, k_2, .., k_n)$. k_i is the weight assigned to the i-th objective. Given a greater k_i value, I_W favors extreme individuals that are closer to the f_i axis in the objective space. Note that I_W is equal to I_H when $\vec{k} = (0, 0, .., 0)$.

This paper uses nine variants of I_W (I_{W1} to I_{W9}) based on nine different combinations of k_1 and k_2 values (Table 1). These value combinations follow the parameter settings in [19]. Note that this paper considers two weight values (k_1 and k_2) because it uses a training problem whose objective space is two dimensional.

Table 1: Nine Variants of I_W

I_W variants	k_1	k_2	I_W variants	k_1	k_2
I_{W1}	10	10	I_{W6}	0	20
I_{W2}	10	0	I_{W7}	30	30
I_{W3}	0	10	I_{W8}	30	0
I_{W4}	20	20	I_{W9}	0	30
I_{W5}	20	0			

3.3 HypE Indicator

I_{HypE} is also an extension to I_H. This indicator places different weights on different portions in the hypervolume that an individual dominates. The hypervolume is divided into multiple portions based on how many other individuals dominate it as well. I_{HypE} of $\vec{x}$ is computed as follows [1].

$$I_{HypE}(\vec{x}) = \sum_{i=1}^{\mu} \frac{1}{i} H_i(\vec{x}) \quad (3)$$

μ denotes the population size (the number of individuals in the population). $H_i(\vec{x})$ denotes the hypervolume that is dominated by $\vec{x}$ and other $(i-1)$ individuals in the population. H_1 is the hypervolume that $\vec{x}$ dominates exclusively. The highest weight (1) is given to H_1. H_2 is the hypervolume that $\vec{x}$ and another individual dominate. The second highest weight ($\frac{1}{2}$) is given to H_2. The lowest weight ($\frac{1}{\mu}$) is given to H_μ, which all individuals in the population dominate.

3.4 Binary ε Indicators

I_ε takes two individuals ($\vec{x}$ and $\vec{y}$) and measures the distance between them on a per-objective basis [21].

$$I_\epsilon(\vec{x}, \vec{y}) = max_{i \in \{1,..,n\}}(f_i(\vec{x}) - f_i(\vec{y})) \quad (4)$$

This paper considers two methods to evaluate the quality of an individual ($\vec{x}$) against the other individuals in the population P. The first method is to sum up I_ε values.

$$I_{\epsilon 1}(\vec{x}) = \sum_{\vec{y} \in P \setminus \{\vec{x}\}} I_{\epsilon}(\vec{y}, \vec{x}) \quad (5)$$

The second method amplifies the influence of dominating individuals over dominated ones.

$$I_{\epsilon 2}(\vec{x}) = \sum_{\vec{y} \in P \setminus \{\vec{x}\}} -e^{-I_{\epsilon}(\vec{y}, \vec{x})/l} \quad (6)$$

l is a scaling coefficient. $l = 0.05$ in this paper, which is a recommended value in [21].

3.5 Binary Hypervolume Indicators

I_{HD} takes two individuals ($\vec{x}$ and $\vec{y}$) and measures the hypervolume dominated by $\vec{x}$ but not by $\vec{y}$ [21].

$$I_{HD}(\vec{x}, \vec{y}) = \begin{cases} H(\vec{x}) - H(\vec{y}) & \text{if } \vec{x} \text{ dominates } \vec{y} \\ H(\vec{x}) - H(\vec{x}) \cap H(\vec{y}) & \text{otherwise} \end{cases} \quad (7)$$

$H(\vec{x})$ denotes the hypervolume that $\vec{x}$ dominates.

Similar to $I_{\epsilon 1}$ and $I_{\epsilon 2}$, this paper considers two variants, I_{HD1} and I_{HD2}, to evaluate the quality of an individual ($\vec{x}$) against the other individuals in the population. $I_{HD1}(\vec{x})$ and $I_{HD2}(\vec{x})$ are computed by replacing $I_{\epsilon}(\vec{y}, \vec{x})$ with $I_{HD}(\vec{x}, \vec{y})$ in Equations 5 and 6, respectively.

3.6 Fuzzy Indicators

I_F is computed based the relationship of the fuzzy Pareto dominance between two individuals ($\vec{x}$ and $\vec{y}$) [10].

$$I_F(\vec{x}, \vec{y}) = \frac{\prod_i min(f_i(\vec{x}), f_i(\vec{y}))}{\prod_i f_i(\vec{x})} \quad (8)$$

Similar to $I_{\epsilon 1}$ and $I_{\epsilon 2}$, this paper considers two variants, I_{F1} and I_{F2}, to evaluate the quality of an individual ($\vec{x}$) against the other individuals in the population. I_{F1} and I_{F2} are computed with Equations 5 and 6, respectively. $l = 0.01$ for I_F in this paper.

3.7 Volume Indicators

I_V is computed as follows [11].

$$I_V(\vec{x}, \vec{y}) = \frac{H(\vec{x}) - H(\vec{y})}{H(\vec{x}) \cap H(\vec{y})} \quad (9)$$

I_V also has two variants, I_{V1} and I_{V2}, which are computed as I_{F1} and I_{F2} are computed.

4. THE PROPOSED BOOSTING METHOD

Algorithm 1 shows the proposed boosting method, which employs Pdi-Boosting. It takes M indicator-based selection operators (S) and aggregates some of them as an ensemble (S^*). This paper uses 19 tournament selection operators that use 19 indicators described in Section 3 ($M = 19$).

The proposed boosting method is carried out through offline training with a multiobjective optimization problem in which Pareto-optimal solutions are known. This training problem is used to generate N_O initial training populations, $\{p_1, p_2, .., p_{N_O}\}$, each of which contains μ individuals (Line 1). These individuals represent randomly-chosen points in the region that the Pareto-optimal solutions dominate in the objective space.

Algorithm 1 The Proposed Boosting Method

Input: $\mathcal{S} = \{s_1, s_2, .., s_M\}$, M indicator-based selection operators

Output: $\mathcal{S}^*$, an ensemble of operators

1: Generate the initial N_O training populations: $\mathcal{P} = \{p_1, p_2, .., p_{N_O}\}$
2: $t = 0, N = N_O, \mathcal{S}^* = \phi$
3: **repeat**
4: $t = t + 1$
5: Each operator s_j performs individual selection N_p times on each training population p_i.
6: Calculate the selection error rate (e_j) for s_j
$e_j = \frac{\sum_{i=1}^{N} I_{ji}}{N}$ where
$I_{ji} = \begin{cases} 0 & \text{if } s_j\text{'s selection is successful on } p_i \\ 1 & \text{otherwise} \end{cases}$
7: Choose an operator s_t^* such that $s_t^* = \arg\min_{s_j \in \mathcal{S}} e_j$ and $s_t^* \notin \mathcal{S}^*$
8: $\mathcal{S}^* = \mathcal{S}^* \cup \{s_t^*\}$
9: $d = N \times (1 - 2e_j)$
10: Let $\mathcal{P}'$ be a set of training populations on which s_t^*'s individual selection is unsuccessful.
11: Let $\mathcal{W}$ be a set of HVR values that s_t^* yields with training populations in $\mathcal{P}'$
12: $D =$ interpolateExtraPopulations($\mathcal{P}'$, $\mathcal{W}$, d)
13: $\mathcal{P} = \mathcal{P} \cup \mathcal{D}$
14: $N = N + d$
15: **until** $e_t < 0.5$
16: **return** $\mathcal{S}^*$

The proposed boosting method iteratively executes a loop (Line 3 to 15) and selects one operator into S^* in each iteration. In each iteration, each of M operators selects an individual N_p times (i.e., N_p individuals in total) from each training population (Line 5). The quality of those N_p individuals is evaluated with the hypervolume ratio (HVR) metric [17]. HVR is computed as the ratio of the hypervolume (HV) of N_p individuals (P^S) to the hypervolume of μ individuals in a training population p_i.

$$HVR(P^S) = \frac{HV(P^S)}{HV(p_i)} \quad (10)$$

HV measures the union of the volumes that a given set of individuals dominate in the objective space [22].

The selection of N_p individuals is said to be *successful* if $HVR(P^S)$ is greater than or equal to a threshold: $\theta < 1$. Given this condition, the selection error of each operator (e_j) is calculated as shown in Lines 6 and 7. Then, the proposed boosting method chooses an operator (s_t^*) that has the lowest selection error (Line 7) and includes the operator in the output ensemble S^* (Line 8).

In Line 9, d is computed as the difference between the number of training populations on which individual selection is successful ($N \times (1 - e_j)$) and the number of training populations on which individual selection is unsuccessful ($N \times e_j$). The proposed boosting method generates d extra training populations that are similar to P', which is a set of training populations on which s_t^*'s individual selection is unsuccessful (Line 12, $|\mathcal{P}'| = N \times e_j$), and adds the extra populations to P (Line 13).

This way, the proposed boosting method dynamically adjusts the number of training populations by interpolating d

populations around $\mathcal{P}'$ so that $|\mathcal{P}'|+d$ becomes equal to the number of populations on which s_t^*'s individual selection is successful. As a result, in subsequent loop iterations, the proposed method favors the operators that perform successful individual selection on interpolated populations.

Algorithm 2 Interpolate Extra Training Populations

```
Input: P' = {p_1, p_2, .., p_m}, m training populations
Input: W = {w_1, w_2, .., w_m}, m HVR values associated
    with the populations in P'
Input: d, the number of populations to be interpolated
Output: P* = {p*_1, p*_2, .., p*_d}, the populations to be inter-
    polated
 1: Sort the populations in P' in ascending order of their
    HVR values
 2: i = 1
 3: while i ≤ d do
 4:   Create new empty population p*_i
 5:   for each individual x in p_i do
 6:     Create new individual x*
 7:     for j = 1 to the total number of objectives do
 8:       f_j(x*) = f_j(x) + N(0, σ^2)
 9:     end for
10:     Add x* to p*_i.
11:   end for
12:   Add p*_i to P*
13:   i = i + 1
14: end while
15: return P*
```

Algorithm 2 shows how to generate d training populations and interpolate them around $\mathcal{P}' = \{p_1, p_2, .., p_m\}$ (`interpolateExtraPopulations()` in Algorithm 1). The m populations in $\mathcal{P}'$ are sorted in ascending order of HVR values (Line 1). This ensures that the populations with smaller HVR values are used more often for interpolation than the populations with higher HVR values when $d < m$. A new population (p_i^*) is generated by modifying the objective values of individuals in $p_i \in P'$ with a normal distribution $\mathcal{N}(0, \sigma^2)$.

5. THE PROPOSED ENSEMBLE-BASED EMOA: BIBEA-P

This section describes an EMOA, called Boosted Indicator Based Evolutionary Algorithm (BIBEA-P), which leverages the boosting method discussed in Section 4.

Algorithm 3 shows BIBEA-P's algorithmic structure, which is based on an existing indicator-based EMOA: IBEA [21]. In the *0*-th generation, μ individuals are randomly generated as the initial population (Line 2). In each generation (g), a pair of individuals, called parents (p_1 and p_2), are chosen from the current population with an ensemble of indicator-based selection operators that Algorithm 1 produces (`ensembleBasedParentSelection()`, Lines 6 and 7).

With the crossover rate P_c, two parents reproduce two offspring with the SBX (self-adaptive simulated binary crossover) operator [6] (Lines 9). Each offspring performs polynomial mutation [5] with the probability P_m (Lines 10 to 15). The boosted parent selection, crossover and mutation operators are repeatedly executed on $\mathcal{P}_g$ until μ offspring are reproduced (i.e., until $|O_g| = \mu$). The offspring ($\mathcal{O}_g$) are combined with the population $\mathcal{P}_g$ to form $\mathcal{R}_g$ ($|R_g| = 2\mu$), which is a pool of candidates for the next-generation individuals (Line 19).

Environmental selection follows offspring reproduction. μ individuals are selected from 2μ individuals in $\mathcal{R}_g$ as the next-generation population $\mathcal{P}_{g+1}$ (`ensembleDrivenEnviSelection()`, Line 20). Environmental selection performs a $(\mu+\mu)$-elitism.

Algorithm 3 The Algorithmic Structure of BIBEA-P

```
 1: g = 0
 2: P_g = initializePopulation(μ)
 3: while g < g_max do
 4:   O_g = ∅
 5:   while |O_g| < μ do do
 6:     p_1 = ensembleBasedParentSelection(S*, P_g)
 7:     p_2 = ensembleBasedParentSelection(S*, P_g)
 8:     if random() ≤ P_c then
 9:       {o_1, o_2} = crossover(p_1, p_2)
10:       if random() ≤ P_m then
11:         o_1 = mutation(o_1)
12:       end if
13:       if random() ≤ P_m then
14:         o_2 = mutation(o_2)
15:       end if
16:       O_g = {o_1, o_2} ∪ O_g
17:     end if
18:   end while
19:   R_g = P_g ∪ O_g
20:   P_{g+1} =ensembleDrivenEnvSelection(R_g, S*)
21:   g = g + 1
22: end while
```

Algorithm 4 Ensemble-based Parent Selection Operator

Input: $\mathcal{S}^* = \{s_1^*, s_2^*, .., s_T^*\}$, an ensemble of T indicator-based selection operators
Input: $\mathcal{P}$, a population of μ individuals
Output: an individual to be used as a parent for crossover
1: Each of T operators selects one individual from the population $\mathcal{P}$ with a v-way tournament. In total, T individuals are selected: $\{x_1, x_2, ..., x_T\}$
2: Calculate the number of votes for each individual x_i as $\varphi_i = \sum_{t=1}^{T} I_{ti}$
$$\text{where } I_{ti} = \begin{cases} 1 & \text{if } s_t^* \text{ selects } x_i \\ 0 & \text{otherwise} \end{cases}$$
3: **return** $x^* = argmax_{x_i}\varphi_i$.

5.1 Ensemble-based Parent Selection

Algorithm 4 shows how the proposed ensemble-based parent selection works (c.f. `ensembleBasedParentSelection()` in Algorithm 3). It takes an ensemble of T indicator-based selection operators S^*, which Algorithm 1 produces.

Each of T operators first selects one individual (i.e., parent candidate) from the population P with a v-way tournament (Line 1). In a v-way tournament, a selection operator randomly draws v individuals from P and chooses the best one based on a quality indicator that the operator uses. The count of votes φ_i ($1 \leq i \leq T$) is assigned to each of selected T individuals (Line 2). Finally, the proposed ensemble-based parent selection operator chooses an individual with the highest vote count as a parent. If more than one individuals have the same highest vote number, one of them is randomly chosen.

5.2 Ensemble-driven Environmental Selection

Algorithm 5 shows how the proposed ensemble-driven environmental selection (`ensembleDrivenEnvSelection()` in Algorithm 3) works. It takes an ensemble of T indicator-based selection operators S^*, which Algorithm 1 produces. It first identified an operator that Algorithm 3 selected in its first loop iteration (s^+) (Line 1). Then, with the indicator (I^+) that s^+ uses, μ individuals are removed from 2μ individuals in $\mathcal{R}_g$ (Lines 2 to 6). Finally, the remaining μ individuals are selected as the next-generation population ($\mathcal{P}_{g+1}$) (Line 8).

Algorithm 5 Boosting-driven Environmental Selection Operator

Input: $\mathcal{R}_g$, a population of 2μ individuals
Input: $\mathcal{S}^* = \{s_1^*, s_2^*, .., s_T^*\}$, an ensemble of T indicator-based selection operators
Output: $\mathcal{P}_{g+1}$, a population of individuals to be used in the next generation

1: $s^+ = s_1^*$
2: **while** $|\mathcal{R}_g| > \mu$ **do**
3: Rank all the individuals in $\mathcal{R}_g$ with I^+, which is the indicator that s^+ uses.
4: Select an individual d that has the worst I^+ value in $\mathcal{R}_g$
5: $\mathcal{R}_g = \mathcal{R}_g \setminus \{d\}$
6: **end while**
7: $\mathcal{P}_{g+1} = \mathcal{R}_g$
8: **return** $\mathcal{P}_{g+1}$

Although environmental selection depends on what the proposed boosting method (Algorithm 3) produces, it does not use all T operators in S^* as parent selection does. It uses only one operator (s_1^*) in S^* because it intends to minimize the degree of randomization in environmental selection.

6. EXPERIMENTAL EVALUATION

This section evaluates BIBEA-P as well as the proposed boosting method. Experiments were configured as shown in Table 6 and conducted with jMetal [8] on a 3.4GHz 64bit Core i7 processor.

Table 2: Experimental Configurations

Parameter	Value
M (Algorithm 1)	19
N_O (Algorithm 1)	300
μ (Algorithms 1, 3 and 5)	100
N_p (Algorithm 1)	20
θ (Algorithm 1)	0.87
σ (Algorithm 2)	0.05
g_{max} (Algorithm 3)	150, 200 or 500
v (Algorithm 4)	2, 3, 4 or 5
Crossover rate	0.9
Mutation rate	1/ (# of decision variables)

This evaluation study uses ZDT1 as a training problem for the proposed boosting method. ZDT1 is the simplest problem in the ZDT family problems [20]. It has a convex Pareto-optimal front in a two dimensional objective space.

ZDT2, ZDT3, ZDT4 and ZDT6 are used as test problems. Each of them has a two dimensional objective space. ZDT2 and ZDT6 are essentially same as ZDT1 in terms of problem design and complexity; however, they have concave Pareto-optimal fronts. ZDT3 and ZDT4 are harder problems than ZDT1. ZDT3 has five discontiguous Pareto-optimal fronts. ZDT4 posesses a large number of (20^9) local optima.

DTLZ family problems, DTLZ1, DTLZ2, DTLZ3, DTLZ4 and DTLZ7 [7], are also used as test problems. All of them are harder problems than ZDT1 (i.e., the training problem in this evaluation study). They have three dimensional objective spaces. DTLZ1 has a continuous and planar Pareto-optimal front. DTLZ2, DTLZ3 and DTLZ4 have continuous and spherical Pareto-optimal fronts. DTLZ7 has four discontiguous Pareto-optimal fronts.

All ZDT and DTLZ problems are configured with the default settings of jMetal. Every experimental result is obtained with 20 independent experiments for ZDT problems and 10 independent experiments for DTLZ problems.

6.1 Evaluation Metrics

This paper uses two evaluation metrics: hypervolume ratio (HVR) and coverage metric ($\mathcal{C}$-metric). HVR is calculated as the ratio of the hypervolume (HV) of non-dominated individuals (D) to the hypervolume of Pareto-optimal solutions (P^*) [17].

$$HVR(D) = \frac{HV(D)}{HV(P^*)} \tag{11}$$

HVR quantifies the optimality and diversity of non-dominated individuals D. A higher HVR indicates that non-dominated individuals are closer to the Pareto-optimal front and more diverse in the objective space.

$\mathcal{C}$-metric compares two sets of non-dominated individuals [23]. Given non-dominated individual sets A and B, $\mathcal{C}(A, B)$ measures the fraction of individuals in B that at least one individual in A dominates:

$$\mathcal{C}(A, B) = \frac{|\{b \in B \mid \exists a \in A : a \succ b\}|}{|B|} \tag{12}$$

6.2 Boosting Overhead

The left half of Table 3 shows a set of indicators that the proposed boosting method chose from 19 indicators with Pdi-Boosting. It also depicts how many training populations were used to choose individual indicators. Note that the number of training populations is initially 300 ($N_O = 300$ in Algorithm 1. See Table 6.) and it gradually grows. Therefore, the proposed boosting method uses different numbers of training populations for selecting different indicators. In total, it used 19,515 training populations.

The right half of Table 3 shows a set of indicators that an AdaBoost-based method chosen [15, 16]. In this method, the number of training populations is fixed. In total, it used 80,000 training populations. (10,000 per indicator was the minimum number of training populations for the AdaBoost method to obtain the best experimental results.)

The number of training populations impacts the overhead of a boosting algorithm (i.e., how long it takes for the algorithm to complete its boosting process.) The boosting overhead was 10 minutes in the proposed boosting method with Pdi-Boosting while it was 18 minutes with AdaBoost.

Thanks to Pdi-Boosting's dynamic adjustment of the number of training populations, the proposed boosting method is 44% faster than an AdaBoost-based method.

Table 3: The Number of Training Populations used by Pdi-Boosting and AdaBoost

Indicator	# of training populations in Pdi-Boosting	Indicator	# of training populations in AdaBoost
$I_{\epsilon 2}$	300	$I_{\epsilon 2}$	10,000
I_{HD2}	450	I_{HD2}	10,000
I_{F2}	686	I_{HypE}	10,000
I_{HypE}	889	I_{WO}	10,000
I_{WO}	1,193	I_{W3}	10,000
I_{W3}	1,619	I_{W6}	10,000
I_{W6}	2,171	I_H	10,000
I_H	2,895	$I_{\epsilon 1}$	10,000
I_{HD1}	3,930		
I_{V1}	5,382		
Total	19,515	Total	80,000
Overhead	10 (mins)	Overhead	18 (mins)

6.3 Evaluation of Ensemble Selection

This section evaluates a boosted indicator that aggregates the ten indicators listed in Table 3 in terms of optimality and diversity. Table 4 shows the average HVR values that five algorithms yield at the last generation in 10 different test problems. The total number of generations in each experiment (g_{max} in Table 6) is 150 in ZDT problems, 500 in DTLZ3 and 200 in the other DTLZ problems. In Table 4, a number in parentheses indicates a standard deviation among different experiments. I_B represents BIBEA-P that uses an ensemble indicator aggregating the ten indicators listed in Table 3. (BIBEA-P uses $I_{\epsilon 2}$ for its environmental selection.) Each of the other four algorithms represents a variant of IBEA [21] that performs parent and environmental selection with an indicator listed in Table 3. For example, I_{HD2} represents a variant of IBEA that uses I_{HD2} for parent and environmental selection. v in Table 4 indicates the size of a tournament in parent selection. In each test problem, 2-way to 5-way tournament selections are examined. A bold number indicates the best result among five algorithms on a per-row basis. The results of other six selected indicators (i.e., I_{WO}, I_{WO},, I_{W2}, I_{W6}, I_H, I_{HD1} and I_{VD1}) are not shown due to the space limitation Their results are significantly worse than the top four selected indicators.

In five of ten test problems (i.e., ZDT2, ZDT4, ZDT6, DTLZ1 and DTLZ3), I_B outperforms the other indicators when $v = 5$. In three other problems (i.e., ZDT1, ZDT3 and DTLZ2), I_B and $I_{\epsilon 2}$ tie when $v = 5$ if HVR values are truncated to two decimal places. Table 4 demonstrates that the proposed boosting method can work with a simple training problem (i.e., ZDT1) and I_B can effectively operate to solve harder test problems.

$I_{\epsilon 2}$ works well in ZDT1, ZDT3, DTLZ2, DTLZ4 and DTLZ7; however, its performance is marginal in DTLZ1 and DTLZ3. In both problems, $I_{\epsilon 2}$ never yields 0.19 or higher HVR. The other three (existing) indicators exhibit similar performance inconsistencies among different problems. For example, I_{F2} performs well in ZDT1 and ZDT2, while it performs poorly in DTLZ4. (It never yields 0.05 or higher HVR in DTLZ4.)

In contrast, I_B's HVR performance is much more consistent among different problems. Its worst HVR is 0.68 (DTLZ4) while $I_{\epsilon 2}$'s worst is 0.09 (DTLZ1), I_{HD2}'s is 0.44 (ZDT4) and I_{F2}'s is 0.01 (DTLZ4).

In summary, Table 4 demonstrates that I_B performs better than, or equally to, existing indicators in HVR (i.e., in optimality and diversity) in all test problems and I_B is more robust and stable than existing indicators under different characteristics in different problems.

6.4 Comparative Evaluation of BIBEA-P

Tables 5 shows the average HVR values that BIBEA-P and five other EMOAs (BIBEA, IBEA-ϵ2, IBEA-HD2, NSGAII and SMS-EMOA) yield at the last generation in 10 different test problems. BIBEA (Boosted Indicator Based Evolutionary Algorithm) is a variant of IBEA that uses an ensemble selection operator constructed with AdaBoost [16]. IBEA-ϵ2 and IBEA-HD2 are variants of IBEA that perform parent and environmental selection with $I_{\epsilon 2}$ and I_{HD2}, respectively [21]. NSGAII is a traditional EMOA that uses dominance ranking in its parent and environmental selection [5]. SMS-EMOA is a steady state EMOA that uses the hypervolume indicator in its environmental selection [2]. All algorithms use a 5-way tournament in parent selection.

In Tables 5, a number in parentheses indicates a standard deviation among different experiments. A bold number indicates the best result among six algorithms. A double star (**) or a single star (*) is placed when a HVR result is significantly different from BIBEA's result based on a single-tail t-test. A double and a single stars are placed with the confidence level of 99% and 95%, respectively.

As shown in Table 5, BIBEA-P yields the best HVR in four of ten test problems (i.e., ZDT2, ZDT4, ZDT6, DTLZ3. BIBEA yields the best HVR in three problems (i.e., DTLZ1, DTLZ4 and DTLZ7). BIBEA-P outperforms BIBEA in four problems. Of one of the four problems (i.e., ZDT6), BIBEA-P outperforms BIBEA with the confidence level of 99%.

BIBEA-P outperforms IBEA-ϵ2 significantly in ZDT4, ZDT6, DTLZ1 and DTLZ3 with the 95% or higher confidence level. It significantly outperforms IBEA-HD2, NSGA-II and SMS-EMOA in seven, six and five problems, respectively. BIBEA-P significantly outperforms all the other five EMOAs in ZDT6. In ZDT3, DTLZ1 and DTLZ4, BIBEA-P's average HVR is not the best among six EMOAs; however, it is not outperformed significantly by the others.

Table 6 compares BIBEA-P with the other five algorithms with $\mathcal{C}$-metric. The first two rows compare BIBEA-P and BIBEA. A bold font face is used to indicate a higher $\mathcal{C}$-metric value between $\mathcal{C}$(BIBEA-P, BIBEA) and $\mathcal{C}$(BIBEA, BIBEA-P). $\mathcal{C}$(BIBEA-P, BIBEA) > $\mathcal{C}$(BIBEA,BIBEA-P) in eight of 10 problems. This means that BIBEA-P outperforms BIBEA in those eight problems. In DTLZ1 and DTLZ3, BIBEA outperforms BIBEA-P; however, they yield very similar $\mathcal{C}$-metric values. The differences are 5.4% in DTLZ1 and 0.1% in DTLZ3.

Note that Table 6 shows BIBEA-P outperforms BIBEA in DTLZ4 and DTLZ7 while BIBEA outperforms BIBEA-P in the average HVR (Table 5). This conflict occurs due to high standard deviations in HVR (Tables 4 and 5).

BIBEA-P outperforms IBEA-ϵ2, IBEA-HD2 and SMS-EMOA in eight, nine and eight problems, respectively. Even when BIBEA-P is outperformed, the difference in $\mathcal{C}$-metric values is not significant.

Table 4: Comparison of I_B and Other Top Four Selected Indicators with HVR

	v	I_B	$I_{\epsilon 2}$	I_{HD2}	I_{HypE}	I_{F2}
ZDT1	2	0.99038(0.00078)	**0.99108** (0.00051)	0.99053(0.00065)	0.99019 (0.00081)	0.98815(0.00069)
	3	0.99114(0.00059)	**0.99124** (0.0005)	0.99108 (0.00052)	0.9872 (0.00133)	0.9863(0.00069)
	4	0.99078(0.00054)	**0.9914** (0.00044)	0.99131 (0.00061)	0.98373 (0.003)	0.98976 (0.0006)
	5	0.99085(0.00055)	**0.9914** (0.00053)	0.99124 (0.00057)	0.98007 (0.00306)	0.99013(0.0007)
ZDT2	2	0.9683(0.02064)	**0.96861** (0.01234)	0.67788 (0.26256)	0.97276 (0.00368)	0.94773(0.04736)
	3	**0.97863**(0.00248)	0.97635 (0.00258)	0.80336 (0.22041)	0.96998 (0.00451)	0.96932(0.01206)
	4	**0.97873**(0.00219)	0.97757 (0.00224)	0.88847 (0.17961)	0.95958 (0.01163)	0.97486(0.00272)
	5	**0.97864**(0.00211)	0.97816 (0.00141)	0.85718 (0.22804)	0.94279 (0.02943)	0.97541(0.00569)
ZDT3	2	0.97186(0.03306)	**0.98468** (0.01757)	0.97633 (0.02599)	0.98584 (0.01706)	0.82823(0.00073)
	3	0.98678(0.01748)	**0.98923** (0.00069)	0.97772 (0.02378)	0.98843 (0.01018)	0.82899(0.0008)
	4	0.98481(0.01768)	**0.98906** (0.00091)	0.98537 (0.00082)	0.98908 (0.00689)	0.82913(0.00052)
	5	0.98279(0.0251)	**0.9892** (0.00125)	0.98569 (0.00098)	0.98277 (0.02218)	0.82927(0.0006)
ZDT4	2	0.89002(0.06255)	0.82759 (0.09139)	0.4487 (0.27688)	**0.95183** (0.03788)	0.82026(0.10946)
	3	0.91844(0.0632)	0.89975 (0.06417)	0.61921 (0.19496)	**0.94363** (0.06164)	0.87938(0.09757)
	4	**0.96153**(0.01557)	0.92762 (0.03617)	0.52386 (0.25191)	0.94837 (0.03878)	0.93339(0.05858)
	5	**0.96446**(0.01789)	0.93968 (0.03962)	0.59782 (0.23131)	0.93607 (0.07498)	0.89258(0.10842)
ZDT6	2	**0.91442**(0.0142)	0.89694(0.01971)	0.86634 (0.02646)	0.90851 (0.01496)	0.90671(0.00992)
	3	**0.95499**(0.00717)	0.93181 (0.00818)	0.93458 (0.01476)	0.94867 (0.00984)	0.9459(0.00824)
	4	**0.97157**(0.0051)	0.94592 (0.01112)	0.95305 (0.01261)	0.96787 (0.00669)	0.96024(0.00577)
	5	**0.979**(0.00362)	0.95166 (0.00771)	0.96303 (0.00709)	0.97581 (0.00445)	0.96884(0.00482)
DTLZ1	2	0.92785(0.01461)	0.16563 (0.16349)	0.87292 (0.1565)	**0.93612** (0.00366)	0.72269(0.31834)
	3	0.9337(0.00307)	0.18356 (0.12278)	0.86789 (0.16297)	**0.93523** (0.0037)	0.91004(0.03724)
	4	0.84968(0.2651)	0.13599 (0.16671)	0.82699 (0.15773)	**0.93057** (0.00657)	0.91907(0.02753)
	5	**0.93431**(0.00477)	0.09898 (0.08299)	0.85456 (0.14999)	0.90112 (0.09922)	0.86101(0.18988)
DTLZ2	2	0.8967(0.00127)	**0.89671** (0.00165)	0.8817 (0.0013)	0.89665 (0.00171)	0.8713(0.003)
	3	0.89635(0.00135)	**0.89722** (0.00055)	0.8815 (0.00075)	0.89561 (0.00174)	0.87548(0.0045)
	4	0.8961(0.00183)	**0.89624** (0.00185)	0.88098 (0.00107)	0.86899 (0.01116)	0.8785(0.00315)
	5	0.89533(0.0014)	**0.8967** (0.00087)	0.88071 (0.00115)	0.75846 (0.0847)	0.87945(0.00234)
DTLZ3	2	**0.8751**(0.01467)	0.15156 (0.11169)	0.67875 (0.21244)	0.88077 (0.01817)	0.8496(0.02864)
	3	**0.87677**(0.03506)	0.12678 (0.09993)	0.79458 (0.13355)	0.8793 (0.00867)	0.84667(0.03259)
	4	**0.88044**(0.01828)	0.18072 (0.13898)	0.81021 (0.12525)	0.77406 (0.06568)	0.86444(0.01944)
	5	**0.88113**(0.0124)	0.13781 (0.05099)	0.81664 (0.06968)	0.67406 (0.10538)	0.8524(0.02157)
DTLZ4	2	0.73641(0.34721)	**0.88301** (0.20706)	0.55533 (0.3879)	0.88276 (0.20657)	0.04929(0.06082)
	3	0.73536(0.25797)	**0.8827** (0.2069)	0.56097 (0.38541)	0.78462 (0.25305)	0.01464(0.03364)
	4	0.7354(0.41662)	**0.88293** (0.20701)	0.61755 (0.39914)	0.83329 (0.23659)	0.00656(0.02075)
	5	0.68672(0.34287)	**0.7853** (0.25371)	0.61014 (0.40272)	0.73481 (0.2574)	0.00211(0.00669)
DTLZ7	2	0.80116(0.08808)	**0.90849** (0.04448)	0.74587 (0.17607)	0.80901 (0.09467)	0.84283(0.05248)
	3	0.80705(0.11318)	**0.90558** (0.04829)	0.71182 (0.1039)	0.80016 (0.11071)	0.85851(0.05549)
	4	0.83449(0.08327)	**0.92182** (0.00907)	0.70199 (0.16297)	0.80508 (0.10569)	0.84186(0.04963)
	5	0.82417(0.07712)	**0.89312** (0.06185)	0.68389 (0.14252)	0.78243 (0.11719)	0.82051(0.07021)

BIBEA-P outperforms NSGA-II in all ten problems. In ZDT6, DTLZ2 and DTLZ7, no individuals of NSGA-II cannot dominate BIBEA individuals. A very limited number of NSGA-II individuals can dominate BIBEA individuals; for example, 0.5% in ZDT1, ZDT2 and ZDT3, 0.4% in DTLZ3, and 0.3% in DTLZ4.

In summary, Tables 4 and 5 demonstrate that Pdi-Boosting is superior than AdaBoost in that it allows BIBEA-P to outperform BIBEA in optimality and diversity. They also illustrate that ensemble indicator based EMOAs outperform existing indicator-based EMOAs and dominance ranking based EMOAs.

7. CONCLUSIONS

This paper proposes and evaluates an ensemble learning method that constructs an ensemble of quality indicators with a novel boosting algorithm called Pdi-Boosting. The proposed method is efficient thanks to its dynamic adjustment of training data. It can work with a simple training problem, and an ensemble of indicators can effectively aid parent selection and environmental selection in order to solve harder problems. An ensemble of indicators outperforms existing individual indicators in optimality, diversity and robustness. The proposed ensemble-based evolutionary algorithm outperforms a well-known dominance-based EMOA and existing indicator-based EMOAs.

8. REFERENCES

[1] J. Bader and E. Zitzler. HypE: An algorithm for fast hypervolume-based many-objective optimization. *Evol. Computat.*, 19(1), 2011.

[2] N. Beume, B. Naujoks, and M. Emmerich. SMS-EMOA: Multiobjective selection based on dominated hypervolume. *Eur. J. Oper. Res.*, 181(3), 2007.

[3] P. Boonma and J. Suzuki. Prospect indicator based evolutionary multiobjective optimization algorithm. In *Proc. IEEE Congress on Evol. Computat.*, 2011.

[4] C. C. Coello. Evolutionary multi-objective optimization: Some current research trends and topics that remain to be explored. *Front. Computat. Sci. China*, 3(1), 2009.

[5] K. Deb, A. Pratap, S. Agarwal, and T. Meyarivan. A fast and elitist multiobjective genetic algorithm: NSGA-II. *IEEE Trans Evol. Computat.*, 6(2), 2002.

[6] K. Deb, K. Sindhya, and T. Okabe. Self-adaptive simulated binary crossover for real-parameter optimization. In *Proc. ACM Int'l Genetic and Evolutionary Computation Conference*, 2007.

[7] K. Deb, L. Thiele, M. Laumanns, and E. Zitzler. Scalable test problems for evolutionary multiobjective optimization. In A. Abraham, R. Jain, and

Table 5: Comparison of BIBEA-P and Other Five EMOAs with HVR

	BIBEA-P	BIBEA	IBEA-ε2	IBEA-HD2	NSGAII	SMS-EMOA
ZDT1	0.99085(0.00055)	0.99124 (0.00073)	**0.99140** (0.00053)**	0.99124 (0.00057)*	0.98490 (0.00137)**	0.99048(6.5E-4)*
ZDT2	**0.97864**(0.00211)	0.97855 (0.00201)	0.97816 (0.00141)	0.85718 (0.22804)*	0.96948 (0.00330)**	0.91286(0.09076)*
ZDT3	0.98279(0.0251)	0.98618 (0.01717)	0.98920 (0.00125)	0.98569 (0.00098)	**0.99284** (0.00202)	0.98882(0.01754)
ZDT4	**0.96446**(0.01789)	0.96062(0.03139)	0.93968 (0.03962)*	0.59782 (0.23131)**	0.95103 (0.04873)	0.71216(0.23092)**
ZDT6	**0.979**(0.00362)	0.97168 (0.00502)**	0.95166 (0.00771)**	0.96303 (0.00709)**	0.93456 (0.01069)**	0.85502(0.02427)**
DTLZ1	0.89533(0.0014)	**0.93482**(0.00364)	0.09898 (0.08299)**	0.85456 (0.14999)	0.46676 (0.46002)**	0.93192(0.06896)
DTLZ2	0.89533(0.0014)	0.89625 (0.00135)	0.89670 (0.00087)	0.88071 (0.00115)**	0.80160 (0.01253)**	**0.91111**(5.6E-4)**
DTLZ3	**0.88113**(0.0124)	0.87064 (0.03315)	0.13781 (0.05099)**	0.81664 (0.06968)**	0.76162 (0.03454)**	0.88058(0.05345)
DTLZ4	0.68672(0.34287)	**0.88277** (0.20642)	0.78530 (0.25371)	0.61014 (0.40272)	0.80650 (0.28387)	0.72147(0.37901)
DTLZ7	0.82417(0.07712)	**0.91760** (0.00504)**	0.89312 (0.06185)*	0.68389 (0.14252)*	0.84875 (0.01250)	0.76956(0.01022)*

Table 6: Comparison of BIBEA-P and Other Five EMOAs with $\mathcal{C}$-metric

	ZDT1	ZDT2	ZDT3	ZDT4	ZDT6	DTLZ1	DTLZ2	DTLZ3	DTLZ4	DTLZ7
$\mathcal{C}$(BIBEA-P, BIBEA)	**0.267**	**0.441**	**0.558**	**0.758**	**0.937**	0.062	**0.079**	0.185	**0.067**	**0.027**
$\mathcal{C}$(BIBEA, BIBEA-P)	0.199	0.114	0.165	0.729	0.137	**0.120**	0.018	**0.186**	0.030	0.011
$\mathcal{C}$(BIBEA-P, IBEA-ε2)	**0.454**	**0.693**	**0.565**	0.623	**0.971**	0.062	**0.084**	**0.299**	**0.098**	**0.032**
$\mathcal{C}$(IBEA-ε2,BIBEA-P)	0.170	0.060	0.154	**0.860**	0.0720	**0.109**	0.014	0.117	0.008	0.005
$\mathcal{C}$(BIBEA-P, IBEA-HD2)	**0.475**	**0.647**	**0.547**	0.690	**0.939**	**0.098**	**0.141**	**1.000**	**0.155**	**1.000**
$\mathcal{C}$(IBEA-HD2,BIBEA-P)	0.139	0.069	0.252	**0.793**	0.103	0.000	0.059	0.000	0.021	0.000
$\mathcal{C}$(BIBEA-P, SMS-EMOA)	**0.851**	**0.900**	**0.644**	**0.888**	**0.991**	0.080	**0.033**	**0.243**	0.020	**0.048**
$\mathcal{C}$(SMS-EMOA, BIBEA-P)	0.057	0.027	0.007	0.594	0.000	**0.124**	0.016	0.148	**0.044**	0.002
$\mathcal{C}$(BIBEA-P, NSGAII)	**0.973**	**0.965**	**0.673**	**0.869**	**0.988**	**0.526**	**0.283**	**0.610**	**0.195**	**0.497**
$\mathcal{C}$(NSGAII,BIBEA-P)	0.005	0.005	0.005	0.615	0.000	0.058	0.000	0.004	0.034	0.000

R. Goldberg, editors, *Evolutionary Multiobjective Optimization*. Springer, 2005.

[8] J. Durillo, A. Nebro, and E. Alba. The jMetal framework for multi-objective optimization: Design and architecture. In *Proc. IEEE Congress on Evolutionary Computation*, 2010.

[9] Y. Freund and R. E. Schapire. A decision-theoretic generalization of on-line learning and an application to boosting. *J. Computat. Syst. Sci.*, 55, 1997.

[10] M. Koppen, R. Vicente-Garcia, and B. Nickolay. Fuzzy-pareto dominance and its application in evolutionary multi-objective optimization. In *Proc. Int'l Conf. on Evol. Multi-criterion Optimization*, 2005.

[11] K. Le and D. Landa-Silva. Obtaining better non-dominated sets using volume dominance. In *Proc. IEEE Congress on Evolutionary Computation*, 2007.

[12] B. Liu, M. B., and A. H.A. Improving genetic classifiers with a boosting algorithm. In *Proc. IEEE Congress on Evol. Computat.*, 2003.

[13] B. Liu, B. McKay, and H. A. Abbass. Feature selection combining genetic algorithm and adaboost classifiers. In *Proc. Int'l Conference on Pattern Recognition*, 2008.

[14] B. Naujoks and H. Trautmann. Online convergence detection for multiobjective aerodynamic applications. In *Proc. IEEE Congress on Evol. Computat.*, 2009.

[15] D. H. Phan and J. Suzuki. Boosting indicator-based selection operators for evolutionary multiobjective optimization algorithms. In *Proc. IEEE Int'l Conference on Tools with Artificial Intelligence*, 2011.

[16] D. H. Phan, J. Suzuki, and I. Hayashi. BIBEA: Boosted indicator based evolutionary algorithm for multiobjective optimization. In *Proc. Asia Pacific Symposium of Intelligent and Evol. Systems*, 2011.

[17] D. A. V. Veldhuizen and G. B. Lamont. Multiobjective evolutionary algorithm test suites. In *Proc. ACM Symposium on Applied Computing*, 1999.

[18] T. Wagner, N. Beume, and B. Naujoks. Pareto-, aggregation-, and indicator-based methods in many-objective optimization. In *Proc. Int'l Conf. Evol. Multi-criterion Optimization*, 2007.

[19] E. Zitzler, D. Brockho, and L. Thiele. The Hypervolume Indicator Revisited: On the Design of Pareto-compliant Indicators Via Weighted Integration. In *Proc. Int'l Conference on Evolutionary Multi-Criterion Optimization*, 2007.

[20] E. Zitzler, K. Deb, and L. Thiele. Comparison of multiobjective evolutionary algorithms: Empirical results. *Evol. Computat.*, 8(2), 2000.

[21] E. Zitzler and S. Kuenzli. Indicator-based selection in multiobjective search. In *Proc. Int'l Conference on Parallel Problem Solving from Nature*, 2004.

[22] E. Zitzler and L. Thiele. Multiobjective optimization using evolutionary algorithms: A comparative study. In *Proc. Int'l Conference on Parallel Problem Solving from Nature*, 1998.

[23] E. Zitzler and L. Thiele. Multiobjective evolutionary algorithms: a comparative case study and the strength pareto approach. *IEEE Trans.Evol. Comput.*, 3(4), 1999.

A New Multi-Objective Evolutionary Algorithm Based on a Performance Assessment Indicator

Cynthia A. Rodríguez Villalobos
Computer Science Department
CINVESTAV-IPN
México, DF
cynthiadriana@gmail.com

Carlos A. Coello Coello*
Computer Science Department
CINVESTAV-IPN
México, DF
ccoello@cs.cinvestav.mx

ABSTRACT

An emerging trend in the design of multi-objective evolutionary algorithms (MOEAs) is to select individuals through the optimization of a quality assessment indicator. However, the most commonly adopted indicator in current use is the hypervolume which becomes very expensive (computationally speaking) as we increase the number of objectives. In this paper, we propose, instead, the use of another indicator calledΔ_p. Although the Δ_p indicator is not Pareto compliant, we show here how it can be incorporated into the selection mechanism of an evolutionary algorithm (for that sake, we adopt differential evolution as our search engine) in order to produce a MOEA. The resulting MOEA (calledΔ_p-Differential Evolution, or DDE) is validated using standard test problems and performance indicators reported in the specialized literature. Our results are compared with respect to those obtained by both a Pareto-based MOEA (NSGA-II) and a hypervolume-based MOEA (SMS-EMOA). Our preliminary results indicate that our proposed approach is competitive with respect to these two MOEAs for continuous problems having two and three objective functions. Additionally, our proposed approach is better than NSGA-II and provides competitive results with respect to SMS-EMOA for continuous many-objective problems. However, in this case, the main advantage of our proposal is that its computational cost is significantly lower than that of SMS-EMOA.

Categories and Subject Descriptors

I.2.8 [**Computing Methodologies**]: Artificial Intelligence—*Problem Solving, Control Methods, and Search.*

General Terms

Algorithms, Theory.

*The second author acknowledges support from CONACyT project no. 103570.

Keywords

Multi-objective optimization, multi-objective evolutionary algorithms, performance assessment indicators

1. INTRODUCTION

A wide variety of evolutionary algorithms (EAs) have been proposed for solving multi-objective optimization problems (MOPs) [7]. Since EAs do not guarantee the optimality of their solution sets, it is of interest to compare their performance. Several quality assessment indicators have been proposed to evaluate and compare the outcome sets of multi-objective evolutionary algorithms (MOEAs). Assuming that a quality assessment indicator provides a good ordering among sets that represent Pareto approximations, the fitness function used to select individuals may be defined in such a way that the chosen indicator is optimized. In fact, the use of performance indicators to guide the search of a MOEA has been a relatively recent trend regarding algorithmic design [2, 13]. The main motivation has been to overcome the poor performance exhibited by Pareto-based selection schemes when dealing with many-objective optimization problems (i.e., MOPs having four or more objectives) [15]. It is worth noting, however, that indicators can be incorporated into a MOEA in different ways, depending of our aim. In the specialized literature, we can find three main approaches to integrate an indicator into a MOEA:

1. **As an archiving algorithm:**
   An indicator is used to decide which subset of the non-dominated solutions are stored in a bounded archive [14, 12].

2. **As a selection mechanism:**
   The objective function is recast as the optimization of an indicator through appropriate selection mechanisms [22, 2, 19].

3. **As a set preference relation:**
   The optimization problem is viewed as a set problem where the search space consists of all possible Pareto set approximations. An indicator can be used to compare such sets [23, 1, 24].

To date, most indicator-based MOEAs rely on Pareto compliant indicators [25]. However, the only unary Pareto-dominance compliant indicator currently known is the hypervolume indicator [5].[1] The main advantage of the hypervolume indicator is that it has been proved that the

[1]The **Hypervolume** (also known as the S metric or the

maximization of this performance measure is equivalent to finding the Pareto optimal set [11]. This has been empirically corroborated [14, 10] and, in fact, the maximization of this indicator also leads to sets of solutions whose spread along the Pareto front is maximized (although the distribution of such solutions is not necessarily uniform). However, the main disadvantage of adopting this indicator is that the best algorithms known to compute the hypervolume have a computational cost which grows exponentially on the number of objectives [3, 4].

In spite of the evident disadvantages of the hypervolume, its nice mathematical properties have triggered an important amount of research, as well as the development of MOEAs whose selection mechanism is based on this indicator (see for example the S Metric Selection-Evolutionary Multiobjective Optimization Algorithm (SMS-EMOA) [2], which bases its selection mechanism on the hypervolume combined with the non-dominated sorting procedure adopted in NSGA-II [8]).

An interesting question, however, is the following: is it possible to develop a selection mechanism based on another (computationally inexpensive) performance indicator that can properly guide the search of a MOEA in an analogous way as the hypervolume does it? Here, we attempt to answer to this question in a positive way. For that sake, we explore the use of theΔ_p indicator which, in spite of not being Pareto compliant, has other properties that can be exploited by a MOEA. As we will see later on, the selection mechanism that is introduced in this paper has a similar performance as that of a representative Pareto-based MOEA (the NSGA-II [8]) and that of a representative hypervolume-based MOEA (SMS-EMOA [2]). Additionally, when the number of objectives is increased, our proposed approach outperforms NSGA-II and remains competitive with respect to SMS-EMOA, but at a much lower computational cost.

The remainder of this paper is organized as follows. We define the basic concepts related to the contents of this paper in Section 2. TheΔ_p indicator is presented in Section 3 while its integration into a MOEA is discussed in Section 4. Section 6 presents our experimental design (indicating a short description of the test problems and performance assessment indicators adopted in our experimental study) and a case study that aims to analyze the scalability of our proposed approach (regarding the number of objectives). Finally, Section 7 provides our conclusions and some possible paths for future research.

2. BASIC CONCEPTS

In multi-objective optimization problems (MOPs), the aim is to find a set of decision variable vectors which represent optimal trade-offs among all the objectives. We assume that each objective function should be minimized.

The most commonly adopted approach for solving MOPs is to compare their decision variable vectors using the Pareto dominance relation.

DEFINITION 1. *Given two decision variable vectors $\vec{x}, \vec{y} \in \mathbb{R}^n$ and a function $F : \mathbb{R}^n \rightarrow \mathbb{R}^k$, $\vec{x}$ dominates $\vec{y}$ ($\vec{x} \prec \vec{y}$) if*

$$\forall i \in \{1, \ldots, k\} \quad f_i(\vec{x}) \leq f_i(\vec{y}) \tag{1}$$

$$\exists j \in \{1, \ldots, k\} \quad f_j(\vec{x}) < f_j(\vec{y}) \tag{2}$$

otherwise $\vec{x} \nprec \vec{y}$

Lebesgue Measure) of a set of solutions measures the size of the portion of objective space that is dominated by those solutions collectively [20].

Within Pareto dominance, we can distinguish between *strong* dominance and *weak* dominance.

DEFINITION 2. *A solution $\vec{x}$ strongly dominates $\vec{y}$ if $\vec{x}$ is strictly better than $\vec{y}$ in all objectives*

DEFINITION 3. *A solution $\vec{x}$ weakly dominates $\vec{y}$ if $\vec{x}$ is better than $\vec{y}$ in at least one objective and is as good as $\vec{y}$ in all other objectives.*

Neither type of Pareto dominance induces a total order in $\mathbb{R}^k$ since some solutions may be *incomparable.* Therefore, most MOPs do not have a single solution but a set of incomparable solutions which is called the *Pareto optimal set.*

DEFINITION 4. *In a MOP, the Pareto optimal set O is defined as*

$$O = \{\vec{x} \in \mathbb{R}^k | \forall \vec{y} \in \mathbb{R}^k \ \vec{y} \nprec \vec{x}\} \tag{3}$$

DEFINITION 5. *Given a MOP and its Pareto optimal set O, the Pareto front is defined as*

$$PF = \{\vec{u} = (f_1(\vec{x}), \ldots, f_k(\vec{x})) | \vec{x} \in O\} \tag{4}$$

The Pareto front of a MOP is bounded by the *ideal* and *nadir* objective vectors

DEFINITION 6. *Given a MOP and its Pareto optimal set O, the ideal objective vector is defined as*

$$f_{ideal} = \left(\inf_{x \in O} f_1(\vec{x}), \ldots, \inf_{x \in O} f_k(\vec{x}) \right) \tag{5}$$

If the ideal objective vector represents an existing solution, then the solution of the MOP is unique.

Analogously, the nadir objective vector is defined as

$$f_{nadir} = \left(\sup_{x \in O} f_1(\vec{x}), \ldots, \sup_{x \in O} f_k(\vec{x}) \right) \tag{6}$$

3. THE Δ_P INDICATOR

The goal of a MOEA is to find a set of solutions that are as close as possible to the true Pareto front of a MOP. It is also desirable that such solutions are well-distributed in objective function space. The quality of the approximation set generated by a MOEA is often evaluated through quality assessment indicators which allow us to perform a quantitative comparison of the performance of several MOEAs. Next, we will discuss a recently proposed performance indicator called Δ_p, which is the one adopted for the work reported here.

TheΔ_p indicator [17], which can be viewed as an averaged Hausdorff distance between an approximation set and the Pareto front of a MOP, is composed of two (slightly modified) quality indicators: Generational Distance (GD) [18] and Inverted Generational Distance (IGD) [6].

DEFINITION 7. *Given an approximation set A and a discretized Pareto front PF= $(p_1, p_2, \ldots, p_{|PF|})$ of a MOP, the (slightly modified) GD indicator is defined as [18, 17]*

$$I_{GD_p} = \left(\frac{1}{|A|} \sum_{i=1}^{|A|} d_i^p \right)^{\frac{1}{p}} \tag{7}$$

where d_i is the Euclidean distance from a_i to its nearest member of PF.

Definition 8. *Given an approximation set A and a discretized Pareto front PF= $(p_1, p_2, \ldots, p_{|PF|})$ of a MOP, the (slightly modified) IGD indicator is defined as [6, 17]*

$$I_{IGD_p} = \left(\frac{1}{|PF|} \sum_{i=1}^{|PF|} \tilde{d}_i^p \right)^{\frac{1}{p}} \tag{8}$$

where d_i is the Euclidean distance from pf_i to its nearest member of A.

Both I_{GD_p} and I_{IGD_p} have (weak) metric properties [17]:

- I_{GD_p} and I_{IGD_p} are non-negative
- I_{GD_p} and I_{IGD_p} are non-symmetric
- I_{GD_p} and I_{IGD_p} don't satisfy the (relaxed) triangle inequality

Definition 9. *Given an approximation set A and a discretized Pareto front PF= $(p_1, p_2, \ldots, p_{|PF|})$ of a MOP, the Δ_p indicator is defined as [17]:*

$$I_{\Delta_p} = \max\left(I_{GD_p}, I_{IGD_p}\right) \tag{9}$$

TheΔ_p indicator has better metric properties than either the GD or the IGD indicators [17]:

- It is positive and symmetric: I_{Δ_p} is a semi-metric.
- If the magnitudes of the sets are bounded, the relaxed triangle inequality is satisfied and I_{Δ_p} is a pseudo-metric.
- If $p = \infty$ then I_{Δ_p} is a metric (the Hausdorffdistance).

TheΔ_p indicator is not Pareto compliant but its properties can be exploited by a MOEA to guide its search in a proper way.

4. OUR PROPOSED APPROACH

The aim of the work reported here was to design a MOEA which attempted to minimize theΔ_p indicator. The idea was, of course, that such an algorithm would be able to operate as traditional MOEAs (i.e., that it would provide solutions as close as possible to the true Pareto front and with a reasonably good distribution in objective function space). In our proposed approach, the MOP is recast as:

$$\min I_{\Delta_p}(P) \tag{10}$$

where P is the population used by a differential evolution algorithm (in its DE/rand/1/bin version) where:

- individual fitness is determined according to an individual's contribution to the indicator
- survival selection is replaced with aΔ_p-based mechanism
- the outcome of the algorithm is a set instead of an individual

4.1 Fitness Assignment

As previously stated, our aim is to minimize theΔ_p indicator

$$I_{\Delta_p} = \max\left(I_{\mathrm{GD}_p}, I_{\mathrm{IGD}_p}\right) \tag{11}$$

which implies the simultaneous minimization of the GD_p and IGD_p indicators.

Therefore, the fitness assignment of an individual must consider its contribution to I_{GD_p} and I_{IGD_p} to properly reflect its contribution to I_{Δ_p}.

4.1.1 Individual contribution to the GD_p indicator

Since the GD_p indicator takes the power mean of the Euclidean distances between the elements of a set A and the Pareto front PF, an individual's contribution must reflect its distance to PF. This leads us to the following definition.

Definition 10. *The contribution of an individual a_i to the GD indicator ($I_{GD}[a_i]$) can be defined in a straightforward manner as:*

$$I_{GD}[a_i] = d_i \tag{12}$$

where d_i is the Euclidean distance from a_i to its nearest member of PF.

The elements of A with lower GD contributions are preferred to those with higher GD contributions.

4.1.2 Individual contribution to the IGD_p indicator

The IGD_p indicator takes the power mean of the Euclidean distances between the elements of the Pareto front PF and a set A. Since I_{IGD_p} considers only the elements of A which are closest to at least one element of PF, some elements of A may not contribute to the value of this indicator while other elements can have several contributions. This leads us to the following definition.

Definition 11. *Let Q be the set of all elements of the Pareto front PF for which $a_i \in A$ is the closest element in A. The contribution of a_i to I_{IGD_p} can then be defined as:*

$$I_{IGD}[a_i] = \begin{cases} \sqrt[p]{\sum_{q \in Q} dist(q, a_i)^p} & Q \neq \emptyset \\ -1 & Q = \emptyset \end{cases} \tag{13}$$

where dist is the Euclidean distance between two points.

The elements of A with higher IGD contributions are preferred to those with lower IGD contributions, since the former often cover larger sections of the Pareto front.

4.1.3 Individual contribution to the Δ_p indicator

An individual's contribution to theΔ_p indicator must consider its contributions to both the GD and the IGD indicators. Since the indicator is to be minimized, individuals with lowerΔ_p contributions should be preferred with respect to those with higherΔ_p contributions.

Definition 12. *Let A be an approximation set for a MOP with Pareto front PF. Given two elements $a_i, a_j \in A$, a_i contributes less than a_j to I_{Δ_p} if one of the following conditions holds:*

1. *a_i contributes to I_{IGD_p} and a_j does not.*

$$I_{IGD}[a_i] > 0 \quad and \quad I_{IGD}[a_j] < 0 \tag{14}$$

2. *a_i contributes more to I_{IGD_p} than a_j*

$$I_{IGD}[a_i] > I_{IGD}[a_j] \quad (15)$$

3. *a_i and a_j contribute equally to I_{IGD_p} but a_i is closer to the Pareto front*

$$I_{IGD}[a_i] = I_{IGD}[a_j] \quad \text{and} \quad I_{GD}[a_i] < I_{GD}[a_j] \quad (16)$$

In our proposed approach, an individual's contribution to the IGD indicator is given more importance than its contribution to the GD indicator since I_{IGD_p} reflects an individual's importance in terms of both convergence and coverage of the Pareto front while I_{GD_p} only reflects its contribution to convergence.

4.2 Reference Set Construction

TheΔ_p indicator needs two sets:

- the *approximation set A*:
  given by the population of the MOEA
- the *reference set R*:
  a (discretized) Pareto front for the MOP

Since the true Pareto front is normally unknown, an approximation must be constructed to be used as the reference set for the MOEA. Some desirable properties for the reference set are the following:

1. All elements in A should be dominated by elements of R.
2. R should be (easily) updated if A is slightly modified.
3. No element in R must (strongly) dominate other elements in the reference set
4. The elements of R should be evenly spaced.

Our proposal for building the reference set is described in Algorithm 1.

Algorithm 1 Reference set construction

1: Approximate the ideal and nadir objective vectors (see Section 4.2.1)
2: Build an upper k-dimensional frame bounded by the ideal and nadir vectors (see Section 4.2.2)
3: Fit the frame to the non-dominated points in A (see Section 4.2.3)
4: Remove duplicated points (see Section 4.2.4)

4.2.1 *Ideal and nadir vector approximation*

The approximate ideal vector is set as the known minimum for each objective function:

$$\vec{b}_i = \left(\min_{\vec{x}\in A} f_1(\vec{x}), \min_{\vec{x}\in A} f_2(\vec{x}), \dots, \min_{\vec{x}\in A} f_k(\vec{x}) \right) \quad (17)$$

where A contains all known non-dominated solutions to the MOP. An element of the approximate ideal vector is updated whenever an improvement is achieved in the corresponding objective function.

The approximate nadir vector is defined using only the non-dominated solutions in the current generation G

$$\vec{b}_n = \left(\max_{\vec{x}\in G} f_1(\vec{x}), \max_{\vec{x}\in G} f_2(\vec{x}), \dots, \max_{\vec{x}\in G} f_k(\vec{x}) \right) \quad (18)$$

To reduce the computational cost of building the reference set too often, an element of the nadir vector approximation is only updated when the corresponding element in $\vec{b}_i$ changed or the difference between the current value and the updated value is "large enough".

4.2.2 *Frame building*

In order to approximate the Pareto front, a box of uniformly distributed points is set bounded by $\vec{b}_i$ and $\vec{b}_n$. However, only the walls of the box which contain the approximate nadir vector are included in the frame. The frame is built by setting k independent $(k-1)$-dimensional walls. A point $\vec{x}$ in the i-th wall should only be added to the frame if

$$\exists \vec{y} \in Q \quad \forall j \in \{1, \dots, k\} \backslash \{i\} \quad f_j(\vec{x}) \le f_j(\vec{y}) \quad (19)$$

where Q is the set of non-dominated solutions in the current population. Since each wall of the frame has some points on the edges of the box, those points will appear duplicated.

The distance between points should be

$$s = \frac{\sum_{j=1}^{k} (b_n[j] - b_i[j])}{kr} \quad (20)$$

where r is the resolution (average number of points on the edges of the frame) of the reference set which is given as a parameter to the MOEA.

4.2.3 *Frame fitting*

Since the frame was built using the nadir point, several points in the frame could be dominated by points in the population. Therefore, the dominated points must be rearranged to ensure that none of the frame points is strongly dominated and that every element in the population is (weakly) dominated by at least one element in the frame.

The reference set is fitted as described in Algorithm 2.

Algorithm 2 Reference set fitting

1: **for** each objective function f_i **do**
2:   **for** each point x on the i-th wall of the frame **do**
3:     $Q \leftarrow \{q \in \text{non-dominated solutions} \,|\, f_m(q) \le x[m]\}$, $m = \{1, \dots, k\} \backslash \{i\}$
4:     $q_{\min} \leftarrow \min_{q\in Q}(f_i(q))$
5:     $x_i \leftarrow b_n[i] - \frac{\lceil b_n[i] - q_{\min}[i] \rceil}{s} s$
6:   **end for**
7: **end for**

4.2.4 *Removing duplicated points*

The fitting proposed before, can lead to several points located in the same position on the reference set. Such points would bias the MOEA towards sections with duplicated points which is evidently, undesirable. Thus, all but one point in a given position are marked as duplicates with only unmarked points contributing to the fitness assignment. The points cannot be completely deleted from the reference set since a future fitting could have those points in different positions.

5. THE ALGORITHM

The full description of our proposed approach (calledΔ_p-*Differential Evolution* (DDE) is shown in Algorithm 3. It is worth remarking that some modifications were done to DE/rand/1/bin to adapt the algorithm for multi-objective optimization using the proposed Δ_p-based selection mechanism:

- The creation and update of the reference set (lines 3 and 18) was included
- Δ_p contributions must be computed considering the objective function values of the population and the reference set (lines 4 and 19)
- The (1+1)-selection mechanism was replaced by an (NP+NP)-selection (lines 17-20)
- The outcome of DE is its final population instead of a single individual (line 22)

Algorithm 3 DE/*rand*/1/*bin* with Δ_p-based selection (DDE)

1: Generate initial population (A) of NP individuals *randomly*
2: Evaluate the objective function for each individual
3: *Initialize the reference set* S
4: *Compute the* I_{Δ_p} *contributions of each individual according to* S
5: **repeat**
6: $\quad \{N\} \leftarrow \emptyset$
7: $\quad$ **for** each individual $\vec{x} \in A$ **do**
8: $\quad\quad$ Pick three distinct individuals $\vec{b}, \vec{c}, \vec{d} \in A$.
9: $\quad\quad$ Pick an index $R \in \{1, \ldots, D\}$
10: $\quad\quad$ **for** $i = 1, \ldots, D$ **do**
11: $\quad\quad\quad$ Pick $r_i \in (0, 1)$ uniformly at random
12: $\quad\quad\quad$ **if** ($i = R$ or $r_i <$CR) **then** $y_i = b_i + F(c_i - d_i)$
13: $\quad\quad\quad$ **else** $y_i = x_i$
14: $\quad\quad$ **end for**
15: $\quad\quad$ $\{N\} \leftarrow \{N\} + \vec{y}$
16: $\quad$ **end for**
17: $\quad$ *Evaluate the objective function for all the generated offspring* N
18: $\quad$ *Update* S
19: $\quad$ *Compute the* I_{Δ_p} contributions *of* $A \cup N$ *according to the updated* S
20: $\quad$ $A \leftarrow$ *the NP individuals which the lowest* I_{Δ_p} *contributions*
21: **until** a stopping criterion is met
22: **return** *the final population*

Our proposed approach assumes that the real Pareto front of the problem is $(k-1)$-dimensional and continuous. Therefore, we don't expect our proposed approach to work well with functions where the Pareto front lost dimensionality or where it is discontinuous.

5.1 Influence of the resolution parameter

The resolution r for the reference set was included as an additional parameter to our proposed approach. This parameter has a strong influence on both the quality of the outcome set of DDE as well as on its computational cost. The main issues to consider are the following:

- If the reference set is too small (i.e., if it has less points than the population), then the quality of the outcome set drastically decreases since it cannot distribute well all the points in the population (the Pareto front would be under-sampled)
- If the reference set is too large (i.e., if it has at least twice as many points as the population), then the computational cost of our approach increases (because of the cost of building and updating a large reference set), while the quality of the outcome set does not improve.

Ideally, the reference set should have approximately the same size as the population for the MOEA since in that scenario, the Pareto front is appropriately sampled for the number of solutions used while maintaining the computational cost as low as possible.

We recommend the value of r to be at least

$$r = \max(3, \sqrt[k-1]{N}) \tag{21}$$

where N is the size of the population since any value lower than 3 would consider only the extreme known values for the functions and any value less than $\sqrt[k-1]{N}$ would under-sample the Pareto front. However, it is important to consider that more points are deleted from the reference set in higher dimensions which implies that, for many-objective problems, the value of r should be larger than the given bound.

6. PERFORMANCE ASSESSMENT

Our proposed DDE was tested on 12 problems from the Zitzler-Deb-Thiele (ZDT) [21] and the Deb-Thiele-Laumanns-Zitzler (DTLZ) [9] test suites. These test problems were adopted with the settings shown in Table 1.

Problem	**# variables**	**# objectives**
ZDT 1-3	30	2
ZDT 4,6	10	2
DTLZ 1	13	3
DTLZ 2-6	12	3
DTLZ 7	22	3

Table 1: Test problem settings

We compared our approach with respect to NSGA-II [8] (which is a Pareto-based MOEA representative of the state-of-the-art) and SMS-EMOA [2] (which is a hypervolume-based MOEA representative of the state-of-the-art) using the hypervolume [20] and the Δ_1 [16] indicators.

6.1 Parameters Settings

30 independent runs of each algorithm were performed with the parameters shown in Table 2. The three MOEAs adopted a population size of 100 individuals and were run during 200 generations.

DDE	**NSGA-II**	**SMS-EMOA**
$F = 1.0$	$p_c = 0.9$	
Cr$= 0.4$	$p_m = 1/\lvert\vec{x}\rvert$	$p_m = 1/\lvert\vec{x}\rvert$
$p = 1.0$	$n_c = 15$	$n_c = 15$
$r = \lceil \sqrt[k-1]{100} \rceil$	$n_m = 20$	$n_m = 20$

Table 2: Parameters used for each MOEA

The outcome sets were compared using the hypervolume indicator [20] and the Δ_1 indicator [16]. For the Δ_1 indicator, a set of ≈ 150 evenly distributed points of the Pareto front was used.

Test problem	I_{Δ_1}			I_H			
	DDE	NSGA-II	SMS-EMOA	DDE	NSGA-II	SMS-EMOA	Reference point
ZDT1	0.004625	0.005314	**0.003912**	0.870584	0.868009	**0.871766**	(1.1, 1.1)
ZDT2	0.004638	0.005488	**0.004093**	0.536988	0.533828	**0.538295**	(1.1, 1.1)
ZDT3	0.008469	**0.006065**	0.007855	0.945797	0.951098	**0.951629**	(0.9, 1.1)
ZDT4	**0.011449**	0.020748	0.053781	**0.854655**	0.845837	0.825166	(1.1, 1.1)
ZDT6	**0.003549**	0.016471	0.008221	**0.502041**	0.4823269	0.494348	(1.1, 1.1)
DTLZ1	**0.678735**	10.2047	1.426136	**1.020308**	0.000000	0.399135	(1.1, 1.1, 1.1)
DTLZ2	**0.058214**	0.074047	0.063697	0.722791	0.690814	**0.757763**	(1.1, 1.1, 1.1)
DTLZ3	**2.561606**	32.001436	11.754814	**103.861710**	0.169759	11.16606	(5.0, 5.0, 5.0)
DTLZ4	**0.058748**	0.165438	0.063790	0.719107	0.650300	**0.757853**	(1.1, 1.1, 1.1)
DTLZ5	0.297309	0.005608	**0.004923**	0.292570	0.437321	**0.439354**	(1.1, 1.1, 1.1)
DTLZ6	**0.009725**	1.379611	0.460537	**0.436414**	0.000000	0.090737	(1.1, 1.1, 1.1)
DTLZ7	0.092193	**0.085428**	0.110085	2.946258	2.933973	**3.041450**	(1.1, 1.1, 7.0)

Table 3: Comparison of the average results obtained by NSGA-II, SMS-EMOA and DDE for the ZDT and DTLZ test problems

6.2 Results

The comparison of results is shown in Table 3. We can see in this table that the values obtained by the three MOEAs are, in most cases, very similar. Thus, and because of the obvious space limitations, we will focus our discussion on three particular types of problems:

- Problems with a discontinuous Pareto front
- Problems in which the Pareto front is not $(k-1)$-dimensional
- Multi-frontal problems

As previously stated, we expected our approach to produce bad outcome sets for problems with discontinuous Pareto fronts with the solutions clustering around the boundaries of the Pareto front. Such a behavior can be observed in DTLZ7 (see Figure 1). However, it is interesting to note that the quality of the outcome sets generated by DDE in this case was not much worse than those produced by either NSGA-II or SMS-EMOA in terms of the chosen indicators.

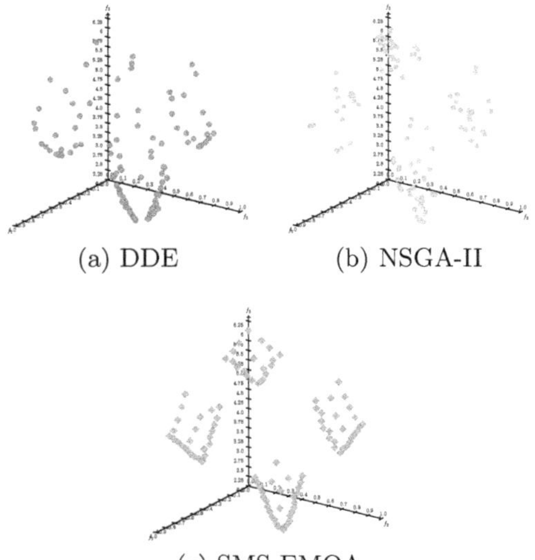

(a) DDE (b) NSGA-II

(c) SMS-EMOA

Figure 1: Graphical results for DTLZ7

We also indicated that our proposed approach was not expected to work well for problems in which the Pareto front loses dimensionality. Both DTLZ5 and DTLZ6 have this feature (see Figure 2). Although it is clear that our approach has difficulties for solving DTLZ5 (which has a bias towards solutions close to the Pareto front) it could easily solve DTLZ6, which is normally considered to be a harder MOP than DTLZ5.

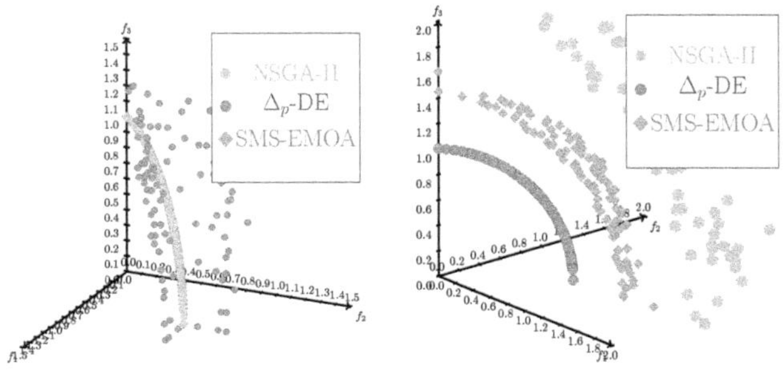

(a) DTLZ5 (b) DTLZ6

Figure 2: Graphical results for DTLZ5 and DTLZ6

Also, our proposed approach seems less prone to get trapped in local optima than both NSGA-II and SMS-EMOA. The results obtained by our approach in highly multi-frontal problems such as DTLZ1 and DTLZ3 (see Figure 3) are significantly better than those obtained by the two other MOEAs with respect to which it was compared.

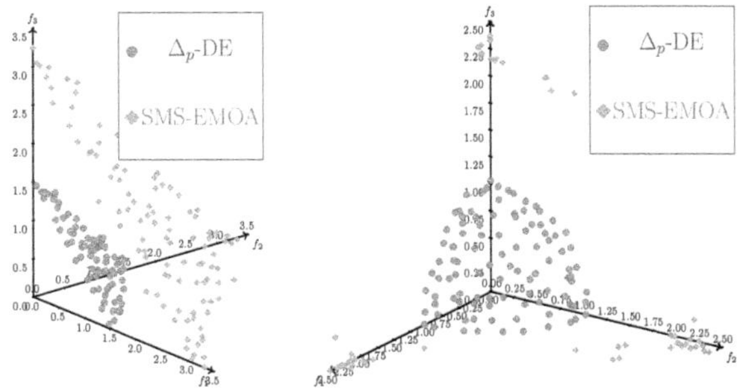

(a) DTLZ1 (b) DTLZ3

Figure 3: Graphical results for DTLZ1 and DTLZ3

6.3 Many-Objective Optimization: A Case Study

In order to evaluate the ability of our proposed approach to deal with many-objective optimization problems, we scaled the DTLZ2 test problem from 2 to 10 objectives, in order to use it as our case study. Again, we compared the performance of our approach to both NSGA-II and SMS-EMOA. In this case, however, only 10 independent runs of each algorithm were performed, mainly because of the high computational cost of SMS-EMOA. For these runs, we used a population of 200 individuals running for 200 generations using the same parameters as before but adjusting the resolution values for DDE as shown in Table 4.

Objectives (k)	2	3	4	5	6	7	8	9	10
Resolution (r)	200	15	6	4		3			

Table 4: Resolution values for DDE

The outcome sets of the algorithms were compared using the exact generational distance indicator (which, due to the geometry of the Pareto front for DTLZ2, can be computed as $\sum_{i=1}^{|NP|}\left(\sqrt{\sum_{j=1}^{k} f_j(a_i)^2} - 1\right)$, the hypervolume indicator(using $\overrightarrow{1.1}$ as the reference point), and the running time of each MOEA.

We can see in Figure 4 how NSGA-II has a quick performance degradation as we increased the number of objectives. This does not occur with SMS-EMOA or with our proposed DDE. However, it is clear that SMS-EMOA is better than our proposed approach in terms of the performance indicators adopted. However, quantitatively, the difference is not significant, since our approach reached only slightly worse results than SMS-EMOA. Our proposed DDE obtained, on average, over 95% of the best hypervolume value found by SMS-EMOA. In terms of computational time, however, there is a significant difference, since our proposed approach required less than 0.1% of the computational time consumed by SMS-EMOA (see Figure 5).

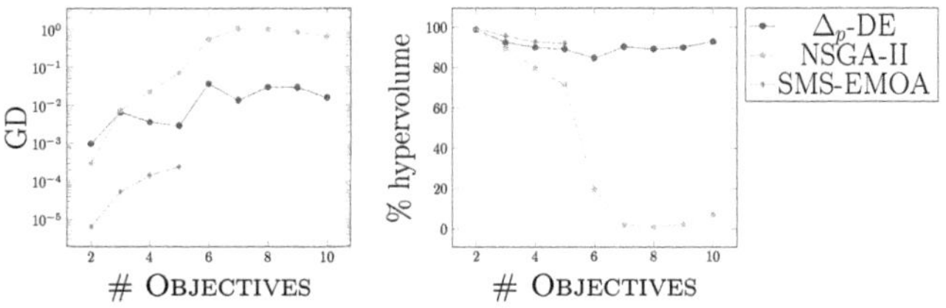

Figure 4: Indicator values for DTLZ2

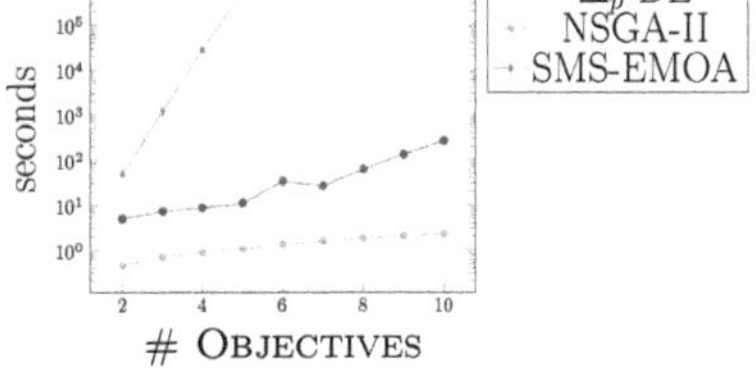

Figure 5: Running time for DTLZ2

These preliminary results lead us to claim that our proposed DDE constitutes a viable alternative for solving MOPs, and we particularly encourage its use in many-objective optimization problems. As we have seen, SMS-EMOA, which is also an indicator-based MOEA, can properly handle many-objective optimization problems. However, its high computational cost can easily make it unaffordable for MOPs having more than 5 objectives. This high computational cost is evidently due to the hypervolume calculation that SMS-EMOA requires.

7. CONCLUSIONS AND FUTURE WORK

We have proposed a MOEA based on the minimization of a performance indicator called Δ_p. Our proposed approach was shown to obtain competitive results when compared to NSGA-II and SMS-EMOA using several test problems and performance indicators taken from the specialized literature.

As we saw in our results, when dealing with problems having two or three objectives, our proposed approach has a similar performance as both NSGA-II and SMS-EMOA. We also saw that in these low dimensionality MOPs, our proposed approach produced significantly better results than NSGA-II and SMS-EMOA in highly multi-frontal MOPs (i.e., problems having many false Pareto fronts). Conversely, the main limitation of our proposed approach is that it is not well-suited for MOPs in which the Pareto front is discontinuous or is not $(k-1)$-dimensional. However, in our experiments, we found the first feature to generate difficulties to NSGA-II and SMS-EMOA as well, while the second feature did not have a significant impact on performance all the time. Nevertheless, these features require more attention and will be the focus of our future work. We believe that it is possible to improve the procedure to construct the reference set, so that we can properly deal with these features, and that will be part of our future work.

When dealing with a MOP having many objectives, our proposed approach performed better than NSGA-II and was outperformed by SMS-EMOA. However, the values of the indicators did not show a significant difference in performance and we showed how our proposed approach was significantly faster than SMS-EMOA as we increased the number of objectives of a MOP. These results are very encouraging, but it is clear to us that a more thorough study of the scalability of our proposed approach is required and that is, indeed, part of our ongoing research.

8. REFERENCES

[1] J. Bader, D. Brockhoff, S. Welten, and E. Zitzler. On Using Populations of Sets in Multiobjective Optimization. In M. Ehrgott, C. M. Fonseca, X. Gandibleux, J.-K. Hao, and M. Sevaux, editors, *Evolutionary Multi-Criterion Optimization. 5th International Conference, EMO 2009*, pages 140–154. Springer. Lecture Notes in Computer Science Vol. 5467, Nantes, France, April 2009.

[2] N. Beume, B. Naujoks, and M. Emmerich. SMS-EMOA: Multiobjective selection based on dominated hypervolume. *European Journal of Operational Research*, 181(3):1653–1669, 16 September 2007.

[3] K. Bringmann and T. Friedrich. Approximating the volume of unions and intersections of high-dimensional geometric objects. In *Proceedings of the 19th International Symposium on Algorithms and*

Computation, pages 436–447, Berlin, Heidelberg, 2008. Springer-Verlag.

[4] K. Bringmann and T. Friedrich. Approximating the Least Hypervolume Contributor: NP-Hard in General, But Fast in Practice. In M. Ehrgott, C. M. Fonseca, X. Gandibleux, J.-K. Hao, and M. Sevaux, editors, *Evolutionary Multi-Criterion Optimization. 5th International Conference, EMO 2009*, pages 6–20. Springer. Lecture Notes in Computer Science Vol. 5467, Nantes, France, April 2009.

[5] D. Brockhoff, T. Friedrich, and F. Neumann. Analyzing Hypervolume Indicator Based Algorithms. In G. Rudolph, T. Jansen, S. Lucas, C. Poloni, and N. Beume, editors, *Parallel Problem Solving from Nature–PPSN X*, pages 651–660, Dortmund, Germany, September 2008. Springer. Lecture Notes in Computer Science Vol. 5199.

[6] C. A. Coello Coello and N. Cruz Cortés. Solving Multiobjective Optimization Problems using an Artificial Immune System. *Genetic Programming and Evolvable Machines*, 6(2):163–190, June 2005.

[7] C. A. Coello Coello, G. B. Lamont, and D. A. Van Veldhuizen. *Evolutionary Algorithms for Solving Multi-Objective Problems*. Springer, New York, second edition, September 2007. ISBN 978-0-387-33254-3.

[8] K. Deb, A. Pratap, S. Agarwal, and T. Meyarivan. A Fast and Elitist Multiobjective Genetic Algorithm: NSGA–II. *IEEE Transactions on Evolutionary Computation*, 6(2):182–197, April 2002.

[9] K. Deb, L. Thiele, M. Laumanns, and E. Zitzler. Scalable Test Problems for Evolutionary Multiobjective Optimization. In A. Abraham, L. Jain, and R. Goldberg, editors, *Evolutionary Multiobjective Optimization. Theoretical Advances and Applications*, pages 105–145. Springer, USA, 2005.

[10] M. Emmerich, N. Beume, and B. Naujoks. An EMO Algorithm Using the Hypervolume Measure as Selection Criterion. In C. A. Coello Coello, A. Hernández Aguirre, and E. Zitzler, editors, *Evolutionary Multi-Criterion Optimization. Third International Conference, EMO 2005*, pages 62–76, Guanajuato, México, March 2005. Springer. Lecture Notes in Computer Science Vol. 3410.

[11] M. Fleischer. The Measure of Pareto Optima. Applications to Multi-objective Metaheuristics. In C. M. Fonseca, P. J. Fleming, E. Zitzler, K. Deb, and L. Thiele, editors, *Evolutionary Multi-Criterion Optimization. Second International Conference, EMO 2003*, pages 519–533, Faro, Portugal, April 2003. Springer. Lecture Notes in Computer Science. Volume 2632.

[12] S. Huband, P. Hingston, L. White, and L. Barone. An Evolution Strategy with Probabilistic Mutation for Multi-Objective Optimisation. In *Proceedings of the 2003 Congress on Evolutionary Computation (CEC'2003)*, volume 3, pages 2284–2291, Canberra, Australia, December 2003. IEEE Press.

[13] H. Ishibuchi, N. Tsukamoto, and Y. Nojima. Iterative Approach to Indicator-Based Multiobjective Optimization. In *2007 IEEE Congress on Evolutionary Computation (CEC'2007)*, pages 3967–3974, Singapore, September 2007. IEEE Press.

[14] J. Knowles and D. Corne. Properties of an Adaptive Archiving Algorithm for Storing Nondominated Vectors. *IEEE Transactions on Evolutionary Computation*, 7(2):100–116, April 2003.

[15] J. Knowles and D. Corne. Quantifying the Effects of Objective Space Dimension in Evolutionary Multiobjective Optimization. In S. Obayashi, K. Deb, C. Poloni, T. Hiroyasu, and T. Murata, editors, *Evolutionary Multi-Criterion Optimization, 4th International Conference, EMO 2007*, pages 757–771, Matshushima, Japan, March 2007. Springer. Lecture Notes in Computer Science Vol. 4403.

[16] O. Schütze, X. Esquivel, A. Lara, and C. A. C. Coello. Measuring the Averaged Hausdorff Distance to the Pareto Front of a Multi-objective Optimization Problem. Technical Report TR-OS-2010-02, CINVESTAV, 2010.

[17] O. Schütze, X. Esquivel, A. Lara, and C. A. C. Coello. Measuring the Averaged Hausdorff Distance to the Pareto Front of a Multi-objective Optimization Problem. *IEEE Transactions on Evolutionary Computation*, 2012. (to appear)

[18] D. A. V. Veldhuizen. *Multiobjective Evolutionary Algorithms: Classifications, Analyses, and New Innovations*. PhD thesis, Department of Electrical and Computer Engineering. Graduate School of Engineering. Air Force Institute of Technology, Wright-Patterson AFB, Ohio, May 1999.

[19] T. Wagner and H. Trautmann. Integration of Preferences in Hypervolume-Based Multiobjective Evolutionary Algorithms by Means of Desirability Functions. *IEEE Transactions on Evolutionary Computation*, 14(5):688–701, October 2010.

[20] E. Zitzler. *Evolutionary Algorithms for Multiobjective Optimization: Methods and Applications*. PhD thesis, Swiss Federal Institute of Technology (ETH), Zurich, Switzerland, November 1999.

[21] E. Zitzler, K. Deb, and L. Thiele. Comparison of Multiobjective Evolutionary Algorithms: Empirical Results. *Evolutionary Computation*, 8(2):173–195, Summer 2000.

[22] E. Zitzler and S. Künzli. Indicator-based Selection in Multiobjective Search. In X. Y. et al., editor, *Parallel Problem Solving from Nature - PPSN VIII*, volume LNCS 3242, pages 832–842, Birmingham, UK, September 2004. Springer-Verlag.

[23] E. Zitzler, L. Thiele, and J. Bader. SPAM: Set Preference Algorithm for Multiobjective Optimization. In G. Rudolph, T. Jansen, S. Lucas, C. Poloni, and N. Beume, editors, *Parallel Problem Solving from Nature–PPSN X*, pages 847–858. Springer. Lecture Notes in Computer Science Vol. 5199, Dortmund, Germany, September 2008.

[24] E. Zitzler, L. Thiele, and J. Bader. On Set-Based Multiobjective Optimization. *IEEE Transactions on Evolutionary Computation*, 14(1):58–79, February 2010.

[25] E. Zitzler, L. Thiele, M. Laumanns, C. M. Fonseca, and V. G. da Fonseca. Performance Assessment of Multiobjective Optimizers: An Analysis and Review. *IEEE Transactions on Evolutionary Computation*, 7(2):117–132, April 2003.

Local Preference-inspired Co-evolutionary Algorithms

Rui Wang
Department of Automatic Control and Systems Engineering
University of Sheffield &
Depart of Systems Engineering
National University of Defense Technology
Sheffield, UK
cop10rw@sheffield.ac.uk

Robin C. Purshouse
Department of Automatic Control and Systems Engineering
University of Sheffield
Sheffield, UK
r.purshouse@sheffield.ac.uk

Peter J. Fleming
Department of Automatic Control and Systems Engineering
University of Sheffield
Sheffield, UK
p.fleming@sheffield.ac.uk

ABSTRACT

Preference-inspired co-evolutionary algorithms (PICEAs) are a new class of approaches which have been demonstrated to perform well on multi-objective problems (MOPs). The good performance of PICEAs is largely due to its clever fitness calculation method which is in a competitive co-evolutionary way. However, this fitness calculation method has a potential limitation. In this work, we analyze this limitation and propose to implement PICEAs within a local structure (LPICEAs). By using the local structure, the benefits of local operations are incorporated into PICEAs. Meanwhile, the limitation of the original fitness calculation method is solved. In details, the candidate solutions are firstly partitioned into several clusters according to a clustering technique. Then the evolutionary operations, i.e. *selection-for-survival* and *genetic-variation* are executed on each cluster, separately. To validate the performance of LPICEAs, LPICEAs are compared to PICEAs on some benchmarks functions. Experimental results indicate LPICEAs significantly outperform PICEAs on most of the benchmarks. Moreover, the influence of LPICEAs to the tuning of the parameter k, i.e. the number of clusters used in LPICEAs is studied. The results indicate that the performance of LPICEAs is sensitive to the parameter k.

Categories and Subject Descriptors

I.2.8 [**Genetic algorithms**]: preferences/co-evolutionary algorithm – *Working principles of evolutionary computing*

Keywords

Preferences, Co-evolutionary, Local structure, Cluster

1. INTRODUCTION

Many real-world problems are expressed as multi-objective problems (MOPs), since they naturally have two or more objectives that must be optimized simultaneously. Generally, the optimal solution of MOPs is not a single one but a set of trade-off solutions. Multi-objective evolutionary algorithms (MOEAs) become increasingly popular on solving MOP. Since its population based nature is particularly useful for approximating trade-off surfaces in a single run [5].

To date, many different MOEAs have been proposed [26]. For example, Pareto-dominance relation based algorithms, e.g. NSGA-II [6] and SPEA2 [30]; indicator (hypervolume) based algorithms, e.g.. IBEA [28], SMS-EMOA [2] and HypE [1]; scalarizing function based algorithms, e.g. MSOPS [13] and MOEA/D [26] . It is widely recognized those Pareto-dominance based algorithms perform well on MOPs with 2 or 3 objectives. However, its search ability is highly deteriorated when optimizing many-objective problems (MOPs with more than 3 objectives) [24]. Although indicator based algorithms have high search ability even on many-objective problems, the computation load of hypervolume calculation exponentially increases as the number of objectives increases [17], which significantly inhibit its application. However, it should be noted that HypE [1] is an exception which uses the Monte Carlo sampling method to estimate the hypervolume value so that the computation cost is less severe.. The scalarizing function based algorithms have a competitive performance on both 2, 3 and many-objective problems [12, 16].

Very recently, a new class of MOEAs, i.e. Preferences-inspired co-evolutionary algorithms (PICEAs) was proposed by Purshouse *et. al* [23]. PICEAs evolve a family of preferences to guide the candidate solutions to approximate the Pareto-optimal front. Both the preferences and candidate solutions are optimized in an evolutionary manner. In PICEAs, instead of using Pareto dominance relation as search engine, a unique co-evolution based fitness assignment strategy is applied. The algorithms have been demonstrated to perform well on both bi-objective and many objective problems [23].

In PICEAs the evolutionary operations, i.e. *selection-for-survival* and *genetic-variation* are executed on the whole population, i.e. global operation. The global operation has been demonstrated to offer many advantages to MOEAs. It can drive the search towards Pareto optimal front more effectively and efficiently. However, a potential problem is that global operation may disregard some solutions that, although are not globally non-dominated currently, have the potential to increase the diversity of the entire population and make more contribution in the subsequent evolution [25]. In order to avoid the above problem and tackle one limitation of the fitness assignment strategy used in PICEAs (which would be analyzed in Section 2), in this paper we study how to implement PICEAs within a local structure, i.e. LPICEAs and focus on the locality of selection and variation.

Various strategies have been proposed to accomplish the local operations for MOEAs. A direct way is to do the local operations on neighboring individuals in the objective space. The earliest studies of this type of approaches are [7, 10] in which individuals whose distance is farther apart than a value mating is banned from recombination. Ishibuchi and Shibata proposed to do the tournament selection on two individuals with a close distance [15]. In another way, the local operation could be executed on individuals with a similar search direction in the objective space. The related approaches are [14, 18, 26]. An issue of these approaches is how to assign uniformly the search effort towards all search directions. Apart from these approaches, we could also divide the objectives themselves into several sub-objectives and do the evolutionary operations on these sub-problems independently. See [22] for details.

In LPICEAs, a simple yet effective local strategy is applied. The evolutionary operations *selection-for-survival* and *genetic-variation* are executed on the neighboring solutions in the objective space. Specifically, we apply a clustering technique to partition the individuals into a fixed number of clusters. Individuals in the same cluster are defined as neighbors. The two evolutionary operations are then implemented on each single cluster. The effect of the local structure is validated by comparing LPICEAs with PICEAs on the leading WFG [11] test problems with 2 and 4 objectives.

The remainder of this paper is organized as follows: in Section 2 the general PICEAs are introduced and the limitation of the fitness assignment strategy is analyzed. Section 3 elaborates how to implement PICEAs within a local structure. The experimental setup, experimental results and a further discussion are provided in Section 4. Finally, Section 5 concludes the paper.

2. PREFERENCE-INSPIRED CO-EVOLUTIONARY ALGORITHMS

In PICEAs preferences are used to generate approximation sets for a posteriori decision-making, rather than representing true articulations of decision-maker preferences for a priori or progressive optimization. The preferences are evolved as a basis for guiding the candidate solutions to converge to the Pareto optimal front [23]. Various preferences, e.g. goals, search directions, priorities from the decision maker can be applied for PICEAs. The existing one algorithm of this type, i.e. PICEA-g employs goals as preferences, where 'g' represents goals. It was demonstrated that PICEA-g not only performs well on bi-objective but also shows a promising performance on many-objective optimization problems [23].

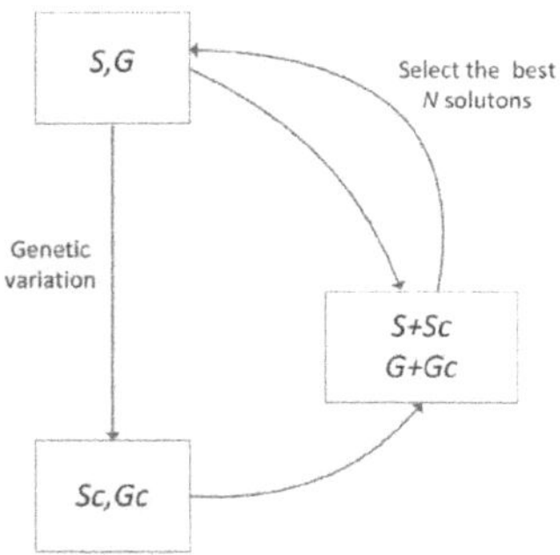

Figure 1. The flow chart of PICEA-g

In PICEA-g two populations, i.e. candidate solutions and preferences are co-evolved in the optimization process. The algorithm is implemented within a $(\mu+\lambda)$ elitist framework, as shown in Figure 1. Specifically, a population of candidate solutions and preference sets, S and G, of fixed size, N and $NGoal$, are co-evolved for a fixed number of generations. In each generation t, parents $S(t)$ are subjected to genetic variation operators to produce N offspring, $Sc(t)$. Simultaneously, $NGoal$ new preference sets, $Gc(t)$, are randomly re-generated based on the initial bounds. $S(t)$ and $Sc(t)$, and $G(t)$ and $Gc(t)$ are then pooled respectively and the combined population is sorted according to the fitness. Truncation selection is applied to select the best N solutions as new parent population, $S(t+1)$ and $G(t+1)$.

In PICEA-g, the fitness of candidate solutions and preferences is calculated in a competitive way. Candidate solutions gain fitness by dominating a particular set of goals, but the fitness contribution must be shared between other solutions that also dominate those goals. Goals only gain fitness by being dominated by a candidate solution, but the fitness is reduced the more times the goals are dominated by other solutions in the population. Such fitness assignment strategy is also introduced in [20] where targets are used as preferences. According to [20, 23], the formula of calculating fitness of candidate solution, s and preferences, g are defined as follows:

$$F_s = \sum_{g \in G \cup Gc} \frac{1}{n_g} \tag{1}$$

where n_g is the number of solutions that satisfy preference g. Note that if s does not satisfy any g then the F_s of s is defined as 0.

$$F_g = \frac{1}{1+\alpha} \tag{2}$$

$$\alpha = \begin{cases} 1, & n_g = 0 \\ \dfrac{n_g - 1}{2N-1}, & otherwise \end{cases} \tag{3}$$

where N is the number of candidate solutions. Readers are referred to [23] for more details about the fitness calculation.

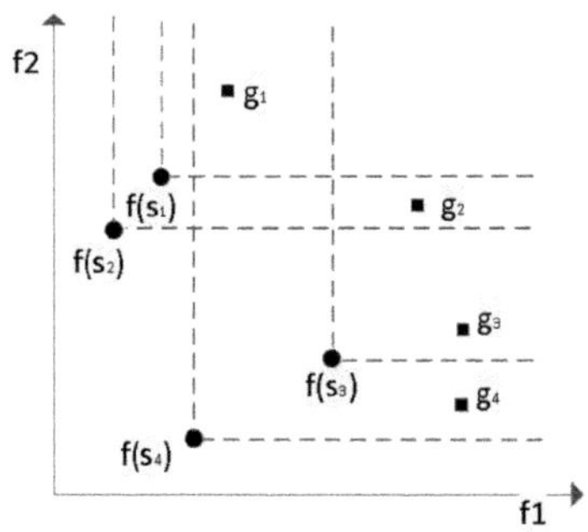

Figure 2. A simple bi-objective minimization example

Since this fitness assignment is based on a weak Pareto dominance relation. Solutions with higher fitness are only sure to be worse than (dominated by) solutions with smaller fitness. Therefore the fitness calculation method may disregard some non-dominated solutions. Take a bi-objective minimization problem with 4 candidate solutions and 4 preferences as an example. See Figure 2. According to formula (1), (2) and (3), the fitness of s_1 s_2 s_3 and s_4 are 0.33, 0.67, 0.83 and 2.17, respectively. Based on the fitness, s_3 and s_4 are considered as the best solutions, which will be selected for the next generation. However, obviously, s_2 and s_4 are the individuals that are expected to be retained in the population set (they are non-dominated). Upon closer examination, such a problem can be solved simply by doing local selection. Details is introduced in Section 3.

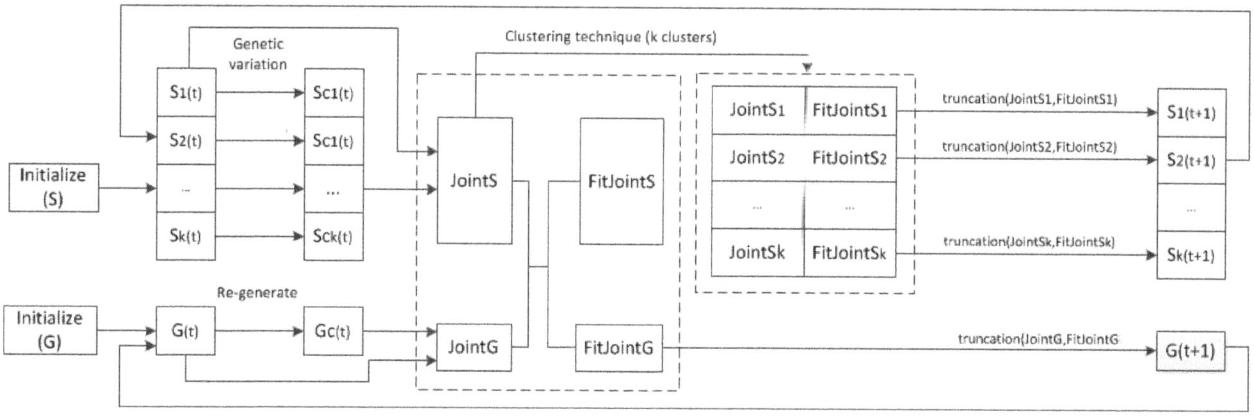

Figure 3. The flow chart of LPICEAs.

3. LOCAL PREFERENCE-INSPIRED CO-EVOLUTIONARY ALGORITHMS

In this section we elaborate how to implement PICEAs within the local structure. We choose PICEA-g as the basic PICEA and the local structure based algorithm is denoted as LPICEA-g. The core process of LPICEA-g is presented in Figure 3. The pseudo-code of LPICEA-g is provided in ALGORITHM 1.

From Figure 3, we can see that similar to PICEA-g, a population of candidate solutions and preference sets, S and G are co-evolved. However, in the process of assigning the fitness, the joint candidate solutions, $JointS$, i.e. Parents, $S(t)$ and their offspring, $Sc(t)$ are firstly partitioned into k clusters, i.e. $JointS_k$. The number k is defined at the beginning of the optimization. The candidate solutions in each cluster are sorted separately according to their fitness, i.e. $FitJointS_k$. The operation of *selection-for-survival*, i.e. truncation, is executed on each $JointS_k$ to select the best several solutions as new parent candidate solutions, $S_k(t+1)$, After that genetic variations are executed on each $S_k(t+1)$ separately to produce new offspring, $Sc_k(t+1)$.All these solutions $S_k(t+1)$ and $Sc_k(t+1)$ are pooled together to compose the new $JointS(t+1)$. The process continued till the stopping criterion is satisfied. This local operation could also be implemented on preferences and would be studied in future. Note that the fitness calculation is the same as that used in PICEA-g and the fitness is calculated before dividing the candidate solutions into different clusters.

In ALGORITHM 1, the function termination is currently implemented as a simple maximum generation number, T. The goal_generator randomly generates goal vectors directly in objective space, within bounds defined by the vectors of ideal and anti-ideal performance (variation operators have not been implemented for the goals). According to [5], local operations should be used in a probabilistic manner, and after a predefined number of generations Therefore Rate_generate is implemented as $rate = 1 - gen / T$. Local operation is applied only if $rate < rand$, $rand$ is a randomly generated number. The function multiset_union is to combine the population together. The function Partition is used to partition the current population into different clusters.

There are many clustering algorithms such as connectivity based clustering, centroid based clustering, distribution based clustering, and density based clustering [21]. In this study we use the Hierarchical clustering [19] which is one of the connectivity based clustering methods. The core idea is that objects being more related to nearby objects than to objects farther away. Thus, the clusters are formed by connecting objects according to their distances. E.g., Euclidean distance, squared Euclidean distance, chebychev distance, Mahalanobia distance cosine similarity. etc.

ALGORITHM 1: Local structure based preference-inspired co-evolutionary algorithm (LPICEA-g)

```
[S,G]= initialize(N, NGoal)
Sc = genetic_variation(S)
Gc = goal_generator(NGoal)
[JointS, JointG]= multiset_union(S, Sc, G, Gc)
JointF = objective_function(JointS)
While Not termination(S)
  [FitJointF,FitJointG] = fitness(JointF,JointG)
  rate = Rate_generate(gen)
  if rate<rand
    (JointF_i, JointS_i ,index)=Partition(JointF, JointS, k)
    FitJointS_i=index_select(FitJointS, index)
    For i = 1 to k
      [S_i, FS_i] = truncation_selection(JointS_i, JointF _i,
    FitJointS_i)
    End
    [S, FS] = multiset_union (S_i,FS_i)
  Else
    [ S,FS] = truncation_selection(JointS, JointF,FitJointS)
  End
  G = truncation_selection(JointG, FitJointG)
  if rate<rand
    For i = 1 to k
      Sc_i = genetic_variation(S_i)
    End
    Sc = multiset_union (Sc_i)
  Else
    Sc = genetic_variation(S)
  End
  FSc = objective_function(Sc )
  [JointF,JointS] = multiset_union(FS, FSc, S, Sc)
  Gc = goal_generator(NGoal)
  JointG = multiset_union(G,Gc)
End While
```

Apart from this, we also need to define the linkage criterion. Several choices are available such as single-single-linkage clustering (the nearest distance), complete linkage clustering (the furthest distances), average-linkage clustering (the un-weighted average distance) and ward-linkage clustering (the inner squared distance). Readers are referred to [21] for more details about the clustering algorithms.

In this study we use chebychev function to measure the distances between the solutions and choose the ward-linkage clustering as the linkage criteria. Before computing the chebychev distance, the solutions are, S normalized by the formula (4) which is to avoid the inuence caused by the scale of objective values.

$$S = (S - \mu_S) / \sigma_S \quad (4)$$

where μ_S stands for the mean value of S and σ_S represents the standard deviation of S.

Recall the example shown in Figure 2, the fitness of s_1 and s_2 are smaller than those of s_3 and s_4, however, in LPICEAs, s_1 and s_2, s_3 and s_4 will be partitioned into two clusters due to their similarity in the objective space. The operation of *selection-for-survival* is executed on each cluster, separately, which enables the individuals s_2 and s_4 to be propagated into the next generation.

It has been demonstrated that doing genetic variation especially, recombination on similar parents is more effective and so can produce more fruitful offspring [25]. In this study the operation of genetic variation is executed on solutions in the same cluster, which means *genetic variation* is implemented on similar solutions in objective space. Note that we assume that solutions that are nearby in the objective spaces are also close to each other in the decision space. We understand that it is not the case for all the problems. However the probability is high for most of problems.

Overall, in LPICEA-g the two operations, *selection-for-survival* and *genetic variation* are implemented on the neighboring solutions in the objective space. The neighbors are determined by the Hierarchical clustering approach. Executing *selection-for-survival* locally can compensate the limitation of fitness assignment method of PICEA-g. Executing *genetic variation* locally can produce more effective offspring. Therefore, LPICEA-g is expected to have a better performance than PICEA-g. Besides, it is obvious that this local structure can be extended on other PICEAs or even any MOEA and this would be studied in future.

4. EXPERIMENT

To demonstrate the effect of local structure, LPICEA-g is compared to PICEA-g on some benchmarks. The experimental setup is presented in 4.1, the experimental results are discussed in 4.2 and a further discussion is provided in 4.3.

4.1 Experimental Setup

To benchmark the performance of the MOEAs, the leading WFG test suit [11] from WFG2 to WFG9 for *M=2* and *4*-objective instances are used as test problems. We use WFGX-Y to represent the problem WFGX with Y objectives. In all cases, WFG parameters, *the position parameter* and *the distance parameter* are set to 18 and 14, respectively, and so the decision variable number, *var* is 32.

Both PICEA-g and LPICEA-g are implemented within an $(\mu + \lambda)$ elitist framework. During the comparison, the population size of candidate solutions, N is set to 200, the number of preferences, *NGoal* is set to $M \times 100$, where M is the number of objectives. The number of clusters, k is set to be equal to M. Simulated binary crossover (SBX) and polynomial mutation (PM) with standard settings (the same as in NSGA-II) [6] are applied for genetic variation. See Table 1.

To evaluate the performance of the MOEAs, we use *hypervolume* [29], which measures the volume of the *M* dimensional region in objective space enclosed by the obtained non-dominated solutions and a dominated reference point. Obtained Pareto front showing a higher value of *hypervolume* can be considered as a better set of

Table 1. General parameters settings

Parameters	Values
Generations, T	200
SBX	$p_c = 1, \eta_c = 15$
PM	$p_m = 1/\mathrm{var}, \eta_m = 20$

solutions from the convergence and diversity viewpoints. The *hypervolume* is calculated using the method and software developed by Fonseca and colleagues [8]. To provide additional information separately on convergence, the coverage *C metric* [29] is used. Let us denote *A* and B the sets of non-dominated solutions found by two algorithms. *C(A,B)* gives the fraction of solutions in *B* that are dominated at least by one solution in *A*. Readers are refers to the paper [31] to find more details of the performance indicators.

4.2 Experiment Analysis

4.2.1 Statistical treatment

For each problem, a number of 20 000 function evaluations are performed in each single algorithm run and 50 are executed. The initial populations are generated randomly for every replication of every algorithm on every problem instance. The approximation sets used in the comparisons are non-dominated solutions in the offline archive of each replication. The performance metrics (*hypervolume and C metric*) are calculated for each approximation set. The reference point, *anti-ideal* for computing *hypervolume* is $(2i+1),\ i = 1, 2, \cdots M$.

We firstly report the averages and the standard deviations of indicators across replications. The best one is in **boldface**. Then the non-parametric statistical approach introduced in [3] is conducted. We apply the Mann-Whitney (M-W) rank-sum two-sided comparison procedure at the 95% confidence level to see whether the two algorithms are significantly different or not. The symbol '<', '=' or '>' means PICEA-g is statistically worse, equal or better than LPICEA-g at 5% level.

Additionally, Box plots are used to visualize the distribution of the 50 performance metric values for the associated problems. The upper and lower ends of the box are the upper and lower quartiles, while a thick line within the box encodes the median. Dashed appendages summarize the spread and shape of the distribution. Outlying values are marked as '+'.

4.2.2 Results

Figure 4 and Table 2, Figure 5 and Table 3 show comparison results of PICEA-g and LPICEA-g in terms of *C Metric* for 2 and 4-objective WFG tests, respectively. Labels '1' and '2' in each rectangle of Figures 4 and 5 represent *C*(PICEA-g, LPICEA-g) and *C*(LPICEA-g, PICEA-g), respectively.

From Tables 2 and 3 we can easily observe that the average value of C(PICEA-g, LPICEA-g) is smaller than that of C(LPICEA-g, PICEA-g) on all the test problems except for WFG2-4 where the average value of PICEA-g is smaller. Also, according to the non-Parameter statistical test results, LPICEA-g performs a significantly better convergence than PICEA-g at 95% confidence level on all the 2-objective problems and 6 out of 8 4-objective problems. On WFG2-4 PICEA-g outperforms LPICEA-g. On WFG3-4 the two algorithms have comparable convergence. Moreover, seen from Figures 4 and 5 it is obvious that the median value of C(PICEA-g, LPICEA-g) is lower than C(LPICEA-g, PICEA-g) on 15 out of all the 16 test problems. Such results indicate that LPICEA-g can achieve a better Pareto approximation set in terms of convergence than PICEA-g. In other words, the local structure works effectively on PICEA-g, which can drive the search towards a better Pareto front.

Besides, the standard variance of the C(PICEA-g, LPICEA-g) is larger than C(LPICEA-g, PICEA-g) on most of the problems. Also, the comparison results of LPICEA-g and PICEA-g on WFG2-2 and WFG2-4 are converse which indicate that the local structure may exhibit some difficulties on solving problems like WFG2.

Table 2. The mean /std *C Metric* values of PICEA-g (A) and LPICEA-g (B) on 2-objective WFG tests.

WFG	C(A,B)	C(B,A)	
2	**0.2721**/0.2543	0.5724/0.2427	<
3	**0.2244**/0.2484	0.4967/0.3035	<
4	**0.1675**/0.1066	0.5589/0.1688	<
5	**0.1743**/0.1058	0.3021/0.0949	<
6	**0.3435**/0.3254	0.4732 /0.3416	<
7	**0.1739**/0.1098	0.5308/0.1628	<
8	**0.2779**/0.1446	0.6020/0.1568	<
9	**0.1233**/0.1654	0.5718/0.3534	<

Table 3. The mean /std *C Metric* values of PICEA-g (A) and LPICEA-g (B) on 4-objective WFG tests.

WFG	C(A,B)	C(B,A)	
2	0.0976/0.0788	**0.0652**/0.0520	>
3	**0.0231**/0.0151	0.0290/0.0217	=
4	**0.0127**/0.0089	0.0442/0.0216	<
5	**0.0095**/0.0060	0.0318/0.0138	<
6	**0.0265**/0.0249	0.0382/0.0211	<
7	**0.0169**/0.0131	0.0449/0.0216	<
8	**0.0283**/0.0186	0.1343/0.0952	<
9	**0.0080** /0.0068	0.0773/0.0521	<

The hypervolume comparison results of PICEA-g and LPICEA-g are provided in Tables 4 and 5. For 2-objective problems, the average hypervolume values presented in Table 4 indicate that LPICEA-g gives the best performance on all tests except for WFG2-2, where PICEA-g shows a larger mean hypervolume value. The results can also be confirmed by the non-parameter statistical test, PICEA-g is significantly inferior to LPICEA-g on 7 out of the 8 bi-objective WFG benchmarks. On WFG2-2, PICEA-g acts comparably with LPICEA-g.

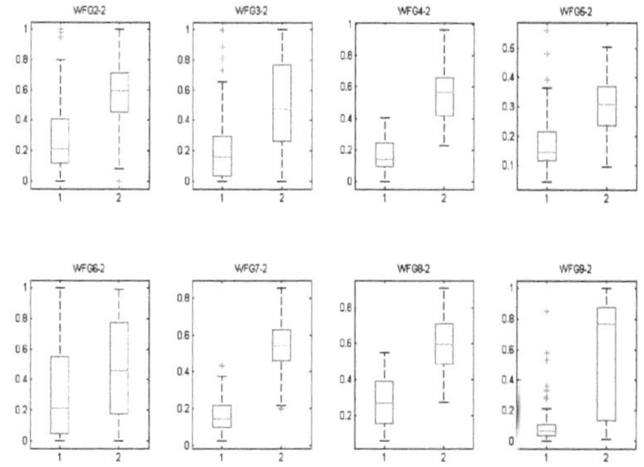

Figure 4. Box-plots of the *C metric* values on 2-objective WFG tests.

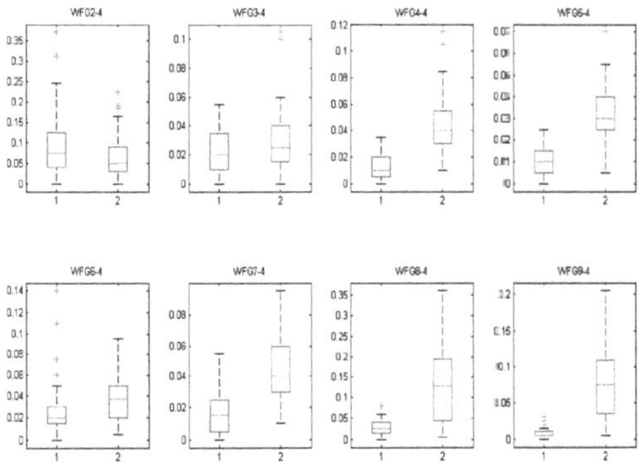

Figure 5. Box-plots of the *C metric* values on 4-objective WFG tests..

Table 4. The mean/std *hypervolume* values of MOEAs on 2-objective WFG tests.

	PICEA-g	LPICEA-g	
2	**0.6002**/0.0128	0.5965/0.0056	=
3	0.6943/0.0052	**0.6992**/0.0049	<
4	0.5376/0.0054	**0.5541**/0.0040	<
5	0.5179/0.0033	**0.5266**/0.0029	<
6	0.5105/0.0055	**0.5176**/0.0059	<
7	0.4637/0.0130	**0.4792**/0.0125	<
8	0.3594/0.0174	**0.3792**/0.0261	<
9	0.4954/0.0147	**0.5161**/0.0187	<

With respect to 4-objective WFG benchmarks, LPICEA-g continually gives the highest average hypervolume value on all tests except for WFG2-4 where the average value of PICEA-g is slightly larger. According to the non-parameter statistical test results LPICEA-g outperforms PICEA-g on 5 out of 8 test problems. On WFG2-4, WFG3-4 and WFG6-4 PICEA-g has a comparable performance with LPICEA-g.

Table 5. The mean/std *hypervolume* values of MOEAs on 4-objective WFG tests.

	PICEA-g	LPICEA-g	
2	**0.7988**/0.0038	0.7951/0.0057	=
3	0.8658/0.0068	**0.8672**/0.0075	=
4	0.7507/0.0061	**0.7662**/0.0072	<
5	0.7222/0.0050	**0.7383**/0.0036	<
6	0.7178/0.0139	**0.7184**/0.0120	=
7	0.7521/0.0120	**0.7697**/0.0139	<
8	0.5643/0.0064	**0.5947**/0.0197	<
9	0.6292/0.0067	**0.6544**/0.0135	<

Overall, according to the above comparison results, we can find that LPICEA-g performs better than PICEA-g for most of the benchmarks in terms of the selected performance metrics. It indicates that the local structure is effective and efficient. In addition, it should be noted that LPICEA-g does not act better than PICEA-g on WFG2 test instance, which is the only test problem with a disconnected Pareto optimal front [11]. The reason may be that the clustering approach used in this study is not effective and the candidate solutions are partitioned into different clusters, inappropriately. This issue will be carefully studied in future.

4.2.3 Discussion

In this section we firstly provide a further analysis on the effect of the local structure. Secondly, the influence of LPICEA-g to the turning of parameter k is studied.

4.2.3.1 The effect of local structure

The experimental results indicate LPICEA-g acts a better performance than PICEA-g. The reason might be that the local structure is helpful to reduce the formation of lethal [7, 9]. To validate our hypothesis, we check how many offspring are better than their parents for PICEA-g and LPICEA-g, respectively. We plot the change of *C(offspring, Parents)* and the hypervolume of offspring over parents on the left and right of Figure 8, respectively..

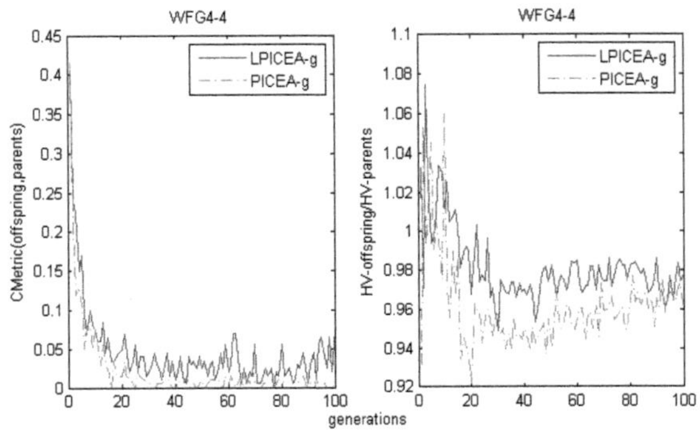

Figure 8. The comparison results for WFG4-4

In Figure 8 the *C(offspring, Parents)* of LPICEA-g is higher than PICEA-g along the search process. Around 5% offspring dominate their parents. However, the value is less than 2% for PICEA-g. The ratio of the *hypervolume* of offspring to their parents is around 98% for LPICEA-g, 96% for PICEA-g. The results indicate that local operations enable the algorithm to generate more fruitful offspring.

4.2.3.2 The tuning of parameter k

The empirical comparison has identified that LPICEA-g performs relatively better than PICEA-g. In LPICEA-g, a pre-defined value k =2, 4 are used for 2 and 4-objective problems, respectively. However, we do not know whether such settings are the best choices. It is important to study the influence of LPICEA-g to the tuning of parameter k and so to provide a level of validation to our findings.

In a similar way to the original set of experiments described in 4.1. WFG problems with 2 and 4 objectives are used as the test problem. 20 000 function evaluations are taken as the stopping criterion. LPICEA-g with different k is executed on each test problem for 50 times. Table 6 presents the settings of k . Figures 9 and 10 box plot the distribution of hypervolume results for LPICEA-g with different k . $k = 1$ stands for PICEA-g.

Table 6. The parameter setting of k

parameter	Value
N	200
M	2, 4
k	1, 2, 3, 4, 5, 6, 7, 8, 9, 10, 11, 12, 13, 14

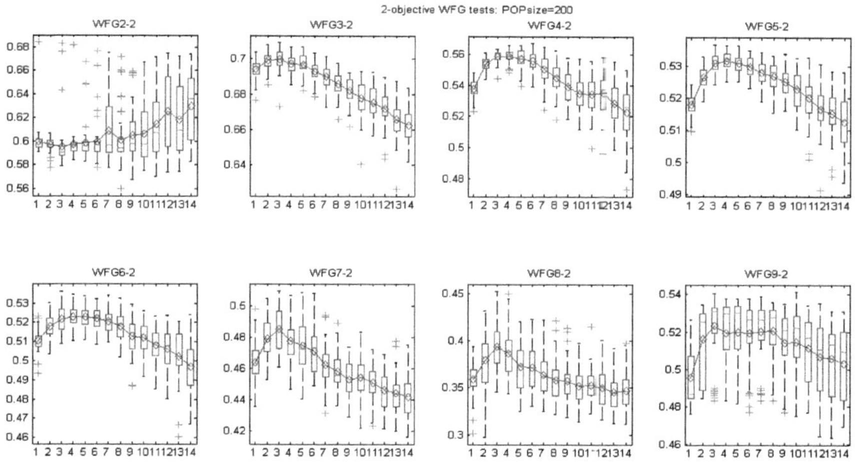

Figure 9. The hypervolume results of LPICEA-g with different k (2-objective)

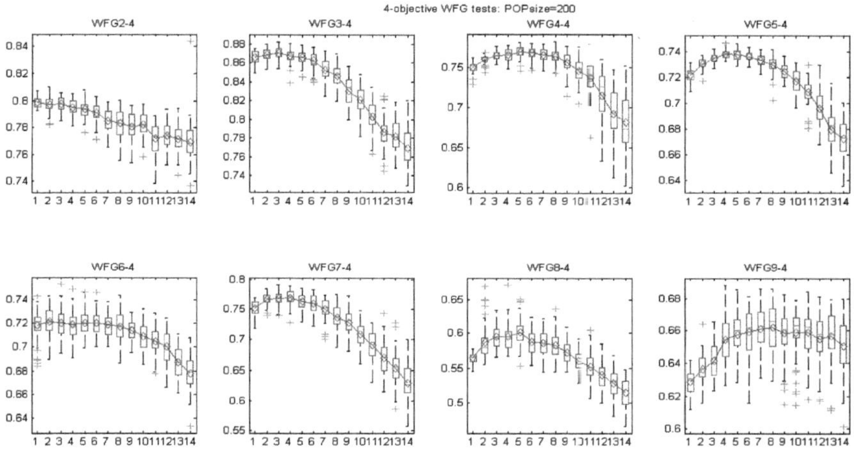

Figure 10. The hypervolume results of LPICEA-g with different k (4-objective)

According to the results in Figures 9 and 10, firstly, we can observe that it is not the case that the more clusters LPICEA-g uses, the better LPICEA-g performs. The reason is that with a fixed population size, if k is set to a large number then the number of solutions in each cluster may be very small. Certainly, the algorithm cannot find a good global Pareto optimal front. Secondly, $k = 2$ and $k = 4$ are good settings for 2 and 4-objective WFG tests however, they are not the best settings. Thirdly, for some problems, e.g. WFG2-4, LPICEA-g is not able to offer a better performance for all the selected settings of k .

All in all , various settings of k may result in different performance of LPICEA-g. From Figures 9 and 10 it is suggested that with population size of 200, $k = 3$ is relatively a better setting for 2-objective problems and so is $k = 5$ for 4-objective problems. Besides, apart from the problem dimension, intuitively, we think an appropriate setting of k may also be related to the population size used in the search. However, it is beyond the research scope of this paper but would be studied in future.

5. CONCLUSION

The promising preference-inspired co-evolutionary algorithms are firstly implemented within a local structure. To accomplish this purpose, we apply a clustering technique to partition the evolutionary population into a number of clusters. Then the evolutionary operations (*selection-for-survival and genetic-variation*) are executed separately on each cluster. Experimental results indicate that such strategy works effectively on PICEAs. Moreover, the tuning of parameter, k , i.e. the number of clusters is attempted. The results show that the performance of LPICEA-g is different for various settings of k . Roughly, $k = 3,5$ are good settings for 2 and 4-objective problems.

As for future research, the first important issue is to investigate how to set an appropriate value for parameter k . In other words, parameter k may need to be changed in the evolution process and we need to find how to adjust it automatically. Secondly, other clustering techniques should be considered to do the partition of the solutions. Thirdly, the local structure should be extended on other MOEAs.

6. ACKNOWLEDGMENTS

The authors would like to thank the anonymous reviewers. The first author would also like to thank for the National Science Foundation of China (No. 70971132)

7. REFERENCES

[1] Bader, J. and Zitzler, E. 2011. HypE: an algorithm for fast hypervolume-based many-objective optimization. *Evolutionary computation*. 19, 1 (Jan. 2011), 45-76.

[2] Beume, N. et al. 2007. SMS-EMOA: Multiobjective selection based on dominated hypervolume. *European Journal of Operational Research*. 181, 3 (Sep. 2007), 1653-1669.

[3] Carrano, E.G. et al. 2010. A Multicriteria Statistical Based Comparison Methodology for Evaluating Evolutionary Algorithms. *Evolutionary Computation, IEEE Transactions on*. 99 (2010), 1–23.

[4] Coello, C.A.C. 2006. 20 years of evolutionary multi-objective optimization: what has been done and what remains to be done. *Computational Intelligence: Principles and Practice* (2006), 73–88.

[5] Coello, C.A.C. et al. 2007. MOEA Local Search and Coevolution. Evolutionary algorithms for solving multi-objective problems. Springer-Verlag. 131-174.

[6] Deb, K. et al. 2002. A fast and elitist multiobjective genetic algorithm: NSGA-II. *IEEE Transactions on Evolutionary Computation*. 6, 2 (Apr. 2002), 182-197.

[7] Fonseca, C.M. et al. 1993. Genetic algorithms for multiobjective optimization: Formulation, discussion and generalization. *Proceedings of the fifth international conference on genetic algorithms* (1993), 416.

[8] Fonseca, C.M. et al. 2006. An Improved Dimension-Sweep Algorithm for the Hypervolume Indicator. *2006 IEEE International Conference on Evolutionary Computation*. (2006), 1157-1163.

[9] Goldberg, D.E. 1989. *Genetic Algorithms in Search, Optimization and Machine Learning*. Addison-Wesley.

[10] Hajela, P. and Lin, C.-Y. 1992. Genetic search strategies in multicriterion optimal design. *Structural Optimization*. 4, 2 (Jun. 1992), 99-107.

[11] Huband, S. et al. 2006. A review of multiobjective test problems and a scalable test problem toolkit. *IEEE Transactions on Evolutionary Computation*. 10, 5 (Oct. 2006), 477-506.

[12] Hughes, E.J. 2007. MSOPS-II: A general-purpose Many-Objective optimiser. *2007 IEEE Congress on Evolutionary Computation*. (Sep. 2007), 3944-3951.

[13]Hughes, E.J. 2001. Multiple single objective pareto sampling. *The 2003 Congress on Evolutionary Computation, 2003. CEC '03*. 4, (2001), 2678-2684.

[14] Ishibuchi, H. and Murata, T. 1998. A multi-objective genetic local search algorithm and its application to flowshop scheduling. *Systems, Man, and Cybernetics, Part C: Applications and Reviews, IEEE Transactions on*. 28, 3 (1998), 392–403.

[15] Ishibuchi, H. and Shibata, Y. 2003. An Empirical Study on the Effect of Mating Restriction on the Search Ability of EMO Algorithms. *Evolutionary MultiCriterion Optimization Second International Conference EMO 2003* (2003), 433-477.

[16] Ishibuchi, H. et al. 2009. Evolutionary many-objective optimization by NSGA-II and MOEA/D with large populations. *Proceedings of the 2009 IEEE International Conference on Systems, Man, and Cybernetics* (San Antonio, TX, USA, May. 2009), 1820-1825.

[17] Ishibuchi, H. et al. 2008. Evolutionary many-objective optimization: A short review. *2008 IEEE Congress on Evolutionary Computation (IEEE World Congress on Computational Intelligence)* (Hong Kong, Jun. 2008), 2424-2431.

[18] Jaszkiewicz, A. 2002. Genetic local search for multi-objective combinatorial optimization. *European journal of operational research*. 137, 1 (2002), 50–71.

[19] Jiang, C.Y. et al. 1993. Hierarchical clustering. *October*. 1 (1993), 1-4.

[20] Lohn, J.D. et al. 2002. Comparing a coevolutionary genetic algorithm for multiobjective optimization. *Proceedings of the 2002 Congress on Evolutionary Computation. CEC'02* (2002), 1157-1162.

[21] Prasad, H. and Punithavalli, M. 2010. A Review on Data Clustering Algorithms for Mixed Data. *Global Journal of Computer Science and Technology*. 10, 5 (2010), 43-48.

[22] Purshouse, R. and Fleming, P. 2003. An adaptive divide-and-conquer methodology for evolutionary multi-criterion optimization. *Evolutionary Multi-Criterion Optimization* (2003), 72–72.

[23] Purshouse, R. et al. 2011. Preference-driven co-evolutionary algorithms show promise for many-objective optimization. *Evolutionary Multi-Criterion Optimization* (2011), 136–150.

[24] Purshouse, R.C. and Fleming, P.J. 2007. On the Evolutionary Optimization of Many Conflicting Objectives. *IEEE Transactions on Evolutionary Computation*. 11, 6 (Dec. 2007), 770-784.

[25] Sato, H. et al. 2007. Local dominance and local recombination in MOEAs on 0/1 multiobjective knapsack problems. *European Journal of Operational Research*. 181, 3 (Sep. 2007), 1708-1723.

[26] Zhang, Q. and Li, H. 2007. MOEA/D: A multiobjective evolutionary algorithm based on decomposition. *Evolutionary Computation, IEEE Transactions on*. 11, 6 (2007), 712–731.

[27] Zhou, A. et al. 2011. Multiobjective evolutionary algorithms: A survey of the state of the art. *Swarm and Evolutionary Computation*. 1, 1 (Mar. 2011), 32-49.

[28] Zitzler, E. 2004. Indicator-based selection in multiobjective search. *Parallel Problem Solving from Nature-PPSN VIII* (2004), 1-11.

[29] Zitzler, E. and Thiele, L. 1999. Multiobjective evolutionary algorithms: a comparative case study and the strength Pareto approach. *IEEE Transactions on Evolutionary Computation*. 3, 4 (1999), 257-271.

[30] Zitzler, E. et al. 2001. SPEA2□: Improving the Strength Pareto Evolutionary Algorithm. *Computer Engineering*. (2001), 1-21.

[31] Zitzler, E. et al. 2003. Performance assessment of multiobjective optimizers: an analysis and review. *IEEE Transactions on Evolutionary Computation*. 7, 2 (2003), 117-132.

On the Relationship Between Environmental and Morphological Complexity in Evolved Robots

Joshua E. Auerbach
Morphology, Evolution and Cognition Lab
Department of Computer Science
University of Vermont
Burlington, VT 05401
joshua.auerbach@uvm.edu

Josh C. Bongard
Morphology, Evolution and Cognition Lab
Department of Computer Science
University of Vermont
Burlington, VT 05401
jbongard@uvm.edu

ABSTRACT

The principles of embodied cognition dictate that intelligent behavior must arise out of the coupled dynamics of an agent's brain, body, and environment. While the relationship between controllers and morphologies (brains and bodies) has been investigated, little is known about the interplay between morphological complexity and the complexity of a given task environment. It is hypothesized that the morphological complexity of a robot should increase commensurately with the complexity of its task environment. Here this hypothesis is tested by evolving robot morphologies in a simple environment and in more complex environments. More complex robots tend to evolve in the more complex environments lending support to this hypothesis. This suggests that gradually increasing the complexity of task environments may provide a principled approach to evolving more complex robots.

Categories and Subject Descriptors

I.2.9 [**Computing Methodologies**]: Artificial Intelligence—*Robotics*

General Terms

Experimentation

Keywords

Evolutionary Robotics, Morphological Complexity

1. INTRODUCTION

According to the principles of embodied cognition intelligent behavior arises out of the coupled dynamics between an agent's body, brain and environment [2, 6, 9, 26]. This suggests that the complexity of an agent's control policy (brain) and physical body (morphology) should scale proportionally to the complexity of its task environment. This link between control and morphology has been studied [25], however the relationship between environmental complexity and morphological complexity is not well understood.

Evolutionary robotics (ER) [14,23], the application of evolutionary algorithms to the design and optimization of robot control policies and/or morphologies, provides a framework for investigating this relationship. While most evolutionary robotics projects have restricted themselves to optimizing control strategies for human designed or bio-mimicked robot body plans, evolutionary algorithms may also be used to design complete robots: physical morphologies in addition to control policies. Evolving morphology in addition to control has the advantage of being able to discover body plans uniquely suited to a machine's given task environment rather than suffering from the design biases of human engineers.

This idea of allowing an evolutionary algorithm to control both the morphologies and controllers of simulated machines in virtual environments to produce adaptive behavior was first introduced by Sims [30]. Sims' was followed by other studies (e.g. [1, 3, 5, 7, 8, 13, 15, 17, 19, 21, 22, 32]) which also explored evolving both the morphologies and control policies of robots in virtual environments. These studies varied in a number of meaningful ways including their underlying genetic encodings, the parts with which the robots were constructed, the evolutionary algorithms employed, and the tasks investigated. However, by far the most commonly investigated task in this line of research has been locomotion over flat terrain: how far a robot is able to displace itself over flat ground in an allotted amount of time.

While interesting results have come from investigating this task it suffers from its simplicity. Relatively simple morphologies of just a few cuboids or spheres are all that is needed to be successful. However, it is of great interest how morphological complexity scales in more complex task environments, therefore additional task environments must be investigated. Previous studies have looked at evolving robots in more challenging task environments (e.g. [18]), but because these studies used body plans composed of cuboids, like Sims' system, there was a low ceiling on the maximum complexity of their evolved morphologies.

The current study aims to investigate the relationship between environmental and morphological complexity in a more principled way in order to test the hypothesis that the morphological complexity of a robot increases commensurately with the complexity of its task environment. While

GECCO'12, July 7–11, 2012, Philadelphia, Pennsylvania, USA.

it draws inspiration from the previous studies mentioned above, the evolutionary system presented here has several advantages which make it better suited to studying this issue.

One advantage concerns the genetic encoding employed and the manner in which robot morphologies are modeled. As has been demonstrated in the past [16,17] generative and developmental encodings offer demonstrable benefits over direct encodings for evolving robot morphologies. Accordingly, the morphologies in this study are created from a specific generative encoding that has been shown to possess a host of advantages over other encodings: Compositional Pattern Producing Networks (CPPNs) [33][1]. This is similar to what was done in [3,5], however in lieu of building robots out of spherical components via a growth procedure as is done in [3,5] morphologies are instead created out of triangular meshes (trimeshes) based on sampling a CPPN output at regular intervals over a region of space. The flexibility of trimeshes allows for the creation of a greater diversity of morphologies than is possible with cuboids or spheres (see Figures 1 and 4 for examples of morphologies evolved with the current system).

Another advantage of the current system is the genetic algorithm employed. Many advances have been made in developing more successful evolutionary algorithms since Sims' work, which should allow for searching the space of robot morphologies more effectively. Specifically, in this research, populations of CPPN genomes are evolved using CPPN-NEAT: an extension of the widely used NeuroEvolution of Augmenting Topologies (NEAT) [34] algorithm. Some of the advantages of CPPN-NEAT are presented in the next section.

A final advantage worth mentioning is the vast amount of computational resources that many modern researchers have access to. These resources are necessary to run large numbers of physical robotics simulations at small enough step sizes to produce physically plausible results. All the experiments presented in this paper are carried out on a 7.1 teraflop supercomputing cluster. Without access to such a distributed computing system one single evolutionary run from one single experiment would take multiple days to complete on a standard personal computer. But, when using the cluster, an entire experiment (of 100 runs) can be run in less than one day thus allowing for experimentation with a large number of environments within which enough runs may be conducted to produce statistically significant results.

The remainder of this paper is organized as follows: the next section further describes the CPPN encodings used, describes how they evolve and how they produce actuated robots. A description of the different simulated environments in which robots are evolved then follows. Next, results are presented which capture how different environments affect the complexity of the robot morphologies that evolve inside them. This is followed by a discussion of how the complexity of a robot body plan may be calculated using geometric properties and information theoretic measures. These techniques are then applied to the evolved robot body plans and relationships between environmental and morphological complexity are examined. The paper finishes with concluding remarks and a discussion of how the ideas presented in this paper may be extended in future work.

[1]For more on the specific advantages of CPPNs as a genetic encoding the reader is directed to [3–5,10,12,31,33].

2. METHODS

2.1 CPPNs

Compositional Pattern Producing Networks (CPPNs) [33] are a form of artificial neural network (ANN). However, CPPNs differ from traditional ANNs in several important ways. Unlike traditional ANNs where every internal node has the same activation function (such as a sigmoid or a step function) CPPN nodes can take on one of several activation functions from a predefined set. This function set often includes functions that are repetitive such as sine or cosine as well as symmetric functions such as Gaussian, thus allowing for motifs seen in natural systems: symmetry, repetition, and repetition with variation. Additionally CPPNs are often used as a generative system to encode some other object of interest e.g. pictures [27], 3D structures [4,11], robot morphologies [3,5] or traditional ANNs [31], as opposed to being employed directly as a control architecture as ANNs typically are. Here CPPNs are used as such a generative encoding to produce actuated robot body plans. A more in depth description of CPPNs is beyond the scope of this paper; the reader is referred to [33] for further details.

2.2 Evolutionary Algorithm

In this study CPPN-NEAT [33] is the algorithm used to evolve CPPNs. CPPN-NEAT is an extension of the state of the art NeuroEvolution of Augmenting Topologies (NEAT) [34] method of neuro-evolution. NEAT and by extension CPPN-NEAT begins with small networks (those without any internal or hidden nodes) and gradually increases the complexity of the networks over time through the addition of new nodes and links. Additionally the population is divided into "species" for the purpose of promoting genotypic diversity and allows novel structural innovations time to mature. This systematic way of increasing network complexity as needed should lend itself well to studying how morphologies increase in complexity when evolving inside different environments. A more thorough description of the NEAT and CPPN-NEAT algorithms also falls outside the bounds of this paper, so the reader is directed to [33,34] for additional details.

2.3 Building Robots from CPPNs

In previous studies [3,5], robots were constructed out of spherical components from evolving CPPNs by means of an iterated growth procedure. This procedure involved starting at a specific initial point and attaching spheres to grow outwards by means of querying the CPPN genome locally and placing newly created spheres in a priority queue whereby they could be selected as attachment points for additional spheres. This process would repeat until a complete robot was grown.

While promising results were produced by the system presented in those papers it has several drawbacks. In many cases the additional indirection added by the growth procedure prevents desirable features of the CPPNs' outputs – such as symmetry and repetition – from being realized in the resulting morphologies. Moreover, while spheres are easy to physically simulate due to their single points of contact such that morphologies with a small number of spheres can be cheaply simulated, the computational costs become too large (even on a cluster) when trying to model suffi-

Figure 1: The control environment and a sampling of the experimental environments with robots that evolved to locomote successfully in each. The ground is a high friction surface, while the blue "blocks of ice" have very low friction. To view videos of these robots in action visit `http://tinyurl.com/GECCO2012-Videos`

ciently complex physical shapes with spheres. Because of these considerations an alternative method is employed in this work.

In lieu of the growth procedure just described the current study employs a voxel based method to create morphological components out of triangular meshes (trimeshes) similar to what is done for the creation of 3D shapes in [11]. A regular grid is placed over a region of 3D-space which defines the presence of voxel locations. In the current work this region extends from -1 to 1 (inclusive) in each dimension and grid lines are placed at intervals of 0.2. This yields a total of 11 grid lines in each dimension for a total of 1331 voxels.

A candidate CPPN is iteratively queried with the (x, y, z) Cartesian coordinates at every voxel location except for the extrema in each direction. Voxel locations that exceed a predefined output threshold (0.5 in this case) are considered to contain matter, while those that do not exceed this threshold are considered to be devoid of matter. All voxels lying on one of the extrema ($|x| = 1$ or $|y| = 1$ or $|z| = 1$) are given output value 0 to ensure that the final triangular meshes have completely enclosed surfaces. Once the CPPN has been queried for every voxel location the Marching Cubes algorithm [20] is employed to create triangular meshes from the underlying voxel data. Specifically an enclosed triangular mesh is created for each connected voxel component which defines the exterior surface of a single physical shape. It is these triangular meshes which are sent to the physics simulator where they define the exterior surface of a solid object and are imbued with mass. As far as the authors are aware this is the first instance of physically simulating evolved, rigid body robots composed of triangular meshes.

Since the purpose of this study is to investigate how different task environments affect the shapes of evolved morphologies, a number of simplifications are used in order to concentrate on the physical shapes of the evolved robots and control for other factors that may influence their performance. From the multiple enclosed trimesh components that could be produced when querying a single CPPN only one of these (the largest in terms of number of triangles) is used in the resulting robot. This single component is copied and reflected across the x-axis. The resulting components (the original and its mirror image) are then spread apart by 0.2 units and a capsule of this length is placed between them such that it connects their two closest points. The two trimesh components each connect to this capsule by means of a hinge joint. These joints have rotation normals of $(1, 0, 0)$ and $(0, 0, -1)$ such that the joints rotate through the robot's coronal and sagitall planes respectively. Reflecting and copying a single component like this ensures that all robots have the same degrees of freedom and ensures that the robots are all bilaterally symmetric (which should make locomotion easier) while at the same time it allows for a vast number of different morphologies due to the flexibility of the trimesh model.

The two degrees of freedom of each robot are actuated by means of coupled oscillators. Each of the two oscillators is parameterized by several parameters: amplitude, period, and phase shift. These six parameters (three parameters apiece for each of the two joints) are directly encoded in the genome of the evolving robots as floating point numbers so that the genome is in actuality a CPPN plus a six dimensional floating point array. These floating point numbers are recombined and mutated in exactly the same manner as CPPN link weights except that since every individual possesses these parameters crossover is possible in all instances of sexual reproduction. Values for these parameters are constrained to predefined ranges: amplitude, $a \in [\frac{\pi}{4}, \frac{3\pi}{4}]$ (so that the hinge rotates between $-a$ and a radians), period $\in [250, 1500]$ simulation time steps (or equivalently $[2, 12]\%$ of the total evaluation time) and phase shift $\in [-1, 1]$ periods. Each parameter has a mutation probability of 0.1, which was chosen experimentally.

Encoding the control parameters in this fashion is done to keep the controllers as simple as possible so that fitness is primarily dictated by the physical form of the robots while at the same time allowing for diverse enough behavior so that the robots can succeed in the different task environments.

2.4 Selecting desirable robots

The focus of this study is on how varying the complexity of task environments affects the complexity of evolved robot morphologies. Towards this aim a simple task is chosen which can be accomplished with more or less difficulty in a variety of environments. Specifically, like in previous work, the task investigated here is maximizing directed displacement in a fixed amount of time, though this is done across a range of environments and not just on flat ground.

A candidate robot morphology (triangular mesh) and accompanying control parameters are sent to a physics simulator[2] and allowed to act for a fixed number of simulation time steps. Since trimeshes can be arbitrarily shaped and, unlike spheres, may simultaneously contact the environment at several points it is necessary to use a much smaller step size than has been used in previous work in order to get physically realistic behavior. Specifically, a step size of 0.001s is used in this work. Because of this smaller step size a propor-

[2]Simulations are conducted in the Open Dynamics Engine (`http://www.ode.org`), a widely used open source, physically realistic, simulation environment.

tionally larger number of time steps are needed to achieve the same effective simulation length. Here robots are evaluated for $T = 12500$ time steps.

After the robot has completed its time in the simulator its fitness is calculated. How exactly this fitness is calculated takes some care, because evolution often finds ways to "cheat" naïve fitness functions especially when the task environment is difficult. For example, if fitness only considers the positions of the robot's center of mass, C, and takes fitness as $C(T)_x - C(0)_x$ where $C(t)_x$ is the x-coordinate of the robot's center of mass at time t and T is the simulation length then in environments where locomotion is difficult evolution will tend to find solutions where C is initially raised far off the ground so that its displacement can be maximized by falling forward. This is a local optimum in this fitness landscape. Similarly, if one tries to eliminate this cheating by only considering the trailing point of the robot so that fitness is $\min p(T)_x - \min p(0)_x$ where $\min p(t)_x$ is the smallest x-coordinate across all points on the robot at time t falling forward can still be an effective solution (and is still a local optimum) in difficult environments if morphologies are created which have backwards protrusions and thus make $\min p(0)_x$ as small as possible.

In light of these considerations the fitness employed in all environments in this research is $\min p(T)_x - \max p(0)_x$. With this fitness function falling forward will not be rewarded because the maximum fitness that can be achieved by pivoting about a single point will be 0 and so a robot must actually displace its whole body forward to be rewarded.

2.5 Exploring environments

As mentioned previously the goal of this study is to investigate how varying the complexity of task environments affects the complexity of evolved robots. To accomplish this goal, robots are evolved in a range of environments with tunable parameters that can effectively increase or decrease the difficulty of the task. For each environment investigated 100 independent evolutionary runs of CPPN-NEAT are run for 500 generations with a population size of 150. The implementation of CPPN-NEAT, the parameter settings, and the CPPN activation functions are the same as those used in [5] except for the addition of the floating point array encoding the control parameters, and an improved selection mechanism[3].

The first environment in which robots are evolved in is flat, high friction ground similar to previous work. The robots evolved in this simple environments are considered control cases to compare with robots evolved in other environments. Subsequent environments are more complex: they all consist of an infinite series of low friction rectangular solids ("blocks of ice") over which a robot must locomote. These "ice blocks" are constructed such that it is impossible for a robot to gain purchase by moving over their upper surfaces but must instead reach into the gaps between the blocks to propel themselves forward. This requires the evolution of morphologies with appropriate physical forms. These "icy" environments vary according to two parameters: the height of the blocks and the spacing between the blocks. Each of these parameters varies from 0.025 units to 1.6 units exponentially for a total of $7 * 7 = 49$ different environments. The exponential scaling is used in order to cover a range of parameters which produce qualitatively different environments. Figure 1 shows a sampling of these environments and robots that evolve inside them.

[3]The authors were made aware through personal correspondence of a bug in the selection mechanism in previous versions of the HyperNEAT C++ distribution. The code was patched to fix this bug (and thus behave as described in the literature) before the current experiments were run.

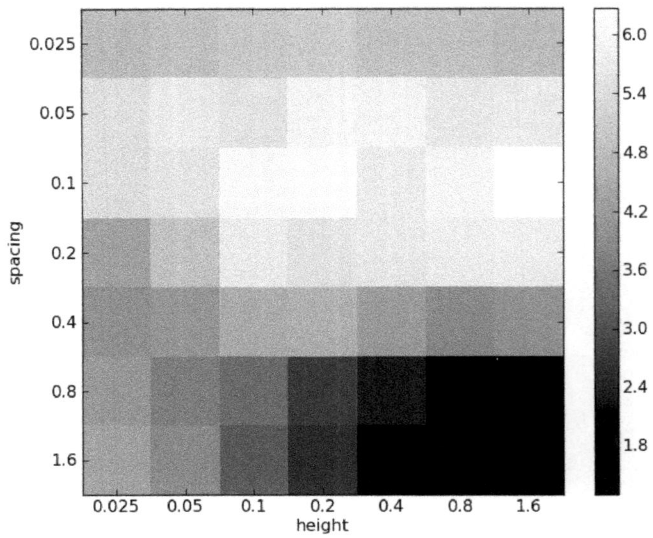

Figure 2: Mean distance achieved (in arbitrary ODE units) by best individual in final generation taken across the 100 independent runs in each of the 49 experimental environments. For comparison the mean distance achieved from the 100 independent runs in the control environment is 5.09 units.

3. RESULTS

After completing the 100 run in the control environment and another 100 runs for each of the 49 experimental environments (for a total of $50 * 100 = 5000$ evolutionary runs) the most obvious question becomes: how difficult are these different experimental environments? Or, put another way, how successful is this evolutionary system at producing locomoting robots in each of these environments?

Figure 2 shows the mean distance that the best of run individuals are able to locomote (taken across the 100 independent runs) in each experimental environment. This figure demonstrates that there is a clear relationship between these environmental parameters and the difficulty of the task. Specifically, starting in the lower right of this matrix where both the spacing and the height of blocks are large the task becomes very difficult and the robots all become stuck in the gaps unable to successfully locomote. Keeping the spacing constant and decreasing the block height gradually makes the task easier as the robots are able to navigate over these smaller blocks and therefore displace far enough to be considered successfully locomoting. Once the height has been reduced to 0.025 units the blocks are so small that the environment becomes very similar to flat ground and in fact distances achieved by robots in the lower left environments are not significantly different from those of the control environment, nor are the morphologies in this environment significantly different from those of the control environment (see below).

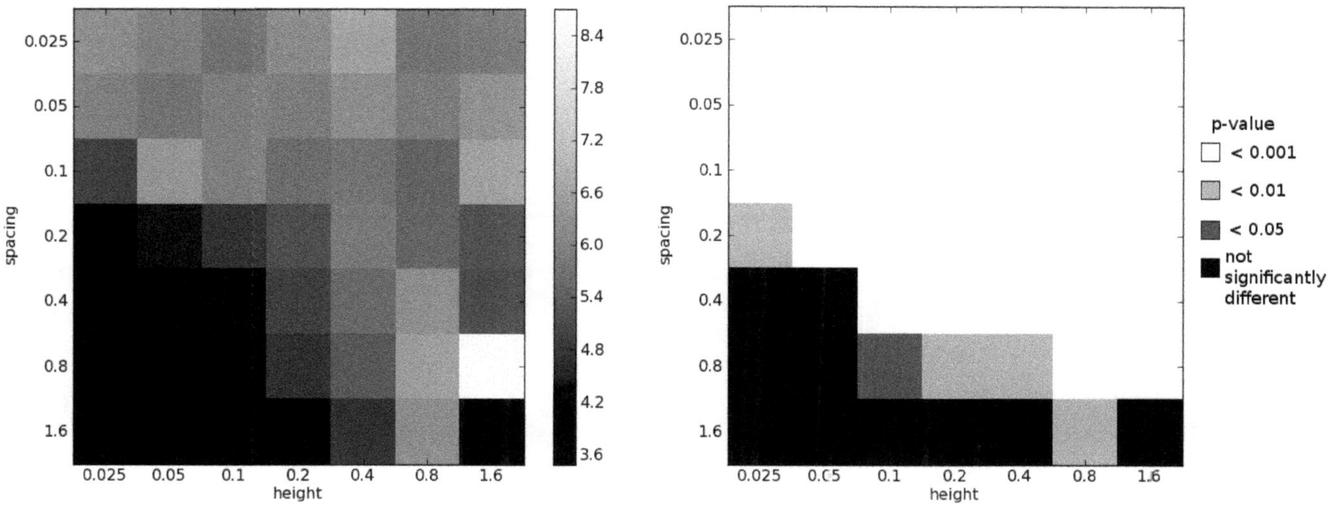

Figure 3: *Left*: Mean ratio between volume of morphology's AABB and volume of morphology itself for each of the experimental environments. The best of run robots from the control experiment have a mean of 3.58 for this ratio, similar to the black square in this plot. *Right*: Significance of the difference of this ratio in each experimental environment compared to the control environment. The ratio is significantly greater (morphologies are significantly less space filling) on average in the vast majority of experimental environments. There are no experimental environments in which this ratio is significantly smaller than that of the control. All p-values calculated using the Mann-Whitney U test.

As the spacing between the blocks is reduced the robots are no longer able to behave as they would on flat ground, but instead must find ways to move along the tops of the blocks while finding means of gaining purchase by reaching into the gaps. The height of the blocks loses importance in this part of the parameter space but still has an effect (though opposite to when the spacing is large). Here the general pattern is for taller blocks to make the task easier, probably because taller blocks result in a greater volume of space whereby the robot can reach into the gaps to gain purchase. Finally at the top of the matrix, when the spacing is smallest block height ceases to have an impact as no matter what forms the robots evolve to they can not reach very far into the gaps.

For a better understanding of how the evolved robots behave in each of these environments it is helpful to watch them in action. For this purpose, videos of robots evolved in each environment are available on the web at `http://tinyurl.com/GECCO2012-Videos`.

4. DISCUSSION

It is clear that different environments in this parameterization present the evolutionary system with varying degrees of difficulty, but do they also select for different sorts of morphologies? And if so, can these differences be quantified?

One simple way to study this question is to consider how space filling the evolved morphologies are. This can be done by computing the ratio of the volume of a morphology's Axis Aligned Bounding Box (AABB) to the volume of that morphology itself[4].

Figure 3 shows the mean values of this ratio, once again taken across the 100 best of run individuals from each experimental environment. Also plotted is how significantly different this ratio is, on average, in each experimental environment when compared to the best of run individuals from the control environment. In the majority of experimental environments this ratio is significantly greater from that of the robots in the control experiment. This demonstrates that these environments do in fact influence the morphologies of the robots which evolve inside them in quantifiable ways: becoming less space filling than those evolved in the control environment for a large portion of the parameter space. Additionally Fig. 3 (left) shows how (at least) one aspect of morphology gradually changes as one moves through this environmental parameter space. This lends support to the chosen parameterization being a good one for the purpose of studying how the morphologies of robots are affected by the environment in which they evolve.

It is clear that the morphologies which evolve in these environments vary in quantifiable (and significant) ways across this parameter space. The question now becomes: do some or all of these environments actually select for more complex morphologies than those that evolve to locomote over flat ground?

There are many ways one might think to quantify the complexity of an evolved morphology. Different measures of how space-filling a morphology is such as the AABB ratio presented above or its surface area to volume ratio or measures of how concave a morphology is (such as the ratio of a morphology's volume to that of the convex hull of its points) may all hint at how complex a morphology is. However, each of these measures may be deceived by relatively simple body shapes.

[4]For simplicity all morphological measures are computed on the single enclosed trimesh object that is produced by Marching Cubes for a CPPN, i.e. the reflected copy of this trimesh and the connecting capsule are not considered

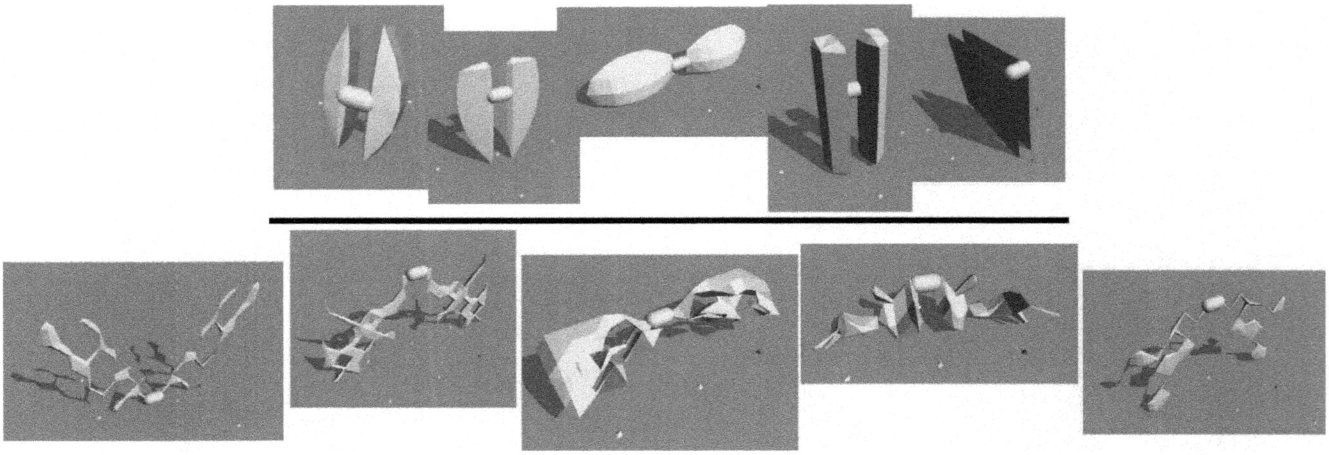

Figure 4: The five morphologies with smallest (*top*) and largest (*bottom*) values of H_Δ across all best of run individuals from all environments (experimental and control). The morphologies with high H_Δ values are clearly more complex than those with small H_Δ values.

4.1 Entropy of curvature

Instead, it is useful to think about the complexity of a body shape in information theoretic terms. One commonly used measure of complexity is Shannon's Entropy [28], which measures the information content of a random variable. Recent work [24,35] has demonstrated how notions of Shannon Entropy can be applied to measuring the complexity of a 3D object by considering the curvature of the object as a random variable. In fact, quantifying the complexity of 3D objects in this way has been shown to strongly correlate with human observers notions of complexity [35]. In the space below the building blocks of computing this measure are presented, and the reader is referred to [24] and [35] for more in depth discussions of their theoretical underpinnings.

Given a random variable x with a probability density function (PDF) $p(x)$, entropy H is defined as

$$H = -\int_{-\infty}^{\infty} p(x)\log p(x)\,\mathrm{d}x \tag{1}$$

where $p(x)$ is a continuous function. If instead $p(x)$ is discretized such that $p_i = \int_{x_{i-1}}^{x_i} p(x)\,\mathrm{d}x$ where the x_is are specific values of x then H can be formulated discretely as

$$H = -\sum_i p_i \log p_i \tag{2}$$

which is the formulation employed here.

But, what is the random variable x on which H will be calculated? Following [24,35] x will be a measure of Gaussian curvature of the points on a body shape. Since the body shapes here are built out of triangular meshes the points at which this curvature is non-zero are precisely the vertices of the triangular mesh. Specifically, for each vertex j in a trimesh the angle excess Φ_j is calculated as

$$\Phi_j = 2\pi - \sum_i \phi_i \tag{3}$$

where ϕ_i is the internal angle at j of each triangle i of which j is a vertex. This angle excess Φ_j has a direct relationship to the Gaussian curvature at that point [24]. This will be the variable on which entropy is calculated.

Following the calculation of Φ_j for every vertex a PDF $p(\Phi)$ is estimated by placing the values of Φ_j into discrete bins of uniform width (Δ) and counting the number of Φ_j samples that fall into each bin. This results in a discrete set of probabilities p_i, and Equation 2 can be used to arrive at an estimate of entropy that depends on the chosen Δ, denoted here H_Δ[5].

Does H_Δ calculated in this way capture the complexity of evolved morphologies as has been demonstrated in previous work? To answer this question H_Δ is calculated for all 5000 best of run individuals from all environments (experimental and control). Out of those 5000 the five morphologies which have the lowest value for this measure and the five morphologies which have the highest value for this measure are selected. Images of these morphologies are shown in Figure 4. Looking at these two sets of morphologies most everyone would agree that those with high H_Δ values appear more complex than those with low H_Δ values. In light of this observation and the previous work in this area it is concluded that H_Δ does a good job of measuring morphological complexity.

With the knowledge that the complexity of an evolved morphology can be adequately quantified, focus shifts to how the complexity of these morphologies varies from the simple control environment to the more complex parameterized experimental environments. From studying Figure 5 one can see that in total the experimental environments tend to select for more complex morphologies than those which evolve in the control environment. Additionally, there is a suggestive pattern across the parameter space where environments in the upper right half of the matrix are much more

[5]The choice of Δ greatly impacts the results of this calculation. If Δ is too large the majority of samples will fall into the same bin and all information is lost. If Δ is too small then the majority of samples will fall into independent bins and H_Δ reduces to a function of the number of vertices n. In general there is no optimum Δ, and since the trimesh morphologies considered here have much fewer vertices than those of [24] a correspondingly larger bin width must be used. In all calculations presented here a bin width $\Delta = \frac{\pi}{10}$ is used, chosen as a reasonable value by visually inspecting histograms of varying bin widths.

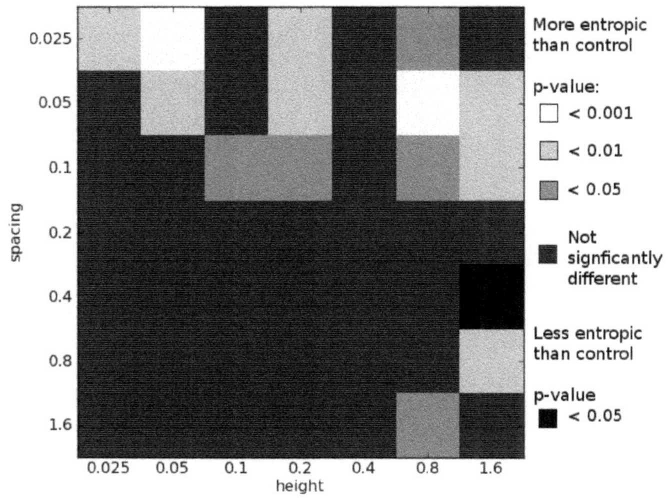

Figure 5: The ways in which morphologies from experimental environments are more, less, or equally complex than those evolved in the control environment. Plot is based on comparing the H_Δ values for best of run individuals in each experimental environment to the H_Δ values for the best of run individuals in the control environment. The more complex experimental environments tend to select for more complex morphologies: there are many experimental environments where significantly more complex morphologies evolve, while only one experimental environment where significantly less complex morphologies evolve. All p-values calculated using the Mann-Whitney U test.

likely to produce complex morphologies, and this coincides with where the AABB ratios are most significantly different from the control experiment. The upper right of the matrix contains the environments with narrow gaps and higher obstacles, and thus present the most different task from the control environment, so it makes sense that this is where the most different morphologies would evolve. In addition, it makes sense that additional complexity would be needed to succeed in these environments because morphologies with more simple sphere or block like components are unable to reach into the gaps to gain purchase. Therefore evolution must find more complex morphologies to be successful.

5. CONCLUSION

This work has investigated the relationship between environmental and morphological complexity in evolved robots. Using an information theoretic measure of morphological complexity, known to correlate with human perceptions of complexity, it was demonstrated that many complex environments create evolutionary pressures which lead to the evolution of more complex body forms than those of robots evolved in the simple, flat ground environment traditionally investigated. This lends support to the hypothesis that the morphological complexity of a robot should increase commensurately with the complexity of its task environment.

A number of simplifications were made so that the analyses could be focused on the shape of the evolved morphologies. These simplifications included limiting the morphologies to a specific configuration of connectivity with a single connected trimesh reflected and copied and connected via hinge joints to an intermediary capsule, and using an open loop control strategy of coupled oscillators with a small number of evolvable parameters. While the robots evolved in this manner were able to successfully locomote in the majority of environments investigated it would be interesting to investigate how removing these simplifications would affect the presented results. Perhaps with a more sophisticated controller and/or a greater number of degrees of freedom it would be possible to evolve robots which succeed in the most challenging environments or that are able to succeed in other environments without such an increase in morphological complexity: could increased control complexity supplant the need for increased morphological complexity? However, quantifying the complexity of such robots will require extending the entropy measure presented here to take into account additional factors such as the number and placement of additional degrees of freedom and the complexity of their controller architectures.

The estimation of probability density functions used here in calculating H_Δ could also be improved. As mentioned above, the chosen method depends heavily on selecting a good bin width Δ. Alternative means of estimating a PDF such as kernel density estimation [29] may provide a better means of calculating this measure and will be investigated in future research.

Finally, it will be interesting to see how the morphologies of evolved robots vary in other environments not experimented with in this work. Do certain environments drive an increase in morphological complexity while others drive an increase in complexity of the control strategy or sensory system? Could measuring the complexity of robots while they are evolving be used to inform the evolutionary search process in a meaningful way? Could environments co-evolve along with morphologies much like natural environments change over time, and therefore implicitly drive the evolution of complexity in a more principled way? All of these are fruitful areas for future research.

6. ACKNOWLEDGMENTS

This work was supported by National Science Foundation Grant PECASE-0953837 and DARPA M3 grant W911NF-1-11-0076.

The authors also acknowledge the Vermont Advanced Computing Core which is supported by NASA (NNX 06AC88G), at the University of Vermont for providing High Performance Computing resources that have contributed to the research results reported within this paper.

7. REFERENCES

[1] A. Adamatzky, M. Komosinski, and S. Ulatowski. Software review: Framsticks. *Kybernetes: The International Journal of Systems & Cybernetics*, 29(9/10):1344–1351, 2000.

[2] M. Anderson. Embodied Cognition: A field guide. *Artificial Intelligence*, 149(1):91–130, 2003.

[3] J. E. Auerbach and J. C. Bongard. Dynamic Resolution in the Co-Evolution of Morphology and Control. In *Artificial Life XII: Proceedings of the Twelfth International Conference on the Simulation and Synthesis of Living Systems*, 2010.

[4] J. E. Auerbach and J. C. Bongard. Evolving CPPNs to Grow Three-Dimensional Physical Structures. In *Proceedings of the Genetic and Evolutionary Computation Conference (GECCO)*, 2010.

[5] J. E. Auerbach and J. C. Bongard. Evolving Complete Robots with CPPN-NEAT: The Utility of Recurrent Connections. In *Proceedings of the Genetic and Evolutionary Computation Conference (GECCO)*, 2011.

[6] R. D. Beer. The dynamics of brain-body-environment systems: A status report. In P. Calvo and A. Gomila, editors, *Handbook of Cognitive Science: An Embodied Approach*, pages 99–120. Elsevier, 2008.

[7] J. Bongard and R. Pfeifer. Repeated structure and dissociation of genotypic and phenotypic complexity in Artificial Ontogeny. *Proceedings of The Genetic and Evolutionary Computation Conference (GECCO 2001)*, pages 829–836, 2001.

[8] J. C. Bongard. Evolving modular genetic regulatory networks. In *Proceedings of The IEEE 2002 Congress on Evolutionary Computation (CEC2002)*, pages 1872–1877, 2002.

[9] R. Brooks. *Cambrian intelligence.* MIT Press Cambridge, Mass, 1999.

[10] J. Clune, B. Beckmann, C. Ofria, and R. Pennock. Evolving Coordinated Quadruped Gaits with the HyperNEAT Generative Encoding. In *Proceedings of the IEEE Congress on Evolutionary Computing*, pages 2764–2771, 2009.

[11] J. Clune and H. Lipson. Evolving 3d objects with a generative encoding inspired by developmental biology. In *Proceedings of the Eleventh European Conference on Artificial Life (ECAL)*, pages 144–148, 2011.

[12] J. Clune, R. T. Pennock, and C. Ofria. The sensitivity of hyperneat to different geometric representations of a problem. In *Proceedings of the Genetic and Evolutionary Computation Conference*, 2009.

[13] P. Eggenberger. Evolving morphologies of simulated 3D organisms based on differential gene expression. *Procs. of the Fourth European Conf. on Artificial Life*, pages 205–213, 1997.

[14] I. Harvey, P. Husbands, D. Cliff, A. Thompson, and N. Jakobi. Evolutionary robotics: the sussex approach. *Robotics and Autonomous Systems*, 20:205–224, 1997.

[15] G. Hornby and J. Pollack. Body-brain co-evolution using l-systems as a generative encoding. *Proceedings of the Genetic and Evolutionary Computation Conference (GECCO-2001)*, pages 868–875, 2001.

[16] G. Hornby and J. Pollack. Evolving L-systems to generate virtual creatures. *Computers & Graphics*, 25(6):1041–1048, 2001.

[17] M. Komosinski and A. Rotaru-Varga. Comparison of different genotype encodings for simulated three-dimensional agents. *Artif. Life*, 7(4):395–418, 2002.

[18] N. Lassabe, H. Luga, and Y. Duthen. A new step for artificial creatures. In *Proceedings of 1st IEEE Conference on Artificial Life (IEEE-ALife âĂŹ07)*, pages 243–249. IEEE Press, 2007.

[19] H. Lipson and J. B. Pollack. Automatic design and manufacture of artificial lifeforms. *Nature*, 406:974–978, 2000.

[20] W. E. Lorensen and H. E. Cline. Marching cubes: A high resolution 3d surface construction algorithm. *SIGGRAPH Comput. Graph.*, 21:163–169, August 1987.

[21] H. H. Lund and J. W. P. Lee. Evolving robot morphology. *IEEE International Conference on Evolutionary Computation*, pages 197–202, 1997.

[22] C. Mautner and R. Belew. Evolving robot morphology and control. *Artificial Life and Robotics*, 4(3):130–136, 2000.

[23] S. Nolfi and D. Floreano. *Evolutionary Robotics: The Biology,Intelligence,and Technology.* MIT Press, Cambridge, MA, USA, 2000.

[24] D. Page, A. Koschan, S. Sukumar, B. Roui-Abidi, and M. Abidi. Shape analysis algorithm based on information theory. In *Image Processing, 2003. ICIP 2003. Proceedings. 2003 International Conference on*, volume 1, pages I – 229–32 vol.1, sept. 2003.

[25] C. Paul. Morphological computation: A basis for the analysis of morphology and control requirements. *Robotics and Autonomous Systems*, 54(8):619–630, 2006.

[26] R. Pfeifer and J. Bongard. *How the Body Shapes the Way We Think: A New View of Intelligence.* MIT Press, 2006.

[27] J. Secretan, N. Beato, D. B. D'Ambrosio, A. Rodriguez, A. Campbell, J. T. Folsom-Kovarik, and K. O. Stanley. Picbreeder: A case study in collaborative evolutionary exploration of design space. *Evolutionary Computation Journal*, pages 373–403, 2011.

[28] C. E. Shannon. A mathematical theory of communication. *Bell system technical journal*, 27, 1948.

[29] B. W. Silverman. *Density estimation: for statistics and data analysis.* London, 1986.

[30] K. Sims. Evolving 3D morphology and behaviour by competition. *Artificial Life IV*, pages 28–39, 1994.

[31] K. Stanley, D. D'Ambrosio, and J. Gauci. A Hypercube-Based encoding for evolving Large-Scale neural networks. *Artificial Life*, 15(2):185–212, 2009.

[32] K. Stanley and R. Miikkulainen. A taxonomy for artificial embryogeny. *Artificial Life*, 9(2):93–130, 2003.

[33] K. O. Stanley. Compositional pattern producing networks: A novel abstraction of development. *Genetic Programming and Evolvable Machines*, 8(2):131–162, 2007.

[34] K. O. Stanley and R. Miikkulainen. Evolving neural networks through augmenting topologies. *Evolutionary Computation*, 10:2002, 2001.

[35] S. Sukumar, D. Page, A. Koschan, and M. Abidi. Towards understanding what makes 3d objects appear simple or complex. In *IEEE Conference on Computer Vision and Pattern Recognition CVPR 2008, Sixth IEEE Workshop on Perceptual Organization in Computer Vision (POCV)*, 2008.

A Manifold Operator Representation for Adaptive Design *

Jacob Beal
Raytheon BBN Technologies
Cambridge, MA, USA 02138
jakebeal@bbn.com

Hala Mostafa
Raytheon BBN Technologies
Cambridge, MA, USA 02138
hmostafa@bbn.com

Annan Mozeika
iRobot Corporation
Bedford, MA, USA 01730
amozeika@irobot.com

Benjamin Axelrod
iRobot Corporation
Bedford, MA, USA 01730
baxelrod@irobot.com

Aaron Adler
Raytheon BBN Technologies
Cambridge, MA, USA 02138
aadler@bbn.com

Gretchen Markiewicz
Raytheon BBN Technologies
Cambridge, MA, USA 02138
gmarkiew@bbn.com

ABSTRACT

Many natural organisms exhibit canalization: small genetic changes are accommodated by adaptation in other systems that interact with them. Engineered systems, however, are typically quite brittle, making design automation extremely difficult. We propose to address this problem with a generative representation of design based on manifold operators. The operator set we propose combines the intuitive simplicity of top-down rewrite rules with the flexibility and distortion tolerance of bottom-up GRN-based models. An embryogeny specified using this representation thus places constraints on a developing design, rather than specifying a fixed body plan, allowing canalization processes to modulate the design as it continues to develop. We demonstrate our ideas in the domain of electromechanical design and validate them with simulations at different levels of abstraction.

Categories and Subject Descriptors

D.2.2 [**Software Engineering**]: Design Tools and Techniques; I.2.9 [**Artificial Intelligence**]: Robotics

General Terms

Design

Keywords

Morphogenetic Engineering, Generative Design, Implicit Embryogeny, Generative Representation, Functional Blueprints

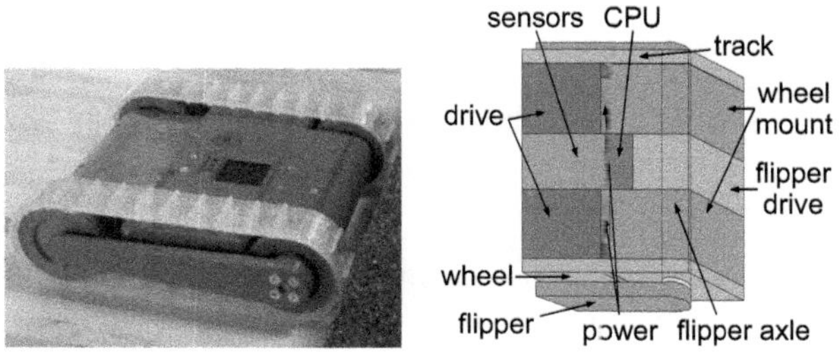

(a) miniDroid (b) Partly developed embryo

Figure 1: We investigate embryogeny as a representation for adaptable structures using the example of a "miniDroid" robot (a), beginning by developing a body plan (b) from an undifferentiated egg.

1. INTRODUCTION

When human engineers make modifications to a design, not all parameters are treated equally. Instead, a design expert typically begins by addressing only the parameters most critical to the desired modification. Constraints between the elements that are modified and other parts of the design then imply other changes, which may ripple throughout the entire design. In fact, human engineers consider many of these implicit changes to not be changes at all, but in fact to be *keeping the same design*.

This suggests that design evolvability by any automated system, from evolutionary algorithms to knowledge-based design tools, might be greatly enhanced by using a representation capturing relations exploited by a human designer. This would allow each element to adjust its phenotype for compatibility with other elements it interacts with.

In natural biological organisms, the processes of morphogenesis adapt structure to environment remarkably well on both an individual and evolutionary time scale. Significantly for our purposes, small genetic or somatic changes can produce cascading effects during development in other systems that interact with them. This ability to accommodate small changes without causing related components to fail is termed *canalization* [29]. Great strides have been made in understanding the building blocks of biological adaptivity and the ties between morphogenesis and evolution [9, 19], and there have been a number of systems that apply ideas from morphogenesis to particular aspects of design (see Section 2). No clear framework has yet been developed, however, for exploiting morphogenetic principles in the creation of general engineered systems.

In this paper, we present a generative representation for

*Sponsored by DARPA under contract W91CRB-11-C-0052; views and conclusions contained in this document are those of the authors and not DARPA or the U.S. Gov't.

GECCO'12, July 7-11, 2012, Philadelphia, Pennsylvania, USA.

electromechanical system designs, using as an example a small ground robot, the "miniDroid" (Figure 1). Generative representations have the advantages of being compact and capable of representing highly complex phenotypes. Such representations are typically implemented either as top-down rewrite rules or bottom-up cellular models. The former has the advantage of being more intuitive to craft, while the latter exhibit more tolerance to distortions. Our encoding has the best of both worlds because it is rule based, but the rules invoke manifold operators that are robust to distortions (executing correctly regardless of the geometry).

Our approach promotes canalization; the result of our embryogeny is not the final body plan, but a web of constraints and relations among design parameters. This might be applied to both the form of a body and its controller, though in this paper we restrict ourselves to considering only the form. This affords more freedom to the design process to adapt the design by changing key parameters and having the rest be derived in accordance with the constraints. We suggest that this may allow for more flexible and efficient designs, where much of the process of adaptation can be carried out autonomously.

We instantiate our morphogenetic model framework with a candidate basis set of five manifold geometry operators, inspired by common processes in the embryogeny of animals. Such programs might then be integrated together with functional blueprints [1, 3] to facilitate design adaptation. Finally, we use the miniDroid for preliminary validation of this approach, creating a program for development of a robot body plan and testing the approach with simulations at several levels of abstraction.

2. RELATED WORK

Automated design of electrical and mechanical systems has long been a topic of interest. While there has been much work in the area (e.g., [8], [16], [14]), it has faced significant obstacles from the complexity of searching the space of possible designs. A primary aim of our work is a principled reduction of this design space.

This aim matches the goals of "morphogenetic engineering" as proposed by Doursat [12] and for robotics in [18] and [28]. Initial work towards a framework for morphogenetic engineering has been laid out for evolvable pattern formation in [11]. Meng et al.'s morphogenetic approach [26] to modular robotics combines a rule-based controller to generate desired patterns with a simulated genetic regulatory network to coordinate the configuration of robot modules. A more formal mathematical model can be found in [25], though the representational consequences are not explored.

An embryogeny is the process of growth that defines how a genotype is mapped to a phenotype [6]. Several works advocate the use of indirect mappings (also known in the Evolutionary Computing literature as implicit embryogeny) from genotype to phenotype (e.g., [6], [15], [17]). The genotype in this case is a generative encoding of the rules that govern the development of an individual. Generative encodings have the advantages of being compact and capable of representing highly complex phenotypes. This is due to parts of the genome being reused during development across time and space. Implicit embryogeny is implemented either as top-down rewrite rules or bottom-up cellular models. In subsequent sections, we elaborate on the similarities between our approach and each of these two approaches.

(a) iRobot Warrior (b) iRobot PackBot

(c) iRobot SUGV (d) iRobot LANdroid

Figure 2: Families of engineered systems often exhibit "phylogenetic" relationships similar to those of natural organisms.

A number of specialized languages for shape formation have been inspired by morphogenesis. For example, chemical gradients are the basis of Nagpal's Origami Shape Language [27], which produces deformable geometric patterns, and Coore's Growing Point Language [10], which forms topological patterns using a model of plant tropisms. Likewise, Kondacs' model of pattern formation [21] creates regenerable patterns using a model of cell reproduction and apoptosis. However, such languages have been specialized and hard to apply to the design of realistic engineered systems.

Regardless of the specifics of the representation, genetic algorithms are typically used as the design process that modifies a genome to achieve a desired form/function. An alternative is offered by functional blueprints [1, 3], an engineering approach in which a system is specified according to its desired performance, with programs to incrementally adjust structure to improve performance when the goals are not met. The representation we provide in this paper is well-suited for interaction with either genetic algorithms or functional blueprints.

3. EMBRYOGENY CAN ENCODE DESIGN PARAMETER RELATIONS

In any engineered system, some parameters strongly influence overall system design, while others can be derived by an expert human designer from the interaction of the key parameters. To better understand how these sort of systematic relations might be exploited, we focus on the example of electromechanical systems, and in particular the the family of products that the iRobot corporation has derived from their original PackBot system (Figure 2), and a new "miniDroid" design based on the same architecture (Figure 1(a)). Although these robots span a wide range of sizes and applications, all of them share a base body plan, including paired treads each driven by two wheels, flippers coaxial with one wheel, and a top-mounted sensor/manipulator package. The loose similarity to natural phylogenetic families suggests that the natural world may yield hints toward a design representation that facilitates such variation.

Consider a simple modification to the miniDroid which, like all robots in the PackBot family, uses its flippers to climb over obstacles. When a designer increases the miniDroid's

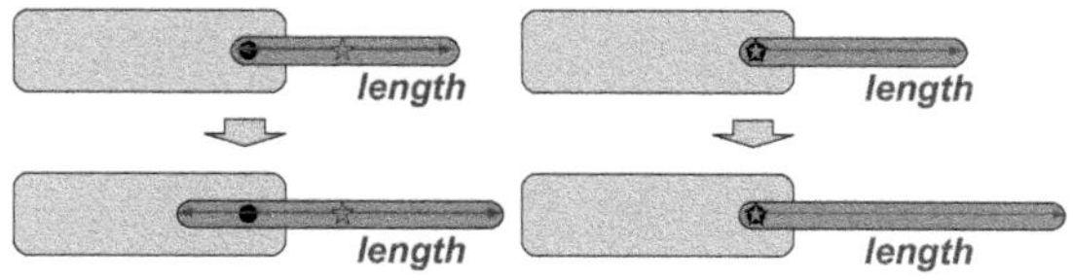

(a) Part-Centric (b) Interface-Centric

Figure 3: Coordinate systems can implicitly encode design: interface-centric coordinates let a miniDroid flipper extend outward when lengthened.

flipper length (e.g., to climb over slightly taller obstacles) should the flipper extend symmetrically around its geometric center (Figure 3(a)), away from its attachment point (Figure 3(b)), or some combination thereof? The answer is intuitive to a human designer, but a self-adapting design must have some way of representing this relationship.

This is potentially a severe problem: engineered designs have extremely high numbers of parameters: even a simple beam is described by at least nine parameters (side lengths, position, and orientation). Only a few of these parameters are key, while most are constrained by their relationship to key parameters. Natural systems, however, must solve this problem in the embryogenies that create their forms, since evolution acts through relatively independent incremental changes to very few parameters at a time.

In animals, the process of embryogenesis effectively specifies a hierarchy of spatial relationships and coordinate systems that constrain how changes can occur. For example, when an arm is lengthened, it extends further out from the body, rather than attempting to invade into the body.

We thus look to embryogeny as a means of encoding relationships between design parameters, defining it as a partially ordered sequence of operations over a spatial computer that convert a simple initial "egg" into a "mature" structure. It is important to note that although the systems we design are not going to be physically built using a developmental process, we still need to simulate this process because it generates by-products (e.g., various coordinate systems local to tissues, tissue specialization hierarchies, and simulated physical interactions between tissues) that guide the maintenance of a design's integration as its components are being changed, whether by a human designer, an evolutionary algorithm, or an online process for repair and adaptation.

4. DEVELOPMENTAL REPRESENTATIONS

We now propose a representation of embryogeny using a candidate basis set of manifold geometry operators, then demonstrate how this can be applied to develop the body plan of a miniDroid. For reasons of space, we give only a high-level description of the operators and the implementations we have constructed. Full details can be obtained from the MADV release online at `http://madv.bbn.com`.

4.1 Manifold Operators

In natural systems, a vast array of mechanisms are used to develop the form of an organism. From this panoply, we extract five simple abstract manifold geometry operators for measuring, segmenting, and modifying manifolds. This is not necessarily the "best" set of operators, but for preliminary work, we minimize the complexity of the model in order to simplify analysis of its capabilities and implications.

We formulate these as operators on continuous manifolds, rather than simpler Euclidean geometric operators, so that they can tolerate topological distortions. Thus when a structure's shape and size are changed (either by changes to its antecedents or by physical interaction with other structures), the operators should still produce qualitatively similar effects, promoting canalization. These operators can be applied to either the entire structure or to any substructure (viewed as a submanifold), and affect surrounding tissues only indirectly, as a byproduct of physical interaction.

Figure 4 illustrates our set of manifold operators:

- **coordinatize(0-region, 1-region)**: This operator computes a local coordinate system between two regions, ranging from 0 in one region linearly to 1 in the other region. It is based on the use of chemical gradients to polarize tissues, and most particularly on those where the signal is the ratio of two chemicals.

- **latch(region, type)**: The latch operator differentiates a region into a component type. This operator is analogous to determination of cell fate in a biological system, such as the determination of limb fields.

- **scale(region, scale-factor)**: The scale operator takes a region and increases or decreases its scale proportionately along one or more axes. This is inspired by directed proliferation, such as is used in the construction of limb buds.

- **connect(source-region, destination-region)**: This operator extends a new region from a source region along a near-shortest path to a destination region. It is based on cell migration, particularly the migration of tissue sheets, and on the extension of cell processes such as axons. We have tentatively specified that only the closest point in the source will connect, and that the width of the connection will be proportional to the size of the smaller region.

- **speckle(region, expected-separation)**: The speckle operator selects a set of small regions filling the space, each region determined randomly and separated by an expected distance from all others nearby. This is inspired by symmetry-breaking processes, such as those used to create hair follicles.

When composed using arithmetic, branching, and function definition, we believe that this set of manifold operators may be sufficient to express most arbitrarily complex adaptable structures (though they are not space-time universal [2]). Many other biological mechanisms can also be expressed as composites of these operators: for example, recruitment can be expressed as coordinatize followed by latch.

4.2 Example: miniDroid Body Plan

To validate the plausibility of our candidate operators, we have created a draft developmental sequence for the body plan of a miniDroid, which is likely to also apply well to other members of the PackBot family. The sequence begins with a cuboid egg (to better match current engineered systems and manufacturing processes), and uses all operators except for speckle. Our developmental sequence can be viewed in terms of eight stages, shown in Figure 5, though execution may proceed somewhat asynchronously:

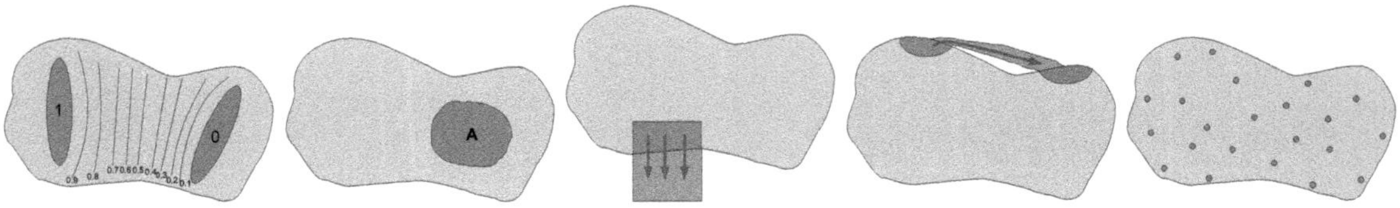

(a) Coordinatize (b) Latch (c) Scale (d) Connect (e) Speckle

Figure 4: Candidate manifold geometry operators to be a basis set for developing electromechanical designs.

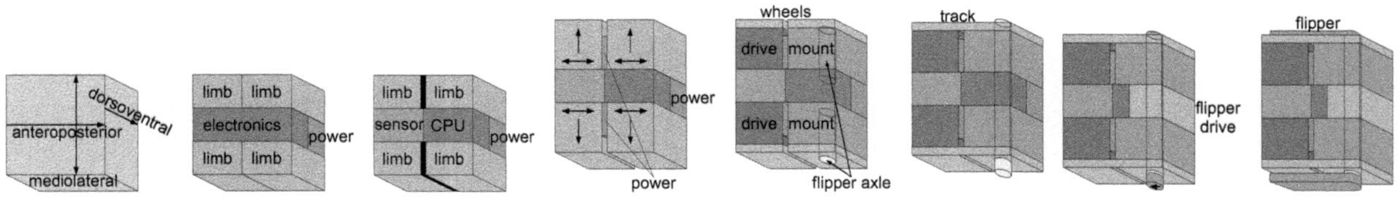

(a) Stage 1 (b) Stage 2 (c) Stage 3 (d) Stage 4 (e) Stage 5 (f) Stage 6 (g) Stage 7 (h) Stage 8

Figure 5: Approximate developmental stages of a miniDroid (or other PackBot family member) body plan.

- Stage 1: basal coordinates are created, along anteroposterior, dorsoventral, and mediolateral axes. **Operators: coordinatize**
- Stage 2: basal coordinates are used to partition the robot into coarse body plan, with the exterior latching into "skin." **Operators: latch**
- Stage 3: the electronics region differentiates along the anteroposterior axis into sensor and CPU regions. The boundary between limb buds recruits nearby material to form a gap between anterior and posterior limbs. **Operators: coordinatize, latch**
- Stage 4: limb buds scale themselves out of the body, then establish a proximodistal axis and local centromedial axis. The power region recruits inter-limb gap material. **Operators: coordinatize, latch, scale**
- Stage 5: distal section of limb buds differentiates into wheels. Proximal section of front limb buds differentiates into drive. For rear limb buds, the flipper axle differentiates using the centromedial axis, and the proximal section of the limb bud differentiates into a passive mounting point. The wheels will round themselves later, as the body scales up. **Operators: latch**
- Stage 6: flipper axles scale in and out, meeting in the center. Wheel edges connect tracks between wheels. **Operators: scale, connect, latch**
- Stage 7: flipper axles scale outwards to form the flipper drive, pressing away nearby sections of CPU and power. Distal sections of axle differentiate into flipper buds and form a new anteroposterior axis. **Operators: scale, coordinatize, latch**
- Stage 8: flippers scale from buds. **Operators: scale**

At Stage 8, the complete body plan has been formed. Each of the sections can now refine its details, while scaling up to reach the mature size and component scale relations specified by its genotype. The connectivity relations developed in the body plan constrain this scaling process, resolving implicit parameters: for example, if the flipper grows longer it can only do so by lengthening the portion not attached to the axle, and if the overall body grows wider, the wheel and motor assemblies will be carried outward along with the expansion. Meanwhile, power and signal wires connect the CPU, batteries, and motors using the connect operator, a process similar to innervation in vertebrates.

Together, these processes should produce a design similar to that of the miniDroid. Integration with a (semi)autonomous design process, such as an evolutionary algorithms or functional blueprints, should be possible by placing the scaling parameters and/or embryogeny under control of the design process.

5. IMPLEMENTATION

To begin validation of our approach, we have implemented simulations at four different levels of abstraction:

- At the highest level of abstraction, a tissue-level simulator demonstrates flexible application of manifold operators using an asynchronous rule system.
- Refining to a cellular model, we demonstrate that using manifold operators allows a design to maintain coherent inter-component relations even if the adaptation process subjects it to severe distortions.
- A soft-body simulation demonstrates the ability to compute adhesion, displacement, and penetration of components at reasonable computational cost, enabling physics-based resolution of component layout.
- Finally, adaptive refinement of details under feedback control is demonstrated with a chemotactic wiring model.

Each of these demonstrates a different aspect of how our morphogenetic approach enables canalization of a developing design. Having demonstrated that each requirement of the system is individually reasonable, the next obvious step will be to integrate them to produce a single system that completely constrains the realization of design phenotypes.

5.1 Tissue-Level Models

In the previous section, we proposed a set of manifold operators for representing development. The tissue-level model

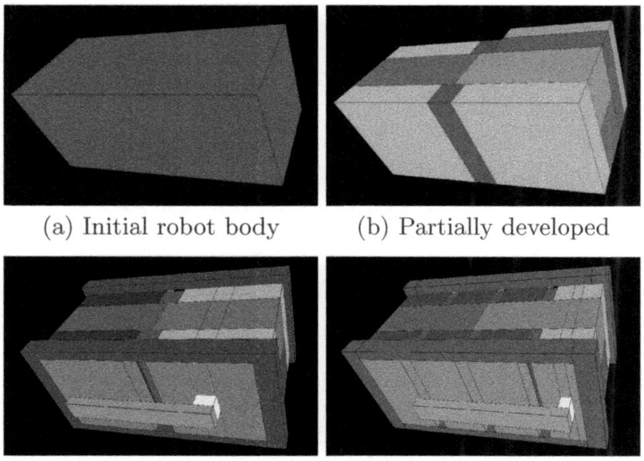

(a) Initial robot body (b) Partially developed

(c) Four wheeled robot (d) Eight wheeled variant

Figure 6: (a) The initial robot body is (b) updated using the set of development rules to create either (c) a four or (d) eight wheeled robot (wheels are unrounded green boxes).

demonstrates how these can be combined into a flexible embryogeny through asynchronous rule execution.

For this simulation, we implemented a prototypical specification of embryogeny, executor, and visualizer in Java. The simulation uses a coarse-grained representation of cell collectives (tissues), where all cells carry out the same function, analogous to biological tissues. Each tissue contains a set of body part labels (e.g., "flipperBud"), a geometry specifying its shape, and a means of converting between its own coordinate system and others.

The tissues are manipulated by a set of developmental rules. Our choice of asynchronous rules for a representation is inspired by naturally occurring genetic regulatory networks (GRNs): both of these have the useful property of separating execution conditions (promoter sequence of GRNs, preconditions of rules) from actions (encoded protein/nucleic-acid complexes of GRNs, post-conditions of rules). The rules are thus loosely coupled, reducing the need for explicit ordering constraints on their execution. As in other generative design systems, iteration and conditional execution are implicit and arise out of the interaction of the rules.

In our representation, a rule applies to any tissue that matches the rule's preconditions. An executor starts firing the developmental rules on an undifferentiated robot body ('egg'), breaking ties in arbitrary order. As rules differentiate and manipulate parts of the body, other rules become applicable. A rule's effects are a sequence of manifold operators from the basis set given in 4.1.

A difference between our developmental rules and traditional re-write rules is that ours operate in the context of a physics simulator that places physical constraints on their effects. Another important difference is that our rules can have non-local triggers and effects (e.g., a rule involving scaling can result in attached tissues being dragged along).

We have implemented a miniDroid embryogeny, which uses 12 rule skeletons that are parameterized into 23 rules that carry out the 8 developmental stages described in the previous section. Currently, our rules avoid operations that would require interactions between tissues, e.g., penetrating other tissue. Our work to support such interactions is described in Sections 5.2 and 5.3. The rules produce a body plan of a robotic "embryo" made up of various "organs" like limbs, flippers and wheels. We were careful to keep the rules oblivious to absolute dimensions and positions, a task that was facilitated by the use of the manifold operators. Figure 6 shows the initial body (6(a)) and the body-plan after embryogeny (6(c)). An example of the adaptability of our encoding is shown in Figure 6(d), which shows an eight-wheeled variant created by changing the single parameter specifying the number of body segments (pairs of wheels).

The body plan is not yet the final design, but effectively encodes constraints on the design parameters, allowing many implicit parameters to be resolved by means of the geometric and topological relationships established in the elaborated manifold developed by executing these rules. For example, the CPU and batteries are inside the body, though their relative positions within are not fixed, and the flippers are attached at the axle, so if they are made longer, they can only grow outward away from the axle.

Although rule-based generative encodings have been widely used (e.g., [17], [20], [23]), we note that our encoding and the resulting phenotypes are very different from those of prior systems. Existing approaches develop systems consisting of large numbers of simple repeated structures. For example, in Framsticks [20], the body of a robot is composed of a set of interconnected simple elements called sticks. The simplicity, uniformity and large numbers of these system building blocks allow the rewrite rules significant freedom in manipulating the structure. Most electromechanical designs, however, like the miniDroid, are made of parts that are highly heterogeneous and tightly coupled. Our rules therefore cannot arbitrarily rewrite the body, but need a representation like ours, which allows parts to maintain particular physical and topological relationships as they differentiate.

5.2 Cellular Models

Computing arbitrary distortion of manifolds at the tissue level is extremely challenging due to the difficulty of analytically representing and manipulating arbitrary geometries, so we demonstrate the distortion tolerance of manifold operators using a cellular simulation instead. We implemented this model in the Proto [4] spatial computing language. In Proto, a program is specified in terms of geometric computations and information flow on a continuous manifold, then compiled to generate a local program that approximates the global specification. Because our proposed manifold operators were deliberately selected to be compatible with such transformations, the local programs produced from them are simple and could be readily transformed into a GRN representation.[1] Proto thus links tissue-level representations, such as those discussed in the previous section, with cellular models where it is simpler to represent approximate topological distortions.

We have implemented the first five stages of the miniDroid embryogeny, from the initial coordinatization of the initial body through the scaling and differentiation of limb buds. While the Proto implementation does not represent rules (we instead transform the dependencies into flow control), its manifold representation allows the program to execute under distortion on a wide range of alternate manifolds—a

[1]In fact, Proto programs have already been transformed into actual biological GRNs [5].

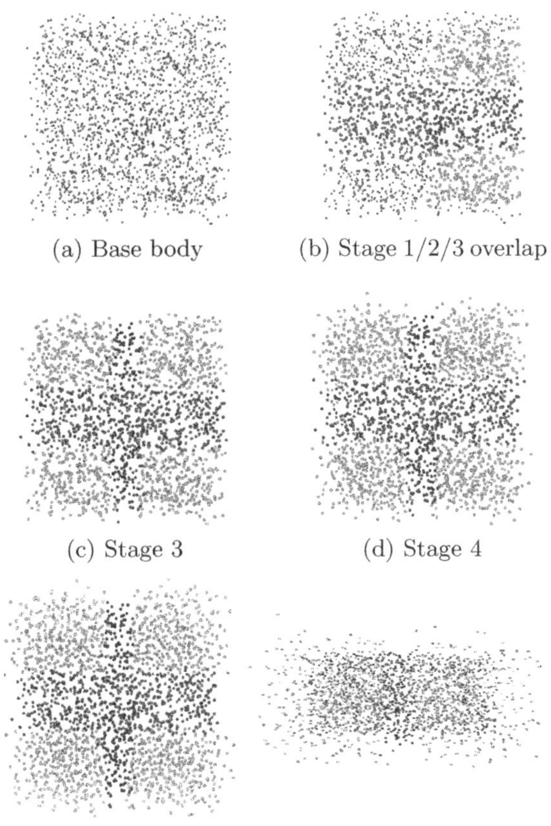

(a) Base body (b) Stage 1/2/3 overlap

(c) Stage 3 (d) Stage 4

(e) Stage 5 (f) Stage 5, side view

Figure 7: Stages 1 to 5 of body-plan development executed in fine-grained Proto models. From the initial body (a), the spreading coordinate systems trigger differentiation (b) into the base components (c). The limb buds then scale outward (d) and differentiate into wheels, motors, and mounts (e,f).

critical capability for emulating the adaptivity exhibited by natural morphogenesis. The continuous model of distributed execution also provides a natural path toward using blending to resolve conflicts between rules.

Figure 7 shows snapshots of embryogeny executing on a model of 2000 cells distributed through a rectilinear 3D volume of space. Figure 8 compares the result of execution the same program with different initial conditions, showing the inherent geometric adaptation of the program.

Notice that the operators of the embryogeny are able to execute both asynchronously and simultaneously, and that the manifold representation allows the program to produce sensible results even on a radically distorted underlying manifold. The mathematical nature of manifold geometry thus provides one form of canalization: whenever a region of space is transformed, the coordinate fields created by coordinatize operators transform along with it, and any subsequent operator that is applied to that region is transformed to match as a consequence.

Although our model is "cellular," it is very different from the cellular models discussed in works on implicit embryogeny, which tend to be more bio-mimetic, capturing low-level biological processes like GRNs and cell-level interactions (e.g., the work by Eggenberger [13] implements concepts like cell division, death and induction at the cell and GRN level). The question often addressed in the literature is how to go from low-level interactions to the desired global behavior/structure. The answer typically relies on an external element (e.g., fitness function in a genetic algorithm) to assess the collective behavior/structure arising out of the interactions. This assessment is then used as a guide to make changes to the low-level interactions that hopefully (though not directly) move the system closer to its goal. Our approach differs in that in our cellular model, we compile the desired global behaviors into low-level interactions, instead of the other way around. This greatly simplifies the problem, allowing us to develop more complex morphologies than those in the literature (e.g., [7], [13], [22]).

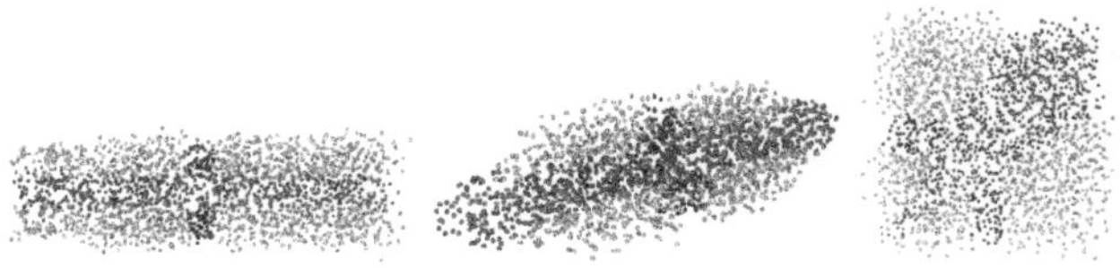

Figure 8: Proto's manifold model allows embryogeny to automatically adapt to execute on changed underlying spaces. Shown (l to r) are execution on a flat egg, an ovoid egg, and twisted coordinates.

5.3 Soft-Body Tissue Interaction

In many cases, developing components may try to move relative to connected components or to move into occupied space. The adaptability of our manifold representation allows many such conflicts in design layout to simply be resolved physically, by having tissues push, pull, shear, and penetrate one another, much like biological tissues. This promotes canalization by allowing structures to develop in a dynamically adjusted physical context (using the distortion tolerance discussed in the previous section), rather than forcing all geometric conflicts to be resolved in the developmental program. For example, in Stage 6 of miniDroid development, the flipper axles scale outward, penetrating the wheels (Figure 5(f)), which means that the wheel program need not be modified to allow for the development of flippers.

Implementing this interaction requires a soft-body simulation, which must be computationally inexpensive enough to be practical. We are not attempting to simulate tissue interactions in a way that is necessarily biologically plausible. We need only to represent tissues in a way that allows them to flexibly interact during growth operations.

As a first case study we simulated a tissue scaling operator penetrating into an adjacent tissue with the focus being on how the penetrated tissue responds (Figure 9), analogous to the flipper axle/wheel interaction described above. The axle must push up against the inner walls of the wheels; the wheel gives way elastically up to a point and then begins to plastically deform, allowing the flipper axle to penetrate. After investigating several representations of tissues, node based tissue representations have produced the most desirable results. Nodes (cells) were uniformly distributed throughout the volume contained by a surface mesh (initial state). The cells are outfitted with several interactions which allow the tissue to retain shape when under no external forces (from

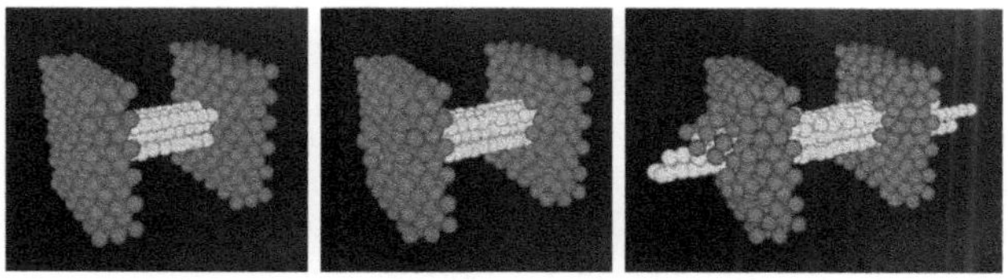

(a) Initial State (b) Deformation (c) Penetration

Figure 9: Soft-body model of a shaft growing axially between two wheels (a), that deform outward (b), then are penetrated and deform plastically (c).

adjacent tissues) while allowing deformation to occur (plastically and elastically) when external forces are applied. A low resolution representation of the miniDroid has been implemented using the node based tissue representation.

Simulations were implemented using MASON, a Java-based multi-agent simulator [24]. Our interaction models use directed growth, implemented by assigning a growth vector $\boldsymbol{\lambda}$ to each class of cells (tissue type). The growth rate for each cell is computed from a neighborhood vector $\boldsymbol{\eta}$, which we define as the distance-weighted centroid of the N cells within distance M of the position of the current cell:[2]

$$\boldsymbol{\eta} = \sum_{i}^{N} \frac{\mathbf{x} - \mathbf{x_i}}{||\mathbf{x} - \mathbf{x_i}||} \quad (1)$$

where $\mathbf{x}$ is the position of the current cell, $\mathbf{x_i}$ is its ith neighbor, and $||\ ||$ denotes vector length. The growth, or aging, rate for a particular cell, Γ, is the dot product of $\boldsymbol{\eta}$ and $\hat{\boldsymbol{\lambda}}$:

$$\Gamma = \boldsymbol{\eta} \cdot \hat{\boldsymbol{\lambda}} \quad (2)$$

where $\hat{\boldsymbol{\lambda}}$ is the normalized vector. A cell splits to create a child when its age reaches a certain threshold. The child is placed at a random location in a sphere of radius $\boldsymbol{\lambda}$, centered around the parent. Then the parent's location adjusted so that their centroid of the pair matches the parent's original location.

Directed growth is not enough to maintain tissue shape, so intercellular interactions are also directed according to $\boldsymbol{\lambda}$. We modeled three inter-cellular forces: 1) a strong repellent force when two cells are overlapping, 2) a weak attractive force between cells of the same class within some small distance, and 3) a weak repellent force between cells of different classes within some small distance. All three of these forces are governed with the same underlying equation:

$$\mathbf{f_{type_{ij}}} = (\mathbf{x_i} - \mathbf{x_j})\frac{-f_{max_{type}}}{(r_i + r_j)} + f_{max_{type}} \quad (3)$$

where r_i and r_j are the two cell radii, and $f_{max_{type}}$ is the maximum value for that force type.

We found these forces to be necessary to keep groups of the same cell type together, and prevent too much mixing between types. These forces are then summed over neighbors as follows:

$$\mathbf{F} = \sum_{i}^{N}((\mathbf{f_{1_i}} + \mathbf{f_{2_i}} + \mathbf{f_{3_i}}) \cdot \hat{\boldsymbol{\lambda}})\frac{(\mathbf{x} - \mathbf{x_i})}{||\mathbf{x} - \mathbf{x_i}||} \quad (4)$$

[2]We found stability was improved by limiting the maximum number of neighbors in the calculation.

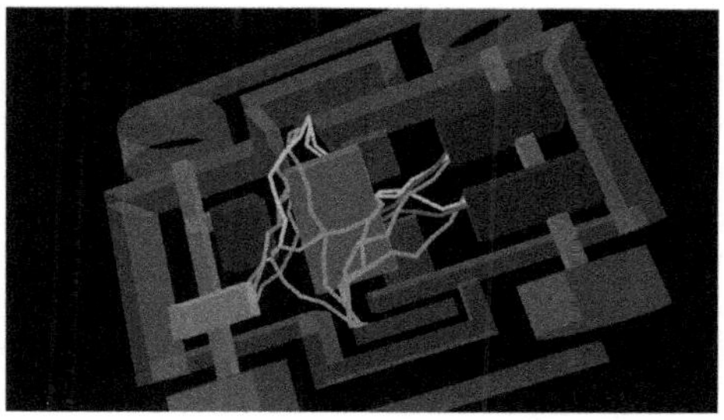

Figure 10: Wiring model executing in a simulated miniDroid interior. Components are modeled as rectangles, with wires routing around obstacles.

This ensures that motion due to inter-cellular forces is more pronounced in the directions that align with $\boldsymbol{\lambda}$.

Finally, we also ensure that cells that do not become too dense by killing off cells with high forces exerted on them. This also aids in deformation and penetration when cell classes collide.

Our simulation method is efficient, requiring only $O(nN)$ computation, where n is the number of cells and N the neighborhood size, but can still be much improved.

5.4 Wiring Models

The connect operator enables another form of canalization that is also quite important in biological organisms: the integration of systems that initially develop separately. An important example of this is the chemotactic process by which neurons grow axons to reach appropriate target cells in an organism's developing nervous system. Because this integration happens as a feedback process, perturbations such as congenital extra fingers or toes are simply integrated into the system and become functional.

With the miniDroid, wiring components to the CPU and power supply presents an analogous problem. We implemented a self-stabilizing connect operator in Proto, and used it to implement autonomous wiring design for the miniDroid. The connect operator is implemented by having its destination emit a chemical whose diffusion forms a gradient that propagates through penetrable tissue only (i.e., around solid obstacles like motors). The source follows this gradient back to the destination, forming a near-shortest path between them. Because the computation is self-stabilizing, when the structure changes the path automatically adjusts as well.

The wiring model for the miniDroid uses 9 connect operators to create 15 wires connecting the motors, CPU, batteries, and flipper encoder. Figure 10 shows the wiring model executing on a 4,000 cell approximation of a miniDroid interior, in which wires successfully connect signal, power, and ground between the batteries, CPU, encoder, and motors.

This demonstrates a fourth form of canalization enabled by our manifold operators, in which a functional blueprint acts during embryogeny to ensure functionality of a design by actively modifying it toward specified goals as it develops.

6. CONTRIBUTIONS AND FUTURE WORK

We have presented a morphogenetic engineering framework for simplifying design adaptation. This simplification is due to implicit design parameters being derived from key parameters, made possible by encoding the design constraints in our implicit embryogeny. We also proposed a basis set of manifold operators for representing distortion-tolerant embryogeny, and applied them to the example of the miniDroid. We further demonstrated the plausibility of this approach with four simulations at various levels of abstraction: models of tissue-level development, cellular development under distortion, soft-body component interaction, and wiring design. One measure of success of our design tool is comparing the size of the design space (e.g., in terms of the number of parameters a design process can manipulate) to the size of the space explored by our framework. Preliminary results show a dramatic decrease in the search space.

Three clear directions for future work follow from the work presented in this paper: first, integration of our simulations to produce a complete mapping from genotype to adapted phenotype. Second, integration with (semi)autonomous design adaptation methods such as evolutionary algorithms or functional blueprints, and quantification of the benefits of incorporating morphogenetic constraints. Finally, and on a more general level, theoretical investigation of how use of morphogenetic models modifies a fitness landscape.

7. ADDITIONAL AUTHORS

Additional authors: Kyle Usbeck (Raytheon BBN Technologies, email: kusbeck@bbn.com)

8. REFERENCES

[1] A. Adler, F. Yaman, J. Cleveland, and J. Beal. Morphogenetically assisted design variation. In *Int'l Conference on Morphological Computation*, 2011.

[2] J. Beal. A basis set of operators for space-time computations. In *Spatial Computing Workshop*, 2010.

[3] J. Beal. Functional blueprints: An approach to modularity in grown systems. *Swarm Intelligence*, 5(3), 2011.

[4] J. Beal and J. Bachrach. Infrastructure for engineered emergence in sensor/actuator networks. *IEEE Intelligent Systems*, pages 10–19, March/April 2006.

[5] J. Beal, T. Lu, and R. Weiss. Automatic compilation from high-level languages to genetic regulatory networks. *PLoS ONE*, 2011.

[6] P. Bentley and S. Kumar. Three ways to grow designs: A comparison of embryogenies for an evolutionary design problem. In *GECCO*, 1999.

[7] J. C. Bongard and R. Pfeifer. Repeated structure and dissociation of genotypic and phenotypic complexity in artificial ontogeny. In *GECCO*, pages 829–836, 2001.

[8] M. I. Campbell, J. Cagan, and K. Kotovsky. A-design: An agent-based approach to conceptual design in a dynamic environment. *Research in Engineering Design*, 11:172–192, 1999.

[9] S. B. Carroll. *Endless Forms Most Beautiful*. W. W. Norton & Company, 2005.

[10] D. Coore. *Botanical Computing: A Developmental Approach to Generating Interconnect Topologies on an Amorphous Computer*. PhD thesis, MIT, 1999.

[11] R. Doursat. Organically grown architectures: Creating decentralized, autonomous systems by embryomorphic engineering. In R. Wurtz, editor, *Organic Computing*, pages 167–200. Springer-Verlag, 2008.

[12] R. Doursat. Morphogenetic engineering weds bio self-organization to human-designed systems. *PerAda Magazine*, 2011.

[13] P. Eggenberger. Evolving morphologies of simulated 3d organisms based on differential gene expression. pages 205–213. MIT Press, 1997.

[14] M. P. J. Fromherz, D. G. Bobrow, and J. de Kleer. Model-based computing for design and control of reconfigurable systems. *AI Magazine*, 24(4), 2003.

[15] T. Gordon and P. Bentley. Towards development in evolvable hardware. In *NASA/DoD Conference on Evolvable Hardware, 2002*, pages 241 – 250, 2002.

[16] S. P. Hoover and J. R. Rinderle. A synthesis strategy for mechanical devices. *Research in Engineering Design*, 1:87–103, 1989.

[17] G. S. Hornby and J. B. Pollack. Creating high-level components with a generative representation for body-brain evolution. *Artificial Life*, 8:223–246, 2002.

[18] Y. Jin and Y. Meng. Morphogenetic robotics: An emerging new field in developmental robotics. *IEEE Transactions on Systems, Man, and Cybernetics, Part C: Applications and Reviews*, 41(2):145–160, 2011.

[19] M. W. Kirschner and J. C. Norton. *The Plausibility of Life: Resolving Darwin's Dilemma*. Yale University Press, 2005.

[20] M. Komosinski. *Framsticks: a platform for modeling, simulating and evolving 3D creatures*, chapter 2, page 37–66. Springer, New York, first edition, 2005.

[21] A. Kondacs. Biologically-inspired self-assembly of 2d shapes, using global-to-local compilation. In *IJCAI*, 2003.

[22] S. Kumar and P. J. Bentley. Computational embryology: past, present and future. In *Advances in evolutionary computing: theory and applications*, pages 461–477. Springer Verlag (UK, 2003.

[23] A. Lindenmayer. Mathematical models for cellular interaction in development: Parts I and II. *Journal of Theoretical Biology*, 18:280–315, 1968.

[24] S. Luke, C. Cioffi-Revilla, L. Panait, K. Sullivan, and G. Balan. Mason: A multi-agent simulation environment. *Simulation*, 82(7):517–527, 2005.

[25] B. MacLennan. Models and mechanisms for artificial morphogenesis. In *Natural Computing, Proceedings in Information and Communications Technology*, volume 2, 2010.

[26] Y. Meng, Y. Zhang, and Y. Jin. A morphogenetic approach to self-reconfigurable modular robots using a hybrid hierarchical gene regulatory network. In *International Conference on the Synthesis and Siumulation of Living Systems*, 2010.

[27] R. Nagpal. *Programmable Self-Assembly: Constructing Global Shape using Biologically-inspired Local Interactions and Origami Mathematics*. PhD thesis, MIT, 2001.

[28] R. O'Grady, A. L. Christensen, C. Pinciroli, and M. Dorigo. Robots autonomously self-assemble into dedicated morphologies to solve different tasks. In *AAMAS*, 2010.

[29] C. H. Waddington. Canalization of Development and the Inheritance of Acquired Characters. *Nature*, 150(3811):563–565, November 1942.

A Cell-based Developmental Model to Generate Robot Morphologies

Sylvain Cussat-Blanc
DEMO Lab, Volen National Center for Complex System - Brandeis University MS018
415 South street, Waltham, MA 02454, USA
cussat@brandeis.edu

Jordan Pollack
DEMO Lab, Volen National Center for Complex System - Brandeis University MS018
415 South street, Waltham, MA 02454, USA
pollack@brandeis.edu

ABSTRACT

This paper presents a new method to generate the body plans of modular robots. In this work, we use a developmental model where cells are controlled by a gene regulatory network. Instead of using morphogens as in many existing works, we evolve a more flexible "hormonal system" that controls the inputs of the regulatory network. By evolving the regulatory network and the hormonal system in parallel with a blind watchmaker, we have generated various virtual robots with interesting inherent properties such as regularity and symmetry. The prototypes of the robotic blocks that will be used to actually build the real machines are also presented in this paper.

Categories and Subject Descriptors

I.2.9 [**Artificial Intelligence**]: Robotics

Keywords

Modular robots, Cell-based developmental model, Gene regulatory network, Hormonal system, Body plans

1. INTRODUCTION

Modular robots built over the last several years have gotten more and more complex. Usually based on cubic blocks, they embed complex mechatronics to make them more accurate, more efficient and more diversified [25]. In this domain, the "Molecube" may be seen as an example. First based on a cube able to turn around its central axis to demonstrate limited self-replication, Lipson and his team went on to develop new modules to build more complex machines [26]. For example, we can cite the gripper modules able to pick up objects, the wheel cubes, the camera cubes, etc. To control these blocks, a neural network is then evolved. However, the user has to imagine the morphology of the robots by himself. It means that, in case of modification of the machine's purpose, a human has to redesign the morphology of the robot before evolving its controller. In 2007, Christensen proposed a robotic approach where the behavior of the machine, also composed of rotating cubic blocks, is strongly linked to its morphology [5]. Indeed, instead of having a fixed morphology, the robot is self-reconfiguring in order to accomplish its function. This method generates a very interesting property: generated robots are capable of self-healing, as multicellular organisms are.

On the other side, many works have been done in simulation to generate virtual modular robots. The first major work evolving realistic virtual robots is Karl Sims in 1994 [24]. It took another six years before evolved robots took a step from virtual to reality [18]. Sims used a graph-based genotype-phenotype map to generate a morphology controlled by a neural network, while Lipson & Pollack directly evolved the morphology. Both systems are coevolved so that the controller is as much as possible adapted to the morphology. L-Systems have also been used for the same purpose. Komosinski has made one of the most advanced work in this domain. Here again, a neural network is coevolved with the morphology generator (a L-System) to produce artificial robots. More recently, artificial Gene Regulatory Networks (GRN's) appear to be able, at the first hand, to generate complex morphologies when they control a developmental model [11, 3] and, at the second hand, to control different kinds of agents [16, 19]. Schramm was even able to grow a digital aquatic worm that moves by oscillation generated by the same regulatory network [22].

However, few of these works have been designed to actually build a real robot. With this idea in mind, Hornby proposed a model where a L-System is evolved to control a "turtle" factory which could produce a virtual robot controlled by a neural network [14]. Here, the best robots have actually been built by hand and were capable of moving like the virtual robots.

The main motivation of this paper is to use a cell-based developmental system driven by a gene regulatory network to generate real robot morphologies. To present this new method to generate robots' body plans, the paper is organized as follows. The next section presents the prototypes of real robotic blocks that will be used to build the robots. Section 3 presents the developmental model, the gene regulatory network and the hormonal system. In section 4, the blind watchmaker interactive evolutionary method is described. Section 5 presents a set of results obtained with this model and proposes a discussion about the complexity of the morphologies and the emergent properties obtained such as regularity and symmetry. The paper concludes with possible extensions of this work.

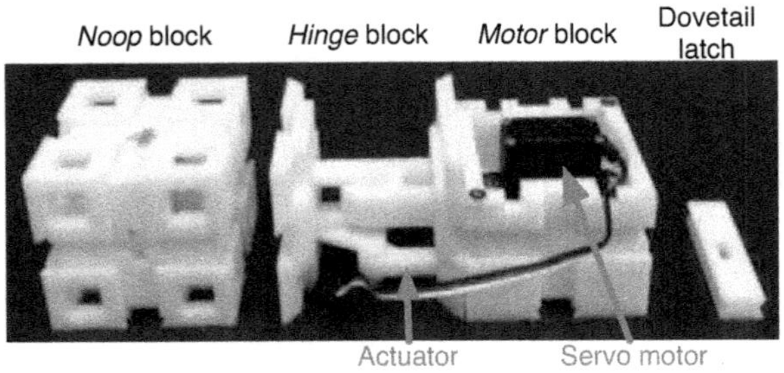

Figure 1: The robots are composed of three different blocks (from left to right): a *noop* block, a *hinge* block and a *motor* block. Blocks are tied together by the use of dovetail *latches* inserted between the blocks.

2. THE ROBOTIC BLOCKS

In this work, we took inspiration from living organisms to design our machine. An organism is usually comprised of billions of functional units: the cells. Cells can have various functions (neural, muscular, etc.). Thus, our machine uses multiple blocks that have different functions. The blocks must be easy to assemble to be able to conceive an automatic assembly process. When a machine is built, its morphology will not evolve anymore (as many grown living beings do not modify their morphology). With this constraint, the blocks do not need a dynamic linking and unlinking system. Finally, each block must be cheap to produce to keep the robot's overall cost low.

With all these requirements, we have designed each block as a cube, scaled to 2 inches (about 5cm) per side. As presented in figure 1, three different units are used in the work: (1) A *noop* block is used to build the structure of the robots (such as bones are the structure of the body). This block does not have any function, except the capacity to be linked to other blocks. (2) A *hinge* block can rotate around a central axis within the range $[-\pi/3; \pi/3]$. This block does not move by itself, but can be actuated by a neighboring motor block through two actuators, as tendons are actuating a real articulation. (3) A *motor* block actuates the *hinge* block. The actuators protubing from the hinge blocks are tied to the motor so that the motor can actuate the hinge.

This choice to separate the hinge and the motor comes from a biological observation. In Nature, most articulations and muscles are separated. They are linked together with tendons. With this method, muscles can have various shapes and sizes, according to local constraints (space, needed strength, etc.). We decided to use this idea for our building blocks for two main reasons. First, motors are usually the heaviest parts of the robots. Modifying the position of the motors in the robot can modify its center of mass, which can be relevant. Secondly, we can also imagine the possibility to increase the strength of a joint by having multiple motors actuating the same hinge (as multiple muscular cells actuate the same articulation).

Because, our robotic system does not reconfigure itself since each block's position is given by the evolved body plan of the robot (its morphology), we can keep the linking system as simple as possible. As presented in figure 1, it consists in a dovetail latch slipped between two blocks.

These blocks are currently at the stage of prototypes but are close to a final version. A 3-D printer is used to produce the plastic structure of the blocks and the dovetail latches. Servo motors (Futaba S3102) are embedded in the motor blocks and are linked to the hinge block via the actuators. These actuators are still the main issue of realization: they need to be strong, light and inelastic. Three solutions have been tested: using nylon strings, steel strings or having the actuators embedded to the hinge, as presented in figure 1. Because the two first solutions provide very unprecise movement due to the complexity of the strings' length calibration, the last solution should be the one adopted for the final robots. It requires a more elaborated conception of the hinge blocks but strongly simplify the assembly process of the blocks and increase the precision of the movement of the global articulation.

To produce the plans of the robots, we propose a novel approach based on a developmental model in which cells are controlled by a gene regulatory network coupled to a novel hormonal system. In comparison to other methods such as Graphtals or L-Systems, this approach has the advantage to be biologically plausible. Moreover, some properties such as regularity and symmetry emerge from the system, without any prior encoding. The next section presents this model.

3. THE DEVELOPMENTAL MODEL

3.1 The cells and their environment

The developmental model is based on cells that act in a 3-D discrete environment. Each cell has a unique identifier given at its birth, a division plan and a position in the environment. Two main types of cells are available: (1) *undifferentiated* cells or *stem* cells that can divide as much as they want to and (2) *differentiated* cells coming from a specialization of a stem cell to one of the three following types of cells: *B-cells*, *H-cells* or *M-cells*. When a cell is differentiated, it cannot divide anymore. The use of stem cells to drive the organism's growth has already been successfully used to developed complex shapes by Fontana in [12].

At each time step of the simulation, the stem cells can perform one of the following actions:

- *Symmetric division*: when a stem cell performs this action, a new stem cell is positioned in the position of the mother cell while the mother cell migrates in direction to its division plan. Whereas the mother cell keeps the same identifier, the new cell receives a new unique one. Its initial division plan is oriented as its mother's one.

- *Asymmetric division*: a stem cell can divide to create a new differentiated cell. In this case, the mother cell first produces an exact copy (same internal state) of itself in the direction indicated by its division plan. While the newly created cell stays a stem cell, the mother cell differentiates to a *B-cell*. Thus, this cell cannot divide anymore.

- *Differentiation*: a stem cell can become a *B-cell*. Because a differentiated cell cannot divide, this action stops the proliferation of a stem cell.

- *Rotation*: a cell can reorient its division plan. When it choses this action, it can turn in one of the four following directions: *right*, *left*, *top* or *bottom*. While turning, the cell stays at the exact same position.

- *Special division*: a cell can divide asymmetrically twice during one time step. In this case, it first produces a *H-cell* at the initial position, a *M-cell* one voxel away from the initial position in the direction of its division plan and a copy of itself two voxels away.

Naturally, two cells cannot be in the same voxel of the environment. To satisfy this requirement, all inconsistent actions are disabled at a time step of the growth. For example, if a cell wants to divide, the position in direction of the division plan is first checked. If the position is not free (in other words, already occupied by another cell), the division is disabled. The cell will have to choose another action. At least two actions are guaranteed to be always available: *rotation* and *differentiation*. Indeed, both actions only affect the cell itself: no new voxels are necessary.

After the growth of the organism from a single cell to a connected set of cells, each cell is translated to a robotic block: *B-cells* and *stem cells* are interpreted as *noop* blocks, *M-cells* produce *motor* blocks, and, finally, *H-cells* produces *hinge* blocks.

To evaluate the morphologies generated, a virtual robot is built and dropped down in a 3-D physics environment. This simulator is used to visualize the produced robots before actually building them. We use the well-known Bullet physics engine coupled with OpenGL for the graphic visualization.

To select an action, cells are using a gene regulatory network. The next section details our model based on a simplification of Banzhaf's GRN [1].

3.2 The gene regulatory network

3.2.1 Background on GRN's

In Nature, each cell of a living organism has a gene regulatory network (GRN) that controls its behavior. The possible actions are coded by genes in its DNA and their expressions are controlled by the regulatory network [8]. The GRN uses external proteic signals from the cell's environment to activate or inhibit the transcription of genes. Cells can collect external signals thanks to protein sensors localized on the cell membrane. The expression of genes determines the cell's behavior.

Artificial regulatory networks are based on the same principle. Torsten Reil was one of the first to propose a biologically plausible simulation of a GRN [20]. He defined the genome as a bit string. In his model, each gene started with the particular sequence of 4 bits, named the "promoter". The dynamics of this regulatory network is very close to Banzhaf's, detailed below.

Banzhaf proposed an artificial regulation network model strongly inspired by real gene regulation [1]. The aim of this model was to study the behaviors generated by a biologically plausible regulatory network. He has generated many random bit strings and observed various behaviors from oscillators to faster or slower transitory patterns.

Regulatory networks have been proven successful to grow cell based artificial creatures with more or less complex morphologies [11, 10, 15]. More recently, regulatory networks have also been used as behavior generators to solve the pole balancing problem [19] or to control a foraging virtual robot [16]. Schramm also used a GRN to control the morphology development and the behavior of swimming worms [22].

However, no real robotic application has been yet proposed for this system. Our work proposes to use a simplification of Banzhaf's regulatory network to control the cells of our developmental model.

3.2.2 Presentation of Banzhaf's regulatory network

Banzhaf's GRN may be currently one of the best models. It has been designed to be as close as possible to a real gene regulatory network. As DNA is composed of a sequence of nucleotides, Banzhaf's network is encoded within a sequence of bits. As a real gene starts with the particular sequence of nucleotides, a gene in Banzhaf's network starts with a particular sequence of 8 bits named the "promoter". A gene is then encoded next to this sequence by 5 32-bit integers, named the "sites". This mechanism allows the generation of a variable number of genes in a fixed size chromosome. However, as in Nature, it also generates a certain amount of noncoding DNA, the probability to have a promoter being very low (2^{-8}). This noncoding DNA (98% of human DNA) is thought to be used in Nature to protect the genome from mutation by lowering the probability that a mutation will affect a coding nucleotide.

Banzhaf's model has not been designed to be evolved nor to control any kind of agent. However, Nicolau used an evolution strategy to evolve the GRN to control a pole-balancing cart [19]. Even if the cart behavior has been shown consistent within its environment, the evolution of the GRN has been an issue. In our opinion, the difficulty of the evolution is due to: (1) the *noncoding DNA* and (2) the *dynamics* of the network. The next section details these two points and proposes a possible adaptation of the model to be more efficient as a computational model.

3.2.3 Adaptation of Banzhaf's model to an efficient computational model

Encoding of the network

As presented above, the *noncoding DNA*, which may have positive benefits in natural systems, impedes the evolution of artificial GRNs.

To get rid of the noncoding DNA, we propose a new encoding of the network. In our model, each protein is encoded as an indivisible component composed of four attributes:

- The protein *identifier* coded as an integer between 0 and p. The upper value p of the domain can be changed in order to control the precision of the GRN. In Banzhaf's work, p is equal to 32, which is the size of a site. In our work, we have decided to increase the precision by setting p to 64.

- The *enhancer identifier* coded as an integer between 0 and p. The enhancer identifier is used to calculate the enhancing matching factor between two proteins.

- The *inhibitor identifier* coded as an integer between 0 and p. The inhibitor identifier is used to calculate the inhibiting matching factor between two proteins.

- The *type* determines if the protein is an *input* protein (whose concentration is given by the environment of the regulatory network and which regulates other proteins but is not regulated), an *output* protein (whose concentration is used as output of the network and who is regulated but does not regulate other proteins) or a *regulatory* protein (internal protein that regulates and is regulated by other proteins).

The GRN is defined as a set of these proteins. A GRN can have a variable number of proteins. To be evolved, the GRN is encoded in a genome defined as a variable length chromosome of indivisible proteins. Each protein is encoded within four integers: three between 0 and p for the three different identifiers and one between 0 and 2 for the type of the protein. If an evolutionary algorithm has to evolve this chromosome, the modification operators have to be redefined. First, the *crossover* consists in exchanging subparts of two different networks. Because proteins are indivisible, the crossover points have to be chosen between two proteins. It ensures the integrity of each sub-network. The local connectivity is thus kept. Only new links between the different sub-networks are created. The *mutation* can be applied in three equiprobable ways: *mutating an existing protein* by randomly changing one of its four integers, *adding a new protein* randomly generated or *removing one protein* randomly chosen in the network.

Dynamics of the network

The *dynamics* of the network is, in our opinion, a crucial point that determines the reactivity of the network. In Banzhaf's network, the enhancing dynamics of each protein are given by the following equation:

$$e_i = \frac{1}{N}\sum_{j}^{N} c_j e^{\beta u_j^+ - u_{max}^+}$$

where e_i is the enhancing value for a protein i, N is the number of proteins in the network, c_j is the concentration of protein j, u_j^+ is the enhancing matching factor between protein i and protein j (calculated by counting the number of different bit of the proteins signatures) and u_{max}^+ is the maximum enhancing matching factor observed. β is a control parameter described later. The modification of the concentration of a protein i is then given by the differential equation $dc_i/dt = \delta(e_i - h_i)c_i - \Phi$, where e_i is the enhancing signal previously presented, h_i is the inhibiting signal (calculated exactly as the enhancing signal by using inhibiting matching factors instead of the enhancing matching factors), c_i is the current concentration of the protein i and Φ is a function that keeps of the sum of all protein concentrations equal to 1.

As presented in this last equation, the evolution of the concentration of a protein i is directly related to its current concentration. In other words, if a protein's concentration appears to be null, this protein will never be produced anymore. This is problematic because, in the case of a computational model, it means that an output completely disabled at a particular time of the simulation will never be activated anymore. With this observation, we propose to change the differential equation by the following one:

$$\frac{dc_i}{dt} = \frac{\delta(e_i - h_i)}{\Phi}$$

With this new equation, the current concentration of the protein i does not intervene anymore. The scaling function is also divided instead of subtracted in order to have a more proportional scaling factor.

With this new encoding and these new dynamics, the regulatory network should be easier to evolve and more reactive to its environment. Next section presents how this regulatory network is embedded within the cells of our developmental system.

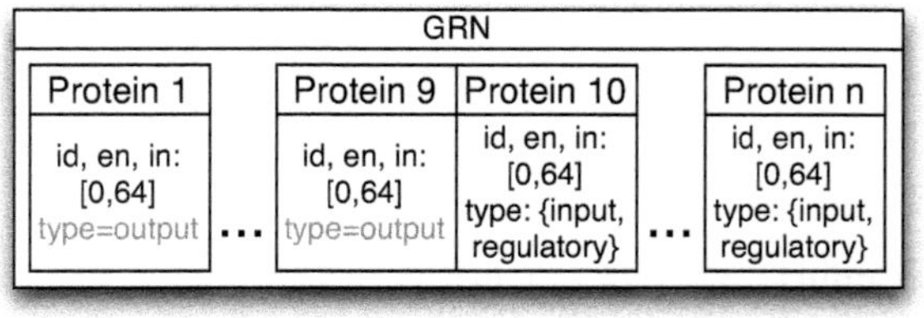

Figure 2: The chromosome that encodes the GRN is subdivided into two parts: the first nine proteins are output proteins and the remainder of the chromosomes encodes input and regulatory proteins.

3.2.4 Encapsulation into the cells

Cells have 5 different actions: *symmetric division*, *asymmetric division*, *differentiation*, *division plan reorientation* (rotation) and *special division*. However, if a cell choses to rotate, it also has to decide in which direction it wants to (left, right, top or bottom). To encode this in the GRN, we decided to subdivide the outputs into two groups of output proteins: the first group contains 5 output proteins that match with the 5 possible actions and the second group contains 4 output proteins that encodes the 4 possible rotation directions when the rotation is selected in the first group of proteins. Thus, 9 output proteins are necessary to encode the possible actions of the cells.

As illustrated by figure 2, these 9 output proteins are encoded at the beginning of the genome. Their three identifier (protein, enhancer and inhibitor) can be mutated but the type cannot. The remaining elements of the genome are composed of 25% of input proteins and 75% of regulatory proteins (empirically chosen[1]). It can be mutated and crossed over as previously presented.

At each step of the simulation, the cells execute the regulatory network for 25 steps (found to be within reasonable range during prelimanery tests) and select the action corresponding to the maximum protein concentration of the first 5 proteins: if the first protein has the maximum concentration, the cell divides symmetrically, if the second protein has the maximum concentration, the cell divides asymmetrically and so on. When the *rotation* action is chosen, it gives access to the second group of output proteins. The cell calculates the maximum value of the last 4 output proteins' concentrations to determine in which direction to turn.

The coefficients β and δ presented in the dynamics model are also encoded in the genome. They modify the dynamics of the network. β affects the importance of the matching factor and δ affects the level of production of the protein in the differential equation. The lower both values, the smoother the regulation. At the opposite, the higher the values, the more sudden the regulation. Both values are encoded as a second independent chromosome that only contains both values. They are coded with double-precision floats in [0.5; 2] (empirically chosen[1]).

Finally, we must provide inputs to the regulatory network in order to be able to select an action at every time step of the growth. In most developmental models, cells can produce morphogens such as in [17, 15]. They are informative molecules that diffuse in the environment and are the in-

[1]Empirically chosen values have been determined by a series of pre-tests to find a reasonable range.

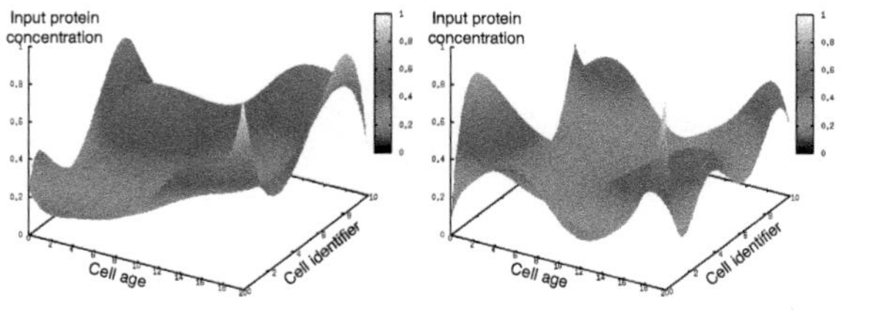

Figure 3: Examples of generated inputs with Bézier surfaces. They show the diversity of signal we can obtain by using this generative method.

puts of the GRN. In few other models, the morphogens are hand-coded in the environment [4, 7]. This method is less realistic than the first one but strongly reduces the complexity of the simulation. Because of its complexity, the first method generally leads to simple shapes such as 2-D colored rectangles, 2-D salamanders or 3-D tubes. The second method make possible to generate more complex 3-D colored structures such as cubes, diamonds or spheres. In this work, we choose an intermediate solution. Cells have a hormonal system that produces the inputs of the regulatory network. The next section details this system.

3.3 The hormonal system

The genotype of our developmental model also describes a novel hormonal system. This hormonal system generates the inputs to the gene regulatory network based on the timestep and index number of the cell. In order to be efficient, each input protein of the GRN must have a different hormonal production profile that provides the concentration of the input protein all along the simulation. Moreover, this profile must also be different for each stem cell in the organism. Indeed, if all the cells would have the same profile, it would not allow any variation of their behaviors: they would all perform the same sequence of actions. In summary, the concentration c_i of an input protein i is related to two parameters: the current time step t of the simulation and the identifier of the cell in which the concentration is calculated.

Many models of artifical hormones exist in the literature. From those applied to robotics, we can cite AHHS used to control the behavior of Symbrion and Replicator reconfigurable robots [13]. Here, an hormone is diffusing throught the robot and is used for local communication purpose.

Thus, the hormonal profile of an input protein can be coded by a 3-D surface. The first two dimensions of the surface correspond to the simulation time in abscissa and the identifier of the cells in ordinate. The third dimension gives the concentration of the corresponding input protein's concentration according to the two first dimensions. The global hormonal system is thus defined as a set of p 3-D surfaces. Each surface is associate with the identifier of the input protein (which varies between 0 and p, p being the precision of the GRN).

To generate these surfaces, we used Bézier's algorithm [2]. Originally used to design car bodyworks, it allows the generation of a surface by the mean of a given set of checkpoints. In this work, we use a Bézier surface of order ($n = 10, m = 10$). This order corresponds to the number of checkpoints. For a (10, 10) order surface, $(10+1)*(10+1) = 121$ checkpoint $k_{i,j}$ are necessary. With these checkpoints, the z coordinate of every point of coordinate (x, y, z) of the surface is given by the following equation:

$$z = \sum_{i=0}^{n=10} \sum_{j=0}^{m=10} B_i^n(x) B_j^m(y) k_{i,j}$$

where $B_i^n(x)$ is the Bernstein polynomial:

$$B_i^n(x) = \frac{n!}{i!(n-i)!} x^i (1-x)^{n-i}$$

Figure 3 presents some examples of randomly generated surfaces using this method. They show the diversity of possible landscape generated with only 121 checkpoints.

Each possible input protein must have a Bézier surface assigned. To do so, we have decided to allocate a surface to each possible protein identifier. When the identifier of an input protein is changed by mutation to another value, a new surface is thus assigned. With this method, p surfaces are necessary for a GRN of precision p (a protein identifier is coded with an integer between 0 and p. Here $p = 64$). To encode this system into the genome, the checkpoints are encoded in the third chromosome that consists in a common set of $121 * p$ double-precision floats. Each value can vary in the range $[-1.0; 1.0]$. This chromosome can be classically crossed over and mutated. In order not to overflow the regulatory network with the input proteins, the input concentrations given by Bézier surfaces are normalized between 0 and 0.05.

3.4 Summary of the model

To summarize, cells are acting in a 3-D discrete environment. Stem cells can divide symmetrically, asymmetrically or twice in the same time step to produce an articulation. They can also reorient their division plan and differentiate to *B-cells*. To control their developmental behavior, cells have a gene regulatory network coupled to a hormonal system. We have proposed an adaptation of Banzhaf's well-known GRN to make it more efficient for computational purposes.

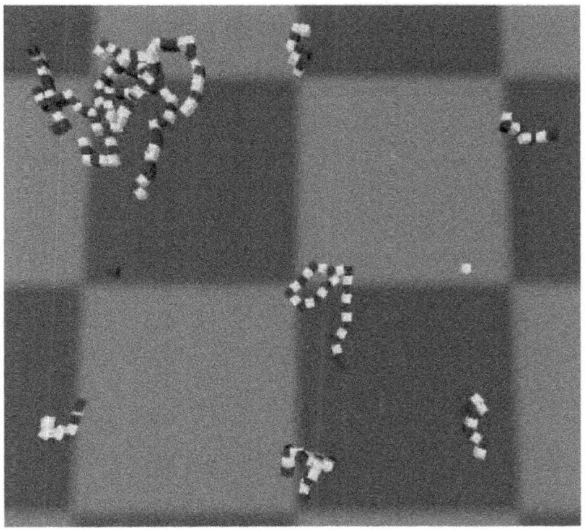

Figure 4: 9 robots evolve at the same time in the physics simulator. A 6-second phase oscillator generates the robots' movements. The user can select the robot that he wants to evolve. The evolution only consists in mutating 10% of the genome. Spacing between robots has been reduced for this particular picture.

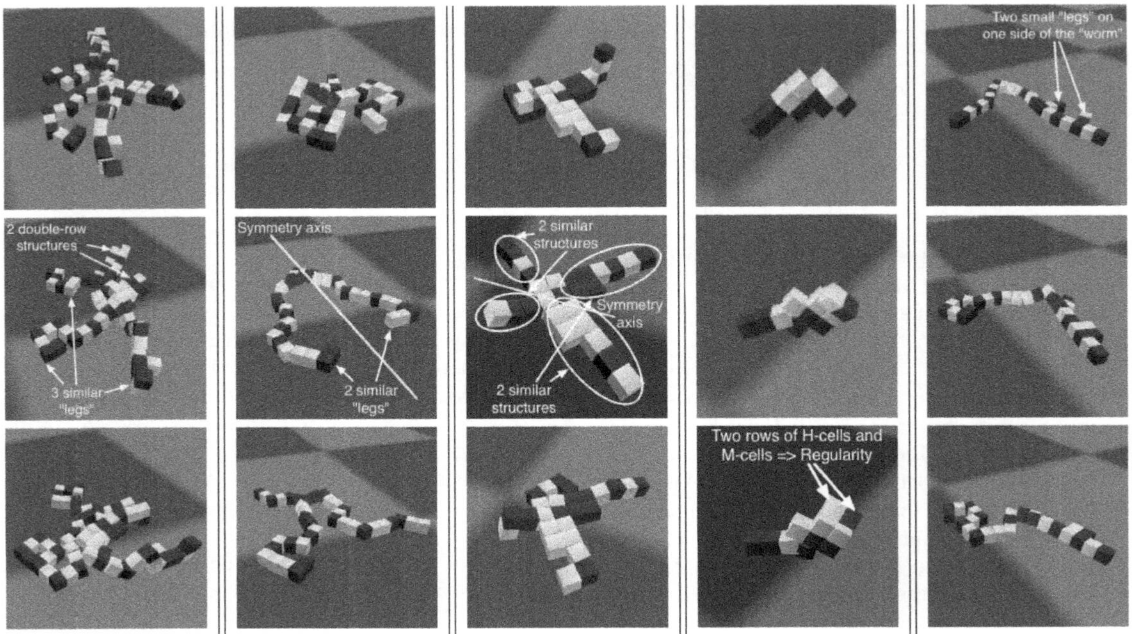

Robot R1	Robot R2	Robot R3	Robot R4	Robot R5
Generation 9	Generation 11	Generation 14	Generation 14	Generation 30

Figure 5: Examples of robots obtained in a single run of the blind watchmaker. Generated robots are complex and diversified, especially in few generations with few individuals evaluated at each generation (9 robots only).

The hormonal system uses Bézier surfaces to generate the inputs to the GRN. Each input protein is produced by a hormone, a 3-D surface indexed by the simulation time and the cell identifier.

In order to evolve the organisms (and thus the robots' body plan), both systems are encoded in a genome composed of three independent chromosomes: the first chromosome encodes a set of indivisible proteins used to build the architecture of the GRN, the second chromosome encodes the dynamics parameters and the third chromosome encodes the checkpoints necessary to generate the hormonal system's Bézier surfaces.

In order to evaluate the complexity of possible morphologies generated by this model, we have decided to use a Blind WatchMaker instead of a classical evolutionary algorithm. The aim is to study the capacity of the GRN to inherently produce properties that other models usually include such as symmetry or regularity. We also want to verify that our system is able to generate a wide variety of morphologies keeping in mind its possible evolution with an evolutionary algorithm.

4. EVOLUTION OF THE ROBOTS: THE BLIND WATCHMAKER

The Blind WatchMaker is an interactive evolutionary method first proposed in 1986 by Richard Dawkins [9]. He originally used this method to sustain the theory of natural evolution using a pedagogical model called *biomorphs*, fractal-like creatures generated with a small set of genes. This method gave birth more recently to the field of interactive evolution. Many applications are nowadays based on this principle to solve various problems. It has for example been used with genetic programming to generate realistic camouflage [21], or with HyperNeat to generate 2-D pictures [23] or 3-D shapes [6].

In this work, we first generate 9 random genomes. The developmental model is then executed to generate the corresponding virtual robots. When the robots are created, they are dropped down in the physics simulator in 9 different points of the environment so that they cannot interact with one another. Figure 4 illustrates nine random robots evolving in the physics simulator. In this particular experiment, we have limited the number of developmental steps to 20 and the number of stem cells to 10 in order to control the scale of morphologies. Later, these limits will be needed based on the actual availability of robotic cells, but might be based on simulating biologically plausible mechanisms.

During the first 5 seconds, the robots do not move in order to stabilize their structure on the floor. Then, to make the robots move in the environment, an oscillator controls the movement of every hinge of the robots: they rotate clockwise for 3 seconds (the rotation angle of a hinge cannot be above $-\pi/3$) and then counterclockwise for 3 seconds (within a $\pi/3$ limit). A third of the oscillators are inverted: when it should turn clockwise, an inverted hinge actually turns counterclockwise and vice versa. Even though this method generates simple movements, it is sufficient to visualize the potential of the generated morphologies.

The user can use window controls to navigate from a robot to another to observe its movement and its properties. The user can also select the robots he wants to evolve. The application then generates 9 new robots by mutating 10% of the selected robot's genome. We have decided not to use the crossover operator to enhance the diversity of generated robots. For the same reason, the mutation rate has been deliberately chosen high.

With this method, we have generated a pool of diversified robots. The next section presents some of them and discusses properties of robots obtained.

5. RESULTS AND DISCUSSION

Figure 5 presents 5 robots obtained during the same run of the interactive evolutionary algorithm. These examples show the diversity of morphologies obtained.

The first observation we can make about these robots is the capacity of the regulatory network to generate robots of different sizes. The GRN is able to generate as well small robots (such as robot R4) or bigger ones (such as R1 or R2). This is mainly possible by using the differentiation action that stops the proliferation of the stem cells.

Moreover, interesting properties emerge during the evolution. After only 9 generations, the robot R1 already presents some regularity in its morphology. We call a *regularity* a set of cells with the same organization (relative positioning and differentiation of the cells) that appears at different places in the organism. For example, the robot R1 is composed of 3 similar "legs" and two identical structure build with double-row structure of cells (see the second picture of R1 on figure 5). The robot R2 also has some regularities. It is composed of 2 long "legs" of the same size. The same observation can be done on robots R3 and R5 (2 small legs on one side for the robot R5).

In some cases, these regularities can be very interesting: on the robot R4, it produces a double row of H-cells and M-cells, which generates a double joint in the robot. This structure multiplies the strength of the resulting joint. Figure 6 presents the growth sequence of the robot R4. The double-row cell structure appears at the beginning of the growth, from step 1 to 3. The initial cell first divides. Then both cells perform the same actions for 2 steps, before changing their behaviors, certainly because of a change in the hormone profile of some input proteins at this particular point of the simulation. While the first cell produces the left part of the robot, the second cell quickly stops its development after few more (parasitic) reorientations of its division plan.

As proven by the blind watchmaker approach, some of the robots can be symmetric such as robots R2 and R3 on figure 5. This property is particularly interesting because it is usually expected in robot's morphologies. A symmetric machine will have more chances to be stable. The symmetry seems to be achieved using a similar method which achieves regularity – but with a rotation before two equivalent sequences of actions are performed.

The use of a developmental model to generate robot body plans seems to be a promising approach. Some desirable properties such as regularity and symmetry is easily obtained with this system. As presented above, we have obtained these properties in few generations with a very small population. This is not necessarily the case in works based on HyperNEAT or L-Systems which requires many more generations of evolution. Moreover, the hormonal system provides for much more creativity than a classical morphogens production regulated by the GRN. For now, the profiles of the hormone are encoded in the genome, but we could easily imagine using hormones and morphogens simultaneously. Morphogens produced by the cells could, for example, control the production profile of the hormones.

Step	Cell 1	Cell 2	Cell 3	Cell 4	Organism
0	Birth				
1	SyD2	Birth			
2	TurnB	TurnB			
3	SpD	SpD			
4	SyD3	TurnB	Birth		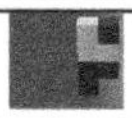
5	TurnB	TurnB	SyD4	Birth	
6	TurnB	Diff	Diff	TurnB	
7	TurnB	-	-	Diff	
8	SpD	-	-	-	
9	AsD	-	-	-	
10	Diff	-	-	-	

Figure 6: Actions performed by the stem cells only. Each line corresponds to a growth step. Signification of the acronyms: SyDx=Symmetric division to create a new cell x; AsD=Asymmetric Division, SpD=Special division, Diff=Differentiation and Turn$B$=Turn to Bottom

6. CONCLUSION AND PERSPECTIVES

This paper presents an innovative system to generate robot body plans. It is based on a developmental model in which cells are controlled by a gene regulatory network. We have based our GRN model on Banzhaf's by modifying the encoding of the GRN into a chromosome without any non-coding DNA and by modifying its dynamics. The resulting GRN is easier to evolve and is more adapted to a computational purpose. Instead of using morphogens as in most developmental models, we have decided to provide input to the GRN using a hormonal system which is differentiated by the cell identifier, the input protein, and the simulation time. These hormone profiles are generated by the use of Bézier surfaces controlled by a finite set of 121 checkpoints which are evolved with the GRN.

We have produced various virtual robots by evolving in the same time the GRN and the hormonal system with a blind watchmaker. Resulting robots have various sizes, from small to very large, and two interesting properties emerge from the systems: many creatures have regularities in there morphologies, such as "legs" or double-joints, and some of them are symmetric. This is possible because of the oscillations, which is a well-known property of GRN system.

We anticipate much future work on this model. First, we have to produce more robotic blocks and actually build the virtual robots into reality. The prototypes of the robotic blocks already exist but the building of a whole robot will likely require some modifications and re-engineering of the robotic blocks (actuators, motors, dovetail latches, etc.) as well as cause constraints to be added to the physics simulator (motor strength, block friction, etc.).

The joints' controllers are also something we have to work on. They only consist of oscillators moving the joints clockwise and then counterclockwise. Two main solutions are currently considered to improve the controller. First, we can imagine that the same GRN also controls the joints when the growth of the robot is finished. This method has already been applied with success by Schramm in [22]. The second solution could be to plug a neural network or an equivalent method to the joints. Here, two solutions are possible: at the first hand, the neural network and the developmental model can be evolved at the same time or, at the second hand, it can be evolved after the evolution of the morphology.

In order to generate efficient robots, their genomes will have to be evolved by an evolutionary algorithm. The fitness function continues to be the main issue, as the field needs to move beyond linear movement in a simulated environment. To have other kinds of morphologies, we are considering including complexity, symmetry and regularity measures to the fitness function as well as utilizing multi-objective techniques for the co-evolution of body and behavior.

7. REFERENCES

[1] W. Banzhaf. Artificial regulatory networks and genetic programming. *Genetic Programming Theory and Practice*, pages 43–62, 2003.

[2] P. Bézier. *Numerical control; mathematics and applications.* John Wiley & Sons, 1972.

[3] J. Bongard and R. Pfeifer. Evolving complete agents using artificial ontogeny. *Morpho-functional machines: The new species (designing embodied intelligence)*, pages 237–258, 2003.

[4] A. Chavoya and Y. Duthen. A cell pattern generation model based on an extended artificial regulatory network. *Biosystems*, 94(1-2):95–101, 2008.

[5] D. Christensen. Experiments on Fault-Tolerant Self-Reconfiguration and Emergent Self-Repair. In *IEEE Symposium on Artificial Life (ALIFE'07)*, pages 355–361, 2007.

[6] J. Clune, B. E. Beckmann, P. K. McKinley, and C. Ofria. Investigating whether hyperneat produces modular neural networks. In *Proceedings of the 12th annual conference on Genetic and evolutionary computation*, GECCO '10, pages 635–642. ACM, 2010.

[7] S. Cussat-Blanc, N. Bredeche, H. Luga, Y. Duthen, and M. Schoenauer. Artificial gene regulatory networks and spatial computation: A case study. In *Proceedings of the European Conference on Artificial Life (ECAL'11).* MIT Press, Cambridge, MA, 2011.

[8] E. H. Davidson. The regulatory genome: gene regulatory networks in development and evolution. *Academic Press*, 2006.

[9] R. Dawkins. The blind watchmaker. *Longman Scientific & Technical*, 1986.

[10] R. Doursat. Organically grown architectures: Creating decentralized, autonomous systems by embryomorphic engineering. *Organic Computing*, pages 167–200, 2008.

[11] P. Eggenberger. Evolving morphologies of simulated 3d organisms based on differential gene expression. In *Proceedings of the Fourth European Conference on Artificial Life*, pages 205–213. MIT Press, 1997.

[12] A. Fontana. Devo co-evolution of shape and metabolism for an artificial organ. *Artificial Life XII, H. Fellermann et al., Eds. Boston: MIT Press*, pages 16–23, 2010.

[13] H. Hamann, J. Stradner, T. Schmickl, and K. Crailsheim. A hormone-based controller for evolutionary multi-modular robotics: From single modules to gait learning. In *IEEE Congress on Evolutionary Computation*, pages 1–8, 2010.

[14] G. Hornby, H. Lipson, and J. Pollack. Generative representations for the automated design of modular physical robots. *Robotics and Automation, IEEE Transactions on*, 19(4):703–719, 2003.

[15] M. Joachimczak and B. Wróbel. Evo-devo in silico: a model of a gene network regulating multicellular development in 3d space with artificial physics. In *Proceedings of the 11th International Conference on Artificial Life*, pages 297–304. MIT Press, 2008.

[16] M. Joachimczak and B. Wróbel. Evolving Gene Regulatory Networks for Real Time Control of Foraging Behaviours. In *Proceedings of the 12th International Conference on Artificial Life*, 2010.

[17] J. Knabe, M. Schilstra, and C. Nehaniv. Evolution and morphogenesis of differentiated multicellular organisms: autonomously generated diffusion gradients for positional information. *Artificial Life XI*, 11:321, 2008.

[18] H. Lipson and J. Pollack. Automatic design and manufacture of robotic lifeforms. *Nature*, 406:974–978, 2000.

[19] M. Nicolau, M. Schoenauer, and W. Banzhaf. Evolving genes to balance a pole. *Genetic Programming*, pages 196–207, 2010.

[20] T. Reil. Dynamics of gene expression in an artificial genome - implications for biological and artificial ontogeny. *Advances in Artificial Life*, 1999.

[21] C. Reynolds. Interactive evolution of camouflage. *Artificial Life*, 17(2):123–136, 2011.

[22] L. Schramm, Y. Jin, and B. Sendhoff. Emerged coupling of motor control and morphological development in evolution of multi-cellular animats. *Advances in Artificial Life: Darwin Meets von Neumann*, pages 27–34, 2011.

[23] J. Secretan, N. Beato, D. B. D Ambrosio, A. Rodriguez, A. Campbell, and K. O. Stanley. Picbreeder: evolving pictures collaboratively online. In *Conference on Human Factors in Computing Systems*, CHI '08, pages 1759–1768. ACM, 2008.

[24] K. Sims. Evolving 3d morphology and behavior by competition. *Artificial Life IV*, pages 28–39, 1994.

[25] M. Yim, W. Shen, B. Salemi, D. Rus, M. Moll, H. Lipson, E. Klavins, and G. Chirikjian. Modular self-reconfigurable robot systems [grand challenges of robotics]. *IEEE Robotics & Automation Magazine*, 14(1):43–52, 2007.

[26] V. Zykov, W. Phelps, N. Lassabe, and H. Lipson. Molecubes Extended: Diversifying Capabilities of Open-Source Modular Robotics. In *International Conference on Intelligent RObots and Systems, Self-Reconfigurable Robots Workshop (IROS 08)*, 2008.

Distance Measures for HyperGP with Fitness Sharing

Jan Drchal
Czech Technical University in Prague
Faculty of Electrical Engineering, Department of Computer Science and Engineering
Karlovo náměstí 13, 121 35 Praha 2
Czech Republic
drchajan@fel.cvut.cz

Miroslav Šnorek
Czech Technical University in Prague
Faculty of Electrical Engineering, Department of Computer Science and Engineering
Karlovo náměstí 13, 121 35 Praha 2
Czech Republic
snorek@fel.cvut.cz

ABSTRACT

In this paper we propose a new algorithm called HyperGPEFS (HyperGP with Explicit Fitness Sharing). It is based on a HyperNEAT, which is a well-established evolutionary method employing *indirect encoding* of artificial neural networks. Indirect encoding in HyperNEAT is realized via special function called Compositional and Pattern Producing Network (CPPN), able to describe a neural network of arbitrary size. CPPNs are represented by network structures, which are evolved by means of a slightly modified version of another, well-known algorithm NEAT (NeuroEvolution of Augmenting Topologies). HyperGP is a variant of HyperNEAT, where the CPPNs are optimized by Genetic Programming (GP). Published results reported promising improvement in the speed of convergence.

Our approach further extends HyperGP by using *fitness sharing* to promote a diversity of a population. Here, we thoroughly compare all three algorithms on six different tasks. Fitness sharing demands a definition of a *tree distance measure*. Among other five, we propose a *generalized distance measure* which, in conjunction with HyperGPEFS, significantly outperforms HyperNEAT and HyperGP on all, but one testing problems. Although this paper focuses on *indirect encoding*, the proposed distance measures are generally applicable.

Categories and Subject Descriptors

I.2.6 [**Artificial Intelligence**]: Learning—*Concept learning, Connectionism and neural nets*

General Terms

Algorithms, Experimentation

Keywords

HyperGP, HyperNEAT, GP, fitness sharing, tree distance measures, artificial neural networks, indirect encodings

1. INTRODUCTION

Increasing availability of parallel computation allows for simulation of large-scale neural networks. Classical training algorithms (such as back-propagation, second order optimization and evolutionary computation) suffer from poor convergence caused by the large dimension of the optimized, *directly encoded*, weights.

A counterpart to the direct encoding is an *indirect encoding* (or a *generative encoding*). The idea of the indirect encoding is inspired by the Nature where a relatively short genome encodes for a highly complex brain (and the rest of the body). This immense compression of information is, among others, facilitated by repeating motifs found at all scales of magnification. This involves repetition or more precisely repetition with variation and diverse kinds of symmetries. A similar compression can be employed in Evolutionary Computation, effectively reducing a dimensionality of the optimization problem and possibly making it solvable.

In [12], Fréderic Gruau presented *Cellular Encoding*, which was inspired by embryogenesis. He has demonstrated evolution of artificial neural networks representing the XOR function of arbitrary number of inputs. Biological Gene Regulatory Networks were inspiration for [8] while Discrete Cosine Transformation is used to compress neural network weights in [16].

HyperNEAT [5, 10], is another state-of-the-art *indirect encoding* scheme. Here, a *final network* is indirectly encoded using a special function called CPPN (Compositional and Pattern Producing Network). In original HyperNEAT, CPPNs are represented by models resembling common Artificial Neural Networks, although different types of computational nodes are used to reflect the need to encode the aforementioned regular patterns. The *base algorithm* used to evolve CPPNs is a slightly modified version of a well-known Neuro-evolutionary algorithm NEAT [23]. In [2], Buk et al. presented a derivative algorithm named HyperGP, where NEAT, being the *base algorithm* for HyperNEAT, was replaced by GP (Genetic Programming) [22]. The results, although limited to a single domain, have shown a substantial improvement in a speed of a convergence. HyperGP represents CPPNs by trees (or more specifically forests to facilitate multiple outputs) using nodes very similar to those used in original HyperNEAT.

In this paper, we present an extension to HyperGP called HyperGPEFS (HyperGP with Explicit Fitness Sharing), where HyperGP is further extended by *fitness sharing* [17]. We will use abbreviation GPEFS for our *base algorithm*. Fitness sharing is a so-called *niching algorithm* [17]. Niching methods were originally designed to find multiple optima of multimodal functions. In other contexts they were used to promote diversity of population during evolutionary run (as in NEAT [23]). Every niching method requires the existence of a *distance measure* describing a pairwise similarity of members in a population. Here, we experiment with six different such measures. We compare HyperNEAT, HyperGP and HyperGPEFS on six different tasks. Furthermore, we compare all three *base algorithms* and *distance measures* on direct encoding domains, namely a Symbolic Regression and a Maze Navigation task, to study, whether there are any observable differences when different *distance measures* are employed. The results shown are promising as GPEFS significantly outperformed GP and NEAT on all testing problems with an exception of one.

The paper[1] is organized as follows. Section 2 describes the theoretical background. Section 3 introduces HyperGPEFS algorithm as well as six tree distance measures. Section 4 describes the test problems and the experimental setup. Section 5 discusses the results. Final section concludes the paper.

2. BACKGROUND

2.1 HyperNEAT

HyperNEAT algorithm was introduced in [5, 10] it was already applied to many domains, namely: game playing [11], robot control tasks [2, 5, 7] or visual processing [10].

HyperNEAT works in a following way: at first, one have to decide for the structure of a *final network* (number and types of neurons and possible connections), also each neuron is assigned coordinates. Such template is called the *substrate*. Second, NEAT algorithm is used to evolve the CPPNs. The CPPN in HyperNEAT has a form of a common neural network, with an exception of using diverse nodes with special transfer functions which are either symmetric (e.g., absolute value, Gaussian function), periodic (e.g., Sin, Cos) or of a different type (e.g., sigmoid, to represent nonlinearities) to reflect the above mentioned regularities found in living creatures. Third, the *final network* is constructed with the same structure as the *substrate*. The CPPN is then used to determine synaptic weights of all possible connections found in the *substrate*. The coordinates of both interconnected neurons are fed into the CPPN's inputs, the CPPN then outputs their connection weight. The connection is not expressed in *final network* if the weight's absolute value is below a given threshold. Fourth, the *final network* is evaluated on a problem domain to get the fitness value and provide a feedback to NEAT.

By using neuron coordinates, HyperNEAT can exploit a geometry of a problem. For example, when applied to checkers, it actually gets notion of which square is adjacent to which square, and in which direction [11]. An important feature of HyperNEAT is that its substrate can be scaled to higher resolutions approximately preserving its inner structure and function [5, 10].

NEAT [23] (NeuroEvolution of Augmenting Topologies) is an algorithm originally developed for evolution of both parameters (weights) and topology of artificial neural networks. It was later enhanced to produce the CPPNs with heterogenous nodes for HyperNEAT algorithm instead of producing the neural networks directly. It works with genomes of variable size. NEAT introduced a concept of *innovation numbers*, which are gene labels allowing effective genome alignment in order to facilitate crossover-like operations. Moreover, innovation numbers are used for computation of a genotypical distance measure of two individuals. The distance measure is needed by niching evolutionary algorithm, which is a core of NEAT. Because NEAT evolves networks of different complexity (sizes) niching was found to be necessary for a protection of new topology innovations. An important NEAT property is the *complexification* – it starts with simple networks and gradually adds new neurons and connections.

The niching algorithm used in NEAT is *Explicit Fitness Sharing* [17] (EFS) as it uses a genotypical distance measure. Fitness sharing reduces the fitness of an individual given the number of similar individuals (similar individuals form a niche) in the population. The version used in NEAT divides the population into mutually exclusive niche (species). When a new individual is to be assigned to a species it goes through a list of the already existing species and is always compared with an individual designated as the *species' representative*. The comparison is done via evaluation of a distance measure. If the two individuals are similar enough (their distance is below a predefined *speciation threshold* δ) the new individual is assigned to the species, otherwise, it tries the next one in the list. If no species is compatible enough, a new one is created and the individual becomes its *representative*. This approach proved to be sufficient for NEAT and has a better time complexity than common EFS which compares all pairs of individuals in the population.

2.2 HyperGP

HyperGP [2] is a modification of HyperNEAT, where NEAT is replaced by GP. It was shown to be superior in a speed of convergence to NEAT on a simulated robotic task.

In this paper, we use a slightly simplified version of GP as a *base algorithm* for HyperGP, omitting a commonly used crossover operator as it was shown to decrease performance in [2]. More specifically, to create a new generation, we employ a tournament selection (tournament of size 2) to select N (the population size) parents. Each selected parent then produces a single offspring. Algorithm continues by sorting all $2N$ individuals by their fitness and successively reduces their number back to N, keeping only the fittest.

The initial population is created using the *grow method* [22]. The depth of trees is limited to avoid bloating. We use two types of mutations: a *structural mutation* selects a random node in a tree and replaces it by a random subtree again using the *grow method* or replaces the node by a random node of the same arity. A *parametric mutation* selects a random constant node (if exists) and applies a Cauchy mutation [24] to it. A newly created random constant node is initialized by a random value from a selected interval.

2.3 GP, Fitness Sharing and Distance Measures

The idea to use Fitness Sharing together with GP is not new. Approaches mostly differ in a choice of a distance measure. In [18] a *phenotypic* measure is used with promising

[1]Note, that the paper is supported by additional materials including a detailed experimental setup, full results and source codes, visit: `http://neuron.felk.cvut.cz/~drchaj1/`.

results: less generations or smaller populations are needed to solve selected tasks. In [9] a configurable *genotypic* measure is proposed leading to significantly smaller evolved trees than those evolved with plain GP. An interesting approach [14] uses a simple *genotypic* measure which only compares for exact equality or inequality of the trees, the algorithm then uses a modification of Fitness Sharing called the Structure Fitness Sharing.

Other references to tree distance measures are studies of GP population diversity [3, 19], Multi-Objective Evolutionary Algorithm for GP bloat reduction [6] and others [1, 13, 21]. A nice overview of tree distance measures can be found also in [20].

3. OUR APPROACH

3.1 HyperGPEFS

An idea to use EFS together with HyperGP comes from the fact, that it was successfully used in NEAT but also in other contexts, see 2.3. Although GP does not employ complexification as NEAT (all trees up to maximum depth are permitted, even in the initial generation), it still works with *parametric* and *structural* mutations. When a structural mutation introduces a new promising structure EFS should be able to protect it through speciation in a similar way as it does in NEAT.

HyperGPEFS is a simple combination of both HyperGP and HyperNEAT. It takes genome encoding, mutation operators and the way of creation of the initial generation from HyperGP. Speciation and selection is, on the other hand, taken from NEAT (for more details, see [23]). In our implementation, we use an adaptive *speciation threshold* δ: it is doubled when a number of species exceeds the target number of species, otherwise it is divided by 2.

3.2 Distance Measures for HyperGPEFS

Unlike in NEAT which works with general graphs it is much simpler to design a time efficient distance measure for trees. The following list contains distance measures which we used for HyperGPEFS. Note the single letter abbreviations in brackets that will be used below.

1. **Innovation Numbers (I)**: We propose this genotypic tree distance measure as a counterpart to distance measure used in NEAT [23]. Similar approach, although adapted for crossover operators, can be found in [19] . A unique *innovation number* is assigned to each node in a tree. Whenever a *structural mutation* adds new nodes to the tree, new *innovation numbers* are generated by an ever increasing counter. As GPEFS uses vastly different structural mutation operators (growing random subtrees) compared to NEAT, we do not use any kind of innovation memory. The distance limited to interval $[0, 1]$ is defined as:

    (a) Let I_p and I_q be the sets containing the innovation numbers of the trees p and q,

    (b) then $d(p, q) = 1 - 2\frac{|I_p \cap I_q|}{|I_p|+|I_q|}$.

2. **Node Count (N)**: It is based on *pseudo-isomorphs* [3]. Simple genotypic distance measure uses a relative difference of the number of nodes. The relative difference is defined as:

$$d_r(x, y) = \frac{|x - y|}{max(|x|, |y|)}.$$

    the **N** distance is then defined as:

$$d(p, q) = d_r(n(p), n(q)),$$

    where the function $n(x)$ gives the number of nodes of a tree with the root x. This measure is limited to interval $[0, 1]$.

3. **Tree Description (D)**: An extended version of the **N** measure, defined as:

$$d(p, q) = \frac{1}{4}(d_r(n(p), n(q)) + d_r(l(p), l(q)) + d_r(c(p), c(q)) + d_r(d(p), d(q))),$$

    takes also the number of leaves $l(x)$, constants $c(x)$ and the depth $d(x)$ of trees into account. It is again limited to $[0, 1]$.

4. **Generalized (G)**: The generalized distance measure, covers many already published approaches, it is mostly inspired by [9]. It allows to change behavior according to parameters. At first, all node types are partitioned to sets $A_0, A_1, A_2, \ldots$, where $A_0 = \{NIL\}$ contains only a special NIL node and A_1 is reserved for constants. Prior to the computation of the distance between two trees p and q, we compute R_{pq}: the absolute range of constant values of both the trees p and q[2]. Then we define an auxiliary function to compute the distance between two node types $x \in A_i$ and $y \in A_j$:

$$d'(x, y) = \begin{cases} 0 & \text{if } x = y \text{ (note, this implies } i = j), \\ C\frac{|x-y|}{R_{pq}} & \text{if } i = j = 1, \\ 1 & \text{otherwise.} \end{cases}$$

    Finally, the generalized measure is defined as:
    $d(p, q) = d'(p, q)$ if neither p, nor q have descendants
    $d(p(s_1, \ldots, s_n), q(t_1, \ldots, t_m)) = d(q(t_1, \ldots, t_m), p(s_1, \ldots, s_n))$
    for $m < n$, $d(p(s_1, \ldots, s_n), q(t_1, \ldots, t_m)) = d'(p, q) + \max(\alpha, \delta_{pq})\frac{1}{K}\left(\sum_{i=1}^{n} d(s_i, t_i) + \beta \sum_{j=n+1}^{m} d(NIL, t_j)\right)$ for $n \leq m$, where

    (a) constant $\alpha \in \{0, 1\}$ decides whether to descend into subtrees, when nodes have different types (descends when $\alpha = 1$),

    (b) constant $\beta \in \{0, 1\}$ decides whether to include information concerning the missing subtree in one of the trees (includes when $\beta = 1$),

    (c) δ_{pq} is the Kronecker delta,

    (d) constant $C \geq 0$ controls the influence of constants (for $C = 0$ constants are not taken into account),

    (e) constant $K > 0$ controls the influence of a node depth in the tree (for $K = 1$ the node depth does not matter).

Table 1 shows settings of the **G** measure which reflect previously published measures.

[2]The approach in [9] uses constant value range of the whole population.

Table 1: Generalized (G) tree distance measure. Known parameter settings.

α	β	C	K	Close or equal to
0	0	0	1	[13]
1	0	0	1	[6]
0	0	0	$2 \times$ arity	[21]
1	1	multiple	multiple	[1, 9]

5. **Phenotypic (P)**: This is an only representative of *phenotypic* distance measures [20] (fitness sharing which uses *phenotypic* measure is often called *implicit*). This measure does not compare trees, but rather their outputs for the same input vector. More precisely, it computes an average square difference of trees' outputs over all input vectors.

6. **Random (R)**: The distance between two trees is defined as a random number from interval $[0, 1)$ using uniform distribution. This special measure was defined as a control treatment.

Note, that although this section dealt with tree distance measures, in fact we evolve forests with HyperGPEFS to allow CPPNs with multiple outputs. The distance between two forests is then computed as an average of distances between corresponding trees.

4. EXPERIMENTAL SETUP

4.1 Introductory Problems, Direct Encoding

In this subsection, we present Symbolic Regression and Maze Navigation problems used to compare the *base algorithms* (NEAT, GP, GPEFS) without Hyper extension. All subsequent problems are aimed to examine their properties on indirectly encoded problems. Such experiments will be helpful to show, whether there is a difference in a choice of the right distance measure for direct and indirect encoding domains.

Symbolic Regression

The first, most straightforward problem is Symbolic Regression, the test functions are in Table 2. The equations are divided into four groups according to their dimensionality (the number of inputs). They were selected from a larger set, of which they presented the most diverse behaviors. Note, that the equation 4D-V was obtained by solving a problem described in 4.4 by HyperGP. The 1D, 2D and 3D functions were sampled in a hypercube having minimum and maximum coordinates -10 and 10, 4D used boundaries of -1 and 1. We have used 20 equidistant samples in each dimension for 1D, 7 for 2D and 3D and 5 for 4D. The fitness is computed using *Mean Squared Error* as $1/(1+MSE)$ which lies in $(0, 1]$. The problem was considered to be solved, when target fitness 0.95 was reached. Note, neither testing nor validation sets were used.

Maze Navigation

Maze navigation (Figure 1) presents a *deceptive task* to show abilities to overcome local extremes. The problem is a simple target approach, where a simulated robot tries to navigate through a maze from a starting position to a target one.

Table 2: Symbolic Regression functions.

ID	Function
1D-F	$1.5x_1^3 + 2.3x_1^2 - 1.1x_1 + 3.7$
1D-H	$0.1x_1^2 + 0.2\sin(x_1)$
2D-I	$1.5x_1x_2^2 + 2.3x_1x_2 - 1.1x_2^2$
2D-K	$x_1x_2^2 + x_1x_2 - x_2^2$
3D-E	$1.5x_1x_2 + 2.3x_1 + x_2x_3 - 1.1x_3$
3D-H	$1.5x_1x_2^2x_3 + 2.3x_1x_2x_3 - 1.1x_2 + 5.3$
3D-K	$x_1x_2^2x_3 - x_1x_2 + x_2x_3$
4D-C	$1.5x_1x_2x_3x_4$
4D-F	$1.5x_1x_2x_3 + 2.3x_1 - 1.1x_2 - 1.1x_4$
4D-G	$1.5x_1x_2^2x_3x_4 + 2.3x_1 - 1.1x_2$
4D-V	$e^{-1.36709x_2^2}x_1\left(2.43454e^{-x_3^2} - 0.393788\sin(1 - x_1)\right)$

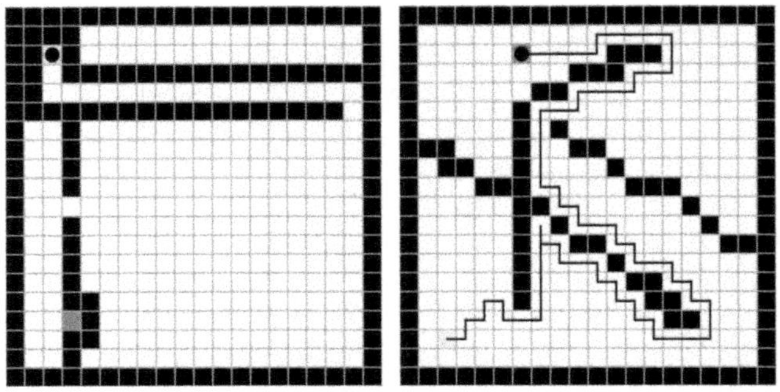

Figure 1: MAZE-1 (left), MAZE-2 (right) maps. MAZE-2 shows a possible solution. Both tasks are deceptive as there are local extremes in a proximity of the global one.

Fitness is derived from the Manhattan distance between the robot and the target after 150 steps. We have used not only two different maps, but for each map also different types of sensors. For MAZE-1 the sensors were: distance to target, binary wall sensors (1 step ahead, ahead-left, ahead-right) and binary target detection (ahead, left, right and behind). For MAZE-2 we have used four wall range finders instead of three wall detection sensors. The controller has a single output: for output values less than -0.5 the robot turns left and advances, for values greater than 0.5 it turns right and advances, otherwise it makes only a step forward. The problem was considered to be solved if and only if the robot reaches the target.

4.2 Bit Permutation

Bit permutation is a set of three problems which are similar to the Bit Mirroring in [4]. All possible combinations of inputs (0s and 1s) were tested. In this paper we did experiments with $n = 6$ inputs/outputs (64 possibilities). The fitness is computed as a number of all correct output bits over all test patterns (in contrary to [4].) The problem was considered to be solved when all input patterns generated correct output patterns. The substrate is composed of two layers of neurons (input and output). Nodes in each layer are placed equidistant (with a distance 1). A bias neuron (having coordinate 0) is connected to all output neurons. The CPPN has therefore 2 outputs. The three problems are:

Figure 2: Mobile Robot Navigation map with road (fast) and grass (slow) surfaces. Two white squares determine starting positions.

Bit Reverse Bits $1, 2, \ldots n$ labeled from the LSB to the MSB: $o_j = i_{n-j+1}$, for $j \in \{1, 2, \ldots, n\}$.

Bit Shift Logical shift to the right: $o_n = 0$, $o_j = i_{j+1}$, for $j \in \{1, \ldots, n-1\}$.

Bit Rotate Circular shift to the right: $o_j = i_{j+1} \mod n$, for $j \in \{1, \ldots, n\}$.

4.3 Parity Problem

In this experiment we evolve a network computing odd parity. The function has n inputs (in our case 4) and a single output. The substrate is similar to the previous one, although we added a biased hidden layer (CPPN with 4 outputs). A *final network* must give correct answers for all 16 test cases.

4.4 Visual Discrimination

As presented in [10], the task is to detect the larger object of two objects, projected on a two-dimensional array of input neurons. Unlike in the original experiment which used two layer 2D substrate of 11×11 neurons we have used 5×5. The problem was considered to be solved only for success in all test cases – highest precision possible was needed.

4.5 Mobile Robot Navigation

In the last experiment, we have employed ViVAE (Visual Vector Agent Environment) [2, 7]. The task was to evolve a robotic controller to drive two robots on a map (See Figure 2) at a maximum possible speed. The best strategy is to drive on a side of a road to avoid collisions. The problem was considered to be solved when the fitness reached 0.797 (value found experimentally).

4.6 Parameter Settings

The size of population was set to 100, the maximum number of generations was 1000 (for Mobile Robot Navigation they were set to 100 and 50) for all algorithms (GP, GPEFS and NEAT). All experiments were repeated for 200 times with an exception of the Mobile Robotic Navigation, which was repeated for 20 times, only.

We have used the same node types for all experiments. In the case of NEAT they were: Bipolar Sigmoid, Sin, Linear and Gaussian. For GP and GPEFS: Add, Multiply, ArcTan, Sin and Gaussian. For GP and GPEFS the maximum tree depth was 5. Note, that other parameter settings, e.g., mutation rates, as well as their detailed explanation are available at the paper support page (see above).

To test the properties of the generalized distance measure, we did experiments for all 24 combinations of $\alpha \in \{0, 1\}$, $\beta \in \{0, 1\}$, $C \in \{0, 1\}$ and $K \in \{1, 2, 10\}$, we will write these configurations as tuples, e.g., $(1, 0, 1, 2)$, in the following text.

5. RESULTS

Figures 3 and 4 show the results of experiments comparing NEAT, GP and GPEFS (with all distance measures). Note that only the best out of 24 configurations of the **G** measure are shown (results for different settings are discussed below).

The figures show that with an exception of the Parity problem, the most successful approach is GPEFS with the **G** measure: whenever the **G** is the single best, it is also significantly[3] better compared to the second best (for Bit rotate the difference is not significant). Plain GP performs significantly best on the Parity problem.

The Random (**R**) measure shows very interesting results, in many cases it is comparable to other measures, or even significantly outperforms them (e.g., **I** on 1D-H and 4D-C, **N** on 3D-E, **N** and **D** on the Visual Discrimination). Another interesting discovery is that the **R** measure significantly beats plain GP in some cases (e.g., 1D-H, 4D-F, Maze Navigation, Bit Reverse or Visual Discrimination).

The **I** measure is the second best for Visual Discrimination and Bit Shift (significantly better than the third one), but in many cases it is mediocre or even fails (e.g., 4D-G, 4D-V or Maze Navigation). The only *phenotypic* measure **P** does not perform well on any of problems (although, on 3D-K it looks like the second best, this is not significant). The measures **N** and **D** show comparable performance on many tasks.

Compared to the other algorithms, NEAT does not perform especially well on any task. It was able to significantly outperform GP and GPEFS with **P** measure on the MAZE-2, It was also significantly better than **P** measure on Visual Discrimination. We have run another set of experiments with NEAT (all problems except Mobile Robot Navigation) having population doubled to 200 and with doubled maximum number of generations to 2000. Only in a single case of MAZE-1 for doubled population size, the results significantly improved (but still not enough to outperform GPEFS).

The following experiments deal with GPEFS using Generalized measure **G**. With the exception of Mobile Robot Navigation, all 24 parameter settings were tested (see 4.6). The K (for $K > 1$ the deeper the node is in a tree the smaller influence it has on a distance) parameter shown to be the most influential with respect to the performance. We have decided to aggregate all parameters according to the K (this makes $\frac{24}{3}200 = 1600$ experiments for each of the three values of K).

The results are presented in Figures 5 and 6. With exceptions of 3D-E ($K = 2$ is significantly the best) and 3D-K ($K = 1$ is insignificantly better than $K = 2$) the distance measure performs best for $K = 1$ significantly, on direct encoding domains. On indirect encoding domains, the situation is different. Bit Reverse gives balanced results. The same goes for Visual Discrimination (not true for $K = 10$ where the performance drops). For Bit Shift the trend is

[3]We use Fisher's Exact test (two-tailed, significance level 5%) to compare the numbers of successful experiments.

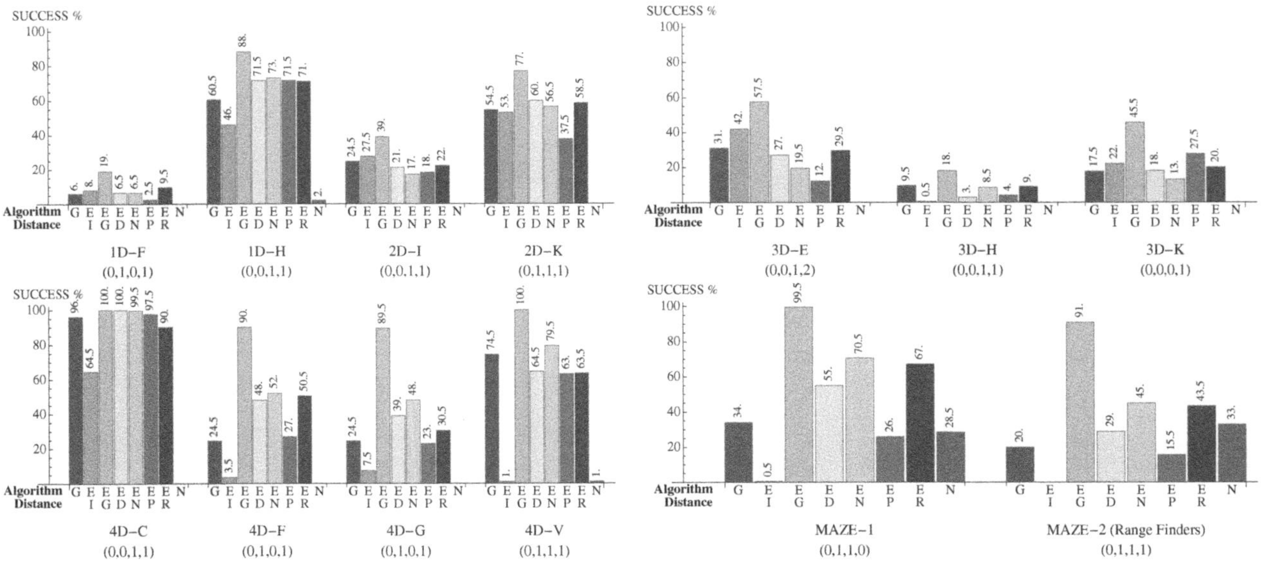

Figure 3: Comparison of base algorithms on all directly encoded problems. Percentual success rate out of 200 experiments each. The first row below bars determines a base algorithm (G (GP), E (GPEFS), N (NEAT)), second row a distance measure. The tuples below problem names show the settings of α, β, C and K for generalized distance measure. Note, that GPEFS with generalized distance measure performs best for all cases.

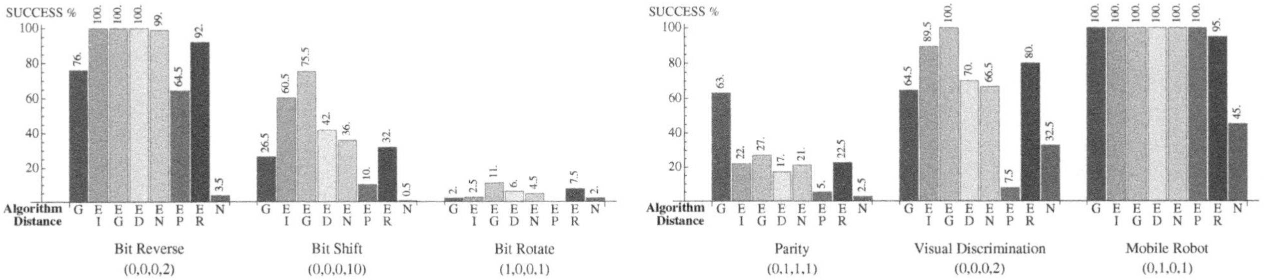

Figure 4: Comparison of base algorithms on all indirectly encoded problems. Percentual success rate out of 200 experiments each. The first row below bars determines a base algorithm (G (GP), E (GPEFS), N (NEAT)), second row a distance measure. Again, GPEFS with generalized distance measure performs best for all cases with an exception of Parity where GP is the winner.

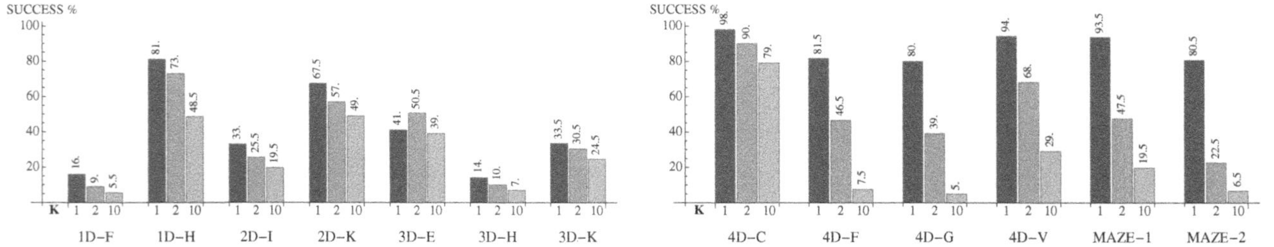

Figure 5: Results on GPEFS with generalized measure G on all directly encoded problems, aggregated for different values of K. Each bar shows the successful rate over 1600 experiments. The value of $K \in \{1, 2, 10\}$ is shown below the corresponding bars. With a single exception of 3D-E Symbolic Regression problem $K = 1$ (depth of nodes does not matter) is the best setting.

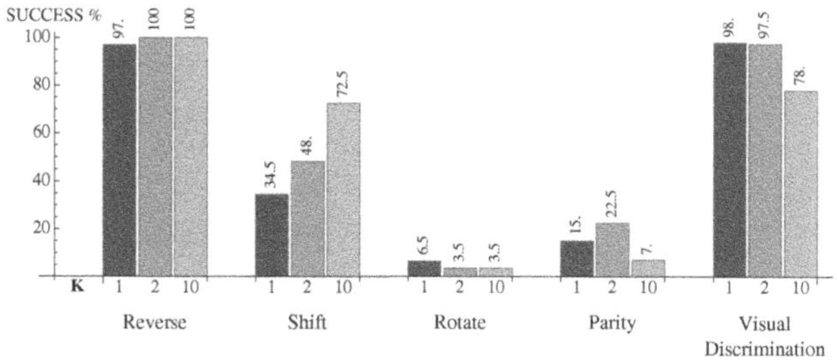

Figure 6: Results on HyperGPEFS with G measure, aggregated for different values of K. In contrast with directly encoded problems the influence of K is problem-dependent.

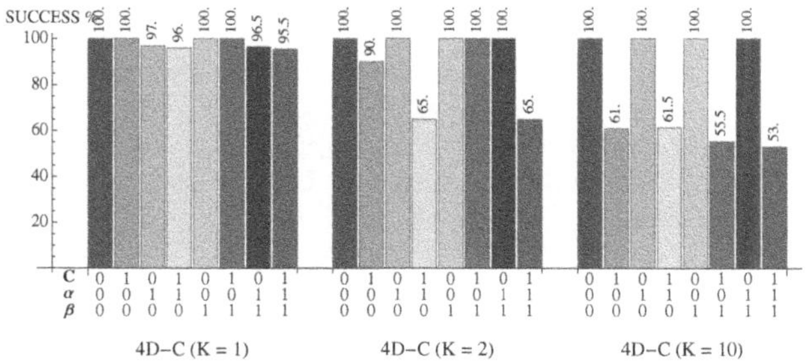

Figure 7: GPEFS with G measure on 4D-C Symbolic Regression problem. Performace drops for increasing parameter K while considering differences of random constant values ($C = 1$).

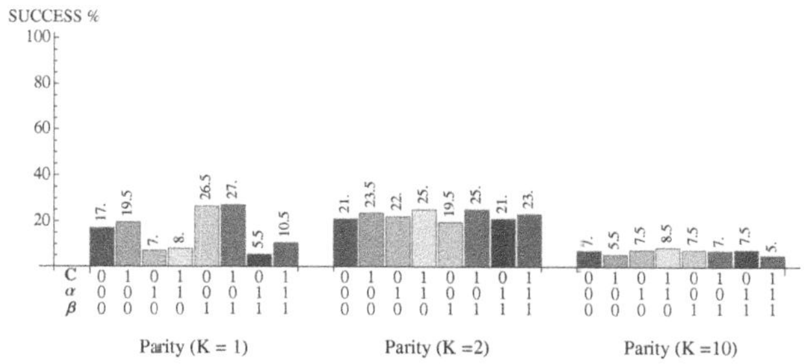

Figure 8: HyperGPEFS with G measure on the Parity problem, showing influence of α and β parameters for $K = 1$. Note the drop of success rate for $K = 1$ and $\alpha = 1$.

opposite, $K = 10$ gives significantly best results. For Parity, setting $K = 2$ significantly outperforms the others.

An interesting trend was discovered for many of direct encoding domains (see Figure 7). For increasing K the constant C increases its importance: for $C = 1$ (takes the difference of random constants into account) the performance dramatically drops compared to the same setting with $C = 0$ (random constant values are ignored). This effect is even stronger for Maze Navigation, where the success rates drop even below 1% (data not shown, but available on the support web page).

The parameter α (enables/disables a comparison of subtrees with different root node types) had even less influence on a performance than the K or C. Figure 8 shows evident drop of success rate on the Parity for enabled descent ($\alpha = 1$) for $K = 2$ and $K = 10$ the effect vanishes. We have observed similar trends for 3D-E and 3D-K problems (data not shown).

We have found the last parameter β (take or not the size and shape of subtrees missing in one of the trees into account) to be the least important of all. Figure 8 shows an increase of performance on the Parity for $K = 1$, $\alpha = 0$ and $\beta = 1$ (significant for $C = 0$ but not for $C = 1$).

6. CONCLUSIONS

The main contribution of this paper is the novel algorithm HyperGPEFS which replaces NEAT in HyperNEAT by GP with Explicit Fitness Sharing (GPEFS). We tested six different *tree distance measures* for GPEFS on six problems of which four used *indirect encoding* and two *direct encoding*. Most important results were:

- GPEFS significantly outperformed GP and NEAT on all problems with an exception of Parity, where GP was a winner (with roughly double success rate).
- The most successful *tree distance measure* for GPEFS was the generalized measure **G** at all cases. We have studied its four parameters and found that the most important parameter is the K which decides whether to count with node depth in a tree. For other three parameters we have found cases in which their change leads to a significant difference in performance. In all cases of *directly encoded* problems we have found, that the best results are obtained when the depth of a node is not taken into account ($K = 1$), this contradicts results in [15].
- Other tested distance measures have shown diverse results on different problems. Interestingly, in many cases their performance was significantly worse than the performance of the random measure **R**. It implies, that the wrong choice of a *distance measure* can even have a disruptive effect on convergence. GPEFS with the **R** measure was also observed to outperform plain GP in some cases. The worst results were given by the *phenotypic* measure **P**.
- The innovation number based measure **I** inspired by the distance measure used in NEAT has shown very diverse results for different problems: from being the second best to complete failure, where other measures performed well.
- NEAT has shown significantly better results than GP on a single problem only (*direct encoding*, MAZE-2). For all *indirect encoding* problems GP was superior which supports results in [2]. Our estimation is that this is caused by a larger search-space for NEAT as it has to optimize more random constants than a comparable tree. Also, some of the tested problems demanded high accuracy (e.g., Symbolic Regression) which might be disadvantageous for NEAT. This has to be, however, thoroughly examined in the future.

As for future work, we plan to experiment with more types of *tree distance measures*, particularly with edit-distance based measures [20]. We also plan to find out reasons which led to results on the Parity, where GP outperformed both other methods which employ niching. Another research should be done on importance of crossover for both GP and GPEFS.

7. ACKNOWLEDGMENTS

This research has been supported by the Ministry of Education,Youth and Sports of the Czech Republic as a part of the institutional development support at the CTU in Prague.

8. REFERENCES

[1] V. C. Bhavsar and H. Boley. A Weighted-Tree Similarity Algorithm for Multi-Agent Systems in e-Business Environments. *Computational Intelligence*, 20(4):584–602, 2004.

[2] Z. Buk, J. Koutnik, and M. Snorek. NEAT in HyperNEAT Substituted with Genetic Programming. *Adaptive and Natural Computing Algorithms*, 5495:243–252, 2009.

[3] E. Burke, S. Gustafson, G. Kendall, and N. Krasnogor. Advanced Population Diversity Measures in Genetic Programming. In *Parallel Problem Solving from Nature PPSN VII*, number 2439 in Lecture Notes in Computer Science, pages 341–350. Springer-Verlag, 2002.

[4] J. Clune, K. O. Stanley, R. T. Pennock, and C. Ofria. On the Performance of Indirect Encoding Across the Continuum of Regularity. *IEEE Transaction On Evolutionary Computation*, 15(3):346–367, 2011.

[5] D. B. D'Ambrosio and K. O. Stanley. A Novel Generative Encoding for Exploiting Neural Network Sensor and Output Geometry. In *Proceedings of the 9th Annual Conference on Genetic and Evolutionary Computation - GECCO '07*, pages 974–981, New York, NY, USA, 2007. ACM Press.

[6] E. D. De Jong, R. A. Watson, and J. B. Pollack. Reducing Bloat and Promoting Diversity using Multi-Objective Methods. In *Proceedings of the Genetic and Evolutionary Computation Conference GECCO 2001*, pages 11–18. Morgan Kaufmann, 2001.

[7] J. Drchal, J. Koutnik, and M. Snorek. HyperNEAT Controlled Robots Learn How to Drive on Roads in Simulated Environment. In *CEC'09 Proceedings of the Eleventh conference on Congress on Evolutionary Computation*, pages 1087–1092, Trondheim, 2009. IEEE Press.

[8] P. Eggenberger-Hotz. Creation of Neural Networks Based on Developmental and Evolutionary Principles. In *In Proceedings of the International Conference on Artificial Neural Networks*, pages 337–342. Springer-Verlag, 1997.

[9] A. Ekárt and S. Z. Németh. A Metric for Genetic Programs and Fitness Sharing. In *Proceedings of the European Conference on Genetic Programming*, volume 1802 of *Lecture Notes in Computer Science*, pages 259–270, Berlin, Heidelberg, 2000. Springer Berlin Heidelberg.

[10] J. Gauci and K. O. Stanley. Generating Large-Scale Neural Networks Through Discovering Geometric Regularities. In *Proceedings of the 9th Annual Conference on Genetic and Evolutionary Computation - GECCO '07*, pages 997–1004, New York, NY, USA, 2007. ACM Press.

[11] J. Gauci and K. O. Stanley. Autonomous Evolution of Topographic Regularities in Artificial Neural Networks. *Neural Computation*, 22(7):1860–1898, 2010.

[12] F. Gruau. *Neural Network Synthesis Using Cellular Encoding And The Genetic Algorithm.* PhD thesis, Ecole Normale Supirieure de Lyon, France, 1994.

[13] Y. Hasegawa and H. Iba. Multimodal Search with Immune Based Genetic Programming. In *Lecture Notes in Computer Science*, volume 3239, pages 330–341, Berlin, Heidelberg, 2004. Springer Berlin Heidelberg.

[14] J. Hu, K. Seo, S. Li, Z. Fan, R. C. Rosenberg, and E. D. Goodman. Structure Fitness Sharing (SFS) For Evolutionary Design By Genetic Programming. In *GECCO 2002 Proceedings of the Genetic and Evolutionary Computation Conference*, pages 780–787. Morgan Kaufmann Publishers, 2002.

[15] C. Igel and K. Chellapilla. Investigating the Influence of Depth and Degree of Genotypic Change on Fitness in Genetic Programming. In *Proceedings of the Genetic and Evolutionary Computation Conference*, pages 1061–1068, Orlando, FL, USA, 1999. Morgan Kaufmann.

[16] J. Koutnik, F. Gomez, and J. Schmidhuber. Evolving Neural Networks in Compressed Weight Space. In *Proceedings of the 12th Annual Conference on Genetic and Evolutionary Computation - GECCO '10*, page 619, New York, New York, USA, 2010. ACM Press.

[17] S. W. Mahfoud. A Comparison of Parallel and Sequential Niching Methods. In *In Proceedings of the Sixth International Conference on Genetic Algorithms*, pages 136–143. Morgan Kaufmann, 1995.

[18] R. I. B. McKay. An Investigation of Fitness Sharing in Genetic Programming. *The Australian Journal of Intelligent Information Processing Systems*, 7(1/2):43–51, 2001.

[19] N. F. Mcphee. Analysis of Genetic Diversity Through Population History. In *Proceedings of the Genetic and Evolutionary Computation Conference*, pages 1112–1120. Morgan Kaufmann, 1999.

[20] T. H. Nguyen and X. H. Nguyen. A Brief Overview of Population Diversity Measures in Genetic Programming. In *Proceedings of the Third AsianPacific workshop on Genetic Programming*, pages 128–139, 2006.

[21] S.-H. Nienhuys-Cheng. Distance Between Herbrand Interpretations: A Measure for Approximations to a Target Concept. In *ILP '97 Proceedings of the 7th International Workshop on Inductive Logic Programming*, pages 213–226. Springer-Verlag London, 1997.

[22] R. Poli, W. B. Langdon, and N. F. Mcphee. *A Field Guide to Genetic Programming.* Number March. Published via http://lulu.com, 2008.

[23] K. O. Stanley. *Efficient Evolution of Neural Networks through Complexification.* PhD thesis, The University of Texas at Austin, 2004.

[24] X. Yao, L. Yong, and L. Guangming. Evolutionary Programming Made Faster. *IEEE Transactions on Evolutionary Computation*, 3:82—-102, 1999.

Complex and Diverse Morphologies Can Develop from a Minimal Genomic Model

Jose David Fernández
Research Group in Biomimetics, Department of Computer Science, University of Málaga, Severo Ochoa 4, 29590 Málaga, Spain
josedavid@geb.uma.es

Francisco J. Vico
Research Group in Biomimetics, Department of Computer Science, University of Málaga, Severo Ochoa 4, 29590 Málaga, Spain
fjv@geb.uma.es

René Doursat
Research Group in Biomimetics, Department of Computer Science, University of Málaga, Severo Ochoa 4, 29590 Málaga, Spain
doursat@yahoo.com

ABSTRACT

While development plays a critical role in the emergence of diversity, its mechanical and chemical actions are considered to be inextricably correlated with *genetic control*. Since in most extant species the complex growth from zygote to adult organism is orchestrated by a complex gene regulatory network (GRN), the prevalent view is that the evolution of diverse morphologies must result from the evolution of diverse GRN topologies. By contrast, this work focuses on the unique effect of developmental processes through an abstract model of self-regulated structure *without* genetic regulation—only modulation of initial conditions. Here, morphologies are generated by a simple evolutionary algorithm searching for the longest instances of unfolding dynamics based on *tensegrity* graphs. The usual regulatory function of the genome is taken over by physical constraints in the graphs, making morphological diversity a pure product of structural complexification. By highlighting the potential of structural development, our model is relevant to both "structuralist" biological models and bio-inspired systems engineering.

Categories and Subject Descriptors

J.3 [**Life and medical sciences**]: Biology and genetics; I.2.8 [**Artificial Intelligence**]: Problem Solving, Control Methods, and Search—*Heuristic methods*; G.1.6 [**Numerical Analysis**]: Optimization—*Global optimization*

General Terms

Algorithms, Design

Keywords

computational biology, evolutionary development, morphogenesis, indirect encoding, tensegrity

1. INTRODUCTION

The phenotype of a multicellular organism is generated by a complex developmental process, which transforms a single fertilized cell, the zygote, into a living architecture composed of millions to trillions of cells. This process is a fascinating self-made choreography of precisely timed events, during which cells in the growing organism spontaneously divide, modify their physicochemical properties, and arrange into layers and tissues, themselves folding into increasingly complicated shapes to form organs and appendages [9]. The recent discipline of *evolutionary developmental biology*, or "evo-devo", studies development from an evolutionary perspective (and vice-versa). It examines how phenotypic variation arises from the interplay between the physics of growth and both genetic and environmental variations. Evo-devo takes the viewpoint that morphological trends in evolution are biased to a large extent by developmental mechanisms [1], re-interpreting the traditional but simpler concept of "phenotypic plasticity" [7]. It also applies to some unicellular organisms, albeit at the molecular scale [11].

In this context, *genetic regulatory networks* (GRNs) are emerging as a unifying operating concept [5]. A GRN model postulates that the genome can be described as a vast and complex network of interacting genes, promoting and repressing each other's expression through the intermediation of produced proteins that bind to specific regulatory sites on the DNA. Abstracting out the convoluted pathways and feedback loops between genes, RNA, proteins and metabolites, the state of a GRN can be formalized as a set of "transcription levels" on each gene-node—in the simplest of cases, a binary graph. It can be conceptualized as a dynamical system that follows different trajectories in state space, typically landing on fixed-point or limit-cycle attractors. Each attractor-subset of genes can then be interpreted as a cell type with precise behavior and properties [19]. Since the discovery of the *homeobox* genetic toolkit, development is construed as a complex process tightly modulated by an underlying GRN model: large-scale, coordinated changes in the phenotype are a more or less direct consequence of small, localized changes in the regulation of the developmental process [7], be they genetic [36] or environmental [38] changes.

1.1 Reinstating Development

However, while the detailed knowledge of genomic sequences enables scientists to pinpoint where and when different genes are expressed in the embryo, it is insufficient to understand how the organism builds itself [27]. Regulating and regulated genes of a GRN are separated in reality by the major gap of *development*, which comprises cellular biomechanics and chemical signaling. To fill this gap, evo-devo researchers describe developmental processes as a *coupling* between GRNs and the physical properties of the organisms [7, 9]. The aim of the present work is to focus on the latter, specifically the ability of *tensegrity* structures (see Section 2.1) to generate a wide diversity of forms.

Complex morphologies can be generated by developmental processes. Mechanical cues (strain, compression, bending forces, etc.) play a key role in development by modulating cell differentiation, influencing the direction of growth, and, of special interest here, deforming tissues [13]. Even late-stage (post-embryogenesis) events, such as the folding of the mammalian gut, are primarily determined by mechanical dynamics [33]. Geometrically, the typical embryogenesis of a triploblastic animal consists of a set of complex and precisely timed developmental steps, which dynamically change the physical properties of the cells, the surrounding extracellular matrix and the differential adhesiveness among cells and between cells and other substrates [9].

At a mechanical level, several types of morphogenetic processes can be distinguished, such as cell sheets growing in a given direction, or cells detaching from these sheets and migrating to create new groups. Some of the most common morphogenetic processes include "invagination", in which a sheet of cells folds inward, possibly resulting in the folded cells detaching to form another sheet (e.g., the neural tube), and "branching", in which a tube recursively branches off into a fractal-like pattern (e.g., lung organogenesis [16] or vasculogenesis [21]).

1.2 Relegating Genetic Control

In sum, for evo-devo, biological development consists of a precise spatio-temporal cascade of developmental stages in which morphodynamic physical processes are continually regulated by the genome at multiple levels [27]. Rewinding the course of evolution, however, one can make the hypothesis that in the beginnings of multicellular life the morphologies of organisms might have been essentially generated by physical processes and their environmental conditions, while it is only later that gene regulation had stepped in and taken control [29]. In this paradigm, morphologies made their first appearance as a contingent, but deterministic, result of physicochemical constraints, after which new layers of regulation mechanisms encoded in the DNA helped stabilize these pre-existing developmental processes and expose them to genetic variation and natural selection.

The present study broadly belongs to *artificial development* (AD), an emerging field at the crossroads of computational biology, artificial life and evolutionary computation that studies computational models of development toward various scientific and engineering applications [35]. Typically, the use of evolutionary methods to conduct a parameter search or stochastic optimization becomes especially difficult when the individuals are *complex systems*, i.e. made of a large number of interacting components, because of their high dimensionality (number of degrees of freedom). As a new avenue of bio-inspiration, AD therefore offers interesting approaches to encode complex problems in a compact way, *via* a developmental or generative stage. AD genomes are cases of "indirect" encodings whose size is significantly smaller than "direct" encodings [35], thus greatly improving the efficiency of evolutionary algorithms (despite the added developmental calculation).

However, the introduction of a developmental stage adds a new layer of complexity in some cases. In most AD models, indirect encoding remains a complex interaction between the genotype (often a GRN) and the developing phenotype, for example in generative architectures based on L-system grammars [14], Framsticks robots using genetic programming [20] or path-follower creatures produced by graph rewriting [22]. Some researchers have investigated more complex and biologically realistic models of developing phenotypes with the intention of minimizing the size and complexity of the genotype even further to make it more amenable to evolutionary methods [8]. In this context, our study represents an exploration of how small the genetic component of an AD model can become, while also keeping structural principles simple and still enabling an evolutionary search to solve a problem—in this case, give rise to a diversity of morphologies. To this aim, we use tensegrity structures, as explained in the next section.

2. MECHANICAL MODEL

2.1 The Potential of Tensegrity

Historically, many definitions of tensegrity structures have been proposed [18]. Most of them are variations on the original definition by Snelson [34] and Fuller [10], respectively the creator and namer of this concept (from a contraction of "tensional integrity"). The most generic definition of tensegrity involves a structure composed of compression-bearing rigid elements (rods) isolated from each other and connected by a network of tensioned cables (springs), such that the sum of forces acting on each vertex is null [25] and the structure is maintained in mechanical equilibrium. The balance of strains and compressive forces sustained by each tensegrity element is called the *self-stress* of the structure and characterizes the high structural resilience of the whole. Combined with an exceptionally high rigidity-to-mass ratio, all these properties make tensegrity an object of active study with numerous applications in architecture, civil and mechanical engineering [25].

The last decade has also seen many applications of tensegrity structures to robotics. They comprise the design of control systems in walking robots by analytical [12] or evolutionary [31] methods, the optimization of the dynamical response of articulated wing frameworks [2], the reliance on large-scale couplings and nonlinear dynamics in tensegrity to achieve locomotion with minimal control [32], and the design of ballistic structures able to withstand landing impacts by minimizing the effects of compression shocks [23].

The concept of tensegrity has also been extensively used in biology, notably by Ingber at the molecular and cellular levels [15]. His proposal that the cytoskeleton can be modeled as a dynamic tensegrity structure has led to a new explanation of several properties of cells and tissues in terms of tensegrity properties, in particular:

- the exceptional resilience of the cytoskeleton [3] as an effect of uniform load distribution in tensegrity structures;
- the complex mechanical response of the cell [15, 4] to deformation and substrate-dependent shape change;

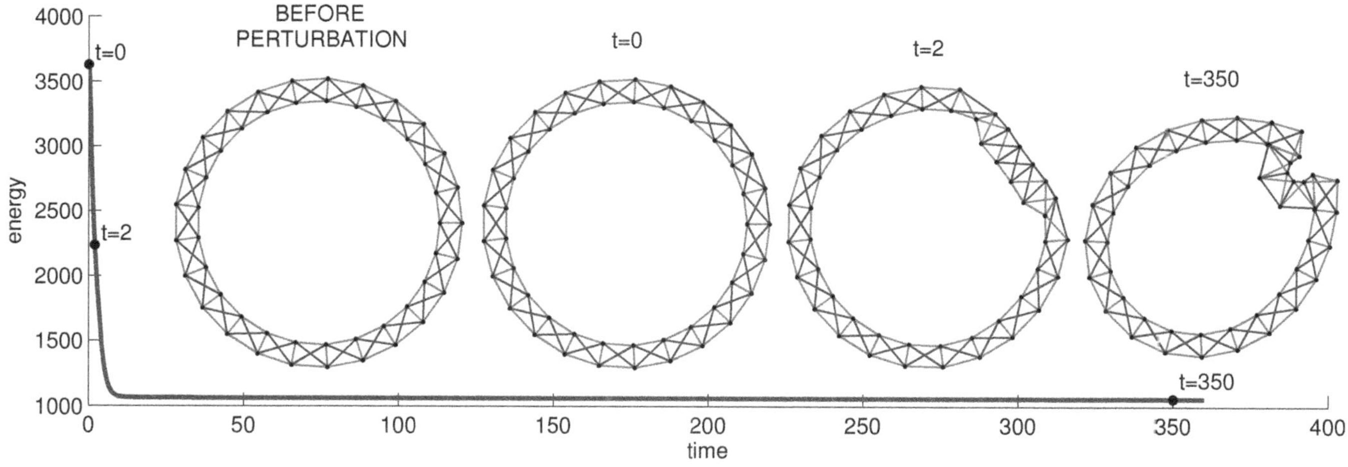

Figure 1: A 2D circular sheet of cells modeled as an elastic tensegrity structure (see text). A morphogenetic event (invagination) is triggered by shortening the peripheral elastic links of a group of neighboring cells [30]. During the subsequent relaxation process, the structure reaches a new equilibrium state. Three snapshots are shown: start of simulation ($t = 0$), midway folding ($t = 2$), and final state ($t = 350$). Blue plot: total energy as a function of time (notice the sharp drop).

- the conversion of mechanical signals into biochemical responses, or "mechanotransduction" relying on force distribution throughout the cytoskeleton [17].

These properties have important consequences on development, too. As sheets of cells expand and cells assemble in specific locations, they become subject to forces and strains that provide mechanical cues, which in turn eventually affect the timing of the growth stages. The tensegrity properties of the cytoskeleton are critical in supporting this whole process [24].

2.2 A Circular Sheet of Cells

In this section, we describe a model of development with minimal genetic control based on tensegrity structures. Since the elements of a tensegrity structure store potential energy, the structure can find itself in an unstable state. If the balance of forces is perturbed beyond a certain threshold, whether by shape deformation or modification of the stress properties of the elements, the structure will "snap" to accommodate these new constraints. It will then settle again into a lower-energy state possibly characterized by a very different shape, dissipating potential energy in the process.

Our work exploits this propensity to "catastrophic" state change or "phase transition" exhibited by tensegrity structures under certain stress conditions. It is inspired by a simple 2D developmental model of invagination [26, 30], in which a circular sheet of cells is modeled as a closed chain of cellular cytoskeletons. Each cell's cytoskeleton consists of six overdamped elastic edges: four external edges arranged in a quadrilateral plus their two diagonals. These quadrilaterals are then merged together to form a circular elastic network representing a closed sheet of cells (Figure 1, first structure). As a whole, the sheet constitutes a self-stressed tensegrity structure potentially capable of settling into multiple configurations of compressed and strained elements. For example, to provoke an invagination process in one region of the cell sheet, it is sufficient to shorten the resting length of the outer elastic links in that region (Figure 1, second to fourth structures). This shows that a very simple and localized genetic signal controlling only a few cytoskeletal features is able to induce a dramatic phenotypic change.

We adopt a similar 2D structure (see Figure 2b) as a starting point for the present evolutionary study, leaving aside its origins as a cell sheet model. Instead, we construe it from now on as an abstract model of morphogenetic processes, by which shapes can undergo a complex but well-ordered series of morphological transformations (keeping in mind that some transformations might not be topologically possible in more realistic 3D structures). We show that elastic tensegrity networks are able to rearrange themselves under minimal genetic control and give rise to a diverse array of morphologies. Such behavior makes these structures good candidates to represent the physical substrate of complex development, whether in biological modeling or in bio-inspired engineering.

3. EVOLUTIONARY DEVELOPMENT

An evolutionary algorithm is used to explore the parameter space of morphogenetic tensegrity processes. The information comprised in each gene of an individual is interpreted as a *local or global perturbation* to be applied to its structure at a given developmental stage—here, the initial circular sheet common to all individuals. Thus the genome does not represent the layout of the organism, but scheduled sequence of *changes* in the internal balance of forces. These changes accumulate potential energy in the structure, and new arrangements of cells emerge from their subsequent expression and unfolding. In summary, to evaluate an individual, the initial structure is first modified according to its genome, then goes through a physical relaxation process, which may include one or several abrupt transitions, until it stabilizes into a new shape. The evaluation is the measure of the "quality" of this morphogenetic process, as it will be explained below.

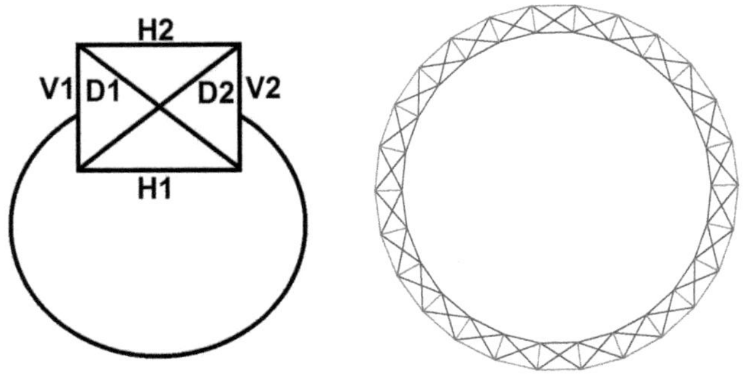

(a) (b)

Figure 2: (a) The six elastic links composing each quadrilateral cell. (b) Circular tensegrity structure of 26 connected cells used as the common initial state of all morphogenetic processes. The V_2 link of each cell is superimposed on the V_1 link of its neighbor clockwise. H1's resting length is *smaller* than its length in the circle, while H2's is *longer* (see Appendix). Compressed links are red, stretched ones are blue.

3.1 Individuals

We denote by H_1, H_2, V_1, V_2 D_1, and D_2 the six types of elastic links of a single quadrilateral cell (Figure 2a), and by L_{ij} an instance of (undirected) link between two vertices i and j. The force exerted by L_{ij} on i at any time is given by $\mathbf{F}^e_{ij} = -k_{ij}(d_{ij} - l_{ij})\mathbf{u}_{ij}$, where k_{ij} is a positive stiffness coefficient, l_{ij} the resting length of link L_{ij}, d_{ij} its current length (absolute values), and $\mathbf{u}_{ij}$ a unit vector oriented from j to i. The initial structure is in equilibrium, i.e. $\mathbf{F}^e_i = \sum_j \mathbf{F}^e_{ij} = \mathbf{0}$ for all i.

Each cell in the initial sheet structure is indexed by an integer $c \in [1, 26]$. The genome of a structure is encoded in a list of variable length, where each perturbation element is represented by a quintuple denoted (c_a, c_b, S, T, x) with the following definitions:

- c_a and c_b are two integer *indices* in the range $[-5, 30]$ such that the perturbation is applied only to the cells that verify $c \in [\min(c_a, c_b), \max(c_a, c_b)] \cap [1, 26]$
- S is a *subset* of link types $\{H_1, H_2, V_1, V_2, D_1, D_2\}$ such that, inside each cell c, the perturbation is applied only to the categories of links listed in S
- T is a rule type *symbol* from the set $\{K, R, K_f, R_f\}$ and x is a real-valued coefficient in $[0, 2]$, such that:
  - if $T = K$, the link's stiffness k is multiplied by x
  - if $T = R$, its resting length l is multiplied by x
  - if $T = K_f$, same effect as K; in addition, l is also readjusted such that the force value $F^e = -k(d - l)$ is unchanged (under the link's current length d)
  - if $T = R_f$, same effect as R using coefficient x' instead of x such that: if $x > 1$ then $x' = x$ for a compressed link ($l > d$) and $x' = 1/x$ for a stretched link ($l < d$), and conversely for $x < 1$; in addition, k is also readjusted such that F^e is unchanged.

All perturbations coded in the genome are applied to the initial circular sheet in the order they appear in the list, then the structure is left free to rearrange itself. Note that, while perturbations of types K_f and R_f leave the balance of forces seemingly unchanged, they significantly alter "undercover" the mechanical response of affected links to subsequent perturbations, thus greatly influencing the developmental process. Finally, after all perturbations have been applied, links of stiffness k lower than a given threshold are discarded because they play no significant role in the dynamics. Likewise, the values of k or l are limited to given maximum values to prevent the system from becoming unstable.

A remark about the computational size of the genome: since c_a, c_b, S and T can each be represented by one byte, and x is a double-precision floating-point variable, a perturbation can be encoded in just 12 bytes (or even 11, if S and T are crammed into a single byte). Therefore, with typical evolved genomes containing 2 to 5 perturbations, their size ranges from 10 to 25 variables, or 24 to 60 bytes. Thus the "minimality" of the genome in this work can be understood as referring to its small size as well as the simplicity of the mapping.

3.2 Evaluation

Denoting the position of vertex i by $\mathbf{P}_i$, we can write $d_{ij} = \|\mathbf{P}_i - \mathbf{P}_j\|$ and $\mathbf{u}_{ij} = (\mathbf{P}_i - \mathbf{P}_j)/d_{ij}$. The equation of motion of i then reads $\ddot{\mathbf{P}}_i = \mathbf{F}^e_i + \mathbf{F}^v_i$, where $\mathbf{F}^e_i$ is the sum of elastic forces:

$$\mathbf{F}^e_i = -\sum_{j=1}^{N} A_{ij} k_{ij} \left(\|\mathbf{P}_i - \mathbf{P}_j\| - l_{ij}\right) \frac{\mathbf{P}_i - \mathbf{P}_j}{\|\mathbf{P}_i - \mathbf{P}_j\|}$$

($A_{ij} = 1$ or 0 denoting the existence or absence of L_{ij}) and $\mathbf{F}^v_i = -\mu \dot{\mathbf{P}}_i$ is a linear damping force, with $\mu = 0.1$.

After perturbing the circular sheet according to the genome of an individual, the resulting structure is generally unstable and its numerical simulation requires a fourth-order Runge-Kutta integrator with time step $\Delta t = 0.01$. We calculate the total energy of the system $E = E_k + E_p$, where $E_k = \frac{1}{2} m \sum_i \|\dot{\mathbf{P}}_i\|^2$ is the kinetic energy of the vertices and

$$E_p = \frac{1}{2} \sum_{i,j=1}^{N} A_{ij} k_{ij} \left(\|\mathbf{P}_i - \mathbf{P}_j\| - l_{ij}\right)^2$$

is the potential energy stored in the elastic links. Typical coefficient values are $m = 1$ and $k_{ij} = 20$, making E_k of the order of 10% of E in the very first steps of the relaxation, then at best a fraction of 1% of E on the long run (Figure 3). As E decreases over time, we stop the relaxation process when the rate of energy loss $|\dot{E}|$ drops below a given threshold, meaning that the structure is close to its final stable configuration.

In a simple metastable system such as the invagination process of Figure 1, the relaxation from the initial to the final state was following an exponential-looking energy curve, characterized by a sharp drop before a slow decrease. There, the potential energy was spent in one shot. However, tensegrity structures are also able to exhibit much longer and more complex transformations, consisting of a diverse *sequence* of developmental stages and qualitative transitions (Figure 3). In order to encourage this diversity, we propose to detect the transitions through the conspicuous *accelerations* that they produce in the energy loss rate, then use them to count

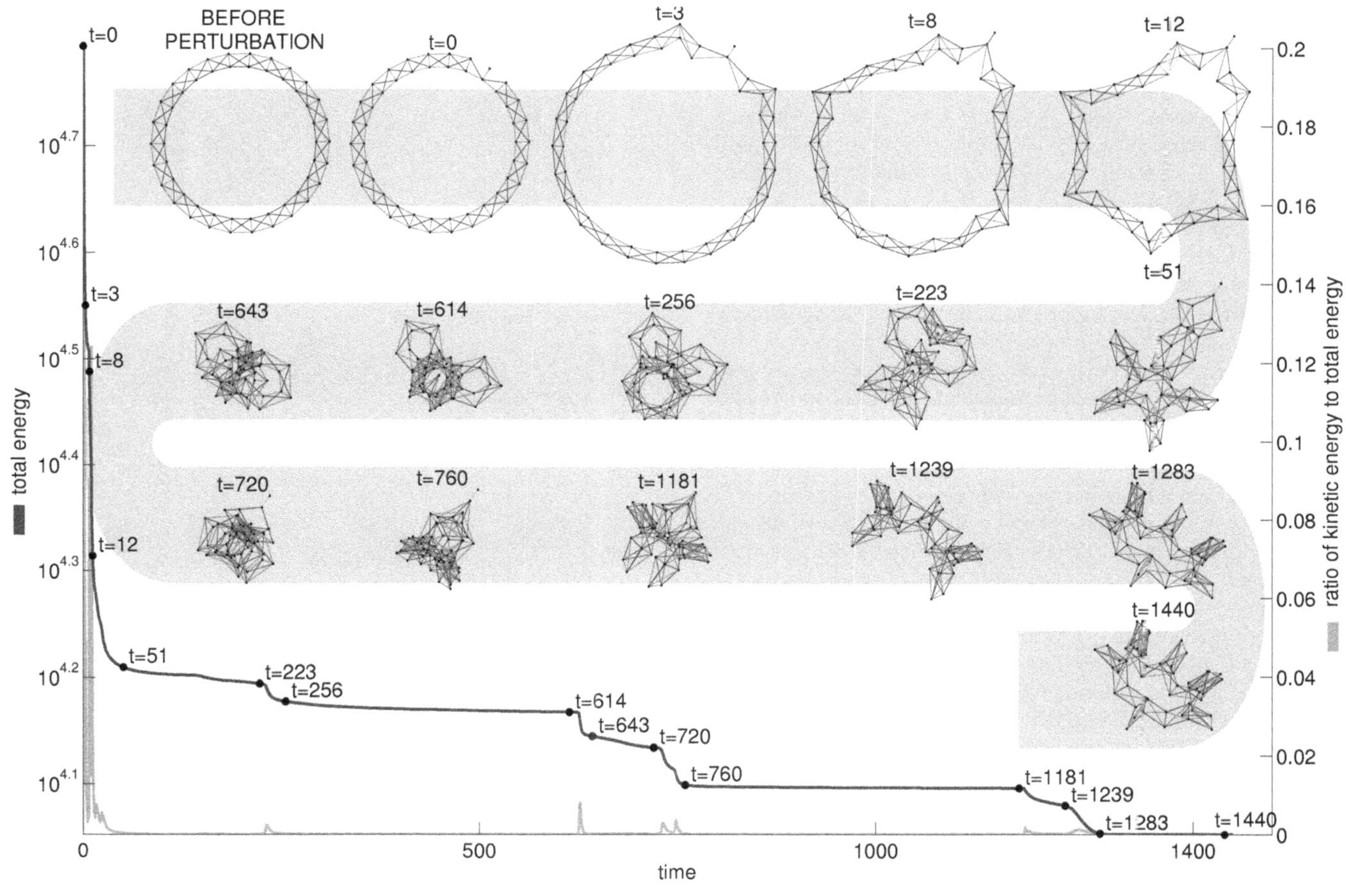

Figure 3: An example of developmental process with minimal genetic control. See the text for details.

the number of developmental steps (energy plateaus), their size and distribution, which will allow us to design a fitness or measure of "quality" of the process.

Staircase steps in the energy curve $E(t)$ appear as peaks and valleys in its first derivative $\dot{E}(t)$. We count only the peaks in energy rate that have a maximal value greater than a given threshold. Let a_q be the time of peak q, b_{q-1} and b_q the times of the valley flats before and after a_q, and $d_q = E(b_{q-1}) - E(b_q)$ the energy drop corresponding to peak q. Denoting by $\mathbf{D}'$ the complete sequence of energy drops in decreasing order of magnitude: $\mathbf{D}' = (d'_1 > \cdots > d'_n)$, we first discard its largest component d'_1 (in most cases the initial peak: $d'_1 = d_1$), viewing it as an outlier. Then, we rescale the values in the reduced set with respect to the second maximum d'_2 and define the fitness f as the sum of these values:

$$f = \sum_{k=2}^{n} \frac{d'_k}{d'_2}$$

Therefore, by attempting to maximize this function, the goal is to favor long and complex developmental processes characterized by an energy profile made of multiple steps of similar size.

3.3 Selection

Randomly generated individuals are unlikely to produce complex developmental processes and diverse morphologies. For this reason, we used the following evolutionary protocol:

1. First, 100 individuals are randomly generated and evaluated. This set constitutes the initial population.
2. Then, the following steps are repeated 500 times:
   - 2.1 individuals from the current population are selected through a size-4 tournament, with elitism, to generate a new population (i.e., the best individual is automatically copied, while the other individuals compete in randomly chosen groups of 4)
   - 2.2 some individuals of the new population are mutated and re-evaluated.

Three types of mutations affecting the list of "perturbation" genes (c_a, c_b, S, T, x) are possible:

- delete a randomly chosen gene
- change the value of a randomly chosen component of a randomly chosen gene
- insert a randomly created gene at a randomly chosen location in the gene sequence.

Each mutation is applied to each individual with probability 0.05. The initial 100 individuals contain exactly two randomly created genes, in such a way that the first perturbation gene is always global (i.e., the interval defined by c_a and c_b includes $[1, 26]$ completely), while the second perturbation gene is always localized to 5 cells or less (i.e., $|c_a - c_b| \leq 5$).

4. EXPERIMENTAL RESULTS

Through several runs of the above evolutionary algorithm, we found many examples of long processes containing multiple developmental steps. A sizable fraction of these cases were discarded because, for example, the structure would collapse into a small area and make it difficult to visualize a shape. Since the heuristics only relies on an indirect criterion (maximizing f), some processes did not resemble any sequence of developmental steps. In numerous other examples, however, the structure did not collapse upon itself and even exhibited interesting bilateral symmetry. In symmetric structures, shape creation could be followed visually as different segments of the cell sheet folded in various ways and gave rise to a wide variety of transient and final morphologies. Figure 3 is illustrative of two typical properties of a "successful" developmental process:

- Developmental steps are characterized by periods of smooth changes separated by sudden transformations, during which potential energy is rapidly converted to kinetic energy, then dissipated, causing a drop in total energy. In most cases, these transitions correspond to sudden reversals in the positions of the extremities of one or several elastic links. The plots of Figure 3 show the typical staircase profile of total energy over time (blue line), $E(t)$, and the ratio of kinetic energy (green line), $E_k(t)/E(t)$ (drops in the former coinciding with peaks in the latter).
- The structure undergoes dramatic rearrangements. Snapshots of the different stages of development are also shown in Figure 3. The gray path indicates their chronological order. Each snapshot is taken just before or after one of the transition steps characterized by a sudden energy drop (times are indicated on the figures and the corresponding locations on the plot).

In this typical example, two regimes in the dynamics of $E(t)$ can be clearly distinguished:

- An initial phase where most of the energy is dissipated in a fraction of time. This first and intense "snap" corresponds to the setup of the developmental process, modulated by the local and global genomic perturbations that were stored in the structure.
- A much longer regime during which the remaining energy is dissipated in much smaller quantities (the vertical axis in Figure 3 is a logarithmic scale to show these steps better). This "slow" regime corresponds to the developmental process proper and embodies the essential differences between examples.

The initial conditions of this example are configured by the following genome, composed of a global perturbation followed by two local perturbations:

$$(1, 26, \{H_1\}, R, 2.145)$$
$$(1, 1, \{H_2, D_1\}, K, 0.0)$$
$$(2, 2, \{H_2, D_2\}, K, 0.0)$$

Global perturbations have the effect of introducing a significant amount of potential energy and destabilizing the initial structure. Local perturbations canalize the destabilized structure into an specific developmental path by modulating the location and dynamics of the initial catastrophic events (reversals of elastic links).

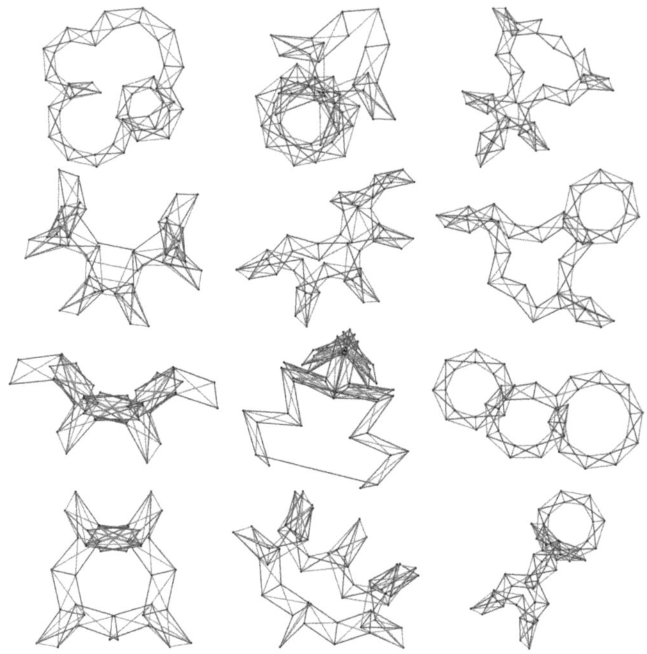

Figure 4: Various examples of final morphologies produced by different developmental processes, exhibiting more or less symmetry. All these morphologies are generated from the same initial structure (Figure 2b) by modulating the perturbations applied to that structure.

Many examples of final, stable morphologies have been evolved. As shown in Figure 4, they strikingly differ from each other, although they all originate from the same initial cell sheet structure through folding.

5. DISCUSSION

In this study, we proposed a model of development able to give rise to a diversity of morphologies under minimal genetic control. While it is common to consider that, in most cases, a complex genetic control is necessary to guide an equally complex developmental process, essentially by intervening at bifurcation points to switch on and off distinct, heterogeneous phases (see, e.g., [6]), our model represents an extreme example of self-controlled physical structure. No GRN is needed to guide the unfolding of its dynamics, since the properties of metastable tensegrity modulate themselves the sequence of transformation steps. After perturbation in a few specific points, the structure follows a complex sequence of morphological rearrangements and state transitions before settling down into a final configuration.

This whole process is enabled by the "self-stress" features of the circular sheet used as the initial state of the model. This structure is stable in geometric configurations that correspond to local minima of the energy function (see Section 2.1), and the role of the perturbations specified by an individual's genome is precisely to alter the shape of this energy function. This drives the structure into a developmental path (a trajectory in phase space), where each step is a consequence of the geometric changes created in previous steps, until a new balance of forces is attained. Although our primary goal was to study development as such, this method can also be seen as a new way to generate novel tensegrity structures (see Section 2.1 for other methods).

5.1 Relevance to Biological Modeling

With respect to evo-devo, we believe that the significance of our model is to cast a new light on the question still little addressed in today's predominant gene-centric view of biology: Can organisms also be the product of complex physico-chemical developmental processes not (necessarily or always) controlled by complex underlying genetics? This question was mostly investigated by the "structuralist" school of theoretical biology, which can be traced back to Goethe, D'Arcy Thompson, and Waddington (before or during the advent of genetics and its modern synthesis with evolution). Later, in the genomic era, it was most actively pursued and defended by Kauffman [19] and Goodwin [11] under the banner of *self-organization*, argued to be a greater force than *natural selection* in the production of viable diversity.

Each element of our tensegrity graphs influences the stress state of the other elements in convoluted, nonlinear ways, creating the conditions for enhanced developmental effects, while only a small amount of genetic information is sufficient to encode structural perturbations. This can also be seen in unicellular organisms whose complex cytostructure develops from an undifferentiated stage. A classical example is Goodwin's model of *Acetabularia* [11], a genus of green algae in which the genome does not explicitly code for the branching "bracts" (rings of little leaflike elements) of a growing cell. These bracts are only the indirect result of a set of physical initial conditions, which can be modulated by the genome to produce different morphologies in different species. This represents a real-life example of developmental process primarily based on the physical properties of the developing structure, as in our model.

As seen in Figure 3, one tensegrity individual is characterized by its typical sequence of variation steps, or "signature", of its energy over time. These steps are "catastrophic" geometric events, in the sense of René Thom's theory [37], frequently involving reversals of the elastic links, which cause a self-propagating cascade of dramatic jumps in the balance of forces. In Kauffman's interpretation of Waddington's epigenetic landscapes, cell types are metastable states of the cell's genetic regulatory network [19]. The morphodynamics described in this work could thus be considered a purely physical analog of Kauffman's metaphor, at an abstract level of self-organization. A metastable morphology represents a "transient attractor" in the physical dynamics of the structure, as it visits these attractors before arriving in its final state.

Although our model is not related to any real-world biological system, it represents a proof of concept that complex developmental processes do no always need to be controlled by genetics but can largely self-regulate by relying on the physical properties of growing tissues [28]. In this respect, it lends support to the hypothesis that, in the beginnings of multicellular life, organismal development was under little to no genetic regulation [29], instead being guided by structural constraints.

5.2 Relevance to Bio-inspired Engineering

From the point of view of evolutionary computation and systems design, the aims of artificial development are to discover and improve algorithms by leveraging self-organizational processes to code complex solutions with small genomes [8]. Yet, even in this field especially suited to the design of "embodied" agents, a common assumption is that generating architectures complex enough to be capable of spontaneous innovation requires direction from a complex GRN or GRN-like mechanisms distinct from the physical model proper. As mentioned in Section 1.2, many AD models choose to support complexity in the development by a relative complexity in its recipe [8, 14, 20, 22, 6].

Our developmental model is purely "ballistic" in the sense that genetic control is limited to providing perturbations to an initial metastable structure. In this respect, it represents a proof of concept that AD-based evolutionary algorithms [35] can encode solutions to form-finding problems in extremely concise ways. Earlier explorations of this concept [8] have used more complex genetic machinery, which we could avoid here by using tensegrity structures.

Naturally, starting from this minimal base, it would be also perfectly possible to extend the model and reintroduce more genetic information. For example, one could allow perturbations to be triggered not only at the beginning of development but at later times, too, through various physical parameters. This would certainly allow for an even more complex and more reactive growth dynamics, better resembling real-world biological development.

6. REFERENCES

[1] W. Arthur. *Biased embryos and evolution*. Cambridge University Press, 2004.

[2] H. Bart-Smith, K. W. Moored, S. A. Taylor, and T. K. Bliss. Optimization of a tensegrity wing for biomimetic applications. In *Proceedings of the 45th IEEE Conference on Decision and Control*, pages 2288–2293, 2006.

[3] C. Brangwynne, F. Mackintosh, S. Kumar, N. Geisse, J. Talbot, L. Mahadevan, K. Parker, D. Ingber, and D. Weitz. Microtubules can bear enhanced compressive loads in living cells because of lateral reinforcement. *Cell Biology*, 173:733–745, 2006.

[4] M. F. Coughlin and D. Stamenović. A tensegrity structure with buckling compression elements: application to cell mechanics. *Journal of Applied Mechanics*, 64(3):480–486, 1997.

[5] E. H. Davidson. Emerging properties of animal gene regulatory networks. *Nature*, 468(7326):911–920, 2010.

[6] R. Doursat. *Organic Computing*, chapter Organically Grown Architectures: creating Decentralized, Autonomous Systems by Embryomorphic Engineering, pages 167–199. Springer, 2008.

[7] M. J. West-Eberhard. Phenotypic plasticity and the origins of diversity. *Annual Review of Ecology and Systematics*, 20(1):249–278, 1989.

[8] P. Eggenberger. Genome-physics interaction as a new concept to reduce the number of genetic parameters in artificial evolution. In *Proceedings of the 5th IEEE Congress on Evolutionary Computation*, volume 1, pages 191–198, 2003.

[9] G. Forgács and S. Newman. *Biological physics of the developing embryo*. Cambridge University Press, 2005.

[10] B. Fuller. *Synergetics: explorations in the geometry of thinking*. Macmillan, 1975.

[11] B. Goodwin. *How the leopard changed its spots: the*

evolution of complexity. Princeton University Press, 2001.

[12] A. Graells Rovira and J. M. Mirats Tur. Control and simulation of a tensegrity-based mobile robot. *Robotics and Autonomous Systems*, 57(5):526–535, 2009.

[13] J. Henderson and D. Carter. Mechanical induction in limb morphogenesis: the role of growth-generated strains and pressures. *Bone*, 31(6):645–653, 2002.

[14] G. S. Hornby, H. Lipson, and J. B. Pollack. Generative representations for the automated design of modular physical robots. *IEEE Transactions on Robotics and Automation*, 19(4):703–719, 2003.

[15] D. Ingber. Cellular tensegrity: defining new rules of biological design that govern the cytoskeleton. *Journal of Cell Science*, 104(3):613–627, 1993.

[16] D. Ingber. Mechanical control of tissue morphogenesis during embryological development. *Developmental Biology*, 50:255–266, 2006.

[17] D. Ingber. Cellular mechanotransduction: putting all the pieces together again. *The FASEB Journal: Official Publication of the Federation of American Societies for Exp. Biology*, 20(7):811–827, 2006.

[18] S. Juan and J. Miratstur. Tensegrity frameworks: static analysis review. *Mechanism and Machine Theory*, 43(7):859–881, 2008.

[19] S. A. Kauffman. *The Origins of Order: self-Organization and Selection in Evolution*. Oxford University Press, USA, 1993.

[20] M. Komosinski and A. Rotaru-Varga. Comparison of different genotype encodings for simulated 3D agents. *Artificial Life*, 7(4):395–418, 2001.

[21] T. Kowaliw and W. Banzhaf. Augmenting artificial development with local fitness . In *Proceedings of the 2009 IEEE Congress on Evolutionary Computation*, pages 316–323, 2009.

[22] D. Lobo. *Evolutionary development based on genetic regulatory models for behavior-finding*. PhD thesis, Universidad de Malaga, 2010.

[23] D. Lobo and F. J. Vico. Evolutionary development of tensegrity structures. *Biosystems*, 101(3):167–176, 2010.

[24] T. Mammoto and D. E. Ingber. Mechanical control of tissue and organ development. *Development*, 137(9):1407–1420, 2010.

[25] R. Motro. *Tensegrity: structural systems for the future*. Butterworth-Heinemann, 2003.

[26] J. Muñoz, V. Conte, and M. Miodownik. Stress-dependent morphogenesis: continuum mechanics and truss systems. *Biomechanics and Modeling in Mechanobiology*, 9(4):451–467, 2010.

[27] G. Müller and S. Newman, editors. *Origination of organismal form: beyond the gene in developmental and evolutionary biology*. The Vienna series in theoretical biology. MIT Press, 2003.

[28] C. Nelson, R. Jean, J. Tan, W. Liu, N. Sniadecki, A. Spector, and C. Chen. Emergent patterns of growth controlled by multicellular form and mechanics. *Proceedings of the National Academy of Sciences of the United States of America*, 102:11594–11599, 2005.

[29] S. Newman. *Origination of organismal form: beyond the gene in developmental and evolutionary biology*, chapter From physics to development: the evolution of morphogenetic mechanisms, pages 221–240. In Muller and Newman [27], 2003.

[30] G. Odell, G. Oster, P. Alberch, and B. Burnside. The mechanical basis of morphogenesis: epithelial folding and invagination. *Developmental Biology*, 85(2):446–462, 1981.

[31] C. Paul, V. F. Cuevas, and H. Lipson. Design and control of tensegrity robots for locomotion. *IEEE Transactions on Robotics*, 22(5):944–957, 2006.

[32] J. A. Rieffel, F. J. Valero-Cuevas, and H. Lipson. Morphological communication: exploiting coupled dynamics in a complex mechanical structure to achieve locomotion. *Journal of The Royal Society Interface*, 7(45):613–621, 2010.

[33] T. Savin, N. A. Kurpios, A. E. Shyer, P. Florescu, H. Liang, L. Mahadevan, and C. J. Tabin. On the growth and form of the gut. *Nature*, 476(7358):57–62, 2011.

[34] K. Snelson. Continuous tension, discontinuous compression structure (US patent 3169611), 1965.

[35] K. Stanley and R. Miikkulainen. A taxonomy for artificial embryogeny. *Artificial Life*, 9(2):93–130, 2003.

[36] G. Struhl. A homoeotic mutation transforming leg to antenna in Drosophila. *Nature*, 292(5824):635–638, 1981.

[37] R. Thom. *Structural stability and morphogenesis*. Addison Wesley Publishing Company, 1989.

[38] C. H. Waddington. Genetic assimilation of the Bithorax phenotype. *Evolution*, 1:1–13, 1956.

APPENDIX

The initial structure contains two concentric rings of 26 equally spaced vertices of mass $m = 1$. The radius of the inner ring is 61.5107152186897, and the outer ring 72.1497004210614. All elastic links have a stiffness of $k = 20$ and the following actual and resting lengths:

link	d	l
H_1	14.8285948251829	13.975
H_2	17.3933707403416	20.15
D_1, D_2	19.2641442449179	18.1264008079376
V_1, V_2	10.6389852023717	11.0406139435269

The exact gene values in the initial genome are:

$(1, 26, \{H_1\}, R, 2.14494510765828)$
$(1, 1, \{H_2, D_1\}, K, 0.0)$
$(2, 2, \{H_2, D_2\}, K, 0.0)$

The simulation was carried out in floating arithmetic with double precision, using the Dorman-Prince method (integrator `ode45` in `MATLAB`™).

Co-evolution of Morphology and Control of Soft-bodied Multicellular Animats

Michał Joachimczak
Systems Modelling Laboratory, IOPAN
Powstańców Warszawy 55
Sopot, Poland
mjoach@gmail.com

Borys Wróbel
Systems Modelling Laboratory, IOPAN
Sopot, Poland
Evolutionary Systems Laboratory, UAM
Poznań, Poland
Institute for Neuroinformatics, UZh & ETHZ
Zurich, Switzerland
wrobel@evosys.org

ABSTRACT

We present a platform that allows for co-evolution of development and motion control of soft-bodied, multicellular animats in a 2-dimensional fluid-like environment. Artificial gene regulatory networks (GRNs) with real-valued expression levels control cell division and differentiation in multicellular embryos. Embryos develop in a simulated physics environment and are converted into animat structures by connecting neighboring cells with elastic springs. The springs connecting outer cells form the external envelope which is subject to fluid drag. Both the developmental program and motion control are encoded indirectly in a single linear genome, which consists of regulatory regions and regions that code for regulatory products (some of which act as morphogens). We applied a genetic algorithm to co-evolve morphology and control using a fitness measure whose value depends on distance traveled during the evaluation phase. We obtained various emergent morphologies and types of locomotion, some of them showing the use of appendages.

Categories and Subject Descriptors

I.2.8 [**Artificial Intelligence**]: Problem Solving, Control Methods, and Search—*Heuristic methods*; F.1.1 [**Computation by Abstract Devices**]: Models of Computation—*Self-modifying machines*; J.3 [**Life and medical sciences**]: Biology and genetics

General Terms

Algorithms, Design, Experimentation

Keywords

Artificial Embryogenesis, Body-brain co-evolution, Development, Evolution of locomotion, Evolution of morphology, Gene Regulatory Networks, Generative and Developmental Systems, Genetic Algorithms, Soft-body animats

1. INTRODUCTION

Co-evolution of morphology and movement control is one of the most active research areas of Artificial Life. Progress in this area is driven by the desire to shed light on how co-evolution of body and control shaped the form of biological organisms, and also by the hope that the creative power of artificial evolution can be used to discover novel morphologies and control methods which would be difficult to conceive using other engineering approaches.

Ever since the landmark paper by Karl Sims [23], there have been many proposals for how to use generative or developmental processes to evolve animats (e.g., [9, 14, 18]), but often with high level abstractions of biological development, and large components (such as parameterized shapes) connected with joints. This is effective from the engineering point of view, but very far from biology. Although a considerable progress has been achieved recently in using lower-level approaches, inspired by biological gene regulatory networks (GRNs), for modeling evolution of development (e.g., [5, 15, 10, 12]), there are only a handful of models for the evolution of multicellular animats with such a low-level approach. For example, Bongard and Pfeifer [1] used artificial GRNs to evolve morphologies and neural networks of animats moving on a plane (cells were connected by rotating joints). Eggenberger Hotz [6] demonstrated how GRN-controlled multicellular animats can move without a neural network, thanks to the adhesive forces between cells reshaping the morphology. Several recent animat models (e.g., [17, 13, 26, 16, 20] are based on spring-massed systems, perhaps drawing inspiration from the landmark work of Terzopoulos et al. [25]. However, some of these models do not use GRNs [17, 13, 26] or are not developmental [26].

The platform described in this work allows for evolution of GRN-controlled development in a 2-dimensional (2-D) simulated physical environment. The final structure of an animat is defined as a spring-mass system in the form of a planar graph, in which nodes represent masses (cells) and edges act as springs. The regions of the body determined by edges are prevented from collapsing through internal pressure. These regions behave like pressurized chambers and form a kind of "hydrostatic skeleton". Each cell in the final structure is capable of actuation by contracting and expanding its springs, which reduces or enlarges neighboring regions. The resulting soft-bodied, highly flexible structure relies both on the actuators and internal elasticity to generate forces that drive movement. Both the developmental programs and the way movement is controlled are encoded indirectly in biologically-inspired genomes. During evolution animats are selected only for their ability to swim in a virtual environment, so neither the type of morphology nor the controller are externally enforced.

Our work was driven by the desire to create a model of co-evolution of form and function, but the results are relevant for the emerging field of soft-bodied robotics. This field has seen considerable progress in recent years: physical robots with fluid/air filled cavities driven by expanding and contracting actuators [24, 22], robots inspired by caterpillars [19], octopuses [3], and starfish [22], and models of entirely amorphous, locally expanding morphologies [8].

2. EMBRYOGENETIC MODEL

We adopted the model of the genome, GRN, and multicellular development from our earlier work [12]. Our platform strives for biological realism. The animat phenotype is a result of interactions taking place on multiple levels of abstraction. On the lowest level, the interactions between products and promoters, encoded in a linear genome, determine the GRN topology. Products continuously build up and degrade in cells and their level determines cell division and differentiation. The final body shape is the result of physical interactions between cells, which freely move in 2-D space with simulated physics as the embryo develops. Finally, the movement of the animat results from interactions between distributed control, the physical structure of the animat, and the properties of the simulated environment.

2.1 Genome and GRN

Our model of the genome was inspired by the work of Eggenberger Hotz [5], but with some important differences discussed in our previous papers [10, 12, 11]. A genome is a list of genetic elements, divided into three classes: (i) genes, coding for products (transcription factors, TFs), which can act only in one cell or diffuse to other cells (and act as morphogens), (ii) regulatory regions (promoters), and (iii) "special elements" which are used as inputs and outputs of the network (Fig. 1). The genome is parsed sequentially. Regulatory units are formed whenever a series (one or more) of promoters is followed by a series of genes. Regulatory units form the nodes in the GRN. When a unit is active, all genes that belong to it are expressed at the same level.

Each genetic element has several fields (numbers). Affinity between products and promoters is determined using a metaphor of chemical affinity between biological informational macromolecules (proteins and nucleic acids). Two fields (real numbers) specify a point in continuous R^2 "affinity space". Affinities depend on distances between points corresponding to genetic elements. The smaller the distance, the higher the weight (maximum weight, set to 10, for zero distance). The weights decrease exponentially with distance, up to a cut-off value (at which the weight is zero) to prevent full connectivity. Other fields of the genetic elements define their class and their "sign" (the result of multiplication determines if a product-promoter interaction corresponds to inhibition or activation). Since regulatory units can have multiple promoters and multiple products, any two nodes in

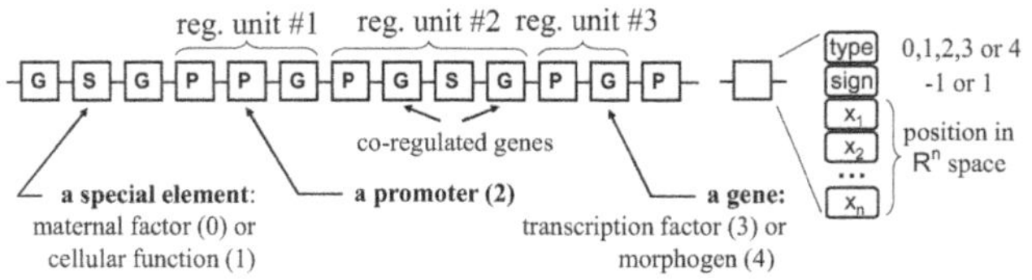

Figure 1: The structure of the genetic elements and the linear genome. Each element consists of a type field (the numbers in parenthesis in the descriptions below the graph indicate types), a sign field, and an ordered set of N real values which is used to determine affinity to other elements; $N = 2$ was used in this paper.

the graph can be connected by several edges. Our approach does not enforce limits on the size of regulatory graph or the number of types of TFs which can be encoded in the genome.

Product concentrations are updated in discrete time steps. First, activation of each promoter of the given regulatory unit is calculated as a weighted sum of concentrations of products which have affinity to this promoter. Then, the sum of the activities of all the promoters is used to calculate the rate at which products of this regulatory unit are produced or degraded:

$$\Delta L = (\tanh \frac{A}{2} - L)\Delta t \qquad (1)$$

where Δt is the time step (0.05 was used), L is the current concentration of the product, and A is the sum of activation of all promoters for this regulatory unit. The formula ensures that all product concentrations remain within $[0, 1)$.

Special elements, which encode the inputs and outputs of the GRN, are treated like TFs (for inputs) or like if they were regulatory units with one gene (for outputs). The activation of outputs is determined by the concentration of TFs that have affinity to a particular special element. The model includes six cellular actions, associated with outputs: cell division, cell rotation, modification of cell size (which affect development), and three actions that modify oscillation parameters (which affect movement; explained below). Four inputs can be used: a signal of "1" (a TF with a constant maximum concentration; this is similar to a bias input in neural networks), and three substances ("maternal morphogens") diffusing from three sources in the 2-D physical space in which development occurs. Evolution determines what inputs and outputs are actually used in a given GRN.

2.2 Developmental process

Development starts from a single cell (Fig. 2). All cells have the same GRN, encoded by the genome. Cells occupy real-valued positions in 2-D space and behave as soft circular objects in a simulated fluid-like environment. After each division, physical forces cause now overlapping cells to repel each other and to gradually drift apart. Coherent structure of the embryo is maintained by an adhesive force that makes close-by cells stick to each other.

Development is guided by diffusive substances, which include not only the three maternal morphogens, but also morphogens which can be produced by cells. In our simplified, grid-less diffusion model, the level of a diffusing product at

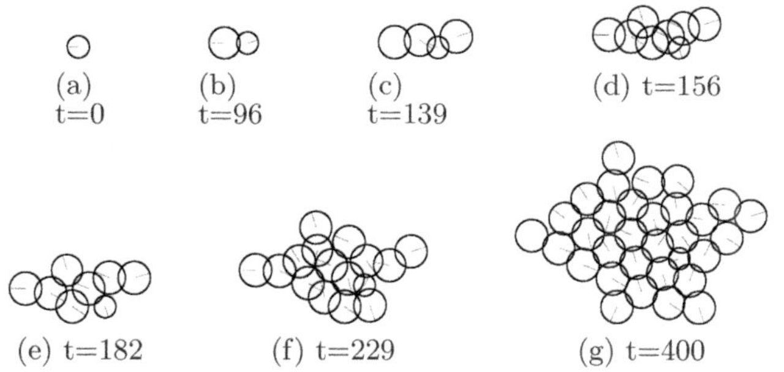

Figure 2: Example of a developmental process. The panels (a-g) show the development of the animat in Fig. 7b, 6a at indicated simulation time steps, (d) shows cells that have just divided, but were not yet pushed away by physical forces, this process took about 30 time steps (e). Cells are represented as circles, short lines indicate the direction of the orientation vector.

a given location is a function of distance and the historic concentration of this morphogen at its source.

Cell division occurs when the level of a product coded by the special element associated with this action reaches the threshold of 0.9. Each cell maintains its orientation vector, used to determine the direction towards which a new cell will be placed at division. The daughter cells inherit all the TF concentrations and the direction of the orientation vector from their mothers. At division, the daughter is placed in close proximity to the mother, and the orientation vector of the daughter is rotated proportionally to the activation level of the associated GRN output (maximum expression, 1, corresponds to a rotation angle of 2π). If a mother cell expresses the gene responsible for size increase, the radius of a new cell may be up to 50% larger. We enforced a hard limit for the size of the embryo of 32 cells, with the exception of one series of evolutionary runs in which up to 64 cells were allowed. This limitation can be seen as stemming from the strict limits on the resources available to the embryo.

3. PHENOTYPIC REPRESENTATION

After the development ends, the obtained morphology is transformed into the animat structure. The first step of this transformation is the formation of the edges connecting the centers of adjacent outer cells. This outline forms the external surface of the animat (Fig. 3). In our model of a fluid-like environment, it is only the outline that generates drag. The overall shape of an animat is maintained by all of its cells, connected with damped springs.

To obtain the internal structure of an animat, a graph of connectivity between cells is computed. The vertices correspond to cell centers; edges connect neighboring cells. Importantly, only the positions of cell centers in the developed embryo are taken into account, and not cell radii (but the radii determine the final positions of centers during development). Thus, the connectivity graph of the animat structure is determined entirely by cell positions, which are indirectly encoded in the genome.

We use Gabriel graphs [7] as a notion of point proximity. For P points in the plane, any two points a and b are connected by an edge if and only if the disc with the diameter

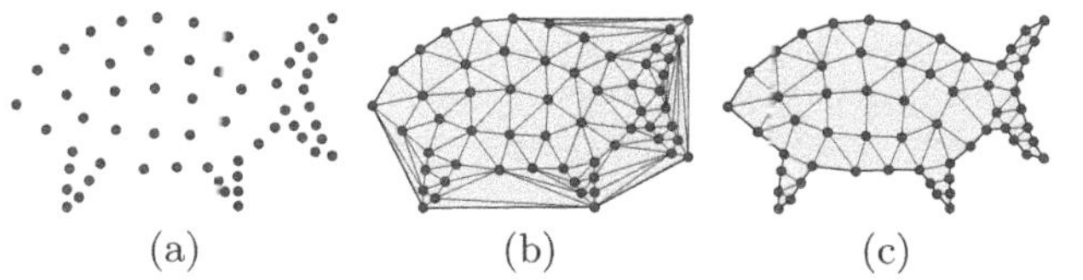

Figure 3: Algorithmic transformation of a set of points into the structure of the animat: (a) cell centers at the end of developmental phase, (b) a Delaunay triangulation, (c) a Gabriel graph (final structure).

ab does not contain any other point of P. A Gabriel graph can be obtained from a Delaunay graph by removing edges that do not fulfil the above criterion.

Actuation is achieved by modifying the resting lengths of the springs. Each cell (vertex) can contract or extend the length of the springs (edges) connected to it. The result is shrinkage or expansion of the regions around this cell. The effect exercised by two cells connected to the same spring is additive. Each cell is characterized by three parameters describing its pattern of oscillation: amplitude, phase and frequency. These three parameters are influenced by the corresponding GRN outputs. The state of the outputs at the end of development is used to set parameters for each cell. The parameters remain fixed during evaluation of locomotion.

The resting length of each spring is modified according to:

$$L = (1 + a_1 \sin(f_1 t + \phi_1) + a_2 \sin(f_2 t + \phi_2)) \cdot L_0 \quad (2)$$

where a_1, a_2 are the evolved amplitudes of the two connected cells (scaled to the interval between 0 and 0.2), f_1, f_2 are the evolved frequencies of oscillation, and ϕ_1, ϕ_2 are evolved phase shifts (from 0 to 2π). To prevent sudden changes in resting length for cells with non-zero phase shift at the start of simulation, such cells postpone their activity for up to half of their period, so that the resting length is always modified gradually from its equilibrium value.

4. PHYSICS SIMULATION

The structure of the animat is simulated in the physical environment as a set of small, circular masses (cells) connected by damped springs. All cells have identical mass. Each spring has a resting length determined during creation of the animat. The forces acting on cells connected by springs are calculated according to Hooke's law with damping (with the same values of the elasticity and damping coefficient for all the springs).

The body is divided into regions (polygons formed by edges) which act as pressurized chambers and oppose excessive compression to prevent collisions of internal nodes with springs. The chambers provide the animats with a form of hydrostatic skeleton. At the time of creation of the morphology, the area S_0 for each region is computed and pressure is assumed to be in equilibrium. If during actuation a body region becomes smaller or larger, a pressure force will act along the normal of each edge defining this region:

$$F_p = c_p \cdot L \cdot (1 - \frac{S}{S_0}) \quad (3)$$

where F_p is the pressure force acting outward along the normal of the edge that is considered, L is the length of this edge, S and S_0 represent the current and original surface area of this region, while c_p is the global pressure coefficient, controlling resistance to compression.

We used a simplified model of fluid drag [20, 21] which assumes that the fluid is stationary and that the force acting on a single edge belonging to the outline of the body is a sum of tangential and normal drag components for the motion of this edge. Thus, to calculate drag, the motion of the edge is split into its normal and tangential components v_T and v_N:

$$F_T = -d_T \cdot L \cdot sgn(v_T) \cdot (v_T)^2 \quad (4)$$

$$F_N = -d_N \cdot L \cdot sgn(v_N) \cdot (v_N)^2 \quad (5)$$

where d_T and d_N are the drag coefficients for tangential and normal drag of unit length edge. Since the animat structure is not rigid and the lengths of the springs change dynamically, the direction of motion of a given edge is understood as the direction of movement of its center. The calculated force is then divided by two and applied to the nodes associated with the given edge. Penetration of an edge by a cell is not allowed and results in an elastic collision. This could happen, for example, when protruding parts of the morphology hit each other or bend to collide with the external surface of the animat.

We used the Bullet library [2] for physics simulation. Because this library is best suited to rigid body simulations, we used it only for the integration of cell movement. Forces related to the damped spring-mass system described above were calculated externally to the library.

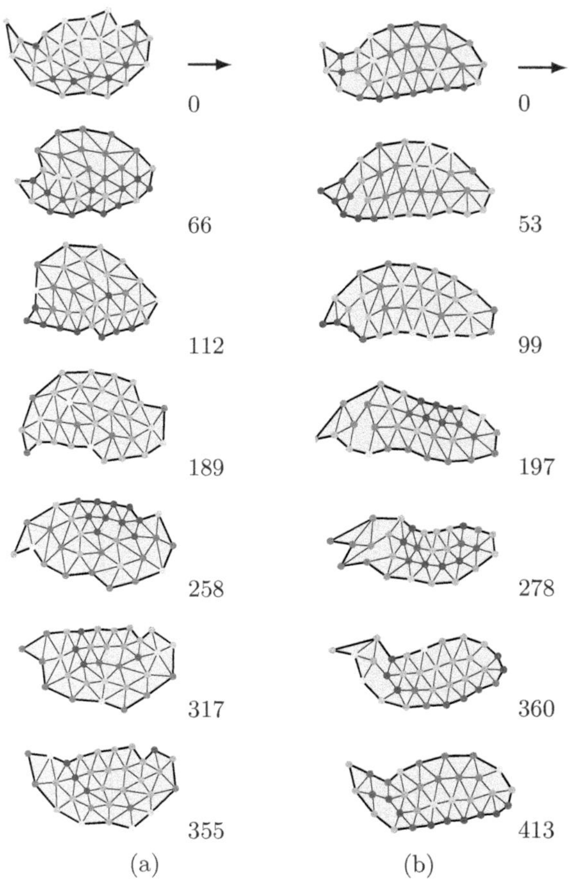

Figure 4: Snapshots of a single motion cycle of two undulating individuals propelling themselves in a high drag ($d_N = 10$) fluid environment. Node color indicates whether the cell is contracting or expanding its springs (red: expansion, blue: contraction, green: neutral). Numbers indicate the time steps in the cycle. The direction of movement is rightwards.

5. GENETIC ALGORITHM AND FITNESS EVALUATION

Genetic operators in our system can change element type, sign, or coordinates. The change of coordinates moves the point that corresponds to the element in a random direction in affinity space by a distance drawn from a normal distribution. In addition, duplications and deletions of series of elements are allowed.

We employed a genetic algorithm with a population size of 100, elitism, tournament selection, and multipoint crossover for sexual reproduction (for 20% of the individuals in each generation). Tournament selection was performed on two randomly drawn individuals. To avoid premature convergence, the probability of selection of the fitter individual was initially equal to 0.8 and continuously increased to 1 over the first 1000 generations. The initial populations were generated randomly, by creating individuals with 10 regulatory units, each containing a single promoter and a single product. To assess individual fitness, animats were placed in the simulated physical world and simulated for a fixed number of time steps (4000 or 8000 in some experiments). The fitness awarded to an individual was equal to the straight-line distance traveled by the animat's center of mass from its initial location. Evolutionary runs were terminated after no improvement over 500 generations was detected (the total number of generations was usually around 5000, and rarely above 10000).

To promote faster evolution, we introduced criteria which individuals had to meet to take part in the creation of the next generation. The regulatory graph (the GRN) had to contain a path between at least one input and the outputs associated with division and oscillations. Animats were required to have at least three cells. The last division had to occur at least 100 time steps before the end of development (which was simulated for 400 time steps in total). This condition is necessary to allow the morphology to expand after the last division (see Fig. 2). The initial random individuals were generated until the criteria were fulfilled and then placed in the initial population. Typically, this required a few hundred tries for each random individual.

6. RESULTS: EVOLUTION OF SWIMMING

We evaluated the ability of our approach to co-evolve morphology and control under different environmental conditions, varying the settings for normal/tangential drag coefficients (the latter was always 1/200 of the former). We have run 10 independent evolutionary runs for each setting.

In almost all cases, the factor responsible for an increase of cell sizes during development was found to be expressed at the maximum level, resulting in the largest morphologies possible. This may be because we rewarded the absolute distance traveled, not the distance relative to animat size, so it is beneficial to be large.

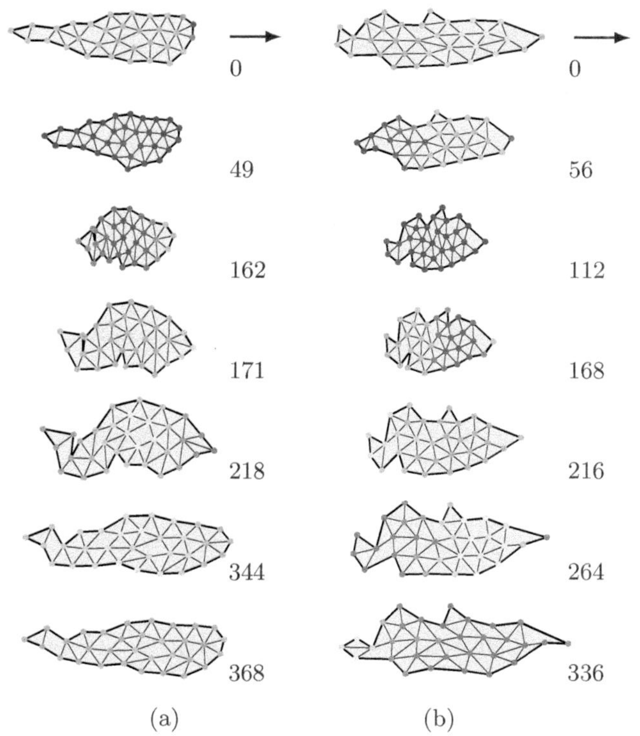

Figure 5: Snapshots of a single motion cycle of two individuals propelling themselves through asymmetric contractions in a moderate drag environment ($d_N = 2$). Node color indicates whether the cell is contracting or expanding its springs (red: expansion, blue: contraction, green: neutral). Numbers indicate the time steps in the cycle. The direction of movement is rightwards.

The best individuals (for all settings) would propel themselves using either waves of contractions traveling through the body or synchronous contractions of the whole structure. The frequency of contractions evolved to reinforce the oscillations coming from the elastic properties of the physical structure of the animat.

We could identify three main strategies of evolved locomotion, but many of the best individuals displayed a combination of two modes. One class consists of animats with bodies elongated in the direction of motion and moving by undulation which results from waves of contractions propagating through the body in a direction perpendicular to the direction of movement (Fig. 4)[1]. In 10 independent runs with a high drag coefficient ($d_N = 10$), half of the best individuals in 10 independent runs, including the two best solutions overall, moved by undulation. This strategy appeared, but mostly mixed with other strategies, among the best solutions when the drag was moderate (when $d_N = 2$, four out of 10 used undulation, three mixed it with other strategies, see below), and rarely if at all when the drag was low ($d_N = 0.5$; only one mixed strategy involved limited undulation, see below).

The second mode of locomotion is also employed by elongated individuals, but instead of undulating, their bodies contract along the direction of motion because the cells oscillate synchronously. An expansion of the animat structure generates asymmetric drag. The front of the body becomes pointy, while the back becomes flat due to drag, which further increases drag because most surfaces are orthogonal to the direction of expansion (Fig. 5). During the contraction, the drag is almost equal at the front and at the back (Fig. 5a; note how the "tail" becomes perpendicular to the direction of motion during expansion while it is aligned during contraction). This type of locomotion was the most successful when drag coefficients were moderate ($d_N = 2$: six best individuals in 10 independent runs, one of them with undulation), but emerged in all environmental settings ($d_N = 0.5$: one out of 10; $d_N = 10$: two out of 10).

Perhaps the most interesting mode of locomotion was obtained in experiments with the lowest drag coefficients: under these conditions, animats often evolved protrusions ("appendages"; in nine out of 10 runs with $d_N = 0.5$, in one of these nine the best strategy was mixed with some undulation). When the drag coefficients were moderate, protrusions appeared, but only in strategies mixed with undulation ($d_N = 2$: in two out of 10). When the coefficients were high ($d_N = 10$), protrusions also appeared (in four out of 10), but the movement strategy was less clear or (in one of these four best individuals) mixed with undulation.

The best individuals which use protrusions propel themselves by extending them and generating thrust while the protrusions are pulled backwards (Fig. 6). Although fins *sensu stricto* cannot exist in 2-D, the overall appearance is similar. Movement results from the fact that the protrusions are fully extended when moving backwards (generating thrust) but are contracted during their return. We have observed a clear tendency to place the protrusions symmetrically. In 32-cell structures protrusions are often built from one cell extending beyond the main outline of the body and become more pronounced only due to dynamic changes in shape during motion. Much more clearly defined protrusions, consisting of multiple cells (Fig. 6b), emerged when the cell limit was increased to 64 cells and the drag was put at an even lower value ($d_N = 0.2$, under these conditions nine out of 10 best individuals used protrusions, but one had a mixed strategy, using a "tail", the remaining one used only the "tail"). In most of 32- and 64-cell individuals employing this mode of locomotion the wave of contractions allowing for movement travels from the back towards the front of the animat.

More detailed analysis of the best individuals revealed that the amplitude and frequency of the oscillations is rarely differentiated between cells. We observed some successful individuals who had cells with slightly different frequencies of oscillations, but the motion of these animats was usually efficient only during a very limited period of time. In particular, their motion would quickly become inefficient when the simulation was extended beyond the lifespan they experienced during the evaluation phase of the genetic algorithm.

The amplitude of oscillation almost universally evolved to be close to maximum for all cells. This could be because there is no cost to actuation. Using maximum amplitudes of oscillations is a way to perform the most work against the fluid drag. Because the whole structure is connected and energy is easily transferred along the springs, even the contractions of internal cells add to the forces acting on external surfaces. On the other hand, the differentiation of phase

[1]Supplementary videos of animat behaviors are available at: `http://www.evosys.org/gecco12animats`

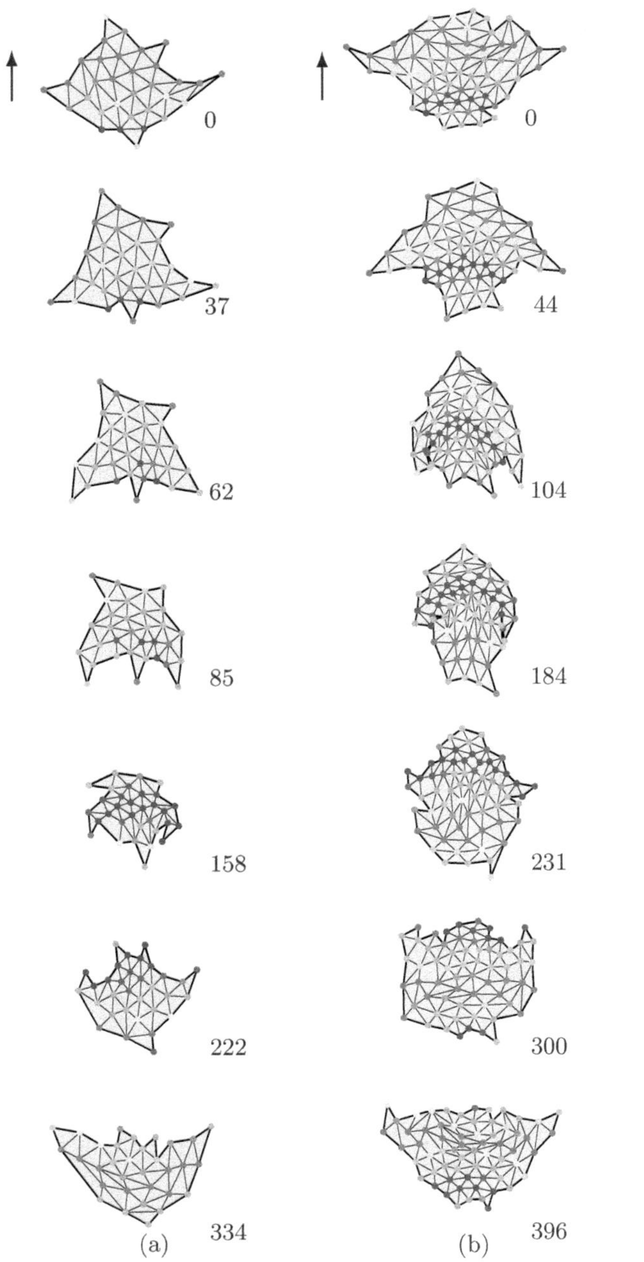

Figure 6: Snapshots of two individuals propelling themselves with the use of symmetric protrusions in an environment with low fluid drag. Panel (a): an individual with 32 cells, evolved under $d_N = 0.5$, (b): with 64 cells (b), $d_N = 0.2$. Node color indicates whether the cell is contracting or expanding its springs (red: expansion, blue: contraction, green: neutral). Numbers indicate the time steps in the cycle. The direction of movement is upwards.

did evolve. For example, the perpendicular wave traveling through the body in Fig. 4a is a direct result of the fact that cells differ in phase in the direction perpendicular to the direction of movement (Fig. 7a). For the individual seen in Fig. 6a, most springs contract and expand in synchrony and there is no smooth phase gradient (Fig. 7b). However, because a line of cells at the back is strongly shifted in phase,

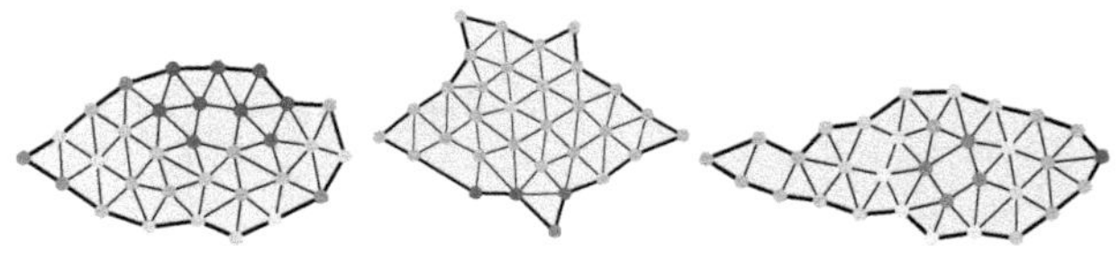

(a) 1.42π (b) 1.27π (c) 0.29π

Figure 7: Example of evolved cell oscillation phase shifts. Panel (a): the individual in Fig. 4a, (b): in Fig. 6a, (c): in Fig. 5a. All animats are displayed in their initial, equilibrium states. Color range is normalized on each picture and the maximum value of phase shift in each individual (corresponding to the red node) is indicated.

a wave of contractions travels through the body during locomotion. For the individual in Fig. 5a, the phase differences are small, and springs contract and expand almost at the same time (Fig. 7c, note the low maximum phase shift).

7. RESULTS: EVOLUTIONARY HISTORY

The fitness function we employed implicitly rewards size, so the best individuals we obtained always had the maximum number of cells that was allowed. Early generations were populated by animats in which all springs contracted and expanded in synchrony and with similar amplitude. Combined with asymmetries in the morphology, these oscillations would allow for some movement.

Analysis of the best fit individuals over generations suggests that initially the winning morphology changes rapidly. In all the runs, entirely new combinations of morphology and control sweep through the population for the first hundreds of generations, until the winning mode of locomotion emerges. For most of the remaining evolutionary history, small improvements of control and morphology would prevail (this stage would often take more than 10 000 generations). Only rarely would the best morphology change after many thousands of generations (this was the case for the history of the individual shown in Fig. 4a, whose mode of locomotion became the best after generation 8914, replacing an individual in the class of motion shown on Fig. 5). Whenever a significant morphological change would occur, it was quickly followed by a steep improvement in fitness, spanning about 100 generations. Some of these improvements corresponded to refinements of morphology, but mostly to adjustments of control to exploit new body structures.

For example, the history of the run that gave rise to the individual in Fig. 4b (Fig. 8) reveals that after two thousand generations, a large change in the winning morphology occurred. This morphology was quickly refined to its final state in less than 200 generations. The path for a final series of improvements was initiated around generation 3100, by modifying the control to a non zero, non uniform phase shift among cells. Further refinements took over 3500 generations, without any morphological change.

A fragment of another evolutionary history (Fig. 9) shows that the most radical improvements after generation 200 were driven by morphological changes. The winning morphological type appeared very early, about generation 340. Along the way, the final winning morphology already seen in generation 250 would be at least once out-competed by a related morphology in generation 263, only to reappear as the winning solution in generation 292.

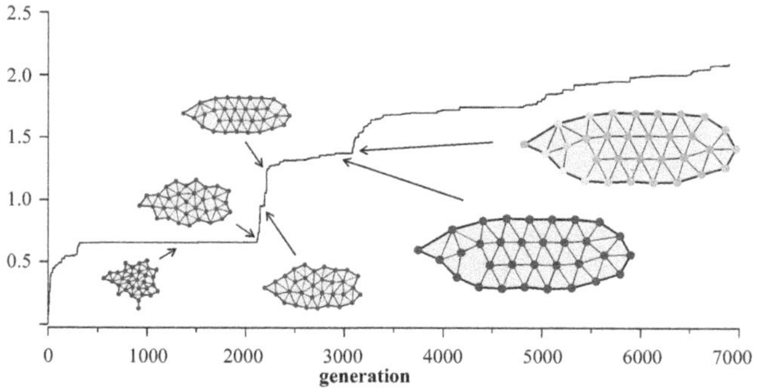

Figure 8: Fitness of the best individuals in the evolutionary run that ended with the animat in Fig. 4b. The last two individuals (which were the best around generation 3000) are shown enlarged and with cells colored to illustrate the change in oscillation phase shift among the cells, which was no longer zero afterwards.

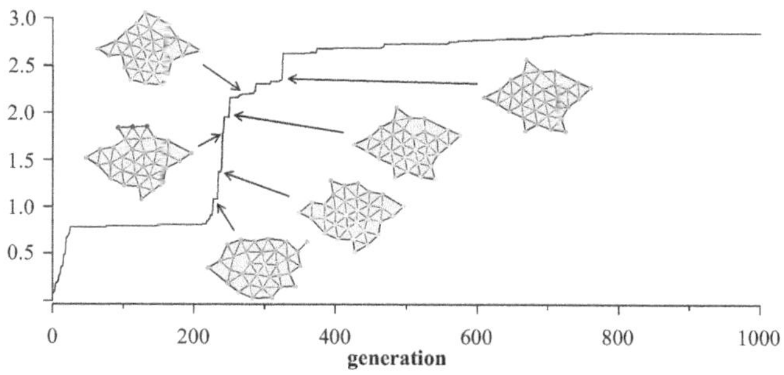

Figure 9: Fitness of the best individuals in the evolutionary run that ended with the animat in Fig. 6a. Multiple changes to the winning morphology occur during about 100 generations.

7.1 Conclusions and future work

We present in this paper a model of the evolution of GRN-controlled development of multicellular bodies which form soft-bodied animats able to move in a fluid-like environment. Our model has similarities with the one presented by Schramm et al. [20], who evolved GRNs which controlled development of 2-D animats (with springs and masses) promoting elongated shape in the fitness function. In contrast to this previous work, we do not promote any particular morphology nor the type of locomotion. Both are encoded indirectly, in one linear genome. We have shown that various combinations of morphology and control, with various modes of locomotion, emerge in environments with different drag coefficients. We observed that high drag promotes movement employing undulations while lower drag promotes symmetric appendages. We found that our method of converting the multicellular embryo into a mass-spring structure with a hydrostatic skeleton generates a wide range of interesting and relatively complex morphologies with different methods of locomotion despite the use of low numbers of cells. Importantly, the approach we employed to generate the final animat structure is based only on a set of points which is later outlined with an external "skin" and divided into elastic regions. This method provides a simple and useful approach to generate animat morphologies in other generative multicellular systems. It could also be easily extended to 3-D.

The observation that most changes in morphologies occur during initial generations suggests that most of the later morphological changes are highly detrimental. We have also observed that novel morphologies quickly improve in fitness thanks to the readjustments to control. Our observations suggest that the genetic algorithm might benefit from niching. Protecting novel morphologies until evolution has the time to adjust the control could prevent the loss of some morphologies with potential for supporting even better locomotion than we observed, but which were lost because our simple genetic algorithm did not allow their lineages enough time to adjust control.

One clear direction for future work is to allow for active control of the animats during locomotion. In the present version of our system, the GRN controls only the development. If the GRN continued to function beyond development, direct control of spring contractions would be possible. The cells could also communicate during that time through diffusive factors (similar to morphogens acting during development). It would be interesting to investigate if such communication influences the sustainability of behavior over time or its robustness to external disruptions and if the addition of sensors would allow for directional swimming. The relative ease with which the GRN model used here could actively control behavior of unicellular organisms sensing food gradients has been evaluated in our earlier work [11].

We chose Gabriel graphs as our initial approach to specify animat internal structure because they are a fast and non-parametric way to generate non convex structures and because they allow the generation of interesting patterns of connectivity which are not limited to triangle meshes. Obviously, this is just one of many possible notions of point proximity. Computational geometry provides many comparable methods that might be worth exploring in further work. For example, connections could be generated between nodes only if they are within a certain distance. Another approach would be to compute the outline of the body through α-shapes [4], a method that would additionally allow the generation of hollow structures. Alternative methods may become useful when the number of cells is increased and a more fine-grained definition of shape becomes possible.

In future work, the stiffness of the springs could also be put under genetic control, so that some parts of the animat would be more soft and some more rigid. We also plan to investigate evolution of locomotion in an environment with a surface with ground friction and gravity. Our preliminary results show that such an environment promotes evolution of primitive appendages. We would also like to introduce the notion of energy efficiency as a part of the fitness function. We hope that introducing the cost of actuation will introduce an evolutionary pressure to employ only some of the cells as actuators and to leave others to be passive but elastic elements of the structure which allow energy transfer along the body.

8. ACKNOWLEDGMENTS

We acknowledge the support by the Polish Ministry of Science and Education (project N519 384236,N303 291234), the Tri-city Academic Computer Center (TASK), and the Interdisciplinary Center for Molecular and Mathematical Modeling (ICM, University of Warsaw; project G33-8). We are grateful to Rene Doursat and Taras Kowaliw for discussions, and to Roman Bauer, Sabina Pfister and Adrian Whatley for critically reading the manuscipt.

9. REFERENCES

[1] J. C. Bongard and R. Pfeifer. Evolving complete agents using artificial ontogeny. In F. Hara and R. Pfeifer, editors, *Morpho-functional Machines: The New Species*, pages 237–258. Springer Japan, 2003.

[2] Bullet Physics library 2.79. http://www.bulletphysics.org, 2011.

[3] M. Calisti, M. Giorelli, G. Levy, B. Mazzolai, B. Hochner, C. Laschi, and P. Dario. An octopus-bioinspired solution to movement and manipulation for soft robots. *Bioinspir. Biomim.*, 6(3):036002+, 2011.

[4] H. Edelsbrunner, D. Kirkpatrick, and R. Seidel. On the shape of a set of points in the plane. *IEEE T. Inform. Theory.*, 29(4):551–559, 1983.

[5] P. Eggenberger Hotz. Evolving morphologies of simulated 3D organisms based on differential gene expression. In *Artificial Life IV*, pages 205–213. MIT Press, 1997.

[6] P. Eggenberger Hotz. Asymmetric cell division and its integration with other developmental processes for artificial evolutionary systems. In *Artificial Life IX*, pages 387–393. MIT Press, 2004.

[7] K. R. Gabriel and R. R. Sokal. A new statistical approach to geographic variation analysis. *Syst. Zool.*, 18(3):259–278, 1969.

[8] J. D. Hiller and H. Lipson. Evolving amorphous robots. In *Artificial Life XII*, pages 717–724. MIT Press, 2010.

[9] G. S. Hornby and J. B. Pollack. Body-brain co-evolution using l-systems as a generative encoding. In *Proceedings of the Genetic and Evolutionary Computation Conference (GECCO 2001)*, pages 868–875. Morgan Kaufmann, 2001.

[10] M. Joachimczak and B. Wróbel. Complexity of the search space in a model of artificial evolution of gene regulatory networks controlling 3D multicellular morphogenesis. *Adv. Complex Syst.*, 12(3):347–369, 2009.

[11] M. Joachimczak and B. Wróbel. Evolving gene regulatory networks for real time control of foraging behaviours. In *Artificial Life XII*, pages 348–355. MIT Press, 2010.

[12] M. Joachimczak and B. Wróbel. Evolution of the morphology and patterning of artificial embryos: scaling the tricolour problem to the third dimension. In *ECAL 2009: Proceedings of the 10th European Conference on Artificial Life*, volume 5777 of *Lecture Notes in Computer Science*, pages 33–41. Springer, 2011.

[13] H. Komatsu, Y. Hashimoto, Y. Chen, and H. Ohashi. An evolvability-enhanced artificial embryogeny for generating network structures. In *Proceedings of the Genetic and Evolutionary Computation Conference (GECCO 2008)*, pages 835–842. ACM, 2008.

[14] M. Komosinski and A. Rotaru-Varga. Comparison of different genotype encodings for simulated three-dimensional agents. *Artif. Life*, 7(4):395–418, 2002.

[15] S. Kumar and P. Bentley. Biologically inspired evolutionary development. In A. Tyrrell, P. Haddow, and J. Torresen, editors, *Evolvable Systems: From Biology to Hardware*, volume 2606 of *Lecture Notes in Computer Science*, chapter 6, pages 57–68. Springer Berlin / Heidelberg, 2003.

[16] D. Lobo and F. J. Vico. Evolution of form and function in a model of differentiated multicellular organisms with gene regulatory networks. *Biosystems*, 102(2-3):112–123, 2010.

[17] S. Lucas. Evolving spring-mass models: a test-bed for graph encoding schemes. In *2002 World Congress on Computational Intelligence - WCCI'02*, volume 2, pages 1952–1957. IEEE, 2002.

[18] T. Miconi. Evosphere: Evolutionary dynamics in a population of fighting virtual creatures. In *IEEE Congress on Evolutionary Computation*, pages 3066–3073. IEEE, 2008.

[19] J. Rieffel, B. Trimmer, and H. Lipson. Mechanism as mind: what tensegrities and caterpillars can teach us about soft robotics. In *Artificial Life XI*, pages 506–512. MIT Press, 2008.

[20] L. Schramm, Y. Jin, and B. Sendhoff. Emerged coupling of motor control and morphological development in evolution of multi-cellular animats. In *Proceedings of the 10th European Conference on Artificial Life (ECAL2009)*, volume 5777 of *Lecture Notes in Computer Science*, pages 18–26. Springer, 2011.

[21] M. Sfakiotakis and D. P. Tsakiris. Simuun : A simulation environment for undulatory locomotion. *Int. J. Model. Simul.*, 26:350–358, 2006.

[22] R. F. Shepherd, F. Ilievski, W. Choi, S. A. Morin, A. A. Stokes, A. D. Mazzeo, X. Chen, M. Wang, and G. M. Whitesides. Multigait soft robot. *Proc. Natl. Acad. Sci. U. S. A.*, 108(51):20400–20403, 2011.

[23] K. Sims. Evolving virtual creatures. In *Proceedings of the 21st annual conference on Computer graphics and interactive techniques*, SIGGRAPH '94, pages 15–22. ACM Press, 1994.

[24] E. Steltz, A. Mozeika, N. Rodenberg, E. Brown, and H. M. Jaeger. Jsel: Jamming skin enabled locomotion. In *IEEE/RSJ International Conference on Intelligent Robots and Systems (IROS 2009)*, pages 5672–5677, 2009.

[25] D. Terzopoulos, X. Tu, and R. Grzeszczuk. Artificial fishes: autonomous locomotion, perception, behavior, and learning in a simulated physical world. *Artif. Life*, 1(4):327–351, 1994.

[26] G. Turk. Sticky Feet: evolution in a multi-creature physical simulation. In *Artificial Life XII*, pages 496–503. MIT Press, 2010.

An Evo-Devo Approach to Architectural Design

Daniel Richards
Manchester Institute for Research and Innovation in Art & Design
Manchester Metropolitan University
Manchester M15 6BG, UK
D.Richards@mmu.ac.uk

Nick Dunn
Manchester Institute for Research and Innovation in Art & Design
Manchester Metropolitan University
Manchester M15 6BG, UK
N.Dunn@mmu.ac.uk

Martyn Amos
School of Computing, Mathematics & Digital Technology
Manchester Metropolitan University
Manchester M1 5GD, UK
M.Amos@mmu.ac.uk

ABSTRACT
We present a developmental genotype-phenotype growth process, or embryogeny, which is used to evolve, *in silico*, efficient three-dimensional structures that exhibit real-world architectural performance. The embryogeny defines a sequential assembly of architectural components within a three-dimensional volume, and indirectly establishes a regulatory network of components based on the principles of gene regulation. The implicitly regulated phenotypes suggest advances for the automatic design of physical structures, by improving scalability of the genotype encoding and embedding real-world constraints. We demonstrate that our model can evolve novel, yet efficient, architectural structures which exhibit emergent shape, topology and material distribution. Finally, we compare evolved structures against a "hand-coded" solution to illustrate that our model produces competitive results without prior knowledge of the design solution or direct human guidance.

Categories and Subject Descriptors
I.2.11 **[Distributed Artificial Intelligence]**; J.5 **[Arts and Humanities]**: Architecture; J.6 **[Computer-aided Engineering]**: Computer-aided Design (CAD).

Keywords
Artificial Embryogeny, Morphogenetic Engineering, Architectural Design, Self-Organization, Computational Design Synthesis.

1. INTRODUCTION
The physical properties of natural morphologies are extraordinary. Through complex processes of self-organization and evolution, nature is able to assemble extremely efficient material structures that are economical, multifunctional and exhibit magnitudes of complexity that greatly surpass anything we can currently design. Architects and engineers have often taken inspiration from nature; today, in the face of rapid climate change and urbanization, they seek new bio-inspired methods of designing "sustainable" performance-oriented architectural form.

Traditional "form-first" design approaches often consider real-world performance, such as structural integrity or solar gains, late in the design process. Consequently, the structures produced are often wasteful in their use of material and composed of many mono-functional sub-systems which render them far less "sustainable" and "integrated" than the complex material structures found in nature. An emerging alternative design paradigm, often termed computational design synthesis, seeks to invert the traditional approach [1-4]. Our proposed method extends this field of research by using bio-inspired computation to transform physical parameters from *passive* attributes into *active* properties that shape development. Rather than being ascribed to form post-design, features such as material properties, fabrication constraints and environmental performance are allowed to influence the early development and synthesis of form. Our ultimate goal is *automatic self-organization* of real-world components into efficient architectural morphologies. We use an evolutionary algorithm (EA) with a novel developmental genotype-phenotype encoding to construct highly integrated three-dimensional structures that exhibit competitive real-world performance, and express emergent shape, topology and material distribution.

Computational design synthesis research has demonstrated *semi-automated* models that use performance simulations to inform the early development of form [1,2,5]. However, these methods are limited to addressing relatively simple design problems, since they require the manual design, modification and interpretation of *parameterized design representations* in response to performance analysis. Parameterized representations have proved successful when applied to late-stage optimization, but they assume a prior understanding of the design problem, so that key parameters can be identified and encoded before computation is applied. To progress existing research and eventually address complex design problems (where prior understanding of the solution is unavailable) we require *open-ended design representations* [6,7] that allow the topology of solutions to be modified throughout an evolutionary "design" process. Existing application of open-ended representations within architectural design has been limited, yet it is argued that the ability to integrate simulation and performance analysis with such representations will facilitate the self-organization of extremely integrated, performance-driven structures [8-10].

This paper presents a novel developmental representation that is *explicitly* defined, yet *implicitly* [20] regulated using an indirect genotype-phenotype mapping inspired by genetic regulatory networks. The developmental mapping is combined with a simple evolutionary algorithm (EA) to construct an evo-devo model, and used to demonstrate the self-organization of efficient architectural structures without the aid of a designer.

GECCO'12, July 7–11, 2012, Philadelphia, Pennsylvania, USA.

The paper is structured as follows: In Section 2 we review related work that utilizes developmental or generative encodings within EAs to construct performance-oriented structures. In Section 3 we present the genotype encoding and developmental mapping process. Section 4 describes our experimental results, and we conclude in Section 5 with a summary and discussion of further research challenges and opportunities.

2. RELATED WORK

Evolutionary computation has been widely applied to design and engineering for the post-design optimization of parameterized (fixed topology) design representations (see Kicinger, *et al.* for an extensive overview [11]). Existing attempts to integrate EAs into the early stages of design have focused upon either the iterative design and "calibration" of parameterized representations to enhance architectural performance [12-13], or the use of generative, open-ended representations for the creative exploration of formal possibilities [14-16]. However, the successful application of EAs to synthesize *shape, topology* and *material distribution* for the self-organization of highly integrated architectural form has not, until now, been demonstrated. Existing work has demonstrated that open-ended representations can produce *well-performing* structures without the need for *well-defined* parameterized representations. Shea *et al.* use an open-ended representation based on shape grammars to evolve novel truss structures early in the design process [17], and Funes and Pollack demonstrate a grammar-based encoding to evolve structurally robust Lego structures [18]. This research illustrates the successful use of open-ended representations to encode and evolve physical structures; however, these models require a direct genotype-phenotype mapping process, which has proved to be less effective at finding good solutions as design problems increase in scale and complexity [6,18]. To improve scalability, the use of bio-inspired developmental growth processes, or *embryogenies*, has been proposed as a means of indirectly mapping from genotype (encoding) to phenotype (structure) [19-21].

Explicit embryogenies [20], which use indirect grammar-based representations, have been used to evolve three-dimensional structures for architectural design. O'Reilly and Hemberg demonstrate the evolution of grammar-based three-dimensional surfaces within a simulated environment [15]. von Mammel and Jacob present a swarm-based grammar system for evolving architectural forms [22], O'Neil *et al.* use grammatical representations to evolve simple architectural shelter designs [23], and Rieffel *et al.* use a graph-based encoding for finding and optimizing large irregular tensegrity structures [24]. The major limitation of existing explicit embryogenies, when applied to architectural design, is inclusion of real-world performance. Firstly, evolved forms often exhibit "unbuild-able" intersecting geometries, as Sims found in his work on early virtual creatures [25]. Secondly, the inclusion of real-world materiality, construction logic and spatial performance has been limited in existing works, often necessitating evolved forms be fabricated as small scale 3D printed objects [6,26] or remain in silico [22,23].

Implicit embryogenies [20], which utilize bio-inspired regulatory networks to *activate* and *suppress* genes within a developmental representation, have also been used to evolve structures. Eggenberger demonstrates a model of gene regulation that is combined with a genetic algorithm (GA) to evolve "multicellular" three-dimensional shapes [27]. Bongard and Pfeifer use a genetic regulatory model to simultaneously evolve three-dimensional morphologies and neural controls of computational agents within a simulated environment [28]. Miller presents a developmental cellular model to evolve two-dimensional graphics that are able to self-repair when damaged [29]. Hiller and Lipson use a compositional pattern positioning network to evolve amorphous robot morphologies [30] and Yogev *et al.* apply a developmental embryogeny to evolve three-dimensional structures to support simulated structural loadings [31]. The advantages of implicit embryogenies for real-world architectural design problems are twofold. Firstly, implicit embryogenies have been shown to scale efficiently [20], and are therefore suitable for solving complex design problems. This is significant, because existing attempts to bridge the "reality gap" between computational self-organization and real-world fabrication necessitate parameterized or one-to-one open-ended representations [17-18] that are inherently limited to simple design problems. Secondly, real-world design problems are necessarily constrained by fabrication technologies and the physical properties of available components. We suggest that implicit representations can successfully utilize real-world assembly logic, material properties and sizing of components to ensure the development of diverse - yet "build-able" - phenotypes. This can be achieved using developmental regulatory processes inspired by *gene expression, gene repression* and *programmed cell death* (see Section 3).

The developmental design methodology presented in this paper uses an implicitly regulated genotype-phenotype mapping, inspired by genetic regulatory networks, to evolve multifunctional architectural morphologies from a programmable library of architectural components.

3. EMBRYOGENY

The design of our encoding has two principle advantages. Firstly, it allows diverse structures to be represented using small amounts of information. Secondly, it is modular, so can be easily reused to evolve novel libraries of architectural components in response to variable performance criteria. To accomplish this, the genotype encoding takes inspiration from encoding mechanisms in evolutionary developmental biology. The embryogeny defines a *developmental growth process* whereby structural nodes are used to sequentially define a network of material components that constitute a larger architectural structure.

3.1 Genotype Encoding

During the *developmental embryogeny*, characteristics of nodes are used to assemble three-dimensional structures using various material components from the predefined libraries. Within the two predefined libraries there are three types of geometry and nine different classes of material that nodes can use to create material connections. The three types of geometry are: struts between nodes to form branching structures (Fig 1d), struts connecting multiple nodes in a clockwise sequence to form rings (Fig 1e) and surfaces connecting exactly three nodes to form petal-like components (Fig 1f). The nine material classes represent nine different sheet-cut aluminum components which differ in width and cross-sectional area (Fig 2a). Surfaces between nodes are achieved by bending aluminum sheets and connecting at structural seams (Fig 2b). Each material class offers a different trade-off between weight, cost and structural strength, allowing nodes to construct a diverse array of material connections. Each genotype comprises a string of integers which define the behavior of a population of nodes within a three-dimensional volume. Figure 1 and Figure 2 describe the genotype in detail.

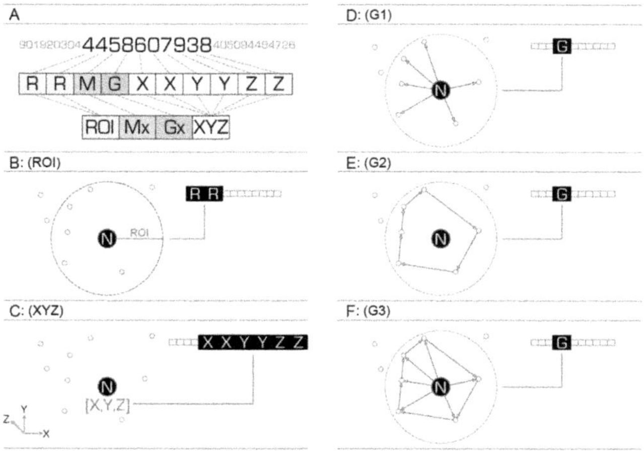

Figure 1. Genotype structure: (A) Each node is described by 4 genes, which define 4 aspects of its development: ROI, M, G and [X,Y,Z]. (B) The *range of influence* (ROI), a radial dimension, described by a 2 digit gene (in the range 0-99), within which nodes can perceive, communicate and connect to other nodes. (C) The *position* of the node within 3D space as described by a 6-digit gene (each digit in the range 0-9) that defines the Cartesian coordinates [XX,YY,ZZ]. (D-F) The library of *geometry types*, G, that the node uses to construct structural connections within its ROI. This is specified using a 1 digit gene (in the range 0-9) to select either: G1,G2 or G3.

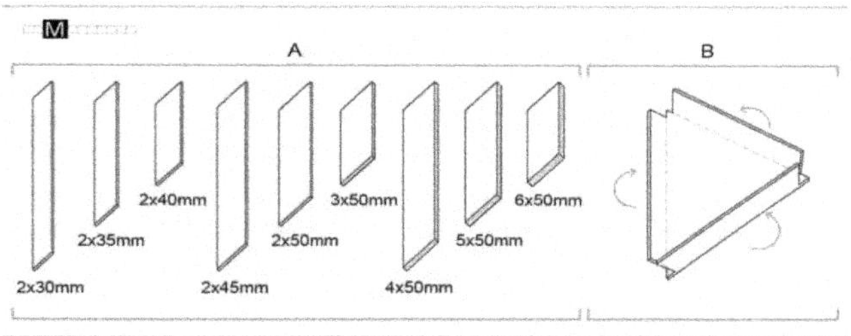

Figure 2. Library of material classes. (A) The *material properties*, M, of connections the node can create. Each nodes' M is defined using a 1 digit gene (in the range 0-9) to select a connection type from the predefined library of components. (B) Surfaces are created by bending aluminum sheets and connecting at structural seams.

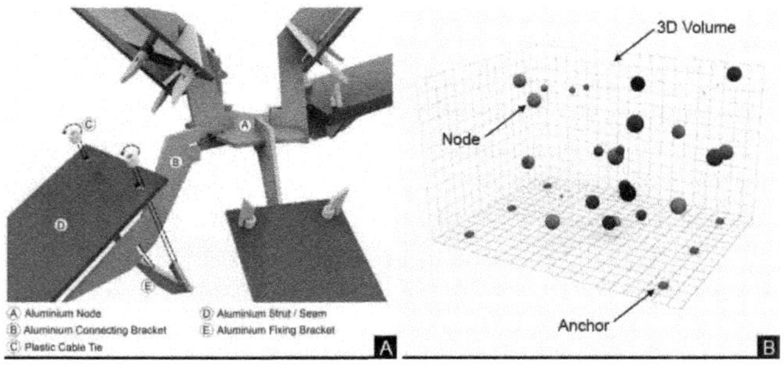

Figure 3. (A) Parametrically defined node detail. (B) The model comprises a collection of nodes within a 3D volume and predefined anchor points.

The length of material connections is controlled by each node's ROI. Nodes which have large ROI values can effectively "see" further, and may subsequently construct longer connections between potentially greater numbers of nodes. All components can be fabricated by cutting 1mm sheet aluminum on a CNC milling machine, therefore the maximum ROI is defined by the maximum dimensions of the CNC mill. Joints between material connections (structural members) are constructed using a *parametrically* defined fixing detail, which may also be cut from sheet aluminum (Fig 3a). In addition to node-node connections, nodes are also able to construct material connections between various anchor points within the three-dimensional volume, which transmit loads directly to a ground surface. Fig 3b illustrates the model set-up with six anchor points defined.

3.2 Developmental Mapping

We now describe the developmental embryogeny to decode the genotype and produce a set of *assembly instructions* that can be used to construct complex three-dimensional structures. In this context, "assembly instructions" simply describe the behavior of individual nodes. Each node operates as a genetic switch that, when activated, constructs local material connections with other nodes within its ROI; thus the local behavior of nodes collectively defines the larger three-dimensional structure. However, as material connections have structural depth and weight, there can only ever be one connection between any two nodes, in order to prevent intersecting geometry. This requires a *sequential growth* of material connections, in a hierarchical fashion defined by node index. This means that the order in which nodes construct material connections is significant, and makes the entire assembly process operate as a primitive genetic regulatory network. Material connections that are constructed by the early growth of nodes indirectly activate or suppress the growth of subsequent connections via processes of *positive* and *negative regulation.*

Within biological systems, positive and negative regulation is observed in the complex processes of gene expression [32]. Put simply, genes are switched "on" or "off" by the existence or non-existence of specific proteins (in reality, genes are rarely binary). If a gene is switched "on", or *expressed*, a protein is produced, which will in turn control the expression or repression of other genes through positive regulation. Conversely, if the gene is switched "off", or *repressed*, no protein is transcribed which influences the expression or repression of other genes, known as negative regulation. Whilst existing work has used biologically analogous models of gene regulation to evolve complex morphologies [27,28], our model makes no such attempt to accurately model genetic regulatory networks. However, it does utilize the basic mechanisms of positive and negative regulation to produce three-dimensional structures that are highly sensitive to nodal behavior via a complex network of regulatory dependencies.

In order for nodes to establish connections and dependencies (topology), each node is given a small *memory space* in which it stores information about other nodes to which it is currently connected. Before each node constructs connections between itself and nodes within its ROI, the node first checks that it does not *already* have an imprint of each node (analogous to a protein) in its memory space (analogous to a cis-regulatory region of DNA). If the node finds an imprint then no connection is made, but if no imprint exists then a new material connection is grown, and each node exchanges a copy of their node index in order to prevent further connections being made.

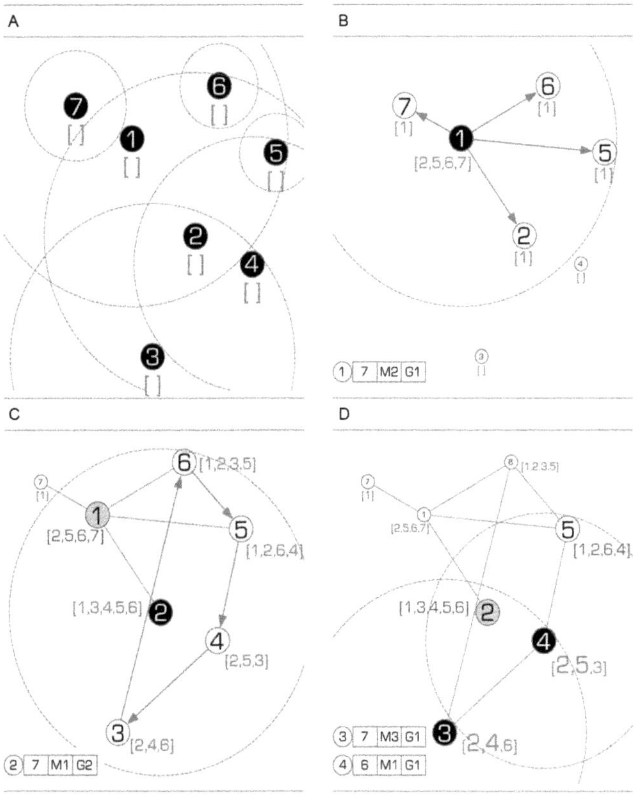

Figure 4. Developmental growth. (A) Shows a random arrangement of nodes with empty memory spaces. (B) Node 1 grows G1 connections between itself and nodes within its ROI. (C) Node 2 grows G2 connections between surrounding nodes – omitting Node 1 as it already has a connection. (D) Nodes 3 and 4 have been repressed by Node 2's earlier growth.

Figure 4 illustrates the developmental growth process using 7 nodes. For clarity, the nodes are set within a two-dimensional space, and each node is defined by 3 genes which control: ROI, material class and geometry type. Each node's memory space is illustrated as square brackets to demonstrate how information is exchanged during assembly. Figure 5 illustrates how small changes to node characteristics provide significant alterations to the phenotype structures.

Following the sequential assembly process, two further operations are performed to remove unbuild-able components from the structure, using a procedure inspired by the biological process of programmed cell death (PCD) [33]. Figure 6 illustrates the process of PCD in detail.

By combining the developmental embryogeny with a standard GA we are able to evolve multifunctional three-dimensional structures that exhibit emergent shape, topology and material distribution. In the next Section, we describe our experimental results.

4. EXPERIMENTAL RESULTS

We test our *evo-devo* model on a simple experimental design problem. The problem was to "design" an economical, free-standing structure that can provide controlled (passive) solar shading to a space during the summer months and must be fully fabricated using 1mm CNC cut aluminum sheets. To address this design problem we limited the maximum build volume of structures to 2000 x 1500 x 1100mm and the amount of nodes to 30 based upon initial trials.

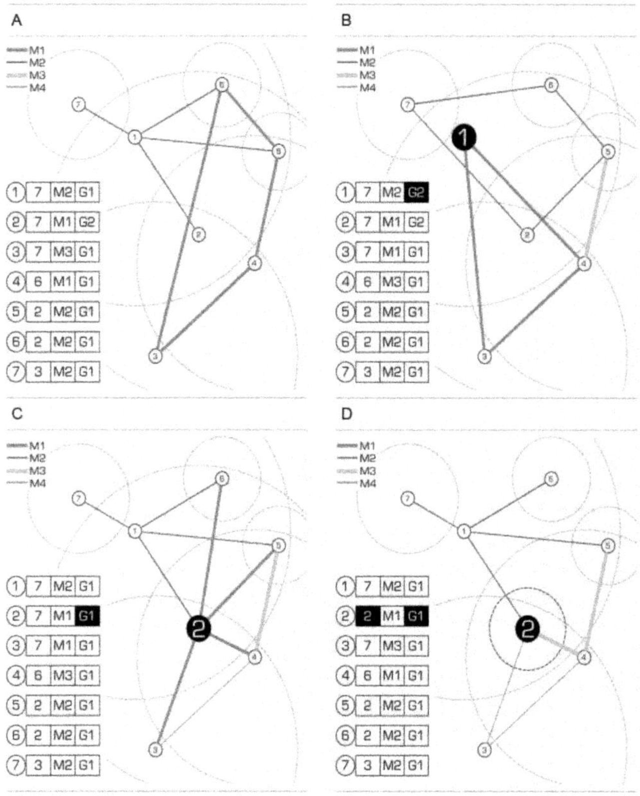

Figure 5. Phenotype variability. Small changes to node ROI or geometry type dramatically influence phenotype formation through positive and negative regulation. (A) Phenotype produced from Fig 4. (B) Mutation of Node 1 geometry type – G1 to G2. (C) Mutation of Node 2 geometry type – G2 to G1. (D) Mutation of Node 2 ROI – ROI = 7 to ROI = 2.

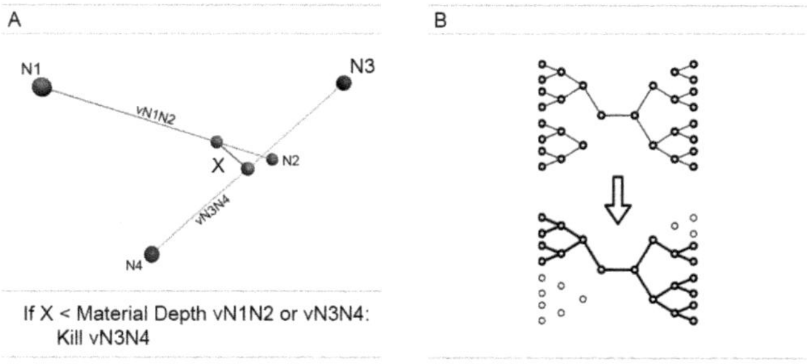

Figure 6. Programmed cell death. (A) Following the developmental growth process, if any components intersect the last component to be formed initiates an automatic suicide program and is deleted. (B) Following the intersection test a connectivity test is used to identify and remove any components which are disconnected from the main structure.

We designed two libraries of components that can be fabricated using 1mm aluminum sheeting (Fig 2) and programmed the maximum ROI of nodes to correspond with the maximum cutting dimensions of our CNC mill (840 x 900mm). This approach allows us to represent "build-able" three-dimensional structures with a 120-gene genotype (300 digits in the range 0 9) using our developmental embryogeny.

To provide a baseline for comparison, we hand-designed a solution, shown in Fig 7.

4.1 Fitness Function

The fitness of each phenotype is calculated using the weighted sum of four performance measures: Firstly, we considered the *average nodal deflection* of structures under loading. Secondly, we measured the *average height* of structural nodes. Thirdly, *total fabrication cost* was considered, based on material usage, and finally, we used a measure of daily *solar performance*.

Structural fitness (StF) is calculated using physical simulation (see Implementation). The average combined deflection in [x,y,z] position of structural nodes (AvD) is compared with an acceptable nodal deflection value (AcD) and an unacceptable deflection value (UaD) that defines the breaking point of the component when subjected to a combination of dead weight of structure and an imposed 0.2KN wind loading (1):

$$\mathrm{StF} = 1 - \left(\frac{\mathrm{AvD - AcD}}{\mathrm{UaD - AcD}} \right) \quad (1)$$

$$\text{If } \mathrm{StF} > 1 : \mathrm{StF} = 1, \text{ If } \mathrm{StF} < 0 : \mathrm{StF} = 0$$

Height fitness (HeF) is defined by the average height of structural nodes (AvH) in relation to the maximum build volume height (BvH). In this experiment, tall models are favored in an attempt to consider how accommodation requirements of structures might be evolved in larger models. (2):

$$\mathrm{HeF} = \frac{\mathrm{AvH}}{\mathrm{BvH}} \quad (2)$$

The total fabrication cost (CoF) is defined by the required amount of aluminum sheeting (ReA) to fabricate the structure. This is compared against a defined fabrication budget (FaB) and a maximum overspend allowance (MoS). For illustrative purposes the FaB = £300 and MoS = £500 for this experiment (3):

$$\mathrm{CoF} = 1 - \left(\frac{\mathrm{ReA - FaB}}{\mathrm{MoS - FaB}} \right) \quad (3)$$

$$\text{If } \mathrm{CoF} > 1 : \mathrm{CoF} = 1, \text{ If } \mathrm{CoF} < 0 : \mathrm{CoF} = 0$$

Solar fitness (SoF) is defined by the average differentiation (AvDiff) of each solar analysis grid cell and a desired measure of solar performance (DeS). Full exposure of any grid cell during analysis returns 2400 KWh. For illustrative purposes DeS = 1500KWh in this experiment (4):

$$\mathrm{SoF} = 1 - \left(\frac{\mathrm{AvDiff - DeS}}{2400 - \mathrm{DeS}} \right) \quad (4)$$

$$\text{If } \mathrm{SoF} < 0 : \mathrm{SoF} = 0$$

Finally, the overall fitness of each phenotype (F) is calculated by the weighted sum of StF, HeF, CoF and SoF. The relative weightings correspond to the importance of each performance-based attribute in the architectural solution (5):

$$\mathrm{F} = \left(\frac{\mathrm{StF} \cdot \mathrm{w1} + \mathrm{HeF} \cdot \mathrm{w2} + \mathrm{CoF} \cdot \mathrm{w3} + \mathrm{SoF} \cdot \mathrm{w1}}{4.5} \right) \quad (5)$$

$$\mathrm{w1} = 1.5;\ \mathrm{w2} = 1;\ \mathrm{w3} = 0.5$$

4.2 Implementation

The model is implemented with Python on a 2.7GHz 8-core Windows OS with 6GB RAM, using a combination of COM, OLE and DDE servers to tie together three commercial CAD packages: *3DS Max, Multiframe 3D* and *Ecotect*.

3DS Max is used to create three-dimensional geometry and construction details via a COM server using the inbuilt scripting language *Maxscript*.

Multiframe 3D is used to perform structural analysis of structures using finite element analysis (FEA). Structural data is input using an OLE server and used to accurately define the material properties and imposed physical forces upon phenotypes. Nodes are considered as rigid joints during analysis, whereas anchor points and nodes with a height value of zero are defined as fixed to the ground surface. Results of the FEA return the total deflection for each node in response to the dead weight of the structural components and optional live loadings that can be imposed on all nodes and structural members by a designer.

Ecotect is used to perform basic solar analysis using a .dxf model exported from 3DS Max, and is operated by python using a DDE server and the inbuilt scripting language *Luc*. An analysis grid is placed on the ground plane of the defined volume, and each grid cell measures how much solar radiation it is exposed to over a specified time period. In these experiments, the solar duration is between the hours of 10:00 to 14:00 from 1st June to 31st August and the location is Manchester, UK. Results of the solar analysis return the average daily solar radiation experienced at each cell, and is used to determine the deviation from an idealized (uniform) radiation value that is defined in the fitness function of the GA.

4.3 GA Parameters

Population size = 100, generations = 60, runs = 10, selection type = tournament, tournament size = 5, crossover type = one-point, crossover rate = 100% and mutation rate = 0.005%.

4.4 Results

We now present the results obtained over 10 runs of the GA and compare them against the human designed, "hand coded" solution. The hand coded solution uses the same material and construction details as the evolved models, and was designed using a traditional *form-first* approach. A simple arch was proposed using 6x50mm aluminum members, and then clad using non-structural aluminum panels. Each panel has a different sized aperture. South facing panels have small apertures to allow shading, whereas north facing panels have larger apertures to reduce material costs.

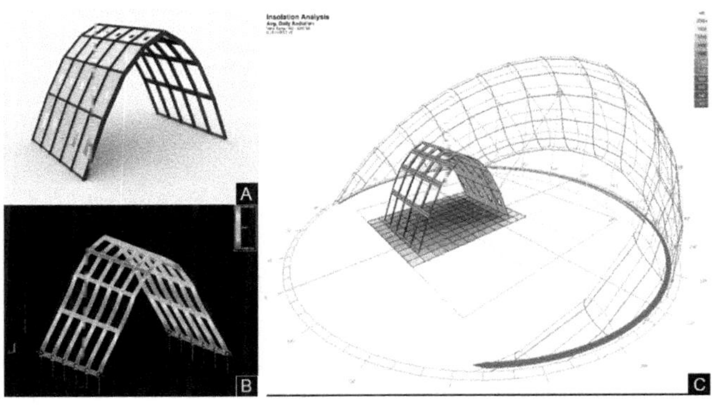

Figure 7. (A) Hand coded solution. (B) FEA structural deformation analysis. (C) Solar analysis.

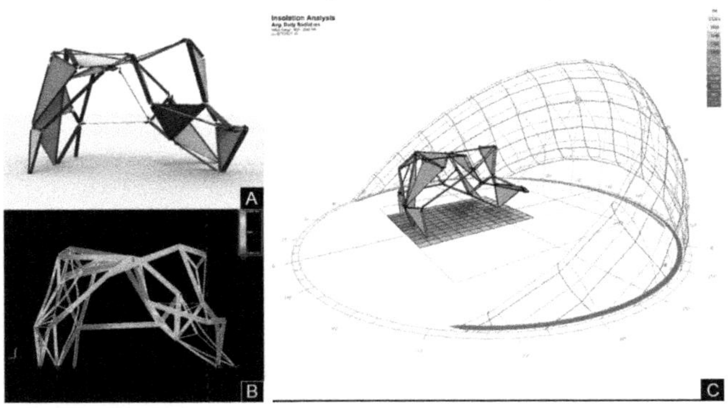

Figure 8. (A) Typical evolved solution. (B) FEA structural deformation analysis. (C) Solar analysis.

Figure 9 presents a comparative analysis of the hand coded structure against the (average) fitness of the best performing evolved structures over 10 runs. The hand coded performance breaks down as follows: structural fitness = 1, solar fitness = 0.75, height fitness = 0.58, cost fitness = 0.49 and overall fitness = 0.77. In comparison the (best) evolved structures over 10 runs have the following (average) performance: structural fitness = 0.92, solar fitness = 0.61, height fitness = 0.43, cost fitness = 1 and overall fitness = 0.72.

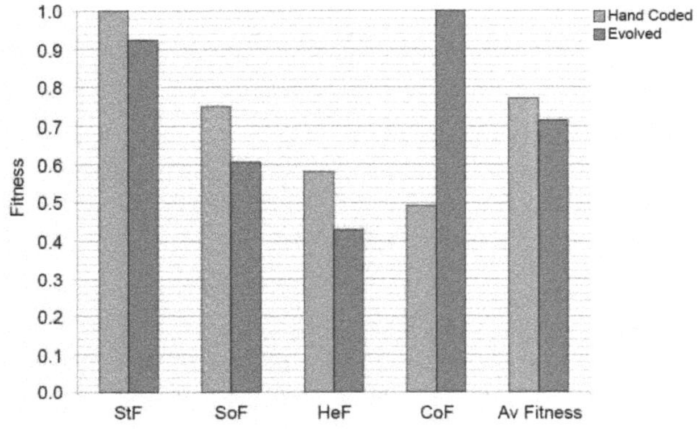

Figure 9. Comparative fitness analysis

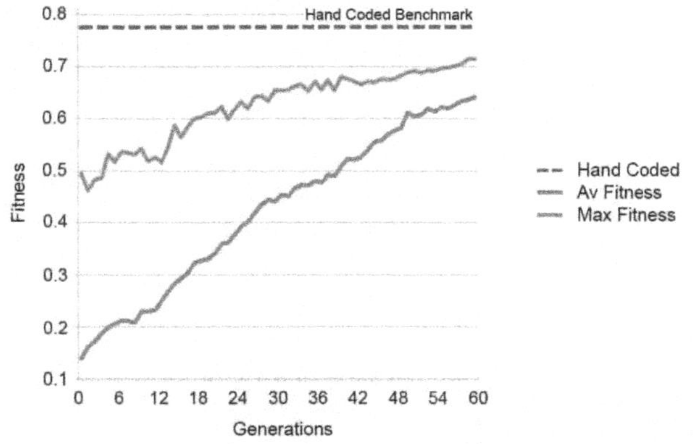

Figure 10. Average and maximum fitness over 10 runs

Figure 10 illustrates how the results of the GA converge in comparison to the hand coded fitness benchmark. Although we note that the average fitness is still rising when the runs were terminated, this was due to the time required for evaluation of each generation (the simulations are extremely processor-intensive). Future work will extend the number of generations to further investigate convergence properties, and assess whether the structural benefits obtained from longer runs are outweighed by the additional computational resources required.

4.5 Analysis

Figure 9 demonstrates that our evolved structures exhibit competitive fitness in comparison to the hand coded solution. After 60 generations the evolved structures obtain fitness only 6.5% below the hand-coded benchmark (Fig 10). Significantly they achieve this *without* prior knowledge of the solution or direct human guidance.

In this experiment, initial structures generated by random search provide extremely poor structural performance (Fig 11a-b). Consequently our fitness function was used to reward structural integrity to facilitate the evolution of build-able structures (Fig 9). Figure 10 shows that the maximum fitness derived from a random search is relatively high, suggesting that an exhaustive search may produce well performing structures. However, this is somewhat deceptive and highlights the challenge of designing a fitness function which can effectively communicate our *design intent* for real-world structures. Figure 11c-f illustrates structures derived by random search that exhibit relatively high fitness values (around 0.5). These structures do not provide well "rounded" architectural performance. However, they do exhibit good *structural performance* and *material economy,* which allows them to obtain deceptively high overall fitness values.

For the purpose of addressing this simple performance-based design problem, our fitness function facilitates the synthesis of shape, topology and material distribution to produce novel architectural solutions (Fig 12). However, we argue that non-trivial design problems will require *implicit* methods of describing *design intent,* so that real-world characteristics, such as structural integrity and material economy, become *emergent* properties that do not require *explicit* definition within the fitness function. We consider these in more detail in the following discussion.

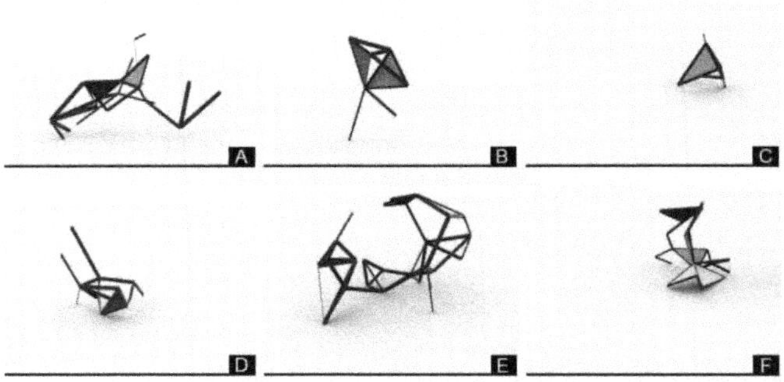

Figure 11. Structures generated by random search.

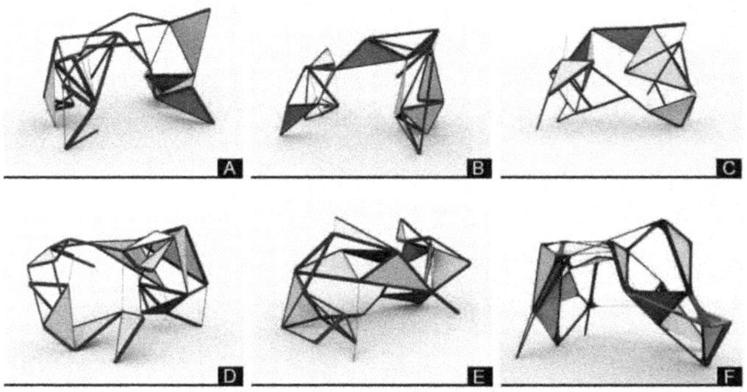

Figure 12. Examples of evolved structures

4.5.1 *Evolved Formal Traits*

During our experiments, evolved structures exhibited three *emergent*, recurring *formal traits*. Firstly, we observed the evolution of primitive *arch formations* (Fig 13a). Arch-shaped structures were assigned higher height fitness (HeF) due to the method of analysis, and were often *cheaper* to fabricate, since they eliminated unnecessary components from the middle of the three-dimensional volume. Secondly, we observed the evolution of *north-south differentiation* in structures. The north sides of structures often evolve to be structurally robust (Fig 13a left) which allows the south side of structures (Fig 13 right) to become structurally dependent, effectively "leaning up" against the robust north side. This formal trait was beneficial to structural performance, but also allowed the south sides of structures to express more numerous "petal-like" surface components in order to enhance solar shading. Thirdly, we observed *dual functionality* of surface components, to both enhance solar performance and improve structural integrity. Figure 13b-d illustrates the structural stresses imposed upon a typical arch structure. On the south (right) side of the structure, surface components are efficiently supported to increase shading. However, we also see surface components being utilized in areas of high structural stress to enhance *structural integrity*. This can be seen in Figure 13d on the north (left) side of the structure.

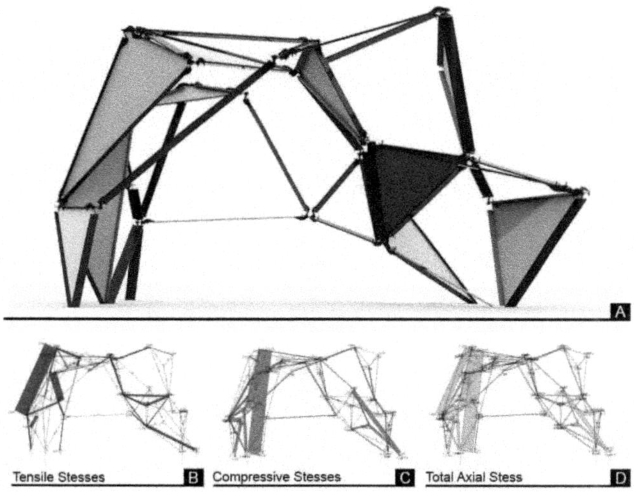

Figure 13: (A) Emergent arch formation. (B) Tensile stresses. (C) Compressive stresses. (D) Total axial stresses.

5. SUMMARY AND FUTURE WORK

We have presented a developmental genotype-phenotype mapping process and used it to self-organize a programmable library of architectural components in response to real-world performance objectives. Our results demonstrate a proof-of-principle that our evo-devo model can automatically synthesize shape, topology and material distribution, *in silico*, to produce functional architectural structures that are comparable to simple human designed solutions. This method extends the field of computational design synthesis and suggests that an evo-devo approach to architectural design may provide a way of breaking through the "glass ceiling" imposed by existing semi-automated design processes.

We claim this ability to automatically synthesize performance-driven architectural form via self-organizing processes is novel, and could open up entirely new territories for *sustainable design* of complex architectural structures.

Four key areas require further research before we can successfully apply *programmable self-organization* to non-trivial, physical architectural design problems.

Firstly, the current implementation of our model is dependent upon commercial CAD software packages to run performance analysis. The primary benefit of using existing CAD packages is (1) the validity of results and (2) they provide a useful medium for interdisciplinary communication. However, the central drawback is dramatically increased computation time. Each run of our model takes around 72 hours to complete. Consequently, the results presented have been limited to 60 generations and simply capture the beginning of evolutionary development. Future work requires the development of faster computational processes for the structural and environmental analysis of three-dimensional structures.

Secondly, the developmental representation provides a significant reduction in genotype size by reusing information during the regulatory developmental embryogeny. However, there is potential to further reduce genotype sizing and improve scalability of the model by utilizing *grammatical encodings* to generate node values, instead of relying upon fixed length string genomes.

Thirdly, the principal advantage of our developmental representation is the ability to integrate the physical properties of architectural components and evolve real-world performance for three-dimensional structures. However, evolved structures are currently analyzed as fully assembled morphologies that, in reality, would require additional scaffolding during construction. Further work is required to consider how physical incremental assembly of architectural components can be managed, and ultimately automated.

Finally, future work in this domain will explore how localized perturbations of nodes, in response to structural deflection analysis, can be introduced into the developmental embryogeny so that fundamental real-world properties (such as structural integrity) can be completely removed from our fitness function. We suggest that the ability to *implicitly* select structures which exhibit *essential* performance attributes will be critical for addressing non-trivial design problems in future works. However, we also believe that *implicit selection* via localized perturbations might allow additional useful properties, such as structural robustness (in response to damage), to emerge "for free". Such developmental representations that allow fundamental physical properties to emerge "for free" could facilitate the production of increasingly efficient, multifunctional and sustainable architectural morphologies using an automatic process of programmable self-organization.

6. ACKNOWLEDGMENTS

Daniel Richards is supported by a Ph.D. studentship from the Manchester Institute for Research and Innovation in Art and Design (MIRIAD).

7. REFERENCES

[1] Hensel, M. Menges, A. Weinstock, M. 2010. *Emergent Technologies and Design: Towards a Biological Paradigm for Architecture*, Routledge: Oxon.

[2] Oxman, N. 2010. *Material-based Design Computation*. Doctoral Thesis, MIT.

[3] Menges, A. Ahlquist, S. 2011. *Computational Design Thinking*. Sussex: Wiley.

[4] Oxman, R.: 2010. New Structuralism: Design, Engineering and Architectural Technologies. *Architectural Design*, 80(4), 14-23.

[5] Fleischmann, M. Lienhard, J. Menges, A. 2011. Computational Design Synthesis: Embedding Material Behaviour in Generative Computational Processes. In *Proceedings for eCAADe 2011*, (Ljubljana, Slovenia, September 21-24). 759-767.

[6] Hornby, G. 2004. Functional Scalability through Generative Representations: The Evolution of Table Designs. *Environment and Planning B*, vol 3. 569-587.

[7] Bentley, P. J. 2007. Climbing through Complexity Ceilings. In Burke, A. Tierney, T.(eds). *Network Practices: New Strategies in Architecture and Design*. New York: Princeton University Press. 178-197.

[8] Menges, A.: 2007. Computational Morphogenesis. In *Proceedings for ASCAAD 2007*, (Egypt, November 28-30). 725-744.

[9] Roudavski, S. 2009. Towards Morphogenesis in Architecture. *International Journal of Architectural Computing*, 7(3).345-374.

[10] Ulieru, M. Doursat, R. 2011. Emergent engineering: A radical paradigm shift. *International Journal of Autonomous and Adaptive Communications Systems,* 4(1). 39-60

[11] Kicinger, R. Arciszewski, T. and Jong, K. 2005. Evolutionary Computation and Structural Design: a Survey of the State of the Art, *Computers and Structures*, Vol 83. 1943-1978.

[12] Cladas, L. 2008. Generation of energy efficient architecture solutions applying GENE_ARCH: An evolution-based generative design system, *Advanced Engineering Informatics*, 22(1). 59-70

[13] Turrin, M. Buelow, P.V. Stouffs, R. and Kilian, A. 2010, Performance-Orientated Design of Large Passive Solar Roofs, In *Proceedings for eCAADe 2010*, Zurich, 321-330.

[14] Janssen, P. Frazer, J.H. Ming-Xi, T. 2002, Evolutionary Design Systems and Generative Design Processes, *Applied Intelligence*, 16(2). 119-128.

[15] O'Reilly, U. M. Hemberg, M. 2007. Integrating Generative Growth and Evolutionary Computation for Form Exploration. *Genetic Programming and Evolvable Machines*, 8(2). 163-186.

[16] Clune, J. Lipson, H. 2011. Evolving Three-Dimensional Objects with a Generative Encoding Inspired by Developmental Biology, In *Proceedings for ECAL 2011*, Paris, 141-148.

[17] Shea, K. Aish, R. Gourtovai, M. 2005. Towards Integrated Performance-Driven Generative Design Tools. *Automation in Construction*, vol 14. 253-264.

[18] Funes, P. and Pollack, J. 1998. Evolutionary Body Building: Adaptive Physical Designs for Robots, *Artificial Life*, Vol 4(4). 337-357.

[19] O.Stanley, K. Miikkulainen, R. 2003. A Taxonomy of Artificial Embryogeny, *Artificial Life*, Vol 9(2). 93-130.

[20] Bentley, P.J. And Kumar, S. 1999. Three Ways to Grow Designs: A Comparison of Embryogenies for an Evolutionary Design Problem, In *Proceedings for GECCO '99*, Florida. 35-43.

[21] Bentley, P. Kumar, S. (eds). 2003. *On Growth, Form and Computers*. London: Elsevier.

[22] von Mammel, S. Jacob, C. 2008. Evolutionary Swarm Design of Architectural Idea Models. *In Proceedings for GECCO '08*, (Atlanta, July 12-16). 143-150.

[23] O'Neill, M. McDermott, J. Swafford, J. M. Byrne, J. Hemberg, E. Brabazon, A. Shotton, E. McNally, C. Hemberg, M. 2010. Evolutionary Design using Grammatical Evolution and Shape Grammars: Designing a Shelter. *International Journal of Design Engineering*, 3(1). 4-24.

[24] Rieffel, J. Valero-Cuevas, F. Lipson, H. 2009. Automated Discovery and Optimisation of Large Irregular Tensegrity Structures, *Computers and Structures*, Vol 87. 368-379.

[25] Sims, K. 1994. Evolving 3D Morphology and Behavior by Competition, *Artificial Life*, Vol 1(4). 353-372.

[26] Lipson, H. and Pollack, J. 2000. Automatic Design and Manufacture of Robotic Lifeforms, *Nature*, Vol 406. 974-978.

[27] Eggenberger, P. 1997. Evolving Morphologies of Simulated 3D Organisms based on Differential Gene Expression, *CEC03*, Vol 1. 191-198.

[28] Bongard, J. and Pfeifer, R. 2003. Evolving Complete Agents using Artificial Ontogeny, In Hara, F. and Pfeifer, R (Ed), *Morpho-Functional Machines: The New Species (Designing Embodied Intelligence),* Springer Verlag: Berlin. 237-258.

[29] Miller, J. 2004. Evolving a Self-repairing, Self-regulating, French Flag Organism. In *Proceedings for GECCO '04*, (Washington, June 26-30). 129-139.

[30] Hiller, J.D. Lipson, H. 2010. Evolving Amorphous Robots. In *Proceedings for Alife XII*, (Odense, August 19-23). 717-724.

[31] Yogev, O. Shapiro, A. A. Antonsson, E. K. 2010. Computational Evolutionary Embryogeny. *IEEE Transactions on Evolutionary Computation*, 14(2). 301-325.

[32] Watson, J. D. Baker, T. A. Bell, S. P. Gann, A. Levine, M. Losick, R. 2007. *Molecular Biology of the Gene*. New York: Benjamin Cummings.

[33] Raff, M.C. 1992. Social controls on cell survival and cell death. *Nature*, Vol 356. 397-400.

Morphologies of Self-Organizing Swarms in 3D Swarm Chemistry

Hiroki Sayama
Collective Dynamics of Complex Systems Research Group
Binghamton University, State University of New York
P.O. Box 6000, Binghamton, NY 13902-6000, USA
sayama@binghamton.edu

ABSTRACT

A three-dimensional version of the Swarm Chemistry model is presented. Self-organization and morphogenesis of heterogeneous swarms in the 3D model were compared to those in the original 2D version. It was observed that the resulting patterns generally had remarkable robustness against dimensionality change, while some swarms were susceptible to the change. Further experiments showed that it was often sufficient to make minimal parameter adjustments in order to recover the original topological and dynamical properties of those susceptible swarms in 3D, although the dependence on parameters varied case by case with no generic parameter mapping between 2D and 3D.

Categories and Subject Descriptors

I.2.11 [**Artificial Intelligence**]: Distributed Artificial Intelligence—*Multiagent systems*; I.6.6 [**Simulation and Modeling**]: Simulation Output Analysis; I.6.3 [**Simulation and Modeling**]: Applications

General Terms

Experimentation

Keywords

swarms, artificial life, artificial chemistry, swarm chemistry, morphology, spatial dimensions, 3D

1. INTRODUCTION

Self-organization, development and morphogenesis in biological systems are inherently spatial, where spatial dimensions play a crucial role in determining how those dynamical processes take place. In the literature of Morphogenetic Engineering [6], various kinds of computational models of self-organization and morphogenesis have been proposed, mostly using either 2D space [2, 11, 1, 8, 3] or 3D space [10, 22, 9]. However, few studies addressed the robustness and sensitivity of a particular morphogenetic system against changes in the dimensionality of space in which it operates.

This paper reports a comparative study on the effects of spatial dimensionality on self-organizing morphogenetic collective systems by using a newly developed three-dimensional version of Swarm Chemistry [14, 20]. Morphologies of self-organizing swarms in the 3D Swarm Chemistry model was compared to their original 2D counterparts to illustrate their robustness and sensitivity against the 2D-3D dimensional changes.

The rest of the paper is organized as follows. In the next section, the Swarm Chemistry model and its 3D implementation are described. In Section 3, two experiments and their results are discussed: one with the original parameter settings and the other with revised parameter settings. Then Section 4 concludes the paper with discussions of the implications, limitations and future directions.

GECCO'12, July 7–11, 2012, Philadelphia, Pennsylvania, USA.

2. MODEL

2.1 Original Model: Swarm Chemistry

Swarm Chemistry [14, 20] is an artificial chemistry [5] model that can demonstrate self-organization of dynamic patterns of kinetically interacting heterogeneous particles. A swarm population in Swarm Chemistry consists of a number of simple self-propelled particles moving in a continuous two-dimensional space. Each particle can perceive average positions and velocities of other particles within its local perception range, and change its velocity in discrete time steps according to the following kinetic rules (adopted and modified from the rules in Reynolds' Boids [13]; see Fig. 1):

- If there are no other particles within its local perception range, steer randomly (*Straying*).
- Otherwise:
  - Steer to move toward the average position of nearby particles (*Cohesion*, Fig. 1(a)).
  - Steer toward the average velocity of nearby particles (*Alignment*, Fig. 1(b)).
  - Steer to avoid collision with nearby particles (*Separation*, Fig. 1(c)).
  - Steer randomly with a given probability (*Randomness*).
- Approximate its speed to its own normal speed (*Self-propulsion*).

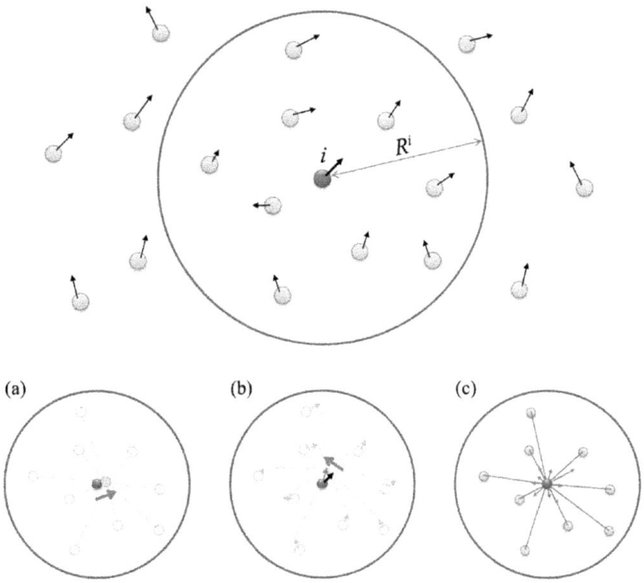

Figure 1: Kinetic interactions between particles (from [20]). Top: Particle i senses only positions and velocities of nearby particles within distance R^i. Bottom: (a) Cohesion. Particle i accelerates toward the center of mass of nearby particles. (b) Alignment. Particle i steers to align its orientation to the average orientation of nearby particles. (c) Separation. Particle i receives repulsion forces from each of the nearby particles whose strength is inversely related to distance.

These rules are implemented in the algorithm given in Fig. 2. Kinetic parameters used in this algorithm are listed and explained in Table 1.

Each particle is assigned with its own kinetic parameter settings that specify preferred speed, local perception range, and strength of each kinetic rule. Particles that share the same set of kinetic parameter settings are considered of the same type. Particles do not have a capability to distinguish one type from another; all particles look exactly the same to each other.

For a given swarm, specifications for its macroscopic properties are indirectly and implicitly woven into a list of different kinetic parameter settings for each swarm component, called a *recipe*, (Fig. 3) [14], which would be hard to obtain through conventional design methods but can be obtained heuristically through interactive evolutionary methods [14, 15, 4].

Computational exploration using evolutionary methods demonstrated that mixtures of multiple kinetically distinct types of particles usually undergo spontaneous mutual segregation, often leading to the formation of multilayer structures, and they may additionally show more dynamic macroscopic patterns, including linear motion, rotation, oscillation, chaotic motion, and even complex mechanical or biological-looking structures and behaviors [14, 20].

The Swarm Chemistry model has recently been extended to realize several different phenomena, such as morphogenesis and self-repair [20, 16] and spontaneous evolution [17, 18, 19]. In this paper, only its most basic version [14] is considered.

```
97 * (226.76, 3.11, 9.61, 0.15, 0.88, 43.35, 0.44, 1.0)
38 * (57.47, 9.99, 35.18, 0.15, 0.37, 30.96, 0.05, 0.31)
56 * (15.25, 13.58, 3.82, 0.3, 0.8, 39.51, 0.43, 0.65)
31 * (113.21, 18.25, 38.21, 0.62, 0.46, 15.78, 0.49, 0.61)
```

Figure 3: Example of a recipe, formatted as a list of kinetic parameter sets of different types within a swarm (from [20, 16]). Each row represents one type, which has a number of particles of that type at the beginning, followed by its parameter settings in the format of $(R^i, V^i_n, V^i_m, c^i_1, c^i_2, c^i_3, c^i_4, c^i_5)$.

2.2 Making It 3D

Translation of the original 2D Swarm Chemistry model into a 3D version was a straightforward task. As seen in Fig. 2 and Table 1, nothing in the model parameters or the simulation algorithm assumed a particular spatial dimensionality. The revision of the simulator software was therefore largely just to include the third dimension in position and velocity variables. The codes were written in Java 1.6, based on the original Swarm Chemistry simulator source codes available from the project website [21].

Visualization of swarms required some major modifications, however. For this study, 3D visualization was implemented using primitive Java graphics drawing functions only, without any advanced 3D graphics rendering API such as Java3D or OpenGL. This choice was made primarily in the interest of visualization speed. The 3D Swarm Chemistry simulator internally maintains three separate lists for the same set of particles, each sorted by their x-, y- or z-coordinate, which are utilized in its neighbor detection algorithm. Therefore, the 3D visualization was easily achieved by simply drawing particles in the order given in the z-coordinate list (with appropriately rescaled particle size and a little highlight added to each particle) without additional computation for overlap detection. More advanced, aesthetic 3D graphics rendering is beyond the scope of this paper at this point.

3. EXPERIMENTS

3.1 Experiment I: Comparison between 2D and 3D

In the first set of computational experiments, the dynamics of swarms were simulated in 3D space using the recipes originally designed for the 2D model, then it was observed how similar the resulting patterns were to their original 2D morphologies. The recipes published on the project website [21] were used for this purpose. The spatial dimensionality (2D or 3D) was the only experimental variable, while all other model parameters were kept constant. Similarities of 2D and 3D patterns were assessed primarily through visual inspection by a human observer, taking into account both topological structures and dynamical behaviors.

Figures 4, 5 and 6 show the results of simulations. Out of seventeen recipes tested, ten successfully produced in 3D space, without any parameter adjustments, the topological structures and dynamical behaviors that were very similar to those in 2D (Fig. 4). Their actual dynamic movements can be simulated online on the project website [21]. The

for all $i \in$ particles **do**
  $N \leftarrow \{j \neq i$ that satisfies $|\vec{x}_j - \vec{x}_i| < R^i\}$ // Finding other particles within its local perception range
  if $|N| = 0$ **then**
    $\vec{a} \leftarrow (r_{\pm.5}, r_{\pm.5})$ // Straying
  else
    $\langle\vec{x}\rangle \leftarrow \sum_{j \in N} \vec{x}_j/|N|$ // Calculating the average position of nearby particles
    $\langle\vec{v}\rangle \leftarrow \sum_{j \in N} \vec{v}_j/|N|$ // Calculating the average velocity of nearby particles
    $\vec{a} \leftarrow c_1^i(\langle\vec{x}\rangle - \vec{x}_i) + c_2^i(\langle\vec{v}\rangle - \vec{v}_i) + c_3^i \sum_{j \in N}(\vec{x}_i - \vec{x}_j)/|\vec{x}_i - \vec{x}_j|^2$ // Cohesion, alignment and separation
    if $r < c_4^i$ **then**
      $\vec{a} \leftarrow \vec{a} + (r_{\pm 5}, r_{\pm 5})$ // Randomness
    end if
  end if
  $\vec{v}_i' \leftarrow \vec{v}_i + \vec{a}$ // Acceleration
  $\vec{v}_i' \leftarrow \min(V_m^i/|\vec{v}_i'|, 1) \cdot \vec{v}_i'$ // Prohibiting overspeed
  $\vec{v}_i' \leftarrow c_5^i(V_n^i/|\vec{v}_i'| \cdot \vec{v}_i') + (1 - c_5^i)\vec{v}_i'$ // Self-propulsion
end for
for all $i \in$ particles **do**
  $\vec{v}_i \leftarrow \vec{v}_i'$ // Updating velocity
  $\vec{x}_i \leftarrow \vec{x}_i + \vec{v}_i$ // Updating location
end for

Figure 2: The algorithm used to simulate the behavior of particles (from [20]). $\vec{x}_i$, $\vec{v}_i$ and $\vec{v}_i'$ are the location, the current velocity, and the next velocity of the i-th particle, respectively. $\vec{a}$ is a local variable temporarily used to represent an acceleration. r and $r_{\pm p}$ represent random numbers taken from $[0, 1]$ and $[-p, +p]$, respectively.

Table 1: Kinetic parameters involved in the simulation of particle behavior (from [14]). Unique values are assigned to these parameters for each particle i as its own kinetic properties.

Name	Min	Max	Meaning	Unit
R^i	0	300	Radius of local perception range	pixel
V_n^i	0	20	Normal speed	pixel step^{-1}
V_m^i	0	40	Maximum speed	pixel step^{-1}
c_1^i	0	1	Strength of cohesive force	step^{-2}
c_2^i	0	1	Strength of aligning force	step^{-1}
c_3^i	0	100	Strength of separating force	$\text{pixel}^2\ \text{step}^{-2}$
c_4^i	0	0.5	Probability of random steering	—
c_5^i	0	1	Tendency of self-propulsion	—

observed robustness of swarm morphology may result from the simplicity of particle interaction rules adopted in the Swarm Chemistry model.

In the meantime, the other seven recipes resulted in either too dispersed (Fig. 5) or too aggregated (Fig. 6) morphologies in 3D, compared to their original ones in 2D. Statistical comparison of kinetic parameter values in the recipes between Figs. 4, 5 and 6 did not detect any statistically significant difference between those categories (Table 2), although there was a slight indication that the swarms that dispersed in 3D might have more particles per type than others (Table 2: column n) and that the swarms that were successful in maintaining their original properties in 3D might have longer perception ranges than others (Table 2: column R).

3.2 Experiment II: Adjusting Experimental Parameters

The second set of experiments was to search for minor parameter adjustments that could make the susceptible swarms shown in Figs. 5 and 6 recover their original topological and dynamical properties in 3D space. Because many parameters were involved in each swarm (as shown in Fig. 3), the search space would be large if exhaustive exploration were attempted. To simplify the exploration effort, only a few selected parameters were systematically varied. The parameters to be varied were chosen based on the following analytical consideration.

First, one of the major differences between 2D and 3D from an individual particle's perspective is in the number of nearest neighbors. In 2D space, particles tend to self-organize into hexagonal lattices, making the number of nearest neighbors six. In 3D space, on the other hand, particles naturally form hexagonal close-packed structures, in which the number of nearest neighbors to each particle is twelve. While this change does not affect cohesion or alignment force, it does affect separation force (see Fig. 2, line 8 for mathematical details). This implies the possibility that the separation force might be much stronger in 3D than in 2D. To correct this potential problem, reducing the coefficient of separation force c_3 into half of its original value was adopted as one of the experimental conditions tested.

Second, it was recognized through numerical analysis that the average distance between nearby particles in their initial random distribution was about 1.5 to 3 times longer in 3D than in 2D, because of the existence of one more dimension. This would make aggregation of particles relatively more difficult in 3D. To correct this problem, two more experimental conditions were tested: doubling the perception range R, and shortening the length of an edge of a cube that represents the particles' initial random distribution range, named L, into half of its original value.

Moreover, combinations of the above three parameter adjustments were also tested, making the total number of experimental conditions seven. In each condition, one of the swarms shown in Figs. 5 and 6 was simulated five times to assess the reproducibility of resulting patterns.

The results are summarized in Table 3. Successful parameter adjustments were found for four ("Blobs", "Pulsating Eye", "Multicellularity" and "No, Wait – This Way") out of the seven recipes experimented. It was clearly observed that the sensitivity to parameter adjustments varied significantly across different recipes, indicating that there would be no generic parameter mapping between 2D and 3D. Finally, each of the remaining three recipes ("Recombining Blobs", "Wedding Ring" and "Chaos Cells") was further examined individually by trial-and-error manual parameter editing. As a result, successful parameter adjustments were discovered for the latter two. The morphologies of those six revised swarms after respective parameter adjustments are shown in Fig. 7. Those parameter adjustments were all minor, only involving changes in just a few parameters.

For the last unsuccessful recipe ("Recombining Blobs"), no parameter adjustment has been discovered yet to reproduce its 2D morphology in 3D. A unique property of this particular recipe is that the resulting patterns it creates in 2D space shows a very fluctuating, dynamic behavior, including irregular fusion and fission of wandering blobs, which was somewhat similar to spatio-temporal chaos found in other complex systems models (e.g., [12]). It may be the case that such fluctuating designs depend significantly on a fine balance between multiple parameters and hence are most susceptible to any major changes, including those in spatial dimensionality.

4. CONCLUSIONS

In this paper, the effects of spatial dimensionality difference upon morphologies of self-organizing swarms were investigated through numerical simulations of the newly developed 3D Swarm Chemistry model. A majority of the recipes tested successfully produced morphologies in 3D that were similar to their original ones in 2D, even without any parameter adjustments, which demonstrated their remarkable robustness against the dimensional change from 2D to 3D. While other recipes had difficulty in maintaining the morphologies in 3D, parameter adjustments for their recovery were found for most cases. All the adjustments involved changes in values of no more than two parameters, i.e., the adjusted parameter settings were fairly close to their original ones in a high dimensional parameter space.

In the meantime, the directions of those parameter adjustments for susceptible swarms varied from recipe to recipe. No generic parameter mapping from 2D to 3D that could conserve topological and dynamical properties of the resulting patterns was identified (yet). One potential explanation of this observation is the high nonlinearity in the genotype-phenotype mapping in Swarm Chemistry. The relationships among kinetic parameters are not uniform and may change in different ways when the spatial dimensionality is changed. If a genotype (recipe) relies on some subtle balance among its parameters, its phenotype (self-organizing pattern) is likely to be affected by the spatial dimensionality change, and how to correct it would depend on many non-trivial factors.

This study still has limitations. One apparent problem is how to evaluate the topological/dynamical similarity of morphologies between 2D and 3D in a more rigorous, objective way. In this paper, simple visual inspection was used, though a more mathematical, quantitative measurement would be desirable. The application of persistent homology analysis [7, 23] is currently being considered for this purpose. Another direction of future work is to conduct mathematical analysis of the relationships between the three primary kinetic parameters (c_1, c_2 and c_3) in both 2D and 3D settings using a simplified mathematical model in order to find theoretical connections between morphologies in those two different spatial dimensions. Such analytical work

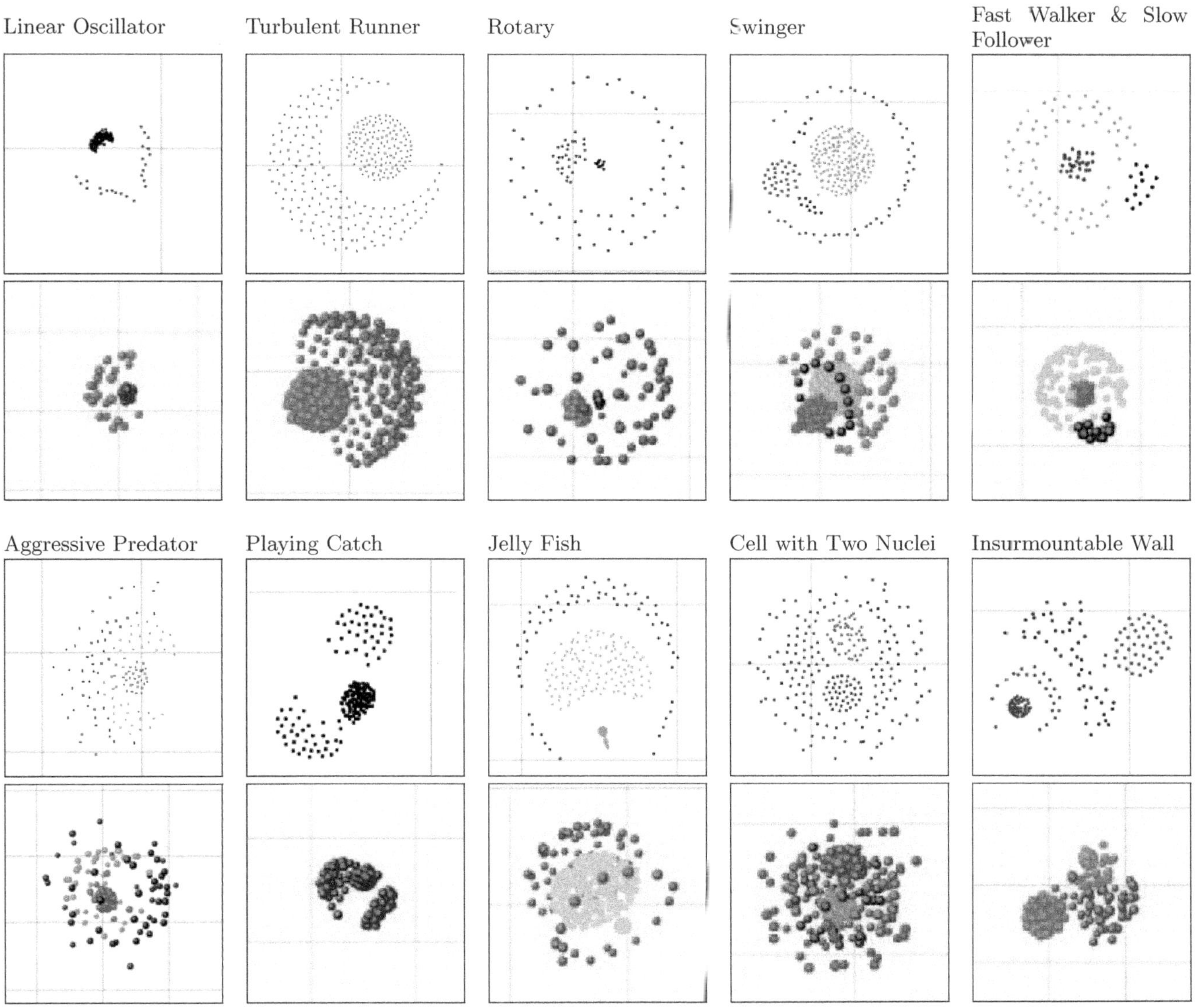

Figure 4: Morphologies created from recipes that can maintain similar topological and dynamical properties in both 2D (top) and 3D (bottom). Gray grid lines are references drawn at regular intervals to show the relative scale of the swarms. All the recipes used in this paper were designed using the 2D version of the Swarm Chemistry software. The recipes can be found on the Swarm Chemistry website [21].

Parameter	n	R	V_n	V_m	c_1	c_2	c_3	c_4	c_5
Overall mean	63.85	179.03	10.03	21.65	0.58	0.42	40.06	0.2	0.51
Fig. 4 mean	55.47	199.61	10.35	22.79	0.56	0.39	37.87	0.21	0.52
Fig. 5 mean	95.45	143.42	10.19	15.55	0.72	0.55	47.25	0.16	0.59
Fig. 6 mean	56.89	144.79	8.63	24.81	0.5	0.39	39.58	0.2	0.38
ANOVA p-value	*0.082*†	*0.073*†	0.726	0.141	0.181	0.325	0.692	0.63	0.313

Table 2: Statistical comparison of average parameter values in the recipes between Figs. 4, 5 and 6. n **is the number of particles of the same type in a recipe. † indicates weakly significant difference (**$p < 0.1$**).**

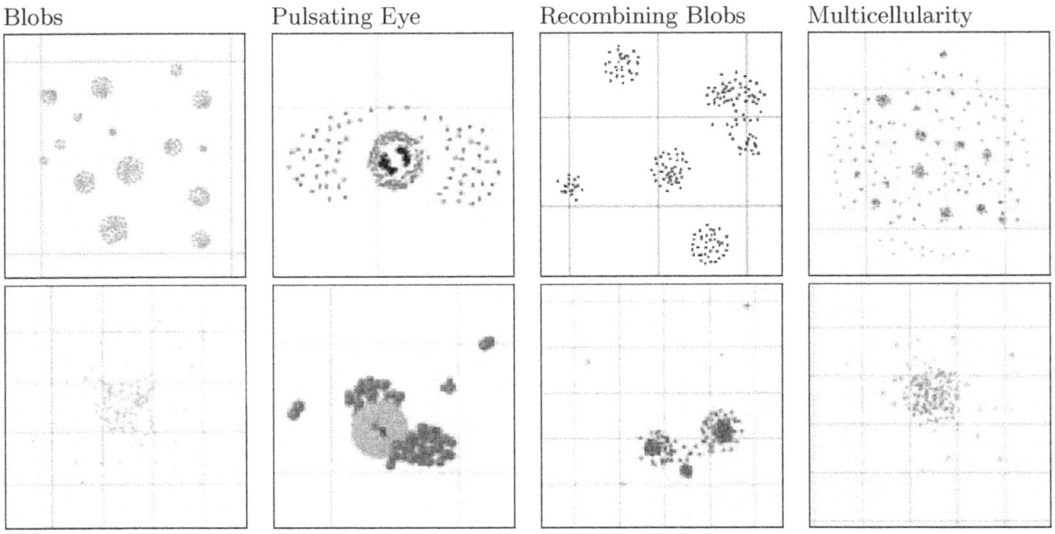

Figure 5: Morphologies created from recipes that produce more dispersed structures in 3D (bottom) than their original ones in 2D (top).

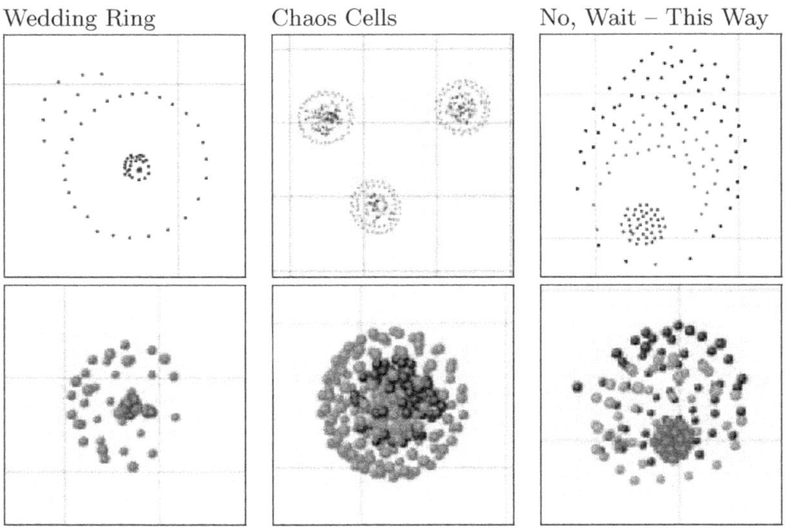

Figure 6: Morphologies created from recipes that produce more aggregated, static structures in 3D (bottom) than their original ones in 2D (top).

Parameter Setting			Recipe						
c_3 halved	R doubled	L halved	Blobs	Pulsating Eye	Recombining Blobs	Multi-cellularity	Wedding Ring	Chaos Cells	No, Wait – This Way
✓			·	·	·	·	·	·	◯
	✓		○	◯	·	○	·	·	◯
		✓	○	◯	○	○	·	·	·
✓	✓		○	◯	·	·	·	·	·
✓		✓	◯	◯	·	○	·	·	◯
	✓	✓	·	◯	·	◯	·	·	◯
✓	✓	✓	·	◯	·	◯	·	·	·

Table 3: Results of parameter adjustment experiments. Each recipe was simulated five times under each parameter setting. Markers indicate that topological/dynamical properties similar to the original ones in 2D were recovered in 3D four times or more (◯), one to three times (○), or never (·).

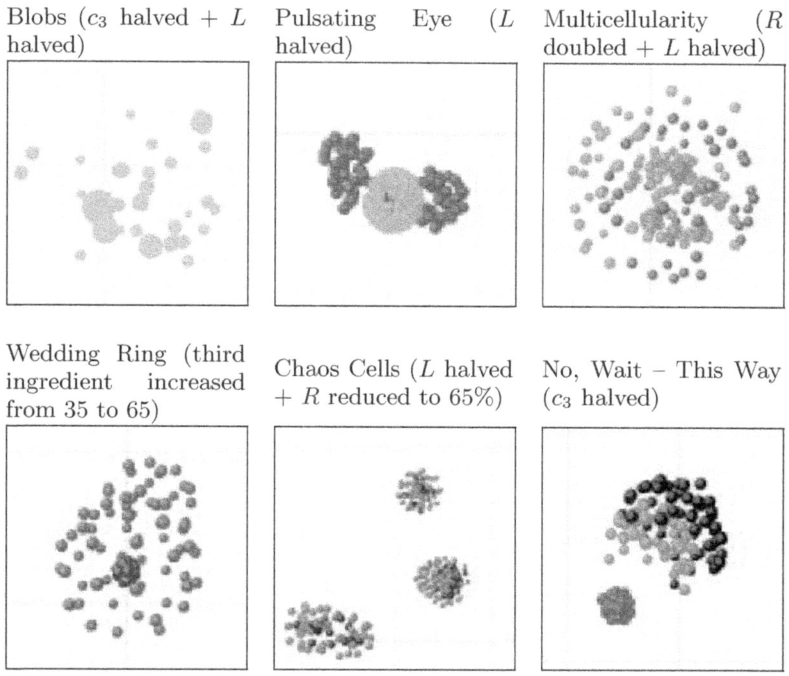

Figure 7: Morphologies created after successful parameter adjustments.

may also elucidate the possibility of unique morphologies that could arise only in 3D but not in 2D (and vice versa).

5. REFERENCES

[1] Arbuckle, D. J. and Requicha, A. A. G. 2010. Self-assembly and self-repair of arbitrary shapes by a swarm of reactive robots: algorithms and simulations. *Autonomous Robots* **28**, 197-211.

[2] Bai, L., Eyiyurekli, M., and Breen, D. E. 2008. Automated shape composition based on cell biology and distributed genetic programming. In *GECCO '08 Proceedings of the 10th Annual Conference on Genetic and Evolutionary Computation.* ACM.

[3] Bhalla, N., Bentley, P. J., and Jacob, C. 2010. Evolving physical self-assembling systems in two-dimensions. In *Evolvable Systems: From Biology to Hardware*, pp.381-392. Lecture Notes in Computer Science 6274, Springer.

[4] Bush, B. J. and Sayama, H. 2011. Hyperinteractive evolutionary computation. *IEEE Transactions on Evolutionary Computation* **15**, 424-433.

[5] Dittrich, P., Ziegler, J., and Banzhaf, W. 2001. Artificial chemistries - A review. *Artificial Life* **7**, 225-275.

[6] Doursat, R., Sayama H., and Michel, O., eds. *Morphogenetic Engineering: Toward Programmable Complex Systems.* Springer/NECSI Studies on Complexity Series, Springer. In press.

[7] Edelsbrunner, H., Letscher, D., and Zomoridan, A. 2002. Topological persistence and simplification. *Discrete & Computational Geometry* **28**, 511-533.

[8] Liu, W. and Winfield, A. F. T. 2010. Autonomous morphogenesis in self-assembling robots using IR-based sensing and local communications. In *Swarm Intelligece*, pp.107-118. Lecture Notes in Computer Science 6234, Springer.

[9] Meng, Y., Zhang, Y., and Jin, Y. 2011. Autonomous self-reconfiguration of modular robots by evolving a hierarchical mechanochemical model. *IEEE Computational Intelligence Magazine* **6(1)**, 43-54.

[10] Murata, S., Yoshida, E., Kamimura, A., Kurokawa, H., Tomita, K., and Kokaji, S. 2002. M-TRAN: Self-reconfigurable modular robotic system. *IEEE/ASME Transactions on Mechatronics* **7**, 431-441.

[11] O'Grady, R., Christensen, A. L., and Dorigo, M. 2009. SWARMORPH: Multirobot morphogenesis using directional self-assembly. *IEEE Transactions on Robotics* **25**, 738-743.

[12] Pearson, J. E. 1993. Complex patterns in a simple system. *Science* **9**, 189-192.

[13] Reynolds, C. W. 1987. Flocks, herds, and schools: A distributed behavioral model. *Computer Graphics* **21(4)**, 25-34.

[14] Sayama, H. 2009. Swarm chemistry. *Artificial Life* **15**, 105-114.

[15] Sayama, H., Dionne, S., Laramee, C., and Wilson, D. S. 2009. Enhancing the architecture of interactive evolutionary design for exploring heterogeneous particle swarm dynamics: An in-class experiment. In *Proceedings of the Second IEEE Symposium on Artificial Life*, pp.85-91. IEEE.

[16] Sayama, H. 2010. Robust morphogenesis of robotic swarms. *IEEE Computational Intelligence Magazine* **5(3)**, 43-49.

[17] Sayama, H. 2010. Swarm Chemistry evolving. In *Artificial Life XII: Proceedings of the Twelfth International Conference on the Synthesis and Simulation of Living Systems*, pp.32-33. MIT Press.

[18] Sayama, H. 2011. Seeking open-ended evolution in Swarm Chemistry. In *Proceedings of the Third IEEE Symposium on Artificial Life*, pp.186-193. IEEE.

[19] Sayama, H. and Wong, C. 2011. Quantifying evolutionary dynamics of Swarm Chemistry. In *Advances in Artificial Life, ECAL 2011: Proceedings of the Eleventh European Conference on Artificial Life*, pp.729-730. MIT Press.

[20] Sayama, H. Swarm-based morphogenetic artificial life. In *Morphogenetic Engineering: Toward Programmable Complex Systems*. Springer/NECSI Studies on Complexity Series, Springer. In press.

[21] Sayama, H. *Swarm Chemistry website.* http://bingweb.binghamton.edu/~sayama/Swarm-Chemistry/. Accessed on January 27th, 2012.

[22] Werfel, J. and Nagpal, R. 2008. Three-dimensional construction with mobile robots and modular blocks. *International Journal of Robotics Research* **27**, 463-479.

[23] Zomorodian, A. and Carlsson, G. 2005. Computing persistent homology. *Discrete & Computational Geometry* **33**, 249-274.

Linkage Neighbors, Optimal Mixing and Forced Improvements in Genetic Algorithms

Peter A.N. Bosman
Centrum Wiskunde & Informatica (CWI)
P.O. Box 94079
1090 GB Amsterdam
The Netherlands
Peter.Bosman@cwi.nl

Dirk Thierens
Department of Computer Science
Utrecht University
3508 TB Utrecht
The Netherlands
D.Thierens@uu.nl

ABSTRACT

Recently, the Linkage Tree Genetic Algorithm (LTGA) was introduced as one of the latest developments in a line of EA research that studies building models to capture and exploit linkage information between problem variables. LTGA was reported to exhibit excellent performance on several linkage benchmark problems, mainly attributed to use of the LT linkage model. In this paper we consider a technique called Forced Improvements (FI), that allows LTGA to converge to a single solution without requiring an explicit, diversity-reducing, selection step. We further consider a different linkage model, called Linkage Neighbors (LN), that is more flexible, yet can be learned equally efficiently from data. Even with the simplest learning approach for configuring the LN, better results are obtained on the linkage benchmark problems than when the LT model is used. However, on weighted MAXCUT (a combinatorial optimization problem), very poor results are obtained and a more involved multiscale LN variant is required to obtain a performance near that of LTGA. Our results underline the advantage of processing linkage in a single model on multiple scales as well as the importance of also considering problems other problems than common linkage benchmark problems when judging the merits of linkage learning techniques.

Categories and Subject Descriptors

G.1 [**Numerical Analysis**]: Optimization; I.2 [**Artificial Intelligence**]: Problem Solving, Control Methods, and Search

General Terms

Algorithms, Performance, Experimentation

Keywords

Genetic Algorithms, Estimation-of-Distribution Algorithms, Linkage learning, Optimal Mixing

GECCO'12, July 7–11, 2012, Philadelphia, Pennsylvania, USA.

1. INTRODUCTION

Linkage learning is a key research topic in evolutionary computation, the goal of which is to identify, during optimization, key linkage relations between variables, meaning that these variables should be considered jointly when generating new solutions because it leads to more efficient optimization [14]. Good, linkage-friendly variation operators can be engineered for specific problems. The complexity of real-world problems however typically requires taking a perspective of black-box optimization (BBO), i.e. making no assumptions on the optimization problem. Because engineering good variation operators beforehand is then not possible, linkage learning becomes of great importance.

A very recent EA that learns and exploits linkage is the Linkage Tree Genetic Algorithm (LTGA) [12, 13, 6]. LTGA exhibits excellent performance on several benchmark problems, outperforming a variety of well-known EAs from the literature. The LT linkage model has great value as it can be learned from data efficiently via hierarchical clustering and can represent variable linkages at different levels, from the smallest sets (i.e. singletons) of linked variables to the set of all variables. It however also has drawbacks. A LT is always fully built every generation and fully traversed in the generation of every new solution. Moreover, a LT model has limited ability to represent overlapping building blocks. We will therefore consider a different type of linkage model that is more flexible: the Linkage Neighbors (LN). The LN can naturally represent overlapping building blocks and can be learned from data at least as efficiently as a LT, i.e. in $\mathcal{O}(nl^2)$ time where l is the number of problem variables and n the population size. Furthermore, learning a LN can be parallelized in a straightforward manner.

2. PROBLEMS AND EXPERIMENTS

Because we illustrate our findings throughout the paper, we first present the optimization problems that we consider and the manner in which we perform experiments.

2.1 Optimization problems

We consider three common linkage benchmark problems and one well-known NP-hard problem, all of which need to be maximized. First is the well-known onemax problem:

$$f_{\text{Onemax}}(\boldsymbol{x}) = \sum_{i=0}^{l-1} x_i$$

The second function is the mutually exclusive, additively decomposable composition of the well-known order-k deceptive trap functions [3]. We consider subfunctions with $k = 5$:

$$f_{\text{Trap5}}(\boldsymbol{x}) = \sum_{i=0}^{(l/k)-1} f^{\text{sub}}_{\text{Trap-k}}\left(\sum_{j=ki}^{ki+k-1} x_j\right)$$

where

$$f^{\text{sub}}_{\text{Trap-k}}(u) = \begin{cases} 1 & \text{if } u = k \\ \frac{k-1-u}{k} & \textit{otherwise} \end{cases}$$

It is commonly known that the EA needs to detect and process the linkage groups pertaining to the deceptive subfunctions in order for optimization to proceed efficiently [14].

The third function is the nearest-neighbour overlapping, additively decomposable composition of predetermined, but completely random subfunctions of length k, which is essentially a NK-landscape [7]. We consider subfunctions of length 5 and the maximum overlap of 4 (corresponding to a shift of 1 where the next subfunction starts), but without wraparound:

$$f_{\text{NK-S1}}(\boldsymbol{x}) = \sum_{i=0}^{l-k} f^{\text{sub}}_{\text{NK}}\left(\boldsymbol{x}_{(i,i+1,\ldots,i+k-1)}\right)$$

where $f^{\text{sub}}_{\text{NK}}\left(\boldsymbol{x}_{(i,i+1,\ldots,i+k-1)}\right)$ is a pre-determined, but randomly chosen value in $[0;1]$.

The combinatorial optimization problem we consider is weighted MAXCUT that is defined given an weighted undirected graph with a set of l vertices $V = \{v_0, v_1, \ldots, v_{l-1}\}$, a set of edges E between the vertices, and a weight w_{ij} for each edge $(v_i, v_j) \in E$. The goal in weighted MAXCUT is to split V into two sets such that the combined weight of all edges that are thereby cut, i.e. running between vertices in different sets, is maximized. By introducing a single binary variable x_i for every vertex that indicates if vertex v_i is either in set 0 or set 1, the function to be optimized is therefore:

$$f_{\text{weighted MAXCUT}}(\boldsymbol{x}) = \sum_{(v_i,v_j)\in E} \begin{cases} w_{ij} & \text{if } x_i \neq x_j \\ 0 & \textit{otherwise} \end{cases}$$

We encode this problem in a straightforward manner, i.e. using the binary problem variables x_i directly in the representation that the EA optimizes over. Benchmark sets of various types and sizes of problem instances exist in literature, but because we want to be able to perform a controlled scalability analysis, we generated our own instances. For problem sizes $l \in \{6, 12, 25, 50, 100\}$ we generated fully connected graphs, i.e. graphs having precisely $\frac{1}{2}l(l-1)$ edges. To set the weights, we follow the approach by Rubinstein [10] to obtain interesting instances and choose them randomly following a β distribution with parameters $\alpha = 100$, $\beta = 1$ and scaled to the range of $[1;5]$. For each problem size, we generate 10 instances. The maximum problem size was chosen such that the exact optimizer BIQMAC [9] could provide optimal solutions within reasonable time.

2.2 Experimental setup

For every problem and every population size that we consider, we perform 100 independent runs of an EA. We say that an EA solved the problem if at least 99 of these runs converged to either the global optimum or a predefined sufficiently close approximation. Moreover, instead of stopping when the optimum is reached, we run EAs until convergence (all solutions are the same) because we feel this is more realistic in practice where the optimum is not known beforehand and one typically collects outcomes upon termination.

For NK-S1, we have generated 100 instances per problem size randomly. The 100 independent runs are performed on 100 different, but always the same 100, instances per dimensionality. For weighted MAXCUT however, every problem instance is considered separately as is more typical of combinatorial optimization literature. The reason for this is that specific instances may be easy or hard and their properties may be interesting to study separately. Therefore, for weighted MAXCUT 100 independent runs are performed per problem instance per dimensionality. Note that this alters the interpretation of the min-max error bars that we will show where we aggregate per problem size. For weighted MAXCUT these min-max error bars will be much larger.

A key performance indicator for the performance of EAs on a certain type of problem is scalability, i.e. how do the required resources (population size and number of required evaluations) increase as the problem gets bigger. To study this, we determine, for various problem sizes, the minimally required population size to solve the problem. To do so, we perform a bisection search in which, starting from population size 1, the population size is doubled until the problem is solved and subsequently a binary search is performed in the range between the last two tested population sizes. Because this process is still subject to noise rooted in the stochastic nature of EAs, we perform 10 independent bisection searches for every problem size (and in case of weighted MAXCUT, for every problem instance).

3. LINKAGE MODELING AND MIXING

Having a tunable linkage model in an EA to match the structure of the optimization problem most often comes down to identifying groups of variables that together make an important contribution to a solution's quality. Here we first consider a general formulation of such models and then describe a canonical EA outline that uses such a model. The most recent version of LTGA follows the same outline [13].

3.1 The FOS model and the LT instance

As a general model we consider the *family of subsets* (FOS), denoted $\mathcal{F}$. A FOS contains subsets of a certain set S. Moreover, subsets may appear more than once (which is potentially the case for the linkage neighbors, see Section 4.1), making a FOS a multiset that consists of elements of $\mathcal{P}(S)$, i.e. the powerset of S. In our case, the main set S is the set of all problem variable indices, i.e. $\{0, 1, \ldots, l-1\}$. A FOS $\mathcal{F}$ can be written as $\mathcal{F} = \{\boldsymbol{F}^0, \boldsymbol{F}^1, \ldots, \boldsymbol{F}^{|\mathcal{F}|-1}\}$ where $\boldsymbol{F}^i \subseteq \{0, 1, \ldots, l-1\}$, $i \in \{0, 1, \ldots, |\mathcal{F}|-1\}$. For representing linkage to be used in a mixing operator, it is convenient to ensure a FOS is complete in the sense that every problem variable index is contained in *at least* one subset in $\mathcal{F}$, i.e. $\forall i \in \{0, 1, \ldots, l-1\} : \left(\exists j \in \{0, 1, \ldots, |\mathcal{F}|-1\} : i \in \boldsymbol{F}^j\right)$. In this manner, when performing variation following subsets in $\mathcal{F}$, no variable is left out of the process.

The linkage tree (LT) is a specific type of FOS. The LT is a hierarchical model that represents the outcome of a hierarchical clustering procedure started from all l singleton sets, with the exception that the top level, i.e. all variables in a single cluster, is excluded. For any subset $\boldsymbol{F}^i$ with more than one variable, there are subsets $\boldsymbol{F}^j$ and $\boldsymbol{F}^k$ such that

$F^j \cap F^k = \emptyset$, $|F^j| < |F^i|$, $|F^k| < |F^i|$ and $F^j \cup F^k = F^i$. Different from most linkage models in literature, variables can thus both be independent and dependent in the same model. A LT somewhat represents a path through dependency space, from the univariate, all-independent state to the full, all-jointly-dependent state. To learn a LT from data, a hierarchical clustering procedure can be used that iteratively merges the two sets that are the most similar. Both the combined subset as well as its constituent subsets are then in the LT FOS. For details, see [12, 13, 6]. Given a data set of size n, a straightforward implementation takes $\mathcal{O}(nl^3)$ time, asymptotically similar to the model-building complexity of most well-known EDAs that can effectively process higher-order linkage information. However, using a less straightfoward alternative approach the LT can also be built in $\mathcal{O}(nl^2)$ time [4].

3.2 Optimal Mixing

Instead of fully creating new solutions first and only then evaluating fitness, in Optimal Mixing (OM) [13] an existing parent solution is chosen and cloned first. Then, during variation, each time a partial solution is generated, such as is the result of crossing over a part from another parent as reminiscent of GAs or sampling values for a subset of variables as reminiscent of EDAs, this part is used in the full solution that was cloned. If this leads to the solution being improved, the improved solution is kept, otherwise the solution is left unchanged. Variation continues, each time testing whether newly generated partial solutions lead to improvements. Thus, during variation the quality of a solution monotonically improves. The reason for calling this operation optimal mixing is due to its inception in the original LTGA [12] where a two-parent crossover operator was used following the LT with intermediate evaluations to check for improvements. Given only two parents, with OM all building blocks as described in the FOS wind up in one of the two parents, so mixing can be said to be optimal. However, randomly selecting a new donor parent for each element in the FOS, which was called Genepool Optimal Mixing (GOM) was recently found to generally be a more efficient manner of OM because this removes the covariance inherent in using the same two parents for the entire operation [13].

The use of OM increases selection pressure in a building-block-wise manner instead of on an entire solution basis, the latter of which is a source of noise in deciding well between building blocks that increases the required population size. It is mostly because of OM that the LTGA requires only very small population sizes compared to most EDAs.

3.3 Forced Improvements

Using the ingredients of the above subsections, a canonical EA can be constructed. Recently, such a canonical EA was formulated and called Optimal Mixing Evolutionary Algorithm (OMEA) [13]. However, at the end of each generation, an additional tournament selection operation with tournament size 2 was performed on the offspring to ensure convergence by logistic growth of the optimal solutions over multiple generations. This further allowed for fair comparison with a GA and EDA approach with similar convergence properties. However, the additional selection step reduces the diversity faster than needed. We therefore propose to not use this additional selection step. However, we do perform tournament selection to select the solutions to use in

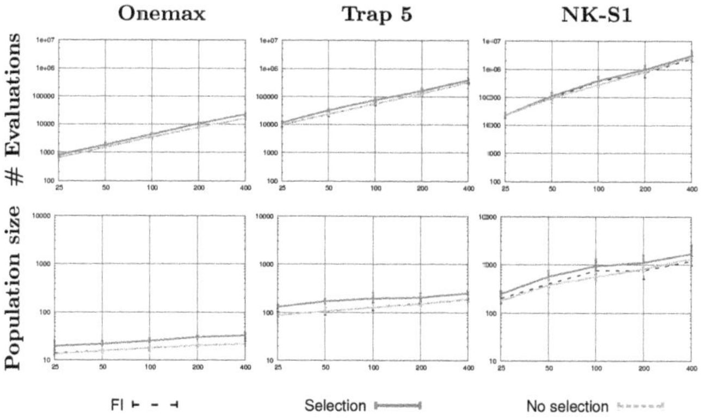

Figure 1: Scalability of LTGA variants.

learning the linkage model. This can be seen as a form of a reweighting scheme before learning, which is known to be beneficial [11]. Optimal mixing however then proceeds to work on the original population rather than on the selection. In Figure 1 an improved performance of LTGA can indeed be seen on the linkage benchmark problems.

Although the results on the linkage benchmark problems inspire confidence, it is important to realize that (real-world) problems may contain (many) local optima and/or symmetries. Solutions in the population may then become divided over multiple basins of attraction and progress may deteriorate in each of these basins because variation is attempted between solutions located in different basins. It is then further hard to detect when the EA should halt. On various instances of weighted MAXCUT we observed such undesirable behavior for LTGA without selection. One approach to deal with this is to introduce niching, which can be done in a variety of ways. Although potentially effective, it is however nontrivial to select the right number of niches or, alternatively, the niche radius. We therefore consider a different means of focusing selection on a single optimum to pursue. If a solution could not be improved by OM, an additional OM operation is performed on that solution but now with the currently known best solution as the donor. However, as soon as an improvement is detected, this forced-improvement (FI) OM operation is stopped. One advantage is that adding FI doesn't continuously increase the selection pressure and reduce population diversity further, but that this only happens if a solution couldn't be improved anymore anyway. Also, it puts a very specific additional pressure on the convergence phase, namely a directed convergence, through linkage space, toward the best solution found so far. With this approach we indeed observed efficient convergence on all our weighted MAXCUT instances. Moreover Figure 1 shows that the impact on LTGA's performance on the linkage benchmark problems is slim to none.

3.4 Genepool Optimal Mixing EA

Figure 2 provides an overview in pseudo-code of the Genepool Optimal Mixing Evolutionary Algorithm (GOMEA), now updated with FI. We shall use this general outline to study the Linkage Neighbors (LN) linkage model.

4. LINKAGE NEIGHBORS

Although LTGA exhibits excellent performance [6, 13], the LT model still has limitations. Most notably, although

```
GOMEA //population size n, problem size l
for i ∈ {0,1,...,n−1} do
  P_i ← CreateRandomSolution()
  EvaluateFitness(P_i)
while ¬TerminationCriterionSatisfied do
  x^best ← arg max_{x∈P}{fitness[x]}
  S ← TournamentSelection(P, n, 2)
  LearnModel(S)
  for i ∈ {0,1,...,n−1} do
    O_i ← FI-GOM(P_i)
  P ← O
```

```
FI-GOM(x)
b ← o ← x; fitness[b] ← fitness[o] ← fitness[x]; improved ← false
for i ∈ {0,1,...,|F|−1} do
  p ← Random({P_0, P_1, ..., P_{n−1}})
  o_{F^i} ← p_{F^i}
  if o_{F^i} ≠ b_{F^i} then
    EvaluateFitness(o)
    if fitness[o] > fitness[b] then
      b_{F^i} ← o_{F^i}; fitness[b] ← fitness[o]; improved ← true
    else
      o_{F^i} ← b_{F^i}; fitness[o] ← fitness[b]
if ¬improved then
  for i ∈ {0,1,...,|F|−1} do
    o_{F^i} ← x^best_{F^i}
    if o_{F^i} ≠ b_{F^i} then
      EvaluateFitness(o)
      if fitness[o] > fitness[b] then
        b_{F^i} ← o_{F^i}; fitness[b] ← fitness[o]; improved ← true
      else
        o_{F^i} ← b_{F^i}; fitness[o] ← fitness[b]
    if improved then breakfor
if ¬improved then
  o ← x^best; fitness[o] ← fitness[x^best]
```

Figure 2: Pseudo-code for GOMEA where FI-GOM is the genepool optimal mixing operator with forced improvement for a single solution.

it is capable of modeling overlapping linkage relations, these are always organized in a hierarchical fashion, where the lower-order constituents of a linkage set are mutually exclusive. For this reason we study a different linkage model.

4.1 Linkage Neighbors FOS

The concept of the Linkage Neighbors (LN) model is to focus on each problem variable separately and determine its (nearest) neighbors in terms of linkage. Thus, for each variable X_i there is a set in the FOS that contains X_i and its linkage neighbors. The potential to model overlapping building blocks with the LN is greater than with the LT. For instance, for two building blocks consisting of variable indices $[0, 1, 2]$ and $[1, 2, 3]$ respectively, the linkage tree can only represent this overlap by putting all variables together, i.e. $[0, 1, 2, 3]$ and at a lower level also include either $[0, 1, 2]$ and $[3]$ or $[0]$ and $[1, 2, 3]$. In any case, indices 2 and 3 can only appear in one of either sets. In the LN model however, overlap can be represented by $[0, 1, 2]$, $[1, 2, 0, 3]$, $[2, 1, 0, 3]$ and $[3, 2, 1]$ where in each set the second to last variable are linkage neighbors of the first variable.

In addition to the increased ability to represent overlap, there is also a conceptual motivation for the LN model. In optimization, each problem variable needs to be set in a certain manner. To set this value correctly, the values for its linkage neighbors need to be taken into account. Therefore, for each variable we need to know its linkage neighbors.

To prevent introducing a bias when considering the l LN sets, the place where variable i and its neighbors appear in the FOS should be randomized. In learning the LN FOS we therefore ensure this happens every generation.

4.2 Learning the LN FOS

In this subsection we discuss different ways to learn the LN model from data. For each of the proposed ways, each set of neighbors for each variable can be determined completely independently, which makes parallelization of building a LN model straightforward. In contrast, parallel model building (or linkage learning) is nontrivial for many existing models.

4.2.1 Independence threshold

The simplest idea to determine the linkage neighbors of X_i is to test, for each X_j, $j \neq i$, whether X_i and X_j are linked. To decide this from data, a common approach is to use statistical hypothesis testing. Here, we use the well-known likelihood-ratio test [2] which can be used to decide whether one probability distribution is a better fit than another probability distribution. The likelihood-ratio test is the most powerful test to decide this [2]. A better fit means a higher likelihood, or equivalently, a lower negative log-likelihood (NLL). Nested models are required for the likelihood-ratio test, meaning that one probability distribution can be obtained by imposing restrictions on the other probability distribution, which is exactly what we are dealing with here. In our case, the distributions to compare are $P(X_i, X_j)$, i.e. the joint distribution as the non-restricted version of $P(X_i)P(X_j)$, i.e. the factorized probability distribution. If the joint distribution is a better fit, then the variables can validly be said to be dependent.

The test statistic is $-2\log\{\mathcal{L}(P(X_i)P(X_j))/\mathcal{L}(P(X_i, X_j))\}$ where $\mathcal{L}$ is the well-known likelihood function for probability distributions over random variables $\boldsymbol{X}$ given n data points $\boldsymbol{x}_i$, $i \in \{0, 1, \ldots, n-1\}$, i.e. $\mathcal{L}(P(\boldsymbol{X})) = \prod_{i=0}^{n-1} P(\boldsymbol{X} = \boldsymbol{x}_i)$. As in any form of statistical hypothesis testing, the test statistic follows a certain distribution and in order to determine the outcome of the test, a range of values can be determined for the test statistic where the hypothesis is accepted or rejected. Moreover, the likelihood-ratio test statistic has a fixed number of degrees of freedom, namely the difference in the the number of parameters for the tests [15]. Given that we are only interested in testing for pairs of variables, this means that a single threshold value should suffice. However, this is not necessarily the case for linkage detection in an EA. The data from which the distributions are estimated, comes from a process in which variation and selection are used. If stochastic random variables are independent, collecting independently and identically drawn (iid) samples will work well with a single predefined threshold value for the test statistic exactly because the data are iid. But although in an optimization problem (i.e. in the fitness function) variables may actually have an independent contribution, like in the onemax function, the data that are used to estimate the distributions from are influenced by selection and variation. These operators can skew the observed distributions and introduce a form of noise for the distribution estimation process. Ultimately, this may cause variables that are independent in the fitness function to appear to be more dependent in the population than they actually are, see also [8]. In the case of the likelihood-ratio test this results in a higher value for the test statistic. This then means that a single,

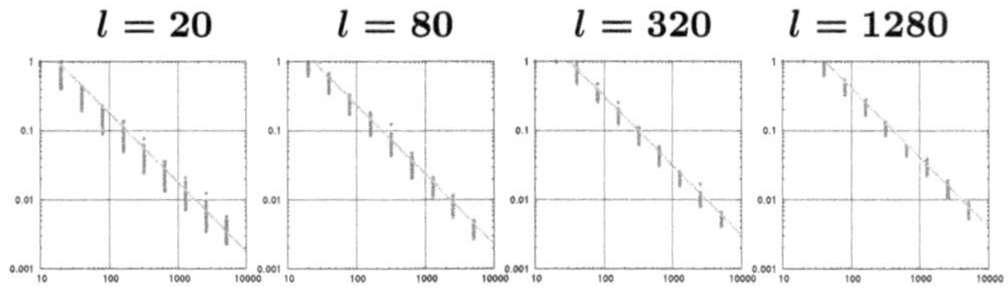

Figure 3: The independence threshold and the maximum MI values in 100 runs of univariate GOMEA on onemax as a function of population size.

predefined threshold doesn't suffice because the more variables a problem has, the larger the potential amount of noise. For this reason we will perform an experimental analysis on one of the simplest optimization functions with completely independent and equally scaled variables: onemax.

However, before considering such an analysis, we first point out the similarity with the very commonly used notions of entropy and more importantly, mutual information (MI) in linkage learning. To this end we first note that in obtaining maximum-likelihood estimates for probability distributions, often the NLL is minimized rather than that the likelihood is equivalently maximized. Because the NLL is often seen as an error function, we write it as $\mathcal{E}(P(\boldsymbol{X})) = -\log(\mathcal{L}(P(\boldsymbol{X})))$ and we rewrite the likelihood-ratio test statistic as $-2\log(\mathcal{L}(P(X_i)P(X_j))) + 2\log(\mathcal{L}(P(X_i, X_j))) = -2\mathcal{E}(P(X_i)P(X_j)) + 2\mathcal{E}(P(X_i, X_j))$. Moreover, it is not hard to see that $\mathcal{E}(P(X_i)P(X_j)) = \mathcal{E}(P(X_i)) + \mathcal{E}(P(X_j))$ and thus that we can further rewrite the test statistic as $2\mathcal{E}(P(X_i, X_j)) - 2\mathcal{E}(P(X_i)) - 2\mathcal{E}(P(X_j))$. It can be shown (see e.g. [1]) that, if maximum-likelihood estimates are used, the NLL of the estimated distribution equals n times entropy, i.e. $\mathcal{E}(P(\boldsymbol{X})) = nH(\boldsymbol{X})$. We thereby then obtain $2n(H(X_i) + H(X_j) - H(X_i, X_j))$, which is thus to say that the test statistic is just $2n$ times the value of the MI between random variables X_i and X_j, i.e. $2nMI(X_i, X_j)$. So instead of finding a threshold value for the likelihood-ratio test, we can equivalently find a threshold for MI, which is actually the same type of information with which the linkage tree in the LTGA can be built [12, 13, 6] and the marginal product model in advanced EDAs such as ECGA [5].

To determine what threshold to use with GOMEA, we ran GOMEA on onemax with a univariate FOS, i.e. $\mathcal{F} = \{\{0\}, \{1\}, \ldots, \{l-1\}\}$, which is the desired linkage model on this particular problem. Then, for different population sizes and dimensionalities $l \in \{10, 20, 40, 80, 160, 320, 640, 1280\}$ we performed 100 independent runs and measured for each run the highest observed MI between any two variables during the entire run. From this, a threshold of $\theta^{MI\text{-}indep} = 10l^{0.2}/n$ was determined. This threshold and the observed MI values are shown in Figure 3. When multiplied by n, this is a threshold for the likelihood-ratio test, which then indeed not varies with the population size, but does need to grow slightly with the dimensionality.

The use of the independence threshold $\theta^{MI\text{-}indep}$ provides a first, base $O(nl^2)$ learning algorithm for the LN model: for each variable X_i, determine its linkage neighbors as all X_j, $i \neq j$ for which $MI(X_i, X_j) \geq \theta^{MI\text{-}indep}$.

4.2.2 *Dependence-ratio threshold*

The use of $\theta^{MI\text{-}indep}$ alone may still lead to undesirable models. The main reason for this is that even if variables are only very weakly dependent, their MI will rise above $\theta^{MI\text{-}indep}$. It may consequently happen that the sets in the FOS grow very large if the order of dependencies in the problem isn't very clearly bounded. It might therefore be beneficial to consider a second threshold that only accepts dependencies that are of a certain minimal strength. Because the strength of possible dependencies may differ in scale per variable, we propose to look for a ratio threshold $\theta^{MI\text{-}ratio} \in [0; 1]$ that accepts variable X_j to be a neighbor of variable X_i if $(MI(X_i, X_j) - \min_k\{MI(X_i, X_k)\})/(\max_k\{MI(X_i, X_k)\} - \min_k\{MI(X_i, X_k)\}) \geq \theta^{MI\text{-}ratio}$. Note that this ratio threshold will be used jointly with the independence threshold, i.e. variable X_j is accepted to be a neighbor of variable X_i only if $MI(X_i, X_j) \geq \theta^{MI\text{-}indep}$ holds *additionally*. The only problem then is how to set $\theta^{MI\text{-}ratio}$ properly because for this there isn't a clear definition like that of independence. We therefore propose three different approaches and evaluate their respective merits experimentally.

Fixed threshold selection. Use a single, predetermined value for $\theta^{MI\text{-}ratio}$ for every X_i.

Random threshold selection. Use a newly uniformly randomly drawn value in $[0; 1]$ for $\theta^{MI\text{-}ratio}$ for every X_i.

Adaptive threshold selection. For every X_i, divide the range $[\min_k\{MI(X_i, X_k)\}; \max_k\{MI(X_i, X_k)\}]$ into k bins and place each variable X_j in its respective bin according to its MI with X_i. The last bin now contains all variables with which X_i has the strongest linkage relation. Note that this bin always has at least one variable. It is expected that often, most of the variables will end up in lower bins. Therefore, start from the last bin and iteratively move to the lower bins. Check if the number of variables in the next bin is lower or higher than the previous bin. As long as this number decreases, we are still in the tail of the strongest dependencies and these bins are accepted. However, as soon as this number starts to grow again, a new cluster of linkage relations is found and we stop, setting $\theta^{MI\text{-}ratio}$ so that the values in this bin are no longer accepted. We used a fixed number of $k = 10$ bins.

4.3 Experiments

The performance of LN-GOMEA with forced improvements, which, for short, we will refer to as LNGA (Linkage Neighbors Genetic Algorithm), on the common linkage benchmark problems is shown in Figure 4. Even using the simplest learning approach in the LNGA, i.e. only using the $\theta^{MI\text{-}indep}$, already provides the best results on each of the common benchmark problems, even outperforming LTGA. This is somewhat surprising, given the relatively extreme simplicity and low-order runtime complexity of learning the LN model. This is however also indicative that the common benchmark problems may be too easy when it comes to linkage learning. Especially finding the partitions in the trap functions using MI in GOMEA is not hard. As soon as the partitions are driven to their optimal and suboptimal attractors (typically in the first one or two generations), the MI is exactly 1 for all dependent variables and 0 for all non-dependent variables. Any arbitrary threshold is capable of finding this separation. Indeed, as can be seen in Figure 4, for any value of $\theta^{MI\text{-}ratio}$, including random values, the same performance is obtained on the trap functions.

It is a different story on the overlapping NK-landscapes however. Clearly, the order of interaction that needs to be modeled is still nicely limited because even using only

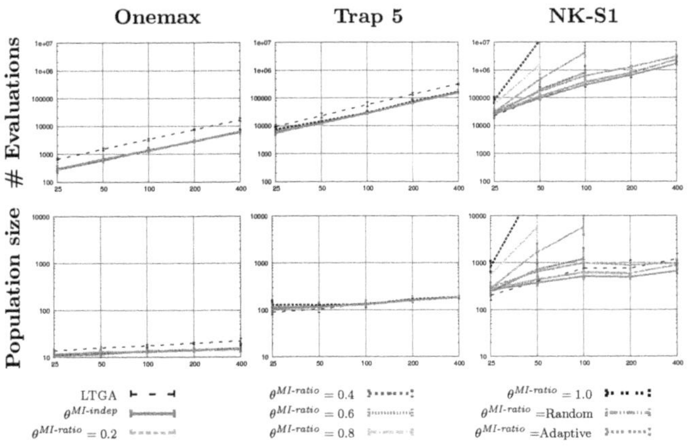

Figure 4: Scalability of LNGA variants.

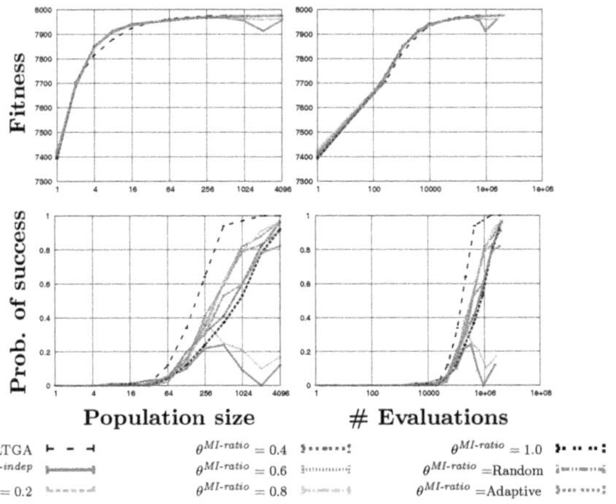

Figure 5: Performance of LNGA variants on a single 100-dimensional instance of weighted MAXCUT.

$\theta^{MI\text{-}indep}$ the problem is solved most efficiently. But, if $\theta^{MI\text{-}ratio}$ is set too high even and only the very strongest dependencies are selected, the LNGA breaks down. For a given variable, its most important linkage neighbors now do not have all similar and extremely high MI values like is the case in the trap functions. From the excellent performance however it can be concluded that for NK-S1 there still is a natural cutoff point that provides the required linkages. Moreover, $\theta^{MI\text{-}indep}$ already fits this bill.

As pointed out before, the common benchmark problems all have strong dependencies beween only a limited number of variables. For some of the weighted MAXCUT instances that we consider however, this is not the case. Therefore, as the population size increases, the statistical evidence for variables to be dependent accumulates and increasingly many linkage neighbors are identified when considering only $\theta^{MI\text{-}indep}$. Consequently, the LNGA with this learning approach breaks down if the population size increases, as can be seen in Figure 5. If additionally a random value for $\theta^{MI\text{-}ratio}$ is used or the adaptive scheme is used, the LNGA does not break down in a similar fashion. Out of these two, the adaptive scheme is the most efficient, but it is not *as* efficient as is the LTGA. What appears to be the main reason for this is the hierarchy in the LT model and not just the fact that it incorporates smaller-order linkages whereas the LN model has either random-order linkages or medium-order linkages (via the adaptive approach). This can be seen in Figure 7 where the performance of GOMEA is also shown in which a fixed structure is used: every set of two variables for which there is an edge in the graph in the MAXCUT instance, which in our case means all pairs of variables. In this configuration GOMEA is also capable of solving the problem to optimality reliably, but it requires even more function evaluations than LNGA with medium-order linkages or random-order linkages. The population size is very small however because of the relatively large (quadratic) number of sets in the FOS, resulting in extensive optimal mixing. The LTGA, that models lower-order (as in GOMEA-fixed), medium-order (as in LNGA) linkages, as well as high-order linkages, performs much better.

5. MULTISCALE LINKAGE NEIGHBORS

The results so far indicate that modeling linkages at multiple scales is important in GOMEA. Although the hierarchical structure as used in the LTGA is a natural manner of doing so, it is still limited in its ability to represent overlapping dependencies. In this section we therefore consider a multiscale variant of the LN model. This additionally allows us to validate the hypothesis that representing linkages at multiple scales can be beneficial compared to representing linkages at a single scale, even if they are allowed to overlap.

5.1 Multiscale Linkage Neighbors FOS

We extend the LN model to the Multiscale Linkage Neighbors (MLN) model by allowing multiple linkage sets to exist in the FOS per problem variable. Moreover, these sets can be ordered as inclusive subsets, i.e. a set in such an ordering is a subset of the next set.

5.2 Learning the MLN FOS

As a basis we consider the same approach as in the LNGA using $\theta^{MI\text{-}indep}$. We then progressively subdivide the accepted linkage neighbors. We consider 4 alternative approaches that all have the same computational complexity.

Linear decomposition. For a linkage neighborhood of X_i of k variables (neighbors and X_i itself), we consider all k subsets that are obtained by iteratively excluding a variable. To determine the ordering in which to drop the variables, we sort the variables on their MI values with X_i. To prevent requiring $\mathcal{O}(l\log(l))$ time in this phase, we use bucket sort with l buckets that are equidistantly created between the minimum and maximum MI among all accepted linkage neighbors (i.e. not among all variables $j \neq i$ as for $\theta^{MI\text{-}ratio}$ from Section 4.2.2). If multiple variables end up in a single bucket, they are not sorted further because they are considered to be of similar importance. Finally, because very large sets of linkage neighbors no longer contribute much to mixing and improving solutions and are only expected to reduce diversity without further benefit, we start the shrinking process from the strongest-linked $\lfloor l/2 \rfloor$ variables if the number of accepted linkage neighbors is larger than $\lfloor l/2 \rfloor$.

Exponential decomposition. Instead of decreasing the sizes of the subsets linearly, decrease the size exponentially by a factor of 2.

Bucket-linear decomposition. Perform a bucket sort with $\sqrt{n}$ buckets without sorting the buckets (i.e. perform histogram binning). Then, for each variable X_i, include a set in the FOS that iteratively grows over all $\sqrt{n}$ buckets, each

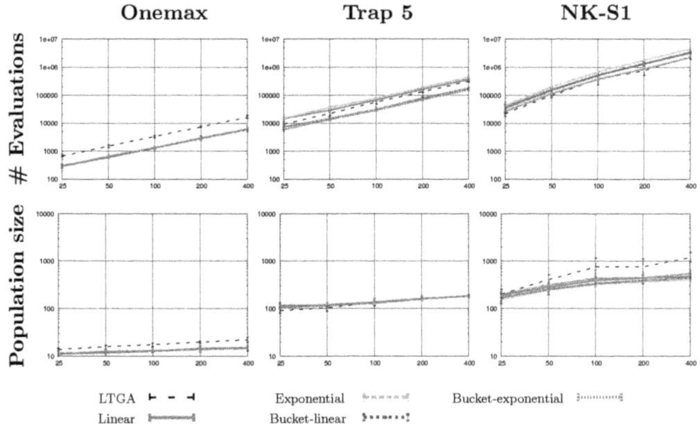

Figure 6: Scalability of MLNGA variants.

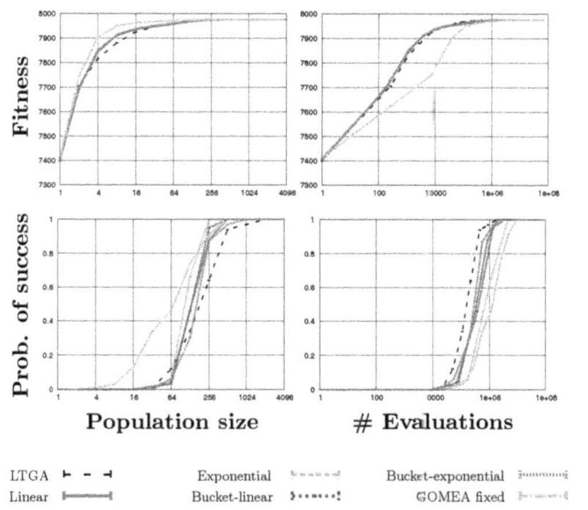

Figure 7: Performance of MLNGA variants on a single 100-dimensional instance of weighted MAXCUT.

time including all variables in a bucket. If a bucket results in including more than $\lfloor l/2 \rfloor$ variables, the variables in that bucket are not included and learning stops. The algorithm starts with the subset of X_i together with all variables in the last bucket (associated with the highest MI values). The reason for $\sqrt{n}$ buckets is that entropy (used within MI) is essentially an average (over all $\log(P(\boldsymbol{X} = \boldsymbol{x}_i))$. Because the standard deviation over different possible data sets coming from the same source decreases with the square root of the sample size, so the number of bins should therefore grow at most with $\mathcal{O}(\sqrt{n})$.

Bucket-exponential decomposition. The buckets are still regarded in order of decreasing MI, but instead of increasing the sizes of the subsets bucket by bucket, a new subset is only introduced if the number of variables in all prior buckets is at least twice the number of variables in the previously added subset.

5.3 Experiments

The performance of the MLN-GOMEA with forced improvements, which, for short, we will refer to as MLNGA (Multiscale Linkage Neighbors Genetic Algorithm), on the linkage benchmark problems is shown in Figure 6. Different from the LNGA variants, none of the MLNGA variants fail on any of the common linkage benchmark problems due to the expression of linkage relations on multiple scales. Moreover, because of $\theta^{\textit{MI-indep}}$, all MLNGA variants perform the same on onemax, outperforming LTGA. On the trap functions there is a clear difference between the variants that use a bucket-wise decomposition and a sorting-order wise decomposition in favor of the former. The reason for this is that the bucket-wise decomposition brings along a certain degree of adaptation to the observed MI values. In case of the trap functions almost all MI values are either very small or very large. As a result, all variables linked to variable X_i end up in the same bucket and are consequently included in exactly one FOS set. In the other variants however this set is always unnecessarily subdivided. On NK-S1, the best performing variant is the one with the bucket-exponential decomposition. Although expanding all buckets in MLNGA works, the number of sets in the FOS is more than is needed. The same can be said for the linear decomposition versus the exponential decomposition of the sorted neighbors.

Most of these observations extend to the weighted MAXCUT problem. In Figure 7 it can be seen that no MLNGA variant breaks down like some LNGA variants do. Thus, this empirically validates our hypothesis that representing linkages at multiple scales can be beneficial. The MLNGA variant with bucket-exponential decomposition of the linkage neighbors is the most efficient MLNGA variant.

We conclude our experimental analysis with a scalability analysis of the best variants of LNGA and MLNGA on weighted MAXCUT where the value to reach (VTR) is either 95% or 100% of the optimum. The VTR is computed per instance separately as $VTR = ARV + 0.95(OPT - ARV)$ where OPT is the optimal value for the instance and ARV is the average random value computed over many randomly sampled solutions. We use ARV rather than 0 because often $ARV \gg 0$, which would make it look fairly easy to reach a close approximation of the optimum if 0 were used. In Figures 5 and 7 the ARV is similar to the average fitness value that can be observed for all EAs with population size 1. In Figure 8 the best variants are shown for weighted MAXCUT as well as for the common benchmark problems.

The finally selected variants of LNGA and MLNGA exhibit excellent performance on the linkage benchmark problems, performing similar or better than LTGA in terms of population size and number of evaluations. On weighted MAXCUT however, when targeting the true optimum, the LN model is clearly less efficient. Moreover, on this problem LTGA outperforms MLNGA as the problem size increases. The scale-up of MLNGA is quite similar in shape to that of the GOMEA with the fixed linkage structure containing only all variable pairs. The worse behavior, compared to LTGA, of MLNGA may therefore well be a result of the large number of small linkage sets in the MLN model or the fact that the singletons aren't always in the FOS.

6. CONCLUSIONS

We have introduced and experimentally analyzed a new linkage model, called Linkage Neighbors (LN), to use in Optimal Mixing Evolutionary Algorithms (OMEAs). An advantage of the LN model compared to the Linkage Tree (LT) model is that it is well-suited to represent overlapping linkage relations. The use of a pair-wise likelihood-ratio test proved to be sufficient to configure the LN for a set of common linkage benchmark problems, even resulting in better performance than when the LT model is used. However, because the LN model can only represent a single list of

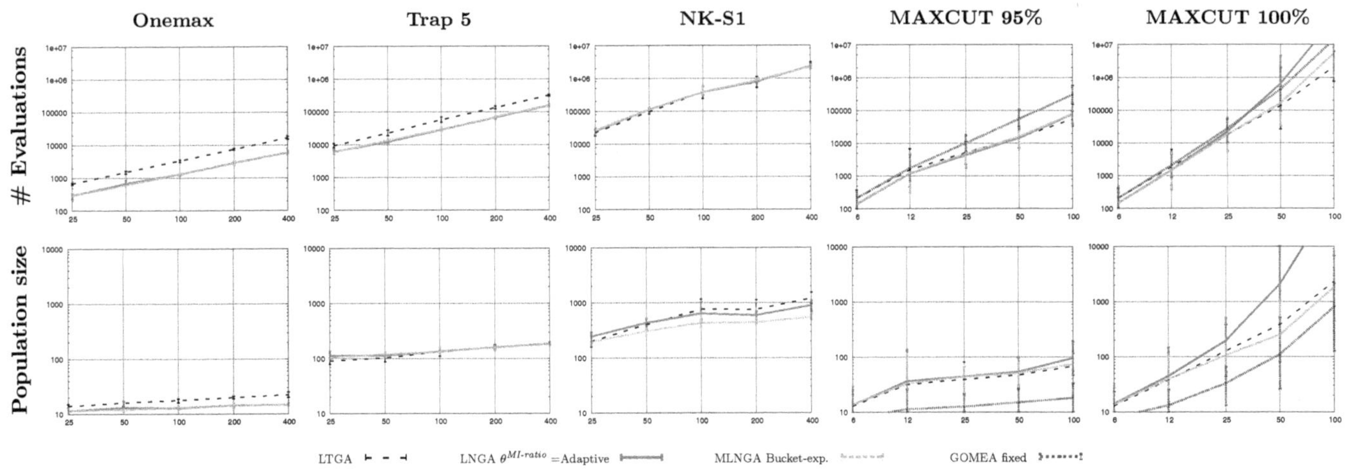

Figure 8: Scalability of LTGA, LNGA, MLNGA and GOMEA-fixed variants on all problems.

linkage neighbors per problem variable and a problem may exhibit dependencies at more levels than (very) strong and (very) weak (or independent), a better overall performance can be obtained using a multiscale subdivision of the LN model. This is indicative that representing linkages at multiple scales can be beneficial compared to representing linkages at a single scale, even if they are allowed to overlap.

Although more flexible than the LT model, the LN and MLN models still admit learning algorithms with efficient $\mathcal{O}(nl^2)$ runtime complexity. Moreover, the proposed algorithms perform binning of mutual information values independently for each variable, making parallelization straightforward. Although these properties make the LN and MLN models interesting to study further, results on weighted MAXCUT indicate that the LT model still offers a superior way of configuring a multi-scale linkage model. Therefore, it might alternatively be interesting to study the use of concepts introduced in this paper to adjust the LT model.

Because we were still able to improve upon the results of LTGA on the common linkage benchmark problems using the LN and MLN models inspite of the larger degrees of freedom, improvements may also be obtained by building a FOS via the selection of subsets from the powerset of all variables directly. This may however be hard to do while keeping the runtime complexity of the learning algorithm low. In future research we shall further explore this avenue.

Finally, we also showed that within OMEAs, the use of forced improvements via optimal mixing with the best known solution whenever optimal mixing with random solutions doesn't lead to an improvement, establishes efficient convergence without requiring additional population-wise selection and without losing diversity too quickly.

7. REFERENCES

[1] P. A. N. Bosman and D. Thierens. Negative log–likelihood and statistical hypothesis testing as the basis of model selection in IDEAs. In A. Feelders, editor, *Proceedings of the Tenth Belgium-Netherlands Conference on Machine Learning — BENELEARN 2000*, pages 109–116, Tilburg, 2000. Tilburg University.

[2] D. R. Cox and D. V. Hinkley. *Theoretical Statistics.* Chapman and Hall, London, 1974.

[3] K. Deb and D. E. Goldberg. Sufficient conditions for arbitrary binary functions. *Annals of Mathematics and Artificial Intelligence*, 10(4):385–408, 1994.

[4] I. Gronau and S. Moran. Optimal implementations of UPGMA and other common clustering algorithms. *Information Processing Letters*, 104(9):205–210, 2007.

[5] G. R. Harik, F. G. Lobo, and K. Sastry. Linkage learning via probabilistic modeling in the extended compact genetic algorithm (ECGA). In M. Pelikan et al., editors, *Scalable Optimization via Probabilistic Modeling: From Algorithms to Applications*, pages 39–61. Springer–Verlag, Berlin, 2006.

[6] M. Pelikan, M. W. Hauschild, and D. Thierens. Pairwise and problem-specific distance metrics in the linkage tree genetic algorithm. In *Proceedings of the Genetic and Evolutionary Computation Conference — GECCO–2011*, pages 1005–1012, New York, New York, 2011. ACM Press.

[7] M. Pelikan, K. Sastry, D. E. Goldberg, M. V. Butz, and M. Hauschild. Performance of evolutionary algorithms on NK landscapes with nearest neighbor interactions and tunable overlap. In *Proceedings of the Genetic and Evolutionary Computation Conference — GECCO–2009*, pages 851–858, New York, New York, 2009. ACM Press.

[8] E. Radetic and M. Pelikan. Spurious dependencies and EDA scalability. In *Proceedings of the Genetic and Evolutionary Computation Conference — GECCO–2010*, pages 303–310, New York, New York, 2010. ACM Press.

[9] F. Rendl, G. Rinaldi, and A. Wiegele. Solving Max-Cut to optimality by intersecting semidefinite and polyhedral relaxations. *Math. Programming*, 121(2):307, 2010.

[10] R. Y. Rubinstein. Cross-entropy and rare events for maximal cut and partition problems. *ACM Transactions on Modeling and Computer Simulation*, 12(1):27–53, 2002.

[11] F. Teytaud and O. Teytaud. Why one must use reweighting in estimation of distribution algorithms. In G. Raidl et al., editors, *Proceedings of the Genetic and Evolutionary Computation Conference — GECCO–2009*, pages 453–460, New York, New York, 2009. ACM Press.

[12] D. Thierens. The linkage tree genetic algorithm. In *Parallel Problem Solving from Nature — PPSN XI*, pages 264–273, Berlin, 2010. Springer–Verlag.

[13] D. Thierens and P. A. N. Bosman. Optimal mixing evolutionary algorithms. In *Proceedings of the Genetic and Evolutionary Computation Conference — GECCO–2011*, pages 617–624, New York, New York, 2011. ACM Press.

[14] D. Thierens and D. E. Goldberg. Mixing in genetic algorithms. In *Proceedings of the 5th International Conference on Genetic Algorithms*, pages 38–47, San Francisco, CA, 1993. Morgan Kaufmann Publishers Inc.

[15] S. S. Wilks. The large-sample distribution of the likelihood ratio for testing composite hypotheses. *The Annals of Mathematical Statistics*, 9:60–62, 1938.

Efficient Filters for the Simulated Evolution of Small Sorting Networks

Drue Coles
Department of Mathematics, Computer Science and Statistics
Bloomsburg University of Pennsylvania
Bloomsburg, PA 17815
dcoles@bloomu.edu

ABSTRACT

A sorting network is a mathematical model of an oblivious sorting algorithm—that is, a sorting algorithm in which all comparisons take place in a fixed order at predetermined positions in the list.

The search for sorting networks of optimal size is an old problem. Asymptotically optimal networks of size $O(n \log n)$ are known, where n is the number of inputs, but the hidden constants are enormous. Genetic algorithms have been used to tackle this problem in a number of studies since the early 1990s, often focusing on the historically interesting case of 16 inputs. In this special case, the best known bound of 60 comparisons has been attained, but often through the use of a particular, highly structured, initial sequence of comparisons that narrows the search space by filtering out all but a small core of input sequences.

We make explicit the concept of a filter—a fixed sequence of comparisons to be extended to a sorting network through a stochastic process—and present a new construction for any perfect square number of inputs. In the case of 9 inputs, we extend the filter to a sorting network of size 25, attaining the best known bound. For 16 and 25 inputs, we present a simple GA variant that extends the filter to produce small sorting networks with highly regular structure.

Categories and Subject Descriptors

I.2.8 [**Problem Solving, Control Methods, and Search**]: [Heuristic methods]; F.2 [**Nonnumerical Algorithms and Problems**]: [Sorting and searching]

Keywords

Sorting networks, genetic algorithms, simulated evolution

1. INTRODUCTION

A comparison network can be viewed as a sequence of integer pairs, each pair indicating the positions in a list of two elements to be compared and, if out of order, swapped.

GECCO'12, July 7–11, 2012, Philadelphia, Pennsylvania, USA.

A sorting network is a comparison network that sorts every possible input sequence.

The standard visual representation of a sorting network, shown in Figure 1, is motivated by its potential realization in hardware. The horizontal lines represent wires that carry data from left to right. Vertical lines denote comparators, logic gates that test the values on two wires and swap them if they are out of order. The shaded regions indicate groups of comparators that, having disjoint inputs, can operate in parallel. The size of a sorting network is defined to be the number of comparators, and its depth (or delay) is a measure of its comparison-level parallelism: the maximum number of comparators incident to a common wire.

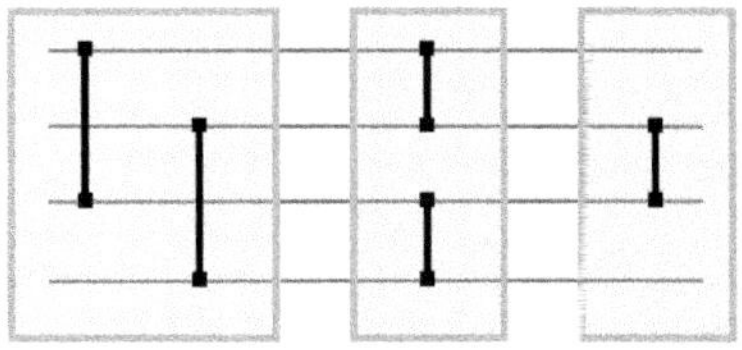

Figure 1: Sorting network of size 5 and depth 3

The original interest in sorting networks arose from their realization in hardware, but they also have applications to secure multiparty computation (see Maurer [12] for a short overview of this subject). SMC protocols enable distributed parties to compute a function on their combined inputs while keeping their individual inputs secret.

The correctness of a sorting network can be verified by examining its behavior on binary inputs. In particular, the zero-one principle asserts that a comparison network sorts all input sequences if and only if it sorts all binary sequences [11].

Knuth uses $\hat{S}(n)$ to denote the smallest possible size of a sorting network on n wires, and $\hat{T}(n)$ the smallest possible depth [11]. $\hat{S}(n)$ is known precisely only for $n \leq 8$ and $\hat{T}(n)$ for $n \leq 10$. It remains an open problem to improve the bounds on these functions for larger n.

Constructions by Hand.

In 1962, Bose and Nelson [3] gave a general construction that for 16 wires requires 65 comparisons. Two years later, Batcher [2] and, independently, Floyd and Knuth [7] found a general construction (known today as Batcher's odd-even merging network) that requires only 63 comparisons for 16 wires. As recounted by Knuth [11], G. Shapiro discovered a sorting network on 16 wires with 62 comparisons in 1969 and, later that year, M. W. Green found one with only 60 comparisons. This stands today as the best known bound on optimal size for 16 wires. All of these constructions were devised without the aid of computers.

The AKS network, an infinite family of sorting networks obtained from expander graphs, appeared in 1983 [1]. It has optimal size $O(n \log n)$ and depth $O(\log n)$, but the constants of proportionality hidden by the O-notation are enormous. The construction has been greatly simplified [14, 15], but Batcher's odd-even merging network, though not asymptotically optimal, is better for input sizes of practical interest.

Genetic Algorithms.

GAs were first used in connection with sorting networks by Hillis [9] in 1992, who generated a sorting network on 16 wires with 61 comparisons. Though not optimal, it was used as a proof of concept for the use of computer-based search methods to find small sorting networks. Hillis implemented an analog of diploid genotypes as they occur in nature, which allowed for the possibility of dominant and recessive genes. Fitness was measured as the fraction of sample inputs that were correctly sorted. The population of networks evolved on a two-dimensional grid with local mating.

Noting that most of the small sorting networks on 16 wires began with the same 32 comparisons (first seen in Green's network), Hillis fixed these comparisons in the population and did not allow recombination or random mutation to change them. This strategy, or some variation of it, has since been used in a number of other works (e.g., [4, 5]).

A novel feature of Hillis' work concerned the sampling of inputs for fitness evaluation. Test suites consisting of 10-20 binary strings were allowed to co-evolve on the same grid. Their fitness was a measure of how frequently the local sorting networks failed to sort them. Hillis observed "waves of epidemic and immunity" that prevented the population from settling into static neighborhoods of networks stuck in local optima.

More recently, hybrid genetic algorithms have been used, combining genetic operators with local search heuristics. For example, Choi and Moon [4, 5, 6] were able to produce 16-input sorting networks with 60 comparisons. Juillé [10] matched this result using a simulated evolution technique called "evolving non-determinism". This technique applied to the 13-input case produced a sorting network with only 45 comparisons, improving the previously best known upper bound of $\hat{S}(13) \leq 46$.

The fitness of a comparison network is typically measured during the selection process by sampling binary inputs and counting those that are correctly sorted by the network. Theoretical results indicate that sampling is necessary since the problem of verifying the correctness of arbitrary sorting networks is Co-$\mathcal{NP}$ Complete [13].

Green Filter.

Let $\mathcal{G}$ denote the comparison network obtained from the first 32 comparisons of Green's network (see Figure 2). As mentioned above, various pure and hybrid genetic algorithms have been devised to produce 16-input sorting networks by extending $\mathcal{G}$. This approach allows the evaluation of fitness to be derandomized: $\mathcal{G}$ produces only 151 unsorted binary output sequences, so it suffices to check how many of these sequences are sorted by the extention. For this reason we call $\mathcal{G}$ a *filter*: it reduces the set of binary inputs that must be considered in evaluating an extension to (ideally) a very small subset. Henceforth, we refer to $\mathcal{G}$ as the Green filter.

Knuth [11] described the behavior of $\mathcal{G}$ in a natural way (noting that no natural interpretation of the remaining 28 comparisons in Green's network is apparent). Imagine the wire indices 0-15 as characteristic vectors σ_i for a set of four elements and let y_i denote the output of $\mathcal{G}$ on wire i. Then we have $y_j \leq y_k$ whenever $\sigma_j \subseteq \sigma_k$. The latter condition can be tested programmatically by $j \mid k = k$, where the pipe symbol | denotes bitwise OR. This construction is easily generalized to the case of 2^r wires for any $r > 1$.

A natural question arises and inspires our work in the next two sections: can the performance of genetic algorithms for producing small sorting networks be enhanced by using a different filter?

2. SQUARE FILTER

For each integer $n > 1$ we define the $n \times n$ matrix M_n by $M_n(i, j) = in + j$ for $0 \leq i, j \leq n - 1$. Figure 3 shows M_4.

We define the *square filter* $\mathcal{F}_n$ on n^2 wires in two stages:

1. For each column of M_n, add comparators to sort the n values on the wires indexed by the column entries.

   (For example, the k-th column in Figure 3 corresponds to the k-th group of 5 comparisons shown in Figure 4.)

2. Repeat (1) using the rows of M_n instead of the columns.

Thus we embed $2n$ copies of a sorting network on n wires into a comparison network on n^2 wires. The construction is shown for $n = 4$ in Figure 4 and an equivalent construction obtained by rearranging independent comparisons is shown in Figure 5.

We will see below that $\mathcal{F}_4$ produces 53 unsorted binary outputs. This compares favorably with $\mathcal{G}$ in the sense that 28 comparisons are needed to extend $\mathcal{G}$ to a sorting network of size 60, and each of these 28 comparisons must make an average "contribution" of $151/28 = 5.39$ sorted outputs. The square filter, on the other hand, requires an additional 20 comparisons, so each comparison needs to make an average contribution of only $53/20 = 2.65$ sorted outputs. Of course, this does not guarantee that a genetic algorithm extending $\mathcal{F}_4$ is more likely to find sorting network than one extending $\mathcal{G}$; for one thing, the measure of average contribution fails to account for favorable correlations in the output set of a filter. The utility of a filter can be demonstrated empirically, however, and we do this in the next section.

The size of $\mathcal{G}$ is easily calculated, but the size of $\mathcal{F}$ depends on the subnetworks used in the embedding. The following theorem enumerates the binary outputs of $\mathcal{F}$.

THEOREM 1. *The square filter $\mathcal{F}_n$ produces $\binom{2n}{n}$ distinct binary outputs.*

PROOF. Let $A_i = 0^{n-i}1^i$. We order the symbols A_i by their index i; for example, $0011 < 0111$. Since stage 2 of the construction of $\mathcal{F}_n$ sorts consecutive blocks of size n, it is clear that any output of the filter can be expressed as a sequence $\mathcal{A} = A_{i_1}, \ldots, A_{i_n}$.

Suppose $\mathcal{A}$ contains consecutive symbols A_i and A_{i+1} with $A_i > A_{i+1}$. This means that there is an index j such that $A_i(j) = 1$ and $A_{i+1}(j) = 0$. But this is impossible because

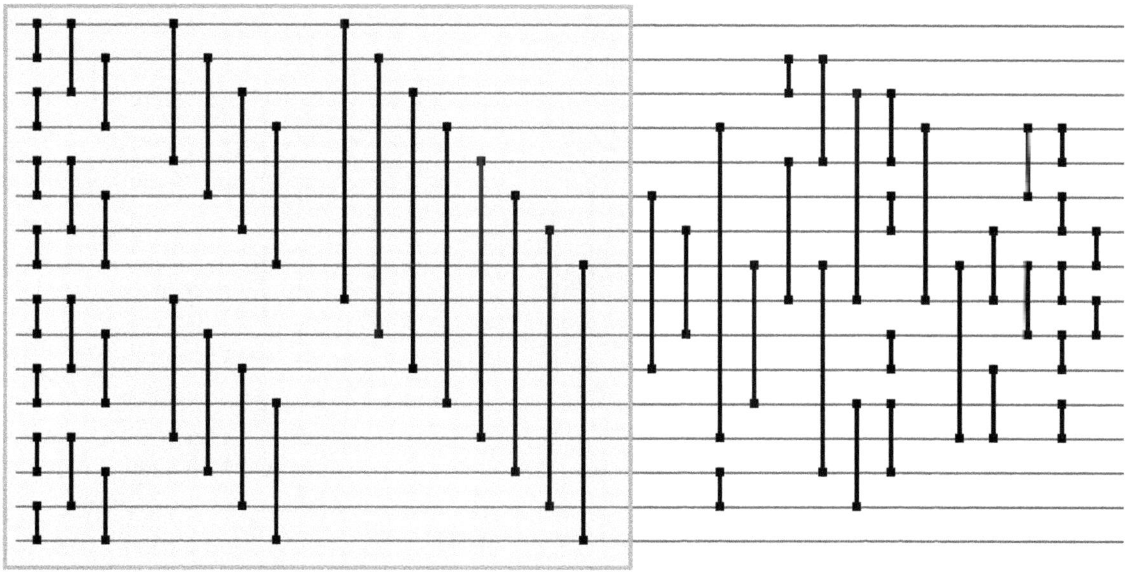

Figure 2: Green's sorting network with $\mathcal{G}$ shaded

$$\begin{pmatrix} 0 & 1 & 2 & 3 \\ 4 & 5 & 6 & 7 \\ 8 & 9 & 10 & 11 \\ 12 & 13 & 14 & 15 \end{pmatrix}$$

Figure 3: M_4

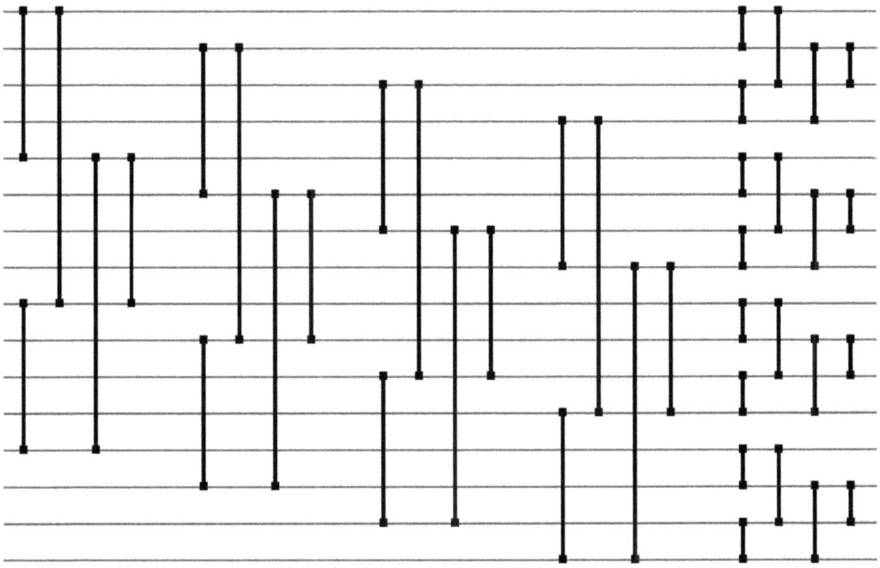

Figure 4: The filter $\mathcal{F}_4$. The first 4 groups of 5 comparisons correspond to the columns of M_4 and the last four groups (shown vertically stacked) correspond to the rows.

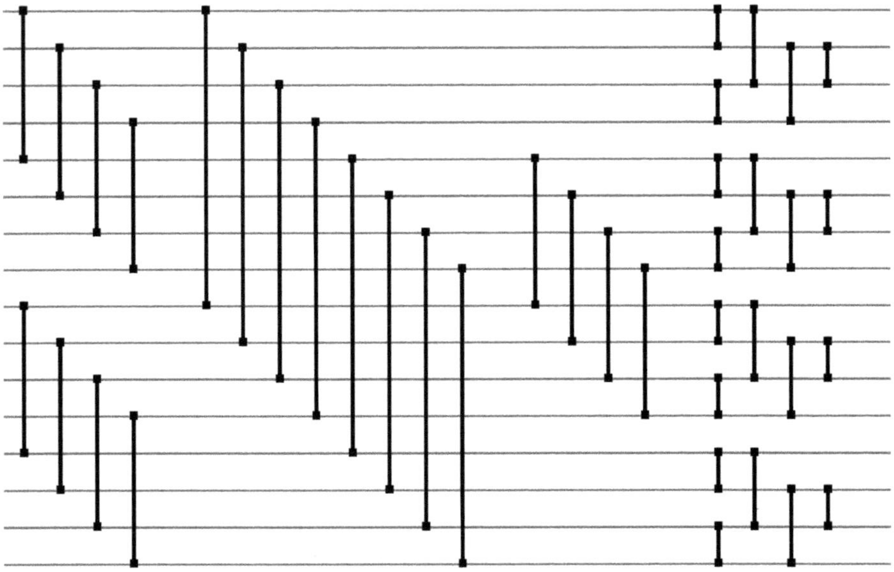

Figure 5: Equivalent to filter $\mathcal{F}_4$

these two bits are compared in Stage 1. It follows that the symbols A_i in the output sequence $\mathcal{A}$ must appear in sorted order. The number of possible such sequences is just the number σ_n of non-decreasing length-n sequences of integers $0, \ldots, n$:

$$\sigma_n = \sum_{i_0=0}^{n} \sum_{i_1=i_0}^{n} \cdots \sum_{i_n=i_{n-1}}^{n} 1. \qquad (1)$$

Note that σ_n is also the number of lattice paths from $(0, 0)$ to (n, n) using increments $(0, 1)$ and $(1, 0)$. The height of the j-th horizontal step corresponds to a specific index i_j in equation (1). These lattice paths correspond to binary strings of length $2n$ having as many 0's (right steps) as 1's (upward steps), and of these there are $\binom{2n}{n}$. $\square$

Thus $\mathcal{F}_4$ produces $\binom{8}{4} = 70$ binary outputs. There are 17 sorted binary sequences of length 16, and each of these moves unaltered through a comparison network. So subtracting these from the 70, we see that $\mathcal{F}_4$ produces 53 unsorted binary outputs, as mentioned earlier.

The binary outputs of both $\mathcal{F}$ and $\mathcal{G}$ always begin with 0 and end with 1, so genetic algorithms attempting to extend these filters may ignore all comparisons involving the first or last positions of the input sequence.

$\mathcal{F}_3$ has 18 comparisons. We were able to extend it by hand to a sorting network of size 25 (see Figure 6), matching the best known construction for 9 wires (which, as seen in Figure 7, has a more irregular structure).

3. GENETIC ALGORITHMS

In this section, we describe a simple genetic algorithm variant that extends the square filter to sorting networks on 16 and 25 wires. In the 16-wire case, a sorting network of size 61 is obtained in a majority of runs. We implemented a variety of local search heuristics to reduce the size to 60, but without success. Note, however, that these are the only known sorting networks on 16 wires of size ≤ 62 for which

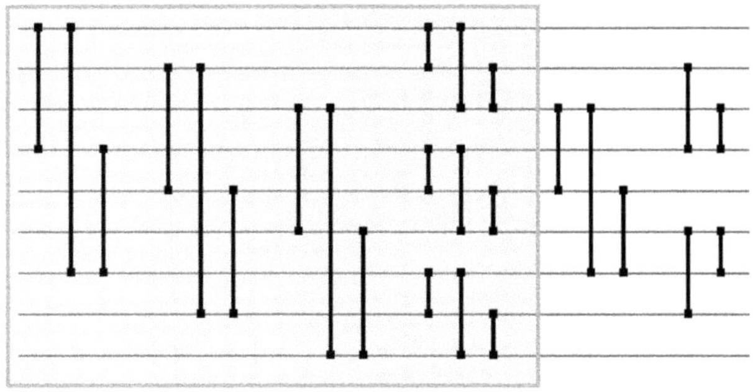

Figure 6: $\mathcal{F}_3$ (shaded) extended to a sorting network

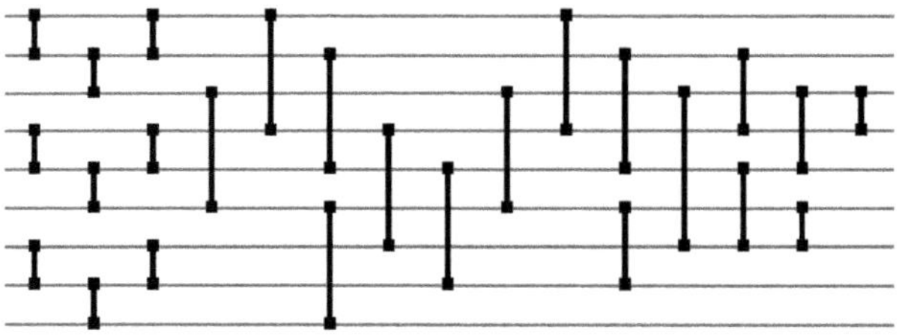

Figure 7: Smallest known sorting network on 9 wires

such a long initial sequence of comparisons (the filter) admits a general high-level description.

We will refer to the number of distinct unsorted binary outputs generated by a comparison network as its *deficiency*. This is the cost function used by our genetic algorithm to evaluate comparison networks.

Chromosomes are represented by sequences of integers (genes), each of which denotes a wire index. Comparators are determined by consecutive pairs of genes. Chromosomes in the initial population are obtained by selecting each gene independently and uniformly at random.

Selection works as follows:

1. The population is sorted by deficiency.

2. Each network N produces two pairs of offspring by being paired with its adjacent left and right neighbors (with wraparound). These four offspring along with a copy of N are sorted by deficiency, and the individual of lowest deficiency among these five will replace N in the next generation.

Offspring are produced using standard random one-point crossover. The crossover rate is 100%, but if the crossover point occurs after the last gene then the resulting offspring will be identical to the parents. There is no mutation. Each run of the GA continues until there are no improvements in the lowest deficiency for 50 consecutive generations.

16 Wires.

In 100 independent trials, we evolved a population of 50,000 networks of size 21 as extensions of $\mathcal{F}_4$. In 52 of these trials, sorting networks were obtained. The filter has 40 comparisons, so the new sorting networks have size 61 (efforts to obtain smaller sorting networks in this way were unsuccessful). An example is shown in Figure 8. Recall that Batcher's odd-even sorting network has 63 comparisons.

The comparisons in the extension in the unshaded region of Figure 8 are enumerated as follows (reading left-to-right within successive rows):

03-09	02-08	06-12	03-06	07-13	05-08	09-12
01-04	07-10	03-05	07-09	02-04	11-14	03-04
05-08	10-12	06-08	09-10	11-13	07-08	11-12

Wires are indexed from 0 (top wire) to 15 (bottom wire).

25 Wires.

We evolved a population of 80,000 random comparison networks, each with 52 comparisons, to obtain a network that sorts the outputs of $\mathcal{F}_5$. The filter has 90 comparisons, so the size of the resulting sorting network was 142. A hill climbing procedure (described below) was used to reduce the size of this network to 138 while retaining sortability. The resulting extension of $\mathcal{F}_5$ is shown in Figure 9 and its comparisons are enumerated as follows (with the numbering convention used above):

04-20	02-10	14-22	01-05	08-16	19-23	04-12
16-20	12-16	17-20	09-21	03-15	09-17	08-12
03-06	09-15	18-21	02-05	06-10	14-18	19-22
03-05	07-11	13-17	19-21	04-07	17-20	07-09
07-10	14-17	08-11	13-16	04-07	17-20	04-06
18-20	04-05	08-10	14-16	19-20	09-11	13-15
09-10	11-13	14-15	07-08	12-13	11-12	

The best known construction also has size 138, and others (such as Bose-Nelson) have size 154. For the 25-input case, our construction is the first achieved by a genetic algorithm (in fact, previous work on the use of GAs for producing small sorting networks has focused exclusively on 9-16 inputs).

The hill climbing procedure used to reduce the size of the sorting network from 142 to 138 comparisons operated as follows: each comparison was deleted to obtain a network with one less comparison but which no longer sorts perfectly, and each such network was altered by one-point mutation in each possible way. If perfect sortability was restored in any of the smaller mutated networks, the process was repeated on the mutant. We obtained no further improvements after size 138, and the GA has not yet produced other instances of larger-than-optimal sorting networks that can be reduced by the hill climber to 138 or fewer comparisons.

4. DEFICIENCY OF RANDOM FILTERS

Define $\delta_n(k)$ to be the smallest possible deficiency of a comparison network of size k on n wires. We know that $\delta_{16}(40) \leq 53$ since the square filter on 16 wires has size 40 and deficiency 53. Also, $\delta_{32}(16) \leq 151$ by the Green filter.

As a preliminary step toward a deeper investigation of δ, a problem that may hold independent mathematical interest, we consider here the deficiency of random networks of size 40 on 16 wires. We tested purely random networks as well as networks evolved by the genetic algorithm of the previous section from an initially random population.

For the first experiment, we evolved a random population of 1,000,000 networks on 16 wires with 40 comparisons. The lowest deficiency obtained in this way was 279.

The genetic algorithm produced somewhat better results though was extremely slow since deficiency was used as the cost function (rather than approximating deficiency through sampling). Populations of 500 comparison networks were evolved with crossover, selection, and other parameters as specified in Section 3. The lowest deficiency obtained in this way was 193. Although the simple GA variant used here was able to extend the square filter to small sorting networks, it is not effective at *creating* filters of any reasonable quality.

5. CONCLUSION AND OPEN PROBLEMS

The GA of Hillis [9] exploited the fact that most small sorting networks on 16 wires known at the time began with the first 32 comparisons of Green's sorting network. He fixed this initial segment in the population and did not allow it to be altered by recombination or mutation. In this article, we made explicit the general concept of a filter as a comparison network that transforms the space of all binary inputs to a small set of binary outputs. Given a particular filter, the search for small sorting networks is reduced to a search for comparison networks that merely sort the outputs of the filter. We provided a simple construction, the square filter $\mathcal{F}_n$ on n^2 wires, that produces $\binom{2n}{n}$ binary outputs.

A GA variant was implemented to extend the filter on 16 wires to produce sorting networks of size 61. The same GA produced a small sorting network on 25 wires that, after improvements by a local greedy heuristic, yielded a sorting network of size 138 — the smallest size known to be possible, and the only such result obtained by a GA.

The highly regular structure of the filter and the abundant symmetry in Figure 9 hint at the possibility of identifying and generalizing functional substructures that might be used in a deterministic family of sorting networks. This symmetry might also be exploited by a GA, perhaps by identifying individual genes with symmetric subnetworks. Graham and Oppacher showed that GAs tend to produce small sorting networks more efficiently if the populations are initialized with symmetric pairs of comparators [8], although in their study the pairs are not preserved by crossover and mutation.

We leave it as an open problem to determine bounds on the deficiency function $\delta_n(k)$. As a special case, it would be interesting to determine if the Green filter and the square filter are optimal: do $\delta_{16}(32) = 151$ and $\delta_{16}(40) = 53$ hold?

Another direction for future work in this area would be to find new examples of low-deficiency filters and extend them

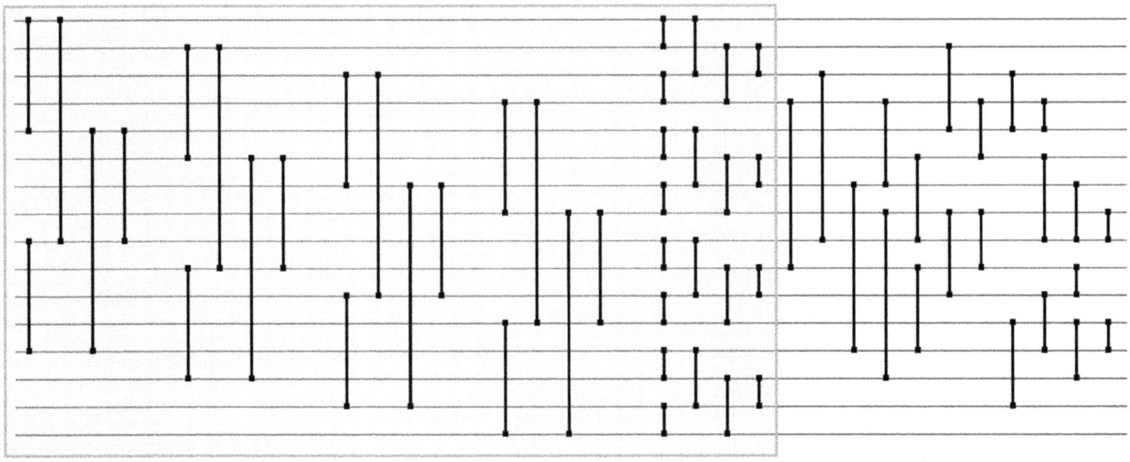

Figure 8: A new sorting network on 16 wires with 61 comparators ($\mathcal{F}_4$ shaded).

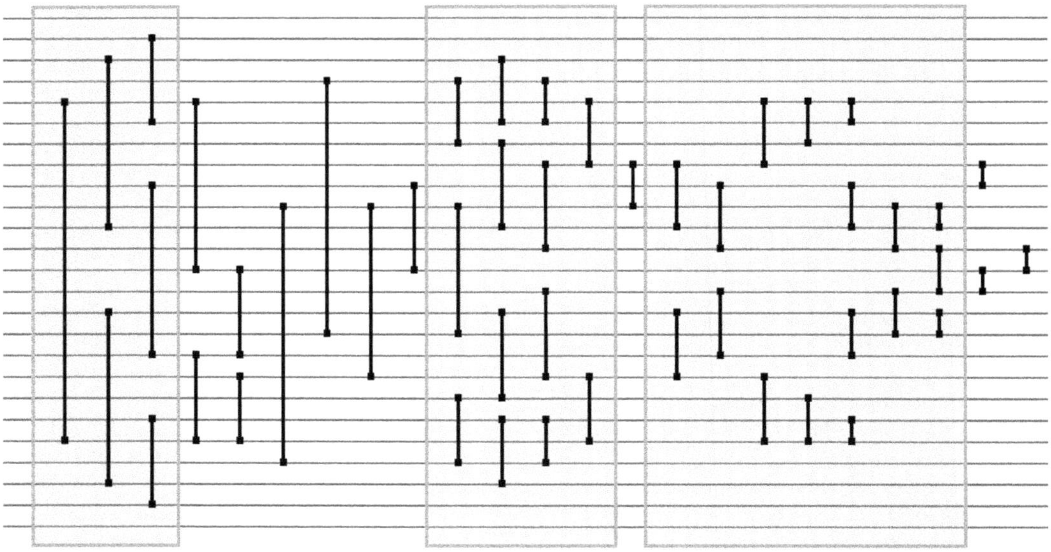

Figure 9: Extension to $\mathcal{F}_5$ yielding sorting network of size 138. Note the symmetry in the shaded regions.

to sorting networks through the use of genetic algorithms or other random search techniques. Statistical analysis of these networks may reveal common features that can be exploited to create new families of sorting networks. The use of genetic algorithms to extend efficient filters may also help to improve known bounds on the optimal sizes of sorting networks for specific input lengths.

6. ACKNOWLEDGMENTS

The author gratefully acknowledges the thoughtful and helpful suggestions of the referees.

7. REFERENCES

[1] M. Ajtai, J. Komlós, and E. Szemerédi. An $O(n \log n)$ sorting network. *Combinatorica*, 3:1–19, 1983.

[2] K. E. Batcher. Sorting networks and their applications. In *AFIPS Spring Joint Computer Conference*, volume 32, pages 307–314, New York, NY, 1968. ACM.

[3] R. C. Bose and R. J. Nelson. A sorting problem. *JACM*, 9:282–296, 1962.

[4] S. S. Choi and B. R. Moon. A hybrid genetic search for the sorting network problem. In *GECCO-2001: Proceedings of the Genetic and Evolutionary Computation Conference*, pages 258–265, San Francisco, CA, USA, 2001. Morgan Kaufmann Publishers Inc.

[5] S. S. Choi and B. R. Moon. More effective genetic search for the sorting network problem. In *GECCO-2002: Proceedings of the Genetic and Evolutionary Computation Conference*, pages 335–342, San Francisco, CA, USA, 2002. Morgan Kaufmann Publishers Inc.

[6] S. S. Choi and B. R. Moon. A graph-based Lamarckian-Baldwinian hybrid for the sorting network problem. *IEEE Trans. Evolutionary Computation*, 9(1):105–114, 2005.

[7] R. W. Floyd and D. E. Knuth. Improved constructions for the Bose-Nelson sorting problem. *Notices of the Amer. Math. Soc.*, 14:283, 1967.

[8] L. Graham and F. Oppacher. Symmetric comparator pairs in the initialization of genetic algorithm populations for sorting networks. *Congress on Evolutionary Computation (CEH-06) and IEEE World Congress on Computational Intelligence (WCCI-06)*, pages 2845–2850, 2006.

[9] W. D. Hillis. Co-evolving parasites improve simulated evolution as an optimization procedure. In C. Langton, C. Taylor, J. D. Farmer, and S. Rasmussen, editors, *Artificial Life II*, 1992.

[10] H. Juillé. Evolution of non-deterministic incremental algorithms as a new approach for search in state spaces. In *Proceedings of the 6th International Conference on Genetic Algorithms*, pages 351–358, San Francisco, CA, USA, 1995. Morgan Kaufmann Publishers Inc.

[11] D. E. Knuth. *The Art of Computer Programming. Vol 3. Sorting and Searching.* Addison-Wesley, Reading, MA, 1973.

[12] U. Maurer. Secure multi-party computation made simple. *Discrete Applied Mathematics*, 154(2):370–381, 2006.

[13] I. Parberry. Single-exception sorting networks and the computational complexity of optimal sorting network verification. *Mathematical Systems Theory*, 23(2):81–93, 1990.

[14] M. Paterson. Improved sorting networks with $O(\log N)$ depth. *Algorithmica*, 5(1):65–92, 1990.

[15] J. Seiferas. Sorting networks of logarithmic depth, further simplified. *Algorithmica*, 53(3):374–384, 2009.

An Empirical Approach to the Measurement of Interchromosomal Distances in the Genetic Algorithm

Robert Collier
School of Computer Science
University of Guelph
Guelph, Ontario, Canada
collierr@uoguelph.ca

Mark Wineberg
School of Computer Science
University of Guelph
Guelph, Ontario, Canada
mwineber@uoguelph.ca

ABSTRACT
Data visualizations, population diversity measurements, and cluster analyses are all invariably constructed from measures of distance or dissimilarity, and it is recognized that any measure of the distance between points should represent the manner and ease with which an algorithm or process can move from one point towards another. For the genetic algorithm, this traversal is largely accomplished by mutation and recombination, but in spite of this, measures like the Hamming distance and the edit distance are still used to assess the distance between population members. This represents a significant problem, because these measures were not designed with the genetic algorithm in mind and they do not consider how the genetic operators will actually traverse genotypic space. The need for distance measures to be accurate and representative cannot be overstated, but for the complex traversals of the genetic algorithm, it is exceedingly difficult to determine whether one measure is any more representative than another. To address this need, this paper will introduce an empirical approach to distance measurement, and since the resultant values are derived from actual traversals, the distance measured is guaranteed representative, and can be used as a baseline against which other measures can be evaluated.

Categories and Subject Descriptors
I.2.8 [**Artificial Intelligence**]: Problem Solving, Control Methods, and Search – *Heuristic methods.*

General Terms
Algorithms, Measurement

Keywords
genetic algorithm, distance measure, Monte Carlo simulation

1. INTRODUCTION
The merits associated with the use of distance measures are well established [1], but the need for those measures to be both accurate and representative cannot be overemphasized. With measures of distance being defined such that they reflect the length of the shortest path between two points in a state space, measures that are not representative of the manner in which the same state space will be traversed can yield misleading results. This would be analogous to an onboard navigational system reporting a straight-line Euclidean distance between points, instead of the length of the physical route that must be travelled. Although such an oversight might seem unlikely, the predominant approach to measuring the distance between the binary genotypes often used in genetic algorithms is the Hamming distance, and it is not difficult to demonstrate that this measure is not representative of the manner in which the genetic operators traverse solution spaces [5]. Since several exploratory applications are constructed from distance measures, the use of unrepresentative measures can be detrimental. Consequently there is a definite need for measures that are demonstrably representative of the manner in which the space will be traversed, and therein lies the difficulty – the complexity (and stochasticity) of the operators severely complicates the characterization of how of the genetic algorithm actually traverses genotypic space [2], making it difficult to find nontrivial traversals suitable for calibration.

The main contribution of this paper is the development of an empirical distance measure. It has been established that distance can be effectively measured by observing randomly generated traversals (as in [7,8]), so the proposed empirical measure will determine the distance between genotypes by observing actual traversals by typical operations. Consequently, the distance reported will be accurate [9], and representative of the manner in which that distance would be traversed. Although such a measure is too computational expensive to be used in every application, the distances measured are ideal for the calibration and evaluation of other measures. We believe that the work presented here represents a crucial stage in the development of representative distance measures, specific to the genetic algorithm, that will be used to significantly advance the different approaches to data visualization, population diversity measurement, and cluster analysis.

The remainder of this paper is divided into three major sections, preceding the final summaries. Since the genotypic space is often very difficult to conceptualize, Section 2 describes how the proposed empirical measure was modeled from a real-world geometric construction, before describing the actual technique in detail. Although the traversals generated by the proposed empirical measure correspond to traversals that can be made using mutation and recombination, Section 3 offers a theoretical analysis of the validity of the approach. Finally, to illustrate the application of the proposed empirical measure, Section 4 describes the comparative evaluation of the Hamming distance against an overly-simplistic, but more representative, alternative measure.

GECCO'12, July 7–11, 2012, Philadelphia, Pennsylvania, USA.

2. EMPIRICAL MEASURE DESIGN

The use of a drafting compass to construct a bounding (circular) subplane associated with a fixed compass radius serves as an effective analogy for the proposed empirical approach. The act of turning a drafting compass is an exhaustive (continuous) exploration of all possible angles at which a mechanism capable of two-dimensional motion might proceed, and the mechanism defined by the mutation and recombination operators of a genetic algorithm can be used similarly. This exploratory mechanism can be to identify the genotypic subspace that can be reached by the application of the variational operators (to some origin genotype). As such, this geometric construction analogy is quite valuable for exploring the foundational concepts from which the empirical distance measure was developed.

2.1 Geometric Construction Analogy

A drafting compass has one leg fixed to a point C_0 on the surface of a finite plane and the angle between the legs of the compass is fixed such that the compass radius is representative of the distance that could be traversed by a mechanism within a fixed interval of time T. By turning the compass, a circular subplane C_1 centered on the origin is identified such that the distance from the origin to any point in the subplane C_1 is no more than the radius and, thus, each point in the subplane can be reached by the mechanism in T units of time or less, while all points outside the subplane cannot be reached within T units of time.

If the compass is then used to identify one additional subplane of the same radius centered at each point i within the subplane C_1, the union of these additional subplanes also identifies a circular subplane, denoted C_2 and centered at the origin, such that the distance from the origin to any point within the subplane C_2 can be reached by the mechanism in question in 2T units of time or less. Consequently, every point that can be reached from the origin requiring either T or 2T units of has been identified. Naturally, this approach can be repeated until the amount of time (expressed as an integer multiple of T) required by the mechanism to traverse the distance from the origin to any reachable point in the plane has been determined. The geometric construction process is depicted in Figure 1.

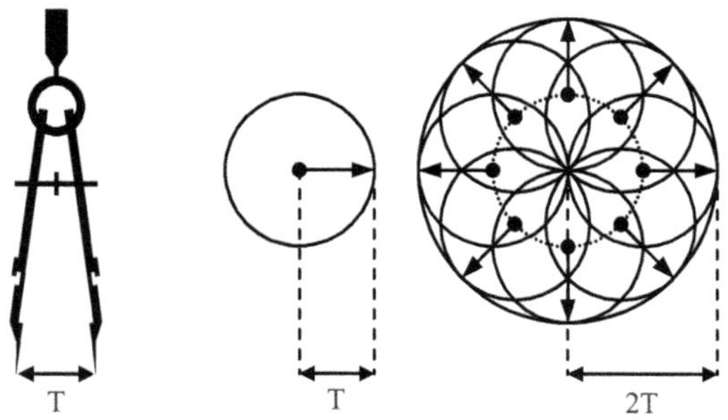

Figure 1. A drafting compass of fixed width can be used to identify a circular subplane of the same radius; the points within can then be used to identify a subplane of twice the radius with the same center.

It is not difficult to extend the preceding geometric construction analogy from a continuous, two dimensional space to a discrete, binary, four-dimensional hypercubic space that is more easily equated with a genotypic space. Assuming a genotypic space of four bit candidate solutions, a mechanism defined using only a single bit flipping operator and origin genotype ■■■■, the hypercubic genotypic space and first subspace identified by the process described are depicted in Figure 2.

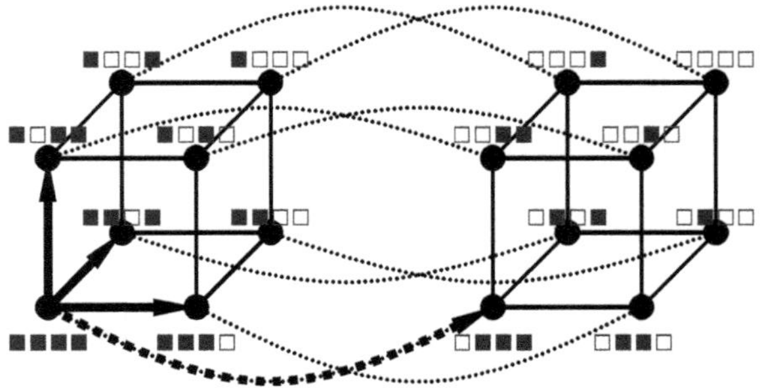

Figure 2. With an operator that only flips a single bit and origin ■■■■, the proposed approach would identify {■■■□, ■■□■, ■□■■, □■■■} to be nearest the origin.

If the proposed approach is then reapplied to the same space with each element of the first subspace as a possible origin, the second subspace can be identified, as depicted in Figure 3.

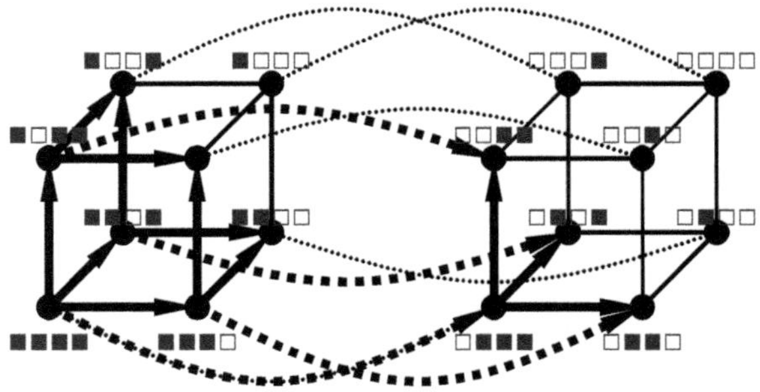

Figure 3. Using the first subspace (from Figure 2) as the next set of possible origins, the approach would identify {■■□□, ■□■□, ■□□■, □■■□, □■□■, □□■■} as next nearest the origin.

It should be evident that there is a direct correspondence between the Hamming distance that separates each genotype from the origin and the membership of that same genotype to an indexed subspace. It is also clear that the proposed methodology can be used to effectively measure genotypic spatial distances, by constructing the geodesic (i.e., shortest path) through genotypic space that could be traversed by the operator available.

Unfortunately, as traversals made by a genetic algorithm also employ a binary operator (recombination) and probabilistic applications, the possible 'directions' through genotypic space associated with the exploratory mechanism are much more difficult to define. As a clarifying example, recombining ■■■■ and □□□□ can produce the genotype ■□□■ as an offspring, even though the Hamming distance between ■■■■ and ■□□■ is greater than one – this clearly demonstrates that the Hamming distance does not reflect traversals made by recombination and, consequently, this distance does not reflect the manner in which genotypic space is traversed by the genetic algorithm.

For this investigation, the uniform recombination operator and a probabilistic and independent bit-flipping mutation operator were used. It should be emphasized that every member of the population of a genetic algorithm is, essentially, subjected to both mutation and recombination each generation. For a population of ρ binary genotypes of length λ, there are as many possible mutations as there are members of the complete genotypic space (S), which, assuming the absence of any infeasible genotypes, is of cardinality 2^λ. Furthermore, as every uniform recombination between genotypes of length λ can be uniquely identified by a crossover mask of length λ, there are also, at most, 2^λ possible recombination operations between each pair.

This entails that any one genotype that could be selected to undergo recombination could be paired with any member of the current population of ρ members. Consequently, for a given genotype (designated as the origin genotype) there are $\rho 2^\lambda$ recombination operations (of which some may be functionally equivalent). The result is $2^\lambda \cdot \rho 2^\lambda$ (= $\rho 2^{2\lambda}$) possible applications of the exploratory mechanism that could be applied to any genotype. It follows, then, that if an origin genotype and its descendants (created after each generation of the genetic algorithm) are analogous to entities moving through the space of possible genotypes, then each of the $\rho 2^{2\lambda}$ possible operations that could be applied to the origin genotype establishes a direction in which the motion through genotypic space can proceed. Furthermore, since the state of the population is actually expected to change after every generation of the genetic algorithm, the set of possible directions will also change each generation. Consequently, the path (starting with the origin) traversed through genotypic space would be most accurately represented as a curve.

As it would require an intractable number of calculations to exhaust the set of possible directions after each generation) the proposed approach would consider only those directions defined by the mutation of the origin and/or the recombination of the origin with a member of the current population. Using the previous analogy, this would be a traversal that was tangential to the curved-path traversal described above. Since the offspring are observed without actually being added to the current population, the available population is fixed and, thus, the direction of the tangent line does not change. To further reduce the complexity, a Monte Carlo simulation based approach to the exploration of the different possible directions was also favoured.

The proposed approach would repeatedly subject the origin genotype and a member of the population to both a randomly selected recombination operation and a randomly selected mutation operation. The set of resultant genotypes would then be considered representative of the set of possible genotypes that can be reached by a single application of the exploratory mechanism. This is analogous to the identification of the first circular subplane by the drafting compass, in the preceding analogy. It is then possible, through repeat application of this approach, to establish a sequence of concentric, contoured zones, similar to the contoured representation of land relief that are often employed in topographic maps.

The first zone (designated C_0) would contain only the origin and the second zone (designated C_1) would contain the genotypes that are most likely to be produced from the origin and the population. The likelihood is based on the frequency of produced genotypes by the Monte Carlo process, and since any genotype can potentially be produced (due to the nature of the mutation operator), a statistical significance test is used to determine which chromosomes produced will be considered a part of zone C_1. These genotypes are considered the first nearest to the origin. Analogous to the creation of the second circle from points contained in the first circle using the geometric compass, all members of zone C_1 are now considered possible origin genotypes for the creation of zones $C_2, ..., C_n$. Zones $C_2, ..., C_n$. would then contain those genotypes designated the second nearest, third nearest, … and n^{th} nearest to the origin, respectively. In so doing, an ordinal distance measure has been constructed, where all genotypes that are members of zone C_i but are not also members of zone C_{i-1} can be assigned a distance value of i.

Although the process by which a representative sample of the possible 'directions' the exploratory mechanism might use to traverse genotypic space has been established, there are properties of the geometric construction described previously that are not shared by the genetic algorithm. These must be adapted for an empirical measure that pertains specifically to traversals made by the genetic algorithm.

2.2 Adaptation to the Genetic Algorithm

The first application of the drafting compass to delineate distance in geometric space results in a single circular subplane. This subplane contains the set of points that are separated from the origin by a distance that is less than or equal to a single compass width. It could also be stated that this subplane contains the points that could be considered the nearest neighbours of the origin, and from these points a random neighbour (and, thus, a random direction) could be selected.

However, since it is possible to apply mutation and recombination operators to an origin genotype such that any other genotype of the same length is the result, this entails that every genotype is, in fact, a neighbour of the origin. That being said, it is accepted that the mutation and recombination operators of the genetic algorithm do not produce the uniformly random selection of one of the 2^λ genotypes that could be considered neighbours, and may, in fact, not produce certain genotypes if their appearance would violate a constraint on the problem. Since the genotypes that might be produced after a single application of the genetic operators are each generated with varying degrees of likelihood, the process described in the analogy could only be adapted for use with the genetic algorithm if the neighbouring genotypes that are more likely to appear are assigned membership to a zone that is designated a lesser distance from the origin. This is consistent with the way neighbour structures in the search space can be derived from the genetic operators [6].

To clarify, consider a mechanism defined entirely by a point mutation operator that independently and probabilistically (probability < 0.5) flips each bit of a four bit genotype. From an origin ■■■■, it is technically possible to apply this operator once and produce any four bit binary genotype. However, the four genotypes for which only a single bit differs (i.e. ■■■□, ■■□■, ■□■■, and □■■■) would each be the result with a probability of $(0.25)(0.75)^3$, while the six genotypes for which exactly two bits differ (i.e. ■■□□, ■□■□, ■□□■, □■■□, □■□■, and □□■■) would be the result with the lesser probability $(0.25)^2(0.75)^2$. Consequently, it would be more reasonable to consider the former four genotypes to be nearer the origin than the latter six. Furthermore, the proposed Monte Carlo simulation based approach will only yield observations that can be used to approximate these probabilities, and thus it is necessary to use a statistical significance testing technique to determine the set of genotypes that should be assigned membership to each of the contoured zones.

Also contrary to the drafting compass analogy is the observation that, following the identification of zone C_1, it is not immediately obviously which genotypes should be subjected to the genetic operators to determine contoured zone C_2. To clarify, in the drafting compass analogy the first circular subplane C_1 was centered upon the origin point C_0 and the circular subplane that would be created by the union of subplanes constructed using the points of C_1 (with $C_0 \subseteq C_1$) as central points would, in fact, be equivalent to the union of subplanes constructed using the points of the set difference $C_1 \setminus C_0$ as possible points of origin. Similarly, in determining C_3, the union of subplanes created from center points from the one of the sets C_2, $C_2 \setminus C_0$, and $C_2 \setminus C_1$ would all be identical. Although this result could be construed as indicating that that the set of operators need only be applied to those genotypes belonging to the furthest contoured zone from the origin genotype, this is not the case for the genetic algorithm. This result is, in fact, a consequence of the subadditivity property (i.e. the satisfaction of the triangle inequality) of the two dimensional Euclidean distance associated with the geometric construction analogy. Since the distance between the origin and a point in contoured zone C_{i+2} cannot exceed the sum of the distance between a point in C_i and a point in C_{i+1} and the distance between that point in C_{i+1} and the point in C_{i+2}, there is no reason to include the points in C_i in the determination of C_{i+2}. It must, however, be emphasized that the triangle equality does not hold for a distance defined as a function of both mutational and recombination measures of distance.

Finally, although the analogous geometric construction did not constrain the compass width, it must also be stressed that the repeated application of the genetic operators does not typically result in a traversal of genotypic space in what would be considered a single 'direction'. Mutation and recombination operations are determined probabilistically each generation and the state of the population in the current generation determines the possible offspring that might be produced by recombination. It could thus be concluded that, since the population is expected to change each generation, a single generation represents the longest period of time that the mechanism can be guaranteed not to change direction. This would, in the context of the analogy, place a constraint on the width of the drafting compass; in the context of empirical distance measurement for the genetic algorithm, only a single generation of the exploratory mechanism can be applied when constructing each contoured zone. With respect to the considerations and constraints presented in this section, an empirical approach to the measurement of the genotypic spatial distances, representative of the manner in which the genotypic space is actually traversed by the recombination and mutation genetic operators used by the genetic algorithm, can finally be introduced.

2.3 Empirical Distance Measurement

The following pseudocode summarizes the process, inspired by the geometric construction analogy, by which genotypic spatial distances can be measured empirically. It should be noted that the mutation and recombination operations applied by the proposed approach must adhere to any constraints pertaining to the feasible region of genotypic space. It should also be noted that when no additional genotypes can be added to the current contoured zone, it indicates that every genotype that remains is not likely to be reached (over the course of a single generation) with the operators available.

Algorithm 1. Empirical Distance Measurement

```
/*                    Input Variables
<origin> is a genotype that is designated to be the point
of origin, from which the distances will be measured
<population> is a multiset of genotypes corresponding to
the state of the current population
<genotype> is an array of binary genotypes of a given
length (taken from the set of all possible genotypes, S),
with the 0th element designated as the initial point of
origin; it has Boolean attribute <measured> representing
whether or not that genotype has been assigned membership
to a zone; it has also has integer attribute <count> to
record the number of times it appears each iteration
                      Other Variables
<zone> is an array of objects representing each contoured
zone; it has a real attribute <quotient> representing the
fraction of the total number of Monte Carlo trials that
will use the genotypes of that zone as possible points of
origin for the traversal
<reachable> is the set of genotypes with nonzero
appearance frequencies that are not assigned to a zone */

// the origin is assigned membership to zone 0
<genotype>[0].<measured> = true
<zone>[0].<quotient> = 1.0
i = 1
until |<zone>[i-1]| = 0
  <genotype>[1 to |S-1|].<count> = 0

  // for each genotype in an established zone
  for j = 0 to i
    for <origin> ∈ <zone>[j]
      for k = 1 to <zone>[j].<quotient> ÷ |<zone>[j]|
        // apply the operators and record the result
        <member> = randomly_select_member(<population>)
        <mask> = randomly_generate_crossover_mask()
        <result> = recombine(<origin>, <member>, <mask>)
        <result> = mutate(<result>)
        <genotype>[<result>].<count>++

  <reachable> = descending-sort-by-count(<genotype>)
  for j where <genotype>[j].<included> = true
    <reachable> = <reachable> \ <genotype>[j]

  // add most frequent genotype to the current zone
  for j = 1 to |<reachable>|
    until significant_count_difference(1, j+1)
    <zone>[i] = zone[i] ∪ <reachable>[j]

  // the quotient for each zone is recalculated
  for j = 0 to i
    <zone>[j].<quotient> = 0
    for k = 0 to |S-1|
      if <genotype>[k] ∈ <zone>[j]
        <zone>[j].<quotient>+= <genotype>[k].<count>

  normalize <zone>[0..i].<quotient>
  i++
```

Since the number of Monte Carlo trials to be performed will not change after each iteration, the total number of trials is divided amongst the reachable genotypes according to the frequency with which they have appeared in previous iterations. At this point, every reachable genotype represents a possible origin from which the distance must be calculated. These genotypes are subjected to random applications of the genetic operators and the resulting genotype appearance frequencies are tallied. Finally, genotypes are sorted in descending order by appearance frequency and statistical significance testing (between genotypes sorted into adjacent positions against a binomial distribution as the null hypothesis) is used to identify the subset of genotypes constructed with the highest frequency, identifying the next contoured zone.

3. EMPIRICAL MEASURE VALIDATION

It should be evident from the pseudocode that the proposed approach to empirical distance measurement is not simply a generalized implementation of the genetic algorithm. It should also be noted that the proposed approach is not merely a measure of the observance of a random walk. A random walk between two locations cannot be guaranteed to terminate without the imposition of an upper bound on the number of steps permitted, and in those instances, distance between the locations (as traversed by the random walk) would be most accurately reported as infinite. The proposed empirical measure, on the other hand, is guaranteed to terminate after a set number of Monte Carlo trials, ultimately predicting concentric contoured zonal 'neighbourhoods' around an origin genotype. Although this is not entirely unlike computing the transition probabilities between all possible pairs of genotypes (such that genotypes associated with transformations of lesser likelihoods are mapped to more distant neighbourhoods), there are subtle (but not inconsequential) differences that preclude using only state transition probabilities.

The infinite population model [4] of the simple genetic algorithm facilitates the conceptualization of the evolutionary mechanism as the product of two state transition matrices – one associated with selection and another associated with the two genetic operators, mutation and recombination. The model also abstracts the finite population of genotypes simulated in a typical genetic algorithm into an infinite population that can be represented as a row vector. Although the function of the selection mechanism is recognized to be dependent on the evaluation function being optimized, the infinite population model does facilitate an investigation of the different probabilities that are associated with random traversals by the genetic operators (with the provision that the available current population, defining the range of the recombination operator, is known). It is relatively simple to derive the state transition probabilities associated with the mutation operator that probabilistically flips each bit of a genotype independently. In contrast, since uniform recombination is a binary operator, it is impossible to express the likelihood that one genotype will be recombined into another independent of the probabilities with which each genotype in the current population might serve as an operand (i.e. be selected as a parent).

Since the approaches by which this limitation might be circumvented exceeds the scope of this paper, it must suffice to state that it is also possible to derive the state transition probabilities [3,10] associated with every possible recombination operation. The matrices for both the mutation and recombination operations can then be combined to derive a matrix representation of the exploratory mechanism of the genetic algorithm. This is referred to as the mixing matrix in the infinite population model [4], and this state transition matrix representation of the exploratory mechanism closely matches the intuition about the distances between genotypes that could be traversed in a single generation by the genetic operators. It can be observed, for instance, that the component matrix associated with mutation is independent of the current population. The matrix associated with recombination, on the other hand, is specified entirely by the current population. The state transition matrix representation of the explorative component accurately conveys the likelihood that one genotype could be subjected to the mutation and recombination operators of a genetic algorithm (for a single generation) and produce another genotype as offspring. It must, however, be emphasized that the genetic algorithm is not expected to navigate genotypic space using traversals of a single generation - ideally, a measure of the traversable distance between genotypes should reflect more than traversals of length 0 and 1.

As a clarifying example, the transition probability matrix associated with the transformation of genotype ■■■■ into □□□□, without a mutation operator and using recombination operators defined by a nonexistent population would, naturally, be a zero matrix. If, however, two genotypes ■■□□ and □□■■ were added to the population, two traversals of length 2 are introduced that can effect the transformation of genotype ■■■■ into □□□□. In spite of the fact that the recombination operation alone can now achieve the traversal from genotype ■■■■ to □□□□, the state transition matrix associated with the explorative component of the evolutionary mechanism would still specify the transition probability between genotypes ■■■■ and □□□□ as 0. This would, naturally, be addressed by raising the transition matrix to an exponent of the number of applications of the mechanism; it is then possible to compute the probability that one genotype can be transformed into another within a specified number of iterations.

Although it might be tempting to use this approach to compute transition probabilities associated with traversals of increasing lengths and attempt to compute an expected transition probability, the authors emphasize that transition probabilities are not equivalent to distance measures. The simple, five state example depicted in Figure 4 below can be used to effectively differentiate the two approaches.

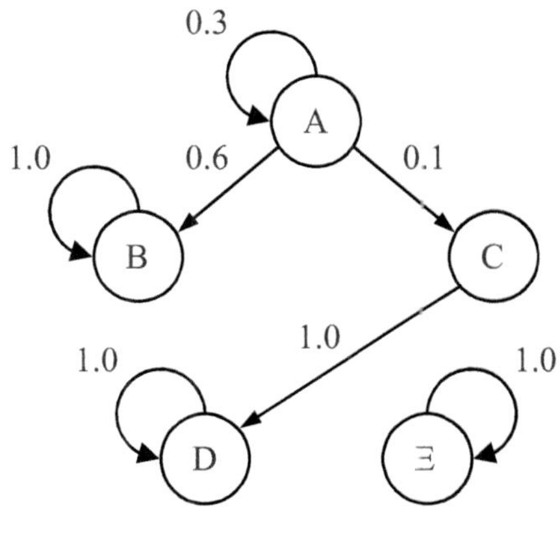

Figure 4. A simple, five state example.

Firstly, it is observed that even though the distance from A to itself should have a value of 0, the transition probability is 0.3. This point aside, it is also observed that the probability associated with the transitions from A to D and from A to E have the same probability, in spite of the fact that the distance from A to E cannot ever be traversed (since no path connects those states). Although this could be addressed by squaring the corresponding transition matrix, the product of a state vector corresponding to state A (i.e., [1.0, 0.0, 0.0, 0.0, 0.0]) with the squared transition probability matrix would be [0.09, 0.78, 0.03, 0.10, 0.00], suggesting that the distance from A to C is somehow more difficult to traverse than the distance from A to D, even though C must be reached before D can be entered and must, therefore, be a lesser distance from A.

Of course transition probability matrices could be used (as part of a more complex approach) to gather measurements that would be equivalent those gathered by the proposed empirical distance measure. This approach was investigated and it was determined (using a correlation analysis) that each distinct iteration of the empirical measurement algorithm does reproduce the behaviour expected by the product of an initial population vector and the transition probability matrix, provided that any nonmaximal values of the product vector are reduced to 0 (as would be expected if the population size could only be guaranteed to support the most likely avenues of traversal). This correlation (between the distance rankings that are specified by adapted state transition matrix approach and those that are specified using the proposed empirical distance measure) is depicted in Figure 5 for an origin genotype ■■■■■■■■ and the explorative component established by a population comprised entirely of genotypes ■■■■■■■□, ■■■■■■□□, ■■■■■□□□, and ■■■■□□□□.

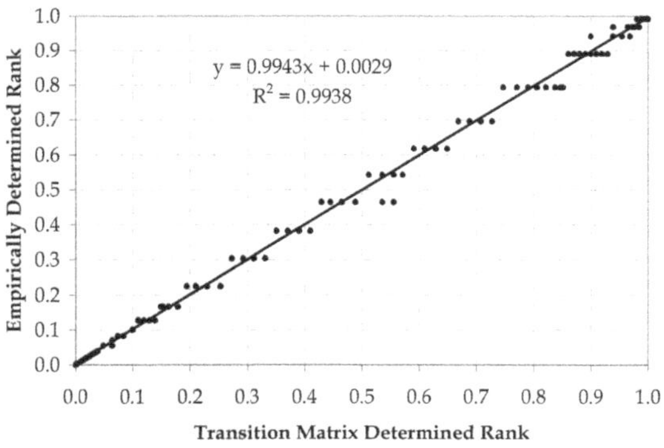

Figure 5. The correlation between the rankings generated by a state transition matrix against those generated by the proposed empirical approach. The strong correlation coefficient is evidence that the empirical approach is valid, and parallels a true genetic algorithm.

Given that transition probabilities could conceivably be used to replicate the behaviour of the empirical distance measure, it should be stressed that the ability of the empirical distance measure to function in the absence of transition probabilities can often prove beneficial. Using the proposed approach, it will be possible for developers exploring new genetic operators to determine the neighbourhood structures induced by those operators without needing to determine the exact transition probabilities. It could also be used as a means to empirically verify proposed transition probabilities, which are often subtle and hard to calculate.

In further validation of the suitability of the empirical approach, if the measure is specified such that only mutation is employed, then, as the Hamming distance is suitable for traversals conducted by mutation alone, the empirically determined ranking of should be strongly correlated with the Hamming distance. As evidenced by Figure 6, the distance rankings that are assigned by each approach are identical, emphasizing that the empirical approach is truly representative of the actual manners in which genotypic space can be traversed (and is, thus, suitable for establishing a baseline against which other measures can be calibrated and evaluated).

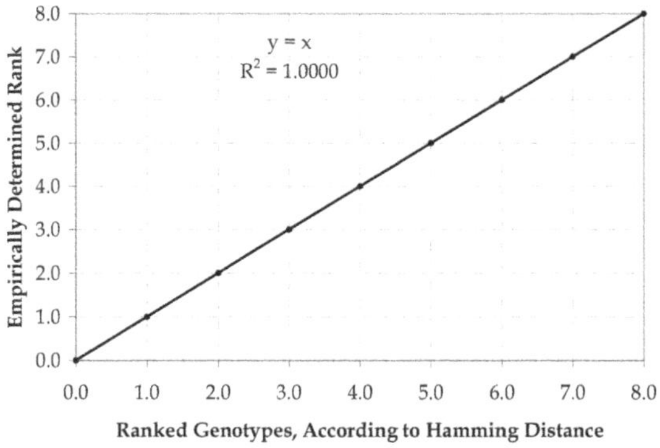

Figure 6. The ranking of genotypes according to their Hamming distance from the origin and by the empirical approach (for an evolutionary mechanism comprised entirely of a mutation operator) are identical.

4. COMPARATIVE EVALUATION

Having established the validity of the proposed approach to empirical distance measurement, it is now possible to evaluate the representativity of distance measurement approaches that require less computational expense; although it has been demonstrated that the empirical measure is representative of the manner in which genotypic space will be traversed, this approach was designed primarily to facilitate the evaluation of other more efficient (but possibly less rigorous) measurement approaches.

The Hamming distance is arguably the most common approach to genotypic spatial distance measurement, but for a measure of distance to be representative of the manner in which genotypic space is traversed by the genetic algorithm, it must reflect traversals by the recombination operator as well as the mutation operator. As such, an alternative (albeit equally simple) measure has been developed for this investigation: the Euclidean distance to the target genotype from the centroid of the population (i.e. the centroid of the set of genotypes that could be used as operands for a recombination operation). Where the Hamming distance is calculated between two genotypes, this simple alternative would be the Euclidean distance between the arithmetic mean of the population and the target genotype. Although it may seem counterintuitive to measure the distance between the origin and the target without considering the origin explicitly, consider that the shortest traversable distance from a location in Manhattan (New York) to London is defined almost entirely by the distance between New York's John F. Kennedy International Airport and the London Heathrow Airport. This distance (between the major airports) would also be highly representative of the shortest traversable distance to London from Queens (New York), Brooklyn (New York), etc.

While this approach is not entirely unreasonable, it must be strongly emphasized that the authors are not suggesting this measure for real-world application – it is introduced here only as a point of reference against which the Hamming distance can be compared. It should also be noted that the Euclidean distance measure described above remains a measurement of the genotypic spatial distance, and is not a measurement defined over phenotype space. The binary genotypes that are frequently used to represent candidate solutions are not real-valued phenotypes and, thus, the Euclidean distance between the phenotypes of candidate solutions would be undefined. That being said, the proposed alternative is not the Euclidean distance between real-valued candidate solutions, but is rather the distance between points in a continuous space interpolated from the discrete binary genotype space – the former representing a binary genotype and the latter being the average value for each genotypic dimension across the population (i.e. the population centroid).

For the following exemplary comparison of the Hamming distance and the Euclidean distance from the population centroid, it is conjectured that the latter will be more representative than the former for genotypic traversals of nontrivial length, because the former offers no consideration for the state of the current population. The comparison was conducted for binary genotypes of length eight, with the same population used previously (establishing the possible operands for a recombination operation), composed of exactly four genotypes: ■■■■■■■□, ■■■■■■□□, ■■■■■□□□, and ■■■■□□□□. Recognizing that the exploratory mechanism of the genetic algorithm includes a recombination operator used to traverse genotypic space in a manner not reflected by the Hamming distance, it is not surprising to observe, as in Figure 7, that the ranking of genotypes by their Hamming distance from the origin does not match the empirically determined rankings. The comparatively stronger correlation between the distance from the centroid and the empirical distance is depicted in Figure 8, corroborating the prediction that a measure that includes consideration for the state of the current population will outperform a measure that does not. Finally, as it might be difficult to deduce the correlation strengths between the rankings determined by each approach from Figures 7 and 8, Figure 9 is also included on the following page. With an R^2 of 0.22, the poor performance of the Hamming distance as a representative measure is very evident, to the point that the use of the Hamming measure is little better than randomly guessing the distance. Contrarily, an R^2 of 0.941 indicates that the ranks assigned by the Euclidean distance from the centroid match the empirically determined results much more closely.

It must be emphasized that the poor performance of the Hamming distance was not unexpected – the Hamming distance was originally designed for use in signal processing, and the Hamming distance between binary strings does not reflect the distance (between the corresponding binary genotypes) that would be traversed by the operators of the genetic algorithm. If, for instance, a population comprised entirely of genotypes ■■■■■■■■ and □□□□□□□□ (in a 1:1 ratio) was subjected to a uniform recombination operation with probability 0.5, the probability that ■■■■■■■■ will be recombined with a member of the population and produce ■□■□■□■□ as an offspring is identical to the probability of producing ■■■■■■■□ as an offspring instead; this is in spite of the fact that the Hamming distance from ■■■■■■■■ to ■□■□■□■□ is four while the Hamming distance from ■■■■■■■■ to ■■■■■■■□ is one. Even so, given that the Hamming distance remains a predominant approach to genotypic spatial distance measurement, it is perhaps surprising that the Hamming distance measure performed as poorly as it did. However, it is important to recognize that this conclusion was the result of a preliminary study, with a small (and selected) population. Consequently, no firm conclusions should be drawn of the universality of these findings: neither from the strong performance of the centroid distance, nor from the excessively weak performance of the Hamming distance.

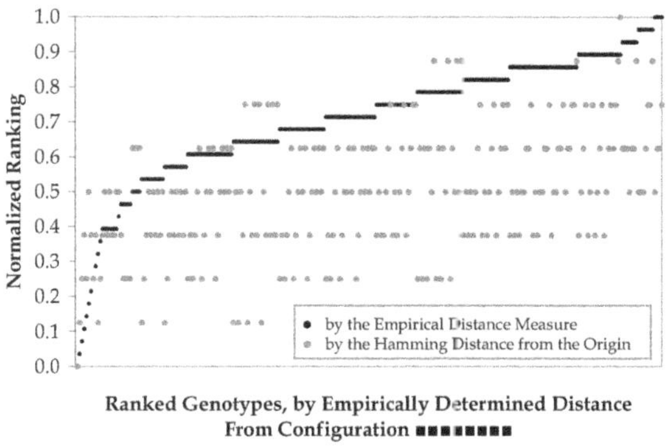

Figure 7. It is evident that the ranking by Hamming distance from the origin is not as representative of the manner in which the space is actually traversed.

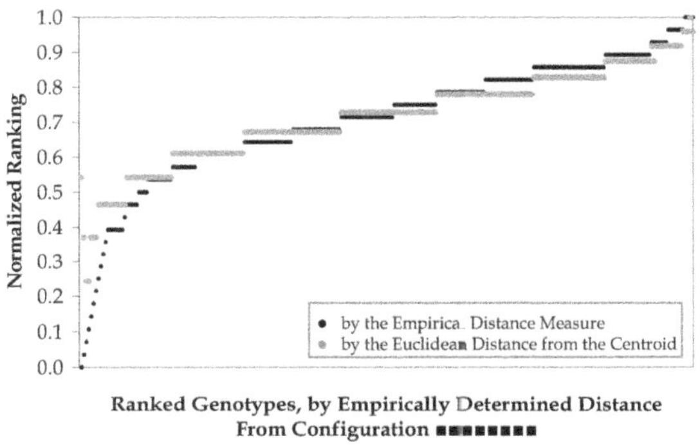

Figure 8. Although a ranking by distance from the population centroid is more representative in general, it is not representative of traversals of a short distance since these are easily traversed without recombination.

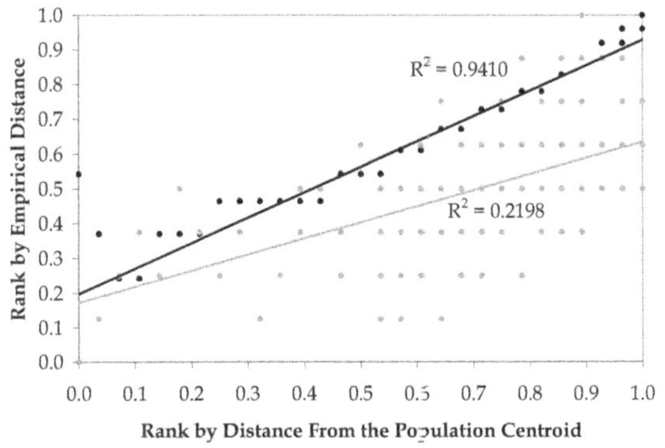

Figure 9. The correlation between the rankings determined empirically, against the ranking of genotypes by the Hamming distance (black) and the distance from the population centroid (gray).

This example has been solely used to demonstrate the utility of the empirical measure, where the results would be non-trivial but still match expectations. Finally, please note that although the analyses were conducted for genotypes of relatively short length, the evaluation function independence of the explorative component of the genetic algorithm (i.e., the mutation and recombination operators, in the absence of selection) yields results that are highly generalizable. It should not surprise the reader that the proposed measure can be computed without fitness function information, because the Hamming distance itself is also fitness function independent (since both the Hamming distance and the empirical distance between two binary strings can be computed without any knowledge of what each of the strings represents).

5. SUMMARY AND CONCLUSIONS

The contributions of this paper can be summarized as follows:

1. An original approach to the measurement of the distance traversed by the operators of the genetic algorithm (using an ordinal measure) was derived from a geometric analogy. This represented a highly intuitive approach to constructing traversals of predetermined, nontrivial distance, and the technique was carefully adapted for empirically measuring distances as they would be traversed by genetic algorithms.
2. To complement the intuitive nature of the proposed measure, the technique was demonstrated to be consistent with the behaviour of a theoretical model of the genetic algorithm. The validity of the technique was also assessed empirically using a state transition matrix example and a single-bit flipping mechanism (which, in this case, performed as expected by precisely replicating the Hamming distance).
3. Finally, the use of the technique was demonstrated with a comparison of the Hamming distance and a simplistic, but more representative, alternative measure. It is well established that the Hamming distance does not reflect traversals by the genetic operators, and the results of the comparative evaluation were consistent with this.

The proposed approach, analogous to a straightforward geometric construction in two dimensions, permits the partitioning of genotypic space into concentric zones, centered on an origin genotypeα. The membership of a genotype β in the ith zone indicates that the length of a traversal from α to β is expected to be greater than a traversal from α to a genotype in the $i\text{-}1^{th}$ zone, but less than a traversal from α to a genotype in the $i+1^{th}$ zone. It is also expected that any traversals starting at α and ending in the ith zone are expected to be the same length. The membership to a zone can, thus, be used to rank genotypes according to their distances from the origin genotype. Although this measure should not to be confused with the more rigorous 'metric' definition (since it can be demonstrated that neither the symmetry nor the subadditivity conditions is upheld), it is invaluable as a basis against which other measures of genotypic spatial distance can be comparatively evaluated. As the empirical approach was designed to emulate a generalized instance of the genetic algorithm (rather than replicate it precisely) the representativity of the results was thoroughly assessed before it was applied in a comparison of the Hamming distance and a simplistic alternative measure. The analysis demonstrated that the Hamming distance is not representative of the genotypic spatial distance that would need to be traversed by the genetic algorithm - a result that is in accord with theoretical analyses.

Representative measures of distance are essential to the development of data visualizations, diversity assessment techniques, and cluster analyses. Unfortunately, it is quite unremarkable to observe the use of an unrepresentative measure in an effort to reduce complexity or computational expense. The application of the Hamming distance as a measure of the distance traversed by the genetic algorithm is one such usage, and the prevalence of this approach impedes the development of novel, more representative measures. Furthermore, the complexity of the genetic algorithm prevents the construction of predetermined, nontrivial traversals that could be used for the calibration and evaluation of novel measures. Consequently, the development and acceptance of novel measures is obstructed, and it was these issues that motivated the development of an empirical approach to the measurement of the distance. The introduction of this measure should facilitate the development and validation of novel measures of genotypic spatial distance, and this will, in turn, lead to more reliable and representative applications.

6. ACKNOWLEDGMENTS

The authors wish to acknowledge partial funding for this research by the Natural Sciences and Engineering Research Council of Canada (NSERC).

7. REFERENCES

[1] U.-M. O'Reilly. "Using a Distance Metric on Genetic Programs to Understand Genetic Operators," in Proceedings of 1997 IEEE International Conference on Systems, Man, and Cybernetics. IEEE Press, vol. 5, pg. 4092-4097, 1997.

[2] T. Jones. Evolutionary Algorithms, Fitness Landscapes, and Search. Ph.D. Thesis, University of New Mexico, Albuquerque, NM, 1995.

[3] A. Nix and M. Vose. "Modeling Genetic Algorithms with Markov Chains," Annals of Mathematics and Artificial Intelligence, Springer Netherlands, vol. 5, pp. 79-88, 1992.

[4] M. Vose. The Simple Genetic Algorithm: Foundations and Theory. MIT Press, Cambridge, MA, 1998.

[5] J. Culberson. "Mutation-Crossover Isomorphisms and the Construction of Discriminating Functions," Evolutionary Computation, vol. 2, pp. 279-311, 1995.

[6] A. Moraglio and R. Poli. "Topological Interpretation of Crossover," in Proceedings of the Genetic and Evolutionary Computation Conference. Springer, vol. 3102, pp. 1377-1388, 2004.

[7] L. Yen, D. Vanvyve, F. Wouters, et al. "Clustering Using a Random Walk Based Distance Measure," in Proceedings of the 13th European Symposium on Artificial Neural Networks. pp. 317-324, 2005.

[8] D. Harel and Y. Koren. "On Clustering Using Random Walks," in Proceedings of the 21st Conference on Foundations of Software Technology and Theoretical Computer Science. Springer, vol. 2245, 2001.

[9] L. Vanneschi, S. Gustafson, and G. Mauri. "Using Subtree Crossover Distance to Investigate Genetic Programming Dynamics," in Proceedings of the 9th European Conference on Genetic Programming. Springer, 2006.

[10] C. Reeves and J. Rowe. Genetic Algorithms: Principles and Perspectives: A Guide to GA Theory. Kluwer Academic Publishers, 2002.

Depictions of Genotypic Space for Evaluating the Suitability of Different Recombination Operators

Robert Collier
School of Computer Science
University of Guelph
Guelph, Ontario, Canada
collierr@uoguelph.ca

Christian Fobel
School of Computer Science
University of Guelph
Guelph, Ontario, Canada
cfobel@uoguelph.ca

Gary Grewal
School of Computer Science
University of Guelph
Guelph, Ontario, Canada
ggrewal@uoguelph.ca

Mark Wineberg
School of Computer Science
University of Guelph
Guelph, Ontario, Canada
mwineber@uoguelph.ca

ABSTRACT

When the genetic algorithm recombines two parent genotypes, the differences between them define a genotypic subspace, and any offspring produced should be confined to this subspace. Although this might seem insignificant, those recombination (or crossover) operators that violate this principle can direct a search away from the region (in genotypic space) that contains the two parent genotypes. This is contrary to the task for which the recombination operator was originally developed and can be detrimental, so this paper introduces a visualization that can be used to detect violations of this principle. The methodology also inspired the development of a different approach to recombining permutations, and a brief case study shows that an alternative recombination operator that does not violate this principle can be used to achieve a performance improvement over previous attempts to optimize Field-Programmable Gate-Array placements using a genetic algorithm. We believe that this technique will be invaluable for developing additional recombination operators.

Categories and Subject Descriptors

I.2.8 [**Artificial Intelligence**]: Problem Solving, Control Methods, and Search – *Heuristic methods.*

General Terms

Algorithms, Measurement, Theory

Keywords

genotypic space visualization, genetic algorithm, recombination.

1. INTRODUCTION

One of the most significant differences between the genetic algorithm and other meta-heuristics is the use of a recombination (or crossover) operator. When the genetic algorithm was first popularized by Holland's work [1] in 1975, he stated that one-point crossover would function such that "each of the ... schemata instanced by the resultant arises from a potentially useful manipulation of schemata already in the pool (those instanced by [the parents])". Equivalently, it was the objective of this operator to generate only those offspring that would explore variations on the subspace defined by the parent genotypes being recombined.

This represents a fundamental property that should govern the behaviour of all recombination operators - *the differences that exist between a pair of parent genotypes defines a genotypic subspace, and any offspring genotype produced from a legitimate recombination of these parent genotypes should be confined to this subspace.* Although the adherence of an operator to this principle might appear trivial when binary genotypes are being recombined, when operators are designed for other (i.e., non-binary) genotypic representations, the locations (in genotypic space) corresponding to the possible offspring are not always considered. Consequently, some recombination operators violate this principle and produce offspring that do not truly represent a variation defined by the two parent genotypes [5].

This can severely hinder the progress of the genetic algorithm – it is recognized [2] that the appeal of recombination is largely the capacity to produce new combinations of features that are already present in the population, but the offspring produced by improper recombination can actually direct the search away from the region that contains the parents. As a result, the recombination operator begins to function as an untuned macromutation operator, to the detriment of the genetic algorithm.

The main contribution of this paper is the development of an intuitive visualization technique that can be used to easily detect violations of this principle. By carefully constructing a two-dimensional representation of genotypic space, the position of every possible offspring genotype (produced from a given recombination operator) can be depicted relative to the positions of the two parent genotypes. It is then possible to conclude, at a glance, if the given recombination operator will violate this principle and produce an offspring that is not a legitimate recombining of the two parents. This paper demonstrates the proposed approach with many different operators for recombining binary and permutation-type genotypes. Since the common partially-mapped recombination operator was shown to violate the aforementioned principle (both here and in [5]), this paper also includes a case study, where the visualization was used to motivate the use of a geometric crossover operator for recombining the possible placements of Field-Programmable Gate-Arrays. This novel approach exhibited a demonstrable improvement in performance.

Since the primary objective of data visualization is to facilitate the acquisition of insight [3] and since the technique described in this paper revealed several violations of a governing principle, we believe that the visualization technique described in this paper will be an invaluable tool in the development of future recombination operators.

The remainder of this paper is organized into five major sections. Section 2 explores the common intuition surrounding recombination and provides valuable insight concerning the adherence or violation of the aforementioned principle. Section 3 will describe the proposed visualization technique, exemplifying it with the common recombination operators. The technique is explored further in Section 4, where a case study (in which the visualization was successfully applied) is presented. Finally, an alternative operator, described in the context of the proposed depictions of genotypic space, is presented and tested in Section 5, with conclusions summarized in Section 6.

2. CONCERNING RECOMBINATION

It is often forgotten that the express purpose of the recombination operator is to shift the algorithm from a greater tendency to perform exploration in the early generations (i.e., to evaluate points in the genotypic space that have not yet been visited by the population) to a greater tendency to perform exploitation in the later generations (i.e., use the genotypes already contained in the population to determine the optimal). Just as much of the established genetic algorithm terminology has its origins in biology, the crossover operation was named after the biological process of crossing-over, defining "an interchange of genes or segments between homologous chromosomes." In contrast with a technique like simulated annealing, where the shift from exploration to exploitation is accomplished explicitly, it is the effect that the current level of population diversity has on the range of the recombination operator that accomplishes this shift in the genetic algorithm.

This is trivially exemplified by the fact that the uniform recombination of two binary genotypes between which there is a maximal Hamming distance (i.e., the two parent genotypes are complementary binary strings) is capable of producing any binary genotype as an offspring, while the application of the same recombination operator to a pair of identical binary strings is incapable of generating offspring that are any different from the initial parent genotype.

Stated simply, the magnitude of the effect of recombination varies directly with the diversity of the population to which it is applied, and since it is widely recognized that the use of a proportional selection strategy results in a trend of decreasing population diversity over time [4], the range of possible offspring of the recombination operator is reduced, diminishing the tendency of the genetic algorithm to explore the search space.

The implicit restriction that two parent genotypes, when recombined, should only produce offspring that are contained in the genotypic subspace defined entirely by those parents, is consistent with the common intuitions about crossing-over in nature. Consider, for example, the recombination of two organisms, where the former possesses a single gene that is expressed as a blue-eyed trait while the latter possesses a different gene (for the same allele) that is expressed as a brown-eyed trait; although human eye colour is polygenic, it is not unreasonable to pose an example where a single trait is expressed by a single gene. Notwithstanding the possibility of a mutation that can change eye color, and independent of the expression of any other gene, it should not be possible to produce an offspring that exhibits something other than blue or brown eyes.

Thus, it follows that if two parents are depicted in a representative multi-dimensional scaling of genotypic space as being separated by some distance Δ, the sum of the distances between the offspring and each of its parents should not exceed Δ. If an offspring was separated from the first parent by a distance of Δ and was not equal to the second parent, it can be deduced that the traversal of genotypic space by recombination was affected by a gene that is different from both parents and would, thus, actually represent a mutation. It can be concluded that a proper recombination operation should produce an offspring whose structure is a function of the parent genotypes alone and, thus, should be contained in the genotypic subspace defined only by its parents.

It should be noted that the effectiveness of recombination is not universally accepted by the research community. There have been several analyses [6–7] that have compared the performance of a genetic algorithm that does employ a recombination operator against a genetic algorithm or evolutionary system that does not employ any recombination operator. In these analyses, when the genetic algorithm that does use recombination is outperformed by the genetic algorithm that does not, it is interpreted as evidence that the usefulness of the binary recombination operators is dubious, or perhaps equivalent to a macromutation operator. Notwithstanding these conclusions, it should be noted that when an offspring genotype is produced by the recombination of two parent genotypes and is not contained in the genotypic subspace defined by these parent genotypes (i.e., the recombination operator has violated the governing principle described above), the appearance of the offspring could correspond to a macromutation and could, quite possibly, be detrimental to the function of the evolutionary mechanism.

3. DEPICTING GENOTYPIC SPACE

3.1 Constructing the Visualization

Experienced researchers will immediately recognize that when two binary genotypes are selected to function as the parents of a recombination operation, if the bit located in the genotype of the first parent, at some index *i*, is the same as the bit located in the genotype of the second parent at index *i*, any offspring produced by a one-point, two-point, shuffle, or uniform crossover operation will not have a genotype value at *i* that differs from that of either parent. Equivalently, each of the possible offspring is a member of the highest order schema that contains both parent genotypes. Although this property should be apparent to experience researchers, it can be visualized, for a specified pair of genotypes, by the meaningful representation of the complete genotypic space of solutions as a two dimensional arrangement of points.

Naturally, before the high-dimensional genotypic space can be represented with fewer dimensions, it is necessary to determine the neighbourhood structure of the space by selecting a useful measure of the genotypic spatial distance that separates two genotypes. Since it is reasonable to state that two genotypes are adjacent if one can be transformed into the other (and vice versa) using a single application of the mutation operator, a mutational distance measure (such as the Hamming distance measure, appropriate for binary genotypes) is used to construct the low-dimensional representation of genotypic space.

Having selected a suitable measure of mutational distance from which a neighbourhood structure can be derived, it is first necessary to assign each element of the genotypic space a value according to the number (and, if necessary, likelihood) of mutations necessary to produce the element if the first parent genotype is selected as the point of origin. For binary genotypes of length λ, this defines $\lambda+1$ sets of genotypes, at Hamming distances 0, 1, 2, ..., λ from the first parent, respectively. If the length λ has a value of 4, with the first parent genotype 0000, the set of genotypes at Hamming distance 0 has cardinality 1 and contains only the element 0000, while the set of genotypes at Hamming distance 1 has cardinality 4 and contains only the elements {0001, 0010, 0100, 1000}, etc. Having established these sets, it can now be stated that an element of the set corresponding to a length λ' can only be transformed (with only a single bit flipped during a mutation operation) into an element of either the set corresponding to length λ'-1 or the set corresponding to length λ'+1. Contrarily, it is not possible for any element to be transformed (with a single application of the mutation operator) to another element of the same set. It is then possible to sort the elements of each set by assigning a value to each element according to the mutational distance that must be traversed to produce that element if the second parent genotype is selected as the point of origin.

By this methodology, each genotype is assigned two values, equivalent to its mutational distance from the first and second parents, respectively. The genotypes can then be depicted using a sequence of diagonals (directed from the top-left to the bottom-right), where the genotype that is separated from the first and second parents by mutational distances X and Y, respectively, is depicted as an element of the Xth diagonal and enumeratively distanced from the center of that diagonal according to distance Y – a design decision made to contribute to the intuitiveness of the resulting depiction. For a length λ of 4 and the first and second parent genotypes 000000 and 000111, respectively, the sequence of diagonals is depicted in Fig. 1.

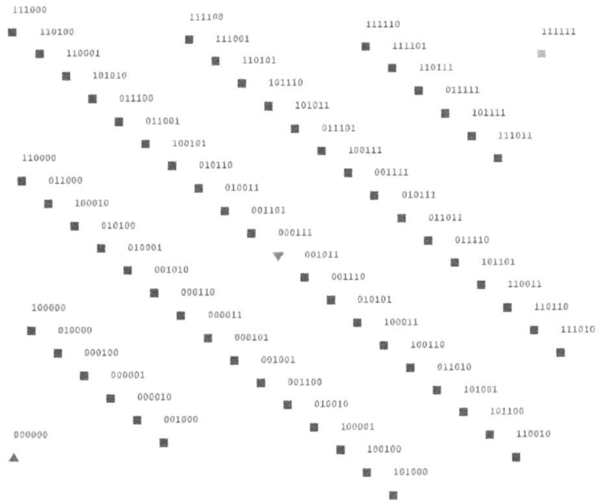

Figure 1. A representation of genotypic space, with two parents, and the complement of the first parent, highlighted.

By arranging the representations of each genotype in a sequence of diagonals (using the methodology described in the preceding paragraph), the first parent is depicted in the bottom left, the genotype (or genotypes) from which it is maximally distant (which, if the genotypes are binary strings, is the complement) is depicted in the top right, and the second parent is represented by the point that intersects the Δth diagonal with the straight-line path from the first parent to its complement. Furthermore, the genotypic subspace defined by the legitimate recombination of the first and second parents (under the assumption that a clone of either the first or second parent would not be considered a recombination) would be entirely contained between the 1st and the $\Delta\text{-}1^{th}$ diagonal, exclusively.

It should be apparent that each point used in this approach to representing genotypic space corresponds to a genotype that may or may not be one of the possible offspring of the first and second parent genotypes. Naturally, it is possible to iterate through all possible applications of a recombination operator between the two parents (and, if necessary, iterate through different sets of parents) and indicate on the depiction whether or not each genotype is a possible offspring. It follows, then, that if a recombination operator was to produce an offspring that was not confined to the genotypic subspace defined by its parent genotypes (and, in so doing, violate the governing principle of recombination described earlier), at least one genotype belonging to the union of the all diagonals between the Δth and the λth would be indicated. This is illustrated in Fig. 2, below.

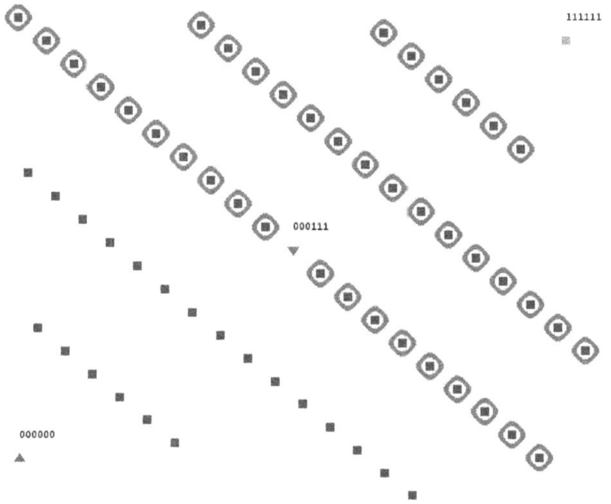

Figure 2. The representation of genotypic space from Fig. 1., adapted to indicate the set of possible offspring genotypes that would correspond to a violation of the principle.

Finally, since each of the depictions created using the preceding method would correspond to the recombination of a specific pair of genotypes, it would be necessary (for any generalizable conclusion) to overlay each depiction corresponding to the recombination of a first parent genotype with any other genotype that is separated from the first by a mutational distance λ. Since the diagonal (or pair of diagonals) with the largest cardinality will always depict the genotypes that are maximally distant from both the first parent and its complement, the visualization from which the most insight can be gathered would be constructed from the recombination of the first parent with every genotype from a diagonal with the largest cardinality.

For the one-point recombination of binary genotypes with a length λ of 4 (and a first parent genotype 0000), the methodology described above would produce Fig. 3, top. As noted previously, this operator was designed to preclude the creation of offspring that are not members of the highest order schema to contain both parents; consequently, it is not surprising that Fig. 3, top, does not indicate a violation of the governing principle described earlier. Contrast this with a hypothetical (and naive) recombination operator that flips the first binary digit of the offspring of a uniform recombination operator. Fig. 3, bottom, was produced for this operator using the same methodology described above, and it is clear from the depiction that this operator has violated the principle described earlier and should be considered suspect.

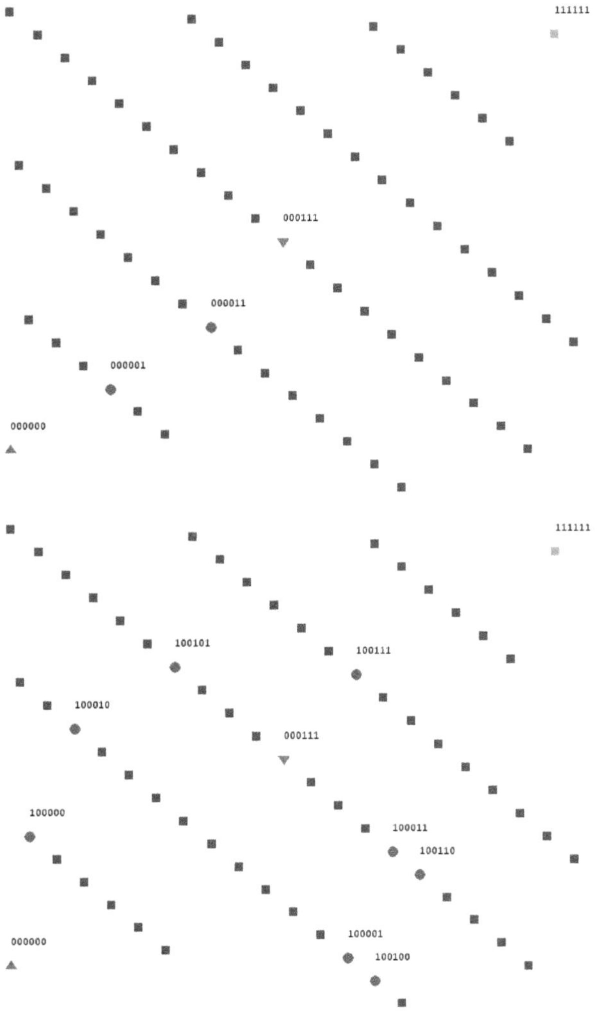

Figure 3. The offspring that could be produced (from parent genotypes 000000 and 000111) by using the one-point recombination operator (top) and by using an operator that performs uniform recombination and then flips the first bit (bottom). The latter operator should not be considered a legitimate recombination operator.

Having demonstrated the approach by which these intuitive visualizations can be constructed, it remains to demonstrate how these depictions can be used to evaluate the validity of different recombination operators.

3.2 Binary Genotype Recombination

Of the specific recombination operators mentioned previously, the two-point, shuffle, and uniform recombination operators have not yet been used for constructing one of the proposed visualizations – these are included as Fig. 4, top, middle, and bottom, for a length λ of 4 and a first parent genotype 0000.

As anticipated, none of the depictions in Fig. 4 has indicated a violation of the principle described earlier. However, as the next subsection will illustrate, several of the recombination operators applied to permutation genotypes (specifically the partially-mapped, order-based, and position-based crossover operators) do not adhere to this principle and should be used with caution.

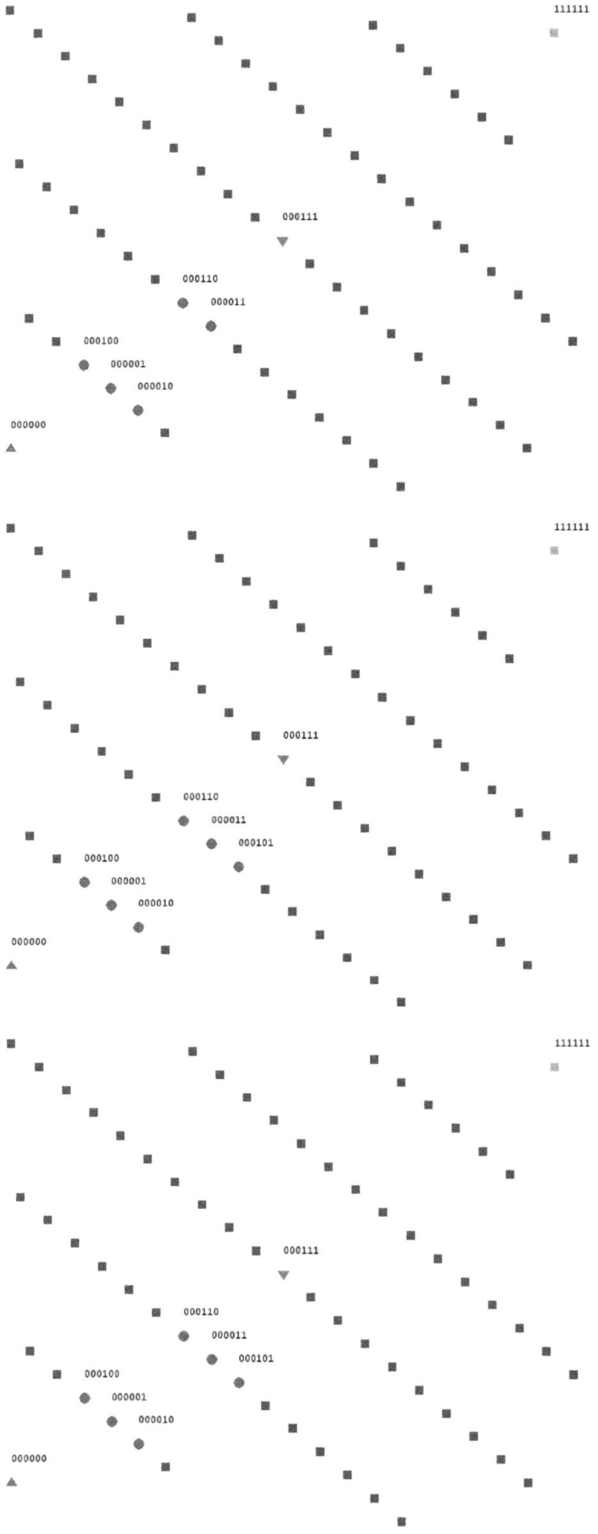

Figure 4. The offspring that could be produced (from parent genotypes 000000 and 000111) by using the two-point recombination operator (top), the shuffle recombination operator (middle), and the uniform recombination operator (bottom) operators. Contrast these with the depiction in Fig. 3 (top) of the offspring that could be produced by using the one-point recombination operator.

3.3 Permutation Genotype Recombination

For binary genotypes, offspring are assigned positions (in the representation) according to their Hamming distances from the two parent genotypes. This produces a visualization that depicts the traversal of genotypic space in an intuitive manner – namely that the result of a single mutation of a parent genotype will be assigned a position that is proximate to the location of the parent. By arranging the representation thusly, it is easy to conceptualize the crossover of a subset of genes (differing between the two parents) as a sequence of mutation operations applied to one of the parents. For example, if 000000 and 111111 are recombined to produce offspring genotype 000011, 000011 is depicted (and can be conceptualized) as though it were the mutation of the 5th and 6th bit of the first parent (or, equivalently, the mutation of the first four bits of the second parent). This approach facilitates the notion that the distance between two parent genotypes can be traversed using either (or both) of the genetic operators.

Thus, when applying the proposed visualization approach to a non-binary genotype, it is first necessary to establish the operation that will define the distance between pairs of genotypes. Where the Hamming distance was equivalent to the number of mutation operations necessary to transform one binary genotype into another, there are several mutation operations suitable for application to permutation genotypes [8]. Since the exchange of the values at two randomly selected positions in a permutation is probably the most logical approach to mutating permutations, the distance measured between permutations (for constructing the visualization) will be a count of the number of exchange operations necessary to transform one permutation into another. It follows, then, that a permutation genotype does not have a single complement. The sequence (1, 2, 3), for example, is as distant (in terms of the number of necessary exchanges) from sequence (2, 3, 1) as it is from sequence (3, 1, 2). Consequently, when the genotypes are first arranged by their distance from the first parent (with the most distant genotypes assigned to the top-right corner), several genotypes will be placed along the diagonal that is maximally distant from the point corresponding to the first parent.

3.3.1 Partially-Mapped Recombination

Probably the most common approach to the recombining of permutations is the partially-mapped recombination operator [8], where an attempt is made to exchange a subsequence of the permutation of one parent with that of the other to form a novel sequence. Naturally, this approach will frequently create a sequence that is not, itself, a valid permutation, and in circumventing this problem, partially-mapped recombination constructs a mapping of the individual elements of the subsequence of the first parent with the corresponding elements of the subsequence of the second parent. This mapping is then used to translate the first and second parents into two distinct offspring.

Although this does ensure that the offspring generated from valid permutations will themselves be valid, the set of possible offspring is not confined to the solution subspace specified by the parents, constituting a violation of the principle described earlier. This can be detected by applying the proposed visualization technique to the permutations (1, 2, 3, 4, 5) and (4, 5, 2, 1, 3), and the result is included in Fig. 5. Since it is evident that the representation (4, 3, 5, 1, 2) was assigned to the third diagonal, its distance from the first parent would be covered by three exchange operations. However, since it is also separated from the second parent by several operations, it is not truly a recombination of the parents – it has been subjected to an operation that made it more distant from the first parent without bringing it nearer the second.

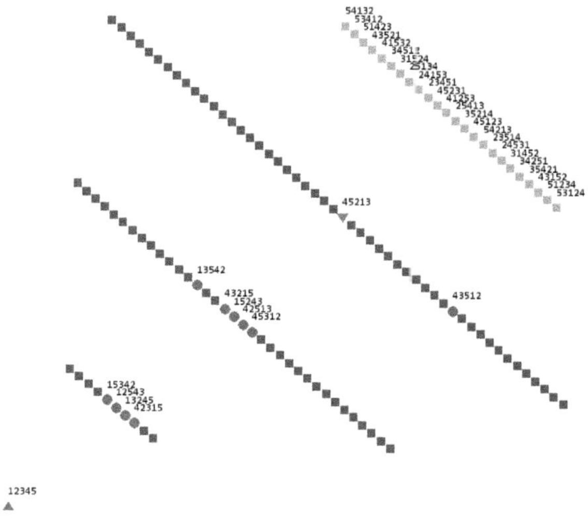

Figure 5. The possible offspring associated with the partially-mapped recombination of (1, 2, 3, 4, 5) and (4, 5, 2, 1, 3).

3.3.2 Order-Based Recombination

Unlike partially-mapped recombination, the lesser-known order-based recombination operator attempts to exchange data by transmitting the relative ordering of some subset of the integers of the permutation [8]. To clarify, a set of indices are randomly selected (independently, from a uniform distribution) to specify a subset of the integers of each permutation, and the ordering of those integers in one parent is imposed on a copy of the other parent to create the offspring. Although this approach differs dramatically from partially-mapped recombination, this operator also violates the aforementioned principle. The application the proposed visualization technique to the same permutations in the previous example is included in Fig. 6 and indicates that several genotypes are possible offspring in spite of the fact that they are not confined to the subspace defined by the parent genotypes.

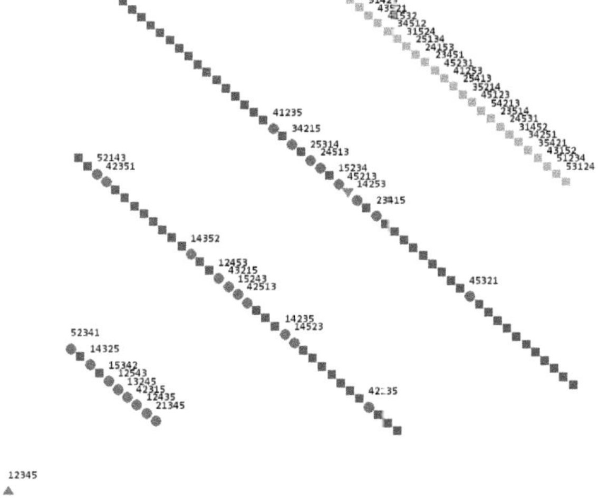

Figure 6. The possible offspring associated with the order-based recombination of (1, 2, 3, 4, 5) and (4, 5, 2, 1, 3).

Although there are several other common approaches to recombining of permutations that violate the principle described earlier, it would exceed the scope of this paper to include the necessary depictions for each of them. Thus, having demonstrated that the proposed visualization approach can be used to detect violations of the principle mentioned earlier, the next section will present a case study where the same methodology was used to explore whether the use of typical permutation recombination operators might be partially responsible for the relatively poor performance of the genetic algorithm at optimizing the placements of Field-Programmable Gate-Arrays. To provide further evidence in support of the hypothesis that the violations of the principle mentioned earlier are (at least partially) responsible for the relatively poor performance of the genetic algorithm, a different recombination operator, motivated directly from the previous depictions of genotypic space, was explored as an alternative.

4. INVESTIGATING FPGA PLACEMENT

Field-Programmable Gate-Array (FPGA) technology is essential to electronics companies, as it allows for the implementation of digital systems without the costs, risks, and delays associated with application specific integrated circuits. Although the optimization of FPGA placements has been previously attempted [9–11] using genetic algorithms, these approaches have met with limited success. Since genetic algorithms are frequently able to outperform single-point optimization techniques, the relatively poor performance of the genetic algorithm at FPGA placement surprised the authors and motivated an exploratory investigation into any factors might account for the relatively poor performance. Since the proposed visualization technique was successfully applied in this investigation, uncovering the problems associated with the common approaches to permutation recombination, the results of this investigation are presented here as a case study. Fig. 7 depicts the fundamental components of the Island Style FPGA architecture [12], including the programmable interconnect network as well as the tiles that contain at least one configurable logic block or I/O block.

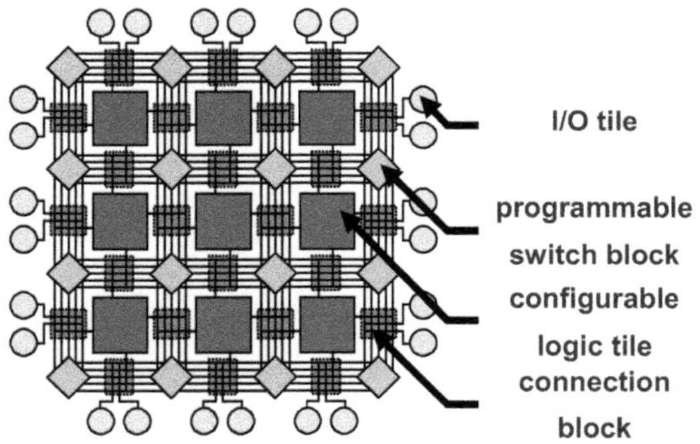

Figure 7. The Island Style Field Programmable Gate Array architecture.

FPGA placement begins with an architecture definition (defining the layout, number and capacity of tiles) along with a netlist of logic blocks (which includes configurable logic blocks and I/O pads) and the interconnections between them for the circuit to be placed. The result of placement is the physical assignment of all blocks and pads in the netlist to the target FPGA architecture. Although the minimization of critical-path delay and power are important objectives, when performing placement the most basic objective is to minimize the total wire-length [13] required to connect all blocks as defined in the netlist. The genetic algorithm represents one possible approach to the task of minimizing the wire-length, by maintaining a population of valid candidate solutions to an FPGA placement problem and then subjecting this population to processes that emulate the evolutionary ideas of natural selection.

4.1 Genetic Algorithm Approach

The first step in implementing a genetic algorithm is to determine an appropriate technique for representing candidate solutions. This representation will define the space of candidate solutions to be searched, and the topology of this space must be considered before the genetic operators (mutation and recombination) are selected. For the task of optimizing the placement of M logic blocks in a region of N possible configurable tiles, it should be noted that a simplification of the FPGA placement problem could be considered equivalent to the task of selecting M tiles (one for each logic block to be placed) out of the N available tiles. Consequently, the most common approaches to representation (for this problem) employ a sequence of integers to either specify the element of the set of tiles that is associated with each block [14], or to specify the element of the set of blocks that is associated with each empty tile [10].

Our analysis opted for the latter representation, using a sequence of N integers to represent each placement such that each integer was taken from the interval [-1, M), with values between 0 and M corresponding to the logic block with the same index, and the value -1 corresponding to every tile to which a block has not been assigned. This is essentially a permutation of integers (wherein any duplicate values of -1 are permitted) and is demonstrated in Fig. 2. While there are many other approaches to the representation of a candidate solution to an FPGA placement problem, and the representation selected will most certainly impact the effectiveness of the different genetic operators, we selected the permutation representation for our experiment because of its widespread usage in the research community.

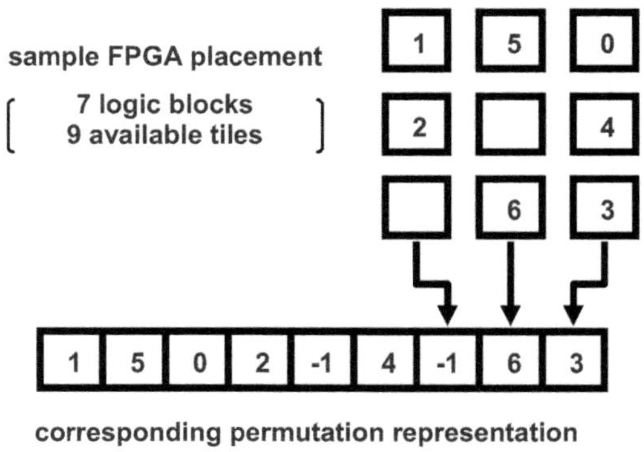

Figure 8. A permutation representation of the assignment of 7 blocks to the 9 tiles of an FPGA.

Naturally, since candidate solutions were to be represented using permutation genotypes, the most common genetic operators for permutations were investigated. It was at this point that the proposed visualization technique indicated that the typical partially-mapped, order-based, and position-based recombination operators would each violate the governing principle described earlier. It was conjectured that these violations might be partially responsible for the relatively poor performance exhibited by the genetic algorithm when solving FPGA placement problems, so an alternative operator (suitable for application to permutation genotypes) was developed. This operator, referred to herein as confined-swap recombination, was designed so as to preclude violation of the principle described earlier, with no additional computational expense.

5. CONFINED-SWAP RECOMBINATION

A swapping path is operationally defined for this case study as a sequence of exchange operations, from one parent to another such that each subsequent exchange operation produces an offspring that is further from the first parent and nearer to the second parent. With this definition, a confined-swap recombination operation will only produce offspring that belong to at least one of the unique swapping paths that connect one parent to another.

The operator first iterates over the two parent representations to identify the differences between them that could conceivably be exchanged to produce the offspring. A one-to-one and onto relation is then defined between the corresponding values of the subsequence of each parent, and then random elements of the set of ordered pairs (i.e., exchange operations) defined by this relation are selected and applied. Following the application of each exchange operation, the relation is updated to reflect any changes to the index of a value that was affected by the operation. In so doing, regardless of the number of individual exchanges performed, the representation of the offspring solution will never be moved to a position that is further from the first parent without also being moved closer to the second parent. The pseudocode for the proposed confined-swap operator is presented in Algorithm 1.

Algorithm 1. Confined-Swap Recombination

```
given parents P and P' of length N
struct V = {value; to; from;}
for i = 1:N
 if P(i) <> P'(i)
  add P(i) to V
for i = 1:N
 if P(i) <> P'(i)
  V(P(i)).from = i
  V(P'(i)).to = i
until enough elements crossed over
 random select an element E of V
 swap E.from with E.to
 V(E.to) = E.from
end
```

It must be emphasized that the time complexity associated with this operator is no worse than that of partially-mapped recombination (i.e., O(N) where N is the representation length). However, as this form of recombination only performs exchanges that move the possible offspring representation nearer to the second parent by the same distance they are moved further from the first parent, the set of possible offspring will never exit the subspace specified by the parents.

With a recombination operator that adheres to the aforementioned principle while remaining suitable for application to permutation representations of candidate solutions to the FPGA placement problem, it remained to verify the conjecture that the use of this operator would result in a performance improvement over the use of other permutation recombination operators. For a valid evaluation of the proposed operator, a control genetic algorithm was implemented (with two member tournament selection and standard exchange mutation) for each of the confined-swap, partially-mapped, and order-based recombination operators. Having established that the partially-mapped recombination operator fails to uphold a hypothetically crucial principle, the order-based operator was included only to provide an additional point of reference.

Each of the three recombination operators was tasked with the FPGA placement optimization problem associated with each of 14 different MCNC [15] benchmarks, using bounding box wire-length cost [13] to evaluate fitness. The results conclusively demonstrated, with an extremely high level of statistical significance (i.e., all p-values remaining less than 0.001 after Bonferonni post hoc correction) that the use of the confined-swap operator on permutation representations of candidate FPGA placement problem solutions universally resulted in a substantial improvement over the performance of partially-mapped recombination, which was, itself, demonstrably superior to order-based recombination. These results are summarized in Table 1.

Table 1. Mean best performance for each operator.

	Recombination Operator		
Benchmark	Confined-Swap	Partially-Mapped	Order-Based
alu4	467.04 ± 11.57	523.24 ± 2.97	538.03 ± 2.27
apex2	726.90 ± 6.71	796.95 ± 5.03	817.63 ± 3.52
apex4	388.31 ± 3.82	435.26 ± 2.58	447.30 ± 3.59
bigkey	688.57 ± 8.09	758.49 ± 4.69	781.25 ± 2.97
Des	681.07 ± 7.16	765.00 ± 3.69	776.00 ± 3.22
diffeq	525.28 ± 8.67	578.66 ± 3.44	597.13 ± 2.52
Dsip	502.98 ± 5.56	561.99 ± 3.23	572.62 ± 1.79
elliptic	1865.36 ± 30.89	2047.57 ± 10.34	2111.28 ± 6.85
ex5p	328.03 ± 2.43	365.71 ± 2.25	376.76 ± 2.45
misex3	443.48 ± 3.37	495.15 ± 3.19	508.47 ± 1.62
s298	612.98 ± 15.96	644.52 ± 3.85	673.97 ± 3.04
Seq	648.30 ± 10.55	700.40 ± 3.57	717.57 ± 3.18
Spla	2049.92 ± 25.17	2138.41 ± 8.42	2205.09 ± 8.10
tseng	303.99 ± 3.03	349.39 ± 3.06	359.35 ± 3.33

To further illustrate the performance improvement that was achieved through the use of the alternative recombination operator, Fig. 10 below depicts the best performance achieved by each of the three operators implemented (the confined-swap, partially-mapped, and order-based recombination operators, respectively) on each of the MCNC benchmarks tested, with the results normalized such that the best operator receives a score of zero while the worst receives a score of one. The normalized standard deviation is also depicted, but should not be interpreted as a confidence interval – all statistical significance testing was conducting using the nonparametric version of the student t-test (i.e., a student t-test performed on the ranks associated with each value), ensuring the validity of the comparison.

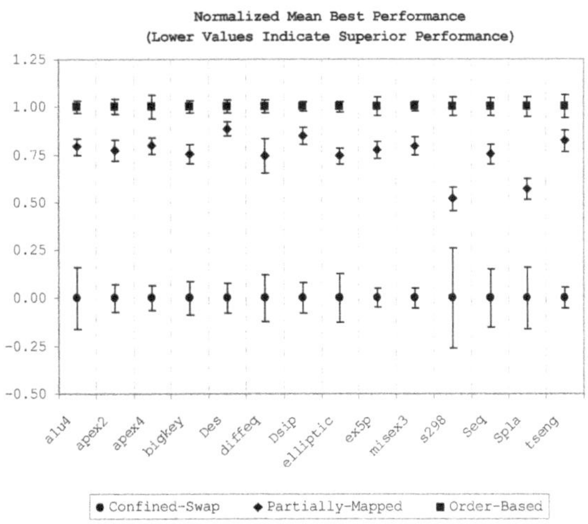

Figure 10. A normalization of the best fitness achieved using each of the three recombination operators (confined-swap, partially-mapped, and order-based) on each of the 14 MCNC benchmarks.

6. CONCLUSIONS

Based on the results of the comparative evaluation described in the previous section, the case study conclusively demonstrated that the alternative recombination operator can be used to achieve a significant performance improvement over that which can be achieved by partially-mapped crossover. Since the proposed visualization technique provides both the motivation and intuition for this operator, this case study clearly demonstrates that these visualizations can be applied, by both designers and practitioners, in the development of genetic algorithms that are more consistent with the principles of the original design.

Although the representation of high-dimensional genotypic spaces is fraught with complications, the proposed construction of a two-dimensional scatter representation, where genotypes are depicted relative to the absolute positions assigned to parent genotypes, provides a simple and intuitive methodology for determining the range of possible offspring that can be produced with a given operator. This represents an efficient and effective approach for detecting significant (and often detrimental) deviations from the expected behaviour of a recombination operator, and we believe that the visualization we have developed (and successfully applied) will be an invaluable tool in the advancement of the genetic algorithm.

7. ACKNOWLEDGMENTS

The authors wish to acknowledge partial funding for this research by the Natural Sciences and Engineering Research Council of Canada (NSERC).

8. REFERENCES

[1] J. Holland, Adaptation in Natural and Artificial Systems, 1975.

[2] J. Culberson. "Mutation-Crossover Isomorphisms and the Construction of Discriminating Functions," Evolutionary Computation, vol. 2, no. 3, pp. 279-311, 1995.

[3] J. van Wijk. "The Value of Visualization," in Proceedings of IEEE Visualization, 2005, pp. 79-86.

[4] D. Goldberg, Genetic Algorithms in Search, Optimization, and Machine Learning. Addison-Wesley Publishing, Inc., 1989.

[5] A. Moraglio, R. Poli. "Topological Crossover for the Permutation Representation," Intelligenza Artificiale, vol. 5, no. 1, pp. 49-70, 2011.

[6] D. Fogel and L. Stayton. "On the Effectiveness of Crossover in Simulated Evolutionary Optimization," Biosystems, vol. 32, no. 3. pp. 171-82, 1994.

[7] J. Schaffer and L. Eschelman. "On Crossover as an Evolutionarily Viable Strategy," in Proceedings of the 4th International Conference on Genetic Algorithms, pp. 61-68, 1991.

[8] M. Buckland, AI Techniques for Game Programming, 1st ed. Course Technology PTR, 2002.

[9] M. Rubio-Solar, M. A. Vega-Rodriguez, J. M. S. Perez, A. Gomez-Iglesias, and M. Cardenas-Montes, "A FPGA Optimization Tool Based on a Multi-island Genetic Algorithm Distributed over Grid Environments," in Cluster Computing and the Grid, IEEE International Symposium on, Los Alamitos, CA, USA, 2008, pp. 65-72.

[10] M. Yang, A. Almaini, and P. Wang, "FPGA placement optimization by two-step unified Genetic Algorithm and Simulated Annealing algorithm," Journal of Electronics (China), vol. 23, no. 4, pp. 632-636, Jul. 2006.

[11] P. Jamieson, "Persistent CAD for in-the-field Power Optimization," in ERSA, 2010, pp. 267-270.

[12] W. Wolf, FPGA-based system design. Prentice Hall, 2004.

[13] V. Betz and J. Rose, "VPR: a new packing, placement and routing tool for FPGA research," in Field-Programmable Logic and Applications, 1997, pp. 213-222.

[14] P. Jamieson, "Revisiting Genetic Algorithms for the FPGA Placement Problem," International Conference on Genetic and Evolutionary Methods, 2010.

[15] S. Yang, "Logic synthesis and optimization benchmarks user guide version 3.0," MCNC, Jan, 1991.

Estimating the Evolution Direction of Populations to Improve Genetic Algorithms

Andrea De Lucia[1], Massimiliano Di Penta[2], Rocco Oliveto[3], Annibale Panichella[1]
[1]University of Salerno, Via Ponte don Melillo - 84084 Fisciano (SA), Italy
[2]University of Sannio, Viale Traiano - 82100 Benevento, Italy
[3]University of Molise, C.da Fonte Lappone - 86090 Pesche (IS), Italy
adelucia@unisa.it, dipenta@unisannio.it, rocco.oliveto@unimol.it, apanichella@unisa.it

ABSTRACT

Meta-heuristics have been successfully used to solve a wide variety of problems. However, one issue many techniques have is their risk of being trapped into local optima, or to create a limited variety of solutions (problem known as "population drift"). During recent and past years, different kinds of techniques have been proposed to deal with population drift, for example hybridizing genetic algorithms with local search techniques or using niche techniques. This paper proposes a technique, based on Singular Value Decomposition (SVD), to enhance Genetic Algorithms (GAs) population diversity. SVD helps to estimate the evolution direction and drive next generations towards orthogonal dimensions. The proposed SVD-based GA has been evaluated on 11 benchmark problems and compared with a simple GA and a GA with a distance-crowding schema. Results indicate that SVD-based GA achieves significantly better solutions and exhibits a quicker convergence than the alternative techniques.

Categories and Subject Descriptors

I.2.8 [**Computing Methodologies**]: Artificial Intelligence - Problem Solving, Control Methods, and Search—*Heuristic methods*

General Terms

Algorithms, Experimentation.

Keywords

Genetic Algorithms, Singular Value Decomposition.

1. INTRODUCTION

In past and recent years, meta-heuristics have been proven to be very successful to deal with problems that could not be solved analytically, e.g., NP-complete problems. Despite that, a challenge many researchers have is to efficiently solve highly dimensional problems—where the number of local optima increases exponentially with the problem dimension—and for which an optimization algorithm may be trapped in the local optima of the objective function.

Since the 1960s, several stochastic optimization techniques inspired to the natural evolutionary process, called evolutionary algorithms, have received considerable attention for solving such kinds of complex problems. Genetic Algorithms (GAs), one of the most popular algorithm in this class, is a simple stochastic search technique introduced by Holland [11] in the 1970s. GAs have been successfully applied in several fields of science and engineering (e.g., fuzzy systems, neural networks), and offer several practical advantages such as conceptual simplicity, robustness to dynamic changes and flexibility. The intrinsic parallelism of GAs, due to multiple evolving solutions (i.e., individuals of a population) mitigates, but does not completely solve, the risk of being trapped into local optima. The difficulty of finding the global optimum can be due to inability of standard GA to identify the best direction of evolution and to accelerate the evolution in different directions [7]. Thus, solving high dimensionally problems with multiple local solutions remain a challenge for researchers.

In recent years considerable effort has been dedicated to improve the efficiency of GA in terms of convergence rate and solution accuracy. In order to reach such a goal previous studies suggest to (i) combine GA with a complementary local search technique [7] (e.g., simulated annealing), (ii) modify standard genetic operators [13], or (iii) use niche techniques [19]. Incorporating a local search method within a GA can improve the search performance; indeed, a hybrid algorithm should find a balance between exploration and exploitation, in order to solve global optimization problems. Since the division of the hybrid's time between the two methods influences the efficiency and the effectiveness of the search process, designing a well balanced hybrid GA is an important issue [7]. Diversity preserving techniques are very useful for increasing diversity between individuals within population with the aim at improving the performance of GA for multimodal and locally multimodal problems. However, these techniques push only for the diversity of individuals, thus they reduce the probability to converge to some local optimum without increasing the convergence speed of GAs [20].

In this paper, we propose the use of a linear algebra technique, the Singular Value Decomposition (SVD) [21], to (i)

GECCO'12, July 7-11, 2012, Philadelphia, Pennsylvania, USA.

estimate the current *evolution direction* of a population and (ii) drive the next generations along orthogonal directions. In particular, for evolution direction we intend the direction along which the best individuals of population are evolving in the genotype space across two different generations. From a theoretical point of view, the estimated current evolution direction can be used to improve the convergence speed of a GA for convex problem where the convergence rate of standard GAs is very low [23]. In addition, driving the next generations along directions that are orthogonal with respect to the current evolution direction improves the probability of converging to a global optimum. In summary, the main contributions of this paper can be summarized as follows:

1. the paper introduces the concept of evolution direction, into a genotype space, of a population across different generations;
2. the paper presents an approach to evaluate the evolution direction across different generations. Such an approach is based on linear algebra principles and theorems;
3. the paper defines an intuitive approach for accelerating the evolution of future generations along orthogonal directions.

We have investigated the effectiveness of the proposed algorithm by solving 11 benchmark test functions having 50 dimensions each. Both convex unimodal and high-dimensional multimodal functions are considered in the conducted case study to make the results generalizable. The achieved results indicate the (statistically significant) superiority of the proposed GA as compared to a standard GA and a GA enriched with a distance-crowding schema.

The rest of the paper is organized as follows. Section 2 provides background information about two fundamental aspects of our work: the population drift problem and SVD. Section 3 presents the proposed approach to estimate the evolution direction and identify an orthogonal sub-population of individuals with respect to the current population. Section 4 presents the design and the results of our numerical experiment, while Section 5 concludes the paper highlighting directions for future work.

2. BACKGROUND

This section provides background information about two fundamental aspects of our work: the population drift problem in GAs and the SVD, which is used to estimate the evolution direction.

2.1 Genetic Algorithms and Population Drift

The optimization problem considered in this paper can be formalized as follows:

$$\begin{array}{lll} \textit{minimize} & f(x) = f(x_1, x_2, \ldots, x_n) & \\ \textit{subject to} & x_i^{\min} \leq x_i \leq x_i^{\max} & i = 1, 2, \ldots, n \end{array}$$

where $f(x)$ denotes the objective function, $x = (x_1, \ldots, x_n)$ is a variable vector defined in $\mathbb{R}^n$, while $x^{\min} = (x_1^{\min}, \ldots, x_n^{\min})$ and $x^{\max} = (x_1^{\max}, \ldots, x_n^{\max})$ define the feasible solution space. The domain of x_i is denoted by $[x_i^{\min}; x_i^{\max}]$ and the feasible solution space by $[x^{\min}; x^{\max}]$.

Conceptually, the problem consists in finding a solution—within the space of possible solutions—that provides the minimum value for the objective function. When the search space becomes large, and the objective function depends on the problem dimension, there is need for using a specific technique to find the global optimum. To this aim, a GA tackles the problem by means of its intrinsic parallelism, i.e., having multiple solutions (individuals) evolving in parallel to explore different parts of the search space. The pseudo code of a simple GA (as described by Goldberg [8]) is:

Algorithm 1 Simple Genetic Algorithm

```
1: i ← 0;
2: generate P_i;
3: evaluate P_i;
4: while not (termination condition) do
5:     apply crossover and mutation on P_i to yield C_i;
6:     evaluate C_i;
7:     select P_{i+1} from P_i and C_i;
8:     i ← i + 1;
9: end while
```

where P_i and C_i are *parents* and *offspring* of the ith generation respectively.

GA is a stochastic search technique based on the mechanism of natural selection and natural genetics. The search starts with a random population (2) where each individual represents a solution to the global optimization problem. The population evolves through subsequent generations and, during each generation, the individual are evaluated (3) using a fitness function to be optimized. To create next generation, new individuals (*offspring*) are generated by either (i) recombining two individuals from the current generation using the *crossover* operator; and (ii) modifying individuals using the *mutation* operator (5). A new generation is made by selecting—according to the fitness values—some parents and offspring in order to keep the population size constant (7). Best individuals have higher probability to survive in the next generation.

When solving a global optimization problem using GAs, it is generally difficult to maintain the diversity of the solutions with the risk to be trapped in a local optimum of the search space. Indeed, a GA tends to create a limited number of group of solutions (*niches*), that are close to each other in the criterion space, leaving the rest of the search space empty and sparsely populated. This phenomenon is known as *population drift* (or *genetic drift*) [17].

Niching methods, based on the mechanism of *natural ecosystems*, have been proposed to reduce the population drift resulting from the selection operator in the standard GA [11, 5]. They maintain population diversity and allow the GA to investigate many search sub-spaces in parallel.

The *fitness sharing method* is probably one of the most known and used niching technique. It was originally introduced by Holland [11] and further formalized by Goldberg and Richardson [9]. Fitness sharing modifies the fitness function by reducing the payoff in densely populated regions. Using such an approach each individual's fitness value is decreased by an amount nearly equal to the number of similar individuals in the population.

Another approach to deal with the population drift is the *crowding method* [5], that inserts new individuals in the population by replacing similar individuals. In the standard crowding method [5, 19], an offspring replaces the most similar individual (in terms of genotypic comparison) taken from a randomly drawn subpopulation of size *cf* (*crowding factor*) from the global population. Mahfoud [14] improved the standard crowding schema by introducing competition between children and parents of identical niches. After crossover and mutation, each child replaces the nearest parent if the child has a higher fitness.

Even if the crowding method can mitigate the population drift problem, it has been originally designed for finding multiple, distinct solutions to multimodal optimization problems. Harik *et al.* [10] proposed the Restricted Tournament Selection (RTS) to adapt standard tournament selection for multimodal optimization. RTS initially selects two elements from the population to undergo crossover and mutation. After recombination, a random sample of *cf* individuals is taken from the population as in standard crowding.

We share with the aforementioned approaches the need to have a population with individuals having different characteristics aiming at mitigating the population drift problem. However, differently from previous approaches, the proposed approach does not analyze single population. We propose to estimate the evolution direction (considering several populations) in order to enrich the population with new individuals that allow the investigation of completely different search sub-spaces.

2.2 Singular Value Decomposition

In this section we assume a familiarity with the basic terminology of linear algebra and refer the reader to [21] for a more complete coverage.

Two vectors x and y are orthogonal if $x^T y = 0$, where x^T demotes the transpose of vector x. In two or three-dimensional space this simply means that the vectors are perpendicular. Let A be a $m \times n$ matrix where m and n are arbitrary, a *Singular Value Decomposition* (SVD) of A is a factorization [21]:

$$A = U \Sigma V^T$$

where $U \in \mathbb{R}^{m \times m}$ and $V \in \mathbb{R}^{n \times n}$ are orthonormal matrices and $\Sigma \in \mathbb{R}^{m \times n}$ is a diagonal matrix. In addition, the diagonal entries σ_j of Σ are non negative and in non-increasing order. Thus, $\sigma_1 \geq \sigma_2 \geq \cdots \geq \sigma_r \geq 0$ where $r = \min(m, n)$. The m columns of U, called *left singular vectors*, are orthonormal eigenvectors of AA^T while the n columns of V, called *right singular vectors*, are orthonormal eigenvectors of $A^T A$, and Σ is a diagonal matrix containing the square roots of eigenvalues from U or V in descending order.

The SVD of a matrix A is typically computed in two steps [21]. In the first step, the matrix is reduced to a bi-diagonal matrix[1]. The computational complexity of this step is $\mathcal{O}(m \cdot n^2)$, assuming that $m > n$. In the second step, an iterative method is applied to compute the SVD of the bi-diagonal matrix. This method requires $\mathcal{O}(n)$ iterations, where each iteration has a complexity of $\mathcal{O}(n)$. Thus, the overall cost of SVD is $\mathcal{O}(m \cdot n^2)$ [22].

SVD is a factorization of a real or complex matrix, with many useful applications in different fields. In numerical analysis, the SVD provides a measure of the effective rank of a given matrix [21], while in statistics and time series analysis, the SVD is particularly useful tool for finding least-squares solutions and approximations [12]. The properties of SVD can be successfully used in image processing for compression and noise reduction [16], as well as in Information Retrieval to deal with linguistic ambiguity issues [6].

SVD has also been employed for characterizing protein molecular dynamics trajectories [18]. Similar to this work, we propose to integrate SVD in a GA to (i) estimate the evolution direction of a population and (ii) add to the population individuals with different characteristics, allowing the GA to explore many search sub-spaces in parallel.

[1] A bi-diagonal matrix is a matrix with non-zero entries along the main diagonal and either the diagonal above or the diagonal below.

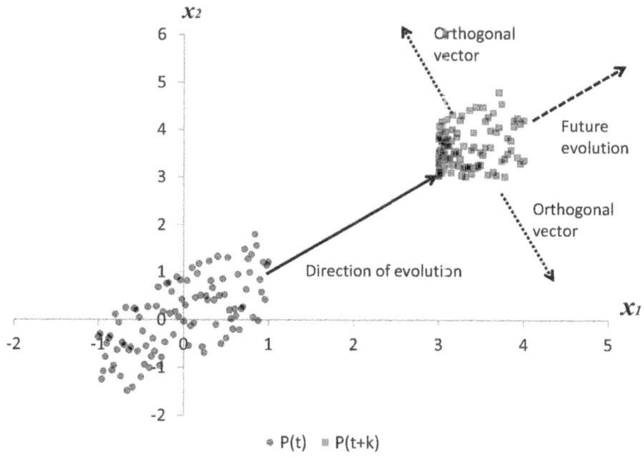

Figure 1: Geometrical representation of the evolution direction and its orthogonal vectors.

3. EVOLUTION DIRECTION OF POPULATIONS

This section describes how to estimate the evolution direction of a population across different GA generations, aiming at improving the performance of simple GAs. We first discuss on the utility of estimating where a population is evolving in the search space and how such information can be used for generating sub-populations with orthogonal evolution, i.e., containing individuals with different characteristics. Then, we describe an approach, based on SVD, for computing (i) the evolution direction and (ii) sub-populations with an orthogonal evolution. Finally, we present and discuss the SVD-based GA.

3.1 Why Estimating the Evolution Direction

During the evolution of a GA, best individuals have higher probability to be selected for generating offspring individuals using crossover and mutation operators. Since these operators are intrinsically based on randomness, it would not be possible to clearly identify the evolution direction of the GA. However, it is possible to identify where the best individuals of population are evolving in the genotype space (or search space) across two different generations. We can define such movements of individuals within genotype space as *evolution direction*. Figure 1 shows an example of the evolution direction of a population after k generations in a two dimensions optimization problem. It is important to note that we are not interested in measure the evolution direction of each individual; instead, we are rather interested in measuring the main evolution direction of the whole population or the best part of it.

For an optimization problem characterized by a continuous feasible region with only lower and upper bounds, estimating such direction for an optimization problem can be useful for:

1. accelerating the next generation along the current direction of evolution in order to improve the convergence speed for convex problems where the convergence rate of a simple GA is very low;
2. driving the next generation along directions that are orthogonal with respect to the current evolution direction adding to the population new individuals. This allows the investigation of completely different search sub-spaces reducing the probability of a GA to be trapped in local optima of the objective function.

All these considerations suggest that the evolution direction can be used for modeling an evolutionary preserving diversity technique. Indeed, most used preserving diversity techniques try to increase population diversity using only information about the current generation, without extracting any information about how population is evolving. Another important aspect to be highlighted is that the evolution direction should be estimated in the genotype space to separate the complexity of the estimation method from the complexity of the fitness function.

The next section describes an approach to compute the evolution direction within genotype space using the SVD factorization.

3.2 How to Estimate the Evolution Direction

In this paper we propose to use the SVD for estimating the evolution direction and generate sub-populations of individuals with an orthogonal evolution direction as compared to the individuals of the current population. The basic idea is that a population of solutions P provided by GA at generation t can be viewed as an $m \times n$ matrix

$$P_t = \begin{bmatrix} p_{1,1} & p_{1,2} & \cdots & p_{1,n} \\ p_{2,1} & p_{2,2} & \cdots & p_{2,1} \\ \vdots & \vdots & \ddots & \vdots \\ p_{m,1} & p_{m,2} & \cdots & p_{m,n} \end{bmatrix}$$

where n is the problem dimensionality, i.e. the number of independent variables, m is the population size and the generic entry $p_{i,j}$ denotes the values of the variable x_j in the ith individual. SVD can be applied on such a matrix $(P_t = (U_t \cdot \Sigma_t \cdot V_t^T))$ for identifying and ordering the dimensions along which the individuals exhibit the most variation. In particular, we suggest to use *eigenvalues* and *eigenvectors* obtained applying SVD on the matrices representing the populations of two different generations. The goal is to estimate the current *evolution direction* of the population across different generations and driving the future generations along orthogonal directions.

In this context, the column vectors of V represent the main directions along which a population is distributed, while the diagonal elements of Σ represent the *importance* of each main direction v_j for the population distribution. Since the diagonal elements $\sigma_{i,i}$ of Σ are in descending order, the correspondent vectors $V = \{v_1, v_2, \ldots, v_n\}$ are sorted according to their importance. Thus, the population exhibits the first largest variation along the direction v_1, the second largest variation along the direction v_2, and so on.

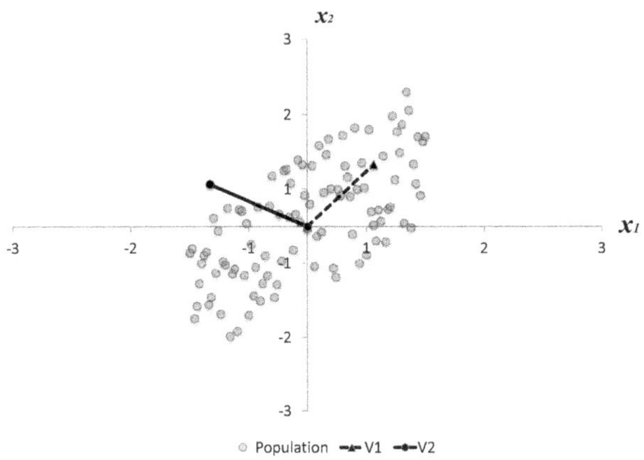

Figure 2: Graphical interpretation of SVD.

Figure 2 shows a population in a two-dimensional space and the correspondent column vectors of V. It can be noted how the right singular values of V, i.e., the column vectors v_1, v_2 in the figure, represent the main directions (eigenvectors) along which the population is distributed. It is also important to note that v_1, v_2 are two orthonormal vectors, thus they represent only the main directions of P without bringing information about how important they are. Such information is provided by the diagonal elements σ_1 and σ_2 in Σ that measure the importance (eigenvalues) of the main directions for such a population. As it can be seen in the example of Figure 2, the population exhibits the largest variation along v_1 ($\sigma_1 \geq \sigma_2$) confirming the theoretical definition of SVD.

Clearly, different populations have different SVD factorizations. Thus, a simple way to estimate the directions along which a population is evolving after k generations consists of comparing the decomposition $\{\Sigma_t, V_t\}$ at generation t with $\{\Sigma_{t+k}, V_{t+k}\}$ at generation $t+k$. Formally, let $P_t = (U_t \cdot \Sigma_t \cdot V_t^T)$ and $P_{t+k} = (U_{t+k} \cdot \Sigma_{t+k} \cdot V_{t+k}^T)$ be two SVD factorizations of a population at two different generations t and $t+k$, respectively. We can define the following matrices:

$$\overline{V} = V_{t+k} - V_t$$

$$\overline{\Sigma} = \Sigma_{t+k} - \Sigma_t$$

where $\overline{V}$ estimates the *direction* along which the population is evolving (*evolution direction*) and $\overline{\Sigma}$ measures the *magnitude* of the evolution. Starting from these matrices it is possible to generate a new population P^*_{t+k} having a direction of evolution that is orthogonal to actual one as follows:

$$P^*_{t+k} = U_{t+k} \cdot (\Sigma_{t+k} + \overline{\Sigma}) \cdot (V_{t+k} + Orth(\overline{V}))^T$$

where $Orth(\overline{V})$ is a matrix whose column vectors are unit and orthogonal with respect to column vectors of $\overline{V}$, i.e., $Orth(\overline{v_i})$ is orthogonal to $\overline{v_i}$ for $i = 1 \ldots n$. Since the number of orthogonal column vectors is infinite, a good choice would be to randomly generate such vectors.

Assuming that all individuals in the initial population are feasible solutions, every time the orthogonal population P^*_{t+k} is computed there might be several new individuals that violate one or more constraints of the optimization problem.

Table 1: List of test functions used in our numerical experiment. The number of variables is $n = 50$.

Test Function	Equation	Solution Space
Rastrigin's function	$f_1(x) = \sum_{i=1}^{n} (x_i^2 - 10 \cos(2 \pi x_i) + 10)$	$[-5.12; 5.12]^n$
Ackley's function	$f_2(x) = -20\, exp \left(-0.2 \sqrt{\frac{1}{n} \sum_{i=1}^{n} x_i^2}\right) - \exp\left(\frac{1}{n} \sum_{i=1}^{n} \cos(2 \pi x_i)\right) + 20 \exp(1)$	$[-32; 32]^n$
Griewangk's function	$f_3(x) = \frac{1}{4000} \sum_{i=1}^{n} x_i^2 - \prod_{i=1}^{n} \cos \frac{x_i}{\sqrt{i}} + 1$	$[-600; 600]^n$
Generalized penalized functions 1	$f_4(x) = \frac{\pi}{n} \left\{10 \sin^2(\pi y_i) + \sum_{i=1}^{n-1} (y_i - 1)^2 [1 + 10 \sin^2(\pi x_{i+1})] + (y_n - 1)^2 \right\} + \sum_{i=1}^{n} u(x_i, 10, 100, 4)$	$[-50; 50]^n$
	$u(x_i, a, k, m) = \begin{cases} k(x_i - a)^m & x_i > a \\ 0 & -a \leq x_i \leq a \\ k(-x_i - a)^m & x_i < -a \end{cases}, \quad y_i = 1 + \frac{1}{4}(x_i + 1)$	
Generalized penalized functions 2	$f_5(x) = \frac{1}{10} \left\{\sin^3(3 \pi x_i) + \sum_{i=1}^{n-1} (x_i - 1)^2 [1 + \sin^2(3 \pi x_{i+1})] + (x_n - 1)^2 [1 + \sin^2(2 \pi x_n)]; \right\} + \sum_{i=1}^{n} u(x_i, 5, 100, 4)$	$[-50; 50]^n$
Normalized Rana function	$f_6(x) = \frac{\sum_{i=1}^{n-1} \left((x_{i+1} + 1) \cos \sqrt{\lvert x_{i+1} - x_i + 1 \rvert} \sin \sqrt{\lvert x_{i+1} - x_i + 1 \rvert} + (x_i + 1) \cos \sqrt{\lvert x_{i+1} - x_i + 1 \rvert} \sin \sqrt{\lvert x_{i+1} - x_i + 1 \rvert}\right)}{n}$	$[-500; 500]^n$
Sphere model	$f_7(x) = \sum_{i=1}^{n} x_i^2$	$[-100; 100]^n$
Schwefel's Problem 2.22	$f_8(x) = \sum_{i=1}^{n} \lvert x_i \rvert + \prod_{i=1}^{n} \lvert x_i \rvert$	$[-10; 10]^n$
Schwefel's Problem 2.21	$f_9(x) = \max \{\lvert x_i \rvert, i = 1, 2, \ldots, n\}$	$[-100; 100]^n$
Schwefel's Problem 1.2	$f_{10}(x) = \sum_{i=1}^{n} \left(\sum_{j=1}^{n} x_j\right)^2$	$[-100; 100]^n$
Schwefel sin root function	$f_{11}(x) = \sum_{i=1}^{n} -x_i \sin \sqrt{\lvert x_i \rvert}$	$[-512; 512]^n$

We push these individuals p^* back into the feasible region as follows:

$$p_i^* = \begin{cases} x_i^{\min} & p_i^* \leq x_i^{min} \\ p_i^* & x_i^{min} \leq p_i^* \leq x_i^{max} \\ x_i^{\max} & p_i^* \geq x_i^{max} \end{cases} \qquad i = 1 \ldots n$$

3.3 SVD-based GA

Based on the observations made in previous section, we propose to modify the general structure of a simple GA as follows:

Algorithm 2 SVD-based Genetic Algorithm

$t \leftarrow 0$;
generate P_t;
$oldGen \leftarrow P_t$;
evaluate P_t;
while not (termination condition) **do**
  apply crossover and mutation on P_t to obtain C_t;
  evaluate C_t;
  select P_{t+1} from P_t and C_t;
  if mod(t,k)=0 **then**
    sort P_{t+1} according to their fitness value;
    $lastGen \leftarrow P_{t+1}$;
    generate P_{t+1}^* applying SVD on 50% of the best individuals of *oldGen* and *lastGen*;
    replace 50% worst individuals of P_{t+1} with P_{t+1}^*;
    $oldGen \leftarrow P_{t+1}$;
  end if
  $t \leftarrow t + 1$;
end while

where $mod(t, k) = 0$ denotes the modulo operation (i.e., the remainder of the division t/k), and k represents the number of generations between two populations to be considered for computing the orthogonal sub-population P_{t+1}^* (*SVD-Frequency*). Let N be the total number of generations; the sub-population P_{t+1}^* will be computed $\lfloor N/k \rfloor$ times, i.e., each k generations.

With the aim of estimating the evolution direction as much accurately as possible, we suggest to compute such an orthogonal population considering only the 50%[2] best individuals of the two populations P_t and P_{t+k} and then to replace the worst 50% individuals of the last generation P_{t+k} with the new (generated) orthogonal sub-population.

It is important to note that the proposed SVD-based GA estimates the evolution direction within the genotype space, thus the use of SVD does not require further fitness function evaluations. Moreover, the computational complexity of SVD is polynomial with respect to the population size and the number of variables—as described in Section 2.2—and does not depend on the complexity of the fitness function.

4. EMPIRICAL EVALUATION

This section reports the design and results of an experiment aiming at analyzing the benefits of the proposed SVD-GA as compared to other GAs. Specifically, we compared the proposed SVD-GA with a simple GA as described by Goldberg [8], and a GA with a distance crowding schema (DC-GA) as defined by De Jong [5].

The implementation of all the algorithms is based on the MATLAB's Global Optimization Toolbox [15]. For the DC-GA and GA algorithms we used the routine *ga*, while parameter values described in Section 4.2 are set using *gaoptimset*. The proposed SVD-GA algorithm is also implemented in Matlab by customizing the routine *ga*. In all three alternatives the *elitist selection* was used, which allows some of the better individuals from the current generation to carry over to the next generation unaltered [1].

4.1 Test Functions

The three algorithms have been experimented on 6 multimodal and 5 unimodal benchmark functions [2, 13, 23] reported in Table 1. For some of them the Matlab imple-

[2]We empirically identified such a value using a trial-and-error process.

mentation is available online[3]. Functions $f_1 - f_6$ are multimodal functions where the number of local minima increases exponentially with the problem dimension (i.e., the number of independent variables). Instead, functions $f_7 - f_{11}$ are high-dimensional unimodal problems that, because of their convexity, cause poor or slow convergence of the optimization algorithms to a single global minimum. All the benchmark functions considered in our case study are deemed to be representative of difficult classes of problems for many optimization algorithms (including evolutionary algorithms) [2, 13, 23].

It is worth noting that for unimodal functions, it is more useful to analyze the convergence rates than the final results of fitness function. Instead, for multimodal function, the final results are much more important since they represent the ability of an optimization algorithm to escape from local optima and moves toward (near) global optimum.

For all benchmark functions we set the problem dimension (n) to 50 in order to increase the difficulty in obtaining the global optimum. Note that previous works usually set such a number to 30 [2, 13, 23].

4.2 GA Parameter Settings

For each of the experimented GA, we adopted the same parameter values or scheme as done in previous studies (for example [13]):

Population size: we choose a moderate population size. We set $p = 100$ that is equal to twice the problems dimension.

Initial population: for each of test function the initial population is uniformly and randomly generated within the solution spaces reported in Table 1.

Number of generations: we select different number of generations that vary on the basis of the different problem complexities. Table 2 also reports the maximum number of generations for each test functions.

Fitness scaling function: we adopt a fitness scaling rank scheme, that scales the raw scores based on the rank of each individual instead of its score. The rank of an individual is its position in the sorted scores: the rank of the best individual is 1, the next most fit is 2, and so on.

Crossover function: we use arithmetic crossover with probability $P_c = 0.60$.

Mutation function: we use a uniform mutation function with probability $P_m = 0.02$ for f_1 and f_8 that have a lower search space, while $P_m = 0.05$ is used for all the other functions.

Stopping criterion: if the fitness value of the best individual cannot be further optimized in the subsequent 50 generations, then the execution of the GA is stopped.

Elitism: the number of individuals in the current generation that are guaranteed to survive to the next generation is 2.

SVD-Frequency: orthogonal sub-populations are generated by SVD every two generations (i.e., $k = 2$). This parameter applies only for SVD-GA.

[3]http://www.maths.uq.edu.au/CEToolBox/node3.html

4.3 Data Collection and Analysis

We run the three algorithms 50 times, on each test function. For each run, we store the number of generations and the best values achieved. Once collected all the data, we computed the descriptive statistics (i.e., median, mean, and standard deviation) of the best values achieved in each run.

We also statistically compare the results achieved by SVD-GA and the other two GAs on each test functions. The statistical analysis is used to test the following null hypothesis:

> *There is no difference between the best values achieved by SVD-GA and GA (or DC-GA) when solving the test problem f_i.*

where $i = 1 \ldots 9$. To compare samples from two data sets (e.g., the best values achieved in each run by the SVD-GA and GA) and test our hypotheses, we use the Wilcoxon Rank Sum test [4]. In all our statistical tests we consider p-values < 0.05 as statistically significant, i.e., we accept a 5% chance of rejecting a null hypothesis when it is true [4]. However, since three pairwise tests are necessary (simple GA vs SVD-GA, simple GA vs. DC-GA, and SVD-GA vs. DC-GA), we reject the null hypothesis if all p-values are smaller than $\frac{0.05}{3} = 0.016$, i.e., we correct p-values using the Bonferroni correction [4]. Other than testing the hypotheses, we also estimate the magnitude of the difference between performances achieved by two GAs. To this aim, we use the Cohen d effect size [4]. For dependent samples (to be used in the context of paired analyses) it is defined as the difference between the means (M_1 and M_2), divided by the standard deviation of the (paired) differences between samples (σ_D):

$$d = \frac{M_1 - M_2}{\sigma_D}$$

The effect size is considered *small* for $0.2 \leq d < 0.5$, *medium* for $0.5 \leq d < 0.8$ and *large* for $d \geq 0.8$ [3]. We chose the Cohen d effect size as it is appropriate for our variables and given the different levels (small, medium, large) defined for it, it is quite easy to be interpreted.

4.4 Analysis of the Results

Table 2 reports the performances of the three experimented GAs, namely SVD-GA, DC-GA, and GA. As can be seen, the mean function values of SVD-GA are very close to the optimal ones and the values of the standard deviation are small. These results indicate that SVD-GA can find optimal or close-to-optimal solutions, and its solution quality is quite stable.

Comparing the SVD-GA performances with traditional GAs, it is easy to note that our approach turns out to be very useful for highly dimensional multimodal problems where the number of local optima is very high. Table 2 shows how SVD-GA provides solutions that are several orders of magnitude lower than those of simple GA. Indeed, it provides more accurate global optimum for the functions $f_1 - f_6$ demonstrating the ability to surf on the search space with lower probability to be trapped in local optima. This result confirms our theoretical finding: *producing orthogonal sub-populations using SVD represents a preserving diversity technique robust and effective.*

Moreover, the proposed GA has higher convergence speed for unimodal functions $f_7 - f_{11}$ than the others. With the same number of generations, SVD-GA provides solutions

Table 2: **Performances of SVD-GA, a GA with distance crowding (DC-GA), and a simple GA.**

f	Generations	SVD-GA			DC-GA			Simple GA			f_{min}
		Median	Mean	St. dev.	Median	Mean	St. dev.	Median	Mean	St. dev.	
f_1	1,000	0	0	0	0.08	0.56	0.86	0.08	0.46	0.76	0
f_2	500	8.88×10^{-16}	2.45×10^{-15}	1.95×10^{-15}	0.55	0.53	0.25	0.57	0.62	0.35	0
f_3	500	6.17×10^{-10}	8.96×10^{-10}	8.99×10^{-10}	0.47	0.49	0.11	0.49	0.50	0.10	0
f_4	500	1.23×10^{-11}	3.40×10^{-11}	1.11×10^{-10}	0.03	0.06	0.06	0.03	0.08	0.12	0
f_5	500	3.71×10^{-10}	4.89×10^{-10}	4.27×10^{-10}	0.30	0.34	0.19	0.33	0.34	0.17	0
f_6	1,500	-470.24	-473.32	9.37	-455.10	-454.69	8.28	-457.68	-456.83	8.91	-512.27
f_7	500	6.41×10^{-167}	7.20×10^{-152}	5.09×10^{-151}	1.32	1.43	0.51	1.37	1.38	0.41	0
f_8	500	1.59×10^{-74}	4.17×10^{-66}	2.48×10^{-66}	0.58	0.60	0.13	0.58	0.59	0.10	0
f_9	500	1.99×10^{-81}	6.93×10^{-65}	4.90×10^{-64}	2.82	2.81	0.42	2.79	2.82	0.40	0
f_{10}	1,000	9.43×10^{-39}	5.85×10^{-03}	1.75×10^{-02}	929.23	916.41	213.43	854.45	883.09	200.04	0
f_{11}	1,000	-20,949.12	-20,915.17	71.62	-20,454.17	-20,394.24	244.17	-20,356.95	-20,329.81	250.98	-20,949.14

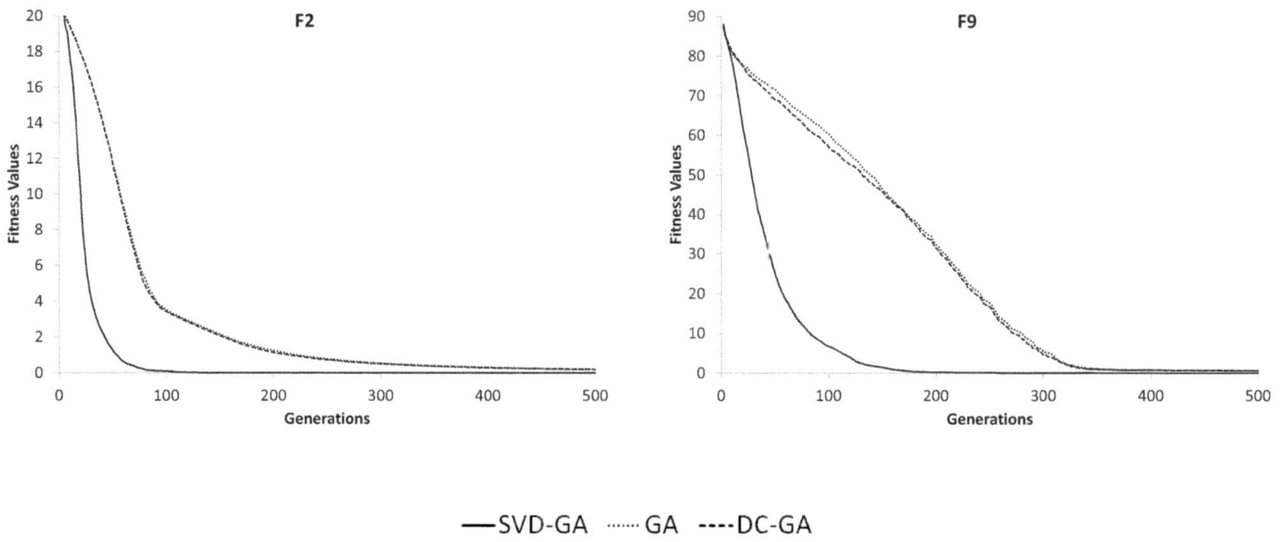

Figure 3: Comparison between convergence speeds of SVD-GA, GA, DC-GA.

that are several orders of magnitude lower than the simple GA, regardless of whether the distance crowding schema is adopted or not. A particular case is represented by the function f_{10} that is a highly convex unimodal function. For that function the convergence speed of the simple GAs is very low. In particular, after 1,000 generations the mean function value achieved by the SVD-GA is lower than 0.01 (very close to 0 that represents the global optimum), while DC-GA and GA provide mean function values greater than 900 and 850, respectively. This indicates that *the use of SVD for estimating the evolution direction of the population increases the convergence speed of GA for convex problems accelerating the evolution.*

To provide further evidence of the benefits provided by the proposed approach, Figure 3 compares the mean values (across the 50 runs) of the best fitness values for f_2 (a multimodal function) and f_9 (a convex unimodal function) achieved by the three algorithms at each generation of the evolutionary process. As for f_2 it can be seen how SVD-GA quickly converges (only 100 generations are required), while the other two algorithms have a lower convergence rates and are still trapped in some local optima after 400 generations. Turning to f_9, it is easy to note how SVD-GA converges to unique global optimum in less than 200 generations, while GA and DC-GA employ more than 300 generations to converge to a near optimum value. It is worth noting that in both cases the improvement achieved by distance crowding is negligible when compared with the convergence speed improvement achieved by SVD-GA. The same graphs related to the test functions show consistent results and are not shown due to space limitation.

The results discussed above are also confirmed by the statistical analysis. Table 3 reports the results of the Wilcoxon rank sum test and the Cohen d effect size. Since in all the cases the p-values are smaller than 0.016, we can reject our null hypotheses, concluding that the fitness function values provided by SVD-GA are statistically better than values achieved by both DC-GA and GA. In addition, the magnitude of the improvement (measured by the effect size) is *large* in 9 out of 11 cases. In the other two cases, the effect size is *medium* when comparing SVD-GA with the other GAs on the function f_1, and when comparing SVD-GA with DC-GA on the function f_4.

5. CONCLUSION AND FUTURE WORK

The paper introduced the concept of *evolution direction* across different generations of a GA, and explained how to use such an information to (i) improve the convergence speed of GA and (ii) increase diversity of population driving evolution in completely different search sub-spaces. Based on

Table 3: Results of the Wilcoxon tests.

f	SVD-GA *vs.* DC-GA		SVD-GA *vs.* Simple GA	
	p-value	effect size	p-value	effect size
f_1	< 0.001	0.61	< 0.001	0.66
f_2	< 0.001	2.07	< 0.001	1.74
f_3	< 0.001	4.55	< 0.001	4.92
f_4	< 0.001	0.63	< 0.001	0.90
f_5	< 0.001	1.77	< 0.001	2.06
f_6	< 0.001	1.24	< 0.001	1.25
f_7	< 0.001	2.78	< 0.001	3.37
f_8	< 0.001	4.68	< 0.001	5.88
f_9	< 0.001	6.68	< 0.001	7.01
f_{10}	< 0.001	4.29	< 0.001	4.41
f_{11}	< 0.001	2.05	< 0.001	2.28

that, the paper proposed an approach based on Singular Value Decomposition (SVD) to compute the evolution direction and identify orthogonal sub-populations of individuals.

The proposed SVD-based GA has been used to solve 11 benchmark functions having 50 independent variables each. Results achieved from 50 independent runs for each test function indicated the higher convergence speed for unimodal problems of SVD-GA as compared to a simple GA, and a GA with a distance crowding schema. Also, for the same number of generations of the two alternative approaches, SVD-GA provides solutions that are several order of magnitude better. Moreover, it provides better global optimum values for multimodal problems, demonstrating the ability to surf on search space with lower probability to be trapped in local optima.

There are a number of directions for future work. First, we will replicate the study considering other benchmark functions and different genetic operators. Second, we will apply the proposed algorithm on different kinds of optimization problems, for example constrained global optimization problems with non-linear constraints. Moreover, since our approach does not require any modification of genetic operations, it can be combined with other enhancing strategies (as for example hybrid genetic algorithms). Finally, we will investigate whether the evolution direction is useful for solving multi-objective optimization problems where diversity techniques are really important for producing a wider Pareto front.

6. REFERENCES

[1] C. W. Ahn and R. Ramakrishna. Elitism-based compact genetic algorithms. *IEEE Transactions on Evolutionary Computation*, 7(4):367 – 385, 2003.

[2] K. Chellapilla. Combining mutation operators in evolutionary programming. *IEEE Transactions on Evolutionary Computation*, 2(3):91 –96, 1998.

[3] J. Cohen. *Statistical power analysis for the behavioral sciences.* Lawrence Earlbaum Associates, 2nd edition, 1988.

[4] W. J. Conover. *Practical Nonparametric Statistics.* Wiley, 3rd edition, 1998.

[5] K. A. De Jong. *An analysis of the behavior of a class of genetic adaptive systems.* PhD thesis, University of Michigan, 1975.

[6] S. Deerwester, S. T. Dumais, G. W. Furnas, T. K. Landauer, and R. Harshman. Indexing by latent semantic analysis. *Journal of the American Society for Information Science*, 41(6):391–407, 1990.

[7] T. A. El-Mihoub, A. A. Hopgood, L. Nolle, and A. Battersby. Hybrid genetic algorithms: A review. *Engineering Letters*, 13(2):124–137, 2006.

[8] D. E. Goldberg. *Genetic Algorithms in Search, Optimization and Machine Learning.* Addison-Wesley Longman Publishing Co., Inc., 1st edition, 1989.

[9] D. E. Goldberg and J. Richardson. Genetic algorithms with sharing for multimodal function optimization. In *Proceedings of the Second International Conference on Genetic Algorithms on Genetic algorithms and their application*, pages 41–49, Cambridge, MA, USA, 1987. Lawrence Erlbaum Associates.

[10] G. Harik. Finding multimodal solutions using restricted tournament selection. In *Proceedings of the Sixth International Conference on Genetic Algorithms*, pages 24–31, Pittsburgh, PA, USA, 1995. Morgan Kaufmann.

[11] J. H. Holland. *Adaptation in Natural and Artificial Systems.* University of Michigan Press, 1975.

[12] N. Holter, A. Maritan, M. Cieplak, N. Fedoroff, and J. Banavar. Dynamic modeling of gene expression data. In *Proceedings of the National Academy of Sciences of United States of America*, volume 98, pages 1693–1698, 2001.

[13] Y.-W. Leung and Y. Wang. An orthogonal genetic algorithm with quantization for global numerical optimization. *IEEE Transactions on Evolutionary Computation*, 5(1):41 –53, 2001.

[14] S. W. Mahfoud. Niching methods for genetic algorithms. Technical report, Illinois Genetic Algorithms Laboratory, 1995.

[15] MATLAB. *version 7.10.0 (R2010b).* The MathWorks Inc., Natick, Massachusetts, 2010.

[16] J. A. Richards. *Remote Sensing Digital Image Analysis.* Springer-Verlag, 1993.

[17] A. Rogers and A. Prügel-Bennett. Genetic drift in genetic algorithm selection schemes. *IEEE Transactions on Evolutionary Computation*, 3(4):298–303, 1999.

[18] T. Romo, J. Clarage, D. Sorensen, and G. N. J. Phillips. Automatic identification of discrete substates in proteins: singular value decomposition analysis of time-averaged crystallographic refinements. *Proteins*, 22:311–321, 1995.

[19] B. Sareni and L. Krähenbühl. Fitness sharing and niching methods revisited. *IEEE Transactions on Evolutionary Computation*, 2(3):97–106, 1998.

[20] S. N. Sivanandam and S. N. Deepa. *Introduction to Genetic Algorithms.* Springer Publishing Company, Incorporated, 1st edition, 2007.

[21] G. Strang. *Introduction to Linear Algebra.* Wellesley-Cambridge Press and SIAM, 4th edition, 2009.

[22] L. N. Trefethen and D. Bau III. *Numerical linear algebra.* Society for Industrial and Applied Mathematics, 1997.

[23] X. Yao, Y. Liu, and G. Lin. Evolutionary programming made faster. *IEEE Transactions on Evolutionary Computation*, 3:82–102, 1999.

Linkage Tree Genetic Algorithms: Variants and Analysis

Brian W. Goldman
Natural Computation Laboratory
Department of Computer Science
Missouri University of Science and Technology
Rolla, Missouri, U.S.A.
brianwgoldman@acm.org

Daniel R. Tauritz
Natural Computation Laboratory
Department of Computer Science
Missouri University of Science and Technology
Rolla, Missouri, U.S.A.
dtauritz@acm.org

ABSTRACT

Discovering and exploiting the linkage between genes during evolutionary search allows the Linkage Tree Genetic Algorithm (LTGA) to maximize crossover effectiveness, greatly reducing both population size and total number of evaluations required to reach success on decomposable problems. This paper presents a comparative analysis of the most prominent LTGA variants and a newly introduced variant. While the deceptive trap problem (Trap-k) is one of the canonical benchmarks for testing LTGA, when LTGA is combined with applying steepest ascent hill climbing to the initial population, as is done in all significant LTGA variations, Trap-k is trivially solved. This paper introduces the deceptive step trap problem (StepTrap-k,s), which shows the novel combination of smallest first subtree ordering with global mixing (LTS-GOMEA) is effective for black box optimization, while least linked first subtree ordering (LT-GOMEA) is effective on problems where partial reevaluation is possible. Finally, nearest neighbor NK landscapes show that global mixing is not effective on problems with complex overlapping linkage structure that cannot be modeled correctly by a linkage tree, emphasizing the need to extend how LTGA stores linkage to allow the power of global mixing to be applied to these types of problems.

Categories and Subject Descriptors

I.2.8 [**Artificial Intelligence**]: Problem Solving, Control Methods, and Search; I.2.6 [**Artificial Intelligence**]: Learning

General Terms

Algorithms

Keywords

LTGA, Linkage Learning, Deceptive Trap, Deceptive Step Trap, Nearest Neighbor NK Landscapes, Optimal Mixing

1. INTRODUCTION

Linkage learning has been shown to benefit the performance of evolutionary algorithms and a variety of linkage algorithms have been developed which use non-tree structures [3]. The canonical Linkage Tree Genetic Algorithm (LTGA) variant was introduced in 2010 [7, 8] with two promising additional variants being introduced in 2011 [5, 9]. The basis for all LTGA variants is the identification of linked substructures in the genome by examining the entropy in the current population and representing those linkages as a hierarchical tree. Each node in the tree represents a cluster of linked genes and the children of each node are non-overlapping subsets of their parent. To exploit the linkage information, LTGA performs a multistage crossover designed to allow for significant exploration without disrupting interdependent genes. The LTGA variants differ in the exact method for how they construct their linkage tree, apply it during crossover, and select parents on which to perform crossover; there has been little analysis of the advantages and disadvantages of these options. Furthermore, most of the work done with LTGA employs Steepest Ascent Hill Climbing (SAHC) on the initial population to help the initial tree construction, the effects of which warrant further investigation. Table 1 shows the principal differences between the LTGA variants in terms of option combinations. To aid in explaining how LTGA works and how all of these option combinations affect evolution, a running example is presented which uses the population in Table 2. These example individuals are evaluated using a trap-like fitness function in which the gene loci *abc*, *def*, and *ghi* are evaluated as groups, such that the gene configuration of 111 results in the best fitness and 000 the second best.

The next few sections provide an introduction to how LTGA works and explain the rationale driving each of the different option combinations. The effects of each LTGA option are discussed and some experimental evidence is provided to support this discussion. To isolate the effects of each, a new LTGA variation consisting of a unique option combination is introduced. Also, a new benchmark is introduced in Section 7 to better understand how LTGA exploits the local search on the population. Finally, Section 9 summarizes the findings and indicates which variant is best under what circumstances.

2. INITIAL POPULATION

In LTGA's canonical form, the initial population undergoes SAHC before starting evolution. In each SAHC iteration, all of an individual's neighbors are evaluated. If any

Dimension	Options
Initial Population	Random / SAHC
Clustering	Full / Pairwise
Subtree Ordering	Least Linked First / Smallest First
Crossover	Two-Parent / Global Mixing / Global Best Next
Variations	**Options Used**
Original [8, 7]	SAHC, Full, Least Linked First, Two-Parent
Original+	SAHC, Pairwise, Least Linked First, Two-Parent
Pairwise [5]	SAHC, Pairwise, Smallest First, Two-Parent
LT-GOMEA [9, 1]	SAHC, Pairwise, Least Linked First, Global Mixing
LTS-GOMEA	SAHC, Pairwise, Smallest First, Global Mixing

Table 1: Existing variations on LTGA

of those neighbors are better than the current individual, then the best neighbor replaces it. SAHC continues until no improvement can be found. On binary problems, the SAHC neighborhood consists of all individuals within one bit flip of the original individual. One reason why LTGA uses SAHC on the initial population is to discover linkage information [5]. The linkage tree is constructed using all of the individuals in the current population and is built before any type of selection occurs. As a result, if SAHC is not performed on the initial population and no other steps are taken, LTGA attempts to determine the linkage of randomly generated genes. Not only does this create a meaningless tree, [5] argues that applying those trees can be very harmful to the search's success. If SAHC is not used, they suggest some form of selection be performed prior to the initial tree creation, such as tournament selection. Table 2 provides an example of how SAHC application can discover linkage information. After SAHC is applied to the randomly initialized individuals, the linked groups are clearly visible.

Using SAHC on the initial population can result in on the order of μN^2 evaluations, where μ is population size and N is genome size. On some problems it is possible to do partial reevaluation such that neighbors of an individual can be evaluated at a much lower cost than a brand new individual [1]. In such cases, the total number of SAHC iterations is counted, which requires on the order of μN steps. As a promising offset to SAHC's cost based on population size, [1] shows how performing local search can reduce the population size required to achieve success.

	Initial	After SAHC
Individual 1	100010001	000000000
Individual 2	101100100	111000000
Individual 3	010011010	000111000
Individual 4	001001110	000000111

Table 2: Example population before and after SAHC

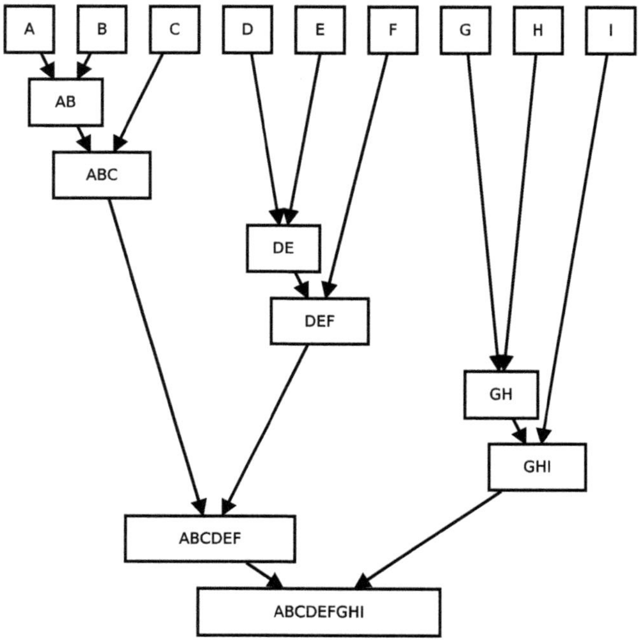

Figure 1: Example Linkage Tree

3. CONSTRUCTING TREES

LTGA stores linkage information as a tree. Each node in the tree represents a cluster of genes that LTGA believes to be linked. A tree is built by first creating a subtree with one node for each locus in the genome. LTGA then iteratively joins the two subtrees that it considers the most linked (with ties broken stochastically) into a binary tree whose root contains all of the loci of both subtrees. As a result, the number of subtrees is reduced by one each iteration, meaning the total number of nodes in the final tree is one less than twice the number of dimensions.

Figure 1 provides an example linkage tree construction for the running example. When constructing this tree, the first merge combines a and b. In the next iteration, LTGA can combine any of the remaining individual loci with each other, as well as with the newly created subtree ab, but it can no longer combine loci with just a or b. This represents one of the limitations of LTGA, since it is unable to fully capture a relationship such as a linked to b and b linked to c without a linked to c. The closest approximation LTGA can make to this type of linkage is if a is more tightly linked to b than b is to c, then the linkage tree can contain both ab and abc, which is one of the primary advantages of a tree representation over simple clusters. Also, since LTGA rebuilds the linkage tree each generation, changes in the population can allow it to shift priorities, for instance from ab to bc. It is important to note that the tree provided in Figure 1 is not the only one that can be constructed for this population and that LTGA contains no bias based on where loci are positioned in the genome. LTGA also has no bias on merging larger or smaller subtrees first.

3.1 Cluster Distance

The linkage between genes is determined using the normalized variation of information, defined by Eq. 1, where D is the distance between clusters C_i and C_j, and H is the entropy of a cluster, as given by Eq. 2. S represents all possible strings that cluster C can be, and $p_c(s)$ is the fraction of the current population that has cluster C set to s.

$$D(C_i, C_j) = 2 - \frac{H(C_i) + H(C_j)}{H(C_i \cup C_j)} \quad (1)$$

$$H(C) = -\sum_{s \in S} p_c(s) \log(p_c(s)) \quad (2)$$

As a result, $D(C_i, C_j)$ provides the ratio of the entropy of the clusters separately to the clusters joined. The minimum distance is achieved when for each s in C_i there is exactly one s' in C_j such that all individuals who have s also have s'. This method of calculating distance, measures how well the contents of one cluster can predict another, which implies they are linked.

Using the example population in Table 2 after SAHC and starting after the first merge, the distance between the cluster ab and the clusters c and d is calculated as follows. For cluster ab, $p_{ab}(00) = \frac{3}{4}$, $p_{ab}(11) = \frac{1}{4}$, and all other possible strings for ab never occur in the population. Both c and d have $p(0) = \frac{3}{4}$ and $p(1) = \frac{1}{4}$. This means that the numerator in Eq. 1 will be the same for both $D(ab, c)$ and $D(ab, d)$ and also that all three clusters have the same value for H. Joined, $p_{abc}(000) = \frac{3}{4}$ and $p_{abc}(111) = \frac{1}{4}$ for abc and $p_{abd}(000) = \frac{2}{4}$, $p_{abd}(110) = \frac{1}{4}$ and $p_{abd}(001) = \frac{1}{4}$ for abd. Because the entropy for abd is higher than abc, the distance value for ab to c will be lower, and LTGA will choose to join abc first.

3.2 Pairwise Approximation

In the original LTGA variant [8, 7], hereafter referred to simply as Original, the method given in Section 3.1 was used to merge all clusters. However, a follow up paper showed that this method does not scale well, as calculating the entropy between all possible clusters becomes very time consuming when solving high-dimensional problems [5]. To overcome that problem, that paper proposed an estimation method, provided in Eq. 3.

$$D'(C_i, C_j) = \frac{1}{|C_i| \cdot |C_j|} \sum_{c_i \in C_i} \sum_{c_j \in C_j} D(c_i, c_j) \quad (3)$$

Instead of finding the entropy of an entire cluster, this measure only finds the entropy between all pairs of loci in the population. For clusters of sizes greater than one, this finds the average of the pairwise entropy for all loci in C_i with all loci in C_j. While the intent behind this metric was to reduce the time complexity used to construct trees, in which it succeeded, using the pairwise distance also led to a drop in the population size and number of evaluations required to achieve success on a number of problems [5]. The first algorithm to use this method is hereafter referred to as Pairwise, and Original using this method is called Original+.

4. CROSSOVER

The linkage tree is used to perform crossovers that do not disrupt gene linkage, while still exploring the search space. Each subtree in the linkage tree is used as a crossover mask, such that all of the genes in that subtree's cluster are crossed between the parents. When creating a single offspring, all of the crossover masks are used sequentially. Crossovers that create an improvement are kept, while detrimental changes are discarded. As was discussed in the context of LT-GOMEA [9, 1], this incremental change can be seen as a form of local search. Since the leaves of the linkage tree each contain a single locus, LTGA's crossover will mimic a simple hill climber as well as bit flip mutation.

Parents	111000000	000111000	Changes Kept?
abcdef	000111000	111000000	No
ghi	111000000	000111000	No
gh	111000000	000111000	No
def	111111000	000000000	Yes
de	111001000	000111000	No
abc	000111000	111000000	No
ab	001111000	110000000	No
Single Bit Crossover Here			

Table 3: Two parent crossover with least linked first ordering as used by Original. Shading indicates which genes were crossed.

Tables 3–6 provide examples of how LTGA performs crossover for different variants. The left column in each shows which subtree cluster is in use, the middle column(s) show how the offspring are being modified, and the right column indicates if the changes are kept or reverted before applying the next crossover. Each offspring is created through a series of $2N - 2$ crossovers. This includes all crossovers of length one and all other subtrees in the linkage tree. The root of the tree, which contains all of the loci, is not crossed because it will not create any new individuals.

Since the most linked genes are clustered first and are treated as a unit in all further clustering, few crossovers will occur that disrupt their linkage. For instance, the two genes that have the minimum distance (tightest linkage) will be merged first. All other clusters will either contain both genes or neither, so only two of the $2N - 2$ crossovers act on one gene but not the other. Conversely, pairs of clusters with the highest distance (weakest linkage) will be merged last, allowing many crossovers to mix their gene values. In the example, a and b were the first merged cluster, meaning that only their leaf nodes can perform a crossover that splits their values, while a and g are not linked until the root of the linkage tree, and as a result the subtrees a, g, ab, abc, gh, ghi, and $abcdef$ can all freely mix their gene values.

In LTGA, crossover occurs inside all clusters, with the potential of increasing their entropy, making it less likely to form them in the future without impacting diversity. This allows LTGA to recover from some amount of confusion of gene linkages, unlike nonhierarchical crossover.

4.1 Repeated Evaluations

If no preventative measures are taken, LTGA will create an immense number of duplicate individuals. For example, 14 of the 32 individuals created in Table 4 are duplicates of either individuals created during this crossover or of the original parents. As a slight prevention, all of the published LTGA variants avoid evaluating individuals that are identical to their parents, or at least make no mention of deviating from the original LTGA formulation that did this. While

Parents	111000000	000111000	Changes Kept?
Single Bit Crossover Here			
ab	001000000	110111000	No
de	111110000	000001000	No
gh	111000000	000111000	No
abc	000111000	111000000	No
def	111111000	000000000	Yes
ghi	111111000	000000000	No
abcdef	000000000	111111000	No

Table 4: Two parent crossover with smallest first ordering as used by Pairwise. Shading indicates which genes were crossed.

Clone	111000000	Changes Kept?
abcdef	000000000	No
ghi	111000111	Yes
gh	111000001	No
def	111111111	Yes
de	111001111	No
abc	000111111	No
ab	001111111	No
Single Bit Crossover Here		

Table 5: Global mixing crossover with least linked first ordering as used by LT-GOMEA. Shading indicates which genes were crossed.

Clone	111000000	Changes Kept?
Single Bit Crossover Here		
ab	001000000	No
de	111110000	No
gh	111000110	No
abc	000000000	No
def	111111000	Yes
ghi	111111111	Yes
abcdef	000000111	No

Table 6: Global mixing crossover with smallest first ordering as used by LTS-GOMEA. Shading indicates which genes were crossed.

helpful, this does not catch all of the duplicates. For this study, no individual is evaluated twice. This provides an accurate gauge of how many unique evaluations each LTGA variant uses and removes any bias against LTGA variants that are more likely to create duplicate individuals.

4.2 Subtree Ordering

The order in which subtrees are used to perform crossover is one of the primary differences between LTGA variants. In Original and LT-GOMEA, subtrees are applied in least linked first order. In this ordering, the crossover masks are stored in a stack. All of the individual loci are pushed randomly onto the stack. During each iteration of tree construction, the newly formed cluster is also pushed onto the stack. Table 3 shows the ordering for the running example. Since *abcdef* was the last cluster to be merged, it is the first to be applied. The focus of this ordering is for crossover to perform solution refining. The initial crossovers are likely to be large and will be based on the least amount of information in the linkage tree. These steps provide search space exploration. The more linked LTGA believes a cluster of genes to be, the more likely it believes that keeping those genes together will allow for an individual to improve by crossing them. As such, this method starts with the least predictable crossovers, followed by something very similar to local search, bringing the solution to a local optima.

Pairwise employs an alternative subtree ordering which sorts the clusters based on size instead of linkage, with equal sized clusters applied in random order. This method is more akin to optimizing the parts of the problem you know the most about before using the optimized pieces to make larger changes. Table 4 provides an example for this ordering. Smallest first is not the direct opposite of least linked first. One major difference is that least linked first has the potential to deal with the same set of genes in a number of sequential crossovers, where as in smallest first that is very unlikely. In the example, *de* and *gh* are crossed after *ab* and before *abc*, which means if there is a linkage between *ab* and either *de* or *gh* that was previously undiscovered, this ordering has the potential to try it before modifying *c*.

4.3 Parent Selection

In Original and Pairwise, all crossovers for a single offspring are based on two parents, similar to canonical Genetic Algorithms (GAs). To create each child, two parents are selected at random. For each cluster in the linkage tree, two children are created by swapping the genetic material of the parents for that cluster. If either of the children created in one step of the crossover are better than the best of the parents, both of the parents are replaced by the children before continuing on to the next subtree. This method of replacement ensures that the genetic diversity inside a single crossover is unchanged, as whatever patterns existed in the parents before crossover will still exist after. Often this has a polarizing effect, as the best parent is likely to improve by taking the best parts of the weaker. After all of the linkage clusters have been applied, the best child created during the entire process is copied into the next generation. This means that each parent pairing creates a single child. As LTGA uses generational survivor selection, to achieve a steady population size parents must participate in creating more than one offspring each generation. Since parents are modified during the creation of their offspring, subsequent offspring created by the same parent will benefit from the learning performed during the creation of their first. Tables 3 and 4 provide examples for this type of crossover.

The LTGA variant Linkage Tree Global Optimal Mixing Evolutionary Algorithm (LT-GOMEA) differs from Original and Pairwise by performing crossover in a method more similar to Estimation of Distribution Algorithms than GAs. Instead of selecting two parents to pull genetic material from, LT-GOMEA starts by cloning a single parent to initialize the child. For each subtree crossover mask, LT-GOMEA chooses a random parent from the population to donate genetic material to the child for that mask. If the child is improved, the changes will be kept, otherwise they are reverted. While it is not explicitly stated as part of LT-GOMEA, the donated genetic material is assumed here to not be identical to the child's gene values, as doing so would waste a chance at improving the individual. Tables 5 and 6 provide examples of performing global mixing crossover using the population provided in Table 2.

A variant to LT-GOMEA was proposed in [1] which tried all possible donations for each crossover before choosing to keep any. This change allows LTGA to perform a steepest ascent local search on each subtree cluster for each individual, finding the global next best. Unfortunately, doing so incurs significant overhead and causes premature convergence due to large subtrees copying so much of an individual as to allow the current best individual to spread too rapidly.

5. EXPERIMENTS

While most of the permutations listed in Table 1 are valid ways to configure an LTGA, this paper focuses on the variants most likely to achieve interesting results. From the work with LT-GOMEA and Pairwise, it appears that subtree ordering and crossover represent the ways in which the state-of-the-art LTGA variations differ. To examine the effects of these variations, empirical test results are presented for all four combinations of least linked first linkage, smallest first linkage, two parent crossover, and global mixing, which are represented by Original+, Pairwise, LT-GOMEA, and the novel combination Linkage Tree Smallest First Global Mixing Evolutionary Algorithm (LTS-GOMEA). While global next best is an option for crossover, [1] tested LT-GOMEA against global next best and found it to be sufficiently inferior to not warrant further investigation.

In order to ensure a minimal population size, each LTGA variant was tuned to each problem using a modified version of bisection [6]. In order to remove operator bias and further generalize the method, the bisection used here starts by setting the initial population size to the minimum possible for the algorithm, which in this case is two. It then proceeds by testing to see if its guess meets the success criteria. If not, then it doubles its guess and tries again. Once the criteria are met, the current guess is used as the maximum population size and the previous guess is the minimum population size for bisection. This ensures the starting minimum is below the population size required and the starting maximum is at least as high as required. In this instance, the required success rate was 24 of 25 runs finding the global optimum. When actually gathering experimental results, all experiments used 100 runs.

To reduce the noise generated by the initial population, a set of individuals was created for each run of each population size on each problem. These sets of individuals were then all optimized using SAHC. Having all versions of LTGA share initial populations for the same population size facilitates examining how each algorithm utilizes the information in those populations. Furthermore, any difference in population size is then more clearly indicative of a need for different initial information, and not just caused by random chance.

6. DECEPTIVE TRAP

The canonical benchmark for LTGA is the deceptive trap (Trap-k) problem [2], which divides the genome into separate traps of length k bits. Each trap is scored using Eq. 4, where t is equal to the sum of the bit values in the trap.

$$trap(t) = \begin{cases} k-1-t, & t<k \\ k, & t=k \end{cases} \tag{4}$$

N=50	Population Size	Rarest Trap Count	Local Search Steps	Evals To Success (Standard Dev.)
Original+	26	1.94	513.93	1946.53 (481.90)
LT-GOMEA	26	1.94	513.93	21.31 (5.55)
Pairwise	26	1.94	513.93	2200.38 (468.01)
LTS-GOMEA	26	1.94	513.93	89.81 (0.48)
N=100				
Original+	24	1.52	922.33	6134.35 (1244.64)
LT-GOMEA	24	1.52	922.33	47.91 (10.19)
Pairwise	24	1.52	922.33	6794.50 (1307.67)
LTS-GOMEA	24	1.52	922.33	179.82 (0.48)
N=150				
Original+	32	2.26	1827.23	15430.62 (2625.32)
LT-GOMEA	32	2.26	1827.23	79.65 (14.06)
Pairwise	32	2.26	1827.23	15507.38 (2577.15)
LTS-GOMEA	32	2.26	1827.23	269.78 (0.48)

Table 7: Deceptive Trap Results, k=5

Each trap is fully deceptive, in that all non-optimal values lead away from the global optimum of all ones toward the local optimum containing all zeros. As a result, any crossover that affects less than a complete trap will likely cause both individuals to move away from the global optima. This need to preserve linkage, coupled with trap independence, makes Trap-k an ideal proof of concept benchmark for LTGA.

LTGA needs an initial population that contains the optimized value for each trap in at least one individual to find the global optima, as the deceptive nature of each trap makes creating the optimized value during evolution unlikely. Local search on the deceptive trap function ensures that all traps in all individuals are initialized to either the optimum (all ones) or the local optimum (all zeros). LTGA's first benefit is the complete removal of entropy for each trap. Independent of trap size, after local search all traps will contain less than one bit of information. As a result, when LTGA builds the gene clusters, all genes in a trap will have the minimum possible distance from each other. Furthermore, when performing a crossover using a subset of the cluster (i.e., a subtree of size less than k), new trap values cannot be created as there is no way to change less than k bits in any individual to improve its fitness. Thus, the only way for LTGA to lose track of a trap's grouping is if the entire population agrees on the value between two traps. In such an event it is still unlikely that LTGA will create a trap with a value other than all ones or all zeros. When performing a crossover that contains one or more complete traps, LTGA's behavior changes depending on the type of crossover in use. The final best offspring of Original and Pairwise, using two-parent crossover, will contain all of the optimized traps that started in either individual. LT-GOMEA and LTS-GOMEA will solve even faster, as after all complete traps have been crossed over, the individual produced will contain all optimized traps that exist anywhere in the population. The second benefit of local search for LTGA is the increased number

N=49	Population Size	Rarest Trap Count	Local Search Steps	Evals To Success (Standard Dev.)
Original+	64	1.83	1486.62	2148.50 (571.09)
LT-GOMEA	64	1.83	1486.62	13.41 (3.43)
Pairwise	64	1.83	1486.62	2454.71 (579.23)
LTS-GOMEA	64	1.83	1486.62	90.91 (0.27)
N=98				
Original+	78	1.76	3541.38	12983.56 (2990.20)
LT-GOMEA	78	1.76	3541.38	31.89 (7.08)
Pairwise	78	1.76	3541.38	14082.40 (2884.49)
LTS-GOMEA	78	1.76	3541.38	181.92 (0.26)
N=147				
Original+	80	1.57	5410.32	27150.74 (5581.73)
LT-GOMEA	80	1.57	5410.32	53.68 (11.26)
Pairwise	80	1.57	5410.32	30189.41 (4738.40)
LTS-GOMEA	80	1.57	5410.32	272.96 (0.17)

Table 8: Deceptive Trap Results, k=7

N=50	Population Size	Rarest Trap Count	Local Search Steps	Evals To Success (Standard Dev.)
Original+	73	8.66	414.4	13744 (2925.2)
LT-GOMEA	67	8.09	383.1	9643 (2606.3)
Pairwise	74	9.43	422.3	13475 (2901.1)
LTS-GOMEA	49	5.34	278.2	11192 (2163.7)
N=100				
Original+	86	9.78	893.7	46579 (7085.9)
LT-GOMEA	84	9.41	874.1	32533 (4820.6)
Pairwise	97	11.42	1011.6	50669 (7921.5)
LTS-GOMEA	62	6.32	642.7	36272 (4755.3)
N=150				
Original+	101	11.35	1520.8	91652 (13411.8)
LT-GOMEA	96	10.64	1449.6	58591 (7269.7)
Pairwise	107	12.54	1610.5	100951 (14306.7)
LTS-GOMEA	73	7.31	1103.0	68129 (10462.3)

Table 9: Deceptive Step Trap Results, k=5, s=2

of optimized traps in the starting population. The probability of a trap containing an optimal value in a single individual increases from $\frac{1}{2^k}$ to $\frac{k+1}{2^k}$, since SAHC will not change randomly generated optimized traps, and will improve all traps with a single incorrect bit to the optimum.

Tables 7 and 8 provide the experimental results for the LTGA variations on Trap-5 and Trap-7, respectively. As expected, the algorithms required the same initial population size, due to their identical requirements on the existence of optimized traps. Population size predictably increases with problem size, with the exception of $N = 50$ to $N = 100$, where the population size decreases. This minor drop is likely a bisection tuning artifact, which relies on stochastic processes to set the population size. The rarest trap count value given for each problem is the average number of individuals in the initial population containing the optimized version of the trap with the lowest frequency of individuals containing its optimized version over all successful runs.

The LTGA variants vary in the number of evaluations after local search that each requires to achieve success. Most notably, both versions using global mixing (LT-GOMEA and LTS-GOMEA) require far less than either form of two-parent crossover. When performing global mixing, each crossover mask that contains exactly one trap will result in the child having the optimized version of that trap after crossover. This is because the child either has the optimized version, and therefore no chance to improve for that crossover mask, or the suboptimal version and will therefore randomly select a parent with the only other genetic material for that crossover mask: the optimized value. Since two-parent crossover can only create offspring containing the optimized traps from its two parents, multiple crossovers are required to build individuals such that when they are paired, at least one has the optimized value for all traps. The difference between LT-GOMEA and LTS-GOMEA is trivial in this case, as the difference is how many crossover masks are tried before all single trap masks are applied. In LTS-GOMEA there will be $2N - \frac{N}{k}$ subtrees with a size less than or equal to k, as opposed to LT-GOMEA where, depending on tree construction, there can be as few as $2\frac{N}{k} - 1$ subtrees with less than or equal linkage to the single trap subtrees. These formulas are near perfect predictors of the experimental number of evaluations found in Tables 7 and 8.

7. DECEPTIVE STEP TRAP

The artificial nature of the Trap-k problem, as exploited by SAHC, makes LTGA's performance on this benchmark an unlikely predictor of its ability on more realistic problems. In order to create a very similar problem to Trap-k that cannot be exploited as much by SAHC, the creation of StepTrap-k,s as defined in Eq. 5 is proposed. Similar to Trap-k, StepTrap-k,s uses a series of non-overlapping trap functions, where each trap is scored using the sum of the bits set to one. The optimal value for each trap is all ones, with a local optimum of all zeros. All other configurations improve monotonically as they approach all zeros. The only difference between normal Trap-k and StepTrap-k,s is that StepTrap-k,s includes plateaus of length s. If s is set to one, then StepTrap-k,s is identical to Trap-k. For $s > 1$, up to $s-1$ bits can change without a change in the fitness of non-optimal traps. By modifying Trap-k to StepTrap-k,s and setting s=2, SAHC will still create optimized traps at the same probability as in Trap-k, but it will leave the majority of traps in some partial state between all zeros and all ones. As such the loss of entropy for each trap will not be as extreme as in normal Trap-k, making LTGA more prone to clustering errors.

$$step\_trap(t) = \left\lfloor \frac{(k-s) \pmod s + trap(t)}{s} \right\rfloor \quad (5)$$

Tables 9 and 10 provide the experimental results for each

N=49	Population Size	Rarest Trap Count	Local Search Steps	Evals To Success (Standard Dev.)
Original+	120	4.30	535.6	36033 (4756.3)
LT-GOMEA	135	4.66	599.0	34349 (5035.3)
Pairwise	147	5.76	654.4	42689 (5746.5)
LTS-GOMEA	117	4.18	521.4	39870 (6170.5)
N=98				
Original+	233	8.71	1841.0	180075 (17685.8)
LT-GOMEA	197	7.20	1549.5	130998 (16004.0)
Pairwise	265	10.26	2090.6	222781 (25374.9)
LTS-GOMEA	143	4.37	1127.0	147621 (15173.7)
N=147				
Original+	256	9.58	2899.9	371343 (35206.8)
LT-GOMEA	317	12.17	3596.4	292347 (35440.8)
Pairwise	309	11.97	3509.9	485905 (50916.7)
LTS-GOMEA	200	6.61	2268.3	319875 (27276.5)

Table 10: Deceptive Step Trap Results, k=7, s=2

variation of LTGA on the StepTrap-k,s problem using s=2 with k set to 5 and 7 respectively. Unlike the uniform population sizes found on Trap-k, all LTGA variants needed a different sizes on StepTrap-k,s. For all N and k tested, LTS-GOMEA was the least destructive to existing optimized traps, and was therefore able to achieve the global optima with the smallest population sizes.

To understand why global mixing with smallest first ordering is the least destructive to existing optimized traps, we first need to examine how optimal mixing is able to lose an optimized trap. Incorrectly linked crossovers can include parts of multiple traps. If, when performing these crossovers, the amount that some of the traps improve is greater than the fitness lost by breaking one of the other traps, the change is still kept. Consider the example where a, b, c, and z are incorrectly linked. The first three are part of one trap that is not at either optima in the parents, and the fourth is part of another trap which one of the parents has optimized. The crossover abc improves its trap by increasing its fitness two points, which offsets the crossover of z, which decreases its trap value one point. As a result, the optimized trap is lost. Smallest first ordering is sometimes able to avoid this problem by making minimal changes first. In the example, if any of a, b or c are linked before all three are combined with z and crossing that subtree can achieve even a single point of fitness increase, then when crossing $abcz$ there will no longer be enough improvement to offset the damage.

Conversely, because smallest first is more likely to push individual traps to their local optima before performing larger crossovers, it is less likely that larger crossovers that include partial traps will make enough of an improvement to be considered successful. This means that until better linkage information is found, most of the larger crossovers in smallest first ordering will likely be wasted. Least linked does not have this problem, and in fact the most tightly linked crossovers at the end of search are more likely to make improvements, and help prevent wasted evaluations. As an indirect added bonus, every successful crossover reduces the entropy of most if not all of the traps it effects, making the next generation's linkage tree more accurate. This is because as traps are pushed to the extremes, StepTrap-k,s approaches the Trap-k problem, which is very easy for LTGA to solve, as shown in Section 6.

Two-parent crossover is even more likely to destroy optimized traps than global mixing, as shown in Tables 9 and 10. While two-parent crossover can have all of the same flaws as global mixing for optimized trap destruction, it can also lose a trap due to parent pairing. If two parents are paired such that the worse parent has an optimized trap in a location the better parent does not, and no crossover exists that can move that trap without significantly damaging the other parent, that genetic material can be lost. It is possible that this explains why smallest first does not help Pairwise as much as LTS-GOMEA, as even though crossover is not directly destroying traps, the inability for Pairwise to move traps between parents is resulting in their loss. One final consideration about the trade off between LT-GOMEA and LTS-GOMEA is the inclusion of the initial search steps as evaluations. If either is applied to a problem where partial reevaluation is not an option, the number of evaluations required for local search will be about N times larger than the number of local search steps. LTS-GOMEA's smaller population size allows it to solve all of the StepTrap-k,s problems except N=49 in less evaluations than LT-GOMEA if local search evaluations are included.

Similar to normal Trap-k, if LTGA is able to correctly link each trap independently before all optimized versions of any trap are lost, it is very unlikely that any LTGA variant will fail to reach the global optimum. This is because any crossover that moves a single trap from one parent to another can only improve that trap's fitness, which will shift the population toward both extremes, again making it resemble Trap-k. The only way to lose an optimized trap now would be to cross multiple traps into a child, where more traps are made optimal than are made non-optimal. Smallest first ensures that any crossover that moves multiple traps will first optimize the individual traps, which again reduces the likelihood of this happening. Two-parent crossover is also unlikely to have this issue as, independent of what order traps are crossed, optimal traps that are lost in one step can be reclaimed in subsequent crossovers with the same parent or will be optimized before they can contribute to a lost optimized trap.

8. NEAREST NEIGHBOR NK

NK landscapes are a set of randomly generated benchmark problems [4]. An NK landscape is defined by the number of dimensions used (N), the number of other genes each gene relies on to calculate its own fitness (k), the epistasis table defining the linkages between genes, and N randomly generated fitness functions which determine the fitness of each collection of linked genes. Nearest neighbor NK landscapes are a subset of NK landscapes in which each gene is linked to the k genes that directly follow it, with the final genes wrapping around. This subset is of interest for testing LTGA as it contains overlapping blocks of genes with varying levels of linkage. Furthermore, by utilizing dynamic programming it is possible to determine the optimal value for nearest neighbor NK landscapes in polynomial time [10].

N=30	Population Size	Local Search Steps	Evals To Success (Standard Dev.)
Original+	132	1038.06	8253.86 (3473.91)
LT-GOMEA	131	1039.16	7743.29 (4804.82)
Pairwise	110	867.97	7144.20 (3426.76)
LTS-GOMEA	151	1219.60	10634.28 (5112.47)
N=40			
Original+	323	3286.34	33141.11 (12757.48)
LT-GOMEA	501	5102.29	36300.81 (21529.69)
Pairwise	250	2549.38	28875.14 (10652.87)
LTS-GOMEA	317	3233.64	40525.74 (16589.45)
N=50			
Original+	383	4786.59	67280.11 (22403.78)
LT-GOMEA	393	4905.07	60809.10 (24655.13)
Pairwise	371	4636.94	69266.90 (21912.95)
LTS-GOMEA	276	3451.42	62564.14 (19336.66)

Table 11: NK Results, k=5

Table 11 shows the results of each LTGA variant tested on nearest neighbor NK using k=5. Unlike the previous two benchmarks, Pairwise was able to outperform both global mixing strategies on N=30 and N=40 in both population size and total number of evaluations. Original+ was also able to achieve a lower number of evaluations on N=40. The most likely cause is LTGA's inability to capture overlapping dependencies inherent in nearest neighbor NK. When performing two-parent crossover, all donated information comes from the same individual. As such, any partial improvements made to a child are more likely to work well with subsequent crossovers with the same parent as both sets of genes were effective together in at least that parent.

When performing global mixing, no similar linkage exists between donated information. As a result, global mixing attempts to combine genetic material from many different parents, with only a limited ability to keep linked information together. Individuals created in this way are less likely to be an improvement over the existing individual, and will therefore be a wasted evaluation. The increased population size is likely a symptom of premature convergence caused by this inability to generate good solutions.

The reason why N=40 switches which type of mixing is most effective is probably because as the number of problem variables increases but the amount of overlap stays constant, the effect of incorrect linkage is lessened. This may explain why both global mixing variants were able to reduce their required population size from N=40 to N=50.

9. CONCLUSIONS

Using the Trap-k problem to test the different variations of LTGA provides little to no information, as SAHC converts a very difficult problem into a trivial one for any type of LTGA. In order to provide a better benchmark for non-overlapping linked genes, this paper introduces the StepTrap-k,s problem, which modifies the traditional Trap-k to contain fitness plateaus of width s. These plateaus prevent SAHC from pushing all traps to the extremes, providing a much more challenging problem for LTGA.

This new problem reveals global mixing's ability to converge faster and use smaller population sizes than two-parent crossover. By applying the smallest crossover masks first, LTGA better avoids destroying existing optimized structures in the population when incorrect linkage occurs at the expense of needing more search evaluations. As a result, on non-overlapping linkage problems where local search cannot exploit partial reevaluation, the novel LTGA variant LTS-GOMEA, which uses smallest first ordering, may outperform LT-GOMEA, which uses least linked first ordering.

Testing the LTGA variants on nearest neighbor NK landscapes provides insight to how each variant handles linkage styles less suited to tree structures. On problems with lots of overlap, the two-parent variants seem to perform better than global mixing due to the inherent linkage between subsequent crossovers between the same two parents. As global mixing is able to significantly outperform two-parent crossover in all other instances, improving how LTGA stores linkage information to allow for better representation of overlap is a very important next step for making LT-GOMEA and LTS-GOMEA more generally applicable.

10. REFERENCES

[1] P. Bosman and D. Thierens. The roles of local search, model building and optimal mixing in evolutionary algorithms from a BBO perspective. *GECCO*, pages 663–670, 2011.

[2] K. Deb and D. Goldberg. Analyzing deception in trap functions. *In Proceedings of FOGA II: the Second Workshop on Foundations of Genetic Algorithms*, pages 93–108, 1992.

[3] G. R. Harik, F. G. Lobo, and K. Sastry. *Linkage learning via probabilistic modeling in the extended compact genetic algorithm.* Springer–Verlag, Berlin, 2006.

[4] S. Kauffman. The origins of order: self organization and selection in evolution. *Oxford University Press*, 1993.

[5] M. Pelikan, M. Hauschild, and D. Thierens. Pairwise and problem-specific distance metrics in the linkage tree genetic algorithm. *GECCO*, pages 1005–1012, 2011.

[6] K. Sastry. Evaluation-relaxation schemes for genetic and evolutionary algorithms. Master's thesis, University of Illinois at Urbana-Champaign, Department of General Engineering, 2001.

[7] D. Thierens. Linkage tree genetic algorithm: first results. *GECCO*, pages 1953–1957, 2010.

[8] D. Thierens. The linkage tree genetic algorithm. *Parallel Problem Solving from Nature*, pages 264–273, 2010.

[9] D. Thierens and P. Bosman. Optimal mixing evolutionary algorithms. *GECCO*, pages 617–624, 2011.

[10] A. H. Wright, R. K. Thompson, and J. Zhang. The computational complexity of N-K fitness functions. *IEEE Trans. on Evolutionary Computation*, 4(4):373–379, 2000.

Image Segmentation using a Genetic Algorithm and Hierarchical Local Search

Mark Hauschild
Missouri Estimation of Distribution Algorithms Laboratory (MEDAL)
Dept. of Mathematics and Computer Science
University of Missouri at St. Louis
mwh308@umsl.edu

Sanjiv Bhatia
Dept. of Mathematics and Computer Science
University of Missouri at St. Louis
sanjiv@acm.org

Martin Pelikan
Missouri Estimation of Distribution Algorithms Laboratory (MEDAL)
Dept. of Mathematics and Computer Science
University of Missouri at St. Louis
pelikan@cs.umsl.edu

ABSTRACT

This paper proposes a hybrid genetic algorithm to perform image segmentation based on applying the q-state Potts spin glass model to a grayscale image. First, the image is converted to a set of weights for a q-state spin glass and then a steady-state genetic algorithm is used to evolve candidate segmented images until a suitable candidate solution is found. To speed up the convergence to an adequate solution, hierarchical local search is used on each evaluated solution. The results show that the hybrid genetic algorithm with hierarchical local search is able to efficiently perform image segmentation. The necessity of hierarchical search for these types of problems is also clearly demonstrated.

Categories and Subject Descriptors

I.2.8 [**Artificial Intelligence**]: Problem Solving, Control Methods, and Search; I.4.6 [**Segmentation**]: Partitioning; G.1.6 [**Numerical Analysis**]: Optimization

General Terms

Algorithms, Applications, Performance

Keywords

genetic algorithms, image segmentation, local search

1. INTRODUCTION

Image segmentation is the process of dividing an image into multiple distinct segments. It is one of the most important applications in computer vision and image processing. Good image segmentation can be used to help emphasize boundaries and locate distinct objects in images and is often used as a preliminary step in computer vision. Unfortunately, segmentation is also one of the most difficult tasks in image processing.

This paper focuses on image segmentation of grayscale images using the q-state Potts model. While this model has been used in the past to perform image segmentation, the previous methods either used a Monte Carlo approach that takes exponential time as image size increases [5, 11, 14, 15], used Markov random fields [1] or directly applied the q-state model to the original image itself [2]. In this paper, the input image is used to generate a set of weights for a q-state spin glass. Then candidate solutions are evolved based on these set of weights using a genetic algorithm (GA). The candidate solution that results in the lowest spin glass energy is the final image segmentation returned by the algorithm.

While GAs have been used on an almost endless variety of problems [8], using a GA for image segmentation presents an interesting challenge. Even relatively small images have a large number of data points compared to most GA applications. This can lead to long convergence times as well as an increased cost to crossover and fitness functions. To help alleviate these problems, it is helpful to use a population as small as possible. We achieve this by using two methods. First, a steady-state genetic algorithm is used to help preserve diversity. Second, a powerful local search is needed to allow a small population size, both to ensure a small initial population size is sufficient and to decrease the convergence time to an adequate solution. A hierarchical local search is used with the steady-state GA to create a powerful hybrid GA capable of performing image segmentation. In addition, we note that it is possible for two segmented images to have the same physical regions. To overcome this problem, a transformation is used to map different candidate solutions to the same region assignments when performing crossover.

The paper is organized as follows. Section 2 describes the q-state Potts model and how we transform the input image into a set of weights. Section 3 decribes the hybrid GA used to evolve candidate image segmentations. Section 4 covers the experimental setup as well as the experimental results. Finally, section 5 summarizes and concludes the paper.

2. Q-STATE POTTS MODEL

Spin glasses are prototypical models for disordered systems and have played a central role in statistical physics during the last three decades [3, 7, 10, 17]. A simple model to describe a finite-dimensional Potts spin glass is typically arranged on a regular 2D or 3D grid where each node i corresponds to a spin s_i and each edge $\langle i, j \rangle$ corresponds to a coupling between two spins s_i and s_j. Each edge has a real value $J_{i,j}$ associated with it that defines the relationship between the two connected spins. In general, the computational task is to find an assignment of spins such that it minimizes the total energy of the system.

In this paper, the first step to our goal is to map a grayscale image to a set of spin glass weights. First we convert the grayscale image into a set of weights using a method similar to reference [14]. The weight $J_{i,j}$ between neighboring pixels at locations i and j (spins) is given by:

$$J_{i,j} = 1 - \frac{\Delta_{i,j}}{\theta \bar{\Delta}} , \tag{1}$$

where $\Delta_{i,j}$ is the absolute grayscale difference between the neighboring pixels in the original image and $\bar{\Delta}$ is the average difference between neighboring pixels in the entire image. From this equation, we see that if the difference between pixels i and j is large, then the corresponding weight parameter $J_{i,j}$ will be low. On the other hand, the closer the values of pixels i and j, the closer the weight will be to 1.

The overall goal is to minimize the energy of the q-state spin glass. Using the Kronecker δ function (which is 1 if the values are equal and 0 othrwise), energy is defined as

$$E = - \sum_{\langle i,j \rangle} J_{i,j} \delta_{\sigma_i \sigma_j} , \tag{2}$$

The strength of the interaction is given by the weight $J_{i,j}$. However, the two spins only interact if they are nearest neighbors and are in the same spin state since $\delta_{\sigma_i, \sigma_j}$ is the Kronecker δ function.

Once given a set of weights, it is now possible to segment our image by assigning each pixel in a new image to one of a range of possible grayscale colors corresponding to unique regions and then, finding the set of assignments to such regions that minimize the energy E. This works since using the set of weights and trying to minimize the overall energy of the system yields a high probability that neighboring pixels that are nearly the same shade of grayscale values in the input image will be assigned to the same region in the segmented image. On the other hand, if two neighboring pixels are of very different gray scale levels they will most likely be placed into different regions in the segmented image result.

3. ALGORITHM

The steady-state genetic algorithm (GA) [8, 9] evolves a population of candidate solutions typically represented by strings of a fixed length. In this paper the candidate solutions will be of size n, where n is equal to the number of pixels in the image, with the cardinality of the string equal to the number of q-states. The initial population is generated at random according to a uniform distribution over all of those strings. Each iteration starts by randomly selecting two parents and then variation operators such as crossover are used to create a new solution. The new candidate solution is then incorporated into the population using a replacement operator. The run is terminated when some termination criteria has been met. The basic steady-state GA procedure is laid out in Algorithm 1.

In this work, we have used two different variation operators. The first, the *crossover* operator, described in Section 3.1, swaps a rectangular section between the two images with a transformation applied before crossover to ensure that the segment color schemes are consistent between the two parents. Then, we apply the *mutation* operator, with each character of the solution string having a probability of $1/n$ (where n is the number of pixels in the image) to be assigned randomly to one of the regions. Finally, a hierarchical local searcher is used on each solution when it is evaluated to improve performance. If the new candidate solution is of higher fitness than the least fit parent solution, it replaces the least fit parent solution in the population.

Algorithm 1 Steady-state GA pseudocode

```
g ← 0
generate initial population P(0)
while (not done) do
  select two parents a and b randomly from the population
  generate new individual c by crossover of a and b
  perform mutation on new individual
  if Fitness(b) > Fitness(a) then
    Swap(a,b)
  end if
  if Fitness(c) > Fitness(b) then
    b ← c
  end if
  g ← g + 1
end while
```

3.1 Crossover Operator

The goal of our crossover operator is to take parent images a and b and create a new image c that incorporates elements of both the parent images. First, we randomly select a pivot pixel as the pixel that will be in the center of the rectangular region. For an image of size x columns and y rows, a rectangular region of size $\sqrt{x/2}$ columns and $\sqrt{y/2}$ rows is used, centered on the pivot pixel. This region size was used to ensure that the crossed over region was relatively small as image size increased, to minimize disruption during crossover. Then, from image a, add those pixels in the rectangular region to image c and all other pixels in c are set to the values in image b.

The application of this crossover operator without any transformation leads to a poor quality to the new child. This is because the individual segmented images can be essentially segmented the same but be done using different numbered assignments. Figure 1 shows two simple segmented images, segmented between black, white, and gray. It is clear that using a rectangular crossover between these two images would result in a poor child solution. To attempt to alleviate this problem, we perform a transformation on the rectangular region from image a to keep its region assignments as similar as possible to b before adding it to the new individual c. This transformation is created using the possible region assignments $q \in \{0 \dots r\}$. For each pixel in the entire images a and b at each stage, we calculate the conditional probability that given a source pixel in a that is assigned to a state q_m, the probability that in b it is assigned to a state q_n. An example of one of these conditional probability tables is given in Table 1. In this table, the columns represent assignments in image a and the rows represent an assignment in image b, with the values in the table repre-

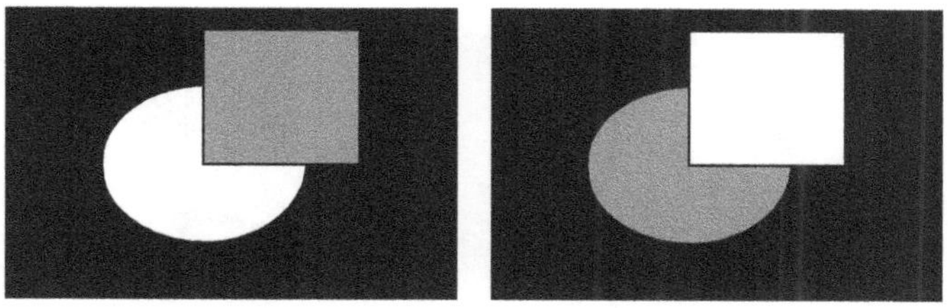

(a) Image a (b) Image b

Figure 1: Two images with identical segmented regions but different region assignments.

	$p = 0$	$p = 1$	$p = 2$	$p = 3$
$p = 0$	0.7902	0.0022	0.0989	0.1998
$p = 1$	0.0828	0.0162	0.0603	0.0532
$p = 2$	0.0505	0.6261	0.4766	0.6950
$p = 3$	0.0765	0.3554	0.3641	0.0520

Table 1: Example conditional probability table generated during crossover that shows the probability that a pixel p in image a is assigned to a different state in image b.

senting the conditional probability that a pixel in image a is of value p in image b.

We use a greedy algorithm to create the transformation from image a to b. All the pixels taken from the target rectangular region in a are mapped to the highest conditional probabilities of their region assignment in b before being added to the new individual c. Referring back to Figure 1, it is clear that the best transformation from image a to b would be to map all white pixels to gray and all gray pixels to white. In this way, the disruption to similar regions in a and b is minimized when combined in c. For a more complex example,using the data in Table 1, the highest conditional probability results in assigning segment 0 of image a to segment 0 of image b. The next highest assigns segment 2 of image a to segment 3 of b. Continuing on, the final transform array is $T = [0, 1, 3, 2]$.

3.2 Hierarchical Local Search

Due to the large number of variables in each solution string, it is important that a local search be used with the GA to allow us to use a smaller population and to ensure quick convergence to an adequate solution. Initially, a simple deterministic hill climbing (DHC) local search was used. This hill climbing algorithm would find the largest possible fitness gain by changing any single variable. This process is repeated until no single variable change would lead to an improvement.

From other works on local search in spin glasses [13], a dramatic increase in segmented image quality was expected. For example, it might be expected that local search would expand a region to cover an entire monocolored region of an image. Unfortunately, this was not the case. Instead, the local search repeatedly got stuck in many poor local optima.

Figure 2a shows a simple example image of only 3 shapes with the exact same color in all shapes. Figure 2b shows the segment assignment after an individual is randomly initialized. Figure 2c shows the segmentation after the application of DHC. We see in this image that instead of assigning the

(a) Initial image

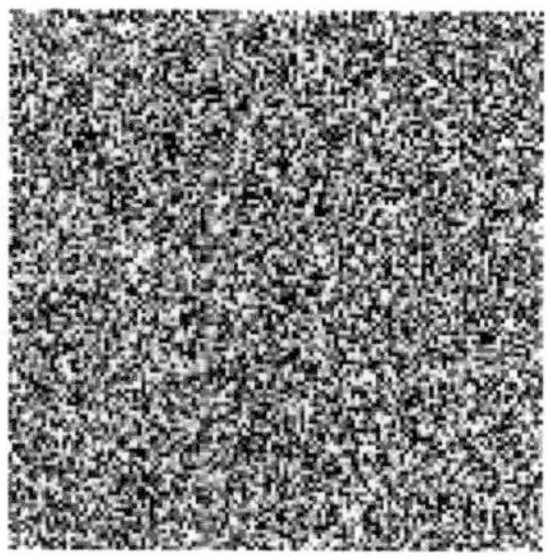

(b) Random segmentation

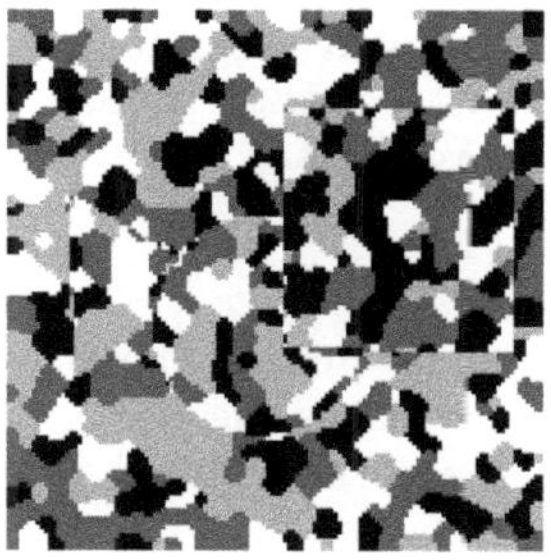

(c) Segmentation after DHC

Figure 2: An image containing 3 monocolor shapes and its corresponding randomly initialized segmentation and the segmentation result after DHC. Note that local search gets stuck in many poor local optima.

monocolored area to the same region, the local search gets stuck and the final assignments are many different patchy areas that are of the same color.

Figure 3 shows the reason for the local search getting stuck in poor local optima. Figure 3 shows a subset of a segmented image where the original image is all of the same color. This implies that assignments to adjacent segments that are the same have zero cost and all others have the same penalty. The local search has assigned the lower diagonal part of the image to gray. However, at this point, the local search gets stuck. This is due to a having 3 neighbors that give penalties (due to being of different segment assignments when the underlying color was the same). If a is assigned to gray, those 3 penalties go away but an additional 5 extra penalty terms are added. With different segmented solutions containing many patches assigned to various regions even in same color areas, this resulted in the crossover operator having poor performance.

Examining Figure 2a led us to consider a hierarchical local search. The hierarchical local search algorithm works by initially performing DHC. Then, all contiguous colored regions are identified and treated as a single region assignment. The local search is then performed again, this time attempting to assign each region to a new color and seeing the fitness gain. The assignment that leads to the highest fitness gain is then taken, which usually leads to region merges. This process is then repeated with the new set of regions. The overall process terminates when no region, when fully assigned to a new color, leads to a fitness gain.

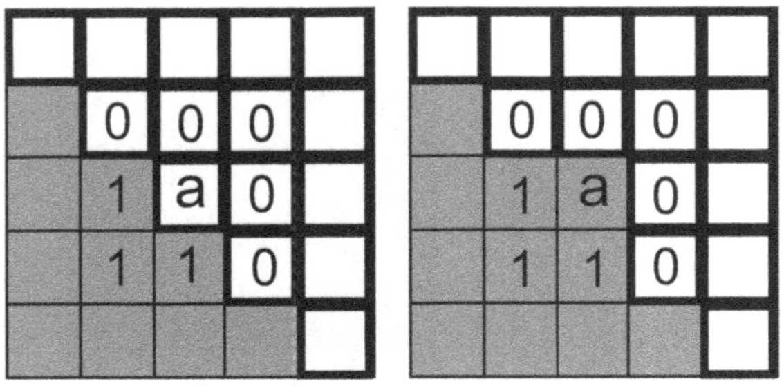

(a) Before a (b) After a

Figure 3: A subset of a segmented image with associated penalties to fitness before and after a is switched between regions.

Figure 4 shows several steps of the hierarchical search in action. We see that over time, the hierarchical search merges regions together and eventually, leads to the same color areas being completely covered by the same region assignment as we might have expected initially from just using DHC. In Figure 4a, it is hard to perceive the original shapes. However, by *step* = 50 in Figure 4b the shapes begin to become clear. After the final hierarchical search step, the original image is much more noticeable but clearly more work needs to be done than simply the hierarchical local search.

To further emphasize the necessity of local search, the GA was run on the 3 shapes image with different local search methods with the population set to 50 initial randomly generated solutions. Figures 5 shows the resulting image segmentations at generation $g = 1$, $g = 100$ and $g = 1000$ using no local search, DHC and the hierarchical local searcher. Figures 5a-c are the results using no local search and even after 1000 generations there is little to distinguish the final segmentation from the initial segmentation result. Using DHC in Figures 5d-f, we do see that as the generations increase, the segmented regions are getting larger, so the image is slowly converging to the solution. Even for $g = 1000$ however, the segmentation is of poor quality and it is very hard to distinguish the shapes in the initial image. When the GA is run with the hierarchical search as in Figures 5g-i, we see a dramatic improvement, with the GA able to find the optimal solution in 100 generations. We also explored performance with and without region maps and while we would expect the lack of region mapping to hurt good segmentations, the hierarchical local searcher seems to be more important than a crossover that minimizes disruption.

This hierarchical search process is considerably more computationally expensive than simple DHC. However, when determining the gain or loss in fitness from switching the color assignment of a region, it is only necessary to check the gain along the border between different regions. This is because internal to the same region, switching it entirely to a different color does not change the overall fitness value for that region. In addition, as the hierarchical local search progresses and changes in some region's color result in merged regions, some boundary pixels become internal pixels and are no longer considered. Also of note is that only the initial hierarchical local searches require many steps since the individual regions become much simpler after the initial search.

While this paper uses hierarchical region merging to improve local search results, Duarte et al. [6] used hierarchical region merging to improve the final results of image segmentation.

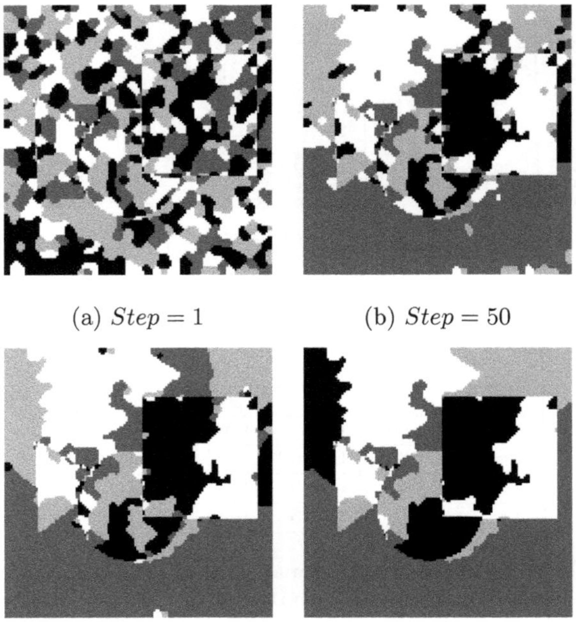

(a) *Step* = 1 (b) *Step* = 50 (c) *Step* = 100 (d) *Step* = 143

Figure 4: Several steps of the hierarchical local search as it merges regions together over time. *Step* = 1 is after the first merge of a region and *step* = 143 is after the final region merge with no other region merges giving any gains.

4. EXPERIMENTS

This section covers both the experimental setup used for the hybrid GA and the resulting segmented images.

4.1 Experimental Setup

For an image of x columns and y rows, the GA evolves strings of size $n = xy$. The values of each individual variable in the string can be set to $q \in \{0 \ldots r - 1\}$, where r is the maximum number of different region assignments. In this paper, we have used the value $r = 4$, setting the cardinality of the variables in the solution strings to 4. While it is possible to set r to other values, higher cardinality results in a slower search and $r = 4$ was shown to be sufficient in size to segment all images tested. The initial population for all experiments was set at $N = 50$ to ensure that sufficient diversity was in the initial population, with all candidate solutions being initialized to random values. The hybrid GA was run for 1000 generations. All input images were converted to 8-bit grayscale to contain 256 distinct gray levels and this image was then used to generate a weights matrix for fitness evaluation.

4.2 Results

In this subsection, we examine two different digital photographs and the resulting segmentations after running the hybrid GA on them. In addition, we examine the segmented

(a) $g = 1$ no ls

(b) $g = 100$ no ls

(c) $g = 1000$ no ls

(d) $g = 1$ DHC

(e) $g = 100$ DHC

(f) $g = 1000$ DHC

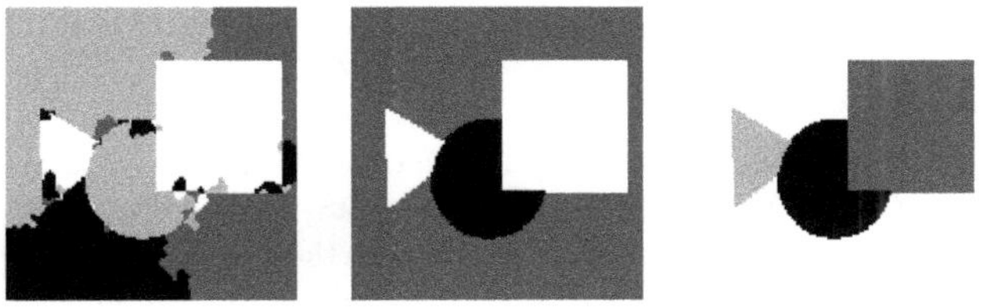

(g) $g = 1$ HLS

(h) $g = 100$ HLS

(i) $g = 1000$ HLS

Figure 5: Resulting best fitness segmentations on the 3 shapes image after runs of the GA to different numbers of generations using no local search, DHC and hierarchical local search (HLS).

image after coloring the regions depending on the average color of that segment in the original image. Finally, we examine the two images segmented using meanshift segmentation and compare the results to the hybrid GA segmentation.

Figure 6a shows a digital photograph of a house of size 150×100 pixels. The resulting segmented image found by the GA is shown in Figure 6b. In this image, we can see many distinct shapes corresponding to distinct regions in the original image. Finally, Figure 6c shows the segmented image with each segment colored by the average color of that segment in the original image. The average colored segmented image looks very similar to the original image except with much more clearly defined areas.

Figure 7 shows the digital image of a dog on a sofa of size 160×128 pixels. Figure 7b shows the resulting segmented image after running the GA. While this segmentation is not as clear as the results in the previous case, the averaged color image in Figure 7c shows more clearly defined edges than in the original image.

For comparison the two images were segmented using meanshift segmentation with the quantization-based method [4], one of the current strongest segmentation algorithms. Figure 8a is intermediate result of the segmentation of the house image showing the borders between regions. Figure 8b is the final segmentation result with 17 colors. There is a strong similarity between the two segmentation

(a) Initial image

(b) Segmented image

(c) Image with each segment identified by its average color

Figure 6: An image of a house, the resulting final segmentation using the hybrid GA, and then a segmented image with each segment colored by its average color in the original image.

results in Figure 7c and Figure 8b. Many large regions have been segmented in much the same way between algorithms. For example, the doors and driveway are easily identified in both, as well as different areas of the roof.

Figure 9 shows the results of meanshift segmentation on the dog on a couch image, with Figure 9a showing the region boundaries identified. Figure 9b shows the final results of the segmentation into 22 colors. One notable difference between the two algorithms can be seen in the intermediate results shown in Figure 7b and Figure 9a, with the dog divided into many more regions by the meanshift algorithm. Much as with the house image, the final results of segmentation are very similar, with major regions differentiated in both images.

5. SUMMARY AND CONCLUSIONS

This paper describes a hybrid GA to perform image segmentation on gray scale images. First, the images were transformed to a set of weights for the q-state Potts spin glass model, which can then be used to calculate the quality of an image segmentation of the original image. A hierarchical local search was used to improve solution quality upon each evaluation. A rectangular region crossover operator was used to generate new candidate segmentations, with the region transformed to ensure that the regions combined in the new candidate solution followed the same approximate region color scheme. The hybrid GA was then used to evolve candidate solutions of segmented images. The results show that the hybrid GA is able to efficiently generate segmented images of high quality.

This paper shows that while using a GA on images can be difficult due to the large number of variables and many local optima, it is still possible to overcome these problems using a powerful local search method such as the hierarchical local search used in this paper.

(a) Initial image

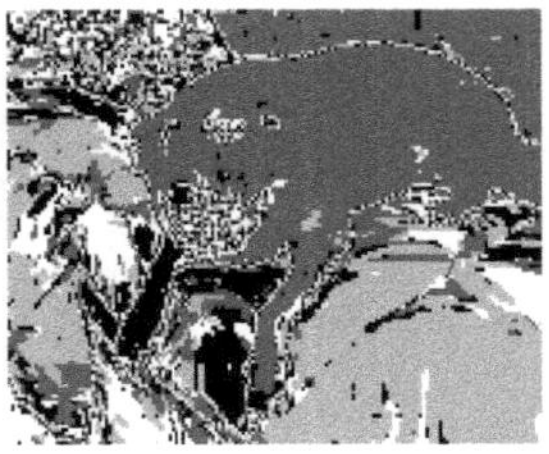

(b) Segmented image

(c) Image with each segment identified by its average color

Figure 7: An image of a dog on a sofa, the resulting final segmentation using the hybrid GA, and a segmented image with each segment colored by its average color in the original image.

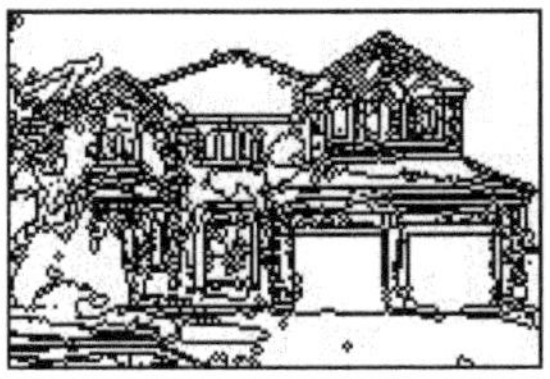

(a) Intermediate

(b) Final

Figure 8: Intermediate results and final results of meanshift segmentation on the house image segmented into 17 colors.

One of the key findings of this paper is the necessity of hierarchical local search on this type of problem. Since simple local search has often been shown to improve performance on many problems in GAs, a similar result was expected on image segmentation. However, the simple local search often led to a degradation of performance as monocolor regions were divided up into small regions. By moving to the hierarchical search that merged regions together, suddenly the local search resulted in dramatic improvements. This finding has implications beyond image segmentation, as simple local searches are used in many hybrid GAs and it is possible that they could benefit from a hierarchical local search. In particular, problems involving local search on images or spin glasses could be prime candidates for hierarchical local search.

There are several other key areas for future work. First, more powerful crossover operators should be examined and tested to see if they can improve the convergence time to a good solution. Then, different inhibition terms [12, 16] could

(a) Intermediate

(b) Final

Figure 9: Intermediate results and final results of meanshift segmentation on the dog on couch image segmented into 26 colors.

be used to emphasize contrast in the resulting segmented images. It is also important to study the effects of population size on the quality of the obtained image segmentation and the efficiency of the search.

Acknowledgments

This project was sponsored by the National Science Foundation under CAREER grant ECS-0547013 and IIS-1115352 and by the University of Missouri in St. Louis through the High Performance Computing Collaboratory sponsored by Information Technology Services, and the Research Award and Research Board programs. Any opinions, findings, and conclusions or recommendations expressed in this material are those of the author(s) and do not necessarily reflect the views of the National Science Foundation, the Air Force Office of Scientific Research, or the U.S. Government.

6. REFERENCES

[1] P. Andrey and P. Tarroux. Unsupervised segmentation of markov random field modeled textured images using selectionist relaxation. *Pattern Analysis and Machine Intelligence, IEEE Transactions on*, 20(3):252–262, mar 1998.

[2] F. W. Bentrem. A Q-ising model application for linear-time image segmentation. *Central European Journal of Physics*, 8:689–698, Jan. 07 2009.

[3] K. Binder and A. Young. Spin-glasses: Experimental facts, theoretical concepts and open questions. *Rev. Mod. Phys.*, 58:801, 1986.

[4] D. Comaniciu and P. Meer. Robust analysis of feature spaces: color image segmentation. In *CVPR '97: Proceedings of the IEEE Computer Society Conference on Computer Vision and Pattern Recognition.*, pages 750 –755, jun 1997.

[5] X. Descombes, M. Moctezuma, H. Maître, and J.-P. Rudant. Coastline detection by a Markovian segmentation of SAR images. *Signal Process.*, 55:123–132, November 1996.

[6] A. Duarte, A. Sánchez, F. Fernández, and A. S. Montemayor. Improving image segmentation quality through effective region merging using a hierarchical social metaheuristic. *Pattern Recogn. Lett.*, 27(11):1239–1251, Aug. 2006.

[7] K. Fischer and J. Hertz. *Spin Glasses.* Cambridge University Press, Cambridge, 1991.

[8] D. E. Goldberg. *Genetic algorithms in search, optimization, and machine learning.* Addison-Wesley, Reading, MA, 1989.

[9] J. H. Holland. *Adaptation in natural and artificial systems.* University of Michigan Press, Ann Arbor, MI, 1975.

[10] M. Mezard, G. Parisi, and M. Virasoro. *Spin glass theory and beyond.* World Scientific, Singapore, 1987.

[11] J. P. Neirotti, S. M. Kurcbart, and N. Caticha. Superparamagnetic segmentation by excitable neural systems. *Phys. Rev. E*, 68:031911, Sep 2003.

[12] R. Opara and F. Wörgötter. A fast and robust cluster update algorithm for image segmentation in spin-lattice models without annealing – visual latencies revisited. *Neural Comput.*, 10:1547–1566, August 1998.

[13] M. Pelikan. *Hierarchical Bayesian optimization algorithm: Toward a new generation of evolutionary algorithms.* Springer-Verlag, 2005.

[14] S. Peng, B. Urbanc, L. Cruc, B. T. Hyman, and H. E. Stanley. Neuron recognition by parallel potts segmentation. *Proceedings of the National Academy of Sciences*, 100(7):3847–3852, 2003.

[15] K. Tanaka. Statistical-mechanical approach to image processing. *Journal of Physics A: Mathematical and General*, 35(37):R81, 2002.

[16] C. von Ferber and F. Wörgötter. Cluster update algorithm and recognition. *Phys. Rev. E*, 62:R1461–R1464, Aug 2000.

[17] A. Young, editor. *Spin glasses and random fields.* World Scientific, Singapore, 1998.

Off-Line Building Block Identification

Detecting Building Blocks Directly from Fitness without Genetic Algorithms

Hsuan Lee
Taiwan Evolutionary Intelligence Laboratory
Department of Electrical Engineering
National Taiwan University
hsuanlee@teilab.ee.ntu.edu.tw

Tian-Li Yu
Taiwan Evolutionary Intelligence Laboratory
Department of Electrical Engineering
National Taiwan University
tianliyu@cc.ee.ntu.edu.tw

ABSTRACT

This paper aims at detecting the existence of *building blocks* directly from the fitness function without performing genetic algorithms. To do so, this paper extends the convergence time model and the gambler's ruin model so they can be applied to a larger variety of problems. With proposed models, the number of fitness evaluations can be estimated for both of these two cases: (1) some genes are transferred together in crossover (treated as a building block); (2) the genes are transferred separately. Therefore, we can compare the number of fitness evaluations and detect the existence of building blocks for a large family of fitness functions without actually performing a genetic algorithm.

Categories and Subject Descriptors

F.2.m [**Analysis of Algorithms and Problem Complexity**]: Miscellaneous; G.1.6 [**Numerical Analysis**]: Optimization; I.2.8 [**Artificial Intelligence**]: Problem Solving

Keywords

Genetic Algorithms, Building Blocks, Problem Decomposition, Convergence Time, Population Sizing, Number of Fitness Evaluations

1. INTRODUCTION

The term *building block* (BB) has long been widely used in genetic algorithms (GA) without formal definition. In recent researches, there are different interpretations to the term. One of them is interpreted as how the fitness function is defined. In this point of view, a BB is a separable part of the fitness function. Another interpretation focuses on how a GA solves the problem. In this case, a BB is a block in the optimal structure with which GAs perform the most efficiently [5]. The latter one is more practical for two reasons: (1) In some problems, there are no separable blocks in the definition of fitness function; (2) a sub-function in the fitness function does not necessarily have to be transferred together in crossover for best performance. For instance, we can define the *OneMax problem* of length ℓ as several blocks of smaller *OneMax problems*. The problem is still the same and the optimal structure for crossover is still treating the chromosome as ℓ individual bits. Throughout this paper, we define the term BB as a block of the crossover structure with which GAs require the smallest number of fitness evaluations ($\mathcal{N}_{fe}$) to solve the problem.

The ultimate goal of this work is to detect BB in any problem definition. In this paper, we start out with (m,k)-*unitary problems* [5]. An (m,k)-*unitary problem* is defined as m non-overlapping sub-problems of order k. The length of the problem ℓ is $m \times k$. The fitness of a chromosome $X(x_1 x_2 x_3 \ldots x_\ell)$ is defined as

$$f(X) = \sum_{i=0}^{m-1} g\left(u\left(x_{g_{i1}} x_{g_{i2}} x_{g_{i3}} \ldots x_{g_{ik}}\right)\right) \quad , \qquad (1)$$

where $u(X)$ is the unitary function that compute the number of 1s in a bit string. $g_{i1} \ldots g_{ik}$ are the k genes in group i. They do not have to be consecutive genes. We target this family of problems because many test problems in the field of GA fall into this family. For example, the *OneMax problem* is defined by

$$g(u) = u \qquad (2)$$

and the (m,k)-*trap problem* [6] is defined by

$$g(u) = \begin{cases} 1 & \text{if } u = k \\ 0.9 \times \left(1 - \frac{u}{k-1}\right) & \text{otherwise} \end{cases} \quad . \qquad (3)$$

Other problems in this family that we test with will be introduced later in this paper. The problem we want to solve in this paper is: given a $g(u)$, we want to know if the sub-problem actually forms a BB.

For the time being, people cannot decide the optimal structure for crossover before they have run a GA with all candidate crossover structures. For each structure to be tested, enormous computation is required to find the minimum population size, convergence time and therefore the $\mathcal{N}_{fe}$ for this specific structure. This process is extremely time consuming. In this paper we propose a new convergence time model and a new population sizing model to estimate the $\mathcal{N}_{fe}$ for two different crossover structures: uniform crossover and uniform BB-wise crossover. With the proposed models we can decide efficiently the better crossover structure for the (m,k)-*unitary problem* family. BBs can be defined accordingly. In short, given the definition of a fitness function, we are able to identify BBs with which this problem can be solved with the least $\mathcal{N}_{fe}$.

GECCO'12, July 7-11, 2012, Philadelphia, Pennsylvania, USA.

This paper is organized as follows: In Section 2, we show some existing models for estimating convergence time and minimum population size. In Section 3, we show some modifications and some new derivations that can be used to estimate the $\mathcal{N}_{fe}$ for any problem in the *(m,k)-unitary problem* family. The results of these models are compared with experiment results in Section 4. Finally, in Section 5, we show how the tools introduced in this paper can be applied to a wider range of problems, other than the *(m,k)-unitary problem* family.

2. BACKGROUND KNOWLEDGE

There is a lot of existing work that predict the behavior of GAs [1, 3, 4, 6, 7, 8, 9]. We introduce briefly three existing models in this section: the convergence time model [10], the gambler's ruin model [8] and the Markov chain model [4, 9]. Their strengths and limits are compared in the end of this section.

2.1 Convergence Time Model

Thierens' convergence time model [10] estimates the number of generations it takes for a GA to converge to all 1s for *OneMax problem*. The model assumes an infinitely large population and perfect mixing. Under such assumptions, the difference of the mean fitness between two generation is $\overline{f(t+1)} - \overline{f(t)} = I(t)\sigma(t)$, where $\overline{f(t)}$ is the average fitness at generation t, $\sigma(t)$ is the standard deviation of fitness at generation t and $I(t)$ is the selection intensity at generation t. For tournament selection with selection pressure of 2, $I(t) \approx 0.57$ for any t [2]. Both $\overline{f(t)}$ and $\sigma(t)$ can be expressed as a function of the portion of correct genes in the population at generation t, $p(t)$

$$p(t+1) - p(t) = I\sqrt{\frac{p(t)\left(1-p(t)\right)}{\ell}} \quad . \tag{4}$$

Solving the above equation yields the approximate convergence time

$$\tau = \left(\frac{\pi}{2} - \sin^{-1}\left(2P_0 - 1\right)\right)\frac{\sqrt{\ell}}{I} \quad , \tag{5}$$

where P_0 is the possibility that a gene is assigned the correct value initially. $P_0 = \frac{1}{2}$ if the initial chromosomes are randomly assigned without bias.

2.2 Gambler's Ruin Model

The gambler's ruin model introduced by Harik et. al. [8] finds the probability that a block drifts to the *best* schema, the schema with the highest fitness value, for a given population size. Or inversely, it estimates the minimum population size needed for a GA to converge to the best schema successfully. The model focuses on the proportion of the best schema in the population. For an *(m,k)-decomposable problem*, which can be decomposed to m independent blocks of size k, the proportion of the best schema starts at $\frac{1}{2^k}$. The population gets one new copy of the best schema when the best schema wins over a worse schema in selection and loses one copy otherwise. The gambler's ruin model views the GA as a series of growing and losing of the best schema until the best schema takes up the entire population or it is entirely lost. The model gives an estimation of the population size needed for a GA to converge to the best schema.

$$n = \frac{2^k \ln(\alpha)}{\ln\left(\frac{1-p}{p}\right)} \quad , \tag{6}$$

where α is the probability that a BB fails to converge to the best schema and p is the probability that the best schema wins over a worse schema in selection.

2.3 Markov Chain Model

The works of Davis and Nix [4, 9] model the search process of the GA with a Markov chain. In a bit string problem that has ℓ genes, there are 2^ℓ possible chromosomes. A state is obtained by distributing a total of n individuals into these 2^ℓ possible chromosomes. Therefore, there are $H_n^{2^\ell}$ (n-multicombination from set of size 2^ℓ) possible states. $V(t) = [P_1(t), P_2(t), \ldots, P_{H_n^{2^\ell}}(t)]^T$ is a $H_n^{2^\ell}$ dimensioned vector that holds the probability for each state at time t. The effects of selection, crossover and mutation are modelled as Markov transfer matrices. Since there are $H_n^{2^\ell}$ states, the Markov transfer matrix M is a $H_n^{2^\ell}$ by $H_n^{2^\ell}$ matrix. The probability vector for each generation can be obtained from $V(t) = M^t V(0)$.

In the $H_n^{2^\ell}$ states, there are 2^ℓ states where the entire population has one identical chromosome. If mutation is not used in GAs, these 2^ℓ states can be seen as *attractors*: once the GA gets into one of these states, it can never escape from this state since the entire population has already converged. Let these 2^ℓ attractor states be the first 2^ℓ of the total $H_n^{2^\ell}$ states and the state in which all chromosomes are the best chromosome be the first state. Then the expected value of the convergence time can be obtained from the summation

$$\sum_{t=0}^{\infty}\left(t\sum_{i=1}^{2^\ell}\left(P_i(t) - P_i(t-1)\right)\right) \quad . \tag{7}$$

Similarly, the probability that the population converges to chromosome with the highest fitness value is given by

$$P_{success} = \frac{P_1(\infty)}{\sum_{i=1}^{2^\ell} P_i(\infty)} \quad . \tag{8}$$

The minimum population size is the smallest population size n such that $P_{success}$ is higher than a threshold.

2.4 The Need for Model Modification

In this paper, we need to estimate the minimum population size and the convergence time for both crossover structures on all the problems in the *(m,k)-unitary problem* family. Existing models cannot satisfy our needs.

The convergence time model estimates the convergence time for simple problems. In these problems, the average and variance of fitness are formulated as functions of the proportion of the best schema in the population. However, when sub-optimal schemata also contribute fitness to the chromosome, the existing convergence time model cannot be used. In such cases, we have to know the proportion of all schemata, not only the proportion of the best schema.

The gambler's ruin model gives precise estimation of the minimum population size for most problems when uniform

BB-wise crossover is used. When uniform crossover is performed within a BB, the gambler's ruin model cannot be applied.

The Markov chain model is complete and precise in estimating the minimum population size and convergence time for all problems and all crossover structures. However, it is extremely computation heavy. For a bit string problem of length ℓ and a population size of n, the size of the matrix is $H_n^{2^\ell}$ by H^{2^ℓ}. It exceeds the computation power of existing machines for a simple problem of length 100 and population size 1000, requiring a 10^{30000} by 10^{30000} matrix, let alone the time complexity.

3. $\mathcal{N}_{FE}$ ESTIMATION

In the previous section, Section 2.4, we have explained that existing models cannot serve our purpose in comparing the $\mathcal{N}_{fe}$ for different crossover structures. New models have to be created. In this section we introduce three models to estimate the convergence time and the minimum population size for uniform crossover and uniform BB-wise crossover. In other words, we test two different crossover structures: m blocks of size k and ℓ blocks of size 1. The perfect model for (m,k)-*unitary problem* is clearly one of these two. We use tournament selection with a selection pressure of 2 throughout the derivations and experiments of this work.

3.1 Reduced Markov Chain Model

In Section 2.3, we have shown that the Markov chain model is a precise model but it is also too complex to be used realistically. Here we show a simplification of the Markov chain model that can be used on (m,k)-*decomposable problems*. Instead of keeping track of the distribution on the entire 2^ℓ possible chromosomes, we only maintain the distribution of 2^k schemata in a block. For uniformly scaled problems, this simplification is valid since every blocks in a chromosome should go through similar states at the same time. The simplification reduces the number of states from $H_n^{2^\ell}$ to $H_n^{2^k}$. The size of the transfer matrix is therefore reduced to $H_n^{2^k}$ by $H_n^{2^k}$.

3.1.1 Definition

A **state** s_i of the reduced Markov chain model is defined as a unique distribution of the population of size n into 2^k possible schemata. Each state s_i has a unique distribution vector N_i. $N_i = [n_{i1}, n_{i2}, \ldots, n_{i2^k}]^T$, where $\sum_{x=0}^{2^k} n_{ix} = n$. There are $H_n^{2^k}$ states. The **probability vector** $V(t)$ is a $H_n^{2^k}$ dimensioned vector $V(t) = \left[p_{s_1}(t), p_{s_2}(t), \ldots, p_{s_{H_n^{2^k}}}(t)\right]^T$, where each $p_{s_i}(t)$ is the probability that the GA resides at state s_i at time t. The **transfer matrix** M is a $H_n^{2^k}$ by $H_n^{2^k}$ matrix, where each element m_{ij} is the probability that s_i transfers to s_j after one generation. The matrix is combined from the **selection matrix** and the **crossover matrix** if crossover is performed within a block. If crossover is not performed within a block, the **transfer matrix** is the **selection matrix**.

3.1.2 Selection

For any given state s_i, the average and variance of fitness is given by the equation:

$$E(f)_{s_i} = \sum_{x=0}^{2^k} \frac{n_{ix}}{n} f_x \tag{9}$$

$$Var(f)_{s_i} = \sigma_{s_i}^2 = \sum_{x=0}^{2^k} \frac{n_{ix}}{n} (f_x - E(f)_{s_i})^2 \quad , \tag{10}$$

where f_x is the fitness of schema x. When the problem is uniform scaled, we can assume that the variance of fitness of other $m-1$ blocks are the same as this block. Therefore, the probability of choosing schema x when x and y are compared is given by

$$p_{x,y} = \Phi\left(\frac{f_x - f_y}{\sqrt{2(m-1)}\sigma_{s_i}}\right) \quad , \tag{11}$$

$\Phi(x)$ is the CDF for normal distribution. The probability of selecting a schema x for state s_i is

$$p_x = \frac{n_{ix}^2}{n^2} + 2\sum_{y \neq x} p_{x,y} \frac{n_{ix} n_{iy}}{n^2} \quad . \tag{12}$$

Finally, the probability of transferring from state s_i to state s_j can be derived

$$m_{sij} = \frac{n!}{\prod n_{jx}!} \prod_{x=0}^{2^k} p_x^{n_{jx}} \quad . \tag{13}$$

m_{sij} is the element (i,j) of the **selection matrix** M_s.

3.1.3 Crossover

Crossover affects the distribution of schemata only when uniform crossover is used, rather than uniform BB-wise crossover. Consider the crossover of two schemata y and z, the probability that they produce a schema x after crossover is given by

$$p_{x,y,z} = \frac{1}{2^{D(y,z)}} F(x,y,z) \quad . \tag{14}$$

$D(y,z)$ is the Hamming distance of schemata y and z. If x is identical to the bits where y and z are identical, $F(x,y,z) = 1$; otherwise $F(x,y,z) = 0$. For example, if $y = 1010$ and $z = 1100$ then $F(x,y,z) = 1$ *if and only if* x =1**0.

The probability of creating a schema x after *crossover* is given by

$$p_x = \sum_{y=0}^{2^k} \sum_{z=0}^{2^k} p_{x,y,z} \frac{n_{iy} n_{iz}}{n^2} \quad . \tag{15}$$

Similar to *selection*, the probability of transferring from state s_i to state s_j is

$$m_{cij} = \frac{n!}{\prod n_{jx}!} \prod_{x=0}^{2^k} p_x^{n_{jx}} \quad . \tag{16}$$

m_{cij} is the element (i,j) of the **crossover matrix** M_c.

3.1.4 Application

At this point, with the **selection matrix** and **crossover matrix** at hand, we can derive the schema distribution at any time t for both cases: uniform crossover and uniform BB-wise crossover. In the case of uniform crossover,

$V(t)$ is given by $V(t) = (M_c M_s)^t V(0)$. If uniform BB-wise crossover is used, $V(t)$ is given by $V(t) = M_s^t V(0)$. For both cases, the convergence time is given by Equation 7 and the minimum population size is given by Equation 8, as introduced in Section 2.3. By comparing the $\mathcal{N}_{fe}$ $n \times t$, we can know if the block of size k should be treated as a BB or not. Although this model has been greatly reduced from the original Markov chain model, it is still too complex for computation. Further simplification is needed.

3.2 Expected Distribution Model

Instead of keeping track of the probability of each possible state as in the previous section, we use only one expected distribution to represent the situation at time t. In this model, an infinitely large population is used. Since we are dealing with unitary functions, only $k+1$ groups are maintained to represent the number of ones in a block, instead of 2^k groups in the previous section.

3.2.1 *Definition*

A **distribution vector** is a $(k+1)$ dimensioned vector. $V(t) = [p_0(t), p_1(t), \ldots, p_k(t)]$, where $p_x(t)$ is the proportion of the population that has x 1s in the block. At time 0, when the population is initialized randomly, the initial expected distribution is given by

$$p_x(0) = \frac{C_x^k}{2^k} \quad . \tag{17}$$

3.2.2 *Selection*

Selection in expected distribution model is similar to that in the Markov chain model. First we have to know the variance of fitness at time t by Equation 10. When the problem is uniform scaled, we can assume that the fitness variances of other $m-1$ blocks are the same as this block. The expected proportion of group x after selection is given by

$$p_x(t+1) = p_x^2(t) + 2\sum_{y \neq x} p_x(t)p_y(t)\Phi\left(\frac{f_x - f_y}{\sqrt{2(m-1)}\sigma_t}\right) \quad . \tag{18}$$

3.2.3 *Crossover*

When the population is infinitely large, uniform crossover performs similarly as population-wise random shuffling. In this case, we can use population-wise random shuffling for simpler derivation. The probability that a gene is 1 is given by

$$p_{one}(t) = \sum_{x=0}^{k} x p_x(t) \quad . \tag{19}$$

After *crossover*, these 1s are redistributed into the population. Therefore, the proportion of group x after crossover becomes

$$p_x(t+1) = p_{one}^x(t)\left(1 - p_{one}(t)\right)^{k-x} C_x^k \quad . \tag{20}$$

3.2.4 *Application*

The expected population distribution for every generation is calculated by applying the transformation functions iteratively, with or without crossover, to the initial expected population. When one group takes up most of the population (say, 99%), the population is converged. The number of generations for the model to reach this criteria is the convergence time of the GA. In most of the situations, the population converges to the best schema. For some problems, when uniform crossover is used, the population might converge to a sub-optimal schema. In this case, we say that the population is *trapped* at the sub-optimal schema.

Although this model is generation-by-generation simulation, it is efficient. The time complexity for this method is $O(k^2\sqrt{\ell})$, which is much faster than actually performing a GA. It gives a precise estimation to the convergence time as well. We will show the results of this model and compare them to the experiment results of GAs in Section 4.1.

3.3 Extended Gambler's Ruin Model

Harik's gambler's ruin model can be applied to problems when uniform BB-wise crossover is used and give tight upper bounds of the minimum population size. Here we modify the model to estimate the minimum population size when uniform crossover is used within a block. Also, we can slightly improve the precision when for uniform BB-wise crossover.

The gambler's ruin model considers only the threat from the second best schema. However, many other competitors are worse than the second best schema. We consider the probability that the best schema wins a tournament in selection when it is compared to all other schemata, not only the second best. After selection of the first generation

$$p_k(1) = p_k^2(0) + 2p_k(0)(1 - p_k(0))p_d \quad . \tag{21}$$

Therefore, the probability that the best schema wins over other schemata during selection is

$$p_d = \frac{p_k(1) - p_k^2(0)}{2\left(p_k(0) - p_k^2(0)\right)} \quad . \tag{22}$$

We substitute p in Equation 6 with p_d and get

$$n = \frac{2^k \ln(\alpha)}{\ln\left(\frac{1-p_d}{p_d}\right)} \quad . \tag{23}$$

For the gambler's ruin model to be applied to uniform crossover, the growth of p_{one} after selection is inspected.

$$p_{one}(1) = p_{one}^2(0) + 2p_{one}(0)(1 - p_{one}(0))p_d' \quad , \tag{24}$$

where p_d' is the probability that a 1 can be distinguished from a 0 after selection. Similar to p_d,

$$p_d' = \frac{p_{one}(1) - p_{one}^2(0)}{2\left(p_{one}(0) - p_{one}^2(0)\right)} \quad . \tag{25}$$

Substitute p in Equation 6 with p_d' gives the minimum population size n' when uniform crossover is used

$$n' = \frac{2\ln(\alpha)}{\ln\left(\frac{1-p_d'}{p_d'}\right)} \quad . \tag{26}$$

In the following section, Section 4.2, we will show how this estimation works compared to the experiment results of GAs.

4. EXPERIMENTS

In this section, we show the estimations of the expected distribution model and the extended gambler's ruin model, compared to experiment results of GAs. All the problems that we have tested with belong to the (m,k)-*unitary problem* family. The fitness function of the (m,k)-*unitary problem* family is defined in Equation 1. Different core function

$g(u)$ produces different problems. In this work, we have tested with the core functions defined in Table 1.

Table 1: Core functions used in this paper.

problem	definition
OneMax	$g(u) = u$
OneMaxExp	$g(u) = e^u$
OneMaxLog	$g(u) = \ln(u+1)$
NIAH	$g(u) = \begin{cases} 1 & \text{if } u = k \\ 0 & \text{otherwise} \end{cases}$
Trap	$g(u) = \begin{cases} 1 & \text{if } u = k \\ 0.9 \times \left(1 - \frac{u}{k-1}\right) & \text{otherwise} \end{cases}$

4.1 Expected Distribution Model

In this set of experiments, we show how precise the expected distribution model is in predicting the search path of GAs. Figure 1 shows the expected distribution of each generation compared to GA results. In all four problems shown, $(m, k) = (100, 5)$. We can see in the figures that when uniform BB-wise crossover is used, the entire population converges to the best schema $(u = k)$ in both problems. When uniform crossover is used in the *(m,k)-trap problem*, the population gets trapped at a sub-optimal schema $(u = 0)$. Also, from the figure, we can see that the expected distribution model predicts the search path of GAs precisely.

Figure 2 shows the convergence time for each problems. $k = 5$ for all problems except for *Trap2*, where $k = 2$. *Trap2* and *Trap5* are both defined as in Table 1, with different block sizes k. An large population is used to get the experiment values of convergence time and an infinitely large population is used in the estimation of convergence time. From the figure we can see that there's a constant ratio between the estimated and the experimented convergence times. Since such ratios for uniform crossover and uniform BB-wise crossover are the same, this error does not affect our detection for BBs.

4.2 Extended Gambler's Ruin Model

This set of experiments test the accuracy of the extended gambler's ruin model. Figure 3 shows the estimated and experimented probability that a BB converges to the best schema when different population sizes are used. When we use uniform crossover on the *(m,k)-trap problem*, the problem cannot be solved, no matter how large the population is. The *(m,k)-trap problem* can be solve with uniform crossover only when the selection pressure is high enough and an exponentially large population is used, but that is beyond the scope of this work. The theoretical lines are the results of Equation 6 and the equation comes from a simplification that is valid only when p is much larger than q or when the size of population is very large. This causes the error in the experiments shown in Figure 3 when n is small. This work needs only the minimum population size with which a GA can converge to the global optimum, so this error does not affect the detection of BBs.

Figure 4 shows the estimated and experimented minimum population size for different problem sizes. There is always a difference between the minimum population size estimated by the extended gambler's ruin model and the minimum

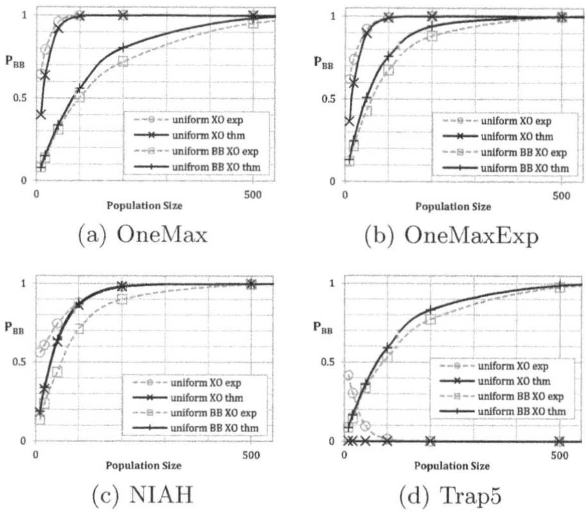

Figure 3: Estimated and experimented success rate that a BB converges to the best schema. $(m, k) = (100, 5)$ **in all experiments.**

population size obtained from bisection. This difference is sensitive to the choice of α in Equation 6. Similar to convergence time, this error is minor since the error is identical in both crossover structures and therefore cancels each other. In this set of estimations, α is set to $\frac{1}{\ell}$.

4.3 Models Combined

In this section, we combine the results of two models and estimate the $\mathcal{N}_{fe}$. Figure 5 shows $\mathcal{R}$, the ratio of $\mathcal{N}_{fe}$, for different population sizes. $\mathcal{R}$ is defined as

$$\mathcal{R} = \frac{n_{uni} t_{uni}}{n_{uniBB} t_{uniBB}} \quad . \tag{27}$$

The values of n_{uni} and n_{uniBB} are calculated from Equations 26 and Equation 23. The values of t_{uni} and t_{uniBB} are acquired with the method introduced in Section 4.1. When $\mathcal{R} > 1$, the GA works better if the block is considered a BB in crossover; when $\mathcal{R} < 1$, the GA works better if bits in a block are transferred separately in crossover. In short, a block in the *(m,k)-unitary problem* should be considered a BB *if and only if* $\mathcal{R} > 1$. With the criteria and Figure 5, we can assert that a block in the *OneMax problem*, the *OneMaxExp problem* and the *OneMaxLog problem* should not be considered a BB while a block in the *Trap problem* should be considered a BB. The *NIAH problem* is more tricky. When m is small, the minimum population size is bounded by BB supply so GAs work better when genes are transferred separately. When m is large, $\mathcal{R}$ becomes larger than 1 and GAs work better if a block is treated as a BB. We can see in Figure 5 that our models are accurate, except for the *NIAH problem* when problem size is small. The reason for this error is that, when the problem size of *NIAH* is small, the minimum population size is bounded by BB supply and BB supply is not considered in our models.

Here, we test this ratio $\mathcal{R}$ with *B-Trap problem* [5]. The *B-Trap Problem* is similar to the *Trap problem* except that it uses the Bézier curve with a parameter α to control the extent of deception. The core function of *B-Trap problem*

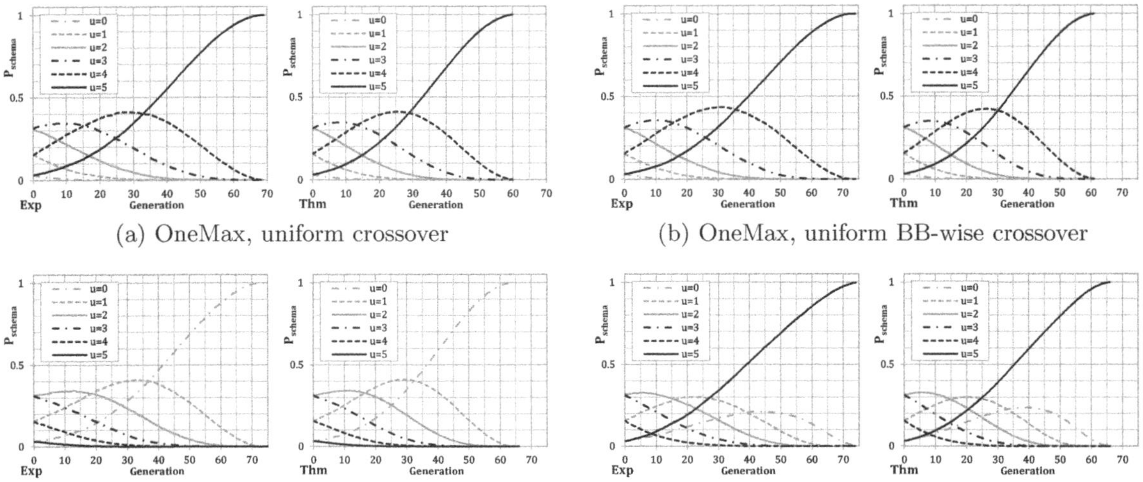

(a) OneMax, uniform crossover (b) OneMax, uniform BB-wise crossover

(c) Trap, uniform crossover (d) Trap, uniform BB-wise crossover

Figure 1: Estimated and experimented distribution of schemata in each generation.

can be defined as

$$g(u) = 0.9 - 1.8t + 1.9t^2 \quad , \tag{28}$$

where t is the root of the equation

$$u = k(1-2\alpha)t^2 + 2k\alpha t \tag{29}$$

that resides in the range $[0, 1]$. The *B-Trap problem* is least deceptive when $\alpha = 0$ and most deceptive when $\alpha = 1$. The fitness curve of the *B-Trap problem* with $k = 5$ is shown in Figure 6.

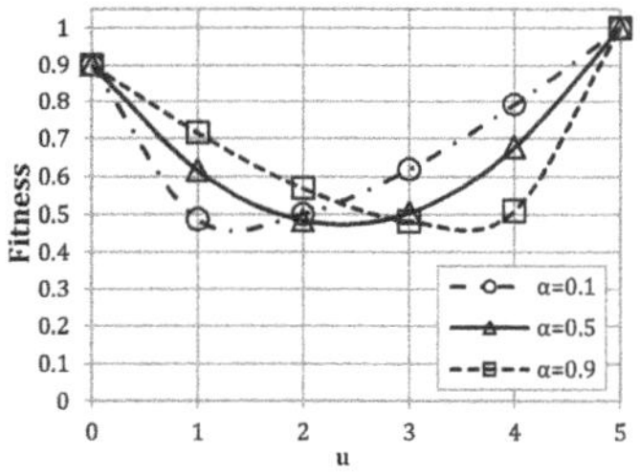

Figure 6: Fitness curve of the *B-Trap problem*.

The ratio $\mathcal{R}$ for different α is shown in Figure 7. $(m, k) = (100, 5)$ for this experiment. When $\alpha < 0.42$, $\mathcal{R}$ is smaller than 1. In this case, the block should not form a BB. When $0.42 < \alpha < 0.6$, the GA works better if the block is considered a BB. When α is greater than 0.6, the *B-Trap problem* becomes deceptive and the block must be considered a BB; otherwise the problem cannot be solved without an exponentially large population and a high selection pressure.

5. EXTENDIBILITY

In the previous sections, we have shown a way to estimate the convergence time and minimum population size for (m,k)*-unitary problems* when uniform crossover or uniform BB-wise crossover is used. The models introduced in this work can be used to a larger range of (m,k)*-decomposable problems* than the (m,k)*-unitary problem* family. Generally speaking, each of the 2^k schemata can have a different fitness value, as in the case of (m,k)*-landscape problem.* The only modification to the expected distribution model would be changing the number of groups from $k + 1$ to 2^k. We have done some preliminary work that uses only $k + 1$ groups to estimate the $\mathcal{N}_{fe}$ of (m,k)*-landscape problems.* The fitness value of a group is the average fitness of its member schemata. We generated 10000 random (m,k)*-landscape problems* and see how many of them form BBs. From Figure 8, we can see that about 50% random subproblems (m,k)*-landscape problem* form a BB ($\mathcal{R} > 1$), and a small portion of them are deceptive ($\mathcal{R} \to \infty$).

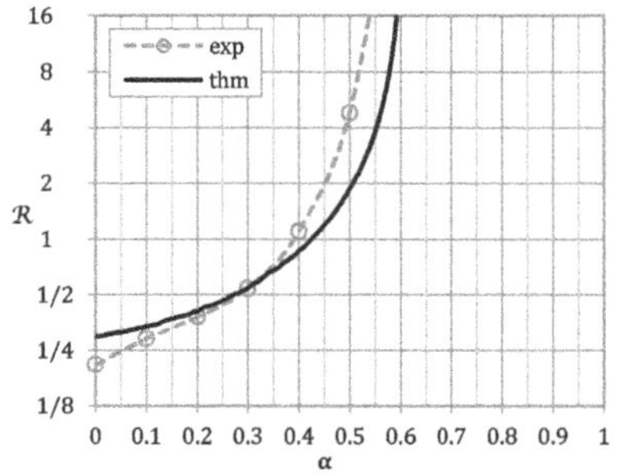

Figure 7: The $\mathcal{N}_{fe}$ ratio $\mathcal{R}$ for different α in *B-Trap problem*. $(m, k) = (100, 5)$ for all α.

Throughout this work, we focus on off-line BB detection. That is, we can detect the existence of BBs if the fitness function is given. However, the values in the derivations of our model can be acquired in GA run-time. Therefore, the models we propose in this paper can also be used to detect BBs in GA run-time.

6. CONCLUSION

This paper proposed a method to decide if a sub-function in a given fitness function should be considered a BB. To do so, we proposed three models to estimate the $\mathcal{N}_{fe}$ for both crossover structures: uniform crossover and uniform BB-wise crossover. The expected distribution model estimates

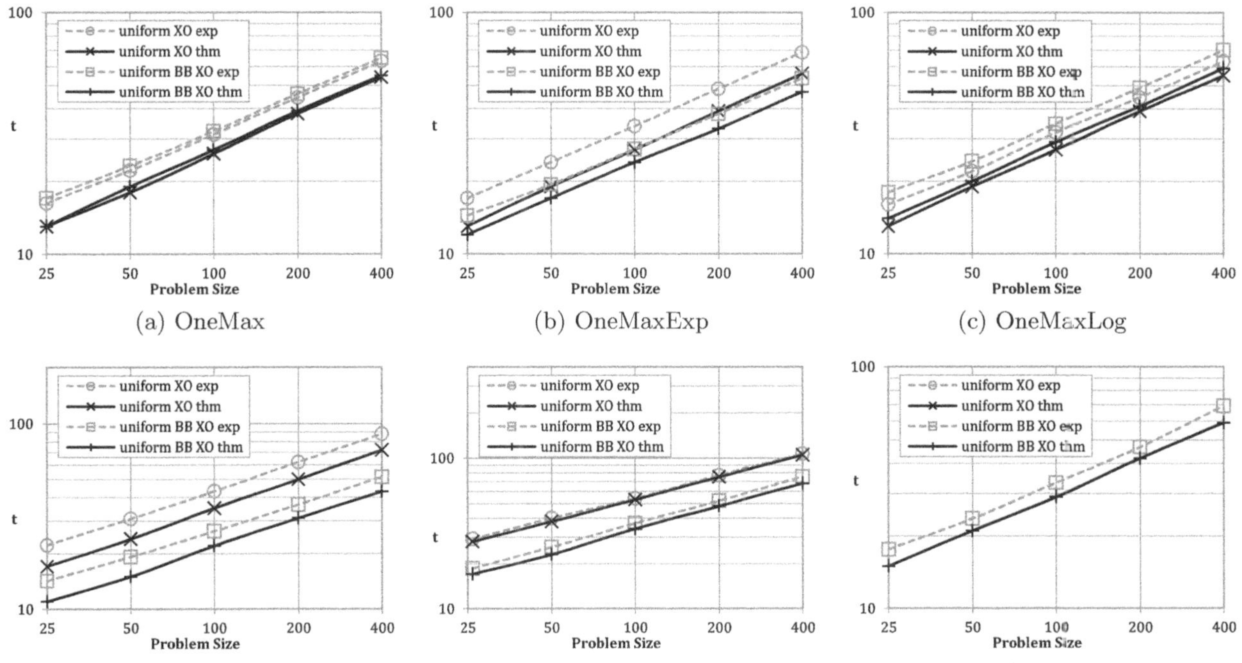

(a) OneMax (b) OneMaxExp (c) OneMaxLog

(d) NIAH (e) Trap2 (f) Trap5

Figure 2: The estimated and experimented convergence time for different problem sizes.

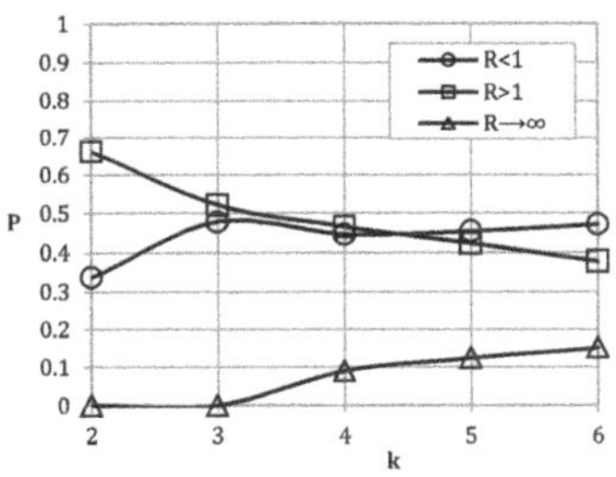

Figure 8: The probability that a block in the (m,k)-*landscape problem* forms a BB for different sub-problem size k.

the number of generations that a GA requires to converge; The extended gambler's ruin model estimates the minimum population size for a GA to converge to the optimal rather than other sub-optimal solutions. The expected $\mathcal{N}_{fe}$ is the product of the expected number of generations and the expect minimum population size.

Our models are general. They can be applied to most of the problems in the (m,k)-*unitary problem* family, which contains most of the decomposable problems that recent GA researches test with. Our models are accurate, according to the experiment results. Our models are also efficient: we only need $O(k^2\sqrt{\ell})$ operations to estimate the $\mathcal{N}_{fe}$ for both crossover structures. It is a huge improvement compared to the original way that actually runs a GA, which takes up $O(n\log(n)\sqrt{\ell})$ operations for bisection.

7. REFERENCES

[1] H. Asoh and H. Mühlenbein. On the mean convergence time of evolutionary algorithms without selection and mutation. *Parallel Problem Solving from Nature*, 866:88–97, 1994.

[2] T. Blickle and L. Thiele. A mathematical analysis of tournament selection. In *International Conference on Genetic Algorithms*, pages 9–16, 1995.

[3] A. Ceroni, M. Pelikan, and D. E. Goldberg. Convergence-time models for the simple genetic algotihm with finite population. Technical report, Illinois Genetic Algorithms Lab, 2001.

[4] T. E. Davis and J. C. Principe. A markov framework for the simple genetic algorithm. *Evolutionary Computation*, 1:269–288, 1993.

[5] K.-C. Fan, T.-L. Yu, and J.-T. Lee. Interaction detection by nfe estimation: A practical view of building blocks. Technical report, National Taiwan University, 2011.

[6] D. E. Goldberg, K. Deb, and J. H. Clark. Genetic algorithms, noise, and the sizing of populations. *Complex Systems*, 6:333–362, 1991.

[7] D. E. Goldberg, K. Sastry, and T. Latoza. On the supply of building blocks. *Proceedings of the Genetic and Evolutionary Computation Conference*, pages 336–342, 2001.

[8] G. Harik, E. Cantú-Paz, D. E. Goldberg, and B. L. Miller. The gambler's ruin problem, genetic algorithms, and the sizing of populations. *Evolutionary Computation*, 7:231–253, 1999.

[9] A. E. Nix and M. D. Vose. Modeling genetic algorithms with markov chains. *Annals of Mathematics and Artificial Intelligence*, 5:79–88, 1992.

[10] D. Thierens and D. E. Goldberg. Convergence models of genetic algorithm selection schemes. *Parallel Problem Solving from Nature*, 866:119–129, 1994.

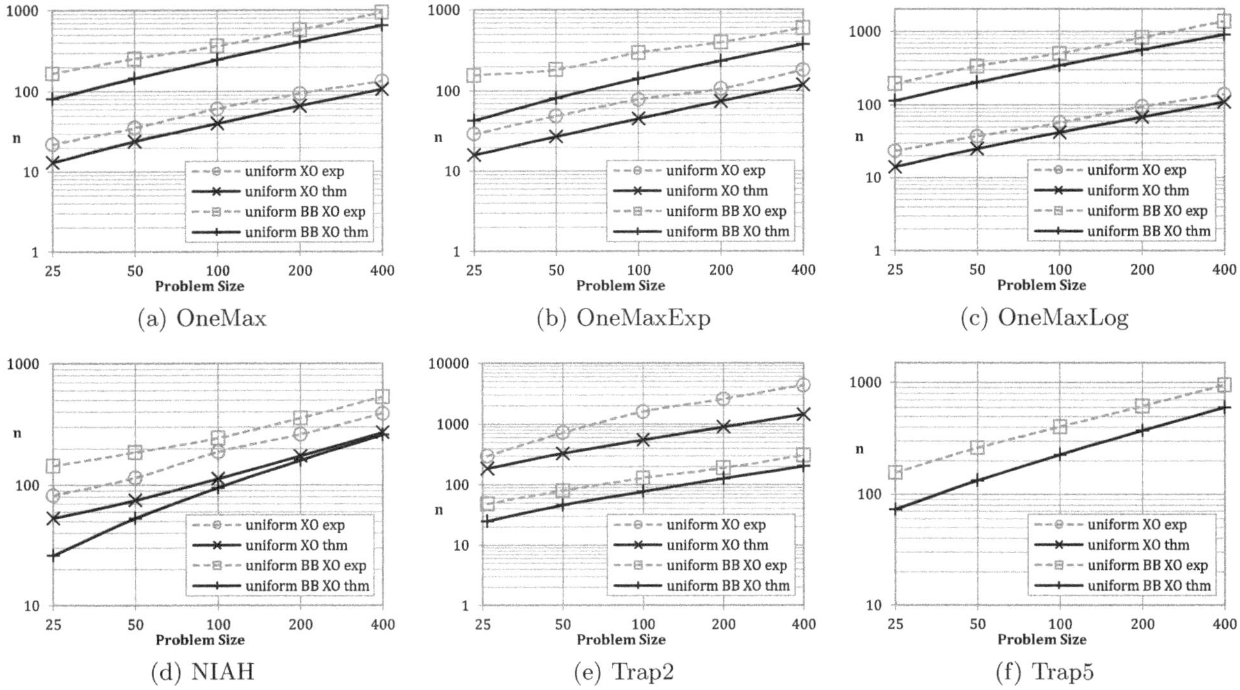

Figure 4: The estimated and experimented minimum population size for different problem sizes.

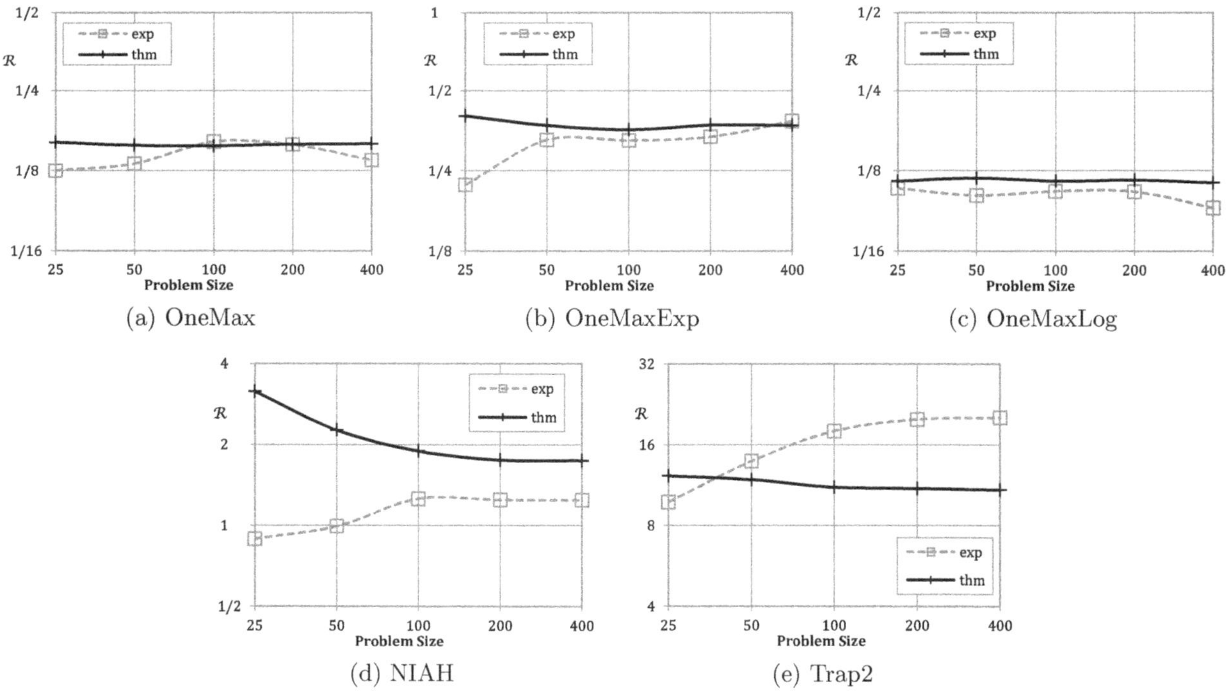

Figure 5: The estimated and experimented ratio of $\mathcal{N}_{fe}$ for different problem sizes.

Runtime Analysis of Convex Evolutionary Search

Alberto Moraglio
CERCIA, University of Birmingham
Birmingham B15 2TT, UK

Dirk Sudholt
University of Sheffield
Sheffield S1 4DP, UK

ABSTRACT

Geometric crossover formalises the notion of crossover operator across representations. In previous work, it was shown that all evolutionary algorithms with geometric crossover (but with no mutation) do a generalised form of convex search. Furthermore, it was suggested that these search algorithms could perform well on concave and approximately concave fitness landscapes. In this paper, we study the runtime of a generalised form of convex search on concave fitness landscapes. This is a first step towards linking a geometric theory of representations and runtime analysis in the attempt to (i) set the basis for a more general/unified approach for the runtime analysis of evolutionary algorithms across representations, and (ii) identify the essential matching features of evolutionary search behaviour and landscape topography that cause polynomial performance. Our convex search algorithm optimises LeadingOnes in $O(n \log n)$ fitness evaluations, which is faster than all unbiased unary black-box algorithms.

Categories and Subject Descriptors

F.2.2 [**Analysis of Algorithms and Problem Complexity**]: Nonnumerical Algorithms and Problems

Keywords

Geometric crossover, recombination, runtime analysis, convex search, pure adaptive search

1. INTRODUCTION

For the No Free Lunch (NFL) theorem [20], no search algorithm is better than any other on all fitness landscapes. This implies that any non-futile theory of search algorithms that aims at proving performance better than random search has to focus on a restricted class of search algorithms and on a corresponding "well-matched" restricted class of fitness landscapes. Matching classes of search algorithms and fitness landscapes is an important open problem in the field.

GECCO'12, July 7–11, 2012, Philadelphia, Pennsylvania, USA.
Copyright 2012 ACM 978-1-4503-1177-9/12/07 ...$10.00.

The class of evolutionary algorithms (EAs) with geometric crossover [11] encompasses and formalises many well-known representation-specific EAs [9]. In recent work [10], Moraglio showed that this class of algorithms (without mutation) does a generalised/abstract form of convex search. The unity in behaviour of EAs across representations calls for a single class of fitness landscapes well-matched to them all – a matching that goes beyond the specific representation. Well-matched "topographic features" of fitness landscapes are those essential features that can be exploited by the common "behavioural features" characterising this class of search algorithms, and produce good search performance. Intuition on continuous spaces suggests that convex search may be well-matched with functions which have a globally concave trend (when maximising). There is some formal evidence that this intuition is correct and that it extends naturally to general metric spaces [10].

Runtime analysis is the standard approach to analyse analytically algorithmic performance. In the last decade it has been applied, with an ever increasing success, to randomised search heuristics and it is establishing itself as a leading theory [14, 1]. Despite its success, it has been difficult to analyse EAs with population and crossover, although there are some results [4, 5, 16, 2, 6]. Furthermore, the analysis is done on a per-algorithm-and-per-problem basis, and approaches that have worked on a algorithm-problem pair do not usually transfer to others. Clearly, a more general approach to determine the performance of a *class* of algorithms on a *class* of problems would be a major progress.

In this paper, we start studying the runtime of a generalised form of convex search on concave fitness landscapes. This is a first step towards linking a geometric theory of representations and runtime analysis in the attempt to set the basis for a more general/unified approach for the runtime analysis of evolutionary algorithms across representations.

We strip to the bare essentials both the specific class of evolutionary algorithms and the matching class of problems considered. Whereas both algorithms and problems are not by themselves of practical interest/relevance, they allow us to identify the essential matching features of evolutionary search behaviour and landscape topography that cause polynomial performance, on problems on which Pure Random Search (PRS) runs in exponential time. Interestingly, their simplicity allows us to draw tight links with the work on Pure Adaptive Search (PAS) [15], an *ideal* algorithm which has been studied since the eighties and which presents an exponential speed-up on PRS on almost all problems. The main open challenge about PAS is finding how to implement it efficiently. We will also discuss how the results presented here could be extended, in the future, to EAs in actual use and to interesting combinatorial optimisation problems, making this line of theory potentially relevant to practice.

2. ABSTRACT CONVEX EVOLUTIONARY SEARCH

We give some necessary definitions and previous results[1] from [10]. For each definition, we give the general version for a generic metric space, and the corresponding definition specialised to the Hamming distance on binary strings (obtained by substituting the Hamming distance in the general definition, and rephrasing the outcome in terms on representation-specific language, i.e., binary strings, bits and schemata).

A recombination operator is a *geometric crossover* if, for some metric, all offspring are in the metric segment between their parents, for any pair of parents. Many well-known recombination operators across representations are geometric crossovers, e. g., all mask-based crossovers on binary strings are geometric crossovers w. r. t. Hamming distance.

A set of points in a metric space is *geodetically convex* if all metric segments between any two points in the set are entirely contained in the set. In the Hamming space on binary strings, geodetically convex sets coincide with schemata.

The *metric convex hull* of a set of points in a metric space is the smallest geodetically convex set that includes the set. In the Hamming space on binary strings, the metric convex hull of a set of binary strings is the smallest schema (with the least number of '*' symbols) matching all those strings.

Regardless of the specific metric space and associated representation, and of the specific fitness landscape considered, all evolutionary algorithms with geometric crossover (and selection and replacement) but with no mutation do a form of *convex search* (see Figure 1). The term *co*() denotes the metric convex hull operator, and P_n, P'_n and P_{n+1} are the current population, the set of selected parents, and the offspring population, respectively. Figure 1 shows that the convex hull of the population of offspring is always included in the convex hull of the population of parents. So, the overall search forms a nested chain of convex hulls of populations reducing in size with time. Specifically for the Hamming space, this result says that once a bit is fixed in a population to a certain value (i.e., 0 or 1) that bit will stay fixed in all subsequent populations, or equivalently, that the smallest schemata spanning subsequent populations are increasingly more specific (they can only lose '*' symbols).

On the Euclidean space, intuition suggests that convex search may do well on (approximately) concave functions when maximising [2] (see Figure 2). Various traditional notions of concave function can be generalised to general metric spaces, hence to combinatorial spaces associated with any representation, by replacing the notion of (Euclidean) segment with that of metric segment in the original definitions. However, caution is needed, as the resulting generalisation may not be suitable for combinatorial spaces (only degenerate landscapes on combinatorial spaces may be encompassed

[1]The framework in this section may look related to the field of Convex Optimisation, but it differs fundamentally from it. See [10] for a discussion of the differences.

[2]In this work, we assume maximisation on concave landscapes. Analogous considerations hold unchanged for minimisation on convex landscapes.

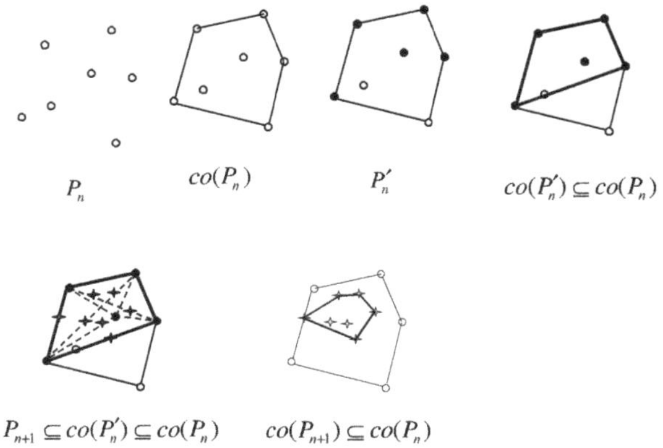

Figure 1: Convex evolutionary search.

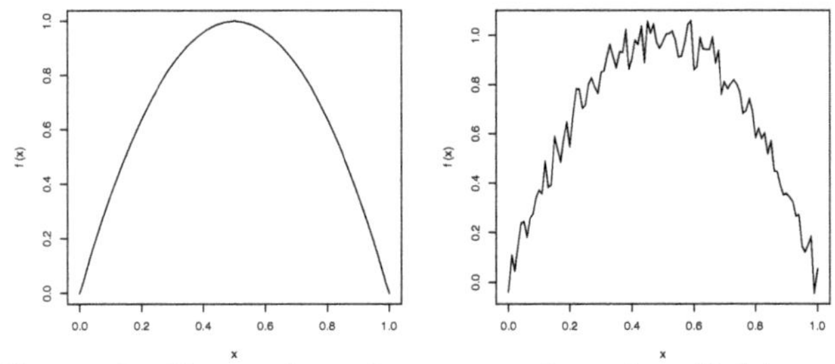

Figure 2: Examples of concave function (left) and function with a concave trend (right).

by the definition, e.g., only flat landscapes). The following well-behaved generalisations were proposed in [10]:

Average-concave landscapes for all $x, y : z \sim U([x, y])$, $E[f(z)] \geq (f(x) + f(y))/2$.

Quasi-concave landscapes for all $x, y : z \in [x, y], f(z) \geq \min(f(x), f(y))$.

They specialise to the space of binary strings with the Hamming distance by considering the Hamming segment in their definition. It can be shown that the OneMax problem is average-concave and average-convex (i.e., it is average-affine), and the LeadingOnes problem is quasi-concave.

Adding an ϵ-bounded perturbation function to the above definitions, we obtain *approximately average-concave* and *approximately quasi-concave* landscapes: $E[f(z)] \geq (f(x) + f(y))/2 - \epsilon$ and $f(z) \geq \min(f(x), f(y)) - \epsilon$. Any function is approximately average/quasi concave for ϵ large enough.

In [10] it was shown that, *regardless of the specific metric, on average/quasi concave landscapes, convex search with geometric crossover and selection produces steady improvements*: for any population, the average/worst fitness of the next population is in expectation/deterministically no worse than the average/worst fitness of the given population (even without selection). This result degrades graciously as the landscape becomes less concave (for increasing ϵ). Whereas this result in general does not imply neither convergence to the optimum nor efficient performance, it is a strong one-step performance result that holds across all representations.

In the reminder, we investigate the possibility of a general runtime analysis of evolutionary algorithms on concave landscapes *across representations* starting from the result above. Is a general result possible *regardless of the underlying space*? Does convex search on concave landscapes have exponentially better runtime than random search *regardless of the underlying space*? If not, what are the features of the underlying space which affect critically the runtime, making it change from polynomial to exponential? In order to start answering these questions we need further assumptions on the specific algorithm, landscape and performance measure.

3. ALGORITHM, LANDSCAPE AND PERFORMANCE MEASURE

We strip to the bare essentials both the specific class of EAs and the matching class of problems considered. This will allow us to pinpoint the essential mechanism that links matching features of evolutionary search behaviour and landscape topography to polynomial performance, on problems on which random search runs in exponential time.

3.1 Algorithm

The search algorithm considered is the Convex Search Algorithm (Algorithm 1). This is an *abstract/representation-independent* algorithm as it is well-defined over any metric space, as all its algorithmic elements are well-defined on any metric space. The *metric convex hull uniform recombination* returns an offspring sampled uniformly at random from the (metric) convex hull formed by its parents. This recombination operator is a multi-parental recombination operator which like geometric crossover performs a convex search when used in a EA without mutation, regardless of the specific underlying space and representation.

Algorithm 1 Convex Search Algorithm

```
Input: k: population size
Output: individual in the last population

Initialise Population Uniformly at Random
while Population has not converged to the same individual do
    Rank individuals on fitness
    if there are at least two fitness values in the current population
    then
        remove all individuals with the worst fitness
    end if
    Apply k times Metric Convex Hull Uniform Recombination to
    the remaining individuals to create the next population
end while
return any individual in the last population
```

The specific convex hull recombination for binary strings with Hamming distance can be formally obtained by plugging in the Hamming distance in the general definition of metric convex hull recombination. It can then be turned into an operational (i.e., algorithmic) definition by re-writing the operator in terms of manipulation of the underlying representation (binary strings). This turns the geometric description into a description of how to act on the parent binary strings to obtain the offspring. These two are different descriptions of the same operator. The operational description of the uniform convex hull recombination for the Hamming space is shown in Algorithm 2.

Algorithm 2 Binary Uniform Convex Hull Recombination

```
for each position in the binary strings do
    if all parents have 1 or 0 at that position then
        the offspring has 1 or 0 at that position, respectively
    else
        (if there is at least a 1 or at least a 0)
        the offspring has 1 or 0 at that position with probability 0.5
    end if
end for
```

The (abstract) Convex Search Algorithm can be formally specified to the Hamming space by replacing the Metric Uniform Convex Hull Recombination with the Binary Uniform Convex Hull Recombination, obtaining the Binary Convex Search Algorithm. This is a variant of Genetic Algorithm with Gene Pool Recombination, with a recombination which does not depend on the frequency of 0s and 1s at each position, and with a particular type of truncation selection.

3.2 Landscape

In section 2, we have considered two types of generalisations of concave landscapes, average-concave and quasi-concave, and their approximately concave extensions. These landscapes are "well-matched" with Convex Evolutionary Search *at an abstract level* because there the average/worst fitness of the offspring population is not worse than the average/worst fitness of the parent population *irrespective of the underlying specific metric and representation*. In this work, we focus on quasi-concave landscapes leaving the analysis of the other notions of concave landscapes to future work.

We define *(canonical) fitness-level sets* as follows. Assume that the codomain of the fitness function is finite, with values $a_0 < a_1 < \cdots < a_q$. Then for $0 \leq i \leq q$ we define the level set L_i as $\{x \in S\colon f(x) \geq a_i\}$ (slightly abusing the term *level set* as L_i includes higher levels). All these level sets form a nested chain of sets by construction: $L_0 \supsetneq L_1 \supsetneq \cdots \supsetneq L_q$. In particular, $L_0 = S$. The sets $(L_0 \setminus L_1), (L_1 \setminus L_2), \ldots, L_q$ form a *fitness-level partition* in the sense defined by Wegener [19].

The following properties hold for quasi-concave landscapes irrespective of the underlying metric and representation:

1. If f is quasi-concave: for all sets $C \subseteq S$, if $z \in \mathrm{co}(C)$ then $f(z) \geq \min\{f(x) \mid x \in C\}$.
2. A landscape f is quasi-concave iff all level sets are (metric) convex sets.

A direct consequence of the first property is that the convex hull recombination on quasi-concave landscapes returns offspring whose fitness is not worse than those of any of its parents, for any underlying metric and representation.

The second property allows us to characterise quasi-concave landscapes constructively: a landscape is quasi-concave iff it is a "Tower of Hanoi" of convex sets. This property is interesting when considered together with combinatorial spaces because they give rise to discrete sets of fitness values. This allows us to check quasi-concavity of a landscape by checking the convexity of all level sets one by one. Also, we can use this property to construct any quasi-concave function for any representation and metric space.

We illustrate this for the Hamming space on binary strings. The idea is to iteratively build a nested chain of convex level sets and subsequently increase fitness values for inner sets. We start from the largest level set and assign the same minimum fitness to all points. We then choose a convex subset of the current fitness level as next fitness level and increase the fitness of all points therein. The process is iterated by further dividing the next fitness level, and so on.

For example, for any x_0 matching the schema `******`, we initially assign, say, $f(x_0) := 0$. Consider the convex subset `0*****` of `******` and let us assign to any x_1 matching this schema fitness values of 1, i.e., $f(x_1) := 1$. So, the quasi-concave function we will obtain has fitness 0 for any string starting with 1 and fitness strictly larger than 0 for any string starting with 0. Now consider the fitness level

0*****. We choose the convex subset 01**1* of 0***** to have fitness value 2, and then choose a further convex subset in 01**1*, and so on. The procedure ends when a convex set with a single element is reached, or earlier, so obtaining a landscape with a plateau. As the LEADINGONES landscape can be built in this way, it is a quasi-concave landscape. It is possible to show that ONEMAX is not a quasi-concave landscape because its level sets are Hamming balls, which unlike Euclidean balls, are not geodetically convex.

Quasi-concave landscapes are a rather nice class of landscapes, potentially solvable efficiently. However, it is easy to see that the NEEDLE landscape belongs to this class. This shows that this class, in the worst case, is intractable by any search algorithm that does not know a priori information about the position of the needle. What makes NEEDLE intractable is that convex fitness levels are too few and shrink too fast. Therefore we restrict the class of quasi-concave landscapes as follows. A *polynomial quasi-concave landscape* is a quasi-concave landscape with:

1. the number $q+1$ of fitness levels is polynomial in n (problem size, $n = \log(|S|)$).
2. the rate between sizes of successive fitness levels is an inverse polynomial: $r := \min\{|L_{i+1}|/|L_i| \mid 0 \leq i < q\} \geq 1/\text{poly}(n)$.

A polynomial quasi-convex landscape has two characteristic parameters q and r. It is easy to verify that LEADINGONES is a polynomial quasi-concave landscape (it has n fitness levels, and for each level the area of the next level is half of the area of the previous level), whereas NEEDLE is a quasi-concave landscape but not polynomial quasi-concave (it has only two fitness levels, but the area of the second level is exponentially smaller than that of the first level).

3.3 Performance Measures

We say that Convex Evolutionary Search has converged when the whole population contains copies of the same search point. As the algorithm does not always converge to the optimum, we are interested in estimating the probability that the algorithm converges to a global optimum (PC). We also look at the runtime conditional on convergence (RT). A lower bound on PC and a deterministic upper bound on RT give an upper bound on the expected time a global optimum is found when restarts are used. Restarting Convex Evolutionary Search after RT generations yields an upper bound of RT/PC on the expected total number of generations.

The number of function evaluations is by a factor of k larger than the number of generations. The former might be a more fair performance measure as it excludes the possibility that a polynomial number of generation is achieved by means of an exponentially large population. So we are most interested in settings where k·RT/PC is polynomial.

The class of search algorithms and fitness landscapes considered are well-defined for any underlying metric space and associated representation. In their definitions, the underlying space appears as a parameter, so the class of search algorithms and fitness landscapes can be considered as functional forms that can be instantiated to a specific space by functional application to it. At an abstract level, we could imagine that an abstract search algorithm is "run" on an abstract fitness landscape *before* specifying the underlying specific space in both algorithm and landscape, obtaining a performance that is itself a functional form on the underlying space, i.e., in which the underlying space appears as a parameter. This functional way of interfacing general and specific results allows us to separate neatly the part of the analysis which is valid for any underlying space and associated representation (i.e., a general theory essentially resulting from matching the abstract notions of convexity of the search algorithm and the concavity of the landscape), and pinpoint which particular features of the underlying space and representation have an effect on the performance. The space-specific values of these features can then be measured and plugged in the general expression of the runtime result, as any other parameter, to obtain the specific runtime for the specific space. This way of shaping a theory has the benefit of systematising/automatising the runtime analysis for any new space and associated representation.

4. PURE ADAPTIVE SEARCH

Pure Adaptive Search (PAS) (see Algorithm 3) is an ideal algorithm, which is in general not implementable efficiently, that has been studied analytically since the 80s in the field of Global Optimisation. This search algorithm requires a search operator able to sample offspring uniformly at random in the level set corresponding to the fitness of the best solution found so far. As Pure Random Search (PRS), which at each iteration samples offspring uniformly at random in the entire search space, the performance of PAS does not depend on the structure of the space S but only on the frequency distribution of the values in the range of the objective function f. This makes PAS a representation-independent algorithm, well-defined on any metric space and across representations. PAS has a well-developed general theory [21], which essentially says that on almost all functions, PAS is exponentially better than PRS. This result is conceptually interesting because it shows that the two simple ingredients of (i) getting at each step better offspring, and (ii) getting them uniformly distributed in the improving set are *sufficient conditions* to produce an exponential speed up on random search performance, very generally, on any search space and virtually on any problem. Interestingly, the result above holds also for a number of relaxations of PAS which are closer to implementable algorithms, e.g., Hesitant Adaptive Search [21]. In this algorithm offspring can land in the improving fitness level only with a certain probability, and the probability distribution of the offspring may deviate from uniformity (in some restricted ways).

Algorithm 3 Pure Adaptive Search

```
1: Pick an initial point X_0 uniformly at random.
2: i = 0
3: while optimum not found do
4:     Generate X_{i+1} uniformly at random on the level set S_i = {x :
       x ∈ S, f(x) ≥ f(X_i)} (improving set).
5:     i = i + 1
6: end while
```

The big challenge about PAS is being able to find efficient implementations of it. Looking for general efficient implementations of PAS working on any problem is a chimera, as it would imply RP = NP. So, it makes sense to look for specific efficient implementations of PAS when applied to restricted classes of problems. This objective can be approached the other way around: starting from a randomised search heuristic and a class of problems and showing that the search heuristic can be seen as an implementation of PAS for that class of problems. This would at the same time (i) give a general and fundamental explanation of why that specific search heuristic is efficient on the class of problems considered (i.e., because it can be reduced to PAS) (ii) show that PAS is implementable efficiently for a specific class of problems (i.e., because the specific search heuristic can be implemented efficiently). In this work, we will show that convex search on concave landscapes is essentially an implementation of PAS, linking for the first time the PAS framework to Evolutionary Algorithms.

The following theorem gives the runtime of PAS and PRS on the particular class of function considered in this study.

THEOREM 1. *Consider fitness levels* $L_0, \ldots, L_q$ *and let* $r := \min\{|L_{i+1}|/|L_i| \mid 0 \le i < q\}$ *as well as* $s := \max\{|L_{i+1}|/|L_i| \mid 0 \le i < q\}$.

The expected running time of PAS is at most q/r. *In particular, the expected running time of PAS on any polynomial quasi-concave landscape is polynomial.*

The expected running time of PRS is at least s^{-q}. *If* $s = 1 - \Omega(1)$ *and* $q = n^{\Omega(1)}$ *this time is exponential.*

PROOF. The expected runtime of PAS can be upper bounded by $1/\Pr(L_1 \mid L_0) + 1/\Pr(L_2 \mid L_1) + \cdots + 1/\Pr(L_q \mid L_{q-1})$. As each term is at most $1/r$, we get an upper bound of q/r. For any polynomial quasi-concave landscape we have $q \le \text{poly}(n)$ and $1/r \le \text{poly}(n)$, hence we get a polynomial upper bound.

The hitting probability of PRS can be written as $\Pr(L_0) \cdot \Pr(L_1 \mid L_0) \cdot \cdots \cdot \Pr(L_q \mid L_{q-1})$, which is upper bounded by s^q. The expected hitting time of PRS is hence at least s^{-q}. □

5. RUNTIME ANALYSIS OF CONVEX EVOLUTIONARY SEARCH

In this section we first propose a general runtime result for convex search on quasi-concave landscapes that holds across spaces and representations. This result applies in principle to *any* metric space and representation. In order to illustrate its applicability, we show how the general result can be specialised to determine the runtime of convex search on quasi-concave landscapes for three specific spaces: Boolean spaces endowed with the Hamming distance, the space of integer vectors endowed with the Hamming distance, and the space of integer vectors endowed with Manhattan distance.

Before presenting the formal statement and proof of the general result, we give an informal description of the idea. The reasoning to determine the runtime of a successful convex search is as follows. The initial population comprises a number of points sampled uniformly at random from the search space (i.e., L_0). Then selection is applied which removes all points in the population with the worst fitness value. The remaining points are typically uniformly distributed at random on L_1 (by rejection sampling).

If the convex hull of these selected points covers L_1 completely, the convex hull recombination of these points generates the offspring population uniformly at random on L_1. The mentioned condition is met with high probability on combinatorial spaces provided the population size is sufficiently large[3]. Then the cycle is repeated, until the optimum has been found. Assuming that the convex hull of the selected points at a previous level always covers the next level (or, in rare cases, a further one), the algorithm always conquers a new fitness level at each iteration. Then, the runtime of the algorithm is bounded by the number of non-optimal fitness levels, q. As the algorithm performs uniform sampling on each traversed fitness-level set, in such a successful run, this makes the link to PAS explicit.

Note that the only space-specific element in this reasoning is the (worst-case) probability that a convex set in the specific space is covered by the convex hull of a number of points sampled uniformly at random in the convex set. This probability is important as it affects the required size of the population for the optimum to be reached with high probability, and it can be passed as the only required space-specific parameter to the general runtime expression.

5.1 A General Runtime Bound

We formalise these ideas. With regard to a given metric space, we say that a set P *covers* a set C if $\text{co}(P) \supseteq C$.

DEFINITION 2. *Given a metric space* $M = (S, d)$, *let* $\mathbf{C_M}$ *be the set of all geodetically convex sets on* M. *We define* $\text{P}_M^{\text{Cov}}(m)$ *as the worst-case probability that the convex hull of the set* P *of* m *points drawn uniformly at random from a geodetically convex set* $C \in \mathbf{C_M}$ *covers entirely the set* C:

$$\text{P}_M^{\text{Cov}}(m) = \min_{C \in \mathbf{C_M}} \Pr(\text{co}(P) = C \mid P = U_m(C)).$$

Note that the worst-case covering probability is monotone in the number of samples m as additional samples can only increase the convex hull:

$$\forall m' \ge m \colon \text{P}_M^{\text{Cov}}(m') \ge \text{P}_M^{\text{Cov}}(m).$$

The following lemma gives a lower bound on the probability that the next fitness level is covered completely.

LEMMA 3. *Assume fitness levels* $L_0, \ldots, L_q$ *where* $r = \min\{|L_{i+1}|/|L_i| \mid 0 \le i < q\}$. *Consider a (parent) population* P'_t *and suppose for some fitness level* $0 \le i < q$ *we have* $\text{co}(P'_t) = L_i$. *Let the new population* P_{t+1} *result from k-times Metric Convex Hull Uniform Recombination of* P'_t *and let* $P'_{t+1} = \text{sel}(P_{t+1})$ *be the next parent population. The probability that* $\text{co}(P'_{t+1}) = L_j$ *for some* $i < j \le q$ *is at least*

$$\text{P}_M^{\text{Cov}}\left(\frac{kr}{4}\right) - \exp\left(-\frac{9kr}{32}\right).$$

PROOF. Let j be the largest index such that $P_{t+1} \subseteq L_{j-1}$. (Typically $j = i + 1$.) Note that all offspring are still distributed uniformly in L_{j-1}. And as $P_{t+1} \cap (L_{j-1} \setminus L_j) \neq \emptyset$, selection will remove all points in $L_{j-1} \setminus L_j$, leading to $\text{sel}(P_{t+1}) \subseteq L_j$. The probability of covering L_j is at least $\text{P}_M^{\text{Cov}}\left(\frac{kr}{4}\right)$, provided that at least $\frac{kr}{4}$ offspring are in L_j.

The probability for this event can be estimated by standard Chernoff bounds [13]. The expected number of offspring in L_j is $k|L_j|/|L_{j-1}| \ge kr$. The probability that less than $kr/4$ offspring fall in L_j is at most

$$\exp\left(-kr \cdot (3/4)^2 \cdot 1/2\right) = \exp\left(-\frac{9kr}{32}\right).$$

The claim then follows by the union bound. □

[3]On continuous spaces, this condition is never met. However, this condition is sufficient and not necessary to guarantee that the optimum is reached. So, this does not necessarily imply that the convex search algorithm cannot be efficient on continuous spaces.

Lemma 3 easily generalises, using that all probabilities for covering different fitness levels are independent and taking the union bound for error probabilities $\exp\left(-\frac{9kr}{32}\right)$. We also take into account the probability of covering L_0 in the initialisation. It is at least $\mathrm{P}_M^{\mathrm{Cov}}(k) \geq \mathrm{P}_M^{\mathrm{Cov}}\left(\frac{kr}{4}\right)$.

THEOREM 4. *Assume a quasi-concave fitness function on any metric space M with fitness levels $L_0, \dots, L_q$ where $r = \min\{|L_{i+1}|/|L_i| \mid 0 \leq i < q\}$. The Convex Search Algorithm with population size k finds a global optimum within q generations and kq fitness evaluations with probability at least*

$$\left(\mathrm{P}_M^{\mathrm{Cov}}\left(\frac{kr}{4}\right)\right)^{q+1} - q \cdot \exp\left(-\frac{9kr}{32}\right).$$

5.2 Boolean Spaces & Hamming Distance

We specialise the general runtime result to the space of binary strings endowed with the Hamming distance HD. The specialised result is the runtime of the convex search algorithm specialised to this space (the convex search algorithm with the binary uniform convex hull operator, Algorithm 2) on the quasi-concave landscape specialised to this space (the class of binary landscapes presented in section 3.2).

We first bound the probability of covering any set.

LEMMA 5. *For $M = (\{0,1\}^n, \mathrm{HD})$ and $m \in \mathbb{N}$ we have*

$$\mathrm{P}_M^{\mathrm{Cov}}(m) \geq (1 - 2^{-m+1})^n.$$

PROOF. For every geodetically convex set $C \in \mathbf{C_M}$ for the specific case of $M = (S, \mathrm{HD})$ a necessary requirement for the convex hull of m points uniformly drawn in C not covering C is that there is a bit that is fixed to the same value in all m samples. The probability for fixing a specific bit is 2^{-m+1} as the bit needs to be set to either 0 or 1 in all m uniform samples. The probability that no bit is fixed is $(1 - 2^{-m+1})^n$. □

Then the bound from Theorem 4 simplifies as follows.

THEOREM 6. *Let $M = (\{0,1\}^n, \mathrm{HD})$ and the assumptions for Theorem 4 hold. Then the Convex Search Algorithm finds a global optimum within at most q generations and kq fitness evaluations with probability at least*

$$\left(1 - 2^{-\frac{kr}{4}+1}\right)^{n(q+1)} - q \cdot \exp\left(-\frac{9kr}{32}\right)$$

$$\geq 1 - (q+2)n \cdot 2^{-\frac{kr}{4}}$$

where the second bound requires $2^{\frac{kr}{4}-1} \geq n(q+1)$.

PROOF. The first bound follows directly from Theorem 4 by plugging in Lemma 5. If $2^{\frac{kr}{4}-1} \geq n(q+1)$ we use $(1-x)^y \leq 1 - xy/2$ for $0 \leq xy \leq 1$ [7, Lemma 1] to estimate $(1-2^{-\frac{kr}{4}+1})^{n(q+1)} \leq (q+1)n \cdot 2^{-\frac{kr}{4}}$. We also have $2^{-kr/4} \geq e^{-9kr/32}$ since $2^{-1/4} \geq e^{-9/32}$. Further, $q \leq n$ as at least one bit is fixed with every fitness level. So $q + (q+1)n \leq (q+2)n$. Putting everything together gives the second bound. □

In particular, we can easily derive how large the population must be in order to guarantee that Convex Evolutionary Search with restarts finds a global optimum. If $k \geq 4\log(2(q+2)n)/r$, the probability bound from Theorem 4 is at least $1/2$. This gives the following.

COROLLARY 7. *If $k \geq 4\log(2(q+2)n)/r$ then Convex Evolutionary Search restarting after q generations finds a global optimum within $2q$ expected generations and $2kq$ expected fitness evaluations.*

On polynomial quasi-concave landscapes, as both q and $\frac{1}{r}$ are polynomial in n, the number of generations and the population size are polynomial. For LEADINGONES $q = n$ and $r = 1/2$, so with $k \geq 8\log(2(n+2)n) \approx 16\log n$ the expected number of generations with restarts is at most $2n$.

COROLLARY 8. *Convex Evolutionary Search with population size $k = 8\log(2(n+2)n)$ and restarts optimises LEADINGONES in $O(n \log n)$ function evaluations.*

This is remarkable as EAs using only mutation need at least $\Omega(n^2)$ function evaluations [17]. The same holds for all unary unbiased black-box algorithms [8], whereas binary black-box algorithms run in time $O(n \log n)$ [3].

5.3 Integer Vectors & Hamming and Manhattan Distances

We give two more examples of specialisation of the general runtime result. We consider two metric spaces on the same set: the Hamming distance HD and the Manhattan distance MD on integer vectors $S_d = \{0, 1, \dots, d-1\}^n$, a natural space e. g. for colouring problems [18].

Before presenting the specialisation of the runtime, we explain the specialisation to these spaces in order to understand the space-specific forms of the convex search algorithm and the class of quasi-concave landscapes. Both metrics are product metric spaces; distances between two vectors can be written as a dimension-wise sum of (unidimensional) distances between their elements in each dimension. The unidimensional distance corresponding to the Manhattan distance is the absolute value of the difference between two integers, and for the Hamming distance is the "discrete" distance over a set of integers, which is 1 for any two different integers, and 0 otherwise. The product structural property of these spaces allows us to build geometric elements (e.g., segments) in these spaces by doing the cartesian product of uni-dimensional segments across all dimensions.

Space structure: For (S_d, HD), the neighbourhood graph associated with each dimension is a clique with d nodes as any two non-coinciding integers (i.e, nodes) are at distance one (i.e., they are direct neighbours and connected by an edge). The neighbourhood structure of (S_d, HD) is the cartesian product of clique graphs across dimensions. For (S_d, MD), the neighbourhood graph associated with each dimension is a line graph of d nodes (i.e, an integer line ranging from 0 to $d-1$). The neighbourhood structure of (S_d, MD) is the cartesian product of line graphs across dimensions (i.e., "discretised" hyper-boxes).

Segment: For (S_d, HD), unidimensional segments are edges, i.e., degenerate segments that are made of only the end-points of the segments. For (S_d, MD), unidimensional segments are integer intervals delimited by the end-points of the segments. The segments in (S_d, HD) and (S_d, HD) are the cartesian product of the unidimensional segments across dimensions. E.g., for (S_d, HD), the segment between $(0,2,1)$ and $(2,2,0)$ are the vectors obtained by $\{0,2\} \times \{2\} \times \{0,1\} = \{(0,2,0), (0,2,1), (2,2,0), (2,2,1)\}$. For (S_d, MD), the segment between the same vectors is obtained by $\{0,1,2\} \times \{2\} \times \{0,1\} = \{(0,2,0), (0,2,1), (1,2,0), (1,2,1), (2,2,0), (2,2,1)\}$.

Geometric crossover: A geometric crossover on product spaces can be seen as the vector-wise aggregation of geometric crossovers acting on each dimension, each one defined on the distance associated with each dimension [12]. So, for (S_d, HD), any mask-based crossover on integer vectors is a geometric crossover, as a segment in each dimension is an edge (i.e., it comprises only the end-points of the segment). For(S_d, MD), geometric crossovers are component-wise blend-crossovers in which each position in the offspring can take intermediate integer values between the values of parents at that position, as a segment in each dimension is the integer interval bounded by the values of the end-points.

Convex set: A convex set on a product space is the cartesian product of unidimensional convex sets across dimensions. For (S_d, HD), for a dimension, the set of all (unidimensional) convex sets are all sub-cliques of the neighbourhood graph of that dimension. Convex sets on the entire space can be represented as generalised schemata in which there are special symbols indicating all possible superpositions of values in $\{0, 1, \dots, d-1\}^n$. E.g., on an alphabet with values in $\{0, 1, 2\}$ generalised schemata use the values $0, 1, 2$ and the special symbols $*_{01}, *_{02}, *_{12}, *_{012}$, each one denoting the superposition of the values appearing in its index. For example, the generalised schema $0 *_{01} *_{02} 2$ matches the vectors $0002, 0102, 0022, 0122$. For (S_d, MD), like for the Hamming space on binary strings, convex sets coincide with segments, i.e., they are integer hyper-boxes. Notice instead that in (S_d, HD) not all convex sets are segments.

Quasi-concave landscapes: We can derive the specific class of quasi-concave landscapes for any space by piling-up a nested chain of convex sets. For (S_d, HD), this translates to creating functions using a recursive construction analogous to the one in section 3.2 for the Hamming space on binary strings but using generalised schemata instead. Notice however, that unlike the case of binary strings, not every successive level fixes a '*' symbol to specific value, but it may simply reduce the degree of freedom of a '*' symbol, e.g., "fixing" $*_{012}$ to $*_{01}$. For (S_d, MD), piling-up a nested chain of convex sets translates into piling-up hyper-boxes from the largest to the smallest. E.g., on two-dimensional vectors, these landscapes are traditional quasi-concave functions with rectangular or squared levels, whose domain is restricted to integer values.

Convex hull: We can derive the convex hull from its definition and the notion of convex set. For (S_d, HD), the convex hull of a set of integer vectors is the most specific generalised schema matching all vectors. For (S_d, MD), the convex hull of a set of integer vectors (i.e., points) is the smallest hyper-box covering all points.

Uniform convex hull recombination: We can derive this operator from the notion of convex hull. For (S_d, HD), it is the operator that at each position returns, with the same probability, any value that occurs in that position in the parents at least once. This corresponds to sampling uniformly the most specific generalised schemata matching all parent vectors. For (S_d, MD), it is the operator that at each position (i.e., dimension) returns with the same probability any value in the interval between the minimum and maximum values of the parents in that position. This corresponds to sampling the hyper-box uniformly, as this can be achieved by sampling uniformly at random each coordinate (within the specified range that allows to cover all parents).

We now specify the runtime to the space (S_d, HD).

LEMMA 9. *For $M = (S_d, \text{HD})$ and $m \in \mathbb{N}$ we have*

$$\mathrm{P}_M^{\mathrm{Cov}}(m) \geq 1 - dn\left(1 - \frac{1}{d}\right)^m \geq 1 - dn \cdot \exp\left(-\frac{m}{d}\right).$$

PROOF. The worst case is attained for covering the whole space S_d. We cover S_d if in every component of the integer vector every value is present in at least one sample. For each dimension we need all values because to cover a clique graph (i.e., a unidimensional subspace of S_d) we need all nodes (i.e., values) in the clique.

For a fixed component this corresponds to the well-known coupon collector's problem: we are drawing m coupons (integer values) uniformly at random and are interested in the probability that we have at least one coupon of each kind.

This gives rise to the following tail bound. The probability of one fixed value not appearing in m draws is $(1 - 1/d)^m$. The probability that this does not happen for any value is at most $d \cdot (1 - 1/d)^m$ by the union bound. Taking the union bound over n processes on all bits, we get a probability of at most $dn \cdot (1 - 1/d)^m$ that S_d is not covered. □

Then the bound from Theorem 4 simplifies as follows, the second bound being derived as in Theorem 6.

THEOREM 10. *Let $M = (\{0, 1, \dots d-1\}^n, \text{HD})$ and the assumptions for Theorem 4 hold. Then the Convex Search Algorithm finds a global optimum within at most q generations and kq fitness evaluations with probability at least*

$$\left(1 - dn \cdot \exp\left(-\frac{kr}{4d}\right)\right)^{q+1} - q \cdot \exp\left(-\frac{9kr}{32}\right)$$
$$\geq 1 - (q+2)dn \cdot \exp\left(-\frac{kr}{4d}\right)$$

where the second bound requires $\exp\left(\frac{kr}{4d}\right) \geq dn(q+1)$.

COROLLARY 11. *If $k \geq 4d\ln(2(q-2)dn)/r$ then Convex Evolutionary Search restarting after q generations finds a global optimum within $2q$ expected generations and $2kq$ expected fitness evaluations.*

On polynomial quasi-concave landscapes, if $d \leq \text{poly}(n)$, we get polynomial expected numbers of generations and fitness evaluations for appropriate population sizes.

For the space (S_d, MD) we get similar results.

LEMMA 12. *For $M = (S_d, \text{MD})$ and $m \in \mathbb{N}$ we have*

$$\mathrm{P}_M^{\mathrm{Cov}}(m) \geq 1 - 2n\left(1 - \frac{1}{d}\right)^m \geq 1 - 2n \cdot \exp\left(-\frac{m}{d}\right).$$

PROOF. The worst case is attained for covering S_d. We cover S_d if in every component of the integer vector both values 0 and $d-1$ are present in at least one sample. The probability of one fixed value not appearing in m samples is $(1 - 1/d)^m$. The probability that this does not happen for both values and n components is at most $2n \cdot (1 - 1/d)^m$. □

THEOREM 13. *Let $M = (\{0, 1, \dots, d-1\}^n, \text{MD})$ and the assumptions for Theorem 4 hold. Then the Convex Search Algorithm finds a global optimum within at most q generations and kq fitness evaluations with probability at least*

$$\left(1 - 2n \cdot \exp\left(-\frac{kr}{4d}\right)\right)^{q+1} - q \cdot \exp\left(-\frac{9kr}{32}\right)$$
$$\geq 1 - 2(q+2)n \cdot \exp\left(-\frac{kr}{4d}\right)$$

where the second bound requires $\exp\left(\frac{kr}{4d}\right) \geq 2n(q+1)$.

COROLLARY 14. *If $k \geq 4d\ln(4(q+2)n)/r$ then Convex Evolutionary Search restarting after q generations finds a global optimum within $2q$ expected generations and $2kq$ expected fitness evaluations.*

6. SUMMARY AND FUTURE WORK

Two important open challenges in the Evolutionary Computation field are (i) finding out on what class of landscapes a certain search algorithm performs well and why, and (ii) devising a more systematical approach to runtime analysis to obtain results that hold for *classes* of search algorithms on *classes* of problems. In this work, we have proposed a novel framework that is a first step towards addressing jointly both challenges. The framework put together a geometric theory of representations and runtime analysis to determine systematically the performance *across, in principle, all spaces and representations* of a population-based evolutionary algorithm with a form of population-wide convex recombination on a class of concave landscapes. Runtime analysis at this level of generality is possible because at its core relies on abstract properties of convex search and of concave landscapes common to all underlying spaces and representations.

The general runtime expression is parametrised on a single space-dependent feature, the worst-case probability of covering convex sets. It can be determined on specific spaces and plugged in the general expression to determine the runtime of the space-specific pair of search algorithm and fitness landscape. We have illustrated this for three spaces and obtained polynomial runtime bounds for polynomial quasi-concave landscapes. We also showed that convex search can be regarded as pure adaptive search on concave landscapes. This is the ultimate cause behind the polynomial runtime of convex search on concave landscapes across representations.

Remarkably, for LeadingOnes convex search turned out to be faster than all unbiased unary black-box algorithms, including EAs using only mutation [8, 17]. This further demonstrates the potential of convex search and population-based EAs.

There is plenty of future work, in at least three directions of investigation. The first direction is to extend the theory to encompass evolutionary algorithms used in practice with standard forms of crossover, selection and mutation. This seems to be possible as EAs with standard operators approximate the convex search behaviour considered in this study. The second direction is to extend the theory to encompass a larger family of fitness landscapes, in particular approximately concave landscapes, and study how the degree of approximation to concavity affects the runtime. From preliminary study, it seems that performance could degrade gracefully as the approximation becomes less good. Furthermore, we would like to determine to what extent interesting non-toy problems fit this framework. There seems to be hope as fitness landscapes associated with well-known combinatorial problems have been shown empirically to have some form of "global concavity". We would like to develop an analytical methodology to recognise that a certain problem provably fits a certain class of concave landscapes. Clearly, NP-Hard problems can be expected to fit a polynomially solvable class of fitness landscapes only with respect to some relaxed target (e.g., approximation complexity, parametrized complexity). Finally, as third line of investigation, we would like to specialise the results to other representations (e.g., continuous and permutation spaces), and devise a general approach for easily determining the required space-specific convexity feature, using known results from convexity on graphs.

Acknowledgments: The authors thank Jon Rowe and a reviewer for helpful comments. This research was supported by EPSRC grants EP/I010297/1 and EP/D052785/1.

7. REFERENCES

[1] A. Auger and B. Doerr, editors. *Theory of Randomized Search Heuristics – Foundations and Recent Developments.* World Scientific, 2011.

[2] B. Doerr, E. Happ, and C. Klein. Crossover can provably be useful in evolutionary computation. *Theoretical Computer Science*, 425(0):17–33, 2012.

[3] B. Doerr, D. Johannsen, T. Kötzing, P. K. Lehre, M. Wagner, and C. Winzen. Faster black-box algorithms through higher arity operators. In *Proc. of FOGA '11*, pages 163–172. ACM Press, 2011.

[4] T. Jansen and I. Wegener. On the analysis of evolutionary algorithms—a proof that crossover really can help. *Algorithmica*, 34(1):47–66, 2002.

[5] T. Jansen and I. Wegener. Real royal road functions—where crossover provably is essential. *Discrete Applied Mathematics*, 149:111–125, 2005.

[6] T. Kötzing, D. Sudholt, and M. Theile. How crossover helps in pseudo-Boolean optimization. In *Proc. of GECCO '11*, pages 989–996. ACM Press, 2011.

[7] J. Lässig and D. Sudholt. General scheme for analyzing running times of parallel evolutionary algorithms. In *Parallel Problem Solving from Nature (PPSN 2010)*, pages 234–243. Springer, 2010.

[8] P. K. Lehre and C. Witt. Black box search by unbiased variation. In *Proc. of GECCO '10*, pages 1441–1448, 2010.

[9] A. Moraglio. *Towards a Geometric Unification of Evolutionary Algorithms.* PhD thesis, University of Essex, 2007.

[10] A. Moraglio. Abstract convex evolutionary search. In *Proc. of FOGA '11*, pages 151–162. ACM Press, 2011.

[11] A. Moraglio and R. Poli. Topological interpretation of crossover. In *Proc. of GECCO '04*, pages 1377–1388. Springer, 2004.

[12] A. Moraglio and R. Poli. Product geometric crossover. In *Parallel Problem Solving from Nature (PPSN 2006)*, pages 1018–1027. Springer, 2006.

[13] R. Motwani and P. Raghavan. *Randomized Algorithms.* Cambridge University Press, 1995.

[14] F. Neumann and C. Witt. *Bioinspired Computation in Combinatorial Optimization – Algorithms and Their Computational Complexity.* Springer, 2010.

[15] N. R. Patel, R. L. Smith, and Z. B. Zabinsky. Pure adaptive search in Monte Carlo optimization. *Mathematical Programming*, 4:317–328, 1988.

[16] D. Sudholt. Crossover is provably essential for the Ising model on trees. In *Proc. of GECCO '05*, pages 1161–1167. ACM Press, 2005.

[17] D. Sudholt. General lower bounds for the running time of evolutionary algorithms. In *Parallel Problem Solving from Nature (PPSN 2010)*, pages 124–133. Springer, 2010.

[18] D. Sudholt and C. Zarges. Analysis of an iterated local search algorithm for vertex coloring. In *Proc. of ISAAC '10*, pages 340–352. Springer, 2010.

[19] I. Wegener. Methods for the analysis of evolutionary algorithms on pseudo-Boolean functions. In R. Sarker, X. Yao, and M. Mohammadian, editors, *Evolutionary Optimization*, pages 349–369. Kluwer, 2002.

[20] D. H. Wolpert and W. G. Macready. No free lunch theorems for optimization. *IEEE Transaction on Evolutionary Computation*, 1(1):67–82, 1996.

[21] Z. B. Zabinsky. *Stochastic Adaptive Search for Global Optimization.* Kluwer Academic, 2003.

Dynamic Segregative Genetic Algorithm for Optimizing the Variable Ordering of ROBDDs

Cristian Rotaru
"Al. I. Cuza" University of Iaşi, Faculty of Computer Science
Gen. Berthelot 5, Iaşi, Romania
cristian.rotaru@infoiasi.ro

Octav Brudaru
"Gh. Asachi" Technical University of Iaşi
D. Mangeron 53, Iaşi, Romania
brudaru@tuiasi.ro

ABSTRACT
In this paper an efficient dynamic segregative genetic algorithm for optimizing variable order in Reduced Ordered Binary Decision Diagrams is presented. The approach integrates a basic genetic algorithm and uses a feature function in order to define a similarity measure between chromosomes. Subpopulations of individuals, formed by applying a clustering procedure in the feature space, are explored in parallel by multiple copies of the basic genetic algorithm. A communication protocol preserves the similarity inside each subpopulation during the evolution process. The redundant exploration of the search space is avoided by using a tabu search associative memory. Genetic material from yet unexplored regions of the search space is managed and organized in order to explicitly guide the search process to yet undiscovered local optima. The experimental evaluation of the algorithm uses classical benchmark problems, known to be very difficult. Experiments suggest that our approach has a better performance in terms of stability and quality of the solution, when compared to other heuristics, such as local search methods, basic genetic algorithms, a cellular genetic algorithm and even the static segregative genetic algorithm that was the starting point of this work. The quality of the distributed implementation and the communication protocol are thoroughly analyzed.

Categories and Subject Descriptors
I.2.8 [**Artificial Intelligence**]: Problem Solving, Control Methods and Search – *heuristic methods.*

General Terms
Algorithms

Keywords
segregative genetic algorithm, feature space, associative tabu search memory, search space management, similarity preserving communication protocol, extensive exploration, intensive exploitation, distributed implementation.

GECCO'12, July 7–11, 2012, Philadelphia, Pennsylvania, USA.
Copyright 2012 ACM 978-1-4503-1177-9/12/07...$10.00.

1. INTRODUCTION
We propose a new method to optimize the variable order in Reduced Ordered Binary Decision Diagrams (ROBDDs). ROBDDs are data structures that represent canonical forms for Boolean functions. An ROBDD is an acyclic graph with respect to some order of the input variables and satisfying a set of properties. The size of the ROBDD is the number of non-terminal nodes and it is proven that it strongly depends on the order of the variables ([1]). The goal is to minimize this size. One important application of ROBDDs is in digital circuit design – a smaller size of the ROBDD that represents a Boolean function describing a circuit transfers directly to a smaller chip size. Other applications include: symbolic model checking; formal verification of combinatorial circuits; analysis of sequential systems.

The methods used to tackle the problem are both exact and approximate. The most successful exact approaches are based on the branch-and-bound paradigm and use the lemma proven in [2]. The heuristic approaches are categorized in two types: static and dynamic methods. Static methods use application specific information, for example the structure of the evaluated combinatorial circuit, to build good variable orders before constructing the ROBDD ([3]). Dynamic methods improve the size of an ROBDD by modifying the order of variables. Basic approaches are described in [4] and [5]. [6] presents "the sifting heuristic", a specialized local search technique based on hill-climbing. [7] describes a method based on simulated annealing and [8] introduces the use of genetic algorithms, further developed in [9]. Hybrid approaches are described in [10] and [11]. [12] introduces a novel method for optimizing the variable order, a cellular genetic algorithm with parallel evolving and communicating grids. This method employs multiple populations to explore the search space and uses a similarity preserving communication protocol to transfer high quality genetic material between subpopulations, in order to boost the quality of the solution.

In [13] the authors describe an initial variant of a segregative genetic algorithm for the problem of optimizing the variable order of ROBDDs. The segregative approach defines a similarity measure between chromosomes. The measure is computed in a feature space obtained by attaching feature vectors to chromosomes. Large numbers of individuals are organized in subpopulations, by applying a clustering procedure in the feature space. The search space is explored by means of a basic genetic algorithm (BGA) on each subpopulation. Depending on computational resources, multiple subpopulations can be explored in parallel. A communication protocol is used to maintain the similarity inside each subpopulation during the evolution. A tabu search associative memory is introduced in order to avoid redundant exploration of the search space.

In this paper an improved version of the algorithm described in [13] is proposed. Some of the components of the approach are revised to deliver better performance. The main improvement is the introduction of the management of yet unexplored regions of the search space. The algorithm in [13], called Static Segregative Genetic Algorithm (SSGA), generates a large initial population, divides it in a fixed number of subpopulations and explores these subpopulations. Chromosomes that occur during the evolution process and are not similar with any subpopulation are included in some subpopulation, but usually they do not have the power to guide the search process towards the newly discovered region of the search space. The new approach explicitly manages chromosomes from these regions, by dynamically creating subpopulations that will be later explored by the BGA. The approach is called Dynamic Segregative Genetic Algorithm (DSGA). Some of the ideas used by the approach can be also found in [14].

The structure of the paper is the following: Section 2 describes the problem; Section 3 briefly describes the BGA; Section 4 presents the translation from genotype to phenotype; Section 5 details all aspects of the segregative approach; Section 6 presents the extensive experimental evaluation of the method; Section 7 summarizes some conclusions and future work directions.

2. OPTIMIZING THE ORDER OF VARIABLES FOR ROBDDS

This section formally describes the ROBDD data structure and the problem of optimizing the variable order. The importance of variable ordering is briefly underlined.

Let BF: $B^n \rightarrow B^m$, $B = \{0,1\}$ be a Boolean function that outputs m values. Let π be a permutation of the n input variables, $\pi = (v_1,v_2,\ldots,v_n)$, $v_i \in B$, $i = 1,\ldots,n$.

An Ordered BDD (OBDD) for BF with respect to π is a directed acyclic graph with the following properties ([15]): i) it has exactly two terminal nodes, labeled with 0 and 1, respectively; ii) each nonterminal node is labeled by a variable v_i, $0 < i \leq n$ and has two out-edges labeled with 0 and 1, respectively; iii) the order in which the variables appear on any path in the graph respects the order π. The number of nonterminal nodes in the graph represents the size of the OBDD and is the value that must be minimized.

The structure called Reduced OBDD (ROBDD) is obtained by applying reduction rules to an OBDD with a fixed variable order, further reducing the size of the graph ([15]). A ROBDD is a canonical form for BF. The size of the structure strongly depends on the fixed order. In [1] it is proven that optimizing the order of variables is NP-complete and finding the best order is NP-hard.

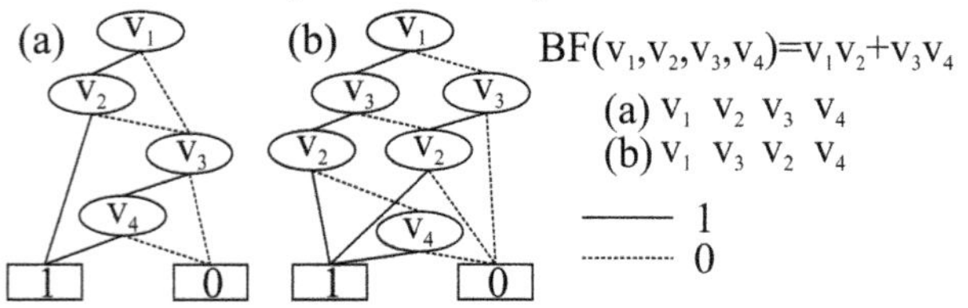

Figure 1. Dependence of the size of the ROBDD on the order of variables

Figure 1 illustrates the effect of using different orders of variables when building ROBDDs for a simple Boolean function. For two slightly different orders the sizes of the corresponding ROBDDs differ substantially.

3. BASIC GENETIC ALGORITHM

The method used to explore subpopulations in the context of the segregative approach can be any population based method for which a similarity measure between individuals can be defined. The method used in this paper is the genetic algorithm described thoroughly in [16].

A chromosome represents a permutation of the input variables of BF, denoted $x = (x_1,x_2,\ldots,x_n)$, $x_i \in \{v_1,\ldots,v_n\}$, $i=1,\ldots,n$. The fitness of a chromosome, denoted $f(x)$, is the size of the ROBDD obtained by using x as the order of variables. The size of the initial population, denoted pop_sz, is directly proportional to the number of variables, n, as a consequence of an empirically determined rule. The initial population is generated randomly.

The algorithm applies an elitist selection for survival. The offspring compete with the current generation. The best pop_sz individuals with respect to fitness value are kept in the next generation.

The method uses two crossover operators, described in [9], and three mutation operators, described in [17]. [16] shows that using several operators yields better results than applying only one operator for crossover and one for mutation. The common characteristic of all genetic operators is that the similarity between parents and offspring grows with the number of generations, assuring the convergence of the algorithm. The probabilities to apply crossover and mutation, denoted p_{CX} and p_M respectively, are empirically initialized and dynamically controlled during the evolution process, by means of a measure of the variability of the population. The variability is computed each generation as the distribution of fitness values over the entire population. The probabilities are adjusted in order for the variability to match a predefined objective function. This function ultimately defines the balance between exploration and exploitation. In [16] specific equations are presented and the effects of several objective functions are thoroughly examined.

The algorithm stops when the variation of the average fitness of the population stagnates: $|avg\_fit(k) - avg\_fit(k-1)|/avg\_fit(k) < T_{stop}$ holds true for N_{stop} consecutive generations, where $avg\_fit(k)$ is the average fitness of the population at generation k, and T_{stop} a small threshold value.

4. FEATURE SPACE

The capacity of the segregative algorithm to manage individuals during the evolution process depends on the measure of similarity defined between individuals. As mentioned before, a chromosome represents a permutation of the input variables. This representation does not support a straightforward definition of a measure of similarity. In order to define the similarity between two individuals, a real valued feature vector is computed for each chromosome. The vector, denoted $\varphi(x)$, is computed when the chromosome x is evaluated. The measure of similarity between two chromosomes x and x' is defined as the Euclidean distance in $\mathbb{R}^n$ between the corresponding feature vectors, $\| \varphi(x) - \varphi(x') \|$.

Two methods to compute the feature vector are described below, both used to define the similarity between chromosomes in [12] and [13]. Let x be a chromosome. One option is to use the structural information of x, as permutation of the input variables. The obtained feature vector, denoted $\varphi_1(x)$, is defined as: $\varphi_1(x) = (\alpha_1,\ldots,\alpha_n)$, where $\alpha_i = x_i/[n(n+1)/2]$, $i = 1,\ldots,n$. $\varphi_1(x) \in \mathbb{R}^n$ and $\Sigma\alpha_i = 1$. Another option is to capture the cost based characteristics of x. The second feature vector, denoted $\varphi_2(x)$, is defined as: $\varphi_2(x) =$

$(\lambda_1,\ldots,\lambda_n) \in \mathbb{N}^n$, where λ_i represents the number of nodes on the i-th level of the graph corresponding to the ROBDD.

The extensive experimental evaluations of the algorithms described in [12] and [13] show that using the feature vector φ_1 yields more stable but poorer quality results than using φ_2. In all cases, by using φ_2, the stability of the results decreases slightly, while the quality improves substantially. All experimental results further presented in this paper are obtained by using φ_2, denoted simply φ from now on.

5. THE SEGREGATIVE ALGORITHM

This section describes the elements of the segregative approach and how they work.

5.1 Search space exploration by subpopulations

The segregative algorithm employs multiple copies of the BGA to explore the search space. At any particular moment, each copy evolves a given subpopulation. Subpopulations are clusters of similar chromosomes, with regard to the feature vector φ, and are representative for some region of the search space. Depending on available computational resources, a number p of subpopulations are explored in parallel. During the evolution process, the segregative approach discovers and explores various well defined regions of the search space and intensifies the search in promising regions by applying the BGA. A communication protocol preserves the similarity inside the evolved subpopulations. The approach avoids redundant exploration of regions of the search space and manages yet unexplored regions of the search space. This is done by means of the control components of the algorithm, which will be later detailed. The segregative algorithm acts as a collector of various local optima from different regions of the search space.

5.1.1 Initializing the subpopulations

Initially, a large population, denoted P_{init}, is randomly generated. All chromosomes are evaluated and the feature vectors are computed. A clustering algorithm is used to split the set of feature vectors in S similar groups, $Cl_1,\ldots,Cl_S \subset \mathbb{R}^n$, with the centroids $\phi_1,\ldots,\phi_S \in \mathbb{R}^n$. The initial subpopulations are represented by the preimages of the clusters from the feature space, in the representation space, $P_i = \varphi^{-1}(Cl_i)$, $i = 1,\ldots,S$. The subpopulations are sent to the component of the algorithm Q_{NEW} that will distribute them to the copies of BGA, for exploration. The activity of Q_{NEW} will be later detailed.

Experiments show that the *c-means* clustering algorithm offers good results in terms of speed and accuracy. The Davies-Bouldin index for the quality of the clustering solution was used to determine a good value for the number of clusters, S.

5.1.2 Control components

The control components of the algorithm are used to define the behavior of the method. The following subsections will detail: the tabu search associative memory, the management of yet unexplored and unknown regions of the search space, and the archive that stores promising individuals occurred during the evolution process. Several focused scenarios involving communications between components of the algorithm and subpopulations will be presented. A later subsection will detail all aspects regarding the communication protocol.

5.1.2.1 Tabu search associative memory

The tabu search associative memory, denoted TS_{AM}, is a control component introduced in order to avoid the redundant exploration of regions of the search space. As previously mentioned, the BGAs evolve subpopulations of individuals that induce clusters of feature vectors in the feature space. A subpopulation SP has a corresponding centroid in the feature space, $\phi_{SP} \in \mathbb{R}^n$, and a cluster radius, $\rho_{SP} \in \mathbb{R}$, which are computed when the clustering algorithm is applied. The centroid captures the features off all individuals in the cluster and is computed by the clustering algorithm. The radius is set as the maximum distance between any feature vector in the cluster and the centroid. When the evolution process on SP is finished, the pair (ϕ_{SP},ρ_{SP}) is sent to TS_{AM}. At some moment in the execution of the segregative algorithm, TS_{AM} stores s pairs (ϕ_{sp},ρ_{sp}), where ϕ_{sp} is the centroid of some explored subpopulation sp and ρ_{sp} is the radius of the cluster. The associative feature of this memory comes from the fact that it does not store chromosomes from different regions of the search space; it only stores centroids which capture the characteristics of many individuals from the corresponding regions.

Let x be a chromosome received by TS_{AM} from a copy of the BGA. The communication protocol between subpopulations currently explored by copies of BGA ensures that x does not belong to any of those subpopulations. The function of TS_{AM} is to decide whether x belongs to an already explored region of the search space or not. If for some $j \in \{1,\ldots,s\}$, $\| \varphi(x) - \phi_j \| \le \rho_j$ holds, then x belongs to an already explored region and is discarded, otherwise x belongs to an yet unexplored or unknown region and it is sent to Q_{NEW}.

5.1.2.2 Management of the search space

The component that manages yet unexplored and unknown regions of the search space, denoted Q_{NEW}, contains two collections of individuals: PQ_{NEW} and U_{NEW}.

PQ_{NEW} is a priority queue of yet unexplored clusters of individuals. PQ_{NEW} stores the centroids and radiuses of the clusters and also a small number of representative chromosomes that will be used to start the evolution process on the subpopulation. The subpopulations are scored with the average fitness of these individuals. When a copy of the BGA finishes the evolution process on the assigned subpopulation, it will receive from PQ_{NEW} the best subpopulation to explore. PQ_{NEW} is initialized with the initial subpopulations, $P_1,\ldots,P_S$.

U_{NEW} is a large collection of chromosomes from unknown regions of the search space. Let x be a chromosome received by Q_{NEW} from TS_{AM}. x does not belong to any subpopulation that is currently or was already explored. If x is similar enough with some cluster from PQ_{NEW} it will be stored in the small population of that cluster if it is good enough, or it will be discarded. If not, x is stored in the unstructured collection U_{NEW}. Initially, U_{NEW} is empty. When the size of U_{NEW} reaches a high enough value, 1000–2000 chromosomes, denoted M_{UNEW}, the same clustering procedure described in the initialization phase is applied, U_{NEW} is emptied, and the resulting subpopulations are appended to PQ_{NEW}.

Q_{NEW} is the component that ensures the dynamic character of the approach by managing and organizing new genetic material produced during the evolution process on subpopulations. The segregative algorithm stops when PQ_{NEW} and U_{NEW} are empty and all copies of the BGA finish the execution on the assigned subpopulation.

5.1.2.3 Archive

The last component of the segregative approach is also a collection of chromosomes. The archive stores the elite of individuals from explored subpopulations, meaning 5–10% of the individuals from the last generation. The selection of the BGA being elitist, these are the best chromosomes produced by the evolution process on those subpopulations.

The main benefit of the archive is an alternative method to initialize the segregative method: it offers the means for efficiently restarting the algorithm, by including the high quality chromosomes from the archive in the primordial large population. This procedure can be correlated with keeping the information stored by TS_{AM} in consecutive runs of the algorithm, which can accelerate the discovery and exploration of new regions of the search space.

5.1.3 *Communication protocol*

Data transfer occurs between currently explored subpopulations, subpopulations and control components and between control components of the segregative algorithm. The communication between different entities defines their behavior and ensures the functionalities of the segregative method.

Each data transfer has a source and a destination. The source entity places data in a buffer at the destination. In order not to overwhelm the communication with processing times, data accumulates in buffers and all entities involved process their buffers every R evolution stages, counting all copies of the BGA. Effects of varying this value will be presented in the experimental evaluation section.

5.1.3.1 *Data transfer at subpopulation level*

Data transfer that originates in a subpopulation is intended to preserve the similarity inside that subpopulation. Offspring created by means of genetic operators are either kept in the subpopulation, or sent to other subpopulations or control components, if they are not similar enough with the current subpopulation.

Let BGA_i be the copy of the BGA, which currently evolves the subpopulation SP_i. Let ϕ_i be the centroid of the cluster induced by SP_i in the feature space and ρ_i the radius of this cluster. Let x be a chromosome generated during the evolution process on SP_i.

If $\| \phi_i - \varphi(x) \| \leq \rho_i$, then x is similar enough to the individuals in SP_i and is included in the evolution process performed by BGA_i.

If $\| \phi_j - \varphi(x) \| \leq \rho_j$ holds for some $j \in \{1,\ldots,p\}, j \neq i$, then x is similar with the currently explored subpopulation SP_j and it will be included in the evolution process performed by BGA_j. BGA_j receives such chromosomes in a buffer, denoted Buf_j.

If none of the above cases hold, then x is not similar with any currently explored subpopulation and it will be sent to TS_{AM}.

At the end of the evolution process on SP_i, the pair (ϕ_i,ρ_i) is sent to TS_{AM} and the elite of the current population is sent to the archive. The copy of the BGA that performed the exploration of SP_i will receive another subpopulation from Q_{NEW}, if available.

5.1.3.2 *Data transfer at control component level*

TS_{AM} receives chromosomes from the copies of the BGA in the buffer denoted B_{TSAM}. Let x be such an individual. If TS_{AM} decides that x belongs to an already explored region of the search space, then x is discarded, otherwise it is sent to Q_{NEW}.

Q_{NEW} receives individuals from TS_{AM} in the buffer denoted B_{QNEW}. The chromosomes are either discarded, or stored in the initial population of some cluster in PQ_{NEW}, or in U_{NEW}. Whenever a copy of the BGA finishes the exploration on some subpopulation, Q_{NEW} extracts the best subpopulation from PQ_{NEW} and sends it to the BGA for exploration.

5.2 Execution of the algorithm

This section summarizes the execution steps of the copies of BGA and of the control components of the segregative algorithm. The procedures include the functionalities of all entities and the data flows previously detailed.

5.2.1 *Execution of the BGA*

1. receive subpopulation SP from Q_{NEW}: individuals to initialize the population, centroid and radius of the cluster induced in the feature space, (ϕ_{SP},ρ_{SP}).
2. initialize the evolution stage, $st = 1$; initialize the current population $pop(1)$; empty the buffer, $Buf = \emptyset$.
3. while not stopped do:
   - 3a. $st = st + 1$;
     if $st \% R = 0$ then $pop(s) = pop(s-1) \cup Buf$, $Buf = \emptyset$;
     else $pop(s) = pop(s-1)$.
   - 3b. apply genetic operators, evaluate offspring, and compute feature vectors; for each new individual x:
     - $pop(s) = pop(s) \cup \{x\}$ or
     - send x to another currently explored subpopulation or
     - send x to TS_{AM}.
   - 3c. apply selection on $pop(s)$; update centroid and radius.

5.2.2 *Execution of the segregative algorithm*

1. initialize P_{init}; obtain $P_1,\ldots,P_S$ by clustering;
   $PQ_{NEW} = \{P_1,\ldots,P_S\}$; $U_{NEW} = \emptyset$.
2. $TS_{AM} = \emptyset$.
3. while PQ_{NEW} and U_{NEW} are not empty:
   - 3a. if a copy of the BGA is free and PQ_{NEW} is not empty
     - choose the best subpopulation from PQ_{NEW} and send it to the BGA;
     - the copy of the BGA starts the evolution process.
   - 3b. when a copy of the BGA finishes the exploration of a subpopulation:
     - send the centroid and radius of the completed cluster to TS_{AM};
     - update the archive.
   - 3c. every R generations, TS_{AM} checks the chromosomes in B_{TSAM} and either discards them or sends them to Q_{NEW}.
   - 3d. every R generations, Q_{NEW} processes the chromosomes in B_{QNEW} and discards them, or stores them in some cluster in PQ_{NEW}, or stores them in U_{NEW}.
   - 3e. when U_{NEW} reaches the size M_{UNEW}, or U_{NEW} is not empty and PQ_{NEW} is empty, apply the clustering procedure on the feature vectors of the individuals in U_{NEW}, obtain the similar subpopulations in the representation space and append them to PQ_{NEW}, empty U_{NEW}.

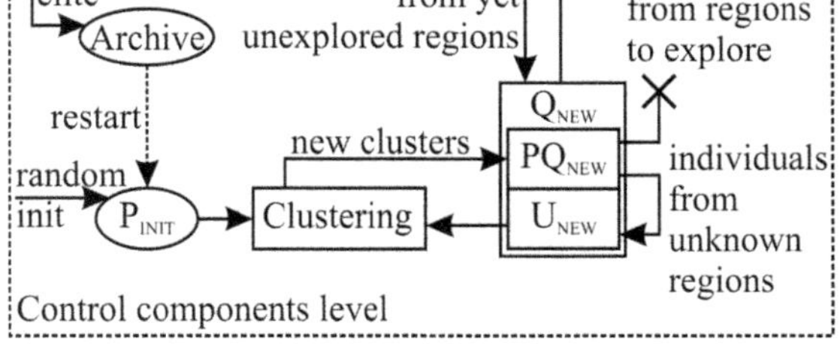

Figure 2. Functional diagram of the segregative algorithm

6. EXPERIMENTAL EVALUATION

The experiments are designed to study the stability and quality of the solution obtained by the segregative approach. Comparisons with the single population genetic algorithm, the cellular genetic algorithm from [12], the static segregative genetic algorithm from [13] and other heuristic approaches are extensively described below. Other experiments study the quality of the distributed implementation and the efficiency of the communication protocol.

The experimental evaluation uses well known benchmark problems from the LGSynth91 dataset, found at [21]. The instances are divided into three categories, depending on their size: small – *cm85a*, *cm163a*, *cu*, *alu4*, *s1494*, *vda*, *misex3*; medium – *apex2*, *apex7*, *cordic*, *ttt2*; and large instances – *i3*, *apex6*.

The optimal solution is known for most of the instances and is denoted *bk*. The reported indicators are the following: best found solution (*bf*), the average (*m*), standard deviation (σ) and unitized risk (σ/m) for the absolute error ($bf - bk$). The column titled In/Out presents the number of input and output variables of the Boolean function, respectively.

The CUDD library ([22]) was used in order to build the ROBDD associated with an order of variables and to compute the fitness and feature vector φ_2, which is used in all experiments.

6.1 Parameter tuning

The parameters of the basic genetic algorithm are the ones which gave the best results in [16]. The values are empirically set. The extensive experimental evaluation in [16] analyzes the effect of different choices for all parameters. The following values are used in [16] to produce the results reported in the performance evaluation and are also used in the segregative approach. The size of the population, *pop_sz,* is set to 50 for the small and medium problem instances, and to 50 and 100 for the large instances. p_{CX}, the probability of the crossover operator, is initialized to 0.6. p_M, the probability of the mutation operator, is initialized to 0.35. The objective function for the variability of the population, used to control p_{CX} and p_M, is an exponential periodic function. The parameters used to define the stopping condition are: $N_{stop} = 20$ and $T_{stop} = 0.001$.

The experiment designed to determine a suitable size for the primordial population, P_{init}, consists in running the algorithm on some of the test instances (*alu4*, *cordic* and *apex6*) with different values, ranging from 200 to 10000, and checking for statistically significant differences between the averages of the absolute error (*m*), obtained on each instance. Both Wilcoxon Signed-Rank non-parametric test and the two-tailed t-test with assumed unequal variances showed ($p < 0.01$) that values ranging from 2000 to 200 chromosomes produce a decrease in stability and quality of the solution. Values ranging from 2000 to 10000 revealed no significant difference. This proves the efficiency of the component Q_{NEW} that successfully manages the exploration of unknown regions of the search space, compensating for a poor initial genetic pool. The size P_{init} is set to 2000 individuals. As showed in [13], the static segregative genetic algorithm requires an initial population of size at least 5000 to deliver best performance. M_{UNEW}, the maximum size of the unstructured population U_{NEW}, is set to 1000 chromosomes ($|P_{init}| / 2$).

Various values for the communication period, *R*, are tested: 2, 4, 8, 10 and 12 evolution stages. Detailed results are presented in the section concerning the evaluation of the distributed implementation. The value used for generating the results in the performance evaluation is 8.

In conclusion, most of the parameters of the approach are set to known best suitable values, the rest are determined by means of a limited statistical analysis. As the results obtained by using these settings are very promising, a further in-depth analysis of the parameters and dependencies between them is not included in this work. Future research should devise experiments and procedures to determine if the whole ensemble of parameters, for the BGA and control components of the DSGA, can be fine-tuned against each other to deliver even better performance for the segregative approach.

6.2 Performance evaluation

For the performance evaluation, a computer with an AMD Athlon X4 630 processor was used. As this processor has 4 physical cores, 4 copies of the BGA ran in parallel. For each problem instance, the algorithm was executed 30 times.

6.2.1 *Quality and stability*

The reported indicators are presented in Table 1.

Table 1. Performance evaluation of the DSGA

Instance	In/Out	*bk*	*bf*	*m*	σ	σ/m
cm85a	11/3	28	28	0	0	-
cm163a	16/5	26	26	0	0	-
cu	14/11	32	32	0	0	-
alu4	14/8	350	350	0	0	-
s1494	14/25	369	369	0	0	-
vda	17/39	478	478	0	0	-
misex3	14/14	478	478	0	0	-
apex2	39/3	-	303	305.5	2.063	0.0067
apex7	49/37	-	214	215	1.114	0.0051
cordic	23/2	42	42	0	0	-
ttt2	24/21	107	107	0	0	-
i3	132/6	133	133	0	0	-
apex6	135/99	498	506	20.16	7.985	0.3959

The segregative method finds the optimal solution in all runs on all small and medium instances, for which the optimal value is known. This happens also for one of the large instances (*i3*). For the second large instance, *apex6*, which is the most difficult one, the results are very close to the optimal value. The standard deviation and unitized risk prove the high stability of the method which replicates the same or very close results in nearly all runs.

6.2.2 *Comparison with other heuristic methods*

The first comparison focuses on some simple search procedures and other more complex heuristics from the literature. As published results are not available in a systematic manner, only the best found solution is reported on some of the small and medium instances. Table 2 present the comparison with the following methods: the sifting heuristic ([6]); the genetic algorithm described in [8]; depth first search, breadth first search, fault simulation ([18]); level and fanin heuristics ([19]); fanout heuristic ([20]). The results show that the DSGA offers results at least as good as or better than these approaches.

Table 2. Comparison with other heuristics

Inst.	sift	GA[8]	DSGA	Inst.	sift	GA[8]	DSGA
cm85a	36	28	28	alu4	602	350	350
cm163a	28	26	26	s1494	388	370	**369**
cu	35	32	32				

Inst.	dfs	bfs	fsim	lvl	fin	fout	DSGA
vda	529	3647	533	2733	515	533	**478**
ttt2	190	171	234	163	170	186	**107**

The second comparison is a more detailed one with the following methods: the basic genetic algorithm used in the segregative approach (BGA), the static segregative genetic algorithm from [13] (SSGA) and the best variant of the cellular genetic algorithm from [12] (CGA). As all methods behave very well on the small instances, only the results for the medium and large instances are reported.

Table 3 presents the comparison with the BGA. In order to achieve a fair comparison, an execution of the BGA that contributes to the computation of the reported parameters consists actually of multiple executions followed by an aggregation of the results. The number of executions depends on the available computation time, which is set for each instance as the average execution time of the DSGA on that instance.

Table 3. Comparison with BGA

Method	BGA			DSGA		
Instance	*bf*	*m*	*σ*	*bf*	*m*	*σ*
apex2	312	352	54	303	305.5	2.063
apex7	215	240	11	214	215	1.114
cordic	42	5.3	3.6	42	0	0
ttt2	107	4.1	5.4	107	0	0
i3	157	35.4	12	**133**	**0**	**0**
apex6	561	84.8	22	**506**	**20.16**	**7.985**

Table 3 shows that both quality and stability of the solution are significantly higher in the case of the DSGA, especially on the most difficult instances. This fact proves some of the qualities of the segregative approach compared to the single population genetic algorithm. In the case of the DSGA, the stability of the solution is an explicit goal of the approach, achieved by a systematic exploration of the search space. The search procedure is guided by well-defined characteristics of the search space and the intensification of the search is more focused on clearly defined regions. The method avoids being trapped in local optima by using the tabu search memory. The quality of the solution, best found and average, shows that the efficient search process achieved by the DSGA compensates for the weak performance of the BGA.

Table 4 presents the comparison with the two other multi population approaches: SSGA and CGA.

Table 4. Comparison with SSGA and CGA

Meth.	SSGA			CGA			DSGA		
Inst.	*bf*	*m*	*σ*	*bf*	*m*	*σ*	*bf*	*m*	*σ*
apex2	304	315	3.6	309	318.6	7.2	303	305.5	2.06
apex7	214	227	3.5	214	225.3	11	214	215	1.12
cordic	42	1.3	1.0	42	0.1	0.3	42	0	0
ttt2	107	1.5	1.1	107	0.4	0.8	107	0	0
i3	138	9.7	3.1	133	0	0	**133**	**0**	**0**
apex6	536	55.9	9.6	508	38.6	13	**506**	**20.16**	**7.98**

The SSGA is a primitive version of the DSGA, having the same main purpose: a systematic exploration of the search space that focusses on solution stability and aims at improving the quality by exploring various local optima. The CGA is an intermediate design between the single population genetic algorithm and the segregative approach. The merit of the approach is the communication between parallel evolving populations that considerably boosts the quality of the solution. The results suggest that the DSGA performs better than both other approaches in terms of stability and quality of the solution.

All reported results are obtained in similar conditions: each algorithm was executed 30 times for each instance, on the same processor type. The parameters for the components of the BGA that are incorporated in all approaches are the same. Both Wilcoxon Signed-Rank non-parametric test and the two-tailed t-test with assumed unequal variances proved ($p < 0.01$) the statistical significance of the differences between the averages of the absolute error (*m*), on each problem instance.

The results of the t-test for the comparison with the CGA are the following: *apex2* – $t(34) = -9.623$, $p < 0.001$; *apex7* – $t(30) = -5.321$, $p < 0.001$; *cordic* – $t(29) = -1.795$, $p = 0.083$; *ttt2* – $t(29) = -3.067$, $p < 0.005$; *apex6* – $t(45) = -6.623$, $p < 0.001$. The statistical significance of the differences proves the quality of the main components introduced by the segregative design: the exploration of the search space by subpopulations, the communication protocol that preserves the similarity of the explored subpopulations and the tabu search associative memory.

The results for the comparison with the SSGA are the following: *apex2* – $t(47) = -12.885$, $p < 0.001$; *apex7* – $t(35) = -17.832$, $p < 0.001$; *cordic* – $t(29) = -6.966$, $p < 0.001$; *ttt2* – $t(29) = -7.426$, $p < 0.001$; *i3* – $t(29) = -16.909$, $p < 0.001$; *apex6* – $t(54) = -16.091$, $p < 0.001$. The tests confirm that the newly introduced component Q_{NEW}, that represents the main difference between DSGA and SSGA, produces significant differences in the quality of the solution obtained by the algorithm.

6.3 Evaluation of the distributed implementation

This section presents results regarding the efficiency of the distributed implementation and details several aspects regarding the communication protocol at different levels of the segregative approach.

6.3.1 Efficiency of computations

Four copies of the BGA were run in parallel on a four-core processor. The measures used to evaluate the quality of the distributed implementation are the following: the parallel computing time, denoted T_p – the maximum execution time for any processor; the efficiency of processors utilization, denoted E_c – $E_c = T_s / (p \times T_p)$, where T_s is the sequential execution time and p is the number of processors, $p = 4$.

The values are computed as averages over all executions of the algorithm that produced the results reported in the performance evaluation section and are grouped according to the size of the problem instances: small – $T_p = 5.2$ seconds, $E_c = 0.9$; medium – $T_p = 22.5$ seconds, $E_c = 0.94$; large – $T_p = 70.3$ seconds, $E_c = 0.97$.

The parallel time, in each processor, mainly consists of the fitness evaluation. The reported times are quite small taking into account the size of the problems and the complexity of building the ROBDD for a chromosome. Also, the algorithm explores many subpopulations during the process. An immediate advantage of the segregative approach is that the parallel time can be reduced by running more copies of the BGA in parallel, without any further changes.

As comparison, [10] reports the following execution times for three different exact methods, for some of the test instances, in seconds: *cordic* – 1.93 / 1.35 / 1.29; *ttt2* – 435 / 345 / 362. Results for execution times of exact methods on the large instances are not available.

Decreases in the value of E_c are obtained only by synchronizations during communication. The values, very close to 1, prove the efficiency of the communication protocol, which does not load the computations of the copies of BGA and control components with unnecessary overhead. The presented values are obtained with a communication rate, R, of 8 evolution stages, counting all copies of the BGA. Higher values for R, such as 10 and 12, produced almost the same results. Smaller values, such as 2 and 4, yielded worse processor utilization on small instances, where computations are very fast and a more intense communication overwhelms the system. In terms of quality and stability of the solution, different values for R do not produce significantly different results. As an empiric rule, R should be set to $p \times 2$ or $p \times 3$. Both Wilcoxon Signed-Rank non-parametric test and the two-tailed t-test with assumed unequal variances were applied to check the statistical significance of the differences between the averages of the absolute error (m) and E_c, obtained on each test instance, for the tested values for R. Only R was varied, all other parameters were the same as the ones used in the performance evaluation. All tests confirmed the presented conclusions with $p < 0.01$.

6.3.2 *Communication issues*

This subsection presents some issues regarding data flows at different levels of the segregative approach, in order to illustrate the effects of the communication protocol. All data corresponds to an execution on the *cordic* problem instance. The parameters are the same as the ones used in the performance evaluation.

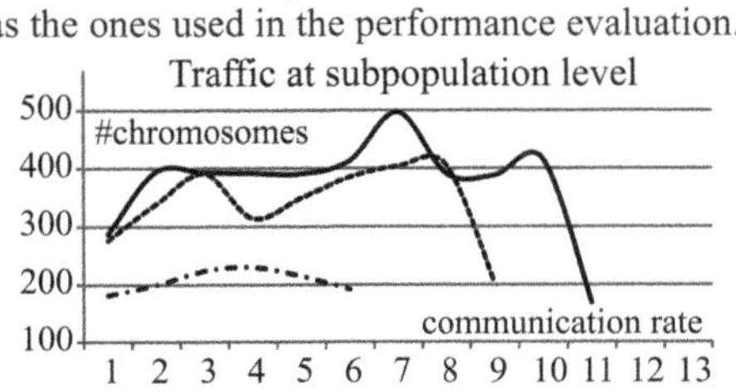

Figure 3. Data flows at subpopulation level

Figure 3 presents the number of chromosomes transferred by three parallel evolving subpopulations towards the fourth one. The moments of communication are multiples of the communication period, R. The dynamic adjustment of the genetic operator rates makes the communication at subpopulation level hard to predict. The data does not indicate a classical communication pattern for algorithms with multiple populations, such as an intense communication in the beginning of the evolution and then a decreasing trend towards the end.

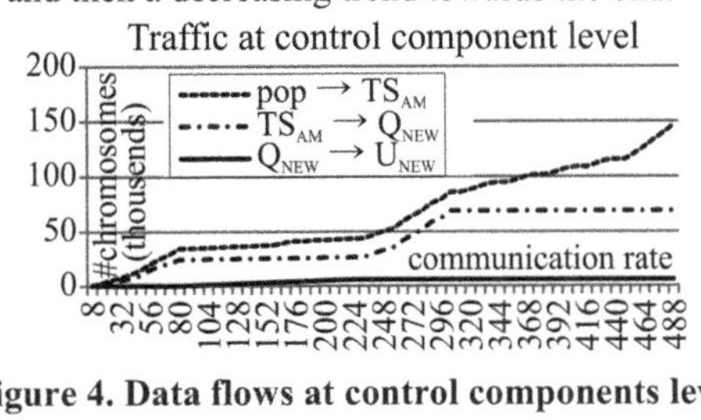

Figure 4. Data flows at control components level

Figure 4 presents the traffic towards and between the control components of the segregative algorithm. The values on each of the three graphs represent the total amount of transferred chromosomes until some evolution stage, counting all copies of the BGA. The dotted line represents the number of chromosomes transferred by the copies of the BGA towards TS_{AM} (chromosomes which are not similar to any of the four currently explored subpopulations. The intensity of the communication is correlated with the intensity of the traffic at subpopulation level. Lower data flows between currently explored subpopulations produce a more intense transfer towards TS_{AM}. The dash-dot line represents the amount of chromosomes that are transferred by TS_{AM} towards Q_{NEW} (chromosomes that do not belong to any explored region of the search space). The traffic is more intense in the beginning of the execution, which is to be expected, taking into account that the exploration history recorded by TS_{AM} is initially void and becomes larger and larger during the execution. As the algorithm converges, the transfer towards Q_{NEW} stagnates. The solid line represents the amount of chromosomes that are stored by Q_{NEW} in U_{NEW}, the large unstructured population with individuals from unexplored regions of the search space. The trend is similar to the previously described one: the communication is more intense in the beginning of the execution and stagnates as the algorithm converges.

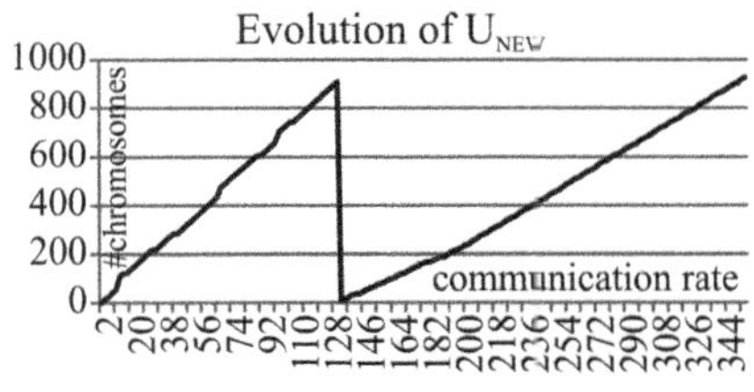

Figure 5. Amount of chromosomes entering U_{NEW}

Figure 5 depicts the evolution of the number of chromosomes in U_{NEW}. U_{NEW} is initially empty and it receives individuals until it reaches the maximum size, M_{UNEW}. After that the clustering procedure is applied and U_{NEW} is emptied. As the exploration performed by the algorithm becomes more extensive, U_{NEW} gets filled up more slowly.

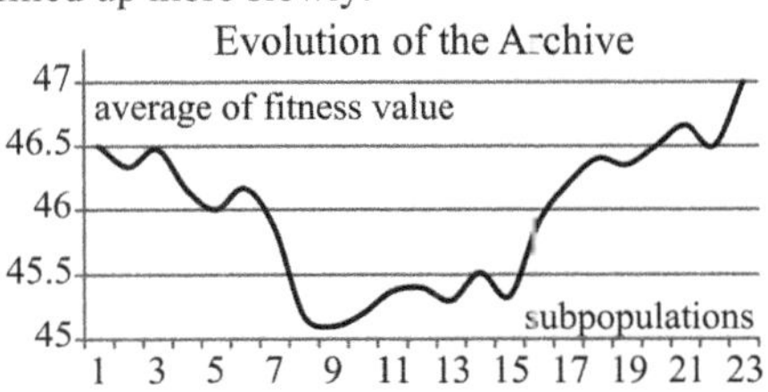

Figure 6. Average fitness in the Archive

Figure 6 presents the average fitness of the individuals in the archive, computed after the evolution of some subpopulation is finished and the archive is updated. Because of the random initialization of P_{init}, the initial values represent, in general, low fitness values. The values improve during the execution. The quality decreases towards the end because the algorithm also explores low quality subpopulations. The trend of the evolution suggests that PQ_{NEW} handles well the prioritization of subpopulations which are sent to the copies of BGA for exploration.

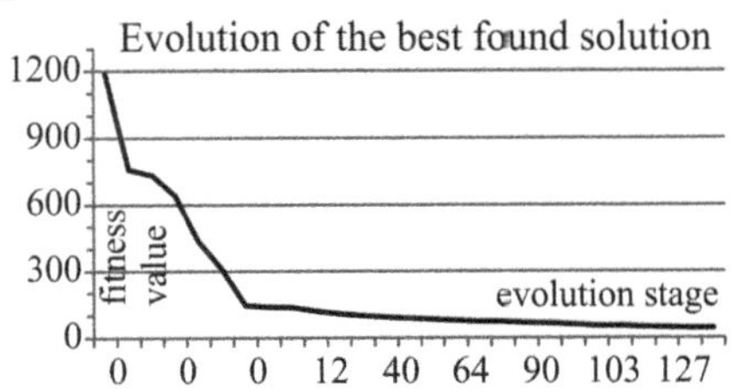

Figure 7. Evolution of the best found solution

Figure 7 presents the evolution of the best found solution during the execution of the algorithm. The starting value is of low quality, due to random initialization. The method greatly improves the solution, and very fast. Constant improvement towards the end of the evolution underlines the capacity of the algorithm to escape local optima.

7. CONCLUSIONS AND FUTURE WORK

In this paper a highly efficient dynamic segregative genetic algorithm for optimizing the order of variables in ROBDDs was presented. The approach deals with both representation and feature space. The exploration of the search space is achieved by evolving many subpopulations of individuals, which are induced by clustering in the feature space. The design of the algorithm is general and can incorporate any population based heuristic, as long as a similarity measure between individuals can be defined. An efficient communication protocol is introduced in order to maintain similarity inside the explored subpopulations and to focus the search on well-defined regions of the search space. The approach systematically avoids being trapped in local optima by using a tabu search associative memory. The exploration capabilities of the method are enhanced by a component that manages individuals from yet unexplored regions of the search space. Large quantities of promising individuals are managed and organized in subpopulations, in order to guide the search process towards newly discovered regions of the search space. The approach has a high potential for distributed computing and can be easily extended to solve problem instances in short time or to successfully solve very large instances that are intractable with exact methods.

Extensive evaluation on difficult benchmark problems shows a high level of performance of the algorithm in terms of quality and stability of the solution. Comparisons with single and multi-population heuristics are presented. The efficiency of the communication protocol and that of a distributed implementation are thoroughly analyzed.

Future research directions are focused on: devising a better feature vector, in order to better discriminate between highly similar individuals; integration of the branch-and-bound paradigm by evolving embryos instead of chromosomes; parameter tuning.

8. ACKNOWLEDGMENTS

Special thanks to Dr. Rüdiger Ebendt, Institute of Transportation Systems, Berlin, German Aerospace Center, for his support and for providing us with his ROBDD parser, based on CUDD package. All the experiments included in this paper were performed using this parser.

Cristian Rotaru acknowledges that this work was partially supported by the European Social Fund in Romania, under the responsibility of the Managing Authority for the Sectorial Operational Programme for Human Resources Development 2007-2013, Grant POSDRU/88/1.5/S/47646.

9. REFERENCES

[1] Bollig, B., Wegener, I. 1996. *Improving the variable ordering of OBDDs Is NP-complete*. IEEE Trans. on Computers, vol. 45, p. 993–1002.

[2] Friedman, S. J., Supowit, K. J. 1990. *Finding the optimal variable ordering for BDDs*. IEEE Trans. on Comp., vol. 39, p. 710–713.

[3] Fujii, H., Ootomo, G., Hori, C. 1993. *Interleaving based variable ordering methods for OBDD*. Int'l Conf. on CAD, p. 38–41.

[4] Meinel, C., Slobodova, A. 1997. *Speeding up variable reordering for OBDDs*. Int'l Conf. on Computer Design, p. 338–343.

[5] Panda, S., Somezi, F. 1995. *Who are the variables in your neighborhood*. Int'l Conf. of CAD, p. 74–77.

[6] Rudell, R. 1993. *Dynamic variable ordering for ordered binary decision diagrams*. Int'l Conf. of CAD, p. 42–47.

[7] Bollig, B., Lobbing, M., Wegener, I. 1995. *Simulated annealing to improve variable orderings for OBDDs*. Int'l Workshop on Logic Synth., p. 5b:5.1–5.10.

[8] Drechsler, R., Becker, B., Göckel, N. 1996. *A genetic algorithm for variable ordering of OBDDs*, IEEE Proceedings, 143(6), p. 363–368.

[9] Lenders, W., Baier, C. 2005. *Genetic algorithms for variable ordering problem of BDDs*. Lect. Notes in Comp. Sc., Springer, p. 1–20, vol. 3469/2005.

[10] Ebendt, R., Günther, W., Drechsler, R. 2005. *Combining ordered best-first search with branch and bound for exact BDD minimization*. IEEE Trans. on CAD of Integ. Circuits and Syst. 24(10), p. 1515–1529.

[11] Brudaru, O., Ebendt, R., Furdu, I. 2010. *Optimizing variable ordering of BDDs with double hybridized embryonic genetic algorithm*. Proc. of The 12th Int. Symposium on Symb. and Num. Algorithms for Sc. Comp., Synasc 2010, p. 167–173.

[12] Rotaru, C., Brudaru, O. 2012. *Multi-grid cellular genetic algorithm for optimizing variable ordering of ROBDDs*. Proc. of the 2012 IEEE Congress on Evolutionary Computation, IEEE CEC 2012, in press.

[13] Brudaru, O., Rotaru, C., Furdu, I. 2011. *Static segregative genetic algorithm for optimizing variable ordering of ROBDDs*. Proc. of The 13th Int. Symposium on Symbolic and Numeric Algorithms for Scientific Computing, Synasc 2011, p. 222–229.

[14] Brudaru, O., Rotaru, C. 2010. *Dynamic segregative genetic algorithm for assembly lines balancing*. Proc. of The 12th Int. Symposium on Symbolic and Numeric Algorithms for Scientific Computing, Synasc 2010, p. 229–236.

[15] Bryant, R.E. 1986. *Graph-based algorithms for Boolean function manipulation*. IEEE Trans on Comp. 35(8), p. 667–691.

[16] Furdu, I., Brudaru, O. 2009. *New hybrid genetic algorithm with adaptive operators and variability target for optimizing variable order in OBDD*. Proc. of "Gh. Vranceanu" Int'l Conference on Mathematics and Informatics ICMI 2, nr. 2 , p.156–172, vol. 19/2009.

[17] Goldberg, D.E. 1989. *Genetic algorithms in search, optimization and machine learning*, Addison Wesley.

[18] Butler, K.M., Ross, D., Kapur, R., Mercer, M.R. 1991. *Heuristics to compute variable orderings for efficient manipulation of OBDDs*. Proc. of the 28th ACM/IEEE Design Autom. Conf., p. 417–420.

[19] Malik, S., Wang, A.R., Brayton, R.K., Sangiovanni-Vincentelli, A. 1988. *Logic verification using BDDs in a logic synthesis environment*. Proc. of the ACM/IEEE Int. Conf. on Computer Aided Design, p. 6–9.

[20] Fujita, M., Fujisawa, H., Kawato, N. 1988. *Evaluation and improvements of Boolean comparison method based on BDDs*. Proc. of the ACM/IEEE Int. Conf. on Computer Aided Design, p. 2–5.

[21] http://cadlab.cs.ucla.edu/~kirill/, accessed June 2010.

[22] CUDD package URL: vlsi.colorado.edu/~fabio/CUDD.

How Long Should We Run in Dynamic Optimization?

Briseida Sarasola*
E.T.S. Ingeniería Informática
Bulevar Louis Pasteur s/n
Málaga, Spain
briseida@lcc.uma.es

Enrique Alba
E.T.S. Ingeniería Informática
Bulevar Louis Pasteur s/n
Málaga, Spain
eat@lcc.uma.es

ABSTRACT

The problem of measuring performance in dynamic optimization is still an open issue. The most popular procedure consists of choosing one measure from the standard evolutionary optimization domain, such as the best fitness in the current population, and averaging it across the number of generations (sometimes, the number of periods). Generally, it is assumed that the measure of our election has been sufficiently exposed to the changing landscape, although there is no way of actually checking whether this exposition has taken place or not. Our purpose is proposing here for the first time a way of determining how long we should run our experiments in order to get meaningful conclusions in a changing environment after a representative number of changes. The new stopping condition is based on the convergence of the chosen measure for the dynamic problem at hand, thus globally useful.

Categories and Subject Descriptors

G.1.6 [**Numerical Analysis**]: Optimization; I.2.8 [**Artificial Intelligence**]: Problem Solving, Control Methods, and Search—*Heuristic Search*

General Terms

Performance

Keywords

Dynamic Optimization, Metaheuristics, Stop Condition

1. INTRODUCTION

Measuring the performance of metaheuristics in the field of dynamic optimization (DO) is not a trivial issue. Many measures have been proposed, being the most popular ones those based on the best fitness average and the best fitness error average [6]. In dynamic problems, reporting the final fitness value is not significant, since the problem has probably changed many times and this final value is only related to the last problem landscape. Therefore, the usual approach is reporting the average of several fitness values, which are related to the different dynamic subproblems. However, it is generally accepted that these measures can capture the algorithmic performance only partially [16]. Therefore, additional measures concentrate on further aspects of the algorithm behavior such as stability, diversity, recovery rate, etc. The situation is however that they are not usually reported in those studies belonging to the DO field that do not specifically deal with performance measures.

An important question that is inherent to measuring performance in DO is how long we should simulate the changing problem. Many dynamic optimization problems (DOPs) require an algorithm that is able to provide and update good solutions for many dynamically changing scenarios during an unbounded period of time. However, the simulation time in the experimental phase is logically limited for practical reasons. We consider therefore that it is essential to determine how long a DOP should be simulated so that we obtain results that are representative for the whole problem dynamics. In the static domain, algorithms are run either a fixed number of evaluations, or until the best found solution has converged to a quality solution [14]. However, in the dynamic domain it is generally meaningless to stop when the algorithm has converged to a good solution, since the environment may continue changing and the current optimum may become obsolete. The vast majority of works in DO report results after up to 100 changes in the environment (sometimes even much below this value). This parameter is very seldom analyzed, and what may happen after the last period stays unknown and uncared for.

Our objective in this paper is providing a way to design a stopping condition that makes the algorithm stop when it has been sufficiently exposed to the problem dynamics. The idea is that an averaged measure, such as those used in the DO domain, should converge to a stable value after calculating it for a certain number of problem changes. In fact, according to the law of large numbers, the average of a random sample converges to the expected value if the sample size is large enough, thus, in order to make a truly scientific work researchers need to care about what is a "large enough" number of metric values. To test our proposal, we pick four well-known adaptations of a standard generational genetic algorithm (GA) for dynamic environments and a well-known benchmark in the moving peaks problem.

*Corresponding author.

GECCO'12, July 7-11, 2012, Philadelphia, Pennsylvania, USA.

It should be noted that we refer to convergence as the mathematical notion of a sequence of values approaching a limit, where the values are the averaged fitness measures that are usually used in dynamic optimization. Therefore, we do not use the term "convergence" to allude to population convergence in evolutionary algorithms, nor to refer to convergence speed as the number of evaluations required to obtain an accurate solution. Although it might be desirable to determine, independently from the algorithm and the performance measure, what are "representative problem dynamics" for a given dynamic optimization problem, we consider that studying the convergence of the fitness average can provide relevant information about the process through which the fitness average was obtained. It is important to emphasize that we are only able to evaluate algorithms through performance measures; therefore, acquiring supplementary knowledge about the measure behavior can help us understand the algorithm performance over a DOP (Fig. 1 summarizes this explanation).

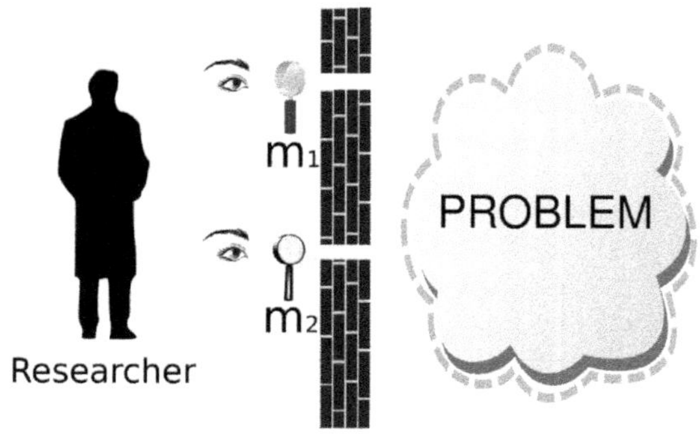

Figure 1: Information about the algorithm performance is obtained through performance measures. In this example, measures m_1 and m_2 provide different insights into the behavior of an algorithm over a problem.

In addition, a DOP is often considered an open-ended optimization problem, i.e. it keeps changing for an indefinite period of time. However, some DOPs are defined using a specific time limit, requiring thus to be simulated for a prearranged number of evaluations, generations, changes, or amount of time. In this case, it is obviously not necessary to determine how long we should simulate the problem, although we expect our convergence measure to provide additional information when averaged fitness measures are used.

Finally, the DO domain comprises different types of problems that can be classified according to several criteria, such as the way the optimum moves [9], the types of uncertainty [8], and the change features [3]. In this work, we deal with a real-valued, non-cyclic, periodically changing fitness function. However, using fitness averages is a very popular approach in most dynamic open-ended problems and our past experience shows that these measures behave very similar across most problem types, including different problem representations (i.e. binary, integer, and real), cyclic and non-cyclic problems, DOPs with diverse frequency and severity values, etc.

This article is organized as follows. Section 2 presents a survey of the best well-known performance measures in the literature, and discuss their strong and weak points for DO. Our proposal is described in detail in Section 3, and the experimental study is analyzed in Section 4. Finally, Section 5 draws some conclusions and lines of future work.

2. LITERATURE REVIEW

This section describes some of the current existing measures for DOPs in the literature and summarizes the most important studies in this area. See [6] for a detailed and up-to-date state of the art in this topic.

The first approaches to measuring the algorithm performance in dynamic optimization were offline and online performances [5, 7]. They both involve calculating fitness averages for the whole execution: offline performance is averaged using the best solution at each time (most typically, at each generation, although it may be measured at the end of each period), while online performance takes into account all solution evaluations in one execution (see Eq. 1, 2, where E is the total number of evaluations in one run and N is the number of generations). Often, offline performance is also referred to as Best-of-Generation Average ($\overline{BOG}$).

$$p_{online} = \frac{1}{E} \cdot \sum_{e=1}^{E} f(solution_e) \tag{1}$$

$$p_{offline} = \overline{BOG} = \frac{1}{N} \cdot \sum_{n=1}^{N} f(gen\_best\_solution_n) \tag{2}$$

Branke [3] specifically adapted offline performance to dynamic problems by calculating it using the best solution seen in the current period (since last change occured in the environment). Branke's measure equals the former one if an elitist algorithm is used or if the problem changes in each generation. In [11], Morrison proposes Collective Mean Fitness (F_C), a variation of offline performance that asserts that, if the algorithm runs for a sufficient number of generations and if a sufficient number of runs is performed, the collective mean fitness F_C closely approximates the total mean fitness F_T of the algorithm in that problem instance, where F_T is the average best-of-generation over an infinite number of generations (see Eq. 3, where M is the number of runs). However, no clue is provided about how many generations and runs are "a sufficient number".

$$F_C = \frac{1}{M}\frac{1}{N} \cdot \sum_{m=1}^{M}\sum_{n=1}^{N} f(gen\_best\_solution_n) \tag{3}$$

A number of error-based measures have also been proposed (e. g. relative error, offline error, mean fitness error, etc.). They are useful only when it is possible to know the optimum fitness for each changing landscape; this excludes many complex and/or real life problems.

Offline performance and offline error are the most popular ones in the DO domain. Their advantage is to provide a single value which summarizes the algorithm behavior. However, they do not contribute to any further analysis on specific features of dynamic problems: in fact, several algorithms may obtain similar fitness averages through different search behaviors [1]. For this reason, several ways of measuring other aspects of DOPs have been proposed.

One of these aspects is diversity. Entropy [19], and more often, the Hamming distance [22] have been widely used to measure population diversity in DOPs. Morrison and De Jong [12] proposed Inertia as a method to efficiently measure diversity. The advantage of their method is being able to compute it with linear complexity, as opposed to the quadratic complexity in most pair-wise methods.

Another two aspects are stability and ε-reactivity, which were introduced by Weicker in a systematic study about the usefulness of performance measures in dynamic optimization problems [18]. Accuracy, stability, and ε-reactivity are proposed as key features. Existing performance measures from the literature were reviewed and a new window based performance measure was proposed. Two algorithms, a standard GA and a hypermutation GA, were evaluated using a moving peaks bechmark. The study showed that the best fitness average is the best performance measure for problems with moderate fitness severity, while some deficiencies existed for problems without coordinate transitions (in this case, the window based measure was preferred).

Although the convergence in DO has not yet been addressed, one related issue is the evolvement of the averaged fitness performance measure. A measure named β-degradation takes into account the improving / degrading trends in the best-of-generation fitness, as a way of anticipating the performance of the algorithm as the problem changes [2].

Closely related domains are performance measures used in dynamic multiobjective optimization [4, 17] as well as in dynamic constrained optimization [15]. We encourage the reader to consult the referenced studies for further information on these two related fields.

3. A CONVERGENCE INDEX FOR DO

In this section we introduce a way to detect whether an averaged measure has converged to a stable value or not. We aim at designing a convergence index that can be applied to any of the fitness and error averages used in the DO domain, as well as to any of the measures that are reported as an averaged value across the number of generations or periods.

As explained in the previous section, the usual way of reporting performance in DO is averaging the fitness or the error during the execution. In the remainder of this work we use the average best-of-generation fitness (Eq. 2), since it is the most general term and it is also very popular in the literature. However, the discussion can be extended to collective mean fitness, since they are calculated in a similar way and provide almost identical results. We have excluded online performance from our discussion as it is not used in recently published works. We will not discuss in this article error-based measures either since they can hardly be applied in real world problems (i.e. those problems where it is not possible to know the optimum), but our convergence measure could also be applied to them if needed.

In the DO domain, algorithms are often run for a short number of changes (e.g. 10, 20, 50, 100) and conclusions are extracted from these periods (sometimes they are even shown merely as graphs [1, 2]). What may happen after this fixed number of periods remains unknown. An additional and related problem is the fact that several algorithms may achieve the same BOG average after a fixed number of periods following different search behaviors. The problem here is that the same final value is used to conclude that the algorithms are similar, but they are not.

A way to overcome these difficulties is running the algorithm long enough. The problem is determining what "long enough" means quantitatively, which can be different for different problems and algorithms. As previously discussed, it can be desirable to run the algorithm until the measure of our choice has converged to a stable state. In order to address this problem, we propose to incorporate the measure average into the stopping condition.

In the following subsections, the convergence index is defined (Section 3.1), we show an example and a figure to illustrate how it works (Section 3.2), and we detail its strengths and weaknesses (Section 3.3).

3.1 Definition

Let $r_{\overline{BOG},t}$ be the ratio of the current best-of-generation average to the past best-of-generation average at time $t-\omega$.

$$r_{\overline{BOG},t} = \frac{\overline{BOG_t}}{\overline{BOG_{t-\omega}}} \tag{4}$$

where $\overline{BOG_{t-\omega}}$ is used as the reference value to compare with: in order to determine whether the measure is now stable or not, it must be compared with a previous value; $0 < \omega < t$ is used to determine the length of the temporal window considered: if ω is 1, the reference value is the immediately former generation; if it is greater than 1, more distant generations are used.

Let S_g be the set of stable $r_{\overline{BOG},t}$ measurements defined as follows:

$$S_g = \{t \mid 1-\varepsilon < r_{\overline{BOG},t} < 1+\varepsilon\} \tag{5}$$

where $\varepsilon \gtrsim 0$ is a small value that must be set by the researcher and it is used to decide whether $r_{\overline{BOG}}$ is stable or not; the smaller ε, the stricter the convergence condition.

The convergence index I_c is defined as Eq. 6:

$$I_c = \frac{|S_g|}{n_g} \geq R_c \tag{6}$$

where $n_g > 0$ is the number of times that the measure has been averaged and $R_c < 1$ is the desired convergence rate. Since $|S_g| \leq n_g$, I_c is always in the interval $[0, 1]$.

Convergence is thus calculated using the number of times that the average measure is considered stable. An averaged measure is stable when it changes very little compared to the former measured value. In this way, we provide a new stopping condition (Eq. 6) that can also be used as a way to measure convergence in DO. The researcher needs to set only the constants ω, ε and R_c, which denote the length of the temporal window, the threshold to consider a $r_{\overline{BOG}}$ value as stable, and the stopping condition, respectively.

3.2 Example

Figure 2 shows an example of the behavior of these parameters when we run an Evolutionary Algorithm over a general problem. In the top figure, the running BOG and the $\overline{BOG}$ are shown. As we can see, the BOG is the actual fitness, which changes whenever a change happens in the environment. $\overline{BOG}$ fluctuates in a smoother way, following the changes in the best-of-generation fitness. The bottom figure shows the running I_c until it reaches the convergence rate $R_c = 0.95$ (which was set as stopping condition here). The ratio $r_{\overline{BOG}}$ is also displayed (calculated using $\omega = 2$). The shaded area around $r_{\overline{BOG}} = 1$ represents the interval in which $r_{\overline{BOG}}$ is considered stable (i. e. $(1 \pm \varepsilon$, $\varepsilon = 0.05)$.

In addition to the final I_c, two intermediate points are also marked with vertical lines in both figures, namely $I_c = 0.85$ and $I_c = 0.90$. At these two points the $\overline{BOG}$ has not yet converged.

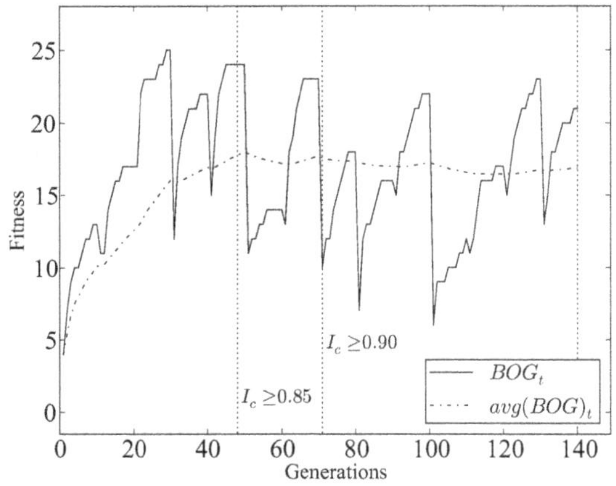

(a) Running BOG and $\overline{BOG}$ of an EA over a general DOP with changes every 10 generations.

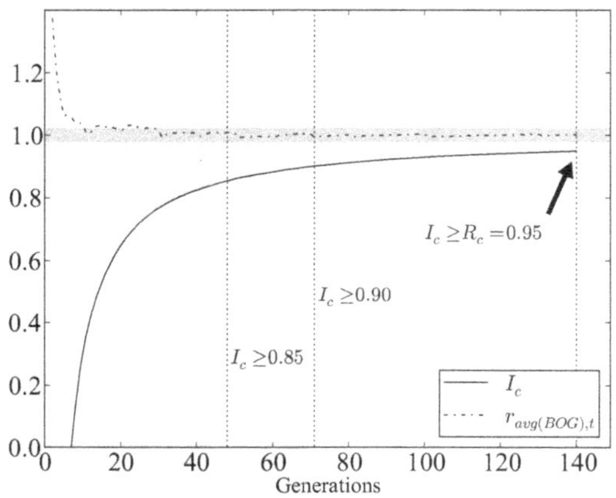

(b) Running ratio $r_{\overline{BOG}}$ and I_c, which is calculated using $\varepsilon = 0.05$ and $\omega = 2$.

Figure 2: Parameters that take part in the convergence index I_c. The stopping condition is $I_c \geq R_c = 0.95$. In addition, two intermediate I_c values are also marked.

3.3 Strengths and Weaknesses Analysis

In order to see how and where to use our convergence index, it is necessary to understand its strengths and weaknesses. The most evident advantage of using I_c is using a systematic method to decide when to stop a dynamic problem, instead of taking this decission in an arbitrary way. In addition, even when it is used with a predefined stop condition such as the number of periods, it informs about the level of convergence achieved by the averaged fitness/error measure, providing thus additional and valuable information on the behavior of the algorithm during the search. Finally, it is also useful when less periods than the usual $p = 100$ are required; in this case, it would be possible to save computation time without losing significant information, which is specially relevant in hard computing problems.

Some weaknesses should also be taken into account, so that we can provide solutions for them. Some average measures could converge too slowly when solving some problem instances using a given algorithm, so that it could be unfeasible to let this algorithm run for such a long time. A way to overcome this issue is adding a second stop condition based on the maximum number of periods, generations or evaluations, and reporting the $\overline{BOG}$ together with the convergence value achieved by the I_c. In a similar way, the measure could converge too fast (e.g. if the problem is not hard and the change frequency is low); in this case, it could be necessary to add another stop condition based on the minimum number of changes for the simulation. A second matter is the fact that it is necessary to set three parameters: ω, ε, and R_c. We suggest to use $\omega \in [10, 100]$, $\varepsilon \leq 0.05$, and $R_c \geq 0.95$.

4. EXPERIMENTAL VALIDATION

This section is aimed at closely examining the usage of several predefined stop conditions based on the number of periods (changes) as well as our own modified stop condition.

4.1 Benchmark Description

There are several benchmark problems for DO, such as the dynamic bit-matching, dynamic royal road, moving parabola, time varying knapsack problem, etc. Since we want to illustrate the new stopping condition, the election of the problem is not important. In this paper, we focus on one of the most widely used benchmark problem for DO: the moving peaks problem (MPP) [3]. This problem is very popular in the DO literature and has been recently addressed using advanced algorithms [13, 21]. The moving peaks' aim is to have an artificial multidimensional landscape consisting of several peaks where the height, width, and position of each peak is altered every time a change in the environment occurs. The cost function for N dimensions and m peaks has the following form:

$$F(\vec{x}, t) = \max\{B(\vec{x}), \max_{i=1\ldots m} P(\vec{x}, h_i(t), w_i(t), \vec{p}_i(t))\} \quad (7)$$

where $B(\vec{x})$ is a time-invariant "base" landscape, and P is the function defining a peak shape, where each of the m peaks has its own time-varying parameter height (h), width (w), and location ($\vec{p}$). Every certain number of evaluations, the height and width of every peak are changed by adding a random Gaussian variable. The location of every peak is changed by a vector v of fixed length s. A parameter λ determines if a peak change depends on the previous move or not. If $\lambda = 0$ then each change is completely random, while for $\lambda = 1$, the peak will always move in the direction of the former change.

We use a problem configuration that corresponds closely to the standard settings proposed by Branke. We use a plane defined in $(0, 100) \times (0, 100)$ with 5 dimensions and 10 peaks. The peak heights are in the interval [30, 70] and the widths in [0.001, 0.2]. The height change severity is set to 7.0 and the width change severity to 0.01. Changes occur every 1000 evaluations and $\lambda = 0$. Three different period lengths $\Delta e = \{500, 1000, 5000\}$ (measured in evaluations)

Table 1: Best-of-generation results after four stop conditions: 100, 500, and 1000 changes in the environment, as well as after $\overline{BOG}$ convergence is achieved.

(a) Ranking of algorithms. The asterisk * in the columns $p = 500$ indicates a tie between two algorithms.

Rank	Stopping condition							
	$p = 100$		$p = 500$		$p = 1000$		Conv.	
	Algorithm	Sum	Algorithm	Sum	Algorithm	Sum	Algorithm	Sum
1	genGA+ri	5	genGA+ri	5	genGA+mri	5	genGA+mri	3
2	genGA+mri	6	genGA+me	7	genGA+me	6	genGA+ri	7
3	genGA	9	genGA*	9	genGA+ri	8	genGA+me	8
4	genGA+me	10	genGA+mri*	9	genGA	12	genGA	13

(b) Average Best of Generation fitness.

Stopping condition	Instance	genGA	genGA+me	genGA+ri	genGA+mri
$p = 100$	MPP-e-500	4.8639e+01$_{\pm 3.6e+00}$	4.7634e+01$_{\pm 4.0e+00}$	4.8185e+01$_{\pm 3.7e+00}$	4.8057e+01$_{\pm 4.5e+00}$
	MPP-e-1000	4.8206e+01$_{\pm 4.4e+00}$	4.8798e+01$_{\pm 3.8e+00}$	4.9455e+01$_{\pm 4.2e+00}$	4.9039e+01$_{\pm 3.3e+00}$
	MPP-e-5000	4.9714e+01$_{\pm 3.7e+00}$	5.0019e+01$_{\pm 4.4e+00}$	5.0087e+01$_{\pm 3.8e+00}$	5.0304e+01$_{\pm 3.9e+00}$
$p = 500$	MPP-e-500	4.8654e+01$_{\pm 1.9e+00}$	4.8911e+01$_{\pm 2.0e+00}$	4.8670e+01$_{\pm 1.9e+00}$	4.8146e+01$_{\pm 1.5e+00}$
	MPP-e-1000	4.9294e+01$_{\pm 1.8e+00}$	4.9277e+01$_{\pm 2.1e+00}$	4.9300e+01$_{\pm 2.0e+00}$	4.9245e+01$_{\pm 2.0e+00}$
	MPP-e-5000	4.9468e+01$_{\pm 1.9e+00}$	4.9949e+01$_{\pm 2.0e+00}$	5.0329e+01$_{\pm 2.3e+00}$	5.1015e+01$_{\pm 2.1e+00}$
$p = 1000$	MPP-e-500	4.8992e+01$_{\pm 1.2e+00}$	4.9038e+01$_{\pm 1.6e+00}$	4.8774e+01$_{\pm 1.4e+00}$	4.9166e+01$_{\pm 1.3e+00}$
	MPP-e-1000	4.9148e+01$_{\pm 1.4e+00}$	4.9615e+01$_{\pm 1.7e+00}$	4.9453e+01$_{\pm 1.6e+00}$	4.9375e+01$_{\pm 1.5e+00}$
	MPP-e-5000	4.9469e+01$_{\pm 1.2e+00}$	4.9842e+01$_{\pm 1.7e+00}$	5.0177e+01$_{\pm 1.6e+00}$	5.0532e+01$_{\pm 1.8e+00}$
Conv.	MPP-e-500	4.8613e+01$_{\pm 1.1e+00}$	4.9064e+01$_{\pm 1.2e+00}$	4.9083e+01$_{\pm 8.1e-01}$	4.9137e+01$_{\pm 9.5e-01}$
	MPP-e-1000	4.9237e+01$_{\pm 9.3e-01}$	4.9556e+01$_{\pm 1.4e+00}$	4.9249e+01$_{\pm 9.5e-01}$	4.9787e+01$_{\pm 1.0e+00}$
	MPP-e-5000	4.9520e+01$_{\pm 1.8e+00}$	4.9869e+01$_{\pm 2.0e+00}$	4.9949e+01$_{\pm 1.8e+00}$	5.1180e+01$_{\pm 2.5e+00}$

are considered. The dataset has then three instances: *MPP-e-500*, *MPP-e-1000*, and *MPP-e-5000*.

4.2 Algorithm Description

In this section, our aim is to validate the convergence index using a set of widely known algorithms in the DO field. To this end, we use an elitist generational genetic algorithm (genGA) as well as three strategies which adapt metaheuristics to dynamic environments: explicit memory (me) [10], random immigrants (ri) [7], and both memory and immigrants (mri) [20]. These three adaptations to dynamic environments are popular in the literature and they have been applied to a wide range of problems. This results in four algorithms: genGA, genGA+me, genGA+ri, genGA+mri. The population size is set to 100 individuals in the case of genGA, 90 individuals plus 10 additional individuals in the memory for genGA+me, 90 individuals plus 10 additional random generated individuals for genGA+ri, and 80 plus 10 memory individuals plus 10 random generated individuals for genGA+mri (we assign different population sizes in order to preserve the number of evaluations in each generation). Parent selection is done by binary tournament; uniform crossover probability p_c equals 0.6, and mutation probability for each solution bit is $p_m = 1/L$, where L is the length of the real-valued string.

4.3 Experimental Settings

We are using in this paper $\overline{BOG}$. Since the best result is known in the MP problem, the offline error could be used and the conclusions we draw would be almost the same. However, we prefer to illustrate our approach in the most general case, using offline performance since it is not always possible to know the error when we work with real life problems. Algorithms are implemented using Java 1.5 and the experiments are run in a pool of Debian machines. Each algorithm is run 100 times on each instance with each stopping condition.

We also perform statistical significance tests in our study, since not only being quantitative is a must in DO today, but statistical validation is mandatory to assess that our claims are not due to random fluctuations of the algorithms. We check if the data follow a Gaussian distribution using the Kolmogorov-Smirnov test. If the answer is positive, we perform a Levene test to check the homocedasticity (homogeneity of the variances). If the Levene test is positive, we do an ANOVA test to compare the means; otherwise we perform a Welch test. If the data does not follow a normal distribution, we use a Kruskal-Wallis test. All these tests use a level of confidence of 95 %.

4.4 A Study on Convergence in DO

In this subsection we present how the conclusions we draw about performance in dynamic optimization can vary when we simulate a dynamic problem over a different number of periods. This is an undesired scenario, but a frequent one in the literature up to now because researchers do not face it in existing articles. We analyze the results obtained after 100, 500, and 1000 changes in the environment ($p = \{100, 500, 1000\}$), as well as after the index I_c has converged to R_c.

The numerical results are shown in Table 1. Table 1a presents a summary of the results in terms of ranking positions (the first, the best). Each algorithm is ranked according to the following method: algorithms are sorted according to their position in $\overline{BOG}$ performance $(1, 2, 3, 4$ from best to worse) for each instance; then each algorithm positions are

Table 2: Average number of periods for each algorithm run using $I_c \geq R_c$ as stopping condition.

Problem	GA	GA+me	GA+ri	GA+mri
MPP-e-500	$5643.55_{\pm 654.20}$	$5146.21_{\pm 599.08}$	$4521.67_{\pm 613.78}$	$5028.06_{\pm 646.07}$
MPP-e-1000	$3195.63_{\pm 404.09}$	$2924.14_{\pm 419.62}$	$2968.30_{\pm 420.30}$	$2870.84_{\pm 409.24}$
MPP-e-5000	$699.32_{\pm 142.18}$	$619.90_{\pm 134.76}$	$715.67_{\pm 148.50}$	$601.28_{\pm 132.79}$

Table 3: Convergence index I_c after 100, 500, and 1000 changes in the environment, as well as after convergence is achieved.

Periods	Instance	GA	GA+me	GA+ri	GA+mri
	MPP-e-500	$0.065_{\pm 0.07}$	$0.087_{\pm 0.09}$	$0.071_{\pm 0.10}$	$0.085_{\pm 0.08}$
100	MPP-e-1000	$0.166_{\pm 0.10}$	$0.173_{\pm 0.12}$	$0.157_{\pm 0.13}$	$0.153_{\pm 0.10}$
	MPP-e-5000	$0.646_{\pm 0.10}$	$0.687_{\pm 0.09}$	$0.671_{\pm 0.10}$	$0.685_{\pm 0.10}$
	MPP-e-500	$0.455_{\pm 0.07}$	$0.494_{\pm 0.06}$	$0.527_{\pm 0.06}$	$0.485_{\pm 0.06}$
500	MPP-e-1000	$0.680_{\pm 0.05}$	$0.713_{\pm 0.04}$	$0.704_{\pm 0.03}$	$0.713_{\pm 0.04}$
	MPP-e-5000	$0.927_{\pm 0.01}$	$0.938_{\pm 0.01}$	$0.930_{\pm 0.02}$	$0.940_{\pm 0.01}$
	MPP-e-500	$0.724_{\pm 0.04}$	$0.746_{\pm 0.04}$	$0.756_{\pm 0.03}$	$0.746_{\pm 0.03}$
1000	MPP-e-1000	$0.837_{\pm 0.02}$	$0.855_{\pm 0.02}$	$0.852_{\pm 0.02}$	$0.855_{\pm 0.02}$
	MPP-e-5000	$0.965_{\pm 0.01}$	$0.968_{\pm 0.01}$	$0.966_{\pm 0.01}$	$0.969_{\pm 0.01}$
	MPP-e-500	$0.950_{0.00}$	$0.950_{0.00}$	$0.950_{0.00}$	$0.950_{0.00}$
Conv.	MPP-e-1000	$0.950_{0.00}$	$0.950_{0.00}$	$0.950_{0.00}$	$0.950_{0.00}$
	MPP-e-5000	$0.950_{0.00}$	$0.950_{0.00}$	$0.950_{0.00}$	$0.950_{0.00}$

summed up in one single value; finally, the algorithms are ranked according to the sum of positions they have achieved (an asterisk * denotes a tie between two or more algorithms). Table 1b reports the best-of-generation average $\overline{BOG}$ for each problem and each instance, according to the four different stop conditions.

Using the number of periods as the stop condition.

First we start by analyzing the case of stopping after 100 changes in the problem (standard stop condition in the literature). According to the resulting ranking of $\overline{BOG}$, the best algorithm is genGA+ri, followed by genGA+mri, genGA, and genGA+me in this order. These results suggest that the memory we are using does not help the algorithm to find better solutions, since genGA+mri and genGA+me obtain worse results than genGA+ri and genGA, respectively.

Second, we run the algorithms for a longer time ($p = 500$ is the new stopping condition). As we can see in the ranking table, genGA+ri is still the best algorithm, but genGA+me overtakes genGA and genGA+mri as the second best algorithm. Algorithms genGA and genGA+mri tied (they scored the same value in the sum of positions). In this case, we may conclude that the algorithm with a memory a random immigrants performs poorly and is not able to improve the results obtained by the standard genGA.

Third, we let the algorithms run still longer (stop after 1000 changes in the environment). Now the best algorithms are genGA+mri for instances *MPP-e-500* and *MPP-e-5000*, and instance genGA+me in *MPP-e-1000*. In this case, considering the ranking scores, genGA+mri is the best algorithm, followed by genGA+me, genGA+ri, and genGA.

In summary, the conclusions are different for each of the three predefined stopping conditions. For example, the algorithm genGA+me provides the worst results after 100 changes, but it is the second best one after 500 and 1000 changes; genGA and genGA+mri may be seen as algorithms that provide solutions of similar quality after 500 changes, while they would be seen respectively as the worst and the best algorithm after 1000 changes.

Using the convergence index as the stop condition.

Now we analyze what happens when we force the algorithms to run until they achieve convergence on the $\overline{BOG}$ measure. For that purpose, we use the stopping criterion defined in Section 3, using $\varepsilon = 0.01$, $R_c = 0.95$, and $\omega = 100$. These values have been fixed in a preliminary experimental study.

The ranking is shown in the last column of Table 1a and the results for each instance are detailed in the last three rows of Table 1b. In this case, genGA+mri is the best algorithm for each instance, so it occupies the first place in the ranking table. The second, third, and fourth algorithms are genGA+ri, genGA+me, and genGA in this order. These results are the most similar ones to the results obtained after simulating 1000 changes in the dynamic problem (but not 100 nor 500 changes), which suggests that $p = 1000$ is closer to the number of periods needed when using our convergence index as stopping condition. These algorithms need a longer exposition to the dynamic landscape (longer than the standard number of $p = 100$). The convergence index I_c provides a way of detecting how long is "long enough".

Number of periods to achieve convergence.

In Table 2 we show how many periods are needed for each algorithm in order to reach $\overline{BOG}$ convergence. When comparing the number of periods that each algorithm needs to run to achieve convergence, it can be seen that, the faster the problem changes, the higher the number of periods the algorithm should be executed. In the rapidly changing instance (*MPP-e-500*), the algorithms need around 5000 periods to converge (according to our experimental settings, where the values of R_c, ε, and ω have been previously set). The instance which changes every 1000 evaluations requires that algorithms are exposed to around 3000 periods of the changing landscape before we can assure their convergence. Finally, only the slowest changing instance ($\Delta e = 5000$) does not require to run the algorithms for the maximum prefixed value we have considered in this work ($p = 1000$): around 700 periods is enough to ensure convergence. As already explained in this article, convergence refers here to the stabilization of the average fitness measure (and not convergence to the optimum value).

Analyzing I_c on its own.

It is also possible to analyze the $\overline{BOG}$ convergence even when we are not using it as the stop condition. This could be needed if $\overline{BOG}$ converge very slowly, as well as in problems that must be necessarily run using another stop condition.

Table 3 shows the value of the convergence index at the final generation for each stop condition, problem, and algorithm. As it can be seen regarding the first two stopping conditions, simulating 100 and 500 changes in the environment is insufficient to achieve a good convergence value, specially when the changes in the environment are very frequent. When the simulation is performed for 1000 changes, I_c values are above 0.70 in the rapidly changing instance, above 0.90 when changes happen every 1000 evaluations, and above 0.95 in the slowly changing instance. We consider that $I_c > 0.90$ is probably a good convergence index, although deeper mathematical analysis is needed in this case. It can also be noticed that, for instance *MPP-e-5000* and $p = 1000$, the algorithms achieve a higher convergence rate than our own fixed $R_c = 0.95$. This means that, when using a predefined number of periods, all algorithms run for too short in all instances except in the slowest changing instance when the fixed number of periods is 1000. For the sake of completeness, we also include the value of the convergence index when we use it as the stopping condition (as expected, $I_c = R_c = 0.95$ for all algorithms and instances).

Figure 3 shows an example of how our I_c is much more significant and informative than the best-of-generation average when it comes to giving information about the convergence of the fitness average. Figure 3a (above) shows how $\overline{BOG}$ evolves while the problem changes, while Figure 3b (below) shows the evolution of the convergence index I_c during the same time. It can be seen that 100 periods is an insufficient number of changes if we want to obtain a stable average (there is a high loss of the best-of-generation average just around $p = 100$ in the x-axis). Fixing R_c (the stopping condition of I_c) at 0.95 is a decision which depends on how much computational time is available and how sure we want to be about the convergence of the average fitness.

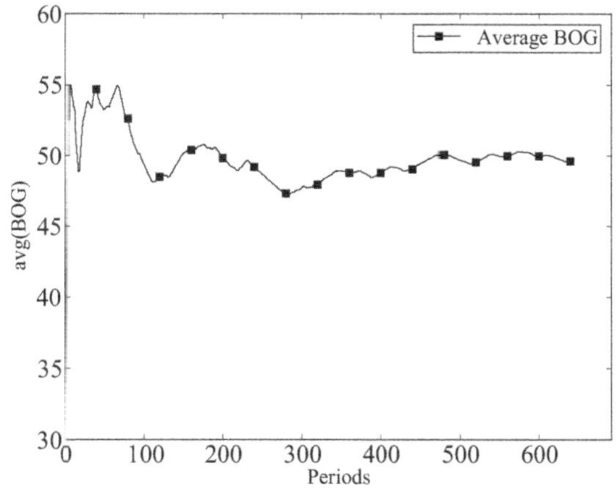

(a) Running best-of-generation average $\overline{BOG}$.

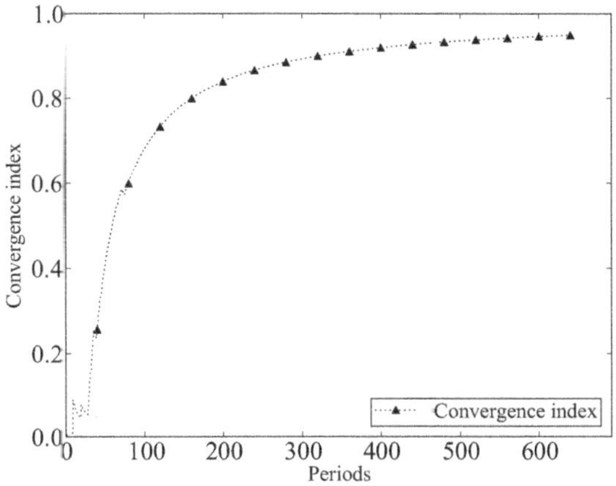

(b) Running convergence index I_c.

Figure 3: Evolution of $\overline{BOG}$ (above) and I_c (below) of genGA on *MPP-e-5000* (median trace).

5. CONCLUSIONS AND FUTURE WORK

This article presents a study on the problem of average fitness convergence in dynamic optimization. We have discussed the problems associated with using a predefined (and arbitrary) number of periods as stopping condition, and we propose a new convergence index which can be used as a new stopping condition. We show that the usual number of periods $p = 100$ can be insufficient to expose the algorithms to the dynamic landscape, since different conclusions may be drawn depending on how long we let the algorithm run. We think that the usual simulation length in dynamic optimization problems should be questioned and, in any case, should not be a predefined parameter which is never disputed. Using I_c in the stop condition makes it possible to design more reliable experiments. It also helps to gain additional insights about the algorithm behavior, even when it is used independent of the stopping condition.

Future work includes deeper analysis of the mathematical properties and the parameter sensitivity of this convergence index. Another research line is to study the convergence of DO measures when using different GAs as well as other families of metaheuristic algorithms. We are also interested in analyzing and comparing the convergence of the algorithms in other DOPs.

6. ACKNOWLEDGMENTS

Authors acknowledge funds from the Spanish Ministry of Sciences and Innovation European FEDER under contract TIN2008-06491-C04-01 (M* project) as well as TIN2011-28194 (RoadMe project), and CICE, Junta de Andalucía under contract P07-TIC-03044 (DIRICOM project). Briseida Sarasola is supported by grant AP2009-1680 from the Spanish government.

7. REFERENCES

[1] E. Alba and B. Sarasola. ABC, a new performance tool for algorithms solving dynamic optimization problems. In *IEEE Congress on Evolutionary Computation*, pages 1–7, 2010.

[2] E. Alba and B. Sarasola. Measuring fitness degradation in dynamic optimization problems. In

European Conference on the Applications of Evolutionary Computation, 2010.

[3] J. Branke. *Evolutionary optimization in dynamic environments*. Kluwer Academic Publishers, 2002.

[4] M. Cámara, J. Ortega, and F. de Toro. Performance measures for dynamic multi-objective optimization. *Bio-Inspired Systems: Computational and Ambient Intelligence*, I(5517):760–767, 2009.

[5] H. G. Cobb and J. J. Grefenstette. Genetic algorithms for tracking changing environments. In *5th International Conference on Genetic Algorithms*, pages 523–530, 1993.

[6] C. Cruz, J. González, and D. Pelta. Optimization in dynamic environments: a survey on problems, methods and measures. *Soft Computing - A Fusion of Foundations, Methodologies and Applications*, 15:1427–1448, 2011.

[7] J. J. Grefenstette. Genetic algorithms for changing environments. In *Parallel Problem Solving from Nature*, pages 139–146, 1992.

[8] Y. Jin and J. Branke. Evolutionary optimization in uncertain environments-a survey. *IEEE Trans. Evolutionary Computation*, 9(3):303–317, 2005.

[9] Y. Jin and B. Sendhoff. Constructing dynamic optimization test problems using the multi-objective optimization concept. In *EvoWorkshops*, volume 3005 of *LNCS*, pages 525–536. Springer, 2004.

[10] N. Mori, S. Imanishi, H. Kita, and Y. Nishikawa. Adaptation to changing environments by means of the memory based thermodynamical genetic algorithm. In *7th International Conference on Genetic Algorithms*, pages 299–306, 1997.

[11] R. Morrison. Performance measurement in dynamic environments. In *GECCO Workshop on Evolutionary Algorithms for Dynamic Optimization Problems*, pages 5–8, 2003.

[12] R. W. Morrison and K. A. D. Jong. Measurement of population diversity. In *Selected Papers from the 5th European Conference on Artificial Evolution*, pages 31–41, London, UK, 2002. Springer-Verlag.

[13] I. Moser and R. Chiong. Dynamic function optimisation with hybridised extremal dynamics. *Memetic Computing*, 2(2):137–148, 2010. 10.1007/s12293-009-0027-6.

[14] A. J. Nebro, J. J. Durillo, C. A. C. Coello, F. Luna, and E. Alba. A study of convergence speed in multi-objective metaheuristics. In *Parallel Problem Solving from Nature*, pages 763–772, 2008.

[15] T. T. Nguyen and X. Yao. Continuous dynamic constrained optimisation - The challenges. *IEEE Transactions on Evolutionary Computation*, 2011.

[16] W. Rand and R. Riolo. Measurements for understanding the behavior of the genetic algorithm in dynamic environments: a case study using the shaky ladder hyperplane-defined functions. In *Workshops on Genetic and evolutionary computation*, pages 32–38, 2005.

[17] E. Tantar, A.-A. Tantar, and P. Bouvry. On dynamic multi-objective optimization, classification and performance measures. In *IEEE Congress on Evolutionary Computation*, pages 2759–2766, 2011.

[18] K. Weicker. Performance measures for dynamic environments. In *Parallel Problem Solving from Nature*, volume 2439, pages 64–73. 2002.

[19] M. Wineberg and F. Oppacher. Enhancing the ga's ability to cope with dynamic environments. In *Genetic and Evolutionary Computation Conference*, pages 3–10, 2000.

[20] S. Yang. Genetic algorithms with memory- and elitism-based immigrants in dynamic environments. *Evolutionary Computation*, 16(3):385–416, 2008.

[21] S. Yang and C. Li. A clustering particle swarm optimizer for locating and tracking multiple optima in dynamic environments. *Evolutionary Computation, IEEE Transactions on*, 14(6):959–974, dec. 2010.

[22] S. Yang and R. Tinós. A hybrid immigrants scheme for genetic algorithms in dynamic environments. *International Journal of Automation and Computing*, pages 243–254, 2007.

Enhancing the Virtual Loser Genetic Algorithm for Dynamic Environments

Anabela Simões*
Coimbra Polytechnic
Rua Pedro Nunes - Quinta da Nora
3030-199 Coimbra, Portugal
abs@isec.pt

Ernesto Costa
CISUC, University of Coimbra
Polo II - Universidade de Coimbra
3030-290 Coimbra - Portugal
ernesto@dei.uc.pt

ABSTRACT

In recent years, several memory schemes have been used in Evolutionary Algorithms (EAs) for dynamic optimization problems (DOPs). The Virtual Loser Genetic Algorithm (VLGA), recently proposed, uses a novel type of associative memory to deal with DOPs. This memory scheme memorizes past errors concerning the performed mutations and uses this information to create new individuals when a change in the environment occurs. In this paper the VLGA is further investigated in order to enhance its performance in different types of DOPs: the influence of an important parameter is analyzed, and the interaction between the memory scheme and the use of immigrants is also investigated. A novel immigrant scheme is proposed and compared with the random immigrants approach. The results show that the investigated methods significantly enhance the previous version of the VLGA for cyclic and random environments.

Categories and Subject Descriptors

I. [**Computing Methodologies**]: ARTIFICIAL INTELLIGENCE—*Problem Solving, Control Methods, and Search*

General Terms

Algorithms, Experimentation, Performance

Keywords

Evolutionary Algorithms, Dynamic Environments, Memory, Associative Memory, Virtual Loser

1. INTRODUCTION

Evolutionary Algorithms (EAs) are a class of metaheuristic algorithms inspired by principles of natural evolution, such as selection and population genetics. The use of EAs for dynamic optimization problems (DOPs) has been widely explored in the last decade. The main goal in the design of EAs for DOPs is to avoid the premature convergence of the population, allowing the EAs to track and to adapt to the changing environment. In this context, several approaches have been developed for EAs to address DOPs. These approaches include maintaining and reintroducing diversity during the run [3], [4], memory schemes [7], [10], using multi-populations [2] or the prediction of the next change [8]. Memory-based EAs are beneficial when past situations reappear in the future. This way, memorized solutions can help the EA to readapt to the new conditions [2]. Different types of memory have been investigated in the literature: direct memory approaches, associative memory, memory schemes using immigrants and hybrid approaches [10]. This paper is centered in associative memory, which stores the best individual from the population and additional information about the environment. This information is used to create new individuals every time a change occurs [10]. Different types of associative memory have been proposed in the past: Yang [10] introduced an associative memory scheme inspired by Baluja's population-based incremental learning (PBIL) algorithm. In this memory scheme, the best solution in the population together with a probability vector, which represents the current environment, is stored in the memory. When a change is detected, the probability vector associated with the best memory sample is used to create new individuals. Other PBIL's inspired associative memory scheme were investigated in [12] and [11]. Barlow [1] investigated a memory-enhanced EA to the dynamic job shop scheduling problem. This memory-based EA uses a classifier-based memory for abstracting and storing information about schedules, that is used to build similar schedules at future times. In previous work [9] a novel form of associative memory has been proposed for EAs dealing with DOPs. The method, called the Virtual Loser Genetic Algorithm (VLGA), creates a vector of inhibitions during the evolutionary process, which contains knowledge about errors that were performed. This vector, called *the virtual loser*, is a template of the unfit individuals of the population evolved between two consecutive changes and is stored in the memory associated to the best individual of the corresponding population. When a change occurs, this knowledge about previous errors is used to create new individuals to reintroduce into the population. The underlying metaphor is that the new solutions should be as different as possible from the virtual loser, in order to avoid repetition of past errors. The obtained results showed that the VLGA, for cyclic environments, outperformed other methods. Nevertheless, when ap-

*also belongs to CISUC

GECCO'12, July 7–11, 2012, Philadelphia, Pennsylvania, USA.

plied to random environments the performance of the VLGA decreased and, in some situations, was worse than other algorithms [9]. In this paper the VLGA is further investigated to improve its adaptability in dynamic environments. The main goal is to enhance the previous version of the VLGA increasing its performance for cyclic, and especially for random environments. First, the influence of the number of bits to mutate in the new individuals created using the virtual loser vector (parameter β) is deeply analyzed. Second, the interaction between the memory scheme and the use of immigrants is also analyzed. An innovative approach to create immigrants from the virtual loser vector is investigated and compared with Grefenstette's random immigrants method [4].

The rest of the paper is organized as follows: the next section describes the *Virtual Loser Genetic Algorithm* for DOPs and how virtual loser immigrants are created and used in combination with the memory. Section 3 details the experimental setup used in this work. The experimental results and analysis are presented in Section 4. Section 5 concludes the paper and some considerations are made about future work.

2. THE VIRTUAL LOSER GA

The virtual loser scheme was proposed by Sebag et al. [5] and was tested in static function optimization, using a $(\mu + \lambda)$-ES, assuming that the fitness landscape was fixed and that the fitness of an individual was independent from the other individuals in the population. The knowledge stored in the virtual loser vector was used by a mutation operator, called flee-mutation, that created offspring derived from the parents. The virtual loser was used to compute different mutation probabilities to a selected number of bits in such a way that the 'bad' mutations performed in the past were avoided. In [9] the same metaphor was adapted to be used in DOP, resulting in a new associative memory-based GA, called Virtual Loser Genetic Algorithm (VLGA). The proposed mechanism uses a vector denoted by *the virtual loser* which memorizes past errors of evolution in order to avoid (inhibit) their future occurrence. This idea resembles to that of Tabu Search, but instead of memorizing a list of past individuals to avoid, which would only reflect a small part of the search space, uses a tractable and general description of past errors. The virtual loser vector (VL) is initialized at the beginning of the run (or whenever a change happens) and is updated at every generation until a change is detected in the environment. The virtual loser is initialized by analyzing the bits of the best individual of the population and the corresponding bits in the worst individuals of the population. For instance, in Table 1, A is the best individual, B, C and D, the worst individuals (adapted from [5]). The VL calculates, for each position, the percentage of bits of the worst individuals that differ from the corresponding bit in the best individual. For instance, bit 1 was always different in the unfit solutions when compared with the best one. This means that the high fitness of A can be due to bit 1 equal to 1 and this value should be preserved. Contrariwise, nothing can be said about the influence of bit 3 in the fitness of A, since this bit has the same value for all individuals. In the future, when applying mutation to solution A, bit 3 should be more affected than bit 1. So, for the first bit the mutation should be strongly inhibited and the opposite for the third bit. At every generation, the VL is updated by relaxation from a fraction η of the worst individuals in the current population. The relaxation factor γ is used to update VL as follows (eq. 1): $\text{VL}(t+1) = (1-\gamma) \times \text{VL}(t) + \gamma \times d\text{VL}$, where dVL is a vector measuring, at position i, the difference between the bits of a fraction η of the worst individuals and the best individual. The memory is updated whenever a change occurs. The relevant information stored in memory refers to the population before the change. This information consists of the pair $< B^{p-1}, \text{VL}^{p-1} >$, where B^{p-1} is the best individual of the population before change and VL^{p-1} is the VL vector evolved until the generation before change. When the environment changes, the memory is reevaluated according to the new environment and the best memory point $< B^m, \text{VL}^m >$ is retrieved. The solution B^m and the associated VL^m vector are used to create a set of $\alpha \times p$ new individuals, that will replace the worst individuals in the population. The parameter $\alpha \in [0, 1]$ is called associative factor and determines the number of individuals created from the memory when a change happens. To create those new individuals, each bit of B^m is mutated according to a certain probability, calculated using VL^m and the value of the gene. The probability to mutate a bit B_i^m is given by: $P_i = 1 - \text{VL}_i^m$ (eq. 2). For the example illustrated in Table 1 and for $B^m = [111111]$, $P = [0.00; 0.33; 1.00; 0.33; 0.33; 0.67]$.

Table 1: Creating the virtual loser

bit	1	2	3	4	5	6	Fitness
A	1	1	1	1	1	1	high
B	0	0	1	0	0	1	low
C	0	0	1	1	1	1	low
D	0	1	1	0	0	0	low
VL	1.00	0.67	0.00	0.67	0.67	0.33	

Two mechanisms for creating the new individuals I from B^m are investigated: probabilistically and tournament-based. Let $\beta \times L$ (L is the chromosome length) be the number of potential bits to mutate in B^m. In the probabilistic VLGA (VLGAp), $\beta \times L$ bits are randomly selected and each bit i ($i = k_1, k_2, ..., k_X$) is mutated according the value of P_i, and using the ith allele from B^m: if $rand(0,1) < P_i$ then $I_i = 1 - B_i^m$. In the tournament-based VLGA (VLGAt), three bits are randomly selected and the one with the highest value of P_i is the winner of the tournament. The winner bit is always mutated. This process is repeated $\beta \times L$ times. Moreover, after a change, the VL is reinitialized using the procedure illustrated in Table 1. Then, at every evolutionary step, after selection, crossover and mutation, the VL is updated using eq. 1 until the occurrence of the next change. In this paper, in order to enhance the performance of the VLGA, one additional step is included in the algorithm: the introduction, at every generation, of new individuals (immigrants) into the population. The proposed approach uses the VL vector to create a percentage r_i of individuals from the current best individual. These immigrants can be created using either the probabilistic or the tournament method for selecting the percentage β of bits to mutate. The VLGA using this mechanism will be denoted by VLGAp_vli and VLGAt_vli. Our approach will be compared with the random immigrants approach, and for this case, the VLGA will be referred as VLGAp_ri and VLGAt_ri. In both cases, the created immigrants replace the worst individuals of the population. Figure 1 presents the pseudo code of the VLGA.

```
Function VLGA
  L: chromo. length        n: n. of individuals
  p: pop. size             m: mem. size
  β: % of bits to mutate
  α: assoc. factor         r_i: % of immigrants
  γ: relax. factor         η: fraction of worst

t = 0;
Initialize and Evaluate(P(0))
Initialize and Evaluate(M(0))
VL(t) = initVL(P(t))
repeat
  Preserve best individual from P(t-1)
    if change is detected then
      //Update Memory
      B' = best from P(t-1)
      VL' = updateVL(VL^p(t-1), P(t-1), γ, η, p)
      M(t) = UpdateMemory(B', VL')
      //Retrieve Memory
      Retrieve B^m(t) and VL^m(t) from memory
      I(t) = CreateNewInd(B^m(t), VL^m(t), α, β, L, p)
      P(t) = ReplaceWorst(P(t), I(t), α, p)
      // Reinitialize VL
      VL^p(t) = initVL(P(t))
  P'(t) = Selection(P(t))
  Crossover(P'(t))
  Mutation(P'(t))
  P(t+1) = P'(t)
  Evaluate(P(t+1))
  Evaluate(M(t+1))
  //eq. 1
  VL^p(t+1) = updateVL(VL^p(t), P(t+1), γ, η, p)
  if virtual loser immigrants then
    P(t+1) = Immi_vl(P(t+1), VL^p(t+1), β, r_i, L, p)
  if random immigrants then
    P(t+1) = Immi_rnd(P(t+1), r_i, p)
  t = t+1
until stop_condition
```

Figure 1: Pseudo code for the VLGA

3. EXPERIMENTAL DESIGN

3.1 Dynamic Test Environments

The dynamic environments to carry out our experimentation were created using Yang's Dynamic Optimization Problems (DOP) generator [10]. This generator allows the construction of different dynamic environments from any binary-encoded stationary function using the bitwise exclusive-or (XOR) operator. The characteristics of the change are controlled by two parameters: the speed of the change, r, that is the number of function evaluations between two changes, and the magnitude of the change, ρ, that controls how different is the new environment from the previous one. The DOP generator can construct three types of dynamic environments: cyclic, cyclic with noise and random. In this work we constructed two types of environments: cyclic and random. For each type of DOP, the parameter r was used with 1000 and 5000. The ratio ρ was set to different values in order to test different levels of change: 0.1 (a light shifting) 0.2, 0.5 and 1.0 (severe change). A random change was also tested concerning severity. For this case, the new environment has no relation with the previous one. Two binary-encoded problems were selected as the stationary functions: the 0-1 Knapsack (KP) and the Royal Road F1 function (RRF1). Those benchmark problems were transformed from static to dynamic using the DOP generator, described before.

3.2 Parameters Setting

In the experiments, ten GAs were investigated using the above constructed DOPs: the standard GA (SGA), the Hypermutation GA (HGA) proposed by [3], the Random Immigrants GA (RIGA) [4], the Associative Memory Genetic Algorithm (AMGA) investigated in [10] and the different versions of the Virtual Loser Genetic Algorithm (VLGAp and VLGAt) detailed in the previous section. In the following sections VLGAp_vli and VLGAt_vli denote the VLGA using the virtual loser immigrants; VLGAp_ri and VLGAt_ri designate the VLGA using random immigrants. Standard parameters were used for all GAs: generational replacement with elitism of size one, tournament selection with tournament of size two, uniform crossover, with probability $p_c = 0.7$ and flip mutation with $p_m = 0.01$. Binary representation was used with chromosomes of length 100 for the KP and 64 for the RRF1. The associative factor α for the AMGA, the VLGAp and the VLGAt was set to 0.5. The hypermutation rate used in the HMGA was 0.2. The ratio of immigrants was set to 0.2. All algorithms used a global number of individuals $n = 100$. When using immigrants, n was set to $n = \frac{100}{1+r_i}$, since that the $r_i \times n$ immigrants were also evaluated every generation. The memory size for AMGA and VLGA was set to $m = 0.2 \times n$. For the VLGA, the relaxation factor γ was set to 0.02, the fraction η of the worst individuals was 0.5. The number of bits to mutate per individual was exhaustively tested: this number is a percentage β of the chromosome length. In this paper β was tested with values varying from 0.1 to 1.0 with increments of 0.1. The *similar* replacing strategy proposed by [2] was used to replace a memory solution when the maximum capacity for the memory is attained. For each experiment of an algorithm, 50 runs were executed. Each algorithm was run for a number of generations corresponding to 200 environmental changes. The overall performance used to compare the algorithms was the offline performance [2] averaged over 50 independent runs, executed with the same random seeds.

4. EXPERIMENTAL RESULTS

The results presented in this section were statistically validated using the nonparametric Friedman's ANOVA test at a 0.01 level of significance. After this test, the multiple pair wised comparisons were performed using the Nemenyi procedure with Bonferroni correction. The notation used in the statistical results tables is $s+$, $s-$ and $\sim$, when the first algorithm is significantly better than, significantly worse than, or without statistical evidence with the second algorithm, respectively.

4.1 Analyzing the influence of β

In previous work, VLGA used $\beta = 1.0$. This means that the number of bits to mutate using either the probabilistic or the tournament-base methods is equal to the chromosome length. This value allowed the VLGA to obtain good results for cyclic environments, but poor results were attained in random environments [9]. The use of a higher value for β was motivated by the fact that, mutating all the bits using the VL information, memorized errors were avoided by the creation of fittest individuals. This assumption was proved, but a side effect was observed: the diversity of the population decreased and a high number of individuals presented similar genotypes. As shown in [6], when using memory, usually, a lower population's diversity does not affect the performance of the EA because the memorized solutions are very effective for this type of environments. For random environments memory is not so effective and consequently extra diversity in the population is required. So, in order to see how this parameters influences the performance of VLGAp and VLGAt, both algorithms were run using different values for β. Tables 4 and 5 show the results obtained using β from 0.1 to 1.0 for VLGAt (for VLGAp, the results were equivalent). The values marked with bold are statistically better when compared with the worst values (usually $\beta = 1.0$). For cyclic environments, the use of $\beta = 1.0$ leads the VLGA to the worst results. Lower values for β are usually better and, as β increases, the performance of the VLGA decreases. These results indicate that few mutations in the best memory individual when a change is detected are enough to create fittest individuals for the new environment. For random environments this relation is not so evident, but in general $\beta = 0.1$ is better than $\beta = 1.0$. In fact $\beta = 0.1$ guarantees the best results in the majority of the analyzed situations, showing that the fitness of the individuals is increased by mutating only a small fraction of the bits of the best memory solution.

4.2 Comparing VLGA with the peer algorithms

This section compares the VLGA using $\beta = 0.1$ with the peer algorithms. Figure 3 and Table 2 show the results obtained for the KP in cyclic and random environments and Figure 4 and Table 3 for the RRF1 problem. The statistical results refer only to the comparison of the proposed method with the peer algorithms. From the plots and statistical analysis result that, for cyclic environments, the performance of VLGA is significantly better than SGA, HGA, RIGA and AMGA. The few exceptions occur in the RRF1 in slower environments ($r = 5000$) with light severity of change ($\rho = 0.1$). This is understandable, as for $r = 5000$ the algorithm has more time to evolve and for light changes, keeping individuals from previous environments can be advantageous. Comparing the two versions of VLGA, the results show that, in cyclic environments, in general, VLGAt and VLGAp have no statistical difference. Only when $\rho = 1.0$ and $\rho = rnd$ in the KP, VLGAp is better than VLGAt. For random environments, the use of $\beta = 0.1$ improved the results obtained in [9], but in general the results have no statistical difference when compared with the peer algorithms. Only when $\rho = 1.0$ and for some $\rho = rnd$ for the KP, VLGAp and VLGAt are better than the peer algorithms. It is important to observe that the random environment is in fact cyclic for $\rho = 1$ (as every bit is changed in each period, i.e., the environment is repeated every two periods), what explains the obtained results.

4.3 Results using Immigrants

Tables 6 and 8 compare the results obtained using random immigrants and virtual loser immigrants in VLGAp and VLGAt for the dynamic KP. For the RRF1 the results are in Tables 7 and 9. The comparisons are made with the peer algorithm that obtained the best results (AMGA). The results show that the use of Grefenstette's random immigrants in both VLGAs don't provide any significant advantage to the algorithms. For the KP the performance using or not using random immigrants are identical and for the RRF1, the performance of VLGAs in most situations decreases when random immigrants are included. Nevertheless, the results of VLGAp_ri and VLGAt_ri, in cyclic environments, are still significant better than AMGA, and for random environments the results are similar to the ones described in the previous section. On the other hand, the use of virtual loser immigrants significantly enhances the performance of VLGAp and VLAGt either in cyclic and random environments, especially in the KP. The enhancement of the performance using virtual loser immigrants is more evident in the VLGAt. As the tables show, VLGAt_vli is in general significant better than VLGAt and AMGA, for both cyclic and random environments. The use of virtual loser immigrants in VLGAp enhances the performance of the algorithm for cyclic environments with light changes and outperforms AMGA in most situations. In random environments, VLGAp_vli is better than VLGAp and AMGA for the KP, but the same is not observed in the RRF1. These results show that the inclusion, at every generation, of new individuals, created using the VL information and avoiding the bad mutations previously performed, enhances the performance of the VLGA. Figure 2 shows an example of how VLGAt and VLGAt_vli evolves over time, for the KP in cyclic and random environments.

Table 2: Statistical Results for the Dynamic KP

$\alpha = 0.5$	Cyclic									
	$r = 1000$					$r = 5000$				
$\rho \Rightarrow$	0.1	0.2	0.5	1.0	rnd	0.1	0.2	0.5	1.0	rnd
VLGAp - SGA	$s+$	$s+$	$s+$	$s+$	$s+$	$s+$	$s+$	$s+$	$s+$	$s+$
VLGAp - HGA	$s+$	$s+$	$s+$	$s+$	$s+$	$s+$	$s+$	$s+$	$s+$	$s+$
VLGAp - RIGA	$s+$	$s+$	$s+$	$s+$	$s+$	$s+$	$s+$	$s+$	$s+$	$s+$
VLGAp - AMGA	$s+$	$s+$	$s+$	$s+$	$s+$	$s+$	$s+$	$s+$	$s+$	$s+$
VLGAp - VLGAt	$\sim$	$\sim$	$\sim$	$s+$	$s+$	$\sim$	$\sim$	$\sim$	$\sim$	$s+$
VLGAt - SGA	$s+$	$s+$	$s+$	$s+$	$s+$	$s+$	$s+$	$s+$	$s+$	$s+$
VLGAt - HGA	$s+$	$s+$	$s+$	$s+$	$s+$	$s+$	$s+$	$s+$	$s+$	$s+$
VLGAt - RIGA	$s+$	$s+$	$s+$	$s+$	$s+$	$s+$	$s+$	$s+$	$s+$	$s+$
VLGAt - AMGA	$s+$	$s+$	$s+$	$s+$	$s+$	$s+$	$s+$	$s+$	$s+$	$s+$
$\alpha = 0.5$	Random									
	$r = 1000$					$r = 5000$				
$\rho \Rightarrow$	0.1	0.2	0.5	1.0	rnd	0.1	0.2	0.5	1.0	rnd
VLGAp - SGA	$s-$	$s-$	$s+$	$s+$	$s+$	$s-$	$s-$	$s+$	$s+$	$s+$
VLGAp - HGA	$\sim$	$s-$	$\sim$	$s+$	$\sim$	$\sim$	$\sim$	$\sim$	$s+$	$\sim$
VLGAp - RIGA	$s-$	$s-$	$\sim$	$s-$	$s+$	$\sim$	$\sim$	$\sim$	$s+$	$\sim$
VLGAp - AMGA	$s-$	$s-$	$s+$	$s+$	$s+$	$s-$	$\sim$	$\sim$	$s+$	$s+$
VLGAp - VLGAt	$\sim$	$\sim$	$\sim$	$s+$	$\sim$	$\sim$	$\sim$	$\sim$	$\sim$	$\sim$
VLGAt - SGA	$s-$	$s-$	$s+$	$s+$	$s+$	$s-$	$s-$	$s+$	$s+$	$s+$
VLGAt - HGA	$s-$	$s-$	$\sim$	$s+$	$s+$	$\sim$	$\sim$	$\sim$	$s+$	$s+$
VLGAt - RIGA	$s-$	$s-$	$\sim$	$s+$	$s+$	$\sim$	$\sim$	$\sim$	$s+$	$s+$
VLGAt - AMGA	$s-$	$s-$	$\sim$	$s+$	$s+$	$\sim$	$\sim$	$\sim$	$s+$	$s+$

Table 3: Statistical Results for the Dynamic RR1

$\alpha = 0.5$	Cyclic									
	$r = 1000$					$r = 5000$				
$\rho \Rightarrow$	0.1	0.2	0.5	1.0	rnd	0.1	0.2	0.5	1.0	rnd
VLGAp - SGA	$s+$	$s+$	$s+$	$s+$	$s+$	$\sim$	$s+$	$s+$	$s+$	$s+$
VLGAp - HGA	$s+$	$s+$	$s+$	$s+$	$s+$	$s+$	$s+$	$s+$	$s+$	$s+$
VLGAp - RIGA	$s+$	$s+$	$s+$	$s+$	$s+$	$\sim$	$s+$	$s+$	$s+$	$s+$
VLGAp - AMGA	$s+$	$s+$	$s+$	$s+$	$s+$	$\sim$	$s+$	$s+$	$s+$	$s+$
VLGAp - VLGAt	$s-$	$s+$	$\sim$	$\sim$	$\sim$	$\sim$	$\sim$	$\sim$	$\sim$	$\sim$
VLGAt - SGA	$s+$	$s+$	$s+$	$s+$	$s+$	$\sim$	$s+$	$s+$	$s+$	$s+$
VLGAt - HGA	$s+$	$s+$	$s+$	$s+$	$s+$	$s+$	$s+$	$s+$	$s+$	$s+$
VLGAt - RIGA	$s+$	$s+$	$s+$	$s+$	$s+$	$\sim$	$s+$	$s+$	$s+$	$s+$
VLGAt - AMGA	$s+$	$s+$	$s+$	$s+$	$s+$	$\sim$	$s+$	$s+$	$s+$	$s+$
$\alpha = 0.5$	Random									
	$r = 1000$					$r = 5000$				
$\rho \Rightarrow$	0.1	0.2	0.5	1.0	rnd	0.1	0.2	0.5	1.0	rnd
VLGAp - SGA	$s-$	$\sim$	$s+$	$s+$	$\sim$	$s-$	$s-$	$s+$	$s+$	$\sim$
VLGAp - HGA	$\sim$	$\sim$	$\sim$	$s+$	$\sim$	$\sim$	$s-$	$\sim$	$s+$	$\sim$
VLGAp - RIGA	$\sim$	$\sim$	$\sim$	$s+$	$\sim$	$\sim$	$s-$	$\sim$	$s+$	$\sim$
VLGAp - AMGA	$\sim$	$\sim$	$\sim$	$s+$	$\sim$	$\sim$	$\sim$	$\sim$	$s+$	$\sim$
VLGAp - VLGAt	$\sim$	$\sim$	$\sim$	$\sim$	$\sim$	$\sim$	$\sim$	$\sim$	$\sim$	$\sim$
VLGAt - SGA	$s-$	$\sim$	$s+$	$s+$	$\sim$	$s-$	$s-$	$s+$	$s+$	$\sim$
VLGAt - HGA	$\sim$	$\sim$	$\sim$	$s+$	$\sim$	$\sim$	$s-$	$\sim$	$s+$	$\sim$
VLGAt - RIGA	$\sim$	$\sim$	$\sim$	$s+$	$\sim$	$\sim$	$s-$	$\sim$	$s+$	$\sim$
VLGAt - AMGA	$\sim$	$\sim$	$\sim$	$s+$	$\sim$	$\sim$	$\sim$	$\sim$	$s+$	$\sim$

Table 4: Effect of β in VLGAt for the Dynamic Knapsack

	r	ρ	$\beta=0.1$	$\beta=0.2$	$\beta=0.3$	$\beta=0.4$	$\beta=0.5$	$\beta=0.6$	$\beta=0.7$	$\beta=0.8$	$\beta=0.9$	$\beta=1.0$
CYCLIC	1000	0.1	**1771.70**	1771.33	1770.45	1769.65	1767.41	1767.20	1765.75	1764.75	1764.11	1764.08
		0.2	**1772.06**	1769.50	1768.72	1766.87	1765.97	1764.22	1762.76	1762.03	1763.28	1760.73
		0.5	**1767.26**	1767.62	1764.02	1761.86	1762.12	1761.37	1760.81	1761.04	1761.84	1761.04
		1.0	**1787.85**	1783.93	1775.04	1764.69	1763.20	1764.25	1763.25	1766.88	1766.39	1766.58
		rnd	**1790.13**	1781.07	1775.32	1765.25	1763.14	1762.78	1764.72	1764.50	1763.85	1767.16
	5000	0.1	**1791.19**	1790.64	1789.29	1789.30	1788.49	1788.23	1788.22	1787.31	1787.10	1786.80
		0.2	**1790.57**	1790.30	1789.37	1788.42	1787.61	1786.86	1786.27	1785.66	1783.80	1785.11
		0.5	**1792.77**	1791.32	1790.73	1789.00	1787.32	1786.87	1786.73	1784.81	1785.00	1786.37
		1.0	**1815.12**	1813.71	1812.33	1812.56	1811.44	1801.62	1797.25	1791.91	1792.97	1793.10
		rnd	**1812.85**	1813.72	1813.11	1813.11	1812.28	1806.31	1792.70	1791.81	1792.30	1791.60
RANDOM	1000	0.1	**1764.46**	1764.63	1764.65	1764.83	1763.73	1763.14	1763.10	1762.80	1763.12	1762.02
		0.2	**1759.41**	1759.41	1759.07	1758.88	1758.95	1758.31	1758.24	1757.13	1757.25	1757.82
		0.5	**1752.91**	1752.21	1751.82	1751.67	1750.60	1750.20	1750.06	1749.42	1749.77	1749.83
		1.0	**1787.50**	1782.47	1773.80	1765.07	1764.07	1764.56	1763.35	1765.18	1765.30	1765.95
		rnd	**1754.13**	1753.99	1753.26	1751.60	1751.62	1750.65	1750.70	1750.11	1750.91	1750.71
	5000	0.1	1786.86	1786.56	1785.96	1786.34	1786.19	1785.71	1785.71	1785.69	1786.03	1785.53
		0.2	1779.37	1779.53	1779.42	1778.85	1779.38	1778.91	1779.00	1779.06	1779.50	1778.89
		0.5	1771.05	1770.82	1771.33	1771.39	1771.39	1771.00	1770.83	1771.05	1770.93	1770.83
		1.0	**1815.22**	1812.97	1812.35	1812.77	1810.63	1796.50	1798.56	1794.38	1792.82	1791.25
		rnd	1773.22	1773.70	1773.48	1773.02	1773.74	1773.27	1773.32	1772.74	1773.00	1772.72

Table 5: Effect of β in VLGAt for the Royal Road F1

	r	ρ	$\beta=0.1$	$\beta=0.2$	$\beta=0.3$	$\beta=0.4$	$\beta=0.5$	$\beta=0.6$	$\beta=0.7$	$\beta=0.8$	$\beta=0.9$	$\beta=1.0$
CYCLIC	1000	0.1	**28.48**	27.20	27.54	25.88	24.76	22.94	23.33	22.88	22.06	21.57
		0.2	**29.74**	28.36	28.31	26.52	23.02	23.69	21.73	19.75	21.44	22.19
		0.5	**35.51**	34.15	32.10	27.33	27.19	26.79	27.11	27.52	27.39	26.18
		1.0	**45.21**	43.41	42.01	42.07	41.37	41.64	40.30	41.82	41.58	41.76
		rnd	42.89	42.42	41.24	40.76	42.52	42.60	42.14	41.43	41.68	42.72
	5000	0.1	**52.14**	52.86	50.64	49.82	50.21	50.24	49.47	48.84	49.85	47.95
		0.2	**54.57**	52.65	49.29	46.61	44.53	42.62	42.65	43.15	43.85	42.04
		0.5	**59.39**	59.56	59.80	58.24	54.65	56.81	59.34	55.80	53.60	53.66
		1.0	63.92	63.47	62.77	62.88	62.62	62.47	62.37	61.41	62.51	62.19
		rnd	63.28	63.17	63.11	62.75	62.30	61.83	62.20	62.43	62.18	62.98
RANDOM	1000	0.1	**22.07**	22.03	22.04	21.07	21.11	21.39	21.16	20.32	21.27	20.36
		0.2	**14.14**	13.81	13.75	14.00	13.51	13.79	13.39	12.91	13.22	12.94
		0.5	10.72	10.94	10.00	10.24	10.00	9.82	9.88	9.74	9.54	9.69
		1.0	**46.11**	43.07	41.30	41.59	41.92	40.60	41.74	41.65	41.95	40.54
		rnd	11.46	11.35	11.68	11.26	11.15	11.18	11.27	11.07	10.77	10.72
	5000	0.1	**51.20**	50.53	50.59	49.87	49.84	50.65	50.59	50.03	50.00	49.63
		0.2	35.00	35.43	35.69	34.99	35.26	35.17	34.94	35.36	35.28	35.57
		0.5	22.68	21.85	22.20	22.06	22.38	22.43	22.35	22.39	22.29	22.15
		1.0	63.45	62.92	63.03	62.19	62.19	62.52	62.82	61.11	61.85	62.09
		rnd	24.73	24.46	24.97	24.18	24.02	24.44	25.43	24.55	24.72	24.62

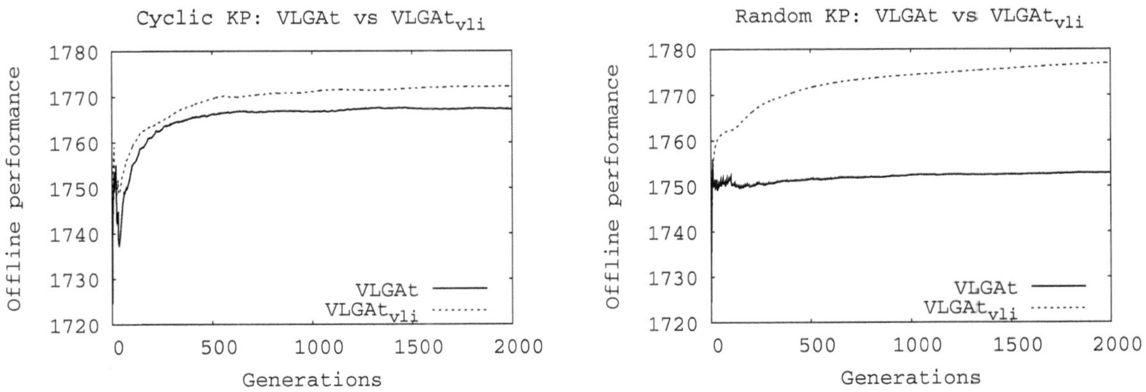

Figure 2: Offline performance of VLGAt with and without virtual loser immigrants (Knapsack)

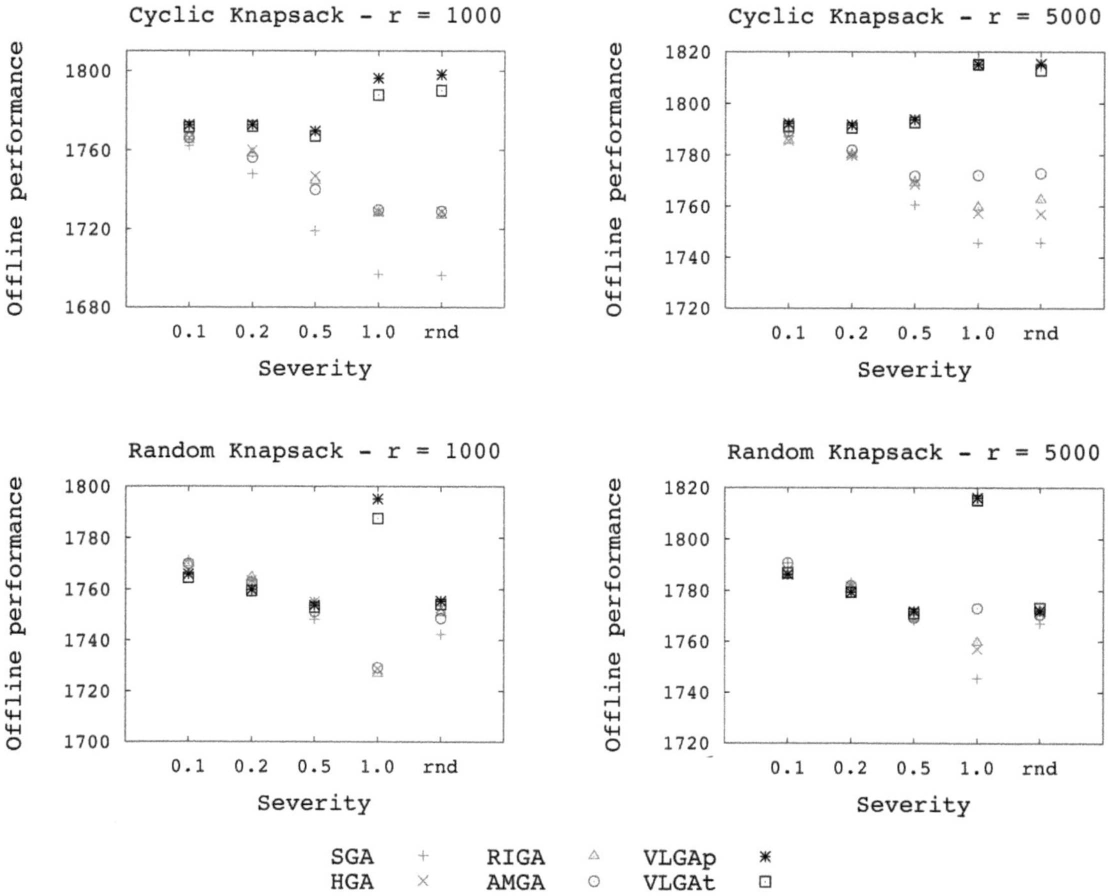

Figure 3: Offline performance for the dynamic Knapsack

Table 6: Results using Random and Virtual Loser Immigrants for the Dynamic Knapsack

	r	ρ	AMGA	VLGAp	VLGAp_ri	VLGAp_vli	VLGAt	VLGAt_ri	VLGAt_vli
CYCLIC	1000	0.1	1766.16	1772.79	1770.18	1776.84	1771.70	1770.73	1776.85
		0.2	1756.29	1772.86	1768.62	1776.01	1772.06	1768.75	1776.52
		0.5	1740.01	1769.64	1768.52	1779.06	1767.26	1766.81	1772.20
		1.0	1729.74	1796.25	1796.88	1798.01	1787.85	1787.02	1790.60
		rnd	1729.05	1798.13	1794.84	1797.24	1790.13	1787.70	1788.85
	5000	0.1	1789.32	1792.26	1789.32	1797.26	1791.19	1789.15	1794.90
		0.2	1781.93	1791.71	1789.98	1799.58	1790.57	1789.37	1794.85
		0.5	1771.78	1793.82	1793.28	1807.38	1792.77	1793.09	1795.49
		1.0	1772.06	1815.19	1815.02	1817.06	1815.12	1814.07	1809.28
		rnd	1772.76	1815.35	1815.64	1816.78	1812.85	1813.52	1810.06
RANDOM	1000	0.1	1769.91	1765.82	1763.30	1769.34	1764.46	1763.47	1772.09
		0.2	1762.71	1759.82	1757.35	1762.10	1759.41	1758.39	1765.36
		0.5	1751.22	1753.74	1751.16	1756.39	1752.91	1752.23	1758.07
		1.0	1729.22	1795.13	1796.91	1797.80	1787.50	1789.20	1788.52
		rnd	1748.57	1755.45	1751.92	1757.82	1754.13	1752.62	1760.03
	5000	0.1	1790.80	1786.28	1785.28	1791.82	1786.86	1785.23	1791.11
		0.2	1781.93	1779.37	1777.39	1784.76	1779.37	1778.10	1784.97
		0.5	1769.35	1771.85	1768.95	1776.81	1771.05	1769.90	1777.02
		1.0	1773.08	1816.04	1816.03	1815.84	1815.22	1813.82	1810.24
		rnd	1770.61	1772.02	1771.85	1779.52	1773.22	1772.70	1779.31

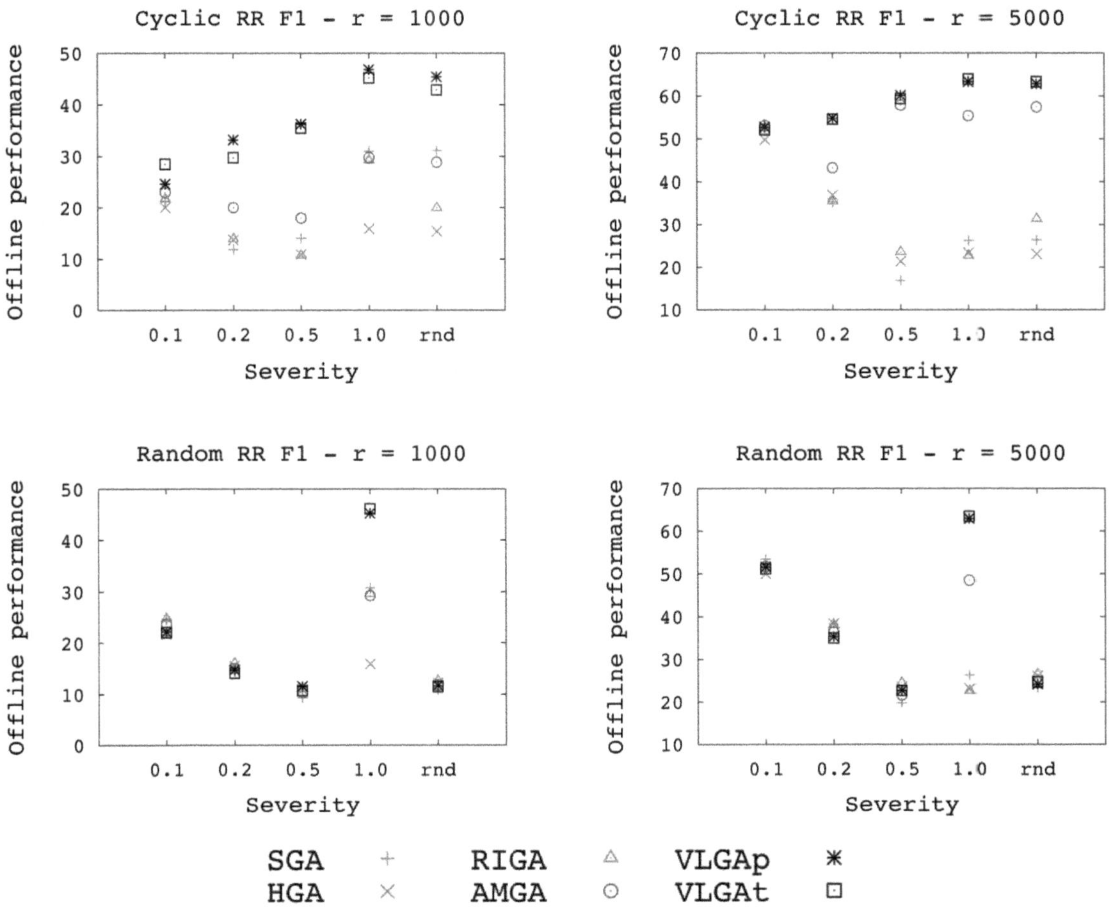

Figure 4: Offline performance for the dynamic Royal Road F1

Table 7: Results using Random and Virtual Loser Immigrants for the Dynamic RR1

	r	ρ	AMGA	VLGAp	VLGAp_ri	VLGAp_vli	VLGAt	VLGAt_ri	VLGAt_vli
CYCLIC	1000	0.1	22.99	24.60	23.06	23.75	28.48	28.02	34.75
		0.2	20.04	33.19	27.88	29.73	29.74	31.81	37.70
		0.5	17.99	36.26	33.02	32.88	35.51	35.12	35.62
		1.0	29.78	46.81	46.43	43.26	45.21	44.07	43.02
		rnd	28.85	45.42	43.16	45.51	42.89	43.31	44.16
	5000	0.1	53.08	52.73	51.39	51.02	52.14	49.62	53.69
		0.2	43.26	54.80	50.64	48.51	54.57	51.95	55.21
		0.5	57.89	60.16	59.84	55.72	59.39	57.90	59.19
		1.0	55.42	63.35	63.21	60.25	63.92	63.32	61.06
		rnd	57.44	62.82	62.52	60.29	63.28	62.22	60.62
RANDOM	1000	0.1	23.66	22.18	18.33	18.97	22.07	20.38	28.38
		0.2	15.05	14.74	11.82	9.92	14.14	12.86	17.83
		0.5	10.33	11.51	8.81	6.87	10.72	9.85	12.88
		1.0	29.23	45.24	43.42	41.76	46.11	46.41	47.02
		rnd	11.83	11.66	9.96	8.13	11.46	10.71	11.90
	5000	0.1	51.72	51.58	49.10	48.03	51.20	49.67	54.71
		0.2	36.40	35.31	31.85	29.40	35.00	33.27	38.45
		0.5	21.64	22.73	19.87	16.88	22.68	20.31	22.99
		1.0	48.50	62.94	63.23	60.16	63.45	63.27	62.75
		rnd	24.80	24.23	22.85	19.60	24.73	23.40	24.95

Table 8: Statistical Results for the KP - immigrants

$\alpha = 0.5$	Cyclic									
	$r = 1000$					$r = 5000$				
$\rho \Rightarrow$	0.1	0.2	0.5	1.0	rnd	0.1	0.2	0.5	1.0	rnd
VLGAp_ri - VLGAp	∼	s−	∼	∼	s−	s−	∼	∼	∼	∼
VLGAp_ri - AMGA	s+	s+	s+	s+	s+	s+	s+	s+	s+	s+
VLGAp_vli - VLGAp	s+	s+	s+	∼	∼	s+	s+	s+	s+	∼
VLGAp_vli - AMGA	s+	s+	s+	s+	s+	s+	s+	s+	s+	s+
VLGAt_ri - VLGAt	∼	s−	∼	∼	∼	∼	∼	∼	∼	∼
VLGAt_ri - AMGA	s+	s+	s+	s+	s+	s+	s+	s+	s+	s+
VLGAt_vli - VLGAt	s+	s+	s+	∼	∼	s+	s+	s+	s−	∼
VLGAt_vli - AMGA	s+	s+	s+	s+	s+	s+	s+	s+	s+	s+
$\alpha = 0.5$	Random									
	$r = 1000$					$r = 5000$				
$\rho \Rightarrow$	0.1	0.2	0.5	1.0	rnd	0.1	0.2	0.5	1.0	rnd
VLGAp_ri - VLGAp	∼	∼	s−	∼	s−	∼	∼	s−	∼	∼
VLGAp_ri - AMGA	s−	s−	∼	s+	∼	s−	∼	∼	s+	∼
VLGAp_vli - VLGAp	s+	s+	s+	∼	s+	s+	s+	s+	∼	s+
VLGAp_vli - AMGA	∼	∼	s+	s+	s+	∼	s+	s+	s+	s+
VLGAt_ri - VLGAt	∼	∼	∼	∼	∼	∼	∼	∼	∼	∼
VLGAt_ri - AMGA	s−	s−	∼	s+	s+	∼	∼	∼	s+	s+
VLGAt_vli - VLGAt	s+	s+	s+	∼	s+	s+	s+	s+	s−	s+
VLGAt_vli - AMGA	s+	s+	s+	s+	s+	∼	s+	s+	s+	s+

Table 9: Statistical Results for the RRF1 - immigrants

$\alpha = 0.5$	Cyclic									
	$r = 1000$					$r = 5000$				
$\rho \Rightarrow$	0.1	0.2	0.5	1.0	rnd	0.1	0.2	0.5	1.0	rnd
VLGAp_ri - VLGAp	∼	s−	s−	∼	∼	∼	s−	∼	∼	∼
VLGAp_ri - AMGA	s+	s+	s+	s+	s+	∼	s+	s+	s+	s+
VLGAp_vli - VLGAp	∼	∼	s−	s−	∼	∼	s−	s−	∼	∼
VLGAp_vli - AMGA	s+	s+	s+	s+	s+	∼	s+	∼	s+	s+
VLGAt_ri - VLGAt	∼	∼	∼	∼	∼	s−	s−	∼	∼	∼
VLGAt_ri - AMGA	s+	s+	s+	s+	s+	s−	s+	∼	s+	s+
VLGAt_vli - VLGAt	s+	s+	∼	∼	s+	∼	∼	∼	∼	s−
VLGAt_vli - AMGA	s+	s+	s+	s+	s+	∼	s+	s+	s+	s+
$\alpha = 0.5$	Random									
	$r = 1000$					$r = 5000$				
$\rho \Rightarrow$	0.1	0.2	0.5	1.0	rnd	0.1	0.2	0.5	1.0	rnd
VLGAp_ri - VLGAp	s−	s−	s−	∼	s−	s−	s−	s−	∼	∼
VLGAp_ri - AMGA	s−	s−	s−	s+	s−	s−	s−	s−	s+	∼
VLGAp_vli - VLGAp	s−	s−	s−	s−	s−	s−	s−	s−	∼	s−
VLGAp_vli - AMGA	s−	s−	s−	s+	s−	s−	s−	s−	s+	s−
VLGAt_ri - VLGAt	s−	s−	∼	∼	∼	s−	s−	∼	∼	∼
VLGAt_ri - AMGA	s−	s−	∼	s+	∼	s−	s−	∼	s+	∼
VLGAt_vli - VLGAt	s+	s+	s+	∼	∼	s+	s+	∼	∼	∼
VLGAt_vli - AMGA	s+	s+	s+	s+	∼	s+	s+	∼	s+	∼

5. CONCLUSIONS AND FUTURE WORK

This paper proposes different techniques to enhance a previously proposed associative memory-based GA called VLGA to address DOPs. Two different versions of VLGA were analyzed: a probabilistic, denoted by VLGAp and a tournament based, called VLGAt. In order to enhance the performance of VLGA, especially in random environments, where the previous versions presented poor performances when compared with other algorithms, extra experimentation and additional steps were included in the algorithm. First, an exhaustive variation of the parameter β was made to assess the best value to use either in cyclic or random environments. Second, the associative memory used in VLGA was combined with the insertion immigrants. A new mechanism to create immigrants was proposed and compared with the well known scheme proposed by Grefenstette (random immigrants). The proposed method used the virtual loser vector to create immigrants from the best individual of the population (virtual loser immigrants). From the experimental results on a series of dynamic benchmark problems, the following conclusions can be drawn. First, the parameter β influences the results and a correct choice for this parameter can significantly improve the performance of VLGA. Nevertheless, even using the best choice for β the enhancement on the performance of VLGAp and VLGAt for random environments was not sufficient to outperform the peer algorithms. Second, the insertion of random immigrants in VLGAp and VLGAt didn't confer any advantage to the algorithms: similar performances were obtained, and sometimes it was observed a negative effect. Third, the proposed virtual loser immigrants scheme significantly enhanced the performance of VLGAp and VLGAt, for cyclic and random environments. The proposed mechanism allowed VLGAp and VLGAt to outperform the peer algorithms in cyclic environments. For random environments, this enhancement was always observed in the Knapsack Problem, but less evident for the RR F1. For future work we intend to investigate the use of a mechanism for automatically adjust the value of β during the run. Also, the influence of other parameters, such as γ and η will be analyzed. Finally, more problems must be included in the experiments.

6. REFERENCES

[1] G. J. Barlow and S. F. Smith. A memory enhanced evolutionary algorithm for dynamic scheduling problems. In *Applications of Evolutionary Computing*, LNCS 4974, pages 606–615, Springer 2008.

[2] J. Branke. Evolutionary Optimization in Dynamic Environments. Kluwer Academic Publishers, 2002.

[3] H. G. Cobb. An Investigation into the Use of Hypermutation as an Adaptive Operator in Genetic Algorithms having Continuous, Time-Dependent Nonstationary Environments. *TR AIC-90-001*, Naval Research Laboratory, 1990.

[4] J. J. Grefenstette. Genetic Algorithms for Changing Environments. In R. Männer and B. Manderick (ed), *Proceedings of PPSN II*, pages 137–144, 1992.

[5] M. Sebag, M. Schoenauer, C. and Ravisé. Toward civilized evolution: Developing inhibitions. In Bäck, Thomas (ed), *Proceedings of ICGA-97*, pages 291–298. San Francisco, CA: Morgan Kaufmann, 1997.

[6] A. Simões and R. Carvalho and J. Campos and E. Costa. A Study on Population's Diversity for Dynamic Environment. *Proceedings of ICANNGA 2011*, LNCS 6593, pages 300–309. Springer-Verlag, 2011.

[7] A. Simões and E. Costa. Variable-size Memory Evolutionary Algorithm to Deal with Dynamic Environments. M. Giacobini and et al. (eds), *Applications of Evolutionary Computing*, LNCS 4448, pages 617–626, Springer-Verlag, 2007.

[8] A. Simões, E. Costa. Prediction in Evolutionary Algorithms for Dynamic Environments using Markov Chains and Nonlinear Regression. In *Proceedings of GECCO 2009*, pages 883–890. ACM Press, 2009.

[9] A. Simões and E. Costa. Virtual Loser Genetic Algorithm for Dynamic Environments. C. Di Chio et al. (eds), *Applications of Evolutionary Computing*, LNCS 7248, pages 539–548, Springer-Verlag, 2012.

[10] S. Yang. Explicit Memory Schemes for Evolutionary Algorithms in Dynamic Environments. In S. Yang et al. (eds). *Evolutionary Computation in Dynamic and Uncertain Environments*, pages 3–28. Springer-Verlag, 2007.

[11] S. Yang and H. Richter, H. Hyper-learning for Population-based Incremental Learning in Dynamic Environments. *Proceedings of CEC 2009*, pages 682–689, IEEE Press, 2009.

[12] S. Yang and X. Yao. Population-based Incremental Learning with Associative Memory for Dynamic Environments. *IEEE Transactions on Evolutionary Computation*, Nij 12(5), pages 542–561, IEEE Press, 2008.

A Genetic Algorithm for Designing Neural Network Ensembles

Symone G. Soares
Institute of Systems and Robotics (ISR-UC), Department of Electrical and Computer Engineering (DEEC-UC), University of Coimbra, Pólo II, 3030-290 Coimbra, Portugal
symonesoares@isr.uc.pt

Carlos H. Antunes
Department of Electrical and Computer Engineering (DEEC-UC) and INESC Coimbra, University of Coimbra, Pólo II, 3030-290 Coimbra, Portugal
+351239851040
ch@deec.uc.pt

Rui Araújo
Institute of Systems and Robotics (ISR-UC), Department of Electrical and Computer Engineering (DEEC-UC), University of Coimbra, Pólo II, 3030-290 Coimbra, Portugal
rui@isr.uc.pt

ABSTRACT

Ensemble Methods (EMs) are sets of models that combine their decisions, or their learning algorithms, or different data to obtain good predictions. The motivations are the possibility of improving the generalization capability and the overall system performance. However, several issues are at stake in EM development, such as the design of models that disagree as much as possible on the same data, the selection of some of them and their optimal combination to enhance the robustness of the ensemble. Since there is no unified procedure to implement these steps, this paper proposes a new methodology to design Neural Network (NN) ensembles using a Genetic Algorithm (GA). Firstly, a set of NNs with high degree of diversity is produced. The aim is to draw a different training data set for each NN by applying bootstrap. The architecture of the NN is selected by varying the number of hidden neurons, activation functions and initialization of weights. Secondly, a GA is employed to select both the best subset of NNs and the optimal combination strategy for ensuring the accuracy and the robustness of the ensemble. Experiments on well-known data sets are reported to evaluate the effectiveness of the proposed methodology.

Categories and Subject Descriptors

I.2.6 [**Artificial Intelligence**]: Learning—*Connectionism and neural nets*; I.2.8 [**Artificial Intelligence**]: Problem Solving, Control Methods, and Search—*Heuristic methods.*

General Terms

Algorithms, Performance, Design.

Keywords

Ensemble Methods, Neural Networks, Genetic Algorithms.

1. INTRODUCTION

Ensemble Methods (EMs) are sets of models that combine in some way their decisions, or their learning algorithms, or different data to achieve accurate predictions. Research has shown that an EM is generally more accurate than any single model, and the effectiveness of EMs has been shown in different benchmark data sets [7, 3, 19, 6, 2]. Neural Network (NN) ensembles have been widely investigated for both classification and regression problems. The main motivations are the possibility of improving the generalization capability and the overall system performance. Theoretical and empirical investigations have revealed that a good EM is one in which the models make different errors on the same data point [3]. Nowadays EMs represent one of the main research lines in Machine Learning [21].

In general, the design of an EM can be divided into three main steps: generation of candidate models, selection of some of them, and combination of them to produce the output of the EM. Since there is no unified procedure to implement these steps, different approaches including metaheuristics have been proposed for automatic development of EMs [4].

For example, the Genetic Algorithm based Selective Ensemble (GASEN) trains NNs using bootstrap for increasing the diversity and then employs a Genetic Algorithm (GA) to select an optimum subset of NNs to constitute the ensemble. In this approach each NN is assigned a weight derived from the marginal improvement in the *fitness* associated with including this NN in the ensemble. Then the NNs whose weights are higher than a predefined threshold are selected to be included in the ensemble [27]. However, the NNs have fixed architectures and the combination strategies are limited by simple average and weighted average for regression and classification, respectively.

An automatic design of Neural Network Ensemble using Evolutionary Learning and Negative Correlation Learning (EENCL) is presented in [19]. Negative Correlation Learning (NCL) creates negatively correlated NNs using a correlation penalty term in the error function to encourage specialization and cooperation among the NNs. EENCL does not explore the linear combination between the NNs and the NN architectures are also predefined. Bayesian Artificial Immune System (BAIS) is an immune-inspired methodology to design EM of NNs with better generalization performance when compared to EENCL. BAIS introduces diversity in the architecture of the individual NNs. However, only one type of combination is performed to aggregate the NNs [8].

This paper proposes a new methodology to design neural network ensembles for regression problems using GA. In the first phase, a set of NNs with high diversity degree is produced. For each NN, the proposed approach generates a different training data set by applying bootstrap and then selects the best NN architecture by varying the number of hidden neurons, activation functions and initialization of weights. In the second phase, a GA is employed to select both the best subset of NNs and the optimal type of combination for them. The individuals of the population are coded as a sequence of bits that contains information about the subset of NNs and the type of combination to aggregate them. For each individual the optimal combination strategy is determined to ensure the accuracy and robustness of the EM. Experiments on two well-known data sets are performed to evaluate the effectiveness of the proposed methodology.

The work is organized as follows. In Section 2, important issues for creating an EM are outlined. Section 3 reports the key issues in EM. Section 4 details the proposed methodology, named as Genetic Algorithm for Designing Neural Network Ensembles (GA-NNE). The experimental results are reported and analyzed in Section 5. Finally, Section 6 contains some concluding remarks.

2. CREATING AN ENSEMBLE METHOD

The combination strategy of the EM is of fundamental importance. Optimal combination can enhance the robustness and accuracy of an EM. In this paper, robustness is defined as the capability of the EM to perform well on new data points. The scope of this paper is restricted to the combination at the prediction level. Let us assume an initial data set $\mathbf{D}_{init} = \{(\mathbf{x}_i, y_i)\}_{i=1}^{k}$ of size k, where $\mathbf{x}_i \in \mathbb{R}^{v\times 1}$ (v is the number of input variables) and y_i is an output variable. $\mathbf{D}_{init}$ is split as a training data set $\mathbf{D}_{train} = \{(\mathbf{x}_i, y_i)\}_{i=1}^{k_1}$, a validation data set $\mathbf{D}_{valid} = \{(\mathbf{x}_i, y_i)\}_{i=1}^{k_2}$, and a testing data set $\mathbf{D}_{test} = \{(\mathbf{x}_i, y_i)\}_{i=1}^{k_3}$, of size k_1, k_2 and k_3, respectively, where $k = k_1 + k_2 + k_3$.

Bootstrap [9] is applied on the training data set to create a different training data set for each NN. Bootstrap can be used to expand upon a single realization of a distribution or to generate a data set that can provide a better understanding of the mean and variability of the original unknown distribution [15]. Several studies have applied bootstrap in EM modeling to create diverse models [10]. In this case, each NN of the ensemble is trained with a bootstrapped data set from the training data set.

Assuming a set of n NNs for implementing an EM, the proposed approach trains each NN j using a different bootstrapped data set. This is done by random drawing k_1 times with replacement from the training data set. The performance of an NN j is evaluated by the Mean Square Error (MSE) between the estimated output $f_j()$ and real output y using the validation data set.

After training and evaluation, the NNs are aggregated using the predictions of the testing data set. Considering n the number of NNs in the ensemble and $F()$ the output of the EM, the proposed combinations are:

1. *Mean*: the output of the EM is obtained as the average of all models' predictions:

$$F(\mathbf{x}_i) = \frac{1}{n}\sum_{j=1}^{n} f_j(\mathbf{x}_i). \quad (1)$$

2. *Trimmed Mean*: the output of the EM is calculated as the trimmed mean of all models' outputs. This approach removes the lowest models' outputs and highest models' outputs before calculating the *mean*, avoiding extreme values of the outputs. For $P\%$ trimmed mean, the *mean* is obtained by excluding $P\%/2$ from highest models' outputs and $P\%/2$ from lowest models' outputs. (This paper sets $P\%$ as 10%).

3. *Median*: the output of the EM is equivalent to the median among all the NNs' outputs:

$$F(\mathbf{x}_i) = \underset{j=1,\ldots,n}{\text{median}}\{f_j(\mathbf{x}_i)\}. \quad (2)$$

4. *Weighted Mean*: the output of the EM is obtained by taking a weighted sum of the NNs' outputs, where each weight w_j of a NN j is based on its accuracy. Here the accuracy of each NN is determined by the MSE using the validation data set. The EM's output is expressed as:

$$F(\mathbf{x}_i) = \sum_{j=1}^{n} w_j \cdot f_j(\mathbf{x}_i). \quad (3)$$

Each weight w_j is determined by [8]:

$$w_j = \frac{\text{adjusted MSE}_j}{\sum_{k=1}^{n}\text{adjusted MSE}_k}, \quad (4)$$

where

$$\text{adjusted MSE}_j = 1 - \text{average MSE}_j, \quad (5)$$

and

$$\text{average MSE}_j = \frac{\text{MSE}_j}{\sum_{k=1}^{n}\text{MSE}_k}. \quad (6)$$

The performance of the EM is evaluated by the MSE between the estimated output $F()$ and the actual output y using the test data set MSE^{test}.

3. KEY ISSUES IN ENSEMBLE METHODS

Diversity is one of the key issues for the success of Ensemble Methods (EMs). Empirical results reveal that the performance of an EM is related to the diversity and accuracy of the models [5]. In the development of EMs, the information about diversity can be taken into account; i.e. the system may or may not explicitly try to optimize some metric of diversity during the design of the EM. These two approaches are classified as *explicit* and *implicit* diversity methods, respectively.

Bagging (short for **B**oostrap **Agg**regation Learn**ing**) uses an *implicit* method. It randomly samples the training data by bootstrap to produce a different data set for each model [2]; at no point a measurement is taken to promote diversity. Bagging has proved to be a popular technique in many fields of application [6, 15]. Boosting performs an *explicit* method. It manipulates the training data distributions to ensure diversity in the set of models [11]. However, it is not guaranteed to be the "right" form of diversity.

According to Brown et al. [3], the diversity of the EM can be dealt with in three main ways: (*i*) by starting the learning with different conditions; (*ii*) by varying the set of models; and (*iii*) by modifying the trajectory used by the components in the search space.

The first way (*i*) aims to diversify the initial components of the individual models. For example, for EMs of NNs starting each NN with a different initialization of weights can increase the probability of continuing in a different trajectory with respect to the other NNs. Since usually the NNs are not diverse enough, this approach generally does not achieve good results [4].

The second approach (*ii*) attempts to alter the set of models available to the EM: firstly by manipulating the training data set that it receives (e.g., k-*fold cross-validation* [22], Bagging, Boosting or noise injection [10]); and secondly by modifying the model architecture itself (e.g., NNs with different architectures or different activation functions) or designing EM with heterogeneous learning algorithms (e.g., Bayesian, RBF NNs and Support Vector Machines) [6].

The last category of approaches to achieve diversity (*iii*) aims to alter the way the search space is traversed, leading different NNs to converge to different hypotheses. This technique can be subdivided into: evolutionary methods and penalty methods. The most popular penalty method for encouraging diversity in EMs is the NCL proposed by Liu et al. [18]. It introduces a correlation penalty term into the cost function of the NNs so that each NN minimizes its error together with the error correlation within the EM. Evolutionary algorithms can also evolve a population of NNs using some heuristic to maintain the diversity of the population. In [17] a multi-objective evolutionary approach is proposed to explore both accuracy and diversity between the members of the EM.

Evolutionary methods and penalty methods can also be hybridized. In [19], a penalty term is used to explore the interaction and diversity between the NNs and the evolutionary method addresses the issue of automatic determination of the number of NNs of the EM.

Evolutionary methods and other meta-heuristic optimization approaches, such as Genetic Algorithms [27], Particle Swarm Optimization [26] and Bayesian Artificial Immune System [8], have been used to select the best subset of models among a set of base models. In this setting some issues are at stake, such as how to produce the individual models, how to evaluate the performance of the models and what selection strategy to be performed [21].

Moreover, the way to aggregate the different outputs of the models is crucial to enhance the performance [24] and to balance the diversity between the models of the EM. However, most selection methods for ensembles consider a single combination strategy.

In order to address all the reported issues on the development of EMs, the proposed work performs (*i*) and (*ii*) to achieve diversity and, consequently, good generalization capability. The aim is to produce NNs using different training data sets by bootstrap and then choose the best architecture of each NN by varying the neurons of the hidden layer, the initialization of weights and the activation functions. Moreover, a GA is employed to select the best subset of NNs and the optimal combination strategy for them.

4. PROPOSED METHODOLOGY

The proposed method, named GA-NNE, aims to build neural network ensembles using a GA as detailed in Algorithm 1. Firstly, a set of candidate NNs with a high degree of diversity is produced. Then the GA is employed to select both the best subset of NNs to join the ensemble and the best type of combination for aggregating the NNs. Each individual of the population represents an ensemble to be implemented.

Algorithm 1 Genetic Algorithm for Designing Neural Network Ensembles (GA-NNE)

Input n: number of candidate NNs.

1. Divide the data set into training data set, validation data set and testing data set; generate n copies from the training data set and apply bootstrap on the n training data sets.
2. Select n NNs for each manipulated training data set; the topology of each NN is chosen among a number of NNs based on the performance of the validation data set.
3. Set $t \leftarrow 1$. Consider c the number of bits that represents the types of combinations, randomly produce an *initial population* P_1 with m individuals of size $(n+c)$.
4. Evaluate the *fitness* of all individuals of P_1 using all available types of combinations.
5. Assign to each individual of P_1 the best type of combination based on the *fitness*.
6. **Repeat:**
   (a) Perform Roulette Wheel *Selection* to choose $p_s^{\%}$ of the individuals of P_t.
   (b) Apply *crossover* on the selected individuals to produce a population of offspring O_t.
   (c) Randomly *mutate* $p_m^{\%}$ of the individuals of O_t on the first n bits (the *model* part).
   (d) Calculate the *fitness* of all individuals of O_t using all available types of combinations.
   (e) Assign to each individual of O_t the best type of combination based on the *fitness*.
   (f) *Select* individuals for the next generation $(t+1)$:
      i. Consider a temporary population $P'_t \leftarrow (O_t \cup P_t)$ and P_{t+1} the population for the next generation;
      ii. *Elitism*: assign to P_{t+1} the e individuals of P'_t with the best *fitness*;
      iii. Perform Roulette Wheel *Selection* on P'_t to select $(m-e)$ individuals for P_{t+1}.
   (g) Set $t \leftarrow t+1$.

   until $t = maxgenerations$;

As described in Section 2, the data set is split into training data set, validation data set and testing data set. Assuming that the aim is to produce n candidate NNs, these are trained using bootstrap data sets from the training data set. The NNs are implemented with one hidden layer using Multilayer Perceptron Neural Network (MLP NN) by Levenberg-Marquardt (LM) algorithm [13]. LM algorithm has become a standard technique for non-linear problems, widely adopted in a broad range of applications. It is a combination of the steepest descent and the Gauss-Newton methods.

The topology of each NN is chosen among a number of NNs based on the MSE of the validation data set. The number of NNs is obtained by varying the number of neurons in the hidden layer (from 1 to 10); two activation functions (linear and fast hyperbolic tangent) for the hidden layer and output layer; and three different initializations of weights. These techniques for initialization of weights are:

1. randomize the initial weights with a small number in an interval of $[-1/ni, 1/ni]$, where ni is the number of neuronal inputs [16];
2. Nguyen-Widrow initialization method, where the initial weights are set according to the NN learning [20];
3. uniform random initialization method in the interval of $[-0.5, 0.5]$ [25];

The encoding of the chromosomes is binary, as displayed in Figure 1. The representation is composed by two parts: *models* and *type of combination*. The first part contains information about the subset of NNs for composing the ensemble. Considering a set of n NNs $\{net_1, \ldots, net_n\}$, each *locus* of the *model* part is related to the absence "0" or presence "1" of a model net_j in the ensemble. The second part refers to the type of combination to be used for aggregating the subset of models. Assuming that the number of types of combinations is z, the number of bits c to represent them is given by $c = \lceil \log_2^z \rceil$, where $\lceil x \rceil$ is the smallest integer not lower than x. As reported in Section 2, the number of types of combinations is four: *mean*, *trimmed mean*, *median* and *weighted mean*; their binary representations being "00", "01", "10" and "11", respectively.

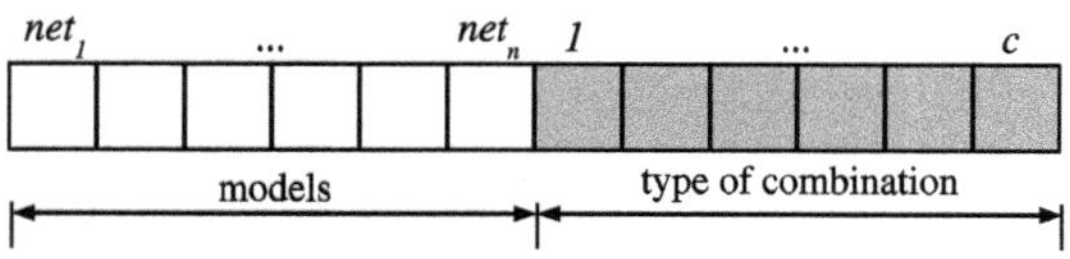

Figure 1: Binary Representation of a Chromosome.

Figure 2 displays an example of a chromosome representation using a set of ten models $\{net_1, \ldots, net_{10}\}$. Figure 2a shows the binary encoding of the chromosome. Figure 2b displays the decoding of the same chromosome. The final subset of NNs $\{net_1, net_4, net_6, net_7, net_8, net_{10}\}$ is selected according to the binary bits on the *model* part. In this example, the selected combination strategy is *mean* (i.e. "00").

Other important issue is to define the *fitness* function. This work considers $1/\text{MSE}^{test}$ as fitness function, where $1/\text{MSE}^{test}$ is calculated as described in Section 2. In Algorithm 1, step (3) produces an initial population P_1 with m individuals. In step (4), P_1 is evaluated by the *fitness* function using all available types of combinations. In step (5), for each individual of P_1, the best type of combination is assigned based on the *fitness*. The combination is an important step for designing a robust ensemble, and this approach ensures that the ensemble will be always built using the optimal combination.

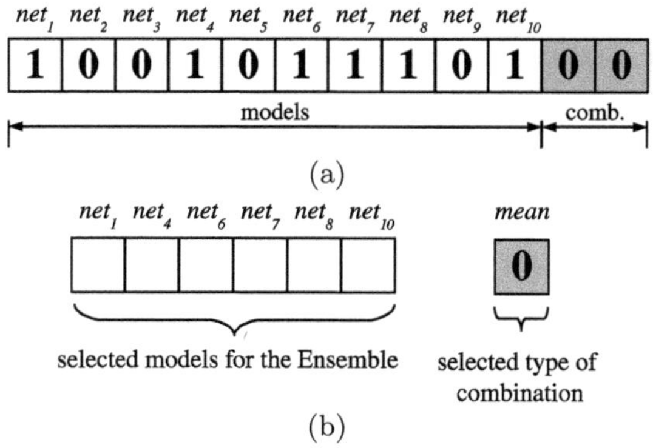

Figure 2: Example of a Chromosome - (a) Binary Chromosome Representation; (b) Decoding the Chromosome.

In step (6), the proposed GA loops over t generations to make the population evolve. In sub-step 6a $p_s^{\%}$ of the individuals of P_t are chosen using Roulette Wheel *Selection*. This selection method picks an individual of P_t to be a parent with a probability proportional to its *fitness*.

In sub-step 6b, the selected parents are combined to form a population of offspring O_t. The best results have been achieved with uniform crossover using a random mask, where two parents ($parent_1$ and $parent_2$) produce two offspring ($offspring_1$ and $offspring_2$). The crossover is only performed on the bits of the *model* part. A mask is a vector of binary bits with length n. When the bit in the mask is "0", the corresponding bit in $parent_1$ is passed to $offspring_1$ and the corresponding bit in $parent_2$ is passed to $offspring_2$. When the bit in the mask is "1", the corresponding bit in $parent_1$ is passed to $offspring_2$ and the corresponding bit in $parent_2$ is passed to $offspring_1$ [14].

In sub-step 6c, $p_m^{\%}$ of random individuals of O_t are selected to be mutated only on the *model* part. The aim is to change randomly one or more bits of each individual to foster diversity. In sub-step 6d and sub-step 6e, O_t is evaluated and the best type of combination is assigned to each individual as described above.

An important issue is to pick the individuals for the next generation $(t+1)$. The computational experiments revealed that elitism provides better results. The algorithm selects e individuals with best *fitness* of both populations O_t and P_t, and then it assigns these e individuals to the next generation population P_{t+1}, where P_{t+1} has size m. The other $(m-e)$ individuals are chosen by Roulette Wheel *Selection*. After t generations, the best individual of the population of the last generation is chosen as the solution to the problem.

5. EXPERIMENTAL RESULTS

To evaluate the performance of the proposed methodology, several experiments have been carried out and their results are summarized below.

5.1 Data Set Descriptions

The tests are performed using two data sets available on Luís Torgo's website [23]: Boston Housing and Friedman.

Friedman is a nonlinear prediction problem [12]. It is an artificial data set with 10 independent predictor variables $\mathbf{x} = [x_1, x_2, \dots, x_{10}]$ each of which is uniformly distributed over $[0, 1]$. The function is given by:

$$y = 10\sin(\pi x_1 x_2) + 20\left(x_3 - \frac{1}{2}\right)^2 + 10x_4 + 5x_5 + \epsilon \,. \quad (7)$$

The dimensionality of the covariance space is increased, so that instead of one noise ϵ, there are now more five independent variables $x_6, \dots, x_{10}$. The data set includes 40768 samples.

The Boston Housing is a well-known data set [1]. The goal is to predict housing values in areas of Boston. The data set contains 13 input variables (mainly socio-economic), 1 output variable (median housing price) and 506 samples.

The tests are evaluated using 10-*fold cross-validation*, where each data set is split into 10 subsets. The result is the average of the results of the 10 subsets. So each subset is in turn used as testing data set while the samples of the other 9 subsets are randomly divided as a training data set (90%) and a validation data set (10%). Therefore, results of MSE^{test} using 10-*fold cross-validation* are given by averaging the MSE of all 10 testing subsets.

5.2 Experiment 1 - Candidate Models

Before starting the experiments, it is important to evaluate the performance of the individual NNs. For this purpose, tests were done by varying the number of neurons in the hidden layer. Other parameters were set according to popularity, such as, Nguyen-Widrow method as initialization of methods, fast hyperbolic tangent as activation function for the hidden layer and linear as activation function for the output layer. Figure 3 displays the accuracy of the NNs, where the MSE is calculated using 10-*fold cross-validation.*

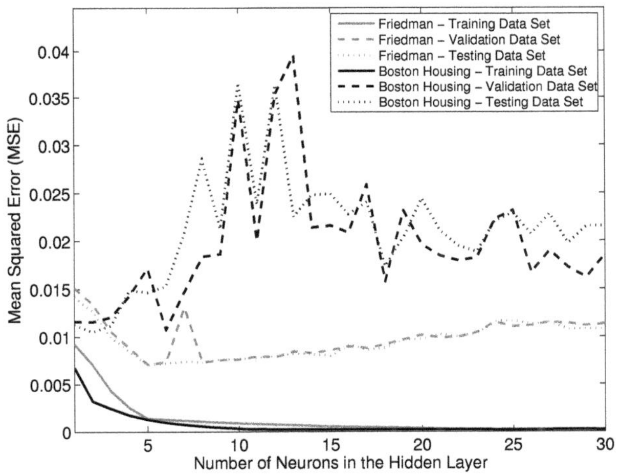

Figure 3: Performance of the Individual NNs.

According to the results provided by the individual NN, it can be seen that the performance on unseen data (e.g. validation and testing data set) is poor when compared to the training data set. Moreover, NNs with lower number of neurons in the hidden layer have better generalization capability.

A set of 20 candidate NN models is generated using only steps (1) and (2) of Algorithm 1. The training of the NNs stops when the MSE on the training data set reaches 10^{-4} or the number of iterations reaches 500.

Table 1 reports the MSE on the testing data set if all the candidate models are used to design ensembles. In this paper, we refer to this technique as *Ensembling All*, i.e. it aggregates all the models of the ensemble without performing the optimization technique to select the best subset of models. The candidate models are employed to design ensembles using *mean*, *trimmed mean*, *median*, and *weighted mean* as type of combination. In the Friedman data set, all the types of combinations have the same performance. In the Boston Housing data set, *trimmed mean* outperforms the other types of combinations.

Table 1: Results of MSE^{test} using *Ensembling All*. In the table, all the MSE values have been multiplied by 10^3.

Data Set	Type of Combination			
	mean	tr. mean	median	wt. mean
Friedman	2.100	2.100	2.100	2.100
Boston H.	5.000	4.900	5.100	5.000

5.3 Experiment 2 - GA-NNE

In this approach, Algorithm 1 was implemented to select the best subset of NNs and the best type of combination. The models of the *Ensembling All* using 20 NNs are also employed here as candidate models. Several experiments were performed by varying the GA parameters, such as number of the mutated bits (1 and 2), the mutation probability $p_m^{\%}$ (5%, 10% and 15%), the selection probability $p_s^{\%}$ (60% and 100%) and the number of individuals of the population (20, 40 and 60). The crossover probability is 1. The number of individuals selected by elitism was set as 1.

Table 2 and Table 3 show the experimental results of the GA-NNE using the Friedman and Boston Housing data sets on 20 runs. For both data sets, some characteristics are noticed. For example, 1 mutated bit has inferior results when compared to 2 mutated bits; mutation probability of 10% has the same performance when compared to mutation probability of 15%, and these probabilities outperform a probability of 5%; selection probability of 60% is more efficient than selection probability of 100%; and, improvements are observed when the number of individuals increases from 20 to 40 and 60.

Figure 4 shows the GA properties of the run with *min* value of the experiment with best performance for Friedman and Boston data set. On Table 2 and 3, these runs are displayed in bold and they have values of 1.788 and 2.431, respectively. *Mean* is the average of the MSE^{test} of all individuals of the population in a generation (i.e. 1/*fitness*) and *Best* is the best value of MSE^{test} of all individuals of the population in a generation. As it can be seen, no improvements are shown after generation 500 for the Friedman and 700 for the Boston Housing. The percentages of selection of each type of combination on all runs are reported in Table 4. For both data sets *median* is the best strategy.

Table 2: Experimental Results of the GA-NNE Using the Friedman Data Set. In the table, all the MSE values have been multiplied by 10^3.

No. of Mutated bits	1	1	2	2	2	2	2	2
Mutation Probability ($p_m^{\%}$)	5%	5%	5%	5%	5%	5%	10%	15%
Selection Probability ($p_s^{\%}$)	60%	100%	60%	100%	60%	60%	60%	60%
No. of Individuals (m)	20	20	20	20	40	60	20	20
Mean	1.798	1.799	1.794	1.794	**1.792**	1.792	1.793	1.793
S.D.	0.004	0.003	0.003	0.002	**0.002**	0.002	0.002	0.001
Min	1.790	1.795	1.788	1.788	**1.788**	1.788	1.788	1.788
Max	1.806	1.808	1.802	1.798	**1.797**	1.799	1.797	1.797

Table 3: Experimental Results of the GA-NNE Using the Boston Housing Data Set. In the table, all the MSE values have been multiplied by 10^3.

No. of Mutated bits	1	1	2	2	2	2	2	2
Mutation Probability ($p_m^{\%}$)	5%	5%	5%	5%	5%	5%	10%	15%
Selection Probability ($p_s^{\%}$)	60%	100%	60%	100%	60%	60%	60%	60%
No. of Individuals (m)	20	20	20	20	40	60	20	20
Mean	2.502	2.503	2.455	2.457	2.443	2.442	2.440	**2.440**
S.D.	0.037	0.042	0.019	0.016	0.010	0.009	0.008	**0.005**
Min	2.458	2.455	2.431	2.439	2.431	2.431	2.432	**2.431**
Max	2.594	2.607	2.510	2.494	2.459	2.460	2.461	**2.452**

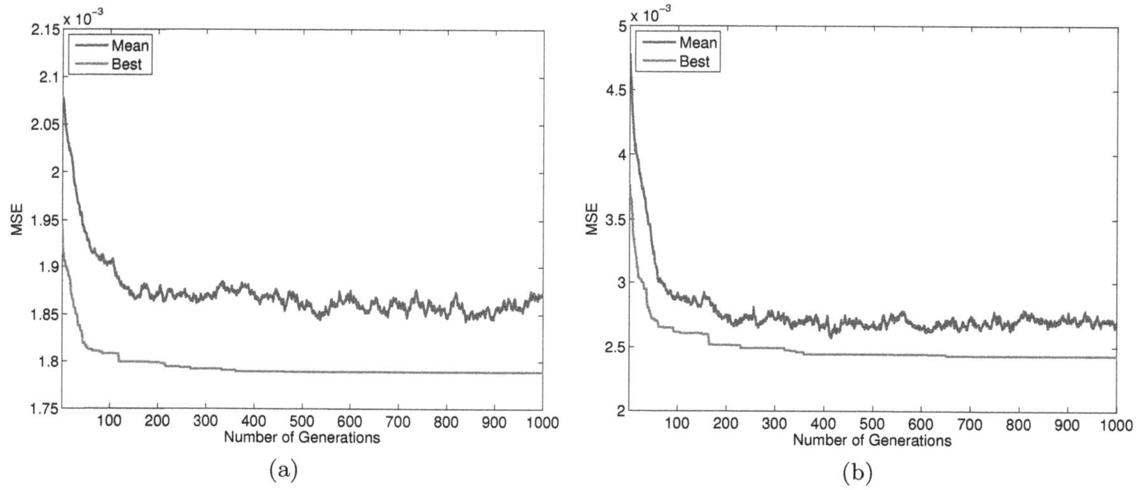

Figure 4: Mean of the fitness of the population and the fitness of the best individual of the population on a generation - (a) Friedman data set; (b) Boston Housing data set.

Table 4: GA-NNE - Percentage of Selection of the Types of Combinations.

Data Set	Type of Combination			
	mean	tr. mean	median	wt. mean
Friedman	1.00%	0.00%	**93.50%**	5.50%
Boston H.	10.00%	0.00%	**79.50%**	10.50%

5.4 Experiment 3 - Comparisons of the Strategies for Ensembling

In this Subsection, the proposed methodology GA-NNE is compared to Bagging, *Ensembling All* and GASEN. In Bagging, the ensemble is composed by 100 NNs trained using bootstrap resampling from the training data set. The NNs are trained with Levenberg-Marquardt algorithm and they have fixed architecture (MLP NN) and parameters. In this paper, these parameters are set as: 5 neurons in the hidden layer; initialization of weights proposed by Kasabov et [16]; fast hyperbolic tangent activation function in the hidden layer; linear function in the output layer; the training stops when the value of the MSE on the training data set reaches 10^{-4}. The combination strategy is *mean*.

GASEN is an approach for selecting models from a set of available NNs to constitute an ensemble using the GA. This method selects NNs to be included in the ensemble based

Table 5: Experimental Results of Different Methods Using the Friedman Data Set. In the table, all the MSE values have been multiplied by 10^3.

MSE^{test}	Bagging	*Ensembling All*				GASEN	GA-NNE
		mean	tr. mean	median	wt. mean		
Mean	7.501	2.100	2.100	2.100	2.100	1.927	**1.792**
S.D.	0.022	-	-	-	-	0.035	**0.002**
Min	7.466	-	-	-	-	1.870	**1.788**
Max	7.543	-	-	-	-	1.980	**1.797**

Table 6: Experimental Results of Different Methods Using the Boston Housing Data Set. In the table, all the MSE values have been multiplied by 10^3.

MSE^{test}	Bagging	*Ensembling All*				GASEN	GA-NNE
		mean	tr. mean	median	wt. mean		
Mean	7.849	5.000	4.900	5.100	5.000	6.349	**2.440**
S.D.	0.107	-	-	-	-	0.876	**0.005**
Min	7.666	-	-	-	-	5.461	**2.431**
Max	8.059	-	-	-	-	9.015	**2.452**

on the evolving weights. Initially, the NNs are assigned as random weights and finally the approach selects those NNs which have weights higher than a predefined threshold λ to join the ensemble. The tests are performed using the code available at the website [27]. The number of candidate NNs is 20. Other parameters are set to the default values: NNs trained with Backpropagation; MLP architecture with one hidden layer; 5 neurons in the hidden layer; hyperbolic tangent sigmoid as activation function in the hidden layer; linear function in the output layer; stopping criterion when the number of epochs reaches 100; number of individuals of the population equal to 20; threshold (λ) for selecting the NNs as 1/20.

Table 5 and Table 6 report the main results for both Friedman and Boston Housing data sets. For Bagging and GASEN the experiments involved 20 runs. In *Ensembling All*, the results of the ensemble using 20 NNs are reported, i.e. the same results obtained in Subsection 5.2. The strategy with best performance is displayed in bold in Table 5 and Table 6.

For both data sets, Bagging presents worse results when compared to the other approaches. This can be explained as follows. Firstly, the diversity of the ensemble is achieved just by manipulating the training data set. Secondly, no selection method is employed to choose the best subset of NNs and type of combination. On the other hand, *Ensembling All* has better performance when compared to Bagging. The success of *Ensembling All* is explained by the two levels of diversity: (*i*) by using different initializations of weights and (*ii*) by altering the set of NNs accessible to the ensemble (i.e. by manipulating the data set and varying the architectures of the NNs).

With respect to the Friedman data set, GASEN has better generalization capability than *Ensembling All*. On the contrary, for the Boston Housing data set, GASEN has worse performance when compared to *Ensembling All*. This reveals that, in some cases, it is better ensembling all models than applying a selection method. However, GASEN has smaller computational cost than *Ensembling All*. In *Ensembling All*, the search for the best NN architecture in a pool of available NNs has an expensive time cost.

The experiments reveal that a subset selection of models when combined with a selection of the type of combination (e.g. GA-NNE) can produce good results in comparison with ensemble all models (e.g. *Ensembling All*). Moreover, as can be observed, GA-NNE outperforms GASEN, because GASEN designs an ensemble using only one type of combination and with NNs that have fixed architectures.

The average number of ensemble models used by GASEN and GA-NNE is presented in Table 7, where the results are obtained over the 20 runs. From the experimental results, it can be seen that GASEN selects less models for ensembling when compared to GA-NNE.

Table 7: Average Number of Models in the Ensemble.

Data Set	GASEN	GA-NNE
Friedman	**4.160**	5.325
Boston H.	**4.895**	4.985

6. CONCLUSIONS

Ensemble Methods (EMs) of Neural Networks (NNs) are powerful techniques for improving the generalization capabilities and overall system performance. However, several issues are at stake in EM development, such as generation of candidate NNs that disagree as much as possible on the same data point, the selection of some NNs and the optimal combination to enhance the robustness of the EM.

Since there is no unified procedure to implement these steps, this paper proposed a methodology for automatic design of NN ensembles using Genetic Algorithm (GA), named GA-NNE. Firstly, a set of NNs with high degree of diversity is designed. Secondly, a GA is employed to select both the best subset of NNs and the optimal type of combination for them.

This paper compared GA-NNE with other approaches, such as Bagging, *Ensembling All* and GASEN. The tests using two well-known data sets have shown the effectiveness of the GA-NNE. The experiments have shown that our approach outperforms other methodologies. This is explained by the high diversity degree of the NNs. The diversity is achieved by using NNs with different numbers of hidden neurons, activation functions, initializations of weights and training data sets. The selection of the optimal type of combination was fundamental to enhance the accuracy and robustness of the EM.

7. REFERENCES

[1] D. A. Belsley, E. Kuh, and R. E. Welsch. *Regression Diagnostics: Identifying Influential Data and Sources of Collinearity.* Wiley, 1980.

[2] L. Breiman. Bagging predictors. *Machine Learning*, 24(2):123–140, August 1996.

[3] G. Brown, J. Wyatt, R. Harris, and X. Yao. Diversity creation methods: A survey and categorisation. *Information Fusion*, 6(1):5–20, 2005.

[4] P. A. D. Castro and F. J. V. Zuben. Learning ensembles of neural networks by means of a bayesian artificial immune system. *IEEE Transactions on Neural Networks*, 22(2):304–316, February 2011.

[5] A. Chandra, H. Chen, and X. Yao. Trade-off between diversity and accuracy in ensemble generation. In Y. Jin, editor, *Multi-Objective Machine Learning*, volume 16 of *Studies in Computational Intelligence*, pages 429–464. Springer Berlin / Heidelberg, 2006.

[6] A. L. V. Coelho and D. S. C. Nascimento. On the evolutionary design of heterogeneous bagging models. *Neurocomputing*, 73(16-18):3319–3322, 2010.

[7] T. G. Dietterich. Ensemble methods in machine learning. In J. Kittler and F. Roli, editors, *Proceedings of the First International Workshop on (MCS 2000) Multiple Classifier Systems*, volume 1857, pages 1–15. Springer-Verlag, 2000.

[8] S. Dondeti, K. Kannan, and R. Manavalan. Genetic algorithm optimized neural networks ensemble for estimation of mefenamic acid and paracetamol in tablets. *Acta Chimica Slovenica*, 52:440–449, 2005.

[9] B. Efron and R. J. Tibshirani. *An Introduction to the Bootstrap.* Chapman & Hall, New York, 1993.

[10] L. Fortuna, S. Graziani, and M. G. Xibilia. Comparison of soft-sensor design methods for industrial plants using small data sets. *IEEE Transactions on Instrumentation and Measurement*, 58(8):2444–2451, August 2009.

[11] Y. Freund and R. Schapire. A short introduction to boosting. *Japanese Society for Artificial Intelligence*, 14(5):771–780, 1999.

[12] J. H. Friedman. Multivariate adaptive regression splines. *The Annals of Statistics*, 19(1):1–67, 1991.

[13] M. T. Hagan, H. B. Demuth, and M. Beale. *Neural Network Design.* PWS Publishing, Boston, MA, USA, 1996.

[14] R. L. H. S. E. Haupt. *Practical Genetic Algorithms.* Wiley-Interscience, 2 edition, 2004.

[15] Y. Jia and T. B. Culver. Bootstrapped artificial neural networks for synthetic flow generation with a small data sample. *Journal of Hydrology*, 331(3-4):580–590, 2006.

[16] K. N. Kasabov. *Foundations of Neural Networks, Fuzzy Systems, and Knowledge Engineering.* MIT Press, Cambridge, MA, USA, 1st edition, 1996.

[17] S. Khakabimamaghani, F. Barzinpour, and M. R. Gholamian. A high diversity hybrid ensemble of classifiers. In *2010 2nd International Conference on Software Engineering and Data Mining (SEDM)*, pages 461–466, June 2010.

[18] Y. Liu and X. Yao. Ensemble learning via negative correlation. *Neural Networks*, 12:1399–1404, 1999.

[19] Y. Liu, X. Yao, and T. Higuchi. Evolutionary ensembles with negative correlation learning. *IEEE Transactions on Evolutionary Computation*, 4(4):380–387, November 2000.

[20] D. Nguyen and B. Widrow. Improving the learning speed of 2-layer neural networks by choosing initial values of the adaptive weights. In *IJCNN International Joint Conference on Neural Networks 1990*, volume 3, pages 21–26, June 1990.

[21] M. Re and G. Valentini. Ensemble methods: A review. In *Data Mining and Machine Learning for Astronomical Applications*, pages 1–40. Chapman & Hall, 2011. (in press).

[22] M. Ries, O. Nemethova, and M. Rupp. Performance evaluation of mobile video quality estimators. In *Proceedings of the 15th European Signal Processing Conference*, pages 159–163, September 2007.

[23] L. Torgo. *Regression Datasets.* Laboratory of Artificial Intelligence and Decision Support (LIAAD), University of Porto, 2011. `http://www.liaad.up.pt/~ltorgo/Regression/DataSets.html`.

[24] J. Torres-Sospedra, M. Fernandez-Redondo, and C. Hernandez-Espinosa. A research on combination methods for ensembles of multilayer feedforward. In *IEEE International Joint Conference on Neural Networks, 2005. IJCNN '05. Proceedings 2005*, volume 2, pages 1125–1130, July-August 2005.

[25] J. Škutová. Weights initialization methods for mlp neural networks. *Transactions of the VŠB - Technical University of Ostrova, Mechanical Series*, LIV(2):147–152, 2008.

[26] T. Yu-Bo and X. Zhi-Bin. Particle-swarm-optimization-based selective neural network ensemble and its application to modeling resonant frequency of microstrip antenna. In *Microstrip Antennas*, pages 69–82. InTech, April 2011.

[27] Z.-H. Zhou, J. Wu, and W. Tang. Ensembling neural networks: Many could be better than all. *Artificial Intelligence*, 137(1-2):239–263, 2002.

Crossover Speeds Up Building-Block Assembly

Dirk Sudholt
Department of Computer Science
University of Sheffie d
Sheffield S1 4DP, U<

ABSTRACT

We re-investigate a fundamental question: how effective is crossover in combining building blocks? Although this has been discussed controversially for decades, we are still lacking a rigorous and intuitive answer. We provide such answers for royal road functions and ONEMAX, where every bit is a building block. For the latter we prove that a simple GA with uniform crossover is twice as fast as the fastest EA using only standard bit mutation, up to small-order terms. The reason is that crossover effectively turns neutral mutations into improvements by combining the right building blocks at a later stage. Compared to mutation-based EAs, this makes multi-bit mutations more useful. Introducing crossover changes the optimal mutation rate on ONEMAX from $1/n$ to $(1+\sqrt{5})/2 \cdot 1/n \approx 1.618/n$. Similar results are proved for k-point crossover. Experiments and statistical tests confirm that our findings apply to a broad class of building-block functions.

Categories and Subject Descriptors

F.2.2 [**Analysis of Algorithms and Problem Complexity**]: Nonnumerical Algorithms and Problems

Keywords

Crossover, recombination, building-block hypothesis, runtime analysis, mutation rate

1. INTRODUCTION

Ever since the early days of genetic and evolutionary algorithms, researchers have wondered when and why crossover is an effective search operator. It has been folklore that crossover is useful if it can combine building blocks, i. e., schema of high fitness, to give better solutions [14]. But, as Watson and Jansen [23] put it, *there has been a considerable difficulty in demonstrating this rigorously and intuitively.*

Many attempts at understanding crossover have been made in the past. Mitchell, Forrest, and Holland [14] presented so-called *royal road* functions as an example where, supposedly, genetic algorithms outperform other search algorithms due to the use of crossover. Royal roads divide a bit string into disjoint blocks. Each block makes a positive contribution to the fitness in case all bits therein are set to 1. Blocks thus represent schemata, and all-ones configurations are building blocks of optimal solutions. However, the same authors later concluded that simple randomized hill climbers performed better than GAs [6, 15].

Runtime analysis has become a major area of research that can give rigorous evidence and proven theorems. However, studies so far have eluded the most fundamental setting of building-block functions. Crossover was proven to be superior to mutation only on constructed artificial examples like Jump_k [9, 12] and "Real Royal Road" functions [10, 18], the H-IFF problem [2], coloring problems inspired by the Ising model from physics [5, 19], and the all-pairs shortest path problem [3, 22, 17]. H-IFF [2] and the Ising model on trees [19] consist of hierarchical building blocks. But none of the above papers addresses single-level building blocks in a setting as simple as royal roads.

Watson and Jansen [23] presented a constructed building-block function and proved exponential performance gaps between EAs using only mutation and a GA. However, the definition of the internal structure of building blocks is complicated and artificial, and they used a tailored multi-deme GA to get the necessary diversity. With regard to the question on how GAs combine building blocks, their approach does not give the intuitive explanation one is hoping for.

This paper presents such an intuitive explanation, supported by rigorous analyses. We consider royal roads and other functions composed of building blocks, such as monotone polynomials. $\text{ONEMAX}(x) = \sum_{i=1}^{n} x_i$ is a special case where every bit is a building block. We give rigorous proofs for ONEMAX and show how the main proof arguments transfer to broader classes of building-block functions. Experiments support the latter. Our main results are as follows.

1. We show that on ONEMAX a simple (μ+1) GA with uniform crossover and standard bit mutation is at least twice as fast as *every* evolutionary algorithm (EA) that only uses standard bit mutations (up to small-order terms). More precisely, the expected number of function evaluations decreases from $e \cdot n \ln n - O(n)$ to $e/2 \cdot n \ln n + O(n)$. The reason for this speedup is that the GA can store a neutral mutation in the population (a mutation not altering the parent's fitness), along with the respective parent. It can then use crossover to combine the good building blocks between

these two individuals, improving the current best fitness. In other words, crossover can capitalize on mutations that have both beneficial and disruptive effects on building blocks.

2. The use of uniform crossover leads to a different optimal mutation rate on OneMax. While for mutation-based EAs $1/n$ is the optimal mutation rate [26], the above-mentioned GA has an optimal mutation rate of $(1+\sqrt{5})/2 \cdot 1/n \approx 1.618/n$ (ignoring small-order terms). This is because introducing crossover makes neutral mutations more useful and larger mutation rates increase the chance of a neutral mutation. Optimality is proved by means of a matching lower bound on the expected optimization time of the (2+1) GA that applies to *all* mask-based crossover operators (where each bit value is taken from either parent). Using the optimal mutation rate, the expected number of function evaluations is $1.19n \ln n \pm O(n \log \log n)$.

3. These results are not limited to uniform crossover or the absence of linkage. The same (2+1) GA using k-point crossover, for arbitrary k, has a similar performance, but it performs slightly worse on OneMax.

4. The reasoning for OneMax carries over to other functions with a clear building block structure. Experiments reveal similar performance differences as on OneMax for royal road functions and random polynomials with unweighted, positive coefficients. This is largely confirmed by statistical tests.

The first result, the analysis for uniform crossover, is remarkably simple and intuitive. It gives direct insight into the working principles of GAs. Its simplicity also makes it very well suited for teaching purposes. And in this case simplicity implies robustness and versatility: the analysis can easily be carried over to other, similar GAs.

Note that randomized local search (RLS) [4]—flipping a single bit in every step—is still faster than the GA as it needs time $n \ln n + O(n)$ on OneMax [4]. But as it cannot escape from local optima, we are more interested in global optimizers like EAs using standard bit mutation.

2. PRELIMINARIES

We measure the performance of the algorithm with respect to the number of function evaluations performed. For steady-state algorithms this equals the number of generations (apart from the initialization). Note that the number of generations can be decreased by using offspring populations or parallel evolutionary algorithms [13]. But this significantly increases the computational effort within one generation, so the number of function evaluations is a more fair and widely used measure.

Looking at function evaluations is often motivated by the fact that this operation dominates the execution time of the algorithm. Then the number of function evaluations is a reliable measure for wall clock time. However, the wall clock time might increase when introducing crossover as an additional search operator. Also when increasing the mutation rate, more pseudo-random numbers might be required. Jansen and Zarges [11] point out a case where this effect leads to a discrepancy between the number of function evaluations and wall clock time. This concern must be taken seriously when aiming at reducing wall clock time. However, each implementation must be checked individually in this respect [11]. Therefore, we keep this concern in mind, but still use the number of function evaluations in the following. We also use the term *optimization time* synonymously.

In our aim to show that crossover is beneficial, we first need to define the GA we are considering. For building-block like functions like OneMax recombining a high-fitness solution with a low-fitness one seems unlikely to produce an offspring which is better than both parents. We also know from previous studies [7, 25, 20] that exploitation is crucial and large populations are of little use when minimizing the number of function evaluations. In fact, for OneMax the author proved that among all evolutionary algorithms that start with one random solution and only use standard bit mutations the expected number of function evaluations is minimized by the simple (1+1) EA [20].

Contrarily, when using crossover to speed up optimization we obviously need a population with some diversity. The following (μ+1) GA performs exploitation in the same way as the (1+1) EA. For generating offspring only the current best search points are chosen as parents. However, it can store multiple individuals in the population if they share the same current best fitness. This adds diversity to the evolution without compromising on the exploitation capabilities of the algorithm, compared to the (1+1) EA. We call the parent selection "greedy" because it is a greedy strategy to choose the current best search points as parents. For the same reason, we refer to the GA as "greedy (μ+1) GA". The greedy (μ+1) GA avoids storing duplicates in the population to prevent identical search points from clustering.

Algorithm 1: Greedy (μ+1) GA with mutation rate p for maximizing $f\colon \{0,1\}^n \to \mathbb{R}$.

Initialize population $\mathcal{P}$ of size $\mu \in \mathbb{N}$ u. a. r.
while *true* **do**
  Choose y_1, y_2 with maximal fitness in $\mathcal{P}$ u. a. r.
  Obtain y' by a crossover of y_1 and y_2.
  Flip each bit in y' independently with probability p.
  Choose $z \in \mathcal{P}$ with minimal fitness in $\mathcal{P}$ u. a. r.
  if $f(y') \geq f(z)$ and $y' \notin \mathcal{P}$ **then** $\mathcal{P} := \mathcal{P} \setminus \{z\} \cup \{y'\}$.
end

Note that "greedy" parent selection can be simulated by tournament selection with a large tournament size, ranking selection with a high selection pressure, or by using fitness-proportional selection and re-scaling the fitness values exponentially, as done in [16]. In this sense the greedy (μ+1) GA is similar to other commonly used GAs with a high selection pressure. It is plausible that results for the greedy (μ+1) GA also hold similarly for other, similar GA variants.

As only one new search point is generated in each generation, the optimization time equals the number of generations until a global optimum is found. As crossover operator we will use both uniform crossover and k-point crossover in the following. For k-point crossover we assume that the roles of first and second parent are chosen uniformly at random.

3. UNIFORM CROSSOVER IS TWICE AS FAST AS MUTATION

We show that the greedy (μ+1) GA is at least twice as fast as every evolutionary algorithm using only mutation.

Regarding the latter, the author recently proved the following lower bound on the running time of a very broad class of *mutation-based EAs* [21]. It covers all possible selection mechanisms, parent or offspring populations, and even parallel evolutionary algorithms. We slightly rephrase this result.

THEOREM 1 (SUDHOLT [21]). *Let $n \geq 2$ and $2^{-n/3} \leq p \leq \frac{1}{\sqrt{n}\log n}$. Every EA that uses only standard bit mutation with mutation rate p to create new solutions has expected optimization time at least*

$$\frac{\min\{\ln n, \ln(1/(p^2 n))\} - \ln\ln n - 3}{p(1-p)^n}$$

on ONEMAX *and every other function with a unique optimum. For $p = 1/n$ this is at least*

$$en\ln n - en\ln\ln n - 3en.$$

The greedy (μ+1) GA can cut the dominant term of the running time in half, for the standard mutation rate $p = 1/n$. The precise result is more general.

THEOREM 2. *Let $\mu \geq 2$ and $n \geq 2$. The expected optimization time of the greedy (μ+1) GA with uniform crossover and mutation rate p on* ONEMAX *is at most*

$$\frac{\ln(n^2 p + n) + 1 + p}{p(1-p)^{n-1} \cdot (1+np)} + \frac{8n}{(1-p)^n}.$$

For $p = 1/n$ we get an upper bound of

$$\frac{e}{2} \cdot n\ln n + 35n.$$

The main difference between the upper bound for the (μ+1) GA and the lower bound for all mutation-based EAs is an additional factor of $1 + pn$ in the denominator of the upper bound. This is a factor of 2 for $p = 1/n$ and an even larger gain for larger mutation rates.

PROOF OF THEOREM 2. The simplification for $p = 1/n$ is easy, so we only prove the first, general bound. We consider canonical fitness levels, i. e., the i-th fitness level contains all search points with fitness i. We estimate the time spent on each level i, i. e., when the best fitness in the current population is i. For each fitness level we consider two cases. The first case applies when there is only a single elitist. The second one reflects the setting after a neutral mutation has been made and there is more than one elitist.

Case $i.1$**:** Assume there is a unique search point in the population with current best fitness i. Note that then greedy parent selection selects this parent twice, so the greedy (μ+1) GA simply performs a mutation. The GA leaves this case for good if either a better search point is created or if it creates another search point with i ones.

The probability for the former event is at least $(n-i) \cdot p(1-p)^{n-1}$ as there are $n-i$ suitable 1-bit flips. The probability for the latter event is at least $i(n-i) \cdot p^2(1-p)^{n-2}$ as it is sufficient to flip one of i 1-bits and one of $n-i$ 0-bits. The probability of leaving this case is thus at least

$$\begin{aligned}&(n-i) \cdot p(1-p)^{n-1} + i(n-i) \cdot p^2(1-p)^{n-2}\\ &\geq p(1-p)^{n-1} \cdot (n-i)(1+ip).\end{aligned}$$

The expected time spent together in all cases $i.1$ is hence bounded by

$$\frac{1}{p(1-p)^{n-1}} \cdot \sum_{i=0}^{n-1} \frac{1}{(n-i)(1+ip)} \quad (1)$$

which can be estimated as follows. Separating the summand for $i = n-1$, we get

$$\begin{aligned}&\frac{1}{p(1-p)^{n-1}} \cdot \left(\sum_{i=0}^{n-2} \frac{1}{(n-i)(1+ip)} + \frac{1}{1+(n-1)p}\right)\\ \leq\ &\frac{1}{p(1-p)^{n-1}} \cdot \left(\int_{i=0}^{n-1} \frac{1}{(n-i)(1+ip)}\, \mathrm{d}i + \frac{1+p}{1+np}\right).\end{aligned}$$

We use equation 3.3.20 in [1] to simplify the integral and get

$$\begin{aligned}&\frac{1}{p(1-p)^{n-1}} \cdot \left(\left[\frac{1}{1+np} \cdot \ln\left(\frac{1+ip}{n-i}\right)\right]_0^{n-1} + \frac{1+p}{1+np}\right)\\ =\ &\frac{1}{p(1-p)^{n-1}} \cdot \left(\frac{\ln(np+1-p)+\ln(n)}{1+np} + \frac{1+p}{1+np}\right)\\ \leq\ &\frac{\ln(n^2p+n)+1+p}{p(1-p)^{n-1} \cdot (1+np)}.\end{aligned}$$

Case $i.2$**:** Assume there is more than one search point of best fitness i in the population. Then there is a probability of at least 1/2 of selecting two different parents. Let these have Hamming distance $2d$ and let X denote the number of 1-bits among these positions in the offspring. Note that X is binomially distributed with parameters $2d$ and 1/2 and its expectation is d. We estimate the probability of getting a surplus of 1-bits as this leads to an improvement in fitness. This estimate holds for any $d \in \mathbb{N}$. Since $\text{Prob}(X < d) = \text{Prob}(X > d)$, we have

$$\begin{aligned}\text{Prob}(X > d) &= \frac{1}{2}\left(1 - \text{Prob}(X = d)\right)\\ &= \frac{1}{2}\left(1 - 2^{-2d}\binom{2d}{d}\right) \geq \frac{1}{4}.\end{aligned}$$

Mutation keeps all 1-bits with probability at least $(1-p)^n$. Together, the probability of increasing the current best fitness is at least $1/8 \cdot (1-p)^n$. The total expected time spent in all cases $i.2$ is hence at most $8n \cdot (1-p)^{-n}$.

Summing up all expected times yields the result. □

It is remarkable that the waiting time for successful crossovers in Cases $i.2$ is only of order $O(n)$. This shows how effective crossover is in recombining building blocks. With a more detailed analysis the constant in the term $35n$ for $p = 1/n$ can be decreased to $e\ln(5) \leq 4.38$. Hence, for realistic problem dimensions n the time spent in all Cases $i.2$ is negligible, compared to the time spent in all Cases $i.1$.

Note that the result applies to arbitrary population sizes $\mu \geq 2$. In fact, more than two elitists can only increase the chance of recombining two different elitists. Non-elitists are never selected as parents and can be ignored. Also note that the proof is really simple as it uses only elementary arguments and it is fully self-contained. Actually, this simplicity makes the analysis quite robust. It easily transfers to other GA variants. For instance, using a fixed crossover probability to determine whether crossover is applied only affects the analysis of Cases $i.2$. If the crossover probability grows faster than $1/\log n$ and $p = \Theta(1/n)$, we still get the same dominant term in the running time bound. Also adaptations to other parent selection operators, variants where there is no mutation after crossover, or crossover creates two offspring instead of one are possible.

Our analysis has revealed that neutral mutations can help to escape from the first case. Even though these mutations do not immediately yield an improvement, crossover is very efficient in exploiting the gained diversity by combining two current elitists. It can capitalize on mutations that have both beneficial and disruptive effects on building blocks.

An interesting consequence is that this affects the optimal mutation rate on ONEMAX. For EAs using only standard bit mutations Witt [26] recently proved that $1/n$ is the optimal mutation rate for the (1+1) EA on all linear functions. Recall that the (1+1) EA is the optimal mutation-based EA (in the sense of Theorem 1) on ONEMAX [21].

For mutation-based EAs on ONEMAX neutral mutations are neither helpful nor detrimental. With crossover neutral mutations now become helpful. Increasing the mutation rate increases the likelihood of neutral mutations. In fact, we can easily derive better upper bounds from Theorem 2 for slightly larger mutation rates, thanks to the additional term $1 + np$ in the denominator of the upper bound.

Consider mutation probabilities $p = c/n$ for some positive constant c. Using asymptotically smaller or larger mutation rates lead to worse performance [8, 26]. Using $(1-c/n)^{n-1} \geq e^{-c} - O(1/n)$ for every constant $c > 0$, the upper bound from Theorem 2 simplifies to

$$\frac{n \ln n}{c \cdot e^{-c} \cdot (1+c)} + O(n). \qquad (2)$$

This leads to the following.

COROLLARY 3. *The asymptotically best running time bound for the greedy (μ+1) GA from Theorem 2 is obtained for $p = (1+\sqrt{5})/(2n)$. For this choice the upper bound is*

$$\frac{e^{(\sqrt{5}+1)/2}}{\sqrt{5}+2} \cdot n \ln n + 35n \approx 1.19 n \ln n + 35n.$$

4. THE OPTIMAL MUTATION RATE

In order to prove that the result from Corollary 3 is indeed optimal, we need to establish a matching lower bound. The following result applies to population size $\mu = 2$ and all mask-based crossovers, where each bit value is taken from either parent. This includes uniform crossover, k-point crossover and even biased operators like bit-wise OR.

THEOREM 4. *Consider the greedy (2+1) GA with mutation rate $0 < p \leq 1/(\sqrt{n} \log n)$ using an arbitrary mask-based crossover operator. Its expected optimization time on ONEMAX is at least*

$$\frac{\min\{\ln n, \ln(1/(p^2 n))\} - O(\log\log n)}{(1 + \max_k\{\frac{(pn)^k}{k!k!}\}) \cdot p(1-p)^n}.$$

Before giving the proof, note that for $p = c/n$, $0 < c \leq 4$ constant, $\max_k\{\frac{(pn)^k}{k!k!}\} = pn$ and the lower bound is

$$\frac{n \ln n}{c \cdot e^{-c} \cdot (1+c)} - O(n \log\log n).$$

This matches the upper bound (2) up to small order terms, showing that the new term $1 + c$ in the denominator of the bound from Theorem 2 was not a coincidence. For $p > 4/n$, the lower bound is at least

$$(e + \Omega(1)) \cdot n \ln n.$$

Together, this establishes the optimal mutation rate for the greedy (2+1) GA on ONEMAX.

THEOREM 5. *For the greedy (2+1) GA with uniform crossover on ONEMAX mutation rate $p = (1+\sqrt{5})/(2n)$ minimizes the expected number of function evaluations, up to small-order terms.*

For the proof of Theorem 4 we use the following lower-bound technique based on fitness levels by the author [21].

THEOREM 6 (SUDHOLT [21]). *Consider a partition of the search space into non-empty sets $A_1, \dots, A_m$. For a search algorithm $\mathcal{A}$ we say that it is in A_i or on level i if the best individual created so far is in A_i. If there are $\chi, u_i, \gamma_{i,j}$ for $i < j$ where*

1. *the probability of traversing from level i to level j in one step is at most $u_i \gamma_{i,j}$ for all $i < j$,*
2. *$\sum_{j=i+1}^{m} \gamma_{i,j} = 1$ for all i, and*
3. *$\gamma_{i,j} \geq \chi \sum_{k=j}^{m} \gamma_{i,k}$ for all $i < j$ and some $0 \leq \chi \leq 1$,*

then the expected hitting time of A_m is at least

$$\sum_{i=1}^{m-1} \text{Prob}(\mathcal{A} \text{ starts in } A_i) \cdot \chi \sum_{j=i}^{m-1} \frac{1}{u_j}. \qquad (3)$$

PROOF OF THEOREM 4. We prove a lower bound for the following sped-up GA instead of the original greedy (2+1) GA. Whenever it creates a new offspring with the same fitness, but a different bit string as the current best individual, we assume the following. The algorithm automatically performs a crossover between the two. Also, we assume that this crossover leads to the best possible offspring in a sense that all bits where both parents differ are set to 1 (i.e., the algorithm performs a bit-wise OR). That is, if both search points have i 1-bits and Hamming distance $2k$, then the resulting offspring has $i + k$ 1-bits.

Due to our assumptions there is always a single best individual. For this reason we can model the algorithm by a Markov chain representing the current best fitness.

The analysis follows a lower bound for EAs on ONEMAX [21, Theorem 9]. As in [21] we consider the following fitness-level partition that focuses only on the very last fitness values. Let $\ell = \lceil n - \min\{n/\log n, 1/(p^2 n \log n)\}\rceil$. Let $A_i = \{x \mid |x|_1 = i\}$ for $i > \ell$ and A_ℓ contain all remaining search points. We know from [21] that the GA is initialized in A_ℓ with probability at least $(1 - 1/\log n)$ if n is large enough.

The probability $p_{i,i+k}$ that the sped-up GA makes a transition from fitness i to fitness $i + k$ equals

$$\begin{aligned} p_{i,i+k} = {} & \text{Prob}(k \text{ more 0-bits than 1-bits flip}) + \\ & \text{Prob}(k \text{ 0-bits and } k \text{ 1-bits flip}) \end{aligned}$$

According to [21, Lemma 2], for the considered fitness levels $i > \ell$ the former probability is bounded by

$$p^k(1-p)^{n-k} \cdot \frac{(n-i)^k}{k!} \cdot \left(1 + \frac{3}{5} \cdot \frac{i(n-i)p^2}{(1-p)^2}\right).$$

The latter probability is bounded by

$$\begin{aligned} & \text{Prob}(k \text{ 0-bits flip}) \cdot \text{Prob}(k \text{ 1-bits flip}) \\ \leq {} & \frac{(n-i)^k}{k!} \cdot p^k(1-p)^{n-i-k} \cdot \frac{i^k}{k!} \cdot p^k(1-p)^{i-k} \\ \leq {} & \frac{(n-i)^k}{k!} \cdot p^k(1-p)^n \cdot \frac{(pn)^k}{(1-p)^{2k} \cdot k!}. \end{aligned}$$

Together, $p_{i,i+k}$ is at most

$$(p(n-i))^k(1-p)^n\left(1+\frac{3}{5}\cdot\frac{i(n-i)p^2}{(1-p)^{2+k}}+\frac{(pn)^k}{(1-p)^{2k}\cdot k!k!}\right).$$

We need to find variables u_i and $\gamma_{i,i+k}$ along with some $0 \le \chi \le 1$ such that all conditions of Theorem 6 are fulfilled. Abbreviate $M := \max_k\left(\frac{(pn)^k}{k!k!}\right)$ and define

$$u'_i := p(1-p)^n(n-i)\left(1+\frac{3}{5}\cdot\frac{i(n-i)p^2}{(1-p)^3}+\frac{1}{(1-p)^2}\cdot M\right)$$

and

$$\gamma'_{i,i+k} := \left(\frac{p(n-i)}{(1-p)^2}\right)^{k-1}.$$

Observe that, for every $k \in \mathbb{N}$,

$$\begin{aligned}
&u'_i\gamma'_{i,i+k}\\
&\ge p^k(1-p)^n(n-i)^k\left(1+\frac{3}{5}\cdot\frac{i(n-i)p^2}{(1-p)^{1+2k}}+\frac{1}{(1-p)^{2k}}\cdot M\right)\\
&\ge p^k(1-p)^n(n-i)^k\left(1+\frac{3}{5}\cdot\frac{i(n-i)p^2}{(1-p)^{2+k}}+\frac{(pn)^k}{(1-p)^{2k}\cdot k!k!}\right)\\
&\ge p_{i,i+k}.
\end{aligned}$$

In order to fulfill the second condition in Theorem 6, we consider the following normalized variables: $u_i := u'_i \cdot \sum_{j=i+1}^{n}\gamma'_{i,j}$ and $\gamma_{i,j} := \frac{\gamma'_{i,j}}{\sum_{j=i+1}^{n}\gamma'_{i,j}}$. As $u_i\gamma_{i,j} = u'_i\gamma'_{i,j} \ge p_{i,j}$, this proves the first condition of Theorem 6.

Following the proof of Theorem 9 in [21], it is easy to show that for $\chi := 1 - \frac{1}{(1-p)^2\log n}$ we get $\gamma_{i,j} \ge \chi\sum_{k=j}^{m}\gamma_{i,k}$ for all i, j with $j > i$. This establishes the third and last condition. In addition, we get

$$\sum_{j=i+1}^{n}\gamma'_{i,j} \le \frac{1}{1-\frac{1}{(1-p)^2\log n}},$$

which implies (omitting intermediate steps)

$$\begin{aligned}
u_i &\le p(1-p)^n\cdot(n-i)\cdot\frac{1}{1-\frac{1}{(1-p)^2\log n}}\\
&\quad\cdot\left(1+\frac{3}{5}\cdot\frac{i(n-i)p^2}{(1-p)^3}+\frac{1}{(1-p)^2}\cdot M\right)\\
&\le p(1-p)^n\cdot(n-i)\cdot\frac{1+M}{1-\frac{8}{5(1-p)^3\log n}}.
\end{aligned}$$

Invoking Theorem 6 and recalling that the first fitness level is reached with probability at least $1-1/\log n$, we get a lower bound of

$$\begin{aligned}
&\left(1-\frac{1}{\log n}\right)\chi\sum_{i=\ell}^{n-1}\frac{1}{u_i}\\
&\ge\left(1-O\!\left(\frac{1}{\log n}\right)\right)\frac{1}{1+M}\cdot\frac{1}{p(1-p)^n}\sum_{i=\ell}^{n-1}\frac{1}{n-i}.
\end{aligned}$$

Bounding $\sum_{i=\ell}^{n-1}\frac{1}{n-i} \le \ln(\min\{n, 1/(p^2n)\}) - \ln(\log n)$ as in [21] and absorbing all small-order terms in a $-O(\log\log n)$ term gives the claimed bound. $\square$

We also ran experiments to see whether the outcome matches our inspection of the dominating terms in the running time bounds for realistic problem dimensions. We chose $n = 1000$ bits and recorded the average optimization time over 100 runs. The mutation rate p was set to c/n with $c \in \{0.1, 0.2, \ldots, 4\}$. The result is shown in Figure 1.

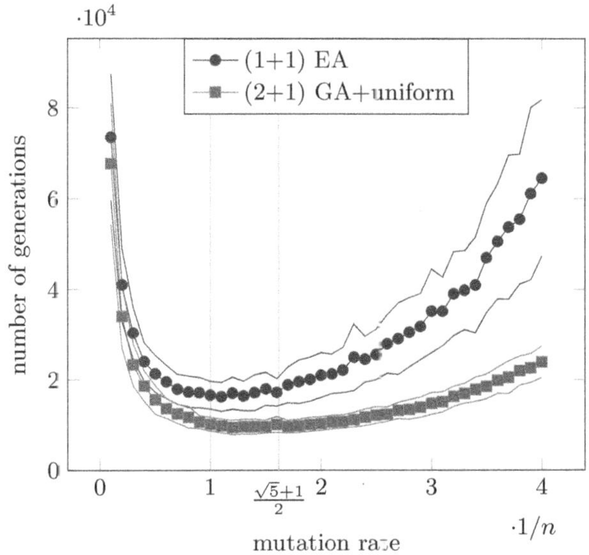

Figure 1: Average optimization times for the (1+1) EA and the greedy (2+1) GA with uniform crossover on OneMax with $n = 1000$ bits. The mutation rate p is set to c/n with $c \in \{0.1, 0.2, \ldots, 4\}$. The thin lines show mean $\pm$ standard deviation.

One can see that for every mutation rate the greedy (2+1) GA has a lower average optimization time. As predicted, the performance difference becomes larger as the mutation rate increases. The optimal mutation rates for both algorithms match with minimal average optimization times. Note that also the variance/standard deviation was much lower for the GA for higher mutation rates. Preliminary runs for $n = 100$ and $n = 10000$ bits gave very similar results. More experiments and statistical tests are given in Section 6.

5. K-POINT CROSSOVER

For k-point crossover, with arbitrary k, we get a similar upper bound. Preliminary experiments indicated that the greedy (2+1) GA with k-point crossover, for $k \in \{1, 2\}$, performs slightly worse than the one with uniform crossover. In fact, the upper bound derived in the following turns out to be slightly worse than the one for uniform crossover.

For uniform crossover we have seen that populations containing two search points of equal fitness are beneficial as uniform crossover can easily combine the good "building blocks". For k-point crossover it can happen that in such a population the two search points differ in two bits, and their bit positions are quite close. Then 1-point crossover has a high probability of taking both bits from the same parent. In order to recombine those building blocks, the cutting point has to be chosen in between the two bit positions. A similar effect occurs for 2-point crossover also if the two bit positions are on opposite ends of the bit string.

The following lemma gives a lower bound on the probability that k-point crossover combines the right building blocks on OneMax, if two parents are equally fit and differ in two bits. The lemma and its proof are of independent interest.

Lemma 7. *Assume two search points x, y with $x_i = 1, x_j = 0, y_i = 0, y_j = 1$ for $i, j \in \{1, \ldots, n\}$ and $x_s = y_s$ for $s \notin \{i, j\}$. The probability of k-point crossover of x, y, with $1 \le k < n - (n \bmod 2)$, creating an offspring with a larger number of 1-bits is at least $\min\{|i-j|, n-|i-j|\}/(2n)$. For odd k it is even at least $\min\{|i-j|/(2n), 1/4\}$.*

Proof. W.l.o.g. $i < j$. Abbreviate $d := j - i$. With probability $1/2$ the prefix is taken from x. Assume that $k \le (n-1)/2$; if not, we exchange the roles of cutting points and non-cutting points.

There are $n-1$ or n possible cutting points, depending on whether k is odd or even. Let $N \in \{n-1, n\}$ denote this number. We identify cutting points with bits such that cutting point a results in two strings $x_1 \ldots x_a$ and $x_{a+1} \ldots x_n$. We say that a cutting point a separates i and j if $a \in \{i, \ldots, j-1\}$. The claim now follows from showing that the number of separating cutting points is odd with twice the claimed probability.

Let X be the random variables that describes the number of cutting points separating i and j. This variable follows a hypergeometric distribution: it is equivalent to the following urn model with red and white balls. The urn contains N balls, d of which are red. We draw k balls uniformly at random, without replacement. Then X describes the number of red balls drawn. We have

$$p_{\text{even}}^{(k)} = \sum_{x \text{ even}} \text{Prob}(X = x) = \sum_{x \text{ even}} \frac{\binom{d}{x}\binom{N-d}{k-x}}{\binom{N}{k}}$$

describing the probability that X is even and an analogous probability $p_{\text{odd}}^{(k)}$. Consider

$$p_{\text{even}}^{(k)} - p_{\text{odd}}^{(k)} = \sum_{x=0}^{k} (-1)^x \cdot \text{Prob}(X = x) = \sum_{x=0}^{k} (-1)^x \cdot \frac{\binom{d}{x}\binom{N-d}{k-x}}{\binom{N}{k}}.$$

An analysis of this function shows that for $d \le N/2$ and all $k \in \mathbb{N}$ we have

$$p_{\text{even}}^{(k)} - p_{\text{odd}}^{(k)} \le p_{\text{even}}^{(1)} - p_{\text{odd}}^{(1)} = \frac{\binom{d}{0}\binom{N-d}{1}}{\binom{N}{1}} - \frac{\binom{d}{1}\binom{N-d}{0}}{\binom{N}{1}} = \frac{N-2d}{N}.$$

Hence $p_{\text{odd}}^{(k)} \ge p_{\text{even}}^{(k)} - (N-2d)/N$ and along with $p_{\text{even}}^{(k)} + p_{\text{odd}}^{(k)} = 1$ we get

$$p_{\text{odd}}^{(k)} \ge 1 - p_{\text{odd}}^{(k)} - \frac{N-2d}{N}$$

which is equivalent to

$$p_{\text{odd}}^{(k)} \ge \frac{1}{2} - \frac{N-2d}{2N} = \frac{d}{N}.$$

If k is even (and so $N = n$), we can handle the case $d \ge N/2$ in the same fashion, exchanging the roles of red and white balls. If the number of red balls is odd, so is the number of white balls, and vice versa. This results in the same bound for $p_{\text{odd}}^{(k)}$: $p_{\text{odd}}^{(k)} \ge \frac{N-d}{N} = \frac{n-d}{n}$.

For odd k, we observe that for $d \ge N/2$

$$p_{\text{even}}^{(k)} - p_{\text{odd}}^{(k)} \le 0.$$

This implies $p_{\text{odd}}^{(k)} \ge 1/2$ and hence the claim. □

Using this lemma, we get the following upper bound.

Theorem 8. *The expected optimization time of the greedy (2+1) GA with mutation rate $p = c/n$, $0 < c \le 2$ constant, and k-point crossover, $1 \le k < n - (n \bmod 2)$, on OneMax is at most*

$$\left(\frac{1}{ce^{-c} \cdot (1+c)} + \frac{2c}{3+3c}\right) \cdot n \ln n + O(n).$$

Compared to the upper bound for uniform crossover, this upper bound is by a term of $\frac{2c}{3+3c} \cdot n \ln n$ larger. For $c = 1$ we get a leading constant of $e/2 + 1/3$, i. e., a time bound of about $1.69 n \ln n + O(n)$. The analysis is more complicated as we can evolve elitists that differ in more than 2 bits, and then it is complicated to figure out which cutting points lead to a fitness improvement. Also the calculations are quite lengthy. For these reasons we only sketch the proof.

We again estimate the time spent on each fitness level i, i. e., when the best fitness in the current population is i. As before, we again consider cases $i.1$ and $i.2$, the former reflecting a single elitist individual on level i and the latter dealing with two elitists. The expected time spent in all Cases $i.1$ is estimated as in the proof of Theorem 2:

$$\frac{n \ln n}{c \cdot e^{-c} \cdot (1+c)} + O(n).$$

A further condition for Case $i.2$ now is that the Hamming distance between the two individuals must be 2. If the two differ in more than 2 bits, it is hard to estimate the probability of k-point crossover creating an improvement. We therefore consider further "error" states $i.1$-error and $i.2$-error that are reached in case unlikely events happen that make an analysis very difficult.

Error state $i.1$-error is reached from Case $i.1$ when a new elitist is created that differs in more than two bits from its parent. On high fitness levels this is unlikely as two 0-bits and two 1-bits need to flip, and 0-bits are particularly rare. The GA can escape from the error state by selecting the same parent twice and thus simulating a mutation that improves the fitness. As the state is rarely reached, the expected time spent in all states $i.1$-error can be bounded by

$$\frac{c^3 n}{3(1-c/n)^3} = O(n).$$

The time in Case $i.2$ is estimated as follows. We know that a new elitist has been created by mutation flipping a 0-bit and a 1-bit. The position of these bits is chosen uniformly at random among all 0-bits and all 1-bits, respectively. We get the following statement about the distance between these bit positions in the bit string. The proof is omitted.

Lemma 9. *For any $x \notin \{0^n, 1^n\}$ let i, j be bit positions chosen uniformly among all 1-bits and 0-bits in x, resp. Then the random variable $\min\{|i-j|, n-|i-j|\}$ stochastically dominates the uniform distribution on $\{1, \ldots, n/4\}$.*

We pessimistically assume the uniform distribution for the random variable $\min\{|i-j|, n-|i-j|\}$. Conditional on this random variable, we then invoke Lemma 7 to get a probability of crossover creating an improvement. In addition, we take into account that the GA is able to simulate a mutation, and this can also lead to an improvement. (Relying only on crossover would give a $\Theta(n \log n)$ bound.) Together, the expected time in all Cases $i.2$ can be bounded by

$$\frac{2\ln(1+4c)}{c/n \cdot (1-c/n)^n} + \frac{8n \ln\left(\frac{1+4c}{2ec}\right)}{(1-c/n)^n} = O(n).$$

Whenever the GA is in Case $i.2$ and the current population is changed towards a different pair of elitists, the above random variable $\min\{|i-j|, n-|i-j|\}$ is replaced by a new instantiation, possibly drawn under different circumstances than before. This interferes with the above analysis, so in our Markov chain model of cases we make a transition to $i.2$-error. Relying on crossover for escaping is difficult as we do not know the Hamming distance and the differing bit positions between elitists. Also a successful crossover can be followed by a disruptive mutation, and this is likely to change the current elitists even further. So, we only count on simulating a mutation to leave this state. The total time spent in all states $i.2$-error can be bounded by

$$\frac{2c}{3+3c} \cdot n \ln n + O(n).$$

Summing up all expected times gives the claimed bound.

6. ROYAL ROADS AND MONOTONE POLYNOMIALS

So far, our theorems and proofs have been focused on OneMax only. This is because we do have very strong results about the performance of EAs on OneMax at hand. However, the insights gained stretch far beyond OneMax. Royal road functions generally consist of larger blocks of bits. All bits in a block need to be set to 1 in order to contribute to the fitness; otherwise the contribution is 0. All blocks contribute the same amount to the fitness, and the fitness is just the sum of all contributions.

The fundamental insight we have gained for neutral mutations also applies to royal road functions. If there is a mutation that completes one block, but destroys another block, this is a neutral mutation and the offspring will be stored in the population of the greedy (μ+1) GA. Then crossover can recombine all finished blocks in the same way as for OneMax. The only difference is that the destroyed block may evolve further. More neutral mutations can alter bits in the destroyed block. Then the population can be dominated by many similar solutions, and it becomes harder for crossover to find a good pair for recombination. However, as crossover has generally a high probability of finding improvements, the last effect probably plays only a minor role.

A theoretical analysis of general royal roads up to the same level of detail as for OneMax is harder, but not impossible. So far results on the more general class of monotone polynomials have only been asymptotic [24]. For now, we use experiments to see whether the performance is similar to that on OneMax. We use royal roads with $n = 1000$ bits and block size 5, i. e., we have 200 pairwise disjoint blocks of 5 bits each. We also consider random monotone polynomials. Instead of using disjoint blocks, we use 1000 monomials of degree 5 (conjunctions of 5 bits): each monomial is made up of 5 bit positions chosen uniformly at random, without replacement. This leads to a function similar to royal roads, but "blocks" are broken up and can share bits; bit positions are completely random. Figure 2 shows the average optimization times in 100 runs on all these functions, for the (1+1) EA and the greedy (2+1) GA with uniform, 1-point, and 2-point crossover. We chose the last two because k-point crossovers for odd k treat ends of bit strings differently from those for even k.

On OneMax both k-point crossovers are better than the (1+1) EA, but slightly worse than uniform crossover. This is in accordance with the theoretical results. For royal roads the curves are very similar. The difference between the (1+1) EA and the greedy (2+1) GA is just a bit smaller. For random polynomials there are visible differences, albeit smaller. Mann-Whitney U-tests tests confirm that wherever there is a noticeable gap between the curves, there is a statistically significant difference on a significance level of 0.01.

For small mutation rates c/n the tests were not significant. For larger c (mostly $c \geq 0.9$) all differences between the (1+1) EA and all greedy GAs were statistically significant. For OneMax the difference between uniform crossover vs. k-point crossover was significant, while for royal roads and random polynomials it was not. There were no significant differences between 1-point and 2-point crossover.

These findings give strong evidence that the insights drawn from the analysis on OneMax transfer to broader classes of functions where building blocks are assembled.

7. CONCLUSIONS

We have demonstrated rigorously and intuitively that crossover can speed up building block assembly on OneMax, with evidence that the same holds for a broad class of functions. The basic insight is that neutral mutations can lead to a successful recombination at a later generation. This effect makes the greedy (μ+1) GA twice as fast as every mutation-based EA on OneMax, with regard to the expected number of function evaluations (up to small-order terms). This applies to uniform crossover and to k-point crossover, the latter leading to slightly worse performance guarantees.

Another intriguing conclusion following naturally from our analysis is that the optimal mutation rate changes from $1/n$ to $(1+\sqrt{5})/2 \cdot 1/n \approx 1.618/n$ when using uniform crossover. This is simply because neutral mutations and hence multi-bit mutations become more useful. Experiments are in perfect accordance with the theoretical results for OneMax. For other functions like royal roads and random polynomials they indicate that the performance differences also hold in a much more general sense.

Our results give novel, intuitive and rigorous answers to a question that has been discussed controversially for decades.

In the future, we would like to extend the analysis to monotone polynomials and to other, common GA variants with high selection pressure. Also investigating weighted building blocks, like in linear functions, is an interesting topic for future work.

Acknowledgment: This work was partially supported by EPSRC grant EP/D052785/1.

8. REFERENCES

[1] M. Abramowitz and I. A. Stegun. *Handbook of Mathematical Functions with Formulas, Graphs, and Mathematical Tables.* Dover, New York, ninth Dover printing, tenth GPO printing edition, 1964.

[2] M. Dietzfelbinger, B. Naudts, C. Van Hoyweghen, and I. Wegener. The analysis of a recombinative hill-climber on H-IFF. *IEEE Transactions on Evolutionary Computation*, 7(5):417–423, 2003.

[3] B. Doerr, E. Happ, and C. Klein. Crossover can provably be useful in evolutionary computation. *Theoretical Computer Science*, 425(0):17–33, 2012.

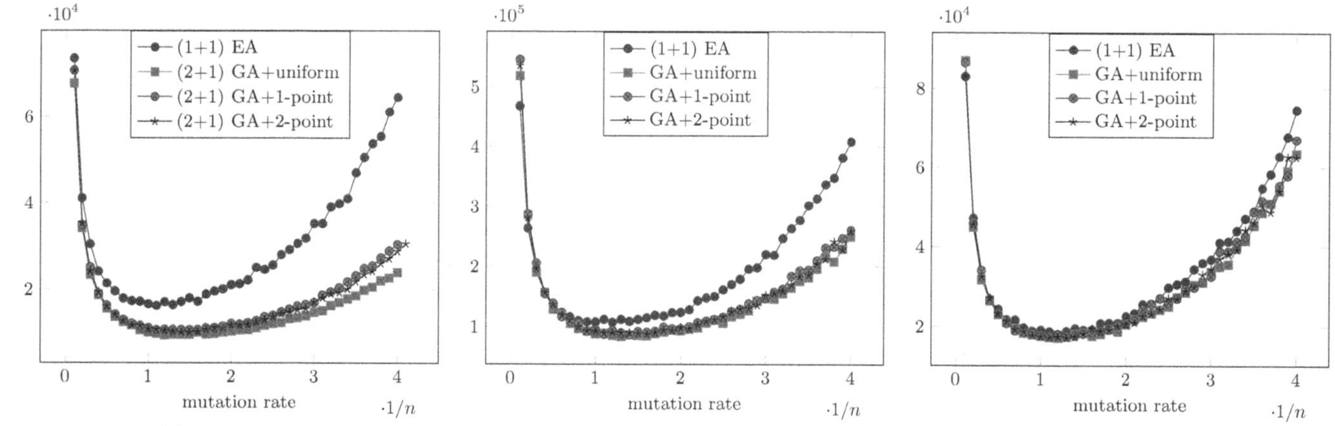

(a) OneMax (b) Royal road (c) Random polynomials

Figure 2: Average optimization times for (1+1) EA and the greedy (2+1) GA with various crossover operators on functions with $n = 1000$ bits: OneMax, a royal road function with block size 5, and random polynomials with 1000 unweighted monomials of degree 5. The mutation rate p is set to c/n with $c \in \{0.1, 0.2, \ldots, 4\}$.

[4] S. Droste, T. Jansen, and I. Wegener. On the analysis of the (1+1) evolutionary algorithm. *Theoretical Computer Science*, 276:51–81, 2002.

[5] S. Fischer and I. Wegener. The one-dimensional Ising model: Mutation versus recombination. *Theoretical Computer Science*, 344(2–3):208–225, 2005.

[6] S. Forrest and M. Mitchell. Relative building block fitness and the building block hypotheses. In *Proc. of FOGA 2*, pages 198–226. Morgan Kaufmann, 1993.

[7] T. Jansen, K. A. De Jong, and I. Wegener. On the choice of the offspring population size in evolutionary algorithms. *Evolutionary Computation*, 13:413–440, 2005.

[8] T. Jansen and I. Wegener. On the choice of the mutation probability for the (1+1) EA. In *PPSN '00*, volume 1917, pages 89–98. Springer, 2000.

[9] T. Jansen and I. Wegener. On the analysis of evolutionary algorithms—a proof that crossover really can help. *Algorithmica*, 34(1):47–66, 2002.

[10] T. Jansen and I. Wegener. Real royal road functions—where crossover provably is essential. *Discrete Applied Mathematics*, 149:111–125, 2005.

[11] T. Jansen and C. Zarges. Analysis of evolutionary algorithms: from computational complexity analysis to algorithm engineering. In *Proc. of FOGA '11*, pages 1–14. ACM, 2011.

[12] T. Kötzing, D. Sudholt, and M. Theile. How crossover helps in pseudo-Boolean optimization. In *Proc. of GECCO '11*, pages 989–996. ACM Press, 2011.

[13] J. Lässig and D. Sudholt. General scheme for analyzing running times of parallel evolutionary algorithms. In *PPSN '10*, pages 234–243. Springer, 2010.

[14] M. Mitchell, S. Forrest, and J. H. Holland. The royal road function for genetic algorithms: fitness landscapes and GA performance. In *Proc. of the 1st European Conference on Artificial Life*, pages 245–254. MIT Press, 1992.

[15] M. Mitchell, J. H. Holland, and S. Forrest. When will a genetic algorithm outperform hill climbing? In *Advances in Neural Information Processing Systems*, pages 51–58. Morgan Kaufmann, 1994.

[16] F. Neumann, P. S. Oliveto, and C. Witt. Theoretical analysis of fitness-proportional selection: landscapes and efficiency. In *Proc. of GECCO '09*, pages 835–842. ACM Press, 2009.

[17] F. Neumann and M. Theile. How crossover speeds up evolutionary algorithms for the multi-criteria all-pairs-shortest-path problem. In *Proc. of PPSN '10*, pages 667–676. Springer, 2010.

[18] T. Storch and I. Wegener. Real royal road functions for constant population size. *Theoretical Computer Science*, 320:123–134, 2004.

[19] D. Sudholt. Crossover is provably essential for the Ising model on trees. In *Proc. of GECCO '05*, pages 1161–1167. ACM Press, 2005.

[20] D. Sudholt. General lower bounds for the running time of evolutionary algorithms. In *PPSN '10*, pages 124–133. Springer, 2010.

[21] D. Sudholt. A new method for lower bounds on the running time of evolutionary algorithms. *ArXiv e-prints*, 2011. Available from `http://arxiv.org/abs/1109.1504`.

[22] D. Sudholt and C. Thyssen. Running time analysis of ant colony optimization for shortest path problems. *Journal of Discrete Algorithms*, 2012. To appear.

[23] R. A. Watson and T. Jansen. A building-block royal road where crossover is provably essential. In *Proc. of GECCO '07*, pages 1452–1459. ACM, 2007.

[24] I. Wegener and C. Witt. On the optimization of monotone polynomials by simple randomized search heuristics. *Combinatorics, Probability and Computing*, 14:225–247, 2005.

[25] C. Witt. Runtime analysis of the (μ+1) EA on simple pseudo-Boolean functions. *Evolutionary Computation*, 14(1):65–86, 2006.

[26] C. Witt. Optimizing Linear Functions with Randomized Search Heuristics - The Robustness of Mutation. In *Proc. of STACS '12*, pages 420–431, 2012.

Author Index

Volume 1 Pages: 1–696

Volume 2 Pages: 703–1357

www.ingramcontent.com/pod-product-compliance
Ingram Content Group UK Ltd.
Pitfield, Milton Keynes, MK11 3LW, UK
UKHW051455290926
15471UKWH00008B/1214

9 781450 319447